THIRTY-NINT

KOVELS' ANTIQUES & COLLECTIBLES PRICE LIST

FOR THE 2007 MARKET

ILLUSTRATED

RANDOM HOUSE REFERENCE

NEW YORK TORONTO LONDON SYDNEY AUCKLAND

 Published in the United States by Random House Reference, an imprint of The Random House Information Group, a division of Random House, Inc., New York, and simultaneously in Canada by Random House of Canada Limited, Toronto.

Please address inquiries about electronic licensing of any products for use on a network, in software or on CD-ROM to the Subsidiary Rights Department, Random House Information Group, fax 212-572-6003.

This book is available for special discounts for bulk purchases for sales promotions or premiums. Special editions, including personalized covers, excerpts of existing books, and corporate imprints, can be created in large quantities for special needs. For more information, write to Random House, Inc., Special Markets/Premium Sales, 1745 Broadway, MD 6-2, New York, NY or email *specialmarkets@randomhouse.com.*

Visit the Random House Reference Web site: *www.randomhouse.com*

Library of Congress Cataloging-in-Publication Data is available.

Printed in the United States of America

ISBN-10: 0-375-72185-1
ISBN-13: 978-0-375-72185-4

10 9 8 7 6 5 4 3 2 1

THIRTY-NINTH EDITION

BOOKS BY RALPH AND TERRY KOVEL

American Country Furniture, 1780–1875

A Directory of American Silver, Pewter, and Silver Plate

Kovels' Advertising Collectibles Price List

Kovels' American Antiques, 1750–1900

Kovels' American Art Pottery

Kovels' American Silver Marks, 1650 to the Present

Kovels' Antiques & Collectibles Fix-It Source Book

Kovels' Antiques & Collectibles Price List

Kovels' Bid, Buy, and Sell Online

Kovels' Book of Antique Labels

Kovels' Bottles Price List

Kovels' Collector's Guide to American Art Pottery

Kovels' Collectors' Source Book

Kovels' Depression Glass & Dinnerware Price List

Kovels' Dictionary of Marks—Pottery & Porcelain

Kovels' Guide to Selling, Buying, and Fixing
Your Antiques and Collectibles

Kovels' Illustrated Price Guide to Royal Doulton

Kovels' Know Your Antiques

Kovels' Know Your Collectibles

Kovels' New Dictionary of Marks—Pottery & Porcelain

Kovels' Price Guide for Collector Plates, Figurines,
Paperweights, and Other Limited Editions

Kovels' Quick Tips—799 Helpful Hints
on How to Care for Your Collectibles

Kovels' Yellow Pages: A Resource Guide for Collectors

The Label Made Me Buy It: From Aunt Jemima to Zonkers—
The Best-Dressed Boxes, Bottles, and Cans from the Past

INTRODUCTION

This is the thirty-ninth year *Kovels' Antiques & Collectibles Price List* has been published. The book is still written by its original authors, Ralph and Terry Kovel, and has the same reliable content. This edition has hundreds of color photographs and product logos, about 45,000 prices, and dozens of tips about care. All of the antiques and collectibles priced here are bought and sold in the American market.

READ THIS FIRST

This is a book for the collector. We check prices, visit shops, shows, and flea markets, read hundreds of publications and catalogs, check online services and the Internet, and decide which antiques and collectibles are of most interest to most collectors. We concentrate on the average pieces, but some high-priced items are included so you will realize that some rarities are very valuable.

Examples of furniture, silver, Tiffany, or art pottery may sell for more than $40,000; we list a few. The highest price in this book is $89,125 for a Tiffany lamp with a green and mottled geometric shade with raised dots. The lowest price is 25 cents for a Belfry Farms milk bottle cap. Most pieces we list cost less than $10,000. We also include the weird and the wonderful. This year you can find a red dynamite detonating box for $115, a 5-inch-long blown glass model of a leech used for teaching for $1,150, a bull rider's groin protector for $120, and Elvis Presley's hair, authenticated and sealed in a plastic container, for $8,722. The smallest items in the book are a ⅞-inch celluloid Ballistite & Empire pin for $90 and another ⅞-inch pin, picturing a dead duck and advertising Dead Shot Smokeless Powder, for $98. The biggest item is a nineteenth-century eight-panel Chinese lacquered screen, 9 feet 3 inches by 13 feet, for $15,860.

Prices are up in some categories: Georg Jensen silver, majolica, baskets (especially those from Nantucket or rare American Indian examples), teapots, Roseville's Juvenile line, exceptional celluloid toys, and anything Popeye that's in excellent condition. Advertising items, especially those from the early 1900s or before, are rising in price. Modern textiles continue to sell well. The furniture by "name" designers of the 1960s to 1990s is selling for thousands, even hundreds of thousands, of dollars. And American art pottery pieces by Rookwood, Grueby, and even Marblehead and North Dakota School of Mines are still selling for high prices. England's Moorcroft Pottery, De Morgan, Martin Brothers, and majolica by known factories are all expensive. Garden antiques and collectibles continue to interest collectors at all levels of the market, from $25 vintage clay pots to $1,000 cast-iron statues of dogs. All of the many pottery and porcelain lines decorated with flowers are selling. Viktor Schreckengost, the Cowan artist who made the Jazz bowl, is 100 years old this year. Anything he designed, from dinnerware to bicycles, is up in price. Less-than-perfect antiques and collectibles, like repaired bottles or art pottery, are selling at about 80 percent of the price of a perfect piece—if they are rare. But Arts and Crafts furniture, especially pieces by Gustav Stickley, must have original finish to sell at a high price. New research seems to show that eighteenth- and early nineteenth-century pieces may have an old but not original finish. It is difficult to determine what is original, so there is somewhat less emphasis on condition of finish unless the piece is museum-quality. Prices at large, well-advertised auctions look high when compared to presale estimates, but if you take a closer look you'll find that estimates in general are about the same as last year—although there seems to be an increase in unsold items. On eBay, estimates are often very low because the seller pays a fee to eBay based on the estimated price, not the final price. In general, Internet auction prices are still dropping, although many more large auction houses are selling on land and online at the same time, giving them an international customer base.

Most items in our original book were made before 1860. Today we have pieces made as recently as the 1990s, and there is great interest in furniture, glass, and ceramics made since 1950.

The book is kept at about 900 pages so you can carry it to sales. Prices are from the American market for the American market. Few European sales are reported. We take the editorial privilege of not including prices we think result from "auction fever."

All photographs and prices are new, except pictures that are pattern examples in Depression Glass and Pressed Glass. Antiques and collectibles pictured are items that were offered for sale. Whenever computer-generated spaces appear, we fill them with new tips about care of collections, security, and other useful information. Don't discard this book. Old Kovels' price books should be saved for future reference and for tax and appraisal information.

The prices in this book are reports of the general antiques market. Every price in the book is new. We do not estimate or "update" prices. Prices are asking prices; a buyer may have negotiated to a lower selling price. No price is an estimate. If a price range is given, at least two identical items were offered for sale at different prices. Price ranges are found only in categories like Pressed Glass, where identical items can be identified. If the price is from an auction, it includes the buyer's premium, but like all the prices, it does not include sales tax.

If you are selling your collection, do not expect to get retail value unless you are a dealer. Wholesale prices for antiques are usually 50 percent of retail prices. The antiques dealer must make a profit or go out of business. Internet auction prices are less predictable. Because of the international audience and "auction fever," prices can be higher or lower than retail.

RECORD PRICES

Every year the media reports record prices because a million-dollar table makes a great story. They tend to ignore the everyday prices of collectibles. We report the records because it is always nice to dream that Grandma's vase *could* be worth a fortune. Just remember, it is as likely as winning the lottery. These are the prices for the rarest and the best this past year.

ADVERTISING

Leaded glass sign: $19,800 for a California Steam Beer stained leaded glass sign, multicolored glass panels, 74 x 21½ in.

Mr. Peanut display: $35,750 for a three-dimensional Mr. Peanut store display figure, standing, holding cane, black top hat, papier-mâché, 1920s, 50 in.

Potlid: $13,966 for a "Bear's Grease Manufacturer" round potlid made by Mayer Brothers, picturing the interior of a room where bear's grease is being prepared, double-line border, outer margin with maker's name, inscription "Clayton & Co.'s Real Bear's Grease, 58 Watling St., London," c.1850.

CLOCKS & WATCHES

Simon Willard lighthouse clock: $744,000 for a lighthouse clock in a painted white tin case with glass dome, original brass bell and alarm mechanism, inscribed on the waist panel, "Simon Willard's Patent, Roxbury," c.1825.

FURNITURE

Boston side chair: $464,000 for a Chippendale carved mahogany side chair, Boston, c.1770, 37¾ inches.

Byrdcliffe chiffonnier: $207,000 for a Byrdcliffe oak chiffonnier, c.1904, with the colony's lily cypher oil paintings in the front panels, signed by Hermann Dudley Murphy, remnants of original transparent green stain, original bronze hardware, branded BYRDCLIFFE 1904, 27¼ x 38½ x 14¾ inches.

Chair set: $2,144,000 for a set of six Queen Anne figured maple plain yoke-back side chairs with rush seats and scalloped skirts, made in Philadelphia, attributed to William Savery, c.1760.

Seed chest: $75,900 for a pine and poplar seed chest, attributed to John Boyer, 22 drawers, hinged slant lid opens to fitted interior with three compartments, feather graining, porcelain pulls, one drawer with pencil inscription "Anna B. Stauffer, Brickerville," mid to late 19th century, 22½ x 18⅜ inches.

GLASS

American engraved historical glass: $9,625 for a colorless pressed and cut tumbler engraved with a view of the Bank of Pennsylvania in Philadelphia, c.1840, 4⁷⁄₁₆ x 3⅛ inches.

Plated Amberina vase: $27,600 for a New England Plated Amberina vase with pinched sides and four-fold rim, 4 inches.

Sandwich glass tulip vase: $22,000 for a Boston & Sandwich tulip vase, brilliant deep violet blue with white marbling, octagonal base, wafer construction, c.1855, 10¼ inches.

MISCELLANEOUS

American Indian art object: $800,000 for an Upper Missouri River man's quilled and pony-beaded hide shirt, probably Blackfoot, mid 19th century, 57 inches long.

American Indian basket: $336,250 for a Paiute multicolored small-mouth globular basket, "Tina Charlie, 1929," curving sides decorated with three panels of stacked triangles, concentric linear devices, bands of triangles, stepped diamond lozenges with alternating dark and light sewing material, 10¼ inches high x 20½-inch diameter.

Candlebox: $744,825 for a pine candlebox with sliding lid, incised, painted red, white, and blue, decorated with demilune rainbow banding, potted tulips, chickens, and paisley corners, molded base, c.1840, 6½ x 12¼ x 9½ inches.

Canvas-constructed decoy: $132,250 for the Old Squaw drake decoy by Lothrop Holmes with original paint and patina, canvas construction over wire-frame body, c.1875, 14 inches.

Guitar without celebrity association: $268,000 for a Gibson solid-body electric guitar, Les Paul model, Kalamazoo, Michigan, 1959, signed, ink stamped "9 0871," 17 15/16 inches, with later Gibson case.

Individual Nantucket basket: $115,000 for an open, handleless Nantucket lightship basket with heart-carved stave ends protruding through hoops in the rim, crisscross rim wrap, two concentric circles in base, c.1875, 4 x 9⅛ inches.

Marie Zimmermann box: $117,500 for a hand-carved wooden box by Marie Zimmermann on ivory ball feet, painted green, blue, red, and yellow with black outlining, decorated with studded cabochon jewels of amethyst and semiprecious quartz, purple silk-lined interior, cast bronze handles and hinges, with Egyptian designed hasp, c.1920, 10 x 12½ x 8⅝ inches.

Vinyl lunch box: $2,645 for the 1967 Chuck Wagon vinyl lunch box by Mattel, shows cowboy making breakfast, side panel with two different headshots of cowboy, 7 x 8¾ x 4 inches.

Walt Disney celluloid from *Pinocchio*: $12,925 for a 1940 Walt Disney gouache on celluloid from *Pinocchio* depicting the Blue Fairy dubbing Jiminy Cricket as Pinocchio's conscience, applied to an airbrushed background, matted and framed, 5½ x 6 inches with mat.

Weather vane: $1,080,000 for the gilt-molded copper and sheet-iron weather vane "Goddess of Liberty," wearing a liberty cap and holding an American flag, made by William Henis, Philadelphia, mid 19th century, 30 inches.

PAINTING

American portrait: $21,296,000 for the oil-on-canvas portrait *George Washington at Princeton,* by Charles Willson Peale, 1779, with General Washington standing with the Battle of Princeton in the background and the flags of the captured Hessians at his feet, signed and dated in the lower left, 96½ x 61½ inches. Also a record for any single-owner sale of Americana.

PAPER

Disney poster: $138,000 for a Mickey Mouse poster, *The Mad Doctor,* United Artists, 1933, one-sheet (27 x 41 inches), one of only two copies known to exist.

Octavo edition of John James Audubon's *Birds of America*: $132,000 for the first octavo edition of John James Audubon's *Birds of America, from Drawings Made in the United States and Their Territories,* seven volumes, 500 hand-colored lithographic plates, 19th century.

Original comic book cover art: $195,500 for the original cover art for *Batman* No. 11, cover dated June–July 1942, by artists Fred Ray and Jerry Robinson, featuring Batman, Robin, and their arch-nemesis, the Joker.

Single unused postcard: $12,650 for a c.1898 unused postcard advertising Waverly Bicycles, artwork designed by Alphonse Mucha (Czech, 1860–1939).

PHOTOGRAPHY

Any 20th-century photograph at auction (tie): $822,400 for the Edward Weston photograph "The Breast," a warm-toned platinum print, signed, titled, and dated 1923 in pencil, 1921, 7⅜ x 9⅜ inches. Setting the same record and also setting a record for the artist: $822,400 for the Dorothea Lange photograph "White Angel Breadline," flush-mounted, signed and dated 1933 in ink on the image, 13¼ x 10¼ inches.

Adams, Ansel, photographs: $352,000 for a sequence of five Ansel Adams photographs of the San Mateo County coast, titled "Surf Sequence," mounted and signed in pencil, with the Ansel Adams, Carmel, California, studio stamp (BMFA 11), 10⅞ x 13⅛ inches each.

Curtis, Edward S., photographs: $1,416,000 for the Edward S. Curtis large-format photogravures *The North American Indian,* Portfolios 1–20, Volumes 1–20, 1907–30, each approximately 15½ x 11 inches.

POTTERY & PORCELAIN

Clement Massier "Mushroom" Vase: $100,000 for a Clement Massier "Mushroom" vase, made in Golfe-Juan, France, c.1897–99, 13¾ inches high x 8-inch diameter.

Dennis Chinaworks/Tuffin piece: $27,353 (£15,720) for a "March of the Penguins'" vase, designed by Sally Tuffin, resembling an iceberg with a spiraling slope and no fewer than 40 individually modeled black and white birds edging their way down closer to the sea, 7 inches.

Denver Denaura vase: $9,600 for a Denver Denaura squat vase carved with fish, underwater flora, and cresting waves, covered in dark green vellum glaze, considered the best known example of Denaura and the only hand-signed piece by William Long, 11 x 5½ in.

George Jones quail game dish: $57,500 for a George Jones full-nest quail game dish with turquoise ground, 13½ inches.

George Ohr: $84,000 for a vase by George Ohr with two ribbon handles, red and green mottled glaze, and stamped G.E. OHR, Biloxi, Mississippi, 8½ x 5¾ inches.

Meissen bantam cocks: $508,800 for a pair of Meissen porcelain figures of bantam cocks, each bird holding a turquoise berry in its beak and standing on a leaf-shaped base, plumage painted in a kakiemon-style palette (milk-white porcelain decorated with multicolored glazes), c.1732, 7¾ inches high x 9½ inches long and 7⅝ inches high x 9 inches long.

Newcomb College vase: $96,000 for a Newcomb College vase carved by Sadie Irvine, pine trees with green needles on blue trunks, blue green and ivory ground, 1909, 15¼ x 7½ in

Rockingham County pottery: $25,300 for a 5-gallon stoneware churn attributed to Emanuel Stuter, Rockingham County, Virginia, decorated with freehand cobalt blue chicken on front, two applied handles, galleried rim, c.1880, 18¼ inches high.

Royal Worcester vases by George Owen: $102,000 for a pair of Royal Worcester vases and stoppers reticulated by George Owen, pierced and gilt-beaded, with gilt crowned mark for 1906, model No. 871, 9 inches.

SILVER & OTHER METALS

Any escutcheon/Pennsylvania wrought iron: $42,120 for a wrought-iron door escutcheon in the form of an Indian head with feathered headdress, 18th century, 8¼ inches.

Cast-iron doorstop: $38,500 for a Halloween Girl cast-iron doorstop of a young girl in her Halloween costume holding a jack-o'-lantern, by Littco Products, Littlestown, Pennsylvania, 13⅞ 7x 8¾ inches.

Doorknob: $9,234 for a standing elk doorknob with the manufacturer's name, Russell & Erwin, on the reverse and with the patent date, June 6, 1870, stamped into the shank.

Hitching post: $46,000 for a cast-iron "Chinaman" hitching post, painted, late 19th century, 48 inches.

SPORTS

Babe Ruth and Lou Gehrig signed baseball: $98,000 for a baseball signed by Babe Ruth and Lou Gehrig.

Jim Thorpe autograph: $28,000 for the 1940s Jim Thorpe single signed autographed baseball.

TOOLS

Hand tool: $20,240 for an ax head, c.1650, with one side picturing the portrait of a bearded man and the other side a fighting cock.

TOYS, DOLLS, & GAMES

Celluloid Mickey Mouse and Pluto: $10,450 for a celluloid Mickey Mouse Cowboy on Pluto toy, wooden rocking base, wearing original paper hat, windup, early 1930s, with original box, Japan, 8 x 7½ inches.

Dinky No. 108 "Joe 90" in fluorescent orange: $2,661 for a Dinky No. 108 "Joe 90" rare-issue Sam's Car finished in fluorescent orange, lemon interior, with keyless clockwork motor, original box, and inner pictorial stand.

Girl Skipping Rope bank: $57,500 for the J. & E. Stevens cast-iron mechanical bank, Girl Skipping Rope, c.1890.

Popeye rowboat toy: $28,000 for Popeye the Sailor mechanical rowboat toy, manufactured by Hoge, windup, original oars and rudder, in original box, copyright 1935 King Features Syndicate, 15 x 8 inches.

A NOTE TO COLLECTORS

You already know this is a great overall price guide for antiques and collectibles. Each entry is current, every picture is new, and all prices are accurate.

New this year is a Kovel electronic publication designed to keep you up-to-the-minute in the world of collecting. Things change quickly. Important sales produce new record prices. Fakes appear. Rarities are discovered. To keep up with developments, you can read *Kovels on Antiques and Collectibles,* our monthly newsletter. It is now available in two forms, a print edition that is mailed and an electronic edition that is emailed. Both have the same current information on collecting. They are filled with color photographs, about forty per issue. The newsletter reports prices, trends, auction results, Internet sales, and other news for collectors *as it happens.* For a free printed sample of *Kovels on Antiques and Collectibles,* fill out and mail the postage-paid postcard at the back of this book. Our Web site takes electronic subscriptions and also offers FREE pricing information, lists of publications and sources, news, and more. Visit www.kovels.com to keep up on the buy-sell world of antiques.

HOW TO USE THIS BOOK

There are a few rules for using this book. Each listing is arranged in the following manner: CATEGORY (such as Pressed Glass), OBJECT (such as vase), DESCRIPTION (as much information as possible about size, age, color, and pattern). Some types of glass, pottery, and silver are exceptions to this rule. These are listed CATEGORY, PATTERN, OBJECT, DESCRIP-

TION. All items are presumed to be in good condition and undamaged, unless otherwise noted. In most sections, if a maker's name is easily recognized, like Gustav Stickley, we include it near the beginning of the entry. If the maker is obscure, the name may be at the end.

Many of the general glass entries are in special categories: Glass-Art, Glass-Blown, Glass-Bohemian, Glass-Contemporary, Glass-Midcentury, and Glass-Venetian. Major glass factories are listed under factory names. Well-known types of glass, such as Cut, Pressed, Depression, Carnival, etc., can be found in their own categories. You will find silver flatware in either Silver Flatware Plated or Silver Flatware Sterling. There is also a section for Silver Plate, which includes coffeepots, trays, and other plated pieces. Most solid or sterling silver is listed by country, so look for Silver-American, Silver-Danish, Silver-English, etc. Silver jewelry is listed under Jewelry. Most pottery and porcelain is listed by factory name, such as Weller; by item, such as Calendar Plate; in sections like Dinnerware or Kitchen; or in a special section, such as Pottery-Art, Pottery-Contemporary, Pottery-Midcentury, etc.

We made several editorial decisions. A butter dish is a "butter." A salt dish is called a "salt" to differentiate it from a saltshaker. It is always "sugar and creamer," never "creamer and sugar." Political collectors often refer to "pinbacks," the round celluloid or tin pins decorated with candidates' names and faces. We use the word "button" instead of "pinback." The word "button" is also used when referring to fasteners on clothing. Where one dimension is given, it is the height; if the object is round, the dimension is the diameter. The height of a picture is listed before width. Glass is clear unless a color is indicated.

This book does *not* include price listings for fine art paintings, antiquities, stamps, coins, or most types of books. *Big Little Books* and similar children's books *are* included. Comic books are listed only in special categories like Superman, but original comic art and cels *are* listed in their own categories.

Prices for items pictured can be found in the appropriate category. Look for the matching entry with the abbreviation "Illus."

Prices are reported from all parts of the United States, Canada, and Europe, then converted to U.S. dollars at the rate of exchange at the time of the sale. The average rate of exchange between June 2005 and June 2006 was about $0.85 U.S. to $1 Canadian and $1.23 U.S. to ¤1 (one Euro). Prices are from auctions, shops, Internet sales, and shows. Every price is checked for accuracy, but we are not responsible for errors.

We cannot answer your letters asking for price information, but please write if you have any requests for categories to be included in future editions or any corrections to the paragraphs or prices.

When you see us at shows and flea markets, stop and say hello. Don't be surprised if we ask for your suggestions. You can write to us at P.O. Box 22200-K, Beachwood, Ohio 44122, or visit us at our Web site, www.kovels.com.

RALPH & TERRY KOVEL
July 2006

ACKNOWLEDGMENTS

We give special thanks to those who helped us with pictures and deeds: Allard Auctions; Auction Team Köln; Aumann Auctions; Bertoia Auctions; Brunk Auctions; Christie's; Conestoga Auction Co.; Craftsman Arts & Crafts Auctions; Doyle New York; Early's Auction Co.; Freeman's 200; Glass-Works Auctions; Green Valley Auctions; Hake's Americana & Collectibles; Heritage-Slater Americana; Jackson's International Auctioneers & Appraisers; James D. Julia; Majolica Auctions (Michael Strawser); Mastro Auctions; McMasters Harris Auction Co.; Morphy's Auctions; Neal Auction Co.; New Orleans Auction Galleries; Norman C. Heckler & Co.; Rago Arts & Auctions Center; Random Treasures Auction; Randy Inman Auctions; Robert C. Eldred Co.; Skinner; Smith House Toys & Auction Co.; Sotheby's; Tom Harris Auctions; Woody's Auctions.

To the others in the antiques trade who knowingly or unknowingly contributed to this book, we say "thank you": 4th Dimension Collectibles; 20th Century Art & Design; Absentee Auctions; Adams Auction Co.; Aleph-Bet Books; American Bottle Auctions; American Cut Glass Association; American Political Items Collectors; Anderson Auctions; Andre Ammelounx; Ark Antiques; Baker's International Antiques & Collectibles; BBR Auctions; Behold (Larry Gottheim); Bottles & Bygones World; Burton Country Village Antiques; Carlton Antique Toys; Charlton Hall Galleries; Cincinnati Art Galleries; Clars Auction Gallery; Coffman's Antiques Market; Copake Auction; Cottone Auctions; Country Classic Antiques; Crown Jewels of the Wire; Cyr Auction Gallery; Daguerreian Society; Daniel Auction Co.; Delmarva Acquisitions & Appraisals; Dianne Vetromile; Disney–Just Just Kids Nostalgia; DuMouchelles; Early American History Auctions; Faganarms; Fairfield Auction; Federation of Historical Bottle Collectors; Fenton Art Glass Collectors of America; Fox Auctions; Frank and Grace Zuest; Frank H. Boos Gallery; Frank's Antiques & Auctions; Galley at Knotty Pine; Garth's Arts & Antiques; Gene Harris Auctions; George H. Labarre Galleries; Gisela Antiques; Great Antique Bottles; Greg and Barbara Hall; Harold R. Nestler; Hartley's Antiques; Heisey Collectors of America; Hi+Lo Modern; High Desert Books, Bottles & Collectibles; Hoosier Peddler; Hummel Collector's Club; Ian & Graemes Bottles; International Antiques Mall; Ivey-Selkirk Auctioneers; Jantiques & Collectibles; Joy Luke Fine Arts Brokers & Auctioneers; Joyce Porcelli Art Gallery; Just Art Pottery; Keystone Toy Trader; Lang's Sporting Collectables; Last Moving Picture Co.; Leslie Hindman Auctioneers; Live Free or Die Antique Tool Auctions; Livingston's Auction; Los Angeles Modern Auctions; Manion's International Auction House; McMurray Antiques & Auctions; Metz Superlative Auction; Michael Ivankovich Antiques & Auction Co.; Monsen & Baer; Mystic Light of the Aladdin Knights; National Association for Milk Bottle Collectors; National Bottle Auction; Nelson Rarities; New England Antiques Journal; Noel Barrett Antiques & Auctions; North Country Bottle Shop; Northeast Auctions; O.J. Club; Old Barn Auction; Old

Sleepy Eye; Old Toy Shop; Old Toy Town; Old World Auctions; One Man's Junk; Only Mint (Harvey K. Rainess); Page Button Auctions; Paper & Advertising Collectors' Marketplace; Past Pleasures Antiques; Peggy McClard Antiques; Petroleum Collectibles; Pewter Collectors Club of America; Phoenix Militaria Corp.; Pook & Pook; Potties Specialists Auctions; R.O. Schmitt Fine Arts; Rachel Davis Fine Arts; Rich Penn Country Store & Advertising; Richard Opfer Auctioneering; RJG Antiques; Robert Edward Auctions; Ron Smith; RSL Auction Co.; Ruby Lane; Russ Cochran's Comic Art Auction; Schrager Auction Galleries; Second Childhood NYC; Seeck Auctions; Showcase Antique Center; Sloans & Kenyon Auctioneers & Appraisers; Smith and Jones Pottery Auctions; Sold USA Auctions; Southern Folk Pottery Collectors Society; Steeplechase Antiques; Steve Butler; Strawser's Auction; Swann Galleries Auctioneers; Tea Leaf Club International; Team's Tiffany Treasures; Ted Kromer Antique Shows; Theriault's; Thomaston Place Auction Galleries; TIAS; Toothpick Bulletin; Touch of Glass; Toy Shop; Trade Card Place Auction; Trader Fred's Toys of Yore; Tradewinds Auctions; Treadway Gallery; Treadway/Toomey Galleries; Treasures of the Talking Wire; Vicki and Bruce Waasdorp; Waddington's; Wayne and Phyllis Hilt; Weschler's; White House Treasures; William Morford Auctions; Willis Henry Auctions.

We thank those at Random House Reference for working through the unique way we write this price book. Our editor Rahel Lerner was a pleasure to work with. David Naggar, president of Random House Information Group; Sheryl Stebbins, vice president and publisher of Random House Reference; Elizabeth Bennett, publishing director; Celeste Sollod, editorial director; Patricia Dublin and Beth Levy, associate managing editors; William Tracy, editorial assistant; Lisbeth Dyer, senior production editor; Lisa Montebello, production manager; Fabrizio LaRocca, creative director; and Geraldine Sarmiento, designer, all worked together to create the new look of this book. Merri Ann Morrell at Precision Graphics has solved the problems of computer printing, digital photos, and other electronic questions. She deserves a double thank you for her work.

The details and hard work required to record prices, assemble photos and information, check accuracy and spelling, and solve many other problems are all done by our staff first. We thank Carmie Amata, Lisa Bell, Linda Coulter, Grace DeFrancisco, Marcia Goldberg, Evelyn Hayes, Katie Karrick, Kim Kovel, Liz Lillis, Heidi Makela, Tina McBean, Nancy Saada, Julie Seaman, June Smith, and Cherrie Smrekar. Pictures come from many sources and they are all sized, positioned, and digitally enhanced by Karen Kneisley, our picture editor. Gay Hunter has kept the records and led the group for years and continues to keep us on schedule. She reads every word and even corrects our spelling errors. She solves the problems of changing information and changing technology. We thank all of them. We know that the book is a group effort even though our names appear on the cover.

A. WALTER made pate-de-verre glass under contract at the Daum glassworks from 1908 to 1914. He started his own firm in Nancy, France, in 1919. Pieces made before 1914 are signed *Daum, Nancy* with a cross. After 1919 the signature is *A. Walter Nancy*.

Bookends, Amber, Squirrel Resting On Green Mottled Base, Signed, 5 x 4 3/4 In. 8625.00
Bowl, Green, Yellow, Blue, Signed, 3 3/4 In. 1553.00
Bowl, Iguana, Black Amethyst, Terra-Cotta Bowl, Signed, 3 1/2 x 6 3/4 In. 345.00
Bowl, Locusts, Pinecones, Brown, Green, Blue, Signed, 3 1/2 In. 8912.00
Bowl, Yellow To Orange, Green Leaves, Brown Berries, 7 In. 4600.00
Change Dish, Beetle Form, Brown & Black, Yellow Tray, Signed, 4 x 3 1/2 In. 2645.00
Change Dish, Scarab Form, Brown & Black, Green Tray, Signed, 5 In. 3565.00
Dish, Fish Swimming In Pond, Concentric Waves, Green, 7 x 5 In. 6038.00
Figurine, Frog On Pedestal, Light To Medium Green, Mottled Green, Purple, Signed, 2 In. 3450.00
Figurine, Nude Woman Sleeping On Flowing Leaf Bed, Tree Trunk, Signed, 9 x 6 1/2 In. 8050.00
Figurine, Seal On Rock, Yellow, c.1910, 6 1/2 In. 1434.00
Figurine, Woman, Seated, Hugging Knees, c.1919, 4 In. 1076.00
Lamp, Wrought Iron, Edgar Brandt, c.1920, 16 x 6 1/4 In. 9600.00
Paperweight, Butterfly, Green Base, Oval, Nancy, 1 1/2 x 4 x 3 1/4 In. 3000.00
Tray, Blue, Yellow & Brown Inclusions, Leaf, Blossom, Berries, Nancy, 5 x 2 1/2 In. 1850.00
Tray, Brown & Black Beetle, Lavender Shaded To Ocher, Signed, 3 x 9 In. 2185.00
Tray, Green Base, Mottled Yellow, Orange Molded Fish, Signed, 5 1/2 In. 810.00
Tray, Henri Berge, c.1920, 13 1/2 x 7 1/4 In. 9600.00
Vase, Pottery, Trees, Signed, Nancy, 9 1/2 In. 1800.00

ABC plates, or children's alphabet plates, were most popular from 1780 to 1860, but are still being made. The letters on the plate were meant as teaching aids for children learning to read. The plates were made of pottery, porcelain, metal, or glass. Mugs and other items were also made with alphabet decorations.

Cup, Rabbit, Stangl, 2 5/8 x 4 1/4 In. 55.00
Plate, 2 Rabbits, Alphabet Border, Signing Alphabet, Aynsley, 8 1/4 In. 550.00
Plate, 3 Dutch Children, Sign Language, Anysley & Co., Blue Transfer, 1800s, 6 1/2 In. 110.00
Plate, American Sports Base Ball Striker & Catcher, 6 1/4 In. 303.00
Plate, Animal Decal, Cartoon, Lord Nelson Pottery, Staffordshire, England, 7 In. 35.00
Plate, Bull Hunt, Staffordshire, 7 3/4 In. 66.00
Plate, Fox Hunt, Blue Transfer, 7 1/4 In. 320.00
Plate, Girl & Boy Playing Hoops, Tin, Late 1800s, 3 In. 210.00
Plate, Hen & Chicks, Glass, 6 In. 55.00
Plate, Higbee, Vaseline, Moser Glass Company, 6 1/2 In. 30.00
Plate, Hotel Brighton, Staffordshire, 7 1/2 In. 175.00
Plate, Ice Cream, Glass, Federal Glass Co., Columbus, Ohio, c.1900, 5 3/4 x 4 3/8 In. 140.00
Plate, Jointed Wooden Dolls, Sign Language, Green Transfer, H. Aynsley, 1800s, 6 1/2 In. 165.00
Plate, Owl Classroom, Sign Language, Blue Transfer, H. Aynsley, 1800s, 6 1/2 In. 220.00
Plate, Rabbits, In Sunday's Best Clothes, Pink Transfer, Aynsley, 8 1/4 In. 440.00
Plate, Rub A Dub Dub, 3 Men In A Tub, Ironstone, Wood & Sons, Early 1900s, 7 In. 39.00
Plate, Sancho Panza & Dapple, Frosted Center, Glass, 1880s, 6 In. 95.00
Plate, Steeplechase, Blue Transfer, Diamond Shape Center, White, 7 1/4 In. 275.00
Plate, Tea Party, Sign Language, H. Aynsley, 1800s, 6 1/2 In. 248.00
Plate, Who Killed Cock Robin, Tin, Late 1800s, 7 3/4 In. .... 95.00 to 120.00

ABINGDON POTTERY was established in 1908 by Raymond E. Bidwell as the Abingdon Sanitary Manufacturing Company. The company started making art pottery in 1934. The factory ceased production of art pottery in 1950.

Bookends, Horse Head, Black, 6 1/2 In. 100.00
Bowl, Center, Shell, Blue Gray, 3 x 12 x 7 3/4 In. 35.00
Bowl, Shell, Sea Green, No. 533, 1940-48, 11 1/4 x 8 In. 35.00
Console, 2 Acanthus Leaf Handles, High Gloss, Blue, No. 564, 2 1/2 x 11 x 7 In. 15.00
Console, Blue, No. 532, 1941-50, 3 3/4 x 14 1/2 In. 25.00
Console, High Gloss, Yellow, 5 3/4 x 14 1/2 x 4 1/3 In. 40.00
Console, Multicolored, Flower, Gold Gilt Trim, 17 x 7 In. 50.00

Cookie Jar, Choo-Choo, Green Roof, Wheels, No. 651, 11 3/4 In. 52.00
Cookie Jar, Cookie Time, No. 653, 9 x 8 In. 185.00
Cookie Jar, Hippo, 1940s, 8 1/4 In. ....252.00 to 295.00
Cookie Jar, Little Old Lady, c.1940, 9 In. 238.00
Cookie Jar, Teepee, 11 1/2 In. 308.00
Figurine, Pelican, Fish In Mouth, Satin White, 4 3/4 In. 75.00
Flowerpot, High Gloss, White, Ribbed, No. 151, 5 In. 25.00
Planter, Fan Shape, Ribbon, Light Blue, 4 1/2 x 8 In. 27.50
Planter, Ruffled Edge, 2 x 7 x 10 1/2 In. 8.00
Tile, Coolie, Asian Man, Sitting Among Bamboo, Yellow, Square, 1937, 5 In. 195.00
Vase, 2 Handles, High Gloss, Blue, No. 522, 8 3/4 In. 50.00
Vase, 2 Handles, High Gloss, White, Art Deco, No. 114, 9 3/4 In. 75.00
Vase, 2 Handles, White, No. 515, 7 In. 28.50
Vase, 2 Handles, Yellow, 10 x 8 In. 45.00
Vase, Blue, No. 118, 1940-46, 10 x 6 1/2 In. 34.00
Vase, Blue, No. 325, 1934-47 .... 40.00
Vase, Blue, White Flowers, No. 563, 8 3/4 In. 60.00
Vase, Cornucopia, High Blue, White Flower, No. 569, 4 3/4 In. 50.00
Vase, Deco Style, No. 154, 9 In. 70.00
Vase, Double Cornucopia, White, No. 482, 11 In. 35.00
Vase, Dusty Blue, No. 117, 1938-49, 9 3/4 In. 45.00
Vase, Fan, Blue, No. 513, 9 x 9 1/2 In. ....38.00 to 45.00
Vase, Flowers, Gold Decoration, No. 557, 10 1/2 In. 125.00
Vase, Glossy White, Art Deco, Squared Handles, Greek Key, Cylinder, 9 3/4 x 6 1/2 In. 60.00
Vase, Glossy, Gray, No. 101, 9 1/2 x 6 1/4 In. 85.00
Vase, High Gloss, Yellow, Art Deco, Handle, c.1940, 9 3/4 x 6 3/8 In. 55.00
Vase, Ornate Handles, Ribbed, Green, 8 3/4 In. 26.00
Vase, Pillow, Blue, Art Deco, Sailing Ship, No. 494, c.1940, 7 x 6 3/8 x 3 In. 40.00
Vase, Red, Buttressed Handles, Shou Pattern, High Gloss, No. 103, 10 x 6 In. 115.00
Vase, Ribbon, Aqua Green, No. 462, 1939-50, 4 x 7 1/2 In. 34.00
Vase, Scalloped, Low, Dusty Rose, Matte, No. 564, 1942-50, 2 3/4 x 11 In. 32.00
Wall Pocket, Morning Glory, Blue, Shiny, No. 377, 8 1/2 x 6 1/4 x 4 In. 45.00
Window Box, Aqua, Matte, No. 437, c.1938-50, 3 x 10 x 3 3/4 In. 36.00

ADAMS china was made by William Adams and Sons of Staffordshire, England. The firm was founded in 1769 and became part of the Wedgwood Group in 1966. The name "Adams" appeared on various items through 1998. All types of tablewares and useful wares were made. Other pieces of Adams may be found listed under Flow Blue and Tea Leaf Ironstone.

Bowl, Adams' Rose, 2 7/8 x 5 In. 11.00
Creamer, Adams' Rose, Black & Brown Rainbow, Spatter, Staffordshire, c.1840, 3 1/2 In. 215.00
Cup & Saucer, Adams' Rose, Red, Purple, Spatter, Staffordshire, c.1840 .... 1315.00
Plate, Adams' Rose, Blue, Spatter, Staffordshire, c.1840, 8 3/4 In., 6 Piece 568.00
Plate, Soup, Adams' Rose, Red, Green, Blue, Rainbow, Spatter, Staffordshire, c.1840, 10 In. 359.00
Platter, Adams' Rose, Blue, Spatter, Staffordshire, c.1840, 12 1/2 In. 655.00
Platter, Adams' Rose, Multicolored, Scalloped Rim, 17 1/4 x 14 In. 1045.00
Platter, Jedburgh Abbey, River, Flower Border, Blue Transfer, 13 1/4 x 17 In. 460.00
Tea Bowl & Saucer, Adams' Rose, Blue, Spatter, Staffordshire, c.1840 .... 190.00
Tea Bowl & Saucer, Adams' Rose, Green, Spatter, c.1840 .... 777.00
Teapot, Adams' Rose, Purple, Blue-Black, Brown, Rainbow, Spatter, c.1840, 6 In. 390.00

ADVERTISING containers and products sold in the old country store are now all collectibles. These stores, with the crackers in a barrel and a potbellied stove, are a symbol of an earlier, less hectic time. Listed here are many of the advertising items. Other similar pieces may be found under the product name, such as Planters Peanuts. We have tried to list items in the logical places, so large store fixtures will be found under the Architectural category, enameled tin dishes under Graniteware, paper items in the Paper category, etc. Store fixtures, cases, signs, and other items that have no advertising as part

of the decoration are listed in the Store category. For more information, see *Kovels' Advertising Collectibles Price List.* The early Dr Pepper logo included a period after "Dr," but it was dropped in 1950. We list all Dr. Pepper items without a period so they alphabetize together.

Ad, Cream Of Wheat Is Ready, J.M. Flagg, Frame, c.1908, 10 x 14 In. 17.00
Ad, Cream Of Wheat, Mail Goes, N.C. Wyeth, Frame, c.1907, 10 x 14 In. 17.00
Ad, Time To Re-Tire Get A Fisk, Paper Lithograph, Frame, c.1926, 13 1/2 x 11 In. 90.00
Ashtray, Antikamnia, Woman Sitting In Rocker, Tin Lithograph, 3 1/4 x 4 3/4 In. 154.00
Ashtray, DuPont Electroplating Division, Oval, 5 3/4 In. 41.00
Ashtray, Great Falls Select Fine Beer, Red Pyro Glaze, Milk Glass, Round, 5 1/4 In. 12.00
Ashtray, Kuntz's Old German Lager, Enamel, Yellow, Rectangle 30.00
Ashtray, Lucky Strike Cigarettes, Ceramic, Cigarette Pack, 5 1/4 x 4 1/4 In. 100.00
Ashtray, Rolls-Royce, Spirit Of Ecstasy, Round Base, c.1930, 5 x 5 1/2 In. 470.00
Bag, Buffalo Corn Gluten Feed, 100 Pounds Net, Gunny Sack, 1800s 58.00
Bag, Carter's Seed Peanuts, Heavy Duty, 50 Lb., 33 x 18 1/2 In. 53.00
Bag, Maine Champion Potatoes, Walter Reed, Fort Fairfield, Maine, Burlap 12.00
Banner, Buffalo Bill's Wild West In Town, Textile, 16 x 24 In. 1390.00
Banner, Dr. Daniels' Medicines For Your Stock, Cloth, 10 3/4 x 23 1/2 In. 1760.00
Banner, Fish Hook Chewing Tobacco, Canvas, Fisherman, Holds Hooks, 29 x 61 In. 300.00
Banner, Kinney Bros., Sweet Caporal, Butterflies, Frame, 1888, 31 x 20 In. 2040.00
Banner, Lee Jeans, Cloth, Gold 90.00
Banner, Marble's Game Getter Gun, Specialties For Sportsmen, c.1900, 33 In. 419.00
Banner, Wm. S. Kimball, High Grade Cigarettes, Ballet Queens, 1888, 33 x 18 In. 3285.00
Basket, Miller's Furniture, Carnival Glass, Open Edge, Marigold 40.00
Bin, Bacon Stickney & Co. Gun Powder, 13 1/4 x 13 1/2 x 19 1/2 In. 84.00
Bin, Beech-Nut Chewing Tobacco, Tin Lithograph, 8 1/2 x 10 x 8 In. 468.00
Bin, Blue Tiger Chewing Tobacco, 5 Cent, Blue, Lorillard, 11 1/2 x 8 x 6 In. 990.00
Bin, Nic Nac Tobacco, Dog, Tobacco Pack, 12 x 8 In. 1540.00
Bin, Sweet Cuba Tobacco, Tin, 8 x 9 1/2 In. 963.00
Bin, W.H. Granger Coffee, Country Store, 19 1/2 x 13 In. 580.00
Bin, Woodson Spice Co., Roasted Coffee, 50 Pound, Hinged Lid, 23 x 15 x 15 In. 825.00
Books may be included in the Paper category.
Booklet, Jell-O, Girl, Holding Box Of Jell-O, 1912 .... 15.00
Booklet, Jell-O, Girl, Holding Fruit Basket, 1920 .... 10.00
Booklet, Moth Proof Closets For Your Home, Mitchell Mfg., Alabama, 2 Pages 10.00
Booklet, Mullens Celebrated Hornets Nest Liniment, Charlotte, N.C., 4 Pages 15.00
Booklet, S.A. Millard & Co., Clayville, N.Y., 1879, 3 Pages 15.00
Bottles are listed in their own category.
Bottle Carrier, Nehi Soda, 6-Pack, Cardboard, Bottle Master, Atlanta, 1949 .... 10.00
Bottle Carrier, Watkins, Wood, Metal Handle, 2 Drawers, 9 x 21 In. 120.00
Bottle Openers are listed in their own category.
Bottle Topper, 7Up, Fresh Up, Boy, In Beanie, Cardboard, 1949, 8 x 5 In. 12.00
Bottle Topper, Enjoy A 7Up Float, Green Arrow 26.00
Bowl, Isaac Benesch & Sons, Carnival Glass, Amethyst, Ruffled Edge 275.00
Bowl, Ogden Furniture, Carnival Glass, Amethyst, Ruffled Edge 700.00
Bowl, Zodiac, Sunray DX Oil Company, Prairie Green, Frankoma, 7 In. 33.00
Box, see also Box category.
Box, Allen's Foot-Ease, Yellow, Black, Cardboard, June 30, 1906, 8 x 14 x 3 In. 154.00
Box, Alphabets Crackers, ZuZu Clown, Block Shape, Nabisco, 3 x 3 x 3 In. 99.00
Box, Auto Brand Shirts, Cardboard, Car, Lewis Meier Co., 19 x 11 x 2 In. 230.00
Box, Babe Ruth Underwear, Cardboard, 9 3/4 In. 605.00
Box, Babe Ruth Underwear, Contents, 1930s 897.00
Box, Beer, J. Rapp & Son., S.F., Red Paint, Holds Quarts, 24 x 7 In. 120.00
Box, Black Hawk Soap, Wood, Hinged Lid, Labels, Rock Island, Ill., 4 1/2 x 14 In. 300.00
Box, Celebrated Oregon Kidney Tea, Horses, Canoe, Hoyt Chemical Co., 4 x 2 In. 187.00
Box, Cereal, Albers Pearls Of Wheat, Prospector, Cardboard, 3 Lb., 7 x 5 In. 253.00
Box, Cereal, Atlas Oats, Cardboard, Image Of Atlas, Yellow Ground, Red Letters, 7 1/2 In. 120.00
Box, Cereal, Blue Jay Rolled Oats, Cardboard, 3 Lb., 9 3/4 x 5 1/2 In. 690.00
Box, Cereal, Dacotah Rolled Oats, Indian, Andrew Kuehn Co., 7 Oz., 9 1/2 x 5 1/2 In. 908.00

Advertising, Box, Display, Bull Dog Jar Rubbers, Red, Double Lip, Cardboard, 12 x 10 x 7 In.

Advertising, Box, Display, Ferry Seeds, Flower Seeds, Label, Oak, 9 3/4 x 11 1/2 In.

Advertising, Box, Display, Union Leader Tobacco, Smoke Or Chew, Cardboard, 12 x 9 1/2 In.

Box, Cereal, Kamp, Rolled Oats, Cardboard, 3 Lb., 9 1/2 x 5 1/2 In. 550.00
Box, Cereal, Kellogg's Corn Flakes, Pep, Krumbles, Red, Black, c.1939, 11 x 7 x 3 In. 55.00
Box, Cereal, Poehler Rolled Oats, Cardboard Lithograph, Bar Image, 9 1/2 x 5 In. 100.00
Box, Cereal, Rolled Oats, Scout Cabin, Cardboard, 9 1/2 x 5 1/2 In. 330.00
Box, Cereal, Ube See Oatmeal, Girl Smiling, Cardboard, 3 Lb., 9 1/2 x 5 1/2 In. 220.00
Box, Cover, National Remedy Co., N.Y., Japanese Oil, Wood, Dovetailed, 9 x 11 3/4 In. 75.00
Box, Curtis' Zapote Gum, Split Lid, 7 1/4 x 8 In. 253.00
Box, Daisy Air Rifles, 1/2 Doz. 1000 Shot, Wood, Plymouth, Mich., 5 x 38 x 7 In. 104.00
Box, Diamond Crystal Salt Co., Shaker Sister, Salt Holder, Pine, 12 x 17 In. 470.00
Box, Display, Bull Dog Jar Rubbers, Red, Double Lip, Cardboard, 12 x 10 x 7 In. . . . . *ILLUS* 303.00
Box, Display, Cameron & Cameron's Fatima Cigarettes, 17 1/4 x 13 1/2 In. 330.00
Box, Display, Cigar, Kalamazoo Bats, 4 For 10 Cents, c.1887, 14 x 8 x 5 In. 1045.00
Box, Display, Ferry Seeds, Flower Seeds, Label, Oak, 9 3/4 x 11 1/2 In. . . . . *ILLUS* 231.00
Box, Display, Gold Tip Gum, Cardboard, 20 Boxes, 4 3/4 x 6 In. 358.00
Box, Display, Hershey's, Almond Milk Chocolate, 7 1/2 x 5 3/4 In. 75.00
Box, Display, Smart Gum, Peppermint, Cardboard, 20 Packs, 3 1/2 x 6 x 4 1/4 In. 358.00
Box, Display, Stickney & Poor's Pure Mustard, Extra Fine, Wood, 12 x 15 In. 358.00
Box, Display, Union Leader Tobacco, Smoke Or Chew, Cardboard, 12 x 9 1/2 In. . . . . *ILLUS* 1018.00
Box, Display, Wrigley's Nips Gum, Inside Glass Lid, 8 3/4 x 13 1/4 x 6 1/4 In. 358.00
Box, Display, Yueta Chewing Gum, Paper Over Cardboard, Glass, 5 x 8 1/2 x 1 In. 77.00
Box, Dr. Herrick's Sugar Coated Pills, Man, Wood, Oval, Wrapper, 2 In. 154.00
Box, Dr. Kilmer's Swamp Root, Kidney Liver & Bladder Cure, Wood, 10 x 11 In. 154.00
Box, Dr. King's New Discovery For Consumption, Wood, 18 x 22 x 9 In. 60.00
Box, Dr. Miles Nervine, Restorative, 2-Faced Man, Wood, Dovetailed, 11 x 9 x 9 1/2 In. 120.00
Box, Duble-Heder Ice Cream Cake Cones, Maryland Baking Co., 1934, 4 x 7 In. 315.00
Box, Electric Brand Bitters, 2 Doz., Small, Wood, 11 x 17 1/2 x 10 In. 77.00
Box, Fairbanks Gold Dust Washing Powder, Twins, Lever Bros., 8 3/4 x 6 In. 72.00
Box, Falstaff Beer, Cardboard, Staples, 12 Bottle Capacity, 10 x 12 x 16 In. 12.95
Box, Faultless Pepsin Gum Chips, 3 x 1 1/2 x 3/8 In. 187.00
Box, Frank Miller's Peerless Blacking, Uncle Sam Shaving, Wood, 3 x 12 x 9 In. 235.00
Box, Fresh Up With 7Up, Santa Fe, Mexico, White, Red, Temple Mfg., 4 x 19 x 12 In. 14.00
Box, Gamble's Small Arms Ammunition, Wood, 16 1/2 x 5 7/8 x 5 1/4 In. 120.00
Box, Hegeman & Co.'s Camphor Ice, For Sore Lips, Chapped Hands, 2 1/2 x 2 In. 120.00
Box, Hollingshead's, Hoof Packing, Contents, 5 x 4 3/4 x 2 1/2 In. 230.00
Box, Malt-Nutrine, Greatest Of Tonics, Anheuser-Busch, Wood, 10 x 15 x 6 In. 66.00
Box, Marshall's Prepared Cubeb For Catarrh, Paper Lithograph, 3 1/2 x 7 1/4 In. 157.00
Box, Murine Eye Remedy, For Eyes That Need Care, Wood, Dovetailed, 4 1/2 x 7 In. 275.00
Box, Nabisco Clowns Cookie, Animal Cracker Type, String Handle, 1930s, 3 x 5 In. 115.00
Box, Nesbitt California Orange Soda, Wood, Metal Corners, For 24 Bottles, 1966 . . . . 61.00
Box, Peters High Velocity, 12 Gauge, Wood, 14 1/2 x 9 1/2 x 9 In. 49.00
Box, Portland Cracker Co., Wood, 14 x 15 1/2 In. 468.00
Box, Psychine, Greatest Of Tonics, T.A. Slocum Co., Wood, Dovetailed, 12 x 10 1/2 In. 88.00
Box, Remington Express, 20 Gauge, Wood, 8 1/2 x 15 x 8 In. 47.00
Box, Remington Shur Shot, 20 Gauge, Wood, 14 3/4 x 8 1/4 x 7 3/4 In. 23.00

To remove a crayon mark from paper, coat it with a thin layer of rubber cement, let it dry, then rub it off.

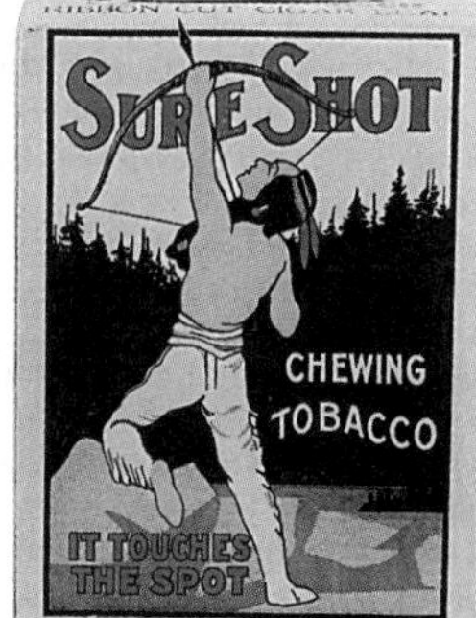

Advertising, Box, Sure Shot Tobacco, 2-Sided, Cardboard, 13 x 10 3/8 x 7 3/4 In.

Box, Remington UMC Nitro, Wood, 13 1/2 x 6 x 5 1/4 In. 30.00
Box, Remington UMC, Metallic Cartridge, Wood, 14 3/8 x 7 3/4 x 6 1/8 In. 23.00
Box, Remington UMS Nitro Club, 16 Gauge, Wood, 14 3/4 x 9 x 8 1/4 In. 42.00
Box, Security Stock Powder, Farmer, Animals, $1.00 Per Package, 10 1/2 x 7 1/2 In. 580.00
Box, Seed, D.M. Ferry & Co., 11 1/2 x 7 In. 193.00
Box, Seed, E.J. Bowen, Girls Planting Seeds, Wood, 9 x 11 x 7 1/2 In. 358.00
Box, Seed, Ferry, Choice Flower Seeds, Children, Garden, Wood, 9 x 11 x 7 In. 209.00
Box, Seed, Lewis Atwood & Son, Selected Seeds, Winterport, Me., 1800s 165.00
Box, Seed, Mandeville & King Co. Flower, Wood, Paper Lithograph, 4 x 19 In. 145.00
Box, Seed, Mandeville & King Co., 12 x 4 1/2 In. 65.00
Box, Seed, Portland Flower, Couple Playing Lawn Tennis, 7 3/8 x 9 5/8 x 5 In. 255.00
Box, Seed, Rice's Flower, Oak, 9 1/2 x 11 x 6 1/2 In. 330.00
Box, St. Jacob's Oil, Great German Remedy, Wood, Stenciled, Lid, 5 x 7 x 7 In. 70.00
Box, Sure Shot Tobacco, 2-Sided, Cardboard, 13 x 10 3/8 x 7 3/4 In. .... *ILLUS* 908.00
Box, Sylvan Chewing Gum, Cardboard, Lithograph, 2 Piece, 6 1/4 x 3 3/8 x 1 1/2 In. 440.00
Box, Tobacco, Log Cabin, Paper Over Wood, Hinged, Black Man, Log Cabin, 1870s 880.00
Box, Tobacco, Old Virginia Log Cabin, Wood, c.1880, 16 x 14 1/2 x 9 1/4 In. 770.00
Box, Tongaline For Rheumatism, Neuralgia, Wood, Dovetailed, 8 1/2 x 11 1/2 x 7 In. 64.00
Box, Warner's Safe Cure, Keep In A Cool Place, Wood, Dovetailed, 13 x 9 x 10 In. 104.00
Box, Warner's White Wine & Tar, Best Cough Remedy On Earth, Wood, 13 x 20 x 9 In. 154.00
Box, Watkin's Remedies, J.R. Watkin's Med. Co., Wood, 15 x 25 x 10 In. 59.00
Box, Western Super X, 410 Gauge, Wood, 14 1/4 x 6 1/4 x 5 1/2 In. 89.00
Box, Winchester Nublack, 20 Gauge, Wood, 14 1/4 x 8 1/2 x 7 3/4 In. 23.00
Box, Winchester Repeater, 410 Gauge, Wood, 14 3/8 x 11 3/8 x 5 5/8 In. 172.00
Box, Winchester Super Speed, 410 Gauge, Wood, 14 x 5 3/4 x 5 1/2 In. 99.00
Box, Winchester, Short Rim, 22 Gauge, Wood, 15 1/2 x 11 3/4 x 4 3/4 In. 23.00
Broom Holder, Garland Stoves, Ranges, Somers Bros., Tin Lithograph, 4 1/2 x 5 In. 358.00
Broom Holder, Wilbur's Cocoa, Image Of Can With Cupid Stirring Cocoa, 4 x 2 In. 300.00
Broom Rack, Schmidt's Blue Ribbon Bread, 3 Loaves, Masonite, 2-Sided, 30 x 25 In. 145.00
Bullet Board, Nosler, 30 Bullets, Elk, 9 1/2 x 17 In. 288.00
Cabinet, Baby Ruth, Butterfinger, Curtis Candy, Maple, 1930s, 22 x 16 3/4 x 11 In. 136.00
Cabinet, DeLaval Cream Separators, Tin Lithograph, Oak, 25 3/4 x 17 3/4 In. 1265.00
Cabinet, Diamond Dyes, Children With Balloon, Tin Lithograph, c.1908, 24 x 15 In. 1870.00
Cabinet, Diamond Dyes, Fairy, 10 Cents, Wells & Richardson, 30 5/8 x 24 In. 3300.00
Cabinet, Diamond Dyes, Governess, Wells & Richardson, c.1906, 30 x 22 x 10 In. 382.00
Cabinet, Dr. Daniels' Veterinary Medicines, Oak, Tin Door Panel, 22 x 8 x 29 In. 2645.00
Cabinet, Dr. Daniels' Veterinary Medicines, Tin Lithograph, Embossed, 27 x 21 In. 5170.00
Cabinet, Dr. J.N. Norwood's Veterinary Medicines, Counter, 29 x 18 x 8 1/2 In. 1155.00
Cabinet, Dr. Lesure's Veterinary Medicines, Horse's Head, 27 x 7 In. ....3575.00 to 5610.00
Cabinet, Humphrey's Homeopathic Specifics, Maple, Red Stain, Tin Panel, 21 x 10 In. 4025.00
Cabinet, Milwards, Needles, 3 Drawers, Walnut, Glass Panels, c.1875, 22 x 9 1/2 In. 575.00
Cabinet, Munyon's Homeopathic Home Remedies, Tin Lithograph, 11 x 14 In. 1485.00
Cabinet, R.J. Reynolds, Tobacco, Oak, Walnut Finish, Line Inlay, Glass Doors, 14 x 14 In. 288.00
Cabinet, Remington, 22 Caliber, Wood, Glass Front, 5 Columns, 10 x 9 1/4 In. 283.00

Cabinet, Remington, Fine American Made Pocket Knives, Glass, 1930s, 12 x 29 In. 206.00
Cabinet, Sergeant's Dog Medicines, Boy, Dog, 1930s, 14 x 12 x 6 1/2 In. 1155.00
Cabinet, Spool, Clark's O.N.T., 2 Drawers, Walnut, 8 x 22 In. 255.00
Cabinet, Spool, Clark's, Mile-End Thread, 2 Drawers, Ruby Glass Inserts, 22 x 14 In. 300.00
Cabinet, Spool, J. & P. Coats', Oak, Leather Inserts, 4 Drawers, 12 x 29 In. 220.00
Cabinet, Squibb Aspirin, Mirror Front, Wood, Display, 1930s, 13 x 9 1/2 In. 385.00
Cabinet, Whitlock's Medicines, Wood, Tin Signs, 25 x 14 x 11 3/4 In. 2090.00
Calendars are listed in their own category.
Can, B&L Oysters, Bivalve Oyster Packing Co., Gal. 23.00
Can, Home Oil Co., Litho Pry Lid, Crimped Seam, Race Car Image, 4 1/2 x 3 3/8 In. 413.00
Can, Nyoil, Whaling Scene, Stencil Labels, Painted, Plastic Cap, Spout, 3 Oz. 61.00
Can, Yellow Cab Cigars, Tin Lithograph, Orange Ground, 1920s, 5 1/2 x 2 5/8 In. 1073.00
Candy Wrapper, Planters Nickel Dessert, Waxy Paper, 5 5/8 x 7 7/8 In. 143.00
Canisters, see introductory paragraph to Tins in this category.
Cards are listed in the Card category as card, advertising.
Carton, Dr. Hess Heave Powder, Farmer With Horse, Contents, 7 x 4 In. 77.00
Carton, Lucky Strike Cigarette, World War II, 10 Packs, 4 1/2 x 11 x 3 In. 253.00
Carton, Talbott's Little Giant Poultry Regulator, Animals, Contents, 6 1/2 x 4 In. 297.00
Carton, Talbott's Rheumatic Remedy For Dogs, Label, Wood, Contents, 2 x 1 3/4 In. 495.00
Case, Display, Case XX Cutlery, Glass Front, Wood, 2 Shelves, 18 x 16 x 10 In. 86.00
Case, Display, Case XX Limited Edition, 8 Knives, Walnut, 24 1/2 x 13 x 8 1/2 In. 462.00
Case, Display, Case XX, 7 Knives, 24 x 12 In. 578.00
Case, Display, Charms, 11 Luscious Flavors, Glass, Wood, 8-Sided, 6 x 12 1/2 In. 1265.00
Case, Display, E.C. Simmons Keen Kutter, Oak, Glass, Electric, c.1940, 42 x 50 In. 460.00
Case, Display, Hammer Brand Knives, 10 Knives, N.Y. Knife Co. 866.00
Case, Display, Hanson Drill Bits, 1950s 150.00
Case, Display, Ingersoll Watch, 6 Watches, Gold Stencil, c.1900, 9 1/2 In. 504.00
Case, Display, John Primble, 12 Pocketknives, c.1950, 18 1/2 x 17 3/4 x 9 In. 774.00
Case, Display, Keen Kutter Knives, Glass, Metal Top, Bottom, Early 1900s, 42 x 7 In. 300.00
Case, Display, Keen Kutter, 12 Padlocks, 27 1/4 x 7 In. 380.00
Case, Display, Marbles Gun Sights, 19 Sights, Walnut, Nickel Plated, 4 x 11 In. 2734.00
Case, Display, Matchbox, Models Of Yesteryear, 16 Cars, Locking Rear Storage 1250.00
Case, Display, Oriental Powder Mills Gunpowder, 4 Bottles, 15 x 10 1/2 In. 690.00
Case, Display, Remington Cutlery, c.1923, 14 x 30 1/2 x 8 In. 100.00
Case, Display, Remington DuPont Knives, Wood, 18 Knife Slots, 17 1/2 x 10 In. 326.00
Case, Display, Remington Kleanblade, 6 Drawers, Wires, 14 x 30 3/4 x 10 1/2 In. 150.00
Case, Display, Shapleigh's, Mahogany, Glass Front, 9 Compartments, 9 3/4 x 15 In. 178.00
Case, Display, Tobacco, Wood, Glass On 3 Sides, Counter, 23 x 15 In. 99.00
Case, Display, Universal Cutlery, Wood, Glass, Brown Paint, 15 x 25 1/4 x 9 In. 40.00
Case, Display, Winchester, Walnut, 2 Doors, 24 Pigeon Holes, 22 x 19 x 11 In. 712.00
Chair, Lone Jack Cigarettes, Wood, Folding, 33 x 16 x 14 In. 1210.00
Change Receiver, see also Tip Tray in this category.
Change Receiver, Brunhoff El Sidelo Cigars, Reverse Painted Glass, 2 x 7 In. 90.00
Change Receiver, Cuban Seal Cigar, 5 Cents, Roulette Wheel, Tin Lithograph, 2 x 7 In. 1045.00
Charger, Red Raven, Woman Hugging Raven, Metal, c.1900, 24 In. 2750.00
Cigar Band, Hans Wagner, c.1910 .... 1160.00
Cigar Box, Al Simmons, 1930s, 10 Cigar Size 139.00
Cigar Box, B.F. Honsinger, Baseball, c.1897, 2 3/4 x 8 x 5 In. 1276.00
Cigar Box, Cy Young, Sweet Home Co., c.1910, 2 1/4 x 8 1/4 x 5 In. 6380.00
Cigar Box, Diamond King, Wood, 1891, 4 1/4 x 10 x 5 In. 1624.00
Cigar Box, Doylestown Giants, Picture, c.1900 .... 335.00
Cigar Box, E.J. Reardon & Bros' Supreme Court, 1890, 8 x 4 1/2 x 4 In. 452.00
Cigar Box, Edd Roush, Wood, c.1920, 2 1/2 x 9 x 5 1/4 In. 1160.00
Cigar Box, Forbes Field, c.1909, 1 1/4 x 6 1/2 x 3 In. 1392.00
Cigar Box, Goal, Height Of Success, c.1901, 1 3/4 x 9 1/4 x 6 In. 580.00
Cigar Box, Gold Mining, Cabin Shape, Wood, Label, 5 1/2 x 8 1/2 x 4 3/4 In. 1375.00
Cigar Box, Home Run, Wood, 1905, 2 1/2 x 8 x 4 3/4 In. 1624.00
Cigar Box, Honus Wagner Hand Made Long Filler, c.1898, 2 1/2 x 9 x 5 1/4 In. 5510.00
Cigar Box, Joe Tinker, Mild Havana, Wood, 1 1/2 x 9 1/2 x 5 1/4 In. 580.00
Cigar Box, Lucky Strike, Wood, Green Label, 8 x 9 x 5 1/2 In. 468.00
Cigar Box, Mordecai Brown, c.1910, 5 1/2 x 5 1/4 x 6 1/2 In. 2610.00

Cigar Box, Mungos, S. Davis & Sons, 1880s, 2 1/2 x 8 1/2 x 5 In. 1624.00
Cigar Box, National Sport, H. Buech, 1880s, 2 3/4 x 8 3/4 x 5 In. 4640.00
Cigar Box, Our Club, Panatelas, Wood, c.1883, 2 3/4 x 2 1/2 x 4 3/4 In. 1160.00
Cigar Box, Racing Car, Hinge, Brass, Cedar, 1910s, 2 3/4 x 5 1/2 x 9 In. 517.00
Cigar Box, Safe Hit, Wood, 1890s, 4 1/2 x 8 x 5 In. 1624.00
Cigar Box, Sebring's Special, c.190s, 2 1/2 x 8 1/4 x 4 1/2 In. 3190.00
Cigar Box, Short Stop, 1870s, 3 1/2 x 10 1/2 x 4 3/4 In. 696.00
Cigar Box, Three Bagger, Wood, 1910, 2 3/4 x 5 1/2 x 14 1/2 In. 348.00
Cigar Box, Upmann's All Nations, Uncle Sam, 1885, 4 1/2 x 8 1/2 x 2 1/2 In. 498.00
Cigar Box, Yellow Cab, Cardboard, 7 In. 77.00
Cigar Cutter, Boston Trade, Factory, Chas. Odence, Metal Case, Wood Base, c.1880, 6 In. 385.00
Cigar Cutter, Building, Clock Tower, Red, Yellow, Green, Tin, Bing Lithograph, c.1880, 12 x 7 In. 495.00
Cigar Cutter, Cigars-Dubuque, Iowa, Myers, Cox & Co., Nickel Plated Iron, Wood Base, 3 x 6 In. 302.00
Cigar Cutter, General Greene, Cast Iron, 1890s, 7 1/2 x 5 1/4 x 3 3/4 In. 2310.00
Cigar Cutter, Liquor Bottle, Silver Plated, Brass Cap, Stores Matches, Early 1900s, 7 In. 155.00
Cigar Cutter, Old Crow Cigars, Pig, Cast Iron, 5 3/4 x 6 1/4 x 4 1/4 In. 1980.00
Cigar Cutter, Optimo Cigars, Chrome, Cast Iron, Counter, 6 3/4 x 9 1/4 In. 2640.00
Cigar Cutter, Padlock, Push Handle, Brass, Green Patina, Marked, DBGM 1623984, 4 In. 145.00
Cigar Cutter, Pig, Curly Tail, Base, Bronzed Cast Iron, For & Woodworth, 4 x 7 1/2 In. 415.00
Cigar Cutter, Red Lion, Figural, Cast Iron, Nickel Plated, 8 In. 2200.00
Cigar Cutter, Revolver, Nickel Plated, Wood Trim, Early 1900s, 4 In. 358.00
Clicker, Moxie Man Pointing Finger, Drink Moxie, 1 1/4 In. 400.00
Clicker, Virginia Lee Doughnuts, Metal, 4 1/2 In. 30.00
Clocks are listed in their own category.
Coaster, Ballantine Beer, Watches Your Belt Line, Round, 1957, 3 1/2 In. 3.00
Coaster, Budweiser, King Of Bottled Beer, Clydesdales, 8-Sided, 1938, 4 In. 28.00
Coaster, Carling Black Label, Cleveland, Ohio, Square, 1956, 3 In. 4.00
Coaster, Gettelman Milwaukee Beer, It's True, Red, White, Square, 1964, 3 1/2 In. 3.00
Coaster, Goetz Country Club Beer, Round, 1940 .... 14.00
Coaster, Have You Made The Budweiser Test, Scalloped Edge 8.00
Coaster, It's The Age Of Acme, Fine Beer Since 1860, San Francisco, 1936-43 .... 15.00
Coaster, Kinsgbury Beer, Fit For A King, 4 Kings, Singing, Square, 1955, 3 1/2 In. 8.00
Coaster, Michelob Draught Beer, Budweiser, Keg Shape, 1941, 4 In. 8.00
Coaster, Rheingold Beer, Backside Of 2 Cowboys On Horses, Round, 1942, 4 In. 14.00
Coaster, Silver Top Beer, Duquesne Brewing Co., Pittsburgh, 1938, 4 In. 150.00
Coaster, Yusay Premium Pilsen Beer, Chicago, Oval, 1958, 3 1/2 In. 4.00
Coffee Bin, Golden Rio, Tin, Lift-Up Lid, Applied Brass Handle, Late 1800s, 28 x 20 In. 764.00
Container, Borden's Malted Milk, Metal, Dome Lid, 9 In. 275.00
Container, Borden's, Improved Malted Milk, Ribbed Glass, Vitrolite, Metal Lid, 8 In. 1100.00
Container, Carnation Malted Milk, Milk Glass, Metal Lid, Red & Green Letters, 9 In. 469.00
Container, Carnation Malted Milk, Porcelain, Enameled, Metal Cover, 9 1/2 x 6 In. 523.00
Container, Columbia Lice Powder, Animals, Yellow, Red, Black, Cylindrical, 7 x 3 In. 209.00
Container, Coors Golden Malted Milk, Stoneware, Metal Lid, 9 In. 302.00
Container, Cover, Carnation Malted Milk, Porcelain, Tin, 5 7/8 x 9 1/2 In. 280.00
Container, Dr. Dent's Dog Remedies, Label, Wood, Cylindrical, Sealed, Contents, 3 In. 176.00
Container, Milkose Malted Milk, Glass, Domed Metal Lid, 10 In. 264.00
Container, Thompson's Malted Milk, Double Malted, Porcelain Over Metal, 6 In. 360.00
Container, Thompson's Malted Milk, Porcelain, Enamel, 10 x 5 1/2 In. 743.00
Cooler, Eskimo Pie, Eskimo Legs, Thermos, Norwich, Conn., 1930, 16 x 7 3/4 In. 835.00
Cooler, Eskimo Pie, Real Ice Cream Enrobed In Chocolate, Blue, 15 In. 3400.00
Counter Felt, Case Brothers Cutlery Company, Little Valley, N.Y., 10 1/4 x 12 In. 59.00
Counter Felt, Dead Shot Smokeless, Falling Duck, 11 5/8 x 9 1/2 In. ....231.00 to 415.00
Counter Felt, DuPont Powders, 9 1/8 x 11 In. 148.00
Counter Felt, Laflin & Rand Infallible Smokeless, Frame, 12 1/4 In. 356.00
Counter Felt, Peters Cartridges, World's Records, 11 x 13 1/2 In. 593.00
Counter Felt, Peters Shells & Cartridges, Moose, Square, 10 3/4 In. 890.00
Counter Felt, Union Metallic Cartridge Co., Quail, 11 1/4 x 13 3/8 In. 1054.00
Counter Felt, Winchester, Repeating Rifles, Shotguns, Ammunition, 11 x 13 1/2 In. 476.00
Crock, Heinz Preserved Peaches, Label, Stoneware, 8 1/4 x 4 1/4 In. 660.00
Crock, Heinz Quince Jelly, Label, Stoneware, 7 3/4 x 4 In. 852.00
Crock, Heinz Tomato Preserves, White, Lid, Label, Stoneware, 8 3/8 x 5 1/2 In. 990.00

Advertising, Dispenser, Cherri Bon, Original Pump, Ceramic, 14 In.

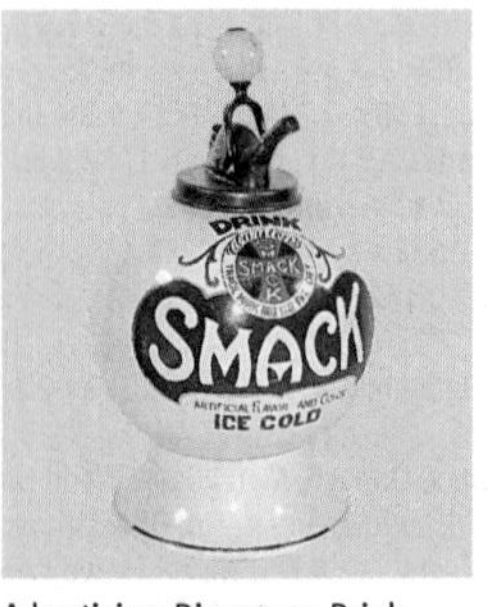

Advertising, Dispenser, Drink Clayton's Smack, Original Pump, Ceramic, 16 In.

Advertising, Dispenser, Drink Dixie-Flip, Wonder Drink, Horseshoe Pump, Ceramic, 16 In.

Crock, Heinz, Preserved Strawberries, Label, Lid, Stoneware, 5 7/8 x 4 5/8 In. 852.00
Crock, Stenciled James Hamilton & Co., Cobalt Blue Vines, Lines, 3 Gal., 13 5/8 In. 440.00
Crumb Scraper Set, Mardi Gras Tea & Coffee, Tin Lithograph, 2 Piece, 6 1/2 x 7 In. 798.00
Dispenser, Albers Root Beer, Barrel, Blue Letters, 14 In. 132.00
Dispenser, Alka-Seltzer, Be Wise, Alkasize, Tin, Metal Base, Turn Wheel, 14 1/2 In. 470.00
Dispenser, Armour's Veribest Root Beer, White, Blue Letters, 15 In. 1210.00
Dispenser, Bromo-Seltzer, Blue Bottle, Cup, Glass, 23 x 8 x 6 In. 440.00
Dispenser, Bromo-Seltzer, Blue Bottle, Glass, Blue Glass Base, 17 In. 522.00
Dispenser, Buckeye Root Beer, 5 Cents, Satyrs, Ginger Plunger Cap, 15 In. 2860.00
Dispenser, Buckeye Root Beer, Black Ceramic, Gold Lettering, 14 In. 468.00
Dispenser, Buckeye Root Beer, Black, 15 In. 1650.00
Dispenser, Buckeye Root Beer, Gnomes 4760.00
Dispenser, Buckeye Root Beer, Syrup, 16 x 8 In. 2200.00
Dispenser, Buckeye Root Beer, Tree Branch Letters, Cleve. Fruit Juice, 1970s, 15 In. 3080.00
Dispenser, Buckeye Root Beer, Tree Stump Form, Brown, White Letters, 15 In. 550.00
Dispenser, Cardinal Cherry, Cherries, Leaves, Branches, Embossed, 12 In. 5500.00
Dispenser, Carnation Hot Chocolate, Metal, Plastic, 1950s, 8 In. 220.00
Dispenser, Cherri Bon, Original Pump, Ceramic, 14 In. . . . . *ILLUS* 23750.00
Dispenser, Cherri Bon, Red, Green, White Letters, Horseshoe Pump, 14 In. 25320.00
Dispenser, Cherry Chic, J. Hungerford Smith Co., Buffalo, N.Y., Gold Details, 14 In. 12100.00
Dispenser, Cherry Smash, Always Drink, Ceramic, c.1900, 10 1/2 x 9 In. 2316.00
Dispenser, Cherryallen's Red Tame Cherry, Frosted Globe, Marble Base, 22 In. 2750.00
Dispenser, Cherryallen's Red Tame Cherry, Glass, Marble Base, Brass Pole, 19 In. 825.00
Dispenser, Christo Cherry Drink, 5 Cents, Cherries, Barrel, 16 In. 4180.00
Dispenser, Christo Ginger Ale, Richmond, Va., White, Light Blue, Gold, 16 In. 990.00
Dispenser, Citro-The Thirst Quencher, 5 Cents, Yellow Lemon, Silver Letters, 14 In. 770.00
Dispenser, Crawford's Cherry Fizz, It's Jake-A-Loo, Horseshoe Pump, 16 In. 9620.00
Dispenser, Daggett's Orangeade, Green Glass Base, Spigot, Lid, 15 In. 522.00
Dispenser, Dixie-Flip, Wonder Drink, Fruit, Leaves, Horseshoe Pump, 16 In. 37400.00
Dispenser, Douglas Root Beer, Barrel, 13 In. 1100.00
Dispenser, Dr Pepper, Drink Dr Pepper, White, Scalloped Rim, Urn, 17 In. 26400.00
Dispenser, Dr. Swett's Root Beer, 5 Cents, Light Blue Letters, Barrel, 16 In. 7150.00
Dispenser, Dr. Swett's Root Beer, On The Market 75 Years, Boy, Tree Stump, 14 In. 6160.00
Dispenser, Dr. Swett's, Stoneware, 7 x 21 1/2 In. 140.00
Dispenser, Drink Almond Smash, Phila., Ball Style Pump, 15 In. 9900.00
Dispenser, Drink Birchola, Ceramic, Painted Birch Leaves, Original Pump, 14 In. 1430.00
Dispenser, Drink Birchola, Keg, Stand, 16 In. 1650.00
Dispenser, Drink Birchola, Leaves, Branches, Round, Horseshoe Pump, 15 In. 1650.00
Dispenser, Drink Bowey's Old Style Root Beer, Key, Wood Stand, Spigot, 13 In. 660.00
Dispenser, Drink Brazilla, Red, White, Blue, Barrel, 16 In. 990.00
Dispenser, Drink California Iron Port, 5 Cents, Man, World On Shoulders, 16 In. 11000.00
Dispenser, Drink Cannons Grape Punch, Grapes, Horseshoe Pump, 16 In. 12100.00
Dispenser, Drink Cherry-Julep, 15 In. 3740.00
Dispenser, Drink Clayton's Smack, Original Pump, Ceramic, 16 In. . . . . *ILLUS* 17250.00

Dispenser, Drink Dal-O, 5 Cents, White, Red, Gold, Burden Mfg. Co., East Liverpool, Oh., 15 In. 3300.00
Dispenser, Drink Dixie-Flip, Wonder Drink, Horseshoe Pump, Ceramic, 16 In. .... *ILLUS* 34750.00
Dispenser, Drink Fan-Taz, Drink Of The Fans, Pennant Winner, 5 Cents, Baseball Form 27500.00
Dispenser, Drink Fowler's Root Beer, 5 Cents, Ceramic, Original Pump, 14 In. 1540.00
Dispenser, Drink Grape Smash, It's Delicious, Grapes, Horseshoe Pump, Porcelain Knob, 15 In. .. 3520.00
Dispenser, Drink Grape-Julep, 15 In. 3520.00
Dispenser, Drink Grapefruitola, 5 Cents, Yellow, Green, Red Letters, 1913, 15 In. 34100.00
Dispenser, Drink Green River, Syrup, Yellow & Green, Spigot, 16 In. 691.00
Dispenser, Drink Ironport, You'll Like It, 5 Cents, White, 16 In. 18150.00
Dispenser, Drink Kel-Ola, Flowers, 15 In. 3850.00
Dispenser, Drink Mo-Pep, Barrel, 14 In. 1100.00
Dispenser, Drink Parfay, It's Refreshing, Red, White, Gold Trim, 14 In. 2530.00
Dispenser, Drink Phos-Ferrone, Wonder Werker Mechanism, Vitrolite, Multiplex Faucet, 29 In. 2970.00
Dispenser, Drink Red Keg, Pure Wholesome, 5 Cents, Barrel, Red, Green, 15 In. 3190.00
Dispenser, Drink Ubet, Brown, Green, 15 In. 5500.00
Dispenser, Drink Ver-Ba, It's Safe & Sane, 5 Cents, 15 In. 1980.00
Dispenser, Drink Viccola The Famous Drink, 5 Cents, Horseshoe Pump, 16 In. 2750.00
Dispenser, Emerald Isle, Glass, Clambroth Milk Glass Base, 13 1/2 x 7 1/2 In. 853.00
Dispenser, Eskimo Pie Ice Cream Bars, Cast Metal, Counter, 1920s, 16 x 8 In. 1850.00
Dispenser, Fowler's Cherry Smash, Always Drink Cherry Smash, 5 Cents, 14 In. 2860.00
Dispenser, Fowler's Cherry Smash, Always Drink, Our Nation's Beverage, 16 In. 385.00
Dispenser, Fowler's Cherry Smash, Etched Ruby Glass, Clamp, Spigot, 14 In. 825.00
Dispenser, Fowler's Cherry Smash, Red Glass Globe, Counter, 15 In. 224.00
Dispenser, Fowler's Root Beer, 5 Cents, The Best, Red Letters, Round, 15 In. 2090.00
Dispenser, Getz Blend Root Beer, Red, White, Blue, Gold, C.F.G. Co., 1920, 13 In. 4290.00
Dispenser, Ginger-Mint Julep, Barrel, Horseshoe Pump, Porcelain Knob, 15 In. 605.00
Dispenser, Gleason Fruit Juices, Urn, Hand Painted, 26 In. 4400.00
Dispenser, Grape Crush, Pressed Glass, Purple, Embossed Grapes, Leaves, 14 x 7 In. 1265.00
Dispenser, Grape Kola, 5 Cents, Grapes, White, Gold Letters, Urn, 22 In. 2420.00
Dispenser, Green River, Embossed Glass, Chrome Holder & Lid, 14 In. 715.00
Dispenser, Green River, Milk Glass, Etches, 15 In. 1870.00
Dispenser, Green's Muscadine Punch, Red, White, Green, Gold Trim, Barrel, 16 In. 660.00
Dispenser, Hershey's Hot Fudge Sundae, Metal, Heat Dial, Pot Insert, 9 1/2 In. 179.00
Dispenser, Hires Root Beer, 5 Cents, Boy, Mettlach, Villeroy & Boch, 19 In. .... *ILLUS* 61000.00
Dispenser, Hires Root Beer, Barrel, 1930, 27 In. 616.00
Dispenser, Hires Root Beer, Boy In Bib, Urn, Base, Spigot, 19 In. 66000.00
Dispenser, Hires Root Beer, Drink Hires, 5 Cents, Barrel, Red Letters, 16 In. 1650.00
Dispenser, Hires Root Beer, Drink Hires, It's Pure, Hourglass, Red Letters, 12 In. 495.00
Dispenser, Hires Root Beer, Drink Hires, It's Pure, Hourglass, White, Red, 15 In. 660.00
Dispenser, Hires Root Beer, Munimaker, Marble, Milk Glass Globe, 35 x 16 In. 7700.00
Dispenser, Hires Root Beer, Pottery, 13 1/2 In. 604.00
Dispenser, Hires, Round, Milk Glass, Vitrolite Base, 23 In. 4540.00
Dispenser, Howel's Orange-Julep, 5 Cents, 15 In. 2090.00
Dispenser, Howel's Orange-Julep, Horseshoe Pump, Porcelain Ball, 16 In. 3080.00
Dispenser, Hunter's Root Beer, Barrel On Tree Stump, Lid & Spigot, 13 In. 825.00
Dispenser, Indian Rock Ginger Ale, 5 Cents, White Porcelain, Indian Scene, 16 In. 13200.00
Dispenser, Jersey Cream Perfect Drink, White Porcelain, Gold Leaf Design, 15 In. 2090.00
Dispenser, Jersey Cream, White, Gold Embossed, 15 In. 2420.00
Dispenser, Jim Dandy Root Beer, Red, Green Letters, Gold Trim, Pump, 15 In. 44000.00
Dispenser, Johnston's Cold Fudge, Blue Crockery, Galvanized Lid, 8 In. 143.00
Dispenser, Lash's Grapefruit Drink, Green Glass, Black Amethyst Base, Label, 13 In. 467.00
Dispenser, Lash's Orangeade, Pressed Glass, Milk Glass Base, Label, Spigot, Lid, 18 In. 880.00
Dispenser, Liberty Root Beer, Big Stein, 5 Cents, Wood Keg, Claw Foot Base, 14 In. 770.00
Dispenser, Liberty Root Beer, Try A Stein, It's Fine, Red & Blue Letters, 14 In. 2420.00
Dispenser, Liggett's Grape Juice, Bunches Of Grapes, Spigot, 13 In. 3190.00
Dispenser, Magnus Concordia Punch, Porcelain Over Metal, California, 14 In. 3190.00
Dispenser, Magnus Lime Rickey, Ceramic Bowl, Iron Base & Frame, Label, 14 In. 2970.00
Dispenser, Magnus Root Beer, Barrel Shape, Milk Glass, Aluminum Clamp, 15 x 6 In. 358.00
Dispenser, Magnus Root Beer, It's Fine In The Stein, Metal, Porcelain, 14 In. 935.00
Dispenser, Magnus Root Beer, White, Barrel, Blue, Gold Letters, 16 In. 715.00
Dispenser, Marrowfood Makes Rich Red Blood, 5 Cents, Horseshoe Pump, 16 In. 17600.00

Advertising, Dispenser, Hires Root Beer, 5 Cents, Boy, Mettlach, Villeroy & Boch, 19 In.

Advertising, Dispenser, So. Cas. Co. Orange Ale, Horseshoe Pump, Ceramic, 16 In.

Dispenser, Massey's Root Beer, Barrel, 5 Cents, Refreshing, 15 In. 2750.00
Dispenser, Menlo Root Beer, Pure & Good, Barrel, White, Red, Blue, 15 In. 880.00
Dispenser, Mission Grapefruitade, Ice Cold, Metal, Rubber Craft Lid, Footed, 16 In. 1540.00
Dispenser, Mission Orange, Real Fruit Juice, Black Glass Base, Rubber Lid, 13 1/2 In. 336.00
Dispenser, Mission Orangeade, Ice Cold, Metal, Rubber Craft Lid, Footed, 16 In. 1870.00
Dispenser, Mission Real Fruit Juice, Frosted Green Glass, Metal Base & Lid, 13 In. 660.00
Dispenser, Mission Real Fruit Juice, Frosted Pink Glass, Metal Base & Lid, 13 In. 660.00
Dispenser, Moar, The Juicy Grape Drink, 5 Cents, Grapes, Glass Bottle, 19 In. 3190.00
Dispenser, Montelaise Vigorola, Invigorating Beverage, Horseshoe Pump, 15 In. 11000.00
Dispenser, Moutarde De Dijon, Jigoin Ceramic Co., France, c.1930, 15 x 10 1/2 In. 759.00
Dispenser, Moxie, Etched Glass, Pedestal Base, 22 In. 880.00
Dispenser, Murray's Old Fashioned Root Beer, Barrel, Tree Stump, Cordley & Hayes, 12 In. 605.00
Dispenser, Nesbitt's Citrus Fruit Product, Frosted Green Base, Decals, 13 In. 275.00
Dispenser, Nesbitt's Grapefruit, Counter, Clamp, Label, 18 In. 232.00
Dispenser, Nesbitt's Orange, Counter, Clamp, Label, 18 In. 187.00
Dispenser, Nesbitt's, Pink Glass, Embossed, Pat. 1926, Gal., 9 1/2 In. 132.00
Dispenser, Orange Crush, Black Glass Base, Frosted Globe, Metal Lid, c.1910, 17 In. 495.00
Dispenser, Orange Crush, Brown Glass, Embossed, Label, Chrome Pump, 13 In. 440.00
Dispenser, Orange Crush, Green Porcelain Lid, Chrome Base, 15 In. 330.00
Dispenser, Orange Julep, 5 Cents, Barrel, Mueller-Keller, 16 In. 4070.00
Dispenser, Orange Julep, Stoneware, Pump, 14 1/2 x 9 1/2 In. 3410.00
Dispenser, Pokagon, American Indian, Orange Transfer, 15 In. 1760.00
Dispenser, Port Wine, Ceramic, Barrel Shape, White, Green Stripes, Gold Design 44.00
Dispenser, Rich Root Beer, 5 Cents, Maid Of Honor, Label, Rochester, N.Y., 16 In. 2750.00
Dispenser, Richardson's Liberty Beer, Barrel On Tree Stump, 13 In. 770.00
Dispenser, Richardson's Liberty Drinks, Art Deco, Black Amethyst Base, 11 In. 242.00
Dispenser, Rochester Root Beer, Barrel On Tree Stump, 13 In. 550.00
Dispenser, Rochester Root Beer, Mug Form, Etched Glass, 14 In. 632.00
Dispenser, Rosary Root Beer, 5 Cents, Barrel, Mueller-Keller, Horseshoe Pump, 16 In. 3740.00
Dispenser, Schuster's Root Beer, Brown & White, Barrel, 15 In. 550.00
Dispenser, So. Cas. Co. Orange Ale, Horseshoe Pump, Ceramic, 16 In. .... *ILLUS* 25750.00
Dispenser, Steins Famous Root Beer, White, Red & Green Letters, Horseshoe Pump 7700.00
Dispenser, Texberry, Barrel, Red, White, Gold, Horseshoe Pump, Ball, 16 In. 990.00
Dispenser, Treet, Cased Iridescent Glass, Black Letters, 14 In. 3190.00
Dispenser, Triple XXX Cola, 5 Cents, It Satisfies, Barrel, 15 In. 2530.00
Dispenser, Ward's Lemon Crush, Ceramic, Yellow, 1920s, 11 1/2 x 13 1/2 In. .... 1466.00 to 1932.00
Dispenser, Ward's Lemon Crush, Lemon Shape, Stoneware, 14 x 11 x 7 In. 1430.00
Dispenser, Ward's Lime Crush, 13 In. 4290.00
Dispenser, Ward's Orange Crush, Figural, Orange, Flowered Base, 14 In. 1320.00
Dispenser, World's Greatest Health Drink Liquid Force, Blue, Pink, Yellow, 16 In. 9825.00
Dispenser, Zipp's Cherri-O, 5 Cents, Barrel, Bird Drinking, 15 In. 4180.00
Dispenser, Zipp's Root Beer, 5 Cents, Barrel, Man Serving Root Beer, 15 In. 2320.00
Dispenser, Zipp's Root Beer, Barrel, White, Red Letters, 15 In. 7540.00
Display, Ace Comb, 25 Cents, Wood, 3 Drawers, 4-Sided, 10 x 9 In. 190.00
Display, Alfred Dunhill Of England, Pipe Stand, 1900s 395.00
Display, American Flyer, Boy, Santa Claus, Train Set, Cardboard, 1920, 60 In. 26400.00
Display, Athlo Medicines, Street Scene, Trifold, Cardboard, 18 7/8 x 22 1/2 x 7 In. 605.00
Display, Beech-Nut Chewing Tobacco, Yankee Stadium, 1926, 38 x 60 In. 4930.00

Display, Beech-Nut Cough Drop, 5 Cent, Counter, Pressed Tin, Litho, 10 1/2 In. 209.00
Display, Blue Ribbon Cigar, Easel Back, Cardboard Lithograph, c.1900, 30 x 17 In. 27.00
Display, Bus Brand Fuse, Tin Lithograph, Fuses, 13 1/4 x 18 1/4 x 5 In. 231.00
Display, Carborundum Pocket Hone, Tin Lithograph, 4 Boxes, 10 x 11 1/2 In. 2145.00
Display, Carborundum Razor Strop Dressing, Tin Litho, Easel Back, 9 3/8 x 13 In. 2200.00
Display, Carborundum, Knife Sharpening Stones, Hone, Tin Lithograph, 10 x 11 1/2 In. 1375.00
Display, Cattaraugus, Better Quality Knife, 32 Holders, 13 x 24 1/4 x 7 In. 283.00
Display, Collier Shot Tower, Glass, Lead Shot, Various Sizes, 9 1/2 In. 1424.00
Display, Diamond Edge Pocket Knives, 36 Slots, Counter, 10 1/2 x 20 1/2 In. 113.00
Display, Diamond Inks, 3 Tiers, Shelf, Wood, Tapered, 16 x 15 In. 198.00
Display, Dollar Knife, 33 Metal Hangers, Wood, 13 x 20 3/4 x 5 1/2 In. 445.00
Display, Drink Birchola 5 Cents, Horizontal Keg Shape, 16 In. 2530.00
Display, Edison Mazda Lamps, You Can't Buy A Better Lamp, Woman, Bulb, c.1930, 28 x 16 In. 580.00
Display, Edison Mazda, Die Cut Cardboard, Window, Bulb Holder, 26 1/2 x 34 In. 798.00
Display, Ground Spices, Maxfield & Seabury Co., Cinnamon, 15 x 16 1/2 In. 176.00
Display, Gulfspray Insect Killer, Can, Cardboard Lithograph, c.1940, 12 x 11 In. 121.00
Display, Harmony Tobacco, Slice Cut Pipe Tobacco, Man, Can, 10 x 10 x 3 5/8 In. 154.00
Display, Heineken Beer, Light-Up Windmill, Mechanical, 1930s 1250.00
Display, Hohners Harmonicas, 21,000,000 Sold, Clockwork Base, Revolves, 32 In. 470.00
Display, If It's Remington It's Right, Pocket Knife, Counter, 12 x 13 In. 850.00
Display, Jar Rubbers, Canning, Bulldog, 24 Original Boxes, 12 x 10 In. 300.00
Display, Jar, Ramon's Pills, Clear, ABM Lip, Glass Lid, Counter, 9 3/4 In. 90.00
Display, Jefferson Union Glass Fuses, Blindfolded Man Driving, Tin, 10 x 7 x 3 In. 358.00
Display, Ko-Pak-Ta Toasted Nuts, 5 Cents, Natives, Metal, Glass, Light-Up, 17 In. 224.00
Display, Marble's Gun Sights, Metal, Glass, c.1940, 7 1/2 x 12 In. 242.00
Display, Matchbox Models, 16 Cars, Locking Storage 1250.00
Display, Nature's Remedy, NR Tablets, Men, Women, Trifold, Cardboard, 28 x 54 In. 660.00
Display, Nature's Remedy, NR To-Night, Trifold, Cardboard, 1930s, 28 x 50 In. 385.00
Display, Northwest Airlines Timetable Holder, Metal, 1930s, 6 1/2 x 4 3/8 x 3 In. 330.00
Display, Peggen Medicinal, Cardboard, Easel Back, 15 3/8 x 11 In. 413.00
Display, Post Sugar Crisp Cereal, Cardboard, Leo Durocher, 1955, 20 In. 425.00
Display, Radiotron Village, Cardboard, Stand-Up Figures, Easel Back, 11 x 20 In. 3520.00
Display, RCA Radio Tubes, Radiotron, Tested Free, Parrish, Die Cut, 26 x 19 In. 1210.00
Display, RCA Radiola, Christmas Santa, Die Cut Cardboard, 1931, 39 3/4 x 53 In. 358.00
Display, Reddy Kilowatt Your Electric Servant, Plywood, c.1943, 5 x 12 x 18 In. 500.00
Display, Reddy Kilowatt, Red & White, Wood, 1940s, 25 In. 500.00
Display, Sensation Cigar, Girl, Kipp Cigar Co., 50 Count, 5 1/8 x 5 1/2 In. 880.00
Display, Shredded Wheat, Cardboard, Wheat Specimen Bottles, 14 x 19 1/2 In. 120.00
Display, Silver Birch Gum, Hickman's, 5 Cents, 1920s, 5 1/4 x 6 3/8 x 4 1/4 In. 633.00
Display, Smith Bros. Cough Drops, Tin Lithograph, 10 5/8 x 4 x 3 3/8 In. 990.00
Display, Solarine Metal Polish, Racing Scene, Cardboard, Insert, 22 x 38 In. 1595.00
Display, Star Nail Cup & Sorter, Cast Iron, c.1860 .... 150.00
Display, Stollwerck Cocoa, Die Cut, Tin Lithograph, 20 5/8 x 9 1/2 In. 2530.00
Display, Towle's Log Cabin, Cardboard, Figural, Folding, 15 x 15 x 10 In. 550.00
Display, Westinghouse Mazda Lamps, Jackie Cooper, Cardboard, 1932, 39 x 32 In. 390.00
Display, Whistle Steel Hand, Bottle, 3 1/2 x 10 In. 730.00
Display, Zenith Transistor Radios, Cardboard, Die Cut, Easel Back, 13 1/2 x 12 In. 300.00
Display Board, Hornady Bullets, c.1980, 14 1/4 x 22 1/4 In. 170.00
Display Board, Hornady Bullets, Composition, Wood, 1970s, 15 1/2 x 21 In. 192.00
Dolls are listed in their own category.
Door Ornament, Dr. D. Jayne's Sanative Pills For Liver Complaints, Iron, 5 x 7 1/2 In. 12.00
Door Push, Ask For A Crush, Natural Flavor, Natural Color, Embossed, 26 1/2 In. 77.00
Door Push, Black Caps, For Treating Gonorrhea, Safety Remedy Co., c.1900s, 10 x 4 In. 110.00
Door Push, Brunswick Balk Collender Co. Makers, Brass, 1880-90s, 3 x 9 In. 95.00
Door Push, Buckingham Tobacco, Embossed, Porcelain, 3 x 32 In. 255.00
Door Push, Buvez Pepsi-Cola Glace, Porcelain Over Pressed Steel, France, 32 In. 66.00
Door Push, Dr. Caldwell's Syrup Pepsin, Family Laxative, Blue, Yellow, 6 x 3 3/4 In. 470.00
Door Push, Dr. King's Cure For Consumption, Porcelain, 7 x 3 1/2 In. 1100.00
Door Push, Grain Belt Beer, From Perfect Brewing Water, 1964, 30 In. ....60.00 to 125.00
Door Push, Orange Crush, Round, Porcelain, 5 In. 1400.00
Door Push, Orange Crush, Tin Lithograph, 13 1/2 x 3 1/2 In. 330.00

Door Push, Orange-Ade, Bottle, Embossed, Tin Lithograph, 10 x 3 1/2 In. 130.00
Door Push, Polar Bear Tobacco, Porcelain, 6 1/2 x 3 7/8 In. 798.00
Door Push, Polar Bear Tobacco, Porcelain, 7 1/4 x 3 1/2 In. 990.00
Door Push, Polar Bear Tobacco, Porcelain, Black Ground, White Bear, 7 x 3 In. 1300.00
Door Push, Read & White, Dress Clothing Rental Agency, Black, White, Porcelain, 6 x 3 In. 230.00
Door Push, Star Naphtha, Laundry Soap, Porcelain, 6 1/4 x 3 5/8 In. 230.00
Door Push, Towle's Log Cabin Syrup, Tin, Girl Holding Oversize Can, 6 x 3 In. 2100.00
Door Push, Yeast Foam, Porcelain, 6 x 3 3/4 In. 1210.00
Dose Glass, C.O. Fauda Pharmacy Remedies & Pharmaceuticals, Etched, 2 3/4 In. 22.00
Dose Glass, Dr. Harter's, Embossed Bottle In Crescent, 8-Sided, 3 In. 49.00
Dose Glass, Dr. Petzold's German Bitters, 3 1/4 In. 38.00
Fans are listed in their own category.
Fan Pull, Totem Cigar, Totem Pole, 5 Cents, Die Cut, Cardboard, String, 6 1/2 x 6 In. 690.00
Feeder, Archer Booster Feeds, Archer, Red, White, Blue, 17 1/2 In. 45.00
Figure, Bulldog, Lollipop, Plaster, 7 In. 99.00
Figure, Conestoga Wagon, Pfeiffer Beer, Wood, Fabric, 1959, 11 x 18 x 7 In. 125.00
Figure, Dog, Morses Pure Pops, Holds 22 Suckers, Chalkware, 6 1/2 x 5 In. 330.00
Figure, Hamm's Beer Bear, Frying Fish, Porcelain, 1979, 5 1/2 In. 45.00
Figure, Hunter Ale, Spelter, Original Patina, 14 In. 358.00
Figure, Mountain Dew, Willy The Hillbilly, Vinyl, Plush, 1965, 20 In. 165.00
Figure, Nipper, RCA Dog, Cast Iron, White, 13 1/2 x 13 1/4 x 6 1/2 In. 410.00
Figure, Polar Bear, Papier-Mache, Label, Old King Cole, Canton, Ohio, 20 x 38 x 12 In. 978.00
Figure, RCA Nipper Dog, Papier-Mache, Oversized, 36 x 14 x 35 In. 1045.00
Figure, Red Raven, Old King Cole Papier-Mache Works, 12 x 5 In. 1760.00
Figure, Reddy Kilowatt, Your Electric Servant, Wood, 1940s, 18 x 5 x 12 In. 500.00
Figure, Schmidt's Brewery, 1930s, 10 In. 975.00
Figure, Speedy Alka-Seltzer, Vinyl, 1960s, 8 In. 500.00
Figure, Turtle, Christo Cola, Nation's Joy Drink, Iron, Celluloid Shell, 2 1/2 In. 225.00
Gum Wrapper, Greenback Chewing Gum, Paper, Currency Design, Eagle, 4 x 2 In. 80.00
Hat, Champ Hat For A Champ, Box, Salesman's Sample, 5 In. 45.00
Hat, Dobb's Fifth Avenue Hats, Octagonal Box, Salesman's Sample, 5 In. 39.00
Holder, Ice Cream, McLarens Real Cake Cones, Glass, Metal Hinged Lid & Base, 18 In. 715.00
Hot Fudge Warmer, Bowie's Co., Metal, 7 In. 100.00
Humidor, Benson & Hedges, Rosewood, Brass Bound, England, Early 1900s, 15 x 12 In. 650.00
Humidor, Briggs, Tobacco Barrel, Wood, 7 In. 28.00
Jar, American League Perfectos, Hand Made, Paper Label, Embossed, 7 1/2 In. 1210.00
Jar, Beggs Liver Pills, Etched Glass, Dakota Globe, Ground Stopper, 13 In. 1045.00
Jar, Borden's Malted Milk, Metal Lid, 9 x 6 1/2 In. 715.00
Jar, Chico's Spanish Peanuts, 5 Cents, Tin Lid & Base, c.1925, 11 x 8 In. .... 335.00 to 690.00
Jar, Cover, Columbia Candy, Tiffin Glass, 1950s, 15 In. 80.00
Jar, Cover, Tom's Original 5 Cent Peanut .... 39.00 to 56.00
Jar, Dakota Cylinder Candy, Tiffin Glass, 1950s, 23 1/2 In. 136.00
Jar, Jumbo Peanut Butter, Elephant Shape, Tin Lid, Frank Tea & Spice, c.1900, 3 In. 175.00
Jar, Jumbo Peanut Butter, Screw Lid, Bail Handle, Frank Tea & Spice Co., Cinc., 2 Lb. 145.00
Jar, M. Kopp Manufacturing Confectioner, Salt Lake, Utah, 4-Sided, 10 x 4 In. 155.00
Jar, Malted Grape-Nuts, Metal Cover, 7 3/4 x 6 In. 770.00
Jar, Rare Piece Cigars, Embossed, Paper Label, 7 1/2 In. 275.00
Jar, Schepp's Cocoanut, Embossed, Cocoanut Finial, 6 1/2 x 5 1/2 In. 220.00
Jar, Sharpe & Dohme Lozenges, Ground Stopper, Raised Label, 11 1/2 In. 110.00
Jar, Tobacco, Stenciled Fine Maccoboy, c.1870, 9 7/8 In. 95.00
Jigsaw Puzzle, Adams Gum, Woman, Red Coat, Black Fur, Gum Wrapper Premium, 1930s 180.00
Kickplate, Free Land Overalls, Porcelain, c.1940, 10 x 30 In. 305.00
Kickplate, Star Tobacco, Sold Hear, Porcelain, 1930s, 12 x 24 In. 275.00
Knife Sharpening Stone, Easy Credit Terms, Nude, Celluloid, Oval, 2 3/4 x 2 In. 660.00
Label, Beer, Alt Heidelberg Bock Beer, Burnished Gold, Unused, 1933-50, 3 x 4 In. 15.00
Label, Beer, Altes Double Bock, Man Riding Goat, 1952, 12 Oz. 15.00
Label, Beer, Bosch Bock, 1952, 32 Oz. 7.00
Label, Beer, Columbia Pale Ale, Burnished Silver, Green, Unused, 1933-50, 3 x 4 In. 7.00
Label, Beer, Columbia, Burnished Gold, Unused, 1933-50, 11 Oz., 2 7/8 x 4 1/8 In. 15.00
Label, Beer, Columbia, Burnished Gold, Unused, 1933-50, 11 Oz., 3 x 3 5/8 In. 7.00
Label, Beer, Du Bois Bock, 2 Goats, Butting Heads, 1946, 12 Oz. 5.00

Label, Beer, Fox Deluxe, Fox Hunter, Blowing Horn, 1954, 16 Oz. 4.00
Label, Beer, Golden Pheasant, Sebewaing, 1960, 12 Oz., 3 1/4 x 4 1/4 In. 1.00
Label, Beer, Renner Old German Style Lager, Man, Holding Glass, 1938, 12 Oz. 20.00
Label, Beer, Schmidt Extra Special, 1967 .... 12.00
Label, Beer, Tam O' Shanter Ale, Dry Hopped, Orange Ground, 12 Oz. 11.00
Label, Beer, Tech, Pittsburgh, Pa., Plaid Ground, 1945, 12 Oz. 3.00
Label, Beer, Townsend Lager Beer, Port Townsend Brewing, Wash., c.1906-16 .... 4.00
Label, Beer, Townsend Lager Beer, Unused, c.1906-16 .... 3.00
Label, Cigar Box, Zep Cigar, Los Angeles Zeppelin, Square, Early 1900s, 4 1/2 In. 115.00
Label, Food, Burnham Brand Early Evergreen Corn, Embossed, 9 x 3 3/4 In. 15.00
Label, Whiskey, Federal League Bourbon, Baseball Batter, c.1915 .... 118.00
Lamps are listed in the Lamp category.
Lander's, Tin, Painted, Children, Eating At Picnic Table, 8 In. 66.00
Lapel Pin, Ask For Winchester Nublack, 2 In. .... 134.00 to 162.00
Letter Opener, Blackburn-Shaw, Ambulance Service, Wood Handle, Metal Blade, 9 In. 35.00
Letter Opener, Compliments Of W Atlee Burpee & Co., Lima Bean Handle, Celluloid, 8 In. 34.00
Letter Opener, Glyco, Heroin, Compliments Of Martin H. Sith Co., 1880-1900 .... 79.00
Light Globe, American Flyer, Milk Glass, Red Letters, Silver Base, Electric 385.00
Lunch Box, Dan Patch Cut Plug, Swing Handles, 4 1/4 x 7 In. 300.00
Lunch Box, Dixie Kid Cut Plug, Black Baby, Nall & Williams, 3 3/4 x 8 x 5 1/4 In. 415.00
Lunch Box, Dixie Kid, White Kid Version, Tin, Tobacco Box, Yellow Ground, 3 x 8 In. 925.00
Lunch Box, Dixie Queen Tobacco, Metal Handle, Tin, 4 1/4 x 7 3/4 x 5 1/8 In. 155.00
Lunch Box, Pedro Smoking Tobacco, Tin Lithograph, 4 x 8 x 5 1/4 In. 330.00
Lunch Box, U.S. Marine Tobacco, Sailor, Battleship, Tin, 4 5/8 x 7 1/2 x 4 3/8 In. 660.00
Lunch Box, Warnick & Brown Tobacco, Farmer, Gentleman, Folding Handles, 5 x 7 3/4 x 4 In. 40.00
Lunch Box, Winner Cut Plug, Smoke & Chew, Tin Lithograph, 4 1/4 x 7 3/4 x 5 1/4 In. 468.00
Lunch Boxes are also listed in their own category.
Matchbook, 7Up, Peacock, 1930s-40s 4.00
Matchbook, Ask For Richbrau Beer, Richmond, Va., c.1939 .... 3.00
Matchbook, Bromo-Seltzer, 1930s-40s 3.00
Matchbook, Budweiser, Compliments Of Club Bar, Cordova, Alaska, c.1939 .... 2.00
Matchbook, Budweiser, St. Louis, Mo., c.1939 .... 2.00
Matchbook, Butte Beer, Pale, Special, 1941 .... 12.00
Matchbook, Century Beer, Ph. Schneider, Trinidad, Colo., 1930s-40s 8.00
Matchbook, Cliquot Club, 1930s-40s 2.00
Matchbook, Clock Ale, Waterbury, Conn., Art Deco, 1930s-40s 7.00
Matchbook, Falstaff, Bottle, Cone Top Can, 1949 .... 5.00
Matchbook, Hamm's Beer, Bear Rolling Log In Water, 1957 .... 5.00
Matchbook, Kessler Brewing Co., Moose Club, Deer Lodge, Mont., c.1939 .... 3.00
Matchbook, Mason's Root Beer, 1930s-40s 3.00
Matchbook, Old German Beer, 1930s-40s 4.00
Matchbook, Pabst Blue Ribbon, Father's Day, Blue, White, 1940 .... 8.00
Matchbook, Regal Pale, San Francisco, c.1939 .... 2.00 to 3.00
Matchbook, Richbrau Beer, Richmond, Va., 1930s-40s 4.00
Matchbook, Schlitz, John Frederick, Wholesaler, Chicago, Ill., 1955, Large Format 6.00
Matchbook, Schlitz, World's Fair, New York, 1939 .... 2.00
Matchbook, Tivoli Beer, Paul's Liquors, Denver, Colo., 1945 .... 3.00
Matchbook, Uneeda Biscuit, 1930s-40s 3.00
Matchbook, Younger's Beer, Get Younger Every Day, Edinburgh, Scotland, 1956 .... 12.00
Menu Board, Enjoy Fairmont Ice Cream, Interchangeable Flavor Labels, 23 In. 165.00
Menu Board, Imperial Whiskey, Self-Framed Tin, Red, Special Today, 17 In. 17.00
Menu Board, Nature's Remedy, Better Than Pills For Liver Ills, Tin, 23 x 17 In. 176.00
Menu Board, Royal Crown, Embossed, Tin Lithograph, 1940s, 20 x 28 In. .... 85.00 to 224.00

Advertising mirrors of all sizes are listed here. Advertising pocket mirrors range in size from 1 1/2 to 5 inches in diameter. Most of these mirrors were given away as advertising promotions and include the name of the company in the design.

Mirror, Angelus Marshmallows, Angel, Oval 28.00
Mirror, Barry's Tricopherous Hair Tonic, Celluloid, Woman Pouring Tonic, 3 x 2 In. 2860.00
Mirror, Bee Hive Overalls Best Maid, Woman In Overalls, Oval, 2 3/4 x 1 3/4 In. 220.00

Advertising, Pail, E.K. Pond Co., Toyland Brand Peanut Butter, 4 3/4 x 4 3/8 In.

Advertising, Pot Scraper, American-Maid Bread, Die Cut, Bread Loaf Shape, 1 3/4 x 3 In.

Mirror, Beeman's Pepsin Gum, Good For Digestion, Man, Bearded, 2 In. Diam. 145.00
Mirror, Buckeye Fence, Good The Whole Year Round, 4 Women, Celluloid, 2 1/8 In. 520.00
Mirror, California Fig Bitters, Man, Bald, Beard, X-Rated, 1 5/8 In. Diam. 687.00
Mirror, Columbia Tool Steel Co., Clarite, Round, 2 1/4 In. 20.00
Mirror, Cook Bros. Pianos, Holland, Mich., Round, 2 1/4 In. 15.00
Mirror, Gay-Ola, Woman & Cola, Celluloid, 1910, 2 In. 440.00
Mirror, Horlick's Malted Milk, Woman, Cow, Round, Celluloid . . . . .27.00 to 30.00
Mirror, Jacob Bertsch, Jackson, Ohio, Round, 2 1/4 In. 30.00
Mirror, Master Polish, For Boots & Shoes, Walnut Frame, 8 1/2 Diam. 210.00
Mirror, Old Manse Maple Syrup, Canadian Sap, It's Lickin Good, Celluloid, 2 In. 385.00
Mirror, Osborn's Ice Cream Parlor, Kansas City, Mo., Round, Pocket, 2 1/8 In. 385.00
Mirror, Ryan's Pure Beers, Indian, Headdress, Celluloid, Round, Syracuse, N.Y., 2 1/8 In. 135.00
Mirror, Sanspariel Dress Shirts, Night Robes, Pajamas, Beveled, Stand, c.1900, 15 In. 275.00
Mirror, Swift's Pride Soaps & Washing Powder, Celluloid, Pocket, 2 3/4 In. 660.00
Mirror, Thirsty Or Not You'll Enjoy Grapette Soda, c.1950, 16 x 8 In. 330.00
Mirror, Topless Female Holding Bow & Arrow, H. Fee & Co., Celluloid, 2 3/4 In. 350.00
Mirror, Trolley, Little Rock Railway, Celluloid, 2 3/4 x 1 3/4 In. 4400.00
Mirror, Tums For The Tummy, Orange, Blue, White, Chain, Easel, Self-Framed, 16 x 8 In. 275.00
Mirror, Victor, Celluloid, Nipper & Machine Image, Pocket, 1 3/4 x 2 3/4 In. 250.00
Mixer, Hires, Malted Milk, Porcelain, Cast Iron, Windup, 13 In. 770.00
Mug, Dr. Swett's Original Root Beer, Brown & Blue, Ivory Ground, Stoneware, 6 In. 265.00
Mug, Hires Root Beer, Blue & Gray, Stoneware, Bark Handle, 5 1/2 In. 275.00
Mug, Hires Root Beer, Boy, Mug, Caldon Ware, England, 4 In. 120.00
Mug, Hires Root Beer, Boy, Mug, Drink Hires Root Beer, Germany, 4 1/4 In. 130.00
Nail Apron, Winchester Store, Dodson Hdw Co, Alvin, Texas 225.00
Oil Dispenser, Bowser & Co., Nickel, Brass, Salesman's Sample, c.1901, 8 x 5 In. 1100.00
Package, Lime Kiln Club Tobacco, Contents, c.1920, 4 1/4 x 2 1/2 x 1 In. 385.00
Pail, Adams Peanut Butter, Pumpkin Color, Crown In Center, Pail Handle, Lb. 365.00
Pail, Big Sister Peanut Butter, Witch, Broom, Lithograph, Lb., 3 1/2 x 3 3/4 In. 525.00
Pail, E.K. Pond Co., Toyland Brand Peanut Butter, 4 3/4 x 4 3/8 In. . . . . ***ILLUS*** 275.00
Pail, J.D. Foster, Santa Claus, Tin Lithography, 3 1/2 In. 550.00
Pail, Mastiff Plug Cut Tobacco, Leather Handle, 16 Oz., 5 1/4 x 6 x 4 In. 3960.00
Pail, Morrell Peanut Butter, Children, Maypole, Handle, Tin Lithograph, 14 Oz., 3 3/8 x 4 In. 580.00
Pail, Newton Tea's Peter Rabbit Peanut Butter, Rabbits, Frogs, Lb., 3 3/4 x 3 5/8 In. 745.00
Pail, Oyster, Pride Of Chesapeake, Gal., 7 1/4 x 6 3/4 In. 360.00
Pail, Pickaninny Brand Peanut Butter, F.M. Hoyt, Lb., 3 1/2 x 3 3/4 In. 275.00
Pail, Red Seal Peanut Butter, Old King Cole, Newton Tea Co., Tin, 4 x 4 In. 280.00
Pail, S.C. Smith & Co., Family Brand Coffee, Soldered, Stenciled, 7 x 4 3/8 In. 360.00
Pail, School Boy Peanut Butter, Bail Handle, 2 Lb., 4 1/4 x 4 1/2 In. 59.00
Pail, Squirrel Peanut Butter, Tin Lithograph, 3 1/2 x 3 3/4 In. 495.00
Pail, Uncle Remus Syrup, Corn & Pure Georgia Can, Paper Label, 9 Lb. 250.00
Pamphlet, Sharples Separator, Just Week-Day Sense, 1905, 12 Pages 10.00
Patch, Carling Black Label Beer, Red Ground, Tilted Label Design, Square, 4 x 3 In. 2.00

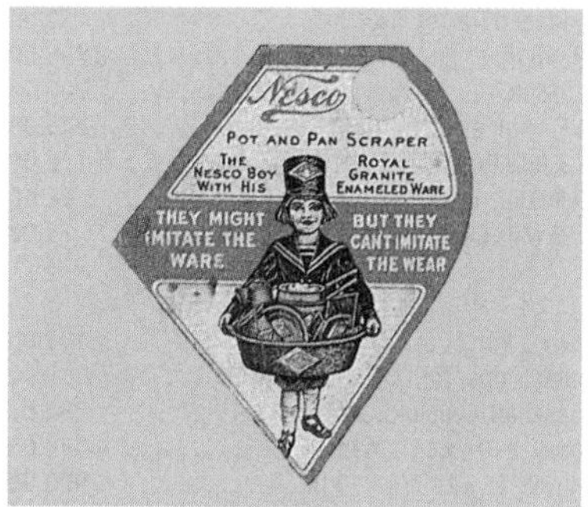

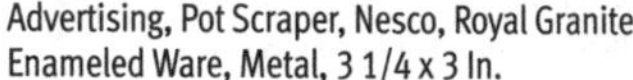
Advertising, Pot Scraper, Nesco, Royal Granite Enameled Ware, Metal, 3 1/4 x 3 In.

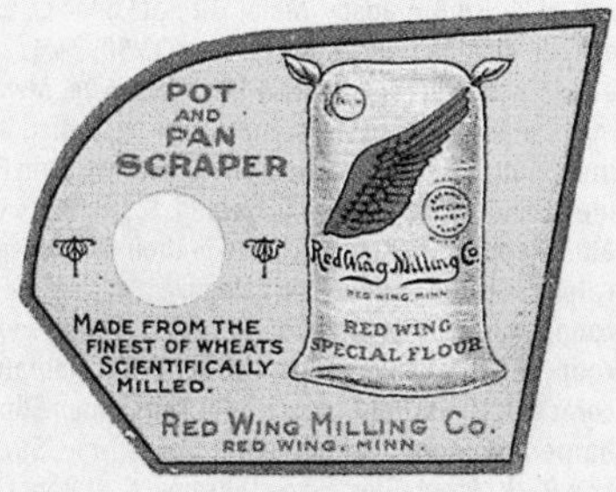

Advertising, Pot Scraper, Red Wing Special Flour, Metal, 2 1/4 x 3 1/4 In.

Patch, Fabric, Bob's Big Boy, Stitched Double Burger, 1950s, 2 3/4 In. 15.00
Patch, Olympia Beer, Yellow Letters, Border, Rectangular, 4 x 2 In. 2.00
Pennant, Marble's, Felt, Gun, Axe, 38 x 10 In. 249.00
Pin, Ballistite & Empire, World's Best, Celluloid, Round, 7/8 In. 90.00
Pin, Ceresota Flour, Boy, Cutting Bread, Celluloid, 1 In. 16.00
Pin, Dead Shot Smokeless Powder, Dead Duck, Boston, 7/8 In. 98.00
Pin, Dead Shot Smokeless Powder, Dead Duck, T.F. Moore Co., 1 1/4 In. 125.00
Pin, Dead Shot Smokeless Powder, Falling Duck, Round, 1 In. 120.00
Pin, Dr Pepper, 10-2-4, Man, Top Hat, Pince-Nez Spectacles, Bottle, 3/4 In. 45.00
Pin, DuPont Smokeless Cartridges, Dogs, Celluloid, 1 In. 130.00
Pin, DuPont Smokeless Powder, Quail, Celluloid, Round, 1 In. 45.00
Pin, Globe Poultry Feed, Rooster On Globe, Make 'Em Lay, 1 In. 36.00
Pin, Long Beach Festival Of The Sea, September 1908, 2 1/8 In. 1265.00
Pin, Peters Cartridges, Triangle Of Bullets, Celluloid, 7/8 In. 89.00
Pin, Peters Shells & Cartridges, Bastian Bros., 7/8 In. 85.00
Pin, Peters Shells, Round, 7/8 In. 64.00
Pin, Port Huron Threshing Engine, Celluloid, 1 1/2 In. 250.00
Pin, Scout Stocking, Linen Clad, Celluloid, 1 In. 10.00
Pin, Sharples, Tubular Cream Separators, Different From The Others, Celluloid, 1 In. 22.00
Pin, Silver Quill Chicken Feed, Blue Bonnet Girl, Celluloid, 1 In. 11.00
Pin, Underwood Unequaled, Typewriter, Celluloid, 1 In. 15.00
Pin, Vote For Ferguson's Honey Bread, Celluloid, 1 In. 10.00
Pin, Winchester Guns & Cartridges, Wonderful Topperweins, 1 1/4 In. 130.00
Pin, Winchester Shotgun Shells & Shotguns, Whitehead & Hoag 45.00
Pin, Winchester Shotgun Shells, Celluloid, Round, c.1896, 1 In. 65.00
Pin, Winchester, C.G. Spencer, Model 1897 Rifle, Oval, 1 In. 290.00
Pin, Winter's Bread, Speed Gibson, Pilot, Red Ground, Celluloid, Round, 1 In. 25.00
Pin, Worcester Salt, Train, Standard For Quality, Celluloid, 1 In. 15.00
Plaque, Colt's Armory, God Created Man, Colt Made Them Equal, Brass, 1886, 10 x 4 In. 858.00
Plate, Duff Gorden, Tin Lithograph, Vienna Art, 10 1/8 In. 300.00
Plate, Eat Paradise Sodas, Amethyst, Carnival Glass, 6 In. 300.00
Plate, Fern Brand Chocolates, Carnival Glass, Amethyst, Handgrip 500.00
Plate, Fred Krug Brewing Co., 50th Anniversary, China, 2-Sided, 1859-1909, 9 3/4 In. 80.00
Plate, Rood's Chocolates, Carnival Glass, Amethyst, 6 In. 3400.00
Postcard, Gold Dust Twins, Santa Clothes, Yuletide Verse 460.00
Pot Scraper, American-Maid Bread, Die Cut, Bread Loaf Shape, 1 3/4 x 3 In. .... *ILLUS* 264.00
Pot Scraper, Anthony's Holsum Bread, Metal, 2 3/4 x 3 3/8 In. 965.00
Pot Scraper, Junket, Makes Milk Into Delicious Dessert, Metal, 2-Sided, 3 x 3 In. 255.00
Pot Scraper, Nesco, Royal Granite Enameled Ware, Metal, 3 1/4 x 3 In. .... *ILLUS* 187.00
Pot Scraper, Red Wing Special Flour, Metal, 2 1/4 x 3 1/4 In. .... *ILLUS* 660.00
Powder Keg, Oriental Powder Mills, Wood, Stenciled Label, Paper Label, 25 Lb. 468.00
Price Board, Lowney's Cocoa, Chalkboard, Wood Frame, 2-Sided, 33 x 15 In. 2420.00
Print, Kenteria Havana Cigars, Dogs Playing Poker, Oak Frame, 15 In. 28.00

Printing Plate, John Deere, Don't Let Your Equipment, Bandaged Tractor, 6 x 6 In. 50.00
Rack, Hillerich & Bradsby, Metal, 12 Bat Capacity, c.1939, 48 In. 1856.00
Rack, Remington Guns, Knotty Pine, c.1950, 34 1/2 x 12 5/8 In. 200.00
Rack, Winchester Flashlights & Batteries, Wire, Metal, 14 Flashlights, 25 x 14 In. 1246.00
Ring, Cannon, Gabby Hayes, Brass, Spring, Puffed Wheat & Rice Premium, c.1951 .... 132.00
Ruler, Blotter & Calendar, Seasons Greetings, Sam Fox, Celluloid, 1931, 2 x 8 In. 55.00
Ruler, Sanitary Tinning Co., Cleveland, O., Retin Ice Cream & Milk Cans, Metal Edges 15.00
Salt & Pepper Shakers are listed in their own category.
Scales are listed in their own category.
Scoop, James Lutted, Buffalo, N.Y., Glass, Embossed, 6 1/2 x 3 In. 187.00
Scoop, Lutted's Cough Drops, Use Lutted's Celebrated Cough Drops, Tin, 2 3/4 In. Diam. 165.00
Scorecard, Hires, Put-Out Route For Thirst, Josh Slinger, Baseball, Celluloid, 3 x 2 In. 385.00
Sharpening Stone, Carborundum, Saves Time, Saves Money, 2 3/4 x 11 1/4 In. 348.00
Shoe Rack, Raven Gloss Shoe Dressing, Cast Iron, Oak, Mirror, 15 x 12 3/4 x 12 In. 900.00
Shoebox, Mother Goose, Child's, 1950s, 4 x 7 In. 55.00
Sign, 7Up, Bottle Cap, White Ground, Green, Red, 1970s, 8 1/2 In. 8.00
Sign, 7Up, You'll Like It, It Likes You, Light-Up, 6 1/2 x 11 x 28 In. 140.00
Sign, A&P Grocery, Porcelain, Red Ground, White, 1950s, 9 In. 475.00
Sign, Abdulla Superb Cigarettes, Tin, 1910s, 30 x 20 In. 430.00
Sign, Acme Boots, Paul Newman, 1958, 20 x 12 1/2 In. 380.00
Sign, Adams Pepsin Tutti-Frutti, Blue, Silver, Cardboard, 11 3/4 x 15 3/4 In. 385.00
Sign, Aladdin Lamp, Yellow, Red, Black, White, Cardboard Lithograph, 14 x 56 3/4 In. 220.00
Sign, All-Star Line-Up For Men, Marilyn Monroe, Cardboard, 1951, 13 x 11 In. 1095.00
Sign, Allen & Ginter's, Virginia Brights Cigarettes, 1890s, 28 x 19 1/2 In. 1276.00
Sign, Allen's Red Tame Cherry, Cardboard, 2-Sided, Die Cut, Hanger, 6 x 6 In. 415.00
Sign, Alpha Cement, Hazlett & Chase, Cobalt Blue & White, Porcelain, 18 x 60 In. 130.00
Sign, Alpha Ice Cream, Sundae, Cookies, McPherson Creamery, Tin Litho, 13 x 13 In. 385.00
Sign, Alt Heidelberg, Columbia Brewing, Tacoma, Cardboard, Frame, 16 3/4 x 13 In. 25.00
Sign, Alt Heidelberg, Pale Beer, Cardboard, Composition Frame, 13 x 16 3/4 In. 25.00
Sign, American Eagle Fire Insurance, Porcelain, 14 1/2 x 15 In. 255.00
Sign, American Express Co., Money Orders, Foreign Drafts, Porcelain, 2-Sided, 13 x 17 In. 385.00
Sign, American Surety Co., Surety On Bonds, Blue, White, Porcelain, 10 x 15 In. 300.00
Sign, Apothecary, Tin, W.T. Co., 6 x 25 In. 1150.00
Sign, Arm & Hammer Soda, Snowy Owl, Self-Framed, 14 3/4 x 11 1/4 In. 89.00
Sign, Arrow Beer, Matchless Body, Earl Moran, Frame, c.1940, 28 x 17 1/2 In. 175.00
Sign, Ask For Davidson's Breads, They're Different, Porcelain, 4 x 16 In. 525.00
Sign, Ask For Gargoyle Mobiloil, Porcelain, c.1930, 24 x 19 In. 440.00
Sign, Baker's Cocoa, Pure, Delicious, Nutritious, Woman Carrying Tray, Tin, 18 x 13 In. 1705.00
Sign, Ballistite & Empire, Woman Hunter, c.1910, 26 5/8 x 13 3/4 In. 2610.00
Sign, Beech-Nut Chewing Tobacco, Embossed, Porcelain, 10 x 22 In. 855.00
Sign, Beeman's Pepsin Gum, Girl, Goose, Cardboard, Embossed, Die Cut, 16 x 9 In. 495.00
Sign, Belmont Orange Bud, A Fruit Drink, Self-Framed, Embossed, 19 1/2 In. 66.00
Sign, Betsy Ross Cigar, 5 Cents, Betsy Ross, Tin Lithograph, Self-Framed, 24 x 20 In. 5390.00
Sign, Big Loaf Bread, Really Big, Really Good, Porcelain, 22 x 44 In. 275.00
Sign, Billy Boy Tobacco, Embossed, Die Cut, Cardboard, Cowgirl, Frame, 12 x 10 In. 1870.00
Sign, Black Cat Hosiery, We've Got 'Em For Sale, Cat, Paper, E.K. Elledge, 12 x 18 In. 275.00
Sign, Black Cat Shoe Dressing Scribbler, 7 1/2 x 10 In. 575.00
Sign, Black Cat Stove Polish, Outshines 'Em All, Cat, Bottle, Paper, Metal, 16 x 11 In. 690.00
Sign, Black Flag, Newsboy With Paper, War Declared, 23 1/4 x 18 In. 635.00
Sign, Borden's Pioneer Evaporated Cream, Prospector, 2-Sided, Cardboard, 8 x 5 In. 330.00
Sign, Brahmans, Bull, Blue, White, Yellow, Porcelain, 54 x 48 In. 300.00
Sign, Brazil Brewing Co., Porcelain, Embossed, Curved Corners, 20 x 13 In. 2750.00
Sign, Brookfield Rye, Tin, Girl In Thin Gown Holding Bottle Of Liquor, 23 In. 3850.00
Sign, Brotherhood Tobacco, Chewing, Smoking, Train, 2 Men, Cardboard, Frame, 30 x 21 In. 1595.00
Sign, Brown's Jumbo Bread, Tin Lithograph, Die Cut, 13 x 15 In. 470.00
Sign, Budweiser, King Of Beers, Tin Over Cardboard, 1948, 17 1/2 x 15 In. 185.00
Sign, Bull Durham Smoking Tobacco, Couple Kissing, Umbrella, Paper, 30 x 22 In. 2320.00
Sign, Bull Durham, Black Boys On Swing, Cardboard, Hanger, Die Cut, 11 1/2 x 9 In. 1705.00
Sign, Bull Stud Service, Guernsey Bull, Pay At Time Of Service, Wood, 14 x 32 In. 530.00
Sign, Burma Shave, This World Of Toil & Sin, Red, White, Tin Lithograph, 3 x 6 In. 905.00
Sign, Butter-Nut Bread, Red, Yellow, Black, Tin Lithograph, 5 1/2 x 27 In. 120.00

Sign, Camel Cigarettes, Joe Camel, Neon, 25 x 19 x 6 In. 168.00
Sign, Camel, Genuine Taste, Neon, 27 x 22 In. 22.00
Sign, Camel, In Prime Condition, Football Player, Frame, 1930s, 47 x 34 In. 948.00
Sign, Camera Shape, Yellow Paint, Tin, 11 x 17 In. 2990.00
Sign, Carter's Union Made Overalls, Porcelain, 6 x 15 In. 3190.00
Sign, Caution To Cyclists, Dangerous To Proceed Without Refreshment, 27 x 20 In. 415.00
Sign, Chas. W. Cramer Law Office, Hand Pointing, Black, Gold, Painted, Wood, 30 In. 275.00
Sign, Cherry Smash Soda, Tin On Cardboard, Chain Hung, 2 Piece, 18 x 8 3/4 In. 770.00
Sign, Chesterfield, Dean Martin & Jerry Lewis Sound Off For, 1952, 22 x 21 In. 5656.00
Sign, Chesterfield, Sinatra, Like Your Pleasure Big?, c.1957, 22 x 21 In. 1015.00
Sign, Cigarettes, Allen & Ginter, Richmond Straight Cut, c.1910, 12 x 16 In. 495.00
Sign, Cigarettes, Allen & Ginter, Richmond, Straight Cut No. 1, c.1890, 18 x 28 In. 415.00
Sign, Clay-Grant Pharmacy, Metal, Glass, Light-Up, 5 x 9 1/2 In. 100.00
Sign, Clement Paris, Cycles & Automobiles, L.C. Bombled, c.1905, 37 x 51 In. 1350.00
Sign, Cole's Peruvian Bark & Wild Cherry Bitters, Porcelain, 6 x 16 In. 880.00
Sign, Colgate's Dental Powder, Easel Back Cardboard, c.1898, 12 x 10 In. 2970.00
Sign, Colonial Club 5 Cent Cigar, Brunette Woman In Large Hat, 22 x 17 In. 810.00
Sign, Colorado's Best Flour, Pride Of The Rockies, Paper, 18 x 36 In. 55.00
Sign, Colt 45, Inverted Horseshoe, Yellow, Blue, Neon, 17 x 22 In. 44.00
Sign, Columbia Brewing Co., Lady Liberty Clad In Stars & Stripes, Tin, 13 In. 4715.00
Sign, Columbian Beer, Extra Pale, Tennessee Brewing Co., Embossed, 17 x 14 In. 240.00
Sign, Condition Counts, Dog Chow Keeps Us That Way, Cardboard, c.1939, 12 x 16 In. 440.00
Sign, Congress Playing Cards, c.1903, 18 1/2 x 12 1/4 In. 405.00
Sign, Cornell Wood Board, 2-Sided, Flange, Porcelain, Red, White, Black, 9 x 18 1/4 In. 385.00
Sign, Corner Shop, Corset Specialists, Free Fitting Service, Early 1900s, 49 x 11 In. 265.00
Sign, Cow Ease Vet, Man Spraying Cow, Tin Lithograph, Chain Hung, 4 x 14 3/4 In. 6600.00
Sign, Cream Of Wheat, Boy Eating, Paper Lithograph, Frame, 33 1/2 x 22 3/4 In. 910.00
Sign, Cresco Biscuits, 2 Black Kids Hunting, Cardboard, Embossed, Easel, 10 x 6 In. 358.00
Sign, Crosman Bros. Seeds, Stone Lithograph Paper, Boy On Seed Box, 31 x 25 In. 1320.00
Sign, Crossett Shoe, Makes Life Walk Easy, C.S. Betts, Smithfield, 28 x 19 In. 192.00
Sign, Crown Quality Ice Cream, Anderson & Patterson, Tin Lithograph, 28 x 20 In. 715.00
Sign, Crystal Rock Beverages Ginger Ale, Bottle, Tin Lithograph, 23 x 8 1/4 In. 35.00
Sign, Cunard's White Star Cruise Ship Line, Queen Mary, Paper Litho, 21 x 34 In. 525.00
Sign, D & M Baseball Equipment, Cardboard, c.1910-15, 20 x 20 In. 2310.00
Sign, D.M. Ferry & Co. Standard Seeds, Paper Lithograph, c.1898, 28 x 19 In. 525.00
Sign, Dad's Root Beer, Genuine Old Fashioned Draft, Red, Yellow, Blue, Tin Litho, 11 x 14 In. 358.00
Sign, Deer Run Whiskey, Stag, Landscape, Tin Lithograph, Self-Framed, 12 In. Diam. 550.00
Sign, DeLaval Cream Separators, Tin Lithograph, Self-Framed, 27 1/2 x 18 In. 4950.00
Sign, Detroit Stove Works, Tin, 38 x 13 In. 710.00
Sign, Devilish Good Cigar, 5 Cents, None Better, Children Smoking, Tin Litho, Chain, 10 x 14 In. 300.00
Sign, Doell Gunsmith's, Pine, Wrought Iron, Painted, Gilded, 108 x 12 1/2 In. 19200.00
Sign, Dr Pepper, Drink A Bite To Eat, Celluloid Over Tin, 5 3/4 x 7 3/4 In. 450.00
Sign, Dr Pepper, Good For Life, Porcelain, 10 1/2 x 26 1/2 In. 900.00
Sign, Dr Pepper, Good For Life, Tin Lithograph, 2-Sided, Flange, 10 x 17 1/2 In. 800.00
Sign, Dr. D. Jaynes Family Medicines, Flemish Bride, Frame, 24 x 19 3/4 In. 385.00
Sign, Dr. Hess Vet, Poultry Medicine, 26 x 21 In. 855.00
Sign, Dr. Kendall's Blackberry Balsam, Paper, 21 x 40 In. 28.00
Sign, Dr. Leonard, Wood, Painted, Gilt Lettering, Black Ground, 8 x 31 In. 530.00
Sign, Dr. Morse's Root Pills, Indian, Teepees, Cardboard, Trifold, 27 1/2 x 42 In. 360.00
Sign, Dr. Scholl's Foot Comfort Service, Porcelain, 2-Sided Flange, 12 x 22 In. 165.00
Sign, Dr. Swett's Root Beer, Great Health Beverage, Victorian Woman, Tin Litho, 15 In. 825.00
Sign, Drink Cheer Up, Delightful Beverage, Tin, Die Cut Flange, c.1950, 12 x 10 In. 275.00
Sign, Drink Fowler's Cherry Smash, Red, White, Green, Tin Over Cardboard, 18 In. 630.00
Sign, Drink Hires In Bottles, Woman, Holding Glass, Cardboard, c.1918, 21 x 15 In. 330.00
Sign, Drink Moxie, Man Pointing, Hanging, 1950s, 8 1/2 x 11 In. 76.00
Sign, Drink Moxie, Soda Syrups, Tin, Embossed Over Cardboard, 19 x 13 1/4 In. 7260.00
Sign, Drink Nehi, In All Popular Flavors, Cardboard, 1940s, 21 1/2 x 13 1/2 In. 1100.00
Sign, Drink Queen Cola, It's Different & Better, Embossed, 25 In. 330.00
Sign, Drink Ward's Orange Crush, Tin, Embossed, c.1930, 9 x 19 1/2 In. 660.00
Sign, Drug Store, Die Cut, Porcelain, Tenn. Enamel Mfg. Co., Nashville, c.1920, 24 x 96 In. 935.00
Sign, Duke's Mixture, Roll Of Fame, Enamel, Multicolored, 8 x 5 1/4 In. 170.00

Sign, DuPont Ballistite, Green Wing Teal, 1913, 30 x 19 In. 3870.00
Sign, DuPont, Shoot Ballistite, Hunter, Pipe, Shorebirds, Charles De Feo, 30 x 19 In. 6490.00
Sign, DuPont, Shoot DuPont Powders, 2 Dogs Looking Sideways, Tin, 1903, 28 x 23 In. 4125.00
Sign, DuPont, Shoot DuPont Powders, Dog, Duck, Edmund Osthaus, 1904, 31 x 21 In. 1980.00
Sign, Duquesne, There's Only One, Man, Woman, Dog, 1957, 17 x 22 1/2 In. 60.00
Sign, E. Bement & Sons Steel Plows, Farmer Plowing, Paper Lithograph, 26 x 20 In. 550.00
Sign, Edgeworth Extra High Grade Smoking Tobacco, Tin Lithograph, 11 x 27 In. 715.00
Sign, Edgeworth Tobacco, High Grade, Men, Pipe, Cardboard, 24 x 18 1/2 In. 495.00
Sign, Edgeworth Tobacco, Its Quality Never Changes, Cardboard Lithograph, Trifold, 32 x 40 In. 440.00
Sign, El Moriso 5 Cent Cigar, Cardboard, Counter, 13 1/2 x 10 1/4 In. 22.00
Sign, Elgin Watch, My Elgin's All Right, Boy, Watch, Wood, Litho, c.1910, 22 x 15 In. 410.00
Sign, Elgin Watches, Cardboard, Father Time Holding Watch, 28 x 20 3/4 In. 690.00
Sign, Elk Hats, Elk, Wood, 21 x 15 In. 410.00
Sign, Emblem Cigarettes, U.S. Cavalry Officer, Paper Lithograph, Frame, 23 x 17 In. 660.00
Sign, Enjoy Orange Crush, Button, Celluloid Over Cardboard, 9 In. Diam. 145.00
Sign, Ernst Ruehl, Home Builders, Embossed, Tin Lithograph, Real Estate, 14 x 19 In. 2200.00
Sign, Evinrude & Elto Outboard Motors, Tin, 1940s, 12 x 24 In. 347.00
Sign, Evinrude Outboard Motors, Neon, 13 x 23 In. 770.00
Sign, Eye-Se Beverage, Flavors You Will Like, Call It Icy, Tin Lithograph, 13 x 23 In. 145.00
Sign, F.R. Rice Mercantile Cigar Co., Agent Cigar, Porcelain, 3 x 24 In. 1100.00
Sign, Fairbank's Gold Dust Washing Powder, Black Twins, Cardboard, 11 x 21 In. 410.00
Sign, Falstaff, Trophy Cup Shape, Light-Up, 1955, 20 In. 60.00
Sign, Fanny Edel Plug Cut, St. Nick, Cardboard, Die Cut, Embossed, 10 x 7 In. 715.00
Sign, Father John's Medicine, Girl, Bottle, Cardboard Lithograph, c.1930, 35 In. 78.00
Sign, Fits-U Optical Shop, Tin, Flange, 1930s, 11 x 9 In. 635.00
Sign, Florida Water, Reverse Painted Glass, N.Y., 1800s, 20 1/2 x 24 1/2 In. 265.00
Sign, Fly Paper, Tanglefoot, Cardboard, Baby Covered With Flies, 9 x 16 In. 2860.00
Sign, French War Relief, Black & White, Early 20th Century, 36 1/2 x 96 In. 55.00
Sign, Fresh Up With 7Up, Tin, 1954, 18 x 54 1/2 In. 90.00
Sign, Frostlene Frosting, Gypsy Holding Cake, Tin, Embossed, c.1900, 27 x 19 In. 3500.00
Sign, Fuller & Warren Co., Stoves, Ranges, Paper, 41 x 27 In. 1550.00
Sign, Gail & Ax Navy Tobacco, Man With Foot On Box, Paper, Frame, 41 x 31 1/2 In. 1540.00
Sign, Gem Razors & Blades, Holiday Gifts, Wreath, Red Bow, Cardboard, 38 x 30 In. 77.00
Sign, George Washington Cut Plug, String, Cardboard, Die Cut, 2-Sided, 9 x 9 In. 605.00
Sign, George Washington Tobacco, We Sell A Full Package, Die Cut, Oval, 11 x 8 In. 230.00
Sign, Gibbons Beer, Season's Greetings, Wreath, Cardboard, 1937, 20 In. 125.00
Sign, Gillette Super Speed Razor, Casey Stengel, Cardboard, 1953, 44 x 37 In. 1327.00
Sign, Gillette, Razor, Blade Box, Round, Porcelain, Flange, c.1930, 19 1/2 x 22 In. 4070.00
Sign, Golden Guernsey Milk, 11 3/4 x 17 In. 80.00
Sign, Goldwaite's Golden Gum, Paper, Art Nouveau Style Woman, 22 x 20 In. 350.00
Sign, Good Humor Ice Cream, Porcelain, Graphic Ice Cream Bar, 18 x 26 In. 1705.00
Sign, Grain Belt Beer, Cold Grain, Tin Over Cardboard, 1978, 6 x 29 In. 10.00
Sign, Grain Belt Beer, Friendly Bottled Keg Beer, Cardboard, Frame, 1936, 20 x 16 In. 340.00
Sign, Grain Belt Beer, Go With The Grain, Foil Over Cardboard, 1978, 10 x 19 In. 10.00
Sign, Grain Belt Beer, In Cap Sealed Cans, Cardboard, Frame, 1938, 11 x 9 1/2 In. 135.00
Sign, Granulated 54 Tobacco, Secret Of Contentment, Man, Desk, 7 x 9 In. 330.00
Sign, Grape-Nuts, For Energy, Dizzy Dean, Pamphlet Holder, Cardboard, c.1935, 26 x 22 In. . ***ILLUS*** 493.00
Sign, Grapette Soda, Thirsty Or Not, Cardboard, Die Cut, Easel, 1940s, 19 x 18 In. 140.00
Sign, Great Majestic Ranges, Ed. Fitzgerald, Tin, 19 1/2 x 9 1/4 In. 600.00
Sign, Green River Whiskey, Cardboard, Frame, 19 3/4 x 24 1/2 In. 224.00
Sign, Green Spot, A Real Fruit Drink, 5 Cents, Tin Lithograph, 2-Sided, 21 x 18 In. 385.00
Sign, Gunsmith's, Double Barrel Shotgun Shape, Wood, Painted, 1800s, 83 1/2 In. 575.00
Sign, Haas Bros. Gall Cure, Blue, Yellow, Porcelain, 3 x 24 In. 255.00
Sign, Haas, Extra Pale Beer, Enjoy Top Quality, Cardboard, 1942, 8 x 17 In. 65.00
Sign, Hamm's Beer, Bear, Lying On 12 Pack, 1975, 13 x 10 In. 16.00
Sign, Hamm's Beer, Now In Cans, Frame, 1936, 7 x 19 In. 75.00
Sign, Hamm's, Neon, c.1970, 24 In. 150.00
Sign, Harding's Ice Cream, Malted Milk, 20 Cents, Sealtest Stamp, Frame, c.1930, 44 x 11 In. 715.00
Sign, Harris Takes In Washing, Fetch 'Em Yours, Man, Woman, Yellow, Black, Tin, 13 x 20 In. 360.00
Sign, Hauenstein's Beer, Season's Greetings, Cardboard, 1941, 11 x 14 In. 140.00
Sign, Hazel Club, Tru Orange, Flange Tin Lithograph, 2 x 14 x 20 In. 112.00

Sign, Helmar Turkish Cigarettes, Cardboard, Frame, Girl In Pointed Hat, 29 x 21 In. 415.00
Sign, Hershey's Syrup, Plus Milk, Topping For Many Desserts, Cardboard, c.1937, 45 x 30 In. 410.00
Sign, Hi-En Premium, Beer With Cheer, Chalk, Round, 1962, 13 In. 60.00
Sign, Hills Bros. Tea & Coffee, Curved, Red Ground, San Francisco, 18 x 12 In. 3080.00
Sign, Hires Root Beer, Barrel, Tin Lithograph, Embossed, 65 x 47 1/2 In. 60.00
Sign, Hires Root Beer, Drink Hires In Bottles, Tin Lithograph, c.1950, 35 In. Diam. 220.00
Sign, Hires Root Beer, With Roots-Barks-Herbs, Bubble Glass, Light-Up, Frame, 16 In. 660.00
Sign, Hires Root Beer, Woman In Red Dress, Die Cut Cardboard, 10 x 49 In. 225.00
Sign, Hires, Woman Drinking Soda, Cardboard, 15 x 21 In. 900.00
Sign, Hodson, Superior Pork Butcher, Pig Shape, 1880s, 37 x 58 In. 5540.00
Sign, Hoffman House Bouquet Cigar, Children, Dressing Screen, Lithograph, 17 1/2 x 13 In. 2200.00
Sign, Hoffman's Stein Club Cigars, Men Playing Poker, Tin Lithograph, 19 x 27 In. 4070.00
Sign, Home Of Arculeo's Ice Cream Supreme, Wood, Painted, 18 3/4 x 60 In. 179.00
Sign, Home Run Cigarettes, Batter, Catcher, Baseball Uniform, 1910, 12 x 18 In. 3740.00
Sign, Honest Scrap Tobacco, Cardboard, 22 1/4 x 30 1/4 In. 1980.00
Sign, Honey Moon Smoking Tobacco, Couple In Canoe, Cardboard, Frame, 12 x 22 In. 800.00
Sign, Honey Moon Tobacco, Couple Sledding, Cardboard Trolley Sign, 12 x 22 In. 360.00
Sign, Hood's Ice Cream, Die Cut Flange, 2-Sided, Cow, 19 1/8 In. 3300.00
Sign, Hood, Enamel Paint, Sheet Metal, Oval, 30 x 48 In. 52.00
Sign, Humphrey's Homeopathic Remedies, Nude, Lion, Cardboard Litho, c.1900, 14 x 17 In. 132.00
Sign, Humphrey's Specifics, Red, Black, Gold, Reverse Glass, Frame, 30 1/2 x 22 In. 2640.00
Sign, Hy Quality Coffee, Girl On Swing, Cardboard, Die Cut, 34 1/2 x 16 1/2 In. 1595.00
Sign, Imperial Club Cigar, Embossed, Tin Lithograph, 10 x 13 3/4 In. 230.00
Sign, Imperials Cigarettes, Man Smoking, Porcelain, 2-Sided, Flange, 21 x 14 In. 770.00
Sign, Improved Hickok Calcium Burner, Hanging Burner, Wood, c.1900, 48 x 24 In. 935.00
Sign, Indian Crown Cigars, Indian Chief, Tin Lithograph, 15 x 20 3/4 In. 1870.00
Sign, Indian Rock Ginger Ale, Indian, Tin Lithograph, Embossed, 11 1/2 x 35 1/2 In. 560.00
Sign, Iron Fireman, Automatic Coal Burner, Shoveling Robo-Man, 11 7/8 In. 240.00
Sign, Ivory Soap, Girl Cleaning Dolls In Washtub, 21 3/4 x 16 1/2 In. 470.00
Sign, J. Chalifoux Spring Traps, Lures Hide Stretchers, Wood, Painted, 12 x 36 In. 440.00
Sign, J.A. Cigars, Blue, Yellow, White, Porcelain, 3 1/2 x 21 In. 220.00
Sign, J.H. Baad Coal Man, Boy Holding Piece Of Coal, Multicolored, Tin, 19 3/4 x 3 In. 80.00
Sign, Jackie Coogan, The Kid, Holding Shoe, France, c.1921, 50 x 38 In. 625.00
Sign, John Paul Jones Whiskey, Temptation Of St. Anthony, 1890, 20 In. 765.00
Sign, Keen Kutter Tools, General Hardware, Hillsboro, Kansas, Metal, 9 3/4 x 27 In. 115.00
Sign, Keen Kutter Tools, Saw, Ax, Enamel, Tin, 7 1/2 x 21 In. 189.00
Sign, Keen Kutter Tools, Sell & Sons, Pittsburg, Girard, Metal, 9 3/4 x 27 3/4 In. 59.00
Sign, Keepsake Diamond Rings, Genuine Registered, Mirror, Blue, Neon, 11 x 25 In. 415.00
Sign, Kellogg's Korn Klun, Higher Yielding, Red, Blue, Tin, Embossed, 28 x 20 In. 110.00
Sign, Kendall's Spavin Cure, Paper, 1880s, 28 x 22 In. 6160.00
Sign, Kis-Me Gum, Tin Over Cardboard, 7 5/8 x 6 In. 850.00
Sign, Klondike Cough Nuggets, 5 Cents, Cardboard, 6 3/4 x 10 In. 910.00
Sign, Kodak Developing & Printing, Porcelain, 2-Sided, 14 x 20 In. 690.00
Sign, Kuntz's Lager, Tin, Embossed, Frame, 26 x 20 In. 6500.00
Sign, L.O. Ryan Law Office, Sand Finish, Gold Lettering, Painted, 9 1/2 x 27 In. 55.00
Sign, La Neva Cycles, Airplane, Tin, Self-Framed, c.1948, 14 x 19 In. 230.00
Sign, Laundry, 2 Girls Doing Doll's Laundry, Paper Lithograph, 21 x 13 In. 686.00
Sign, Levi Strauss & Co., 24 x 36 In. 350.00
Sign, Liner Package Foods, Ocean Liner, Celluloid Over Tin, Chain Hanger, 6 x 8 In. 90.00
Sign, Lionel Electric Trains, Enamel, c.1930, 9 x 12 In. 1459.00
Sign, Lipton Tea, Drink & Enjoy, Sold In Air Tight Cans Only, 2-Sided, 9 x 16 In. 855.00
Sign, Long's Ox-Heart, Chocolates, Cocoa, Embossed, Porcelain, 5 1/8 x 25 In. 1540.00
Sign, Lorillard Climax Plug Tobacco, Cardboard, Die Cut, 14 1/2 x 6 In. 550.00
Sign, Lovell Diamond Bicycles, Embossed, Lithograph, Oak Frame, c.1895, 23 x 17 In. 935.00
Sign, Lucky Strike Cigarette, Harry Heilmann, Trolley Car, 1928, 11 x 20 In. 3770.00
Sign, Lucky Strike Cigarette, Harry Heilmann, Trolley Car, c.1925, 11 x 21 In. 6400.00
Sign, Lucky Strike Cigarette, Lloyd Waner, Trolley Car, c.1928, 11 x 21 In. 3615.00
Sign, Lucky Strike Cigarette, Tony Lazzeri, Trolley Car, 1920s, 11 x 21 In. 8529.00
Sign, Lucky Strike, Red Grange, It's Toasted, Mat, Frame, 1930s, 23 x 17 3/4 In. 4815.00
Sign, Magic Yeast, Great Raiser, Die Cut Straight Razor, Cardboard, 14 1/2 x 7 In. 965.00
Sign, Maillard's Chocolate, Cocoa, Tin Lithograph, 22 x 16 1/4 In. 2310.00

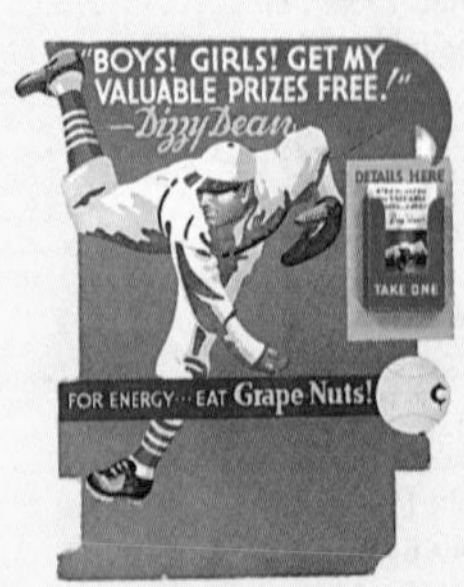

Advertising, Sign, Grape-Nuts, For Energy, Dizzy Dean, Pamphlet Holder, Cardboard, c.1935, 26 x 22 In.

Advertising, Sign, Ted's Creamy Root Beer, Cardboard, Easel, Mat, Frame, 1950s, 16 x 21 In.

Sign, Makomb Finer Brooders, We Sell Energee Chicks, Frame, Tin, 36 x 60 In. 300.00
Sign, Marlin Firearms Co., Cowboy, Boulder, P. Goodwin, c.1890, 23 x 14 In. 1945.00
Sign, Marquette Club, Man, Holding Bottle, Embossed, Die Cut, 1940s, 11 x 8 In. 58.00
Sign, Mavis Chocolate Drink, Cardboard, Die Cut, 29 x 18 In. 385.00
Sign, Max Factor, Hollywood, Claudette Colbert, 1940s, 40 x 26 In. 470.00
Sign, Max Factor, Hollywood, Pan-Stick, Rita Hayworth, Cardboard, 1948, 40 x 25 In. 690.00
Sign, Max Factor, Hollywood, Rita Hayworth, Cardboard, 1947, 42 x 30 In. 1485.00
Sign, Mayo's Smoking Tobacco, Embossed Porcelain, Die Cut Pipe, 6 x 16 In. 1155.00
Sign, Mayo's Tobacco, Mayo's Plug, Cock O' Walk, Rooster, Porcelain, 13 x 6 In. 1825.00
Sign, McCormick Mowers, Best In World, 1900, 16 x 22 In. 330.00
Sign, Mecca Cigarette, Girl In Hat, Frame, 19 3/4 x 11 In. 550.00
Sign, Member Texas, Southwestern Cattle Raisers Ass'n. Inc., Porcelain, 10 x 20 In. 190.00
Sign, Millinery & Fancy Goods, Gold, Black, Frame, Pine, Mid 1800s, 34 x 14 In. 4850.00
Sign, Milton R. Ziehn, The Tailor, Black, Silver Lettering, 1800s, 22 1/2 x 67 In. 800.00
Sign, Modern Service, Barber Pole, Red, Blue, Curved, Porcelain, Bob White Sign Co., 48 In. 605.00
Sign, Mom Always Buys Hershey's Ice Cream, Kids Eating, Cardboard, 32 x 37 In. 55.00
Sign, Mother Parker's Tea & Coffee, Tin, 19 x 47 In. 975.00
Sign, Moxie, Boy, Dog, Cardboard, Easel Back, 1927, 20 x 12 In. 275.00
Sign, Moxie, Drink Moxie, Frank Archer Pointing, Tin, Die Cut, 2-Sided, 6 In. 1595.00
Sign, Moxie, Red, Yellow, White, Black, 2-Sided, Flange, Tin, 9 x 18 In. 240.00
Sign, Moxie, Soda Jerk's Head, Tin Lithograph, Die Cut, 6 3/4 x 4 1/2 In. 578.00
Sign, Murad Turkish Cigarette, Woman Holding Box Of Cigarettes, 39 x 29 In. 1230.00
Sign, My Elgin's All Right, Child, Holding Pocket Watch, Wood, 22 x 15 In. 360.00
Sign, National Stove Ranges, Furnaces, Excelsior Stove & Mfg., Tin, 12 x 36 In. 495.00
Sign, National Stoves & Ranges, Curve, Porcelain, 17 x 24 In. 160.00
Sign, Nature's Remedy, All Vegetable Laxative, Porcelain, Self-Framed, 17 x 23 In. 770.00
Sign, Nature's Remedy, Mortar, Pestle, Mirrored, Reverse Glass, Frame, 25 x 18 In. 2750.00
Sign, Netherland Ice Cream, Dutch Boy & Girl Holding Cone, Tin, 1930s, 26 In. 660.00
Sign, Neverslips, Red Tip Horse Shoes, Horse Head, 2-Sided, Die Cut, 11 3/4 x 10 In. 495.00
Sign, New Amsterdam Amber, Yellow, Orange, Neon, 32 x 12 In. 45.00
Sign, New Size Old Virginia Cheroots, 3 For 5 Cents, Cardboard, 1920s, 13 x 19 In. 248.00
Sign, New Standard Egg Case, Best Egg Carrier On The Market, c.1890, 8 x 10 In. 18.00
Sign, Newman's Baking Powder, Cardboard, Embossed, Die Cut, 10 1/2 x 6 In. 220.00
Sign, Nichol Cola, America's Taste Sensation, Tin, Embossed, 36 In. 88.00
Sign, North Coast Bus, Embossed, Round, 12 In. 1018.00
Sign, NuGrape, Tin Lithograph, Embossed, 13 3/4 x 5 In. 525.00
Sign, Nylotis Talcums, Woman, Talc On Arm, Cardboard, Easel, 6 x 15 1/2 In. 155.00
Sign, O-Pee-Chee Chewing Gum, Oh So Good, Tin Lithograph, Embossed, 4 x 5 1/2 In. 578.00
Sign, Office Of Clipper Mower & Reaper Co., N.Y.C., 1869, 5 x 8 In. 15.00
Sign, Ohio Farmers Insurance Co., Embossed Porcelain, 2-Sided, 13 1/2 x 18 In. 745.00
Sign, Old Gold Cigarettes, Carole Lombard, Cardboard, 1934, 42 x 30 1/2 In. 406.00
Sign, Old Gold Cigarettes, Love At First Light, Glass, Chain, c.1920, 7 1/2 x 13 7/8 In. 880.00
Sign, Old Gold Cigarettes, Not A Cough In A Carload, Chain Hung, Glass, 7 1/2 x 15 In. 605.00

Sign, Omar Turkish Blend Cigarettes, Multicolored Litho, 25 x 18 In. 560.00
Sign, Optometrist, Keenan & Buck, Sheet Copper Spectacles, Iron, Enamel, 37 x 38 In. 2585.00
Sign, Orange Crush, Feel Fresh, Tin Lithograph, 11 5/8 x 15 3/4 In. 336.00
Sign, OshKosh B'Gosh, Uncle Sam, Cardboard, Metal Edge, c.1920, 13 x 30 In. 525.00
Sign, Our Soda, True Fruit Flavors, Girl, Paper, Frame, J. Hungerford Smith, 12 x 18 In. 935.00
Sign, Owl Cigar, 5 Cents, 2-Sided, Tin Lithograph, Round, Hanger, 8 In. 1075.00
Sign, Ox-Heart Cocoa, We Sell Ox-Heart Cocoa, Blue, Red, Porcelain, 7 x 20 In. 1320.00
Sign, Ozite Carpet, Johnny Carson, Early 1960s, 24 3/8 x 66 1/2 In. 509.00
Sign, Pabst Blue Ribbon Beer, Red, White, Blue, Neon, Box, 12 x 36 In. 100.00
Sign, Palmolive Shaving Cream, Man, Tube, Box, Die Cut, Easel Back, 12 x 9 In. 55.00
Sign, Passing Show Cigarettes, Cork Tipped Virginia, Man, Top Hat, Porcelain, 16 x 9 In. 495.00
Sign, Paul Jones Rye Whiskey, Old Farmer, Bottle, Self-Framed, 1905-10, 28 x 22 In. 1045.00
Sign, Paul Jones Whiskey, Girl & 2 Cows, Wood, 20 x 14 In. 715.00
Sign, Pearl Lager Beer, Best Of Texas, Tin Over Cardboard, 1951, 9 x 13 In. 60.00
Sign, Peters Ammunition, Cowboy, Grizzly Bear, 1930, 30 1/2 x 20 In. 1425.00
Sign, Peters Ammunition, Raging Bear, Frame, 21 x 13 In. 2185.00
Sign, Peters Big Game Ammunition, Elk, Rock, Phillip R. Goodwin, 30 x 20 In. 570.00
Sign, Peters Big Game Ammunition, Elk, Wilderness, Phillip R. Goodwin, 30 x 20 In. 910.00
Sign, Peters Loaded Shells, Steel Belongs, Pheasants, c.1940, 30 x 20 In. 1780.00
Sign, Piedmont Cigarettes, Cigarette Of Quality, Blue, White, 9 1/2 x 18 In. 78.00
Sign, Piedmont Cigarettes, People By Staircase, Tin Lithograph, 1916, 24 x 30 In. 470.00
Sign, Piper Heidsieck Tobacco, 10 Cents, Paper Lithograph, Frame, 12 x 15 In. 230.00
Sign, Pippins Co., Cigars, Porcelain, 3 1/2 x 21 In. 935.00
Sign, Play Tom Thumb Golf, Enamel On Metal, Round, 1930s, 42 In. 569.00
Sign, Pleasantview Rooms & Meals, Baths, Biddeford Pool, Metal, 35 3/4 x 50 In. 978.00
Sign, Plow Boy Tobacco, Man On Plow Smoking Pipe, Cloth, Frame, 15 x 9 In. 580.00
Sign, Plummer's, Hats Caps & Furs, Blue Ground, White Letters, 2 Parts, 6 3/4 x 53 1/2 In. 1650.00
Sign, Polar Bear Tobacco, Chew Polar Bear, Blue, White, Porcelain, 5 x 8 1/2 In. 550.00
Sign, Pope Bicycle, Lady Handing Woman Flowers, Paper, Frame, 23 x 16 In. 580.00
Sign, Postal Telegraph, 8 7/8 x 8 3/8 In. 1375.00
Sign, Power City Baking, Hazle Maid Bread, Cupcakes, Celluloid, Round, 9 In. 415.00
Sign, Pratt's Food, Horses & Cattle, Pratt's Official Chart, Paper Lithograph, 22 x 27 3/4 In. 1020.00
Sign, Pratt's Poultry Regulator, Chicken Breeds, Frame, 21 x 27 1/2 In. 525.00
Sign, Pub, Woodstock Arms, 2-Sided, Early 20th Century, 39 x 28 x 1 3/4 In. 708.00
Sign, Puretest Rubbing Alcohol, Football Players, Frame, 1930s, 38 x 25 In. 1635.00
Sign, Rainier Aged Beer & Ale, Ducks, Composite, Self-Framed, 1943, 16 x 11 In. 135.00
Sign, Raleigh 903, Gene Tierney, Cardboard, 1946, 30 x 20 In. 679.00
Sign, Range Eternal, 2 Gifts She Will Never Forget, Family, Engman-Matthews, 1900s, 34 x 24 In. . 360.00
Sign, RCA Radiotron, A Good Idea, Parrish, Die Cut, Easel Back, 8 5/8 x 20 In. 495.00
Sign, Reach Baseball Gloves, Mitt, 11 x 8 In. 1595.00
Sign, Reach For Sunbeam Bread, Tin, Embossed, c.1960, 19 x 55 In. 825.00
Sign, Red Goose Shoes, Porcelain, Red Neon, 1940s, 36 In. 1790.00
Sign, Red Indian Tobacco, Must Have It, 5 Cts., Paper Lithograph, 31 x 25 x 21 In. 1265.00
Sign, Red Man Cigar Leaf, First In America, c.1920, 18 x 12 In. 390.00
Sign, Red Man Tobacco, First In America, Aviator, Indian, 1930s, 39 x 26 1/2 In. 626.00
Sign, Red Man Tobacco, Paper, Indian Holding Tobacco Pack, 19 1/4 x 13 In. 1210.00
Sign, Red Rock Ginger Ale, Cowgirl With Gun, Glass Over Paper, Chain, 10 x 5 In. 440.00
Sign, Regal Supreme Beer, Jailbreak, Frame, 1951, 13 x 17 1/4 In. 425.00
Sign, Regal Supreme Beer, Wrestlers, Frame, 1951, 13 x 17 1/4 In. 425.00
Sign, Remington 22 Cal. Rifles, Die Cut, Easel, 30 x 10 In. 237.00
Sign, Remington Arms, UMC, 3 Setters In Window, Matte, Frame, 24 x 17 In. 1575.00
Sign, Remington Game Loads, Grouse, Die Cut, Hanger, Lynn Boque Hunt, 10 x 11 In. 800.00
Sign, Remington Metallic Cartridges, Deer, Die Cut, Easel, 15 x 10 In. 490.00
Sign, Remington, Wetproof Shells, Ducks, Paper, Stand-Up, 1923, 40 x 26 In. 1430.00
Sign, Rental Service, Choctaw Machinery Co., Indian, Porcelain, 6 x 6 In. 578.00
Sign, Rev-O-Noc Sporting Goods, Baseball, Golf, Fishing, Hunting, 13 x 19 In. 3600.00
Sign, Revere Liquid Paint, 4 Stacked Graduated Barrels Shape, 2-Sided, 52 In. 2300.00
Sign, Rice's Popular Flower Seeds, Girl With Pot, Paper Lithograph, 30 x 20 In. 1870.00
Sign, Richmond Straight Cut Cigarettes, Tin, Oval, c.1900, 29 x 23 In. 465.00
Sign, Ridder Farm, Milk Cream, Round, Raised Porcelain, Farm Image, 24 In. 470.00
Sign, Royal Crown Cola, Bottle, Red, Yellow, Brown, Tin Lithograph, Frame, 1936, 36 x 16 In. 220.00

Sign, Royal Crown Cola, Red, White, Blue, Metal, 51 3/4 x 25 3/4 In. 175.00
Sign, Ruby Ring, Most Complimented Stocking In America, Packer, 37 x 26 In. 226.00
Sign, S & H Green Stamps, Green, White, Red, Black, Tin, 3 Piece, 40 x 35 1/2 In. 25.00
Sign, Safety First, Drink Pluto Water, Celluloid, Hanger, Round, 6 In. 285.00
Sign, San-Nap-Pak, Hours Of Extra Protection, Woman, Clock, c.1920, 23 x 17 In. 200.00
Sign, Santa Claus Soap, St. Nick, Fairbanks, Sack Of Toys, Paper, 25 x 19 In. 385.00
Sign, Satin Skin Powder & Cream, Woman Holding Fan, 25 Cents, Paper, c.1903, 42 x 28 In. 65.00
Sign, Say Burgie, Truly Fine Pale Beer, Burgermeister, Light-Up, Pre 1940, 13 x 19 In. 150.00
Sign, Say Hires, Boy, Bib, Pointing, Cardboard, Self-Framed, Oval, 24 x 20 In. 1870.00
Sign, Schlitz Brewery, Globe, Blue, White, Porcelain, 13 x 14 1/2 In. 770.00
Sign, Schlitz, Can That Opens Like Bottle, Cardboard, Easel, 1935, 12 x 10 In. 68.00
Sign, Schlitz, Enjoy The Best, Picnic, Cardboard, Easel, 1936, 12 x 10 In. 68.00
Sign, Schmidt Beer, Canada Geese, Frame, 1979, 18 x 26 In. 45.00
Sign, Schmidt's City Club Beer, Light-Up, Reverse On Glass, 1938, 6 1/2 x 27 In. 725.00
Sign, Score Board, 7Up, Masonite, 11 1/2 x 21 In. 672.00
Sign, Scotch Irish Whiskey, Reverse Paint On Glass, 1800s, 72 In. 220.00
Sign, Scott Atwater Outboard Motors, Sales, Service, Reverse Painted, 12 x 26 In. 468.00
Sign, Seal Of North Carolina Smoking Tobacco, Wells & Hope, c.1880, 32 x 23 In. 27500.00
Sign, Seilheimer's Ginger Ale, Porcelain, 10 3/4 x 18 1/2 In. 280.00
Sign, Seneca Cameras & Roll Film, 2-Sided, Flange, 1910-20, 14 x 15 In. 6600.00
Sign, Shac, For Everybody's Headache, 8 Faces, Paper, Frame, 19 x 39 In. 1045.00
Sign, Sharp & Dohmes Medicinal Products, Reverse Painted Glass, Frame, 12 x 25 In. 1210.00
Sign, Shawnee Fire Insurance, Chief Tecumseh, Tin Lithograph, 20 x 13 1/2 In. 1375.00
Sign, Ship Us Your Furs, United States Fur Co., Unwelcome Surprise, 1930s, 21 x 15 In. 710.00
Sign, Skates! Skates!, A.M. Gardner Hardware Co., Boston, 1890s, 6 x 7 In. 25.00
Sign, Smith & Wesson Revolvers, Man, On Horse, Mat, Frame, 1920s, 29 x 25 In. 1485.00
Sign, Sober-Up Drink, Sober-Up It's A Life Saver, Cardboard, 1950s, 14 x 19 In. 165.00
Sign, Soda Mint Gum, For Your Stomach's Sake, Woman On Chair, Paper, 15 5/8 x 12 5/8 In. 770.00
Sign, Soda, Wood, Painted, Applied Molding, Orange Lettering, 1900s, 14 x 50 In. 940.00
Sign, Springfield Tractor, Farmer On Tractor, Paper Lithograph, 12 x 15 1/4 In. 1650.00
Sign, Squires Pork Products, Pig On Box, Arlington Sausage, Die Cut, Cardboard, 13 x 8 In. 520.00
Sign, Squirrel Brand Salted Peanuts, Paperboard, 12 x 11 In. 125.00
Sign, Squirrel Brand Salted Peanuts, Squirrel, Tin, Cardboard, Die Cut, 12 x 11 In. 265.00
Sign, Star Brand Shoes, Yellow, Red, Black, Tin, W.F. Brower & Co., 12 x 23 In. 130.00
Sign, Star Tobacco, Sold Here, Yellow, Blue, White, Brown, Metal, c.1900, 12 x 24 In. 360.00
Sign, Star Tobacco, Sold Here, Yellow, Brown, Blue, Porcelain, 12 x 24 In. 275.00
Sign, Stars & Stripes, Red, White, Blue, Shield Form, Porcelain, 4 1/2 x 3 7/8 In. 240.00
Sign, Sterling Salt, Lithograph, Cardboard, 1940s 125.00
Sign, Stevens Fire Arms, Give Universal Satisfaction, Tin, Self-Framed, 6 x 12 In. 4630.00
Sign, Storz Beer, Scrolling, Light-Up, 1953, 22 In. .... 88.00 to 110.00
Sign, Storz Brewing Company, And Pass The Ammunition, 1942, 19 x 22 In. 360.00
Sign, Stroh's Brewery Co., 3-Dimensional, 10 1/2 x 5 1/2 x 13 1/2 In. 999.00
Sign, Stroh's Brewery Co., GOP National Convention, 1980, 21 1/2 x 14 In. 175.00
Sign, Sunoco Gas Station, Rest Room, Men, Ladies, 4 1/8 x 9 1/8 In., Pair 1595.00
Sign, Sunshine Tobacco, Indian Chief, Leather, c.1910, 42 x 46 In. 1799.00
Sign, Swain's Drugs, Soda Fountain, Postcards, New Hampshire, 95 x 25 In. 4315.00
Sign, Swan Pencil Co., Pencil, Aldebaran, Yellow, 6-Sided, Wood, 32 x 2 In. 680.00
Sign, Sweet Caporal Cigarettes, Woman, Cardboard, Frame, Kinney Bros., 12 x 8 3/4 In. 230.00
Sign, Sweet-Orr Overalls, Clothes To Work In, Porcelain, 2-Sided, 18 x 18 In. 1485.00
Sign, Swift's Ice Cream, Blue, White, Porcelain, 2-Sided, 18 x 24 In. 550.00
Sign, Swim In A Jantzen, Paper, c.1920, 17 x 25 In. 440.00
Sign, Ted's Creamy Root Beer, Cardboard, Easel Back, 1950s, 20 x 30 In. 3190.00
Sign, Ted's Creamy Root Beer, Cardboard, Easel, Mat, Frame, 1950s, 16 x 21 In. .... *ILLUS* 877.00
Sign, Ted's Ice Cream, White Lettering, Blue Ground, Wood, Painted, 5 x 81 In. 176.00
Sign, Theodore Distler Plumbing & Heating, Wood, Painted, 22 x 107 In. 415.00
Sign, Thirsty Or Not!, Enjoy Grapette, Smiling Woman, Cardboard, 31 x 20 In. 105.00
Sign, Thirsty?, Just Whistle, Boy, Running With Bottle, Frame, 1939, 26 x 14 In. 415.00
Sign, Thomas Ryan Brewery, Sparkling Cream Ales, Tin Lithograph, 22 x 33 1/2 In. 5610.00
Sign, Tippecanoe Quack Medicine, Warner's Safe Co., 9 3/4 x 22 In. 468.00
Sign, Tivoli White Ribbon, Drink Of Delight, Bottle, Blue, White, Tin Lithograph, 14 x 19 In. 330.00
Sign, Travelers Accident Insurance, Accident Tickets, Blue, White, Porcelain, 3 3/4 x 7 In. 385.00

Sign, Try Rice's Seeds, Vegetables, As Good As Any, Better'n Some, Paper, 30 x 20 In. 880.00
Sign, Tums, For The Tummy, Quick Relief, 10 Cents, Porcelain, Self-Framed, 17 x 23 In. 1430.00
Sign, UMC Shot Shells, Quails, Flying, 29 1/4 x 15 In. 1215.00
Sign, UMC Smokeless Shot Shells, Puppies In Vest, 1904, 24 3/4 x 15 In. 4746.00
Sign, UMC, Bull's Eye, Bull Head, Tin, Flange, 26 1/2 x 18 1/2 In. 4139.00
Sign, Uneco Radio Tubes, Textured, Canvas, 12 3/4 x 14 3/4 x 13 3/4 In. 155.00
Sign, Union Made Cigar, Have A Good One, Men At Cigar Counter, Wood, 15 x 21 In. 440.00
Sign, Union Shield, Painted, Red, White, Blue, Light Bulb Border, Electric, 49 x 36 In. 4700.00
Sign, United Pajama, Victorian Scene, Kaufman & Strauss, Tin, Embossed, 17 x 11 In. 3100.00
Sign, United Service Motors, Porcelain, Light-Up, 1950s, 36 In. 840.00
Sign, US Cartridge Co., Black Shells, Romax, Climax, Ajax, Tin, Fluted, 9 x 13 1/4 In. 119.00
Sign, US Cartridges, Shot Shells, Mountain Lion, Die Cut, Easel Back, 1923, 30 x 40 In. 1660.00
Sign, US Shot Shells, Load For Every Purpose, Puppies, Dog, Dead Duck, 31 x 20 In. 1246.00
Sign, W. Davies, Draper, Licensed Dealer In Tea, Coffee, Snuff, Tobacco, Late 1800s 880.00
Sign, W.F. Sellers & Co., South Bend Watches, Tin Lithograph, 9 3/4 x 27 1/2 In. 230.00
Sign, Walk-Over Shoes, Fall Favorites, Football Player, Cardboard, Easel, 1910s 235.00
Sign, Walter Plumb & Son, Hide Skin Fat & Wool Market, Early 1900s, 9 x 15 In. 118.00
Sign, Walter's Barber Shop, Painted Red & White Striped, Wood, c.1900, 6 x 40 In. 3200.00
Sign, Ward Collars, Die Cut, Cardboard, 12 x 7 1/2 In. 275.00
Sign, Warner's Safe Yeast, 2 Indians Paddling Canoe, 29 1/2 x 13 1/2 In. 1345.00
Sign, Watkins Products, Blue, White, Porcelain, 7 1/2 x 19 1/2 In. 110.00
Sign, We Sell Cigarettes, Smoke Kool, Penguin, Tin, Embossed, 26 In. 45.00
Sign, We Want Juniata Ice Cream, Easel Back, 1940s, 10 x 12 In. 110.00
Sign, Wellingtons, Studio Of Taxidermy, Sandwich, N.H., 22 1/2 x 30 1/2 In. 405.00
Sign, Wells Fargo & Co., Bankers & Express Forwarders, Enamel On Steel, 12 x 24 In. 100.00
Sign, Western Ammunition, Bob White, Lynn Bogue Hunt, c.1925, 24 x 15 1/2 In. 1130.00
Sign, Western Super-X, Boy Holding Rifle, Target, Die Cut, 1933, 26 x 19 In. 830.00
Sign, Western Super-X, Boys Target Shooting, Die Cut, Easel, 16 x 12 In. 356.00
Sign, Western Union, Porcelain, Chain Hung, 2 3/4 x 13 In. 210.00
Sign, Western Xpert 22s, Super-X 22s, Die Cut, 15 1/4 x 12 In. 89.00
Sign, White House Coffee, Cardboard, Embossed, 14 x 10 In. 385.00
Sign, White Label Cigar, 10 x 13 3/4 In. 358.00
Sign, White Orchid Cigar, Mechanical, Victorian Woman, Moving Eyes & Mouth 4400.00
Sign, White Rock, World's Best Table Water, Psyche, Tin Lithograph, 8-Sided, 14 In. 1650.00
Sign, White Rock, World's Best Table Water, Winged Woman, Self-Framed, 14 In. 360.00
Sign, Wilson Football Equipment, Cardboard, Die Cut, 1940s, 27 x 25 In. 430.00
Sign, Winchester Cartridges & Guns, Antlers, Dead Ducks, Tin, Alexander Pope, 36 x 30 In. 6050.00
Sign, Winchester Repeating Shotguns, Hunting Dogs, c.1910, 30 3/8 x 16 1/2 In. 1520.00
Sign, Winchester, For Sale Here, Bear Dogs, Painted Frame, 32 x 41 1/2 In. 7000.00
Sign, Winchester, New Rival Shotgun Shells, Game Bird, Die Cut, 10 x 9 3/4 In. 1060.00
Sign, Winchester, Shoot 'Em & Avoid Trouble, Self-Framed, 25 x 33 In. 4720.00
Sign, Winchester, Shooting Holidays Are Here, Die Cut, Easel, 29 x 22 In. 260.00
Sign, Winchester, Short Hair Pointers, c.1910, 29 1/2 x 16 1/2 In. 1190.00
Sign, Window Display, Reach Baseball Glove, Cardboard, 2 Players, c.1910, 8 x 11 In. 880.00
Sign, Window, Popsicle Pet Frozen Treats, Different Color Popsicles, 1940, 9 x 8 In. 140.00
Sign, Winston, Finer Flavor!, Finer Filter!, Tin, 22 In. 22.00
Sign, Wonder Grape Drink, 5 Cents, Bunch Of Grapes, Tin, c.1920, 14 x 19 In. 470.00
Sign, Wood Street Garage, 252 E. Wood St., Decatur, Black Boy, Mule, Ithaca, 1900, 48 In. 740.00
Sign, World Series, Louisville Slugger, 1931, 12 1/2 x 19 In. 250.00
Sign, Wrigley's Doublemint, Cardboard, Die Cut, Easel, 13 1/2 x 10 1/2 In. 880.00
Sign, Wrigley's Gum, Beveled, Tin Over Cardboard, 6 x 13 In. 745.00
Sign, Wrigley's Spearmint Gum, Buy The Best, The Flavor Lasts, Tin, 17 1/2 x 9 In. 550.00
Sign, Wrigley's Spearmint Gum, Package, Trademark Character, 7 1/2 x 11 In. 275.00
Sign, Yellow Kid 5 Cent Cigars, Kid In Center, Black, Red Trim, Cardboard, 1890s 1500.00
Sign, Yellow Kid Big Bubble, 1 Cent, Cardboard, Die Cut, 5 x 7 In. 1320.00
Sign, Yellow Kid Cigar, Paper, Brucker & Boghien, c.1910, 8 1/4 x 4 1/2 In. 70.00
Slate Board, Dr Pepper, Painted Clock, 34 x 28 In. 225.00
Smock, Keen Kutter, Red & White Stripes, 15 1/2 x 21 1/2 In. 115.00
Smoke Stand, Colorado Fina Cigars, Black Boy, Barrels, Austria, Majolica, 1880s, 7 1/2 In. 315.00
Stickpin, Ask For Winchester Nublack, Shotgun Shell Shape, 2 x 1 In. 110.00
Strawholder, Drink Grape Smash, Painted, 2-Sided, 11 1/2 In. 1320.00

Strawholder, Drink Hires, Cast Iron, White Paint, Ruby Glass Inserts, 1911, 5 1/2 x 10 In. 4070.00
Strawholder, Grape Smash, Glass, Hinged Metal Lids, Purple Painted Letters, 9 1/2 In. 1980.00
Strawholder, Hires, 5 Cents, Iron, 4 Green Panels, 1911, 5 1/2 x 10 In. 3300.00
Strawholder, Jersey-Creme, Pressed Glass, Hinged Lid, 4 x 10 In. 520.00
Stringholder, Post Toasties, Bully For Breakfast, Round, 1915-20, 11 1/2 In. 330.00
Stringholder, Red Goose Shoes, Goose Silhouette About Metal Frame Holder 3400.00
Sugar & Creamer, Borden's, Elsie & Elmer, Figural, Lid, Original Box, 1950s, 5 In. 225.00
Sugar & Creamer, Elsie & Elmer, Ceramic, 5 1/4 In. 100.00
Tap Knob, Blatz Pilsener, Chrome, Footed Base, Enamel Inlaid Brass Insert, 1946 .... 90.00
Tap Knob, Erlanger Deluxe, Tin, Celluloid, Chrome, 1937 .... 150.00
Tap Knob, Iron City, 1-Piece Ball, Chrome, Enamel Inlaid Brass Insert, 1939 .... 100.00
Tap Knob, Krueger Extra Light Dry Beer, c.1950 .... 65.00
Tap Knob, Manz Beer, Philadelphia Brewing Co., Bakelite, Celluloid Insert, 1949 .... 120.00
Tap Knob, Ortlieb's Ale, Bakelite, 2-Piece, Metal Base, Celluloid Insert, 1939 .... 50.00
Tap Knob, Schlitz, Enamel Insert, Chrome 50.00
Tap Knob, Stegmaier Beer, Wilkes-Barre, Pa., Chrome, Porcelained Brass Insert, 1948 .... 65.00
Tap Knob, Yankee Premium Beer, Chrome, Porcelained Brass Insert, 1945 .... 120.00
Thermometers are listed in their own category.

Advertising tin cans or canisters were first used commercially in the United States in 1819 and were called *tins*. The English language is sometimes confusing. Today the word *tin* is used by most collectors to describe many types of containers, including food tins, biscuit boxes, roly poly tobacco containers, gunpowder cans, talcum powder sprinkle-top cans, cigarette flat-fifty tins, and more. Beer Cans are listed in their own category. Things made of undecorated tin are listed under Tinware.

Tin, Ace High Spice, Thyme, Airplane Over Water, Lithograph, 3 1/4 x 2 5/8 x 1 1/4 In. 600.00
Tin, Adams Pepsin Gum, American Chicle, Lithograph, 6 x 6 1/2 x 4 3/4 In. 385.00
Tin, Adams Silver Roll, Pedestal, 8 1/2 x 4 3/4 In. 2420.00
Tin, Air Float Corylopsis Of Japan Talcum Powder, Asian Woman, 4 1/2 In. 90.00
Tin, Air Float Talcum Powder, Woman, Pink Flowers, Talcum Puff Co., 4 5/8 In. 33.00
Tin, Air Float Talcum Powder, Woman, Sample, Talcum Puff Co., 2 1/8 In. 60.00
Tin, All American Cigars, Lincoln, Washington, Franklin, Lithograph, 5 x 5 In. 468.00
Tin, Allen & Ginter's Genuine Louisiana Perique, Black, Gold, Hinged Lid, 4 x 3 In. 135.00
Tin, Altex, Condom, 1 3/4 x 2 1/4 x 1/4 In. 330.00
Tin, American Blend Tobacco, Indian Village Scene, Germany, 4 1/2 x 3 x 7/8 In. 800.00
Tin, American Eagle Tobacco, Hinged Lid, 1 1/2 x 2 5/8 x 7/16 In. 110.00
Tin, American Eagle, Bare Breasted Woman Hugging Eagle, Pocket, 2 3/8 x 3 5/8 In. 800.00
Tin, Anza Coffee, Culture Ripened Coffee, Roasted & Packed By George C. Buell & Co., 6 In. 15.00
Tin, Apache Trail Cigars, Indian On Horse, 50 Count, Multicolored, 5 3/4 x 6 1/8 x 4 1/8 In. 1595.00
Tin, April Showers Talcum Powder, Cheramy, Green, Pink, White, Cap, Contents, 4 1/4 In. 30.00
Tin, Aristocrat, Condom, Lithograph, 1 5/8 x 2 3/8 x 3/8 In. 770.00
Tin, Arthur's Shaving Powder, Lithograph, 4 x 1 3/4 In. 745.00
Tin, Attraction Wafers, Cupid, Indian, F.B. Crouch, 4 1/2 x 2 In. 550.00
Tin, Austin Powder Company, Gunpowder, 6 x 4 In. 660.00
Tin, Baker's Nursery Talcum Powder, Baby On Stork, Lithograph, 6 x 2 x 1 In. 198.00
Tin, BB Special High Grade Coffee, Pittsburgh, Pa., 5 Lb. 195.00
Tin, Berma Coffee, Distinctive Quality, Grand Union Co., N.Y., Lb., 6 In. 18.00
Tin, Big Ben Tobacco, British Landmark, Lithograph, Pocket, 4 1/2 x 3 x 7/8 In. 880.00
Tin, Big Ben Tobacco, Brown Horse, Red Ground, 4 1/4 In. 30.00
Tin, Bismoline Toilet Powder, A.A. LeFevre Co., 4 x 2 1/2 In. 1155.00
Tin, Black Fox Cigar, London, Canada 700.00
Tin, Blanke's Mojav Coffee, Small Cap, 2 Lb., 7 x 5 1/4 In. 635.00
Tin, Blue Plate, Blue Willow China Graphics, With Shortening, 20 x 16 In. 225.00
Tin, Blue Plate, Blue, White, With Shortening, 14 1/2 x 13 In. 180.00
Tin, Bone, Eagle & Co., Menthol Cough Drops, Reading, Pa., Screw-On Lid, 7 1/2 x 5 In. 198.00
Tin, Bone, Eagle & Co., Red Cough Drops, Red, Yellow, Screw-On Lid, 5 Lb., 7 x 5 In. 630.00
Tin, Bouquet Roasted Coffee, Lb. 95.00
Tin, Bowl Of Roses Tobacco, 7/8 In. 190.00
Tin, Bowl Of Roses Tobacco, 1 1/2 In. 200.00

Advertising, Tin, Crawford, Fairy House Bank, Biscuit, Mabel Lucie Attwell, 1934, 8 In.

Advertising, Tin, Huntley & Palmers, Cabinet, Biscuit, 1911, 7 1/4 In.

Tin, Boye Stainless Oil, Stencil Painted, Plastic Spout, 3 Oz. 11.00
Tin, Browning Gun Oil, Pewter Top, Plastic Cap, 4 7/8 In. 392.00
Tin, Buckingham Cut Plug Smoking Tobacco, 5 x 5 In. 47.00
Tin, Bulger Cigarette Tobacco, Round, 4 3/4 In. 16.00
Tin, Bull Durham Smoking Tobacco, Tin Lithograph, Pocket, 4 x 3 x 1 In. 3960.00
Tin, Cabot's Lubri-Tasgon, Yellow, Black, Stencil, Cylindrical, Pint, 5 1/2 In. 37.00
Tin, Cadette Tooth Powder, Tin Soldier, Lithograph, 7 3/8 x 1 1/4 In. 358.00
Tin, Candy, Nursery Rhymes, Thomas Lamb, Lithograph, 3 1/4 x 4 1/2 In. 265.00
Tin, Carmen Brand Latex Condoms, Seminude Woman, Round, 1 5/8 x 5/8 In. 230.00
Tin, Chamberlains Tooth Powder, Blue, White, Des Moines, Ia., 4 1/8 In. 330.00
Tin, Charm Of The West Tobacco, Spaulding & Merrick, 2 1/2 x 3 1/2 In. .... 358.00 to 415.00
Tin, Colgate's Antiseptic Dental Powder, To Cleanse & Whiten The Teeth, 3 5/8 In. 255.00
Tin, Colgate's Baby Talc Powder, Baby Holding Tin, 6 In. 70.00
Tin, Colgate's Baby Talc, Real Boric Powder, Contents, Sample, Box, 2 1/2 In. 88.00
Tin, Colgate's Dactylis Talc Powder, Woman, 6 In. 20.00
Tin, Colgate's Dactylis Talc Powder, Woman, Sample, 2 1/8 In. 20.00
Tin, Columbia Healing Powder, F.C. Sturtevant Co., Hartford, Contents, Oval, 4 1/2 In. 45.00
Tin, Corona Athlete Chewing Gum, Pineapple, Hinged Lid, Yellow, Red, 1 x 3 1/4 x 3/8 In. 80.00
Tin, Country Club, Snyder & Son's, 5 1/2 x 5 x 5 In. 230.00
Tin, Cow & Gate Milk Food, Laughing Baby, Wearing Crown, Lid, Blue, White 25.00
Tin, Crawford, Fairy House Bank, Biscuit, Mabel Lucie Attwell, 1934, 8 In. .... *ILLUS* 140.00
Tin, Cub Shoe Polish, Best In Town, Round, Lithograph, 1 x 3 In. 550.00
Tin, Cushman's Menthol Balm, Antiseptic Ointment, Green, Red, Black, Box, 3 x 1 3/4 In. 165.00
Tin, Cy Young Cigar, Mild Havana Blend, c.1910, 5 x 5 In. 4930.00
Tin, Cy Young Cigar, Portrait, Front & Back, 1905-10 .... 3410.00
Tin, Dandy Gum Co., Pepsin Chewing Gum, Girl, 1 7/8 x 1/2 In. 635.00
Tin, De-Luxe Condom, Blue Ribbon, German Shepherd, 1 5/8 x 2 1/8 x 1/4 In. 300.00
Tin, Dermacilia Ointment, Man Sitting At Desk, Red, White, Blue, 2 3/8 In. Diam. 358.00
Tin, Dixie Queen Plug Cut, Lithograph, 6 1/2 x 5 In. 330.00
Tin, Dixie Queen Tobacco, Woman, Lithograph, 6 1/2 x 4 3/4 In. 300.00
Tin, Dorsella Milk Food, Smiling Baby, Blue, Cream, Lid 35.00
Tin, Dr. A.C. Daniels Antiseptic Dusting Powder, 25 Cents, Contents, Lithograph, 4 In. 330.00
Tin, Dr. A.C. Daniels Antiseptic Dusting Powder, 50 Cents, Contents, Lithograph, 5 In. 255.00
Tin, Dr. E.L. Graves Unequaled Tooth Powder, For Health & Beautiful Teeth, 4 1/8 In. 88.00
Tin, Dr. Herman's Valiant Talcum Powder, For Toilet Use, Baby, Embossed, 5 7/8 In. 188.00
Tin, Dr. Hess Medicated Powder, Red, Orange, Black, 25 Cents, Oval, Contents, 4 Oz., 5 1/4 In. 70.00
Tin, Dr. I.W. Lyon's Perfect Tooth Powder, Cleansing & Beautifying The Teeth, 3 5/8 In. 49.00
Tin, Dr. J. De Pratis, Hamburg Figs, Red, Black, California, 3 1/2 x 2 1/4 In. 121.00
Tin, Dr. J.D. Kellogg's Asthma Remedy, Northrop & Lyman, Toronto, 4 7/8 x 2 x 1 3/4 In. 35.00
Tin, Dr. Scholl's Foot Powder, Antiseptic & Deodorant, Yellow, Blue, Contents, 6 In. 45.00
Tin, Dr. Scott's Electric Safety Razor, Arm, Lightning Bolts, Lithograph, 1 x 2 1/4 In. 440.00
Tin, Dr. T.L. Stephens Celebrated Chemical Eye Salve, White, Blue, Wrapper, 1 x 3/4 In. 130.00
Tin, Drako Coffee, Duck, Lithograph, Lb. 635.00
Tin, Dref's Gout & Rheumatism, Yellow, White, Adopted July 1, 1916, 3/4 x 2 In. 28.00
Tin, Drummer Coffee, Can't Be Beat, Drum, Cup Of Coffee, Lb., 3 5/8 x 5 1/4 In. 410.00
Tin, Dunwoody's Facial Soap, Girl Holding Can, 4 7/8 x 2 1/8 In. 440.00
Tin, DuPont Superfine FFFg Gun Powder, 1924, 6 x 4 In. 33.00

Advertising, Tin, Huntley & Palmers, Ink Stand, Fox Hunting, Biscuit, 1928, 9 1/4 In.

Advertising, Tin, Huntley & Palmers, Literature, Biscuit, 1901-02, 6 1/4 In.

Tin, E.C. Shotgun Powder, No. 1, Orange, 5 1/2 x 3 1/2 x 1 1/2 In. 39.00
Tin, Eagle Violet Borated Talcum Powder, Eagle, Eagle Supply Co., 4 3/4 In. 93.00
Tin, Eclectic Herbs, Barks, Roots & Gums, 100 Day Treatment, 2 3/8 x 4 x 2 In. 44.00
Tin, Eclectic Mixture, Pace Co., Women Image, Tin Lithograph, Hinge, 3 3/8 x 4 1/2 In. 330.00
Tin, Edgeworth Ready Rubbed Pipe Tobacco, Lithograph, Pocket, 4 1/4 x 3 x 1 In. 495.00
Tin, Elephant Salted Peanuts, Superior Peanut Co., Cleveland, 4 x 4 x 2 In. 88.00
Tin, Erasmic Co., Kiddy Powder, 2 1/2 x 7/8 x 3/4 In. 230.00
Tin, F.J. Kellogg's Obesity Food Tablets, Yellow, Black, 2 5/8 x 2 In. 240.00
Tin, Fairy Marshmallows, Rueckheim Bros. & Eckstein, Chicago, 8 x 17 x 11 In. 187.00
Tin, Fiendoil, Stencil Painted, Plastic Spout, Cap, 3 Oz. 34.00
Tin, Forest & Stream Tobacco, Fishing Scene, Lithograph, 4 1/4 x 3 x 7/8 In. 495.00
Tin, Fort Henry Brand Lard, Weimer Packing Co., Orange, Black, Wheeling, W. Va., 4 Lb. 60.00
Tin, Fountain Tobacco, Victorian Fountain, Covington, Ky., 6 3/8 x 5 1/4 In. 198.00
Tin, Four Roses, Tin Lithograph, Liggett & Myers Co., Pocket, 4 1/2 x 3 x 7/8 In. 523.00
Tin, Frismuth's Tobacco, Lithograph, Pocket, 4 x 3 3/8 x 1 In. 5060.00
Tin, Full Dress Pipe & Cigarette Tobacco, Sears & Roebuck & Co., 4 1/4 x 3 x 1 In. 630.00
Tin, Game Tobacco, Fine Cut, Jno. J. Bagley & Co., Quails, 7 1/2 x 11 1/2 In. 1980.00
Tin, Gardenia Bouquet Talcum Powder, Romney Distributors, No Cap, 7 Oz., 8 In. 16.00
Tin, Gardenia Bouquet Talcum Powder, Woman, White, Lavender, 6 In. 14.00
Tin, George Washington Cut Plug, RJ Reynolds, 4 1/2 x 8 3/4 In. 40.00
Tin, Glove Powder, Blue, White, Sears Roebuck & Co., 3 x 5/8 In. 45.00
Tin, Gobblers, Latest Smoke, Lithograph, 5 x 5 In. 470.00
Tin, Gold Dust Tobacco, Gold Miners, Worth Its Weight In Gold, Lithograph, 4 x 3 x 1 In. 4950.00
Tin, Golden Rule Tea, W Co., Paper Label, 5 Lb., 10 1/2 In. 75.00
Tin, Golf Girl Talcum, Victorian Woman Golfer, Label, 8 5/8 x 2 1/2 In. 965.00
Tin, Goodrich Drug Co., Velvetina, Talcum Powder, Tin Lithograph, 5 x 2 1/4 In. 155.00
Tin, Hales Midget Popcorn, Milwaukee, Wis. 90.00
Tin, Hand Made Globe Tobacco, Lithograph, 4 x 3 3/8 In. 330.00
Tin, Harrison Candy, Peter Rabbit, Hinged Lid, Handle, 3 1/8 x 6 1/8 x 3 7/8 In. 130.00
Tin, Hershey Cocoa, Paper Label, 3 1/4 x 3 x 1 3/4 In. 209.00
Tin, Hiawatha Tobacco, Rectangular, 4 Oz. 105.00
Tin, Himrod's Asthma Powder, Influenza, Rose Cold, Nasal Catarrh, Label, 3 1/2 x 2 In. 38.00
Tin, Hindoo Granulated Plug, Lithograph, Strater Brothers, 3 1/2 x 3 1/2 x 2 In. 745.00
Tin, Hires Instant Soluble Coffee, Tan, Off-White, Yellow, 2 3/8 x 2 3/4 In. 130.00
Tin, Hoadleys Phosphate Tablets, Hinged Lid, Glass Panels, Somers Bros., 1879, 5 Lb. 715.00
Tin, Home Run Cigar, Federal Tin Co., Baltimore, Md., c.1905, 6 x 4 1/4 In. 3480.00
Tin, Home Safety Razor, Eastman & Drauss Co., 2 x 3 x 1 5/8 In. 385.00
Tin, Home-Run Stogie, 3 For 5 Cents, c.1910, 6 x 4 1/4 In. 2610.00
Tin, Honey Girl Violet Talcum Powder, Woman, Embossed, 6 In. 90.00
Tin, Honeymoon Tobacco, Penn Tobacco Co., Man, Moon 165.00
Tin, Howard's Perfection Oil, Screw-On Lid, 4 5/8 x 3 5/8 In. 125.00
Tin, Hummer Spices, Paprika, Hummingbird, T.C. Newburn Spice Mills, 3 x 2 5/8 In. 880.00
Tin, Huntley & Palmers, Cabinet, Biscuit, 1911, 7 1/4 In. .... *ILLUS* 392.00
Tin, Huntley & Palmers, Ink Stand, Fox Hunting, Biscuit, 1928, 9 1/4 In. .... *ILLUS* 336.00
Tin, Huntley & Palmers, Literature, Biscuit, 1901-02, 6 1/4 In. .... *ILLUS* 56.00
Tin, Huntley & Palmers, Purse Shape, Bark Pattern, Biscuit, 1902, 7 In. .... *ILLUS* 168.00
Tin, Huntley & Palmers, Slyvan Hornsby, Biscuit, 1908-09, 8 In. .... *ILLUS* 224.00

Advertising, Tin, Huntley & Palmers, Purse Shape, Bark Pattern, Biscuit, 1902, 7 In.

Advertising, Tin, Huntley & Palmers, Slyvan Hornsby, Biscuit, 1908-09, 8 In.

Tin, Jacob & Cos Cream Crackers, 10 x 6 1/2 x 3 In. 55.00
Tin, Jam-Boy Coffee, Lithograph Of Boy Eating Jelly Sandwich, Lb. 410.00
Tin, Jap Rose Toilet Talcum Powder, Woman, Yellow, Black, Red, Kirk, Chicago, 6 In. 30.00
Tin, JBL Rectal Soap, Tyrell's Hygienic Institute, Blue, Red, White, 3 1/4 x 1 1/8 In. 104.00
Tin, Jim Dandies Peanuts, Tin Lithograph, Kids Playing Ball, 10 Lb., 11 x 7 1/2 In. 2090.00
Tin, John Bird Companies Bar Harbor Mocha & Java, Tole, 22 x 13 1/4 In. 430.00
Tin, Kathleen Talc, Woman, Butterflies, 6 In. 20.00
Tin, Kendall's Blister, Horse, Paper Label, Contents, 2 1/2 Diam. 90.00
Tin, Kickapoo Salve, Bison, Orange, Black, Kickapoo Indian Medicine Co., 1 7/8 In. 60.00
Tin, King George Tobacco, Crest, Frishmuth Bro. & Co., 4 1/4 x 3 1/8 x 1 In. 385.00
Tin, Lacassia Labs Army Brand, Foot Power, 4 1/2 x 2 1/4 x 1 3/4 In. 255.00
Tin, Laflin & Rand, Crane, Marsh, Lithograph, Orange Ground, 1901, 6 x 4 x 1 In. 855.00
Tin, Lanus Bros., Edgeworth Tobacco, Lithograph, Pocket, 4 1/4 x 3 x 1 In. 176.00
Tin, Little Elf Coffee, Elf Carrying Tray, Bursley & Co., Fort Wayne, Lb. 670.00
Tin, Long's Covered Wagon Syrup, 5 Lb., 6 x 7 x 4 In. 1155.00
Tin, Lovell's Black Pete Toffee, Red, Yellow, Black, Paper Label, 9 3/4 In. 155.00
Tin, Lucky Curve, Plug Cut, Tobacco, 1920s, 4 1/4 x 6 3/4 x 4 1/2 In. 350.00
Tin, Lucky Star Smoking Tobacco, Von Eickens, Red, Blue, Gold, Lithograph, 4 x 3 x 1 In. 410.00
Tin, Lucky Strike Cigarettes, Lithograph, Round, 3 1/4 x 2 5/8 In. 525.00
Tin, Lucky Strike Tobacco, Baseball Graphics, Rectangular, c.1910 . . . . 525.00
Tin, Lucky Strike Tobacco, Lithograph, 4 1/4 x 3 x 1 In. 45.00
Tin, Lucky Strike, Inset Lid, White Ground, 4 1/4 x 3 x 1 In. 550.00
Tin, Lucky Strike, Roll Cut Tobacco, Lithograph, Contents, c.1910, Pocket, 4 3/8 x 3 In. 265.00
Tin, Lutteds Candy, Horse Drawn Sleigh, Santa, Toys, Lithograph, 4 x 6 1/8 x 2 1/4 In. 550.00
Tin, Macfarlane Lang, House That Jack Built, Biscuit, 1934-36, 6 1/2 In. . . . . *ILLUS* 112.00
Tin, Mammy's Favorite Coffee, C.D. Kenny Co., Handle, Tin Lithograph, 4 Lb., 11 x 6 In. 469.00
Tin, Mansco Perfumer Baby Talc, Child, Ball, Toys, Tin Lithograph, 6 x 2 1/4 x 1 1/4 In. 190.00
Tin, Massatta Talc, Asian Woman, Laxell, 1 7/8 In. 60.00
Tin, May Queen Tobacco, Topless Woman, Landscape, J.G. Flint Co., 2 3/8 x 3 3/4 x 1/2 In. 300.00
Tin, Mazaawatte Tea, We'se Done Had Our Mazaawatte, Black Boy, 1800s, 8 1/2 In. 175.00
Tin, Mellowmints, Cover, Brandle & Smith Co., 6 1/2 x 8 1/4 In. 55.00
Tin, Mohawk Chief, 50 Count, Red Ground, Lithograph, 5 1/2 x 6 1/4 x 4 1/4 In. 2035.00
Tin, Montgomery Ward Co., Java & Mocha Coffee, 1905, 5 Lb. 205.00
Tin, Moscos Great Peruvian Catarrh Cure, Indians Digging, Blue, White, Label, 1 1/2 In. 120.00
Tin, Moscos Great Peruvian Catarrh Cure, Multicolored, Lithograph, 1 1/2 In. 154.00
Tin, Mother's Mustard Plasters, First Aid For Household, Hinged Lid, 3 3/4 x 5 In. 55.00
Tin, Mt. Hood Antiseptic Tooth Powder, Red, Label, Williams Pharmacy, 3 1/2 In. 210.00
Tin, Mule Kick Waste Pipe Cleaner, Round, 1931, 3 1/2 In. 18.00
Tin, My Baby's Talcum, Sears & Roebuck Co., 6 2 1/4 x 1 1/4 In. 200.00
Tin, National Licorice, Red, Black, Gold, Hinged Lid, Glass Front, 5 Lb. 120.00
Tin, Navy Smoking Tobacco, G.W. Gail & Ax, Baltimore, Blue, Black Letters, Gold Lid, 7 1/2 In. 175.00
Tin, Neilson's Jersey Brand Cocoa, Sample, Oz., 2 1/8 x 1 3/8 In. 40.00
Tin, Newton's Heave, Cough, Distemper, Indigestion Cure, Horse & Driver, 7 x 3 1/2 In. 220.00
Tin, Nigger Shoe Polish, Stork Carries Black Baby In Swaddling, Lithograph, 2 3/4 In. 180.00
Tin, Nyals Tooth Powder, The Perfect Dentifrice, Red, Yellow, Gold, 4 1/8 In. 275.00
Tin, Nylotis Rose Talcum Powder, Tapered, 1914, 5 1/8 In. . . . . 27.00 to 50.00
Tin, Old Tavern Coffee, Key Wind, Lithograph, Lb., 3 1/2 x 5 1/8 In. 385.00

Advertising, Tin, Parein, Thatched Cottage, Biscuit, France, 1930-35, 7 1/4 In.

Advertising, Tin, Macfarlane Lang, House That Jack Built, Biscuit, 1934-36, 6 1/2 In.

Tin, Orcico Brand Cigar, Orrison Co., Western Images, 5 1/2 x 6 1/4 x 4 1/8 In. 265.00
Tin, Oregon Kidney Tea, Stark Medicine, 5 x 3 1/2 In. 715.00
Tin, Paint, I'm Blac-It, King Of Black Enamels, Tin Lithograph, Prewar, 3 1/2 In. 50.00
Tin, Parein, Thatched Cottage, Biscuit, France, 1930-35, 7 1/4 In. . . . . *ILLUS* 84.00
Tin, Parke Davis Hypodermic Tablets, 5 Vials, Green, Blue, Sample, Detroit, 2 x 1 In. 190.00
Tin, Patterson Bros., Whip Brand Ready Rolled Tobacco, 3 1/2 x 2 5/8 In. 525.00
Tin, Pedro Smoking Tobacco, King Of Spades, Wm. S. Kimball & Co., 6 1/2 x 4 7/8 In. 605.00
Tin, Peek Frean & Co., Biscuit, Hummingbirds, Dragonflies, Flowers, London, 8 In. 125.00
Tin, Perfumed Borated Talcum Powder, Baby, Red, White, Cylindrical, 4 In. 44.00
Tin, Peter Rabbit Baby Powder, 6-Sided, 3 5/8 In. 120.00
Tin, Peter Rabbit Baby Powder, Lithograph, 3 3/4 x 4 1/4 In. 468.00
Tin, Peter Rabbit Talc, Lithograph, 3 1/2 x 4 1/4 x 1 3/8 In. 275.00
Tin, Pipe Major Tobacco, Brown & Williamson, Lithograph, 4 1/2 x 3 In. 210.00
Tin, Players Cigarettes, Navy Cut Mild, 5 7/8 x 4 1/4 x 5/8 In. 10.00
Tin, Police Foot Powder, Lithograph, 4 3/4 x 2 1/2 In. 1320.00
Tin, Pomade, Georgia Brown, Mulatto Black Man & Woman, 1940s, 1 1/2 In. 30.00
Tin, Popper's Ace, 10 Cents, Airplane, Lithograph, 50 Count, 5 1/2 x 5 In. 440.00
Tin, Ralston's Climax Hoof Ointment, Trainer Working A Horse, 3 1/2 x 3 1/2 In. 358.00
Tin, Rawleigh's Tooth Powder, Cleans, Whitens, Polishes & Preserves, 3 Oz., 4 1/2 In. 358.00
Tin, Red Wolf Coffee, Ridenour-Baker Co., Yellow Ground, Red Graphics, 4 x 5 In. 90.00
Tin, Regal Smoking Tobacco, Imperial Tobacco Co., 4 x 3 3/8 x 1 1/4 In. 360.00
Tin, Reynaldo Brand Cigar, Tin Lithograph, 5 x 5 1/4 In. 660.00
Tin, Robertson's Confectionery, Chubby Face Boy Scout, Toronto 650.00
Tin, Rodeo Coffee, Winnipeg, 5 Lb. 1900.00
Tin, Roly Poly, Dixie Queen, Dutchman, Lithograph, 7 x 6 In. 745.00
Tin, Roly Poly, Dixie Queen, Mammy, Corncob Pipe, Lithograph, 7 x 6 In. 1595.00
Tin, Roly Poly, Dixie Queen, Satisfied Customer, Man, Smoking Pipe, 7 x 6 In. 1210.00
Tin, Roly Poly, Dixie Queen, Singing Waiter, Lithograph, 7 x 6 In. 550.00
Tin, Roly Poly, Dixie Queen, Store Keeper, Lithograph, 7 x 6 In. 1760.00
Tin, Roly Poly, Mayo's Cut Plug, Scotland Yard, Lithograph, 7 x 6 In. 880.00
Tin, Rose Of Kansas Coffee, Pry Lid, Lb., 3 3/4 x 5 1/4 In. 3520.00
Tin, Royce's Improved Talcum Powder, For The Nursery, Toilet & Complexion, 4 3/4 In. 130.00
Tin, Rumford Baking Powder, Rumford, Rhode Island, 4 7/16 In. 20.00
Tin, Rust Parker Co., Table King, Coffee, Lithograph, Pry Lid, Lb. 330.00
Tin, San Tox After Shave Talcum Powder, De Pree Co., 4 1/2 In. 20.00
Tin, San Tox Baby Talcum Powder, De Pree Co., 5 5/8 In. 27.00
Tin, Sana-Dermal Talc, 4 3/4 x 2 1/2 x 1 7/8 In. 468.00
Tin, Sanitol Talc, Woman, Flowers, Tin Lithograph, 2 1/4 x 1 1/4 x 3/4 In. 130.00
Tin, Sanitol Tooth Powder, Cleanses The Teeth, Blue, White, 4 1/8 In. 90.00
Tin, Sanitol Tooth Powder, Free Sample, Prevents Tooth Decay, It's Antiseptic, 2 1/4 In. 95.00
Tin, Sanitol Violet-Elite Talcum Powder, Woman, Blue, Red, White, Sample, 2 1/8 In. 88.00
Tin, Schotten & Co., Golden Days Coffee, Lithograph, 2 Lb., 6 3/8 x 6 1/4 In. 230.00
Tin, Scissor Cigarette, Red Ground, White Scissors, 2 7/8 x 1 1/2 x 3/8 In. 175.00

Tin, Score Card Cigar, c.1910, 5 1/4 x 3 1/2 In. 1275.00
Tin, Scottie Cigars, Dog, Red, Yellow, White, Lithograph, 50 Count, 5 1/4 x 4 1/2 In. 297.00
Tin, Scully's Skookum Syrup, Lithograph, 10 Lb., 11 x 6 x 4 In. 255.00
Tin, Seal Of North Carolina Tobacco, 2 Women, Cornucopia, Lithograph, 6 x 5 In. 255.00
Tin, Shasta Coffee, 2 Lb., 7 x 5 In. 690.00
Tin, Silver Knight Condoms, Disease Preventative, Lithograph, 1 1/2 x 2 In. 660.00
Tin, Sir Walter Raleigh, Grayish Tan Ground, Black Image Of Sir Walter, 3 x 3 In. 1500.00
Tin, Ski-Hi Brand Cigar, Bi-Wing Plane Image, Paper Label, 5 1/4 x 5 1/2 In. 798.00
Tin, Slippery Elm Lozenges, Yellow, Black, Hinged Lid, Glass Front, 5 Lb. 550.00
Tin, Spratt's Flea & Insect Powder, St. Bernard, 6 In. 22.00
Tin, Squibb's Unscented Talcum, White, Gold, 5 3/4 In. 60.00
Tin, Stork Oysters Thompson & Co., Grasonville, Md., Gal. 65.00
Tin, Strong Heart Coffee, Indian Image, Lithograph, 1 Lb., 5 3/4 x 4 1/4 In. 300.00
Tin, Sunset Trail Cigars, 5 Cent, Man, Woman, On Horses, 50 Count, 5 1/2 x 6 x 4 In. 468.00
Tin, Sunset Trail Cigars, Cowboy, Cowgirl, Lithograph, 5 3/8 x 6 1/8 x 4 1/8 In. 440.00
Tin, Sunshine Coffee, Little Girl With Umbrella, Tin Lithograph, 5 3/4 x 4 1/4 In. 440.00
Tin, Sure Shot Chewing Tobacco, Indian, Hinged Lid, Porcelain Knob, 8 x 15 In. 410.00
Tin, Swansdown Coffee, Swan, Tin Lithograph, Pry-Lid, 6 1/4 x 4 1/4 In. 358.00
Tin, Sweet Burley Tobacco, Spaulding & Merrick, Yellow, Red, Gold, Lithograph, 11 x 8 In. 230.00
Tin, Sykes Comfort Powder, 2 Girls, Skin Healing Powder, 4 3/8 In. 35.00
Tin, Talcum Puff Co., Air-Float Talc, Lithograph, 4 1/2 x 2 1/8 In. 65.00
Tin, Tavern Coffee, Closset & Devers, Canister, 6 x 4 1/4 In. 3520.00
Tin, Three Bee Brand Blacking & Stove Polish, Image Of Children, 4 x 2 In. 145.00
Tin, Tiny-Tot Toilet Powder, Made Expressly For Babies, United Drug Co., 3 3/4 In. 45.00
Tin, Toffee, Black Pete, Licorice, Big Lipped Black Pete Logo, Paper Label, 9 3/4 In. 166.00
Tin, Torpedo Special Short Cut Smoking Tobacco, Pocket 3750.00
Tin, Toy Talc Cop., Bear, Figural, Embossed, Composition, 5 5/8 x 2 1/2 In. 230.00
Tin, Trout Line Smoking Tobacco, Fly Fisherman, Lithograph, Pocket, 3 3/4 x 3 1/4 In. 495.00
Tin, Turkey Brand Coffee, A.J. Kasper Company, 3 Lb., 11 In. 880.00
Tin, Turkey Coffee, Wild Turkey, A.J. Kasper Co., Tin Lithograph, 3 Lb., 10 1/2 x 5 1/2 In. 740.00
Tin, U.B. Bray Co., Lead Spout, Cap, Green Paint, Unopened, 4 Oz. 15.00
Tin, Uniform Cut Plug Tobacco, Sailor, Lithograph, 3 x 6 1/8 x 3 7/8 In. 385.00
Tin, Vesta Coffee, Image Of Coffee Plant, McClinton-Trunkey, 5 3/4 x 4 1/2 In. 1750.00
Tin, Veteran Coffee, Civil War Officer, Lithograph, 5 3/4 x 4 1/2 In. 255.00
Tin, Victory Gum, Indian, Arab On Horse, Tin, Embossed Lithograph, 11 x 6 x 4 In. 176.00
Tin, Visano Oxygen Tooth Powder, Werner Chem. Co., 3 3/4 In. 770.00
Tin, W. & R. Jacob, Ice Skaters, Christmas Cake, Octagonal .... ***ILLUS*** 28.00
Tin, Watkins Antiseptic Healing Powder, Blue, Gold, White, 50 Cents, 6 3/4 In. 95.00
Tin, Watkins Perfumed Talcum Powder, 15 Cents, 3/8 Cent Series, 1914 Stamp, 4 1/8 In. 60.00
Tin, Watkins Talcum Powder Man, Sample, Am. Can 11A, Oval, 1 7/8 In. 80.00
Tin, Weldon Cube Cut Smoking Tobacco, S.S. Pierce Co., Yellow, Blue, 3 5/8 x 3 1/2 In. 230.00
Tin, Whip Ready Rolled, Lithograph, 8-Sided, 5 1/2 In. 385.00
Tin, White House Coffee, Dwinell-Wright Co., 9 1/4 x 5 1/2 In. 18.00
Tin, White Rose Tooth Soap, Man, Horse, Red, Black, Charles Wright Smith, 3 1/2 x 2 In. 265.00
Tin, Yellow Cab Cigar, 5 5/8 x 5 1/2 In. 3025.00
Tin, Yucatan Gum, American Chicle Co., Yellow, Red, Black, Tin Lithograph, 6 x 6 5/8 x 5 In. 385.00

Advertising tip trays are decorated metal trays less than 5 inches in diameter. They were placed on the table or counter to hold either the bill or the coins that were left as a tip. Change receivers could be made of glass, plastic, or metal. They were kept on the counter near the cash register and held the money passed back and forth by the cashier. Related items may be listed in the Advertising category under Change Receiver.

Tip Tray, Baby Ruth, Curtis Candy Co., Reverse Painted On Glass, 6 1/4 In. 120.00
Tip Tray, Bartholomay, Rochester, N.Y., Woman On Bird, Clouds, 4 In. 165.00
Tip Tray, Best In The West National Brewing Co., Cowboy On Horse, 4 In. 1210.00
Tip Tray, Booth Bros. Dutch Woman & Little Girl Carrying Water, Blue & White, 4 In. 55.00
Tip Tray, Borden's, Malted Milk In Square Package, Woman Holding Tray, Tin, 4 In. 440.00
Tip Tray, Carnation Chewing Gum, Lithograph, Round, 4 3/8 In. 120.00
Tip Tray, Castelberg's, Victorian Woman, Round, 1907, 4 1/4 In. 115.00

Tin signs and cans will fade from ultraviolet rays coming in a window. Cover the window with Plexiglas UF-1 or UF-3 to keep the rays away from your collection.

Advertising, Tin, W. & R. Jacob, Ice Skaters, Christmas Cake, Octagonal

Tip Tray, Cigar, Warwick, The Wenham Cigar Co., Tobacco Color, 6 In. 248.00
Tip Tray, Cottolene, Lithograph, Child, Woman Slaves Working In Cotton Field, 4 In. 60.00
Tip Tray, Eye-Fix, Great Eye Remedy, Woman, Cherub, Lithograph, 4 1/4 In. 550.00
Tip Tray, Frank Jones Homestead Ale, Emblem In Center, Red & Black, 5 In. 110.00
Tip Tray, Goebel, Dutch Girl Carrying Water, Blue & White Ground, 1900s, 4 1/4 In. 30.00
Tip Tray, Gold Seal Urbana Wine Co., Bottle, Lake In Background, Brown Edge, 6 In. 55.00
Tip Tray, Graphite Brand Paint, Pressed Aluminum, 4 1/2 x 3 1/8 In. 130.00
Tip Tray, Hernan Cortex, Famous Explorer, 6 In. 305.00
Tip Tray, Hupfel Brewing Company, Factory Scene, Horses & Carriages, 1890s, 6 In. 330.00
Tip Tray, Indianapolis Brewing Co., Lieben's Gold Medal Beer, Bottle, Red Ground, 5 In. 140.00
Tip Tray, King's Pure Malt, Waitress In White With Tray, 6 In. 55.00
Tip Tray, Miller High Life, Gold & Green Border, Trapezoid 20.00
Tip Tray, Moxie, Victorian Woman, I Just Love Moxie Don't You, 1906, 6 In. 385.00
Tip Tray, Moxie, Woman Drinking Beverage, 1906, 6 In. 250.00
Tip Tray, National Beer, Best In West, Cowboy, On Horse, Round, 4 3/8 In. 1760.00
Tip Tray, National Cigar, Classic Woman Image With Numerous Bands Around Rim, 6 In. 195.00
Tip Tray, Red Raven, Victorian Lady With Bird, 1900, 3 1/2 x 2 1/2 In. 400.00
Tip Tray, Roi-Tan, Perfect Cigar, Man & Woman At Table With Box, 6 In. 20.00
Tip Tray, Schmauss Garden Cafe, Tin Lithograph, 6 In. 255.00
Tip Tray, Schnecksville State Bank, Woman Fishing, Large Hat, Green & Black, 6 In. 165.00
Tip Tray, Shawmut Furniture Co., Lathrop, Ga., Woman, Long Hair, Tin Lithograph, 4 In. 100.00
Tip Tray, Use Big Jo Flour, Woman, Wabasha Rolling Mill Co. 70.00
Tip Tray, White Rock, The World's Best Table Water, Girl By Brook, Black & Red, 6 In. 140.00
Tip Tray, Woodland Whiskey, Crigler & Crigler, Victorian Woman, c.1910, 4 In. 115.00
Tray, Tip, see Tip Trays in this category.
Tray, A. Gettelman, Milwaukee, Hand Holding Glass, 1936, 13 In. 75.00
Tray, Adler Brau, Geo. Walter's, Round, Appleton, Wisc., 1945, 12 In. 120.00
Tray, Advance Stove Works, 13 1/2 x 11 In. 125.00
Tray, American Ice Cream, Ice Cream Sundae, Tin Lithograph, 17 1/2 x 11 1/2 In. 230.00
Tray, Artic Ice Cream, Polar Bear, Cream Supreme, Icebergs, Tin Lithograph, 13 1/2 In. Diam. 715.00
Tray, Ballantine & Sons, Ales & Beers, Tin, Keg Shape, 6 In. 100.00
Tray, Beck's Bier, Beck's Brauerei, Bremen, Germany, 1961, 13 In. 19.00
Tray, Benham's Ice Cream, Brownies Eating Ice Cream, Tin Litho, Beach Co., 13 x 10 1/2 In. 1540.00
Tray, Blatz, Milwaukee's Finest Bottled Beer, Round, 12 In. 15.00
Tray, Buckeye Root Beer, Cleveland Grape Juice, Mug, Jug, Bottle, Jar, Tin, 13 x 13 In. 495.00
Tray, Budweiser, King Of Beers, Red, Round, 1951, 13 In. 40.00
Tray, Carlsburg, Old Man, Holding Stein, Round, 13 In. 12.00
Tray, Central Brewing Co., Factory, Oval, 1906, 13 5/8 x 16 1/2 .... 2850.00
Tray, Central Brewing Co., Tin Lithograph, Factory Scene, Frame, 12 5/8 x 16 In. 2310.00
Tray, Coors, Snow Covered Mountains, Round, 13 In. 10.00
Tray, Crown Beer, Woman, Bonnet, Flowers, Bartels Brewing Co., c.1910 .... 315.00
Tray, Cunningham's Ice Cream, Factory Behind The Product, Tin Lithograph, Oval, 15 x 18 In. 300.00
Tray, Daeufer's, Pilsner Glass, Round, 1941, 12 In. 95.00
Tray, Dawson's Ale & Beer, Man & Woman At Table, Round, 1943, 12 In. 125.00
Tray, Delicia Ice Cream, Factories In Mineral Wells, Tin Lithograph, 1925, 13 x 13 In. 495.00

Tray, Diploma Beer, Everytime, Clipped Corner Shape 25.00
Tray, Dr Pepper, King Of Beverages, Free From Caffeine & Drugs, Tin, Oval, 13 1/2 x 16 1/2 In. 825.00
Tray, Dr Pepper, King Of Beverages, Medallion & Eagle Border, Waco, Tin, 10 x 13 In. 1100.00
Tray, Drink Mathie's, On The Level, Lacquered, Round, 1908, 13 In. 1150.00
Tray, Drink Pittsburg Union Club Whiskey, Woman, Grapes, 16 3/4 x 13 3/4 In. 336.00
Tray, Eagle Shoe, T. Pariseau Shoe Store, Manchester, Oval, Pressed Steel, 16 1/2 In. 110.00
Tray, Eichler's Beer, New York, N.Y., Round, 1936, 12 In. 25.00
Tray, Falstaff, Premium Quality Beer, Round 15.00
Tray, Fox Head 400, Famous Waukesha Water, Fox Head, Round, 1947, 13 In. 135.00
Tray, Graupner's, Elfenweiss, Factory Scene, Round, 1914, 12 In. 1350.00
Tray, Hamm's, Perplexed Bear, Born In Land Of Sky Blue Waters, Round, 1970, 13 In. 35.00
Tray, Hampden, Waiter, Round, 1937, 13 In. 123.00
Tray, Harris-Hart, Girl & Polar Bear, White & Brown, Tin Lithograph, 1920s 75.00
Tray, Harvard, Has What It Takes, Round, 1939, 13 In. 46.00
Tray, Hayfield Whiskey, Man Drinking, Smoking, Tin Lithograph, 10 1/8 In. 231.00
Tray, Hires Root Beer, 5 Cents, Lithograph, Round, 12 1/4 In. 5610.00
Tray, Hires Root Beer, Boy, Mug, At Soda Fountains, In Bottles Carbonated, Tin, 13 In. Diam. 825.00
Tray, Hires Root Beer, Just What The Doctor Ordered, 5 Cents, 1914, 13 In. Diam. 742.00
Tray, Hires Root Beer, Kid Holding Stein, Yellow Rim, Tin Lithograph, 12 1/8 In. Diam. 660.00
Tray, Hires Root Beer, Things Is Getting Higher, Hires Are Still A Nickel A Trickle, Tin, 13 In. 440.00
Tray, Hires Root Beer, Tin, 10 1/2 x 13 1/4 In. 280.00
Tray, Hires Root Beer, Woman, Green Shirt, Tin, Haskell Coffin, 13 x 10 1/2 In. 248.00
Tray, Hoffman's Ice Cream, Kewpies Eating Ice Cream, Tin Lithograph, 13 In. 220.00
Tray, Jersey-Creme Soda, Victorian Girl, The Perfect Drink, Tin Lithograph, 12 In. 408.00
Tray, Jersey-Creme, Perfect Drink, 5 Cents, Elk In Forest, 13 1/4 In. Diam. 187.00
Tray, Jersey-Creme, Perfect Drink, Victorian Woman In Plumed Bonnet, 12 In. Diam. 990.00
Tray, Kist, Orange Border, Bottle, Pinup Girl, Sailboat, 13 1/4 x 10 1/2 In. 179.00
Tray, Kreamy Ice Cream, Banana Split, Tin Lithograph, 13 In. Diam. 360.00
Tray, Lakeside Grape Juice, Bottle, Grapes, Tin Lithograph, 13 1/2 In. Diam. 412.00
Tray, Leinenkugel's, Indian Maiden, Round, 1957, 12 In. 28.00
Tray, Miller High Life, Girl In Moon, Round, 1913, 13 In. 550.00
Tray, Miller High Life, Girl In Moon, Round, 1954, 12 In. .... 35.00 to 65.00
Tray, Miller High Life, Woman On Moon, Round, 12 In. 60.00
Tray, National Brewing Co., Tin Lithograph, Cowboy, Bottle, 16 5/8 x 13 5/8 In. 3630.00
Tray, New Yorker Beer & Ale, Innkeeper, 4 Men At Table, Round, 1936, 12 In. 45.00
Tray, Noaker Ice Cream, Tin, Lithograph, c.1915, 13 In. 770.00
Tray, Old Style Beer, Old World Village, Round, 1967, 12 In. 15.00
Tray, Olympia Beer, Horseshoe, Waterfall, Black Ground, Round, 13 In. 20.00
Tray, Olympia Beer, It's The Water, Horseshoe, White, Cream, Round, 13 In. 25.00
Tray, Olympia Brg. Co., Tum Water, Blue Ground, Round, c.1905, 12 In. 125.00
Tray, Olympia Brg. Co., Tum Water, Green Ground, Round, Pre Prohibition, 12 In. 95.00
Tray, Olympia, It's The Water, Round, 1978, 13 In. 18.00
Tray, Oneida Brewing Co., Indian Chief, Porcelain, 12 In. 495.00
Tray, Orange Crush, Crushy Image, Yellow, Blue, Orange, 13 In. 145.00
Tray, Orange Crush, Crushy In Center, Oranges, Tin Lithograph, 13 x 10 1/2 In. 210.00
Tray, Orange Julep, Girl In Swimsuit, Holding Umbrella, Tin Lithograph, 10 1/2 x 13 In. 220.00
Tray, Pabst Blue Ribbon, Bartender, 3 Glasses On Arm, Nutron Plastic, 13 1/2 In. 12.00
Tray, Pabst Brewery, It's Time For Pabst, Round, 1936, 12 In. 85.00
Tray, Peerless Ice Cream, Boy Eating Cone, Ice Cream Sundae, Flowers, Tin Lithograph, 13 In. 440.00
Tray, Piel's Beer, Bert & Harry Piels, Round, 1957, 13 In. 30.00
Tray, Piel's Light Beer, Gnome, Round, 1953, 12 In. 35.00
Tray, Polar Maid Ice Cream, Woman, Children, Blue & White, Tin Lithograph, 1916, 13 In. Diam. 550.00
Tray, Producers Pride Ice Cream, Ice Cream Sundae, Tin Lithograph, 17 1/2 x 11 1/2 In. 230.00
Tray, Rainier Beer, Chrome, Oval, Pre Prohibition, 12 x 16 In. 60.00
Tray, Rainier Pale Beer, Woman, Holding Glass, Pre Prohibition, 13 1/4 x 10 1/2 In. 95.00
Tray, Red Raven, Ask The Man, Woman, Hugging Raven, Tin Lithograph, Round, 12 In. 550.00
Tray, Rheingold Beer, What No Rheingold Beer?, Hunter, Black Boy, Lithograph, 12 In. 110.00
Tray, Rheingold Extra Dry, Brooklyn, N.Y., Round, 13 1/4 In. 20.00
Tray, Sanborn's Kidney & Liver Vegetable Bitters, Tin Lithograph, 12 x 1 1/2 In. 1595.00
Tray, Schlitz Beer, Round, 1954, 13 In. 28.00
Tray, Schlitz, Schlitzerland Map, Round, 1957, 12 In. .... 40.00 to 45.00

Tray, Schuller's Ice Cream, Girl In Ice Cream Bucket, Tin Lithograph, 12 In. Diam. 1540.00
Tray, Schuster's Root Beer, It's Healthful, Boy, Girl, Dog, Tin Lithograph, 13 In. 1040.00
Tray, Standard Brewing Co., Execution Of 38 Sioux Indians, Round, c.1900, 12 In. 290.00
Tray, Stegmaier Gold Medal Beer, Since 1857, Finest Of Beer, Round, 1955, 12 In. 25.00
Tray, Stegmaier's Quality Beers, Wilkes-Barre, Pa., Round, 13 1/2 In. 30.00
Tray, Superior Ice Cream, Finishing Touch, Woman Eating Ice Cream, Tin, 1821, 13 In. Diam. 330.00
Tray, Tom Moore Cigars, Photo In Center, Green & White, 4 1/4 In. 250.00
Tray, Tru Blue Ale, Blue Boy, Round, 1943, 12 In. 125.00
Tray, Tuborg Gold Label, Copenhagen, Denmark, Round, 11 3/4 In. 15.00
Tray, Utica Club, Pilsner Beer, Cream Ale, Woman's Hand, Round, 1952, 12 In. 20.00
Tray, Utica Club, West End Brewing Co., Round, 12 In. 35.00
Tray, Valley Forge Beer & Rams Head Ale, Adam Scheidt, Round, 11 1/2 In. 30.00
Tray, Valley Forge Beer, Washington's Headquarters, Round, 1952, 12 In. 45.00
Tray, Walter's, Premium Beer, Mountains, White Ground, Red Trim, Round, 1962, 12 In. 49.00
Tray, Ward's Ice Cream, Mother, Son Eating Treats, Tin, K & S Litho, c.1900, 13 1/2 In. Diam. 410.00
Tray, Weld's Ice Cream, Health & Happiness In Every Spoonful, Tin Lithograph, 13 1/2 In. Diam. 75.00
Tray, Yuengling's Ice Cream, Waitress, Tin Lithograph, Haskell Coffin, 13 In. Diam. 550.00
Tray, Yuenling's Fine Beer, Ale, Porter, Woman, Drinking From Glass, Round, 12 In. 25.00
Tray, Zipp's Cherri-O, Drink Zipp's Cherri-O, 5 Cents, Tin Lithograph, 12 In. 1980.00
Urn, Bardwell's Root Beer, Center Ring, Stoneware, Cobalt Blue, Stamped, BPOE, 11 x 19 In. 1540.00
Wall Hanging, Esky, Esquire Magazine, Relief Painted, 1940s, 6 3/4 x 10 x 2 1/2 In. 250.00
Wallet, Antikamnia, Leather, Blue, White, 6 x 7 In. 49.00

AGATA glass was made by Joseph Locke of the New England Glass Company of Cambridge, Massachusetts, after 1885. A metallic stain was applied to New England Peachblow, which the company called Wild Rose, and the mottled design characteristic of agata appeared. There are a few known items made of opaque green with the mottled finish.

Bowl, 6-Crimped Scalloped Rim, 8 In. 518.00
Celery Vase, Corset Shape, Tight Crimped Rim, 6 In. 345.00
Cruet, Blue & Gold Staining, Alabaster Stopper, Handle, 6 In. 1495.00
Cuspidor, Woman's Ruffled Rim, Paper Label, 5 In. 1035.00
Dish, Cover, Green Opaque, Egg Shape, Amethyst Veining, Gold Trim, Applied Finial, 6 In. 4255.00
Pitcher, Amethyst & Gold Stain, Egg Shape, Square Mouth, Reeded Handle, 7 In. 5465.00
Pitcher, Gold, Blue Staining, Bulbous, Square Mouth, Alabaster Reeded Handle, 6 1/2 In. 2013.00
Punch Cup, Blue & Gold Stain, Loop Handle, 2 1/2 In. 489.00
Punch Cup, Gold Stain, 2 1/2 In. 144.00
Saltshaker, Pillar Mold, Stain, 4 In. 2070.00
Tankard, Blue & Gold Stain, 8 1/4 In. 4428.00
Toothpick, Inverted Tricornered Rim, 2 1/4 In. 520.00
Tumbler, 3 3/4 In. 316.00
Tumbler, Amber & Blue Stain, 3 3/4 In. 230.00
Tumbler, Amethyst Spots, 3 3/4 In. 460.00
Tumbler, Cylindrical, Glossy, 3 3/4 In. 173.00
Tumbler, Green Opaque, Veining, 3 1/2 In. 518.00
Vase, Amethyst Stain, Bulbous, Crimped Collar, 3-Fold Rim, 3 3/4 In. 2015.00

AKRO AGATE glass was made in Clarksburg, West Virginia, from 1932 to 1951. Before that time, the firm made children's glass marbles, which are listed in this book in the Marble category. Most of the glass is marked with a crow flying through the letter *A*.

Apothecary Jar, Cover, Black, 6 1/2 x 3 3/4 In. 43.00
Ashtray, Clam Shell, Brown, Marbleized, 4 x 3 3/4 In. 7.00
Ashtray, Hotel Lincoln, N.Y., Pumpkin, 1 x 4 In. 260.00
Ashtray, Leaf, Orange, Marbleized, 4 x 3 In. 5.00
Bell, Blue, 5 1/2 In. 100.00
Bowl, Cereal, Transparent Topaz, Interior Panel, 3 3/8 In. 30.00
Bowl, Handles, Pumpkin, 2 3/4 x 9 In. 130.00
Creamer, Transparent Green, Interior Panel, 1 1/4 In. 75.00
Cup, Opaque Green, Octagonal, 1 1/2 In. 9.00

Cup, Pumpkin, Octagonal, 1 1/4 x 2 In. 20.00
Cup, Transparent Blue, Concentric Ring, 1 3/8 In. 65.00
Cup & Saucer, Transparent Topaz, Interior Panels, 1 1/4-In. Cup 32.00
Drink Set, Play-Time, Opaque Green, Octagonal, Box, Child's 7 Piece 175.00
Flowerpot, Blue, Marbleized, 5 1/8 x 5 7/8 In. 90.00
Flowerpot, Blue, Ribbed Top, 2 5/8 In. 10.00
Lamp, Wall, Ivory, 7 1/8 x 6 1/2 In. 90.00
Pitcher, Transparent Topaz, Stippled Band 42.00
Planter, Narcissus, Green, Marbleized 40.00
Planter, Pumpkin, Scalloped Top, 4-Footed, 4 x 8 1/2 x 4 1/2 In. 28.00
Plate, Opaque Blue, Octagonal, 4 1/4 In. 8.00
Powder Jar, White, 6 1/8 In. 190.00
Saucer, Opaque Pink, Octagonal, 3 3/8 In. 4.00
Saucer, Transparent Green, Stipple Band 10.00
Sugar, Transparent Topaz, Interior Panel, 1 3/8 In. 60.00
Sugar & Creamer, Transparent Blue, Stacked Disc, 2 x 3 3/8 In. 80.00
Tea Set, Little American Maid, Transparent Blue, Stipple Band, No. 1000, Box, 11 Piece 800.00
Teapot, Cover, Concentric Ring, Blue, 3 x 2 3/8 In. 40.00
Teapot, Cover, Transparent Topaz, Interior Panel, 2 5/8 In. 95.00
Urn, Orange, Marbleized, Square Foot 12.00
Vase, Daffodil, Green, Marbleized, 4 1/4 x 4 1/2 In. 20.00
Vase, Tiger Lilly, Orange, Marbleized, 4 1/2 x 5 In. 10.00

ALABASTER is a very soft form of gypsum, a stone that resembles marble. It was often carved into vases or statues in Victorian times. There are alabaster carvings being made even today.

Bust, Beatrice, A. Cipriani, Italy, Late 1800s, 13 3/4 In. 265.00
Bust, Beatrice, Marble Bodice, Marble Slab Base, Late 1800s, 12 3/4 In. 646.00
Card Tray, Warrior Head Medallion, Bronze Pedestal Base, 5 1/4 x 5 In. 200.00
Ewer, Fluted Body, Carved Leaves, Dragon Wing Handle, Square Base, c.1850, 22 In., Pair 3200.00
Figurine, Dog, Retriever, Brown Glass Eyes, Octagonal Plinth Base, 13 x 15 In. 265.00
Figurine, Dove On Rock, Detachable Dove, 11 3/4 In. 650.00
Figurine, Tiger, Green & White, Crystal Eyes, 12 x 20 In. 1350.00
Figurine, Young Girl, With Frog, Marble Plinth, Signed, S. Della E. Figli, Italy, 24 In. 1935.00
Sculpture, Mask Of Dante, Wearing Laurel Wreath, c.1860, 8 1/4 x 7 In. 695.00
Urn, Cover, Bouquets, Curled Ribbons, Acanthus, Continental, c.1890, 25 x 6 In., Pair 1000.00
Urn, Cover, Fruit Garlands, Square Base, Mounted As Lamps, Italy, 22 x 7 In., Pair 1880.00
Vase, Down-Turned Lip, Leaf Shape Lip, Round Base, Continental, 1800s, 14 x 9 1/2 In. 235.00

ALUMINUM was more expensive than gold or silver until the 1850s. Chemists learned how to refine bauxite to get aluminum. Jewelry and other small objects were made of the valuable metal until 1914, when an inexpensive smelting process was invented. The aluminum collected today dates from the 1930s through the 1950s. Hand-hammered pieces are the most popular.

Atomizer, Carnival, Turquoise Cap, Cameo, Star & Diamond, 4 In. 35.00
Bookmark, Egg-O-See, Heart Shape, Forget-Me-Nots, 2 1/2 x 2 In. 40.00
Bootjack, Longhorn Steer, Painted Eyes & Nose, Ricardo, 10 3/4 x 5 In. 9.50
Cake Server, Carry-All, Westbend, 1950s, 7 1/2 x 14 1/4 x 11 1/2 In. 20.00
Canister Set, 1940s, 10 In., 4 Piece 35.00
Canister Set, Bakelite Cover, Kromex, 6 1/2-In. Sugar Canister, 4 Piece 35.00
Canister Set, Bakelite Handle, Everbrite, Italy, 8 Piece 25.00
Coffee Server, Mayfair, No. 7200, Wood Handle, L. Guild, Kensington, c.1940, 10 In. 60.00
Coffeepot, Percolator, Bakelite Handle, Wear-Ever, 8 Cup 50.00
Coffeepot, Percolator, Craftmaster Products Corp., Hillside, N.J., 4 Cup 18.00
Coffeepot, Percolator, Electric, Windsor, Japan, Box, 1960s, 10 Cup 9.00
Coffeepot, Percolator, No. 212 & No. 240, 3-Footed, Bakelite Handle, Farberware 45.00
Coffeepot, Range Top, Percolator, Mirro, 7 1/2 x 8 In., 7 Cup 15.00
Dish, Cover, Flowers, 2 Handles, 3 1/2 x 9 In. 18.00
Frying Pan, Divided, Bakelite Handle, Everedy Co. 18.00
Grease Can, Copper Color, Black Lid, Strainer, West Bend, 5 1/8 In. 12.00

Ice Bucket, Cover, Tongs, Hammered, Gailstyn 15.00
Ice Bucket, No. 5008, Everlast, Hand Hammered, 10 x 6 x 8 In. 62.00
Lazy Susan, Art Deco, Wilson Specialties, 17 In. 50.00
Lazy Susan, Fruits, Ruffled Edges, Cromwell, 15 In. 49.00
Mixing Bowl, Handle, Spout, Mirro, 11 1/2 x 5 1/4 In. 20.00
Mug Set, Barber Shop Quartet, Mirro, 4 x 3 1/4 In., 4 Piece 20.00
Pitcher, Dairy, No. 580, Wood Handle, Wear-Ever, 19 x 12 In. 80.00
Pitcher, Ice Lip, No. 983, Everlast, Hammered, Forged, 9 In. 25.00
Pitcher, Ice Lip, Twisted Handle, BW Buenilum, 7 In. 30.00
Pitcher, Measuring, No. 5262, Wear-Ever 27.50
Pitcher, Water, Ice Lip, Ear Handle, Everlast, 8 In. 55.00
Pitcher Set, Juice, 6 Tumblers, Multiple Colors, Kromax, 5 1/2-In. Pitcher, 7 Piece 80.00
Plaque, 2 Parakeets, Rene P. Chambellan, Alcoa, 12 1/4 x 8 3/4 In. 826.00
Server, 3 Tiers, Center Post, Gailstyn, 12 1/2 x 13 1/4 In. 39.00
Silent Butler, Art Deco Design, Canterbury, Hammered, 11 1/4 x 5 3/4 In. 30.00
Silent Butler, Roses, Everlast, 11 1/2 In. 22.00
Spice Set, Black Plastic Cover, Shaker Insert, Kromex, 1960s, 8 Piece 45.00
Teakettle, Cast, Wood Handle, Jefferson Aluminum Detroit Ware, 11 In. 56.00
Teakettle, Club Aluminum, 4 x 7 1/4 In. 35.00
Teapot, Wood Handle, A-143, Griswold, 6 1/2 x 5 1/4 In. 30.00
Tray, Condiments, Glass Insert, No. 462, Rodney Kent, 12 x 5 1/2 In. 65.00
Tray, Deer, Hammered, Continental Mark, 18 1/2 x 12 1/2 In. 75.00
Tray, Divided, Ruffled Edge, Farber & Shlevin, 10 x 10 1/4 In. 33.00
Tray, Flower Edge, Wilton, Columbia, Pa., 12 In. 38.00
Tray, Flowers, Square, Everlast, Hammered, 14 3/4 x 14 3/4 In. 50.00
Tray, Flying Goose Handles, Hand Wrought, No. 713, Shup Laird 55.00
Tray, Fruit, Hammered, 21 1/2 x 12 In. 85.00
Tray, Grasshopper Design, Wendell August Forge, 11 In. 195.00
Tray, Pinecones, Marked 530, Wendell August Forge, 9 x 6 3/4 In. 25.00
Tray, Raised Handles, No. 572, Continental Solder Co., 13 1/4 x 7 1/4 In. 55.00
Tray, Seahorses, No. 605, Turned Handles, Wendell August Forge, 14 1/4 x 8 3/4 In. 50.00
Trivet, Hand Forged, Everlast, 4 x 5 In. 22.00
Tumbler, Anodized, Red, 1950s, 7 1/4 In. 9.00
Tumbler, Magenta, Lime, Copper, Gold, Sunburst, 5 3/4 In., 4 Piece 23.00
Water Set, Flamingo, Hammered, Nasco, Italy, 1950s, 7 Piece 35.00
Water Set, Pitcher, Tumblers, Multicolored, Sunburst, 8-In. Pitcher, 4 3/4-In. Tumbler, 5 Piece 45.00

AMBER, see Jewelry category.

AMBER GLASS is the name of any glassware with the proper yellow-brown shading. It was a popular color just after the Civil War and many pressed glass pieces were made of amber glass. Depression glass of the 1930s–50s was also made in shades of amber glass. Other pieces may be found in the Depression Glass, Pressed Glass, and other glass categories. All types are being reproduced.

Ashtray, Moon & Star, Round, L.E. Smith, 1 1/2 x 8 In. 35.00
Basket, Thumbprint, Ruffled, 8 In. 25.00
Box, Round, Hinged Cover, 5 In. 50.00
Cake Stand, Thumbprint, Footed, 2 3/8 x 11 In. 25.00
Candleholder, Moon & Star, L.E. Smith, 4 1/2 In. . . . . .12.00 to 30.00
Compote, L.E. Smith, 6 1/2 x 6 In. 27.00
Compote, Pedestal, Lotus Blossom, Indiana Glass, 7 1/2 x 6 In. 30.00
Compote, Scalloped Rim, 8 x 5 In. 10.00
Creamer, 6 Oz., 4 In. 5.00
Dish, Hen On Nest Cover, Painted Red Comb, 5 1/2 x 7 In. 15.00
Figurine, Horse, Right Hoof Raised, 6 x 5 In. 25.00
Goblet, Moon & Star, L.E. Smith, 8 In. 6.00
Pitcher, Inverted Thumbprint, 2 Qt., 8 In. 15.00
Pitcher, Trees, Flowers, 9 1/2 x 5 In. 25.00
Saltcellar, Pedestal Base, Square, 2 x 1 1/2 In. 12.50
Saltshaker, Polka Dot, 2-Piece Top, Hobbs Brockunier, 1885-90 . . . . . 45.00
Tumbler, Hobnail, 6 x 4 1/2 In. 13.00

AMBERINA is a two-toned glassware made from 1883 to about 1900. It was patented by Joseph Locke of the New England Glass Company, but was also made by other companies. The glass shades from red to amber. Similar pieces of glass may be found in the Baccarat, Libbey, and Plated Amberina categories. Glass shaded from blue to amber is called *Blue Amberina* or *Bluerina*.

Beverage Set, Inverted Thumbprint, Late 19th Century, 7 1/2 In., 8 Piece 206.00
Celery Vase, Diamond-Quilted, Scalloped Rim, 6 1/4 In. 460.00
Celery Vase, Inverted Thumbprint, Ruffled Edge, 6 1/4 In. 120.00
Condiment Set, Salt, Pepper, Mustard, Spoon, Silver Plated Frame, Twisted Handle, 7 In. 575.00
Cruet, Inverted Thumbprint, Amber Handle, Faceted Stopper, 5 3/4 In. ....230.00 to 345.00
Cruet, Inverted Thumbprint, Applied Handle, Faceted Stopper, 5 3/4 In. 200.00
Cruet, Inverted Thumbprint, Oval, Swirled Ribs, Applied Swirl Handle, 5 In. 259.00
Ewer, Pedestal Foot, 9 3/4 In. 150.00
Mustard, Inverted Thumbprint, Applied Flip Lid, Handle, Spoon, 4 In. 720.00
Pitcher, Inverted Thumbprint, Amber Reeded Handle, 8 1/2 In. 100.00
Pitcher, Inverted Thumbprint, Clear Reeded Handle, 7 In. 200.00
Pitcher, Tankard, Optic Ribbed, Applied Handle, 7 In. 430.00
Pitcher, Water, Diamond-Quilted, Applied Reeded Handle, Late 1800s, 9 In. 206.00
Pitcher, Water, Optic Ribbed, Applied Amber Handle, 8 In. 173.00
Pitcher, Water, Pink Flowers, Gold Tracery, Ribbed, Amber Handle, 10 In. 430.00
Pitcher, Water, Reverse, Diamond Optic, 10 Lobes, Square Mouth, Clear Handle, 10 In. 290.00
Sauceboat, Daisy & Button, Hobbs, c.1885, 6 In., 6 Piece 489.00
Sugar & Creamer, Inverted Thumbprint, Square Mouth, Amber Reeded Handle, 4 1/2 In. 748.00
Toothpick, Inverted Thumbprint, Hat Shape, 2 In. 489.00
Tumble-Up, Inverted Thumbprint, 7 1/2 In., 2 Piece 518.00
Tumbler, 3 3/4 In. 29.00
Tumbler, Lemonade, Swirled Ribs, 5 1/4 In. 100.00
Vase, Bulbous, Swirled, Gold Enameled, Bird, Leaves, Amber Rigaree Rim, Feet, 8 1/2 In. 201.00
Vase, Diamond-Quilted, Raspberry Prunts, Rigaree Collar, Bulbous, Pinched, 8 In. 1840.00
Vase, Lily, Optic Ribbed, Scalloped Rim, 8 In. 660.00
Vase, Pinched, Tricornered, Everted Rim, Amber Rigaree Collar, 6 In. 400.00
Waste Bowl, Silver Plate Frame, Optic Pattern, 4 x 3 1/4 In. 230.00

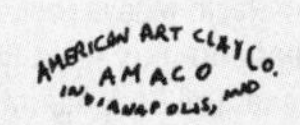

AMERICAN ART CLAY Company of Indianapolis, Indiana, made a variety of art pottery wares, especially vases, from about 1930 to after World War II. The company used the mark AMACO, as well as the company name. Do not confuse this company with an earlier art pottery firm from Edgerton, Wisconsin, called the American Art Clay Works.

Figurine, Flamenco Dancer, White High Glaze, Deco, 8 In. 225.00
Nappy, Handles, Blue High Glaze, 8 In. 200.00
Vase, Alligator Glaze, 10 In. ....190.00 to 250.00

AMERICAN DINNERWARE, see Dinnerware.

AMERICAN ENCAUSTIC TILING COMPANY was founded in Zanesville, Ohio, in 1875. The company planned to make a variety of tiles to compete with the English tiles that were selling in the United States for use in fireplaces and other architectural designs. The first glazed tiles were made in 1880, embossed tiles in 1881, faience tiles in the 1920s. The firm closed in 1935 and reopened in 1937 as the Shawnee Pottery.

Border Tiles, Cuenca, Chinese Floral Pattern, 3 x 6 In., 14 Piece 176.00
Fireplace Surround, Cattails, Lilies, Birds, 18 6-In. Tiles, 36 x 36 In. 900.00

AMETHYST GLASS is any of the many glasswares made in the dark purple color of the gemstone called amethyst. Included in this category are many pieces made in the nineteenth and twentieth centuries. Very dark pieces are called *black amethyst* and are listed under that heading.

Bowl, Pedestal Base, 8 x 7 1/2 In. 38.00

Bowl, Ruffled Edge, 3 3/4 x 8 In. 22.00
Bowl, Ruffled Edge, 5 x 11 In. 38.00
Salt, Swan, 2 1/4 x 4 x 2 1/4 In. 15.00
Shoe, Bow Slipper, Scroll & Lattice, 2 1/4 x 1 5/8 x 4 1/2 In. 16.00
Vase, Enameled, Flowers, Ruffled Edge, 8 In. 125.00
Vase, Trumpet, Polished Bottom, Pontil, 8 In. 110.00

AMPHORA pieces are listed in the Teplitz category.

ANDIRONS and related fireplace items are included in the Fireplace category.

ANIMAL TROPHIES, such as stuffed animals, rugs made of animal skins, and other similar collectibles made from animal, fish, or bird parts, are listed in this category. Collectors should be aware of the endangered species laws that make it illegal to buy and sell some of these items. Any eagle feathers, many types of pelts or rugs (such as leopard), ivory, and many forms of tortoiseshell can be confiscated by the government. Related trophies may be found in the Fishing category. Ivory items may be found in the Scrimshaw or Ivory categories.

Antler Carving, Oni Demon, Japan, 1800s, 5 1/2 In. 1763.00
Baboon Head 350.00
Big Horn Sheep, Full Body Mount 1800.00
Birds, On Branches, Taxidermy, Glass Dome, Victorian, 15 1/2 x 9 In. 230.00
Boar Head, Mounted, 19 x 16 In. 146.00
Bobcat, Full Body Mount .... 250.00 to 400.00
Brown Bear, Full Body Mount, 8 Ft. 6 In. 7000.00
Buffalo, Full Body Mount 2500.00
Buffalo Head, Stuffed, Late 1900s, 32 x 27 x 23 In. 489.00
Coyote, Full Body Mount, On Base, 27 x 44 In. 110.00
Dahl Sheep, Shoulder Mount .... 800.00 to 1300.00
Dinosaur Egg 400.00
Elk, Shoulder Mount .... 800.00 to 1150.00
Emu, Full Mount, On Base, 52 x 42 In. 110.00
Fallow Deer, Full Mount, 57 x 52 In. 220.00
Greater Kadu Head, By Johnas Bros., 66 x 37 In. 330.00
Gun Rack, Moose Feet, Birch Plaque, 14 x 29 In., Pair 14.00
Hippopotamus Tusk, Row Of Elephants, Japan, Early 1900s, 10 1/2 In. 147.00
Hyena, Full Body Mount, Africa .... 525.00 to 700.00
Impala, Full Body Mount, Africa 450.00
Moose, Shoulder Mount .... 1500.00 to 2300.00
Moose Horns, On Shield Shaped Plaque, Velvet, Early 1900s, 51 x 34 In. 345.00
Oriole, Ornithological Tableau, Wax Fruit, Glass Dome, Victorian, 13 In. 206.00
Oryx Head, Shoulder Mount With Horns, Jonas Bros., c.1959, 41 x 16 In. 110.00
Rug, Buffalo .... 625.00 to 775.00
Rug, Coyote 175.00
Rug, Leopard Skin, Faux Spots, Open Mouth, Cast Teeth, c.1930, 60 x 38 In. 500.00
Rug, Mountain Lion 1250.00
Rug, Polar Bear 3000.00
Rug, Raccoon, 35 x 26 In. 39.00
Rug, Zebra Skin, 5 Ft. 4 In. x 8 Ft. 9 In. 275.00
Rug, Zebra Skin, Black Felt Liner, c.1915, 9 Ft. 7 In. x 6 Ft. 10 In. 1116.00
Rug, Zebra, Africa .... 1050.00 to 1300.00
Skull, Bison, Horns, On Stand, 18 In. 3000.00
Tooth, Tiger's, Carved, Buddha On Top, 3 1/2 In. 440.00
Tooth, Tyrannosaurus Rex 110.00
Tusk, Mammoth, 37 Lb. 2800.00
Wolverine, Full Body Mount 700.00

ANIMATION ART collectibles include cels that are painted drawings on celluloid needed to make animated cartoons shown in movie theaters or on TV. Hundreds of cels were made, then photographed in sequence to make a cartoon showing moving figures. Early examples made by the Walt Disney Studios are popular with collectors today. Original sketches used by the artists are also listed here. Modern animated cartoons are made using computer-generated pictures. Some of these are being produced as cels to be sold to collectors. Other cartoon art is listed in Comic Art and Disneyana.

Cel, Fred Flintstone, Dino, TV Commercial, Post Fruity Pebbles, 10 x 13 In. 39.00
Cel, Jungle Book, Baloo & King Louie, Matte, Frame, 1967, 8 x 10 3/4 In. 2039.00
Cel, Snow White, Candle, Hand Painted, 1937, 7 3/4 x 10 1/2 In. 3697.00
Drawing, Simpsons, Homer, 6 Drawings, 6 x 4 In. 88.00

ANNA POTTERY was started in Anna, Illinois, in 1859 by Cornwall and Wallace Kirkpatrick. They made many types of utilitarian wares, bricks, drain tiles, and giftware. The most collectible pieces made by the pottery are the pig-shaped bottles and jugs with special inscriptions, applied animals, and figures. The pottery closed in 1894.

Anna Pottery

Pig, Henry Bromschwig & Co. Importers, Salt Glaze, 3 3/4 x 6 1/2 In. 6425.00

APPLE PEELERS are listed in the Kitchen category under Peeler, Apple.

ARCHITECTURAL antiques include a variety of collectibles, usually very large, that have been removed from buildings. Hardware, backbars, doors, paneling, and even old bathtubs are now wanted by collectors. Pieces of the Victorian, Art Nouveau, and Art Deco styles are in greatest demand.

Bracket, Carved, Acanthus Leaves, 8 1/4 x 12 In., Pair 148.00
Capital, Marble, Leaf & Scroll Carved, Chamfered Corners, 15 1/2 x 19 In., Pair 1469.00
Column, Oak, Egg & Dart Molding, Tapered, 94 x 16 In. 2185.00
Cross, Copper, Verdigris, 44 1/2 x 29 1/2 In. 795.00
Cupola, Zinc, Sheet Metal, Arrow, Compass Points, Directional, 24 x 66 In. 1150.00
Curtain Rod, Finials, Pressed Glass, Opaque Blue, Pontil, Brass Connectors, 6 In., Pair 110.00
Door, Carved, Flower Filled Vases, Birds, Islamic Calligraphy, India 885.00
Door, Interior, Bamboo, Ink Painting, Calligraphy, Frame, Japan, 69 x 40 In. 235.00
Door, Interior, Paneled, France, 19th Century, 95 1/2 x 48 3/4 In. 295.00
Door, Iron Transom, Slatted, Raised Panels, 125 x 48 In., Pair 2350.00
Door, Walnut, Iron, Molded Frame, Continental, 1800s, 114 x 48 In., Pair 2350.00
Door Handle, Brass, Lion Motif, Spain, 7 x 5 In., Pair 105.00
Door Handle, Iron, Thumb Latch, Tulip Shape Plate, Pa., 1700s, 16 In. 578.00
Doorframe, Wood, Sages, Scholars, Chinese, Late 1800s, 87 x 42 In. 646.00
Doorknob, Cranberry Cut To Clear, Mercury Lining, 2 In., Pair 935.00
Doorknocker, Brass, Butterfly, Rosa May Pickard, Patented May 11, 1926 1320.00
Doorknocker, Brass, Cottage, Nichols House, 1780, Sarah W. Symonds, Salem, Mass. 1870.00
Doorknocker, Brass, Lion's Masque, Regency Style, Regal, England, 8 1/4 In. 381.00
Doorknocker, Brass, Sphinx, Vase Shape, c.1915, 8 1/4 x 4 1/2 In. 70.00
Doorknocker, Iron, Cardinal, On Branch, Painted, Hubley, 5 x 2 7/8 In. *ILLUS* 504.00
Doorknocker, Iron, Ivy, Embossed Basket, 4 1/2 In. 99.00
Doorknocker, Iron, Rose, Pink, 3 Buds, Green Leaves, Painted, 5 x 3 In. *ILLUS* 1568.00
Doorknocker, Iron, Wallace Nutting, 6 x 5 In. 550.00
Doorknocker, Iron, Woodpecker, Painted, Hubley, 2 3/4 x 3 3/4 In. 224.00
Doorknocker, Parrot, Embossed, Feathers, On Branch, Medallion, Hubley, 4 3/4 In. 275.00
Eagle, Zinc, On Dome, Raised Wings, Beak Extended, Weathered, Gilding, 30 x 16 In. 805.00
Elevator Door, Iron, Vertical Rods, Horizontal Bars, Scrolls, c.1890, 84 x 41 In., Pair 604.00
Fence, Iron, Open Work, Flower & Leaf Scrolls, 8 Sections, 40 x 59 In. 1210.00
Figure, Molded Zinc, Serpent, Winged, Body & Legs Of Bird, Paint Trace, 15 x 17 In. 588.00
Finial, Gilt, Swan Shape, Beaded Necklace, 15 x 17 In., Pair 3099.00
Finial, Iron, Pineapple, Gold Paint, 12 In., Pair 131.00
Finial, Iron, Pyramid, 4-Sided, Ball Top, c.1865, 12 x 12 1/2 In., Pair 330.00
Fireplace Surround, Faux Marble, Black, Grain Painted, N.Y., c.1850, 66 x 50 In. 2650.00
Frieze, Hardwood, Carved, Car Race, Spectators, 6 Panels, c.1920, 22 x 59 In. 1684.00
Gate, Iron, Birds, Animals, Leaves, Scrolls, 1800s, 82 x 72 In., Pair 2760.00
Gate, Iron, Scrolls, Attached Ornaments, 84 x 35 1/2 In., Pair 2588.00

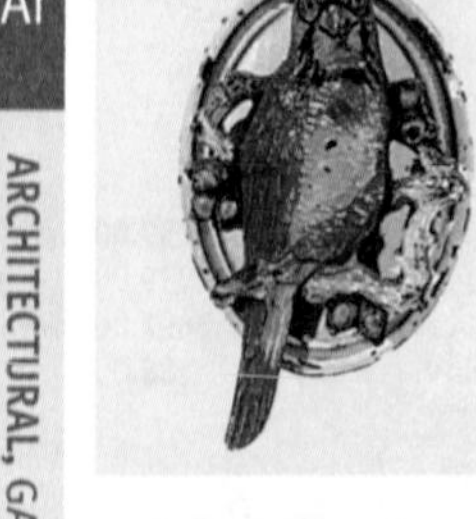

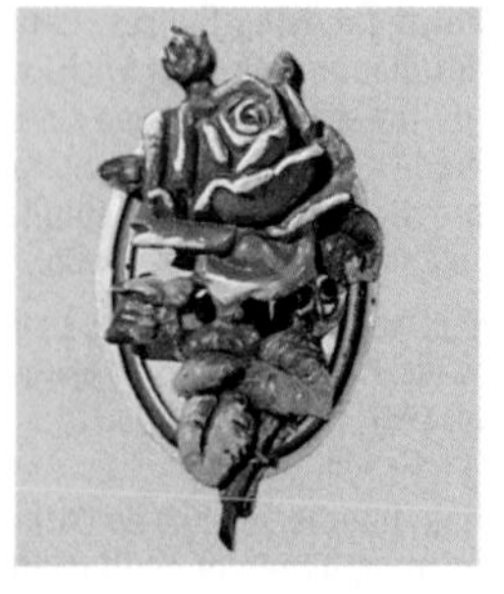

Architectural, Doorknocker, Iron, Cardinal, On Branch, Painted, Hubley, 5 x 2 7/8 In.

Architectural, Doorknocker, Iron, Rose, Pink, 3 Buds, Green Leaves, Painted, 5 x 3 In.

Gate, Iron, Trefoils, Fleur-De-Lis, Gothic Revival, c.1850, 115 x 63 In., Pair 6756.00
Gate, Wood, Crisscross Design, Peg Construction, 18th Century, 33 x 22 In. 1350.00
Gazebo, Columns, Figures, Cast Metal, Gilt, 19th Century, 13 x 5 3/4 x 5 In. 400.00
Grate, Demilune, Iron, Scrolled, Leaves, 19th Century, 17 1/4 x 34 1/4 In. 176.00
Grille, Iron, Stylized Basket, Scroll-Like Flowers, Borders, 40 x 33 1/2 x 5 In. 115.00
Hinge, Iron, Scrolled Ends, 31 1/2 In., Pair 173.00
Hinge, Iron, Tulip Bud, Snake Shape, c.1800, 29 In., Pair 5750.00
Hinge, Iron, Tulip, Cutout Heart, 25 1/2 In. 4140.00
Hinge, Spiked, Flared Ends, c.1800, 30 1/4 In., Pair 3220.00
Lavabo, Iron, Lion Head Spout, Wall Mount, 32 x 25 In. 518.00
Louver, Pine, 4-Panel, Diagonal, Green Paint, Early 1800s, 12 1/2 x 67 In. 1058.00
Mantel, Greek Revival, Painted, c.1850, 58 x 72 In. 675.00
Mantel, Maple, Carved, Molded Top, Corbels, c.1900, 47 x 57 x 11 In. 330.00
Mantel, Marble, Carrara, Carved Bust, Serpentine Top, Fruit, Shells, 49 x 72 In. 5875.00
Mantel, Oak, Applied Wreaths, 51 x 60 x 9 In. 201.00
Mantel, Oak, Turned Spindles, Beaded Panel, 68 x 58 In. 210.00
Mantel, Wood, Neoclassical, Dentil Moldings, Carved Swags, Bows, Shells, 91 1/2 In. 275.00
Newel Post, Iron, Pinecone Shape, c.1920, 15 In., Pair 702.00
Ornament, Iron, Star Finial, Arcs, Scrolls, Leaves, Wooden Base, Maryland, 36 In. 230.00
Overmantel Mirror, Belle Epoque, Flowers, Acanthus Pierced, c.1880, 68 x 42 In. 3760.00
Overmantel Mirror, Belle Epoque, Trophy Crest, Garlands, Late 1800s, 52 x 37 In. 1528.00
Overmantel Mirror, Carved Oak, Rococo Style, Scrolled, Carved Frame, 63 x 40 In. 472.00
Overmantel Mirror, Faux Wood, Louis XV Style, 61 x 42 In. 412.00
Overmantel Mirror, Federal Style, Flowers, Applied Leaf, c.1920-30, 23 x 54 1/2 In. 275.00
Overmantel Mirror, Georgian, Leaves, Vines, C-Scrolls, 72 x 50 In. 3055.00
Overmantel Mirror, Gesso Crest, Flowers, Fluted Columns, Beveled, 51 x 54 1/2 In. 495.00
Overmantel Mirror, Gilt, Arched Top, Shell Crest, c.1850, 76 x 41 In. 1763.00
Overmantel Mirror, Gilt, Federal Style, Eglomise, 27 1/2 x 63 In. 3600.00
Overmantel Mirror, Gilt, Federal, 5 Sections, c.1810, 41 x 56 In. 3819.00
Overmantel Mirror, Gilt, Gessoed Crest, Flowers, Leaves, Fluted Columns, 51 x 54 In. 495.00
Overmantel Mirror, Gilt, Louis XVI Style, Trophy Crest, 1800s, 57 x 49 In. 4818.00
Overmantel Mirror, Gilt, Spherules, Eagle, Divided Mirror, c.1810, 62 x 36 In. 823.00
Overmantel Mirror, Giltwood, Arched Crest, Leaf Scroll, Georgian, c.1735, 37 x 14 In. 2115.00
Overmantel Mirror, Giltwood, Louis XIV Style, Strapwork Cartouches, 91 x 47 In. 6756.00
Overmantel Mirror, Giltwood, Louis XVI Style, c.1890, 62 3/4 x 49 1/2 In. 1180.00
Overmantel Mirror, Giltwood, Rococo Revival, Napoleon III, Carved, 61 1/2 x 41 In. 3055.00
Overmantel Mirror, Walnut Burl, Victorian, Gold Liner, 29 x 36 In. 525.00
Overmantel Mirror, Walnut, Art Nouveau, Flowers, Beveled, c.1890, 50 x 40 In. 189.00
Panel, Applied Scrolls, Bull's-Eye Rosettes, White Overpaint, 46 x 49 In. 550.00
Post, Iron, Black Paint, Leaf & Vine Decoration, Gold Eagle, 83 In. 269.00
Post, Iron, Tapered, Fluted Shaft, Gold & Black, Pineapple Finial, 77 1/2 In. 269.00
Railing, Faux Marble, Bulbous Baluster, 30 x 70 In. 2200.00
Shutters, Maple Leaf Cutouts, Louvers, Blue Paint, 52 x 33 In., Pair 230.00
Tieback, Gilt Brass, Rosette, c.1825, 5 In., 6 Piece 1000.00
Tieback, Gilt Brass, Rosette, Victorian, c.1850, 3 3/4 x 3 3/4 In., 4 Piece 411.00
Tieback, Gilt Bronze, Napoleon III, 1865-80, 9 1/2 x 5 In., Pair 588.00
Trim, Walnut, Figures, Nuts, Leaves, Renaissance Style, 32 x 4 1/2 In., Pair 960.00

Valance, Door, Oak, Stick & Ball, Hanging Finials, 10 x 52 In., Pair . . . 140.00
Ventilator Panel, Carved, Painted, Battle Scene, Temple, Gilding, 14 x 13 In. . . . 146.00

AREQUIPA POTTERY was produced from 1911 to 1918 by the patients of the Arequipa Sanatorium in Marin County, north of San Francisco. The patients were trained by Frederick Hürten Rhead, who had worked at the Roseville Pottery.

Bowl, Applied Seashells, Blue, Crystalline Matte Glaze, Impressed, 8 1/8 In. . . . 805.00
Vase, Blue, Gray, Tan, Ivory Matte Glaze, Squeezebag Design At Shoulder, 6 In. . . . 11400.00
Vase, Embossed Cattails, Crackle Tan Glaze, 7 1/2 In. . . . 2500.00
Vase, Incised Linear Design, Green Matte Glaze, Shouldered, 5 In. . . . 2800.00
Vase, Iridescent Orange, 3 1/2 x 3 In. . . . 495.00
Vase, Squat, Globular, 7 Floral Medallions, Blue Over Brown, BCI, 2 1/2 x 4 3/4 In. . . . 1065.00
Vase, Stylized Floral Squeezebag Decoration, Blue, Tan Matte Glaze, 6 In. . . . 11115.00

ARGY-ROUSSEAU, see G. Argy-Rousseau category.

ARITA is a port in Japan. Porcelain was made there from about 1616. Many types of decorations were used, including the popular Imari designs, which are listed under Imari in this book.

Bowl, Bell Shape, Bat, Humorous, Blue, White, 4 Character Mark, 1800s, 4 3/4 In. . . . 127.00
Bowl, Transfer, Hand Painted Designs, Japan, c.1900, 9 3/4 In. . . . 35.00
Charger, Koransha Ware, Multicolored, Fan Panels, 1868-1911, 18 1/2 In. . . . 1116.00
Charger, Painted, Bird, Flowers, Red Ground, Late 1800s, Japan, 18 1/2 In. . . . 145.00
Dish, Flowers, 3 Friends Border, Blue, White, 1800s, 7 3/4 In., 8 Piece . . . 1955.00
Plate, Ho Bird Center, Karakusa, Blue, White, 1800s, 7 1/4 In., 10 Piece . . . 374.00
Vase, Palace, Inverted Pear Shape, Dome Cover, Children, Playing, Late 1800s, 38 In. . . . 1150.00

ART GLASS, see Glass-Art category.

ART NOUVEAU is a style of design that was at its most popular from 1895 to 1905. Famous designers, including Rene Lalique and Emile Galle, produced furniture, glass, silver, metalwork, and buildings in the new style. Ladies with long flowing hair and elongated bodies were among the more easily recognized design elements. Copies of this style are being made today. Many modern pieces of jewelry can be found. Additional Art Nouveau pieces may be found in Furniture or in various glass categories.

Vase, Cameo Glass, Gilt Thistle, Chipped Ice Ground, c.1900, 25 1/2 In. . . . 1315.00
Vase, Painted Stylized Poppy, Ceramic, Bronzed Metal Base, Norich, 16 x 6 1/2 In. . . . 1880.00
Vase, Plaster, Woman, Flower, Goldtone Finish, 19 x 8 In. . . . 94.00

ART POTTERY, see Pottery-Art.

ARTS & CRAFTS was a design style popular in American decorative arts from 1894 to 1923. In the 1970s collectors began to rediscover Mission furniture, art pottery, metalwork, linens, and light fixtures from this period. The interest has continued. Today everything from this era is collectible, including jewelry, graphics, and silverware. Additional items may be found in the Furniture category, various glass categories, etc.

Bowl, Silver, Hand Hammered, Shallow, Boat Shape, 2 Scroll Feet, 5 3/4 In. . . . 439.00
Desk Set, Lamp, Hammered Aluminum, Penholders, Letter Racks, Calendar, 41 x 15 In. . . . 764.00
Vase, Dragonflies, Green Over Rose Matte Glaze, 1914, 7 In. . . . 345.00

AURENE glass was made by Frederick Carder of New York about 1904. It is an iridescent gold, blue, green, or red glass, usually marked *Aurene* or *Steuben*.

AURENE

Bowl, Blue, 8-Fold Rim, 10 In. . . . 978.00
Bowl, Blue, Pedestal, Signed, 8 In. . . . 575.00
Bowl, Centerpiece, Gold, Optic Ribbing, Applied Pedestal Foot, 12 In. . . . 1035.00
Bowl, Gold, Blue, Purple Highlights, Steuben, 12 3/4 In. . . . 865.00
Bowl, Gold, Egg Shape, Inverted Rim, 10 In. . . . 1898.00
Bowl, Gold, Red Highlights, Signed, 10 x 3 1/2 In. . . . 978.00

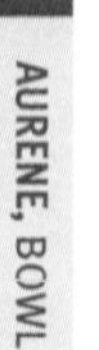

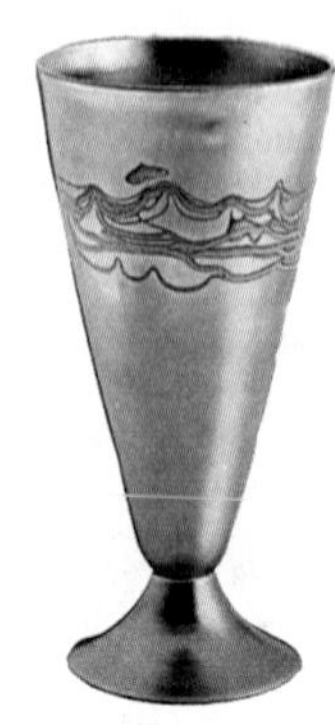

Never allow water to evaporate in a glass vase. It will leave a white residue that may be impossible to remove.

Aurene, Vase, Blue, Gold Threading, Conical, Footed, 10 In.

Bowl, Green, Gold, Red Highlights, Steuben, 8 In. 290.00
Candlestick, Gold, Twisted Stem, Disc Foot, No. 686, Signed, 8 In., Pair 1495.00
Compote, Blue, Chalice Shape, Steuben, Signed, 8 In. 920.00
Compote, Gold, Blue Highlights, Steuben, Signed, 6 In. 518.00
Compote, Gold, Steuben, Signed, 7 In. 805.00
Compote, Gold, Twisted Stem, Applied Cabochons, 7 In. 2300.00
Console, Blue, Calcite, Center Interior, Flared, Stretched Rim, 10 1/4 In. 1495.00
Console, Blue, Disc Shape, Inverted Rim, 3 Applied Feet, 12 In. .... 1035.00 to 1208.00
Cup & Saucer, After Dinner, Blue, Signed 460.00
Decanter, Gold, Melon Ribbed, Flame Stopper, 11 1/2 In. 1725.00
Finger Bowl, Gold, Underplate, Scalloped Rim, Signed, 6 In. 405.00
Goblet, Gold, Cone Shaped Body, Applied Prunts, Rigaree, Threaded Pedestal, 5 3/8 In. 805.00
Jar, Potpourri, Perforated Cover, Blue, Green, Gold, Purple Highlights, 5 1/2 In. 1495.00
Lamp, 2-Light, Gold, Baluster Standard, Square Shades, 23 In. 1610.00
Lamp Base, Pink, Shouldered, Acanthus Leaf, Footed, Steuben, 11 1/2 In. 1150.00
Nappy, Blue Aurene, Tricornered, Inverted Rim, Loop Handle, Signed, 5 In. 690.00
Nappy, Blue, 4-Footed, Flared, Ruffled Edge, 6 In. 575.00
Nut Dish, Gold, Scalloped Rim, 5 In. 460.00
Perfume Bottle, Gold, Bulbous, Stopper, Steuben, 3 3/4 In. 1150.00
Perfume Bottle, Gold, Cone Shaped, Teardrop Stopper, Steuben, 7 1/4 In. 1150.00
Perfume Bottle, Gold, Cylindrical, Teardrop Stopper, Steuben, 7 1/2 In. 920.00
Perfume Bottle, Gold, Melon Ribbed, Blue, Teardrop Stopper, Steuben, 4 1/2 In. 1265.00
Salt, Gold, Footed, Flared Rim, 1 1/2 In. 230.00
Salt, Gold, Red, Platinum Highlights, 3 In., 3 Piece 865.00
Shade, Bell Shape, Green, Gold Heart & Vine, 14 In., Pair 3680.00
Shade, Gold, Honeycomb, Signed, Fleur-De-Lis, Steuben, 5 In., 4 Piece 1095.00
Shade, Helmet Shape, Gold, Ribbed, Red, Platinum Highlights, Matte, 10 3/4 x 4 1/4 In. 1265.00
Sherbet, Underplate, Gold, Blue, Purple Highlights, 5 1/4 x 3 1/2 In. 210.00
Vase, Blue, 4 Bud Holders, Pinched Waist, Flared, Pinched Rim, 7 1/4 In. 920.00
Vase, Blue, Bulbous, Footed, c.1920, 5 1/2 In. 155.00
Vase, Blue, Footed, 8 In. 400.00
Vase, Blue, Gold Threading, Conical, Footed, 10 In. .... ***ILLUS*** 3107.00
Vase, Blue, Gold, Bulbous, Circular Rim, Foot, Pulled Fistoons, 8 1/4 In. 1495.00
Vase, Blue, Purple, Green Highlights, Ribbed, Steuben, 6 In. 805.00
Vase, Blue, Urn Shape, 10 1/2 In. 2030.00
Vase, Gold, Blue At Foot, Raspberry Center, Gold Iridescent Interior, Steuben, 6 3/4 In. 604.00
Vase, Gold, Egg Shape, Rolled Rim, 2 1/2 In. 460.00
Vase, Gold, Flower Form, Twisted Stem, Bulbous, Ruffled Edge, 12 1/2 In. 3819.00
Vase, Gold, Flower Shape, Baluster Stem, Crimped Rim, 8 1/2 In. 2990.00
Vase, Gold, Green Hearts & Vine, Baluster, 4 1/2 In. 2390.00
Vase, Gold, Optic Ribbed, Flared Rim, Footed, 8 In. 575.00
Vase, Gold, Red, Blue Highlights, Bulbous, Shouldered, 8 1/2 In. 1150.00
Vase, Gold, Tall Neck, Wide Ruffled, Stretched Rim, Dimpled Base, 6 3/4 In. 2588.00
Vase, Jack-In-The-Pulpit, Gold, Scalloped Rim, Footed, 6 In. 978.00
Vase, Stick, Gold, Bulbous, Flared Rim, Green Pulled Feathers, 7 In. 805.00

Vase, Tree Trunk, 3-Prong, Blue, Platinum Highlights, 6 In. 863.00
Vase, Tree Trunk, 3-Prong, Gold, 10 In. 1495.00
Vase, Tree Trunk, Blue, 3-Prong, 6 1/4 In. 1725.00
Vase, Trumpet, Gold, Rolled Edge, Steuben, 6 In. 575.00

AUSTRIA is a collecting term that covers pieces made by a wide variety of factories. They are listed in this book in categories such as Royal Dux, or Porcelain.

AUTO parts and accessories are collectors' items today. Gas pump globes and license plates are part of this specialty. Prices are determined by age, rarity, and condition. Signs and packaging related to automobiles may also be found in the Advertising category. Lalique hood ornaments will be listed in the Lalique category.

Air Compressor, S.M. Sorensen Co., N.Y., c.1900, 9-In. Wheel, 18 1/2 In. 690.00
Bottle, Esso Extra Motor Oil, Pyro Label, Cylindrical, 18-Sided, London, Pt., 12 In. 54.00
Bottle, Esso Oil, Embossed, Clear, ABM, Cylindrical, 22-Sided, Qt., 15 In. 69.00
Bottle, Penn Drake Motor Oil, Super, Lid, Paper Label, c.1940, Qt. 21.00
Bottle, Shell Motor Oil, Canada, 1933, Imperial Qt., 15 1/4 In. 87.00
Bottle, Sunoco Oil, Metal Spout, Front Labels, Qt., 13 5/8 x 4 In. 60.00
Can, Pennzoil, United Airlines Plane, Tin, c.1950, 5 Qt. 120.00
Can, Sunoco Motor Oil, Handi-Can, 1955, 2 1/2 Gal. 395.00
Can, Texaco Motor Oil, White Ground, Red Letters, 5 Gal., 16 In. 198.00
Cigarette Case, Mercedes Benz, Woman Holding Car, Silver, 1920s, 3 1/2 x 2 3/4 In. 2714.00
Cowl Light, Favrile, Nickel Silver Body, 1920s, 4 In., Pair 388.00
Cup, Trop-Artic Motor Oil & Gasoline, Tin Lithograph, 2 3/4 x 3 3/4 In. 415.00
Display, Bowers Tire Repair, Metal, 6 Compartments 185.00
Display, Edison Mazda, Cabinet, Lights, Porcelain, 16 x 7 x 7 1/2 In. 688.00
Display, Westinghouse Lamps, Mazda Automobile Lamps, Wood, Tin, 24 x 19 In. 235.00
Figurine, Spirit Of Ecstasy, Rolls-Royce, Bisque, Wood Base, 1979, 9 In. 995.00
File Cabinet, Pegasus, Metal, 15 x 10 x 7 In. 65.00
First Aid Kit, Phillips 66, Plastic 18.00
Gas Pump, Gulf, 1950s, 90 In. 1232.00
Gas Pump, Red Crown, 1915, 10 Ft. 2240.00
Gas Pump, Shell, 1950s, 77 In. 950.00
Gas Pump, Texaco, Model 390, 1950s, 34 In. 670.00
Gas Pump Globe, American, Metal 310.00
Gas Pump Globe, Amoco, Metal 448.00
Gas Pump Globe, Ashland Plus A, Plastic 168.00
Gas Pump Globe, Cities Service Koolmotor, Clover Shape, 15 In. 728.00
Gas Pump Globe, Shell, Metal 225.00
Gas Pump Globe, Sinclair Dino Supreme, Plastic 168.00
Gas Pump Globe, Sinclair H-C, Glass, 13 1/2 In. 280.00
Gas Pump Globe, Skelly Keotane 280.00
Gas Pump Globe, Standard Flame, Glass 615.00
Gas Pump Globe, Texaco Black Border, Plastic 56.00
Gas Pump Globe, Texaco Diesel Chief, Gill Body, 14 In. 840.00
Gas Pump Globe, Texaco Sky Chief, 14 In. 500.00
Gas Pump Globe, Tydol Ethyl, c.1945 .... 965.00
Hat, Texaco Fire Chief, Plastic, 1960s, 14 In. 55.00
Headlamp, Arclite, Carbide, Self-Generating, H. Miller & Co., England, 1906, 11 x 11 In. 950.00
Headlight, Carbide, Self-Generating, Bleriot, France, 8 5/8 x 11 x 13 3/4 In. 2085.00
Headlight, King Of Road, Lucas & Co., No. 664, Brass, Carbide Gas, 1907, 14 1/4 In., Pair 1058.00
Hood Ornament, Austro Daimler, Chrome Plated, Nickel Over Brass Cap, Early 1930s, 4 In. 285.00
Hood Ornament, Ballerina, Le Gui, Wind Driven, Nickel Silver, France, Late 1920s, 7 In. 285.00
Hood Ornament, Boar, Military Helmet, Brass, 1914-18, 4 In. 759.00
Hood Ornament, Boy, Crying, Oh Tis Hot, J. Reeves, 1924, 3 3/4 In. 590.00
Hood Ornament, Eagle, Soaring, Bronze, c.1920, 15 1/2 In. 355.00
Hood Ornament, Elephant, Brass, Chromium Plated, C. Charles, France, c.1920, 4 1/2 In. 690.00
Hood Ornament, Gargoyle, Wings, Bronze, c.1920, 6 1/2 x 4 3/4 In. 679.00
Hood Ornament, Goddess Head, Wings, Brass, Gold Patina, Buick, 1927, 3 x 4 1/2 In. 785.00
Hood Ornament, Goddess, Chrome Plated, Mappin & Webb, c.1922, 7 In. 2397.00
Hood Ornament, Man In Moon, Nickel Plated, c.1920, 2 1/2 In. 430.00

Hood Ornament, Penguin, Nickel Plated, c.1927, 7 1/4 In. 588.00
Hood Ornament, Racehorse, Brass, Chromium Plated, c.1925, 3 3/4 In. 235.00
Hood Ornament, Ram, Belier, Opalescent Glass, Sabino, France, Early 1930s, 9 1/4 In. 590.00
Hood Ornament, Speed, Glass, Chrome Mount, Red Ashay, England, c.1930, 8 1/2 In. 4375.00
Hood Ornament, Victoire, Persons Majestic Co., Worcester, Mass., 1930s, 10 In. 4025.00
Horn, Boa Constrictor, Flexible, Coiled Body, Black Rubber Bulb, England, 1905, 48 In. 1549.00
Horn, Boa Constrictor, Head, Metal, Green Eyes, Martin Signal, Germany, 1909, 12 x 6 3/4 In. 690.00
Horn, Boa Constrictor, Head, Silver, Red Eyes, Martin Signal, Germany, 1905, 11 3/4 x 6 1/2 In. 1280.00
Lamp, Rear, Oil, Brass, Red Lens, G. Ducellier, Paris, 1902, 10 x 6 In. 569.00
Lamp Set, To Get You Home, Brass, Paraffin, Mahogany Box, c.1905, 15 x 6 x 10 In., 3 Piece 2840.00
License Plate, California, 1963, Yellow On Black 10.00
License Plate, New York, 1930s-40s, Slow Down & Live In Spring Valley, Yellow On Black 15.00
License Plate, Pennsylvania, 1955, Blue On Yellow 15.00
License Plate, Puerto Rico, 1965-66, Yellow On Black 12.00
License Plate, Texas, 1958, White On Black 10.00
Light, Rear Signal, Chromium, Steel, 3 Bulbs, Red, Amber, Green, c.1930, 5 x 4 x 4 1/4 In., Pair 259.00
Mirror, Wells Chevrolet Co., Heart Of Auto Row, Celluloid, c.1920, 1 3/4 x 2 3/4 In. 255.00
Oil Can, Checker Motor Oil, Men Playing Checkers, Race Car, 5 1/2 x 4 In. 360.00
Oil Can, Efficiency Gas Oil, Hand Soldered, Tin Lithograph, Yellow, Blue, White, 7 x 8 x 3 In. 990.00
Oil Can, Kenmore, Aero Craft Motor Oil, Airplane, Race Car, 5 1/2 x 4 In. 690.00
Oil Can, Mobile, Gargoyle Brand, Artic, Tin Lithograph, Cone Shape, 12 1/4 x 4 In. 385.00
Oil Can, United Co-Op, Farm Scene, 2 Gal., 10 1/2 x 8 5/8 x 5 5/8 In. 120.00
Oil Dispenser, Service Stations, Nickel Over Brass, Bower & Co., 1901, 8 x 5 In. 475.00
Oiler, Brass, 7 Capsules, Screw Down Cap, c.1900, 16 In. 1148.00
Poster, Ford, Universal Car, 4 People Try To Grab Car, c.1900, 62 x 48 In. 1635.00
Poster, Gladiator, Automobiles, Cycles, Car Race In Ancient Rome, c.1920, 51 x 67 In. 1685.00
Poster, Moteur Romain, Man, Woman, In Vehicle, Early 1900s, 57 1/2 x 41 1/2 In. 835.00
Poster, Mustang, The First Generation, Pictures Models From 1964-73, Square, 24 In. 80.00
Poster, Renault, Bilancourt, Seine, 1920s, 47 x 62 1/2 In. 950.00
Sign, Atlantic Imperial, Pressed Aluminum, Shield Shape, 11 1/2 In. 39.00
Sign, Atlantic, Porcelain, 13 In. 145.00
Sign, Automobile Motorists Mutual Insurance, Metal, Oval, Red, White, Blue, 36 x 60 In. 230.00
Sign, Automobile, Profile, Cast Iron, Cutout, 1903, 33 1/2 x 17 3/4 In. 920.00
Sign, Champion, Dependable, Spark Plug Service, Flange, 18 In. 130.00
Sign, Chevrolet, Bel Air, 4-Door Station Wagon, Green, Cardboard, 1955, 18 1/2 x 32 In. 400.00
Sign, Chevrolet, Two-Ten Club Coupe, Red, Yellow Ground, Cardboard, 1955, 18 1/2 x 32 In. 360.00
Sign, Delco Batteries, Red, White, Blue, Metal Lithograph, 62 3/4 x 18 1/2 In. 100.00
Sign, Delco Batteries, Red, White, Blue, Metal Lithograph, Made In U.S.A., 70 1/2 x 18 1/2 In. 190.00
Sign, Fire Chief, Texaco, Fire Helmet, Porcelain, 18 In. 176.00
Sign, Flying A Service, Wings, Tin, Embossed, Enamel, 55 x 42 In. 1210.00
Sign, Gasco Gasoline, Shell Oil, Bird, Porcelain, 12 In. 4510.00
Sign, Globe Gasoline, John P. Hanson, Red, White, Blue, Metal, Wood Back, Frame, 36 x 122 In. 550.00
Sign, Good Gulf, White, Orange, Blue, Porcelain, 11 In. 99.00
Sign, Goodyear Tires & Battery Service, Blue, Yellow, White, Red, Embossed, Tin, 30 x 24 In. 310.00
Sign, Goodyear Tires, Tin, Embossed, c.1901, 27 1/2 x 39 1/2 In. 10150.00
Sign, Gulf Salesman's Sample, Outdoor, Light-Up, Gas Station, Metal Base, Pole, 21 x 7 In. 523.00
Sign, Gulftane, White Ground, Orange & Navy Blue Bands, Porcelain, 8 1/2 x 11 3/8 In. 85.00
Sign, Mobilgas, Red Pegasus, Porcelain, Wire Hanger, 13 x 15 In. 95.00
Sign, Pennzoil, Safe Lubrication, Pressed Tin, Yellow Ground, 2-Sided, Oval, 16 1/2 In. 187.00
Sign, Phillips 66, Red, White, Black, Porcelain, 2-Sided, Shield Form, c.1960, 47 x 47 In. 230.00
Sign, Quaker State Motor Oil, Porcelain, 1/2 Round, U.S.A. Donasco 3/82, 2-Sided, 29 x 26 In. 200.00
Sign, Rolls-Royce, Best Car In World, Glass, Gilt Frame, 1907, 26 1/2 x 39 1/4 In. 2245.00
Sign, Rolls-Royce, RR, Silver Paper, Black Print, c.1950, 37 x 21 In. 345.00
Sign, Shell, Lubrication, Modern Upkeep Service, Porcelain, 12 1/4 x 12 1/4 In. 2640.00
Sign, Signal Oil & Gas Co., Lubester, Porcelain, Round, 6 1/8 In. 825.00
Sign, Texaco Motor Oil, 2-Sided, Harlequin, Tin, 21 1/2 In. 176.00
Sign, Texaco Motor Oil, Ford, Porcelain, 15 In. 330.00
Sign, Texaco, Fire Chief Gasoline, Porcelain, White Ground, Red & Green, 1962, 18 x 12 In. 115.00
Sign, Texaco, Red Star, Green T, Porcelain, Round, 12 In. 248.00
Sign, Texaco, Red Star, Porcelain, Round, 24 In. 330.00
Sign, Texaco, Sky Chief Su-Preme Gasoline, Wire Hanger, Porcelain, 3-5-62, 18 In. 125.00

Sign, Texaco, Small Star, Red, White, Black, Green, Porcelain, 2-Sided, Hexagon, 53 x 85 In. 360.00
Sign, Texaco, Star, Red, Green, White, Black, Porcelain, 2-Sided, c.1954, 72 In. Diam. 300.00
Sign, Tydol's Flying A Pump, Round, Porcelain, 10 In. 463.00
Sign, Wil-Flo Motor Oil, At 30 Degrees Below, 17 1/2 x 23 1/4 In. 3960.00
Sign, Willard Batteries, Red, White, Black, Metal Lithograph, AM Sign Co., 58 1/2 x 16 1/4 In. 195.00
Thermometer, Champion Spark Plug, World's No. 1 Seller, Celluloid, 24 In. 77.00
Tin, Atlantic Oil, Lithograph, Gagged Parrot, Qt., 8 x 3 1/2 In. 550.00
Trunk, Packard, 39 1/2 x 20 1/2 x 17 1/2 In. 468.00
Vanity, Silver, Enamel, Tortoiseshell, Early 20th Century, 7 1/2 x 3 3/4 x 5 1/4 In. 819.00
Water Can, Top Bail Handle, Side Handle, Green Ground, Texaco, 22 In. 55.00
Wrench, Ford, Adjustable 25.00

AUTUMN LEAF pattern china was made for the Jewel Tea Company beginning in 1933. Hall China Company of East Liverpool, Ohio, Crooksville China Company of Crooksville, Ohio, Harker Potteries of Chester, West Virginia, and Paden City Pottery, Paden City, West Virginia, made dishes with this design. Autumn Leaf has remained popular and was made by Hall China Company until 1978. Some other pieces in the Autumn Leaf pattern are still being made. For more information, see *Kovels' Depression Glass & Dinnerware Price List.*

Bowl, 7 1/2 In. 42.00
Bowl, Fruit, Hall, 5 1/2 In. 11.95
Bowl, Hall, 6 In. 14.74
Bowl, Jewel Tea Ware, Hall, 5 1/2 In. 9.00
Bowl, Vegetable, Ruffled, Hall, 9 In. 110.00
Butter, Cover, Hall, Lb., 4 x 9 5/8 x 5 1/2 In. .... 500.00 to 600.00
Cake Plate, Hall, 9 1/2 In. 20.00
Cake Stand, Brass Foot, Hall, Box, 3 1/2 x 9 In. 275.00
Casserole, Hall, 3 x 7 In. 29.50
Coffeepot, Electric 400.00
Custard Cup, 2 x 3 1/2 In. 5.00
Marmalade, Underplate, Hall, 6 1/8 In. 30.00
Mixing Bowl, Hall, 3 1/2 x 6 1/4 In. 24.00
Mixing Bowl, Hall, 4 x 7 1/2 In. 35.00
Mixing Bowl, Hall, 5 x 9 In. .... 35.00 to 45.00
Pie Bird, Hall, 5 x 2 In. 30.00
Pitcher, Ball Shape, Hall, 9 x 8 In. 70.00
Pitcher, China Specialties, Child's, 2 1/4 In. 40.00
Pitcher, Ice Lip, 3 1/4 In. 40.00
Pitcher, Jewel Tea, Hall, 5 1/2 In. 68.00
Plate, 9 In. 20.00
Plate, Bread & Butter, Hall, 7 In. 11.95
Reamer, China Specialties, Child's, 1 x 3 In. 50.00
Rolling Pin, China Specialties, 15 In. 66.00
Salt & Pepper, 1 3/4 In. 30.00
Saucepan, 6 x 13 3/4 In. 100.00
Saucer, Hall, 6 In. .... 6.00 to 9.95
Soup, Cream, Hall, 4 1/2 In. 36.00
Teapot, Aladdin, China Specialties, 2 3/4 x 4 1/2 In. 38.00

AVON bottles are listed in the Bottle category under Avon.

AZALEA dinnerware was made for Larkin Company customers from 1918 to 1941. Larkin, the soap company, was in Buffalo, New York. The dishes were made by Noritake China Company of Japan. Each piece of the white china was decorated with pink azaleas.

Bowl, Dessert, 5 1/4 In. 8.50
Bowl, Shell Shape, 3 5/8 x 7 1/8 In. 430.00
Cake Plate, 2 Handles 45.00
Candy Jar, Cover, 6-Sided, 5 1/8 x 3 7/8 In. .... 599.00 to 850.00
Casserole, Cover, 10 In. 50.00
Creamer & Sugar, Gold Finial, 4 3/8 x 6 3/8-In. Sugar, 3 5/8 x 5 5/8-In. Creamer 190.00

Cup & Saucer 16.50
Dish, Mayonnaise, Footed 22.00
Gravy Boat, Attached Underplate, 3 1/8 x 9 x 5 7/8 In. .... 40.00 to 45.00
Mayonnaise Set, Bowl, Plate, Ladle, 1 3/4 x 4-In. Bowl, 5 1/2-In Plate, 5-In. Spoon, 3 Piece .. 75.00 to 95.00
Mustard, Spoon, 2 1/2 x 3 3/4-In. Jar, 3 1/4-In. Spoon 140.00
Plate, Dinner, 9 3/4 In. .... 15.00 to 20.00
Plate, Salad, 7 1/2 In. .... 12.00 to 20.00
Plate, Salad, Square, 7 5/8 In. 60.00
Platter, 14 x 10 1/2 In. 55.00
Relish, 2 Sections, 1 1/2 x 8 1/2 x 5 In. 65.00
Sugar & Creamer, 2 3/8 x 6 1/8-In. Sugar, 3 5/8 x 3 7/8-In. Creamer 85.00
Vase, Bud, Fan Shape, 5 1/2 In. 250.00

BACCARAT glass was made in France by La Compagnie des Cristalleries de Baccarat, located 150 miles from Paris. The factory was started in 1765. The firm went bankrupt and began operating again about 1822. Cane and millefiori paperweights were made during the 1845 to 1880 period. The firm is still working near Paris making paperweights and glasswares.

Candelabrum, 7-Light, Spiral Turned Arms, Cabochons & Prisms, 23 x 15 In. 3525.00
Candlestick, Hurricane, 16 In., Pair 819.00
Compote, Cut Flutes, Alternating Clear & Frosted, Scalloped Rim, c.1873, 4 3/4 x 7 In. 450.00
Cup & Saucer, Cut Diamond Point Base, Engraved Flowers, Stippled Ground, 7 In. 110.00
Decanter, Swirl, 8 In. 160.00
Figurine, Panther, Lying Down, 3 1/4 x 10 1/4 In. 320.00
Figurine, Penguin, 4 1/2 In. 235.00
Figurine, Snowman, 4 In. 80.00
Mustard, Cover, Spoon, Cut Facets, 1950s, 4 1/2 In. 150.00
Paperweight, Cinquefoil Garland, Millefiori, 2 x 3 In. 495.00
Paperweight, Millefiori, Concentric, 2 x 2 3/4 In. 220.00
Paperweight, Sulphide, Will Rogers, Star Cut Amber Ground, 2 3/4 In. 35.00
Perfume Bottle, Bichara, Chypre, Clear, Frosted, Label, c.1913, 6 In. 1200.00
Perfume Bottle, Corday, Femme Du Jour, Black Crystal, Gold, Silk Box, c.1926, 4 In. 1440.00
Perfume Bottle, Cut Diamond, Atomizer, Leather Case, 3 x 1 1/4 x 2 3/4 In. 77.00
Perfume Bottle, Elizabeth Arden, Cyclamen, White, Clear, Jeweled Pin, Box, c.1938, 6 In. 6000.00
Perfume Bottle, Ferragamo, Giglio, Limited Issue, Clear, Bronze Neck, Suede Box, 1961, 6 In. 960.00
Perfume Bottle, Forest, Ming Toy, Clear Crystal, Gold, Enameled Detail, c.1924, 4 3/8 In. 10200.00
Perfume Bottle, Houbigant, Subtilite, Crystal, Engraved, Box, c.1919, 3 1/4 In. 540.00
Perfume Bottle, Pleville, Flamme De Gloire, Clear Crystal, Box, 1920s, 4 1/4 In. 2400.00
Perfume Bottle, Ramses IV, 1919, 4 1/2 In. 6573.00
Perfume Bottle, Reflexions Ciro Paris, 5 In. 195.00
Perfume Bottle, Shalimar, Blue Glass Stopper, Foil Label, France, c.1930, 1/2 Oz. 55.00
Perfume Bottle, Ybry, Amour Sauvage, Black Crystal, Enameled Cover, c.1929, 2 1/2 In. 1080.00
Perfume Bottle, Ybry, Devinez, Butterscotch Crystal, Cased, Stopper, Tassel Box, c.1927, 2 In. 900.00
Powder Box, Cover, Cranberry Cut To Clear, Signed, 3 x 5 In. 350.00
Sculpture, Face, 5 In. 145.00
Vase, Stick, Serpent, Molded Beetle, Frosted, Clear, Signed, 8 1/2 In. 600.00

BADGES have been used since before the Civil War. Collectors search for examples of all types, including law enforcement and company identification badges. Well-known prison or law enforcement badges are most desirable. Most are made of nickel or brass. Many recent reproductions have been made.

Agent, Texas Alcoholic Beverage Commission, Round, Raised Star, c.1930 .... 100.00
Cab Driver, Yellow Cab Co., Inlaid Cloissone, Enameling, 2 1/8 x 2 In. 413.00
Civil Official Rank, Silk, Quail, Metal Wrapped Threads, 12 x 11 In., Pair 165.00
Deputy Sheriff, Lake County, Illinois, 5-Point Star, Eagle, Holding Banner 74.00
Deputy Sheriff, Madison County, Ind., State Of Indiana, 6-Point Star, 2 In. 57.00
Fireman, 1st Ass't Engineer For Round Lake V.F.D., Eagle, Fire Truck 19.00
Fireman, Boeing Security, Wichita, State Of Kansas, Silver Tone, 2 x 1 3/4 In. 51.00
Fireman, Chief, Shelbyville, Indiana, Nozzle, Horn, 1920s, 2 x 1 3/8 In. 55.00

Fireman, Division Of Training, Providence, R.I., Early 1900s, 2 3/4 x 2 In. 235.00
Fireman, Essex County Fire Brigade, England 16.00
Fireman, Fire Police Association, Servants Of Brotherhood, Penn., Round, 1949, 2 In. 24.00
Fireman, Forest Fire Warden, Maine, Chief, Round, 2 In. 44.00
Fireman, Honorary Exempt Sons 23rd Ward, Eagle, Crossed Horns, 2 1/4 x 1 1/2 In. 307.00
Fireman, Lawrence Fire Lines, Fire Dept Badge, Admit Through 179.00
Game Warden, State Of Colorado, 2 1/4 x 1 3/4 In. 165.00
Hat, Firefighting, New Phila., Pa., 1940s, 1 3/4 In. 25.00
Official, Rank, Silk, Embroidered, Pheasant, Chinese, Late 1800s, 11 1/2 x 11 In. 76.00
Ontario Department Of Lands & Forests, Coat Of Arms, Maple Leaves, 1 3/4 x 1 1/2 In. 76.00
Pacific Plant Protection, Sergeant, 3 x 2 In. 20.00
Parker Security Systems, 7-Point Star, Bear, 3 In. 28.00
Patrolman, U.S. Naval Training Center Police, Sampson, N.Y., Sterling, 2 1/2 In. 60.00
Police, Alberta Provincial, King's Crown, Coat Of Arms, Maple Leaves, 2 x 1 1/2 In. 127.00
Police, CTA, Chicago Transit Authority, Spread Winged Eagle, C.H. Hanson 46.00
Police, Detroit, Special Patrolman, 1940s 59.00
Police, Erie County, New York, Auxiliary, Patrolman, Nickel Plated 31.00
Police, Indian Motorcycle Company, Special Police, 2 3/4 x 2 1/2 In. 50.00
Police, Indian Police, Wind River, Wyo., Bear, 6-Point Star, 2 1/4 In. 15.00
Police, International Ass'n Of Chiefs Of Police, Sterling, Enamel, Golden Gate, 2 x 1 5/8 In. 140.00
Police, Plantation, Georgetown County, S.C., Runaway Slave Patrol, 1858, 2 x 2 In. 105.00
Police, Policia Federal, Republica Argentina, Rooster, Woman's Profile, Rays, 2 In. 18.00
Police, Portland, Star In Circle, National Stamp & Seal Works, Portland, Ore., 3 In. 205.00
Police, Reserve, Captain, City Of New York, Eagle, 3 x 2 1/4 In. 30.00
Police, Southern Pacific Railroad, Nickel Plated, 1920s, 2 3/4 x 2 In. 158.00
Ranger, Forest Reserve Dist., Cook County, Trees, 6-Point Star, Blackington 238.00
Ranger, U.S. Bureau Of Mines, L.A. Stamp & Sty Co., L.A., Cal., 2 In. 169.00
Sheriff, Maryland State Sheriff's Association, Gold Plated, 5-Point Star 30.00
Trooper, Department Of Public Safety, Texas, Round, c.1930 .... 178.00

BANKS of metal have been made since 1868. There are still banks, mechanical banks, and registering banks (those that show the total money deposited on the face of the bank). Many old iron or tin banks have been reproduced since the 1950s in iron or plastic. Some old reproductions marked Book of Knowledge or John Wright, or Capron are listed. Pottery, glass, and plastic banks are also listed here. Mickey Mouse and other Disneyana banks are listed in Disneyana. We have added the M-numbers based on *The Penny Bank Book: Collecting Still Banks* by Andy and Susan Moore and the R numbers based on *Coin Banks by Banthrico* by James L. Redwine.

4 Tower, Cast Iron, J. & E. Stevens, M 1121 .... 242.00
Airplane, Spirit Of Saving, Aluminum, 8 In. ....382.00 to 441.00
Airplane, Spirit Of St. Louis, White Metal, Blue Paint, Afros-Fe Co., M 1423, 2 1/4 x 7 7/8 In. 235.00
Andy Gump, Seated, Reading Newspaper, Cast Iron, Painted, Arcade, M 217, 4 3/8 x 2 7/8 In. 1410.00
Apple, Cast Iron, Painted, Kyser & Rex, M 1621, c.1882, 4 x 5 1/2 In. 660.00
Apple, Stoneware, Multicolor Glaze, 2 In. 72.00
Apple, Stoneware, Painted Accents, 3 In. 230.00
Baby In Cradle, Cast Iron, Green & Gold, Nickel Plated, M 51, 3 1/4 x 4 In. 2705.00
Baby In Cradle, White, Cast Iron, Yellow, Gold, Modern, 3 3/8 In. 130.00
Bank Building, City Bank, With Chimney, M 1101, 7 1/2 In. 1065.00
Bank Building, Columbia Magic Savings, Nickel Plated, Magic Introduction Co., M 1065, 5 1/4 In. 175.00
Bank Building, Crown With Tower, Cast Iron, Red, Green, J. & E. Stevens, M 1230, 3 1/4 x 2 3/4 In. 2233.00
Bank Building, Eagle With Ball, Cast Iron, M 1133, 10 3/4 x 5 1/2 In. 2468.00
Bank Building, Home Savings, Dog Finial, Iron, J. & E. Stevens, M 1237, 5 3/4 In. 120.00
Bank Building, State Bank, Cast Iron, Kenton, M 1078, 8 In. 770.00
Bank Building, State Bank, Cast Iron, Kenton, M 1080, 5 7/8 x 4 5/8 In. 176.00
Bank Building, State Bank, Cast Iron, Kenton, M 1085, 3 x 2 In. 130.00
Bank Building, Tower Bank, Cast Iron, Kyser & Rex, M 1198, 6 7/8 In. ....1320.00 to 2645.00
Barrel, White City, Puzzle Savings Bank, Barrel Of Money, Cast Iron, Nicol, M 916, 5 x 3 3/8 In. ... 190.00
Baseball On 3 Bats, Cast Iron, Hubley, M 1608, 5 1/4 In. ....1528.00 to 1870.00
Baseball Player, Cast Iron, A.C. Williams, 1920, M 19, 5 1/2 In. 785.00

Baseball Player, Cast Iron, Gold, White, Red Paint, A.C. Williams, M 18, 5 3/4 In. 500.00
Baseball Player, Cast Iron, Painted, A.C. Williams, 1909, M 20, 5 3/4 In. 215.00
Baseball Shape, Detroit Tigers, Mobil's Pegasus, Glass, 3 1/2 In. 99.00
Basket, Steel, Paper Label, M 915, 2 1/2 In. 28.00
Basket Of Corn, Cast Iron, Handles, J.M. Harper, c.1907, M 575, 2 1/2 x 3 1/4 In. 2200.00
Basketball, Tin, Round, Spiral Logo, Gene Bosch Design, Chein, 1970s, 4 1/2 In. 225.00
Be Wise & Save Owl, Cast Iron, Painted, A.C. Williams, M 598, 4 7/8 x 6 In. 170.00
Bear, Begging, Cast Iron, M 715, 5 3/8 In. 56.00
Bear, Mean, Standing, Cast Iron, Painted, Hubley, M 1683, 6 1/4 In. 130.00
Bear, On Hind Legs, Cast Iron, John Harper, M 710, 6 1/8 In. 176.00
Bear, Seated On Log, Cast Iron, M 714, 7 In. 765.00
Bear, Stealing Honey, Cast Iron, England, M 1308, 7 In. 130.00
Bear, Stealing Pig, Cast Iron, A.C. Williams, M 693, 5 1/2 In. 825.00
Bear, Teddy, On 4 Feet, Cast Iron, Arcade, M 694, 2 1/2 x 3 7/8 In. 250.00
Beaver, Cast Iron, Painted, Stamped, W-S S In Triangle, Canada, M 750, 2 1/2 x 8 In. 7740.00
Beehive, Cast Iron, Painted, Industry Shall Be Rewarded, Kyser & Rex, M 683, 2 3/8 In. 1060.00
Beehive, Pottery, Mottled Glaze, 3 3/4 In. 250.00
Bell, Liberty Bell, Glass, Amber, 4 3/8 In. 47.00
Billiken, A.C. Williams, 1909, M 74, 4 1/4 x 2 1/2 In. 295.00
Billiken, Cast Iron, A.C. Williams, M 74, 4 In. 35.00
Billy Bounce, Cast Iron, Painted, Hubley, M 15, 4 3/4 In. 500.00
Bird On Stump, Cast Iron, Painted, A.C. Williams, M 664, 4 3/4 x 4 3/4 In. 440.00
Black Man, Bust, Bow Tie, Porcelain, Mouth Coin Slot, 6 1/2 In. 440.00
Black Man's Head, Red Collar, Pottery, 3 3/4 In. 130.00
Black Man's Head, White Collar, Pottery, 4 1/2 In. 130.00
Blackpool Tower, Silvered Lead, Germany, 4 1/2 x 3 1/2 In. 118.00
Boast, Battleship Maine, Cast Iron, Grey Iron Casting, M 1440, 5 In. 336.00
Boat, Barge, Green, Blue, Cast Iron, Yellow Red Paint, Kyser & Rex, M 1453, 1 1/4 x 5 3/4 In. 9990.00
Boat, Battleship Maine, Cast Iron, Grey Iron Casting, M 1440, 4 5/8 x 4 1/2 In. 470.00
Boat, Battleship Maine, Cast Iron, J. & E. Stevens, M 1439, 6 x 10 1/4 In. 2000.00
Boat, Battleship Oregon, Cast Iron, J. & E. Stevens, M 1450, 3 7/8 x 4 7/8 In. ....224.00 to 410.00
Boat, Battleship Oregon, Cast Iron, J. & E. Stevens, M 1452, 4 7/8 x 6 In. 190.00
Boat, Fortune Ship, Cast Iron, Red Paint, M 1457, 4 1/8 x 5 3/8 In. 2350.00
Boat, Gunboat, Cast Iron, Painted, Blue, White, Kenton, M 1462, 2 3/4 x 8 1/2 In. 529.00
Boat, Steamboat, Cast Iron, A.C. Williams, M 1459, 2 1/2 x 7 1/2 In. 190.00
Boy Scout, Cast Iron, A.C. Williams, M 45, 6 In. 196.00
Boy Scout, Scarf, Buckle, Cast Iron, Gold Paint, Canada, M 46, 5 3/4 In. 255.00
Boy Scout, Scarf, Buckle, Cast Iron, Painted, Hubley, M 47, 5 3/4 In. 825.00
Brownie, A Brownie Is Thrifty, Plastic, Gold, Paint, M 1640, 6 x 4 1/4 In. 155.00
Buffalo, Cast Iron, Red Paint, Arcade, M 560, 3 1/8 x 4 3/8 In. ....84.00 to 117.00
Buffalo Head, Pottery, Rose Glaze, Stamped Austria, 3 1/4 In. 60.00
Bugs Bunny At Barrel, Lock & Key, Alloy Metal, Moss, Box, M 270, 5 1/2 x 5 3/4 In. 175.00
Building, Belfry, Cast Iron, Painted, Kenton, M 1233, 8 x 3 5/8 In. 4348.00
Building, Boston State House, Cast Iron, Red, White, Blue, Smith & Egge, M 1209, 6 3/4 x 5 In. 3408.00
Building, Bungalow, Porch, Cast Iron, Nickel Plated, Grey Iron Casting, M 999, 3 3/4 In. 360.00
Building, Bureaux Caisse, Cast Iron, Gold Paint, France, M 1137, 10 x 6 In. 510.00
Building, Castle, 2 Towers, John Harper, M 1114, 7 In. 880.00
Building, Castle, Cast Iron, Kyser & Rex, M 954, 3 x 2 3/4 In. 3175.00
Building, Colonial House, Cast Iron, Painted, A.C. Williams, M 992, 4 x 3 7/8 In. 116.00
Building, Columbia Tower, Cast Iron, Grey Iron Casting, M 1118, 6 7/8 x 3 1/8 In. 2700.00
Building, Columbia, Cast Iron, Copper & Gold Finish, Kenton, M 1073, 8 3/4 x 7 In. 1290.00
Building, Columbia, Silver, Blue, Cast Iron, Kenton, M 1069, 4 1/2 x 3 1/2 In. 646.00
Building, Crown, Cast Iron, Copper & Gold, J. & E. Stevens, M 1227, 3 x 2 1/2 In. 456.00
Building, Crown, Footed, Cast Iron, Painted, M 1151, 4 7/8 x 4 1/4 In. 670.00
Building, Cupola, Cast Iron, Painted, J. & E. Stevens, M 1145, 5 1/2 x 4 1/4 In. 850.00
Building, Cupola, Cast Iron, Painted, Red Roof, J. & E. Stevens, M 1147, 3 1/4 x 2 5/8 In. 145.00
Building, Cupola, Cast Iron, Painted, Red, Silver Roof, J. & E. Stevens, M 1147, 3 1/4 x 2 5/8 In. .. 336.00
Building, Domed Mosque, Cast Iron, Grey Iron Casting, M 1177, 4 1/2 In. 56.00
Building, Eiffel Tower, Cast Iron, England, M 1075, 10 3/8 x 5 1/4 x 5 1/4 In. 3995.00
Building, Flat Iron, Cast Iron, Kenton, M 1159, 8 1/4 x 4 3/4 In. 2235.00
Building, Independence Hall Tower, Cast Iron, Enterprise, M 1202, 9 1/2 In. 450.00

Building, Independence Hall, Cast Iron, Enterprise, M 1242, 10 In. 310.00
Building, Jarmulowsky, Cast Iron, J. & E. Stevens, M 1086, 7 3/4 x 2 1/8 In. 6555.00
Building, Log Cabin, Black Banjo Player & Dancer, Tin Lithograph, Chein, 3 In. ....392.00 to 420.00
Building, Log Cabin, Cobalt Blue, Coin Slots In Door, Stoneware, c.1840, 4 1/4 x 3 3/4 In. 2640.00
Building, Log Cabin, W.H. Harrison & Hard Cider Campaign, Stoneware, c.1840, 4 1/4 x 3 3/4 In. . 2640.00
Building, Palace, Cast Iron, Painted, Ives, 8 x 8 1/4 In. 1320.00
Building, Penthouse, Cast Iron, A.C. Williams, M 1234, 5 7/8 x 2 1/2 In. 1725.00
Building, Skyscraper, Four Towers, Cast Iron, A.C. Williams, M 1239, 4 1/2 In. 85.00
Building, U.S. Treasury, Cast Iron, Painted, Grey Iron Casting, M 1053, 3 1/4 x 3 1/4 In. 605.00
Bulbous, Pointed Finial, Yellowware, Mottled Glaze, 5 In. 440.00
Bull, Aberdeen Angus, Aluminum, M 555, 4 1/8 x 7 3/8 In. 80.00
Bus, Double-Decker, Cast Iron, Painted, M 1490, 2 1/4 x 3 1/2 In. 850.00
Bust, David Lloyd George, Cast Iron, England, M 7, 5 3/4 x 4 In. 3408.00
Camel, Cast Iron, Painted, A.C. Williams, M 767, 7 1/4 x 6 1/4 In. 529.00
Camel, Cast Iron, Painted, A.C. Williams, M 768, 4 3/4 x 3 7/8 In. 225.00
Camel, Kneeling, Trunk On Back, Cast Iron, Kyser & Rex, M 770, 2 1/2 x 4 3/4 In. 1234.00
Camel, Oriental, 2 Camels, Cast Iron, M 769, 3 3/4 x 5 3/8 In. 500.00
Camel, With Pack, Composition, M 771, 4 In. 85.00
Cannon, Cast Iron, Red, Green, Hubley, M 1425, 3 x 6 7/8 In. 2585.00
Captain Kidd, Cast Iron, Painted, M 38, 5 5/8 x 4 1/8 In. ....275.00 to 295.00
Car, 4 Passenger, Cast Iron, Green, Red Tires, A.C. Williams, M 1487, 3 1/2 x 6 3/4 In. 1880.00
Car, Armored, Red, Gold, Cast Iron, A.C. Williams, M 1424, 3 3/4 x 6 3/4 In. 3642.00
Car, Limousine Cab, Cast Iron, Yellow, Green, White Tires, Arcade, M 1480, 3 1/2 x 8 In. 5522.00
Car, Model-T, Driver, Passenger, Cast Iron, Black, White Tires, Arcade, M 1484, 4 x 6 5/16 In. 3525.00
Car, Yellow Cab, Arcade, c.1920, M 1489, 4 1/4 x 7 1/2 In. 690.00
Cash Register, Junior, Cast Iron, J. & E. Stevens, M 930, 4 1/4 x 3 1/2 In. 295.00
Cat, Kitty, Pink Bow, Cast Iron, Hubley, M 349, 4 3/4 In. 60.00
Cat, Lindys, Seated, Looking Up, Alloy, M 371, 4 3/4 x 4 1/2 In. 180.00
Cat, Pottery, Scroddled, England, 5 In. 470.00
Cat, Seated, Painted Red, Cast Iron 470.00
Cat, With Bow, Cast Iron, Black, White, Yellow, Hubley, M 350, 4 1/8 In. 175.00
Cat Head, Porcelain, c.1900, 2 In. 415.00
Chicken In Nest, Stoneware, Mottled Green Glaze, Center Loop Handle, 5 1/2 In. 319.00
Child, Crying In Washtub, Purple Glaze, Pottery, 3 1/2 In. 70.00
Church, Chein, Tin, 4 In. 30.00
Clock, Money Saver, Cast Iron, Steel, Arcade, M 1544, 3 1/2 In. 165.00
Clock, Save Your Pennies, Cast Iron, Arcade, M 1545, 3 1/2 In. 235.00
Clock, Street Clock, Cast Iron, A.C. Williams, M 1548, 6 x 2 1/2 In. 735.00
Clock, Time Is Money, Cast Iron, Tin, H.C. Hart, M 1555, 4 7/8 In. 325.00
Clown, Cast Iron, Gold Paint, A.C. Williams, M 211, 6 1/4 In. 100.00
Clown, Cast Iron, Silver Paint, A.C. Williams, M 211, 6 3/4 In. 25.00
Clown, Crooked Hat, Cast Iron, M 210, 6 3/4 In. 1060.00
Clown, Multicolored, Tin, Saalheimer & Strauss, Germany 4115.00
Clown Head, White, Brown, Porcelain, Schierholz, 5 In. 255.00
Cockatoo, White Metal, Painted, M 656, 5 In. 365.00
Columbia World Expo, Globe, On Base, Cast Iron, M 779, 5 In. 940.00
Cow, Holstein, Cast Iron, White, Arcade, M 544, 2 1/2 x 4 5/8 In. 500.00
Cow, Milking, On Platform, Cast Iron, Multicolored, J. & E. Stevens, M 540, 4 1/4 In. 1295.00
Detroit Tigers, Pottery, Stanford, 3 x 3 x 7 In. 929.00
Dewitt Clinton Railroad Train, Steam Engine, 4 Cars, Lead, 1930, M 1477, 2 1/8 x 7 In. 375.00
Dime, Ladd & Tilton, Established 1859, Portland, Oregon, Celluloid, 2 1/4 x 1/2 In. 155.00
Dog, Basset Hound, Gold Finish, Cast Iron, A.C. Williams, M 380, 3 1/8 In. 795.00
Dog, Boston Bulldog, Black, White, Red, Chain Collar, Cast Iron, Hubley, M 413, 4 3/8 x 5 5/8 In. .. 420.00
Dog, Bulldog, Ceramic, Padlock, Key, 7 In. 45.00
Dog, Cutie, Black, Red Collar, Seated, Cast Iron, Hubley, M 414, 3 7/8 In. 130.00
Dog, English Bulldog, Cast Iron, Hubley, M 396, 3 7/8 In. 106.00
Dog, Fido, Hubley, 5 In. 88.00
Dog, Husky, Cast Iron, Grey Iron Casting, M 411, 5 In. 530.00
Dog, Labrador Retriever, Black, Red, Gold Collar, Cast Iron, M 412, 4 1/2 x 6 In. 200.00
Dog, Lost Dog, Seated, Cast Iron, H.L. Judd, M 407, 5 3/8 In. 645.00
Dog, Pug, Seated, Cast Iron, Painted, Kyser & Rex, M 405, 3 1/2 In. 190.00

Dog, Scottie, Black, Red, Cast Iron, Hubley, M 419, 4 7/8 x 6 In. 220.00
Dog, Scottie, Black, Standing, Cast Iron, Hubley, M 435, 3 1/4 In. 140.00
Dog, Scottie, Fala, White, Seated, Cast Iron, M 430, 2 3/4 In. 200.00
Dog, Scottie, Tiny, Seated, Black, Cast Iron, M 428, 3 1/8 In. 295.00
Dog, Spaniel Head, Brown Over Yellow Glaze, Stoneware, 4 1/2 In. 220.00
Dog, Spaniel, Begging, Lead, M 361, 5 In. 310.00
Dog, Spaniel, Black & White, Cast Iron, Hubley, M 418, 3 3/4 x 6 In. 140.00
Dog, Spaniel, Pack On Back, Cast Iron, M 438, 5 1/2 x 8 In. 200.00
Dog, Spaniel, Pottery, Brown Glaze, Molded, Orange, Slot In Back, 5 3/8 In. 440.00
Dog, Spaniel, Stoneware, Albany Slip Glaze 1045.00
Dog, Spitz, Gold Finish, Cast Iron, Grey Iron Casting, M 409, 4 1/4 In. 380.00
Dog, St. Bernard, Pack, Cast Iron, A.C. Williams, Large, M 437, 5 1/2 In. .... 55.00 to 85.00
Dog, St. Bernard, Pack, Cast Iron, Painted, A.C. Williams, Small, M 439, 3 3/4 x 5 1/2 In. 95.00
Dog, Wirehaired Terrier, Cast Iron, Hubley, M 422, 4 5/8 In. 145.00
Dolphin, Sailor In Boat, Anchor, Cast Iron, Gold Finish, Grey Iron Casting, M 33, 4 1/2 In. 470.00
Donkey, Large, Cast Iron, Painted, A.C. Williams, M 500, 6 3/4 x 6 1/4 In. 270.00
Donkey, Small, Cast Iron, Gold Paint, Arcade, M 499, 4 1/2 x 4 5/8 In. 60.00
Donkey, Small, Cast Iron, Gray Paint, Arcade, M 499, 4 1/2 x 4 5/8 In. 36.00
Donkey, Small, Cast Iron, Silver Finish, Arcade, M 499, 4 1/2 x 4 5/8 In. 60.00
Dreadnaught, Shaking Hands, Flags, Ship, Cast Iron, England, M 1314, 7 x 7 1/2 In. 1060.00
Duck, On Tub, Top Hat, Hubley, M 616, 5 1/2 In. 130.00
Duck, Round, Cast Iron, Yellow, Orange Paint, Kenton, M 619, 4 x 4 7/8 In. 240.00
Dutch Boy, Gold Finish, Cast Iron, Grey Iron Casting, M 17, 6 3/4 In. 705.00
Dutch Boy, On Barrel, Cast Iron, Hubley, M 180, 6 In. 30.00
Dutch Girl, Gold Finish, Cast Iron, Grey Iron Casting, M 16, 6 In. 705.00
Dutch Girl, With Flowers, Cast Iron, Hubley, M 183, 5 1/4 In. 130.00
Eagle, Wisconsin's Historic War Eagle, Silver Finish, Cast Iron, M 678, 2 7/8 In. 1528.00
Eggman, Gold Finish, Cast Iron, Arcade, M 108, 4 1/8 In. 2585.00
Elephant, Bent Knee, Cast Iron, Painted White, Kenton, M 447, 3 1/2 x 4 7/8 In. 223.00
Elephant, Chariot, Cast Iron, Gold, Blue, Yellow, Red, Hubley, M 479, 4 3/4 x 6 7/8 In. 470.00
Elephant, Circus, Seated, Raised Trunk, Cast Iron, Hubley, c.1940, 3 7/8 In. 132.00
Elephant, Howdah, Cast Iron, A.C. Williams, M 477, 3 1/2 In. .... 53.00 to 84.00
Elephant, Howdah, Large, Cast Iron, A.C. Williams, M 474, 4 7/8 x 6 3/8 In. 70.00
Elephant, Howdah, Small, Cast Iron, A.C. Williams, M 459, 3 x 4 In. 242.00
Elephant, Howdah, Stiff Legs, Cast Iron, Harris Toy Co., M 469, 3 1/2 x 4 1/4 In. 529.00
Elephant, Howdah, Tiny, Cast Iron, A.C. Williams, M 457, 2 1/2 x 3 In. 48.00
Elephant, On Bench, On Tub, Cast Iron, Painted, A.C. Williams, M 486, 3 7/8 In. 84.00
Elephant, On Tub, Cast Iron, Painted, A.C. Williams, M 484, 5 3/8 In. 121.00
Elephant, On Wheels, Cast Iron, A.C. Williams, M 446, 4 1/2 In. 605.00
Elephant, Seated, Turned Trunk, Cast Iron, Gold Finish, M 445, 4 1/4 In. 294.00
Elephant, Tucked Trunk, Cast Iron, Green, Arcade, M 472, 2 3/4 x 4 5/8 In. 91.00
Elephant, Tucked Trunk, Cast Iron, Red, Arcade, M 472, 2 3/4 x 4 5/8 In. 91.00
Elephant, With Ball, Lead, M 485, 3 In. 616.00
Elephant, With Blanket, Cast Iron, Gold Finish, Red, Kenton, M 487, 3 1/8 x 5 In. 1998.00
Elmer Fudd, Barrel, Alloy Metal, Multicolored, Moss, Box, M 306, 5 1/2 x 5 3/4 In. 441.00
Encyclopedia, Our 10 Cents A Day, Tin, Blue, Werner Co. 200.00
Family Safe, Cast Iron, Black, Bronze Dog, Pat. 1858, 12 x 13 x 10 In. 1540.00
Fire Alarm, Red, White, To Send Fire Alarm Pull, Cast Iron 188.00
Football Player, Cast Iron, Gold Finish, A.C. Williams, M 11, 5 7/8 In. 325.00
Foxy Grandpa, Cast Iron, Painted Silver, Red Vest, Hubley, 1920, M 320, 5 1/2 In. 165.00
Foxy Grandpa, Cast Iron, Turnpin, Wing, 1900, M 320, 5 1/2 In. 245.00
Fruit Basket, Puzzle, Cast Iron, Nicol, M 919, 2 3/4 x 3 1/2 In. 470.00
Gas Pump, Cast Iron, Red Paint, M 1485, 5 3/4 x 2 1/8 In. 176.00
Gas Stove, Save Your Money, Cast Iron 110.00
Gator Eating Black Man, Pottery, 6 In. 28.00
General Butler, Cast Iron, J. & E. Stevens, M 54, 6 1/2 In. 2350.00
General Pershing, Cast Iron, Grey Iron Casting, M 150, 7 3/4 In. 30.00
General Pershing Bust, Cast Iron, Grey Iron Casting, M 157, 1918, 7 3/4 In. 145.00
General Sheridan, On Horse, Base, Cast Iron, Arcade, M 50, 4 x 2 3/8 In. 558.00
Gingerbread House, Silver Plate, Denmark, 3 3/4 In. 198.00
Give Me A Penny, Black Man, Cast Iron, Wing U.S.A., M 167, 5 1/2 In. 305.00

Give Me A Penny, Turnpin, Cast Iron, Painted, Wing, U.S., M 167, 5 5/8 In. ....220.00 to 400.00
Golliwog, Cast Iron, Porcelain Finish, John Harper, M 85, 6 In. 225.00
Hamm's Bear, Porcelain, 1973 .... 185.00
Head, Man Smoking Pipe, Long Nose, Stocking Cap, Stoneware, Salt Glaze, 6 1/4 In. 110.00
Heckyl, Wood, Hand Painted, Tag, Key, Terrytoones, CBS Films, 8 In. 155.00
Hippo, Cast Iron, M 718, 2 x 5 1/4 In. 3335.00
Horse, Beauty, Cast Iron, Arcade, 1932, M 532, 4 1/8 x 4 3/4 In. 275.00
Horse, On Tub, Cast Iron, Black Paint, Orange Blanket, A.C. Williams, M 509, 5 1/4 In. 96.00
Horse, Prancing, Cast Iron, Painted, M 517, 4 1/4 x 4 7/8 In. 36.00
Horse, Prancing, With Belly Band, Cast Iron, Painted, M 506, 4 1/2 x 5 In. 196.00
Horse, Work Horse, Cast Iron, Arcade, M 533, 4 In. 28.00
House, Chimneys, Windows, Stoneware, Red Glaze, Yellow, Green, 1903, 6 3/4 x 5 3/8 In. 550.00
Ice Cream Freezer, North Pole, Cast Iron, Grey Iron Casting, M 1371, 4 1/4 x 2 5/8 In. 385.00
Independence Hall, Cast Iron, 1876, M 1211, 6 3/8 x 11 In. 3800.00
Indian, Bust, With Headdress, Lead, Yosemite National Park, M 227, 3 1/8 In. 335.00
Indian Family, Cast Iron, J.M. Harper, M 224, 3 5/8 x 5 1/8 In. 2070.00
Kelvinator, Cast Iron, Arcade, M 1338, 4 In. 168.00
Liberty Bell, N.P.M.A., Proclamation Text, J.M. Harper, c.1906, 3 7/8 In. 605.00
Liberty Bell, Sesquicentennial, Grey Iron Casting, 1926, M 782, 4 In. 45.00
Lion, Ears Up, Cast Iron, Turnpin, Painted, A.C. Williams, M 757, 3 5/8 x 4 1/2 In. 30.00
Lion, Tail Between Legs, Cast Iron, Painted, M 764, 3 x 5 1/4 In. 48.00
Lion, Tail Left, Cast Iron, Painted, Hubley, M 763, 3 3/4 x 5 3/8 In. 60.00
Lion, Tail Right, Cast Iron, A.C. Williams, M 754, 5 In. 55.00
Little Red Riding Hood, Safe, J.M. Harper, c.1907, M 25, 5 1/6 In. 3300.00
Log Cabin, Birds, Figures, Stoneware, Green Glaze, Cream, 5 1/8 x 6 In. 2640.00
Log Cabin, Raccoon On Roof, Stoneware, Cobalt Blue, Thomas Haig Jr., Phila., c.1846 .... 18150.00
Log Cabin, Raccoon, Coin Slot In Door, Stoneware, Glazed, 1850, 4 1/2 In. 3080.00
Main Street Trolley, With People, Cast Iron, A.C. Williams, M 1471, 7 In. 170.00
Mammy, Hands On Hips, Cast Iron, Hubley, M 176, 5 1/4 In. 198.00
Mammy, With Spoon, Cast Iron, Painted, A.C. Williams, M 168, 5 7/8 In. 302.00
Man, In Barrel, Arms, Legs, Face On Lid, Cast Iron, J. & E. Stevens, M 282, 3 5/8 In. 2468.00
Man, In Barrel, Cast Iron, Brown, H.L. Judd, M 909, 2 3/4 x 2 In. 210.00
Man, Seated, Hat, Holding Pitcher, Pottery, Brown Glaze, 4 1/2 In. 85.00
Mary & Little Lamb, Cast Iron, Painted, M 164, 4 3/8 In. 485.00

Mechanical banks were first made about 1870. Any bank with moving parts is considered mechanical. The metal banks made before World War I are the most desirable. Copies and new designs of mechanical banks have been made in metal or plastic since the 1920s. The condition of the paint on the old banks is important. Worn paint can lower a price by 90%.

Mechanical, Acrobat, Kicks Clown, Stands On Head, Pushes In Coin, J. & E. Stevens, c.1883 .... 1045.00
Mechanical, Afghanistan, Herat, Cast Iron, Mechanical Novelty Works, New Britain, Ct., c.1885 .... 3760.00
Mechanical, Artillery, Cast Iron, Bronze Plated, Coin Trap, Shepard Hardware, c.1892 ....525.00 to 1456.00
Mechanical, Artillery, Red Coat, Cast Iron, J. & E. Stevens, c.1900 .... 1058.00
Mechanical, Bad Accident, Black Man, Wagon, Iron, J. & E. Stevens, c.1891, 10 In. ....1064.00 to 3190.00
Mechanical, Bank Teller, Cast Iron, Painted, J. & E. Stevens, c.1880, 7 x 4 1/2 In. 940.00
Mechanical, Bear, Red & White Striped Pants, Tin, Saalheimer & Strauss, Germany 4115.00
Mechanical, Billy Goat, Brass, J. & E. Stevens, c.1910 .... 265.00
Mechanical, Bomb 'n' Bank, Coins Drop From Airplane Into Cylinder, 1940s 1293.00
Mechanical, Bonzo, Tin, Saalheimer & Strauss, Germany 3290.00
Mechanical, Bowling Bank, Richards, 1950s 795.00
Mechanical, Boy & Bulldog, Cast Iron, H.L. Judd 2467.00
Mechanical, Boy On Trapeze, Cast Iron, c.1891, J. Barton Smith, 9 1/4 In. ....1045.00 to 9500.00
Mechanical, Boy Scout Camp, Cast Iron, Painted, J. & E. Stevens ....2016.00 to 16450.00
Mechanical, Boys Stealing Watermelons, Cast Iron, Kyser & Rex, c.1894 .... 2800.00
Mechanical, Breadwinners, Honest Labor, Cast Iron, Painted, J. & E. Stevens, c.1886 .... 14100.00
Mechanical, British Soldier At Drum, Fur Hat, Painted, Schuco, Germany, c.1930 .... 2938.00
Mechanical, Bulldog, On Carpet, Cast Iron, Brown, J. & E. Stevens, 1880 ....1430.00 to 2240.00
Mechanical, Butting Ram, Man Thumbs Nose, Cast Iron, Painted, Wagner & Zweibel, Wisconsin .. 9300.00
Mechanical, Cabin Bank, Yellow, Black Figure, Cast Iron, J. & E. Stevens, 4 x 3 In. ....660.00 to 1500.00

Mechanical, Calamity, 3 Colliding Football Players, Cast Iron, J. & E. Stevens, c.1904 .... 22800.00
Mechanical, Cat & Mouse, Cast Iron, Painted, J. & E. Stevens, Pat. 1891, 11 1/2 In. ....4480.00 to 4620.00
Mechanical, Cat Sailboat, Richards, 1950s 1500.00
Mechanical, Chief Big Moon, Cast Iron, Silver Stripe, J. & E. Stevens, c.1899 ....935.00 to 8960.00
Mechanical, Chimpanzee, Cast Iron, Kyser & Rex, 1880 .... 2016.00
Mechanical, Chimpanzee, Seated, Mouth Waggles, Pot Metal 410.00
Mechanical, Chinaman, Reclining, Cast Iron, Painted, J. & E. Stevens 8325.00
Mechanical, Chronometer, Cast Iron, Painted, Register, Penny 3290.00
Mechanical, Circus Ticket Collector, Standing At Barrel, Cast Iron, H.L. Judd 2470.00
Mechanical, Circus, Clown & Cart, Cast Iron, Shepard Hardware, 1887 .... 9520.00
Mechanical, Clown On Globe, Cast Iron, Tan, J. & E. Stevens, 1890 .... 4480.00
Mechanical, Clown On Globe, Does Handstand, Cast Iron, Painted, J. & E. Stevens, 9 In. .1760.00 to 1850.00
Mechanical, Clown On Globe, Yellow Base, Cast Iron, J. & E. Stevens, Box ....9350.00 to 12925.00
Mechanical, Creedmoor, Man Shooting At Tree, Cast Iron, Painted, J. & E. Stevens ....705.00 to 770.00
Mechanical, Cupola, Circular, Cast Iron, Green, J. & E. Stevens, 1872 .... 1905.00
Mechanical, Darktown Battery, Iron, Painted, J. & E. Stevens, c.1888, 7 1/2 x 10 In. ....1760.00 to 4125.00
Mechanical, Dentist, Cast Iron, Mid 20th Century, 6 1/2 x 9 In. 310.00
Mechanical, Dentist, Pulling Tooth From Man's Mouth, Cast Iron, J. & E. Stevens, 1880 .... 8250.00
Mechanical, Dinah, Black Woman, Cast Iron, Yellow Shirt, John Harper, 1911 ....499.00 to 1763.00
Mechanical, Dinah, Black Woman, Red & White Shirt, Aluminum, England ....130.00 to 242.00
Mechanical, Dog Tray, Cast Iron, Painted, Kyser & Rex, Philadelphia, c.1885 .... 3880.00
Mechanical, Eagle & Eaglets, Cast Iron, Gray, J. & E. Stevens, 1883 .... 4760.00
Mechanical, Elephant & 3 Clowns, Cast Iron, J. & E. Stevens, c.1883 ....990.00 to 3910.00
Mechanical, Elephant, 3 Stars, Cast iron, Painted, c.1880, 5 x 9 In. 930.00
Mechanical, Elephant, Pull Tail, Cast Iron, Painted Gray, Red, Hubley, c.1930 .... 1116.00
Mechanical, Fisherman's Luck, Richards, 1950s 1295.00
Mechanical, Fortune Horse Race, Lithographed Tin, Norton Bros., Patent 1897 .... 8800.00
Mechanical, Freedmens Bureau, Now You See It, Now You Don't, Wood, Painted, 3 Drawers 1880.00
Mechanical, Frog On Rock, Cast Iron, Kilgore, c.1920s 2240.00
Mechanical, Frog On Round Base, Cast Iron, J. & E. Stevens, c.1872 .... 1800.00
Mechanical, Frog On Round Base, Cast Iron, Red Lattice, J. & E. Stevens, c.1872 .... 2990.00
Mechanical, Frogs, Two, Cast Iron, Painted, J. & E. Stevens, c.1882, 9 In. ....1045.00 to 1540.00
Mechanical, Gem, Dog & Building, Cast Iron, Painted, H.L. Judd, c.1878 .... 605.00
Mechanical, George Washington At The Rappahannock, Cast Iron, John Wright, Box 380.00
Mechanical, Girl In Victorian Chair, Cast Iron, Painted, W.S. Reed 2350.00
Mechanical, Girl Skipping Rope, Cast Iron, J. & E. Stevens, c.1890 ....28200.00 to 57500.00
Mechanical, Grenadier, Cast Iron, John Harper, c.1890 .... 1058.00
Mechanical, Hall's Excelsior, Cashier, Cast Iron, Painted, J. & E. Stevens, 5 1/2 x 4 In. 820.00
Mechanical, Harlequin, Second Casting, Cast Iron, J. & E. Stevens, c.1907 .... 12100.00
Mechanical, Harold Lloyd, Tin, Saalheimer & Strauss, Germany, c.1920 ....1530.00 to 5320.00
Mechanical, Horse Race, Flanged Base, Cast Iron, Painted, J. & E. Stevens, c.1871 .... 3760.00
Mechanical, Humpty Dumpty, Cast Iron, Painted, Shepard Hardware, c.1884 .... 720.00
Mechanical, I Always Did 'Spise A Mule, Jockey, Iron, Painted, J. & E. Stevens, c.1879 . . .1645.00 to 6500.00
Mechanical, Indian & Bear, Cast Iron, Painted, J. & E. Stevens, c.1883 .... 2937.00
Mechanical, Joe Socko, Boxers, Tin, Straits Corp., 1930s 205.00
Mechanical, John Bull's Money Box, Dog, Barrel, Iron, Painted, Sydenham & McOustra, c.1909 ... 7150.00
Mechanical, Jolly Nigger, Cast Iron, J. & E. Stevens 185.00
Mechanical, Jolly Nigger, Fixed Eyes, Cast Iron, England 106.00
Mechanical, Jolly Nigger, Red Shirt, Cast Iron, Original Paint, Shepard Hardware, 7 In. ....330.00 to 353.00
Mechanical, Jolly Nigger, Top Hat, Cast Iron, John Harper ....495.00 to 880.00
Mechanical, Key, Golden Gate, Aluminum, William J. Somerville, 5 1/2 In. 385.00
Mechanical, Kick Inn, Mule Kicks Coin In House, Wood, Paper Label, Melvisto Novelty Co., c.1921 . 90.00
Mechanical, Leap Frog, Cast Iron, Painted, Shepard Hardware, c.1891 .... 4112.00
Mechanical, Lighthouse, Cast Iron, Painted, c.1890, 10 3/8 x 6 3/8 In. 765.00
Mechanical, Lion & 2 Monkeys, Cast Iron, Kyser & Rex, c.1883 ....1070.00 to 5320.00
Mechanical, Lion & Monkeys, Single Peanut Variety, Cast Iron, Kyser & Rex, c.1883 .... 880.00
Mechanical, Little Joe, Cast Iron, John Harper 336.00
Mechanical, Magic Bank, Cast Iron, Painted, J. & E. Stevens, 6 In. ....1650.00 to 3200.00
Mechanical, Magician, At Table, J. & E. Stevens, Cast Iron .... *ILLUS* 3360.00
Mechanical, Mary Roebling Trenton Trust, Cast Iron, Grey Iron Casting, Box, c.1963 .... 4500.00
Mechanical, Mason, Brick Layer & Carrier, Cast Iron, Shepard Hardware ....2420.00 to 13800.00

Bank, Mechanical, Magician, At Table, J. & E. Stevens, Cast Iron

Bank, Mechanical, Tammany, Gray Pants, Cast Iron, J. & E. Stevens, 1873 Patent

Bank, Mechanical, Trick Pony, Cast Iron, Shepard Hardware, 1885 Patent

Mechanical, Minstrel, Black Boy, Sticks Out Tongue, Tin, Germany, 7 x 4 In. 705.00
Mechanical, Minstrel, Tin, Saalheimer & Strauss, Germany, Type 1 .... 820.00
Mechanical, Monkey & Coconut, Cast Iron, Painted, J. & E. Stevens, 8 1/2 In. 8020.00
Mechanical, Monkey & Parrot, Tin, Saalheimer & Strauss, Germany 820.00
Mechanical, Monkey Bank, Organ Grinder & Monkey, Cast Iron, Painted, Hubley ....605.00 to 1645.00
Mechanical, Monkey With Tray, Sitting On Cage, Tin Lithographed, Germany 560.00
Mechanical, Monkey, Coin In Stomach, Cast Iron, S.S. & S.D. Tallman, Bridgeport, Ct., c.1882 .... 2115.00
Mechanical, Mosque, Building, H.L. Judd, 1880s 3800.00
Mechanical, New Bank, Guard Exits Door, Cast Iron, Painted, J. & E. Stevens, 6 x 4 1/2 In. 1045.00
Mechanical, Novelty Bank, Cast Iron, Brown, J. & E. Stevens, 1873 .... 3200.00
Mechanical, Olympic Coliseum, Cast Iron, John Wright 4800.00
Mechanical, Olympic Towers, Cast Iron, John Wright 1800.00
Mechanical, Organ Bank, Cat & Dog, Cast Iron, Painted, Kyser & Rex ....1650.00 to 3055.00
Mechanical, Organ Bank, Monkey, Cast Iron, Painted, Medium, Kyser & Rex ....1100.00 to 2700.00
Mechanical, Organ Grinder & Bear, Cast Iron, Painted, Kyser & Rex, 1890s ....4348.00 to 5600.00
Mechanical, Owl, Slot In Book, Cast Iron, Painted, Kilgore, 1930s 500.00
Mechanical, Owl, Turns Head, Cast Iron, J. & E. Stevens, Pat. 1880 ....460.00 to 1800.00
Mechanical, Paddy & The Pig, Cast Iron, Book Of Knowledge, 1960s 255.00
Mechanical, Paddy & The Pig, Cast Iron, Painted, J. & E. Stevens, c.1885 .... 3175.00
Mechanical, Paddy & The Pig, Green Coat, J. & E. Stevens, c.1885 .... 3920.00
Mechanical, Panorama, Building, Picture Window, Cast Iron, J. & E. Stevens, 1876 .... 6720.00
Mechanical, Penny On The Drum, St. Dunstans, Box, 1948 .... 295.00
Mechanical, Penny Pineapple, Hawaii Gains Statehood In 1958, Cast Iron, John Wright 295.00
Mechanical, Pig At Drum, Key Wind, Schuco 880.00
Mechanical, Pig In Highchair, Cast Iron, Nickel Plated, J. & E. Stevens, 1897 ....795.00 to 1116.00
Mechanical, Postman, Puts Coin In Letter Box, England, 1927 .... 385.00
Mechanical, Professor Pug Frog's Great Bicycle Feat, J. & E. Stevens 16500.00
Mechanical, Punch & Judy, Cast Iron, Large Letters, Painted, Shepard Hardware ....3290.00 to 4250.00
Mechanical, Punch & Judy, Tin, Painted, Burnett Limited, England 1645.00
Mechanical, Rabbit, Small, Standing, Holding Ball, Cast Iron, Lockwood 1292.00
Mechanical, Reclining Chinaman, Blue Pants, Cast Iron, J. & E. Stevens, Pat. 1882 .... 13200.00
Mechanical, Ronald Reagan, Tip O'Neill, Cast Aluminum, 2 1/2 x 5 3/4 x 9 1/2 In. 445.00
Mechanical, Rooster, Cast Iron, Painted, Kyser & Rex, 6 In. 635.00
Mechanical, Royal Trick Elephant, Tin, Germany, c.1912, 4 1/2 In. 1456.00
Mechanical, Santa Claus At Chimney, Cast Iron, Painted, Shepard Hardware ....2675.00 to 4935.00
Mechanical, Sentry, Soldier Lifts Rifle, Tin 3525.00
Mechanical, Shoot The Chute, Cast Iron, Wood Box, J. & E. Stevens 8225.00
Mechanical, Snake & Frog In Pond, Tin, Painted, Germany 2940.00
Mechanical, Speaking Dog, Cast Iron, J. & E. Stevens, c.1900, 7 1/2 In. 235.00
Mechanical, Speaking Dog, Cast Iron, Painted, John Harper Ltd. 1175.00
Mechanical, Speaking Dog, Cast Iron, Painted, Shepard Hardware ....980.00 to 1410.00
Mechanical, Springing Cat, Lead, Painted, Charles A. Bailey 19975.00
Mechanical, Squirrel, Tree Stump, Cast Iron, Novelty Works 3920.00
Mechanical, Stump Speaker, Black Man, Hat, Cast Iron, Shepard Hardware, 10 In. .....2585.00 to 2750.00

Mechanical, Sunny Boy Money, Aluminum, England, Box, 5 1/2 In. 415.00
Mechanical, Tammany, Brown Pants, Blue Coat, Cast Iron, J. & E. Stevens, 12-23-1873 . . . .335.00 to 440.00
Mechanical, Tammany, Gray Pants, Cast Iron, J. & E. Stevens, 1873 Patent . . . . . . *ILLUS* 2240.00
Mechanical, Teddy & The Bear, Cast Iron, J. & E. Stevens, Box 14560.00
Mechanical, Teddy & The Bear, Cast Iron, J. & E. Stevens, Pat. 1907 . . . . . .1265.00 to 2714.00
Mechanical, Tennis, Billie Jean King & Bobby Riggs, c.1970 . . . . . . 325.00
Mechanical, Thing, Addams Family, Battery Operated, Poynter Products, Box, 1964, 4 3/4 In. 1190.00
Mechanical, Thrifty Tom's Jigger Bank, Tin, Ferdinand Strauss, Pat. May 24, 1910 . . . . . . 2350.00
Mechanical, Trick Dog, 6 Part Base, Clown, Hoop, Barrel, Cast Iron, Hubley, 1880s . . . . . .950.00 to 1725.00
Mechanical, Trick Dog, Solid Base, Clown, Hoop, Barrel, Cast Iron, Hubley, 1920s . . . . . . .200.00 to 558.00
Mechanical, Trick Pony, Cast Iron, Shepard Hardware, 1885 Patent . . . . . . *ILLUS* 2800.00
Mechanical, Try Your Weight, Tin, Painted, Germany 470.00
Mechanical, U.S. Bank Building, Eagle Finial, Pedestal Base, J. & E. Stevens, 9 1/2 In. 1210.00
Mechanical, Uncle Sam, Cast Iron, Shepard Hardware, Pat. 1886, 11 In. . . . . . .1980.00 to 13200.00
Mechanical, Volunteer, Cast Iron, John Harper, England 5175.00
Mechanical, Weeden's Plantation Darky, Dancing Lessons 1 Cent, Tin, 1880s, 5 1/2 In. .1210.00 to 2860.00
Mechanical, William Tell, Aluminum, Painted, Australia 793.00
Mechanical, William Tell, Cast Iron, Painted, J. & E. Stevens, 1890s, 7 x 11 In. . . . . . .460.00 to 990.00
Mechanical, World's Fair, Columbus & Indian, Cast Iron, J. & E. Stevens 1730.00
Mechanical, Zoo, Animals In Windows, Cast Iron, Painted, Kyser & Rex, c.1884 . . . . . . 3640.00
Mechanics & Farmers Savings Bank, Bridgeport, Conn., Celluloid, Round, 2 1/2 In. 39.00
Minuteman, Cast Iron, Painted, Hubley, M 44, 6 In. 185.00
Money Bag, $100,000, Cast Iron, M 1262, 3 5/8 x 4 1/4 In. 295.00
Monument, Bunker Hill Monument, Cast Iron 11750.00
Moravian Melon, Green, Orange, Red, 1825-50, 5 1/2 In. 1400.00
Mosque, Cast Iron, M 1174, 3 In. 28.00
Mulligan Policeman, Cast Iron, Hubley, M 177, 5 3/4 In. 300.00
Multiplying, Cast Iron, Painted, Interior Mirrors, J. & E. Stevens, M 1184, 6 1/2 x 4 In. 1320.00
Mutt & Jeff, Cast Iron, Painted, A.C. Williams, M 157, 4 1/4 x 3 1/2 In. 100.00
North Pole, Ice Cream Freezer, Cast Iron, Grey Iron Casting, M 1371, 4 In. 280.00
Orange Shape, Pottery, Late 1800s, 3 In. 145.00
Owl, On Stump, Cast Iron, Vindex, M 597, 4 1/4 x 2 1/2 In. . . . . . .195.00 to 250.00
Pail, Prosperity, Tin, Pink, Swing Handle, Chein, 1950s, 2 1/4 x 3 In. 225.00
Parlor Stove, Reliable, Cast Iron, Schneider & Trencamp, M 1356, 5 3/4 In. 300.00
Pear, Pottery, Painted Accents, 3 3/4 In. 385.00
Penguin, Glass, 29 Cents, 8 In. 100.00
Pickaninny, Cast Iron, England, M 171, 5 In. 225.00
Pig, Chubby Pig, White Metal, M 641, 4 In. 28.00
Pig, Curled Tail, Hair Strip, Punched Eyes, Stoneware, Green Glaze, 7 1/2 In. 28.00
Pig, Decker's Iowana, Cast Iron, Gold Paint, M 603 . . . . . .56.00 to 65.00
Pig, Glass, Hands Clasped Behind Back, 7 3/4 In. 20.00
Pig, I Made Chicago Famous, Black, Iron, Arcade, c.1900, 4 In. 193.00
Pig, Pottery, Brown Alkaline Glaze, Sponge, c.1890, 5 1/2 In. 550.00
Pig, Razorback, Stoneware, Brown Alkaline Glaze, c.1850, 2 1/2 x 5 In. 37400.00
Pig, Seated, Cast Iron, A.C. Williams, M 582, 3 In. 56.00
Pig, Stoneware, Mottled Brown, Green Sponge, c.1880, 3 1/4 In. 525.00
Pig, Stoneware, Mottled Glaze, Early 20th Century, 5 1/2 In. 59.00
Pig, Wise, Thrifty, Hubley, Cast Iron, M 609, 6 1/2 In. 130.00
Policeman Bust, Gold Finish, Every Copper Helps, Cast Iron, England, M 71, 4 3/4 In. 410.00
Red Goose Shoes, Cast Iron, 3 1/2 In. 605.00
Register, Barrel, Dime Register, Cast Iron, Kyser & Rex, 4 x 2 1/2 In., 10 Cents 118.00
Register, Bean Pot, Cast Iron, 3 1/2 In., Nickel 155.00
Register, Buddy L Savings & Recording, Steel, 6 1/2 In., Quarter 190.00
Register, Clown & Monkey Daily Dime, Tin Lithograph, 2 1/2 In., Dime 125.00
Register, Imperial 3 Coin, Bronze, 3 7/8 x 2 3/8 In., Nickels, Dimes & Quarters 410.00
Register, National Recording, Cast Iron, Copper Flash, 7 1/4 In., Dime 440.00
Register, National Recording, Cast Iron, Gold Finish, 7 1/4 In., Dime 225.00
Register, National, Cash Register, Tin, Eagle, Red, White, Blue, Three Coin, 5 3/4 In. 129.00
Register, Pail, Cast Iron, Kyser & Rex, 3 In., Penny 120.00
Register, Penny Saver, Cash Register, Cast Iron, Penny 140.00
Register, Prudential Registering, 10 Cent Deposit, Cast Iron, Dime 295.00

Register, Prudential Registering, 25 Cent Deposit, Cast Iron, Quarter 265.00
Register, Uncle Sam's, Cash Register Shape, Steel, Durable Toy & Novelty, 4 1/2 In., Nickel 20.00
Register, Uncle Sam's, Cash Register Shape, Steel, Durable Toy & Novelty, 6 1/4 In., 3 Coin 35.00
Reindeer, Large, Cast Iron, Gold Paint, A.C. Williams, M 737, 9 1/2 In. 100.00
Reindeer, Small, Cast Iron, Green Paint, A.C. Williams, M 736, 6 1/4 In. 100.00
Safe, Arabian, Cast Iron, Kyser & Rex, M 882, 4 1/2 x 4 1/4 In. 120.00
Safe, Cast Iron, Painted, J. & E. Stevens, M 869, 3 1/4 In. 85.00
Safe, Globe, Combination, Red & White, Cast Iron, U.S., M 808, 5 1/4 x 4 In. 999.00
Safe, Royal Safe Deposit, Cast Iron, Black Paint, 6 x 5 1/4 In. 120.00
Safe, Safe Deposit, Black Paint, Henry C. Hart, Detroit, 1885, 5 In. 155.00
Safe, Security Safe Deposit, Cast Iron, Kyser & Rex, M 891, 4 In. .... 66.00 to 88.00
Safety Locomotive, Cast Iron, Cow Catcher, Light, Cast Iron, M 1476, 3 1/4 x 1 1/2 x 5 3/4 In. 280.00
Sailor, Cast Iron, Hubley, M 28, 5 1/2 In. 336.00
Santa, Save A Smile, Cast Iron, M 60, Wall Mount, 7 1/4 In. 448.00
Santa With Tree, Cast Iron, Hubley, M 61, 6 In. 2520.00
Savings, Black Jocomo, Painted, Washington Slave Boy Hitching Post, 1888, 7 In. 65.00
Service Station, Esso, Imperial, Plastic, 2 x 6 x 3 In. 35.00
Shmoo, Blue, Plastic 50.00
Shriner's Hat, Syria Potentate, Steel, Red, Black Tassel, M 1395, 4 In. 40.00
Silo, Marietta Silo Saves You Money, Cast Iron, M 1246, 5 1/2 In. 385.00
Snow Crest Bottle, Bear Shape, Glass, Tin Lid, Salem, Mass. 30.00
Snowman, Copeland, Aluminum, White, Black, Copeland Refrigerators, M 96 .... 235.00
Soccer, Tin, Round, Spiral Logo, Gene Bosch Design, Chein, 1970s 225.00
Songbird, On Stump, Cast Iron, M 664, 5 In. 336.00
Space Heater, Flowers, Cast Iron, England, M 1094, 6 1/2 x 3 7/8 In. 175.00
Statue Of Liberty, Cast Iron, A.C. Williams, M 1164, 6 In. 270.00
Statue Of Liberty, Cast Iron, Painted, Kenton, M 1165, 6 3/8 In. 365.00
Tally-Ho, Cast Iron, M 535, 4 1/2 In. 110.00
Three Wise Monkeys, Cast Iron, A.C. Williams, M 743, 3 1/4 x 3 1/2 In. 235.00
Toby, Delft, Multicolored, 8 In. 80.00
Tomato, Pottery, 4 3/4 In. 415.00
Turkey, Cast Iron, A.C. Williams, M 587, 3 1/2 In. 165.00
Two Faced Black Boy, A.C. Williams, 1901, M 83, 4 1/8 x 3 1/8 In. 450.00
U.S. Mail Box, Cast Iron, Hanging, A.C. Williams, M 856, 5 In. 30.00
Universal Stoves Ranges & Furnaces, Globe, Tin, Lithograph, Box, 4 x 3 1/4 x 2 In. 495.00
Urn Shape, Birth, Stoneware, White Glaze, Tan, Rope Handles, Cone Finial, 5 5/8 In. 360.00
Vault, Fidelity Trust, Cast Iron, J. Barton Smith, M 903, 6 1/2 In. 355.00
Watch Me Grow Tall, Man With Hat, Tin, 9 In. Tall When Full 65.00
Whizzo The Clown, Slush Metal, Banthrico, R 59, 6 1/2 In. 56.00

BANKO is a group of rustic Japanese wares made in the nineteenth and twentieth centuries. Some pieces are made of mosaics of colored clay; some are fanciful teapots. Redware and other materials were also used.

Humidor, Elephant In Barrel, Green, Red Staves, Elephant Head Cover, 8 x 5 1/2 In. 375.00
Jar, Cover, Butterflies, Flowers, Textured Scallops, Beaded Cover, Round, 2 1/2 x 4 In. 350.00
Nodder, Monkey, Wearing Vest, Holding Pipe & Tobacco Pouch, 6 x 5 In. 695.00
Plate, White Bamboo, Volcanic Gray Ground, Oval, 7 1/2 In. 325.00
Sake Bottle, 3 Friends, Prunus, Pine, Bamboo, 1700s, 10 In. 325.00
Teapot, Boy Riding Elephant, Flowered Blanket, Bamboo Handle, 1900s, 7 x 4 1/2 In. 375.00
Teapot, Cranes, Flowers, Bird Finial, Twisted Branch Handle, 5 x 7 1/2 In. 710.00
Teapot, Iris, Butterflies, Gray Ground, Bamboo Handle, 1967, 6 x 5 In. 120.00
Teapot, Raised Flowers, Enameled Stems & Leaves, Cane Handle, Signed, 4 3/4 x 5 3/4 In. 195.00
Teapot, Shell, Crusted Green & White Sea Foam, Wire Wrapped Vine Handle, 1920s, 6 In. 475.00
Teapot, Tomato, 3 Monkeys, Leaf Cover, 4 x 6 1/2 In. 499.00
Vase, Landscape With Cranes, 6-Sided, 6 1/2 In. 220.00

BARBED WIRE was first patented in 1867. Collectors want eighteen-inch samples.

7 Samples, Shadowbox Frame, 28 x 36 In. 30.00
10 Samples, On Wood, Rope Frame, 1875-98 Wire, 11 1/2 x 12 In. 20.50

21 Samples, Mounted On Texas Shape Plaque, 1868-85 Wire, 16 x 16 In. 46.00
Brinkerhoff Riveted Splicer, Shadowbox Frame, 8 x 24 In. 13.00

BARBER collectibles range from the popular red and white striped pole that used to be found in front of every shop to the small scissors and tools of the trade. Barber chairs are wanted, especially the older models with elaborate iron trim.

Chair, Imitation Leather, Iron, Child's, 24 In. 11.00
Chair, Kochs, Oak, c.1910-20 .... 4675.00
Chair, Koken, Enameled, Hydraulic Base, c.1925, 49 x 25 x 34 In. 145.00
Chair, Koken, Shaving Straps, Adult, 51 In. 1568.00
Chair, Walnut, Iron, Serpentine Back, Scrolled Legs, Archer Manufacturing Co., 40 x 21 In. 500.00
Hair Clippers, Shapleigh Hardware Co., No. 14T, Box, 1930s, 3 1/4 x 5 1/4 In. 55.00
Lamp, Barber Pole Globe, Electric, Porcelain Top, Bottom, 34 In. 505.00
Pole, Black & White, Acorn Finials, Original Paint, Iron Mounting, 19th Century, 34 In. 825.00
Pole, Carved, Painted, Green, Blue, Red, Silver, 40 In. 345.00
Pole, Cyclo, Cast Iron, Globe Topper, 80 In. 3190.00
Pole, Double, Metal, Lighted, 86 In. 1680.00
Pole, Glass, Wall, Wood Mounted, Koken, 35 In. 896.00
Pole, Louvered Finial, Baluster Turned Column, Red, White Candy Stripe, 75 In. 5750.00
Pole, Painted, Red, White, Blue, Gold, Acorn Finial, Wood, 36 In. 720.00
Pole, Pine, Red, White, Blue, Acorn Finial, Vase Turning, Stepped Base, 77 In. 3105.00
Pole, Tapered, 2-Sided, Cut From 1-In. Stock, Cape Cod, c.1860, 75 x 8 In. 4850.00
Pole, Turned, Painted, Yellow, Red, White, Blue, Gesso Undercoat, 31 x 8 In. 3335.00
Shaving Paper Vase, Cobalt Blue, Gold Flowers, Polished Rim, 7 3/8 In. 950.00
Sign, Barber Shop, Porcelain, Enamel Flange, 1 1/2 x 12 x 24 In. .... 140.00 to 225.00

BAROMETERS are used to forecast the weather. Antique barometers with elaborate wooden cases and brass trim are the most desirable. Mercury column barometers are also popular with collectors. It is difficult to find someone to repair a broken one, so be sure your barometer is in working condition.

A. Carrier, Belle Epoque, Greek Maiden, Clock, Cast Iron, Late 1800s, 37 x 21 x 10 In. 7050.00
Advertising, Dunlop, Der Erfinder Des Pneumatik, Reverse On Glass, 1913, 18 1/4 x 12 In. 569.00
Aneroid, Chelsea Timepiece, Thermometer, Mahogany, Edwardian, Early 1900s, 31 In. 150.00
Banjo, Lione & Co., 12-In. Silvered Dial, 46 In. 2585.00
Banjo, Lione & Tomali, Mahogany, String Inlay, Georgian, England, 41 x 21 In. 980.00
Banjo, Mahogany, Flower & String Inlay, Brass Face, Marked, Rochester, 38 1/2 In. 880.00
Banjo, Maple Case, Humidity Meter, Thermometer, Level, 43 In. 1035.00
Banjo, Thorpe Turnbridge & Wells, Mahogany Case, Thermometer, England, 36 In. 460.00
Barograph, Julien P. Friez, No. 30, Clockwork Drum, Mahogany Case, Baltimore, 11 In. 410.00
Canti Warranted, Mahogany, Circular Brass Plaque, England, 1800s, 39 1/4 In. 1680.00
D. Davis Optician, Mahogany, String Inlay, 2 Dials, Convex Mirror, Glasgow, 44 In. 1800.00
George III Style, Siglezze, Mahogany, Shell & Flower Inlay, London, 38 In. 1200.00
IM Hof, Weather Station, 4-Dial, Hygrometer, Gold Plated Case, c.1960, 4 3/4 In. 195.00
James W. Queen & Co., Watch Form, Brass Case, 3 In. 235.00
John M. Merrick & Co., Rosewood, Worcester, Mass., c.1857, 39 In. 825.00
Mahogany Inlay, Shaped Case, Inlaid Floral Rosettes, Conch Shells, 39 In. 1530.00
Marine, R.N. Disterra, Fortin Type, Brass, Bow Front, Gimbal Mount, 37 In. 295.00
Nautical, Bell, Ship's, Cast Bronze, U.S. Navy, Stamped, 20th Century, 9 In. 120.00
Nautical, Marine, Plath Of Hamburg, 43 x 4 1/2 x 5 1/2 In. 1035.00
R.N. Disterra, Marine, Brass, 37 In. 295.00
Ship's, H.A. Clum, Rochester, N.Y., 8-In. Silvered Dial, 44 In. 2938.00
Stick, Mahogany, Brass Screw Construction, Half Glass Tube, Paper Scale, 42 In. 460.00
Stick, Rosewood, Gardner & Co., Beveled Glass, Thermometer, Glasgow, c.1840, 36 In. 1200.00
Stick, Thermometer, H. Hughes & Sons, Brass Case, Iron Gimbal Bracket, 37 In. 200.00
Stick, Thermometer, J.G. West & Co., Oak, London, c.1875, 39 In. 840.00
Stick, Thermometer, P. Cox, Bone Register, Oak Trunk, Scroll Pediment, London, 40 In. 470.00
Thermometer, Castle, Fox In Clothes, Greeting Ducks, Wood, Swiss, c.1880, 17 x 13 In. 1085.00
Thermometer, IM Hof, 8-Day Clock, Time, Alarm, Gold Plated Case, c.1960, 4 In. 39.00
Thermometer, J. Tadeo, New York, Federal, Mahogany, Boxwood Inlay, 38 x 10 In. 1175.00

Thermometer, Laboratory, Henry J. Green, Fortin-Type, Type 4, Brass Tube, N.Y., 44 In. 470.00
Thermometer, Louis XVI Style, Lyre Form Crest, Giltwood, 19th Century, 37 x 19 3/4 In. 1000.00
Thermometer, Louis XVI Style, Ormolu, Diana, Ribbon, Hunt, France, 1900s, 19 In. 2115.00
Thermometer, Walnut, Brass, Glass, Leaves, Victorian, 19 x 9 x 1 3/4 In. 140.00
W. Walz, Holosteric, Bone Thermometer, 6 In. 155.00
Watch Form, James W. Queen, Lacquered Brass Case, Silvered Scale, Pocket, 2 In. 235.00
Wheel, Georgian Style, Mahogany, Swan's Neck Cresting, Convex Mirror, 38 In. 705.00
Wheel, J.G. West & Co., Oak, Renaissance Revival, England, Late 1800s, 36 1/2 In. 175.00
Wheel, Thermometer, George III Style, Painted, Swan's Neck, c.1875, 37 1/2 In. 410.00
Wheel, Thermometer, Hygrometer, Georgian Style, Mahogany, Swan's Neck, c.1900, 40 In. 294.00
Wheel, Thermometer, Mahogany, Swan's Neck Crest Over Hygrometer, 1800s, 38 In. 705.00
Wheel, Victorian, Rosewood, Onion Top, Mirror Roundel, Late 1800s, 40 1/4 In. 323.00

BASEBALL collectibles are in the Sports category, except for baseball cards, which are listed under Baseball in the Card category.

BASKETS of all types are popular with collectors. American Indian, Japanese, African, Shaker, and many other kinds of baskets can be found. Of course, baskets are still being made, so the collector must learn to tell the age and style of the basket to determine the value.

2 Red Rows, Green Row, Wrapped Handle, Lancaster County, 1800s, 15 1/2 x 14 x 13 1/2 In. 140.00
Bobbin, 3 Tiers, Splint, Herringbone Weave, Green, Red Bands, 13 x 9 1/2 x 41 1/2 In. 978.00
Buttocks, 52 Staves, Round Top, Arched Handle, 13 1/2 x 15 In. 316.00
Buttocks, Bentwood Handle, Patina, 8 x 5 1/4 In. 175.00
Buttocks, Splint, Oak, Bentwood Handle, 3 x 3 1/4 In. 110.00
Buttocks, Splint, Oak, Round, Red, Bentwood Handle, 10 x 11 In. 190.00
Buttocks, Splint, Round, Red Dyed Weave, Bentwood Handle, 10 x 11 In. 190.00
Buttocks, Splint, Walnut Finish, 60 Ribs, Abbeyville, S.C., 18 1/2 x 17 In. 405.00
Cheese, Splint, Oak, Open Weave Handle, Reinforced Rim, Oval, 5 1/2 x 12 x 9 In. 155.00
Cheese, Splint, Round, Hexagonal Sided Basket, Openwork, 7 1/2 x 20 1/2 In. 235.00
Cheese, Splint, Round, Hexagonal Weave, 5 3/4 x 22 1/2 In. 198.00
Cheese, Splint, Round, New York, c.1875, 14 x 4 1/2 In. 1950.00
Chest, Coiled, Rye Straw, Cover, Straight Sides, 9 1/2 x 17 x 11 1/2 In. 85.00
Coiled, Rye Straw, Footed, Handles, Tapered Sides, 5 1/4 x 14 x 8 In. 155.00
Coiled, Rye Straw, Openwork Rim, Footed Base, 4 3/4 x 10 1/2 In. 154.00
Cover, Painted, Green, Blue, Salmon, Yellow, 18 x 12 In. 2070.00
Drying, Coiled, Rye Straw, Round, 4 x 22 1/2 In. 145.00
Egg, Split, Oak, Pointed Shoulder, 15 1/2 x 17 x 12 In. 403.00
Field, Round, Rye Straw, Tapered Sides, Woven Side Handles, 7 1/2 x 5 In. ....415.00 to 3410.00
Fruit, Coiled, Tapered Sides, Woven Handles, 5 x 13 1/2 x 10 1/4 In. 195.00
Gathering, Oyster, Tapered Sides, Raised Bottom, Bentwood Handles, 12 x 14 12 In. 240.00
Ikebana, Splint, Bamboo, Egg Shape, Entwined Handle, Japan, Early 1900s, 14 1/2 In. 460.00
Ikebana, Splint, Bamboo, Egg Shape, Entwined Handle, Japan, Early 1900s, 18 1/2 In. 316.00
Ikebana, Splint, Bamboo, Melon Shape, Ring Handles, Japan, Early 1900s, 9 In. 120.00
Maple, Ash, Round, Shaped Bentwood Hinged Handle, Marked, APR 1880, 13 1/2 x 12 In. 345.00
Market, Splint, Rectangle, Bentwood Handle, Pine Base, Tapered Sides, 12 x 16 x 12 In. 165.00
Nantucket, Lightship, Free Form, Flared Sides, Carved Wooden Ears, 1860-80 .... 8050.00
Nantucket, Purse, Carved Seagull On Lid, Carved Pin Closure, 7 x 8 1/2 In. 200.00
Nantucket, Purse, Hinged Handle, Ivory Knobs, Wood Base, Whale, 1900s, 6 3/4 x 10 1/2 In. 200.00
Nantucket, Purse, Oval, Lid, Jose Formosa Reyes, 1960s, 11 x 9 1/2 x 7 In. 3840.00
Nantucket, Round, Splint, Cane, Incised Star, Bentwood Handle, 1987, 10 1/2 x 10 1/2 In. 165.00
Nantucket, Turned Wooden Base, Swing Handle, 13 x 6 In. 345.00
Nantucket, Turned Wooden Bottom, 12 x 14 In. 750.00
Nantucket, Wood Base, Wood Swing Handle, 4 1/2 x 9 1/2 In. 635.00
Nantucket Style, Round, Splint, Cane, Bentwood Handle, P. O'Connell, 1987, 10 1/2 In. 165.00
Nantucket Style, Splint Swing Handle, 1800s, 5 x 8 In. 185.00
Orchard, 2 Handles, Green Paint, 21 In. 825.00
Oval, Corncobs, Wire Frame, c.1925, 9 x 6 1/2 x 8 1/2 In. 300.00
Picket Fence, Old Blue Paint, Twisted Wire, Metal Band, 24 x 7 In. 1095.00
Picnic, Hawkeye Refrigerator, Hickory, Bamboo, 15 x 21 In. 58.00
Potato Stamp Decoration, Handle, Miniature 375.00
Rectangle, Coiled, Rye, Tapered Sides, Footed, 2 Handles, 5 1/4 x 14 x 8 In. 155.00

Rye, Cover, Round, Bulbous, 11 3/4 x 15 In. 415.00
Splint, 2 Handles, 2 Colors, Double Wrapped Top, 9 x 14 In. 230.00
Splint, 2 Handles, Stamp Decoration, 12 1/2 x 5 In. 50.00
Splint, 2 Swing Handles, 21 x 26 x 8 In. 316.00
Splint, Ash, Rectangle, Curled Fancy Weave, Dyed Green, 4 x 12 x 10 In. 28.00
Splint, Ash, Rectangle, Dyed Banding, Bentwood Handles, 6 1/2 x 12 1/2 x 8 1/2 In. 275.00
Splint, Ash, Rectangle, Red, Yellow Dyed, 6 1/4 x 19 x 15 In. 105.00
Splint, Ash, Rectangle, Straight Sides, Carved Bentwood Handles, 6 1/2 x 12 1/2 x 8 1/2 In. 275.00
Splint, Ash, Round, Red, Green Bentwood, Twig Ribs, God's Eye Handle, 8 1/2 x 10 In. 190.00
Splint, Ash, Round, Rim, Hexagonal Weave, Bentwood Handle, 14 3/4 x 13 1/4 In. 99.00
Splint, Ash, Round, Tapered Sides, Green Dyed Bands, Bentwood Handles, 7 x 14 1/2 In. 105.00
Splint, Band, Red Paint, Handle, 9 1/2 In. 66.00
Splint, Cheese, Oval, Open Weave Handle, 5 1/2 x 12 x 9 In. 154.00
Splint, Cover, Patina, 19th Century, 17 1/2 In. 80.00
Splint, Goose Feather, Blue Paint, New England, c.1875, 27 x 16 In. 1150.00
Splint, Half Circle, Rib, God's Eye Bentwood Handle, 14 1/2 x 15 1/2 x 9 In. 385.00
Splint, Handles, Double Wrapped Top, 11 x 15 In. 173.00
Splint, Oak, Cover, Rectangle, 12 x 27 x 16 1/2 In. 130.00
Splint, Oak, Green Ribs, Red Weave, Bentwood Handle, Round, 8 1/2 x 10 In. 85.00
Splint, Oak, Handle, Virginia, Early 1900s, 2 1/4 x 2 1/4 In. 990.00
Splint, Oak, Handle, Virginia, Early 1900s, 3 3/8 x 3 1/2 In. 485.00
Splint, Oak, Oval, Straight Sides, Reinforced Rim, 5 3/4 x 14 1/2 x 11 1/2 In. 30.00
Splint, Oak, Rectangle, Straight Sides, Bentwood Handle, Shellac, 8 1/4 x 14 x 10 In. 165.00
Splint, Oak, Round, Ribs, Dyed Green, Red Weave, Carved Bentwood Handle, 8 1/2 x 10 In. 85.00
Splint, Oak, Square, Reinforced Rim & Corners, Tapered Sides, Pine Base, 10 3/4 x 12 1/2 In. 30.00
Splint, Oak, Straight Sides, Bentwood Handle, Shellac, 8 1/4 x 14 x 10 In. 165.00
Splint, Oak, Tapered, Bentwood Handle, Round, 11 1/2 x 12 1/2 In. 95.00
Splint, Oval, Rib, Cane, God's Eye Weave, Bentwood Handle, Wood Hinges, 7 1/4 x 11 1/2 In. 94.00
Splint, Potato Stamp Design, 2 Bentwood Handles, 1800s, 5 1/2 x 21 x 12 In. 518.00
Splint, Round, 2 Handles, Wrapped Top, 13 x 4 In. 173.00
Splint, Round, Tapered Rib, Oak, Bentwood Handle, 11 1/2 x 12 1/2 In. 94.00
Splint, White Oak, Blue Paint, Page Co., Va., Early 20th Century, 9 3/8 In. 2970.00
Splint, Woven, Bentwood Handle, 17 1/2 x 8 In. 175.00
Splint, Woven, Painted Salmon, Round, Carved Handles, Blue Bands, 1800s, 7 x 17 In. 2705.00
Splint, Woven, Round, Green Paint, Tapered Sides, Swing Handle, 8 x 12 In. 705.00
Splint Rib, Half Circle, God's Eye Bentwood Handle, 14 1/2 x 15 1/2 x 9 In. 385.00
Swing Handle, Signed Lord, Double Wrapped Top, 8 In. 288.00
Table, Rye Straw, Openwork Bands, Tapered Sides, 4 1/4 x 9 1/2 In. 255.00

BATCHELDER products are made from California clay. Ernest Batchelder established a tile studio in Pasadena, California, in 1909 and expanded until 1916. Then he built a larger factory with a new partner. The Batchelder-Wilson Company made all types of architectural tiles, garden pots, and bookends. The plant closed in 1932. In 1936 Batchelder opened Batchelder Ceramics, also in Pasadena, and made bowls, vases, and earthenware pots. He retired in 1951 and died in 1957. Pieces are marked *Batchelder Pasadena* or *Batchelder Los Angeles*.

BATCHELDER
LOS ANGELES

Fountain, 2 Sections, Children Playing Hand Flutes, Rabbits, Trees, 31 x 19 x 12 In. 7638.00
Tile, Birds In Stylized Leaves, Deeply Carved, 6 In. 510.00
Tile, Pinecones, Gray, Brown, Impressed Mark, 6 In. 720.00
Tile, Stylized Rose, Leaves, Blue Engobe, 8 3/4 In. 410.00
Vase, Blossoms, Green Charcoal Glaze Over Terra-Cotta, Semimatte, 14 x 7 In. 805.00

BATMAN and Robin are characters from a comic strip by Bob Kane that started in 1939. In 1966, the characters became part of a popular television series. There have been radio and movie serials that featured the pair. The first full-length movie was made in 1989.

Bank, Ceramic, Hands On Hips, Japan, 1966, 7 In. 90.00
Batboat, No. 1003, Corgi Jr., On Card, 1967, 4 x 6 1/2 In. 185.00
Batcave, Command Center, Box, Kenner, 1993, 12 1/2 x 23 In. 63.00

Batmobile, Batman Forever, Lights Up, Fires Missiles, Battery Operated, Kenner, 1995, 8 x 17 In. . . 21.00
Batmobile, Die Cast, Corgi, Box, No. 267, 1974 . . . . 134.00
Batmobile, Lighted Engine, Tin, Battery Operated, ASC, Box, 11 In. 1320.00
Batmobile, Plastic, Simms, Box, 1966, 8 1/2 In. 20.00
Batmobile, Wood, No Wheels, Marx, 25 In. 3920.00
Bottle, Milk, Catwoman, Feisty Feline, Multicolored ACL, Square, Warner Bros., Qt. 28.00
Button, Bat Kids Fan Club, Batman, White, Purple, Black, 1960s, 2 1/2 In. 21.00
Button, Ron Riley's Batman Club, White, Black, Red, 1966, 2 1/4 In. 7.00
Figure, Batman, Die Cast Metal, Mego, Box, 1977, 5 1/2 In. 52.00
Lunch Box, Batman & Robin, Metal, Purple Border, Bottle, Aladdin, 1966 . . . . 76.00 to 85.00
PEZ Dispenser, Cape, Blue, No Feet, Austria 82.00
PEZ Dispenser, Penguin, Purple Stem, 1978 . . . . 84.00
Puppet, Plastic Base, Kohner, 1969, 4 x 1 3/4 In. 618.00
Record, Catwoman's Revenge, Power Records, Size 45 But Plays 33 1/3, Sealed, 1975 . . . . 57.00
Robot, Tin, Battery Operated, Fairylite, Japan, 12 In. 1155.00
Wristwatch, Robin, Silver Luster Dial, Black Leather Strap, Timex, 1978, 1-In. Dial 186.00

BAUER pottery is a California-made ware. J.A. Bauer bought Paducah Pottery in Paducah, Kentucky, in 1885. He moved the pottery to Los Angeles, California, in 1909. The company made art pottery after 1912 and dinnerwares marked *Bauer* after 1929. The factory went out of business in 1962.

Bowl, Jade, Ruffled, Matt Carlton, 3 3/4 x 7 1/4 In. 225.00
Bowl, Textured Brown Exterior, Glossy Green Interior, Tracy Irwin, 16 1/2 In. 125.00
Cal Art Line, Planter, Swan, Satin Pink, 11 1/2 In. 145.00
Carafe, Green, Wood Handle, 9 1/4 In. 95.00
Compote, Pumpkin, Satin Beige, Tracy Irwin, 5 1/2 x 7 7/8 In. 90.00
Flower Bowl, Glossy Green On Buff Clay, 2 3/4 x 6 7/8 In. 175.00
Flower Bowl, Matte Green On Buff Clay, 7 3/4 In. 165.00
Flowerpot, 16 Swirl, Olive Green, 10 7/8 x 12 3/4 In. 120.00
Flowerpot, Saucer, Spanish, Orange, 9 1/2 x 11 5/8 In. 160.00
Flowerpot, Stand, Biltmore, Tan Speckle, 11 x 20 In. 150.00
Jardiniere, Orange, 5 1/2 x 6 7/8 In. 160.00
Mixing Bowl, No. 12, Blue Speckle, 9 1/2 In. 95.00
Monterey, Fruit Bowl, Ring, 3-Footed, 10 1/4 In. 185.00
Pitcher, Whiteware, Wheel Thrown, Matt Carlton, 5 1/4 In. 495.00
Planter, Swan, Satin Ivory, 10 In. 85.00
Ring, Bowl, Orange, 9 3/4 In. 185.00
Ring, Carafe, Yellow, Stopper, 10 In. 150.00
Ring, Chop Plate, Yellow, 12 1/2 In. 125.00
Ring, Vase, Cylindrical, Red Brown, 6 In. 110.00
Ring, Vase, Jade Green, Matt Carlton, 5 In. 650.00
Strawberry Jar, Orange, 4 1/4 In. 395.00
Vase, Black, Wheel Thrown, Fred Johnson, 5 1/2 In. 295.00
Vase, Carnation, Cobalt Blue, Matt Carlton, 6 1/2 In. 325.00
Vase, Corsage, Gray, Lava Glaze, Russel Wright, 5 x 4 In. 315.00
Vase, Dark Green Glaze, Matt Carlton, 6 In. 325.00
Vase, Fan Shape, Jade Green, Matt Carlton, 5 7/8 In. 250.00
Vase, Light Blue, Matt Carlton, 5 3/4 In. 450.00
Vase, Matte Green, Gloss White Interior, Wheel Thrown, Matt Carlton, 7 1/4 In. 325.00
Vase, Pink, Tulip Form, Handles, Marked, 10 In. 60.00
Vase, Swirls, Gloss Green, Matt Carlton, 8 1/2 In. 350.00

BAVARIA is a region in Europe where many types of porcelain were made. In the nineteenth century, the mark often included the word *Bavaria*. After 1871, the words *Bavaria, Germany*, were used. Listed here are pieces that include the name *Bavaria* in some form, but major porcelain makers, such as Rosenthal, are listed in their own categories.

Plate, Portrait, Cupid, Lovers, Transfer, Mitterteich, Early 1900s, 10 3/4 In. 200.00
Plate, Portrait, King Ludwig II, Richmond Bavaria, Early 1900s, 12 In. 104.00

BEADED BAGS are included in the Purse category.

BEATLES collectors search for any items picturing the four members of the famous music group or any of their recordings. Because these items are so new, the condition is very important and top prices are paid only for items in mint condition. The Beatles first appeared on American network television in 1964. The group disbanded in 1971. Ringo Starr and Paul McCartney are still performing. John Lennon died in 1980. George Harrison died in 2001.

Bank, Yellow Submarine, Figural, John, Paul, George, Ringo, Composition, 1968, 7 In., 4 Piece ... 1585.00
Bobbin' Head Car Mascot Set, Box, 1964, 4 Piece ... 1086.00
Button, Flasher, I Love Paul, 2 1/2 In. ... 66.00
Button, I Love The Beatles, White, Blue, Red, 1964, 3 1/2 In. ... 115.00
Button, I Still Love The Beatles, Red, White, Blue, 1964, 3 1/2 In. ... 22.00
Button, I've Got My Beatles Movie Tickets, Have You?, Celluloid, 3 In. ... 15.00
Button Set, Flicker, I Love, Paul, John, Ringo, George, 1960s, 2 1/2 In., 5 Piece ... 149.00
Charm, John, Paul, George, Ringo, Yellow, Red, Blue, Orange, Plastic, 1960s, 1 1/4 In., 4 Piece ... 49.00
Display, Abbey Road, Cardboard, Die Cut, Stand-Up, Frame, 1969, 32 x 25 In. ... 522.00
Doll Set, Inflatable, 1966, 4 Piece ... 250.00
Harmonica, Hohner, Box, On Card, c.1965 ... 512.00
Lunch Box, Yellow Submarine, 4 Beatles In Submarine, Metal, Thermos, 1968 ... 280.00
Model Set, Revell, Box, 1964, 4 Piece ... 2243.00
Mug, Group Photograph, Ceramic, NEMS, c.1964, 4 5/8 In. ... 370.00
Nodder, Bobb'n Head Beatles, Instructions, Car Mascots, Box, 1964, 4 Piece ... 1115.00 to 1634.00
Paper Sculpture Kit, Yellow Submarine, Beatles, Craft Master, 1968, 18 x 15 In. ... 315.00
Pin, Tie Tack, Ringo, Press-Initial Corp., Card, 1964, 3/4 In. ... 27.00
Poster, Arrivano I Beatles, Technicolor Techniscope, Spain, 1964, 54 x 39 In. ... 353.00
Poster, Beatles Come To Town, 1963, 41 x 27 In. ... 900.00
Poster, Beatles Come To Town, 1964, 42 x 28 In. ... 427.00
Poster, Beatles, Blue Brick Wall, London Palladium, 1964, 31 1/4 x 23 3/4 In. ... 1350.00
Poster, Hard Day's Night, Linen, United Artists, 1964, 81 x 41 In. ... 708.00 to 1485.00
Poster, Rubber Soul, 12 Brand New Songs, 1965, 34 x 22 1/4 In. ... 1044.00
Poster, Sensational Inside Story, Exclusive, Sunday People, c.1964, 29 x 19 3/8 In. ... 569.00
Print, London Palladium, Royal Command Performance, 1963, Louis F. Dow, Frame, 1964 ... 82.00
Ticket Stub, Shea Stadium, Blue, August 23, 1966, 1 1/2 x 3 1/2 In. ... 154.00
Tote Bag, Luggage Tag, Beatles To U.S.A., TWA, Red, August, 1965 ... 2581.00
Towel, Beach, Yeah! Yeah! Yeah!, Beatles, In Swimsuits, 33 1/2 x 59 In. ... 336.00
Toy, Paint By Numbers, Paint Your Own Beatle Kit, Artistic Creations, 1960s ... 485.00
Tray, Portraits, Signatures, 4-Sided, Steel, Stamped, MTM, England, 1960s, 13 In. ... 116.00
Tumbler, Portraits, Facsimile Signatures, Gold Rim, c.1964, 5 1/2 In. ... 140.00

BEEHIVE, Austria, or Beehive, Vienna, are terms used in English-speaking countries to refer to the many types of decorated porcelain bearing a mark that looks like a beehive. The mark is actually a shield, viewed upside down. It was first used in 1744 by the Royal Porcelain Manufactory of Vienna. The firm made porcelains, called *Royal Vienna* by collectors, until it closed in 1864. Many other German, Austrian, and Japanese factories have reproduced Royal Vienna wares, complete with the original shield or *beehive* mark. This listing includes the expensive, original Royal Vienna porcelains and many other types of beehive porcelain. The Royal Vienna pieces include that name in the description.

Bowl, Classical Women, After Angelica Kaufmann, Pink, Black Border, 9 In. ... 294.00
Bowl, Cover, Lady Portrait, Magenta, Gilt Highlights, Bird Handles, Royal Vienna, Early 1900s, 6 In. 525.00
Dish, 2 Women, Mountains, Blue Border, Oval, Royal Vienna, 5 x 6 In. ... 322.00
Dish, Girl, Kneeling, 2 Baskets, Late 1800s, 6 1/2 x 11 1/4 In. ... 120.00
Ewer, Cobalt Blue, Scene, Fairy On Rock Ledge, Gold Stencil, Royal Vienna, 11 In. ... 2500.00
Ewer, Handles, Green Ground, Pink Rose, Gold Stencil, Royal Vienna, 4 1/2 In. ... 450.00
Jar, Cover, Women In Large Hats, Cobalt Blue, Gold Stenciling, 7 1/2 In., Pair ... 250.00
Plate, Aeneas, Royal Vienna, Early 20th Century, 9 1/2 In. ... 235.00
Plate, Odysseus & Telemachus, Gilt, Multicolored, K. Burklen, c.1915, 11 In. ... 70.00

Plate, Portrait, Bust Of Woman In Costume, Cobalt Blue Rim, Gilt, 9 1/2 In., Pair 646.00
Tea Caddy, Augustus & Cleopatra, Abra, 2-Sided, Royal Vienna, c.1900, 5 1/2 In. 475.00
Urn, Cover, Mythological, Magenta, Teal, Gilt, Pedestal, Royal Vienna, 1900s, 36 1/2 In. 1200.00
Urn, Cover, Romeo & Juliet Scene, Cobalt Blue, Gilt, Royal Vienna, c.1900, 17 1/2 In. 650.00
Urn, Lady Playing Harp, Gilt Handles, Luster, Royal Vienna, Early 20th Century, 12 In. 850.00
Urn, Mythological Scene, Cobalt Blue, Gilt, Plinth Base, Royal Vienna, 7 1/2 In., Pair 425.00
Urn, Woman, Doves, Cherub, Handles, Royal Vienna, 7 1/16 In. 865.00
Vase, 2 Handles, Cobalt Blue, Lebrum II Portrait, Gold Highlights, Royal Vienna, 9 In. 650.00
Vase, Classical Scene, People In Courtyard, Landscape, 3-Footed, Royal Vienna, 1900s, 6 3/4 In. . 275.00
Vase, Cover, Achilles, Diana, Hector, Thetis, Stand, Handles, Shouldered, Oval, 45 In., Pair 43475.00
Vase, Cover, Gamboling Putti, Gilt, Claret Ground, 2 Handles, c.1815, 8 3/4 In. 94.00
Vase, Cover, Porcelain, Cobalt Blue, Stand, Titled Scene, Triumph Of Love, Vienna, 14 In. 1410.00
Vase, Portrait, Flowers, Leaves, Metallic Ground, Gilt, c.1900, 15 x 18 In. 1116.00
Vase, Queen Louise Of Prussia, Gilt Handles, Royal Vienna, c.1900, 9 3/4 In. 1200.00
Vase, Woman & Fairies In Flower Field, Cobalt Blue, 12 1/2 In. 475.00
Vase, Woman, Flowers, Scrolling, Gray Green Ground, Royal Vienna, 5 In. 575.00
Wall Pocket, Blue Transfer, Flowers, Vines, Manila, 4 3/4 x 4 1/2 x 2 In. 54.00

BEER BOTTLES are listed in the Bottle category under Beer.

BEER CANS are a twentieth-century idea. Beer was sold in kegs or returnable bottles until 1934. The first patent for a can was issued to the American Can Company in September of that year; and Gotfried Kruger Brewing Company, Newark, New Jersey, was the first to use the can. The cone-top can was first made in 1935, the aluminum pop-top in 1962. Collectors should look for cans in good condition, with no dents or rust. Serious collectors prefer cans that have been opened from the bottom.

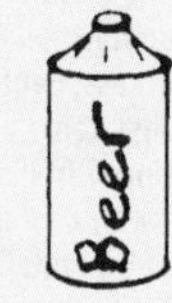

ABC Extra Pale Dry, Flat Top, Red, White, Blue, 1958, 12 Oz. 85.00
Aero Club Pale Select, Cone Top, High Profile, 1953, 12 Oz. 315.00
Alpine Pilsner, Fox Deluxe Brewing, Mich., Bottom Opened, Flat Top, 1955, 12 Oz. 320.00
Badger, Wisconsin Badgers Football Schedule, Tab Top, Bottom Opened, 1983, 12 Oz. 4.00
Ballantine XXX Ale, Flat Top, Bottom Opened, 1957, 12 Oz. ....20.00 to 25.00
Barbarossa, Red Top Brewing Co., High Profile, Cone Top, 1952, 12 Oz. 625.00
Billy, Tab Top, Top Opened, 1978, 12 Oz. 7.00
Blatz, Blue Christmas, Flat Top, Top Opened, 1957, 12 Oz. 180.00
Blatz, Flat Top, Bottom Opened, 1957, 12 Oz. 14.00
Blatz Old Heidelberg, High Profile, Cone Top, Pre 1950, 12 Oz. 130.00
Buckeye Sparkling Dry, High Profile, Cone Top, 1956, 12 Oz. 263.00
Carling Black Label, Cleveland, Flat Top, 1955, 10-12 Oz. 15.00
Casey's Lager, Duke Snider, Tab Top, Bottom Opened, 1971, 12 Oz. 9.00
Chief Oshkosh, Supreme Pilsener, High Profile, Cone Top, 1953, 12 Oz. 224.00
Coors Banquet, Flat Top, 1951, 12 Oz. 35.00
Drewry's Extra Dry, Sports, Purple, Flat Top, Air Sealed, 1953, 12 Oz. 175.00
Falstaff, Omaha, Neb., Flat Top, Top Opened, 1959, 12 Oz. 18.00
Falstaff, Omaha, Neb., High Profile, Cone Top, 1949, 12 Oz. ....90.00 to 115.00
Fighting Wildcats, Kentucky Football, Tab Top, Bottom Opened, 1982, 12 Oz. 8.00
Gettelman Rathskellar, High Profile, Cone Top, 1953, 12 Oz. 165.00
Great Lakes Premium, Flat Top, Bottom Opened, 1952, 12 Oz. 225.00
Hamm's, Blue Ground, Red Letters, Flat Top, Top Opened, 1962, 12 Oz. 14.00
Heileman's Old Style Lager, Monks Brewing, Low Profile, 1935, 12 Oz. 300.00
Horton Ale, Cap, Low Profile, Cone Top, 1940 .... 750.00
Iron City, Penn State Football, Tab Top, Bottom Opened, 1974, 12 Oz. 60.00
Iron City, Pittsburgh Steelers, Tab Top, Bottom Opened, 1979, 12 Oz. 4.00
Label, Tivoli Brewing Co., 1950s, 3 x 3 1/2 In. 11.00
Lion Special Pilsener, Zebra, Tab Top, Bottom Opened, South Africa, 1974, 12 Oz. 8.00
Lucky Lager, Bottom Opened, c.1956 .... 25.00
Miller High Life, Black Ground, Flat Top, Keglined Block, c.1955, 12 Oz. ....65.00 to 75.00
Miller High Life, Flat, Rolled, 1940s 30.00
Milwaukee's Best, Flat Top, Bottom Opened, 1960, 12 Oz. 17.00
Old Milwaukee, Schoolhouse, Blue, Red, Yellow, Flat Top, Bottom Opened, 1937, 12 Oz. 2000.00
Old Milwaukee, White, Red, Soft Top Lid, Flat Top, Top Opened, 1962, 12 Oz. 20.00

Old Topper Snappy Ale, Cone Top, J-Spout, 1938, 12 Oz. 67.00
Pabst Blue Ribbon, Milwaukee, Wisc., Red, White, Blue, Flat Top, Top Opened, 12 Oz. 14.00
Pabst Blue Ribbon, Peoria, Ill., White, Blue, Flat Top, Bottom Opened, 1955, 12 Oz. 45.00
Pfeiffer Premium, Canadian Geese, Flat Top, Bottom Opened, 1954, 12 Oz. 250.00
Rainier Special Export, Low Profile, Cone Top, 1936, 12 Oz. 200.00 to 325.00
Schlitz, Cone Top, High Profile, Pre 1950, 12 Oz. 95.00
Schlitz, Made Milwaukee Famous, Milwaukee, Flat Top, Rolled, Air Sealed, 1960, 10 Oz. 45.00
Schlitz, Made Milwaukee Famous, Tampa, Fla., Flat Top, Rolled, Air Sealed, 1958, 12 Oz. 85.00 to 110.00
Schmidt, Ice Fisherman, Tab Top, Top Opened, St. Paul, Minn., 1969, 12 Oz. 7.00
Stag, Carling Brewing, Flat Top, Bottom Opened, 1958, 12 Oz. 21.00 to 28.00
Sun Valley, East Idaho Brewing, High Profile, Cone Top, 1953, 12 Oz. 945.00
Sunshine Premium Beer, Reading, Pa., Flat Top, Air Sealed, 1963, 12 Oz. 65.00
Tennent's Lager, Tennent's Girls, Tab Top, Bottom Opened, Scotland, 1974, 12 Oz. 10.00 to 15.00
Wisconsin Premium Quality Beer, Flat Top, Bottom Opened, 1956, 12 Oz. 45.00
Yuengling, Red Ground, Cone Top, High Profile, 1952, 12 Oz. 192.00

BELL collectors collect all types of bells. Favorites include glass bells, figural bells, school bells, and cowbells. Bells have been made of porcelain, china, or metal through the centuries.

Brass, Hand Pumper Fire Truck, Wrought Iron Support, Red Paint, 10 x 40 In. 1035.00
Brass, Hand, Nickel Plated, Embossed Schafferstown, U.B. Church, 1851-1919, 4 In. 135.00
Brass, Harness, Center Bell, 2 Smaller Bells, Iron Frame, Mounted On Stand, 21 In. 385.00
Bronze, Cast Iron, Call, Rotating, Victorian, 6 1/2 In. 200.00
Bronze, Flower Trellises, Japan, 1800s, 8 In. 176.00
Church Tower, Cast Iron, c.1880, 28 x 39 In. 527.00
Iron, Yoke, Upright, Clapper, c.1900, 18 In. 118.00
Plantation, Cast Iron, White & Silver Paint, No. 26, Yoke, Rope Wheel, 16 x 25 In. 6465.00
Rumbler, Robert, Wells, Bronze, No. 26, Wiltshire, England, c.1760, 4 1/4 In. 595.00
School, Brass, 10 In. 46.00
Sleigh, 29 Bells, Strap, Buckle, 87 In., 2 3-In. Bells 259.00
Smoke, Blown Glass, Gauffered, Kerosene, Applied Ring Hanger, 1860-90, 8 x 6 1/8 In. 35.00
Smoke, Blown Glass, Gauffered, Kerosene, Fiery Opalescent, Gilt, 1860-90, 8 x 6 In. 88.00

BELLEEK china was made in Ireland, other European countries, and the United States. The glaze is creamy yellow and appears wet. The first Belleek was made in 1857. All pieces listed here are Irish Belleek. The mark changed through the years. The first mark, black, dates from 1863 to 1890. The second mark, black, dates from 1891 to 1926 and includes the words *Co. Fermanagh, Ireland*. The third mark, black, dates from 1926 to 1946 and has the words *Deanta in Eirinn*. The fourth mark, same as the third mark but green, dates from 1946 to 1955. The fifth mark, green, dates from 1955 to 1965 and has an R in a circle added in the upper right. The sixth mark, green, dates after 1965 and the words *Co. Fermanagh* have been omitted. The seventh mark, gold, was used from 1980 to 1993 and omits the words *Deanta in Eirinn*. The eighth mark, introduced in 1993, is similar to the second mark but is printed in blue. The word *Belleek* is now used only on the pieces made in Ireland even though earlier pieces from other countries were sometimes marked *Belleek*. These early pieces are listed by manufacturer, such as Ceramic Art Co., Haviland, Lenox, Ott & Brewer, and Willets.

Basket, Trefoil, Openwork, Flower Buds, 2 1/4 x 6 1/4 In. 176.00
Creamer, Leaves, Black Mark, 3 1/2 In. 60.00
Dinner Set, Shamrock Pattern, Pitcher, Cake Plate, Vase, Place Setting, 11 Piece 234.00
Figurine, Dog On Pillow, Green Mark, c.1950, 4 3/4 In. 60.00
Frame, Shell, White, Oval, 1st Mark, Black, 6 1/2 In. 1150.00
Loving Cup, Song Of Hiawatha, Indian Lovers Scene, Love Is Sunshine, c.1897, 6 1/2 In. 470.00
Mug, Gussie Motter, 1897, 5 1/2 In. 69.00
Pitcher, Cider, Signed, 5 1/2 In. 130.00
Pitcher, Fruit, Hand Painted, c.1900, 6 x 8 In. 205.00
Sugar & Creamer, Bamboo Type Pattern, Vine Handles, 4th Mark, Green, 3 In. 80.00

Sugar & Creamer, Shamrock Pattern, Basket Mold, 2nd Mark, Black 58.00
Tumbler, Tapered, Fluted, Pointed Ribs, Gold Top Rim, 1st Mark, Black, 1863-90, 4 1/2 In. 58.00
Vase, Baluster Shape, Hand Painted, Cascading Peonies, c.1900, 21 In. 1870.00
Vase, Basket, Center Handle, Rose Vine, Daisies, 2nd Mark, Black, 4 1/4 x 6 In. 230.00
Vase, Flowers, Cylindrical, Hand Painted, 7 3/4 x 2 1/4 In. 176.00
Vase, Frog, Cream, Black Highlights, 4 1/2 In. 360.00
Vase, White, Woman's Head Upper Border, Tree Lower Border, Hand Painted, 8 1/2 In. 235.00

BENNINGTON ware was the product of two factories working in Bennington, Vermont. Both the Norton Company and the Lyman Fenton Company were out of business by 1896. The wares include brown and yellow mottled pottery, Parian, scroddled ware, stoneware, graniteware, yellowware, and Staffordshire-type vases. The name is also a generic term for mottled brownware of the type made in Bennington.

Baking Dish, Flint Enamel, 8-Sided, Raised Rim, A Mark, 8 3/4 x 11 1/4 In. 400.00
Candlestick, Flint Enamel, 8 In. 220.00
Candlestick, Flint Enamel, Amber, Olive Green, Blue, 8 1/2 In. 1090.00
Churn, Cobalt Blue Decoration, Oval, Dasher, E. & L.P. Norton, 17 In. 1095.00
Churn, Deer, Tree, House, J. & E. Norton, c.1855, 3 Gal., 16 In. 8800.00
Churn, Leaf, Cobalt Blue, E. Norton & Co., 4 Gal. 440.00
Churn, Lid, Cobalt Blue Flowers, Julius Norton, 4 Gal. 440.00
Churn, Plume, Cobalt Blue, E. & L.P. Norton, 5 Gal. 825.00
Coffeepot, Helmet Cover, Spout, Handle On Rib, Blue, Green, Flint Enamel, 13 1/4 In. 2415.00
Cream Pot, Deer, Fence, Tree, J. & E. Norton, c.1855, 3 Gal., 12 In. 8800.00
Cream Pot, House, Deer, Trees, Fence, Cobalt Blue, J. & E. Norton, c.1855, 13 In. 13750.00
Creamer, Alternate Rib Pattern, Flint Enamel, 5 1/2 In. 1035.00
Creamer, Tulip & Heart Pattern, Green Highlights, Flint Enamel, Signed, 6 In. 720.00
Crock, Chicken Pecking Corn, Blue, J. & E. Norton, c.1861, 2 Gal., 9 In. 6050.00
Crock, Deer & House, Blue, J. & E. Norton, c.1855, 3 Gal., 10 1/2 In. 6600.00
Crock, Thistle Flower, Blue, J. & E. Norton, c.1855, 6 Gal., 13 1/2 In. 690.00
Cuspidor, Flint Enamel, A Mark, 3 3/4 x 8 In. 145.00
Cuspidor, Flint Enamel, Diamond Pattern, Amber, Green, 8 1/4 x 4 1/2 In. 145.00
Cuspidor, Glazed, Impressed Mark, Vermont, 1858, 9 3/4 In. 120.00
Figurine, Deer, Flint Enamel, Spill Holder Bases, Coleslaw Leaves, 11 x 10 1/2 In. 1150.00
Figurine, Lion, Flint Enamel, Coleslaw Mane, Holding Ball In Paw, Amber, Green, 12 In., Pair 7590.00
Figurine, Lion, Flint Enamel, Facing Right, Amber, Blue Glaze, Lyman Fenton, c.1849, 11 x 19 In. ... 18400.00
Figurine, Poodle, Holding Basket, Coleslaw Fur, Topknot, 10 1/2 x 8 3/4 In., Pair 3450.00
Foot Warmer, Flint Enamel, Molded Scroll Decoration, Paneled Back, 8 1/2 In. 259.00
Humidor, Flint Enamel, Lid Impressed, 1849 Mark 140.00
Jar, Canning, Bird, Blue, J. Norton & Co., c.1861, 10 1/2 In. 965.00
Jardiniere, Fern Leaves, 2 Parts, 12 In. 300.00
Jug, Bird On Leaf, Stoneware, J. Norton & Co., c.1861, 2 Gal., 13 In. 1760.00
Jug, Dotted Plume, Blue, E. & L.P. Norton, c.1880, 3 Gal., 15 In. 155.00
Jug, Flower, Blue, J. & E. Norton, c.1855, 2 Gal., 13 In. 385.00
Jug, Flower, Cobalt Blue, Oval, L. Norton, Gal. 300.00
Jug, Flower, Cobalt Blue, Oval, Norton & Fenton, 3 Gal. 330.00
Jug, Flower, Double, Blue, J. & E. Norton, c.1855, 2 Gal., 13 1/2 In. 440.00
Jug, Flower, Ocher, Oval, L. Norton & Son, c.1833, 3 Gal., 15 1/2 In. 1980.00
Jug, Flower, Stylized, Dotted, J. & E. Norton, c.1855, 3 Gal., 14 In. 1925.00
Jug, Leaf, Blue, Dotted, E. & L.P. Norton, c.1880, 2 Gal., 13 In. 300.00
Jug, Leaf, Cobalt Blue, Impressed Label, E. & L.P. Norton, 11 1/4 In. 130.00
Jug, Leaf, Cobalt Blue, J. & E. Norton, 3 Gal. 140.00
Jug, Leaf, Freehand Blue Slip, Strap Handle, Norton, 4 Gal., 17 In. 259.00
Jug, Parrot, Freehand Blue Slip, Strap Handle, J. Norton, 2 Gal., 13 1/2 In. 690.00
Jug, Rough & Ready, Zachary Taylor, c.1850, 12 3/4 x 13 In. 4632.00
Paperweight, Figural, Flint Enamel, Reclining Spaniel, Rectangular Base, 4 1/2 x 3 In. 400.00
Pitcher, Alternate Rib, Green, Rockingham Glaze, c.1849, 10 In. 230.00
Pitcher, Flower Spray, Paneled, Rockingham Glaze, Norton & Fenton, Vt., 8 3/4 In. 949.00
Pitcher, Molded Grapevines, Hunt Scene, Hound Handle, Rockingham Glaze, 10 In. 375.00
Teapot, Flint Enamel, Olive Green, Individual, c.1970, 5 3/4 In. 460.00
Toby Jug, Ben Franklin, Boot Handle, Rockingham Glaze, 5 3/4 In. 230.00

Toby Jug, Grapevine Handle, Rockingham Glaze, 6 In. 259.00
Vase, Cottage, Multicolored Biscuit Panels, 8 1/2 In., Pair 230.00
Vase, Tulip, Flint Enamel, Green, Blue, Raised Ribs, 9 In. 920.00
Washbowl, Pitcher, Flint Enamel, Alternate Rib, Blue, Green, Yellow, 14 & 13 In. 1440.00

BERLIN, a German porcelain factory, was started in 1751 by Wilhelm Kaspar Wegely. In 1763, the factory was taken over by Frederick the Great and became the Royal Berlin Porcelain Manufactory. It is still in operation today. Pieces have been marked in a variety of ways.

Cup & Saucer, Commemorative, Blue, Gold, Maerz, 1818 7985.00
Plaque, Banishment Of Hagar & Ishmael, E. Heyn, c.1900, 11 3/8 x 13 1/4 In. 8815.00
Plaque, Classically Draped Young Girl, Holding Lamb, Seated, Oval, Late 1800s, 11 In. 6390.00
Plaque, Psyche Mourning, Frame, 5 3/4 x 4 In. 1955.00
Plaque, Young Woman, Kneels Beside Girl With Pitcher, 7 x 4 1/2 In. 3276.00
Plaque, Young Woman, Long Hair, Diaphanous Gown, Giltwood Frame, Ginner, 6 3/4 x 5 In. 1610.00
Plate, Country Hills, People, Trees, Gold Border, 1815, 9 1/2 In. 5810.00
Plate, Documentary Botanical, 1817, 9 3/4 In. 18875.00
Plate, House, People, Horse, Cart, Trees, Gold Border, 1817-23, 9 3/4 In. 10165.00
Plate, House, Porch, People, Horses, Gold Border, 1817-23, 9 1/2 In. 14520.00
Plate, Military, 3 Officers Talking, Camp, Soldiers On Horses, 1803-13, 9 1/2 In. 24685.00
Plate, Topographical, Building, Lawn, Trees, People, Gold Border, 1817-23, 10 In. 10165.00
Plate, Topographical, Canal, Building, People, Trees, Gold Border, 1817-22, 9 3/4 In. 5080.00
Tea & Coffee Set, Micro Mosaic, Gold Ground, 1817-23, 5 3/4-In. Teapot 17425.00
Vase, Flowers, Gold Details, 1817-23, 16 In. 12340.00

BESWICK started making earthenware in Staffordshire, England, in 1936. The company is now part of Royal Doulton Tableware, Ltd. Figurines of animals, especially dogs and horses, Beatrix Potter animals, and other wares are still being made.

Ashtray, 3 Dogs, No. 916, 2 1/4 In. 35.00
Ashtray, 5 Dogs, No. 869, 2 x 6 In. 95.00
Character Jug, Barnaby Rudge, 4 1/2 In. 95.00
Character Jug, Mr. Bumble, No. 2032, 1966-73, 5 In. 80.00
Character Jug, Tony Weller, Second Version, No. 281, 7 In. 150.00
Creamer, Mr. Micawber, No. 674, 1940s, 3 1/4 In. 40.00
Face Jug, Mr. Micawber, No. 310, Pre 1930, 9 In. 275.00
Face Jug, Scrooge, No. 372, Pre 1930, 7 In. 275.00
Figurine, Bulldog, No. 1731, 1960-72, 2 1/2 In. 40.00
Figurine, Cat, Ginger, No. 1867, 1963-70, 8 1/2 In. 90.00
Figurine, Cat, White, Blue Eyes, No. 1886, 4 In. 103.00
Figurine, Cheshire Cat, No. 2480, Royal Doulton Tableware Ltd., 1974, 1 1/2 In. 350.00
Figurine, Collie, No. 1814, 1962-75, 3 1/4 In. 55.00
Figurine, Elephant, No. 974, 4 3/4 In. 60.00 to 65.00
Figurine, Horse, Lying Down, No. 915, 3 1/8 x 4 7/8 In. 90.00
Figurine, Hunca Munca, BP-2, 1955-72, 2 3/4 In. 154.00
Figurine, Labrador Retriever, Black, Glossy, No. 3062B, 8 1/4 x 5 1/2 In. 125.00
Figurine, Leopard, 4 7/8 x 11 5/8 In. 190.00
Figurine, Miss Moppet, BP-3b, 1974-85, 3 In. 79.00
Figurine, Mr. Jeremy Fisher, Spotted Legs, BP-3a, c.1973, 3 In. 145.00
Figurine, Mrs. Rabbit & Bunnies, P2543, BP-3, 3 5/8 x 2 In. 75.00
Figurine, Mrs. Tittlemouse, P1103, 1948, 4 In. 100.00
Figurine, Panda, Standing, 2 1/4 x 3 In. 25.00 to 40.00
Figurine, Pig, No. 832, Arthur Gredington, Pre 1972, 3 1/4 In. 55.00
Figurine, Piglet, Trotting, No. 834, 1940-71, 1 1/2 In. 25.00
Figurine, Scottish Terrier, 3 x 4 1/2 x 6 3/4 In. 115.00
Figurine, Siamese Cat, Lying, No. 1558A, 1958-63, 4 1/2 x 7 1/4 In. 95.00 to 115.00
Figurine, Tailor Of Gloucester, P1108, 3 1/2 In. 75.00
Figurine, Yorkshire Terrier, Laughing, No. 2102, 1967-72, 3 In. 125.00
Figurine, Yorkshire Terrier, No. 1944, 3 3/8 x 4 1/8 In. 90.00
Figurine Set, Cat Orchestra, Gray, 1945-73, 2 In., 4 Piece 235.00
Group, Mr. Benjamin Bunny & Peter Rabbit, P2509, BG-3b, 4 In. 150.00
Jug, Scenic, A Midsummer's Night's Dream, No. 1366, 1955-72, Hallam & Orwell, 8 1/2 In. 185.00

Bicycle, Schwinn, Panther, 1950s

Bicycle, Tricycle, Steelcraft, 1940s

Plate, Christmas In England, No. 2393, 1972, 8 x 8 In. .37.00 to 40.00
Plate, Christmas In Mexico, No. 2419, 1973, 8 x 8 In. .37.00 to 40.00
Relish, Leaf, Green, 2 Orange Flowers, c.1920, 12 1/2 x 5 1/4 In. 16.00
Salt & Pepper, Sairey Gamp & Mr. Micawber, 1939-73, 3 1/2 In. 62.00
Sugar, Tony Weller, No. 673, 1940s, 2 3/4 In. 45.00
Sugar & Creamer, Pecksniff, No. 1129, No. 1117, 3 1/2 In. 85.00
Teapot, Sairey Gamp, No. 691, 1939-73, 5 3/4 In. 125.00

BETTY BOOP, the cartoon figure, first appeared on the screen in 1931. Her face was modeled after the famous singer Helen Kane and her body after Mae West. In 1935, a comic strip was started. Her dog was named Bimbo. Although the Betty Boop cartoons ended by 1938, there was a revival of interest in the Betty Boop image in the 1980s and new pieces are being made.

Ashtray, Betty & Bimbo, Ceramic, Fleischer Studios, Japan, 4 In. 175.00
Ashtray, Hand Painted, In Relief, Nippon, Blue Rising Sun Mark, c.1910, 3 3/4 In. 355.00
Blanket, Fleischer Studios, 1930s, 12 x 16 In. 110.00
Button, Betty Boop, Standing, Drawn Stage Drapes, Celluloid, c.1931, 1 1/4 In. 2935.00
Doll, Composition, Cloth Dress, Heart Decal, Cameo Doll Co., 1930s, 12 In. 4760.00
Doll, Composition, Jointed, Green Dress, Shoes, Fleischer Studios, 12 In. 300.00
Figurine, Celluloid, Elastic String, Movable Arms, 6 In. 350.00
Figurine Set, Betty Boop Playing Instruments, Bisque, Fleischer Studios, Box, 3 1/2 In., 4 Piece 1500.00
Nodder, Celluloid, Windup, Fleischer Studios, Box, 1930s, 7 In. 2500.00
Soap Set, The Picture Outlasts The Soap, Fleischer Studios, 2 3/4 x 5 1/2 In., 3 Piece 140.00
Tea Set, Tan, Luster, Japan, 1930s, 3 1/2-In. Teapot, 5 Piece 220.00
Toy, Acrobat, Betty Boop Moves On Metal Rod, Windup, Celluloid, C.K. Co., Box, 9 In. 1800.00
Toy, Stroller, Betty & Mickey Mouse, Folding, Tin, Rico Toy Co., 1930s, 11 In. 1345.00
Toy, Whirligig, Jolly Betty, Windup, Celluloid, Japan, Box, 1930s, 10 1/2 In. .7500.00 to 8400.00

BICYCLES were invented in 1839. The first manufactured bicycle was made in 1861. Special ladies' bicycles were made after 1874. The modern safety bicycle was not produced until 1885. Collectors search for all types of bicycles and tricycles. Bicycle-related items are also listed here.

Banner, Racing, Grand Victorian, Wanderlust, Germany, 1905, 35 x 18 In. 626.00
Boneshaker, Cast Iron, Wood Seat, Velvet Cushion, Double Spoked, 1800s, 30 x 22 In. 415.00
Boneshaker, Michaux, Bronze Acorn Counter Balanced Pedals, 36-In. Front Wheel 5500.00
Bugle, New Model 3, Henry Keat & Sons, London, Brass, Nickel Mouthpiece, 8 In. 1100.00
Button, League Of American Wheelmen, 2 Bicyclists, Celluloid, 1 In. 15.00
Button, Member Fisk Bicycle Club, Celluloid, 1 In. 15.00
Button, Royal, Bicycle Wheel, Wild Cat, Celluloid, Stud, 1 In. 15.00
Colson, Commander, Wilbur Henry Adams, 1936 5225.00
Columbia, Boycycle, Sidewalk Style, c.1920, 27 In. 140.00
Columbia, High Wheel, Columbia Special, c.1880, 54 In. 1320.00

Columbia, Man's, Chainless, 2-Speed, Goodyear Speedway Tires, 1905 .... 1980.00
Columbia, Model 46, Girl's, Tall Frame, Pneumatic Safety, Wooden Chain Guard Fender 330.00
Columbia Five Star, Model 5636, Boy's, Jet-Rider, Horn Tank, Goodyear Tires, 1950s 360.00
Cross Frame, Ewart Chain, Safety, Hard Tires, c.1889, 20-In. Wheels, Child's 4400.00
Elgin, Bluebird, French Blue, Chrome, Teardrop Pedals, Allstate Whitewalls, 1936 .... 11000.00
Grand Rapids Bicycle Co., Clipper, Hard Tires, Safety, Convertible, 1892, 26-In. Front Tire 4125.00
Hartford Cycle Co., Scorcher, Man's, Pneumatic Safety, Downswept Handlebar, c.1894 .... 525.00
High Wheel, Curved Handlebar, Stirrup Grips, D. Rudge, 1885, 46 In. 4675.00
High Wheel, Eagle, Light Roadster, L.B. Gaylor, Stamford, Conn., c.1890, 51-In. Wheel 11550.00
High Wheel, Strap Steel, Quick Change Front Wheel, c.1890, 28-In. Wheel 1100.00
High Wheel, Thomas, Bayliss, Open Head Model, Curved Handlebars, c.1883, 52 In. 2200.00
Iver Johnson, Lovell Diamond, Pneumatic Safety, Rover Frame, 1893, 30-In. Wheels 1980.00
Lamp, Miller, Model 4A, Carbide, Miller & Co., Birmingham, 19th Century 45.00
Manton & Smith, Boy's, Blue Enamel, Chrome Fenders, 2 Whitewall Tires, 1939 .... 3850.00
Mercury, F26, Pod Carrier, Crash Bars, Rocket Ray Lamp, Maroon, Red, c.1949 .... 990.00
Monarch 1, Silver King, Hex Tube, Cheese Grater Rack, Snake Belly Tires, 1948 .... 1210.00
Monark, Silver King Flo-Cycle, Steel Spring Leaf Suspension, Butterfly Stand, c.1937 .... 2640.00
Murray, Monterey, Girl's, Burgundy, Label, Murray Ohio Mfg. Co., Lawrenceburg, Tenn. 175.00
Overman Wheel Co., Credenda, Woman's, Hard Tires, Chicopee Falls, Mass., c.1891 .... 1045.00
Poster, La Pareoline, Obturateur Perpetuel, Tire, 2 Cyclists, c.1902, 47 1/2 x 35 In. 1150.00
Poster, Peugeot, Success Sans Precedent, France, 1900, 73 x 49 1/2 In. 950.00
Poster, Snell, American Cycles, Man, In Tuxedo, Riding Bike, France, c.1900, 47 x 32 In. 1115.00
Rambler, Model 772, Safety, Corbin Duplex Coaster Brake, Attached Tire Pump, 1903 .... 550.00
Roadmaster, Supreme, Girl's, Black, White, Skirt Guard, Lobdell Horizontal Sprung Saddle 2750.00
Rollfast, Royal Flyer, Balloon Tires, Black & Cream, Red Stripes, D.P. Harris Co., 1936 .... 745.00
Ross, Balloon, Blue, White, Convertible, Training Wheels, c.1960, 16 In. 60.00
Schwinn, Black Phantom, Boy's, Balloon Style, c.1950s 660.00
Schwinn, Panther, 1950s .... *ILLUS* 952.00
Schwinn, Woody, Cruiser, Balloon Style, Whitewalls, 7-Speed Hub, Chrome Fenders 220.00
Scooter, Skudder Ball Bearing Car, Seesaw Footboard, Janesville Products, No. 1 .... 305.00
Scooter, Tricycle, Buddy L, Pump Action, Disc Wheels 605.00
Seesaw, Clown's, 1 Direction Gear Drive, 1930s, 8 Ft. 6 In. 770.00
Shelby, Flying Cloud, Chrome Tank, Blue & Red Fenders, Lamp, c.1930 .... 495.00
Shelby, Ideal No. 11, Woman's, Pneumatic Safety, Oil Lamp, Wood Fender, c.1890 .... 415.00
Sidewalk, Colson, Speed Bike, c.1920, Child's 44.00
Tandem, Morrow Coaster Brake, Steel Clad Rims, c.1898 .... 275.00
Tricycle, Monark, Silver King, Aluminum, c.1939 .... 825.00
Tricycle, Scout Runner, Child's 255.00
Tricycle, Steelcraft, 1940s .... *ILLUS* 504.00
Tricycle, Tiller, Gendron Wheel Co., 19th Century, 20-In. Rear & 12-In. Front Wheels 415.00
Tricycle, Tiller, Pedal Drive, Child's, c.1895, 26-In. Rear Wheels 275.00
Unicycle, Stand, Columbia, c.1950, 40 In. 25.00
Victor, Model C, Overman Wheel Co., Chicopee, Mass., c.1890 .... 7425.00
Wolff-American, Duplex, 3-Wheel Sociable, 2 Side-By-Side Seats, New York, 1896 .... 1925.00

BING & GRONDAHL is a famous Danish factory making fine porcelains from 1853 to the present. Underglaze blue decoration was started in 1886. The annual Christmas plate series was introduced in 1895. Dinnerwares, stoneware, and figurines are still being made today. The firm has used the initials B & G and a stylized castle as part of the mark since 1898. The company became part of Royal Copenhagen in 1987.

B&G KJØBENHAVN
MADE IN DENMARK

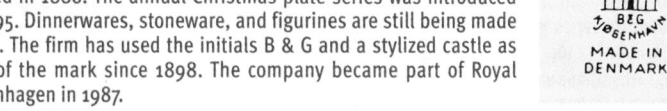

Figurine, Bison, c.1980, 18 1/2 In. 1058.00
Figurine, Cat, Lying Down, c.1915, 7 In. 470.00
Figurine, Dog, Japanese Chin, c.1950, 6 3/4 In. 295.00
Figurine, Farmer, 2 Horses, A. Locher, c.1935, 9 1/2 In. 590.00
Figurine, Fox, c.1950, 12 In. 235.00
Figurine, Guillemot, Jens Peter Dahl-Jensen, c.1920, 7 1/4 In. 380.00
Figurine, Lion On Rock, Lauritz Jensen, c.1955, 7 3/4 In. 380.00
Figurine, Lioness, c.1950, 9 In. 295.00

If you like vases of fresh flowers, buy custom-cut pieces of glass to protect the table and chest tops from water stains.

Bing & Grondahl, Vase, Cover, Blue & Gray Leafy Branches, Low Relief, Luster Base, 14 In.

Figurine, Little Match Girl, c.1935, 3 1/2 In. 120.00
Figurine, Llama, Early 1900s, 5 In. 176.00
Figurine, Monkey, c.1940, 6 3/4 In. 235.00
Figurine, Monkey, Gray, c.1930, 14 1/2 In. 705.00
Figurine, Monkey, I.P. Irminger, c.1984, 3 1/8 In. 120.00
Figurine, Monkey, Tortoise, Dahl-Jensen, c.1980, 5 In. 175.00
Figurine, Panther, L. Jensen, c.1930, 7 1/2 In. 499.00
Figurine, Penguin, On Rock, A. Locher, c.1950, 18 In. 1410.00
Figurine, Puma, Dahl-Jensen, c.1935, 10 In. 176.00
Figurine, Snail, c.1935, 4 1/8 In. 560.00
Figurine, Tiger & Cub, c.1930, 11 In. 1058.00
Figurine, Tiger, Laurits Jensen, c.1975, 9 1/2 In. 825.00
Group, Deer Nursing Fawn, Knud Max Moller, c.1921, 6 In. 470.00
Group, Lioness & Cub, L. Jensen, c.1930, 12 1/2 In. 529.00
Group, Monkeys, c.1935, 5 1/2 In. 295.00
Paperweight, Boy, Nude, On Rectangular Base, c.1950, 4 1/2 In. 235.00
Plate, Christmas, 1901, Three Wise Men From The East 180.00
Plate, Christmas, 1904, View Of Copenhagen 175.00
Plate, Christmas, 1905, Anxiety Of The Coming Christmas Night 164.00
Plate, Christmas, 1906, Sleighing To Church On Christmas Eve 41.00
Plate, Christmas, 1907, Little Match Girl 76.00
Plate, Christmas, 1910, Old Organist 75.00
Plate, Christmas, 1911, First It Was Sung By Angels 66.00
Plate, Christmas, 1912, Going To Church On Christmas Eve 110.00
Plate, Christmas, 1913, Bringing Home Yule Tree 155.00
Plate, Christmas, 1915, Chained Dog Getting Double Meal 93.00
Plate, Christmas, 1917, Arrival Of Christmas Boat 51.00
Plate, Christmas, 1918, Fishing Boat Returning Home For Christmas 56.00
Plate, Christmas, 1919, Outside The Lighted Window 62.00
Plate, Christmas, 1920, Hare In Snow 60.00
Plate, Christmas, 1921, Pigeons In Castle Court .... 41.00 to 57.00
Plate, Christmas, 1923, The Royal Hunting Castle, Ermitage 96.00
Plate, Christmas, 1925, Child's Christmas .... 29.00 to 58.00
Plate, Christmas, 1927, Skating Couple 58.00
Plate, Christmas, 1931, Arrival Of Christmas Train 59.00
Plate, Christmas, 1936, Royal Guard Outside Amalienborg Castle 60.00
Plate, Christmas, 1937, Arrival Of Christmas Guests 85.00
Plate, Christmas, 1946, Commemoration Cross 46.00
Plate, Christmas, 1947, Dybbol Mill 44.00
Tray, 2 White Mice, c.1955, 3 In. 206.00
Vase, 3 Panels, Vertical Lines, Stoneware, Valdemer Petersen, 1940s, 5 In. 285.00
Vase, Cover, Blue & Gray Leafy Branches, Low Relief, Luster Base, 14 In. .... *ILLUS* 9600.00
Vase, Magnolia, Pink Ground, c.1935, 11 1/2 In. 150.00
Vase, Oval, Coastal Landscape, Boating Figures, Sophus Jensen, 12 x 31 In. 295.00

BINOCULARS of all types are wanted by collectors. Those made in the eighteenth and nineteenth centuries are favored by serious collectors. The small, attractive binoculars called *opera glasses* are listed in their own category.

Airguide, 4 x 32, 60A, Chicago, USA, Leather Case 55.00
Asahi Optical, 7 x 50, 7.1 Field, Pentax Prism, Coated Optics, Case, Strap, Japan 33.00
Bardou & Fils Paris, 1860s, 6 1/2 x 4 1/2 In. 22.00
Bausch & Lomb, 6 x 30, Leather Case, U.S. Army Signal Corps, 6 1/2 x 4 1/4 In. 67.00
Bausch & Lomb, 7 x 50, U.S. Navy, BU Ships, Mark 28, Strap, Case, 1943 .... 120.00
Bausch & Lomb, 7 x 50, Zephyr, Strap, 1930s 40.00
Biascope Wollensak, 6 x 58 mm., Rochester, Pat Applied For, 3 1/4 x 3 1/4 x 3 3/8 In. 95.00
Carl Zeiss, 15 x 50, Jena, Pentekarem, Case, Germany, c.1970 .... 168.00
Carl Zeiss, 16 x 40, Jena, Telsexor, Case, Pre 1940 .... 180.00
Carl Zeiss, 6x, Jena, Original Leather Case, 1913 .... 126.00
Carl Zeiss, 8 x 30, Jena, Deltrentis, 6 1/2 x 9 In. 55.00
Dienstglas, 6 x 30, Case, Leather Strap, Germany, World War II 80.00
H. Sanders, Brass, Gutta Percha, Leatherette, Case, Shoulder Strap, Montreal, 1860s 195.00
Hensoldt Wetzlar, 8 x 30, Dienstglas, German Federal Armed Forces, Rubber Coated, 1960s 50.00
Leitz, 7 x 20, Trinovid Model, Green, Case 125.00
Lemaire Fabt, Paris, Gutta Percha Focus Wheel, 1860s, 6 1/2 In. 189.00
Max Balbeck, No. 765432, Prism, 4x Magnification, Folding, 1920 .... 350.00
Signal Glass Day & Night, Enamel Body, Gutta Percha Knob, Leatherette, 1860s 195.00
Universal Camera Corp., 6 x 30, U.S. Navy, Buships, Mod. O, Leather Strap, Case, 1943 .... 46.00
Vendome, Paris, Leather Covered, 6 In. 95.00
Westinghouse, 7 x 50, Coated Opticals, US Military M-15, Leather Case, 1944, 8 In. 225.00

BIRDCAGES are collected for use as homes for pet birds and as decorative objects of folk art. Elaborate wooden cages of the past centuries can still be found. The brass or wicker cages of the 1930s are popular with bird owners.

Aluminum, Glass, Red, Round, Toys, 1950s 350.00
Brass, Art Cage Mfg. Co., N.Y.C., 19 x 14 In. 450.00
Brass, Hand Painted Butterfly & Dragonflies Art Cage Co., c.1929 .... 300.00
Brass, Mesh Seed Guard, Beehive Shape, Maxwell, 14 x 14 In. 200.00
Canary, Brass, Classic Style, John Maxwell, N.Y., 12 x 13 1/2 x 9 In. 250.00
Canary, Brass, Glass, Art Deco, Acid Etched Pattern Slide-Out Tray, 12 x 8 1/2 x 15 In. 400.00
Canary, Brass, Pagoda, Arabesque Pattern, Hendryx, c.1910, 15 x 12 In. 750.00
Cathedral, Dome Over 4 Porticos, Stand, Mahogany, 83 x 26 x 26 In. 3995.00
Finch & Canary, Brass Wire, Osborn, Hudson Street, N.Y.C., Late 1800s, 12 x 12 x 10 In. 250.00
Ginykage, England, 15 x 16 x 14 In. 95.00
Parrot, Brass, Perch, Cups, On Stand, Hendryx, New Haven, Conn., c.1907, 64 In. 2000.00
Parrot, Brass, Toy, Swing Perch, Victorian, 30 x 21 1/2 In. 800.00
Tin, Green & Blue Paint, Slide Door, Swing Perch, 13 In. 35.00
Victorian, Tin, Painted, 16 In. 66.00

BISQUE is an unglazed baked porcelain. Finished bisque has a slightly sandy texture with a dull finish. Some of it may be decorated with various colors. Bisque gained favor during the late Victorian era when thousands of bisque figurines were made. It is still being made. Additional bisque items may be listed under the factory name.

Centerpiece, Swan, Portugal, c.1940, 11 x 8 x 17 In. 59.00
Figurine, Car, Putti Driver, Woman, c.1902, 7 1/2 x 7 In. 355.00
Figurine, Foxy Grandpa, Blue Striped Suit, 8 1/2 In. 35.00
Figurine, Girl, Seated, Bonnet, Basket, Karl Schneider, Germany, 7 In. 550.00
Figurine, Girl, Seated, Hat, Cat, Plate, Bread, Bare Feet, Blue Intaglio Eyes, 7 In. 250.00
Figurine, Girl, With Puppy, Victorian, c.1890, 12 1/2 x 4 In. 105.00
Figurine, Koko The Clown, 4 In. 95.00
Figurine, Man, Seated, Pipe, Signed, Mougin, 2 Impressed Marks, 1900, 6 1/2 In. 300.00
Figurine, Nude Woman On Tiptoe, Leg Extended, Balancing Gold Ball, Germany, 1940, 9 In. 1570.00
Figurine, Nude Woman Seated Holding A Rose, Arm Extended, Germany, 5 In. 1065.00

Figurine, Nude Woman Standing On Base, Black Stockings, Heeled Shoes, Germany, 8 In. 1512.00
Figurine, Nude Woman Tossing Ball, Sculpted Hair, c.1940, Germany, 9 In. 1570.00
Figurine, Nude Woman, Head, Arms Extended Backward, Germany, 9 In. 530.00
Figurine, Renaissance Lady, Lace Hat, Bodice, Corset, Locket, Early 1900s, 17 In. 380.00
Figurine, Wealthy Automobile Driver, Sheepskin Coat, c.1906, 7 3/4 In. 620.00
Figurine, Woody Woodpecker Triple Portrait, Armstrong, Signed Walter Lantz, 7 x 4 In. 235.00
Lotus Bowl, Turquoise Glaze, Pooled To Cavetto, Ormolu Tripod, c.1850, 4 1/2 In. 820.00
Madonna, Fired Gold Accents, Porcelain, Sweden, 14 In. 295.00
Plaque, Relief, Figural, Multicolored Decoration, Classical Scenes, c.1900, 10 x 15 In. 529.00

BLACK memorabilia has become an important area of collecting since the 1970s. The best material dates from past centuries, but many recent items are also of interest. F & F is the mark used on plastic made by Fiedler & Fiedler Mold & Die Works, Inc. in the 1930s and 1940s. Objects that picture a black person may also be listed in this book under Advertising; Tin; Bank; Bottle Opener; Cookie Jar; Doll; Salt & Pepper; Sheet Music; Toy; etc.

Ashtray, Black Boy Wrestles Open Mouthed Gator, Painted, Japan, c.1950, 4 3/4 In. 65.00
Ashtray, Black Face Bottom, Ceramic, Embossed Relief, Painted, 1880s, 5 1/2 In. 85.00
Ashtray, Blackamoor, Bisque, Stylized, Moorish Prince, Painted, 1880s, 5 1/4 In. 95.00
Ashtray, Holder, Blackamoor, Flower, Basket, Bisque, Majolica, 1880s, 5 1/4 In. 75.00
Ashtray, Man Eating Watermelon, Ceramic, 6 In. 56.00
Ashtray, Startled Black Man, Aluminum, Hand Painted, Germany, 1890s, 4 1/2 In. 105.00
Banner, Aunt Jemima Pancakes, Coming, In Person, Cloth, 34 x 25 In. 176.00
Book, 10 Little Niggers, David Brett, Dean & Son, London, c.1910 .... 600.00
Bowl, Punch & Sambo, Ceramic, Hand Painted, Great Britain, Early 1900s, 4 In. 95.00
Box, Aunt Jemima's Baking Powder, Wood, Paper Label, Howell Mfg. Co., 6 x 14 1/2 In. 220.00
Box, Candy, Amos 'n' Andy, Ain't Dat Sumptin, 5 Cents, Cardboard, Lithograph, 12 x 20 In. 248.00
Box, Heide's Black Kids, Cardboard, 5 Lb., 6 3/4 x 10 1/4 In. 415.00
Box, Pickaninny Jelly Beans, Jelly Bean Airship, Blacks, Wood, 17 x 20 x 13 In. 440.00
Broadside, Minstrel, Paper Lithograph, Ethiopian Serenaders, 1850s, 18 In. 240.00
Candy Box, Black Jack Minstrel, Strums Banjo, Lithographed Cardboard, Box, 8 1/4 In. 55.00
Cigar Holder, Happy Black Boy, Holding Melon Slice, Sitting By Tree Stump, Prewar, 5 In. 110.00
Cigarette Holder, Black Girl With Firewood, Bisque, Hand Painted, Austria, 1880s, 5 1/4 In. 95.00
Cigarette Holder, Sambo & Pig, Porcelain, Painted, Big Lipped Sambo, Prewar, 6 1/2 In. 45.00
Cigarette Holder, Stylized Black Babies In Loincloths, Prewar Japan, 5 3/4 In. 85.00
Cleaning Polish, All Purpose, Lazy Black Man, Sleeping Pig Logo, 1920s, 6 1/4 In. 85.00
Cookie Jars are listed in the Cookie Jar category.
Cup, Naughty Nigger, 2 Boys, Poem, Painted, 14K Trim, Signed, Leslie Irving, 1900s, 3 In. 140.00
Cup & Saucer, Boy Trying To Catch Rooster, 14K Gold Trim, Germany, 1900s, 4 1/2 In. 90.00
Decanter, Bellhop, Ceramic, Painted, Deco Style, Head Removes To Pour, Prewar, 5 In. 95.00
Decanter, Cannibal, Big Ears, Plated Lip Woman, Painted, Japan, Prewar, 10 1/4 In. 65.00
Dispenser, Black Snow Baby, Blue Trim, Holds Ice Cone For Cigarettes, 1900s, 3 In. 90.00
Dispenser, Cigarette, Exaggerated Black Man Wears Barrel, Germany, 1920s, 8 1/4 In. 55.00
Display, Aunt Jemima Pancake Flour, Aunt Jemima On Swing, 2-Sided, 1900s, 17 x 9 In. 520.00
Display, Aunt Jemima Pancake Flour, Climber, Die Cut, Cardboard, 2 Piece, 13 x 6 In. 2640.00
Doll, Babyland Rag, Jointed Shoulders, Hips, Original Clothes, Bruckner, 1901, 13 In. 275.00
Doll, Beecher, Stockinet, Painted & Embroidered, Calico Dress, 1895, 20 In. 1065.00
Doll, Bisque Shoulder Head, Sculpted Hair, Glass Eyes, Muslin, Bisque Limbs, Germany, 20 In. ... 1430.00
Doll, Bisque Socket Head, Brown, Flirty Eyes, Painted Features, Fleecy Hair, Jointed, 10 In. 1100.00
Doll, Bisque Socket Head, Brown, Sculpted Hair, Composition, Gebruder Heubach, 9 In. 1760.00
Doll, Bisque Socket Head, Brown, Sleep Eyes, Hair, Composition, Ball Jointed, Kestner, 11 In. 6875.00
Doll, Bisque Socket Head, Brown, Sleep Eyes, Teeth, Mohair, Jointed, Kuhnlens, 7 In. 798.00
Doll, Bisque Socket Head, Ebony, Painted Hair, c.1910, 14 In. 1320.00
Doll, Boy, Composition Flange Head, Cloth Body, Disc-Jointed Hips, Original Clothes, 13 In. 330.00
Doll, Cloth, Wool Hair, Brows, Needle Sculpted Nose, Button Eyes, Clothes, Earrings, 11 In. 405.00
Doll, Golliwog, Girl, Glitter Earrings, Bowtie, 6 In. 45.00
Doll, Golliwog, Girl, Hand Knitted Face & Outfit, Great Britain, Prewar, 13 In. 30.00
Doll, Golliwog, Stuffed Fabric, Plastic Eyes, Striped Shirt, Yellow Vest, Great Britain, 13 1/2 In. 45.00
Doll, Nut Head, Carved Nose, Painted Facial Features, Fleecy Hair, Muslin Body, 9 In. 358.00

Doll, Plastic, Socket Head, Flirty Eyes, Wig, Jointed Shoulders & Hips, 17 In. 825.00
Doll, Rag, White Blouse, Head Scarf, Patterned Skirt, 13 In. 345.00
Doll, Vargas, Young Man, Bags Of Cotton, New Orleans, Early 1900s, 6 1/2 In. 105.00
Doll, Wood, Carved Features, Gesso Over Wood Hair, Dowel Jointed, 12 In. 1540.00
Doll, Wool, Needle Sculpted Head, Embroidered Features, Curacao, Early 1900s, 31 In. 355.00
Dominoes, Double Nine Nubian, Stylized, Etched, Crown Dominoes, Box, 1900s, 12 1/2 In. 85.00
Egg Holder, Black Boy Emerges From Cracked Egg, Hand Painted, Bisque, 1890s, 3 In. 90.00
Eggcup, Golliwog Holding Up Egg Carrier, Ceramic, 1920s, 2 3/4 In. 80.00
Eggcup, Golliwog, Robertson's Golden Shred, Painted, Molded, Box, 2 3/4 In., Pair 110.00
Figurine, 2 Children Jumping Rope, Wood, Jointed Arms, Glass Eyes, Platform Base, 11 In., Pair 1095.00
Figurine, 3 Boys, With Musical Instruments, Terra-Cotta, 13 In. 3360.00
Figurine, Amos, Andy & Son, Seated On Watermelon, Chalkware, Premium, 1930s, 7 1/2 In. 455.00
Figurine, Amos, Pewter, Hand Painted, Premium, 5 In. 120.00
Figurine, Angel, Chalkware, Painted, Exaggerated Features, Gold Highlights, 1920s, 4 1/2 In. 65.00
Figurine, Aunt Jemima, Hands On Hips, Iron, Hand Painted, Littco 950.00
Figurine, Banjo Neck, All Coons Look Alike To Me, Chalkware, 19 1/2 In. 270.00
Figurine, Black Boy Riding Gator Eating Watermelon, Bisque, Painted, Austria, 1890s, 6 In. 120.00
Figurine, Blackamoor, Serving Aristocrats, Porcelain, Hand Painted, 10 In. 95.00
Figurine, Boy Eating Watermelon, Bisque, 4 In. 56.00
Figurine, Boy Eating Watermelon, Celluloid, Arms Move, 5 In. 56.00
Figurine, Boy On Potty, Bisque, 3 In. 56.00
Figurine, Boy Smoking Pipe, Bisque, 5 In. 56.00
Figurine, Boy With Gator, Terra-Cotta, 8 In. 28.00
Figurine, Boy, Girl, Sitting In Rustic Chairs, Bisque, 5 In., Pair 56.00
Figurine, Cannibals & Teddy, Pottery, Painted, Gilner Pottery, 1951, 4 1/2 In., 2 Piece 55.00
Figurine, Children Under Palm Tree, Bisque, 5 In. 560.00
Figurine, Couple Eating Ice Cream, Bisque, 4 x 5 In. 168.00
Figurine, Dancing Couple, Bisque, 5 In. 112.00
Figurine, Dancing Rastus, Talking Machine Spinning Activates, Articulated, 7 In. 120.00
Figurine, Dream Of Paradise, Chickens Walk Into Smiling Black's Mouth, Chalk, 1910, 7 In. 160.00
Figurine, Fisherman, Porcelain, 5 In. 56.00
Figurine, Girl, Exaggerated, Dressed As A Lady, Picks Up Dress, Germany, 1890s, 9 In. 166.00
Figurine, Golliwog, On Watermelon, Painted, Folk Art, 8 In. 35.00
Figurine, Jockey In Tobacco Barrel, Terra-Cotta, Painted, Austria, 1880s, 7 In. 295.00
Figurine, Man In Clown Outfit, Bisque, 7 In. 28.00
Figurine, Minstrel, Bisque, 8 1/2 In., Pair 110.00
Figurine, Minstrel, Little Musician, Porcelain, Painted, Boy, Top Hat & Tails, Accordion, 4 In. 60.00
Figurine, Minstrel, Open Mouth, Playing Accordion, Bisque, Austria, 1890s, 4 1/2 In. 110.00
Figurine, Minstrel, Tree Branch Chair, Playing Cymbals, Bisque, Austria, 1880s, 6 1/2 In. 95.00
Figurine, Performing Coons, Dancing Darkies, Cardboard, 1900s, 6 In., 4 Piece 190.00
Figurine, Potty, Black & White Babies On Potty, Bisque, Hand Painted, Germany, 4 1/2 In. 85.00
Figurine, Seated Minstrel, Meissen, Bisque, Hand Painted, Austria, 1880s, 5 In. 105.00
Figurine, Slave Woman, Tambourine Banjo, Hand Carved, Mahogany, 1880s, 16 In. 210.00
Figurine, Snowflake, Bisque, Movable Eyes, Oscar Hitt, Germany, 2 7/8 In. 90.00
Figurine, Soldiers, Gambling, Exaggerated Features, Ceramic, Painted, Prewar, 5 1/2 In. 95.00
Figurine, Stork & Baby, Black Baby Pops Out Of Watermelon, Prewar, 8 1/2 In. 95.00
Game, Beat The Drums, Bakelite, Exaggerated Images, Electric Game Co., 1956, 4 3/4 In. 90.00
Game, Golliwog Ring Toss, Noddy's Ring, 11 Golliwog Pals, Spears, England, 1960, 13 In. 120.00
Game, Pinball, Uncle Remus, Brer Rabbit, Lithograph, Graphic Board, 16 In. 110.00
Game, Snake Eyes, Selchow & Richter, Box, 1950s, 14 1/2 In. 65.00
Hearth Brush, Golliwog, Sticking Out Tongue, Wood, Horsehair Bristles, 22 In. 1065.00
Humidor, Baby Crawling, Bare Bottom, Hand Painted, Terra-Cotta, Austria, 1880s, 5 1/4 In. 220.00
Humidor, Beer Drinking Black Boy, Ceramic, Majolica, Austria, 1880s, 7 1/2 In. 365.00
Humidor, Black Man Barrel Head, Bisque, Austria, 1880s, 4 1/2 In. 165.00
Humidor, Blackamoor, Ceramic, Hand Painted, 7 In. 120.00
Humidor, Boy's Head, Straw Hat, Bisque, 6 In. 225.00
Humidor, Bust, Smiling Boy Fez, Terra-Cotta, Bernard Bloch, Austria, 1880s, 5 1/2 In. 160.00
Humidor, Man, White Hat, 6 In. 505.00
Jigger, Articulated, Folk Art Arms, Swing Jointed, Floor Dancer, Early 1900s, 12 In. 95.00
Jug, Folk Art, Black Face, Exaggerated Features, Bug Eyes, Thick Lips, Black Ace Jug, 6 In. 45.00

Juicer, Man's Head, Wide Open Mouth, White Hat, Porcelain, Bavaria 195.00
Lamp, Chalkware, Barefoot Black Boy Carving Watermelon, 1870s, 15 In. 30.00
Lampshade, Family In Buckboard, 5 Black Cowboys In Rodeo, 6 1/2 In. 30.00
Lantern Set, Li'l Nigger Boys, 10 Derogatory Stories, Painted, England, 3 1/2 x 3 1/2 In. 140.00
Lighter, 2 Faces, Smirking Black Man, Mechanical, Silver Plated, Japan, Prewar, 3 1/4 In. 75.00
Makeup, Blackface Minstrel, Cardboard Aluminum Tube, Box, 1.25 Oz., 5 In. 60.00
Milk Bottle, Chocolate, Pyrograph, Smiling Black Kids, 9 1/2 In. 55.00
Minstrel Set, Die Cut, Paper Lithograph, Guitar, Accordion, Bone Player, 1880s, 3 Piece 55.00
Mug, Porcelain, Exaggerated Black Man, Melon Slice, Painted, Germany, 1900, 5 In. 110.00
Mug, Shaving, Ceramic, Painted, Exaggerated, Black Man, Singing, Bavaria, 1880s, 4 3/4 In. 188.00
Nodder, Bellhop, Big Ears, Blue Shirt, White Pants, Red Cap, Bisque, Prewar Japan, 3 3/4 In. 111.00
Nodder, Black Boy, Grinning, Hand On Hip, Posable Head, 1920s, 3 1/2 In. 85.00
Nodder, Pickaninny, Riding Turtle, Head, Tail Move, Bisque, Painted, Japan, Prewar, 4 In. 110.00
Nodder, Schoolboy, Barefoot Black Student, Bisque, Hand Painted, 5 1/2 In. 166.00
Nodder, Schoolboy, Holding Chalkboard, Hand Painted, Bisque, Austria, 1880s, 5 1/2 In. 110.00
Paint Box, Circus, Golliwogs, Lithograph, Children With Animals, 14 In. 35.00
Pencil Box, Koh-I-Noor, Black Man, Spear & Shield, Cardboard, Lithograph, 7 1/4 In. 105.00
Pipe Tamper, Hagenhaur, Brass, Deco Figure, Exaggerated Naked Boy, Austria, 2 3/4 In. 85.00
Pitcher, Mammy, Porcelain, Crossed Bug Eyes, Exaggerated Features, Germany, 3 1/4 In. 90.00
Pitcher, Pickaninny, Exaggerated Bug-Eyed Golliwog, Schafer & Vater, 1880s, 3 1/2 In. 135.00
Pitcher, Sambo & Molly, Gold Trimmed Top, Painted, Regal Pottery, 3 1/4 In. 145.00
Planter, Babies On Log, Ceramic, Hand Painted, Germany, 1920s, 6 3/4 In. 90.00
Planter, Li'l Black Boy, Runs From Angry Turkey, Porcelain, Japan, 1920s, 4 In. 30.00
Planter, Li'l Black Boy, Walks Down Street With Sausages, Porcelain, Japan, 1920s, 4 In. 30.00
Plaque, Pickaninny Baby, Pottery, Relief Face, Scared Black Baby, 4 1/4 In. 45.00
Plaque, Sambo, Grinning, Ceramic, Exaggerated Big Lips, Bug-Eyed, Grinning, 5 1/2 In. 55.00
Plate, Currier & Ives, Loading Cotton On The Miss., Slave Working & Dancing, 1940s, 10 In. 85.00
Plate, Grinning Black Man, Exaggerated, New Orleans Souvenir, Germany, 1890, 3 1/4 In. 166.00
Plate, Little Niggers, Under Tree, Fallen Coconut, 1900s, 5 1/2 In. 156.00
Plate, Nursery, Black Hunter, Bird On Rifle, Where's Dat Bird?, England, 1920s, 5 1/2 In. 100.00
Poster, Minstrel, Knights Of Columbus Catholic Daughters, Cardboard Litho, 1916, 21 In. 380.00
Puppet, Clown, Wood, Jointed, Painted, Cloth Coat Over Vest, Striped Pants, 28 1/2 In. 1840.00
Puppet, Minstrel, Wood, Carved, Painted, Articulated Head, Arms, Legs, Box, 14 In. 105.00
Puppet, Wood, Painted, Hinged Knees & Elbows, Cloth Shirt & Pants, 13 In. 1095.00
Puzzle, Boo Boogey Mans, 3 Missionaries Stranded With 3 Cannibals, Cardboard, Box, 4 In. 70.00
Puzzle, Dixie Pickaninny, Cabin Scene, Black, Melons, Pigs, Cardboard Lithograph, 10 In. 75.00
Puzzle, Golliwog & Friends, Fuzzy The Fireman, Paper Lithograph, Wood, Box, 8 In. 40.00
Puzzle, Golliwog, Arm & Leg Torn Off By Pit Bull Puppy, Wood, Painted, Box, 6 1/2 In. 30.00
Puzzle, Golliwog, Moon Express Meets Moon Man, Paper Lithograph, Wood, Box, 8 In. 40.00
Puzzle, Negertjes, The Niggers, Sambo Scene, Wood, Simplex Holland, 1930s, 8 In. Diam. 147.00
Rattle, Black Baby's Head, Celluloid, Painted, Germany, 1900s, 6 In. 135.00
Salt Spoon, Sterling Silver, Embossed, Grinning Boy Eating Watermelon, Early 1900s, 2 In. 95.00
Slave Bracelet, Brass, England, c.1700-1820, 2 3/4 In. 55.00
Smoke Set, Black Boy Holding Assorted Baskets, Porcelain, Hand Painted, 12 3/4 In. 370.00
Smoke Set, Black Boy Offering Cheroots, Bisque, Hand Painted, Austria, 1880, 8 In. 345.00
Smoke Set, Black Boy On Log, Hand Painted, Hat Holds Matches, Germany, 1880s, 8 In. 185.00
Smoke Set, Black Jockey, On Fence, Holds Cigarillos, Majolica, 1880s, 6 3/4 In. 245.00
Smoke Set, Ceramic, Black Man, On Knees, Matches Come Out Behind, 1890s, 5 In. 135.00
Smoke Set, Cigar Dispenser, Black Minstrel, Bamboo Holders, Majolica, 1880s, 8 1/2 In. 190.00
Smoke Set, Cigar Smoking Boy, Sitting On Pillow & Rug, Ceramic, Hand Painted, Majolica, 1880s . 105.00
Smoke Set, Minstrel, Playing Accordion, Leaf Covered Baskets, Bisque, Austria, 1880s, 8 In. 266.00
Smoke Set, Nubian Queen, Leaning On Wall, Majolica, Austria, 1880s, 5 3/4 In. 305.00
Smoke Set, Sleeping Boy Holding Pipe, Log Ashtray, Majolica, 1880s, 6 In. 290.00
Smoke Set, Watermelon Boy, Match Holder & Strike, Ceramic, Painted, Austria, 1880s, 7 1/2 In. . 314.00
Smoke Stand, Black Man Eating Watermelon, 3 Baskets, Ceramic, Painted, Austria, 1880s, 6 In. . 300.00
Smoke Stand, Girl With Vase, Seated, Blue Hat, Ceramic, Hand Painted, Austria, 1880s, 7 In. 266.00
Soap, Light & Shade, Using Dreydoppel Soap From Black To White, c.1892, 5 1/2 In. 120.00
Spoon, Helena Ark, Twisted Handle, Embossed Torso, Grinning Black Man, Alligator, 6 In. 120.00
Spoon, Sterling, 3 Coons, Louisiana, Landmarks, State Seal, Engraved, Embossed, 1900s, 4 In. .. 120.00
Spoon, Sterling, Enamel, Boy, Peach Tree, Melon Bowl, Charles Crankshaw, 1900s, 4 In. 222.00

Spoon, Sterling, Enamel, Boy, Watermelon, Slave, Cotton Bale, Engraved, Marion, S.C., 1900s, 4 In. 180.00
Spoon, Sterling, Engraved, Black Boy Eating Melon, Alligator, On Handle, 1908, 5 3/4 In. 166.00
Spoon, Sterling, Engraved, Grinning Boy Eating Watermelon, On Handle, 1900s, 2 1/4 In. 120.00
Spoon, Sterling, Engraved, New Orleans & Alligator, Sleeping Black Man, 1900s, 4 1/4 In. 175.00
Spoon, Sterling, Engraved, Who Said Watermelon, Black Boy On Fence, 1900s, 4 In. 166.00
Spoon, Sterling, Grinning Man, Cotton, Alligator, Helena, Ark., Twisted Handle, 1900s, 5 3/4 In. 166.00
Spoon, Sterling, Old Kentucky Home, Gilbert Verso, Engraved, Triton & Girardet, 1901, 5 3/4 In. 150.00
Tin, Candy, Graphic Logo, Black Boy In Ornate Bellboy Uniform, Fruit Tray, 9 1/4 In. 95.00
Tin, Pancake, Aunt Jemima, Quaker Limited Edition, 1983, 6 In. 13.00
Toothbrush, Deluxe Darkie, Smiling Minstrel On Label, Regular, Unopened, 6 1/2 In. 20.00
Toothpick, Coon Chicken Inn, Bell Hop's Head, M.L. Graham, 6 In. 165.00
Vase, Black Milkmaid, Standing Under Fruit Tree, Bisque, Hand Painted, Austria, 1890s, 4 3/4 In. 121.00

BLENKO GLASS COMPANY is the 1930s successor to several glassworks founded by William John Blenko in Milton, West Virginia. In 1933, his son, William H. Blenko Sr., took charge. The company made a line of reproductions for Colonial Williamsburg. They are still in business and are best known today for their decorative wares and stained glass.

Ashtray, Orange Yellow Amber, Ridged, 2 x 6 In. 12.00
Barber Bottle, Clear Crackle Glass, Hobs, Screw-On Metal Cap, 8 In. 45.00
Beaker, Clear Crackle, 4 Ruby Red Leaves, c.1950, 7 1/4 In. 125.00
Beaker, Clear Crackle, 4 Turquoise Blue Leaves, Pontil, 9 1/2 x 6 In. 135.00
Bowl, Clear Crackle, Applied Blue Raspberries, Pontil, 2 1/2 x 11 1/2 In. 115.00
Bowl, Green, Footed, 6 1/2 x 16 In. 145.00
Bowl, Orange, Crackle, Hand Blown, Ruffled Edge, 4 x 8 1/2 In. 45.00
Cake Plate, Clear, Sunflower, 3-Footed, 13 In. 35.00
Cooler, Wine, Cowboy Hat Shape, 7 1/2 x 16 In. 75.00
Decanter, Crackle, Amethyst, No. 920, Winslow Anderson, 1950s, 22 3/4 In. 295.00
Figurine, Owl, Amber, Sticker, 7 x 5 1/2 In. 75.00
Lamp, Dark Olive Green, 3-In. Finial, 28 1/4 x 11 In. 395.00
Paperweight, Mushroom, Green Yellow, 3 1/2 x 4 1/2 In. 45.00
Pitcher, Amber, Crackle, 6 In. 38.00
Pitcher, Amber, Crackle, 9 In. 75.00
Pitcher, Emerald Green, Double Side Spouts, c.1960, 8 x 6 1/4 x 3 In. 45.00
Pitcher, Tangerine, Joel Meyers, c.1950, 9 1/2 In. 65.00
Pitcher, Tangerine, Optic, 10 1/2 In. 95.00
Tile, Green, 8 x 8 In. 25.00
Vase, Amber, Tortoiseshell, 13 x 8 In. 100.00
Vase, Amberina, Pulled, Twisted, 20 x 8 In. 150.00
Vase, Aqua Blue, Vertical Lines, Buttons At Base, Horizontal Waves, Pulled Rim, 33 In. 200.00
Vase, Crackle, 3 Applied Yellow Rosettes, 7 1/2 x 4 1/4 In. 110.00
Vase, Crackle, 4 Applied Blue Rosettes, 9 1/2 x 7 1/2 x 7 1/2 In. 135.00
Vase, Ear, Crackle Glass, Vertical Ribs, 1950s, 7 1/2 x 5 In. 325.00
Vase, Globe, Topaz, No. 9632, 10 In. 85.00
Vase, Hat Shape, Crackle, Green, Foil Sticker, 2 1/2 x 4 1/2 In. 59.00
Vase, Lavender, Pulled Rim, 1960s, 40 In. 250.00
Vase, Olive Green, Pulled Asymmetrical Rim, Diamond Base, 36 In. 200.00
Vase, Sea Green, Applied Twists, 11 x 6 In. 75.00
Vase, Wheat, 12 x 8 In. 60.00

BLOWN GLASS, see Glass-Blown category.

BLUE GLASS, see Cobalt Blue category.

BLUE ONION, see Onion category.

BLUE WILLOW, see Willow category.

BOCH FRERES factory was founded in 1841 in La Louviere in eastern Belgium. The wares resemble the work of Villeroy & Boch. The factory is still in business.

Bathroom Set, 1920s, 10-In. Pitcher, 14-In. Bowl, 2 1/2 x 5-In. Soap Dish, 9-In. Dish 600.00
Bowl, Center, Ormolu Mounted, Earthenware, France, Early 1900s, 14 1/2 In. 353.00

Bowl, Deer, Blue, Green, White, Charles Catteau, c.1925, 11 In., Pair 2400.00
Bowl, Large Red, Yellow, Blue Flowers, Painted Over Glaze, Low, Keramis, 11 In. 130.00
Bowl, Teardrop Shape, Art Deco, Black, Gold Stripes, Red Spots, 5 1/2 x 9 1/2 In. 75.00
Box, Leaves, Crackle Ground, Rectangular, Charles Catteau, c.1925, 5 1/2 In. 285.00
Garniture, Jar, Cover, Vases, Delft Flowers, c.1860, 11 1/2-In. Jar, 3 Piece 285.00
Platter, Deer, Blue, Green, White, Charles Catteau, c.1925, 15 In., Pair 1800.00
Tile, Heraldic Eagles, Indigo, Yellow, Brown, Cuerda Seca, Green, 8 In., Pair 118.00
Vase, 4 Antelopes, Leaves, Grass, Enamel, Crackle Ground, Marked, 9 In. 1725.00
Vase, Antelopes, Crackle Ground, Flat Sides, 9 1/4 In. 1265.00
Vase, Black & White Spirals, Green & Blue Marbleized Ground, Charles Catteau, 7 In. 400.00
Vase, Deer, Blue, Green, White, Charles Catteau, c.1925, 9 1/4 In., Pair 1200.00
Vase, Deer, Blue, Green, White, Charles Catteau, c.1925, 13 In., Pair 1920.00
Vase, Deer, Blue, Green, White, Charles Catteau, c.1925, 19 1/4 In., Pair 4200.00
Vase, Egg Shape, Ruffled Rim, Loop & Dot Design, Brown, Cream, 1920s, 10 In. 245.00
Vase, Egg Shape, Ruffled Rim, Loop & Dot Design, Cream, Peach, 1920s, 10 In. 264.00
Vase, Embossed Overlapping Fans, Ivory Glaze, Signed, 11 1/2 In. 125.00
Vase, Flowers, Mottled, Ivory, Brown, Art Deco, Belgium, 11 1/2 x 7 1/2 In. 885.00
Vase, Incised, Vertical Bands, Circles, Charles Catteau, 1920s, 9 1/2 In. 660.00
Vase, Multicolored Stylized Flowers, Signed, Art Deco, 10 1/2 In. 300.00
Vase, Oxblood, Metal Mount, Logo, 11 1/2 In., Pair 374.00
Vase, Pillow, Art Deco, Cuerda Seca, Turquoise, Indigo Deer, White Ground, 9 In. 705.00
Vase, Stylized Flowers, Yellow Ground, Signed, Art Deco, 6 1/2 In. 255.00

BOEHM is the collector's name for the porcelains of Edward Marshall Boehm. In 1953 the Osso China Company was reorganized as Edward Marshall Boehm, Inc. The company is still working in England and New Jersey. In the early days of the factory, dishes were made, but the elaborate and lifelike bird figurines are the best-known ware. Edward Marshall Boehm, the founder, died in 1961, but the firm has continued to design and produce porcelain. Today, the firm makes both limited and unlimited editions of figurines and plates.

Bowl, Fluted, White, No. 705, Late 1950s, 3 x 11 In. 125.00
Figurine, Arabian Camel & Calf, Bisque, 1978, 13 1/4 x 12 1/2 In. 1170.00
Figurine, Arctic Tern, Limited Edition, No. 78, 19 x 22 In. 819.00
Figurine, Baby Blue Jay, No. 436, 4 1/2 In. ....135.00 to 165.00
Figurine, Barn Owl, American Owl Collection, Bisque, 5 1/4 In. 117.00
Figurine, Chickadee, Holly Branch, No. 40427, 5 1/2 In. 320.00
Figurine, Chipmunk, Sitting, 3 In. 250.00
Figurine, Crested Flycatcher On Sweetgum, No. 488, 18 3/4 In. 600.00
Figurine, Dogwood Branch, No. 300-45, 12 In. 300.00
Figurine, Giant Panda, 1974, 6 In. 225.00
Figurine, Goldfinch Chick, No. 448, 4 1/2 In. 140.00
Figurine, Junco, 2 Birds, Branches With Berries, Snow, No. 400-12, 11 1/2 In. 350.00
Figurine, Kingfisher, Bisque, 9 x 9 In. 410.00
Figurine, Lion, Lying Down, Crossed Front Paws, 8 1/2 In. 235.00
Figurine, Mallards, Bisque, No. 406, 10 3/4 In., Pair 530.00
Figurine, Owl, 24K Gold Glaze, Diamond Eyes, 1978-80, 4 1/2 In. 500.00
Figurine, Panda, Cub, Bamboo, Bisque, Oriental Wooden Base, c.1974, 6 In. 230.00
Figurine, Peace Rose, Bisque, 5 x 9 In. 205.00
Figurine, Queen Elizabeth Roses Branch, No. 37, 1980, 7 In. 175.00
Figurine, Rabbits, Bisque, 5 1/2 & 3 1/2 In., Pair 235.00
Figurine, Ring Necked Pheasants, Bisque, Limited Edition, No. 409, 8 1/2 x 12 1/2 In., Pair 527.00
Figurine, Roufous Hummingbirds On Icelandic Poppy, No. 487, 14 3/4 In. 500.00
Figurine, Royal Duet, Roses, Bisque, Limited Edition, 6 1/4 x 6 In. 235.00
Figurine, Tree Peony, Bisque, 7 x 8 In. 470.00
Figurine, Varied Buntings, No. 481, 22 In. 750.00
Figurine, Verdins, Birds In Branches, No. 400-02, 1969, 9 In. 675.00
Figurine, Wood Thrush, No. 4445, 4 1/4 In. 125.00
Figurine Set, Wise Men, Bethlehem Collection, 3 Piece 450.00
Plaque, Coach & Four, W. Smith Leeds, Horse Drawn Carriage, Frame, 11 x 13 3/4 In. 643.00
Plate, Brandy, Roses Of Excellence, Gold Rim, Hamilton Collection, 1983, 11 In. 60.00

Plate, Canvasback, Water Birds Of North America, Box, 1981, 11 In. 60.00
Plate, Eastern Chipmunks, Woodland Wildlife, Blue & Gold Border, Lenox, 1976, 10 3/4 In. 66.00
Plate, Peace Rose, Award Winning Roses, 10 3/4 In. .... 28.00 to 78.00
Plate, Prairie Grouse, Gold Rim, Game Birds Of North America, 11 In. 56.00
Plate, Raccoons, Woodland Wildlife, Gold & Blue Border, Lenox, 1973, 11 In. 60.00
Plate, Raccoons, Woodland Wildlife, Gold & Blue Border, Lenox, Box, 1973, 11 In. 80.00
Plate, Snowy Owl, Hamilton Collection, Box, 11 In. 45.00
Plate, Willow Partridge, Gold Rim, Game Birds Of North America, 11 In. 56.00

BOHEMIAN GLASS, see Glass-Bohemian.

BONE includes those articles made of bone not listed elsewhere in this book.

Fid, Whalebone, Macrame, Ring Turned, Fist Finial, Sailor Made, 1800s, 3 5/8 x 3/8 In. 60.00
Figurine, Basket Seller, Oval Base, Chinese, 1900s, 12 1/2 x 7 In. 470.00
Figurine, Fisherman On Sea Dragon, Fish, Pole, Hat, Pipe, Pouch, 21 1/2 x 17 1/2 x 28 In. 1095.00
Group, 2 Mythical Figures Riding Sea Turtle, Wood Base, 22 1/4 x 11 1/4 x 16 1/2 In. 750.00
Pie Crimper, Fluted Wheel, Decorated Handle, 1800s, 6 1/4 In. 110.00

BONE DISHES were considered a necessary part of a table setting for the Victorian table. The crescent-shaped dish was kept at the edge of the dinner plate so the bones removed from the fish could be stored away from the uneaten food. Some bone dishes were made in more fanciful shapes and many resemble fish.

Branches & Leaves, Inset Landscape, Brown Transfer, Edge, Malkin & Co., Burslem, England, 6 In. 20.00
Chintz, Red Transfer, 6 1/4 In. 22.00
Fish, Blue & White, Gold Trim, 4 1/2 x 3 1/2 In. 35.00
Fish, Purple & Gold Border, Shaped Edge, Continental, 6 x 4 1/2 In. 52.00
Fish, Underwater Landscape, Fishing Net, Coral, Painted, Raised Gold Trim, 6 3/4 In. 20.00
Floral Transfer, Brown, Edge, Malkin & Co., Burslem, England, c.1885, 7 In. 18.00
Green Flowers, Beaded & Scrolled Border, W.H. Grindley & Co., 6 3/4 x 4 In., 4 Piece 23.00
LaBelle, Flow Blue, Wheeling, 1893-1910, 6 3/8 x 3 3/8 In. 125.00

BOOKENDS have probably been used since books became inexpensive. Early libraries kept books in cupboards, not on open shelves. By the 1870s bookends appeared, especially homemade fret-carved wooden examples. Most bookends listed in this book date from the twentieth century. Bookends are also listed in other categories by manufacturer or material. All bookends listed here are pairs.

Abraham Lincoln, Iron, 6 x 4 1/4 In. 40.00
Abraham Lincoln, Lincoln Memorial, Copper Clad, Jennings Brothers, 7 In. 230.00
Airplane Glider, White Metal, 5 3/8 x 6 1/2 In. 110.00
American Eagle, Iron, Gilt, 7 x 5 In. 35.00
Amish Man & Woman, Iron, Painted, 4 1/2 In. 80.00
Anvil Shape, Bronze, Carl Aubock, Austria, 3 3/4 x 6 1/4 In. 1121.00
Boxer, Bradley & Hubbard, 1930s, 5 3/4 In. 395.00
Boy Reading, Cast Iron, 5 1/4 x 6 5/8 In. 30.00
Cannon, Brass, Mahogany Base, 5 1/2 In. 145.00
Cape Cod Fisherman, Patinated Iron, Connecticut Mfg. Co., 5 1/2 In. 69.00
Cherub Leaning On Book, White Metal, 6 1/4 In. 50.00
Clown, White Metal, 6 5/8 x 3 1/4 In. 140.00
Dante, Patinated Iron, Bradley & Hubbard, 5 3/4 In. 35.00
Dante & Beatrice, Electroformed, Armor Bronze Co., 7 In. 46.00
Discus Thrower, Copper Clad, Jenning Brothers, 7 In. 90.00
Dog, Cocker Spaniel, Red Painted Collar, Hubley, 6 1/4 In. 193.00
Dog, Russian Wolfhound, Iron, 5 1/4 x 6 1/8 In. 140.00
Dog, Scottie, Cast Iron, Marked, No. 5217, 5 x 5 In. .... *ILLUS* 28.00
Dog, Seated, Bronzed Plaster, 8 1/2 In. 265.00
Dog, Setter, At Point, Iron, 4 1/4 x 5 1/2 In. 224.00
Dog, Setter, At Point, Iron, Painted, Hubley, 8 In. 160.00
Dog, Wirehair Fox Terrier, Iron, Bradley & Hubbard, 5 3/8 x 9 1/2 In. 112.00
Dog, Wirehair Fox Terrier, Iron, Hubley, 5 x 5 3/4 In. 225.00

Bookends, Dog, Scottie, Cast Iron, Marked, No. 5217, 5 x 5 In.

Bookends, Dutch Couple, Kissing, Cast Iron, Marked, Hubley, No. 332, 4 3/4 x 4 1/2 In.

Dutch Couple, Kissing, Cast Iron, Marked, Hubley, No. 332, 4 3/4 x 4 1/2 In. .... *ILLUS* 196.00
Dutch Milkmaid, Plated Iron, 6 1/2 In. 46.00
Edgar Allan Poe, Cast Iron, Bradley & Hubbard, 6 1/8 x 4 1/8 In. 1456.00
Egyptian Head, Composition, Hand Painted, Gilded, Hirsh, 8 1/4 x 4 1/2 In. 165.00
Egyptian Temple, Patinated Iron, Bradley & Hubbard, 5 In. 69.00
Elephant, Bronze, Wood Base, Brass Plate, 20th Century, 10 7/8 x 6 In. 7800.00
Elephant Head, Bronze, Brown Patina, B. Johnson, c.1927, 6 x 4 1/2 In. 1880.00
Eve, Brass, 7 1/8 x 6 1/8 In. 280.00
Falcon, Alabaster, 7 In. 45.00
Flower Basket, Chrysanthemum, Iron, 6 1/4 x 4 1/2 In. 390.00
Fountain, Cast Iron, 5 3/4 x 4 In. 28.00
Geometric, Brass, Chased, Repousse, Robert R. Jarvie, 5 x 6 In. 675.00
Girl, Reading, Cast Iron, 5 1/2 x 6 1/8 In. 28.00
Golfer, Swinging, Caddy, Iron, 5 1/2 x 3 3/4 In. 85.00
Hammered Copper, Tooled Medallion, Old Mission Koppercraft, 5 In. 270.00
Hands, Brass, Carl Aubock, c.1950, 5 In. 1080.00
Horse, Iron, 6 x 6 In. 35.00
Huckleberry Finn, Iron, 12 1/4 x 9 3/8 In. 1456.00
Indian, Holding Spear, Bronzed Metal, JB 1699, 9 1/2 In. 345.00
Indian, Kneeling, Dog, Spelter, Bronze Patina, C. Vieth, c.1900, 7 x 5 1/2 x 5 1/2 In. 835.00
John Alden Figure, Puritan, Bronze, Patinated, 9 In. 380.00
Library, Bookshelves, Iron, 5 1/8 x 4 3/8 In. 336.00
Lily Pad, Cattails, L-Shape, Bronze, McClelland Barclay, 4 1/4 x 3 x 3 3/4 In. 259.00
Lion, Lying Down, Bradley & Hubbard 86.00
Lion, Standing, Bronze, Gift House, Inc., 5 3/4 In. 46.00
Man, Woman, Oriental, Fan, Bronze, 4 3/4 In. 69.00
Medallion, Minerva, Relief, Plated Iron, 4 3/4 In. 25.00
Monkeys, Copper Overlay, Bronze Finish, 4 1/2 In., Pair 59.00
Muse Of Drama, Iron, Hubley, 5 3/4 In. 50.00
Nude Dancers, White Metal, Patinated, 4 1/2 In. 58.00
Nymph, Dryad, Hubley, 5 1/2 x 4 1/2 In. 250.00
Owl, On Book, Metal, Patinated, 1900s, 12 1/4 In. 295.00
Pegasus, Brass, 7 1/2 In. 86.00
Reading Girl, Midfield Parish Design, Blue Dress, Black Base, 6 x 5 3/4 In. 88.00
Science, Study, Patinated Iron, 5 3/4 In. 46.00
Sea Gull, Waves, White Metal, Patinated, 7 1/4 In. 80.00
Victory, Bronze, 5 In. 58.00
Village Blacksmith, Bronze, 5 In. 40.00
Whipper Inn, Hubley, 4 3/4 In. 50.00
Woman, Curtseying, Iron, 7 1/2 In. 196.00
Woman, Nude, Dancing, Tambourine, Copper Electroplated, Iron, 5 1/4 x 5 1/4 In. 448.00
Woman, Nude, Greyhounds, Iron, 7 In. 505.00

Woman, Nude, Holding Books, Earthenware, Brown Glaze, R.P. Bringhurst, c.1900, 6 1/2 In. 575.00
Woman, Nude, Holding Drape, Brass Electroplated, Iron, 6 3/4 In. 140.00
Woman, Nude, In Clouds, Iron, 5 3/4 x 5 1/2 In. 196.00
Zinnias, Embossed, Iron, 5 1/4 In. 85.00

BOOKMARKS were originally made of parchment, cloth, or leather. Soon woven silk ribbon, thin cardboard, celluloid, wood, silver, tortoiseshell, and metals were used. Examples made before 1850 are scarce, but there are many to be found dating before 1920.

Comfort Soap, It's All Right, Child, Wearing Glass, Reading Book, 7 x 2 In. 34.00
Eat Egg-O-See, Aluminum, Heart Shape, 2 x 2 1/2 In. 40.00
Hoyt's German Cologne, Child, White Hat, Rubifoam For Teeth, E.W. Hoyt & Co., 4 1/2 In. 9.00
Kirk Johnson & Co., Pianos & Organs, Lebanon, Pa., Girl, Dress, Roses, Victorian, 6 x 2 In. 15.00
Montana, Souvenir, Brass, Enamel, Case, 3 1/2 x 1 1/2 In. 17.00
Mrs. Tiggy-Winkle, Beatrix Potter, Woven Silk, Cash's Of England, Unopened, 8 1/2 In. 12.00
Rabbit, Toye Kenning & Spencer, Box, England, 3 1/2 x 1 1/4 In. 40.00
Sandalwood, Elephant Finial, 2 1/2 In. 20.00
TV Guide, Television Set, Knobs, Metal 65.00
Washington, Evergreen, Chinook Words, Silk, c.1900, 1 7/8 x 6 1/2 In. 30.00
World Confederation For Physical Therapy, Sterling Silver, 3 7/8 x 3/4 In. 110.00

BOSSONS character wall masks (heads), plaques, figurines, and other decorative pieces are made by W.H. Bossons, Limited of Congleton, England. The company was founded in 1946 and closed in 1996. Dates shown are the date the item was introduced.

BOSSONS

Plaque, Chrysanthemum, 14 In. 55.00
Plaque, Raccoon In Tree, 12 1/4 x 4 In. 65.00
Wall Figure, Peon, 1963 ..... 275.00
Wall Mask, Abduhl 100.00
Wall Mask, Albanian ..... 35.00 to 100.00
Wall Mask, Beefeater, 1960 ..... 125.00
Wall Mask, Betsy Trotwood, 1964 ..... 100.00
Wall Mask, Bill Sikes, 1981 ..... 100.00
Wall Mask, Chef 105.00
Wall Mask, Cheyenne, Red Jacket, Box 180.00
Wall Mask, Coolie, 1963 ..... 105.00 to 149.00
Wall Mask, Eskimo 105.00
Wall Mask, Himalayan, 1966, 5 x 3 1/2 x 2 In. 39.00
Wall Mask, Jock, 5 1/2 In. ..... 48.00 to 65.00
Wall Mask, Mr. Pickwick, 1964 ..... 65.00 to 125.00
Wall Mask, Old Salt, 1971, 5 x 4 x 3 In. 39.00
Wall Mask, Oldtimer, 1977 ..... 80.00
Wall Mask, Paddy, 1969 ..... 100.00
Wall Mask, Persian, 5 In. ..... 30.00 to 110.00
Wall Mask, Rawhide, 1967, 6 1/2 In. 65.00
Wall Mask, Romany, Man, Playing Accordion, 1st Model 200.00
Wall Mask, Saracen, 1960, 7 In. ..... 100.00 to 165.00
Wall Mask, Sarah Gamp, 1964 ..... 100.00
Wall Mask, Scrooge, 1981 ..... 100.00
Wall Mask, Sikh, 1966 ..... 100.00
Wall Mask, Welsh Lady, 1966 ..... 110.00

BOSTON & SANDWICH CO. pieces may be found in the Lutz and Sandwich Glass categories.

BOTTLE collecting has become a major American hobby. There are several general categories of bottles, such as historic flasks, bitters, household, and figural. ABM means the bottle was made by an automatic bottle machine after 1903. Pyro is the shortened form of the word *pyroglaze,* an enameled lettering used on bottles after the mid-1930s. This form of decoration is also called ACL or applied color label. For more bottle prices, see the book *Kovels' Bottles Price List* by Ralph and Terry Kovel.

Avon started in 1886 as the California Perfume Company. It was not until 1929 that the name *Avon* was used. In 1939, it became Avon Products, Inc. Avon has made many figural bottles filled with cosmetic products. Ceramic, plastic, and glass bottles were made in limited editions.

Avon, Alaskan Moose After Shave, 1974 .... 14.00
Avon, Bay Rum After Shave, Anniversary Bottle, Box, 1981, 5 In. 10.00
Avon, Betsy Ross, Sonnet Cologne, Contents, 1976, 5 1/2 In. 12.00
Avon, Collectors Club Convention, Pottery, Box, 1973, 6 1/4 In. 60.00
Avon, Decanter, Bell, Cotillion Cologne, 1968, 5 In. 12.00
Avon, Decanter, Old-Time Radio, Liquid Hair Lotion, 1972, 5 Oz., 4 3/4 In. 10.00
Avon, Little Bo Peep, Sweet Honesty Cologne 10.00
Avon, Skin Freshener, Purple, Box, 4 Oz. 20.00
Barber, Amethyst, Gold, Yellow Enamel, Pontil, Tooled Rolled Lip, Art Nouveau, 7 3/4 In. 210.00
Barber, Bay Rum, Milk Glass, Hand Painted, 9 In. 125.00
Barber, Bay Rum, Milk Glass, Painted Multicolored Flowers, Cylindrical, Pontil, 8 1/2 In. 415.00
Barber, Bay Rum, White, Flowers, Crown Top, Stopper, 10 In. 140.00
Barber, Blue Latticinio, Turquoise Stripes, Flared Lip, Porcelain Spout, Pontil, 8 1/2 In. 210.00
Barber, Blue Opalescent, Spiral Ribs, Polished Pontil, 6 3/4 In. 450.00
Barber, Blue, White Looping, Nailsea Type, 7 1/4 In. 140.00
Barber, Bohemian Style, Ruby Red To Clear 250.00
Barber, Brilliantine, Cobalt Blue, Ribs, Orange, Yellow, Enamel, Ground Lip, Metal Cap, 4 3/8 In. .. 90.00
Barber, Children Playing Badminton, Cobalt Blue, Mary Gregory Type, 8 1/4 In., Pair 420.00
Barber, Cobalt Blue, Bird, Flowers, Leaves, Gold Paint, Silvertone Metal Top, 8 3/4 In. 195.00
Barber, Cobalt Blue, Gold, Yellow Enamel, Pontil, Tooled Rolled Lip, Art Nouveau, 7 3/4 In. 225.00
Barber, Fishnet Ribs, White, Blue, Red, Green, Pontil, Tooled Lip, 8 3/4 In. 125.00
Barber, Fishnet Ribs, White, Red, Venetian Glass, Pontil, Tooled Lip, 8 3/4 In. 125.00
Barber, Frosted Amber, T. Noonan & Co., Barbers Supplies, 9 In. 176.00
Barber, Hobnail, Amethyst, 7 In. 245.00
Barber, Milk Glass, Multicolored Flowers, Opalescent, Hair Tonic, Cylindrical, 8 5/8 In. 300.00
Barber, Milk Glass, Opalescent, Multicolored Flowers, Toilet Water, Pontil, 8 1/2 In. 440.00
Barber, Milk Glass, Painted Multicolored Flowers, Metal Closure, 10 3/8 In. 450.00
Barber, Millefiori, Bulbous, Long Neck, Stopper, 9 In. 190.00
Barber, Millefiori, Green, Puce, Flared Lip, Porcelain Spout, Pontil, 8 1/2 In. 275.00
Barber, Millefiori, Red Ground, Flared Lip, Porcelain Spout, 8 1/2 In. 275.00
Barber, Millefiori, Red, Green, Blue, Pink, Flared Lip, Porcelain Spout, Pontil, 8 1/2 In. 250.00
Barber, Pink & White, Fluted, Bulbous, 9 In. 200.00
Barber, Pink & White, Swirled To Left, 4-Sided, 10 1/2 In. 385.00
Barber, Pink Opalescent, Ribs, Bulbous, 8 1/2 In. 300.00
Barber, Porcelain, Painted Multicolored Flowers, Flanged Lip, Square, 8 3/4 In. 50.00
Barber, Purple Amethyst, White Enamel, Ribs, Pontil, Sheared, Tooled Lip, 1885-1925, 7 7/8 In. .. 190.00
Barber, Rainbow Millefiori, Flared Lip, Pontil, 8 1/2 In. 210.00
Barber, Vaseline, Opalescent & Flower Design, Silvertone Top, 8 1/2 In. 195.00
Barber, White Latticinio, Multicolored Stripes, Flared Lip, Porcelain Spout, 8 1/2 In. 220.00
Barber, White, Blue Bow & Letters, Red Stripes, Flared Lip, Shampoo, 9 In. 30.00
Barber, Yellow & White, Swirled To Left, Bulbous, 8 1/2 In. 385.00
Barber, Yellow Green, Gold, Yellow Enamel, Pontil, Tooled Rolled Lip, Art Nouveau, 7 3/4 In. 225.00
Beam, Model A, Ford, 1928 Model, Sport Coupe, Box 125.00
Beam, Oregon Centennial, Beaver, Trees, River, Fisherman, 1959 .... 25.00
Beer, A. Gettelman Brewing Co., Private Mold, Machine Crown, Wis., Pt., 9 1/2 In. 5.00
Beer, A.B.C. Sparkling Lager, E.C. Rosche, Albany, N.Y., Blob Top, 1894, 14 Oz. 50.00
Beer, Alabama Brewing Co., San Francisco, Amber, Hutchinson, Split 50.00
Beer, Albion Burnell & Co., S.F. Brewery, 7Up Green, Crown Top, Split 650.00
Beer, Alpen Brau Beer, Columbia Brewing Company, Paper Label, Qt. 15.00
Beer, Anchor Brewing Co., San Francisco, Special Christmas Ale, 1987 .... 10.00
Beer, Anheuser-Busch, Amber, Sloping Collar, Split 1000.00
Beer, Anheuser-Busch, Logo, Eagle, A, Harrisburg Bottling Works, Amber, Crown Top 39.00
Beer, Ballantine's Extra Porter, Green, 1914, Bomber Size, 22 Oz. 85.00
Beer, Bay View Brewing Co., Seattle, Wash., Green 225.00
Beer, Berkshire Ale, Green, Yellow ACL, 1955, 8 Oz. 3.00

Beer, Blatz, Private Mold, Embossed, Machine Crown, Wis., 1/2 Pt., 8 3/4 In. 2.00
Beer, Bohemian Bock, Spokane, Wash., c.1938 .... 30.00
Beer, Brown Stout, B, Grass Green, Applied Sloping Collar, Iron Pontil, 6 5/8 In. 112.00
Beer, Buffalo Brewing Co., S.F., Agency, Clear, Original Stopper, Split 160.00
Beer, Burgermeister Pale Ale, San Francisco, 1947, 11 Oz. 20.00
Beer, C.D. Postel, S.F., Cal., Embossed Sheaf Of Wheat, Deep Amber, c.1884, Qt. 500.00
Beer, Chas. Grove, Brown Stout, Green, Double Tapered Collar, Squat, Pontil 145.00
Beer, Chesapeake Brewing Co., Tooled Crown, Private Mold, Md., Pt., 9 1/2 In. 12.00
Beer, Christian Moerlein Brewing, Old Jug Lager, Stoneware, Pre Prohibition, Qt., 10 1/2 In. 85.00
Beer, Consumer's Brewing Co., Embossed, 1909, 12 Oz. 11.00
Beer, D. Davis, 12-Sided, Blue, Applied Top, 10 In. 2900.00
Beer, Des Moines Brewing Co., Amber, Porcelain Stopper, Pre Prohibition, 1/2 Gal. 50.00
Beer, Dr. Cronk, B & C, Blue, 12-Sided, Embossed, Iron Pontil, 10 In. 4900.00
Beer, Dr. Cronk, Blue, Applied Top, Embossed, Iron Pontil, 10 In. 3300.00
Beer, Eldorado Brewing, Stockton, Cal., Amber, Blob, Pre Prohibition, Pt. 25.00
Beer, Emil T. Raddant Brewing Co., Shawano, Wisc., Brown, Embossed, 1900, 12 Oz. 25.00
Beer, Enterprise Brewing Co., S.F., Cal., Amber, Pre Prohibition, 1/2 Pt. 30.00
Beer, Erie Brewing Co., Baltimore Loop, Plate Mold, Embossed, Pa., Pt., 9 1/2 In. 10.00
Beer, Falstaff Brewing Corp., Paper Label, Pre 1950 .... 15.00
Beer, Fehr's X/L, Cincinnati, Ohio, Brown, Paper Label, Crown Top, 1960, 12 Oz. 9.00
Beer, Gambrinus Bottling Co., San Francisco, Cal., Amber, Blob Top, Split 30.00
Beer, Gambrinus Bottling Co., San Francisco, Light To Medium Amber, Lady's Leg Neck, Pt. 50.00
Beer, Gambrinus Brewing, Portland, Oregon, Brown, Embossed Slug Plate, 1896, 24 Oz. 65.00
Beer, Geo. W. Hoxie's Premium Beer, Hand Tooled, Applied Top, Olive Amber, 1861, 10 Oz. 158.00
Beer, Globe, San Francisco, Amber, Barrel Shape, Handle, 1933-38, 1/2 Gal. 60.00
Beer, Goetz Country Club, Wood Arrow Through Bottle, Novelty, 9 1/4 In. 35.00
Beer, Hancock & Melvin, Stoneware, Cobalt Blue Shoulder, Spout, 10 1/2 In. 385.00
Beer, Hauenstein New Ulm, Brown, Paper Labels, Crown Top, 1966, 12 Oz. 7.00
Beer, Honolulu Brewing Co., Honolulu H.T., Green Tint, Qt. 80.00
Beer, Hoster, Columbus, Ohio, Aqua, 1903, 12 Oz. 13.00
Beer, J. Gahm, Yellow, Olive Tone, Mug Base, Blob Top, Lightning Stopper, 9 3/4 In. 220.00
Beer, J. Proll Bottling Works, U.S. Lager, S.F., Amber, Sloping Collar, Split 425.00
Beer, J.H. Rainville, Suncook, N.H., Embossed, Blob Top, 1891, 12 Oz. 30.00
Beer, John Stanton Brewing Co., Troy, N.Y., Emerald Green, Porcelain Stopper, Pt. 85.00
Beer, John Wielands Export, S.F., Red Amber, Sloping Collar 120.00
Beer, Leisy Brewing Co., Tooled Crown, Plate Mold, Ill., Qt., 11 1/2 In. 20.00
Beer, Los Angeles Brew. Co., Blob, Plate Mold, Embossed, Qt., 11 1/4 In. 22.00
Beer, M.S. Johns, Sapphire Blue, Open Pontil, Applied Top, 7 1/2 In. 1900.00
Beer, Maryland Brewing Co., Tooled Crown, Private Mold, Embossed, Pt., 9 In. 6.00
Beer, Milwaukee Waukesha Brew. Co., Tooled Crown, Private Mold, Pt., 9 1/4 In. 9.00
Beer, N. Cervelli, 615 Francisco St., S.F., Amber, Blob Top, Split 140.00
Beer, Neef's, Registered, Aqua, Embossed, 1916, 12 Oz. 10.50
Beer, Neuweiler's, Cream Ale, Green, Paper Label, 1938, 12 Oz. 12.00
Beer, Pacific Bottling Co., S.F., J Monogram, Light Amber, Sloping Collar, Qt. 140.00
Beer, Philadelphia Bottling Co., Lager Beer, Amber, Sloping Collar, Qt. 1200.00
Beer, Propp's Brewing, Tupper Lake, N.Y., Brown, 1900, 12 Oz. 32.00
Beer, Prospect Brewing Co., Philadelphia, Amber, Blob, Bent Neck, 1/2 Pt. 20.00
Beer, Rainier, Seattle Brewing & Malting Company, Amber, Blob Top, Applied Lip, 1/2 Pt. 45.00
Beer, Red Top Ale, Red Top Brewing Co., Cincinnati, Ohio, Paper Label, Pre 1950 .... 20.00
Beer, S.F. Stock Brewing, San Francisco, Cal., Amber, Sloping Collar, Pt. 475.00
Beer, Salt Lake City Brewing Co., Blob, Plate Mold, Embossed, 1/2 Pt., 7 3/4 In. 350.00
Beer, San Jose Bottling Co., San Jose, Amber, Applied Sloping Collar, Pt. 180.00
Beer, Sparkling Cream Ale, XXX, N.H., Blob Top, Wire Closure, Labels, 1902, 12 Oz. 135.00
Beer, Sunset Bottling Co., San Francisco, Cal., Amber, Sloping Collar, Split 70.00
Beer, Terre Haute Brewing Co., Private Mold, Embossed, Machine Crown, Pt., 9 1/2 In. 5.00
Beer, Theodore Lutger & Co., San Jose, Cal., Green, Blob Top, Qt. 210.00
Beer, Union Brewing & Malting Co., S.F., Cal., Amber, Pt. 30.00
Beer, Voight Brewing, Embossed, 1906, 12 Oz. 20.00
Beer, Wm. S. Kinch & Co., Patterson, N.J., Orange Amber, Applied Mouth, 7 3/4 In. 101.00
Beer, Wysser's Brewery, Mauch Chunk, Pa., Amber, Crown Top, Mug Base, 9 1/2 In. 20.00
Beer, Zieger 520, Brown, Paper Labels, 1943, 12 Oz. 14.00

Bininger, A.M. & Co., 19 Broad St., N.Y., Barrel, Gold Amber, Double Collar, Pontil, 8 In. 247.00
Bitters, African Stomach, Yellow Amber, Sloping Collar ....224.00 to 325.00
Bitters, Atwood's Jaundice, Citron Green, 12-Sided, Tooled Lip, 1890-1910, 6 1/4 In. 530.00
Bitters, Atwood's Jaundice, Georgetown, Mass., Aqua, 12-Sided, Open Pontil, 6 1/8 In. 220.00
Bitters, Baker's Orange Grove, Strawberry Puce, Sloping Collar, 9 1/2 In. 1680.00
Bitters, Begg's Dandelion, Amber, Rounded Shoulders, Sloping Collar, 7 In. 80.00
Bitters, Brown's Celebrated Indian Herb, Brown, Chocolate Amber, 1867 .... 1000.00
Bitters, Brown's Celebrated Indian Herb, Yellow, Amber, Sheared, Rolled Lip, 12 In. 672.00
Bitters, Caldwell's Great Tonic, Medium To Deep Amber, Pontil, c.1870, 12 3/4 In. 390.00
Bitters, Carl Mampe Berlin, Elephant, Light Olive Green, Square, Applied Lip, 6 1/8 In. 125.00
Bitters, Castilian, Amber, Tapered, Cylindrical, Flanged Applied Top, 10 1/8 In. 1200.00
Bitters, Chamberlain & Co., Von Hopfs Curacoa, Des Moines, Amber, Sloping Collar, 7 3/4 In. 60.00
Bitters, Cooley's Anti Dyspeptic, Aqua, Pontil, Applied Mouth, Paneled, 1840-60, 6 1/4 In. 1345.00
Bitters, Dingens Bros., Napoleon Cocktail, Drum Shape, Pontil, Applied Mouth, 10 In. 8960.00
Bitters, Dr. A. S. Hopkins Union Stomach, Yellow, Amber, Green, Square, Applied Lip, 9 1/2 In. 375.00
Bitters, Dr. Boyce's Tonic, Aqua, 12-Sided, Cylinder, Waterbury, Vt., 8 In. 110.00
Bitters, Dr. C. W. Roback's Stomach, Yellow Amber, Barrel, 1865-75, 9 1/4 In. 364.00
Bitters, Dr. C.D. Warner's, Reading, Mich, Gold Amber, Semi-Cabin, Double Collar, 1880, 9 3/4 In. 110.00
Bitters, Dr. E.P. Eastman's, Yellow Dock, Aqua, Iron Pontil, Applied Mouth, c.1850, 8 In. 2240.00
Bitters, Dr. Hoofland's German, Dyspepsia & Liver Complaint, Aqua, 1860-70, 8 In. 45.00
Bitters, Dr. Hostetter's Stomach, Yellow Amber, 4-Sided, Sloping Collar, 9 In. 200.00
Bitters, Dr. Langley's Root & Herb, Amber, Embossed Panel, 6 In. 95.00
Bitters, Dr. Langley's Root & Herb, Green, Cylindrical, Applied Doughnut Lip, 8 3/8 In. 200.00
Bitters, Dr. Mowe's Vegetable, Lowell, Mass., Aqua, Drippy Applied Top, 10 x 4 In. 425.00
Bitters, Dr. Petzold's Genuine, German, Amber, Ribs, Applied Top, Short Blob, 1862, 10 In. 325.00
Bitters, Dr. Petzold's Genuine, German, Light Amber, Oval, Applied Lip & Ring, 1862, 10 In. 400.00
Bitters, Dr. Petzold's Genuine, German, Orange Amber, Ribs, Applied Top, 1862, 10 3/4 In. 415.00
Bitters, Dr. R. T. Hylton's Wild Cherry Tonic, Milk Glass, Square, Flanged Lip, 1867, 9 In. 5500.00
Bitters, Dr. Soule's Hop Bitterine, Topaz, Cabin, 4-Sided, Sloping Collar, 9 3/8 In. 610.00
Bitters, Dr. Stephen Jewett's Celebrated Health, Restoring, Blue, Aqua, Pontil, c.1850, 7 In. 785.00
Bitters, Drake's Plantation, 6 Log, Amber, 1862-70, 10 1/8 In. 146.00
Bitters, Drake's Plantation, 6 Log, Cherry Puce, Sloping Collar, Patented 1862, 10 In. 385.00
Bitters, Drake's Plantation, 6 Log, Citron Green, 1862, 10 In. 11650.00
Bitters, Drake's Plantation, 6 Log, S.T., Applied Sloping Collar, 1860, 9 3/4 In. 1210.00
Bitters, Drake's Plantation, 6 Log, Strawberry Puce, 1860, 9 3/4 In. 165.00
Bitters, Drake's Plantation, 6 Log, Yellow Citrine, 1860, 9 3/4 In. 1540.00
Bitters, Drake's Plantation, 6 Log, Yellow, 1862, 9 3/4 In. 1210.00
Bitters, F. Brown Boston Sarsaparilla & Tomato, Aqua, Oval, Double Collar, Pontil, 9 1/2 In. 165.00
Bitters, F. Brown, Sarsaparilla & Tomato, 60 Star, Aqua, Open Pontil, Applied Top, Oval, 9 In. 300.00
Bitters, Ferro Quina Stomach, Amber, Tooled Lip, 1890-1900, 3 3/4 In. 672.00
Bitters, Fish, W.H. Ware, Gold Amber, Patented 1866, 1866-80, 11 5/8 In. 165.00
Bitters, Fish, W.H. Ware, Yellow, Amber, Olive, 1866-75, 11 5/8 In. 1456.00
Bitters, G.C. Blake's, Anti. Despeptic, Aqua, Oval, Pontil, Applied Mouth, c.1850, 7 3/8 In. 1065.00
Bitters, Gen'l Frank Cheatham's, Amber, Semi-Cabin, 1865-70, 10 In. 8960.00
Bitters, German Hop, Reading, Mich., Semi-Cabin, Yellow Amber, Applied Collar, 1872, 9 1/2 In. 100.00
Bitters, Greeley's Bourbon, Barrel, Deep Puce, Applied Square Lip, 9 1/4 In. 675.00
Bitters, Hagan's, Golden Yellow, 3-Sided, Arched, Applied Sloping Collar, c.1870, 9 7/8 In. 580.00
Bitters, Hagan's, Yellow, Olive Amber, 3-Sided, Applied Top, 9 7/8 In. 3300.00
Bitters, Hall's, E.E. Hall New Haven, Orange Amber, Barrel, 9 3/8 In. 670.00
Bitters, Hertrich's, Yellow Olive Green, Ten Pin, Double Collar, Bulbous, 9 1/4 In. 336.00
Bitters, Holtzermann's Patent Stomach, Red, Orange, Amber, Cabin, Tooled Lip, 9 7/8 In. 280.00
Bitters, Holtzermann's, Cabin, 4-Roof, Light Amber, 9 3/4 In. 190.00
Bitters, Hutchings Dyspepsia, Aqua, Iron Pontil, Applied Mouth, 1840-60, 1/2 In. 896.00
Bitters, J. Walker's Vinegar, Green, Applied Mushroom Lip, 8 1/2 In. 375.00
Bitters, John Moffat, Phoenix, Olive Green, Rectangular, Applied Lip, Open Pontil, 5 1/2 In. 1000.00
Bitters, John W. Steele's Niagara Star, Root Beer Amber, Cabin, 4-Sided, Applied Mouth, 10 1/4 In. 1120.00
Bitters, Kaiser Wilhelm, Sandusky, O., Lady's Leg, Clear, 10 1/2 In. 69.00
Bitters, Kimball's Jaundice, Yellow Amber Olive, Sloping Collar, Iron Pontil, 6 7/8 In. 1870.00
Bitters, Litthauer, Hartwig, Kantorowicz, Yellow, Green, Fish, 6-Point Star, c.1900, 10 In. 420.00
Bitters, National, Ear Of Corn, Gold Amber, Applied Sloping Collar, 1867 Patent, 12 1/8 In. 300.00
Bitters, National, Ear Of Corn, Pink Puce, 1867-75, 12 1/2 In. 6160.00

Bitters, National, Ear Of Corn, Yellow Amber, 1867-75, 12 1/2 In. 840.00
Bitters, National, Ear Of Corn, Yellow Topaz, 1867-75, 12 5/8 In. 2350.00
Bitters, New York Hop Bitters Co., Flag, Aqua, Square, Tapered Lip, Bubbles, 9 1/2 In. 85.00
Bitters, Old Dr. Warren's Quaker, Flint & Co., Prov., R.I., Aqua, 10 In. 79.00
Bitters, Old Home, Laughlin, Smith & Co., Wheeling, Gold Amber, Semi-Cabin, 10 In. 2210.00
Bitters, Old Homestead Wild Cherry, Cabin, Amber, 9 5/8 In. ....400.00 to 450.00
Bitters, Old Homestead Wild Cherry, Cabin, Gold Amber, Sloping Collar, 9 1/4 In. 500.00
Bitters, Old Sachem & Wigwam Tonic, Barrel, Blue, Aqua, Olive Striation, 1862-70, 10 In. 6160.00
Bitters, Old Sachem & Wigwam Tonic, Barrel, Gold Amber, Applied Square Collar, 9 1/4 In. 400.00
Bitters, Old Sachem & Wigwam Tonic, Barrel, Light Topaz, 9 1/4 In. 440.00
Bitters, Oxygenated For Dyspepsia, Asthma, General Debility, Blue, Aqua, 7 5/8 In. 612.00
Bitters, Peychaud's American Aromatic, New Orleans, La., Amber, Applied Collar, Fifth 60.00
Bitters, Romaine's Crimean, W. Chilton & Co., Olive Yellow, Cabin, Sloping Collar, 10 In. 7250.00
Bitters, Seaworth, Lighthouse, Aqua, Tooled Sloping Collar, 11 1/4 In. 580.00
Bitters, Simon's Centennial, George Washington, Medium Red Amber To Yellow Amber, 10 In. 4760.00
Bitters, Sol Frank's Panacea, Frank Hayman & Rhine, Lighthouse, Golden Amber, 10 1/4 In. 469.00
Bitters, Sunny Castle Stomach, Light To Golden Amber, Square, Tooled Lip, 9 In. 125.00
Bitters, Taylor's Trade Mark, Green, Applied Lip, Qt., 12 In. 250.00
Bitters, Tippecanoe, H.H. Warner & Co., Amber, 9 In. 190.00
Bitters, Travellers, Embossed Man, Amber, Concave Paneled, 1834, 1870, 10 3/4 In. 9500.00
Bitters, Ulmer's Mountain Ash, New German Remedy, Aqua, Oval, Paneled, Pontil, c.1850, 7 In. 1120.00
Bitters, Vermo Stomach, Tonic & Appetizer, Square, Lip Ring, 9 1/2 In. 20.00
Bitters, W & Co., Pineapple Shape, Yellow, Olive Green, Pontil, Double Collar, 8 3/4 In. 6160.00
Bitters, West India Stomach, Gold Amber, Sloping Collar, Paper Label, WIM Co., 8 1/2 In. 1330.00
Bitters, Whitwell's Temperance, Green, Aqua, Pontil, Applied Mouth, 1840-60, 7 1/4 In. 450.00
Bitters, William Allen's Congress, Blue Green, Semi-Cabin, Applied Mouth, c.1870, 10 In. 3080.00
Bitters, William Allen's Congress, Green, Indented Panels, Applied Top, 10 In. 3300.00
Black Glass, English, Mallet, Olive Amber, Pontil, Applied String Lip, 8 1/4 In. 215.00
Black Glass, Kidney, Yellow, Olive Green, Flat Sided, Pontil, String Lip, 7 In. 1120.00
Black Glass, Onion, Mallet, Olive Green, Pontil, Applied String Lip, 7 1/2 In. 100.00
Black Glass, Onion, Olive Amber, Pontil, Sheared Mouth, Applied String Lip, 5 3/8 In. 560.00
Black Glass, Onion, Olive Green, Pontil, Sheared Mouth, Applied String Lip, 6 1/4 In. 1905.00
Black Glass, Onion, Pancake, Yellow, Olive Green, Pontil, Applied String Lip, 5 3/4 In. 560.00
Black Glass, Onion, Yellow, Olive Green, Pontil, Applied String Lip, 7 5/8 In. 950.00
Blown, Aquamarine, Oval Base, Sloping Collar, Portrait, 10 x 5 1/2 x 4 In. 11.00
Blown, Aquamarine, Oval, Swirled Ribs, 8 1/4 x 4 1/2 In. 55.00
Blown, Chestnut, Olive Green, Pontil, Applied Lip, 1780-1810, 5 In. 500.00
Blown, Chestnut, Olive Green, Pontil, Applied Lip, Bubbles, 5 5/8 In. ....616.00 to 728.00
Blown, Chestnut, Olive Yellow, Open Pontil, Applied Lip, Bubbles, 6 1/8 In. 450.00
Blown, Chestnut, Olive Yellow, Open Pontil, Bubbles, Swirls, Paddle Marks, 10 In. 780.00
Blown, Globular, Olive Yellow, Open Pontil, Applied String Lip, 11 In. 310.00
Blown, Globular, Ruby, Applied Ring, c.1850, 10 3/4 x 9 In. 33.00
Blown, Globular, Yellow, Olive Green, Open Pontil, Applied Lip, 9 1/2 In. 1568.00
Blown, Globular, Yellow, Olive Green, Pontil, Applied Lip, 1790-1820, 11 1/2 In. 990.00
Blown, Globular, Yellow, Olive Green, Pontil, Sheared Mouth, Applied String Lip, 11 In. 504.00
Blown, Jar, Lavender, Rolled Neck, 4 3/4 In. 175.00
Cherry Smash, Glass, Nickel Cup, 12 In. 605.00
Coca-Cola bottles are listed in the Coca-Cola category.
Cosemtic, Vanda Captiva Bath Oil, Gold-Colored Cap, Orlando, Florida, 2 Oz. 15.00
Cosmetic, Ayer's Hair Vigor, Cobalt Blue, Stopper, 8 In. 20.00
Cosmetic, Ayer's Hair Vigor, Cobalt Blue, Glass Stopper, Label, c.1910 .... 110.00
Cosmetic, Ayer's Hair Vigor, Cobalt Blue, Tooled Lip, Tam Stopper, 2 3/4 In. 785.00
Cosmetic, B.F. Fish's Hair Restorative, San Francisco, Aqua, Applied Mouth, 7 1/4 In. 495.00
Cosmetic, Barry's Tricopherous For Skin & Hair, Aqua, Open Pontil, 6 In. 35.00
Cosmetic, Beahore's For Dandruff, Amber, Reverse Painted Label, 7 1/2 x 2 3/4 In. 525.00
Cosmetic, Bear's Oil, Blue Aqua, Open Pontil, Rolled Lip, 2 3/4 In. ....146.00 to 168.00
Cosmetic, Camm's Spanish Hair Preservative, Aqua, Open Pontil, Oval, Applied Top, 6 In. 220.00
Cosmetic, D.P. Brown Salve, Buffalo, N.Y., 12-Sided, Yellow, Olive Amber, 1 1/4 In. 305.00
Cosmetic, Dr. Chaussier's Empress, Cobalt Blue, Striations, Applied Mouth, 7 5/8 In. 616.00
Cosmetic, Dr. Grave's Tooth Powder, Paper Label, Contents, c.1900, 4 In. 210.00
Cosmetic, Dr. Leon's Hair Renewer, Purple, Amethyst, Tooled Mouth, 7 1/4 In. 950.00

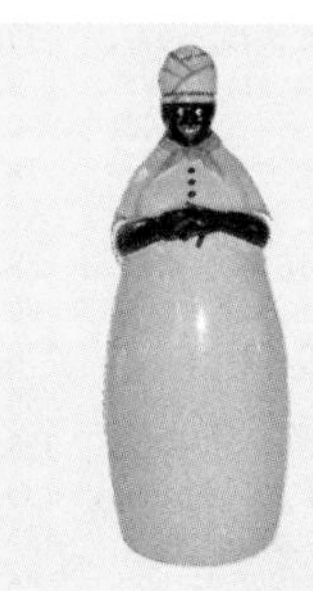

Bottle, Figural, Black Woman, Yellow Dress, Ceramic, Marked, Robj Paris, 10 In.

Bottle, Figural, Senorita, Holding Jug, Milk Glass, Paint, Mexico, 1920-40, 11 1/2 In.

Cosmetic, Dr. Tebbetts' Hair Regenerator, Pink Amethyst, Applied Double Collar, 7 5/8 In. . .365.00 to 392.00
Cosmetic, Dr. Tebbetts' Physiological Hair Regenerator, Red Puce, Blue, Aqua, Pontil, Pt. 48.00
Cosmetic, E.S. Russell's Castanaine For Hair, Scalp, Skin, Yellow Amber, Oval, 6 7/8 In. 390.00
Cosmetic, Heberlings Cream Lotion, Narrow Neck & Mouth, Cover, Label, 5 1/2 In. 15.00
Cosmetic, Hood's Tooth Powder, C.I. Hood & Co., Lowell, Mass., 3 1/2 In. 10.00
Cosmetic, Jerome's Hair Color Restorer, Cobalt Blue, Flared Lip, 6 1/2 In. 560.00
Cosmetic, Jerome's Hair Color Restorer, Olive Yellow, Open Pontil, Flared Lip, 6 5/8 In. 530.00
Cosmetic, John Hart & Co. Hair Tonic, Amber Heart, Applied Double Collar, 7 1/4 In. 670.00
Cosmetic, Kickapoo Sage Hair Tonic, Cobalt Blue, Tooled Lip, 4 1/2 In. 157.00
Cosmetic, Lavona Hair Tonic, Original Lid, Box, 1906, 4 1/2 In. 18.00
Cosmetic, Lombard & Cundall Hair Tonic, Aqua, Pontil, Applied Double Collar, 6 1/2 In. 100.00
Cosmetic, Louden & Co. Hair Dye, No. 2, Aqua, Open Pontil, Rolled Lip, 3 In. 179.00
Cosmetic, Lucky Tiger Hair Tonic, Contents, 14 Oz. 9.00
Cosmetic, Mascara For The Hair, Cornucopia, Clear, Embossed, Oval, 9 1/2 In. 68.00
Cosmetic, Phalon's Chemical Hair Invigorator, N.Y., Light Aqua, Pontil, 5 1/2 In. 26.00
Cosmetic, Pierce's Rosetta Hair Tonic, Boston, Mass., Blue, Aqua, Pontil, Double Collar, 6 In. 475.00
Cosmetic, Shampoo, Cobalt Blue, Tooled Lip, Bent Neck, Finger Grooves, Cremex, 7 3/4 In. 190.00
Cosmetic, W.C. Montgomery's Hair Restorer, Amber, Embossed, 7 1/2 In. 16.00
Cosmetic, W.C. Montgomery's Hair Restorer, Black Amethyst, Double Collar, 7 5/8 In. 336.00
Cosmetic, White's Hair Restorative, Aqua, Oval, Open Pontil, Sloping Collar, 6 3/8 In. 135.00
Cosmetic, Wilson's Hair Colorer, Aqua, Open Pontil, Rolled Lip, 5 In. 90.00
Cosmetic, Wood's Tooth Powder, Nathan Wood & Son, Portland, Me., Cork, 3 1/4 In. 13.00
Cure, Dr. C.C. Roc's Liver Rheumatic & Neuralgic, Knoxville, Tenn., 8 In. 35.00
Cure, Dr. Craig's Original Kidney & Liver Cure For Bright's Disease, Amber, 9 1/2 In. 3850.00
Cure, Dr. D.B. Vincent Magic Cough, San Francisco, Aqua, Applied Mouth, 7 In. 300.00
Cure, John Bull Extract Of Sarsaparilla, Rochester, N.Y., Aqua, 9 1/2 In. 29.00
Cure, Piso's, Hazeltine & Co., Yellow Olive Green, 4 Indented Panels, 5 1/4 In. 15.00
Cure, S.B. Catarrh, Smith Bros., Aqua, Tooled Single Collar, c.1900, 8 In. 40.00
Cure, Spark's Kidney & Liver, Camden, N.J., Amber, Sample Size, 4 In. 29.00
Cure, Warner's Safe Kidney & Liver, Rochester, Amber, Double Collar, 9 1/2 In. 30.00
Cure, Warner's Safe, Amber, Blob Top, Embossed, Oval, 40 Oz., 11 1/4 In. 1200.00
Cure, Warner's Safe, Melbourne, London, Toronto, Rochester, Yellow, 9 1/2 In. 300.00
Decanter, 16 Ribs, Cobalt Blue, Twisting Swirls, Sheared, Tooled Lip, 12 In., Pair 336.00
Decanter, Blown, 3-Piece Mold, Open Pontil, No Stopper, 8 x 4 In. 66.00
Decanter, Blown, Flowers, Bulbous, Tooled Inward-Rolled Mouth, Pontil, Stopper, Qt. 770.00
Decanter, Clipper Ship, 1876, Etched, Open Pontil, Stiegel Type, 7 1/2 In. 120.00
Decanter, Keene, Blown, 3-Piece Mold, Geometric, Olive Green, Open Pontil, 7 3/4 In. 1210.00
Decanter, Vaseline, Painted Gold Flowers, Bulbous Bottom, 3 Neck Rings, Stopper, 13 In. 200.00
Demijohn, Blue Green, Bulbous, Dip Mold, 1 1/2 Gal., 14 1/2 In. 69.00
Demijohn, Emerald Green, Sheared Lip, Applied Neck, Wicker Holder, 21 1/4 In. 112.00
Demijohn, Forest Green, Squat, 3-Piece Mold, Kick-Up, Applied Lip, Gal., 14 1/2 In. 48.00
Demijohn, Golden Yellow, 2-Piece Mold, Oval Base, Applied Sloping Collar, Pontil, 8 1/4 In. 82.00
Demijohn, Green, Smooth Base, 24 x 15 In. 66.00
Demijohn, Light Green, Smooth Base, Applied Top, 12 3/4 x 4 1/4 In. 22.00
Demijohn, Olive Green, Wicker Holder, Handles, 20 x 11 In. 55.00
Demijohn, Olive Yellow, Cylinder, Open Pontil, Applied Top, 18 In., 2 Gal. 79.00
Demijohn, Olive Yellow, Heart Shape, 4-Piece Mold, Pontil, 1830-60, 19 In., 4 Gal. 159.00

Demijohn, Yellow Citron, Cylinder, Wicker Holder, Handles, Qt., 12 1/2 In. 35.00
Figural, Alligator, Milk Glass, Pontil, Sheared, Tooled Mouth, 10 In. 170.00
Figural, Baby In Basket With Grapes, Clear, Tooled Top, 13 In. 60.00
Figural, Basket, Aqua, Pontil, Rolled Lip, Label, France, 3 1/8 In. 78.00
Figural, Bather, Clear, Pontil, Tooled Mouth, Stopper, France, 1880-1915, 11 3/4 In. 56.00
Figural, Bear Face, Frosted Clear Glass, Amethyst, Sheared, Tooled Lip, 1890-1915, 10 In. 179.00
Figural, Bear, Milk Glass, Applied Mouth, Label, Russia, 1890-1910, 11 In. 90.00
Figural, Bear, On Pole, Frosted Black Glass, Pontil, Tooled Mouth, France, 1880-1910, 13 1/2 In. . . 730.00
Figural, Birdcage, Teal Blue, Gold Paint, 1920-35, 4 3/4 In. 56.00
Figural, Black Woman, Yellow Dress, Ceramic, Marked, Robj Paris, 10 In. .... *ILLUS* 358.00
Figural, Bust Of Man, Clear, Pontil, Tooled Mouth, Continental, 1910-20, 5 1/8 In. 235.00
Figural, Bust, Poincare, Milk Glass, Metal Base & Lid, France, 1890-1910, 13 In. 495.00
Figural, Chick Hatching From Egg, Milk Glass, Gold Paint, 1880-1910, 3 1/8 In. 56.00
Figural, Child In Rocker, Milk Glass, Sheared, Ground Lip, 1880-1910, 5 1/8 In. 390.00
Figural, Child, Butterfly, Clear, Sheared, Ground Lip, 1890-1915, 5 3/4 In. 78.00
Figural, Child, Hands In Pockets, Clear, Tooled Mouth, 1890-1915, 6 7/8 In. 78.00
Figural, Chinese Man, Opalescent Milk Glass, Ground Lip, Metal Screw Cap, 1890-1915, 4 1/4 In. 246.00
Figural, Clam, Cobalt Blue, Pontil, Sheared, Tooled Lip, 1850-65, 4 In. 280.00
Figural, Clock, Milk Glass, Tooled Lip, France, 1880-1910, 12 In. 110.00
Figural, Cluster Of Grapes, Cobalt Blue, Sheared, Ground Lip, Brass Chain, 5 1/2 In. 100.00
Figural, Cockatoo, Black Amethyst, Sheared, Ground Lip, Continental, 1890-1910, 13 1/2 In. 210.00
Figural, Country Woman, Apron, Bare Feet, Yellow Tint, Ground Stopper, 1900-25, 12 1/2 In. 70.00
Figural, Duck, Clear, Tooled Mouth, 1880-1915, 3 1/8 In. 135.00
Figural, Duck, Opaque White, Atterbury, 1871 Patent, 11 1/2 In. 99.00
Figural, Eagle's Claw Holding Ball, Clear, 3-Piece Mold, 1880-1900, Qt., 14 In. 39.00
Figural, Ear Of Corn, Yellow Amber, Applied Mouth, 1860-75, 9 7/8 In. 728.00
Figural, Egyptian Sphinx, Frosted, Clear, Pontil, Tooled Mouth, 6 7/8 In. 125.00
Figural, Fish, Crackle Glass, Cork, Amber, Applied Mouth, St. Julian Wine Co., Detroit, 5 x 8 In. 125.00
Figural, General De Brigade, Porcelain, Robj, 10 In. 1410.00
Figural, La Cantinere, Porcelain, Robj, 12 1/2 In. 2585.00
Figural, Le Muscadin Ou L'Incroyable, Porcelain, Robj, 12 1/2 In. 4406.00
Figural, Legionnaire, Porcelain, Robj, 9 3/4 In. 3055.00
Figural, Man Holding Bag, Broom, Clear, Sheared Lip, 1890-1915, 7 1/2 In. 56.00
Figural, Man-In-The-Moon, Yellow Amber, Amethyst Base, Spout, 12 In. 770.00
Figural, Monkey, Seated, Milk Glass, Tooled Mouth, 1890-1910, 4 1/2 In. 365.00
Figural, Nude Venus, Blue Frosted, Plastic Base, Marked, Creme De Violet, 10 1/4 In. 66.00
Figural, Paysanne Revolutionnaire, Porcelain, Robj, 10 1/2 In. ....2468.00 to 3290.00
Figural, Peace Pipe, Clear, Ground Top, 8 1/2 In. 59.00
Figural, Pig, Standing, Yellow Glaze, 6 1/4 In. 105.00
Figural, Santa Claus, Green Milk Glass, Loaded Bag, 8 In. 90.00
Figural, Senorita, Holding Jug, Milk Glass, Paint, Mexico, 1920-40, 11 1/2 In. .... *ILLUS* 88.00
Figural, Snake & Skull, Bisque, Stopper, 9 In. 200.00
Figural, Soaky Set, Monsters, Colgate Palmolive, 4 Piece .... *ILLUS* 728.00
Figural, Soaky, He Man, Plastic, Shampoo, Mattel, 1983, 9 1/4 In. 2.00
Figural, Soaky, Top Cat, Plastic, Bubble Bath, 10 In. 45.00
Figural, Soldier Sitting On Cannonballs, Carnival Glass, Tooled Mouth, Continental, 7 3/8 In. 160.00
Figural, Uncle Sam, Flaccus Ketchup Sampler, Tooled Top, 1900-20, 5 1/8 In. 198.00
Figural, Violin, Cornflower Blue, Hand-Tooled Sheared Lip, 7 1/2 In. 25.00
Figural, Vodka, Bearded Russian, Red Coat, Porcelain, Robj, 11 3/4 In. 1175.00
Figural, Whisk Broom, Milk Glass, Tooled Mouth, Dust Remover, 1890-1915, 6 3/8 In. 505.00
Flask, 10 Diamonds, Gold Amber, Sheared Mouth, Pontil, 4 7/8 In. 835.00
Flask, 14 Ribs, Molded, Clear Green, Sheared, Tooled Lip, Pontil, 6 1/8 In. 125.00
Flask, 24 Ribs, Amber, Applied Handle, Top, Pontil, c.1845, 8 In. 470.00
Flask, 24 Ribs, Sheared Lip, Pontil, c.1820-30, 8 1/4 In. 176.00
Flask, 24 Ribs, Vertical, Gold Amber, Sheared Mouth, Pontil, 5 In. 250.00
Flask, 26 Ribs, Medium To Dark Amber, Pinched Waist, Molded, c.1845, 8 1/4 In. 440.00
Flask, Anchor & Phoenix, Baltimore Glass Works, Aqua, Applied Double Collar, 1865, Pt. 110.00
Flask, Anchor Sheaf Of Grain, Yellow, Olive, Baltimore Glass Works, 1865-75, 1/2 Pt. 2130.00
Flask, Banjo Player, Pale Green, Sheared Mouth, Chapman's Maryland Glass Works, 1855, 1/2 Pt. 209.00
Flask, Cannon, A Little More Grape, Capt. Bragg, Apricot, Sheared Mouth, Pontil, 1/2 Pt. 500.00
Flask, Chestnut, Olive Green, Applied Lip, Elongated, Open Pontil, 1800-30, 4 1/4 In. 1320.00

Switch dishwasher detergent brands periodically. This helps to keep the inside of the dishwasher and the dishes free of any chemical buildup.

Bottle, Figural, Soaky Set, Monsters, Colgate Palmolive, 4 Piece

Flask, Chestnut, Yellow Olive, Painted Sailboat Scene, Outward-Rolled Mouth, Pontil, 5 3/4 In. ... 945.00
Flask, Copper Puce, Double Collar Mouth, 1860-80, Qt. ... 390.00
Flask, Corn For The World, Baltimore Monument, Orange Amber, c.1880 ... 560.00
Flask, Corn For The World, Golden Amber, Applied Mouth, Qt. ... 850.00
Flask, Corn For The World, Teal Blue, Applied Mouth, Qt. ... 6720.00
Flask, Cornucopia & Urn, Blue Green, Sheared Mouth, Pontil, Pt. ... 715.00
Flask, Cornucopia & Urn, Blue Green, Sheared Mouth, Tubular Pontil, 1/2 Pt. ... 660.00
Flask, Cornucopia & Urn, Blue Green, Sheared Mouth, Tubular Pontil, Pt. ... 660.00
Flask, Cornucopia & Urn, Honey Amber, 1/2 Pt., 5 1/2 In. ... 200.00
Flask, Cornucopia & Urn, Olive Amber, Sheared Mouth, Pontil, 1830-48, Pt. ... 99.00
Flask, Cornucopia & Urn, Olive Green, Flared Sheared Lip, Open Pontil, 6 3/4 In. ... 77.00
Flask, Cornucopia & Urn, Yellow Amber, Sheared Mouth, Open Pontil, 1/2 Pt. ... 110.00
Flask, Double Eagle, Aqua, Corrugated, Applied Lip, 1860-68, 8 1/2 In. ... 360.00
Flask, Double Eagle, Aqua, Cunningham, Civil War Era, 7 5/8 x 4 In. ... 120.00
Flask, Double Eagle, Aqua, Open Pontil, Sheared Lip, Pt. ... 440.00
Flask, Double Eagle, Aqua, Open Pontil, Sheared, Tooled Lip, 1830-35, Pt. ... 280.00
Flask, Double Eagle, Aqua, Sheared Mouth, Open Pontil, Pt. ... 275.00
Flask, Double Eagle, Grass Green, Calabash, Sloping Collar, Pontil, Qt. ... 220.00
Flask, Double Eagle, Olive Green, Pontil, Sheared Lip, 1/2 Pt. ... 448.00
Flask, Double Eagle, Ribbed, Green, Pt., 8 In. ... 230.00
Flask, Eagle & Anchor, Blue Aqua, Applied Lip, 1855-75, Pt. ... 168.00 to 280.00
Flask, Eagle & Anchor, Yellow, New London Glassworks, Pt. ... 3600.00
Flask, Eagle & Banner, Yellow, Green, Iron Pontil, Calabash, Qt. ... 415.00
Flask, Eagle & Coffin, Aqua, Open Pontil, Sheared, Tooled Lip, 1825-35, 1/2 Pt. ... 336.00
Flask, Eagle & Coffin, Green, Pt., 6 1/4 In. ... 175.00
Flask, Eagle & Cornucopia, Amber, Sheared Mouth, Pt. ... 120.00
Flask, Eagle & Cornucopia, Olive Green, Sheared Mouth, Pontil, 1830-42, Pt. ... 110.00
Flask, Eagle & Cornucopia, Yellow, Brown, Open Pontil, Embossed, Pt. ... 390.00
Flask, Eagle & Flag For Our Country, Eagle, Facing Left, Aqua, Pontil, 7 In. ... 275.00
Flask, Eagle & Flag, Apple Green, Open Pontil, Sheared, Tooled Lip, 1825-75, Qt. ... 260.00
Flask, Eagle & Flag, Aqua, Open Pontil, Sheared, Tooled Lip, 1825-35, Qt. ... 200.00
Flask, Eagle & Flag, Pale Aqua, Sheared Lip, Pontil, Pt. ... 200.00
Flask, Eagle & Grapes, Blue Aqua, Open Pontil, Sheared, Tooled Lip, 1825-35, Qt. ... 280.00
Flask, Eagle & Grapes, Green Aqua, Open Pontil, Sheared Lip, Qt. ... 220.00
Flask, Eagle & Indian Shooting Bird, Blue, Aqua, Applied Mouth, Qt. ... 336.00
Flask, Eagle & Louisville, Aqua, Ribbed, Applied Lip, Qt. ... 250.00
Flask, Eagle & Louisville, Green Aqua, Pontil, 1840s, Pt., 6 7/8 In. ... 335.00
Flask, Eagle & Oak Tree, Aqua, Open Pontil, Sheared Lip, Embossed, Pt. ... 325.00
Flask, Eagle & Scroll, Aquamarine, Sheared Lip, 1850-60, Pt., 6 3/4 In. ... 100.00
Flask, Eagle & Willington, Red Amber, Applied Double Collar, Qt. ... 420.00
Flask, Eagle & Willington, Yellow Green, Sheared Mouth, Pontil, Pt. ... 605.00
Flask, Eagle & Willington, Yellow Olive Green, Applied Double Collar, 1/2 Pt. ... 336.00
Flask, Eagle & Willington, Yellow, Old Amber, Applied Double Collar, Qt. ... 616.00
Flask, Eye Opener, Milk Glass, Ground Lip, Metal Screw-On Cap, 1890-1915, 5 1/8 In. ... 179.00
Flask, For Pike's Peak, Prospector & Eagle, Blue Aqua, Applied Ring Lip, Pt. ... 280.00

Flask, For Pike's Peak, Prospector, Eagle, Aqua, Qt. 220.00
Flask, General Lafayette & Eagle, Pale Aqua, Kensington Glass Works, Pt., 6 1/2 In. 285.00
Flask, General Taylor Never Surrenders, Capt. Bragg., Aqua, Pontil, Sheared Lip, 1/2 Pt. 390.00
Flask, General Taylor Never Surrenders, Yellow, Green, Pontil, Pt. 4900.00
Flask, Geo. W. Robinson, Blue Aqua, Sheared Lip, Applied Neck Ring, 1/2 Pt. 200.00
Flask, Horseman & Hound, Aqua, Sheared Lip, Pontil, Qt., 8 In. 165.00
Flask, Horseman & Hound, Golden Yellow, Double Collar, Pt. 358.00
Flask, Horseman & Hound, Strawberry Puce, Sloping Collar, Smooth Base, Pt. 2975.00
Flask, Hunter & Fisherman, Amber, Applied Tapered Lip, Pontil, c.1860, Qt. 330.00
Flask, Hunter & Fisherman, Aqua, Open Pontil, Double Collar, Qt. 200.00
Flask, Hunter & Fisherman, Blue Green, Sloping Collar Mouth, Tubular Pontil, Qt. 390.00
Flask, J.D. Heise & Co., S.F., Amber, Shoofly, Applied Sloping Collar, 1/2 Pt. 2800.00
Flask, Jackson & Eagle, Green Aqua, Sheared Mouth, Pontil, J.T. & Co., Pt. 880.00
Flask, Jenny Lind & Glasshouse, Blue Green, Embossed, Calabash, Pontil, Qt. 775.00
Flask, Jenny Lind & Glasshouse, Blue, Green, Calabash, Pontil, Double Collar, S. Huffsey 2350.00
Flask, Klondyke Nugget, Ground Lip, Metal Screw-On Cap, 1900-15, 5 7/8 In. 110.00
Flask, Kossuth & Tree, Olive Yellow, Calabash, Open Pontil, Applied Mouth, 1855-60 . . . . 785.00
Flask, Kossuth & Tree, Yellow Topaz, Sloping Collar, Pontil, Qt. 945.00
Flask, Kossuth & Tree, Yellow Topaz, Sloping Double Collar, Pontil, 1845-60, Qt. 358.00
Flask, Lafayette & Dewitt Clinton, Olive Green, Pontil, Sheared, Tooled Lip, Pt. 505.00
Flask, Lafayette & Eagle, Open Pontil, Sheared Lip, Embossed, Pt. 550.00
Flask, Lafayette & Liberty, Aquamarine, Sheared Mouth, Pontil, 1824-25, Pt. 8250.00
Flask, Lafayette & Liberty, Yellow Amber, Pontil, Sheared, Tooled Lip, 1/2 Pt. 1680.00
Flask, Lafayette & Liberty, Yellow Olive Amber, Pontil, Sheared, Tooled Lip, 1/2 Pt. 896.00
Flask, Liberty, Eagle & Willington, Golden Amber, Sloping Collar, 1860-73, Qt. 1150.00
Flask, Lilienthal & Co., Amber, Crown, Teardrop, Screw Cap, Pt. 300.00
Flask, Livingston & Co., S.F., 25 & 27 Fremont St., Yellow Amber, Tooled Lip, Pt. 3400.00
Flask, Lowell Railroad & Eagle, Olive, Oval Panels, c.1840, 6 3/4 In. 646.00
Flask, Masonic & Crossed Keys, Yellow Olive, Sheared Mouth, Coventry Glass Works, 1/2 Pt. 37400.00
Flask, Masonic & Eagle, Aqua, Open Pontil, Sheared, Tooled Lip, Pt. 280.00
Flask, Masonic & Eagle, Aquamarine, Sheared Mouth, Pontil, Midwest, 1/2 Pt. 495.00
Flask, Masonic & Eagle, Golden Yellow Amber, Sheared Mouth, Pontil, Shepard & Co., Pt. 1650.00
Flask, Masonic & Eagle, Green Aqua, Sheared Mouth, Pontil, N.E.G. Co., Pt. 470.00
Flask, Masonic & Eagle, Yellow Amber Olive, Sheared Mouth, Pontil, 1825, Pt. 358.00
Flask, Masonic & Eagle, Yellow Olive, Sheared Mouth, Pontil, Keene, Pt. 297.00
Flask, Masonic & Seeing Eye, 6-Point Star, Olive Green, Sheared Mouth, Pontil, Stoddard, Pt. 1540.00
Flask, Milk Glass, Ground Lip, Metal Screw-On Cap, 1890-1915, 4 5/8 In. 269.00
Flask, Monument & Fell's Point, Strawberry Puce, Sheared Mouth, Pontil, 1/2 Pt. 450.00
Flask, Monument Liberty & Union, Aqua, Open Pontil, Sheared Lip, Embossed, Pt. 500.00
Flask, Monument, A Little More Grape, Aqua, Sheared Lip, Pontil, 1/2 Pt. 950.00
Flask, Monument, A Little More Grape, Copper Puce, Open Pontil, 1/2 Pt. 8300.00
Flask, Nailsea Type, Milk Glass, Red & Blue Loopings, Tooled Mouth, Pontil, 1840-60, 6 1/2 In. 660.00
Flask, Pantaloon Eagle & Cornucopia, Olive Amber, Sheared Mouth, Pontil, Pt. 7700.00
Flask, Pink & White, Swirled, Pontil, 5 3/4 In. 165.00
Flask, Pitkin Type, 30 Ribs, Broken Swirl, Light Amber, Open Pontil, Midwest, 6 1/2 In. 660.00
Flask, Pitkin Type, 30 Vertical Ribs, Green, Gray, Open Pontil, 6 7/8 In. 900.00
Flask, Pitkin Type, 32 Broken Ribs, Swirled To Left, Emerald Green, Open Pontil, 6 1/2 In. 650.00
Flask, Pumpkinseed, Life Preserver, 2 Stars, Embossed, 1/4 Pt. 69.00
Flask, Pumpkinseed, Log Cabin, Billy Winters, Portland, Ore., Pt. 900.00
Flask, Pumpkinseed, Phoenix Bourbon, Embossed Phoenix, 1/2 Pt. 180.00
Flask, Pumpkinseed, Pocket Watch, Winder, Loop, Milk Glass, Embossed Face, 5 1/4 In. 440.00
Flask, Pumpkinseed, Ribs, Clear, Diamond, A. Colburn Co., 1/4 Pt. 59.00
Flask, Pumpkinseed, Spider Web & Sunburst, Golden Yellow Amber, Pt. 79.00
Flask, Saddle, Olive Green, Flat, Oval, Concave Back, Round Bottom, Applied Collar, 8 In. 55.00
Flask, Scroll, Amber, Applied Mouth, Red Iron Pontil, Pt. 900.00
Flask, Scroll, Amber, Sheared Mouth, Tubular Pontil, 1/2 Pt. 1320.00
Flask, Scroll, Amber, Sheared, Tooled Lip, Open Pontil, 1/2 Pt. 1120.00
Flask, Scroll, Aqua, Sheared Lip, Iron Pontil, c.1855-65, 6 1/2 In. 55.00
Flask, Scroll, Aqua, Sheared Lip, Pinched Waist, Open Pontil, Qt. 775.00
Flask, Scroll, Blue Aqua, Waisted, Open Pontil, Sheared, Tooled Lip, Pt. 560.00
Flask, Scroll, Blue Green, Sheared Lip, Iron Pontil, 1/2 Pt. 1430.00

Flask, Scroll, M'Carty & Torreyson, Pale Blue, 7 1/4 In. 978.00
Flask, Scroll, Olive Green, Sheared Lip, Pontil, Pt. 1540.00
Flask, Scroll, Teal Blue, Sheared, Tooled Lip, Pontil, Pt. 4480.00
Flask, Scroll, Yellow Green, Applied Mouth, Iron Pontil, Qt. 1540.00
Flask, Scroll, Yellow Green, Sheared Mouth, Pontil, 1845-60, Pt. 2975.00
Flask, Scroll, Yellow Green, Sheared, Tooled Lip, Open Pontil, Pt. 950.00
Flask, Scroll, Yellow, Iron Pontil, Sheared Lip, Qt. 3900.00
Flask, Sheaf Of Grain, Aqua, Open Pontil, Sheared Lip, Qt. 365.00
Flask, Sheaf Of Grain, Olive Green Amber, Double Collar, Pt. 165.00
Flask, Sloop & Bridgetown, New Jersey, Aqua, Open Pontil, Sheared Lip, 1/2 Pt. 465.00
Flask, Sloop & Star, Aqua, Sheared Mouth, Open Pontil, 1/2 Pt. 110.00
Flask, Spring Garden & Anchor, Apricot, Applied Mouth, c.1875, 1/2 Pt. 1345.00
Flask, Stag & Willow Tree, Aqua, Open Pontil, Sheared, Tooled Lip, Pt. 280.00
Flask, Success To The Railroad, Golden Amber, Pontil, 1830-50, Pt. 550.00
Flask, Success To The Railroad, Olive Green, Sheared, Tooled Lip, Open Pontil, Pt. 476.00
Flask, Success To The Railroad, Tan, Olive, Open Pontil, Pt. 550.00
Flask, Success To The Railroad, Yellow Olive, Sheared Mouth, Pontil, Pt. 445.00
Flask, Success To The Railroad, Yellow Olive, Sheared Mouth, Tubular Pontil, Pt. 420.00
Flask, Success To The Railroad, Yellow, Olive Amber, Sheared, Pontil, Pt. 450.00
Flask, Summer & Winter, Blue Green, Sloping Collar, Pontil, Qt. 370.00
Flask, Summer & Winter, Copper Topaz, Applied Double Collar, Pt. 1568.00
Flask, Summer & Winter, Yellow Amber, Pontil, Double Collar, Qt. 2600.00
Flask, Summer & Winter, Yellow Green, Applied Double Collar, Pt. 672.00
Flask, Sunburst, Aqua, Open Pontil, Sheared Lip, Embossed, Pt. 550.00
Flask, Sunburst, Aqua, Open Pontil, Sheared, Tooled Lip, 1/2 Pt. 310.00
Flask, Sunburst, Forest Green, Sheared Lip, Pontil, Pt. 2090.00
Flask, Sunburst, Green Aqua, Open Pontil, Sheared Lip, 1/2 Pt. 440.00
Flask, Sunburst, Olive Green, Pontil, Sheared, Tooled Lip, Pt. 530.00
Flask, Sunburst, Olive Yellow, Sheared Lip, Pontil, Pt. 4675.00
Flask, Sunburst, Yellow, Olive Green, Open Pontil, Sheared, Tooled Lip, Pt. 450.00
Flask, Two Men Arguing, Cobalt Blue, Pontil, Sheared, Tooled Lip, 1/2 Pt. 840.00
Flask, Union, Clasped Hands & Eagle, Amber, Applied Ring, Pt. 325.00
Flask, Union, Clasped Hands & Eagle, Aqua, Open Pontil, 1/2 Pt. 165.00
Flask, Union, Clasped Hands & Eagle, Citron, Applied Collar, Qt. 1000.00
Flask, Union, Clasped Hands & Eagle, Orange Amber, Applied Collar, A & Co., Qt. 425.00
Flask, Washington & Eagle, Aqua, Pt. 175.00
Flask, Washington & Eagle, Blue, Green, Open Pontil, Sheared Lip, Pt. 3900.00
Flask, Washington & Eagle, Green, Pontil, Sheared, Tooled Lip, 1825-35, Qt. 150.00
Flask, Washington & Fells Point, Green, Pt., 7 In. 200.00
Flask, Washington & Jackson, Aqua, Pontil, Sheared, Tooled Lip, 1829-35, Pt. 200.00
Flask, Washington & Jackson, Olive Amber, Sheared Mouth, Pontil, Pt. 220.00
Flask, Washington & Monument, Aqua, Pontil, Sheared, Tooled Lip, 1829-35, Pt. 365.00
Flask, Washington & Taylor, Apricot, Applied Mouth, Smooth Base, 1849-55 .... 448.00
Flask, Washington & Taylor, Aqua, Open Pontil, Sheared Lip, Pt. 300.00
Flask, Washington & Taylor, Aqua, Sheared Mouth, 8 1/4 In. 510.00
Flask, Washington & Taylor, Cobalt Blue, Pontil, Qt. ....2750.00 to 3360.00
Flask, Washington & Taylor, Cobalt Blue, Sheared Lip, Pontil, Pt. 2100.00
Flask, Washington & Taylor, Emerald Green, Applied Mouth, c.1855, Qt. 560.00
Flask, Washington & Taylor, Emerald Green, Sheared Lip, Qt. 3080.00
Flask, Washington & Taylor, Honey Amber, Sheared Mouth, Pontil, Pt. 1210.00
Flask, Washington & Taylor, Plum Amethyst, Sheared Lip, 1860-70, Pt. 3020.00
Flask, Washington & Taylor, Sapphire Blue, Applied Lip, Qt. 7280.00
Flask, Washington & Taylor, Teal Blue, Sheared, Tooled Lip, Pontil, Pt. 1120.00
Flask, Washington & Taylor, Yellow Amber, Open Pontil, Sheared, Tooled Lip, Pt. 840.00
Flask, Washington & Taylor, Yellow Olive, Applied Mouth, c.1855, Qt. 1344.00
Flask, Washington & Tree, Aqua, Calabash, Open Pontil, Qt. 365.00
Flask, Will You Take A Drink, Duck, Aqua, Applied Mouth, 1860-70, Pt. 250.00
Flask, Will You Take A Drink, Duck, Blue, Aqua, Applied Ring Lip, 1/2 Pt. 775.00
Flask, Zanesville City Glass Works, Yellow, Amber, Strap Sides, Pt. 950.00
Food, D. Ghiradelli & Co., San Francisco, Aqua, Applied Mouth, 6 1/4 In. 66.00
Food, Green, Cylindrical, Tapered, Applied Lip, S.F., Calif., 11 1/4 In. 2420.00

Food, H. J. Heinz Pat, Number 150, Incised, Clear, 24 Oz., 12 In. 25.00
Food, Log Cabin Syrup, Liberty Bell, Bicentennial, 1976, 8 x 4 1/2 x 2 1/2 In. 8.00
Food, Molded, Clear, 16 Ribs, Twisting Swirls, Pontil, Applied Neck Ring, 5 In. 78.00
Food, My Wife's Salad Dressing, Citron, Swirled Neck Design, 7 3/4 In. 40.00
Food, Storage, Emerald Green, Red Iron Pontil, Applied Double Collar, 17 In. 235.00
Food, T.A. Bryan & Co.'s Perfection Tomato Sauce, Baltimore, Yellow Amber, 8 3/8 In. 112.00
Food, Yellow Amber, Cylindrical, 3-Piece Mold, Outward Rolled Mouth, Stoddard, 8 1/4 In. 770.00
Fruit Jar, A. Stone & Co., Phila., Aqua, Applied Mouth, Internal Neck Threads, Lid, Qt. 390.00
Fruit Jar, Atlas E-Z Seal, Olive Green, Glass Lid, Wire Closure, Pt. 12.00
Fruit Jar, Ball Ideal, Bust Of Fisher, Fisher Years, Clear, 1941-46, Qt. 50.00
Fruit Jar, Ball Perfect Mason, Leaning Letters, Aqua, Pt. 12.00
Fruit Jar, Bamberger's, Always Busy Store, Newark, Aqua, Zinc Lid, Pt. 135.00
Fruit Jar, Battleship Maine & Morro Castle, Milk Glass Insert Lid, Eagle, Band Closure 290.00
Fruit Jar, Bloeser, Aqua, Glass Lid, Embossed, Clamp 300.00
Fruit Jar, Clark's Peerless, Aqua, Lid, Wire Closure, Pt. 8.00
Fruit Jar, Cloud Crown, Crown Emblem, Aqua, Qt. 4.00
Fruit Jar, Cohansey Glass Mfg. Co. Pat. Mar 20 '77, Barrel, Aqua, Qt. 115.00
Fruit Jar, Crown Imperial, Lid, Zinc Band, Aqua, Pt. 8.00
Fruit Jar, F.A. & Co., Applied Mouth, Blue Aqua, Qt. 70.00
Fruit Jar, Gem, Plain Monogram, Square O, Aqua, Midget 150.00
Fruit Jar, Gilberds Improved, Star, Aqua, Glass Lid, Wire Clamp, Qt. 145.00
Fruit Jar, Globe, Yellow Amber, Glass Lid, Iron Clamp, Qt. 125.00
Fruit Jar, Globe, Yellow Amber, Lid, Wire Closure, Ground Lip, Qt. 125.00
Fruit Jar, Globe, Yellow Amber, Squat, Ground Mouth, Wire & Iron Clamp, 1/2 Pt. 15400.00
Fruit Jar, Globe, Yellow, Patented May 25, 1886, Lid, Closure, Qt. 239.00
Fruit Jar, Griffen's Patent, Oct. 7 1862, Aqua, Glass Lid, Iron Cage Clamp, Qt. 135.00
Fruit Jar, J.J. Squire 2, Patd. Octr 18th, 1864 & Mar 7th, 1865, Aqua, Ground Mouth, Lid, Qt. 715.00
Fruit Jar, Knowlton Vacuum, Star, Aqua, Qt. 25.00
Fruit Jar, Lafayette, Aqua, 3-Piece Glass & Metal Stopper, Pt. 390.00
Fruit Jar, Leotric, In Circle, Aqua, Qt. 5.00
Fruit Jar, Lightning Putnam 59, Trademark, Golden Yellow, Cylindrical, 1880-95, Qt. 88.00
Fruit Jar, Magic Fruit Jar, Wm. McCully & Co., Aqua, Ground Mouth, June 6th 1866, Qt. 715.00
Fruit Jar, Mason's 2 Patent Nov 30th 1858, Aqua, 1/2 Gal. 20.00
Fruit Jar, Mason's CFJCo Patent Nov 30th 1858, Olive Green, Qt. 100.00
Fruit Jar, Mason's Cross Patent Nov 30th 1858, Green, Qt. 10.00
Fruit Jar, Mason's Cross Patent Nov 30th 1858, Yellow Amber, Zinc Lid, Qt. 179.00
Fruit Jar, Mason's Patent Nov 30th 1858, Aqua, Ground Lip, Qt. 3.00
Fruit Jar, Mason's Patent Nov 30th 1858, Aqua, Zinc Lid, Midget 18.00
Fruit Jar, Mason's Patent Nov 30th 1858, Aquamarine, Ground Lip, 1/2 Gal. 30.00
Fruit Jar, Mason's Patent Nov 30th 1858, Deep Olive, Smooth Lip, Screw Top, 1900-10, Qt. 805.00
Fruit Jar, Mason's Patent Nov 30th 1858, Hourglass, Aqua, Midget 90.00
Fruit Jar, Mason's Patent Nov 30th 1858, Yellow Amber, Midget 2050.00
Fruit Jar, Mason's Patent Nov 30th 58, Ball Jar, Christmas, Aqua, Lid, Pt. 140.00
Fruit Jar, Mason's Patent Nov 30th, 1858, Amber, Zinc Lid, Qt. 415.00
Fruit Jar, Mason's Patent Nov. 30th 1858, Tobacco Amber, Zinc Lid, 1/2 Gal. 220.00
Fruit Jar, Mason, Ball Blue, Zinc Lid, Pt. 6.00
Fruit Jar, Millville Atmospheric, Aqua, 68 Oz. 125.00
Fruit Jar, Mission Trade, Bell, W.J. Latchford Co., Los Angeles, California, Aqua, Qt. 18.00
Fruit Jar, P. Lorillard, Amber, Glass Lid, No Clamp, Qt. 10.00
Fruit Jar, Potter & Bodine's, Patent April 13th, 1858, Barrel Shape, Wax Seal Lip, Qt. 1100.00
Fruit Jar, Royal, Green Aqua, Lid, Qt. 350.00
Fruit Jar, Safety Seal Made In Canada, Clear, Lightning Beaded Neck Seal, Pt. 2.00
Fruit Jar, Safety Valve Pat. May 21 1895, Greek Key, Clear, 1/2 Gal. 60.00
Fruit Jar, Safety, Yellow Amber, Ground Lip, Glass Lid, Wire Bail, Qt. 179.00
Fruit Jar, Smalley's Crown, Royal Trade Mark, Nu-Seal, Clear, Qt. 9.00
Fruit Jar, Sun Trade Mark, Circle, Aqua, Glass Lid, Metal Yoke Clamp, Qt. 134.00
Fruit Jar, Sure Seal, Made For L. Bamberger & Co., Ball Blue, Lid, Pt. 40.00
Fruit Jar, Sure Seal, Made For L. Bamberger & Co., Ball Blue, Lid, Qt. 35.00
Fruit Jar, Swayzee's Improved Mason, Aqua, 1/2 Gal. 15.00
Fruit Jar, The Hero, Yellow Amber, Ground Mouth, Tin Lid, Patd Nov 26, 1867, Qt. 8400.00
Fruit Jar, Trademark Lightning Putnam, U.S. Patent Office, Aqua, 1/2 Pt. 15.00

Fruit Jar, Trademark Lightning, Aqua, Qt. 4.00
Fruit Jar, Trademark Lightning, Yellow, Blown In Mold, Sheared, Ground Lip, 1880-1910, 7 1/2 In. 70.00
Fruit Jar, Wears Jar, In Stippled Oval, Clear, Pt. 7.00
Fruit Jar, White Crown Mason, Aqua, 1/2 Gal. 8.00
Gemel, Blown, Marbled, White Loopings, Flattened Egg Shape, c.1875, 11 x 4 1/4 In. 77.00
Gin, Case, Amber, Applied Flared Lip, Open Pontil, 10 In. 140.00
Gin, Case, Yellow, Olive Amber, Open Pontil, Applied Mouth, 10 In. 146.00
Gin, Case, Yellow, Olive Green, Open Pontil, Applied Mouth, 10 7/8 In. 213.00
Gin, I.A.I. Nolet, Schiedam, Case, Olive Green, Tapered, Dutch, 9 In. 77.00
Gin, J.T. Daly Club House, Case, Amber, Applied Flared Lip, Iron Pontil, 9 1/2 In. 700.00
Gin, Van Den Bergh & Co., Case, Olive Green, Bell, Shoulder Seal, Applied Top, 11 1/2 In. 99.00
Ginger Beer, Barker's, Cambridge, Stoneware, 2-Tone, 6 1/2 In. 24.00
Ginger Beer, Campbell Praed & Co., Home Brewed, Unicorn, Stoneware, 2-Tone, 6 3/4 In. 49.00
Ginger Beer, J. Macintyre & Co., Number 2, Salt Glaze, 8 1/2 In. 15.00
Ginger Beer, Julius Peters, Bull, Stoneware, 2-Tone, Champagne Shape, 8 In. 49.00
Ginger Beer, Wrexham's Fermented Stone, Goat, Stoneware, 2-Tone, 6 3/4 In. 59.00
Globular, Aqua, Blown, 24 Ribs, Swirled, Pontil, Zanesville, 7 1/2 In. 403.00
Glue, Mucilage, 8-Sided, Aqua, Thin Flared-Out Lip, Open Pontil, 1840-60, 3 1/8 In. 165.00
Glue, Sanford's Ink & Library Paste, Qt. 15.00
Household, Blacking, Osborn's Liquid Polish, Aqua, Rolled Lip, c.1850s, 3 3/4 In. 850.00
Household, Dazzle Detergent, Amber, c.1949, 32 Oz., 9 1/4 In. 10.00
Household, Kinning's Bleuing, Rochester, N.Y., Aqua, Sheared Lip, Round, 6 In. 8.00
Household, Little Bo-Peep Ammonia, Post 1900, 7 3/4 In. 10.00
Ink, 6-Sided, Aqua, Sloping Shoulders, Blown In Mold, Sheared Lip, 2 In. 17.00
Ink, 8-Sided, Aqua, Tipper, Cutaway Base, Blown In Mold, Sheared Lip, 2 3/4 In. 24.00
Ink, 8-Sided, Blue Aqua, Pontil, Sheared, Inward-Rolled Lip, 1840-60, 1 3/4 In. 200.00
Ink, 16 Vertical Ribs, Olive Amber, Disc Mouth, Pontil, 1830-73, 1 5/8 x 2 5/8 In. 10450.00
Ink, A.B. Laird's, 8-Sided, Blue Green, Open Pontil, Inward-Rolled Lip, 1840-60, 2 1/8 In. 4480.00
Ink, Blackwood & Co., Igloo, Aqua, Blown In Mold, Sheared Lip, London, 2 1/2 In. 40.00
Ink, Blown, Geometric, 3-Piece Mold, Olive Amber, Pontil, Tooled Mouth, 1815-30, 1 3/4 In. 125.00
Ink, Blown, Geometric, 3-Piece Mold, Olive Amber, Pontil, Tooled Mouth, 2 5/8 In. 200.00
Ink, Blown, Geometric, 3-Piece Mold, Olive Yellow, Pontil, Tooled Mouth, 1815-30, 2 In. 235.00
Ink, Blown, Geometric, 3-Piece Mold, Yellow Amber, Pontil, Tooled Mouth, 1815-35, 1 1/2 In. 310.00
Ink, Blown, Geometric, 3-Piece Mold, Yellow Olive Green, Pontil, Tooled Mouth, 1815-35, 1 1/2 In. 224.00
Ink, Cannon, Aqua, Blown In Mold, Applied Lip, 3 3/4 In. 35.00
Ink, Carter's, Cathedral, 6-Sided, Cobalt Blue, Pour Spout, Paper Label, 10 1/2 In. 410.00
Ink, Carter's, Cathedral, Cobalt Blue, Master, 12 1/2 In. 80.00
Ink, Carter's, Green, 3-Piece Mold, Pt. 75.00
Ink, Carter's, Inky Racer, 2 Square Bottles, Amber, Clear, Box, 2 3/4 x 3 In. 230.00
Ink, Carter's, Inx, Woman, Blond Hair, Glasses, Holding Rolling Pin, 3 1/2 In. 110.00
Ink, Cone, Blue, Open Pontil, Rolled Lip, 2 1/2 In. 1450.00
Ink, Cone, Green, Open Pontil, Rolled Lip, 2 3/8 In. 800.00
Ink, De Halsey, Patente Light, Olive Green, Pontil, 3 x 3 1/2 In. 275.00
Ink, Dormay, Red, England, 1920s, 2 In. 10.00
Ink, E. Waters, Troy, N.Y., Aqua, Open Pontil, Applied Top, 3 x 1 3/4 In. 253.00
Ink, Farley's, N.Y., Yellow Olive, Octagonal, Sheared Mouth, Pontil, 1 3/4 In. 1330.00
Ink, Geometric, Olive Green, Open Pontil, 1 1/2 x 2 1/2 In. .... 175.00 to 187.00
Ink, Harrison's Columbian, 8-Sided, Aqua, Open Pontil, 1 3/4 In. 66.00
Ink, Harrison's Columbian, 8-Sided, Aqua, Open Pontil, Applied Mouth, 1840-60 .... 560.00
Ink, Harrison's Columbian, Cylindrical, Cobalt Blue, Open Pontil, Applied Mouth, 9 5/8 In. 3360.00
Ink, Hollidge, Boat, Green, 2 Pen Rests, Blown In Mold, Sheared Lip, 2 In. 19.00
Ink, House, Doors, Windows, Aqua, Hand Tooled Lip, 2 5/8 In. 440.00
Ink, J. & I. E. M., Igloo, Yellow Topaz, Offset Neck, Tooled Mouth, 1 3/4 x 1 1/8 In. .... 1000.00 to 1500.00
Ink, J.J. Field, 8-Sided, Aqua, Embossed, Long Neck, Sheared Lip, 3 In. 20.00
Ink, K. & T. M., Tent, Aqua, Round, Ribbed Shoulders, Pen Rest, 2 1/2 In. 39.00
Ink, Lyon's, Cobalt Blue, Tooled Lip, 1880-95, 2 7/8 In. 235.00
Ink, Lyon's, Cotton Reel, Aqua, Blown In Mold, Sheared Lip, 3 In. 25.00
Ink, P. & J. Arnold's Writing Fluid, Denby Pottery, Salt Glaze, Stoneware, c.1862, 32 Oz., 7 In. 60.00
Ink, Rexall Fountain Pen, Square, Clear, Dovetailed Wood Box, 10 x 8 x 6 In., 1 Dozen 300.00
Ink, S. Fine Black, Cylindrical, Yellow Green, Inward Rolled Mouth, Pontil, 2 7/8 In. 780.00
Ink, S.S. Stafford's, Cobalt Blue, Pour Spout, Qt., 9 1/2 x 3 1/4 In. .... 75.00 to 90.00

Ink, S.S. Stafford's, Teal Green, Qt. 75.00
Ink, S.S. Stafford's, Teal, Tooled Sloping Collar, Pour Spout, Paper Label, 1880-1900, 10 In. 55.00
Ink, Shaw's Inks Are Best, 8-Sided, Aqua, Blown In Mold, Sheared Lip, 3 In. 35.00
Ink, Sheaffer's Skrip, Blue Black, Partial Contents, Box, 2 Oz. 15.00
Ink, Sheaffer's Skrip, Washable Blue, No. 42, Lid, Label, Built-In Inkwell, 2 Oz. 10.00
Ink, Square, Cobalt Blue, Blown In Mold, Sheared Lip, Faceted Shoulders, 2 In. 29.00
Ink, Stephens, Cotton Reel, Aqua, Blown In Mold, Applied Lip, 2 1/2 In. 29.00
Ink, Stoddard, Umbrella, Root Beer Amber, Pontil, 2 1/2 x 2 1/4 In. 295.00
Ink, Teakettle, 6-Sided, Milk Glass, Painted Flowers, Tapered, 2 1/2 In. 725.00
Ink, Teakettle, 8-Sided, Amethyst, Brass Cap, 2 In. 250.00
Ink, Teakettle, 8-Sided, Amethyst, Concave, Brass Mouth Ring, 2 In. 475.00
Ink, Teakettle, 8-Sided, Concave Panels, Center Disc, Cobalt Blue, 2 1/4 In. 465.00
Ink, Teakettle, 12-Sided, Cobalt Blue, Pontil, Sheared, Ground Lip, Metal Cap, 2 1/4 In. 224.00
Ink, Teakettle, Blue, Pumpkin, Long Spout, Ground Lip, 1 3/4 In. 1000.00
Ink, Teakettle, Cobalt Blue, Sheared, Ground Lip, 1875-95, 1 5/8 In. 390.00
Ink, Umbrella, 8-Sided, Amber, Pontil, Elongated Neck, Stoddard, 2 1/2 In. 305.00
Ink, Umbrella, 8-Sided, Amber, Rolled Lip, Pontil, 2 1/2 In. 700.00
Ink, Umbrella, 8-Sided, Amber, Sheared Lip, Stoddard Style, Pontil, 2 1/2 In. 180.00
Ink, Umbrella, 8-Sided, Amethyst, Inward-Rolled Lip, 1855-65, 2 1/2 In. 1680.00
Ink, Umbrella, 8-Sided, Blue Green, Inward-Rolled Lip, Open Pontil, 2 3/8 In. 89.00
Ink, Umbrella, 8-Sided, Blue Green, Open Pontil, Inward Rolled Lip, 1840-60, 2 5/8 In. 365.00
Ink, Umbrella, 8-Sided, Blue Green, Open Pontil, Rolled Lip, 2 1/4 In. 160.00
Ink, Umbrella, 8-Sided, Cobalt Blue, Rolled Lip, 2 1/2 In. 750.00
Ink, Umbrella, 8-Sided, Cornflower Blue, Square Collar Lip, 2 In. 325.00
Ink, Umbrella, 8-Sided, Green, Rolled Lip, Open Pontil, 1840-1855, 2 In. 88.00
Ink, Umbrella, 8-Sided, Green, Rolled Lip, Open Pontil, 2 1/2 In. 200.00
Ink, Umbrella, 8-Sided, Light Emerald Green, 2 3/8 In. 88.00
Ink, Umbrella, 8-Sided, Midnight Blue, Inward Rolled Mouth, Tubular Pontil, 2 3/8 In. 1770.00
Ink, Umbrella, 8-Sided, Olive Green, Open Pontil, Inward Rolled Lip, 1840-60, 2 1/2 In. 672.00
Ink, Umbrella, 8-Sided, Olive Green, Pontil, Stoddard, 2 1/2 In. 77.00
Ink, Umbrella, 8-Sided, Olive Green, Rolled Lip, Pontil, 2 1/2 In. 450.00
Ink, Umbrella, Blue, Green, Open Pontil, Rolled Lip, 3 1/8 x 2 5/8 In. 950.00
Ink, Umbrella, Cobalt Blue, Tubular Open Pontil, Rolled Lip, 2 15/16 x 3 In. 7200.00
Ink, United Drug Co. Fountain Pen, Aluminum Top, Label, Rexall, 5 1/8 In. 12.00
Ink, W. Thomas & Co., Dark Aqua, Tooled Lip, Smooth Base, Indented Panel, 2 3/8 In. 35.00
Ink, Wiltshire's, Aqua, Indented Panel, Tooled Lip, 3 In. 25.00
Jar, Aquamarine, Cone Top, Sheared & Tooled Mouth, Pontil, 6 x 5 In. 605.00
Jar, Battery, Sapphire Blue, Rectangular, Ground Mouth, Condit Hanson & Co., 8 x 9 1/4 x 5 7/8 In. 990.00
Jar, Candy, Cover, Gum Drops, Black & Gold Letters, Bulbous, Pedestal Base, 19 In. 1870.00
Jar, Candy, Cover, Horehound, Black & Gold Letters, Bulbous, Pedestal Base, 20 In. 880.00
Jar, Candy, Cover, Lemon Drops, Black & Gold Letters, Bulbous, Pedestal Base, 19 In. 1320.00
Jar, Candy, Cover, Licorice, Black & Gold Letters, Bulbous, Pedestal Base, 19 In. ....660.00 to 1760.00
Jar, Candy, Cover, Taffy, Black & Gold Letters, Bulbous, Pedestal Base, 20 In. 930.00
Jar, Cutting & Co., San Francisco, Aqua, Wax Sealer, Qt. 1300.00
Jar, Golden Amber, Cylindrical, Sheared & Tooled Rim, Pontil, 1830-50, 10 x 6 1/2 In. 1430.00
Jar, Goofus Glass, Embossed Flowers, Birds, Sheared, Ground Lip, 12 1/2 In. 90.00
Jar, Honey, Aqua, Pontil, Rolled Lip, Bees, Beehive, 7 1/4 In. 215.00
Jar, Maxwell House Coffee, Embossed, Pebbly, 1 Lb. 15.00
Jar, Milk Pail, Blue, Ground Mouth, Tin Collar, Lid & Wire Handle, 1880-88, 4 3/8 In. 770.00
Jar, Milk Pail, Yellow Topaz, Ground Mouth, Applied Tin Collar, Wire Handle, Tin Lid, 1887, 4 1/4 In. 605.00
Jar, Mucilage, 8-Sided, Aqua, Whimsy, Inward-Rolled Lip, Open Pontil, 1840-60, 3 In. 1320.00
Jar, Mustard, Barrel, Olive Amber, Applied Mouth, 3 7/8 In. 146.00
Jar, Peanut Butter, Clear, Elephant Standing, Lid, 3 1/4 In. 390.00
Jar, Storage, Blue Green, Pontil, Tooled, Flared Mouth, 6 3/8 In. 110.00
Jar, Storage, Yellow Amber, Pontil, Rolled Lip, 9 3/8 In. 110.00
Jar, Tobacco, Yellow, Barrel, Sheared, Ground Lip, Metal Lid, Bail, Wooden Handle, 7 1/4 In. 190.00
Jar, Wrigley's Doublemint Gum, Ground Top, Paper Label, 11 1/2 In. 360.00
Jar, Yellow Olive, Cylindrical, Tooled, Wide Flared Mouth, Pontil, 12 x 7 1/2 In. 770.00
Medicine, Apothecary, Clear, Blown, Pontil, Applied Foot, Ground Folded Rim, Stopper, 7 3/4 In. ... 78.00
Medicine, Apothecary, Clear, Tooled, Ground Lip, Columbia, 13 3/4 In. 310.00
Medicine, Apothecary, Cobalt Blue, Applied Rings, Hammered Copper Lid, 1820-40, 12 In. 220.00

Medicine, Apothecary, Cobalt Blue, Pontil, Rolled Lip, Stopper, 11 3/8 In. 215.00
Medicine, Apothecary, Compound Oxygen, Starkey & Palen, Phila., Cobalt Blue, 9 In. 69.00
Medicine, Apothecary, Cover, Clear, Applied Blue Banding, Finial, Pontil, c.1850s, 8 1/2 In....... 385.00
Medicine, Apothecary, Milk Glass, Flowers, Gold Lettering, Bromuro, Azahar, 7 3/4 In. 215.00
Medicine, Ayer's Cherry Pectoral, Aqua, Rectangular, Lowell, Mass., 7 1/2 In. 14.00
Medicine, Bininger's Old Dominion, Wheat Tonic, Olive Yellow, 1855, 9 3/4 In. 616.00
Medicine, Brant's Purifying Extract, M.T. Wallace & Co., Aquamarine, Pontil, 10 In. 358.00
Medicine, Bumstead's Worm Syrup, Applied Square Mouth, 4 1/2 In......................... 35.00
Medicine, C. Brinkerhoff Health Restorative, Yellow Olive, Beveled Corners, c.1850, 7 In. 852.00
Medicine, Caldwell's Syrup Pepsin, Blown In Mold, Applied Lip, 3 In. 6.00
Medicine, Clarke Stanley's Snake Oil Liniment, Embossed, Contents, Label, Box, 6 1/2 In. 358.00
Medicine, Clemen's Indian Tonic, Geo. W. House, Aqua, Oval, Tooled, Label, 5 5/8 In............ 690.00
Medicine, Dr. B. Ober's Compound Extract Of Mountain Ash, Aqua, Pontil, Flared Lip, 7 In. 800.00
Medicine, Dr. Belding Medicine Co., Tested Years, Blue, White, Box, Minneapolis, Minn., 9 In. 65.00
Medicine, Dr. Browder's Compound Syrup, Indian Turnip, Aqua, Open Pontil, Applied Top, 7 In. ... 390.00
Medicine, Dr. Cronk, Blue, 12-Sided, Iron Pontil, Applied Top, Embossed, 10 In. 5500.00
Medicine, Dr. Denig's Cough Balsam, Contents, Box, Mother & Baby Graphics, 6 1/2 In. 55.00
Medicine, Dr. Gordak Jelly Of Pomegranate, Preparate, Green, Aqua, Pontil, Oval, 6 7/8 In. 245.00
Medicine, Dr. Hoofland's Balsamic Cordial, Aqua, Pontil, Paneled, Flanged Lip, 6 3/4 In. 280.00
Medicine, Dr. J. Blackman's Genuine Healing Balsam, Clear, 8-Sided, Open Pontil, 5 5/8 In....... 70.00
Medicine, Dr. J.H. Mclean's Tar Wine Lung Balm, Label, Contents, Flyer, Box, 5 1/4 In............ 176.00
Medicine, Dr. Kelling's Pure Herb, Aqua, Open Pontil, Cylindrical, 6 3/8 In. 365.00
Medicine, Dr. Keyser's Blood & Searcher, Pittsburgh, Aqua, Round Collar, 1865-75, 9 In. 110.00
Medicine, Dr. Kilmer's Swamp Root Kidney Remedy, Sample, 4 1/4 In. 10.00
Medicine, Dr. Ordway's Celebrated Pain Destroyer, Flared Lip, Open Pontil, Label, 5 In........... 132.00
Medicine, Dr. Perry's Last Chance Liniment, Aqua, Applied Square Lip, 5 3/4 In. ....55.00 to 145.00
Medicine, Dr. Pettit's American Eye Water, Black & White, Wrapper, Buffalo, N.Y., 4 In............ 90.00
Medicine, Dr. R. Goodale's Catarrh Remedy, Blue, Aqua, Tubular Pontil, Applied Lip, 6 In......... 415.00
Medicine, Dr. Robbins' Tecumseh, Rheumatic, Boston, Mass., Blue, Open Pontil, 4 5/8 In........ 5000.00
Medicine, Dr. Rose's, Philadelphia, Teal, Sheared Inward Rolled Mouth, Pontil, Rectangular, 5 In. . 305.00
Medicine, Dr. S.A. Weaver's Canker & Salt Syrup, Aqua, Oval, Iron Pontil, Applied Mouth, 9 1/2 In. 179.00
Medicine, Dr. Seth Arnold's Cough Killer, Aqua, 5 In....................................... 20.00
Medicine, Dr. Thatcher's Liver & Blood Syrup, Yellow Green, Rectangular, 3 1/2 In. 75.00
Medicine, Dr. Thompson's Eye Water, 1/2 Gr. Opium, Sealed, 4 In. 110.00
Medicine, Drs. Ivan & Hart, New York, 8-Sided, Aquamarine, Pontil, Applied Mouth, 7 In. 1008.00
Medicine, E. Bringhurst's Essences, Clear, Pink, Gray, Beveled, Pontil, Rolled Lip, 5 In. 90.00
Medicine, Fairchild's Sure Remedy, Aqua, Open Pontil, Applied Mouth, 7 7/8 In................ 100.00
Medicine, Foster's Terp-Heroin, Amber, 6 3/4 In... 220.00
Medicine, G.W. Merchant Chemist, Lockport, N. Y., Blue Green, Pontil, Applied Mouth, 5 In. 336.00
Medicine, G.W. Merchant Chemist, Lockport, N. Y., Green, Pontil, Applied Mouth, 5 In. 670.00
Medicine, G.W. Merchant Chemist, Lockport, N. Y., Teal Blue, Iron Pontil, Sloping Collar, 7 In. 1230.00
Medicine, Gargling Oil, Lockport, N.Y., Emerald Green, Applied Sloping Collar, 7 3/8 In. 200.00
Medicine, Gargling Oil, Lockport, N.Y., Teal, 5 1/4 In....................................... 35.00
Medicine, Hazard & Caswell, Chemists, Newport, R.I., Aqua, 10 In. 19.00
Medicine, Healy & Bigelow, Indian Head, War Bonnet, Aqua, 8 1/2 In. 45.00
Medicine, Herrick's Germain Horse Liniment, Aqua, Paneled, 9 In. 40.00
Medicine, Hooker's English Remedy, W.H. Hooker & Co., Sole Agents, Cobalt Blue, 4 3/4 In. 39.00
Medicine, J.B. Wheatley's Compound Syrup, Dallasburgh, Ky., Aqua, Pontil, 1855, 6 In. ...110.00 to 180.00
Medicine, John Bull's King Of Pain, New York, Aqua, Open Pontil, Indented Panels, 5 In. 390.00
Medicine, John G. Hazzard & Co. Chemists, New York, Red Amber, Square, 7 1/4 In. 25.00
Medicine, Judson's Cherry & Lungwort, Blue Aqua, Open Pontil, Applied Mouth, 8 3/8 In. 840.00
Medicine, Karnak, Cork, Partial Contents, Box, 8 1/4 In. 15.00
Medicine, Kennedy's Salt Rheum Ointment, Aqua, Bulbous, Open Pontil, Rolled Lip, 2 In. 180.00
Medicine, Kopp's Baby's Friend, 1/8 Gr. Sulphate Morphine, Label, Box, 6 3/4 In. 330.00
Medicine, L.Q.C. Wishart's Pine Tree Tar Cordial, 1859, Blue Green, Square, 9 5/8 In. 330.00
Medicine, Linden Cough Balsam, Aqua, Stopper, Box, 6 1/4 In. 90.00
Medicine, Louden & Co.'s Indian Expectorant, Philadelphia, Aqua, Oval, 7 1/4 In............... 120.00
Medicine, Morse's Celebrated Syrup, Blue Green, Oval, Pontil, Applied Mouth, 9 1/2 In. 3080.00
Medicine, Moxie Nerve Food, Lowell, Mass., Patented, Cork, Early 1900s, 10 In. 185.00
Medicine, Mrs. E. Kidder's Dysentery Cordial, Green, Pontil, Cylindrical, 7 3/4 In. 3900.00
Medicine, Mrs. Metler's Dysentery Cordial, Aqua, Paneled, Tubular, Pontil, 6 3/4 In. 220.00

Medicine, Munyon's Germicide Solution, Green, Rectangular, 3 1/2 In. 25.00
Medicine, Mustang Liniment, Blue Aqua, Iron Pontil, Cylindrical, Mexico, 7 3/8 x 2 3/4 In. 440.00
Medicine, Myers Rock Rose, New Haven, Aqua, Sloping Collar, Iron Pontil, 9 1/4 In. 469.00
Medicine, Nerve & Bone Liniment, Yellow Green, Tubular, Open Pontil, Cylindrical, 3 7/8 In. 550.00
Medicine, Norwich Pharmacy Company, Cork Stopper, 7 In. 105.00
Medicine, Owl Drug Co., San Francisco, Embossed Owl, Teal Green, Applied Mouth, 8 In. 90.00
Medicine, Parke Davis Aloin Compound, 100 Gelatin Coated Pills, Label, 4 1/2 In. 40.00
Medicine, Price's Glycerin, Cobalt Blue, 4-Sided, Tapered, Partial Contents, Label, 7 1/2 In. 165.00
Medicine, Prof. H.K. Flagg's Balm Of Excellence, Aqua, Embossed, Pontil, Applied Top, 5 In. 280.00
Medicine, Queru's Cod Liver Oil, Aqua, Open Pontil, Outward Rolled Lip, 5 1/2 In. 100.00
Medicine, Red Cherry Cough Syrup, Label, Contents, Box, 7 1/4 In. 35.00
Medicine, Red Raven Splits, Green, Label, Contents, Metal Cap, Allegheny Co., Pa., 12 In. 38.00
Medicine, Rohrer's Expectoral Wild Cherry Tonic, Amber, Applied Mouth, 10 1/2 In. 310.00
Medicine, Rohrer's Expectoral Wild Cherry Tonic, Yellow Amber, Applied Mouth, 10 5/8 In. 390.00
Medicine, Sanford's Extract Of Hamamelis Or Witch Hazel, Cobalt Blue, Square, 11 In. 670.00
Medicine, Sanford's Extract Of Witch Hazel, Sapphire Blue, Applied Lip, 9 3/8 In. 325.00
Medicine, Scarpa's Oil For Deafness, Aqua, 6-Sided, Flared Lip, Open Pontil, 2 1/2 In. 450.00
Medicine, Shaker Cherry Pectoral Syrup, Aqua, Open Pontil, Applied Mouth, 5 3/8 In. 100.00
Medicine, Shaker Syrup No. 1, Canterbury, N.H., Aqua, Pontil, Beveled Panels, 7 1/2 In. 365.00
Medicine, Sulphume For Skin & Blood, Woman, Flyer, Partial Contents, Box, Boston, 8 In. 60.00
Medicine, Swaim's Panacea, Philada, Blue Green, Sloping Collar, 1860-70, 7 1/2 In. 390.00
Medicine, Swaim's Panacea, Philada, Lime Green, Pontil, Applied Lip, 8 In. 225.00
Medicine, Swaim's Panacea, Philada, Medium Green, 12 Indented Panels, Double Collar, 8 In. 358.00
Medicine, Swaim's Panacea, Philada, Olive Green, Applied Sloping Double Collar, 8 In. 310.00
Medicine, Taylor's Best, Cobalt Blue, 6-Sided, Cucumber Shape, Iron Pontil, 8 1/4 In. 1008.00
Medicine, Urquhart's Cholera Cordial, Aqua, 1860-70, 5 1/2 In. 22.00
Medicine, Vaughn's Vegetable Lithontriptic Mixture, Buffalo, Aqua, Applied Sloping Collar, 8 In. . . 660.00
Medicine, W.T. Wenzell, San Francisco, Aqua, Oval, Applied Square Lip, 5 1/2 In. 33.00
Medicine, Warner's Safe Diabetes Cure, Rochester, N.Y., Gold Amber, Oval, Double Collar, 9 1/2 In. 70.00
Medicine, Warner's Safe Kidney & Liver Remedy, Rochester, Orange Amber, 9 3/4 In. 40.00
Milk, Abbotts Alderney Dairies, Ribbed, Embossed, Round, Pt., 9 In. . . . . . 25.00 to 40.00
Milk, Allendale Dairy, Deposit, Red ACL, 1950, Qt. 5.00
Milk, America First Last Always, Eagle, Blue & Red War Slogan, ACL, Elmira, N.Y., Qt. 415.00
Milk, Ayrshire, Ken Ayr Farms, Brown & Green ACL, Round, Qt. 127.00
Milk, Beck's Dairy, Marshalltown, Ia., ACL, Round, Qt. 45.00
Milk, Bill's Milk Depot, Aurora, Colorado, Cow, ACL, Qt. 85.00
Milk, Bisgrove Dairy, Audubon, N.Y., Orange, Black, ACL, Square, Qt. 19.00
Milk, Bolte's Dairy, Seymour, Embossed, Round, Pt. 500.00
Milk, Borden's, Red ACL, Square, Qt. 15.00
Milk, Borden's, Ribs, Embossed, Round, 1/2 Pt. 6.00
Milk, Borden's, Ruby, Embossed, 8 1/2 x 3 3/4 In. 1705.00
Milk, Bowman Dairy Company, Chicago, Ill., Embossed, 1/2 Pt. 30.00
Milk, Brookfield, Baby Top, Baby Face In Neck, Qt., 9 1/2 In. 15.00
Milk, Cambridge Dairy, P. Young & Son, Denver, Est. 1892, Building, Orange & Black Letters, Qt. . . 85.00
Milk, Cardy's Dairy, Roswell, New Mex., Painted, Red Letters, Slug, Qt. 45.00
Milk, Casey Dairy, Cortland, New York, Green Spot, Green Circle, 1/2 Pt. 10.00
Milk, Cloverleaf Dairy, Springfield, Missouri, Red & Green ACL, Square, Qt. 25.00
Milk, Cole's Diamond Dairy, Port Jervis, N.Y., ACL, Cream Top, 9 1/2 In. 15.00
Milk, Columbia Dairy Farm, Faloma, Oregon, Embossed, Round Slug, Qt. 35.00
Milk, Conewago Dairy, ACL, Orange, Yellow, Qt. 12.00
Milk, Creamer, Crowley's Dairy, Maroon ACL, Square 45.00
Milk, Creamer, Ewells XL Dairy, Squared Mouth, Tin Closure, 1/2 Pt. 100.00
Milk, Creamer, Westwood, California, Westwood Creamery, 1930s, 4 1/4 x 2 In. 28.00
Milk, Culver Military Academy, Embossed, Round, 1/2 Pt. 330.00
Milk, Dairy Delivery Co., San Francisco, Rolled Edge, 1/2 Pt. 100.00
Milk, Dairylea, Dairymen's League, Embossed, Round, Pt. 7.00
Milk, Dean's, Cleveland Hts., Ohio, Orange ACL, Square, Squat, 1/2 Pt. 5.00
Milk, DeLaval, Embossed, Round, Pt. 20.00
Milk, Duncan & Beery, Winfield, Kansas, ACL, Round, Qt. 75.00
Milk, Edgewood, Girl's Head, Ice Cream Cone, ACL, Red, Orange, Black, Qt. 19.00
Milk, Estes Park Creamery, Estes Park, Colo., Girl On Horse, ACL, Squat, Qt. 125.00

Milk, Ezell Mackie Dairies, Purity Pasteurized Product, Embossed, 1/2 Pt. 15.00
Milk, Fairlea Farms, Ice Cream, Try It, Red Letters, Square, c.1960, Qt., 9 3/4 In. 18.00
Milk, Fischl's Dairy, Manitowoc, Wis., Red ACL, Cream Top, Qt. 24.00
Milk, Foremost, White ACL, Policeman, Children, Contoured, Netting Design, c.1940, Pt.......... 21.00
Milk, Gay's Dairy, Pinellas Park, Fla., Red ACL, Qt., 9 1/2 In. 9.00
Milk, Gloucester Milk Co., Embossed, Round, Qt. 8.00
Milk, Gray's Greeley, Colo., Only Home Owned Dairy, Painted, Dark Red, 1/2 Pt. 45.00
Milk, Grisham Dairy, Tipton, Embossed, Round, Qt. 425.00
Milk, Heisler's Cloverleaf Dairy Inc., Tamaqua, Pa., Baby, Green ACL, Square, 8 Oz. 51.00
Milk, Hershey Estates Local Farms, Hershey, Pa., Red & Green ACL, Square, Qt. 19.00
Milk, Hoffman's, In Any Season Serve Delicious Hot Or Cold Chocolate Milk, Pt. 19.00
Milk, Hottle Fisher Dairy, Strasburg, Va., Qt. 260.00
Milk, Isaly's Swiss Dairymen, Red ACL, Tall, Round, Qt. 10.00
Milk, J.P. Murawski, Southington, Conn., Yellow ACL, Qt. 110.00
Milk, Jersey Creamery, 1413 Park St., Alameda, Rolled Edge, Tin Closure, 1/2 Pt. 160.00
Milk, Kingston Milk Distributors, Embossed, Round, Canada, Qt. 12.00
Milk, Kline Dairy, Logansport, Embossed, Round, 1/2 Pt. 525.00
Milk, L.B. Haines, Hurffville, N.J., Embossed, Round, Tall, Qt. 9.00
Milk, Lake Placid Club Dairy, Club Farm Heavy Cream, Embossed, Round, Cap, Pt. 70.00
Milk, Lancaster Creamery, Boy, For Mothers Who Care, Amber, White ACL, Qt. 19.00
Milk, Martin Hill Dairy, H.H. Hottle, Strasburg, Va., Qt. 475.00
Milk, Maurer's Wayside Dairy, Mt. Carmel, Pa., Red ACL, Round, Qt. 11.00
Milk, Meadow Brook Dairy, Green River, Wyo., Slug Plate, Qt. 85.00
Milk, Merced Dairy, Solomon Bros., 1507 Broderick St., 10-Pin Shape, Tin Closure, Pt. 100.00
Milk, Mid Valley Farm Dairy, Green ACL, Square, Qt. 19.00
Milk, Millbrae California Milk Co., Folsom & 21st Sts., S.F., 10-Pin Shape, Pt. 120.00
Milk, Mission Ranch, Phoenix, Arizona, ACL, Dark Brown, 1/2 Pt. 35.00
Milk, O.H. Reddick, Seymour, Embossed, Round, Qt. 330.00
Milk, Okla. A & M College, Cowboy, Horse, Blue, ACL, 1/2 Pt. 195.00
Milk, Ottawa Dairy, Embossed, Round, Canada, Qt. 12.00
Milk, Parry Dairy, Forty Fort, Wyoming Valley, Pa., Clear, ACL, Cap, Qt., 8 3/4 In. 7.50
Milk, Pet Pasteurized, Red ACL, Square, Qt. 22.00
Milk, Plains Dairy, Cheyenne, Wyoming, Frontier Days, Black ACL, Round, Qt. 37.00
Milk, Quaker Maid Dairy Products, Pa., Embossed, Round, 1/2 Pt. 6.00
Milk, Queensboro Farm Products Inc., Long Island, N.Y., Wide Mouth, 16 Oz. 85.00
Milk, R.J. Gagnon, Waterville, Me., ACL, Round, 1/2 Pt. 25.00
Milk, R.S. Balenger Shady Side Dairy, Bunker Hill, Pt. 275.00
Milk, Red Bud Dairy Farm, Cole Bros., Stephenson, Va., Pt 625.00
Milk, Red Bud Dairy Farm, Cole Bros., Stephenson, Va., Qt. 500.00
Milk, Royal Oak Dairy, Taste The Difference, Silk Screen Label, 10 1/4 In. 15.00
Milk, Russells' Farm Dairy, Winchester, Va., Qt. 250.00
Milk, San Mateo County Dairy, 10-Pin Shape, Pt. 100.00
Milk, Sheffield Sealtest, Red ACL, Round, Squat, Qt. 12.00
Milk, Shenandale Dairy, Elkton, Va, Qt. 425.00
Milk, Sherman Dairy Co., South Haven, Mich., Orange ACL, Square, Qt. 25.00
Milk, Skyland Dairy, Luray, Va., Qt. 325.00
Milk, Skyline Farms, Grade A Dairy Products, Lincoln, Neb., Red ACL, Square, Qt. 8.00
Milk, Steward's, Thermopolis, Wyo., World's Largest Hot Springs, ACL, Round, Qt. 250.00
Milk, Sunny Slope Dairy, 9 3/4 In. 19.00
Milk, Sunnyside, Geo. P. Kern Dairy Co., Pt. 225.00
Milk, Sunrise Dairy, Gastonia, N.C., Boy Carrying Bottle, Red Letters, Square, c.1951, Qt. 18.00
Milk, Thackston Dairy, Yankee Doodle Verse, Maroon ACL, Tall, Round, 1940s, Qt. 50.00
Milk, Thatcher's Dairy, Martinsburg, W.V., Qt. 140.00
Milk, Tilton Dairy Farms, Asbury Park, N.J., Embossed, Round, Qt. 20.00
Milk, Try Gold Guernsey, Dairymen's Association Ltd., Honolulu, ACL, Squat, Qt. 125.00
Milk, United Farmers Co-Operative, Boston, Mass., Red Letters, Cream Top, Qt. 50.00
Milk, United Milk Co., S.F., Amber, 10-Pin, Rolled Edge, Qt. 275.00
Milk, University Of Georgia, George Washington, Red ACL, Round, Qt. 160.00
Milk, Velvet Cream & Dairy Products, Reno, Nev., Red ACL, Tall, Round, 1940s, 1/2 Pt. 11.00
Milk, Warner Bros., Bugs Bunny, Only 10, 200 Made, Multicolor ACL, Square, Qt. 28.00
Milk, Whitcomb's Farms, Littleton, Mass., Baby Face, Qt. 212.00

Milk, White Oak Dairy, Tree, 2 Cows, Orange ACL, Embossed Diamond, 1/2 Pt. 12.00
Milk, Winnisimet Dairy, Tiverton, R.I., Amber, White ACL, Indian Head, Square, Qt. 10.00
Milk, Winnisquam Farms, Waterbury, Amber, White ACL, Square, Qt. 12.00
Milk, Zapp's Dairy, That Good Flavor, ACL, Round, Qt., 9 1/2 In. 12.00
Mineral Water, A.W. Rapp's Improved Patent, New York, Blue Green, 6 3/4 In. 336.00
Mineral Water, A.W. Rapp, N.Y., Cobalt Blue, Iron Pontil, Applied Blob Mouth, 7 3/4 In. 286.00
Mineral Water, Alburgha, Gold Amber, Applied Double Collar, Qt. 1064.00
Mineral Water, Alburgha, Yellow Amber, Applied Double Collar, Qt. 1456.00
Mineral Water, Blatz Gold Star Carbonated, Green, Label, 1924, 11 1/2 In. 40.00
Mineral Water, Blount Springs, Cobalt Blue, Applied Mouth, 1870-80, 8 7/8 In. 179.00
Mineral Water, Blount Springs, Natural Sulphur Water, Monogram, Cobalt Blue, 7 5/8 In. 160.00
Mineral Water, Blue Mountain Forest, Cobalt Blue, Tooled Mouth, 10 In. 246.00
Mineral Water, Broughton & Chase, Rochester, N.Y., Sapphire Blue, Blob Top, 7 1/2 In. 210.00
Mineral Water, Buffalo Lithia, Blue Green, Cylindrical, Square Collar, 9 3/4 In. 250.00
Mineral Water, C.B. Hale, Camden, N.J., Blue Green, Sloping Double Collar, Pontil, 7 1/4 In. 168.00
Mineral Water, C.B. Hale, Camden, N.J., Emerald Green, Sloping Double Collar, Pontil, 7 In. 336.00
Mineral Water, Caladonia Spring, Yellow Amber, Applied Double Collar, Qt. 505.00
Mineral Water, Caledonia Spring, Wheelock, Vt., Yellow Amber, Sloping Collar, 1870, Qt. 479.00
Mineral Water, Campbell Mineral Spring Co., Blue Aqua, Double Collar, Qt. 896.00
Mineral Water, Chalybeate, Light To Medium Green, Applied Blob Lip, 7 3/4 In. 330.00
Mineral Water, Champion Spouting Spring, Blue Aqua, Swirls, Pt. 150.00
Mineral Water, Chattolanee Water, Chattolanee, Md., Aqua, 1/2 Gal. 69.00
Mineral Water, Clarke & Co., Blue Green, Iron Pontil, Applied Double Collar, Qt. .... 310.00 to 336.00
Mineral Water, Clarke & White, New York, Forest Green, Applied Sloping Double Collar, Pt. 55.00
Mineral Water, Clarke & White, New York, Yellow Olive Amber, Sloping Double Collar, Pt. 135.00
Mineral Water, Congress & Empire Spring Co., Blue Green, Double Collar, Pt. 90.00
Mineral Water, Congress & Empire Spring Co., Emerald Green, Double Collar, 9 In. 785.00
Mineral Water, Congress & Empire Spring Co., Forest Green, Embossed Cross, Pt. 160.00
Mineral Water, Congress & Empire Spring Co., Large E, Emerald Green, Pt. 45.00
Mineral Water, Congress & Empire Spring Co., Olive Green, Double Applied Collar, Pt. 180.00
Mineral Water, Excelsior Spring, Yellow Green, Hand Tooled Lip, Embossed, Qt. 415.00
Mineral Water, G.W. Weston & Co., Olive Green, Sloping Double Collar Mouth, Qt. 160.00
Mineral Water, Gleason & Cole, Olive Yellow, Iron Pontil, Sloping Collar Mouth, 7 3/4 In. 728.00
Mineral Water, Guilford Spring, Blue Green, Double Collar, 1865-75, Qt. 100.00
Mineral Water, Hanbury Smith, Vichy Water, Olive Yellow, Sloping Collar, Pt. 146.00
Mineral Water, Hand & Murtha, Aqua, Sloping Collar, Iron Pontil, 1840-60, 7 3/8 In. 896.00
Mineral Water, Harris, S, Albany, Blue Green, Sloping Collar, Deep Kick-Up, 7 1/4 In. 1065.00
Mineral Water, Hawthorn Spring, Emerald Green, Saratoga, N.Y., Pt., 7 1/4 In. 99.00
Mineral Water, Highrock Congress Spring, Amber, Double Applied Collar, Embossed, Qt. 450.00
Mineral Water, Highrock Congress Spring, C & W, Saratoga, Teal Blue, Sloping Collar, Pt. 525.00
Mineral Water, Highrock Congress Spring, Yellow Amber, Sloping Double Collar, Qt. 335.00
Mineral Water, Hutchinson & Co., Blue, Cylindrical, Iron Pontil, Blob Top, 7 1/8 In. 650.00
Mineral Water, Hutchinson & Co., Sapphire Blue, Cylindrical, Iron Pontil, 7 1/4 In. 500.00
Mineral Water, I.G. Powell, Honesdale Glass Works, Pa., Blue Green, Iron Pontil, 7 In. 390.00
Mineral Water, Iodine Spring, Old Amber, Applied Double Collar, 1865-85, Qt. 1568.00
Mineral Water, J. & W. Coles, Cobalt Blue, Iron Pontil, Applied Blob Mouth, 7 3/8 In. 420.00
Mineral Water, John Clarke, N.Y., Olive Amber, Pontil, Applied Double Collar, Pt. 310.00
Mineral Water, John Clarke, N.Y., Olive Amber, Pontil, Applied Double Collar, Qt. 200.00
Mineral Water, Lamoille Spring, Yellow Gold Amber, Applied Double Collar, 1865-75, Qt. 160.00
Mineral Water, Lynch & Clarke, New York, Olive Green, Applied Double Collar, 7 3/8 In. 330.00
Mineral Water, Lynde & Putnam, Teal Blue, Iron Pontil, Applied Blob Mouth, 7 1/8 In. 269.00
Mineral Water, M.T. Crawford, Blue, Violet, Pontil, Applied Blob Mouth, 7 5/8 In. 840.00
Mineral Water, Minnequa, Bradford Co., Amber, Applied Double Lip, Qt. 725.00
Mineral Water, Minnequa, Bradford Co., Aqua, Applied Top, Pt. 390.00
Mineral Water, Minnequa, Bradford Co., Orange Amber, Qt. 170.00
Mineral Water, Missisquoi A Springs, Woman & Papoose, Yellow, Olive Green, Qt. 420.00
Mineral Water, Missisquoi A Springs, Yellow Amber, Applied Double Collar, 1870-75, Qt. 150.00
Mineral Water, Missisquoi A Springs, Yellow Green, Applied Double Collar, 1865-70, Qt. 235.00
Mineral Water, Pavilion & United States Spring Co., Saratoga, N.Y., Emerald Green, Pt. 165.00
Mineral Water, Saratoga Spring Co., Yellow Green, Drippy Applied Top, Pt. 190.00
Mineral Water, Saratoga Star Spring, Amber, Pt., 7 1/2 In. 110.00

Mineral Water, Saratoga Vichy Spouting Spring, Aqua, Applied Top, Embossed, Qt. 220.00
Mineral Water, Seitz & Bros., Premium, Easton, Pa., Cobalt Blue, 8-Sided, Blob Top, 7 1/4 In. 785.00
Mineral Water, Seitz & Bros., Sapphire Blue, 8-Sided, Iron Pontil, Blob Mouth, 7 1/8 In. 390.00
Mineral Water, Sheldon A Spring, Sheldon, Vt., Red Amber, Sloping Double Collar, Qt. ..2800.00 to 3080.00
Mineral Water, Shell Rock Spring, Aqua, 5 Pints Bottled At The Spring, 11 1/2 x 1 1/2 In. 35.00
Mineral Water, Southwick & Tupper, Blue Green, 10-Sided, Pontil, Blob Mouth, 7 5/8 In. 840.00
Mineral Water, Tweddle's Celebrated, Blue Green, 7 1/4 In. 476.00
Mineral Water, Vermont Spring, Blue, Green, Applied Double Collar, 1865-75, Qt. 125.00
Mineral Water, Vichy, Patterson, Forest Green, Applied Top, 1/2 Pt. 200.00
Mineral Water, W.W. Lappeus, Albany, Teal Blue, 3-Piece Mold, Sloping Collar, Pontil, 7 In. 785.00
Mineral Water, Washington Spring Co., Bust Of Washington, Emerald Green, 1868-89, 8 In. 880.00
Mineral Water, Wm. H. Weaver, Belvidere, Slug Plate, Blue Green, Blob Top, Pontil, 7 1/4 In. 1568.00
Mineral Water, Wm. H. Weaver, Hackettstown, Slug Plate, Blue Green, Blob Top, Pontil, 7 3/8 In. . 450.00
Mineral Water, Wm. W. Lappeus, Cobalt Blue, Iron Pontil, Applied Blob Mouth, 7 In. 1120.00
Nursing, A1 Hygienic Feeder, Clear, Tablespoon & Ounce Gradations 30.00
Nursing, Allenbury, Semi-Banana Shape, Gradations On Base, c.1890 .... 50.00
Nursing, Grip-Tight, Curved, Embossed, Box, Pre 1910, 7 In. 135.00
Oil, Edison Battery Oil, Made In U.S.A., Thomas A. Edison, Bloomfield, N.J., 4 Oz., 4 In. 8.00
Oil, Heisey, Old Sandwich, Stopper, 8 1/2 x 3 In. 130.00
Onion, Squat, Green, 7 In. 144.00
Pattern Molded, Honeycomb, Round Lip, 9 1/2 x 4 1/2 In. 175.00
Pepper Sauce, Emerald Green, Ribs, 9 In. 45.00
Perfume bottles are listed in their own category.
Pickle, 6-Sided, Leaf, Blue Green, Indented, Outward-Rolled Lip, 12 7/8 In. 2200.00
Pickle, 6-Sided, Leaf, Blue Green, Rolled Lip, 13 1/8 x 5 In. 550.00
Pickle, 7 Vertical Lobes, 16 Flutes, Blue Green, Tooled Lip, Iron Pontil, 1845-60, 11 1/2 In. 880.00
Pickle, 8-Sided, Leaf, Aqua, Iron Pontil, Rolled Lip, 10 3/4 x 4 1/2 In. 725.00
Pickle, Blue Aqua, Draped Shoulder, Iron Pontil, Rolled Lip, 11 1/4 In. 146.00
Pickle, Cathedral, Aqua, 3 Balls, Open Pontil, Outward Rolled Lip, 9 1/8 In. 325.00
Pickle, Cathedral, Aqua, 8-Sided, X Hatch, Open Pontil, Rolled Lip, 8 5/8 x 3 In. 700.00
Pickle, Cathedral, Aqua, Outward-Rolled Lip, 1865-75, 11 1/2 In. 165.00
Pickle, Cathedral, Aqua, Outward-Rolled Lip, Iron Pontil, 11 1/2 In. 1100.00
Pickle, Cathedral, Aqua, Outward-Rolled Lip, Tubular Pontil, 7 1/2 In. 2090.00
Pickle, Cathedral, Aqua, Rolled Lip, Crown Mark On Base, 14 3/4 In. 45.00
Pickle, Cathedral, Aqua, Trefoils, Outward Rolled Lip, c.1850, 11 1/2 In. 190.00
Pickle, Cathedral, Aquamarine, Single Collar, 1860-70, 13 3/4 In. 595.00
Pickle, Cathedral, Beveled Corners, Gothic Arches, Medium Green, Iron Pontil, 8 5/8 In. 408.00
Pickle, Cathedral, Blue Aqua, Diamond Geometrics, 1/2 Pt. 45.00
Pickle, Cathedral, Blue Aqua, Iron Pontil, Rolled Lip, 12 In. 504.00
Pickle, Cathedral, Blue Aqua, Oval Panels, Leaf, Pt. 100.00
Pickle, Cathedral, Blue Green, Rolled Lip, 11 3/4 In. 390.00
Pickle, Cathedral, Green, Applied Lip, 11 1/2 In. 800.00
Pickle, Cathedral, Green, Applied Lip, 14 In. 1500.00
Pickle, Cathedral, Green, Applied Lip, Neck Ring, Iron Pontil, 11 3/4 In. ....475.00 to 650.00
Pickle, Cathedral, Green, Blue, Rolled Lip, Embossed, 1/2 Gal. 2200.00
Pickle, Cathedral, Light Green, 13 7/8 x 4 In. 450.00
Pickle, Cathedral, Light Green, Applied Lip, Iron Pontil, 7 1/2 In. 275.00
Pickle, Cathedral, Teal Green, 14 In. 255.00
Pickle, Crosshatch, Tubular Open Pontil, Rolled Lip, Square, 6 In. 170.00
Pickle, Keyhole, Blue Aqua, Neck Ring, Applied Lip, Iron Pontil, 9 In. 700.00
Pickle, Scrolled Leaf, Aqua, Rolled Lip, Embossed, Square, 11 3/4 x 4 In. 900.00
Pickle, Tin Lid, Bail Handle, 15 x 9 In. 88.00
Pickle, W.K. Lewis & Co., Blue Aqua, Iron Pontil, Applied Mouth, 10 3/4 In. 560.00
Pickle, Wells Miller & Provost, Blue Green, Square, Applied Collar, Pontil, 11 3/4 In. 400.00
Poison, Admiralty, Cobalt Blue, Arrow, N, Blown In Mold, Applied Lip, Square, 1 Oz., 4 1/2 In. 85.00
Poison, Ammonia, Caution Poisonous Not To Be Taken, Beehive, 6 1/4 In. 35.00
Poison, Bright Green, Tooled Lip, Vertical Ribs, Cylindrical, Stopper, 6 3/4 In. 40.00
Poison, Carbolene Disinfectant, Aqua, Oval, Tooled Lip, 6 1/4 In. 20.00
Poison, Carbolic Acid, Cobalt Blue, Oval, 6 1/2 In. 25.00
Poison, Clarkes Clear Fluid Ammonia, Aqua, Offset Neck, 9 In. 40.00
Poison, Cobalt Blue, Skull Shape, Embossed, c.1894, 3 1/2 In. 1323.00

Poison, Cobalt Blue, Triangular, Cross-Stitching, Embossed, 5 1/8 In. 325.00
Poison, Cobalt Blue, Triangular, Embossed Mesh Design, U.D.C.O., 3 1/2 x 1 1/2 In. 110.00
Poison, Coffin, Gold Amber, Tooled Round Collar, Norwich 16A, 7 1/2 In. 13250.00
Poison, Coffin, Pointed Diamonds, Cobalt Blue, Embossed, 3 7/16 In. 130.00
Poison, Coffin, Pointed Diamonds, Cork, Labels, 4 7/8 In. 1400.00
Poison, Diamond & Lattice, Blue Green, Cylindrical, Tooled Lip, 4 5/8 In. 310.00
Poison, Diamond & Lattice, Cobalt Blue, Cylindrical, 3 7/8 In. 100.00
Poison, Dykemas, C.L.G. Co., Grass Green, Irregular Hexagon, Tooled Ring Top, 6 In. 2275.00
Poison, Embalmer's Supply Co., Clear, Square Squat, 8 1/2 In., 1/2 Gal. 45.00
Poison, Embalming Fluid, Rochester Germicide, Flared Lip, Patent 1883, 8 1/2 In. 125.00
Poison, F.A. Thompson & Co., Detroit, Coffin, Light Yellow Amber, Tooled Lip, 3 In. 425.00
Poison, Formalin, Hand Holding Scythe, Cuming Smith & Co., Red Amber, Vertical Ribs, 8 In. 200.00
Poison, Killgerm Disinfectant, Poisonous Not To Be Taken, Aqua, Oval, 6 1/2 In. 20.00
Poison, Lyon's Powder, Golden Amber, Open Pontil, Rolled Lip, 4 3/8 In. 190.00
Poison, Lyon's Powder, Olive Green, Open Pontil, Rolled Lip, 4 3/8 In. 308.00
Poison, Lyon's Powder, Pink Amethyst, Shaded, Open Pontil, Rolled Lip, 4 1/4 In. 190.00
Poison, Lysol Boots, All British, Green, Stars, Embossed, Blown In Mold, Applied Lip, 4 In. 39.00
Poison, Manchester Royal Infirmary, Green, 6-Sided, 7 1/2 In. 35.00
Poison, Not To Be Taken, Aqua, Ribbed, 9 In. 25.00
Poison, Not To Be Taken, Embossed, Cobalt Blue, 6-Sided, 6 3/4 In. 25.00
Poison, Olive Green, Horizontal Ribs, Irregular Hexagon, 5 1/2 In. 240.00
Poison, Owbridge's Embrocation Hull, Cobalt Blue, 6-Sided, 5 In. 35.00
Poison, Plynine Limited Household Ammonia, Green, 11 In. 40.00
Poison, Skull & Crossbones, Cobalt Blue, Embossed, Ribs, Tooled Lip, 3 1/4 In. 70.00
Poison, Skull & Crossbones, Green, 6-Sided, Tooled Lip, Germany, 8 1/2 In. 150.00
Poison, Skull & Crossbones, Star, Yellow Amber, Oval, Tooled Lip, 4 3/4 In. 840.00
Poison, Tippers Animal Medicines, Cobalt Blue, Cylindrical, 7 1/2 In. 195.00
Poison, Vulcanizing Fluid, Metal Cap, Keystone Rubber & Mfg. Co., Erie, Pa., 5 x 2 1/4 In. 125.00
Sarsaparilla, Compound Extract, Clear, Rectangular, Lowell, Mass., 8 1/2 In. 7.00
Sarsaparilla, Custer's Extract, Aqua, 1880-90, 9 1/8 In. 146.00
Sarsaparilla, Dr. J. Townsend's, New York, Aqua, Tubular, Open Pontil, Square, 9 5/8 In. 1650.00
Sarsaparilla, Dr. Thompson's, New York, Teal Blue, Iron Pontil, Applied Mouth, 9 3/4 In. 1345.00
Sarsaparilla, Dr. Townsend's, Albany, N.Y., Olive Green, Sloping Collar, Pontil, 9 1/2 In. 330.00
Sarsaparilla, Dr. Townsend's, Albany, N.Y., Yellow Green, Square, 9 1/2 In. 225.00
Sarsaparilla, Dr. Townsend's, Albany, N.Y., Yellow Olive, Tapered Lip, Pontil, c.1850, 9 3/4 In. 240.00
Sarsaparilla, Dr. Wynkoop's, Cobalt Blue, Pontil, Applied Mouth, 10 1/4 In. 4200.00
Sarsaparilla, F. Gleason, Sapphire Blue, 10-Sided, Flat Panels, Iron Pontil, 7 5/8 In. 1900.00
Sarsaparilla, Joy's, Edwin W. Joy Co., San Francisco, Blue Aqua, 1890s, 8 1/2 In. 45.00
Scent, Amber, Heart & Fleur-De-Lis, Pontil, Pewter Crown Cap, France, 3 1/2 In. 202.00
Scent, Aqua, Oval, Pinched Center, Pontil, Sheared, Tooled Lip, Applied Rigaree, 2 In. 365.00
Scent, Blue, Swirled Ribs, Oval, 2 3/4 x 1 1/2 In. 28.00
Scent, Clear, Cobalt Blue Overlay, Cut Glass, Sheared, Polished Lip, Stopper, 3 1/4 In. 168.00
Scent, Clear, Cobalt Blue Overlay, Polished Pontil, Sheared, Tooled Lip, 3 In. 110.00
Scent, Clear, Gray Tone, Column, Open Pontil, Flared Lip, Embossed, 8 3/8 In. 165.00
Scent, Clear, Pinched Waist, Pontil, Sheared, Tooled Lip, Applied Rigaree Bands, 2 1/2 In. 125.00
Scent, Cobalt Blue & White Swirl, Sandwich, 3 3/8 In. 165.00
Scent, Cobalt Blue, Concentric Ring, Pontil, Tooled Lip, 2 1/4 In. 225.00
Scent, Cobalt Blue, Cut Glass, Waffle, Pontil, Sheared, Polished Lip, 3 1/8 In. 110.00
Scent, Cobalt Blue, Flat Oval, Ribbed Shoulder, Waist, Raised Band, Ground Mouth, 2 1/8 In. 300.00
Scent, Cobalt Blue, Molded, Ribbed, 3 In. 165.00
Scent, Cobalt Blue, Olive Yellow Overlay, Herringbone, Pontil, Sheared, Ground Lip, 2 In. 135.00
Scent, Honeycomb, Plain Oval, Pear Form, Cobalt Blue, Sheared Mouth, Pontil, 2 3/4 In. 825.00
Scent, Milk Glass, Gray Blue, Column, Open Pontil, Flared Lip, Embossed, 8 3/8 In. 775.00
Scent, Milk Glass, Open Pontil, Pheasant, Flowers, Cylindrical, 13 1/2 In. 550.00
Scent, Opalescent Electric Blue, Octagonal, Pinched Waist, Metal Screw Lid, 2 3/8 In. 520.00
Scent, Porcelain, Couple Seated In Meadow, Landscape, 2 1/2 In. 120.00
Scent, Seahorse, Clear, Copper Wheel-Cut Letter, Pontil, Tooled Lip, Applied Rigaree, 4 In. 670.00
Scent, Seahorse, Clear, Teal Blue Applied Rigaree, Pontil, Tooled Lip, 2 1/4 In. 110.00
Scent, Seahorse, Clear, White Bands, Pontil, Tooled Lip, Applied Rigaree, 4 3/4 In. 670.00
Scent, Seahorse, Clear, White, Blue, Puce Bands, Pontil, Tooled Mouth, Applied Rigaree, 2 5/8 In. 1008.00
Scent, Seahorse, Cobalt Blue, White Bands, Pontil, Tooled Mouth, Rigaree, 2 3/4 In. 530.00

Scent, Sunburst, Sapphire Blue, Beaded Edge, Pontil, 1820-40, 2 3/4 In. 765.00
Scent, Sunburst, Shield Form, Cobalt Blue, Sheared Mouth, Pontil, 2 5/8 In. 220.00
Scent, Water Lilies, Dragonfly, Teardrop, Red Ground, Screw Cap, Cameo, 3 1/4 In. 3335.00
Scent, Yellow, Amber, Heart & Fleur-De-Lis, Pontil, Pewter Crown Cap, France, 3 1/2 In. 728.00
Seal, Black Glass, Olive Amber, Pontil, Applied Double Collar, England, 1770-90, 11 In. 364.00
Seal, Class Of 1846, W, Yellow Olive, Applied Collar, Ring, Iron Pontil, Qt. 495.00
Seal, E.I.J. Whiskey, Yellow Olive, Applied Collar, Ring, Iron Pontil, 1845-60, Qt. 1980.00
Seal, F. & Co. Whiskey, New York, Inverted Cone, Yellow Amber, Double Collar, Pontil, 16 In. 3850.00
Seal, H. Rickett's & Co., Olive Green, Pontil, Double Collar, 3-Piece Mold, England, 11 In. ..170.00 to 179.00
Seal, Nathan Bros. Whiskey, Amber, Lip, Crosshatch, c.1860-75, 7 1/2 In. 190.00
Seltzer, Belfast, San Francisco, Green, ACL, Qt. 30.00
Seltzer, Cosley Bottling Co., Green, Ribs, Dubuque, Iowa, 12 In. 55.00
Seltzer, Mimi Seltzer Co., Blue Glass, Chrome, Art Deco, Czechoslovakia 100.00
Seltzer, Red Dragon, New York, Green, Cylindrical, 2 3/4 In. 30.00
Snuff, Agate, Almond Shape, Brown, Dark Bands, Stopper, Chinese, 1800s, 3 In. 143.00
Snuff, Agate, Birds, Flowering Tree, Turquoise Inlaid Base, Chinese, 1800s, 2 1/2 In. 355.00
Snuff, Agate, Butterscotch, Square, Stopper, 19th Century, 2 1/2 In. 176.00
Snuff, Agate, Embellished Figures, Interior Decoration, 2 1/2 In. 1755.00
Snuff, Agate, Flask Shape, Blue Tracery, Brown Banding, Hardstone Stopper, 3 In. 75.00
Snuff, Agate, Flask Shape, Carved, Fish, Lotus, Camellia, Banded, Red Glass Stopper, 2 1/2 In. ... 114.00
Snuff, Agate, Flask Shape, Relief Carving, Face, Boy Holding Cabbage, Quartz Stopper, 3 In. 145.00
Snuff, Agate, Gray, Black Marking, 1800s, 2 1/4 In. 235.00
Snuff, Agate, Honey, Flowers, 144 Label, 1800s, 2 1/4 In. 150.00
Snuff, Agate, Horse, High Relief, 171 Label, c.1800, 2 1/4 In. 5875.00
Snuff, Agate, Monkey, Horse, 125 Label, Chinese, c.1800, 2 1/2 In. 2115.00
Snuff, Agate, Moss, Gilt Wirework Overlay, Coral, Turquoise, Mongolia, 3 1/2 In. 295.00
Snuff, Agate, Rounded Flask Shape, Cloudy Translucent, Amethyst Stopper, 3 In. 125.00
Snuff, Agate, Sparrow, Hawk In Tree, Rectangular, Glass Stopper, 2 3/4 In. 1380.00
Snuff, Amethyst, Bird, Tree, Mother-Of-Pearl, Flat Oval, Malachite Stopper, 2 1/2 In. 230.00
Snuff, Amethyst, Cicada, Stone Stopper, 2 1/4 In. 865.00
Snuff, Carnelian, Buddha's Hand, Citron, 19th Century, 2 1/4 In. 380.00
Snuff, Carnelian, Goldfish Shape, Chinese, 1800s, 2 1/4 In. 264.00
Snuff, Cinnabar, Children, Landscape, Sunken Relief, Spade Shape, Amber Stopper, 2 In. 390.00
Snuff, Cinnabar, Figural Landscape, Spade Shape, Rose Quartz Stopper, 2 3/4 In. 115.00
Snuff, Coral Glass, Flattened Flask Shape, Pine, Deer, Pavilion, 19th Century, 2 1/2 In. 349.00
Snuff, Coral, Birds, Trees, Animals, Chinese, 1800s, 2 1/4 In. 3055.00
Snuff, Enamel, Crane & Pine Tree, Metal Spoon, Chinese, 1800s, 2 3/4 In. 250.00
Snuff, Glass, Brown, Overall Enamel Decoration, Figures, Flowers, Chinese, 2 1/8 In. 2635.00
Snuff, Glass, Brown, Red Overlay, Monkeys, Lion Epaulets, Hardstone Stopper, Chinese, 3 In. 270.00
Snuff, Glass, Chinese Elder & Child, Reverse Painted, 2 x 1 3/4 x 1 1/4 In. 33.00
Snuff, Glass, Chocolate Amber, Square, Open Pontil, Tooled, Flared Lip, 4 1/4 In. 390.00
Snuff, Glass, Coral Color, Double Gourd, Carved Gourds & Vines, 3 In. 376.00
Snuff, Glass, Double Gourd, Aubergine Overlay, Hydra, Bat, Chinese, 3 In. 380.00
Snuff, Glass, Dragon, Opalescent Ground, Oval, Quartz Stopper, 2 In. 2070.00
Snuff, Glass, Enameled Bird, Lotus, Flattened Oval, Chinese, 3 In. 585.00
Snuff, Glass, Flask Shape, Red Body, 2 Hydra, Amber Overlay, Agate Stopper, Chinese, 3 In. 180.00
Snuff, Glass, Green, Rectangular, Chamfered Corners, Tooled, Flared Lip, Pontil, 4 1/2 In. 660.00
Snuff, Glass, Honey Amber, Stoddard, Square, 3 3/4 x 2 3/8 In. 48.00
Snuff, Glass, Man On Horse, Attendant, Palace, White, Silver Top, Chinese, 1800s, 2 1/2 In. 1116.00
Snuff, Glass, Olive Amber, Square, Paneled, Pontil, Tooled, Flared Lip, 5 3/4 In. 560.00
Snuff, Glass, Olive Green, Square, Beveled Panels, Open Pontil, Tooled, Flared Lip, 5 In. 615.00
Snuff, Glass, Olive Yellow, Rectangular, Sheared, Open Pontil, c.1790-1820, 6 In. 210.00
Snuff, Glass, Orange Amber, Square, Pontil, Tooled, Flared Lip, 3 1/2 In. 365.00
Snuff, Glass, Plum Amethyst, Tooled, Flared Lip, Pontil, Rectangular, Beveled Corners, 4 1/4 In. 1650.00
Snuff, Glass, Red Cut To White, Chinese, 2 3/4 In. 380.00
Snuff, Glass, Turquoise, Yellow, Ruby, Pink Flowers, Leaves, Snowflakes, Stopper, 2 3/4 In. 560.00
Snuff, Glass, Yellow Amber, Rectangular, Panels, Pontil, Flared Lip, 5 In. 500.00
Snuff, Glass, Yellow, Olive Amber, 8-Sided, Open Pontil, Tooled, Flared Lip, 4 In. 840.00
Snuff, Ivory, Archaic Bronze Shape, Chinese, Late 1800s, 2 1/2 In. 646.00
Snuff, Ivory, Bamboo Shoot, Stopper, 3 1/2 In. 325.00
Snuff, Ivory, Figural Landscape, Temple Vase Shape, Stopper, 3 1/4 In. 635.00

Snuff, Ivory, Scholar, Peacock, Red, White, Spade Shape, Stopper, 4 1/4 In. 635.00
Snuff, Ivory, Texts, Flowers, Lacquer Inlay, Chinese, 1800s, 3 In. 2820.00
Snuff, Ivory, Woman Carrying Basket, Head Stopper, 3 3/4 In. 138.00
Snuff, Ivory, Woman, Multicolored, Japan, Early 1900s, 4 1/2 In. ....294.00 to 355.00
Snuff, Jade, Bird, Lotus, Green, White, Mock Handles, Rectangular, Ruby Stopper, 2 In. 1610.00
Snuff, Jade, Blue, Gray, Pavilion, Seal, 19th Century, 2 1/2 In. 590.00
Snuff, Jade, Flowers, White, Ruby Glass Stopper, Chinese, c.1800, 2 1/2 In. 5288.00
Snuff, Jade, Frog, 3-Legged, Green, Red Area, Chinese, 1800s, 2 1/2 In. 880.00
Snuff, Jade, Goldfish On Lily Pad, Red, Green Marking, Chinese, 1800s, 2 1/2 In. 5580.00
Snuff, Jade, Green, Melon Shape, 1800s, 2 1/2 In. 470.00
Snuff, Jade, Hawk, Pine Tree, Blue Lavender, Stopper, 2 1/4 In. 259.00
Snuff, Jade, Heart Shape, Hollowed Form, c.1800, 2 1/2 In. 355.00
Snuff, Jade, Moss On Snow, Apple Green, White Ground, Stopper, 19th Century, 2 In. 235.00
Snuff, Jade, Mottled, Tapered, Flattened, Carved Mask Mock Ring Handles, 3 1/4 In. 235.00
Snuff, Jade, Mutton Fat, Brown, White, Oval, Jadeite Stopper, 2 In. 430.00
Snuff, Jade, Mutton Fat, Dragon In Clouds, Glass Stopper, 3 In. 518.00
Snuff, Jade, Nephrite, Rectangular, Glass Stopper, 2 1/2 In. 805.00
Snuff, Jade, Peach Shape, Gray Yellow, Jadeite Top, 1800s, 2 In. 705.00
Snuff, Jade, Raised Panel, Gray, White, Rectangular, Agate Stopper, 2 1/4 In. 115.00
Snuff, Jade, Swirling Bat, White, Oval, Glass Stopper, 2 In. 690.00
Snuff, Jade, Turtle Shape, c.1800, 2 1/2 In. 590.00
Snuff, Jade, Vase Shape, White, Foo Dog Masks, 1800s, 2 In. 1410.00
Snuff, Lacquer On Metal, Women, Black Ground, Spade Shape, Stopper, 4 In. 1080.00
Snuff, Lapis Lazuli, Carved Dragon, Gemological Institute Of America Note, 3 In. 700.00
Snuff, Lapis Lazuli, Coral Top, Square, Brass, 19th Century, 2 1/4 In. 440.00
Snuff, Lapis Lazuli, Dragon, Mock Ring Handles, Spade Shape, Coral Stopper, 2 1/2 In. 1610.00
Snuff, Monkey, 1800s, 2 1/2 x 1 1/2 In. 300.00
Snuff, Overlay, Emerald Green, Early 1900s, 2 3/4 In. 29.95
Snuff, Porcelain, Bird, Flower, Agate Stopper, 2 In. 130.00
Snuff, Porcelain, Brocade, Bow Leaf, Glass Stopper, 2 1/2 In. 138.00
Snuff, Porcelain, Demon Queller, Famille Noire, Cylindrical, Coral Stopper, 2 1/4 In. 375.00
Snuff, Porcelain, Double, Grasshopper, 4 Characters, Amber Stoppers, 1 3/4 In. 259.00
Snuff, Porcelain, Dragon, 5 Claw, Blue Underglaze, Coral Stopper, 6 Characters, 3 1/4 In. 115.00
Snuff, Porcelain, Dragon, Pearl, Blue, White, Wood Stopper, 4 Characters, 2 3/4 In. 510.00
Snuff, Porcelain, Dragon, Phoenix, Spade Shape, 4 Characters, 3 1/4 In. 375.00
Snuff, Porcelain, Figural Landscape, Flat Oval, Turquoise Ground, Coral Stopper, 2 In. 460.00
Snuff, Porcelain, Flowers, Pilgrim, Flask Form, Gilt Handles, Stopper, 4 Characters, 2 3/4 In. 518.00
Snuff, Porcelain, Foo Dog, Flat Oval, Jade Stopper, 4 Characters, 2 3/4 In. 150.00
Snuff, Porcelain, Hand Painted Flowers, Jade Lid, Spoon, Chinese, 3 In. 125.00
Snuff, Porcelain, Leaf Shape, Chinese, Late 1800s, 3 1/4 In. 355.00
Snuff, Porcelain, Painted Figures, 4 Characters, 3 1/2 In. 1290.00
Snuff, Porcelain, Pear Shape, Mask Handles, Ivory Stopper, 3 In. 228.00
Snuff, Porcelain, Underglaze, Red, Blue, Warrior Scene, Cylindrical, Stopper, 3 In. 145.00
Snuff, Porcelain, Wolf In Pine Tree, White-On-White, Jade Stopper, 2 1/2 In. 175.00
Snuff, Porcelain, Women, Children In Pavilion, White-On-White, Stopper, 2 3/4 In. 460.00
Snuff, Quan Yin On Horseback, Attendants, Famille Noire, 4 Characters, 2 1/3 In. 520.00
Snuff, Rock Crystal, Butterfly, Lotus, Spade Shape, Stone Stopper, 2 1/2 In. 127.00
Snuff, Rock Crystal, Crabs, Lobsters, Blue Stone Stopper, 2 1/4 In. 115.00
Snuff, Rock Crystal, Crane, Pine Tree, Spade Shape, Rose Quartz Stopper, 1 3/4 In. 130.00
Snuff, Rock Crystal, Dragon, Cloud, Rectangular, Glass Stopper, 2 3/4 In. 230.00
Snuff, Rock Crystal, Gourds, Vines, Leaves, Relief, Fruit Form, Glass Stopper, 2 3/4 In. 130.00
Snuff, Rock Crystal, Sage, Deer, Peach Tree, Prunus, Bird, Spade Shape, Stone Stopper, 2 In. 460.00
Snuff, Rose Quartz, Bat Lying On Double Gourd, Glass Stopper, 1 1/2 In. 345.00
Snuff, Rose Quartz, Bird, Prunus, Spade Shape, Jade Stopper, 2 1/2 In. 105.00
Snuff, Silver, Enameled, Pear Shape, Flowers, Ring Handles, Chinese, 1800s, 2 3/4 In. 235.00
Snuff, Silver, Lappet, Temple Jar Shape, Rose Quartz Stopper, 2 1/2 In. 518.00
Snuff, Straw Olive Yellow, Chamfer Corners, Flared Lip, c.1840-55, 4 1/4 In. 230.00
Snuff, Tourmaline, Pink, Bird, Pine Tree, Flat Oval, Stopper, 2 1/2 In. 575.00
Snuff, Tourmaline, Pink, Horse, Maiden, Flower Ground, Spade Shape, Stopper, 2 3/4 In. 2400.00
Snuff, Tourmaline, Pink, Leaf, Spade Shape, Rose Quartz Stopper, 2 1/4 In. 1150.00
Snuff, Wood, Carved, Japan, 4 1/4 In. 200.00

Snuff, Wood, Silver Mount, Turquoise, Coral, Lapis, Mongol Type, Chinese, 1800s, 3 1/2 In. 120.00
Soda, 7Up, Bicentennial, Liberty Bell, First Rung July 8, 1776, Beverage Management, 1975 ..... 1.00
Soda, 7Up, Bubble Girl, 1949, 7 Oz. 12.00
Soda, 7Up, Portland, Oregon, 1952, 7 Oz., 8 In. 5.00
Soda, American Soda Works, S.F., Aqua, Embossed Flag, Blob Top 30.00
Soda, Aspinock, Red & White ACL, Indian, Putnam, Conn., 1942, 12 Oz. 21.00
Soda, B & G, San Francisco, Blue, 10-Sided Base, Blob Top, Iron Pontil 425.00
Soda, B.R. Lippincott & Co., Stockton, Blue, 10-Sided Base, Iron Pontil, Blob Top 850.00
Soda, Bailey Boys Pop, Marshalltown, Iowa, 1912-52, 8 Oz. 45.00
Soda, Bartlett Water, White, Blue, Brown ACL, Lake County, Cal., 1951, 7 Oz. 6.00
Soda, Bay City Soda Water Co., S.F., Star, Cobalt Blue, Blob Top, 7 In. 140.00
Soda, Bay City Soda Water Co., S.F., Star, Sapphire Blue, Blob Top .... 220.00 to 300.00
Soda, Beehive Beverages, White ACL, Brigham City, Utah, 1969, Qt. 5.00
Soda, Ben's Bubbling Beverages, White ACL, Oberlin, Kan., 1947, 7 Oz. 23.00
Soda, Benicia Steam Soda Works, Gustav Gnauk, Citron To Lime, Hutchinson, 1895, 6 3/4 In. 330.00
Soda, Big Chief, Embossed Indian, Square, Early 1900s, 9 1/4 In. 46.00
Soda, Breig & Schafer, S.F., Aqua, Embossed Fish, Blob Top 40.00
Soda, Buffalo Ginger Ale, Columbia, S.C., Aqua, Straight Sides, 1930s, 6 1/2 Oz., 8 5/8 In. 8.00
Soda, Buffum's Porter, Blue Aqua, Inverted Cone Mouth, Iron Pontil, 7 5/8 In. 225.00
Soda, Calandra, Red & White ACL, Clear, Fresno, Ca., 1955, 9 Oz. 3.00
Soda, Carpenter & Cobb, Blue, Green, 10-Sided, Iron Pontil, Applied Blob Top, 7 5/8 In. 896.00
Soda, Cassin's English Aerated Waters, Green, Round Bottom, Blob Top, 9 1/2 In. 550.00
Soda, Champagne Mead, Blue Aqua, 8-Sided, Blob Top, c.1871 .... 100.00
Soda, Classen & Co., Sparkling, Crossed Anchors, Blue, Applied Square Lip 130.00
Soda, Cledon's Limel'lo, Paper Under Glass, Cap, 13 In. 410.00
Soda, Cleo Cola, Red & White ACL, Clear, 1938, 12 Oz. 240.00
Soda, Cottle Post & Co., Eagle, Portland, Ore., Phoenix Bird, Blue Green, 1877-81, 7 In. 295.00
Soda, Cream Soda, Taylor & Wilson, Aqua, Blob, 6 In. 79.00
Soda, Dana Beverages, White & Red ACL, Diamonds, Clear, Cleveland, 1956, 8 Oz. 7.00
Soda, Dillon Beverages, Orange & White ACL, Bronco, Dillon, Montana, 1940, 12 Oz. 10.00
Soda, Dr Pepper, 10 2 4, Red & White ACL, 1950s, 8 1/4 In. 5.00
Soda, Drink Christo Cola, 5 Cents, Painted Letters, Applied Lip, 11 x 3 1/4 In. 360.00
Soda, Durham's Hi-Tide, Red, White & Blue ACL, Ship, 1955, 8 Oz. 4.00
Soda, Esquire, ACL, Horse & Rider, Atlanta, Ga., 1947, 7 Oz. 5.00
Soda, Frostie Root Beer, ACL, 1973, 16 Oz. 3.00
Soda, Frostie Root Beer, By 7Up, Contents, Cap, Jasper, Alabama, 1950s, 10 Oz. 10.00
Soda, Geo Eagle, Blue Green, Sloping Collar, Iron Pontil, 7 In. 840.00
Soda, Grape-Julep, Paper Under Glass Label, 13 In. 440.00
Soda, Grapette, Imitation Grape Soda, ACL, Clear, Contents, 1960s, 6 Oz. 5.00
Soda, Grapette, Rome, Ga., Camden, Ark., c.1946, 6 Oz. 2.00
Soda, Groves & Whitnall, Salford, England, Amber, Embossed Side, Codd, 10 Oz. 30.00
Soda, H. & V.B., Newton, N.J., Emerald Green, Sloping Double Collar, 7 1/4 In. 448.00
Soda, H. Nash & Co. Root Beer, Cincinnati, Cobalt Blue, 8-Sided, Applied Lip, 9 In. 1800.00
Soda, Hall Of Waters, White & Green ACL, Excelsior Springs, Mo., 1948, 7 Oz. 6.00
Soda, Hippo, Embossed Writing, Nov. 2, 1926, Patent, 13 Oz., 9 1/2 In. 13.00
Soda, Hires Root Beer, ACL, 1948, 12 Oz. 4.00
Soda, Hires Root Beer, Old Time Flavor, Made By Hires Since 1876, 1958, 12 Oz. 10.00
Soda, Ho-Vie, 5 Cents, Enameled Label, Applied Lip, Metal Cap, 12 1/2 x 3 1/4 In. 330.00
Soda, Hollywood, Red & White ACL, Stars, Albuquerque, N.M., 1951, 10 Oz. 4.00
Soda, Hudson Hot Rod Root Beer, ACL, Brown, Contents, 1947, 7 Oz. 15.00
Soda, It's Julep Time, ACL, Glenn's Beverage Co., Champaign-Urbana, Ill., 1950, 10 Oz. 11.00
Soda, J. & A. Dearborn, N.Y., Sapphire Blue, Blob Top, Iron Pontil, 7 1/8 In. 258.00
Soda, J. Esposito Koca Nola, Washington Ave., Phila., Straw Yellow, Hutchinson, 8 In. 1568.00
Soda, J. Marbacher, Easton, Pa., Improved, M, Blue Green, Blob Top, Iron Pontil, 7 1/4 In. 200.00
Soda, J. Wise, Allentown, Pa., Cobalt Blue, Sloping Collar, 6 7/8 In. 200.00
Soda, James Lingard, S. Lingard, Salford, England, Narrow Neck, Aqua, Codds Patent, c.1880, 6 Oz. 25.00
Soda, James Wise, Allentown, Pa., c.1860, 7 3/8 x 2 1/2 In. 150.00
Soda, John Johnston, New York, Teal Blue, Blob Top, Iron Pontil, 1840-60, 7 1/2 In. 950.00
Soda, L.E. Rousse, Philada., Emerald Green, Iron Pontil, 7 1/8 In. 75.00
Soda, Lazy-B Beverages, Hi Pardner, Red & White ACL, Clear, 1951, 10 Oz. 10.00
Soda, Leigh & Co., Salford, England, Amber, Globe, Codd, 6 Oz. 25.00

Soda, MacFuddy, White, Green & Red ACL, Scotsman, Mich., 1941, 10 Oz. 12.00
Soda, Mason's Diet Beverages, Orange, White & Blue ACL, Clear, 1964, 10 Oz. 5.00
Soda, Mason's Root Beer, Yellow & Red ACL, Grand Rapids, Mich., 1949, 10 Oz. 4.00
Soda, Mountain Dew, ACL, Hillbilly, 1966, 10 Oz. 8.00
Soda, Moxie, Orange & White ACL, Authority Of Moxie, Boston, Mass., 1954, 7 Oz. 7.00
Soda, Myopia Club Beverage, Blue & White ACL, Isington, Mass., 8 Oz. 153.00
Soda, Nehi Beverage, Lansing, Mich., Yellow & Red Label, 1956, 7 Oz. 8.00
Soda, Nehi Beverage, Portland & Salem, Oregon, Red & White Label, 1956, 9 Oz. 8.00
Soda, Nesbitt's, Los Angeles, 1940s, 10 Oz. 2.00
Soda, Orange Crush, 1970, 10 Oz. 10.00
Soda, Orange Crush, Brown, Orange Diamond Label, Contents, 1974, 7 Oz. 2.00
Soda, Orange Crush, Clear, Meridian, Miss., Pat'd July 20, 1920, 6 Oz. 3.00
Soda, Orange Crush, Clear, Ribbed, 1920s, 7 Oz. 7.00
Soda, Orange Crush, Clear, Ribs, Embossed, Pat'd July 20, 1920, 6 Oz. 5.00
Soda, Orange Crush, Embossed, Emerald Green, Horizontal Ribs, 1920, 7 Oz., 8 3/4 In. 74.00
Soda, Owen Casey, Eagle Soda Works, Sac City, Apple Green, Sloping Collar, 7 1/2 In. 308.00
Soda, Owen Casey, Eagle Soda Works, Sac City, Cobalt Blue, Blob Top, 7 1/2 In. 213.00
Soda, P. Kellett, Newark, N.J., Emerald Green, Sloping Collar, Pontil, 6 3/4 In. 179.00
Soda, P. Kellett, Newark, N.J., Ice Blue, Blob Top, Iron Pontil, 7 3/8 In. 112.00
Soda, Patio Diet Cola, ACL, Contents, 1964, 8 Oz. 5.00
Soda, Paul Bunyan Beverages, Paul Sez It's Tops, Red, Green & White ACL, 1951, 7 Oz. 295.00
Soda, Phillip's Soda Water Co., S.F., Aqua, Blob Top 120.00
Soda, Pioneer Soda Water, S.F., Embossed Bear, Aqua, Crown Top 80.00
Soda, Pioneer Soda Works, W In Shield, Aqua, Blob Top 20.00
Soda, Quiky, Yellow ACL, Green, Ribbed Middle, 1956, 7 Oz. 23.00
Soda, R.W. & S.L., White, Green, Embossed, Screw Stopper, London, Early 1900s, 9 1/8 In. 35.00
Soda, Rancho, Black & White ACL, Cowboy, Needles, Cal., 1948, 10 Oz. 6.00
Soda, Red Bird Beverages, Red & White ACL, Hays, Kan., 1949, 8 Oz. 7.00
Soda, Red Rock Cola, Red & White ACL, Vancouver, Wash., 1948, 10 Oz. 2.00
Soda, Royal Crown Cola, Paper Label, Return For The Deposit, Screw Cap, c.1974, 32 Oz. 3.00
Soda, S.S. Knickerbocker, Cobalt Blue, 10-Sided, Iron Pontil, Sloping Collar, 7 1/4 In. 213.00
Soda, Spraul's Beverages, Red & White ACL, Roman Man, Troy, Ohio, 1950, 10 Oz. 10.00
Soda, Sprite, Contents, Early 1970s, 10 Oz. 2.00
Soda, Sprite, Sugar Free, Yellow ACL, Rocky Mountain Nat'l. Park, 1979, 10 Oz. 9.00
Soda, Squeeze, Boy & Girl, ACL, Pinched Design, Adams, Mass., 1960, 8 Oz. 10.00
Soda, Squeeze, Boy & Girl, Black & White ACL, Fairmont, W. Va., 1948, 8 Oz. 10.00
Soda, Squirt, Yellow & Red ACL, Green, W.Va., 1947, 7 Oz., 8 In. 3.00
Soda, Stienke Kornahrens, Green, 8-Sided, Applied Tapered Lip, Iron Pontil, 1850-60, 8 In. 330.00
Soda, Stienke T. Kornahrens, Cobalt Blue, 8-Sided, Applied Tapered Lip, Iron Pontil, 8 1/4 In. 660.00
Soda, Strawberry-Julep, Paper Under Glass Label, 13 In. 440.00
Soda, Stromeyer's Grape Punch, Paper Under Glass Label, Cap, 13 In. 210.00
Soda, Sun Drop, Dale Earnhart, Rookie Of The Year, NASCAR Series 1, Contents, 1979, 12 Oz. 6.00
Soda, Sunny Side, Green & White ACL, Clear, Oklahoma City, 1968, 10 Oz. 7.00
Soda, Sunrise Cola, Buy With Confidence, Drink With Pleasure, Havre, Mont., 1959, 10 Oz. 3.00
Soda, Sunrise Cola, Buy With Confidence, Drink With Pleasure, 1968, 7 Oz. 10.00
Soda, T & H, Sonoma, Cal., Aqua, Hutchinson, c.1877 .... 500.00
Soda, T. Burkhardt, Braddock, Pa., Olive Yellow, Hutchinson Collar, 1895, 6 3/4 In. 495.00
Soda, Tab, White ACL, By Coca-Cola, 1964, 7 Oz. 4.00
Soda, Thrill, Blue & White Label, 1940s, 9 1/4 In., 9 Oz. 15.00
Soda, Tolls Beverages, Blue & White ACL, LA Beverage Co., 7 Oz. 158.00
Soda, Tolls Beverages, Refresh With Tolls, Red & White ACL, 10 Oz. 90.00
Soda, Triple AAA Root Beer, Contents, 1946, 12 Oz. 11.00
Soda, Union Glass Works, Phila., Blue Green, Blob Top, Iron Pontil, c.1850, 7 1/4 In. 135.00
Soda, Upper, Dunsmuir, Cal., Aqua, Tooled Crown Top, c.1900, 8 In. 60.00
Soda, Valentine & Vreeland, Newark, N.J., Cobalt Blue, Blob Top, 7 3/8 In. 213.00
Soda, Vance's, White & Green ACL, Cowboy, Logan, West Virginia, 1966, 16 Oz. 18.00
Soda, VanHorn & Sawtell, New York, 4-Sided, W.T. Co., U.S.A., c.1870, 9 1/2 In. 125.00
Soda, Vernor's, Yellow & Green ACL, Gnome, Detroit, Mich., 1957, 8 Oz. 4.00
Soda, Vess Cola, ACL, Contents, Lid, Martins Ferry, Ohio, 1955, 10 Oz. 5.00
Soda, Vincent's Sparkling Ginger Ale, Green, White & Red ACL, Deer, 1948, 28 Oz. 20.00
Soda, W. Eagle, Canal St., N.Y., Philadelphia, Porter, 1860, Blue Green, 7 In. 246.00

Soda, W. Morton, Trenton, N.J., W, Blue Green, Applied Mouth, Iron Pontil, 7 1/8 In. 90.00
Soda, W. Morton, Trenton, N.J., W, Deep Blue Green, Blob Top, Iron Pontil, 7 1/4 In. 200.00
Soda, W. Ryder, Newark, N.J., Slug Plate, Teal Green, Double Collar, Iron Pontil, 6 5/8 In. 280.00
Soda, Ward's Orange-Crush, Painted Label, Metal Cap, Applied Top, 12 1/2 x 3 1/4 In. 715.00
Soda, Washington Beverages, Brown, Beige, 7 Oz. 155.00
Soda, Whistle, Bethlehem, Pa., Raised Diamond Pattern, 1926, 6 1/2 Oz., 8 3/4 In. 3.00
Soda, Whistle, Thirsty? Just Whistle, Blue & White ACL, Clear, 1949, 10 Oz. 5.00
Soda, White Rock Orange, Paper Label, Contents, Cap, 7 Oz., 7 In. 20.00
Storage, Green, Tapered Shoulder, Folded Rim, c.1875, 13 1/2 In. 130.00
Storage, Olive Green, Tapered Shoulder, Flared Rim, c.1850, 10 1/4 In. 77.00
Storage, Olive Green, Tapered Shoulder, Flared Rim, c.1850, 12 1/4 In. 130.00
Storage, Olive Green, Tapered Shoulder, Flared Rim, c.1850, 13 In. 145.00
Target Ball, Amber, 3-Piece Mold, Diamond, 2 1/2 In. 110.00
Target Ball, Amber, 7 Rings, Sheared Lip, 2 1/2 In. 730.00
Target Ball, Bogardus, Olive Yellow, Sapphire Blue, Sheared Lip, Pat. April 10, 1877, 2 In. 2800.00
Target Ball, Bogardus, Sapphire Blue, Sheared Lip, Pat. April 10, 1877, 2 1/2 In. 2800.00
Target Ball, Bogardus, Tobacco Amber, Diamond Pattern, Sheared Lip, Pat. April 10, 1877, 2 In. .. 9520.00
Target Ball, Cobalt Blue, Cylindrical, 2-Piece Mold, Outward-Flared Mouth, c.1890, 2 1/2 In. 80.00
Target Ball, Cobalt Blue, Square Pattern, 3 x 3 In. 270.00
Target Ball, Cobalt Blue, Square Pattern, English Type, 3 x 3 1/2 In. 150.00
Target Ball, Cobalt Blue, Square Pattern, Sheared Lip, 2 1/2 In. 135.00
Target Ball, Ira Paine's Filled Ball, Yellow Amber, 3-Piece Mold, Pat. Oct 23, 1877, 2 In. 336.00
Target Ball, Light To Medium Cobalt Blue, Blown, 5-Piece Mold, Sheared Mouth, 2 5/8 In. 55.00
Target Ball, Tie Breaker, Blue, 2 In. 250.00
Target Ball, Van Gutsem, Cobalt Blue, Diamond Pattern, Sheared Lip, 2 1/2 In. 112.00
Target Ball, Yellow Amber, Shaded, 5-Piece Mold, Sheared Lip, 2 1/2 In. 78.00
Tonic, Dr. Jones Red Clover, Golden Amber, c.1885, 8 1/4 In. 135.00
Tonic, Dr. Smith's Columbo, Sunken Panel, Amber, Tooled Collar, 1885-95, 9 In. 75.00
Tonic, Herba Blood Purifier & Stomach, Yellow Amber, c.1895, 9 1/2 In. 165.00
Tonic, Mara Nova, Boston, Mass., Green Aqua, Double Collar, 1890-1900, 8 1/3 In. 25.00
Tonic, Mexican, Embossed, Amber, 8-Sided, Tapered Collar, 1890-1900, 11 In. 75.00
Tonic, Ross's Aromatic, J.R.R. & Co., Amber, Applied Tapered Collar, 8 3/4 In. 95.00
Tonic, Wait's Wild Cherry, Great Tonic, Amber, Tooled Lip, Fifth 70.00
Vinegar, White House, 2 Handles, Crackled Cabbage Rose Pattern, Cork, 9 1/2 In. 30.00
Vinegar, White House, Ballerina, Green, Glass Stopper, Filigree Decoration, Qt. 300.00
Whiskey, Amber, Applied Handle, 8 3/4 x 3 1/2 In. 33.00
Whiskey, Amber, Oval, Applied Sloping Collar, Handle, Rigaree, Pontil, 1850-65, 6 In. 143.00
Whiskey, B&B Old Glen, 907 Columbus Ave., N.Y., Square, Qt. 19.00
Whiskey, Backbar, Paul Jones Rye, Pinch, Clear, Enamel, Man Pouring, Stopper, 8 1/4 In. 112.00
Whiskey, Backbar, Perrine's, Bulbous, Ribs, Glass Stopper, 10 1/2 In. 79.00
Whiskey, Backbar, Victorian Woman, Fluted Base, Flared, W.N. Walton Pat. Sept. 23/62, 10 In. ... 230.00
Whiskey, Backbar, Yellow Amber, Coin Spots, Pontil, Tooled Mouth, 11 In. 280.00
Whiskey, Bear Grass Bourbon, Braunschweiger & Co., S.F., Light Amethyst, Tooled Top, Fifth 250.00
Whiskey, Chestnut Grove, C.W., Amber, Pontil, Applied Ringed Mouth, Handle, 9 In. 190.00
Whiskey, Chestnut Grove, C.W., Tobacco Amber, Pontil, Applied Seal, Mouth, Handle, 9 In. 260.00
Whiskey, Chestnut Grove, Wharton's, Cobalt Blue, Teardrop, Applied Mouth, 1850, 5 In. 728.00
Whiskey, Cobalt Blue, 3-Piece Mold, Applied Mouth, 1855-75, 11 1/8 In. 728.00
Whiskey, Columbian Kentucky Bourbon, Cavagnaro, San Francisco, Cal., Amber, Fifth 1700.00
Whiskey, Cut Glass, Intaglio & Bull's-Eye Patterns, 12 In. 165.00
Whiskey, Davy Crockett Pure Old Bourbon, Amber, Tooled Lip, Fifth 150.00
Whiskey, Duffy Malt, Amber, Short Neck, Patd Aug 24, 1886, Fifth, 10 1/4 In. 15.00
Whiskey, Duffy Malt, Rooster, Crescent, Saloon, 214 Jefferson St., Louisville, Pig Form, 7 1/2 In. .. 2330.00
Whiskey, E.G. Booz's Old Cabin, Medium Amber, 1840, 7 5/8 In. 7840.00
Whiskey, E.G. Booz's Old Cabin, Root Beer Amber, 1840, 7 7/8 In. 3920.00
Whiskey, E.L.B. Bevan, Pittston, Pa, Amber, Octagonal, Embossed, Stars, 7 1/2 In. 3575.00
Whiskey, Ferdinand Westheimer & Sons Distillers, Cincinnati, Square, Squat, Swirled Neck, 9 In. . 27.00
Whiskey, Genesta, Gold Hill Liquor Co., Cincinnati, Ohio, 5 1/4 In. 15.00
Whiskey, Good Night, Man In Nightcap, Opalescent Milk Glass, Metal Cap, 4 1/8 In. 112.00
Whiskey, Good Old Bourbon, In A Hog's, Amber, Hand Tooled Lip, 6 3/4 In. 365.00
Whiskey, Good Ole Rye, In A Hog, S, Pig Form, Milk Glass, Blue, Green, Red Splotches, 8 1/2 In. .. 2090.00
Whiskey, H.F. & B., N.Y., Strawberry Puce, 6-Sided, Sloping Collar, c.1870, 11 In. 36.00

Whiskey, Hollywood, Amber, Qt., 11 1/2 In. 19.00
Whiskey, Jesse Moore & Co., Louisville, Ky., Amber, Sloping Collar, Fifth 140.00
Whiskey, Jug, Schiedam Gin, Imported, Shield, 16-Sided, Concave, Snake-Head Handle 1350.00
Whiskey, Milshire Dry Gin, Square, 3 1/8 In. 12.00
Whiskey, Mullins & Crigler Distillers Office, Covington, Ky., Clear, 10 1/2 In. 14.00
Whiskey, Nabob, Green, 4-Piece Mold, Glob Top, Kick-Up, 1870-80 .... 395.00
Whiskey, Nathan Bros., Philad., Yellow Amber, Bulbous, Applied Flared Mouth, 7 1/4 In. 515.00
Whiskey, Night Cap, Man In Nightcap, Opalescent Milk Glass, 4 1/8 In. 200.00
Whiskey, Old Quaker, 3 5/8 In. 8.00
Whiskey, Renz's Blackberry Brandy, San Diego, Amber, Sloping Collar, c.1880, Fifth 2090.00
Whiskey, Rosedale O.K., Siebe Bros. & Plagemann, Amber, Glob Top, 11 1/2 In. 1250.00
Whiskey, Royal Halburton, Town Crier, Green Coat, Red Scarf, c.1976, 13 3/4 x 5 In. 35.00
Whiskey, Simmond's Nabob, Pure KY Bourbon, Orange Amber, 4-Piece Mold 1200.00
Whiskey, Strawberry Puce, Barrel, 1865-75, 9 3/8 In. 530.00
Whiskey, Theodore Netter, Barrel, Cobalt Blue, Embossed, 5 7/8 In. 500.00
Whiskey, Truet Jones & Arrington, Dew Drop, Root Beer Amber, Tapered Cylinder, 10 In. 896.00
Whiskey, Udolpho Wolfe's Aromatic Schnapps, Schiedam, Olive Yellow, Applied Lip, 9 1/2 In. 130.00
Whiskey, Udolpho Wolfe's Aromatic Schnapps, Schiedam, Orange Puce, Sloping Collar, 8 1/2 In. .. 190.00
Whiskey, Udolpho Wolfe's Aromatic Schnapps, Yellow Olive Green, Pontil, 1855, 7 7/8 In. 390.00
Whiskey, Udolpho Wolfe's Schiedam Schnapps, Sea Green, Square, Sloping Collar, Pontil, 8 In. .. 187.00
Whiskey, Wharton's, Yellow Amber, Pour Spout, Applied Handle, Curl, 1865-75, 10 1/4 In. 715.00
Whiskey, William Foust, Distiller, Pure Rye, Glen Rock, Pa., Amber, Strap Flask, Pt. 200.00
Wine, Mallet, W.R., 1752, Yellow Olive, Sheared Mouth, String Rim, Pontil, 7 5/8 In. 3025.00
Wine, Mallet, Yellow Olive, Sheared Mouth, String Rim, Pontil, 1700-40, 8 3/4 In. 1210.00
Wine, Pickering Dodge, Yellow Green, Sloping Collar, Pontil, 10 In. 725.00
Wine, Welch's, Milk Glass, White, Spatter Paint Look, 1955, 11 In. 39.00
Wine, Yellow Olive, Cylindrical, Applied Sloping Collar, Pontil, 10 1/2 In. 1040.00
Wine, Yellow Olive, Painted Ship Scene, Bulbous, Sheared Mouth, Ring, Pontil, 10 3/4 In. 2530.00

BOTTLE CAPS for milk bottles are the printed cardboard caps used since the 1920s. Crown caps, used after 1892 on soda bottles, are also popular collectibles. Unusual mottoes, graphics, and caps from bottlers that are out of business bring the highest prices.

Alta Crest Farm Products, Quality Goes In, Before Name Goes On, Cow 2.00
Arethusa Farm, Guernsey Light Cream, Litchfield, Conn. 4.00
Belfry Farms, RD 2, Norristown, Pa., 1 3/4 In. .... .25
Black's Dairy, Raw Chocolate Milk, Millerstown, Pa. 41.00
City Dairy, Niles, Mich., Milk Is Health, Metal, Cardboard 1.50
Cleary Dairy, Grade A, Pasteurized, Whole Milk, Green Edge, Salem, Oregon 35.00
Crown, $1000 Beer, A. Gettelman Brewing Co., Milwaukee, 1953 .... 15.00
Crown, 7Up, Fido Dido Set, Green Ground, 5 Piece 7.00
Crown, Acme Beer & Ales, Kork-N-Seal, 1940s 5.00
Crown, Altes Golden Lager, 1956 .... 16.00
Crown, Beaver State Beer, 1939 .... 9.00
Crown, Boston Light Ale, Red Ground, Lighthouse, 1950 .... 35.00
Crown, Buffalo Rock Ginger Ale, Cork Lined 31.00
Crown, Cardinal Beer, Peerless Brewing Co., Washington, Mo., 1941 .... 40.00
Crown, Clown Root Beer, Cork Lined, 1940s 5.00
Crown, Cream Ale, Louis F. Neuweiler's & Sons, Allentown, Pa., 1941 .... 35.00
Crown, Drewrys Mountie Pep, Red Ground, 1938 .... 18.00
Crown, Dutch Hendricks, Skiatook, Okla., Red & Blue On White 118.00
Crown, Evervess, Sparkling Water, Cork Caps, 4 Piece 8.00
Crown, Felix Orange Dry, 1 1/4 In. 18.00
Crown, Fisher Beer, Black, Gold, White, Crown, 1956 .... 25.00
Crown, Fizz Whiz, Red Seal, Pat. No. 2903148 .... 4.00
Crown, Give Me Gipps Beer, Red Letters, 1954 .... 35.00
Crown, Hamm's Orange Drink, Orange Ground, 1920 .... 17.50
Crown, Lemon-Lime Crush, Cork Lined, 1940s 1.75
Crown, Malt Marrow, Red Letter, Green Ground, 1941 .... 5.60
Crown, Nehi Cherry, Cork Lined, Unused, 1930s 4.95
Crown, Nehi Cola, Cork Lined, Red, Yellow, Louisville, Ky., 1930s 5.00

Crown, Nehi Ginger Ale, Cork Lined, Unused, 1930s 7.00
Crown, Nehi Peach, Cork Lined, Unused, 1930s 6.50
Crown, Nesbitt's Lemon Soda, Cork, Yellow Ground, Green Letters 3.50
Crown, Palecola, Cork, Yellow Ground, Orange Letters, Rim 12.00
Crown, Pickwick Ale, Haffenreffer & Co., Boston, Crown, 1946 .... 8.00
Crown, RC Cola, Worth 1 Cent, Save-A-Seal, Cork Lined 2.00
Crown, Rooney's Pilsener, General Braddock Brewing, Braddock, Pa., Crown, 1937 .... 16.00
Crown, Simba Carbonated Beverage, Cork Lined, Coca-Cola Bottling, Seattle, Wash. 6.50
Crown, Stegmaier Gold Medal Beer, For Cone Top Can, 1947 .... 14.00
Crown, Vartray Water Company, Red Letters, White Ground, Buffalo, N.Y., 1890 .... 7.00
Crown, White Rock Quinine Water Q-9, Cork Lined, Unused, Los Angeles, Cal. 24.00
Crown, Yusay Pilsen Beer, Eagle, Red, White, Blue, 1958 .... 13.00
DeLaval, Christmas, Wreath, Tree, Red Bow, 1 13/16 In. 5.00
Dell Dale Farm Inc., Black Letters, Aluminum .... .20
Edwin Schultz Dairy, Pure Milk, Montello, Wis. 13.00
Fenn Dairy, Whipping Cream, Kent, O. 3.00
Grant's Dairy, Elmer, N.J., 2-Color, 1 3/4 In. .... .50
Hoopingarner Dairy, Good Morning, Here's Your Milk, Cardboard, Unused 1.50
Japan Attacks US Fleet At Pearl Harbor, 1941, 1 1/4 In. .... .75
Jersey Raw Cream, Gardnerville, Nevada 33.00
Korean War Begins, 1950, 1 1/4 In. .... .75
Lone Pine Farms, Hanover, N.J., Sunrise, 2-Color, 1 3/4 In. .... .25
M. Burns Dairy Products, Six Lakes, Mich. 26.00
Maplewood Dairy, Hudson Falls & Franville, N.Y., 1 3/4 In. .... .25
McCloud Dairy, McCloud, Ca., Mountain, Yellow, Brown 12.55
Med-O Bloom, Homogenized, Pasteurized Milk, Kokomo, Ind. 41.00
Merry Christmas, Happy New Year, Santa Claus, Red, Green 43.00
National Dairy, Sour Cream, Whiting, Ind. 1.85
Norman's Dairy, Jewett City, Conn., Approved Milk, 1 1/4 In. .... .50
Peters Dairy, Oriskany Falls, N.Y., Red Letters, White Ground, 2 Piece 2.00
Plains Dairy Cream, Cheyenne, Wyo. 61.00
Pure Guernsey Milk, Bottled On Farm, Metal Ring 2.50
Puritan Dairy, Perth Amboy, N.J., 2-Color, 1 3/4 In. .... .50
S.W. Higbee, 3 Percent B.F. Whole Milk, T.B. Tested, Jeffersonville, O. 11.50
Shimko's Good Rich Milk, Strong, Pa., Orange, White 1.50
Walker's Folly Dairy, Melfa, Va., Skim Milk, Red Letters, 1 3/4 In. .... .25
Willow Brook Farm, Cortland, N.Y., 2 Piece 3.00
Windley Raw, Pantego, North Carolina 26.00

BOTTLE OPENERS are needed to open many bottles. As soon as the commercial bottle was invented, the opener to be used with the new types of closures became a necessity. Many types of bottle openers can be found, most dating from the twentieth century. Collectors prize advertising and comic openers.

7Up, You Like It, It Likes You, Embossed, Wall Mount, Starr X, Brown Co. .... 2.00 to 8.50
Alligator, Biting Black Boy, Cast Iron, 2 1/2 x 4 In. 25.00
Alligator, Cast Iron, 1 1/4 x 6 1/8 In. 196.00
Alligator, Head Up, 2 1/2 x 5 1/8 In. 196.00
Alligator & Boy, Cast Iron, 2 3/4 x 3 7/8 In. 450.00
Alligator & Boy, Hands Up, Cast Iron, 3 x 4 1/2 In. 390.00
Baseball Player, Leisy Beer, Cleveland, Ohio, Flat, 1914, 3 1/4 In. 46.00
Bathing Girl, Old Style Lager, Butte Brewing, Flat, 2 7/8 In. 53.00
Black Americana, Bowtie, Cast Iron, Wall Mount, 4 1/8 x 3 5/8 In. 25.00
Black Caddy, Nickel Plated, Cast Iron, 5 13/16 x 1 7/8 In. 1455.00
Black Man, Cast Iron, Wilton, 4 In. 130.00
Black Man, Drunk, Holds On Palm Tree, Germany, 1920s, 4 In. 120.00
Blatz Pilsener, Beer Bottle Shape, 1943, 4 In. 20.00
Burgomaster, Fitzgerald Bros., Troy, N.Y., Flat, Embossed Bottle, 1938, 3 1/8 In. 15.00
Canada Goose, Cast Iron, 1 11/16 x 3 5/8 In. 84.00
Cathy Coed, Girl With Books, Cast Iron, 4 1/2 In. 336.00
Cold Spring Lager, Sunbury, Pa., 4 In. 18.00

Bottle Opener, Cowboy, Guitar, Souvenir, Hamburg, N.Y., John Wright Co., 4 3/4 x 3 In.

Bottle Opener, Foundry Man, Cast Iron, John Wright Co., 3 1/8 x 2 5/8 In.

Cowboy, Drunk By Cactus, 3 3/4 x 2 5/8 In. 560.00
Cowboy, Guitar, Cast Iron, 4 3/4 x 3 1/8 In. 110.00
Cowboy, Guitar, Souvenir, Hamburg, N.Y., John Wright Co., 4 3/4 x 3 In. .... *ILLUS* 56.00
Cowboy, Hanging On Signpost, Cast Iron, John Wright Co., 4 x 2 1/2 In. 70.00
Cowboy, In Chaps, Cast Iron, 4 1/2 x 2 3/4 In. 670.00
Donkey, Metal, 3 In. 15.00
Drewrys Beer, Big D, Wood Handle, 1936, 4 In. 12.00
Drink Nehi, Knife, 5 Cents, Leg Shape, High Heel Shoe, Brass, 3 1/4 In. 10.00
Drink Nehi, Knife, Lady's Boot, 5 Cents, Quality Beverages, Brass Color, 3 3/8 In. 26.00
Elephant, Sitting Up, Cast Iron, Painted, 3 1/2 In. 55.00
Enjoy Grapette, Thirsty Or Not, 3 3/4 In. 5.00
Evervess Sparkling Water, Pepsi-Cola Co., Reseal Cap, 3 5/8 x 1 1/8 In. 12.00
Faux Jewels, Mother-Of-Pearl Discs, Leaves, Vines, Goldtone, 4 1/2 In. 17.00
Fish, Tail Up, Cast Iron, 2 5/16 x 4 5/8 In. 196.00
Fitger's Rex Beer, Duluth, Minn., Celluloid Handle, 1952, 4 1/4 In. 20.00
Foundry Man, Cast Iron, John Wright Co., 3 1/8 x 2 5/8 In. .... *ILLUS* 336.00
Four Eyes Man, Cast Iron, John Wright Co., 3 15/16 x 4 1/16 In. .... *ILLUS* 168.00
Four Eyes Woman, Cast Iron, Wilton, 4 In. 55.00
Freddie Frosh, Cast Iron, 4 x 2 In. 336.00
Fresh Up With 7Up, Cap Catcher, Wall Mount, Box, 1940s, 6 x 2 1/2 In. 77.00
Fresh Up With 7Up, Consolidated Cork Corp., Brooklyn, N.Y., 3 3/8 In. 7.00
Grand Prize Lager Beer, Wall Mount, 1946 .... 7.00
Gunther's, Word For Quality Beer, Prestopener, Electro-Chemical Engraving Co., 2 1/4 In. 32.00
Hand, Making Okay Sign, Handy Way To Order Ballantine, Flat, 1954 .... 10.00
Hanging Drunk, Cast Iron, Wall Mount, 5 x 3 1/2 In. 168.00
Horsehead, Curved, Sterling Silver, Hermes, 4 In. 360.00
Iron City Beer, Over The Top Style, 1939, 4 1/4 In. 5.00
Iroquor's Beer & Ale, Brass, Buffalo, N.Y. 125.00
Mac's Elec., Balko, Oklahoma, Screwdriver, 6 1/2 In. 10.00
Mad Hatter, Cast Iron, Wilton, 5 1/2 In. 132.00
Man, 4 Eyes, Cast Iron, Wilton, 4 In. 55.00
Mermaid, Compliments Lebanon Bottling Works, 4 In. 18.00
Miller High Life, Beer Can Shape, Retractable Can Piercer, 1960, 1 3/4 In. 18.00
Nehi, Knife, Lady's Boot, Remington, Silver Color, 3 1/4 In. 41.00
Nehi, Wall Mount, Starr, New Port News, Va., 1925, 4 In. 47.00
North Star Lager, Red Ribbon Beer, Mathie Ruder Brewing, Spoon End, 1943, 7 3/4 In. 25.00
Nude Woman, Cast Iron, 8 In. 95.00
Orange Crush, Starr X, Wall Mount, Metal, 3 1/4 x 2 3/4 In. 36.00
Ortlieb's Premium Lager Beer, Cap Lifter, Wood Handle, Green, 1942, 4 1/2 In. 13.00
Paddy, Pledgemaster, Cast Iron, 3 7/8 x 2 1/4 In. 390.00
Palm Tree, Drunk, Straw Hat, Cast Iron, John Wright Co., 4 1/4 x 2 1/2 In. .... *ILLUS* 168.00
Parrot, Cast Iron, 5 5/8 x 3 In. .... 84.00 to 95.00
Parrot, Ocean City, Md., Can Punch, Cast Iron, John Wright, 5 In. 165.00
Parrot, On Perch, Cast Iron, 4 1/2 In. 30.00
Patty Pep, Cheerleader, Cast Iron, 4 In. 670.00
Pelican, Gray, White, Cast Iron, 3 3/8 x 3 3/4 In. 84.00

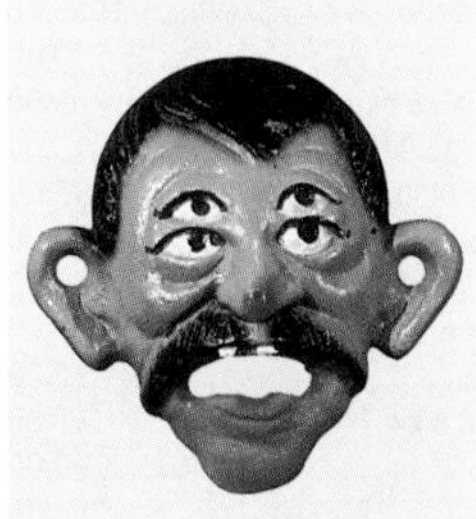

Bottle Opener, Four Eyes Man, Cast Iron, John Wright Co., 3 15/16 x 4 1/16 In.

Bottle Opener, Palm Tree, Drunk, Straw Hat, Cast Iron, John Wright Co., 4 1/4 x 2 1/2 In.

RC Royal Crown Cola, Go Fresher, Wire, 3 1/2 x 1 1/2 In. 1.00
Robin Hood Beer, Fontenelle Brewing, Bottle Shape, Vaughan, Chicago, 1940, 4 In. 12.00
Rooster, Iron, Painted, Red, Yellow, Black 125.00
Royal Crown Cola, Best By Taste-Test, C.M.I., Vaughan, 3 x 1/2 In. 3.75
Royal Crown Cola, Starr X, Brown Mfg. Co., Newport News, Va., Box, 3 In. 21.00
Ruppert Beer, Metal, 1940s Style, 3 1/4 In. 15.00
S-K Lager Beer, Retractable, Prestopener, Electro-Chemical Engraving Co., 1935, 2 1/4 In. 60.00
Schlitz, Bottle Shape, Over The Top Style, 1936, 4 In. . . . . .25.00 to 60.00
Schmidt's City Club, Cap Lifter, Wood Handle, Red, 1939, 4 1/2 In. 17.50
Shasta Spring Water, Shriner's Victory Convention, Flat, Sword Shape, 1946, 3 In. 25.00
Sommelier Bartender, Figural, Metal, Corkscrew, Signed, 8 x 3 In. 60.00
Souvenir, Made From Duralumin Used In Construction Of Airship Akron, 1934 . . . . 53.00
Storz Beer, Omaha, Neb., Celluloid Handle, 1953, 4 1/4 In. 17.60
Toast To The Host, International Toasts, Can Opener, Aluminum, Italy 12.99
Top Hat, Brass, 2 In. 40.00
Whistle, Starr X, Wall Mount, Cast Metal, 1925, 4 In. 80.00
White Rock Sparkling Beverages, Vaughan, Chicago . . . . .2.00 to 3.75

BOXES of all kinds are collected. They were made of thin strips of inlaid wood, metal, tortoiseshell, embroidery, or other material. Additional boxes may be listed in other sections, such as Advertising, Ivory, Shaker, Tinware, and various Porcelain categories. Tea Caddies are listed in their own category.

3 Hand Painted Sides, Pincushion Top, Lined Drawer, Tramp Art, c.1920, 6 x 7 x 7 In. 875.00
Alms, Church Shape, William IV, London Missionary Society, 1832, 12 x 9 x 15 In. 6000.00
Apple, Pine, Tricornered, Green & Red Paint, New Hampshire, c.1840, 15 x 4 1/2 In. 2650.00
Apple, Poplar, Painted, Tulips, Hearts, Dovetailed, Square Nails, 10 1/2 x 10 1/2 x 4 In. 1035.00
Apple, Wood, Blue Paint, Tapered Sides, Square Nail, Screw, 5 1/4 x 15 1/4 x 10 1/4 In. 605.00
Apple, Wood, Painted, Tapered Sides, Seaweed, Nailed, 3 1/4 x 11 1/2 x 11 3/4 In. 275.00
Applied Paper Animal, Hinged Lid, Shells, 7 x 9 1/2 x 5 1/2 In. 290.00
Bakelite, Round, Yellow, Green, Marbled, Cube Knob, 4 Feet, 4 3/4 x 4 1/4 In. 410.00
Band, Blue Paint, Wood Pin, 4 3/8 x 8 1/2 In. 303.00
Band, Finger Joints, Blue Paint, Stenciled, Pumice, 3 x 6 5/8 In. 1045.00
Band, Finger Joints, Copper Fasteners, Round, 1 3/8 x 2 1/4 In. 45.00
Band, Finger Joints, Copper Tack Fasteners, Round, 1 3/8 x 2 3/4 In. 39.00
Band, Finger Joints, Nail Fasteners, Oval, 2 x 6 x 4 1/2 In. 60.00
Band, Flowers, Blue, Brown, 11 1/2 x 7 In. 460.00
Band, Flowers, Side Arms, Center Loop Handle, Shaped Lid, Scandinavia, 6 1/4 x 11 1/4 In. 305.00
Band, Pine, Blue Paint, 4 3/8 x 8 1/2 In. 305.00
Band, Red Painted, Wood Pin, 3 x 6 1/4 In. 187.00
Band, Tulips, Hearts, Flowers, Wood Peg, Painted Red Ocher Ground, Lid, 3 x 7 x 5 In. 88.00
Band, Wallpaper, Flower, Bird, Oval, 9 1/2 x 13 1/2 x 10 1/2 In. 990.00
Band, Wallpaper, Flowers, Blue Ground, 1840 Newspaper Lined, 5 x 12 x 9 In. 715.00
Band, Wallpaper, Flowers, Geometric, Blue, Green, Red, 10 x 13 1/4 x 10 1/4 In. 275.00
Band, Wallpaper, Flowers, Geometric, Green, Browns, White Ground, 5 x 11 3/4 x 9 In. 220.00
Band, Wallpaper, Heart Shape, Red & Green Flowers, Gray Ground, Lydia Benn, 4 1/4 In. 1035.00

Band, Wallpaper, Landscape, Horse, Rider, Dogs, Church, String Handle, 11 1/2 x 18 x 13 3/4 In. . 1045.00
Band, Wallpaper, Oval, 3 x 5 1/2 x 3 In. 290.00
Band, Wallpaper, Rectangular, Castle Garden N.Y., Rustic Bridge, c.1840, 15 x 16 In. 705.00
Band, Wallpaper, Ship, Prosperity To Our Commerce, Multicolored, Oval, Lid, 11 1/2 x 18 In. 2310.00
Band, Wallpaper, Wood, Flowers, White Ground, Blue, Green, Pink, 10 x 14 3/4 In. 495.00
Band, Walnut, Carved, Coffered Panel, Scallop Shell, Scrolls, Putti, 21 x 43 x 19 In. 1530.00
Band, Walnut, Dovetailed, Sectioned Interior, Leather Handle, Hinged Lid, 11 x 25 x 13 In. 60.00
Band, Wood Peg, Tulips, Hearts, Fern, Multicolored, Red Ocher Paint, 3 1/4 x 6 1/2 In. 187.00
Band, Wood Strips, Rectangular, 2 1/8 x 1/2 x 4 1/4 In. 110.00
Bentwood, Flowers, Multicolored, Red Ground, Carved Latches, Scandinavia, 6 x 4 1/4 In. 145.00
Bentwood, Iron Tacks, Green Paint, Red Dots, 5 3/4 x 2 3/4 In. 2760.00
Bentwood, Oval, Painted, Single Fingers, Copper Tacks, 6 x 3 In. 290.00
Bentwood, Tulip, Painted, 6 x 14 x 9 1/4 In. 195.00
Bible, Oak, Carved, England, 18th Century, 8 x 26 x 16 1/2 In. 200.00
Bible, Oak, Carved, Queen Anne, Initials & Date, England, AF 1713 .... 850.00
Bible, Pine, Red Paint, Dovetailed, Wire Hinges, Lid, Early 1800s, 10 1/4 x 26 x 13 In. 470.00
Bible, Pine, Slant Front, 1600s, 11 x 20 x 17 In. 760.00
Bird's-Eye Maple, Wallpaper Interior, Lift Lid, Early 1800s, 5 x 12 x 6 1/4 In. 489.00
Blue & Yellow, Brass & Iron Hardware, Dovetailed, Dome Lid, Mass., c.1805, 18 x 9 In. 6800.00
Blue Paint, Tilton, N.H. Label, 24 1/2 x 13 1/4 x 10 3/4 In. 518.00
Bride's, Bentwood, Bands, 2 Women, Oval, Decoupage Lithograph Lid, 18 x 12 x 7 In. 605.00
Bride's, Bentwood, Painted, Couple Dancing, Draped Banner, Flowers, Oval, 7 x 18 In. 748.00
Bride's, Bentwood, Painted, Figures, Flowers, German Inscription, Pa., 7 1/2 x 19 x 12 In. 805.00
Bride's, Folk, Painted, Scandinavia, 16 3/4 In. 440.00
Brown Sponge Decoration, Iron Bail Handle, Dome Lid, 11 1/2 x 27 14 In. 173.00
Bucher, Painted, Tulips, M. Schemel Inscription, Lancaster Co., Penn., 2 3/8 x 9 x 8 In. 4480.00
Camphorwood, Brass Bound, 6 Compartments, Bracket Molded Base, 8 x 14 x 9 1/2 In. 175.00
Candle, Brown Paint, Dovetailed, Slide Lid, Raised Panel Lid, 6 x 12 x 8 1/2 In. 155.00
Candle, Cherry, Dovetailed, Slide Lid, Beaded Edge Panel, Chip Carved, 7 x 12 In. 405.00
Candle, Curly Maple, Dovetailed, Slide Lid, Heart Shape Finger Groove, 6 x 10 In. 546.00
Candle, Grain Painted, Lift Lid, New England, 10 1/2 In. 358.00
Candle, Oak, Dark Finish, Slide Lid, Shaped Crest, England, 15 3/4 In. 115.00
Candle, Painted, Carved Eagle, Sliding Box, 1860s, 6 x 12 In. 110.00
Candle, Painted, Dovetailed, Gouge Finger Pull, Serrated Edge, Slide Lid, 5 1/2 x 12 x 7 In. 130.00
Candle, Painted, Dovetailed, Gouge Finger Pull, Slide Lid, Raised Panel Lid, 6 x 12 x 8 5/8 In. 155.00
Candle, Painted, Stenciled, Dots, Flowers, Geometrics, 1803, 5 1/2 x 14 In. 5378.00
Candle, Pine, Double Canted, Nails, Red Paint, Cutout Lid, Wall, c.1845, 17 x 11 In. 3450.00
Candle, Pine, Red Wash, Slide Lid, Beveled Lid, 9 x 5 1/4 x 4 In. 290.00
Candle, Tulips, Urns, Incised, Molded Base, Penn., 1800s, 5 x 14 1/2 In. 2510.00
Candle, Wall, Pine, Dry Scraped Finish, Square Nails, Lollipop Finial, 12 3/8 x 11 5/8 In. 805.00
Candle, Wall, Tin, Black Paint, Cylindrical, 19th Century, 8 1/4 x 13 1/2 In. 235.00
Candle, Walnut, Dovetailed Case, Applied Molding, Slide Lid, 11 3/4 x 5 3/4 In. 345.00
Candle, Wood, Green Paint, Hinged Slant Lid, Lock, 19th Century, 15 1/2 In. 99.00
Cantonese, Lotus Medallion, Figures In Pavilion, Enamel, Round, Blue, 13 x 16 1/2 In. 325.00
Chart, Pine, Red Wash, Dovetailed, Hinged Thumb Molded Lid, 10 x 51 x 9 1/2 In. 705.00
Cheese, Chrome Yellow Paint, Round, Softwood, Nails, 6 1/2 x 20 In. 80.00
Cheese, Softwood, Nail, Yellow Paint, Round, 6 1/2 x 20 In. 80.00
Cherry, Carved, Rosettes, Hearts, Fans, Geometric Chip Carved Borders, Early 1800s, 5 x 10 In. 470.00
Child's, Pin, Applied Molding, 16 x 25 x 11 In. 200.00
Coffer, Oak, Hinged, Rectangular Top, Inset Carved Panels, Stile Feet, 31 x 23 x 53 In. 571.00
Collar, Pine, Birch Bark, Quill, 6 In. 290.00
Cosmetic, Brass, Pastoral Ruins, Hand Painted, Early 19th Century, 5/8 x 1 1/2 In. 145.00
Curly Maple, Dovetailed, Brass Keyhold Escutcheon, 16 1/2 x 10 x 9 In. 374.00
Curly Maple, Oak, Contemporary, Dovetailed, Bracket Feet, Bernard Harter, 11 x 8 In. 345.00
Cutlery, Fruitwood, Green Paint, 1800s, 6 1/2 x 10 1/2 x 7 1/2 In. 165.00
Cutlery, Wood, Divided, Old Brown Paint, 19th Century, 13 In. 65.00
Desk, Lap, Black Lacquer, Mother-Of-Pearl & Abalone Inlaid Flowers, Fitted, 3 x 11 x 8 In. 350.00
Desk, Lap, Campaign, Burlwood, Mahogany, Brass Inlay, Fitted Interior, 6 x 14 x 9 In. 380.00
Desk, Lap, Mahogany, Rosewood, Brass Shield Escutcheon, Slant Lid, 4 x 16 x 9 1/2 In. 5405.00
Desk, Lap, Rosewood, Mother-Of-Pearl Vining Border, Fitted Interior, 6 x 18 x 10 In. 590.00
Document, Dutch Mulberry Veneered, Silvered Brass Mounted, Dome Lid, 3 3/4 x 9 3/4 In. 250.00

Document, Hide Lid, Leather Trim, Brass Studs, Dome Lid, 19th Century, 11 3/4 x 7 In. 55.00
Document, Leather Covered, Brass Hardware, Rosehead Nails, 18th Century, 8 In. 235.00
Document, Pine, Brass Bail Handle, Lock Plate, Dome Lid, 1800s, 16 In. 1045.00
Document, Pine, Brown Paint, Green, Yellow Banding, Molded Base, Lid, 18 x 8 x 6 In. 375.00
Document, Pine, Grapes, Vines, Leaves, Mustard Paint, 11 In. 715.00
Document, Pine, Mustard Paint, Iron Hasp Lock, Brass Bail Handle, Dome Lid, 15 x 7 1/2 x 7 In. .. 345.00
Document, Pine, Red, Black, Yellow Graining, Bail Handles, Stenciled Initials S.S., 18 x 7 In. 405.00
Document, Swags, Tassels, New England, Early 1800s, 5 1/2 x 11 3/4 x 7 1/4 In. 2390.00
Document, Tin, Birds, Painted, Brass Handle, Dome Lid, 1800s, 7 x 9 1/2 x 5 In. 468.00
Document, Wood, Iron Lock Plate & Latch, Dome Lid, 19th Century, 14 1/4 In. 80.00
Document, Wood, Mother-Of-Pearl & Whalebone Inlay, Flower, Heart, 1800s, 4 x 11 x 8 In. 805.00
Dovetailed, Slide Lid, Raised Paneled Lid, Gouged Finger Pulls, 5 3/4 x 19 1/2 x 8 In. 330.00
Dragon, Mother-Of-Pearl Inlay, Lacquer, Gold, Korea, 11 3/4 In. 1265.00
Dresser, Bronze Edge, Hinged, Flowers, Musicians, Chateau Des Tuileries, 3 1/2 x 9 x 6 In. 575.00
Dresser, Flowers, Man, Lute, Woman, Hand Painted, Hinged, P.G. Paris, 2 x 7 x 3 3/4 In. 518.00
Dresser, Lacquered, Serpentine, Oval Mirror, Removable Boxes, Lid, 29 1/4 x 20 1/4 In. 1680.00
Dresser, Notched Tier, Center Panels, Green Velvet, Ormolu, Mirrored Lid, 6 1/4 x 3 1/2 x 3 In. 121.00
Dresser, Notched Tier, Circular & Star, Brass Side Handles, Fabric Lined, 1913, 5 x 8 x 5 In. 132.00
Dresser, Onyx, Bronze, Pietra Dura, Dome Lid, 4 3/4 x 6 x 4 In. 345.00
Dresser, Woman, Cherubs, Brass Clasp, Velvet Lining, Celluloid Lid, 1890s, 8 3/4 x 5 1/2 In. 201.00
Dynamite Detonating, Red Paint, 14 1/2 In. 115.00
Egg, Red Paint, Prime Patent Egg Case, 10 x 7 x 9 In. 345.00
Embroidered, Fountain, Birds, Trees, Insects, Ball Feet, England, c.1640, 6 x 9 x 4 In. 6500.00
Enamel, Before Marriage, After Marriage, Husband & Wife Profiles, 18th Century, 1 x 2 In. 350.00
Enamel, Copper Patch, Oval, Pink Scallop Base, Black Inscription, White Lid, c.1790, 2 In. 175.00
Enamel, Silver, Hinged, Austria, c.1920, 2 x 3 In. 527.00
Enamel, White Ground, Painted, Bird, Flowers, France, 1 1/2 x 2 3/4 x 1 1/2 In. 117.00
Fan, Burl, Brass Inlay, Blue Tufted Silk Lined, Ivory String Inlay, Victorian, 2 1/2 x 13 x 4 In. 195.00
File, Wood, Painted Flowers, 3 Shaped Sides, Arts & Crafts, A.C. Nowell, 11 x 5 In. 450.00
Firewood, Storage, Pine, Blue Paint, Large, 19th Century 150.00
Flowers, Orange, Green, Peach Enamel, Flat Bottom, Rounded Sides, Lid, 2 1/2 x 5 In. 795.00
Flowers, Yellow, Sponge Highlights, Peg Construction, Dome Lid, 9 1/4 x 18 1/2 x 11 In. 605.00
Gilt, Brass Argente, Interlocking Crescent Shapes, Round, Art Deco, Rischmann, 3 x 8 In. 587.00
Gilt Bronze, Round, 1st Empire Style, Porcelain Portrait Empress Josephine, 1 x 3 5/8 In. 499.00
Glass, Amber Cut To Clear, Oval, Lid, 5 3/4 In. 50.00
Gold, Flower Repousse, Pierced, Ruby, Emerald Colored Inset, India, 18th Century, 1 3/4 x 1 In. ... 2235.00
Grain Painted, Flat Lid, New England, 5 x 19 x 11 In. 80.00
Handling, Poplar, Dovetailed Case, Cutout Crest, Drawer, Red Paint, Slant Lid, 12 x 18 In. 115.00
Hat, Wallpaper Covered, Flowers, Birds, Black, Yellow, White, 9 1/2 x 13 1/2 x 10 1/2 In. 990.00
Hat, Wallpaper Covered, Geometric, Flowers, Newspaper Lined, Rectangular, 3 3/4 x 11 x 9 In. ... 110.00
Hat, Wallpaper Covered, Grand Canal Scene, Ship, Multicolored, Oval, 11 1/2 x 17 1/2 x 14 In. ... 2310.00
Hat, Wallpaper Covered, Top Hat, Newspaper Lined, Oval, 9 1/2 x 14 1/2 x 12 1/2 In. 635.00
Hide, Leather Hinge, Handle, Iron Latch, Brass Tag, Dome Lid, 1834, 6 3/8 x 12 1/4 x 7 In. 235.00
Humidor, Brass Inlaid & Mounted, Stand, Rectangular, Early 1900s, 33 x 21 In. 646.00
Humidor, Copper, Hammered, Curled Riveted Handle, Cedar Lined, G. Stickley, 6 x 7 x 5 In. 2940.00
Humidor, Mahogany, Brass Bound, 11 1/2 x 19 1/2 x 13 In. 690.00
Humidor, Mahogany, Carved, Scrolls & Garlands, Cabriole Legs, Glass Lined, 8 x 9 x 16 In. 580.00
Humidor, Mahogany, Metal Lined, Brass Bound, Benson & Hedges, 10 1/4 x 16 x 13 In. 575.00
Incense, Porcelain, Powder Blue Decoration, Chinese, 1700s, 4 In. 295.00
Jewelry, Art Glass, Blue To Clear, Round, Hinged, 3 1/2 In. 200.00
Jewelry, Art Glass, Yellow, Round, Hinged, 4 In. 125.00
Jewelry, Bronze, Italian Baroque, Velvet Lined, 4 1/2 x 6 1/2 x 4 1/2 In. 445.00
Jewelry, Burl Wood, Malachite, Bronze Gilded, Engraved Flowers, c.1870, 5 x 12 x 9 In. 275.00
Jewelry, Gilt Brass, Steel, Mother-Of-Pearl, Neorenaissance, Napoleon III, 3 1/4 x 6 3/4 In. 205.00
Jewelry, Gilt Bronze, Porcelain, Woman, Red Cap, Long Hair, Germany, Late 1800s, 2 1/2 x 8 In. ... 2400.00
Jewelry, Mirror Front, 4 Drawers, 4 Pigeonholes, Pa., c.1815, 17 x 12 x 11 1/4 In. 1265.00
Jewelry, Pigeon Blood, Round, Hinged, Brass Feet, 4 1/2 In. 160.00
Jewelry, Rosewood, Mother-Of-Pearl, Casket Shape, William IV, c.1840, 14 x 15 x 11 In. 1765.00
Jewelry, Silver, Heart Shape, Garlands, Cartouches, Howard & Co., N.Y., c.1903, 2 3/4 x 7 1/4 In. .. 840.00
Jewelry, Venetian Gilded, Lacquered, Inset Stones, Plaster Details, Claw Feet, c.1900, 9 x 8 In. ... 90.00
Knife, Banded, Inlaid Mahogany, Thomas Sheraton, Edwardian, c.1900, 14 x 10 In., Pair 1410.00

Knife, Cherry, Molded Base, Molded Edge, Slant Lid, 1900s, 17 3/4 x 13 x 7 3/4 In. 230.00
Knife, Georgian, Slant Front, Mahogany, Marquetry Band, Brass Mounted, 13 x 9 In. 820.00
Knife, Mahogany, Cornucopia Inlay, George III, Early 1800s, 14 3/4 x 8 1/2 x 11 3/4 In. 295.00
Knife, Mahogany, Inlaid, Serpentine Front, Compass Star, Sloped List, Late 1700s, 12 x 8 In. 1058.00
Knife, Mahogany, Satinwood Inlay, Serpentine Front, Slant Lid, c.1830, 14 x 9 In., Pair 1998.00
Knife, Mahogany, Serpentine Front, Silver Escutcheon, George III, 9 x 7 3/4 x 14 In. 530.00
Knife, Mahogany, Star Inlay, Serpentine, Federal, Early 1800s, 14 1/2 x 9 1/4 In., Pair 4115.00
Knife, Pine, Painted, Maroon, Red Cherries, Yellow Flowers, 9 x 12 x 5 In. 200.00
Leather, Green, Silver Overlay, Putti, Clouds, Monogram, 1 3/4 x 5 x 3 3/4 In. 390.00
Leather, Hinged, Painted, Courtyard, Chinese, 6 1/4 x 15 x 8 1/2 In. 146.00
Letter, Khatam, Persian, Inlaid, Geometric Design, 17 3/4 x 12 3/4 In. 410.00
Lift Top, Light & Dark Barber Pole Inlaid Border, 6 1/2 x 14 x 6 In. 145.00
Lock, Oak, Initials MWI, Jacobean, 1684, 10 x 27 x 15 In. 558.00
Lock, Oak, Iron Bound, Side Handles, Continental, 1600s 380.00
Mahogany, Bird's-Eye Maple Veneer, Geometric Shapes, Sailor Made, Hinged Lid, 5 x 10 In. 1175.00
Mahogany, Bleached, Dovetailed, Ditty Box Interior, Lift Lid, England, 8 x 13 1/2 x 7 In. 290.00
Mahogany, Carved, Lion & Shield, Dome Lid, c.1900, 3 x 12 1/2 x 5 1/2 In. 110.00
Mahogany, Chest, 2 Drawers, Scrolled Feet, 9 7/8 x 10 1/4 x 5 1/4 In. 248.00
Mahogany, Geometric Inlaid Borders, Inlaid Star, Hinged Lid, 19th Century, 6 x 6 In. 295.00
Mahogany, Inlaid Lid, Fitted Interior, Lift Lid, 5 1/2 x 13 1/2 x 9 1/2 In. 290.00
Mahogany, Token O Love, Turned Barrel Shape, Stenciled Gilt, Late 1800s, 6 In. 150.00
Mahogany Veneers, Lift Lid, 4 1/2 x 13 x 8 1/2 In. 200.00
Malachite, Molded Draped Maiden, Square, Lid, 3 1/2 In. 518.00
Malachite, Molded Flowers, 3 Muses Playing Instruments On Lid, Czechoslovakia, 5 In. 1035.00
Malachite, Molded Nudes Swimming, Round, Lid, 4 In. 430.00
Marble, Malachite Clad, Green, 1800s, 2 3/4 x 3 1/2 x 5 1/4 In. 235.00
Money, Merchant's, Oak, Brass Escutcheons, Stylized Crowns, 3 Sections, Coin Slots, 1700s 395.00
Oak, Carved Panel, Diamond & Flower Medallions, Stretcher Frame, England, 32 x 31 In. 980.00
Oak, Copper, Marked, Charles Rohlfs, Arts & Crafts, c.1900, 1 3/4 x 7 5/8 x 4 1/4 In. 6000.00
Painted, Birds, Flowers, Line Borders, Bail Handle, Dome Lid, 16 x 11 In. 776.00
Painted, Blue Ground, Dovetailed, Leather Hinges, Dome Lid, 1810, 4 5/8 x 7 3/4 x 4 In. 440.00
Painted, Blue Ground, Multicolored Flowers, Tin Hasp, Wire Hinges, Dome Lid, 4 x 3 In. 805.00
Painted, Blue, Iron Hasps & Lock Plate, Dome Lid, 19th Century, 11 x 24 x 12 In. 388.00
Painted, Dome Lid, New England, 19th Century, 12 x 28 x 14 In. 600.00
Painted, Dovetailed, Wood Peg, Till, Leather Hinge, Dome Lid, 1810, 4 1/2 x 7 3/4 x 4 1/4 In. 440.00
Painted, Flowers, Slide Lid, Swiss, 1800s, 4 1/4 x 9 1/2 x 5 In. 99.00
Painted, Geometric, Concentric Rectangles, Green, Yellow, Salmon, 31 x 16 x 11 In. 8625.00
Painted, Hinged Lid, Circles, Geometric Patterns, 1900s, 6 x 14 1/2 x 9 In. 200.00
Pantry, 3 Fingers, Round, Green Paint, 10 1/8 x 4 1/2 In. 405.00
Pantry, Banded, Painted, Pennsylvania Style Folk Art, Oval, 1800s, 6 1/2 In. 195.00
Pantry, Bentwood, Red Paint, Oval, 10 1/2 x 8 3/4 x 5 In. 430.00
Pantry, Blue Paint, Lap, Nails, 12 In. 175.00
Pantry, Blue Paint, Lid, H. Stratton, New England, 1800s, 7 x 16 1/2 In. 1100.00
Pantry, Carved, Fish, Trees, 2 x 3 1/2 In. 575.00
Pantry, Dark Green Paint, 7 1/2 x 3 1/2 In. 290.00
Pantry, Green Paint, Lap, Nails, 6 1/2 In. 200.00
Pantry, Oval, Fingers, Natural Finish, c.1869, 3 1/2 x 2 1/2 In. 259.00
Pantry, Oval, Straight Joint, Copper Tacks, Branded Hingham, 4 1/4 x 6 In. 85.00
Pantry, Oval, White Painted Cinnamon, 6 1/2 x 5 x 2 1/2 In. 3220.00
Pantry, Putty Paint, Lap, Nails, 13 1/2 In. 345.00
Pantry, Round, Dark Green Paint, Branded ES, 6 1/2 x 2 2/3 In. 85.00
Pantry, Round, Fingers, Natural Finish, 6 1/2 x 3 3/4 In. 145.00
Pantry, Round, Flowers, Leaves, 1800s, 3 x 6 In. 145.00
Pantry, Round, Lilac Paint, 9 1/2 x 5 In. 978.00
Pantry, Round, Putty Paint, 6 x 2 3/4 In. 259.00
Peacock, Flared Feathers, Hammered, Chased, Circular, Dome Lid, F. Marshall, 3 x 5 In. 2100.00
Pencil, Reg'lar Fellers, Partial Contents, Eagle Co., 1930s, 8 1/2 x 6 In. 85.00
Pencil, Willie Whopper, Cardboard, Eagle Pencil Co., 1934, 8 1/2 In. 39.00
Penwork, Sarcophagus Shape, Leaves, Landscape, Brass Handles, Paw Feet, Regency, 5 x 7 In. 940.00
Pigskin, Hinged, Chinese, c.1900, 12 x 30 x 20 In. 146.00
Pill, Enameled, Gilt, Classical Male, Caduceus, Phoenix, Oblong Lid, 1 1/4 x 2 1/4 x 1 1/4 In. 405.00

Pine, Basswood, Painted, Black On Red Sponging, Dome Lid, 18 x 9 x 9 In. 2013.00
Pine, Blanket Chest Shape, Painted, Flowers, Pinstripes, 1800s, 6 1/4 x 9 x 6 1/4 In. 1076.00
Pine, Brown Paint, Tulips, Buds, Stars, Hinged Lid, Dated 1831, 7 1/2 x 14 x 8 In. 359.00
Pine, Brown Vinegar Fans, Mustard Ground, 33 x 17 x 13 In. 230.00
Pine, Dovetailed, Painted, Black Ground, Flowers, Sailboat, Girl On Swing, 11 x 6 In. 4370.00
Pine, Dovetailed, Turned Legs, Lock, Key, c.1840, 8 1/2 x 13 1/8 x 6 1/2 In. 525.00
Pine, Graining, Brass Handle, 1842 Newspaper Lined, J.C.B. Kimball, 20 x 10 x 8 In. 230.00
Pine, Mahogany, Dovetailed, Vinegar Grained Paint, Red, Yellow, Dome Lid, 13 x 9 In. 575.00
Pine, On Stand, Molded Edges, Square Tapered Legs, Hinged Lid, 28 x 22 x 15 In. 895.00
Pine, Oval, 3 Fingers, Iron Tack Fasteners, Silk Lined, Brown Stain, Lid, 2 3/4 x 7 3/8 In. 235.00
Pine, Painted, Blue, White, Recessed Panels, Stars, Hinged Lid, 15 x 37 x 15 In. 3585.00
Pine, Painted, Buds, Blossoms, Leafy Branch, Wire Hinged Lid, 3 3/4 x 11 x 8 3/4 In. 880.00
Pine, Painted, Faux Bois Tiger Maple Graining, Hinged Lid, 3 3/8 x 10 1/2 In. 120.00
Pine, Painted, Flowers, Compass, Red Ground, Yellow, Lift Lid, 1800s, 8 1/2 x 16 x 7 1/2 In. 908.00
Pine, Painted, Hinged, Hex Designs, Pa., Late 1700s, 5 x 12 3/4 x 12 In. 3300.00
Pine, Painted, Multicolored, 6-Point Star, Salmon Paint, Hinged Lid, 6 x 12 In. 590.00
Pine, Pierced Peaked Backboard, Painted, Wall, 19th Century, 7 1/4 x 12 7/8 In. 295.00
Pine, Poplar Till, Painted, Blue, Orange Stars, Corners, c.1860, 9 x 16 x 12 In. 468.00
Pine, Poplar, Hinged Lid, Gray Paint, Running Wheel, c.1830, 6 1/2 x 10 x 6 In. 1980.00
Pine, Red Paint, Dovetailed Case, Thumb Notches, Slide Lid, 15 1/2 x 6 3/8 In. 635.00
Pine, Red Paint, Flowers, 1842, 6 1/2 x 14 x 10 In. 175.00
Pine, Red, Black Grain Painted, Red Roses, Green, Yellow Tole Style Vining, Lid, 18 x 9 x 8 In. 460.00
Pine, Red, White, Blue Tulips, Flowers, Green Ground, Wire Hinges, Dome Lid, 4 3/8 x 3 In. 374.00
Pine, Square Nails, Butt Hinges, Wall, Lift Lid, Initial R, Pennsylvania, c.1855, 10 x 15 In. 2250.00
Pine, Yellow Paint, Black Transfers, Landscapes, Agriculture, Figures, 7 x 10 x 17 3/4 In. 230.00
Pipe, Cedar, Black Paint, Backboard, Molded Front Panel, Black Over Salmon, 24 x 7 In. 529.00
Pipe, Cherry, Dovetailed, Sliding Beveled Edge Lid, Bernard Harter, 5 5/8 x 17 1/4 In. 115.00
Pipe, Cherry, Pierced Shaped Backboard, Lower Drawer, Early 1800s, 22 x 6 x 5 In. 4820.00
Pipe, Cherry, Poplar, Scrolled Cutout Sides, Crest, Dovetailed Drawer, Red Stain, 18 1/2 In. 8050.00
Pipe, Pine, Carved, Gray Paint, Cutout Pierced Heart Backboard, c.1800, 19 x 5 In. 3410.00
Poplar, 2 Drawers, Dovetailed, c.1830, 8 1/2 x 12 1/2 x 7 1/4 In. 745.00
Poplar, Dovetailed, Painted, Turned Feet, Slide Lid, 8 3/4 x 13 1/4 x 7 3/4 In. 550.00
Poplar, Stenciling, Black Ground, Birds Guarding Eggs, Flat Lid, 13 x 9 x 8 In. 375.00
Puzzle, Salmon Paint, Turned, 8 In. 520.00
Quillwork, Rectangular, 1800s, 10 1/2 In. 46.00
Red & Black Grained, Dome Lid, Maine, 28 x 14 x 11 In. 403.00
Red Paint, Decorated, Dome Lid, 14 x 7 x 6 In. 144.00
Rosewood, Brass Inlay, Satin & Paper Lined, Bun Feet, William IV Style, 6 x 12 x 9 In. 499.00
Rosewood, Gaming, Cards, Counters, George W. Williams, N.Y., c.1850, 11 3/4 x 10 1/2 In. 1165.00
Rosewood, Mother-Of-Pearl, Metal Banding, Victorian, 1 1/34 x 8 1/2 x 4 3/4 In. 95.00
Rosewood, Pail Shape, Chinese, 1800s, 9 3/4 In. 355.00
Rosewood, Sarcophagus Shape, Grain Painted, Hinged Lid, Maine, c.1850, 5 x 11 x 8 In. 120.00
Round, Flat, Painted Still Life On Lid, 1900s, 13 1/4 x 2 1/8 In. 230.00
Salt, Painted, Red Ground, Rosehead Nail, Peg Hinges, Cutout Crest, Slant Lid, 17 x 11 x 11 In. ... 800.00
Softwood, Divided Panel, Flower, Compass Star, Dome Lid, 6 1/2 x 3 1/2 x 3 In. 88.00
Softwood, Dovetailed, Orange Paint, Chamfered Lid, Slide Lid, 4 3/4 x 9 5/8 x 7 1/2 In. 660.00
Softwood, Dovetailed, Painted, Wire Hinges, Dome Lid, 8 3/4 x 20 x 9 1/2 In. 1210.00
Stationery, Exotic Woods, Inlaid Rectangles, Hinged Writing Slope, Fitted Interior, 9 x 15 In. 646.00
Storage, Green, Black Paint, Gilt Decoration, Lift Lid, Initialed G.G.W., 19th Century 259.00
Storage, Oak, Dovetailed, Brass Bound, Brass Handles, Hinged Lid, Metal Lined, 14 x 51 In. 155.00
Storage, Pine, Dovetailed, Red Paint, 1800s, 11 x 29 1/2 x 17 In. 195.00
Storage, Pine, Poplar, Maple, Joined Panels, Hinged Lid, c.1720, 10 1/4 x 25 1/2 x 28 1/4 In. 1765.00
Stylized Flowers, Leaves, Champleve, Enameled, Gilt Brass, Slag Glass, c.1900, 7 x 4 1/2 In. 406.00
Tabernacle, Carved, Giltwood, Arched Door, Relief Figure Of Christ, 27 1/2 x 25 In. 2585.00
Tabernacle, Gilt Bronze, Round Door, Silvered Mother-Of-Pearl, 12 x 34 In. 765.00
Tantalus, Exotic Wood, Brass Mounted, 3 Compartments, Decanters, England, 11 3/4 x 9 1/4 In. . 445.00
Tantalus, Kingwood, Jewel Encrusted, Napoleon III, Late 1800s, 13 x 10 1/2 x 9 1/2 In. 530.00
Tantalus, Marquetry, Side Loop Handles, Slant Lid, Holland, c.1840, 13 3/4 x 12 x 9 1/2 In. 840.00
Tantalus, Rosewood, 3 Bottles, Silver Plate Mounted Frame, Mappin & Webb, 14 x 16 In. 230.00
Tantalus, Rosewood, Brass Inlay, Ebonized, Decanters, Napoleon III, c.1865, 10 1/2 x 13 In. 825.00
Tiger Maple, Drawer, Lift Top, 1800s, 7 1/2 x 13 x 8 3/4 In. 315.00

Tin, Swags, Leaves, Painted, Dome Lid, Penn., 1800s, 5 1/2 x 8 5/8 In. 510.00
Tobacco, Brass, Copper, Boar Hunt, Verse, Oval, Holland, c.1773, 5 3/4 In. 380.00
Treen, Round, Red Over Mustard, Lid, Poplar, 6 1/4 x 6 3/4 In. 2645.00
Treen, Turned, Mustard Paint, Lid, 4 In. 575.00
Utility, Hardwood, Turned Handle, Center Divider, 4 1/4 x 13 In. 66.00
Wall, 3 Pockets, Heart Shape, Geometric, Round Nail, 13 1/2 x 7 3/4 x 3 1/2 In. 130.00
Wall, Pine, Dovetailed, Scalloped Crest, Divided, Blue Paint, Slant Lid, 13 x 10 In. 290.00
Wall, Walnut, Pine, Cutout Scrolled Crest, Dividers, Slant Lift Lid, 13 x 7 x 11 In. 1150.00
Wallpaper Covered, Pink & Blue, Dome Lid, New England, c.1800, 9 In. 2450.00
Walnut, Sloping Lift Top, Dovetailed, 19th Century, 9 3/4 x 13 3/4 x 7 In. 1035.00
White Birch, Stenciled, 19th Century, 5 1/4 x 7 In. 120.00
Wood, 3 Drawers, Scrolled Ribbon Front, Shaped Backsplash, 9 1/2 x 9 1/2 x 9 In. 415.00
Wood, Flowers, Swirl, Red Ground, Scandinavia, 6 1/2 x 10 1/4 x 6 In. 750.00
Wood, Inlaid Flowers, Figure, Lid, Korea, 1800s, 8 1/4 x 14 x 9 In. 2280.00
Wood, Ivory Inlay, Boy Reading, Girl Knitting, Tree, Head, Hand, Heart, 8 x 13 x 8 In. 2245.00
Wood, Mustard & Brown Paint, Slant Lid, 34 x 34 x 18 In. 1265.00
Wood, Painted, Marked, Ship Napoleon, 10 x 16 x 11 In. 230.00
Wood, Painted, Tulip, Trees, Jacob Webber Attribution, Penn., c.1845, 2 1/4 x 4 In. 1555.00
Wood, Tray Top, Pine, Blue Gray Paint, Stenciled, Metal Bin Edging, 28 x 20 In. 750.00
Work, Black, Carnelian Red, Gilt, 8-Sided, Drawer, Lift-Out Tray, Chinese, c.1835, 7 x 16 In. 1880.00
Writing, Lacquered, Figures, Gold Work, 9 In. 2350.00
Writing, Lacquered, Women, Landscapes, Persia, 19th Century, 9 In. 2350.00
Writing, Regency, Calamander, Wood, Brass Bound, Ink Bottles, c.1825, 6 1/2 x 16 In. 825.00
Writing, Regency, Mahogany, Brass Bail Handles, Ink Bottles, c.1820, 5 3/4 x 14 In. 470.00
Writing, Regency, Mahogany, Cut Brass, Inlaid, Secret Compartments, c.1810, 6 3/4 x 16 In. 600.00
Writing, Rosewood, Brass Bound, Leather Surface, Gilt Decoration, 7 1/4 x 18 x 10 In. 290.00
Writing, Table Top, Slant Lid, Poplar, Ocher & Brown Grain, Cutout Feet, 12 x 10 1/2 In. 115.00
Writing, Traveling, Lacquered, Gilded, Figural Inset Panels, c.1900, 4 x 12 x 10 In. 165.00

BOY SCOUT collectibles include any material related to scouting, including patches, manuals, and uniforms. The Boy Scout movement in the United States started in 1910. The first Jamboree was held in 1937. Girl Scout items are listed under their own heading.

Ax, Camp, Plumb, Hickory Handle, 3 1/4 x 5 1/4-In. Head 25.00
Bear Cub Scout Book, New York, 1948, 156 Pages 12.00
Booklet, Archery, Merit Badge Series, New Brunswick, N.J., 1965, 32 Pages 6.00
Booklet, Zoology, Merit Badge Series, New Brunswick, N.J., 1966, 48 Pages 5.00
Cub Scout Guidebook, New Brunswick, 1956, 18 Pages 6.00
Game, American Boy, Milton Bradley, Board, Box, 1920s 110.00
Knife, Remington, 4 In. 140.00
Lamp, Montpelier, 1 Out Of Every 4, 1933, 16 In. 560.00
Neckerchief Slide, Continental Camporee, Leather, 1959 .... 5.00

BRADLEY & HUBBARD is a name found on many metal objects. Walter Hubbard and his brother-in-law, Nathaniel Lyman Bradley, started making cast iron clocks, tables, frames, andirons, lamps, chandeliers, sconces, and sewing birds in 1854 in Meriden, Connecticut. The company became Bradley & Hubbard Manufacturing Company in 1875. Charles Parker Company bought the firm in 1940. Their lamps are especially prized by collectors.

BRADLEY & HUBBARD MFG. CO.

Cuspidor, Dragon, Cast Iron, Brass Wash, Step On Head To Raise Shell, 5 1/2 x 11 1/2 In. 470.00
Desk Set, Copper, Tooled Leaf Design, 3 Piece 120.00
Inkwell, Bronze, Art Nouveau, c.1900, 8 1/2 In. 104.00
Lamp, Bridge, Cast Iron, Patinated Metal, Early 1900s, 46 In. 170.00
Lamp, Copper Base, Burmese Glass Shade, Red, Copper Scrolling, 18 x 12 In. 1495.00
Lamp, Gone With The Wind, Brass Base, Glass Shade, 18 In. .... *ILLUS* 140.00
Lamp, Kerosene, Banquet, Milk Glass Shades, 26 x 12 In., Pair 275.00
Lamp, Metal Overlay Shade, Slag Glass, 16 In. .... *ILLUS* 392.00
Lamp, Oil Lamp Base, Copper, Brass, Caramel Shade, Flowers, Electrified, 13 In. 235.00
Lamp, Parlor, Hanging, Brass, Iron Hanger, Opal Shade, Late 1800s, 33 In. 176.00

Bradley & Hubbard, Lamp, Gone With The Wind, Brass Base, Glass Shade, 18 In.

Bradley & Hubbard, Lamp, Metal Overlay Shade, Slag Glass, 16 In.

Lamp, Round Base, Brass, Iron, Helmet Shade, 50 1/2 In. 173.00

BRASS has been used for decorative pieces and useful tablewares since ancient times. It is an alloy of copper, zinc, and other metals. Additional brass items may be found under Bell, Candlestick, Tool, or Trivet.

Bed Warmer, Cross & Sunburst Engraving, Turned Wood Handle, Early 1800s, 42 In. 60.00
Bed Warmer, Pierced, Engraved, Turned Wood Handle 150.00
Bed Warmer, Punched Bird, Flowers, Turned Handle, 19th Century, 46 In. 270.00
Bed Warmer, Wood, Turned, Grain Painted Shaft, Hinged Cover, Punch Rosette, 42 1/2 In. 165.00
Box, Pandan, Fish Shape, South India, 1800s, 12 In. 325.00
Cannon Model, Cast Iron Wheels, Wood, Sheet Iron Carriage, Turned Barrel, 23 x 10 In. 315.00
Cannon Model, On Frame, Wheels, 8 In. 90.00
Casket, Napoleon III, Renaissance Style, Gilt, Chased, Clambroth, Faux Lapis Glass, 6 x 9 In. 765.00
Chest, Raised Designs, Pheasant, Lion, 3 1/2 x 4 1/2 x 6 In. 295.00
Cigarette Box, Horseless Carriage, 1890s, 3 3/4 x 5 1/4 x 2 1/2 In. 470.00
Coal Hod, Regency Style, Ebonized Tin, Tapered Sides, Paw Feet, 14 x 14 1/2 x 12 In. 205.00
Coal Scoop, Ivory Handle, England, 1800s, 15 In. 205.00
Coal Scuttle, Shovel, Handles, Tin Lined, Walnut Feet, 18 x 11 x 18 In. 115.00
Coffeepot, Dovetailed Construction, Wooden Handle & Finial, England, c.1800 .... 350.00
Collar, Dog, Inscribed, John Wedgwood, Late 18th Century, 3 3/4 In. 1295.00
Collar, Dog, Scalloped Lock & Bell, Inscribed Stephen Old's Dog Dash, England, 1700s 595.00
Cribbage Board, Scalloped Edges, 4 Ball Feet, Inscribed Thos Tailor, 1827 .... 385.00
Document Seal, Wood Handle, Initials, Beehive, 1765 .... 295.00
Doorbell Pull, Chain, Victorian, c.1900 .... 380.00
Doorknocker, Lady, In Flower Garden, 3 In. 330.00
Dressing Table Set, Gilt, Blue Enamel, Molded, Scrolling Leaves, Reed Borders, c.1900 .... 1935.00
Flower Stand, Pierced, Gilt, Glass Insert, 2 Handles, France, c.1915, 4 1/2 x 16 In. 1410.00
Foot Warmer, Oval, Pierced Cover, Swing Handle, Dutch, Mid 18th Century, 11 1/2 In. 410.00
Footman, Paw Feet, 13 x 16 x 12 In. 290.00
Frame, Victorian, Embossed Designs, 11 In. 35.00
Head, Buddha, Marble Base, Thailand, 7 In. 590.00
Incense Burner, Stand, Chinese, c.1900, 13 In. 380.00
Jamb Hooks, Classical, Urn Shape Finials, Early 19th Century, 3 1/4 & 2 3/4 In., 2 Pairs 470.00
Jardiniere, Foo Dog Handles, Rectangular Panels, Bas-Relief Animals, Chinese, 8 In., Pair 470.00
Jardiniere, Hammered, Flared, Bulbous Neck, Flattened Square Base, Arts & Crafts, 17 In. 480.00
Measure Set, Tavern, Handle, England, 19th Century, Quart, Pint, 1/2 Pt., 3 Piece 850.00
Mortar & Pestle, 2 Angular Handles, 5 In. 120.00
Mortar & Pestle, Jewels, 8 1/2 x 8 In. 2420.00
Pipe Tongs, Extension, England, 18th Century 350.00
Planter, Open Lily Pad, Vines & Leaves, Frog Inside, Patinated, Footed, 7 x 19 x 13 In. 230.00
Planter, Oriental Style, Foo Dog Ring Handles, c.1950, 12 x 19 In. 105.00
Plaque, Hammered, Scarab Design, 9 1/2 x 8 1/2 In. 220.00
Plaque, Memorial, Portrait, Abraham Lincoln, 9 x 6 In. 35.00
Plaque, William Shakespeare, Angels, Round, France, 38 In. 115.00
Ring, Airline Hostess, Adjustable, Young Woman, Enclosed By Stars, 1936 .... 600.00
Samovar, Bulbous, Faceted, Leaf Handles, Paw Feet, 19 1/2 In. 1534.00

Sconce, Feathered Top, 3 Scrolled Arms, Electric, 27 1/4 x 18 x 11 In. 920.00
Sculpture, Fantasy Car, Marble Base, Emmanuel Zurini, c.1900, 18 1/2 In. 2714.00
Shower Ring, Victorian, Chain Pull Valve Shower Head, c.1900, 74 x 26 In. 1763.00
Skimmer, Flat Wrought Iron Handle, Stamped, J. Schmidt 1848, 19 1/2 x 5 1/4 In. 248.00
Stringholder, Gilt, Leather, Cylindrical, 1st Empire Style, Scissors, France, 4 1/4 x 3 1/4 In. 646.00
Tieback, Drapery, Gilt, Louis XI Style, France, Late 19th Century, 13 1/2 In., 4 Piece 500.00
Wax Jack, Pierced Base, Thumb Hold, Round Drip Pan, Center Spring, Snuffer, 5 1/2 In. 390.00

BRASTOFF, see Sascha Brastoff category.

BREAD PLATE, see various silver categories, porcelain factories, and pressed glass patterns.

BRIDE'S BASKETS OR BRIDE'S BOWLS were usually one-of-a-kind novelties made in American and European glass factories. They were especially popular about 1880 when the decorated basket was often given as a wedding gift. Cut glass baskets were popular after 1890. All bride's baskets lost favor about 1905. Bride's baskets and bride's bowls may also be found in other glass sections. Check the index at the back of the book.

BRIDE'S BASKET, Blue, White, Ruffled Edge, Rogers Silver Plated Frame, c.1857, 9 x 8 1/2 In. 895.00
Blue Thumbprint, White, Ruffled Edge, Silver Plated Frame 345.00
Cranberry, Cherub & Bird Frame, Gilt Metal, 6 x 8 In. 99.00
Cranberry, Ruffled Vaseline Rigaree Edge, Silver Plated Frame 165.00
Cranberry Opalescent, Cased To White, Silver Plated Frame, 5 In. 330.00
Crystal, Pressed Glass, Etched Flowers, 10 x 8 In. 75.00
Diamond Quilted Mother Of Pearl, Ruffled, Flowers, Quadruplate Frame, Webster & Co., 12 In. 575.00
Jadeite, Applied Handle, Moser, 8 1/2 x 5 In. 25.00
Laurel Ridge, Quadruple Plate, Fluted Pie Crust Edge, 1893 .... 225.00
Opalescent Amethyst Bowl, White Flowers, Reticulated Metal Frame, 10 1/2 In. 325.00
Red, Fluted, Brass Frame, c.1940 .... 225.00
Silver, Pierced & Flower Design, Monogram, Reed & Barton, 5 1/4 x 15 x 11 In. 1055.00
Silver Plate, Indented Shell Shape, Ball & Claw Feet, Morning Glory Handle, 5 x 3 In. 39.00
Vaseline Glass, Ruffled Edge, Silver Plated Basket Frame, Stourbridge 325.00
White, Pink Interior, Quilted, Folded & Ruffled Rim, Silver Plated Frame, 11 In. 230.00
BRIDE'S BOWL, Blue, Rose Vase, Silver Plated Frame, Meriden, 14 3/4 x 11 1/2 In. 1295.00
Blue Over White, Enamel Flowers, Silver Crested Edge, c.1900, 4 x 10 In. 135.00
Pink Over Green, Cased, Silver Plated Frame, 10 1/2 x 12 In. 250.00

BRISTOL glass was made in Bristol, England, after the 1700s. The Bristol glass most often seen today is a Victorian, lightweight opaque glass that is often blue. Some of the glass was decorated with enamels.

Mantle Set, Opaline Urn, 2 Vases, Red Stemmed Flowers, Leaves, c.1900, 12 & 9 1/2 In. 90.00
Vase, Blown, Enamel Overlay, Flowers, 11 x 4 In., Pair 59.00
Vase, Enameled, Iris Decoration, Pink Ground, 19th Century, 12 In., Pair 95.00
Vase, Flowers, Opaque Blue, Enameled, Late 1800s, 14 In., Pair 104.00
Vase, Stick, Bulbous, Dutch Windmill, 11 In. 58.00
Vase, Stick, Yellow, Stemmed Daisies, Leafy Branches, Bird, Banded, 9 In., Pair 86.00

BRITANNIA, see Pewter category.

BRONZE is an alloy of copper, tin, and other metals. It is used to make figurines, lamps, and other decorative objects. Bronze lamps are listed in the Lamp category. Pieces listed here date from the eighteenth, nineteenth, and twentieth centuries.

Basin, Leaf Edge, Lotus Petals, Spring Rain Hall, Japan, 1800s, 12 1/2 In. 265.00
Bookends, McCartan, E., Figural, Hide & Seek, 8 3/4 In. 1530.00
Bowl, Isihara, T., Mermaid Creating Whirlpool, Japan, Early 1900s, 9 1/2 In. 489.00
Bust, Athena, Classical, Malachite Veneer Base, Continental, 15 3/4 In. 2470.00
Bust, Calverley, Charles, Sir Walter Scott, Brown Patina, c.1896, 16 In. 1175.00
Bust, Ceccarelli, Silvio, Benito Mussolini, Italy, c.1930, 22 1/2 In. 956.00
Bust, Diosi, Ernest, Bust, Race Car Driver, 10 1/4 x 7 1/2 In. 7530.00
Bust, Diosi, Ernest, Motorcycle Racer, c.1900, 11 x 9 1/2 In. 5140.00
Bust, Lady Of Fashion, Patinated, Square Marble Base, France, 11 x 7 In., Pair 1645.00

Bust, Mythological, Man, Bird On Chest, Cast, Wooden Round Base, 1900s, 4 In. 80.00
Bust, Oesten, Race Car Driver, Gladenbeck, Germany, c.1920, 6 x 12 In. 2635.00
Bust, Renaissance Girl, 19th Century Girl, Gilt, 10 In., Pair 590.00
Bust, Vanderstraeten, Georges, Gilt, Ivory Face, Marble Base, 8 1/2 In. 1320.00
Bust, Volck, Frederick, Gen. Robert E. Lee, Marble Base, 1863, 19 x 12 In. 4115.00
Cachepot, Lions, Monkeys, Bulls, Green Patina, 1900s, 12 1/2 x 21 3/4 In., Pair 4800.00
Calling Card Holder, Gothic Revival, Fence, Column, c.1830, 12 In., Pair 380.00
Candlestick, Winged Griffins, Marble Base, 10 1/2 x 6 In., Pair 635.00
Carriage Step, Silvered, Winged Goddess, Scroll & Leaf Backplate, France, 1800s, 12 x 6 In. 750.00
Censer, 3-Footed, Stump, Oval, Loop Handles, Chinese, 5 In. 230.00
Censer, 6 Character Mark, Tripod, Patina, Chinese, 3 x 4 1/2 In. 316.00
Censer, Cover, 4 Bird Head Legs, Lion Finial, Japan, Late 19th Century, 14 1/4 In. 230.00
Censer, Cover, Champleve Enamel, Dragon Handles, Square, Shishi, Japan, 1800s, 23 In. 1295.00
Censer, Egg Shape, Gold Splashed, Upright Loop Handles, Tripod, Chinese, 4 1/2 In. 1120.00
Censer, Oblong, Panels, Rectangular Handles, Japan, 18th Century, 3 3/4 x 5 1/2 In. 590.00
Censer, Squat, Oval, Jade Plant, Lion's Head Handles, 6 In. 240.00
Centerpiece, Sevres Style, Gilt, Cobalt Blue Ground, 7 3/4 x 17 1/4 In. 6000.00
Cornice, 2 Sections, Bracket Corner, Gilt, Gesso, 150 x 24 x 16 In. 980.00
Crucifix, Corpus, Brushed Aluminum, Ebonized, Bronze Base, Art Deco, c.1930, 22 In. 700.00
Crucifix, Processional, Medallions Of Evangelists, Gilt, Silvered, Molded, 90 In. 1028.00
Dish, Car, Gordon Bennett, 2 Handles, France, c.1899, 17 x 10 1/2 In. 1115.00
Epergne, Louis XVI Style, Putti, Flowers, Cut Glass Trumpet Vase, Patinated, Gilt, 27 In., Pair 3995.00
Finial, Animal Head, Triangular, Persia, 3 1/4 In. 294.00
Garniture Set, Louis XVI Style, Gilt, Carrara Marble, Clock, Candlesticks, 10 1/2 In. 1645.00
Garniture Set, Mantel, Gilt Bronze, Cased, Porcelain Dial, 4-Light Candelabra, 20 In. 2855.00
Garniture Set, Temple Clock, Onyx, Green, Ormolu Mounted, France, Early 1900s, 3 Piece 1116.00
Girdle Hook, Stylized Dragon, Lotus Pod Inlay, Inlaid Gilt, 4 1/4 In. 690.00
Incense Burner, Elephant, Chinese, 33 x 30 In. 4680.00
Jardiniere, Flower, 6 Lobe, 3 Cherry Blossom Feet, Japan, 1800s, 11 In. 405.00
Jardiniere, Norrstrom, Carl Hjalmar, Fisherman, Wife, Sea Monster, Gilt, 7 1/2 x 15 3/4 In. 660.00
Jardiniere, Putti, Horned Lion Supports, Round, Patinated, 28 x 45 In., Pair 4406.00
Jardiniere, Vine Handles, Base, Chinese, c.1900, 7 1/2 x 10 In. 320.00
Lamp Base, Buddha Head, Formal Headdress, Wooden Stand, Thailand, 34 In., Pair 940.00
Lamp Base, Tripod Base, Griffin Mounts, Scrolled Feet, 15 1/2 x 6 3/4 In. 460.00
Masque, Medusa, Shrieking, Patinated, High Relief, Louis XVI Style, 18 x 14 In., Pair 1530.00
Medallion, Portrait, George Washington, Gilded, Cast Bronze, Late 1800s 7050.00
Mortar, Dark Patina, Flower Panels, Date, 1667, 7 x 5 In. 350.00
Mortar & Pestle, Russia, 1800s, 6 1/2 In. 70.00
Pedestal, Renaissance Revival, Bacchus Masques, Square, 29 1/2 x 13 In., Pair 1528.00
Planter, Relief Lotus Meanders, Chinese, 19th Century, 15 1/2 x 10 1/2 In. 590.00
Plaque, 4 Elephants, Japan, 19th Century, 19 In. 590.00
Plaque, Adam-Salomon, Woman, Profile, Bonnet, c.1848, 19 1/2 x 15 1/2 In. 510.00
Plaque, Barbedienne, F., Bas Relief, 9 Muses, Inscription, Giltwood Frame, 7 x 28 In. 1225.00
Plaque, Buddha, Lesser Deities, Double Sided, Low Relief, Cambodia, 1800s, 5 In. 115.00
Plaque, Meunier, Constantin, Miner, Rectangular, c.1875, 12 3/4 x 10 In. 226.00
Plaque, Military Scene, Napoleonic Era, Erotic, Early 20th Century, 7 x 4 3/4 In. 530.00
Plaque, Woman, Horse, 2 Dogs, France, 12 1/2 x 9 1/2 In. 145.00
Plate, Mandarin Ducks, Flowering Tree, Bamboo Edge, Japan, 19th Century, 9 1/2 In. 235.00
Sculpture, Abbot, Seated On Double Lotus Throne, 6 1/2 In. 3175.00
Sculpture, Alligator, Patinated, 1900s, Life Size, 31 x 88 x 28 In. 7050.00
Sculpture, Amodio, Bacchus, Naples, 1800s, 22 1/2 x 10 In. 1116.00
Sculpture, Apollo, Lions, Seated, Playing Lyre, Marble Base, Art Deco, 18 x 22 1/2 In. 2350.00
Sculpture, Arab Painting China, Carpet, Austria, 5 1/2 x 6 1/2 In. 1405.00
Sculpture, Ariadne On Panther, Stepped Marble Base, 8 In. 865.00
Sculpture, Barbedienne, F., Apollo, Russet Patina, Round Base, 24 3/4 In. 3230.00
Sculpture, Barillot, E., Piper, In Medieval Dress, Marked, c.1890, 8 In. 355.00
Sculpture, Bear, Gilt, Rectangular, Onyx Base, France, c.1900, 2 1/2 In. 270.00
Sculpture, Bergman, F.X., Turkish Dancer, Cold Painted, Marble Base, c.1900, 8 1/4 In. 945.00
Sculpture, Bodhisattva, Standing, Lotus Plinth, Japan, 18th Century, 33 1/2 In. 3835.00
Sculpture, Bonheur, Isidore Jules, Standing Cow, 1800s, 7 1/4 In. 2830.00
Sculpture, Bormann, Wilhelm, Child, Cat On Shoulder, Patina, Germany, Signed, 12 1/2 In. 780.00

Sculpture, Boxer, Green Patina, Walnut Plinth Base, 3 1/2 x 7 x 5 In. 900.00
Sculpture, Boy & Girl In Jester Outfits, Boy With Mandolin, Green Marble Base, 6 In. 1495.00
Sculpture, Bryant, Nanna M., Lovers, Signed, c.1910, 13 1/2 x 11 In. 480.00
Sculpture, Buddha, Gilt, Thai, 19th Century, 13 In. 355.00
Sculpture, Buddha, Infant, On Lotus Base, Gilt, Chinese, 10 In. 460.00
Sculpture, Buddha, Seated On Lotus Throne, Chinese, 9 1/2 In. 1440.00
Sculpture, Buddha, Seated, Holding Carnelian Flower, Gilt, Tibet, 1700s, 4 1/4 In. 4680.00
Sculpture, Bull, Charging, Japan, 1800s, 16 In. 1175.00
Sculpture, Caesar Augustus, Marble Base, Grand Tour, c.1900, 15 1/2 In. 645.00
Sculpture, Cape Buffalo, Wood Base, 13 x 7 In. 230.00
Sculpture, Car, 2 Figures, On Quartz Base, c.1900, 3 x 1 In. 390.00
Sculpture, Car, Racing, Marble Base, Early 1900s, 3 x 8 x 2 In. 1115.00
Sculpture, Carbonell, Manuel, With The Wind, Marble Base, Mid 1900s, 41 1/2 In. 3525.00
Sculpture, Carvin, Louis, Hunting Dog, In Long Grass, Marble Base, c.1910, 6 x 8 1/4 In. 508.00
Sculpture, Cecioni, Adriano, Boy With Cockerel, c.1863, 40 In. 7200.00
Sculpture, Charpentier, Alexandre, Wrestlers, Black Patina, 25 In. 7200.00
Sculpture, Cleopatra's Needle, Copper Plate, 15 1/4 In. 2415.00
Sculpture, Clodion, Dancing Bacchantes, Satyr, France, 30 1/2 x 16 In. 6325.00
Sculpture, Crane, Open Beak, Raised Leg, Standing On Lily Pad, c.1912, 15 In. 220.00
Sculpture, Crayfish, Japan, Early 1900s, 12 In. 259.00
Sculpture, Cupid Playing Lute, Draped Book, Plinth Base, Black Patina, 37 1/2 In. 2700.00
Sculpture, D'Aste, Joseph, Fete Au Village, Women, Children, Stone Base, 18 1/4 In. 2115.00
Sculpture, Dallin, Cyrus Edwin, Appeal To The Great Spirit, 18 1/4 x 16 1/2 In. 860.00
Sculpture, Daruma Seated, Shakudo Eyes, Gold Belt, Japan, 19th Century, 3 1/2 In. 2820.00
Sculpture, David With Sling, Marble Base, c.1900, 23 In. 1405.00
Sculpture, Davis, Earle, Best Friends, Marble Base, 1900s, 10 1/2 In. 819.00
Sculpture, Davis, Earle, On The Prowl, Marble Base, 1900s, 10 In. 366.00
Sculpture, Davis, Earle, Raging Bull, Wood Base, 1900s, 10 1/2 In. 175.00
Sculpture, Deer, Brown Patina, Mahogany Base, 15 5/8 x 19 1/2 In. 405.00
Sculpture, Deihle, G., Athlete, Holding Wreath, Propeller, Germany, c.1914, 12 In. 1530.00
Sculpture, Deming, Edwin Willard, Polar Bear, Standing, Roman Bronze Works, 14 x 9 In. 1989.00
Sculpture, Diana The Huntress, Brown Patina, 23 1/2 In. 775.00
Sculpture, Disciple, Kneeling, Praying Hands, Lacquered, Gilt, Thailand, 28 1/4 In. 2125.00
Sculpture, Discus Thrower, Brown Patina, 19 In. 1888.00
Sculpture, Divinity Seated On Pedestal, Burma, 19th Century, 7 In. 205.00
Sculpture, Dog, Reclining, Black Marble Base, France, 13 x 29 1/2 In. 400.00
Sculpture, Dragon, 19th Century, Japan, 19 In. 4700.00
Sculpture, Drouot, Edouard, Woman Beside Birdbath, Marble Base, 30 In. 7638.00
Sculpture, Dubois, Paul, Le Courage Militaire, Brown Patina, 34 In. 7800.00
Sculpture, Dumaige, Etienne Henry, Musical Dancers, 1800s, 21 3/4 In. 1785.00
Sculpture, Dying Gladiator, Marble & Slate Base, Grand Tour, Late 1800s, 7 In. 265.00
Sculpture, Egret, Standing On Vegetation, Gilt, 12 5/8 In. 2585.00
Sculpture, Elephant, Attacked By Two Tigers, Ivory Tusks, Japan, c.1890, 16 In. 705.00
Sculpture, Elephant, Fighting Rhino, Wooden Base, 15 1/2 x 7 In. 115.00
Sculpture, Elephant, Ivory Tusks, Japan, Signed, c.1890, 17 In. 470.00
Sculpture, Elephant, Ivory Tusks, Wood Stand, Japan, Late 19th Century, 13 x 16 1/2 In. 660.00
Sculpture, Elephant, Standing, Lowered Trunk, Japan, 1800s, 15 1/2 In. 1080.00
Sculpture, Erte, Aphrodite, c.1986, 19 In. 3600.00
Sculpture, Erte, Coquette, c.1985, 18 In. 3350.00
Sculpture, Falguiere, J.A., Neoclassical Male, Rouge Marble Plinth, 1800s, 31 In. 3220.00
Sculpture, Foo Dog, Chinese, c.1850, 18 In., Pair 2240.00
Sculpture, German Imperial Soldier, Signed, P. Bellaira Co., Berlin, 11 In. 495.00
Sculpture, Gladiator, Shield, Short Sword, Grand Tour, c.1900, 13 5/8 In. 764.00
Sculpture, God Of Longevity, Holding Staff, Japan, Early 1900s, 11 In. 380.00
Sculpture, Goddess Of Mercy, Chinese, 19th Century, 7 3/4 In. 765.00
Sculpture, Gotz, I., Nude Woman Fixing Hair, Golden, Brown Patina, Signed, 16 In. 635.00
Sculpture, Gotze, M., Nude Woman, Crouching, Hand On Lips, Marble Base, Signed, 18 In. 630.00
Sculpture, Hackstock, Karl, Boy, Smoking, Marble Base, Germany, 12 3/8 In. 470.00
Sculpture, Hagenauer, African Nude, Kneeling, Wood Base, c.1930, 9 In. 1885.00
Sculpture, Hand, After Rodin, Black Marble Plinth, 39 x 21 1/2 In. 4480.00
Sculpture, Hawks, Rachel, Child Standing Over Sundial, 1917, 7 3/4 In. 2468.00

Sculpture, Head, Buddha, Northern Thai, 19th Century, 8 1/2 In. 385.00
Sculpture, Heikka, E.E., Old Time Prospector, c.1936, 12 1/2 x 5 x 15 In. 1150.00
Sculpture, Herzel, Paul, Standing Dog, 6 1/2 x 6 1/2 In. 405.00
Sculpture, Hopkins, Mark, Eagle Dancer, 1900, 21 1/2 In. 366.00
Sculpture, Hopkins, Mark, Treehouse, 1900s, 16 In. 458.00
Sculpture, Hunting Dog, Cast, Hollow, Green Patina, 17 x 9 1/4 In. 345.00
Sculpture, Indian On Horse, Brown, Green Patina, 18 1/2 x 16 In. 635.00
Sculpture, Jouve, Paul, Monkey, Gilt, Marble Base, 6 5/8 x 6 1/2 In. 4036.00
Sculpture, Jurojin On Mountain, Crashing Waves, Gold, Silver Inlay, Japan, 1800s, 15 In. 410.00
Sculpture, Kauba, Carl, Sioux Chief, Quartz Base, Brown Patination, 19 In. 6730.00
Sculpture, Kowalczewski, Paul Ludwig, Millwright, Germany, c.1900, 18 In. 1340.00
Sculpture, La Faguays, Pierre, Nude, Outstretched Bird, Marble Base, 1920s, 21 In. 4900.00
Sculpture, Lange, Richard, Mercedes Grand Prix Racer, c.1914, 13 1/2 x 6 In. 5415.00
Sculpture, Levasseur, H., Napoleon Bonaparte, Dark Brown Patina, Inscribed Base, 25 In. 5100.00
Sculpture, Lizard, Open Mouth, Outstretched Legs, Curled Tail, 4 1/2 x 11 In. 115.00
Sculpture, Lukeman, Henry Augustus, Reclining Nude, Brown Patina, Signed, c.1916, 6 In. 1765.00
Sculpture, Marioton, Eugene, Peasant Farmer Family, Couple & Baby, 31 1/2 In. 4450.00
Sculpture, Marque, Albert, Mother & Child Playing, Bronze Base, France, 12 In. 5600.00
Sculpture, Martel, Jan & Joel, Bird, Stylized, Paris, 13 x 8 1/2 In. 4720.00
Sculpture, Melani, S., Nude With Birds, Marble Base, 1900s, 21 x 32 In. 2300.00
Sculpture, Ment, Pierre Jules, Goats, Marble Base, Late 1800s, 6 x 10 1/4 In. 475.00
Sculpture, Mercury, Marble Base, Grand Tour, Early 1900s, 16 1/4 In. 325.00
Sculpture, Mercury, Zephyr Masque, Patinated, Grand Tour, 35 In. 2230.00
Sculpture, Milles, Ruth, Dutch Girl, 10 In. 765.00
Sculpture, Moigniez, Jules, Pheasant With Salamander, France, 1800s, 20 x 11 In. 234.00
Sculpture, Monk, Seated, Prayerful Pose, Chinese, 5 In. 345.00
Sculpture, Moreau, Mathurin, La Rosee, Allegorical Woman, Late 19th Century, 36 In. 4406.00
Sculpture, Moreau, Mathurin, Madonna, Holding Book, Child Kneeling, France, 19 x 15 In. 2760.00
Sculpture, Moroccan Falconer, Upraised Arm, Patinated, Marble Plinth, 26 x 24 In. 1410.00
Sculpture, Noh Actor, Silver Inlay, Japan, 13 In. 1645.00
Sculpture, Novacek, Raymond, Abstract Form, Rectangular, Base, c.1950, 41 x 18 In. 1600.00
Sculpture, Omerth, Georges, Soldier, Standing, Lighting Pipe, Signed, 12 1/2 In. 880.00
Sculpture, Osborne, James, Greyhound, Racing, Elliptical Stepped Base, 10 1/2 In. 1760.00
Sculpture, Pheasant, Extended Tail, Multicolored Paint, Austria, 3 1/2 In. 316.00
Sculpture, Pheasant, Signed, Hodo, Japan, 19th Century, 23 In. 3819.00
Sculpture, Philippe, Paul, Awakening, Gilt, Nude Woman, Early 1900s, 10 1/4 In. 520.00
Sculpture, Phoenix On Cloud, Spread Wings, Gilt, Korea, 3 1/2 In. 635.00
Sculpture, Picault, Emile Louis, Musketeer, Drinking, Late 1800s, 25 x 11 In. 1058.00
Sculpture, Pilet, Leon, Cleopatra, Egyptian Revival, Parcel Gilt, 11 1/2 In. 2938.00
Sculpture, Poertzel, Otto, Snake Charmer, Ivory, c.1925, 10 3/4 In. 14400.00
Sculpture, Preiss, Ferdinand, Girl, Ivory Head & Hands, 8-Sided Base, c.1930, 6 1/2 In. 1795.00
Sculpture, Quan Yin, Seated, Wearing Crown, Chinese, 8 1/4 In. 300.00
Sculpture, Rabbit, Vienna, Multicolored, Gilt, Pompeiian Bronze Company, Late 1800s, 5 In. 2230.00
Sculpture, Rancoulet, Ernest, Woman, Fan, Wood Pedestal, c.1900, 71 In. 4800.00
Sculpture, Romanelli, Camel, 2 Humps, Patinated, c.1925, 30 x 39 In. 6000.00
Sculpture, Ronalezemki, P., Warrior, Hand Over Eyes, Signed, 14 In. 1650.00
Sculpture, Ruff, Ander, Woman, Art Nouveau, c.1890, 6 In. 510.00
Sculpture, Sadaksari, Seated On Lotus Throne, Copper Base, 3 1/4 x 2 5/8 In. 546.00
Sculpture, Samurai Warrior, Barefoot, Drawn Swords, 1900s, 16 1/2 In. 145.00
Sculpture, Schildt, Gary, Bull & Rider, c.1965, 11 x 5 In. 518.00
Sculpture, Sears, Philip Shelton, Male Diver, 31 In. 5580.00
Sculpture, Shao Lao, Standing, Chinese, 20th Century, 10 1/2 In. 355.00
Sculpture, Shrady, Henry Merwin, Horse's Head, 15 1/4 x 14 In. 2300.00
Sculpture, Sphinx, Brown Patina, 19th Century, 8 In. 355.00
Sculpture, St. Roland, Boy Carrying Girl, Societes Des Bronzes De Paris, 1800s, 29 In. 1175.00
Sculpture, Szekely, Pierre, Nude Woman, Holding Hair, Hungary, 1900s, 15 In. 936.00
Sculpture, Tantric, Deity, 4 Headed, Multi-Armed, Consort, Gilt, Tibetan, 38 In. 1760.00
Sculpture, Tharel, Leon, Idle Fiddle, Boy Napping, Violin, c.1900, 7 3/8 x 7 3/4 In. 1295.00
Sculpture, The Athlete, Nude Man, Continental, c.1900, 10 x 11 In. 405.00
Sculpture, Thornycroft, Warrior, Carrying Wounded Youth, 1877, 27 In. 9600.00
Sculpture, Tiger, Burlwood Base, Japan, 1868-1911, 31 In. 2350.00

Sculpture, Tofanari, Sirio, Bull, Cow, Calf, Signed, Founders Mark, Italy, 13 1/2 x 29 x 11 In. 4095.00

Sculpture, Venus, Draped, 19th Century, 24 3/4 In. 2705.00

Sculpture, Vez, C., Dancer, Original Patina, Signed, 20th Century, 13 In. 598.00

Sculpture, Villanis, Emmanuele, Lola Cavalliera Rusticana, France, c.1900, 25 1/2 In. 1755.00

Sculpture, Volk, Leonard, Abraham Lincoln, Emancipation Proclamation, 1891, 33 In. 7345.00

Sculpture, Warrior On Horseback, Cyrillic Signature, Russia, c.1875, 6 x 5 1/4 In. 1680.00

Sculpture, Water Buffalo, With Horns, Cast, Walnut Base, Signed, 24 1/2 In. 1150.00

Sculpture, Woman Seated With Dog, Oval Onyx Base, Painted, Art Deco, 10 x 6 1/2 In. 295.00

Sculpture, Wuertz, Emiel, Bust Of A Muse, 1896 465.00

Sculpture, Zachara, Bernadetta, Centaur, Woman, Wood Base, 1981, 11 1/2 x 17 1/2 In. 527.00

Sculpture, Zorach, William, First Steps, 7 x 4 In. 4200.00

Sculpture, Zorach, William, Head Of A Young Woman, 15 x 10 In. 1800.00

Tazza, Fratin, Christopher, 2 Playing Bears On Stem, Brown Patina, c.1896, 6 In. 1175.00

Tazza, Renaissance Style, Napoleon III, Tripodal Base, Standing Putti, Gilt, 8 x 7 In., Pair 1997.00

Tray, Art Nouveau, Vines, Leaves, Lizard, Handles, Oval, Early 1900s, 15 In. 450.00

Tray, Mounted, Parcel Gilt, Lapis Lazuli, Asian Style, France, 4 1/2 x 26 x 16 In. 6000.00

Vase, Baluster, 5 Cranes, Moonlight, Tripod Base, Silver Details, Japan, 1800s, 8 1/4 In. 1150.00

Vase, Bamboo Shape, 2 Monkey Handles, Japan, 1800s, 8 In. 235.00

Vase, Bird In Flowering Tree, Japan, 1800s, 13 1/2 In. 1058.00

Vase, Birds, Foo Dogs, Loop Handles, Chinese, 9 1/4 In., Pair 354.00

Vase, Cover, Anthropomorphic, Rhinoceros Handles, Foo Dog Finial, 1900s, 11 1/2 In. 700.00

Vase, Double Gourd Shape, Inlaid Dragons, Cranes, Japan, 1800s, 10 1/2 In., Pair 920.00

Vase, Dragons, Foo Dog Heads, Taotie Marks, Ring Handles, 14 In. 1000.00

Vase, Dragons, Globular, Flared Neck, Chinese, 19th Century, 11 3/4 In. 440.00

Vase, Dragons, Signed, Japan, 19th Century, 9 3/4 In. 380.00

Vase, Ecclesiastic, Madonna & Child, Apostles, Cylindrical, c.1900, 7 3/8 In. 176.00

Vase, Egg Shape, Crane, Lotus Leaf & Flower, Japan, Late 19th Century, 14 In. 885.00

Vase, Elephant, Flowers, Jewels, Mongolia, c.1800, 17 1/2 x 12 1/2 In. 2006.00

Vase, Fish, Japan, 20th Century, 9 1/2 In. 646.00

Vase, Herons, Bulbous, Japan, Late 1800s, 17 1/2 x 10 1/2 In. 1175.00

Vase, Inverted Pear Shape, 5 Dragon Feet, Japan, Late 19th Century, 23 1/2 In. 1095.00

Vase, Silver Inlay, Quatrefoil, Egg Shape, Bird Handles, Chinese, 1800s, 12 In. 1298.00

Vase, Teardrop Shape, Mixed Metal Bird, Wisteria, Japan, Late 19th Century, 9 1/2 In. 1035.00

Vase, Wisteria, Butterflies, Mixed Metal Inlay, Flared, Japan, c.1900, 9 In. 1998.00

BROWNIES were first drawn in 1883 by Palmer Cox. They are characterized by large round eyes, downturned mouths, and skinny legs. Toys, books, dinnerware, and other objects were made with the Brownies as part of the design.

Book, Brownie Yearbook, Palmer Cox, McLoughlin Bros., N.Y., 1895 450.00

Book, Brownies & Prince Florimel, Cox Inscription, Century, N.Y., 1918, 246 Pages 600.00

Book, Brownies At Home, Century, N.Y., 1893, 144 Pages 750.00

Booklet, Rhyme & Reason, Clark's Spool Cotton, 1890s, 4 3/4 x 3 1/4 In., 12 Pages 250.00

Candlestick, Majolica, Policeman, Figural, Palmer Cox, Continental, 8 3/4 In. 748.00

Card, Advertising, Even Change & Henry Clay Cigars, Giant Cigar 17.00

Card, Advertising, Sporting Life, Brownie On Bicycle 30.00

Sign, Lambertville Boots, Rubber Footwear, Brownies, Tin Lithograph 375.00

Stamp Set, No. 1401, Baumgarten & Company, Box, Early 1900s 195.00

BRUSH Pottery was started in 1925. George Brush first worked in 1901 in Zanesville, Ohio. He started his own pottery in 1907, but it burned to the ground soon after. In 1909 he became manager of the J.W. McCoy Pottery. In 1911, Brush and J.W. McCoy formed the Brush-McCoy Pottery Co. After a series of name changes, the company became The Brush Pottery in 1925. It closed in 1982. Old Brush was marked with impressed letters or a palette-shaped mark. Some new pieces are being marked in raised letters or with a raised mark. Collectors favor the figural cookie jars made by this company. Because there was a company named Brush-McCoy, there is great confusion between Brush and Nelson McCoy pieces. See McCoy category for more information.

Buffalo Pottery Deldare, Candlestick, Colonial Scene, Marked, 9 In., Pair

Buffalo Pottery Deldare, Ewer, Tavern & Village Scenes, Signed, Stiller, 1908, 12 1/2 In.

Figurine, Frog, Green, Ivory, Black, 8 In. 450.00
Umbrella Holder, Greek Key, Silken Green Matte, 21 x 10 In. 518.00
Vase, Art Vellum, Swan, Handle, Rose, 5 In. 20.00

BRUSH MCCOY, see Brush category and related pieces in McCoy category.

BUCK ROGERS was the first American science fiction comic strip. It started in 1929 and continued until 1967. Buck has also appeared in comic books, movies, and, in the 1980s, a television series. Any memorabilia connected with the character Buck Rogers is collectible.

Badge, Buck Rogers, Spaceship Commander, Brass, 1 3/4 In. 410.00
Badge, Chief Explorer, Brass, Red Enamel, Cream Of Wheat, 1936-39, 1 1/2 In. 195.00
Badge, Solar Scout Member, 2 Ray Guns, Brass, Cream Of Wheat, 1936-39, 1 1/2 In. 104.00
Badge, Spaceship Commander, Brass, Cream Of Wheat, 1936-39, 1 5/8 In. 195.00
Book, Buck Rogers & The Overturned World, Better Little Book, No. 1474, Whitman, 1941 .... 42.00
Book, Strange Adventures In Spider Ship, 3 Pop-Up Pictures, Pleasure Books, 1935 .... 500.00
Disintegrator Combat Set XZ-40, XZ38 Pistol, XZ39 Holster, 1930s 1327.00
Pencil Box, Cardboard, American Pencil Co., c.1936, 1 1/4 x 4 x 8 1/2 In. 140.00
Pocket Watch, Buck Rogers, Wilma Deering, 2 In. 679.00
Toy, Sonic Ray Pistol, Box, 1952 .... 449.00

BUFFALO POTTERY was made in Buffalo, New York, after 1902. The company was established by the Larkin Company, famous manufacturers of soap. The wares are marked with a picture of a buffalo and the date of manufacture. Deldare ware is the most famous pottery made at the factory. It has either a khaki-colored or green background with hand-painted transfer designs.

BUFFALO POTTERY, Bowl, Art Deco, Stylized Tulip, Cobalt Blue, Burgundy, Ivory, 3 1/4 x 8 1/4 In. .. 60.00
Bowl, Lake Scene, Signed, C. Harris, Abino, 1912, 3 1/2 x 8 In. 980.00
Pitcher, 2 Sailors, Lighthouse, Cobalt Blue, Marine, 9 x 9 In. 230.00
Pitcher, Cinderella Riding Horse Drawn Carriage, 1907, 6 1/2 x 7 1/4 In. 200.00
Pitcher, Fox Hunt, Whirl Of The Town, Man, Dog, Horses, 7 x 6 In. 1265.00
Pitcher, Geranium, Yellow, Orange, Mauve, Green, Purple, 6 1/4 x 7 1/2 In. 80.00
Pitcher, Holland, 4 Girls Knitting, Woman Working In Field, 1907, 6 x 7 In. 290.00
Pitcher, Indian On Horseback, Bison Hunt, 6 3/4 x 8 In. 315.00
Pitcher, Lady Glorianna Kneeling On Hillside, Standing, 9 1/4 x 9 In. 460.00
Pitcher, Landing Of Roger Williams, 1906, 6 1/3 x 7 In. 290.00
Pitcher, Robin Hood, Bow & Arrow, White Glaze, 8 1/4 x 6 In. 300.00
Pitcher, Roosevelt Bears, At Circus, Home, Auto Ride, 1907, 8 x 8 In. 1495.00
Pitcher, Triumph, Blue Poppy, Repeat, Bulbous, 5 1/4 x 6 1/2 In. 306.00
Pitcher, Whaling Ship, 1907, 6 1/4 x 7 In. 690.00
Plaque, Desert Scene, 1912, 13 1/2 In. 2645.00
Plate, George Washington, Bicentennial Anniversary, 10 1/2 In. 1150.00
Plate, Sailing Ships, Peach Glaze, Olive, Tan, Signed, C. Harris, 1912, 7 1/4 In. 290.00
Plate, Sailing Ships, Waves, Peach Glaze, Abino, Signed, C. Harris, 1912, 6 1/4 In. 200.00
BUFFALO POTTERY DELDARE, Bowl, Fallowfield Hunt, Breakfast At 3 Pigeons, 5 1/4 x 12 In. 805.00
Bowl, Fern, Ye Village Street, Woman, Toddler, Man, Couple, 3 1/2 x 8 1/2 In. 400.00

Bowl, Ye Village Tavern, Men Drinking, 1908, 3 3/4 x 9 In. 175.00
Candleholder, Village Scene, Circular Handle, Signed GHS, 5 1/4 In. 315.00
Candlestick, Colonial Scene, Marked, 9 In., Pair . . . . *ILLUS* 360.00
Candlestick, Village Scene, Ink Mark, Signed, W.F., 9 1/4 x 5 1/4 In. 300.00
Chamberstick Holder, Village Scene, 3 Men, Signed, GHS, 1925, 6 1/2 x 6 1/4 In. 575.00
Creamer, Breaking Cover, Huntsmen, Dogs, 1908, 2 3/4 x 4 1/2 In. 175.00
Creamer, Dr. Syntax & Dairymaid, Signed, E. Missel, Emerald, 1911, 3 1/4 x 5 In. 316.00
Cup & Saucer, Fallowfield Hunt, Landscape, Signed, L. Palmer 145.00
Cup & Underplate, Fallowfield Hunt, Ivory, Emerald 316.00
Ewer, Tavern & Village Scenes, Signed, Stiller, 1908, 12 1/2 In. . . . . *ILLUS* 480.00
Mug, Dr. Syntax Made Free Of Cellar, Broel, Emerald, 1911, 4 1/2 x 5 In. 375.00
Mug, Fallowfield Hunt, Man, Dogs, Riders, Signed, M. Broel, 1909, 4 1/2 x 5 In. 259.00
Pitcher, Dr. Syntax Stopt By Highwaymen, Robbery Scene, Emerald, 6 x 5 1/2 In. 1035.00
Pitcher, Great Controversy, All You Have To Do, 1908, 12 In. 220.00
Pitcher, To Spare An Old Broken Soldier, AR, 1909, 8 x 7 In. 300.00
Pitcher, Which He Returned With A Curtsey, Signed, Gerhardt, 1908, 6 x 5 1/2 In. 316.00
Plate, 5 Peacocks On Vine, Yellow Feathers, Emerald, 1911, 8 1/4 In. 2990.00
Plate, Dr. Syntax Introduction To Courtship, B. Willon, Emerald, 1911, 9 1/4 In. 375.00
Plate, Dr. Syntax Losing His Way, Emerald, 1911, 9 1/4 In. 546.00
Plate, Dr. Syntax Making A Discovery, Gerhardt, Emerald, 1911, 3 1/2 In. 115.00
Plate, Dr. Syntax Presenting A Floral Offering, Sauter, Emerald, 1911, 6 1/4 In. 105.00
Plate, Dr. Syntax Pursued By Bull, Sauter, Emerald, 1911, 9 In. 920.00
Plate, Fallowfield Hunt, Rider Fallen From Horse, Steiner, 1908, 6 1/4 In. 105.00
Plate, Fallowfield Hunt, The Death, Dogs, Captured Fox, 1909, 8 1/2 In. 105.00
Plate, Yankee Doodle, Colonial Men On Road, Ink Mark, 1909, 10 In. 1725.00
Plate, Ye Olden Times, Men Walking On Boardwalk, 1909, 8 1/2 In. 46.00
Plate, Ye Village Street, Men Walking On Street, Ink Mark, 1908, 7 1/4 In. 46.00
Relish, Ye Olden Times, Signed, Delaney, 1908, 2 x 12 In. 375.00
Sugar, Breaking Cover, 6-Sided, Huntsmen, 1908, 1 3/4 x 6 In. 635.00
Tankard, Dr. Syntax To Becky's Hand, Newman, Emerald, 1911, 12 x 7 In. 145.00
Tankard, Fallowfield Hunt, Supper, Signed, Ball, 1908, 12 1/4 x 7 In. 805.00
Tankard, Great Controversy, Signed, Palmer, 1909, 13 x 8 In. 690.00
Teapot, Cover, Village Scene, Small Boy & Grandmother, 1925, 5 3/4 x 9 In. 175.00
Tile, Dr. Syntax Taking Possession, E. Missel, Emerald, 1911, 6 In. 375.00
Tray, Calling Card, Dr. Syntax Robbed Of His Property, Broel, Emerald, 1911, 7 In. 316.00
Tray, Dancing Ye Minuet, Dancing Couples, Signed W. Foster, 1908, 12 x 9 In. 316.00
Tumbler, The Start, The Return, Hunters, 1917, H. Clum, 4 x 3 In., 2 Piece 1495.00
Vase, Art Nouveau, White Daisy, Leaves, Butterfly, Emerald, 6 3/4 x 3 1/2 In. 978.00
Vase, Butterflies, Grapes, Leaves, Signed, W. Foster, Emerald, 1911, 13 x 5 1/2 In. 375.00
Vase, Ye Village Schoolmaster, Emerald, 8 1/2 x 6 1/2 In. 345.00
Wall Plaque, Dr. Syntax Sketching Lake, M. Gerhardt, Emerald, 1911, 12 In. 1150.00
Wall Plaque, Ye Lion Inn, 3 Men, House Border, Signed, L. Anna, 12 In. 201.00

BUNNYKINS, see Royal Doulton category.

BURMESE GLASS was developed by Frederick Shirley at the Mt. Washington Glass Works in New Bedford, Massachusetts, in 1885. It is a two-toned glass, shading from peach to yellow. Some pieces have a pattern mold design. A few Burmese pieces were decorated with pictures or applied glass flowers of colored Burmese glass. Other factories made similar glass also called *Burmese*. Related items may be listed in the Fenton category, the Gundersen category, and under Webb Burmese.

Bowl, Centerpiece, Pink, Ruffled Edge, 11 3/4 x 3 3/4 In. 748.00
Bowl, Oval, Diamond-Quilted, Tricornered Rim, Raspberry Prunt, Footed, 5 In. 1725.00
Candlestick, Baluster, Diamond-Quilted, Scalloped Bobeche, Melon Ribbed, Footed, 8 In. 2705.00
Condiment Set, Salt, Pepper, Mustard, Ribbed, Silver Plated Stand, 8 1/2 In., 3 Piece 540.00
Cruet, Melon Ribbed, Applied Yellow Handle, Stopper, 6 1/2 In. . . . . 345.00 to 460.00
Cruet, Pillar, Faceted Stopper, 6 1/2 In. 520.00
Cup & Saucer, Queen's Pattern, Blue, Yellow, White & Green Flowers, Gold Handle 175.00
Epergne, 3 Fairy Lamps, Bud Vases, Enameled, Berries, Leaves, Branches, 10 In. 5175.00
Ewer, Enameled, Flying Swallows, Verse, Applied Handle, 11 In. 9490.00

Pitcher, Oval, Applied Handle, 4 1/2 In. 633.00
Pitcher, Oval, Applied Handle, 6 3/4 x 8 In. 575.00
Pitcher, Tankard, Applied Loop Handle, 7 In. 518.00
Punch Cup, Flattened Hobnail, Applied Handle, Glossy, 2 3/4 In. 460.00
Spooner, Pinched Rim, Glossy, 4 3/4 In. 200.00
Sugar, Wishbone Feet, Raspberry Prunt, 3 1/2 In. 575.00
Sugar & Creamer, Scalloped Rim, Wishbone Feet 750.00
Syrup, Enameled, Silver Plated Top, 6 In. 1700.00
Syrup, Yellow & White Flowers, Silver Plated Rim & Lid, Repousse Butterflies, 6 In. 4600.00
Toothpick, Applied Rigaree Around Neck, Ruffled Edge, 2 1/2 x 3 In. 635.00
Toothpick, Enameled Daisies, Tricornered Rim, 2 In. 489.00
Tumbler, 3 1/2 In., Pair 175.00
Tumbler, Lemonade, Diamond-Quilted, Applied Loop, Handle, Glossy, 4 3/4 In. ....200.00 to 316.00
Vase, Applied Feather & Poppies, Square Crimped & Folded Rim, 5 In. 3450.00
Vase, Enameled Blue & Cream Flowers, Green Leaves, Double Gourd Shape, 6 1/2 In. 690.00
Vase, Enameled Daisies, Leaves, Bulbous, Tricornered Rim, Footed, 14 In. 3740.00
Vase, Enameled Flower Clusters, Vines, White, Yellow, 11 3/4 In. 865.00
Vase, Enameled Flowers, Leaves, Pink, Yellow, Orange, 9 1/2 In. 690.00
Vase, Enameled Leaves, Vines, Flowers, 7 In. 1265.00
Vase, Enameled Prunus Blossoms, White Beading, Gourd Shape, 12 In. 920.00
Vase, Enameled Purple & White Orchids, Green Stems, Gourd Shape, Gold Trim, 8 In. 1095.00
Vase, Enameled Violets, White Beading, Bulbous, Squared Crimped Rim, Handles, 4 1/2 In. 1210.00
Vase, Enameled Wild Roses, Gold, Vines, 9 7/8 In. 1150.00
Vase, Flattened Hobnail, Applied Wavy Rigaree, Pinched Neck, Scalloped Rim, 4 In. 805.00
Vase, Glossy, Pillow Shape, 6 1/2 x 13 In. 550.00
Vase, Gold & Copper Enameled Bamboo, Bulbous, 12 In. 805.00
Vase, Gourd Shape, Pulled Neck, 8 1/4 In. 175.00
Vase, Jack-In-The-Pulpit, 11 In. 520.00
Vase, Jack-In-The-Pulpit, Crimped & Ruffled Rim, 15 In. 575.00
Vase, Lily, 16 1/2 In. 865.00
Vase, Lily, 18 In. 920.00
Vase, Lily, Ruffled Edge, 9 3/4 In. 405.00
Vase, Oval, Stain, Egyptian Scene, Standing Deer, Pyramid Oasis, 4 1/2 In. 764.00
Vase, Stick, Enameled Blue Zipper Pattern, Bulbous Base, 8 In. 460.00
Vase, Stick, Enameled Daisies, Bulbous Base, 10 In. 1495.00
Vase, Stick, Enameled Flowers, Hawthorne Pattern, Bulbous Base, 12 In. 1150.00
Vase, Stick, Enameled Flowers, Leaves, Gold Rings, Bulbous Base, 10 In. 1840.00
Vase, Stick, Queen's Decoration, Daisies, 8 In. ....1840.00 to 2415.00
Vase, Tricornered Rim, 3 Reeded Feet, Oval, 6 1/2 In. 890.00
Vase, Trumpet, Glossy, Ruffled Edge, Metal Holder, 10 In. 520.00
Vase, Urn Shape, Handles, Footed, 6 1/2 In. 520.00

BUSTER BROWN, the comic strip, first appeared in color in 1902. Buster and his dog, Tige, remained a popular comic and soon became even more famous as the emblem for a shoe company, a textile firm, and other companies. The strip was discontinued in 1920. Buster Brown sponsored a radio show from 1943 to 1955 and a TV show from 1950 to 1956. The Buster Brown characters are still used by Brown Shoe Company, Buster Brown Apparel, Inc., and Gateway Hosiery.

Bank, Buster Brown & Tige, A.C. Williams, 5 1/2 In. 130.00
Bank, Horse, Buster Brown & Tige, Good Luck Horseshoe, Cast Iron, Arcade, 4 1/2 In. 605.00
Button, Buster Brown, Blue Ribbon Shoes, Buster, Tige, Celluloid, 1 In. 15.00
Button, Buster, Tige, Celluloid, 1 1/2 In. 138.00
Button, You Can't Buster Brown Hose Supporter, Buster, Tige, Celluloid, 1 In. 10.00
Cigar Box, 2 For 5 Cents, Man In Chair, Label, Wood, 9 1/8 x 9 x 3 In. 420.00
Comic Strip Blueprint, Buster Brown On The Farm, Copyright 1905 .... 85.00
Game, Cloth Party, 12 Neckties, Selchow & Righter, Box, c.1905, 29 x 25 In. 75.00
Game, Target, Beach Bag, Paper Lithograph On Wood, Bliss, c.1910, 24 x 10 In. 1455.00
Marbles, Brown Shoe Co., Stetmeier's Shoe Store, St. Louis, Unopened 72.00
Match Holder, Buster Brown Bread, Tin Lithograph Of Buster & Tige At Table, 7 In. 950.00

Pin, Morton's Buster Brown Bread, Hughie Jennings, 1909 .... 679.00
Sign, Buster Brown Apple, For Sale Here, Buster, Tige, Cardboard, Frame, 14 x 14 In. 2750.00
Toy, Buster In Cart, Pulled By Tige, Cast Iron, Kenton, c.1910 .... 450.00

BUTTER CHIPS, or butter pats, were small individual dishes for butter. They were the height of fashion from 1880 to 1910. Earlier as well as later examples are known.

Brown Transferware, Flowers, c.1870, 2 3/4 x 2 3/4 In. 30.00
Country Home, Blue, Woods, England, 3 In. 5.00
Flow Blue, Gold Overlay, 3 3/8 In. 43.00
Flow Blue, Touraine Pattern, Stanley Pottery, England, c.1898 .... 65.00
Gold Leaf Border, Scalloped Rim, Round, England, 1890-1910, 3 1/4 In. 14.00
Hostessware, No. 207, Pacific Pottery, 3 1/8 In. 35.00
Ironstone, Flower Border, Alfred Meakin, England, c.1890, 2 1/2 In. 28.00
Normandy Pattern, Johnson Brothers, England, c.1900, 3 In. 65.00
Oakland Blue, John Maddock & Sons, England, 2 1/2 x 2 1/2 In. 5.00
Pineapple, Leaves, Stylized, Half Round, Scrubbed Finish, Inset Handle, 3 1/4 x 7 In. 175.00
Scalloped Rim, Mellor & Taylor, England, Round, 1880-1900, 3 In. 12.00
Stoneware, Dogwood Flower Border, Green Trim, Round, England, 1910-30, 3 In. 16.00
Stoneware, White, 2 Green Lines, Gold Band, Round, England, 1910-25, 3 1/2 In. 12.00
Union Pacific Railroad, Winged Streamliner, Restaurant Ware, Sterling/Trenton China Co. 24.00
Warwick Pattern, John Maddock, England, 3 In. 20.00
West Point Logo, Restaurant Ware, Scroll Border, Round, 1930s, 3 1/8 In. 42.00

BUTTER MOLDS are listed in the Kitchen category under Mold, Butter.

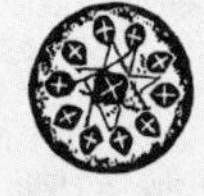

BUTTON collecting has been popular since the nineteenth century. Buttons have been known throughout the centuries, and there are millions of styles. Gold, silver, or precious stones were used for the best buttons, but most were made of natural materials, like bone or shell, or from inexpensive metals. Only a few types are listed for comparison.

2 Faces, Turn It Up, Turn It Around, 1700s 1018.00
Go To Davis Cooch, Wedding Rings, Guinea Gold, 4 Center Holes 55.00
Grasshopper, Mica, Reverse Painted, 1700s, Large 1210.00
Heraldic, Silver Plate, Eagle Crest, Firmin & Sons, London, Box, c.1800, 1 In., 6 Piece 323.00
Hot Air Balloon, Flags, Medium, 1700s 633.00
Ivory, Nene Erisalle, Queen Accepting Flower Arch Angel, Hand Painted, c.1738 .... 715.00
L. Wacher De Gruier, Man With Walking Stick, Watercolor, 1700s 275.00
Lady's Head, Carved Pearl, Paste Ivory Border, Cooper Back, Medium 935.00
Man's Portrait, Young, Blond, Hand Painted, Ivory Paste Border, Signed 2145.00
Militia, Canada British, From Lieutenant Gowan, Montgomery's Tavern, 1837, 16 In. 328.00
Mother-Of-Pearl Cabochons, Pinshank Center, Steel Back, 1700s 615.00
Plastic, Asian Face, 3/4 x 1 In., 4 Piece 68.00
Washington Inaugural, Long Live The President, Linked States, 1789, 1 3/8 In. 5700.00

BUTTONHOOKS have been a popular collectible in England for many years but are now gaining the attention of American collectors. The buttonhooks were made to help fasten the many buttons of the old-fashioned high-button shoes and other items of apparel.

18K Gold, Eagle's Head Mark, France, c.1870, 2 3/4 In. 270.00
Agate, Scotland, 2 3/4 In. 195.00
Bakelite Handle, c.1900, 7 In. 10.00
Bog Oak, Jockey, Cap, Victorian, 5 1/2 In. 295.00
Celluloid Handle, 8 In. 5.00
Commonsense Shoe Store, Chester, Pa., Folding, 4 1/2-In. Open, 2 1/4-In. Closed 18.00
Ivory Handle, France, 6 1/2 In. 12.00
Metal, Black Paint, Twist Handle, Flat Top, Victorian, 12 In. 35.00
Metal, Folding, Mandoline, 4-In. Open, 2 1/2-In. Closed 11.00
Mother-Of-Pearl Handle, 3 3/4 In. 32.00
P.E. Carlson Company Of Chicago, Butterfly, Slightly Curved, 3 1/2 x 3/4 In. 5.00
Robert Peschke, 5 1/8 In. 12.50

Steel, Folding, c.1900, 4 1/2-In. Open, 2 3/4-In. Closed 17.00
Steel, Queen Quality Shoes 3.00
Sterling Silver, Amethyst Top, Victorian, 5 1/2 In. 115.00
Sterling Silver, Art Nouveau, Unger Brothers, Dauphine, 1903 Patent, 8 1/2 In. 225.00
Sterling Silver, Beaded Shield, 9 3/4 In. 110.00
Sterling Silver, Birks, 7 In. 40.00
Sterling Silver, Celtic Knot, 3 1/4 In. 125.00
Sterling Silver, ELZ, Gorham, 5 7/8 In. 48.00
Sterling Silver, Flowers, M&H 25.00
Sterling Silver, Hourglass Shape, Beaded Edge, Sheila, Victorian, 6 1/4 In. 95.00
Sterling Silver, Man, Playing Mandolin, Woman, Seated, 11 In. 38.00
Sterling Silver, Repousse, Anchor Hallmark, 4 1/2 In. 125.00
Walk-Over Shoe, Folding, 4 1/2-In. Open, 2 1/2-In. Closed 22.00

CALENDARS made to hang on the wall or to be displayed on a desk top have been popular since the last quarter of the nineteenth century. Many were printed with advertising as part of the artwork and were given away as premiums. Calendars with guns, gunpowder, or Coca-Cola advertising are most prized.

1892, Hood's, Sarsaparilla, 7 Children, 7 In. Diam. 44.00
1895, Winchester, 2 Hunters, Dead Bear, December, 27 x 14 1/2 In. 1940.00
1899, Hood's, American Girl, 9 1/2 x 6 1/2 In. 27.00
1900, Laflin & Rand Powder Co., Elk, Full Pad, 6 x 3 1/2 In. 940.00
1901, Seymour R. Church, Baseball, July To December, 19 1/2 x 23 3/4 In. 3190.00
1903, Marlin Repeating Rifles & Shotguns, Antelope, Pocket, 6 x 4 1/4 In. 1305.00
1904, Marlin Firearms, Repeating Rifles & Shotguns, Man Hunting, Cardboard, 6 x 3 1/2 In. 1018.00
1906, Bristol Steel Rods, Men Fishing, Oliver Kemp, 20 1/4 x 15 1/4 In. 375.00
1906, Deering Harvesters, Woman, Orchard, 20 1/4 x 13 1/8 In. 225.00
1906, Horton Mfg., Full Pad, Frame, 20 1/2 x 18 1/2 In. 2970.00
1909, Peters Cartridge Co., First Lesson Steady, G. Muss-Arnolt, 27 1/4 x 14 In. 1130.00
1910, Lambertville Rubber Co., Snag Proof, Woman, Rifle, 12 x 8 1/8 In. 150.00
1910, Winchester, Dawn At Open Season, 1910, 29 3/4 x 18 3/4 In. 4500.00
1912, Deering, Woman, Horse, May To December, 23 1/2 x 13 3/8 In. 279.00
1912, Pacific Brewing & Malting, Full Pad, Frame 1485.00
1913, Selby Loads, California Quail, E.W. Currier, November, December 3108.00
1916, Winchester, 2 Men, Dog, Mountain, Phillip R. Goodwin, 30 1/4 x 15 1/4 In. 1130.00
1917, Wallace Nutting, Partial Pad, 6 1/2 x 12 In. 35.00
1918, Hercules Powder Company, Not This Trip, Old Pal, 29 5/8 x 13 In. 230.00
1918, Peters Cartridge Co., Hunter, Dogs, July Page 1515.00
1921, Remington UMC, Geese, Fox, 28 1/2 x 15 In. 980.00
1921, Western, Devotion, Hunter, Dog, Behind Tree, Full Pad, 30 1/8 x 15 1/8 In. 665.00
1923, 2 Men, Dogs, Full Pad, Starts December 1922, 28 1/2 x 15 In. 825.00
1923, Remington UMC, 2 Hunters, Dogs, Leaving Store, Full Pad, 28 1/2 x 15 In. 840.00
1923, Winchester, A.B. Hudelson Gen. Merc., North Powder, Ore., Philip R. Goodwin, 19 x 10 In. 440.00
1924, Peters Cartridge Co., Game Birds, G. Muss-Arnolt, Full Pad, 29 1/4 x 13 In. 1780.00
1924, Peters Cartridge Co., Hunting Dogs, G. Muss-Arnolt, July, 30 x 14 In. 1068.00
1924, Western Ammunition, Saving The Day, Hunters Waking Up, 32 x 14 3/4 In. 2772.00
1925, Remington, Let'er Rain, Man, In Boat, 28 1/2 x 15 In. 1130.00
1925, Western Ammunition, Pointers & Setters, A. Russell, December, 27 1/2 x 13 In. 1485.00
1925, Winchester, Lowell Moore Hdwe. Company, Poore Dogs, Full Pad 1790.00
1926, Peters Cartridge Co., Quails In Field, Partial Pad, 29 3/8 x 13 1/4 In. 1500.00
1927, Alfred C. Handley Auto Electrical Shop, Indian Woman, On Rock, Canoe, 46 x 21 1/2 In. 360.00
1927, Hercules Powder, Man, Dog, William Eaton, November, 29 1/8 x 13 In. 267.00
1927, Western Ammunition, Interference, Full Pad, 29 1/2 x 15 In. 1425.00
1928, Hercules Powder Company, This Trip We All Go, Man, Boy, Dog 550.00
1928, Western Ammunition, Snow Geese, Lynn Bogue Hunt, 28 1/2 x 15 In. 285.00
1929, Peters Cartridge Co., Ducks, July Page, 28 1/8 x 15 In. 580.00
1929, Rexall, Kuykendalls Drug Store, Landscape View From Patio, Pomeroy, Wash., 46 x 22 In. 110.00
1929, Winchester, As Good As The Gun, Full Pad, 20 3/8 x 10 In. 485.00
1929, Winchester, As Good As The Gun, Hollen & Sons Hdwr., 20 x 10 In. 990.00
1930, Hazard Smokeless Powder, Boy, Dog, June To December, 6 1/4 x 4 1/2 In. 949.00

1930, Peters Cartridge Co., Mountain Lion, Hunter, 35 1/2 x 17 In. 1155.00
1930, Peters Cartridge Co., Mountain Lion, Hunter, Full Pad, 32 1/2 x 13 1/2 In. ....1968.00 to 2049.00
1931, Peters Cartridge Co., Pheasants, Lynn Bogue Hunt, 32 x 13 1/2 In. ....265.00 to 475.00
1931, St. Louis Cardinals, Matted, Frame, 2 Cardinals, Players, 15 x 34 In. 1540.00
1931, US Shot Shells, Cartridges, Old Hunter, Dog, 31 3/8 x 16 In. 1190.00
1932, Edison Mazda, CR Herzberg, Omaha, Parrish, 7 x 9 1/2 In. 358.00
1932, Hercules Powder, Stowaways, W.B. Humphrey, December, 30 x 13 In. 268.00
1936, Hercules Powder, Days End, No Pad, 30 1/4 x 13 In. 42.00
1937, Great Northern Railway, Empire Builder, Indian, Headdress, 34 x 16 In. 69.00
1938, Brown & Bigelow Calendar Co., Disney Monthly Scenes, 16 1/2 x 9 In. 520.00
1938, Meyer & Rasmussen Inc., Cotton Yarns, P.R. Goodwin, Full Pad, 45 x 21 In. 186.00
1940, Hercules Powder, Pioneers, June To December Pages, 30 x 13 In. 115.00
1946, DuPont Explosives, Dog, Ariel, Full Pad, 30 x 15 In. 115.00
1947, Maas & Steffen Co., Furs, Struggle For Existence, Full Pad, 26 3/8 x 13 1/2 In. 565.00
1951, Hercules Powder, Hunter, Dog, Plummer, Partial Pad, 30 1/4 x 13 In. 408.00
1952, Tom Cuffs Gulf Service Station, Mt. Carmel, Pa. 14.00
1954, Marilyn Monroe, Nude, Golden Dreams, Leanders Automotive Service, 24 x 11 In. 120.00
1954, Mt. Katahdin, Greetings From Maine, J. Carleton Bicknell, 4 x 5 1/2 In. 45.00
1955, Marilyn Monroe, Nude, Sweet Dreams, 17 x 10 1/2 In. 132.00
1957, Hercules Powder Company, Pheasant Hunting In Oregon, F. Ludekens, 30 x 13 In. 90.00
1958, Gutwein Hybrids, Boy, Man, Fishing, Dog, 23 1/2 x 11 In. 28.00
1961, Jayne Mansfield, Eagle Line, 33 x 16 In. 236.00
1979, Ruger, Man, Canoe, Rifle, James M. Triggs, Frame, 23 1/2 x 18 1/2 In. 34.00
1980, Tom's Toasted Peanuts, Old Truck, 18 7/8 x 12 In. 50.00

CALENDAR PLATES were very popular in the United States from 1906 to 1929. Since then, plates have been made every year. A calendar and the name of a store, a picture of flowers, a girl, or a scene were featured on the plate.

1909, H.C. Paulsen Co., Jewelers, Sonora, Calif., Rose, Homer Laughlin 69.00
1910, Compliments Of Schuler, Knox Co., Sisson, Calif., Carnation McNichol, 9 In. 25.00
1910, Pink Roses, Gold Rim, C.F. Company, Warranted, Crown, 8 3/4 In. 35.00
1911-12, Compliments Of Henry Fauss, General Merchandise, Craven, So. Dak., 8 1/2 In. 50.00
1915, Panama Canal, Compliments Of D. Trozzo Co., Pittsburgh, Dresden, 7 1/2 In. 30.00
1953, Debutante, Homer Laughlin 25.00
1953, Jubilee Line, Homer Laughlin 8.00
1953, Merry Christmas From Gately's, 10 In. 35.00
1958, Windmill, Gold On White, Taylor Smith Taylor, 10 In. 18.00
1962, Finke Monument Co., Wentzville, Mo. 8.00
1962, Zodiac, God Bless This House, Blue, Meakin 24.00
1963, Windmill, Taylor Smith Taylor, 10 In. 16.00
1966, Liberty Bell, Declaration Of Independence, Green, Royal Staffordshire 16.00
1969, Currier & Ives, Royal China Co., 10 In. 18.00
1969, Zodiac, God Bless This House, Brown, Meakin 18.00
1970, 4 Sports, 8-Sided, 10 In. 14.00
1973, Taylor Smith Taylor, 10 1/4 In. 18.00
1974, Zodiac, Green Edges, Gold Letters, 10 1/2 In. 20.00
1975, Children's Games, 5th In Series, Wedgwood, 10 In. 30.00

CAMBRIDGE GLASS Company was founded in 1901 in Cambridge, Ohio. The company closed in 1954, reopened briefly, and closed again in 1958. The firm made all types of glass. Their early wares included heavy pressed glass with the mark *Near Cut*. Later wares included Crown Tuscan, etched stemware, and clear and colored glass. The firm used a C in a triangle mark after 1920. Some Cambridge patterns may be included in the Depression Glass category.

Allegro, Cordial, Paisley Etching 75.00
Apple Blossom, Ashtray, Gold Krystol, 3 In. 20.00
Apple Blossom, Bowl, Gold Krystol, Oval, 4-Toed, 12 In. 45.00
Apple Blossom, Vase, Amber, 10 In. 150.00

Blossom Time, Candlestick, 2-Light, Etched, 6 In. 10.00
Blossom Time, Cocktail Shaker, Etched, 48 Oz. 85.00
Blossom Time, Vase, Ebony, Gold Encrusted, Footed, 9 In. 325.00
Blossom Time, Vase, Hat, 9 In. 200.00
Blue Jay, Flower Frog, 5 1/2 In. 130.00
Bluebell, Vanity Box, Cover 60.00
Caprice, Banana Bowl, 4-Toed, 15 In. 70.00
Caprice, Bowl, Salad, Cupped, LaRosa, 13 In. 250.00
Caprice, Candlestick, 2-Light, Keyhole, Moonlight Blue, Alpine, 6 In., Pair 80.00
Caprice, Candlestick, 2-Light, Prisms, 7 1/2 In., Pair 100.00
Caprice, Candlestick, 3-Light, Oval, 9 1/2 In. 45.00
Caprice, Candlestick, Alpine, Prisms, 7 In., Pair 40.00
Caprice, Candlestick, LaRosa, Alpine, No. 70, Pair 189.00
Caprice, Candlestick, Moonlight Blue, 3-Light 110.00
Caprice, Candlestick, Moonlight Blue, Prism, 7 In., Pair 65.00
Caprice, Candlestick, Prisms, Sterling Silver Flowers, 7 In., Pair 40.00
Caprice, Candlestick, Smoke, 2-Light, 6 In. 175.00
Caprice, Cheese Stand 65.00
Caprice, Creamer, Mulberry 35.00
Caprice, Dish, Mayonnaise, Sections, Moonlight Blue, 2 Ladles 275.00
Caprice, Ice Bucket, Moonlight Blue, Alpine, Chrome Handle & Tongs 200.00
Caprice, Jam Jar, Moonlight Blue, Bulbous, Clear Cover 250.00
Caprice, Plate, 4-Toed, 11 1/2 In. 30.00
Caprice, Relish, Moonlight Blue, Alpine, 3 Sections, 8 In. 35.00
Caprice, Sugar & Creamer, LaRosa, Medium 45.00
Caprice, Vase, Ball, Amber, 8 1/2 In. 95.00
Caprice, Vase, Ball, Amethyst, 4 1/2 In. 55.00
Caprice, Vase, Ball, Moonlight Blue, Crimped, 8 1/2 In. 300.00
Carmen, Decanter, Pinch, Clear Stopper, 36 Oz. 75.00
Carmen, Ivy Ball, Clear Keyhole & Foot, 8 In. 70.00
Carmen, Ivy Ball, Clear Stem & Foot, 6 1/2 In. 75.00
Carmen, Nut Cup, 4-Toed, 3 In. 30.00
Carrara, Doorknob, Octagon 80.00
Chantilly, Celery & Relish, 3 Sections, 4-Toed, 12 In. 15.00
Cherub, Candlestick, Gold Krystol, Pair 1700.00
Cleo, Batter Jug, Cover, Amber 250.00
Cleo, Bowl, Peach-Blo, Decagon, 2 Handles, 10 In. 30.00
Cleo, Sandwich Tray, Amber, Center Handle, 11 In. 20.00
Crown Tuscan, Candlestick, Dolphin, 2-Light, 5 In., Pair 195.00
Crown Tuscan, Candy Box, Cover, 3 Sections, Gold Encrusted, 8 In. 30.00
Crown Tuscan, Compote, Charleton Enamel Roses & Harbor Scene, 7 1/2 In. 65.00
Crown Tuscan, Flower Frog, Shell, Charleton Enamel Roses, Gold Encrusted, 7 1/2 In. 105.00
Crown Tuscan, Vase, Bud, Charleton Enamel Roses, Gold Encrusted, Footed, 10 In. 85.00
Crown Tuscan, Vase, Bud, Gold Encrusted, Chintz No. 2 Etch, Footed, 10 In. 135.00
Decagon, Ice Bucket, Royal Blue, Chrome Handle & Tongs 105.00
Diane, Jam Jar, Cover, Etched, 8 Oz. 55.00
Diane, Lamp, Hurricane, No. 1603, Etched, Pair 375.00
Diane, Pitcher, Emerald, Etched 585.00
Diane, Relish, Round, 5 Sections, 10 1/2 In. 45.00
Diane, Stein, Etched, 14 Oz. 65.00
Diane, Vase, Crown Tuscan, Gold Encrusted, 5 In. 120.00
Draped Lady, Flower Frog, Emerald, 13 In. 197.00
Draped Lady, Flower Frog, Emerald, Oval Base, 8 1/2 In. 385.00
Draped Lady, Flower Frog, Mandarin Gold, 8 1/2 In. 130.00
Draped Lady, Flower Frog, Peach-Blo, 8 1/2 In. 110.00
Ebony, Bottle, Etched Bath Salts, Gold Encrusted 295.00
Ebony, Bottle, Etched Hand Lotion, Gold Encrusted 295.00
Ebony, Candlestick, 2-Light, Gold Encrusted, Blossom Time Etch, 6 In., Pair 175.00
Ebony, Candy Box, Cover, Blossom Time Etch, 3-Toed, 6 1/2 In. 250.00
Ebony, Compote, Charleton Gold Roses, 6 1/2 In. 140.00
Ebony, Compote, Decagon, Sterling Silver Overlay, 7 In. 85.00

Ebony, Cordial, 1 Oz. 55.00
Ebony, Creamer, Plainware, Footed, Etched Glue Chip 100.00
Ebony, Sandwich Tray, Center Handle, White Gold Encrusted, Gloria Etch, 11 In. 110.00
Ebony, Swan, Signed, 4 1/2 In. 85.00
Elaine, Vase, Keyhole, 10 In. 85.00
Everglade, Sandwich Plate, Amber, 3-Toed, 15 In. 75.00
Everglade, Sandwich Plate, Willow Blue, Etched, 3-Toed, 15 In. 85.00
Fernland, Celery Dish, Near Cut, 10 In. 15.00
Fernland, Compote, Near Cut, 7 In. 30.00
Georgian, Candy Box, Cover, Smoke 40.00
Gloria, Nut Cup, 4-Toed, 3 In. 50.00
Gyro-Optic, Fishbowl, Aquaria, Footed, Amber, 10 In. 200.00
Gyro-Optic, Jug, Amethyst, 20 Oz. 50.00
Helio, Cheese & Cracker Set, 10 In. 65.00
Helio, Vase, Ball, Gold Encrusted, 4 3/4 In. 155.00
Heron, Flower Frog, 12 In. 150.00
Jefferson, Goblet, Emerald, 10 Oz., Pair 10.00
Jefferson, Sherbet, Moonlight Blue, 6 Oz. 30.00
Laurel Wreath, Relish, 3 Sections, 4-Toed, 11 In. 25.00
Mah-Jong Etch, Jug, Cover, Overnight, Gold Encrusted 650.00
Mandarin Gold, Nut Cup, Gold, 4-Toed, 3 In. 40.00
Marjorie, Punch Set, Bowl, 12 Cups 110.00
Martha Washington, Compote, Carmen, Footed, Rockwell Sterling Overlay, 5 1/2 In. 230.00
Martha Washington, Sugar & Creamer, Milk Glass 20.00
Minerva, Compote, Gold Stippled Rim, 6 In. 40.00
Mt. Vernon, Compote, Amber, Clear Stem & Foot, 6 In. 45.00
Mt. Vernon, Decanter, Stopper, 40 Oz. 50.00
Mt. Vernon, Ivy Ball, Footed, Heatherbloom, 4 1/2 In. 45.00
Mt. Vernon, Sherbet, Violet, 6 1/2 Oz. 195.00
Nude, Ashtray, Carmen, Clear Stem & Foot 310.00
Nude, Ashtray, Royal Blue 345.00
Nude, Candlestick, Crown Tuscan, 9 In., Pair 375.00
Nude, Claret, Carmen, 4 1/2 Oz. 200.00
Nude, Claret, Royal Blue, Clear Stem & Foot, 4 1/2 Oz. 175.00
Nude, Cocktail, Pink, Clear Stem & Foot, 3 Oz. 235.00
Nude, Cocktail, Smoke Crackle, Clear Stem & Foot, 3 Oz. 1050.00
Nude, Cocktail, Tahoe Blue, Clear Stem & Foot, 3 Oz. 375.00
Nude, Compote, Carmen, Clear Stem & Foot, 7 In. 225.00
Nude, Compote, Cupped, Amethyst 290.00
Nude, Compote, Flared, Royal Blue 335.00
Nude, Compote, Flared, Royal Blue, Clear Stem & Foot, 7 In. 300.00
Nude, Compote, Shell, Crown Tuscan, 7 In. 95.00
Nude, Compote, Shell, Mandarin Gold 510.00
Nude, Cordial, Amethyst, Clear Stem & Foot, 1 Oz. 500.00
Nude, Cordial, Carmen, Clear Stem & Foot, 1 Oz. 825.00
Nude, Cordial, Forest Green, Clear Stem & Foot, 1 Oz. 375.00
Nude, Dish, Mint, Carmen, Clear Stem & Foot 900.00
Nude, Goblet, Satin Stem, Sterling Silver Overlay 500.00
Nude, Saucer, Champagne, Satin Stem, Optic Bowl, Monogram 100.00
Nude, Wine, 3 Oz. 265.00
Portia, Bowl, Oblong, 4-Toed, 12 In. 55.00
Portia, Candy Box, Cover, 7 In. 95.00
Portia, Relish, Crown Tuscan, Gold Encrusted, Sections, 3 Handles, 8 In. 35.00
Portia, Relish, Gold Krystol, 3 Sections, 3 Handles, 8 In. 45.00
Primrose, Bowl, 7 1/4 In. 70.00
Primrose, Compote, 6 In. 40.00
Primrose, Vase, Cylinder, Gold Band Laurel Wreath Overlay, 10 In. 65.00
Radiant Rose, Tumbler, Whiskey, 3 Oz. 60.00
Ram's Head, Bowl, Amethyst, Gadroon Rim 230.00
Rosalie, Dish, Mayonnaise, Underplate, Amber, Oval, 6 1/2 In. 55.00
Rose Point, Butter, Cover, 5 1/2 In. 110.00

Rose Point, Candlestick, Leaf, 6 1/2 In., Pair 400.00
Rose Point, Candy Dish, Cover, Etched 135.00
Rose Point, Celery & Relish, Gold Encrusted, Etched, 3 Sections, 4-Toed, 12 In. 100.00
Rose Point, Compote, 5 1/2 In. 45.00
Rose Point, Compote, Blown, 5 3/8 In. 45.00
Rose Point, Compote, Sterling Filigree Rim, Sterling Around Foot, 8 1/2 In. 250.00
Rose Point, Cruet Set, Oil & Vinegar 225.00
Rose Point, Dish, Mayonnaise, Ladle, Gold Encrusted, Footed 55.00
Rose Point, Dish, Mayonnaise, Underplate, Gold Encrusted 65.00
Rose Point, Goblet, Amethyst, 9 Oz. 75.00
Rose Point, Ice Tub, Sterling Silver Base, Etched 255.00
Rose Point, Jug, Ball, Etched, No. 3400 .... 200.00
Rose Point, Marmalade, Cover, Ladle, 8 Oz. 90.00
Rose Point, Vase, Star Base, Etched, 6 In. 256.00
Seashell, Bowl, Tahoe Blue, 3-Toed, 10 In. 550.00
Seashell, Compote, Milk Glass, 8 1/2 In. 45.00
Seashell, Relish, Pearl Mist, 3 Sections, 4-Toed, 9 In. 15.00
Shell, Flower Frog, Windsor Blue, 7 1/2 In. 245.00
Sonata, Bowl, Carmen, Oval, 10 1/2 In. 65.00
Swan, Dish, 4 1/2 In. 40.00
Swan, Dish, 8 1/2 In. 70.00
Swan, Dish, Crown Tuscan, 3 In. 35.00
Swan, Dish, Emerald, Signed, 3 In. 45.00
Swan, Dish, Gold Krystol, 3 In. 30.00
Swan, Dish, Peach-Blo, 3 In. 40.00
Tally-Ho, Bowl, Salad, Forest Green, 2 Sections 25.00
Tally-Ho, Cordial, Mocha, 1 Oz. 60.00
Tally-Ho, Ice Bucket, Chrome Handle, Etched, Valencia 50.00
Tally-Ho, Plate, Salad, Carmen, Rockwell Sterling Overlay, 8 In. 225.00
Tally-Ho, Salad Set, Royal Blue Blow, 2 Sections, Footed, 18 In. 365.00
Tally-Ho, Vase, Top Hat, Amber, 10 1/2 In. 100.00
Valencia, Urn, Cover, Etched 350.00
Virginian, Cake Salver, 10 1/2 In. 90.00
Wildflower, Bonbon, 2 Handles, 2 1/2 x 8 1/4 In. 23.00
Wildflower, Nut Cup, 4-Toed, 3 In. 75.00

CAMBRIDGE POTTERY was made in Cambridge, Ohio, from about 1895 until World War I. The factory made brown glazed decorated artwares with a variety of marks, including an acorn, the name *Cambridge*, the name *Oakwood*, or the name *Terrhea.*

Mug, Handle, High Glaze, Alpena, Michigan Logo, 4 7/8 In. 45.00
Pitcher, Flowers, High Standard Glaze, Gold Trim, Grafton, North Dakota, Logo, 4 5/8 In. 60.00
Planter, Laurella, Embossed Vine & Bow, Blue Glaze, 5 1/2 In. 31.00
Vase, Flowers, High Standard Glaze, Manitowoc, Wisconsin, Logo, 4 5/8 In. 65.00

CAMEO GLASS was made in much the same manner as a cameo in jewelry. Parts of the top layer of glass were cut away to reveal a different-colored glass beneath. The most famous cameo glass was made during the nineteenth century. Signed cameo glass pieces are listed under the glasswork's name, such as Daum or Galle.

Biscuit Jar, Red Satin, Apple Blossoms, 7 1/4 x 6 In. 1780.00
Bowl, Amber, Purple, F. Decorchemont, 3 x 6 In. 6520.00
Bowl, Centerpiece, Pink, Red, Grapevine, Opal Squared Rim, c.1930, 7 In. 470.00
Bowl, Green, Orange, Brown, Lozenge Shape, F. Decorchemont, 3 3/8 x 3 1/8 In. 4346.00
Bowl, Yellow, Acid Cut, Art Deco, Edouard Cazaux, France, c.1915, 5 1/2 x 13 In. 1290.00
Charger, Enameled, Ruby Overlay, Water Fowl, Grasses, Monogrammed Medallion, 11 In. 175.00
Decanter, Gold Grape Leaves, Frosted Ground, Spelter Flip Lid, Lion, Shield, France, 10 In. 430.00
Finger Bowl, Underplate, Stems, Leaves, Flowers, 5 1/2 In. 550.00
Lamp Base, Red, Sunflowers, Footed, Oval, England, 4 In. 345.00
Tazza, Blue, Geometric Designs, F. Decorchemont, 6 x 7 1/2 In. 7140.00
Vase, Blue, Opaque Flowers, Leaves, Reverse Butterflies, Oval, 6 1/4 In. 1840.00

Vase, Cascading Branches, Leaves, Buds, Flowers, Red Ground, Shouldered, 6 In. 2015.00
Vase, Citrine, Flowers, Leaves, Stems, Wheat Stalks, Tapered, Flared Rim, 8 In. 290.00
Vase, Flowers, Leaves, Double Band Borders, Burgundy, England, 5 1/2 In. 1555.00
Vase, Ivory, Oval, Shouldered, Cascading Branch, Border, Webb & Son, 6 1/4 In. 865.00
Vase, Mottled Yellow, Green Iris, Bulbous Bottom, Tapered Neck, Crois Mare, 11 In. 635.00
Vase, Orange Geometric Design, Frosted Ground, Bulbous Neck, Flared Rim, Honesdale, 14 In. ... 1840.00
Vase, Ostriches, White, Mottled, Amethyst Ground, 12 1/4 In. 805.00
Vase, Prussian Blue, Apple Blossom, Bulbous, England, 7 In. 805.00
Vase, Prussian Blue, Egg Shape, Flower Cutting, Shouldered, England, 5 3/4 In. 805.00
Vase, Red Cased, Morning Glories, Gourd Shape, England, 6 In. 1150.00
Vase, Roses, Ruby Overlay, Baluster, E. Michel, c.1900, 8 3/4 In. 6573.00
Vase, Trees, Mountains, Red & Black Overlay, Baluster, De Frez, c.1890, 6 1/4 In. 598.00
Vase, Women, Birds, Wisteria, Green, Caramel, Amethyst Overlay, Kelsey, 12 In. 230.00

CAMPAIGN memorabilia is listed in the Political category.

CAMPBELL KIDS were first used as part of an advertisement for the Campbell Soup Company in 1906. The kids were created by Grace Drayton, a popular illustrator of the day. The kids were used in magazine and newspaper ads until about 1951. They were presented again in 1966; and in 1983, they were redesigned with a slimmer, more contemporary appearance.

Advertisement, 3 Kids Running, 1954, 12 1/4 x 9 1/2 In. 13.00
Advertisement, They Always Eat Better, Chicken Noodle Soup, 1965, 13 x 10 In. 8.00
Advertisement, Tomato Soup, Kids, Carrying Sign, 1914, 14 x 5 1/2 In. 6.00
Bank, Cast Iron, Gold Paint, A.C. Williams, M 163 .... 96.00
Bank, Cast Iron, Painted, A.C. Williams, M 163 .... 250.00
Bell, Fishing Buddies, Fenton, 1984, 6 x 3 1/2 In. 54.00
Bell, Music Box, Joy To The World, Fenton, 1984, 6 1/4 x 3 3/4 In. 95.00
Cookie Jar, Nodder, Spoon & Fork Inserts, Davar, 10 1/4 In. 650.00
Doll, Bicentennial Clothes, Box, 1976, Pair 195.00
Doll, Girl, Composition, 6-Piece Body, 12 In. 224.00
Doll, Vinyl, Movable Head, Arms, Legs, Tags, World Doll, 1984, 17 In., Pair 140.00
Mug, Girl, Plastic, Melmac Melamine, 1970s, 2 5/8 x 3 1/4 In. 6.00
Mug, M'm M'm Good, Westwood International, 1989 .... 3.00 to 5.00
Ornament, Kids & Santa, 1980 .... 6.00
Ornament, Kids, Hanging Stockings On Mantel, 6th In Series, Box, 1985 .... 12.00
Postcard, Boy, Batting, Verse, 10 Cents A Can 144.00
Salt & Pepper, Plastic, F & F Mold & Die Works, Dayton, Ohio, c.1950, 4 1/2 In. 80.00
Stringholder, c.1950, 6 3/4 In. 395.00
Wristwatch, Leather Strap, Centurion, Swiss, 1982 .... 30.00

CANDELABRUM refers to a candleholder with more than one arm to hold many candles; a candlestick is designed to hold one candle. The eccentricity of the English language makes the plural of candelabrum into candelabra.

2-Branch, Iron, Elephant Medallion, Edgar Brandt, 13 x 9 1/2 In., Pair 10620.00
2-Branch, Neoclassical Style, Prism Drops, 28 3/4 In., Pair 1112.00
2-Branch, Silver Plate, Scrolling, Cut Glass, Bobeches, Prism Drops, 4 x 15 In, Pair 585.00
2-Branch, Silver, Pomegranate, Georg Jensen, Denmark, Post 1945, 8 1/2 In. 8955.00
2-Light, Brass, Stepped, Round Base, Scroll Branches, 1700s, 6 1/2 x 7 1/4 In., Pair 865.00
2-Light, Bronze, After Moreau, Male & Female Dionysian Herms, 13 3/8 In., Pair 380.00
2-Light, Bronze, Dore, Napoleon III, c.1860, 13 1/2 In., Pair 1120.00
2-Light, Copper, Twisted Stem, Notched Bobeche, Footed, Handicraft Shop, 9 In. 210.00
2-Light, Gilt Bronze, Champleve Enamel, Square Column, Urn Finial, 13 In., Pair 1625.00
2-Light, Gilt Bronze, Louis XV Style, Adjustable Damask Screen, France, 22 In. 1060.00
2-Light, Scroll Arms, Stepped Circular Base, Lettner, c.1950, 6 In., Pair 1600.00
2-Light, Silver, C-Scroll Arms, Baluster Stem, Dwarf, Continental, c.1900, 8 In., Pair 410.00
2-Light, Silver, Trumpet Sconce, Flower Stem Arm, La Paglia, International Sterling, 7 3/4 In., Pair . 1880.00
2-Light, Wrought Iron, Spanish Colonial, Strap Iron Base, 57 x 17 x 16 In. 370.00
3-Branch, Bronze, Crystal, France, 11 x 9 In., Pair 530.00
3-Branch, Flowers, Prisms, Removable Bobeche, 9 1/4 x 12 1/4 In., Pair 65.00

3-Branch, Ormolu, Winged Figure, Electrified, France, 1800s, 21 In., Pair 4400.00
3-Branch, Red Enamel, Copper Vase Shape, Pedestal Base, Victorian, 15 1/2 x 9 In. 85.00
3-Branch, Scroll Branches, Silver, Ortega, Mexican, 13 x 18 In., Pair 1055.00
3-Branch, Silver, Flowers, Arabesque, 1920-40, 17 x 14 In., Pair 2115.00
3-Light, Bronze, Flowering Tree, Bird, Rocks, Chinese, Early 1900s, 14 1/2 In. 200.00
3-Light, Bronze, Silvered, Jean Despres, 1900s, 8 1/4 x 9 7/8 In. 7760.00
3-Light, Cut Glass, Anglo-Irish, Late 1800s, 23 1/4 In., Pair 1115.00
3-Light, Gilt Bronze, Cherubs, Patinated, Marble, 17 1/2 In., Pair 4800.00
3-Light, Gilt Bronze, Earthenware, France, c.1900, 14 In., Pair 880.00
3-Light, Gilt Bronze, Marble, Empire Style, Classical Herm Stem, 17 1/2 In., Pair 1295.00
3-Light, Gilt Bronze, Marble, Louis XVI Style, Caryatid Support, 21 x 8 In., Pair 2820.00
3-Light, Pressed Glass, Scroll Arms, Flower Cups, 6-Sided Foot, Czechoslovakia, 15 x 13 In., Pair .. 382.00
3-Light, Scroll Branch Arms, Turned, Square Form, Footed, Barker Ellis, 16 x 13 1/2 In., Pair 410.00
3-Light, Sheffield Plate, Regency, Shell, Acanthus, Early 1800s, 19 1/2 x 18 In., Pair 1715.00
3-Light, Silver Plate, Convertible, 14 1/2 x 16 In., Pair 117.00
3-Light, Silver Plate, Convertible, 15 x 12 1/2 In., Pair 470.00
3-Light, Silver Plate, Convertible, England, 18 x 16 1/2 In., Pair 265.00
3-Light, Silver Plate, Flowers, Leaves, c.1850, 23 1/2 In., Pair 405.00
3-Light, Silver Plate, Georgian Style, William Adams, England, 1900s, 15 x 14 In., Pair 175.00
3-Light, Silver Plate, Gilt, Reed & Barton, 12 1/4 x 19 1/4 In. 176.00
3-Light, Silver Plate, Lobed, Square Base, Scrolling Arms, 13 x 11 1/2 In., Pair 120.00
3-Light, Silver Plate, Scroll Branches, Barker Ellis, 16 In., Pair 410.00
3-Light, Silver Plate, Sheffield, 20 In., Pair 819.00
3-Light, Silver Plate, Sheffield, c.1820, 21 1/2 x 16 1/2 In. 265.00
3-Light, Silver, 2 Scroll Arms, Knopped Hexagonal Base, c.1937, 18 In., Pair 3100.00
3-Light, Silver, Convertible, Gorham, 11 1/4 In., Pair 234.00
3-Light, Silver, Cornucopia Branches, Germany, Early 1900s, 10 1/2 In., Pair 440.00
3-Light, Silver, Georgian Style, Weighted, 15 In., Pair 175.00
3-Light, Silver, Marked Miyata, 20th Century, 15 In., Pair 235.00
3-Light, Silver, Triple Knop Sconce, Baluster Stem, Redlich & Co., c.1950, 9 1/4 In., Pair 764.00
3-Light, Silver, Weighted, Swag & Scroll, Gorham, 13 In., Pair 519.00
3-Light, Tin, Weighted, Cone Shape Base, Crimped Drip Pan, 1800s 248.00
4-Branch, Brass, Animals, Flowers, Leaves, Hagenauer, Austria, 1930s, 10 1/2 In. 7730.00
4-Branch, Glass, Baluster Stem, Petal Shape Base, Waterford, 14 x 23 1/2 In. 800.00
4-Light, Brass, Carved Marble, 16 1/2 x 10 In., Pair 295.00
4-Light, Bronze, Patinated, 4-Part Base, England, Late 1800s, 28 1/2 x 18 In. 940.00
4-Light, Chromium, Art Deco, France, c.1930, 9 1/2 In., Pair 295.00
4-Light, George III, Round Base, Knopped Stem, Victorian, 16 1/4 In., Pair 5805.00
4-Light, Gilt Bronze, Louis XVI Style, Early 1900s, 18 3/4 In., Pair 880.00
4-Light, Gilt Bronze, Patinated, Nike, Restauration Style, France, 24 1/4 In., Pair 3290.00
4-Light, Gilt Bronze, Restauration, Reeded Standards, Orpheus, France, 21 In., Pair 2585.00
4-Light, Gilt Metal, Louis XVI Style, Cherubs, C-Scroll Arms, Late 1800s, 33 In., Pair 410.00
4-Light, Leaf Molded & Scrolled Arms, Shaped Foot, France, c.1850, 19 In., Pair 7638.00
4-Light, Marble, Bronze, Napoleon III, Levillain, Barbedienne, 25 In., Pair 5400.00
4-Light, Sevres Porcelain, Bronze, c.1880, 23 In., Pair 1520.00
5-Branch, Silver Plate, Grapevine, 3-Footed, c.1850, 28 1/4 In. 1245.00
5-Light, Brass, Center Cup, 4 Scrolling Arms, Turned, M On Bottom, 16 In., Pair 100.00
5-Light, Bronze, 4 Arms, Winged Victory Figure, Ormolu, French Empire, Pair 6040.00
5-Light, Bronze, White Marble, France, 1800s, 20 In., Pair 936.00
5-Light, Crystal, Gilt Metal, France, 21 x 9 In., Pair 1055.00
5-Light, Cut Glass, Prisms, Paneled, Tapered Hollow Post, Octagonal Platform, 24 x 18 1/2 In. 635.00
5-Light, Sheffield Plate, Flame Finial, Armorial, Late Georgian, 1800s, 26 x 22 1/2 In. 1645.00
5-Light, Silver Plate, Georgian Style, Ellis Barker, 21 In., Pair 805.00
5-Light, Silver Plate, Scrolling Arms, Hartford Sterling Co., c.1925, 24 x 15 In., Pair 763.00
5-Light, Silver, Putto, Neo-Greque Style, Meriden, 15 In. 175.00
5-Light, Silver, Reeded Stem, Lazarus Posen, Germany, c.1900, 18 3/4 In., Pair 2470.00
5-Light, Silver, Thistle Sconce, Downswept Arms, Roger Williams, 1900s, 10 1/2 In., Pair 940.00
6-Light, Brass, Deux Couleurs, Rouge Royale Marble, Electrified, France, c.1900, 27 In., Pr. 2230.00
6-Light, Gilt Bronze, 3-Paw Base, Columnar Shaft, Grapevine Arms, 23 1/2 In., Pair 384.00
6-Light, Gilt Bronze, Louis XVI Style, Christofle, Paris, c.1900, 27 1/4 In., Pair 7200.00
6-Light, Gilt Bronze, Putto & Bouquet, Napoleon III, Louis XVI, 40 x 15 In. 2820.00

6-Light, Gilt Metal, Scrolling Branches, White Molded Glass Flowers, 28 In., Pair 510.00
6-Light, Silver, Scroll Branch Arms, Continental, 17 1/4 In. 670.00
7-Light, Bronze, Gilt, Jesus, Mary, Joseph, 3-Sided Base, 19 x 20 In., Pair 440.00
7-Light, Gilt Bronze Mounted, Verde Antico Marble, Louis XVI Style, 58 In. 6460.00
7-Light, Parcel Gilt Wood, Iron, Painted Green, Neoclassical Style, 90 In., Pair 5170.00
7-Light, Silver Plate, 3 Women, Serpentine Arms, England, c.1875, 24 1/2 In., Pair 4115.00
8-Light, Gilt Bronze, Scrolled, Maidens, Patinated, c.1885, 34 In., Pair 4800.00
13-Light, Cut Glass, 2 Tiers, 6 Scrolled Arms, Cup, Bobeches, Prisms, 33 x 23 In. 635.00
Chromium Plated Brass, J. Robert F. Swanson, c.1947, 25 x 21 x 6 In. 3600.00
Figural, Depicting Woman, With Dog, Germany, c.1900, 16 In. 382.00
Girandole, 4-Light, Gilt Bronze, Brass, Cut Glass, Louis XVI, 22 x 13 1/2 In., Pair 3055.00
Girandole, Gilt Bronze, Dolphin Form, Prisms, Marble Base, 15 In., Pair 2350.00

CANDLESTICKS were made of brass, pewter, glass, sterling silver, plated silver, and all types of pottery and porcelain. The earliest candlesticks, dating from the sixteenth century, held the candle on a pricket (sharp pointed spike). These lost favor because in times of strife the large church candlesticks with prickets became formidable weapons, so the socket was mandated. Candlesticks changed in style through the centuries, and designs range from classic to rococo to Art Nouveau to Art Deco.

Bell Metal, Continental, 7 1/2 In. 80.00
Blown Glass, Blue Opaque, Petal Top, Dragon Head Serpent Stem, 8 x 4 3/4 In., Pair 50.00
Blown Glass, Blue, Clambroth, Petal Top, Dolphin Stems, Square Base, 11 In., Pair 130.00
Blown Glass, Flared Rim, 6-Ring Beehive Decoration, 1810-35, 10 x 3 In. 1375.00
Blown Glass, Opaque White, Crucifix Top, Graduated Hexagonal Base, 10 x 4 In. 45.00
Blown Glass, Opaque, Crucifix Stem, Hexagonal Raised Base, Top, 11 1/2 x 4 1/2 In. 55.00
Blown Glass, Stepped Bases, Rounded Corners, 8 1/2 In., Pair 175.00
Blown Glass, Vaseline, Petal Top, Hexagonal Stem, Flared Base, 7 x 4 In. 165.00
Bluejohn, Derbyshire, Spar Stem, Slate Sconce, Base, 7 1/8 In., Pair 1058.00
Brass, Altar, Renaissance Style, Tapered Shaft, 3-Sided Base, 19th Century, 34 In., Pair 800.00
Brass, Baluster Shaft, Octagonal Base, Empire, 8 3/4 x 3 5/8 x 3 1/4 In. 99.00
Brass, Baluster Shaft, Octagonal Base, Empire, 10 x 4 1/8 x 4 1/4 In. 110.00
Brass, Baluster Shafts, Square Base, Cut Corners, c.1850, 8 7/8 In., Pair 175.00
Brass, Baluster Stem, Octagonal Base, 19th Century, 14 In., Pair 206.00
Brass, Baluster Stem, Square Footed Base, Tooled Rings, 8 1/2 In. 345.00
Brass, Baluster, Urn Shape Candlecup, England, Early 1800s, 10 x 4 1/2 In. 35.00
Brass, Beehive Shape, Late 1800s, 12 In., Pair 185.00
Brass, Beehive, Cut Square Corner Base, Push-Up, 1800s, 12 In., Pair 315.00
Brass, Beehive, Turned Shafts, Round Base, 9 1/2 In., Pair 55.00
Brass, Butterfly Reflector, Etched Flowers, Petal Cups, 21 1/2 In., Pair 60.00
Brass, Classical, 3-Footed, Portrait Panels, Tapered Column, Urn Base, 22 1/2 In. 275.00
Brass, Cold Painted Metal, Parakeet, Dome Foot, Early 1900s, 8 In., Pair 1295.00
Brass, Dome Base, Base Molding, Turned Baluster Column, 9 1/2 In. 400.00
Brass, Dome Base, Molded Base, Drip Pan, Baluster Column, 1700s, 8 1/4 In., Pair 400.00
Brass, Elongated Candle Cups, Baluster Shaft, Cushion Base, 8 7/8 In., Pair 295.00
Brass, Empire, Baluster Shaft, Octagonal Base, 8 3/4 x 3 5/8 x 3 1/4 In., Pair 99.00
Brass, Gothic Style, Oval Niches, 3-Footed, Openwork, 19 1/2 x 8 x 8 In. 345.00
Brass, Mission Style, Square Pedestal Base, 7 1/2 x 3 In., Pair 44.00
Brass, Multi-Knopped Stem, Dome Foot, Trefoil Feet, Continental, c.1800, 20 In., Pair 325.00
Brass, Neoclassical, Ionic Columns, 2 Females Busts, Continental, 10 3/4 In., Pair 705.00
Brass, Paste, Gothic Style, Fraefel & Co., Swiss, 1800s, 14 3/4 In., Pair 180.00
Brass, Petal Base, Seamed Construction, England, 18th Century 395.00
Brass, Queen Anne, Singe Petal, Cylinder Candle Cup, 7 1/2 In. 175.00
Brass, Queen Of Diamonds, 11 1/2 In., Pair 288.00
Brass, Rose Brass, Column, Louis Philippe, Mid 1800s, 8 1/2 In., Pair 352.00
Brass, Round Base, Push-Up, 1800s, 10 3/4 In., Pair 200.00
Brass, Silvered, Cylindrical Sockets, Fluted Baluster Stem, Late 1800s, 10 In., Pair 175.00
Brass, Tapered Column, Bottom Ribbing, Oval Base, 6 1/4 In., Pair 140.00
Brass, Tommi Parzinger, Sunburst Bobeche, Dorlyn Silversmiths, 7 In., Pair 266.00
Brass, Turned Columns, Scalloped Square Base, 7 1/4 In., Pair 145.00

Bronze, 4 Art Nouveau Heads At Top, Enameled Flowers, Flared Base, 8 In. 840.00
Bronze, Bulbous Cup, Stick Stem, Disc Foot, Arts & Crafts, 14 In. 240.00
Bronze, Cherub, Tripod, Pricket, 17 x 5 1/2 In., Pair 520.00
Bronze, Figure, Aesthetic On Seashell, Holding Basket Over Head, Japan, 12 In., Pair 2350.00
Bronze, Friffoul, Newark, N.J., c.1900, 10 3/8 In., Pair 59.00
Bronze, Gilt Bronze, Molded Foliate Sockets, Baluster Stems, France, 11 In., Pair 408.00
Bronze, Gothic Style Pricket, 2 Seated Figures, 37 x 10 1/2 x 10 1/2 In. 800.00
Bronze, Patinated, Gilt, Winged Caryatid, Empire, France, 1800s, 8 7/8 In., Pair 470.00
Bronze, Pricket, Hexagonal Bobeche, Faceted Stem, Arches, Gothic Style, 34 In., Pair 1410.00
Bronze, Seahorse Design, E.T. Hurley, 12 3/4 In., Pair 3600.00
Bronze, Shaped Cup, Stick Stem, Palm Leaf Design On Foot, Bradley & Hubbard, 24 In. 900.00
Ceramic, Parrot On Stumps, Rococo Style, Brass Sockets, Bases, 15 x 9 x 7 1/2 In., Pair 1840.00
Chamber, Brass, Side Ejectors, Secured & Patent, 4 5/8 In., Pair 145.00
Chamber, Scalloped Rim, Saucer, Bobeche, Shells, 3-Footed, c.1748, 4 In. 2645.00
Chamber, Silver, Scalloped Edge Saucer, Flame Top Snuffer, c.1839, 2 3/4 In. 545.00
Chamber, Silver, Tortoise Shell, Heart Shape Saucer, Finger Ring, Holder, 5 In. 690.00
Composition, Gilded, Archangels, Round Platform Base, 16 x 4 1/2 In., Pair 55.00
Copper, Round Base, Tubular, Flower Blossom Cup, Leaves, H.G. Cleaveland, 16 In., Pair 1500.00
Copper Tube, Alligator, Jonathan Bonner, 1986, 4 x 14 In., Pair 945.00
Enamel, Multicolored, White Ground, Flowers, Staffordshire, Late 1700s, 9 1/8 In., Pair 410.00
Gilt, Pricket, Lobed Standard, Tripod Base, Italy, Late 1700s, 24 x 7 In., Pair 1469.00
Gilt Gesso, Pricket, Baroque Style, Baluster Stem Ending, 27 1/2 In., Pair 1058.00
Glass, 21-Rib Baluster Socket, 16 Rib Base, Clear, Flint, Aqua Tint, Inward Rim, 3 3/8 In. 2530.00
Glass, Blue, Opaque, Petal Shape Top, Dragon Head Stem, Rounded Base, 8 In., Pair 50.00
Glass, Clambroth Stem, Cornflower Blue Socket, Acanthus Leaf, 11 In. 460.00
Glass, Cobalt Blue, Applied Socket, Inward Folded, Tooled Rim, 1840-65, 4 In. 385.00
Glass, Crucifix, Amber, New England, 9 1/4 In. 45.00
Glass, Electric Blue, Pewter Bobeche, Electric Blue, 11 In. 165.00
Glass, Green, Iridized, Archimede Seguso, Oval Gold Foil Label, 19 1/4 In., Pair 1410.00
Glass, Hexagonal Panels, Sanded Clambroth Base, Cornflower Blue, 8 1/4 In., Pair 230.00
Glass, Hexagonal, Opaque Blue, Sanded Finish, 6 7/8 In., Pair 115.00
Glass, Vaseline, Petal Top, Flared Base, Thumbprint, 7 x 4 3/8 In. 198.00
Glass, White, Opaque, Crucifix Shape Stem, Hexagonal Raised Base, Top, 11 1/2 In., Pair 55.00
Glass, White, Opaque, Crucifix Top, Graduated Hexagon Base, 10 x 4 In. 44.00
Glass Shade, Blown, Engraved, Telescoping, c.1850, 20 1/4 In., Pair 880.00
Hog Scraper, Brass, Wedding Ring, Push-Up, Stamped Fisher, 7 1/8 In. 518.00
Hog Scraper, Lip Hanger, Soldered Brass Rings, Push-Up, 6 In., Pair 259.00
Hog Scraper, Tin, Flared Top, Base, Push-Up, 6 1/2 x 3 7/8 In. 60.00
Iron, Griffin, Finger Hook, 6 x 6 x 3 In., Pair 220.00
Iron Pendant, Ratchet Trammel, Square Base, Pivoting Candlestick, Holder, 32 1/2 To 53 In. 265.00
Ivory, Amber, Olla Shape Candlecup, Cylindrical Stem, Square Base, France, 10 In., Pair 590.00
Maple, Turned, Pewter Candlecup, Ball Finial, 19th Century, 32 1/2 In. 235.00
Marble, Ormolu, Columnar, Cherub, Louis XVI Style, Late 1800s, 7 1/2 In., Pair 940.00
Metal Alloy, George III, c.1760, 10 1/2 In., Pair 445.00
Parcel Gilt Wood, Carved, Multicolored, Putto Masque, Baroque Style, 13 In. 1290.00
Pewter, Pricket, Baluster, Turned Knop, 3-Sided Concave Base, 3 Ball Feet, 56 In., Pair 2230.00
Pewter, Tudric, 4-Sided, Pierced Base, Archibald Knox, Liberty, 13 x 6 In. 6465.00
Porcelain, Gilt Brass Mounted, Sevres Style, Blue Ground, Flowers, Birds, Paris, 10 1/4 In., Pair . . 1290.00
Rock Crystal, Ormolu, Leaf Molded Nozzle, Trim, Louis XVI Style, 7 1/2 In., 4 Piece 3055.00
Sabbath, Bombe Base, Acanthus Leaves, Knopped Column, 15 1/2 In., Pair 370.00
Sconce, 2-Arm, Gilded, Figural, Cast Resin, Holder, 14 x 11 In., Pair 77.00
Sheffield Plate, Acanthus Leaf Cup, Goodman Gainsford & Fairbairn, c.1800, 8 1/8 In., Pair 530.00
Sheffield Plate, Baluster Stem, Fluted Corners, George III, 9 1/2 x 4 1/4 In., Pair 470.00
Sheffield Plate, Georgian, Fluted Column, Gadroon Bobeche, Square Base, 13 In., Pair 705.00
Sheffield Plate, Regency, Telescoping, Thistle, Blagden, Hodgson, 1820s, 10 1/2 In., Pair 175.00
Sheffield Plate, Regency, Urn Shape Candlecup, Matthew Boulton, c.1810, 16 1/4 x 7 1/2 In. . . . 645.00
Silver, 6-Shell Foot, Flute & Shell Stem, George III, c.1765, 10 In., Pair 3885.00
Silver, Adam Style, Flowers, Quatrefoil Bobeche, Shreve, c.1900, 14 1/4 In., Pair 2390.00
Silver, Adam Style, Weighted, Udall & Ballou, 11 In., 4 Piece 1150.00
Silver, Arms Of George III, 10 1/4 In., Pair 9438.00
Silver, Blossom Cups, Hammered, Raised Square Base, William Dodge, 3 In., Pair 1200.00

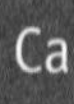

Candlestick, Silver, Fluted, Shells, Boar's Head Cup, Ebenezer Coker, c.1763, 10 In., Pair

Candy Container, Barney Google, Glass, Paint, Tin Closure, 4 In.

Silver, Chamber, Gadroon Borders, Robert Salmon, London, George III, 1800 .... 936.00
Silver, Classical Revival, Fluted, Leaftip Sconces, Monogram, Poland, 12 In., Pair 705.00
Silver, Corinthian Column, Bead Border Stepped Base, Victorian, 10 In., 4 Piece 2516.00
Silver, Corinthian Fluted Stems, Ireland, c.1775, 12 In., Pair 8270.00
Silver, Dome Foot, Trumpet Shape, Eagles, Leaves, Gorham, c.1925, 12 In., Pair 2629.00
Silver, Ellis-Barker Silver Co., England, 20 1/2 In., Pair 995.00
Silver, Flower Shape Nozzle, Pear Shape Stem, Rocaille Scrolls, Russia, 1895, 13 In., Pair 765.00
Silver, Fluted Column, Corinthian Top, Square Base, Gorham, 7 1/2 x 3 1/4 In., Pair 440.00
Silver, Fluted Columns, Stepped Base, Family Crest, England, 1768, 11 x 4 3/4 In., Pair 2530.00
Silver, Fluted, Shells, Boar's Head Cup, Ebenezer Coker, c.1763, 10 In., Pair .... ***ILLUS*** 3884.00
Silver, Fourteenth Century Pattern, Hammered, Shreve, c.1909, 9 1/2 In., Pair 1554.00
Silver, Francis I, Flowers, Fruits, Reed & Barton, c.1907, 10 In., Pair 2270.00
Silver, George I, 6-Sided Base, Samuel Wastell, London, 1717, 7 1/4 In. 6000.00
Silver, George I, Baluster, 6-Sided Base, Matthew Cooper I, London, 1716, 7 In., Pair 8400.00
Silver, George II, Bobeches, England, 1753, 10 In., 4 Piece 12500.00
Silver, George V, Scrolled Handle, Chamber, London, c.1910, 5 1/4 x 6 In., Pair 1175.00
Silver, Georgian Style, Weighted, Corinthian Capital Sconce, Gorham, 1907, 8 1/4 In., Pair 470.00
Silver, Oval Bobeche, Tapered Stem, Weighted, Gorham, 1900s, 9 1/4 In., 4 Piece 705.00
Silver, Repousse, Weighted, Thistle Sconce, S. Kirk & Son, 1903-24, 10 In., Pair 1528.00
Silver, Retro Style Bowl Shape, Footed, Sanborns, Mexico, c.1950, 3 In., Pair 176.00
Silver, Square Base, I.F.S. Ltd., England, 12 In., Pair 295.00
Silver, Square Base, Warsaw Marks, 1900s, 12 In., Pair 530.00
Silver, Square Column Shape, Leaf Sockets, Nozzles, Stepped Base, c.1928, 4 Piece 1258.00
Silver, Taper, Bell Shape Sconce, Flower Foot, Continental, 1900s, 6 3/4 In., Pair 200.00
Silver, Taper, Trumpet, Slender, S-Shaped Base, Michelsen, Denmark, c.1950, 5 In., Pair 350.00
Silver, Tapered Reeded Stem & Base, John Green & Co., Sheffield, 13 In., Pair 2350.00
Silver, Tapered, Strap Handle, Round Base, Chamber, Kalo, 3 x 4 In. 995.00
Silver, Weighted, Mauser, 10 In., 4 Piece 1150.00
Silver, Weighted, Reeded Nozzles, Stepped Foot, Black Starr & Frost, 1900s, 8 In., Pair 235.00
Silver, Wood Base, C.E.T., Birmingham, England, c.1910, 4 In., Pair 58.00
Silver Plate, Adam Style, Rams' Heads, Swags, Detachable Nozzle, 11 3/4 In., 4 Piece 2700.00
Silver Plate, Arts & Crafts, Hammered, Fluted Columns, Meriden, 10 5/8 In., Pair 80.00
Silver Plate, Circular, Pierced Leaf, Reed & Barton, c.1900, 11 3/4 In., Pair 320.00
Silver Plate, Cylindrical, Removable Bobeches, Robert R. Jarvie, 8 1/8 In., Pair 1600.00
Silver Plate, Georgian Style, Corinthian Column, Gorham, 1916, 10 1/2 In., 4 Piece 590.00
Silver Plate, Gothic, Romanesque Style, Monumental Pricket, 49 x 12 1/2 In. 920.00
Silver Plate, Knopped Tapered Stem, Sheffield, c.1820, 10 In., 4 Piece 629.00
Silver Plate, Openwork, Baluster, Flowers, Pairpoint, 9 1/2 In., Pair 460.00
Silver Plate, Sheffield, Removable Bobeche, 12-Sided Base, 10 3/4 In., Pair 200.00
Silver Plate, Swid Powell, Open Geometric, Italy, 9 In., Pair 345.00
Steel, Enamel, Brass Cup, Disk Shade, 4 Legs, Holder, Raymond M. Price, 40 In. 355.00
Tin, Cylindrical, Shaped Crest, Lift Lid, Holder, 6 3/4 x 11 3/4 In. 115.00
Traveling, Silver, Chamber, Dominick & Haff, Repousse Flower Box, 3 1/4 In. 1495.00
Wood, Painted, Pricket, 18th Century, 34 1/2 x 9 x 8 In. 1095.00
Wrought Iron, Brass, Tripod Scrolled Base, 69 x 22 In., Pair 1058.00
Wrought Iron, Wood, Spiral, Adjustable, 18th Century, 7 3/8 In. 235.00

CANDLEWICK items may be listed in the Imperial and Pressed Glass categories.

CANDY CONTAINERS have been popular since the late Victorian era. Collectors have long favored the glass containers, but now all types, including tin and papier-mache, are collected. Probably the earliest glass container sold commercially was the Liberty Bell made in 1876 for sale at the Centennial Exposition. Thousands of designs were made until the cost became too high in the 1960s. By the late 1970s, reproductions were being made and sold without the candy. Containers listed here are glass unless otherwise described. A Belsnickle is a nineteenth-century figure of Father Christmas. Some candy containers may be listed in Toy or in other categories.

Acorn, Original Closure ... 965.00
Airplane, Liberty Motor, Flag, Clear Glass, Tin ... 1980.00
Airplane, Patent 113053, Paper Label, Original Closure ... 22.00
Airplane, Spirit Of Goodwill, 80 Percent Paint, Original Prop, Original Closure ... 94.00
Airplane, US P-51 ... 33.00 to 39.00
Amos 'n' Andy, Blue Jacket, Red Jacket, Yellow Wheels, 4 1/2 In. ... 275.00 to 385.00
Barney Google, Glass, Paint, Tin Closure, 4 In. ... *ILLUS* 392.00
Barney Google & Ball, Glass, c.1927, 3 1/2 In. ... 175.00
Barney Google & Ball, Green, Original Closure ... 385.00
Baseball, Baseball Bank, Plastic Stand, Original Closure ... 28.00
Baseball Player, Glass Jar, Yellow Screw Top, Painted ... 1880.00
Baseball Player On Base, Painted, Metal Cap, Original Closure ... 605.00
Basket, Rooster Head, Round, Hot Pink, Celluloid, 3 1/4 x 2 3/4 In. ... 79.00
Basket, Wire Handle, Original Closure ... 28.00
Bell, Fancy School, Original Closure ... 770.00
Birdcage, Original Bail, Closure ... 105.00
Bisque Poupee Head, Enamel Eyes, Mohair, Carton Body, Papier-Mache Box, 9 In. ... 3960.00
Boat, Battleship On Waves, Tin Replacement Closure ... 83.00
Boat, Miniature Battleship, Red Stacks, Contents, Paper Label, Metal Closure ... 110.00
Boat, Queen Mary, Original Closure ... 28.00
Bottle, R.D. Rawlings, Light Green, Torpedo Soda Bottle, No Closure ... 33.00
Boy Riding Pig, Papier-Mache, Bisque, Movable Arms, Waving Hat, 4 x 5 In. ... 336.00
Buddy Bank, Marx ... 385.00
Bureau, Partial Paint, Original Mirror, No Closure ... 220.00
Bus, Chicago, Painted, Original Closure ... 633.00
Bus, Greyhound, 80 Percent Paint, Original Wheels, Closure ... 523.00
Bus, New York-San Francisco, Original Closure ... 825.00
Bus, Victory Lines Special, Painted, Original Closure ... 121.00
Camera On Tripod, c.1913, 5 In. ... 316.00 to 660.00
Candlestick, Handles, Souvenir Of St. John's N.F., Ruby Flashed, Original Closure ... 415.00
Candlestick, Sunshine, Contents, Original Closure, Box ... 578.00
Cannon, 2 Wheel Mount, No. 2, Original Tin, Original Closure ... 330.00
Cannon, Rapid Fire Gun, Embossed Tin Top, Instructions, Original Closure ... 385.00
Cannon, U.S. Defense Field Gun No. 17, Contents, Original Closure ... 415.00
Car, Flat Top, Tassels, Maroon Paint, Original Closure ... 195.00
Car, Limousine, Pat Ap'ld For, Green Paint, Original Closure ... 130.00
Car, Limousine, Rear Trunk, Tire, Partial Red Paint, Original Closure, 1/2 Oz. ... 60.00
Car, Limousine, West Spec. Co., Green Wheels, Original Closure ... 138.00
Car, Sedan, 6 Vents, Radiator Cap, Painted, Original Closure ... 120.00 to 130.00
Car, Streamlined, Red Paint, No Closure ... 88.00
Car, Streamlined, Yellow Paint, No Closure ... 80.00
Car, Taxi, Green, Original Closure ... 825.00
Car, Taxi, Yellow, Original Closure ... 908.00
Car, V.G. Co. Coupe, Metal Wheels, Contents, Original Closure ... 715.00
Car, V.G. Co. Sedan, Yellow Paint, Original Wheels, Closure ... 195.00
Careful Chubby D. Cop, Contents, Box ... 305.00
Carpet Sweeper, Baby Sweeper, Original Tin, Wheels, Closure ... 525.00
Carpet Sweeper, Dolly Sweeper, Painted, Original Tin, Wheels, Closure ... 578.00
Cash Register, Original Closure ... 415.00
Cat, Papier-Mache, Spring Neck, Tail, Arm, Plays Instrument, Black, Germany, 12 In. ... 1650.00

Chauffeur, Pumpkin Head, Glass, 4 In. 450.00
Chicken, On Oblong Basket, Victory Glass Co., 1930s, 3 x 2 x 1 3/4 In. .... 60.00 to 65.00
Chicken, Round Base, No Paint, Original Closure 415.00
Chicken, Round Sagging Base, No Paint, Original Closure 1100.00
Clock, Alarm, Original Closure 275.00
Clock, Glass, Gold Finish 95.00
Clock, Lynne, Plastic, Boy & Girl Under Umbrella, Contents, Original Closure 415.00
Clock, Mantel, No Bank Slot, Partial Paint, Original Closure 80.00
Clock, Mantel, Paint, Bank Slot Not Knocked Out, Original Closure 105.00
Clock, Milk Glass, Tin Closure .... *ILLUS* 280.00
Clock, Milk White, Paint, Souvenir, Emery, S.D., Original Closure 190.00
Clown, Papier-Mache, Cardboard, Germany, c.1930, 7 1/2 In. 90.00
Clown, Wheelbarrow, Flywheel Drive, Lithograph, Pair 2292.00
Coach, Parlor Car, New York Central RR, Purple Tinted Glass, Original Closure 358.00
Coal Car, Overland Limited, Original Wheels, Closure 385.00
Condiment Set, Rainbow Candy, Original Closure 50.00
Condiment Set, Vanstyle, Clear Glass, Original Closure 44.00
Dagger, Glass, Original Closure 99.00
Dirigible, Los Angeles, Paint, Original Closure 165.00
Dirigible, Los Angeles, Victory Glass, Early 1900s, 6 In. 170.00
Display Case, Paint, Original Paper Sticker, Original Closure 308.00
Dog, Amber, Oblong Base, No Closure 110.00
Don't Park Here, No Paint, Original Closure 110.00
Don't Park Here, No. 2, No Paint, Original Closure 187.00
Don't Park Here, No. 2, Paint Traces, Original Closure 250.00
Don't Park Here, Partial Paint, Original Closure 130.00
Drum, Candy Filled Bank, Paint, Original Closure 688.00
Duck, Large Bill, Paint Traces, Original Closure 95.00
Duck In Sailor Outfit, Composition, 10 In. 250.00
Duck On Nest, Clear Glass, Yellow, Red, Blue Paint, Metal Screw On Lid, 2 3/4 In. 420.00
Elephant, G.O.P., Partial Paint, Original Closure 330.00
Fanny Farmer Yacht, 11 In. 95.00
Fat Boy On Drum, Paint, Original Closure 303.00
Felix, Mitten Hands, Partial Paint, Original Closure 470.00
Felix, On Pedestal, No Paint, Original Closure 2310.00
Felix The Cat, Roly Poly, Papier-Mache, Rope Tail, Whiskers, 5 1/2 In. 1565.00
Felix The Cat, Roly-Poly, Papier-Mache, Rope Tail, Head Removes, 1922, 6 In. 1655.00
Fire Engine, 1914 Stough, Original Wheels, Original Closure 50.00
Fire Engine, Fire Dept. No. 99, Paint Traces, No Closure .... 28.00 to 35.00
Fire Engine, Ladder Truck, Paint, Contents, Original Wheels, Sticker, Closure 305.00
Fire Engine, Little Boiler No. 2, Original Closure 60.00
Flossie Fisher's Bed, Paint, Original Closure 1430.00
Flossie Fisher's Chair, Cat & Rabbit On Seat, Paint, Original Closure .... 495.00 to 688.00
Flossie Fisher's Dresser, Paint, Original Closure 1980.00
Flossie Fisher's Sideboard, Paint, Original Closure 660.00
Foxy Doctor Play Set, 5 Bottles, Contents, Original Closure 300.00
Frog, Leaping, Spring Action, Lithograph, Green, Cream, Black, Georg Fischer 345.00
Gas Pump, Gas 23 Cents Today, Paint Traces, Original Closure 209.00
George Washington On Horseback, Centennial 3200.00
Goblin Head, Partial Paint, Original Closure 385.00
Gun, Amber, Sunken Panel, No Closure 28.00
Gun, Cambridge Automatic, Small Opening, Original Closure 110.00
Gun, Kolt, Type 1, Paint, Original Closure 45.00
Happy Hooligan, Composition Eyes, Eyes Jiggle, Germany, 1915, 9 3/4 In. 395.00
Happy Hooligan, Molded Composition, Eyes Jiggle, Germany, c.1915, 5 In. 395.00
Helicopter, 2 Blades, Contents, Sticker, Original Closure 110.00
Horn, Clarinet, Paper Label, Original Closure 39.00
Horn, Musical Clarinet, No. 515A, Contents, Original Closure 495.00
Horn, Trumpet, Clear Glass, No Closure 35.00
Horn, Trumpet, Milk Glass, Bear Decal, Germania Souvenir, Original Closure 90.00
Hot Doggie, Blue, Original Closure 965.00

Candy Container, Clock, Milk Glass, Tin Closure

Candy Container, Submarine, Glass, Tin Lithograph Flag, Periscope, Closure, 5 In.

Hot Doggie, Clear, No Paint, Original Closure 578.00
Hot Doggie, Partial Brown Paint, Original Closure 825.00
House, Paint Traces, Replacement Closure 50.00
Independence Hall, Bank, Sandwich Glass, Kirchner, 7 1/2 In. 275.00
Independence Hall, Original Closure 248.00
Irishman With Hat, Slotted Closure, Original Closure 4400.00
Iron, Electric, Original Cord, Paper Plug, Closure 50.00
Iron, Flat, Paint, Contents, Original Closure 880.00
Jack-O'-Lantern, Paint, Metal Rim . . . . . . 220.00 to 440.00
Jack-O'-Lantern, Popeyed, Paint, Bail, Original Closure 385.00
Jack-O'-Lantern, Popeyed, Paint, No Bail, Original Closure 525.00
Kiddie Kar, Paint Traces, Replacement Closure 60.00
Lamp, Chamberstick, Original Shade, Closure 3410.00
Lamp, Christmas Lamp, Partial Label, Replaced Shade, Original Closure 495.00
Lamp, Easter, Yellow Chick, Wire Frame, Replaced Shade, Original Closure 3960.00
Lamp, George Washington, Blue Painted Tin, Original Shade, Contents, Closure 770.00
Lamp, Hobnail, Contents, Basket Weave Shade, Original Closure 690.00
Lamp, Hurricane, Screw-On Plain Chimney, Replacement Closure 250.00
Lamp, Library, Contents, Original Closure 635.00
Lamp, Ribbed Base, Souvenir Of Springfield, Mass, Original Shade, Contents 95.00
Lamp, Ringed Candlestick Base, Red Cap, Contents, Original Shade, Closure 605.00
Lamp, Ringed Candlestick Base, White Cap, Contents, Original Shade 550.00
Lamp, Tin Shade, Contents, Paper Sticker, Original Closure 28.00
Lantern, Barn Type No. 1, Ruby Flashed, No Bail, Philadelphia, Original Closure 110.00
Lantern, Dec 20 1904, Bail 35.00
Lantern, Magnifying Lens, Chain, Original Closure 44.00
Lantern Shape, Ruby Stained, 6 In. 120.00
Lawn, Porch Swing, Green Tin Swing Seat, Red Stand, Contents 468.00
Lawn, Porch Swing, Red Tin Swing Seat, Red Stand, Contents 220.00
Lawn Swing, Original Tin, Purple Tinted Glass, Original Closure 715.00
Liberty Bell, Amber, Bail, Original Closure 28.00
Liberty Bell, Clear, Bail, Original Closure 28.00
Liberty Bell, Clear, Contents, Bail Hanger, Original Closure 55.00
Liberty Bell, Contents, Partial Label, Crown Straps, Original Closure . . . . . . 105.00 to 253.00
Liberty Bell, Original Shaker Top Closure 61.00
Locomotive, 999, Man In Window, Original Closure . . . . . . 22.00 to 39.00
Locomotive, Jent. Glass Co., No. 888, Original Wheels, Original Closure 77.00
Locomotive, Lithographed Closure No. 1, Original Closure 16.50
Locomotive, Lithographed Closure No. 2, Original Closure 16.50
Locomotive, Little No. 23, Original Closure 66.00
Locomotive, Small Plain Screw Cap, Original Friction Type Closure 61.00
Locomotive, Small, Plain, Screw Cap, Friction Cap Type, No Closure 50.00
Mailbox, Clear Glass, Green Paint, Original Closure 286.00

Mailbox, Milk Glass, Silver Paint, Original Closure 358.00
Mailbox, Silver Paint, Souvenir Dubui, IA, Original Closure 193.00
Man On Motorcycle, Side Car, No Paint, Original Closure 220.00
Milk Bottle Carrier, Anco Candy, 4 Original Caps, Original Closure . . . . . 110.00 to 330.00
Milk Bottle Carrier, Dairy Sweets, 3 Original Caps, Original Closure 605.00
Milk Bottle Carrier, No Closure 27.00
Milk Cart, Post Cart, Lithographed, Yellow, Germany 230.00
Monkey Lamp, Original Closure 248.00
Mr. & Mrs. Bunny, Papier-Mache, Glass Eyes, Removable Heads, 9 In., Pair 578.00
Mug, Child's Tumbler, Original Closure . . . . . 248.00 to 385.00
Mule Pulling 2 Wheeled Barrel, Driver, Paint, Original Closure 66.00
My Southern Mammy Decorations, Contents, Original Closure 440.00
Naked Elfin Child, Original Closure 121.00
Nursing Bottle, Flat Oval, Contents, Original Closure 35.00
Opera Glass, Plain Panels, Clear, Original Closure 66.00
Opera Glass, Plain Panels, Paint, Original Closure 55.00
Opera Glass, Swirl Ribs, Original Closure . . . . . 77.00 to 120.00
Opera Glass, Victor, Original Closure 176.00
Opera Glass, Victor, Original Closure, Box 605.00
Pencil, Baby Jumbo, Original Label, Original Closure 50.00
PEZ, 1-Eyed Monster, Austria, c.1968 . . . . . 50.00
PEZ, Asterix, Blue Stem 1500.00
PEZ, Baloo, Red Head, No Feet 650.00
PEZ, Bullwinkle, Brown Stem, No Feet, Yellow Hinge, Austria. 255.00
PEZ, Bullwinkle, Yellow Antlers, 1960s 246.00
PEZ, Bullwinkle, Yellow Stem, 2 Orange Candy Pack, Sealed, 1960s 695.00
PEZ, Captain Hook, No Feet, 1960s 25.00
PEZ, Cockatoo, Red, Yellow Beak, 3.9 Austrian Stem, Thin Feet 711.00
PEZ, Pluto, Round Head, Movable Ears, No Feet, Hong Kong, 1960s 10.00
PEZ, Pony Go Round, Brown Head, Black Bridle, Red Stem . . . . . 77.00 to 84.00
PEZ, Pony, Orange Head, White Hair, Blue Stem, No Feet, 1970s 77.00
PEZ, Ringmaster, No Feet, Austria, 1970s 385.00
PEZ, Stewardess, Blue Stem, Pink Inner Sleeve, No Feet, Austria 82.00
PEZ, Thor, Black Stem, No Feet, Patent 3.9, Austria . . . . . 379.00 to 400.00
PEZ, Yosemite Sam, Blue Stem, Painted Steers & Horseshoes On Stem, Continental 2.00
Phonograph, Glass Record Type, Paint Traces, Original Closure 143.00
Planetorium, Original Closure 825.00
Policeman On Pumpkin, Paint, Original Closure 2310.00
Powder Horn, Bubble End No. 2, Original Closure 27.00
Powder Horn, Contents, Original Closure 33.00
Powder Horn, Hanger, Original Closure 27.00
Produce Cart, Ice Cream, Steam Dairy, Decorated, Lithograph, Germany 229.00
Pumpkin Head Jr. Policeman, Partial Paint, Replacement Closure 248.00
Pumpkin Head Policeman, No Paint, Original Closure 385.00
Pumpkin Head Witch, No Paint, Original Closure 275.00
Purse, Ruby Flashed Panel, Original Closure 413.00
Purse, Souvenir, Patton, Pa., Original Closure 660.00
Puss In Boots, Milk Glass, 1915-30, 3 In. 45.00
Rabbit, Aluminum Ears, Original Closure 1650.00
Rabbit, Basket On Arm, Paint Traces, Original Closure 77.00
Rabbit, Basket On Dome, Paint, Original Closure . . . . . 341.00 to 715.00
Rabbit, Crouching, Brown Paint, Original Closure 605.00
Rabbit, Eating Carrot, No Closure 17.00
Rabbit, Eating Carrot, T.H. Stough, 1947, 5 In. 60.00
Rabbit, Emerging From Tree Trunk, West Bros., Replaced Shade, Original Closure 2860.00
Rabbit, Feet Together, Round Nose No. 2, Paint Traces, Original Closure 523.00
Rabbit, Feet Together, Round Nose, No Paint, Contents, Original Closure 88.00
Rabbit, Forepaws Next To Body, Paint, Original Closure 44.00
Rabbit, In Egg Shell, No Paint, Original Closure 39.00
Rabbit, In Egg Shell, Victory Glass, Early 1900s, 5 1/4 In. 145.00
Rabbit, Laid Back Ears, Paint Traces, No Closure 44.00

Rabbit, Laid Back Ears, Partial Paint, Blue Head, Replacement Closure 209.00
Rabbit, Legs Apart, Clear Glass, Paint Traces, Original Closure ....105.00 to 248.00
Rabbit, Mother & Daughter, Original Closure 635.00
Rabbit, Pushing Chick In Shell Cart, Paint, Original Closure 688.00
Rabbit, Running On Log, Paint, Original Closure 358.00
Rabbit, Turquoise Blue, Paint, ABM Lip, Metal Closure, c.1930, 5 1/2 In. 125.00
Rabbit, Wearing Hat, Paint Traces, Original Closure 1017.00
Rabbit, Wheelbarrow, Paint, Original Closure 440.00
Racer, 12, Paint, Contents, Original Closure 550.00
Racer, 6, No. 2 On Grill, Repainted Silver, Replacement Closure 55.00
Racer, 6, No. 4 On Grill, Original Closure 60.00
Radio, Tune In, Paint Traces On Horn & Dials, Original Closure 70.00
Radio, Tune In, Repainted Horn, Original Closure 77.00
Rocking Horse, Clown Rider, Clear, Paint Traces, Replacement Closure 50.00
Rocking Horse, Original Closure 110.00
Rocking Settee, Paint, Original Closure 690.00
Rolling Pin, Original Parts, Original Closure 198.00
Rooster, Crowing, Paint, Original Closure 95.00
Safe, Clear, Original Closure ....110.00 to 165.00
Safety First, Green Tint, No Closure 145.00
Safety First, Partial Paint, Original Closure 165.00
Santa Claus, Banded Coat, Partial Paint, Original Closure ....72.00 to 85.00
Santa Claus, Carrying Stack Of Sticks, Papier-Mache, Germany, 6 In. 115.00
Santa Claus, Germany, Repaired Aluminum Cap, Original Closure 358.00
Santa Claus, Leaving Chimney, Paint Traces, Original Closure ....55.00 to 60.00
Santa Claus, Paneled Coat, Original Closure ....72.00 to 77.00
Santa Claus, Papier-Mache, Felt, 2 Piece, Germany, 11 In. 485.00
Santa Claus, Plastic Head, Partial Paint, Contents, Original Closure 45.00
Santa Claus, Sleigh, Reindeer, Papier-Mache 1380.00
Santa Claus, Square Chimney, Partial Paint, Replacement Closure 80.00
Santa Claus, Standing By Chimney, Papier-Mache, Germany, 10 In. 35.00
Skookum, By Tree Stump, Repainted, Replacement Closure 94.00
Soda Fountain, Yellow, Cups, Box 66.00
Soldier, By Tent, Painted Soldier, Partial Tent Paint, Original Closure 2750.00
Soldier, With Sword, Paint Traces, Original Closure 770.00
Soldier, With Sword, Partial Red Paint, No Closure 440.00
Space Doctor Play Set, 4 Bottles, Contents, Original Closure ....275.00 to 300.00
Spark Plug, Horse, Paint, Replacement Closure 155.00
Statue Of Liberty, Metal Casting Hole, Original Closure 3300.00
Stop & Go, Yellow Flags, All Original Parts, Original Closure 660.00
Submarine, Glass, Tin Lithograph Flag, Periscope, Closure, 5 In. .... ***ILLUS*** 1904.00
Suitcase, Bail, Original Closure ....22.00 to 27.00
Suitcase, Milk Glass, Bear Decal, Souvenir, Fairbanks, Bail, Original Closure 99.00
Swan Boat, Rabbit & Chick, Partial Paint, Original Closure 825.00
Swan Boat, Rabbit & Chick, Victory Glass, Early 1900s, 4 1/4 In. 920.00
Sweetone, Yellow, Complete Label ....110.00 to 121.00
Tank, Man In Turret, Green Paint, Contents, Original Closure 33.00
Tank, U.S. Army, No Closure 16.00
Telephone, Bell & Crank, Replaced Receiver, Original Bell, Crank, Closure 303.00
Telephone, Pewter Top No. 2, Aqua Tint, Replaced Receiver, 5 1/2 x 2 1/2 In. 88.00
Telephone, Pewter Top, Marked R-7, Receiver, Original Closure 33.00
Telephone, Redlick's Cork Top, Original Bell, Receiver, Closure 578.00
Telephone, Redlick's Screw Top, Cork Top, Bell, Original Closure 308.00
Telephone, Redlick's Small Screw Top, Receiver, Holder, Original Closure 94.00
Telephone, West Bro's 1907, Wood Receiver, Line's Busy Sticker, Original Closure 39.00
Telephone, Wood Transmitter No. 3, Contents, Sticker, Receiver, Original Closure 110.00
Toonerville Depot Line, Partial Paint, Original Closure 688.00
Train, Molded Glass, Tin Lithograph Cap, 4 In. 195.00
Truck, Ice, Jitney Bus Body, Replaced Seats, Original Tin Canopy 176.00
Trunk, Round Top, Clear, Original Closure 72.00
Trunk, Round Top, Milk Glass, Partial Paint, Original Closure 85.00

Trunk, Round Top, Milk Glass, Souvenir, Almena, Kan., Original Closure 120.00
Trunk, Round Top, Milk Glass, Souvenir, Cranville, Original Closure 105.00
Turkey, Gobbler, No Paint, Replacement Closure 66.00
Turkey, Papier-Mache, 6 1/2 In. 40.00
Uncle Sam, By Barrel, Partial Paint, Original Closure 198.00
Uncle Sam, By Barrel, Tin Screw Cap, 1918, 4 In. 310.00
Village, 5 & 10 Cent Store, Original Insert, Original Clip 1100.00
Village, Bungalow, Original Insert, Clip 440.00
Village, Church, Steeple, Original Insert, No Clip 145.00
Village, Log Cabin, Original Insert, Original Clip 305.00
Village, Railroad Station, Original Insert, No Clip 198.00
Village, Tudor House, No Insert, Green Roof 105.00
Village, Tudor House, Original Insert, Clip, Red Roof 495.00
Wagon, U.S. Express, Original Tin, Parts, Red Repainted, Original Closure 715.00
Washing Machine, Little Miss, Red, Marx 77.00
Washing Machine, Pretty Maid, White, Decal, Marx 88.00
Watch, Circle Back, Paper Face, Fancy Embossed Back, No Closure 209.00
Watch, Original Strap, Fob, Box, Closure 495.00
Well, Ye Olde Oaken Bucket, Paint, Original Bail, Closure 60.00
Wheelbarrow, Original Wheel, Replacement Closure 27.00
Wheeled, Plastic, Clown, Pumpkin Men, 1940s 280.00
Whip, Contents, Original Closure 3520.00
Wild Willie Western, Contents 523.00
Windmill, Candy Guaranteed, Solid Base, Original Blades, Original Closure 825.00
Windmill, Dutch Windmill, Original Blades, No Closure 27.00
World Globe On Stand, Our Country, Original Closure 209.00

CANES and walking sticks were used by every well-dressed man in the nineteenth century, but by World War I the style had changed. Today canes are used by few but the infirm. Collectors prize old canes made with special features, like hidden swords, whiskey flasks, or risqué pictures seen through peepholes. Examples with solid gold heads or made from exotic materials are among the higher-priced canes. See also Scrimshaw.

4-Leaf Clovers, Jeweled Rock Crystal Knob, Engraved, 18K Collar, Ebony Shaft, 1800s, 37 In. 9800.00
Animal Motif, Hand Carved, Painted Canes, Mexico, c.1950, 35 x 36 In., Pair 146.00
Art Glass, Smoke Color, Twisted Internal Design, 1880s, 39 In. 185.00
Ball Knob, 24K Gold Wire Inlay, Flowers, Ebony Shaft, Bronze Ferrule, Ladies, 36 In. 375.00
Boar's Tusk, Silver Ferrule, Wood Shaft, Rubber Tip, 36 1/2 In. 316.00
Fruitwood Knob, Bulldog Head, Malacca Shaft, Metal Ferrule, Automated, Vienna, 35 In. 1840.00
Gamers, Ivory, Built-In Container, 5 Small Dice, Ebony Shaft, England, 19th Century, 34 In. 690.00
Gold Knob & Eyelets, Flowers, Engraved, Tortoiseshell Shaft, Gilt Ferrule, M De L, 1800s, 36 In. 4140.00
Ivory, 14K Gold Band, Rubber Tip, Hook Handle, Slightly Curved Shaft, 38 3/4 In. 1035.00
Ivory, Cockatiel Head, Glass Eyes, 6-Sided Bamboo Shaft, Bronze Ferrule, Vienna, 1800s, 36 In. 460.00
Ivory, Coiled Snake On Snakewood Shaft, 19th Century, England, 37 In. 1265.00
Ivory, Frog Playing Drum, Swamp Oak Shaft, Metal Ferrule, 19th Century, 34 1/2 In. 2185.00
Ivory, L Handle, Gold, Quartz, Enamel, Scrolls, Chains, Case, c.1860, 33 3/4 In. 8960.00
Ivory, Monkey Chasing Rat, Carved, Japanese Characters, Bamboo Form Shaft, 35 In. 355.00
Ivory, Monkeys, Intertwined Chain, Cherry Shaft, Japan, c.1900, 37 1/4 In. 1120.00
Ivory, Squirrel Nibbling Acorn, Branch, Malacca Shaft, Brass Ferrule, 1800s, 38 1/2 In. 3220.00
Ivory, Thousand Faces, Gold Gilt Collar, Tropical Wood Shaft, c.1890, 34 2/3 In. 2128.00
Ivory, Whale, American Eagle, Whalebone Snake Shaft, c.1840, 36 1/3 In. 11200.00
Ivory, Woman, Seminude, Seated, Harp, Scroll, Ivory Ferrule, Late 1800s, 34 In. 1765.00
Jade, Crocodile Eating Cane, Malacca, Metal Shaft, Ferrule, Gilt Collar, Engraved, 38 In. 7480.00
Malachite, Ball Knob, Ebony Shaft, Silver Collar, Bronze Ferrule, 1900s, 37 1/2 In. 520.00
Novelty, Brass, Telescope, 3-Draw, Ball Top, Wood Shaft, Brass Tip, 34 In. 520.00
Novelty, Mahogany, Violin, Tau Handle, Horsehair Bow, c.1860, 33 7/8 In. 5600.00
Novelty, Pepperbox Pistol, Crook Handle, Tropical Wood Shaft, Belgium, c.1895, 33 3/4 In. 4920.00
Novelty, Silver, Watch, Ball Handle, Scrolls, Flowers, Malacca Shaft, Holuska, c.1890, 36 In. 2800.00

Porcelain, Dog, Tau Handle, Gold Gilt Collar, Ebony Shaft, c.1880, 35 1/4 In. 5880.00
Porcelain, Saint Cloud, Flowers, Silver Collar, Malacca Shaft, France, 1700s, 34 2/3 In. 4480.00
Presentation, Gold Filled Knob Handle, Millard To Cyrus Fillmore, c.1870, 36 1/4 In. 5040.00
Silver, Automobile, Ebony Shaft, Brass Tip, France, c.1912, 35 3/4 In. 1115.00
Stone Knob, Pink, Veined, Rosewood Shaft, Mascot, 19th Century, 36 In. 345.00
Sword, Antler Handle, Boxwood Sheath, 1850-70 .... 336.00
Sword, Knobby Shaft, Bentwood Handle, Brass Ferrule, 1 Blade, Spain, c.1870, 27 In. 525.00
Walking Stick, Carved Tip, Girl Holding Muff, Ivory Head, Bamboo Shaft, 34 In. 200.00
Walking Stick, Carved, Painted, Animals, Figures, Patriotic Symbols, Togus, Me., 32 3/4 In. 940.00
Walking Stick, Gold Handle, Gold Plated Top, Ebonized Shaft, c.1859, 36 In. 264.00
Walking Stick, Rabbit, Cedar, Glass Eyes, Brass Tip, 1920s, 35 In. 280.00
Walking Stick, Snakes, Crisscross Designs, Hand Carved, c.1885, 35 In. 660.00
Walking Stick, Whalebone, Baleen, Carved, Massachusetts, 33 1/2 In. 1898.00
Whale Ivory, Mahogany Shaft, Octagonal, Ebony Handle, 19th Century, 30 In. 400.00
Whalebone, Handle Only, Women Rope Design, Sailor Carved, 1800s, 4 3/4 x 3/4 In. 500.00
Wood, Ball Top, Spiraling Snake, Bird, People, Tools, Folk Art, 30 In. 240.00
Wood, Locomotive, Inscriptions, 8-Sided, c.1850, 34 In. 1035.00
Wood, Polar Bear, L Handle, Malacca Shaft, Tiffany & Co., c.1895, 33 1/2 In. 11760.00
Wood, Snake, Faux Knots, Green Stripes, Brown, Black, Paint, 34 1/2 In. 85.00

CANTON CHINA is a blue-and-white ware made near the city of Canton, in China, from about 1785 to 1895. It is hand decorated with Chinese scenes. Canton is part of the group of porcelains known today as Chinese Export Porcelain.

Basket, Undertray, Riverscape, Triple Border, 10 1/4 In. 850.00
Bidet, Mahogany Wooden Stand, Waisted Oval Shape, Brass Spigot, c.1820, 20 x 14 In. 1058.00
Bowl, Cover, Berry Finial, Burst Glaze, 8 x 9 In. 316.00
Bowl, Dragon Center, Intricate Design, Enamel, Signed, 19th Century, 9 x 2 1/2 In. 495.00
Bowl, Riverscape, 19th Century, 4 1/2 x 9 1/2 In. 649.00
Bowl, Riverscape, 19th Century, 10 In. 649.00
Bowl, Riverscape, Scalloped, 19th Century, 8 1/4 In. 415.00
Bowl, Scalloped, 19th Century, 10 1/4 In. 770.00
Bowl, Shallow, Round, 19th Century, 2 x 11 In. 118.00
Bowl, Square, Cut Corner, 1800s, 4 1/2 x 10 1/2 In. 865.00
Bowl, Vegetable, Cover, 18th Century, 10 1/2 In. 295.00
Bowl, Vegetable, Cover, Pinecone Knop, Rectangular, 4 3/4 x 7 x 8 3/8 In. 235.00
Bowl, Vegetable, Cover, Riverscape, 19th Century, 9 x 7 1/4 In. 250.00
Candlestick, Lotus Flower, Leaf, Electrified, 1800s, 14 1/4 In. 499.00
Candlestick, Pair, 12 In. 295.00
Charger, Bamboo Decoration, Footed, Shallow, 13 1/2 In. 345.00
Charger, Riverscape, 19th Century, 12 1/4 In. 325.00
Chestnut Basket, 18th Century, 3 1/2 x 9 3/8 In. 380.00
Cider Jug, Cover, Riverscape, 19th Century, 7 In. 1300.00
Cider Jug, Twisted Handle, Foo Dog Finial, 7 In. 2990.00
Creamer, Helmet Form 275.00
Dish, Buildings, Water, Boats, Deep, Oval, 11 3/4 In. 358.00
Dish, Cover, Flowers, Nut Finial, 1800s, 8 1/2 x 10 1/2 In. 58.00
Dish, Cover, Lozenge, 11 x 10 In., Pair 385.00
Dish, Leaf Form, 7 1/8 In. 200.00
Dish, Shrimp, Flat Handle, 10 1/2 x 10 In. .... *ILLUS* 489.00
Dish, Shrimp, Orange Peel Glaze, Shallow Rim, 9 1/2 x 10 1/4 In. 105.00
Fruit Basket, Undertray, Reticulated, Early 1800s, 4 7/8 x 11 In. 2000.00
Garden Seat, 8-Sided, Bulging Sides, Flowers, Scrolled Leaves, 1800s, 18 3/4 In. 1645.00
Ginger Jar, Landscape, 1800s, 6 3/4 In., Pair 449.00
Ginger Jar, Men Fishing, House, Water, Flat Cover, 1800s, 8 x 8 In. 460.00
Jar, Cover, 1800s, 6 3/4 In., Pair 920.00
Jar, Square, Raised Rim, Mounted As Lamp, Carved Wooden Base, Cap, 31 1/2 In. 1530.00
Mug, Strap Handle, Intertwined Handles, Cylindrical, 1800s, 4 1/2 x 4 In. 315.00
Mug, Syllabub, Entwined Lapped Handles, Married Cover, Child's 235.00
Pie Dish, Round, 9 1/4 In. 345.00

Rubber cement solvent has many uses. Put a few drops on a paper towel and rub off ink smudges, adhesive tape glue, or label glue from glass or porcelain.

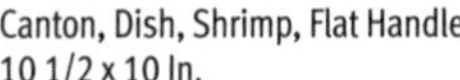

Canton, Dish, Shrimp, Flat Handle, 10 1/2 x 10 In.

Pie Plate, 1800s, 10 1/2 In. 375.00
Pitcher, Cider, Cover, Foo Dog Finial, 1800s, 8 In. 865.00
Plate, Hot Water, Octagonal, 19th Century, 1 5/8 x 10 3/8 In. 150.00
Plate, Soup, Riverscape, 19th Century, 8 3/4 In., 8 Piece 385.00
Platter, 18th Century, 10 1/8 x 13 In. 585.00
Platter, Buildings, Water, Bridge, Trees, c.1850, 18 1/2 x 14 3/4 In. 978.00
Platter, c.1900, 16 1/4 x 20 In. 936.00
Platter, Chamfered, Rectangular, 19th Century, 12 1/2 x 15 1/2 In. 176.00
Platter, Cover, Riverscape, 1800s, 11 1/2 In., Pair 560.00
Platter, Cut Corner, 15 3/4 x 13 In. 690.00
Platter, Cut Corner, 1800s, 12 x 14 1/2 In. 290.00
Platter, Cut Corner, Buildings, Mountains, Water, Boat, 1800s, 10 1/2 x 13 In. 290.00
Platter, Cut Corner, c.1850, 8 1/4 x 11 1/4 In. 345.00
Platter, Deep, 17 x 14 In. 1150.00
Platter, Nesting, Riverscape, 19th Century, 12 1/2 & 10 3/4 In., 2 Piece 325.00
Platter, Orange Peel Glaze, 14 1/4 x 17 1/4 In. 518.00
Platter, Riverscape, 19th Century, 12 1/4 In. 295.00
Platter, Riverscape, 19th Century, 15 1/2 In. 355.00
Platter, Riverscape, 19th Century, 19 In. 445.00
Platter, Riverscape, 8-Sided, 1800s, 15 1/2 In. 355.00
Platter, Well & Tree, Riverscape, 17 In. 708.00
Sauceboat, Riverscape, 19th Century, 3 1/2 x 8 In., 3 Piece 708.00
Serving Bowl, Square, Cut Corner, Early 19th Century, 4 1/2 x 9 1/2 x 9 1/2 In. 825.00
Serving Dish, 1800s, 10 1/4 x 9 1/4 In. 315.00
Serving Dish, Cover, Cut Corner, Nut Finial, 8 x 9 1/4 In. 315.00
Sugar & Creamer, 2 Loop Handles, Dome Cover, Nut Finial, 4 In. 86.00
Teapot, Cover, Strap Handle, 5 x 7 In. 290.00
Teapot, Cover, Strap Handle, 7 x 9 1/4 In. 315.00
Tray, Ice Cream, 2 x 7 1/4 x 14 In. 325.00
Tureen, Cover, Boar's Head Handles, Nut Finial, Footed, 8 1/2 x 14 In. 2530.00
Tureen, Cover, Chinese House, Water, Boar's Head Handles, 8 In. 605.00
Tureen, Cover, Early 19th Century, 9 x 10 1/2 In. 205.00
Tureen, Cover, Rectangular, Cut Corner, Boar's Head Handles, 1800s, 9 x 13 1/2 In., Pair 1265.00
Tureen, Cover, Rectangular, Stem Knop, Boar's Head Handles, Early 1800s, 8 1/2 x 8 1/2 In. 646.00
Tureen, Cover, Riverscape, Boar's Head Handles, 12 1/2 In. 770.00
Tureen, Sauce, Underliner, Boar's Head Handles, Footed Base, Cut Corner, 5 x 7 In. 690.00
Tureen, Soup, Cover, Boar's Head Handles, c.1850, 8 3/4 x 13 3/4 In. 1438.00
Tureen, Soup, Cover, Undertray, Boar's Head Handles, 1800s 1550.00
Urn, Early 20th Century, 23 x 9 1/4 In., Pair 700.00
Vase, Bottle Shape, Leaves, Electrified, 1800s, 14 In. 823.00
Vase, Cover, Figures, Courtyard, Foo Dog Finial, 14 3/4 In., Pair 558.00
Vase, Lobed, Tapering, Dragon, Flowers, Turquoise Ground, c.1890, 9 1/2 x 7 In. 645.00
Vase, Spill, Dragons, Leaves, 1800s, 8 1/8 In., Pair 147.00
Vase, Tapered, Flat Panel Sides, Birds, Flowers, Dot Field, Elephant Handles, 17 In., Pair 2115.00

CAPO-DI-MONTE porcelain was first made in Naples, Italy, from 1743 to 1759. The factory moved near Madrid, Spain, reopened in 1771, and worked to 1834. Since that time, the Doccia factory of Italy acquired the molds and is using the crown and N mark. Societe Richard Ceramica is a modern-day firm often referred to as Ginori or Capo-di-Monte. This company uses the crown and N mark.

Box, Putti, Chariot, God, Goddess, Blue Crown, Oval, c.1875, 4 1/2 x 9 1/2 x 6 In. 690.00
Box, Vanity, Putti, Birds, Scrolls, Brass Mounted, Elliptical, 4 x 7 x 5 In. 528.00
Figurine, Man & Woman, White, 9 x 3 1/2 In., Pair 110.00
Mug, Cover, Embossed, Classical Scenes, Early 20th Century, 8 In. 147.00
Mug, Men & Women Amidst Grapes & Leaves, Blown Out, 4 3/4 In. 115.00
Plaque, Adam & Eve, Angel, Ebony, Hardstone, 8-Sided Frame, Late 1800s, 20 x 17 In. 644.00
Pot De Creme Set, Richard Ginori, Italy, 12 Piece 175.00
Tray, Figures, Trees, Shaped Edge, c.1800, 12 x 15 In. 585.00
Tureen, Sauce, Putti Finials, Painted, Gilt, Garlands, 2 Handles, 9 In., Pair 922.00
Urn, Mask Handles, Putti On Dolphin, Mermaids, Square Base, Late 1800s, 12 3/4 In. 115.00
Vase, Classical Scenes, Relief, Reticulated, 11 1/2 In., Pair 82.00
Vase, Garniture, Multicolored, 2 Handles, Cover, Classical Figures, 22 x 11 In. 1410.00

CAPTAIN MARVEL was introduced in February 1940 in Whiz comic books. An orphan named Billy Batson met the wizard, Shazam, and whenever he said the magic word he was transformed into a superhero. A movie serial was released in 1940. The comic was discontinued in 1954. A second Captain Marvel appeared in 1966, a third in 1967. Only the original was transformed by shouting *Shazam*.

Bank, Dime Register, Opens At $5.00, Metal, Square, c.1948, 2 5/8 In. 138.00
Bust, Bowen, Box, 1970s, 5 1/2 In. .... 16.00 to 35.00
Comic Book Art, Shazam, No. 4, Page 9, C.C. Beck, 15 x 10 In. 365.00
Figure, Alex Ross Kingdom Come, Unopened, Box, 7 In. 10.50
Figure, Kingdom Come, DC Direct Line, 6 1/4 In. .... 6.00 to 8.00
Figure, Paper, Captain Marvel Jr., Ski Jump, Reed & Assoc., Envelope, 1944, 10 x 7 In. 35.00
Figure, Paper, Uncut, Fawcett Publications, Envelope, 1944 .... 29.00
Figure Set, Captain Marvel, Mary, Jr., Punch-Out, Unused, Fawcett, 1945 .... 35.00
Figurine, Music Box, Captain Marvel Shazam, Red Outfit, Yellow Cape, 1970s, 5 1/2 In. ..... 16.00 to 45.00
Film, Captain Marvel & Death Ship, Republic Pictures, Box, Super 8, 8 mm 13.00
Key Chain, Captain Marvel Club, Round, 1946 .... 25.00
Kit, Captain Marvel Jr. Ski Jump, Paper, Punch Out, Reed & Associates, 1944, 8 x 10 In. 7.00
Magic Flute, Cardboard, Plastic, Metal, Lee Tex, On Card, 1946, 4 3/4 In. 81.00
Pennant, Felt, Blue, Silk Screen, c.1946, 8 x 14 1/2 In. 140.00
Picture Puzzle, One Against Many, 10 Cents, Reed & Assoc., Envelope, 1944, 10 x 7 In. 35.00
Punch-Out, Die Cut, Unused, Samuel Lowe Co., 1942, 11 3/4 x 8 1/2 In. 395.00
Punch-Out Set, Paper, Mary Marvel, Marvel Jr., Captain Marvel, 1945 .... 12.50
Ring, Rocket Raider Compass, Enameled Sides, 1946 .... 400.00
Toy, Car, Racing, No. 2, Windup, Automatic Toy Co., N.Y., 1947, 4 In. 72.00
Toy, Car, Racing, No. 3, Windup, Automatic Toy Co., N.Y., 1947, 4 In. 54.00
Tumbler, Shazam, Pepsi Super Series, 1976, 6 1/2 In. 4.00
Tumbler, Shazam, Pepsi Super Series, 1978, 6 1/2 In. 2.00

CAPTAIN MIDNIGHT began as a network radio show in September 1940. The first comic book appeared in July 1941. Captain Midnight was really the aviator Captain Albright, who was to defeat the Nazis. A movie serial was made in 1942 and a comic strip was published for a short time. The comic book Captain Midnight ended his career in 1948. Radio premiums are the prized collector memorabilia today.

Badge, Secret Squadron Decoder, Photograph 58.00
Book, Big Little Book, Flip Book, Captain Midnight, 1942, 5 In., 454 Pages 55.00
Book, Captain Midnight & Secret Squadron, Better Little Book, 1941 .... 10.00 to 15.00
Book, Captain Midnight & Sheik Jomak Khan, Better Little Book .... 11.00 to 18.00
Code Key, Brass, Die Cut, 1949, 3/4 In. 186.00
Decoder, SS, Brass Case, Plastic Wheel, 1949, 2 1/4 In. 80.00

Decoder, SS, Whistle, Plastic, 1947, 1 3/4 In. 73.00
Manual, Secret Squadron New Official Code & Manual, 1948, 16 Pages 20.50
Medal, Spinner, Membership, Flight Patrol, Brass, Skelly Oil Logo, 1940, 1 1/2 In. .... 5.00 to 23.00
Membership Kit, Code Book, Membership Card, Letter, Mailer, 1955-56 .... 129.00
Mug, Ovaltine, Plastic, Red, Insert, Decal, 1953, 3 x 3 In. .... 12.50 to 27.00
Mug, Shake-Up, Orange, Blue Dome Top, Wander Co., Chicago, 5 x 2 In. 45.00
Mystery Dial Code-O-Graph, Master Code, Super Code, 1941, 2 1/4 x 1 1/2 In. .... 20.00 to 78.00
Photograph, Skelly Oil, 7 1/2 x 5 3/4 In. 12.00
Photomatic Decoder Badge, Secret Squadron, Picture, 2 1/8 x 1 5/8 In. 76.00
Playsuit, U.S. Flight Commander, Aviator Ace Badge, Collegeville 175.00

CARAMEL SLAG, see Imperial Glass category.

CARDS listed here include advertising cards (often called trade cards), greeting cards, baseball cards, playing cards, and others. Color photographs were rare in the nineteenth century, so companies gave away colorful cards with pictures of children, flowers, products, or related scenes that promoted the company name. These were often collected and stored in albums. Baseball cards also date from the nineteenth century, when they were used by tobacco companies as giveaways. Gum cards were started in 1933, but it was not until after World War II that the bubble gum cards favored today were produced. Today over 1,000 cards are issued each year by the gum companies. Related items may be found in the Postcard and Movie categories.

Advertising, A. S. T. Black Tipped Shoes, New Planet 15.00
Advertising, Atlantic & Pacific Tea Co., James Garfield, Palette Shape, 1880s, 10 1/2 In. 419.00
Advertising, Atmore's Mince Meat Plum Pudding, Boy, Girl With Pudding 9.00
Advertising, Babbitt's Soap, Spirit Of 1776, 19 x 26 In. 12.00
Advertising, Baseball Comic, Curver 22.00
Advertising, Baseball Comic, Get Back 26.00
Advertising, Baseball Comic, Great Expectations 22.00
Advertising, Baseball Comic, Home Run 34.00
Advertising, Baseball Comic, Victor & Vanquished 26.00
Advertising, Beymer Bauman & Co., White Lead Paint, Folding, Testimonials 20.00
Advertising, Broadhead Dress Goods, Dressed Up Children, Folding 13.00
Advertising, Brooks Spool Cotton, Thread In Tug Of War, Goat 11.00
Advertising, Burdock Blood Bitters, 3 People On Toboggan 22.00
Advertising, Burdock Blood Bitters, Momma Dog Washing Pups 15.00
Advertising, Catlin's Old Style Smoking Tobacco, Mother Spanking Son 13.00
Advertising, Cigarette, Irish Place Names, Leather Box, 25 Piece 52.00
Advertising, Cole's Great New York & New Orleans Circus, Sepia, 7 x 3 7/8 In. 50.00
Advertising, Dobbins' Electric Soap, Whining Schoolboy 9.00
Advertising, Domestic Sewing Machine, Black Family In Wagon With Machine 10.00
Advertising, Domestic Sewing Machine, Globe Metamorphic 17.00
Advertising, Dr. Haas' Alterative, Horse About To Start, 1883 .... 83.00
Advertising, Dr. Haas' Alterative, Runaway Horse, 1883 .... 77.00
Advertising, Dr. Hartshorn's Cough Balsam, Ice Hockey Players 100.00
Advertising, Dr. Morse's Indian Root Pills, Indian, Bear, 1883 Calendar 15.00
Advertising, Durham Smoking Tobacco, Bismarck, Ben Butler, Mechanical 35.00
Advertising, Enterprise Lawn Sprinklers, Soaked Punster 28.00
Advertising, Erie Stove Co., Woman Eating Apple, Tambourine, Erie, Pa., 6 1/2 x 4 1/2 In. 14.00
Advertising, Garland Stoves, Parlor Stove Metamorphic, 4 Panels 20.00
Advertising, Gold Medal Sarsaparilla, Harrison & Cleveland, 1892, 3 5/8 x 7 In. 38.00
Advertising, Granite Iron Ware, Girl, Pitcher On Winter Ice, 1884 .... 9.00
Advertising, Granite Iron Ware, Milkmaid, Pail, Where Are You Going My Pretty Maid 13.00
Advertising, Great American Tea Company, Early 1900s, 2 1/4 x 4 1/4 In. 15.00
Advertising, H. Harwood & Sons, Base Balls & Bats, National Game, 1871, 4 1/2 x 3 1/4 In. 3770.00
Advertising, Haas Hog & Poultry Remedy, Our Family Remedy, I Will Insure Your Hogs, 1882 .... 50.00
Advertising, Herrod's Shoes, Black Boy Watching Chicks In Shoe, 1883 .... 12.00
Advertising, Higgins' German Laundry Soap, 7 Card Series 41.00

Card, Greeting, Valentine, Cut Cobweb Center, Country Scene, Watercolor, Pull String, 4 In.

Card, Greeting, Valentine, Cutwork, Watercolor & Scherenschnitte, Verse, 12 In.

Card, Greeting, Valentine, Token Of Love, Lace, Embossed, Cobweb, 7 x 5 In.

Advertising, Hoyt & Co. Foods, Girl, 1893 Calendar, Lowell, Mass., 5 1/2 x 3 1/2 In. 15.00
Advertising, Inter Ocean Newspaper, Newsboys Peddling Papers 56.00
Advertising, J. P. Alley's Hambone 5 Cent Cigars, Black Aviator, Hanging, 7 In. 53.00
Advertising, Jackson's Best Chewing Tobacco, Donkey Gets Chew Of Tobacco, Animated 31.00
Advertising, Jolly Nigger Bank, Lithograph, For Sale By Pratt & Co. 413.00
Advertising, Jolly Nigger Toy Savings Bank, 5 In. 275.00
Advertising, Kendall's Spavin Cure, Cured Horse Finishing Time Trial 15.00
Advertising, Kicking Mule Bank, Blue Printing, White Ground, 5 1/2 In. 77.00
Advertising, Lamb Wire Fence, Escaped Lion & Lamb 13.00
Advertising, Lorillard's Splendid Plug Tobacco, Storm, Weather Flags 19.00
Advertising, Mathew's Flavoring Extracts, Lincoln & Tad, Albumen Photograph, 4 x 2 In. 345.00
Advertising, Merchant's Gargling Oil, Fallen Skating Couple, Mechanical, 1892 .... 39.00
Advertising, New American Stove 37.00
Advertising, Pace's Best Tobacco, Boy Trying To Retrieve Baseball 9.00
Advertising, Pfister's NYC Pool & Billiard Room, Man Breaks Overhead Lamp 24.00
Advertising, Plum Long Cut Tobacco, Child Smelling Flower, 8 x 4 1/2 In. 9.00
Advertising, President Suspenders, Bryan & McKinley Buying Suspenders, Corning, N.Y. 30.00
Advertising, Punch & Judy Toy Savings Bank, c.1890 .... 176.00
Advertising, Rapid Transit Soap, Elevated Railroad In City, Horse Drawn Traffic 276.00
Advertising, RCA Victor, Nipper The Dog 475.00
Advertising, Shole's Insect Exterminator, Fable Of The Ox 13.20
Advertising, Soapine, Mouse Trap, Hold-To-Light 62.00
Advertising, Soapine, Washing Black, White Whales 17.00
Advertising, Sulphur Bitters, Mrs. President Cleveland 20.00
Advertising, T.E. Wood's Art Assn. Oil & Pastel Portraits, 1882, 4 x 2 1/2 In. 15.00
Advertising, Tansill's Punch & Old Rip Cigars, 2 Piece 13.00
Advertising, Veggie People, White Plume Celery, 1887 .... 20.00
Advertising, Warner's Safe Cure & Safe Yeast & Safe Pills, c.1887, 5 x 3 1/2 In. 35.00
Advertising, Warner's Safe Yeast, 2 Children, Bedroom, Large Can Of Yeast, 5 1/2 x 4 In. 45.00
Advertising, Warner's Safe Yeast, Victorian Woman, Children, Maid, 5 x 3 3/4 In. 14.00
Advertising, Warner's Safe Yeast, Woman, Can, Building, 5 1/2 x 4 In. 45.00
Advertising, Warner's Safe Yeast, Woman, Holding Baby, 5 1/2 x 4 In. 45.00
Advertising, Washburn Crosby Coarse Bran, Cattle Eating From Bags 18.00
Advertising, Western & Southern Life Insurance Co., Black Girl With Flowers 18.00
Advertising, Wheeler Bicycles, People Riding Bicycles, 3 Piece 17.00
Advertising, Willimantic Spool Cotton, Bridge, Cables, Ships 9.00
Baseball, Bill Mazeroski, Topps, No. 323, 1963 .... 407.00
Baseball, Frank Robinson, Topps, No. 35, 1957 .... 725.00
Baseball, Johnny Bench, All-Star Rookie, Topps, No. 95, 1969 .... 493.00
Baseball, Nolan Ryan, Topps, No. 220, 1973 .... 335.00
Baseball, Phil Rizzuto, Bowman, No. 8, 1948 .... 598.00
Baseball, Ralph Kiner, Rookie, Leaf, No. 91, 1948 .... 725.00
Baseball, Roberto Clemente, Topps, No. 50, 1973 .... 228.00
Baseball, Stan Musial, Topps, No. 150, 1959 .... 304.00

Do not hide a key outside the house, not even in a key-holding stone. Burglars are smart.

Carlsbad, Ewer, Iridescent Glaze, Applied Gold Trailing Leaf Handle, Signed, 7 1/2 In.

Baseball, Topps Wax Pack, 5 Cents, 1st Series, Unopened, 1952 .... 4427.00
Baseball, Topps, 1966, 598 Cards 2766.00
Basketball, Bill Russell, Fleer, No. 62, 1961-62 .... 966.00
Basketball, K.C. Jones, Fleer, No. 22, 1961-62 .... 658.00
Basketball, Michael Jordan, Fleer, No. 57, 1986-87 .... 1558.00
Boxing, Sugar Ray Robinson, Leaf, No. 64, 1948 .... 725.00
Football, Jerry Rice, Rookie, Topps, 1986 .... 2637.00
Football, Jim Brown, Topps, No. 28, 1962 .... 725.00
Football, Jim Thorpe, Topps All-American, No. 37, 1955 .... 875.00
Football, Otto Graham, Bowman, No. 45, 1950 .... 658.00
Football, Roger Staubach, Rookie, Topps, No. 200, 1972 .... 250.00
Football, Terry Bradshaw, Rookie, Topps, No. 156, 1971 .... 449.00
Football, Topps Wax Pack, Unopened, 1965 .... 3136.00
Greeting, Valentine, Cobweb Center, Cherub, Swan, Watercolor, Lace, Fringe, c.1850, 7 x 5 In. 410.00
Greeting, Valentine, Cobweb Center, Flowers, Verse, Love Knot, Man Proposing, 10 x 8 In. 765.00
Greeting, Valentine, Cobweb Center, Woman In Heart, Flowers, Verse, 10 x 8 In. 500.00
Greeting, Valentine, Cut Cobweb Center, Country Scene, Watercolor, Pull String, 4 In. .... *ILLUS* 1880.00
Greeting, Valentine, Cutwork, Watercolor & Scherenschnitte, Verse, 12 In. .... *ILLUS* 5500.00
Greeting, Valentine, Octagonal, Hand Drawn, Catherine Kinig, Frame, 1839, 12 In. 1018.00
Greeting, Valentine, Puppy With String Tied To His Tail, 1950s, 4 x 8 In. 15.00
Greeting, Valentine, Puzzle Purse, Frame, c.1845, 25 In. 12000.00
Greeting, Valentine, Token Of Love, Lace, Embossed, Cobweb, 7 x 5 In. .... *ILLUS* 147.00
Hockey, Bobby Orr, O-Pee-Chee, No. 129, 1972-73 .... 800.00
Playing, Bicycle, Walnut Box, 2 Compartments, Gladiator & Bicycle Race On Lid, 7 x 5 In. 130.00
Playing, Centenary Of First U.S. Postage Stamps, Herman Herst Jr., Box, 1947, 2 Decks 90.00
Playing, Globe, Round, I.N. Richardson, Boston, Mass., Box, 1874, 3 1/4 In., 52 Cards 540.00
Playing, Knuckle Down, 1906, 2 Decks 770.00
Playing, Samuel Hart & Co., N.Y., c.1885, 52 Cards 300.00
Playing, Waterproof Playing Card Co., Boston, Round, c.1890, 52 Cards 374.00
Playing, Winchester, 12 Gauge Shell Shape, Man On Horse, Unopened 23.00

CARDER, see Aurene and Steuben categories.

CARLSBAD is a mark found on china made by several factories in Germany, Austria, and Bavaria. Many pieces were exported to the United States. Most of the pieces available today were made after 1891.

Biscuit Jar, Cover, Blue Iris, Leaves, Scalloped Rim, 6 1/2 x 5 In. 70.00
Bowl, Portrait, Woman, 9 1/4 In. 125.00
Bowl, Vegetable, Cover, Marx & Gutherz, c.1885-98, 11 x 7 1/4 In. 200.00
Bowl, Vegetable, Cover, Roses, Leaves, Gold Trim, Scalloped, c.1900, 7 x 9 1/2 In. 85.00
Bowl, Vegetable, Cover, Roses, Vines, Gold Trim, 7 x 12 In. 45.00
Bread Plate, Pink Carnations, 24K Gold Filigree, 6 In. 18.00
Ewer, Iridescent Glaze, Applied Gold Trailing Leaf Handle, Signed, 7 1/2 In. .... *ILLUS* 510.00
Oyster Plate, Pink Dahlias, 5 Wells, c.1900, 8 1/4 In. 100.00
Plate, Courting Couple, Multicolored Transfer, Stamped, 14 1/2 In., Pair 235.00

Plate, Dinner, Flowers, Vines, Marx & Gutherz, Late 1800s, 9 1/2 In. 50.00
Plate, Luncheon, Flowers, Vines, Marx & Gutherz, c.1900, 8 1/4 In. 40.00
Plate, Portrait, Bust Of Napoleon, Green, Scalloped Edge, Gold Accents, 7 In. 700.00
Plate, Serving, Handles, Flowers, Gold Trim, 2 x 10 In. 149.00
Platter, Marx & Gutherz, c.1885-98, 2 1/4 x 17 1/2 x 9 1/4 In. 174.00
Soup, Dish, Flowers, Vines, Marx & Gutherz, c.1900, 9 1/2 In. 45.00
Tray, Hand Painted, 8 3/4 In. 40.00

CARLTON WARE was made at the Carlton Works of Stoke-on-Trent, England, beginning about 1890. The firm traded as Wiltshaw & Robinson until 1957. It was renamed Carlton Ware Ltd. in 1958. The company went bankrupt in 1995, but the name is still in use.

Compote, Bell, Flowers, Leaves, Wiltshaw & Robinson, 1930s, 7 In. 547.00
Vase, Bird Of Paradise & Tree, Butterflies, Wiltshaw & Robinson, 1930s, 4 3/4 In. 358.00
Vase, Bird Of Paradise, Leaves, Wiltshaw & Robinson, 1930s, 8 In. 320.00
Vase, Red Flambe, Egg Shape, Weeping Willows, Prunus Tree, Early 1900s, 10 1/8 In. 588.00
Vase, Sketching Bird, Trees, Wiltshaw & Robinson, 1930s, 8 In. 448.00

CARNIVAL GLASS was an inexpensive, iridescent, pressed glass made from about 1907 to about 1925. More than 1,000 different patterns are known. Carnival glass is currently being reproduced. Additional pieces may be found in the Northwood category.

Acanthus, Bowl, Ruffled Edge, Smoke 55.00
Acanthus, Chop Plate, Marigold 85.00
Acanthus, Chop Plate, Smoke 375.00
Acorn, Bowl, Ruffled Edge, Marigold 10.00
Acorn Burrs, Berry Bowl, Master, Amethyst .... 145.00 to 155.00
Acorn Burrs, Butter, Amethyst 300.00
Acorn Burrs, Creamer, Amethyst 55.00
Acorn Burrs, Pitcher, Green 185.00
Acorn Burrs, Punch Set, Amethyst, 8 Piece 1500.00
Acorn Burrs & Bark pattern is listed here as Acorn Burrs.
Amaryllis pattern is listed here as Tiger Lily.
American Beauty Roses pattern is listed here as Wreath of Roses.
Apple Blossom, Berry Set, Enameled, Blue, 7 Piece 225.00
Apple Blossom, Table Set, Enameled, Blue, 4 Piece 700.00
Apple Blossom, Tumbler, Enameled, Blue .... 85.00 to 105.00
Apple Blossom Twigs, Bowl, Ruffled Edge, White 85.00
Apple Blossom Twigs, Plate, Marigold, 9 In. 145.00
Apple Blossom Twigs, Plate, Peach Opalescent, 9 In. 200.00
Apple Tree, Tumbler, Blue, 4 In. 15.00
April Showers, Vase, Marigold, 11 In. 50.00
Arched Flute, Toothpick, Wisteria 275.00
Argonaut Shell pattern is listed here as Nautilus.
Asters, Rose Bowl, Blue, 5 In. 60.00
Asters, Vase, Marigold, Square Mouth, 5 In. 375.00
Aurora Pearls, Bowl, Crimped & Ruffled Edge, White Opalescent, 12 In. 500.00
Australian Emu, Sauce, Ruffled Edge, Amethyst 175.00
Australian Kingfisher, Bowl, Ruffled Edge, Amethyst 200.00
Autumn Acorn, Bowl, Ruffled Edge, Green 95.00
Autumn Acorn, Bowl, Ruffled Edge, Marigold 18.00
Autumn Acorn, Plate, Green, 9 In. 600.00
Band Of Stars, Wine Set, Marigold, 7 Piece 75.00
Banded Medallion & Teardrop pattern is listed here as Beaded Bull's-Eye.
Basket Of Roses, Bonbon, Amethyst 210.00
Basketweave, Basket, Open Edge, Ruffled, Aqua 45.00
Basketweave, Basket, Ruffled Edge, Aqua 70.00
Basketweave, Basket, Ruffled Edge, Cherry Red 325.00
Basketweave, Basket, Ruffled Edge, Ice Blue 400.00
Basketweave, Basket, Ruffled Edge, Ice Green 195.00
Basketweave, Basket, Ruffled Edge, Marigold 10.00
Basketweave, Basket, Ruffled Edge, Powder Blue, Marigold Iridescence 135.00

Basketweave, Basket, Ruffled Edge, Vaseline, Marigold Iridescence 70.00
Battenburg Lace No. 1 pattern is listed here as Hearts & Flowers.
Battenburg Lace No. 2 pattern is listed here as Captive Rose.
Battenburg Lace No. 3 pattern is listed here as Fanciful.
Beaded Acanthus, Pitcher, Milk, Marigold 70.00
Beaded Bull's-Eye, Vase, Marigold, 6 1/2 In. 65.00
Beaded Bull's-Eye, Vase, Marigold, 10 In. 30.00
Beaded Cable, Rose Bowl, Amethyst .... 50.00 to 55.00
Beaded Cable, Rose Bowl, Aqua Opalescent 250.00
Beaded Cable, Rose Bowl, Blue 175.00
Beaded Cable, Rose Bowl, Marigold .... 35.00 to 40.00
Beaded Cable, Rose Bowl, White 225.00
Beaded Medallion & Teardrop pattern is listed here as Beaded Bull's-Eye.
Beaded Shell, Mug, Amethyst .... 30.00 to 40.00
Beaded Shell, Pitcher, Marigold 600.00
Beaded Shell, Tumbler, Marigold 45.00
Beaded Spears, Pitcher, Marigold 215.00
Beaded Star, Rose Bowl, Marigold 10.00
Beaded Star & Snail pattern is listed here as Constellation.
Beauty, Vase, Bud, Amethyst 5.00
Bells & Beads, Bowl, Crimped & Ruffled Edge, Peach Opalescent, 7 In. 70.00
Bells & Beads, Bowl, Ruffled Edge, Amethyst, 7 In. 65.00
Big Basketweave, Vase, Blue, 11 In. 175.00
Big Fish, Bowl, Crimped & Ruffled Edge, Marigold 625.00
Bird & Grape, Wall Pocket, Marigold 120.00
Birds & Cherries, Bonbon, Green 60.00
Birds & Cherries, Compote, Ruffled Edge, Amethyst 30.00
Birds On Bough pattern is listed here as Birds & Cherries.
Birmingham Age Herald, Plate, Amethyst, 9 In. 2000.00
Blackberry, Basket, Open Edge, Blue 50.00
Blackberry, Basket, Open Edge, Marigold 25.00
Blackberry, Basket, Open Edge, White, 2 Sides Up 135.00
Blackberry, Bowl, Ruffled Edge, Amethyst, 7 In. 60.00
Blackberry, Compote, Amethyst, Miniature 40.00
Blackberry, Compote, Blue, Miniature .... 30.00 to 50.00
Blackberry, Compote, Green, Miniature 115.00
Blackberry, Compote, Marigold, Miniature 115.00
Blackberry, Hat, Open Edge, Ruffled, Green 140.00
Blackberry, Vase, Open Edge, Marigold, 7 1/2 In. 950.00
Blackberry & Rays, Compote, Ruffled Edge, Amethyst 300.00
Blackberry & Rays, Compote, Ruffled Edge, Green 145.00
Blackberry A pattern is listed here as Blackberry.
Blackberry B pattern is listed here as Blackberry Spray.
Blackberry Spray, Hat, Ruffled Edge, Red 70.00
Blackberry Wreath, Bowl, Crimped & Ruffled Edge, Amethyst, Satin, 7 In. 55.00
Blackberry Wreath, Sauce, Ruffled Edge, Marigold 50.00
Blossomtime, Compote, Ruffled Edge, Amethyst .... 120.00 to 135.00
Blossomtime, Compote, Ruffled Edge, Marigold 115.00
Blueberry, Pitcher, Marigold 350.00
Blueberry, Pitcher, White 700.00
Broken Arches, Punch Set, Amethyst, 8 Piece 350.00
Broken Arches, Punch Set, Marigold, 6 Piece 225.00
Brooklyn Bridge, Bowl, Ruffled Edge, Marigold 155.00
Bull's-Eye & Beads, Vase, Blue, 13 In. 235.00
Bushel Basket pattern is listed here as Basket.
Butterfly, Bonbon, Amethyst .... 25.00 to 55.00
Butterfly, Bonbon, Marigold 25.00
Butterfly, Bonbon, Ribbed Back, Amethyst 175.00
Butterfly & Berry, Berry Set, Blue, 5 Piece 160.00
Butterfly & Berry, Hatpin Holder, Marigold 850.00
Butterfly & Berry, Table Set, Blue, 4 Piece 400.00

Butterfly & Cable pattern is listed here as Springtime.
Butterfly & Fern, Pitcher, Water, Blue 425.00
Butterfly & Fern, Tumbler, Blue 65.00
Butterfly & Grape pattern is listed here as Butterfly & Berry.
Butterfly & Plume pattern is listed here as Butterfly & Fern.
Butterfly & Stippled Rays pattern is listed here as Butterfly.
Butterfly & Tulip, Bowl, Square, Footed, Amethyst 850.00
Buzz Saw, Cruet, Stopper, Green, 4 In. 300.00
Buzz Saw, Cruet, Stopper, Green, 6 In. 175.00
Buzz Saw, Pitcher, Water, Marigold, Small 55.00
Buzz Saw, Tumbler, Marigold 25.00
Cabbage Rose & Grape pattern is listed here as Wine & Roses.
Cactus Leaf Rays pattern is listed here as Leaf Rays.
Captive Rose, Blue, 9 In. 225.00
Captive Rose, Bonbon, Marigold 70.00
Captive Rose, Bowl, Crimped & Ruffled Edge, Amethyst 75.00
Captive Rose, Bowl, Crimped & Ruffled Edge, Green 115.00
Captive Rose, Bowl, Ruffled Edge, Blue 85.00
Captive Rose, Compote, Crimped & Ruffled Edge, Amethyst 45.00
Captive Rose, Plate, Amethyst, 9 In. 400.00
Captive Rose, Plate, Green, 9 In. 275.00
Captive Rose, Plate, Marigold, 9 In. 550.00
Carolina Dogwood, Bowl, Peach Opalescent 65.00
Castle, Shade, Hanging, Marigold 145.00
Cattails & Fish pattern is listed here as Fisherman's Mug.
Cattails & Water Lily pattern is listed here as Water Lily & Cattails.
Chatelaine, Tumbler, Amethyst 95.00
Checkerboard, Tumbler, Amethyst 175.00
Checkerboard, Tumbler, Marigold 250.00
Cherries, Bowl, Ice Cream, Amethyst 105.00
Cherries, Bowl, Ice Cream, Marigold, Satin, 7 In. 75.00
Cherries, Bowl, Ruffled Edge, Amethyst, 9 In. 250.00
Cherries, Plate, Crimped Edge, Amethyst, 6 In. 185.00
Cherries, Plate, Crimped Edge, Peach Opalescent, 6 In. 75.00
Cherries, Sauce, Ruffled Edge, Amethyst, 6 In. 55.00
Cherries & Holly Wreath pattern is listed here as Cherry Circles.
Cherries & Mums pattern is listed here as Mikado.
Cherry, Spooner, Green, 4 In. 110.00
Cherry & Cable, Tumbler, Marigold 125.00
Cherry Chain, Bowl, Ice Cream, White, 10 In. 30.00
Cherry Chain, Plate, Blue, 6 In. 30.00
Cherry Chain, Plate, Marigold, 6 In. 45.00
Cherry Circles, Bonbon, Blue .... 30.00 to 55.00
Cherry Circles, Bonbon, Marigold 25.00
Cherry Wreathed pattern is listed here as Wreathed Cherry.
Christmas Cactus pattern is listed here as Thistle.
Christmas Plate pattern is listed here as Poinsettia.
Christmas Rose & Poppy pattern is listed here as Six Petals.
Chrysanthemum, Bowl, Ruffled Edge, Footed, Black Amethyst, 10 In. 210.00
Chrysanthemum, Chop Plate, Marigold 550.00
Chrysanthemum, Chop Plate, Smoke 1200.00
Chrysanthemum Wreath pattern is listed here as Ten Mums.
Circle Scroll, Pitcher, Marigold 305.00
Classic Arts, Vase, Marigold, 7 1/2 In. 325.00
Cobblestone, Bowl, Ruffled Edge, Amethyst 250.00
Coin Dot, Bowl, Deep, Red, 7 In. 900.00
Coin Spot, Compote, Ruffled Edge, Lime Green 45.00
Coin Spot, Compote, Ruffled Edge, Marigold .... 10.00 to 30.00
Coin Spot, Compote, Ruffled Edge, Peach Opalescent .... 20.00 to 45.00
Colonial Lady, Vase, Amethyst 425.00
Columbine, Pitcher, Enameled, Blue 450.00

Columbine, Pitcher, Enameled, Green 450.00
Concave Diamonds, Tumbler, Celeste Blue 30.00
Concave Diamonds, Tumbler, Vaseline 85.00
Concord, Bowl, Ruffled Edge, Marigold 185.00
Concord, Plate, Marigold, 9 In. 750.00
Constellation, Compote, Ruffled Edge, Marigold .... 55.00 to 70.00
Constellation, Compote, Ruffled Edge, White 30.00
Coral, Plate, Marigold, 9 In. 600.00
Corinth, Vase, Amethyst, 10 In. 15.00
Corinth, Vase, Aqua, 10 In. 25.00
Corinth, Vase, Jack-In-Pulpit, Blue Opal, 8 1/2 In. 205.00
Corinth, Vase, Jack-In-Pulpit, Helios Green, 9 1/2 In. 85.00
Corinth, Vase, Jack-In-Pulpit, Marigold Iridescence, 9 1/2 In. 115.00
Corn, Bottle, Green 215.00
Corn, Vase, Ice Green 315.00
Cosmos & Cane, Berry, Honey Amber, 4 In. 25.00
Cosmos & Cane, Bowl, Headdress Interior, Square, Honey Amber 70.00
Cosmos & Cane, Chop Plate, Honey Amber 500.00
Cosmos & Cane, Compote, Punch Bowl Shape, Honey Amber 175.00
Cosmos & Cane, Compote, Punch Bowl Shape, Marigold 190.00
Cosmos & Cane, Compote, Punch Bowl Shape, White 185.00
Cosmos & Cane, Dish, Honey Amber, Tricornered, 9 In. 200.00
Cosmos & Cane, Rose Bowl, Whimsy, Cuspidor Shape, Honey Amber 1200.00
Cosmos & Cane, Rose Bowl, Whimsy, Volcano Shape, Marigold 1400.00
Cosmos & Cane, Table Set, Honey Amber, 4 Piece 600.00
Cosmos & Cane, Tumbler, White 95.00
Courthouse, Bowl, Ruffled Edge, Amethyst, Radium Iridescence .... 700.00 to 800.00
Crab Claw, Water Set, Marigold, 5 Piece 155.00
Curled Rib, Vase, Jack-In-Pulpit, Smoke, 8 In. 165.00
Curved Star, Bowl, Cover, Marigold 45.00
Curved Star, Bowl, Marigold, 5 In. 10.00
Curved Star, Vase, Blue, 9 1/2 In. 875.00
Curved Star, Vase, Marigold, 9 1/2 In. 165.00
Dahlia, Pitcher, Water, Marigold 700.00
Dahlia, Pitcher, Water, White, Gold Flowers 425.00
Dahlia, Sugar & Creamer, Cover, Amethyst 65.00
Dahlia, Table Set, White, 4 Piece 625.00
Dahlia, Tumbler, Marigold 80.00
Dahlia, Tumbler, White 125.00
Daisy & Drape, Vase, Inward Rim, Marigold 250.00
Daisy & Plume, Candy Dish, Berry Interior, Footed, Marigold 35.00
Daisy & Plume, Compote, Ruffled Edge, Amethyst 40.00
Daisy & Plume, Rose Bowl, Berry Interior, Footed, Amethyst 55.00
Daisy & Plume, Rose Bowl, Berry Interior, Footed, Marigold 45.00
Daisy & Plume, Rose Bowl, Footed, Smoke 105.00
Daisy & Plume, Rose Bowl, Green 25.00
Daisy Band & Drape pattern is listed here as Daisy & Drape.
Daisy Cut, Bell, Marigold 250.00
Daisy Web, Hat, 2 Sides Up, Amethyst 450.00
Daisy Wreath, Bowl, Ruffled Edge, Blue Opalescent 150.00
Daisy Wreath, Bowl, Ruffled Edge, Peach Opalescent 85.00
Dandelion, Pitcher, Water, Tankard, Green 650.00
Dandelion, Tumbler, Amethyst 125.00
Dandelion, Tumbler, Ice Blue 205.00
Dandelion Variant pattern is listed here as Paneled Dandelion.
Deep Grape, Compote, Green 2000.00
Diamond & Cable pattern is listed here as Fentonia.
Diamond & Fan, Pitcher, Milk, Marigold 10.00
Diamond & Rib, Jardiniere, Whimsy, Flared, Marigold 15000.00
Diamond & Rib, Vase, Funeral, Green, 17 In. 1800.00
Diamond & Rib, Vase, Funeral, Marigold, 20 In. 500.00

Diamond Band pattern is listed here as Diamonds.
Diamond Cut Shields, Water Set, Marigold, 7 Piece 145.00
Diamond Daisy, Tumbler, Marigold 35.00
Diamond Daisy, Water Set, Marigold, 8 Piece 205.00
Diamond Lace, Pitcher, Water, Amethyst .... 135.00 to 250.00
Diamond Lace, Tumbler, Amethyst .... 35.00 to 55.00
Diamond Lace, Water Set, Amethyst, 7 Piece 475.00
Diamond Point, Vase, Amethyst, 9 In. 95.00
Diamond Point, Vase, Blue, 10 In. 225.00
Diamond Point, Vase, Marigold, 9 In. 55.00
Diamond Point & Daisy pattern is listed here as Cosmos & Cane.
Diamond Point Variant, Vase, Marigold, 6 In. 155.00
Diamond Points, Vase, Emerald Green, 9 In. 1500.00
Diamond Points, Vase, Squat, Blue, 7 1/2 In. 265.00
Diamonds, Pitcher, Green 325.00
Diamonds, Pitcher, Marigold 150.00
Diamonds, Tumbler, Green 80.00
Dianthus, Pitcher, Tankard, Enameled, Ice Green 375.00
Dianthus, Pitcher, Tankard, Enameled, White 300.00
Dianthus, Tumbler, Enameled, Ice Green 85.00
Diving Dolphins, Bowl, Ruffled Edge, Amethyst 95.00
Dogwood & Marsh Lily pattern is listed here as Two Flowers.
Dogwood Spray, Bowl, Ruffled Edge, Dome Foot, Peach Opalescent .... 30.00 to 50.00
Double Dutch, Cuspidor, Whimsy, Footed, Marigold 1300.00
Double Loop, Creamer, Blue 225.00
Double Loop, Sugar, Blue 55.00
Double Star, Pitcher, Marigold 425.00
Double Star, Tumbler, Marigold 110.00
Double Stem Rose, Bowl, Ruffled Edge, Dome Foot, Amethyst 210.00
Double Stem Rose, Bowl, Ruffled Edge, Dome Foot, Celeste Blue 425.00
Double Stem Rose, Bowl, Ruffled Edge, Dome Foot, White 85.00
Dozen Roses, Bowl, Footed, Amethyst 450.00
Dragon & Lotus, Bowl, Crimped & Ruffled Edge, Amethyst 70.00
Dragon & Lotus, Bowl, Crimped & Ruffled Edge, Green 70.00
Dragon & Lotus, Bowl, Crimped & Ruffled Edge, Peach Opalescent 450.00
Dragon & Lotus, Bowl, Crimped & Ruffled Edge, Red 728.00
Dragon & Lotus, Bowl, Ice Cream, Blue .... 20.00 to 45.00
Dragon & Lotus, Bowl, Ice Cream, Cherry Red, Iridescence 900.00
Dragon & Lotus, Bowl, Ruffled Edge, Amber 135.00
Dragon & Lotus, Bowl, Ruffled Edge, Amethyst 115.00
Dragon & Lotus, Bowl, Ruffled Edge, Green 50.00
Dragon & Lotus, Bowl, Ruffled Edge, Marigold .... 35.00 to 60.00
Dragon & Lotus, Bowl, Ruffled Edge, Powder Blue, Marigold Iridescence 85.00
Dragon & Lotus, Plate, Blue, 9 In. 1500.00
Dragon & Strawberry, Bowl, Ruffled Edge, Footed, Marigold 550.00
Dragon Tongue, Bowl, Footed, Ruffled Edge, Marigold, 10 In. 2000.00
Drapery, Candy Dish, Ice Blue .... 95.00 to 115.00
Drapery, Rose Bowl, Amethyst 170.00
Drapery, Rose Bowl, Aqua Opalescent .... 165.00 to 225.00
Drapery, Vase, Amber, Footed, 10 In. 40.00
Drapery, Vase, Marigold, 7 1/2 In. .... 50.00 to 75.00
Drapery Variant, Vase, Amethyst, 8 1/2 In. 215.00
Eagle Furniture Co., Plate, Amethyst, 6 In. 300.00
Egyptian Band pattern is listed here as Round-Up.
Egyptian Queen, Vase, Marigold, 7 1/2 In. 350.00
Elks, Plate, Parkersburg, Blue, 1914, 8 In. 2100.00
Emaline pattern is listed here as Zipper Loop.
Embroidered Mums, Bowl, Ribbed Back, Ruffled Edge, Amethyst 325.00
Embroidered Mums, Bowl, Ribbed Back, Ruffled Edge, Blue .... 225.00 to 300.00
Embroidered Mums, Plate, Ice Green, 9 In. 800.00
Embroidered Mums, Plate, Ribbed Back, Ice Green, 9 In. 1300.00

Enameled Freesia, Pitcher, Tankard, Marigold 225.00
Enameled Freesia, Tumbler, Marigold 85.00
Estate, Perfume, Smoke 275.00
Fan, Gravy Boat, Peach Opalescent 60.00
Fan & Arch pattern is listed here as Persian Garden.
Fanciful, Bowl, Ruffled Edge, Marigold 45.00
Fanciful, Plate, Amethyst, 9 In. .... 195.00 to 900.00
Fanciful, Plate, Blue, 9 In. 450.00
Fantail, Berry Bowl, Marigold, Master 35.00
Fantasy pattern is listed here as Question Marks.
Fashion, Tumbler, Amethyst 275.00
Fashion, Tumbler, Smoke 85.00
Feather & Heart, Pitcher, Amethyst 250.00
Feather & Heart, Pitcher, Marigold 450.00
Feather & Heart, Tumbler, Amethyst 65.00
Feather & Heart, Tumbler, Marigold 75.00
Feather & Hobstar pattern is listed here as Inverted Feather.
Feather Stitch, Bowl, Ruffled Edge, Blue 95.00
Feathered Scroll pattern is listed here as Feathered Serpent.
Feathered Serpent, Berry Set, Marigold, 7 Piece 50.00
Feathered Serpent, Sauce, Ruffled Edge, Amethyst 15.00
Feathers, Vase, Amethyst, 10 In. 65.00
Feathers, Vase, White, 8 In. 475.00
Featherstitch, Bowl, Ice Cream, Aqua 135.00
Featherstitch, Bowl, Ruffled Edge, Blue 25.00
Fenton's Butterfly pattern is listed here as Butterfly.
Fentonia, Pitcher, Blue 400.00
Fentonia, Tumbler, Blue 85.00
Fern, Compote, Ruffled Edge, Amethyst 75.00
Fern, Compote, Ruffled Edge, Green .... 85.00 to 100.00
Fern, Compote, Ruffled Edge, Marigold 25.00
Field Flower, Pitcher, Water, Green 265.00
Field Thistle, Plate, Marigold, 6 In. 185.00
Field Thistle, Sauce, Celeste Blue, 5 In. 475.00
Field Thistle, Vase, Marigold, 8 1/2 In. 145.00
File, Pitcher, Marigold 1000.00
File, Tumbler, Marigold 50.00
File, Vase, Marigold, 5 1/4 In. 225.00
File & Fan, Compote, Ruffled Edge, Peach Opalescent 40.00
Fine Cut & Roses, Candy Dish, Aqua Opalescent, Butterscotch Iridescence 145.00
Fine Cut & Roses, Candy Dish, Ice Blue 200.00
Fine Cut & Roses, Rose Bowl, Amethyst .... 40.00 to 55.00
Fine Cut & Roses, Rose Bowl, Fancy Interior, Horehound 275.00
Fine Cut & Roses, Rose Bowl, Ice Blue .... 35.00 to 40.00
Fine Cut & Roses, Rose Bowl, Marigold 50.00
Fine Cut & Star pattern is listed here as Star & File.
Fine Rib, Vase, Cherry Red, 9 1/2 In. 295.00
Fine Rib, Vase, Dark Red, 11 In. 200.00
Fine Rib, Vase, Ice Green, 9 In. 300.00
Fine Rib, Vase, Powder Blue, Marigold Iridescence, 9 In. 115.00
Fine Rib, Vase, Sapphire, 10 In. 250.00
Fine Rib, Vase, Vaseline, Marigold Iridescence, 10 In. .... 175.00 to 225.00
Fish & Flowers pattern is listed here as Trout & Fly.
Fisherman's Mug, Amethyst 30.00
Fisherman's Mug, Peach Opalescent 800.00
Fishnet, Epergne, Peach Opalescent .... 165.00 to 225.00
Fishscale & Beads, Plate, Marigold, 7 In. 35.00
Fishscale & Beads, Plate, White, 7 In. 75.00
Flashing Star, Water Set, Marigold, 7 Piece 175.00
Fleur-De-Lis, Bowl, Dome Foot, Crimped & Ruffled Edge, Green, Radium Iridescence 275.00
Fleur-De-Lis, Bowl, Marigold 5.00

Floral & Diamond Point pattern is listed here as Fine Cut & Roses.
Floral & Grape, Pitcher, Amethyst 225.00
Floral & Grape, Pitcher, Blue 155.00
Floral & Grape, Sauce, Footed, Green 45.00
Floral & Grapevine pattern is listed here as Floral & Grape.
Floral & Optic, Cake Plate, Footed, Red 475.00
Floral & Optic, Cake Plate, Footed, White 70.00
Floral & Sunburst, Bowl, Straight Sides, Blue, 5 In. 115.00
Flower Pot pattern is listed here as Butterfly & Tulip.
Flowering Almonds pattern is listed here as Peacock Tail.
Flowers & Frames, Bowl, Ruffled Edge, Dome Foot, Amethyst 195.00
Fluffy Bird pattern is listed here as Peacock.
Fluffy Peacock, Pitcher, Blue 550.00
Fluffy Peacock, Pitcher, Marigold 300.00
Fluffy Peacock, Tumbler, Blue 105.00
Fluffy Peacock, Tumbler, Marigold 70.00
Flute, Compote, Marigold 30.00
Flute, Salt, Marigold, Master 20.00
Flute, Toothpick, Amethyst .... 30.00 to 70.00
Flute, Toothpick, Marigold 40.00
Flute & Cane, Pitcher, Milk, Marigold 35.00
Folding Fan, Crimped & Ruffled Edge, Peach Opalescent 15.00
Formal, Hatpin Holder, Marigold 175.00
Four Flowers, Bowl, Ruffled Edge, Olive Green 75.00
Four Flowers, Plate, Ice Green, 9 In. 475.00
Four Flowers, Plate, Peach Opalescent, 6 In. .... 65.00 to 80.00
Four Pillars, Vase, Aqua Opalescent, 10 In. 25.00
Four Pillars, Vase, Ribbed, Olive Green, 11 In. 20.00
Four Seventy Four, Pitcher, Marigold 130.00
Freefold, Vase, Amethyst, 11 1/2 In. 95.00
Frosted Block, Rose Bowl, Marigold 8.00
Fruit Salad, Punch Set, Marigold, 8 Piece 350.00
Fruits & Flowers, Bonbon, Amethyst 45.00
Fruits & Flowers, Bonbon, Blue 95.00
Fruits & Flowers, Sauce, Ruffled Edge, Amethyst 35.00
Garland, Rose Bowl, Blue .... 45.00 to 95.00
Good Luck, Bowl, Pie Crust Edge, Basketweave Back, Marigold 275.00
Good Luck, Bowl, Pie Crust Edge, Ribbed Back, Blue 325.00
Good Luck, Bowl, Pie Crust Edge, Ribbed Back, Marigold .... 225.00 to 475.00
Good Luck, Bowl, Ruffled Edge, Basketweave Back, Amethyst 165.00
Good Luck, Bowl, Ruffled Edge, Ribbed Back, Amethyst 275.00
Good Luck, Bowl, Ruffled Edge, Ribbed Back, Blue .... 155.00 to 250.00
Good Luck, Bowl, Stippled, Ruffled Edge, Ribbed Back, Blue .... 400.00 to 500.00
Good Luck, Plate, Basketweave Back, Amethyst 325.00
Good Luck, Plate, Basketweave Back, Green, 9 In. .... 500.00 to 525.00
Good Luck, Plate, Ribbed Back, Marigold, 9 In. 350.00
Good Luck, Plate, Ribbed Back, Marigold, Pink Iridescence, 9 In. 1000.00
Grand Thistle, Tumbler, Amber 90.00
Grape & Cable, Banana Boat, Blue 95.00
Grape & Cable, Banana Boat, Green 175.00
Grape & Cable, Banana Boat, Ice Blue 135.00
Grape & Cable, Berry Bowl, Green, Master 75.00
Grape & Cable, Berry Set, Amethyst, 7 Piece 120.00
Grape & Cable, Berry Set, Green, 7 Piece 145.00
Grape & Cable, Bonbon, Amethyst .... 60.00 to 65.00
Grape & Cable, Bonbon, Blue 180.00
Grape & Cable, Bowl, Ice Cream, Footed, Amethyst 10.00
Grape & Cable, Bowl, Pie Crust Edge, Basketweave Back, Amethyst 85.00
Grape & Cable, Bowl, Ruffled Edge, Basketweave Back, Marigold, 11 In. 55.00
Grape & Cable, Bowl, Ruffled Edge, Ice Blue, 7 In. 300.00
Grape & Cable, Bowl, Salad, Ruffled Edge, White 275.00

Grape & Cable, Candle Lamp, Green 600.00
Grape & Cable, Candle Lamp, Marigold, Flared Shade 1000.00
Grape & Cable, Cologne, Amethyst .... 175.00 to 225.00
Grape & Cable, Cologne, Green 300.00
Grape & Cable, Cologne, Stopper, Amethyst 300.00
Grape & Cable, Cuspidor, Whimsy, Amethyst 4000.00
Grape & Cable, Dish, Sweetmeat, Cover, Amethyst 85.00
Grape & Cable, Hatpin Holder, Amethyst .... 135.00 to 205.00
Grape & Cable, Hatpin Holder, Green .... 200.00 to 325.00
Grape & Cable, Hatpin Holder, Ice Blue 350.00
Grape & Cable, Hatpin Holder, Marigold 225.00
Grape & Cable, Pin Tray, Amethyst 195.00
Grape & Cable, Pin Tray, Green .... 185.00 to 275.00
Grape & Cable, Pitcher, Amethyst 190.00
Grape & Cable, Pitcher, Marigold 145.00
Grape & Cable, Pitcher, Tankard, Ice Green 1350.00
Grape & Cable, Pitcher, Tankard, Marigold 300.00
Grape & Cable, Plate, Basketweave Back, Amethyst, 9 In. .... 110.00 to 115.00
Grape & Cable, Plate, Footed, Marigold, 9 In. 30.00
Grape & Cable, Plate, Green, 9 In. 105.00
Grape & Cable, Plate, Handgrip, Amethyst, 6 In. .... 75.00 to 155.00
Grape & Cable, Plate, Marigold, 9 In. 55.00
Grape & Cable, Plate, Stippled, Old Rose Distillery, Ribbed Back, Green, 9 In. 375.00
Grape & Cable, Powder Jar, Amethyst 275.00
Grape & Cable, Powder Jar, Green .... 105.00 to 215.00
Grape & Cable, Punch Set, Amethyst, Small, 8 Piece 350.00
Grape & Cable, Punch Set, Amethyst, Small, 10 Piece 450.00
Grape & Cable, Punch Set, Marigold, Banquet, 8 Piece 1600.00
Grape & Cable, Punch Set, Stippled, Blue, 10 Piece 1500.00
Grape & Cable, Sauce, Ruffled Edge, Amethyst, 6 In. 30.00
Grape & Cable, Sauce, Ruffled Edge, Blue, 6 In. 190.00
Grape & Cable, Sauce, Ruffled Edge, Green, 6 In. 30.00
Grape & Cable, Shade, Candle, Marigold 450.00
Grape & Cable, Tray, Dresser, Amethyst 260.00
Grape & Cable, Tumbler, Whiskey, Amethyst 185.00
Grape & Cable, Water Set, Amethyst, 7 Piece 105.00
Grape & Cable, Water Set, Tankard, Amethyst, 7 Piece 350.00
Grape & Gothic Arches, Table Set, Blue, 4 Piece .... 300.00 to 475.00
Grape & Gothic Arches, Tumbler, Custard 15.00
Grape & Gothic Arches, Water Set, Blue, 7 Piece 550.00
Grape & Gothic Arches, Water Set, Green, 5 Piece 600.00
Grape & Gothic Arches, Water Set, Marigold, 5 Piece 95.00
Grape Arbor, Pitcher, Tankard, Ice Blue .... 100.00 to 500.00
Grape Arbor, Water Set, Tankard, Marigold, 6 Piece 325.00
Grape Delight pattern is listed here as Vintage.
Grape Leaves, Bowl, Ruffled Edge, Green 65.00
Grape Wreath, Bowl, Green, 7 In. 70.00
Grapevine Diamonds pattern is listed here as Grapevine Lattice.
Grapevine Lattice, Bowl, Ruffled Edge, Amethyst, 7 In. 145.00
Grapevine Lattice, Bowl, Ruffled Edge, White, 6 In. 35.00
Grapevine Lattice, Pitcher, Tankard, Marigold 375.00
Grapevine Lattice, Pitcher, Tankard, White 650.00
Grapevine Lattice, Plate, Amethyst, 7 In. 2000.00
Grapevine Lattice, Tumbler, Marigold 30.00
Grapevine Lattice, Tumbler, White 95.00
Grapevine Lattice, Water Set, Tankard, Amethyst, 7 Piece 400.00
Greek Key, Bowl, Ruffled Edge, Basketweave Back, Amethyst 115.00
Greek Key, Bowl, Ruffled Edge, Dome Foot, Marigold 45.00
Greek Key, Bowl, Ruffled Edge, Ribbed Back, Marigold 105.00
Greek Key, Pitcher, Tankard, Marigold 600.00
Greek Key, Plate, Basketweave Back, Marigold, 9 In. 600.00

Greek Key, Plate, Ribbed Back, Marigold, 9 In. 750.00
Greek Key, Tumbler, Marigold 80.00
Hanging Cherries, Compote, Amethyst 600.00
Hanging Cherries, Creamer, Amethyst 50.00
Hattie, Bowl, Deep, Marigold 10.00
Hattie, Bowl, Deep, Smoke .... 75.00 to 105.00
Hattie, Chop Plate, Marigold 1700.00
Heart & Vine, Bowl, Crimped & Ruffled Edge, Amethyst 85.00
Heart & Vine, Bowl, Ruffled Edge, Amethyst 40.00
Heart & Vine, Plate, Marigold, Spector's Department Store, 9 In. 525.00
Hearts & Flowers, Bowl, Pie Crust Edge, Ribbed Back, Ice Blue 375.00
Hearts & Flowers, Bowl, Pie Crust Edge, Ribbed Back, Marigold 525.00
Hearts & Flowers, Bowl, Ruffled Edge, Ribbed Back, Amethyst 300.00
Hearts & Flowers, Bowl, Ruffled Edge, Ribbed Back, Blue 250.00
Hearts & Flowers, Bowl, Ruffled Edge, Ribbed Back, Ice Blue .... 145.00 to 275.00
Hearts & Flowers, Bowl, Ruffled Edge, Ribbed Back, Marigold 225.00
Hearts & Flowers, Compote, Ruffled Edge, Amethyst 135.00
Hearts & Flowers, Compote, Ruffled Edge, Aqua Opalescent .... 225.00 to 700.00
Hearts & Flowers, Compote, Ruffled Edge, Blue .... 125.00 to 225.00
Hearts & Flowers, Compote, Ruffled Edge, Ice Green 475.00
Hearts & Flowers, Compote, Ruffled Edge, Marigold .... 105.00 to 165.00
Hearts & Flowers, Compote, Ruffled Edge, Powder Blue Opalescent 3250.00
Hearts & Flowers, Compote, Ruffled Edge, White .... 65.00 to 100.00
Hearts & Flowers, Plate, Marigold, Pink Iridescence, Ribbed Back, 9 In. 825.00
Hearts & Flowers, Plate, Ribbed Back, Amethyst, 9 In. 850.00
Hearts & Flowers, Plate, Ribbed Back, Marigold, 9 In. 710.00
Heavy Grape, Bowl, Lime Green, 6 In. 20.00
Heavy Grape, Bowl, Ruffled Edge, Blue, 7 In. 850.00
Heavy Grape, Chop Plate, Amber 60.00
Heavy Grape, Chop Plate, Amethyst .... 390.00 to 550.00
Heavy Grape, Chop Plate, Marigold 70.00
Heavy Grape, Plate, Amethyst, 8 In. .... 145.00 to 250.00
Heavy Grape, Plate, Green, 8 In. 25.00
Heavy Grape, Punch Bowl, Base, Marigold 425.00
Heron & Rushes pattern is listed here as Stork & Rushes.
Hobnail, Banana, Blue Opalescent 130.00
Hobnail, Cuspidor, Amethyst 300.00
Hobnail, Pitcher, Amethyst 1700.00
Hobnail, Pitcher, Blue 4250.00
Hobnail, Rose Bowl, Amethyst 210.00
Hobnail Swirl, Rose Bowl, Amethyst 185.00
Hobnail Swirl, Rose Bowl, Marigold 175.00
Hobnail Swirl, Vase, Green, Radium Iridescence, 10 In. 350.00
Hobnail Swirl, Vase, Marigold, 11 In. 295.00
Hobstar, Pickle Castor, Marigold 350.00
Hobstar & Feather, Punch Set, Marigold, 10 Piece 1000.00
Hobstar & Feather, Rose Bowl, Amethyst, Large 1500.00
Hobstar & Fruit, Sauce, Ruffled Edge, Blue Opalescent 135.00
Hobstar & Fruit, Sauce, Ruffled Edge, Peach Opalescent 45.00
Hobstar & Shield, Water Set, Marigold, 7 Piece 125.00
Hobstar & Torch pattern is listed here as Double Star.
Hobstar Flower, Compote, Ruffled Edge, Amethyst 45.00
Holly, Bowl, Crimped & Ruffled Edge, Amber 75.00
Holly, Bowl, Ice Cream, Green 105.00
Holly, Bowl, Ice Cream, Marigold 35.00
Holly, Bowl, Lime Green 65.00
Holly, Bowl, Ruffled Edge, Amber 145.00
Holly, Bowl, Ruffled Edge, Marigold 25.00
Holly, Bowl, Ruffled Edge, Powder Blue, Marigold Iridescence 85.00
Holly, Bowl, Ruffled Edge, White 60.00
Holly, Compote, Goblet Shape, Lime Green Opalescent 450.00

Holly, Compote, Ruffled Edge, Amethyst . . . 60.00
Holly, Compote, Ruffled Edge, Green . . . 90.00
Holly, Compote, Ruffled Edge, Lime Green, Marigold Iridescence . . . 65.00
Holly, Compote, Ruffled Edge, Marigold . . . 20.00
Holly, Hat, 2 Sides Up, Red . . . 800.00
Holly, Hat, Ruffled Edge, Red . . . 185.00
Holly, Hat, Square, Marigold . . . 30.00
Holly, Plate, Blue, 9 In. . . . 185.00 to 300.00
Holly, Plate, Green, 9 In. . . . 600.00
Holly, Plate, Light Marigold, 9 In. . . . 55.00
Holly, Plate, Marigold, 9 In. . . . 155.00 to 165.00
Holly, Rose Bowl, Blue . . . 125.00
Holly & Berry, Bowl, Ruffled Edge, Amethyst . . . 100.00
Holly & Berry, Bowl, Ruffled Edge, Peach Opalescent . . . 30.00
Holly Spray pattern is listed here as Holly Sprig.
Holly Sprig, Bonbon, Amethyst, Satin . . . 85.00
Holly Sprig Variant, Bowl, Marigold, Crimped Edge, 7 In. . . . 155.00
Holly Whirl, Bowl, Ruffled Edge, Amethyst, 10 In. . . . 135.00
Homestead, Chop Plate, Amber . . . 3500.00
Homestead, Chop Plate, Pastel Marigold . . . 800.00
Honeycomb & Beads, Dish, Tricornered, Amethyst . . . 145.00
Honeycomb Collar pattern is listed here as Fishscale & Beads.
Horse Medallions pattern is listed here as Horses' Heads.
Horses' Heads, Bowl, Footed, Blue . . . 125.00
Horses' Heads, Bowl, Footed, Lime Green, Marigold Iridescence . . . 205.00
Horses' Heads, Bowl, Footed, Marigold . . . 55.00
Horses' Heads, Bowl, Ice Cream, Marigold . . . 30.00
Horses' Heads, Bowl, Ruffled Edge, Footed, Amethyst . . . 375.00
Horses' Heads, Bowl, Ruffled Edge, Footed, Green . . . 235.00 to 250.00
Horses' Heads, Bowl, Ruffled Edge, Marigold . . . 60.00
Horses' Heads, Plate, Marigold, 7 In. . . . 130.00
Horses' Heads, Rose Bowl, Marigold . . . 85.00
Imperial Fruit, Pitcher, Amethyst . . . 450.00
Imperial Fruit, Punch Set, Amethyst, 8 Piece . . . 2700.00
Imperial Fruit, Tumbler, Amethyst . . . 75.00
Imperial Grape, Bowl, Ruffled Edge, Amethyst . . . 195.00 to 235.00
Imperial Grape, Carafe, Amethyst . . . 150.00
Imperial Grape, Cup & Saucer, Amethyst . . . 45.00
Imperial Grape, Pitcher, Amethyst . . . 125.00
Imperial Grape, Pitcher, Marigold . . . 50.00
Imperial Grape, Plate, Amber, 9 In. . . . 1050.00
Imperial Grape, Plate, Amethyst, 6 In. . . . 105.00
Imperial Grape, Plate, Green, 6 In. . . . 20.00 to 30.00
Imperial Grape, Plate, Marigold, 6 In. . . . 45.00
Imperial Grape, Tumbler, Marigold . . . 10.00
Intaglio pattern is listed here as Hobstar & Feather.
Interior Of Cherries & Mums pattern is listed here as Mikado.
Inverted Feather, Biscuit Jar, Green . . . 120.00 to 185.00
Inverted Feather, Parfait, Marigold . . . 10.00
Inverted Strawberry, Candlestick, Marigold, Pair . . . 325.00
Inverted Strawberry, Compote, Marigold, Small . . . 850.00
Inverted Strawberry, Cuspidor, Green . . . 525.00
Inverted Strawberry, Cuspidor, Marigold . . . 315.00
Inverted Strawberry, Powder Jar, Green . . . 170.00
Inverted Strawberry, Rose Bowl, Amethyst, Large . . . 325.00
Inverted Strawberry, Spooner, Amethyst . . . 250.00
Inverted Strawberry, Sugar, Cover, Amethyst . . . 375.00
Inverted Strawberry, Sugar, Cover, Marigold . . . 250.00
Iris, Compote, Ruffled Edge, Amethyst . . . 40.00 to 90.00
Iris, Compote, Ruffled Edge, Blue . . . 95.00
Iris, Compote, Ruffled Edge, Marigold . . . 30.00

Iris, Goblet, Buttermilk, Marigold 30.00
Isaac Benesch, Bowl, Ruffled Edge, Amethyst 375.00
Jeweled Heart, Plate, Smooth Rays Interior, Crimped Edge, Amethyst, 6 In. 135.00
Jeweled Heart, Tumbler, Marigold 85.00
Kimberly pattern is listed here as Concave Diamonds.
Kittens, Bowl, Cereal, Blue 315.00
Kittens, Bowl, Cereal, Marigold .... 105.00 to 315.00
Kittens, Bowl, Cereal, Powder Blue, Marigold Iridescence 250.00
Kittens, Bowl, Ruffled Edge, Blue 185.00
Kittens, Bowl, Ruffled Edge, Marigold 145.00
Kittens, Cup & Saucer, Blue 400.00
Kittens, Cup & Saucer, Marigold 245.00
Kittens, Cup, Marigold 65.00
Kittens, Dish, 2 Sides Up, Marigold .... 90.00 to 195.00
Kittens, Dish, 4 Sides Up, Amethyst 255.00
Kittens, Dish, 4 Sides Up, Marigold 180.00
Kittens, Toothpick, Marigold 75.00
Kittens, Vase, Blue 300.00
Kittens, Vase, Marigold 145.00
Labelle Elaine pattern is listed here as Primrose.
Labelle Poppy pattern is listed here as Poppy Show.
Labelle Rose pattern is listed here as Rose Show.
Lattice & Grape, Pitcher, Tankard, Blue 275.00
Lattice & Grape, Pitcher, Tankard, Marigold 135.00
Lattice & Grape, Tumbler, Blue 10.00
Lattice & Grape, Water Set, Tankard, Marigold, 6 Piece 135.00
Lattice & Grapevine pattern is listed here as Lattice & Grape.
Lattice & Poinsettia, Bowl, Ruffled Edge, Footed, Ice Blue 1050.00
Lattice & Poinsettia, Bowl, Ruffled Edge, Ribbed Back, Footed, Amethyst 325.00
Lattice & Poinsettia, Bowl, Ruffled Edge, Ribbed Back, Footed, Blue 350.00
Lattice & Points, Bowl, Ruffled Edge, Amethyst 55.00
Lattice & Points, Bowl, Ruffled Edge, Marigold 10.00
Lattice & Points, Bowl, Ruffled Edge, White 30.00
Leaf & Bands, Nut Dish, Footed, Green 30.00
Leaf & Beads, Plate, Flared, Rayed Interior, Green, 9 In. 65.00
Leaf & Beads, Rose Bowl, Amethyst 175.00
Leaf & Beads, Rose Bowl, Aqua Opalescent, Butterscotch Iridescence .... 200.00 to 245.00
Leaf & Beads, Rose Bowl, Lime Green Opalescent 1800.00
Leaf & Beads, Rose Bowl, Marigold 55.00
Leaf & Little Flowers, Compote, Green, Radium Iridescence 220.00
Leaf Chain, Bowl, Clambroth, 9 In. 10.00
Leaf Chain, Bowl, Ruffled Edge, Amethyst, 7 In. 75.00
Leaf Chain, Bowl, Ruffled Edge, Blue, 9 In. 70.00
Leaf Chain, Bowl, Ruffled Edge, Red, 7 In. 425.00
Leaf Chain, Plate, Blue, 7 In. .... 75.00 to 135.00
Leaf Chain, Plate, Blue, 9 In. 330.00
Leaf Chain, Plate, Marigold, 7 In. .... 25.00 to 75.00
Leaf Chain, Plate, Marigold, 9 In. 1700.00
Leaf Columns, Vase, Green, 11 In. 135.00
Leaf Columns, Vase, Ice Blue, 10 In. 300.00
Leaf Columns, Vase, Sapphire, 10 In. 825.00
Leaf Columns, Vase, Squat, Amethyst, 6 In. 195.00
Leaf Columns, Vase, Squat, Green, 7 In. 215.00
Leaf Medallion pattern is listed here as Leaf Chain.
Leaf Pinwheel & Star Flower pattern is listed here as Whirling Leaves.
Leaf Rays, Nappy, Peach Opalescent 10.00
Leaf Rays, Nappy, Ruffled Edge, Amethyst 10.00
Leaf Rays, Nappy, Tricornered, Amethyst 30.00
Leaf Rays, Nappy, White 15.00
Leaf Tiers, Tumbler, Marigold 60.00
Lily Of The Valley, Pitcher, Tankard, Blue 1600.00

Lily Of The Valley, Tumbler, Blue 225.00
Lily Of The Valley, Tumbler, Marigold 500.00
Lined Lattice, Vase, Amethyst, 8 1/2 In. 145.00
Lined Lattice, Vase, Footed, Amethyst, 12 In. 185.00
Lined Lattice, Vase, Lavender, 10 In. 135.00
Lined Lattice, Vase, Squat, Peach Opalescent, 4 1/2 In. 220.00
Lined Lattice, Vase, White, 9 In. 95.00
Lined Lattice, Vase, White, 10 In. 65.00
Lions, Bowl, Ice Cream, Marigold 50.00
Lions, Bowl, Ruffled Edge, Marigold . . . . 65.00 to 70.00
Lions, Plate, Marigold, 7 1/2 In. 1064.00
Little Beads, Compote, Ruffled Edge, Peach Opalescent 15.00
Little Fishes, Berry Bowl, Master, Footed, Marigold 95.00
Little Fishes, Bowl, Ice Cream, Footed, Blue 300.00
Little Fishes, Sauce, Ruffled Edge, Footed, Amethyst 95.00
Little Flowers, Bowl, Amethyst, 10 In. 55.00
Little Flowers, Bowl, Ruffled Edge, Green, Satin, 7 In. 25.00
Little Flowers, Bowl, Ruffled Edge, Marigold, 7 In. 40.00
Little Flowers, Chop Plate, Marigold . . . . 1100.00 to 2500.00
Little Stars, Bowl, Ruffled Edge, Marigold, Satin, 7 In. 185.00
Loop & Column pattern is listed here as Pulled Loop.
Looped Petals pattern is listed here as Scales.
Lotus & Grape, Bowl, Ruffled Edge, Green 85.00
Lotus & Grape, Plate, Amethyst, 9 In. 1150.00
Lotus & Grape, Plate, Green, 9 In. 500.00
Lotus Land, Bonbon, Amethyst 400.00
Lovely, Bowl, Footed, Green 1100.00
Lucille, Water Set, Blue, 7 Piece 300.00
Luster Rose, Bowl, Ruffled Edge, Footed, Smoke, 8 In. 35.00
Luster Rose, Fernery, Footed, Blue 65.00
Luster Rose, Tumbler, Amethyst 105.00
Luster Rose, Tumbler, Powder Blue 30.00
Luster Rose, Water Set, Amethyst, 5 Piece 400.00
Magnolia & Poinsettia pattern is listed here as Water Lily.
Magnolia Drape, Pitcher, Enameled, Marigold 80.00
Maine Coast pattern is listed here as Seacoast.
Many Fruits, Punch Set, Marigold, 8 Piece 350.00
Many Stars, Bowl, Crimped & Ruffled Edge, Green, Radium Iridescence 600.00
Many Stars, Bowl, Ruffled Edge, Amethyst, Radium Iridescence 450.00
Marilyn, Pitcher, Amethyst 375.00
Marilyn, Tumbler, Amethyst 75.00
Mary Ann, Vase, Amethyst 20.00
Maryland pattern is listed here as Rustic.
Melinda pattern is listed here as Wishbone.
Melon & Fan pattern is listed here as Diamond & Rib.
Memphis, Punch Set, Marigold, 8 Piece 800.00
Mikado, Compote, Marigold 155.00
Mikado, Compote, Ruffled Edge, Blue 475.00
Milady, Tumbler, Blue 90.00
Miniature Morning Glory, Vase, Amethyst, 5 In. 325.00
Miniature Morning Glory, Vase, Amethyst, 7 In. 105.00
Miniature Morning Glory, Vase, Flared Rim, Green, 4 1/4 In. 140.00
Miniature Morning Glory, Vase, Marigold, 5 In. 30.00
Miniature Morning Glory, Vase, Marigold, 7 In. . . . . 10.00 to 40.00
Miniature Morning Glory, Vase, Marigold, 8 1/2 In. 10.00
Miniature Morning Glory, Vase, Smoke, 7 1/2 In. 40.00
Mirrored Lotus, Rose Bowl, Marigold 450.00
Moonprint, Bowl, Ruffled Edge, Marigold . . . . 25.00 to 45.00
Moonprint, Compote, Footed, Marigold 45.00
Morning Glory, Vase, Amethyst, 7 In. 180.00
Morning Glory, Vase, Funeral, Amethyst, 13 In. 625.00

Morning Glory, Vase, Funeral, Amethyst, 16 In. 300.00
Morning Glory, Vase, Jack-In-The-Pulpit, Marigold, 9 In. 35.00
Morning Glory, Vase, Smoke, 6 1/2 In. 400.00
Multi Fruit & Flowers pattern is listed here as Many Fruits.
Mums & Greek Key pattern is listed here as Embroidered Mums.
Nautilus, Vase, Amethyst, 6 1/4 In. 400.00
Nesting Swan, Bowl, Ruffled Edge, Amethyst, Satin 145.00
Nesting Swan, Bowl, Ruffled Edge, Green, Satin 190.00
Nesting Swan, Bowl, Ruffled Edge, Marigold, Satin 65.00
Nine Sixteen, Vase, Blue, 16 In. 75.00
Nippon, Bowl, Pie Crust Edge, Ribbed Back, Amethyst 200.00
Nippon, Bowl, Pie Crust Edge, Ribbed Back, Ice Blue 235.00
Oak Leaf & Acorn pattern is listed here as Acorn.
Octagon, Butter, Cover, Amethyst 105.00
Octagon, Compote, Aqua 130.00
Octet, Bowl, Ruffled Edge, Dome Foot, Amethyst 50.00
Octet, Bowl, Ruffled Edge, Dome Foot, Green 115.00
Ohio Star, Pitcher, Tankard, White 105.00
Old Fashion Flag pattern is listed here as Iris.
Open Rose, Bowl, Amber, 9 In. .... 25.00 to 45.00
Open Rose, Plate, Amber, 9 In. 85.00
Open Rose, Plate, Amber, 10 In. 65.00
Open Rose, Plate, Amethyst, 9 In. 1700.00
Optic & Button, Pitcher, Marigold 145.00
Orange Peel, Sherbet, Peach Opalescent, Souvenir, Dover & Foxcroft, Maine 105.00
Orange Tree, Bowl, Ice Cream, Blue 200.00
Orange Tree, Bowl, Ice Cream, Marigold .... 25.00 to 35.00
Orange Tree, Bowl, Ruffled Edge, Green 155.00
Orange Tree, Bowl, Ruffled Edge, White 75.00
Orange Tree, Creamer, Blue 55.00
Orange Tree, Goblet, Marigold 10.00
Orange Tree, Hatpin Holder, Blue .... 100.00 to 185.00
Orange Tree, Hatpin Holder, Green 105.00
Orange Tree, Loving Cup, Blue 525.00
Orange Tree, Loving Cup, Marigold .... 145.00 to 275.00
Orange Tree, Mug, Amethyst 20.00
Orange Tree, Mug, Aqua, Marigold Iridescence 145.00
Orange Tree, Mug, Blue .... 25.00 to 40.00
Orange Tree, Mug, Cherry Red 450.00
Orange Tree, Mug, Lavender 25.00
Orange Tree, Mug, Marigold 8.00
Orange Tree, Pitcher, Footed, Blue 195.00
Orange Tree, Plate, Amethyst, 9 In. 1100.00
Orange Tree, Plate, Blue, 9 In. .... 450.00 to 475.00
Orange Tree, Plate, Green, 9 In. 1200.00
Orange Tree, Plate, Marigold, 9 In. .... 150.00 to 215.00
Orange Tree, Plate, White, 9 In. .... 105.00 to 200.00
Orange Tree, Powder Jar, Amethyst .... 225.00 to 375.00
Orange Tree, Powder Jar, Blue .... 100.00 to 120.00
Orange Tree, Powder Jar, Marigold 50.00
Orange Tree, Punch Set, Blue, 9 Piece 375.00
Orange Tree, Punch Set, Marigold, 6 Piece 175.00
Orange Tree, Sherbet, Ruffled Edge, Marigold, Whimsy 75.00
Orange Tree, Tumbler, Footed, Blue 75.00
Orange Tree, Water Set, Blue, 8 1/2 In., 5 Piece 294.00
Orange Tree & Cable pattern is listed here as Orange Tree Orchard.
Orange Tree Orchard, Water Set, Blue, 6 Piece 750.00
Oriental Poppy, Pitcher, Tankard, Marigold 175.00
Oriental Poppy, Water Set, Tankard, Amethyst, 7 Piece 600.00
Palm Beach, Banana Boat, Amethyst .... 80.00 to 145.00
Palm Beach, Pitcher, Honey Amber 325.00

Palm Beach, Vase, Amethyst, Pinched Top, Whimsy, 7 In. 650.00
Paneled Bachelor Buttons pattern is listed here as Milady.
Paneled Dandelion, Pitcher, Tankard, Amethyst 70.00
Paneled Dandelion, Tumbler, Amethyst 45.00
Paneled Dandelion, Tumbler, Blue 15.00
Paneled Dandelion, Water Set, Blue, 7 Piece 500.00
Pansy, Bowl, Ruffled Edge, Amethyst 205.00
Pansy, Bowl, Ruffled Edge, Lavender 85.00
Pansy, Bowl, Ruffled Edge, Marigold 35.00
Panther, Berry Bowl, Master, Marigold 75.00
Panther, Bowl, Centerpiece, Footed, Marigold 400.00
Panther, Sauce, Footed, Blue 50.00
Panther, Sauce, Footed, Marigold 10.00
Panther, Sauce, Ruffled Edge, Footed, Marigold ....25.00 to 30.00
Parlor Panels, Vase, Squat, Marigold, 7 In. 115.00
Pastel Swan, Salt, Celeste Blue ....8.00 to 10.00
Pastel Swan, Salt, Ice Green 15.00
Pastel Swan, Salt, Marigold 95.00
Pastel Swan, Salt, Peach Opalescent 55.00
Pastel Swan, Salt, Souvenir, Devils Lake, N.D., Amethyst 95.00
Peach, Berry Bowl, White, Gold Enameled 65.00
Peach, Spooner, White 65.00
Peach, Sugar, Cover, White 85.00
Peach, Water Set, Blue, 5 Piece 700.00
Peacock, Bowl, Master Berry, Amethyst, Radium Iridescence 425.00
Peacock, Sauce, Ruffled Edge, Amethyst, Radium Iridescence 75.00
Peacock & Dahlia, Bowl, Ice Cream, Lime Green, Marigold Iridescence, 7 In. 55.00
Peacock & Grape, Bowl, Ice Cream, Footed, Marigold 20.00
Peacock & Grape, Bowl, Ruffled Edge, Amethyst 50.00
Peacock & Grape, Bowl, Ruffled Edge, Lime Green 60.00
Peacock & Grape, Plate, Footed, Marigold, 9 In. ....250.00 to 350.00
Peacock & Grape, Plate, Marigold, 9 In. ....700.00 to 1750.00
Peacock & Urn, Bowl, Ice Cream, Amethyst ....400.00 to 500.00
Peacock & Urn, Bowl, Ice Cream, Marigold 300.00
Peacock & Urn, Bowl, Mystery, Crimped & Ruffled Edge, Green, Satin 130.00
Peacock & Urn, Compote, Aqua ....85.00 to 95.00
Peacock & Urn, Compote, Blue 85.00
Peacock & Urn, Compote, Marigold ....30.00 to 46.00
Peacock & Urn, Compote, Ruffled Edge, Lime Green, Marigold Iridescence 65.00
Peacock & Urn, Compote, Ruffled Edge, White 45.00
Peacock & Urn, Plate, Marigold, 6 In. 500.00
Peacock & Urn, Plate, White, 9 In. 220.00
Peacock & Urn, Sauce, Amethyst 35.00
Peacock & Urn, Sauce, Ice Cream, Amethyst ....65.00 to 85.00
Peacock & Urn, Sauce, Ice Cream, Blue ....95.00 to 135.00
Peacock & Urn, Sauce, Ice Cream, Ice Blue 150.00
Peacock & Urn, Sauce, Ice Cream, Marigold ....55.00 to 65.00
Peacock At The Fountain, Berry Bowl, Master, Marigold 95.00
Peacock At The Fountain, Bowl, Fruit, Ruffled Edge, Amethyst 425.00
Peacock At The Fountain, Bowl, Marigold 135.00
Peacock At The Fountain, Compote, Ruffled Edge, Blue 300.00
Peacock At The Fountain, Creamer, Green 400.00
Peacock At The Fountain, Pitcher, White 125.00
Peacock At The Fountain, Punch Set, White, 8 Piece 1600.00
Peacock At The Fountain, Tumbler, Amethyst 13.00
Peacock At The Fountain, Tumbler, Electric Blue 45.00
Peacock At The Fountain, Tumbler, Ice Blue 65.00
Peacock At The Fountain, Water Set, Marigold, 6 Piece 215.00
Peacock Eye & Grape pattern is listed here as Vineyard.
Peacock On Fence pattern is listed here as Peacocks.
Peacock Tail, Berry Set, Amethyst, 7 Piece 145.00

Peacock Tail, Bowl, Crimped & Ruffled Edge, Green 50.00
Peacock Tail, Compote, Ruffled Edge, Blue 40.00
Peacock Tail, Compote, Ruffled Edge, Green 50.00
Peacock Tail, Compote, Ruffled Edge, Marigold 15.00
Peacock Tail, Plate, Marigold, 6 In. 195.00
Peacocks, Bowl, Ribbed Back, Pie Crust Edge, Amethyst ....400.00 to 525.00
Peacocks, Bowl, Ribbed Back, Pie Crust Edge, Blue ....350.00 to 725.00
Peacocks, Bowl, Ribbed Back, Pie Crust Edge, Marigold ....165.00 to 200.00
Peacocks, Bowl, Ribbed Back, Ruffled Edge, Aqua Opalescent, Butterscotch Iridescence 1000.00
Peacocks, Bowl, Ribbed Back, Ruffled Edge, Green ....475.00 to 500.00
Peacocks, Bowl, Ruffled Edge, Aqua Opalescent, 8 3/4 In. 880.00
Peacocks, Bowl, Stippled, Pie Crust Edge, Ribbed Back, Blue 450.00
Peacocks, Plate, Ice Green, 9 In. 475.00
Peacocks, Plate, Ribbed Back, Green, 9 In. 900.00
Peacocks, Plate, Ribbed Back, Ice Green, 9 In. ....250.00 to 355.00
Peacocks, Plate, Ribbed Back, Marigold, 9 In. 275.00
Peacocks, Plate, Stippled, Ribbed Back, Blue, 9 In. ....250.00 to 700.00
Peacocks, Plate, White, 9 In. ....109.00 to 150.00
Peacocks, Stippled, Bowl, Ribbed Back, Pie Crust Edge, Marigold ....135.00 to 225.00
Peacocks, Stippled, Plate, Ribbed Back, Marigold, 9 In. 600.00
Persian Garden, Bowl, Fruit, Base, Amethyst 450.00
Persian Garden, Bowl, Ice Cream, White, 11 In. 130.00
Persian Garden, Plate, Amethyst, 6 In. 210.00
Persian Garden, Plate, Marigold, 6 In. ....35.00 to 40.00
Persian Medallion, Berry Set, Green, 7 Piece 175.00
Persian Medallion, Bonbon, Blue 50.00
Persian Medallion, Bonbon, Marigold 20.00
Persian Medallion, Bowl, Crimped & Ruffled Edge, Green, 10 In. ....135.00 to 140.00
Persian Medallion, Bowl, Ruffled Edge, Amethyst, 10 In. 90.00
Persian Medallion, Chop Plate, Blue 275.00
Persian Medallion, Compote, Ruffled Edge, Amethyst, Small ....65.00 to 135.00
Persian Medallion, Hair Receiver, Blue 170.00
Persian Medallion, Hair Receiver, Marigold 135.00
Persian Medallion, Plate, Amethyst, 6 In. 175.00
Persian Medallion, Plate, Blue, 9 In. 600.00
Persian Medallion, Plate, Marigold, 6 In. ....35.00 to 40.00
Persian Medallion, Plate, Marigold, 9 In. ....275.00 to 400.00
Persian Medallion, Rose Bowl, Blue 110.00
Petal & Fan, Plate, Crimped Edge, Amethyst, 6 In. ....265.00 to 425.00
Petal & Fan, Plate, Crimped Edge, Peach Opalescent, 6 In. 155.00
Petal & Fan, Sauce, Crimped Edge, Amethyst 75.00
Petal & Fan, Sauce, Ruffled Edge, Peach Opalescent 35.00
Peter Rabbit, Bowl, Ruffled Edge, Green 1100.00
Phlox, Pitcher, Amethyst 300.00
Pillow & Sunburst, Bowl, Ruffled Edge, Amethyst 15.00
Pinched Swirl, Vase, Peach Opalescent, 6 In. 30.00
Pine Cone, Bowl, Ice Cream, Blue, 7 In. ....20.00 to 35.00
Pine Cone, Bowl, Ice Cream, Green, 6 1/2 In. 195.00
Pine Cone, Plate, Blue, 7 In. 165.00
Pine Cone, Plate, Dark Amber, 7 In. 400.00
Pine Cone, Plate, Green, 6 In. 45.00
Pine Cone Wreath pattern is listed here as Pine Cone.
Pineapple, Creamer, Amethyst 45.00
Plaid, Bowl, Ice Cream, Blue, 6 1/2 In. ....50.00 to 80.00
Plaid, Bowl, Ice Cream, Marigold 100.00
Plain Jane, Basket, Amethyst 145.00
Plain Jane, Basket, Ice Green 80.00
Plain Jane, Basket, Marigold Milk Glass 125.00
Plain Jane, Basket, White 10.00
Poinsettia, Pitcher, Milk, Marigold ....35.00 to 65.00
Poinsettia & Lattice, Bowl, 3-Footed, Ice Blue 1232.00

Poinsettia & Lattice, Bowl, Footed, Blue 672.00
Poinsettia & Lattice, Bowl, Ruffled Edge, Footed, Blue 600.00
Pond Lily, Bonbon, Marigold 18.00
Pond Lily, Bonbon, White 55.00
Pony, Bowl, Ruffled Edge, Amethyst 85.00
Pony Rosette pattern is listed here as Pony.
Poppy, Compote, Green 250.00
Poppy, Dish, Pickle, Aqua 1800.00
Poppy, Dish, Pickle, Blue 225.00
Poppy, Dish, Pickle, Green 135.00
Poppy, Dish, Pickle, Ice Blue 125.00
Poppy, Dish, Pickle, Marigold 75.00
Poppy Scroll pattern is listed here as Poppy.
Poppy Show, Bowl, Ruffled Edge, Ice Green 1300.00
Poppy Show, Plate, Blue, 9 In. 1250.00
Poppy Show, Plate, Marigold, 9 In. 1050.00
Poppy Show, Plate, White, 9 In. .... 350.00 to 375.00
Poppy Show, Vase, Marigold 525.00
Princess Lace pattern is listed here as Octagon.
Propeller, Compote, Ruffled Edge, Green 55.00
Propeller, Vase, Footed, Marigold, 7 1/2 In. 80.00
Pulled Loop, Vase, Blue, 10 1/2 In. 75.00
Puzzle, Bonbon, Marigold 40.00
Puzzle, Bonbon, Peach Opalescent 15.00
Puzzle, Compote, Handles, Peach Opalescent, 7 1/2 In. 70.00
Question Marks, Compote, Crimped Edge, Amethyst 155.00
Question Marks, Compote, Crimped Edge, Peach Opalescent .... 40.00 to 85.00
Question Marks, Plate, Footed, Marigold 75.00
Question Marks, Plate, Footed, White 100.00
Question Marks, Plate, White, Whimsy 210.00
Raindrops, Bowl, Ruffled Edge, Dome Foot, Amethyst 210.00
Raspberry, Compote, Ruffled Edge, Marigold, Small 20.00
Raspberry, Gravy Boat, Amethyst 65.00
Raspberry, Pitcher, Green 325.00
Raspberry, Pitcher, Milk, Amethyst 180.00
Raspberry, Pitcher, Milk, Marigold .... 125.00 to 195.00
Raspberry, Pitcher, White, Satin 1100.00
Raspberry, Tumbler, Amethyst 10.00
Ribbon Tie, Bowl, Ruffled Edge, Marigold 15.00
Ripple, Vase, Blue Green, 10 In. 125.00
Rising Sun, Water Set, Marigold, 6 Piece .... 145.00 to 300.00
Rose & Ruffles pattern is listed here as Open Rose.
Rose Bouquet, Bonbon, White, Handles 175.00
Rose Garden, Vase, Marigold, 9 1/2 In. 400.00
Rose Garden, Vase, Rectangular, Blue, 5 In. 175.00
Rose Garden, Vase, Rectangular, Blue, 7 1/2 In. 600.00
Rose Shell, Bowl, Ice Green 1000.00
Rose Show, Bowl, Ruffled Edge, Aqua Opalescent 750.00
Rose Show, Bowl, Ruffled Edge, Blue Opalescent 205.00
Rose Show, Bowl, Ruffled Edge, Green 500.00
Rose Show, Bowl, Ruffled Edge, Ice Blue 375.00
Rose Show, Bowl, Ruffled Edge, Marigold 125.00
Rose Show, Bowl, Ruffled Edge, White 260.00
Rose Show, Plate, Amethyst, 9 In. 550.00
Rose Show, Plate, Blue, 9 In. 1350.00
Rose Show, Plate, Marigold, 9 In. .... 700.00 to 1050.00
Rose Show, Plate, White, 9 In. .... 125.00 to 175.00
Rose Spray, Compote, Green Ice 45.00
Rose Tree, Bowl, Ruffled Edge, Blue 900.00
Roses & Loops pattern is listed here as Double Stem Rose.
Rosette, Bowl, Ruffled Edge, Amethyst 165.00

Rosette & Prisms pattern is listed here as Rosette.
Round-Up, Bowl, Ruffled Edge, Blue 125.00
Round-Up, Bowl, Ruffled Edge, Peach Opalescent 40.00
Round-Up, Plate, Blue, 9 In. . . . . . 200.00 to 350.00
Rustic, Vase, Amethyst, 15 In. 165.00
Rustic, Vase, Amethyst, 17 In. 155.00
Rustic, Vase, Crimped Edge, Marigold, 8 In. 30.00
Rustic, Vase, Marigold, 16 In. 40.00
Rustic, Vase, Marigold, 18 In. 675.00
Sailboat & Windmill pattern is listed here as Sailboats.
Sailboats, Sauce, Red 300.00
Sailboats, Sauce, Ruffled Edge, Lime Green, Marigold Iridescence 35.00
Sailboats, Sauce, Ruffled Edge, Marigold 10.00
Sailboats, Sauce, Ruffled Edge, Powder Blue, Marigold Iridescence 65.00
Sailboats, Sauce, Ruffled Edge, Powder Blue, Silvery 35.00
Scales, Bowl, Ruffled Edge, Blue Opalescent 45.00
Scales, Bowl, Ruffled Edge, Marigold Milk Glass 35.00
Scales, Compote, Ruffled Edge, Green 35.00
Scales & Greek Key, Bowl, Ruffled Edge, Dome Foot, Green, Radium Iridescence 20.00
Scroll Embossed, Bowl, Deep, Amethyst 45.00
Scroll Embossed, Compote, Amethyst, Miniature 125.00
Scroll Embossed, Plate, Amethyst, 9 In. . . . . . 265.00 to 300.00
Scroll Embossed, Plate, Green, 9 In. . . . . . 30.00 to 65.00
Scroll Embossed, Sauce, Ruffled Edge, File Back, Smoke 55.00
Scroll Embossed, Sauce, Ruffled Edge, Marigold 8.00
Scroll-Cable pattern is listed here as Estate.
Sea Lanes pattern is listed here as Little Fishes.
Seacoast, Pin Tray, Amethyst 950.00
Seacoast, Pin Tray, Marigold 1500.00
Seaweed, Bowl, Crimped & Ruffled Edge, Amethyst, Satin 275.00
Shasta Daisy, Pitcher, Enameled, Ice Green 300.00
Shasta Daisy, Tumbler, Enameled, Ice Green 95.00
Shell & Sand, Bowl, Marigold 35.00
Shell & Sand, Bowl, Ruffled Edge, Amethyst 235.00
Shell & Sand, Plate, Green 65.00
Shell & Wild Rose pattern is listed here as Wild Rose.
Shriner's, Champagne, New Orleans, 1910 . . . . . 35.00
Shriner's, Champagne, Rochester, 1911 . . . . . 35.00
Singing Birds, Berry Bowl, Master, Marigold 55.00
Singing Birds, Berry Set, Amethyst, 5 Piece 75.00
Singing Birds, Mug, Amethyst . . . . . 40.00 to 85.00
Singing Birds, Mug, Green 195.00
Singing Birds, Mug, Stippled, Marigold 65.00
Singing Birds, Pitcher, Amethyst 300.00
Singing Birds, Pitcher, Marigold 250.00
Singing Birds, Tumbler, Marigold 35.00
Singing Birds, Water Set, Green, 7 Piece 600.00
Single Flower, Bowl, Ruffled Edge, Enameled, Peach Opalescent 70.00
Six Petals, Bowl, Crimped & Ruffled Edge, Peach Opalescent 70.00
Ski Star, Banana Boat, Crimped Edge, Footed, Peach Opalescent 400.00
Ski Star, Basket, Dome Foot, Handle, Peach Opalescent 75.00
Ski Star, Bowl, Footed, Amethyst 168.00
Ski Star, Bowl, Ruffled Edge, Peach Opalescent 65.00
Ski Star, Plate, Handgrip, Footed, Peach Opalescent 175.00
Smooth Panels, Vase, Squat, Marigold, 7 In. 15.00
Smooth Rays, Bowl, Ruffled Edge, Marigold Milk Glass 20.00
Snow Fancy, Sauce, Marigold, 4 In. 5.00
Soldiers & Sailors, Illinois, Plate, Blue, 7 In. 2400.00
Soldiers & Sailors, Illinois, Plate, Marigold, 7 In. 2000.00
Soutache, Bowl, Crimped & Ruffled Edge, Dome Foot, Peach Opalescent 45.00
Spirilex, Vase, Peach Opalescent, 10 In. 85.00

Springtime, Berry Set, Amethyst, 7 Piece 275.00
Springtime, Berry Set, Marigold, 6 Piece 150.00
Springtime, Butter, Cover, Green 325.00
Square Diamond, Vase, Blue, Rectangular, 8 3/4 In. 275.00
Stag & Holly, Bowl, Ice Cream, Amber 155.00
Stag & Holly, Bowl, Ruffled Edge, Ball-Footed, Marigold .... 100.00 to 225.00
Stag & Holly, Bowl, Ruffled Edge, Spatula Foot, Blue .... 55.00 to 150.00
Stag & Holly, Bowl, Ruffled Edge, Spatula Foot, Marigold .... 55.00 to 75.00
Stag & Holly, Rose Bowl, Marigold 140.00
Star, Bowl, Marigold, 10 In. 10.00
Star, Chop Plate, Marigold, 15 In. 35.00
Star & Fan, Cordial Set, Marigold, Bottle, Underplate, 6 Cordials 165.00
Star & File, Rose Bowl, Marigold 25.00
Star Medallion, Pitcher, Milk, Marigold 25.00
Star Of David, Bowl, Ruffled Edge, Amethyst 175.00
Star Of David & Bows, Bowl, Dome Foot, Ruffled Edge, Amethyst .... 50.00 to 105.00
Star Of David & Bows, Bowl, Dome Foot, Ruffled Edge, Green 40.00
Star Of David Medallion pattern is listed here as Star of David & Bows.
Starfish, Compote, Ruffled Edge, Peach Opalescent 60.00
Starflower, Pitcher, Blue 400.00
Stippled Clematis pattern is listed here as Little Stars.
Stippled Diamond & Flower pattern is listed here as Little Flowers.
Stippled Leaf pattern is listed here as Leaf Tiers.
Stippled Leaf & Beads pattern is listed here as Leaf & Beads.
Stippled Posy & Pods pattern is listed here as Four Flowers.
Stippled Rays, Bowl, Ruffled Edge, Marigold, 7 In. 95.00
Stippled Rays, Bowl, Ruffled Edge, Reverse Amberina, 7 In. .... 95.00 to 175.00
Stippled Rays, Compote, Ruffled Edge, Ice Green 65.00
Stippled Rays, Plate, Marigold, 6 In. .... 10.00 to 45.00
Stippled Rays, Sauce, Amethyst 20.00
Stippled Rays, Sauce, Ruffled Edge, Amberina 35.00
Stippled Rays, Sugar, Lime Green 10.00
Stippled Strawberry, Bowl, Ruffled Edge, Ribbed Back, Amethyst 195.00
Stippled Strawberry, Plate, Basketweave Back, Green, 9 In. 1100.00
Stork & Rushes, Pitcher, Amethyst 300.00
Stork & Rushes, Punch Set, Marigold, 8 Piece 300.00
Stork & Rushes, Tumbler, Blue 40.00
Stork & Rushes, Water Set, Blue, 7 Piece 685.00
Strawberry, Bonbon, Amber 65.00
Strawberry, Bonbon, Blue 125.00
Strawberry, Bonbon, Lime Green 225.00
Strawberry, Bowl, Basketweave Back, Ruffled Edge, Amethyst 70.00
Strawberry, Bowl, Basketweave Back, Ruffled Edge, Marigold 65.00
Strawberry, Bowl, Pie Crust Edge, Amethyst 105.00
Strawberry, Bowl, Pie Crust Edge, Basketweave Back, Marigold 185.00
Strawberry, Bowl, Ruffled Edge, Green 75.00
Strawberry, Compote, Ruffled Edge, Marigold, Radium Iridescence 235.00
Strawberry, Plate, Amethyst, 9 In. 120.00
Strawberry, Plate, Basketweave Back, Green, 9 In. 105.00
Strawberry, Plate, Basketweave Back, Marigold, 9 In. 85.00
Strawberry Scroll, Pitcher, Marigold 2100.00
Strawberry Scroll, Tumbler, Marigold 80.00
Strawberry Wreath, Bowl, Crimped Edge, Amethyst, 8 In. 165.00
Strawberry Wreath, Bowl, Square, Amethyst, 9 In. 410.00
Stream Of Hearts, Compote, Ruffled Edge, Marigold .... 45.00 to 85.00
Sunflower pattern is listed here as Dandelion.
Sunflower, Bowl, Ruffled Edge, Spatula Foot, Marigold 35.00
Sunflower & Wheat pattern is listed here as Field Flower.
Target, Vase, Amethyst, 8 1/2 In. 50.00
Target, Vase, Blue, 11 1/2 In. 105.00
Target, Vase, Marigold, 12 In. 25.00

Tartan, Bowl, Cover, Marigold 10.00
Teardrops pattern is listed here as Raindrops.
Ten Mums, Bowl, Crimped & Ruffled Edge, Blue 165.00
Thin Rib, Vase, Amethyst, 10 In. .... 40.00 to 65.00
Thin Rib, Vase, Green, 9 1/2 In. 125.00
Thin Rib, Vase, Green, 12 In. .... 170.00 to 195.00
Thin Rib, Vase, Jack-In-Pulpit, Green, 8 In. 150.00
Thin Rib & Drape, Vase, Marigold, 5 In. 30.00
Thistle, Banana Boat, Blue 205.00
Thistle, Bowl, Crimped & Ruffled Edge, Amethyst 100.00
Thistle, Bowl, Crimped & Ruffled Edge, Green 115.00
Three Fruits, Bowl, Basketweave Back, Pie Crust Edge, Amethyst 85.00
Three Fruits, Bowl, Basketweave Back, Ruffled Edge, Marigold 35.00
Three Fruits, Bowl, Ruffled Edge, Stippled, Footed, Amethyst 195.00
Three Fruits, Bowl, Ruffled Edge, Stippled, Footed, Lime Green Opalescent 1100.00
Three Fruits, Bowl, Stippled, Ruffled Edge, Ribbed Back, Marigold 50.00
Three Fruits, Bowl, Stippled, Ruffled Edge, Ribbed Back, White .... 200.00 to 250.00
Three Fruits, Plate, Amethyst, 9 In. .... 60.00 to 105.00
Three Fruits, Plate, Basketweave Back, Amethyst, 9 In. .... 115.00 to 175.00
Three Fruits, Plate, Basketweave Back, Marigold, 9 In. 155.00
Three Fruits, Plate, Green, 9 In. .... 100.00 to 200.00
Three Fruits, Plate, Stippled, Ribbed Back, Amethyst, 9 In. 185.00
Three Fruits, Plate, Stippled, Ribbed Back, Blue, 9 In. .... 375.00 to 800.00
Three Fruits, Plate, Stippled, Ribbed Back, Marigold, 9 In. .... 105.00 to 165.00
Thumbprint & Oval, Vase, Marigold 375.00
Tiger Lily, Pitcher, Blue, Imperial 175.00
Tiger Lily, Pitcher, Blue, Riihimaki 425.00
Tiger Lily, Pitcher, Marigold, Imperial .... 35.00 to 105.00
Tiger Lily, Tumbler, Amethyst, Imperial 85.00
Tiger Lily, Tumbler, Blue, Imperial 135.00
Tiger Lily, Tumbler, Marigold, Imperial .... 25.00 to 35.00
Tiger Lily, Water Set, Blue, Imperial, 7 Piece 325.00
Toronado, Vase, Amethyst, Small 475.00
Town Pump, Amethyst 625.00
Tree Trunk, Vase, Amethyst 225.00
Tree Trunk, Vase, Blue, 10 In. 220.00
Tree Trunk, Vase, Funeral, Elephant Foot, Amethyst, 13 In. 1100.00
Tree Trunk, Vase, Green, 11 In. 115.00
Tree Trunk, Vase, Green, 13 In. 425.00
Tree Trunk, Vase, Plunger Base, Green, 13 In. 1600.00
Tree Trunk, Vase, Plunger Base, Marigold, 14 In. 600.00
Tree Trunk, Vase, Sapphire, 9 1/2 In. 600.00
Tree Trunk, Vase, Squat, Amethyst, 6 In. 30.00
Tree Trunk, Vase, Squat, Green, 7 1/2 In. 55.00
Trout & Fly, Bowl, Crimped & Ruffled Edge, Amethyst 600.00
Trout & Fly, Bowl, Crimped & Ruffled Edge, Marigold, Radium Iridescence 325.00
Trout & Fly, Bowl, Ice Cream, Amethyst, Satin 500.00
Trout & Fly, Bowl, Ruffled Edge, Green, Satin 825.00
Twins, Berry Bowl, Ruffled Edge, Smoke 20.00
Two Flowers, Bowl, Deep, Blue 75.00
Two Flowers, Bowl, Ruffled Edge, Footed, Marigold 50.00
Two Flowers, Sauce, Ruffled Edge, Footed, Lime Green 25.00
Two Fruits, Bonbon, Sections, Blue 70.00
Two Fruits, Bonbon, Sections, Marigold 25.00
Venetian, Bowl, Green, 10 1/2 In. 950.00
Vineyard, Pitcher, Peach Opalescent 425.00
Vining Leaf, Vase, Footed, Marigold, 6 In. 135.00
Vining Leaf, Vase, Footed, Marigold, 8 1/2 In. 105.00
Vintage, Bowl, Nut, Amethyst 35.00
Vintage, Bowl, Ruffled Edge, Cherry Red, Silver Iridescence, 9 In. 700.00
Vintage, Bowl, Ruffled Edge, Green, 4 1/2 In. 35.00

Vintage, Bowl, Ruffled Edge, Red, 9 In. 325.00
Vintage, Epergne, Amethyst 210.00
Vintage, Plate, Amethyst, 7 In. 85.00
Vintage, Plate, Blue, 7 In. 155.00
Vintage, Plate, Green, 6 In. 275.00
Vintage, Plate, Marigold, 6 In. 155.00
Vintage, Powder Jar, Marigold 35.00
Vintage, Rose Bowl, Amethyst .... 30.00 to 65.00
Vintage, Rose Bowl, White .... 35.00 to 55.00
Water Lily, Ruffled Edge, Footed, Marigold 10.00
Water Lily, Sauce, Footed, Green 70.00
Water Lily, Sauce, Ruffled Edge, Footed, Aqua 145.00
Water Lily, Sauce, Ruffled Edge, Footed, Blue, Silver Iridescence 70.00
Water Lily, Sauce, Ruffled Edge, Footed, Lime Green, Marigold Iridescence .... 25.00 to 180.00
Water Lily, Toothpick, Marigold 15.00
Water Lily & Cattails, Pitcher, Marigold 450.00
Water Lily & Cattails, Tumbler, Marigold 50.00
Western Thistle, Water Set, Blue, 7 Piece 350.00
Whirling Leaves, Bowl, Green, 10 In. 150.00
Whirling Leaves, Bowl, Tricornered, Crimped Edge, Green, Radium Iridescence 450.00
White Oak, Tumbler, Marigold 50.00
Wild Grapes pattern is listed here as Grape Leaves.
Wild Rose, Bowl, Footed, Blue, 9 In. 95.00
Wild Rose, Bowl, Footed, Marigold, 9 In. 85.00
Wild Strawberry, Bowl, Ruffled Edge, Amethyst, 10 In. 95.00
Wild Strawberry, Bowl, Ruffled Edge, Ice Blue, 10 In. 650.00
Wild Strawberry, Bowl, Ruffled Edge, Lime Green, 10 In. 1050.00
Wild Strawberry, Plate, Handgrip, Green, 8 In. 125.00
Windflower, Bowl, Ruffled Edge, Amethyst 95.00
Windflower, Nappy, Handle, Amethyst 40.00
Windflower, Nappy, Handle, Ice Green 115.00
Windflower, Nappy, Handle, Marigold 8.00
Windflower, Plate, Marigold, 9 In. 65.00
Windmill, Pitcher, Milk, Marigold 40.00
Windmill, Tumbler, Amethyst 75.00
Windmill, Water Set, Marigold, 7 Piece 75.00
Windmill Medallion pattern is listed here as Windmill.
Wine & Roses, Goblet, Blue 50.00
Wine & Roses, Pitcher, Cider, Marigold 175.00
Wishbone, Bowl, Pie Crust Edge, Amethyst, 10 In. 150.00
Wishbone, Bowl, Ruffled Edge, Footed, Amethyst .... 90.00 to 110.00
Wishbone, Bowl, Ruffled Edge, Footed, Ice Green 850.00
Wishbone, Bowl, Ruffled Edge, Green, 10 In. 175.00
Wishbone, Epergne, Green 600.00
Wishbone, Plate, Footed, Amethyst, 9 In. 260.00
Wishbone, Tumbler, Marigold 115.00
Wishbone & Spades, Plate, Amethyst, 6 In. .... 135.00 to 275.00
Wishbone & Spades, Plate, Souvenir, White Creek, Wis., Peach Opalescent, 6 In. 305.00
Wishbone & Spades, Sauce, Ruffled Edge, Peach Opalescent 45.00
Woodlands, Vase, Black River Falls, Wis., Marigold, 5 In. 205.00
Wreath Of Roses, Bonbon, Green 50.00
Wreath Of Roses, Bonbon, Marigold 20.00
Wreath Of Roses, Compote, Ruffled Edge, Blue 35.00
Wreath Of Roses, Compote, Ruffled Edge, Green 40.00
Wreath Of Roses, Compote, Ruffled Edge, Marigold 10.00
Wreath Of Roses, Punch Set, Vintage Interior, Green, 5 Piece 450.00
Wreath Of Roses, Punch Set, Vintage Interior, Marigold, 8 Piece 400.00
Wreath Of Roses, Rose Bowl, Marigold 10.00
Wreathed Cherry, Bowl, Oval, Amethyst, 10 In. .... 55.00 to 80.00
Wreathed Cherry, Pitcher, Marigold 350.00
Wreathed Cherry, Sauce, Oval, White, 5 In. 25.00

Wreathed Cherry, Table Set, Marigold, 4 Piece 225.00
Wreathed Cherry, Tumbler, Marigold 30.00
Zig Zag, Bowl, Crimped & Ruffled Edge, Amethyst, Radium Iridescence 245.00
Zipper Loop, Lamp, Finger, Marigold, 5 In. 1500.00
Zipper Loop, Lamp, Marigold, 9 In. 475.00
Zipper Stitch, Cordial Set, Marigold, 8 Piece 225.00

CAROUSEL or merry-go-round figures were first carved in the United States in 1867 by Gustav Dentzel. Collectors discovered the charm of the hand-carved figures in the 1970s, and they were soon classed as folk art. Most desirable are the figures other than horses, such as pigs, camels, lions, or dogs. A jumper is a figure that was made to move up and down on a pole; a stander was placed in a stationary position.

Horse, Carved, Painted, Left Front Leg Bent Up, Frederick Heyn Attribution, 44 x 56 In. 5750.00
Horse, Jumper, Jewels, Spiral Brass Stand, C.W. Parker, Leavenworth, c.1917, 59 In. 2530.00
Horse, Jumper, Lowered Head, Wood, Cropped Tail, Mane, 52 In. 1293.00
Horse, Jumper, Wood, Carved, Painted, Pine Frame, Early 20th Century, 47 x 53 In. 940.00
Horse, Prancing, Allan Herschell, Tonawanda, New York, Early 1920s 1500.00
Horse, Running, Wood, Carved, Painted, Bent Front Legs, Blue Blanket, 38 x 52 In. 1725.00
Horse, Standing, Fiberglass, Contemporary, 1 Raised Foot, 59 In. 413.00
Horse, Standing, Pine, Brown, Horsehair Tail, Charles W. Looff, c.1890, 46 x 53 In. 9600.00
Horse, Wood, Composition, Painted, Black Mane, Multicolored Saddle, 1800s, 53 x 50 In. 1175.00
Horse, Wood, Glass Eyes, Repainted, Tail, Stirrups, 46 x 38 In. 1456.00
Lion, Standing, Wood, Carved, Early 20th Century, 37 1/2 x 45 In. 1763.00
Mask, Mounted, Iron, Painted Faces, Depicts 4 Winds, Bethlehem, Pa., 11 In. 935.00
Pig, Pine, Painted, Pink Bow, Brass Rod, Herschell-Spillman, c.1912, 72 x 46 In. 20400.00
Rounding Board, Curved, Carved Egg & Dart Borders, Painted, 24 x 124 1/2 In., Pair 470.00

CARRIAGE means several things, so this category lists baby carriages, buggies for adults, horse-drawn sleighs, and even strollers. Doll-sized carriages are listed in the Toy category.

Baby Buggy, Oak, Iron Frame, Wooden Spoke Wheels, Painted, Leather, 36 x 24 x 55 In. 499.00
Baby Buggy, Roll Sides, Adjustable Foot Rest, Iron Wheels, Victorian, 36 x 45 x 22 In. 60.00
Baby Buggy, Walnut, Carved Flowers, Vinyl Bonnet, Metal Frame, Porcelain Handle, c.1920 .... 495.00
Baby Buggy, Wicker, Chrome Fenders, Moon Hubcaps, Germany, c.1950, 34 x 21 x 54 In. 100.00
Baby Buggy, Wicker, Hood, Lloyd Loom Products, Mich., c.1917, 31 x 34 In. 100.00
Cart, Pull, Wicker Seat, Spoke Wheels, Curled Suspension Springs, Leather, 25 x 20 In. 138.00
Stroller, Heywood, Wicker, Parasol Top, Gardner, Mass., Victorian, c.1880, 32 x 45 x 19 In. 1150.00
Stroller, Oak, Convertible, High Chair, Turned Spindles, Fiber Seat, c.1910, 41 x 18 x 21 In. 1175.00
Stroller, Wicker Sides, Metal Frame, Fold-Up Canopy, 1910-20, 34 x 52 x 14 In. 35.00
Stroller, Wicker, Wood Wheels, 1920s, 30 x 16 x 29 In. 45.00

CASH REGISTERS were invented in 1884 because an eye on the cash was a necessity in stores of the nineteenth century, too. John and James Ritty invented a large model that resembled a clock and kept a record of the dollars and cents exchanged in the store. John Patterson improved the cash register with a paper roll to record the money. By the early 1900s, elaborate brass registers were made. About World War I, the fancy case was exchanged for the more modern types.

Michigan, Amount Purchased Crest, 15-Key, Leaf Design, 18 x 14 x 17 In. 375.00
National, Model 5, Brass, Polished, Lacquered, c.1900, 21 x 8 1/4 In. 1265.00
National, Model 104, Oak Drawer, Rings Up To 399.99, 1904-08, 30 x 28 In. 880.00
National, Model 313, 15-Key, Bronze, Early 1900s 715.00
National, Model 324, Bronze, 22 In. 728.00
National, Model 332, Bronze, 17 x 16 1/2 In. 230.00
National, Model 332, Oak, Cast Nickel, 21 In. 1210.00
National, Model 333, Bronze, 1892-98, 17 x 17 In. 230.00
National, Model 336, Bronze 560.00
National, Model 416, 26-Key, Bronze, 1908-15 .... 785.00

National, Model 442-E-XX, Bronze, Oak Base, Marble Till, Electric, c.1915 .... 1106.00
National, Model 445, 36-Key, Bronze, Amount Purchased Marquee, c.1915 .... 470.00
National, Model 452, 45-Key, Bronze, c.1915 .... 785.00
National, Model 452-20, Oak, 2 Drawers, 6 Clerk, Keys, Crank, c.1915, 31 x 23 In. 410.00

CASTOR JARS for pickles are glass jars about six inches in height, held in special metal holders. They became a popular dinner table accessory about 1890. Each jar had a top that was usually silver or silver plate. The frame, also of a silver metal, had a handle that arched above the jar and a hook that held a pair of tongs. By 1900, the pickle castor was out of fashion. Many examples found today have reproduced glass jars in old holders. Additional pickle castors may be found in the various Glass categories.

Pickle, Amethyst, Enameled, Gilt Metal Stand, Victorian 1100.00
Pickle, Cranberry, Enameled Flowers, Squat Silver Plated Frame, 4 In. 395.00
Pickle, Cranberry, Optic Ribbed, Albany Silver Plated Frame, 11 In. 600.00
Pickle, Daisy & Button, Amber, Silvered Metal Frame, 9 3/4 In. 115.00
Pickle, Daisy & Button, Canoe Shape, Bryce, Silver Plated Frame, 8 In. 725.00
Pickle, Daisy & Button, Meriden Frame, Victorian, 10 1/2 In. 115.00
Pickle, Daisy & Button, Vaseline, Rockford Frame, Victorian, 12 In. 200.00
Pickle, Inverted Thumbprint, Cobalt, Enameled White & Yellow Daisies, Metal Caddy, 10 In. 690.00
Pickle, Shaded Pink Satin Glass, Enameled Flowers, Oval Handle, Tongs, 9 In. 695.00

CASTOR SETS holding just salt and pepper castors were used in the seventeenth century. The sugar castor, mustard pot, spice dredger, bottles for vinegar and oil, and other spice holders became popular by the eighteenth century. These sets were usually made of sterling silver. The American Victorian castor set, the type most collected today, was made of silver plated Britannia metal. Colored glass bottles were introduced after the Civil War. The sets were out of fashion by World War I. Be careful when buying sets with colored bottles; many are reproductions. Other castor sets may be listed in various porcelain and glass categories in this book.

2 Bottles, Clear Satin, Star Cut Base, Metal Finial, Silver Plated Frame, Wilcox 345.00
3 Bottles, Cranberry, Cruet, Salt & Pepper 700.00
3 Bottles, Daisy & Button, Silvered Metal Frame, Victorian, 10 In. 46.00
4 Bottles, Baluster Shape, Round Foot, Sterling Silver, George II/III, c.1759, 5 In. 615.00
4 Bottles, Cranberry Cut To Clear, Silver Plated Frame 500.00
4 Bottles, Cut, Sheffield Plate Holder, Ct. & Co., c.1892, 8 1/2 In. 495.00
4 Bottles, Waffle, Square, Silver Plated Frame, Wood Handle 125.00
5 Bottles, Cut Panels, Square Silver Plated Frame, Minnehaha Falls, N.Y. 155.00
5 Bottles, Inverted Thumbprint, Cranberry, Wm. Rogers Frame, 15 In. 750.00
5 Bottles, Thomas & Jabez Daniel, England, c.1773, 8 In. 645.00
6 Bottles, Daisy & Button, Vaseline, Rogers Meriden Frame, 18 1/2 In. 950.00
6 Bottles, Daisy & Button, Vaseline, Silver Plated Frame, Rogers Meriden, Victorian, 19 In. 950.00
6 Bottles, Engraved Glass, Mythological Silver Plated Frame, Meriden, 20 In. 230.00
6 Bottles, Optic Swirl, Cranberry, Silver Plated Revolving Frame, 20 In. 675.00
7 Bottles, Silver Plated Frame, Birmingham, c.1860, 6 1/2-In. Bottles, 11 1/2 In. 950.00

CATALOGS are listed in the Paper category.

CAULDON Limited worked in Staffordshire, Great Britain, and went through many name changes. John Ridgway made porcelain at Cauldon Place, Hanley, until 1855. The firm of John Ridgway, Bates and Co. of Cauldon Place worked from 1856 to 1859. It became Bates, Brown-Westhead, Moore and Co. from 1859 to 1862. Brown-Westhead, Moore and Co. worked from 1862 to 1904. About 1890, this firm started using the words *Cauldon* or *Cauldon Ware* as part of the mark. Cauldon Ltd. worked from 1905 to 1920, Cauldon Potteries from 1920 to 1962. Related items may be found in the Indian Tree category.

Plate, Dinner, Black & Gold Banded Rim, 10 1/4 In., 8 Piece 380.00
Punch Bowl, Blue, White, Roses, Garden, Sailboats, Mountains, England, 7 1/2 In. 431.00

CELADON is the name of a velvet-textured green-gray glaze used by Chinese, Japanese, Korean, and other factories. The name refers both to the glaze and to pieces covered with the glaze. It is still being made.

Bottle, Mae Byong, Gray Green Glaze, Korea, 1500s, 10 1/2 In. 529.00
Bowl, Cover, Jade, Dragon Chasing Pearl Of Wisdom, Band Of Bats & Clouds, 6 In. Diam. 7000.00
Bowl, Deep, Flared Sides, Short Foot Ring, Korea, Koryo Dynasty, 7 In. 590.00
Bowl, Louis XV Style, Gilt Bronze Mounted, Crackled, 8 1/2 x 7 In. 764.00
Brush Holder, Flowers, Reticulated, Korea, 1800s, 5 In. 11750.00
Brush Washer, Jade, Mughal Style, Quatrefoil, Carved Lotus Heads, Ram's Head Handle, 5 In. 2124.00
Cachepot, Geometric Designs, Gakuseki, Japan, 6 In. 530.00
Charger, Floral Incised Center, Barbed, Ming Dynasty, 13 In. 425.00
Charger, Fluted Border, Flower Center, Chinese, Yuan Dynasty, 13 1/2 In. 1888.00
Ewer, Phoenix Form, Blue, Japan, 9 In. 1058.00
Figurine, Pig, Brown & Russet Inclusions, 17th Century, 2 1/2 x 1 1/4 In. 250.00
Ginger Jar Set, Round, Wooden Knop Cover, Painted, 1800s, 9 x 9 In., 3 Piece 295.00
Jar, Geometrics, Mishima Style, Slip Filled, Yatsuhiro Ware, Japan, 1800s, 13 1/2 In. 176.00
Planter, Rectangular, Painted, Footed, Chinese, 3 3/8 x 6 1/2 x 10 In. 145.00
Plate, 2 Flowers, Buds, Famille Rose, Blue Seal Mark, 8 In. 400.00
Tureen, Blue Decoration, Chinese, 19th Century, 8 1/2 x 9 1/2 In. 80.00
Umbrella Stand, Flower Scrolls, Japan, c.1900, 24 1/2 In. 529.00
Vase, Aquatic Animals & Fish, Relief Decoration, c.1900, 23 1/2 In. 4950.00
Vase, Baluster, Flowers, Ming Style, Chinese, 16 1/2 In. 530.00
Vase, Blue Decoration, 2 Handles, 19th Century, 13 3/4 x 7 In., Pair 295.00
Vase, Carved Leaf, Flowers, 6 1/2 x 3 In. 345.00
Vase, Crackle Glaze, Double Gourd, Late 18th Century, 15 In. 1300.00
Vase, Egg Shape, Elongated Neck, Animal Handles, Chinese, Qing Dynasty, 11 In. 1003.00
Vase, Egg Shape, Flowers, Japan, 10 1/2 In. 295.00
Vase, Flowers, Molded, Lung Chuan Style, 24 In. 1175.00
Vase, Kuan Style, Triple Gourd Shape, Phoenix Handles, Chinese, 1700s, 10 In. 1880.00
Vase, Lotus Scrolls, Chinese, 1800s, 16 1/2 In. 441.00
Vase, Louis XVI Style, Flowers, Gilt Bronze Shaped Handles & Base, 33 x 15 In., Pair 12925.00
Vase, Mounted As Lamp, Chinese, 15 1/2 x 28 In., Pair 1638.00
Vase, Pottery, Square, Chinese, 3 7/8 x 7 1/2 In. 580.00
Vase, Square, Flared Neck, Splayed Foot, Chinese, 12 1/2 In. 354.00
Vase, Yen Yen, Flowers, Chinese, Qing Dynasty, 16 In. 384.00

CELLULOID is a trademark for a plastic developed in 1868 by John W. Hyatt. Celluloid Manufacturing Company, the Celluloid Novelty Company, Celluloid Fancy Goods Company, and American Xylonite Company all used celluloid to make jewelry, games, sewing equipment, false teeth, and piano keys. The name *celluloid* was often used to identify any similar plastic. Celluloid toys are listed under Toy.

Baby Rattle, Christmas Stocking, Red Teething Ring, 1910-20, 4 1/2 x 2 1/2 In. 130.00
Collar Box, Roses, Blue Ground, Brass Closure, Pink Lining, 3 3/4 x 7 In. 179.00
Comb, Victorian, Fancy 60.00
Dresser Set, Pearlized, Green Swirl, Rhinestones, Pearls, Pyramid, 10 Piece 75.00
Hair Comb, Flower, Art Nouveau Design, Cabochons, 3 3/4 x 4 1/2 In. 87.00
Photograph Album, Boy, Kneeling On Pillow, Kissing Girl, Music Box, 12 x 9 1/2 In. 375.00
Photograph Album, Pony Express Rider, Leaves, Brass Clasp, 8 1/4 x 10 3/4 In. 208.00
Shaving Box, Kneeling Boy, Offering Apple To Girl, Scrollwork, Mug, Mirror 165.00
Tissue Holder, Ivory Ground, Embossed & Painted Kitten, 1950s, 3 x 4 1/2 In. 45.00

CELS are listed in this book in the Animation Art category.

CERAMIC ART COMPANY of Trenton, New Jersey, was established in 1889 by J. Coxon and W. Lenox and was an early producer of American Bélleek porcelain. It became Lenox, Inc. in 1906. Do not confuse this ware with the pottery made by the Ceramic Arts Studio of Madison, Wisconsin.

Dresser Jar, Belleek, Enameled Gold, Flowers, Tracery, 3 x 2 1/4 In. 250.00

Infant Feeder, Belleek, Flowers, Hand Painted, c.1900, 3 In. 144.00
Jug, Belleek, Flowers, Hand Painted, c.1900, 4 In. 75.00
Mug, Grapevines, Dragon Handle, Belleek, c.1910, 5 3/4 x 4 1/8 In. 175.00

CERAMIC ARTS STUDIO was founded about 1940 in Madison, Wisconsin, by Lawrence Rabbett and Ruben Sand. Their most popular products were expensive molded figurines. The pottery closed in 1955. Do not confuse these products with those of the Ceramic Art Co. of Trenton, New Jersey.

Figurine, Gay 90's Man, With Dog, 7 In. 60.00
Figurine, Tom Cat, White, Persian, 5 In. 42.00
Head Vase, Lotus, Asian Man, Black Hair, 8 In. 145.00
Head Vase, Woman, Bonnie, Brown Hair, Green Eyes, 7 1/4 In. 175.00
Vase, Wing-Sang, Lu-Tang, Bamboo Back, White Coat, 7 In., Pair 175.00
Vase, Wing-Sang, Lu-Tang, Bamboo Back, Yellow Coat, 7 In., Pair 125.00
Vase, Wing-Sang, Yellow Coat, Bamboo Back, 7 In. 65.00

CHALKWARE is really plaster of Paris decorated with watercolors. One type was molded from Staffordshire and other porcelain models and painted and sold as inexpensive decorations in the nineteenth century. This type is very valuable today. Figures of plaster, made from about 1910 to 1940 for use as prizes at carnivals, are also known as chalkware. Kewpie dolls made of chalkware will be found in their own category.

Figurine, Cat, 1800s, 5 1/4 In. 825.00
Figurine, Cat, Hollow Molded, Painted, Early 19th Century, 15 In. 2640.00
Figurine, Cat, Multicolored Decoration, 19th Century, 15 1/2 In. 7475.00
Figurine, Cat, Reclining, Apricot, Green Painted Eyes, Black Whiskers, 10 1/4 In. 30.00
Figurine, Cat, Seated, Black & Red Paint, 6 1/2 In. 316.00
Figurine, Cat, Sitting, 19th Century, 15 In. 2640.00
Figurine, Deer, Red, Sprayed Silver Highlights, Gray Antlers, Black Hooves, 15 x 16 In. 230.00
Figurine, Dog, Poodle, Red & Black Spots, Brown Ears, 8 In. 173.00
Figurine, Dog, Poodle, Standing, Brown Paint, Yellow, Red Traces, 4 1/4 In. 345.00
Figurine, Dog, Poodle, Standing, Moke, Multicolored, 7 1/2 x 6 x 3 1/2 In. 165.00
Figurine, Dog, Reclining Greyhound, Rectangular Base, Red Brown Wash, 1800s, 11 x 7 1/2 In. 2530.00
Figurine, Dog, Spaniel, Gold Rim, Multicolored, Starburst, 7 1/2 x 5 1/2 x 3 In. 605.00
Figurine, Dog, Spaniel, Seated, Multicolored, 5 1/2 x 4 x 2 1/2 In. 385.00
Figurine, Dog, Spaniel, Standing, Pinwheel Starburst, Rectangular Base, 7 1/2 x 5 1/2 In. 605.00
Figurine, Dove, Perched On Stump, Yellow Paint, Red Berries, Leaves, 10 In. 230.00
Figurine, Falcon On Rock, Multicolored, 7 1/4 x 4 x 2 3/4 In. 165.00
Figurine, Parrot, Red, Black, 8 In. 403.00
Figurine, Parrot, Sitting On Plinth & Ball, Yellow, Green, Red Wings, 1800s, 13 3/4 In., Pair 1265.00
Figurine, Rooster, Flared Tail, 1800s, 8 In. 8800.00
Figurine, Rooster, Green, Yellow, Orange, 6 1/4 In. 403.00
Figurine, Rooster, Pronounced Tail Feathers, Paint Traces, 7 1/4 In. 200.00
Figurine, Rooster, Yellow, Black, Red Decoration, 19th Century, 7 1/2 In. 4140.00
Figurine, Squirrel, Eating Nut, Round Base, Green, Tan, 6 1/2 In. 316.00
Figurine, Stag, Reclining, Smoke, Painted, 9 1/4 x 8 1/2 x 4 In. 220.00
Whistle, Pig Shape, Tail Is Whistle, Side Slot, Purple, Red, Hanging Loop, 2 1/2 In. 115.00

CHARLIE CHAPLIN, the famous comic and actor, lived from 1889 to 1977. He made his first movie in 1913. He did the movie *The Tramp* in 1915. The character of the Tramp has remained famous, and in the 1980s appeared in a series of television commercials for computers. Dolls, candy containers, and all sorts of memorabilia with the image of Charlie's Tramp are collected. Pieces are being made even today.

Bank, Charlie By Barrel, Glass, Borgfeldt, 1920s, 4 In. .... 59.00 to 382.00
Bank, Glass, Painted 410.00
Candy Container, Smith, Paint, Original Closure 715.00
Full Figure, Cane In Hand, Tin Lithograph, Clockwork, Box, Germany, 6 3/4 In. 1760.00
Movie Poster, Gold Rush, United Artists, Re-release, 1941, 36 x 14 In. 266.00

The old cord on a vintage phone adds value. Green cords are best. Other old forms are twisted cords, brown cords, or patterned cords called rattlesnakes.

Charlie Chaplin, Toy, Cloth Suit, Hat, Fake Fur Hair, Schuco, Germany, c.1920, 6 1/2 In.

Movie Poster, Modern Times, Linen Back, 1936, 62 x 110 In. 944.00
Pencil Box, Tin Lithograph, Henry Cline, 7 3/4 x 2 1/4 x 3/4 In. 75.00
Toy, Charlie On Telephone, Tips Hat, Germany, c.1920, 7 In. 1345.00
Toy, Cloth Suit, Hat, Fake Fur Hair, Schuco, Germany, c.1920, 6 1/2 In. . . . . *ILLUS* 784.00
Toy, Figure, Cast Iron Feet, Tin, Windup, B&R Co., 1925, 8 1/2 In. 1790.00
Toy, Hat Tipper, Tin Lithograph, England, 1950s, 4 In. 193.00
Toy, Pop Gun, Buy Your Auto Supplies At Roses Used Car, 1914, 6 x 11 In. 325.00
Toy, Spinner, Umbrella Spins, Tin Lithograph, Embossed, 5 In. 55.00
Toy, WWII Soldier, Composition, Metal Shoes, Uniform, Windup, Walking, 12 In. 168.00

CHARLIE MCCARTHY was the ventriloquist's dummy used by Edgar Bergen from the 1930s. He was famous for his work in radio, movies, and television. The act was retired in the 1970s.

Bank, Charlie McCarthy, Feed Me I Save You Money, Composition, c.1930, 9 1/2 In. 165.00
Birthday Card, Talks, No. 8247, White & Wycoff Mfg., 5 1/2 x 4 In. 18.00
Dummy, Composition, Detective Outfit, Effanbee, Box, 1938, 20 In. 745.00
Dummy, Composition, Tuxedo, Effanbee, Box, 1938, 20 In. 743.00
Toy, Benzine Buggy, Tin, Windup, Marx, 1938, 8 In. . . . . .330.00 to 560.00
Toy, Charlie & Mortimer Snerd, Private Car, Tin Lithograph, 1939, 16 In. 1344.00
Toy, Charlie, Tin, Windup, Vibrates, Mouth Opens & Closes, Marx, 1938, 8 In. 330.00
Toy, Crazy Car, Tin Lithograph, Clockwork, Marx, c.1939, 7 3/4 In. 353.00
Toy, Drummer, Mortimer Snerd, Parade Dress, Bass Drum, Clockwork, 8 1/2 In. 660.00
Toy, Mortimer Snerd, Crazy Car, Head Spins, Tin, Windup, Marx, 1938, 7 1/2 In. 476.00
Toy, Mortimer Snerd, Crazy Car, Tin, Windup, Marx, 1937, 7 1/2 In. 595.00
Toy, Mortimer Snerd, Crazy Car, Tin, Windup, Marx, 1939, 7 1/2 In. 476.00
Toy, Mortimer Snerd, Tin, Windup, Vibrates, Marx, Box, 1939, 6 1/2 In. . . . . .468.00 to 605.00
Toy, Mouth, Chin Moves, Celluloid, Windup, C&K, Japan, Box, 1930s, 7 In. 675.00
Toy, Private Car, Charlie & Mortimer, Tin, Windup, Marx, 1939, 16 In. . . . . .1155.00 to 2255.00

CHELSEA porcelain was made in the Chelsea area of London from about 1745 to 1769. Some pieces made from 1770 to 1784 are called Chelsea Derby and may include the letter *D* for *Derby* in the mark. Ceramic designs were borrowed from the Meissen models of the day. Pieces were made of soft paste. The gold anchor was used as the mark, but it has been copied by many other factories. Recent copies of Chelsea have been made from the original molds. Do not confuse Chelsea porcelain with Chelsea Grape, a white pottery with luster grape decoration.

Bowl, Reticulated, c.1770, 3 x 8 In. 450.00
Candlestick, Child Holding Basket, Flowers, Gilt Trim, Anchor Mark, 7 3/8 In., Pair 374.00
Dish, Flower, Insect, 3 1/2 In. 49.00
Figurine, Italian Beggar, c.1754, 8 1/8 In. 11947.00
Figurine, Minerva, Owl Mask, Derby, Chelsea Derby, 1770-75, 10 1/2 In. 1500.00
Figurine, Peasant, Folded Arms, Black Hat, c.1754, 7 1/2 In. 9887.00
Group, Gardener & Companion, Spade, Flower Basket, 1758-60, 6 1/4 In. 4500.00

Tureen, Cover, Lettuce, Red Anchor Mark, c.1755, 5 1/8 In. 10800.00

CHELSEA GRAPE pattern was made before 1840. A small bunch of grapes in a raised design, colored with purple or blue luster, is on the border of the white plate. Most of the pieces are unmarked. The pattern is sometimes called *Aynsley* or *Grandmother*. Chelsea Sprig is similar but has a sprig of flowers instead of the bunch of grapes. Chelsea Thistle has a raised thistle pattern. Do not confuse these Chelsea patterns with Chelsea Keramic Art Works, which can be found in the Dedham category, or with Chelsea porcelain, the preceding category.

Bowl, Fruit, Adderleys, England, 1 x 6 In. 20.00
Cup, Adderleys, England, 2 5/8 x 3 5/16 In. 25.00
Cup & Saucer, Paneled, c.1820, 2 3/4-In. Cup, 5 3/4-In. Saucer 45.00
Cup Plate, c.1820, 4 In. 35.00
Plate, Bread & Butter, Adderleys, England, 6 In. 15.00
Saucer, Adderleys, England, 5 3/8 In. 6.00
Waste Bowl, c.1820, 3 3/8 x 6 3/4 In. 80.00
CHELSEA SPRIG, Cup & Saucer, Adderleys, England, 3 x 4-In. Cup, 6 1/4-In. Saucer 48.00

CHINESE EXPORT porcelain comprises all the many kinds of porcelain made in China for export to America and Europe in the eighteenth, nineteenth, and twentieth centuries. Other pieces may be listed in this book under Canton, Celadon, Nanking, and Rose Medallion.

Basin, Famille Verte, Youth, Qilin, Crane, Goldfish, Leaves, Qing Dynasty, 15 In. 1121.00
Basket, Handles, Undertray, Blue & White Brocade Monogram, 1700s, 9 In. 690.00
Basket, Peonies, Pierced Sides, Famille Rose, 2 Handles, c.1750, 15 In. 5400.00
Bottle, Famille Rose, Square, Rooster, Branches, Fish, Crab, Lobster, 10 1/2 In. 944.00
Bowl, 6-Character Seal Mark, Ruby Back, Blue Lanterns, 6 In. 646.00
Bowl, Blue & White, Aster Blossoms, Leaves, 8 Radial Panels, 5 1/8 In. 354.00
Bowl, Blue & White, Flowers, Scrolling Leaves, 11 In., 4 Piece 354.00
Bowl, Blue & White, Flowers, Scrolling Leaves, Bats, 19th Century, 15 1/2 In. 180.00
Bowl, Blue, Gilt, Flowers, Early 19th Century, 10 1/4 In. 575.00
Bowl, Blue, White, 6-Character Seal, Lotus, 6 In. 1295.00
Bowl, Blue, White, Qing Dynasty, 16 1/2 In. 10620.00
Bowl, Cabbage Leaf, Butterflies, Shaped Rim, Flowers, Gilt Trim, 5 x 10 1/2 In. 750.00
Bowl, Copper Red & Blue, 2 Deer Under Pine Tree, 1736-96, 7 1/4 In. 3835.00
Bowl, Cover, Cut Corner, 3 Landscape Reserves, Blue, White, 1800s, 4 1/2 x 9 1/4 In. 805.00
Bowl, Cover, Famille Rose, Flowers, 6 Compartments, 1821-50, 7 1/2 In. 530.00
Bowl, Cut Corner, Bird & Butterfly, 19th Century, 9 1/2 x 4 3/4 In. 430.00
Bowl, Famille Rose, Flower Sprays, 5 3/8 In. 2360.00
Bowl, Famille Rose, Flower, 1723-35, 13 In. 945.00
Bowl, Famille Rose, Flowers, Apple Green Ground, 1736-95, 7 In. 3068.00
Bowl, Famille Rose, Garland & Wreath Border, c.1800, 4 x 9 In. 575.00
Bowl, Famille Rose, Masonic, 10 1/2 In. 1180.00
Bowl, Famille Rose, Millefleurs, 19th Century, 6 x 9 In. 885.00
Bowl, Famille Rose, Rooster, Flowers, 1875-1908, 5 1/4 In. 945.00
Bowl, Famille Verte, Mythical Beasts, Footed, 3 5/8 x 7 1/2 In. 230.00
Bowl, Figural Decoration, Flower Interior, 1700s, 11 1/4 In. 460.00
Bowl, Figure, Calligraphy, Famille Rose, Iron Red Seal Mark, 1821-50, 6 In. Diam. 400.00
Bowl, Figures, Lattice, Central Medallion, Gilt Trim, 5 x 11 1/2 In. 2070.00
Bowl, Fish, Famille Jaune, 19th Century, 16 x 18 In., Pair 7080.00
Bowl, Fish, Riverscape, Carved Wood Stand, Famille Verte, 14 In. 1534.00
Bowl, Flowers, Incised Apple Green Ground, Famille Rose, Marked, 1736-95, 5 3/4 In. 400.00
Bowl, Green Fitzhugh, Leaf Reserves, Black Enamel, 1800s, 10 3/4 In. 765.00
Bowl, Imperial Yellow, Blue Mark, 1662-1722, 5 In. 1300.00
Bowl, Peaches, Bats, Waves, Famille Rose Enamel, 19th Century, 6 1/2 In. 264.00
Bowl, Ship, British Flag, Flowers, 11 In. 575.00
Bowl, Swatow, Blue & White, Deer, Bird, Butterflies, Double Ring, 15 1/2 In. 560.00
Bowl, Vegetable, Cover, Bird & Butterfly Pattern, 9 1/2 In. 345.00

Bowl, Vegetable, Cover, Diamond Shape, Clipper Ships On Lid, Gilt Berry Finial, 9 x 4 In. 400.00
Box, Cover, Famille Rose, 12 In. 3835.00
Brush Washer, 2 Quatrefoils, Bird, Lotus, Peony, Faux Bois Ground, 3 In. Diam. 275.00
Brush Washer, Famille Verte, 2 Dragons Chasing Pearl Of Wisdom, Interior Crab, 4 1/4 In. Diam... 500.00
Brushpot, Blue & White, Figures, Cylindrical, 7 In. 445.00
Brushpot, Famille Rose, 2 Dragons Chasing Pearl Of Wisdom, Clouds, 5 1/2 In. 445.00
Brushpot, Famille Rose, Cylindrical, Figures, Landscape, 1723-35, 4 3/4 In. 1180.00
Brushpot, Famille Rose, Cylindrical, Immortal, Attendant, 1723-35, 4 In. 1890.00
Brushpot, Famille Rose, Hexagonal, 4 Seasons, Scholar's Objects, 5 x 4 In. 2006.00
Brushpot, Famille Verte, Cylindrical, Riverscape, 1800s, 5 1/4 In. 413.00
Brushpot, Famille Verte, Figures Fighting, 1662-1722, 6 1/2 x 7 3/4 In. 850.00
Butter Tub, Cover, Famille Rose, Floral Sprays, Gilt Band, c.1770, 3 x 5 In. 705.00
Cachepot, Famille Jaune, 20th Century, 9 1/2 In., Pair 1062.00
Cachepot, Famille Rose, Lion's Head Handles, Flowers, 9 1/2 In., Pair 1410.00
Cachepot, Rose Bouquets, Garlands, Serpentine Rim, Handles, Footed, 7 x 9 In. 2350.00
Censer, 2 Dragons Chasing Pearl Of Wisdom, Bombe, 8 In. 2000.00
Censer, Cover, Cloisonne, Enamel, Flowerhead, Leaves, 10 3/4 x 11 In. 9440.00
Censer, Famille Rose, Deer, Flowers, 10 In. 1060.00
Censer, Rock Crystal, Beast Head Handles, Loose Rings, Birds, Prunus, 4 x 8 5 5/8 In. 3335.00
Censer, Stand, Tripod, Loop Handles, Lotus Leaves, 3-Footed, 7 In. 388.00
Charger, Blue & White, Butterflies, Peonies, Fretwork Border, 1800s, 15 In. 470.00
Charger, Blue & White, Flowers, 15 1/2 In. 885.00
Charger, Blue & White, Riverscape, Barbed Rim, 15 In. 1416.00
Charger, Blue & White, Scalloped Rim, Flowers, 18 In. 294.00
Charger, Blue & White, Shallow Well, Wide Lobed Rim, 13 3/4 In. 345.00
Charger, Famille Rose, Flowers, Butterflies, Birds, 1800s, 13 1/2 In. 495.00
Charger, Famille Rose, Flowers, Fence, 14 1/2 In. 1180.00
Charger, Monogrammed M, Gilt Floral Sprays & Edge, Oval, 21 1/2 In. 3819.00
Charger, Multicolored, Gilding, Cranes, Flowers, 3-Lobe Border, Wood Stand, 18 In. 350.00
Chestnut Dish, Underplate, Blue & White, 1700s, 4 x 10 1/2 &11 In. 585.00
Creamer, Cover, Orange Fitzhugh, 19th Century, 3 1/2 In. 500.00
Cup, Bird In Flowering Tree, Famille Rose, 2 1/2 x 4 1/4 In. 590.00
Cup, Center Medallion, 2 Flying Bats, Waves, Peach Bloom, Stem, 4 1/2 x 5 3/4 In. 750.00
Cup & Saucer, Iron Red Grisaille, Gilding Monogram, Mantled Shield, c.1785-90 .... 4800.00
Cup & Saucer Set, Gold & Sepia Armorial Decoration, 10 Piece 375.00
Dish, Armorial, 18th Century, 9 In., 9 Piece 410.00
Dish, Covered Jar, Blue & White 18th Century 146.00
Dish, Famille Rose, 2 Men Under Flowering Tree, Fence, 6 In. 400.00
Dish, Famille Rose, Deer & Bats Under Pine Tree, Blue Seal Mark, 6 In. 425.00
Dish, Famille Verte, Flowers, Fluted Rim, 1662-1722, 6 In., Pair 826.00
Dish, Flowers, Salmon & Cobalt Blue Band, 1800s, 7 3/4 In. 118.00
Dish, Phoenixes, 8 Character, 20th Century, 8 1/2 In. 3290.00
Dragons Chasing Pearl Of Wisdom, Green, Yellow, 4 1/8 In., Pair 7170.00
Figurine, Bird, Famille Rose, Electrified, 19th Century, 17 1/2 In. 410.00
Figurine, Birds, Famille Rose, 19th Century, 14 In. 1120.00
Figurine, Buddha, Standing, Famille Rose Enamel Decoration, 1800s, 12 In. 999.00
Figurine, Dignitary, Robed Man Seated In Horseshoe Chair, 13 x 6 1/2 x 5 1/2 In. 5290.00
Figurine, Foo Dog On Pedestal, Multicolored Glazes, 38 x 13 x 20 1/4 In., Pair 2995.00
Figurine, Guanyin & Attendant, Lapis Lazuli, Blue, 3 1/2 In. 500.00
Figurine, Guanyin, Flowing Robes, Seated On Braided Mat, 9 1/2 x 5 x 4 1/4 In. 431.00
Figurine, Immortal, Robe, Pointed Beard, Jui Scepter, Quartz, Qing Dynasty, 10 1/2 In. 800.00
Figurine, Phoenix Bird, Rockwork Base, Famille Rose Enamel, 21 In., Pair 1116.00
Figurine, Rooster, Famille Rose, 16 In., Pair 384.00
Figurine, Woman Holding Stringed Instrument, Coral, Wood Base, 11 1/2 x 2 1/4 In. 1265.00
Fishbowl, Famille Rose, Flowers, Blue Ground, c.1745, 16 x 24 In. 6600.00
Fishbowl, Quatrefoils With Figures, Powder Blue Ground, Famille Rose, 12 1/4 In. Diam. 650.00
Flask, Moon Shape, Famille Jeune, Enamel, Leaves, Dragon, Lizard Handles, 1800s, Pair 705.00
Fruit Cooler, Green Fitzhugh, 20th Century, 10 In., Pair 1180.00
Ginger Jar, Blue & White, Oval, Dome Lid, Blue Underglaze, 10 In., Pair 940.00
Ginger Jar, Blue, Wheel Thrown, 19th Century, 7 1/2 x 7 In. 99.00
Ginger Jar, Famille Rose, Pink Peonies, 19th Century, Pair 293.00

Hat Holder, Famille Rose, Flowers, Cutout, 6-Sided, Qing Dynasty, 19th Century, 11 In. 150.00
Hunt Bowl, Hunt Scene, Grisaille Exterior, 1700s, 15 3/8 In. 8815.00
Jar, Black, Oval, Ribbed Body, Loop Handles, 8 3/4 In. 239.00
Jar, Blue & White, Flowers, Oval, 8 In., Pair 649.00
Jar, Blue & White, Flowers, Oval, Shaped Cartouches, 7 In. 500.00
Jar, Cover, Birds, Wisteria, Peony Blossoms, Dome Lid, 9 1/2 In., Pair 765.00
Jar, Cover, Famille Rose, Figures, Water, Turtles, 19th Century, 11 In. 150.00
Jar, Cover, Famille Rose, Shepherdess, Seated, Tree, 3 Goats, 1723-35, 6 1/2 In. 2000.00
Jar, Cover, Famille Verte, 100 Antiques, Birds, Flowers, 1800s, 11 In. 410.00
Jar, Cover, Green Fitzhugh, 2 Handles, 1700s, 5 In. 265.00
Jar, Famille Verte, Baluster, Women, Children In Garden, 20th Century, 11 In. 1000.00
Jar, Peacock, Blackbirds, Flowers, Aqua, White, Multicolored, Oval, 9 In. 470.00
Jug, Cider, Orange Peel Glaze, Intertwined Handle, Gilt Trim, 9 In. 230.00
Jug, Cover, Gilt & Cobalt Blue Bands, Reeded & Twisted Handle, Dog Finial, 12 In. 1295.00
Mug, Barrel Shape, Applied Handle, Flower Decoration, 6 x 4 3/4 In. 358.00
Mug, Blue Fitzhugh, 1800s, 4 In. 489.00
Mug, Famille Rose, Flower Sprays, 1800s, 5 In. 345.00
Pitcher, Imari Style Decoration, Birds, Fish, Flowers, 1700s, 8 1/2 In. 588.00
Pitcher, Milk, Enameled Interior Court Scene, Gold Spout & Handle, 4 3/4 In. 176.00
Planter, Painted Wood Grain, Black, Russet, Yellow, Green, 5 1/2 x 5 1/2 In., Pair 8625.00
Plaque, Famille Rose, Flowers, Calligraphy, 14 3/4 x 9 1/2 In. 200.00
Plate, Armorial, Mertins Impaling Peck, Flower Border, c.1725, 8 3/4 In. 1528.00
Plate, Armorial, Octagonal, Gilt, Enamel, Loof Of Amsterdam, c.1765, 9 In. 646.00
Plate, Armorial, Shield, Oliphant Impaling Browne, Trellis, c.1790, 8 In. 325.00
Plate, Bird & Butterfly Pattern, 10 1/2 In., 9 Piece 259.00
Plate, Blue & White, Lotus Petal, Scalloped, 9 In. 944.00
Plate, Blue & White, Radiating Aster Blossoms, Scalloped Rim, 8 1/2 In. 500.00
Plate, Butterfly, Flowers, Green, White, 10 In., 6 Piece 266.00
Plate, Covered Cup, Tea Bowl, Chrysanthemum Pattern, 18th Century, 3 Piece 234.00
Plate, Dinner, Blue & White, Fitzhugh, 19th Century, 9 1/2 In., 8 Piece 1650.00
Plate, Famille Export, Peonies, Butterflies, Green Lattice Border, 8 In., 8 Piece 940.00
Plate, Famille Jaune, Calligraphy, Yellow Ground, Key Fret Rim, 1875-1908, 9 In., Pair 649.00
Plate, Famille Rose, Dragon, Pagoda, Tree, Gilt Highlights, c.1800, 9 In., Pair 295.00
Plate, Famille Rose, Flowers, 1736-95, 9 In., Pair 590.00
Plate, Famille Rose, Flowers, 8-Sided, Qianlong Period, 9 In. 384.00
Plate, Famille Rose, Flowers, Bats, Clouds, 1700s, 9 1/4 In. 646.00
Plate, Famille Rose, Multicolored Enamel, Flower Urn Center, 9 In., 8 Piece 1410.00
Plate, Famille Verte, 3 Birds Over Garden, Flower & Bird Border, 8 3/4 In. 600.00
Plate, Famille Verte, Kakiemon Flowers, Lotus Petal Shape, 1662-1722, 8 3/4 In. 445.00
Plate, Green Fitzhugh, 19th Century, 10 In., Pair 415.00
Plate, Orange Fitzhugh, 9 3/4 In. 710.00
Plate, Peony Bouquet, Magenta, Turquoise, c.1730, 8 3/4 In., Pair 720.00
Plate, Red Garland Border, 18th Century, 8 7/8 In. 146.00
Plate, Soup, Blue & White, Riverside Landscapes, Floral Scroll Borders, 8 1/2 In. 150.00
Plate, Soup, Famille Verte, Flowers, 1662-1722, 8 1/2 In., Pair 560.00
Plate, Swagged Crest, Red Monogram, Blue & Gilt Border, 9 3/4 In., 12 Piece 2115.00
Plate & Soup Set, Bamboo, Flower Sprigged Border, 9 & 8 3/4 In., 12 Piece 2820.00
Platter, Armorial, Caulfield Arms Impaling Talbot, Motto, c.1802, 19 In. 2468.00
Platter, Armorial, Oval, Gilt, Purple Bowknot, Early 19th Century, 17 3/4 In. 1175.00
Platter, Blue & White, Fitzhugh, Oval, 19th Century, 19 In. 1535.00
Platter, Blue & White, Riverscape, c.1780, 16 In. 590.00
Platter, Central Pinwheel Roundel, 18th Century, 20 In. 1150.00
Platter, Orange Peel Glaze, Cobalt Blue Landscape, Scallop Borders, 14 x 11 In. 460.00
Platter, Tobacco Leaf Pattern, Scalloped, Oval, c.1775-85, 15 In. ....6600.00 to 7800.00
Platter, Tobacco Leaf Pattern, Scalloped, Oval, c.1775-85, 16 1/2 In. 9000.00
Pot De Creme Set, Blue, White, 1800s, 3 In., 6 Piece 374.00
Punch Bowl, Armorial, Blue Border, Monogram, Flowers, Late 1700s, 14 1/4 In. 880.00
Punch Bowl, Bronze Stand, Famille Rose, Mandarin, 10 x 18 3/4 In. 4025.00
Punch Bowl, Cabbage, 6 1/2 x 15 7/8 In. 1880.00
Punch Bowl, Famille Rose, Bird, Butterfly, Roman Key Border, c.1850, 5 1/2 x 12 3/4 In. 920.00
Punch Bowl, Famille Rose, Gold Trim, Panels, Figures In Domestic Scenes, 15 In. 1410.00

Punch Bowl, Famille Rose, Oval Reserve Panels, Sepia Landscapes, 16 In. 3055.00
Punch Bowl, Famille Verte, Flower Vignettes, Interior Bands, 5 1/2 x 12 In. 796.00
Punch Bowl, Flowers, Laurel Swag Border, Gilt Trim, Late 1700s, 11 1/4 In. 529.00
Punch Bowl, Flowers, Shells, Leaf Scrolls, Early 1800s, 4 3/4 x 11 1/8 In. 295.00
Punch Bowl, Foo Dogs, Bats, Insects, Fruit, 11 1/2 x 5 In. 6000.00
Punch Bowl, Green Fitzhugh, Eagle, Shield, 17 1/2 x 7 1/2 In. 590.00
Sauceboat, Tobacco Leaf Pattern, Fluted, Oval, c.1775-85, 8 1/2 In. 5100.00
Saucer, Famille Rose, 4 Multicolored Carp, Flowers, c.1800, 8 7/8 In. 245.00
Saucer, Man Smoking, Gilt Border, 1700s, 6 In. 118.00
Saucer, Warriors On Horseback, Hunting Scene, Blue, White, Gilt, 7 1/2 In., Pair 615.00
Service, Sepia, Gilt Flower Spray, Leaf Borders, 12 Piece 1800.00
Serving Dish, Blue & White, Fitzhugh, Oval, 11 1/2 In. 354.00
Shaker, Painted Rosebuds, Gold Rimmed Cover, 2 In. 40.00
Tazza, Famille Verte, Flowers, 1662-1722, 4 x 10 1/2 In. 1298.00
Tea Service, Iron Red, Gilding, Flower Basket, Sprigs, Leaf Border, 60 Piece 1680.00
Tea Service, Sepia, Gilt Flower Spray, Line, Dot Border, Tea Bowls, Saucers, 53 Piece 1320.00
Tea Set, Famille Rose, Flowers, Gilt Ground, c.1890, Miniature, 2-In. Teapot, 7 Piece 340.00
Teapot, Blue & White, Flower Heads, Scrolled Leaves, Upright Handle, 6 1/2 In. 1180.00
Teapot, Blue & White, Globular, 2 Cartouches, Bird, Flowers, 7 In. 2125.00
Teapot, Blue & White, Melon Shape, 19th Century, 6 1/2 In. 80.00
Teapot, Cover, Famille Rose, Blue Ground, 1800s, 2 3/4 In. 290.00
Teapot, Famille Rose, People In Court, 1700s, 7 In. 325.00
Teapot, Silver Mounts, 18th Century, 8 1/2 In. 645.00
Tray, Black Lacquer, Gilt Mandarins In Garden, 24 x 19 In. 646.00
Tray, Spoon, 2 Deer, 18th Century, 4 1/2 In. 160.00
Tureen, Blue & White, Riverscape, Boar Head Handles, c.1800, 12 In. 385.00
Tureen, Blue & White, Riverscape, Twist Handles, Pinecone, Branches, 14 1/4 In. 1770.00
Tureen, Cover, Famille Rose, Mandarin, 12 1/2 x 11 In. 325.00
Tureen, Famille Rose, Boar Form, 15 1/2 In. 750.00
Tureen, Sauce, Blue & White, Fitzhugh, 19th Century, 9 In. 470.00
Tureen, Sauce, Green Fitzhugh, c.1820, 7 1/2 In., Pair 3300.00
Tureen, Sauce, Stand, Tobacco Leaf Pattern, Scalloped, Oval, c.1775-85, 8 In. 7800.00
Tureen, Soup, Cover, Famille Rose, Flowers, 1875-1908, 9 1/4 In. 118.00
Tureen, Stand, Famille Rose, Flowers, Foo Dog Finial, 1700s, 14 1/2 In. 3055.00
Tureen, Undertray, Cover, Entwined Handles, Bird, Butterfly, Flower, 14 In. 949.00
Tureen, Undertray, Famille Rose, Cabbage Leaf, 20th Century, 15 In. 649.00
Urn, Landscape, Gilt Trim, Pistol Handles, Mounted As Lamp, c.1800, 14 In. 1058.00
Vase, 2 Dragons Chasing Pearl Of Wisdom, Yellow, Green, Aubergine, 15 In. 765.00
Vase, 2 Fish, Blue Monochrome, Qing Dynasty, 18th Century, 10 1/2 In. 1200.00
Vase, 4 Figural Panels, Famille Verte, 16 In. 445.00
Vase, Baluster, Famille Verte, Mounted As Lamp, 1800s, 18 3/4 x 7 1/4 In. 1135.00
Vase, Beaker, 2 Figural Panels, Flower Alternate, 1800s, 7 1/2 In., Pair 125.00
Vase, Beaker, Blue & White, Pagoda, Flower Heads, Scrolling Leaves, 13 In. 885.00
Vase, Beaker, Decorated Border, Salmon, c.1900, 9 1/2 In. 345.00
Vase, Blue & White, Flowers, Butterfly, Oval, 15 In. 413.00
Vase, Blue & White, Plum Branches, Blue Wash Cracked Ice Ground, 17 1/2 In. 3658.00
Vase, Blue & White, Stylized Dragon, 1736-96, 17 1/2 In. 2950.00
Vase, Bombe Shape, Iridescent Green, 17 In. 777.00
Vase, Bottle, Copper Red Glaze, 13 1/2 In. 9560.00
Vase, Bulbous, Flared Top, Flowers, Birds, Trees, c.1850, 24 In. 489.00
Vase, Champleve Enamel Grapevines, Baluster, Dragon Head Handles, 17 In., Pair 1762.00
Vase, Copper Red Glaze, Oval, Peach Form Handles, Electrified, 10 1/2 In. 359.00
Vase, Court Scene, Foo Dog, Ring Handles, Iron Red, Gold, 14 In. 826.00
Vase, Courtiers, Gilt Borders, 1700s, 18 In., Pair 3819.00
Vase, Cover, Famille Rose, Flowers, Phoenix, Foo Dog Finials, 45 1/2 In., Pair 1534.00
Vase, Cover, Famille Rose, Stand, Baluster, Dragons, Peonies, 1800s, 12 1/2 In. 499.00
Vase, Cover, Famille Verte, Hexagonal, Brocade, Electrified, 18th Century, 11 In., Pair 590.00
Vase, Cover, Louis XVI Style, Bronze Dore Mounts, Flower, Butterflies, 14 1/2 In. 590.00
Vase, Cover, Phoenix & Foliage Decoration, Gold Trim, Tao-Kuang, 13 In. 176.00
Vase, Dragon Design, Red, Gold, Bottle Form, Qianlong Mark, 12 In. 2300.00
Vase, Dragon, Phoenix, Green, Iron Red, Gu Form, 13 In. 227.00

Vase, Dragons, Claire De Lune, Blue, Gold, 7 In., Pair ... 750.00
Vase, Famille Noir, Enamel On Biscuitware, Flowering Prunus Tree, 28 In. ... 2115.00
Vase, Famille Rose, 100 Bat, Oval, Elongated Neck, Iron Red 6-Character Mark, c.1910, 16 1/2 In. 3000.00
Vase, Famille Rose, Baluster, Dragon Handles, 1800s, 15 x 8 1/4 In., Pair ... 643.00
Vase, Famille Rose, Baluster, Figures, Flowers, Foo Dog Handles, 14 x 8 In., Pair ... 3308.00
Vase, Famille Rose, Birds Perched On Flowering Branches, Oval, Waisted Neck, 1736-95, 14 In. .. 180.00
Vase, Famille Rose, Bombe Center, Birds, Flowers, 1796-1820, 19 x 9 In., Pair ... 944.00
Vase, Famille Rose, Cabbage Leaf Form, Insects, 19th Century, 15 In. ... 1300.00
Vase, Famille Rose, Cabbage Leaf, Butterfly, 1800s, 15 1/2 In. ... 3186.00
Vase, Famille Rose, Double Gourd, Dragon, Qianlong Mark, 1900s, 10 1/2 In. ... 385.00
Vase, Famille Rose, Dragon Appliques, Court Scenes, Flowers, 1800s, 24 1/2 In. ... 705.00
Vase, Famille Rose, Figural, Landscape, 22 1/4 In., Pair ... 1770.00
Vase, Famille Rose, Garden Settings, Floral Panels, 20th Century, 24 In. ... 118.00
Vase, Famille Rose, Hand Painted Panels, 20th Century, 12 In., Pair ... 206.00
Vase, Famille Rose, Landscape, Enameled Designs, Early 1900s, 9 In. ... 940.00
Vase, Famille Rose, Millefleur, 4-Character Iron Red Hallmark, 1820-50, 15 In. ... 3750.00
Vase, Famille Rose, Riverscape, Bottle Form, 1662-1722, 8 1/4 In. ... 2600.00
Vase, Famille Rose, Warriors, Bird, Flower Borders, Dragon Appliques, 19th Century, 24 In. ... 1645.00
Vase, Famille Verte, Dragons, Square, 1800s, 24 In. ... 705.00
Vase, Famille Verte, Figural, 18th Century, 16 In. ... 500.00
Vase, Famille Verte, Figures, Trees, 156 In. ... 375.00
Vase, Famille Verte, Shaped Cartouches, Weathered Rock, Flowers, Insects, 9 x 8 1/2 In. ... 316.00
Vase, Famille Verte, Yen, Yen, Kylin & Carp, Flower Borders, 19th Century, 17 3/4 In. ... 2350.00
Vase, Flambe, Oval, Copper Red Glaze, 9 1/2 In. ... 240.00
Vase, Flowers, Birds, 4-Character Iron Red Mark, 10 In. ... 1900.00
Vase, Flowers, Birds, Footed, c.1905, 11 1/2 x 9 In. ... 165.00
Vase, Flowers, Vines, Figures, Pistol Handle, Mounted As Lamp, Early 1800s, 12 In. ... 1058.00
Vase, Foo Dog Handles, Birds, Flowers, c.1920, 18 x 9 In. ... 110.00
Vase, Frolicking Boys Decoration, Tao-Kuang, Rouge-De-Fer Mark, 11 In., Pair ... 705.00
Vase, Garlic Shaped Mouth, Dragon On Shoulder, Lang Yao, 9 1/2 In. ... 440.00
Vase, Gilt, Flowers, Black, Baluster Form, Electrified, 15 1/2 In. ... 657.00
Vase, Gray Crackle Glaze, Stylized Animal Handles, Oval, Qing Dynasty, 11 1/2 In. ... 150.00
Vase, Immortals, Crane Roundels, Prunus Tree, 19th Century, 9 1/2 In. ... 500.00
Vase, Imperial Yellow, Incised Flowers, Oval, Elephant Head Handles, Qing Dynasty, 7 1/2 In. ... 1600.00
Vase, Multicolored, Dragon, Flowers, 16 3/4 In. ... 145.00
Vase, Mythical Beasts Playing In Waves, Green, Yellow, Purple, Famille, 12 1/3 In., Pair ... 1495.00
Vase, Rouleau, Figures, Rocky Landscape, Famille Verte, Qing Dynasty, 17 In. ... 1535.00
Vase, Taotie Mask, Flowers, Gu Form, 15 In., Pair ... 945.00
Warming Dish, Orange Peel Glaze, Cobalt Blue, Gilt Flowers, 9 1/2 x 12 1/2 In. ... 115.00
Washbasin, Enamel, Bat Exterior, Flower Garden Interior, c.1900, 13 3/8 In. ... 235.00
Washbasin, Famille Rose, Female Immortal, Deer, Bamboo Grove, Medallions, 16 In. ... 105.00
Washbasin, Famille Rose, Flower Spray, Bird, Blossoms, Orange Ground, 5 1/4 x 14 3/4 In. ... 147.00
Water Bottle, Famille Rose, Blue Underglaze Flower, Roe Borders, 9 In. ... 235.00
Water Dropper, Peach Bloom, 6 Characters, 3 3/4 In. ... 448.00
Wine Cup, 2-Character K'ang His, Green Dragons, Yellow Ground, 1 x 1 3/4 In., Pair ... 2115.00
Wine Pot, Peach Form, Purple, Turquoise Glaze, 19th Century, 5 In. ... 765.00

CHINTZ is the name of a group of china patterns featuring an overall design of flowers and leaves. The design became popular with English makers about 1928. A few pieces are still being made. The best known are designs by Royal Winton, James Kent Ltd., Crown Ducal, and Shelley. Crown Ducal and Shelley are listed in their own sections.

Clyde, Teapot, Underplate, Royal Winton, 6 x 10 1/4-In. Teapot, 5 3/4-In. Plate ... 525.00
DuBarry, Sugar, Open, James Kent, 2 1/8 x 3 In. ... 60.00
Hazel, Plate, Black Ground, Square, Royal Winton, 7 In. ... 140.00
Heather, Jam Jar Set, Lord Nelson, 4 1/2-In. Jar, 4 Piece ... 190.00
Julia, Nut Dish, Royal Winton, 1930s, 5 3/4 In. ... 130.00
Lorna Doone, Cake Stand, 4-Sided, Aluminum Center Handle, W.R. Midwinter, c.1937 ... 105.00
Lorna Doone, Tea Tray, Royal Tudorware, Barton Brothers, c.1937, 8 3/4 In. ... 170.00
Marina, Teacup & Saucer, Lord Nelson, 1930s, 2 3/4 x 3 1/2-In. Cup, 5 3/4-In. Saucer ... 128.00
Marina, Teacup & Saucer, Lord Nelson, 1930s, Demitasse ... 88.00

Marina, Vase, Bud, Lord Nelson 195.00
Marion, Butter, Cover, Royal Winton, 2 1/2 x 5 x 3 1/4 In. 150.00
Marion, Cake Plate, Pedestal, Footed, Green Ground, Royal Winton, 3 x 8 1/2 x 8 1/2 In. 375.00
Marion, Cup & Saucer, Royal Winton 110.00
Marion, Jam Jar, Cover, Royal Winton, 4 x 2 1/2 In. 140.00
Marion, Nut Dish, Tab Handles, Square, Royal Winton, 1 1/4 x 4 In. 75.00
Maytime, Teacup & Saucer, Crown Bone China Co., c.1950 .... 100.00
Melody, Plate, Royal Crown, 9 In. 215.00
Midwinter Coral, Sugar Shaker, 6 x 2 1/2 In. 150.00
Mille Fleurs, Dish, B. Ford & Co., Burslem, England, 6 1/4 In. 50.00
Old Cottage, Cup & Saucer, Royal Winton, 1937 .... 115.00
Old Foley, Bonbon, Pedestal Base, Scalloped Rim, James Kent, c.1935 .... 70.00
Pansy, Candy Dish, Gold Trim, Lord Nelson, c.1940, 1 1/4 x 6 3/4 x 4 1/2 In. 70.00
Queen Anne, Cake Stand, Chrome Center Handle, Royal Winton, 1936-40 .... 128.00
Rose, Plate, Gold Trim, Norcrest, 10 In. 29.00
Rose Time, Salt & Pepper, Tray, Nelson Ware, 3-In. Shakers, 6 1/2-In. Tray 188.00
Rosina, Cup & Saucer, 2 1/2-In. Cup, 5 1/2-In. Saucer 85.00
Royal Brocade, Creamer, Gold Trim, Lord Nelson, 1930s, 1 1/2 x 3 In. 60.00
Royal Brocade, Salt & Pepper, Tray, Nelson Ware, 1910-28, 3-In. Shaker, 6 1/2-In. Tray 168.00
Royal Brocade, Sugar & Creamer, Lord Nelson, 2 1/8-In. Sugar, 3-In. Creamer 175.00
Royal Brocade, Teacup & Saucer, Lord Nelson, 1930s, 2-In. Cup, 4-In. Saucer 58.00
Somerset, Mustard Pot, Cover, Ascot Shape, Royal Winton, 1932, 2 1/2 In. 130.00
Somerset, Sugar, Conical, Royal Winton, 2 x 4 In. 95.00
Springtime, Plate, Wikinson, 8 In. 45.00
Summertime, Ashtray, Royal Winton, 4 1/4 In. 65.00
Summertime, Teapot, Royal Winton 180.00
Sunshine, Honey Pot, Royal Winton, 3 3/4 In. 90.00
Victorian Rose, Jar, Cover, Burleigh Staffordshire, 7 In. 100.00

CHOCOLATE GLASS, sometimes mistakenly called caramel slag, was made by the Indiana Tumbler and Goblet Company of Greentown, Indiana, from 1900 to 1903. It was also made at other National Glass Company factories. Fenton Art Glass Co. also made chocolate glass from about 1907 to 1915. More recent pieces have been made by Imperial and others.

Biscuit Jar, Cover, Cactus, Greentown, 8 In. 145.00
Cactus, Biscuit Jar, Cover, Greentown, c.1902, 8 x 5 1/2 In. 185.00
Cactus, Master Berry Bowl, Greentown, 1900-03, 3 1/2 x 8 1/4 In. 145.00
Cactus, Syrup, No Cover, Greentown, c.1902, 5 1/4 In. 39.00
Leaf Bracket, Berry Bowl, Greentown, 2 x 4 3/4 In. 60.00
Leaf Bracket, Nappy, Handle, Greentown 110.00
Majestic, Compote, Jelly, National Glass, McKee, c.1897, 5 3/8 x 5 1/4 In. 695.00
Outdoor Drinking Scene, Mug, Greentown, 4 1/2 x 3 In. 125.00
Squirrel, Greentown .... *ILLUS* 590.00
Syrup, Cord & Drapery, Greentown, Late 1800, 6 1/2 In. 175.00

CHRISTMAS collectibles include not only Christmas trees and ornaments listed below, but also Santa Claus figures, special dishes, and even games and wrapping paper. A Belsnickle is a nineteenth-century figure of Father Christmas. A kugel is an early, heavy ornament made of thick blown glass, lined with zinc or lead, and often covered with colored wax. Christmas cards are listed in this section under Greeting Card. Christmas collectibles may also be listed in the Candy Container category. Christmas trees are listed in the section that follows.

Badge, Waving Santa, Toy Bag, Meet Me At Yeagers, Philadelphia, Celluloid, 1 1/4 In. 29.00
Bandanna, Printed, Santa Claus, 4 Different Corner Block Motifs, 26 x 16 In. 259.00
Bell, Poinsetta, Mom & Dad 1983 On Reverse, Porcelain, Hallmark, 3 In. 5.00
Belsnickle, Cardboard, Red Painted Robe, Mica Flecks, Black Base, Feather Tree, 11 In. 403.00
Belsnickle, Papier-Mache, Gold Coat, Holding Feather Tree, 11 1/4 In. 825.00
Belsnickle, Papier-Mache, Lavender Coat, Feather Tree With Berry, Mica Cover, 7 1/2 In. 715.00

Chocolate Glass, Squirrel, Greentown

Christmas, Belsnickle, Papier-Mache, Yellow Robe, Feather Tree, 9 1/2 In.

Christmas, Toy, Santa Claus, Roly Poly, Schoenhut, 9 In.

Belsnickle, Papier-Mache, Seafoam Green Coat, Feather Tree, Mica Cover, 10 In. 1210.00
Belsnickle, Papier-Mache, Yellow Robe, Feather Tree, 9 1/2 In. . . . . *ILLUS* 616.00
Belsnickle, Santa Claus, Figure, German Composition, Early 1900s, 3 x 10 1/2 In. 529.00
Belsnickle, White Suit, Holding Feather Tree, Composition, Germany, c.1910, 10 1/2 In. 529.00
Blocks, English Sovereigns, Wood, Paper Lithograph, Slide Lid Box, McLoughlin Bros., 6 x 11 In. . . 33.00
Book, Night Before Christmas, 7 Metal Bells, Saalfield, Akron, 1946 . . . . 300.00
Book, Rudolph The Red Nosed Reindeer, Montgomery Ward, Robert L. May, 1939 . . . . 135.00
Button, Christmas Tree, Rhinestones, Multicolored, Goldtone Setting, 2 1/2 In. 7.00
Button, Santa Claus, Chandler & Rudd Co., Celluloid, 1 In. 69.00
Button, Santa Claus, Christmas Greetings From Harris', Celluloid, 1 In. 19.00
Button, Santa Claus, In Chimney, I Am At Jordan Marsh Co.'s, Celluloid, 1 1/4 In. 73.00
Button, Santa Claus, Lobel's, For Christmas Gifts, Celluloid, 1 3/4 In. 28.00
Button, Santa Claus, Meet Me At The Hub, Celluloid, 1 In. 94.00
Button, Santa Claus, On Rocking Horse, Pull Bell Santa Moves, Plastic, c.1960, 3 3/4 In. 9.00
Button, Tree Ornament, Bow, Red & Green Enamel, Goldtone, Marked Gerry's, 1 5/8 In. 6.00
Candle, Plastic, Lighted, 3 Candles, Marked Empire Made In USA, 13 x 5 In. 10.00
Candy Containers are listed in the Candy Container category.
Earrings, Holiday Wreath, Dangling Bells In Center, Clip-On, Box, 1 1/8 In. 5.00
Figure, Angels, Kissing, Porcelain, 3 3/4 In., Pair 4.00
Figure, Choir Girls Holding Song Book, Porcelain, Red Ink Mark, Japan, 3 In. 8.00
Figure, Christmas Holly Frog, Nightcaps, Holly, Lefton, 2 1/2 In., Pair 13.00
Figure, Noel Angel Choir, 4 Boys Holding Letter Of Noel, 1950s, 3 3/4 In., 4 Piece 18.00
Figure, Santa Claus, Celluloid, Fur Trim, Feather Tree, Japan, Box, 6 3/4 In. 150.00
Figure, Santa Claus, Composition, Germany, 10 In. 81.00
Figure, Santa Claus, In Sleigh, Reindeer, Composition, Felt, Fur Beard, Germany, 8 In. 80.00
Figure, Santa Claus, In Sleigh, Reindeer, Molded Paper Face, Cotton Beard, Felt Suit, 10 In. 92.00
Figure, Santa Claus, Papier-Mache, Cardboard Base, Jointed Arms, Painted, Felt, Germany, 10 In. . 80.00
Greeting Card, Christmas Greetings, Hand Colored Scene, Wallace Nutting, c.1920, 6 x 5 In. 28.00
Greeting Card, Paul Jacoulet, Hokkan-Zan, Coree, Folder, Yellow Cover Design 259.00
Greeting Card, Paul Jacoulet, Le Bonze Errant, Coree, Folder, Yellow Cover Design 180.00
Greeting Card, Paul Jacoulet, Orchidees Blanche, Jaluit, Folder, Green Cover Design 374.00
Greeting Card, Paul Jacoulet, Souvenirs D'Autrefois, Japon, Folder, Yellow Cover Design 173.00
Greeting Card, VFW, Veterans Of Foreign Wars, Box Of 19 Cards, 1970s, 7 x 5 In. 3.00
Handkerchief, Crocheted Lace Trim, Machine Embroidered, Candles, 11 In. 6.00
Plates that are limited editions are listed in the Collector Plate category or in the correct factory listing.
Postcard, Children, Sleeping Under Tree, Raphael Kirchner, Paris 80.00
Postcard, Happy & Bright Christmas, Santa Claus, Sleigh, Hold-To-Light, Mallick 230.00
Postcard, Happy Christmas, Santa Claus, Angels, Hold-To-Light, Mallick 259.00
Postcard, Jolly Christmas, Santa Claus, Red Suit, Hold-To-Light 259.00
Postcard, Merry Christmas, Santa Claus, Children, Windmill, Hold-To-Light 200.00
Postcard, Santa Claus, Tree, Children, Raphael Kirchner 546.00
Puzzle, Santa Claus Travels, Cube, Cardboard, Lithograph, Box, 1897, 13 1/2 x 11 In. 798.00
Puzzle, Santa Claus, The Night Before Christmas, Cardboard, Lithograph, Box, McLoughlin Bros . . 578.00
Santa Claus, Head, Papier-Mache, Large 35.00

Santa Claus, Papier-Mache, White Coat, Tree, Basket Of Toys, Germany, 15 In. 400.00
Santa Claus, Sleigh, Presents, Tree, Papier-Mache, 12 In. 190.00
Shaker, Mrs. Claus, Spaghetti Trim On Apron, Holly Leaf, Japan, 3 3/4 In. 7.00
Snowman, Snow Globe Belly, Snow, Angel & Deer Inside, Hong Kong, c.1965, 4 3/4 In. 18.00
Stocking, E.T., Felt, Tree, Star, 1982, 15 In. 11.00
Toy, Balloon Santa, Tin, Windup, Alps, 9 1/2 In. 33.00
Toy, Jack-In-The-Box, Santa Claus, Papier-Mache, Germany 55.00
Toy, Magic Snowman, Battery Operated, Box, Insert, 1950s 225.00
Toy, Santa Claus, Composition, Roly Poly, 1910, 8 In. 495.00
Toy, Santa Claus, Happy, Tin, Fabric, Plush, Battery Operated, Z Co., Box, 12 In. 165.00
Toy, Santa Claus, Nodder, Runs In Circles, Tin, Celluloid, Masudaya, Occ. Japan, Box, 3 3/4 In. 72.00
Toy, Santa Claus, On Sled, Tin, Celluloid, Windup, Mitsushima, Occupied Japan, Box, 7 In. 138.00
Toy, Santa Claus, Rabbit Fur Beard, Windup, Composition, Germany, 6 In. 275.00
Toy, Santa Claus, Roly Poly, 1910, 4 1/4 In. 275.00
Toy, Santa Claus, Roly Poly, Schoenhut, 9 In. .... ***ILLUS*** 616.00
Toy, Santa Claus, Tin, Celluloid, Cast Iron, Windup, Occupied Japan, Box, 6 In. 385.00
Toy, Santa Claus, Walker, Cast Iron Feet, Box, Occupied Japan 764.00
Toy, Sleigh, Santa, 2 Reindeer, Cast Iron, Swirling Rudders, Swan Heads, Hubley, 16 3/4 In. 1540.00
Toy, Sleigh, Santa, Cast Iron, Kyser & Rex, 13 In. 3901.00

CHRISTMAS TREES made of feathers and Christmas tree decorations of all types are popular with collectors. The first decorated Christmas tree in America is claimed by many states, including Pennsylvania (1747), Massachusetts (1832), Illinois (1833), Ohio (1838), and Iowa (1845). The first glass ornaments were imported from Germany about 1860. Dresden ornaments were made about 100 years ago of paper and tinsel. Manufacturers in the United States were making ornaments in the early 1870s. Electric lights were first used on a Christmas tree in 1882. Character light bulbs became popular in the 1920s, bubble lights in the 1940s, twinkle bulbs in the 1950s, plastic bulbs by 1955. In this book a Christmas light is a holder for a candle used on the tree. Other forms of lighting include light bulbs. Other Christmas memorabilia is listed in the preceding section.

Aluminum, 94 Branches, Evergleam, Box, 72 In. .... 500.00 to 542.00
Aluminum, 94 Branches, Revolving Color Projector, Evergleam, Box, 72 In. 825.00
Aluminum, Rotating, Musical Stand, Color Wheel, Evergleam, 84 In. 570.00
Bubble Light, 18 Lights, Green Model, Noma, c.1948, 23 In. 305.00
Bubble Light, 21 Lights, C-7, Noma, 38 In. 357.00
Color Wheel, 4 Colors, Colormagic, Motorized, Compco Corp., Box 55.00
Color Wheel, Deluxe Model, 4 Colors, Penetray, Box, 12 In. 86.00
Color Wheel, Motorized, 4 Colors, Norelco, Box 76.00
Feather, Berries, 10 Branch Layers, Wood Base, West Germany, 66 In. 585.00
Feather, Red Berries, Flame Resistant, Cube Base, U.S. Zone Germany, 32 In. 178.00
Feather, Wrapped Trunk, Red Berries, Wooden Base, West Germany, 11 1/2 In. 115.00
Fence, Cast Iron, Double Gates, J.E. Stevens, 1880, 10 Piece 425.00
Fence, Folk Art, Angels, Donkeys, Trees, Stars, c.1900, 14 1/2 x 12 In. 330.00
Fluorescent, 7 Lights, Sylvania Lamp, Royal, Box 80.00
Garland, Gold, Indoor, Outdoor, Vinyl, Non-Tarnishing, Weatherproof, Flameproof, Box, 15 Ft. 10.00
Kugel, Blown Glass, Green, Germany, 8 In. 75.00
Kugel, Glass, Blue, Round, Embossed Tin Mount, Swivel Ring Hanger, 9 1/2 In. 99.00
Kugel, Glass, Grape Cluster, Gold, Brass Mount, Ring Hanger, 4 x 2 3/4 In. .... 88.00 to 110.00
Kugel, Glass, Green, Egg Shape, Brass Mount, Ring Hanger, 7 x 5 In. 99.00
Light, Cat & The Fiddle, Milk Glass, Marked SK14 Japan, 3 3/4 In. 12.50
Light Set, 7 Different Disney Characters, Paramount, Original Box, 1950s 255.00
Light Set, 7 Lights, Plastic Holders, Red & Green String, ClemCo Lighting, N.J., Box, c.1935 .... 15.00
Light Set, Bakelite Holders, Noma Electric Corp., N.Y., Box, 1939 .... 20.00
Light Set, Bubble, 7 Lights, Sylvania, Box .... 18.00 to 39.00
Light Set, Drum Covers, 10 Lights, Box, 1960s 26.00
Light Set, Holly Twinkle Lite, Lamps Twinkle At Random, Box 108.00
Light Set, Mickey & Minnie Mouse, Pluto, Mazda Lamps, Noma, Box, 1935-38 .... 110.00
Light Set, Zelco, 8 Bulbs, Cloth Cord, Zell Bros. Mfg. Co., Box, c.1925 .... 104.00

Don't try to restore old ornaments. A little damage and wear adds to the charm of old Christmas ornaments. Restoration lowers value.

Christmas Tree, Stand, Painted Tin, 3 Dwarfs, Hatchets, Mushroom Support, 9 x 12 In.

Ornament, Angel On Cloud, Felt, Paper Label, Russberrie & Co., Tiawan, 3 1/2 In. 4.00
Ornament, Angel, Stained Glass, Handmade, 4 In. 5.00
Ornament, Baby's First Christmas, Carriage, Plastic, Hallmark, Box, 1981, 3 3/4 In. 41.00
Ornament, Ball, 3-D Scene, Trees, Santa Claus, Sleigh, Reindeer, Plastic, c.1960, 3 1/2 In. 5.00
Ornament, Banjo, Stamped Cardboard, Silvered, Gold Strings, Dresden, 5 1/4 In. 1870.00
Ornament, Basket Of Flowers, Glass, Metal Top, Marked Japan, Paint, 1 3/4 In. 4.00
Ornament, Bell, Mercury Glass, Metal Cap, Shiny Brite Made In U.S.A., 2 1/4 In. 3.00
Ornament, Bird, Glass, Hand Blown, Germany, 1950s, 4 1/2 In. 18.00
Ornament, Cat, Glass, Brown, Hand Painted, Czechoslovakia, c.1920, 3 1/2 x 2 In. 35.00
Ornament, Dog, White, Black, Red Collar, Hand Painted, Dresden, 2 3/4 In. 358.00
Ornament, Elephant, Howdah, Stamped Cardboard, Silvered, Dresden, 3 In. 2750.00
Ornament, Frog, Green, Red, Metallic Pain, Dresden, 2 In. 2090.00
Ornament, Girl, Reproduction Of Hummel By Schmid, 1984, 4 1/4 In. 13.00
Ornament, Goose, Running, White, Stamped Cardboard, Dresden, 2 3/4 In. 468.00
Ornament, Grape Cluster, Glass, Cobalt Blue, Germany, Victorian, 4 x 1 3/4 In. 21.00
Ornament, Horse Drawn Trolley, Stamped Cardboard, Dresden, 5 3/4 In. 2750.00
Ornament, Mercury Glass, Bell Shape, Pink & Green Stripes, 1 3/4 In. 16.00
Ornament, Merry Christmas, Glass, Ball, Hallmark, Box, 1981 .... 6.50
Ornament, Moon Face, Pressed Cardboard, Gold Finish, Dresden, 3 1/8 In. 275.00
Ornament, Our First Christmas Together, Ball, Hallmark, Box, 1979 .... 41.00
Ornament, Pickle Shape, Gold Tone Cap, Green, Germany, 4 1/2 In. 22.00
Ornament, Pinecone, Glass, Frosted, Blown, 4 In., 14 Piece 110.00
Ornament, Pinecone, Glass, Metal Top, Marked Made In U.S. Of A., 2 3/4 In. 4.00
Ornament, Pink Tree, Clear Glass Globe, West Germany, 3 3/4 In. 36.00
Ornament, Ring Necked Pheasant, 3rd In Series, Hallmark, Box, 1984 .... 17.00
Ornament, Rooster, Pressed Cardboard, Dresden, 3 1/2 x 3 1/4 In. 1540.00
Ornament, Santa Claus, Children, Basket, 2-Sided, Dresden, 3 3/4 In. 1100.00
Ornament, Santa Claus, Cotton, Tree In Hand, Paper Face, Bag, 4 3/4 In. 275.00
Ornament, Santa Claus, Glass, Silvered, Blown, Frosted Trim, 3 1/2 In., 6 Piece 55.00
Ornament, Santas, Holding Hands, Tree, Hand Blown, Painted, Poland, 1950s, 5 x 3 In. 22.00
Ornament, Spaceman, Mercury Glass, Early 1900s, 4 1/2 x 2 1/2 In. 132.00
Ornament, Spirit Of Christmas, Santa In Airplane, Hallmark, Box, 1982 .... 17.00
Ornament, Swiss Chalet, Stamped Cardboard, Silvered, Dresden, 2 x 1 3/4 In. 3850.00
Ornament, Tin Soldier, Pressed Tin, Hallmark, Box, 1982 .... 7.00 to 8.00
Ornament, Wolf, Stamped Cardboard, Dresden, 4 3/8 In. 165.00
Ornament Set, Cardboard, 3-D, Surf Laundry Detergent Premium, Unused, 1952 .... 24.00
Ornament Set, Comic Characters, Wood, Unbreakable, Jaymar, Box, 10 Piece 330.00
Ornament Set, Shiny Bright, Balls, Glass, Box, 12 Balls 18.00
Stand, Cast Iron, Crosshatch Design, c.1900, 5 1/ 2 x 17 In. 75.00
Stand, Illuminated, Mazda Lamps, Metal, No. 6549, 3 Legs, Box, 1930s, 9 In. 36.00
Stand, Lifetime, Metal, Box, 8 x 5 In. 25.00
Stand, Painted Tin, 3 Dwarfs, Hatchets, Mushroom Support, 9 x 12 In. .... ***ILLUS*** 252.00
Stand, Receptacles, Outlets, Painted Green, Cast Iron, Peerless, 1930s 410.00
Stand, Rotating, For Aluminum Tree, 4 Colors, Evergleam, Box 610.00

Topper, Angel, On Cloud, Plastic, Gold Foil Base, National Tinsel, 1950s, 7 In. 50.00
Topper, Mercury Glass, Green, Gold Stars, Glitter, 12 In. 30.00
Topper, Santa Glo, Illuminated, Noma, Box, 8 1/2 In. 56.00

CHROME items in the Art Deco style became popular in the 1930s. Collectors are most interested in high-style pieces made by the Connecticut firms of Chase Brass & Copper Co. and Manning-Bowman & Co.

CHASE

Bell, Chase, Canterbury, Bakelite Handle, Harry Laylon 55.00
Candy Box, Chase, Eden, Harry Laylon, 4 3/4 x 3 In. 25.00
Canister Set, Flour, Sugar, Coffee, Tea, Everedy, 4 Piece 55.00
Cocktail Shaker, Chase, Glass, Blue Moon Doric, Bakelite, 12-In. Shaker, 3-In. Glass 500.00
Cocktail Shaker, Cylindrical, Turned Walnut Finial, Italy, 1920s, 10 In. 113.00
Cocktail Shaker, Manhattan, Polished, Norman Bel Geddes, Revere, Box, 13 1/4 In. 944.00
Cocktail Stand, Ferris Wheel, Glasses, Manhattan Cocktail Shakers, Bel Geddes, 24 In. 7080.00
Coffee Set, Bakelite Handles, Manning-Bowman, 1930s, 13 1/2-In. Pot, 3 Piece 125.00
Coffee Set, Red Bakelite Handles, Art Deco, No. 800, United, 3 Piece 350.00
Coffee Set, Tray, Krome Kraft, Bakelite Handles, Farber, 12-In. Pot, 19-In. Tray, 4 Piece 250.00
Humidor, Chase, Art Deco, 5 1/2 x 5 1/4 In. 99.00
Ice Bucket, Tongs, Antartica, Russel Wright, Chase, 7 1/2 In. 175.00
Ice Bucket, Tongs, Hammacher Schlemmer 29.00
Percolator, Bakelite Handle, Foreman Bros., 12 In. 135.00
Pitcher, Cocktail, Cover, Empire Pattern, Bakelite Finial & Stopper, Revere, 12 1/2 In. 1455.00
Salt & Pepper, Skyway, Chase, c.1940, 1 1/4 x 1 3/8 In. .... 30.00 to 35.00
Sandwich Plate, Quiet Pool, Lurelle Guild, 1934, 13 In. 55.00
Sauce, Chase, Viking, Walter Von Nessen 55.00
Sugar & Creamer, Alfonso Lanelli, Sunbeam, 1940s 30.00
Sugar & Creamer, Art Deco, Cordiality Tray, Frederick Preiss, Revere, 12 1/4-In. Tray 32.00
Sugar & Creamer, Tray, Art Deco, No. 2420, Irwinware, 9-In. Tray 18.00
Sugar & Creamer, Tray, Daphne, Revere, c.1939, 9 1/4 x 3 3/4 In. Tray 25.00
Sugar & Creamer, Tray, Revere, 11 1/4-In. Tray, 2 3/8-In. Creamer, 2 1/4-In. Sugar 68.00
Syrup, Chase, Russel Wright 105.00
Table Chef, Chase, Walter Von Nessen Handle 146.00
Tidbit, 2 Tiers, Art Deco, Riviera, Box, 11 x 13 In. 30.00
Tidbit, Folding, Chase, 8 x 15 x 11 In. 150.00
Tray, Art Deco, Catalin Handles, Feet, Manning-Bowman, c.1928 .... 246.00
Vase, Penthouse, Art Deco, Manning-Bowman, c.1934 .... 145.00

CIGAR STORE FIGURES of carved wood or cast iron were used as advertisements in front of the Victorian cigar store. The carved figures are now collected as folk art. They range in size from counter type, about three feet, to over eight feet high.

Bust, Hiawatha, Bear Claw Necklace, Plaster, 20 x 13 In. 627.00
Indian, 3 Feathers, Gold Color Necklace, Star On Green Sash, c.1940, 60 In. 2200.00
Indian, Carved, Painted, Feathered Headdress, Holding Knife, 800s, 78 In. 16100.00
Indian, Carved, Painted, Plume Headdress, New Base, 1800s, 69 In. 24150.00
Indian, Hand To Forehead, Headdress, Plaster, Early 1900s, 58 In. 1210.00
Indian, Holding Tobacco Leaves, Cigar, Cast Zinc, W. Demuth & Co., 81 In. 27600.00
Indian, Lying Down, Red Indian Cut Plug, Ceramic, 1900s, Countertop 1320.00
Indian, With Dog, Cast Zinc, Painted, 19th Century, 78 In. 63250.00
Indian, Woman, Feathered Headdress, With Tobacco Leaves, Box, 79 x 34 In. 28200.00
Indian, Woman, Tabletop, 37 In. 5290.00
Scottish Argyle Drummer, Wood, Carved, Red, White, Black Paint, 41 In. 300.00

CINNABAR is a vermilion or red lacquer. Pieces are made with tens to hundreds of thicknesses of the lacquer that is later carved. Most cinnabar was made in the Orient.

Bowl, Imperial, Gilded Mount, 6 Characters, 1735-96, 8 1/4 In., Pair 21150.00
Box, 2 Tiers, Flowers, Hardstone Plaque, Chinese, Early 1900s, 12 1/2 x 9 x 4 In. 590.00
Box, Cover, Bird On Flowering Prunus Branch, Brocade Ground, Carved, 4 1/4 In. Diam. 140.00
Box, Cover, Hunting Scene, Diaper Ground, Carved, 6 3/4 In. 300.00
Box, Dragons, Pearls, Fruit, Flowers, Chinese, 1800s, 11 In. 1530.00

Box, Dragons, Pearls, Square, Chinese, 1800s, 7 3/4 In., Pair 1175.00
Snuff Bottle, Carved, Bone Spoon, Chinese, 2 5/8 x 1 7/8 In. 95.00
Vase, Carved, Landscaped Panels, Plum Blossoms, Leaves, Baluster, 16 In. 763.00
Vase, Landscapes, Flower Borders, Chinese, 1800s, 24 In., Pair 7640.00

CIVIL WAR mementos are important collectors' items. Most of the pieces are military items used from 1861 to 1865. Be sure to avoid any explosive munitions.

Apothecary Box, Wood, Compartments, Bottles, N.B. Drewry, Surgeon, 30th Georgia, 1863 .... 4025.00
Artificial Leg, Iron, Wood Peg, Hard Rubber Base, John Logan, Mo., 33 x 5 In. 110.00
Artillery Pass Box, Leather, Brass Rivets, Strap, Wood Block Bottom, Cylindrical, 9 x 5 In. 690.00
Belt, Louisiana Enlisted, Leather, Brass Buckle, Pelican In Nest, Laurel Wreath, Stars 8050.00
Belt, Sword, South Carolina Officer's, Brass Buckle, Palmetto Tree, NP Ames 14950.00
Belt Buckle, 2nd Ohio Volunteer, Infantry, Brass, Applied Nickel Plated No. 2 .... 55.00
Belt Plate, Confederate, GM, Georgia Militia, Mottled Brass Patina, 2 Piece 7475.00
Binoculars, LeMaire Of Paris, 6 x 5 1/2 In. 415.00
Boots, Cavalry 230.00
Box, Wood, Sponge, Stenciled, Ordnance Officer, Atlanta Arsenal, Georgia, 38 x 20 In. 1150.00
Bridle Rosettes, US Artillery, Brass, Intertwined USA On Front, Pair 175.00
Buttons, Rubber, National Rubber Co., 1851 Patent, 8 Piece 35.00
Calipers, Engineer's, Iron, Stamped A. Richards, c.1865 .... 750.00
Camp Chair 165.00
Canteen, Bull's-Eye, Original Cover, Cloth Strap 300.00
Canteen, Confederate, Cedar Wood, Iron Bands & Straps, Spout, Linen Sling, 7 1/4 In. 4600.00
Canteen, Confederate, Rattan Wicker Cover, 8 x 5 In. 195.00
Canteen, Drum Shape, Domed Sides, Iron Bands, Carrying Strap, Wood, 9 1/2 x 6 In. 575.00
Canteen, Union, Cloth Cover, Sling, 8 In. 400.00
Cap, Forage, Union, Crossed Sabers, Company Letter I, Regimental No. 2, Chinstrap 6900.00
Carpet Bag, Leather Handles, Lock, Key, J.H. Menges, Columbia, Pa., 18 x 16 In. 575.00
Cartridge Box, Leather, Brass Plate, SNY, State Of New York 520.00
Cartridge Box, Leather, Lead-Filled Plate, US, Marked, Longley & Co., Lewiston, Me., 1862 .... 980.00
Coat, Frock, Confederate Veteran's, Lt. Col. Of Kentucky, Gray, Double Breasted Buttons 1800.00
Coat, Frock, Union, 1st Lieutenant's, Blue Wool, 9 Eagle I Buttons, Shoulder Crests 6325.00
Coat, Frock, Union, New York Captain's, Blue Wool, Captain's Shoulder Boards 4600.00
Coat, Great, Union, Infantry, Sky Blue Wool, Cape, Gold Buttons, Dated Sept. 20, 1864 .... 5463.00
Crutch, Wood, John Logan, Mo., 48 x 5 In. 116.00
Drum, 2 Sticks, Samuel Lowman, 5th Maryland Volunteers, Union Drum Mfg. Co. 3658.00
Drum, Dixie White Olaf, William Sempf, N.Y., c.1860, 16 x 8 3/4 In. 489.00
Drum, Snare, Wood, Rope, Label, Boston Drum Factory, 61 Court St., Elias Howe, Agent, 12 In. 1150.00
Epaulets, Naval Staff Officer's, Silver Bullion Roped Fringe, Shadow Box 525.00
Fife, Ebony, 2 Rings, Metal Ends, 16 1/2 In. 145.00
Fife, Rosewood, Liver Ditson & Co., Barton, Mass., 17 In. 198.00
Hat, Hardee, Crossed Cavalry Insignia, Jeff Davis Pin, Yellow Cord, Label 9200.00
Hat, Slouch, Blue, Embroidered Patch, 190 GAR, Officer Cord, T. Dalton, N.Y. 489.00
Haversack, Artillery, Leather, Roller Buckle, Stamped US Watervliet Arsenal, 14 x 14 In. 750.00
Jacket, Shell, Artillery, Union, Blue Wool, Eagle On Collar & Cuffs, Plaid Lining 3165.00
Kepi, City Hospital Ambulance Surgeon, Brass Eagle Buttons 230.00
Knife, Bowie, Blacksmith Made, D-Guard, Strap Guard, Confederate, 16 1/2-In. Blade 950.00
Knife, Bowie, D-Guard, Forged From File, Confederate, Leather Scabbard, c.1863, 23 3/8 In. 7345.00
Knife, Mess, Tinned Blade, Bone Grip, Patina, Lamson Goodnow & Co., 6 1/4 In. 95.00
Map, Army Of Potomac, 1862 .... 65.00
Medical Kit, Dr. John Duff Brown, Ivory Handles, Confederate, 5 1/2 x 9 1/2 In. 2485.00
Medicine Case, Alligator Skin Bag, 43 Glass Vials, Boerick & Tafel, N.Y., 7 x 7 x 16 In. 660.00
Money Belt, Officer's, Leather, Woven Strap, 7 Pouches, c.1862, 3 1/2 x 28 1/2 In. 345.00
Powder Horn, Incised Design, Prancing Horse, Brass Tacks, Domed Plug, 1860, 17 In. 1100.00
Saber, Cavalry, Palmetto, Ames Model 1840, Marked Columbia, S.C., Scabbard, 36 In. 8400.00
Saber, U.S. Cavalry Officer's, Etched, Eagle, Flag, Ribbon, E Pluribus Unum, 35 In. 3500.00
Saddle, Cavalry, Model 1859 McClellan, Brass Tag, Allegheny/US/Arsenal, 1864 .... 6325.00
Saddle, Valise, Black Leather, Skirts, Straps, Embossed US Shield, Model 1859, 15 In. 3740.00
Saddle Blanket, Penn. Medical Officer's, Tarred Canvas, Blue Wool, Leather, Gold Braid 3160.00
Saddle Blanket, Union Officer's, Blue Felt, Silver Cloth Stars & Edging, 33 x 22 In. 489.00

Saddle Pack, Confederate, Brown Leather, Tooled Flower, Round, Straps, Buckle, Handles 575.00
Saddlebag, Leather, Sewn, Roller Buckle, Crow's Foot Strapping, Virginia, 14 x 12 In., Pair 575.00
Sash, Non-Commissioned Officer's, Red Worsted, Knot & Tassel Ends, 84 In. 690.00
Sash, Officer's, Red Silk, Knot & Tassel Ends, 108 x 4 In. 800.00
Surgeon's Kit, Wood, 3 Tiers, Fitted Interior, 27 Tools, Key 4888.00
Sword, Artillery, Confederate, Short Blade, Cast Brass Handle, 25 In. 195.00
Sword, Artillery, Etched Eagle, Marked NP Ames, Springfield, 1841, 19-In. Blade 1035.00
Sword, Calvary, Single Edge Blade, Emerson & Silver, Wrapped Handle, 42 In. 248.00
Sword, Cutlass, Naval, Verdigris Pommel, Leather Grip, Stamped NC, Ames, Model 1860 .... 690.00
Sword, Dress, Cast Brass Hilt, Sharkskin Handle, Scabbard, G.A.R., 1800s, 34 1/2 In. 165.00
Sword, Model 1850, Staff & Field Officer, Etched Blade, Steel Scabbard, 32 In. 2050.00
Sword, Officer's, Etched Blade, Sharkskin Grip, Scabbard, Ames, Model 1850, 31 In. 2700.00
Sword, Officer's, Single Edge, Acid Etched, Stamped, Cast Brass, Wrapped Handle, 38 In. 330.00
Sword, Single Edge Blade, Leather Wrapped Handle, Brass Hilt, Chelmsford, Mass., 42 1/2 In. ... 320.00
Telescope, Brass, Leather Covered, Marked CSA, Unfolded 16 1/2 In. 978.00

CKAW, see Dedham category.

CLAMBROTH glass, popular in the Victorian era, is a grayish color and is somewhat opaque, like clam broth. It was made by several factories in the United States and England.

Salt, 4-Lobe Bowl & Foot, Oval, c.1840, 2 1/4 x 3 1/8 In. 605.00
Salt, Stag Horn, 32-Ray Base, 1835-50, 1 3/4 x 2 x 3 1/8 In. 66.00
Vase, Trumpet, 14 In. 230.00

CLARICE CLIFF was a designer who worked in several English factories after the 1920s, including A.J. Wilkinson Ltd., Wilkinson's Royal Staffordshire Pottery, Newport Pottery, and Foley Pottery. She is best known for her brightly colored Art Deco designs, including the "Bizarre" line. She died in 1972. Reproductions have been made by Wedgwood.

Alpine, Bowl, Stepped, Black, Cream, Landscape Interior, Square, 11 x 11 x 3 1/2 In. 1135.00
Bizarre, Bowl, Landscape, Latona, Backstamp, 1930, 16 In. 1645.00
Bizarre, Bowl, Multicolored, Landscape, Tree, Latona Pattern, 1930, 16 In. 1655.00
Bizarre, Vase, Cream Ground, Landscape, Patina Country Pattern, 1930, 10 In. 1295.00
Bizarre, Vase, Orange Poppies, Stepped Form, Signed, 7 1/2 In. 780.00
Cowslip, Teacup & Saucer, Green, Cream, 2 1/4 x 5 & 5 In., Pair 720.00
Crocus, Box, Cover, Circular, Newport Pottery, c.1930, 5 1/4 In. 320.00
Flying Swan, Vase, 3 Holes, Multicolored, 6 1/4 In. 1315.00
Geometric, Teapot, Cover, Green, Cream, Orange, 4 1/2 In. 359.00
Geometric Flowers, Candlestick, 2 1/2 In., Pair 448.00
Goldstone, Vase, Flower, Beetle, Handle, 7 1/2 x 3 3/4 In. 239.00
Inspiration, Basket, Blue, Pink, Footed, Handle, 15 In. 2150.00
Inspiration, Vase, Stepped, Aqua, 7 1/2 In. 720.00
Inspiration Lily, Bowl, Stepped, Aqua, 4 1/2 x 12 1/2 x 12 1/2 In. 840.00
Latona, Vase, Stained Isis, Multicolored, 10 In. 3465.00
Leaf Tree, Plate, Orange, Green, 7 1/2 In. 480.00
Melon, Fantasque Bizarre, Bowl, Newport Pottery, c.1930, 5 In. 210.00
Patina, Vase, Landscape, Multicolored, Mushroom, 5 1/2 x 4 1/4 In. 780.00
Patina, Vase, Tree, Notched Rim, Multicolored, 6 In. 895.00
Pine Grove, Beaker, Trees, Black, Cream, Orange Interior, 5 In. 299.00
Sliced Fruit, Bowl, Octagonal, 4 1/2 x 9 1/2 In. 448.00
Sungold, Planter, Geometric, Multicolored, 7 1/2 In. 510.00

CLEWELL ware was made in limited quantities by Charles Walter Clewell of Canton, Ohio, from 1902 to 1955. Pottery was covered with a thin coating of bronze, then treated to make the bronze turn different colors. Pieces covered with copper, brass, or silver were also made. Mr. Clewell's secret formula for blue patinated bronze was burned when he died in 1965.

Bowl, Pottery, Copper Clad, Bulbous, Original Patina, Marked, 9 In. 780.00
Vase, Copper Clad, Raised, Incised, Patina, 6 3/4 In. 1645.00

Vase, Copper Clad, Tooled Clover Design, Flattened Form, 6 1/4 In. 600.00
Vase, Copper Clad, Verdigris, Baluster, Flared Rim, 12 1/2 x 7 In. 470.00
Vase, Copper Clad, Verdigris, Squat Base, Straight Neck, Flared Rim, Handles, 7 x 7 1/2 In. 1295.00
Vase, Leaf Blade, Green On Green, 4 3/4 In. 80.00
Vase, Pottery, Copper Clad, Shouldered, Flared, Original Patina, Marked, 11 In. 2510.00
Vase, Pottery, Copper Clad, Squat, Original Patina, Marked, 4 1/2 In. 1435.00
Vase, Raised Flowers, Copper Clad, Tapered, Original Patina, 6 In. 538.00

CLIFTON POTTERY was founded by William Long in Clifton, New Jersey, in 1905. He worked there until 1909 making lines including *Crystal Patina* and *Clifton Indian Ware.* Clifton Pottery made art pottery until 1911 and then concentrated on wall and floor tile. By 1914 the name had been changed to Clifton Porcelain and Tile Company. Another firm, Chesapeake Pottery, sold majolica marked *Clifton Ware.*

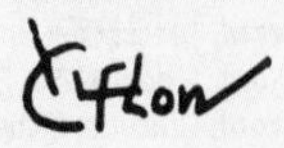

Pitcher, Cover, Indian Ware, Black Geometric, Red Ground, 8 In. 50.00
Teapot, Indian Ware, Black Geometric, Red Ground, Squat, 5 x 11 In. 50.00
Vase, Green Glaze, 2 Angular Handles, 1906, 11 In. 150.00
Vase, Indian Ware, Dark Red Arches, Red Ground, 11 1/2 In. 150.00
Vase, Red Brown, Dark Brown Geometric, Marked, Arkansas 205, Cinerary Olla, 6 1/2 In. 300.00
Vase, Squat, Pueblo Viejo Tribe, Upper Gila Valley, 7 3/4 x 12 1/2 In. 646.00
Vase, Yellow & Green Crystalline Drip Glaze, White Ground, Bulbous Base, 7 1/2 In. 360.00

CLOCKS of all types have always been popular with collectors. The eighteenth-century tall case, or grandfather's clock, was designed to house a works with a long pendulum. In 1816, Eli Terry patented a new, smaller works for a clock, and the case became smaller. The clock could be kept on a shelf instead of on the floor. By 1840, coiled springs were used and even smaller clocks were made. Battery-powered electric clocks were made in the 1870s. A garniture set can include a clock and other objects displayed on a mantel.

Advertising, Aspinall's Enamel, Baird, c.1895, 30 1/2 In. 728.00
Advertising, Belle Bourbon, Cast Iron, Bell Shape, Bronzed Finish, Late 1800s, 12 1/2 In. 235.00
Advertising, Borden's Milk & Cream, Elsie, Curved Glass, Gold Frame, 15 1/2 In. 165.00
Advertising, Chew Friendship Cut Plug, Chewing Mouth, 5 x 4 1/8 x 2 1/2 In. 1650.00
Advertising, Columbia Bicycles, Curved Lens Glass, Chrome Bezel, Light-Up, 1940s, 12 In. 578.00
Advertising, Damaskeene Razor, Bearded Man Shaving, Holding Baby, 21 x 27 1/2 In. 330.00
Advertising, Deckers Iowana, World's Best Hams & Bacons, Oak, Paper Dial, c.1910, 14 In. 90.00
Advertising, Dr Pepper, Thanks, Call Again, Reverse On Glass 3360.00
Advertising, Eibners Ice Cream, Since 1883, Red, White, Blue, Double Bubble, Round, 16 In. 330.00
Advertising, Eveready Batteries, Mahogany Frame, Electric, c.1940, 13 1/4 In. 33.00
Advertising, Falstaff Beer, 1956, 19 x 19 In. 116.00
Advertising, Garfield Tea, Cures Constipation, Walnut, Seth Thomas, c.1890, 27 1/2 In. 1120.00
Advertising, Goulding's Manures, Are The Best, New Haven, c.1915, 30 x 18 In. 1680.00
Advertising, Goulding's Manures, Best For Crops, Black, Embossed, New Haven, 32 In. 1905.00
Advertising, Griswold Mfg. Co., Erie, Pa., Frying Pan, Cast Iron, 14 5/8 In. 4406.00
Advertising, Hires Root Beer, Wall, Original Glass Lens, 15 In. 190.00
Advertising, Iroquois Beer, Ale, Double Bubble, Electric, Light-Up, Round, c.1960 .... 275.00
Advertising, Jolly Tar Pastime, John Finzer & Bros., Edw. F. Baird, c.1910, 30 1/2 In. 1120.00
Advertising, Keen Kutter, Round, c.1940, 19 In. 305.00
Advertising, Keen Kutter, Square, c.1950, 14 1/2 In. 390.00
Advertising, Lucky Strike Tobacco, R.A. Patterson Tob. Cos., Paper Dial, Wood, Round, 16 In. 385.00
Advertising, Lucky Strike, Rosewood Case, New Haven, c.1915, 25 x 16 In. 1230.00
Advertising, Lucky Strike, Rosewood Veneer, 8-Day, New Haven, c.1910, 25 In. 336.00
Advertising, Lucky Strike, School, 8-Day, New Haven, c.1920, 24 1/2 In. 530.00
Advertising, Milkmaid Milk, Now's The Time To Buy It, Pendulum, Baird Style, 17 1/2 In. 460.00
Advertising, Monell's Teething Cordial, Baird, c.1892, 30 x 18 In. 2520.00
Advertising, Mt. Lassen Beverages, Pressed Aluminum, Glass, 24 In. 250.00
Advertising, Old Mr. Boston Whiskey, Flask Shape, Metal Case, 8-Day, Gilbert, 1900s, 22 x 10 In. 306.00
Advertising, Packard, Yellow Neon, 1950s, 26 In. 1790.00
Advertising, Quaker State Motor Oil, Lights Up, Plastic, Black Numbers, 1984 .... 95.00
Advertising, Rexall For Reliability, Blue, Yellow, White, Curved Glass, 15 In. 100.00

Advertising, Rexall, Bisma-Rex, Relieves, Soothes, Yellow, Blue, White, Plastic, Round, 16 In. 190.00
Advertising, Sauer's Flavoring Extracts, Mahogany, 8-Day, New Haven, c.1910, 42 In. ...530.00 to 1400.00
Advertising, Sliptivity Oil, C.C. Snowdon, Calgary, Edmonton, Winnipeg, Vancouver, c.1925, 10 In. 560.00
Advertising, Time Cutlery, Remington DuPont, Pressed Front, 24 x 18 In. 115.00
Advertising, Tivoli Beer, Round, 20 In. 275.00
Advertising, Triangle Brand Shoes, Gilbert Clock Co., 5 x 6 In. 55.00
Advertising, Vanner & Prest's Molliscorium, 8-Day, Baird Clock Co., c.1890, 31 In. 1090.00
Alarm, Organ Grinder, Animated, Waterbury Clock Co., c.1910, 3 3/4 x 3 3/4 In. 130.00
Alarm, Topsy, Blinking Eye, Louisiana Old Time Syrup, Working, 5 In. 450.00
Alarm, Winchester Store, 6 x 4 In. 810.00
American Clock Co., Iron Front, Painted, Time, Strike, Alarm, c.1850, 16 x 13 In. 390.00
Angel & Trumpet, Gilded Bronze, 8-Day, Thread Suspension, c.1840, 19 1/2 x 24 In. 4750.00
Anniversary, Dome, Brass, Enamel, c.1920, 12 In. 99.00
Ansonia, 2 Sailors Turning Ship's Wheel, 8-Day, Time & Strike, 17 In. 2465.00
Ansonia, Alarm, Echo, Animated, Boy Hammers Bell, c.1880, 7 1/2 x 4 In. 2016.00
Ansonia, Arcadia, Ball Swing, 8-Day, c.1905, 31 1/2 In. 8120.00
Ansonia, Bagdad, Walnut, 50 In. 4400.00
Ansonia, Berkeley, Black, Painted, Time, Strike, Alarm, 22 x 13 1/2 In. 110.00
Ansonia, Capitol, Wall, Regulator, Oak Case, 8-Day Spring, Time & Strike, c.1900, 53 In. 896.00
Ansonia, Dawson, Regulator, Crystal, Brass Case, 8-Day, Time & Strike, c.1914, 9 1/4 In. 475.00
Ansonia, Dorval, Regulator, Crystal, Brass Case, 8-Day, Time & Strike, c.1914, 8 3/4 In. 195.00
Ansonia, Elysian, Regulator, Crystal, Brass, Glass, 8-Day, Gong Strike, c.1915, 16 1/2 In. 895.00
Ansonia, Etruscan, No. 1, Cast Spelter, Bronze Finish, 8-Day, Time & Strike, c.1874, 18 In. 275.00
Ansonia, Gallery, Oak, 8-Day, Time & Strike, c.1900, 16 In. 140.00
Ansonia, Macbeth, Shelf, Cast Metal Case, 8-Day, Time & Strike, c.1904, 11 1/2 In. 448.00
Ansonia, Marbleite, Shelf, Hard Rubber, 8-Day, Time & Strike, c.1883, 11 1/2 In. 280.00
Ansonia, Niobe, Oak Case, 38 In. 1650.00
Ansonia, Pompeii, Shelf, Iron Case, 8-Day, Time & Strike, c.1904, 10 3/4 In. 390.00
Ansonia, Pulford, Porcelain Dial, Oak Case, 8-Day, Time & Strike, c.1904, 13 1/4 In. 78.00
Ansonia, Queen Elizabeth, Oak Case, 8-Day, Time & Strike, c.1901, 37 In. 896.00
Ansonia, Regulator B, Oak Case, 8-Day, c.1905, 31 1/2 In. 280.00
Ansonia, Regulator, Crystal, Brass, 10 3/4 x 6 1/2 In. 259.00
Ansonia, Regulator, Crystal, No. 6, Cobalt Blue, Gold Trim, c.1914, 17 1/2 In. 4430.00
Ansonia, Regulator, Jeweler's, No. 17, Oak Case, 96 In. 8800.00
Ansonia, Regulator, Mahogany, Classical Style, 8-Day, 2-Weight, Chime, 1800s, 30 x 16 In. 350.00
Ansonia, Rosalind, Shelf, Iron Case, Enameled, 8-Day, Time & Strike, c.1904, 12 In. 335.00
Ansonia, School, Mahogany, Terry Patent Calendar, c.1870, 24 In. 1900.00
Ansonia, Shelf, Apollo, Faux Tortoiseshell, 8-Day, Time & Strike, c.1901, 16 1/4 In. 615.00
Ansonia, Shelf, Black Enameled Metal Case, c.1900, 9 In. 92.00
Ansonia, Shelf, Figural, George Dilby, World War I Commemorative, Spelter, 20 In. 330.00
Ansonia, Shelf, Greek, Ebonized, 2-Train Movement, N.Y., Late 1800s, 15 In. 88.00
Ansonia, Shelf, Man, Compass, Paper, Round Clock, Gold Paint, 13 1/2 x 17 1/2 x 7 1/2 In. 460.00
Ansonia, Shelf, Mercury, Metal Case, Porcelain Dial, 8-Day, Time & Strike, c.1894, 15 In. 500.00
Ansonia, Swing, No. 2, Doll, 30-Hour, c.1900, 8 In. 1000.00
Ansonia, Wall, Cherry Case, 47 In. 7425.00
Ansonia, Wall, Oak, Brass Trimming, 8-Day, 2-Weight, c.1904, 46 1/2 In. 5600.00
Art Deco, Deer, Rectangular Base, Metal, Patinated, Onyx, France, c.1930, 12 1/4 In. 170.00
Arthur Pequegnat Clock Co., School, Oak, Canada, 26 x 16 In. 530.00
Atkins, School, Short Drop, Time Only, c.1875, 25 x 15 In. 670.00
Austrian, Grand Sonnerie, Walnut, Scroll Engraved, Movement Replaced, c.1880, 50 In. ... *ILLUS* 1792.00
Bachelard Terrond De Alliez, Shelf, Grand Sonniere, Pinwheel, Calendar, 8-Day, c.1825, 11 In. .. 2910.00
Banjo, Chelsea, Perry's Victory, Mahogany, 8-Day, Willard, c.1925, 42 In. 1008.00
Banjo, Chelsea, Reverse Painted Tablet, Boston State House, Bigelow & Kennard, 32 In. 635.00
Banjo, E. Howard & Co., No. 5, Cherry Case, 8-Day, Iron Weight, c.1875, 29 In. 1905.00
Banjo, E. Howard & Co., No. 5, Grained Case, Pendulum, Weight, c.1875, 29 In. 2800.00
Banjo, Elmer Stennes, O.O.B. 880.00
Banjo, Elmer Stennes, Weight Driven, 24 K Gold Plated 1430.00
Banjo, Federal, Mahogany, Brass Mounts, Weight, Pendulum, 30 1/2 x 10 x 4 In. 400.00
Banjo, Federal, Mahogany, Gilt Gesso, Ball & Eagle Finial, Brass Bezel, 40 In. 1175.00
Banjo, G.D. Hatch, Rosewood Case, 8-Day, Weight Driven, c.1860, 33 1/4 In. 1456.00
Banjo, Gold Rope-Twist Trim, Brass Fittings, Eagle Finial, Reverse Glass Panels, Roses, 34 In. 230.00

Clock, Austrian, Grand Sonnerie, Walnut, Scroll Engraved, Movement Replaced, c.1880, 50 In.

Clock, Banjo, Pine, Rosewood Veneer, E. Howard Movement, Repro, c.1930, 39 In.

Clock, Carriage, Brass, Cloisonne, Day, Date, Alarm, Stike, Repeat, Japan, c.2002, 8 1/4 In.

Banjo, Howard & Davis, Boston, No. 4, Cherry Case, Lighthouse Tablet, c.1850, 32 In. 1232.00
Banjo, Howard & Davis, Rosewood Case, c.1860, 38 x 15 1/2 In. 2520.00
Banjo, M. Cheney, Walnut Case, Weight Driven, Painted Dial, Montreal, 1830s, 37 1/2 In. 1050.00
Banjo, Mahogany, Reverse Painted, Brass Side Arms, 8-Day, Strike Lever, 32 x 8 x 3 In. 410.00
Banjo, New Haven, Winetka, Mahogany Case, 8-Day, Time & Strike, c.1929, 18 1/2 In. 224.00
Banjo, Pine, Rosewood Veneer, E. Howard Movement, Repro, c.1930, 39 In. .... *ILLUS* 2532.00
Banjo, Samuel Abbott, Grand Piano Movement, Scenic Tablet, Stenciled Leaves, 40 In. 5825.00
Banjo, Seth Thomas, Blackstone, Wood, Painted, Eagle Finial, 8-Day, c.1932, 18 3/4 In. 196.00
Banjo, Simon Willard, Mahogany Case, T-Bridge Movement, 33 1/4 In. 4025.00
Banjo, Waltham, Walnut, 2 Ships, Eagle Finial, 8-Day, c.1930, 42 In. 3360.00
Banjo, Waterbury, Gilt, Hull Glass 1870.00
Barr, Executive Model Battery, Cherry Base, Silvered Dial, Dome, c.1939, 10 1/2 In. 225.00
Bawo & Dotter, Shelf, H & H Monastery, English Chiming, 15 x 19 1/2 In. 525.00
Becker, Gustav, Alt Deutsch, 8-Day, Spring Movement, Arch Dial, Eagle Finial, c.1900, 46 In. 1036.00
Becker, Gustav, Box, Oak Case, 8-Day, Time & Strike, Porcelain, Brass, c.1910, 20 In. 140.00
Becker, Gustav, Grand Sonnerie, Walnut, 3-Weight, Engraved Tulips, c.1885, 49 1/2 In. 1540.00
Becker, Gustav, Regulator, Vienna, Walnut, Late 1800s, 32 x 16 x 6 1/2 In. 120.00
Beehive, Iron Front, Mother-Of-Pearl Inlay, Time & Strike, c.1850, 15 x 9 In. 448.00
Beers, Lester, Shelf, Pillar & Scroll, Mahogany Veneer, 30-Hour, c.1970, 31 In. 590.00
Bell, John, Burnley, Skeleton, 2-Fusee, Bell Strike, Wood Base, No Dome, c.1860, 17 1/2 In. 2240.00
Berliner, Wall, Swinging Arm, 36 In. 770.00
Biedermeier, Wall, Regulator, Mahogany, Scalloped Door, 30-Day, Austria, c.1840, 42 In. 7800.00
Birge & Fuller, Double Steeple, Wagon Spring, Walnut, 4-Candle, 26 In. 2750.00
Birge & Fuller, Mahogany Veneer, Cornice Shelf, 8-Day, Time & Strike, c.1845, 39 In. 950.00
Black Forest, Carved, Eagles, Sheep, Rabbit, Fox, 44 In. 6050.00
Black Forest, Cuckoo, Bird, Flowers, Brass, 30-Hour, 18 1/2 x 14 x 7 In. 138.00
Black Forest, Cuckoo, Hand Carved, Quail, Grape, Leaf, 30-Hour, 18 1/2 x 16 1/2 x 7 1/2 In. 385.00
Black Forest, Cuckoo, Shelf, 30-Hour, 17 x 11 x 7 In. 170.00
Black Forest, Cuckoo, Stag Pediment, Crossed Rifles, Birds, Rabbit, Cast Iron Weights, 48 In. 1150.00
Black Forest, Shelf, Walnut, Carved, Deer & Bocage On Rockwork, Outswept Base, 24 x 18 In. 1440.00
Black Forest, Trumpeter & Cuckoo, Deer Head, 1/4-Strike, 3-Weight, c.1890, 33 In. 2800.00
Black Starr & Frost, Shelf, Mahogany Case, 8-Day, Time & Strike, 13 In. 110.00
Black Starr & Frost, Travel, Sterling Silver, 8-Day, Leather Case, 3 1/8 x 2 3/4 In. 315.00
Blinking Eye, Black Man Grins, Plastic, Second Hand Move, Counter Pendulum, 4 1/2 In. 100.00
Blondeau, Regulator, Restoration, Rosewood, Inlaid, c.1820, 21 1/4 x 11 1/2 x 8 In. 7200.00
Boardman, Chauncey, Shelf, 8-Day, Fusee, President's House 825.00
Boardman & Wells, Shelf, Mahogany Veneer, 30-Hour, Wood Dial, c.1840, 26 In. 106.00
Boiler Room, Enameled Metal, Bakelite, 8-Day, Lever Movement, England, c.1910, 7 In. 67.00
Boname, Shelf, Marble, Brass, France, 17 3/4 x 13 1/2 In. 935.00
Boston Clock Co., Shelf, Art Nouveau, Mahogany, Peaked Case, Early 1900s, 10 1/4 In. 355.00
Boudoir, Marble, Ormolu, Ram, Porcelain Dial, France, c.1900, 7 1/2 In. 560.00
Bracket, 1/4 Strike, 2 Gongs, Silk Thread Suspension, Neufchatel, Swiss, c.1790, 37 In. 3696.00
Bracket, Bell Top, Carved, 4-In. Dial, France, 12 In. 220.00
Bracket, Ebonized Case, Arched, Gilt Columns, Flame Finials, 3-Fusee, 8-Bell, England, 18 In. 2350.00

Bracket, Ebonized Case, Ormolu, 3-Fusee, 8-Bell, 1/4-Chime, 2 Tunes, England, c.1890, 28 In. . . . 2910.00
Bracket, Mahogany Case, 3-Fusee, 8-Bell, 5-Gong, Chimes, Shreve, Crump & Low, 27 In. 4250.00
Bracket, Walnut Case, Burnished Steel, Silent Dial, Sweep Second Hand, 18 x 11 x 7 1/2 In. 2990.00
Bracket, Werner Deponirt Patent, Calendar, Germany, c.1890, 15 In. 2350.00
Bradley & Hubbard, Colonial Man, Blinking Eye, Cast Iron, c.1857, 16 In. 2800.00
Bradley & Hubbard, John Bull, Blinking Eye, Cast Iron, c.1865, 17 In. 1790.00
Bradley & Hubbard, Sambo, Holding Banjo, Blinking Eye, 30-Hour, Cast Iron, 16 In. 1905.00
Bradley & Hubbard, Topsy, Blinking Eye, 30-Hour, Cast Iron, c.1865, 16 3/4 In. 3470.00
Brass, 2-Piece Frame, Engraved Cornucopia, Urns, Fruit Baskets, Caryatids, 5 1/8 x 4 In. 1035.00
Brass, Looping Movement, Flower On Stem, 8-Day, 15 Jewels, Swiss, c.1950, 5 3/4 In. 39.00
Brass, White Enamel Dial, Blue Ground, Giltwood, Eagle Surmount, 21 x 14 In. 1325.00
Breguet, Carriage, Pepose Works, Key 7280.00
Breguet & Fils, Carriage, Brass Gorge Case, Repeater, Alarm, Engraved Top Glass, 7 1/4 In. 6160.00
Brewster & Ingrahams, Mahogany Veneer, 8-Day, Rack Strike, Repeater, c.1845, 20 In. 616.00
Brewster & Ingrahams, Shelf, Rosewood, Onion Top, Steeple Finials, 8-Day, Time & Strike, 20 In. 2128.00
Bridgeport Brass Co., Shelf, Walnut Case, 8-Day, Time & Strike, c.1880, 24 In. 390.00
Brown, J.C., Shelf, Column & Cornice, Mahogany Veneer, 8-Day, Time & Strike, c.1848, 32 In. 840.00
Burlingham, D.C., Wall, Mahogany Case, 8-Day, Fusee, England, c.1890, 14 1/2 In. 650.00
Butler, Roman M., Shelf, Mahogany Veneer, 8-Day, Time & Strike, c.1835, 39 1/4 In. 476.00
Camerer Cuss & Co., Oak, Architectural, 8-Day, Fusee, c.1890, 44 In. 1905.00
Carriage, Brass, Cloisonne, Day, Date, Alarm, Stike, Repeat, Japan, c.2002, 8 1/4 In. . . . . . . *ILLUS* 90.00
Carriage, Brass, Corinthian Columns, Beveled-Edge Glass Panels, 5 1/2 In. 1438.00
Carriage, Brass, Grand Sonnerie, Alarm & Repeat, France, c.1900, 7 1/4 In. 1680.00
Carriage, Brass, Lift Panel, Porcelain Dial, Promoli & Hausberg, c.1835, 5 In. . . . . *ILLUS* 5600.00
Carriage, Brass, Oval, Engraved Geometrics, Scroll Handle, Grand Sonnerie, France, 8 In. 3360.00
Carriage, Brass, Paris, 4 x 7 1/2 x 3 1/2 In. 710.00
Carriage, Brass, Time & Strike, Travel Case, France, c.1845, 6 In. 810.00
Carriage, Empire Style, Green Japanned, Griffins, Late 1800s, 9 1/4 In. 295.00
Carriage, Gilt Brass, Bell Strike, White Enamel Dial, Repeater, c.1900, 5 1/2 In. 2245.00
Carriage, Gilt Brass, White Enamel Dial, Bell Below, Alarm, Beveled Glass Case, 1900, 6 In. 265.00
Carriage, L'Epie Fondie, Brass, Glass, Repeater, France, 1939, 5 1/4 In. 1035.00
Carter, L.F. & W.W., Calendar, Double Dial, Rosewood, 8-Day, Time & Gong, c.1865, 26 In. 2070.00
Carter, L.F. & W.W., Shelf, Rosewood Case, B.B. Lewis Calendar, 33 In. 880.00
Cartier, Alarm, 14K Gold, Square, Macassar Base, Triptych Box, Art Deco, 4 x 4 x 3 In. 1880.00
Chelsea, Desk, Drake, Bronze Case, 8-Day, Black Finish, Beveled Glass, c.1930, 6 In. 140.00
Chelsea, Desk, Hancock, Brass Case, 8-Day, c.1924, 4 In. 335.00
Chelsea, Desk, Raleigh, Bronze Case, 8-Day, Beveled Glass, c.1939, 8 In. 335.00
Chelsea, Desk, Standish, Brass Case, 8-Day, c.1930, 10 In. 700.00
Chelsea, Mahogany, Carved, 8-Day, Barometer, Thermometer, Hygrometer, c.1952, 39 In. 1008.00
Chelsea, Pendulum Regulator, No. 1, Oak, Weight Driven, c.1902, 34 In. . . . . .1570.00 to 2016.00
Chelsea, Shelf, Walnut, 8-Day, Time & Strike, c.1970, 12 1/2 In. 390.00
Chelsea, Ship's Bell, Copper, Patinated, c.1915, 8 3/4 x 17 In. 660.00
Chelsea, Ship's Bell, Mahogany, Brass Case & Bezel, Silvered Dial, 8-Day, c.1952, 9 In. 615.00
Cope, William, School, 2-Fusee, Painted Dial, Nottingham, England, c.1860, 28 In. 900.00
Couaillet, Shelf, Regulator, Crystal, 9 In. 415.00
Courtin, Shelf, Marble, Bronze, France, 15 In. 880.00
Cuckoo, Eagle & Deer, Carved, 34 In. 770.00
Cuckoo, Walnut, Vine, Singing Bird, Continental, Late 1800s, 12 3/4 x 10 3/4 In. 646.00
Cuckoo, Wood, 3 Weights, Swiss, 17 In. 80.00
Cuckoo & Quail, 3-Train, 1/4 Striking, 3 Flute Assemblies, Germany, c.1910, 38 In. 3585.00
Daniel Pratt's & Son, Office Regulator, Oak, 8-Day, Weight, Eastman, c.1895, 34 In. 2240.00
Davall, Lantern, Brass Case, 8-Day, Passing Strike, c.1937, 11 3/4 In. 390.00
Delagrave, C.H., World Time, Ebonized Case, 8-Day, Time & Strike, c.1900, 18 In. 840.00
Deniere, Shelf, Marble, Regulator, Crystal, Paris, 14 1/2 In. 1100.00
Dogs Attacking Boar, 2 Rabbits, Leaves, Swiss, 1880, 28 x 18 1/2 x 5 In. 5750.00
Drew, William, Shelf, George III Style, Mahogany, Brass Mounted, c.1865, 24 x 16 In. 1000.00
Drocourt, Carriage, Brass Case, Beveled Glass, Grand Sonnerie, Repeater & Alarm, 7 1/2 In. 2800.00
Duverdrey & Bloquel, Tall Case Shape, Mahogany, 8-Day, 11 Jewels, c.1910, 11 1/2 In. 196.00
Electrique Brillie, Metal Case, Painted Dial, Battery, France, c.1914, 21 1/2 In. 308.00
Eli Bartholomew & Co., Mahogany, Sea Battle, Mirror Glass, c.1825, 35 In. . . . . *ILLUS* 441.00
Eli Terry & Sons, Mahogany, 30-Hour, Pillar & Scroll, 1818-24, 31 In. . . . . *ILLUS* 2115.00

Clock, Carriage, Brass, Lift Panel, Porcelain Dial, Promoli & Hausberg, c.1835, 5 In.

Clock, Eli Bartholomew & Co., Mahogany, Sea Battle, Mirror Glass, c.1825, 35 In.

Clock, Eli Terry & Sons, Mahogany, 30-Hour, Pillar & Scroll, 1818-24, 31 In.

Elliott, F.W., Mahogany Case, 8-Day, Time & Strike, Bailey Banks & Biddle, c.1900, 20 In. 616.00
Eterna, Desk, 8-Hour, Silver, Guilloche Enamel, Bun Feet, France, 1900s, 2 1/4 In. 646.00
Eureka, Shelf, Model No. 4440, Mahogany Inlay, Electric, England, c.1910, 11 3/4 In. 445.00
Farmer, Pushing Wheelbarrow, Spelter, 30-Hour, Alarm, France, c.1900, 10 In. 1008.00
Feishtinger, C.W., Calendar, Double Dial, Walnut, 8-Day, Time & Strike, c.1894, 22 In. 1595.00
Forestville, Beehive, Rosewood, Piecrust Ripple, 8-Day, Time & Strike, Alarm, 19 In. 2465.00
Forestville, Column & Cornice, Mahogany, 8-Day, Time & Strike, Bird Tablet, 34 In. 840.00
French, Brass, Painted, Hot Air Balloon, 1846, 9 1/2 In. 645.00
French, Lyre, Ebonized, Gilt, 20 In. 690.00
French, Man & Bicycle, Alabaster Case, 8-Day, Pendulum, c.1900, 15 1/2 In. 840.00
French, Ormolu, Bronze, Marble, Cherub, 8-Day, c.1880, 12 In. 1008.00
French, Ormolu, Marble, 2 Putti, Temple Designs, Revolving Dials, c.1875, 17 1/4 In. 9070.00
French, Shelf, Cast Brass, Porcelain Dial, 8-Day, Time & Strike, 19 In. 365.00
French, Shelf, Louis XVI Style, Gilt Bronze, 8-Day, Silk Suspension, c.1850, 12 In. 670.00
French, Shelf, Lyre Shape, Rosewood, Satinwood Inlay, Knight's Armor, 8-Day, 23 1/2 In. 2800.00
French, Shelf, Mahogany Case, Double Escape Wheel, 8-Day, Time & Strike, c.1890, 14 In. 670.00
French, Shelf, Marble, Perpetual Calendar, Thermometer, Barometer, 8-Day, c.1890, 16 In. 785.00
Frodsham, Charles, Desk, Porcelain Panels, Greek Scenes, c.1885, 12 In. 2800.00
Frodsham, Charles, Shelf, George III Style, Ebonized, Lifting Handle, Victorian, 19 1/2 In. 1410.00
G. Nelson, Rosewood Face, Aluminum Hour Markers & Hands, Round, 13 In. 1680.00
Gallery, Oak, Japan, 9 In.-Dial, 14 In. 84.00
German, Calendar, Multi-Dial, Black Case, Day, Month & Date Rollers, c.1890, 18 In. 525.00
German, Picture Frame, Gypsy Dancer, Wood Case, 30-Hour, Time & Strike, c.1880, 15 In. 225.00
Gien, Porcelain, White & Rose, Cartouche, Cherubs, Flowers, Enamel Dial, 10 x 9 In. 325.00
Gilbert, Kitchen, Oak, Gingerbread Decoration, Victorian, 20 In. 120.00
Gilbert, Oak, Champion M, 16 1/2 x 15 In. 170.00
Gilbert, Ogee, 30-Hour, c.1880, 25 x 15 In. 56.00
Gilbert, Regulator, No. 3, Walnut Case, 48 In. 1870.00
Gilbert, School, Slant Drop, Rosewood Case, c.1870, 25 x 17 In. 168.00
Gilbert, Wm. L., Amphion, Walnut, 8-Day, Time & Strike, c.1885, 26 In. 1120.00
Gilbert, Wm. L., Mitra, Walnut, 8-Day, Time & Strike, c.1891, 22 1/2 In. 560.00
Gilbert, Wm. L., Office Drop Calendar, Maranville Patent, 34 In. 2530.00
Gilbert, Wm. L., Regulator, No. 11, Walnut, 8-Day, 2-Weight, c.1891, 50 In. 4200.00
Gilbert, Wm. L., Shelf, Curfew, Enamel Over Wood, 8-Day, Time & Strike, c.1915, 17 1/2 In. 196.00
Gilbert, Wm. L., Shelf, No. 411, Porcelain, Blue, Flowers, 8-Day, Time & Strike, c.1898, 11 In. . . . 225.00
Gilbert, Wm. L., Winstead Gothic Extra, 30-Hour, Rosewood Veneer, c.1875, 17 1/4 In. 146.00
Gilbert Clock Co., Shelf, Oak, Classical Roman Style, Winstend, Conn., 15 x 22 In. 350.00
Gillett & Johnston, Wall, Regulator, Brass Dial, Digital Reading, 2-Weight, c.1900, 61 In. 4590.00
Girl, Bronze, Gold Plated, Ormolu, 8-Day, Bell Strike, c.1875, 14 1/2 In. 560.00
Globe, 4 Gilt Bronze Women, Robes, 8-Day, Cut Pinion, Continental, c.1955, 13 x 6 In. 1290.00
Gravity, Rack, Germany, c.1955, 4-In. Dial, 23 In. 190.00
Gravity, Ratcheted Upright, Barbell Pendulum, England, c.1921, 11 In. 336.00
Griesbaum, Karl, Peddler & Whistler, 30-Hour, Pendulum, Arched Dial, c.1960, 13 In. 1467.00
Grivolas, 4-Glass Case, Porcelain Dial, Pendule 400 Jours, c.1915, 11 In. 925.00

Gubelin, Marble, Red Lacquered Dial, Silvered Bronze Mount, 9 1/2 x 8 5/8 In. 2328.00
Gubelin, World Time, Gilt & Brass Case, 8-Day, 24 Cities, c.1950, 5 3/4 In. 308.00
Hamburg American, Cottage, Hardwood Case, 30-Hour, Time & Alarm, c.1875, 14 1/4 In. 190.00
Hermes, Revolving, Silver, Brass, Calendar, Thermometer, Compass, Barometer, 3 5/8 In. 1840.00
Horolovar, Dickory Dickory Dock, Mouse, 8-Day, Box, c.1965, 24 In. 728.00
Hotchkiss, Spencer, Shelf, Empire Style, Full Column, Mahogany, c.1830, 36 In. 785.00
Hour, Charles, Barometer, Thermometer, 4-Glass Case, Wanamaker, c.1900, 11 1/2 In. 925.00
Hour, Charles, Shelf, Marble, 8-Day, Time & Bell, Grogan Co., France, c.1900, 12 1/4 In. 560.00
Howard, E. & Co., Regulator, No. 10, Walnut Case, 8-Day, Weight Driven, c.1874, 34 In. 3640.00
Howard, E. & Co., Regulator, No. 11, Keyhole, 8-Day, Weight, c.1880, 32 In. 8400.00
Howard, E. & Co., Wall, Marble Front, 28 In. 2549.00
Howard, No. 36, Wall, Regulator, Jewelers, Walnut, Mercurial Pendulum, 75 1/2 In. 46750.00
Howard, No. 66, Wall, Slave, 16-In. Dial 3286.00
Howard Miller, Asterisk, Yellow Enameled Metal, Black Hands, G.Nelson, 10 In. 410.00
Howard Miller, Ball, No. 4755, Multicolored Balls, G. Nelson, c.1948, 13 In. 1140.00
Howard Miller, Ball, No. 4755, Salmon Color, G. Nelson, c.1948, 13 In. 480.00
Howard Miller, Basket Weave, Round, G. Nelson, c.1955, 12 In. 540.00
Howard Miller, Black, Orange Blocks, Yellow Enameled Metal, Red Second Hand, 11 1/4 In. 1175.00
Howard Miller, Eye, G. Nelson, c.1954, 30 In. 4320.00
Howard Miller, Moon Dial, Mahogany, Broken Arch Pediment, Weight Driven, 94 x 31 In. 1640.00
Howard Miller, Pretzel, G. Nelson, c.1955, 18 In. 1680.00
Howard Miller, Roman Numerals, Round, G. Nelson, c.1958, 14 In. 180.00
Howse, Charles, Bracket, 2-Fusee, 8-Day, Time & Strike, c.1777, 16 1/2 In. 4760.00
Imhof, Desk, Gotham, Brass, 8-Day, 15 Jewel, c.1955, 6 3/4 In. 78.00
Ingraham, Doric, Candy Stripe, Maple, Walnut, 30-Hour, Time & Strike, c.1880, 16 In. 560.00
Ingraham, E. & Co., School, Regulator, Boston Model, Oak, 8-Day, c.1920, 32 In. 448.00
Ingraham, Kitchen, Walnut, Silvered Decoration In Door, Victorian, 22 In. 150.00
Ingraham, Oak, Gingerbread, Golden Oak Case, c.1890, 21 x 14 In. 56.00
Ingraham, School, Hartford Model, Long Drop, Oak, c.1900, 32 x 17 In. 308.00
Ingraham & Co., Shelf, Empire, Walnut, 8-Day, Time & Strike, c.1885, 18 In. 756.00
Ithaca Bank, No. 2, Wall, Walnut, 48 In. 2200.00
Ithaca Calendar, Double Dial, c.1875, 26 x 12 In. 1230.00
Ithaca Calendar, No. 10, Farmers, Walnut, 30-Day, Double Dial, c.1874, 21 In. 670.00
Ithaca Calendar, No. 11, Octagon, Walnut, Double Dial, c.1880, 21 In. 925.00
Ithaca Calendar, Walnut Case, Carved, H.B. Horton, 20 1/4 In. 1870.00
J. Mancer & Co., Table, 3-Fusee, 1/4 Chime, 8 Bells, England, c.1890, 24 1/2 In. 3080.00
Jahresuhrenfabrik, Gilt Case, 400-Day Disc, Torsion Pendulum, c.1902, 11 In. 420.00
Japy, Freres, Cartel, Cast Bronze, 8-Day, Time & Strike, c.1880, 20 In. 450.00
Japy Freres, Calendar, Marble Case, 2 Dials, 8-Day, Time & Strike, c.1890, 16 In. 1456.00
Japy Freres, Garniture Set, Marble, 8-Day, Time & Strike, Rancoulet, c.1896, 30 In., 3 Piece 950.00
Japy Freres, Gilt Bronze, Champleve Enamel, Marble Base, c.1875, 23 In. 4200.00
Japy Freres, Regulator, Crystal, 8-Day, Time & Gong Strike, c.1900, 8 3/4 In. 785.00
Japy Freres, Regulator, Crystal, Brass, 8-Day, Time & Gong, Oval, c.1900, 10 1/2 In. 448.00
Japy Freres, Regulator, Crystal, Brass, 8-Day, Time & Strike, c.1900, 11 1/2 In. 476.00
Japy Freres, Regulator, Crystal, Ormolu, Enamel, 8-Day, Time & Gong, c.1900, 15 1/2 In. 1510.00
Japy Freres, Shelf, Brass, Glass, 2 Doors, Portrait On Ivory Pendulum Bob, R. Ricard, 12 In. 575.00
Japy Freres, Shelf, Figures In 18th-Century Costume, Porcelain, c.1890, 12 x 9 1/2 In. 276.00
Japy Freres, Shelf, Paris Porcelain, Knight, Gilt, Flowers, 1800s, 20 x 11 1/4 x 5 1/2 In. 295.00
Jefferson Electric, Mystery, Goldtone Case, c.1955, 9 In. 35.00
Jerome, Chauncey, Iron Front, c.1850, 20 x 12 In. 390.00
Jerome, Chauncey, Shelf, Ogee, Mahogany Veneer, 30-Hour, Time & Strike, c.1850, 25 1/2 In. 84.00
Jerome, Chauncey, Shelf, Paris Model, Brass, Porcelain, Dome, Botsford Patent, c.1850, 11 In. ... 756.00
Jerome & Company, Steeple, Miniature 56.00
Jeromes & Darrow, Shelf, Wooden Works, c.1842, 38 x 19 1/2 In. 1065.00
Johnson, William, Shelf, Rosewood Grain, 4 Columns, Double Fusee, 30-Hour, c.1845, 19 In. 1345.00
Junghans, Art Nouveau Woman, Draped, Holding Pendulum & Clock, 13 In. 430.00
Junghans, Batboy, Swinging Mystery, Bronzed Spelter, c.1905, 19 In. ....560.00 to 1090.00
Junghans, Black Boy, Guitar, Animated, Germany, c.1890, 4 1/4 x 9 1/2 In. 1760.00
Junghans, Bracket, Walnut, 8-Day, Quarter Strike, 2 Gongs, c.1900, 21 3/4 In. 505.00
Junghans, Elephant, Swinging Arm, 8-Day, c.1905, 11 In. 1120.00
Junghans, Max Bill, Ceramic, White, Timer, 10 x 6 1/2 In. 826.00

If you find a clock with a complete, original paper label, add 35% to the value. A damaged porcelain clock face lowers the value by 20% to 30%.

Clock, McClintock, Alarm, Chrome, Light Green Marbleized Catalin, Art Deco, 5 1/2 In.

Junghans, Monkey Business, Blinking Eye, Open Book, Pedestal Base, 9 1/4 In. ....765.00 to 1064.00
Junghans, Onion Boy, Swinging Arm, Porcelain Dial, c.1905, 11 In. 868.00
Junghans, Onion Boy, Swinging Arm, Spelter, 8-Day, c.1900, 15 1/2 In. 1230.00
Junghans, Shelf, Mahogany Case, Westminster Chime, c.1910, 17 In. 420.00
Knox, Archibald, Pewter, Copper, Enamel, England, 1902-05, 7 1/2 In. 5240.00
Knox, Archibald, Travel, Pewter, Leaves, Tudric, Round Face, England, Early 1900s, 4 In. 615.00
Knox, Archibald, Tudric, Pewter, Enameled Cabochons, England, c.1902-05, 8 In. 3495.00
Kroeber, F., Regulator, No. 30, Walnut, Turned Columns, 8-Day, New York, c.1880, 41 In. 2690.00
Lashley, Edward, School, Oak, 2-Fusee, c.1850, 45 In. 1568.00
LeCoultre, Atmos, Brass, 15 Jewels, Perpetual, Never Wind, c.1956, 9 In. 450.00
LeCoultre, Atmos, Brass, Glass Panel, 9 x 8 1/4 In. 410.00
LeCoultre, Atmos, Cube-Shape Movement, Brass, Glass, 1900s, 9 1/4 In. 470.00
LeCoultre, Atmos, Presentation, Engraved Brass Plaque, c.1957, 9 In. 450.00
LeCoultre, Desk, Gilt Brass, Silvered Brass Dial, 8-Day, c.1950, 7 1/4 In. 65.00
LeCoultre, Shelf, Atmos, Presentation, Brass, Perpetual, c.1964, 9 1/4 In. 450.00
LeCoultre, Shelf, Brass, Glass, Perpetual Motion, 9 1/2 x 7 In. 468.00
Lenox, Travel, Bronze, Mother-Of-Pearl, Leather Case, Swiss, c.1900, 3 In. 230.00
Lenzkirch, Shelf, Regulator, Crystal, 9 1/2 In. 600.00
Lenzkirch, Shelf, Walnut, Bronze Trim, 8-Day, Germany, c.1890, 12 1/2 In. 700.00
LeRoy, Horoger Du Roy, Shelf, Lyre Shape, 8-Day, Time & Strike, c.1910, 15 1/2 In. 1736.00
LeRoy, Skeleton, Portico, 2-Train, Bell Strike, Grid Pendulum, No Dome, c.1850, 20 In. 5600.00
Lighthouse, Platform, 8-Day, Bronze Patina, France, c.1880, 20 In. 590.00
Lovers, Ormolu, Silk Suspension, Bell Strike, France, c.1830, 19 In. 1456.00
Lux, Country Scene, Pendulette, 6 1/4 In. 358.00
Lux, Golfer, Pendulette, 7 In. 905.00
Macomb Co., Shelf, Calendar, Old Movement, New Case, 28 In. 660.00
Mammy, Blinking Eye, Second Hand Move Acorn Counter, Pendulum, 7 1/4 In. 90.00
Man, Shovel, Flower Bouquet, Spelter, Gold Paint, France, c.1890, 12 In. 360.00
Man On Chair, Books, Rosewood Plinth, Gilt Brass, Inlaid & Blown Glass Dome, France, 1855 .... 880.00
Marti, Regulator, Crystal, Champleve, 12 In. 935.00
Marti, Samuel, Regulator, Crystal, Oval, Cloisonne Trim, Mercury Pendulum, c.1900, 11 In. 785.00
Marti, Shelf, Lyre, Ebonized Wood Case, 8-Day, Time & Strike, c.1880, 23 In. 1008.00
Marti & Cie, Lyre, Marble, Ormolu, Porcelain Dial, c.1890, 23 In. 5320.00
Marti & Cie, Marble, 2 Dials, 8-Day, Time & Strike, Calendar, c.1890, 16 In. 1905.00
Marti & Cie, Marble, Perpetual Calendar, Barometer, 8-Day, c.1890, 19 3/4 In. 1625.00
Marti & Cie, Regulator, Crystal, Brass, 8-Day, Time & Gong, Oval, c.1900, 11 In. 530.00
Martinot, Boulle Style, 8-Day, Time & Strike, c.1870, 33 In. 4200.00
Marton & Gain, Skeleton, 2-Train Fusee, Walnut Base, No Dome, Spain, c.1975, 17 In. 1120.00
McClintock, Alarm, Chrome, Light Green Marbleized Catalin, Art Deco, 5 1/2 In. .... *ILLUS* 325.00
Meiji, Wall, Black Lacquered Case, 8-Day, Time & Strike, c.1948, 15 1/2 In. 30.00
Molle, Shelf, Brass, Architectural Case, Horse, Bell, Paris, c.1860, 14 x 7 In. 880.00
Mougin, Shelf, Lyre, Marble, Gilt, Porcelain Dial, 8-Day, Bell Strike, c.1890, 24 In. 645.00
Muller, Baseball Players, Iron Face, Wood Case, 1876, 16 x 13 In. 4930.00
Munger & Benedict, Mahogany Veneer, 8-Day, Time & Strike, c.1832, 39 In. 1900.00
Mystery, Glaneuse Statue, Swinging Pendulum, Spelter, France, c.1900, 25 In. 3580.00

Mystery, Woman, Gown, Swinging Pendulum, Spelter, Patinated, France, c.1890, 20 In. 2520.00
New Haven, Glass Case, Porcelain Dial, 30-Hour, Round, c.1910, 5 In. 390.00
New Haven, School, Time, Strike, Calendar, Oak Case, Short Drop, 25 x 16 In. 335.00
New Haven, Shelf, Arts & Crafts, Oak, Batwing Hinges, 14 1/4 x 11 1/2 x 5 1/2 In. 144.00
New Haven, Shelf, Harvard Pattern, Cut Glass, 8 x 9 1/2 In. 385.00
New Haven, Shelf, Ogee, Reverse Painted Lyre, Mahogany Veneer, 18 1/4 x 11 3/4 In. 145.00
New Haven, Shelf, Walnut, Calendar, 8-Day, Time & Strike, c.1885, 34 1/2 In. 1680.00
New Haven, Whitney, Wall, Mahogany, 8-Day, Time & Strike, c.1932, 30 1/2 In. 145.00
Novelty, Animated Monk, Bell Ringer, France, Metal, 14 In. 550.00
Novelty, John Bull, Blinking Eye, 16 In. 168.00
Novelty, Shelf, Minstrel, Black, Blinking Eye, 1-Day, Germany, c.1910, 9 In. 1960.00
Oriental Style, Wooden Case, Painted, Gilt, Pagoda, Water Birds, 8 1/2 In. 520.00
Oswald, Genie, Blinking Eye, Composition, Germany, c.1935, 9 In. 730.00
Oswald, Scottie, Googly Eyes, Wood, c.1930, 6 x 5 1/2 In. 145.00
Owens, George, Wall, Regulator 1100.00
Payne, Balloon, Mahogany, 8-Day, Time & Strike, Convex Dial, c.1810, 29 1/2 In. 2130.00
Pinwheel, Regulator, Burled Walnut, 70 In. 2970.00
Pinwheel, Regulator, Jewelers, 84 In. 3960.00
Poole, Melrose, Mortise Case, Silvered Dial, Battery, Morse Products, c.1932, 10 In. 195.00
Portico, Black Marble, Gilt Bronze Pendulum, Classical Mounts, France, c.1830, 19 x 10 In. 2115.00
Portico, Louis Philippe Style, Gilt Bronze, Alabaster, Flowerhead Pendulum, 18 x 9 x 5 In. 940.00
Portico, Louis Philippe, Marble, Gilt Bronze Mounted, 4 Columns, 2 Birds, c.1835, 18 In. 2230.00
Redier, A., Office, Ebonized Pine, 30-Day, Time & Calendar, Porcelain Dial, c.1875, 14 In. 896.00
Regulator, Berliner Style, Germany, 29 In. 550.00
Regulator, Brass, Enamel, France, 11 1/4 In. 978.00
Regulator, Crystal, Champleve, Onyx, France, 13 1/2 In. 1100.00
Regulator, Crystal, Mercury Pendulum, Onyx, Marble, Ormolu, France, c.1900, 13 In. 2015.00
Regulator, Crystal, Year, 4 Glass Panels, Mercury Pendulum, 1-Fusee, Germany, c.1900, 10 3/4 In. 2910.00
Regulator, Vienna, Ebonized Case, Porcelain Dial, 6-Day, 1-Weight, Austria, 32 In. 1680.00
Regulator, Vienna, Oak, Late 1800s, 41 In. 439.00
Regulator, Vienna, Walnut Finish Case, Turned Decoration, 19th Century, 32 In. 176.00
Regulator, Vienna, Walnut, 1-Weight, Austria, c.1880, 35 In. 630.00
Regulator, Vienna, Walnut, 2-Weight, Austria, c.1880, 50 In. 756.00
Regulator, Vienna, Walnut, 3-Train, Chiming Movement, Peaked Case, c.1900, 46 In. 645.00
Regulator, Vienna, Walnut, Ebonized Trim, 2-Weight, Pendulum, Germany, c.1890, 44 In. 2185.00
Regulator, Walnut, Domed Top, Applied Woman's Bust, Late 1800s, 34 In. 206.00
Regulator, Walnut, Ebonized, 3-Weight, Chime, Folkl Josef Debreczenben, c.1870, 48 In. 825.00
Rempe, No. 26, Oak Case, Self-Winding, Painted Dial, c.1903, 43 In. 1900.00
Riggs & Brother, Carriage, Repeater, Philadelphia, 7 1/2 In. 1238.00
Royal Vienna, Dome, Porcelain Case, 4 Columns, French Works, 17 In. 4070.00
School, Drop Octagon, Calendar, 8-Day, Time & Gong Strike, Oak, Germany, c.1900, 27 In. 700.00
School, Warren Sevenoaks, Oak, Round, Pendulum, Key, 18 In. 150.00
Serin, Edouard, Globe, World Time, 8-Day, Bell Strike, c.1880, 19 In. 4480.00
Sessions, Dickory Dickory Dock, Model 5, Oak, 30-Hour, c.1910, 15 1/2 In. 672.00
Seth Thomas, Adamantine, 8-Day, Time & Strike, Black & Tan Case, c.1893, 10 In. 168.00
Seth Thomas, Chime, No. 14, Mahogany Veneer, 8-Day, 1/4 Chime, 5 Bells, 14 In. 756.00
Seth Thomas, Chime, No. 101, Mahogany, 4 Bells, Sonora Chime, 25 1/2 In. 2576.00
Seth Thomas, Column, Rosewood Veneer, 8-Day, Time, Strike, Alarm, c.1875, 16 1/4 In. 450.00
Seth Thomas, Dundee, Mahogany Veneer, 8-Day, Time & Strike, c.1917, 10 1/4 In. 225.00
Seth Thomas, Eclipse, Walnut Case, 8-Day, Time & Strike, c.1890, 24 In. 336.00
Seth Thomas, Empire, No. 11, Regulator, Crystal, 4 Glass Panels, c.1910, 14 In. 560.00
Seth Thomas, Empire, No. 15, Regulator, Crystal, 8-Day, Time & Strike, c.1910, 15 In. 475.00
Seth Thomas, Fashion Model, Double Dial, Walnut Case, c.1880, 27 x 15 In. 3360.00
Seth Thomas, Figural, Rebecca At Well, 8-Day, Time & Strike, c.1870, 17 In. 360.00
Seth Thomas, Gallery, Round, 30-Day, 17 1/2 In. 1265.00
Seth Thomas, Garfield, Walnut Case, 8-Day, Time & Strike, c.1886, 29 In. 2690.00
Seth Thomas, Globe, Drop Octagon, School, Oak, 8-Day, Time Only, c.1900, 32 In. 616.00
Seth Thomas, Kitchen, Victorian, Walnut, Incised Decoration, Stenciled Gilt Glass, 23 In. 118.00
Seth Thomas, Newark, Walnut Case, 8-Day, Time & Strike, Alarm, c.1887, 22 In. 250.00
Seth Thomas, Oregon, 8-Day, Time & Strike, Cathedral Gong, c.1884, 19 1/2 In. 310.00
Seth Thomas, Pillar & Scroll, Folk Art Tablet, 30-Hour, 2-Weight, c.1820, 32 In. 2800.00

Seth Thomas, Pillar & Scroll, Mahogany, 30-Hour, Time & Strike, 31 In. 1120.00
Seth Thomas, Regulator, Calendar, Weight Driven, Rosewood Case, c.1862, 43 x 18 In. 1645.00
Seth Thomas, Regulator, No. 2, Oak Case, c.1910, 34 In. 2128.00
Seth Thomas, Regulator, No. 2, Oak, 1-Weight, Pendulum, c.1900, 36 In. 2015.00
Seth Thomas, Regulator, No. 2, Oak, 8-Day, c.1890, 34 In. 1230.00
Seth Thomas, Regulator, No. 2, Oak, 8-Day, Weight Driven, 36 In. 1680.00
Seth Thomas, Regulator, No. 20, Mahogany, c.1910, 14-In. Dial, 62 In. 8960.00
Seth Thomas, School, Oak Case, Painted Dial, Glass Door, c.1909, 10 In. 325.00
Seth Thomas, School, Regulator, Oak, c.1900, 36 In. ....259.00 to 690.00
Seth Thomas, Shelf, Eastlake, Ebonized Case, Inlaid, Chip-Carved Crest, Late 1800s, 14 1/2 In. .. 440.00
Seth Thomas, Shelf, Mahogany Frame, Conn., 11 1/2 x 14 x 7 3/4 In. 590.00
Seth Thomas, Shelf, Marble & Slate Case, Lion's Head Handles, 19th Century, 10 In. 150.00
Seth Thomas, Shelf, Pillar & Scroll, Mahogany Case, Colonial House, 32 x 17 1/4 In. 1955.00
Seth Thomas, Tambour, Mahogany, c.1950, 8 x 17 In. 55.00
Seth Thomas & Sons, Shelf, Figural, Huntress, No. 8023, 20 In. 1345.00
Seymour Williams & Porter, Shelf, Triple Decker, 35 In. 385.00
Shelf, 8-Day, Time & Gong, H. Desprez Panels, France, c.1890, 10 3/4 In. 530.00
Shelf, Art Deco, Green Onyx, Electric, 8 x 12 x 3 In. 135.00
Shelf, Art Deco, Woman, Seated, Holding Bird, 8-Day, Marble, Spelter, France, c.1920, 10 In. 250.00
Shelf, Arts & Crafts, Oak, Hammered Copper Base, Geometric, 8-Day Movement, 7 x 12 In. 2468.00
Shelf, Black Slate, Bronze Lion's Head Handles, 8-Day, Time & Strike, 13 x 21 x 9 In. 195.00
Shelf, Brass, Porcelain Panel, Dial, Continental, 16 x 8 In. 175.00
Shelf, Brass, Vincenti Movement, Gorge Case, Fluted Columns, France, Early 1900s, 9 5/8 In. 355.00
Shelf, Ebonized Rosewood, Gilt Brass, Engraved Brass Dial, Architectural, 18 In. 968.00
Shelf, Empire, Bronze Dore, France, c.1810, 15 In. 4012.00
Shelf, Federal, Mahogany, Inlaid, Veneered, c.1810, 34 3/4 x 11 1/4 x 6 1/4 In. 7200.00
Shelf, Figural, Lounging Women, Spelter, Marble, France, 24 In. 1540.00
Shelf, Figural, Spelter Reclining Woman, Marble Platform Base, Cast Legs, 1800s 935.00
Shelf, Figural, Woman, Alabaster, France, 23 In. 2475.00
Shelf, French Empire, Mahogany, Classical Gilt Bronze Figural Ormolu Mounts, 8-Day 825.00
Shelf, French Style, Brass Mounted, Red Lacquer Trim, Key Wind, 12 x 6 x 3 In. 120.00
Shelf, French Style, Bronze, Porcelain, Enamel, Footed, c.1900, 17 In. 468.00
Shelf, Gilded Metal, White Onyx, Classical Figure, 8-Day, Time, Victorian 358.00
Shelf, Gilded Spelter, Painted Porcelain, 8-Day, Time & Gong, France, c.1890, 15 In. 475.00
Shelf, Gilt Bronze, Turquoise Ground, Garlands, Urn Finial, Top-Shaped Feet, 20 In. 2245.00
Shelf, Gilt Bronze, White Enamel Dial, Flower, Leafy Panels, Cupid, 1800s, 15 In. 1450.00
Shelf, Glass Case, Applied Top, Cherubs, Gilbert, 10 In. 145.00
Shelf, Kitchen, Walnut, Ebony Highlights, 21 1/2 x 14 1/2 In. 140.00
Shelf, Louis XVI Style, Enamel, Ormolu, 2-Train, 1/2 Strike, c.1900, 15 In. 590.00
Shelf, Lyre, Wood, Gilt Mountings, 8-Day, Time & Bell Strike, France, c.1875, 20 1/2 In. 1680.00
Shelf, Marquetry, Inlaid, Austria, 18 In. 550.00
Shelf, Metal Case, Black Enameled, Beveled Glass Door, Marble, c.1900, 10 x 15 In. 150.00
Shelf, Musical, 1-Day, Skeleton Dial, 2 Tunes, Gilt, Silvered, Dome, Austria, c.1820, 19 In. 2576.00
Shelf, Napoleon III, Gilt Bronze, Cobalt Blue Ground, Porcelain, 19th Century, 23 In. 8400.00
Shelf, Oak, Leaves, Flowers, Masked Faces, Brass Face, 8-Gong Chime, Germany, 22 x 14 In. 2700.00
Shelf, Porcelain Case, Embossed Rococo Mold, Hand Painted Florals, c.1900, 13 In. 175.00
Shelf, Porcelain, Gilt Bronze, Royal Blue, Cherubs, Flowers, Gilt, Sevres, 31 In. 5097.00
Shelf, Porcelain, Scrolled, Flower Spray, Pendulum, 13 1/2 In. 295.00
Shelf, Rosewood, China Pilasters, Swiss, 13 x 11 In. 138.00
Ship's Wheel, Brass, Silvered Dial, Jeweled Lever, Rear Wind, 8 In. 450.00
Skeleton, 1-Fusee, Gothic Frame, Brass Movement, No Dome, England, c.1900, 16 In. 756.00
Skeleton, 1-Fusee, Moon Hands, Scroll Frame, Glass Dome, England, c.1875, 14 In. 1790.00
Skeleton, 2-Fusee, 2 Bells, 1/4 Strike, Fretted Dial, No Dome, England, c.1870, 21 In. 6160.00
Skeleton, Brass Works, Scrolling, Fleur-De-Lis Finials, Fusee Movement, Dome, 16 In. 750.00
Skull, Rotating Eye, Molded Composition, Germany, c.1920, 4 In. 840.00
Smith & Goodrich, Wall, Lyre, Mahogany, 8-Day, Original Tablet, Bristol, Conn., 28 In. 8400.00
Sperry, Henry, Shelf, Papier-Mache, 8-Day, Time & Strike, c.1850, 16 In. 500.00
Steeple, 8-Day Time, Strike, Etched, Frosted Glass, 20 x 9 3/4 x 4 1/4 In. 140.00
Steeple, Walnut, 30-Hour, Time & Alarm, c.1870, 15 3/4 x 9 In. 110.00
Stennes, Elmer O., Girandole, 1-Weight, Gilt Case, Aurora Glasses, c.1973, 44 In. 9520.00

Stennes, Elmer O., Girandole, 8-Day, Weight, Gold Leaf, Boston Wharf Tablets, c.1968, 44 In. 4480.00
Stennes, Elmer O., Lyre, Mahogany, Weight Driven, c.1972, 46 In. 7000.00
Swinging Arm, 2 Figures, Canister Type, 8-Day, France, c.1895, 24 In. 3470.00
Swinging Arm, Figural, Woman, Globe, 35 In. 330.00
Swinging Arm, Moreau, Fleur De Mai, France, 39 In. 4180.00
Swinging Doll, Alabaster, 8-Day, Time Only, Skeleton Front Plate, France, c.1890, 9 1/4 In. 728.00
Swinging Doll, Alabaster, Brass Trim, 8-Day, France, c.1900, 9 In. 390.00
Swinging Doll, Time Only, Gilt White Metal Case, Love Birds, France, c.1890, 12 In. 785.00
Tall Case, 8-Day, Strike, Mahogany, Arched Painted Dial, Early 1800s, 87 In. 1335.00
Tall Case, Aaron Brokaw, Federal, Mahogany, Veneer, Swan's-Neck Cresting, c.1815, 95 In. 9990.00
Tall Case, C. Shedden, Mahogany, Painted Face, Postman On Horse, Cottage, Perth, 85 In. 3055.00
Tall Case, Cherry, Poplar, Ogee Feet, Scalloped Aprons, c.1824, 89 In. 2070.00
Tall Case, Chippendale, Mahogany, 2-Train, Brass, Etched Steel Dial, 98 In. 4995.00
Tall Case, Chippendale, Walnut, Broken Pediment, Pa., Late 1700s, 91 x 19 x 12 In. 3885.00
Tall Case, Country, Walnut, Bonnet Top, Brass-Capped Pilasters, Urn Finials, 19 x 91 In. 2530.00
Tall Case, Daniel Seddon, Oak, 8-Day, Rolling Moon, Frodsham, England, c.1820, 86 In. 2130.00
Tall Case, David Seip, Cherry, 30-Hour, 91 1/2 In. 5060.00
Tall Case, Elliott, Oak, Ornately Carved, 97 In. 6600.00
Tall Case, Father Time, Animated Grandfather, 2-Weight, Calendar, Oak Case, 84 In. 3410.00
Tall Case, Federal, Cherry, Inlaid, Swan's-Neck Pediment, Pa., Early 1800s, 96 1/4 In. 8965.00
Tall Case, Federal, Cherry, Scrolls, Flowers, Painted Face, c.1815 .... 3346.00
Tall Case, Federal, Mahogany, Arched Face Door, Painted Face, 94 1/4 In. 6575.00
Tall Case, Federal, Mahogany, Maple, Veneer, New York, c.1815 .... 8400.00
Tall Case, French Provincial, 20th Century, 82 1/2 x 21 x 13 1/2 In. 225.00
Tall Case, French Provincial, Striking Movement, Round Enamel Dial, 1800s, 86 In. 620.00
Tall Case, Gazo San Juan Bautista, Alder Wood, Carved, 1980, 110 In. 6600.00
Tall Case, George III, Burl Walnut, String Inlaid Mahogany, Painted Face, 83 In. 3819.00
Tall Case, George III, Mahogany, Silver Face, Brass Accents, c.1800, 90 x 19 In. 2000.00
Tall Case, George III, Pine, Painted Oriental Scenes, 3 Spherical Finials, Stepped Plinth, 84 In. 2645.00
Tall Case, George IV, Crossband Mahogany, c.1825, 91 1/4 In. 3220.00
Tall Case, George IV, Mahogany, Millidge, Edinburgh, Scotland, 7 1/4-In. Dial, 42 In. 3000.00
Tall Case, Georgian, Oak, Panel Door, Pedestal Base, c.1800, 75 x 17 1/2 x 8 1/2 In. 355.00
Tall Case, Gothic Style, Glazed Door, Sunburst Dial, 81 x 21 x 12 1/2 In. 649.00
Tall Case, Hepplewhite, Cherry, Reeded Columns, Curved Top, c.1780, 84 x 18 In. 2115.00
Tall Case, Herschede, Oak, Molded Cornice, Moon Phase Dial, 96 x 28 In. 3795.00
Tall Case, John G. Schmid, Mahogany, Double Scroll Cresting, Phila., c.1820, 91 In. 3885.00
Tall Case, John Heintzlman, Chippendale, Walnut, 8-Day, Broken Arch, Manheim, Pa., 95 In. 4950.00
Tall Case, John Heintzlman, Walnut, 8-Day, Astragal Door, Painted Metal Dial, 95 In. 4950.00
Tall Case, John Howard, New Brentford, Cream Ground, Painted Oriental Scenes, 84 In. 6169.00
Tall Case, Lenzkirch, Regulator, Vienna, Walnut, 94 In. 3960.00
Tall Case, Louis XV, Walnut, Fruit Basket, Late 1700s, 104 In. 4115.00
Tall Case, Mahogany, Double Scrolls, Painted Face, Moon Phases, 95 1/4 In. 4780.00
Tall Case, Mahogany, Westminster Chime, 70 1/2 In. 3024.00
Tall Case, Oak, 30-Hour, Arched Brass Dial, Lutterworth, England, c.1740, 80 In. 1960.00
Tall Case, Oxley, Inlaid, Norwich, c.1770, 99 In. 6050.00
Tall Case, Peter Miller, Cherry, Mahogany Finish, Double Scroll Cresting, Pa., 1800s, 97 In. 5676.00
Tall Case, Regency, Mahogany, Inlaid, Arched Hood, 2-Train Movement, 86 In. 2468.00
Tall Case, Rosewood, Marquetry, Flowers, Hills, Scandinavia, 1920s, 72 x 16 x 9 1/2 In. 4560.00
Tall Case, Samuel Berry, Bonnet Top, Arched Door, Block Base, Chinoiserie, London, 83 In. 4700.00
Tall Case, Samuel Stephens, George III, Chinoiserie, 2-Weight, Striking Bell, c.1790, 79 In. 2940.00
Tall Case, Self Winding Clock Co., Walnut, N.Y., 82 1/2 In. 965.00
Tall Case, Sell & Morall, Mahogany, Swan's-Neck Pediment, Liverpool, 93 x 23 x 9 1/2 In. 1610.00
Tall Case, Seth Thomas, Mahogany, Broken Arch Pediment, Moon Dial, 81 x 19 In. 760.00
Tall Case, Silas Hoadley, Grain Painted, Eagle On Dial 615.00
Tall Case, Silas Hoadley, Painted Dial, 2 Brass Weights, Wooden Works, Stars, 91 x 19 In. 1955.00
Tall Case, Silas Hoadley, Pine, Painted, Multicolored Gilt Dial, c.1825, 90 In. 11750.00
Tall Case, Silas Hoadley, Pine, Wooden Works, Plymouth, 77 1/4 In. 345.00
Tall Case, Stennes, Elmer O., Rocking Ship, 2-Weight, c.1971, 60 In. 3470.00
Tall Case, Walnut, Brass Works, Painted Hound, Flower Sprigs, 94 In. 805.00
Tall Case, Walnut, Double Scroll, Ball & Spire Finials, Arched Face Door, 92 In. 2629.00

Tall Case, Waterbury, No. 6, Standing Regulator 3630.00
Tall Case, Waterbury, No. 77, Mahogany, 3/4 Fluted Columns, Pendulum, 86 x 29 In. 1725.00
Tall Case, Whiting, Red & Black Graining, Red Base, Bracket Feet, Cove Molded, 86 In. 2015.00
Tall Case, William IV, Mahogany, Carved, 1/4 Column, Polished Steel Face, 1820, 79 x 17 x 8 In. .. 7050.00
Tall Case, Woller, William IV, Mahogany, Rope-Turned Columns, c.1830, 94 x 26 x 10 In. 4406.00
Tambour, Mahogany Case, Fusee Movement, Germany, c.1905, 20 1/4 In. 785.00
Telechron, Electric, Burlwood Veneer, Chrome Bands, G. Rohde & H. Miller, 7 x 13 In. 2240.00
Tennis Player, Ball, Glass, Brass, Hand Painted Dial, 2 3/4 In. 248.00
Terry, Eli & Samuel, Shelf, Federal, Mahogany, Veneer Pillar & Scroll, c.1827, 31 x 18 In. 1295.00
Terry, S.B., Column & Cornice, 8-Day, Brass Works, Paw Feet, c.1840, 38 3/4 In. 3470.00
Terry, Samuel, Pillar & Scroll, Eglomise Panel, c.1830, 32 x 17 In. 1290.00
Terry & Andrews, Shelf, Iron Case, Painted, 8-Day, Time & Strike, c.1850, 14 In. 420.00
Tezuka, Dog, Blinking Eye, 30-Hour, Brass Movement, c.1948, 9 In. 140.00
Tezuka, Owl, Blinking Eye, 30-Hour, Brass Movement, c.1948, 10 1/2 In. 168.00
Thomas, G., World Time, Globe, Equator Time Ring, 8-Day, France, c.1890, 12 In. 3920.00
Thuret, Shelf, Louis XIV Style, Boulle, 2-Train, 1/2 Strike, Cupid, c.1900, 19 1/4 In. 1410.00
Thwaites & Reed, Ben Franklin Limited Edition, Brass, Metal, London, c.1957 .... 320.00
Thwaites & Reed, Skeleton, Brass, Chimes, Pendulum, Bell Jar Cover, Green Marble Base, 11 In. . 635.00

Tiffany clocks that are part of desk sets made by Louis Comfort Tiffany are listed in the Tiffany category. Clocks sold by the store, Tiffany & Co., are listed here.

Tiffany & Co., Bracket, Mahogany, 8-Day, Westminster, 4 Gongs, France, c.1900, 17 1/2 In. 895.00
Tiffany & Co., Carriage, Gilt Brass, Glass, France, 4 3/4 x 3 x 2 1/2 In. 520.00
Tiffany & Co., Carriage, Time, Strike, Repeat, Reeded Columns, Drocourt, c.1900, 7 3/4 In. 3300.00
Tiffany & Co., Louis XVI Style, Woman, Lion, Gilt Bronze, Marble, France, c.1900, 28 In. 7800.00
Tiffany & Co., Partners, Brass, Marble Base, Double Dial, 8-Day, 1930s, 5 3/4 In. 310.00
Tiffany & Co., Shelf, Black Marble Case, 8-Day, Time & Strike, Japy Freres, c.1890, 8 In. 250.00
Tiffany & Co., Shelf, Mahogany Case, Beveled, Line Inlay, Bubble Glass Door, 11 In. 288.00
Tiffany & Co., Shelf, Marble, 8-Day, Time & Strike, Japy Freres & Cie, c.1900, 9 1/2 In. 207.00
Tiffany & Co., Shelf, Marble, Gilt Figures, 8-Day, Time & Strike, Marti & Cie, c.1890, 16 In. 1905.00
Tiffany & Co., Shelf, Moorish Design, 3/4 Columns, Onion-Shape Tops, P. Marti & Cie, 16 x 11 In. . 1495.00
Time Recorder, International, Oak, 65 In. 1540.00
Travel, Pink Leather Case, Mid 20th Century, 4 x 4 In. 29.00
United Metal Goods, Model A Car & Gas Pump, Light-Up, Brooklyn, 16 In. 65.00
Vignon, G., Shelf, Marble, Bronze, Ormolu, Birds, Arrows, Paris, 13 In. 635.00
Wag-On-Wall, Shaped Face, Flowers, Cream Ground, Male Figures, 19 x 12 In. 3408.00
Wall, Art Nouveau, Walnut, Grand Sonnerie, 3-Weight, Quarter Strike, 44 In. 2060.00
Wall, Eastlake Style, Walnut Case, Key Wind Brass Works, Germany, c.1900, 36 x 13 In. 205.00
Wall, Eglomise, Wood, Germany, 19th Century, 14 In. 945.00
Wall, Enameled Face, Roman Numerals, Painted Flowers, Pendulum, Windup, France, 55 In. 575.00
Wall, Federal, Mahogany, Bird's-Eye Maple Veneer, Cornice, Eglomise Tablet, 20 In. 2350.00
Wall, Johnson Service Co., French Pinwheel, Milwaukee, Wisc., Oak 1650.00
Wall, Mahogany, Ebonized, Scrolling, Glazed Door, Roman Numerals, 33 x 18 x 5 In. 355.00
Wall, Oak, Fusee Carved, 8 Bells, England, 37 In. 4070.00
Wall, Porcelain Dial, Pendulum, Cameo, Beveled Glass, Pillared Doors, c.1890 .... 295.00
Wall, Regulator, Celluloid Face, Brass Works, Pendulum, Key, Weights, Germany, 43 x 19 In. 489.00
Wall, Regulator, Jewelers, Walnut, 83 In. 1760.00
Wall, Regulator, Shell Carved, Ormolu Mounted Cornice, Brass Mounts, 57 x 18 x 7 In. 690.00
Wall, Regulator, Standard, Oak, 75 1/2 In. 990.00
Wall, Regulator, Vienna, 1-Weight, 38 In. 715.00
Wall, Renaissance Revival, Walnut, Bird, Tree, Chime, Continental, Late 1800s, 37 x 14 In. 145.00
Wall, Thermometer, Barometer, Hand Carved, 1875 .... 880.00
Wall, Walnut, Bird, Vine, Flower Inlay, Dogs, Key Wind, Pendulum, 31 x 16 1/2 x 5 In. 690.00
Wall, Walnut, Grand Sonnerie, Fluted Columns, 3-Weight, Austria, c.1880, 50 In. 1790.00
Waltham, Abbot Lyre, 8-Day, 1-Weight, c.1925, 43 In. 11200.00
Waltham, School, Mahogany, Painted Dial, Molded Frame, 11 1/2-In. Dial 1840.00
Waltham, Shelf, Mahogany, 8-Day, Flowers, c.1930, 13 1/4 In. 125.00
Waltham, Shelf, Walnut, 8-Day, Time & Strike, c.1925, 10 3/4 In. 280.00
Warren Telechron Co., Master Clock, Type B 2090.00
Waterbury, Calendar, No. 28, Oak, 8-Day, c.1891, 40 1/2 In. 3875.00
Waterbury, Calendar, No. 33, Oak, 40 1/2 In. 1100.00
Waterbury, Calendar, No. 43, Walnut, 29 In. 935.00

Waterbury, Calendar, No. 44, Pressed Oak, 8-Day, Time & Strike, c.1891, 24 In. 590.00
Waterbury, Delft-Type Case, Windmill, Blue, 30-Hour, c.1900, 9 3/4 In. 195.00
Waterbury, Gallery, c.1890, 27 In. 1120.00
Waterbury, Henshaw, Pressed Oak, 8-Day, Time & Strike, c.1906, 22 In. 300.00
Waterbury, Keating, Calendar, Oak, 8-Day, c.1900, 33 In. 2465.00
Waterbury, No. 54, Wall, 2-Weight, Oak, 59 In. 1760.00
Waterbury, Regulator, No. 18, Oak, 2-Weight 1100.00
Waterbury, Regulator, No. 80, Oak, Drop Case, 2-Weight, Deadbeat Escapement, c.1915, 41 In. .. 4480.00
Waterbury, Regulator, No. 83, Oak, 30-Day, Double Spring, c.1914, 41 1/2 In. 1120.00
Waterbury, School, Walnut, Short Drop, Time & Strike, Ireland, 20 1/2 x 14 1/2 In. 110.00
Waterbury, Shelf, Art Nouveau, Brass Works, Open Escapement, c.1898, 12 x 6 In. 206.00
Waterbury, Study, No. 4, Oak, 8-Day, Time & Strike, c.1893, 22 3/4 In. 1120.00
Waterbury, Tavernes, Regulator, Crystal, 8-Day, Time & Strike, c.1915, 9 1/2 In. 470.00
Wegelin, Gilt Bronze, Porcelain, Painted, Courting Couple, Garden, c.1900, 7 In. 6000.00
Weinberg, Frederick, Model EH3, Red Arms, White Balls, 1950s, 22 1/2 In. 960.00
Welch, Arditi, Gale's Perpetual Calendar, 27 1/4 In. 935.00
Welch, E.N., Beehive, Ripple Front, 19 In. 1430.00
Welch, E.N., Black Lacquer, Adamantine, 8-Day Time, Strike, c.1902, 10 x 15 In. 110.00
Welch, E.N., Empire Style, Reverse Painted Tablet, Capitol Building, 18 3/4 In. 150.00
Welch, E.N., Porcelain, Hand Painted, Birds, Flowers, Blue, Green Ground, 1881, 6 In. 605.00
Welch, E.N., Porcelain, Hand Painted, Birds, Flowers, Ivory Ground, 1881, 6 In. 385.00
Welch, E.N., Porcelain, Hand Painted, Birds, Flowers, Pink, Yellow Ground, 1881, 6 In. 525.00
Welch, E.N., Regulator, No. 11, Mahogany, 30-Day, Double Spring, c.1889, 60 In. 5376.00
Welch, E.N., Regulator, Wall, Rosewood, 2-Weight, c.1860, 40 In. 3416.00
Welch, E.N., Regulator, Walnut, 60 In. 3575.00
Welch, E.N., Shelf, Albani, Marble, 8-Day, Time & Strike, c.1889, 14 1/2 In. 365.00
Welch, E.N., Verdi, Wall, Rosewood Veneer, 8-Day, Time & Strike, c.1880, 31 In. 1064.00
Welch, Parepa, 22 1/2 In. 495.00
Welch Spring, Double Dial, Rosewood Case, B.B. Lewis Perpetual Calendar, 32 x 16 In. 950.00
Welch Spring, Regulator, Rosewood, Round Top, 8-Day, Spring Driven, c.1880, 26 In. 950.00
Welch Spring, Shelf, Rosewood, Turned Columns & Finials, 8-Day, c.1880, 18 In. 1345.00
Williams, David L., Regulator, Tavern, 8-Day, Grain Painted, c.1865, 34 In. 2070.00
Windmill, Animated, France, 16 1/2 In. 1540.00
Windmill, Bronze, Lattice Blades Turn, Barometer Dial, France, 19 In. 5040.00
Winterhalder & Hoffmeier, Mahogany, 8-Day, 2 Fusee, Chime, Germany, c.1900, 14 In. 2410.00
Winterhalder & Hoffmeier, Rosewood Veneer, 8-Day, Time & Strike, c.1900, 12 3/4 In. 390.00
Wise Old Owl, Rotating Eye, Carved Wood, Germany, c.1930, 9 1/2 In. 560.00
Woman, Kneeling, Praying, Bronze, Ormolu, France, c.1830, 11 1/2 In. 560.00
Zappler, Crown Verge Movement, 1-Day, Dome, Austria, c.1820, 3 1/2 In. 1008.00
Zenith, Child On Clock Tower, Royal Copenhagen, Early 1900s, 9 3/8 In. 880.00
Zodiac Watch Co., Desk, 15 Jewels, Brass Case, Box, c.1970, 7 3/4 In. 100.00

CLOISONNE enamel was developed during the tenth century. A glass enamel was applied between small ribbons of metal on a metal base. Most cloisonne is Chinese or Japanese. Pieces marked *China* are twentieth-century examples.

Bottle, Snuff, Trigrams, Cloud Border, Chinese, 1800s, 3 In. 1116.00
Bowl, Shallow, Flowers, Chinese, 1900s, 15 In. 189.00
Bowl, Stylized Lotus Flowers, Turquoise Ground, 1800s, 7 1/4 In. 176.00
Bowl, Stylized Lotus, Turquoise Ground, 19th Century, 5 x 10 1/2 In. 2585.00
Box, Casket Shape, Silver, Elizabeth Copeland, c.1915, 3 3/4 x 7 1/2 x 5 1/4 In. 66000.00
Box, Cover, Egg Shape, Ho Bird, Paulownia, Japan, Late 19th Century, 6 1/2 In. 920.00
Box, Cover, Goat Shape, Sliding Glass Top, Chinese, 4 x 4 3/4 x 2 1/4 In., Pair 643.00
Box, Egg Shape, Wirework, Butterflies, Flowers, Blue, Ando Jube, Early 1900s, 5 3/4 In. 978.00
Box, Flower Pattern Fans, Bracket Feet, Late 19th Century, 2 1/4 x 3 3/4 x 4 3/4 In. 575.00
Box, Flowers, Turquoise Ground, Lobe Forms, 2 1/2 x 4 1/2 In. 118.00
Box, Incense, Cranes, Clouds, Lotus, Ju-I Lappets, Chinese, 1800s, 5 In. 147.00
Box, Oval, Flower Rondel Design, Late 19th Century, 3 3/4 In. 96.00
Box, Rectangular, Maple Leaf Design, Ando, Late 19th Century, 5 1/4 In. 2760.00
Candlestick, Brass, Chinese, 20th Century, 10 1/4 In., Pair 35.00
Censer, Elephant Shape, 20th Century, 10 In., Pair 200.00

Censer, Elephant, Mask, Chinese, 7 1/2 In. 826.00
Censer, Elephants, Chinese, 10 In., Pair 500.00
Censer, Lid, 2 Gilt Foo Dog & Ring Handles, Foo Dog Finial, Oval, 3-Footed, 1800s, 7 In. 425.00
Censer, Passion Flowers, Mask Legs, Squirrel Handles, Blue Ground, 3 3/4 x 6 In. 805.00
Charger, Central Medallion, Phoenix, Flying, Wave Pattern, 1800s, 18 In. 470.00
Charger, Phoenix, Flower Border, Japan, Late 19th Century, 12 In. 150.00
Charger, Sparrow, Peony, Japan, Late 19th Century, 11 3/4 In. 90.00
Cup, 8-Sided, Passion Flower, Japan, c.1850, 3 1/2 In. 259.00
Ewer, Celadon Jade Plaques, Final, Chinese, 14 1/2 In. 1000.00
Ewer, Lid, Flowers, Celadon Jade Plaques & Finial Inset, Late 19th Century, 14 1/2 In. 1100.00
Figure, Buddha, Floral Robe, 23 In. 450.00
Figure, Chariots, Flowers, Blue Ground, Chinese, 14 1/2 In., Pair .... 450.00 to 826.00
Figure, Rooster, Turquoise Ground, Multicolored Decoration, Oval Plinth Base, 39 x 19 In. 480.00
Figure, Water Buffalo, Chinese, 8 In., Pair 649.00
Figure, Water Buffalo, Early 20th Century, 8 In., Pair 750.00
Jar, 100 Birds Decoration, Flowers, Birds, Turquoise, Wood Base, 20 1/2 In. 490.00
Jar, Chinese, c.1910, 5 1/2 In., Pair 146.00
Jar, Chrysanthemums, Brass Colored Top & Bottom Rim, 12 x 7 In., Pair 115.00
Jar, Cover, Dragons, Phoenix, Flowers, Oval, 4 1/4 In. 11160.00
Jar, Cover, Leaves, Flowers, Butterfly, Black Ground, 3-Footed, Extended Handles, Japan, 3 1/4 In. 690.00
Jar, Dragon, Kylin, Phoenix, Flowers, Globular, 3-Footed, Japan, 5 1/2 In. 700.00
Jar, Egg Shape, Bird, Flowering Tree, Hayashi Kodenji, Japan, Late 19th Century, 6 In. 1840.00
Jar, Flowers, Birds, Blue Ground, Vertical Brass Band Decoration, 10 In., Pair 400.00
Jar, Red, Fans, Birds, Stippled Ground, Wood Cover, Ivory Man Finial, 13 3/4 In. 345.00
Jardiniere, Bronze, Aesthetic Movement, France, Late 1800s, 14 1/2 x 11 3/4 In. 940.00
Jarlet, Baluster, Black Field, Bird, Prunus, Iris, Flowers, 1900s, Japan, 7 In. 95.00
Jarlet, Square Body, Waisted Feet, Floral Panels, Blossoms, 5 In., Pair 4310.00
Joss Stick Holders, Water Buffalo, Champleve, c.1900, 8 3/4 In. 575.00
Lion, Plinth Base, Multicolored, Gilded, Chinese, 1800s, Pair 820.00
Ornament, Mantel, Lyre Shape, Brown Onyx, Fleur-De-Lis Finials, 18 In., Pair 1645.00
Panels, Figures, Landscape, Calligraphy, c.1800, 28 1/2 x 8 1/2 In., 4 Piece 9000.00
Planter, Yellow, Lotus Blossoms, Leaves, Oval, Lobed, Gold Rim & Foot, 5 x 10 In. 95.00
Plaque, Loquat Tree, Black Ground, Brown Border, Flowers, Japan, 19th Century, 12 1/4 In. 235.00
Plate, Butterfly, Flower, Scroll, Japan, Late 19th Century, 9 1/2 In. 120.00
Plate, Exotic Birds, Holding Beads, Central Lotus, Turquoise, Japan, 9 5/8 In. 520.00
Plate, Porcelain, Flowers, Butterflies, Birch Bark, Japan, 19th Century, 11 1/2 In. 940.00
Rooster, Round Base, Blue Ground, Multicolored, c.1950, Pair 175.00
Teapot, Globular, Lotus, Scroll, Gilt Handle, Spout, Chinese, 1800s, 4 3/4 In. 1650.00
Teapot, Insect, Flower, Blue Ground, Oval, 7 In. 660.00
Tray, Butterflies, Flowers, Square 9 1/4 In. 650.00
Urn, Arts & Crafts, Bulbous, Hibiscus Flowers, Leaves, Brass, c.1910, 6 In., Pair 325.00
Urn, Cover, Blue Ground, Floral Reserves, Teakwood Base, Chinese, 1800, 39 x 19 In. 2225.00
Urn, Cover, Bronze, Mask Handles, Central Geometric Band, c.1900, 14 In. 90.00
Urn, Green Ground, Dogwood Blossoms, Gilt Highlights, Chinese, 15 In., Pair 295.00
Vase, 6-Sided, Red & White Flowers, Blue Ground, Adachi Kinjiro, Late 19th Century, 6 In. 450.00
Vase, Ando Manner, Orchid, Cream Ground, Japan, 1900s, 11 1/4 In. 360.00
Vase, Baluster Shape, Serpent Head Handles, Mounted As Lamp, Chinese, 11 1/2 In. 295.00
Vase, Bird In Flowering Tree, Japan, 1868-1911, 12 In. 480.00
Vase, Bird, Flower, Baluster Shape, Blue Ground, 14 In. 1800.00
Vase, Bird, Flower, Black Ground, Japan, Late 19th Century, 3 3/4 In. 920.00
Vase, Bird, Flower, Blue Ground, Foot, Rim, Japan, Late 19th Century, 9 1/2 In., Pair 230.00
Vase, Bird, Flower, Fuji, Blue Ground, Japan, Late 19th Century, 7 In., Pair 1560.00
Vase, Bird, Flower, Teardrop Shape, 6 In., Pair 115.00
Vase, Bird, Flying, Green, Chinese, 1800s, 15 In., Pair 530.00
Vase, Birds On Flowering Tree, Silver Wire Technique, Ando, Japan, c.1920, 12 1/2 In. 2938.00
Vase, Birds, Chrysanthemum, Silver Wire Technique, Japan, 20th Century, 10 In., Pair 1295.00
Vase, Birds, Irises, Green Ground, Turquoise Blue Interior, 9 3/4 In., Pair 7820.00
Vase, Birds, Wisteria, Blue, Silver Wire Technique, Japan, Early 1900s, 10 In., Pair 1765.00
Vase, Blue Ground, Flower & Birds Decoration, c.1900, 5 3/4 In., Pair 350.00
Vase, Bottle, Blue Ground, Lotus, Crane, Champleve Band, 1700s, 24 In., Pair 4935.00

Vase, Branches, Green, Pear Shape, 8 Sides, Beast-Head Handles, 6 x 3 x 3 In., Pair 345.00
Vase, Bud, Cylindrical, Kingfisher On Irises, Dark Ground, Scroll Base, 7 In. 370.00
Vase, Bud, Fish Design, Japanese, 19th Century, 6 In. 1287.00
Vase, Butterfly, Flower, Black Ground, Japan, Late 19th Century, 6 1/2 In. 60.00
Vase, Carp, Gray, Turquoise Blue Ground, 10 In. 4700.00
Vase, Celadon Green, Brass Base, Korea, 9 3/4 In. 690.00
Vase, Crane, Blue Ground, Ginbari, Pine Tree Mark, Japan, Late 19th Century, 4 3/4 In. 720.00
Vase, Cranes, Camellias, Blue Ground, Shouldered, Flared Rim, 12 3/4 x 7 In., Pair 520.00
Vase, Cranes, Landscape, Pink, Lavender, Orange Peonies, 12 1/4 In., Pair 115.00
Vase, Cranes, Turquoise, Cracked Ice Ground, Japan, 19th Century, 6 1/4 In. 325.00
Vase, Dove, Blue Ground, Transparent, Japan, Late 19th Century, 4 3/4 In. 259.00
Vase, Dragon, Red, Blue Ground, Hayashi Kodenji Attribution, Late 19th Century, 3 3/4 In. 635.00
Vase, Dragons, Emblems, Phoenix, Kylin, Oval, Diamond Shape Mouth, Japan, 8 1/2 In. 2585.00
Vase, Egg Shape, Crane, Red Ground, Japan, Late 19th Century, 3 3/4 In. 480.00
Vase, Egg Shape, Squat, Crane, Black Ground, Japan, Late 19th Century, 6 3/4 In., Pair 575.00
Vase, Emblems, White Ground, Animal Mask Handles, Japan, 19th Century, Square 8 In. 529.00
Vase, Exotic Bird, Dragon Handles, Japan, c.1900, 14 In. 120.00
Vase, Flower, Butterfly, Green Ground, Japan, Late 19th Century, 7 1/4 In. 100.00
Vase, Flowering Trees, Coast, Silver Wire Designs, Gonda Hirosuke, 7 1/4 In. 765.00
Vase, Flowers, Blue Ground, Globular, Flared Neck, Japan, 19th Century, 7 1/2 In. 590.00
Vase, Flowers, Green, Ando Ginbari, Japan, Early 1900s, 9 1/2 In. 115.00
Vase, Flowers, Precious Objects, 10 1/4 In. 425.00
Vase, Flowers, Transparent, Hattori Todasaburo, Japan, Late 19th Century, 3 1/2 In. 510.00
Vase, Hexagonal Panel, Narrow Neck, Landscape, Bird Panels, Japan, 9 3/4 In. 5265.00
Vase, Inaba Style, Birds, Bamboos, Silver & Gold Wirework, Late 19th Century, 7 In. 1150.00
Vase, Indian Club Shape, Swallow, Wisteria, Transparent, Late 19th Century, 24 1/2 In. 1150.00
Vase, Inverted Pear Shape, Cicada Design, Gray Blue Ground, Late 19th Century, 2 3/4 In. 1380.00
Vase, Inverted Pear Shape, Crane, Ota Jinoei, Japan, Late 19th Century, 3 In. 450.00
Vase, Inverted Pear Shape, Mount Fuji, Japan, Late 19th Century, 2 1/4 In. 300.00
Vase, Inverted Pear Shape, Phoenix, Butterfly, Japan, Late 19th Century, 7 1/4 In. 115.00
Vase, Inverted Pear Shape, Phoenix, Dragon, Blue Ground, Late 19th Century, 7 1/2 In. 240.00
Vase, Inverted Pear Shape, Transparent, Iris, Hattori Tadasaburo, Late 19th Century, 4 In. 1380.00
Vase, Lotus Scrolls, Turquoise Ground, Bronze, Wire, 7 3/8 x 3 x 2 1/2 In. 403.00
Vase, Morning Glories, Dark Blue Ground, Shouldered, 10 In. 420.00
Vase, Orchids, Apricot Ground, Japan, Early 1900s, 9 In. 560.00
Vase, Passion Flower, Bat, Bronze, Square, Hu Form, 6 1/4 In. 420.00
Vase, Passion Flower, Blue Ground, Inverted Pear Shape, 7 1/4 In. 2040.00
Vase, Pheasants, Quail, Sparrows, Flowers, Silver Mounts, Japan, 1800s, 8 3/4 In., Pair 3290.00
Vase, Phoenixes, Dragons, Globular, Flared Neck, Japan, 1868-1911, 18 In., Pair 880.00
Vase, Red, Multicolored Flowers, Slender Neck, 10 1/2 x 5 1/2 In. 50.00
Vase, Rooster, Hen, Deep Blue Ground, Tapered, Long Neck, 6 1/4 In., Pair 4600.00
Vase, Seed Form, Bird, Flowers, Blue Ground, Japan, Late 19th Century, 4 1/2 In. 420.00
Vase, Seed Form, Hydrangea, Transparent, Ota Tameshiro, Late 19th Century, 4 3/4 In. 200.00
Vase, Seed Form, Melon Ribbed, Transparent, Irios, Japan, Late 19th Century, 4 3/4 In. 1150.00
Vase, Stylized Lotus, Garlic Shape Mouth, Globular, China, 20th Century, 12 1/2 In. 120.00
Vase, Tapered, Flowers, Butterfly, Olive Green Ground, 3 x 3 In. 100.00
Vase, Tripod, Ding Shape, Lotus Cover, Dragons, Yellow, Bracket Handles, 39 1/2 In. 810.00
Vase, White & Pink Peony Design, Blue Ground, Stand, 12 In., Pair 176.00
Vase, Wisteria, Olive Green Ground, Japan, 1868-1911, 10 In. 825.00
Water Pipe, Leaves, Black Ground, 12 In. 132.00

CLOTHING of all types is listed in this category. Dresses, hats, shoes, underwear, and more are found here. Other textiles are to be found in the Coverlet, Movie, Quilt, Textile, and World War I and II categories.

Busk, Corset, Wooden, Carved, Stained Design, Harriet Hutchkins Enos Crocker, c.1846, 14 In. ... 374.00
Coat, Black, Embroidered, Gold Thread, Flowering Branches, Chinese 200.00
Coat, White Wool, Plastic Buttons, 1960s, Pierre Cardin, Size 10 .... 2160.00
Dealer's Outfit, Harold's Club, Vest, Pants, Cummerbund, Apron, 1950s, Size Medium 75.00
Dress, Bonnet, Mourning, Black Silk, Tan Cotton Lining, Baleen Busks, Civil War 316.00
Dress, Linen, Embroidered Bands, Sash Belt, 28-In. Waist, 60-In. Length .... *ILLUS* 360.00

Old furs oxidize and change color. Dark furs darken, light furs turn yellow, brown furs often turn reddish brown.

Clothing, Dress, Linen, Embroidered Bands, Sash Belt, 28-In. Waist, 60-In. Length

Dress, Paper, Souper, Campbell Soup, Andy Warhol, c.1966 .... 509.00
Gloves, Lace, Fingers Out, Ruffled Wrist, White, 1940s 55.00
Greatcoat, Russian Officer's, 13th Narvski Hussars, c.1910, 63 3/4 x 57 In. 10160.00
Helmet, Armor, Leather, Horsehair Plume, Monogram, Europe, Late 1800s 1115.00
Jeans, Denim, Men's, Tuf-Nut Westerns, Original Tags, 1950s, Size 30 x 34 In. 200.00
Mittens, Amish, Wool, Pink, Dog Applique, Flannel Lining, 1930s 300.00
Mittens, Buffalo Hide, Early 1880s 110.00
Mittens, Knit, Arrow Pattern, Green, Red, Amish, 11 x 6 In. 330.00
Mittens, Knit, Purple, Red, Amish, 10 x 6 In. 330.00
Raincoat, Brown, Plastic, A-Line, Knee Length, Pierre Cardin, 1960s, Size 10 .... 710.00
Robe, Dragon, Gold Embroidery, Blue Ground, 19th Century 2468.00
Robe, Embroidered, Flowers, Orange Ground, Chinese, Early 1900s, Woman's 440.00
Robe, Silk, Magenta, Gold Boteh, Persia, 18th Century 558.00
Robe, Silk, Purple, Appliqued Forbidden Stitch Birds, Flowers, Brass Buttons, Chinese 330.00
Sari, Silk, Brocade, Flower Heads, Square Reserves, Burgundy, Gold, Turquoise, India, c.1900 .... 770.00
Scarf, Aloha Hawaii, United States Navy, White Stain, Gold Fringe, 21 x 21 In. 18.00
Scarf, Silk, Columbus Discovering America, Multicolored, Hermes 235.00
Scarf, Silk, Yellow Abstract Design On Cream Ground, Emilo Pucci, 1960s, 28 x 28 In. 300.00
Shawl, Paisley, Scotland, 19th Century, 118 x 51 In. 415.00
Shoes, Leather, High Top, Woman's, Salesman's Sample, 5 In., Pair 805.00
Shoes, Penny Loafer, Black Leather, G.H. Bass, 1960s, Size 7 .... 45.00
Shoes, Penny Loafer, Black Leather, G.H. Bass, 1960s, Size 7 1/2 .... 50.00
Skirt, Silk, Purple, Embroidered Butterflies, Chinese 110.00
Skirt, Silk, Red, Appliqued Tassels, Bronze Bells, Chinese 767.00
Skirt, Silk, White, Quilted Padding, Chinese 2715.00
Slipper, Ball, Woman's, Cream Satin, Medium Heel, New England, 1750-70 .... 2500.00
Socks, Battery Heated, Winchester, Box, Pair 11.00
Uniform, Air Force Academy Cadet, Hat, Jacket, Trousers, 1970s 55.00
Uniform, U.S. Military Academy, Blue Wool, Ivory Trim, Silver Buttons, 1880s, Medium 130.00

CLUTHRA glass is a two-layered glass with small air bubbles and powered glass trapped between the layers. The Steuben Glass Works of Corning, New York, made it in 1920. Victor Durand, of Kimball Glass Company in Vineland, New Jersey, made a similar glass from about 1925. Durand's pieces are listed in the Durand category. Related items are listed in the Steuben category.

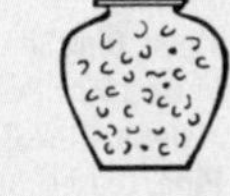

Finger Bowl, Amethyst, 2 5/8 x 5 In. 285.00
Vase, Amethyst, No. 2683, 8 In. 1900.00
Vase, Blue, Squared Shoulder, Flared Rim, 10 1/2 In. 660.00
Vase, Green Over White, Cylindrical, Signed, 10 In. 230.00
Vase, Lavender, Tapered, Flared Rim, 10 In. 1035.00
Vase, Pink Over White, Shouldered, Flared Rim, 6 1/4 In. 1035.00
Vase, Pink, Bulbous, Flared Rim, 10 1/4 x 10 In. 1006.00
Vase, Rose, No. 2683, 8 In. 2200.00
Vase, Rose, Urn Shape, 2 Opalescent M Handles, 11 In. 2300.00

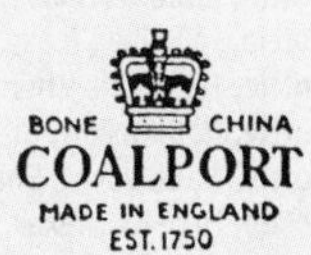

COALPORT ware has been made by the Coalport Porcelain Works of England from 1795 to the present time. Early pieces were unmarked. About 1810–25 the pieces were marked with the name *Coalport* in various forms. Later pieces also had the name *John Rose* in the mark. The crown mark has been used with variations since 1881. The date 1750 is printed in some marks, but it is not the date the factory started. Some pieces are listed in Indian Tree.

Basket, Reticulated, Turquoise Ground, Flowers, Oval, c.1810, 10 1/8 In. 3000.00
Plaque, Flowers, Urn Vase, Oval, Stephen Lawrance, 1824, 14 3/4 In. 9600.00
Plate, Dinner, Floral Basket Decoration, Mid 20th Century, 10 1/2 In., 12 Piece 82.00
Plate, Painted Center, Flower Garden Basket, Gilt, Blue Surround, 8 1/2 In., Pair 426.00
Platter, Oriental Flowers & Leaves, Scalloped Border, 14 In. 200.00
Potpourri, Loch Earn, 3 Handles, Painted, Flower Panels, Gilt, Blue Ground, 5 1/2 In. 871.00
Teapot, Cover, Stand, Oval, Fluted, Gilt Leaves, Cobalt Blue Borders, Early 1800s, 10 In. 294.00
Vase, Pink Ground, Gold Leaves, c.1890, 6 In., Pair 825.00
Vase, Pink Ground, Raised Flowers Relief Design In Gold, 1890, 6 In. 810.00

COBALT BLUE glass was made using oxide of cobalt. The characteristic bright dark blue identifies it for the collector. Most cobalt glass found today was made after the Civil War. There was renewed interest in the dark blue glass in the late 1930s and dinnerwares were made.

Butter, Cover, Inverted Thistle Pattern, Flame Finial, 6 x 7 3/4 In. 49.00
Dresser Box, Cover, Deer, Flowers, Silver Overlay, Round, 2 1/2 x 4 In. 185.00
Figurine, Shoe, Woman's, Beaded Band On Toe & Around Edges 45.00
Jar, Cover, Embossed Stars, 3-Terrier Dog Finial, Round, Art Deco, 5 x 4 1/2 In. 350.00
Mustache Cup & Saucer, Gold Flowers & Leaves In Cartouche 110.00
Pitcher, Pinched Neck, Flared Rim, 2 Pt., 5 1/2 In. 22.00
Punch Set, 1930s, 5 1/4 x 10 3/4-In. Bowl, 7 Piece 277.00
Vase, Baluster Shape, Clear Reeded Handles, 10 In. 90.00
Vase, Bud, Ruffled Edge, Clear Foot, 8 1/2 In. 24.00
Vase, Jack-In-The-Pulpit, 10 In. 85.00
Vase, Swirled & Fluted Sides, 9 Petal Feet, 5 1/4 x 2 3/4 In. 65.00
Vase, Swirled Optic Rib, Bulbous, Tapered, Rolled Rim, 1930s, 5 In. 25.00

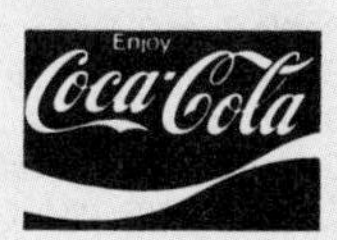

COCA-COLA was first served in 1886 in Atlanta, Georgia. It was advertised through signs, newspaper ads, coupons, bottles, trays, calendars, and even lamps and clocks. Collectors want anything with the word *Coca-Cola*, including a few rare products, like gum wrappers and cigar bands. The famous trademark was patented in 1893, the *Coke* mark in 1945. Many modern items and reproductions are being made.

Ashtray, Pull Match, 1930s, 7 In. 2640.00
Bag Holder, Sprite Boy, For Home Refreshment, Coca-Cola, c.1949, 16 x 40 In. 605.00
Bank, Bottle Shape, Plastic, 24 x 7 In. 15.00
Bank, Dispenser, Refresh Yourself, Ice Cold, Battery Operated, Tin, 1950s, 10 x 7 x 5 In. 385.00
Bank, Dispenser, Tin, Plastic, Battery Operated, Linemar, Box, 9 1/2 In. 965.00
Bank, Soda Machine Shape, 5 Cents, M.S.R., Box, 7 1/4 In. 80.00
Bank, Soda Machine Shape, Red, Bottles, 1950s, 5 1/2 In. 110.00
Blotter, Chewing Gum, Cardboard, Early 1900s, 3 3/4 x 9 In. 615.00
Blotter, Chewing Gum, Cardboard, Early 1900s, 4 x 6 In. 1120.00
Blotter, Good, Button, Sprite Boy, Bottle, 1953, 3 3/8 x 7 1/2 In. 15.00
Book, Alphabet Book Of Coca-Cola, 1928 .... 750.00
Bookmark, Hilda Clark, Cardboard, Embossed, Frame, 1903, 6 x 2 In. 358.00
Bookmark, Lillian Nordica, Drink Coca-Cola, 5 Cents, Frame, 1904, 6 x 2 In. 1100.00
Bottle, Albany, N.Y., Light Aqua, Straight-Sided, c.1905, 6 1/2 Oz., 7 1/2 In. 10.00
Bottle, Cabbage Patch Kids, 1988, 10 Oz. 49.00
Bottle, Centennial, Gold Plated, Draw String Bag, 1986, 7 3/4 In. 50.00
Bottle, Chipley, Georgia, Straight-Sided, 1900-15 .... 2211.00
Bottle, Coatsville Bottling Works, 1922, 6 Oz., 7 1/2 In. 17.00
Bottle, Diamond Embossed, 1960s, Pt. 13.00

Bottle, Edwards Sodas, Coca-Cola Bottling Co., Newark, Ohio, Patd. Nov. 1923, 6 1/2 Oz. 22.00
Bottle, Fall River, Mass., Deer, Antlers, Straight-Sided, 1900-15, 8 Oz., 9 In. 24.00
Bottle, Florida Panthers, Inaugural Season, Coca-Cola Classic, Unopened, 1994, 8 Oz. 3.00
Bottle, Hobbleskirt, Green, Coca-Cola Trademark Registered, Pat'd Nov 16 1915, 6 Oz. 35.00
Bottle, Hobbleskirt, Smoky, Thick Bottom, Pat'd Nov 16 1915, 6 Oz. 111.00
Bottle, Houston, Texas, Nov. 15, 1915, 8 In. 10.00
Bottle, John Smoltz, Cy Young Award, Unopened, 1996, 8 Oz. 4.00
Bottle, Kroger 100 Anniversary, 1883-1983, 10 Oz. 8.00
Bottle, Memphis, Tenn., Amber, Brown Arrow, c.1911, 7 1/2 In. 24.00
Bottle, Mexico, Copa Del Mundo USA 94, Crown Cap, Vinyl Cover, Contents, 355 Ml., 7 In. 45.00
Bottle, Milledgeville, Ga., Hobbleskirt, Blue Green, 1-In. Thick Base, Nov. 16, 1915 .... 175.00
Bottle, Muskegon, Mich, Pat'd Dec 25, 1923, 6 Oz. 28.00
Bottle, Norton, Kansas, Green, 1967, 6 1/2 Fl. Oz. 10.00
Bottle, Olympics, Barcelona, 1992, 8 Oz. 3.00
Bottle, Petersburg, Va., Aqua Green, Straight-Sided, 1900-15, 8 1/2 Oz. 31.00
Bottle, President Bush Inauguration, Jan. 20, 2005 ....35.00 to 39.00
Bottle, Royal Wedding, Lady Diana Spencer, Prince Of Wales, July 29, 1981 .... 45.00
Bottle, Soda Water, Centerville, Iowa, c.1926, 6 Oz. 35.00
Bottle, South Dakota Centennial, Mt. Rushmore, Contents, 1989, 10 Oz. 10.00
Bottle, St. Louis Cardinals Champs, 1996, 8 Oz. 3.00
Bottle, Super Bowl XVIII, Coke Is It!, Tampa, Fla., Contents, January 22, 1984, 10 Oz. 3.00
Bottle, Sylacauga, Ala., Dark Green, Straight-Sided, Script, 1915, 6 1/2 Oz. 500.00
Bottle, Syrup, Drink Coca-Cola, Embossed, Painted Wreath, Metal Cap, c.1910, 12 1/2 x 3 1/4 In. . 605.00
Bottle, Tallahassee, Fla., Green, Patented November 6, 1923, 6 1/2 Oz., 8 In. 5.00
Bottle, University Of Mississippi, 1848-1998, 8 Oz. 3.00
Bottle Cap, Apollo NASA Series, No. 1, 2, 3, 4 & 5, 5 Piece 7.00
Bottle Cap, Chicago, Ill., Cork Lined, 1930s, 6 Oz. 23.00
Bottle Cap, Los Angeles, Cork Lined, 1930s, 6 Oz. 6.00
Bottle Cap, Salem Depot, N.H., Cork Lined, c.1920, 6 Oz. 7.00
Bottle Cap, Test, Aluminum, Rip Cap, For 6 Oz. Bottle 9.00
Bottle Opener, Cap Catcher, Sprite Boy, Brown Mfg. Co., Box, 1943 Patent, 8 x 3 In. 155.00
Bottle Opener, Drink Bottled Coca-Cola, Nude Mermaid, Wichita, Kans., Metal, 3 In. 120.00
Bottle Opener, Drink Coca-Cola, Consolidated Cork Corp., Brooklyn, N.Y., 3 3/8 x 1 In. ....7.00 to 13.00
Bottle Opener, Drink Coca-Cola, Starr X, Wall Mount, Brown Co., N. News, Va., 1925 Patent . . .15.50 to 22.00
Bottle Opener, Have A Coke, Drink Coca-Cola, It's The Real Thing, Enjoy Coca-Cola 3.00
Bottle Opener, Juo Coca-Cola Jaakylmana, Olympics, Finland, 1952, 3 1/2 In. 25.00
Bottle Opener & Ice Pick 169.00
Bridge Set, Playing Cards, Girl Drinking Coke, 1943 .... 240.00
Calendar, 1898, Girl With Blue Dress, Delicious & Refreshing, Matte, Frame, 13 x 7 1/4 In. 28600.00
Calendar, 1899, Hilda Clark, Writing Letter, Matte, Frame, 13 x 7 1/4 In. 9515.00
Calendar, 1907, Girl With Green Dress, Drink Coca-Cola, Matte, Frame, 14 x 7 In. 13200.00
Calendar, 1914, Betty, Self-Framed, 32 1/4 x 13 In. 1680.00
Calendar, 1917, Constance, August Page, Matte, Frame, 24 1/2 x 11 1/2 In. 523.00
Calendar, 1921, Autumn Girl, 32 x 12 In. 504.00
Calendar, 1922, Summer Girl, Matte, Frame, 32 x 12 In. 7700.00
Calendar, 1923, Flapper Girl, Matte, Frame, 34 1/4 x 21 1/2 In. 280.00
Calendar, 1925, Girl At Party, September To December Pages, 24 x 12 In. 495.00
Calendar, 1932, Old Oaken Bucket, Norman Rockwell, December Page, Frame, 28 x 15 In. 798.00
Carrier, 4-Pack, Cardboard, Red 7.00
Carrier, 6-Pack, Aluminum, Handle, 5 x 8 In. 26.00
Carrier, Drink Coca-Cola In Bottles, Red Letters, Metal Corners, Chattanooga, 1962 .... 8.00
Carrier, Drink Coca-Cola, Aluminum, Red Wood Handle, Acton Mfg., 1950 .... 76.00
Carrier, Drink Coca-Cola, Enjoy Coke, Aluminum, 1950s, 8 x 7 1/2 x 5 In. 51.00
Carrier, Grocery Cart, Enjoy Coca-Cola While You Shop, Metal, 2 1/2 x 6 In. 39.00
Carrier, Wood, Wings, c.1940, 5 1/4 x 7 1/2 x 7 3/4 In. 196.00
Change Receiver, Drink Coca-Cola, 5 Cents, Reverse Glass, Round, Empire, c.1907, 7 In. 2970.00
Cigarette Lighter, Bottle Shape, Plastic, Metal Cap, 1950s, 2 1/2 In. ....11.25 to 28.00
Clock, Coca-Cola In Bottles, Rocking Bottle, Neon, Light-Up, Swihart, c.1948, 20 In. 6600.00
Clock, Drink Coca-Cola In Bottles, Wood Frame, c.1939, 16 x 16 In. 470.00
Clock, Drink Coca-Cola, Sign Of Good Taste, Red, White, Cleveland, 1950s, 34 x 36 In. 3300.00
Clock, Drink Coca-Cola, Take Home A Carton, Neon, Light-Up, 1930s, Countertop 13750.00

Clock, Ideal Brain Tonic, Baird, c.1893, 30 x 18 In. 13440.00
Clock, Regulator, Delicious, Refreshing, 5 Cents, Oak Case, Ingraham, c.1905, 31 x 17 In. 1430.00
Clock Radio, Cooler Shape, Red, 1950s 770.00
Cooler, Airline, Red, 1940-50, 13 x 18 In. 520.00
Cooler, Airline, Red, 1950s, 12 x 17 x 6 In. 385.00
Cooler, Floor Model, Lower Space For Refill Bottles, 30 x 36 In. 145.00
Cooler, Glascock, 17 1/2 x 17 1/2 x 30 In. 616.00
Cooler, Salesman Sample, Closed Front, 8 1/2 x 11 x 9 In. 3080.00
Cooler, Salesman Sample, Drink Coca-Cola, Red, White, c.1939, 10 x 12 In. .... 1650.00 to 1950.00
Coupon, Free Drink, Cardboard, Opera Star, Hilda Clark, 2 x 3 3/8 In. 525.00
Crate, Drink Coca-Cola In Bottles, Painted, Yellow, Red, 18 1/2 x 11 3/4 In. 9.00
Crate, Enjoy Coca-Cola, Wood, 24 Bottle Holes, Red, 1971 .... 13.00
Crate, Wood, 24 Miniature Bottles, Louisville, Ky., c.1930, 4 x 6 In. 850.00
Cup & Saucer, Drink Coca-Cola, Taylor Smith, 1930s 1430.00
Dish, Pretzel, 3 Bottles, Aluminum, c.1930, 4 1/4 x 8 In. 175.00
Dispenser, Drink Coca-Cola, Brown Glass, Chrome Lid, Multiplex Faucet Co., c.1930, 18 In. 2530.00
Dispenser, Drink Coca-Cola, Dole Deluxe, 1947-51, 20 x 21 x 11 In. 410.00
Dispenser, Drink Coca-Cola, Ice Cold, Red, White Letters, Clamp, 23 x 10 In. 330.00
Dispenser, Syrup, Urn, Lid, Base, c.1900, 22 In. 3080.00
Display, Bottle, Christmas, Light Green, Cap, 1923, 20 In. 308.00
Door Pull, Drink Coca-Cola, Be Really Refreshed, Fishtail, Metal, 1960s, 8 x 4 In. 275.00
Door Pull, Have A Coke, Bottle Shape, Plastic, Metal, 1950s, 8 In. .... 340.00 to 440.00
Door Push, Come In, Have A Coca-Cola, Porcelain, 1930s, 11 3/4 x 3 1/2 In. 468.00
Door Push, Thanks Call Again For A Coca-Cola, Porcelain, Canada, 1940s, 14 x 4 In. 300.00
Door Push, Thanks Call Again For A Coca-Cola, Red, Yellow, White, Porcelain, 1930s, 11 1/2 x 4 In. 495.00
Fan, Drink Carbonated Coca-Cola In Bottles, 5 Cent, 1900-05, 15 In. 550.00
Fan, Sprite Boy, Bottle, Have A Coke, Compliments Of Local Coca-Cola Bottling Co., 1950s, 16 In. .. 165.00
Festoon, Umbrella Girls, Frame, 1918, 32 x 65 In. 1100.00
Globe, Ceiling, Milk Glass, Red Logo, 1930s, 9 x 14 In. 1100.00
Globe, Milk Glass, Frosted, Schoolhouse, 1930s, 11 In. 660.00
Jar, Cover, Chewing Gum, 1903-05, 11 1/2 In. 950.00
Kickplate, Drink Coca-Cola, Fountain Service, Porcelain, 1950s, 12 x 29 In. 358.00
Kickplate, Drink Coca-Cola, Porcelain, Green & Red, 1931, 10 x 30 In. 630.00
Kickplate, Drink Coca-Cola, Sold Here Ice Cold, Porcelain, 1930s, 12 x 31 In. 715.00
Kickplate, Drink Coca-Cola, Tin, Embossed, 1934, 11 x 35 In. 1155.00
Menu, Hilda Clark, 2-Sided, 1903, 6 x 4 In. 1760.00
Menu Board, Drink Coca-Cola, Metal, 1950s, 20 x 72 In. 220.00
Menu Board, Tin, Masonite, 1950s, 17 1/4 x 29 1/4 In. 200.00
Menu Board, Tin, Wood, Masonite, 1939, 14 x 26 3/4 In. 840.00
Mirror, Cat, Cardboard, 1920s, 2 1/2 x 2 1/2 In. 468.00
Mirror, Drink Coca-Cola, 5 Cents, Woman, Holding Glass, Oval, 1914, 2 3/4 In. 435.00
Mirror, Drink Coca-Cola, Woman Holding Glass, Oval, 1907, 2 3/4 In. 459.00
Mirror, Good To The Last Drop, Victorian Woman, Celluloid, Oval, 1908, Pocket 1100.00
Notepad, Coca-Cola Company, Woman, Glass, Celluloid, 1902, 5 x 2 1/2 In. 825.00
Notepad, Hilda Clark, Celluloid, 1903, 5 x 2 1/2 In. 715.00
Plate, Sandwich, Knowles, 1931, 7 1/4 In. .... 220.00 to 248.00
Playing Cards, Airplane Spotter, Box, c.1943 .... 90.00
Playing Cards, Drink Coca-Cola In Bottles, Hund & Eger Bottling Co., Box, c.1930s 770.00
Postage Stamp Holder, Celluloid, 1902, 2 1/2 x 1 1/2 In. 415.00
Postcard, Coca-Cola Girl, Drink Delicious Coca-Cola, 1910, 5 1/2 x 3 1/2 In. 578.00
Postcard, Motor Girl, Drink Bottled Coca-Cola, 1911, 5 1/2 x 3 1/2 In. 495.00
Radio, Bottle Shape, Plastic, 1970s 21.00
Radio, Cooler, Drink Coca-Cola, Ice Cold, c.1950, 5 x 12 In. 1045.00
Record, Rum & Coca-Cola Fox Trot, Vaughn Monroe, 78 RPM 15.00
Scooter, 1960s .... *ILLUS* 392.00
Service Emblem, Booker Design, 3 Green Stones, 15 Year 44.00
Sheet Music, Rum & Coca-Cola, Andrews Sisters, 1944 .... 12.00
Sheet Music, Rum & Coca-Cola, Jeri Sullavan, 1944, 2 Pages 7.00
Sign, All Set At Our House, Boy, Holding 6-Pack, Cardboard, Trolley, 11 x 28 In. 358.00
Sign, Bobby Jones, Cardboard, 1947, 15 x 13 In. 523.00
Sign, Bottle, Aluminum, Die Cut, 1951, 16 In. .... 120.00 to 220.00

Coca-Cola, Scooter, 1960s

Coca-Cola, Sign, Drink Coca-Cola, Ice Cold, 2-Sided, Tin, 22 1/2 x 22 1/2 In.

Sign, Bottle, Porcelain, Die Cut, 1940s, 12 In. 143.00
Sign, Bottle, Tin, Embossed, Raised Frame, 1952, 36 x 18 In. 330.00
Sign, Bring Home Coca-Cola, Snowman, Coke Bottle, 1957, 27 x 16 In. 910.00
Sign, Cap, Bottle, Coca-Cola, Enamel On Metal, c.1950, 24 In. 350.00
Sign, Cap, Bottle, Coca-Cola, Porcelain, c.1950, 36 In. 520.00
Sign, Cap, Drink Coca-Cola In Bottles, Arrow, Tin, 1953, 12 In. 525.00
Sign, Cap, Drink Coca-Cola In Bottles, Tin, 1953, 16 In. 715.00
Sign, Cap, Drink Coca-Cola, Arrow, Tin, 1950s, 12 In. . . . . . 468.00 to 495.00
Sign, Cap, Drink Coca-Cola, Red, White, Porcelain, c.1950, 24 In. 605.00
Sign, Cap, Drink Coca-Cola, Tin, 1957, 16 In. 358.00
Sign, Cap, Hand Holding Coke Bottle, White Ground, Aluminum, c.1950, 16 In. 220.00
Sign, Circus Scene, Woman, Clown, Dog, Boy, Frame, 1936, 50 x 30 In. 1045.00
Sign, Coca-Cola Belongs, Man, Woman, Grill, Basket, Frame, 1942, 30 x 50 In. 635.00
Sign, Coca-Cola Gum, Dutch Boy, Cardboard, Easel Back, 1914-16, 8 x 5 1/2 In. 24200.00
Sign, Coca-Cola, Between Bites, Ham Sandwich, Cardboard, 1933, 20 1/2 x 10 1/4 In. 1210.00
Sign, Coca-Cola, Figural Porcelain, 5 1/2 x 19 In. 770.00
Sign, Coca-Cola, Great Together, Hot Dog, Cardboard, 1932, 20 x 10 In. 1210.00
Sign, Coca-Cola, Sign Of Good Taste, Tin, Flange, 1960, 15 x 18 In. 330.00
Sign, Coca-Cola, Take Home A Carton, Tin, c.1942, 20 x 21 In. 400.00
Sign, Coca-Cola, Take Home A Carton, Tin, Sidewalk, 1959, 28 x 20 In. 798.00
Sign, Coca-Cola, Tin Lithograph, Embossed, 1930, 19 5/8 In. 1650.00
Sign, Coke Time, Drink Coca-Cola, Woman, Sunglasses, 1955, 27 x 16 In. 385.00
Sign, Come & Get It, Ice Cold, Drink Coca-Cola, Black Boy, 1956, 20 x 36 In. 798.00
Sign, Drink A Bottle Of Coca-Cola & Be Lucky, 5 Cents, Cardboard, c.1920, 11 x 14 In. 300.00
Sign, Drink Coca-Cola, 4 Women, Hats, 4 Seasons, Trolley, 1923, 9 3/4 x 19 1/2 In. 3740.00
Sign, Drink Coca-Cola, Bathing Girl, Blue Diamond, Cardboard, Die Cut, 1940, 22 x 25 In. 2090.00
Sign, Drink Coca-Cola, Bottle, Red, Yellow, Brown, White, Metal, Self-Framed, 1940s, 18 x 54 In. . . 385.00
Sign, Drink Coca-Cola, Bottle, Tin, Embossed, 1931, 12 1/2 x 4 1/2 In. 440.00
Sign, Drink Coca-Cola, Bottle, Tin, Embossed, Frame, c.1950, 19 x 54 In. 185.00
Sign, Drink Coca-Cola, Bottle, Tin, Lithograph, Embossed, c.1931, 13 1/2 x 6 In. 690.00
Sign, Drink Coca-Cola, Cigars, Candy, Stationery, Porcelain, 2-Sided, Hanging, c.1930, 53 x 46 In. . 1760.00
Sign, Drink Coca-Cola, Delicious & Refreshing, Flapper, 1920s, 20 x 12 In. 440.00
Sign, Drink Coca-Cola, Fountain Service, 1930s, 14 x 27 In. 1100.00
Sign, Drink Coca-Cola, Fountain Service, Green, Yellow, Red, White, Porcelain, 4 1/2 x 8 In. 3740.00
Sign, Drink Coca-Cola, Fountain Service, Porcelain, 1941, 14 x 21 In. 825.00
Sign, Drink Coca-Cola, Fountain Service, Ribbon, Porcelain, 1950s, 12 x 28 In. . . . . . 495.00 to 1018.00
Sign, Drink Coca-Cola, Ice Cold, 2-Sided, Tin, 22 1/2 x 22 1/2 In. . . . . . *ILLUS* 392.00
Sign, Drink Coca-Cola, Ice Cold, Tin, Flange, 1953, 22 x 17 In. . . . . . 330.00 to 358.00
Sign, Drink Coca-Cola, Lunch With Us, Light-Up, Brunhoff, 1930s, 14 x 12 In. 4950.00
Sign, Drink Coca-Cola, Metal, Plastic, Halo Light, Round, 16 In. 525.00
Sign, Drink Coca-Cola, Pause & Refresh, Waterfall, Light-Up, 1940s, 19 1/2 In. 1210.00
Sign, Drink Coca-Cola, Play Refreshed, 4 Football Players, 1950s, 24 x 40 In. 7130.00
Sign, Drink Coca-Cola, Red Dispenser, Yellow Ground, Porcelain, 2-Sided, 1940, 26 x 25 In. 1320.00

Sign, Drink Coca-Cola, Sign Of Good Taste, Bottle, 1960s, 54 x 18 In. 525.00
Sign, Drink Coca-Cola, Sign Of Good Taste, Button, Tin, 1950, 12 In. 330.00
Sign, Drink Coca-Cola, Sprite Boy, Aluminum, 1940, 53 x 17 In. 1760.00
Sign, Drink Coca-Cola, Tin, Flange, 1946, 20 x 24 In. ....330.00 to 413.00
Sign, Drink Coca-Cola, Woman Holding Glass, Green Dress, Mirror, 2 3/4 In. 435.00
Sign, Drink Coca-Cola, Woman, Bathing Suit, Frame, 1939, 50 x 30 In. 798.00
Sign, Extra Bright Refreshment, Woman, Umbrella, Reproduction Frame, 1955, 20 x 36 In. 440.00
Sign, Face The Sun Refreshed, Woman, Frame, Canada, 1941, 50 x 30 In. 770.00
Sign, Fountain Service, Porcelain, 22 1/2 x 25 1/2 In. 3920.00
Sign, Fountain, Porcelain, Enamel, 2-Sided, 27 x 28 In. 2800.00
Sign, Have A Coke, Bottle, Red, White, Yellow, Brown, Enamel, Metal, Frame, c.1948, 54 x 18 In. .. 440.00
Sign, Have A Coke, Cheerleader, Frame, 1946, 20 x 36 In. 550.00
Sign, Have A Drink Of Coca-Cola, Deliciously Refreshing, Trolley, 1912, 11 x 21 In. 11550.00
Sign, Hospitality, Woman, 3 Bottles On Tray, Frame, 1948, 27 x 56 In. 550.00
Sign, Ice Cold Coca-Cola Sold Here, Round, Tin, Embossed, Frame, 1933, 20 In. 1045.00
Sign, Ice Cold Coca-Cola Sold Here, Sidewalk, Matte, Frame, 1934, 28 x 20 In. 360.00
Sign, Ice Cold Coca-Cola Sold Here, Tin, 2-Sided, Flange, Late 1920s, 11 x 16 In. 2090.00
Sign, Ice Cold, Cup, Aqua Ground, Tin, 1960s, 20 x 28 In. 1155.00
Sign, Ice Cold, Cup, Stripes, Tin, 1960s, 28 x 20 In. 1100.00
Sign, Ice Cold, Sign Of Good Taste, Bottle, Tin, Sidewalk, 1960, 20 x 28 In. 385.00
Sign, Join Me, Drink Coca-Cola, Fencer, Frame, 1947, 27 x 16 In. 770.00
Sign, Lunch Refreshed, Drink Coca-Cola, Waitress, Frame, 1947, 27 x 16 In. 2200.00
Sign, Now For A Coke, Woman, Bathing Suit, Gil Elvgren, Frame, 1951, 20 x 36 In. 1650.00
Sign, Pause, Drink Coca-Cola, Clown, Ice Skater, Frame, 1950, 27 x 16 In. 1375.00
Sign, Pick Up 12, White Ground, Pilaster, 1954, 41 x 16 In. ....1980.00 to 3960.00
Sign, Play Refreshed, Drink Coca-Cola, Tennis Player, Frame, 1949, 27 x 16 In. 1430.00
Sign, Play Refreshed, Have A Coke, Woman, Bathing Suit, Cooler, Frame, 1948, 20 x 36 In. 550.00
Sign, Play Refreshed, Woman, On Carousel, Frame, 1948, 50 x 30 In. 935.00
Sign, Please Pay When Served, Plastic, Metal, Glass, Price Brothers, 1940s, 13 x 19 In. 1650.00
Sign, Policeman, Slow School Zone, Iron, 1950s, 62 In. 2800.00
Sign, Policeman, Slow School Zone, Thank You, Resume Speed, 2-Sided, 1962, 60 x 30 In. 3740.00
Sign, Red Grange, Cardboard, 1947, 15 x 13 In. 250.00
Sign, Refresh Yourself, Cheerleaders, Matte, Frame, 1953, 20 x 36 In. 358.00
Sign, Refreshment Right Out Of The Bottle, Woman, Car, 1942, 50 x 30 In. 1430.00
Sign, Serve Coke At Home, 6-Pack, Pilaster, 1947, 41 x 16 In. 415.00
Sign, Slow School Zone, Girl Running With Books, Wood, c.1960, 48 In. 500.00
Sign, So Easy To Carry Home, Woman, In Rain, 1942, 27 x 16 In. 880.00
Sign, Take Home A Carton Of Quality Refreshment, 6-Pack, Pilaster, 1954, 41 x 16 In. ....770.00 to 1870.00
Sign, Take Home A Carton, Easy To Carry, Cardboard, Matte, Frame, 1937, 31 1/4 x 13 In. 1375.00
Sign, Take Home A Carton, Tin, Embossed, 1942, 20 x 21 In. 400.00
Sign, Take Home A Carton, Tin, Embossed, 6-Pack Bottles, 20 x 21 In. 400.00
Sign, Things Go Better With Coke, Bottle, Tin, Self-Framed, c.1964, 54 x 18 In. ....385.00 to 467.00
Sign, Tomese Coca-Cola En Botellitas, 6 Cents, Tin, Embossed, c.1908, 12 x 36 In. 1540.00
Sign, Ty Cobb, Cardboard, 1947, 15 x 13 In. 635.00
Sign, We Sell Coca-Cola, Part Of Every Day, Served Ice Cold, Cardboard, Frame, c.1942, 15 x 22 In. . 580.00
Sign, Woman Aviator, Patriotic Theme, Cardboard Lithograph, c.1940, 27 x 43 In. 3960.00
Sign, Women Basketball Players, Cardboard, Ornate Frame, 1938, 32 1/4 x 21 1/4 In. 6845.00
Straw Dispenser, Delicious & Refreshing, Nickel Steel Lid, Early 1950s, 11 1/4 In. 70.00
Thermometer, Bottle Shape, Coca-Cola, Die Cut, Embossed, 1930s, 17 x 5 In. ....220.00 to 275.00
Thermometer, Bottle Shape, Embossed, c.1930, 15 1/2 x 5 In. 330.00
Thermometer, Bottle, Tin, 1950s, 16 3/4 x 5 1/4 In. 70.00
Thermometer, Buvez Coca-Cola, La Soif N'a Pas De Saison, Porcelain, 1939, 18 x 6 In. 415.00
Thermometer, Christmas Bottle, 16 3/4 x 5 In. 245.00
Thermometer, Drink Coca-Cola In Bottles, Red Ground, Robertson, 1950s, 12 In. 165.00
Thermometer, Drink Coca-Cola, 2 Bottles, Gold Ground, c.1941, 16 x 7 In. 715.00
Thermometer, Drink Coca-Cola, Be Really Refreshed, Round, Pam, 1959, 12 In. 935.00
Thermometer, Drink Coca-Cola, Delicious & Refreshing, Tin, 1939, 16 x 6 1/2 In. 358.00
Thermometer, Drink Coca-Cola, Girl Drinking Coke, Tin, Lithograph, c.1939, 16 x 6 1/2 In. 325.00
Thermometer, Drink Coca-Cola, Green Border, Red Center, Round, Pam, 1948, 12 In. 825.00
Thermometer, Drink Coca-Cola, Red Ground, Round, Robertson, 1950s, 12 In. 90.00
Thermometer, Drink Coca-Cola, Sign Of Good Taste, Red Ground, Robertson, 1957, 12 In. 745.00

Thermometer, Drink Coca-Cola, Thirst Knows No Season, Masonite, 1944, 17 x 7 In. . . . . . .358.00 to 715.00
Thermometer, Drink Coca-Cola, Tin, Lithograph, Embossed, 15 3/4 x 7 In. 410.00
Thermometer, Sign Of Good Taste, Red, White, Cigar Shape, Enamel On Tin, c.1957, 30 x 8 In. . . . 715.00
Thermometer, Things Go Better With Coke, White, Round, Robertson, 1964, 12 In. 358.00
Tip Tray, 1903, Hilda Clark, Delicious, Refreshing, Gold Border, 4 In. 4510.00
Tip Tray, 1909, Exhibition Girl, 6 1/4 x 4 1/2 In. 385.00
Tip Tray, 1913, Hamilton King Girl, Oval, 6 x 4 1/4 In. 1634.00
Tip Tray, 1914, Betty, 6 x 4 1/4 In. 248.00
Tip Tray, 1916, Elaine, 6 x 4 1/4 In. 138.00
Tire Rack, Enjoy Coca-Cola While We Check Your Tires, 2-Sided, 1960, 33 x 17 In. 1650.00
Toy, Dispenser, Drink Coca-Cola, Red, White, 4 Glasses, Box, 9 x 12 1/2 In. 120.00
Toy, Stove, Green, Electric, 1930s, 9 x 8 1/2 x 4 1/2 In. 2860.00
Toy, Truck, Coca-Cola Lorry, No. 37, Matchbox, Lesney, Box, 1956 . . . . 80.00
Toy, Truck, Delicious, Refreshing, 2 Wood Crates, 20 Bottles, Handcart, Marx, c.1954 . . . . 250.00
Toy, Truck, Drink Coca-Cola In Bottles, Marx, Box, 1950s, 4 1/2 x 12 1/2 x 5 1/4 In. 596.00
Toy, Truck, Painted, Metalcraft, 1930s, 10 1/2 In. 690.00
Toy, Truck, Pressed Steel, Metalcraft, 1930s, 11 In. 415.00
Toy, Truck, Pressed Steel, Metalcraft, Partial Box, 1930s, 12 In. 1320.00
Toy, Truck, Sprite Boy, Red Cab, Yellow Back, Marx, 1950s 880.00
Toy, Truck, Wood, Yellow, Buddy L, 1948, 19 In. 2310.00
Toy, Truck, Yellow, Marx, Box, 1950s, 10 3/4 In. 193.00
Tray, 1914, Betty, Oval, 12 x 15 In. 955.00
Tray, 1916, Elaine, 19 x 8 1/2 In. . . . . . . .220.00 to 550.00
Tray, 1921, Autumn Girl, Tin, 13 1/4 x 10 1/2 In. 728.00
Tray, 1923, Flapper Girl, Tin, 13 1/4 x 10 1/2 In. . . . . . . .168.00 to 312.00
Tray, 1925, Party Girl, 13 1/4 x 10 1/2 In. . . . . . . .176.00 to 395.00
Tray, 1926, Couple Golfing, 13 1/4 x 10 1/2 In. 330.00
Tray, 1927, Soda Jerk, 13 1/4 x 10 1/2 In. . . . . . . .450.00 to 605.00
Tray, 1929, Girl In Yellow Swimsuit, 13 1/4 x 10 1/2 In. . . . . . . .280.00 to 385.00
Tray, 1930, Swimsuit Girl, 10 1/2 x 13 1/4 In. . . . . . . .670.00 to 740.00
Tray, 1930, Telephone Girl, Tin, 13 1/4 x 10 1/2 In. . . . . . . .310.00 to 350.00
Tray, 1931, Barefoot Boy, Norman Rockwell, 13 1/4 x 10 1/2 In. . . . . . . .1232.00 to 1320.00
Tray, 1934, Weismuller & O'Sullivan, 10 1/2 x 13 1/4 In. . . . . . . .358.00 to 660.00
Tray, 1935, Madge Evans, 13 1/4 x 10 1/2 In. 336.00
Tray, 1936, Hostess, 13 1/4 x 10 1/2 In. 168.00
Tray, 1937, Running Girl, 13 1/4 x 10 1/2 In. . . . . . . .165.00 to 728.00
Tray, 1938, Girl At Shade, Tin, 13 1/4 x 10 1/2 In. . . . . . . .168.00 to 358.00
Tray, 1939, Springboard Girl, 13 1/4 x 10 1/2 In. 168.00
Tray, 1940, Sailor Girl, 10 1/2 x 13 1/4 In. 224.00
Tray, 1941, Skater Girl, 13 1/4 x 10 1/2 In. . . . . . . .198.00 to 500.00
Tray, 1942, 2 Girls At Car, 13 1/4 x 10 1/2 In. . . . . . . .220.00 to 504.00
Tray, 1950, Girl With Wind In Hair, 13 1/4 x 10 1/2 In. 112.00
Tray, 1953, Menu Girl, 13 1/4 x 10 1/2 In. 56.00
Tray, 1957, Girl With Umbrella, Canada, 13 x 10 1/2 In. 330.00
Vending Machine, Drink Coca-Cola In Bottles, Refresh Yourself, Late 1940s, 74 x 35 x 20 In. 350.00
Vending Machine, Vendolator, Model 33, Bottles, Red, 10 Cent, 1950s, 52 In. 770.00
Vending Machine, Vendolator, Model V-27, 10 Cent, 1940s, 24 x 27 x 19 In. 990.00
Watch Fob, Girl, Holding Glass, Relieves Fatigue, 5 Cent, Brass, Gold Wash, c.1907, 2 In. 232.00
Watch Fob, Girl, Holding Glass, Relieves Fatigue, 5 Cent, Silver, c.1907, 2 In. 187.00

COFFEE MILLS are also called coffee grinders, although there is a difference in the way each grinds the coffee. Large floor-standing or counter-model coffee mills were used in the nineteenth-century country store. Small home mills were first made about 1894. They lost favor by the 1930s. The renewed interest in fresh-ground coffee has produced many modern electric mills and hand mills and grinders. Reproductions of the old styles are being made.

Clawson & Clark, No. 1, Duplex, Cast Iron, Orange Paint, Sept. 28, 1886, 13 In. 522.00
Enterprise, 2 Flywheels, Eagle Stencil, Eagle Finial, Orange, Blue, 35 x 22 1/2 In. 1045.00
Enterprise, 2 Wheels, Lid, Eagle Finial, Cast Iron, Wooden Base, 23 1/2 x 17 In. 1050.00
Enterprise, No. 7, Stenciled, Drawer, Porcelain Pull, 20 x 15 In. 98.00

Enterprise, No. 8, 2 Wheels, Cast Iron, Wood Drawer, Table Top, 15 In. 1320.00
Enterprise, No. 9, Red Open Hopper, Wooden Drawer, Oct. 21, 1873 .... 320.00
Enterprise, No. 12, New Eagle Finial, 32 x 25 In. 770.00
Parker & White, Wall Mount, Tin Hopper, Iron, Lid, Wood, 1833-43, 8 1/4 x 6 In. 196.00
Star Mill, No. 20, Iron, Nickel Plated Hopper, 1885, 73 x 42 In. 3450.00

COIN SPOT is a glass pattern that was named by the collectors for the spots resembling coins, which are part of the glass. Colored, clear, and opalescent glass was made with the spots. Many companies used the design in the 1870–90 period. It is so popular that reproductions are still being made.

Barber Bottle, Blue Opalescent, Shaker Top, 7 1/8 In. 110.00
Lamp Base, Oil, Cranberry Opalescent Top, Victorian, 8 1/2 In. 425.00
Pitcher, Cranberry, Reeded Handle, 8 In. 150.00

COIN-OPERATED MACHINES of all types are collected. The vending machine is an ancient invention dating back to 200 B.C., when holy water was dispensed in a coin-operated vase. Smokers in seventeenth-century England could buy tobacco from a coin-operated box. It was not until after the Civil War that the technology made modern coin-operated games and vending machines plentiful. Slot machines, arcade games, and dispensers are all collected.

Arcade, Baffle Ball, 10 Shots, 1 Cent, 1940s, 22 x 22 x 10 In. 785.00
Arcade, Bally, Skill Score, Golf, Tennis, Bowing, 5 Cent, 71 x 27 x 19 In. 336.00
Arcade, International Mutoscope Co., Hockey, 1930s, 36 x 43 x 23 In. 2245.00
Arcade, Rock-Ola, World Series, c.1937, 53 x 41 In. 37700.00
Arcade, Vending Machine Co., Whiz Ball, 6 Chutes, Oak, 17 In. 410.00
Ballpoint Pen, Oak Manufacturing, 25 Cent, 1960 .... 45.00
Ballpoint Pen, Victor, Vendorama, 10 Cent, 1962 .... 50.00 to 157.00
Ballpoint Pen, Victor, Vendorama, 25 Cent, Wood, 1962 .... 146.00
Ballpoint Pen Refill, Victor, 5 Cent, Key, 1938-50 .... 134.00 to 168.00
Baseball, 1 Cent, Tecumseh Mfg., Wood, Metal, Glass, 16 1/4 x 10 1/4 In. 2145.00
Baseball, Flip Game, 1 Cent, Oak, Pine Case, Pressed Aluminum, 17 In. 1100.00
Bicycle Race, Mermod Freres, No. 641, 30 x 41 x 28 In. 21150.00
Billiard Table, Victorian Style, 1 Cent, c.1920 .... 3630.00
Cigarette, 1 Cent, Metal, Red Window Frame, Shelf, 8 x 6 x 6 1/4 In. 160.00
Condom, Advance Machine, 25 Cent, Wall Mount, Yellow, 31 x 4 x 6 In. 39.00
Condom, Harmon Amco, 25 Cent, Wall Mount, White 50.00
Crane, International Mutoscope Reel, Electric Traveling, Crane, 1940s, 71 In. 5600.00
Crane, International Mutoscope Reel, Red Top Crane, 1931-39 .... 7150.00
Crane, Scientific Machine, Panama Digger, Wood, Marquee, c.1934, 65 x 18 In. 3080.00
Fortune Teller, Marital, Benedict Co., 1 Cent, Happy Home, c.1905, 66 In. 3850.00
Gum, Ad-Lee Co., E-Z, Celluloid, Cast Iron, c.1908, 23 x 9 x 9 In. 1155.00
Gum, Automatic Clerk, Mansfield's Pepsin, Etched Glass, Iron, c.1902, 12 In. 990.00
Gum, Baker Boy, Maniken Vendor Co., 1928-29, 16 x 9 In. .... 6710.00 to 7700.00
Gum, Ford, Twin, Iron, Chrome, Glass, Stand, 40 1/2 In. 150.00
Gum, Norris, Master No. 2, Gooseneck, Porcelain, 1923-25, 16 In. 500.00
Gum, Norris, Master, Penny, Nickel, Porcelain, Green, Cream, c.1923, 16 In. 300.00
Gum, Northwestern, Golf, Oak Case, 15 In. 935.00
Gum, Northwestern, Mouthy Marvin, 25 Cent 125.00
Gum, Pulver, Traffic Cop, 1 Cent, Porcelain, Red, White, Key, 21 In. 730.00
Gum, Pulver, Woody Woodpecker, 1 Cent, Porcelain, 21 In. 1760.00
Gum, Pulver, Yellow Kid, 1 Cent, Too Choos, Red, White, 21 In. 459.00
Gum, Roth's Pansy, Oak Frame, Steel, Iron, c.1905, 20 In. 7150.00
Gum, Spearmint, Pressed Steel, Cast Iron, Yellow, 28 In. 330.00
Gum, Wrigley's Spearmint, 1 Cent, Metal, Wall Mount, 20 x 6 In. 135.00
Gum, Zeno, 1 Cent, Porcelain, Yellow, Black, c.1908, 17 In. .... 300.00 to 650.00
Gum, Zeno, Oak, Iron, Paper Decal, c.1902, 17 In. 825.00
Gumball, Advance, Model D, 1 Cent, 1912-22 .... 100.00
Gumball, Atlas Master, 5 Cent, 1951, 16 In. 35.00
Gumball, Bluebird Products, Universal, 1 Cent, 1915, 12 In. 370.00

If garage windows are painted, burglars won't be able to tell if cars are home or not. Use translucent paint to get light in the closed garage.

Coin-Operated Machine, Gumball, Columbus, Model 34, 1 Cent, Cast Iron, 1936

Gumball, Columbus, Model 34, 1 Cent, Cast Iron, 1936 .... *ILLUS* 515.00
Gumball, Columbus, Model A, Cast Iron, 1908-20, 16 In. 336.00
Gumball, Ford, Chrome, Glass, 11 1/2 In. .... 44.00 to 66.00
Gumball, Gabriel, Pot Metal, Plastic, 16 In. 22.00
Gumball, Hart, 1 Cent, Key, c.1950, 11 In. 106.00
Gumball, Norris, Master No. 77, Fantail, Penny, Nickel, Porcelain, 1933, 16 In. 1735.00
Gumball, Norris, Master, 1 Cent, Porcelain, Red, Key, c.1923, 16 In. 426.00
Gumball, Victor, Baby Grand, 5 Cent, Wood Case, Iron, c.1940, 13 x 7 In. .... 39.00 to 90.00
Gumball, Victor, Topper 1/2 Cabinet, 1 Cent, Key, c.1950, 15 1/2 In. 85.00
Gumball, Victor, Topper, 1 Cent, c.1950, 15 1/2 In. .... 56.00 to 132.00
Gumball, Victor, Vendorama, 25 Cent, Extra Front, 18 1/2 In. 39.00
Gumball, William Michael, 1 Cent, Cast Iron, Key, c.1930, 11 1/2 In. 590.00
Lighter Fluid, Serv-A-Liter, 1 Cent, 1928, 17 1/2 x 6 In. 770.00
Lighter Fluid, Van-Lite, Gas Pump Shape, Red Paint, 1 Cent, c.1940, 18 1/2 In. 660.00
Matches, Columbus, Model 25, 1 Cent, Cast Iron, 1915-28, 12 x 8 In. 145.00
Music Box, Criterion, Double Comb, Crank-Wind, 20 1/2-In. Disc, 85 In. 8225.00
Music Box, Cuendet, No. 7803, 8 Tunes, 6 1/2-In. Cylinder, 17 1/4 In. 880.00
Music Box, Monopol Automatic, Chalet, 32 Discs, 18 In. 7640.00
Music Box, Nicole Freres, Polyphon, Penny, Walnut Case, c.1900, 33 x 24 x 15 In. 5320.00
Music Box, Poylphon, Terra-Cotta Automaton Figure, Savoyard, 11 1/4-In. Disk, 69 In. 31725.00
Music Box, Regina, Mahogany Case, 12 Tunes, 27-In. Disc, 62 In. 16450.00
Music Box, Symphonion, Gabrinus, Wooden King, 11 3/4-In. Disc, 45 In. 10000.00
Music Box, Symphonion, Walnut Case, c.1897, 13 5/8-In. Disc, 23 In. 2350.00
Music Box, Symphonion, Walnut Case, Discs, 25 1/4-In. Disc, 80 In. 11750.00
Mutoscope, American Mutoscope Biograph, Clamshell, c.1895, 33 In. 2350.00
Mutoscope, Clamshell, Cast Iron, Painted, c.1895, 78 In. 3575.00
Mutoscope, Dempsey vs. Tunney, Iron, Late 1920s, 54 In. 4425.00
Mutoscope, Indian, Eagle, Beachy Keen, Iron, c.1900, 76 In. 13585.00
Mutoscope, International, JMK15, Tin, Dancing Woman Reel, 1939-40, 53 In. 1175.00
Mutoscope, International, Reel Only, No. 1, Pursuit & Gun Case 380.00
Nickelodeon, 25 Cent, Mahogany, Griffin Legs, Stained Glass, 54 x 63 In. 3080.00
Nut, Silver King, Hot Nut, Ruby Glass Top, Light-Up, 1947, 15 1/2 In. .... 390.00 to 410.00
Parking Meter, Cast Iron, 1930s 252.00
Peanut, Bloyd Mfg., Lucky Boy, 1 Cent, Keys, 1937, 15 In. 170.00
Peanut, D. Robbins Co., Empire, 1 Cent, 1932, 16 1/2 In. 365.00
Peanut, Great States, Sel-Mor, Model E, 1 Cent, 1938, 15 In. 280.00
Peanut, Mills, Little Perfection, Metal Base, Lid, Chicago, Ill., 1912, 21 In. 12100.00
Peanut, National Novelty, 1 Cent, c.1910 .... 756.00
Peanut, Northwestern, Model 33, 1 Cent, Porcelain, Black, Keys, 1933, 16 In. 370.00
Peanut, Northwestern, Model 33, Porcelain, Red, Key, 1933, 16 In. 190.00
Peanut, Northwestern, Model 40, 1 Cent, Porcelain, Red, 1940, 13 1/2 In. 269.00
Peanut, Northwestern, Model 49, 1 Cent, Key, 1949, 16 In. 50.00
Peanut, Northwestern, Peanut Merchandiser, Porcelain, White, 1920s, 17 1/2 In. 4590.00
Peanut, Oak Mfg., Acorn, Penny, Nickel, Chrome, Red, Key, 1947-50 .... 45.00

Peanut, Regal, 1 Cent, Key, Plastic Cylinder Globe, c.1940, 12 In. 39.00
Peanut, Regal, Hot Nut, 5 Cent, Plastic Top, c.1950 .... 118.00
Peanut, Simmons, Model A, 1 Cent, Porcelain, Green, 1930-34, 16 In. 495.00
Peanut, Stewart & McGuire, Penny, Nickel, c.1935, 18 3/4 In. 570.00
Perfume, Bull Head, 1 Cent, Iron, Black Paint, Wall Mount, 1902-10, 14 In. 3525.00
Pinball, Big Guns, Art Deco, 52 In. 495.00
Pinball, Gottlieb, Humpty Dumpty, Wood Legs, Floor Model, c.1947 .... 1210.00
Pinball, World Series, Wood, 36 In. 550.00
Pistachio, Columbus, Model M, 1 Cent, 8-Sided, Green, Porcelain, 1928, 14 In. 420.00
Popcorn, Gold Metal Product Co., Metal, Floor Model, 59 In. 660.00
Slot, Bally, Sparkplug, Horse Race, 5 Cent, 1924, 13 1/2 x 15 In. 3300.00
Slot, Buckley, Bones, 25 Cent, Oak, Cast Aluminum, 26 In. 880.00
Slot, Caille, Ben Hur, 1 Wheel, 5 Cent, 1908-10, 21 In. 3740.00
Slot, Caille, Centaur, 5 Cent, Mahogany Case, 66 In. 39600.00
Slot, Caille, Dough Boy Bell, 10 Cent, c.1936 .... 825.00
Slot, Caille, Dough Boy Bell, 25 Cent, c.1936 .... 1650.00
Slot, Caille, Grand Prize, 4 Reel, 5 Cent, 1930-39 .... 1045.00
Slot, Caille, Silver Cup, Cast Iron, Nickel Plated, 1909-15, 20 In. 17600.00
Slot, Caille, Superior Jackpot, 5 Cent, 1926-32 .... 1652.00
Slot, Groetchen Tool, Columbia, Deluxe, 5 Cent, 1936 .... 825.00
Slot, Groetchen, Columbia Bell, 10 Cent, 3 Reel, 1946 .... 560.00
Slot, Jennings, Rockaway, 1 Cent, Oak, Aluminum, c.1931, 22 In. .... 1540.00 to 2420.00
Slot, Jennings, Silver Moon Chief, 10 Cent, 1938-41 .... 935.00
Slot, Jennings, Standard Chief, 10 Cent, 1946, 26 In. 1345.00
Slot, Mills Bursting Cherry, 5 Cent, Oak, Nickel, 25 In. 1210.00
Slot, Mills, 777 Hightop, 25 Cent, Wood, Cast Metal, 1947, 27 In. 1540.00
Slot, Mills, Baseball, 5 Cent, Oak, Cast Aluminum, 1929-30, 26 In. 7150.00
Slot, Mills, Black Cherry Bell, 25 Cent, c.1945, 26 In. .... 1100.00 to 1980.00
Slot, Mills, Blue Bell, 10 Cent, Wood, Cast Metal, c.1949, 27 In. 935.00
Slot, Mills, Bursting Cherry, 10 Cent, 1937, 26 In. 1650.00
Slot, Mills, Bursting Cherry, 25 Cent, Oak, Nickel Cabinet, 26 In. 385.00
Slot, Mills, Castle Front, 5 Cent, 1933-36, 26 x 16 In. 1760.00
Slot, Mills, Chrome Bell, Diamond Front, Guaranteed Jackpot, 5 Cent, 1933-46 .... 2200.00
Slot, Mills, Elk, Cast Iron Case, Original Marquee, 18 1/2 In. 5500.00
Slot, Mills, Extraordinary, 5 Cent, c.1933, Floor Model 2860.00
Slot, Mills, Golden Falls, 5 Cent, Key, c.1945, 26 In. 1456.00
Slot, Mills, Golden Nugget, 25 Cent, Oak, Cast Metal, c.1947, 26 In. 1100.00
Slot, Mills, Hi Top, 25 Cent, 3 Reel, c.1940 .... 1064.00
Slot, Mills, O.K. Gum Vender, Oak, Iron, 3 Reel, c.1912, 58 x 17 In. 8250.00
Slot, Mills, Operator Bell, 25 Cent, Oak, Cast Aluminum, 1910-25, 24 In. 1430.00
Slot, Mills, Operator Bell, Iron Case, Side Gum Vendor, c.1911 .... 9075.00
Slot, Mills, Poinsettia, 5 Cent, 3 Reel, c.1928, 25 x 16 In. 925.00
Slot, Mills, Poinsettia, 25 Cent, 3 Reel, c.1928, 25 x 16 In. 1625.00
Slot, Mills, Puritan Baby Bell Vendor, Gumball, 1 Cent, c.1932, 11 x 9 In. 940.00
Slot, Mills, Silent Bell, War Eagle, 25 Cent, Oak, Metal, c.1931, 27 In. 990.00
Slot, Mills, Silent Gooseneck, Lion Front, Table Top, 1931-32 .... 3850.00
Slot, Mills, War Eagle, 10 Cent, c.1931 .... 2800.00
Slot, Mills, Wild Deuces, 25 Cent, Oak, Cast Metal, c.1938, 27 In. 1870.00
Slot, Pace, Comet, 10 Cent, c.1932, 25 x 16 In. 1760.00
Slot, Rock-Ola, 5 Jacks, 1 Cent, Oak Case, Aluminum, c.1930, 20 In. 1210.00
Slot, Watling, Blue Seal, 5 Cent, c.1928 .... 1760.00
Slot, Watling, Rol-A-Top, 5 Cent, Oak, Cast Metal, c.1936, 29 In. 1430.00
Slot, Watling, Rol-A-Top, 25 Cent, c.1936, 29 In. 3960.00
Slot, Watling, Treasury Twin Jackpot, Mint Vendor, 5 Cent, c.1936 .... 19580.00
Slot, Watling, Twin Jackpot, Torch, 1 Cent, c.1930 .... 1810.00
Stamp, Abbey Vending Supply, Stampmaster, 10 & 25 Cent 11.00
Stamp, Abbey, U.S. Postage, 10 & 25 Cent, Key, 14 x 8 x 5 1/2 In. 17.00
Stamp, Mills Novelty, Postage, Oak, Aluminum, c.1915, 22 x 10 In. 4620.00
Stamp, Postage Stamp Machine Co., 5 & 10 Cent, 14 x 10 x 7 In. 39.00
Stamp, U.S. Postage, Continental 200, Porcelain, 22 x 10 x 15 In. 39.00
Stamp, U.S. Stamps, In Sanitary Folders, 25 & 10 Cent, 15 In. 28.00

Trade Simulator, Baseball, Playing Field, 1920-30, 17 1/2 In. 600.00
Trade Stimulator, Ad-Lee, King's Horses, 1 Cent, c.1933, 21 In. 2310.00
Trade Stimulator, Baker, Lucky Strike, Ball Gum, Wheel, 1 Cent, c.1941, 8 x 13 In. 475.00
Trade Stimulator, Daval, Buddy, Gumball, Cigarette, 1 Cent, 1940-46 .... 300.00
Trade Stimulator, Daval, Reel 21, Gumball, Red, Iron, c.1936, 9 x 11 x 8 In. 375.00
Trade Stimulator, Groetchen, Ball Gum, 1 Cent, 3 Reel, 1935 .... 525.00
Trade Stimulator, Groetchen, Liberty, Token Payout, Cigarette Reels, 5 Cent, 1940 .... 240.00
Trade Stimulator, Groetchen, Liberty, Token Payout, Sports Reels, 5 Cent, 1940 .... 275.00
Trade Stimulator, Imp, Cast Metal, Blue Paint, 1927-40, 6 In. 150.00
Trade Stimulator, Jennings, Target, 1 Cent, Aluminum, Indians, c.1926, 18 x 13 In. 1485.00
Trade Stimulator, Keeney & Sons, Magic Clock Gum Vendor, Wood, c.1930, 15 In. .... 469.00 to 499.00
Trade Stimulator, Kicker & Catcher, Mahogany Case, c.1950, 17 1/2 In. 495.00
Trade Stimulator, Milk Bottle, Coin Drop, Aluminum, 17 1/2 x 12 In. 435.00
Trade Stimulator, Peo Manufacturing, Baseball, 1 Cent, 1931-39 .... 1430.00
Trade Stimulator, Roulette, Cigar, 1895, 24 In. 1875.00
Trade Stimulator, Shipman Mfg., Spin It, Horse Race, 4 Cent, c.1937, 11 x 7 In. 269.00
Vending, A.M. Walzer, Moderne Vendor, Hershey, 1 Cent, 1930, 18 In. 157.00
Vending, Berger, Restored, c.1902, 19 In. 11000.00
Vending, Chicago Gum & Candy Co., Gem, 5 Cent, 1925, 15 1/2 In. 125.00
Vending, Dixie Vortex, Dixie Cup, 1 Cent, Glass Tube, 33 In. 615.00
Vending, Harmon Amco, Sanitary Napkin, 10 Cent, c.1923, 34 x 4 1/2 In. 39.00
Vending, Honey Breath Balls, 4 For 1 Cent, Banner, Nickel Plated, Glass, 13 In. 6720.00
Vending, Jolly Pops, Those Good Suckers, 1 Cent, Red, 20 x 10 In. 800.00
Vending, Lucky Eggs, Flintstones, Animated, 25 Cent, 57 x 27 x 25 In. 56.00
Vending, National, Magna Vendor, 16-Sided Glass Globe, Aluminum, c.1934, 15 In. 520.00
Vending, Northwestern, Merchandiser 31, 1 Cent, Cast Iron, 1931 .... 100.00
Vending, Oak Mfg., Gumball, Baseball Cards, 1950s, 28 x 13 In. 1980.00
Vending, Oak Mfg., Oak Premiere, Gumball & Card, 2 Cent, 1956, 13 1/2 In. 300.00
Vending, Parker Pencil, Cast Iron, Pressed Steel, 9 In. 1100.00
Vending, Postcard, Mutoscope, Goofy Giggles, 10 Cent, 1940s, 79 x 18 In. 315.00
Vending, Pulver, Chocolate, Cocoa, Gum, Porcelain, Iron, c.1904, 25 In. 9900.00
Vending, Razor Blades, 10 Cent, Key, 19 x 13 3/4 x 8 1/2 In. 615.00
Vending, Victor, Super Mart, 5 Cent, 1956 .... 23.00
Vending, Victor, Super V, 10 Cent, 1954, 15 In. 60.00
Vendor, Lenox Mfg., Toilet Paper, Iron, Gilt Stencils, c.1891, 9 1/2 In. 9990.00

COLLECTOR PLATES are modern plates produced in limited editions. Some may be found listed under the factory name, such as Bing & Grondahl, Royal Copenhagen, Royal Doulton, and Wedgwood.

Anri, Christmas, 1978, Ferrandiz, Leading The Way, Frame, 9 In. 64.00
Anri, Christmas, 1979, Moss Gatherers Of Villnoess, Frame, 11 1/2 In. 64.00
Anri, Father's Day, 1973, Alpine Father & Children, Frame, 9 In. 38.00
Anri, Mother's Day, 1972, Ferrandiz, Mother Sewing, Frame, 9 In. .... 34.00 to 72.00
Anri, Mother's Day, 1980, Ferrandiz, Spring Arrivals, Frame, 9 In. 72.00
Children Series, DeGrazia, Flower Boy, Box, 1979, 10 In. 166.00
Children Series, DeGrazia, Little Cocopah, Box, 1980, 10 1/4 In. 136.00
Children Series, DeGrazia, White Dove, Box, 10 1/4 In. 105.00
Christmas, 1970, Partridge, Silver Overlay, 8 1/4 In. 8.00
Gorham, 4 Freedoms, Freedom Of Speech, Rockwell, Box, 1976, 10 1/2 In. 64.00
Gorham, Clowns, Julian Ritter, Falling In Love, 1977, 10 In. 163.00
Gorham, Moppets, 1977, Happy Merry Christmas Tree 15.00
Gorham, Norman Rockwell, 1974, Goin' Fishin', Box, 10 1/2 In. 45.00
Gorham, Norman Rockwell, 1978, Ship Ahoy, 8 1/2 In. ....
Holiday, 1981, DeGrazia, A Little Prayer, Christmas Angel, 10 1/4 In. 82.00
Holiday, 1983, DeGrazia, Heavenly Blessings, Box, 10 1/4 In. 40.00
Holiday, DeGrazia, Navajo Madonna, Box, 10 1/4 In. 1100.00
Kaiser, Christmas, 1971, Silent Night, 7 3/4 In. 17.00
Kaiser, Christmas, 1974, Christmas Carolers, 7 5/8 In. 17.00
Kaiser, Christmas, 1977, Three Kings, 7 5/8 In. 42.00
Kaiser, Classic Fairy Tales, Frog King, 1983, 7 1/4 In. .... 35.00 to 40.00
Kaiser, Classic Fairy Tales, Puss In Boots, 7 1/2 In. 44.00

Kaiser, Classic Fairy Tales, Tom Thumb, 1984, 7 1/2 In. 35.00
Kaiser, Mother's Day, 1976, Swan & Cygnets, 7 3/4 In. 18.00
Knowles, American Journey, Westward Ho!, Box, 1987, 8 1/2 In. 35.00
Knowles, Christmas, 1975, Rockwell, Angel With Black Eye, 8 1/4 In. 30.00
Knowles, Christmas, 1978, Rockwell, Christmas Dream, Box, 8 1/4 In. 23.00
Knowles, Christmas, 1982, Rockwell, Christmas Courtship, Box, 8 1/2 In. .... 22.00 to 28.00
Knowles, Christmas, 1983, Children Decorating Tree, Spaulding, 8 1/2 In. 22.00
Knowles, Field Puppies, Missing The Point, Irish Setter, 1988, 8 1/2 In. 35.00
Knowles, Friends I Remember, Fringe Benefits, Box, 1985, 8 1/2 In. 35.00
Knowles, Gone With The Wind, Scarlett, 1978, 8 1/2 In. 130.00
Knowles, Grandparents, Skating Lesson, Box, 1981, 8 1/2 In. 15.00
Knowles, Mother's Day, 1979, Reflections, Rockwell, Box, 8 1/2 In. 30.00
Knowles, Mother's Day, 1981, After The Party, Rockwell, Box, 8 1/2 In. .... 22.00 to 25.00
Knowles, Mother's Day, 1983, Bringing Mom Breakfast, Spaulding, Box, 9 3/4 In. 29.00
Knowles, Norman Rockwell, Heritage, Shipbuilder, 1980, 8 1/2 In. .... 15.00 to 35.00
Knowles, Norman Rockwell, Rediscovered Women, Dreaming In The Attic, 8 1/2 In. 13.00
Knowles, Norman Rockwell, Rediscovered Women, Flirting In Parlor, Box, 8 1/2 In. 36.00
Knowles, Sound Of Music, My Favorite Things, 1986, 8 1/2 In. 18.00
Knowles, Treasured Songs Of Childhood, A Tisket A Tasket, Box, 1988, 8 1/2 In. 29.00
Konigszelt, Christmas, 1979, Adoration, Hedi Keller, Box, 9 1/2 In. 31.00
Konigszelt, Christmas, 1985, Following The Star, Hedi Keller, Box, 9 1/2 In. 32.00
Konigszelt, German Half-Timbered Houses, Middle Franconian, Box, 1986 .... 25.00
Konigszelt, Grimm's Fairy Tales, Rapunzel, Box, 1982, 7 3/4 In. .... 24.00 to 30.00
Konigszelt, Grimm's Fairy Tales, Rumpelstiltskin, Box, 1981 .... 24.00
Konigszelt, Grimm's Fairy Tales, Tale Of Golden Goose, Box, 1984, 8 In. 24.00
Konigszelt, Sulamith's Love Song, Die Musik, Wulfing, Box, 1982, 7 3/4 In. 30.00
Porsgrund, Christmas, 1968, Church 150.00
Porsgrund, Christmas, 1969, Three Wise Men 75.00
Porsgrund, Christmas, 1970, Road To Bethlehem 25.00
Porsgrund, Christmas, 1971, A Child Is Born In Bethlehem 25.00
Porsgrund, Christmas, 1972, 3 Angels Around Christmas Tree 25.00
Porsgrund, Christmas, 1979, Home For Christmas 25.00
Porsgrund, Christmas, 1992, Christmas Tree 60.00
Porsgrund, Father's Day, 1971, Fishing, Box, 5 In. 25.00
Porsgrund, Mother's Day, 1971, Duck & Ducklings, 5 In. .... 13.00 to 26.00
Porsgrund, Mother's Day, 1972, Doe & Fawn, 5 1/4 In. 18.00
Schmid, Bavarian Christmas, 1971, Family Portrait, Box, 9 1/2 In. 38.00
Schmid, Christmas, 1972, Christ In The Manger, Ferrandiz, 8 In. 149.00
Schmid, Christmas, 1975, Raggedy Ann, Gifts Of Love, Box, 7 1/2 In. 38.00
Schmid, Christmas, 1976, Raggedy Ann, Merry Blades, Box, 7 1/2 In. 32.00
Schmid, Christmas, 1977, Raggedy Ann, Christmas Morning, 7 1/2 In. 20.00
Schmid, Mother & Child, Floral, Ferrandiz, 1979, 9 3/4 In. 81.00
Schmid, Music Makers, Flutist, Ferrandiz, Box, 1981, 6 1/2 In. 24.00
Schmid, Paddington Bear, Sandcastles, Box, 1981, 6 3/4 In. 29.00
Western, DeGrazia, Bronco, 1987, 10 1/4 In. 85.00

COMIC ART, or cartoon art, is a relatively new field of collecting. Original comic strips, magazine covers, and even printed strips are collected. The first daily comic strip was printed in 1907. The paintings on celluloid used for movie cartoons are listed in this book under Animation Art.

Cover, 2-Fisted Tales No. 21, EC Library Set, Marie Severin, Watercolor, 1970s, 13 x 9 In. 396.00
Cover Art, Fat & Slat No. 4, Ed Wheelan, Spring, 1948, 18 x 18 In. 1980.00
Cover Art, Moon Girl & The Prince No. 1, Johnny Craig, Fall, 1947, 19 x 13 1/2 In. 8800.00
Drawing, 4 Pages, 2 Of A Kind, Heart & Soul No. 1, Fred Kida, Apr., May 1954, 18 x 12 In. 110.00
Drawing, 6 Pages, Get Lost No. 1, 4-Flush Gordon, Harrison, Andru & Esposito, 1954, 18 x 12 In. 1980.00
Drawing, 7 Pages, Peter & Pinky Visit The Railroads, Burton Geller, 18 x 13 In. 462.00
Drawing, Cover, Moongirl Fights Crime, Man Without A Face, Summer 1949, 19 x 14 In. 1650.00
Drawing, Tiny Tot Comics No. 12, Burton Geller, 19 x 13 1/2 In. 1144.00
Drawing, Winnie The Pooh, Mike Royer, Ink, 8 x 5 In. 55.00
Page, Captain America No. 29, Page 9, Brent Anderson, May 2000, 15 x 9 In. 44.00

Page, Conan The Barbarian No. 163, Page 4, John Buscema, October 1984, 15 x 10 In. 120.00
Page, Connection, Weird Fantasy No. 9, Page 2, Mac Elkin, Sept., Oct. 1951, 18 x 13 In. 187.00
Page, Fat & Slat No. 1, Summer 1947, Page 4, Ed Wheelan, 18 x 13 In. 175.00
Page, Fight No. 67, Fiction House, Page 27, c.1950, 19 x 12 1/2 In. 44.00
Page, Happy Hare & Bruno Bear, Happy Rabbit, Standard Comics, 1940s, 18 x 12 In. 22.00
Page, Konz No. 9, Dell Comics, Page 8, c.1963, 18 x 12 In. 28.00
Page, Pulp Magazines, Love We Forgotted, Bill Elder, Mad No. 30, Dec. 1956, 7 1/2 x 10 In. 363.00
Page, Sunday, Blondie, Chic Young, January 13, 1935, 13 1/2 x 17 In. 830.00
Page, Sunday, Broom Hilda, Russell Myers, September 10, 1972, 12 1/2 x 27 1/2 In. 484.00
Page, Sunday, Captain & The Kids, Rudolph Dirks, August 30, 1964, 15 x 22 1/2 In. 88.00
Page, Sunday, Clarence, Frank Fogarty, May 9, 1948, 16 x 24 1/2 In. 44.00
Page, Sunday, Colonel Potterby & The Duchess, Chic Young, June 16, 1963, 9 x 19 In. 39.00
Page, Sunday, Dawn O'Day In Hollywood, Val Heinz, February 10, 1952, 11 x 25 In. 121.00
Page, Sunday, Fritzi Ritz, Ernie Bushmiller, December 7, 1951, 15 x 22 1/2 In. 110.00
Page, Sunday, Snuffy Smith, Fred Lasswell, March 23, 1941, 11 x 17 1/2 In. 193.00
Page, Sunday, Texas Slim, Ferd Johnson, September 28, 1952, 10 x 23 In. 61.00
Page, Sunday, Tiny Tim, Stanley Link, January 18, 1942, 13 x 19 In. 110.00
Page, Sunday, Tiny Tim, Stanley Link, November 25, 1945, 13 x 19 In. 99.00
Page, Tommy Turtle, Oh, Doctor, Lucky Duck, Standard Comics, c.1951, 18 x 12 In. 25.00
Page, Wonder Warthog Meets Zymotic Zoo-Keeper, Page 6, Shelton, 1967, 13 x 10 In. 363.00
Panel, Back Home Again, Ed Dodd, January 22, 1938, 12 x 12 In. 33.00
Panel, Dennis The Menace, Hank Ketcham, August 13, 1969, 8 x 6 1/2 In. 605.00
Panel, Dennis The Menace, Hank Ketcham, August 18, 1971, 8 x 6 1/2 In. 350.00
Panel, Sunday, Blondie, Chic Young, December 3, 1933, 13 1/2 x 17 In. 726.00
Panel, Sunday, Spooky, Bill Holman, August 8, 1937, 13 x 19 In. 121.00
Panel, Toonerville Folks, Fontaine Fox, July 3, 1930s, 10 x 9 1/2 In. 193.00
Panel, Worry Wart, J.R. Williams, June 21, 1956, 11 x 12 In. 83.00
Panel, Wotta Life, Gaar Williams, September 6, 1933, 13 1/2 x 13 1/2 In. 50.00
Panel Set, Wall-Nuts, Bill Holman, 4 Panels, 1940s, 4 x 13 In. 44.00
Strip, Amazing Spider Man, Stan Lee, Fred Kida, December 23, 1981, 4 1/2 x 14 1/2 In. 44.00
Strip, Archie, Bob Montana, May 30, 1950, 6 x 19 In. 308.00
Strip, Blondie, Chic Young, March 8, 1957, 5 x 17 1/2 In. 165.00
Strip, Boots & Her Buddies, Ed Martin, March 7, 1925, 6 x 24 1/2 In. 77.00
Strip, Bringing Up Father, George McManus, January 27, 1942, 4 x 18 In. 264.00
Strip, Buz Sawyer, Leslie Turner, December 15, 1945, 4 1/2 x 16 In. 116.00
Strip, Dateline Danger, Al McWilliams, April 21, 1970, 5 1/2 x 18 1/2 In. 120.00
Strip, Hagar The Horrible, Dik Browne, December 1, 1975, 3 1/2 x 11 1/2 In. 484.00
Strip, Half Hitch, Hank Ketcham, Inscribed For Jack, June 19, 1970, 5 x 17 In. 44.00
Strip, Harold Teen, Carl Ed, February 20, 1935, 5 1/2 x 20 In. 55.00
Strip, Hatlo's They'll Do It Every Time, Dunn, Scadujo, September 5, 1967, 9 x 12 In. 22.00
Strip, Henry, Carl Anderson, August 17, 1967, 5 1/2 x 20 In. 50.00
Strip, Henry, Carl Anderson, Yellowed Zipatone, August 19, 1967, 5 1/2 x 20 In. 36.00
Strip, Hi & Lois, Dik Browne, Inscribed Best Wishes Jack, June 23, 1969, 5 x 18 In. 88.00
Strip, Kerry Drake, Andriola, Best Wishes To Jack Tippit, July 12, 1967, 6 x 18 1/2 In. 66.00
Strip, Li'l Abner, Al Capp, November 13, 1942, 5 1/2 x 22 In. 240.00
Strip, Li'l Abner, Al Capp, September 4, 1944, 5 1/2 x 22 In. 110.00
Strip, Li'l Abner, January 23, 1973, 5 1/2 x 19 In. 88.00
Strip, Li'l Abner, September 2, 1950, 6 x 22 1/2 In. 110.00
Strip, Little Orphan Annie, Harold Gray, August 15, 1934, 5 1/2 x 20 In. 1320.00
Strip, Nancy, Ernie Bushmiller, August 15, 1964, 5 x 19 In. 99.00
Strip, Nancy, Ernie Bushmiller, January 11, 1946, 5 x 19 In. 120.00
Strip, Nancy, Ernie Bushmiller, June 13, 1941, 5 x 22 In. 132.00
Strip, On Stage, Leonard Starr, August 5, 1965, 5 x 16 1/2 In. 77.00
Strip, Ozark Ike, Ray Gotto, November 18, 1946, 6 x 20 In. 50.00
Strip, Phantom, Wilson McCoy, April 18, 1961, 6 x 21 In. 77.00
Strip, Pogo, Walt Kelly, July 21, 1964, 5 x 18 1/2 In. 330.00
Strip, Pogo, Walt Kelly, March 12, 1958, 4 1/2 x 16 1/2 In. 242.00
Strip, Pogo, Walt Kelly, September 21, 1965, 5 x 18 1/2 In. 165.00
Strip, Rip Kirby, John Prentice, August 26, 1967, 5 x 16 In. 110.00
Strip, Short Ribs, Frank O'Neal, June 6, 1970, 4 1/2 x 20 In. 28.00
Strip, Steve Canyon, Milton Caniff, Inscribed For Cuhnul Tippit, January 25, 1969 .... 220.00

Strip, Steve Canyon, Milton Caniff, Signed For Dodie, February 14, 1983, 5 1/2 x 19 In. 77.00
Strip, Tailspin Tommy, 1928, 6 x 22 In. 120.00
Strip, Terry & The Pirates, George Wunder, May 23, 1949, 6 1/2 x 22 In. 154.00
Strip, Terry & The Pirates, Milton Caniff, November 27, 1946, 6 1/2 x 22 In. 880.00

COMMEMORATIVE items have been made to honor members of royalty and those of great national fame. World's fairs and important historical events are also remembered with commemorative pieces. Related collectibles are listed in the Coronation and World's Fair categories.

Bell, Prince Charles & Lady Diana Wedding, Newhall, 1981, 6 In. 10.00
Bell, Prince Charles & Lady Diana Wedding, Staffordshire, 1981, 6 1/2 In. 20.00
Blanket, Bust Of W.H. Taft, Soldiers, Shields, Woven, Tan, Black, 60 x 60 In. 420.00
Bowl, Mayflower, 350th Anniversary, Scalloped, Aynsley, 1970, 2 x 5 In. 1100.00
Cup & Saucer, King George VI, Queen Elizabeth, Visit U.S., Canada, Paragon, 1939 .... 49.00
Dish, King & Queen, Visit Canada, U.S., Bone China, Aynsley, 1939, 5 1/2 In. 72.00
Handkerchief, Jubilee Of Queen Victoria, Red, Black, 26 x 30 In. 150.00
Mug, Queen Elizabeth's Silver Jubilee, Czechoslovakia, 1977, 3 1/2 x 3 1/4 In. 27.00
Paperweight, Bicentennial, Liberty Bell, Millefiori, Whitefriars, Box, 3 1/8 In. 475.00
Pitcher, Portrait, Christopher Columbus Sighted America, Doulton Lambeth, 6 1/2 In. 58.00
Plate, Bicentennial, Liberty Bell, Carnival Glass, Gold, Indiana Glass, 1976, 8 In. 21.00
Plate, Bicentennial, Portrait Of Liberty, In God We Trust, Fenton, Box, 1975 .... 19.00
Plate, Bicentennial, Washington Crossing Delaware, International Pewter, 9 In. 29.00
Plate, King & Queen, Visit Canada, U.S., Johnson Bros., 1939, 10 1/8 In. 38.00
Plate, Prince Charles & Lady Diana Wedding, Royal Grafton, Box, 1981 .... 24.00
Plate, Prince Charles & Lady Diana Wedding, Wood & Sons, 1981, 10 In. 38.00
Plate, Winston Churchill, Blue, White, Burleigh Ware, 10 1/2 In. 89.00
Postcard, Stamp, Grace Kelly & Prince Rainier Wedding, Black, White, 1956 .... 20.00
Sweets Box, Queen Elizabeth Silver Jubilee, Ceramic, 1 1/2 x 4 x 3 1/2 In. 40.00
Teaspoon, King George, Queen Elizabeth, Visit Canada, Silver Plate, Rogers, 1939 .... 39.00
Tin, King & Queen, Visit Canada, Harry Vincent Ltd., 1939, 2 x 7 x 5 3/4 In. 35.00
Walking Stick, Oak, Silver, Engraved, Timber From John Paul Jones Fleet, 39 In. 388.00

COMPACTS hold face powder. A woman did not powder her face in public until after World War I. By 1920, the beauty parlor, permanent waves, and cosmetics had become acceptable. A few companies sold cake face powder in a box with a mirror and a pad or puff. Soon the compact was designed by jewelers and made of gold, silver, and precious materials. Cosmetic companies began to sell powder in attractive compacts of less valuable metal or plastic. Collectors today search for Art Deco designs, commemorative compacts from world's fairs or political events, and unusual examples. Many were made with companion lipsticks and other fittings.

EEM Co., Art Deco Style, On Ring, Chain, U.S.A., 1 3/4 x 2 1/4 In. 75.00
Enamel, Apollo In Chariot, Classical Gods, Chased Vermeil, Marked 800, 3 x 4 In. 865.00
Enamel, Black, Jadeite, Diamond, Platinum Mount, Round, Art Deco, 2 In. 1175.00
Evans, Enamel, Ivory, Pearls, Round, 2 In. 39.00
Evans, Enamel, Rouge, Powder, Cigarettes, Enamel, 3 5/8 x 2 In. 75.00
Evans, Mother-Of-Pearl, Inlaid Square, Square, 2 1/2 In. 55.00
Guilloche Enamel, Lilac, 1 1/2 In. 395.00
Guilloche Enamel, Mauve, Sterling Silver, 1 5/8 x 1/4 In. 495.00
Guilloche Enamel, Sterling Silver, Brown, Birds, Round, Austria, c.1900, 2 In. 300.00
Hudnut, Goldtone, Enamel Cover, Art Deco, Le Debut, Black 100.00
Mondaine, Velvet, Black, Rhinestones, Strap, N.Y., 4 x 3 In. 130.00
Richard Hudnut, Goldtone, Lipstick Holder, Bag, 3 1/2 x 2 3/8 In. 50.00
Roses, Round, Stratone, England, 3 1/4 In. 16.00
Silver, Enamel, Cartouche Shape, Courting Couple, Italy, Early 1900s, 4 In. 294.00
Silver, Mirror, Art Deco, Elgin American, c.1946, 4 1/2 In. 35.00
Silver, Oval, Stylized Blossom Fob, Georg Jensen USA, New York, 3 x 2 In. 235.00
Sterling Silver, Aztec Designs, Mexico, c.1930, 3 1/2 x 3 1/2 In. 195.00
Sterling Silver, Pillow Top, Quilted, Oval, Majestic Sterling, 2 7/8 x 2 1/4 In. 135.00

Stratnoid Foil, Art Deco, Square, Stratton, England, c.1932, 2 In. 95.00
Stratton, It's Time To Shop, Lulu Guiness, Pouch, Box, 3 1/2 x 2 1/2 In. 175.00
Tortoiseshell, Flower, Hand Painted, Round, 3 7/8 In. 99.00
Volupte, Hand Shape, Goldtone Metal, Powder Puff, Mirror, Burnished Finish, 4 1/2 In. 295.00

CONSOLIDATED LAMP AND GLASS COMPANY of Coraopolis, Pennsylvania, was founded in 1894. The company made lamps, tablewares, and art glass. Collectors are particularly interested in the wares made after 1925, including black satin glass, Cosmos (listed in its own category in this book), Martele (which resembled Lalique), Ruba Rombic (1928–32 Art Deco line), and colored glasswares. Some Consolidated pieces are very similar to those made by the Phoenix Glass Company. The colors are sometimes different. Consolidated made Martele glass in blue, crystal, green, pink, white, or custard glass with added fired-on color or a satin finish. The company closed for the final time in 1967.

Bowl, Chickadee, Green & Peach, 4 x 10 In. 35.00
Bowl, Line 700, Blue, Ormolu Mounted, 10 In. 323.00
Lamp, Katydid, Brown & Green, Satin Custard, 10 1/4 In. 320.00
Sugar Shaker, Cone Pattern, Opaque Green, c.1894, 5 1/2 In. 81.00
Sugar Shaker, Diamond Quilted, Satin, Late 1800s, 3 1/2 In. 115.00
Vase, Bittersweet, Blue, Green & Orange Stain, 10 In. 190.00
Vase, Bittersweet, Brown & Blue Green Stain, 10 In. 60.00
Vase, Bittersweet, Satin Milk Glass, 6 In. 50.00
Vase, Blackberry, Blue Green & Brown Stain, Oval, 7 In. 55.00
Vase, Blackberry, Blue Stain, Satin Milk Glass, Oval, 7 In. 145.00
Vase, Blackberry, Brown Stain, Oval, 7 In. 70.00
Vase, Chrysanthemum, Blue, Flared Neck, 9 In. 55.00
Vase, Chrysanthemum, Metallic Gold On Bright Milk Glass, 12 1/2 In. ....70.00 to 90.00
Vase, Dancing Girls, Nude Women, Satyr, Cream Ground, Tricolor, 12 In. 518.00
Vase, Fern, Pale Blue, Green Leaves, Oval, 7 In. 45.00
Vase, Katydid, Blue & Brown Stain, Satin Milk Glass, 7 In. 90.00
Vase, Leaf Pattern, Pale Blue Leaves, Green Stems, 11 1/2 In. 110.00
Vase, Lovebirds, Blue Green & Pink Stain, Oval, 11 In. 145.00
Vase, Lovebirds, Blue Green, Oval, 6 1/2 In. 70.00
Vase, Lovebirds, Purple Stain, Oval, c.1933, 10 In. 1175.00
Vase, Lovebirds, Satin Custard, Oval, 6 1/2 In. 45.00
Vase, Madonna, Light Blue, White Ground, 10 In. 330.00
Vase, Ruba Rombic, Green, 9 1/4 In. 1645.00
Vase, Screech Owls, Brown, Green Reeds, Satin Custard, 6 In. 125.00

CONTEMPORARY GLASS, see Glass-Contemporary.

COOKBOOKS are collected for various reasons. Some are wanted for the recipes, some for investment, and some as examples of advertising. Cookbooks and recipe pamphlets are included in this category.

Art Of Cookery, Made Plain & Easy, Hannah Glasse, London, 1788 .... 495.00
Better Babies, Pet Milk, 1938, 30 Pages 2.25
Better Homes & Gardens New Cook Book, 5-Ring Binder, 1968, 400 Pages ....32.00 to 57.00
Betty Crocker, New Picture, 5-Ring Binder, 1st Edition, 2nd Printing, 1961, 455 Pages 113.00
Betty Crocker, Outdoor Cook Book, Spiral Bound, 1961, 176 Pages ....7.00 to 20.00
Betty Crocker, Picture Cooky Book, General Mills, 1948, 44 Pages 35.00
Boston Cooking School, Fannie Merritt Farmer, 1933 .... 32.00
Calumet, Happy Times Recipe Book, 1934, 5 3/4 x 4 In., 23 Pages 2.00
Campbell, Easy Ways To Delicious Meals, Hard Cover, Spiral Bound, 1968, 204 Pages 12.00
Carnation, Velvet Blend, Milk-Rich, c.1950, 9 x 6 In., 30 Pages 2.00
Certo, Recipes For Making Better Jams, Jellies & Marmalades, c.1920, 36 Pages 8.00
Chapman Dairy, Soft Cover, c.1920, 10 x 7 In., 34 Pages 12.00
Correct Art Of Candy-Making, Butterick Publishing, 1894, 9 1/2 x 6 3/4 In., 72 Pages 213.00
Crisco, Praise For The Cook, Spiral Binding, 1959 .... 2.00
F.W. McNess' Family Magazine, Cook Book Edition, c.1920, 34 Pages, 9 x 6 In. 13.00
Favorite Hungarian & International Recipes, St. Margaret's, Cleveland, 1988, 9 x 6 In. 153.00

Favorite Recipes, Machiasport Congregational Church, Spiral Bound 15.00
Fleischmann's Yeast, Excellent Recipes For Baking, 1910, 50 Pages, 6 1/4 x 4 3/4 In. 12.00
General Foods, 5th Edition, 1932, 5 1/2 x 8 3/4 In., 370 Pages 22.00
Household Receipts, Baptist Young People's Union, Lawrence, Mass., c.1900, 40 Pages 91.00
Jell-O, It's So Simple, Rockwell Illustrations, 1922, 4 1/4 x 6 1/4 In., 15 Pages 27.00
Jell-O, Maxfield Parrish Illustrations, 1924, 4 1/4 x 6 1/4 In., 17 Pages 104.00
Jell-O, What 6 Famous Cooks Say Of Jell-O, 1912, Pamphlet 37.00
Jell-O, What Salad, What Dessert, Dozens Of Answers, 1928, 22 Pages 5.00
Jell-O & Kewpies, Genesse Pure Food Co., 1915, 6 1/4 x 4 1/4 In., 18 Pages 18.00
Jennie June's American Cookery, American News, 1867, 7 1/2 x 5 In., 343 Pages 250.00
Kenmore Binding Of The American Woman's, 1951, 856 Pages 27.00
Lucy's Notebook, I Love Lucy, Lucy, Ricky, Phillip Morris Tobacco Co., 37 Pages 22.00
Magic Chef Cooking, American Stove Co., 1933, 204 Pages 55.00
Magical Desserts With Whip'n Chill, 44 Pages 5.00
Marshall Field's Gourmet, Taste Of Tradition, Soft Cover, Spiral Bound, 1985, 39 Pages ..123.00 to 184.00
Mary Poppins Magic, C & H Sugar, 1960s, 25 Pages 16.00
Miss Minerva's, De Way To A Man's Heart, Emma Speed Sampson, 323 Recipes, 1931 .... 340.00
Never Fail Cook Book, Ladies Aid Soc., M.E. Church, Wayland, N.Y., 1907, 64 Pages 18.00
New Cooks, By Illuminating Company, 1953 .... 8.00
New Pillsbury Family Cookbook, 1973 ....30.00 to 50.00
Pillsbury, 2nd Grand National 100 Prize Winning Recipes, 1951, 100 Pages 45.00
Pillsbury, 100 Prize-Winning Recipes, 1950, 9 x 6 In., 96 Pages ....25.00 to 49.00
Recipes From Pawley's Island, Waccamaw Episcopal, 1969, 9 x 6 In., 128 Pages 11.00
Tested Recipes, Norwegian Lutheran Memorial Church, Minn., 1950, 129 Pages 15.50
Walter Baker, Dorchester, Mass., 1914, 64 Pages 27.00

COOKIE JARS with brightly painted designs or amusing figural shapes became popular in the mid-1930s. Many companies made them and collectors search for cookie jars either by design or by maker's name. Listed here are examples by the less common makers. Major factories are listed under their own names in other categories of the book, such as Abingdon, Brush, Hull, McCoy, Metlox, Red Wing, and Shawnee. See also the Disneyana category.

Aunt Jemima, Plastic, Red Dress, F & F, 12 In. 305.00
Baby Huey, China, 1960s, 13 In. 275.00
Big Bird, California Originals, 13 3/4 In. 185.00
Boy Pig With Scarf, American Bisque, 11 1/2 In. 153.00
Chef, National Silver, 10 1/4 In. 115.00
Chinese Monk, Twin Winton, 11 In. 455.00
Clown, Juggler, California Originals, 13 In. 175.00
Dahlia On Orange, Model 700, Hand Painted, Ransburg, 1930-60, 10 x 8 1/2 In. 225.00
Elsie The Cow, In Barrel, 12 1/2 x 6 In. ....158.00 to 168.00
Enameled, Green Glass, Flower, Bow, Metal Rim, Handle, Denmark, 1800s, 6 1/4 In. 106.00
Feed Sack, American Bisque, 1958, 9 1/2 In. ....85.00 to 165.00
Flintstones, The Rubbles, American Bisque, c.1960, 9 1/2 In. 259.00
Fluffy The Cat, American Bisque, 12 x 6 In. 175.00
Gingerbread Man, Los Angeles Potteries 175.00
Hen & Chick, American Bisque, 1950s, 9 In. 259.00
I Am A Cookie Crock, Crocodile, California Originals, 12 x 7 In. 250.00
Kitten On Beehive, American Bisque, 11 3/4 In. 165.00
Little Red Riding Hood, Napco, Japan, 1957, 6 1/2 In. 203.00
Majorette, American Bisque, 1960s, 11 1/4 In. 243.00
Mammy, Ceramic, Brayton Laguna, 12 3/4 In. 266.00
Mammy, Striped Shirt, Bandanna, Apron, Brayton Laguna, 1940s 456.00
Milk Wagon, Donkey, American Bisque, 9 In. ....145.00 to 185.00
Mr. Toodles, Lefton, 1960s, 9 In. 120.00
Noah's Ark, Fitz & Floyd, Box, 18 x 16 x 12 In. 525.00
Ole King Cole, Twin Winton, 11 1/2 In. 144.00
Pig In Baby Diaper, Regal China, 1950s, 11 In. 290.00
Poodle, Gray, Sitting Upright, Pink Bow, Sierra Vista Ceramics, California, 1956, 13 In. 90.00
Poodle At Cookie Counter, Twin Winton, 13 1/2 In. 250.00

Quaker Oats Cover, Regal China, Box, 1978, 9 3/4 x 5 1/4 In. 150.00
Raggedy Ann, California Originals, 13 3/4 In. 245.00
Rastus, Cream Of Wheat Chef, Japan, 10 1/2 In. 306.00
Rhett Butler, Happy Memories Collectibles, Box 565.00
Rooster, American Bisque, 10 3/4 x 8 1/4 In. 135.00
Rooster, Twin Winton, 11 1/2 In. 85.00
Seal On Igloo, American Bisque 200.00
Soldier, American Bisque, 10 1/2 In. 100.00
Tiger Kittens, Robinson Ransbottom, R.R.P. Co., Roseville, Ohio, 10 In. 104.00
Tony The Tiger, 1977, 10 1/2 In. 220.00

COORS ware was made by a pottery in Golden, Colorado, a company founded with the help of the Coors Brewing Company. Its founder, John Herold, started the Herold China and Pottery Company in 1910. The company name was changed in 1920, when Herold left. Dishes and decorative wares were produced from the turn of the century until the pottery was destroyed by fire in the 1930s. The name *Coors* is marked on the back. The company is still in business making industrial porcelain. For more information, see *Kovels' Depression Glass & Dinnerware Price List.*

COORS
U.S.A.

Baker, Rosebud, Blue, 11 x 7 1/4 In. 135.00
Batter Bowl, Rosebud, Green, Long Handle, 8 In. 115.00
Batter Bowl, Rosebud, Long Handle, 12 1/4 In. 165.00
Batter Bowl, Rosebud, Orange, Long Handle, 8 In. 100.00
Batter Bowl, Rosebud, Yellow, Long Handle, 8 1/4 In. 100.00
Bean Pot, Rosebud, Blue, 4 1/4 In. 70.00
Bowl, Cereal, Rock Mount, Orange, 6 3/8 In. 25.00
Bowl, Cereal, Rosebud, Red, 6 1/4 In. 45.00
Bowl, Cereal, Rosebud, White, 6 1/4 In. 50.00
Bowl, Fruit, Rosebud, Blue, Handles 30.00
Bowl, Pudding, Ivory, 5 3/4 In. 75.00
Bowl, Shirred Egg, Rosebud, Green, 6 3/4 In. 50.00
Bowl, Vegetable, Red, 9 1/2 In. 45.00
Cake Knife, Rosebud, Blue, 10 1/14 In. 195.00
Cake Plate, Rosebud, Orange, 11 In. 70.00
Casserole, Cover, Rosebud, Blue, Triple Service, 5 3/4 In. 95.00
Cookie Jar, Flowers, Dusty Rose, Knob Handle, 10 In. 125.00
Cup & Saucer, Mello-Tone, Green 25.00
Custard Cup, Thermo Porcelain, Brown, White Interior, Glencoe, 2 1/4 In. 30.00
Dutch Casserole, Cover, Rosebud, Orange, Green Cover 100.00
Gravy Bowl, Coorado, Ivory 135.00
Mixing Bowl, Rosebud, Blue, 10 1/2 In. 125.00
Mortar & Pestle, White 18.00
Mug, Thermo Porcelain, Green, Lion Decal, 4 5/8 In. 30.00
Mug, Thermo Porcelain, Green, White Interior, Handle, 3 3/4 In. 25.00
Pie Plate, Coorado, Ivory, 10 3/4 In. 140.00
Pie Plate, Rosebud, Blue, 10 1/4 In. 90.00
Pitcher, Rosebud, Ivory, 7 1/2 In. 400.00
Plate, Coorado, Ivory, 6 3/8 In. 35.00
Plate, Coorado, Ivory, 9 3/8 In. 50.00
Plate, Rock-Mount, Blue, 7 1/4 In. 15.00
Plate, Rock-Mount, Green, 9 1/2 In. 20.00
Plate, Rosebud, Blue, 6 1/4 In. 30.00
Plate, Rosebud, Blue, 7 In. 22.00
Plate, Rosebud, Ivory, 6 1/4 In. 50.00
Plate, Rosebud, Orange, 6 1/4 In. 30.00
Platter, Mello-Tone, Green, 15 3/4 In. 75.00
Platter, Rock-Mount, Green, 15 1/2 In. 75.00
Ramekin, Thermo Porcelain, Brown, White Interior, Glencoe, 4 1/2 In. 30.00
Saucer, Rosebud, Orange 12.00
Soup, Dish, Mello-Tone, Blue, 7 1/4 In. 25.00

Soup, Dish, Mello-Tone, Green, 7 1/4 In. 25.00
Vase, Beehive, Blue Satin, White Interior, 5 In. 65.00
Vase, Beehive, Orange Matte Glaze, White Interior, 1930s, 5 x 4 3/4 In. 85.00
Vase, Berthoud, Blue Satin, White, 8 In. 125.00
Vase, Berthoud, Orange Matte Glaze, White Interior, Twisted Rope Handles, 8 x 8 1/4 In. 150.00
Vase, Blue Matte Glaze, White Interior, 6 In. 75.00
Vase, Brighton, White, Green, 8 In. 95.00
Vase, Cripple Creek, Turquoise Matte Glaze, White Interior, 5 3/4 x 4 1/4 In. 80.00
Vase, Evergreen, Ivory Satin, Green, 6 3/4 In. 75.00
Vase, Golden, Blue Satin, Ivory, 5 In. 90.00
Vase, Golden, Ivory Satin, Green, 7 1/4 In. 135.00
Vase, Golden, Orange Matte Glaze, White Interior, 7 1/4 x 8 1/2 In. ....165.00 to 175.00
Vase, Golden, Yellow Glossy Glaze, White Interior, 5 1/2 x 6 1/2 In. 150.00
Vase, Golden, Yellow Glossy Glaze, White Satin, 5 In. 85.00
Vase, Minturn, Blue Matte Glaze, White Interior, 8 1/2 In. 115.00
Vase, Orange, 6 In. 20.00
Vase, Orange, Green Interior, 9 In. 23.00
Vase, Rings, Orange, White Interior, 5 In. 18.00
Vase, Vail, Tan Matte Glaze, Turquoise Interior, Bulbous, Handles, 12 x 4 3/4 In. 425.00

COPELAND pieces listed here are those that have a mark including the word Copeland used between 1847 and 1976. Marks include Copeland Spode and Copeland & Garrett. See also Copeland Spode and Royal Worcester.

Bowl, Flower, Brown, White, W.T. Copeland, c.1850, 9 In. 65.00
Bust, John Milton, Parian, c.1874, 13 3/4 In. 353.00
Bust, Summer, Parian, c.1870, 13 In. 558.00
Bust, Woman, Wearing Veil, Impressed, R. Monte 1861, 14 1/2 In. 4388.00
Compote, Aesop's Fables, Fox & Lion, Green Transfer, Copeland & Garrett, 5 1/2 x 11 In. 1195.00
Cup, Demitasse, Grass, Pink, c.1869 .... 22.50
Cup & Saucer, Demitasse, Aesthetic, Pink, Gold, 1870-85 .... 195.00
Cup & Saucer, Demitasse, Grass, Green, 1869 .... 125.00
Dish, Botanical, Nasturtium, Green Transfer, Copeland & Garrett, 1835, 10 1/2 x 8 In. 300.00
Figurine, Lady Godiva, Parian, Raphaelle Monti Model, c.1876, 21 1/4 In. 1175.00
Figurine, Narcissus, Parian, 1846, 12 In. 1175.00
Figurine, Water Nymph, Seated On Rock, Parian, c.1870, 18 1/4 In. 764.00
Jug, Chamber, Baluster, Japan Pattern, Copeland & Garrett, 1833-47, 14 x 8 1/2 In. 265.00
Plate, Aesop's Fables, Fox & Lion, Copeland & Garrett, c.1835, 10 In. 225.00
Plate, Botanical, Green, White, 8-Sided, Copeland & Garrett, c.1835, 8 1/2 In. 175.00
Plate, Botanical, Roses, 8-Sided, Copeland & Garrett, 1833-47, 8 1/2 In. 275.00
Plate, Dinner, Buckingham Palace, Pink & Gilt Borders, Royal Symbols, c.1833, 9 3/4 In. 122.00
Plate, Imari Pattern, Copeland & Garrett, England, 1800s, 16 Piece 585.00
Plate, Imari, Cobalt, Scalloped Edges, W.T. Copeland & Sons, 1870s, 8 1/4 In. ....26.00 to 28.00
Plate, Luster, 1840s, 10 In. 45.00
Plate, Middle Eastern Theme, W.T. Copeland, 1880, 9 1/2 In. 45.00
Platter, Aesop's Fables, Sow & Wolf, Copeland & Garrett, 1833, 16 1/2 x 13 In. 1250.00
Saucer, Flowers, Gilt, Copeland & Garrett, c.1835, 6 In., Pair 95.00
Serving Dish, Cover, Crown Mark D, c.1849, 11 1/4 In. 325.00
Tureen, Abby Ruins, Purple Transfer, W.T. Copeland & Sons, 1881, 10 x 14 1/2 x 9 In. 325.00
Vase, Animals, Landscape, 2 Lizard Handles, Stand, c.1872, 20 1/4 In., Pair 5150.00

COPELAND SPODE appears on some pieces of nineteenth-century English porcelain. Josiah Spode established a pottery at Stoke-on-Trent, England, in 1770. In 1833, the firm was purchased by William Copeland and Thomas Garrett and the mark was changed. In 1847, Copeland became the sole owner and the mark changed again. W.T. Copeland & Sons continued until a 1976 merger when it became Royal Worcester Spode. Pieces are listed in this book under the name that appears in the mark. Copeland Spode, Copeland, and Royal Worcester have separate listings.

Bowl, Cover, Morning Glory, Handles, 5 1/2 x 8 In. 40.00

Bowl, Fruit, Gainsborough, Black Mark, 5 In. 19.00
Bowl, Fruit, Old Bow, 1 1/4 x 9 1/4 In. 50.00
Bowl, Vegetable, Cover, Old Bow, Grid Mark, 7 x 9 x 11 1/2 In. 85.00
Bowl, Vegetable, Cover, Ruins, 1880, 9 In. 235.00
Bowl, Vegetable, Gainsborough, Oval, 10 3/8 x 7 5/8 In. 60.00
Cake Plate, Gainsborough, Square, 10 In. 85.00
Casserole, Cover, Gainsborough, Round, 6 1/4 x 7 1/2 In. 95.00
Compote, Classical Scenes, c.1910, 2 1/2 x 9 x 12 In., Pair 819.00
Cup & Saucer, Dimity Pattern 35.00
Cup & Saucer, Fleur-De-Lis 75.00
Gravy Boat, Attached Underplate, Old Concord, 5 1/2 x 9 1/2 In. 145.00
Jug, Gainsborough, 20 Oz., 5 1/8 x 6 In. 65.00
Jug, Queen Victoria, Jubilee, 1897, 5 In. 350.00
Jug, Sprigware, Dancing Houris, 3 In. 125.00
Jug, Sprigware, Dancing Houris, White On Blue, 4 3/8 In. 185.00
Jug, Sprigware, Hunters, White On Blue, 3 5/8 In. 165.00
Muffin Pan, Cover, Gainsborough, 3 1/2 x 9 In. 150.00
Pitcher, Italian Pattern, Blue, White, 4 1/2 x 5 In. 200.00
Pitcher, Sprigware, Pub Gentlemen, White On Blue, 6 1/2 In. 265.00
Pitcher, Tower, 5 x 5 1/2 In. 255.00
Plate, Bread & Butter, Gainsborough, 6 3/4 In. 10.00
Plate, Bread & Butter, Sorrento, 6 1/2 In. 12.00
Plate, Dessert, Audley, 1962, 9 In. 28.00
Plate, Dessert, Eden, Grid Mark, 1930s, 9 In. 25.00
Plate, Dessert, Hazel Dell, 8 In. 24.00
Plate, Dessert, Korea, 1945, 9 In. 28.00
Plate, Dessert, Nancy, 1951, 8 3/4 In. 28.00
Plate, Dinner, Beverley, 10 1/4 In. 28.00
Plate, Dinner, Dahlia, A. Ball, Mansard, 1932, 10 1/2 In. 65.00
Plate, Dinner, Gainsborough, 10 1/2 In. 30.00
Plate, Dinner, Highley Tower, Multicolored, c.1900, 10 1/4 In. 120.00
Plate, Dinner, Mayflower, Box, 1970, 10 1/2 In. 150.00
Plate, Dinner, Morning Glory, Mansard, c.1932, 10 3/4 In. 30.00
Plate, Dinner, Peplow, Harrods, 1920s, 10 In. 28.00
Plate, Dinner, Tower, Red Transfer, 10 In. 68.00
Plate, Flower, Scalloped Edge, 1910-20, 8 3/4 In. 48.00
Plate, Flowers, 10 1/2 In., 10 Piece 325.00
Plate, Gilt Pagodas, Red Ground, Late 1800s, 10 1/2 In., 12 Piece 1763.00
Plate, Luncheon, Gainsborough, Green Mark, 9 In. 25.00
Plate, Salad, Chinese Rose, 1937, 7 1/2 In. 16.00
Plate, Salad, Gainsborough, Crescent, 7 x 4 1/8 In. 35.00
Plate, Salad, Gainsborough, Green Mark, 7 3/4 In. 17.50
Plate, Salad, Ruins, Brown, 1880 .... 35.00
Plate, Salad, Sorrento, 8 In. 15.00
Platter, Floral & Check, 1926, 7 x 10 1/2 In. 65.00
Platter, Gainsborough, 10 1/4 x 7 1/2 In. 65.00
Platter, Gainsborough, 14 1/2 x 11 In. 99.00
Platter, Gainsborough, 1930s, 9 1/2 x 12 In. ....65.00 to 85.00
Platter, Green Chintz-Like, 1910, 8 1/2 In. 48.00
Platter, Nancy, 1957, 11 x 14 3/4 In. 95.00
Platter, Polka Dot, 1950s, 7 3/4 x 10 1/4 In. 95.00
Platter, Ruins, Brown, 1880, 13 In. 165.00
Soup, Dish, Floral & Check, Blue, White, 10 1/2 In. 25.00
Soup, Dish, Gainsborough, Rim, 7 1/2 In. 20.00
Soup, Dish, Lyon, Grid Mark, 1930s, 10 1/4 In. 45.00
Soup Set, Jeweled Porcelain, Early 1900s, 9 1/4 In., 24 Piece 3900.00
Stein, Sprigware, Hunters, White On Blue, 7 In. 295.00
Sugar, Cover, Sprigware, Dancing Houris 125.00
Sugar, Gainsborough, 4 In. ....50.00 to 55.00
Tray, Imari Pattern, Incurvate Corners, Fishscale Border, c.1857, 16 x 20 1/2 In. 1528.00
Tureen, Domed Cover, Undertray, Flowers, Blue, White Transfer, 10 1/2 In. 765.00

Copper, Box, Cover, Scarab Finial, Gold Plated, Marked, M. Zimmerman, 4 x 13 x 7 1/4 In.

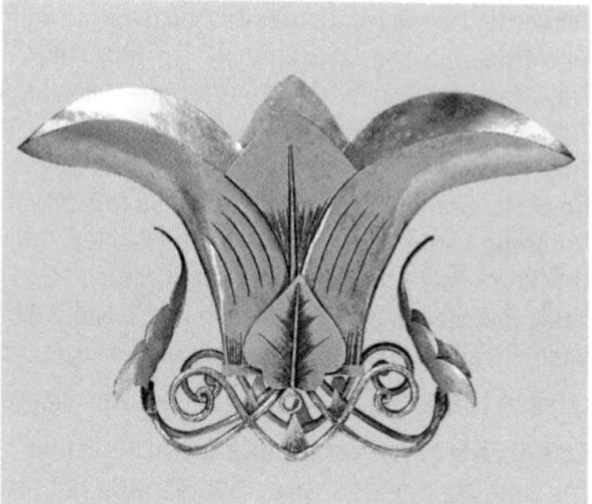

Copper, Vase, Stand, Hammered, Gold Plated, Marked, M. Zimmerman, 11 x 17 In.

COPPER has been used to make utilitarian items, such as teakettles and cooking pans, since the days of the early American colonists. Copper became a popular metal with the Arts & Crafts makers of the early 1900s, and decorative pieces, like desk sets, were made. Other pieces of copper may be found in the Arts & Crafts, Bradley & Hubbard, Kitchen, and Roycroft categories.

Basin, Barber's, Cutout, Broad Rim, Central Boss, England, c.1680 .... 650.00
Bed Warmer, Hinged Cover, Flowers, Pierced, Engraved, Maple Handle, 41 x 11 In. 215.00
Bed Warmer, Punched Bird, Flowers, Mahogany Handle, 19th Century, 43 In. 230.00
Bed Warmer, Punched Star Design, Turned Handle 227.00
Boiler, Cover, Wooden Handles, Inside Rack, 17 1/2 x 27 In., 11 Lb. 148.00
Bowl, Hammered, Cutout Panels, Stylized Blossoms, Handicraft Guild, 2 1/2 x 18 In. 2235.00
Box, Cover, Scarab Finial, Gold Plated, Marked, M. Zimmerman, 4 x 13 x 7 1/4 In. .... *ILLUS* 8225.00
Cauldron, Hammered, Handles, Rustic, c.1870, 20 In. 59.00
Chamberstick, Oak, Carved Feet, Tall Handles, 4-Sided Trays, Rohlfs, c.1901, 10 x 7 1/2 In. 1998.00
Coal Bucket, Arts & Crafts, Wrought Iron Mounted, Patinated, Early 1900s, 11 x 12 1/2 In. 235.00
Desk Set, Hammered, Inset Carved Ivory Medallions, Potter Studio, 5 Piece 3000.00
Dye Pot, Wrought Iron Base, Dovetailed, Bail Handle, 3-Footed, Ring Base, 27 1/2 x 25 In. 385.00
Figure, Crayfish, Repousse, Japan, 19th Century, 8 In. 880.00
Figure, Eagle, Molded, Spread Wing, Standing On Sphere, 19th Century, 69 x 48 In. 4995.00
Figure, Horse, Running, Molded Sheet, Black Paint, Late 1800s, 10 1/2 x 16 In. 499.00
Hand Warmer, Brass Lid, Engraved, Crests, Japan, 19th Century, 7 x 9 In. 175.00
Humidor, Hammered, Original Patina, Round, Old Mission Koppercraft, 6 1/2 In. 510.00
Humidor, Riveted Strap Hinges, Milk Glass Lining, Arts & Crafts, 9 1/2 x 15 x 12 In. 1528.00
Ice Bucket, Hammered, Embossed Ovals, Spade-Shaped Handles, Benedict, 12 x 11 In. 2235.00
Incense Burner, Dragons, Clouds, Repousse, Japan, 19th Century, 8 1/2 In. 325.00
Jardiniere, Hammered, Warty, Arched Folded In Top, Arts & Crafts, 11 x 14 In. 2040.00
Kettle, Apple Butter, Iron Handle, Stamped J.P. Schaum, Lancaster, Pa., 19 x 28 In. 525.00
Kettle, Apple Butter, Molded Rim, Iron Swing Handle, 1800s, 27 In. 130.00
Kettle, Flowers, Butterflies, Gilt, Cylindrical, Japan, 18th Century, 8 In. 176.00
Kettle, Hot Water, Dovetailed, Scorn Lid Finial, England, 1800s, 13 In. 180.00
Kettle, Wrought Iron Bail Handle, 14 x 18 3/4 In. 55.00
Molds are listed in the Kitchen category.
Pitcher, Round Rim, Riveted Handle, Oval, 7 1/4 x 6 1/2 In. 75.00
Plaque, Embossed Tall Trees, Dark Patina, H. Jauchens, 24 x 17 3/4 In. 5875.00
Pot, Cover, Hammered, Tin Lining, Riveted Handles, Gaillard, Paris, 17 1/2 x 23 1/2 In. 499.00
Pot, Cover, Hammered, Wrought Iron Bail Handle, 12 x 13 In. 105.00
Roaster, Chestnut, Brass Handle, England, c.1845, 5 x 21 In. 225.00
Sculpture, Brenner, Bernard, 2 Figures, Embracing, Verdigris Patina, 104 x 56 x 20 In. 6490.00
Shoehorn, Hooked Handle, 18th Century 235.00
Teakettle, Dovetailed, Acorn Finial, 1800s 110.00
Teakettle, Dovetailed, Gooseneck Spout, Swing Handle, E. Miller, 7 In. 300.00

Teakettle, Dovetailed, Gooseneck Spout, Swing Handle, F. Steinman, 8 In. 1650.00
Teakettle, Gooseneck Spout, Dome Lid, Ring Pull, C-Shaped Handle, 9 x 10 x 7 In. 1100.00
Tray, Hammered, Embossed Pods & Leaves, Round, Benedict, 20 1/2 In. 2230.00
Tray, Hammered, Organic Shape, Silver Fish & Lobster, Whiting, c.1880, 5 In. 896.00
Tray, Hammered, Silver Frog In Corner, Aesthetic Movement, Gorham, c.1882, 8 x 6 In. 510.00
Umbrella Stand, Hammered, Riveted Strap Hardware, Gustav Stickley, 27 x 12 1/4 In. 1116.00
Umbrella Stand, Stork, Flowers, Hand Painted, Cylindrical, 22 x 10 In. 520.00
Urn, Tea & Coffee, England, Mid 19th Century, 14 x 14 In. 385.00
Vase, Hammered, Flared, Folded In Rim, Jarvie, 4 1/4 In. 600.00
Vase, Stand, Hammered, Gold Plated, Marked, M. Zimmerman, 11 x 17 In. .... *ILLUS* 21150.00

COPPER LUSTER items are listed in the Luster category.

CORALENE glass was made by firing many small colored beads on the outside of glassware. It was made in many patterns in the United States and Europe in the 1880s. Reproductions are made today. Coralene-decorated Japanese pottery is listed in the Japanese Coralene category.

Vase, Amber, Pedestal Base, 10 In., Pair 75.00
Vase, Fleur-De-Lis, Gold Design, Satin Finish, c.1890, 6 1/4 x 5 1/2 In. 475.00
Vase, Flowers, Ruffled Rim, Victorian, 6 1/2 In. 135.00
Vase, Opaque Cream, Beaded Flower Branches, Butterfly, Footed, Victorian, 4 3/4 In. 150.00
Vase, Pink Rose, Twisted Stem, Green, Gilt, Footed, 8 In. 19.75
Vase, Seaweed, Shell, Flowers, Green, 9 1/2 In. 125.00

CORKSCREWS have been needed since the first bottle was sealed with a cork, probably in the seventeenth century. Today collectors search for the early, unusual patented examples or the figural corkscrews of recent years.

A.B.C. Bohemian Beer, American Brewing Co., Wood Handle, St. Louis, Mo., 1902 .... 125.00
Anheuser-Busch, Bottle Shape, Opens In Middle, Reveals Screw, Nickel Plated, 1905, 2 3/4 In. .. 75.00
Animal Tooth Handle, Sterling Silver Screw, 1800s, 5 In. 351.00
Bullet Shape, Wm. J. Lemp Brewing Co., Williamson Corp., Newark, N.J., 1907 .... 125.00
Champion, Embossed, Nickel Plated, Cast Iron, Wood Handle, 1896, 10 In. 330.00
Henry Schaefer, Iron, Wood Handle, El Reno, Okla., 1909 .... 50.00
Lady's Leg, Striped Stockings, Boots, Celluloid, Germany, 1890s, 5 1/4 x 2 3/4 In. 355.00
Schlitz, Wood Handle, 1915 .... 36.00
Townsend Brewery, Mont., Ring Handle, Wood Sheath, c.1890 .... 125.00

CORONATION souvenirs have been made since the 1800s. Pottery, glass, tin, silver, and paper objects with a picture of the monarchs and date have been sold at many coronations. The pieces that mention King Edward VIII, the king who was never crowned, are not rare; collectors should be sure to check values before buying. Related pieces are found in the Commemorative category.

Ashtray, Queen Elizabeth II, Gold Trim, Square, 1953, 3 1/2 In. 15.00
Bank, Queen Elizabeth II, Crown Shape, 3 1/2 In. 55.00
Booklet, Queen Elizabeth II, Pitkins, 1953 .... 8.00
Charger, King Edward VIII, Paragon, 1936, 12 3/4 In. 325.00
Compact, Queen Elizabeth II, Royal Coat Of Arms, Vanity Fair, 1953, 3 1/2 In. 60.00
Cup & Saucer, Queen Elizabeth, Bone China, Hammersley, 1953 .... 45.00
Dish, King George VI & Queen Elizabeth, Cream Petal Ware, Grundley, 5 In. 35.00
Jug, Queen Adelaide, King William IV, 1831, 5 1/2 In. 650.00
Jug, Queen Victoria, Blue Glaze, 1838 .... 975.00
Mug, King Edward VII, Royal Doulton, 1902 .... 55.00
Mug, King George VI, Fireworks, Eric Ravilious, Wedgwood, c.1937, 4 In. 1037.00
Mug, King George VI, Myott & Son Potters, 1937, 3 1/4 In. 42.00
Mug, King William IV & Queen Adelaide, 1831 .... 850.00
Mug, Queen Elizabeth II, Shelley, 1953, 3 x 4 In. 50.00
Mug, Queen Victoria, Swansea, 1838 .... 1850.00
Pin Tray, Queen Elizabeth II, Bone China, Royal Crown Derby, 1953 .... 25.00

Plate, Czar Nicholas II & Czarina Alexandra, Sarreguemines, 1896, Pair 620.00
Plate, King Edward VII, Queen Alexandra, Porcelain, Pierced, Continental, 1902 .... 125.00
Plate, King George VI & Queen Elizabeth, Pressed Glass, 1937, 9 3/4 In. 158.00
Plate, King George VI, Amber Glass, Pressed, 1937, 9 1/2 In. 96.00
Plate, Queen Elizabeth II, Sepia Photograph, A. Meakin, 1953, 6 1/2 In. 25.00
Plate, Tea, Queen Elizabeth II, Alfred Clough Ltd., 1953, 6 In. 19.00
Tea Caddy, Queen Elizabeth II, Brass, Thermidor, England, 1953 .... 78.00
Teapot, King Edward VII, Porcelain, Continental, 1902 .... 125.00
Teapot, Queen Elizabeth II, Queensware, Embossed, Wedgwood, 1953 .... 328.00
Tin, Biscuit, H.R.H. Queen Elizabeth II, Gray Dunn, Scotland, 1953 .... 20.00
Tin, Biscuit, Queen Elizabeth, Huntley & Palmers, Blue, 1953 .... 21.00
Tin, King George VI & Queen Elizabeth, Peek Freen & Co., 1937, 6 x 4 3/4 x 3 1/2 In. 40.00
Tin, Tea, King George VI, Canadian Tobin's Coronation Blend, Blue, 1937 .... 50.00
Tin, Tea, Queen Elizabeth II, 1953, 6 1/4 x 4 In. 38.00
Tin, Toffee & Chocolate, Queen Elizabeth II, Henry Thorne & Co., 1953, 2 3/4 x 5 1/2 In. 38.00
Tin, Toffee, Queen Elizabeth & Prince Philip, G.W. Horner, 1953, 3 x 5 x 4 1/2 In. 45.00
Tray, King George V, Queen Mary, Coat Of Arms, Porcelain, Austria, 1911, 9 1/2 x 6 1/4 In. 165.00
Vase, King Edward VII, Queen Alexandra, Doulton Lambeth, 1902, 11 In. 550.00
View-Master Reel, Queen Elizabeth, Sawyers Inc., 1953 .... 15.00

COSMOS is a pressed milk glass pattern with colored flowers made from 1894 to 1915 by the Consolidated Lamp and Glass Company. Tablewares and lamps were made in this pattern. A few pieces were also made of clear glass with painted decorations. Other glass patterns are listed under Consolidated Lamp and also in various glass categories. In later years, Cosmos was also made by the Westmoreland Glass Company.

Butter, Cover, Round, 5 1/2 x 8 In. 330.00
Castor Set, 3 Bottles, Glass Base, 7 In. 425.00
Jam Jar, Metal Cover, 2 In. 20.00
Lamp, Electric, Lattice, Multicolored Flowers, Opal Shade, 18 In. 70.00
Pickle Castor, Silver Plated Holder, Victorian 850.00
Pitcher, Flowers, 9 1/8 x 6 1/4 In. 400.00
Pitcher, Pink Neck, 10 In. 170.00
Tumbler, 3 3/4 In. 30.00
Vase, 7 1/2 In. 132.00

COVERLETS were made of linen or wool during the nineteenth century. Most of the coverlets date from 1800 to the 1880s. There was a revival of hand weaving in the 1920s and new coverlets, especially geometric patterns, were made. The earliest coverlets were made on narrow looms, so two woven strips were joined together and a seam can be found. The weave structures of coverlets can include summer and winter, double weave, overshot, and others. Jacquard coverlets have elaborate pictorial patterns that are made on a special loom or with the use of a special attachment. Quilts are listed in this book in their own category.

48 Squares, Embroidered, Black Woman Doing Household Chores, 39 x 55 In. 50.00
Double Weave, Blue, Red, White, Geometric, Pine Tree Border, 80 x 82 In. 460.00
Double Weave, Blue, White, Eagle Corner, Flowers, Birds, Trees, Medallions, 88 x 72 In. 250.00
Double Weave, Blue, White, Pine Tree Borders, Snowflakes, Wool & Silk, 88 x 108 In. 310.00
Double Weave, Grapevine, Starburst, Martha Davis, 1830, 89 x 85 In. 299.00
Double Weave, Red, Blue, Natural, Birds Of Paradise, Flower Urns, 2 Panel, 77 x 82 In. 489.00
Jacquard, 2 Piece, Mount Vernon, Ohio, 89 x 76 In. 201.00
Jacquard, Blue & White, Birds, Tulips Border, 24 Star Medallions, Ohio, 1853, 70 x 86 In. 625.00
Jacquard, Blue, Green, Red, Leaves, Flower Baskets, Sarah Allen, c.1858, 71 x 94 In. 375.00
Jacquard, Blue, White, Birds Feeding Young In Nest, Buildings, 2 Panel, 70 x 86 In. 375.00
Jacquard, Blue, White, Repeating Quatrefoil Center, Bird Border, 1856, 72 x 87 In. 380.00
Jacquard, Capitol, Virtue, Liberty, Independence, c.1876, 83 x 75 In. 360.00
Jacquard, Centennial, Red, Blue, Green, Eagle Spandrels, Memorial Hall Center, Fringe, 74 x 80 In. 290.00

Jacquard, Center Snowflake, Vines, Double Snowflake Border, Lydia Linn, 1843, 84 x 93 In. 300.00
Jacquard, Double Weave, Blue, Natural, Medallions, Ohio, 2 Panel, c.1840, 80 x 80 In. 460.00
Jacquard, Floral Medallions, Corner Blocks, Ardner 1855, 75 x 82 In. 575.00
Jacquard, Medallion, Domed Building, Eagles, Flowers, Blue, White, 1850, 73 x 83 In. 575.00
Jacquard, Medallion, Flower, Bird, Fringe, Late 1800s, 93 x 79 In. 359.00
Jacquard, Medallion, Rose, David Steiner, Penn., c.1850, 95 x 85 In. 1076.00
Jacquard, Medallions, Blue, Red, Natural, Ohio, 2 Panel, 1844, 78 x 90 In. 748.00
Jacquard, Medallions, Borders, Blue, White, Cotton, 2 Panel, c.1852, 8 x 58 In. 590.00
Jacquard, Medallions, Rose, Peacocks, c.1850, 94 x 84 In. 450.00
Jacquard, Navy Blue, Red, Green, Corner Block, 2 Panel, 1838, 78 x 88 In. 865.00
Jacquard, Navy Blue, Sage Green Red, Natural, 2 Panel, 73 x 85 In. 200.00
Jacquard, Octagonal Medallion, Wm. Ney, Penn., c.1840, 82 x 72 In. 330.00
Jacquard, Oval Medallions, Stars, Marked, Cosley, Ohio, 1853, 87 x 77 In. 410.00
Jacquard, Red & Natural, Floral Medallion, Portrait Of George Washington, 1869 . . . . 1090.00
Jacquard, Red, Green, Star Medallions, Tulips, Borders, Buildings, Fringe, 82 x 84 In. 375.00
Jacquard, Red, Navy, Tan, Flowers, Christian Berg, 1844, 92 x 84 In. 550.00
Jacquard, Red, White, Center Medallion, Flower Baskets, 1848, 91 x 83 In. 180.00
Jacquard, Roses, Vines, Fringe, S. Ruter, Trexlertown, 95 x 77 In. 190.00
Jacquard, Snowflake, Starbursts, Flowers, S.B. Musselman, Milford, Bucks Co., No 109, 83 x 92 In. 336.00
Jacquard, Star & Flower, H & A Seifert, Mechanicsburg, 1848, 88 x 94 In. 1035.00
Jacquard, Star Medallion, J. Keagy, Bedford County, Penna., 83 x 90 In. 600.00
Jacquard, Stars, Rose, Leaf, Martin Hoke, York, Pa., 1845, 98 x 86 In. 956.00
Jacquard, Steamboat, Urns, B. Lichtly, Ohio, 1844, 93 x 75 In. 2030.00
Jacquard, Vines, Stars, Roses, Tulips, C. Yordy, 1851, 96 x 81 in. 299.00
Overshot, Geometric, Rust, Navy, Off-White, Wool, Cotton, 2 Panel, 88 x 74 In. 470.00
Overshot, Optical Pattern, 2 Shades Of Blue, 2 Panel, 70 x 86 In. 290.00
Summer & Winter, Wool, Cotton, Weaver Rose, Rhode Island, Late 1800s, 87 x 74 In. 295.00

COWAN POTTERY made art pottery and wares for florists. Guy Cowan made pottery in Rocky River, Ohio, a suburb of Cleveland, from 1913 to 1931. A stylized mark with the word *Cowan* was used on most pieces. A commercial, mass-produced line was marked *Lakeware*. Collectors today search for the Art Deco pieces by Guy Cowan, Viktor Schreckengost, Waylande Gregory, or Thelma Frazier Winter.

Compote, Seahorse, c.1926, 6 1/2 In., Pair 70.00
Flower Frog, Nude Woman, Awakening, 1920s 600.00
Flower Frog, Nude Woman, Dancing, Scarf, 6 3/8 x 5 In. 495.00
Flower Frog, Toadstool, 1925-31, 4 3/4 x 5 1/4 In. 750.00
Lamp Base, Stylized Trees, Green, Blue Ground, Metal Base, 18 In. 240.00
Sculpture, Stylized Head, Black Matte Glaze, Signed, A. Drexel Jacobson, Mark, 14 In. 2400.00
Snack Set, Light Blue, 6-Sided, 2 Piece 105.00
Vase, Blue Luster, 3 3/8 In. 75.00
Vase, Fan, Seahorses, Luster, Larkspur Blue, 1926-28, 8 x 6 In. 200.00
Vase, Green & Brown Matte Glaze, Beehive Shape, Horizontal Ribs, Mark, 8 In. 780.00
Vase, Squirrel, Stork, Pheasant, Blue & Green Glaze, Raised, Bulbous, Impressed Mark, 8 In. 330.00
Vase, Yellow & Mauve Mottled Glaze, Mark, 12 In. 660.00

CRACKER JACK, the molasses-flavored popcorn mixture, was first made in 1896 in Chicago, Illinois. A prize was added to each box in 1912. Collectors search for the old boxes, toys, and advertising materials. Many of the toys are unmarked.

Book, Ben Grows Up, Mini Book 18, Volume 3 . . . . 7.00
Book, Busy, No. 3, Kittens 6.00
Encyclopedia, Birds, No. 1, Blue Jay Cover 5.00
Mug, Blue Logo, c.1960, 3 5/8 x 2 7/8 In. 55.00
Puzzle, Dexterity, Mirror, Rueckheim Bros. & Eckstein, Chicago, 1 1/2 In. 22.00
Puzzle, Man Shooting Basketball Hoops, 2 Metal Balls, Cardboard, 1 1/4 In. 10.00
Puzzle, Pinball, High Flyer, Mother Goose On Goose In The Air 10.00
Puzzle, Pinball, Road Runner, Green 12.00
Toy, Checkers, Goat & Wagon, 1 1/2 In. 88.00
Toy, Felt Patch, Tickle My Fancy 7.00

Toy, Flag Of Freedom, Freedom Forever Hurrah, Tin, Stand-Up, 1940s, 2 1/4 In. 20.00
Toy, Horse & Cart, Angelus Marshmallows, 2 In. 50.00
Toy, Horse & Wagon, Angelus Marshmallows, Tin, 1 x 2 1/4 In. 125.00
Toy, Indian Chief, Peace Pipe, Stand-Up, Nosco, 1950s, 2 In. 5.00
Toy, Prairie Whistle, Warbler Bird Call, Japan, 1950s, 1 In. 12.00
Toy, Rickshaw, 4 1/2 In. 33.00
Toy, Skeezix, Stand-Up, 2 In. 33.00
Toy, Smitty, Stand-Up, 2 In. ....17.00 to 39.00
Toy, Spinner, Red, Blue, World's Famous Confection, Always On Top 95.00
Toy, Teapot, No Cover, 1930s, 1 1/8 In. 7.00
Toy, Toonerville Trolley, c.1922, 1 1/2 In. 413.00
Toy, Truck, Angelus Marshmallows, 2 In. 88.00
Toy, Whistle, Man, Large Mouth, Gold Colored Tin, 2 1/4 In. 34.00

CRACKLE GLASS was originally made by the Venetians, but most of the ware found today dates from the 1800s. The glass was heated, cooled, and refired so that many small lines appeared inside the glass. It was made in many factories in the United States and Europe.

Cigarette Set, Cobalt Blue, Gold Metal Rim, Holder & Ashtray, 1950, 2 Piece 125.00
Cruet, Blue, Hand Blown, Applied Handle, Ball Stopper, Rainbow Glass Co., 7 1/2 In. 55.00
Decanter, Clear Stopper, 11 In. 48.00
Flip Vase, Orange, Hand Blown, Wavy Sides, Rolled Rim, 9 1/2 x 6 1/2 In. 58.00
Hat Vase, Amber, Hand Blown, Pinched Waist, Pilgrim Glass Co., 3 3/4 In. 35.00
Hat Vase, Smoke Charcoal, Hand Blown, Pulled Rim, 4 1/2 x 5 In. 38.00
Lemonade Set, Topaz, Cone Shape, Footed, 7 Piece 300.00
Pitcher, Amberina, Paneled Sides, Kanawha, 16 In. 60.00
Pitcher, Amethyst, Hand Blown, Pilgrim Glass Co., 3 1/4 In. 30.00
Pitcher, Blue, Molded Foot, Kanawha, 5 1/2 In. 28.00
Pitcher, Hand Blown, Ribbed Handle, Ruffled Edge, Pilgrim Glass Co., 4 1/4 In. 30.00
Pitcher, Ruby, Hand Blown, Pilgrim Glass Co., 3 1/4 In. 35.00
Pitcher, Tangerine Orange, Flattened Sides, Pilgrim Glass Co., 9 In. 90.00
Sugar & Creamer, Green, Hand Blown, Pilgrim Glass Co., 2 3/4 In. 45.00
Vase, Chartreuse Yellow, Goblet Shape, Tapered Sides, Ball Base, 1930s, 13 1/2 In. 100.00
Vase, Emerald Green, Squat, Thick Rim, 4 x 4 In. 35.00
Vase, Olive Green, Spherical, Hand Blown, Pinched Rim, Pilgrim Glass Co., 7 1/2 In. 95.00
Vase, Tangerine Orange, Heart Shape, Rainbow Glass Co., 5 1/4 In. 49.00

CRANBERRY GLASS is an almost transparent yellow-red glass. It resembles the color of cranberry juice. The glass has been made in Europe and America since the Civil War. It is still being made, and reproductions can fool the unwary. Related glass items may be listed in other categories, such as Northwood, Rubena Verde, etc.

Box, Round, Hinged Cover, 4 1/4 In. 375.00
Compote, Panel Cut, Van Dyck Rim, 1870s, 9 3/4 In. 510.00
Decanter, Cased, Gold Enameled Stencil, 9 1/4 In. 100.00
Ice Bucket, Art Deco Style, 5 1/2 In. 100.00
Pitcher, Amber Threading, White Looping, Clear Handle, 7 1/2 In. 220.00
Pitcher, Enameled Flower, 8 x 8 1/2 In. 178.00
Pitcher, Herringbone Optic, c.1870, 9 In. 176.00
Pitcher, Melon Ribbed, 8 In. 110.00
Punch Cup, Applied Clear Handle, England, 2 3/4 In., 6 Piece 86.00
Rose Bowl, Hand Blown, Etched, 6 In. 59.00
Salt, Sterling Silver Footed Holder, 3 1/4 In. 90.00
Spooner, Inverted Thumbprint, Enameled, 4 3/4 x 3 In. 121.00
Spooner, Silver Plated Holder, Victorian, c.1870, 8 x 8 In. 146.00
Sugar Shaker, Faceted, Silver Plated, Cover, c.1900, 6 In. 75.00
Sugar Shaker, Silver Plated Cover, c.1900, 6 In. 75.00
Syrup, Inverted Thumbprint, Pewter Top, Hobbs, c.1883, 7 3/4 In. 345.00
Vase, Tapered, Enameled, Ormolu Holder, Italy, Early 1900s, 19 1/4 In., Pair 530.00
Wedding Bell, Cranberry, White Applied Rim, Handle, Finial, 12 In. 110.00

Ceramic pieces that are repaired or with painted decorations should not be soaked in water. Wipe them with a damp cloth. Unglazed pieces should be dusted.

Creamware, Teapot, Cover, Chintz, Ribbons, Zigzags, Entwined Strap Handle, c.1775, 4 1/2 In.

CREAMWARE, or queensware, was developed by Josiah Wedgwood about 1765. It is a cream-colored earthenware that has been copied by many factories. Similar wares may be listed under Pearlware and Wedgwood.

Figurine, Bagpiper, Astbury Type Lead Glaze, Staffordshire, 1700s, 5 In. 2115.00
Figurine, Dog, Pug, Lead Glaze, Staffordshire, 1700s, 3 1/2 In. 1528.00
Figurine, Marc Anthony Reclining, Staffordshire, 12 In. 575.00
Jug, Cover, Multicolored, Hand Painted Roses, Strap Handle, England, c.1770, 7 1/4 In. 350.00
Tea Service, Fluted, Tapered, Green Stripes, Teapot, Creamer, Sugar, England, 3 Piece 1095.00
Teapot, Cover, Chintz, Ribbons, Zigzags, Entwined Strap Handle, c.1775, 4 1/2 In. .... *ILLUS* 21600.00
Tray, Decorated, Reticulated, 11 1/2 x 9 In. 690.00
Vase, Sleeve Shape, Chinese Style, Signed, Early 20th Century, 9 1/2 x 4 In. 440.00
Watch Hutch, Tall Case Clock Form, Lord Nelson Bust, 19th Century, 9 In. 1035.00

CREDIT CARDS, credit tokens, metal charge plates, phone cards, and other similar collectibles that replace money are now part of the numismatic collecting hobby.

Bank Of America, Mastercharge, Expires September, 1980 .... 7.00
BankAmericard, Visa, Bank Of America, Expires September, 1982 .... 5.00
Citibank, Visa, March 1981 To July 1982 .... 5.00
Credicard Instituto Ayrton Senna, MasterCard, Brazil, 1996-99 .... 61.00
Denby's, We Can Be Your Store, White Ground, Blue Letters 19.00
Diners' Club, 1956-59 .... 238.00
Filene's, Light Blue Ground 34.00
Gimbels, Philadelphia & Suburban Stores, Blue, White 65.00
Greater Radisson Hotel, Minneapolis, Minnesota, 3 3/8 x 2 1/8 In. 45.00
Gulf Refining Co., Philadelphia, Metal, Holder, 1930s 11.00
Hilton Carte Blanche, 1960 Expiration 105.00
Lane Bryant Stores, Princess Size 26.00
Midwest Bank Card, Charge-It, Harris Trust & Savings Bank, Chicago, Expires 1970 .... 17.00
Oil City, Yonkers, Old Greenwich, Pelham, Your Car Can't Tell The Difference 26.00
Polk Bros., Revolving Charge, Chicago 16.00
Sinclair Refining Company, Expires 1946, 2 1/2 x 4 In. 16.00
Texas Company, Texaco, National Credit Card, Paper, 1957 2 1/8 x 3 1/2 In. 10.00

CROWN DERBY is the name given to porcelain made in Derby, England, from the 1770s to 1935. Pieces are marked with a crown and the letter *D* or the word *Derby*. The earliest pieces were made by the original Derby factory, while later pieces were made by the King Street Partnerships (1848–1935) or the Derby Crown Porcelain Co. (1876–90). Derby Crown Porcelain Co. became Royal Crown Derby Co. Ltd. in 1890. It is now part of Royal Doulton Tableware Ltd.

Cake Plate, Oval, 1892, 10 1/4 x 8 In. 450.00
Cup & Saucer, Japan Pattern, Demitasse, 3-In. Cup, 5-In. Saucer 85.00

Cup & Saucer, Wentworth, Fluted, Footed, 2 3/8 x 3 3/4-In. Cup, 5 1/2-In. Saucer 65.00
Dish, Imari Pattern, Rectangular, 7 5/8 x 8 7/8 In. 234.00
Eggcup, Derby Posies, 14K Gold Trim, 1 3/4 In. 26.50
Plate, Japan Pattern, 8-Sided, Gilding, 1890-1940, 9 In. 250.00
Plate, Tea, Blue Mikado, Blue, White, 1920s, 6 1/4 In. 35.00
Platter, Blue Printed Crown, 1884, 1 1/2 x 15 1/4 x 13 In., Pair 1380.00
Platter, Gold Vine Platter, 13 1/2 In. 135.00
Platter, Gold Vine, Gold On White, 15 In. 175.00
Platter, Well & Tree, Blue Printed, 1884, 3 x 21 1/2 In. 1265.00
Soup, Cream, Saucer, Gold Vine, 6 3/8-In. Dish, 4 3/4-In. Saucer 40.00

CROWN DUCAL is the name used on some pieces of porcelain made by A. G. Richardson and Co., Ltd., of Tunstall and Cobridge, England. The name has been used since 1916.

CROWN DUCAL WARE ENGLAND

Box, Candy, Cover, Festival, Chintz, 2 x 5 1/4 x 3 1/2 In. 200.00
Charger, Autumn Leaves Charlotte Rhead, 1937-41, 12 1/4 In. 420.00
Cup, Charm, Demitasse 28.00
Cup & Saucer, Blink Bonnie Thistle 28.00
Cup & Saucer, Bristol, 1930s, 3 3/4 In. 24.95
Cup & Saucer, Florentine, 2 3/8-In. Cup, 6-In. Saucer 10.00
Gravy Boat, Attached Underplate, Charm, Gainsborough, Double 52.00
Gravy Boat, Underplate, Blink Bonnie Thistle, 7 3/4-In. Boat, 8 1/2-In. Plate 45.00
Plate, Bread & Butter, Bristol, 1930s, 6 1/4 In. 8.95
Plate, Colonial Times, First Thanksgiving In America, Pink Transferware, 8 In. 49.00
Plate, Floral Basket, Gold Trim, c.1925, 10 1/2 In. 35.00
Plate, Fruit Center, Cobalt Blue Ring, 9 In. 40.00
Plate, Mulberry, Surrender Of Cornwallis To Washington, 1932, 10 1/2 In. 105.00
Plate, Salad, Charm, Gainsborough, 8 In. 14.40
Saucer, Charm, Gainsborough, 6 In. 7.20

CROWN MILANO glass was made by Frederick Shirley at the Mt. Washington Glass Works about 1890. It had a plain biscuit color with a satin finish. It was decorated with flowers and often had large gold scrolls.

Biscuit Jar, Cover, Enameled Flowers, Leaves, 7 In. 920.00
Biscuit Jar, Cover, Enameled, Flowers, Celtic Medallions, 7 1/2 In. 315.00
Biscuit Jar, Flowers, Leaves, Gold Enameled, Ribbed, Twig Shape Handle, 5 In. 748.00
Biscuit Jar, Thistle, Enameled, Silver Plated Collar, Handle, Lid, 10 1/2 In. 405.00
Bowl, Crimped, Enameled Wild Rose, Pairpoint Silver Plated Stand, 10 x 16 1/2 In. 1725.00
Bride's Bowl, Blue & Red Pansies, Tricornered Ruffled Rim, Silver Plated Frame, 11 In. 1495.00
Creamer, Prunus, Gold, Enameled Blue Scrolling, Square, 3 1/2 In. 175.00
Dish, Pickle, Shaded Blue, Embossed, Pedestal Base, 9 In. 1955.00
Ewer, Flowers, Branches, Applied Jewels, Pink, Green, Dragon Handle, 7 1/2 In. 1610.00
Ewer, Gold Outlined Oak Leaves, Acorns, Handle, Footed, 12 In. 1725.00
Lamp, Banquet, Enameled Chrysanthemums, Metal Base, Lion Paw Feet, 31 1/2 In. 575.00
Mustard Jar, Hinged Cover, Forget-Me-Nots, Melon Ribbed, 2 3/4 In. 690.00
Rose Bowl, Enameled Flower Blossoms, Branches, Blue, White, 4 In. 315.00
Rose Bowl, Enameled Flowers, Leaves, Oval, Crimped Rim, 4 1/2 In. 230.00
Rose Bowl, Enameled Mauve, Green, Brown Orchid, 4 3/4 In. 345.00
Rose Bowl, Enameled, Amethyst Foxglove Blossoms, Crimped Rim, 6 1/2 In. 315.00
Spill, Scissor-Cut Rim, Flowers, Gold Trim, 7 In. 690.00
Vase, Enameled Gold Chrysanthemums, Spherical, 4 3/4 x 6 1/2 In. 520.00
Vase, Enameled Roses, Leaves, Conical, Rolled Rim, 9 1/2 In. 460.00
Vase, Enameled Snow Geese Flying, Sunset, Gold Scrolls, Signed, 1880, 14 In. 2600.00
Vase, Flowers, Gold Enameled, Melon Ribbed, Folded, Tricornered Rim, 13 1/2 In. 10350.00
Vase, Flowers, Gold Enameled, Melon Ribbed, Pulled, Folded Rim, 13 In. 1840.00
Vase, Red Roses, Gold Scrolling, Handles, Oval, 4 1/2 In. 400.00
Vase, Stick, 13 1/4 In. 600.00
Vase, Stick, Enameled Flowers, Scrolling, Bulbous Base, 12 1/2 In. 2875.00
Vase, Swirled Body, Enameled & Gold Flowers, 6 In. 1325.00
Vase, Teardrop Shape, 10 1/2 In. 300.00

CROWN TUSCAN pattern is included in the Cambridge glass category.

CRUETS of glass or porcelain were made to hold vinegar, oil, and other condiments. They were especially popular during Victorian times and have been made in a variety of styles since the eighteenth century. Additional cruets may be found in the Castor Set category and also in various glass categories.

Amberina Glass, Swirled Ribs, Amber Handle, Faceted Stopper, 6 1/2 In. 315.00
Bohemian Glass, Amethyst, Moorish, Pinched Sides, Amber Handle & Stopper, 8 In. 1035.00
Glass, Amber, 2 Bottles, Stoppers, Wrought Iron Stand, 8 3/4 x 7 1/2 x 4 In. 100.00
Glass, Broken Column Pattern, Stopper, 6 3/4 In. 175.00
Glass, Cane Pattern, 5 In. 45.00
Glass, Crackle, Cranberry, Double Ball Stopper, Rainbow Glass Company, 6 3/4 In. 100.00
Glass, Feather, 1896 .... 65.00
Glass, Hobnail Pattern, Stopper, Model Flint Glass Co., 1880s, 9 1/4 In. 35.00
Glass, Inverted Thumbprint, Vaseline, Optic Stopper, 5 In. 225.00
Glass, Log & Star Pattern, Stopper, Bellaire, 7 1/4 In. 55.00
Glass, Pattern Molded, Peacock Feather, 8 1/2 In. 65.00
Porcelain, Vinegar, Pearlized Luster, 24K Gold Filigree, Germany, 9 1/2 In. 50.00

CT GERMANY was first part of a mark used by a company in Altwasser, Germany, in 1845. The initials stand for C. Tielsch, a partner in the firm. The Hutschenreuther firm took over the company in 1918 and continued to use the *CT*.

Biscuit Jar, Flowers, Gold Trim, Blue, 7 1/2 In. 75.00
Bowl, Dresser, 24K Gold Flowers, c.1930, 6 1/4 In. 20.00
Chocolate Set, Teal Ground, Hand Painted 395.00
Cup & Saucer, 3-In. Cup, 5-In. Saucer 17.00
Jar, Cover, Wild Roses, Hand Painted, 3 x 3 3/8 In. 38.00
Plate, Floral Rose, 8 1/4 In. 18.00
Plate, Flowers, Gold Luster Rim, Transfer 55.00
Plate, Gilt Trim, 8 1/4 In. 19.00
Plate, Rose, Gold Rim, Transfer, 8 1/4 In. 18.00
Sugar & Creamer, Hand Painted 65.00
Vase, Roses, 6 In. 75.00

CUP PLATES are small glass or china plates that held the cup while a diner of the mid-nineteenth century drank coffee or tea from the saucer. The most famous cup plates were made of glass at the Boston and Sandwich factory located in Sandwich, Massachusetts. There have been many new glass cup plates made in recent years for sale to gift shops or limited edition collectors. These are similar to the old plates but can be recognized as new.

2 Hearts, 2 Arrows, Lyre Border, Deep Blue, 24 Large Scallops, 3 1/2 In. 70.00
4-Leaf Anthemion, Leaf & Dot Border, 24 Bull's-Eyes, Scallop & Point Rim, 3 7/16 In. 143.00
4-Leaf Center, Star Field, Fiery Opalescent, 19 Large Scallops, 3 1/2 In. 80.00
4-Petal Flower & Diamond, Overlapping Circles Border, 60 Scallop Rim, 3 5/8 In. 77.00
8-Petal Starflower, Strawberry Diamond Band, Rope Rim, 3 In. 55.00
12-Rayed Star, Comet Border, 24 Peacock Eye Rim, 3 1/4 In. 275.00
16-Rayed Star, Plain Ground, Uneven Ray Border, Amethyst, 66 Scallop Rim, 3 5/16 In. 55.00
Blown, Gray Tint, Wide Flared Rim, c.1800, 3/4 x 4 1/4 In. 330.00
Diagonal Rib Center, Overlapping Circles Border, Wheat Sheaf Scallop Rim, 3 1/2 In. 358.00
Eagle & Shield, 13 Stars, Rosette & Plume Border, Blue, 44 Scallop Rim, 3 1/4 In. 99.00
Landing Of General Lafayette, Staffordshire, Blue, Impressed, Clews, 3 1/2 In. 460.00
Laurel Wreath Bands, Rope Rim, Top & Bottom, 3 3/4 In. 413.00
Log Cabin, Forget-Me-Not Border, Amber, 66 Scallops, 3 1/4 In. 440.00
Octagon Church, Boston, Blue, Acorn Border, Staffordshire, 4 1/8 In. 2185.00
Plain Center, Flower Basket Border, Fiery Opalescent, Rope Rim, Top & Bottom, 3 3/4 In. 77.00
Sea, Sailboats, Shell Border, Blue, Enoch Wood & Sons, Staffordshire, 3 5/8 In. 400.00
Shield & Rosette, Fiery Opalescent, 10-Sided, Rope Rim, Top & Bottom, 3 1/2 In. 66.00
Ship, Benjamin Franklin, Anchor & Star Border, 48 Scallops, 3 1/2 In. 385.00
Ship, Benjamin Franklin, Anchor Border, Emerald Green, 48 Scallop Rim, 3 1/2 In. 1870.00

Star, Concentric Rings, Leaf & Acorn Border, Swirled Translucent Blue, 3 5/8 In. 990.00
Star In Octagon, Diamond Punty Border, 24 Bull's-Eye Scallops, 3 1/2 In. 187.00

CURRIER & IVES made the famous American lithographs marked with their name from 1857 to 1907. The mark used on the print included the street address in New York City, and it is possible to date the year of the original issue from this information. Earlier prints were made by N. Currier and use that name from 1835 to 1847. Many reprints of the Currier or Currier & Ives prints have been made. Some collectors buy the insurance calendars that were based on the old prints. The words *large*, *small*, or *medium folio* refer to size. The original print sizes were very small (up to about 7 x 9 in.), small (8.8 x 12.8 in.), medium (9 x 14 in. to 14 x 20 in.), large (larger than 14 x 20 in.). Other sizes are probably later copies. Other prints by Currier & Ives may be listed in the Card category under Advertising and in the Sheet Music category. Currier & Ives dinnerware patterns may be found in the Adams or Dinnerware categories.

Abraham Lincoln, Frame, 24 x 18 In. 818.00
Almira, Frame, c.1845, 10 x 14 In. 33.00
American Homestead Spring, Frame, 13 1/2 x 17 In. 661.00
Battle Of Antietam, Frame, c.1862, 12 x 16 In. 374.00
Battle Of New Orleans, Frame, c.1842, 10 x 14 In. 100.00
Bombardment & Capture Of Fort Henry, Tenn., Frame, Small Folio 201.00
Card, Great Dignity Cigars, Boy Turns Down Cigar, 1884 . . . . 72.00
Cares Of A Family, Game Birds, In Field, N. Currier, 26 1/2 x 33 In. 4313.00
Cares Of A Family, N. Currier, Mat, Frame, 20 3/4 x 25 1/4 In. 2860.00
Champion Trotting Stallion Smuggler, Bird's-Eye Maple Frame, 23 x 30 In. 1880.00
Close Finish, Vignette, Rustic Oak Frame, c.1874, 12 x 16 In. 264.00
Going To Pasture Early Morning, Frame, Small Folio 46.00
Grand National Democratic Banner, McClellan, Pendleton, Frame, 1864, 17 x 14 In. 1227.00
High Water In Mississippi, Low Water In Mississippi, Frame, 18 x 28 In., Pair 15865.00
Home Of Washington, Mt. Vernon, Va., Gilt Frame, 16 x 20 In. 288.00
Home To Thanksgiving, Frame, c.1867, 14 3/8 x 24 3/4 In. 1763.00
Jockey's Dream, Hand Colored, 1880, 13 1/4 x 17 1/2 In. 155.00
John Brown The Martyr, Frame, 1870, 19 1/4 x 17 In. 1265.00
Judge Fullerton, Frame, Small Folio 58.00
Life Of A Fireman, Take Up-Man Your Rope, Frame, 21 1/4 x 29 1/2 In. 1783.00
Life Of A Fireman, The New Era, Steam & Muscle, c.1861, 21 3/4 x 30 In. 911.00
My Little Favorite, Frame, c.1850, 12 x 16 In. 39.00
New England Winter Scene, After George Durrie, Frame, 17 x 23 1/2 In. 1898.00
On The Mississippi, Colored, Black Walnut Frame, 9 1/2 x 14 In. 605.00
Roadside Mill, Hand Colored, Mat, Frame, 14 1/2 x 18 3/8 In. 230.00
Robinson Crusoe & His Pets, Hand Colored, Frame, 14 x 17 1/4 In. 173.00
Squall Off Cape Horn, Frame, 10 1/2 x 13 In. 173.00
Steamship City Of Washington, Frame, Small Folio 345.00
Western Farmer's Home, Frame, Small Folio 144.00

CUSTARD GLASS is a slightly yellow opaque glass. It was first made in England in the 1880s and was first made in the United States in the 1890s. It has been reproduced. Additional pieces may be found in the Cambridge, Fenton, Heisey, and Northwood categories. Custard glass is called Ivorina Verde by Heisey and other companies.

Argonaut Shell, Pitcher, Northwood, 8 1/4 x 4 3/4 In. 470.00
Chrysanthemum Sprig, Berry Bowl, 10 1/2 In. 95.00
Chrysanthemum Sprig, Berry Bowl, Blue, Gold Trim, 5 In. 185.00
Chrysanthemum Sprig, Butter, Cover, 7 3/4 In. 175.00
Chrysanthemum Sprig, Creamer, Northwood . . . . .175.00 to 195.00
Chrysanthemum Sprig, Cruet, Stopper, 7 In. 250.00
Chrysanthemum Sprig, Spooner, 4 In. 69.00
Geneva, Spooner, Green Stain, Gold Trim, 4 1/4 x 3 1/2 In. 44.00
Inverted Fan & Feather, Berry Set, 7 Piece 950.00

Louis XV, Berry Bowl, Master 85.00
Louis XV, Pitcher 230.00
Louis XV, Spooner, 4 1/2 In. .... 55.00 to 110.00
Maize is its own category in this book.
Maple Leaf, Toothpick Holder, 2 3/8 x 2 In. 1250.00
Ring Band, Berry Bowl, Enameled Rose 220.00

CUT GLASS has been made since ancient times, but the large majority of the pieces now for sale date from the brilliant period of glass design, 1880 to 1905. These pieces have elaborate geometric designs with a deep miter cut. Modern cut glass with a similar appearance is being made in England, Ireland, and the Czech and Slovak republics. Chips and scratches are often difficult to notice but lower the value dramatically. A signature on the glass adds significantly to the value. Other cut glass pieces are listed under factory names.

Banana Boat, Blue To Clear, Russian, Hobstar, Strawberry Diamond & Cane, 5 1/2 x 12 In. 1045.00
Banana Boat, Engraved Floral, Hobstar & Fan, Blown Out, Pedestal, 6 1/2 x 9 In. 75.00
Banana Boat, McKenna's White Rose, 11 In. 100.00
Basket, Florence Hobstar, Hobstar Base, 13 x 9 1/2 In. 605.00
Basket, Hobstar & Cane, Twist Handle, 6 In. 150.00
Basket, Hobstar, Cane, Diamond, Strawberry Diamond & Fan, Twist Handles, 6 x 8 In. 250.00
Biscuit Jar, Cranberry To Clear, Silver Plated Lid, Bail, 7 In. 240.00
Bowl, Arched Fan, 8 1/4 In. 90.00
Bowl, Centerpiece, Silver Base, Oval, Continental, 19th Century, 10 3/4 x 6 1/2 x 13 1/2 In. 1989.00
Bowl, Clear Button Hobnail, Ray Center, 5 x 9 1/2 In. 250.00
Bowl, Cosmos Star, Signed, Tuthill, 8 In. 550.00
Bowl, Crosscut Diamond, Zipper & Fan, Hobstar Center, Meriden, 8 3/4 In. 60.00
Bowl, Diamond Band, Round Foot, Rolled Rim, England, 1820s, 10 In. 406.00
Bowl, Electra, Straus, 8 In. 125.00
Bowl, Engraved Floral, Green Threaded Border, 8 In. 100.00
Bowl, Engraved Strawberries, Leaves, Sterling Silver Rim, Monogram, 11 In. 201.00
Bowl, Expanding Star, 8-Sided, 9 In. 170.00
Bowl, Fan & Crosshatch Alternating Panels, Fan Cut Rim, Starburst Bottom, 9 In. 175.00
Bowl, Flashed Hobstar, Sterling Silver Rim, 7 1/2 In. 65.00
Bowl, Fruit, Hobstars, Pinwheels, Pedestal, Square Base, 11 x 14 In. 59.00
Bowl, Fruit, Russian Pattern, Brilliant, American, c.1915, 5 x 10 In. 205.00
Bowl, Fruit, Waffle, Strawberry Diamond & Fan, Cupped Rim, 7 In. 1200.00
Bowl, Green To Clear, Intaglio, Fruit, Leaves, Blossoms, 10 x 5 In. 460.00
Bowl, Harvard, Hobstar Center, 3 1/2 x 9 In. 500.00
Bowl, Hobnail, Center Hobstar, 3-Sided, Scalloped Edge, 10 In. 115.00
Bowl, Hobstar & Arched Button, Brilliant, Early 1900s, 9 In. 115.00
Bowl, Hobstar & Cane, Cupped Rim, 9 In. 190.00
Bowl, Hobstar Center, Block, Strawberry Diamond & Fan, Oval, 11 In. 125.00
Bowl, Hobstar, 8-Point, Intaglio Floral, Signed, Tuthill, 8 In. .... 100.00 to 150.00
Bowl, Hobstar, 48-Point, Clark, 7 x 14 In. 2750.00
Bowl, Hobstar, Diamond, Cane & Strawberry Diamond, Signed, Straus, 8 In. 80.00
Bowl, Hobstar, File, Cane & Fan, 8 In. 100.00
Bowl, Hobstar, File, Vesica, Cane & Tusk, 8 In. 150.00
Bowl, Hobstar, Nailhead Diamond, Strawberry Diamond, Pinwheel & Fan, 8 In. 70.00
Bowl, Hobstar, Nailhead Diamond, Strawberry Diamond, Vesica & Star, 10 In. 150.00
Bowl, Hobstar, Nailhead, Strawberry Diamond, Prism & Fan, Oval, 5 x 11 In. 175.00
Bowl, Hobstar, Split Strawberry Diamond Vesicas & Star, 9 In. 50.00
Bowl, Hobstar, Strawberry Diamond & Cane, 9 In. 90.00
Bowl, Hobstar, Strawberry Diamond, Diamond & Cane Vesica, Straus, 4 1/2 x 10 In. 150.00
Bowl, Hobstar, Strawberry Diamond, Zipper, Star, Fan & Tusk, 4 x 9 In. 250.00
Bowl, Hobstar, Vesica, Prism, Nailhead Diamond & Fan, Maltese Cross Center, 8 In. 150.00
Bowl, Intaglio, Oranges & Cherries, 9 In. 165.00
Bowl, Intaglio, Pear, Grapes & Cherries, Signed, Tuthill, 8 In. .... 500.00 to 660.00
Bowl, Middlesex, Square, New England Glass Co., 10 In. 165.00
Bowl, Rembrandt, Clark, 3 1/4 x 8 In. 750.00
Bowl, Rounded Panels, Conforming Arches, Signed, Rogaska, 4 1/2 x 11 In. 69.00

Bowl, Salad, Russian, Square, 9 In. 825.00
Bowl, Strawberry Diamond, Star & Fan, Hobstar Center, 5 x 11 In. 325.00
Bowl, Theodora, Scalloped Edge, 8 In. 1485.00
Bowl, Tulip, Rose & Cane, 4 Sections, Loop Handles, 12 1/2 In. 29.00
Bowl, Vintage, Engraved Grapes, Signed, Tuthill, 9 In. 990.00
Box, Glove, Tulip, 4 x 11 In. 675.00
Brandy Snifter, Amethyst To Clear, Blown, Grapes, Leaves, Fan & Star, 5 In. 59.00
Bread Tray, Hobstar, Cane & Notched Fan, Tab Handles, Signed, Clark, 13 1/2 x 8 In. 850.00
Butter, Cover, Hobstar & Nailhead Diamond, 5 1/2 x 7 1/2 In. ....150.00 to 175.00
Butter, Cover, Strawberry Diamond & Fan, Faceted Finial, 8 x 6 In. 58.00
Cake Plate, 6-Petal Flower, Notched Stem, 6 x 10 In. 495.00
Candlestick, Bull's-Eye, Amber To Clear, 10 x 5 In. 385.00
Candlestick, Flat Panel Cut, Flashed Star Base, Signed, Tuthill, 10 In., Pair 495.00
Candlestick, Notched Stem, Rayed Base, 7 1/2 In. 150.00
Carafe, Hobstar, Block Diamond, Star & Notched Bar, 8 1/4 In. 125.00
Carafe, Water, Hobstar, File & Fan, 8 In. 60.00
Card Tray, Hobstar & Fanned Prism, Pedestal Base, 7 1/2 x 2 3/4 In. 165.00
Celery Tray, Harvard, 13 1/2 In. 66.00
Celery Tray, Hobstar, Cane & Star, Rayed Center, Rolled Rim, 11 In. 30.00
Celery Tray, Hobstar, Strawberry Diamond & Fan, 11 1/2 In. 40.00
Celery Vase, Strawberry Diamonds, Panels, Scalloped Rim, Rayed Base, 8 In., Pair 865.00
Chalice, Amethyst To Clear, Pinwheel, Crosshatch & Fan, Teardrop Stem, 10 1/2 In. 305.00
Chalice, Green To Clear, Cane & Fan, 10 1/4 In. 358.00
Champagne, Ashburton, Polished Pontil, Flint, 5 x 2 3/4 In. ....39.00 to 50.00
Champagne Bucket, Hobstar, Strawberry Diamond & Prism, 7 x 7 1/2 In. 200.00
Cheese Dish, Cover, Hobstar, File, Cane, Prism & Fan, Sections, Silver Finial, 6 x 10 In. 1595.00
Cheese Dish, Cover, Hobstar, Strawberry Diamond & Geometric Star, 6 1/2 x 9 1/2 In. 375.00
Cheese Dish, Cover, Sections, Harvard Pattern, 6 x 8 1/2 In. 550.00
Cheese Dish, Hobstar, Strawberry Diamond & Fan, Hobstar Base, 3 x 10 In. 60.00
Cheese Dome, Ruby To Clear, 7 In. 248.00
Cider Set, Russian Pattern, Tumblers, 7-In. Pitcher, Triple Notched Handle, 9 Piece 605.00
Coffeepot Lid, Florence Hobstar, 2 5/8-In. Opening 160.00
Cologne, Ball Shape, Hobstar, Strawberry Diamond & Fan, Faceted Cut Stopper, 7 In. 70.00
Cologne, Bull's-Eye, Notched Prisms, Hobstars, 7 3/4 x 3 In. 250.00
Cologne, Green To Clear, Hobnail, Stopper, Dorflinger, 6 1/2 In. 715.00
Cologne, Honeycomb, Engraved Floral, Faceted Cut Stopper, Square, 7 In. 150.00
Cologne, Ruby To Vaseline, Crosscut Pattern, 8 In. .... ***ILLUS*** 1600.00
Compote, 8 Panels, Intaglio Floral, Teardrop Stem, 8 3/4 x 7 In. 200.00
Compote, 9 Hobstars, Rayed Star Base, Sterling Rim, C.F. Monroe, 5 x 5 In. 395.00
Compote, Basket Weave, Teardrop Stem, 32-Point Hobstar Scalloped Base, 9 x 9 In. 495.00
Compote, Cobalt Blue To Clear, Baluster Stem, Pontil, 4 1/2 x 8 3/4 In. 110.00
Compote, Drape, Straus, 8 x 9 In. 350.00
Compote, Flashed Hobstar, Vesica, Feathered Prism, Signed, Maple City, 7 3/4 x 8 In. 175.00
Compote, Flower & Ferns, Gravic, Early 1900s, 10 1/2 In. 104.00
Compote, Hobstar, Cane, Strawberry Diamond & Fan, Sections, Hobstar Base, 10 x 8 In. 700.00
Compote, Hobstar, Cane, Strawberry Diamond & Star, Teardrop Stem, 8 x 6 1/2 In., Pair 200.00
Compote, Hobstar, Feathered Fan, 7 x 6 1/2 In. 201.00
Compote, Intaglio, Blackberry, 4 1/2 x 8 In. 660.00
Compote, Intaglio, Grapes & Berries, Teardrop Stem, Tuthill, 4 3/4 x 7 In. 440.00
Compote, Marquis, 18-Point Hobstar Base, Egginton, 6 3/4 x 6 3/4 In. 495.00
Compote, Rolled Rim, Notched Teardrop, Stem, Rayed Base, 9 1/4 In. 90.00
Compote, Ruby To Clear, Clear Stem & Foot, New England, 8 3/4 In. 495.00
Compote, Star & Fan, Brilliant, Hoare, 12 x 6 In. 235.00
Console Set, Cranberry To Clear, 12-In. Pedestal Bowl, 10-In. Candlesticks, 3 Piece 660.00
Cordial, Cupped Bowl, Engraved Swags, Tassels, Stars, Cut Stem, c.1800, 3 1/2 In. 77.00
Cordial, Green, Hexagonal, Scroll, Gold Rim, Germany, 5 1/4 x 1 3/4 In., 6 Piece 375.00
Cordial, Hobstar, Faceted Knop Stem, Scalloped Base, 4 1/4 In., Pair 440.00
Cruet, Buzz Star, Stopper, 4 1/2 In. 165.00
Cruet, Engraved, Flowers, Bowknot, Cylindrical Base, Tapered Neck, Handle, 7 3/4 In. 220.00
Cruet, Ketchup, Hobstar, Gothic Arch & Fan, Crosscut Diamond Stopper, 6 1/2 In. 200.00

Cup & Saucer, Cranberry To Clear, Diamond & Fan 650.00
Decanter, Allover Hobstar, Triple Neck Ring, 13 1/2 x 5 1/4 In. 1095.00
Decanter, Amethyst To Clear, Faceted, Star Base, Faceted Stopper, 12 1/2 In. 175.00
Decanter, Engraved Floral, Embossed Sterling Stopper, 7 In. 170.00
Decanter, Engraved, Eagle, Scroll, Tapered, Monogram, c.1800, Qt., 12 3/4 In. 715.00
Decanter, Engraved, Feathered Swirls, Stars, Tapered, Stopper, c.1800, Qt., 12 In. 175.00
Decanter, Engraved, Flowers, Bowknots, Laurels, Tapered, Stopper, c.1800, 1/2 Pt., 7 In. 605.00
Decanter, Engraved, Flowers, Laurels, Tapered, Stopper, c.1800, Pt., 10 In. 415.00
Decanter, Engraved, Garland, Ovals, Stars, Tapered, Stopper, c.1800, Qt., 11 1/2 In. 220.00
Decanter, Engraved, Leaves, Daisies, Tapered, Heart Shaped Stopper, c.1800, Qt., 11 1/2 In. 440.00
Decanter, Engraved, Rope, Lily-Of-The-Valley, Grapes, Tapered, Stopper, c.1800, Qt., 11 1/4 In. 255.00
Decanter, Engraved, Sprigs, Daisies, Ovals, Swags, Tapered, Stopper, c.1800, Pt., 9 1/2 In. 358.00
Decanter, Engraved, Sprigs, Ovals, Flowers, Tassels, Tapered, Stopper, c.1800, Pt., 9 1/4 In. 209.00
Decanter, Engraved, Sprigs, Ovals, Flowers, Tassels, Tapered, Stopper, c.1800, Qt., 11 In. 220.00
Decanter, Engraved, Sprigs, Ovals, Stars, Tapered, Stopper, c.1800, Qt., 10 1/4 In. 176.00
Decanter, Engraved, Sprigs, Ovals, Swags, Tassels, Tapered, Stopper, c.1800, Pt., 9 1/2 In. 255.00
Decanter, Engraved, Stars, Roundels, Tapered, Stopper, c.1800, Qt., 8 3/4 In. 145.00
Decanter, Engraved, Sunrays, Clouds, Leaves, Monogram, Tapered, c.1800, Pt., 11 In. 660.00
Decanter, Engraved, Swags, Tassels, Stars, Tapered, Stopper, Qt., 11 1/4 In. 523.00
Decanter, Fluted Shoulder & Base, 3 Neck Rings, Flattened Flared Lip, Stopper, 8 1/2 In. 112.00
Decanter, Geometric Hobstar Button, Wafer Base, Pattern Cut Stopper, 12 In. 330.00
Decanter, Hobnail & Lace, Early 20th Century, 9 In., Pair 70.00
Decanter, Hobstar, Fern & Fan, Faceted Ring Neck, 12 In. 225.00
Decanter, Hobstar, File & Fan, 6-Sided Stopper, 10 3/4 In. 250.00
Decanter, Hobstar, Strawberry Diamond, Star & Fan, 6-Sided Stopper, 12 In. 200.00
Decanter, Russian Pattern, Faceted Stopper, Brilliant, Late 1800s, 12 1/2 In. 176.00
Decanter, Ship's, Flutes, Sterling Silver Wheat Stopper, 7 In. 550.00
Decanter, Ships, Hobstar & Fan, Mushroom Shape Hobstar Stopper, 7 In. 425.00
Decanter, Stopper, Harvard & Daisy, Baluster Step Cut Neck, 13 In. 300.00
Decanter, Stopper, White To Cranberry, 16 1/2 In. 110.00
Decanter, Whiskey, Engraved Acorn & Branch, Honeycomb Neck, Stopper, 11 1/2 In. 700.00
Decanter, Whiskey, Hobstar, Strawberry Diamond, Prism & Bull's-Eye, Handle, 11 In. 300.00
Decanter, Whiskey, Hobstar, Strawberry Diamond, Star & Fan, Mushroom Stopper, 14 In. 200.00
Dish, Caviar, Cover, Hobstar & Strawberry Diamond, Cut Finial, 5 1/2 x 8 1/2 In. 900.00
Dish, Caviar, Cover, Strawberry Diamond, Hobstar, Cane, Vesica & Fan, 4 x 5 1/2 In. 450.00
Dish, Mayonnaise, Underplate, Flashed Hobstar, 3 1/4 x 6 1/4 In. 275.00
Ewer, Engraved Fruit, Vines, Elongated Oval, Silvered Metal Mount, WMF, c.1900, 11 1/2 In. 848.00
Ferner, Hobstar, Prism & Fan, Silver Rim, 5 x 10 In. 100.00
Ferner, Prima Donna, 3-Footed, 4 1/2 x 8 In. 300.00
Goblet, Amber To Clear, Cane, Notched Stem, 4 3/4 In., 6 Piece 633.00
Goblet, Blue To Clear, Bull's-Eye & Loop, 6 3/4 In., 6 Piece 330.00
Goblet, Cranberry To Clear, Cane & Bull's-Eye, 8 1/2 In. 55.00
Goblet, Hobstar, Faceted Knop Stem, Scalloped Base, 4 3/4 In. 358.00
Humidor, Cigar, Crosscut Diamond, Strawberry Diamond & Fan, Cut Cover, 8 1/2 In. 400.00
Humidor, Lid, Monarch Pattern, J. Hoare, 9 In. 700.00
Hurricane Shade, Blown, Engraved Garlands, Bezel Edges, 22 In., Pair 3995.00
Ice Bucket, Acme, J. Hoare, 5 1/2 x 5 3/4 In. 275.00
Ice Bucket, Flashed Hobstar, Strawberry Diamond & Fan, Rayed Base, 6 3/4 x 7 1/2 In. 130.00
Ice Bucket, Hobstar, Strawberry Diamond & Fan, Tab Handles, 4 1/4 x 6 In. 450.00
Ice Tub, Hobstar, 1900s, 5 3/4 In. 115.00
Inkwell, Thumbprint, Cane, Brass Collar, Brilliant, England, c.1885, 4 In. 293.00
Jar, Cover, Amethyst To Clear, Punty & Bull's-Eye, Clear Stem, Base, 12 In. 70.00
Jug, Claret, Squat Base, Applied Handle, Sterling Top, Hinged Cover, 6 1/2 x 3 1/2 In. 138.00
Jug, Whiskey, Harvard, Triple Notched Handle, 9 1/2 In. 220.00
Knife Rest, Nailhead Diamond, Strawberry Diamond, Hobstar & Fan, 5 x 2 1/2 In. 225.00
Ladle, Punch, Hobstar, Prism & Fan, Signed J.D. Bergen, 16 In. 375.00
Lamp, Mushroom Shade, Engraved Floral, 2 Sockets, 22 x 12 In. 525.00
Lamp, Mushroom Shade, Hobstar, Strawberry Diamond, Fan & Floral, 23 1/2 x 12 In. 1750.00
Lamp, Mushroom Shade, Hobstar, Strawberry Diamond, Vesica, Prism & Fan, 21 x 12 In. 1200.00
Lamp, Mushroom Shade, Hobstar, Strawberry, Diamond, Prism, Fan, 2 Sockets, 21 x 12 In. 650.00
Nappy, Hobnail, Matching Handles, 3-Sided, 5 In., Pair 20.00

Cut Glass, Cologne, Ruby To Vaseline, Crosscut Pattern, 8 In.

Cut Glass, Punch Bowl, Cranberry To Clear, Crosscut Diamond, 2 Piece, 13 3/4 x 14 In.

Nappy, Hobstar & Nailhead Diamond, Leaf Shape, 7 In. 165.00
Nut Dish, File, Prism & Star, Petticoat Hobstar Base, Footed, 4 1/2 x 7 In. 60.00
Pitcher, Buzz Saw, 1900s, 7 1/4 In. 92.00
Pitcher, Buzz Saw, Early 1900s, 9 3/4 In. 115.00
Pitcher, Cane, File, Star, Hobstar & Fan, Notched Handle, Hobstar Base, 9 In. 175.00
Pitcher, Cider, Strawberry Diamond, Hobstars, Fans, Crosshatching, 7 x 6 1/2 In. 375.00
Pitcher, Engraved Wheat Sheaf, Pattern Cut Handle, Faceted Stopper, 8 1/2 In. 675.00
Pitcher, Hobstar & Lozenge, Ice Lip, 1930s, 9 1/4 In. 510.00
Pitcher, Hobstar Band, Notched Prism Borders, 8 In. 120.00
Pitcher, Hobstar, Crosshatch, Cane & Fan, Triple Notched Handle, 10 In. 250.00
Pitcher, Hobstar, Nailhead Diamond & Strawberry Diamond, 7 3/4 In. 75.00
Pitcher, Honeycomb, Rayed Base, 10 1/2 In. 275.00
Pitcher, Pinwheel, Strawberry Diamond & Fan, 10 1/2 In. 75.00
Pitcher, Tankard, Block, Orb Strawberry Diamond & Cane, Clear Bars, 14 In. 400.00
Pitcher, Tankard, Champagne, Hobstar, Strawberry Diamond & Fan, Notched Handle, 13 1/2 In. .. 550.00
Pitcher, Tankard, Hobstar, Cane & Fan, Triple Notched Handle, Rayed Base, 11 In. 200.00
Pitcher, Tankard, Hobstar, File, Star & Fan, Notched Handle, Embossed Sterling Silver Rim, 11 In. . 880.00
Pitcher, Tankard, Lotus, Eggington, 12 x 6 In. 815.00
Pitcher, Tankard, Sunburst, Pinwheel, Crosshatch, Cane & Fan, 12 1/2 In. 220.00
Pitcher, Thistle, Crosshatching, Triple Notched Handle, Spout, 7 1/2 In. 125.00
Plate, Fuchsia Pattern, Sinclaire, 1 1/4 x 10 In. 375.00
Plate, Green, White To Clear, Double Cut, St. Louis, 8 5/8 In. 99.00
Plate, Hobstar, Crossed Cane Bars, 7 In. 140.00
Powder Box, Hobstar Cover, Prism Cut Base, 5 In. 140.00
Punch Bowl, Base, Alhambra, Intaglio Strapwork Border, Notched Rim, 13 In. 2585.00
Punch Bowl, Base, Amherst, Nailhead Diamonds, Hobstars, Fans, Vesica, 14 In. 1155.00
Punch Bowl, Base, Bolo, J. Hoare, 13 1/2 x 14 In. 1265.00
Punch Bowl, Base, Engraved Daisies, Tulip Shape, 12 x 11 In. 1320.00
Punch Bowl, Base, Fine Hobstar, Crosshatch, Fans, 13 x 14 In. 1155.00
Punch Bowl, Base, Harvard, 12 x 14 In. 345.00
Punch Bowl, Base, Hobstar Clusters, Feathered Fan Accents, 13 1/2 x 15 In. 990.00
Punch Bowl, Base, Pinwheel, Flowers, 10 x 11 In. 345.00
Punch Bowl, Base, Prima Donna, 14 x 15 In. 1760.00
Punch Bowl, Base, Sunbeam, Bergen, 13 x 14 In. 3630.00
Punch Bowl, Cranberry To Clear, Crosscut Diamond, 2 Piece, 13 3/4 x 14 In. .... *ILLUS* 10000.00
Punch Bowl, Flashed Hobstar, Nailhead Vesica & Fan, Meridan, 13 x 14 In. 800.00
Punch Bowl, Hobstar, Strawberry Diamond, Cane & Split Vesica, 13 1/2 x 14 In. 1000.00
Punch Bowl, Hobstar, Strawberry Diamond, Nailhead Diamond & Fan, 7 x 14 In. 275.00
Punch Bowl, Hobstar, Strawberry Diamond, Vesica & Geometric, 13 x 13 1/2 In. 900.00
Punch Bowl, Large Hobstar, Crosshatch, Cane & Star, 7 x 16 In. 825.00
Punch Bowl, Large Hobstars, Crosscut Diamonds & Fans, 7 1/2 x 14 In. 990.00
Punch Bowl, Marlboro Fan, Dorflinger, 13 3/4 In. 345.00
Punch Bowl, Palmetto, Notched Edge, Clark, 7 x 14 In. 2090.00
Punch Bowl, Propeller, Harvard, Hobstar & Split Vesica, 13 1/2 x 11 In. 600.00
Punch Bowl, Shooting Star, Hobstar, Crosshatch, Fans, Notched Scalloped Edge, 7 x 14 In. 440.00
Punch Bowl, Strawberry Diamond, Fan, 12 x 5 3/4 In. 115.00
Punch Bowl, Strawberry Diamond, Hobstars, Prism, Cane & Gothic Arch, 7 1/2 x 14 In. 600.00

Punch Bowl & Stand, Hobstar & Feathered Arch, 1900, 14 In. 2070.00
Punch Cup, Stylized Hobstar & Vertical Cane, Hobstar Base, 3 1/2 In., 9 Piece 850.00
Rose Bowl, 16-Point Hobstar Base, Wood Wheel Finish, c.1890, 8 x 6 In. 695.00
Rose Bowl, Cranberry To Clear, Croesus, J. Hoare, 6 In. 385.00
Rose Bowl, Crosshatch & Fan, Star Cut Base, 8 In. 29.00
Rose Bowl, Hobstar, Strawberry Diamond & Fan, 7 In. 440.00
Rose Bowl, Sunburst, Hobstars, Fine & Fan, 7 In. 578.00
Rose Globe, Interlaced Buzz & Hobstar, Brilliant, Early 1900s, 9 In. 2820.00
Shade, Ball, Allover Cane, 4 3/4 x 9 1/2 In. 58.00
Sugar & Creamer, Canes 55.00
Sugar & Creamer, Cover, Engraved 5-Petal Flower 100.00
Sugar & Creamer, Hobstar, File & Fan, Triple Notched Handles 83.00
Sugar & Creamer, Hobstar, Vesica & Fan, Rayed Base 55.00
Sugar Shaker, Cranberry, Paneled, Victorian, c.1900, 5 1/2 In. 145.00
Sweetmeat Set, Cranberry To Clear, Silver Plated Holder, 5 In. 110.00
Tazza, Starbursts, Shallow Bowl, Brilliant, c.1900, 9 x 7 In. 70.00
Tray, Bangor, 8 Hobstar Vesicas, Prisms, 15 1/2 In. ....*ILLUS* 16000.00
Tray, Expanding Star, Hobstar, 1 1/2 x 11 1/2 In. 2575.00
Tray, Hobstar Clusters, Ray Cut Center, 13 1/2 x 9 In. 350.00
Tray, Hobstar Vesicas, Diamond Crab Claws, Buttons, 14 1/2 In. ....*ILLUS* 10000.00
Tray, Hobstar, File, Star & Fan, Rectangular, Tab Handles, 13 1/2 In. 248.00
Tray, Hobstar, Nailhead Vesica, Clusters, Fans, Diamond Shape, 16 x 9 In. 275.00
Tray, Ice Cream, Expanding Stars, 14 In. 85.00
Tray, Ice Cream, Geometric, Hobstar, Strawberry Diamond, Star & Fan, 15 x 10 1/2 In. 475.00
Tray, Ice Cream, Hobstar, Cane & Fan, 13 1/2 x 8 1/2 In. 300.00
Tray, Ice Cream, Hobstar, Cane & Strawberry Diamond Vesica, 14 x 7 1/2 In. 125.00
Tray, Ice Cream, Hobstar, Vesica, Cane, Strawberry Diamond, Fan, Tab Handles, 14 x 9 In. 275.00
Tray, Ice Cream, Marlboro, Dorflinger, 15 x 11 In. 825.00
Tray, Ice Cream, Princeton, Empire, 13 1/2 x 8 1/2 In. 1250.00
Tray, Ice Cream, Russian Pattern, Brilliant, American, c.1915, 14 x 8 In. 146.00
Tray, Pastry, Hobstar, Cane Vesica, Strawberry Diamond & Stars, 11 1/2 x 7 1/2 In. 165.00
Tumbler, Pokal Style, Engraved Woodland & Castle Scene, 1880s, 15 In. 440.00
Tumbler, Thumbprint, Blue To Clear, 1900s, 4 1/2 In. 69.00
Tumbler Set, Juice, Block Diamond Handle, Dorflinger, 3 In., 4 Piece 10.00
Vase, 28-Point Hobstar, 22 1/4 x 9 In. 2175.00
Vase, Alhambra, Greek Key, Pinched Waist, 14 In. 2310.00
Vase, Alhambra, Pinched Waist, 12 In. 990.00
Vase, Ball, Violet, Hobstar & Crosscut Diamond, Pedestal, Hobstar Foot, 7 In. 110.00
Vase, Ball, Violet, Hobstar & Notched Fan, Hobstar Base, Pedestal, 7 3/4 In., Pair 200.00
Vase, Blue To Clear, Bull's-Eye, Baluster, 14 1/2 In. 200.00
Vase, Emerald Green To Clear, Cane, Hobstar, Diamond & Fan, Pedestal, 6 1/2 In. 175.00
Vase, Engraved Laurel Leaf, Eagle, Optic Ribbed, Gold, 1804-15, France, 18 x 6 1/2 In. 264.00
Vase, Engraved Poppy, Pedestal, 8 1/2 In. 175.00
Vase, Fan, Engraved Rococo Duck, Sterling Silver Foot, 12 1/4 In. 330.00
Vase, Flower Center, Hobstar, Crosshatch, Hobnail & Fan, Notched Neck, 7 1/2 x 9 1/2 In. 330.00
Vase, Geometric, 16-Point Fanned Hobstar Foot, Ruffled Edge, Tuthill, 9 x 5 1/4 In. 775.00
Vase, Green To Clear, Bulbous, Flared Rim, Hollow Blown Pedestal Stem, 9 1/2 x 6 1/2 In. 52.00
Vase, Green To Clear, Bull's-Eye, Notch & Honeycomb, Silver Rim, Footed, 13 In. 990.00
Vase, Hat Shape, Vintage, Ruffled Edge, Tuthill, 7 x 10 In. 770.00
Vase, Hobstar Columns, Prism, Strawberry Diamond & Fan, Pedestal, 12 In. 650.00
Vase, Hobstar, File & Fan, Bull's-Eye & Prism Neck, Flared Rim, 10 In. 495.00
Vase, Hobstar, Pinwheel, Block, Strawberry Diamond & Fan, Bulbous, 10 In. 475.00
Vase, Hobstar, Strawberry Diamond & Fan, Hobstar Chain, Flared, Pinched Waist, 12 In. 100.00
Vase, Hobstar, Strawberry Diamond & Prism, Baluster, 11 1/2 In. 225.00
Vase, Hobstar, Strawberry Diamond, Cane & Star, Tazza Shape, 7 1/2 x 8 In. 375.00
Vase, Hobstar, Strawberry Diamond, Nailhead Diamond, Baluster, 12 In. 750.00
Vase, Hobstar, Strawberry Diamond, Prism & Fan, Baluster, 14 In. 1018.00
Vase, Hobstars With Prism, Bull's-Eye, Strawberry Diamond & Fan, Bowling Pin Shape, 15 1/2 In. . 1320.00
Vase, Hobstars, Strawberry Diamond & Fan, Step Cut Body, 14 In. 800.00
Vase, Intaglio Cut, Engraved, Water Lily, Ribbed, Baluster, c.1885, 19 1/2 In. 998.00
Vase, Intaglio Duck, Flowers, Buds, Leaves, Brass Foot, 9 1/2 In. 3450.00

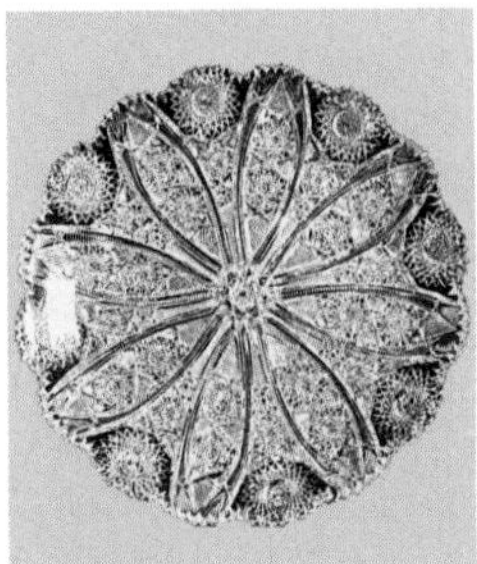
Cut Glass, Tray, Bangor, 8 Hobstar Vesicas, Prisms, 15 1/2 In.

Cut Glass, Tray, Hobstar Vesicas, Diamond Crab Claws, Buttons, 14 1/2 In.

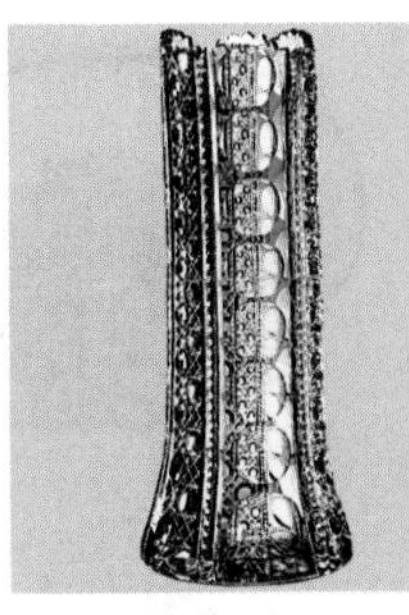
Cut Glass, Vase, Montrose, Cranberry To Clear, Prism, Punty, 10 1/4 In.

Vase, Montrose, Cranberry To Clear, Prism, Punty, 10 1/4 In. .... *ILLUS* 1750.00
Vase, Pinched Waist, Hobstar & Button Chains, Engraved Floral, 12 In. 175.00
Vase, Pinched Waist, Hobstar, Crosshatch, Zipper & Fan, 15 In. 300.00
Vase, Pinched Waist, Hobstar, Strawberry Diamond, Prism & Fan, 14 In. 125.00
Vase, Thumbprint & Zippered Rib, Early 1900s, 10 In. 115.00
Vase, Trumpet, Amethyst To Clear, Harvard Variant, 14 In. 880.00
Vase, Trumpet, Flashed Hobstar, Strawberry Diamond & Fan, 14 In. 140.00
Vase, Trumpet, Green To Clear, Crosscut Diamond, Strawberry Diamond, 12 In. 425.00
Vase, Trumpet, Hobstar, Cane, Bull's-Eye & Fan, Hobstar Base, Tricornered Rim, 12 1/2 In. 250.00
Vase, Trumpet, Russian Pattern, Clear-Cut Buttons, 9 1/2 In. 220.00
Vase, Trumpet, Strawberry Diamond, Fan, Star-Cut Base, 13 3/4 In. 85.00
Vase, Tulip, Bull's-Eye & Prism, 13 3/4 In. 120.00
Vase, Tulip, Harvard, Hobstar & Strawberry Diamond, Knop Stem, 13 1/2 In. 400.00
Vase, Tulip, Heavy Hobstar, Crosshatch, Prism & Fan, Hobstar Base, 14 In. 770.00
Vase, Tulip, Sunburst, Faceted Knob Stem, Scalloped Hobstar Base, 14 1/2 In. 880.00
Vase, Vertical Hobstar Chains, Prism, Strawberry Diamond & Panel, Pedestal, 12 In. 275.00
Vase, Vintage, Intaglio, Tazza Shape, Tuthill, 6 3/4 x 10 In. 180.00
Vase, Violet, Hobstar & Fan, Fan Base, 5 In. 193.00
Vase, Wild Rose, Intaglio, Corseted, Tuthill, 10 In. 660.00
Whiskey Set, Electra, Straus, 9 Piece 200.00
Wine, Cranberry To Clear, Bouquet Drapery, 1910, 9 In. 395.00
Wine, Cranberry To Clear, Crosscut Diamond & Fan, Notched Stem, 4 1/2 In. 220.00
Wine, Cranberry To Clear, Heart, 5 1/2 In. 50.00
Wine, Rhine, Amethyst To Clear, European, 8 In., 4 Piece 75.00
Wine, Russian, Elongated Teardrop Stem, 5 In., 4 Piece 305.00

CYBIS porcelain is a twentieth-century product. Boleslaw Cybis came to the United States from Poland in 1939. He started making porcelains in Long Island, New York, in 1940. He moved to Trenton, New Jersey, in 1942 as one of the founders of Cordey China Co. and started his own Cybis Porcelains about 1950. The firm is still working. See also Cordey.

Bust, God Of Love, Greek Mythology, 9 1/2 In. 590.00
Bust, Victoria, 10 In. 395.00
Figurine, Bunny, Mr. Snowball, 3 1/4 x 4 1/2 In. 100.00
Figurine, Eleanor Of Aquitaine, Katharine Hepburn, 1970s, 13 3/4 In. 2000.00
Figurine, First Flight, 1966, 4 1/2 In. 100.00
Figurine, Madonna With Bird, 1956, 11 1/2 In. 560.00
Figurine, Pheasant, Bisque, Late 1900s, 15 1/2 x 20 In. 468.00
Figurine, Skylark, 6 1/8 In. 420.00
Figurine, Squirrel, Mr. Fluffy Tail, 1965-71, 8 In. 285.00
Figurine, Vireo Building Nest, 7 3/4 In. 740.00
Figurine, Walrus, 4 1/8 In. 95.00

Don't use rubber gloves when washing figurines with protruding arms and legs. The gloves may snag and cause damage.

Czechoslovakia Glass, Lamp, Electric, Fruit Basket, Beaded, 9 1/2 In.

CZECHOSLOVAKIA is a popular term with collectors. The name, first used as a mark after the country was formed in 1918, appears on glass and porcelain and other decorative items. Although Czechoslovakia split into Slovakia and the Czech Republic on January 1, 1993, the name continues to be used in some trademarks.

CZECHOSLOVAKIA GLASS, Dresser Set, Clear Bottles, Blue Stoppers, Dabbers, Tray, 3 In., 3 Piece 460.00
Dresser Set, Clear Bottles, Pink Stoppers, Dabber, Black Tray, 3 Piece 289.00
Dresser Set, Molded Elephants & Flowers, Brown Stain, 7 Piece 5175.00
Lamp, Electric, Fruit Basket, Beaded, 9 1/2 In. .... *ILLUS* 538.00
Lustres, Cranberry, Enameled, c.1930, 12 x 6 In., Pair 410.00
Perfume Bottle, Amber, Hexagonal, Stopper, Dabber, 4 1/2 In. 69.00
Perfume Bottle, Atomizer, Elephant Head, Enameled, 1920s, 4 5/8 In. 720.00
Perfume Bottle, Black, Clear Crystal, Stopper, Silver Neck Mount, Hoffman, 1920s, 7 3/4 In. 3240.00
Perfume Bottle, Black, Clear Intaglio Stopper, Leda & Swan, Pearls, Green Jewels, 6 1/4 In. 1150.00
Perfume Bottle, Black, Clear, Jeweled Metalwork, Hoffman, 1920s, 6 In. 1920.00
Perfume Bottle, Black, Frosted Clear Stopper, Abstract, Dabber, 5 In. 115.00
Perfume Bottle, Black, Frosted Stopper, Molded Nude Dancers, Dabber, Hoffman, 7 1/4 In. 4600.00
Perfume Bottle, Black, Jade, Enameled Holder Set, Black Feet, Dabber, Hoffman, 1920s, 4 1/4 In. 1920.00
Perfume Bottle, Black, Pink Stopper, Enameled Bib, Dabber, 1920s, 4 1/2 In. 180.00
Perfume Bottle, Blue, Clear Intaglio Stopper, Woman Strewing Flowers, Dabber, 5 1/2 In. 805.00
Perfume Bottle, Blue, Intaglio Stopper, Geometric, Dabber, 4 1/2 In. 127.00
Perfume Bottle, Blue, Intaglio Stopper, Woman Fanning, 9 1/2 In. 1510.00
Perfume Bottle, Blue, Jeweled Metalwork, Stopper, 1920s, 4 1/2 In. 780.00
Perfume Bottle, Blue, Stopper, Geometric, 9 3/4 In. 288.00
Perfume Bottle, Bow Shape, Pink Stopper, 1920s, 4 1/2 In. 660.00
Perfume Bottle, Butterfly, Pink, Clear, Jeweled Metalwork, Stopper, 1920s, 2 1/2 In. 330.00
Perfume Bottle, Clear, Art Deco Woman, Intaglio Stopper, Green Jewels, Dabber, Signed, 6 1/2 In. 978.00
Perfume Bottle, Clear, Blue Intaglio Stopper, Tiara, Bluebells, Dabber, 5 1/4 In. 160.00
Perfume Bottle, Clear, Brass Filigree Stopper, Jewels, 5 3/4 In. 110.00
Perfume Bottle, Clear, Dabber, Intaglio Mark, Hoffman, 1920s, 5 1/4 In. 120.00
Perfume Bottle, Clear, Frosted Blue Stopper, Enameled, Jewels, Dabber, 1920s, 7 1/4 In. 1200.00
Perfume Bottle, Clear, Intaglio Stopper, Flower Bouquet In Vase, 5 1/2 In. 184.00
Perfume Bottle, Clear, Intaglio Stopper, Lily-Of-The-Valley, Dabber, 5 In. 115.00
Perfume Bottle, Clear, Molded Stopper, Lady Godiva On Horseback, 6 1/2 In. 2990.00
Perfume Bottle, Clear, Red Intaglio Stopper, Roses, Dabber, 5 1/4 In. 230.00
Perfume Bottle, Cranberry, Mary Gregory Type, Enamel, Gold Ring, Stopper, c.1950, 5 3/4 In. 95.00
Perfume Bottle, Dabber, Screw Lid, 2 1/8 x 1 9/16 In. 125.00
Perfume Bottle, Elephant, Malachite Stopper, Chiseled Finish, Hoffman, 1920s, 5 In. 2240.00
Perfume Bottle, Green Crystal, Jeweled Metalwork, Hoffman, 1920s, 5 1/2 In. 1560.00
Perfume Bottle, Ingrid, Bird Shape, Clear, Frosted, Stopper, Dabber, Hoffman, 1920s, 6 3/4 In. .. 570.00
Perfume Bottle, Irice, Clear, Green, 1920s, 4 In. 570.00
Perfume Bottle, Pale Blue, Hobstar-Cut Disc Stopper, 5 5/8 In. 154.00
Perfume Bottle, Pink, Metalwork, Pearls, Intaglio Stopper, Nude Woman, 8 1/2 In. 1610.00
Perfume Bottle, Pink, Step Cut Stopper, Pink Jewels, 3 In. 374.00

Perfume Bottle, Scimitar Shape, Clear Stopper, Dabber, 6 3/4 In. 115.00
Perfume Bottle, Smoke, Amethyst Intaglio Stopper, Archer, Geese, 4 In. 920.00
Perfume Bottle, Smoke, Molded, Stopper, Flowers, 5 1/4 In. 140.00
Perfume Bottle, Violet, Clear Intaglio Stopper, 2 Dancers, 5 1/2 In. 92.00
Perfume Bottle, Violet, Molded Stopper, Flower, Butterfly Shape, 4 1/2 In. 115.00
Perfume Bottle, Violet, Stopper, Dancer, Abstract, 4 3/4 In. 104.00
Perfume Bottle, Yellow, Clear Intaglio Stopper, Nymph, Flowers, 6 3/4 In. 748.00
Powder Dish, Cover, Clear Molded, Nude Venus, Kneeling Among Fish, 6 1/4 In. 2760.00
Ring Dish, Frosted Clear, Woman Holding Dish On Head, 3 In. 405.00
Vase, Marquetry, Green, Yellow, Blue, Frosted Ground, 9 1/2 In. 460.00
Vase, Marquetry, Stylized Leaves, Orange To Cream Ground, 9 In. 115.00
Vase, Mottled Yellow Ground, Applied Blue Leaf, Branch, 11 1/8 In. 230.00
CZECHOSLOVAKIA POTTERY, Bowl, Ribbed, Berries, Leaves, Stoneware, 1920s, 12 1/2 In. 170.00
Bust, Head Of Woman, Flowers In Hair, Circular Base, 1950s, 13 1/2 In. 245.00
Creamer, Figural, Moose 13.00

D'ARGENTAL is a mark used in France by the Compagnie des Cristalleries de St. Louis. The firm made multilayered, acid-cut cameo glass in the late nineteenth and twentieth centuries. D'Argental is the French name for the city of Munzthal, home of the glassworks. Later they made enameled etched glass.

Jar, Cover, Vines, Flowers, Red Overlay, Yellow Ground, c.1900, 3 1/4 x 3 1/5 In. 598.00
Vase, Berries & Leaves, Russet, Citron Ground, Bulbous Neck, 5 In. 748.00
Vase, Berries, Leaves, Frosted To Brown Ground, 9 1/2 In. 764.00
Vase, Landscape, Trees, Fields, Grasses, Amber, 7 1/2 In. 1190.00
Vase, Leaves, Earth Tones, Camphor Ground, Bulbous, 11 5/8 In. 1180.00
Vase, Lilac, Green, Flowers, Stems, Leaves, Frosted Ground, Signed, 12 3/4 In. 635.00
Vase, Orange, Brown, Flowers, Leaves, Stems, Frosted Yellow Ground, 12 1/4 In. 2245.00
Vase, Plum Tree Branches, Brown, Orange, Oval, c.1930, 12 1/4 In. 1912.00
Vase, Translucent Amber, Leaves, Vines, Flowers, Frosted Ground, 17 In. 2040.00

DANIEL BOONE, a pre–Revolutionary War folk hero, was a surveyor, trapper, and frontiersman. A television series, which ran from 1964 to 1970, was based on his life and starred Fess Parker. All types of Daniel Boone memorabilia are collected.

Book, Daniel Boone, Little Golden, 1st Edition, 1956 .... 10.50
Bottle, Boone Cola, A Boon To Health, Red & White ACL, Spencer, N.C., 7 Oz. 8.85
Card, Indian Chewing Gum, No. 50, 1933 .... 24.00
Card, Pioneer, Look 'N See, No. 55, Topps, 1952 .... 13.00
Figure, Accessories, No. 2060, Marx, Box, 1964, 11 In. 108.00
Film, Return Of Daniel Boone, Bill Elliott, 1941, 16 mm 27.00
Game, Fess Parker's Trail Blazers, Daniel Boone TV Show, Milton Bradley, Box 91.00
Game, Fess Parker, Daniel Boone Wilderness Trail Card Game, Transogram, 1960s 10.00
Knife, Bowie, Brass Guard, Sheath, Case Co., Box, 14 In. 133.00
Knife, Bowie, Family Crest, Stainless Steel Blade, Leather Sheath, Box, 14 In. 128.00
Lunch Box, Metal, Red Trim, Bottle, King-Seeley, 1965, 8 1/2 x 7 x 4 In. .... 50.00 to 60.00
Lunch Box, Metal, Red Trim, No Thermos, King-Seeley, 1965, 8 1/2 x 7 x 4 In. .... 26.00 to 43.00
Lunch Box, Metal, Yellow Trim, Handle, No Thermos, Aladdin, 1965 .... 45.00 to 57.00
PEZ Dispenser, Green Stem, No Feet Version 128.00
Toy, Canoe, Inflatable, Fess Parker's, Indian Head, Unopened, Multiple International, 1965 .... 31.00

DAUM, a glassworks in Nancy, France, was started by Jean Daum in 1875. The company, now called *Cristalleries de Nancy*, is still working. The *Daum Nancy* mark has been used in many variations. The name of the city and the artist are usually both included.

Bottle, Trees, Frosted Ground, Gold Trim, Silver Mounted Ball Stopper, 5 1/4 In., Pair 3880.00
Bowl, Amber Shaded To Orange, Gold Aventurine, Optic Ribbed, Tricornered Ruffled Rim, 8 1/2 In. 230.00
Bowl, Aspen Leaf, Mottled Citron Yellow, Burnt Orange, Cameo, c.1915, 5 3/8 x 10 1/4 In. 1292.00
Bowl, Centerpiece, Green Vine & Leaves, Amethyst Ground, Martele, Oval, Footed, 3 1/2 x 12 In. .. 6325.00
Bowl, Lake, Trees, Yellow, Crimson, Mottled, Cameo, 5 In. 575.00
Bowl, Persimmons, Leaves, Orange, Yellow, Green, Square, Quatrefoil Rim, c.1900, 7 3/4 In. 1795.00
Bowl, Trees, Lake, Oval, 8-Sided, c.1910, 6 1/4 In. 810.00

Bowl, Tulips, Green, Peach, Opalescent White Ground, Cameo, c.1885, 2 1/2 x 4 1/4 In. 1880.00
Bowl, Violets, Green Stems, Leaves, Orange, Green Shading To White, Enameled, 3 1/4 In. 330.00
Box, Cover, Purple, Gold Foil, Applied Ladybug Cabochon, Square, 5 1/2 x 3 In. 1725.00
Box, Dome Lid, Flowers, Leaves, Straight Sides, Cupped Rim, c.1900, 5 1/2 In. 1016.00
Box, Flowers, Enameled Leaves, Amber Mottled Ground, Cameo, Sterling Silver Cover, 3 In. 518.00
Compote, Landscape, Fall, Blue, Yellow & Red, Orange, Boat Shape, Scalloped Rim, 5 In. 2575.00
Creamer, Blossoms, Dragonfly, Leaves, Enameled, Opalescent, Pedestal Foot, Cameo, 4 1/2 In. 5060.00
Cruet, Green, Gold Mistletoe, Frosted Loop Handle, Disc Stopper, Cross Of Lorraine, 6 In. 1265.00
Inkwell, Applied Spider On Cover, Spider Web, 2 Beetles, Glass Insert, 4 3/4 x 3 1/2 In. 6615.00
Jar, Flowers, Leaves, Frosted Ground, Stopper, Cameo, Embossed Metal Cover, 5 In. 1150.00
Lamp, Flowers, Leaves, Ribbed Column, Gourd Shape, Greek Key Foot, Arrows, 32 In. 2588.00
Pitcher, Cranberry, Raised & Gilt Iris, Leaves, Oval, Cameo, Silver Mount, Hinged Lid, 4 1/2 In. 1165.00
Powder Jar, Strawberries, Leaves, Cranberry Over Clear, Metal Embossed Hinged Cover, 5 In. 540.00
Scent Bottle, Enameled Flowers, Vine, Leaves, Village Scene, Stopper, Cameo, 3 1/4 In. 2185.00
Scent Bottle, Pink, Padded, Carved Roses, Brown Stems, Leaves, Cream Ground, 5 1/2 In. 4900.00
Sconce, Marmorean Glass Shade, Gold Inclusions, Iron, 17 1/4 x 11 In., Pair 4956.00
Shade, Curving Vertical Lines, Cobalt Blue, Pink, Flared, c.1900, 15 1/2 In. 660.00
Tray, Leaves, Berries, Orange, Yellow, Red, Brown, Square, Quatrefoil Rim, c.1900, 7 1/2 In. 2390.00
Tumbler, Amethyst To Yellow, Flowers, Spider Web, Barrel Shape, Cameo, 4 3/4 In. 1610.00
Tumbler, Flowers, Rows, Textured Ground, Gold Enameled Border, 4 3/4 In. 978.00
Vase, Amber, Crosshatch, Beaded Bands, Flared, Etched, c.1930, 4 1/2 In. 360.00
Vase, Amethyst To Blue, Mottle, Peacock Feathers, Oval, 6 In. 3740.00
Vase, Amethyst, Foxgloves, Mottled Yellow Ground, Cameo, Signed, 21 1/2 In. 2875.00
Vase, Applied Cranberry Tendrils, Bubbles, Neck Threads, Urn Shape, c.1900, 6 1/4 In. 809.00
Vase, Aventurine, Anthemia, Amber, Etched, Goblet Shape, c.1930, 6 1/2 In. 570.00
Vase, Ball, Ribbed Body, Gold Enameled Embossed Cartouche, Ruffled Edge, 5 1/2 In. 288.00
Vase, Birch Trees, Blue Ground, Pillow Shape, 1 5/8 In. 60.00
Vase, Blue Stylized Flowers, Urn Shape, Cameo, c.1900, 6 3/4 In. 934.00
Vase, Bubbles, Brown Inclusions, 4 Applied Flowers, Baluster, 9 3/4 In. 1699.00
Vase, Cloves, Blossoms, Green, Pink, Tricornered Rim, Cameo, Signed, 14 In. 3450.00
Vase, Cranberry Flowers, Leaves, Gold Enamel, Chipped Ice Ground, 4-Sided, Cameo, 7 In. 635.00
Vase, Cylindrical, Undulating Striations, Stylized Flowers, c.1900, 12 In. 1315.00
Vase, Daisies, Blue, Martele Ground, Pinched Stem, Footed, Cameo, Signed, 9 In. 6900.00
Vase, Enameled Leaves, Berries, Decorated Ground, 4-Sided, Cameo, Signed, 4 3/4 In. 1140.00
Vase, Flowers, Leaves, Amethyst & White, Fire Polished, Martele, Signed, 5 1/4 In. 5750.00
Vase, Flowers, Mottled Yellow, Brown, Green, Cameo, 18 1/4 In. 8225.00
Vase, Flowers, Red, Leaves, Stems, Gold Enameled, Blue Opalescent Ground, Cameo, 20 In. 3510.00
Vase, Flowers, Stems, Leaves, Mottled Amber, Enameled, Yellow Ground, Cameo, 13 In. 5750.00
Vase, Geometric, Mottled Green, Yellow, Pink, Green Handles, Art Deco, Cameo, 14 1/2 In. 863.00
Vase, Gold Speckled, Metal Foil Inclusions, Green, Gray, Internal Decoration, 1925, 23 In. 1163.00
Vase, Grapes, Leaves, Vines, Flared Baluster, Cushion Foot, Knob Stem, c.1890, 15 1/2 In. 2739.00
Vase, Green Peacock Feathers, Padded Centers, Blue Ground, Cameo, Signed, 5 1/2 In. 4900.00
Vase, Landscape, Brown, Green, Yellow Ground, Squat, Cameo, 3 1/2 In. 470.00
Vase, Landscape, Trees, Grasses, Green, Purple, White, Knobbed Stem, Footed, c.1900, 8 3/4 In. . 3346.00
Vase, Landscape, Trees, Lake, Mottled Yellow & Russet Ground, Footed, Signed, 5 1/2 In. 805.00
Vase, Landscape, Trees, Water, Autumn Colors, Cameo, 1905, 24 In. 4024.00
Vase, Landscape, Winter, Enameled Trees, Snowy, Mottled Orange, Yellow Ground, 2 1/2 In. 460.00
Vase, Landscape, Winter, Mottled Orange To Yellow, Oval, Pulled Flared Rim, 5 x 14 In. 12650.00
Vase, Landscape, Winter, Mountain, Stream, Bulbous, Flared Notches, Rim, 9 3/4 In. 7765.00
Vase, Leaves, Thorny Stems, Enameled, Opalescent Ground, Tricornered Rim, Cameo, 12 In. 2300.00
Vase, Lily Of The Valley, Gold Enameled Rim, Cameo, Square, 4 3/4 x 2 In. 750.00
Vase, Lion, Clover, Fleur-De-Lis, Gold Enameled, Shouldered, Cameo, 10 In. 690.00
Vase, Mottled Brown To Yellow, Burnt Orange, 8 Tapered Panels, Flared Rim, 10 1/4 In. 390.00
Vase, Orange Berries, Leaves, Mottled Green To Yellow Ground, Footed, Cameo, Signed, 12 In. 5175.00
Vase, Poppy, Bud, Orange, Stems, Leaves, Cameo, 5 In. 7475.00
Vase, Red Tomatoes, Green Leaves, Vines, Cameo, 19 1/2 In. 5185.00
Vase, Rose Branch, Orange, Red, Thorny Branches, Cameo, 13 In. 2875.00
Vase, Rose Hips, Thorny Branches, Red, Yellow, Green, Cameo, 10 1/2 In. 1035.00
Vase, Spider Web & Bees, Violet Blossoms, Gray, Amber & Yellow, 1900, 15 In. 2530.00
Vase, Stylized Flowers, Leaves, Swirled Ground, Applied Cabochon Centers, Cameo, 15 3/4 In. ... 2013.00
Vase, Swirls, Tangerine, Translucent, Baluster, c.1900, 12 1/4 In. 1435.00

Vase, Thistle, Flowers, Thorny Stems, Leaves, Enameled, Frosted Ground, Signed, 4 1/2 In. 690.00
Vase, Trumpet, Flower Bands, Gold Flecks, Footed, Cameo, Footed, Cameo, c.1900, 7 In. 657.00
Vase, Trumpet, Mottled Blue, Yellow, Cascading Flowers, Knopped Neck, Footed, Cameo, 19 In. ... 5175.00
Vase, White Flowers, Frosted To Mottled Green Ground, Footed, Cameo, Signed, 13 In. 6325.00
Vase, Yellow Blossoms, Enameled Brown Leaves, Mottled Ground, Cameo, 5 3/4 In. 1785.00
Vase, Yellow Poppies, Padded, Green Stems, Leaves, Mottled Ground, Signed, 12 In. 4255.00
Wall Pocket, Orchids, Leaves, Mottled Green Ground, Applied Tendrils, Cameo, 10 1/2 In. 5175.00

DAVENPORT pottery and porcelain were made at the Davenport factory in Longport, Staffordshire, England, from 1793 to 1887. Earthenwares, creamwares, porcelains, ironstone, and other ceramics were made. Most of the pieces are marked with a form of the word *Davenport*.

Cup & Saucer, Genoa Pattern, 16-Panel Saucer, 1840-60 .... 59.00
Jug, Franklin Flying Kite, Purple Transferware, c.1835, 10 In. 425.00
Jug, Hunting, Baluster, Squat, 7 x 9 In. 295.00
Jug, Jardinaire Pattern, Ironstone, Peach Luster Rim, 1805-20, 5 1/2 In. 450.00
Jug, Jardinaire Pattern, Ironstone, Peach Luster Rim, 1805-20, 7 1/2 In. 850.00
Plate, Cambridge, Scalloped, 10-Sided, Ironstone, White, c.1852, 7 1/4 In. 50.00
Plate, Cyprus Pattern, 12 Panels, Ironstone, 1820-50, 9 1/4 In. 49.00
Plate, Floral Pattern, 5-Color Transferware, c.1835, 10 In. 325.00
Plate, Imari Pattern, Orange, Blue, Purple, Gold, c.1825, 8 In. 165.00
Plate, Landscape, Blue, White, Transferware, c.1850, 10 1/4 In. 75.00
Plate, Villagers, Blue Transferware, c.1820, 9 3/4 In. 350.00
Plate Set, Rural Scenes, Blue, White, Gold Highlights, 8 1/2 In., 6 Piece 415.00
Platter, Alpine Amusements, Purple Transferware, c.1835, 14 1/2 In. 525.00
Platter, Chinese Pastime, Blue Transferware, 1820-60, 17 x 14 In. 725.00
Relish, Cyprus Pattern, Mulberry Transferware, c.1845, 9 3/8 x 5 3/8 In. 95.00
Soup, Dish, Muleteer Pattern, 3-Color Transferware, 1835, 10 1/4 In. 275.00
Soup, Dish, Villagers, Transferware, c.1850, 10 In. 250.00
Tureen, Sauce, Cover, Flow Blue, 5 1/2 x 7 1/2 x 4 1/2 In. 489.00
Waste Bowl, Cyprus Pattern, c.1845, 3 1/2 x 5 1/2 In. 95.00

DAVY CROCKETT, the American frontiersman, was born in 1786 and died in 1836. The historical character gained new fame in 1954 when the Walt Disney television show ran a series of episodes featuring Fess Parker as Davy Crockett. Coonskin caps and buckskins became popular and hundreds of different Davy Crockett items were made.

Bank, Dime Register, Metal, Press-Down Trap, Square, 2 5/8 In. 138.00
Cap Gun, Die Cast, Nickel Finish, White Horsehead Grips, Leslie-Henry, 8 1/2 In. 151.00
Cap Gun, Single Shot, 2 Position Safety, Horse Head Grips, Leslie-Henry, 7 3/4 In. 214.00
Caps, Giant Pack Of Roll Caps, Halco Brand, Box, 4 x 5 In., 60 Rolls, 3000 Shots 56.00
Cup, Famous Frontiersman, Milk Glass, Red Graphics, 1786-1836, 3 In. 17.00
Doll, Ginny, Davy Crockett Outfit, Straight Legs, Wig, Rifle, Patch, Vogue, 1955 .... 358.00
Knife, Pocket, Spear Blade, Can Opener, Screwdriver, Celluloid Handles, 3 1/2 In. 25.41
Lunch Box, Tin Lithograph, Holtemp, American Thermos Co., 1955 .... 35.00
Movie Poster, Walt Disney's Davy Crockett, First Release, 1955, 1 Sheet 679.00
Pail, Red Ground, White Interior, Flat Blue Handle, Tin, Ohio Art, 1955, 8 In. 110.00
Play Set, Davy Crockett At Alamo, Unassembled, Louis Marx, Box, 1955 .... 966.00
Play Suit, Box, 1955 .... 416.00
Toy, Knife & Gun, Plastic, Brown, On Card, Multiple Prod., N.Y. 26.00
Wristwatch, Powder Horn Stand, Ingersoll, U.S. Time, Box, c.1955 ....303.00 to 493.00

DE VEZ was a signature used on cameo glass after 1910. E. S. Monot founded the glass company near Paris in 1851. The company changed names many times. Mt. Joye, another glass by this factory, is listed in its own category.

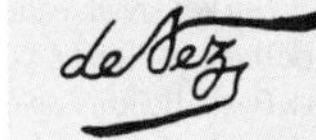

Jar, Cover, Bulbous, Rust, Grapevines, Yellow, c.1910, 4 1/2 In. 715.00
Perfume Bottle, Cameo Glass, Mountains, Yellow, Orange, Citrine, 6 In. 1350.00
Vase, Birds, Lake, Mountains, Blue, Pink, c.1900, 12 In. 1195.00
Vase, Bottle Shape, Frosted Ground, Amethyst Leaves, 1 1/4 In. 175.00
Vase, Brown Flowers, Leaves, Yellow Ground, Bulbous, Tapering Neck, c.1900, 6 In. 390.00

Vase, Enameled, Green, Wolf, Lamb, 8 1/4 In. 635.00
Vase, Frosted, Amethyst Berries, Leaves, Double Corseted, Cameo, Signed, 1 1/4 In. 180.00
Vase, Green, Butterflies, Flowers, Vertical Ribs, Amber, 7 3/4 In. 1200.00
Vase, Mountain Village, Cobalt Blue, Terra-Cotta Red, Opal Sky, 7 1/2 In. 290.00
Vase, Mountains, Trees, Lake, Green, Amber, Early 1900s, 4 1/2 In. 1400.00
Vase, Trees, Sailboats, Lake, Mountains, Elongated Oval, Footed, c.1910, 16 In. 1910.00
Vase, Trees, Water, Mountains, Red, Black, Frosted Ground, 3 1/2 In. 420.00

DECORATED TUMBLERS have been made by Anchor Hocking, Federal, Hazel Atlas, Libbey, and other companies since the 1930s, when the pyroglaze process of printing was introduced. The barware and other glasses feature drinking jokes, characters, or decorative geometric patterns. Swankyswigs are listed in their own category. Decorated tumblers may also be listed in Advertising, Coca-Cola, Pepsi-Cola, and many other categories.

Arby's, B.C. Ice Age, Woman, With Club, Snake, 1981, 5 1/4 In. 6.00
Arby's, Farm In Winter, Horse & Sleigh, Currier & Ives, 1981, 4 5/8 In. 7.00
Arby's, Sleigh Race, Currier & Ives, 1975-76, 4 1/2 In. 7.00
Arby's, Underdog, Bicentennial, 1976, 5 1/8 In. 5.00
Arby's, Zodiac, Gemini, 1976, 16 Oz., 6 1/4 In. 7.00
Brassy & Co., Kentucky Whiskies, San Jose, Cal., Gold Rim, 2 1/8 In. 325.00
Burger King, Star Wars, 1977, 5 5/8 In., 4 Piece .... 27.00 to 51.00
Chicago Lager Beer, San Francisco, 3 1/2 In. 60.00
Dr Pepper, Be A Pepper, Red ACL, 1970s, 12 Oz. 7.00
Kentucky Derby, Frosted, Red & Green Letters, 1971, 5 1/2 In. 22.00
Mackinac Bridge, Michigan, Frosted, Hazel Atlas, 7 In. 10.00
Mazeppa Whiskey, Hilderbrandt-Posner & Co., San Francisco, Gold Rim, 2 In. 130.00
McDonald's, Garfield, Mugs, Jim Davis, 1978, 3 3/8 In., 4 Piece 15.00
McDonald's, Great Muppet Caper, 1981, 5 5/8 In., 4 Piece 13.00
McDonald's, McDonaldland Action Series, 1977, 5 5/8 In., 6 Piece 10.00
Moxie, Drink Moxie, Etched, 4 1/2 In. 40.00
Moxie, Licensed Only For Serving Moxie, Embossed, Early 1900s, 4 1/4 In. 23.00
O! So Good Rieger's Whiskey, Shot Glass, Kansas City, Mo., Shot Glass 25.00
Petty Girls, Seminude, Clothes Disappear When Filled, 1940 .... 125.00
Phoenix Bourbon, 2 1/4 In. 180.00
Pizza Hut, Care Bear, Friend Bear, 1983, 6 In. 20.00
Pizza Hut, Care Bear, Funshine Bear, 1983, 6 In. 10.00
Pizza Hut, Care Bear, Grumpy Bear, 1983, 6 In. .... 6.00 to 9.00
Pizza Hut, Care Bears, 1983, 6 In., 4 Piece .... 14.00 to 20.00
Rusthaller's Gilt Edge, Sacramento Lager, 4 1/2 In. 50.00
Tilbury Carriage, Horse, 3 1/8 In. 12.00
Welch's, Archie & Friends, Original Box, 1971, 6 Piece 90.00
Welch's, Pepe La Pew, Penelope, Looney Tune Collector's Series 2, Cover, 4 In. 10.00
Yosemite Lager, Enterprise Brewery, San Francisco, 3 1/2 In. 90.00

DECOYS are carved or turned wooden copies of birds, fish, or animals. The decoy was placed in the water or propped on the shore to lure flying birds to the pond for hunters. Some decoys are handmade; some are commercial products. Today there is a group of artists making modern decoys for display, not for use in a pond.

Black Duck, Carved, Painted, Inset Glass Eyes, Brand Mark, A. E. Crowell, Mass., 6 x 16 In. 1880.00
Black Duck, Carved, Painted, Inset Glass Eyes, Early 20th Century, 7 x 16 1/2 In. 295.00
Black Duck, Hollow Carved, Delaware River 173.00
Black Duck, Hollow Carved, Tack Eyes, Carved Back, Charles Birch, Virginia 575.00
Black Duck, Hollow, Zeke McDonald, McDonald Island, Mich., c.1900 .... 330.00
Black Duck, Premier Grade, Mason Factory, Mich., 1896-1924 .... 259.00 to 1430.00
Black Duck, Turned Head, Driftwood Base, Russ P. Burr, Hingham, Mass., Miniature 690.00
Black Duck, Weighted, Signed, Charlie Joiner, Md., c.1992, 16 In. 1120.00
Blue-Winged Teal, Herter, Minnesota, 12 1/2 In. 118.00
Blue-Winged Teal, Signed, Horace Graham, Md., c.1960, 13 & 14 In., Pair 390.00

Blue-Winged Teal Hen, Animal Trap Decoy Co. 185.00
Bluebill, Carved, Painted, Rasped Head, Breast, Glass Eyes, A.E. Crowell, Mass., 6 x 14 In. 3055.00
Bluebill Drake, Glass Eyes, Standard Grade, Mason Factory, Mich., 1896-1924 .... 185.00
Bluebill Drake, Premier Grade, Mason Factory, Mich., 1896-1924 .... 1035.00
Bluebill Drake, Turk Piepsenberger, Mich. 290.00
Bluebill Drake, Turned Head, Glass Eyes, William E. Dugan, Martha's Vineyard, Mass. 1095.00
Bluebill Hen, Challenge Grade, Repainted, Mason Factory, Mich., 1896-1924 .... 240.00
Bluebill Hen, Premier Grade, Mason Factory, Mich., c.1910 .... 1540.00
Bluebill Hen, Sam Denny, Upstate N.Y. 400.00
Bluebill Hen, Signed, Jess Urie, Md., c.1965, 13 In. 196.00
Bluebill Hen, Stevens Decoy Co., Weedsport, N.Y., 1880 .... 219.00
Bluebill Hen, William Goffingon, Chincoteague, Va., Late 1930s, 13 1/2 x 7 1/2 x 4 In. 250.00
Bufflehead, 1950s, 12 In., Pair 225.00
Bufflehead, Turned Head, Weighted, Signed, Madison Mitchell, Md., c.1971, 14 In. 450.00
Bufflehead Drake, Dan Brown, Salisbury, Md. 299.00
Bufflehead Drake, Madison Mitchell, Havre De Grace, Md. 46.00
Canada Goose, Carved Wood, Harry Shourds, Tuckerton, N.J., 1871-1920 .... 3300.00
Canada Goose, Carved, Painted, Tack Eyes, A. E. Crowell, Mass., 11 x 21 1/4 In. 1175.00
Canada Goose, Half Size, Signed, Jim Currier, Md., c.1963, 15 In. 950.00
Canada Goose, Painted, Weight, Paul Gibson, Md. 269.00
Canada Goose, Repainted, Mason Factory, Mich., 1896-1924 .... 775.00
Canada Goose, Sheet Metal, Painted, Spike Bottom, 25 x 26 In. 299.00
Canada Goose, Solid Wood Body, Glass Eyes, Painted, Lou Reineri, Virginia, 24 In. 290.00
Canvasback, Flat Bottom, Turned Heads, Signed, Charlie Joiner, Md., c.1971, 16 In., Pair 3640.00
Canvasback, Preening, Signed, Charlie Joiner, Md., c.1968, 14 In., Pair 1570.00
Canvasback, Sink Box, Cast Iron, c.1900, 15 In., Pair 1065.00
Canvasback, Up River Model, Signed, Madison Mitchell, Md., 20 In. 616.00
Canvasback, Wood Wing, Signed, Bob Litzenberg, Md., c.1960, 15 In., Pair 450.00
Canvasback, Wood, Carved, Glass Eyes, Painted, Schmidt, Mich., 16 1/2 In. 175.00
Canvasback, Wood, Carved, Painted, Glass Eyes, Ohio, c.1991, 14 1/2 In. 175.00
Canvasback Hen, Dogbone Weight, Rigged, Upper Bay, Md., Early 1900s, 14 In. 195.00
Canvasback Hen, Painted, Carved Bill, Weight, Tie Eye, Paul Gibson, Md. 230.00
Canvasback Hen, Ralph Reghi, Mt. Clemens, Mich., c.1938 .... 525.00
Canvasback Hen, Wood, Carved, Painted, Glass Eyes, Schmidt, Mich., 16 1/4 In. 1265.00
Chickadee, Driftwood Base, Gordon Clark Jr., Yarmouth, Mass., 1968 .... 259.00
Cinnamon Teal, Turned Heads, Flat Bottom, Signed, Bill Schauber, Md., c.1992, 12 In., Pair 390.00
Cinnamon Teal Drake, Driftwood Base, J. Lapham, Dennisport, Mass., 1959, Miniature 575.00
Cinnamon Teal Drake, J. Lapham, Dennisport, Mass., 4 1/2 In. 660.00
Common Scoter Drake, Driftwood Base, J. Lapham, Dennisport, Mass., 1952, Miniature 835.00
Duck, Black Head, Gray Bill, Yellow Eyes, Lead Weight, Carved, Painted, 1800s 220.00
Duck, Carl G. Malmstrom, 8 1/2 In. 165.00
Duck, Crowell Black, Glass Eyes, A. E. Crowell, East Harwich, Mass., 6 x 17 1/2 In. 1645.00
Duck, Red Head, Black Bill, Yellow Eyes, Carved, Painted, 1800s 220.00
Eider, Driftwood Base, J. Lapham, Dennisport, Mass., Miniature 635.00
Eider Drake, Crossed Wing Tips, Roosevelt Penny, Cape Sable Island, Nova Scotia 99.00
Fish, Brown Trout, Glass Eyes, 10 In. 80.00
Fish, Largemouth Bass, Glass Eyes, Copper Fins, 10 In. 200.00
Fish, Leather Tail, Tin Fins, Carved Gills, Harry Seymour, Bemus, N.Y., c.1885, 6 1/2 In. 3575.00
Fish, Trout, Green, Leather Tail, Tin Fins, Harry Seymour, Bemus, N.Y., c.1885, 7 In. 5060.00
Fish, Whale Shape, Leather Tail, Black, White, Red & White Spots, Lake Chautauqua, 7 In. 220.00
Fish, Yellow, Carved Eyes, Lead Fins, Aluminum Tail, George L. Randall, Box, 7 1/2 In. 59.00
Goldeneye Drake, Louis Schifferl, Green Bay, Wisc. 259.00
Goldeneye Drake, Oval Base, J. Lapham, Dennisport, Mass., 1962, 1/4 Size 865.00
Goldeneye Drake, Repainted, Dodge Factory, Detroit, Mich., 1884-94 .... 210.00
Goldeneye Hen, Carved Wings, Glass Eyes, Luther Nickerson, Cotuit, Mass. 978.00
Goose, Copper Name Tag, Full Size, Horace Graham, Md., c.1960 .... 950.00
Goose, Flying, Mounted On Wooden Plaque, Copper Tag, Bill Schauber, Md., 26 x 35 In. 1570.00
Goose, Mason Factory, c.1910 .... 1210.00
Goose, Raised Wings, Flat Bottom, Signed, Bus Talley, 17 In. 340.00
Goose, Yellow Pine, Black, White Painted, Cast Iron Weights, 13 1/4 x 22 x 7 1/2 In. 520.00
Great Blue Heron, Driftwood Base, Russ P. Burr, Hingham, Mass., Miniature 690.00

Green-Winged Teal Drake & Hen, Mason Factory, Detroit, 1896-1924, 5 In. 1058.00
Harlequin, Signed, Bill Cranmer, N.J., c.1980, 12 In., Pair 560.00
Harlequin Drake, Holger Smith, Mattapoisett, Mass., 1970s 210.00
Harlequin Drake, Hollow, Turned Head, Signed, Fred Hirsch, c.1979, 12 In. 225.00
Loon, Holger Smith, Mattapoisett, Mass., 1970s 400.00
Mallard, Carved, Painted, Inset Glass Eyes, Mason Factory, 1896-1924, 6 1/2 x 16 In., Pair 259.00
Mallard, Drake, Turned Head, Flat Bottom, Bill Cranmer, N.J., 15 In. 615.00
Mallard, Full Size, Signed, Herb Miller, Ship Bottom, N.J., 15 & 16 In., Pair 670.00
Mallard, Mini, Signed, Jess Urie, Md., 6 & 7 In., Pair 110.00
Mallard, Signed, Roger Urie, Rockhall, Md., 7 In., Pair 170.00
Mallard, Turned Heads, Full Size, Signed, Bill Cranmer, N.J., 14 In., Pair 1120.00
Mallard, Weighted, Signed, Jim Pierce, Md., 18 In., Pair 280.00
Mallard, Weighted, Signed, Madison Mitchell, Md., c.1976, 18 In., Pair 1120.00
Mallard Drake, Economy Model, Flat Bottom, Tack Eyes, Animal Trap Co., 15 1/2 In. 60.00
Mallard Drake, Glass Eyes, Standard Grade, Mason Factory, Mich., 1896-1924 .... 345.00
Mallard Drake, Holger Smith, Mattapoisett, Mass., 1970s 90.00
Mallard Drake, Hollow Body, Challenge Grade, Snakey Head, Mason Factory, Mich., c.1910 ...... 2530.00
Mallard Drake, Hollow Carved, Glass Eyes, Wildfowler, Saybrook, Conn., 1939-57 .... 575.00
Mallard Drake, Madison Mitchell, Havre De Grace, Md. 230.00
Mallard Drake, Oval Base, A.E. Crowell, East Harwich, Mass., Miniature 2530.00
Mallard Drake, Turned Head, Ken Harris, Woodville, N.Y., c.1950 .... 440.00
Mallard Hen, A.E. Crowell, Mass., Miniature 2415.00
Meadowlark, Calling, Driftwood Base, Peter Peltz, Mass. 290.00
Merganser, Carved, Painted, Early 20th Century, 6 3/4 x 16 1/2 In. 206.00
Merganser Drake, Carved, Painted, Slotted Head, Iron Weight, Me., c.1910, 7 x 18 1/2 In. 400.00
Old Squaw Drake, Marty Collins, Mattapoisett, Mass. 290.00
Old Squaw Drake & Hen, Signed, Bill Cranmer, N.J., c.1984, 10 & 8 In. 785.00
Owl, Horned, Hollow, Taxidermy Eyes, Signed, Wilbur, 1950s, 21 x 6 In. 3850.00
Pintail, Flat Bottom, Wildfowler, 18 In. 310.00
Pintail, Gunning Birds, Keel, Turned Head, Charlie Joiner, Md., 18 & 15 In., Pair 2016.00
Pintail Drake, Balsa Wood, Glass Eyes, Herter, Minnesota 110.00
Pintail Drake, Hollow, Animal Trap Co., 16 1/2 In. 185.00
Pintail Drake, Signed, Weighted, Hollow, Jim Slack, Pekin, Il., 17 In. 85.00
Plover, Metal Bill, Driftwood Base, Hand Painted, Folk Art, 12 1/2 x 15 1/2 In. 195.00
Red-Breasted Merganser, 1950s Model, Signed, Charlie Joiner, c.1996, 16 In. 2240.00
Red-Breasted Merganser, Carved, Sam Toothacher, Brunswick, Maine, 7 x 16 In. 1410.00
Red-Breasted Merganser, Swimming, Hollow, Raised Wing, Fred Hirsch, 20 In., Pair 505.00
Red-Breasted Merganser Drake, Horsehair Comb, Matt Kowollik, Milford, Ohio 325.00
Redhead, Signed, Madison Mitchell, Md., c.1964, 14 In., Pair 785.00
Redhead, Wing Duck, Weighted, Bob Litzenberg, Elkton, Md., c.1987, 14 & 15 In., Pair 504.00
Redhead Drake, Balsa Wood, Branded GLM, Wildfowler Factory, 1930s, 13 In. 280.00
Redhead Drake, Jasper Dodge, Detroit, Mich., c.1890 .... 440.00
Redhead Drake, Premier Model, Mason Factory, 1896-1924, 14 In. 896.00
Redhead Hen, Premier Grade, Mason Factory, Mich., 1896-1924 .... 690.00
Ring-Necked Drake, Holger Smith, Mattapoisett, Mass., 1970s 115.00
Ruddy Duck Drake, Driftwood Base, J. Lapham, Dennisport, Mass., 1958, Miniature 805.00
Scoter, Carved Eyes, Black, Gus Wilson, Maine, 14 In. 2015.00
Sparrow Hawk, Glass Eyes, Round Base, J. Lapham, Dennisport, Mass. 1150.00
Surf Scoter Drake, Glass Eyes, Driftwood Base, J. Lapham, Dennisport, Mass., Miniature 2015.00
Surf Scoter Drake, Oval Base, J. Lapham, Dennisport, Mass., 1962, 1/4 Size 805.00
Swan, Crackled White & Black Paint, Solid Body, Glass Eyes, Lou Reineri, Virginia, 33 In. 230.00
Swan, Removable Head, Copper Name Tag, Horace Graham, 1960s, 36 In. 1456.00
Swan, Signed, Dave Walker, Md., 24 In. 450.00
Teal Drake & Hen, Glass Set Eyes, Carved Feathers, T.J. Hooker, Nov. 1972, 11 1/2 In. 1035.00
Widgeon, Glass Eyes, H.K. Chadwick, Martha's Vineyard, Mass. 520.00
Widgeon, Half Size, David Blackiston, Md., 8 In., Pair 615.00
Widgeon, Turned Heads, Signed, Bill Cranmer, N.J., c.1981, 8 In., Pair 670.00
Widgeon, Weighted, Signed, Charlie Joiner, Chestertown, Md., 15 In., Pair 1008.00
Wood Duck, Flat Bottom, Oliver Lawson, Crisfield, Md., c.1981, 15 In., Pair 1900.00
Wood Duck, Lead Feet, Driftwood Base, 2 x 6 x 2 In. 415.00
Wood Duck, Turned Heads, David E. Carroll, Chestertown, Md., 14 In., Pair 500.00

DEDHAM Pottery was started in 1895. Chelsea Keramic Art Works was established in 1872 in Chelsea, Massachusetts, by members of the Robertson family. The factory closed in 1889 and was reorganized as the Chelsea Pottery U.S. in 1891. The firm used the marks *CKAW* and *CPUS*. It became the Dedham Pottery of Dedham, Massachusetts. The factory closed in 1943. It was famous for its crackleware dishes, which picture blue outlines of animals, flowers, and other natural motifs. Chelsea Keramic Art Works and Dedham Pottery pieces are listed here.

Azalea, Bacon Rasher, Crackle Glaze, 1 1/2 x 9 1/2 In. 316.00
Azalea, Plate, Crackle Glaze, 6 In. 230.00
Bird In Potted Orange Tree, Plate, Raised Design, Crackle Glaze, Doves, Trees, 8 1/2 In. 375.00
Bird In Potted Orange Tree, Plate, White Doves, Crackle Glaze, Impressed Rabbit, 10 In. 489.00
Butterfly, Plate, 6 1/4 In. 260.00
Cherub, Lamp Base, Crackle Glaze, 5 3/4 x 5 3/4 In. 980.00
Chick, Plate, 8 1/2 In. 4700.00
Clover, Plate, CPUS, 8 1/2 In. 1265.00
Crab, Plate, Blue, 6 In. .... 500.00 to 575.00
Crab, Plate, White Ground, Blue Band, Crackle Glaze, Impressed Rabbit, 8 1/2 In. 489.00
Dolphin, Cup & Saucer, Crackle Glaze, Blue Waves 690.00
Dolphin, Plate, Waves, Crackle Glaze, CPUS, 8 1/2 In. 805.00
Elephant, Pitcher, Crackle Glaze, 5 1/4 x 4 1/4 In. 920.00
Elephant, Rice Cup, Cobalt Blue, Crackle Glaze, 2 x 3 In. 750.00
Elephant, Teapot, Dome Cover, Crackle Glaze, 6 3/4 x 8 1/2 In. 750.00
Fish, Plate, Cobalt Blue Wave, White Crackle Glaze, Stamped, 8 1/2 In. 3450.00
Fish, Plate, Stamped, 8 1/2 In. 3450.00
Grape, Bowl, Reticulated Edge, Grapes Cascading, Stamped, 4 x 8 1/2 In. 400.00
Grape, Pitcher, Angular Handle, 5 x 4 In. 518.00
Grape, Plate, c.1912, 8 1/2 In. 425.00
Grape, Plate, Clusters Extend To Center, Pair, Crackle Glaze, 10 x 7 1/2 In. 200.00
Grape, Plate, Pair, Crackle Glaze, 8 1/2 x 7 1/4 In. 259.00
Horse Chestnut, Charger, Alternating Flowers, Crackle Glaze, Stamped, 12 In. 489.00
Lobster, Plate, Seaweed Design, White Glaze, 6 In. 545.00
Lotus Petal, Bowl, Crackle Glaze, Stamped, 2 1/2 x 5 In. 489.00
Magnolia, Plate, White Glaze, Impressed Rabbit, 10 In. 200.00
Moth, Plate, Alternating Moth & Moon, Raised Design, 8 1/3 In. 690.00
Mushroom, Plate, Crackle Glaze, 8 3/4 In. 748.00
Peacock, Plate, Full Plumage, 6 In. 4890.00
Pilgrim, Flask, Scrolls, Footed, Green, Blue, Brown, CKAW, 5 x 3 3/4 In. 635.00
Pineapple, Plate, Alternating With Raised Flowers, Blue Dots, Crackle Glaze, 8 1/2 In. 575.00
Polar Bear, Plate, Raised Design, Blue Water, Crackle Glaze, Impressed Rabbit, 8 1/2 In. 575.00
Pond Lily, Plate, Raised Design, Crackle Glaze, Impressed Rabbit, 10 In. 290.00
Pond Lily, Plate, Raised Design, White Crackle Glaze, 8 1/4 In. 430.00
Pond Lily, Plate, Soup, Blue Design, Crackle Glaze 175.00
Poppy, Plate, Crackle Glaze, Stamped, Impressed Rabbit, 8 1/2 In. 489.00
Poppy, Plate, Crackle Glaze, White Ground, Raised Design, Impressed Rabbit, 6 In. 920.00
Putty, Goat & Boy, Plate, 9 In. 1265.00
Rabbit, Candlestick Holder Set, Crackle Glaze, 1 3/4 x 3 3/4 In., 4 Piece 635.00
Rabbit, Card Holder, Slot Along Ears, Blue Ink Stamp, 2 1/2 In. 1520.00
Rabbit, Charger, White Crackle Glaze, Maude Davenport, 12 In. 316.00
Rabbit, Coaster, Raised Sides, Recessed Center, Blue Medallion, Crackle Glaze, 4 In. 375.00
Rabbit, Coffeepot, Cover, Square Handle, Elongated Spout, Bulbous, 8 1/2 x 7 In. 1495.00
Rabbit, Creamer, Trumpet Neck, Bulbous, White Ground, 3 1/2 In. 485.00
Rabbit, Cup & Saucer, Crackle Glaze 92.00
Rabbit, Cup, Coffee, Crackle Glaze, Pair, 2 x 5 1/2 In. 115.00
Rabbit, Dish, Soup, Stamped, 1 3/4 x 9 In. 230.00
Rabbit, Eggcup, Crackle Glaze, Blue Stamp, 2 1/2 x 2 In. 259.00
Rabbit, Fish Platter, Crackle Glaze, Oval, Stamped, 12 1/2 In. 805.00
Rabbit, Knife Rest, Crackle Glaze, 3 x 3 1/2 In. 430.00

Rabbit, Mug, Crackle Glaze, Circular Handle, Child's, 5 1/4 x 4 1/4 In. 546.00
Rabbit, Nappy, Crackle Glaze, Stamped, 1 1/2 x 5 1/2 In. 175.00
Rabbit, Oyster Dish, Embossed, Recessed Interior, Crackle Glaze, 4 1/2 In. 920.00
Rabbit, Paperweight, Crackle Glaze, 1 1/2 x 3 In. 1265.00
Rabbit, Pitcher, Side Handle, Crackle Glaze, 9 x 5 1/2 In. 978.00
Rabbit, Plate, 8 1/2 In. 85.00
Rabbit, Plate, Soup, Raised Design, Crackle Glaze, Stamped, Impressed Rabbit, 8 1/4 In. 175.00
Rabbit, Sherbet, Chalice Style, Circular Handles, Crackle Glaze, 3 1/4 x 5 1/2 In. 546.00
Rabbit, Standing, Flower Holder, Cobalt Blue Accents, Dome Shape, 6 3/4 x 4 1/2 In. 2070.00
Rabbit, Stein, Crackle Glaze, Incised, 5 x 5 1/4 In. 430.00
Snowtree, Plate, c.1912, 8 1/2 In. 425.00
Snowtree, Plate, Impressed Rabbit, 10 In. 230.00
Snowtree, Plate, Raised Design, Impressed Rabbit, Crackle Glaze, 6 In. 316.00
Swan, Bacon Rasher, Cattails, Crackle Glaze, 1 1/2 x 9 1/2 In. 405.00
Swan, Charger, Alternating Cattail Stalks, Crackle Glaze, 12 In. 690.00
Swan, Jam Jar, Crackle Glaze, 5 x 4 1/2 In. 690.00
Tapestry Lion, Plate, Raised Lion, Moon, Leaves, Crackle Glaze, Maude Davenport, 10 In. 1380.00
Turkey, Plate, Blue, Crackle Glaze, 10 In. 635.00
Turtle, Bowl, Cobalt Blue, Crackle Glaze, 3 x 6 In. 345.00
Turtle, Paperweight, Dome Shape, Crackle Glaze, 1 3/4 x 4 1/2 In. 1495.00
Turtle, Plate, Blue Crackle Glaze, 6 In. 863.00
Vase, Buff Colored Volcanic Glaze, Hugh Robertson, 10 1/4 x 6 In. 1175.00
Vase, Bulbous, Oxblood Glaze, Green, Hugh Robertson, 6 x 4 In. 1645.00
Vase, Sang De Bouef Thick Glaze, Shouldered, Marked, 10 In. 9000.00
Vase, Shouldered, Thick Green Glaze, Marked, 3 In. 1140.00
Wild Rose, Butter Chip, Crackle Glaze, Blue Stamen To Center, 3 1/2 In. 230.00

DEGENHART is the name used by collectors for the products of the Crystal Art Glass Company of Cambridge, Ohio. John and Elizabeth Degenhart started the glassworks in 1947. Quality paperweights and other glass objects were made. John died in 1964 and his wife took over management and production ideas. Over 145 colors of glass were made. In 1978, after the death of Mrs. Degenhart, the molds were sold. The D in a heart trademark was removed, so collectors can easily recognize the true Degenhart piece.

Bell, Liberty, Bicentennial Chocolate Glass, 1976 .... 15.00
Bell, Liberty, Blue Opalescent, 1976 .... 18.00
Figurine, Baby Shoe, Vaseline, c.1968 .... 25.00
Figurine, Owl On Books, Pink, 3 1/2 In. 25.00
Figurine, Owl, Carnival, Cobalt, 3 5/8 x 2 1/4 In. 125.00
Figurine, Palm, Milk Glass 25.00
Figurine, Pooche, Pre 1965 .... 20.00
Figurine, Tomahawk, Chocolate Slag, 3 3/4 x 2 In. 15.00
Paperweight, 5 Flowers, Multicolored, 1950s, 2 1/2 x 2 1/2 In. 175.00
Paperweight, Flower Bouquet, Multicolored, 1950s, 3 1/4 x 3 1/2 In. 250.00
Paperweight, Single Flower, Blue, 1950s, 3 x 3 In. 250.00
Salt, Bird & Cherry, Blue, 3 In. 15.00
Toothpick, Beaded Oval, Amber Brown, 2 5/8 In. 18.00
Toothpick, Bird, Honey Amber, 1970s 10.00
Toothpick, Forget-Me-Not, Mint Green Slag, c.1972, 2 1/2 In. 25.00

DEGUE is a signature acid-etched on pieces of French glass made in the early 1900s. Cameo, mold blown, and smooth glass with contrasting colored rims are the types most often found.

Bowl, Centerpiece, White Flowers, Amethyst Leaves, Orange, Squat, Cameo, Art Deco, 13 In. 690.00
Vase, Mottled, Clear & Rose, Baluster, Fire Polished, c.1925, 8 3/4 In., Pair 529.00
Vase, Purple, Mottled, Iron Base, 1925, 16 In. 905.00
Vase, Stylized Black Amethyst Flowers, Flared Brown Rim, Frosted, Cameo, 9 1/2 In. 920.00
Vase, Zigzag, Orange, Clear, Bulbous, Flared Rim, c.1920, 7 1/2 In. 508.00
Whiskey, Flower Blossoms, Leaves, Cameo, Signed, 2 In. 145.00

DELATTE glass is a French cameo glass made by Andre Delatte. It was first made in Nancy, France, in 1921. Lighting fixtures and opaque glassware in imitation of Bohemian opaline were made. There were many French cameo glass makers, so be sure to look in other appropriate categories.

Bowl, Centerpiece, Internal Streaks, Amethyst Foot, 3 3/8 x 13 3/4 In. 1250.00
Powder Box, Raspberry Red Flowers, Leaves, Stems, Mottled Pink Ground, Signed, 5 In. 865.00
Vase, Art Deco, Silvered Bronze Holder, c.1930, 7 In. 1200.00
Vase, Flambe, Baluster, Gold Leaf Inclusions, 11 In. 440.00

DELDARE, see Buffalo Pottery Deldare.

DELFT is a tin-glazed pottery that has been made since the seventeenth century. Delft was made in England in the eighteenth century. It is decorated with blue on white or with colored decorations. Most of the pieces sold today were made after 1891, and the name *Holland* usually appears with the Delft factory marks. The word *Delft* appears alone on some twentieth century pottery from Asia and Germany.

Bottle, Flowers, Leaves, Multicolored, England, 1700s, 8 1/2 In. 764.00
Bowl, Bleeding, 2 Pierced Flower Handles, Blue, White, c.1740, 9 1/4 In. 588.00
Bowl, Blue, White, 18th Century, 14 In. 495.00
Bowl, Blue, White, Scrolled Leaves & Flowers, England, c.1740, 9 In. 590.00
Bowl, Cover, Blue, White, Vines, Flowers, England, c.1740, 8 1/2 In. 1765.00
Bowl, Flower Bouquets, Oval Border, 18th Century, 11 3/4 In., Pair 230.00
Bowl, Lobes, Footed, Blue Stylized Flowers, Blue Glaze Ground, England, 2 x 8 5/8 In. 470.00
Charger, Blue Flowers, White Ground, Yellow Band, Saggar Marks, 12 1/4 In. 375.00
Charger, Blue, White Tin, Flowers, Butterfly, Urn With Feathers, 13 3/4 x 2 1/2 In. 633.00
Charger, Blue, White, Flowers, c.1760, 14 In. 295.00
Charger, Blue, White, Flowers, Quilted Border, Parrot With Flower, 13 1/2 x 2 1/4 In. 748.00
Charger, Flower, Windmill, Hand Painted, Metal Form Edge, Early 1900s, 17 1/4 In. 350.00
Charger, Garden, Flowers, Yellow Border, 1800s, 13 1/2 In. 382.00
Charger, Imari Design, Blue, 13 1/2 In. 440.00
Charger, Maiden Holding Ship & Anchor, Scroll Cartouche, Scalloped Rim, Garland, 14 In. 1528.00
Charger, Mimosa, 13 1/2 In. 248.00
Charger, Multicolored Urn, Flowers, Feathers, Hanging Hole, England, 13 3/4 x 2 1/2 In. 978.00
Charger, Peacock Feather Leaf Design, Blue, 13 3/4 In. 415.00
Charger, Queen Mary Of England, c.1690, 13 In. 6500.00
Charger, Scenic, Horse Drawn Carts, Holland, 16 In., Pair 80.00
Clock, Windmills, Pastoral Setting, Gilt Surround, Blue, White, Late 1800s, 13 1/2 In. 780.00
Cornucopia, Bird, Flowering Branch, Liverpool, Wall Hanging, c.1755, 8 1/4 In. 5400.00
Dish, Multicolored, Yellow, Blue, Green, England, 18th Century, 13 1/4 In., Pair 3800.00
Egg Coddler, Base, Blue, Flowers, England, c.1775, 4 1/4 In. 646.00
Jar, Cover, Blue, White, Birds, Flowers, 32 In. 1535.00
Plaque, Harlequin, Blue, White, Scenic, Village, Windmill, 24 In. 1175.00
Plate, Blue, White, Black Lion, Leaf Border, c.1750, 9 In., Pair 2468.00
Plate, Divided Floral Border, Songbird, Blue, Rust, Red, Yellow, Green, 9 In. 375.00
Plate, Green, Blue, Mahogany Red Fruit Border, Parrot, Flowers, 9 In. 546.00
Plate, Oriental Design, Pagodas, Fisherman, Hand Painted, 12 In. 748.00
Plate, Peacock, Holland, First Half 18th Century, 12 3/8 In. 646.00
Plate, Pheasant Perched On Yellow Circle, Flowering Plants, Blue, Green, Marked, 10 In. 1150.00
Plate, Shallot, Lion Standing In Front Of Gate, 1730, Pair 6500.00
Punch Bowl, Blue, White, Early Form, c.1720 .... 850.00
Shaving Basin, Soap Indented, c.1730 .... 395.00
Stein, Multicolored, Pewter Lid, Hinged, 1600s, 9 In. 330.00
Stein, Pewter Lid, J.H.M., Flowers, Multicolored, 1600s, 9 3/4 In. 575.00
Tile, 3 Tall Ships, Multicolored, Cuenca, Horizontal, 4 3/4 x 13 In. 880.00
Tile, Blue, White, 18th Century, 5 x 5 In., 4 Piece 415.00
Tile, Flamingo, Facing Right, Cuenca, Frame, 12 x 4 1/2 In. 411.00
Tile, Tall Ships Fleet, Cuenca, 4 x 16 1/2 In. 470.00
Tobacco Jar, Indian, Smoking Pipe, Blue, White, Holland, c.1750, 10 3/8 In. 3290.00
Tobacco Jar, Indians, Smoking Pipes, Blue, White, Holland, 8 1/8 In. 700.00

Tobacco Jar, Sailor, Smoking Pipe, Brass Cover, Holland, c.1750, 10 1/4 In. 2350.00
Vase, Blue, White, Pyriform, Chinese Style, Late 1700s, 7 1/4 In. 646.00
Vase, Cover, Faceted Baluster Shape, Painted, Gilt, Indianische Blumen, 1700s, 11 In. 435.00

DENTAL cabinets, chairs, equipment, and other related items are listed here. Other objects may be found in the Medical category.

Cabinet, Oak, Drop & Roll Front, 6 Drawers, Trays, Harvard Dental Co., Ohio, 61 In. 3173.00
Chair, Wood Frame, Caned Seat, Back, White Dental Manufacturing, c.1900, 51 In. 560.00
Tooth Key, Double Claw, Steel Shaft, Turned Ebony Handle, 6 In. 235.00
Tooth Key, Single Claw, Locking Pin, Turned Wood Handle, 6 In. 206.00

DENVER is part of the mark on an American art pottery. William Long of Steubenville, Ohio, founded the Lonhuda Pottery Company in 1892. In 1900 he moved to Denver, Colorado, and organized the Denver China and Pottery Company. This pottery, which used the mark *Denver*, worked until 1905 when Long moved to New Jersey and founded the Clifton Pottery. Long also worked for Weller Pottery, Roseville Pottery, and American Encaustic Tiling Company. Do not confuse this pottery with the Denver White Pottery, which worked from 1894 to 1955 in Denver.

Scarab, Green & Tan Matte Glaze, 2 5/8 x 3 5/8 In. 95.00
Vase, Dandelions, Brown Matte Glaze, Signed, L.F. Lonhuda, 7 In. 200.00
Vase, Denaura, Squat Top, Nasturtiums, Green Vellum Glaze, 5 1/4 x 6 1/4 In. 2350.00

DEPRESSION GLASS was an inexpensive glass manufactured in large quantities during the 1920s and early 1930s. It was made in many colors and patterns by dozens of factories in the United States. Most patterns were also made in clear glass, which the factories called *crystal.* If no color is listed here, it is clear. The name *Depression glass* is a modern one. For more descriptions, history, pictures, and prices of Depression glass, see the book *Kovels' Depression Glass & Dinnerware Price List.*

Adam, Bowl, Dessert, Green, 4 3/4 In. 28.00
Adam, Bowl, Vegetable, Oval, Green, 10 In. 53.00
Adam, Pitcher, Pink, 8 In. 49.00
Adam, Plate, Dinner, Square, Green, 9 In. 33.00
Adam, Plate, Salad, Square, Pink, 7 3/4 In. 22.00
Adam, Platter, Oval, Green, 11 3/4 In. 46.00
Adam, Platter, Oval, Pink, 11 3/4 In. 43.00
Adam's Rib, Bowl, Amber, 3 Legs, 6 3/8 x 3 In. 22.00
Adam's Rib, Bowl, Shallow, Amber, 6 1/2 In. 15.00
Adam's Rib, Bowl, Shallow, Pink, 6 1/2 In. 17.00
Adam's Rib, Creamer, Amber, 4 1/4 In. 22.00
Adam's Rib, Cup, Amber, 3 3/8 x 2 1/4 In. 15.00
Adam's Rib, Plate, Luncheon, Amber, 8 1/8 In. 16.00
Adam's Rib, Saucer, Amber, 5 3/4 In. 5.00
Adam's Rib, Sugar, Amber, 3 5/8 In. 22.00
American Sweetheart, Berry Bowl, Monax 9 In. ....77.00 to 85.00
American Sweetheart, Berry Bowl, Pink, 3 3/4 In. 100.00
American Sweetheart, Berry Bowl, Pink, 9 In. 54.00
American Sweetheart, Bowl, Cereal, Pink, 6 In. 17.00
American Sweetheart, Plate, Bread & Butter, Monax, Green Trim, 6 In. 23.00
American Sweetheart, Plate, Dinner, Monax, 9 3/4 In. ....28.00 to 30.00
American Sweetheart, Plate, Salad, Monax, 8 In. 30.00
American Sweetheart, Plate, Salad, Red, 8 In. 150.00
American Sweetheart, Platter, Oval, Monax, 13 In. ....25.00 to 89.00
American Sweetheart, Salver, Pink, 12 In. 28.00
American Sweetheart, Sherbet, Pink, 4 1/4 In. 25.00
American Sweetheart, Soup, Cream, Handles, Monax, 4 1/2 In. 140.00
American Sweetheart, Soup, Dish, Monax, 9 1/2 In. ....95.00 to 115.00
American Sweetheart, Soup, Dish, Pink, 9 1/2 In. 85.00

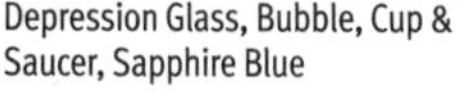
Depression Glass, Bubble, Cup & Saucer, Sapphire Blue

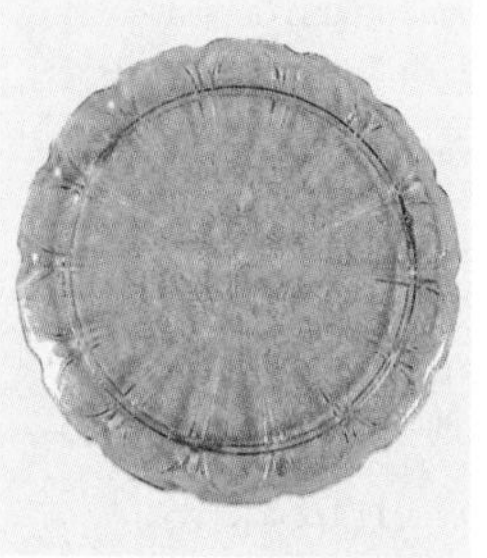
Depression Glass, Cherry Blossom, Cake Plate, 3-Footed, Green

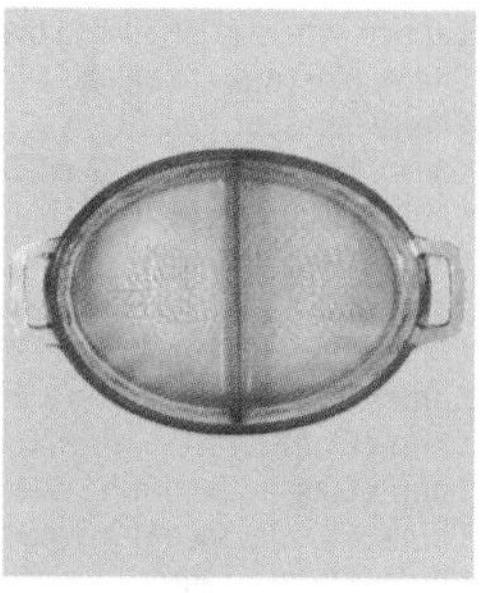
Depression Glass, Floral, Relish, Sections, Handles, Oval, Pink

Apple Blossom pattern is listed here as Dogwood.
Aunt Polly, Sherbet, Iridescent 6.00
Aurora, Bowl, Cereal, Cobalt Blue, 5 3/8 In. 18.50
Aurora, Bowl, Cereal, Pink, 5 3/8 In. 17.00
Aurora, Cup & Saucer, Blue 20.00
Aurora, Plate, Blue, 6 1/2 In. 13.00
Aurora, Sherbet, Cobalt Blue 30.00
Aurora, Tumbler, Cobalt Blue, 10 Oz., 4 3/4 In. .... 13.00 to 29.00
Avocado, Bowl, Handles, Oval, Green, 7 In. 33.00
Avocado, Bowl, Salad, 7 1/2 In. 13.00
Ballerina pattern is listed here as Cameo.
Banded Rib pattern is listed here as Coronation.
Banded Rings pattern is listed here as Ring.
Basket pattern is listed here as No. 615.
Block pattern is listed here as Block Optic.
Block Optic, Berry Bowl, Green, 8 1/2 In. 38.00
Block Optic, Bowl, Cereal, Green, 5 1/4 In. 25.00
Block Optic, Bowl, Salad, Green, 7 1/4 In. 130.00
Block Optic, Bowl, Salad, Pink, 7 1/4 In. 155.00
Block Optic, Console, Rolled Edge, Pink, 11 3/4 In. 110.00
Block Optic, Cup, Green .... 8.00 to 11.00
Block Optic, Goblet, Green, 9 Oz., 5 3/4 In. 35.00
Block Optic, Pitcher, 80 Oz., 8 In. 80.00
Block Optic, Pitcher, Bulbous, Green, 54 Oz., 7 5/8 In. 105.00
Block Optic, Plate, Dinner, Green, 9 In. 28.00
Block Optic, Plate, Luncheon, Green, 8 In. 8.00
Block Optic, Plate, Sherbet, Green, 6 In. 3.00
Block Optic, Plate, Sherbet, Pink, 6 In. 4.00
Block Optic, Sandwich Server, Green, 10 1/4 In. 30.00
Block Optic, Sherbet, Footed, 5 1/2 Oz., 3 1/4 In. 5.00
Block Optic, Sherbet, Footed, 6 Oz., 4 3/4 In. 11.00
Block Optic, Sundae, Ruffled Rim, Footed, Pink, 5 1/2 In. 35.00
Block Optic, Vase, Rubina, 10 1/2 In. 425.00
Bouquet & Lattice pattern is listed here as Normandie.
Bowknot, Cup, Green 10.00
Bowknot, Tumbler, Flared, Green, 10 Oz., 5 In. 27.00
Bubble, Cup & Saucer, Sapphire Blue .... *ILLUS* 12.00
Bullseye pattern is listed here as Bubble.
Cabbage Rose pattern is listed here as Sharon.
Cameo, Bowl, Vegetable, Oval, Yellow, 10 In. 41.00
Cameo, Decanter, No Stopper, Green, 10 In. 180.00
Cameo, Sherbet, Green, 4 7/8 In. 39.00
Cameo, Sugar, Green, 3 1/4 In. 24.00
Cameo, Sugar, Green, 4 1/4 In. 30.00
Candlewick pattern is listed in the Imperial Glass category.

Caprice pattern is included in the Cambridge Glass category.
Cherry Blossom, Cake Plate, 3-Footed, Green ... *ILLUS* 22.00
Cherry Blossom, Cup, Green ... 25.00
Cherry Blossom, Plate, Dinner, Delphite, Hand Painted, 9 In. ... 25.00
Chinex Classic, Bowl, Vegetable, 7 In. ... 27.00
Chinex Classic, Bowl, Vegetable, Flowers, 9 In. ... 32.00
Chinex Classic, Plate, Bread & Butter, Castle, Pink Trim, 6 1/4 In. ... 15.00
Chinex Classic, Plate, Bread & Butter, Flowers, 6 1/4 In. ... 6.00
Chinex Classic, Plate, Bread & Butter, Flowers, Pink Trim, 6 1/4 In. ... 6.00
Chinex Classic, Plate, Dinner, Castle, Blue Trim, 9 3/4 In. ... 19.00
Chinex Classic, Sandwich Server, 11 1/2 In. ... 15.00
Chinex Classic, Sandwich Server, Flowers, 11 1/2 In. ... 26.00
Chinex Classic, Saucer, Flowers, Pink Trim ... 6.00
Circle, Bowl, Green, 8 In. ... 50.00
Circle, Goblet, Green, 8 Oz., 5 3/4 In. ... 13.00
Circle, Plate, Sherbet, Pink, 6 In. ... 5.00
Circle, Sherbet, Green, 3 1/8 In. ... 5.00
Circle, Sherbet, Green, 4 3/4 In. ... 10.00
Circle, Sherbet, Pink, 3 1/8 In. ... 8.00
Circle, Tumbler, Juice, 4 Oz., 3 1/2 In. ... 4.00
Cloverleaf, Bowl, Salad, Green, 7 In. ... 110.00
Cloverleaf, Cup & Saucer, Black ... 19.00
Cloverleaf, Plate, Luncheon, Black, 8 In. ... 15.00
Cloverleaf, Sherbet, Black ... 19.00
Cloverleaf, Sherbet, Green ... 9.00
Colonial, Plate, Dinner, 10 In. ... 32.00
Colonial, Plate, Luncheon, Green, 8 1/2 In. ... 13.00
Colonial, Plate, Luncheon, Pink, 8 1/2 In. ... 12.00
Colonial, Sugar, 4 1/2 In. ... 11.00
Colonial, Tumbler, Footed, Green, 5oz., 4 In. ... 45.00
Colonial, Tumbler, Footed, Pink, 10 Oz., 5 1/4 In. ... 50.00
Colonial Block, Bowl, 4 In. ... 5.00
Colonial Block, Bowl, Green, 4 In. ... 11.00
Colonial Block, Goblet, Green, 5 1/2 In. ... 14.00
Colonial Block, Goblet, Pink, 5 1/2 In. ... 15.00
Colonial Block, Sherbet, Green ... 5.00
Colonial Fluted, Cup, Green ... 9.00
Columbia, Plate, Bread & Butter, 6 In. ... 20.00
Columbia, Plate, Luncheon, 9 1/2 In. ... 10.00
Columbia, Soup, Dish, 8 In. ... 27.00
Columbia, Tumbler, 4 Oz., 2 7/8 In. ... 11.00
Coronation, Berry Bowl, Royal Ruby, 4 1/2 In. ... 9.00
Coronation, Nappy, Royal Ruby, 6 1/2 In. ... 20.00
Craquel, Candy Jar, Cover, Green, 3 1/2 x 4 5/8 In. ... 31.00
Craquel, Plate, Snack, Cloverleaf, Green, 10 1/8 In. ... 16.00
Craquel, Plate, Yellow, 8-Sided, 7 In. ... 12.00
Craquel, Sherbet, 8-Sided Rim, 4 In. ... 7.00
Craquel, Sherbet, 8-Sided Rim, Green, 4 In. ... 16.00
Craquel, Tumbler, Pink, 8 Oz., 4 1/4 In. ... 12.00
Criss Cross, Bottle, Water, 64 Oz., 10 In. ... 48.00
Criss Cross, Butter, Cover Only, 1/4 Lb. ... 14.00
Criss Cross, Reamer ... 19.00
Criss Cross, Reamer, Green ... 45.00
Cube pattern is listed here as Cubist.
Cubist, Butter, Cover Only, Green ... 58.00
Cubist, Candy Jar, Cover, Pink ... 38.00
Cubist, Coaster, Green, 3 1/4 In. ... 10.00
Cubist, Pitcher, Pink, 45 Oz., 8 3/4 In. ... 350.00
Cubist, Sugar, Cover, Green ... 28.50
Daisy pattern is listed here as No. 620.
Dancing Girl pattern is listed here as Cameo.

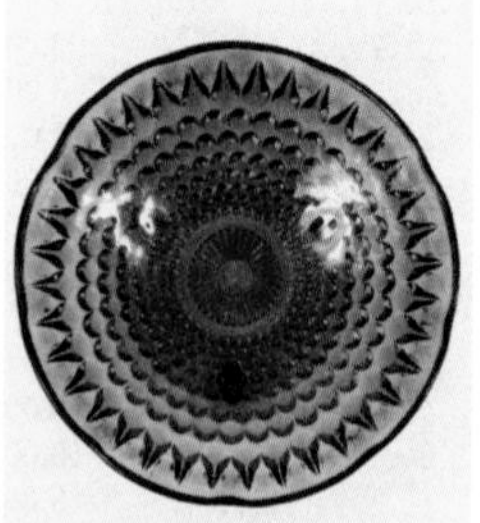

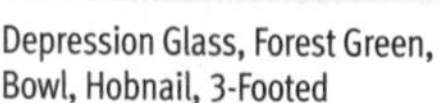
Depression Glass, Forest Green, Bowl, Hobnail, 3-Footed

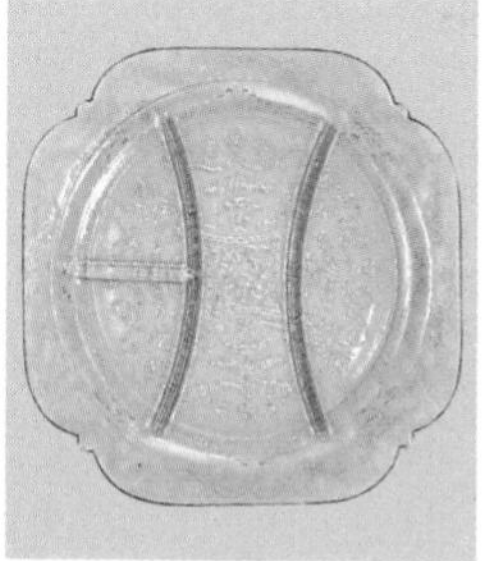

Depression Glass, Madrid, Grill Plate, Amber, 10 1/2 In.

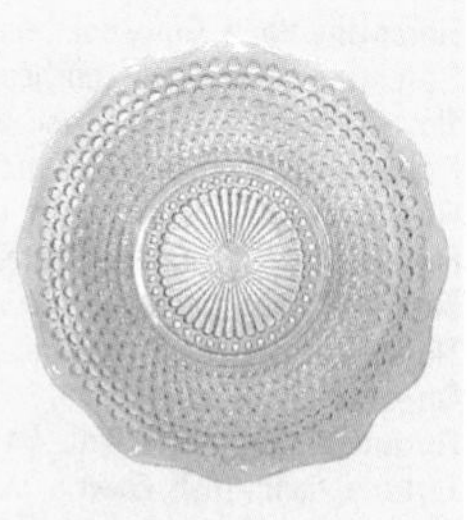

Depression Glass, Moonstone, Bowl, Ruffled Edge, 9 1/2 In.

Delphite, Bowl, Horizontal Ribs, c.1937, 9 3/4 In. 250.00
Delphite, Bowl, Vertical Ribs, 9 In. 175.00
Delphite, Refrigerator Dish, Cover, 4 x 8 In. 155.00
Diamond pattern is listed here as Miss America.
Diana, Bowl, Cereal, Pink, 5 In. 10.00
Diana, Bowl, Fruit, Amber, 11 In. 18.00
Diana, Plate, Dinner, Pink, 9 1/2 In. 20.00
Diana, Platter, Oval, Amber, 12 In. 15.00
Dogwood, Berry Bowl, Pink, 8 1/2 In. 68.00
Dogwood, Bowl, Cereal, Pink, 5 1/2 In. 35.00
Dogwood, Bowl, Fruit, Green, Gold Trim, 10 1/4 In. 295.00
Dogwood, Cup & Saucer, Pink 26.00
Dogwood, Plate, Bread & Butter, Green, 6 In. 12.00
Dogwood, Plate, Luncheon, Pink, 8 In. 7.00
Dogwood, Salver, Monax, 12 In. 25.00
Dogwood, Sherbet, Pink 32.50
Dogwood, Sugar & Creamer, Thick, Footed, Pink, 3 1/4 In. 35.00
Dogwood, Tumbler, Pink, 10 Oz., 4 In. 16.00
Dogwood, Tumbler, Pink, 11 Oz., 4 3/4 In. 32.00
Dogwood, Tumbler, Pink, 12 Oz., 5 In. 77.00
Doric, Berry Bowl, Green, 4 1/2 In. 14.00
Doric, Berry Bowl, Pink, 4 1/2 In. 12.00
Doric, Candy Jar, Cover, Green 60.00
Doric, Pitcher, Green, 32 Oz., 5 1/2 In. 79.00
Doric, Plate, Dinner, Pink, 9 In. 23.00
Doric, Plate, Sherbet, Green, 6 In. 8.00
Doric & Pansy, Creamer, Pink, Child's 39.00
Doric & Pansy, Plate, Sherbet, Ultramarine, 6 In. 10.00
Doric & Pansy, Sherbet, Pink, 6 In. 8.00
Double Shield pattern is listed here as Mt. Pleasant.
Dutch Rose pattern is listed here as Rosemary.
Fine Rib pattern is listed here as Homespun.
Floragold, Berry Bowl, Square, 4 1/2 In. 5.00
Floragold, Bowl, Ruffled Edge, 9 1/2 In. 43.00
Floragold, Butter, Cover Only, 1/4 Lb. 12.00
Floragold, Tumbler, Footed, 10 Oz. 17.00
Floral, Berry Bowl, Green, 4 In. 23.00
Floral, Plate, Dinner, Pink, 9 In. 22.00
Floral, Relish, Sections, Handles, Oval, Green 24.00
Floral, Relish, Sections, Handles, Oval, Pink .... *ILLUS* 30.00
Floral, Tumbler, Lemonade, Footed, Green, 9 Oz., 5 1/4 In. 64.00
Florentine No. 1, Plate, Salad, 8 1/2 In. 9.00
Florentine No. 1, Sherbet 12.00
Florentine No. 2, Berry Bowl, Yellow, 4 1/2 In. 24.00
Florentine No. 2, Butter, No Cover, Yellow 80.00

Florentine No. 2, Creamer 9.00
Florentine No. 2, Gravy Boat, Yellow 65.00
Florentine No. 2, Plate, Luncheon, 8 1/2 In. 8.00
Florentine No. 2, Sherbet, Yellow 10.00
Florentine No. 2, Soup, Cream, Green, 4 3/4 In. 18.00
Florentine No. 2, Soup, Cream, Pink, 4 3/4 In. 20.00
Florentine No. 2, Tumbler, Water, Green, 9 Oz., 4 In. 15.00
Flower & Leaf Band pattern is listed here as Indiana Custard.
Flower Rim pattern is listed here as Vitrock.
Forest Green, Bowl, Hobnail, 3-Footed .... *ILLUS* 8.00
Fortune, Bowl, Handle, Pink, 4 1/2 In. 10.00
Fortune, Candy Dish, Cover 28.00
Fortune, Tumbler, Water, 9 Oz., 4 In. 13.00
Fruits, Cup, Green 10.00
Hairpin pattern is listed here as Newport.
Harpo, Tumbler, Ruby, 10 Oz., 4 1/8 In. 15.00
Hex Optic pattern is listed here as Hexagon Optic.
Hexagon Optic, Cup & Saucer, Green 10.00
Hexagon Optic, Pitcher, Green, 56 Oz., 8 3/8 In. 295.00
Hexagon Optic, Sugar, Closed Handle, Green 7.00
Hexagon Optic, Tumbler, Pink, 9 Oz., 3 3/4 In. 7.00
Hexagon Optic, Tumbler, Ultramarine, 12 Oz., 5 In. 18.00
Hobnail pattern is listed in the Hobnail category.
Homespun, Powder Jar, Cover, Pink 21.50
Homespun, Sherbet 35.00
Homespun, Tumbler, Fired-On Bittersweet, 9 Oz., 4 1/4 In. 11.00
Homespun, Tumbler, Fired-On Green, 9 Oz., 4 1/4 In. 12.00
Homespun, Tumbler, Fired-On Yellow, 13 Oz., 5 In. 14.00
Homespun, Tumbler, Pink, 9 Oz., 4 1/4 In. 15.00
Honeycomb pattern is listed here as Hexagon Optic.
Horizontal Ribbed pattern is listed here as Manhattan.
Horseshoe pattern is listed here as No. 612.
Indiana Custard, Berry Bowl, 5 1/2 In. 11.00
Indiana Custard, Creamer, Footed 16.00
Indiana Custard, Sugar, Footed 15.00
Iris, Berry Bowl, Beaded Rim, Iridescent, 4 1/2 In. 9.00
Iris, Plate, Dinner, 9 1/2 In. 50.00
Iris, Plate, Luncheon, 8 In. 105.00
Iris, Sauce, Ruffled Edge, 5 1/2 In. 7.00
Iris, Sherbet, 2 1/4 In. 25.00
Iris & Herringbone pattern is listed here as Iris.
Jennyware, Mixing Bowl, Pink, 65 Oz., 8 1/4 In. 55.00
Jennyware, Refrigerator Dish, Cover, 32 Oz., 5 3/4 In. 30.00
Jennyware, Salt & Pepper, Ultramarine 60.00
Jubilee, Plate, Luncheon, Topaz, 8 3/4 In. 15.00
Jubilee, Plate, Yellow, Closed Center Flowers, Round, 8 1/4 In. 9.00
Knife & Fork pattern is listed here as Colonial.
Line 300 pattern is listed in the Paden City category as Peacock & Wild Rose.
Little Bo Peep, Mug, Ivory, Red Design, 8 Oz., 3 1/8 x 3 In. 15.00
Little Bo Peep, Plate, Divided, Ivory, Red, Orange & Green Decoration, 7 3/4 In. 40.00
Lorain pattern is listed here as No. 615.
Louisa pattern is listed here as Floragold.
Madrid, Grill Plate, Amber, 10 1/2 In. .... *ILLUS* 10.00
Manhattan, Bowl, Fruit, Handles, 9 1/2 In. 35.00
Manhattan, Candy Dish, 3-Footed, Pink, 6 3/8 In. 14.00
Many Windows pattern is listed here as Roulette.
Martha Washington pattern is included in the Cambridge Glass category.
Mayfair Federal, Cup, Amber 12.00
Mayfair Federal, Grill Plate, 9 1/2 In. 9.00
Mayfair Federal, Plate, Dinner, 9 1/2 In. 12.00
Mayfair Federal, Plate, Dinner, Amber, 9 1/2 In. 17.50

Mayfair Federal, Sugar, Amber 14.00
Mayfair Open Rose, Bowl, Cereal, Pink, 5 1/2 In. .... 25.00 to 35.00
Mayfair Open Rose, Sandwich Server, Handles, Green, 11 1/2 In. 40.00
Mayfair Open Rose, Sherbet, Pink, 3 1/4 In. 17.00
Mayfair Open Rose, Tumbler, Iced Tea, Footed, Pink, 15 Oz., 6 1/2 In. 45.00
Melba, Console, Green, 12 In. 40.00
Miss America, Bowl, Vegetable, Oval, 10 In. 18.00
Miss America, Celery Dish, Pink, 10 1/2 In. 44.00
Miss America, Compote, 5 In. 19.00
Miss America, Grill Plate, 10 1/4 In. 12.00
Miss America, Grill Plate, Pink, 10 1/4 In. 28.00
Miss America, Plate, Dinner, 10 1/4 In. 15.00
Miss America, Relish, 5 Sections, 11 3/4 In. 27.00
Moderntone, Cup, Amethyst 12.00
Moderntone, Juice, Tumbler, Green, 5 Oz., 3 3/4 In. 7.25
Moderntone, Plate, Dinner, 9 In. 5.50
Moderntone, Plate, Dinner, Amethyst, 9 In. 12.75
Moderntone, Plate, Salad, Cobalt Blue, 7 In. 11.25
Moderntone, Plate, Sherbet, 5 7/8 In. 7.00
Moderntone, Plate, Sherbet, Amethyst, 5 7/8 In. 5.00
Moderntone, Saucer, Amethyst 2.25
Moderntone, Soup, Cream, Amethyst, 4 3/4 In. 18.75
Moderntone, Soup, Cream, Cobalt Blue, 4 3/4 In. 22.50
Moderntone, Sugar, Cobalt Blue 12.50
Moonstone, Bowl, Ruffled Edge, 9 1/2 In. .... *ILLUS* 20.00
Moroccan Amethyst, Bowl, Oval, 8 In. 14.00
Moroccan Amethyst, Celery Dish, 9 1/2 In. 16.00
Moroccan Amethyst, Cup & Saucer 5.50
Moroccan Amethyst, Plate, 6 In. 4.75
Mt. Pleasant, Cup & Saucer, Cobalt Blue 20.00
Mt. Pleasant, Grill Plate, Stippled Rim, Black Amethyst, 9 In. 15.00
Mt. Pleasant, Grill Plate, Stippled Rim, Green, 9 In. 12.50
Mt. Pleasant, Plate, Black Amethyst, 7 3/4 In. 14.00
Mt. Pleasant, Saucer, Black Amethyst, Gold Trim, 6 In. 3.50
Mt. Pleasant, Sherbet, Cobalt Blue 17.50
Mt. Pleasant, Tray, Black Amethyst, 10 In. 38.00
Mt. Pleasant, Tumbler, Black Amethyst, 7 Oz., 6 In. 32.00
Mt. Pleasant, Tumbler, Cobalt Blue, 7 Oz., 6 In. 28.00
Mt. Vernon pattern is included in the Cambridge Glass category.
New Century, Butter, No Cover, Green, 6 3/4 In. 40.00
New Century, Cocktail, 3 1/2 Oz., 4 In. 29.00
New Century, Cup 12.50
New Century, Salt & Pepper, Red Tops & Trim 55.00
New Century, Tumbler, Cobalt Blue, 9 Oz., 4 1/4 In. 19.00
New Century, Tumbler, Pink, 9 Oz., 4 1/4 In. 19.00
Newport, Bowl, Pink, 4 3/4 In. 10.00
Newport, Bowl, Platonite, Fired-On Bittersweet, 4 3/4 In. 7.50
Newport, Bowl, Platonite, Fired-On Yellow, 4 3/4 In. 7.50
Newport, Cup, Platonite 4.25
Newport, Plate, Luncheon, Platonite, 8 1/2 In. 3.50
Newport, Soup, Cream, Platonite, Gold Trim 11.00
Newport, Tumbler, Platonite, Fired-On Yellow, 9 Oz., 4 1/2 In. 30.00
No. 601 pattern is listed here as Avocado.
No. 612, Berry Bowl, Green, 9 1/2 In. 44.00
No. 612, Cup, Green 15.00
No. 612, Relish, Yellow, 7 1/2 In. 45.00
No. 612, Saucer, Green 5.00
No. 612, Sherbet, Yellow 18.00
No. 615, Creamer, Green 26.00
No. 615, Plate, Salad, Yellow, 7 3/4 In. 15.00
No. 615, Relish, 4 Sections, Yellow, 8 In. 39.00

No. 618, Cup 10.00
No. 618, Vase, 12 1/2 In. 60.00
No. 620, Bowl, Vegetable, Oval, Amber, 10 In. 20.00
No. 620, Creamer, Amber 8.00
No. 620, Plate, Dinner, Amber, 9 3/8 In. 9.00
No. 620, Plate, Sherbet, Amber, 6 In. 3.00
No. 620, Sherbet, Amber 8.00
No. 620, Soup, Cream, Amber, 4 1/2 In. 12.00
No. 620, Sugar, Amber 9.00
Normandie, Bowl, Cereal, Iridescent, 6 1/2 In. 10.00
Old Cafe, Bowl, Cereal, 5 1/2 In. 20.00
Old Cafe, Candy Dish, Handles, 8 In. 9.00
Old Cafe, Candy Dish, Handles, Pink, 8 In. 14.00
Old Cafe, Olive Dish, Handles, Pink, 6 In. 13.00
Old Cafe, Vase, 7 1/4 In. 25.00
Old English, Tumbler, Amber, 4 1/2 In. 25.00
Old Florentine pattern is listed here as Florentine No. 1.
Open Colony, Bowl, Cereal, 6 3/8 In. 10.00
Open Colony, Plate, Luncheon, Pink, 8 1/4 In. 35.00
Open Rose pattern is listed here as Mayfair Open Rose.
Optic Design pattern is listed here as Raindrops.
Ovide, Berry Bowl, Green, 4 3/4 In. .... 9.00 to 12.00
Ovide, Candy Dish, Cover, Black, 5 3/4 In. 46.00
Ovide, Creamer, Green 10.00
Ovide, Plate, Luncheon, Black, 8 In. 14.00
Ovide, Plate, Luncheon, Green, 8 In. 6.00
Ovide, Salt & Pepper, Black 28.00
Ovide, Salt & Pepper, Green 26.00
Ovide, Sherbet, Black 11.00
Ovide, Sherbet, Green 4.00
Ovide, Tumbler, Black, 9 Oz., 3 3/4 In. 29.00
Ovide, Tumbler, Green, 9 Oz., 4 3/4 In. 29.00
Panel Optic, Refrigerator Jar, Cover, Green, 4 1/8 x 8 3/8 In. 56.00
Parrot pattern is listed here as Sylvan.
Patrician, Berry Bowl, 8 1/2 In. 45.00
Patrician, Berry Bowl, Golden Glo, 5 In. 15.00
Patrician, Berry Bowl, Green, 5 In. 14.00
Patrician, Bowl, Cereal, Golden Glo, 6 In. 29.00
Patrician, Bowl, Vegetable, Oval, Green, 10 In. 40.00
Patrician, Creamer 12.00
Patrician, Grill Plate, 10 1/2 In. 15.00
Patrician, Jam Dish, Amber, 6 3/4 In. 30.00
Patrician, Plate, Luncheon, Amber, 9 In. 14.00
Patrician, Plate, Salad, 7 1/2 In. 13.00
Patrician, Plate, Salad, Golden Glo, 7 1/2 In. 14.00
Patrician, Plate, Salad, Green, 7 1/2 In. 23.00
Patrician, Plate, Sherbet, Golden Glo, 6 In. 10.00
Patrician, Sherbet 10.00
Patrician, Sherbet, Golden Glo 9.00
Patrician, Soup, Cream 17.00
Patrician, Tumbler, 14 Oz., 5 1/2 In. 48.00
Patrician, Tumbler, Golden Glo, 9 Oz., 4 1/4 In. 36.00
Peacock & Wild Rose pattern is listed in the Paden City category.
Petal Swirl pattern is listed here as Swirl.
Petalware, Berry Bowl, Cremax, 9 In. 35.00
Petalware, Berry Bowl, Monax, 9 In. 25.00
Petalware, Berry Bowl, Pink, 9 In. 26.00
Petalware, Bowl, Cereal, 5 3/4 In. 6.00
Petalware, Bowl, Vegetable, Monax, 8 3/4 In. 25.00
Petalware, Cup & Saucer, Cremax, Gold Trim 9.00
Petalware, Cup, Monax 5.00

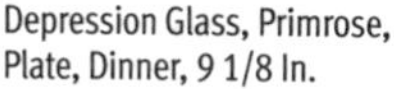
Depression Glass, Primrose, Plate, Dinner, 9 1/8 In.

Depression Glass, Princess, Cup, Green

Depression Glass, Sharon, Berry Bowl, Amber, 5 In.

Petalware, Plate, Monax Florette, 11 In. 29.00
Petalware, Plate, Salad, Cremax, Gold Trim, 8 In. 6.00
Petalware, Plate, Salad, Monax, 8 In. 13.00
Petalware, Platter, Oval, Pink, 13 In. 30.00
Petalware, Salver, Monax, Mountain Flowers, 11 In. .... 40.00 to 45.00
Petalware, Salver, Monax, Pastel Bands, 11 In. 25.00
Petalware, Saucer, Monax Regency 3.00
Petalware, Sherbet 40.00
Petalware, Sherbet, Monax, Mountain Flowers 37.00
Petalware, Soup, Dish, Monax, 7 In. .... 93.00 to 95.00
Petalware, Sugar, Monax, Gold Trim 9.00
Pillar Optic, Cup, Green 16.00
Pillar Optic, Jar, Cover, Oval, Green, 8 In. .... 50.00 to 60.00
Pillar Optic, Pitcher, Tilt, Pink, 8 1/4 In. 50.00
Pillar Optic, Plate, Luncheon, Green, 8 In. 12.00
Pineapple & Floral pattern is listed here as No. 618.
Pinwheel pattern is listed here as Sierra.
Pioneer, Plate, Pink, 8 In. 15.00
Poinsettia pattern is listed here as Floral.
Poppy No. 1 pattern is listed here as Florentine No. 1.
Poppy No. 2 pattern is listed here as Florentine No. 2.
Pretty Polly Party Dishes, see the related pattern Doric & Pansy.
Primrose, Plate, Dinner, 9 1/8 In. .... *ILLUS* 11.00
Princess, Berry Bowl, Green, 4 1/2 In. 36.00
Princess, Bowl, Cereal, Green, 5 In. 47.00
Princess, Bowl, Vegetable, Oval, Green, 10 In. 35.00
Princess, Butter, Cover, Green 110.00
Princess, Cake Stand, Green, 10 In. 40.00
Princess, Candy Dish, Cover, Amber, 6 In. 15.00
Princess, Candy Dish, Cover, Green, 9 In. 70.00
Princess, Cookie Jar, Cover, Pink 82.00
Princess, Cup, Green .... *ILLUS* 15.00
Princess, Cup, Topaz 9.00
Princess, Pitcher, Green, 60 Oz., 8 In. 69.00
Princess, Plate, Dinner, Green, 9 1/2 In. 33.00
Princess, Plate, Dinner, Topaz, 9 1/2 In. 17.00
Princess, Plate, Salad, Green, 8 In. 19.00
Princess, Sherbet, Pink 29.00
Prismatic Line pattern is listed here as Queen Mary.
Provincial pattern is listed here as Bubble.
Queen Mary, Ashtray, Oval, 3 3/4 In. 3.00
Queen Mary, Berry Bowl, 4 1/2 In. 4.00
Queen Mary, Coaster, 3 1/2 In. 3.00
Queen Mary, Compote, 5 3/4 In. 16.00
Queen Mary, Plate, Salad, Embossed Eagle, 8 3/4 In. 15.00

Queen Mary, Tumbler, Juice, Pink, 5 Oz., 3 1/2 In. 16.00
Queen Mary, Tumbler, Water, Pink, 9 Oz., 4 In. 19.00
Rainbow, Bowl, Blue, Deep, 5 1/4 In. 12.00
Rainbow, Bowl, Red, Deep, 5 1/4 In. 12.00
Rainbow, Creamer, Blue 14.00
Rainbow, Creamer, Red 14.00
Rainbow, Pitcher, Ball, Red, 80 Oz. 80.00
Rainbow, Sherbet, Red 14.00
Rainbow, Sherbet, Yellow 14.00
Rainbow, Sugar, Red 14.00
Rainbow, Tumbler, Blue, 10 Oz., 5 1/4 In. 19.00
Rainbow, Tumbler, Green, 9 Oz., 4 1/2 In. 18.00
Rainbow, Tumbler, Green, 10 Oz., 5 1/4 In. 19.00
Rainbow, Tumbler, Red, 10 Oz., 5 1/4 In. 19.00
Rainbow, Tumbler, Yellow, 10 Oz., 5 1/4 In. 19.00
Raindrops, Bowl, 7 3/4 In. 62.00
Raindrops, Tumbler, Green, 3 Oz., 3 In. 7.00
Raindrops, Whiskey, Green, Paneled Bottom, Oz., 1 7/8 In. 7.00
Ribbon, Berry Bowl, Flared Rim, Green, 8 In. 35.00
Ribbon, Bowl, Cereal, Green, 5 In. 55.00
Ribbon, Plate, Luncheon, Green, 8 In. 5.00
Ribbon, Plate, Sherbet, Green, 6 1/4 In. 4.00
Ring, Goblet, Green, 9 Oz., 7 1/4 In. 20.00
Ring, Ice Bucket, Red Yellow Blue Bands, 5 1/2 In. 33.00
Ring, Plate, Luncheon, Yellow, Red, Black Bands, 8 1/4 In. 7.00
Ring, Plate, Sherbet, Green, 6 1/4 In. 4.00
Ring, Sandwich Server, Center Handle 25.00
Ring, Sandwich Server, Center Handle, Green 33.00
Ring, Sherbet, Green, 2 1/8 In. 24.00
Romanesque, Bowl, 8-Sided, Amber, Shallow, 10 1/2 In. 50.00
Romanesque, Bowl, 8-Sided, Black, Shallow, 10 1/2 In. 75.00
Romanesque, Bowl, 8-Sided, Green, Shallow, 10 1/2 In. 63.00
Romanesque, Plate, 8-Sided, Amber, 7 In. 9.00
Romanesque, Plate, Round, Green, 8 In. 10.00
Rope pattern is listed here as Colonial Fluted.
Rose Cameo, Berry Bowl, Green, 4 1/2 In. 18.00
Rose Cameo, Plate, Salad, Green, 7 In. 17.00
Rose Cameo, Sherbet, Green 14.00
Rosemary, Soup, Cream, Green, 5 1/2 In. 35.00
Roulette, Bowl, Green, 9 1/2 In. 32.00
Royal Lace, Bowl, Pink, 3-Footed, 10 In. 70.00
Royal Lace, Bowl, Ruffled Edge, 3-Footed, 10 In. 58.00
Royal Lace, Butter, Cover 80.00
Royal Lace, Cup 11.00
Royal Lace, Saucer, Pink 7.00
Royal Lace, Tumbler, 9 Oz., 4 1/8 In. 17.00
S Pattern, Cup & Saucer 7.00
S Pattern, Grill Plate, 10 1/4 In. 7.00
S Pattern, Plate, Luncheon, Amber Band, 8 1/4 In. 7.00
Sailboat pattern is listed here as Sportsman Series.
Saxon pattern is listed here as Coronation.
Sharon, Berry Bowl, Amber, 5 In. .... *ILLUS* 9.00
Sharon, Berry Bowl, Pink, 5 In. 13.00
Sharon, Berry Bowl, Pink, 8 1/2 In. 40.00
Sharon, Bowl, Cereal, Pink, 6 In. 30.00
Sharon, Bowl, Fruit, Amber, 10 1/4 In. 26.00
Sharon, Bowl, Vegetable, Oval, Amber, 9 1/2 In. 18.00
Sharon, Butter, Cover 44.00
Sharon, Cheese Dish, Cover, 7 1/2 In. 38.00
Sharon, Cup, Pink 15.00
Sharon, Plate, Bread & Butter, Amber, 6 In. 6.00

Sharon, Plate, Bread & Butter, Pink, 6 In. 9.00
Sharon, Plate, Dinner, Amber, 9 In. 11.00
Sharon, Plate, Dinner, Pink, 9 In. 19.00
Sharon, Platter, Oval, Amber, 12 1/2 In. 16.00
Sharon, Saucer, Amber 6.00
Sharon, Sherbet, Amber 12.00
Sharon, Sherbet, Pink 16.00
Sharon, Soup, Cream, Amber, 5 In. 29.00
Sharon, Soup, Dish, Amber, 7 3/4 In. 57.00
Sharon, Soup, Dish, Pink, 7 3/4 In. 57.00
Sharon, Tumbler, Footed, Pink, 15 Oz., 6 1/2 In. 57.00
Sharon, Tumbler, Pink, 9 Oz., 4 In. 45.00
Sierra, Bowl, Cereal, Green 5 1/2 In. 19.00
Spanish Dancers, Tumbler, Black & White, Hazel Atlas, 4 3/4 In. 18.00
Spanish Dancers, Tumbler, Hazel Atlas, 9 Oz., 4 3/4 In. 12.00
Spanish Dancers, Tumbler, Red & White, Hazel Atlas, 4 3/4 In. 19.00
Spanish Dancers, Tumbler, Red, White, Blue & Yellow, Hazel Atlas, 9 Oz., 3 7/8 In. 19.00
Spiral, Berry Bowl, Green, 4 3/4 In. 25.00
Spiral, Cup & Saucer, Green 8.00
Spiral, Plate, Luncheon, Green, 8 In. 4.00
Spoke pattern is listed here as Patrician.
Sportsman Series, Cocktail Mixer, Sailboat 27.00
Sportsman Series, Tumbler, Iced Tea, Band At Top, Sailboat, 5 5/8 In. 13.00
Sportsman Series, Tumbler, Iced Tea, Paneled, Sailboat, 5 5/8 In. 13.00
Sportsman Series, Tumbler, Roly Poly, Sailboat, 2 3/8 In. 12.00
Sportsman Series, Tumbler, Sailboat, Blue, Black & White, 4 5/8 In. 18.00
Sportsman Series, Tumbler, Sailboat, Green, Black & White, 4 5/8 In. 19.00
Sportsman Series, Tumbler, Sailboat, Red, Black & White, 4 5/8 In. 19.00
Sportsman Series, Tumbler, Sailboat, White Boat & Blue Waves, 4 7/8 In. 15.00
Sportsman Series, Tumbler, Sailboat, Yellow, Black & White, 4 5/8 In. 19.00
Sportsman Series, Tumbler, Straight Sides, Sailboat, 3 7/8 In. 15.00
Sportsman Series, Tumbler, Windmill, Blue, White, 3 3/8 In. 15.00
Stippled Rose Band pattern is listed here as S Pattern.
Sun-Ray, Plate, Scalloped Rim, 13 In. 65.00
Sunburst, Berry Bowl, 4 3/4 In. 10.00
Sunburst, Berry Bowl, 8 1/2 In. 25.00
Sunburst, Bowl, 10 3/4 In. 34.00
Sunburst, Plate, Dinner, 9 1/4 In. 16.00
Swirl, Plate, Dinner, Ultramarine, 9 In. 18.00
Swirl, Vase, Footed, Pink, 6 1/2 In. 25.00
Sylvan, Creamer, Green 68.00
Sylvan, Cup, Green 29.00
Sylvan, Plate, Dinner, Green, 9 In. 69.00
Thistle, Bowl, Cereal, Pink, 5 1/2 In. 40.00
Thistle, Cup, Pink 36.00
Thistle, Plate, Luncheon, Green, 8 In. 30.00
Thistle, Plate, Luncheon, Pink, 8 In. 27.00
Threading pattern is listed here as Old English.
Vertical Ribbed pattern is listed here as Queen Mary.
Victory, Bowl, Cereal, Dark Amber, 6 1/2 In. 10.00
Victory, Bowl, Cereal, Green, 6 1/2 In. 14.00
Victory, Bowl, Vegetable, Oval, Green, 9 In. 45.00
Victory, Candleholder, Green, 3 x 4 1/4 In. 18.00
Victory, Compote, Pink, 6 In. 17.00
Victory, Compote, Pink, Gold Trim, 6 In. 17.00
Victory, Console, Green, Gold Trim, 12 In. 48.00
Victory, Creamer, Black 17.00
Victory, Creamer, Green 17.00
Victory, Cup, Dark Amber 8.00
Victory, Cup, Green 8.00
Victory, Plate, Bread & Butter, Green, 6 In. 9.00

Victory, Plate, Dinner, Green, 9 In. 25.00
Victory, Plate, Dinner, Pink, 9 In. 26.00
Victory, Plate, Luncheon, Green, 8 In. 6.00
Victory, Sandwich Server, Center Handle, Cobalt Blue, 10 1/2 In. 78.00
Victory, Sandwich Server, Center Handle, Dark Amber, 10 1/2 In. 30.00
Victory, Sandwich Server, Center Handle, Green, 10 1/2 In. 28.00
Victory, Sandwich Server, Center Handle, Pink, 10 1/2 In. 29.00
Victory, Saucer, Green 5.00
Victory, Saucer, Light Amber 5.00
Victory, Saucer, Pink 5.00
Victory, Sugar, Black 17.00
Vitrock, Bowl, Cereal, 7 In. 19.00
Vitrock, Bowl, Fruit, 6 In. 12.00
Vitrock, Creamer 6.00
Vitrock, Creamer, Yellow 15.00
Vitrock, Cup, Orange & Black Bands 10.00
Vitrock, Plate, Salad, 7 1/4 In. 9.00
Vitrock, Soup, Cream, 5 1/2 In. 6.00
White Ship pattern is listed here as Sportsman Series.
Wild Rose pattern is listed here as Dogwood.
Windmill pattern is listed here as Sportsman Series.
Windsor, Berry Bowl, Green, 4 3/4 In. 10.00
Windsor, Bowl, Cereal, Green, 5 3/8 In. 38.00
Windsor, Chop Plate, Pink, 13 5/8 In. 33.00
Windsor, Plate, Dinner, 9 In. 12.00
Windsor, Plate, Dinner, Pink, 9 In. 27.00
Windsor, Plate, Salad, 7 In. 7.00
Windsor, Plate, Salad, Gold Trim, 7 In. 9.00
Windsor, Relish, 5 Sections, 13 3/4 In. 22.00
Windsor Diamond pattern is listed here as Windsor.

DERBY has been marked on porcelain made in the city of Derby, England, since about 1748. The original Derby factory closed in 1848, but others opened there and continued to produce quality porcelain. The Crown Derby mark began appearing on Derby wares in the 1770s.

Bough Pot, Early 19th Century, 7 1/2 In. 1770.00
Bowl, Painted, Cartouche Scenic Landscape, Early 19th Century, 2 3/4 x 7 In. 295.00
Cup & Saucer, Japan Pattern, 1830-40, 2 x 3 3/4-In. Cup, 5 1/2-In. Saucer 189.00
Dish, Botanical, Lobed, Yellow Border, Gilt, c.1800, 8 1/2 In., Pair 4535.00
Figurine, Amorous Couple, Openwork Base, c.1800, 9 1/2 In. 1500.00
Figurine, Goddess, Cherub, Flowers, 18th Century, 6 In., Pair 489.00
Figurine, Man With Pug, Multicolored Enamel, Gilt Trim, c.1800, 5 1/4 In. 1765.00
Plate, Japan Imari Pattern, 1784-1809, 8 In., Pair 350.00
Plate, Painted, Flower Spray Center, Paneled Border, Blue Ground, c.1825, 8 Piece 530.00
Platter, Heraldic, Crest Over S, Red & Gilt Vine Rim, Oval, c.1800, 12 3/4 In. 176.00
Serving Dish, Shell Shape, Gold, Red, Blue Enamel, Flowers, Garden, 1800s, 9 3/4 In., Pair 265.00
Vase, Farmhouse, Trees, Mountains, Hand Painted, Gilt Decoration, 1782-1820, 3 1/2 In. 300.00
Vase, Foo Dogs, Shouldered Handles, Yellow Ground, Gilt, c.1850, 6 In. 395.00
Vase, Royal Crown, Flowers, Gilt Scroll, Blue Ground, George Jessop, c.1921, 7 In., Pair 1740.00

DICK TRACY, the comic strip, started in 1931. Tracy was also the hero of movies from 1937 to 1947 and again in 1990, and starred in a radio series in the 1940s and a television series in the 1950s. Memorabilia from all these activities are collected.

Badge, Secret Service Patrol, Inspector General, Brass, 1938-39, 2 1/4 In. 450.00
Button, Diamond Theatre Dick Tracy Club, Celluloid, 1 In. 22.00
Coloring Book, 1946, 8 1/2 x 11 In., 96 Pages 45.00
Comic Art, Sunday, On Board, Chester Gould, September 4, 1955, 18 x 27 In. 792.00
Doll, Bonnie Braids, Ideal, Box, Early 1950s, 15 In. 220.00
Figurine, Trench Coat, Head Moves, Open, Close Mouth, Composition, 1930s, 13 1/2 In. 308.00
Game, Target, Revolver, Darts, Marx, Early 1940s, 18 x 18 In. 150.00
Gun, Water, Sub-Machine, Red, Plastic, Tops, Box, 1950s, 12 In. 250.00

Hat, Wool, Miller Bros Hat Co., 1940s, 10 In., Size 7 1/8 .... 138.00
Lamp, Plaster, 3-Dimensional, Shade, Plasto Mfg. Co., 4 1/2 In. 2040.00
Movie Poster, Dick Tracy Meets Gruesome, RKO, 1947, 41 x 27 In. 280.00
Movie Poster, Dick Tracy's Dilemma, Linen, RKO, 1947, 41 x 27 In. 295.00
Movie Poster, Fire Trap, Episode 13, Early 1940s, 41 x 27 In. 815.00
Ring, Brass, Enamel, Premium, Miller Bros Hat Co., 1940s 85.00
Toy, B.O. Plenty, Tin, Windup, Marx, Box, Late 1940s, 8 1/2 In. 595.00
Toy, B.O. Plenty, Tin, Windup, Marx, Late 1940s, 8 1/2 In. .... 154.00 to 225.00
Toy, Squad Car, Battery Operated Light, Marx, 1948, 2 x 11 1/2 In. 255.00
Toy, Squad Car, Spotlight, Tin Lithograph, Clockwork, Marx, c.1950, 11 1/4 In. 176.00
Toy, Squad Car, Tin, Linemar, Box, 8 1/2 In. 303.00
Toy, Squad Car, Tin, Plastic Passengers, Friction, Marx, 1948, 20 In. 195.00
Toy, Telephone, Talking, 10 Phrases, Marx, Box, 1967, 8 1/2 x 8 1/2 x 5 In. 65.00
Trading Card Set, Dick Tracy Caramels, Wrapper, W.H. Johnson Co., 1935, 144 Cards 2320.00

DICKENS WARE pieces are listed in the Royal Doulton and Weller categories.

DINNERWARE used in the United States from the 1930s through the 1950s is listed here. Most was made in potteries in southern Ohio, West Virginia, and California. A few patterns were made in Japan, England, and other countries. Dishes were sold in gift shops and department stores, or were given away as premiums. Many of these patterns are listed in this book in their own categories, such as Autumn Leaf, Azalea, Coors, Fiesta, Franciscan, Hall, Harker, Harlequin, Red Wing, Riviera, Russel Wright, Vernon Kilns, Watt, and Willow. For more information, see *Kovels' Depression Glass & Dinnerware Price List.*

Alice, Jug, Blue Ridge, 6 1/8 x 8 1/2 In. 290.00
American Rose, Plate, Bread & Butter, Paden City Pottery, 6 3/8 In. 3.00
American Rose, Plate, Dessert, Paden City Pottery, c.1949, 5 In. 6.00
American Rose, Soup, Dish, Paden City Pottery, 8 In. 10.00
Apple, Berry Bowl, Skyline Shape, Blue Ridge, 2 1/2 x 8 3/4 In. 33.00
Apple, Gravy Boat, Skyline Shape, Blue Ridge 30.00
Apple, Plate, Dinner, Skyline Shape, Blue Ridge, 10 1/2 In. .... 23.00 to 25.00
Apple, Sugar & Creamer, Cover, Skyline Shape, Blue Ridge 30.00
Apple, Trio, Plate, Dinner, Blue Ridge, 18 In. 18.00
Apple, Trio, Platter, Blue Ridge, 13 In. 28.00
Applejack, Platter, Blue Ridge, 11 1/2 In. 20.00
Autumn Apple, Plate, Dinner, Colonial Shape, Blue Ridge, 10 1/4 In. 12.00
Autumn Harvest, Platter, Taylor, Smith & Taylor, 11 1/2 In. 20.00
Autumn Leaves, Sugar, Cover, Taylor, Smith & Taylor 15.00
Ballerina, Platter, Iris, Universal, 11 1/2 In. 68.00
Ballerina, Platter, Pink, Tab Handles, Universal, 11 1/2 In. 15.00
Ballet, Pie Plate, Iris, Universal, 10 In. 22.00
Ballet, Plate, Dinner, Iris, Universal, 9 7/8 In. 10.00
Ballet, Relish, Iris, 4 Sections, Center Handle, Blue Ridge 150.00
Bells Of Ireland, Cup & Saucer, Harmony House 10.00
Bells Of Ireland, Plate, Dinner, Harmony House, 10 1/2 In. 10.00
Bells Of Ireland, Platter, Harmony House, 11 1/4 In. 25.00
Big Apple, Platter, Blue Ridge, 11 1/2 In. 25.00
Big Blossom, Pitcher, Blue Ridge, 5 3/4 In. 121.00
Bittersweet, Plate, Salad, Blue Ridge, 7 1/2 In. 15.00
Bleeding Heart, Ashtray, Square, Blue Ridge, 3 In. 28.00
Blossom Top, Salt & Pepper, Blue Ridge, 5 1/4 In. 94.00
Blue Lace, Plate, Dinner, Versatile Shape, Taylor, Smith & Taylor, 10 In. 10.00
Blue Moon, Plate, Dinner, Blue Ridge, 10 1/8 In. 48.00
Bluebell Bouquet, Platter, Candlewick Shape, Blue Ridge, 15 In. 28.00
Bouquet, Platter, Johnson Brothers, 13 1/2 x 10 1/2 In. 20.00
Boutonniere, Plate, Dinner, Taylor, Smith & Taylor, 10 In. 13.00
Boutonniere, Relish, Divided, Ever Yours, Taylor, Smith & Taylor 15.00
Boutonniere, Sauceboat, Taylor, Smith & Taylor 13.00
Bow Knot, Bowl, Vegetable, Round, Blue Ridge, 9 In. 20.00

Bow Knot, Platter, Blue Ridge, 13 1/4 x 9 3/4 In. 22.00
Bow Knot, Sugar, Cover, Blue Ridge. 20.00
Break O Day, Platter, Versatile Shape, Taylor, Smith & Taylor, 11 In. 12.00
Briar Rose, Berry Bowl, Homer Laughlin, 5 In. 12.00
Briar Rose, Cup, Homer Laughlin 17.00
Briar Rose, Plate, Bread & Butter, Homer Laughlin, 6 1/4 In. 8.00
Briar Rose, Plate, Dessert, Homer Laughlin, 7 In. 14.00
Briar Rose, Plate, Luncheon, Homer Laughlin, 8 3/4 In. 23.00
Briar Rose, Plate, Salad, Homer Laughlin, 7 3/4 In. 17.00
Briar Rose, Platter, Homer Laughlin, 11 In. 43.00
Briar Rose, Platter, Homer Laughlin, 13 1/2 In. 65.00
Brittany, Bowl, Vegetable, Flowers, Burgundy Band, Homer Laughlin, 9 In. 15.00
Brocatelle, Platter, Taylor, Smith & Taylor, 13 1/2 In. 15.00
Brown Daisy, Bowl, Vegetable, Round, Blue Ridge, 9 In. 18.00
Brown Tulip, Bowl, Cereal, Skyline Shape, Blue Ridge 8.00
Brown Tulip, Bowl, Vegetable, Skyline Shape, Round, Blue Ridge 22.00
Brown Tulip, Casserole, Cover, Blue Ridge, 10 In. 12.00
Brown Tulip, Cup & Saucer, Skyline Shape, Blue Ridge 12.00
Bud Top, Salt & Pepper, Blue Ridge, 5 3/4 In. 94.00
Buttercup, Sugar, Cover, Taylor, Smith & Taylor 9.95
Cambridge Iris, Chop Plate, Handle, Platinum Trim, Universal, 1940s, 14 x 13 In. 40.00
Cameo Rose, Chop Plate, Blue, Harmony House, 12 In. 15.00
Cameo Rose, Plate, Dinner, Blue, White, Harmony House, 10 1/4 In. 10.00
Carnival Vintage, Butter, Cover, Harmony House 20.00
Carnival Vintage, Chop Plate, Harmony House, 12 In. 40.00
Carnival Vintage, Coffeepot, Harmony House, 9 In. 30.00
Cathay, Platter, Taylorstone, Taylor, Smith & Taylor, 11 In. 20.00
Cattail, Casserole, Cover, Universal, 4 1/2 x 8 1/4 In. 45.00
Cattail, Mixing Bowl, Universal, 8 In. 25.00
Celebrity, Platter, Johnson Brothers, 14 1/2 x 11 1/8 In. 35.00
Chelsea Rose, Platter, Johnson Brothers, 13 1/2 In. 35.00
Cherry Bounce, Cup & Saucer, Blue Ridge 16.00
Chinese Princess, Bowl, Fruit, Egg Shell Swing Shape, Homer Laughlin, 5 5/8 In. 9.50
Chinese Princess, Cup, Homer Laughlin 12.50
Chintz, Celery Dish, Blue Ridge 55.00
Christmas Tree, Plate, Dinner, Blue Ridge, 10 1/4 In. ....95.00 to 113.00
Circus, Plate, Dinner, Universal, 10 1/4 In. 18.00
Clara, Pitcher, Blue Ridge, 7 1/2 x 7 In. 60.00
Clematis, Plate, Luncheon, Homer Laughlin, 9 1/4 In. 13.00
Clematis, Soup, Dish, Homer Laughlin 8 In. 14.00
Cock O' The Walk, Bowl, Vegetable, Oval, Blue Ridge 45.00
Cock O' The Walk, Cup & Saucer, Blue Ridge 42.00
Cock O' The Walk, Plate, Blue Ridge, 9 1/4 In. 35.00
Cock O' The Walk, Plate, Bread & Butter, Candlewick Shape, Blue Ridge, 6 1/8 In. 15.00
Columbine, Cup & Saucer, Homer Laughlin 16.00
Corinthian, Bowl, Vegetable, Round, Taylor, Smith & Taylor, 9 1/2 In. 29.00
Coronation Pattern, Dinner Service, Mita Of Japan, Royal M, 180 Piece 295.00
Country Scenes, Sugar, Cover, Taylor, Smith & Taylor 17.50
Crab Apple, Platter, Blue Ridge, 15 1/2 x 11 1/4 In. 50.00
Daisy, Bowl, Vegetable, Blue Ridge, 9 In. 20.00
Daisy, Platter, Candlewick, Blue Ridge, 13 x 10 In. 20.00
Daisy & Hearts, Bowl, Vegetable, Oval, Johnson Brothers, 10 1/4 In. 60.00
Daisy & Hearts, Gravy Boat, Attached Underplate, Johnson Brothers 110.00
Daisy & Hearts, Platter, Oval, Johnson Brothers, 14 1/2 x 10 3/4 In. 80.00
Daisy Chain, Bowl, Salad, Blue Ridge, 2 1/4 x 10 In. 30.00
Day Lily, Bowl, Vegetable, Round, Taylor, Smith & Taylor, 9 In. 27.00
Day Lily, Plate, Dinner, Taylor, Smith & Taylor, 10 In. 11.00
Delta Daisy, Cup & Saucer, Colonial Shape, Blue Ridge 38.00
Demorest, Cup & Saucer, Blue Ridge, Jumbo 95.00
Dogwood, Pitcher, Water, Ice Lip, Universal, 2 Qt., 6 In. 45.00
Dogwood, Plate, Dinner, Salem China, 10 In. 10.00

Dogwood, Soup, Dish, Salem China, 8 1/2 In. 10.00
Dogwood, Teapot, Cover, Homer Laughlin, 5 3/8 In. 78.00
Dorchester, Plate, Dinner, Johnson Brothers, 10 In. 56.00
Dorchester, Plate, Luncheon, Johnson Brothers, 9 In. 23.00
Dorchester, Soup, Dish, Rim, Johnson Brothers, 8 In. 44.00
Dorothy, Berry Bowl, Eggshell, Georgian Shape, Homer Laughlin, 5 In. 7.50
Dorothy, Casserole, Cover, 10 7/8 In. 40.00
Dorothy, Plate, Dinner, Homer Laughlin, 10 In. 10.00
Dutch Petit Point, Bowl, Fruit, Salem China, 5 1/2 In. 15.00
Dutch Petit Point, Cup & Saucer, Salem China 16.00
Dutch Petit Point, Plate, Dinner, Salem China, 9 In. 14.00
Dutch Petit Point, Soup, Dish, Rim, Salem China, 7 1/4 In. 14.00
Easter Parade, Bonbon, Blue Ridge 150.00
Easter Parade, Cake Plate, Maple Leaf Shape, Blue Ridge 125.00
Ellen, Relish, 4 Sections, Center Handle, Blue Ridge, 8 1/2 In. 135.00
English Abbey, Cup & Saucer, Taylor, Smith & Taylor 30.00
English Abbey, Gravy Boat, Underplate, Taylor, Smith & Taylor 45.00
English Abbey, Plate, Bread & Butter, Taylor, Smith & Taylor, 6 1/8 In. 10.00
English Chippendale, Creamer, Red, Johnson Brothers 45.00
English Chippendale, Plate, Salad, Pink, Scalloped Rim, Johnson Brothers, 7 1/8 In. 25.00
English Chippendale, Platter, Red, Johnson Brothers, 1 1/2 x 14 In. 50.00
Fairmede Fruits, Plate, Salad, Blue Ridge, 8 In. 20.00
Ferndale, Creamer, Harmony House 12.00
Ferndale, Serving Bowl, Harmony House, 3 x 9 In. 10.00
Fish, Platter, Johnson Brothers, 20 1/2 In. 490.00
Floating Leaves, Platter, Oval, Johnson Brothers, 12 1/4 In. 38.00
Floral, Relish, Divided, Blue Ridge, 2 7/8 x 8 1/2 In. 150.00
Floral, Teapot, Blue Ridge, 9 1/4 x 8 3/4 In. 280.00
Flowers Of The Dell, Berry Bowl, Jade Shape, Homer Laughlin, 5 In. 15.00
Flowers Of The Dell, Bowl, Vegetable, Cover, Jade Shape, Homer Laughlin 125.00
Flowers Of The Dell, Bowl, Vegetable, Oval, Homer Laughlin, 9 In. ....25.00 to 35.00
Flowers Of The Dell, Cup, Homer Laughlin ....12.50 to 16.00
Flowers Of The Dell, Plate, Dinner, Homer Laughlin, 9 7/8 In. 25.00
Flowers Of The Dell, Plate, Salad, Square, Homer Laughlin, 7 In. 12.00
Flowers Of The Dell, Saucer, Homer Laughlin 7.00
Flowers Of The Dell, Soup, Cream, Homer Laughlin, 6 In. 18.00
Flowers Of The Dell, Soup, Dish, Rim, Homer Laughlin, 8 In. 22.50
Focus, Bowl, Vegetable, Round, Johnson Brothers, 9 In. 22.00
Focus, Creamer, Johnson Brothers 12.00
Focus, Plate, Dinner, Johnson Brothers, 10 3/8 In. 12.00
Fox Grape, Sugar, Blue Ridge 80.00
Foxfire, Plate, Dinner, Blue Ridge, 9 1/2 In. 20.00
French Peasant, Chocolate Pot, Cover, Blue Ridge, 9 x 7 1/2 In. 550.00
French Peasant, Plate, Man, Blue Ridge, 9 3/8 In. 65.00
Friendly Village, Cup & Saucer, Johnson Brothers 19.00
Fruit Fantasy, Plate, Blue Ridge, 9 1/8 In. 22.00
Fruit Punch, Plate, Blue Ridge, 8 1/2 In. 20.00
Fruit Punch, Plate, Dinner, Blue Ridge, 10 In. 25.00
Garland, Berry Bowl, Century Shape, Homer Laughlin, 5 In. 6.00
Garland, Bowl, Vegetable, Oval, Homer Laughlin, 9 In. 25.00
Garland, Plate, Bread & Butter, Homer Laughlin, 6 1/4 In. 6.00
Garland, Saucer, Homer Laughlin 4.00
Garland, Sugar, Cover, Homer Laughlin 19.00
Golden Wheat, Cup, Homer Laughlin 4.00
Golden Wheat, Plate, Bread & Butter, Homer Laughlin, 6 1/8 In. 3.00
Golden Wheat, Plate, Dessert, Homer Laughlin, 7 1/4 In. 4.00
Golden Wheat, Plate, Luncheon, Homer Laughlin, 9 1/4 In. 7.00
Golden Wheat, Soup, Coupe, Homer Laughlin, 8 1/4 In. 7.00
Green Plaid, Bowl, Vegetable, Oval, Blue Ridge 18.00
Green Plaid, Platter, Blue Ridge, 1 3/4 x 7 x 9 1/4 In. 22.00
Green Plaid, Sugar, Blue Ridge 16.00

Greendawn, Plate, Dinner, Johnson Brothers, 10 In. 30.00
Greendawn, Platter, Johnson Brothers, 12 x 9 1/2 In. 40.00
Hacienda, Berry Bowl, Century Shape, Homer Laughlin, 4 7/8 In. 13.00
Ham 'n Eggs, Plate, Blue Ridge, 9 In. 171.00
Harlequin, Sugar, Yellow, Homer Laughlin 9.00
Helen, Pitcher, Blue Ridge, 4 1/2 In. 121.00
Heritage, Bowl, Vegetable, Johnson Brothers, 9 In. 15.00
Heritage Hall, Sugar & Creamer, Johnson Brothers 60.00
Highlander, Coffeepot, Harmony House, 5 Cup 15.00
Homeplace, Plate, Blue Ridge, 9 1/2 In. 138.00
Homespun, Plate, Dinner, Taylor, Smith & Taylor, 10 1/8 In. 15.00
Honolulu, Plate, Salad, Cherries, Blue Ridge, 8 In. 18.00
Honolulu, Plate, Salad, Grapes, Blue Ridge, 8 In. 15.00
Indian Tree, Creamer, Johnson Brothers 20.00
Indian Tree, Platter, Johnson Brothers, 12 x 9 1/2 In. 28.00
Indian Tree, Platter, Johnson Brothers, 14 x 11 In. 32.00
Indian Tree, Teapot, Johnson Brothers, 6 x 10 In. 130.00
Jamaica, Creamer, Empire Shape, Taylor, Smith & Taylor 10.00
Jamestown, Cup & Saucer, Johnson Brothers 22.00
Jubilee Fruit, Plate, Salad, Pears, Blue Ridge, 8 1/4 In. 28.00
Jubilee Fruit, Plate, Salad, Strawberries, Blue Ridge, 8 1/4 In. 22.00
June Bouquet, Platter, Colonial Shape, Blue Ridge, 11 3/4 In. 25.00
Laredo, Bowl, Vegetable, Cover, Johnson Brothers, 7 1/2 In. 40.00
Laurella, Cake Plate, Universal, 11 1/2 In. 35.00
Laurella, Chop Plate, Universal, 11 3/4 In. 15.00
Lazy Daisy, Plate, Salad, Taylor, Smith & Taylor, 7 In. 12.00
Lazy Daisy, Platter, Oval, Taylor, Smith & Taylor, 13 1/2 In. 20.00
Leaf, Celery Dish, Blue Ridge, 11 In. 145.00
Lisa, Creamer, Homer Laughlin 14.00
Lisa, Platter, Oval, Homer Laughlin, 11 3/4 In. 24.00
Lu-Ray, Butter, Cover, Yellow, Taylor, Smith & Taylor 60.00
Lu-Ray, Creamer, Yellow, Taylor, Smith & Taylor 23.00
Lu-Ray, Cup & Saucer, Blue, Taylor, Smith & Taylor 23.00
Lu-Ray, Plate, Dinner, Yellow, Taylor, Smith & Taylor, 10 In. 28.00
Lu-Ray, Plate, Luncheon, Blue, Taylor, Smith & Taylor, 9 In. 18.00
Lu-Ray, Platter, Oval, Pink, 13 1/4 x 9 1/2 In. 42.00
Lu-Ray, Platter, Taylor, Smith & Taylor, 14 1/2 In. 95.00
Lu-Ray, Saucer, Turquoise, Taylor, Smith & Taylor 12.00
Majestic, Plate, Salad, Homer Laughlin, 7 1/4 In. 9.00
Marsh Violet, Plate, Dinner, Taylor, Smith & Taylor, 10 1/4 In. 22.00
Melody Lane, Casserole, Cover, Empire Shape, Taylor, Smith & Taylor 25.00
Mexicana, Berry Bowl, Homer Laughlin, 4 7/8 In. 19.00
Mexicana, Bowl, Vegetable, Oval, Homer Laughlin, 9 In. 35.00
Ming Tree, Plate, Bread & Butter, Blue Ridge, 6 In. 15.00
Mirror Image, Plate, Dinner, Piecrust Shape, Blue Ridge, 10 5/8 In. 22.00
Modern Orchid, Bowl, Dessert, Paden City Pottery, 1940s, 5 1/4 In. 7.00
Modern Orchid, Cup, Paden City Pottery 7.00
Modern Orchid, Platter, Paden City Pottery, 9 In. 10.00
Modern Orchid, Platter, Paden City Pottery, 11 3/4 In. 20.00
Modern Orchid, Platter, Paden City Pottery, 14 In. 29.00
Modern Orchid, Saucer, Paden City Pottery 3.00
Moonglow, Creamer, Harmony House, 3 3/4 x 4 1/4 x 3 3/4 In. 11.00
Mosaic, Serving Bowl, Harmony House, 9 In. 12.00
Moss Rose, Bowl, Vegetable, Universal 9 x 2 1/2 In. 12.00
Moss Rose, Cup, Homer Laughlin 65.00
Mountain Rose, Platter, Candlewick Shape, Blue Ridge, 11 1/2 In. 18.00
National, Cake Plate, Blue Band, Homer Laughlin, 9 In. 15.00
National, Mixing Bowl, Blue Band, Homer Laughlin, 9 In. 22.50
No. C24, Berry Bowl, Cattails, Platinum Trim, Century Shape, Homer Laughlin, 5 In. 9.00
No. C24, Bowl, Vegetable, Cover, Cattails, Homer Laughlin, 10 1/4 In. 80.00
No. C24, Creamer, Cattails, Homer Laughlin 18.00

No. C24, Cup & Saucer, Cattails, Platinum Trim, Century Shape, Homer Laughlin 16.00
No. C24, Platter, Wells Shape, Homer Laughlin, 11 In. 22.00
No. C24, Sugar, Cover, Homer Laughlin 23.00
Nocturne, Bowl, Vegetable, Blue Ridge, 9 1/2 In. 20.00
Nocturne, Plate, Red, Blue Ridge, 9 1/2 In. 20.00
Nora, Platter, Platinum Rim, Harmony House, 12 1/4 In. 13.00
Oakworth, Platter, Oval, Johnson Brothers, 12 1/2 In. 25.00
Old Flower Prints, Platter, Lily & Jasmine, Johnson Brothers, 14 x 11 In. 30.00
Old Mill, Coaster, Johnson Brothers, 4 1/8 In. 12.00
Old Mill, Plate, Bread & Butter, Johnson Brothers, 6 1/4 In. 18.00
Olivia, Bowl, Vegetable, Oval, Homer Laughlin, 9 1/8 In. .... 28.00 to 38.00
Olivia, Plate, Luncheon, Homer Laughlin, 9 1/4 In. 8.00
Olivia, Platter, Oval, Homer Laughlin, 11 1/2 In. 29.00
Opposites, Bowl, Vegetable, Round, Blue Ridge, 9 1/4 In. .... 33.00 to 35.00
Opulence, Pitcher, Alice Shape, Blue Ridge, 6 1/4 x 8 3/4 In. 175.00
Orient, Soup, Dish, Harmony House, 7 1/2 In. 10.00
Oriental Flower, Bowl, Vegetable, Round, Ballerina Shape, Universal, 8 In. 9.00
Pansy Trio, Pitcher, Spiral, Blue Ridge, 7 In. 165.00
Pastoral, Bowl, Fruit, Taylor, Smith & Taylor, 5 3/4 In. 16.00
Peachbloom, Sugar, Johnson Brothers, 2 7/8 In. 20.00
Pebbleford, Bowl, Vegetable, Sunburst, Taylor, Smith & Taylor, 9 In. 12.00
Pebbleford, Pitcher, Pink, Taylor, Smith & Taylor, 8 In. 25.00
Petal Lane, Cup & Saucer, Taylor, Smith & Taylor 15.00
Petal Lane, Plate, Dinner, Taylor, Smith & Taylor, 10 In. 14.00
Petit Point Basket, Bowl, Cereal, Salem China 6 1/4 In. .... 7.00 to 14.00
Petit Point Basket, Casserole, Cover, Salem China, 9 In. 78.00
Petit Point Basket, Cup, Salem China 8.00
Petit Point Basket, Plate, Bread & Butter, Salem China, 6 1/4 In. .... 4.00 to 8.00
Petit Point Basket, Plate, Dinner, Salem China, 9 1/2 In. 14.00
Petit Point Basket, Plate, Salad, Salem China, 7 1/4 In. 7.00
Petit Point Basket, Platter, Salem China, 11 1/4 In. 19.00
Petit Point Bouquet, Platter, Paden City Pottery, 12 In. 25.00
Petite Fleur, Creamer, Johnson Brothers 15.00
Pinkie, Platter, Blue Ridge, 11 3/4 In. 20.00
Plantation Ivy, Plate, Dinner, Blue Ridge, 9 1/2 In. 17.00
Platinum Garland, Bowl, Fruit, Harmony House, 5 1/2 In. 18.00
Platinum Garland, Plate, Salad, Harmony House, 7 3/4 In. 27.00
Platinum Garland, Soup, Dish, Harmony House, 7 3/4 In. 27.00
Poinsettia, Bowl, Tab Handle, Blue Ridge, 7 In. 55.00
Poinsettia, Bowl, Vegetable, Round, Blue Ridge, 9 3/8 In. 35.00
Poinsettia, Cup & Saucer, Blue Ridge 38.00
Poinsettia, Plate, Salad, Blue Ridge, 7 1/4 In. 15.00
Poppies, Bowl, Vegetable, Blue Ridge, 9 1/2 In. 38.00
Poppy, Bowl, Cereal, Pink, Universal, 8 In. 10.00
Poppy, Gravy Boat, Johnson Brothers 35.00
Poppy, Platter, Universal, 13 3/8 x 10 7/8 In. 20.00
Poppy Plate, Dinner, Pink, Universal, 10 In. 15.00
Quilted Fruit, Creamer, Blue Ridge 20.00
Random Leaves, Plate, Dinner, Taylor, Smith & Taylor, 10 1/4 In. 10.00
Red Rooster, Plate, Blue Ridge, 9 1/2 In. 75.00
Red Tulip, Chop Plate, Blue Ridge, 12 In. 45.00
Regency, Cup & Saucer, White, Johnson Brothers 15.00
Regency, Plate, Dinner, Green, Johnson Brothers, 9 7/8 In. 20.00
Regency, Plate, Luncheon, Johnson Brothers, 9 3/4 In. 14.00
Regency, Relish, Oval, White, Platinum Trim, Johnson Brothers, 8 In. 20.00
Rhapsody, Platter, Blue Ridge, 13 1/2 x 10 In. 23.00
Rita, Creamer, Taylor, Smith & Taylor 15.00
Riviera, Bowl, Fruit, Light Green, Homer Laughlin, 5 1/4 In. 14.00
Riviera, Bowl, Fruit, Mauve Blue, Homer Laughlin, 5 1/4 In. 14.00
Riviera, Butter, Red, Homer Laughlin, 1/2 Lb. 125.00
Riviera, Butter, Yellow, Homer Laughlin, 1/2 Lb. 125.00

Riviera, Casserole, Cover, Mauve Blue, Homer Laughlin 140.00
Riviera, Creamer, Yellow, Homer Laughlin 13.00
Riviera, Cup, Light Green, Homer Laughlin 10.00
Riviera, Cup, Mauve Blue, Homer Laughlin 11.00
Riviera, Plate, Bread & Butter, Light Green, Homer Laughlin, 6 1/4 In. 9.00
Riviera, Plate, Bread & Butter, Mauve Blue, Homer Laughlin, 6 1/4 In. 9.00
Riviera, Plate, Bread & Butter, Red, Homer Laughlin, 6 1/4 In. 9.00
Riviera, Plate, Dinner, Light Green, Homer Laughlin, 9 5/8 In. 19.00
Riviera, Plate, Luncheon, Light Green, Homer Laughlin, 9 In. 14.00
Riviera, Saucer, Yellow, Homer Laughlin 6.00
Riviera, Soup, Dish, Light Green, Homer Laughlin, 8 In. 27.00
Rooster, Ashtray, Blue Ridge, Square, 3 In. 35.00
Rooster, Bowl, Vegetable, Oval, Blue Ridge, 9 1/2 In. 50.00
Rooster, Plate, Motto, Blue Ridge, 6 1/8 In. 249.00
Rosalinda, Creamer, Homer Laughlin 19.00
Rosalinda, Cup & Saucer 25.00
Rosalinda, Plate, Dinner, Homer Laughlin, 9 5/8 In. 35.00
Rosalinda, Plate, Luncheon, Homer Laughlin, 8 3/4 In. 19.00
Rosalinda, Soup, Dish, Homer Laughlin, 7 3/4 In. 24.00
Rose, Cup & Saucer, Paden City Pottery 10.00
Rose, Plate, Bread & Butter, Paden City Pottery, 6 1/4 In. 4.00
Rose, Plate, Luncheon, Paden City Pottery, 8 1/4 In. 8.00
Rose, Platter, Oval, Taylor, Smith & Taylor, 13 1/2 In. 30.00
Rose, Platter, Paden City Pottery, 13 3/4 in. 35.00
Rose Chintz, Cup, Pink, Johnson Brothers, 3 1/4 In. 33.00
Rose Marie, Creamer, Blue Ridge 63.00
Rosedawn, Bowl, Cereal, Johnson Brothers, 6 1/4 In. 18.00
Rosedawn, Cup & Saucer, Johnson Brothers 20.00
Rosedawn, Plate, Luncheon, Johnson Brothers, 9 In. 21.00
Rosette, Bowl, Vegetable, Harmony House, 9 1/2 In. 28.50
Rosette, Gravy Boat, Harmony House 56.00
Rosette, Platter, Harmony House, 15 1/2 In. 44.00
Rosewood, Platter, Homer Laughlin, 11 1/2 In. 27.00
Samantha, Bowl, Dessert, Salem China, 5 1/4 In. 6.00
Samantha, Bowl, Vegetable, Salem China, 9 In. 24.00
Samantha, Creamer, Salem China 9.00
Samantha, Cup & Saucer, Salem China 9.00
Samantha, Plate, Bread & Butter, Salem China, 6 In. 4.00
Samantha, Plate, Dinner, Salem China, 10 In. 9.00
Samantha, Salver, Salem China, 12 In. 25.00
Samantha, Soup, Dish, Salem China, 8 In. 8.00
Samantha, Sugar, Cover, Salem China 14.00
Savoy, Plate, Dinner, Johnson Brothers, 10 3/4 In. 12.00
Sculptured Fruit, Pitcher, Blue Ridge, 32 Oz., 6 1/2 In. 95.00
Sculptured Fruit, Pitcher, Blue Ridge, 7 In. .... 125.00 to 130.00
Sea Shell, Casserole, Cover, Taylor, Smith & Taylor, 8 In. 50.00
Sea Shell, Plate, Dinner, Taylor, Smith & Taylor, 10 1/4 In. 11.00
Sea Shell, Platter, Taylor, Smith & Taylor, 13 1/2 In. 30.00
Sea Shell, Soup, Dish, Taylor, Smith & Taylor, 8 In. 13.00
Serenade, Pitcher, Spiral, Blue Ridge, 6 1/8 In. 165.00
Shasta Daisy, Gravy Boat, Taylor, Smith & Taylor 23.00
Shasta Daisy, Plate, Dinner, Taylor, Smith & Taylor, 10 1/8 In. 12.00
Shell Crest, Plate, Tab Handle, Paden City Pottery, 10 1/2 In. 20.00
Shell Crest, Platter, Paden City Pottery, 14 In. 25.00
Shell Crest, Platter, Paden City Pottery, 16 In. 30.00
Silver Design, Platter, Oval, Taylor, Smith & Taylor, 13 1/2 In. 33.00
Simone, Serving Bowl, Harmony House, 9 1/8 In. 22.00
Songbirds, Plate, Salad, Blue Ridge, 8 1/4 In. 139.00
Spiderweb, Snack Tray, Lug Handles, Blue Ridge, 10 1/2 In. 25.00
Spray, Bowl, Cereal, Piecrust Shape, Blue Ridge, 6 In. 12.00
Spring Wreath, Bowl, Fruit, Homer Laughlin, 1948, 5 In. 7.00

Spring Wreath, Bowl, Vegetable, Cover, Homer Laughlin, 8 In. 69.00
Spring Wreath, Bowl, Vegetable, Homer Laughlin, 8 In. 25.00
Spring Wreath, Plate, Bread & Butter, Homer Laughlin, 6 1/4 In. 5.95
Spring Wreath, Platter, Oval, Homer Laughlin, 12 In. 19.00
Spring Wreath, Platter, Oval, Homer Laughlin, 15 1/4 In. 55.00
Spring Wreath, Sauceboat, Homer Laughlin, 8 1/4 In. 25.00
Spring Wreath, Soup, Dish, Homer Laughlin, 8 1/4 In. 12.50
Staffordshire Bouquet, Plate, Dinner, Johnson Brothers, 9 3/4 In. 15.00
Staffordshire Bouquet, Plate, Salad, Johnson Brothers, 7 3/4 In. 15.00
Stanhome Ivy, Plate, Dinner, Blue Ridge, 9 1/2 In. 15.00
Sugar & Spice Blue, Plate, Bread & Butter, Johnson Brothers, 7 In. 13.00
Sugar & Spice Blue, Platter, Oval, Johnson Brothers, 12 1/4 In. 45.00
Summertime, Celery Dish, Blue Ridge, 6 1/2 x 11 In. 99.00
Symphony, Bowl, Fruit, Chartreuse, Harmony House, 5 1/2 In. 12.00
Symphony, Cup & Saucer, Gray, Harmony House 10.00
Symphony, Plate, Bread & Butter, Gray, Harmony House, 6 1/4 In. 12.00
Symphony, Plate, Luncheon, Pink, Harmony House, 9 1/4 In. 18.00
Symphony, Soup, Dish, Chartreuse, Harmony House, 7 3/4 In. 14.00
Symphony, Soup, Dish, Pink, Tab Handle, Harmony House, 1 1/2 x 7 In. 11.00
Tally Ho, Plate, Dinner, Stirrup Cup, Johnson Brothers, 10 1/2 In. 60.00
Tally Ho, Plate, Dinner, The Meet, Johnson Brothers, 10 1/2 In. 60.00
Tally Ho, Platter, The Kill, Johnson Brothers, 20 x 15 In. 399.00
Tangerine, Coffeepot, Harmony House, 8 Cup, 9 In. 20.00
Tartan, Sugar, Cover, Harmony House 15.00
Temp Pica, Bowl, Dessert, Homer Laughlin, 6 In. 7.00
Temp Pica, Bowl, Vegetable, Homer Laughlin, 9 In. 24.00
Temp Pica, Soup, Dish, Homer Laughlin, 8 1/4 In. 13.00
Thanksgiving Turkey, Plate, Blue Ridge, 10 1/2 In. 218.00
Thistle, Platter, Candlewick Shape, Blue Ridge, 14 x 11 1/4 In. 23.00
Triumph, Soup, Dish, Rim, Empire Shape, Taylor, Smith & Taylor 10.00
Tulip Time, Platter, Johnson Brothers, 16 x 12 1/4 In. 85.00
Tulips In Lace, Bowl, Vegetable, Candlewick Shape, Blue Ridge, 9 In. 26.00
Tutti Frutti, Cup & Saucer, Blue Ridge, Jumbo 95.00
Verna, Cake Plate, Maple Leaf Shape, Handle, Blue Ridge, 10 x 10 In. .... 65.00 to 125.00
Vintage, Gravy Boat, Johnson Brothers, 8 In. 25.00
Virginia Rose, Berry Bowl, Cosmos, Homer Laughlin, 5 1/4 In. 8.00
Virginia Rose, Bowl, Vegetable, Tulips In Basket, Homer Laughlin, 8 1/4 In. 33.00
Virginia Rose, Saucer, Homer Laughlin 2.00
Virginia Rose, Saucer, Tulips In Basket, Homer Laughlin 4.00
Virginia Rose, Soup, Dish, Fluffy Rose, Homer Laughlin, 8 1/2 In. 12.00
Weathervane, Platter, Blue Ridge, 13 1/2 In. 50.00
Weathervane, Platter, Oval, Taylor, Smith & Taylor, 14 In. 15.00
Wembley, Creamer, Harmony House 20.00
Wembley, Platter, Harmony House, 14 1/4 x 10 1/8 In. 60.00
Wild Cherry, Soup, Dish, Tab Handle, Blue Ridge, 7 In. 24.00
Wild Quince, Plate, Dinner, Taylor, Smith & Taylor, 10 In. 15.00
Wild Rose, Platter, Rose, Taylor, Smith & Taylor, 12 x 8 3/8 In. 35.00
Wild Strawberry, Plate, Blue Ridge, 9 In. 18.00
Wild Turkey, Dinner Service, Johnson Bros., Service For 12 .... 410.00
Winnie, Creamer, Blue Ridge 18.00
Wood Hyacinth, Plate, Dinner, Fascination Shape, Universal, 10 1/4 In. 13.00
Wood Hyacinth, Platter, Fascination Shape, Universal, 12 x 11 In. 23.00
Wood Rose, Creamer, Taylor, Smith & Taylor 19.00
Wood Rose, Gravy Boat, Underplate, Taylor, Smith & Taylor 26.00
Wood Rose, Sugar, Cover, Taylor, Smith & Taylor 23.00
Woodhue, Bowl, Fruit, White, Gold Trim, Harmony House, 5 1/2 In. 18.00
Woodhue, Creamer, Harmony House, 4 x 5 In. 30.00
Woodhue, Cup & Saucer, White, Harmony House 24.00
Wrinkled Rose, Bowl, Vegetable, Oval, Blue Ridge, 9 1/4 x 7 In. 25.00
Wrinkled Rose, Platter, Blue Ridge, 13 In. 20.00
Yellow Rose, Bowl, Paden City Pottery, c.1950, 6 1/4 In. 8.00

Yellow Rose, Plate, Paden City Pottery, 9 1/4 In. 9.00

DIONNE QUINTUPLETS were born in Canada on May 28, 1934. The publicity about their birth and their special status as wards of the Canadian government made them famous throughout the world. Visitors could watch the girls play; reporters interviewed the girls and the staff. Thousands of special dolls and souvenirs were made picturing the quints at different ages. Emilie died in 1954, Marie in 1970, and Yvonne in 2001. Annette and Cecile still live in Canada.

Doll, Annette, Madame Alexander, Composition, Molded Hairpin, Box, 7 1/2 In. .... 385.00 to 468.00
Doll, Annette, Madame Alexander, Composition, Sleep Eyes, Dress, Tag, 14 In. 300.00
Doll, Annette, Madame Alexander, Composition, Wig, Clothes, Pin, Box, 7 1/2 In. 440.00
Doll, Cecile, Madame Alexander, Composition, Original Dress, Pin, 1930s, 8 In. .... 220.00 to 300.00
Doll, Madame Alexander, Composition, Baby, 1936, 7 In., 5 Piece 705.00
Doll, Madame Alexander, Composition, Baby, Jointed, Clothes, Bed, 7 In., 5 Piece 935.00
Doll, Madame Alexander, Composition, Toddler, Dresses, Tags, 7 In., 5 Piece 990.00
Doll, Madame Alexander, Composition, Toddler, Human Hair Wig, 16 In. 450.00

DIRK VAN ERP was born in 1860 and died in 1933. He opened his own studio in 1908 in Oakland, California. He moved his studio to San Francisco in 1909 and the studio remained under the direction of his son until 1977. Van Erp made hammered copper accessories, including vases, desk sets, bookends, candlesticks, jardinieres, and trays, but he is best known for his lamps. The hammered copper lamps often had shades with mica panels.

Bowl, Brass, Hammered, Flared, Cylindrical Foot, Mark, 11 In. 780.00
Desk Set, Copper, Hammered, Blotter, Inkwell, Letter Opener, 5 Piece 1440.00
Jardiniere, Copper, Hammered, Brown & Red, Warty, Rolled Rim, 5 1/2 x 12 1/2 In. 8225.00
Vase, Copper, Hammered, Baluster, Rolled Rim, Windmill Mark, 9 1/2 x 4 In. 2703.00
Vase, Copper, Hammered, Red, Warty, Squat, Folded In Rim, 4 1/4 x 6 In. 5875.00
Vase, Copper, Hammered, Shouldered, Original Patina, Impressed Mark, 5 In. .... 510.00 to 1140.00
Vase, Copper, Hammered, Tapered Shoulder, Rolled Rim, Windmill Mark, 9 x 7 In. 4995.00
Vase, Copper, Hammered, Warty, Original Patina, Impressed Mark, 8 In. 7700.00
Wastebasket, Willow, Woven, Cylindrical, Hammered Copper Trim, 14 x 11 In. 4500.00

DISNEYANA is a collector's term. Walt Disney and his company introduced many comic characters to the world. Collectors search for examples of the work of the Disney Studios and the many commercial products modeled after his characters, including Mickey Mouse and Donald Duck, and recent films, like *Beauty and the Beast* and *The Little Mermaid.*

Ashtray, 3 Little Pigs, Playing Music, Building Wall, Japan, 1930s, 3 In. 46.00
Ashtray, Mickey Mouse Playing Drum, Ceramic, Japan, 1930s, 3 In. 81.00
Ashtray, Mickey Mouse, Lead, Steel, Painted, 4 x 2 3/4 In. 165.00
Ashtray, Minnie Mouse, Singing, Ceramic, Bavaria, 1930s, 3 In. 60.00
Bank, Donald Duck, Dollars & Cents Windows, Lever, Pressed Tin, Marx, 4 In. 200.00
Bank, Donald Duck, Tin Lithograph, Marx, Box, 1950s, 4 x 4 x 2 1/2 In. 306.00
Bank, Dopey, Dime Register, c.1939, 2 1/2 In. 155.00
Bank, Mickey Mouse, Dime Register, c.1939, 2 1/2 In. 385.00
Bank, Mickey Mouse, Jam Jar, Glass, 4-Sided, Tin Lid, Disney Figures, 1930s, 6 In. 80.00
Bank, Mickey Mouse, Metal, Travel Decals, 1930s, 4 x 3 x 1 In. 135.00
Bank, Mickey Mouse, Treasure Chest, Leather, Brass, Key, Zell Products, c.1939, 4 In. 195.00
Bank, Mickey Mouse, Treasure Chest, Tin Lithograph, Japan, 3 1/4 In. 140.00
Bank, Snow White & Seven Dwarfs, Dime Register, Tin Lithograph, 1938s, 2 1/2 In. 135.00
Bank, Uncle Scrooge, Holds Bag Of Money, Slot, Rubber Trap, 1950s, 9 In. 45.00
Banner, Snow White & Seven Dwarfs Jingle Club, Lithograph, Linen, 1938, 35 x 59 In. 4070.00
Book, 3 Caballeros, H. Marion Palmer, Random House, N.Y., 1944 .... 1200.00
Book, 3 Little Pigs, Blue Ribbon, N.Y., 1933 .... 450.00
Book, Bambi, Flip Book, Whitman, 1942 .... 46.00
Book, Better Little Book, Bambi's Children, Whitman, 1943 .... 45.00

Disneyana, Condiment Set, Mickey & Minnie Mouse, Pottery

Disneyana, Diaper Pail, Donald Duck, Graniteware, 10 In.

Book, Better Little Book, Donald Duck, Forgets To Duck, Whitman, 1939 . . . . . 45.00
Book, Better Little Book, Donald Duck, Green Serpent, Whitman, 1947 . . . . . 45.00
Book, Better Little Book, Mickey Mouse, Dude Ranch Bandit, Flip Book, Whitman, 1943 . . . . . 60.00
Book, Better Little Book, Mickey Mouse, Stolen Jewels, Whitman, 1949 . . . . . 80.00
Book, Better Little Book, Mickey Mouse, The Treasure Hunt, Flip Book, Whitman, 1941 . . . . . 80.00
Book, Big Little Book, Blaggard Castle, Whitman, 1934 . . . . . 127.00
Book, Big Little Book, Mickey Mouse, Pluto Racer, Whitman, 1936 . . . . . 58.00
Book, Big Little Book, Silly Symphony Stories, Donald Duck, Peter Pig, Whitman, 1936 . . . . . 69.00
Book, Big Little Book, The Bat Bandit, Whitman, 1946 . . . . . 230.00
Book, Mickey Mouse Crusoe, Whitman, 1936, 70 Pages 475.00
Book, Mickey Mouse, No. 4, 25 Cents, McKay, 1934 . . . . . 500.00
Book, Walt Disney's Clock Cleaners, Whitman, Racine, 1938 . . . . . 375.00
Book, Walt Disney's Donald Duck, Whitman, Racine, 1935 . . . . . 800.00
Book, Walt Disney's Ferdinand The Bull, Whitman, Racine, 1938 . . . . . 250.00
Book, Wise Little Hen, Walt Disney Enterprises, 1937 . . . . . 250.00
Book Bag, Snow White & Seven Dwarfs, Character Graphics, 1940s-50s 110.00
Bookends, Snow White & Doc, Chalk, 1930s, 7 In. 190.00
Bottle, Mickey Mouse, Ginger Ale, Green Glass, Label, 1930s, 8 In. 199.00
Bowl, Candy, Fantasia, Nymphs, Ceramic, Vernon Kilns, c.1940, 7 In. 120.00
Bowl, Mickey Mouse, Horace, Minnie, China, Bavaria, 1930s, 5 In. 139.00
Bowl, Sneezy & Grumpy, Ceramic, Wadeheath, 1930, 6 1/2 In., Child's 92.00
Box, Mickey Mouse Cookies, 1937, 5 In. 305.00
Box, Pinocchio Chewing Gum, Display, 8 1/2 In. 305.00
Box, Snow White & Seven Dwarfs Candy Pops, 8 In. 77.00
Bracelet, Mickey & Pluto Hunting, Mickey & Minnie Having Picnic, Enamel, 1930 . . . . . 133.00
Calendar, 1939, Brown & Bigelow, 12 x 10 In., 4 Sheet 385.00
Camera, Deluxe Mick-A-Matic, No. 880, Child Guidance, Box, 1960s 130.00
Camera, Mickey Mouse, Brownie Target, Box, 5 In. 2970.00
Can, Donald Duck Grapefruit & Orange Juice, 1942, Qt., 7 In. 50.00
Can, Donald Duck Orange Juice, Qt., 7 In. 55.00
Cane, Mickey Mouse Handle, Wood, Fun-E-Flex, 1930s, 34 In. 275.00
Canister, Donald Duck 3 Minute Oats, Cardboard, 1943-45, 7 In. 120.00
Cap, Mickey Mouse, Beverages Premium, Felt, Purple, Bottle Cap Mounts, 10 x 5 In. 115.00
Cel, see Animation Art category.
Clock, Alarm, Donald Duck, Head Bobs, Box, Bayard, France, Metal, 1960s, 4 1/2 In. 139.00
Clock, Alarm, Mickey Mouse, Head Bobs, Box, Bayard, France, Metal, 1960s, 4 1/2 In. 127.00
Clock, Alarm, Mickey Mouse, Metal, Electric, Animated, Ingersoll, 1930s, 4 x 4 x 3 In. 357.00
Clock, Alarm, Mickey Mouse, U.S. Time, 4 1/2 In. 66.00
Clock, Donald Duck, Square, Metal, Windup, Head Bobs, Glen Clock, c.1950, 5 In. . . . . . 115.00 to 493.00
Condiment Set, Mickey & Minnie Mouse, Pottery . . . . . *ILLUS* 784.00
Cookie Jar, Alice In Wonderland, 1950s, 7 In. 85.00
Cookie Jar, Bull Dog Cafe, Treasure Craft Disney, 13 1/2 In. 40.00
Cookie Jar, Mickey Mouse Club, 12 1/4 In. 12.00
Cup, Mickey Mouse, Pluto, China, Wade Heath & Co., Box, 3 In. 220.00
Cup, Mickey Mouse, Waving At Birds, China, 1930s, 2 1/4 In. 58.00
Diaper Pail, Donald Duck, Graniteware, 10 In. . . . . . *ILLUS* 252.00
Dish, Bambi, Thumper, Friends, Ceramic, Evan K. Shaw, 1940s, 5 1/2 In. 58.00

Dish, Christmas Tree Shape, Mickey Mouse Center, Japan, 6 x 5 In. 7.00
Dish, Donald Duck, China, 3 Sections, 1930s, 8 In. 58.00
Dish, Food Warmer, Donald Duck, Sections, Ceramic, 1950s, 6 In. 46.00
Disneykins, Pinocchio, Snow White, Dumbo, Marx, Box, c.1961, 12 1/2 x 5 1/2 In. 230.00
Display, Cardboard, 20 Plastic Figurines, Marx, 1950s 550.00
Display, Cars, Sport, Mickey, Donald, Goofy, Cardboard, Easel Back, Empire, 8 x 11 In. 259.00
Display, Disneykins Store, Castle, Cardboard, Plastic Figures, Marx, 1960, 13 x 15 x 3 In. 253.00
Display, Disneykins Store, Pinocchio, Easel Back, Die Cut, Marx, 1920, 12 x 16 In. 680.00
Display, Donald Duck Icy-Frost Twins, 8 In. 80.00
Display, Ingersoll Rings, 10 Sterling Silver Rings, 4 Mickey, 6 Donald, 11 x 8 1/4 In. 385.00
Display, Mickey Mouse Pencil Sharpener, Cardboard, Easel, 8 Sharpeners, 1930s, 11 x 8 In. 1650.00
Display, Pocket Watch, Mickey Mouse, 6 Watches, Bradley, Boxes 660.00
Display, Snap-Eeze Store, Figaro, Dopey, Cardboard, 4 Boxes, Marx, 1960s, 12 x 14 In. 285.00
Display, Snap-Eeze Store, Pluto, Mickey, Cardboard, 4 Boxes, Marx, 1960s, 12 x 14 In. 155.00
Display Board, Ingersoll, 10 Watches, 20th Birthday, 1948, Adult 4400.00
Display Card, Rings, Sterling Silver, $1.50, Adjustable, Ingersoll, c.1945 .... 715.00
Doctor Kit, Donald Duck, Suitcase, Medical Supplies, Hassenfeld Bros., 1950s 146.00
Doll, Alice, Plastic, Sleep Eyes, Original Clothes, Booklet, Madame Alexander, 8 In. 85.00
Doll, Danny The Little Black Lamb, Blue Ribbon Pin, 1948, 12 In. 190.00
Doll, Donald Duck, Cowboy, Composition, Knickerbocker, 1938-41, 9 1/2 In. ....6600.00 to 6720.00
Doll, Donald Duck, Russian Costume, Composition, Tag, Knickerbocker, 1938-41, 10 In. 3575.00
Doll, Donald Duck, Sailor, Angry, Velvet Body, Oilcloth Feet, Bill, Krueger, c.1936, 16 In. 1008.00
Doll, Donald Duck, Stuffed, Long Bill, Oilcloth Eyes, Collar, Velveteen, Argentina, 10 In. 195.00
Doll, Donald Duck, Tag, Knickerbocker, 1936-41, 18 1/2 In. 495.00
Doll, Dumbo, Knickerbocker, 1941, 8 1/2 In. 95.00
Doll, Ferdinand The Bull, Composition, Tag, Knickerbocker, 1938-41, 9 In. 204.00
Doll, Jiminy Cricket, Composition, Jointed, Knickerbocker, 1940, 10 In. 385.00
Doll, Jiminy Cricket, Jointed, Wood, Ideal, 1940, 8 1/2 In. ....385.00 to 510.00
Doll, Ludwig Von Drake, Talking, Tape, Gund, Box, 1961, 15 In. 115.00
Doll, Mickey Mouse, Cowboy, Composition, Clothes, Knickerbocker, 1935, 9 1/2 In. 2520.00
Doll, Mickey Mouse, Felt, Dean Rag Book Co., Borgfeldt, c.1930, 8 1/2 In. 358.00
Doll, Mickey Mouse, Felt, Tags, Ear Button, Steiff, c.1931, 4 1/2 In. 2860.00
Doll, Mickey Mouse, Neck Tag, Knickerbocker, 1935, 12 In. 523.00
Doll, Mickey Mouse, Oilcloth Face, Blue Plants, Borgfeldt, c.1934, 10 In. 1230.00
Doll, Mickey Mouse, Stuffed, Cowboy, Composition, Knickerbocker, c.1936, 12 1/2 In. 2800.00
Doll, Mickey Mouse, Stuffed, Rat Nose, Rubber Tail, Knickerbocker, 1930s, 11 In. 645.00
Doll, Mickey Mouse, Stuffed, Steiff, c.1931, 6 1/2 In. 530.00
Doll, Mickey Mouse, Stuffed, Steiff, c.1931, 19 In. 7150.00
Doll, Mickey Mouse, Stuffed, Toothy Grin, Dean Rag Book Co., 1930s, 9 In. 310.00
Doll, Mickey Mouse, Velvet, Red Painted Mouth, Paper Tag, Steiff, c.1931, 9 In. 2800.00
Doll, Mickey Mouse, Velvet, Satin Gloves, Charlotte Clark, c.1935, 18 In. 1900.00
Doll, Minnie Mouse, Felt, Dean Rag Book Co., Borgfeldt, c.1930, 8 In. 525.00
Doll, Minnie Mouse, Felt, Steiff, c.1931, 6 In. 1100.00
Doll, Minnie Mouse, Satin Gloves, Hat, Underwear, Corduroy Shoes, c.1935, 18 In. 1568.00
Doll, Minnie Mouse, Stuffed, Cloth, Felt, Flower In Hat, Lars, Italy, 15 1/2 In. 560.00
Doll, Minnie Mouse, Stuffed, Flower, Skirt, Hang Tag, Borgfeldt Nifty, 1930s, 11 In. 1000.00
Doll, Minnie Mouse, Stuffed, Toothy Grin, Skirt, Dean's Rag Book Co., c.1930, 7 In. 820.00
Doll, Pinocchio, Composition, Tag, Crown Toy Mfg., 1940, 11 In. 310.00
Doll, Pinocchio, Composition, Tag, Knickerbocker, 1940, 13 In. 323.00
Doll, Scrooge McDuck, Cloth, Felt, Lars, Italy, 21 In. 330.00
Doll, Snow White, Composition Shoulder Head, Wrist Tag, Ideal, c.1938, 18 In. 440.00
Doll, Timothy Mouse, Stuffed, Crown Novelty Co., 1940, 19 In. 81.00
Doll Set, Snow White & Seven Dwarfs, Chad Valley, 12 & 8 In., 8 Piece 990.00
Doll Set, Snow White, Knickerbocker, 1930s, 12 1/2 In. 1155.00
Drum, Mickey Mouse, Donald Duck, Wood, Paper, Tin, Noble & Cooley, 6 1/2 In. 140.00
Drum, Mickey Mouse, Happy Hak, Cardboard, Tin, No. 601, 1950s, 6 1/4 In. 157.00
Drum, Mickey Mouse, Parade, Tin, Ohio Art, 1930s, 6 1/2 In. 115.00
Drum, Mickey Mouse, Tin Lithograph, Ohio Art, 1930s, 6 In. 255.00
Drum Set, Mickey Mouse, Tin, Paper, 32 x 32 In. 115.00
Egg Holder, Mickey Mouse, Porcelain, 1930s 165.00
Figurine, Alice In Wonderland, Ceramic, Label, 1940s, 6 In. 315.00

Disneyana, Figurine, Donald Duck, Leaning On Arm, 1940s, 5 In.

Disneyana, Figurine, Grumpy, Beswick, 1930s, 3 1/2 In.

Disneyana, Figurine, Minnie Mouse, Leaning On Broom, American Pottery, 1940s, 6 In.

Figurine, Big Bad Wolf, Bisque, 1930s, 3 1/2 In. 29.00
Figurine, Centaur, Fantasia, Ceramic, Vernon Kilns, c.1940, 10 In. 415.00
Figurine, Centaurette, Fantasia, Ceramic, Vernon Kilns, c.1940, 8 In. 495.00
Figurine, Clarabelle, Bisque, 1930s, 5 In. 569.00
Figurine, Daisy Duck, Playing Flute, Ceramic, Japan, 5 In. 75.00
Figurine, Donald Duck, Angry, Clay, 6 1/2 In. 75.00
Figurine, Donald Duck, Bill In Air, Bisque, 1930s, 3 In. 46.00
Figurine, Donald Duck, Bugle, Bisque, 3 In. 95.00
Figurine, Donald Duck, Ceramic, Hagen-Renaker, 1960s, 1 1/2 In. 69.00
Figurine, Donald Duck, Fun-E-Flex, Wood, c.1935, 3 In. 380.00
Figurine, Donald Duck, Fun-E-Flex, Wood, c.1935, 5 In. 715.00
Figurine, Donald Duck, Hands On Hips, Bisque, 1930s, 4 1/2 In. 145.00
Figurine, Donald Duck, Leaning On Arm, 1940s, 5 In. .... *ILLUS* 115.00
Figurine, Donald Duck, Long Bill, Rubber, Seiberling Co., 1930, 6 1/2 In. 195.00
Figurine, Donald Duck, Painted, Glazed, Zaccagnini, c.1947, 4 1/2 x 5 1/2 x 9 In. 2300.00
Figurine, Donald Duck, Playing Violin, Bisque, 1930s, 4 1/2 In. 350.00
Figurine, Donald Duck, Riding Scooter, Bisque, 1930s 4 1/2 In. 58.00
Figurine, Donald Duck, Swinging Golf Club, Ceramic, Zaccagnini, 4 1/2 x 5 1/2 x 9 In. 2300.00
Figurine, Faline, Ceramic, 1940s, 7 In. 46.00
Figurine, Ferdinand The Bull, Ceramic, 1930s, 5 In. 195.00
Figurine, Figaro, Ceramic, Geppetto Pottery, 1940s, 4 In. 255.00
Figurine, Giddy The Cat, Bisque, 3 In. 65.00
Figurine, Goofy, Bisque, 1930s, 1 3/4 In. 29.00
Figurine, Goofy, Bisque, 4 In. 125.00
Figurine, Grumpy, Beswick, 1930s, 3 1/2 In. .... *ILLUS* 127.00
Figurine, Honest John, Cane, Handkerchief, Brayton Laguna, c.1939, 3 1/2 x 6 In. 1495.00
Figurine, Horace Horsecollar, Bisque, 1930s, 3 3/4 In. ....69.00 to 150.00
Figurine, Jiminy Cricket, Ceramic, 1940s, 3 1/4 In. 40.00
Figurine, Jiminy Cricket, Pressed Wood, Syroco, 1940s, 5 In. 120.00
Figurine, Jiminy Cricket, With Umbrella, Bendable, Plastic, Marx, Box, 1960s, 5 In. 58.00
Figurine, Mickey & Minnie Mouse, Pluto, Sled, Fun-E-Flex, 10 In. 770.00
Figurine, Mickey & Pluto, Pipe, Bisque, Borgfeldt, Early 1930s, 5 1/2 In. 468.00
Figurine, Mickey Mouse, Brave Little Taylor, Composition, 1940s, 9 In. 109.00
Figurine, Mickey Mouse, Celluloid, Cloth Tail, Japan, 1930, 4 3/4 In. 195.00
Figurine, Mickey Mouse, Celluloid, Label, 1930s, 5 In. 160.00
Figurine, Mickey Mouse, Fun-E-Flex, Borgfeldt, 5 In. 305.00
Figurine, Mickey Mouse, Fun-E-Flex, Wood, Borgfeldt, 1930s, 7 In. 280.00
Figurine, Mickey Mouse, Hands On Waist, Rat Nose, Open Mouth, Lead, 2 1/4 In. 118.00
Figurine, Mickey Mouse, Lollipop Hands, Composition Head, Wire Tail, Wood, 7 1/2 In. 3920.00
Figurine, Mickey Mouse, Lollipop Hands, Wood, Borgfeldt, 1930s, 7 In. 728.00
Figurine, Mickey Mouse, Playing Accordion, 1930s, 5 1/4 In. 175.00
Figurine, Mickey Mouse, Porcelain, Black, White, 3 1/4 In. 195.00
Figurine, Mickey Mouse, Riding Pluto, 1930s, 3 In. 80.00
Figurine, Mickey Mouse, Seiberling Rubber Co., 1930s, 3 1/2 In. 95.00

Disneyana, Figurine, Pegasus, Head Up, Vernon Kilns, 1940, 6 In.

Disneyana, Figurine, Pinocchio, Smiling, American Pottery, 1940s, 6 1/4 In.

Disneyana, Figurine, Snow White, Brayton, 1938, 11 1/2 In.

Figurine, Mickey Mouse, Seiberling Rubber Co., 1930s, 6 In. 145.00
Figurine, Mickey Mouse, Singing, Holding Book, Bisque, 3 1/4 In. 250.00
Figurine, Mickey Mouse, Wearing Derby, Striped Pants, Celluloid, Box, 4 In. 275.00
Figurine, Minnie Mouse, Celluloid, Cloth Tail, Japan, 1930, 4 3/4 In. 193.00
Figurine, Minnie Mouse, Fun-E-Flex, Wood, Borgfeldt, 1930s, 7 In. 395.00
Figurine, Minnie Mouse, Fun-E-Flex, Wood, Fabric Skirt, 1950s, 3 3/4 In. 145.00
Figurine, Minnie Mouse, Holding Box, Bisque, 1930s, 3 In. 58.00
Figurine, Minnie Mouse, Holding Nurse Kit, Bisque, 3 1/4 In. 95.00
Figurine, Minnie Mouse, Leaning On Broom, American Pottery, 1940s, 6 In. .... *ILLUS* 115.00
Figurine, Minnie Mouse, Movable Arms, Bisque, 5 1/4 In. 200.00
Figurine, Pegasus, Fantasia, Ceramic, Vernon Kilns, No. 21, 1940, 6 In. 190.00
Figurine, Pegasus, Fantasia, Flute To Chest, Ceramic, Vernon Kilns, No. 6, 1940, 5 1/2 In. 175.00
Figurine, Pegasus, Fantasia, Hand To Ear, Ceramic, Vernon Kilns, No. 5, 1940, 5 In. 195.00
Figurine, Pegasus, Fantasia, Hand To Heart, Ceramic, Vernon Kilns, 1940, 5 In. 135.00
Figurine, Pegasus, Fantasia, Playing Flute, Ceramic, Vernon Kilns, No. 3, 1940, 5 In. 195.00
Figurine, Pegasus, Head Up, Vernon Kilns, 1940, 6 In. .... *ILLUS* 192.00
Figurine, Pinocchio, Pressed Wood, Syroco, 1940s, 8 In. 135.00
Figurine, Pinocchio, Smiling, American Pottery, 1940s, 6 1/4 In. .... *ILLUS* 194.00
Figurine, Pinocchio, Smiling, Ceramic, Embossed, 6 1/4 In. 195.00
Figurine, Pinocchio, Wood, Pull, Fisher-Price, 1939 .... 525.00
Figurine, Pluto, Doghouse, Fun-E-Flex, Borgfeldt 550.00
Figurine, Snow White, Brayton, 1938, 11 1/2 In. .... *ILLUS* 299.00
Figurine, Tinkerbell, Ceramic, Embossed, Goebel, West Germany, 1959, 8 In. ....135.00 to 278.00
Figurine, Unicorn, Fantasia, Black, Ceramic, Vernon Kilns, No. 13, 1940, 5 1/2 In. 195.00
Figurine Set, 3 Little Pigs, Big Bad Wolf, Tin Lithograph, Box, Linemar, Japan, 4 In. 2475.00
Figurine Set, 3 Little Pigs, Bisque, Borgfeldt, Japan, Box, 3 1/2 In., 3 Piece 342.00
Figurine Set, 3 Little Pigs, Seiberling Rubber Co., Box, 1934, 3 Piece 825.00
Figurine Set, Mickey Mouse, Catcher, Pitcher, Outfielder, Batter, 1930s, 3 In., 4 Piece 602.00
Figurine Set, Mickey Mouse, Flag, Rifle, Sword, 1930s, 3 1/2 In., 3 Piece 205.00
Figurine Set, Mickey, Minnie, Others Play Sax, Accordion, Guitar, 3 In., 3 Piece 359.00
Figurine Set, Snow White & Seven Dwarfs, Bisque, Box, 1930s, 3 & 2 1/2 In., 8 Piece 246.00
Figurine Set, Snow White & Seven Dwarfs, Bisque, Musical, Box, 3 & 2 1/2 In., 8 Piece 257.00
Figurine Set, Snow White & Seven Dwarfs, Bisque, Musical, Box, 7 & 4 1/2 In., 8 Piece 1016.00
Figurine Set, Snow White & Seven Dwarfs, Cast Metal, 2 In., 8 Piece 139.00
Figurine Set, Snow White & Seven Dwarfs, Celluloid, R.W. Kerr, Box, 1930s, 5 In., 8 Piece 825.00
Figurine Set, Snow White & Seven Dwarfs, Ceramic, 1940s, 8 Piece 626.00
Flashlight, Silly Symphonies, Joy-A-Teers, Tin, U.S. Electric Co., 1936, 6 3/4 In. 310.00
Fork & Spoon Holder, Donald Duck, Wood, William Rogers & Son, 1936, 5 1/2 In. 330.00
Game, Cinderella, Board, Wand, Playing Cards, Instructions, Parker Brothers, 1950 .... 58.00
Game, Donald Duck, Bean Bag, Cardboard Target, 3 Bean Bags, Gardner, Box 70.00
Game, Dopey's, Bean Bag, Parker Bros., Box, 1938, 14 x 22 In. ....88.00 to 95.00
Game, Mickey Mouse Bagatelle, First Version, Marks Bros., 1934, 24 In. 248.00
Game, Mickey Mouse, Dominoes, Dragon Backs, Box, Halsam, 1930s, 1 x 2 x 9 In. 130.00
Game, Pinocchio, Board, Playing Pieces, Cards, Instructions, Parker Brothers, 1940 .... 109.00

Game, Shuffled Symphonies, Mickey Mouse, 45 Cards, Box, England, 1930s 80.00
Game, Silly Symphony, Big Bad Wolf Board, Parker Brothers, 1930, 13 x 16 In. 135.00
Game, Silly Symphony, Pied Piper Board, Parker Brothers, 1930, 13 x 16 In. 109.00
Game, Silly Symphony, Red Riding Hood Board, Parker Brothers, 1930s, 13 x 16 In. 110.00
Game, Snow White & Seven Dwarfs, Board, Box, Parker Brothers, 1938 ....133.00 to 350.00
Game, Target, Mickey Mouse Soldier, Popgun, 18 Mickey Target Figures, Marks Bros. 625.00
Game, Target, Mickey Mouse, Dart Gun, 3 Wood Legs, Darts, Cardboard, Marks Bros. 278.00
Game, Target, Mickey Mouse, Dart Gun, Darts, Stand, Graphics, Tin, Lido, 8 x 12 In. 46.00
Game, Target, Snow White & Seven Dwarfs, Cardboard, American Toy, 13 x 19 In. 155.00
Gumball Machine, Mickey Mouse & His Pals, Hamilton Enterprises, 1938-41, 15 In. ...1320.00 to 3781.00
Hanky Set, Mickey & Minnie Mouse, Embroidered, Linen, Label, Box, 7 In., 3 Piece 176.00
Hanky Set, Pinocchio, Embroidered, Box, 1940, 7 In., 3 Piece 135.00
Horn, Pinocchio, Tin, Cohn, 15 In. 70.00
Jigsaw Puzzle, Mickey Mouse, Box, Saalfield, 1930s, 8 x 10 In. 98.00
Lamp, Dopey, Ceramic, Seven Dwarfs Shade, 12 In. 155.00
Lamp, Mickey Mouse Figure, Shade, American Pottery Co. Of L.A., 1940s, 17 In. 1350.00
Lamp, Mickey Mouse, Playing Instrument, Glows Pink, 1942-45, 12 In. 300.00
Lamp, Mickey Mouse, Pressed Tin, Mickey & Pluto Shade, 1935, 11 In. 275.00
Lamp, Snow White, Plaster Base, Painted, Shade, LaMode, 13 1/2 In. 275.00
Lantern, Pluto, Tin, Battery Operated, Linemar, Box, 7 In. 220.00
Lunch Box, Alice In Wonderland, Vinyl, Aladdin, 1974, 3 3/4 x 7 1/4 x 8 3/4 In. 196.00
Lunch Box, Disney Express, Metal, Aladdin, 1979-80 .... 35.00
Lunch Box, Minnie Mouse, Ballerina, Red, Vinyl, Standard Plastic Prod., 8 x 8 3/4 In. ...... *ILLUS* 1587.00
Lunch Box, Zorro, Metal, Bottle, Aladdin, 1958, 4 x 7 x 8 In. 280.00
Magnet Set, Mickey Mouse, Minnie Mouse, Rhumba Rhythm, Box, c.1960, 1 1/4 In. 50.00
Map, Treasure Island, Mickey & Donald's Race, Standard Oil, 1939-20, 20 x 27 In. 115.00
Movie Poster, 101 Dalmatians, 1 Sheet, 1961, 41 x 27 In. 510.00
Movie Poster, Fantasia, 1946, 3 Sheet, 77 1/2 x 41 1/2 In. 460.00
Movie Poster, Moth & Flame, Silly Symphony, Re-release, RKO, 1950, 41 x 27 In. 470.00
Movie Poster, Music Land, Linen, RKO, 1955, 41 x 27 In. 190.00
Movie Poster, Pinocchio, Re-release, 1962, 81 x 41 In. 180.00
Movie Projector, Mickey Mouse, Movie Jecktor Co., N.Y., Box, 1935-37 .... 590.00
Movie Projector, Mickey Mouse, Pressed Steel, 2 Films, Keystone, Box, 1935 .... 1045.00
Moving Picture Machine, Mickey Mouse, Pepsodent, Cardboard, 1938, 7 In. 127.00
Napkin Ring, Mickey Mouse, Celluloid, England, c.1930 .... 275.00
Night-Light, Dopey, Tin, Paper, Kiddy Lite, Micro-Lite, Box, 1938, 3 3/4 In. 336.00
Night-Light, Dopey, Tin, Paper, Kiddy Lite, Micro-Lite, 1938, 3 3/4 In. 105.00
Night-Light, Mickey Mouse, Tin, Paper, Kiddy Lite, Micro-Lite, 3 3/4 In. 224.00
Nodder, Donald Duck, Celluloid, Rubber Band Driven, Stickers, 6 In. 395.00
Nodder, Donald Duck, Lead Pendulum, On Metal Base, Windup, 1930s 1050.00
Nodder, Mickey Mouse, Celluloid, Metal Base, Japan, Box, 1930s, 7 In. 2240.00
Nodder, Mickey Mouse, Celluloid, Windup, Borgfeldt, 1930s, 7 In. ....525.00 to 1250.00
Outfit, Mickey Mouse Explorers Club, Guns, Holster, Hat, L. M. Eddy, Box, 1955 .... 248.00
Pail, Candy Container, March On Parade, Donald, Pluto, Huey, Dewey, Louie, 3 In. 86.00
Pail, Donald Duck & Nephews, Tin Lithograph, Ohio Art, 1938, 3 1/2 In. 120.00
Pail, Donald Duck, Nephews On Tricycles, Tin Lithograph, Ohio Art, 1930s, 5 In. 120.00
Pail, Mickey & Minnie, Pluto Roller Skating, Tin Lithograph, 1930s, 3 1/2 In. 145.00
Pail, Mickey Mouse, Golf Clubs, Ohio Art, 6 x 6 In. 468.00
Pail, Mickey Mouse, Marching Scene, Handle, Happynak, 1930s, 4 1/2 In. 235.00
Pail, Minnie Mouse, Pluto, Pressed Tin, Ohio Art, 1938, 11 In. 200.00
Pail & Shovel, Mickey & Minnie Mouse, Chein, c.1933, 6 In. 440.00
Pail & Shovel, Mickey Mouse, Parade, Beach Scene, Pressed Tin, Ohio Art, 10 In. 770.00
Paint Set, Mickey Shaped Palette, Colored, Transogram, 1952, 10 x 14 In. 45.00
Pencil, Mickey Mouse, Mechanical, Figure, Decal, Inkograph Co., 1930, 5 In. 60.00
Pencil Sharpener, Donald Duck, Celluloid, 3 In. 165.00
Pencil Sharpener, Donald Duck, Long Bill, Celluloid, Japan, 2 1/2 In. 180.00
Pencil Sharpener, Goofy, Catalin Plastic, Scalloped Edge, 1940, 1 1/8 In. 90.00
Pencil Sharpener, Snow White, Celluloid, Japan, 2 1/2 In. 250.00
Pencil Sharpener, Thumper, Catalin Plastic, 1 3/4 In. 285.00
Pillow, Mickey & Minnie Mouse, Piano, Vogue Needlecraft, Square, 17 In. 58.00
Pin, Donald Duck, Dry In Any Weather, Celluloid, Norwich Knitting, 1 1/4 In. 244.00

Disneyana, Lunch Box, Minnie Mouse, Ballerina, Red, Vinyl, Standard Plastic Prod., 8 x 8 3/4 In

Disneyana, Toy, Mickey Mouse, Telephone, Tin, Cardboard, NN Hill Co., 1930s, 9 In.

Pin, Donald Duck, Jams, Jellies, Lithograph, 1 1/8 In. 400.00
Pin, Donald Duck, Wanna Fight, c.1935 .... 450.00
Pin, Mickey Mouse Club, Facing Left, Celluloid, 1930s, 1 1/4 In. 86.00
Pin, Mickey Mouse Globe Trotters, I Eat N.B.C. Bread, Celluloid, 1 In. 30.00
Pin, Mickey Mouse, Back To School, Celluloid, White Ground, 1930, 3/4 In. 58.00
Pin, Mickey Mouse, Celluloid, 1928-30, 3/4 In. 175.00
Pin, Mickey Mouse, Crown, Playing Trumpet, Syroco, 1930s, 1 1/2 In. 60.00
Pin, Mickey Mouse, Fox Park Plaza Theater, Celluloid, 1930s, 1 1/4 In. 120.00
Pin, Mickey Mouse, Ice Cream, Southern Dairies Ice Cream, 1 1/4 In. 715.00
Pin, Mickey Mouse, Waving, Tin Lithograph, 1930s, 4 In. 69.00
Pitcher, Mickey Mouse, Porcelain, 4 In. 125.00
Pitcher, Milk, Bambi, Thumper, Friends, Evan K. Shaw, 1940s, 6 In. 58.00
Planter, Archer, Fantasia, Blue, Vernon Kilns, c.1940, 12 In. 275.00
Planter, Bambi & Thumper, Leeds, 1940s 60.00
Planter, Donald Duck, Leeds, 6 x 6 In. 50.00
Planter, Fish Bowl Shape, Fantasia, Vernon Kilns, c.1940, 6 1/2 In. 198.00
Plate, Donald Duck, 3 Sections, Patriot China, 1930s, 8 In. 60.00
Plate, Mickey Mouse, I Like What You Like, Royal Paragon China, England, 7 In. 330.00
Plate, Mickey Mouse, Playing Accordion, Bavaria, 1930s, 6 In. 140.00
Plate, Mickey Mouse, Playing Drum, China, Bavaria, 1930s, 7 1/2 In. 127.00
Plate, Mickey Mouse, Riding Train, China, Bavaria, 1930s, 6 In. 80.00
Plate, Pluto & Friends, Mothers' Day, Schmid, Box, 1977 .... 45.00
Plate, Sleepy & Sneezy, Wade Heath, 1930s, 8 In. 60.00
Platter, Fantasia, Red, Yellow, Blue, Fairies Fly Among Flowers, Vernon Kilns, 12 In. .... 120.00 to 175.00
Poster, Frontierland, Plaque, Frame, c.1955, 63 1/2 x 43 1/4 In. 3376.00
Poster, It's A Small World, Fantasyland, Plaque, Frame, c.1966, 64 x 44 In. 805.00
Poster, Matterhorn Bobsleds, Plaque, Frame, c.1959, 63 1/2 x 43 1/2 In. 3780.00
Poster, Monorail, Plaque, Frame, c.1959, 63 1/2 x 43 1/2 In. 2346.00
Poster, Peter Pan, Italy, 1953, 28 x 13 In. 236.00
Poster, Rocket Jets, Tommorowland, Plaque, Frame, c.1967, 63 1/2 x 43 1/2 In. 730.00
Poster, United Air Lines, Disneyland, Plaque, Frame, c.1964, 54 1/2 x 34 1/2 In. 549.00
Poster, War Bond, Disney Characters, Spaulding Moss Co., 1940s, 28 x 44 In. 98.00
Pot, Mickey & Minnie, Porcelain, Richard G. Krueger Inc., Germany, 1930s, 6 In. 160.00
Printing Set, Mickey Mouse, Stamp Pad, 13 Rubber Stamps, Handles, 1930s, 11 x 8 In. 275.00
Puppet, Captain Hook, Boot Tops, Hook, Box, 1950s, 16 In. 90.00
Puppet, Peter Pan, Box, 1950s, 16 In. 58.00
Radiator Cap, Mickey Mouse, Chrome, 1940s, 4 In. 470.00
Radio, Mickey Mouse, Art Deco, Emerson, No. 410, 1933, 7 1/4 x 7 x 5 In. .... 1530.00 to 1685.00
Radio, Mickey Mouse, Press Wood, Emerson, No. 411, c.1934 .... 3020.00
Radio, Snow White, Emerson, 1933-40, 8 In. 1792.00
Rattle, Mickey & Minnie Mouse, Musical, England, 1930s, 7 1/2 In. 250.00
Rug, Donald Duck, Bambi, Pluto, Lady & Tramp, 1950s, 44 x 66 In. 80.00
Rug, Donald Duck, Huey, Dewey, Louie, 1950s, 20 x 36 In. 58.00
Rug, Mickey Mouse, Donald Duck, Pluto, 1930s, 20 x 40 In. 370.00
Rug, Snow White & Seven Dwarfs, 1930s, 20 x 40 In. 120.00
Salt & Pepper, Fantasia Mushrooms, Hop, Low, Vernon Kilns, 1940, 3 In. 115.00
Salt & Pepper, Mickey Mouse, Black & White, Germany, c.1933, 2 In. 450.00

Salt & Pepper, Pluto, Gold Trim, Leeds, Late 1940s, 3 1/4 In. 89.00
Salt & Pepper, Tweedle Dee & Tweedle Dum, 1950s, 5 In. 278.00
Scissors, Donald Duck, Handheld Lever, Battery Operated, Linemar, Japan, 6 In. 220.00
Scissors, Mickey Mouse Handle, Tin, 1937, 3 1/4 In. 138.00
Sewing Set, Mickey Mouse, 6 Cardboard Cards, Yarn, Box, 7 x 10 In. 180.00
Shelf, Corner, Mickey Mouse, White & Black Faces, Wood, Folk Art, 23 In. 55.00
Shovel, Sand, Mickey Mouse, Tin Lithograph, Ohio Art, 1930s, 10 In. 175.00
Shovel, Snow, Donald & Nephews, Tin Lithograph, Ohio Art, 1930s, 27 x 7 x 9 In. 280.00
Shovel, Snow, Steel, Wood, Ohio Art, 27 In. 385.00
Sign, Donald Duck Bread, Oven Fresh Flavor, Cardboard, 1945, 21 In. 155.00
Sign, Donald Duck Cola, Paperboard, 1952-55, 26 x 22 In. ....375.00 to 450.00
Sign, Mickey Mouse, Crystal White Soap, Red, Cardboard, Stand-Up, 1936, 30 In. 165.00
Sled, Mickey Mouse & Mouse, Flexible Flyer, Wood, Metal, c.1930, 18 x 28 In. 580.00
Sled, Mickey Mouse, No. 80, Flexible Flyer, 1935, 32 In. 248.00
Soap, 3 Little Pigs, Box, 1930s, 4 x 6 x 1 In., 3 Piece 115.00
Soap, Mickey Mouse & Clarabelle, Toilet Set, Box, 1930, 3 Piece 127.00
Soap, Snow White & Seven Dwarfs, Kerk Guild, 1938, 2 1/4 In., 6 Piece 165.00
Stencil Set, Mickey & Minnie Mouse, Box, 1930 .... 145.00
Tape Measure, Donald Duck, Long Bill, Celluloid, 2 5/8 In. 1018.00
Tea Set, 3 Little Pigs, China, Japan, 13 Piece 58.00
Tea Set, Disneyland, Tin, Box, Chein, 1950s, 13 Piece 153.00
Tea Set, Donald Duck, Tin Lithograph, Box, Chein, 6 Piece 130.00
Tea Set, Donald Duck, Tin Lithograph, Box, Ohio Art, 6 Piece 285.00
Tea Set, Mickey & Minnie Mouse, Tin, Ohio Art, 17 Piece 308.00
Tea Set, Mickey Mouse, Aluminum, 13 Piece 120.00
Tea Set, Mickey's Nephews, Tin Lithograph, Ohio Art, 6 Piece 95.00
Tea Set, Mickey, Minnie, China, Japan, 1930, 21 Piece 185.00
Tea Set, Mickey, Minnie, China, Japan, 1930, 27 Piece 127.00
Tea Set, Pinocchio, Tin, Ohio, 1940, 21 Piece 410.00
Tea Set, Snow White, China, Japan, 16 Piece 155.00
Tile Set, 3 Caballeros, Donald, Joe Carioca, Panchito, 4 In., 3 Piece 115.00
Tin, Mickey Mouse, Biscuit, Round, 7 In. 145.00
Toothbrush Holder, 3 Little Pigs, Playing Music, Building Wall, Bisque, 1930s, 3 1/2 In. 90.00
Toothbrush Holder, Donald Duck, Double, Bisque, 1930s, 4 1/4 In. 330.00
Toothbrush Holder, Donald Duck, Saluting, 1930s, 5 In. 110.00
Toothbrush Holder, Dopey & Doc, Bisque, 1930s, 4 In. 109.00
Toothbrush Holder, Mickey & Minnie Mouse, Bisque, 1930s, 4 1/4 In. 120.00
Toothbrush Holder, Mickey & Minnie, Bisque 325.00
Toothbrush Holder, Mickey Mouse Wiping Pluto's Nose, Ceramic, 1930s, 5 In. ....127.00 to 295.00
Toothbrush Holder, Mickey Mouse, Bisque, Movable Arm, 5 In. 285.00
Toothbrush Holder, Mickey Mouse, Pluto, Borgfeldt, 4 1/2 In. 220.00
Toy, 3 Little Pigs Band, Felt Cover, Tin, Windup, Schuco, 4 1/2 In., 3 Piece 1320.00
Toy, 3 Little Pigs, Laundry Set, Wash Pail, Board, Pressed Tin, Ohio Art 145.00
Toy, 101 Dalmations, Colorforms, Cartoon Kit, 1961 .... 26.00
Toy, Alice & Wonderland Characters, Lithograph On Wood, 10 Piece 2300.00
Toy, Bambi, Rocking Horse, Gong Bell Toy Co., 1956, 29 In. 35.00
Toy, Disney Ferris Wheel, Tin, Windup, Chein, Box, 17 In. 560.00
Toy, Disney Parade Roadster, Windup, Marx 450.00
Toy, Disney Roller Coaster, Tin, Windup, Chein, 19 In. 560.00
Toy, Disneyland, Blocks, Wood, Halsan, Box, 1950s, 7 x 4 1/4 In., 15 Piece 90.00
Toy, Donald Duck Walker, Celluloid, Windup, Box, c.1935, 5 1/2 In. 1115.00
Toy, Donald Duck, Car, Pluto In Back, Sun Rubber, 1940s, 7 In. 90.00
Toy, Donald Duck, Carousel, Celluloid, Japan, Box 6160.00
Toy, Donald Duck, Carousel, Celluloid, Windup, Japan, Box, c.1930s, 7 1/2 x 2 1/2 In. 6160.00
Toy, Donald Duck, Cart, Pull Toy, Fisher-Price, 1937, 20 In. 2080.00
Toy, Donald Duck, Celluloid, Windup, Borgfeldt, 1930s, 3 1/4 In. 385.00
Toy, Donald Duck, Choo Choo, Wood, Pull Toy, Bell, Fisher-Price, 1940s, 9 In. 120.00
Toy, Donald Duck, Dipsy Car, Tin, Windup, Linemar, 5 1/2 In. 280.00
Toy, Donald Duck, Dipsy Car, Tin, Windup, Marx, Box, 5 1/2 In. 715.00
Toy, Donald Duck, Driver, Tin, Plastic, Windup, Marx, Box, 7 In. 635.00
Toy, Donald Duck, Driver, Tin, Windup, Linemar 750.00

Toy, Donald Duck, Drummer, Tin Lithograph, Clockwork, Linemar, Japan, 6 In. 770.00
Toy, Donald Duck, Drummer, Tin, Windup, Marx, Box, 6 In. 470.00
Toy, Donald Duck, Fire Chief, Tin, Windup, Linemar, 5 1/2 In. 1265.00
Toy, Donald Duck, Fireman, Climbing Ladder, Linemar, 14 In. 415.00
Toy, Donald Duck, Fireman, Climbing, Engine, Remote, Linemar, Box, 18 In. 2145.00
Toy, Donald Duck, Goofy, Duet, Tin, Windup, Marx, Box, 1946, 10 In. ....715.00 to 950.00
Toy, Donald Duck, Jack-In-The Box, Wooden Box, Spear Products, 1940s, 5 x 5 x 5 In. 109.00
Toy, Donald Duck, Metal, Plastic, Mouth Opens, Windup, Schuco, Box, 1950 .... 395.00
Toy, Donald Duck, Playing Xylophone, Pull Toy, Fisher-Price, 1938, 11 In. 815.00
Toy, Donald Duck, Quacking, Celluloid, Tin Legs, Windup, Ribbon, Japan, 1930s, 8 1/2 In. 8460.00
Toy, Donald Duck, Race Car, Orange, Tin, No. 5, Windup, MT, 4 In. 248.00
Toy, Donald Duck, Train, Rail Car, Pluto, Windup, Box, 1930s, 6 & 2 1/2 In. 1640.00
Toy, Donald Duck, Trapeze, Celluloid, Japan, Box, 1930s, 8 1/2 In. 1065.00
Toy, Donald Duck, Tricycle, Celluloid, Tin, Cloth British Flag, Japan, Box, c.1934, 5 1/2 x 4 In. 2520.00
Toy, Donald Duck, Tricycle, Celluloid, Tin, Pants, British Flag, Japan, 1930s, 4 x 3 1/2 In. 672.00
Toy, Donald Duck, Walker, Celluloid, Windup, 1930s, 5 1/2 In. 340.00
Toy, Donald Duck, Walker, Long Bill, Celluloid, Windup, 1930s, 5 1/2 In. ....750.00 to 1250.00
Toy, Donald Duck, Whirligig, Tin, Celluloid, Occupied Japan, 8 In. 635.00
Toy, Dopey & Doc, Playing Drum, Pull Toy, Fisher-Price, 1938, 7 In. 815.00
Toy, Dopey, Walker, Tin Lithograph, Clockwork, Box, Marx, 8 1/2 In. ....468.00 to 660.00
Toy, Garden Set, Donald Pushing Mickey Mouse In Wheelbarrow, Salco, Box, 3 In. ....110.00 to 120.00
Toy, Goofy, Gardener, Tin, Windup, Marx, England, 1940s, 7 1/4 In. 550.00
Toy, Goofy, Turns In Circles, Tail Spins, Windup, Linemar 375.00
Toy, Jiminy Cricket, Tux, Umbrella, Clockwork, Box, Tin Lithograph, Linemar, 6 In. 825.00
Toy, Locomotive, 3 Cars, Caboose, Windup, Marx, 15 In., 5 Piece 350.00
Toy, Mickey & Minnie Mouse, Acrobats, Celluloid, Japan, Box, 1930s, 13 In. ....715.00 to 1344.00
Toy, Mickey & Minnie Mouse, Barrel Organ, Salco, England, Box, 1930s, 3 1/2 In. 305.00
Toy, Mickey & Minnie Mouse, Hurdy-Gurdy, Distler, 1930, 6 x 8 In. ....6000.00 to 13200.00
Toy, Mickey & Minnie Mouse, Motorcycle, Tin Lithograph, Clockwork, Tipp & Co., 9 In. 5000.00
Toy, Mickey & Minnie Mouse, On The River, Boat, Die Cast, Salco, Box, 5 1/2 In. 300.00
Toy, Mickey & Minnie Mouse, Piano, Wood, Marx, Box, c.1935, 9 x 10 x 4 3/4 In. 3920.00
Toy, Mickey & Minnie Mouse, Rowboat, Green, Lead, Salco, 5 1/4 In. 535.00
Toy, Mickey & Minnie Mouse, Seesaw, Celluloid, Pendulum, Japan, Box, 6 x 5 In. 3080.00
Toy, Mickey & Minnie Mouse, Seesaw, Umbrella, Celluloid, Windup, 6 x 7 1/2 In. 1230.00
Toy, Mickey & Minnie Mouse, Trapeze, Celluloid, Windup, Occupied Japan, Box, 9 In. 787.00
Toy, Mickey & Minnie, Cart, Tin, Celluloid, Windup, Box, 1930s, 5 1/2 x 4 1/2 In. 4480.00
Toy, Mickey Mouse & Donald Duck, Fire Engine, Tin, Plastic, Battery, MT, Box, 16 In. 209.00
Toy, Mickey Mouse & Donald Duck, Weather Forecaster, Plastic House, Box, 6 In. 99.00
Toy, Mickey Mouse & Pluto, Cart, Tin, Celluloid, Windup, Japan, c.1935, 5 x 3 1/4 In. 896.00
Toy, Mickey Mouse, Acrobat, Trapeze, Borgfeldt, Box, 1930s 1495.00
Toy, Mickey Mouse, Balloon Gun, Kilgore, 8 In. 50.00
Toy, Mickey Mouse, Band, 2 Minnie Mouses, Bisque, Borgfeldt, Box, 1933, 3 1/2 In. 440.00
Toy, Mickey Mouse, Bell, N. Hill Brass Co., 1936, 12 In. 385.00
Toy, Mickey Mouse, Bubble Buster Gun, Blowing Up Balloons, Kilgore Co., 1930s 165.00
Toy, Mickey Mouse, Bubble Buster, Lead, Cast Iron, Label, Kilgore, Box, 1935, 7 3/4 In. 225.00
Toy, Mickey Mouse, Carousel, Celluloid, Metal Base, Japan, c.1930s, 7 1/2 In. 2800.00
Toy, Mickey Mouse, Celluloid, Windup, Japan, Box, 1934, 8 In. 5040.00
Toy, Mickey Mouse, Circus Platform, Tin Lithograph, Painted Wood Wheels, 11 In. 1320.00
Toy, Mickey Mouse, Climbing, Cardboard, Pull String, Dolly Toy Co., 8 In. 4480.00
Toy, Mickey Mouse, Cowboy, On Pluto, Celluloid, Windup, Japan, Box, 1930s, 8 In. 10640.00
Toy, Mickey Mouse, Dipsy Car, Tin, Plastic, Windup, Marx, 5 1/2 In. 280.00
Toy, Mickey Mouse, Dipsy Car, Tin, Windup, Linemar, Box, 5 1/2 In. ....525.00 to 750.00
Toy, Mickey Mouse, Donald Duck & Pluto, Windup, Linemar, Box, 3 Piece, 7 In. 3275.00
Toy, Mickey Mouse, Driver, Tin, Plastic, Windup, Marx, Box, 7 In. ....523.00 to 550.00
Toy, Mickey Mouse, Drummer, Tin, Cloth, Battery Operated, Linemar, 11 In. 1695.00
Toy, Mickey Mouse, Drummer, Wood, Paper, Fisher-Price, 1938, 11 In. 130.00
Toy, Mickey Mouse, Drummer, Wood, Paper, No. 476, Fisher-Price, 1941, 7 1/4 In. ....176.00 to 193.00
Toy, Mickey Mouse, Drummer, Wood, Pull Toy, Fisher-Price, 1950s, 8 In. 69.00
Toy, Mickey Mouse, Handcar, Santa, Tree, Clockwork, Box, Lionel, c.1935, 10 In. 1320.00
Toy, Mickey Mouse, Italian Car, Die Cast, Folding Display Box, Politoys, 1960s, 4 In. 46.00
Toy, Mickey Mouse, Jalopy, Tin, Friction, Linemar, 5 In. 220.00

Toy, Mickey Mouse, Jazz Drummer, Tin Lithograph, Squeeze, Chein, c.1935, 6 3/4 In. ...1045.00 to 2800.00
Toy, Mickey Mouse, Laundry Set, Pail, Board, Hanger, Pressed Tin, Ohio Art, 5 1/2 In. 220.00
Toy, Mickey Mouse, Little Big Wheel, Plastic, Battery Operated, Marx, Box, 1970, 10 In. 80.00
Toy, Mickey Mouse, Magician, Tin, Fabric, Battery Operated, Linemar, Box, 10 In. ....1625.00 to 1760.00
Toy, Mickey Mouse, On Hobbyhorse, Celluloid, Wood, Windup, 1930s, 8 In. 1850.00
Toy, Mickey Mouse, Pop-Up, Wood, 5 In. 66.00
Toy, Mickey Mouse, Race Car, Orange, Tin, No. 5, Windup, MT, 4 In. 305.00
Toy, Mickey Mouse, Rambler, Celluloid, Windup, Borgfeldt, Box, 1930 .... 4428.00
Toy, Mickey Mouse, Rocking Chair, Celluloid, Pluto Pulling Cord, Lithograph, Box, 5 In. 1430.00
Toy, Mickey Mouse, Rocking Horse, Wood, Mengel Co., St. Louis, 1935, 34 In. 220.00
Toy, Mickey Mouse, Skater, Tin, Cloth, Windup, 7 In. 605.00
Toy, Mickey Mouse, Sparkler, Rat Nose, Tin, 5 1/2 In. 330.00
Toy, Mickey Mouse, Spring & Bumper, Ride On, Pontiac, 1937, 36 In. 176.00
Toy, Mickey Mouse, Telephone, Tin, Cardboard, NN Hill Co., 1930s, 9 In. .... *ILLUS* 252.00
Toy, Mickey Mouse, Top, Musical, Pressed Tin, Chein, Box, 9 1/2 In. 120.00
Toy, Mickey Mouse, Top, Tin Lithograph, Graphics, 1930s, 10 In. 214.00
Toy, Mickey Mouse, Train Set, Meteor, Tin Lithograph, Windup, Marx 660.00
Toy, Mickey Mouse, Train, Circus, Lionel, 1930s, 7 In. 349.00
Toy, Mickey Mouse, Train, Express, Airplane, Windup, Marx 750.00
Toy, Mickey Mouse, Trapeze, Tin, Celluloid, Windup, Occupied Japan, Box, 4 1/4 In. 330.00
Toy, Mickey Mouse, Trapeze, Wire Frame, Box, Geo. Borgfeldt Dist., Japan, 8 1/4 In. 660.00
Toy, Mickey Mouse, Tricycle, Pressed Tin, Celluloid, Mechanical, Linemar, Box, 4 In. 358.00
Toy, Mickey Mouse, Tricycle, Tin, Celluloid, Occupied Japan, 4 In. 468.00
Toy, Mickey Mouse, Truck, Mickey's Mousekemovers Moving, Tin, Linemar, 13 In. 330.00
Toy, Mickey Mouse, Twirling Tail, Tin, Windup, 5 1/4 In. 220.00
Toy, Mickey Mouse, Whirligig, On Ball, Celluloid, Windup, 10 In. 1120.00
Toy, Mickey Mouse, Whirligig, On Ball, Wood, Windup, Japan, Box, 1930s, 9 1/2 In. ....2640.00 to 2800.00
Toy, Mickey Mouse, Whirligig, Tin, Celluloid, Occupied Japan, 8 In. 635.00
Toy, Mickey Mouse, Xylophone Player, Tin, Windup, Linemar, 6 1/2 In. 385.00
Toy, Minnie Mouse, Rocker, Tin, Windup, Linemar, Box, 1950s, 7 In. 649.00
Toy, Minnie Mouse, Trapeze, Celluloid, Windup, Borgfeldt, Box, 1930s 460.00
Toy, Minnie Mouse, Wood, Folk Art, 1930s, 12 In. 365.00
Toy, Pecos Bill, Riding Widowmaker, Windup, Marx, Box, 1940, 9 1/2 x 6 1/2 x 4 In. 121.00
Toy, Pinocchio, Acrobat, Tin, Windup, Marx, c.1939, 16 In. ....330.00 to 450.00
Toy, Pinocchio, Marching, Tin, Linemar 100.00
Toy, Pinocchio, Rocks, Eyes Roll, Tin, Windup, Marx, 1939, 8 3/4 In. 248.00
Toy, Pinocchio, Walker, Composition, 10 1/2 In. 88.00
Toy, Pinocchio, Walker, Tin, Windup, Linemar, Box, 6 In. ....523.00 to 550.00
Toy, Pinocchio, Walker, Tin, Windup, Marx, Box, 8 1/2 In. 575.00
Toy, Pinocchio, Whistling, Holding Apple, Ceramic, 1940s, 6 In. 497.00
Toy, Pluto, Nose To Ground, Marx, Late 1930s, 10 In. 198.00
Toy, Pluto, Paper On Wood, Red Wheels, Fisher-Price, 5 1/4 In. 250.00
Toy, Pluto, Playful, Tin, Windup, Linemar, Box, 1955, 5 In. ....440.00 to 550.00
Toy, Pluto, Playful, Tin, Windup, Linemar, Box, 6 In. 550.00
Toy, Pluto, Pop-Up Critter, Fisher-Price, c.1950, 10 1/2 In. 59.00
Toy, Pluto, Roll Over, Tin, Windup, Marx, Box, 1939, 9 In. ....303.00 to 550.00
Toy, Pluto, Tin Lithograph, Windup, Linemar, Japan, Post 1945, 7 In. 220.00
Toy, Pluto, Tricycle, Tin, Celluloid, Windup, Linemar, Box, 3 3/4 In. 650.00
Toy, Pluto, Walker, Moving Head, Whirling Tail, Felt, Windup, Linemar, Box 550.00
Toy, Pluto, Wise, Crouched, Nose To Ground, Leather Ears, Tail, Tin Lithograph Box, 8 In. 385.00
Toy, Professor Von Drake, Walker, Tin, Windup, Linemar, Box, 6 In. ....350.00 to 385.00
Toy, Sand Strainer, Donald Duck & Pluto, Tin Lithograph, Ohio Art, 1930, 8 In. 86.00
Toy, Talkie Jecktor, Mickey Mouse, Electric, 11 Films, 3 78 RPM Records, 1930s, 14 In. 764.00
Toy, Tinker Bell, Musical, Tin Lithograph, Peter Puppet Plaything, Box, 12 x 12 x 16 In. 532.00
Toy, Train Set, Santa Fe & Disneyland, R.R. Tyco, Box, 1955 .... 385.00
Toy, Train, Disneyland Express, Plastic Engine, 3 Tin Cars, Windup, Marx, Box, 12 In. 115.00
Toy, Truck & Trailer, Tin Lithograph, Friction, Box, 4 x 9 x 3 In. 1495.00
Toy, Washtub, Washboard, Clothesline, Clothespins, Ohio Art, 5 1/2 In. 138.00
Tray, Fantasia Mushrooms, Ceramic, Blue, Vernon Kilns, 1940, 6 x 12 x 3 In. 100.00
Tray, Fantasia Mushrooms, Ceramic, Multicolored, Vernon Kilns, 1940, 6 x 12 x 3 In. 185.00
Tray, Fantasia Mushrooms, Ceramic, White, Vernon Kilns, 1940, 6 x 12 x 3 In. 86.00

Tray, Mickey & Minnie Mouse, Tin, 1933, 10 x 8 x 7 In. 595.00
Tumbler, All Star Parade, Big Bad Wolf, 3 Pigs, 1939, 4 1/4 In. 25.00
Tumbler, All Star Parade, Greedy Pig & Colt, 1939, 4 1/4 In. 25.00
Tumbler, All Star Parade, Snow White & Seven Dwarfs, 1939, 4 3/4 In. 35.00
Tumbler, Arctic Trip With Goofy, 1930s, 4 1/4 In. 25.00
Tumbler, Donald & Nephews, Boy Scouts, 1930s, 4 1/4 In. 35.00
Tumbler, Donald Duck, Riding A Burro, 1930s, 4 1/4 In. 25.00
Tumbler, Donald, Snow White, Dopey, Mickey, Bosco Tumbleres, 1930s, 3 1/4 In. 58.00
Umbrella, Donald Duck, 1930, 24 In., Child's 86.00
Wall Hanging, Pinocchio, Geppetto, Lampwick, Giddy, Wood, Syroco, 3 1/2 x 6 In. 200.00
Wall Hanging Set, Pinocchio, Figaro, Jiminy Cricket, School, Cardboard, Dolly Toy Co. 69.00
War Bond Certificate, U.S. Treasury, Color Lithograph, 1940s, 8 x 10 In. 230.00
Watch, Pocket, Big Bad Wolf, Fob, $1.30, Ingersoll, Box, Child's 3575.00
Watch, Pocket, Mickey Mouse, Embossed, Box, Ingersoll, 1930s, 2 In. 1232.00
Watering Can, Donald Duck, Trips Over Brick, Tin Lithograph, Ohio Art, 1938, 3 In. 110.00
Watering Can, Donald Duck, Watering Garden, Tin Lithograph, Ohio Art, 1938, 4 1/2 In. 120.00
Watering Can, Mickey & Minnie Mouse, Tin Lithograph, Ohio Art, 1930, 3 In. 185.00
Wristwatch, Alice In Wonderland, Figurine, Box, 1950s, Child's 440.00
Wristwatch, Bambi, Chrome Case, Ingersoll, 20th Birthday Box, 1948 .... 810.00
Wristwatch, Bongo Bear, Chrome Case, Ingersoll, 20th Birthday Box, 1948 .... 390.00
Wristwatch, Cinderella, Figurine, Box, 1950s, Child's 415.00
Wristwatch, Daisy Duck, Chrome Case, Ingersoll, 20th Birthday Box, 1948 .... 448.00
Wristwatch, Donald Duck, Cardboard Pop-Up Figure, Box, 1940s, Child's 275.00
Wristwatch, Dopey, Chrome Case, Ingersoll, 20th Birthday Box, 1948 .... 280.00
Wristwatch, Goofy, 17 Jewel, Runs Backwards, Helbros, Red Box, 1972 .... 650.00
Wristwatch, Jiminy Cricket, Chrome Case, Ingersoll, 20th Birthday Box, 1948 .... 336.00
Wristwatch, Mickey Mouse, Cardboard Figure, Oval Box, 1940s, Child's 468.00
Wristwatch, Mickey Mouse, Chrome Case, Metal Link Band, Ingersoll, Box, 1933 .... 448.00
Wristwatch, Mickey Mouse, Figurine, Ingersoll, Box, 1950s, Child's 385.00
Wristwatch, Mickey Mouse, Gold Case, Band, Ingersoll, 20th Birthday Box, 1939 .... 500.00
Wristwatch, Mickey Mouse, Plastic Figure, U.S. Time, Ingersoll, Box, c.1958, 5 In. 1206.00
Wristwatch, Mickey Mouse, Rectangular Face, U.S. Time, Ingersoll, Box, 1959, 5 In. 1206.00
Wristwatch, Minnie Mouse, $12.95 Price Tag, Ingersoll, Box, First, Adult's 110.00
Wristwatch, Peter Pan, Chrome Case, Vinyl Band, Mohertus Trading, Box, 1970s 310.00
Wristwatch, Pinocchio, Chrome Case, Ingersoll, 20th Birthday Box, 1948 .... 252.00
Wristwatch, Pluto, Chrome Case, Ingersoll, 20th Birthday Box, 1948 .... 382.00
Wristwatch, Snow White, Figurine, Box 385.00
Wristwatch, Snow White, Girls, Original Cloth Band & Buckle, U.S. Time, 1939 .... 150.00
Wristwatch, Snow White, Ingersoll, Mirror Box, 1950s 995.00
Wristwatch, Snow White, Magic Mirror Box, 1940s 770.00
Wristwatch, Zorro, Hat Stand, Box, 1957 .... 385.00

DOCTOR, see Dental; Medical

DOLL entries are listed by marks printed or incised on the doll, if possible. If there are no marks, the doll is listed by the name of the subject or country or maker. Notice that Barbie is listed under Mattel. G.I. Joe figures are listed in the Toy section. Eskimo dolls are listed in the Eskimo section and Indian dolls are listed in the Indian section. Doll clothes and accessories are listed at the end of this section. The twentieth-century clothes listed here are in mint condition.

A.M., 12, Bisque Socket Head, 15-Piece Body, Ball-Jointed, 28 In. 308.00
A.M., 200, Bisque, Googly, Closed Mouth, 5-Piece Body, Bunny Suit, 1925, 9 In. 950.00
A.M., 253, Nobbi Kid, Bisque Socket Head, Googly Sleep Eyes, Looking Right, 7 1/2 In. 956.00
A.M., 390, Bisque Socket Head, Sleep Eyes, Eyelashes, Composition Body, 18 In. 70.00
A.M., 390, Scottish Boy, Bisque Socket Head, Sleep Eyes, Open Mouth, Mohair Curls, 12 In. 280.00
A.M., 390A, Bisque Head, 20 In. 324.00
A.M., 400, Bisque Head, Character, Sleep Eyes, Composition, Wood, Wardrobe, c.1920, 13 In. 2235.00
A.M., 400, Bisque Socket Head, Glass Eyes, Mohair, Composition, Wood, c.1917, 26 In. 2860.00
A.M., 980, Bisque Socket Head, Set Brown Eyes, Real Lashes, Open Mouth, 17 In. 140.00
A.M., 3500, Bisque Head, Brown Sleep Eyes, Open Mouth, Mohair Wig, Bisque Arms, 18 In. 105.00
A.M., Alma, Bisque Shoulder Head, Open Mouth, Teeth, Sleep Eyes, 22 In. 118.00

A.M., Bisque Dome Head, Bent Limb Baby Body, Sleep Eyes, 16 In. 196.00
A.M., Bisque Head, Blond Hair, Glass Eyes, Jointed Composition, Painted, 27 In. 248.00
A.M., Bisque Head, Blue Googly Sleep Eyes, Mohair Wig, Composition, 6 1/2 In. 719.00
A.M., Bisque Head, Sleep Eyes, Wig, Jointed Composition, Painted Shoes, Socks, 30 In. 165.00
A.M., Bisque Socket Head, Bent Limb Jointed Body, 10 1/4 In. 105.00
A.M., Bisque Socket Head, Brown Eyes, Ball-Jointed Body, c.1894, 15 In. 140.00
A.M., Dream Baby, Bisque Head, Flange Neck, Cloth Body, 15 In. 168.00
A.M., Dream Baby, Bisque Head, Sleep Eyes, Cloth Body, Vintage Clothes, 11 In. 92.00
A.M., Floradora, Bisque Head, Blue Eyes, Open Mouth, Kid Body, 17 In. 80.00
A.M., Floradora, Bisque Head, Brown Eyes, Open Mouth, Kid Body, 21 In. 69.00
A.M., Just Me, Peggy Jean, Bisque Socket Head, Painted, Blond, Blue Eyes, 1930s, 8 In. 825.00
A.M., Just Me, Pursed Mouth, Blue Eyes, 5-Piece Composition Body, 9 1/2 In. 1610.00
A.M., Queen Louise, Bisque Head, Composition, Ball-Jointed, 24 In. 160.00
A.M., Queen Louise, Bisque Head, Sleep Eyes, Wig, 15-Piece Body, 22 In. 112.00
Advertising, Buddy Lee, Phillips 66, 13 In. 415.00
Advertising, Cream Of Wheat Man, Cloth, Holding Bowl, 19 In. 110.00
Advertising, Nabisco Slicker Boy, Composition, 16 x 8 In. 578.00
Advertising, Radiotron Selling Fool, Composition, Wood, Parrish, c.1926, 16 In. 880.00
Alabama Baby, Stockinet Head, Oil Painted, Blue Eyes, Hair, Cloth Body, Knit Coat, 22 In. 2365.00
Alexander dolls are listed in this category under Madame Alexander.
Alt Beck & Gottschalck, 1000, China Shoulder Head, Molded Curly Hair, Cloth Body, 22 In. 225.00
Alt Beck & Gottschalck, 1028, China Shoulder Head, Painted Features, Molded Hair, 25 In. 169.00
Alt Beck & Gottschalck, 1362, Bisque Socket Head, Blue Sleep Eyes, Human Hair, 24 In. 590.00
American Character, Betsy McCall, Plastic, Auburn Wig, Pretty Pac, Clothes, Booklet, 8 In. 365.00
American Character, Sweet Sue Sophisticate, Vinyl, Rooted Hair, Sleep Eyes, Jointed, 14 In. 280.00
American Character, Sweet Sue, Plastic Head, Body, Vinyl Arms, Jointed Knees, 17 1/2 In. 92.00
American Character, Sweet Sue, Vinyl Head, Arms, Jointed Elbows, Blue Nylon Dress, 31 In. 394.00
Annette Himstedt, Fatou, Black Vinyl Socket Head, Cloth Body, Original Clothes, Box, 26 In. 140.00
Annette Himstedt, Lisa, Vinyl Socket Head, Cloth Body, Original Clothes, Box, 26 In. 140.00
Armand Marseille dolls are listed in this category under A.M.
Arranbee, Composition Socket Head, Sleep Eyes, Blond Braids, 5-Piece Body, 16 In. 358.00
Arranbee, Littlest Angel, Vinyl Head, Original Outfits, Vinyl Case, 1958, 11 In. 138.00
Automaton, Acrobat, Papier-Mache, Coin-Operated, c.1933, 65 In. 3408.00
Automaton, American Doughboy, Whistler, Wood, Hand Carved, c.1920, 13 1/2 In. 569.00
Automaton, Arkansas-Trav & Eliza-Jane, Black Man & Woman, Wood, 1900s, 22 In. 880.00
Automaton, Autoperipatetikos, Walking Doll, Papier-Mache Shoulder Head, c.1862, 10 In. 440.00
Automaton, Baseball Player, Whistling, Take Me Out To Ball Game, Griesbaum, c.1955, 16 In. 2800.00
Automaton, Bebe Eventail, Jumeau Bisque Head, Lambert, 1880s, 21 In. 6465.00
Automaton, Bird In Cage, Rectangular Base, Curved Leafy Panels, 5 1/2 x 4 In. 440.00
Automaton, Bisque Swivel Head, Mohair, Papier-Mache, Open Spring Motor, 12 1/2 In. 2233.00
Automaton, Black Figure, Carved, Wooden Base, Tin Platform, c.1870s, 8 In. 646.00
Automaton, Boy Dancing, Sand Toy, Paper Lithograph, France, 6 In. 529.00
Automaton, Bru Jumeau, Bisque Head, Turns, Hands Raise & Lower, 16 In. 1610.00
Automaton, Cat Ballet, Kittens In Tutus, Chromolithograph, Coin-Operated, 10 x 12 In. 1880.00
Automaton, Cat In Churn, One Air, Open Spring Motor, Roullet & Decamps, 10 In. 1175.00
Automaton, Cat, White Fur, Glass Eyes, Fan, Lorgnettes, Roullet & Decamps, c.1910, 13 In. 1175.00
Automaton, Chinese Tea Server, Jumeau Bisque Head, Glass Eyes, Lambert, 18 1/2 In. 2645.00
Automaton, Clown Juggler, Lever Operated, Germany, c.1880, 16 In. 1058.00
Automaton, Clown Playing Mandolin, Bisque Head, Glass Eyes, Wire Arms, 15 In. 4704.00
Automaton, Girl, Knitting, In Chair, 2 Movements, 1 Tune, Roullet & Decamps, c.1895, 17 In. 7840.00
Automaton, Girl, Pet Mouse, 5 Movements, 1 Tune, Rambour, France, c.1895, 17 In. 8288.00
Automaton, Harbor Scene, Chinoiserie, Painted Card, Papier-Mache, c.1880, 20 In. 1295.00
Automaton, Harbor Scene, French Port, 3-Masted Ship, Papier-Mache, c.1860, 21 In. 3525.00
Automaton, Highland Whistler, Bagpipes, Going Barrel Movement, Karl Griesbaum, 14 In. 1295.00
Automaton, Lady Of Court, Alexandre Theroude Attribution, Guillard, France, c.1850, 12 In. 6720.00
Automaton, Man, Whistling, Chip Carved, Griesbaum, Black Forest, Germany, c.1900, 13 In. 1680.00
Automaton, Marquis Monkey Smoker, 8 Movements, Gustave Vichy, c.1880, 25 In. 10640.00
Automaton, Marquise, Bisque Head, 4 Movements, 1 Tune, Leopold Lambert, c.1890, 18 In. 8960.00
Automaton, Monkey Violinist, Barrel Organ, Rosewood, Thibouville Lamy, c.1860, 34 In. 18800.00
Automaton, Monkey, Composition Head, Farkass, France, c.1930, 14 1/2 In. 3819.00
Automaton, Scottish Bagpipe Player, Wood, Hand Carved, Head Moves, Early 1900s, 14 In. 390.00

Automaton, Serenade, 8 Movements, Roullet & Decamps, c.1890, 21 x 16 x 9 In. 11480.00
Automaton, Smiling Black Boy, Banjo, 2 Tunes, 5 Movements, G. Vichy, c.1890, 23 In. 10080.00
Automaton, Spanish Lady, Tambourine, 2 Tunes, 3 Movements, Leopold Lambert, c.1890, 21 In. . 7280.00
Automaton, Spanish Lady, Tambourine, 3-Wheel Platform, Gustave Vichy, c.1880, 10 In. 3470.00
Automaton, Twin Babies, Gebruder Heubach, Manivelle, Early 1900s, 6 x 10 x 2 3/4 In. 2350.00
Automaton, Woman, Lifting Flowers, Waltzing, Bisque, Shoulder Plate, 2 Tunes, G. Vichy, 20 In. . . 3175.00
Automaton, Woman, Walking, Bisque Head, Papier-Mache Body, 12 1/2 In. 2235.00
Averill, Bonnie Babe, Bisque Dome, Flange Head, Sleep Eyes, Composition, 17 In. 675.00
Bahr & Proschild, 244, Indian, Socket Head, Composition Body, Early 1900s, 12 In. 355.00
Bahr & Proschild, 686, Bisque Socket Head, Googly Sleep Eyes, Composition Body, 7 In. 2530.00
Barbie dolls are listed in this category under Mattel.
Belton-Type, 183, Bisque Socket Head, Paperweight Eyes, Wood, Composition, 15 1/2 In. 1155.00
Belton-Type, Bisque Socket Head, Paperweight Eyes, Wood, Composition, 13 In. 1925.00
Belton-Type, Marguerite, Bisque Socket Head, Composition, Wood, 1880s, 10 In. 1175.00
Bergmann dolls are also in this category under Simon & Halbig.
Bergmann, 152, Bisque Socket Head, 5-Piece Bent Limb Body, Louis Wolf, Baby, 19 In. 168.00
Bergmann, 1916, Bisque Socket Head, Sleep Eyes, Real Lashes, Human Hair Wig, 24 In. 365.00
Bergmann, Bisque Socket Head, 15-Piece Ball-Jointed Composition Body, 29 In. 280.00
Bergner, Bisque Socket Head, 3 Faces, Pull String, Composition, Wood, Jointed, c.1892, 13 In. . . . 1100.00
Bisque, Brown, Sleep Eyes, Open-Close Mouth, Molded Teeth, Synthetic Wig, 7 In. 80.00
Bisque, Sleep Eyes, Open Mouth, Stiff Neck, Brown Shoes, Germany, 5 In. 115.00
Bisque Dome Shoulder Head, Paperweight Eyes, Mohair Wig, Kid Body, 11 1/2 In. 1238.00
Bisque Dome Shoulder Head, Paperweight Eyes, Mohair, Cloth Body, Leather Arms, 21 In. 1465.00
Bisque Girl, Blue Glass Sleep Eyes, Jointed Arms, Legs, Black Strap Shoes, 7 In. 115.00
Bisque Head, 15-Piece Composition Body, Germany, 20 In. 196.00
Bisque Head, Googly Sleep Eyes, Closed Mouth, Mohair Wig, Early 1900s, 6 3/4 In. 235.00
Bisque Head, Matted Hair, Sleep Eyes, Jointed Composition, Painted, Germany, 23 In. 248.00
Bisque Head, Molded Wig, Stuffed Cloth Body, China Hands, Feet, Painted Shoes, 17 In. 148.00
Bisque Head, Pierced Ears, Open Mouth, Kid Body, Arms, Legs, Silk Costume, c.1890, 21 In. 118.00
Bisque Head, Sleep Eyes, Teeth, Mohair Wig, 15-Piece Ball-Jointed Body, Germany, 21 In. 280.00
Bisque Head, Sleep Eyes, Wig, Jointed Leather Body, Painted, Germany, 26 In. 305.00
Bisque Shoulder Head, Blond Wig, Composition Body, Germany, 10 In. 265.00
Bisque Shoulder Head, Brown Set Eyes, Synthetic Blond Wig, Jointed Kid Body, 22 In. 173.00
Bisque Shoulder Head, Paperweight Eyes, Mohair, Stroked Eyebrows, Germany, 18 In. 590.00
Bisque Socket Head, Paperweight Eyes, Brush-Stroked Brows, Mohair, 1890, 14 In. 5152.00
Bisque Socket Head, Sleep Eyes, Mohair Wig, Wood, Composition, Jointed, 20 In. 844.00
Bisque Swivel Head, Glass Eyes, Peg-Jointed, Painted Lashes, Mignonette, c.1885, 5 In. 7700.00
Bisque Swivel Head, Kid-Edge Shoulder Plate, Glass Eyes, Closed Mouth, Mohair, 17 In. 6048.00
Bisque Swivel Head, Paperweight Eyes, Cloth Body, Kid Arms, Germany, c.1880, 19 1/2 In. 764.00
Black dolls are also included in the Black category.
Bru Jne, 2 Face Surprise, Bisque, Swiveling Mohair Wig, Jointed, c.1883, 9 In. 10575.00
Bru Jne, Bisque Socket Head, Paperweight Eyes, Human Hair, Composition, Jointed, 27 In. 4802.00
Bru Jne, Bisque Swivel Head, Glass Enamel Eyes, Human Hair, Kid, Gusset-Jointed, Bebe, 12 In. . . 9350.00
Bru Jne, Bisque Swivel Head, Glass Eyes, Mohair, Gusset-Jointed, c.1872, 16 In. 4180.00
Bru Jne, Bisque Swivel Head, Glass Eyes, Mohair, Gusset-Jointed, c.1872, 18 In. 4840.00
Bru Jne, Bisque Swivel Head, Glass Eyes, Mohair, Kid Body, Dowel-Jointed, c.1872, 16 In. 7150.00
Bru Jne, Bisque Swivel Head, Mohair, Kid Body, Wood Arms, Dowel-Jointed, c.1872, 19 In. 4620.00
Bru Jne, Bisque Swivel Head, Shoulder Plate, Enamel Inset Eyes, Mohair, Wood, 16 In. 5720.00
Bruno Schmidt, Tommy Tucker, Bisque Head, Sleep Eyes, Composition, Early 1900s, 11 1/2 In. . . 880.00
Bruno Schmidt, Tommy Tucker, Bisque Socket Head, Sleep Eyes, Molded Hair, 18 In. 338.00
Bucherer, Happy Hooligan, Composition, Metal, Felt Clothes, Posable, Swiss, 8 In. 1018.00
Bucherer, Jeff, Composition, Metal, Hand Painted, Felt Clothes, Posable, Swiss, 6 1/2 In. 125.00
Bucherer, Jiggs, Composition, Metal, Hand Painted, Felt Clothes, Posable, Swiss, 7 In. 820.00
Buddy Lee, Hard Plastic, Painted, Eyes Looking Right, Molded Hair, Jointed Shoulders, 12 In. 197.00
Bye-Lo, Bisque Dome Flange Head, Sleep Eyes, Painted Hair, Cloth Body, 10 In. 450.00
Bye-Lo, Bisque Dome Head, Brown Eyes, Cloth Frog Body, Celluloid Hands, 12 In. 230.00
Bye-Lo, Bisque Dome Head, Sleep Eyes, Cloth Body, Original Clothes, Tag, 16 In. 303.00
Bye-Lo, Bisque Head, Blue Sleep Eyes, Closed Mouth, Cloth Frog Body, 15 In. 175.00
Bye-Lo, Bisque Head, Sleep Eyes, Painted Hair, Cloth Frog Body, 15 In. 242.00
Bye-Lo, Bisque Solid Dome Swivel Head, Painted Hair, Sleep Eyes, Loop-Jointed, 8 In. 605.00
Cameo Doll Co., Pete The Pup, Composition Head, Kaallus, 1930, 10 In. . . . . .140.00 to 525.00

Doll, Cornhusk, Woman, Dress, Lace Collar, Hat, Purse, Fan, Marked, May R. Deschamps

Doll, Cornhusk, Woman With Parasol, Marked, May Deschamps, June, 1979, 10 1/2 In.

Doll, Dorothy Heizer, Fashion Lady, Yarn Hair, Tweed Suit, Marked, 16 In.

Century Doll Co., Bisque Shoulder Head, Sleep Eyes, Real Lashes, Human Hair Wig, Child, 24 In. . . 281.00
Chad Valley, Princess Elizabeth, Stockinet Head, Glass Eyes, Original Wool Coat, 1930s, 18 In. . . . 460.00
Chase, Baby, Stockinet Head, Applied Ears, Textured Painted Hair, Cloth Body, 16 In. 534.00
Chase, Boy, Stockinet Head, Sateen Body, Blue Velvet Suit, Early 1900s, 17 In. 294.00
Chase, Cloth, Painted Blond Hair, Sateen Body, Painted Limbs, 16 In. 150.00
Chase, Hospital Baby, Stockinet, Painted Head, Body, Pierced Nostrils, Ears, c.1930, 20 In. 295.00
Chase, Mammy, Black Cloth, Painted Eyes, Astrakhan Wig, Early 1900s, 17 In. 5875.00
Chase, Stockinet Head, Oil-Painted Face, Stitch-Jointed, c.1910, 20 In. 660.00
Chase, Stockinet Head, Rose Cheeks, Blue Eyes, Cloth Body, Applied Limbs, 30 In. 275.00
Chase, Woman, Stockinet Head, Oil Painted, Sculpted Hair, Stitch-Jointed, 15 In. 1100.00
China Head, Cafe Au Lait, Cloth Body, Leather Arms, Wood Carved Feet, 26 In. 118.00
China Head, Exposed Ears, Black Curly Hair, Blue Painted Eyes, Cloth Body, 15 In. 144.00
China Head, Exposed Ears, Black Hair, Painted Features, Blue Eyes, Cloth Body, 16 In. 127.00
China Shoulder Head, Boy, Curly Hair, Blue Eyes, Closed Mouth, Mid 1800s, 19 1/2 In. 560.00
China Shoulder Head, Covered Wagon, Painted, Molded Black Hair, Cloth Body, 17 1/2 In. 619.00
China Shoulder Head, Flat Top, Painted Features, Blue Eyes, Molded Black Hair, 9 In. 169.00
China Shoulder Head, Flat Top, Painted Features, Blue Eyes, Molded Black Hair, 26 In. 338.00
China Shoulder Head, High Brow, Pink Tint, Painted Features, Blue Eyes, Molded Hair, 22 In. 253.00
China Shoulder Head, Painted Eyes, Hair, Gusset Kid Leather Body, 1850-70, 14 In. 165.00
China Shoulder Head, Painted Eyes, Molded Hair, Cloth Body, Germany, c.1840, 22 In. 1645.00
China Shoulder Head, Painted Features, Molded Curly Hair, Cloth Body, 1880s, 22 1/2 In. 175.00
Cloth, 2-Seam Head, Painted Facial Features, Hair, Mitten Hands, 17 In. 575.00
Cloth, 3-Section Head, Painted Features, Stitch-Jointed Arms, Legs, 16 1/2 In. 546.00
Cloth, Amish, Hide-Covered Head, Featureless Face, Long Neck, Skin Wig, Mitten Hands, 20 In. . . . 200.00
Cloth, Emma Adams, Flat Face, Oil-Painted Features, Muslin Stitch-Jointed, 1893, 19 In. 3300.00
Cloth, Emma Adams, Flat Face, Oil-Painted Features, Stitch-Jointed, 28 In. 3960.00
Cloth, Felt Head, Painted Features, Embroidered, Yarn Hair, Cotton Sateen Body, 19 In. 410.00
Cloth, Flat Face, Painted Features, Yarn Hair, Stitch-Jointed Body, Oilcloth, 17 In. 220.00
Cloth, Girl With Lamb, Stitched Features, Round Pasteboard Base, 6 x 4 1/2 In. 430.00
Cloth, Glass Eyes, Waxed Lower Arms, Mohair Wig, 21 In. 115.00
Cloth, Harold Lloyd, Stuffed, Yours For Happiness On Back, 11 In. 165.00
Cloth, Hickory Nut Head, Linen Body, Inked Features, c.1860s, 3 1/4 In. 175.00
Cloth, Humpty Dumpty, Silk Egg-Shaped Head, Body, Painted Features, Stitch-Jointed, 16 In. 330.00
Cloth, Mask Face, Sleep Eyes, Yarn Hair, Muslin, Stitch-Jointed Body, Mitten Hands, 20 In. 248.00
Cloth, Painted Features, Bobbed Hair, Shoulder, Hip Joints, Costume, 13 In. 615.00
Cloth, Primitive, Carpet Hair, Drawn Facial Features, Stitched Fingers, Dress, 14 1/2 In. 175.00
Cloth, Sateen, Flat Face, Wire Curls, Disc-Jointed, Toddler, 18 In. 715.00
Cloth, Scarecrow From Oz, Sateen Mask Face, Yarn Hair, 1933-40, 17 1/2 In. 1410.00
Cloth, Stockinet Head, Painted Features, Hair, Pouty, 12 In. 1870.00
Cloth, Uncle Wiggily, Brown Muslin, Stitched, Painted Features, Disc Eyes, 17 In. 550.00
Composition Head, Body, Squeaker Box, Pigskin Bellows, Papier-Mache Legs, 9 1/2 In. 195.00
Cornhusk, Woman With Parasol, Marked, May Deschamps, June, 1979, 10 1/2 In. . . . . ***ILLUS*** 173.00
Cornhusk, Woman, Dress, Lace Collar, Hat, Purse, Fan, Marked, May R. Deschamps . . . . ***ILLUS*** 200.00
Cosman Freres, Bisque Socket Head, Paperweight Eyes, Composition, Wood, Jointed, 20 In. 5152.00

Denamur, Bisque Socket Head, Paperweight Eyes, Human Hair, 21 In. 2420.00
Door Of Hope, Bride, Pear Wood Head, Cloth Body, Wood Lower Arms, Satin Clothing, 11 In. 1320.00
Door Of Hope, Buddhist Priest, Pear Wood Head, Cloth Body, Cotton Clothes, 11 1/2 In. 550.00
Door Of Hope, Child, Carved Pear Wood Head, Hands, Feet, Early 1900s, 6 1/2 In. 1998.00
Door Of Hope, Girl, Carved Pear Wood Head, Silk Hair, Cloth Body, Early 1900s, 8 3/4 In. 1058.00
Dorothy Heizer, Fashion Lady, Back Curls, Black Dress, Hat, Suede Heels, Cigarette, 16 In. 1915.00
Dorothy Heizer, Fashion Lady, Back Curls, Tweed Suit, Paisley Scarf, Leather Hat, 16 In. 1465.00
Dorothy Heizer, Fashion Lady, Long Curls, Red Print Cotton Dress, Sandals, Straw Hat, 17 In. 2025.00
Dorothy Heizer, Fashion Lady, Yarn Hair, Tweed Suit, Marked, 16 In. .... *ILLUS* 1430.00
Dream World, Brazilian Dancer, Painted Features, Box, 1940s, 11 In. 72.00
Dressel, 1349, Jutta, Bisque Socket Head, Sleep Eyes, Mohair, Composition, Jointed, 11 1/2 In. .. 660.00
Dressel, 1349, Jutta, Bisque, Sleep Eyes, Blond Wig, Ball-Jointed Body, 25 In. 360.00
Dressel, 1469, Bisque Socket Head, Sleep Eyes, Mohair Wig, Composition, 14 1/2 In. 3850.00
Dressel, 1469, Bisque Socket Head, Sleep Eyes, Mohair, Composition, Ball-Jointed, 14 In. 2750.00
Dressel, Bisque Socket Head, Paperweight Eyes, Composition Body, c.1890, 20 In. 940.00
Effanbee, American Child, Anne Shirley, Composition, Human Hair, Jointed, 20 In. 605.00
Effanbee, American Child, Boy, Composition, Human Hair, Original Clothes, 17 In. 990.00
Effanbee, Black Baby Grumpy, Composition, Molded Hair, 3 Pigtails, Cloth Body, 12 In. 422.00
Effanbee, Bubbles, Composition Head, Arms & Legs, Cloth Body, 1930, 16 In. 330.00
Effanbee, Dy-Dee-Baby, Karakul Wig, 15 In. 56.00
Effanbee, Historical Replica, Later Carolina Settlement, 1685, Floral Overdress, 14 In. 338.00
Effanbee, Mae Starr, Windup Talking Mechanism, Yellow Organdy Dress, 30 In. 506.00
Effanbee, Patsy Ann, Composition, Glass Sleep Eyes, Molded Hair, c.1930, 19 In. 176.00
Effanbee, Patsy Ann, Composition, Sleep Eyes, Mohair Wig, Original Clothes, Box, 19 In. 275.00
Effanbee, Patsy Joan, Composition Socket Head, Sleep Eyes, 5-Piece Body, 15 In. 952.00
Effanbee, Patsyette, Composition, Mohair Wig, Original Clothes, Heart Tag, 9 In. 303.00
Effanbee, Skippy, Solid Dome Composition Head, Wooden Socket, Muslin Body, 14 In. 1344.00
Effanbee, Suzanne, Composition Socket Head, Blue Eyes, Blond, 5-Piece Body, 1940, 14 In. 735.00
Elite Creations, Vickie, Walker, No. 414 Dress, Case, 1950s, 8 In. 60.00
Fashion, Bisque Shoulder Head, Glass Eyes, Mohair, Wood, Dowel-Jointed, France, 18 In. 4592.00
Fashion, Bisque Shoulder Head, Glass Eyes, Painted Lashes, Mohair, France, 13 In. 3136.00
Fashion, Bisque Socket Head, Paperweight Eyes, Mohair Wig, Kid Body, 14 In. 2025.00
Fashion, Bisque Swivel Head, Closed Smiling Mouth, Paperweight Eyes, France, 11 In. 1438.00
Fashion, Bisque Swivel Head, Glass Eyes, Mohair, Wood Body, France, c.1866, 18 In. 6875.00
Fashion, Bisque Swivel Head, Kid Over Wood Body, Mohair Wig, France, 1870s, 16 In. 2820.00
Fashion, Bisque Swivel Head, Shoulder Plate, Glass Eyes, Kid, Wood, France, c.1880, 18 In. 5280.00
Fashion, Bisque, Swivel Head, Gusseted Kid Body, Mohair Wig, 1870s, 12 In. 940.00
Franz Schmidt, 1294, Bisque Socket Head, Glass Eyes, Composition, Baby, c.1915, 21 In. 1100.00
French, Bisque Dome Swivel Head, Glass Eyes, Mohair, Peg-Jointed, 5 1/2 In. 3520.00
French, Bisque Shoulder Head, Glass Eyes, Mohair, Kid Body, Gusset-Jointed, c.1865, 18 In. 7150.00
French, Bisque Socket Head, Matte Complexion, Glass Eyes, Mohair, Papier-Mache, 14 In. 6600.00
French, Bisque Solid Dome Swivel Head, Enamel Eyes, Mohair, Peg-Jointed, 5 In. 2860.00
French, Bisque Swivel Head, Glass Eyes, Human Hair, Wood, Dowel-Jointed, 18 In. 5720.00
French, Bisque Swivel Head, Glass Eyes, Mohair, Peg-Jointed, c.1882, 5 1/2 In. 2090.00
French, Bisque Swivel Head, Kid-Edged Bisque Body, Glass Eyes, Mohair, Peg-Jointed, 7 In. 1792.00
French, Bisque Swivel Head, Kid-Edged Shoulder Plate, Enamel Eyes, Human Hair, 14 In. 3024.00
French, Bisque Swivel Head, Kid-Edged Shoulder Plate, Enamel Eyes, Kid Body, Jointed, 13 In. 4032.00
French, Bisque Swivel Head, Kid-Edged, Mohair, Wood, Metal, Ball-Jointed, c.1863, 17 In. 9350.00
French, Bisque Swivel Head, Kid-Over-Wood Body, Mohair Wig, Stuffed Legs, c.1870, 16 In. 2820.00
French, Bisque Swivel Head, Mohair, Peg-Jointed Limbs, c.1882, 5 1/2 In. 1045.00
French, Brown Bisque Socket Head, Glass Eyes, Fleecy Wig, Composition, Wood, Child, 16 In. 605.00
French, Felt Swivel Head, Pressed Features, Googly Eyes, Mohair, Muslin Body, 17 In. 3248.00
French, Porcelain Shoulder Head, Cameo Face, Painted Eyes, Cloth Body, Snood, 18 In. 4704.00
French, Porcelain Socket Head, Human Hair, Painted Features, Gusset-Jointed, 20 In. 4620.00
French, Porcelain, Glass Enamel Eyes, Human Hair, Kid, Gusset-Jointed, c.1860, 17 In. 3850.00
French, Porcelain, Glass Eyes, Human Hair, Kid, Gusset-Jointed, Stitched Fingers, c.1855, 31 In. .. 5500.00
Freundlich, Sailor, Composition, Painted Features, Praise The Lord Tag, 15 In. 275.00
Freundlich, Soldier, Praise The Lord & Pass The Ammunition, Painted Features, 15 In. 275.00
Frozen Charlie, China, Pink Luster Face, Brown Hair, Comb Prints, 10 In. 400.00
Frozen Charlie, China, Pink Tint, Painted Features, Closed Mouth, Black Hair, 8 1/2 In. 309.00

G.I. Joe figures are listed in the Toy category.

Gaultier, Bisque Socket Head, Cork Pate, Glass Eyes, Composition, Wood, Jointed, 18 In. 6272.00
Gaultier, Bisque Socket Head, Glass Enamel Eyes, Mohair, Gusset-Jointed, 1875, 20 In. 3190.00
Gaultier, Bisque Socket Head, Glass Eyes, Painted Features, Mohair, Composition, Jointed, 10 In. . 8800.00
Gaultier, Bisque Swivel Head, Glass Enamel Eyes, Kid Body, Jointed, Fashion, c.1880, 9 In. 1650.00
Gaultier, Bisque Swivel Head, Glass Enamel Eyes, Mohair, Kid, Gusset-Jointed, Fashion, 20 In. ... 3850.00
Gaultier, Bisque Swivel Head, Glass Eyes, Metal Armature Body, Stockinet, Fashion, 19 In. 5500.00
Gaultier, Bisque Swivel Head, Glass Eyes, Mohair, Gusset-Jointed, Bebe, c.1880, 18 In. 5500.00
Gaultier, Bisque Swivel Head, Glass Eyes, Mohair, Metal Armature Body, Composition, 13 In. 5060.00
Gaultier, Bisque Swivel Head, Glass Inset Eyes, Blond Mohair, Gusset-Jointed, Bebe, 16 In. 6875.00
Gaultier, Bisque Swivel Head, Kid-Edged Shoulder Plate, Enamel Eyes, Muslin, Fashion, 15 In. ... 2352.00
Gaultier, Bisque Swivel Head, Kid-Edged Shoulder Plate, Gusset-Jointed, Fashion, 24 In. 3584.00
Gaultier, Bisque Swivel Head, Paperweight Eyes, Human Hair, Gesland Body, Bebe, 30 In. 6440.00
Gaultier, Bisque Swivel Head, Shoulder Plate, Glass Enamel Eyes, Mohair, Fashion, 14 In. 7700.00
Gaultier, Bisque Swivel Head, Shoulder Plate, Glass Enamel Eyes, Mohair, Fashion, 16 In. 4180.00
Gebruder Heubach dolls are also in this category under Heubach.
Gebruder Heubach, 6894, Bisque Socket Head, Flocked Hair, Composition, Wood, Jointed, 16 In. 1540.00
Gebruder Heubach, 6894, Bisque Socket Head, Pouty Mouth, Molded Hair, Toddler, 14 1/2 In. .. 900.00
Gebruder Heubach, 6969, Bisque Socket Head, Sleep Eyes, Pouty Mouth, Pink Face, 13 In....... 1915.00
Gebruder Heubach, 6969, Somber Face, Composition, Mohair, Boy, Early 1900s, 14 In. 1175.00
Gebruder Heubach, 7977, Baby Stuart, Bisque Socket Head, Intaglio Eyes, Composition, 13 In. .. 2530.00
Gebruder Heubach, 9057, Bisque Head, Painted Hair, Googly Intaglio Eyes 374.00
Gebruder Heubach, Bisque Dome Head, Googly Eyes, Winker, 5-Piece Body, 7 In. 1018.00
Gebruder Heubach, Bisque Head & Body, Googly Eyes, Loop-Jointed, 9 In. 1120.00
Gebruder Heubach, Bisque Head, Composition Shoulder, Flange Neck, Cloth Body, 15 In. 144.00
German, Bisque Dome Swivel Head, Painted Hair, Sleep Eyes, Loop-Jointed, Baby, c.1925, 5 In. .. 660.00
German, Bisque Head & Body, Chinese Man, Painted Features, Slanted Eyes, Peg-Jointed, 4 In. ... 615.00
German, Bisque Head & Body, Soldier, Sculpted Helmet, Blond Hair, Peg-Jointed, 4 In. 615.00
German, Bisque Head, Eggshell Costume, Round Face, Googly Eyes, 4 1/2 In. 840.00
German, Bisque Shoulder Head, Curls, Glass Eyes, Muslin, Stitch-Jointed, c.1880, 12 In. 1100.00
German, Bisque Shoulder Head, Curls, Glass Eyes, Muslin, Stitch-Jointed, c.1880, 20 In. 1540.00
German, Bisque Shoulder Head, Glass Eyes, Muslin, Stitch-Jointed, c.1880, 15 In. 935.00
German, Bisque Shoulder Head, Glass Eyes, Muslin, Stitch-Jointed, c.1880, 17 In. 1980.00
German, Bisque Shoulder Head, Glass Eyes, Muslin, Stitch-Jointed, Man, c.1880, 13 In. 1430.00
German, Bisque Shoulder Head, Sculpted Hair, Glass Eyes, Muslin, Stitch-Jointed, 22 In. 770.00
German, Bisque Shoulder Head, Sculpted Hair, Glass Eyes, Muslin, Stitch-Jointed, 23 In. 1043.00
German, Bisque Shoulder Head, Sculpted Hair, Glass Eyes, Muslin, Stitch-Jointed, 26 In. 2200.00
German, Bisque Shoulder Head, Sculpted Hair, Inset Eyes, Muslin, Stitch-Jointed, 20 In. 1260.00
German, Bisque Shoulder Head, Sculpted Hair, Painted Eyes, Muslin Body, c.1880, 10 In. 660.00
German, Bisque Shoulder Head, Sculpted Hair, Painted Features, Muslin Body, 4 In. 330.00
German, Bisque Shoulder Head, Sculpted Hair, Painted Features, Muslin Body, c.1880, 7 In...... 550.00
German, Bisque Socket Head, 2 Faces, Glass Eyes, Composition, Jointed, c.1890, 15 In.......... 1045.00
German, Bisque Socket Head, Amber Glass Eyes, Painted Asian Features, Black Mohair, 10 In. ... 935.00
German, Bisque Socket Head, Glass Sleep Eyes, Mohair, Peg-Jointed, c.1885, 4 1/2 In. 1430.00
German, Bisque Socket Head, Googly Eyes, Forelock, Sideburns, Teeth, 9 In. 5720.00
German, Bisque Socket Head, Mustache, Composition, Wood, Ball-Jointed, Man, 13 In. 6440.00
German, Bisque Socket Head, Sleep Eyes, Open Mouth, Human Hair Wig, Toddler, 11 In. 340.00
German, Bisque Swivel Head, Enamel Sleep Eyes, Mohair, Peg-Jointed, c.1885, 4 1/2 In......... 1870.00
German, Bisque Swivel Head, Glass Sleep Eyes, Mohair, Peg-Jointed, c.1885, 5 In. 1045.00
German, Bisque, Brown Complexion, Glass Eyes, Fleecy Hair, Loop-Jointed, 4 In. 1790.00
German, Bisque, Brown Complexion, Painted, Jointed, Moorish Costume, 2 1/2 In., Pair 495.00
German, Bisque, Chubby Face, Googly Eyes, Mohair, Loop-Jointed, Fairy, c.1920, 5 1/2 In. 440.00
German, Bisque, Glass Googly Sleep Eyes, Mohair, Jointed, 7 In. 2860.00
German, Bisque, Googly, Character, Loop-Jointed Arms, c.1920, 4 In. 138.00
German, Papier-Mache, Sculpted Hair, Braid, Glass Eyes, Wood Limbs, Woman, c.1840, 31 In. ... 7700.00
German, Papier-Mache, Sculpted Hair, Ears, Chignon, Muslin, Stitch-Jointed, c.1840, 32 In. 4400.00
German, Papier-Mache, Sculpted Hair, Glass Eyes, Muslin, Jointed, Leather Arms, c.1865, 16 In. . 1100.00
German, Papier-Mache, Sculpted Hair, Glass Eyes, Muslin, Jointed, Leather Arms, c.1865, 25 In. . 3740.00
German, Papier-Mache, Shoulder Head, Glass Eyes, Kid Body, Wooden Limbs, c.1830, 23 In. 7700.00
German, Papier-Mache, Shoulder Head, Glass Eyes, Kid Body, Wooden Limbs, c.1840, 21 In. 3410.00
German, Papier-Mache, Shoulder Head, Kid Body, Wood, c.1830, 28 In....................... 6600.00
German, Papier-Mache, Shoulder Head, Sculpted Curls, Kid Body, Wooden Arms, Legs, 24 In. 3190.00

German, Papier-Mache, Shoulder Head, Sculpted Hair, Kid Body, Wooden Arms, Legs, 27 In. 3960.00
German, Papier-Mache, Shoulder Head, Sculpted Side Curls, Wooden Arms, Legs, 22 In. 6160.00
German, Porcelain Shoulder Head, Arms, Glass Eyes, Mohair, Muslin, Stitch Jointed, 19 In. 2090.00
German, Porcelain Shoulder Head, Painted Face, Human Hair, Muslin, Stitch-Jointed, 20 In. 2090.00
German, Porcelain Shoulder Head, Painted Features, Muslin, Stitch-Jointed, 18 In. 1045.00
German, Porcelain Shoulder Head, Sculpted Hair, Painted Features, Boy, 4 1/2 In. 3520.00
German, Porcelain, Sculpted Hair, Ears, Painted Eyes, Muslin, Stitch-Jointed, c.1860, 17 In. 1760.00
German, Porcelain, Sculpted Hair, Glass Enamel Eyes, Muslin, Stitch-Jointed, c.1860, 18 In. 3300.00
German, Porcelain, Sculpted Hair, Glass Enamel Eyes, Muslin, Stitch-Jointed, c.1860, 22 In. 2530.00
German, Porcelain, Sculpted Hair, Painted Eyes, Kid Body, Leather Arms, 9 In. 440.00
German, Porcelain, Sculpted Hair, Painted Eyes, Muslin, Stitch-Jointed, c.1865, 15 In. 825.00
German, Porcelain, Sculpted Hair, Pink Tint, Closed Fists, c.1865, 6 In. 440.00
German, Wax Over Papier-Mache Shoulder Head, Glass Eyes, Muslin, Stitch-Jointed, 20 In. 1705.00
German, Wax Over Papier-Mache Shoulder Head, Glass Eyes, Painted Face, Mohair, 21 In. 1705.00
Gigi, Wax Over Porcelain Swivel Head, Glass Eyes, Closed Mouth, Cloth Body, 26 In. 290.00
Gilbert, Honey West, TV's Private Eye-Full, Box, 1965, 11 1/2 In. 420.00
Grace Corry Rockwell, Pretty Peggy, Bisque Head, Bobbed Hair, Cloth Body, 1926, 15 In. 3565.00
Greiner, Papier-Mache Shoulder Head, Painted, Blue Eyes, Molded Hair, Cloth Body, 21 In. 395.00
Greiner-Style, Papier-Mache Shoulder Head, Painted Eyes, Closed Mouth, Cloth, 26 In. 316.00
Grenier, Papier-Mache, Sculpted Hair, Muslin, Stitch-Jointed, Leather Arms, c.1875, 16 In. 440.00
Grodner Tal, Wood, Gessoed, Painted, Peg Joints, c.1820, 7 1/2 In. 529.00
Gund, Little Lulu, Cloth, Box, 1972, 17 1/2 In. 72.00
Half Dolls are listed in the Pincushion Doll category.
Handwerck, Bebe Ellie, 286, Bisque Head, Composition, Ball-Jointed, 18 In. 230.00
Handwerck, Bebe, Cosmopolite, Sleep Eyes, Open Mouth, Mohair Wig, Original Box, 23 In. 575.00
Handwerck, Bisque Socket Head, Brown Sleep Eyes, Open Mouth, Mohair Wig, 28 In. 506.00
Handwerck, Bisque Socket Head, Sleep Eyes, Real Lashes, Mohair Wig, 28 In. 1015.00
Handwerck, Bisque Socket Head, Sleep Eyes, Teeth, Mohair, Composition, 24 1/2 In. 206.00
Hansi, Haralit Head, Arms, Molded Hair, Painted Features, Blue Eyes, Dimples, 10 In. 200.00
Hansi, Yerri & Gretel, Recapture Of Alsace Commemoration, c.1917, 7 3/4 In. 355.00
Harmus, Bisque Socket Head, Sleep Eyes, Mohair Wig, Wood, Composition, 20 In. 468.00
Hasbro, Junior Miss, Plastic, Sleep Eyes, Sewing Kit, Case, 1957, 7 1/2 In. 60.00
Heine & Schneider, Pressed Cardboard Head, Body, Oil Painted, Muslin Limbs, 18 In. 1650.00
Hertel Schwab, 149, Bisque Socket Head, Sleep Eyes, Composition, Wood, Jointed, 14 In. 5940.00
Hertel Schwab, 165, Bisque Socket Head, Googly Eyes, Wood, Composition, 15 1/2 In. 4070.00
Hertel Schwab, Bisque Socket Head, Googly Eyes, Mohair, Composition, Wood, Jointed, 15 In. ... 7700.00
Hertwig, Bisque Shoulder Head, Googly, Molded Hair, Kid Body, Gusset Joints, 19 In. 95.00
Hertwig, Indian, Bisque, Jointed Shoulders, Painted Features, Flocked Finish, 7 In. 105.00
Heubach dolls are also in this category under Gebruder Heubach.
Heubach, 320, Bisque Socket Head, Sleep Eyes, Human Hair Wig, Baby, 24 In. 280.00
Heubach, Bisque Head, Pierced Nostrils, Composition Baby, Koppelsdorf, Early 1900s, 10 In. 147.00
Heubach, Bisque Head, Sleep Eyes, Open Mouth, Wood, Composition, Koppelsdorf, 18 In. 155.00
Heubach, Bisque Socket Head, 15-Piece Ball-Jointed Body, Kopplesdorf, 24 In. 168.00
Heubach, Bisque Socket Head, Sculpted Bonnet, Composition, Bent Limb, Baby, 9 In. 1430.00
Horsman, 1011, Cowgirl, Composition Head, Latex Body, Original Costume, Box, 1950, 10 In. 149.00
Horsman, Bisque Head, Sleep Eyes, Cloth Body, Composition Hands, Newborn, c.1924, 11 In. ... 460.00
Horsman, Carnival Baby Composition Flange Head, Cloth Body, Original Outfit, 30 In. 70.00
Horsman, Composition, Cloth, Original Marked Clothing, 20 In. 110.00
Ideal, Bud Abbott & Lou Costello, Who's On First, Baseball Uniforms, 1983, 10 In., Pair 520.00
Ideal, Gabby, Gulliver's Travels, Wood, Composition, Ideal, Paramount, 1939, 11 In. ......335.00 to 575.00
Ideal, Harriet Hubbard Ayer, Vinyl Head, Sleep Eyes, Plastic Body, Original Dress, 19 In. 72.00
Ideal, King Little, Gulliver's Travels, Wood, Composition, Jointed, Paramount, 1939, 12 In. 650.00
Ideal, Miss Revlon, Vinyl Head, Green Sleep Eyes, Pink Nylon Dress, 1958, 14 In. 510.00
Ideal, Saucy Walker, Plastic, Green Dress, 1955, 22 In. 40.00
Ideal, Toni, Hard Plastic, Sleep Eyes, Blond, Accessories, Box, c.1950, 14 In. 382.00
Ideal, Toni, Hard Plastic, Sleep Eyes, Platinum Hair, Accessories, Box, 1952, 14 In. 475.00
Indian dolls are listed in the Indian category.
Izannah Walker, Cloth, Oil-Painted Facial Features, Stitch-Jointed, c.1865, 18 In. 9900.00
J.D.K. dolls also may be listed in this category under Kestner.
J.D.K., Baby Jean, Bisque Dome Head, Sleep Eyes, Composition Kestner Body, 17 In. 660.00
Jane Davies, William, Bisque, Swivel Head, Jointed, Sailor Suit, Straw Hat, c.1988, 4 1/2 In. 140.00

Japanese, Samurai, 13 In. 176.00
Jumeau, Bisque Head, Closed Mouth, Paperweight Eyes, Composition, Portrait, 22 1/2 In. 10350.00
Jumeau, Bisque Head, Cork Pate, Human Hair, Cloth Body, Kid Arms, France, c.1870, 18 In. 2585.00
Jumeau, Bisque Head, Cork Pate, Paperweight Eyes, Composition, Bebe, c.1880, 16 In. 2115.00
Jumeau, Bisque Socket Head, Closed Mouth, Paperweight Eyes, Silk Dress, 13 1/2 In. 6038.00
Jumeau, Bisque Socket Head, Cork Pate, Paperweight Eyes, Composition, Jointed, 17 In. 5600.00
Jumeau, Bisque Socket Head, Enamel Inset Eyes, Mohair, Composition, 16 In. 8800.00
Jumeau, Bisque Socket Head, Glass Eyes, Composition, Wood, Ball-Jointed, c.1878, 18 In. 6600.00
Jumeau, Bisque Socket Head, Glass Eyes, Mohair, Composition, Wood, Ball-Jointed, 22 In. 9350.00
Jumeau, Bisque Socket Head, Paperweight Eyes, Composition, Wood, Jointed, Bebe, 9 In. 7700.00
Jumeau, Bisque Socket Head, Paperweight Eyes, Composition, Jointed, Bebe, 26 In. 7280.00
Jumeau, Bisque Socket Head, Paperweight Eyes, Composition, Wood, Box, 14 In. 9075.00
Jumeau, Bisque Socket Head, Paperweight Eyes, Composition, Wood, Jointed, Bebe, 12 In. 5500.00
Jumeau, Bisque Socket Head, Paperweight Eyes, Composition, Wood, Jointed, Bebe, 18 In. 3960.00
Jumeau, Bisque Socket Head, Paperweight Eyes, Composition, Wood, Jointed, Bebe, 25 In. 6875.00
Jumeau, Bisque Socket Head, Paperweight Eyes, Mohair Wig, Composition, Bebe, 28 In. 9075.00
Jumeau, Bisque Socket Head, Paperweight Eyes, Mohair, Composition, Wood, Bebe, 13 In. 7640.00
Jumeau, Bisque Socket Head, Paperweight Eyes, Mohair, Composition, Wood, Bebe, 19 In. 8250.00
Jumeau, Bisque Socket Head, Paperweight Eyes, Mohair, Composition, Wood, Bebe, 22 In. 8800.00
Jumeau, Bisque Socket Head, Sleep Eyes, Composition, Wood, Ball-Jointed, Bebe, 10 In. 7040.00
Jumeau, Bisque Socket Head, Sleep Eyes, Composition, Wood, Jointed, Bebe, c.1886, 15 In. 8250.00
Jumeau, Bisque Swivel Head, Enamel Eyes, Mohair, Kid Body, Gusset-Jointed, 15 In. 4400.00
Jumeau, Bisque Swivel Head, Enamel Eyes, Mohair, Kid Body, Gusset-Jointed, Fashion, 13 In. 4180.00
Jumeau, Bisque Swivel Head, Glass Enamel Eyes, Mohair, Kid, Gusset-Jointed, c.1875, 17 In. 3520.00
Jumeau, Bisque Swivel Head, Glass Eyes, Blond Mohair, Kid, Gusset-Jointed, Fashion, 16 In. 2200.00
Jumeau, Bisque Swivel Head, Glass Eyes, Mohair, Muslin, Stitch-Jointed, Fashion, 28 In. 5280.00
Jumeau, Bisque Swivel Head, Kid-Edged, Paperweight Eyes, Gusset-Jointed, 26 In. 4704.00
Jumeau-Type, Bisque Shoulder Head, Cobalt Blue Eyes, Gusseted Kid Body, 12 In. 1680.00
K * R, 101, Bisque Socket Head, Painted Eyes, Mohair Wig, Wood, Composition, 7 1/2 In. 1760.00
K * R, 101, Marie, Bisque Socket Head, Composition, Wood, Ball-Jointed, c.1910, 12 In. 1760.00
K * R, 114, Gretchen, Bisque Socket Head, Painted Face, Composition, Wood, Jointed, 19 In. 6440.00
K * R, 115, Bisque Socket Head, Pouty, Sleep Eyes, Composition, Wood, Toddler, 15 In. 3740.00
K * R, 115A, Bisque Socket Head, Pouty, Composition, Wood, Jointed, Toddler, 15 In. 4592.00
K * R, 115A, Phillip, Bisque Socket Head, Sleep Eyes, Mohair, Composition, c.1912, 19 In. 2750.00
K * R, 121, Bisque Head, Sleep Eyes, Open Mouth, Skin Wig, Composition, Baby, 25 In. 430.00
K * R, 121, Bisque Socket Head, Teeth, Composition, Wood, Ball-Jointed, Toddler, Boy, 22 In. 2016.00
K * R, 121, Character Baby, S & H Bisque Head, Bent Limb Body, Sleep Eyes, 23 In. 616.00
K * R, 126, Bisque Socket Head, Sleep Eyes, Open Mouth, Mohair Composition, Baby, 13 In. 422.00
K * R, 127, Bisque Socket Head, Glass Eyes, Composition, Wood, Toddler, Boy, 16 In. 1595.00
K * R, 131, Bisque Socket Head, Googly Eyes, Mohair, Composition, Wood, Ball-Jointed, 15 In. 9900.00
K * R, Bisque Socket Head, Brown Face, Fleecy Mohair, Composition, Wood, Jointed, 18 In. 3630.00
K * R, Bisque Socket Head, Brown Sleep Eyes, Mohair Wig, 27 1/2 In. 309.00
K * R, Bisque Socket Head, Glass Sleep Eyes, Teeth, Mohair, Composition Body, 8 In. 880.00
K * R, Bisque Socket Head, Open Mouth, 4 Teeth, Plaid Kilts, 1910, 16 In. 895.00
K * R, Bisque Socket Head, Painted Face, Human Hair, Composition, Wood, Ball-Jointed, 29 In. 5940.00
K * R, Bisque Socket Head, Painted Face, Mohair, Composition, Wood, Ball-Jointed, 18 In. 3410.00
K * R, Bisque Socket Head, Sleep Eyes, Bobbed Mohair, Composition, Wood, Uniform, 17 In. 5775.00
K * R, Bisque Socket Head, Sleep Eyes, Mohair Wig, Jointed, Open Mouth, 22 In. 619.00
K * R, Bisque Socket Head, Sleep Eyes, Mohair, Composition, Wood, Ball-Jointed, c.1915, 31 In. 7975.00
K * R, Bisque Socket Head, Sleep Eyes, Mohair, Composition, Wood, Ball-Jointed, Toddler, 18 In. 2128.00
Kathe Kruse, Boy, Cloth, Painted Features, Swivel Head, Hair, Ski Outfit, 20 In. .... *ILLUS* 935.00
Kathe Kruse, Celluloid, Socket Head, Sleep Eyes, 5-Piece Body, 15 In. 275.00
Kathe Kruse, Cloth, Oil-Painted Features, Stitch-Jointed, 14 In. 1760.00
Kathe Kruse, Cloth, Painted Features, Stitch-Jointed, Disc-Jointed, c.1915, 17 In. 4620.00
Kathe Kruse, Deta, Open-Close Laughing Mouth, Tagged Silk Dress, Bonnet, Box, 14 In. 338.00
Kathe Kruse, Du Mein, Plastic Head, Painted Features, Jointed Cloth Body, 20 In. 395.00
Kathe Kruse, Girl, Cloth, Painted Features, Swivel Head, Hair, Jointed Limbs, 20 In. .... *ILLUS* 825.00
Kathe Kruse, Girl, Plastic, Muslin Body, c.1970, 14 In. 176.00
Kathe Kruse, I, Cloth Head, Cloth Jointed Body, Separate Thumb, 16 1/2 In. 4125.00
Kathe Kruse, IH, Cloth, Human Hair, Original Clothing, Tag, 17 In. 3190.00
Kathe Kruse, Plastic Head, Painted, Human Hair, Muslin Body, c.1970, 14 In. 176.00

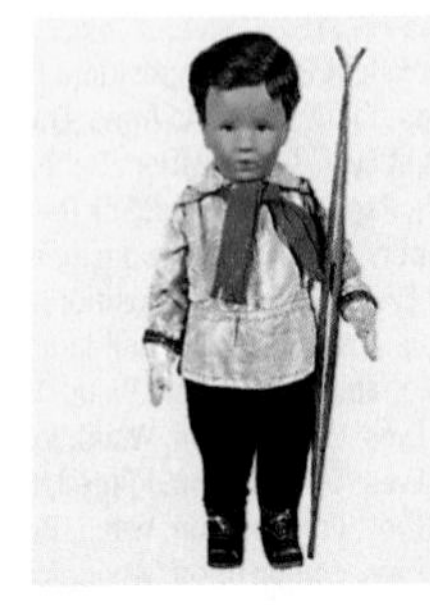

Doll, Kathe Kruse, Boy, Cloth, Painted Features, Swivel Head, Hair, Ski Outfit, 20 In.

Doll, Kathe Kruse, Girl, Cloth, Painted Features, Swivel Head, Hair, Jointed Limbs, 20 In.

Kathe Kruse, Plastic Swivel Head, Cloth Body, Original Clothes, Stoffpuppe Tag, 14 In. 110.00
Kathe Kruse, Smiling Baby, Cloth, Stockinet Head, Painted Hair, Mitten Hands, 13 In. 5225.00
Kathe Kruse, Toni Sabine, Plastic Head, Painted Features, Wig, Cloth Body, Jointed, 18 In. 141.00
Kathe Kruse, VIII, Cloth Swivel Head, Human Hair, Cloth Body, Ethnic Costume, 20 In. 880.00
Kathe Kruse, VIII, Cloth Swivel Head, Human Hair, Cloth Body, Jointed, Original Clothes, 20 In. ... 825.00
Kathe Kruse, VIII, Cloth Swivel Head, Oil Painted, Human Hair Wig, 20 In. 788.00
Kathe Kruse, VIII, Cloth Swivel Head, Painted Cloth Body, Jointed, Original Ski Outfit, 20 In. 935.00
Kathy Redmond, Abigail Adams, Porcelain, Sculpted Features, Flowered Dress, 15 In. 248.00
Kathy Redmond, Elizabeth I, Porcelain, Sculpted Hair, Brocade Gown, Ruff Collar, 16 In. 358.00
Kathy Redmond, Napoleon & Josephine, Porcelain, Molded Hair, Tailored Clothes, 15 & 17 In. ... 358.00
Kestner dolls are also in this category under J.D.K.
Kestner, 102, Bisque Swivel Head, Glass Eyes, Teeth, Peg-Jointed, c.1880, 8 1/2 In. 3630.00
Kestner, 143, Bisque Head, Sleep Eyes, Composition Body, Early 1900s, 13 In. 588.00
Kestner, 143, Bisque Head, Sleep Eyes, Mohair, Composition Body, Early 1900s, 13 1/2 In. 529.00
Kestner, 150, Bisque, Brown Sleep Eyes, Open Mouth, Mohair Wig, Jointed, 10 In. 563.00
Kestner, 154, Bisque Shoulder Head, Plaster Pate, Sleep Eyes, Open Mouth, Mohair Wig, 23 In. .. 338.00
Kestner, 156, Bisque Socket Head, Sleep Eyes, Composition, Wood, Ball-Jointed, 32 In. 2352.00
Kestner, 166, Bisque Shoulder Head, Muslin Body, Molded Eyebrows, Sleep Eyes, 24 In. 176.00
Kestner, 167, Bisque Socket Head, Sleep Eyes, Human Hair, Wood, Composition, 12 1/2 In. 523.00
Kestner, 167, Bisque Socket Head, Sleep Eyes, Open Mouth, Mohair Wig, Jointed, 18 In. 366.00
Kestner, 171, Bisque Socket Head, Set Eyes, Mohair Wig, Wood, Composition, 23 1/2 In. 309.00
Kestner, 171, Bisque Socket Head, Sleep Eyes, Mohair Wig, Wood, Composition, 24 In. 468.00
Kestner, 171, Bisque Socket Head, Sleep Eyes, Mohair Wig, Wood, Composition, Box, 13 In. 523.00
Kestner, 171, Bisque Socket Head, Sleep Eyes, Mohair, Composition, Wood, Ball-Jointed, 26 In. .. 2128.00
Kestner, 174, Bisque Socket Head, Sleep Eyes, Composition, Wood, Ball-Jointed, Child, 14 In. 2128.00
Kestner, 184, Bisque Socket Head, Glass Eyes, Composition, Wood, Ball-Jointed, 12 In. 2420.00
Kestner, 211, Bisque Socket Head, Blue Sleep Eyes, Synthetic Wig, Composition, 22 In. 563.00
Kestner, 241, Bisque Head, Glass Eyes, 4 Teeth, Mohair, Composition, Wood, Ball-Jointed, 25 In. . 5940.00
Kestner, 243, Chinese Baby, Bisque Socket Head, Amber Tint, Brown Eyes, Bent Limbs 4780.00
Kestner, 243, Chinese Baby, Bisque Socket Head, Amber Tint, Sleep Eyes, Teeth, Mohair, 13 In. .. 4290.00
Kestner, Bisque Dome Socket Head, Painted Hair, Sleep Eyes, Open Mouth, Baby, 15 In. 316.00
Kestner, Bisque Head, Skin Wig, Sleep Eyes, Open Mouth, 5-Piece Composition Body, 16 In. 345.00
Kestner, Bisque Head, Sleep Eyes, Mohair Wig, Composition, Wood, Body, c.1880, 15 1/2 In. 2350.00
Kestner, Bisque Shoulder Head, Blue Sleep Eyes, Mohair Wig, Gusseted Kid Body, 19 In. 450.00
Kestner, Bisque Shoulder Head, Sleep Eyes, Open Mouth, Mohair Wig, Kid Body, 20 In. 200.00
Kestner, Bisque Socket Head, Blue Flirty Eyes, Brown Mohair Wig, Composition, 11 1/2 In. 300.00
Kestner, Bisque Socket Head, Glass Eyes, Composition, Wood, Jointed, Size 13, 18 In. 2200.00
Kestner, Bisque Socket Head, Sleep Eyes, Bisque, Composition, Wood, Jointed, c.1890, 17 In. ... 4510.00
Kestner, Bisque Socket Head, Sleep Eyes, Mohair, Composition, Wood, Jointed, Size 10, 15 In. ... 1650.00
Kestner, Bisque Swivel Head, Brown Glass Eyes, Kid-Edged Body, Peg-Jointed, 6 In. 2310.00
Kestner, Bisque Swivel Head, Brown Tint, Fleecy Mohair, Composition, Wood, Jointed, 6 In. 990.00
Kestner, Bisque Swivel Head, Glass Sleep Eyes, Mohair, Peg-Jointed, c.1885, 4 1/2 In. 1870.00
Kestner, Bisque Swivel Head, Mohair, Bisque Body, Peg-Jointed, c.1885, 9 In. 3300.00
Kestner, Bisque Swivel Head, Sleep Eyes, Blond Mohair Wig, Peg-Jointed, 5 1/2 In. 1848.00
Kestner, Gibson Girl, Bisque Shoulder Head, Sleep Eyes, Mohair Wig, Kid Body, 20 In. 1760.00
Kestner, Hilda, Bisque Socket Head, Brown Complexion, Sleep Eyes, Mohair, 10 In. 2800.00
Kestner, Hilda, Bisque Socket Head, Brown Eyes, Composition, Jointed, Toddler, 17 In. 3105.00

Kestner, Hilda, Bisque Socket Head, Brown Sleep Eyes, Skin Wig, Jointed, Toddler, 13 In. 2925.00
Kestner, Hilda, Bisque Socket Head, Glass Eyes, Teeth, Composition, Baby, c.1914, 18 In. 3575.00
Kestner, Hilda, Bisque Socket Head, Sleep Eyes, Open Mouth, 2 Teeth, Baby, 1914, 21 In. 2530.00
Kestner, Hilda, Bisque Socket Head, Sleep Eyes, Teeth, Composition, Jointed, Toddler, 18 In. 6270.00
Kestner, Solid Dome Head, Painted Hair, Sleep Eyes, Open Mouth, Composition, Baby, 22 In. 489.00
Kewpie dolls are listed in the Kewpie category.
Kley & Hahn, Walkure, Bisque Socket Head, Sleep Eyes, Open Mouth, Human Hair Wig, 34 In. ... 395.00
Lenci, Boy, Brown Googly Eyes, Blond Hair, 1925, 17 In. 770.00
Lenci, Boy, Felt Swivel Head, Painted Features, Brown Eyes & Hair, 1930, 12 In. 1250.00
Lenci, Boy, Felt, Sober Face, Mohair, c.1930, 17 In. 646.00
Lenci, Czech Boy, Pressed Felt Swivel Head, Painted Eyes, Looking Left, Mohair Wig, 14 In. 506.00
Lenci, Italian Girl, Felt Swivel Head, Painted Features, Googly, Mohair Braids, 20 In. 1430.00
Lenci, Red Riding Hood, Felt Swivel Head, Blue Eyes, Closed Mouth, 14 In. 600.00
Lenci, Woman, Blue Dotted Apron, Flowered Shawl, Label, 15 3/4 x 6 1/2 In. 920.00
Limbach, Bisque Socket Head, Glass Googly Eyes, Mohair, Composition, Toddler, 8 In. 2860.00
Lynne & Michael Roche, Hannah, Bisque Socket Head, Human Hair Wig, Wood Body, 18 In. 1100.00
Madame Alexander, Agnes, Cloth, Brown Mohair Wig, 1933-40, 15 In. 410.00
Madame Alexander, Alice In Wonderland, 1933-40, 20 In. 499.00
Madame Alexander, Amish Boy, Plastic, Sleep Eyes, Jointed, Wrist Tag, Box, 8 In. 195.00
Madame Alexander, Amy, Composition, Mohair Wig, Original Clothes, Dress Tag, Box, 7 In. 305.00
Madame Alexander, Annabelle, Plastic, Sleep Eyes, 5-Piece Body, 1952, 18 In. 880.00
Madame Alexander, Baby Clown, Plastic, Walker, Pipe Cleaner Dog, 1955, 8 In. 495.00
Madame Alexander, Cissy, Hard Plastic, Wig, Head Turns, Jointed, 1951, 17 1/2 In. 499.00
Madame Alexander, David Copperfield, Molded Felt Face, Blond Wig, Red Hat, 1930s, 16 In. 400.00
Madame Alexander, Easter, Wendy, Plastic, Sleep Eyes, Bent Knees, Original Dress, Tag, 8 In. ... 358.00
Madame Alexander, Elise Ballerina, Hard Plastic, Blue Eyes, Closed Mouth, Jointed, 15 In. 200.00
Madame Alexander, Gold Ballerina, Plastic, Bent Knee Walker, Original Clothes, Tag, 8 In. 195.00
Madame Alexander, Jane Withers, Yellow Dress, Bonnet, Brown Wig, 1937, 13 In. 800.00
Madame Alexander, Jeannie Walker, Composition, Sleep Eyes, Mohair Wig, 13 In. 605.00
Madame Alexander, Kelly, Vinyl, Rooted Blond Hair, Sleep Eyes, Jointed, Dress, Pinafore, 20 In. .. 200.00
Madame Alexander, Korea, Hard Plastic, Dark Skin, Bent Knee, 8 In. 140.00
Madame Alexander, Little Shaver, Painted Cloth Face, Stuffed Cloth Body, Yarn Hair, 17 In. 90.00
Madame Alexander, Marlo Thomas, That Girl, Vinyl, Brown Sleep Eyes, Jointed, 1967, 17 In. 310.00
Madame Alexander, Meg, Hard Plastic, Saran Wig, Sleep Eyes, Margaret Face, Jointed, 14 In. 140.00
Madame Alexander, Nurse, Plastic, Sleep Eyes, Bent Knee, Walker, Jointed, 1956, 8 In. 385.00
Madame Alexander, Quizkin, Hard Plastic, Molded Hair, Sleep Eyes, Nodding Buttons, 8 In. 175.00
Madame Alexander, Southern Belle, Composition, Original Clothes, Dress Tag, Box, 7 In. 165.00
Madame Alexander, Susie Q, Cloth, Yarn Hair, Original Clothes, Wrist Tag, 16 In. 770.00
Madame Alexander, Wendy Visits Ranch, Hard Plastic, Walker, Blond Wig, Sleep Eyes, 8 In. 225.00
Madame Alexander, Winnie Walker, Hard Plastic, Saran Wig, Blue Dress, 24 In. 280.00
Marionette, Memento Mori, Young Man One Side, Skull Other, 18th Century, 31 In. 295.00
Marionettes, Peter Pan & Wendy, Peter Puppets, 1950s, 10 In., Pair 155.00
Martin & Runyon, Walker, Clockwork, 1862 Patent, 10 In. 850.00
Mary Hoyer, Composition, Sleep Eyes, Mohair Wig, Jointed, 1940s, 14 In. 385.00
Mary Hoyer, Hard Plastic, Blond Saran Wig, Sleep Eyes, Jointed Shoulders, Hips, Box, 14 In. 730.00
Mary Hoyer, Hard Plastic, Sleep Eyes, Jointed Shoulders, Hips, Box, c.1954, 14 In. 565.00
Mattel, Barbie, American Girl, Blond Long Hair, Swimsuit, Turquoise Shoes, 1966 .... 350.00
Mattel, Barbie, American Girl, Platinum Blond Hair, Striped Turquoise Swimsuit, Box, 1966 ...... 760.00
Mattel, Barbie, Bubble Cut, Blond, Red Swimsuit, Accessories, Stand, Box, 1962 .... 175.00
Mattel, Barbie, Bubble Cut, Brunette, Black & White Swimsuit, Stand, 1961 .... 110.00
Mattel, Barbie, Bubble Cut, Brunette, Coral Lips, Swimsuit, Accessories, Stand, Box 795.00
Mattel, Barbie, Bubble Cut, Titian Hair, Swimsuit, Accessories, Stand, Box, 1961 ....195.00 to 495.00
Mattel, Barbie, Fashion Queen, Bubble Cut, Case, 16 Partial Outfits 175.00
Mattel, Barbie, Fashion Queen, Swimsuit, Turban, Headband, 3 Wigs, 1963 .... 175.00
Mattel, Barbie, Malibu, Blond Hair, Red Swimsuit, Box, 1978 .... 59.00
Mattel, Barbie, No. 4, Brunette, Ponytail, Black & White Swimsuit, Accessories, Box ......295.00 to 795.00
Mattel, Barbie, No. 5, Blond, Ponytail, Black & White Swimsuit, Accessories, Stand, Box 225.00
Mattel, Barbie, Twist 'n Turn, Ash Blond, Long Hair, Pink 2-Piece Swimsuit, Accessories, Box, 1967 575.00
Mattel, Barbie, Twist 'n Turn, Ash Blond, Swimsuit, Cover-Up, Hairband, 1966 .... 160.00
Mattel, Barbie, Twist 'n Turn, Blond, Swimsuit, Cover-Up, Hairband, 1967 .... 475.00
Mattel, Buffy & Mrs. Beasley, Vinyl, Rooted Hair, Talking, Box, Unopened, 10 In. 195.00

Mego, Laverne & Shirley, Box, 1977, 11 1/2 In., 2 Dolls 80.00
Milliner's, Papier-Mache, Shoulder Head, Apollo Knot Hair, Kid Body, 10 1/2 In. 660.00
Milliner's, Papier-Mache, Shoulder Head, Wood Legs, 1840s, 10 In. 590.00
Milliner's, Papier-Mache, Wood Arms, Legs, Germany, c.1840, 12 In. 470.00
Minerva, Tin Head, Painted, Kid Body, Pin-Jointed, Bisque Hands, Boy, 16 In. 196.00
Morimura Bros., Bisque Head, Sleep Eyes, Mohair Wig, 15-Piece Ball-Jointed Body, 17 In. 140.00
Nancy Ann Storybook, Muffie, Bridesmaid, Plastic, Walker, Tagged Dress, Box, 1956 .... 385.00
Nippon, 4002, Bisque Socket Head, Bent Limb Baby Body, Sleep Eyes, 12 In. 170.00
Norah Wellings, Boy, Felt Swivel Head & Body, Fleecy Hair, Jointed Shoulders, Hips, 31 In. 4980.00
Norah Wellings, Brown Velvet, Pressed, Painted Features, Glass Eyes, Mohair, Jointed, 35 In. 896.00
Norah Wellings, RAF Aviator, Felt Swivel Head, Blue Eyes, Painted Features, 1940s, 29 In. 1795.00
Norah Wellings, Sailor, Felt Swivel Head, Pressed Features, Glass Eyes, Cloth Body, 36 In. 1085.00
Nymphenburg, Porcelain Shoulder Head, Sculpted Features, Jointed, Woman, 16 In. 1210.00
Paper dolls are listed in their own category.
Papier-Mache, Caracul Wig, Swivel Head, Victorian Dress, Hat, 28 In. 785.00
Papier-Mache, Man, Molded Shoulders, Closed Mouth, Cloth Body, 14 1/2 In. 380.00
Papier-Mache, Painted Features, Side Curls, Cloth Body, Wood Legs, Original Dress, 14 In. 825.00
Papier-Mache, Painted Hair, Sculpted Ears, Kid Body, Wood Limbs, Germany, c.1840, 16 In. 1210.00
Papier-Mache, Queen Victoria, Shoulder Head, Glass Eyes, Sculpted Hair, c.1837, 19 In. 2970.00
Papier-Mache, Sculpted Curls, Braids, Turquoise Eyes, Kid Body, Wood Limbs, Germany, 18 In. 1430.00
Papier-Mache, Sculpted Hair, Muslin, Stitch-Jointed, Leather Arms, Germany, c.1860, 16 In. 935.00
Papier-Mache, Shoulder Head, Painted Features, Coiled Braids, Curls, Kid Body, 25 In. 4256.00
Papier-Mache, Shoulder Head, Painted Features, Stuffed Kid Body, Wood Limbs, 1840, 10 In. 588.00
Papier-Mache, Shoulder Head, Painted, Enamel Eyes, Kid Body, Gusset-Jointed, 20 In. 1680.00
Parian, Blond Molded Hair, Sausage Curls, Painted Eyes, China Hands, Leather Boots, 20 In. 215.00
Parian, Molded Snood, Painted Features, Closed Mouth, Cloth Body, Bisque Arms, 19 In. 460.00
Pincushion dolls are listed in their own category.
Plastic Molded Arts, Joanie Walker, Plastic, Sleep Eyes, Kimono, Box, Case, 1950s, 8 In. 165.00
Porcelain, Head Turned To Right, Extended Arm, Sculpted Hair, Comb, Germany, 5 In. 550.00
Poulbot, Bisque Socket Head, Glass Eyes, Red Mohair, Papier-Mache Body, Toddler, 14 In. 9900.00
Puppet, Hand, Mr. Ed, Mattel, 1960s 848.00
Puppet, Henry, Composition, Hand Painted, Red Coat, Yellow Pants, Striped Hat, 12 In. 120.00
Puppet, Punch & Judy, Moving Eyes, Peter Puppet, 1950s 75.00
R. John Wright, Christopher Robin & Winnie The Pooh, Series I, Pressed Felt, c.1987, 18 In. 2420.00
R. John Wright, Eeyore, Wintertime, Taupe Mohair, Snow On Back, Exclusive Edition, 5 In. 523.00
R. John Wright, Hannah, Little Children Series I, Pressed Felt Swivel Head, c.1985, 16 In. 1540.00
R. John Wright, Hans Brinker, Molded Felt, Sculpted Face, Painted, Jointed Knees, 20 In. 2420.00
R. John Wright, Little Prince, Felt Swivel Head, Painted Face, Mohair Wig, Box, c.1984, 16 In. 450.00
R. John Wright, Maria, Character Doll Series, Felt, Brown Cummerbund, 17 In. 1100.00
R. John Wright, Peter, Little Children Series I, Pressed Felt Face, Painted, c.1985, 17 In. 2860.00
R. John Wright, St. Nicholas, Character Doll Series, Molded Felt, Modeled Features, 18 In. 1760.00
Rabery & Delphieu, Bisque Head, Paperweight Eyes, Human Hair Wig, Bebe, 16 1/4 In. 3525.00
Rabery & Delphieu, Bisque Socket Head, Paperweight Eyes, Composition, Wood, Bebe, 20 In. 5500.00
Rabery & Delphieu, Bisque Socket Head, Sleep Eyes, Composition, Wood, Bebe, 10 1/2 In. 4400.00
Radiquet & Cordonnier, Bisque Swivel Head, Cork Pate, Glass Eyes, Mohair, Kid Body, 16 In. 8400.00
Raggedy Ann, Cloth, Yarn Hair, Original Dress, Book, Volland, 1915, 16 In. 880.00
Raggedy Ann, Long Nose, Yarn Hair, Button Eyes, Original Clothes, Georgene, 32 In. 104.00
Raggedy Ann & Andy, Muslin, Averill, 1950s, 20 In., Pair 2340.00
Ravco, Organ Grinder, Pressed Stockinet Head, France, 14 In. 264.00
Recknagel, 21, Bisque Socket Head, 16 In. 168.00
Reliable, Maggie Muggins, Composition, Sleep Eyes, Wig, Original Clothes, Tag, 15 In. 165.00
Remco, I Dream Of Jeannie, Box, 1977, 6 In. 65.00
Revalo, Coquette, Bisque Socket Head, Intaglio Eyes, Wood, Composition, 13 In. 440.00
Rohmer, China Swivel Neck, Gusseted Kid Body, China Arms, Paris, 1860s, 13 In. 3525.00
Rohmer, Porcelain Swivel Head, Glass Enamel Eyes, String Pin, Kid, Fashion, c.1860, 13 In. 5280.00
Rohmer, Porcelain Swivel Head, Mohair, Stuffed, String Pin-Pointed, Fashion, c.1858, 16 In. 4840.00
Rohmer, Porcelain Swivel Head, Wool Wig, Painted Eyes, Stuffed Kid, Fashion, c.1858, 13 In. 3960.00
Rohmer, Porcelain, Pink, Neck Socket, Glass Eyes, Mohair, Kid Body, Jointed, Fashion, 18 In. 5500.00
S & H dolls are also listed here as Bergmann and Simon & Halbig.
S.F.B.J., 237, Soldier, Bisque Socket Head, Composition, Wood, Original Uniform, 17 In. 3850.00
S.F.B.J., Bisque, Composition, Toddler, 27 In. 1035.00

Sasha, Kiltie, Vinyl, Human Hair Wig, 1983 .... 230.00
Sasha, Prince Gregor, Vinyl, Light Brown Hair, Wrist Tag, Certificate, Box 144.00
Sasha, Socket Head, Dark Complexion, Waist Length Blond Hair, 5-Piece Body, Gotz, 16 In. 1120.00
Sasha, Socket Head, Dark Complexion, Waist Length Brunette Hair, 5-Piece Body, Gotz, 16 In. 1008.00
Sasha, Socket Head, Dark Complexion, Waist Length Red Hair, 5-Piece Body, Gotz, 16 In. 1008.00
Schoenau & Hoffmeister, Bisque Head, Sleep Eyes, Open Mouth, Composition Body, 17 In. 115.00
Schoenhut, 204, Wood Socket Head, Carved Hair, Spring Jointed Body, 16 In. 990.00
Schoenhut, 301, Wood, Intaglio Eyes, Blond Mohair Wig, Spring Joints, 1911, 16 In. 770.00
Schoenhut, 308, Wood Socket Head, Mohair Wig, Wood Body, Jointed, 1911, 19 In. 1430.00
Schoenhut, Baby Face, Wood Body, Fully Jointed, Mohair Wig, Boy, 14 In. 230.00
Schoenhut, Barney Google & Spark Plug, 1922, 7 1/2 & 10 x 7 In., 2 Piece 1568.00
Schoenhut, Barney Google, Linen Face, Glass Eyes, Straw Stuffed, Painted, Felt Outfit, 12 In. 295.00
Schoenhut, Barney Google, Molded Head, c.1922, 8 In. 280.00
Schoenhut, Bonzo, Wood, 1920s, 7 In. 2800.00
Schoenhut, Koko The Clown, Ribbon Tag, c.1918, 10 In. 3920.00
Schoenhut, Miss Dolly, Painted Eyes, Open Mouth, Teeth, Mohair Wig, Clothing, 22 In. 294.00
Schoenhut, Wood Dome Head, Sleep Eyes, Celluloid Hands, Bye-Lo Muslin Body, 1925, 14 In. 990.00
Schoenhut, Wood Head, Mohair Wig, Articulated Wood Body, Girl, c.1911, 14 1/2 In. 355.00
Schoenhut, Wood Socket Head, Bobbed Hair, Checkered Dress, 1915, 16 In. 3850.00
Schoenhut, Wood Socket Head, Carved Braids, Intaglio Eyes, Spring-Jointed, 1911, 16 In. 2640.00
Schoenhut, Wood Socket Head, Carved Hair, Intaglio Eyes, Walker, 13 In. 1650.00
Schoenhut, Wood Socket Head, Carved, Mohair, Spring-Jointed, Toddler, Sailor Suit, 13 In. 1100.00
Schoenhut, Wood Socket Head, Intaglio Eyes, Mohair, Spring-Jointed, Boy, 1912, 16 1/2 In. 1980.00
Schoenhut, Wood Socket Head, Mohair Wig, Wood Body, Walker, 1913, 16 In. 468.00
Schoenhut, Wood Socket Head, Painted Blue Eyes, Open Mouth, Mohair Wig, Baby, 15 In. 253.00
Schoenhut, Wood Swivel Head, Mohair, Muslin Body, Wooden Hands, Toddler, 15 In. 660.00
Shirley Temple dolls are included in the Shirley Temple category.
Simon & Halbig dolls are also listed here under Bergmann.
Simon & Halbig, 156, Bisque Socket Head, Sleep Eyes, Wobble Tongue, Wig, Baby, 23 In. 338.00
Simon & Halbig, 550, Bisque Socket Head, Blue Sleep Eyes, Mohair Wig, 21 1/2 In. 563.00
Simon & Halbig, 719, Bisque Swivel Head, Glass Eyes, Eyeliner, Gusset-Jointed, 14 In. 1790.00
Simon & Halbig, 886, Bisque Swivel Head, Kid Edge, Sleep Eyes, Peg-Jointed, 7 1/2 In. 1904.00
Simon & Halbig, 905, Bisque Swivel Head, Solid Dome, Kid Edge, Kid Body, Nun, 14 In. 2800.00
Simon & Halbig, 939, Bisque Socket Head, Paperweight Eyes, Composition, Jointed, 27 In. 4180.00
Simon & Halbig, 940, Bisque Shoulder Head, Brown Sleep Eyes, Synthetic Wig, 23 In. 731.00
Simon & Halbig, 949, Bisque Socket Head, Brown Eyes, Open Mouth, Kid Body, 15 1/2 In. 394.00
Simon & Halbig, 949, Bisque Socket Head, Glass Eyes, Composition, Jointed, 35 In. 4700.00
Simon & Halbig, 950, Bisque Shoulder Head, Glass Eyes, Mohair, Muslin Body, 11 In. 840.00
Simon & Halbig, 1078, Bisque Socket Head, Glass Eyes, Mohair, Composition, Child, 18 In. 2688.00
Simon & Halbig, 1078, Bisque Socket Head, Open Mouth, Synthetic Wig, Jointed, 17 In. 280.00
Simon & Halbig, 1078, Bisque Socket Head, Sleep Eyes, Composition Body, c.1900, 34 In. 470.00
Simon & Halbig, 1079, Bisque Socket Head, Sleep Eyes, Open Mouth, Human Hair Wig, 27 In. 565.00
Simon & Halbig, 1079, Bisque Socket Head, Sleep Eyes, Wood, Composition, 30 In. 715.00
Simon & Halbig, 1159, Bisque Socket Head, Lashes, Human Hair, Composition, Jointed, 21 In. 1792.00
Simon & Halbig, 1159, Bisque Socket Head, Sleep Eyes, Composition, Wood, Jointed, 18 In. 2200.00
Simon & Halbig, 1249, Bisque Socket Head, Set Brown Eyes, Mohair Wig, Jointed, 25 In. 1125.00
Simon & Halbig, 1250, Bisque Shoulder Head, Leather Body, Composition Arms, 1900s, 23 In. 489.00
Simon & Halbig, 1250, Bisque Shoulder Head, Sleep Eyes, Human Hair Wig, Kid Body, 19 In. 169.00
Simon & Halbig, 1279, Bisque Socket Head, Teeth, Composition, Ball-Jointed, Child, 30 In. 2016.00
Simon & Halbig, 1358, Bisque Socket Head, Black, Glass Eyes, Composition, Wood, 15 In. 7150.00
Simon & Halbig, 1428, Bisque Socket Head, Sleep Eyes, Composition, Baby, c.1910, 11 In. 1540.00
Simon & Halbig, Bisque Head, Sleep Eyes, Pierced Ears, Composition, Jointed, 23 In. 220.00
Simon & Halbig, Bisque Socket Head, Amber, Asian Features, Composition, Wood, 15 In. 1320.00
Simon & Halbig, Bisque Socket Head, Brown Face, Sleep Eyes, Composition, Jointed, 11 In. 1792.00
Simon & Halbig, Bisque Socket Head, Sleep Eyes, Composition, Jointed, Fashion, 25 In. 2688.00
Simon & Halbig, Bisque Swivel Head, Glass Eyes, Twill Over Wood Body, c.1875, 13 In. 2970.00
Simon & Halbig, White Bisque Swivel Head, Brown Hair, Blue Glass Eyes, 1875, 10 In. 4725.00
Sonneberg Taufling, Papier-Mache Head, Glass Eyes, Painted Hair, Composition, Wood, 23 In. 2138.00
Steiff, Dutch Boy, Cloth, Glass Eyes, c.1913, 13 In. 355.00
Steiff, Felt, Glass Eyes, Mohair Wig, Jointed Neck, Limbs, c.1940, 13 1/2 In. 646.00
Steiff, Mecki, Mohair Swivel Head, Rubber Face, Ears, Painted Eyes, Smiling Mouth, 21 In. 309.00

Steiff, Woman, Felt, Glass Eyes, Painted Mouth, Mohair Wig, Jointed, 17 In. 105.00
Steiff, Zotti, Felt, Glass Eyes, Closed Mouth, Mohair Wig, Jointed, 1940s, 13 1/2 In. 646.00
Steiner, Bisque Shoulder Head, Glass Eyes, Teeth, Wool Wig, Kid Over Wood, Jointed, 15 In. 9520.00
Steiner, Bisque Socket Head, Enamel Eyes, Brunette Mohair, Bebe, 10 In. 4620.00
Steiner, Bisque Socket Head, Glass Eyes, Mohair, Composition, Jointed, Bebe, c.1890, 10 In. 2310.00
Steiner, Bisque Socket Head, Glass Sleep Eyes, Lever, Human Hair, Composition, Bebe, 29 In. 7975.00
Steiner, Bisque Socket Head, Glass Sleep Eyes, Teeth, Mohair Wig, Composition, Jointed, 14 In. .. 4145.00
Steiner, Bisque Socket Head, Sleep Eyes, Wood, Composition, 19 In. 305.00
Superior Doll Co., Papier-Mache, Blond, Blue Painted Eyes, Woman, 23 1/2 In. 105.00
Swain & Co., Bisque Socket Head, Intaglio Eyes, Composition, Wood, Ball-Jointed, 15 In. 1100.00
Terri Lee, Hard Plastic, Painted Features, Skirt, Blouse, Suitcase Of Clothes, 16 In. 175.00
Terri Lee, Plastic Socket Head, Brown Hair, Cowboy Outfit, 1955, 16 In. 875.00
Terri Lee, Plastic, Painted Features, Blond Wig, Red Dress, Dress Tag, 16 In. 165.00
Thuillier, Bisque Socket Head, Paperweight Eyes, Mohair, Composition, Wood, Jointed, 11 In. 7150.00
Tin Head, Wig, Brown Sleep Eyes, Kid Body, Pin-Jointed, 18 In. 170.00
Unis, 301, Bisque Socket Head, Brown Sleep Eyes, Human Hair, Composition, 24 In. 450.00
Virga, Linda, Black, Plastic, Outfits, Play-Mate School Case, 1955, 8 In. 140.00
Virga, Lucy, Plastic, Sleep Eyes, Mohair Wig, Walker, Clothes, Plaid Case, 1955, 8 In. 140.00
Vogue, Baby Dear, Vinyl, Cloth Body, Original Diaper, New Dress, Bonnet, Tag, 1960, 18 In. 160.00
Vogue, Bride, Sleep Eyes, Walker, Original Clothes, Box, 1956, 8 In. 270.00
Vogue, Cowboy, Plastic, Painted Features, Mohair Wig, 1949, 8 In. 193.00
Vogue, Cynthia, Composition, Sleep Eyes, Jointed, c.1942, 13 In. 220.00
Vogue, Dora Lee, Composition, Sleep Eyes, Blond Braids, Jointed, c.1939, 11 In. 85.00
Vogue, Ginny, Crib Crowd Baby, Hard Plastic, Sleep Eyes, Synthetic Wig, c.1950, 7 1/4 In. 265.00
Vogue, Ginny, Debutante Ginger, Hard Plastic, Red Velvet Dress, Bonnet, 1953 .... 715.00
Vogue, Ginny, Fun Time Ski, Hard Plastic, Braided Wig, Wooden Skis, Box Bottom, 1956 .... 220.00
Vogue, Ginny, Hard Plastic, Blond Wig, Straight Legs, Walker, 5 Outfits, Trunk, c.1955 .... 660.00
Vogue, Ginny, Hard Plastic, Sleep Eyes, Mohair Wig, Strung, c.1950, 7 1/4 In. 355.00
Vogue, Ginny, Kinder Crowd, Blond Braids, Original Clothes, Wrist Tag, Box, 1955 .... 250.00
Vogue, Ginny, Kindergarten Margie, Hard Plastic, Red Wig, Original No. 28 Dress, 1952 .... 745.00
Vogue, Ginny, Tiny Miss June, Hard Plastic, New Underclothes, Dress Tag, 1952 .... 250.00
Vogue, Jill, Bride, Hard Plastic, Auburn Wig, Walker, 1957, 10 1/2 In. 330.00
Vogue, Li'l Imp, Vinyl Head, Sleep Eyes, Rooted Hair, Plastic Body, Tag, Box, 11 In. 149.00
Vogue, Sandra Lee, Skater, Sportswoman Series, Composition, Jointed, Box, 1940s, 14 In. 745.00
Vogue, Skier, Sportswomen Series, Composition, Mohair, Jointed, Box Bottom, 1940s, 14 In. 495.00
Vogue, Sunshine Baby, Composition, Molded Hair, Jointed, 1943-47, 8 In. 110.00
Vogue, Toddles, Composition, Painted Features, Skating Outfit, 8 In. 145.00
Vogue, Valerie, Composition, Googly Eyes, Jointed, Original Clothes, c.1942, 7 In. 165.00
Walkure, Bisque Socket Head, Sleep Eyes, Mohair Wig, Wood, Composition, 27 In. 395.00
Walkure, Bisque Socket Head, Sleep Eyes, Real Lashes, Open Mouth, Mohair Wig, 26 In. 395.00
Wax Head, Human Hair, Cloth Body, England, c.1880, 22 In. 700.00
Wax Head, Human Hair, Cloth Body, Limbs, England, c.1880, 22 In. 705.00
Wax Head, Montanari, Hollow Hands, Feet, Cloth Body, Glass Eyes, 16 1/2 In. 230.00
Wax Head, Sculpted Hair, Bead Eyes, Painted Features, Wood Body, 8 In. 440.00
Wax Head, Shoulder Head, Sleep Eyes, Inserted Wig, Muslin Body, England, 22 In. 990.00
Wax Over Papier-Mache, Black Eyes, Red Velvet Dress, Garnet Necklace, Earrings, 18 In. 196.00
Wax Over Papier-Mache, Sculpted Hair, Enamel Eyes, Muslin Body, Wood Limbs, 13 In. 440.00
Wax Over Papier-Mache, Wire Lever Sleep Eyes, Muslin Body, Stitched-Jointed, c.1860, 15 In. ... 715.00
Wax Over Papier-Mache Domed Head, Flax Hair, Kid Body, Wood Limbs, Man, Germany, 28 In. .. 3960.00
Wax Over Papier-Mache Head, Bald Man, Bead Eyes, Muslin, Stitch-Jointed, 20 In. 1485.00
Wax Over Papier-Mache Slit Head, Mohair Wig, Cloth Body, England, 21 In. 193.00
Wax Over Papier-Mache Swivel Head, Glass Eyes, Muslin, Stitch-Jointed, c.1875, 29 In. 3410.00
Wax Over Plaster Of Paris, 2 Faces, Brunette, Blond, Marked, 20 In. 224.00
Wax Shoulder Head, Arms & Legs, Blue Glass Eyes, Human Hair, Cloth Body, 14 In. 506.00
Wax Shoulder Head, Arms & Legs, Glass Eyes, Mohair, Muslin Body, Child, England, 20 In. 935.00
Wax Shoulder Head, Glass Eyes, Hair, Muslin, England, c.1870, 22 In. 1375.00
Wax Shoulder Head, Glass Eyes, Human Hair, Cloth Body, Wax Arms, Legs, Child, 16 1/2 In. 1690.00
Wax Shoulder Head, Glass Eyes, Inserted Hair, Muslin Body, Woman, England, 17 In. 825.00
Wax Shoulder Head, Glass Eyes, Man, Hair, Brows, Mustache, Muslin Body, England, 16 In. 1350.00
Wax Shoulder Head, Lower Arms & Legs, Set Blue Eyes, Mohair, Cloth Body, 17 In. 605.00
Wooden, Carved Nose, Painted Features, Padded Wire Armature Arms, 8 In. 1210.00

Wooden, Glass Eyes, Mohair Wig, Cloth Lower Body, Arms, England, c.1800, 11 1/2 In. 3055.00
Wooden, Sculpted Nose, Human Hair, Painted, Glass Eyes, Block Body, Jointed, 17 In. 2860.00
Wooden Head, Arms, Glass Eyes, Mohair Wig, Cloth Body, England, 19th Century, 11 1/2 In. 3055.00
Wrestler, Bisque Head, Set Eyes, Human Hair Wig, Molded Boots, Pierced Ears, 8 1/2 In. 3105.00
DOLL CLOTHES, Alexander-Kins, Wendy Loves Being Loved, 3 Outfits, Box, 8 In. 35.00
Baby Annabell, Shirt, Capri Pants, Headband, Zapf, Box 11.00
Barbie, All That Jazz, No. 1848 .... 54.00
Barbie, American Airlines Stewardess, No. 984, 1961-64 .... 85.00
Barbie, Arabian Nights, No. 0874 .... 100.00
Barbie, Black Magic Ensemble, Black Sheath, Cape, Ribbons, Shoes, Globes, No. 1609 .... 130.00
Barbie, Bouncy Flouncy, No. 1805, 1967-68 .... 66.00
Barbie, Brunch Time, No. 1628, 1965 .... 70.00
Barbie, Campus Sweetheart, No. 1616, 1965 .... 128.00
Barbie, Dancing Lights, No. 3437, No Necklace 285.00
Barbie, Dandy Lines, No. 3798, Box, Unopened, 1981 .... 25.00
Barbie, Diva Drive, No. 1615, Package, Unopened, 1965 .... 280.00
Barbie, Evening Splendour, Accessories, No. 961, 1959-62 .... 45.00
Barbie, Extravaganza, Accessories, No. 1844, 1968 .... 119.00
Barbie, Fashion Editor, Accessories, No. 1635, 1965 .... 195.00
Barbie, Flower Wower, No. 1453, Package, Unopened, 1969 .... 56.00
Barbie, Flower Wower, No. 1453, Tag 21.00
Barbie, Fraternity Dance, No. 1638 .... 210.00
Barbie, Fun At Fair, Accessories, No. 1624, c.1965 .... 44.00
Barbie, Golden Glory, No. 1645, 1965-66 .... 81.00
Barbie, Golfing Greats, No. 3413, Package, Unopened 119.00
Barbie, Hawaii, No. 1605, Tag, c.1964 .... 21.00
Barbie, In Holland, No. 823, Leaflet, 1960s 72.00
Barbie, Junior Prom, Accessories, No. 1614, 1965 .... 63.00
Barbie, Lamb 'n Leather, No. 1467, 1970 .... 54.00
Barbie, Let's Dance, Accessories, No. 978 .... 25.00
Barbie, Maxi 'n Mini, No. 1799, Box, Unopened, 1970 .... 200.00
Barbie, Midnight Blue, No. 1617, 1965 .... 130.00
Barbie, Mod Fab City, No. 1874 .... 51.00
Barbie, Mood For Music, No. 940, Box, Unopened 150.00
Barbie, Now Knit, Green Shoes, No. 1452, 1970 .... 21.00
Barbie, On The Avenue, No. 1644, 1965 .... 58.00
Barbie, Orange Blossom, No. 987, Box, Unopened 200.00
Barbie, Patio Party, No. 1692, 1967 .... 67.00
Barbie, Peach Plush, No. 3461 .... 53.00
Barbie, Pepsi Cola, Shirt, Pants, Visor, No. 7756 .... 12.00
Barbie, Picnic Set, No. 967, 1959 .... 70.00
Barbie, Plantation Belle No. 966, 1959-61 .... 62.00
Barbie, Plush Pony, Accessories, No. 1873 .... 79.00
Barbie, Plush Pony, No. 1873 .... 10.50
Barbie, Polka Dots 'n Raindrops, No. 1255, 1966 .... 30.00
Barbie, Poodle Parade, Accessories, No. 1643, 1965 .... 158.00 to 307.00
Barbie, Pretty As A Picture, No. 1652 .... 71.00
Barbie, Rainbow Wraps, No. 1789, Box, Unopened, 1970 .... 160.00
Barbie, Red Flare, No. 939, Unopened 79.00
Barbie, Registered Nurse, Accessories, No. 991, 1961-64 .... 168.00
Barbie, Registered Nurse, No. 991, 1961-64 .... 60.00
Barbie, Saturday Matinee, No. 1615, 1965 .... 280.00
Barbie, Sheath Sensation, Shoes, No. 986, 1961-64 .... 23.00
Barbie, Shimmering Magic, Accessories, No. 1664, 1966-67 .... 260.00
Barbie, Short Set, No. 3481, Box, Unopened, 1971 .... 79.00
Barbie, Slumber Party, No. 1642, 1965 .... 68.00
Barbie, Solo In Spotlight, Accessories, No Microphone, No. 982, 1960-64 .... 30.00
Barbie, Solo In Spotlight, No. 982, Box, 1960-64 .... 527.00
Barbie, Suburban Shopper, No. 969, 1959-64 .... 53.00
Barbie, Sunflower, No. 1683 .... 68.00
Barbie, Theater Date, No. 959, Unopened, 1962 .... 210.00

Bebe, Dress, Blue Flowers, Jumeau Signature, For 18-20 In. Doll 30.00
Bebe, Dress, Hat, Couturier, Ecru Silk, Gold Trim, Bells, Belt 303.00
Chatty Cathy, Socks, White, Cotton, Knit, Mattel .... 11.00 to 14.00
Chatty Cathy, Undies, White, Cotton, Knit, Mattel .... 11.00 to 16.00
Dy-Dee Baby, Dress, Bonnet, Tag, Effanbee, 12 1/2 In. 129.00
Eloise, Loves To Dance, Box, Unopened, Madame Alexander, For 8-In. Doll 29.00
Francie, Altogether Elegant, No. 1242 .... 28.00
Francie, Entertainer, Pink Jumpsuit, No. 1763, c.1965 .... 4.00
Francie, Fur Out, No. 1262, 1966 .... 239.00
Francie, Leather Limelight, No. 1269, 1966 .... 68.00
Francie, Pink Power, No. 1762, Package, Unopened, 1969 .... 65.00
Francie, Shoppin' Spree, No. 1261, Box, Unopened, c.1966 .... 204.00
Francie, Snake Charmer, No. 1245, Tag, 1965 .... 22.00
Francie, Style Setters, No. 1268, 1966 .... 36.00 to 60.00
Francie, Summer Dance Dress, Taffeta, Checkered, Black, White, No. 1291, 1967 .... 34.00
Francie, Tweed-Some, No. 1286 .... 115.00
Francie, Two For The Ball, No. 1232, 1969-70 .... 46.00
G.I. Joe, Green Beret Uniform, Tag, Hasbro, Japan, 1966 .... 19.00
G.I. Joe, Russian Uniform, Hat, Tag, Hasbro, Hong Kong, 1966 .... 22.00
G.I. Joe, Spy Island Uniform, Tag, Hasbro, Hong Kong, 1969 .... 13.00
Ginny Fashion Ensemble, Yellow Dress, Accessories, Box, Vogue, 1984 .... 12.00
Huggums, Sleeper, Footed, Nylon, Pink, Lace Trim, Tag, Madame Alexander 32.00
Ken, Arabian Knights, No. 0774 .... 50.00
Ken, Prince, No. 0772 .... 44.00
Ken, Rally Gear, No. 1429, c.1968 .... 66.00
Ken, Ski Champion, Accessories, No. 798 .... 22.00
Ken, Skin Diver, Accessories, Box, Unopened, 1964 .... 52.00
Ken, Terry Togs Robe, No. 784, Unopened, 1960s 84.00
Ken, U.S. Navy Sailor, No. 796, 1960s 65.00
Pedigree Sindy, Checkmate, Dress, Hat, Shoes, 1984 .... 10.00
Pedigree Sindy, Red Flares, 1970s 20.00
Penny Brite, Sunday Best, 1964 .... 10.00
Sasha, Ballet Outfit, No. 206, Box, Unopened 46.00
Sasha, Blue Slicker, White Boots, No. 804 Duffle, Box, Unused 36.00
Sasha, Red Slicker, Black Boots, No. 802 Duffle, Box, Unused 41.00
Shoes, Brown Leather, Silk Edging, Rosettes, Hook & Eye, Jumeau, 1878, 3 In. 431.00
Shoes, Eden Bebe Brevete, Black Leather, Buttons, Paris, 2 In. 275.00
Shoes, Leather, HL Modes De Paris, Marked 65, Button Closures, France 385.00
Skipper, Ballet Class, No. 1905, Box, Unopened, 1963 .... 199.00
Skipper, Dog Show, No. 1929 .... 54.00
Skipper, Let's Play House, No. 1932, 1963-64 .... 124.00 to 142.00
Skipper, Rolla-Scoot, No. 1940 .... 46.00 to 52.00
Skipper, Silk 'n Fancy, Accessories, Booklet, Original Package, c.1963 .... 68.00
Skipper, Skating Fun, No. 1908, 1960s 61.00
Skipper, Tea Party, No. 1924, Box, Unopened, 1966 .... 320.00
Suzy Cute, Hop Skip & Jump, 1960s 6.00
Tammy, Picnic Party Set, Accessories, Tag, Ideal 14.00
Tammy's Family, Fashion Jeans, Red Sweater, Hanger, On Card, Ideal, 1963 .... 16.00
Tammy's Family, Pepper Tartan, Dress, Accessories, Tag, Ideal 23.00
Tiny Thumbelina, Christening Dress, Hat, Socks, Package, Unopened 11.00
Tiny Thumbelina, Floral Dress, Hat, Socks, Package, Unopened 13.00
Wendy, Ready For Plane Trip, Madame Alexander, No. 452, 1955 .... 62.00
Wendy-Kins, Green Stripe Dress, Panties, 2 Hats, Box, No. 0352, Madame Alexander 128.00

DONALD DUCK items are included in the Disneyana category.

DOORSTOPS have been made in all types of designs. The vast majority of the doorstops sold today are cast iron and were made from about 1890 to 1930. Most of them are shaped like people, animals, flowers, or ships. Reproductions and newly designed examples are sold in gift shops.

Asters, Embossed Leaves, White Painted Wicker Basket, Waverly Studio, 9 In. 55.00

Doorstop, Cat, Tabby, Wrapped Tail, Pedestal Base, Cast Iron, 12 1/2 In., Pair

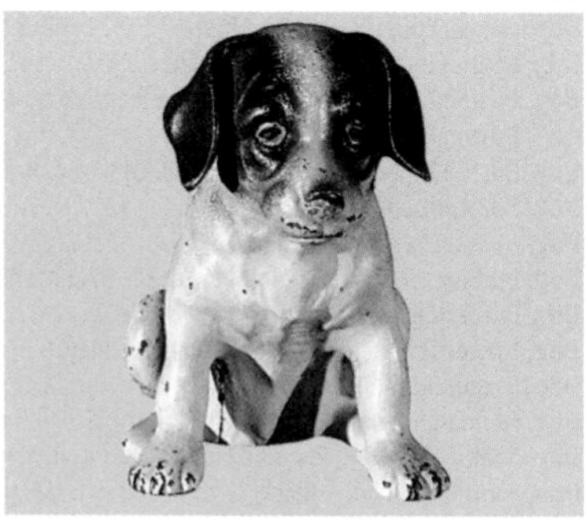

Doorstop, Dog, Beagle Puppy, Cast Iron, Hubley, 7 1/2 x 5 3/8 In.

Aunt Jemima, Blue, White, Cast Iron, Hubley, 1930s 975.00
Basket Of Flowers, Painted, 19th Century, 10 In. 100.00
Basket Of Flowers, Painted, Cast Iron, 9 1/2 In. 90.00
Bathing Beauties, Art Deco, 2 Bathers, Sharing Parasol, Hubley, 9 1/2 x 3 1/2 In. 2090.00
Bathing Beauties, Art Deco, 2 Bathers, Sharing Parasol, Hubley, 10 7/8 x 5 1/4 In. 715.00
Bellhop, Blue Uniform, At Attention, Cast Iron, CJO, 8 7/8 x 4 5/8 In. 415.00
Billy Goat, Full Figure, Black Paint, Cast Iron, 1940s, 5 1/2 x 4 1/2 In. 200.00
Bird Of Paradise, Cast Iron, 5 3/4 x 8 1/2 In. 784.00
Bird Of Paradise, Cast Iron, Feathers, Plumage, 13 3/8 x 7 In. 5600.00
Black Baby In Baby Bootie, Cast Iron, 4 7/8 x 5 1/8 In. 728.00
Blue Jay, Grass, Flowers, Cast Iron, 4 7/8 x 3 3/4 In. 505.00
Bobby Blake, Grace Drayton Design, Hubley, 1930s 950.00
Cat, Black, Cast Iron, 12 1/2 In. 805.00
Cat, Black, Seated, Cast Iron, 9 1/4 In. 450.00
Cat, Black, Seated, Ribbon Around Neck, 11 1/4 In. 260.00
Cat, Black, Yellow Painted Shifty Eyes, Poised Tail, Wedge Back, 7 x 9 In. 660.00
Cat, Gray Tabby, Cast Iron, Hubley, 10 1/4 x 7 7/8 In. 785.00
Cat, Gray Tabby, Cast Iron, Hubley, 11 1/8 x 8 In. 670.00
Cat, Halloween, Black Paint, Cast Iron 165.00
Cat, On Chimney, Cast Iron, 6 1/2 x 4 In. 896.00
Cat, On Pillow, Cast Iron, 8 In. 175.00
Cat, Persian, Green Painted Eyes, Fur Detail, Full Figure, Hubley, 8 1/2 x 6 1/2 In. 275.00
Cat, Pink, Orange Eyes, Composition, 6 5/8 x 4 x 6 1/8 In. 28.00
Cat, Raised Back, Green Eye, Cast Iron, 10 3/8 x 7 1/2 In. 196.00
Cat, Raised Back, Tail Up, Yellow Bow, 13 1/4 x 9 1/4 In. 2520.00
Cat, Sleeping, Red Bow, National Foundry, 3 3/8 x 9 5/8 In. 660.00
Cat, Tabby, Wrapped Tail, Pedestal Base, Cast Iron, 12 1/2 In., Pair . . . . . *ILLUS* 448.00
Charleston Dancers, Cast Iron, Hubley, Signed, Fish Design, 1930s 1250.00
Coach, London Royal Mail, Painted, Cast Iron, 12 In. 45.00
Cockatiel, On Stump, Albany Foundry, 12 1/2 In. 165.00
Cockatoo, On Ball, Cast Iron, 11 3/4 x 5 1/2 In. 670.00
Cockatoo, On Stump, Cast Iron, 14 x 4 1/2 In. 670.00
Colonial Dame, Hubley, 1930s, 8 x 4 1/2 In. 395.00
Cosmos, Vase, No. 455, Cast Iron, Hubley, 17 3/4 In. 605.00
Cottage, Cape Cod, Thatched Roof, Hollyhocks, Vines, Cast Iron, 4 3/4 x 7 1/4 In. 560.00
Cottage, Cast Iron, Slate Roof, Brick Chimneys, Flowers, 4 5/8 x 7 3/8 In. 250.00
Cottage, Fence, Wall Flowers, National Foundry, 7 1/4 In. 140.00
Cottage, Flowers, Trees, Fence, Cast Iron, c.1935, 5 3/4 x 8 In. 325.00
Cottage, Garden, Tiled Roof, Eastern Specialty Mfg. Co., 6 x 9 In. 495.00
Cottage, In Woods, Garden, Wedge Back, Woodland, 8 1/4 In. 385.00
Cottage, Snow Capped, Cast Iron, 7 3/4 x 7 1/8 In. 4480.00
Covered Wagon, Painted, Cast Iron, Late 19th Century, 8 1/2 x 11 3/4 In. 350.00
Daisy Bowl, Flowers, No. 232, Hubley, 1930s 350.00

Dog, Beagle Puppy, Cast Iron, Hubley, 7 1/2 x 5 3/8 In. . . . . *ILLUS* 3080.00
Dog, Boston Terrier, Cast Iron, Hubley, c.1930 . . . . . 295.00
Dog, Boston Terrier, Crying Pup Wiping Tears, Gray, White, Red Collar, Cast Iron, 7 1/2 In. 392.00
Dog, Boston Terrier, Hubley, 1930s 325.00
Dog, Boston Terrier, Standing In Grass, Cast Iron, Bradley & Hubbard, 9 5/8 x 11 3/4 In. 468.00
Dog, Boxer, Hubley, c.1930 . . . . . 325.00
Dog, Bulldog, c.1930 . . . . . 295.00
Dog, Bulldog, Stoneware, Molded, Late 19th Century, 8 1/2 In. 110.00
Dog, Fox Terrier, Cast Iron, 9 3/8 x 9 1/4 In. 450.00
Dog, Fox Terrier, Facing Right, Cast Iron, Hubley, 8 3/4 x 8 1/4 In. 450.00
Dog, Foxhound, White, Black, Brown, Cast Iron, 8 1/2 x 5 3/8 In. 500.00
Dog, German Shepard, Embossed Harness, Green Base, 9 x 7 7/8 In. 140.00
Dog, Scottie, Side By Side, Red Collars, Cast Iron, 5 1/2 x 8 1/2 In. 450.00
Dog, Scottie, Standing, Black, Leather Collar, Full Figured, Hubley, 9 x 10 1/4 In. 385.00
Dog, Sealyham, 2-Piece Casting, Red Collar, Hubley, 17 x 9 In. 1320.00
Dog, Setter, Standing, One Paw Raised, Hubley, 1930s 295.00
Dog, Spaniel, Seated, Rockingham Glaze, Yellowware, 11 In. 300.00
Dog, Terrier, Standing At Attention, 2 Piece, Full Figured, Painted, 7 1/2 x 9 In. 250.00
Dog, Terrier, Welsh Corgi, Cast Iron, Bradley & Hubbard, 8 1/4 x 5 7/8 In. 310.00
Dog, Wirehair Fox Terrier, Cast Iron, Hubley, 7 1/4 x 6 1/4 In. 840.00
Dog, Wirehair Fox Terrier, Cast Iron, Hubley, 13 x 10 1/4 In. 1792.00
Dog & Duck, Nibbling Puppy's Ear, AM Greenblatt, Boston, c.1925, 10 x 8 3/4 In. 1430.00
Drum Major, c.1920-30, 13 1/2 x 6 1/2 In. 950.00
Drum Major, Marching Band, Oversized Baton, Cast Iron, 13 1/2 x 5 In. 330.00
Ducks, 2 Grazing, Nature Setting, Hubley, 8 1/2 In. 550.00
Dutch Girl, Littco, c.1930, Large 950.00
Elephant, Circus, Walking, Painted Blanket, Gray, 5 x 8 In. 250.00
End Of Trail, Cast Iron, 9 5/8 x 9 1/2 In. 170.00
Flower Basket, Cast Iron, Beveled Base, 9 x 7 7/8 In. 225.00
Flower Basket, Cast Iron, Hubley, 10 1/4 x 7 1/2 In. 310.00
Flower Basket, Cast Iron, Hubley, 11 x 6 3/4 In. 275.00
Flower Basket, Lilies Of The Valley, White, Hubley, 10 1/2 x 7 1/2 In. . . . . 303.00 to 440.00
Flower Basket, Pansies, Morning Glories, Cast Iron, 11 1/2 x 7 In. 280.00
Flower Basket, Poppies, Cast Iron, Slant Handle, 10 1/2 x 8 In. 840.00
Flower Basket, Roses, Cast Iron, 11 x 8 In. 450.00
Flower Basket, Roses, Cast Iron, Hubley, 11 In. 110.00
Flower Basket, Tulips, Daffodils, Cast Iron, Hubley, 7 3/4 x 4 3/4 In. 340.00
Flower In Urn, Cast Iron, Wood Base, 7 3/4 x 6 1/4 In. 390.00
Flower Vase, Gladiolas, No. 484, Hubley, 10 x 7 3/4 In. 385.00
Flower Vase, Pink, Yellow, Blue, 8 3/8 x 7 In. 308.00
Flower Vase, Roses, Cornucopia Style, Hubley, 10 1/8 x 8 In. 195.00
Flower Vase, Tulips, Cast Iron, 5/8 x 6 3/4 In. 225.00
Flowerpot, Narcissus, Black & White Stripes, 3-Footed, 7 x 7 In. 250.00
Flowerpot, Nasturtiums, Black & White Stripe, Hubley, 7 1/4 x 6 1/2 In. 220.00
Flowerpot, Tulips, National Foundry, 8 1/4 x 7 In. 550.00
Flowers In Urn, Roses, Cast Iron, Hubley, 6 1/2 x 5 In. 560.00
Fox Head, Brass, Iron, Loop Handle Top, England, Late 1800s, 14 3/4 x 4 3/4 x 5 1/2 In. 440.00
Fruit Basket, Cast Iron, Hubley, 6 7/8 x 6 5/8 In. 165.00
Galleon Shape, Cast Iron, Painted, 6 In., Pair 92.00
Gnome, Bearded Fantasy Character, Casting, 11 In. 220.00
Graf Zeppelin, At Mooring, Light, Cast Iron, 8 3/4 x 12 1/2 In. 670.00
Halloween Girl, Littlestown, Pennsylvania, Cast Iron, Littco, 14 x 8 3/4 In. 38500.00
Horse, Dapple Gray, Leather Saddle, Cast Iron, 10 1/2 In. 390.00
Horse, Palomino, Cast Iron, Hubley, 7 3/4 x 10 3/4 In. 250.00
Horse, Thoroughbred, Chestnut, Flaxen Mane, Tail, Cast Iron, Hubley, 7 3/4 x 10 3/4 In. 450.00
Horseshoe, 4-Leaf Clovers, Good Luck Symbol, Logs, 6 1/2 x 9 7/8 In. 1345.00
House, Cast Iron, 7 1/4 x 12 In. 225.00
House, Edgar Allan Poe Cast Iron, Bradley & Hubbard, 4 x 4 5/8 In. 560.00
House, Edgar Allan Poe Cast Iron, Bradley & Hubbard, 6 x 7 7/8 In. 2130.00
House, Saltbox Stone Fence, Cast Iron, 5 7/8 x 9 1/8 In. 4200.00
House, Sulgrave Manor, Cast Iron, 3 1/2 x 4 3/4 In. 85.00

House, Sulgrave Manor, Cast Iron, 9 1/8 x 10 7/8 In. 1345.00
House, Sulgrave Manor, Home Of George Washington, Cast Iron, 1925, 10 In. 1345.00
Indian Chief, Cast Iron, 6 1/8 x 9 7/8 In. 335.00
Indian Chief, Feathered Headdress, Arrowheads, Cast Iron, 6 7/8 x 7 1/2 In. 1120.00
Indian Chief, Side Profile, Maple Leaf, Cast Iron, 4 3/8 x 3 5/8 In. 250.00
Irises, Purple, Green Leaves, Hubley, No.469, 10 5/8 x 6 3/4 In. 896.00
Knight, Medieval, In Armor, Cast Iron, 13 1/4 x 5 7/8 In. 110.00
Lighthouse, Highland, Cast Iron, 9 x 7 3/4 In. 3360.00
Lion, Full-Bodied, Gold & Silver Repaint, Cast Iron, 9 x 6 1/2 In. 127.00
Little Bo Beep, Cast Iron, Hubley, 7 x 5 1/4 In. 112.00
Major Domo, No. 1249, 1920s, 8 3/8 x 5 1/8 In. 425.00
Mammy, Blue Dress, White Apron, Red Bandanna, Cast Iron, Hubley, 11 In. 1075.00
Mammy, Full Figure, 2 Sections, Classic Pose, Cast Iron, Hubley, 9 x 5 1/2 In. 300.00
Mammy, Hand Painted, Cast Iron, Hubley, 1900s, 10 x 5 In. 975.00
Mammy, Iron, Hand Painted, Hubley, Early 1900s, 10 x 5 In. 975.00
Monkey, Coin Slot In Head, Painted, Cast Iron, 8 In. 360.00
Monkey, Hand Painted, Cast Iron, c.1930, 7 x 5 1/2 In. 750.00
Monkey, Seated, Hand Painted, Cast Iron, 1930s, 7 x 5 1/2 In. 750.00
Old Mill, Stone Bridge, Stream, Winding Lane, Cast Iron, 9 3/4 x 7 1/4 In. 8400.00
Old Salt, Fisherman, Yellow Slicker, Black Hat, Painted, Cast Iron, 5 3/4 In. 55.00
Oriental Man, Lounging Buddha-Esque Man, Ponytail, Sack, 11 x 6 1/2 In. 385.00
Penguin, Yellow, Red, Upturned Head, Marked No. 1, Taylor Cook, 1930, 9 In. 1870.00
Penguins, Double, Cast Iron, 1930, 3 x 3 3/4 In. 560.00
Quail, Original Paint, Cast Iron, Everett '34, Hubley, 7 1/4 In. 690.00
Rabbit, High Society, Black Top Hat, Coat Tails, Albany Foundry, 9 7/8 x 4 3/4 In. 715.00
Ship, U.S. Clipper, American Flag, Ocean Wave Base, CJO 220.00
Stork, Stylized, Wedge Back, Cast Iron, Hubley, 5 x 3 3/4 In. 415.00
Swallows, Singing, Perched On Stump, Berries, 8 1/2 x 7 1/2 In. 990.00
Tavern, In Woods, Red Roof, Woodland Setting, 5 1/4 x 7 1/4 In. 440.00
Teddy Roosevelt, On Horseback, Cast Iron, 10 7/8 x 8 1/2 In. 110.00
Totem Pole, Cast Iron, 8 1/2 x 2 1/4 In. 1792.00
Totem Pole, Owl, Cast Iron, 6 3/4 x 2 3/4 In. 1010.00
Tulips, 2 Tiered, Green Base, Cast Iron, 8 1/4 In. 336.00
Vase, Delphinium, Cast Iron, No. 490, Hubley, 8 3/4 x 7 1/4 In. 275.00
Windmill, Cast Iron, 7 1/4 x 7 1/2 In. ....140.00 to 225.00
Windmill, Cottages, Post, Rail Fence, Cast Iron, 9 7/8 x 11 1/2 In. 1065.00
Woman, Holding Carpet Bag, Sarah Symonds, Bag Marked Phoebe, 12 In. 165.00
Woman, With Hatbox, Flowers, Parasol, No. 30, 6 3/4 In. 248.00
Woman, With Muff, Fur Trimmed Coat, Cast Iron, 9 1/4 x 5 In. 560.00
Young Girl, Flower Basket, Cast Iron, Early 20th Century, 8 To 9 1/2 In., Pair 235.00

DORCHESTER POTTERY was founded by George Henderson in 1895 in Dorchester, Massachusetts. At first, the firm made utilitarian stoneware, but collectors are most interested in the line of decorated blue and white pottery that Dorchester made from 1940 until it went out of business in 1979.

DORCHESTER
POTTERY WORKS
BOSTON, MASS.

Bowl, Butterfly, Ovals, Incised Dots, Blue Body, Sponge, 1 1/2 x 5 1/2 In. 115.00
Bowl, Cereal, Smiling Whale, Sea Gulls, Blue Swirl, 5 3/4 x 2 In. 80.00
Cookie Jar, Cascading Vines, Stylized Branch, Blue Ground, Handles, 9 3/4 x 7 1/2 In. 175.00
Dish, Star, 5-Sided, 8 In. 200.00
Pitcher, Cover, Flat, Half Scroll, Blue Knob, Striped Handle, 4 3/4 x 4 3/4 In. 105.00
Pitcher, Strawberry, Striped Handle, Incised Seed, 3 Leaves, 4 3/4 x 5 1/2 In. 58.00
Sugar, Cover, Sacred Cod, Blue Knob, 4 x 4 1/2 In. 80.00

DOULTON pottery and porcelain were made by Doulton and Co. of Burslem, England, after 1882. The name *Royal Doulton* appeared on their wares after 1902. Other pottery by Doulton is listed under Royal Doulton.

Bowl, Stratford Church, Bulbous, Flared Rim, H. Morr, c.1891, 7 1/2 In. 290.00
Charger, Portrait, Classical Woman, England, c.1885, 12 In. 2115.00
Jar, Cover, Incised, Sterling Rim, Bail, Lambeth, 4 1/2 In. 1840.00

Jardiniere, Blue Rosettes, Doulton Silicon, Lambeth, c.1900, 8 1/4 In. 69.00
Jardiniere, Stoneware, Enamel Glazed Flower, Leaves, Lambeth, Late 1800s, 7 1/2 In. 265.00
Jug, Leaves, Stylized, Silver Mounts, Stoneware, Frances E. Lee, Lambeth, 1876, 5 In. 490.00
Jug, Slater's Patent, Cobalt Blue, Salt Glaze, Lambeth, c.1900, 7 In. 105.00
Pitcher, Nautical, Verses, Blue, Black Transfer, Ironstone, Burslem 165.00
Pitcher, Water, Stoneware, 2-Tone, Brown Glaze, 6 1/2 In. 110.00
Pitcher, Willow, Bulbous, Wide Spout, Handle, Burslem, 11 In. 690.00
Pitcher & Washbowl, Ironstone, Flowers, Leaves, Blue, White, 12 1/2 In. 69.00
Punch Bowl, Willow, Footed, Burslem, 5 x 14 1/2 In. 230.00
Salad Set, Bowl, Fork, Spoon, Handles, Sterling Rim, Lambeth, 4 1/2 x 9 In. 489.00
Teapot, Stoneware, Lambeth, 2-Tone Brown, Signed, 5 In. 50.00
Vase, Baluster, Chrysanthemum, Leaves, Blue, Ocher, Lambeth, c.1890, 12 1/2 x 5 1/4 In. 705.00
Vase, Barbotine, Fruit Trees, Landscape, c.1910, 11 In. 660.00
Vase, Earthenware, Enamel, Gilt, Leaves, Woman, Lyre, Peacock, Late 1800s, 10 1/2 In. 2938.00
Vase, Japanesque Flowers, 2 Handles, Chine, Eliza Simmance, Lambeth, c.1895, 9 1/2 In. 396.00

DRESDEN china is any china made in the town of Dresden, Germany. The most famous factory in Dresden is the Meissen factory. Figurines of eighteenth-century ladies and gentlemen, animal groups, or cherubs and other mythological subjects were popular. One special type of figurine was made with skirts of porcelain-dipped lace. Do not make the mistake of thinking that all pieces marked *Dresden* are from the Meissen factory. The Meissen pieces usually have crossed swords marks, and are listed under Meissen. Some recent porcelain from Ireland, called *Irish Dresden*, is not included in this book.

Candelabrum, 4-Light, Porcelain, Convertible, c.1920, 17 x 10 In., Pair 187.00
Candlestick, Porcelain, Flowers, Woman, Man, Tree, Leaf Base, Early 1900s, 15 3/8 In., Pr. 764.00
Cup & Saucer, Courting Couple, Yellow, Turquoise Flower Panels, Thieme, c.1902 . . . . 150.00
Dish, Hand Painted, Reticulated Sides, 1800s, 8 In. 92.00
Figurine, Gentleman Proposing To Seated Woman, Partial Label, 8 x 8 1/4 In. 315.00
Figurine, Mormoset, Seated, Flowered Stump, Eating Apple, 18th Century, 26 1/4 In. 3760.00
Lamp Base, Urn Shape, Inverted Pear, Flowers, Paw Feet, Electrified, Late 1800s, 23 In. 646.00
Plaque, Portrait, Gypsy Boy Smoking, After Blaas, Frame, Late 19th Century, 24 x 16 In. 2050.00
Plate, Dessert, Silesia, Floral Painted, Gilded Edge, 1 1/2 x 7 3/4 In., 12 Piece 385.00
Vase, Flowers, Scalloped Rim, 15 1/2 In. 497.00
Vase, Gilt, Gourd Shape, Narrow Neck, Multicolored, Late 1800s, 13 x 6 1/2 In., Pair 150.00

DUNCAN & MILLER is a term used by collectors when referring to glass made by the George A. Duncan and Sons Company or the Duncan and Miller Glass Company. These companies worked from 1893 to 1955, when the use of the name *Duncan* was discontinued and the firm became part of the United States Glass Company. Early patterns may be listed under Pressed Glass.

American Way, Candlestick, Petal Feet, Pair . . . . 15.00 to 26.00
Buttons & Bows, Bowl, Yellow Panels, 8 1/2 In. 62.00
Canterbury, Basket, 10 1/2 In. 70.00
Canterbury, Bowl, Turned Down Handles, 13 x 5 3/4 In. 35.00
Canterbury, Candlestick, 6 1/4 In., Pair 60.00
Canterbury, Candy Dish, Cover, Footed, Ruby, 9 x 6 1/4 In. 175.00
Canterbury, Celery Dish, 2 Sections, 10 1/2 x 6 In. 35.00
Canterbury, Dish, Mayonnaise, Underplate, Ladle 18.00
Canterbury, Goblet, 10 Oz. 20.00
Canterbury, Jelly, Footed, 3 3/4 x 5 1/2 In. 18.00
Canterbury, Relish, 3 Sections, 10 1/2 In. . . . . 30.00 to 35.00
Canterbury, Relish, Blue Opalescent, Sections, Handles, 6 In. 49.00
Canterbury, Sugar, Individual 9.00
Canterbury, Torte Plate, 15 In. 78.00
Canterbury, Tumbler, Iced Tea, 13 Oz., 6 1/4 In. 20.00
Canterbury, Vase, Blue Opalescent, Ruffled Edge, 5 1/2 x 7 In. 125.00
Canterbury, Vase, Green, Ruffled Edge, 5 In. 18.00
Caribbean, Bowl, Gold Encrusted, Handles, 6 In. 15.00

Caribbean, Cake Plate, Blue, Handles, 12 In. 75.00
Caribbean, Candlestick, Bobeche & Prisms, 7 3/4 In. 29.00
Caribbean, Cigarette Holder, Ruby, 3 1/2 In. 225.00
Caribbean, Plate, 4-Footed, 12 In. 30.00
Caribbean, Punch Set, Applied Colored Handles, 14 Piece 264.00
Cloverleaf, Plate, 8 In. 12.00
Cloverleaf, Vase, Blue Opalescent, 5 In. 45.00
Dover, Cocktail, Ruby Bowl, Clear Stem & Foot, 3 1/2 Oz., 4 In. 20.00
First Love, Ashtray, 3 1/2 x 2 1/2 In. 15.00
First Love, Champagne, 6 1/2 Oz., 4 3/4 In. 20.00
First Love, Cigarette Box, Cover, 3 x 5 In. 140.00
First Love, Creamer, 3 x 3 In. 24.00
First Love, Plate, 8 In. 29.00
First Love, Relish, Sections, Handles, 6 In. 29.00
First Love, Sugar, 3 x 4 In. 24.00
Hobnail, Basket, Blue Opalescent, 10 x 4 3/4 In. 115.00
Hobnail, Candlestick, 4 In. 16.00
Hobnail, Compote, Ruffled Edge, 6 x 6 In. 25.00
Hobnail, Ivy Ball, Blue Opalescent, 7 x 4 1/2 In. 69.00
Hobnail, Ivy Ball, Ruffled Edge, 7 1/2 In. 95.00
Hobnail, Powder Jar, Pink, 1930s 85.00
Hobnail, Relish, 12 x 6 3/4 In. 35.00
Hobnail, Vase, Flip, Blue Opalescent, Ruffled Edge, 8 x 8 1/2 In. 175.00
Hobnail, Vase, Flip, Green Opalescent, 7 1/4 x 5 In. 40.00
Hobnail, Wine, 3 1/2 Oz., 4 1/4 In. 15.00
Indian Tree, Champagne, 5 Oz., 6 x 4 In. 25.00
Indian Tree, Relish, 3 Sections, 8 In. 25.00
Indian Tree, Tumbler, Iced Tea, Footed, 12 Oz., 6 1/2 In. 19.00
Mardi Gras, Butter, Cover 125.00
Mardi Gras, Salt, Round, 1 1/4 In. 8.00
Mardi Gras, Wine, Flared Rim, 4 1/4 In. 30.00
Pall Mall, Dish, Swan, 7 In. 20.00
Pall Mall, Dish, Swan, 10 In. 45.00
Pall Mall, Dish, Swan, 12 In. ....50.00 to 52.00
Pall Mall, Dish, Swan, Blue Opalescent, 12 In. 175.00
Pall Mall, Dish, Swan, Chartreuse, 7 In. 65.00
Pall Mall, Dish, Swan, Green, 10 In. 75.00
Pall Mall, Dish, Swan, Ruby, 7 1/2 x 11 x 6 3/4 In. 95.00
Plaza, Tumbler, Water, Green, Footed, 5 3/4 In. 15.00
Sandwich, Bowl, Floral, Ruffled Edge, 11 1/2 In. 85.00
Sandwich, Bowl, Salad, 10 In. 65.00
Sandwich, Candlestick, 3 3/4 In., Pair 30.00
Sandwich, Candy Jar, Cover, 8 1/2 In. 100.00
Sandwich, Celery Dish, Bowtie, 10 In. 24.00
Sandwich, Cocktail, 3 Oz., 4 1/2 In. 25.00
Sandwich, Egg Plate, 12 In. ....62.00 to 80.00
Sandwich, Egg Plate, Pink, 12 In. 83.00
Sandwich, Goblet, 9 Oz., 6 In. ....9.00 to 19.00
Sandwich, Relish, Sections, Bowtie, 7 x 4 In. 30.00
Sandwich, Relish, Sections, Handle, 6 In. 25.00
Sandwich, Saucer 4.00
Sandwich, Sherbet, 6 Oz., 4 1/4 In. 12.00
Sandwich, Sugar & Creamer 29.00
Sandwich, Sundae, Footed, 5 Oz., 4 1/2 In. 6.00
Sandwich, Torte Plate, Amber, 12 In. 40.00
Sandwich, Tumbler, 9 Oz., 4 1/2 In. 10.00
Sandwich, Tumbler, Iced Tea, 13 Oz. 28.00
Sandwich, Tumbler, Iced Tea, Footed, 12 Oz. 18.00
Sandwich, Tumbler, Juice, Footed, 5 Oz., 3 3/4 In. 9.00
Sandwich, Wine, 3 Oz., 4 1/4 In. ....14.00 to 20.00
Sanibel, Bowl, Fruit, Pink Opalescent, 6 In. 30.00

Sanibel, Relish, Blue Opalescent, 8 1/2 In. 38.00
Spiral Flutes, Bowl, 12 1/8 In. 45.00
Spiral Flutes, Cup, Amber, After Dinner 16.00
Spiral Flutes, Plate, Luncheon, Green, 8 3/8 In. 15.00
Spiral Flutes, Sherbet, Green, 6 Oz., 5 x 4 In. 15.00
Spiral Flutes, Vase, Green, 10 3/4 In. 35.00
Starred Loop, Pitcher, 8 In. 125.00
Sylvan, Candy Dish, Cover, 8 In. 125.00
Sylvan, Dish, 7 x 6 1/2 In. 8.00
Sylvan, Dish, Swan, Blue Opalescent, 6 x 8 In. 110.00
Sylvan, Dish, Swan, Pink Opalescent, 9 3/4 x 13 In. 195.00
Sylvan, Vase, 6 1/4 x 7 In. 45.00
Sylvan, Vase, Milk Glass, 5 3/4 x 8 1/2 In. 125.00
Tear Drop, Cheese & Cracker Set, Handles, 11-In. Tray, 2 Piece .... 39.00 to 75.00
Tear Drop, Cordial, Oz., 3 3/4 In. 24.00
Tear Drop, Cruet Set, 3 Piece 58.00
Tear Drop, Dish, Sweetmeat, Heart-Shaped Center Handle, 6 1/2 In. 28.00
Tear Drop, Goblet, 10 Oz., 5 3/4 In. 14.00
Tear Drop, Mustard, Cover, 3 In. 28.00
Tear Drop, Nut Dish, Sections, Handles, 6 In. 15.00
Tear Drop, Relish, 3 Sections, Center Handle, 10 In. 22.00
Tear Drop, Relish, Gold Encrusted, Sections, Handles, 6 1/8 In. 25.00
Tear Drop, Relish, Heart Shape Sections, 7 1/2 In. .... 22.00 to 30.00
Tear Drop, Relish, Sections, Handles, 7 In. 18.00
Tear Drop, Sherbet, 6 Oz., 3 3/8 In. 7.00
Tear Drop, Sherbet, 6 Oz., 5 1/8 In. 10.00
Tear Drop, Sugar 13.00
Tear Drop, Sugar & Creamer 20.00
Tear Drop, Tumbler, Whiskey, 2 Oz. 19.00
Terrace, Candlestick, Amber, 3 1/4 In., Pair 65.00
Terrace, Relish, Silver Overlay, Sections, Handles, 6 In. 32.00
Terrace, Sugar & Creamer, Ruby 78.00
Venetian, Bowl, Footed, Ruby, 7 x 10 In. 125.00

DURAND art glass was made from 1924 to 1931. The Vineland Flint Glass Works was established by Victor Durand and Victor Durand, Jr., in 1897. In 1924 Martin Bach, Jr., and other artisans from the Quezal glassworks joined them at the Vineland, New Jersey, plant to make Durand art glass. They called their gold iridescent glass Gold Lustre.

Bowl, Centerpiece, Cobalt Blue, Pulled Feather, Rolled Rim, 12 In. 635.00
Candlestick, Ambergris Ground, Cobalt Pulled Feathers, Flared, Rolled Rim, 5 In., Pair 920.00
Compote, Translucent Canary Yellow, Opal Pulled Feathers Tip, 10 1/2 In. 4715.00
Goblet, Green, White, Citrine, Clear, Pulled Feather, 6 1/2 In. 345.00
Goblet, Ruby, Optic Ribbed, Spanish Yellow Stem, 9 In. 635.00
Lamp, Gold Iridescent, Gold Threading, Embossed Metal Foot, 25 In. 315.00
Lamp Base, Gold Iridescent, Applied Webbing, Baluster, 8 1/4 In. 259.00
Lamp Base, Moorish Crackle, Green, Gold, Bronzed Metal Fittings, 9 In. 230.00
Lamp Shaft, Gold Iridescent, Gold Threading, 8 In. 145.00
Plate, Moorish Crackle, Red, Clear, 6 3/4 In. 40.00
Plate, Ruby, Translucent Cranberry, White Pulled Feathers, Ambergris Ground, 9 3/4 In. 2705.00
Rose Bowl, Gold Iridescent, Rolled Rim, Signed, 7 1/2 In. 575.00
Sconce, Moorish Crackle, Gold Iridescent, Bronze Leaf Cap, Amber Prisms, 22 In. 633.00
Shade, Torchere, Moorish Crackle, Green, White, Gold Iridescent Ground, 8 1/2 In. 635.00
Tazza, Gold Iridescent, Baluster Stem, 6 1/4 In. 690.00
Tazza, Translucent Yellow, Opal Pulled Feathers, Baluster Stem, Footed, 10 1/2 In. 4715.00
Temple Jar, Cover, Marigold Iridescent, Green Tipped Pulled Feathers, Gold Iridescent, 7 1/4 In. 3450.00
Torchere, Gold Iridescent Shade, Green Pulled Feathers, Gesso Base, Pendants, 17 In. 520.00
Urn, Cover, King Tut, Opal, Gold Iridescent Ground, 10 In. 3738.00
Vase, Alabaster, Blue & Gold Hearts, Gold Threading, 4 In. 460.00
Vase, Ambergris Luster, Translucent, White Heart & Vine, 12 In. 520.00
Vase, Ambergris, Canary Yellow Transparent Ground, White Heart, Vine, 7 1/4 In. 375.00

Vase, Ambergris, Canary Yellow, Engraved Flowers, 6 1/2 In. 315.00
Vase, Ambergris, Translucent, Internal Green Pulled Feather, Shouldered, 10 1/4 In. 520.00
Vase, Ambergris, Yellow, Green, Baluster, 9 1/2 In. 230.00
Vase, Amethyst, Bulbous, Ribbed, Slender Neck, Flared Rim, 6 In. 575.00
Vase, Amethyst, Optic Ribbed, Squat, Signed, 6 In. 460.00
Vase, Blue Ground, Blue Heart, Vine, 9 1/2 In. 1840.00
Vase, Blue Ground, Gold Interior, Urn Shape, 7 1/2 In. 2875.00
Vase, Blue Iridescent, Etched Flowers, Butterflies, Shouldered, Signed, No. 1812-7, 7 1/2 In. 1016.00
Vase, Blue Iridescent, Opal Heart & Vine, Shouldered, 8 x 7 1/2 In. 1265.00
Vase, Blue Iridescent, Urn Shape, c.1920, 7 In. 508.00
Vase, Bottle, Green, White, Mottled, Kimble, 6 In. 230.00
Vase, Clear To Cranberry, Pulled Feather, Flowers, Oval, c.1900, 10 In. 896.00
Vase, Cobalt Blue Translucent, White Pulled Feathers, Ambergris Ground, Shouldered, 7 In. 920.00
Vase, Cranberry, Red & White Pulled Feathers, Shouldered, 7 In. 575.00
Vase, Gold Iridescent, Applied Webbing, Narrow Neck, Flared Rim, Bulbous, 7 In. 345.00
Vase, Gold Iridescent, Beehive Shape, Signed, 8 In. 748.00
Vase, Gold Iridescent, Blue Hearts & Vine, Bulbous, Rolled Rim, c.1920, 5 1/2 In. 685.00
Vase, Gold Iridescent, Green, Leaf, Threading, Cream Ground, Yellow, Gold Interior, 7 3/4 In. 978.00
Vase, Golden Orange Iridescent, Shouldered, Flared Rim & Foot, No. 1721, 6 In. 345.00
Vase, Green Ground, Gold Feather, Threaded Rim, 6 In. 520.00
Vase, Green Iridescent, Gold Iridescent Interior, Bulbous, Ribbed, Rolled Rim, 8 In. 4945.00
Vase, Green Iridescent, White Coil, Bulbous Shouldered, 7 In. 920.00
Vase, Green, Clear, Transparent, Engraved Flowers, Pulled Feathers, Baluster, 8 1/2 In. 489.00
Vase, Heart, Vine, Blue Iridescent Ground, 8 1/2 In. 1725.00
Vase, Hearts & Vine, Iridescent Orange Ground, Oval, c.1900, 7 1/4 In. 840.00
Vase, King Tut, Green Iridescent, Gold Iridescent Ground, 6 1/4 In. 1495.00
Vase, King Tut, Marigold Iridescent, Footed, Urn Shape, 8 In. 1380.00
Vase, King Tut, White, Gold Iridescent Ground, c.1915, 14 1/4 In. 2468.00
Vase, Marigold Iridescent, Green Pulled Feathers, Gold Threading, Shouldered, 7 1/4 In. 865.00
Vase, Moorish Crackle, Blue, White, Gold Iridescent, Shouldered, 9 In. 1783.00
Vase, Moorish Crackle, Green, White, Gold Iridescent Ground, 7 3/4 In. 1380.00
Vase, Orange Ground, Hearts & Vine, Oval, c.1900, 7 1/2 In. 1195.00
Vase, Orange Iridescent, Blue, Baluster, c.1900, 8 1/4 In. 840.00
Vase, Orange, Gold Iridescent Ground, Threading, 8 1/2 In. 630.00
Vase, Pink, Red Iridescent, Gold Iridescent Interior, Bulbous, Ribbed, Rolled Rim, 8 1/2 In. 6325.00
Vase, Purple Ground, Pulled Feather, Gold Interior, 8 1/8 In. 2185.00
Vase, Purple Moorish Crackle, Footed, Cylindrical, Signed, 8 1/2 In. 315.00
Vase, Trumpet, Cobalt Blue, White Coil, Flared Rim, 12 In. 690.00
Vase, White Coil, Gold Iridescent, Bulbous, 10 In. 805.00
Vase, White Ground, Blue, Gold Hearts, Applied Webbing, 6 5/8 In. 345.00
Vase, Yellow, White Pulled Feathers, Green Outline, Orange, Gold Ground, Threading, 8 In. 345.00

ELFINWARE is a mark found on Dresden-like porcelain that was sold in dime stores and gift shops. Many pieces were decorated with raised flowers. The mark was registered by Breslauer-Underberg, Inc., of New York City in 1947. Pieces marked *Elfinware Made in Germany* had been sold since 1945 by this importer.

Boot, Flowers, Scalloped Top, Gold Trim, Germany, 5 In. 16.00
Dish, Leaf Shape, Germany, 3 1/2 In. 5.00
Figurine, High Heel Shoe, Forget-Me-Nots, 3 In. 110.00
Shoe, Green Trim, 5 In. 145.00
Toothpick, Goat Pulling Cupid In Cart, 3 x 4 1/4 x 2 1/2 In. 195.00
Trinket Box, Heart Shape, Gold Trim, Germany, 1 x 2 In. 18.00
Watering Can, Spinach, Flowers, Germany, 1920-30, 2 1/4 In. 65.00

ELVIS PRESLEY, the well-known singer, lived from 1935 to 1977. He became famous by 1956. Elvis appeared on television, starred in twenty-seven movies, and performed in Las Vegas. Memorabilia from any of the Presley shows, his records, and even memorials made after his death are collected.

Button, I Like Elvis, Red, White, Blue, Lithograph, Round, 1 In. 15.00

Enamel, Plate, Siamese Cat & Kittens, Black Outline, Turquoise Eyes, Bovano, 9 1/2 In.

Enamel, Plate, Stick Figure, Woman, Flower, Signed, De Pastille, Quebec, c.1965, 4 3/4 In.

Hair, Authenticated, Sealed Plastic Container 8722.00
Movie Poster, Loving You, 1957, 1 Sheet, 27 x 41 In. 342.00
Photograph, Autographed, Inscription, Frame, 1957, 10 x 8 In. 1800.00
Photograph, Autographed, Inscription, G.I. Blues, c.1960, 14 x 11 In. 5295.00
Poster, Extra Special, 3:00 A.M., 1970s, 19 x 16 1/4 In. 679.00
Record, Jailhouse Rock, Dealers' Prevue, 1957, 45 RPM 905.00
Record Sleeve, Elvis, Record, EPA-993, RCA Victor, Autograph, 1956 . . . . . 1090.00
TV Guide, Plain Truth About Elvis Presley, Sept. 8-14, 1956, 7 1/2 x 5 1/4 In. 560.00

ENAMELS listed here are made of glass particles and other materials heated and fused to metal. In the eighteenth and nineteenth centuries, workmen from Russia, France, England, and other countries made small boxes and table pieces of enamel on metal. One form of English enamel is called *Battersea* and is listed under that name. There was a revival of interest in enameling in the 1930s and a new style evolved. There is now renewed interest in the artistic enameled plaques, vases, ashtrays, and jewelry. Enamels made since the 1930s are usually on copper or steel, although silver was often used for jewelry. Graniteware is a separate category, and enameled metal kitchen pieces may be included in the Kitchen category.

Candlestick, Flint Enamel, Round Base, Straight Column, Ring, 6 1/2 In., Pair 1668.00
Compact, Scenic, 2 Lovers, Gilded Silver, Yellow Guilloche, Round, France, 2 1/2 In. 28.00
Dresser Set, Guilloche, Blue, Hairbrushes, Dresser Jars, Perfumes, 6 Piece 290.00
Egg, Faberge, Rosebud, Fitted Blue Velvet Box, Stand, Gilded, Applied Jewels 385.00
Humidifier, Champleve, Maiden, Horse, E.F. Caldwell, Early 1900s, 2 x 7 1/2 x 4 1/4 In. 6000.00
Jardiniere, Flower Design, Champleve, Japan, Late 19th Century, 10 x 10 In. 108.00
Jardiniere, Flying Horse, Kirin, Champleve, Japan, Late 19th Century, 12 x 14 In. 150.00
Miniature, Portrait, Formally Dressed Woman, Brass Frame, Oval Medallion, 2 x 2 1/2 In. 355.00
Mug, Copper Patina, Turquoise Inside, Flattened Handle, Nekrassoff, 3 7/8 In., Pair 90.00
Plaque, Mount Fuji, Japan, 1900s, 10 1/2 x 10 1/2 In. 180.00
Plaque, Still Life, Shaped Decanters, Framed, 11 x 11 In. 59.00
Plate, Bird On White Fence, Blue Ground, Signed, Nekrassoff 80.00
Plate, Daisies, Lady Bug, Green, White Daisies, Bovano, 5 7/8 In. 11.00
Plate, Green, Yellow Highlights, Bovano, 9 In. 19.00
Plate, Indian Kachina Doll, Copper Colored Ground, Annemarie Davidson, 6 In. 13.00
Plate, Modernist Design, Red, Gray Blue, Signed, Marie Thibaudeau, 5 1/2 In. 26.00
Plate, Rabbit In Grass, Norman Brumm, 4 1/2 In. 14.00
Plate, Sea Gulls, Turquoise Ground, Paper Label, Annemarie Davidson, 7 5/8 In. 15.00
Plate, Siamese Cat & Kittens, Black Outline, Turquoise Eyes, Bovano, 9 1/2 In. . . . . . *ILLUS* 13.00
Plate, Specks & Circles, White, Green, Bronze, Brown Sponge Border, Winter, 9 1/2 In. 62.00
Plate, Stick Figure, Woman, Flower, Signed, De Pastille, Quebec, c.1965, 4 3/4 In. . . . . . *ILLUS* 7.00
Plate, Stylized Star, Green Tones, Edwards Star For Gumps, 7 1/4 In. 43.00
Plate, Tree Trunk, Birds, Rabbits, Grass, Green Tones, Margaret Ratcliffe, 7 In. 119.00
Plate, Turquoise, Red Abstract Swirls, Statham, 3 5/8 x 7 7/8 In. 40.00
Plate, White Flowers, Green Leaves, Red Ground, Octagonal, Annemarie Davidson, 6 In. 20.00
Silent Butler, Green & White Abstract Design, Wood Handle, Signed, Nekrassoff, 13 1/2 In. 29.00
Stylized Tree, Black, Gold Ground, Carmen Robichaud, 6 5/8 In. 28.00

Tray, Silhouette, Bonsai Tree, Orange Ground, Annemarie Davidson, 4 x 6 In. . . . . *ILLUS* 150.00
Vase, Champleve, Mounted As Lamp, Bronze Body, Multicolored, Chinese, 26 In. 105.00
Vase, Copper, Gio Ponti, Paoli De Poli, Italy, c.1956, 17 In. 8736.00
Vase, Cover, Painted Mythological Scenes, Silver Gilt, Vienna, Late 1800s, 13 1/2 In. 5400.00
Vase, Dragon, Green, White Ground, Kowaguchi, Japan, Late 19th Century, 4 1/2 In. 748.00
Vase, Urn Shape, Footed, Stone Center, Champleve Enamels, 5 1/2 In. 173.00
Vodka Cup, Silver, Flowers, 2 Blue Dotted Bands, Punch Mark, Russia, 60 Oz., 2 1/4 In. 500.00

ERICKSON glass was made in Bremen, Ohio, from 1943 to 1961. Carl and Steven Erickson designed and made free-blown and mold-blown glass. Best known are pieces with heavy ball bases filled with controlled bubbles.

Ashtray, Amethyst, Controlled Bubbles, 6 In. 65.00
Ashtray, Teal Green, Controlled Bubbles, 5 In. 50.00
Bowl, Green, Free-Form, 7 1/2 In. 60.00
Carafe, Green, Clear, 8 x 3 1/2 In. 110.00
Console, Controlled Bubble Ball Center, 12 In. 475.00
Console, Green, Controlled Bubbles, 4 1/4 x 9 3/4 In. 375.00
Console, Smoky Green, 10 1/2 In. 275.00
Nut Dish, Amethyst, 3 1/2 In. 45.00
Nut Dish, Amethyst, Controlled Bubbles, 3 1/2 In. 145.00
Vase, Amber, 7 In. 65.00
Vase, Bud, Amber, Controlled Bubble Ball Base, 8 In. 45.00
Vase, Bud, Clear Body, Teal Blue, Controlled Bubble Ball Base, 8 In. 45.00

ERPHILA is a mark found on Czechoslovakian and other pottery and porcelain made after 1920. The mark was used on items imported by Ebeling & Reuss, Philadelphia, a giftware firm that is still operating in Pennsylvania. The mark is a combination of the letters *E* and *R* (Ebeling & Reuss) and the first letters of the city, Phila(delphia). Many whimsical figural pitchers and creamers, figurines, platters, and other giftwares carry this mark.

Bowl, Sussex Cheery Chintz, Open Weave, Oval, c.1940, 2 3/4 x 10 x 6 1/2 In. 55.00
Cake Plate, Carnations, Gold Edge, 11 1/2 In. 20.00
Cake Plate, Flower Garlands, Bouquets, Gold Trim, 11 1/4 In. 36.00
Dresser Box, Madame Pompadour, c.1930, 5 1/4 In. 185.00
Figurine, Dog, Beagle Puppy, c.1950, 3 x 3 1/2 In. 21.00
Figurine, Dog, Harlequin Great Dane, 2 x 3 In. 32.00
Figurine, Dog, Japanese Spaniel, 4 x 4 1/2 In. 65.00
Figurine, Old Fisherman, Blue Hat, 5 1/2 x 5 1/2 x 3 In. 40.00
Pitcher, Creamy White Ground, Green Pattern, 5 In. 30.00
Pitcher, Mrs. Gamp, c.1940, 3 In. 14.00
Sugar, Sussex Cheery Chintz, c.1930, 2 1/8 x 2 3/4 In. 26.00
Teapot, Cat, 8 In. 170.00
Teapot, Dog, 8 In. 170.00
Teapot, Elephant, 8 3/4 In. 275.00
Teapot, Pig, c.1930, 7 1/4 In. 265.00
Teapot, Rabbit, 7 3/4 In. 225.00

ES GERMANY porcelain was made at the factory of Erdmann Schlegelmilch from 1861 to 1937 in Suhl, Germany. The porcelain, marked *ES Germany* or *ES Suhl*, was sold decorated or undecorated. Other pieces were made at a factory in Saxony, Prussia, and are marked *ES Prussia*. Reinhold Schlegelmilch made the famous wares marked *RS Germany*.

Cake Plate, Art Nouveau, c.1900, 10 In. 145.00
Candy Dish, Lake, 2 Trees, Hills, Hand Painted, 3-Sided, 3 Handles 68.00
Celery Dish, Green Backstamp, c.1902-38, 1 3/4 x 11 1/2 x 5 1/2 In. 89.00
Vase, Portrait, Woman, Holly Wreath, 1900-10, 11 3/4 In. 170.00

Enamel, Tray, Silhouette, Bonsai Tree, Orange Ground, Annemarie Davidson, 4 x 6 In.

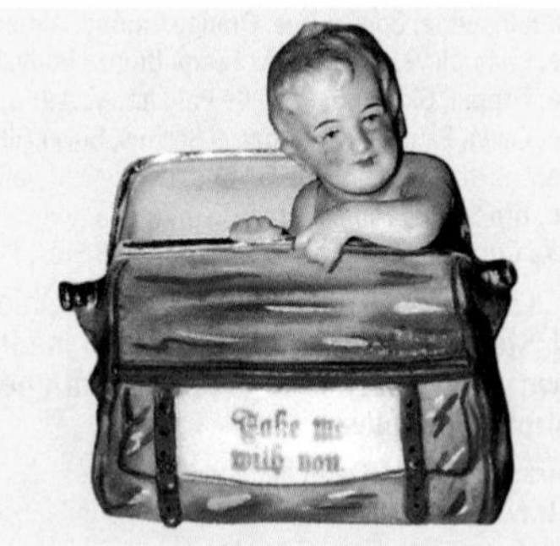

Fairing, Trinket Box, Child, Sitting In Open Suitcase, Red Mark, Germany, 2 3/4 x 3 1/2 In.

ESKIMO artifacts of all types are collected. Carvings of whale or walrus teeth are listed under Scrimshaw. Baskets are in the Basket category. All other types of Eskimo art are listed here. In Canada and some other areas, the term *Inuit* is used instead of Eskimo.

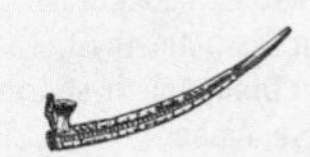

Basket, Aleut, Cover, Bands Of Red & Blue Checks, c.1900, 5 1/4 x 6 1/2 In. 635.00
Basket, Cover, Carved Soapstone Duck, Geometrics, Brown Sealskin Lace, 9 x 11 x 3 In. 633.00
Basket, Cover, Carved Walrus Head Handle, c.1900, 3 1/2 x 4 1/2 In. 1150.00
Basket, Cover, Round, People, Duck, Bird, Geometric Figures, 1900s, 13 x 15 In. 375.00
Basket, Lidded, Yukon River, Geometric Design, Early 20th Century, 7 x 3 1/4 In. 865.00
Basket, Pictorial, Multicolored, Lattice Design, Beetles, 10 In. 480.00
Bowl, Wooden, Painted, Bentwood Lip, Multicolored Trace 1150.00
Doll, Sealskin, Painted Facial Features, Alaska, 1938, 26 In. 315.00
Figure, Bear, Ivory, Sitting, Menacing Teeth, Red & Black Trim, Inuit, 3 1/2 In. 470.00
Kayak, Soapstone, Carved, Paddler, Paddle, Fish, Wood & Bone Implements, Inuit, 20 In. 1295.00
Mask, Cedar, Hand Carved, Flat, White & Gray Ocher, 1970-80, 10 x 7 In. 690.00
Mask, Wood, Carved, Walrus, Tusks, Pierced Mouth, Nostrils, Eyes, Painted, Inuit, 9 In. 1765.00
Pendant, Carved Face, Ivory 200.00
Sculpture, Soapstone, Seal, Tusks, 12 1/2 In. 960.00

FABERGE was a firm of jewelers and goldsmiths founded in St. Petersburg, Russia, in 1842, by Gustav Faberge. Peter Carl Faberge, his son, was jeweler to the Russian Imperial Court from about 1870 to 1914. The rare Imperial Easter eggs, jewelry, and decorative items are very expensive today.

Egg, Tercentenary Of Romanov Dynasty, Green, Maple Box, 1913, 5 3/4 In. 12075.00
Goblet, Wine, Crystal, 11 Piece 527.00
Kovsh, Presentation, Silver, Enameled, Carl Faberge, Pre-Revolution, 3 1/2 x 1 3/4 In. 1925.00

FAIENCE refers to tin-glazed earthenware, especially the wares made in France, Germany, and Scandinavia. It is also correct to say that faience is the same as majolica or Delft, although usually the term refers only to the tin-glazed pottery of the three regions mentioned.

Box, Lid, Fixed Stand, Grape Cluster Shape, Multicolored, Germany, c.1775, 9 1/2 In. 1560.00
Candlestick, Man, Woman, Jar On Head, S. Singer, Wiener Werkstaate, 9 3/4 In., Pair 1535.00
Desk Set, 2 Inkwells, 2 Depressions, Pen, Scrolls, Marked, AM Bologna Italia., 7 x 5 In. 115.00
Ewer, Multicolored, Baluster, Fruit Basket, Ear Handle, Pewter Cover, c.1800, 9 1/2 In. 295.00
Jar, Egg Shape, Birds, Yellow, Blue, Lamp Mount, Continental, 1700s, 11 1/2 In. 1200.00
Jardiniere, Classical Decoration, Painted, Blue, Yellow, Putti, Eagles, c.1900, 13 1/2 In. 425.00
Jardiniere, Round, Renaissance Revival Strapwork, Pink, White, 1800s, 7 1/4 x 9 In. 259.00
Plaque, Enamel, Water Nymphs, Ruffled Rim, France, Early 1900s, 19 3/4 In. 355.00
Plate, Fish, Scalloped Edge, Hand Painted, Central Fish, Floral Border, 10 1/2 In. 220.00
Wall Pocket, Multicolored, Tin Glaze, Bird, Hound Chasing Rabbit, Borders, 11 In., Pair 175.00

FAIRINGS are small souvenir china boxes and figurines that were sold at country fairs during the nineteenth century. Most were made in Germany. Reproductions of fairings are being made, especially of the famous *Twelve months after marriage* series.

Figurine, Cossack On Horseback, 3 1/2 In. 40.00
Figurine, Entertainer, Playing Instrument, Puppet In Basket, 3 1/2 x 1 1/2 In. 140.00
Figurine, Girl On Elephant, 3 1/4 x 3 In. 55.00
Figurine, Girl With Little Dog, 3 3/4 In. 40.00
Group, Arriving Home At 3 In Morning, Wife Beating Husband, 3 1/2 In. 130.00
Group, New Mother & Nurse With Baby, Victorian, 3 x 4 x 2 1/8 In. 350.00
Group, Victorian Woman Allows Man Into Bed, 3 x 3 1/2 x 2 1/8 In. 350.00
Trinket Box, Child, Sitting In Open Suitcase, Red Mark, Germany, 2 3/4 x 3 1/2 In. .... *ILLUS* 115.00
Trinket Box, Lilies-Of-The-Valley, Pietra Dura, Oval, Beading, Hinged Lid, Late 1800s, 5 1/2 In. ... 825.00
Trinket Box, Tortoiseshell, Nickel Inlaid, Florentine Papers, Opaline Glass Feet, 3 x 1 1/2 In. 265.00
Trinket Box, Woman, Field, House, Arts & Crafts, Incised, Multicolored, Russia, c.1900, 7 x 5 In. .. 80.00

FAIRYLAND LUSTER pieces are included in the Wedgwood category.

FAMILLE ROSE, see Chinese Export category.

FANS have been used for cooling since the days of the ancients. By the eighteenth century, the fan was an accessory for the lady of fashion, and very elaborate and expensive fans were made. Sticks were made of ivory or wood, set with jewels or carved. The fans were made of painted silk or paper. Inexpensive paper fans printed with advertising were giveaways in the late nineteenth and early twentieth centuries. Electric fans were introduced in 1882.

Abalone, Silk Net, Bathing Woman, Cupids, Hand Painted, Box, 1800s, 13 3/4 In. 235.00
Advertising, Bebe Jumeau, Chocolat De La Cie, Paper, Wood, France, Late 1800s, 11 3/4 In. 235.00
Advertising, Eutlaw Grocery & Ice Co., Black Family, Reading Bible, Eutawille, S.C., 1950s, 12 In. . 18.00
Advertising, Moet Champagne, Cardboard, Die Cut, Folding, Calendar, 1906, 18 x 10 In. 495.00
Advertising, Moxie, Hand Held, Celluloid, Ivory, Drink Moxie, 1930s, 11 x 7 In. 140.00
Advertising, Simmons Hardware, Keen Kutter Kutlery, Paper, Hatchethandle, 1904, 12 x 8 In. 210.00
Electric, A.C. Gilbert, No. 2017-D, Oscillating, 4 Blades, Art Deco, c.1935 .... 65.00
Electric, Emerson, Type 6250D, 4 Brass Blades, 14 1/2 x 11 1/2 In. 75.00
Electric, Eskimo, Bersted Manufacturing, No. 081002, Turquoise, Bullet Back, 1940s, 11 In. 80.00
Electric, General Electric, 4 Brass 6-In. Blades, Splayed Iron Base, 1924, 7 1/2 In. 140.00
Electric, Wizard, Bersted Manufacturing Co., Fostoria, Ohio, Spider Front, Oscillating, 16 x 15 In... 45.00
Ivory, Carved, Chinese, Gold & Black Lacquered Case, 1800s, 14 In. 940.00
Ivory, Carved, Figures, Garden Scenes, Chinese, 1800s 999.00
Ivory, Carved, Painted Kidskin, Chinoiserie Figures, Scrolls, Frame, 20 1/2 x 24 In. 645.00
Ivory, Carved, Paper, Figures, Brocade Clothes, Chinese, Black Lacquer Case, 1800s 529.00
Ivory, Gilt Filigree, Painted Paper, Figures, Brocade, Chinese, 11 In. 380.00
Ivory, Lacquer, Butterflies, Flowers, Geese, Lotus, Crane, Marsh Grass, Japan, Late 19th Century .. 4315.00
Ivory, Pierced, Carved, Painted, Centaur, Mythological Figures, France, 1800s, 11 x 17 In. 426.00
Ivory Stays, Carved, Pierced, Paper Panels, Figures, Brocade Costumes, Chinese, Case, 1800s ... 825.00
Mother-Of-Pearl, Gauze, Lace, Painted, Man, Woman Alighting From Dinghy, 9 1/2 In. 575.00
Mother-Of-Pearl, Lithographed, Adult & Children, Dancing, Hand Colored, Frame, 17 x 28 In. 290.00
Mother-Of-Pearl, Paper, Painted, Continental, Romantic Scene, c.1905, 9 3/4 In. 489.00
Paper, Tortoiseshell Sticks, Watercolor, 18th Century Courtiers, Charles Douzel, France, 24 In. 649.00
Silk Organza, Ebony Black, France, Late 19th Century, 13 3/4 In. 180.00

FAST FOOD COLLECTIBLES may be included in several categories, such as Advertising, Coca-Cola, Toy, etc.

PATENT MODELS, see Loetz category.

FENTON Art Glass Company, founded in Martins Ferry, Ohio, by Frank L. Fenton, is now located in Williamstown, West Virginia. It is noted for early carnival glass produced between 1907 and 1920. Some of these pieces are listed in the Carnival Glass category. Many other types of glass were also made. Spanish Lace in this section refers to the pattern made by Fenton.

Atlantis, Vase, Iridescent Plum Opalescent, LeVay 210.00

Beaded Melon, Vase, Blue Overlay, 6 1/2 In. 50.00
Beaded Melon, Vase, Cameo Opalescent, 6 In. 35.00
Beaded Melon, Vase, Cameo Satin, 1980s, 6 In. 35.00
Beaded Melon, Vase, Country Cranberry, White Roses, Tricornered Rim, 1982, 6 In. 40.00
Beaded Melon, Vase, Goldenrod, 6 In. 40.00
Beaded Melon, Vase, Painted Violets In The Snow, Tricornered Rim, 6 In. 40.00
Beaded Melon, Vase, Peach Crest, 6 1/2 In. 55.00
Beaded Melon, Vase, Rose Overlay, 5 1/2 In. 30.00
Beaded Melon, Vase, Silver Crest, 6 1/2 In. 60.00
Bicentennial, Compote, Cover, Jefferson Quotes, 1976, 10 1/2 In. 100.00
Bicentennial, Plate, Lafayette & Washington, Lafayette Hotel, Chocolate Glass, Booklet, 1976 .... 45.00
Blue Satin, Compote, Pinwheel 55.00
Blue Satin, Vase, Lovebirds 55.00
Bow & Drape, Vase, Iridescent Dusty Rose, 1980s 45.00
Burmese, Candy Box, Cover, Painted Butterfly 64.00
Burmese, Lamp, Hurricane, Painted Flowers & Butterflies 200.00
Burmese, Lamp, Painted Roses, 20 In. 350.00
Burmese, Pitcher, Painted Dragonfly, 8 In. 168.00
Burmese, Rose Bowl, Painted Leaves 75.00
Burmese, Vase, Painted Roses, 7 In. 95.00
Butterfly & Berry, Vase, Red Slag, 8 1/2 In. 850.00
Buttons & Braids, Tumbler, Blue Opalescent, 3 3/4 In. 90.00
Cameo Satin, Bell, Medallion, Painted Blue Dogwood, 6 1/2 In. 30.00
Cameo Satin, Box, Cover, Painted Blue Dogwood 35.00
Carnival Paisley, Lamp, Plum, Prisms, No. 1245 .... 285.00
Chessie Cat, Bonbon, Footed, Red Carnival, Pair 55.00
Chessie Cat, Candy Dish, Cover, Red Carnival 80.00
Clydesdales, Lamp, 1983-84, 16 In. 350.00
Coin Dot, Barber Bottle, Cranberry, c.1958, 8 1/2 x 4 In. 250.00
Coin Dot, Creamer, Cranberry Opalescent, 4 In. 60.00
Coin Dot, Creamer, Persian Blue Opalescent, 1989, 4 In. 35.00
Coin Dot, Cruet, Cranberry, Stopper, 6 1/2 In. 195.00
Coin Dot, Pickle Castor, Cranberry, Metal Frame, 10 1/2 In. 135.00
Coin Dot, Vase, Blue Opalescent, 8 1/2 In. 65.00
Coin Dot, Water Set, Cranberry Opalescent, Painted Lily Of The Valley, 7 Piece 635.00
Cranberry Opaline, Vase, Bud, Tulip, 8 In. 45.00
Crystal Velvet, Bowl, Basket Weave, 1977 .... 25.00
Custard Satin, Basket, Painted Log Cabin, 8 In. 85.00
Custard Satin, Bell, Medallion, Painted Daisies, 6 1/2 In. 30.00
Custard Satin, Bowl, Persian Medallion 25.00
Custard Satin, Fairy Lamp, Painted Log Cabin 70.00
Custard Satin, Lamp, Hurricane, Painted Log Cabin, Signed, Frederick, 11 In. 190.00
Custard Satin, Lamp, Student, Painted Log Cabin, Signed, Frederick, 21 In. 625.00
Custard Satin, Vase, Painted Log Cabin, 7 In. 60.00
Daisy & Fern, Cruet, Topaz, Stopper, 6 In. 235.00
Daisy & Fern, Decanter, Cranberry Opalescent 250.00
Diamond Optic, Fairy Light, Cranberry Opalescent, Painted Flowers 55.00
Diamond Optic, Vase, Cranberry Opalescent, 6 In. 65.00
Dogwood, Vase, Dusty Rose, 1980s, 8 In. 95.00
Dogwood, Vase, Periwinkle On Blue Burmese, 1985, 11 In. 165.00
Emerald Crest, Cruet Set, Stoppers, Wire Stand, 1950s, 8 1/4 x 7 In. 65.00
Fern, Pickle Castor, Cranberry Opalescent, Bird & Berry Base, Metal Frame, 12 In. 145.00
Figurine, Alley Cat, Burmese Satin, Painted Features, Heart Necklace, 10 1/2 In. ....220.00 to 295.00
Figurine, Alley Cat, Ruby Iridescent, 10 1/2 In. ....65.00 to 75.00
Figurine, Bear, Sitting, Favrene, 1980s 100.00
Figurine, Cat, Painted Poinsettia, 5 In. 49.00
Figurine, Cat, Petal Pink, 1990, 5 In. 30.00
Figurine, Cat, Ruby Amberina, 5 In. 45.00
Figurine, Happiness Bird, Custard, Painted Roses 45.00
Figurine, Happiness Bird, Rosalene, Painted Pink Roses 65.00
French Opalescent, Basket, Pink Handle, Large 95.00

Hearts & Flowers, Bowl, Rosalene, Ice Cream Shape 72.00
Hearts & Vine, Plate, Black Carnival 35.00
Hobnail, Basket, Milk Glass, 12 In. 60.00
Hobnail, Candy Box, Cover, Green Opalescent, Footed, 1954 . . . . . 40.00
Hobnail, Cologne, Milk Glass, Stopper, 6 1/2 x 4 In. 40.00
Hobnail, Cruet, Cranberry Opalescent, 6 1/2 In. 135.00
Hobnail, Decanter, Topaz Opalescent, Cobalt Blue Handle & Stopper 225.00
Hobnail, Mustard Jar, Cover, Spoon, Milk Glass 30.00
Hobnail, Punch Bowl, Green Opalescent, 10 Cups 375.00
Hobnail, Vase, Blue Opalescent, 3-Toed Base, 5 In. 30.00
Hobnail, Vase, Cranberry Opalescent, Flared, 4 In. 38.00
Hobnail, Water Set, Black Iridescent, 7 Piece 175.00
Hobnail, Water Set, Blue Opalescent, 9 Piece 580.00
Hobnail, Water Set, Topaz Opalescent, 8 Matching Tumblers 265.00
Hobnail, Water Set, Topaz Opalescent, 9 Piece 265.00
Lavender Satin, Lamp, Gone With The Wind 800.00
Mermaid, Vase, Amethyst Carnival, 1980s 80.00
Mermaid, Vase, Red, Carnival, Signed, Bill Fenton 200.00
Mosaic, Compote, Amethyst Iridescent, Threading, Oil Spots, 6 1/2 x 10 In. 2300.00
Poppy, Rose Bowl, Lime Sherbet, Large 35.00
Rib Optic, Tumbler, Iced Tea, Blue Opalescent, Dark Blue Handles, 5 1/8 In., 4 Piece 115.00
Rose Satin, Pitcher, Melon Ribbed, Small 60.00
Rose Satin, Rose Bowl 50.00
Rose Satin, Vase, Melon Ribbed, 6 In. 50.00
Silver Crest, Vase, Fan, 12 In. 110.00
Spiral Optic, Vase, Cranberry Opalescent, c.1954, 5 In. 80.00
Spiral Optic, Vase, Cranberry Opalescent, Flared, c.1939 . . . . . 85.00
Stretch Glass, Bowl, Celeste Blue, Optic Ribbed, Footed, c.1920, 11 1/2 In. 59.00
Stretch Glass, Bowl, Swan, Ruby, Ruffled Edge 35.00
Stretch Glass, Candlestick, Florentine Green, 8 1/2 In., Pair 125.00
Stretch Glass, Candy Jar, Cover, Celeste Blue, Grape Etching 20.00
Stretch Glass, Candy Jar, Cover, Florentine Green, Grape Etching 30.00
Stretch Glass, Candy Jar, Cover, Ruby 75.00
Stretch Glass, Vase, Celeste Blue, Paneled, 12 In. 60.00
Stretch Glass, Vase, Celeste Blue, Ring Optic, 14 1/2 In. 200.00
Stretch Glass, Vase, Dolphin, Velva Rose 25.00
Stretch Glass, Vase, Florentine Green, Paneled, 11 In. 30.00
Stretch Glass, Vase, Velva Rose, Roll Optic, 15 In. 185.00
Sunset, Fairy Light, Cameo Satin 50.00
Vasa Murrhina, Vase, Pink, Green, 11 In. 90.00
Vase, Iris, Sand Blasted, Amethyst, 7 1/2 x 3 3/4 In. 60.00
Violet Satin, Lamp, Gone With The Wind 300.00
Water Lily, Candy Dish, Blue Satin, Footed 45.00
Water Lily, Candy Dish, Custard Satin, Footed 45.00
Wheat, Vase, Blue Overlay, 7 3/4 In. 75.00
Wheat, Vase, Honey Amber, 7 3/4 In. 75.00
Wild Rose, Pitcher 175.00
Wild Rose, Vase, Painted Berries, 11 In. 200.00

FIESTA, the colorful dinnerware, was introduced in 1936 by the Homer Laughlin China Co., redesigned in 1969, and withdrawn in 1973. It was reissued again in 1986 in different colors and is still being made. The simple design was characterized by a band of concentric circles, beginning at the rim. Cups had full-circle handles until 1969, when partial-circle handles were made. Harlequin and Riviera were related wares. For more information about Fiesta, its colors and prices, see the book *Kovels' Depression Glass & Dinnerware Price List*.

Celadon Green, Pitcher, Juice, Disk, 30 Oz. 155.00
Chartreuse, Ashtray 60.00
Chartreuse, Bowl, Fruit, 4 3/4 In. . . . . . 45.00 to 65.00

Chartreuse, Chop Plate, 13 In. 50.00
Chartreuse, Chop Plate, 15 In. 55.00
Chartreuse, Cup & Saucer 48.00
Chartreuse, Cup & Saucer, After Dinner 250.00
Chartreuse, Eggcup 88.00
Chartreuse, Jug, 2 Pt. 95.00
Chartreuse, Mug 38.00
Chartreuse, Nappy, 8 1/2 In. 66.00
Chartreuse, Pitcher, Water, Disk, 2 Qt. 125.00
Chartreuse, Plate, Compartment, 10 1/2 In. 31.00
Chartreuse, Sauceboat 27.00
Chartreuse, Shaker, Pair 33.00
Chartreuse, Soup, Cream 66.00
Chartreuse, Sugar, Cover Only 27.00
Chartreuse, Tidbit, 3 Tiers 44.00
Cobalt Blue, Ashtray 50.00
Cobalt Blue, Bowl, Fruit, 11 3/4 In. 209.00
Cobalt Blue, Bowl, Salad, Footed, 12 In. 275.00
Cobalt Blue, Cake Server, Kitchen Kraft 90.00
Cobalt Blue, Candleholder, Bulb, Pair 38.00
Cobalt Blue, Carafe .... 77.00 to 110.00
Cobalt Blue, Chop Plate, 13 In. 41.00
Cobalt Blue, Chop Plate, 15 In. 44.00
Cobalt Blue, Coffeepot, After Dinner 330.00
Cobalt Blue, Compote, 12 In. Diam. 125.00
Cobalt Blue, Compote, Sweets, Tall Stem, 3 3/8 x 5 1/8 In. 121.00
Cobalt Blue, Creamer, Stick 38.00
Cobalt Blue, Cup & Saucer 27.00
Cobalt Blue, Cup & Saucer, After Dinner 50.00
Cobalt Blue, Cup, After Dinner 55.00
Cobalt Blue, Eggcup 60.00
Cobalt Blue, Fork, Kitchen Kraft 55.00
Cobalt Blue, Jar, Cover, Kitchen Kraft, Small .... 145.00 to 235.00
Cobalt Blue, Marmalade .... 135.00 to 165.00
Cobalt Blue, Mixing Bowl, No. 1 .... 110.00
Cobalt Blue, Mustard 155.00
Cobalt Blue, Nappy, 8 1/2 In. 27.00
Cobalt Blue, Nappy, 9 1/2 In. 22.00
Cobalt Blue, Pitcher, Ice Lip, 6 3/8 In. .... 95.00 to 145.00
Cobalt Blue, Pitcher, Water, Disk, 2 Qt. 90.00
Cobalt Blue, Plate, 6 In. 16.00
Cobalt Blue, Plate, 9 In. 26.00
Cobalt Blue, Plate, Compartment, 10 1/2 In. 22.00
Cobalt Blue, Plate, Compartment, 12 In. 33.00
Cobalt Blue, Sauceboat 17.00
Cobalt Blue, Shaker, Pair 35.00
Cobalt Blue, Soup, Cream 71.00
Cobalt Blue, Soup, Onion, Cover .... 440.00 to 580.00
Cobalt Blue, Spoon, Kitchen Kraft 40.00
Cobalt Blue, Sugar & Creamer 38.00
Cobalt Blue, Syrup 300.00
Cobalt Blue, Teapot, 6 Cup 60.00
Cobalt Blue, Teapot, 8 Cup 77.00
Cobalt Blue, Tray, Figure 8 .... 66.00
Cobalt Blue, Tray, Utility 16.00
Cobalt Blue, Tumbler, Juice 35.00
Cobalt Blue, Tumbler, Water 90.00
Cobalt Blue, Vase, 8 In. 408.00
Cobalt Blue, Vase, 10 In. 605.00
Cobalt Blue, Vase, 12 In. 880.00
Forest Green, Ashtray 60.00

Forest Green, Bowl, Dessert, 6 In. 33.00
Forest Green, Bowl, Fruit, 4 3/4 In. 40.00
Forest Green, Casserole 121.00
Forest Green, Chop Plate, 15 In. 55.00
Forest Green, Coffeepot, Cover 295.00
Forest Green, Cup & Saucer ....24.00 to 48.00
Forest Green, Eggcup 82.00
Forest Green, Mug 38.00
Forest Green, Nappy, 8 1/2 In. 55.00
Forest Green, Pitcher, Water, Disk, 2 Qt. 125.00
Forest Green, Plate, 6 In. 33.00
Forest Green, Plate, 10 In. 27.00
Forest Green, Plate, Compartment, 10 1/2 In. 38.00
Forest Green, Platter, Oval, 12 In. 60.00
Forest Green, Sauceboat 60.00
Forest Green, Shaker, Pair 20.00
Forest Green, Soup, Cream 66.00
Forest Green, Tidbit, 3 Tiers 44.00
Gray, Bowl, Dessert, 6 In. ....55.00 to 87.00
Gray, Casserole 121.00
Gray, Chop Plate, 13 In. 28.00
Gray, Coffeepot, Cover 330.00
Gray, Cup & Saucer 48.00
Gray, Cup & Saucer, After Dinner ....250.00 to 275.00
Gray, Eggcup 88.00
Gray, Jug, 2 Pt. 66.00
Gray, Mug 36.00
Gray, Nappy, 8 1/2 In. 18.00
Gray, Pitcher, Water, Disk, 2 Qt. ....125.00 to 135.00
Gray, Plate, 6 In. 38.00
Gray, Plate, 9 In. 17.00
Gray, Plate, 10 In. 22.00
Gray, Plate, Compartment, 10 1/2 In. 16.00
Gray, Platter, Oval, 12 In. 22.00
Gray, Sauceboat 27.00
Gray, Saucer, After Dinner 45.00
Gray, Soup, Cream ....44.00 to 66.00
Gray, Sugar & Creamer 50.00
Gray, Teapot, 6 Cup 165.00
Ivory, Ashtray 50.00
Ivory, Bowl, Fruit, 11 3/4 In. 146.00
Ivory, Candleholder, Bulb, Pair 60.00
Ivory, Candleholder, Tripod, Pair 410.00
Ivory, Casserole ....55.00 to 90.00
Ivory, Chop Plate, 13 In. 44.00
Ivory, Chop Plate, 15 In. ....27.00 to 44.00
Ivory, Coffeepot, After Dinner 440.00
Ivory, Coffeepot, Cover 110.00
Ivory, Compote, Sweets, 12 In. ....80.00 to 110.00
Ivory, Creamer, Stick 27.00
Ivory, Cup & Saucer 27.00
Ivory, Cup & Saucer, After Dinner 60.00
Ivory, Jug, 2 Pt. 77.00
Ivory, Marmalade 145.00
Ivory, Mixing Bowl, No. 2 .... 82.00
Ivory, Mixing Bowl, No. 5 .... 145.00
Ivory, Mixing Bowl, No. 6 .... 155.00
Ivory, Mug 50.00
Ivory, Mustard 133.00
Ivory, Nappy, 8 1/2 In. 22.00
Ivory, Pitcher, Ice Lip, 6 3/8 In. 77.00

Ivory, Pitcher, Water, Disk, 2 Qt. 82.00
Ivory, Plate, 6 In. 16.00
Ivory, Plate, 7 In. 20.00
Ivory, Plate, 9 In. 17.00
Ivory, Plate, Compartment, 10 1/2 In. 22.00
Ivory, Plate, Compartment, 12 In. 38.00
Ivory, Sauceboat 22.00
Ivory, Shaker, Pair 35.00
Ivory, Soup, Cream 58.00
Ivory, Sugar & Creamer 60.00
Ivory, Syrup 275.00
Ivory, Teapot, 6 Cup 66.00
Ivory, Teapot, 8 Cup 55.00
Ivory, Tray, Utility 23.00
Ivory, Tumbler, Juice 28.00
Ivory, Tumbler, Water 60.00
Ivory, Vase, 10 In. 660.00
Ivory, Vase, Bud 55.00
Light Green, Ashtray 38.00
Light Green, Bowl, Dessert, 6 In. 35.00
Light Green, Bowl, Fruit, 4 3/4 In. 126.00
Light Green, Cake Server, Kitchen Kraft 75.00
Light Green, Candleholder, Bulb, Pair 33.00
Light Green, Candleholder, Tripod, Pair 165.00
Light Green, Carafe 110.00
Light Green, Casserole, Kitchen Kraft, 7 1/2 In. 50.00
Light Green, Casserole, Kitchen Kraft, Individual 95.00
Light Green, Chop Plate, 13 In. 31.00
Light Green, Chop Plate, 15 In. 38.00
Light Green, Coffeepot, After Dinner 360.00
Light Green, Coffeepot, Cover 55.00
Light Green, Compote, 12 In. Diam. 77.00
Light Green, Compote, Sweets, Tall Stem, 3 3/8 x 5 1/8 In. 121.00
Light Green, Creamer, Stick 27.00
Light Green, Cup & Saucer 22.00
Light Green, Cup & Saucer, After Dinner 30.00
Light Green, Eggcup 50.00
Light Green, Fork, Kitchen Kraft 66.00
Light Green, Jug, 2 Pt. 82.00
Light Green, Marmalade 135.00
Light Green, Mixing Bowl, No. 3 . . . . . . 55.00
Light Green, Mixing Bowl, No. 4 . . . . . . 155.00
Light Green, Mug 83.00
Light Green, Mustard 125.00
Light Green, Nappy, 8 1/2 In. 27.00
Light Green, Nappy, 9 1/2 In. 27.00
Light Green, Pitcher, Ice Lip, 6 3/8 In. 110.00
Light Green, Pitcher, Syrup 275.00
Light Green, Pitcher, Water, Disk, 2 Qt. . . . . . .66.00 to 77.00
Light Green, Plate, 9 In. 15.00
Light Green, Plate, 10 In. 16.00
Light Green, Plate, Compartment, 10 1/2 In. 23.00
Light Green, Plate, Compartment, 12 In. 38.00
Light Green, Relish Tray, Multicolored Inserts 275.00
Light Green, Salad, Footed, 12 In. 235.00
Light Green, Sauceboat 22.00
Light Green, Shaker, Pair 21.00
Light Green, Soup, Cream 110.00
Light Green, Spoon, Kitchen Kraft 71.00
Light Green, Sugar & Creamer 50.00
Light Green, Teapot, 6 Cup 60.00

Light Green, Teapot, 8 Cup 22.00
Light Green, Tray, Utility 30.00
Light Green, Tumbler, Juice 50.00
Light Green, Tumbler, Water .... 50.00 to 60.00
Light Green, Vase, 10 In. 660.00
Light Green, Vase, 12 In. 605.00
Light Green, Vase, Bud 55.00
Medium Green, Ashtray 132.00
Medium Green, Bowl, Fruit, 4 3/4 In. 410.00
Medium Green, Chop Plate, 13 In. 176.00
Medium Green, Creamer 55.00
Medium Green, Cup & Saucer 66.00
Medium Green, Mug .... 88.00 to 143.00
Medium Green, Nappy, 8 1/2 In. 50.00
Medium Green, Pitcher, Water, Disk, 2 Qt. 520.00
Medium Green, Plate, 6 In. 66.00
Medium Green, Plate, 9 In. 66.00
Medium Green, Plate, 10 In. .... 85.00 to 94.00
Medium Green, Platter, Oval, 12 In. 105.00
Medium Green, Salad, Individual 100.00
Medium Green, Sauceboat 88.00
Medium Green, Shaker, Pair 145.00
Red, Ashtray 38.00
Red, Bowl, Dessert, 6 In. 132.00
Red, Bowl, Fruit, 4 3/4 In. 60.00
Red, Bowl, Fruit, 11 3/4 In. 220.00
Red, Bowl, Salad, Footed, 12 In. 495.00
Red, Cake Plate, Kitchen Kraft 20.00
Red, Cake Server, Kitchen Kraft 100.00
Red, Candleholder, Bulb, Pair 50.00
Red, Candleholder, Tripod, Pair .... 385.00 to 495.00
Red, Carafe .... 100.00 to 130.00
Red, Casserole, Kitchen Kraft, 8 1/2 In. 60.00
Red, Chop Plate, 13 In. 55.00
Red, Chop Plate, 15 In. 70.00
Red, Coffeepot, After Dinner 410.00
Red, Coffeepot, Cover 110.00
Red, Compote, 12 In. Diam. 176.00
Red, Compote, Sweets, Tall Stem, 3 3/8 x 5 1/8 In. 121.00
Red, Creamer, Stick 38.00
Red, Cup & Saucer 27.00
Red, Cup & Saucer, After Dinner 115.00
Red, Fork, Kitchen Kraft 145.00
Red, Jar, Cover, Kitchen Kraft, Large 190.00
Red, Jug, 2 Pt. 95.00
Red, Mixing Bowl, No. 2 .... 143.00
Red, Mixing Bowl, No. 5 .... 66.00
Red, Mug 60.00
Red, Mustard 155.00
Red, Nappy, 8 1/2 In. 38.00
Red, Pie Plate, Kitchen Kraft 22.00
Red, Pitcher, Ice Lip, 6 3/8 In. 100.00
Red, Pitcher, Juice, Disk, 30 Oz. 520.00
Red, Pitcher, Syrup .... 275.00 to 300.00
Red, Pitcher, Water, Disk, 2 Qt. .... 80.00 to 121.00
Red, Plate, 6 In. 46.00
Red, Plate, 7 In. 33.00
Red, Plate, Compartment, 10 1/2 In. 44.00
Red, Plate, Compartment, 12 In. 60.00
Red, Platter, Oval, 12 In. .... 44.00 to 59.00
Red, Relish Tray, 5 Multicolored Inserts 275.00

Red, Salad, Individual 88.00
Red, Sauceboat .... 33.00 to 60.00
Red, Soup, Cream 71.00
Red, Spoon, Kitchen Kraft .... 82.00 to 132.00
Red, Sugar & Creamer 70.00
Red, Teapot, 6 Cup 66.00
Red, Teapot, 8 Cup 100.00
Red, Tidbit, 3 Tiers 88.00
Red, Tumbler, Juice 50.00
Red, Vase, 10 In. 605.00
Red, Vase, 12 In. 1320.00
Red, Vase, Bud .... 77.00 to 88.00
Rose, Ashtray 66.00
Rose, Bowl, Fruit, 4 3/4 In. 16.00
Rose, Casserole 121.00
Rose, Chop Plate, 13 In. 33.00
Rose, Chop Plate, 15 In. 66.00
Rose, Coffeepot, Cover 132.00
Rose, Cup & Saucer 24.00
Rose, Cup & Saucer, After Dinner 220.00
Rose, Eggcup 77.00
Rose, Jug, 2 Pt. 55.00
Rose, Mug 27.00
Rose, Plate, 9 In. 6.00
Rose, Plate, 10 In. 33.00
Rose, Plate, Compartment, 10 1/2 In. 33.00
Rose, Platter, Oval, 12 In. 22.00
Rose, Sauceboat 27.00
Rose, Shaker, Pair 16.00
Rose, Soup, Cream 66.00
Rose, Sugar & Creamer 50.00
Rose, Tumbler, Juice 28.00
Turquoise, Ashtray 33.00
Turquoise, Bowl, Dessert, 6 In. 50.00
Turquoise, Bowl, Fruit, 4 3/4 In. 44.00
Turquoise, Bowl, Salad, Footed, 12 In. .... 190.00 to 200.00
Turquoise, Candleholder, Bulb, Pair .... 38.00 to 77.00
Turquoise, Carafe 160.00
Turquoise, Casserole 100.00
Turquoise, Chop Plate, 13 In. 38.00
Turquoise, Coffeepot, After Dinner 470.00
Turquoise, Coffeepot, Cover .... 77.00 to 82.00
Turquoise, Compote, 12 In. Diam. 82.00
Turquoise, Compote, Sweets, Tall Stem, 3 3/8 x 5 1/8 In. 115.00
Turquoise, Creamer, Stick 44.00
Turquoise, Cup & Saucer 20.00
Turquoise, Cup & Saucer, After Dinner 82.00
Turquoise, Eggcup 50.00
Turquoise, Jug, 2 Pt. .... 55.00 to 90.00
Turquoise, Marmalade 145.00
Turquoise, Mixing Bowl, No. 7 .... 235.00
Turquoise, Mustard 135.00
Turquoise, Nappy, 9 1/2 In. 22.00
Turquoise, Pitcher, Ice Lip, 6 3/8 In. 90.00
Turquoise, Pitcher, Water, Disk, 2 Qt. 72.00
Turquoise, Plate, 7 In. 26.00
Turquoise, Plate, 10 In. 38.00
Turquoise, Plate, Compartment, 10 1/2 In. 23.00
Turquoise, Platter, Oval, 12 In. 47.00
Turquoise, Relish Tray, 5 Multicolored Inserts 250.00
Turquoise, Relish Tray, Side Insert 120.00

Turquoise, Salad, Individual 27.00
Turquoise, Sauceboat . . . . . 16.00 to 33.00
Turquoise, Shaker, Pair 11.00
Turquoise, Soup, Cream . . . . . 110.00 to 125.00
Turquoise, Soup, Onion, Cover 3850.00
Turquoise, Sugar & Creamer 38.00
Turquoise, Syrup 300.00
Turquoise, Teapot, 6 Cup 60.00
Turquoise, Teapot, 8 Cup 77.00
Turquoise, Tray, Utility 23.00
Turquoise, Tumbler, Juice 35.00
Turquoise, Tumbler, Water 77.00
Turquoise, Vase, Bud 44.00
Yellow, Ashtray 44.00
Yellow, Bowl, Dessert, 6 In. 35.00
Yellow, Bowl, Fruit, 11 3/4 In. 100.00
Yellow, Cake Plate, Kitchen Kraft 605.00
Yellow, Cake Server, Kitchen Kraft 90.00
Yellow, Candleholder, Bulb, Pair 50.00
Yellow, Candleholder, Tripod, Pair 275.00
Yellow, Carafe 82.00
Yellow, Casserole 135.00
Yellow, Casserole, Kitchen Kraft, 8 1/2 In. 38.00
Yellow, Chop Plate, 13 In. 31.00
Yellow, Chop Plate, 15 In. 44.00
Yellow, Coffeepot, After Dinner 470.00
Yellow, Coffeepot, Cover 77.00
Yellow, Compote, 12 In. 90.00
Yellow, Creamer, Individual 38.00
Yellow, Creamer, Stick 16.00
Yellow, Cup & Saucer 16.00
Yellow, Cup & Saucer, After Dinner 60.00
Yellow, Eggcup 71.00
Yellow, Fork, Kitchen Kraft 66.00
Yellow, Jug, 2 Pt. 95.00
Yellow, Marmalade 135.00
Yellow, Mixing Bowl, Cover Only, No. 1 . . . . . 930.00
Yellow, Mixing Bowl, Cover Only, No. 3 . . . . . 520.00
Yellow, Mixing Bowl, Cover Only, No. 4 . . . . . 520.00
Yellow, Mixing Bowl, No. 1 . . . . . 165.00
Yellow, Mustard 125.00
Yellow, Nappy, 9 1/2 In. 33.00
Yellow, Pitcher, Ice Lip, 6 3/8 In. 95.00
Yellow, Pitcher, Water, Disk, 2 Qt. 60.00
Yellow, Plate, 6 In. 22.00
Yellow, Plate, 7 In. 17.00
Yellow, Plate, 9 In. 33.00
Yellow, Plate, Compartment, 10 1/2 In. 23.00
Yellow, Plate, Compartment, 12 In. 38.00
Yellow, Relish Tray, 5 Multicolored Inserts 220.00
Yellow, Relish Tray, Center Insert . . . . . 45.00 to 55.00
Yellow, Sauceboat 16.00
Yellow, Soup, Cream . . . . . 110.00 to 125.00
Yellow, Spoon, Kitchen Kraft 82.00
Yellow, Sugar & Creamer 22.00
Yellow, Sugar, Cover . . . . . 16.00 to 22.00
Yellow, Sugar, Individual 47.00
Yellow, Teapot, 6 Cup 66.00
Yellow, Teapot, 8 Cup 85.00
Yellow, Tumbler, Juice 50.00
Yellow, Tumbler, Water 85.00

Yellow, Vase, 12 In. 715.00
Yellow, Vase, Bud 55.00

FINCH, see Kay Finch category.

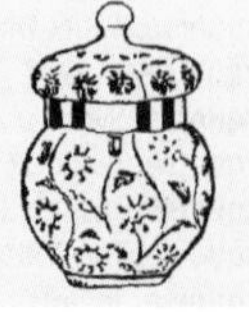

FINDLAY ONYX AND FLORADINE are two similar types of glass made by Dalzell, Gilmore and Leighton Co. of Findlay, Ohio, about 1889. Onyx is a patented yellowish white opaque glass with raised silver daisy decorations. A few rare pieces were made of rose, amber, orange, or purple glass. Floradine is made of cranberry-colored glass with an opalescent white raised floral pattern and a satin finish. The same molds were used for both types of glass.

Spooner, 4 1/2 In. 1200.00
Sugar Shaker, 5 1/2 In. 1495.00
Tumbler, Barrel Shape, 3 3/4 In. 175.00
Vase, 5 In. 1995.00

FIREFIGHTING equipment of all types is wanted, from fire marks to uniforms to toy fire trucks. It is said that every little boy wanted to be a fireman or a train engineer 75 years ago and the collectors today reflect this interest.

Alarm, Oak Case, Brass, 3-Digit Indicator, Windup, Gamewell, 27 In. 2645.00
Bell, Nickel Plated, Iron Bracket, Clapper, 11 In. 295.00
Bucket, Leather, Painted, E.T. Rumery, No. 1, Green, 13 1/2 In. 575.00
Bucket, Leather, Painted, First Church, Chancy Place, Green, Red Rim, 1821, 12 1/2 In. 575.00
Bucket, Leather, Painted, G.O. Fowler, No. 6, Rolled Rim, 12 In. 920.00
Bucket, Leather, Painted, Gilt, Black Lettering, Protector, 17, Red, Gilt, 1800s, 14 In. 380.00
Bucket, Leather, Painted, Green, Decoration, Handle, Calais, Maine, c.1833, 14 In. 5175.00
Bucket, Leather, Painted, Green, Signed, T. Folsom, No. 14, 1803, 14 In. 2400.00
Bucket, Leather, Painted, Green, Stenciled, P. Foster, 17 In. 570.00
Bucket, Leather, Painted, Handle, Sewell Phelps, Boston, 1822, 8 x 13 In. 14500.00
Bucket, Leather, Painted, J. Mansfield, No. 1, Green, Black Rim, 12 3/4 In. 978.00
Bucket, Leather, Painted, J. Pearson, Green, No. 2, 1803, 12 In. 800.00
Bucket, Leather, Painted, Lewis Barnes, No. 1, 1789, 12 In. 3738.00
Bucket, Leather, Painted, Malden Fire Club, 1822, 13 In. 1725.00
Bucket, Leather, Painted, Multicolored, Handle, Ephram Tufts, No. 1, c.1800, 12 1/2 In. 6800.00
Bucket, Leather, Painted, N. White, Black, 14 In. 460.00
Bucket, Leather, Painted, No. 1, Noah P. William, Mutual Fire Club, Roxbury, Mass., 11 In. 2150.00
Bucket, Leather, Painted, Red, Yellow, N.G.P. M.F. Co., Handle, 12 1/2 In. 385.00
Bucket, Leather, Painted, S.A. Ward, No. 2, Red Vine Border, 1827, 10 1/2 In. 1438.00
Bucket, Leather, Painted, T. Parsons, No. 1, 1776, 10 1/2 In. 865.00
Bucket, Leather, Painted, Thomas C. Amory, Gabrielle, Horn, 1806, 12 1/2 In. 3450.00
Bucket, Leather, Painted, Wood Base, Greenish Black, 13 In. 230.00
Bucket, Leather, Putty Colored, Red Trim, Union, Liberty, H. Hill, Beverly, 1826, 12 In. 518.00
Bucket, Leather, Royal Crest, Tapered, Canvas Over Cork Lining, England, 12 1/2 In. 59.00
Cape, Parade, Philadelphia, White, Gold Trim, Late 19th Century, 28 x 48 In. 715.00
Engine Plate, Shield Shape, Engraved, 9 In. 1840.00
Fire Alarm Box, No. 52, Cast Iron, Gamewell, N.Y., 17 In. 235.00
Fire Alarm Key, Boston, To Give An Alarm Pull Hook Down Once Only, Brass Fob, 5 In. 1058.00
Fire Mark, Clasped Hands & 1794, Gold, Black, Baltimore, 1927, 9 3/4 x 10 1/4 In. 575.00
Fire Mark, Convex Oval, Marked F A, Hydrant, Hose, Iron, 1800s, 11 x 7 1/2 In. .... 265.00 to 275.00
Fire Mark, Round, Raised Fire Pump, Lettering, F.I. Co., Cast Iron, 1800s, 14 1/2 In. 325.00
Gong, Indicator, Combination, Gamewell Fire Alarm & Telegraph Co., 39 In. 5290.00
Grenade, Harden's Hand, Fire Extinguisher, Lavender Blue, Footed, Sheared Lip, 5 In. 450.00
Grenade, Harden's Hand, Fire Extinguisher, Turquoise Blue, Sheared Lip, 6 3/4 In. 170.00
Grenade, Harden, 5-Point Star, Blue Green, Sealed 100.00
Grenade, Hayward's Hand, Fire Extinguisher, Aqua, Tooled Lip, Qt., 7 1/2 In. 450.00
Grenade, Hayward's Hand, Fire Extinguisher, Cobalt Blue, Footed, Sheared Lip, 6 In. 390.00
Grenade, Hayward's Hand, Pat. Aug. 8 1871, Olive Yellow, Tooled Lip, 6 1/8 In. 308.00
Grenade, Hazelton's, Chemical Fire Keg, Yellow Amber, Metal Neck Band, 11 1/4 In. 390.00
Helmet, Brass, Greyhound, High Eagle, Front Hammered 630.00
Helmet, Cairns, 8 Comb, Chief Of Dept., Boston, Leather, White 560.00

Helmet, Cairns, Engine 4 PJS-TFD, Leather, Black, Neck Strap 176.00
Helmet, White Leather, High Eagle, Wilson 1380.00
Horn, Brass, Hartford Veteran Firemen, Late Hugh Trumbell, March 9, 1935, 20 1/2 In. 440.00
Horn, Brass, Silk Chord, 7-In. Bell, 15 In. 410.00
Lantern, Brass, Clear Globe, Eclipse, 15 In. 1495.00
Lantern, Wristlet, Volunteer 3, Fixed Globe, Brass Cage, Suspension Ring 1058.00
Nozzle, Brass, A.J. Morse, Boston, 21 1/2 In., Pair 265.00
Nozzle, Brass, Copper, c.1900, 18 In., Pair 70.00
Sector Box, No. 4, Iron, Slant Fist Design, Key, No. 52 Box, Gamewell, 14 In. 235.00
Trumpet, Silver Plated, Flowers, Repousse Bell, 9 1/2-In. Bell, 24 1/2 In. 1880.00
Trumpet, Silver Plated, Presentation, Engraved, c.1872, 22 x 7 1/4 In. 920.00

FIREPLACES were used to cook food and to heat the American home in past centuries. Many types of tools and equipment were used. Andirons held the logs in place, firebacks reflected the heat into the room, and tongs were used to move either fuel or food. Many types of spits and roasting jacks were made and may be listed in the Kitchen category.

Andirons, Arched Base, Penny Feet, 20th Century, 21 1/2 x 15 x 24 In. 69.00
Andirons, Ball Top, Ring Pulls, Joined By Chain, Curved Legs, G. Stickley, 20 x 14 x 25 In. 8225.00
Andirons, Brass, Adam Style, England, 19th Century, 13 x 7 1/2 In. 295.00
Andirons, Brass, Ball Top, Columnar Shaft, Snake Feet, Early 1800s, 17 1/2 In. 227.00
Andirons, Brass, Ball Top, Log Guards, 15 x 25 In. 690.00
Andirons, Brass, Baluster, Scrolled Legs, 1800s, 17 In. 46.00
Andirons, Brass, Cast Columns, Fluted Torches, Flame Finials, 1900s, 21 1/2 In. 105.00
Andirons, Brass, Chippendale, Philadelphia, Penn., c.1780, 20 x 11 In. 2700.00
Andirons, Brass, Double Lemon Top, 8-Sided Body, Penny Feet, Philadelphia, 21 1/2 In. 865.00
Andirons, Brass, Double Lemon Top, Arched Legs, Ball Feet, Federal, c.1800, 19 1/2 In. 575.00
Andirons, Brass, Federal, Urn, Finial, Penny Feet, Philadelphia, c.1775, 13 In. 1950.00
Andirons, Brass, Finial, Iron Saber Shaft, Penny Feet, 22 In. 805.00
Andirons, Brass, Ionic Column, Plinth Base, Faceted Finial, c.1830, 22 In. 1645.00
Andirons, Brass, Iron Belted, Ball Top, Baluster Shafts, 14 1/2 x 12 x 18 1/2 In. 265.00
Andirons, Brass, Iron, Acorn Top, Ball Finials, Baluster Shafts, Early 1800s, 18 x 9 In. 646.00
Andirons, Brass, Iron, American Federal, Knife Blade, Late 1700s, 28 In. 1165.00
Andirons, Brass, Iron, Louis XVI Style, Ionic Columns, Garland, Wreath, 1900s, 14 x 7 In. 59.00
Andirons, Brass, Iron, Scroll Form Openwork Legs, Bun Feet, 21 1/2 x 24 In. 470.00
Andirons, Brass, Iron, Steeple Top, Belted Ball, Slipper Feet, c.1800, 21 x 12 In. 705.00
Andirons, Brass, Iron, Urn, Arched Legs, Philadelphia, Late 1700s, Federal, 28 3/4 In. 4900.00
Andirons, Brass, Magnum, Fire Poker, 28 In. 175.00
Andirons, Brass, Neoclassical, Beehive, 1830-40, 21 1/2 x 10 1/2 x 25 In. 1645.00
Andirons, Brass, Ring & Baluster Rods, Spur Arch, Ball Feet, Empire Style, 15 1/4 In. 200.00
Andirons, Brass, Rococo Style, Urn & Baluster, Raised Anthemion, Tripod Paw Feet, 23 In. 529.00
Andirons, Brass, Seated Dachshunds, 18 x 7 1/2 x 15 1/2 In. 633.00
Andirons, Brass, Steeple Finials, Beaded, Rods, Federal, 20 1/2 x 10 x 21 In. 546.00
Andirons, Brass, Steeple Top, Ball, Shaft, Slipper Feet, J. Davis, Boston, c.1800, 15 1/2 In. 1295.00
Andirons, Brass, Steeple Top, Matching Fire Tools, N.Y., Federal, c.1800, 23 x 11 In. 2400.00
Andirons, Brass, Steeple Top, Spur Legs, Ball Feet, 21 x 22 In. 520.00
Andirons, Brass, Torch & Flame Motif, Federal Style, 27 In. 146.00
Andirons, Brass, Turnings, Log Guards, Ball Feet, 22 x 20 In. 316.00
Andirons, Brass, Wrought Iron, Ball Top, 20th Century, 13 x 17 1/2 In. 189.00
Andirons, Brass, Wrought Iron, England, Late 19th Century, 21 x 12 In. 470.00
Andirons, Brass, Wrought Iron, Urn Top, Baluster Supports, 20 1/2 x 16 1/2 In. 590.00
Andirons, Bronze, Brass, Napoleon III, Gilt Patinated, Columnar, c.1850, 30 x 12 x 21 In. 1175.00
Andirons, Bronze, Geometric Form, Patina, Prairie School, 7 x 20 In. 2290.00
Andirons, Bronze, Iron Figural, Ram's Head, Strap Shape Base, 13 x 20 x 8 In. 825.00
Andirons, Bronze, Louis XV Style, Cherubs, Scroll Base, Lion Mask, Satyrs, 42 x 22 In. 4715.00
Andirons, Bronze, Louis XVI Style, Dogs, Rouge Marble, Flame Finial, 14 x 13 In. 1295.00
Andirons, Bronze, Patinated, Renaissance Style, 19th Century, 49 x 21 In. 3600.00
Andirons, Cast Iron, Baseball Player, c.1910, 20 In. 358.00
Andirons, Chenet, Brass, Ebonized, Graduated Bulb Standards, 1900s, 17 x 41 x 6 In. 142.00
Andirons, Chenet, Gilt Bronze, Louis XV Style, Urn, Scrollwork Base, 25 In. 5100.00

Andirons, Chenet, Lion, Shield, Scrolled Base, Gilt Bronze, c.1850, 14 x 13 1/2 x 6 In. 2585.00
Andirons, Chenet, Louis XV Style, Gilt Brass, Iron, Putto, On Leaf, France, 19 x 14 In. 1175.00
Andirons, Chenet, Louis XVI Style, Dog, Cat, Patinated, Gilt, Late 1800s, 14 x 12 In. 6565.00
Andirons, Iron, American Gothic, Arched, Crocketed, Black, 17 x 8 1/2 x 17 1/2 In. 765.00
Andirons, Iron, Black Man, Squatting, Hands On Knees, 16 1/2 x 10 In. 355.00
Andirons, Iron, Brass, Horse Head Top, Square, Curved Shafts, Early 1900s, 25 1/2 In. 598.00
Andirons, Iron, Dog, Spaniel, Scroll Base, Black Paint, 14 In. 159.00
Andirons, Iron, Figural, Dolphin, 19th Century, 14 1/2 In. 940.00
Andirons, Iron, George Washington, Late 19th Century, 15 1/2 x 18 In. 500.00
Andirons, Iron, Hammered Decoration, Arts & Crafts, 21 x 11 x 22 In. 145.00
Andirons, Iron, Heart Design, Ring Top, Signed EL, Conway, 19th Century, 14 In. 305.00
Andirons, Iron, Hessian Soldier, Striding, Painted Polychrome, 19 1/2 x 20 In. 765.00
Andirons, Iron, Lady Head Tops, 1800s, 13 1/2 x 13 In. 60.00
Andirons, Iron, Owl, 15 In. 110.00
Andirons, Iron, Owl, On Branch, Glass Eyes, Aesthetic, c.1870, 15 1/4 x 9 x 15 In. 590.00
Andirons, Open Spade Top, 4-Sided Shaft, Spread Feet, G. Stickley, 16 x 13 x 22 In. 7638.00
Andirons, Plate Steel, Contemporary, Horse Silhouette, On Hind Legs, 14 1/2 x 11 In. 110.00
Andirons, Steel, Brass, Pierced Flower Finial, 27 In. 1290.00
Andirons, Wrought Iron, Brass, Arched Base, Penny Feet, Columns, 1800s, 17 1/2 In. 230.00
Andirons, Wrought Iron, Dogs, 1940, 19 1/8 x 33 1/8 x 17 1/2 In. 4560.00
Andirons, Wrought Iron, Renaissance Style, Brass, Twisted Uprights, 33 In. 235.00
Andirons, Wrought Iron, Spoked Rondel Finials, Scroll Feet, 1900s, 23 3/4 x 20 1/2 In. 259.00
Andirons & Fender, Brass, Federal, Early 1800s, 20-In. Andirons, 64-In. Fender 826.00
Bellows, Decorated, Mustard, Floral, 18 In. 173.00
Bellows, Fruits, Leaves, Orange, Red, Green, Smoke Ground, Wood, Brass Nozzle, 1800s, 16 In. .. 154.00
Bellows, Turtle Back, Painted, Gold & Black Border, Cattle Under Tree, Brass Nozzle, 15 In. 115.00
Bellows, Turtleback, Yellow Ground, Green, Red Tulips, Brass Nozzle, 18 In. 316.00
Box, Kindling, Mahogany, Faux Bois, Painted, Gougework, Southern, c.1840, 30 x 28 In. 499.00
Chenet, Andirons, Gilt Bronze, Louis XVI Style, Guard Bar, Early 1900s, 18 x 38 In. 295.00
Chenet, Andirons, Gilt Bronze, Louis XVI, Reticulated, Wrought Iron, France, 12 x 18 1/2 In. 940.00
Chenet, Andirons, Gilt Bronze, Rococo Style, Guard Bar, France, 1900s, 11 x 7 1/2 x 4 In. 212.00
Chenet, Andirons, Rococo Style, France, Late 19th Century, 10 x 22 In. 106.00
Coal Bin, Wooden, Brass Carrying Handles, Late Victorian, 24 1/2 x 15 x 12 In. 127.00
Coal Scuttle, Brass, Delft Pottery Handles, 18 x 17 In. 117.00
Coal Scuttle, Brass, Removable Tin Liner, Lift Lid, Wooden Handle, Shovel, 11 x 17 x 14 In. 230.00
Coal Scuttle, Bronze, Embossed Head On Cover, Porcelain Knob, 11 x 15 x 21 In. 138.00
Coal Scuttle, Hinged Top, Removable Container, Handles, Fleur-De-Lis, 18 x 13 x 17 In. 395.00
Coal Scuttle, Tin, Pedestal Base, 19th Century, 17 x 21 In. 35.00
Coal Scuttle, Victorian, Mahogany, Bronze Mounts, Trapezoidal, England, 1800s, 23 x 24 In. 1175.00
Cover, Bronze, 2 Torches, Sun, Branches, Figure, Art Nouveau, Original Patina, 31 x 30 In. 778.00
Crane, Wrought Iron, Scrolling, Long Island, N.Y., 1700s, 20 In. 110.00
Fender, Brass Trimmed Cut Steel, Edwardian, Georgian Style, Early 1900s, 8 x 40 In. 205.00
Fender, Brass, Ball Turned Stanchions, Federal Style, 7 x 42 x 12 In. 220.00
Fender, Brass, Federal, Wire, Crosshatched Design, c.1800, 6 1/2 x 40 1/4 In. 315.00
Fender, Brass, George III Style, Stepped Top, Beehive Stiles, 1800s, 6 x 52 x 14 In. 120.00
Fender, Brass, George III Style, Tubular, Spherule Stiles, 1800s, 10 x 42 x 15 In. 265.00
Fender, Brass, Iron Band Support, 6 x 48 1/2 x 12 1/2 In. 115.00
Fender, Brass, Iron, Lemon Top Finials, Brass Rail, Wirework, Late 1700s, 19 x 63 In. 2235.00
Fender, Brass, Iron, Wire, Brass Rail, Vertical Wire Screen, Scallops, c.1800, 20 x 36 In. 529.00
Fender, Brass, Lion Head Corners, 5 Posts, Acorn Finials, Victorian, 16 x 32 x 8 1/2 In. 138.00
Fender, Brass, Molded Base, Beaded Trim, Draped Wreaths, 72 x 64 x 17 In. 880.00
Fender, Brass, Pierced Decoration, Iron Floor, 6 Stepped Feet, 9 x 44 x 8 In. 518.00
Fender, Brass, Pierced, Serpentine, 6 1/2 x 46 x 7 In. 430.00
Fender, Brass, Rope Twist, 7 Ball Posts, 1800s, 9 x 64 x 15 In. 359.00
Fender, Brass, Sheet Iron, Openwork, Embossed, D-Form, 6 Paw Feet, 8 x 46 In. 265.00
Fender, Brass, Stepped Base, Scrolling, Lobed Urn Finials, Iron Insert, 52 x 14 In. 259.00
Fender, Brass, Wire Mesh, 4 Ball Finials, 3 Ball Feet, 16 1/4 x 31 1/2 In. 145.00
Fender, Brass, Wire, Folding, Swags, Spirals, 24 x 13 In. 1765.00
Fender, Brass, Wirework, Brass Rail, Scroll, Swag, Early 1800s, 10 x 45 In. 500.00
Fender, Brass, Wirework, Steel, Draped Decoration, c.1815, 8 1/2 x 24 In. 290.00
Fender, Bronze, Egyptian Revival, Griffins, Black, Parcel Gilt, France, c.1885, 59 In. 12000.00

Fender, Gilt Bronze, Neoclassical Style, Maiden, Column, Garlands, 1900s, 65 In. 3000.00
Fender, Iron, Hot Twist Rectangular Shape, Birdcage Supports, 1800s, 9 x 15 x 54 In. 195.00
Fender, Metal, Leather Upholstery, Patinated, Early 20th Century, 15 x 60 x 15 In. 415.00
Fender, Wirework, Brass Top Rail, Scrolls, c.1900, 17 x 18 x 46 In. 760.00
Fender, Wrought Iron, Basting Cage, 2 Racks, 18th Century 5060.00
Fireback, Iron, Armorial, Lion, Horse, Fairfax Zane & Marlboro, England, 1900s, 34 x 31 In. 649.00
Fireback, Iron, Bronze Wash, Cherub Riding Angel, 24 3/4 x 20 1/2 In., 2 Piece 359.00
Kettle Shelf, Folding, Wrought Iron, Heart, Curved Pot Handle Rest 600.00
Kettle Tilter, Wrought Iron, 1700s, 32 In. 85.00
Kettle Tilter, Wrought Iron, Idleback Lazy Elbow, Signed, W. Newton, 22 In. 374.00
Log Holder, Iron, Hammered Copper, Riveted Straps, Footed, G. Stickley, 15 x 18 x 29 In. 9990.00
Mantel is listed in the Architectural category.
Meat Warmer, Wrought Iron, Trammel, 2 Hooks, 15 1/2 x 17 x 12 1/4 In. 403.00
Poker, Brass, England, 46 In. 115.00
Poker, Iron, Heart Handle, 18th Century 395.00
Screen, Aesthetic Movement, Ebonized, Parcel Gilt, Leaves, Splayed Feet, 43 x 31 In. 590.00
Screen, Aesthetic, Bronze, Jeweled Leaded Glass, Filigree Arch, c.1880, 35 x 25 In. 1116.00
Screen, Brass, Arched, 20 Glass Panels, Scrolled Feet, Urn Finials, 30 x 20 x 8 1/2 In. 230.00
Screen, Brass, Flower Panel, Hand Stitched, Rope Twist Frame, c.1900, 39 x 28 In. 195.00
Screen, Copper, Hammered, Peacock, Crane, Arts & Crafts, 35 x 34 In. 700.00
Screen, Copper, Hand Wrought, Pierced, Early 1900s, 28 x 42 x 10 In. 819.00
Screen, Empire Style, Mahogany, Ormolu Mounted, Fabric, Late 1800s, 39 x 25 In. 1175.00
Screen, Lady Holding Flag, Dog, 37 x 19 In. 375.00
Screen, Louis XVI Style, Carved, Gilt Wood, c.1870, 45 x 29 x 19 In. 350.00
Screen, Pole, Federal, Mahogany, Inlaid, Silkwork, L'Allegro, Woman, c.1810, 56 In. 825.00
Screen, Pole, Georgian, Mahogany, Silk Inset Panel, Tripod, 1800s, 57 In. 175.00
Screen, Pole, Mahogany, Needlepoint, Flowers, Turned Pedestal, Tripod, 70 x 19 In. 489.00
Screen, Pole, Mahogany, Tapered, Turned, Acorn Finial, Needlework Panel, Regency, 63 In. 1000.00
Screen, Walnut, Needlework, Maltese Cross, 4 Snake Legs, 42 x 27 In. 460.00
Screen, Wrought Iron, Wire Mesh, 3 Panels, Arts & Crafts, 33 x 43 x 12 In. 840.00
Shovel, Wrought Iron, Thumbnail & Star Decoration, Double Rattails, Heart, c.1800, 25 In. 94.00
Spit, Cast Iron, 3 Parts, Tower, Brass Carry Handle, Apron, Spit Rod, Stand, 3 x 31 In. 220.00
Spit, Chippendale, Cast Iron, Clockwork, Brass Handle, 3 Parts, 31 1/2 In. 220.00
Spit, Clock Jack, Key Wind, 1800s, 3 Piece 330.00
Surround, Federal, Brass, Wire, c.1800, 10 1/4 x 39 1/4 In. 546.00
Surround, Marble, Molded Cornice, Egg, Dart Molding, 46 x 59 x 10 In., 4 Piece 3680.00
Surround, Yellow Pine, Stepped Cornice, Frieze, Side Panels, 61 x 71 x 6 In. 1150.00
Tool Set, Brass, Iron, Ring Turned Finials, 19th Century, 11 x 29 1/2 In., 5 Piece 380.00
Tool Set, Copper Patina, Room, Shovel, Tongs, Holder, Bradley & Hubbard, 3 Piece 960.00
Tools, Brass Handles, Baluster & Ball Turned Handles, Iron Shaft, 1800s, 5 Piece 205.00
Tools, Brass, Iron, Steeple Top, Tongs, Shovel, Early 1800s, 32 In. 635.00
Tools, Federal Style, Brass, Urn Top, 1800s, 32 1/2 x 9 1/2 In., 4 Piece 415.00
Trammel, Jack, Wrought Iron 77.00
Trammel, Sliding Bar, Decorated, c.1800, 63 In. 39.00
Trammel, Sliding Bar, Tulips, Whitesmithed, 13 In. 176.00
Trammel, Wrought Iron, Chain, Decorated Hook, 1700s, 81 In. 10.00
Trammel Hook, Wrought Iron, c.1800, 11 In. 11.00
Trammel Hook, Wrought Iron, Twists, c.1800, 10 In. 61.00

FISCHER porcelain was made in Herend, Hungary, by Moritz Fischer. The factory was founded in 1839 and continued working into the twentieth century. The wares are sometimes referred to as *Herend* porcelain.

MF

Basket, Rothschild Bird, Herend, 4 x 10 1/2 In. 295.00
Breakfast Set, Chinese Bouquet Pattern, Green, Gilt Trim, Herend, 9 Piece 410.00
Cachepot, Green Fitzhugh, Herend, 6 x 11 In. 410.00
Figurine, Giraffe, Kangaroo, Herend, 14 1/2 x 6 In., Pair 820.00
Figurine, Hussar, Herend, 15 3/4 In. 700.00
Figurine, Seated Bunny, Herend, 12 In. 700.00
Inkstand, Rothschild Bird, Herend, 4 x 3 1/2 x 6 In. 205.00
Platter, Chinese Rose, Herend, 12 x 16 In. 585.00

Tea Set, Rothschild Bird, Herend 1055.00
Tureen, Chinese Rose, Herend, 10 1/2 x 15 In. 1055.00
Tureen, Cover, Rothschild Bird, Herend, 9 x 13 In. 878.00
Tureen, Cover, Underplate, Black Dynasty, Herend, 14 In. 1062.00

FISHING reels of brass or nickel were made in the United States by 1810. Bamboo fly rods were sold by 1860, often marked with the maker's name. Lures made of metal, or metal and wood, were made in the nineteenth century. Plastic lures were made by the 1930s. All fishing material is collected today and even equipment of the past thirty years is of interest if in good condition with original box.

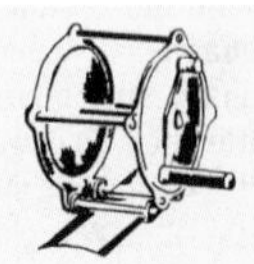

Case, Fly Reel, Geo. Lawrence Co., Leather, Metal Latch, Portland, Ore., 3 1/2 In. 55.00
Catalog, Bristol Steel Fishing Rods, Horton Mfg., 1910, 46 Pages 275.00
Catalog, Bristol Steel Fishing Rods, Horton Mfg., 1919, 32 Pages 578.00
Catalog, Bristol Steel Fishing Rods, String Bound, 12 1/4 x 9 In., 47 Pages 283.00
Catalog, E.F. Payne Rod Co., Highland Mills, N.Y., 1930s, 16 Pages 35.00
Catalog, Thrills Of A Thomas Rod, Bangor, Maine, 1922, 6 x 3 1/2 In., 30 Pages 116.00
Catalog, Winchester, Color, 1924, 5 x 8 In., 32 Pages 110.00
Creel, George Lawrence, Rattan, Split Reed, Leather, Tillamook On Pocket, 10 x 13 In. 1100.00
Creel, McMonies, Lowboy, Split Willow, Leather Trim, Zipper Pocket 880.00
Display, Abbey & Imbrie Lures, Go-Getters, 12 Original Lures, Graphics, 1930s, 11 x 15 In. 392.00
Display, Red's Sure Catch Hooks, 12 Hooks, 50 Cents Each, 1940, Countertop Card 55.00
Float, Innerfloat Tackle Co., Automatic, Metal, Plastic, Box, 3 1/2 In. 36.00
Gaff, Marble's Small Arms Co., Spring Loaded, Metal, Wood Handle, 30 In. 550.00
Jigging Stick, Wood, Fish, Leaves, Trees, Burdett Jacobs, Minn. 660.00
Jigging Stick, Wrapped Handle, Sculptural, Indian, Lake Simcoe, Ontario, Early 1900s 220.00
Knife, Marble's, Metal Finger Ring, 7/8-In. Blade, 5 1/2 In. 305.00
Line Spool, Winchester, Pocahontas, Wood 180.00
Lure, Bud Stewart, Muskrat Fur, Painted Head 80.00
Lure, Clark, Water Scout, No. 402, Black, White, Tack Eyes, Box, 2 1/4 In. 69.00
Lure, Creek Chub, Big Bug Wiggler, 2 1/2 In. 330.00
Lure, Creek Chub, Giant Pikie, No. 2300, Green, White, Glass Eyes, Box, 5 3/4 In. 28.00
Lure, Creek Chub, Husky Pikie Minnow, Red Head, White Body, Box, 6 In. 27.00
Lure, Creek Chub, Musky Champ, Metal, Pikie Scale, Box, 5 In. 110.00
Lure, Creek Chub, Pikie Minnow, Glass Eyes, Cup Rig Hardware, Box, 4 1/2 In. 48.00
Lure, Darby, Spin Head Weedless, Green Back, Instructions, Box, 1930s 495.00
Lure, E. Vom Hofe, Sam's Spoon, Silver Color, 4 In. 28.00
Lure, F.C. Woods, Expert Minnow, 5 Hooks, Green Back, Gold Belly, 1904, 3 5/8 In. 340.00
Lure, Frank Nixon, Aristocrat, Ivoroid, Glass Eyes, Mich., Box, c.1914, 2 1/4 In. 4290.00
Lure, Fred Arbogast, Tin Liz, No. 2, Glass Eyes, Copper & Gold Finish, Box 56.00
Lure, Gee Wiz Bait Co., Frog, Rubber Over Wood Core, Flexible Legs, Box 255.00
Lure, Goble Bait, 2 Joints, 2 Treble Hooks, Tulsa, Okla., Box, 1920s 635.00
Lure, Heddon, Dowagiac Casting, White, Blue Head, Flyer, Box, c.1912, 4 1/2 In. 11110.00
Lure, Heddon, Dowagiac Torpedo Minnow, No. 122, White, Red Glass Eyes, Box, 4 1/2 In. 215.00
Lure, Heddon, Musky Minnow, 5 Hooks, Glass Eyes, 4 Belly Weights, 1910 .... 1320.00
Lure, Heddon, River Runt Spook, Floater, Silver Scale Back, Belly, Black Sides, Box, 2 7/8 In. 25.00
Lure, Heddon, Swimming Minnow, No. 800, Glass Eyes, Box, c.1911, 3 1/4 In. 5500.00
Lure, Heddon, Tadpolly Spook, Plastic, Painted Eyes, Box, 3 In. 21.00
Lure, Hinkley Fish Phantom, Yellow, Gold Spots, c.1897, 2 1/4 In. 75.00
Lure, Joe E. Pepper, Minnow, Revolving, Orange Red, Removable Fins, 1911, Box 5280.00
Lure, Joe E. Pepper, Roamer Bait, Glass Eyes, Rome, N.Y., Cardboard Box, 1 In. 7150.00
Lure, Joe E. Pepper, Underwater Minnow, 5 Hooks, Glass Eyes, Bellyweights, 1905, 3 In. 225.00
Lure, Lowell Calkin, Minnow & Chum Tube, Glass, 2 Compartments, N.J., 1939, 5 In. 660.00
Lure, Pfeffer, Florida Shiner, Brown, Gold Spot Finish, Papers, Box, 5 3/4 In. 415.00
Lure, Pflueger, Globe Bait, No. 3750, Yellow, Box, 3 3/4 In. 89.00
Lure, Pflueger, Globe Bait, No. 3796, Red Head, White Body, Box, 3 3/4 In. 90.00
Lure, Shakespeare, Minnow, 3 Hooks, Glass Eyes, Wood Box, Sliding Lid 1018.00
Lure, Shakespeare, Musky Minnow, No. 53, Glass Eyes, Gem Click Hardware, c.1908 .... 550.00
Lure, Shakespeare, Revolution, Metal, 3 Treble Hooks, 3 In. 358.00
Lure, Silver Creek, Pikaroon, No. 909, Box, 5 1/4 In. 3300.00
Lure, Smithwick, Devil Horse Floater, Snag The Smartest, Unused, Box, 4 In. 20.00

Lure, Welch & Graves, Minnow Tube, N.Y., 1893 Patent, 3 3/4 In. 1210.00
Lure, Winchester, Multi-Wobbler, No. 9203, 3 1/4 In. 60.00
Minnow Bait Cage, Bauman's, Papers, Box, c.1910 .... 5500.00
Minnow Bucket, Cream City, No. 8, Blue, Silver & Gold Fish Stencil 1650.00
Minnow Bucket, Lackawanna, Green, Indian In Canoe, Silver Stencil, 8 Qt. 660.00
Minnow Bucket, Texas, No. 500, Green, Gold, Silver Stencil, 10 Qt. 715.00
Minnow Trap, Camp, Glass, 3 Entry Funnels, Checotah, Okla., 11 In. 179.00
Minnow Trap, McSwain Jr., Glass, Screw-On Lid, Jonesboro, Ark. 85.00
Minnow Trap, Orvis, Glass, Manchester, Vt. 190.00
Minnow Trap, Orvis, Glass, Wire Harness, Perforated Lid, Manchester, Vt. 99.00
Net, C.E. Eveleth, Canoe Cup, Schenectady, N.Y., 1932 .... 605.00
Net, Reinhold, Hemingway Creek, Curly Maple, Trout Model 358.00
Pole, Bamboo, Barrel Reel, Tapered Shaft, Bakelite Inserts, c.1910, 81 1/2 In. 138.00
Reel, B.F. Meek & Sons, Bait Casting, No. 3, Bluegrass, Bone Knob, Leather Case, c.1905 .... 378.00
Reel, B.F. Meek & Sons, Bait Casting, No. 4, Bluegrass, German Silver 825.00
Reel, Barton Alexander & Walker, Brass, Walnut Grasp, c.1870, No. 1 Size, 3 x 2 In. 440.00
Reel, Conroy Bissett & Malleson, Brass, Walnut Handle, Case, c.1875, 2 7/8 x 1 7/8 In. 660.00
Reel, E. Vom Hofe, Matecomber, Model 560, Surf Casting, c.1929, No. 1 Size, 2 1/2 In. 535.00
Reel, E. Vom Hofe, Model 504, Silver, Multiplying, Case, c.1902, 3 5/8 x 1 1/8 In. 2090.00
Reel, E. Vom Hofe, Pat. January 23, 1883, 3 1/4 In. 450.00
Reel, Fin-Nor, Saltwater Fly, No. 3, Left Hand Wind, Pouch, Box, 3 7/8 x 1 In. 385.00
Reel, Hardy, St. George, Trout, Leather Pouch, 2 1/2 x 1/2 In. 600.00
Reel, Hardy, St. John, Salmon, Ribbed Foot, 3 7/8 x 7/8 In. 105.00
Reel, Heddon, Bait Casting, No. 35, Silver, Dual Grasp Handle, 2 x 1 5/8 In. 1870.00
Reel, J. Vom Hofe, Pat. January 14, 1902, 4 1/2 In. 115.00
Reel, J. Vom Hofe, Pat. March 12, 1911, 3 3/4 In. 140.00
Reel, J. Vom Hofe, Trout, German Silver, Rubber, No. 1 Size 1, 2 7/8 x 1 In. 600.00
Reel, J.F. & B.F. Meek, Bait Casting, No. 2, German Silver, 1839-53, 2 x 1 3/4 In. 10450.00
Reel, Leonard-Mills, Trout, Raised Pillar, German Silver, Rubber, 1 7/8 x 1 1/8 In. 2420.00
Reel, Meisselbach, Casting, No. 580, Tripart, Nickel Brass, 80-Yard Spool, Single Crank, c.1909 ... 28.00
Reel, Meisselbach, Expert, No. 17, Cut-Away Gear Plate, Box, 1896 Patent, 3 In. 440.00
Reel, Pflueger, Golden West, Trout, German Silver, 1923 Patent, 2 1/2 x 7/8 In. 375.00
Reel, Talbot, Comet, Bait Casting, Silver, Ivory Handle, 1901 Patent, 7/8 x 1 5/8 In. 506.00
Reel, Union Hardware, Bait Casting, Bakelite Knobs, Jeweled Cam, Level Wind, Box 75.00
Reel, Wheeler & McGregor, Bait Casting, German Silver, 1894 Patent, 2 1/8 x 1 1/2 In. 1375.00
Reel, Winchester, Bait Casting, No. 4228, 60-Yard Spool 119.00
Reel, Winchester, Bait Casting, No. 4253, Nickel, Brass, 80-Yard Spool 178.00
Reel, Yawman & Erbe, Fly, Automatic, Key Wind, Aluminum, 1891 Patent, 3 1/4 In. 85.00
Rod, Abercrombie & Fitch, Fly, 2 Tips, Cork Reel Seat, 7 Ft., 2 Piece 330.00
Rod, Chubb, Fly, Split Bamboo, 2 Tips, Tip Tube, Bag, Display Mount, c.1920, 9 Ft. 140.00
Rod, G.H. Howells, Trout, 2 Tips, Cork Reel Seat, Bag, Case, 1974, 7 1/2 Ft., 2 Piece 3080.00
Rod, Heddon, Fly, Black Beauty, Model 17, 2 Tip, Bag, Tube, 8 1/2 Ft., 3 Piece 275.00
Rod, Orvis, Salmon, Graphite, 1 Tip, Bag, Tube, Butt Extension, 10 Ft., 3 Piece 127.00
Rod, Orvis, Spinning, Superlight, Bag, Tube, Manual, 5 Ft., 2 Piece 360.00
Rod, Orvis, Trout, Battenkill, 2 Tips, Bag, Tube, c.1961, 8 Ft., 2 Piece 335.00
Rod, Phillipson, Paramount, Bait Casting, Chrome Guides, Bag, Tube, 6 Ft., 2 Piece 330.00
Rod, Thomas & Thomas, Trout, No. 4, Midge, 2 Tips, Bag, Tube, 7 Ft., 2 Piece 1980.00
Rod, Thomas, Special Bait, 2 Tips, Down-Locking Reel Seat, c.1920, 8 Ft., 3 Piece 116.00
Rod, Winston, Fly, Steelhead, 2 Tips, Hollow Built, Bag, Tube, 9 Ft., 2 Piece 715.00
Rod, Wright & McGill, Granger, Trout, 2 Tips, Bag, Tube, 1950s, 8 1/2 Ft., 3 Piece 330.00
Rod Case, Abercrombie & Fitch, Leather, Embossed, 55 x 5 In. 220.00
Sign, Better Buy Horrocks Ibbotson, Fish, Fisherman, Die Cut, Cardboard, 27 x 20 In. 140.00
Sign, Fine Fishing Tackle By Shakespeare, Red, Light-Up, 19 In. 880.00
Sign, Wright & McGill Glass Rods, Fish, Fishermen, Cardboard, c.1953, 26 x 21 In. 127.00
Tackle Box, E. Vom Hofe, Brass Hardware, Dec. 22, 74, 10 x 14 1/2 x 8 In. 515.00
Tackle Box, J.W. Gilson, Sportsman, Wood, Laminated, Inside Trays, Stuart, Fla. 160.00
Trophy, Brook Trout Skin Mount, Walnut Plaque, Mohegan Taxidermy, Conn., 14 x 16 In. 55.00
Trophy, Chinook Salmon, Mounted 200.00
Trophy, Marlin, Mounted 150.00
Trophy, Walleye, Mounted .... 150.00 to 175.00

FLAGS are included in the Textile category.

FLASH GORDON appeared in the Sunday comics in 1934. The daily strip started in 1940. The hero was also in comic books from 1930 to 1970, in books from 1936, in movies from 1938, on the radio in the 1930s and 1940s, and on television from 1953 to 1954. All sorts of memorabilia are collected, but the ray guns and rocket ships are the most popular.

Book, Pop-Up, Tournament Of Death, Pleasure Books, 1935 .... 90.00
Book, Power Men Of Mongo, Big Little Book 50.00
Book, Red Sword Invaders, Big Little Book 25.00
Book, Witch Queen Of Mongo, Big Little Book 45.00
Button, Adventures Of Flash Gordon, Buster Crabbe Movie Club, c.1938, 1 1/4 In. 1568.00
Gun, Arresting Ray, Clicker, Marx, 10 x 4 1/2 x 1 1/4 In. 75.00
Gun, Radio Repeater Pistol, Clicker, Tin Lithograph, Louis Marx, 1950s, 10 In. 165.00
Gun, Signal Pistol, Louis Marx & Co., Box, 1935 .... 1155.00
Gun, Sparks, Siren, Red, Green, Marx, 6 1/2 In. 215.00
Gun, Water, Compass, On Card, Esquire Novelty Co., N.J., 1952, 12 x 7 3/4 In. 180.00
Lobby Card, Flaming Torture, Chapter 6, Crabbe & Princess Aura, 1936, 11 x 14 In. 875.00
Lobby Card, Flaming Torture, Chapter 6, Dale Arden, Winged Men, 1936, 11 x 14 In. 215.00
Model Kit, Flash Gordon & Martian, No. 1450, Revell, Box, 1965 .... 105.00
Rocket Fighter, Windup, Metal, Key, Marx, 12 x 4 3/4 In. ....179.00 to 325.00
Space Compass, Esquire Novelty, On Card, c.1951, 2 3/4 x 8 In. 85.00
Wagon, Flash Strat-O-Wagon, Pressed Steel, Wood, Wyandotte, 1940s, 6 In. 105.00
Watch, Pocket, Ingraham, 1950s 60.00
Watch, Precision Time, Box, 1971, 1 1/4-In. Dial 395.00

FLOW BLUE was made in England and other countries about 1830 to 1900. The dishes were printed with designs using a cobalt blue coloring. The color flowed from the design to the white body so that the finished piece has a smeared blue design. The dishes were usually made of ironstone china. More Flow Blue may be found under the name of the manufacturer.

Bowl, Flowers, Garrett & Copeland, 10 In. 155.00
Bowl, Potato, Scalloped, Scinde, Alcock, 10 In. 275.00
Bowl, Scinde, 2 x 10 1/2 In., Pair 230.00
Bowl, Stone Palace, People, Animals, Cauldon, England, 15 x 5 1/2 In. 460.00
Bowl, Tulip Interior, Leaf Outside, 4 1/4 x 7 3/4 In. 60.00
Butter, Cover, Manilla, 8 1/4 In. 230.00
Chamber Pot, Scinde, Alcock, 8 1/2 In. 165.00
Cup & Saucer, Scinde, Alcock, Pair, 4 Piece 138.00
Gravy Boat, Underliner, Scinde, Alcock, 8 1/2 In. 195.00
Ladle, Sauce, Carlton, Winkle, 7 In. 275.00
Ladle, Soup, Scinde, Gold Highlights, Alcock, 12 1/2 In. 1430.00
Pitcher, Madras, Alcock, 8 1/2 In. 200.00
Pitcher, Troy, 6-Sided, Square Spout, Charles Miegh Mark, 8 In. 635.00
Pitcher, Water, Oriental Pattern, 2 Buildings, Flowers, 11 1/4 In. 690.00
Pitcher & Bowl, Scinde, Alcock, 12 1/4 In. 1045.00
Plate, Scinde, Alcock, 8 1/4 In., 4 Piece 165.00
Platter, Beauties Of China, Pagoda, Water, Mellon, Venables & Co., 17 x 13 In. 230.00
Platter, Gothic, John Pratt & Co., 16 1/4 x 12 3/4 In. 115.00
Platter, Kaolin, Podmore, Walker, 17 1/2 x 13 1/2 In. 230.00
Platter, Mandarin, Maddock, 15 3/4 In. 138.00
Platter, Royal Doulton, Watteau Border, 17 1/2 In. 80.00
Platter, Scinde, Alcock, 18 1/4 In. 605.00
Platter, Scinde, Alcock, 20 1/4 In. 1045.00
Platter, Scinde, Oriental Stone, Alcock, 16 1/4 x 12 3/4 In. 290.00
Platter, Scinde, Oriental Stone, Alcock, 20 1/2 x 15 3/4 In. 375.00
Platter, Tonquin, Cut Corner, 13 1/2 x 10 1/4 In. 375.00
Potpourri Jar, Cover, Dragon Handles, 6-Sided, Flowers, Vines, 24 1/2 x 15 In. 2875.00
Razor Box, Cover, Scinde, Alcock, 7 3/4 In. 250.00
Relish, Shell Shape, Scinde, Alcock, 7 1/4 In. 55.00

Serving Dish, 2 Handles, Scinde, 8-Sided, Alcock, 6 1/2 x 12 1/2 In. 1380.00
Shaving Mug, Cherub, Grapes, Raised Decoration, 3 3/4 In. 25.00
Soup, Dish, Scinde, Alcock, 10 1/2 In. 78.00
Sugar, Cover, Scinde, 8 1/4 In. 175.00
Vegetable, Cover, Scinde, Alcock, 13 In. 470.00
Vegetable, Scinde, Alcock, 7 3/4 In. 35.00
Waste Bowl, Scinde, Paneled, Alcock, 5 3/4 In. 55.00

FLYING PHOENIX, see Phoenix Bird category.

FOLK ART is also listed in many categories of this book under the actual name of the object. See categories such as Box, Cigar Store Figure, Paper, Weather Vane, Wooden, etc.

Adam & Eve, Devil In Tree, Wood, Carved, George Lopez, 1969, 18 x 17 In. 1095.00
Alligator, Wood, 33 In. 575.00
Basket, Wire, Lace Heart Shape, 1825, 6 x 8 In. 450.00
Bird Tree, 6 Carved Songbirds On Branches, Patina, 4 1/2 x 7-In. Birds, 18 In. 6800.00
Black Man, Wood, Hand Carved, Boot Stretcher Feet, 1850-99, 70 In. 5142.00
Boat, Wood, Side Wheel, 3 Decks, Carved Figures In Galley, 30 x 31 In. 575.00
Cat, Wood, Carved, Black & White Paint, 19 In. 120.00
Chain, Bird Heads, Wood, Carved, Multicolored 550.00
Clown, Spotted Coat, Holding Hat With Clock Face, Wood, Carved, Painted, 75 x 20 In. 2185.00
Creature, Curled Horns, Tin, David Butler, 1900s, 9 x 17 In. 295.00
Diorama, Bar Scene, Peach Pit, Carved Wood, Brass, Glass, Wooden Case, 8 x 15 1/2 In. 470.00
Diorama, Ship In Tropical Port Of Call, c.1890, 19 x 31 In. 357.00
Dog, German Shepherd, Tan & Black Paint, Wood, 8 3/4 In. 175.00
Eagle, Outstretched Wings, Orb & Plinth Base, Wood, 16 5/8 x 18 In. 1435.00
Eagle, Wood, Painted, Schimmel Style, David Ludwig, York County, Pa., 1900s, 18 In. 550.00
Figure In Barrel, Pine, Carved, Painted, Over The Falls, Niagara Falls, c.1900, 12 1/2 In. 10800.00
Frame, Chip Carved, 11 3/4 x 14 5/8 In. 140.00
Goat, Lying Down, Wood Base, 7 3/4 x 10 1/2 In. 130.00
Gourd, Pickin' De Ole Banjo, Painted, Black Man, Children, Killrell, N.C., 1883, 8 In. 920.00
Hand Gun, Colt SAA, Carved Walnut, Hickory, 6 x 18 In. 115.00
Horse, Black Paint, Gray Detail, Wood, 9 3/4 x 9 In. 230.00
Horse & Rider, Spanish Colonial, Wood, Leather, Metal, Cloth, Glass Eyes, 26 In. 1610.00
Leopard, Crouching, Open Mouth, Black Spots, Green Stripes, Wood, Painted, 11 x 23 In. 805.00
Lion, Carved, Mahogany, Brown Finish, Man, Relief Eyes, Nose, Tail, Ohio, 13 x 6 In. 405.00
Lion, Standing, Mounted On Wood Plank, 19th Century, 1 1/4 x 14 3/4 In. 499.00
Man, In Top Hat, Wood, Painted, Leather Brim, Bead Eyes, Block Base, 14 3/4 In. 1910.00
Monkey, Wood, Carved, Painted, Brass Tail, Round Base, 15 x 9 In. 290.00
Moose, Dog, Carved, Stylized, Burl, Signed L. Johnson, c.1931, 7 x 6 1/2 In. 355.00
Nuestra Senora De La Rosario, Flared Skirt, Crown, Wood, Painted, Rectangular Base, 18 In. 8965.00
Owl Head, Coconut Carved, Taxidermy Glass Eyes, Bear Claw Beak, c.1875, 4 x 5 In. 985.00
Oxen, Brown, White, Black Paint, Wood, 8 x 4 In. 546.00
Panel, Oak, Bird In Tree, Fruit, 24 x 11 1/2 In. 115.00
Pelican, Wobbly Head, Painted, c.1950, 17 1/2 x 15 1/2 In. 110.00
Plaque, Logging, Carved, Polychrome Relief Plaque, Horse, c.1920, 16 1/2 x 14 1/2 In. 205.00
Pole, Red, White & Blue Paint, Uncle Sam, 3 Flags, Wood, 3-Footed Iron Stand, 10 Ft. 2 In. 165.00
Poodle, Painted, Spotted, Pine, Wilhelm Schimmel, Penn., c.1880, 4 x 6 In. 1800.00
Rattlesnake, Wood, Carved, Painted, Oscar Spenser, 54 1/2 In. 315.00
Retablo, Crucifixion Scene, Heaven, Hell, Saints, Adam & Eve, Tin, Painted, Mexico, 10 x 14 In. 940.00
Retablo, St. Christopher & Baby Jesus, Water, Wood, Painted, Tempura, Gesso, 22 x 14 In. 7640.00
Rooster, Perched On Pole, Green, Orange, Paint Black, Leather Wattle, 6 x 19 In. 1016.00
Rooster, Wood, Painted, Schimmel Style, David Ludwig, York County, Pa., 1900s, 6 In. 165.00
Rooster, Wood, Painted, Schimmel Style, David Ludwig, York County, Pa., 1900s, 12 In. 605.00
Sculpture, Monkey Creature, In Rocking Chair, Tin, David Butler, 1900s, 19 x 18 In. 590.00
Sign, Catfish, Wood, Tin, 48 In. 28.00
Statue, John Brown, Wood, Carved, Multicolored, Paint, 76 In. 990.00
Tiger, Devouring Man, Carved, Painted, Wilhelm Schimmel, 5 1/2 x 10 In. 7800.00
Tiger, Papier-Mache, Open Mouth, Swinging Tail, 24 x 45 x 10 1/2 In. 290.00
Turkey On Fence, Fessler, Pa., 34 x 27 x 8 In. 1870.00
Wagon, Conestoga, Oxen, 2 Passengers, Man On Foot, Wood, Metal, Canvas, 25 x 11 In. 170.00

Whatnot Shelf, Hanging, Leather, Pincushion Pads, Birds, Oval Mirror, 13 x 13 In. 430.00
Whimsy, Patriotic, Puzzle Balls, Stars, Square Base, Star Finial, Wood, Painted, 17 In. 5975.00
Whirligig, 2 Figures Sawing, Red & Yellow Propeller, Wood, Zinc, 23 x 29 In. 316.00
Whirligig, 2 Men Sawing, Painted, 14 x 16 In. 220.00
Whirligig, 8 Black, Red Hinged Figures As Pistons, Wood, Wire Shaft, 65 x 45 In. 1150.00
Whirligig, Bicycle, Man, Yellow & Silver Paint, 29 1/4 x 34 In. 230.00
Whirligig, Blue Suited Man, Black Top Hat, Blade Arms, Painted, Late 1800s, 11 In. 900.00
Whirligig, Duck, Wood, Carved, Painted, Iron Wings, Metal Stand, 1900s, 26 x 37 In. 645.00
Whirligig, House, Man, Outhouse, Wood, Feliz A. Breault, Conn., 1948, 25 In. 805.00
Whirligig, Indian Atop Propeller, 4 Paddles, Wide Eyed Expressions, 60 x 21 x 31 In. 355.00
Whirligig, Indian, Carved, Pine, Brave Standing In Canoe, Paddle Arms, 9 1/2 x 16 In. 690.00
Whirligig, Joe Louis, 2 Boxers, Painted, 16 x 19 In. 908.00
Whirligig, Locomotive, Moves Up & Down, Wood, Metal, Painted, 11 x 17 In. 105.00
Whirligig, Man, In Overalls, Black Hat, Tin Brim, Tricolor Paddle Hands, 15 1/4 In. 11213.00
Whirligig, Man, Paddle Arms, Top Hat, Polychrome Paint, 23 In. 385.00
Whirligig, Man, Sawing Wood, Red, White, Windmill, Wood, 25 x 32 In. 480.00
Whirligig, Pheasant, Wood, 1900s, 33 1/2 x 28 1/4 x 6 1/2 In. 330.00
Whirligig, Railroad Hand Cart, 4 Men, Gandy Dancer, Soo Line, Green Bay, Wisc., 22 x 32 In. 748.00
Whirligig, Sailor, Wood, Metal & Wood Hat, Black, White, Nantucket, 13 x 9 1/2 In. 575.00
Whirligig, Windmill, Red, White, Blue, Make-Do Stand 55.00
Wig Stand, Glass, Decalomania, Applied Photos, Painted, Spherical, Trumpet Base, 16 In., Pair 235.00
Woodworker, Seated On Draw Horse, Wood, Jointed Arms, Hips, Cloth Clothes, 10 x 10 In. 300.00
Wreath, Hair, Shadowbox Case, 19th Century, 17 x 7 x 21 In. 117.00

FOOT WARMERS solved the problem of cold feet in past generations. Some warmers held charcoal, others held hot water. Pottery, tin, and soapstone were the favored materials to conduct the heat. The warmer was kept under the feet, then the legs and feet were tucked into a blanket, providing welcome warmth in a cold carriage or church.

Brass, Red Fabric, Charcoal Inside, Lehman Bros., N.Y., 12 x 5 In. 40.00
Brass Lid, Metal Base, Wood, Chaufferette Veilleuse Perfectionnee, Paris, 2 x 10 x 7 In. 80.00
Bronze, Etched, People, Landscape, Chinese, c.1800, 5 x 10 x 8 In. 950.00
Clark Heater, No. 7-D, Drawer, Chicago Flexible Shaft Co., 13 1/2 x 7 x 4 In. 150.00
Copper, Brass Top, Anchor Symbol, Kraussware, Rein Kupfer, 8 1/2 x 11 In. 165.00
Copper, Garantiert Rein Kupfer, 0.75 mm Stark, Germany 68.00
Copper, The Bull Dog, Mesh Handle, 1800s, 4 x 9 In. 250.00
Pottery, SBL Reliable, Doulton Lambeth, 1800s, 6 x 8 In. 185.00
Stoneware, Goodwill's Pat. Aug. 20, 1895 .... 275.00
Tin, Pierced, Wood Frame, 1800-30, 5 1/2 x 9 x 8 In. 105.00
Tin, Pierced, Wood Frame, Circled Heart, 6 x 9 x 7 3/4 In. 110.00
Tin, Punched, Heart, Circle, Wood Frame, Pegged, Wire Latch, Bail Handle, 9 x 7 In. 105.00
Tin, Punched, Heart, Oval, 10 In. 345.00
Tin, Punched, Wood Frame, Wire Bail Handle, 1800s 90.00
Tin, Punched, Wood, Frame, Painted, 1800s 110.00
Wood, Ceramic Tile Top, 6 x 10 x 8 1/2 In. 150.00

FOOTBALL collectibles may be found in the Card and the Sports categories.

FOSTORIA glass was made in Fostoria, Ohio, from 1887 to 1891. The factory was moved to Moundsville, West Virginia, and most of the glass seen in shops today is a twentieth-century product. The company was sold in 1983; new items will be easily identifiable, according to the new owner, Lancaster Colony Corporation. Additional Fostoria items may be listed in the Milk Glass category.

American, Bowl, Trophy, Shaped Handles, 8 1/4 x 12 3/4 In. 65.00
American, Butter, Cover 45.00
American, Cake Plate, Sawtooth Edge, 7 3/4 In. 15.00
American, Cake Stand, 7 x 9 7/8 In. 155.00
American, Candlestick, 2-Light 45.00
American, Candlestick, 6 1/4 In., Pair 70.00
American, Candy Dish, 3-Footed, Large 30.00
American, Candy Jar, Cover, 9 In. 40.00

American, Candy Jar, Cover, Footed, Ruby, 7 1/4 In. 125.00
American, Celery Dish, Oval, 12 In. 35.00
American, Cookie Jar, Cover, 8 3/4 x 5 3/4 In. 295.00
American, Creamer, Individual 8.00
American, Cup & Saucer 8.00
American, Dish, Mayonnaise, Footed, Ladle 55.00
American, Goblet, 10 Oz., 5 1/2 In. 9.00
American, Nappy, Square, Handle, 4 1/2 In. 12.00
American, Nappy, Tricornered, Handle, 5 7/8 In. 12.00
American, Oyster Cocktail, 4 Oz. 11.00
American, Pitcher, Ice Lip, 6 1/2 In. .... 40.00 to 60.00
American, Plate, Bread & Butter, 6 In. 10.00
American, Relish, Sections, Handles, 12 x 5 1/2 In. 20.00
American, Salt & Pepper 20.00
American, Saltshaker 9.00
American, Sherbet, Hexagonal Foot, 4 3/4 In. 9.00
American, Sherbet, Round Foot, 4 1/2 In. 10.00
American, Sugar, Individual 8.00
American, Tumbler, Claret, Footed, 3 Oz. 12.00
American, Tumbler, Iced Tea, 12 Oz., 5 In. 18.00
American, Tumbler, Iced Tea, Footed, 12 Oz., 5 3/4 In. .... 10.00 to 12.00
American, Tumbler, Juice, 5 Oz., 3 3/4 In. 12.00
American, Vase, Bud, Cupped Rim, 6 1/2 In. 15.00
American, Vase, Bud, Ruby, Flared Rim, Footed, 6 In. 75.00
American, Vase, Flared Rim, 7 x 4 3/4 In. 80.00
American, Whiskey 15.00
Baroque, Bonbon, 3-Footed, 6 1/2 In. 15.00
Baroque, Bowl, Salad, 10 In. 35.00
Baroque, Cake Plate, Handles, 12 In. 20.00
Baroque, Candlestick, Bobeche Prisms, Footed, 7 1/2 In., Pair 150.00
Baroque, Console, Rolled Edge, 11 In. 38.00
Baroque, Cruet, 5 3/4 In. 35.00
Baroque, Dish, Pickle, 8 x 4 1/4 In. 14.00
Baroque, Plate, 7 1/2 In. .... 9.00 to 12.00
Baroque, Relish, 3 Sections, 7 1/2 In. 18.00
Baroque, Rose Bowl, 3 1/4 x 3 3/4 In. 32.00
Baroque, Sugar & Creamer 24.00
Baroque, Torte Plate, 14 In. 35.00
Brocaded Acorns, Candlestick, Ice Blue, 3 In., Pair 145.00
Brocaded Acorns, Vase, Lavender, Bulbous, 6 In. 190.00
Brocaded Palms, Bowl, Green, Handle 5.00
Brocaded Palms, Dish, Green, Oval 23.00
Brocaded Poppies, Candlestick, Ice Green, Frosted Top, 3 In., Pair 85.00
Brocaded Poppies, Candlestick, White, 3 In., Pair 85.00
Brocaded Poppies, Compote, Green, Tall 75.00
Brocaded Poppies, Compote, White, Short 70.00
Brocaded Poppies, Compote, White, Twisted Stem, Tall 145.00
Brocaded Poppies, Vase, White, Bulbous, 5 In. 25.00
Century, Plate, Luncheon, 8 1/2 In. 13.00
Century, Tidbit, 3-Footed, 8 In. 18.00
Chintz, Candlestick, 2-Light, 4 x 8 In., Pair 80.00
Chintz, Creamer 19.00
Chintz, Goblet, 9 Oz., 7 1/2 In. 30.00
Coin, Cigarette Holder, Amber, Footed, 3 1/4 In. 17.00
Colony, Bonbon, 3-Footed, 7 In. 17.00
Colony, Candlestick, 3 1/8 In. 25.00
Colony, Candlestick, 3 In., Pair 37.00
Colony, Candlestick, Bobeche & Prisms, 9 3/4 In. 90.00
Colony, Celery Dish, 11 1/2 x 4 1/2 In. 30.00
Colony, Cup & Saucer 9.00
Colony, Ice Tub, Plain Lip, 4 x 7 1/4 In. 245.00

Colony, Sandwich Server, Twisted Center Handle, 11 1/2 In. .25.00 to 35.00
Colony, Sugar & Creamer, Underplate 33.00
Colony, Tumbler, Iced Tea, Footed, 12 Oz., 5 3/4 In. 22.00
Corsage, Cocktail, 3 Oz., 5 In. 20.00
Corsage, Dish, Pickle, Sections, Handles, 8 3/4 x 4 3/4 In. 65.00
Corsage, Plate, 7 1/2 In. 15.00
Cupid, Pitcher, Brocade, 3 Pt., 9 3/8 x 4 5/8 In. 605.00
Diamond Mirror, Castor, Pickle, Royal Mfg. Co. Frame, 4 In. 295.00
Fairfax, Cake Plate, Azure, Open Handles, 10 In. 40.00
Fairfax, Compote, Azure, Lady's Leg Stem, 6 1/2 x 7 1/4 In. 55.00
Fairfax, Cup & Saucer, Amber 10.00
Fairfax, Dish, Sweetmeat, Green, 2 Handles, 6 7/8 In. 15.00
Fairfax, Dish, Sweetmeat, Topaz, 2 Handles, 7 1/4 x 6 In. 9.00
Fairfax, Plate, Dinner, Amber, 9 1/2 In. 20.00
Fairfax, Plate, Dinner, Amber, 10 1/2 In. 25.00
Flame, Candlestick, Bobeche & Prisms, 7 In., Pair 120.00
Iris Ware, Vase, Emerald Green, Square Mouth, Folded Rim, 11 3/4 In. 2975.00
Italian Lace, Bowl, Oval, Gold Trim, 12 1/2 x 7 1/2 In. 55.00
Italian Lace, Candlestick, 2-Light, Gold Trim, 4 1/2 In. 37.00
Jamestown, Wine, Blue, 3 1/2 Oz. 24.00
June, Champagne, 6 Oz. 55.00
Lafayette, Relish, Sections, Regal Blue, Pierced Handles 55.00
Lafayette, Sauceboat, Sections, Amber, Handles, 7 In. 17.00
Leonardo, Salt & Pepper, 5 In. 19.00
Manor, Vase, Green, 5 In. 133.00
Mayfair, Syrup, Cover, Underplate, Green, 5 1/2-In. Syrup 225.00
Meadow Rose, Bowl, Handles, 8 1/2 In. 40.00
Meadow Rose, Candlestick, 3-Light, 5 3/4 x 8 In., Pair 98.00
Midnight Rose, Tumbler, Juice, Footed, 5 Oz. 23.00
Navarre, Candlestick, 2-Light, 4 1/4 In. 28.00
Navarre, Candy Dish, Tricornered, Handle, 4 3/4 In. 20.00
Navarre, Compote, 4 1/2 x 5 1/2 In. 34.00
Navarre, Creamer 68.00
Navarre, Relish, 3 Sections, 12 1/4 x 7 1/2 In. 35.00
Pioneer, Plate, Fruit Center, Green, 12 In. 40.00
Sun Ray, Goblet, 9 Oz., 5 3/4 In. 16.00
Trojan, Candy Dish, Cover, Topaz, 4-Footed 214.00
Versailles, Console Set, Yellow, 14 In., 3 Piece 150.00
Versailles, Tub, Whipped Cream, Pink, Metal Handle, 2 3/4 x 4 3/4 In. 390.00
Versailles, Tumbler, Juice, Green, Footed, 5 Oz., 4 In. 55.00
Virginia, Goblet, Green, 10 Oz., 7 In. 6.00
Wedding Ring, Dish, Mayonnaise, Underplate, Platinum Band 55.00

FOVAL, see Fry category.

FRAMES are included in the Furniture category under Frame.

FRANCISCAN is a trademark that appears on pottery. Gladding, McBean and Company started in 1875. The company grew and acquired other potteries. They made sewer pipes, floor tiles, dinnerwares, and art pottery with a variety of trademarks. In 1934, dinnerware and art pottery were sold under the name Franciscan Ware. They made china and cream-colored, decorated earthenware. Desert Rose, Apple, El Patio, and Coronado were best-sellers. The company became Interpace Corporation and in 1979 was purchased by Josiah Wedgwood & Sons. The plant was closed in 1984 but a few of the patterns are still being made. For more information, see *Kovels' Depression Glass & Dinnerware Price List.*

Antiqua, Plate, Dinner, 10 3/8 In. 16.00
Apple, Bowl, Cereal, 6 In. 27.00
Apple, Bowl, Fruit, 5 1/4 In. 8.00
Apple, Bowl, Vegetable, 8 1/2 In. 90.00

Apple, Bowl, Vegetable, Round, 7 3/4 In. 30.00
Apple, Chop Plate, 12 In. .... 70.00 to 80.00
Apple, Chop Plate, 14 In. .... 140.00 to 195.00
Apple, Cup, Tea 10.00
Apple, Jam Jar, Apple Shape, 4 1/4 In. 600.00
Apple, Mixing Bowl, 6 In. 85.00
Apple, Mixing Bowl, 7 1/2 In. 100.00
Apple, Pitcher, Milk, 6 1/2 In. 75.00
Apple, Pitcher, Water, 8 3/4 In. 125.00
Apple, Plate, Bread & Butter, 6 1/2 In. 8.00
Apple, Plate, Dinner, 10 1/2 In. .... 9.00 to 24.00
Apple, Plate, Salad, 8 1/2 In. .... 7.50 to 15.00
Apple, Plate, Snack, 10 1/2 In. 295.00
Apple, Platter, 12 1/2 In. 38.00
Apple, Platter, 14 In. .... 55.00 to 65.00
Apple, Platter, Turkey, 19 x 13 1/4 In. 295.00
Apple, Relish, 3 Sections, Handles, 11 3/4 In. 97.00
Apple, Relish, Oval, 10 x 4 1/2 In. 35.00
Apple, Saucer 3.00
Apple, Soup, Dish, Rim, 8 1/2 In. .... 14.00 to 25.00
Apple, Teapot, 6 3/4 In. 145.00
Apple, Tidbit, 2 Tier 185.00
Apple, Tidbit, 3 Tier 129.00
Apple, Tumbler, 5 1/4 In. 29.00
Arcadia, Cup & Saucer 25.00
Arcadia Gold, Plate, Dinner, 10 1/2 In. 24.00
Arden, Creamer 22.00
Arden, Gravy Boat, Underplate 40.00
Arden, Sugar & Creamer 25.00
Arden, Sugar, Cover 25.00
Autumn, Bowl, Vegetable, Divided, 13 3/4 x 6 3/4 In. 15.00
Autumn, Pitcher, Milk, 8 1/2 In. 43.00
Autumn, Plate, Salad, 8 In. 4.00
Ballet, Cup & Saucer 20.00
Ballet, Plate, Bread & Butter, 6 1/2 In. 16.00
Birchbark, Plate, Dinner, 10 1/2 In. 34.00
Blue Fancy, Platter, 13 1/4 In. 22.00
Bouquet, Salt & Pepper 50.00
Cafe Royal, Ashtray, Square, 4 3/4 In. 60.00
Cafe Royal, Bowl, Fruit, 6 In. 11.00
Cafe Royal, Butter, Cover 70.00
Cafe Royal, Dish, Heart Shape, 5 3/4 x 5 1/2 In. 50.00
Cafe Royal, Mug, 3 3/4 In. 25.00
Cafe Royal, Salt & Pepper 30.00
Carmel, Cup 6.00
Carmel, Cup & Saucer 14.00
Carmel, Plate, Bread & Butter, 6 3/8 In. 10.00
Carmel, Plate, Salad, 8 In. 12.00
Cloud Nine, Cup & Saucer 10.00
Cloud Nine, Plate, Dinner, White, 10 3/8 In. 19.00
Cloud Nine, Platter, 13 1/4 In. 22.00
Contours Artware, Centerpiece, Amoeba Shape, 16 In. 79.00
Contours Artware, Plate, Bread & Butter, 6 3/8 In. 12.00
Coronado, Bowl, Glacial Blue, 9 In. 60.00
Coronado, Bowl, Vegetable, Oval, Satin Ivory, 12 1/2 x 8 1/2 In. 100.00
Coronado, Casserole, Cover, Satin Ivory, 10 1/2 In. 95.00
Coronado, Chop Plate, Coral, 14 In. 55.00
Coronado, Chop Plate, Ivory, 11 3/4 In. 25.00
Coronado, Console, Ivory, 13 1/2 In. 130.00
Coronado, Plate, Bread & Butter, Turquoise, 6 1/4 In. 8.00
Coronado, Plate, Dinner, Coral, 10 3/8 In. 22.00

Coronado, Plate, Luncheon, Yellow, 9 1/4 In. 6.00
Coronado, Platter, Oval, Satin Ivory, 15 3/4 In. 50.00
Coronado, Platter, Oval, Satin Yellow, 13 x 10 In. 35.00
Coronado, Vase, Coral, 5 1/2 In. 750.00
Coronado, Vase, Ivory, 4 3/8 In. 70.00
Coronado, Vase, Ivory, 6 3/4 In. 80.00
Coronado, Vase, Ivory, Satin, 9 In. 125.00
Country Craft, Plate, Dinner, Blue Skies, 11 In. 20.00
Daisy Wreath, Bowl, Vegetable, 9 1/2 In. 18.00
Daisy Wreath, Casserole, Cover, 2 1/2 Qt., 12 1/2 In. 34.00
Daisy Wreath, Plate, Dinner, 10 3/4 In. 20.00
Del Rio, Plate, Dinner, 10 1/2 In. 15.00
Desert Rose, Ashtray, Oval, 9 In. 90.00
Desert Rose, Baking Dish, 14 x 9 In. 200.00
Desert Rose, Bowl, Cereal, 6 In. 15.00
Desert Rose, Bowl, Salad, 10 In. 49.00
Desert Rose, Bowl, Vegetable, Divided, 2 1/4 x 7 x 10 3/4 In. 33.00
Desert Rose, Bowl, Vegetable, Oval, Divided, 10 3/4 x 7 In. ....33.00 to 65.00
Desert Rose, Bowl, Vegetable, Round, 8 In. 20.00
Desert Rose, Bowl, Vegetable, Round, 9 In. 40.00
Desert Rose, Canister, Cover, 8 x 4 1/2 In. 20.00
Desert Rose, Canister, Tea, 5 3/4 In. 330.00
Desert Rose, Casserole, Cover, 2 1/2 Qt. 400.00
Desert Rose, Chop Plate, 14 In. ....50.00 to 130.00
Desert Rose, Cigarette Box, 3 1/2 x 4 1/2 In. 150.00
Desert Rose, Compote, 4 x 8 In. ....75.00 to 90.00
Desert Rose, Cookie Jar, 9 1/4 In. 245.00
Desert Rose, Cup & Saucer 7.00
Desert Rose, Dish, Oval, 3 Sections, 9 x 7 1/4 In. 160.00
Desert Rose, Ginger Jar, Insert, 4 3/4 x 3 1/4 In. ....350.00 to 500.00
Desert Rose, Gravy Boat, Attached Underplate 40.00
Desert Rose, Grill Plate, 11 In. 95.00
Desert Rose, Mixing Bowl, 3 1/2 x 6 In. 135.00
Desert Rose, Mixing Bowl, 4 1/4 x 7 1/2 In. 145.00
Desert Rose, Mixing Bowl, 4 3/4 x 9 In. 155.00
Desert Rose, Mug, 12 Oz., 4 1/4 In. 45.00
Desert Rose, Napkin Ring Set, 4 Piece 200.00
Desert Rose, Pitcher, Milk, Qt., 6 1/2 In. 75.00
Desert Rose, Pitcher, Water, 2 1/2 Qt., 8 3/4 In. 166.00
Desert Rose, Plate, Dinner, 10 5/8 In. ....8.00 to 25.00
Desert Rose, Plate, Luncheon, 9 1/2 In. 10.00
Desert Rose, Plate, Salad, 8 1/2 In. ....5.50 to 10.50
Desert Rose, Platter, Oval, 8 1/2 x 12 3/4 In. 27.00
Desert Rose, Platter, Oval, 12 3/4 In. 35.00
Desert Rose, Platter, Oval, 14 1/4 In. 52.00
Desert Rose, Porringer, 6 In. 125.00
Desert Rose, Salt & Pepper, Tall, 6 1/4 In. 69.00
Desert Rose, Sugar & Creamer 49.00
Desert Rose, Toast Cover 230.00
Desert Rose, Tumbler, 6 Oz., 3 1/4 x 3 In. 48.00
Desert Rose, Tumbler, 10 Oz., 5 1/4 In. 30.00
Dogwood, Cup & Saucer, Footed 15.00
Dogwood, Plate, Dinner, 10 1/2 In. 14.00
Duet, Bowl, Vegetable, Divided, 8 1/4 In. 20.00
Duet, Mustard, No Cover, 3 In. 19.95
Duet, Plate, Bread & Butter, 6 1/2 In. 5.00
Duet, Plate, Salad, 8 In. 6.00
Duet, Platter, Oval, 13 In. 22.00
Duet, Platter, Oval, 15 In. ....30.00 to 33.00
El Patio, Carafe, Cover, Flame Orange, 7 1/2 In. 145.00
El Patio, Carafe, Cover, Turquoise, 7 1/2 In. ....100.00 to 150.00

El Patio, Casserole, Handle, Cobalt Blue, 8 3/4 In. 25.00
El Patio, Casserole, Handle, Redwood, 8 3/4 In. 20.00
El Patio, Chop Plate, Satin Gray, 14 In. 45.00
El Patio, Cup & Saucer, Glacial Blue 50.00
El Patio, Gravy Boat, Stain Gray 50.00
El Patio, Plate, Artichoke, Turquoise, 3 Sections 125.00
El Patio, Plate, Bread & Butter, Redwood, 6 1/2 In. 6.00
El Patio, Plate, Bread & Butter, Yellow, 6 1/2 In. 5.00
El Patio, Platter, Oval, Turquoise, 11 3/4 In. 47.00
El Patio, Punch Bowl, Gloss White, 6 3/8 x 11 3/4 In. 95.00
El Patio, Sugar & Creamer, Yellow 65.00
El Patio, Tumbler, Apple Green, 3 5/8 In. 25.00
Fern Dell, Bread Tray, 18 x 6 1/2 In. 25.00
Floral, Plate, Dinner, 10 1/2 In. 12.00
Floral, Plate, Salad, 8 1/2 In. 7.00
Floral, Soup, Dish, 7 In. 7.00
Forget-Me-Not, Bowl, Vegetable, Round, 8 3/4 In. 43.00
Forget-Me-Not, Butter, Cover 90.00
Forget-Me-Not, Creamer 33.00
Forget-Me-Not, Cup & Saucer 27.00
Forget-Me-Not, Plate, Dinner, 10 1/2 In. 39.00
Fremont, Gravy Boat, Underplate 120.00
Fremont, Plate, Bread & Butter, 6 3/8 In. 10.00
Fremont, Platter, 12 In. 90.00
Fremont, Platter, 16 In. 130.00
Gingersnap, Bowl, Vegetable, Round, 9 1/2 In. 20.00
Gingersnap, Coffee Mug, 3 3/8 In. 10.00
Gingersnap, Plate, Salad, 8 3/4 In. 8.00
Greenhouse, Bowl, Vegetable, Round, 9 1/2 In. 24.00
Greenhouse, Creamer 20.00
Greenhouse, Platter, Oval, 14 x 11 1/4 In. 30.00
Greenhouse, Sugar, Cover 24.00
Hacienda, Bowl, Vegetable, 9 1/4 In. 30.00
Hacienda, Platter, Oval, 13 1/2 In. 35.00
Hacienda Gold, Coffeepot, Cover, 8 3/4 In. 28.00
Hacienda Gold, Pitcher, 2 1/2 Qt., 7 1/8 In. 30.00
Hacienda Gold, Pitcher, Qt., 6 In. .... 20.00 to 25.00
Hacienda Green, Bowl, Vegetable, 7 3/4 In. 14.00
Hacienda Green, Plate, Bread & Butter, 6 1/2 In. 5.00
Hacienda Green, Plate, Dinner, 10 3/4 In. 8.00
Hacienda Green, Plate, Salad, 8 3/8 In. .... 7.00 to 8.00
Hacienda Green, Saucer 3.00
Ivy, Bowl, Fruit, 5 1/2 In. 35.00
Ivy, Bowl, Vegetable, Round, 7 1/4 In. 55.00
Ivy, Bowl, Vegetable, Round, 8 1/4 In. .... 35.00 to 65.00
Ivy, Cup & Saucer 95.00
Ivy, Plate, Bread & Butter, 6 1/4 In. .... 7.00 to 8.00
Ivy, Plate, Dinner, 10 1/4 In. 40.00
Ivy, Plate, Luncheon, 9 1/4 In. 20.00
Ivy, Platter, Oval, 13 In. .... 45.00 to 100.00
Ivy, Soup, Dish, Footed, 5 1/2 In. 30.00
Ivy, Teapot 290.00
Jamoca, Plate, Salad, 8 3/4 In. 7.00
Jamoca, Platter, Oval, 14 In. 25.00
Kaolena, Ashtray, Yellow, Gold Border, Fan Shape, 7 In. 40.00
Kaolena, Vase, Bud, Flowers, 4-Sided, Flared Rim, 5 1/2 In. 30.00
Larkspur, Bowl, Fruit, 5 In. 3.00
Larkspur, Bowl, Fruit, 6 1/8 In. 12.00
Larkspur, Bowl, Vegetable, 9 1/2 In. 35.00
Larkspur, Chop Plate, 13 In. 24.00
Larkspur, Gravy Boat, Attached Underplate 10.00

Larkspur, Plate, Bread & Butter, 6 1/2 In. 12.00
Larkspur, Plate, Dinner, 10 1/2 In. 19.00
Larkspur, Soup, Dish, 8 3/8 In. 15.00
Madeira, Plate, Dinner, 10 1/2 In. 10.00
Madeira, Platter, Oval, 13 1/2 In. 25.00 to 34.00
Madeira, Sugar & Creamer 25.00
Meadow Rose, Salt & Pepper 50.00
Melrose, Bowl, Vegetable, Oval, 9 x 6 1/2 In. 38.00
Melrose, Plate, Dinner, Platinum Trim, 10 1/4 In. 12.00
Melrose, Platter, 12 1/2 x 9 1/2 In. 36.00
Melrose, Sugar, Cover 20.00
Merry-Go-Round, Casserole, Cover, 8 1/2 In. 40.00
Merry-Go-Round, Cup & Saucer 7.00
Mesa, Creamer, Gold Trim, 2 3/4 x 7 In. 20.00
Mesa, Cup & Saucer 22.00
Mesa, Plate, Bread & Butter, 6 1/4 In. 14.00
Metropolitan, Cup & Saucer, Turquoise, After Dinner 25.00 to 32.00
Mirasol, Plate, Bread & Butter, 7 In. 8.00
Mirasol, Plate, Salad, 8 3/4 In. 13.00
Montecito, Plate, Ruby, 9 3/8 In. 50.00
Montecito, Tumbler, Eggplant, 5 1/4 In. 45.00
Montecito Tumbler, Celadon, 5 1/4 In. 40.00
Moondance, Plate, Dinner, 10 1/2 In. 18.50
Moondance, Plate, Salad, 8 1/2 In. 14.00
Moondance, Platter, Oval, 13 1/2 In. 22.00
Moondance, Saucer 5.00
Oasis, Butter 33.00
Oasis, Plate, Dinner, 10 7/8 In. 25.00
October, Pitcher, 6 3/4 In. 130.00 to 170.00
October, Snack Plate, Square, 8 In. 90.00
Orleans, Bowl, Cereal, 6 1/2 In. 10.00
Padua, Custard Cup 50.00
Padua, Plate, Dinner, 10 1/2 In. 30.00
Padua, Plate, Salad, 9 3/8 In. 25.00
Padua, Sugar, Cover 40.00
Palomar, Plate, Bread & Butter, Gray, 6 1/4 In. 16.00
Palomar, Plate, Salad, Gray, 8 3/8 In. 20.00
Pebble Beach, Bowl, Vegetable, Round, 9 In. 23.00
Pebble Beach, Plate, Dinner, 10 1/2 In. 9.00
Pebble Beach, Plate, Salad, 8 1/2 In. 11.00
Pebble Beach, Platter, Oval, 13 1/2 x 11 1/2 In. 20.00 to 40.00
Pickwick, Platter, Oval, 13 1/2 x 10 In. 12.00 to 16.00
Pink-A-Dilly, Plate, Dinner, 10 1/4 In. 8.00
Pink-A-Dilly, Sugar, Cover 14.00
Poppy, Teapot, Cover 650.00
Poppy, Tumbler, 4 3/4 In. 95.00
Reflections, Butter, Lilac 20.00
Renaissance, Plate, Bread & Butter, Gray, 6 1/4 In. 9.00
Renaissance Gold, Bowl, Vegetable, 9 x 6 1/2 In. 250.00
Renaissance Gold, Cup & Saucer 49.00
Renaissance Gold, Plate, Dinner, 10 5/8 In. 74.00
Renaissance Gold, Plate, Salad, 8 1/2 In. 35.00
Renaissance Gold, Platter, Oval, 15 1/2 x 12 In. 280.00
Rosette, Salt & Pepper 50.00
Rossmore, Plate, Dinner, 10 1/2 In. 12.00
Rossmore, Plate, Salad, 8 3/8 In. 8.00
Sea Sculptures, Plate, Dinner, Nautilus, 10 3/4 In. 12.00
Sierra Sand, Bowl, Vegetable, Round, 9 3/8 In. 26.00
Sierra Sand, Plate, Bread & Butter, 6 3/4 In. 5.00
Sierra Sand, Platter, Oval, 13 3/4 In. 22.00
Sierra Sand, Salt & Pepper 14.00

Simplicity, Soup, Dish, 6 1/4 In. 14.00
Snow Pine, Bowl, Vegetable, Oval, 8 3/4 In. 32.00
Snow Pine, Platter, Oval, 12 1/2 x 9 1/2 In. 32.00
Snow Pine, Soup, Dish, 6 1/4 In. 20.00
Snow Pine, Sugar, Cover 20.00
Southern Blossom, Plate, Dinner, 10 3/8 In. 14.00
Spice, Bowl, Salad, 11 In. 20.00
Spice, Butter, Cover 12.00
Spice, Platter, Oval, 13 3/4 x 10 1/2 In. 25.00
Spice, Platter, Oval, 16 1/2 x 12 1/4 In. 29.00
Spring Song, Gravy Boat, Attached Underplate 35.00
Starburst, Ashtray, Oval, 6 3/4 In. 80.00
Starburst, Bowl, Vegetable, Divided, 8 1/4 In. 40.00
Starburst, Butter, Cover 65.00
Starburst, Chop Plate, Round, 13 1/4 In. 42.00
Starburst, Cruet Set, Covers, Vinegar & Oil, 7 1/2 In., 2 Piece 225.00
Starburst, Jam Dish, Handle, 8 In. 40.00
Starburst, Plate, Salad, 8 In. 19.95
Strawberry, Platter, Oval, 14 1/2 In. 80.00
Strawberry Fair, Bowl, Vegetable, 8 7/8 In. 60.00
Sundance, Bowl, Cereal, 6 1/4 In. 12.00
Sundance, Cup & Saucer, 6 1/4 In. 12.00
Sundance, Plate, Dinner, 10 1/2 In. 14.00
Sundance, Plate, Salad, 8 1/2 In. 10.00
Swingtime, Plate, Dinner, 10 3/8 In. 10.00
Sycamore, Plate, Bread & Butter, 6 1/8 In. 13.00
Tahiti, Bowl, Divided, 10 3/4 In. 37.00
Tahiti, Cup & Saucer 10.00
Tara, Bread & Butter 8.00
Tara, Gravy Boat 35.00
Tara, Plate, Salad, 8 1/8 In. 12.00
Tara, Platter, 12 3/4 x 9 5/8 In. 28.00
Tara, Soup, Dish, 6 1/4 In. 14.00
Tiempo, Casserole, Cover, Sprout, Individual 39.00
Tiempo, Pitcher, Leaf, 2 1/2 Qt., 7 1/2 In. 125.00
Tiempo, Plate, Dinner, Square, Hot Chocolate, 9 3/4 In. 25.00
Tiempo, Plate, Salad, 8 In. 16.00
Tiempo, Platter, Mustard, 13 x 7 3/4 In. 36.00
Tiempo, Soup, Dish, 6 1/2 In. 17.00
Toffee, Creamer 10.00
Tropico, Bowl, Yellow, Gloss, 3-Footed, 9 5/8 In. 65.00
Tropico, Jardiniere, Yellow, 5 3/4 In. 85.00
Tropico, Vase, Redwood, 2 Handles, 5 5/8 In. 50.00
Tulip Time, Bowl, 9 3/8 In. 8.00
Tulip Time, Plate, Dinner, 10 7/8 In. 7.50
Tulip Time, Platter, Oval, 11 1/2 x 9 1/4 In. 16.00
Tulip Time, Platter, Oval, 13 3/4 In. 20.00
Tulip Time, Sugar & Creamer 43.00
Twice Nice, Cup & Saucer 10.00
Whirl-A-Gig, Coffeepot 18.00
Wildflower, Plate, Luncheon, 9 1/2 In. 100.00
Winsome, Bowl, Vegetable, Oval, Divided, 1 7/8 x 10 7/8 x 6 3/8 In. 38.00
Winsome, Dinner, Plate, 10 1/8 In. 11.00
Woodlore, Bowl, Vegetable, Divided, 13 3/4 In. 30.00

FRANKART, Inc., New York, New York, mass-produced nude *dancing lady* lamps, ashtrays, and other decorative Art Deco items in the 1920s and 1930s. They were made of white lead composition and spray-painted. *Frankart Inc.* and the patent number and year were stamped on the base.

Frankart INC

Ashtray, Card Holder, Nude, Jadite Insert, 1932-33 .... 430.00

Ashtray, Nude Pedestal, 23 1/2 x 7 1/4 In. 400.00
Ashtray, Nude Woman, Ball, 1920s, 24 In. 390.00
Ashtray, Nude Woman, Shoulder Stand Position, Glass Insert, 12 In. 470.00
Ashtray, Nude, Outstretched Arms, Green Insert, Jefferson Glass Co., 1928, 10 1/4 x 3 1/2 In. 820.00
Ashtray, Nude, Standing, Frosted Green Glass Ashtray, 24 x 8 3/4 In. 919.00
Bookends, Baby, Curly Hair, On Pillow, Reading Book, Green Paint, 6 1/2 x 5 In. 270.00
Bookends, Cocker Spaniel, Gray, c.1934, 6 1/2 In. 135.00
Cigarette Box Holder, Nude Women, Black 550.00
Lamp, 2 Nude Women, Green Glass Globe, 12 1/4 x 5 In. 1800.00
Lamp, Nude Woman, Arms Thrown Back, 2 Slip Shades, 10 x 8 x 5 1/4 In. 865.00
Lamp, Nude, Green, Moon, Art Deco 1300.00

FRANKOMA POTTERY was originally known as The Frank Potteries when John F. Frank opened shop in 1933. The factory is now working in Sapulpa, Oklahoma. Early wares were made from a light cream-colored clay from Ada, Oklahoma, but in 1956 the company switched to a red burning clay from Sapulpa. The firm makes dinnerwares, utilitarian and decorative kitchenwares, figurines, flowerpots, and limited edition and commemorative pieces. John Frank died in 1973 and his daughter, Joniece, inherited the business. Frankoma went bankrupt in 1990. It was bought by Richard Bernstein in 1991 and is still in business.

Ashtray, Texas Shape, 7 1/4 In. 18.00
Baker, Cover, Mayan-Aztec, Prairie Green, Ada Clay, Individual 10.00
Baker, Cover, Mayan-Aztec, White Sand, Sapulpa Clay, 3 Qt. 35.00
Baker, Cover, Plainsman, Desert Gold, Red Clay, 10 1/2 In. 28.00
Baker, Cover, Plainsman, Desert Gold, Red Clay, 7 1/2 x 10 In. 18.00
Baker, Cover, Plainsman, Prairie Green, Sapulpa Clay, 2 Qt. 25.00
Baker, Cover, Prairie Green, Handle, 4 3/4 x 9 In. 30.00
Baker, Oklahoma, Forest Green, 10 In. 27.00
Baker, Wagon Wheel, Desert Sand, Sapulpa Clay, Individual 35.00
Bean Pot, Cover, Plainsman, Satin Brown, 2 Handles, 5 1/2 In. 40.00
Bowl, Cereal, Plainsman, Prairie Green, Sapulpa Clay, 5 1/2 In. 13.00
Bowl, Cereal, Westwind, Flame, Brown Inside, 5 1/2 In. 9.00
Bowl, Peacock Blue, 11 x 5 x 3 1/2 In. 95.00
Bowl, Prairie Green, Handle, 2 1/2 x 6 In. 15.00
Bowl, Vegetable, Lazybones, Robin Egg Blue, Tab Handles, 10 In. 27.00
Bowl, Vegetable, Plainsman, Divided, Della Robbia White, 14 In. 22.00
Bowl, Vegetable, Robin Egg Blue, 8 1/2 In. 30.00
Bowl, Vegetable, Westwind, Prairie Green, Sapulpa Clay, 7 3/4 In. 14.00
Butter, Cover, Lazybones, Prairie Green 20.00
Butter, Cover, Lazybones, Robin Egg Blue 25.00
Candleholder, Christ The Light, Oral Roberts, Tulsa, 1971 .... 8.00 to 10.00
Candy Dish, Prairie Green, 3 3/4 In. 70.00
Casserole, Cover, Brown Satin, Tab Handles, 4 3/4 x 11 In. 40.00
Casserole, Cover, Desert Gold, 7 1/2 In. 40.00
Casserole, Cover, Sunflower Yellow, 10 In. 35.00
Console, Crescent, Brown Satin, 12 1/2 x 5 In. 50.00
Console, Crescent, Desert Gold, 12 1/2 x 5 In. 50.00
Console, Woodland Moss, Canoe Shape, 13 In. 35.00
Creamer, Ball, Prairie Green 35.00
Creamer, Westwind, Brown Satin 17.00
Cup, Mayan-Aztec, Desert Gold, Pacing Leopard Logo 9.00
Cup, Wagon Wheel, Desert Gold 12.00
Cup & Saucer, Plainsman, Prairie Green 15.00
Dish, Willow Leaf, 1950s, 12 x 6 1/2 In. .... 14.00 to 45.00
Dish, Willow Leaf, Prairie Green, Sapulpa Clay, 7 In. .... 10.00 to 23.00
Figurine, Puma, 7 In. 55.00
Figurine, Swan, 5 1/2 x 8 In. 15.00
Gravy Boat, Brown Satin, 4 1/4 x 6 In. 25.00
Honey Jug, 16 Oz. 17.00

Honey Jug, Cork, Desert Gold, 10 Oz., 6 In. 25.00
Lazy Susan, Della Robbia White, 5 Sections, Ball Bearing Base, 13 In. 40.00
Mug, Brown Speckled Glaze, Sapulpa Clay, 5 1/2 In. 25.00
Mug, Mayan-Aztec, Prairie Green 12.00
Mug, Politcial, Elephant, Nixon, Agnew, Desert Gold, 1973 .... 70.00
Mug, Political, Donkey, Autumn Yellow, 1975 .... 45.00
Mug, Political, Elephant, Donkey, Wisteria, 1983 .... 45.00
Mug, Political, Elephant, Nixon, Agnew, Flame, 1969 .... 35.00 to 85.00
Pitcher, Batter, 66 Oz. 85.00
Pitcher, Blue Gray Jade, 8 In. 27.50
Pitcher, Brown, Bulbous, 5 1/2 In. 20.00
Pitcher, Desert Gold, 7 1/2 x 7 In. 25.00
Pitcher, Flame, 7 1/4 In. 115.00
Pitcher, Iced Tea, Prairie Green, Qt. 50.00
Pitcher, Onyx, Black, 7 1/2 x 4 In. 22.50
Pitcher, Plainsman, Desert Gold, 4 x 4 x 8 In. 30.00
Pitcher, Wagon Wheel, Prairie Green, 2 Qt. 64.00
Planter, Ball Shaped, Red Clay, 8 1/2 In. 30.00
Planter, Satin Brown, Rutile, 4 x 5 1/4 In. 15.00
Planter, Swan, White Sand, 5 1/2 In. 37.00
Plate, Bicentennial, 1974, Battles For Independence, White Sand, 8 1/2 In. 30.00
Plate, Bread & Butter, Plainsman, Brown Satin, 6 1/2 In. 7.00
Plate, Bread & Butter, Plainsman, Desert Gold, Red Clay, 6 In. 9.00
Plate, Christmas, 1968, Flight Into Egypt, Della Robbia White, 8 1/2 In. .... 39.00 to 60.00
Plate, Christmas, 1969, Laid In A Manger, 8 1/2 In. 30.00
Plate, Christmas, 1970, King Of Kings, 8 1/2 In. 30.00
Plate, Christmas, 1971, No Room In The Inn, 8 1/2 In. 40.00
Plate, Christmas, 1972, Seeking The Christ Child, 8 1/2 In. .... 16.00 to 27.00
Plate, Christmas, 1973, Annunciation, 8 1/2 In. 40.00
Plate, Dinner, Lazybones, Prairie Green, 10 In. 20.00
Plate, Dinner, Mayan-Aztec, 10 In. 5.00
Plate, Dinner, Plainsman, Desert Gold, Red Clay, 10 1/2 In. 22.00
Plate, Easter, 1972, Oral Roberts Association, Jesus Is Not Here, He Is Risen .... 15.00 to 50.00
Plate, Indian Chief, Plate, Teal, 7 3/4 In. 9.00
Plate, Oklahoma, Desert Gold, c.1950, 8 1/2 In. 18.00
Plate, Salad, Lazybones, Robin Egg Blue Glaze, 7 In. 14.00
Plate, Salad, Plainsman, Desert Gold, Red Clay, 8 In. 18.00
Plate, Salad, Wagon Wheel, Desert Gold, 7 In. 16.00
Plate, Salad, Wagon Wheel, Prairie Green, 7 In. 15.00
Platter, Mayan-Aztec, Desert Gold, 13 In. 26.00
Platter, Plainsman, Brown Satin, 13 In. 19.00
Salt & Pepper, Mayan-Aztec, Woodland Moss 33.00
Salt & Pepper, Prairie Green, Ringed, Handle, Sapulpa Clay, 4 3/4 In. 15.00
Salt & Pepper, Westwind, 4 In. 12.00
Saucer, Plainsman, Prairie Green 5.00
Saucer, Wagon Wheel, Prairie Green 12.00
Sign, Dealer, Frankoma Pottery, Robin Egg Blue, 2 x 7 In. 138.00
Sugar, Cover, Lazybones, Desert Gold 33.00
Sugar & Creamer, Prairie Green 22.00
Sugar & Creamer, Wagon Wheel, Prairie Green 24.00
Tea Set, Teapot, Onyx Black, Sugar, Creamer, 6-In. Pot, 3 Piece 55.00
Teapot, Cover, Plainsman, Desert Gold, 6 Cup, 7 1/2 In. .... 28.00 to 35.00
Trivet, Butterfly On Flower, Desert Gold, 6 1/4 In. 13.00
Trivet, Liberty Bell, Prairie Green, 6 1/4 In. 22.00
Trivet, Owl, Whoooo Owl, Have A Hootin' Good Day, Desert Gold, 6 1/4 In. .... 10.00 to 32.00
Trivet, Rooster, Blue, 6 1/4 In. .... 34.00 to 53.00
Trivet, Seals Of 5 Civilized Tribes Of Indians In Oklahoma, Prairie Green, 6 1/4 In. .... 23.00 to 35.00
Trivet, Sequoyah, Cherokee Alphabet, Prairie Green, 6 1/4 In. 65.00
Vase, Bud, Crocus, White Sand, c.1943, 8 In. 57.00
Vase, Bud, Snail, Prairie Green, 6 In. 35.00
Vase, Fan Shell, Prairie Green, Ada Clay, 6 In. 38.00

Vase, Flower Frog, Woodland Moss, 5 In. 19.00
Vase, Onyx Black, 2 Handles, 11 x 7 In. 125.00
Vase, Prairie Green, Black Foot, Round, 4 1/2 x 5 In. 27.00
Vase, Prairie Green, Bulbous, Footed, 4 In. 35.00
Vase, Prairie Green, Bulbous, Footed, 8 1/2 In. 35.00
Vase, Ram's Head, Desert Gold, 6 1/2 In. 27.50
Vase, Round, White Sand, 6 1/2 x 4 In. 30.00
Vase, Snail, Black, 6 In. 10.00
Wall Pocket, Phoebe, 7 In. 245.00
Wall Pocket, Phoebe, White Sand, 7 x 5 In. 75.00

FRATERNAL objects that are related to the many different fraternal organizations in the United States are listed in this category. The Elks, Masons, Odd Fellows, and others are included. Also included are service organizations, like the American Legion, Kiwanis, and Lions Club. Furniture is listed in the Furniture category. Shaving mugs decorated with fraternal crests are included in the Shaving Mug category.

American Legion Auxiliary, Ring, Sterling Silver, Woman's, Size 5 .... 20.00
Eagles, Paperweight, Spread Wings, Cast Iron, 5 1/2 In. 55.00
Eastern Star, Salt & Pepper, Masonic Order Of The Eastern Star, Gold Stars, Lefton, 3 1/4 In. 10.00
Eastern Star, Spoon, Sterling Silver, Bible, Vines, Leaves, 5 1/4 In. 30.00
Elks, Clock, Lodge 1245, 11 O'Clock Toast Time, Painted, Tin, Architectural, 40 In. 660.00
Italio-American Baker's Union, Banner, Silk, Needlework, c.1913, 75 x 38 In. 355.00
Knights Of Columbus, Sword, Eagle Pommel, Scabbard, 4th Degree Color Guard, 1950s 280.00
Knights Of Columbus, Sword, Scabbard, Eagle Pommel, Germany, 36 In. 160.00
Knights Of Pythias, Match Safe, 1904 .... 50.00
Knights Of Pythias, Match Safe, Bottom Striker, Pat. Apl. For, 2 1/4 x 1 1/4 In. 36.00
Knights Of Pythias, Robe, Jeweled, Beaded, Cincinnati Regalia Co., c.1900 .... 125.00
Knights Of Pythias, Sword, Dress, Sharkskin Grip, Etched Name, c.1900, 36 1/2 In. 316.00
Knights Of Pythias, Sword, Scabbard, c.1867, 36 In. 175.00
Knights Templar, Paperweight Tile, Wheeling Pottery, Round, 1901, 3 3/4 In. 75.00
Lions Club, Jacket, Corduroy, Black, 39 Pins, Beaverton, Oregon, 1960s, Medium 38.00
Masonic, Charm, Ball, Opens To Cross, 9K Gold, Victorian, 3/4 x 1 In. 485.00
Masonic, Decanter, Glass Engraved, Tapered, Bowknot, Wreath, c.1800, Qt., 11 1/4 In. 440.00
Masonic, Dish, Presentation, Coin Silver, Jones Ball & Poor, 1853, 5 1/2 x 6 3/8 In., 3 Piece 425.00
Masonic, Medallion, Silver, Lodge, No. 811, Amor Honor Et Justitia, 2 1/2 x 2 1/4 In. 2013.00
Masonic, Ring, Secret, Book Style, Double Eagle, 14K Gold, 32nd Degree, Enamel, Size 11 .... 810.00
Masonic, Snuffbox, Masonic Symbols, Iconography, c.1850, 3 1/4 x 1 7/8 In. 539.00
Masonic, Snuffbox, Shoe Shape, Wood, Inlaid Symbols, 1800-50, 3 3/4 In. 540.00
Masonic, Sword, Bone Handle, Scabbard, M.C. Lilly & Co., 1923, 38 3/4 In. 355.00
Masonic, Sword, Officer's, Fred M. Batchelder, Boston, Mass., Early 1900s, 37 In. 335.00
Masonic, Vesta Case, Silver, 2 1/2 x 1 3/4 In. 55.00
Odd Fellows, Postcard, Fraternal Building, Kearney, Missouri, 1930s 12.00
Odd Fellows, Robe, Embroidered Skull & Bones, Black 70.00
Shriner, Letter Opener, AAONMS, Camel, Shriner's Hat, Silver, Adams, 6 In. 35.00
Shriner, Nodder, Composition, Dee Bee Co., Japan, 7 In. 8.00
Shriner, Tile, Symbols, Tube Line Design, Square, Wheeling Tile Co., c.1940, 4 1/4 In. 85.00

FRY GLASS was made by the H. C. Fry Glass Company of Rochester, Pennsylvania. The company, founded in 1901, first made cut glass and other types of fine glasswares. In 1922, they patented a heat-resistant glass called *Pearl Ovenglass*. For two years, 1926–1927, the company made Fry Foval, an opal ware decorated with colored trim. Reproductions of this glass have been made. Depression glass patterns made by Fry may be listed in the Depression Glass category. Some pieces of cut glass may also be included in the Cut Glass category.

FRY GLASS, Bowl, Chicago Pattern, Scalloped Edge, 4 1/4 x 9 In. 440.00
Bowl, Console, Jade Green, Chased Sterling Overlay, Foldover Rim, 4 1/2 x 9 1/2 In. 315.00
Bowl, Vegetable, White, Gold Wheat, 2 3/4 x 8 1/2 In. 9.50

Candlestick, Jade Green, Sterling Overlay, 10 In., Pair 920.00
Casserole, Cover, Opalescent, 1938 Patent, 3 x 8 1/4 In. 55.00
Compote, Amethyst, Crystal, 3 1/2 x 8 In. 180.00
Creamer, Yellow, Cobalt Blue Trim, 4 1/4 x 4 3/4 In. 90.00
Cup & Saucer, Blue, 2 x 4 1/2-In. Cup, 6-In. Saucer 30.00
Loaf Pan, c.1928, 3 x 9 x 4 1/2 In. 20.00
Pitcher, Jade Green Handle, Base, 10 In. 518.00
Reamer, Green, Straight-Sided 45.00
Reamer, Yellow, 2 1/2 x 7 1/2 In. 130.00
Soup, Dish, Flat, Sterling Overlay, 1 1/2 x 7 1/2 In. 230.00
Sugar, Green, Opalescent, 3 x 5 1/2 In. 230.00
Trivet, Pearl, 8 In. 29.00
Tumbler, Fired-On Yellow & Gold Trim, Handle, 12 Oz., 4 3/4 In. 45.00
Tumbler, Pink, Flared, 16 Panels, Footed, 4 1/2 x 3 1/2 In. 12.50
Vase, Bud, Jade Green Connector, 5 1/2 In. 200.00
FRY FOVAL, Bowl, Blue Delft Festoons & Foot, 7 1/2 In. 950.00
Bowl, Blue Delft Trim, Stippled Body, 5 1/4 x 9 1/4 In. 550.00
Bowl, Green Festoons, Egg Shape, Jade Feet, 8 In. 980.00
Bowl, Violet, Egg Shape, 3 Jade Looped Feet, 4 In. 405.00
Candlestick, 3 Blue Delft Wafers & Festoon Looping, Baluster, 12 In., Pair 2875.00
Candlestick, Opal Threading, Jade Wafer, Cylindrical, 10 In., Pair 750.00
Compote, Blue Delft Stem, Pearl Foot, 7 x 6 In. 200.00
Compote, Flared, Blue Delft Rim & Foot, 7 1/2 In. 575.00
Compote, Jade Green Stem, 7 x 6 In. 200.00
Compote, Jade Green Stem, Silver Overlay Rim, 7 x 6 In. 405.00
Compote, Opalescent Bowl & Foot, Blue Delft Stem, 7 In. 290.00
Compote, Pinched Waist, Blue Delft Rim & Foot, 9 1/2 In. 460.00
Compote, Trumpet Form, Scrolling Silver Overlay, 5 In. 460.00
Cup & Saucer, Blue 90.00
Cup & Saucer, Pearl, Delft Handle 95.00
Cup & Saucer, Pearl, Jade Handle, After Dinner 115.00
Custard Cup, Pearl, c.1930, 6 Oz., 2 1/4 In. 12.00
Lemonade, Jade Green Handles, 5 1/2 In., Pair 115.00
Percolator, Opalescent, Cylindrical Coffeepot, 9 In., 4 Piece 259.00
Perfume Bottle, Elongated, Blue Delft Foot, Round Dabber, 8 In. 460.00
Perfume Bottle, Etched Flowers, Jade Intaglio Cuttings & Dabber, 3 1/2 In. 400.00
Perfume Bottle, Flower-Engraved Body, Blue Delft Top, Intaglio Cutting, Dabber, 3 1/2 In. 690.00
Perfume Bottle, Jade Green, Intaglio Cutting, Metal Neck, Cap, Original Dabber 489.00
Sugar & Creamer, Acid Stippled Body, Blue Delft Handles, 3 In. 375.00
Sugar & Creamer, Blue Delft Festoons & Handles 405.00
Sugar & Creamer, Blue Delft Handles, Base, 3-In. Sugar, 2 1/2-In. Creamer 175.00
Tea Set, Delft Spout, Handles & Finial, Silver Rims, 7-In. Pot, 11 Piece 1150.00
Tea Set, Jade Green Spout, Handles & Finial, 6-In. Pot, 11 Piece 575.00
Tea Set, Paneled Dutch Scene, Blue Delft Handles, Silver Overlay, 10 Piece 1380.00
Teapot, Green Trim, 6 x 10 In. 35.00
Tumbler, Lemonade, Pearl, Blue Handle, 5 1/4 In. 150.00
Vase, Blue Delft Base, Flared Rim, 9 x 5 In. 370.00
Vase, Jack-In-The-Pulpit, Jade Rim, 10 1/4 In. 518.00
Vase, Opalescent, Jade Connector, Footed, 8 In. 288.00
Wine, Green Jade Base, Silver Rims, Overlay, Cone Shape, 4 1/2 In., Pair 259.00

FULPER Pottery Company was incorporated in 1899 in Flemington, New Jersey. They made art pottery from 1910 to 1929. The firm had been making bottles, jugs, and housewares from 1805. Doll heads were made about 1928. The firm became Stangl Pottery in 1929. Fulper art pottery is admired for its attractive glazes and simple shapes.

FULPER

Bowl, Blue Flambe, Yellow, Brown, Cobalt Blue Glaze, Flared, Footed, 1910, 4 1/4 x 10 In. 175.00
Candlestick, Blue Flambe, Brown, Crystalline, Oval, 1920, 2 1/2 x 7 1/2 In., Pair 60.00
Candlestick, Mirror Black Flambe Glaze, 11 1/2 In., Pair 560.00
Figurine, Cat, Art Deco, Arched Back, Cucumber Crystalline Glaze, 7 x 8 1/2 In. 765.00

Figurine, Cat, Sleeping, Green Flambe Glaze, Impressed Mark, 3 1/2 x 8 1/2 In. 1295.00
Figurine, Rabbit, White, Pink Glass Eyes, Impressed Mark, 5 1/2 In. 2115.00
Flower Holder, Frog, Antique Green, 2 3/4 x 5 In. 175.00
Flower Holder, Green Matte Glaze, 6 1/2 In. 865.00
Flower Holder, Scarab, Incised, Olive Green Glaze, Blue & Tan, 3 In. 69.00
Lamp, Electric, Free-Form Slag, Glass Insert Shade, 16 1/2 In. 825.00
Lamp, Perfume, Ballerina On Orange Perfume Holder, 6 In. 315.00
Pitcher, Black High Glaze, Silver Sheen, Raised Panels, Handle, Impressed, 5 x 6 1/2 In. 105.00
Pitcher, Copper Dust, Bulbous, Handle, 1916 To 1922, 12 x 7 3/4 In. 920.00
Teapot, Crystalline Glaze, Blue, 7 x 11 x 8 In. 375.00
Urn, Mirror Black To Copper Dust Crystalline Flambe Glaze, 2 Handles, 15 x 7 3/4 In. 940.00
Vase, Black Glaze, Runny, Brown, Gold Crystals, 3 Openwork Handles, 6 3/4 x 4 1/2 In. 290.00
Vase, Blue High Glaze, Matte, Pumpkin Flowers, 3 Looped Handles, 7 1/4 x 9 In. 230.00
Vase, Blue Matte Glaze, Squat, Reticulated Collar, 2 Handles, 6 3/4 In. 315.00
Vase, Blue, Green, Brown Crystalline Glaze, Bulbous, Octagonal, Impressed Mark, 7 1/2 In. 720.00
Vase, Butterscotch Flambe Glaze, 5 5/8 x 9 In. 520.00
Vase, Chinese Blue Flambe Glaze, Baluster, Hammered, 4 Handles, 13 x 11 1/2 In. 2350.00
Vase, Chinese Blue Flambe Glaze, Squat Base, Flaring Neck, 14 x 7 1/4 In. 1175.00
Vase, Chinese Blue Flambe, Cafe Au Lait Crystalline Base, Baluster, 15 x 7 In. 765.00
Vase, Chinese Blue Glaze To Frothy White, Signed, 13 1/2 In. 690.00
Vase, Chinese Blue To Flemington Green Flambe Glaze, Bulbous, 15 1/4 x 7 1/2 In. 529.00
Vase, Cucumber Crystalline Glaze, Ribbed Body, 2 Handles, 6 In. 345.00
Vase, Green & Blue Frothy Glossy Glaze, Cobalt Blue Matte Ground, Tear Shape, 5 1/2 In. 470.00
Vase, Green Semimatte Glaze, Twisted Handle, 3-Footed, 5 1/4 x 8 In. 315.00
Vase, Green, Blue, Rose Ground, Rolled Rim, 3 Handles, 7 x 5 In. 345.00
Vase, Green, Brown Matte Drip Glaze, 5 1/2 In. 290.00
Vase, Leopard Skin Crystalline Flambe, Yellow, Faceted, Collar Rim, 7 1/2 x 6 1/2 In. 650.00
Vase, Moss To Rose Flambe Glaze, Baluster, 17 x 9 1/2 In. 500.00
Vase, Mottled Green, Blue Flambe Glaze, Faceted, Cat's-Eye Base, 9 3/4 In. 410.00
Vase, Mottled Pink & Gray Glaze, Angular Handles, 1920s, 9 1/2 In. 210.00
Vase, Mottled, Runny Purple Glaze, Crystals, 2 Handles, 6 1/4 x 6 1/4 In. 400.00
Vase, Purple, Blue Flambe Glaze, 2 Handles, Label, 6 In. 176.00
Vase, Wisteria Glaze, Squat, 3 Handles, 6 1/4 In. 345.00
Vase, Yellow To Mauve Flambe Glaze, Mushrooms, Embossed, 9 3/4 x 4 1/2 In. 765.00

FURNITURE of all types is listed in this category. Examples dating from the seventeenth century to the 1970s are included. Prices for furniture vary in different parts of the country. Oak furniture is most expensive in the West; large pieces over eight feet high are sold for the most money in the South, where high ceilings are found in the old homes. Condition is very important when determining prices. These are NOT average prices but rather reports of unique sales. If the description includes the word *style*, the piece resembles the old furniture style but was made at a later time. It is not a period piece. Garden furniture is listed in the Garden Furnishings category. Related items may be found in the Architectural, Brass, and Store categories.

Altar, Hanging, 2 Carved, Painted Birds, Hand Wrought Nails, 29 x 25 x 8 1/2 In. 1150.00
Armchairs are listed under Chair in this category.
Armoire, 2-Paneled Doors, Scroll-Carved Apron, France, c.1800, 84 x 53 x 24 In. 6040.00
Armoire, Art Deco, Lime Oak, Brass, Disc Feet, c.1935, 68 x 55 In. 18000.00
Armoire, Baroque Revival, Walnut, 2 Doors, Continental, 78 1/2 x 50 x 20 In. 999.00
Armoire, Brazilian Colonial, Broken Arch Pediment, c.1840, 56 x 25 x 103 In. 410.00
Armoire, Cherry, Paneled Doors, 3 Interior Drawers, Cabriole Legs, 79 x 49 In. 8225.00
Armoire, Chinoiserie, Beech, Bowfront, Damask Veneer, France, c.1915, 76 x 48 In. 295.00
Armoire, Elm, Stepped Cornice, Carved Panel Doors, Continental, 1700s, 77 x 21 In. 3429.00
Armoire, Empire Style, Mahogany, Gilt Bronze Mounts, Arched Mirrored Doors, 82 x 48 In. 3525.00
Armoire, Empire, Mahogany, Bronze Mounted, Flared Cornice, c.1810, 81 x 57 In. 6756.00
Armoire, French Provincial, Oak, Molded Cornice, Carved Doors, 74 x 22 x 52 In. 9525.00
Armoire, French Provincial, Walnut, Early 19th Century, 85 x 53 x 24 In. 1120.00
Armoire, Fruitwood, Runner Feet, Red, Green Finish, Sweden, 80 x 55 In. 3055.00
Armoire, Louis XV Style, Fruitwood, Elm, 2 Doors, c.1850, 83 x 59 In. 4935.00

Furniture, Armoire, Renaissance Revival, Walnut, Bird's-Eye Maple Interior, 112 x 52 x 24 In.

Furniture, Bookcase, G. Stickley, 2 Doors, 3 Shelves, 56 1/2 x 45 1/2 x 13 In.

Armoire, Louis XV Style, Painted, Grilled Upper Panel, Carving, 89 x 60 In. 2000.00
Armoire, Louis XV Style, Pine, Domed, Molded Crest, 99 x 58 x 24 In. 4700.00
Armoire, Louis XV, Cherry, Scrolled Ogee, 74 x 40 x 36 In. 2240.00
Armoire, Louis XV, Fruitwood, 2 Paneled Doors, 1700s, 79 x 48 x 21 In. 825.00
Armoire, Louis XV, Oak, 18th Century, 99 3/4 x 66 x 28 In. 2006.00
Armoire, Mahogany, Mirrored Door, Rod, Hooks, Drawers, 80 x 42 x 25 In. 265.00
Armoire, Mahogany, Plum Pudding, Inlaid, Louisiana, c.1800, 81 x 48 In. 7640.00
Armoire, Mahogany, Scalloped Paneled Doors, Flared Cornice, c.1850, 101 x 71 In. 4115.00
Armoire, Napoleon III, Mahogany, Gilt Brass Mounted, c.1865, 70 x 60 In. 1760.00
Armoire, Neoclassical, Mahogany, 4 Drawers, Beaded Molding, c.1830, 99 x 62 In. 5875.00
Armoire, Neoclassical, Mahogany, Ionic Columns, N.Y., c.1830, 86 x 63 x 29 In. 4700.00
Armoire, Neoclassical, Mahogany, Paneled Doors, 1830-40, 101 x 70 x 25 In. 4400.00
Armoire, Renaissance Revival, Walnut, Bird's-Eye Maple Interior, 112 x 52 x 24 In. .... *ILLUS* 2530.00
Armoire, Spanish Colonial, Fruitwood, 2 Doors, Diamond Panels, 1800s, 70 x 47 In. 2350.00
Armoire, Victorian, Mahogany, Mirrored Doors, Drawer, Late 1800s, 82 x 52 In. 765.00
Armoire, Walnut, Ogee Beaded Cornice, 2-Paneled Doors, Molded Base, 87 x 59 In. 1295.00
Bar, Chase, Art Deco, Demilune, Polychrome, Jazz Orchestra, 43 x 51 x 21 In. 3068.00
Bed, Brass, c.1900, 58 x 56 In. 59.00
Bed, Brass, Tube Construction, Rounded Corners, Castor, c.1900, 59 x 36 x 76 In. 165.00
Bed, Campaign, Iron, Folding, 1800s, 32 x 31 x 74 In. 500.00
Bed, Cherry, Peaked Head & Footboards, Tapered Legs, 48 x 72 1/2 x 35 3/4 In. 145.00
Bed, Directoire, Beech, Painted, France, 41 x 83 In., Pair 1760.00
Bed, Elizabethan Revival, Maple, Turned Symmetrical Arches, c.1850, 52 x 53 In. 470.00
Bed, Federal, Tiger Maple, Scalloped Headboard, Canopy, 78 x 56 x 80 In. 1610.00
Bed, Field, Birch, Red Wash, Folding, High Tapered Posts, Footboard, 76 x 51 x 84 In. 175.00
Bed, Four-Poster, Cherry, Canopy, c.1800, 79 In. 575.00
Bed, Four-Poster, Curly Maple, Rope, 56 x 54 x 72 In. 460.00
Bed, Four-Poster, Federal Style, Mahogany, Canopy, 1900s, 81 x 59 x 84 In. 1060.00
Bed, Four-Poster, Federal Style, Spiral Acanthus Leaves, Pineapple Top, 61 x 36 In. 60.00
Bed, Four-Poster, Federal, Mahogany, Reeded Posts, Arched Headboard, 94 x 56 In. 5290.00
Bed, Four-Poster, Federal, Tiger Maple, Canopy, Scalloped Headboard, Turned Posts 1610.00
Bed, Four-Poster, Federal, Tiger Maple, Vase & Ring Turned Legs, 86 x 54 x 75 In. 3820.00
Bed, Four-Poster, Mahogany, Canopy, Headboard, Carved Posts, 88 x 52 1/2 In. 1430.00
Bed, Four-Poster, Maple Foot Posts, Pine Headboard, Red Paint, 81 x 54 x 72 In. 230.00
Bed, Four-Poster, Neoclassical, Mahogany, Ring Turned, c.1820, 89 x 54 x 71 In. 6465.00
Bed, Four-Poster, Neoclassical, Mahogany, Turned Posts, c.1830, 105 x 58 x 70 In. 2115.00
Bed, Four-Poster, Neoclassical, Maple, Scrolled & Paneled, c.1825, 64 x 79 x 54 In. 1675.00
Bed, Four-Poster, Nutting, No. 836, Tiger Maple, Twin, 60 1/2 In. 660.00
Bed, Four-Poster, Rococo Revival, Rosewood, Cluster Column, Shell Crest, 97 x 58 x 71 In. 8815.00
Bed, Four-Poster, Sheraton, Cherry, Ribbed Foot Posts, 65 x 51 In. 460.00
Bed, Four-Poster, Sheraton, Mahogany, Acanthus Leaves, Spiral Turning, 88 x 53 In. 1430.00
Bed, Four-Poster, Sheraton, Maple & Pine, Acorn Finials, 1800s, 92 x 60 In. 2380.00
Bed, Four-Poster, Sheraton, Painted, Rolled Crest, Blanket Roll, 78 x 76 x 49 In. 575.00
Bed, Four-Poster, Spiral Reeded Posts, Pineapple Finial, c.1825, 94 x 62 x 80 In. 2820.00
Bed, G. Stickley, Horizontal Planks, Through Tenons, 54 x 61 x 80 In. 7640.00
Bed, Half-Tester, Renaissance Revival, Walnut, Anthemion Crest, c.1850, 113 x 64 In. 7640.00
Bed, Iron, Brass, Fleur-De-Lis, Cross, France, 1800s, 56 x 55 x 76 In. 470.00

Bed, Louis Philippe, Satinwood, Scrolled Headboard, Flowers, c.1850, 56 x 71 In. 5875.00
Bed, Louis XVI, Molded Crest Rail, Leaf Carved, Fluted Feet, 51 x 9 x 50 1/2 In. 1415.00
Bed, Maple, Bamboo Turned, Black Rings, Stepped Spindle, 1880, 40 x 77 In. 1210.00
Bed, Maple, Scroll-Cut Headboard, Turned Posts, Acorn Finials, Rope, 76 x 42 x 41 In. 175.00
Bed, Maple, Turned Posts, Headboard, Early 19th Century, 55 x 52 In. 235.00
Bed, Mixed Wood, Scrolled Pediment, Turned Post, Square Rails, 51 x 81 x 57 In. 1060.00
Bed, Poplar, Green Paint, Turned Legs, Arched Headboard, Footboard, Rope, 67 In. 430.00
Bed, Poplar, Posts, Scrolled Headboard, Ball Finials, Rope, 53 1/2 x 54 In. 115.00
Bed, Red Wash, Scalloped Headboard, Cannonball Finials, Rope, 41 x 82 x 41 In. 115.00
Bed, Rococo Revival, Mahogany, Arched Panels, Posts, Strapwork Cartouche, 91 x 59 In. 4400.00
Bed, Settle, Pine, Paneled Apron, Shaped Arms, Hinged Seat, 76 x 19 x 34 In. 1265.00
Bed, Settle, Pine, Red Paint, Rosehead Nails, Beaded Boards, 31 x 53 x 22 In. 1610.00
Bed, Settle, Pine, Wainscot, 18th Century, 35 x 70 x 23 In. 660.00
Bed, Sleigh, Walnut, Arched Paneled & Molded Headboard, c.1850, 41 x 56 In. 529.00
Bed, Tiger Maple, Ball-Top Vase & Ring Turned Posts, Headboard, c.1825, 84 x 48 In. 3410.00
Bed, Walnut, Rope Lacing, Cannonball Finals On Bedposts, Single, 1800 .... 1495.00
Bed Steps, Empire, Mahogany, Figured, 19th Century, 18 x 21 x 21 In. 385.00
Bed Steps, Mahogany, Tooled Leather Tops, Compartment, England, 1800s, 27 x 30 In. 345.00
Bed Steps, Regency, Mahogany, 3 Steps, Leather Inset, Early 1800s, 27 x 28 x 18 In. 1410.00
Bed Steps, Regency, Mahogany, Leather Top, Tapered Legs, c.1820, 29 x 28 x 18 In. 1645.00
Bed Steps, Regency, Mahogany, Leather, Drawer, Cupboard, Early 1800s, 29 x 17 In. 4115.00
Bedroom Set, Blond Wood, King Headboard, Nightstands, Chests, Dresser, 5 Piece 1180.00
Bedroom Set, H. Probber, King, Headboard, Dresser, End Tables, 4 Piece 1120.00
Bedroom Set, Henredon, Maple Veneer, Marble, 5 Piece 3300.00
Bedroom Set, Louis XVI Style, Oak, Armoire, Bed, Cabinet, c.1890, 3 Piece 1170.00
Bedroom Set, Norman Bel Geddes, Enameled Metal, 2 Twin Beds, 8 Piece 1180.00
Bedroom Set, Paul Laszlo, 2 Beds, Nightstand, Vanity, 2 Lamps, Brown Saltman, c.1940 .... 2400.00
Bedroom Set, Teak, Denmark, 14 x 82 x 63-In. Bed, 4 Piece 1400.00
Bedroom Set, Wormley, Mahogany Veneer, Dunbar, 50 x 34-In. Chest, 5 Piece 3420.00
Bench, Beech, Chinese, 19 x 45 x 12 1/2 In. 355.00
Bench, Black Forest, Carved Bears Holding Bench, Branches, Oak Leaves, 37 x 65 In. 4465.00
Bench, Bucket, Pine, 2 Tiers, 20 x 36 In. 130.00
Bench, Bucket, Pine, Poplar, 3 Shelves, Shaped Sides, 18th Century, 52 x 51 x 15 In. 2938.00
Bench, Bucket, Pumpkin Pine, Green Paint Trace, Mortised, Bootjack Ends, 72 x 12 In. 430.00
Bench, Curule, William IV Style, Mahogany, Leather, Leaf Frame, 32 x 61 In. 529.00
Bench, Deacon's, Pine, Chestnut, 1800s, 83 In. 210.00
Bench, Directoire Style, Pine, Padded Seat, Outscrolled Ends, Splayed Legs, 28 x 28 In. 650.00
Bench, Elm, Rectangular, Bamboo Mat, Round Legs, Chinese, 19 1/2 x 44 x 11 In. 295.00
Bench, Empire Style, Bronze, 18 x 72 x 24 In. 6000.00
Bench, Empire Style, Gray Paint, L-Shape, Carved Leaves, Lions Ends, 73 In., Pair 3290.00
Bench, Empire Style, Mahogany, 19th Century, 17 x 23 x 22 In. 1060.00
Bench, Ettore Sottsass, Tubular Steel, Leather, Rubber, 25 x 59 x 20 In. 1000.00
Bench, Fireside, Pine, High Back, Hinged Seat, Compartment, Cutout Feet, 60 x 57 In. 1610.00
Bench, Fireside, Pine, Mortise, Pegged, Arms, Paneled Back, Lift Top, 44 x 56 In. 1265.00
Bench, G. Nelson, No. 6D, Steel Frame, Herman Miller, c.1955, 16 x 72 x 24 In. 1020.00
Bench, G. Nelson, Platform, Birch Slats, Ebonized Wood Legs, 14 x 68 x 18 In. 840.00
Bench, G. Nelson, Platform, No. 4692, Herman Miller, 1947, 14 x 72 x 19 In. 960.00
Bench, G. Stickley, Hall, Shaped Back Stretcher, Back Slats, Arms, 37 x 38 x 18 1/2 In. 1175.00
Bench, George I Style, Walnut, Upholstered, Slip Seat, 1800s, 18 x 38 1/2 x 17 1/4 In. 2240.00
Bench, George III Style, Walnut, Padded, Upholstered, Slip Seat, 1800s, 18 x 20 In. 590.00
Bench, Grain Painted, Scrolled Arms, 1800s, 36 x 76 x 22 In. 415.00
Bench, Grain Painted, Shaped Supports, Cutout Demilune Feet, 15 1/2 x 30 x 11 In. 450.00
Bench, Hall, Oak, Lions, Arms, Molded Base, Compartment, 36 x 58 x 20 In. 1725.00
Bench, Hitchcock, Tiger Maple, Rush Seat, 1830s 4500.00
Bench, Katavolos Littell & Kelley, Glass Top, c.1948, 11 x 62 x 17 In. 1320.00
Bench, Kilim Carpet Upholstery, Gulls, Brick Field, Square Legs, 20 x 37 x 17 In. 558.00
Bench, Ladder Back, Rush Seat, 6 Legs, 34 In. 635.00
Bench, Louis XV Style, Marquetry, Ivory, Scrolled Arms, Lift Seat, 23 x 21 In. 560.00
Bench, Mahogany, Button-Tufted Seat, Cabriole Legs, c.1850, 17 1/2 x 42 x 17 In. 1116.00
Bench, Mahogany, Pink Velvet Upholstered, 20th Century, 37 x 45 3/4 In., Pair 150.00
Bench, Marble, Flowers, Chinese, 1900s, 11 3/4 x 22 x 11 1/2 In. 235.00

Bench, McCobb, No. 1306, Directional, Iron, c.1956, 15 x 20 x 20 In., Pair 1440.00
Bench, Meeting House, Green Paint, 1800s, 96 In. 330.00
Bench, Mission, Oak, Slat Side & Back, California, c.1910, 58 x 37 In. 645.00
Bench, Mustard Paint, Cutout Baseboards, 19th Century, 9 Ft. 110.00
Bench, Neoclassical, Mahogany, Ogee Seat Rail, Scroll Legs, Upholstered, 13 x 49 x 20 In. 2940.00
Bench, Olivier Mourgue, Djinn Series, Airborne International, c.1965, 16 x 50 x 24 In. 660.00
Bench, Open Back, 3 Horizontal Slats, Scroll Arms, France, 39 x 58 x 20 In. 920.00
Bench, Piano, Claw & Ball Feet, Turned Stretchers, c.1900, 19 x 40 In. 120.00
Bench, Pier, Edwardian, Beech, Carved, Celadon Paint, Upholstered, 1900 .... 1725.00
Bench, Pier, Louis XVI Style, Beech, Box Seat, Damask Upholstery, 23 3/4 In. 410.00
Bench, Pine, Blue Paint, Shaped Skirt, Slab Ends, Demilune Cutout Feet, 21 x 66 In. 329.00
Bench, Pine, Bucket, Red Paint, Arched Base Cutouts, Paneled Doors, 36 x 16 x 43 In. 980.00
Bench, Pine, Chamfered Arm Supports, Medallion Handrests, Plank Seat, 54 x 49 In. 575.00
Bench, Pine, Cutout Baseboards, Gray-Green Paint, 19th Century, 6 Ft. 4 In. 88.00
Bench, Pine, Mortised Construction, Red Paint, c.1830, 66 x 19 1/2 In. 2850.00
Bench, Pine, Painted, Plank Supports, Triangular Cutouts, 17 x 78 In. 450.00
Bench, Pine, Painted, Slab Sides, Demilune Ends, 2 Shelves, 46 3/4 x 39 x 12 1/2 In. 1675.00
Bench, Pine, Pegged Construction, Inset Panels, Lift Top Seat, Square Nails, 45 In. 1265.00
Bench, Pine, Red Wash, Scrubbed Top, Scalloped Aprons, Cyma Cutouts, 30 x 9 In. 290.00
Bench, Pine, Stained, Plank Top, Beaded Edge Apron, Hexagonal Legs, 16 x 82 x 10 In. 150.00
Bench, Queen Anne Style, Chinoiserie, 20th Century, 17 x 23 x 19 In. 825.00
Bench, Queen Anne Style, Walnut, Covered Seat, Cabriole Legs 299.00
Bench, R.E. Cahoon Jr., Deacon's, Fruit & Flowers, Mustard Ground, 73 In. 920.00
Bench, Regency Style, Elm, Scrolled Legs, Upholstered, 16 x 19 In., Pair 1410.00
Bench, Regency Style, Mahogany, Inlaid, Upholstered, Scrolled Arms, 28 x 32 In., Pair 940.00
Bench, Regency Style, Mahogany, Padded, Tufted Leather Upholstery, 21 x 48 x 23 In. 1760.00
Bench, Regency Style, Padded, Serpentine Top, Late 1800s, 19 x 39 x 17 In. 325.00
Bench, Rocker, Pine, Spindle Back, Scroll Arms, Front Rail, 29 x 54 In. 330.00
Bench, School, Oak & Pine, Mortise & Peg Construction, 99 x 14 x 33 1/2 In. 545.00
Bench, Serpentine Outline, Bracket Legs, c.1840, 13 x 40 In., Pair 1880.00
Bench, Splayed Legs, Pegged Mortise & Tenon, Chinese, 1700s, 22 1/2 x 49 1/2 In. 195.00
Bench, Stickley Bros., Oak, Slat Back, Upholstered, 38 x 50 x 21 In. 635.00
Bench, Upholstered, Tapered Legs, Dunbar, 27 x 28 x 11 In. 1415.00
Bench, Wagon Seat, Ladder Back, 34 x 18 x 32 1/2 In. 690.00
Bench, Walnut, Hand-Woven Cornhusk Seat, Stretcher Base, Metal Side Rails, 12 x 39 In. 430.00
Bench, Walnut, Lift Top, Early 1800s, 33 x 52 x 17 In. 777.00
Bench, Walnut, Sloping Slab Ends, 2 Hinged Doors, Pa., 1800s, 30 x 72 In. 329.00
Bench, Wicker, White Paint, Wood Top, Reeded Edge, Woven Frieze, 1900s, 19 x 69 In. 275.00
Bench, William IV Style, Mahogany, Suede Seat, 21 x 47 x 22 In., Pair 2230.00
Bench, Window, Cherry, Upholstered Seat, Saber Legs, c.1850, 12 x 38 x 23 In. 910.00
Bench, Windsor, Bamboo Turnings, Plank Seat, Early 1800s, 36 x 74 In. 2510.00
Bench, Windsor, Bow Back, Brown Paint, c.1920, 54 In., Pair 1495.00
Bench, Windsor, Mixed Wood, 25 Spindles, Scrolled Arms, 8 Legs, 33 x 102 In. 825.00
Bench, Windsor, Spindle Back, Green Stencil, B. Breidenbach, 32 x 60 x 14 In. 175.00
Bench, Windsor, Yellow Painted Decorations, Bamboo Turnings, 36 1/2 x 82 In. 4990.00
Bench, Wood, 2 Bears Hold Center Panel, Hiking Bear Panel, Swiss, c.1900, 9 x 18 In. 2840.00
Bench, Wood, Chrysanthemums, Dragons, Arms, Japan, Late 19th Century, 58 x 74 In. 1140.00
Bench, Wormley, Long-John, Walnut, Bentwood Hairpin Legs, Dunbar, 12 x 54 In. 1320.00
Bidet, Restauration, Mahogany, Porcelain Basin, Early 1800s, 32 x 12 x 20 In. 1058.00
Bin, Mixed Wood, Brown Wash, Bookjack Ends, Engraved Panel, 28 x 27 In. 315.00
Bin, Pine, Sloping Hinged Lid, 2 Compartments, 34 1/2 x 47 1/2 x 18 In. 450.00
Bin, William IV, Mahogany, Sloped Lid, Fluted Columns, Turned Feet, 39 x 24 In. 2465.00
Bookcase, Aesthetic Revival, Ebonized, Carved Frieze, c.1875, 68 1/2 x 33 x 16 In. 235.00
Bookcase, Art Deco, Asian Hardwoods, 60 x 33 x 15 In. ....645.00 to 760.00
Bookcase, Art Deco, Rosewood, Inlaid, France, c.1925, 40 x 10 x 44 In. 2075.00
Bookcase, Arts & Crafts, 2 Doors, Gallery Top, 8 Panes, Hammered Copper, 56 x 47 1/2 In. 5875.00
Bookcase, Arts & Crafts, Mullions, Backsplash, Shelves, 56 x 42 In. 999.00
Bookcase, Arts & Crafts, Oak, Dark Stain, Tapered Sides, 6 Shelves, 45 x 18 x 13 In. 259.00
Bookcase, Barrister, Ebonized Oak, Checker Inlay, England, Late 1800s, 81 x 35 In. 470.00
Bookcase, Biedermeier, Fruitwood, Ebonized Trim, 2 Glazed Doors, 72 x 50 In. 2230.00
Bookcase, Blue Paint, Blocked Cornice, Open Shelves, 2-Drawer Base, 73 x 53 In. 765.00

Furniture, Bookcase, G. Stickley, V-Shaped Pulls, Paper Label, 56 x 60 x 13 In.

Furniture, Bookcase, Globe-Wernicke, Oak, Stack, Early 20th Century, 10 x 34 In.

Bookcase, Cherry, Beaded Back Panels, Pullout Drawer, Doors, 6 Panes, 95 x 45 In. 5290.00
Bookcase, English Oak, 2 Doors, Early 20th Century, 73 x 43 1/2 x 17 3/4 In. 945.00
Bookcase, G. Nakashima, Walnut, c.1972, 48 x 36 x 12 In. 6600.00
Bookcase, G. Stickley, 2 Doors, 3 Shelves, 56 1/2 x 45 1/2 x 13 In. .... *ILLUS* 1880.00
Bookcase, G. Stickley, Oak, 2 12-Pane Doors, 56 x 60 x 13 In. 4945.00
Bookcase, G. Stickley, Open Door, 6 Shelves, Arched Toe Board, Columns, 48 x 58 In. 4115.00
Bookcase, G. Stickley, V-Shaped Pulls, Paper Label, 56 x 60 x 13 In. .... *ILLUS* 7638.00
Bookcase, George II Style, Mahogany, Early 20th Century, 47 x 60 x 13 In. 945.00
Bookcase, George III Style, Mahogany, Adjustable Shelves, c.1850, 94 x 135 In. 6460.00
Bookcase, George III Style, Mahogany, Cornice, Astragal Glazed Doors, 81 x 52 In. 3055.00
Bookcase, George III Style, Mahogany, Inlaid, Cylindrical, 1900s, 26 3/4 x 22 In. 325.00
Bookcase, George III, Mahogany, Drawer, Door, c.1790, 49 x 24 x 12 In. 3900.00
Bookcase, George III, Mahogany, Wooden Screws, Drawer, Bun Feet, 1800s, 23 x 23 In. 700.00
Bookcase, George IV, Rosewood, Brass Mounted, Parcel Gilt, c.1820, 38 x 30 In., Pair 7800.00
Bookcase, Georgian Style, Walnut, Oak, Glazed Door, Shell-Carved Cabriole Legs, 76 In. 645.00
Bookcase, Globe-Wernicke, Oak, Stack, Early 20th Century, 10 x 34 In. .... *ILLUS* 411.00
Bookcase, Grain Painted, Dovetailed Case, 3 Drawers, 48 x 42 x 10 In. 6325.00
Bookcase, John Shaw & Son, William IV, Mahogany, c.1835, 71 x 58 In. 7200.00
Bookcase, L. & J.G. Stickley, 2 Doors, 12 Glass Panes, 52 x 12 x 56 In. 6465.00
Bookcase, Lifetime, Door, 4 Shelves, Copper Hardware, 54 x 28 In. 1120.00
Bookcase, Lifetime, Oak, Glass Door, 4 Shelves, 59 x 31 In. 1380.00
Bookcase, Louis Philippe, Mahogany, Glazed Door, c.1850, 48 x 37 In., Pair 3525.00
Bookcase, Macey, Oak, Nut Brown Finish, 4-Stack, Paneled Ends, 63 x 52 In. 1440.00
Bookcase, Mahogany, 20th Century, 75 1/2 x 60 x 17 In. 472.00
Bookcase, Mahogany, 3 Doors, Carved Baluster Posts, Claw Feet, c.1910, 58 x 20 In. 1115.00
Bookcase, Mahogany, Crossbanded, 2 Doors, Shelves, Drawers, 83 1/2 x 48 x 21 In. 1060.00
Bookcase, Mahogany, Marquetry, Arched, Glazed Doors, Drawers, Dutch, 87x 65 In. 4115.00
Bookcase, Mahogany, Molded Cornice, Rosette Corners, 3 Glazed Doors, 59 x 73 In. 2470.00
Bookcase, Neoclassical, Rosewood, Gilt Decoration, Baltimore, c.1820, 91 x 76 In. 7050.00
Bookcase, Oak, 2 Doors, Glass Panes, Adjustable Shelves, 1920s, 78 x 48 In. 1450.00
Bookcase, Oak, 2 Doors, Scroll Carving, Claw Feet, 56 x 48 x 15 In. 546.00
Bookcase, Oak, 3 Doors, Adjustable Shelves, 55 x 59 x 12 1/2 In. 635.00
Bookcase, Oak, Leaf Carved, Flower Medallion, 2 Shelves, 46 x 42 x 13 1/2 In. 200.00
Bookcase, Pearson, 3-Stack, Oak, Leaded Glass Door, 47 x 34 x 13 In. 550.00
Bookcase, Regency Style, Mahogany, Projecting Center Section, 84 x 102 In. 2820.00
Bookcase, Regency Style, Pine, Shelves, Reeding, Lion Masks, Paw Feet, 42 x 58 In. 3055.00
Bookcase, Regency, Mahogany, 2 Doors, Applied Lead Grill Strapping, 51 x 42 In. 1527.00
Bookcase, Regency, Mahogany, Molded Cornice, 2 Doors, Brass Grills, 81 x 59 In. 3055.00
Bookcase, Renaissance Revival, Walnut, 2 Glass Doors, c.1880, 86 x 52 x 23 In. 1520.00
Bookcase, Revolving, Edwardian, Mahogany Inlay, Ogee Feet, c.1900, 31 x 20 In. 1435.00
Bookcase, Walnut, Ogee-Molded Cornice, Glazed Doors, c.1850, 88 x 57 x 13 In. 1175.00
Bookcase, William IV, 3 Arched Glazed Doors Over 3 Paneled Doors, 101 x 64 In. 4400.00
Bookcase-Cabinet, Empire, Ebonized Wood, Bronze Rosettes, 92 x 60 In. 7638.00
Bookcase-Cabinet, George II, Mahogany, c.1750, 100 x 43 x 23 In. 8400.00
Bookcase-Cabinet, L. & J.G. Stickley, Oak, c.1910, 55 x 54 x 12 In. 3840.00
Bookcase-Cabinet, Neoclassical, Mahogany, 4 Doors, 2 Drawers, Boston, c.1830, 83 x 54 In. 3230.00
Bookrack, Adjustable, Scalloped Edge, Red Paint, 1800s, 4 1/4 x 11 3/8 x 9 1/4 In. 740.00

Bookrack, G. Stickley, Extending, Posted & Slatted Ends, 6 x 12 1/2 In. 499.00
Bookrack, Moravian Walnut, Heart Cutout, Early 1800s, 8 x 17 1/4 In. 550.00
Bookrack, Pine, Painted, Mortised Top Shelf, Lyre Supports, Late 1700s, 31 x 26 In. 825.00
Bookstand, Arts & Crafts, Mahogany, Revolving, Early 1900s, 38 x 17 In. 560.00
Bookstand, Mahogany, Dish Top, Book Rest, Cast-Iron Base, Paw Feet, 49 x 15 In. 558.00
Bookstand, Mahogany, String Inlay, 4 Sections, Drawer, Brass Pull, 35 1/2 x 12 x 9 In. 330.00
Bookstand, Roycroft, Little Journeys, Oak, Through-Tenon Shelves, 26 x 26 x 14 In. . . . . . . .520.00 to 980.00
Bracket, Florentine, Gilt, 4 1/2 x 4 x 4 In., Pair 200.00
Bracket, Mahogany, Parcel Gilt, Arched Pediment, Beveled Glass, 18 In. 445.00
Breakfront, Black Lacquer, Chinoiserie, 3 Doors, 3 Drawers, 1900s, 73 x 46 In. 590.00
Breakfront, George III, Mahogany, Glazed Doors, 4 Drawers, c.1815, 92 x 90 In. 8225.00
Breakfront, James Mont, Pickled Oak Veneer, 3 Drawers, Glass Door, 1940s, 71 x 44 In. 1770.00
Breakfront, William & Mary Style, Burl Walnut, Crossbanded, 81 1/2 x 83 In. 4370.00
Breakfront-Bookcase, Edwardian, Mahogany, Domed Cornice, Glazed Door, 77 x 53 In. 2230.00
Breakfront-Bookcase, George III Style, Mahogany, Fluted Frieze, 101 x 170 x 17 In. 6170.00
Breakfront-Bookcase, George III, Mahogany, 3 Drawers, 8 Doors, c.1790, 94 x 84 In. 9400.00
Breakfront-Bookcase, Georgian Style, Pine, Painted, 3 Drawers, 8 Doors, 95 x 85 In. 1528.00
Breakfront-Bookcase, Victorian, Mahogany, Glazed & Paneled Doors, 76 x 65 In. 2115.00
Breakfront-Bookcase, William IV, Mahogany, 4 Glazed Doors, c.1830, 98 x 97 x 23 In. 7050.00
Buffet, 2 Paneled Doors, Crown Molding, Quebec, 1800s, 45 x 38 x 18 In. 1650.00
Buffet, 2 Parts, Marble Top, Mirror Back, 78 x 54 In. 550.00
Buffet, Frankl, Mahogany, Cork, 4 Drawers, 2 Doors, Johnson, 33 x 73 x 21 In. 2830.00
Buffet, French Provincial Style, Cherry, Parquetry, Scalloped Top, 1900s, 40 x 54 In. 120.00
Buffet, French Provincial, Mixed Wood, Drawers, 2 Doors, Shelves, 46 x 48 x 14 In. 1770.00
Buffet, French Provincial, Oak, Shaped Cornice, Panel Doors, Pie Shelf, 91 x 20 In. 712.00
Buffet, G. Nelson, Rosewood, Herman Miller, c.1956, 34 x 19 x 47 In. 4440.00
Buffet, Karl Springer, 4 Doors, Lacquered Goatskin, 1950s, 34 x 72 x 18 In. 5015.00
Buffet, Kurt Ostervig, Rosewood, 4 Sliding Doors, Denmark, 1970s, 43 x 89 x 18 In. 2830.00
Buffet, Louis XV Style, Fruitwood, 2 Drawers, 2 Doors, c.1865, 44 x 53 In. 2585.00
Buffet, Louis XV Style, Fruitwood, Frieze Drawers, Cupboard Doors, 53 x 24 In. 3525.00
Buffet, Louis XV Style, Fruitwood, Mid 19th Century, 41 x 54 x 24 In. 3995.00
Buffet, Louis XV Style, Oak, Cornice, 2 Parts, 1800s, 88 x 54 x 20 In. 5170.00
Buffet, Louis XV Style, Pine, 4 Doors, 2 Parts, 98 x 49 In. 580.00
Buffet, Louis XV Style, Pine, 4 Doors, 2 Parts, c.1890, 95 x 55 In. 2820.00
Buffet, Louis XV Style, Polychrome, 2 Drawers, 3 Doors, c.1890, 42 x 67 In. 2000.00
Buffet, Oak, Carved Crest, Claw Feet, c.1915, 58 x 50 x 23 In. 520.00
Buffet, Pine, Rectangular, Scalloped Shelf, Drawers, Glass Pulls, 44 x 49 x 20 In. 470.00
Buffet, Renaissance Revival, Oak, Carved, Continental, 91 x 69 x 27 In. 710.00
Buffet, Rosewood, 4 Sliding Doors, Dowel Legs, Scandinavia, 47 x 71 x 18 In. 1298.00
Bureau, Chippendale, Birch, Cherry, 4 Drawers, Flat Bracket Base, 35 x 40 x 19 In. 1840.00
Bureau, Chippendale, Mahogany, 4 Drawers, Slant Front, Bracket Base, 41 In. 360.00
Bureau, Chippendale, Slant Front, Birch, 4 Drawers, Conn., c.1780, 43 x 38 x 21 In. 4400.00
Bureau, Chippendale, Walnut Veneer, Serpentine Front, 4 Drawers, 37 x 42 In. 7475.00
Bureau, Cottage, Pine, 4 Drawers, Fruit Shape Pulls, 1800s, 34 x 39 x 17 In. 90.00
Bureau, Cottage, Victorian, 3 Drawers, Oxbow Front, Chamfered Corners, 36 x 44 In. 115.00
Bureau, Drop Front, Lock, Key, 3 Drawers, Continental, 19 x 38 In. 1140.00
Bureau, Federal, Cherry Inlay, 4 Graduated Drawers, c.1810, 41 x 41 In. 2000.00
Bureau, Federal, Cherry, Bird's-Eye Maple Veneer, Bowfront, c.1810-15, 41 x 42 In. 3525.00
Bureau, Federal, Cherry, Inlaid, Swell Front, 4 Drawers, Vermont, c.1790, 35 x 40 In. 1880.00
Bureau, Federal, Cherry, Wavy Birch Veneer, 4 Graduated Drawers, c.1820, 40 x 41 In. 825.00
Bureau, Federal, Mahogany String Inlay, Bowfront, 4 Drawers, 39 x 41 In. 2350.00
Bureau, Grain Painted, 3 Drawers, 29 3/4 x 35 1/2 x 15 3/4 In. 330.00
Bureau, Hepplewhite, Birch, Tiger Maple Band, 4 Drawers, New England, 37 x 37 In. 1320.00
Bureau, Hepplewhite, Cherry, Bowfront, 4 Drawers, 1800s, 31 3/4 x 39 3/4 In. 1980.00
Bureau, Hepplewhite, Mahogany, Cherry, 4 Drawers, French Feet, 33 x 39 x 18 In. 3450.00
Bureau, Painted, Putti, Scrolls, Slant Front, Fitted Interior, Italy, 39 x 40 In. 1645.00
Bureau, Renaissance Revival, Rosewood, 2 Sections, Arched Mirror, 84 x 49 In. 3760.00
Bureau, Sheraton, Bowfront, 6 Drawers, Splashboard, c.1820, 45 x 19 In. 1495.00
Bureau, Sheraton, Mahogany Veneers, Brass Pulls, 4 Drawers, 42 x 52 x 19 In. 460.00
Bureau, Sheraton, Mahogany, Bowfront, 4 Drawers, 37 x 42 3/4 x 22 In. 1705.00
Bureau-Bookcase, Federal, Cherry, 2 Parts, Drawers, Doors, c.1810, 81 x 41 x 19 In. 2300.00

Bureau-Bookcase, George III, Mahogany Inlay, Maple Veneer, 90 x 43 x 22 In. 2350.00
Bureau-Bookcase, George III, Mahogany, Drawer, 4 Doors, c.1780, 98 x 49 In. 11750.00
Bureau-Bookcase, George III, Mahogany, Slant Front, 4 Drawers, 87 x 45 In. 2585.00
Bureau-Bookcase, Georgian, Herringbone, Crossbanded, Slant Front, 1700s, 76 x 35 In. 3820.00
Cabinet, Aesthetic Revival, Gilt, Ebonized, Mirror, 4 Doors, Shakespeare, Byron, 57 x 58 In. 1998.00
Cabinet, Art Nouveau, Oak, Walnut, 4 Doors, 2 Drawers, 2 Parts, 90 x 55 In. 1610.00
Cabinet, Arts & Crafts, Oak, 2 Doors, Leaded, Stained Glass, 2 Drawers, 40 x 14 x 53 In. 470.00
Cabinet, Arts & Crafts, Oak, Applied Backsplash, Window Grates, c.1920, 61 x 42 In. 550.00
Cabinet, Baroque, Walnut, Drawers, Doors, Continental, 50 1/2 x 46 1/2 x 20 In. 1880.00
Cabinet, Biedermeier, Mahogany, Urn Shape, 2 Doors, Turned Base, 28 x 18 In., Pair 1530.00
Cabinet, Black Lacquer, 2 Small Over Large Drawer, Shelf, Chinese, 31 x 26 In., Pair 765.00
Cabinet, Black Lacquer, Graduated, 2-Paneled Doors, Block Feet, 47 x 28 x 17 In. 590.00
Cabinet, Black Lacquered Sides & Base, Double Door, Shelves, Mongolia, 65 x 19 In. 230.00
Cabinet, Black Wood, Dragon Crest, Prunus, Bird, Doors, Chinese, 59 x 30 In. 4600.00
Cabinet, Bread, Louis XV Style, Oak, Fruitwood, Spindles, Carved, 35 x 34 In. 3290.00
Cabinet, Brown Lacquer, 2 Drawers, 2 Doors, Shelf, Chinese, 39 x 42 x 20 In. 649.00
Cabinet, Butler's, Federal, Mahogany, Inlaid, Drawer, 2 Doors, c.1835, 44 x 42 x 22 In. 1645.00
Cabinet, China, Art Deco, Asian Hardwoods, Waterfall, 2 Glazed Doors, 66 x 33 In. 820.00
Cabinet, China, Edwardian, Mahogany, 3 Doors, Reeded Columns, c.1910, 60 x 66 In. 2225.00
Cabinet, China, G. Stickley, Gallery Top, 16-Pane Door, 3 Shelves, 58 x 35 x 13 In. 5875.00
Cabinet, China, Glass & Paneled Doors, Corbels, Northern Furniture, 63 x 44 In. 1880.00
Cabinet, China, L. & J.G. Stickley, 2 Doors, Mullions, Hardware, 44 x 17 x 62 In. 3525.00
Cabinet, China, Limbert, Door, 3 Adjustable Shelves, 24 x 15 x 57 In. 3525.00
Cabinet, China, Oak, Glass, Cornucopia Crest, 67 x 52 x 19 In. 3050.00
Cabinet, China, Victorian, Oak, Drawer, Curved Glass, 68 x 36 In. .... *ILLUS* 1116.00
Cabinet, Corner, Cherry, Glass Door, 2 Paneled Doors, 1800s, 82 x 40 x 22 In. 3400.00
Cabinet, Corner, Eastlake, Ebonized, Paneled Door, Shelf, Columns, 43 1/2 x 36 In. 470.00
Cabinet, Corner, Ebony, Beveled Glass, Mirror Back, 69 x 26 In. 600.00
Cabinet, Corner, Empire Revival, Mahogany, Gilt Bronze, Drawer, Door, 57 x 44 x 24 In. 650.00
Cabinet, Corner, Empire, Mahogany, Marble Top, Frieze Drawer, Cupboard, 43 x 33 In. 2820.00
Cabinet, Corner, Federal, Walnut Inlay, Glazed Door, Shelves, 78 1/4 x 44 x 29 In. 2006.00
Cabinet, Corner, Fruitwood, Marquetry, 4 Doors, 2 Parts, Dutch, 1800s, 89 x 47 x 24 In. 3290.00
Cabinet, Corner, George III Style, Mahogany, Broken Pediment, 70 x 27 In., Pair 646.00
Cabinet, Corner, George III Style, Mahogany, Glazed Door, Paneled Door, 92 In. 1410.00
Cabinet, Corner, Hanging, Cherry, 2 Shelves, Beveled Cornice, 37 x 43 1/2 In. 2185.00
Cabinet, Corner, Hanging, George III Style, Mahogany, Door, 42 x 28 In. 235.00
Cabinet, Corner, Hanging, George III, Mahogany, Acorn & Shell Inlay, 2 Doors, 41 In. 587.00
Cabinet, Corner, Hanging, George Iii, Oak, 2 3-Paneled Doors, Early 1800s, 41 x 42 In. 646.00
Cabinet, Corner, Hanging, Gothic Revival, Oak, Paneled Door, Tracery, 44 x 36 In. 590.00
Cabinet, Corner, Hanging, Pine, 2 Shelves, Glass Door, Grain & Blue Paint, 1800s, 32 In. 110.00
Cabinet, Corner, Louis Philippe, Mahogany, Marble, Triangular, c.1850, 36 x 27 In., Pair 2233.00
Cabinet, Corner, Pine, 2 10-Pane Doors, 2 Paneled Doors, c.1800, 85 x 48 In. 2832.00
Cabinet, Corner, Pine, Dentil Molding, Glazed Door, Paneled Door, 1800s, 80 x 33 In. 1610.00
Cabinet, Corner, Pine, Molded Cornice, 3 Scalloped Shelves, Early 1800s, 49 x 33 In. 325.00
Cabinet, Corner, Regency, Mahogany, Bowfront, Glazed Doors, c.1815, 48 x 30 In. 1527.00
Cabinet, Corner, Walnut, Inlaid, Glazed Door, 2 Paneled Doors, Pa., c.1800, 95 x 44 In. 3885.00
Cabinet, Curly Maple, Pine, Molded Cornice, 2-Paneled Raised Door, 23 x 16 In. 575.00
Cabinet, Display, Art Deco, Mahogany, England, 49 x 10 x 42 In. 152.00
Cabinet, Display, Art Deco, Walnut, 46 x 13 x 45 In. 176.00
Cabinet, Display, Edwardian, Mahogany, Carved, 2 Tall Compartments, Glass Shelves 1045.00
Cabinet, Display, George III Style, Mahogany, 1900s, 101 x 55 x 16 In. 4406.00
Cabinet, Display, George III, Mahogany, Glazed Doors, Shelves, Cornice, 69 x 24 In. 619.00
Cabinet, Display, Louis XV Style, Mahogany, Ormolu, Glass Door, 1800s, 54 x 26 In. 750.00
Cabinet, Display, Mahogany, Glass, Velvet Backing, Tapered Base, 68 x 37 1/2 In. 825.00
Cabinet, Display, Mahogany, Marquetry, 64 1/2 x 25 1/4 x 17 In. 920.00
Cabinet, Display, Mahogany, Molded Top, 2 Glazed Doors, Tapered Legs, 53 x 56 x 13 In. 470.00
Cabinet, Display, Neoclassical, Brass Mounted, Glass Door, Russia, 49 x 27 x 11 In. 2820.00
Cabinet, Display, Rosewood, Chinese, 1800s, 82 x 32 3/4 x 14 1/4 In. 3525.00
Cabinet, Document, Oak, 12 Drawers, Iron Pulls, c.1900, 65 x 26 x 20 In. 645.00
Cabinet, Ebonized, Ormolu Mounted, Boulle, Marble Top, Door, Lock, Key, 42 x 29 In. 1265.00
Cabinet, Edwardian, Mahogany, 2 Doors, Applied Swag & Flags, c.1900, 49 x 50 In. 3055.00

Cabinet, Edwardian, Mahogany, Green Marble Top, Side Cupboards, 36 x 54 In. 3290.00
Cabinet, Elm, 3 Drawers, Tiger Stripe, Chinese, 65 x 20 In. 660.00
Cabinet, Elm, Lacquered, Doors, Shelves, Drawers, Chinese, 65 x 31 x 15 In. 2125.00
Cabinet, Elm, Red Lacquer, Doors, Drawers, Shelves, Chinese, 68 1/2 x 41 1/2 x 20 In. 825.00
Cabinet, Empire, Fruitwood, Demilune Shape, 2 Doors, Drawer, 72 x 32 In. 295.00
Cabinet, Federal, Mahogany, Drawer, Door, Tapered Legs, Early 1800s, 31 x 18 3/4 In. 470.00
Cabinet, French Provincial, Cherry, Marble Top, 28 x 49 x 36 In., Pair 590.00
Cabinet, French Provincial, Fruitwood, 4 Shelves, 2 Drawers, 2 Doors, c.1890, 84 x 55 In. 2585.00
Cabinet, French Provincial, Oak, Inlaid, Marble Top, 2 Doors, Early 1800s, 33 x 27 In. 368.00
Cabinet, Fruitwood, Maple Marquetry, Rosewood Parquetry, 36 1/2 x 35 In. 2585.00
Cabinet, Fruitwood, Marquetry, Glass Shelves, 3 Drawers, 1700s, 73 x 36 x 25 In. 5290.00
Cabinet, G. Nakashima, Kornblut, Walnut, Rosewood, Sliding Doors, 22 x 18 In. 10800.00
Cabinet, George III Style, Mahogany, Stepped Cornice, Cupboards, 84 x 21 x 86 In. 1335.00
Cabinet, George III, Mahogany, Inlaid, 2 Doors, c.1780, 36 x 52 x 23 In. 9000.00
Cabinet, George III, Mahogany, Inlaid, Drawers, Tapered Supports, 15 In., Pair 2000.00
Cabinet, Georgian Style, Mahogany, Limed, Painted, 2 Doors, 1900s, 88 x 39 x 14 In. 1120.00
Cabinet, Georgian Style, Walnut Veneer, 2 Doors, 3 Drawers, 77 3/4 x 44 x 21 1/2 In. 649.00
Cabinet, Georgian, Mahogany, Veneer, Glazed, Bracket Base, c.1800, 85 x 45 x 12 In. 4585.00
Cabinet, Georgian, Mahogany, Veneer, Glazed, c.1765, 91 x 47 x 14 In. 7050.00
Cabinet, Gilt Flowers, Mountain, Figures, Mortised, 2 Doors, Chinese, 25 x 20 x 12 In. 460.00
Cabinet, Gun, Oak, Glazed Door, 2 Paneled Doors, England, c.1890, 88 x 38 In. 1880.00
Cabinet, Hanging, Black Walnut, 18 3/4 x 13 1/2 x 2 1/2 In. 140.00
Cabinet, Hanging, Black, Japanned, Arched Gallery, Mt. Fuji, Wisteria Vines, 28 x 19 In. 499.00
Cabinet, Hanging, French Provincial, Fruitwood, Leaf Scroll, Glazed Door, 23 x 18 In. 146.00
Cabinet, Hanging, George III Style, Mahogany, Arched Cornice, Glazed Door, 24 In. 410.00
Cabinet, Hanging, Italian Baroque, Walnut, Portrait Doors, 30 x 38 In. 3190.00
Cabinet, Hanging, Napoleon III, Inlaid, Ebonized, D-End Top, Late 1800s, 23 x 24 In. 325.00
Cabinet, Hanging, Oak, Raised Panel Door, Molded Top, 2 Shelves, 27 1/4 x 21 1/2 x 7 In. 250.00
Cabinet, Hanging, Pine, 3-Paneled Door, Upholstered Interior, Light, 33 x 26 x 8 In. 236.00
Cabinet, Hardwood, Scroll Brackets, 4 Drawers, 6 Doors, Chinese, 39 x 100 x 21 In. 1530.00
Cabinet, Knoll, Rosewood, Marble Top, 5 Drawers, Chrome Base, 26 x 37 x 18 In. 1890.00
Cabinet, Lacquered, Flowers, 2 Doors, Shelves, Drawers, Chinese, 64 1/2 x 42 x 18 In. 1060.00
Cabinet, Lacquered, Multicolored, 4 Doors, Shelf, 2 Parts, Chinese, 34 x 50 x 16 1/2 In. 590.00
Cabinet, Library, William IV, Mahogany, Glazed Doors, Paneled Doors, 89 x 73 In. 4115.00
Cabinet, Liquor, Oak Case, Fancy Trim, Cut Glass Decanters, 15 x 15 In. 605.00
Cabinet, Louis XIV, Oak, Carved, Paneled, 3 Doors, c.1715, 85 x 48 x 21 In. 3450.00
Cabinet, Louis XV Style, Kingwood, Marble Top, Ormolu, Late 1800s, 38 x 20 In. 1290.00
Cabinet, Louis XVI Style, Mahogany, Marble, 2 Drawers, Doors, c.1890, 39 x 48 In. 2585.00
Cabinet, Louis XVI Style, Satinwood, Rosewood, Mahogany Inlay, 67 x 52 In. 715.00
Cabinet, Map Collector's, Drop Front, Walnut, Mahogany, Parcel Gilt, 59 x 42 In. 12335.00
Cabinet, Metal, White Enamel, Drawer, 2 Doors, Rounded Front, 32 x 31 In., Pair 315.00
Cabinet, Mixed Wood, Diamond Band Inlay, Door, Glass Panels, Shelf, 16 x 9 x 15 In. 115.00
Cabinet, Multicolored, Flower, Vases, 2 Doors, Shelf, Mongolia, 39 x 28 x 15 In., Pair 590.00
Cabinet, Music, Aesthetic Revival, Ebonized, Gilt Incised, Musicians, England, c.1890, 44 x 24 In. 1595.00
Cabinet, Music, Eastlake, Ebonized, Parcel Gilt, 4 Shelves, c.1875, 60 x 21 1/2 In. 588.00
Cabinet, Music, Louis XVI Style, Rosewood, Ormolu Mount, Early 1900s, 62 x 51 In. 2585.00
Cabinet, Music, Mahogany, Veneer, Marquetry, Instruments, Urn, 22 x 15 x 35 1/2 In. 920.00
Cabinet, Music, Neoclassical, Mahogany, 2-Paneled Doors, Brass Handles, 29 x 32 In. 2115.00
Cabinet, Music, Rococo Revival, Rosewood, Mirror, Fruit, Acorns, N.Y., 65 x 30 x 20 In. 4995.00
Cabinet, Napoleon III Style, Black Lacquer, Doors, Shelves, Sevres Plaque, 41 x 66 In. 1116.00
Cabinet, Napoleon III, Ebonized, Ormolu Mounted, Brass, c.1885, 46 x 50 x 20 In. 4800.00
Cabinet, Neoclassical, Cherry, Paneled Doors, Kentucky, c.1840, 93 x 61 x 22 In. 5580.00
Cabinet, Neoclassical, Mahogany, Canted Cornice, Drawers, Doors, Dutch, 80 x 62 In. 8815.00
Cabinet, Oak, 25 Drawers, Lock, 62 x 20 x 16 In. 995.00
Cabinet, P. Evans, Metal Patchwork, Cityscape, 2 Doors, Drawer, 36 x 36 x 20 In. 2125.00
Cabinet, Painted, Basket Of Flowers, Paneled Door, Wrought-Iron Hinges, 26 x 19 In. 259.00
Cabinet, Pine, Drawer, 2 Doors, England, Early 1800s, 48 x 51 x 21 In. 1180.00
Cabinet, Pine, Molded Cornice, Paneled Doors, England, c.1810, 48 x 81 In. 645.00
Cabinet, Polychrome Painted, Continental, 1800s, 37 1/2 x 26 1/2 x 21 1/2 In. 180.00
Cabinet, Polychrome, Domed, Serpentine, Florence, c.1850, 81 x 98 In. 3525.00
Cabinet, Print, Eastlake, Ebonized, Flower Baskets, Handle, Splayed Base, 30 x 23 In. 999.00

Cabinet, Red Lacquer, 2 Doors, 2 Drawers, Shelf, Chinese, 73 x 44 x 31 In. 765.00
Cabinet, Renaissance Revival, Walnut, Drawers, Doors, Italy, 40 x 56 x 28 In., Pair 9990.00
Cabinet, Restauration, Mahogany, Mirrored Doors, 5 Drawers, c.1830, 87 x 54 In. 1765.00
Cabinet, Rococo Revival, Walnut, Drawer, Doors, Philadelphia, c.1850, 44 x 49 x 21 In. 4406.00
Cabinet, Rosewood, 2 Doors, Flat Top, Brass Line Inlay, 34 1/2 x 35 3/4 x 10 3/4 In. 635.00
Cabinet, Rosewood, Green Marble Top, 2 Drawers, 2 Doors, Raised Scrolls, 35 x 53 In. 1295.00
Cabinet, Scholar's, Elm, Fretwork, Carved Doors, Chinese, 76 x 48 x 22 In. 500.00
Cabinet, Secretary, George III, Mahogany, Glazed Doors, Interior Shelves, 82 x 46 In. 306.00
Cabinet, Spice, Chippendale, Cherry, Poplar, Raised Panel Door, 4 Drawers, 20 x 32 In. 575.00
Cabinet, Spice, Chippendale, Figured, Walnut, Pa., c.1780, 22 1/2 x 21 In. 6000.00
Cabinet, Spice, Figured Maple Fronts, 14 Drawers, 17 x 8 x 15 In. 800.00
Cabinet, Spice, Pine, 13 Drawers, Numbers On Drawers, Knobs, 18 1/2 x 6 3/8 x 15 In. 1265.00
Cabinet, Spice, Poplar, Pine, 22 Drawers, Dovetailed, Pennsylvania, c.1845, 26 x 16 In. 5800.00
Cabinet, Spice, Walnut, Paneled Drawers, Reeded Stiles, c.1850, 19 x 17 In. 410.00
Cabinet, Stepped, Burled Veneer, Doors, Bulbous Legs, Modernage, 36 x 48 In. 2360.00
Cabinet, Sycamore, Beech, Pine, Red Paint, 8 Drawers, Wooden Pulls, 18 x 14 x 10 In. 410.00
Cabinet, Tea Utensils, Sliding Doors, 5 Drawers, Japan, 19th Century, 38 x 31 x 13 In. 175.00
Cabinet, Teak, Locking Upper Well, 2 Bottom Doors, Chinese, c.1885, 36 x 28 In. 499.00
Cabinet, Vernis Martin, Gilt, Half Moon, Flat Back, 3 Shelves, 4 Carved Legs, 53 In. 1438.00
Cabinet, Vernis Martin, Gilt, Kidney Shape, Flat Back, 3 Pastoral Scenes, 58 In. 805.00
Cabinet, Victorian, Bamboo, Lacquered, Beveled Mirror, 1800s, 57 1/2 x 27 x 14 In. 1115.00
Cabinet, Victorian, Bowfront, Oak, Curved Glass, Turned Columns, Drawer, 67 x 37 In. 999.00
Cabinet, Victorian, Marble Top, Doors, Shelf, Late 1800s, 31 x 36 x 16 In. 720.00
Cabinet, Victorian, Walnut, Marble Top, Door, Oval Mirror, Drawer, 41 x 29 x 18 In. 980.00
Cabinet, Walnut, Lacquered, 2 Doors, Shelves, Dragon Openwork, Chinese, 34 x 32 In. 530.00
Cabinet, Walnut, Poplar, Molded Cornice, Base, Glass Door, 23 x 8 1/2 x 26 In. 690.00
Cabinet, Wedding, 4 Doors, Grill Work, 3 Drawers, Chinese, 1800s, 78 x 45 In. 660.00
Cabinet, William & Mary Style, Mahogany, Pullout Shelves, 34 x 24 x 15 1/2 In. 235.00
Cabinet, William IV, Mahogany, Molded Cornice, 3 Doors, 75 x 73 x 16 In. 3290.00
Cabinet, Wood, Brass, 2 Sections, 4 Drawers, 2 Doors, Korea, 45 1/2 x 28 1/4 x 13 In. 720.00
Cabinet, Wood, Flowers, Dragons, 2 Drawers, Shelves, Japan, Late 1800s, 90 x 43 In. 2300.00
Cabinet, Wood, Polychrome, Flowers, 2 Drawers, 2 Doors, Mongolia, c.1860, 33 x 26 In. 856.00
Cabinet, Wormley, Cane Sliding Doors, Dunbar, c.1948, 32 x 40 x 13 In. 540.00
Cabinet-On-Case, Continental, 2 Drawers, Door, Carved Flowers, 30 x 10 x 37 In. 1638.00
Cabinet-On-Stand, Black & Gold Lacquer, Chinese Pavilion Decoration, 59 x 31 In. 3290.00
Cabinet-On-Stand, Flemish Style, 2 Doors, Cherub, Spiral Columns, 1658, 65 x 22 In. 2245.00
Cabinet-On-Stand, Queen Anne Style, Black Lacquer, Bowfront, c.1790, 75 x 23 In. 1290.00
Cabinet-On-Stand, Queen Anne Style, Chinoiserie, 2 Doors, Early 1900s, 46 x 46 In. 945.00
Cabinet-On-Stand, Walnut, Multicolored, Birds, Branches, 2 Doors, Chinese, 41 x 32 x 18 In. 470.00
Cabinet-On-Stand, William & Mary, Walnut, Glazed Doors, Drawers, 56 x 39 x 16 In. 1880.00
Candlemold Stand, Pine, 24 Pewter Tubes, Early 19th Century, 19 x 19 1/2 In. 1116.00
Candlestand, Baroque Style, Mixed Wood, Tapestry Cover, 1800s, 29 1/4 x 15 In. 472.00
Candlestand, Black Lacquer, Flowers, Birds, Gold Leaf, Tilt Top, Center Post, 3 Legs, 26 x 20 In. 720.00
Candlestand, Checkerboard Tilt Top, Pedestal, Iron Base, 1800s, 29 x 24 In. 2070.00
Candlestand, Cherry Stain, Molded Rim, Ring Turned, Swelled Pedestal, 29 x 17 In. 1058.00
Candlestand, Cherry, Octagonal Top, Birdcage, Turned Post, 3 Snake Feet, 25 x 20 x 15 In. 115.00
Candlestand, Cherry, Octagonal Top, Spider Legs, 28 1/2 x 22 1/2 x 14 1/4 In. 430.00
Candlestand, Cherry, Oval Top, Inlaid Border, Turned Pedestal, Snake Feet, 29 x 27 x 18 In. 748.00
Candlestand, Cherry, Oval Top, Vase-Turned Pedestal, Spider Legs, Spade Feet, 28 x 23 In. 1035.00
Candlestand, Cherry, Round Tilt Top, Tripod Base, New England, 28 x 20 In. 1095.00
Candlestand, Cherry, Round Top, Bulbous Vase, Turned Support, Tripod Cabriole Legs, 26 x 15 In. 530.00
Candlestand, Cherry, Vase & Ring Turned Support, Tripod Base, 26 x 17 In. 1116.00
Candlestand, Chippendale, Maple, Notched-Corner Top, Cabriole Legs, 17 x 16 In. 1450.00
Candlestand, Chippendale, Walnut, Tilt Dish Top, Birdcage Platform, 29 x 19 In. 1175.00
Candlestand, Colonial Style, Mahogany, Gateleg Base, c.1920, 24 x 24 x 18 In. 200.00
Candlestand, Colonial Style, Oak, Oval Top, Square Post, Chamfered Corners, 27 x 16 In. 115.00
Candlestand, Country, X-Base, 23 1/2 x 14 In. 1780.00
Candlestand, Federal, Cherry, Canted Corners, Baluster-Turned Legs, 29 In. 239.00
Candlestand, Federal, Cherry, Carved, Dish Top, Tripod Cabriole Leg, 27 x 16 3/4 In. 4115.00
Candlestand, Federal, Cherry, Carved, Inlay, Tilt Top, Tripod Base, c.1800, 27 x 14 In. 1295.00
Candlestand, Federal, Cherry, Oblong Top, Vase & Ring Turned Support, 27 x 20 In. 382.00

Furniture, Cabinet, China, Victorian, Oak, Drawer, Curved Glass, 68 x 36 In.

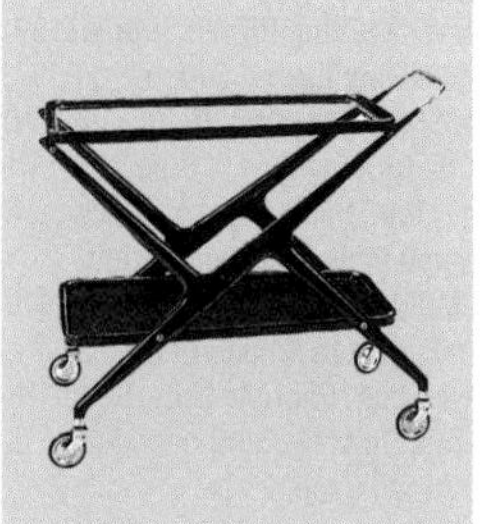
Furniture, Cart, Serving, Aldo Tura, Walnut, Brass Handles, Signed, 29 x 34 x 16 In.

Furniture, Cart, Serving, McCobb, Bleached Mahogany, Carrara Glass Top, 29 x 36 x 19 In.

Candlestand, Federal, Cherry, Octagonal Top, Urn & Ring Turned Support, 28 x 23 x 16 In. 470.00
Candlestand, Federal, Cherry, Oval Tilt Top, c.1800, 28 x 17 x 24 In. 1380.00
Candlestand, Federal, Cherry, Serpentine Top, Ring Turned Support, 27 x 17 x 17 In. 646.00
Candlestand, Federal, Cherry, Shaped, Tilt Top, Tripod Base, Early 1800s, 28 x 24 In. 410.00
Candlestand, Federal, Cherry, Shaped, Tilt Top, Turned Support, 1800s, 28 x 16 In. 705.00
Candlestand, Federal, Cherry, Tilt Top, Shaped Corners, 29 1/4 x 20 In. 290.00
Candlestand, Federal, Cherry, Tilt Top, Vase, Ring Turned Support, Tripod, 26 x 26 x 18 In. 411.00
Candlestand, Federal, Cherry, Vase & Ring Support, Tripod Scroll Leg, 28 x 17 3/4 In. 558.00
Candlestand, Federal, Cherry, Vase & Ring Turned Support, Tripod Base, 29 x 16 In. 765.00
Candlestand, Federal, Cut-Corner Top, Turned Post, 3 Legs, 28 x 20 x 18 In. 230.00
Candlestand, Federal, Mahogany, Cherry Inlay, Vase & Ring Turned Support, 26 x 17 In. 1745.00
Candlestand, Federal, Mahogany, Cherry, Carved, Tilt Top, Tripod Base, 27 x 16 In. 325.00
Candlestand, Federal, Mahogany, Cherry, Rectangular Tilt Top, c.1800, 28 x 21 In. 600.00
Candlestand, Federal, Mahogany, Oval Tilt Top, Tripod Snake Feet, c.1790, 29 x 26 In. 1765.00
Candlestand, Federal, Mahogany, Reeded Edge, Oval, 1800s, 29 x 24 x 16 In. 235.00
Candlestand, Federal, Mahogany, Round, Reeded, Arched Tripod Feet, 29 x 17 In. 175.00
Candlestand, Federal, Mahogany, Shaped Tilt Top, Spider Legs, 29 x 18 x 23 In. 275.00
Candlestand, Federal, Maple, Oval Tilt Top, Turned, Tripod, c.1810, 31 x 12 1/2 In. 325.00
Candlestand, Federal, Walnut, Shaped Top, Arched Spider Legs, 27 x 22 In. 210.00
Candlestand, George III, Mahogany, Serpentine Top, Molded Edge, 25 x 22 x 19 3/4 In. 290.00
Candlestand, Grain Painted, Round Top, Tripod Base, c.1840, 26 x 11 In. 1155.00
Candlestand, Hepplewhite, Cherry, Mahogany, Turned Pedestal, 30 x 16 In. 316.00
Candlestand, Hepplewhite, Cherry, Tilt Top, Pedestal, 3 Arched Legs, c.1800, 32 x 24 In. 575.00
Candlestand, Hepplewhite, Mahogany, Octagonal Top, Spider Legs, Spade Feet, 20 x 13 In. 220.00
Candlestand, Lamp, Iron, 2-Candle, Adjustable, 54 3/4 In. 290.00
Candlestand, Mahogany, Tilt Top, Canted Corners, Reeded Baluster, 31 x 16 In. 120.00
Candlestand, Mahogany, Tilt Top, Vase-Turned Pedestal, Splayed Legs, 28 x 18 x 22 In. 430.00
Candlestand, Maple, Cherry, Round Dish Top, Turned Post, Cabriole Legs, 24 x 15 In. 2585.00
Candlestand, Maple, Tiger Maple, 30 x 22 x 16 In. 375.00
Candlestand, Neoclassical, Mahogany, Carved, Turned Post, c.1825, 26 x 12 1/2 In. 175.00
Candlestand, Neoclassical, Tiger Maple, Oval Chamfered Top, Tripod Base, 27 x 21 In. 645.00
Candlestand, Oak, Twin Candle Arm, Octagonal Base, 3 Legs, c.1800, 31 In. 450.00
Candlestand, Painted, Faux Marble Top, Drawer, Tripod Base, 1800s, 27 x 16 In. 4700.00
Candlestand, Painted, Shaped Top, Cross Shoe Foot Base, c.1800, 28 3/4 x 11 1/2 In. 1650.00
Candlestand, Pine, Turned Post, 3 Curved Legs, 19th Century, 28 x 19 In. 59.00
Candlestand, Queen Anne Style, Mahogany, Fluted Column, 3-Footed, 40 1/2 x 10 In. 165.00
Candlestand, Queen Anne, Cherry, Round Checkerboard Top, Tripod Legs, 27 x 18 In. 1058.00
Candlestand, Queen Anne, Cherry, Square Top, Ring Turned Post, Tripod Base, 27 x 15 In. 1528.00
Candlestand, Queen Anne, Cherry, Urn Turned Shaft, 3 Arched Legs, 27 x 17 In. 460.00
Candlestand, Queen Anne, Mahogany, Dish Tilt Top, Cabriole Legs, 28 x 20 In. 880.00
Candlestand, Queen Anne, Mahogany, Dish Top, Spiral Shaft, 28 1/2 x 24 In. 1295.00
Candlestand, Queen Anne, Mahogany, Shaped Top, Turned Pedestal, 27 x 18 x 18 In. 489.00
Candlestand, Queen Anne, Mahogany, Square Tilt Top, Serpentine, 27 x 19 x 19 In. 1670.00
Candlestand, Queen Anne, Mahogany, Tilt Top, Serpentine, Pedestal, c.1790, 28 x 18 In. 3105.00

Candlestand, Queen Anne, Mahogany, Tilt Top, Tripod Cabriole Base, 28 x 21 1/2 In. 590.00
Candlestand, Queen Anne, Mahogany, Vase & Ring Turned Support, 27 x 16 In. 1175.00
Candlestand, Queen Anne, Maple, Vase & Ring Turned Support, 1700s, 27 x 16 1/2 In. 440.00
Candlestand, Red Paint, Ratchet, Cross Shoe Foot, c.1820, 28 x 24 x 28 In. 4070.00
Candlestand, Red Paint, Rosehead Nails, Turned Post, 1700s, 28 x 19 In. 1430.00
Candlestand, Shaker, Mahogany, Round Top, 3-Part Base, Kentucky, 27 x 14 3/4 In. 2715.00
Candlestand, Sheraton, Mahogany, Turned Pedestal, Reeded Legs, 29 x 21 x 16 In. 520.00
Candlestand, Victorian, Oval, Marble, Molded Edge, 4 Legs, Pedestal Shaft, 29 x 22 In. 145.00
Candlestand, Walnut, Oval Tilt Top, Urn Pedestal, Snake Feet, 1800s, 27 x 20 x 15 In. 840.00
Candlestand, Walnut, Oval Tilt Top, Vase Shaft, Cabriole Legs, Spade Feet, 28 x 15 In. 195.00
Candlestand, Walnut, Round Tilt Dish Top, Birdcage Support, 25 In. 1315.00
Candlestand, Walnut, Tilt Top, Reeded Tripod Base, 29 In. 299.00
Canterbury, Aesthetic Revival, Ebonized Walnut, Parcel Gilt, c.1880, 23 x 23 In. 940.00
Canterbury, Regency Style, Mahogany, Drawer, 4 Sections, 1900s, 21 x 21 x 16 In. 295.00
Canterbury, Regency Style, Mahogany, Drawer, Faux Drawer, Casters, 21 x 15 x 17 In. 350.00
Canterbury, Regency Style, Turned Stiles, Compartments, Grand Rapids Label, 18 x 19 In. 59.00
Canterbury, Regency, Lacewood, Drawer, Tapered Legs, 21 x 17 1/2 x 12 In. 2700.00
Canterbury, Regency, Mahogany, 19 x 18 x 12 In. 5100.00
Canterbury, Regency, Mahogany, c.1815, 21 1/4 x 20 3/4 x 13 3/4 In. 1680.00
Canterbury, Regency, Mahogany, c.1820, 18 x 19 1/4 x 13 1/4 In. 3300.00
Canterbury, Regency, Mahogany, Part Ebonized, c.1815, 18 1/4 x 18 x 12 1/4 In. 3000.00
Canterbury, Victorian, Walnut, Barley Twist Supports, Scrollwork Panel, 19 x 25 In. 765.00
Cart, Serving, Aldo Tura, Walnut, Brass Handles, Signed, 29 x 34 x 16 In. .... *ILLUS* 764.00
Cart, Serving, McCobb, Bleached Mahogany, Carrara Glass Top, 29 x 36 x 19 In. .... *ILLUS* 470.00
Cart, Walnut, 2 Bicycle Wheels, 2 Doors, Divider, 1960s, 19 x 44 x 29 In. 2820.00
Cellarette, Chippendale Style, Mahogany, 8-Sided, Cabriole Legs, Late 1900s, 38 x 15 In. 345.00
Cellarette, George III, Mahogany, Brass Bound, 6-Sided Top, c.1790, 28 x 19 In. 2940.00
Cellarette, Mahogany, Continental, 1800s, 20 1/4 x 17 1/2 x 12 1/2 In. 470.00
Cellarette, Overhang Top, Drawer, Paneled Door, Butterfly Joinery, 33 x 27 x 13 In. 3175.00
Cellarette, Regency, Mahogany, Brass, Hexagonal, Splayed Square Legs, 24 x 19 In. 2350.00
Cellarette, Regency, Mahogany, Octagonal, Lion's-Mask Mounts, On Stand, 45 x 26 In. 3230.00
Cellarette, Regency, Rosewood, Brass Mounted, Lead Lined, c.1805, 21 x 19 In. 6000.00
Cellarette, William IV, Mahogany, Casket Shape, 21 x 21 x 21 In. 1920.00
Cellarette, William IV, Mahogany, Zinc Lining, Casket Shape, c.1850, 28 x 32 x 22 In. 2820.00
Chair, Aalto, No. 31, Arms, Finmar, c.1936, 26 x 24 x 32 In. 6300.00
Chair, Aalto, No. 37, Arms, Artek, 1935-45, 28 x 30 x 36 In. 3120.00
Chair, Aalto, Tank, Upholstered, Cantilevered Base, Arms, Artek, 1940s, 28 x 30 In. 2480.00
Chair, Adams Style, Shieldback, Painted, Cane Seat, Cushion, Arms, 38 x 22 In., Pair 2596.00
Chair, Aesthetic Revival, Black Lacquer, Gold Highlights, Upholstered, 38 x 22 In. 195.00
Chair, Aesthetic Revival, Cherry, Lincrusta Mounted, England, c.1890, 33 In. 645.00
Chair, Andre Arbus, Sycamore, Tall Back, Upholstered, c.1940, 43 x 18 x 16 In., Pair 4800.00
Chair, Arne Jacobsen, Grand Prix, Fritz Hansen, c.1957, 31 x 18 x 17 In., Pair 960.00
Chair, Arne Jacobsen, Pot, Polyurethane, Leather, Steel, F. Hansen, 1940s, 27 In., Pair 9600.00
Chair, Arne Jacobsen, Swan, Wool, Swivels, Tilts, F. Hansen, 30 x 29 In., Pair 3835.00
Chair, Art Deco, Club, Leather, Oak Risers, 32 x 32 In., Pair 1650.00
Chair, Art Deco, Club, Upholstered, Rosewood Veneer, Block Feet, 29 x 32 In., Pair 2480.00
Chair, Art Deco, Tubular Frame, Green Vinyl Seat, Back, Open Arms, 34 x 24 In., Pair 315.00
Chair, Art Deco, Upholstered, Outscrolled Arms, 1900s, 33 x 34 x 36 In., Pair 470.00
Chair, Art Nouveau, Mahogany, Carved Lyre Back, 39 In. 70.00
Chair, Arts & Crafts, Mahogany, Spiral Twist Crest Rail, Arms, Early 1900s, 41 x 24 In. 210.00
Chair, Arts & Crafts, Mahogany, Turned Spindles, Heart Cutout, Owls, Rush Seat, 41 In. 880.00
Chair, Arts & Crafts, Mahogany, Upholstered, Arms, Liberty & Co., c.1905, 28 x 24 In. 400.00
Chair, Arts & Crafts, Oak, Arms, c.1900, 39 x 29 x 26 In. 200.00
Chair, Ash, Ladder Back, Rush Seat, Arms, 1700s 145.00
Chair, B. Mathsson, Eva, Webbing, Karl Mathsson, Sweden, 1960, 33 x 24 x 24 In. 1440.00
Chair, B. Mathsson, Fabric, Leather Straps, Arms, Dux, 38 x 34 x 25 In. 590.00
Chair, Bamboo, Cushion, Padded Back, Anglo-Indian, c.1900, 40 In. 590.00
Chair, Banister Back, 4 Spindles, Shaped Crest, Rush Seat, 42 x 15 In. 400.00
Chair, Banister Back, Black Paint, Half-Turned Spindles, Rush Seat, 41 In. 400.00
Chair, Banister Back, Black Paint, Rush Seat, 43 x 16 In. 400.00
Chair, Banister Back, Black Paint, Shaped Splat, Rush Seat, Mid 1700s, 48 In. 600.00

Chair, Banister Back, Shaped Crest, Rush Seat, Bulbous Turned Front Stretcher, 1700s 190.00
Chair, Baroque Style, Fruitwood, Leather Seat, Columnar Legs, 1800s, 37 x 17 In., Pair 150.00
Chair, Baroque Style, Italy, Arms, 48 x 26 x 24 In., Pair 1265.00
Chair, Baroque Style, Mahogany, Vines, Putto Supports, Leaf-Carved Arms, 52 x 22 In. 1645.00
Chair, Barrel Back, Padded, Upholstered, Loose Seat Cushion, Skirt, 28 x 33 x 33 In. 200.00
Chair, Belter, Rococo, Rosewood, Carved Flowers & Grapes, New York, 42 In. 5100.00
Chair, Bentwood, Arms, Rustic, Early 20th Century, 42 x 22 In. 145.00
Chair, Bentwood, Black Paint, Cane Seat, Backs, Czechoslovakia, 32 x 18 x 20 In. 80.00
Chair, Bergere, Art Deco, Beech, Upholstered, Closed Arms, France, c.1935, 33 In. 499.00
Chair, Bergere, Biedermeier, Upholstered, Tapered Legs, Peg Feet, Closed Arms, 35 x 23 x 27 In. .. 470.00
Chair, Bergere, Carved Seat Rail, Upholstered, Closed Arms, c.1900, 28 x 22 x 21 In. 560.00
Chair, Bergere, Directoire, Fruitwood, Closed Arms, Cushion, Closed Arms, Early 1800s 1880.00
Chair, Bergere, Directoire, Upholstered, Painted, Closed Arms, France, c.1800, 36 x 25 In. 1416.00
Chair, Bergere, Empire Style, Mahogany, Cane, Closed Arms, 41 In., Pair 1880.00
Chair, Bergere, Empire, Mahogany, Cushion, Closed Arms, Early 1800s, 35 1/2 In. 1410.00
Chair, Bergere, George III, Mahogany, Casters, Closed Arms, c.1780 .... 4500.00
Chair, Bergere, Georgian Style, Cane Back, Cushions, Closed Arms, 32 In., Pair 1998.00
Chair, Bergere, Louis XV Style, Carved Crest, Serpentine, Upholstered, 45 x 28 x 29 In. 649.00
Chair, Bergere, Louis XV Style, Leather, Cushion, Closed Arms, 1900s, 37 x 28 In. 1180.00
Chair, Bergere, Louis XV Style, Mahogany, Padded Back, Cushioned Seat, Closed Arms, 36 In. 880.00
Chair, Bergere, Louis XV Style, Padded Back, Closed Arms, Late 1800s, 36 In., Pair 2820.00
Chair, Bergere, Louis XV Style, Scalloped Crest, Padded Back, Closed Arms, 36 In., Pair 3760.00
Chair, Bergere, Louis XVI Style, Cane, Gilt, Closed Arms, 38 In., Pair 3055.00
Chair, Bergere, Louis XVI Style, Fruitwood, Bowed Seat, Lobed Crest, Closed Arms, 36 In. 410.00
Chair, Bergere, Louis XVI Style, Multicolored, Closed Arms, Late 1800s, 40 1/4 In. 1028.00
Chair, Bergere, Louis XVI Style, Painted, Carved Crested Ribbon, Padded, 1800s, Pair 1524.00
Chair, Bergere, Louis XVI Style, White Paint, Upholstered, Fluted Legs, 36 x 24 In., Pair 1645.00
Chair, Bergere, Louis XVI Style, White Paint, Upholstered, Scrolled Arms, 21 In., Pair 1060.00
Chair, Bergere, Napoleon III, Turkish Style, Ebonized Mahogany, Closed Arms, 38 In. 1175.00
Chair, Bergere, Restauration, Mahogany, Dolphins, Closed Arms, Early 1800s, 37 In. 2115.00
Chair, Bergere, Serpentine Frame, Upholstered, Closed Arms, 1900s, 35 x 27 In., Pair 885.00
Chair, Bergere, Wrought Iron, Velvet Seat, Closed Arms, France, c.1900, 37 x 29 In. 235.00
Chair, Biedermeier, Concave Oblong Crest Rail, Tapered Legs, Upholstered, 35 In. 2000.00
Chair, Biedermeier, Fruitwood, Arched Crest, Pierced Splat, Arms, c.1835, 19 In. 470.00
Chair, Biedermeier, Fruitwood, Curved Crest Rail, Fluted Scrolled Splat, Saber Legs, Pair 440.00
Chair, Biedermeier, Fruitwood, Part Ebonized, Scrolled Backrest, c.1820, 18 In., Pair 470.00
Chair, Biedermeier, Walnut, Overupholstered Seat, Scrolled Arms, c.1830, 20 In., Pair 3055.00
Chair, Birch, Upholstered, Arms, c.1925, 34 1/4 In. 7800.00
Chair, Black & Yellow Paint, Banister Back, Shaped Crest, Rush Seat, 18th Century 300.00
Chair, Black Forest, Walnut, Bear, Branch Back, Bears Climb Legs, c.1900, 38 x 18 In. 2465.00
Chair, Black, Red Lacquer, Chinese, c.1880, 45 x 19 x 15 In., Pair 295.00
Chair, Bonet, Hardoy & Kurchan, Butterfly, Tubular Steel, Canvas, Knoll, c.1965 .... 50.00
Chair, Borge Mogensen, Spanish, No. 2226, Oak, Leather, c.1959, 27 x 32 x 22 In. 3600.00
Chair, Bra Bohag, Upholstered, Scandinavia, c.1970 .... 320.00
Chair, Bugatti, Wood, Copper & Pewter Inlay, Round Seat, 49 x 22 In. 4346.00
Chair, Calamander, Padded, Arms, Anglo-Indian, 1800s, 39 x 19 x 28 In., Pair 5580.00
Chair, Campeachy, Mahogany, Carved, Arms, c.1840, 42 x 23 x 19 In. .... *ILLUS* 10869.00
Chair, Campeachy, Walnut, Leather, Acanthus Crest, Scrolled Arms, 1840-50, 42 In. 3525.00
Chair, Charles II Style, Needlepoint, Acanthus Carved, Arms, 1800s, 45 x 25 In. 649.00
Chair, Chinese Chippendale, Black Lacquer, Gilt, Pagoda Shape Crest, Arms, 42 In. 2000.00
Chair, Chinese, Lacquer, Red, Late 19th Century .... *ILLUS* 1180.00
Chair, Chippendale Style, Birch, Brown Stain, Spanish Feet, 20th Century, 38 In., Pair 355.00
Chair, Chippendale Style, Mahogany, Owl-Eye Splat, Open Arms, Late 1800s, 19 In. 529.00
Chair, Chippendale Style, Mahogany, Ribbonback, Scalloped Crest, c.1850 .... 2235.00
Chair, Chippendale Style, Mahogany, Velvet Seat, Brass Tacks, Ribbonback, 38 In. 230.00
Chair, Chippendale Style, Pierced Splat, Needlepoint, Arms, 45 x 23 x 19 1/2 In. 85.00
Chair, Chippendale, Cherry, Rush Seat, Pierced Splat, Heart Cutout, c.1800 .... 275.00
Chair, Chippendale, Mahogany, 4 Pierced Splats With Carved Plumes, Slip Seat 5079.00
Chair, Chippendale, Mahogany, Carved, Scrolled Ear Crest, Pierced Splat, 43 In., Pair 290.00
Chair, Chippendale, Mahogany, Needlepoint Covers, 39 x 20 1/2 x 19 In., Pair 1380.00
Chair, Chippendale, Mahogany, Openwork Splat, Stepped Shoe, Arms, 39 1/2 x 23 In. 978.00

Furniture, Chair, Campeachy, Mahogany, Carved, Arms, c.1840, 42 x 23 x 19 In.

Furniture, Chair, Chinese, Lacquer, Red, Late 19th Century

Chair, Chippendale, Mahogany, Pierced Splat, Arms, 39 x 16 In. 339.00
Chair, Chippendale, Mahogany, Ribboned Splats, Carved Ears, 1700s 248.00
Chair, Chippendale, Mahogany, Serpentine Crest Rail, Slip Seat, Pa., 37 In. 239.00
Chair, Chippendale, Mahogany, Upholstered, Serpentine Crest, Late 1700s, 45 In. 2938.00
Chair, Chippendale, Ribbonback, 3 Horizontal Slats, Rush Seat, 37 x 18 In. 145.00
Chair, Chippendale, Ribbonback, 4 Pierced Slats, Rush Seat, Square Legs, 38 x 18 In. 130.00
Chair, Chippendale, Rush Seat, Pierced Splat, Carved Crest, 39 x 18 In. 259.00
Chair, Chippendale, Solid Wood Seat, Pierced Carved Splat, England, 37 x 18 In., Pair 575.00
Chair, Chippendale, Walnut, Pierced Gothic Splat, Slip Seat, 38 In., Pair 390.00
Chair, Chippendale, Walnut, Scratch Beaded Crest, Vase Splat, c.1780, 39 In. 7638.00
Chair, Chippendale, Walnut, Serpentine Crest, Carved Splat, Arms, c.1770, 39 x 27 In. 5875.00
Chair, Chippendale, Walnut, Serpentine Crest, Gothic Splat, Arms, Phila., c.1770, 38 In. 960.00
Chair, Chrome, Tubular, Red Vinyl Seat, Back Cushion, Wood Armrests, 35 x 25 1/2 In. 200.00
Chair, Club, Art Deco, Burgundy Leather, Black Piping, France, 1930s, Pair 2350.00
Chair, Corner, Chippendale Style, Mahogany, Needlepoint Upholstery, Slip Seat 499.00
Chair, Corner, George II, Mahogany, Carved, Stylized Mask, Scrolling Leaves, 30 In. 286.00
Chair, Corner, George III, Yew, Fruitwood, Rolled Crest, Flat Rounded Arms, 28 x 22 In. 1410.00
Chair, Corner, Georgian Style, Mahogany, 2 Open Splats, Slip Seat, Pad Feet 1410.00
Chair, Corner, Irish Georgian, Elm, Tall Head Rest, Scrolled Arms, Plank Seat, 40 x 21 In. 3055.00
Chair, Corner, Maple, Painted, Turned, Shaped Backrest, Late 1700s, 28 1/2 In. 410.00
Chair, Corner, Oak, Carved Backrest, Arms, 33 x 23 In. 235.00
Chair, Corner, Shaped Crest, Rush Seat, Turned Supports, Curved Arms, 32 1/2 In. 999.00
Chair, Corner, Victorian, Mahogany, Cabriole Legs, 32 x 34 x 26 In. 110.00
Chair, Cypress, Split Oak Seat, Elongated Finials, Tapered Legs, Louisiana, 25 In., Child's 180.00
Chair, Cypress, Woven Seat, Slat Back, Louisiana, Early 1800s, 25 x 17 x 12 In. 529.00
Chair, Danny Ho Fong, Wave Chaise, Tropi-Cal, c.1970, 16 x 24 x 82 In. 2700.00
Chair, Desk, Walnut Base, Upholstered, Tilts, Swivels, 37 x 30 x 28 In. 359.00
Chair, Donald Knorr, Steel, Tubular, Enameled, Painted, Knoll, 1948, 27 3/4 x 22 1/8 In. 6600.00
Chair, Drafting Perch, Robert Probst, Herman Miller, c.1964, 41 x 28 x 10 In. ....540.00 to 720.00
Chair, Drafting, Eames, Aluminum Group, Herman Miller, c.1960 .... 140.00
Chair, Dressing Table, Lucite Swivel Base, 27 1/2 x 19 1/2 x 20 In. 2689.00
Chair, Duncan Phyfe, Mahogany, Ox-Bow Crest Rail, Shaped Splat, Pair 1645.00
Chair, Eames & A. Girard, Fabric, Herman Miller, c.1953, 32 x 25 x 22 In. 2040.00
Chair, Eames, Aluminum Group, Swivels, Arms, Herman Miller, c.1958, Pair 850.00
Chair, Eames, DAR, Fiberglass, Tubular Steel, Herman Miller, c.1950, Pair 700.00
Chair, Eames, DAR, Fiberglass, Tubular Steel, Herman Miller, c.1960 .... 380.00
Chair, Eames, DAW, Fiberglass, Walnut, Steel, Arms, c.1950, 31 x 25 In., Pair 3930.00
Chair, Eames, DAX, Herman Miller, c.1951, 28 x 25 x 24 In. 120.00
Chair, Eames, DAX, Yellow, Zenith Plastics, Herman Miller, c.1951, 28 x 25 x 24 In. 240.00
Chair, Eames, DCW, Bentwood, Red, Aniline Dye, c.1945, 29 In. 600.00
Chair, Eames, Executive Lobby, Leather, Black, Herman Miller, c.1960, 31 x 29 x 24 In. 900.00
Chair, Eames, Executive Lobby, Leather, Purple, Herman Miller, c.1960, 31 x 29 x 24 In. 300.00
Chair, Eames, LCM, Red Analine-Dyed Wood, Herman Miller, c.1946, 27 x 22 x 24 In. 2400.00
Chair, Eames, LCW, Ash Plywood, Ebonized Legs, Herman Miller, c.1952, 22 x 26 In. 1640.00
Chair, Eames, LCW, Ash, Herman Miller, c.1946, 27 x 22 x 24 In. 1080.00
Chair, Eames, LCW, Birch, P. Evans, c.1946, 27 x 22 x 24 In. 1140.00
Chair, Eames, Molded Plywood, P. Evans, c.1945, 15 x 15 x 11 In., Child's 7200.00

Chair, Eames, Time Life Executive, Herman Miller, c.1960 .... 754.00
Chair, Eastlake, Ebonized, Chip Carved, Upholstered, Arms, Late 1800s, 33 In. 560.00
Chair, Edwardian, Mahogany, Carved Crest, Fluted Stiles, Arms, 41 x 23 In., Pair 880.00
Chair, Edwardian, Satinwood, Painted, Flower Garlands, Shieldback, 37 In., Pair 590.00
Chair, Eero Saarinen, Grasshopper, Upholstered, Bentwood, Knoll, 35 x 26 x 32 In. 1534.00
Chair, Eero Saarinen, Womb, Knoll, c.1947, 36 x 39 x 33 In. 1020.00
Chair, Egyptian Revival, Gilt, Painted, Barrel Back, Arms, 40 x 26 x 19 In., Pair 4115.00
Chair, Egyptian Revival, Rosewood, Pharaoh Arms, Late 1800s, 38 x 29 x 27 In. 7638.00
Chair, Empire Style, Mahogany, Parcel Gilt, Scrolled Legs, Arms, 27 x 15 x 23 In. 690.00
Chair, Empire Style, Mahogany, Sphinx, Gilt Bronze, Open Arms, 40 In., Pair 1763.00
Chair, Empire, Gilt Bronze Arm Supports, Bronze Finials, Crest, Pair 1430.00
Chair, Empire, Mahogany, Carved Crest, Down-Swept Arms, Upholstered, 32 3/4 In., Pair 295.00
Chair, Empire, Mahogany, Scrolled Crest, Ormolu Griffin Mount, Arms, 34 1/2 In. 1175.00
Chair, Empire, Maple, Cane, Vase Splat, Scrolled, Cane Seat, 32 x 17 x 16 In. 180.00
Chair, Empire, Shaped Back, Urn Slat, Needlepoint Seat, Saber Legs, 32 x 18 In. 110.00
Chair, Empire, Sheraton, Mahogany, Upholstered, Open Arm, 34 x 23 x 20 In. 440.00
Chair, Empire, Walnut, Carved Back, 32 x 17 x 19 In. 69.00
Chair, English Walnut, Needlepoint, 45 x 18 In., Pair 300.00
Chair, Erberto Carboni, Delfino, Metal, Upholstered, Arflex, c.1954, 33 x 29 In., Pair 2950.00
Chair, Federal Style, Mahogany, Upholstered, Tapered Legs, 48 x 26 x 25 In., Pair 1900.00
Chair, Federal, Mahogany, Carved, Serpentine Crest, Scrolled Arms, c.1790, 47 x 35 In. 7345.00
Chair, Federal, Mahogany, Inlaid, Shieldback, c.1800, 36 1/2 x 19 In. 4406.00
Chair, Federal, Mahogany, Padded, Upholstered, Wing Panels, Arms, 41 x 25 x 22 In. 530.00
Chair, Federal, Tiger Maple, Leaf-Carved Crest, Pierced Splat, Cane Seat, c.1810, Pair 1998.00
Chair, Finn Juhl, Baker, c.1955, 33 x 32 x 25 In. 1800.00
Chair, Finn Juhl, Chieftan, Leather, 38 x 39 x 35 In. 3186.00
Chair, Flemish Baroque, Walnut, Upholstered, Late 1600s, 16 In. 440.00
Chair, Flemish Style, Walnut, Carved, Stretcher Base, Hairy Paw Feet, 19 x 45 In. 345.00
Chair, Flemish Style, Walnut, High Back, Scrolled Feet, Velvet Upholstery, 18 x 49 In. 115.00
Chair, Flemish Style, Walnut, Upholstered, Turned Posts, Arms, 19 In. 445.00
Chair, Florence Knoll, Parallel Bar, Arms, c.1951, 30 x 30 x 30 In. 840.00
Chair, Florence Knoll, Parallel Bar, Stainless Steel, Gold Wool, 30 x 24 In., Pair 1800.00
Chair, Flower-Carved Crest, Needlepoint Upholstered, Arm 127.00
Chair, Folding, Carved, Painted, Name Cora On Crest Rail, Early 1900s, 33 In. 120.00
Chair, French Empire Style, Mahogany, Brass, 34 x 23 x 19 In. 300.00
Chair, French Neoclassical, Open Arm, Female-Carved Arm Supports, 38 x 27 x 22 In. 415.00
Chair, French Regency Style, Fruitwood, Carved, Cabriole Legs, 37 3/4 x 27 x 24 In. 2125.00
Chair, French Restauration, Rosewood, Brass Inlay, Scrolled Arms, Early 1800s, 38 In. 3525.00
Chair, Fritz Hansen, No. 3200, Round Back, c.1961, 28 x 20 x 48 In. 720.00
Chair, Fruitwood, Ladder Back, Turned Stiles, Carved Front Legs, Rush Seats, Pair 210.00
Chair, Fruitwood, Molded Framework, Serpentine Legs, 17 x 34 In. 175.00
Chair, G. Harcourt, Molded Plastic, Upholstered, Metal Base, Swivels, Artifort, 28 In. 1020.00
Chair, G. Nakashima, Conoid, Walnut, Hickory, 1968, 35 1/2 In. 8400.00
Chair, G. Nakashima, Grass Seat, 6-Spindle Back, Dowel Legs, 28 x 24 x 19 In., Pair 3835.00
Chair, G. Nakashima, Mira, English Walnut, 33 1/4 In., Pair 3900.00
Chair, G. Nakashima, Walnut, Hickory Spindles, Arms, 1986, 38 5/8 In. 2700.00
Chair, G. Nakashima, Walnut, Hickory Spindles, Freeform Arm, 1979, 32 5/8 In. 6600.00
Chair, G. Nelson, Coconut, Steel, Orange Vinyl, Herman Miller, 1950s, 32 x 41 x 36 In. ..... ***ILLUS*** 4113.00
Chair, G. Nelson, DFH, A-Frame Base, Herman Miller, c.1956, 32 x 20 x 29 In. 2280.00
Chair, G. Serrurier-Bovy, Oak, Belgium, c.1899, 31 x 17 In. 5678.00
Chair, G. Stickley, Cube, Slats, Loose Cushion, Ivory Vinyl, 29 x 26 x 28 In. 3525.00
Chair, G. Stickley, Morris, 2 Vertical Slats, Leather Sling Seat, Flat Arms, 37 x 30 In. 6465.00
Chair, G. Stickley, No. 2592, 4 Horizontal Slats, Rope, Arms, 32 x 31 x 39 In. 1350.00
Chair, G. Stickley, Tacked-On Leather Seat, Back, Arms, 36 1/2 x 26 x 22 1/2 In. 1115.00
Chair, George I Style, Mahogany, Shaped Crest, Shell-Carved Splat, Arms, 42 In. 1997.00
Chair, George I Style, Walnut, Padded, Upholstered, 1900s, 43 x 22 x 23 In. 266.00
Chair, George II Style, Chippendale, Mahogany, Needlepoint Seat, Cabriole Legs 1060.00
Chair, George II Style, Mahogany, Padded, Upholstered, 1900s, 40 x 33 x 24 In. 470.00
Chair, George II, Mahogany, Quatrefoil Crest, Serpentine Seat, Arms, c.1750, 37 In. 1765.00
Chair, George II, Mahogany, Serpentine Crest, Upholstered, 36 x 22 x 21 In., Pair 4720.00
Chair, George III Style, Leaf-Carved Crest, Medallion, Arms, 37 x 23 x 22 In., Pair 2715.00

Furniture, Chair, G. Nelson, Coconut, Steel, Orange Vinyl, Herman Miller, 1950s, 32 x 41 x 36 In.

Furniture, Chair, Kartell, Molded Plywood, Lacquer, 3 Piece, Joe Columbo, c.1963, 23 x 28 1/2 x 27 In.

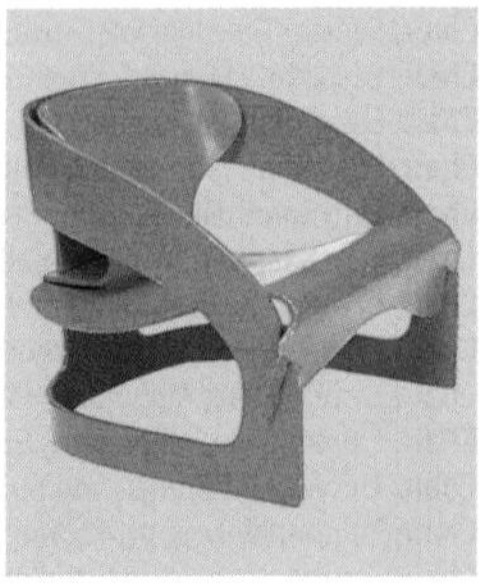

Chair, George III Style, Mahogany, Gothic Arch Back, Arms, Pair 6000.00
Chair, George III Style, Mahogany, Pierced Lattice Back, Arms, Early 1900s, 39 In. 235.00
Chair, George III Style, Mahogany, Wheat Leaf Splat, Slip Seat, Arms, c.1850, 40 In., Pair 590.00
Chair, George III Style, Spoked Backrest, Bowfront Seat, Tapered Legs, Pair 2350.00
Chair, George III Style, Upholstered, Arms, 20th Century, 36 x 31 1/2 x 34 1/2 In. 470.00
Chair, George III, Beech, Painted, Trumpet Splat, Upholstered, 19-In. Seat, Pair 999.00
Chair, George III, Chippendale Style, Mahogany, Padded Seat, Square Legs, Arms, 36 In. 550.00
Chair, George III, Mahogany, Barrel Back, Tufted Upholstery, 35 1/2 x 28 x 28 In. 560.00
Chair, George III, Mahogany, Beaker Splat, c.1800, 17 1/2 In., Pair 590.00
Chair, George III, Mahogany, Crest, Upholstered, Open Arms, 18 1/2 In., Pair 590.00
Chair, George III, Mahogany, Interlacing Ribbon Splat, Late 1700s, 39 In. 880.00
Chair, George III, Mahogany, Ladder Back, c.1775 .... 960.00
Chair, George III, Mahogany, Leather Seat, Arms, Late 1700s, Child's 825.00
Chair, George III, Mahogany, Upholstered, Marlborough Legs, Arms, 38 x 28 x 25 In. 649.00
Chair, George III, Polychrome Paint, Cane Seat, Arms, c.1800 .... 499.00
Chair, George III, Polychrome, Oval Back, Pierced Splat, Arms, Early 1800s, 38 In. 940.00
Chair, Georgian Style, Padded, Shaped Side Panels, Outscrolled Arm, 48 x 34 x 28 In., Pair 1535.00
Chair, Gianfranco Frattini, Sesann, Leather, Chrome, Cassina, 1970, 26 x 40 In., Pair 2006.00
Chair, Gio Ponti, Superleggera, No. 699, Cassina, c.1955, 32 x 16 x 16 In. 960.00
Chair, Gio Ponti, Walnut, Vinyl, Arms, M. Singer & Sons, 1950s, 34 In., Pair 3900.00
Chair, Gothic Revival, Oak, Ebonized Stringing, Scroll Arms, 39 x 20 In., Pair 2645.00
Chair, Gothic Revival, Oak, Upholstered Back, Block Legs, England, c.1890, 44 In., Pair 590.00
Chair, H. Bertoia, Diamond, Knoll, c.1951, 31 x 33 x 28 In. 240.00
Chair, H. Bertoia, Knoll, c.1952, 24 x 16 x 16 In., Child's, Pair 450.00
Chair, H. Probber, Barrel Back, Cane, Vinyl Upholstery, 25 x 33 x 29 In., Pair 2595.00
Chair, Hall, Gothic Revival, Mahogany, Padded Back, Seat, c.1850, 45 In., Pair 765.00
Chair, Hall, Gothic Revival, Walnut, Arched, Pierced Crest, c.1850, 45 x 18 In. 410.00
Chair, Hall, Louis XV Style, Marble Top, Green Accents, 24 x 28 x 40 In. 90.00
Chair, Hall, Pratt & Prince, Burr Elm, Brass Mounted, c.1865, 41 x 22 In., Pair 9600.00
Chair, Hall, Walnut, Stained, Pierced Back, Needlework Seat, England, Early 1700s, 49 In. 820.00
Chair, Hall, William IV, Mahogany, Cartouche Back, Cabriole Legs, c.1830, 36 In., Pair 2056.00
Chair, Hall, William IV, Mahogany, Plank Seat, Pierced Back, c.1840, 36 x 18 In., Pair 960.00
Chair, Hand Painted, Lancaster County, Pa., 19 1/2 x 10 1/4 x 12 In., Child's 1500.00
Chair, Hans Olsen, Upholstered, Arms, c.1950, 33 x 27 x 25 In., Pair 600.00
Chair, Henri II Style, Beech, c.1880, 18 x 16 x 36 In., Pair 530.00
Chair, Hepplewhite Style, Satinwood, Shaped Crest Rails, 1875, 6 Piece 1150.00
Chair, Hepplewhite Style, Shieldback, 19th Century, 37 3/4 x 21 x 17 In., Pair 324.00
Chair, Hepplewhite, Mahogany, Plume, Upholstered, Arms 60.00
Chair, Hepplewhite, Painted, Shieldback, Spindles, Rush Seat, Arms, 37 x 16 In. 1295.00
Chair, Hepplewhite, Pierced Splat, Serpentine Crest Rail, Leather Seat, 38 x 18 In. 60.00
Chair, Hepplewhite, Walnut, Tapered, Upholstered, Stretcher Base, Arms, 17 x 41 In. 635.00
Chair, Horn, Buffalo, Leather Seat, Custer's Last Stand, G.R. Devane Plaque, 44 In. 1150.00
Chair, Horn, Steer, Brass, Checkerboard Upholstered Seat, c.1900, 41 x 17 x 24 In. 1610.00
Chair, Hunting, Oak, Carved, Padded Crest, Storage Space, Needlework, 33 In., Pair 1175.00
Chair, Hunzinger, Walnut, Metal Weave, Arms, c.1870, 37 1/2 In. 690.00
Chair, Ilonka Karasz, Rounded Backrest, Arms, c.1928, 30 x 21 x 20 In. 3600.00
Chair, Irish Chippendale, Mahogany, Eagle's Head Crest, Padded Seat, Arms, 38 1/2 In. 1290.00

Chair, Iron, Padded, 4 Legs, Swivels, American Chair Co., Troy, N.Y., 1850-58 .... 1880.00
Chair, Italian Gondola Style, Bone, Mother-Of-Pearl Inlay, 25 1/2 x 26 x 25 In. 415.00
Chair, Jacobean Style, Mahogany, Scroll, Barley Twist Stiles, Arms, c.1875, 55 x 24 In. 735.00
Chair, Jacobean Style, Oak, Overupholstered, Padded Arms, Ball Handles, 39 x 27 x 24 In. 355.00
Chair, Joe Colombo, Molded Plywood, Orange Lacquer, 3 Sections, c.1963, 28 x 23 In. 1528.00
Chair, Jonathan Singleton, Polished Chrome, Leather, 31 x 39 In. 3835.00
Chair, Jorgen Hovelskov, Harp, Birch, Flag Line Seat, J.C. Snedkeri, 52 x 34 In. 4720.00
Chair, Jules Leleu, Lacquered Metal, Arms, c.1936, 34 1/2 In., Pair 7200.00
Chair, Kartell, Molded Plywood, Lacquer, 3 Piece, Joe Columbo, c.1963, 23 x 28 x 27 In. ... *ILLUS* 1528.00
Chair, Kem Weber, Airline, Arms, c.1934, 32 x 25 x 32 In. 12000.00
Chair, L. & J.G. Stickley, 6 Vertical Slats, Cushion, Arched Rail, Arms, 8 x 26 x 41 In. 1058.00
Chair, L. & J.G. Stickley, Oak, 6-Slat Back, 38 x 20 In. 518.00
Chair, Ladder Back, 3-Slat Back, Splint Seat, Green Paint, Maine, 39 In., Pair 80.00
Chair, Ladder Back, 5 Arched Graduated Rungs, Ball Finials, Rush Seat, Curved Arms 508.00
Chair, Ladder Back, Black Paint, Turned Finials, 5 Arched Splats, 45 x 16 5/8 In. 880.00
Chair, Ladder Back, Painted, Rush Seat, Turned Legs, 7-Stretcher Base, 37 x 18 x 13 In. 130.00
Chair, Ladder Back, Rush Seat, 3 Arched Slats, Ball Finials, Red Paint, 26 1/4 In., Child's 220.00
Chair, Ladder Back, Rush Seat, Turned Legs, Delaware River Valley, Late 1700s, 45 In. 1725.00
Chair, Ladder Back, Sausage Turned, Old Brown Paint, Gilt, 18th Century, 44 In. 2588.00
Chair, Ladder Back, Splint Seat, Arms, Late 18th Century, 48 In. 1295.00
Chair, Lambing, Panel Back, Drawer, Wings, Arms, England, 43 x 21 In. 1840.00
Chair, Le Corbusier, LC 7, Black Tubular Steel, Gray Leather, Swivels, Cassina, 29 In., Pair 900.00
Chair, Limbert, Oak, 3-Slat Back, Cushion, Arms, 36 1/2 In., Pair 1035.00
Chair, Lolling, Chippendale Style, Mahogany, 19th Century, 46 1/2 x 27 1/2 x 30 In. 770.00
Chair, Lolling, Federal, Mahogany, Inlaid, Upholstered Back, Serpentine Crest, 44 In. 15275.00
Chair, Lolling, Mahogany, New England, c.1785, 42 In. 4800.00
Chair, Louis Philippe, Fruitwood, Curved Crest, Padded Back, Seat, Cabriole Legs, 33 In. 295.00
Chair, Louis Philippe, Mahogany, Bowed Seat, Scrolled Arms, c.1835 .... 2350.00
Chair, Louis XIII Style, Elm, Padded, Upholstered, c.1850, 34 1/2 x 19 1/2 In., Pair 826.00
Chair, Louis XIII Style, Mahogany, Upholstered, Scrolling Arms, c.1900, 47 In., Pair 2585.00
Chair, Louis XIV Style, Walnut, Upholstered, Flat Back, Domed, Padded, Arms, 44 In. 1880.00
Chair, Louis XIV, Mahogany, Ribbon-Carved Crest, Tapered Legs, Silk Tapestry, Arms 1265.00
Chair, Louis XV Style, Beech, Upholstered, Serpentine Backrest, Cushion, 28 In., Child's 235.00
Chair, Louis XV Style, Fruitwood, Carved, Padded, Domed Back, 43 In., Pair 499.00
Chair, Louis XV Style, Gilt, Leaf Decoration, Shaped Back, Cane Seat 430.00
Chair, Louis XV Style, Mahogany, Cane, Ormolu Mounted, c.1900, 39 In., Pair 265.00
Chair, Louis XV Style, Multicolored, Padded, Pierced Crest, Arms, c.1890, 40 In., Pair 2230.00
Chair, Louis XV Style, Napoleon III, Rosewood, Ormolu, Upholstered, 38 1/2 In. 352.00
Chair, Louis XV Style, Polychromed, Padded Back, Scrolling Arms, 36 In., Pair 1410.00
Chair, Louis XV Style, Walnut, Arms, Early 20th Century, 40 x 29 x 24 In. 236.00
Chair, Louis XV Style, Walnut, Needlepoint, Arched, Open Arms, c.1910, 38 x 27 In. 825.00
Chair, Louis XV Style, Walnut, Needlepoint, Upholstered, Balloon Seat, Child's 355.00
Chair, Louis XV, Beech, Carved, Upholstered, Flat Back, Scrolling Arms, 1700s, 17 In. 880.00
Chair, Louis XV, Walnut, Padded, Domed Back, Scrolling Arms, Late 1700s, 38 In., Pair 3525.00
Chair, Louis XVI Style, Beech, Upholstered, Tasseled Fringe, 26 1/2 In., Child's 355.00
Chair, Louis XVI Style, Carved, Arms, c.1915, 35 x 26 x 29 In. 265.00
Chair, Louis XVI Style, Carved, Painted, Arms, France, c.1940, 29 x 26 x 38 In., Pair 129.00
Chair, Louis XVI Style, Fruitwood, Upholstered, Medallion Back, Arms, 1800s, 38 In., Pair 1175.00
Chair, Louis XVI Style, Gilt, Polychromed, Arms, Late 1800s, 41 In., Pair 2585.00
Chair, Louis XVI Style, Gilt, Upholstered, Arms, 37 1/2 x 23 1/2 In., Pair 765.00
Chair, Louis XVI Style, Painted, Early 20th Century, 37 x 16 x 15 In. 325.00
Chair, Louis XVI Style, Painted, Parcel Gilt, Ribbon-Carved Backrest 175.00
Chair, Louis XVI Style, Painted, Upholstered Padded Back, Arms, Loose Cushion, Pair 1240.00
Chair, Louis XVI Style, Ribbon Carved, Padded Back, Arms, Sprung Seat, Pair 335.00
Chair, Louis XVI Style, Upholstered, Curved Back, Arms, 1800s 2705.00
Chair, Louis XVI Style, Walnut, Balloon Back, Upholstered, Arms, 190s, 36 x 23 In. 189.00
Chair, Louis XVI Style, Walnut, Floral-Carved Crests, Reeded Columns, 37 In. 1295.00
Chair, Louis XVI Style, Walnut, Upholstered, Curved Back, Arms 118.00
Chair, Lounge, A.J. Donahue, Canadian Coconut, Plywood, Rod Legs, c.1950 .... 945.00
Chair, Lounge, A.J. Donahue, Canadian Coconut, Plywood, Upholstered, Pair 4720.00
Chair, Lounge, Art Deco, Rolled Arms, Loose Cushions, 1930s, 32 x 32 x 31 1/2 In., Pair 2938.00

Chair, Lounge, B. Mathsson, Pernilla, Beech, Fur, Webbing, Sweden, c.1935, 36 x 27 In. 5460.00
Chair, Lounge, B. Mathsson, Pernilla, Laminated Bentwood, c.1934 .... 358.00
Chair, Lounge, Baker, Tufted Back, Velour Upholstery, 30 x 21 x 28 In., Pair 4425.00
Chair, Lounge, Birch, Laminated, 1935-36, 29 7/8 x 24 1/4 In. 9600.00
Chair, Lounge, C. Pollock, Knoll, c.1960, 29 x 25 x 27 In. 1800.00
Chair, Lounge, Clifford Pascoe, Black Cotton Webbing, Blond Wood Frame, 29 x 31 In. 355.00
Chair, Lounge, Donald Deskey, Aluminum, Muslin, Ypsilanti Reed, c.1928, 27 In. 8400.00
Chair, Lounge, G. Nakashima, Conoid, Walnut, Hickory, Rubber, Cushion, 1979, 34 In. 7800.00
Chair, Lounge, G. Nakashima, Free Edge, Writing Arm, Hickory Spindles, 33 In. 9440.00
Chair, Lounge, G. Nakashima, Hickory Spindles, Saddle Seat, Dowel Legs, 33 x 24 In. 5310.00
Chair, Lounge, G. Nakashima, Slatted Back, Tapered Dowel Legs, Armless, 30 x 24 In. 3420.00
Chair, Lounge, Gio Ponti, Upholstered, Dowels, Brass, M. Singer & Sons, 29 x 26 In. 1535.00
Chair, Lounge, Jens Quistgaard, Arms, Dansk, c.1960, 28 x 25 x 28 In. 3900.00
Chair, Lounge, John Widdicomb, Walnut, Castors, Leather, 24 x 25 1/2 x 24 In. 529.00
Chair, Lounge, Le Corbusier, Chrome, Leather, Cassina, 28 x 64 x 22 In. 1298.00
Chair, Lounge, Mario Bruno, Leather, Soronami, 1970s, 35 x 40 x 39 In. 1770.00
Chair, Lounge, Mario Papperzini, Iron, Cushions, Salterini, 36 x 25 x 27 In., Pair 2715.00
Chair, Lounge, Upholstered, Wood Armrests, Tapered Legs, Brass, c.1957 .... 3055.00
Chair, Lounge, W. McArthur, Anodized Aluminum, Upholstered, 1930s, 31 In. 6000.00
Chair, Lounge, W. McArthur, Upholstered, Tubular Aluminum, Arms, 33 x 29 In. 2596.00
Chair, Lounge, Walter Lamb, 2 Seats, Webbing, Tubular Bronze Frame, 35 x 58 In. 6490.00
Chair, Lounge, Wormley, Mahogany, Leather Upholstery, 26 x 30 1/2 x 30 In. 2585.00
Chair, Lounge, Wormley, Upholstered, Tapered Legs, Brass Stretchers, 28 x 28 In., Pair 2950.00
Chair, Lucite, Pink Quilted Silk, Upholstery, Arms, 28 x 31 x 29 In. 8365.00
Chair, Mahogany, Bowed Crest Rail, Saber Legs, Vines, Flowers, Scrolls, Arms, 34 x 22 In. 546.00
Chair, Mahogany, Brass, Marble, Arms, Chinese, c.1835, 34 In., Pair 1175.00
Chair, Mahogany, Carved Crest, Pierced Splat, Serpentine Seat, Upholstered, Pair 550.00
Chair, Mahogany, Carved, Arched Back, Star, Plank Seat, Continental, 39 x 24 x 19 In. 178.00
Chair, Mahogany, Carved, Claw Feet, Scroll Edge, 38 x 22 x 25 In., Pair 355.00
Chair, Mahogany, Carved, Open Frame, Padded Seat, Back, Arms, Late 1700s, Pair 286.00
Chair, Mahogany, Leather Upholstery, Beaded Edge, Brass Tacks, 33 x 25 x 24 In. 415.00
Chair, Mahogany, Sling, Grotesque Face Carving On Back, 37 x 23 In. 175.00
Chair, Mahogany, Upholstered, Padded, Tassels, Late 1800s, 37 In., Pair 880.00
Chair, Mahogany, Vines, Cornucopia, Flowers, Scrolls, Continental, Arms, 35 x 24 x 20 In. 518.00
Chair, Mahogany, Walnut Seat Rail, 37 1/2 x 21 1/2 x 21 In. 405.00
Chair, Maple Black Paint, Banister Back, Ring, Block Turned Stiles, 46 x 18 In. 5750.00
Chair, Maple, Ash, 4 Arched Slats, Ball Finials, Mass., 1700s, 44 1/2 x 17 In. 235.00
Chair, Maple, Ash, Shaped Splats, Rush Seat, Double Stretchers, 42 5/8 x 15 1/2 In. 3819.00
Chair, Maple, Slat Back, Painted, Bulbous Turned Feet, Wooden Wheels, 50 x 18 In. 2705.00
Chair, Marcel Breuer, Plywood, Laminated, Undulated Seat, Isokon, 30 x 24 x 45 In. 7670.00
Chair, Marcel Breuer, Tubular Chrome, Cowhide, Arms, 1928, 32 In., Pair 9600.00
Chair, Maurizio Tempestini, Cushions, Salterini, c.1950, 32 x 29 x 31 In., Pair 1920.00
Chair, McCobb, Velour Upholstery, Arms, Custom Craft, 33 x 29 In., Pair 1650.00
Chair, Metal & Fruitwood Inlaid Panel, Shop Of The Crafters, 37 x 33 x 26 In. .... *ILLUS* 3290.00
Chair, Mies Van Der Rohe, Barcelona, Leather, Steel, X-Base, Knoll, 30 In., Pair 3420.00
Chair, Mogens Voltelen, Copenhagen, Beech, Leather, Denmark, c.1936, 26 x 36 In. 12010.00
Chair, Morris, Corbels, Drop-In Spring Seat, Flat Open Arms, 39 x 33 1/2 x 37 In. 3055.00
Chair, Morris, Oak, Fabric, Claw Feet, Beaded Front, Arms, Dame Stoddard, Boston, Mass. 595.00
Chair, Nana Ditzel, Barrel, Wicker, Tapered Dowel Legs, 29 x 32 x 30 In. 355.00
Chair, Nanna & Jorgen Ditzel, Hanging, R. Wengler, c.1960, 48 x 34 x 27 In. 6960.00
Chair, Napoleon III, Fruitwood, Gilt Bronze Mounted, Upholstered, Arms, 38 In., Pair 4400.00
Chair, Napoleon III, Gilt, Acanthine-Carved Crest, Pierced Splat, c.1850, 37 In., Pair 590.00
Chair, Napoleon III, Gilt, Shaped Crest, Lyre Splat, Padded Seat, 35 1/2 In., Pair 3055.00
Chair, Napoleon III, Mahogany, Carved, Reticulated Crest, Shaped Seat & Back, 50 In. 1175.00
Chair, Napoleon III, Mahogany, Crossed Torches Back, Tassels, c.1865, 36 In., Pair 880.00
Chair, Neoclassical, Lyre Splat, Aubusson Upholstery, Open Arms, Italy, c.1790, Pair 5875.00
Chair, Neoclassical, Mahogany, Arched Splat, Needlepoint, c.1850, 34 In., Pair 825.00
Chair, Neoclassical, Mahogany, Shieldback, Carved, Spade Feet, 38 In. 1998.00
Chair, Neoclassical, Painted, Trumpet Splat, Arms, Italy, Early 1800s, 17 In. 1765.00
Chair, Neoclassical, Tiger Maple, Bowed Crest Rail, Cane Seat, Youth's, 28 In. 206.00
Chair, Neoclassical, Tropical Wood, Sling, Reed Back, Seat, Arms, 1800s, 26 x 26 x 36 In. 3230.00

Furniture, Chair, Metal & Fruitwood Inlaid Panel, Shop Of The Crafters, 37 x 33 x 26 In.

Furniture, Chair, Rococo Revival, Rosewood, Carved Crest, Stanton Hall, 42 1/4 In.

Chair, Nutting, No. 493, Pilgrim, Maple, Rush Seat, 47 x 25 In. 770.00
Chair, Nutting, Spindle Turned, Solid Seat, Arms, Label, 46 In. 555.00
Chair, Oak, Carved Face, Cutout Splat, Needlepoint Sling Seat, c.1890 .... 70.00
Chair, Oak, Carved Lion's Heads, Leaf, Pierced, Tapestry Upholstery, Arm, 44 x 27 In. 195.00
Chair, Oak, Carved, Spoon Back, Baluster Splats, Padded Seat, 52 x 21 x 21 In., Pair 385.00
Chair, Oak, Walnut, Double Slat Back, Plank Seat, Arms, Spain, 51 x 25 x 21 In. 266.00
Chair, Opera, Brass, Tubular, Upholstered Seat, Medallion Back, 33 1/2 In., Pair 230.00
Chair, Orkney Island, Pine, Woven Rush, Stained, Scotland, c.1890 .... 560.00
Chair, Osvaldo Borsani, Upholstered, Flaring Metal Legs, Arms, Techno, 31 x 24 In. 1120.00
Chair, P. Jeanneret, Scissor, Birch, Metal Discs, Plaid Cushions, 29 x 29 In. 840.00
Chair, P. Jeanneret, Scissor, No. 92, Maple, Metal, Webbing, Knoll, c.1960, 29 In., Pair 5400.00
Chair, P. Volther, Corona, Chromed Steel, Plywood, Upholstered, Foam, c.1961 .... 3935.00
Chair, Painted, Open Back, Twist Splat, Serpentine Seat, Curved Arms, Venice, 36 In. 1200.00
Chair, Paul Laszlo, Arms, Brown Saltman, c.1940, 35 x 29 x 32 In., Pair 4200.00
Chair, Paulin, Round, Fiberglass Base, Upholstered, Artifort, 31 x 38 In. 780.00
Chair, Philippe Starck, High Back, Velvet Upholstery, 1 Arm, 54 x 24 In., Pair 765.00
Chair, Piano, Art Nouveau, Mahogany, Satinwood Inlay, 1800s, 39 x 17 x 17 In. 175.00
Chair, Piano, Neoclassical, Mahogany, Arched Legs, N.Y., c.1825, 33 x 14 x 11 In. 2470.00
Chair, Piano, Oak, Ladder Back, 40 x 16 x 19 In. 69.00
Chair, Piano, Rococo Revival, Rosewood, Pierced Scroll Back, Hinged Seat, 48 In. ....940.00 to 2235.00
Chair, Pine, Gray Paint, Cutout Elephant Figure, Stars, Rainbow, 21 x 10 x 12 1/2 In. 120.00
Chair, Planter's, Anglo-Indian Style, Cane, Hardwood, Armrests, Boot Rests, 37 In. 4800.00
Chair, Planter's, Mahogany, Cane, Flat Arms, West Indies, 1800s, 36 x 26 In. 3995.00
Chair, Polychrome, Rush Seat, Arms, Swiss, c.1850, 36 In., Pair 1290.00
Chair, Porter's, George III Style, Leather, Hood, Dome, Brass Tacks, c.1910, 99 x 31 In. 4230.00
Chair, Porter's, Wicker, Arched Sides, Skirt, Armrests, White, 20th Century, 62 x 26 In. 375.00
Chair, Queen Anne Style, Shepherd's Crook Open Arms, Balloon Seat, Pad Feet 560.00
Chair, Queen Anne Style, Upholstered, Arms, c.1925, 37 x 36 x 34 In. 90.00
Chair, Queen Anne Style, Walnut, Shepherd's Crook, Balloon Seat, Open Arms, Pair 558.00
Chair, Queen Anne, 4 Arched Slats, Urn Finials, Rush Seat, Medallion, Arms, 47 In. 575.00
Chair, Queen Anne, Birch, Yoked Molded Crest, Vase Splat, Slip Seat, 42 In. 1530.00
Chair, Queen Anne, Black Paint, Vase Splats, Pad & Biscuit Feet, Rush Seat, 40 In., Pair 200.00
Chair, Queen Anne, Cherry, Spooned Crest Rail, Vase Splat, Rush Seat, 40 In. 410.00
Chair, Queen Anne, Maple, Crest Rail, Splat, Upholstered Slip Seat, c.1760, 40 In. 1998.00
Chair, Queen Anne, Maple, Spoon Crest Rail, Vase Splat, Spanish Feet, 40 In. 705.00
Chair, Queen Anne, Maple, Stretcher Base, Portland, Maine, 42 In. 2200.00
Chair, Queen Anne, Mixed Hardwood, Banister Back, Rush Seat, 17 x 43 In. 315.00
Chair, Queen Anne, Rod Back, 7 Spindles, Turned Posts, Painted, Rush Seat, 1700s 275.00
Chair, Queen Anne, Transitional, Shaped Vase Splat, Rush Seat, Black Paint, 41 x 17 In. 58.00
Chair, Queen Anne, Vase Splat, Turned Stiles, Rush Seat, New England, 41 In., Pair 2700.00
Chair, Queen Anne, Walnut, Carved, Boston, c.1750, 45 1/2 In. 9600.00
Chair, Queen Anne, Walnut, Crest Rail, Vase Splat, Upholstered, 40 x 16 In. 6460.00
Chair, Queen Anne, Walnut, Serpentine Crest Rail, Cabriole Legs, c.1750 .... 2270.00
Chair, Queen Anne, Walnut, Shaped Crest, Vase Splat, Balloon Seat, 41 1/2 In. 6040.00
Chair, Queen Anne, Walnut, Upholstered Seat, Boston, c.1760, Pair 7800.00
Chair, Raffia, Painted Steel, Tom Dixon, 1988, 39 In. 6600.00
Chair, Ray Komai, Plywood, Tubular Metal Legs, J.G. Furniture Systems, 30 x 22 In. 825.00

Chair, Red & Black Graining, Gold & Black Stencils, Eagle, Fruit, 34 In. 175.00
Chair, Red Paint, Banister Back, Molded Crest, Ring Turnings, Arms, 1700s, 44 In. 820.00
Chair, Regency Style, Fruitwood, Parcel Gilt, France, 1800s, 38 x 27 In., Pair 1770.00
Chair, Regency Style, Padded Seat, Upholstered, Arms, c.1850, 43 1/2 In., Pair 1645.00
Chair, Regency Style, Parcel Gilt, 19th Century, 36 x 18 x 17 In., Pair 500.00
Chair, Regency Style, Walnut, Padded, Dome Back, Arms, Late 1800s, 44 1/2 In. 1000.00
Chair, Regency, Fruitwood, Upholstered, Padded Armrests, 34 In., Pair 1770.00
Chair, Regency, Mahogany, Cane Backs, Needlepoint Upholstery, Arms, Pair 635.00
Chair, Regency, Mahogany, Figured, Cushion, Saber Legs, 19th Century, Pair 960.00
Chair, Regency, Mahogany, Green Leather, England, c.1820 6000.00
Chair, Regency, Mahogany, H-Stretcher, Inlaid Stringing, Arms, c.1835, 33 1/2 In. 235.00
Chair, Regency, Mahogany, Rounded Crest, Horizontal Splat, Scrolling Arms, 32 1/2 In. 381.00
Chair, Regency, Mahogany, Spindle Splats, Upholstered Seat, 34 x 22 x 22 In., Pair 1770.00
Chair, Regency, Rosewood, Brass Inlay, Leaf-Carved Splats, Trap Seat, Pair 610.00
Chair, Renaissance Revival, Leather, Bowfront, Cabriole Legs, Claw & Ball Feet, 53 In. 635.00
Chair, Renaissance Revival, Mahogany, Leaves, Fruit, Cupids, Arms, Continental, 1880s 1765.00
Chair, Renaissance Revival, Mahogany, Tufted Red Silk Upholstery, Arms, 1880 705.00
Chair, Renaissance Revival, Oak, Carved North Wind Mask, Lift-Top Seat, 45 In. 529.00
Chair, Renaissance Revival, Oak, Padded Back, Seat, Scrolled Arms, c.1900, 45 x 24 In. 880.00
Chair, Renaissance Revival, Rosewood, Carved, Padded Back, Seat, 1875-85, 40 In., Pair 4995.00
Chair, Renaissance Revival, Walnut, Burl Trim, Carved, Closed Arms, 36 x 30 In. 330.00
Chair, Renaissance Revival, Walnut, Inlaid, Red Velvet, Tufted, Padded, 41 x 25 x 24 In. 590.00
Chair, Renaissance Revival, Walnut, Needlepoint Upholstery, Carved, Arms, Pair 1529.00
Chair, Restauration, Fruitwood, Overupholstered Seat, Arms, France, c.1820, 18 In. 705.00
Chair, Restauration, Walnut, Padded, Outscrolled Back, Arms, c.1815, 35 In., Pair 3055.00
Chair, Ribbon, C. Leonard & F. Stagi, No. CL9, Fiberglass, Chromed Steel, 25 x 37 In. 3420.00
Chair, Robsjohn-Gibbings, Klismos, No. 3, Saridis, Athens, c.1961, 36 x 17 x 30 In. 4800.00
Chair, Rocker, is listed under Rocker in this category.
Chair, Rococo Revival, Beech, Parcel Gilt, Polychrome, Medallion, Open Arm, 37 In. 1116.00
Chair, Rococo Revival, Gilt, Carved, Late 19th Century, 37 1/2 x 18 x 17 In. 355.00
Chair, Rococo Revival, Mahogany, Leaf & Flower Crest, Pierced, Arms, c.1850, 50 x 25 In. 795.00
Chair, Rococo Revival, Meeks, Rosewood, Arms, Stanton Hall, c.1850, 45 x 27 x 22 In. 7638.00
Chair, Rococo Revival, Painted, Parcel Gilt, Upholstered, Flat Back, Cabriole Legs, Arms 295.00
Chair, Rococo Revival, Rosewood, Carved Crest, Stanton Hall, 42 1/4 In. *ILLUS* 4830.00
Chair, Rococo Revival, Rosewood, Laminated, Rosalie Pattern, Scrolled Arms, c.1855 3525.00
Chair, Rococo Revival, Rosewood, Mask & Leaf Backrest, c.1855, Pair 295.00
Chair, Rococo Revival, Rosewood, Oval Back, Upholstered, c.1850, 40 In. 239.00
Chair, Rococo Revival, Rosewood, Rosalie Pattern, Fruit & Flower Crest, c.1850, Pair 2705.00
Chair, Rococo Revival, Rosewood, Rosalie Pattern, Molded Arms, c.1850, 43 x 20 x 21 In. 2820.00
Chair, Rococo Style, Gilt, Oval Back, Padded Seat, Cabriole Legs, 37 1/2 x 18 In. 415.00
Chair, Rococo Style, Shieldback, Arms, 20th Century, 38 3/4 x 26 x 27 In. 355.00
Chair, Rosewood, Arched Crest, Cane Seat, c.1900, 36 x 18 x 17 In., Pair 118.00
Chair, Rosewood, Arched Leaf Crest, Padded Back, Serpentine Seat, c.1850, Pair 410.00
Chair, Rosewood, Carved Vases, Arms, Chinese, 38 x 24 x 19 In. 560.00
Chair, Rosewood, Flowers, Pierced Back, Plank Seat, Chinese, 39 x 25 1/4 x 18 1/2 In. 220.00
Chair, Rosewood, Flowers, Scroll, Carved Apron, Square Legs, Chinese, 39 x 25 x 18 In. 275.00
Chair, Rosewood, Grape, Leaf Back Panel, Bird, Berries, Plank Seat, Arms, Chinese 275.00
Chair, Roycroft, Embossed Leather, Cross Mark, 37 1/2 x 24 x 24 In. *ILLUS* 31725.00
Chair, Rush Seat, 3-Slat Back, Sausage Turnings, Rolled Arms, c.1700, 46 In. 920.00
Chair, Russian Empire, Gilt, Ebonized, Padded, Upholstered, 1800s, Pair 2056.00
Chair, Salmon Paint, Banister Back, 40 1/2 In. 1090.00
Chair, Savonarola, Italian Baroque, Walnut, Carved, Grotesque Masques, 48 In. 1410.00
Chair, Savonarola, Walnut, Leaf-Carved Splats, Slatted Seat, c.1890, 34 x 23 In., Pair 325.00
Chair, Sedan, Rococo Revival, Painted, Gold Brocade, Venice, 72 x 30 In. 2585.00
Chair, Sgabello, Shell Masque, Caryatids, Saddle Seat, Italy, 40 In., Pair 1410.00
Chair, Shaker, Birch, Natural Varnish, 2 Slats, Cane Seat, Yellow Paint Trace, c.1840, 41 In. 4680.00
Chair, Shaker, Birch, Red Brown Stain, 2 Slats, Woven Fiber Seat, Tilters, c.1840, 35 In. 1465.00
Chair, Shaker, Birch, Red Paint, 3 Slats, Shaped Arms, Enfield, 26 In., Child's 11700.00
Chair, Shaker, Maple, Brown, Red Stain, 4 Slats, Rush Seats, Arms, c.1930, 45 1/2 In., Pair 5030.00
Chair, Shaker, No. 1, Tape Seat, Back, Arms, Mt. Lebanon, Child's 220.00
Chair, Shaker, Tilt, Maple, 3 Slats, Dark Stain, Rush Seat, Tilters, c.1840, 41 1/2 In., Pair 3276.00

Furniture, Chair, Roycroft, Embossed Leather, Cross Mark, 37 1/2 x 24 x 24 In.

Furniture, Chair, Step, Shaker, Pine & Birch, Natural Varnish, Enfield, N.H., 21 3/4 In.

Chair, Sheraton Style, Mahogany, Inlay, Upholstered, Open Arms, 1900s, 42 In. 235.00
Chair, Shoeshine, Oak, Table, Marble Top, 1920s 448.00
Chair, Slat Back, Turned, Red Stain, Arms, New England, Late 18th Century, 24 In. 295.00
Chair, Slipper, Mahogany, Finger Carved, Balloon Back, Velvet, 33 1/2 x 23 1/2 In. 149.00
Chair, Slipper, Neogrecque, Cherry, Gilt, Ebonized, Leaf Crest, N.Y., c.1865, 36 In. 1350.00
Chair, Slipper, Queen Anne, Modified, Tiger Maple, Turned Legs, c.1740, 37 In. 295.00
Chair, Slipper, Robsjohn-Gibbings, Mahogany, Brass Legs, Upholstered, 31 x 24 In. 4200.00
Chair, Slipper, Rococo Revival, Rosewood, Laminated, Pierced Back, c.1850, 43 x 16 In. 2115.00
Chair, Slipper, Rococo Style, Rosewood, Carved, Pierced, Waisted Back, 43 In. 355.00
Chair, Smokey Tunis, Matte Paint, Chip-Carved Top, H Base, Upholstered, c.1958 . . . . 2596.00
Chair, Spindles, Round Brass Tacks, Crest, In Memory Of Nana, 19 1/2 In., Child's 345.00
Chair, Step, Shaker, Pine & Birch, Natural Varnish, Enfield, N.H., 21 3/4 In. . . . . *ILLUS* 518.00
Chair, Student's, Heywoodite, Plastic, Tubular Steel, Heywood-Wakefield, c.1965 . . . . 75.00
Chair, Tapio Wirkkala, Nikke, Laminated Birch, Steel, Finland, c.1958, 31 x 18 In. 3276.00
Chair, Tiger Maple, Ladder Back, Arched Crest, Shaped Aprons, Woven Seat, 40 In., Pair 885.00
Chair, Tub, Georgian Style, Mahogany, Continuous Arms, Shaped Seat, Square Legs, Pair 999.00
Chair, Tub, Regency Style, Faux Rosewood, Padded Back, Outscrolled Arms, 33 In., Pair 1525.00
Chair, Tub, Teak, Sibast Mobler, c.1965, Pair 225.00
Chair, Tub, William IV, Mahogany, Downswept Back, Sides, Padded Seat, c.1850, 33 In. 1175.00
Chair, V. Kagan, Reclining, Mahogany, Upholstered, 40 x 28 x 41 In. 8850.00
Chair, V. Kagan, Swivels, Mahogany, Ebonized, Upholstered, 1950s 6000.00
Chair, V. Panton, Cone, No. K1, Fritz Hansen, c.1958, 33 x 23 x 23 In. 480.00
Chair, Victorian Revival, Balloon Back, Flower Crest, Arms, c.1950, 44 x 28 x 33 In. 115.00
Chair, Victorian, Barrel Back, Carved Crest, Velvet Upholstery, Tufted, Arms, 41 x 29 In. 165.00
Chair, Victorian, Carved, Needlepoint Seat, Back, 39 x 21 In. 150.00
Chair, Victorian, Walnut, Carved Crest, Needlepoint Seat, 34 x 17 In. 70.00
Chair, Victorian, Walnut, Finger Carved, Balloon Back, Scroll Sides, Upholstered, 38 In. 110.00
Chair, Victorian, Walnut, Leaf Carved, Cameo Back, Needlepoint Upholstery, Pair 389.00
Chair, Victorian, Walnut, Minerva Head Crest, Open Arm, Upholstered, 43 x 22 In. 195.00
Chair, Victorian, Walnut, Scrolled Armrests, 42 x 34 x 26 In. 115.00
Chair, W. McArthur, Aluminum, Oilcloth, Arms, 32 x 24 x 20 In. 3420.00
Chair, W. McArthur, Aluminum, Tubular, Arms, Hockey-Puck Feet, 1930, 29 In. 2310.00
Chair, Walnut, Balloon Seat, Cabriole Legs, Scrolled Feet, Italy, 43 x 22 x 21 In. 460.00
Chair, Walnut, Carved Back, Scrolled Acanthus Crest, Late 1800s, 45 In. 90.00
Chair, Walnut, Carved Woman's Head Arm Supports, Velvet Upholstery, 35 x 22 In. 165.00
Chair, Walnut, Padded, Arms, England, c.1860, 37 x 27 In., Pair 1645.00
Chair, Walnut, Putti, Leaves, Blackamoor, Arms, Venice, 1800s, 47 x 27 x 23 In. 8225.00
Chair, Walnut, Rose & Scroll Crest Rail, Upholstered, Arms, c.1850, 41 In. 1435.00
Chair, Walnut, Serpentine Back, Upholstered, Continental, Early 1900s, 37 x 27 In. 355.00
Chair, Walnut, Serpentine Crest Rail, Needlepoint Seat, Cabriole Legs, c.1760 . . . . 3885.00
Chair, Walnut, Slip Seat, Pierced Splat, Carved Crest, 1700s, 39 In. 430.00
Chair, Walnut, Turned Finials, Carved Crest, Upholstered, Pair 460.00
Chair, Weaver's, Ladder Back, Maple, Red Paint, Rush Seat, Turned Arms, 35 In. 460.00
Chair, Wegner, Cow Horn, No. JH 505, J. Hansen, c.1952, 29 x 21 x 17 In. 2700.00
Chair, Wegner, Papa Bear, Teak, Upholstered, Dowel Legs, Arms, 39 x 35 x 28 In. 4425.00
Chair, Wegner, Teak, Upholstered, Flared Legs, Arms, J. Hansen, 29 In., Pair 1298.00
Chair, Wegner, Valet, No. PP 250, Teak, J. Hansen, c.1953, 37 In. 4800.00

Chair, William & Mary, Turned, Carved, Brown Paint, Arms, Early 1700s, 51 In. 1528.00
Chair, William & Mary, Upholstered, Scroll-Carved Arms, 53 x 26 In. 86.00
Chair, William IV, Mahogany, Cane Back, Carved Splat, Arms 1019.00
Chair, William IV, Mahogany, Leather Upholstery, Reeded Legs, 31 x 18 x 17 In., Pair 445.00
Chair, William IV, Mahogany, Leather, Padded, Closed Arms, c.1850, 39 In. 1060.00
Chair, Windsor, 5 Spindles, Bamboo Turnings, Mixed Wood, Medallion Crest, 36 In. 405.00
Chair, Windsor, 7 Spindles, Bamboo Turnings, Beaded Bows, 36 1/2 x 16 In., Pair 1725.00
Chair, Windsor, 7 Spindles, Bulbous Turned Legs, Stretchers, Straight Arms, 17 1/2 In. 330.00
Chair, Windsor, Arrow Back, Red Decoration, Yellow Line Detail, 33 In. 115.00
Chair, Windsor, Bamboo Carved, Plank Seat, Arms, 19th Century 165.00
Chair, Windsor, Bamboo Turnings, Straight Crest, Shaped Seat, 16 1/4 In. 70.00
Chair, Windsor, Birdcage, 7 Spindles, Bamboo Turnings, Arms, 34 x 18 In., Pair 690.00
Chair, Windsor, Birdcage, Bamboo Turnings, Black Paint, Arms, 33 x 16 In. 115.00
Chair, Windsor, Birdcage, Plank Seat, Bamboo-Carved Legs, 19th Century 110.00
Chair, Windsor, Black Paint, Continuous Arms, J. Bertine, N.Y., 1790-97, Pair 5980.00
Chair, Windsor, Black Paint, Volute-Carved Arms, Ogee Supports, Turned Stretcher, 1700s 440.00
Chair, Windsor, Bow Back, 7 Spindles, Green Paint, 36 3/4 x 17 In. 215.00
Chair, Windsor, Bow Back, 7 Spindles, Molded Edge Hoop, Saddle Seat, 36 x 18 In. 175.00
Chair, Windsor, Bow Back, 7 Spindles, Pinched Bow, Phila., c.1800, 36 In. 325.00
Chair, Windsor, Bow Back, 8 Spindles, Bamboo Turned Legs, Painted, 37 x 18 In. 175.00
Chair, Windsor, Bow Back, 9 Spindles, c.1800 .... 550.00
Chair, Windsor, Bow Back, Ash, Maple, 7 Spindles, Arms, c.1780, 35 1/2 In. 1880.00
Chair, Windsor, Bow Back, Bulbous Turned Base, Arms, New England, c.1800, 38 3/4 In. 890.00
Chair, Windsor, Bow Back, Elm, Oak, Yew Splat, Arms, c.1825, 42 x 16 x 22 In. 690.00
Chair, Windsor, Bow Back, Mixed Wood, Red Paint, 7 Spindles, Saddle Seat, 36 1/2 In. 805.00
Chair, Windsor, Bow, Spindle Back, Pierced Splat, Bentwood, England, 40 x 22 x 18 In. 490.00
Chair, Windsor, Brace Back, 7 Spindles, Saddle Seat, Splayed Legs, Arms, 37 x 18 In. 290.00
Chair, Windsor, Brace Back, 7 Spindles, Turned Legs, Stretcher, Brown Paint, 34 In. 345.00
Chair, Windsor, Brace Back, Continuous Arm, Saddle Seat, E.B. Tracy, 1700s 358.00
Chair, Windsor, Brace Back, Saddle Seat, Baluster Legs, Bulbous Stretcher, c.1800 .... 840.00
Chair, Windsor, Comb Back, Ash, Maple, Arms, Conn., c.1800, 46 3/4 In. 3000.00
Chair, Windsor, Comb Back, Ash, Saddle Seat, Scroll Knuckle Arms, 1800s, 44 x 22 In. 1880.00
Chair, Windsor, Comb Back, Bulbous Turnings, Arms, Nantucket, c.1800 .... 920.00
Chair, Windsor, Comb Back, Maple, Hickory, Pine, 7 Spindles, 41 In., Arm 5290.00
Chair, Windsor, Comb Back, Mustard Paint, Plank Seat, Scrolled Arms, 18th Century 190.00
Chair, Windsor, Fanback, 7 Spindles, Carved Seat, Splayed Legs, 36 x 16 In. 750.00
Chair, Windsor, Fanback, 7 Spindles, H-Stretcher, Bowed Crest, 37 x 18 In. 635.00
Chair, Windsor, Fanback, 7 Spindles, Shaped Crest, Turned Legs, 35 3/4 In. 690.00
Chair, Windsor, Fanback, 9 Spindles, Shaped Arms, Baluster Arm Posts, 43 In. 4025.00
Chair, Windsor, Fanback, Ash, Maple, Pine, 7 Spindles, Serpentine Crest, 37 In. 410.00
Chair, Windsor, Fanback, Brace Back, 9 Spindles, Saddle Seat, 37 In., Pair 2300.00
Chair, Windsor, Fanback, Bulbous Turnings, Saddle Seat, New England, 1800s 375.00
Chair, Windsor, Fanback, Green Over Red Paint, Plank Seat, Double Front Stretcher, 1700s 165.00
Chair, Windsor, Fanback, Painted, Concave Crest Rail, c.1790, 34 In. 440.00
Chair, Windsor, Fanback, Red Paint, Ring Turned Legs, Shield Seat, 35 1/2 In. 1440.00
Chair, Windsor, G. Stickley, Neoclassical, Mixed Wood, Stretchers, Arms, 44 In., Pair 2115.00
Chair, Windsor, Gothic Revival, Oak, Arched & Pierced Splat, Cabriole Legs, 40 In. 3290.00
Chair, Windsor, High Back, Yew, Winged Crest Rail, William Whitely, London, 48 In. 940.00
Chair, Windsor, Nutting, Bow Back, Saddle Seat, Bulbous Turned Legs 345.00
Chair, Windsor, Nutting, Brace Back, 9 Spindles, Scrolled Ear Crest, Arms, 45 1/2 In. 400.00
Chair, Windsor, Nutting, Fanback, Brace Back, Curving Crest, Scroll Ears, 41 In. 380.00
Chair, Windsor, Nutting, No. 301, Brace Back, 38 x 18 In. ....200.00 to 288.00
Chair, Windsor, Nutting, No. 305, Bamboo Turnings, 39 In. 495.00
Chair, Windsor, Nutting, No. 310, 37 In. 468.00
Chair, Windsor, Oak, Pine, Plank Seat, Bamboo Turnings, 1800s, 34 1/2 x 19 1/2 In., Pair 210.00
Chair, Windsor, Poplar Seat, Mahogany Arms, Splay Legs, Revolving, 34 x 25 x 25 In. 575.00
Chair, Windsor, Sack Back, 7 Spindles, Brown Repaint, Baluster Arm Posts, 35 In. 400.00
Chair, Windsor, Sack Back, 7 Spindles, Knuckle Arms, 18 x 35 In. 2875.00
Chair, Windsor, Sack Back, 7 Spindles, Knuckle Handholds, Turned, 36 In. 940.00
Chair, Windsor, Sack Back, 7 Tapered Spindles, Oval Seat, 43 In. 2645.00
Chair, Windsor, Sack Back, Baluster Legs, Bulbous Stretcher, W. McBride, N.Y., 1800s 1075.00

Chair, Windsor, Sack Back, Black Paint, Arms, 36 In. 690.00
Chair, Windsor, Sack Back, Flared Spindles, Arms, Massachusetts, c.1775, 39 In. 7800.00
Chair, Windsor, Sack Back, Hickory, Ash Bentwood, Shaped Seat, Arms, 34 x 24 In. 1150.00
Chair, Windsor, Sack Back, Hickory, Maple, Walnut, Bentwood, Shaped Seat, 38 In., Arm 748.00
Chair, Windsor, Sack Back, Oak, Hickory, Poplar, 7 Spindles, 16 x 38 1/2 In. 375.00
Chair, Windsor, Sack Back, Oval Seat, Splayed Legs, Arms, Pa., Late 1700s, Pair 1135.00
Chair, Windsor, Step-Down, Painted, 7 Spindles, Bamboo Turned Legs, 36 x 18 In. 46.00
Chair, Windsor, Thumb Back Posts, 4 Spindles, Bamboo Turnings, Gold Stencil, Child's 200.00
Chair, Windsor, Thumb Back, Painted, Bowed Crest Rails, 33 In., Pair 646.00
Chair, Windsor, Thumb Back, Red Paint, Brown Star Panel, 3 Arrow Slats, 33 In. 145.00
Chair, Windsor, Wheel-Carved Splat, Arms, England, 1700s, 37 In. 575.00
Chair, Windsor, Writing Arm, Black Paint, 7 Spindles, Medallion Front, 44 1/2 In. 920.00
Chair, Windsor, Writing Arm, Drawer, Swelled Spindles, c.1780, 28 In. 3525.00
Chair, Windsor, Writing Arm, Maple, Oak, Splayed Base, Shaped Seat, 31 In. 1035.00
Chair, Wing, Chippendale Style, Mahogany, Camelback, Drop-In Seat, 48 x 24 x 22 In. 999.00
Chair, Wing, Chippendale Style, Mahogany, Cushion, Cabriole Legs, 50 x 31 In. 1888.00
Chair, Wing, Chippendale Style, Mahogany, Upholstered, Side Panel, 46 x 31 x 33 In. 500.00
Chair, Wing, Chippendale Style, Upholstered, Cabriole Front Legs, 43 3/4 In. 345.00
Chair, Wing, Chippendale, Mahogany Legs, Red Leather, England, c.1760, 48 In. 3900.00
Chair, Wing, Federal, Mahogany, Upholstered, Marlborough Legs, Late 1700s, 45 In. 530.00
Chair, Wing, George II Style, Mahogany, Needlework, Arms, 1800s, 42 x 32 In. 4720.00
Chair, Wing, George III, Mahogany, Square Legs, Casters, Scrolled Arms, c.1785 .... 1410.00
Chair, Wing, Georgian, Walnut, Crewelwork Upholstery, Cabriole Legs, Pad Feet 2235.00
Chair, Wing, Henredon, Walnut, Cabriole Legs, Pad Feet, 49 In., Pair 890.00
Chair, Wing, Louis XV Style, Beech, Cushion Seat, Scrolled Feet, 1900s, 15 In. 205.00
Chair, Wing, Mahogany, H-Stretcher, Continental, 18th Century 375.00
Chair, Wing, Mahogany, Scrolled Wings, Roll Arms, c.1780, Pair 5975.00
Chair, Wing, Mahogany, Upholstered, 1700s, 46 x 33 x 19 In. 1150.00
Chair, Wing, Queen Anne Style, Colonial Williamsburg, Kittinger, c.1950, 45 x 36 In. 2300.00
Chair, Wing, Queen Anne Style, Crewel Upholstery, Down Cushion, Arms 315.00
Chair, Wing, Queen Anne Style, Mahogany, Rolled Arms, 32 x 19 x 19 In., Child's 920.00
Chair, Wing, Queen Anne Style, Mahogany, Upholstered, Cabriole Legs, c.1900, 48 In. 825.00
Chair, Wing, Queen Anne Style, Mahogany, Upholstered, Cabriole Legs, Pad Feet, 1900s 646.00
Chair, Wood, Carved Crest, Cane Panel, Seat, Ball Finials, 43 1/2 x 19 3/4 x 16 In. 177.00
Chair, Wormley, Cane Back, Upholstered Cushion, Dunbar, 33 x 25 x 23 In. 355.00
Chair, Wormley, Slipper, Flaring Legs, Dunbar, 42 x 25 In., Pair 1416.00
Chair, Wormley, Walnut, Leather Upholstery, Arms, 23 1/2 x 25 x 31 1/2 In., Pair 705.00
Chair & Ottoman, Arne Norell, Inca Series, c.1968, 35 x 36 x 37 In. 1680.00
Chair & Ottoman, Brazilian Rosewood, Leather, 29 1/2 x 39 x 35 In. 3585.00
Chair & Ottoman, Eames, Aluminum Group, No. EA115, Herman Miller, c.1958, 39 In. 1560.00
Chair & Ottoman, Eames, Leather, 31 x 33 1/2 x 36 In. 2390.00
Chair & Ottoman, Eames, No. 670 & 671, Plywood, Leather, Herman Miller, 33 In. 2360.00
Chair & Ottoman, Eames, No. 670 & 671, Rosewood, Leather, c.1956, 31 x 34 x 36 In. 2700.00
Chair & Ottoman, Eero Saarinen, Womb, Knoll, c.1947, 36-In. Chair .... 1200.00 to 3900.00
Chair & Ottoman, Egg Stereo, Lee Chair Corp., c.1975, 52 x 40 x 48 In. .... 960.00 to 1080.00
Chair & Ottoman, G. Nelson, Upholstered, Chrome Legs, Herman Miller, 31 x 30 In. 885.00
Chair & Ottoman, Hans Wegner, Papa Bear, No. AP19, c.1951, 29 x 31 x 33 In. 7200.00
Chair & Ottoman, Horn, Moose Antler Frame, Leather, 46 x 46 x 35 In. 4425.00
Chair & Ottoman, Jan Ekselius, Upholstered, Black, 33 x 24 x 34 In. 1060.00
Chair & Ottoman, Jean Gillon, Wood, Leather, Wood Art Brazil, c.1965, 32 x 37 x 39 In. 3000.00
Chair & Ottoman, Mies Van Der Rohe, Barcelona, No. MR90, Knoll, c.1968, 29 x 31 In. 2400.00
Chair & Ottoman, Pesce, Donna, Foam, UP Series, B&B Italia 2595.00
Chair & Ottoman, Phillip Lloyd Powell, Walnut, Leather, New Hope, 33 x 29 x 31 In. 4130.00
Chair & Ottoman, V. Kagan, No. 175E, Walnut, Chenille Upholstery, 1965, 35 x 30 x 31 In. 10030.00
Chair & Ottoman, Wormley, Down Cushion, Brass D Tag, 28 x 17 x 15 In. 764.00
Chair & Ottoman, Wormley, Upholstered, Wood Base, Dunbar, 33 x 34 In. 1890.00
Chair & Stool, Risom, Army Surplus Webbing, Knoll, c.1942, 30 & 16 In. 960.00
Chair Set, Arne Jacobsen, Ant, Model 3100, Plywood, Steel, Fritz Hansen, 8 .... 1170.00
Chair Set, Art Deco, Tubular Chrome, Red Vinyl Seat, Back, Arms, 32 x 20 In., 4 .... 80.00
Chair Set, Ash Plywood, Molded, Chromed Steel Legs, Glides, 1950, 22 x 29 In., 4 .... 1295.00
Chair Set, Bamboo, Oval Panels, Spindles, Rabbit-Ear Finials, 18 x 36 In., 4 .... 750.00

Chair Set, Beech, Carved, Elephant Head Back, Hoof Feet, Rope Stile, 31 In., 4 .... 4113.00
Chair Set, Beech, Eared Crest, Turned Spindles, England, 36 In., 6 .... 940.00
Chair Set, Beech, Shaped Ladder Back, Rush Seat, 43 In., 10 .... 5405.00
Chair Set, Bergere, Louis XV Style, Cane, Concave Back, Serpentine Rail, 18 In., 4 .... 705.00
Chair Set, Biedermeier, Double Arched Crest, Padded Seat, 33 1/2 x 18 x 16 1/2 In., 6 .... 590.00
Chair Set, Biedermeier, Fruitwood, Arched Crest, Shaped Seat, 1900s, 8 .... 1760.00
Chair Set, Biedermeier, Inlaid Panel, Classical Figures, Saber Legs, 34 In., 6 .... 2205.00
Chair Set, Biedermeier, Rectangular Back, Ebonized, 2 Armchairs, 8 .... 1180.00
Chair Set, Bird's-Eye Maple, Needlepoint Seat, Heart, Spade, Clubs, Diamond, 4 .... 480.00
Chair Set, Burke, Teal, Enameled Seat, Pedestal Base, 1960s, 32 x 19 x 18 In., 5 .... 265.00
Chair Set, Cane Seat, Grain Painted, Vase Splat, Rounded Crest, 1800s, 35 In., 6 .... 980.00
Chair Set, Charles II, Oak, Pierced Leaf Crest, Upholstered Seat, Late 1800s, 43 1/4 In., 4 .... 470.00
Chair Set, Chippendale Style, Mahogany, Earred Crest, Leather Seat, 41 In., 12 .... 5170.00
Chair Set, Chippendale Style, Mahogany, Leaf-Carved Crest, Slip Seat, 1900s, 12 .... 1770.00
Chair Set, Chippendale Style, Mahogany, Leather, 2 Armchairs, 43 x 22 In., 8 .... 5700.00
Chair Set, Chippendale Style, Mahogany, Pierced Splat, 2 Armchairs, 41 In., 12 .... 3290.00
Chair Set, Chippendale Style, Mahogany, Ribbon Splat, Drop Seat, 2 Armchairs, 8 .... 3055.00
Chair Set, Chippendale Style, Mahogany, Shaped Crest, Slip In Seat, 2 Armchairs, 12 .... 3760.00
Chair Set, Chippendale, Birch, Rush Seats, Turned Legs, 17 1/2 x 37 1/2 In., 4 .... 1780.00
Chair Set, Curved Back, Horizontal Slats, Stencil, Rush Seat, 2 Armchairs, 35 In., 5 .... 1668.00
Chair Set, Eames, Aluminum Group, Upholstered, Swivel Base, Herman Miller, 33 In., 4 .... 885.00
Chair Set, Eames, White, Wire, 4-Footed, Herman Miller, c.1952, 34 x 21 In., 4 .... 1440.00
Chair Set, Eero Saarinen, Tulip, Pedestal, Fiberglass, Cast Aluminum, c.1955, 4 .... 302.00
Chair Set, Empire Style, Fruitwood, Ormolu Mounted, Square Legs, 1800s, 6 .... 1645.00
Chair Set, Faux Rosewood, Grained, Stenciled, Maine, c.1850, 32 1/2 In., 6 .... 825.00
Chair Set, Federal Style, Mahogany, Drapery & Leaf Splat, 2 Armchairs, Late 1800s, 8 .... 7170.00
Chair Set, Federal Style, Shieldback, Sheaf Of Wheat, 2 Armchairs, 1900s, 37 In., 8 .... 1840.00
Chair Set, Federal, Mahogany, Upholstered Seats, 34 x 18 x 18 In., 4 .... 935.00
Chair Set, Finn Juhl, Teak, Cane Seat, Dowel Legs, Baker, 31 x 21 x 23 In., 8 .... 2478.00
Chair Set, Finn Juhl, Teak, Scalloped Apron, Leather, Bovirke, 33 x 20 In., 4 .... 1003.00
Chair Set, Frank Lloyd Wright, Heritage Hendredon, c.1956, 32 x 23 1/2 In., 6 .... 1800.00
Chair Set, Frankl, Mahogany, Double X Back, Upholstered Seat, 32 In., 6 .... 2760.00
Chair Set, French Provincial, Fruitwood, Rush Seat, 2 Armchairs, c.1850, 38 In., 8 .... 3760.00
Chair Set, French Provincial, Walnut, Turned Splats, Rush Seat, c.1910, 33 In., 6 .... 235.00
Chair Set, G. Nakashima, Mira, Spindle Back, Spade Seat, 3 Legs, c.1968, 6 .... 8260.00
Chair Set, G. Nakashima, Walnut, Plank Seat, Hickory Spindles, 18 1/2 x 35 1/2 In., 4 .... 8225.00
Chair Set, G. Stickley, Curved Slats, Brown Leather Seat, 39 x 19 In., 4 .... 3055.00
Chair Set, George II Style, Mahogany, Carved Crest, Padded Seat, Cabriole Legs, 4 .... 649.00
Chair Set, George III Style, Mahogany, 2 Armchairs, 1900s, 18 1/2 x 38 In., 8 .... 3525.00
Chair Set, George III Style, Mahogany, Acanthine Splat, 2 Armchairs, 39 3/4 In., 12 .... 1880.00
Chair Set, George III Style, Mahogany, Interlaced Splat, Pad Seat, 2 Armchairs, 38 In., 8 .... 1760.00
Chair Set, George III Style, Mahogany, Ladder Back, 2 Armchairs, 38 In., 12 .... 8225.00
Chair Set, George III Style, Mahogany, Oval Back, Rosette, 2 Armchairs, 38 In., 8 .... 2115.00
Chair Set, George III Style, Mahogany, Shaped & Pierced Crest, c.1900, 38 In., 6 .... 2230.00
Chair Set, George III Style, Mahogany, Shaped Rail, Pierced Splat, Cabriole Legs, 6 .... 3525.00
Chair Set, George III Style, Mahogany, Upholstered, 2 Armchairs, 12 .... 6000.00
Chair Set, George III, Mahogany, Slip Seat, Beaker Splat, c.1780, 4 .... 3055.00
Chair Set, Georgian Style, Owl-Eye Splat, Slip Seat, 2 Armchairs, 1900s, 8 .... 1880.00
Chair Set, Georgian, Mahogany, Serpentine Crest, 2 Armchairs, 1800s, 37 In., 8 .... 5580.00
Chair Set, Gilt Stencil, Cane Seat, Maryland, 6 .... 2200.00
Chair Set, Grain Painted, Decorated, Shaped Crest, Turned Legs, 34 1/2 In., 4 .... 940.00
Chair Set, H. Bertoia, No. 420c, Steel Rod, Bent, Welded, Vinyl Coated, Knoll, c.1950, 4 .... 360.00
Chair Set, H. Probber, Machine-Caned Back, Vinyl Seat, Arms, 34 x 27 x 25 In., 4 .... 470.00
Chair Set, Half Spindle Back, Stencil, Flowers, Leaves, Fruit, Rabbit Ears, 32 In., 6 .... 748.00
Chair Set, Hall, George IV, Mahogany, Painted, Armorial Crest, c.1820, 6 .... 4800.00
Chair Set, Hepplewhite Style, Mahogany, Shieldback, Swag & Feather, 39 In., 12 .... 7050.00
Chair Set, Hepplewhite Style, Satinwood, Shaped Crest, Bellflowers, 2 Armchairs, 8 .... 1150.00
Chair Set, Hepplewhite Style, Shieldback, 2 Armchairs, 6 .... 1225.00
Chair Set, Hitchcock, Gold Stencil, Fruit Basket, Leaves, Cane Seat, 34 In., 4 .... 575.00
Chair Set, Hitchcock, Grain Painted, Flowers, Fruit Basket, 34 In., 6 .... 1955.00
Chair Set, Hitchcock, Painted, Stencil, Carved, Rush Seat, 1 Armchair, 34 In., 6 .... 1555.00

Chair Set, Horizontal Splat, Rear Raking Stiles, Compass Seats, c.1830, 34 In., 8 .... 2115.00
Chair Set, Jacobean Style, Oak, Carved Fleur-De-Lis, Twisted Stiles, Cane Back, 10 .... 4700.00
Chair Set, John Saladino, Leather, Arms, 35 x 24 In., 10 .... 2310.00
Chair Set, Ladder Back, Rush Seat, 2 Armchairs, England, 42 In., 12 .... 1645.00
Chair Set, Ladder Back, Splint Oak Seat, Red Stain, Tenn., Early 1800s, 6 .... 705.00
Chair Set, Limbert, Vertical Black Slats, Arrow Cutout, Leather Upholstery, 36 In., 4 .... 1765.00
Chair Set, Louis XV Style, Medallion Back, 1900s, 40 x 22 x 19 In., 8 .... 1150.00
Chair Set, Louis XVI Style, Mahogany, Brass Mounted, Back Crest, Tapered Legs, 4 .... 355.00
Chair Set, Mahogany Frames, Black Vinyl Seats, 19 x 20 3/4 x 32 In., 6 .... 590.00
Chair Set, Mahogany Graining, Crest Decoration, Balloon Back, 33 3/4 In., 6 .... 2070.00
Chair Set, Michel Cadestin, Georges Laurent, Beaubourg, Steel, Leather, 1976, 29 In., 4 .... 6000.00
Chair Set, Mies Van Der Rohe, Brno, Leather, Chrome, Arms, Knoll, 31 x 23 In., 4 .... 4720.00
Chair Set, Mies Van Der Rohe, Brno, Upholstered, Chrome, Arms, Knoll, 31 x 23 In., 8 .... 3305.00
Chair Set, Moorish, Hardwood, Mosaic Inlay, Arched Back, Slip Seat, 46 x 18 In., 4 .... 2235.00
Chair Set, N. Cherner, Walnut, Turquoise Vinyl Seat & Back, Plycraft, 31 In., 4 .... 2760.00
Chair Set, Neoclassical, Fruitwood, Painted, Lyre Splat, Italy, c.1790, 34 1/2 In., 4 .... 1800.00
Chair Set, Neoclassical, Mahogany, Curved Crest Rail, Upholstered Seat, c.1825, 6 .... 478.00
Chair Set, Neoclassical, Mahogany, Eared Crest, Splat Shell, Slip Seat, 34 In., 4 .... 1410.00
Chair Set, Neoclassical, Mahogany, Flame Veneer Crest, Carved Splat, Slip Seat, 4 .... 2115.00
Chair Set, Neoclassical, Mahogany, Leaf-Carved Splat, Reeded Stiles, 1815-30, 8 .... 5875.00
Chair Set, Neoclassical, Maple, Scrolled Crest, Urn Splat, Cane Seat, c.1825, 34 In., 4 .... 120.00
Chair Set, Neoclassical, Painted, Gilt Striping, Rush Seat, New York, Early 1800s, 8 .... 3525.00
Chair Set, Official's, Shaped Crest, Curved Split, Cane Seat, Chinese, 44 1/2 In., 4 .... 518.00
Chair Set, Painted, Oval Back, Upholstered, Serpentine Seat, England, 1900s, 36 In., 6 .... 590.00
Chair Set, Painted, Paneled Crest, Arrow Spindles, c.1835, 34 In., 6 .... 3290.00
Chair Set, Painted, Pierced Splats, Plank Seat, Rolled Edge, c.1840, 34 In., 6 .... 1410.00
Chair Set, Painted, Plank Seat, Crest Rails, Stenciled Urns, Flowers, 33 x 19 In., 6 .... 748.00
Chair Set, Painted, Shaped Crests, Lyre Splats, Scroll Seat, 33 In., 6 .... 3408.00
Chair Set, Paulin, Tulip, Upholstered Seat & Back, Artifort, 31 In., 4 .... 3400.00
Chair Set, Portuguese Colonial, Mahogany, Oval Palmette Back, Padded Seat, 36 In., 4 .... 3290.00
Chair Set, Primavera, Carved, Bamboo Finish, Woven Fabric, 35 x 23 x 30 In., 6 .... 8962.00
Chair Set, Queen Anne Style, Mahogany, Vase Splat, 2 Armchairs, 38 1/2 In., 12 .... 5287.00
Chair Set, Queen Anne Style, Mahogany, Yoke Crest, Drop Seat, 2 Armchairs, 1900s, 10 .... 4113.00
Chair Set, Queen Anne, Elm, Shaped Crest, Vase Splat, Slip Seat, 4 .... 3408.00
Chair Set, Queen Anne, Walnut, Pierced Splat, Upholstered, Stretchers, 4 .... 3466.00
Chair Set, Raffles, Teak, Cane Seat, Reeded Legs, England, 32 x 21 In., 3 .... 825.00
Chair Set, Regency Style, Mahogany, Carved Rail, Open Tablet Splat, Saber Legs, 12 .... 2115.00
Chair Set, Regency Style, Mahogany, Shaped Crest, Brass Splat, Upholstered, 10 .... 1763.00
Chair Set, Regency, Mahogany, Reeded, 2 Armchairs, England, Early 1800s, 6 .... 1763.00
Chair Set, Regency, Rosewood, Faux Grained, Lyre Splat, 2 Armchairs, c.1815, 32 In., 6 .... 1175.00
Chair Set, Renaissance Revival, Oak, Leaves, Pierced, Cane Seat, 1800s, 40 x 18 In., 6 .... 472.00
Chair Set, Ring Turned Back, Rush Seat, Tapered Supports, 6 .... 619.00
Chair Set, Robin Day, Polyprop, Hille & Co., London, c.1962, 4 .... 125.00
Chair Set, Rococo Style, Oak, Open Back, Slats, Upholstered Seats, 2 Armchairs, 12 .... 1003.00
Chair Set, Rosewood, Plank Seat, Shaped Splat, Turned Stretchers, 17 1/4 In., 6 .... 990.00
Chair Set, Royalchrome, Chrome, Vinyl, Horseshoe, Arms, Royal Metal, 31 x 20 In., 6 .... 253.00
Chair Set, Rush Seat, Cock Fighting, Armrest Crest, Adolph Vandenbroeck, c.1880, 6 .... 358.00
Chair Set, Shaker, Birch, Red & Brown Stained Finish, Cane, Rush Seats, c.1840, 41 In., 6 .... 14040.00
Chair Set, Shaker, Ladder Back, 3 Slats, Splint Seats, Stretchers, 16 In., 4 .... 1045.00
Chair Set, Shaker, Maple, Natural Varnish, 2 Slats, Splint Seats, c.1860, 26 In., 4 .... 4680.00
Chair Set, Sheraton Style, Mahogany, Shaped Crest, 2 Armchairs, 36 1/2 In., 12 .... 3995.00
Chair Set, Sheraton Style, Mahogany, Swag & Bellflower Splat, 37 In., 12 .... 4230.00
Chair Set, Sheraton, Mahogany, Burl Veneer Crest Rail, 1 Arm, 6 .... 2200.00
Chair Set, Spindle Back, 20th Century, 33 In., 4 .... 140.00
Chair Set, Spring Steel, Curved Back, Round Seat, Wrought Legs, Late 1800s, 37 In., 4 .... 930.00
Chair Set, Stefan Siwinski, Tubular Steel, Upholstered, Korina Designs, c.1970, 4 .... 415.00
Chair Set, Thayer Coggin, Faux Leopard, Arms, 4 .... 176.00
Chair Set, Thayer Coggin, Upholstered, Leather, Chrome, 6 .... 380.00
Chair Set, Thonet, Bentwood, Oval, Ring Turned Front Legs, Paper Label, 36 In., 4 .... 316.00
Chair Set, Thonet, Bentwood, Pressed Back, Round Seat, Flared Legs, 33 In., 6 .... 820.00
Chair Set, Tiger Maple, Carved Splat, Rush Seat, Early 19th Century, 4 .... 860.00

Chair Set, Tub, Karl Sorlie & Sonner Sarpseorg, Steel, Upholstered, Sweden, c.1970, 6 .... 450.00
Chair Set, Urn With Wings Crest, White Rush Seat, 32 1/2 In., 4 .... 259.00
Chair Set, Victorian, Mahogany, Carved Splat, Upholstered, Tufted, 7 .... 1070.00
Chair Set, Victorian, Walnut, Cane Seat, 33 x 16 x 17 In., 4 .... 58.00
Chair Set, Victorian, Walnut, Carved, Balloon Back, 1800s, 35 x 19 x 20 In., 6 .... 415.00
Chair Set, Walnut, Ladder Back, Pinecone Finials, Cornhusk Seats, 2 Armchairs, 6 .... 920.00
Chair Set, Walnut, Maple Finish, Patent Leather Upholstery, 28 1/2 x 18 x 19 In., 8 .... 9560.00
Chair Set, Wegner, Teak, Carl Hansen & Son, c.1965, 4 .... 300.00
Chair Set, William IV Style, Broad Crest, Patera Splat, Leather, 2 Armchairs, 37 In., 8 .... 1115.00
Chair Set, William IV, Mahogany, Inlay, Rope Twist Crest, Drop Seat, c.1835, 6 .... 2350.00
Chair Set, Windsor, 1-Board Plank Seat, England, 41 x 25 x 22 In., 6 .... 3165.00
Chair Set, Windsor, 6 Spindles, Bamboo Turnings, Yellow Paint, Grapes, 6 .... 2868.00
Chair Set, Windsor, Arrow Back, Yellow Paint, Decorated, 4 .... 1380.00
Chair Set, Windsor, Bamboo Turnings, Bulbous Legs, Stretchers, 17 1/2 In., 7 .... 330.00
Chair Set, Windsor, Bow Back, 7 Spindles, Saddle Seats, 1800s, 37 1/2 x 18 In., 4 .... 1880.00
Chair Set, Windsor, Bow Back, Black Paint, 7 Spindles, Turned Legs, c.1800, 36 In., 6 .... 5580.00
Chair Set, Windsor, Bow Back, Black Paint, Crest Rails, Spindles, Saddle Seat, 5 .... 3290.00
Chair Set, Windsor, Step-Down, Spindles, Arms, 6 .... 3400.00
Chair Set, Windsor, Thumb Back, Mustard Paint, Fruit, Wm. Fuller, 35 1/2 In., 6 .... 2360.00
Chair Set, Wormley, Ebonized, Tweed Cushion, Arms, Dunbar, 36 x 22 x 20 In., 4 .... 2360.00
Chair-Table, 3-Board Top, Breadboard Ends, Early 1800s, 29 x 52 x 37 In. 2090.00
Chair-Table, Birch, Grain Painted, Red, Round Tilt Top, Shaped Arms, 48 In. 4995.00
Chair-Table, Hardwood, Lift Seat, Rectangular, J. Franklin Miller, Pa., 30 x 47 x 33 In. 635.00
Chair-Table, Maple, Pine, Red Paint, Tilt Top, Late 18th Century, 26 x 51 1/2 In. 6169.00
Chair-Table, Pine, 1600s Elements, Scotland, 48 1/2 x 23 1/2 In. 649.00
Chair-Table, Pine, Red Wash, 4-Board Top, Dished Out Area, 96 x 42 x 29 In. 1610.00
Chair-Table, Pine, Tilt Top, Seat, Drawer, Pa., Early 1800s, 30 x 69 x 40 In. 508.00
Chair-Table, Red Paint, 4-Board Tilt Top, Box Stretcher, Square Legs, 27 x 39 In. 805.00
Chaise Longue, B. & K. Mathsson, Bentwood, Webbing, 36 x 25 x 54 In. 885.00
Chaise Longue, B. Mathsson, Pernilla Series, 35 x 25 x 72 In. 1440.00
Chaise Longue, Cast Aluminum, Sling Seat, Leather Cushions, Eggplant, 17 x 76 x 29 In. 3820.00
Chaise Longue, Eames, ES106, Herman Miller, c.1968, 29 x 17 x 75 In. 3300.00
Chaise Longue, Empire, Mahogany, Ormolu, Early 1800s, 35 x 71 x 33 In. 7640.00
Chaise Longue, G. Harcourt, Cleopatra, Upholstered, Foam, Steel, Artifort, 25 x 74 x 26 In. 885.00
Chaise Longue, Louis XV Style, Painted, 20th Century, 32 x 56 x 24 In. 355.00
Chaise Longue, Louis XVI Style, Mahogany, 6 Fluted & Tapered Legs, 35 x 29 x 57 In. 460.00
Chaise Longue, Louis XVI Style, Mahogany, Dome, Cushion Seat, 47 1/2 x 64 In. 2000.00
Chaise Longue, Mahogany, Cane, Cushions, 6 Turned Legs, England, 18 x 72 In. 2585.00
Chaise Longue, Marcel Breuer, Plywood, Leather, Arms, Late 1950s, 32 x 26 x 51 In. 2596.00
Chaise Longue, New Hope School, Oak Frame, Braided Jute, 33 x 29 x 60 In. 1535.00
Chaise Longue, Rocker, Leather, Chrome, Swivel Base, 1970s, 36 x 24 x 62 In. 2360.00
Chaise Longue, Victorian, Rosewood, Upholstered Button Back, Scrolled Ends, 80 In. 950.00
Chest, 2 Over 4 Drawers, Pivoting Mirror, Carved Posts, 65 x 33 x 18 3/4 In. .... ***ILLUS*** 2400.00
Chest, 3 Drawers, Mahogany, Birch, Nordiska Kompaniet, c.1930, 29 x 35 x 18 In. 8400.00
Chest, Biedermeier, 3 Drawers, Ebonized Top, Pulls, Feet, Lock, 1880-90, 11 x 13 In. 1500.00
Chest, Biedermeier, Maple, Ebony Inlay, 32 Drawers, Plinth Base, 1820, 25 1/2 In. 1295.00
Chest, Black Lacquer, 6 Drawers, Block Feet, Asia, 32 x 47 x 20 In. ....325.00 to 585.00
Chest, Blanket, 6-Board, Hinged Lift Top, Cutout Ends, Vinegar Putty Paint Fan, 21 x 37 In. 2115.00
Chest, Blanket, Baroque, Walnut, Germany, c.1700, 26 x 42 x 24 In. 470.00
Chest, Blanket, Blue Over Red Paint, Bootjack Legs, c.1820, 41 1/2 x 23 x 17 In. 850.00
Chest, Blanket, Blue Paint, 6-Board, Chamfered Lift Top, Cutout Ends, 33 x 60 x 23 In. 529.00
Chest, Blanket, Blue Paint, 6-Board, Poplar, Hinged Lift Top, Early 1800s, 24 x 45 In. 1175.00
Chest, Blanket, Blue Paint, 6-Board, Top Overhang, Rope Handles, 1800s, 18 x 44 In. 235.00
Chest, Blanket, Blue Paint, Dated 1832, 23 x 17 x 46 In. 575.00
Chest, Blanket, Blue Paint, Dovetailed, 2 Drawers, Ball Feet, 29 x 50 x 24 In. 1320.00
Chest, Blanket, Blue Paint, Drawer, Bootjack Ends, 28 1/2 x 41 x 15 In. 2015.00
Chest, Blanket, Blue Paint, Hinged Lid, Bracket Feet, Interior Till, 24 x 49 x 21 In. 450.00
Chest, Blanket, Blue Paint, Lincoln Homestead Scene, Meredith, N.H., 24 x 49 x 18 In. 4025.00
Chest, Blanket, Carved, Woman, Wavy Hair, Oval Crest, England, 29 x 72 12 x 32 In. 1265.00
Chest, Blanket, Chippendale, 2 Drawers, Dovetailed, Lift Top, 42 x 39 18 In. 690.00
Chest, Blanket, Chippendale, Pine, Scalloped, Molding, Bracket Feet, 9 x 5 1/2 In. 430.00

Furniture, Chest, 2 Over 4 Drawers, Pivoting Mirror, Carved Posts, 65 x 33 x 18 3/4 In.

Furniture, Chest, Blanket, Painted, Red, Black, Gold Stencil, Bowl Of Fruit, E.S. 1858, 20 x 37 x 14 In.

Chest, Blanket, Chippendale, Poplar, Painted, Iron Hinges, 46 1/2 x 21 x 25 1/2 In. 690.00
Chest, Blanket, Chippendale, Walnut, Inlaid, 2 Drawers, Late 1700s, 28 x 48 x 23 In. 5875.00
Chest, Blanket, Chippendale, Walnut, Poplar, 2 Drawers, 53 x 22 x 31 In. 978.00
Chest, Blanket, Dome Top, Vinegar & Freehand Paint, House By Lake, 12 x 30 x 15 In. 940.00
Chest, Blanket, G. Stickley, Paneled, Carved Crest, Copper Strapping, 23 x 41 In. 4115.00
Chest, Blanket, Grain Painted, Lift Top, 22 1/4 x 38 x 20 3/4 In. 1725.00
Chest, Blanket, Grained, Turned Feet, 20 x 12 x 14 In. 374.00
Chest, Blanket, Gray Paint, Flower, Molded Edge, 1800s, 14 1/2 x 24 3/4 x 12 1/2 In. 345.00
Chest, Blanket, Green Paint, Bootjack Ends, New England, c.1810, Miniature, 13 In. 3450.00
Chest, Blanket, Jacobean, Oak, Bootjack Ends, Plank Feet, 1600s, 20 x 40 x 14 In. 440.00
Chest, Blanket, Lift Top, 2 Drawers, Bracket Base, 27 x 48 x 22 In. 865.00
Chest, Blanket, Mahogany, Drawers, Stand, Anglo-Indian, 1800s, 33 x 44 x 21 In. 1530.00
Chest, Blanket, Mahogany, Grain Painted, 6-Board, Hinged Lid, Till, c.1810, 26 x 37 In. 765.00
Chest, Blanket, Mustard Paint, Lift Top, 4 Lipped Drawers, c.1820, 38 x 38 In. 730.00
Chest, Blanket, Neoclassical, Walnut, Dovetailed, Ball Feet, c.1830, 21 x 38 x 18 In. 880.00
Chest, Blanket, Painted, Bootjack Ends, Molded Top, 26 x 16 x 45 In. 460.00
Chest, Blanket, Painted, Dovetailed, Iron Lock, Side Handles, 9 3/4 x 24 x 13 1/2 In. 440.00
Chest, Blanket, Painted, Lift Top, Vermont, 36 1/2 x 44 In. 8800.00
Chest, Blanket, Painted, Red, Black, Gold Stencil, Bowl Of Fruit, E.S. 1858, 20 x 37 x 14 In. . *ILLUS* 6600.00
Chest, Blanket, Painted, Rosewood Grain, Square Nails, Iron Lock, Handles, 11 x 26 x 14 In. 440.00
Chest, Blanket, Pecan, Pine, Paneled, Southern U.S., Early 1800s, 20 x 29 x 17 In. 2328.00
Chest, Blanket, Pine, Bootjack Ends, Ditty Box, 1800s, 24 x 36 x 17 In. 200.00
Chest, Blanket, Pine, Dome Top, Dovetailed Corners, c.1840, 19 x 31 x 16 In. 175.00
Chest, Blanket, Pine, Dovetailed Corners, Molded Legs, 1800s, 14 x 37 x 19 In. 230.00
Chest, Blanket, Pine, Dovetailed, Signed Teter K. Lartman, 1868, 38 x 24 In. 345.00
Chest, Blanket, Pine, Drawer, Bracket Base, c.1830, 31 x 43 x 18 In. 316.00
Chest, Blanket, Pine, Drawer, Dovetailed, Brass Hardware, 33 x 39 x 17 In. 460.00
Chest, Blanket, Pine, Floral Panels, Dovetailed, Till, Iron Strap Hinges, 50 x 23 In. 1840.00
Chest, Blanket, Pine, Grain Finished, Lift Top, Turned Feet, Pa., c.1850, 38 1/4 In. 95.00
Chest, Blanket, Pine, Grain Painted, Black Trim & Ball Feet, 24 x 49 1/2 x 22 In. 743.00
Chest, Blanket, Pine, Grain Painted, Burnt Umber, Ocher, Yellow, 6-Board, 18 x 39 x 18 In. 1058.00
Chest, Blanket, Pine, Green Paint Trace, 2 Drawers, 17 x 42 x 45 In. 546.00
Chest, Blanket, Pine, Green Paint, 6-Board, 48 1/2 x 18 x 26 In. 575.00
Chest, Blanket, Pine, Lift Top, 2 Drawers, Bracket Feet, 23 x 42 1/2 x 19 1/4 In. 200.00
Chest, Blanket, Pine, Lift Top, 2 Drawers, Bracket Feet, Thomas Brown, Boston, 43 x 42 In. 690.00
Chest, Blanket, Pine, Lift Top, Ball Feet, Batwing Brasses, 37 x 36 x 18 1/2 In. 605.00
Chest, Blanket, Pine, Molded Bracket Base, Smoke Design, 24 x 52 x 22 1/2 In. 55.00
Chest, Blanket, Pine, Poplar, Black Paint, Scalloped Aprons, 36 x 14 1/2 x 22 In. 2070.00
Chest, Blanket, Pine, Poplar, Red Bands, Tulips, Green, White Combing, 50 x 22 In. 546.00
Chest, Blanket, Pine, Poplar, Till, Dovetailed, Scalloped Apron, Bracket Feet, 23 x 37 In. 400.00
Chest, Blanket, Pine, Poplar, Walnut, 6-Board, Ring Handles, 43 1/2 x 20 In. 690.00
Chest, Blanket, Pine, Red Paint, 6-Board, Ditty Box, Snipe Hinges, 23 x 36 x 16 In. 290.00

Furniture, Chest, Blanket, Poplar, Painted, Lid, Swirl & Fan Design, 22 x 38 x 18 In.

Furniture, Chest, Blanket, Softwood, Grain Painted, Molded Lid, 19th Century, 28 1/2 x 50 1/2 x 24 In.

Chest, Blanket, Pine, Red, Paneled, 6-Board, Molded Edge, c.1830, 26 x 49 x 20 5/8 In. 3760.00
Chest, Blanket, Pine, Robin's-Egg Blue Over Red, Till, Conn., 9 x 4 1/2 x 4 1/4 In. 690.00
Chest, Blanket, Pine, Stencils, Continental, 1700s, 33 1/2 x 62 In. 765.00
Chest, Blanket, Pine, Yellow Paint, J. Weber, Pa., Early 1800s, 4 x 7 x 3 1/2 In. 14400.00
Chest, Blanket, Poplar, Grained, Stencils, Soap Hollow, Till, c.1859, 44 x 23 In. 7190.00
Chest, Blanket, Poplar, Green, Red Sponging, Raised Panels, Scroll Feet, 57 x 30 In. 460.00
Chest, Blanket, Poplar, Molded Top, Lidded Till, Iron Butt Hinges, 23 1/2 x 36 x 19 In. 375.00
Chest, Blanket, Poplar, Molded, Iron Strap Hinges, 3 Drawers, 28 x 50 x 22 1/2 In. 1265.00
Chest, Blanket, Poplar, Painted, Lid, Swirl & Fan Design, 22 x 38 x 18 In. .... *ILLUS* 1155.00
Chest, Blanket, Poplar, Pine, Oak, Black Painted, Unicorns, Tulips, Dovetailed, 15 x 10 In. 345.00
Chest, Blanket, Poplar, Red Paint, Dovetailed, Pine Till, 37 x 18 x 25 In. 750.00
Chest, Blanket, Poplar, Red Paint, Flame Graining, Bracket Base, 42 x 19 x 21 1/2 In. 575.00
Chest, Blanket, Poplar, Red Wash, Molded Edge, Dovetailed, Peg Feet, 31 x 21 In. 230.00
Chest, Blanket, Red Paint, 2 Drawers, Hinged Top, Bracket Feet, 41 x 42 x 17 In. 840.00
Chest, Blanket, Red Paint, 6-Board, 23 x 44 x 18 In. 400.00
Chest, Blanket, Red Paint, Bootjack Ends, 11 x 33 x 16 In. 690.00
Chest, Blanket, Red Paint, Bootjack Ends, Maine, 24 x 41 x 18 In. 115.00
Chest, Blanket, Red Paint, Lid, Horse, Dauphin County, c.1850, 16 x 31 In. 2420.00
Chest, Blanket, Schwenkfelder, Paint, Drawers, Glass Pulls, 1847, 45 x 27 In. 8365.00
Chest, Blanket, Sheraton, Poplar, Blue Paint, Turned Feet, 40 x 17 1/2 In. 1095.00
Chest, Blanket, Softwood, 2 Drawers, Flowers, Tombstone Panel, 25 x 47 x 21 In. 4620.00
Chest, Blanket, Softwood, 2 Molded-Lip Drawers, Ball Feet, 28 1/2 x 50 x 24 In. 1320.00
Chest, Blanket, Softwood, Grain Painted, Molded Lid, 19th Century, 28 1/2 x 50 1/2 x 24 In. *ILLUS* 2200.00
Chest, Blanket, Softwood, Grain Painted, Yellow, Strap Hinges, Ball Feet, 28 x 49 x 23 In. 248.00
Chest, Blanket, Softwood, Painted Center Panel, Strap Hinges, 23 x 54 x 24 In. 495.00
Chest, Blanket, Softwood, Painted Swirls, Yellow Ground, Dovetailed, 26 x 50 In. 1210.00
Chest, Blanket, Softwood, Painted, Bracket Feet, Iron Hinges, Brass Lock, 11 x 24 x 12 In. 1870.00
Chest, Blanket, Softwood, Painted, Dovetailed, Madi Grosin, 1793, 23 x 54 x 24 In. 495.00
Chest, Blanket, Softwood, Red Potato Stamping, Yellow, Pa., 24 x 43 x 22 In. 770.00
Chest, Blanket, Softwood, Sgraffito Style, Strap Hinges, Lock, Key, 26 x 51 x 23 3/4 In. 2420.00
Chest, Blanket, Softwood, Sponged, Dovetailed, York County, 26 x 51 In. 2420.00
Chest, Blanket, Softwood, Tombstone Panel, Lancaster County, 1790s, 26 x 50 In. 3850.00
Chest, Blanket, Sponge Decorated, Lift Top, Bracket Base, 24 x 40 x 20 1/2 In. 460.00
Chest, Blanket, Tombstone Panels, Stars In Circle, Crescent Moon, 25 x 51 x 22 In. 990.00
Chest, Blanket, Walnut, 6-Board, Nailed, Strap Hinges, 18 1/2 x 36 x 13 1/2 In. 525.00
Chest, Blanket, Walnut, Breadboard Top, Iron Butt Hinges, Frame, 21 x 37 In. 978.00
Chest, Blanket, Walnut, Dovetailed, Scalloped Aprons, Bracket Feet, 49 x 20 x 27 In. 1150.00
Chest, Blanket, Walnut, Inset Side Panels, Turned Feet, 12 1/2 x 5 1/2 In. 835.00
Chest, Blanket, Walnut, Molded Edges, 2 Drawers, Iron Strap Hinges, 27 x 51 x 22 In. 2070.00
Chest, Blanket, Walnut, Pine, Lidded Till, Turned Feet, Hinges, Lock, 27 x 49 x 19 1/4 In. 489.00
Chest, Blue Paint, Rope Carving, 2 Bonnet & 2 Side Over 3 Long Drawers, 44 x 47 In. 935.00
Chest, Burl Walnut, 6 Drawers, Molded Edge, England, 1800s, 53 1/4 x 37 In. 770.00
Chest, Campaign, 2 Sections, 42 1/2 x 20 x 39 1/4 In. 235.00

Chest, Campaign, Camphorwood, 3 Part, 5 Drawers, 2 Doors, 1800s, 72 x 38 x 22 In. 5980.00
Chest, Campaign, Camphorwood, Anglo-Indian, c.1850, 43 x 43 x 19 In. 3820.00
Chest, Campaign, Camphorwood, Anglo-Indian, c.1850, 43 x 45 x 23 In. 2940.00
Chest, Campaign, Camphorwood, Ebony, Secretary Drawer, Chinese, 1800s, 44 x 41 In. 485.00
Chest, Campaign, Camphorwood, Leather, Brass Bound, Engraved, J.R. Goodwin, 16 x 36 In. 499.00
Chest, Campaign, Mahogany, Brass Bound, 2 Short Over 3 Long Drawers, 38 x 41 In. 1175.00
Chest, Campaign, Mahogany, Brass Bound, 5 Drawers, England, 1800s, 42 x 36 In. 2240.00
Chest, Campaign, Queen Anne, 2 Parts, 5 Drawers, England, 39 x 37 x 20 In. 600.00
Chest, Camphorwood, Brass Bound, Bracket Handles, 1800s, 12 x 33 x 17 In. 805.00
Chest, Camphorwood, Brass Bound, Bracket Handles, 1800s, 15 x 28 x 14 In. 690.00
Chest, Camphorwood, Dovetailed, Brass Handles, 12 1/2 x 27 1/2 x 13 1/2 In. 400.00
Chest, Cherry, Grain Painted, Molded Cornice, 6 Drawers, 55 x 42 x 19 In. 3450.00
Chest, Cherry, Maple, Old Red Finish, Brass Knobs, Ball Feet, 19 x 10 1/2 In. 949.00
Chest, Cherry, Pine, Cock-Beaded, Paneled Ends, 2 Drawers, 11 1/2 x 9 In. 430.00
Chest, Chippendale Style, Mahogany, Blocked, Serpentine Front, 35 x 43 x 23 1/2 In. 2185.00
Chest, Chippendale Style, Mahogany, Pine, Veneer, 6 Drawers, 50 x 20 x 37 In. 575.00
Chest, Chippendale, Butternut, Chamfered Top, 4 Drawers, 35 x 35 x 17 1/2 In. 1530.00
Chest, Chippendale, Cherry, Bracket Base, 6 Drawers, Late 1700s, 56 x 40 x 19 In. 1840.00
Chest, Chippendale, Cherry, Pine, 2-Board Top, 3 Drawers, Brass, 37 x 45 In. 890.00
Chest, Chippendale, Cherry, Pine, 4 Graduated Drawers, Bracket Feet, 42 x 36 In. 1095.00
Chest, Chippendale, Mahogany, 4 Cock-Beaded Drawers, 35 x 41 In. 1725.00
Chest, Chippendale, Mahogany, 4 Drawers, c.1775, 32 x 29 x 17 In. 2350.00
Chest, Chippendale, Mahogany, 6 Drawers, England, 39 x 44 x 22 In. 920.00
Chest, Chippendale, Mahogany, Figured, 4 Graduated Drawers, Pa., c.1775, 36 x 40 In. 4500.00
Chest, Chippendale, Mahogany, Poplar, 4 Graduated Drawers, 39 x 22 In. 750.00
Chest, Chippendale, Mahogany, Serpentine, 4 Graduated Drawers, c.1780, 32 x 40 In. 11750.00
Chest, Chippendale, Maple, 3 Over 4 Drawers, Dental Molding, Bracket Base, 36 In. 1210.00
Chest, Chippendale, Maple, 4 Drawers, Molded Cornice, c.1785, 37 x 36 In. 2070.00
Chest, Chippendale, Maple, 6 Drawers, Molded Cornice, Brass, c.1785, 55 x 36 In. 8510.00
Chest, Chippendale, Maple, 7 Drawers, Dovetailed, 58 x 36 x 17 In. 2300.00
Chest, Chippendale, Maple, Figured, 2 Short Over 5 Long Drawers, c.1780, 51 x 40 In. 5100.00
Chest, Chippendale, Maple, Molded Cornice, 6 Graduated Drawers, 55 x 38 x 18 In. 5580.00
Chest, Chippendale, Maple, Overhanging Top, 4 Drawers, Late 1700s, 33 x 37 x 20 In. 3820.00
Chest, Chippendale, Maple, Tiger Maple, 3 Short Over 4 Long Drawers, 40 x 36 In. 2000.00
Chest, Chippendale, Maple, Tiger Maple, 4 Graduated Drawers, 36 x 34 x 18 In. 2000.00
Chest, Chippendale, Tiger Maple, 3 Drawers, 36 x 38 x 19 In. 2645.00
Chest, Chippendale, Tiger Maple, 6 Graduated Drawers, Bracket Base, 37 1/2 In. 8800.00
Chest, Chippendale, Walnut, 4 Drawers, Ogee Bracket Feet, 42 In. 4400.00
Chest, Chippendale, Walnut, 5 Drawers, Ogee Feet, Pa., 1700s, 33 x 38 x 21 In. 5380.00
Chest, Chippendale, Walnut, Reeded Columns, Ogee Bracket Feet, 36 x 39 In. 4818.00
Chest, Curly Maple, Bowfront, 4 Drawers, 35 1/2 x 38 1/2 x 21 In. 3738.00
Chest, Dan Johnson, 2 Drawers, Haden Hall, c.1946, 30 x 48 x 20 In. 900.00
Chest, Directoire, Mahogany, Drawers, Gilt Metal Mounts, 6 1/2 In., Pair 1335.00
Chest, Donald Deskey, Black Lacquer, Blond Wood, 5 Drawers, Amodec, 50 x 28 In. 530.00
Chest, Dower, Arts & Crafts, Oak, Cedar Lining, Fluted Plank Legs, 34 1/4 x 47 3/8 In. 865.00
Chest, Dower, Federal, Maple, Cherry, Walnut, 2 Drawers, Lift Top, c.1820, 37 x 24 In. 325.00
Chest, Dower, Oak, 2 Drawers, Animals, Leaves, Continental, 1788, 32 x 59 x 24 In. 1645.00
Chest, Dower, Pine, Hinged Top, 2 Half Drawers, Pinwheels, Fans, 27 x 44 x 22 In. 7638.00
Chest, Dower, Pine, Red Paint, Till, Compass Stars, Bear-Trap Lock, c.1792, 49 x 22 In. 2760.00
Chest, Drop Front, Brass Mount, Bracket, Korea, 24 1/2 x 23 In. 575.00
Chest, Dutch Rococo Revival, Bombe, Red Japanned, 5 Drawers, 1800s, 37 x 38 In. 3290.00
Chest, Edwardian, Satinwood, 5 Drawers, Campaign Style Hardware, 59 x 22 x 20 In. 2585.00
Chest, Empire, Cherry, Drawers, Early 19th Century, 44 x 43 x 21 1/2 In. 470.00
Chest, Empire, Mahogany, 1 Curved & 3 Flat Drawers, Glass Pulls, 45 x 43 x 20 In. 540.00
Chest, Empire, Mahogany, 2 Drawers, Scrolled Feet, 10 x 10 1/4 x 5 In. 250.00
Chest, Empire, Mahogany, 5 Drawers, Harp-Shaped Mirror, 40 In. 220.00
Chest, Empire, Mahogany, 6 Drawers, Gilt Bronze, France, 59 x 33 x 19 In. 7050.00
Chest, Empire, Mahogany, 7 Drawers, Square Posts, 3-Part Backsplash, 40 1/2 In. 385.00
Chest, Empire, Walnut, Cherry, Cherry Veneer, Bonnet Drawer, 51 x 41 x 19 3/4 In. 805.00
Chest, Federal Style, Mahogany, Bowfront, 4 Drawers, 1905, 38 x 43 x 24 In. 2235.00
Chest, Federal Style, Veneer, Graduated Drawers, Baluster Legs, 44 x 39 x 20 In. 355.00

Chest, Federal Style, Walnut, Inlaid, Molded Top, 5 Drawers, 38 x 40 1/2 x 22 In. 2415.00
Chest, Federal, Cherry Inlay, Crossbanded, Mahogany Border, 38 x 43 x 20 In. 529.00
Chest, Federal, Cherry, 4 Beaded Tiger Maple Drawers, Reeded Posts, 37 1/2 In. 840.00
Chest, Federal, Cherry, 4 Graduated Drawers, French Bracket Feet, 44 x 37 In. 2000.00
Chest, Federal, Cherry, 7 Drawers, Molded Cornice, c.1800, 61 x 40 x 20 In. 5079.00
Chest, Federal, Cherry, Birch, Carved, Inlay, Oval Corners, c.1820, 37 x 39 1/2 In. 880.00
Chest, Federal, Cherry, Butternut, Tiger Maple, Inlaid, 4 Drawers, 1800s, 36 x 41 In. 1528.00
Chest, Federal, Cherry, Cherry Veneer, Bowfront, 4 Drawers, c.1800, 38 x 39 x 21 In. 2820.00
Chest, Federal, Cherry, Maple, 4 Drawers, Pa., c.1890, 41 x 41 x 19 In. 1910.00
Chest, Federal, Cherry, Veneer, 6 Drawers, Wood Pulls, 52 x 41 1/2 x 39 In. 5290.00
Chest, Federal, Mahogany Inlay, Bowfront, String & Panel Drawer, c.1800, 40 x 41 In. 5875.00
Chest, Federal, Mahogany, 3 Glove Drawers, 4 Drawers, Early 1800s, 50 x 46 x 24 In. 3175.00
Chest, Federal, Mahogany, 4 Cock-Beaded Drawers, Oval Brasses, 36 x 45 In. 956.00
Chest, Federal, Mahogany, 4 Drawers, Brass Rosette Pulls, Backsplash, 48 x 43 x 20 In. 489.00
Chest, Federal, Mahogany, 5 Drawers, Spiral Side Columns, 41 x 44 In. 300.00
Chest, Federal, Mahogany, Bowfront, 4 Beaded Drawers, French Feet, 39 x 42 x 23 In. 1016.00
Chest, Federal, Mahogany, Bowfront, 4 Drawers, c.1790, 37 x 42 x 26 In. 3300.00
Chest, Federal, Mahogany, Bowfront, 4 Drawers, Gallery Top, Turned Legs, 41 x 39 In. 470.00
Chest, Federal, Mahogany, Figured, Serpentine Front, 4 Graduated Drawers, c.1790 .... 3600.00
Chest, Federal, Mahogany, Inlaid, Bowfront, 4 Drawers, c.1800, 39 x 41 x 21 In. 7768.00
Chest, Federal, Mahogany, Inlaid, Bowfront, c.1810, 37 3/4 x 43 1/4 x 24 1/8 In. 3820.00
Chest, Federal, Mahogany, Mahogany Veneer, Swelled Front, c.1810, 37 3/4 x 41 In. 1410.00
Chest, Federal, Mahogany, Pine, Drawers, Mirror, Glove Drawers, 71 x 19 x 43 1/2 In. 660.00
Chest, Federal, Mahogany, Poplar, Pine, Geometric Inlay, Drawers, 38 x 19 x 20 In. 2415.00
Chest, Federal, Maple, Figured, Bowfront, 4 Drawers, Pa., Early 1800s, 40 x 43 x 20 In. 3107.00
Chest, Federal, Maple, Inlaid Garland, Bowfront, 4 Drawers, c.1800, 36 x 39 In. 11750.00
Chest, Federal, Maple, Inlaid, 4 Drawers, New York, 41 3/4 x 39 x 21 1/2 In. 7200.00
Chest, Federal, Painted, 2 Drawers, Hinged Lift Top, Cutout Feet, Early 1800s, 37 x 37 In. 8225.00
Chest, Federal, Red & Black Paint, Green & Yellow Pinstriping, 44 x 22 x 50 In. 10350.00
Chest, Federal, Red Paint, 4 Drawers, Bethel, Maine, 42 x 19 x 40 In. 805.00
Chest, Federal, Tiger Maple, 4 Drawers, Square Stiles, c.1820, 40 x 44 x 17 3/4 In. 1175.00
Chest, Federal, Walnut, 6 Drawers, Mid-Atlantic, 1800s, 46 x 38 In. 1295.00
Chest, Federal, Walnut, 8 Drawers, Cove-Molded Top, c.1780, 68 x 43 In. 5378.00
Chest, Federal, Walnut, Graduated Drawers, Scalloped Apron, 42 x 42 In. 999.00
Chest, Federal, Walnut, Inlaid, 4 Drawers, Bracket Feet, c.1800, 38 x 42 x 18 In. 1195.00
Chest, Federal, Walnut, Inlaid, 4 Drawers, Cock-Beaded, Mid-Atlantic, 38 x 42 x 21 In. 1998.00
Chest, Federal, Walnut, Line Inlay, 4 Drawers, Pa., c.1800, 41 In. 780.00
Chest, Florence Knoll, Teak, 9 Drawers, c.1951, 30 x 110 x 20 In. 3600.00
Chest, G. Stickley, 2 Over 3 Drawers, Backsplash, Chamfered Sides, 42 x 36 In. 8815.00
Chest, G. Stickley, Oak, 5 Drawers, 33 x 45 x 22 In. 575.00
Chest, George III, Black Lacquer, Parcel Gilt, Polychrome, Early 1800s, 32 x 34 In. 3760.00
Chest, George III, Mahogany, 2 Over 3 Drawers, Bracket Feet, 40 1/2 x 43 1/2 x 19 In. 590.00
Chest, George III, Mahogany, 2 Short Over 3 Long Drawers, Bracket Feet, 36 x 42 In. 1175.00
Chest, George III, Mahogany, 5 Drawers, Gillow Furniture, c.1790, 33 x 36 x 20 In. 5400.00
Chest, George III, Mahogany, 5 Drawers, Inset Columns, Late 1700s, 42 x 47 In. 1765.00
Chest, George III, Mahogany, 6 Drawers, Ogee Bracket Feet, 45 x 44 x 21 In. 1175.00
Chest, George III, Mahogany, 8 Drawers, Bracket Feet, 18th Century, 84 x 45 x 23 In. 2585.00
Chest, George III, Mahogany, Bowfront, 4 Drawers, Bracket Feet, c.1800, 40 x 40 In. 2468.00
Chest, George III, Mahogany, Bowfront, 5 Drawers, Early 1800s, 41 x 42 x 20 In. 3525.00
Chest, George III, Mahogany, Inlaid, Serpentine, 4 Drawers, c.1790, 35 1/4 x 46 1/4 In. 8400.00
Chest, George III, Mahogany, Rectangular Top, 5 Drawers, Late 1700s, 40 x 42 x 22 In. 3525.00
Chest, George III, Mahogany, Rectangular Top, Molded Edge, 5 Drawers, 40 x 38 In. 1410.00
Chest, George III, Mahogany, Serpentine Front, 4 Drawers, 34 x 39 x 22 In. 5400.00
Chest, George III, Mahogany, Straight Front, 8 Short Drawers, 35 x 37 x 21 In. 3058.00
Chest, George III, Satinwood, Bowfront, 5 Drawers, Early 1800s, 40 x 36 x 20 In. 2820.00
Chest, George III, Satinwood, Marble Top, 8 Graduated Drawers, 60 x 26 In. 1410.00
Chest, George IV, Mahogany, Bowfront, 5 Drawers, Reeded Top, c.1810, 39 x 41 In. 1469.00
Chest, Georgian Style, Mahogany, 4 Drawers, Ogee Bracket Feet, 32 x 35 x 19 In. 1765.00
Chest, Georgian Style, Mahogany, Crossbanded, 4 Drawers, c.1900, 42 x 42 x 21 In. 825.00
Chest, Georgian Style, Mahogany, Short Over Long Drawers, Bracket Feet, 32 x 33 In. 705.00
Chest, Georgian, Mahogany, 4 Drawers, c.1800, 34 x 32 x 18 In. 780.00

Chest, Georgian, Oyster Walnut, 4 Drawers, Bracket Base, 30 x 42 x 20 In. 1287.00
Chest, Georgian, Walnut, String Inlay, 5 Drawers, Bracket Feet, Early 1700s, 36 x 39 In. 2468.00
Chest, Grain Painted, 3 Drawers, Splat, Early 1800s, 38 x 38 x 17 In. 585.00
Chest, Grain Painted, Red, 2 Short Over 2 Long Drawers, 16 x 14 In. 1058.00
Chest, Henredon, George II Style, 3 Drawers, Chamfered Corners, 1900s, 25 x 28 In., Pair 650.00
Chest, Hepplewhite, Cherry, 4 Drawers, 36 x 42 x 19 In. 635.00
Chest, Hepplewhite, Cherry, 4 Graduated Drawers, Brass Pulls, 36 x 41 x 17 1/2 In. 990.00
Chest, Hepplewhite, Cherry, 5 Graduated Drawers, Bowfront, 39 In. 1870.00
Chest, Hepplewhite, Cherry, Poplar, Walnut, 4 Drawers, Scalloped Aprons, 42 x 38 In. 980.00
Chest, Hepplewhite, Cherry, String Inlay, Bowfront, French Feet, 20 x 39 x 36 In. 1495.00
Chest, Hepplewhite, Curly Maple, Poplar, 4 Drawers, Cock-Beaded, 19 x 23 In. 690.00
Chest, Hepplewhite, Mahogany, 4 Drawers, Bowfront, Scrolled Apron, 34 x 41 x 20 In. 6670.00
Chest, Hepplewhite, Mahogany, 5 Drawers, Cock-Beaded Edge, c.1810, 40 x 41 In. 880.00
Chest, Hepplewhite, Mahogany, 6 Drawers, Scalloped Apron, 42 x 42 x 21 In. 1265.00
Chest, Hepplewhite, Mahogany, Bowfront, 4 Drawers, c.1800 .... 10500.00
Chest, Hepplewhite, Mahogany, Cherry, Poplar, Inlaid, 4 Drawers, c.1800, 31 x 41 In. 2415.00
Chest, Hepplewhite, Mahogany, Pine, 4 Drawers, c.1790, 40 x 41 In. 1610.00
Chest, Hepplewhite, Mahogany, Pine, Scalloped Apron, 6 Drawers, 40 x 44 x 21 In. 385.00
Chest, Hepplewhite, Maple, Bowfront, Overhanging Top, 4 Drawers, 36 x 32 1/2 In. 575.00
Chest, Hepplewhite, Painted, Grained, Bonnet, 42 x 42 x 18 In. 1035.00
Chest, Louis XV Style, Parquetry, Marble, 5 Graduated Drawers, c.1900, 47 x 32 In. 1410.00
Chest, Louis XV/XVI Style, Parquetry, Marble Top, 2 Drawers, 30 x 14 1/2 In. 295.00
Chest, Mahogany, 3 Dovetailed Drawers, Locks, Black Pulls, Lift-Out Trays, 11 x 8 In. 230.00
Chest, Mahogany, 4 Drawers, Bracket Feet, 18th Century, 34 x 36 x 18 3/4 In. 1300.00
Chest, Mahogany, Bowfront, Cookie Corners, 4 Drawers, 39 x 38 x 19 In. 1208.00
Chest, Mahogany, Bracket Feet, England, 36 1/2 x 20 In. 800.00
Chest, Mahogany, Marble Top, 3 Drawers, D-Shape, 1800s, 35 x 47 x 23 In. 415.00
Chest, Mahogany, Pencil Line Inlay, 4 Drawers, Bracket Feet, Casters, 39 x 41 In. 896.00
Chest, Mahogany, Pine, 2 Over 2 Dovetailed Drawers, Glass Knobs, 16 x 11 In. 230.00
Chest, Maple, 6 Drawers, New England, 54 x 36 In. 2320.00
Chest, Maple, 6 Drawers, Rhode Island, 54 In. 4060.00
Chest, Maple, 6 Graduated Drawers, Bracket Base, N.H., 55 x 36 x 17 1/2 In. 9200.00
Chest, Maple, Molded Edge, Bracket Base, 4 Drawers, Acorn, Leaf Hardware, 37 x 19 In. 1800.00
Chest, Marble Top, 6 Drawers, Bracket Base, Gilt, Metal Mounts, France, 27 x 58 In. 1755.00
Chest, Mixed Wood, 4 Drawers, Rounded Corners, Apron, 1800s, 35 x 36 x 20 In. 270.00
Chest, Mixed Wood, Side Panels, Shaped Apron, 3 Drawers, 35 x 38 1/2 x 17 1/2 In. 708.00
Chest, Mule, George III Style, Burl Walnut, 20th Century, 32 x 60 1/2 x 18 In. 649.00
Chest, Mule, Pine, Old Brown Paint, 2 Drawers, Bun Feet, 41 1/2 x 19 x 33 3/4 In. 1265.00
Chest, Mule, Pine, Vinegar Grain, Dovetailed Drawer, Scalloped Apron, 37 x 31 In. 1325.00
Chest, Neoclassical, Fruitwood Inlay, 2 Drawers, Italy, Early 1800s, 32 x 34 x 20 In. 1880.00
Chest, Neoclassical, Mahogany, Marble Top, Projecting Drawer, 42 x 48 x 24 In. 2820.00
Chest, Neoclassical, Mahogany, Scrolled Gallery, 7 Drawers, c.1830, 66 x 49 In. 2820.00
Chest, Neoclassical, Walnut, Fruitwood, 4 Drawers, Italy, c.1810, 31 x 33 x 17 In. 2585.00
Chest, Neocolonial, Walnut, Molded Cornice, 9 Drawers, 63 x 41 x 21 1/2 In. 3290.00
Chest, Nutting, No. 934, Sheraton, Mahogany, Carved, 4 Drawers, 40 x 42 x 19 In. 4730.00
Chest, Oak, 4 Drawers, Paneled Sides, Bracket Base, 38 x 38 x 24 In. 715.00
Chest, Oak, 4 Over 3 Graduated Long Drawers, 18th Century, 39 x 17 x 31 In. 476.00
Chest, Painted, Gesso, 3 Drawers, Parcel Gilt, Italy, 37 x 46 x 23 In. 5580.00
Chest, Pine, 3 Drawers, Carved Columns, 1800s, 34 x 42 x 23 In. 175.00
Chest, Pine, 4 Drawers, Art Nouveau Pulls, Late 1800s, 35 x 42 x 21 In. 290.00
Chest, Pine, Green Paint, c.1830, 17 1/4 x 17 5/8 x 9 In. 1760.00
Chest, Pine, Inlay, 3 Over 4 Cock-Beaded, Drawers, Kite Escutcheons, 42 x 42 x 20 In. 3910.00
Chest, Pine, Painted, 6-Board, Lift Top, Molding, Cutout Ends, 21 1/2 x 47 x 16 In. 440.00
Chest, Pine, Painted, 6-Board, Molded Lift Top, Dovetailed, Late 1700s, 20 1/2 x 42 In. 880.00
Chest, Pine, Polychrome, 3 Drawers, Bun Feet, Italy, Late 1800s, 39 x 49 In. 3525.00
Chest, Pine, Red Paint, Thumb-Molded Hinged Top, 2 Drawers, 1700s 5290.00
Chest, Pine, Walnut Inlay, Chamfered Backboards, 19th Century, 59 x 40 x 20 In. 6900.00
Chest, Poplar, Green & White Paint, Scalloped Aprons, 45 x 20 x 29 1/2 In. 115.00
Chest, Poplar, Painted, 2 Drawers, Henry Lapp Attribution, 1895, 27 x 48 x 24 In. 165.00
Chest, Poplar, Painted, 6-Board, Molded Lift Top, Cutout Ends, 1800s, 17 x 33 In. 380.00
Chest, Poplar, Pine, Red Paint, 3 Drawers, Arched Cutouts, 10 5/8 x 7 1/4 x 10 3/4 In. 316.00

Chest, Queen Anne Style, Mahogany, 4 Drawers 795.00
Chest, Queen Anne Style, Walnut, Banded, Oyster Veneer Panels, 5 Drawers, 38 x 42 In. 2350.00
Chest, Queen Anne, Cherry, Swan's-Neck Crest, 9 Drawers, c.1780, 82 x 38 In. 12338.00
Chest, Queen Anne, Pine, Carved, Lift Top, Applied Molding, 49 x 38 3/8 x 18 1/2 In. 2235.00
Chest, Queen Anne, Pine, Drawers, Batwing Brasses, 39 3/4 x 18 1/2 x 49 3/4 In. 1380.00
Chest, Queen Anne, Pine, Red Paint, 2 Short Over 4 Long Drawers, 44 x 39 x 19 In. 645.00
Chest, Queen Anne, Walnut, 5 Drawers, Banded, Bun Feet, Late 1700s, 36 x 28 In. 3290.00
Chest, Queen Anne, Walnut, 8 Drawers, c.1740, 52 x 43 In. 4800.00
Chest, Queen Anne, Walnut, Veneer, Double-Arch Molding, c.1760, 73 x 36 In. 4406.00
Chest, Regency, Mahogany, Bowfront, 3 Drawers, Bracket Feet, c.1815, 35 x 38 In. 1290.00
Chest, Regency, Mahogany, Bowfront, 3 Drawers, Early 1800s, 34 x 40 In. 2470.00
Chest, Regency, Mahogany, Bowfront, 5 Drawers, 41 x 39 3/4 x 20 In. 1530.00
Chest, Regency, Mahogany, Bowfront, 5 Drawers, Bracket Feet, 1810, 42 x 42 x 19 In. 1410.00
Chest, Regency, Mahogany, Bowfront, 5 Drawers, Bracket Feet, 40 x 40 x 20 In. 1880.00
Chest, Regency, Mahogany, Bowfront, 5 Drawers, Bracket Feet, c.1815, 39 x 42 In. 1410.00
Chest, Regency, Mahogany, Bowfront, Ebonized String Inlay, 4 Drawers, 35 x 36 In. 2230.00
Chest, Regency, Mahogany, Inlaid, Bowfront, 5 Drawers, c.1815, 42 x 40 3/8 In. 1760.00
Chest, Regency, Mahogany, Inlaid, Bowfront, Pheasant Panels, c.1815, 13 1/2 In. 4230.00
Chest, Regency, Mahogany, Satinwood Banding, 4 Drawers, c.1815, 31 x 41 In. 1290.00
Chest, Rococo Revival, Mahogany, Serpentine, Barley Twist, Continental, 83 x 38 In. 1645.00
Chest, Rococo Style, Mahogany, Marble Top, 3 Drawers, 34 1/4 x 43 1/4 x 21 1/2 In. 470.00
Chest, Rohde, Leatherette, 3 Drawers, Ebonized Feet, Herman Miller, 35 x 45 In., Pair 3185.00
Chest, Rohlfs, 6 Drawers, Signed, 1907, 60 x 33 1/2 x 16 In. .... ***ILLUS*** 12925.00
Chest, Rosewood, Ivory Inlay, Vizagapatam, India, c.1750, 11 x 21 In. 2280.00
Chest, Satinwood Veneer, Bombe, Ormolu Pulls, Mount, Marble Top, 8 x 11 x 5 3/4 In. 460.00
Chest, Seaman's, Brassbound, Chinese Export, Mid 19th Century, 9 x 24 x 12 In. 460.00
Chest, Shaker, Blanket, Pine, Plum Painted Finish, Breadboard Lid, Double Till, 25 x 44 x 18 In. .. 8775.00
Chest, Shaker, Butternut, Low Back, Shaped Stiles, Stretchers, 19th Century, 29 In. 325.00
Chest, Shaker, Storage, Pine, Red Paint, Hinged Lift Lid, Iron Handles, c.1959, 12 x 28 In. 1055.00
Chest, Sheraton, Birch, Painted, 6 Drawers, Shaped Backsplash, 42 x 20 In. 460.00
Chest, Sheraton, Bird's-Eye Maple, Cherry, 4 Drawers, c.1825, 42 x 41 x 22 In. 2749.00
Chest, Sheraton, Cherry, 3 Drawers, Pilasters, 59 x 51 x 22 In. 1290.00
Chest, Sheraton, Cherry, 7 Drawers, Fluted Sides, 1837, 48 x 42 x 21 In. 330.00
Chest, Sheraton, Cherry, Bowfront, 4 Drawers, Dovetailed, Inset Panels, 40 x 39 In. 3220.00
Chest, Sheraton, Cherry, Poplar, 4 Drawers, Beading, 2-Board Top, 43 x 43 x 19 In. 460.00
Chest, Sheraton, Cherry, Poplar, 4 Drawers, Reeded Pilasters, 45 x 44 x 23 In. 405.00
Chest, Sheraton, Mahogany, 4 Crossbanded Drawers, Cookie Corners, 38 x 42 In. 1725.00
Chest, Sheraton, Mahogany, 4 Drawers, Cookie Corners, 40 x 41 x 20 In. 1035.00
Chest, Sheraton, Mahogany, Bowfront, Early 1800s, 48 1/2 x 39 1/2 x 18 In. 1880.00
Chest, Sheraton, Maple, Pine, 4 Drawers, Backsplash, Walnut Pulls, 41 x 41 x 18 In. 385.00
Chest, Sheraton, Pine, 4 Drawers, Scrolled Backsplash, Turned Feet, 37 1/2 In. 240.00
Chest, Softwood, Red & Yellow Paint, 5 Drawers, Early 1800s, 29 x 33 x 22 In. 550.00
Chest, Sugar, Pine, Dovetailed Corners, Lock, 28 1/2 x 25 In. 1600.00
Chest, Sugar, Walnut, 1-Board Top, Applied Molding, Turned Feet, 22 x 43 x 15 In. 2990.00
Chest, Tansu, Elm, 2 Sliding Doors, 2 Drawers, Iron Hardware, Japan, 1800s, 36 x 36 In. 290.00
Chest, Tea, 6-Board, Flower & Leaf Inlay, Dovetail, Till, Iron Handles, 1800s, 19 x 36 In. 949.00
Chest, Tea, 6-Board, Star Inlay, Dovetail, Till, Iron Handles, c.1875, 14 x 25 x 12 In. 545.00
Chest, Tea, Teak, 6-Board, Star & Sting Inlay, Iron Handles, Till, 1800s, 15 x 29 x 15 In. 775.00
Chest, V. Kagan, 8 Drawers, Sculpted Whalebone Base, 32 x 84 x 20 In. 10620.00
Chest, Victorian, Mahogany, 5 Drawers, Rounded Rectangular Top, c.1850, 48 x 48 In. 820.00
Chest, Victorian, Mahogany, Bowfront, 5 Drawers, Bracket Feet, c.1850, 40 x 41 In. 1060.00
Chest, Victorian, Mahogany, Marble Top, Mirror, Oxbow Top Drawer, 43 x 22 x 77 In. 880.00
Chest, Victorian, Mahogany, Plinth Top, 2 Over 3 Drawers, 48 1/2 x 48 x 22 In. 1880.00
Chest, Victorian, Pine, Drawers, Pilasters, Bracket Feet, England, 10 1/2 x 47 x 24 In. 1180.00
Chest, Victorian, Walnut, Hanky Boxes, 3 Drawers, 39 x 36 x 17 In. 115.00
Chest, Walnut, 5 Drawers, Scalloped Skirt, French Feet, 42 x 38 x 18 In. 2468.00
Chest, Walnut, 5 Drawers, Straight Bracket Feet, Pa., c.1785, 38 In. 1195.00
Chest, Walnut, Ebonized, Serpentine Top, 4 Drawers, Plinth Base, 32 x 37 x 21 1/2 In. 558.00
Chest, Walnut, Green Paint, Lift Top, Scalloped, Pa., c.1830, 12 5/8 x 13 3/4 x 9 3/4 In. 1870.00
Chest, Walnut, Molded Cornice, Drawers, Carved Apron, Cabriole Legs, 69 x 41 In. 9560.00
Chest, Walnut, String Inlay, 2 Short Over 3 Graduated Drawers, French Feet, 42 x 38 In. 7368.00

Furniture, Chest, Rohlfs, 6 Drawers, Signed, 1907, 60 x 33 1/2 x 16 In.

Furniture, Confidante, Renaissance Revival, Walnut, Carved Females, 26 x 44 In.

Chest, Walnut, Yellow Pine, Poplar, Cock-Beaded Drawers, 1800s, 62 x 41 x 23 In. 3680.00
Chest, Wedding, 5 Drawers, 2 Doors, Korea, 41 1/2 x 39 1/2 In. 259.00
Chest, Wellington, Burl Walnut, 6 Drawers, England, 1800s, 57 x 38 x 20 In. 945.00
Chest, Wellington, Mahogany, 6 Drawers, Victorian, 63 x 26 In. 1840.00
Chest, William & Mary Style, Oak, 3 Raised-Panel Drawers, 38 x 38 x 21 In. 500.00
Chest, William & Mary, Walnut, Inlaid, 2 Over 3 Drawers, 1600s, 36 x 38 x 23 In. 3820.00
Chest, William IV, Mahogany, 5 Drawers, Holland & Sons, c.1835, 39 x 44 x 23 In. 999.00
Chest, Wormley, MR, Serpentine, Tambour Doors, Dunbar, 36 x 48 In., Pair 4425.00
Chest-On-Chest, Burl Veneer, Brass Mounts, Korea, Early 1900s, 48 x 33 In. 646.00
Chest-On-Chest, Chippendale Style, Cherry, 61 x 39 x 19 In. 470.00
Chest-On-Chest, Chippendale Style, Mahogany, 3 Drawers, 39 x 19 In. 529.00
Chest-On-Chest, Chippendale, Cherry, 3 Short Over 7 Long Drawers, 80 x 38 In. 7768.00
Chest-On-Chest, Chippendale, Mahogany, 8 Drawers, 1700s, 73 x 45 In. 2115.00
Chest-On-Chest, Chippendale, Mahogany, Figured, Carved, Phila., c.1760, 91 x 42 In. 15600.00
Chest-On-Chest, Chippendale, Mahogany, Figured, Scroll Top, Pa., c.1770, 90 x 45 In. 9000.00
Chest-On-Chest, Chippendale, Maple, Carved, Late 1700s, 73 1/2 x 37 1/4 x 21 In. 11750.00
Chest-On-Chest, Chippendale, Walnut, 8 Drawers, c.1800, 73 x 40 In. 10158.00
Chest-On-Chest, George III, Mahogany, 7 Drawers, Late 1700s, 70 x 42 In. 2240.00
Chest-On-Chest, George III, Mahogany, 8 Drawers, Late 1700s, 72 x 42 x 21 In. 880.00
Chest-On-Chest, George III, Mahogany, 8 Drawers, Wave & Dentil Cornice, 71 x 42 In. 2857.00
Chest-On-Chest, Queen Anne, Maple, 8 Drawers, Cabriole Legs, c.1790, 72 x 39 In. 9200.00
Chest-On-Chest, Regency, Mahogany, Inlaid, Bowfront, 8 Drawers, c.1800, 79 x 46 In. 1175.00
Chest-On-Frame, George III, Mahogany, 6 Graduated Drawers, Ireland, 71 x 30 In. 13510.00
Chest-On-Frame, McCobb, Birch, 6 Drawers, c.1960, 34 x 18 x 48 In. 375.00
Chest-On-Frame, Parzinger, Ebonized, Silver Leaf, Drawer, Charak, 36 x 29 In. 8260.00
Chest-On-Frame, Queen Anne Style, Walnut, 2 Doors, 3 Drawers, 1800s, 60 x 41 In. 500.00
Chest-On-Frame, Queen Anne, 6 Drawers, Batwing Pulls, c.1750, 51 x 36 In. 2590.00
Chest-On-Frame, Queen Anne, Walnut, 2 Short Over 4 Graduated Drawers, 42 In. 2645.00
Chest-On-Stand, Sheraton, Yellow Paint, 2 Tiers, 3 Drawers, 36 x 28 x 15 3/4 In. 3220.00
Chiffonnier, Louis XV Style, Marble Top, 5 Drawers, 40 1/2 x 16 1/2 x 12 In. 1180.00
Chiffonnier, Rococo Style, Serpentine Front, Drawers, France, 57 1/2 x 37 x 20 In. 295.00
Coat Rack, Hanging, Oak, Iron Hooks, Beveled Mirror, 20 x 26 In. 140.00
Coat Rack, Jacob & Joseph Kohn, Beech, Center Column, 5 Lights, 96 In. 918.00
Coat Rack, W. McArthur, Anodized Aluminum, Rubber, 1930s, 67 1/4 In. 3600.00
Coffer, Gothic Revival, Oak, Plank Top, Fret-Carved Doors, Plinth Base, 34 x 70 In. 3600.00
Coffer, Oak, Carved, Plank Top, 4-Panel Front, Till, 1600s, 29 x 48 1/2 In. 1035.00
Coffer, Red Paint, Chinoiserie, Fitted Interior, Bracket Feet, 28 x 39 x 27 In. 5170.00
Commode, Biedermeier, Elm, 3 Drawers, Block Feet, 36 x 49 x 25 In. 3995.00
Commode, Block Front, Marquetry Panels, Gilt Bronze, Sebastian Vie, France, c.1790, 39 In. 6190.00
Commode, Bombe, Dutch Rococo, Pine, Serpentine Front, 4 Drawers, 1700s, 32 x 37 In. 3525.00
Commode, Charles X, Mahogany, Ebonized, Gilt Bronze, 36 x 44 x 21 In. 5605.00
Commode, Chippendale Style, Mahogany, Paneled Door, Late 1800s, 30 x 16 In. 120.00
Commode, Corner, Mahogany, Marquetry, Columns, Dutch, 1800s, 33 x 16 x 26 In. 950.00

Commode, Directoire, Cherry, Blocked Front, c.1800s, 34 x 41 In. 2940.00
Commode, Directoire, Mahogany, Crossbanded, 3 Graduated Drawers, 33 x 23 In. 1355.00
Commode, Empire Style, Mahogany, Marble Top, 1800-30, 28 x 16 x 14 In. 1250.00
Commode, Empire Style, Mahogany, Marble Top, Frieze Over 3 Drawers, 38 x 50 In. 3995.00
Commode, Empire, Bird's-Eye Maple, Lift Top, Drawer, Door, 32 x 28 x 16 In. 545.00
Commode, Empire, Fruitwood, Plank Top, 3 Drawers, 35 3/4 x 51 x 23 In. 1300.00
Commode, Empire, Mahogany, Lift Top, 2 Doors, Drawer, 32 x 29 x 18 In. 375.00
Commode, Empire, Mahogany, Marble Top, 4 Drawers, 36 x 54 x 22 In. 4465.00
Commode, Empire, Walnut, 4 Drawers, Column Uprights, c.1810, 40 x 52 In. 1880.00
Commode, French Provincial, Fruitwood, 2 Drawers, Snake Feet, 36 x 49 In. 8225.00
Commode, George III, Japanned, Demilune, Drawer, Tapered Legs, 32 In. 940.00
Commode, George III, Mahogany, Scalloped Gallery, Drawer, Door, 27 x 22 x 22 In. 1530.00
Commode, Italian Neoclassical, Walnut, Inlaid Bands, Starbursts, 5 Drawers, 47 x 52 In. 5875.00
Commode, Louis Philippe Style, Mahogany, Marble Top, 4 Drawers, 33 x 22 In. 676.00
Commode, Louis Philippe, Mahogany, Inlay, Marble Top, 4 Drawers, 1850, 36 x 49 In. 4935.00
Commode, Louis Philippe, Mahogany, Marble Top, 4 Drawers, 34 x 48 x 23 1/2 In. 1060.00
Commode, Louis XV Style, Burl Walnut, Mahogany, Kingwood, Bombe, 32 x 29 In. 2350.00
Commode, Louis XV Style, Fruitwood, Parquetry, Bombe, 28 x 17 x 38 In. 4690.00
Commode, Louis XV Style, Kingwood, Parquetry, Early 1800s, 29 x 20 In. 470.00
Commode, Louis XV Style, Marble Top, 3 Drawers, Serpentine Front, France, 32 x 27 In. 575.00
Commode, Louis XV Style, Marble Top, Gilt Metal Mounts, 2 Drawers, 10 x 12 x 6 In. 1830.00
Commode, Louis XV Style, Marquetry, Marble Top, Bronze Mounted, 19th Century 1535.00
Commode, Louis XV Style, Walnut, 3 Drawers, Serpentine Top, 36 x 27 In. 118.00
Commode, Louis XV Style, Walnut, Marble Top, 3 Drawers, Cabriole Feet, 38 x 48 In. 705.00
Commode, Louis XV, Chinoiserie, Bombe, Ormolu Mounted, 33 x 44 x 19 In. 3760.00
Commode, Louis XV, Faux Marquetry, Marble, Bombe, Early1800s, 35 x 34 x 19 In. 2125.00
Commode, Louis XV, Marble Top, Parquetry, 2 Drawers, 32 1/2 x 30 1/2 x 16 In. 1535.00
Commode, Louis XV, Rosewood, Marquetry Panels, Marble Top, Bombe, 35 In. 2570.00
Commode, Louis XV, Walnut, Planked Top, Scalloped Edge, 1700s, 37 x 51 x 29 In. 8518.00
Commode, Louis XV, Walnut, Serpentine, 6 Drawers, c.1785, 33 x 45 x 25 In. 940.00
Commode, Louis XVI Style, Mahogany, Brass Mounted, Marble Top, 29 x 19 In. 880.00
Commode, Louis XVI Style, Marble Top, Scalloped Front, 2 Drawers, 30 x 22 x 14 In. 945.00
Commode, Louis XVI Style, Walnut, 3 Drawers, Guilloche Borders, 34 x 42 x 18 In. 765.00
Commode, Louis XVI Style, Walnut, 3 Drawers, Shaped Feet, c.1890, 33 x 42 In. 1116.00
Commode, Louis XVI, Mahogany, Brass Mounted, 3 Drawers, Late 1700s, 45 x 52 In. 940.00
Commode, Mahogany, Banded Top, Serpentine Front, Conforming Case, 34 x 41 In. 6168.00
Commode, Mahogany, Drum Shape, Wool Cushion, England, c.1850, 16 x 17 In. 1645.00
Commode, Mahogany, Tray Top, Wavy Gallery, Stand, England, 1800s, 30 x 22 In. 1410.00
Commode, Neoclassical, Mahogany, Marble Top, 3 Drawers, Sweden, 36 x 46 x 24 In. 4995.00
Commode, Painted, Gilt, Female Corner Figures, Drawers, 33 x 39 In. 220.00
Commode, Pine, S.W. Woodward Paintings, Drawer, Door, 28 x 29 x 17 In. 230.00
Commode, Polychrome, Molded Edge, 3 Drawers, Reeded Pilaster, 39 x 49 In. 3525.00
Commode, Polychromed Lacca Povera, Faux Marble, Venice, 36 x 46 x 19 In. 3995.00
Commode, Queen Anne, Pine, 3 Drawers, Applied Decoration, 30 x 26 In. 145.00
Commode, Regency, Kingwood, Ormolu, Marble Top, Bombe, c.1740, 34 In. 5875.00
Commode, Restauration, Mahogany, Marble Top, 4 Drawers, Early 1800s, 38 x 49 In. 2585.00
Commode, Restauration, Mahogany, Marble Top, 4 Drawers, France, c.1840, 39 x 50 In. 2468.00
Commode, Restauration, Walnut, Marble Top, 4 Drawers, 36 x 51 x 22 1/2 In. 1530.00
Commode, Restauration, Walnut, Marble Top, 4 Drawers, Early 1800s, 37 x 48 In. 1880.00
Commode, Restauration, Walnut, Marble Top, 4 Drawers, Early 1800s, 38 x 49 In. 2115.00
Commode, Restauration, Walnut, Marble Top, 4 Drawers, Early 1800s, 38 x 50 In. 2585.00
Commode, Rococo Style, Recessed-Panel Drawers, France, 35 x 56 x 22 1/2 In. 1005.00
Commode, Serpentine, 2 Drawers, Cabriole Legs, Italy, 1700s, 35 x 36 x 23 In. 12075.00
Commode, Venetian Style, Painted, Bombe, Marble Top, 2 Drawers, 35 x 60 x 25 In. 3175.00
Commode, Victorian, Ash, 3 Drawers, Towel Bar, 54 x 30 x 16 In. 145.00
Commode, Victorian, Oak, Grained, Double Towel Bars, 63 x 34 x 19 In. 105.00
Commode, Victorian, Walnut, Drawer, Marble Top, Scalloped Backsplash, 38 x 26 In. 230.00
Commode, Victorian, Walnut, Marble Top, Backsplash, Candlestands, 39 x 30 In. 235.00
Commode, Victorian, Walnut, Marble Top, Burl Panels, 3 Drawers, 40 x 30 x 17 In. 200.00
Commode, Victorian, Walnut, Marble Top, Burl Panels, 39 x 30 x 19 In. 290.00
Commode, Victorian, Walnut, Reeded Columns, c.1880, 31 x 21 x 29 In. 205.00

Furniture, Credenza, Herter Type, Rosewood, Frieze, Marble Top, 42 x 65 x 20 In.

Furniture, Credenza, Victorian, Walnut, Boxwood Inlay, Serpentine Case, 32 x 47 x 14 In.

Commode, Walnut, Bombe, 4 Drawers, Italy, Early 1800s, 33 x 45 x 18 In. 2000.00
Commode, Walnut, Bombe, Bronze Mounts, Continental, Late 1700s, 33 x 49 x 25 In. 6465.00
Commode, Walnut, Figured, Marble Top, 4 Drawers, Italy, 40 x 40 x 23 In. 2585.00
Commode, Walnut, Inlaid, 3 Drawers, Serpentine Sides, Continental, c.1810, 37 x 46 In. 2468.00
Commode, Walnut, Inlaid, 3 Drawers, Shaped Top, Bun Feet, Italy, 1700s, 30 x 25 In. 7050.00
Commode, Walnut, Mahogany, Marble Top, 3 Drawers, Italy, c.1850, 32 x 52 In. 5640.00
Commode, Walnut, Putti, 3 Drawers, Italy, 36 x 58 In. 8120.00
Confidante, Renaissance Revival, Walnut, Carved Females, 26 x 44 In. .... *ILLUS* 2760.00
Counter, Shaker, Tailor's, Pine, 1 Board Top, Pull Out Surface, Door, Drawers, c.1840, 32 x 56 In. . 15210.00
Cradle, Hanging, 4 Interior Mounted Stiles, Knob Finials, 1800s, 16 x 15 x 34 In. 499.00
Cradle, Mahogany, Pine, Hooded, Tapered, 33 x 25 1/2 x 43 In. 288.00
Cradle, Pine, Red Brown Paint, Hood, Shaped Rockers, New England, 27 x 24 x 39 In. 230.00
Cradle, Pine, Red Paint, Hood, Arched Footboard, 37 x 27 In. 290.00
Cradle, Pumpkin Pine, Handmade, c.1860, 16 x 32 x 15 In. 110.00
Cradle, Red Paint, Heart Cutouts, 41 In. 115.00
Cradle, Tiger Maple, Scalloped Headboard, Footboard, Baltimore, 1800s, 23 x 43 In. 1295.00
Cradle, Walnut, Scroll Sides, Cutout Handle Holes, Shaped Rockers, Dovetail, 22 x 40 In. 270.00
Credenza, Boulle, Ebonized, Tortoise Shell, Brass, Medallions, 42 x 51 x 17 1/2 In. 1415.00
Credenza, Florence Knoll, Walnut, c.1960, 29 x 19 x 76 In. 4680.00
Credenza, G. Nelson, Sliding Doors, Herman Miller, c.1950, 26 x 19 x 70 In. 2700.00
Credenza, German Walnut, Burl, Carved, Applied Crest, Arched Opening, c.1880 .... 1650.00
Credenza, Herter Type, Rosewood, Frieze, Marble Top, 42 x 65 x 20 In. .... *ILLUS* 4830.00
Credenza, Knoll, 2 Sliding Doors, Tubular Metal Legs, 31 x 72 x 18 In. 1415.00
Credenza, Knoll, 8 Doors, Steel Base, Enameled Front, 25 x 107 x 18 1/2 In. 3835.00
Credenza, Louis XVI Style, Kingwood, Gilt Bronze, Marble Top, 38 x 89 x 22 In. 2125.00
Credenza, Philip Lloyd Powell, Walnut, 3 Doors, Slate Shelf, 33 x 114 x 20 In. 4425.00
Credenza, Pine, End Panel Drawers, Norway, 1800s, 30 x 34 x 15 In. 200.00
Credenza, Rosewood, 4 Cupboards, Tapered Legs, Scandinavia, c.1965, 32 x 90 In. 565.00
Credenza, Rosewood, Sliding Doors, Scandinavia, c.1965, 30 x 17 x 60 In. 189.00
Credenza, Victorian, Fruitwood, Walnut Inlay, 2 Doors, Paneled, 1875, 41 In. 2465.00
Credenza, Victorian, Walnut, Boxwood Inlay, Serpentine Case, 32 x 47 x 14 In. .... *ILLUS* 823.00
Credenza, Walnut, 2 Drawers, Doors, Woman Finials, Italy, 1800s, 46 x 71 x 24 In. 1765.00
Credenza, Yew, 6 Drawers, 2 Cabinets, 29 x 72 x 18 In. 350.00
Crib, Mahogany, Posts, Acorns, Square Rails, Tapered Legs, 48 x 26 x 51 In. 4400.00
Crib, Regency Style, Mixed Wood, Four-Poster, Turned Spindles, 65 x 50 x 31 In. 502.00
Cupboard, 2 Drawers, 2 Doors, Early 1800s, 48 x 41 x 16 In. 2705.00
Cupboard, Anglo-Indian, Bamboo, Lacquered, Shelf Over Paneled Back, 56 x 20 In. 1290.00
Cupboard, Biedermeier, Mahogany, Marble Top, Urn Shape, Door, c.1850, 29 x 18 In. 880.00
Cupboard, Biedermeier, Mahogany, Vase Shape, 2 Doors, 29 x 18 In., Pair 940.00
Cupboard, Blue Paint, 3-Paneled Doors, Bracket Base, Cornice, 49 x 56 x 15 In. 2310.00
Cupboard, Blue Paint, 4 Doors, Raised Panels, 48 x 20 x 73 In. 3450.00
Cupboard, Bucket Bench, 2 Doors, Conn., 1700s, 56 x 24 x 50 In. 2760.00
Cupboard, Cherry, Mahogany, Drawer, Door, Backsplash, 1800s, 29 x 16 In. 230.00

Cupboard, Cherry, Molded Cornice, 12-Pane Top Door, 2-Paneled Doors, 89 x 35 In. 1840.00
Cupboard, Cherry, Paneled, 5 Drawers, Molded Cornice, Curved Legs, 75 x 49 In. 7640.00
Cupboard, Cherry, Step Back, 3 Drawers, 2 Glazed & 2 Paneled Doors, 87 In. 8965.00
Cupboard, Chimney, Pine, Carved Panel Doors, Beaded Drawers, 1800s, 85 x 39 In. 499.00
Cupboard, Chimney, Pine, Gray Paint, 2 Hinged Doors, Raised Panels, 84 x 18 In. 1530.00
Cupboard, Chippendale, Walnut, Step Back, Pa., c.1770, 81 x 61 In. 4500.00
Cupboard, Corner, Barrel Back, Butterfly Shelves, Paneled Door, Hinges, 34 x 7 3/4 In. 3900.00
Cupboard, Corner, Cherry, 2 Sections, 12-Pane Paneled Doors, 89 x 29 In. 2760.00
Cupboard, Corner, Cherry, 2 Sections, 6-Pane Doors, Ball Feet, 50 x 20 x 89 In. 2875.00
Cupboard, Corner, Cherry, 4 Doors, 2 Drawers, Pa., 1800s, 83 x 58 In. 2310.00
Cupboard, Corner, Cherry, 9-Pane Glass Door, Paneled Lower Door, 41 x 81 In. 2070.00
Cupboard, Corner, Cherry, Glazed Door, 2 Drawers, 2 Paneled Doors, c.1810, 98 x 38 In. 28680.00
Cupboard, Corner, Cherry, Glazed Door, 2 Recessed Paneled Doors, c.1800, 85 x 43 In. 3110.00
Cupboard, Corner, Cherry, Pine, 2 Glazed 2-Paneled Doors, c.1820, 87 x 46 x 22 In. 2820.00
Cupboard, Corner, Faux Tiger Maple, Grained, Glazed, Early 1800s, 88 x 47 In. 11750.00
Cupboard, Corner, Federal, Walnut Inlay, 2 Sections, Pa., c.1800 .... 7800.00
Cupboard, Corner, Flame Graining, Eagles, Flowers, York County, Pa., 86 x 54 In. 4400.00
Cupboard, Corner, George III Style, Mahogany, Bowfront, Shelves, 26 1/2 x 17 In. 325.00
Cupboard, Corner, George III, Mahogany, Demilune, Curved Doors, c.1800, 84 x 30 In. 2585.00
Cupboard, Corner, George III, Mahogany, Inlaid Frieze, Ogee Feet, 82 x 42 In. 5290.00
Cupboard, Corner, Georgian Style, Mahogany, Fluted Stiles, Raised Panels, 100 x 51 In. 940.00
Cupboard, Corner, Hanging, George III, Mahogany, c.1810, 40 x 27 In. 765.00
Cupboard, Corner, Hanging, George III, Mahogany, Paneled Doors, 46 x 33 1/2 In. 570.00
Cupboard, Corner, Hanging, Georgian Style, Mahogany, Bowfront, c.1890, 42 x 24 In. 560.00
Cupboard, Corner, Hanging, Mahogany, Fretwork Frieze, 29 x 25 In. 118.00
Cupboard, Corner, Hepplewhite, Mahogany, String Inlay, Tapered Feet, 32 In. 2185.00
Cupboard, Corner, Painted, 2 Sections, Arched Pediment, 4-Paneled Doors, 86 x 46 In. 1650.00
Cupboard, Corner, Pine, 2 10-Pane Doors, Scalloped Shelves, 97 x 44 x 24 In. 2300.00
Cupboard, Corner, Pine, 2 Arched Doors, Shelves, 103 x 58 In. 3400.00
Cupboard, Corner, Pine, 2 Glazed Doors, 74 x 30 3/8 x 16 In. 1410.00
Cupboard, Corner, Pine, 3 Shelves, Raised Paneled Door, Scalloped, 1800s, 19 x 25 In. 800.00
Cupboard, Corner, Pine, Blue Green Paint, 2 Doors, Cutout Feet, 55 x 78 In. 4025.00
Cupboard, Corner, Pine, Blue Paint, 2 Sections, Raised Panels, 43 x 19 In. 865.00
Cupboard, Corner, Pine, Blue Paint, c.1810, 86 x 44 In. 4600.00
Cupboard, Corner, Pine, Cream, Paneled Doors, Molded Pilasters, 48 x 100 In. 1840.00
Cupboard, Corner, Pine, Flat Cornice, Glazed Door, 80 x 52 x 20 In. 1115.00
Cupboard, Corner, Pine, Paneled Door, Molded Cornice, Early 1800s, 84 x 37 In. 1795.00
Cupboard, Corner, Pine, Paneled Doors, 2 Sections, Scalloped Feet, 42 1/2 x 23 x 91 In. 2185.00
Cupboard, Corner, Pine, Poplar, Grain Painted, 12 Panes Over Panel Door, 45 x 84 In. 2875.00
Cupboard, Corner, Pine, Projecting Cornice, Glazed Door, 2 Shelves, c.1840, 82 x 39 In. 1115.00
Cupboard, Corner, Pine, Red, Yellow, Reeded Molding, Raised Panel Doors, 50 x 79 In. 1610.00
Cupboard, Corner, Red, Yellow Graining, 12-Pane Door, 2-Paneled Doors, 51 x 81 In. 980.00
Cupboard, Corner, Softwood, 12-Pane Door, 2 Sections, Paneled, 83 x 40 x 25 In. 3960.00
Cupboard, Corner, Softwood, 9-Pane Door, Drawer, Bracket Feet, 78 x 44 In. 880.00
Cupboard, Corner, Softwood, Molded Cornice, 2 Doors, Panels, 82 x 47 x 21 In. 2200.00
Cupboard, Corner, Softwood, Raised Paneled Doors, 2 Sections, 83 x 48 x 26 In. 1760.00
Cupboard, Corner, Softwood, Red Paint, 4 Doors, Bracket Feet, 83 x 47 x 21 In. 2200.00
Cupboard, Corner, Walnut, Arched Glazed Doors, Shelves, Drawers, 1800s, 89 x 55 In. 1900.00
Cupboard, Corner, Walnut, Poplar, 8-Pane Doors, Mullions, Tennessee, 94 x 53 x 24 In. 5750.00
Cupboard, Corner, White Paint, 2 Over 2 Paneled Doors, Shelf, 80 x 45 In. 1435.00
Cupboard, Court, Renaissance Revival, Walnut, Doors, Drawers, 1800s, 75 x 49 In. 1880.00
Cupboard, Curly Maple, Gunstock Finish, Mahogany Veneer, Shelves, 45 1/2 In. 520.00
Cupboard, Elizabethan Style, Oak, Rosettes, 2 Drawers, Doors, Shelves, c.1890, 78 x 50 In. 700.00
Cupboard, Elizabethan Style, Walnut, Turned Posts, Rail Galleries, 52 x 43 In. 440.00
Cupboard, Elm, 2 Doors, 11 Drawers, Chinese, 70 x 28 1/4 In. 575.00
Cupboard, Federal, Mahogany, Veneer, Carved, Swan's-Neck Crest, 104 x 48 x 22 In. 7638.00
Cupboard, Federal, Poplar, Painted, 2 Glazed Doors, 1800s, 81 x 42 In. 5050.00
Cupboard, George III Style, Mahogany, Pierced Gallery, 1 Door, 31 x 16 x 13 In. 1116.00
Cupboard, George III, Pine, Red Paint, 2 Drawers, 2 Doors, Late 1700s, 86 x 52 x 15 In. 3290.00
Cupboard, Hanging, 2 Doors, Yellow Graining, Scalloped Ends, 30 x 37 In. 175.00
Cupboard, Hanging, Carved Tiers, Center Door, Arched Applied Panel, 24 x 24 x 14 In. 2640.00

Don't use soap on the bottom of sticking drawers. Eventually it will become sticky. Use paraffin wax.

Furniture, Cupboard, Oak, Enameled Counter, Flour Bin, Early 20th Century, 70 x 40 In.

Cupboard, Hanging, Cherry, Rosewood, Black Ink Graining, Shelves, 35 x 34 In. 1150.00
Cupboard, Hanging, Pine, Blue, Gray Paint, Butterfly Hinges, 14 1/2 x 10 x 6 1/4 In. 9988.00
Cupboard, Hanging, Pine, Dovetailed, Inset Panel Door, 9 Drawers Inside, 20 x 24 In. 1380.00
Cupboard, Hanging, Pine, Gray Paint, 4 Shelves, Raised Panel Door, 39 x 13 x 6 In. 358.00
Cupboard, Hanging, Pine, Paneled, 3 Interior Shelves, Pullout Surface, 47 x 41 In. 645.00
Cupboard, Hanging, Poplar, Red Paint, Mortise & Pegged, Door, 38 x 38 x 13 In. 690.00
Cupboard, Hanging, Red Paint, 2 Drawers, 2 Doors, New Hampshire, 38 x 50 x 12 In. 7480.00
Cupboard, Jelly, Ocher Sponge, 3 Drawers, Pennsylvania, c.1830, 49 x 48 In. 4800.00
Cupboard, Jelly, Pine, 2-Paneled Doors, Plank Top, Early 1800s, 49 x 40 In. 710.00
Cupboard, Jelly, Pine, Blue Paint, 3 Shelves, 2 Raised Panel Doors, 1700s, 76 x 36 In. 2750.00
Cupboard, Jelly, Pine, Poplar, Brown Surface, Bracket Feet, 38 x 20 x 38 In. 489.00
Cupboard, Jelly, Softwood, Drawers, Sunken-Panel Doors, Ball Feet, 53 x 44 x 21 In. 660.00
Cupboard, Jelly, Softwood, Painted, Dovetailed Gallery, 2 Drawers, Doors, 53 x 44 In. 660.00
Cupboard, Jelly, Softwood, Peaked Gallery, Drawers, Panel Doors, 48 x 42 x 16 In. 1045.00
Cupboard, Jelly, Softwood, Yellow Paint, Peaked Gallery, 2 Drawers, Doors, 48 x 42 In. 1045.00
Cupboard, Jelly, Walnut, Cherry, Drawer, Recessed Panel Doors, 54 x 44 3/4 In. 660.00
Cupboard, Louis XV Style, Polychrome, Frieze Door, Paneled Door, 40 x 34 In. 1292.00
Cupboard, Milk, Salmon Paint, Step Back, 3 Shelves, 1800s, 66 x 43 x 25 In. 4290.00
Cupboard, Milk, Softwood, Sunken-Panel Door, Sections, 81 x 38 x 14 3/4 In. 1760.00
Cupboard, Mustard Paint, 2-Paneled Doors, Bun Feet, c.1820, 79 x 58 x 23 In. 1265.00
Cupboard, Napoleon III, Kingwood, Marble Top, 4 Doors, c.1850, 42 x 29 In. 1235.00
Cupboard, Napoleon III, Kingwood, Marble Top, Brass Gallery, c.1865, 31 x 15 In. 705.00
Cupboard, Neoclassical, Egg & Dart Molding, Doors, Scandinavia, 65 x 39 x 23 In. 1770.00
Cupboard, Oak, Enameled Counter, Flour Bin, Early 20th Century, 70 x 40 In. .... ***ILLUS*** 499.00
Cupboard, Oak, Enameled Top, Etched Glass Panels, c.1900, 69 x 47 In. 355.00
Cupboard, Oak, Fan & Floral Carved, 4 Doors, c.1750, 68 x 57 In. 3525.00
Cupboard, Pewter, Pine, Blue Paint, Paneled Doors, Drawers, Shelves, 66 x 22 x 75 In. 4025.00
Cupboard, Pewter, Pine, Painted, Door, 2 Shelves, Pie Shelf, 36 x 12 1/2 x 48 In. 4025.00
Cupboard, Pewter, Pine, Red Stain, Molded Cornice, Shelves, Step Back, 48 x 74 In. 2875.00
Cupboard, Pewter, Yellow Pine, Open, 3 Shelves, Pie Shelf, 46 x 18 x 81 In. 863.00
Cupboard, Pine, 2 Arched Raised Panel Doors, Pennsylvania, c.1810, 113 In. 5290.00
Cupboard, Pine, 2 Concave Shaped Shelves, Hinged Door, Late 1700s, 73 x 47 In. 1880.00
Cupboard, Pine, 2 Scalloped-Panel Doors, 1800s, 81 x 47 x 23 In. 767.00
Cupboard, Pine, 6 Doors Over Blind Door Base, Shelf, c.1835, 78 x 40 x 21 In. 823.00
Cupboard, Pine, Black Paint, Door, Scalloped Apron, Bracket Feet, 17 1/2 x 24 1/2 In. 201.00
Cupboard, Pine, Center Doors, Shelves, Paneled Glass Doors, 78 x 55 x 17 In. 266.00
Cupboard, Pine, Green Paint, 2 Nailed Drawers, Brass Pulls, 3 Paneled Doors, 53 x 69 In. 2300.00
Cupboard, Pine, Paneled Doors, 1800s, 72 x 53 x 13 In. 259.00
Cupboard, Pine, Paneled Doors, Pie Shelf, Rattail Hinges, 1700s, 77 x 40 x 16 In. 525.00
Cupboard, Pine, Step Back, 2 Glass Doors, 2 Wood Doors, 71 x 46 In. 2300.00
Cupboard, Pine, Step Back, Cornice Molding, 3 Shelves, 2 Doors, 1700s, 80 x 59 In. 4315.00
Cupboard, Pine, Step Back, Dark Blue Green Paint, 2 Shelves, Doors, 38 x 19 x 71 In. 460.00
Cupboard, Pine, Step Back, Grain Painted, Projecting Cornice, 80 x 50 x 22 In. 1880.00
Cupboard, Pine, Step Back, Paneled Doors, Bootjack Ends, 79 x 47 In. 1265.00
Cupboard, Polychrome, Parcel Gilt, Marble Top, Italy, Late 1800s, 36 x 28 In., Pair 2820.00

Cupboard, Poplar, Glazed Doors, Painted, Drawers, Mid 1800s, 53 x 52 x 19 In. ... 3290.00
Cupboard, Poplar, Walnut, Step Back, 2 Dovetailed Drawers, 2 Sections, 42 x 19 In. ... 2530.00
Cupboard, Possum Belly, 2 Doors Above, 2 Bins, 2 Drawers, 19th Century, 73 x 42 In. ... 440.00
Cupboard, Projecting Rectangular Top, Beaded Frame, Hinged Door, 59 x 48 x 15 In. ... 1175.00
Cupboard, Red Over Brown Paint, Inset Panels, Chinese, 57 x 24 In. ... 315.00
Cupboard, Red, 2 Doors, 2 Drawers, Dovetailed Top, 52 x 44 x 18 In. ... 2195.00
Cupboard, Shaker, Chimney, Maple, Pine, Red Paint, Raised Panel Door, 56 x 19 In. ... 2225.00
Cupboard, Shaker, Hanging, Maple, Pine, Yellow Ocher Varnish, Panel Door, 2 Shelves, 25 x 18 In. 2106.00
Cupboard, Shaker, Hanging, Pine, Red Paint, Inset Panel Door, 4 Shelves, 29 x 20 x 7 In. ... 1055.00
Cupboard, Shaker, Hanging, Pine, Red Paint, Inset Panel Door, Shelves, Pegs, 26 x 16 In. ... 3805.00
Cupboard, Shaker, Peg Hangers, Butternut, Walnut, Inset Panel Doors, Shelves, 24 x 20 In. ... 12870.00
Cupboard, Shaker, Pine, Poplar, Red Stain, Molded Top, Paneled Doors, 80 x 48 In. ... 2808.00
Cupboard, Shaker, Pine, Pumpkin Wash, Blue Green Inside, 4 Doors, 50 x 40 x 15 In. ... 9200.00
Cupboard, Softwood, 2 Sections, 6-Pane Doors, 80 x 54 x 19 In. ... 2640.00
Cupboard, Softwood, Painted, Yellow Graining, Sunken-Panel Door, 81 x 38 In. ... 1760.00
Cupboard, Spanish Cedar, Poplar, Painted, Glazed & Paneled Doors, 83 x 50 In. ... 8815.00
Cupboard, Victorian, Mahogany, Domed Cornice, Frieze, Swag Carving, 89 x 78 In. ... 1760.00
Cupboard, Walnut, 2 Parts, Scroll Pediment, Glazed Top Door, 1700s, 92 x 45 In. ... 3450.00
Cupboard, Walnut, Carved, 2 Parts, Continental, 1700s, 59 x 25 x 56 In. ... 4315.00
Cupboard, Walnut, Lamb's-Tongue Corners, Beveled Diamond Panels, 46 x 78 In. ... 575.00
Cupboard, Walnut, Poplar, 2 Sections, Mortised, Pinned, 4 Panel Doors, 71 x 16 In. ... 9200.00
Cupboard, Walnut, Step Back, Drop Front Extension, Base, 3 Drawers, c.1845, 81 x 43 In. ... 765.00
Cupboard, Yellow Pine, Poplar, Step Back, Paneled Doors, 47 x 27 x 84 In. ... 1840.00
Daybed, Biedermeier Legs, Blue Paint, Flowers, 31 x 70 In. ... 950.00
Daybed, Cherry, Scrolled Top, Applied Carvings, Molded Panels, 1800s, 38 x 76 In. ... 550.00
Daybed, Elm, Chinese, c.1850, 19 x 83 x 29 In. ... 470.00
Daybed, Empire, Mahogany, Sleigh, Paneled Head, Footboard, Swans, 35 x 32 x 65 In. ... 2585.00
Daybed, G. Nakashima, Walnut, Tapered Plank Legs, 10 x 30 x 72 In. ... 5605.00
Daybed, G. Nelson, No. 5088, Backrest, Herman Miller, c.1947, 26 x 70 x 33 In. ... 1800.00
Daybed, J.M. Young, No. 295, Vertical Slats, Slanted Headrest, Leather Cushions, 78 In. ... 1140.00
Daybed, John Keal, Brown Saltman, c.1958, 32 x 34 x 72 In. ... 1200.00
Daybed, Mies Van Der Rohe, Wood, Chrome, Cushion, Leather, Knoll, 24 x 40 x 79 In. ... 3835.00
Daybed, Neoclassical, Bird's-Eye Maple, Philadelphia, c.1830, 39 x 33 x 75 In. ... 3175.00
Daybed, Richard Stein, No. 700, Upholstered, Knoll, c.1948, 27 x 76 x 36 In. ... 944.00 to 1800.00
Daybed, Walnut, Carved Rosettes, Bud Finials, Velvet Cover, France, c.1900, 77 In. ... 1150.00
Daybed, Wegner, Adjustable, No. 9, Getama, c.1955, 29 x 34 x 78 In. ... 3900.00
Daybed, William & Mary, Carved Scrolls, Arched, Cane Back, 38 3/4 x 68 x 21 In. ... 1265.00
Desk, ABC & Lamb, R.E. Cahoon Jr., 28 1/2 x 24 In., Child's ... 316.00
Desk, Aesthetic Revival, Painted, Part Ebonized, Drawers, 30 x 41 x 23 In. ... 235.00
Desk, Art Deco, 2 Pedestals, Parchment, Oak Feet, Drawer, 2 Doors, France, 30 x 56 In. ... 4425.00
Desk, Arts & Crafts, Drop Front, Oak, 44 x 26 In. ... 115.00
Desk, Arts & Crafts, Oak, 2 Drawers, c.1910, 40 x 30 In. ... 295.00
Desk, Arts & Crafts, Oak, 43 x 30 x 27 In. ... 225.00
Desk, Arts & Crafts, Oak, Center Frieze, Slatted Side Shelves, Grand Rapids, 30 x 43 In. ... 940.00
Desk, Arts & Crafts, Oak, Drawer, Pedestal Book Shelves, Square Legs, 30 1/4 x 36 In. ... 259.00
Desk, Biedermeier, Fruitwood, Leather Inset Surface, Baltic, c.1850, 30 x 58 In. ... 3055.00
Desk, Bleached Wood, Green Leather Inset, 29 x 24 x 44 1/2 In. ... 1555.00
Desk, Butler's, Cherry, Mahogany, 3 Graduated Drawers, Scalloped Skirt, 42 x 40 x 22 In. ... 1955.00
Desk, Butler's, Federal, Drop Front, Mahogany, 3 Drawers, Early 1800s, 45 x 47 In. ... 6169.00
Desk, Butler's, George III, Drop Front, Mahogany, 3 Drawers, c.1800, 44 x 46 In. ... 2585.00
Desk, Butler's, Mahogany, Drawer, 2-Paneled Doors, Inlay, Early 1800s, 44 x 47 In. ... 2950.00
Desk, Butler's, Sheraton Style, Mahogany, 4 Drawers, England, c.1810, 43 x 48 x 22 In. ... 1298.00
Desk, Campaign, Camphorwood, Flap Front, 4 Drawers, 1800s, 40 x 19 x 35 In. ... 5635.00
Desk, Campaign, Mahogany, Pedestal, Gilt Leather Insert, Victorian, 30 x 55 In. ... 4465.00
Desk, Carlton House, Edwardian, Satinwood, Painted, c.1910, 40 x 42 x 24 In. ... 6756.00
Desk, Carlton House, Regency Style, Mahogany, Leather, Early 1900s, 39 x 45 In. ... 1410.00
Desk, Chippendale Style, Slant Front, Mahogany, Cabriole Legs, 26 x 19 1/2 x 13 In. ... 518.00
Desk, Chippendale Style, Walnut, Mahogany, Arched Kneehole, 3 Drawers, 30 x 46 In. ... 1998.00
Desk, Chippendale, Birch, Slat Lid, 4 Drawers, Cock-Beaded, 43 x 40 x 19 In. ... 600.00
Desk, Chippendale, Drop Front, Cherry, 7 Case Drawers, c.1780, 42 1/2 x 40 x 19 In. ... 3525.00
Desk, Chippendale, Drop Front, Mahogany, Claw & Ball Feet, 41 x 21 In. ... 4025.00

Desk, Chippendale, Maple, Mass., c.1780, 40 3/4 x 36 x 19 1/2 In. 5100.00
Desk, Chippendale, Slant Front, Birch, Bracket Feet, 10 Pigeonholes, 5 Drawers, 40 In. 1955.00
Desk, Chippendale, Slant Front, Cherry, 4 Drawers, c.1780, 43 x 40 x 19 In. 1610.00
Desk, Chippendale, Slant Front, Cherry, 4 Drawers, Flat Bracket Base, 41 x 38 x 20 In. 690.00
Desk, Chippendale, Slant Front, Mahogany, 4 Drawers, Boston, 1770-85, 44 x 21 In. 2185.00
Desk, Chippendale, Slant Front, Mahogany, 9 Drawers, Cubbyholes, 42 x 41 x 22 In. 1725.00
Desk, Chippendale, Slant Front, Mahogany, Carved, Reverse Serpentine, 44 x 44 In. 8400.00
Desk, Chippendale, Slant Front, Mahogany, Pigeonholes, 6 Drawers, 43 x 43 1/2 In. 2715.00
Desk, Chippendale, Slant Front, Mahogany, Reverse Serpentine, c.1780, 45 x 44 In. 3600.00
Desk, Chippendale, Slant Front, Pine, Oak, Poplar, Drawers, Cubbyholes, 48 x 43 In. 3795.00
Desk, Chippendale, Slant Front, Tiger Maple, 4 Drawers, Late 1700s, 40 x 30 x 17 In. 7930.00
Desk, Chippendale, Slant Front, Walnut, 4 Drawers, Pa., c.1770, 43 x 40 In. 2990.00
Desk, Chippendale, Slant Front, Walnut, Drawers, Felt Surface, c.1780, 43 x 38 In. 3410.00
Desk, Davenport, Aesthetic Revival, Walnut, England, c.1880, 32 x 28 x 17 In. 440.00
Desk, Davenport, Killarneyware, Inlay, Ireland, c.1860, 40 x 26 In. 815.00
Desk, Davenport, Shanghai Carpenter, Slant Front, 3 Drawers, Chinese, 34 x 21 In. 6038.00
Desk, Davenport, Walnut, Leather, 2 Drawers, Side Doors, England, 1800s, 35 x 25 In. 708.00
Desk, Drop Front, Mahogany, Mirror, Drawer, 48 x 27 x 13 In. 147.00
Desk, Drop Front, Oak, Pine, Shepherd Scene, Leather Surface, 40 x 33 1/2 x 17 In. 1610.00
Desk, Drop Front, Satinwood, Painted, England, c.1900, 37 3/4 x 31 x 18 In. 1650.00
Desk, Drop Front, Walnut, 3 Drawers, 44 x 25 1/2 x 16 In. 259.00
Desk, Drop Front, Walnut, 6 Drawers, Victorian, 68 x 32 x 17 In. 690.00
Desk, Dunbar, Wood Grain Laminate, Marked, 1960s, 29 1/2 x 53 1/2 x 17 1/2 In. .... *ILLUS* 264.00
Desk, Dunbar, Woodgrained Laminate, 3 Drawers, Ring Pulls, c.1960, 53 1/2 x 29 1/2 In. 265.00
Desk, Eames & Saarinen, Red Lion Furniture Co., c.1941, 30 x 21 x 48 In. 7200.00
Desk, Edwardian, Mahogany, String Inlay, Bowed Ends, 4 Drawers, 30 x 35 In. 705.00
Desk, Edwardian, Roll Top, C Roll, Rosewood, Inlaid, Pullout Writing Surface, 25 In. 1620.00
Desk, Elm, 3 Drawers, Butterfly Brasses, 45 x 22 1/2 x 32 In. 1035.00
Desk, Escritoire, Empire Style, Mahogany, Brass Inlay, Marble, Mirror, 49 x 31 In. 1175.00
Desk, Escritoire, Louis XV Style, Fruitwood, Drawers, Cabriole Legs, 29 x 20 x 16 In. 1650.00
Desk, Escritoire, Louis XVI Style, Kingwood, Marble Top, 1800s, 52 x 30 In. 470.00
Desk, Escritoire, Renaissance Style, Walnut, Compartments, 89 x 42 In. 4465.00
Desk, Federal, Mahogany, Inlaid, 2 Doors, 4 Drawers, c.1800, 57 x 41 x 19 In. 2128.00
Desk, Federal, Slant Front, Birch, Interior Drawers, 42 1/2 x 39 3/4 x 18 3/4 In. 1528.00
Desk, Federal, Slant Front, Cherry, Birch, Compartments, Drawers, c.1800, 43 x 41 In. 1410.00
Desk, Federal, Slant Front, Maple, Birch, 4 Drawers, Bracket Feet, Late 1700s, 44 x 41 In. 1410.00
Desk, Federal, Slant Front, Walnut, Late 1700s, 42 x 40 x 21 In. 1910.00
Desk, Finn Juhl, No. 515, Baker, c.1955, 29 x 36 x 65 In. 4200.00
Desk, French Provincial, Slant Front, Walnut, Carved, 2 Drawers, 40 x 47 In. 2350.00
Desk, G. Nakashima, Walnut, 3 Drawers, Pedestal, 29 x 76 x 30 In. 19200.00
Desk, G. Nelson, Roll Top, Action Office, Herman Miller, c.1964, 44 x 32 x 66 In. 1920.00
Desk, G. Nelson, Swag Leg, Gallery Top, Laminate, 3 Drawers, 33 x 42 In. 1416.00
Desk, G. Nelson, Swag Leg, Laminate, Herman Miller, c.1956, 34 x 29 x 39 In. 2880.00
Desk, G. Stickley, Kneehole, Drawer, 2 Half Drawers, 42 x 24 x 29 In. 1410.00
Desk, G. Stickley, Postcard, Shaped Backsplash, Brass Hardware, 36 x 36 In. 1060.00
Desk, George II Style, Burr Maple, Pedestal, 30 x 74 x 48 In. 6000.00
Desk, George II, Slant Front, Walnut Veneer, Pigeonholes, Drawers, 40 x 35 x 18 In. 1650.00
Desk, George III Style, Mahogany, Arched Kneehole, Square Legs, 30 x 41 In. 880.00
Desk, George III Style, Roll Top, C Roll, Satinwood, Inlaid, 39 x 30 x 19 In. 4200.00
Desk, George III Style, Walnut, Kneehole, 5 Drawers, Late 1800s, 30 x 48 In. 705.00
Desk, George III, Slant Front, Mahogany, Drawers, Bracket Feet, 42 x 38 x 23 In. 2006.00
Desk, George III, Slant Front, Mahogany, Gilt Metal Mounted, c.1770, 43 x 45 x 21 In. 3900.00
Desk, George III, Slant Front, Mahogany, Inlaid Fans On Lid, Drawers, 36 x 19 x 31 In. 3400.00
Desk, George III, Slant Front, Mahogany, Kneehole, 38 x 32 x 20 In. 7200.00
Desk, Georgian Style, Mahogany, Double Pedestal, Gilt Tooled Red Leather, 29 x 29 In. 1529.00
Desk, Georgian Style, Slant Front, Mahogany, 3 Drawers, 1800s, 41 x 37 In. 940.00
Desk, Georgian, Slant Front, Walnut, Crossbanded, Inlaid, c.1735, 42 x 36 x 21 In. 3819.00
Desk, Hanging, Walnut, Poplar, Square Nails, Mortise, Pigeonholes, 21 x 27 x 13 In. 290.00
Desk, Hepplewhite, Slant Front, Cherry, Dovetailed, 4 Drawers, Pigeonholes, 37 x 45 In. 1035.00
Desk, Hepplewhite, Slant Front, Cherry, Pine, 3 Drawers, Pigeonholes, 31 1/2 x 43 In. 1725.00
Desk, Jean Prouve, School, Double Chair, Beech Plywood, Steel, 1950s, 31 x 47 x 37 In. 4800.00

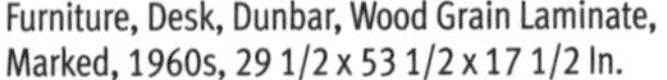

Furniture, Desk, Dunbar, Wood Grain Laminate, Marked, 1960s, 29 1/2 x 53 1/2 x 17 1/2 In.

Furniture, Desk, Roll Top, Oak, Tambour Front, Slide-Out Surface, 19th Century, 40 x 42 In.

Desk, Karl Springer, Parchment, Springer Mfg., c.1975, 29 x 24 x 48 In. 2160.00
Desk, L. & J.G. Stickley, Slant Front, Oak, 3 Drawers, 40 x 29 x 17 In. 1265.00
Desk, Limbert, Oak, Ebony, Arched Backsplash, Gallery Top, Drawer, 35 x 36 x 21 In. 2700.00
Desk, Louis XV Style, Galleried Top, 3 Drawers, Cabriole Legs, 28 x 22 x 48 In. 585.00
Desk, Louis XVI Style, Roll Top, C Roll, Ormolu, Rose Vines, Ribbons, 2 Parts, 42 x 32 In. 1725.00
Desk, Mahogany, Kneehole, 9 Drawers, Mushroom Knobs, 28 1/2 x 30 3/4 x 51 In. 220.00
Desk, Mahogany, Pedestal, Leather Top, 9 Drawers, Victorian, 1800s, 29 x 50 In. 560.00
Desk, Mahogany, Slant Front, 4 Graduated Drawers, Fitted Interior, 39 x 39 In. 1912.00
Desk, Mahogany, Tooled Leather Inset, Drawers, Tapered Legs, 30 x 65 x 28 In. 770.00
Desk, Mahogany, Veneer, Gilt Plaster, Wood Gadrooning, Bronze, 2 Doors 2475.00
Desk, Neoclassical, Roll Top, C Roll, 7 Drawers, 1820-40, 49 x 40 x 23 In. 805.00
Desk, Oak, Pedestal, Plank Top, 4 Drawers, 2 Doors, c.1810, 34 x 50 In. 708.00
Desk, Osvaldo Borsani, Pedestal, 3 Drawers, Clipped Corners, Techno, 30 x 54 In. 1416.00
Desk, Partners, Arts & Crafts, Oak, 8 Dovetailed Drawers, Paneled Ends, 29 x 56 In. 316.00
Desk, Partners, Chippendale Style, Mahogany, Drawers, 1900s, 29 x 53 In. 705.00
Desk, Partners, George III Style, Mahogany, Drawers, 1800s, 30 x 58 In. 4406.00
Desk, Partners, George III, Mahogany, Inset Leather, 8 Drawers, 31 x 58 x 51 In. 5875.00
Desk, Partners, Georgian, Mahogany, Leather Top, c.1800s, 30 x 65 x 34 In. 1298.00
Desk, Partners, Nostell Priory, Mahogany, Oyster Veneer, England, 31 x 82 In. 3055.00
Desk, Partners, Regency Style, Mahogany, Inlaid, Oval Top, 39 x 72 In. 4230.00
Desk, Partners, Regency Style, Mahogany, Leather Surface, Oval, 30 x 71 x 37 In. 3369.00
Desk, Plantation, Slant Front, 2-Paneled Doors, 3 Drawers, 1800s, 53 x 39 In. 805.00
Desk, Protzman, Babinga Wood, Tubular Collection, Herman Miller, c.1970, 30 x 66 In. 1200.00
Desk, Queen Anne, Slant Front, Cherry, Drawer, Cabriole Legs, Pad Feet, 41 x 19 In. 3738.00
Desk, Queen Anne, Slant Front, Tiger Maple, Pine, Stepped Interior, Cubbies, 41 x 35 In. 6455.00
Desk, Regency Style, Mahogany, Pedestal, Oval, Reeded Edge, 8 Drawers, 30 x 71 In. 4406.00
Desk, Regency, Mahogany, Ebony String Inlay, Compartments, 81 x 64 x 168 In. 476.00
Desk, Regency, Mahogany, Parcel Gilt Leather Writing Surface, Drawers, 30 x 61 In. 5170.00
Desk, Risom, Walnut, White Laminate Top, Swing-Out Shelved Door, 26 x 42 In. 660.00
Desk, Rohde, Paldao, Pedestal, Kidney-Shaped Top, Herman Miller, 29 x 52 In. 2360.00
Desk, Roll Top, C Roll, Mahogany, 2 Pedestals, 6 Drawers, 43 x 60 x 32 In. 115.00
Desk, Roll Top, C Roll, Oak, 2 Pedestals, 6 Drawers, 41 x 60 x 34 In. 460.00
Desk, Roll Top, French Victorian, Walnut, Rosewood, 3 Drawers, Reeded Legs, 47 x 51 In. 1410.00
Desk, Roll Top, Oak, Tambour Front, Slide-Out Surface, 19th Century, 40 x 42 In. . . . . . . ***ILLUS*** 588.00
Desk, Roll Top, S Roll, Cherry, 7 Drawers, 52 x 28 In. 345.00
Desk, Roll Top, S Roll, Mahogany, 8 Drawers, 50 x 50 In. 2070.00
Desk, Roll Top, S Roll, Oak, 2 Pedestals, 3 Drawers, Ledger Compartment, 44 x 48 x 30 In. 316.00
Desk, Roll Top, S Roll, Oak, 4 Drawers, Door, 1900-1910, 51 x 54 x 30 In. 880.00
Desk, Roll Top, S Roll, Walnut, Lady's, Victorian, c.1880, 41 x 29 x 44 In. 4500.00
Desk, Roll Top, Walnut, Victorian, 53 x 48 In. 800.00
Desk, Rosewood, Bird, Tree, Marble Dreamstones, Chinese, 1800s, 53 x 41 In. 2350.00
Desk, Satinwood, Brass Mounted, Ebony String Inlay, Kidney Shape, 29 x 41 x 24 In. 2585.00
Desk, Schoolmaster's, Hepplewhite, Slant Front, Pine, Beaded Edge, 44 In. 385.00

Desk, Schoolmaster's, Old Red Paint, 32 x 22 x 41 In. 460.00
Desk, Sheraton, Slant Front, Walnut, Beaded Lid, Old Red Paint, 19th Century, 28 x 28 In. 130.00
Desk, Slant Front, Burl Walnut, 4 Drawers, England, 1700s, 42 x 33 x 19 In. 3000.00
Desk, Slant Front, Cherry, 4 Cock-Beaded Drawers, Late 1700s, 41 x 41 In. 1763.00
Desk, Slant Front, Chippendale, Maple, 4 Drawers, Bracket Base, 19th Century, 38 In. 1980.00
Desk, Slant Front, Fruitwood, Inlaid, 3 Drawers, Italy, Early 1800s, 39 x 44 x 21 In. 2820.00
Desk, Slant Front, Hardwood, Paneled Top, Drawers, Bun Feet, Portugal, 43 x 37 In. 6460.00
Desk, Slant Front, Oak, Drawers, Cabriole Legs, Pad Feet, Iron Locks, 53 x 37 x 22 In. 805.00
Desk, Slant Front, Red Finish, Brass Gallery, 3 Drawers, 30 x 36 1/4 x 20 In. 1208.00
Desk, Slant Front, Walnut, Inlaid, Serpentine, Continental, c.1810, 76 x 49 In. 5875.00
Desk, Spinet, Mahogany, 1930s, 33 x 36 x 20 In. 58.00
Desk, Venetian Rococo Revival, Slant Front, Polychrome, 3 Drawers, 40 x 36 In. 1880.00
Desk, Victorian, Drop Front, Walnut Burl, Pigeonholes, Shelf, 61 x 29 In. 380.00
Desk, Victorian, Drop Front, Walnut, 2 Tiers, Fretwork Bookshelf, 2 Doors, 60 x 29 In. 330.00
Desk, Victorian, Mahogany, Kneehole, 5 Drawers, Late 1800s, 31 x 53 In. 380.00
Desk, Victorian, Mahogany, Pedestal, Leather Top, 9 Drawers, 2 Doors, 29 x 60 In. 999.00
Desk, Victorian, Walnut, Drawer, 2 Doors, Turreted Corners, c.1850, 30 x 56 In. 1060.00
Desk, Wicker, Painted, Drawer, 2 Bookshelves, 34 x 37 In. 295.00
Desk, William IV, Roll Top, C Roll, Mahogany, Leather, 3 Drawers, c.1850, 47 x 60 In. 3290.00
Desk, Wooten, Walnut, Interior Compartments, Swing-Out Pedestals, 31 x 60 x 32 In. 2990.00
Desk, Yew, Chrome, 4 Drawers, X-Stretchers, c.1960, 30 x 72 x 24 In. 999.00
Desk & Chair, Luther Conover, c.1950, 30 x 26 x 50-In. Desk 1440.00
Desk-Bookcase, Chippendale, Drop Front, Cherry, Carved, 2 Hinged Doors, 82 x 39 In. 7050.00
Desk-Bookcase, Roll Top, C Roll, Rococo Revival, Rosewood, c.1865, 102 x 49 x 48 In. 4140.00
Dinette Set, Eero Saarinen, Pedestal Group, Knoll, 2 Armchairs, 78 x 48 In., 9 Piece 7080.00
Dinette Set, Eero Saarinen, Pedestal Group, Laminate, Upholstered, Knoll, 7 Piece 1416.00
Dining Set, Arts & Crafts, Oak, Round, Pedestal Table, Slat Back Chairs, 7 Piece 1380.00
Dining Set, Chrome, Marbled Formica, Vinyl Upholstery, Table, Leaf, 4 Chairs, 1950s 395.00
Dining Set, Federal Style, Cherry, 2 Armchairs, 66 x 42 x 30-In. Table, 7 Piece 320.00
Dining Set, Finn Juhl, Teak, Leather, Niels Vodder, 28 x 49-In. Chair, 7 Piece 4720.00
Dining Set, Frankl, Blond Mahogany, Brown Saltman, 2 Armchairs, 9 Piece 3540.00
Dining Set, French Provincial, Oak, Parquetry, 60 x 37-In. Table, 8 Piece 1170.00
Dining Set, French Provincial, Table, Sideboard, Cabinet, 2 Armchairs, 12 Piece 585.00
Dining Set, Hepplewhite, Mahogany, Hoop Back, Carved Splat, 39 In., 12 Piece 4230.00
Dining Set, Hepplewhite, Mahogany, Table, Sideboard, 6 Shieldback Chairs, c.1930 .... 550.00
Dining Set, Heywood-Wakefield Co., Drop Leaf Table, 6 Chairs, c.1950 .... 1380.00
Dining Set, Koefoeds, Hornslet, Denmark, 60-In. Table, 13 Piece 1055.00
Dining Set, Louis Majorelle, Mahogany, Oak, Rosewood, Inlaid, c.1900, 7 Piece 20400.00
Dining Set, Maximillian, Karp, c.1950, 12 28-In. Chairs, 29 x 53-In. Table 2280.00
Dining Set, Nils Jonsson, Rosewood, China Cabinet, Troeds, c.1965, 8 Piece 945.00
Dining Set, Risom, Pullout Leaves, Velvet Seat, Knoll, 5 Piece 1416.00
Dispenser, Oak, C Roll Tambour Top, S.F. Bowser & Co., c.1900, 58 x 30 In. 385.00
Dresser, American Empire, Burl, 2 Curved & 4 Figured Drawers, Columns, Claw Feet 880.00
Dresser, Borge Mogensen, 4 Drawers, Dowel Legs, 30 x 34 x 18 In. 649.00
Dresser, Chippendale, Maple, Cove-Molded Edge, Drawers, 39 x 36 In. 1175.00
Dresser, Eastlake, Marble Top, Lovebirds, Mirror, Victorian, 88 x 42 x 20 In. 259.00
Dresser, Eliel Saarinen, 4 Drawers, John Stuart, 1940s, 30 x 48 x 21 In. 3600.00
Dresser, Federal, Birch Inlay, 4 Cock-Beaded Drawers, c.1805, 37 1/2 x 38 1/2 In. 999.00
Dresser, Federal, Rosewood, Mahogany, Flame Birch, Bowfront, 4 Drawers, N.H., 42 In. 6465.00
Dresser, G. Stickley, Oak, 2 Drawers, Pivoting Mirror, 52 x 36 x 16 In., Child's 3525.00
Dresser, George III, Mahogany, 4 Drawers, Bracket Feet, c.1775, 32 x 32 In. 3408.00
Dresser, Gothic Revival, Oak, Marble Top, 2 Over 2 Drawers, c.1870, 31 x 47 x 26 In. 825.00
Dresser, James Mont, 6 Drawers, Brass Hardware, Bracket Base, 33 x 64 x 20 In. 4720.00
Dresser, Neoclassical, Bird's-Eye Maple, Oval Mirror, c.1830, 93 x 44 In. 6465.00
Dresser, Neoclassical, Mahogany, Mirror, 4 Drawers, 1800s, 70 x 44 In. 265.00
Dresser, Neoclassical, Mahogany, Mirror, c.1830, 86 x 45 x 23 In. 1880.00
Dresser, Neoclassical, Mahogany, Mirror, Phila., c.1830, 64 x 43 x 24 In. 4700.00
Dresser, Neogrecque, Mahogany, Mirror, Phila., c.1870, 84 x 53 x 18 In. 3230.00
Dresser, Nutting, No. 923, Pine, Door, Shelves, Scroll Top, 73 x 36 x 16 In. 6270.00
Dresser, Oak, 3 Drawers, Mirror, c.1900, 74 x 36 x 17 In. 259.00
Dresser, Renaissance Revival, Walnut, Marble Top, Drop Center, c.1865, 95 x 49 In. 590.00

Dresser, Renaissance Revival, Walnut, Marble Top, Mirror, 3 Drawers, c.1850, 97 x 45 In. 940.00
Dresser, Veneer, 3 Drawers, Round Etched Mirror, Bakelite & Metal Pulls, c.1940 .... 165.00
Dresser, Victorian, Ash, 3 Drawers, Flowers, 75 x 40 x 18 In. 200.00
Dresser, Victorian, Marble Top, Mirror, Late 19th Century, 48 x 23 x 79 In. 585.00
Dresser, Victorian, Oak, 4 Drawers, Mismatched Pulls, Mirror, 70 In. 206.00
Dresser, Victorian, Walnut, 3 Drawers, 2 Hankie Boxes, Mirror, 70 x 40 x 19 In. 259.00
Dresser, Victorian, Walnut, 4 Drawers, Racetrack Molding, 45 x 38 x 18 In. 460.00
Dresser, Victorian, Walnut, 4 Drawers, Swivel Mirror, 70 x 39 x 19 In. 345.00
Dresser, Victorian, Walnut, 5 Drawers, Swivel Mirror, 70 x 43 x 19 In. 175.00
Dresser, Walnut, Flower Basket Crest, Mirror, c.1928, 51 x 22 x 72 In. 140.00
Dresser, Wormley, Bleached Mahogany, Mirror, 2 Cabinets, Drawers, Dunbar, 45 x 60 In. 3835.00
Dry Sink, Copper-Clad Upper Surface, 2 Drawers, Panel Doors, 35 1/2 x 18 x 34 In. 295.00
Dry Sink, Drawer, Storage Door, Scalloped Gallery, Pennsylvania, 36 x 40 In. 695.00
Dry Sink, Lift Top, Blue Paint, c.1820-40, 34 x 18 x 28 1/2 In. 865.00
Dry Sink, Lift Top, Pine, Paneled Door, 1800s, 35 x 35 x 21 In. 635.00
Dry Sink, Lift Top, Red Paint, Mustard Interior, Panel Back, 22 x 32 x 41 1/2 In. 5175.00
Dry Sink, Pine, 2 Drawers, Shelf, 2 Paneled Doors, 1800s, 49 x 39 1/4 x 17 1/4 In. 460.00
Dry Sink, Pine, Brown, Yellow Gallery, 2 Doors, Shelf, 17 x 18 x 10 In. 825.00
Dry Sink, Pine, Door, Shelf, Late 19th Century, 37 x 39 In. 410.00
Dry Sink, Pine, Drawer, Door, Scalloped-Back Gallery, Pennsylvania, 36 x 40 x 15 In. 695.00
Dry Sink, Poplar, Red Wash, Shaped Backsplash, Recessed Doors, 34 x 64 In. 1410.00
Dry Sink, Step Back, Blue Paint, 2 Sections, 42 x 75 x 23 In. 3165.00
Dumbwaiter, Edwardian, Satinwood, Polychrome, 2 Tiers, Late 1800s, 29 x 15 In. 825.00
Dumbwaiter, George III, Mahogany, 2 Tiers, Dish Top, Fluted, Tripod, 33 In. 500.00
Dumbwaiter, George III, Mahogany, 3 Graduated Drop-Leaf Tiers, Tripod, 22 1/2 In. 1410.00
Dumbwaiter, George III, Mahogany, 3 Tiers, Beaded Edge, c.1760, 44 x 24 In. 6000.00
Dumbwaiter, George III, Mahogany, 3 Tiers, c.1865, 44 1/2 x 24 1/2 In. 5700.00
Dumbwaiter, George III, Mahogany, 3 Tiers, Dish Top, 3 Snake Legs, 42 x 25 In. 920.00
Dumbwaiter, George III, Mahogany, Brass Inlay, 3 Tiers, c.1760, 46 x 23 In. 4200.00
Dumbwaiter, George III, Mahogany, c.1865, 44 1/2 x 24 In. 1320.00
Dumbwaiter, Georgian, Mahogany, 2 Tiers, Graduated, Tripod, 29 x 23 In. 295.00
Dumbwaiter, Mahogany, 3 Tiers, Graduated, Dish Top, Tripod, 1800s, 47 x 22 In. 235.00
Dumbwaiter, Mahogany, 3 Tiers, Turned Supports, Tripod, 18th Century, 41 In. 429.00
Dumbwaiter, Queen Anne, Mahogany, 3 Tiers, Dish Top, c.1770, 43 x 24 In. 4200.00
Dumbwaiter, William IV, Mahogany, Telescoping, Triangular Base, 32 x 24 In. 1680.00
Easel, Aesthetic Revival, Ebonized, Carved, Leaf Panels, c.1875, 76 x 23 In. 1175.00
Easel, Eastlake, Ebonized, Parcel Gilt, Spindle Galleries, c.1880, 76 In. 705.00
Easel, Rococo Revival, Mahogany, Carved, Pierced Crest, Adjustable Shelf, 85 In. 235.00
Easel, Victorian, Oak, Adjustable, Triangular Base, Folding, 70 x 21 x 21 In. 750.00
Etagere, Aesthetic Revival, Moorish Style, Ebonized, Inlaid, Glass Door, 57 x 37 In. 2585.00
Etagere, Aesthetic Revival, Parcel Gilt, Ebonized, Mirror Back, c.1875, 76 x 48 In. 3055.00
Etagere, Anglo-Indian, Black Lacquer, Birds & Leaves, 4 Shelves, 43 x 16 In., Pair 1530.00
Etagere, Chippendale Style, Mahogany, Tiered Pagoda, 4 Shelves, Chinese, 69 In., Pair 3290.00
Etagere, Corner, Rococo Revival, Walnut, Carved, 6 Graduated Serpentine Shelves, 67 In. 765.00
Etagere, George IV, Mahogany, 4 Tiers, Drawer, Turned Supports, Casters, 52 x 20 In. 2585.00
Etagere, Hardwood, 2 Sections, Chinese, 64 x 56 1/2 In. 3600.00
Etagere, Louis XIV Style, Glass Shelves, Ivory Finish, c.1950, 66 x 32 x 15 In. 145.00
Etagere, Louis XVI Style, Mahogany, Ormolu Mounted, 4 Shelves, c.1890, 37 x 21 In. 940.00
Etagere, Mahogany, Upper Tier Drawer, Ebonized Supports, France, Late 1800s, 18 In. 475.00
Etagere, Marcel Breuer, No. B75, Steel, Wood, c.1932, 20 x 21 3/4 x 10 In. 3600.00
Etagere, Regency Style, Mahogany, Adjustable Bookrack, Drawer, 51 x 18 In. 120.00
Etagere, Rococo Revival, Rosewood, 2 Doors, Cabochon Cartouches, 64 x 42 In. 1765.00
Etagere, Rococo Revival, Walnut, 3 Graduated Serpentine Shelves, 77 x 45 In. 4230.00
Etagere, Rosewood, 2 Sections, Mirror, Serpentine Front, 88 x 54 x 18 In. 865.00
Etagere, Rosewood, Mirror Back, Inlay, 102 x 60 x 17 In. 3335.00
Etagere, Victorian, Walnut, Dome Top, Mirror, Fruit, Leaves, Drawer, 87 x 49 In. 2128.00
Etagere, Walnut, 2 Parts, 4 Shelves, Panel Door, Plinth Base, Victorian, 73 x 41 x 16 In. 635.00
Fainting Couch, Napoleon III, Gilt, Upholstered, Tufted, 24 x 44 x 96 In. 940.00
Footstool, Black Paint, Yellow Border, Double Pedestal, 16 x 9 In. 120.00
Footstool, Cherry, Poplar, Red Paint, Bootjack Leg Cutouts, Ticking Cover, 10 x 5 In. 200.00
Footstool, Cricket, Wood, Red Paint, 12 In. 35.00

Footstool, French Provincial, Oak, Padded Top, 24 x 19 In., Pair 1325.00
Footstool, G. Stickley, Leather Top, Flared Legs, Square, 4 1/2 x 12 1/12 In. 3175.00
Footstool, G. Stickley, No. 300, Leather Top, Straight Stretchers, 15 x 20 x 16 In. 2235.00
Footstool, George III Style, Mahogany, 18 1/4 x 20 1/4 x 16 1/4 In. 240.00
Footstool, Green Paint, Pineapple, Melon Stencil, Ring Turned Legs, 1900s, 13 x 8 In. 345.00
Footstool, Louis XV Style, Beech, Serpentine Top, Pierced Skirt, Velvet, 16 x 22 In., Pair 1645.00
Footstool, Needlepoint, Acanthus Leaf, Ram's Head, Cabriole Legs, 18 1/2 x 23 x 19 In. 248.00
Footstool, Neoclassical, Carved, Upholstered, Lion Heads, Paw Feet, 19 x 21 1/2 x 17 In. 385.00
Footstool, Neoclassical, Mahogany, Needlepoint Seat, Saber Legs, Square, 13 In. 880.00
Footstool, Neoclassical, Mahogany, Upholstered, Lyre Base, c.1825, 16 x 22 x 18 In. 590.00
Footstool, Painted, Cherries, Strawberries, c.1850, 13 3/4 x 8 1/2 x 9 In. 65.00
Footstool, Pine, Carved, Green & Mustard Paint, Flowers, Leaves, 9 1/2 x 8 1/2 x 17 1/2 In. 940.00
Footstool, Pine, Mustard Paint, Green Band, Line Accents, Red & White Roses, 12 x 9 In. 200.00
Footstool, Pine, Old Blue Paint, Square Nails, Cutout Feet, Sawtooth Ends, 6 x 18 In. 750.00
Footstool, Regency, Rosewood, Gilt Metal Mounted, c.1815, 10 1/4 x 14 x 15 In., Pair 7800.00
Footstool, Victorian, Mahogany, Floral Needlework, Bun Feet, c.1850, 6 x 21 In. 410.00
Footstool, Victorian, Walnut, Hidden Compartment, 15 x 17 In. 240.00
Footstool, Walnut, Hide, Horseshoe Shape, 16 x 14 In. 100.00
Footstool, Windsor, Stretchers, Gold Brocade, Upholstery, 15 x 7 x 10 In. 200.00
Frame, Arts & Crafts, Copper, Sitting Cat Shaped, Oval Picture Opening, 6 In. 450.00
Frame, Arts & Crafts, Line, Leather, Painted Flowers, Yellow, Green, 6 1/4 In. 294.00
Frame, Bronzed Metal, Hammered, Stylized Vine & Leaves, Arts & Crafts, Square, 6 In. 210.00
Frame, Carved, Early 20th Century, 23 x 27 1/2 In. 55.00
Frame, Eastlake, Oak, Painted, Rectangular, Flowers, 28 x 33 In. 120.00
Frame, Oak, Carved, Raised Relief Anchor, Canons, Sword, Cipher, Civil War Era, 12 1/2 In. 195.00
Frame, Pine, Plywood, Red, Black Sponging, Paneled Pilasters, Tom King, 39 x 50 In. 115.00
Frame, Rococo Style, Carved, Gilt, 56 x 45 In. 150.00
Frame, Victorian, Gilt, Bundled Holly Leaves, Berries, 23 1/2 x 29 1/2 In. 90.00
Frame, Victorian, Gilt, Molded Gesso, 3 Liners, c.1880, 9 x 10 1/2 In. 206.00
Frame, Wood, Grain Painted, Early 1800s, 12 x 9 1/8 & 10 1/2 x 13 1/2 In., Pair 440.00
Frame, Wood, Irregular Shape, Applied Hammered Brass Tulips, Arts & Crafts, 7 x 11 In. 390.00
Hall Stand, Art Deco, Aluminum, Mirror, 4 Hooks, Umbrella Stands, France, 79 x 41 In. 700.00
Hall Stand, Arts & Crafts, Bamboo, Glazed, Mirror, Continental, c.1915, 76 x 34 In. 765.00
Hall Stand, Arts & Crafts, Oak, c.1910, 72 In. 150.00
Hall Stand, L. & J.G. Stickley, Oak, Mirror, 4 Coat Hooks, c.1912, 23 x 39 3/4 In. 720.00
Hall Stand, Oak, Carved Leaf & Lollipop Design, Seat, Lift Top, 86 x 45 In. 635.00
Hall Stand, Pine, Carved Panel Sides, Seat, Lift Top, 36 x 32 x 18 In. 175.00
Hall Stand, Renaissance Revival, Bronze, Patinated, Mirror, Hooks, 89 x 50 x 18 In. 4700.00
Hall Stand, Renaissance Revival, Walnut, Marble, Mirror, c.1870, 109 x 54 x 18 In. 6756.00
Hall Stand, Shaped Pediment, Mirror, Marble Top, Drawer, Late 1800s, 92 x 35 x 13 In. 585.00
Hall Stand, Walnut, Walnut Burl, Marble Top, Umbrella Racks, 1880-90, 81 x 35 In. 295.00
Hall Tree, Coalbrookdale, Cast Iron, Rustic Pattern, c.1865, 82 In. 1080.00
Hall Tree, G. Stickley, 2 Tapered Posts, 6 Triple Hooks, Shoe Feet, 71 x 13 x 22 In. 2700.00
Hall Tree, Rustic, 8 Hanging Pegs, 66 In. 940.00
Hall Tree, Victorian, Cast Iron, Tree-Trunk Shape, Reclining Figure Beneath, 82 x 36 In. 3525.00
Hall Tree, Victorian, Cast Iron, White Paint, 2 Cane Holders, 1800s, 80 x 25 In. 650.00
Hat Rack, Mahogany, Brass, Copper, First Mate Plaque, Basket, 5 Hooks, 48 In. 3600.00
Headboard, Wood, Brass-Plated Steel Patches, Spotlights, Sections, 103 x 84 1/2 In. 2235.00
Highboy, Chippendale, Mahogany, Walnut, Pine, Oak, Bonnet Top, 7 Drawers, 80 x 40 In. 635.00
Highboy, Empire Revival, Mahogany, 7 Drawers, Carved Backsplash, 61 x 38 In. 290.00
Highboy, George II Style, Walnut, Broken Pediment, 11 Drawers, c.1910, 91 x 48 In. 5170.00
Highboy, Georgian, Mahogany, 9 Drawers, Cabriole Legs, Pad Feet, 64 x 40 In. 295.00
Highboy, Queen Anne, Cherry, Pine, Carved Fans, 10 Drawers, 66 x 39 x 22 In. 2300.00
Highboy, Queen Anne, Maple, 11 Drawers, New England, c.1750, 74 x 40 x 20 In. 4115.00
Highboy, Queen Anne, Maple, 4 Over 2 Drawers, 3 False Fronts, 39 x 73 In. 7015.00
Highboy, Queen Anne, Maple, Ash, Chestnut, Cabriole Legs, Pad Feet, 9 Drawers, 39 x 67 In. 5175.00
Highboy, Queen Anne, Maple, Pine, Cabriole Legs, Pad Feet, 37 x 39 1/2 x 64 In. 3738.00
Highboy, Queen Anne, Walnut, Inlaid, 8 Drawers, Boston, c.1735, 62 1/2 x 39 In. 10200.00
Highchair, Bentwood, 8 Spindles, Painted, Green, Red, Yellow Bands, 23 x 30 1/2 In. 260.00
Highchair, Plank Seat, Arrow Back Spindles, Green Paint, Flower Crest, 23 1/2 In. 605.00
Highchair, Plank Seat, Barrel Back, Green Paint, Turned Legs, 23 In. 110.00

Highchair, Windsor Style, Phoenix Chair Company 295.00
Highchair, Windsor, Maple, Rod Back, New England, c.1810, 37 3/4 In., Child's 529.00
Highchair, Windsor, Plank Seat, 2 Slats, Red Paint, 22 1/2 x 29 In. 230.00
Humidor, Arts & Crafts, Brass, Stained Glass Inserts, Brass Lid, 8 1/4 In. 58.00
Huntboard, French Renaissance Revival, Carved Oak, Elm, 82 x 60 x 22 In. 1415.00
Huntboard, Southern Pine, Spanish Cedar, Painted, Early 1800s, 46 x 63 x 20 In. 7640.00
Huntboard, Walnut, Cherry, Molded Top, 4 Drawers, Carved Fan, Conn., 34 x 42 In. 1980.00
Huntboard, Yellow Pine, 2-Board Top, 2 Drawers, Pulls, 42 1/2 x 48 x 19 In. 2300.00
Hutch, Louis XIII Style, Oak, 2 Doors, Game, Fruit, c.1880, 86 x 51 In. 880.00
Hutch, Pine, Molded Top, 3 Shelves, 2 Drawers Over Panel Doors, 78 x 48 x 18 In. 750.00
Hutch, Rococo, Fruitwood, Paneled Doors, 2 Drawers, Continental, 75 In. 7050.00
Kas, Anglo-Indian, Teak, Brass Bound, Flared Cornice, 2 Doors, Spiral Feet, 58 x 49 In. 920.00
Kas, Gumwood, 2-Paneled Hinged Doors, Shelves, Drawer, Early 1700s, 79 x 62 In. 22325.00
Kas, Oak, Rosewood, Part Ebonized, Dutch Doors, Putti, Leaves, 1600s, 89 x 66 x 24 In. 2235.00
Kneeler, Prie Dieu, Aesthetic Revival, Padded, Tapered Legs, England, c.1865, 38 In. 205.00
Kneeler, Prie Dieu, Gothic Revival, Oak, Carved, Acanthus Scrolls, 33 x 25 1/2 In., Pair 415.00
Kneeler, Prie Dieu, Napoleon III, Rosewood, Padded Rail, Leaf-Carved Back, 33 In. 440.00
Kneeler, Prie Dieu, Walnut, Faux Bamboo, Padded Rail, Low Seat, France, c.1850, 34 In. 560.00
Lap Desk, Bird's-Eye Maple, Inlaid, Mahogany Molding, 6-Point Star, 3 1/2 x 13 In. 1058.00
Lap Desk, Brass, Mother-Of-Pearl, Rosewood Inlay, Leather Surface, c.1854, 12 x 20 In. 390.00
Lap Desk, Camphorwood, Brass Bound, Tambour Cover, Drawer, Chinese Export, 18 x 16 In. 1208.00
Lap Desk, Curly Maple, Brass Handle, 2 Secret Drawers, 7 3/4 x 21 3/4 x 10 3/4 In. 775.00
Lap Desk, English Oak, Fold-Down Writing Surface, Pigeonholes, 15 x 10 In. 316.00
Lap Desk, Fruitwood, Inlaid, Hinged Lid, Paneled Well, Continental, 1700s, 12 In. 410.00
Lap Desk, George IV, Mahogany, Brass Bound, Leather, c.1835, 22 x 13 In. 880.00
Lap Desk, Mahogany, Dovetailed, Brass Handles, 1800s, 7 3/4 x 20 x 10 1/2 In. 130.00
Lap Desk, Mahogany, Slant Front, Fold Down, Compartments, 14 x 4 1/2 In. 375.00
Lap Desk, Mother-Of-Pearl, Ebony, Brass, Burl, Late 1800s, 5 1/2 x 15 x 10 In. 266.00
Lap Desk, Victorian, Rosewood, Mother-Of-Pearl Inlay, c.1860, 5 1/2 x 15 x 10 In. 720.00
Lap Desk, Walnut, Bird's-Eye Maple Veneer Inlay, 16 In. 130.00
Lap Desk, William IV, Mahogany, 6-Drawer Case, 8 1/2 x 21 1/4 x 12 1/2 In. 530.00
Lap Desk, Wood, Scrimshaw, Foldover Top, Inkwells, Anglo-Indian, 5 x 14 x 10 In. 805.00
Lectern, Lacquer, Black, Gold, Bamboo Design, Drawer, Late 1800s, 19 x 19 In. 315.00
Library Ladder, Regency Style, Mahogany, Folding, 4 Rungs, Brass Treads, 49 x 16 In. 440.00
Library Ladder, Regency, Mahogany, Folding, 4 Rungs, Brass Treads, 48 x 19 In. 646.00
Library Ladder, Victorian, Elm, 7 Rungs, Late 19th Century, 80 In. 440.00
Library Steps, Brown Paint, Turned Supports, Trestle Legs, Casters, 80 x 23 In. 1880.00
Library Steps, Regency Style, Mahogany, Folding, 3 Rungs, Brass Tread, 40 In. .... 295.00 to 350.00
Library Steps, Regency Style, Mahogany, Folding, 4 Rungs, Brass Tread, 48 In. 590.00
Library Steps, Regency Style, Mahogany, Folding, 5 Rungs, Brass Tread, 58 In. .... 998.00 to 1060.00
Library Steps-Chair, Cushion Seat, Crooked Arms, 34 3/4 In. 1880.00
Linen Press, Biedermeier, Cherry, Arched Doors, 3 Drawers, c.1840, 77 x 54 x 22 In. 1765.00
Linen Press, Cherry, Poplar, 3 Parts, Side By Side, Wardrobe, Shelves, 71 x 21 x 85 In. 4315.00
Linen Press, Chippendale, Walnut, Carved, 2 Doors, Recessed Panels, Shelves, c.1780 .... 16450.00
Linen Press, Federal, Cherry, Drawer Over Doors, Chamfered Sides, 49 x 44 In. 2820.00
Linen Press, Federal, Cherry, Inlaid, 2-Paneled Doors, 4 Drawers, c.1800, 79 x 48 In. 5080.00
Linen Press, Federal, Mahogany, Paneled Doors, Southern U.S., c.1810, 89 x 48 In. 8225.00
Linen Press, Federal, Walnut, 2 Paneled Doors, 3 Drawers, Pa., c.1800, 80 x 49 x 22 In. 2030.00
Linen Press, Fruitwood, 19th Century, 77 x 48 In. 5780.00
Linen Press, George II Style, Mahogany, Walnut Veneer, England, 1900s, 76 x 39 In. 740.00
Linen Press, George III Style, Mahogany, Sliding Shelves, 3 Drawers, 80 x 52 In. 4140.00
Linen Press, George III, Mahogany, 2 Doors Over 3 Graduated Drawers, 80 x 48 In. 3185.00
Linen Press, George III, Mahogany, 2 Doors, 4 Drawers, c.1800, 85 x 52 In. 3880.00
Linen Press, George III, Mahogany, 2-Paneled Doors Over 5 Drawers, 76 x 48 In. 3820.00
Linen Press, George III, Mahogany, 3 Drawers, Paneled Doors, c.1800, 83 x 50 In. 3525.00
Linen Press, George III, Mahogany, Ogee Molded Cornice, Paneled Doors, 84 x 52 In. 3525.00
Linen Press, Rococo, Mahogany, 2 Doors, 3 Drawers, Dutch, c.1750, 103 x 61 x 22 In. 6465.00
Linen Press, William IV, Mahogany, 4 Drawers, 2-Paneled Doors, c.1830, 90 x 54 In. 4115.00
Love Seat, Art Deco, Undulated Back, Velvet, 4 Tapered Legs, 36 x 63 In., Pair 4130.00
Love Seat, Dragon Back, Arms, Japan, Late 19th Century, 50 In. 960.00
Love Seat, Harden Furniture Co., Slat Back, Arms 2900.00

Love Seat, Neoclassical, High Back, Gadroon Carved, Brocade Upholstery, 47 x 60 In. 990.00
Love Seat, Victorian, Burl Walnut, Joliet, 42 x 67 In. 650.00
Lowboy, Chippendale Rococo Style, Mahogany, 4 Drawers, c.1876, 32 x 39 In. 2235.00
Lowboy, Chippendale, Oak, Pine, 3 Drawers, 1-Board Top, England, 28 x 32 x 20 In. 545.00
Lowboy, Queen Anne Style, Burl Elm, Elm, 3 Drawers, Cabriole Legs, 1800s, 28 x 30 In. 3055.00
Lowboy, Queen Anne Style, Walnut, Banding, 3 Drawers, 28 3/4 x 28 1/2 x 15 In. 315.00
Lowboy, Queen Anne, Burl Walnut, Shaped Kneehole, Cabriole Legs, 31 x 33 x 19 In. 1890.00
Lowboy, Queen Anne, Cherry, 4 Drawers, Fan Carved, Scalloped Apron, 32 x 34 x 23 In. 4780.00
Lowboy, Queen Anne, Maple, Pine, 1 Over 3 Drawers, Carved Fan Detail, 32 x 33 In. 8625.00
Lowboy, Walnut, 3 Drawers, Scalloped Corners, c.1760, 29 x 34 x 20 In. 2310.00
Mirror, 2 Antler Candleholders, Oval, 53 1/2 x 30 In. 920.00
Mirror, Adam Style, Giltwood, Oval, England, c.1815, 42 1/2 x 33 In. 1997.00
Mirror, Adam, Bilbao Column, Flower Urn, Gilt, Wirework, 26 x 13 In. 2070.00
Mirror, Adam, Giltwood, Bilbao Border, Urn & Flower Cornice, 48 x 19 In. 4945.00
Mirror, Adam, Giltwood, Plaster, 48 x 24 In., Pair 3525.00
Mirror, Adam, Urn Finial, Carved & Gilt Fillets, Swag Draped Base, c.1800, 55 x 18 In. 5750.00
Mirror, Art Deco, Beveled Glass, Black Velvet Trim, Indonesia, 55 x 27 In. 400.00
Mirror, Art Deco, Brass Corner Accents, Arched Pediment, 40 x 65 In. 500.00
Mirror, Art Deco, Giltwood, Carved, Oval, Cornucopia, Flowers, 56 x 49 In. 1290.00
Mirror, Baroque, Giltwood, Acanthine Molding, Italy, c.1800, 72 x 57 In. 4113.00
Mirror, Baroque, Giltwood, Women Blowing Trumpets, Italy, 1700s, 34 x 26 In. 1955.00
Mirror, Baroque, Grotto Style, Fruitwood, Shell & Coral Encrusted, Italy, 50 x 38 In. 4465.00
Mirror, Biedermeier, Burled Walnut, Recessed Inner Frame, Early 1800s, 34 1/4 x 25 1/2 In. 550.00
Mirror, Biedermeier, Mahogany, Peaked Crest, Rosewood Inlay, 32 x 12 In. 360.00
Mirror, Brass, Embossed, Shaped Crest, Beveled, Continental, 23 1/2 x 14 In. 330.00
Mirror, Broken Arch Pediment, Eagle, Scrolls, Flowers, Early 1900s, 61 x 27 In. 1220.00
Mirror, Bronze, Repousse, Classical Figures, Putti, Griffins, 1800s, 24 x 12 In. 90.00
Mirror, Carved, Original Gilt, Italy, 18th Century, 21 x 16 1/2 In. 4250.00
Mirror, Charles X, Ebonized, Parcel Gilt, Scrolls, Leaves, Palmetto, c.1850, 32 x 26 In. 1880.00
Mirror, Charles X, Giltwood, Plaster, Scrolling Leaves, Flowers, c.1835, 54 x 24 In. 1530.00
Mirror, Cheval, Empire, Mahogany, Columns, 2 2-Light Sconces, c.1815, 77 1/2 x 39 In. 4230.00
Mirror, Cheval, George V, Japanned, Crimson Lacquer, Scrolled Pad Feet, 76 x 28 In. 3055.00
Mirror, Cheval, Louis XV Style, Domed, Beveled, Multicolored, c.1910, 72 x 39 In. 1175.00
Mirror, Cheval, Regency Style, Oval, Leaf Carved, Bulb Feet, 57 x 32 x 22 In. 740.00
Mirror, Cheval, Regency, Mahogany, Saber Legs, c.1800, 67 x 31 x 24 In. 2950.00
Mirror, Cheval, Victorian, Mahogany, Turned Posts, Stretcher Platform, 75 x 36 In. 990.00
Mirror, Chinese Chippendale, Silver & Gold Leaf, 20th Century, 69 x 35 1/2 In. 1180.00
Mirror, Chippendale Style, Eagle, 31 x 16 In. 520.00
Mirror, Chippendale Style, Flower Crest, Side Mounts, 49 1/2 x 23 1/4 In. 575.00
Mirror, Chippendale Style, Giltwood, Scrolled Crest, Leaves, c.1800, 44 x 22 In. 805.00
Mirror, Chippendale Style, Mahogany, Giltwood, 20th Century, 47 x 24 In. 500.00
Mirror, Chippendale, Gold Leaf, Gilt Over Gesso, c.1790, 53 x 26 In. 3995.00
Mirror, Chippendale, Mahogany, c.1785, 29 1/2 In. 390.00
Mirror, Chippendale, Mahogany, Carved, Crests, Ode To George Washington, 1800 . . . . 770.00
Mirror, Chippendale, Mahogany, Gilt Gesso, Scrolled Frame, 27 1/2 x 16 In. 380.00
Mirror, Chippendale, Mahogany, Gilt Liner, Fleur-De-Lis Crest, 39 3/4 x 2 1/4 In. 1035.00
Mirror, Chippendale, Mahogany, Gilt Phoenix & Scrolling Vines, 54 In. 720.00
Mirror, Chippendale, Mahogany, Giltwood, Eagle, Carved Leaves & Scrolls, 59 In. 7768.00
Mirror, Chippendale, Mahogany, Giltwood, Scrolled Leaves, 38 1/2 x 20 1/2 In. 590.00
Mirror, Chippendale, Mahogany, Inlaid, Scrolled, c.1790, 38 In. 360.00
Mirror, Chippendale, Mahogany, Molded, Late 1700s, 17 x 10 In. 150.00
Mirror, Chippendale, Mahogany, Parcel Gilt, Scrolled, 27 1/4 x 15 1/2 In. 500.00
Mirror, Chippendale, Mahogany, Parcel Gilt, Scrolled, Reeded, Gilt, c.1800, 22 x 13 In. 380.00
Mirror, Chippendale, Mahogany, Scrolled Crest, Late 1700s, 39 x 19 3/4 In. 295.00
Mirror, Chippendale, Mahogany, Scrolled, c.1800, 19 1/2 In. 200.00
Mirror, Chippendale, Mahogany, Scrolled, Molded Liner, Late 1700s, 25 x 15 In. 295.00
Mirror, Chippendale, Walnut, Pierced Gold Leaf Pediment, Scrolled, c.1780, 40 x 22 In. 1150.00
Mirror, Courting, Reverse Painted, Flower Crest, Marbleized, 17 x 12 In. 1725.00
Mirror, Curtis Jere, Infinity, Porthole, Polished Chrome, 6 x 23 1/2 In. 2360.00
Mirror, Della Robbia Style, Giltwood, Round, 20th Century, 46 1/2 In. 120.00
Mirror, Directoire Style, Giltwood, Carved, 20 Paired Rays, c.1900, 15 In. 470.00

Mirror, Directoire Style, Giltwood, Flower Basket, 1800s, 45 x 25 In. 1530.00
Mirror, Directoire Style, Giltwood, Sunburst, Carved, 12 In. 295.00
Mirror, Directoire Style, Giltwood, Sunburst, Carved, Convex, Italy, 30 In. 1997.00
Mirror, Directoire, Giltwood, Sunburst, Rope Twist, Leaf Carved, 28 x 26 1/2 In. 2230.00
Mirror, Dressing, Bird's-Eye Maple, Austria, c.1900, 74 x 41 x 14 In. 470.00
Mirror, Dressing, Cast Iron, Gilt, Scrolls, Flower Border, Beveled, 22 x 12 1/2 In. 115.00
Mirror, Dressing, Cast Metal, Jenny Lind, Flag, Shield, 1800s, 21 x 15 In. 300.00
Mirror, Dressing, Embossed, Beveled, 11 In. 60.00
Mirror, Dressing, Satinwood, Ebonized Stringing, Oval, Late 1800s, 35 x 27 In. 235.00
Mirror, Egyptian Revival, Gilt Gesso Over Wood, Carved Pilasters, c.1850, 21 x 21 1/2 In. 1800.00
Mirror, Empire, Gold Leaf, Reverse Painted Panel, c.1830, 32 x 16 x 1 1/2 In. 300.00
Mirror, Empire, Mahogany Veneer, Ogee, Signed William Graves, Salem, 30 x 21 In. 55.00
Mirror, Federal Style, Giltwood, Eagle, Laurel Garlands, c.1880, 34 x 24 1/2 In. 1250.00
Mirror, Federal Style, Giltwood, Reverse Painted, Country Manor, 45 x 23 In., Pair 1645.00
Mirror, Federal Style, Giltwood, Reverse Painted, Early 20th Century, 36 1/2 x 22 In. 620.00
Mirror, Federal Style, Reverse Painted, Washington Crossing Delaware, 51 In. 1100.00
Mirror, Federal, Acorn-Drop Finials, Swags, Flowers, 52 x 38 x 8 In. 2070.00
Mirror, Federal, Gilt Gesso, Molded Cornice, Applied Globes, 1800s, 36 x 21 In. 470.00
Mirror, Federal, Gilt Gesso, Wood, Applied Spherules, c.1815, 38 x 16 In. 2940.00
Mirror, Federal, Giltwood, Reverse Painted Panel, Ship, Sea, 33 x 18 In. 489.00
Mirror, Federal, Gold Leaf, Molded Edge, Rectangular, c.1840, 55 x 29 In. 500.00
Mirror, Federal, Mahogany, Reverse Painted, c.1815, 42 1/2 In. 239.00
Mirror, Federal, Mahogany, Reverse Painted, Twisted Pilasters, 23 x 12 1/2 In. 259.00
Mirror, Federal, Mahogany, Veneer, Reverse Painted, Reeded Pilasters, 36 x 18 1/2 In. 1668.00
Mirror, Federal, Parcel Gilt, Acorn Pendant, Ebonized, 2 Parts, 44 3/4 x 27 x 5 In. 770.00
Mirror, Federal, Reverse Painted Tablet, Applied Gilt Half Columns, c.1825, 16 x 32 In. 355.00
Mirror, Federal, Tiger Maple, Carved Cornice, Reeded Column, c.1815, 30 x 18 In. 1295.00
Mirror, French Neoclassical, Reverse Painted, 32 x 26 In. 1290.00
Mirror, George II Style, Mahogany, Parcel Gilt, 31 3/4 x 17 In. 960.00
Mirror, George II, Giltwood, Swan's-Neck Pediment, Eagle Finial, 37 In. 410.00
Mirror, George II, Mahogany, Parcel Gilt, c.1740, 38 1/4 x 22 3/4 In. 1680.00
Mirror, George III Style, Giltwood, Phoenix, 51 x 26 3/4 In., Pair 2070.00
Mirror, George III Style, Mahogany, Parcel Gilt, Scrolled Frame, 1800s, 54 1/2 In. 999.00
Mirror, George III, Mahogany, Parcel Gilt, Fret Carved, Late 1700s, 38 x 19 3/4 In. 120.00
Mirror, Georgian Style, Mahogany, Parcel Gilt, Eagle, Scrolls, 56 x 28 In. 1880.00
Mirror, Georgian Style, Pediment Top, Fruited Scrolling, 62 1/2 x 37 1/2 x 2 In. 415.00
Mirror, Georgian, Flame Mahogany, Gilt, Broken Scrolling, Eagle, 55 x 27 In. 4700.00
Mirror, Georgian, Giltwood, Cornucopia & Leaf Crest, Convex, 1800s, 43 x 25 In. 1645.00
Mirror, Georgian, Walnut, Giltwood, Parcel Gilt, Flower Garlands, c.1835, 39 x 26 In. 2328.00
Mirror, Gesso, Over Wood, Parcel Gilt, Laurel Wreath, 1900s, 42 1/2 In. 265.00
Mirror, Gesso, Over Wood, Pierced Scrolling, Leaves, Late 19th Century, 32 x 28 In. 270.00
Mirror, Gilt Gesso, Over Wood, Early 20th Century, 53 x 39 In. 560.00
Mirror, Giltwood, Beaded, Scrolling Leaves, Square, 78 x 78 In. 470.00
Mirror, Giltwood, Black, Split Baluster, Stenciled, Child, Cat, Garden, c.1830, 32 x 16 In. 560.00
Mirror, Giltwood, Carved, Ebonized, c.1820, 58 1/2 x 46 1/2 x 5 In. 6600.00
Mirror, Giltwood, Carved, Scrollwork, Leaves, Flowers, 37 x 21 In. 270.00
Mirror, Giltwood, Carved, White Washed, 49 x 32 In. 235.00
Mirror, Giltwood, Eagle, Leaf & Scroll Drop, Convex, 33 1/2 x 19 In. 3450.00
Mirror, Giltwood, Laurel Leaf, Acanthus Leaf Corners, France, Late 1800s, 56 x 40 In. 1060.00
Mirror, Giltwood, Leaf Carved, 2 Parts, Continental, 1700s, 83 x 43 In. 2000.00
Mirror, Giltwood, Oval, 20th Century, 45 x 35 In. 140.00
Mirror, Giltwood, Parcel Ebonized, Lion Masque, Dolphins, Convex, 55 x 31 In. 1060.00
Mirror, Giltwood, Reverse Painted, American Flagship, 41 x 23 In. 978.00
Mirror, Giltwood, Seahorse Over Water, Rocks, Scrolled Sides, 41 x 28 x 6 In. 4370.00
Mirror, Giltwood, Square Corner Blocks, Turned Columns, Applied Flowers, 44 x 31 In. 270.00
Mirror, Giltwood, Stepped Cornice, Rosettes, Turned Baluster Sides, 26 x 58 In. 120.00
Mirror, Giltwood, Sunburst, Carved, Molded, Italy, 1700s, 27 1/4 In. 998.00
Mirror, Giltwood, Sunburst, Carved, Stylized Flames, Flower Shaped Center, Italy, 24 In. 590.00
Mirror, Giltwood, Wood, Society For Preservation, Boston, 46 x 25 In. 150.00
Mirror, Girandole, Federal, Giltwood, Eagle On Branch, 3 Candle Arms, 32 In. 420.00
Mirror, Girandole, Giltwood, Seahorse Pediment, 40 In. 6040.00

Mirror, Girandole, Neoclassical, Giltwood, Carved, 46 x 28 In. 3000.00
Mirror, Girandole, Regency, Giltwood, 2 Candle Arms, Convex, 1800s, 33 1/2 In. 3055.00
Mirror, Jean Royere, Lacquered Wood, Silvered Glass, c.1950, 24 x 47 In. 7800.00
Mirror, LaVerne, Brass, Polychrome, Abstract, 1960s, 53 x 34 In. 1415.00
Mirror, Louis XV Style, Giltwood, Decorated Cartouche, Oval, 58 x 38 In. 1645.00
Mirror, Louis XVI Style, Gilt, Flower & Rope Twist Borders, France, 1800s, 29 x 26 In. 350.00
Mirror, Louis XVI Style, Giltwood, Bound Fasces, Ribbon Crest, 36 x 56 In. 2230.00
Mirror, Louis XVI Style, Giltwood, Bowknot, Convex, France, 36 x 16 In. 940.00
Mirror, Louis XVI Style, Giltwood, Cartouche, Trumeau, 1800s, 56 1/2 In., Pair 3304.00
Mirror, Louis XVI Style, Giltwood, Carved, Plaster, Early 1900s, 60 x 34 In. 705.00
Mirror, Louis XVI Style, Giltwood, Leaf & Berry Crest, Late 1800s, 47 x 54 In. 1410.00
Mirror, Louis XVI Style, Giltwood, Pierced Trophy Crest, 1800s, 44 x 32 In. 885.00
Mirror, Louis XVI Style, Painted, Parcel Gilt, Laurel Wreath, 69 x 45 In. 2940.00
Mirror, Mahogany Veneer, Architectural Cornice, Reverse Painted, 18 x 32 In. 175.00
Mirror, Mahogany, Convex, Demilune, Early 1800s, 11 1/2 x 10 1/2 x 3 In. 235.00
Mirror, Mahogany, Fruitwood, Ebonized, Gilt Plaster, Continental, 42 x 33 In. 998.00
Mirror, Mahogany, Gesso Eagle Finial, Flower Drape, 1900s, 30 x 18 In. 193.00
Mirror, Mahogany, Gilt, Scrolled Pediment, Spread-Wing Phoenix Finial, 52 x 26 In. 1650.00
Mirror, Mahogany, Rectangular, 20th Century, 37 3/4 x 41 x 2 In. 236.00
Mirror, Maple, Half Pilasters, Raised Acanthus Leaves, Applied Bird, 40 x 21 1/2 In. 115.00
Mirror, Max Ingrand, Brass, Glass, Fontana Arte, c.1964, 27 3/4 In. 9000.00
Mirror, Napoleon III, Giltwood, Carved, Reticulated Crest, c.1865, 71 x 39 In. 1880.00
Mirror, Napoleon III, Giltwood, Flower Crest, Beaded Frame, c.1865, 56 x 42 In. 1175.00
Mirror, Napoleon III, Giltwood, Flowers, Rectangular, c.1865, 66 x 53 In. 1760.00
Mirror, Napoleon III, Giltwood, Molded & Beaded Frame, Leaves, c.1865, 56 x 40 In. 2115.00
Mirror, Napoleon III, Giltwood, Plaster, Cenotaph, 65 x 34 In. 2350.00
Mirror, Napoleon III, Giltwood, Rope Twist, Leaf Carved, c.1865, 43 x 33 In. 820.00
Mirror, Neoclassical, Curly Maple, Giltwood, Cove Molded, 1800s, 33 x 28 In. 825.00
Mirror, Neoclassical, Giltwood, 1/2 Baluster & Ring, Rosettes, c.1830, 47 x 24 In. 2940.00
Mirror, Neoclassical, Giltwood, Beveled Frame, c.1850, 65 x 35 In. 765.00
Mirror, Neoclassical, Giltwood, Carved, Classical Figures, Rosettes, Leaves, 74 x 35 In. 4406.00
Mirror, Neoclassical, Giltwood, Reverse Painted, Cottage, Lake, Early 1800s, 45 x 24 In. 2470.00
Mirror, Neoclassical, Giltwood, Ripple Molding, Oval, 43 x 27 In. 1175.00
Mirror, Neoclassical, Giltwood, Shell, Flowers, Scroll, 83 x 60 In. 468.00
Mirror, Neoclassical, Giltwood, Urn, Leaves, Oval, c.1865, 59 x 26 In. 880.00
Mirror, Neoclassical, Mahogany Veneer, Gilt Gesso, Carved, Leaves, c.1835, 30 x 54 In. 765.00
Mirror, Neoclassical, Mahogany, Flame Grained, Early 1800s, 45 x 31 In. 1410.00
Mirror, Neoclassical, Mahogany, Giltwood, c.1850, 31 x 22 In. 1116.00
Mirror, Neoclassical, Parcel Gilt, Egg, Dart, 67 x 32 x 6 1/2 In. 1888.00
Mirror, Neoclassical, Stenciled, Ebonized, Lion Masks, Early 1800s, 31 x 16 In. 410.00
Mirror, Neoclassical, Tiger Maple, Reverse Painted, Ship, House, c.1820, 32 x 17 In. 1315.00
Mirror, Neoclassical, Wood, Carved, Silver Leaf, Italy, c.1950, 32 x 8 In. 264.00
Mirror, Neoclassical, Wood, Gilt Gesso, Reverse Painted Tablet, c.1790, 32 x 14 In. 940.00
Mirror, Nutting, Walnut, Good Night Print, 37 x 16 In. 1430.00
Mirror, Oak, Carved, Applied Scroll Crest, Central Finial, 19th Century, 58 x 32 1/2 In. 550.00
Mirror, Oak, Moose & Elk Antlers, 49 x 58 In. 1035.00
Mirror, Oscar Bach, Bronze, Reticulated, Scrolls, Seahorse, 35 x 19 In. 2400.00
Mirror, Pier, Aesthetic Revival, Giltwood, Arched Pediment, Late 1800s, 140 x 45 In. 4465.00
Mirror, Pier, Giltwood, Beveled Frame, Block Corners, Philadelphia, 34 x 52 In. 4115.00
Mirror, Pier, Giltwood, Fluted, Anthemia, Fleur-De-Lis Corners, Divided, 64 In. 5300.00
Mirror, Pier, Giltwood, Gesso, 61 1/2 x 39 1/2 In. 5290.00
Mirror, Pier, Greek Revival, Pediment Top, Fluted Columns, c.1850, 127 x 36 In., Pair 9400.00
Mirror, Pier, Louis XV Style, Gray Paint, Rocaille Crest, Flowers, 122 x 32 In. 940.00
Mirror, Pier, Mahogany, Stepped Cornice, Reeded & Spiral Turned Columns, 54 In. 720.00
Mirror, Pier, Napoleon III, Giltwood, Arched Crest, 106 x 43 1/2 In. 3760.00
Mirror, Pier, Napoleon III, Giltwood, Molded, Beaded, Leaf Carved, c.1865, 52 x 39 In. 1527.00
Mirror, Pier, Neoclassical, Giltwood, 19th Century, 132 x 30 In. 1175.00
Mirror, Pier, Neoclassical, Giltwood, Lotus, Rope, Baltimore, c.1830, 61 x 29 In. 3645.00
Mirror, Pier, Neoclassical, Mahogany, Gilt Bronze Trim, 90 x 25 1/2 In. 2350.00
Mirror, Pier, Neoclassical, Wood, Gilt Gesso, Scrolled Panels, c.1820, 66 x 38 In. 1880.00
Mirror, Pier, Renaissance Revival, Walnut, Maiden's Head Cartouche, 102 x 32 In. 2230.00

Mirror, Pierre Lardin, Giltwood, Silvered Glass, Patinated Metal, c.1940, 45 x 34 In. 5400.00
Mirror, Pine, Brown Paint, Wide Frame, Carved Panels, Gesso Liner, Dutch, 22 x 20 In. 575.00
Mirror, Plaster, On Wood, Gold Paint, Beveled Glass, Rectangular, c.1900, 24 x 48 In. 55.00
Mirror, Queen Anne Style, Black Lacquer, Chinoiserie, 1900s, 38 x 21 In. 295.00
Mirror, Queen Anne Style, Black Lacquer, Chinoiserie, Labarge, 1900s, 59 1/2 In. 679.00
Mirror, Queen Anne Style, Black Lacquer, Gold Flowers, Scroll, 51 x 25 In. 525.00
Mirror, Queen Anne Style, Burl Walnut, Parcel Gilt, Leaf Swags, 1800s, 45 x 24 In. 2115.00
Mirror, Queen Anne Style, Nutting, Mahogany, Bird-Carved Crest, 39 x 15 3/4 In. 865.00
Mirror, Queen Anne, Pine, Ogee Molded, Scalloped-Arch Crest, 17 1/2 x 11 1/2 In. 980.00
Mirror, Queen Anne, Pine, Walnut Veneer, Numbered Drawers, Beveled, 18 1/2 x 15 In. 1265.00
Mirror, Queen Anne-Chippendale, Mahogany, Pine, 18 3/4 In. 440.00
Mirror, Regency Style, Carved, Parcel Ebonized, Gilding, Convex, 42 x 20 In., Pair 4465.00
Mirror, Regency Style, Giltwood, Parcel Ebonized, Carved, Convex, 39 1/2 In. 2115.00
Mirror, Regency, Giltwood, Cove Molded, Oval, Early 1800s, 47 1/2 x 41 In. 1005.00
Mirror, Regency, Giltwood, Globe Border, Bull's-Eye Shape, 23 In. 2350.00
Mirror, Regency, Leafy Crest, Convex, England, Early 1800s, 17 In. 150.00
Mirror, Regency, Shells & Guilloche, Round, England, Early 1800s, 27 In. 1060.00
Mirror, Regency, Wood, Parcel Ebonized, Elephant Tusks, c.1900, 58 x 37 In. 3525.00
Mirror, Rococo Revival, Cove Molded, Leaf Scrolling, Rectangular, 55 x 36 In. 295.00
Mirror, Rococo Revival, Giltwood, Carved Crest, Beaded, Flower Clusters, 40 x 27 In. 940.00
Mirror, Rococo Revival, Giltwood, Pierced Leaves, Continental, 1800s, 54 x 40 In. 2125.00
Mirror, Rococo Revival, Giltwood, Shell & Scroll Border, 27 x 23 In. 206.00
Mirror, Rococo Style, Composition, Shell Pediment, Cornucopia, 48 x 25 In. 1035.00
Mirror, Rococo Style, Gesso Over Wood, Flowers, Oval, 45 1/2 x 33 1/2 x 5 1/2 In. 325.00
Mirror, Rococo Style, Giltwood, Foliated Ribbon & Fruit Borders, 62 x 40 In. 5915.00
Mirror, Rococo Style, Giltwood, Leaf Carved, Pierced Cartouche, 48 x 28 In. 325.00
Mirror, Rococo Style, Giltwood, Oval, France, 20th Century, 44 3/4 x 29 3/4 In. 708.00
Mirror, Rococo Style, Giltwood, Scroll, Flowers, 74 x 56 In. 1170.00
Mirror, Rococo Style, Pine, Parcel Gilt, Multicolored Flowers, 45 x 27 In. 646.00
Mirror, Rococo, Giltwood, Continental, 45 1/2 x 28 In. 1955.00
Mirror, Rococo, Giltwood, Openwork Border, Leaf, C-Scrolls, Italy, c.1750, 44 In. 470.00
Mirror, Rococo, Parcel Gilt, Walnut Inlay, Incised, 1700s, 37 x 17 In. 1175.00
Mirror, Serge Roche, Stained Wood, Tinted Glass, c.1935, 14 3/4 x 29 1/4 In. 9000.00
Mirror, Shaving, Brass, Beveled, Telescopic Brass Arm, Wall Mount, 10 1/2 In. 110.00
Mirror, Shaving, Light & Dark Woods, Stand, 1800s, 21 In., 12 1/2-In. Mirror 1035.00
Mirror, Shaving, Mahogany Veneer, Pine, Brass Paw Feet, Turned Posts, 23 x 8 x 29 In. 230.00
Mirror, Shaving, Rosewood, Brass, Telescopic Arm, Beveled Glass, Wall Mount, 11 In. 110.00
Mirror, Shaving, William IV, Mahogany, c.1830, 27 x 24 In. 355.00
Mirror, Sheraton, Black, Stenciled, Star, Leaf, Flowers, 27 x 14 1/2 In. 375.00
Mirror, Sheraton, Reverse Painted, Chinese Scene, 23 x 12 In. 345.00
Mirror, Sheraton, Reverse Painted, Sea Battle, 31 x 16 In. 375.00
Mirror, Sheraton, Split Spindle, Corner Blocks, Painted, c.1835, 21 x 17 In. 2450.00
Mirror, Tabernacle, Sheraton, Giltwood, Ball Drops, Constitution & Java, 31 x 14 In. 1265.00
Mirror, Tabernacle, Sheraton, Mahogany, Reverse Painted, 2 Parts, 34 x 17 In. 105.00
Mirror, Trumeau, Louis XVI Style, Faux Wood, Textile Insert, 1800s, 85 x 53 In. 2950.00
Mirror, Trumeau, Louis XVI, Beech, Carved, Painted, Putti, 82 x 59 In. 3055.00
Mirror, Trumeau, Neoclassical, Giltwood, Cream Paint, Eagle, Early 1800s, 77 x 34 In. 9105.00
Mirror, Venetian Style, Gilt Scrolled Spandrels, Green Field, Intaglio Cut, 44 1/2 x 34 In. 1265.00
Mirror, Venetian Style, Scrolling Leaves, Cartouche, 1900s, 19 1/2 x 14 1/2 In. 265.00
Mirror, Victorian, Walnut, Inset Gold Leaf, Oval, 39 1/2 x 34 1/2 In. 300.00
Mirror, Walnut, Curved Crest, Rectangular, Early 1900s, 46 x 26 In. 415.00
Mirror, Walter Von Nessen, Skyscraper, Nickeled Bronze, Glass, c.1930, 30 x 40 In. 6600.00
Mirror, William IV, Giltwood, Plaster, Antique Bead Decoration, c.1835, 33 x 21 In. 410.00
Mirror, Wood, Hammered Pewter Overlay, Vine, Flowers, Round, Arts & Crafts, 13 1/2 In. 390.00
Mirror, Wood, Reverse Painted, Mt. Vernon, c.1820, 22 x 11 1/2 In. 828.00
Ottoman, Empire Style, Walnut, Inlaid, Leather Top, Storage Interior, 15 x 32 In., Pair 1410.00
Ottoman, Frank Lloyd Wright, Heritage Hendredon, c.1956, 16 x 27 x 31 In. 540.00
Ottoman, Neoclassical, Mahogany, Carved, Upholstered Top, c.1825, 11 x 22 In., Pair 3525.00
Ottoman, Regency Style, Tufted Upholstery, Ormolu Paw Feet, 10 x 41 x 29 In. 1530.00
Ottoman, William IV Style, Tufted Upholstery, Turned Feet, Casters, 15 x 41 x 41 In. 880.00
Ottoman, William IV Style, Walnut, Padded & Tufted Top, 16 x 40 x 40 In. 1880.00

To remove fresh food stains from upholstery, sprinkle cornmeal on the spot. It will act as a blotter. Vacuum.

Furniture, Recamier, Rococo Revival, Rosewood, Carved Backrest, c.1850, 36 x 39 x 26 In.

Ottoman, William IV, Mahogany, Leather, Padded & Tufted Top, c.1850, 18 x 48 In. 4230.00
Overmantel Mirror, see Architectural category.
Parlor Set, Arts & Crafts, Settee, Rocker, Armchair, Vertical Slats, 3 Piece 4750.00
Parlor Set, Cherry, Upholstered, Sofa, Armchair, c.1905, 35 x 58-In. Sofa, 2 Piece 220.00
Parlor Set, Federal, Cane, Painted, L. Barnes, c.1815, 35 x 53 In., 5 Piece 21600.00
Parlor Set, Gilt, Carved, Cameo Armchairs, Loveseat, Russia, 3 Piece 660.00
Parlor Set, Italian Renaissance Revival, Putti, Griffins, Early 1900s, 3 Piece 4800.00
Parlor Set, Italian Rococo Style, Carved, Scroll, Rocaille Designs, 1900s, 8 Piece 380.00
Parlor Set, Louis XV Style, Wood, Carved, Tapestry, Settee, 2 Armchairs, c.1890, 3 Piece 500.00
Parlor Set, Napoleon III, Rosewood, Ormolu Mount, c.1865, 5 Piece 1880.00
Parlor Set, Renaissance Revival, Rosewood, Carved Crests, Upholstered, 5 Piece 4230.00
Parlor Set, Renaissance Revival, Walnut, Carved Crest, Medallion, c.1880, 43 In. 765.00
Pedestal, Art Nouveau, Mahogany, Beech, Serpentine Top, 51 x 16 In., Pair 529.00
Pedestal, Biedermeier, Fruitwood, Tapered, Fluted, Square Top, Bracket Feet, 42 In., Pair 980.00
Pedestal, Cast Composition, Gold Leaf, White, Corinthian Column, 28 x 16 In. 90.00
Pedestal, Eclectic, Walnut, Bun Feet, Inlaid Geometric Designs, Late 1800s, 19 In. 70.00
Pedestal, Empire Style, Carrara Marble, Curved Top, Ram's Head, Garland, 47 x 12 In. 1645.00
Pedestal, Empire Style, Mahogany, Stone Top, Goat's Head Mounts, 31 x 11 In. 240.00
Pedestal, Faux Malachite Panels, Gilt Molding, Triangular, 1800s, 41 In., Pair 1600.00
Pedestal, Fruitwood, Polychrome, Travertine Top, Fluted Vase-Column, Italy, 50 x 13 In. 720.00
Pedestal, Italian Baroque, Walnut, Leaf-Carved Top, 3 Cupids, Rockwork Base, 24 In. 3525.00
Pedestal, Louis XV Style, Kingwood, Painted, Bombe, Bronze Mount, 1900s, 53 x 13 In., Pair 1410.00
Pedestal, Louis XV Style, Mahogany, Marble Top, c.1900, 42 1/2 x 12 In. 265.00
Pedestal, Louis XVI Style, Fruitwood, Serpentine Top, Fruit, Leaves, 31 x 23 In., Pair 1295.00
Pedestal, Mahogany, Ash, Walnut, Carved Vines, Flowers, Round Top, 38 x 12 In. 805.00
Pedestal, Mahogany, Gilt, Swan, Round Top, 8-Sided Base, c.1825, 41 In., Pair 4995.00
Pedestal, Mahogany, Round Top, Platform Base, c.1905, 17 x 12 In. 95.00
Pedestal, Marble Veneer, Beaded, Fluted, Hexagonal, Continental, 47 x 16 In., Pair 1180.00
Pedestal, Marble, Antique Green, Column, Continental, c.1900, 34 1/2 x 15 1/2 In. 1410.00
Pedestal, Marble, Square Top, Round Column, Square Base, 36 x 14 In., 5 Piece 575.00
Pedestal, Mirror, Black Lacquer, Round, Mid 20th Century, 36 x 18 1/2 In. 560.00
Pedestal, Napoleon III Style, Marble, Square, Bronze Plaques, 45 x 15 In., Pair 2350.00
Pedestal, Neoclassical, Flaring Urn Standard, Leaf, 6-Sided Base, Italy, 41 1/2 In. 560.00
Pedestal, Oak, Barley Twist, Hexagonal Top, 47 3/4 x 16 In. 295.00
Pedestal, Onyx, Green, Turned, Square Top, Plinth Base, 43 x 14 In. 400.00
Pedestal, Regency Style, Bronze Dore, Classical Heads, Scrolls, Tapered, 40 In., Pair 3525.00
Pedestal, Regency Style, Gilt, Raised Flowers, Ram Heads, Paw Feet, 48 In., Pair 805.00
Pedestal, Renaissance Revival, Onyx, Gilt Bronze Mount, Late 1800s, 42 1/2 In. 1175.00
Pedestal, Victorian, Green Marble, Octagonal Base, Molded Flared Top, 43 x 11 In. 250.00
Pedestal, Victorian, Marble Top, Oak, Turned Corner Columns, c.1890, 34 x 16 In. 275.00
Pedestal, Wood, Carved, Green, Gray, Faux Marble, Continental, 50 1/2 x 16 x 16 In. 865.00
Pew, Frank Lloyd Wright, c.1947, 28 x 24 x 21 In. 1440.00
Pew, Oak, Carved Gothic Arches, c.1900, 39 x 50 x 21 In. 175.00
Pew, Pine, Walnut, Straight Back, Scrolled Arms, c.1835, 33 x 111 x 17 In. 165.00
Pie Safe, Hardwood, Pierced Tin Panels, 4 Doors, 2 Drawers, 69 x 39 x 17 In. 489.00

Pie Safe, Hardwood, Pierced Tin Panels, 4 Doors, 2 Drawers, 70 x 39 x 16 In. 259.00
Pie Safe, Mixed Wood, Drawer, 4 Inset Panel Doors, 1800s, 76 x 39 In. 236.00
Pie Safe, Pine, Pierced Tin Panels, 19th Century, 68 x 37 In. 325.00
Pie Safe, Poplar, Pine, Punched, Tin Sides, 2 Shelves, 32 x 17 x 36 In. 720.00
Pie Safe, Poplar, Red Paint, 12 Pierced Tin Panels, Dovetailed Drawer, 39 x 48 In. 1840.00
Pie Safe, Walnut, 2 Drawers Over 2 Doors, 3 Punched Tin Panels, 50 x 38 x 15 In. 1045.00
Pie Safe, Walnut, Drawer, 2 Doors, Punched Tin Panels, 55 x 35 x 17 In. 2415.00
Pie Safe, Walnut, Poplar, Punched Tin, Drawer, 50 x 42 x 17 In. 1610.00
Pie Safe, Walnut, Punched Tin, Pin Wheels, Star Surround, 2 Drawers, 50 x 38 In. 1045.00
Pipe Rack, Drawer, 6 Hooks, Flower Crest, France, 18 3/4 x 7 1/2 In. 1380.00
Plant Stand, 3 Circular Holders, Iron, Jean Royere, c.1939, 25 x 38 x 9 In. 6000.00
Porch Set, Wicker, 2 Settees, 2 Armchairs, Magenta Paint, Cushions, 33 x 53 In. 489.00
Rack, Baking, Brass, Iron, 3 Tiers, Scrolled Supports, 76 x 60 x 17 In. 650.00
Rack, Baking, Regency Style, Wrought Iron, France, 87 x 30 x 14 In. 235.00
Rack, Drying, Herb, Shaker, Maple, Pine, 3 Sections, Hinged, 6 Upright Poles, 41 x 12 x 15 In. 760.00
Rack, Drying, Shaker, Pine, Mustard Paint, Inset Iron Hinges, 3 Rungs, Tapered Leg, 50 x 34 In. ... 878.00
Rack, Drying, Southern Pine, Golden Varnish, Ball Finials, Shoe Feet, 36 x 44 In. 375.00
Rack, Game, Hanging, Scalloped Edge, Tulip Ends, 9 Iron Hooks, 8 1/4 x 33 1/4 In. 316.00
Rack, Magazine, Arts & Crafts, Oak, 4 Shelves, 45 1/4 x 25 3/4 x 15 1/2 In. 115.00
Rack, Magazine, Regency Style, Mahogany, 4 Sections, Drawer, Brass Casters, 21 x 18 x 13 In. ... 275.00
Rack, Magazine, Tree, Wormley, Birch, Walnut Shelves, 28 x 16 x 24 1/2 In. 2350.00
Rack, Towel, Eastlake, Walnut, Dentil Molded Frieze, Flowerhead Corbels, 28 In. 206.00
Rack, Towel, Wood, Chamfered Tapering Supports, Painted, Early 1800s, 36 x 19 In. 235.00
Recamier, French Provincial, Fruitwood, Cane, Cushions, Ball Feet, c.1850, 36 x 26 In. 820.00
Recamier, Louis XV Style, Mahogany, Upholstered, c.1850, 25 x 55 In. 705.00
Recamier, Neoclassical, Mahogany, Boston, Early 1800s, 34 x 66 x 22 In. 3525.00
Recamier, Regency, Faux Wood, Scrolled Back, Arm, Legs, Early 1800s, 34 x 69 x 22 In. 4700.00
Recamier, Rococo Revival, Rosewood, Carved Backrest, c.1850, 36 x 39 x 26 In. .... *ILLUS* 4830.00
Recamier, Victorian, Walnut, Finger Carved, Ribbon Crest, Scrollwork, 46 x 60 x 26 In. 1870.00
Rocker, 3 Arched Slats, Splint Seat, Old Red Paint, Deep Rockers, Turned Arms, 24 In. 200.00
Rocker, 6 Vertical Back Slats, Drop-In Spring Cushion, Maroon Vinyl, 35 x 27 In. 765.00
Rocker, Adirondack, Willow, Oak, c.1900, 41 In. 265.00
Rocker, Arrow Back, Plank Seat, 3 Spindles, Green Paint, Turned Posts, Arms, Legs, 22 In. 115.00
Rocker, Arts & Crafts, Oak, Carved Baseball Game Scene, c.1910, 34 x 24 In. 4510.00
Rocker, Arts & Crafts, Oak, Grand Rapids, Michigan, c.1900, 31 In. 85.00
Rocker, Bentwood, Cane Seat, Arms, 43 x 28 x 32 In. 2360.00
Rocker, Boston, Plank Seat, Black Paint, Yellow Design, 19th Century, Child's 44.00
Rocker, Carolina Style, Cane Back, Seat, Plank Arms, 41 x 25 1/2 x 32 1/2 In., Pair 330.00
Rocker, Cherry, Upholstered, Arched Back, Arms, Shaped Rockers, c.1830, 46 In. 470.00
Rocker, Eames, Fiberglass, Birch Runners, Arms, Zenith, 27 x 25 In. 1650.00
Rocker, Eames, RAR, Herman Miller, c.1951, 27 x 25 x 24 In. 660.00
Rocker, Eastlake Style, Ebonized, Painted Rail, Spindles, Cane Back, Seat, Child's 415.00
Rocker, Eastlake, Mahogany, Serpentine Crest Rail, Cane Seat, 42 x 24 x 34 In. 679.00
Rocker, Federal, Pillow Back, Double Crest, Rush Seat, Arms, Applied Rockers, 41 In. 170.00
Rocker, G. Stickley, Double Horizontal Slats, 5 Vertical Slats, 28 x 29 x 44 In. 2115.00
Rocker, Honduran Mahogany, c.1970, 36 x 22 x 43 In. 2160.00
Rocker, Horn, Plush Seat, Wood Rockers, c.1900, 43 In. 3525.00
Rocker, L. & J.G. Stickley, Oak, 6-Slat Back, 42 1/2 x 17 In. 719.00
Rocker, L. & J.G. Stickley, Slatted Sides, Back, Drop-In Cushion, 37 x 32 x 35 In. 2520.00
Rocker, Ladder Back, 4 Slats, Mortised Posts, Open Arms, 39 x 31 1/2 x 29 In. 2938.00
Rocker, Ladder Back, 4 Slats, Urn Finials, Splint Seat, 18th Century 55.00
Rocker, Ladder Back, Black Paint, 4 Curved Slats, Turned Arms, Legs, 37 1/2 In. 230.00
Rocker, Ladder Back, Black Paint, Sausage Turned, Arms, 1700s 140.00
Rocker, Ladder Back, Mixed Hardwood, Scrolled Ends, Arms, 1700s, 45 x 24 x 23 In. 405.00
Rocker, Ladder Back, Mixed Wood, 5 Splats, Rush Seat, Southern, 44 x 21 x 15 In., Pair 825.00
Rocker, Ladder Back, Red Finish, Potty Seat, 1700s 138.00
Rocker, Ladder Back, Red Wash, Splint Seat, Walnut Arms, 45 In. 115.00
Rocker, Lincoln Style, Maple, Needlepoint Seat, Back, 1800s, 50 x 22 x 34 In. 60.00
Rocker, Maple, Brown Stain, Arched Crest, Vase Splat, Scrolled Arms, 41 In. 430.00
Rocker, Oak, Pressback, Caned Seat, c.1900, 36 In. .... *ILLUS* 59.00
Rocker, Oak, Rattan Herringbone Seat, 46 1/4 x 28 1/2 x 35 1/2 In. 236.00

Furniture, Rocker, Oak, Pressback, Caned Seat, c.1900, 36 In.

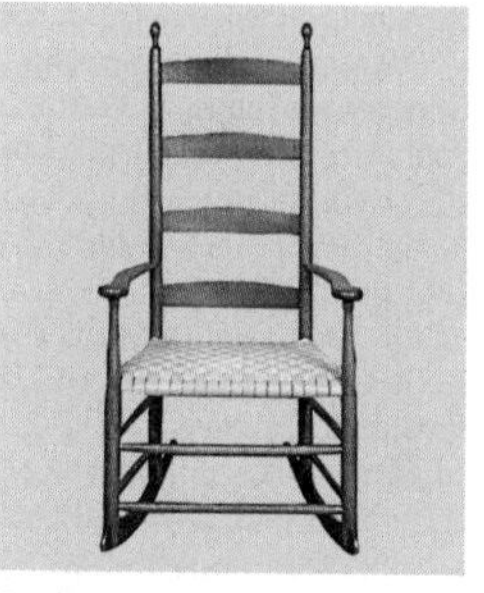
Furniture, Rocker, Shaker, Tiger Maple, Taped Seat, New Lebanon, N.Y., c.1830-40, 46 In.

Furniture, Rocker, Victorian, Oak, Swing-Out Footrest, c.1900, 42 In.

Rocker, Pine, Maple, Spindle Back, Bamboo Turnings, Swept Arms, c.1875, 43 x 22 In. 165.00
Rocker, Plank Seat, Red Paint, Black Graining, Shaped Crest, Bamboo Turnings, 20 1/2 In. 230.00
Rocker, Ralph Rapson, Green Webbing, Armless, Knoll, 29 x 25 x 32 In. 3068.00
Rocker, Ron Arad, Epoxy-Coated Steel, Galvanized Springs, 1981-83, 25 In., Pair 3300.00
Rocker, Sam Maloof School, 7 Back Slats, Saddle Seat, Arms, 51 x 28 x 48 In. 1000.00
Rocker, Sewing, Victorian, Walnut, Cane Seat & Back, Late 19th Century, 35 In. 50.00
Rocker, Shaker, 4 Graduated Slats, Natural Finish, Arms, Ash Splint Seat, c.1840, 42 In. 4095.00
Rocker, Shaker, 4 Slats, Maple, Walnut Stain, Curved Arms, Mushroom Caps, Taped Seat, 43 In. .. 1870.00
Rocker, Shaker, Ladder Back, 3 Slats, Acorn Finials, Tape Seat, Arms, Mt. Lebanon, 34 In. 400.00
Rocker, Shaker, Maple, Ebony Stained Finish, Tan & Cream Taped Back, Seat, c.1890, 38 In. 1346.00
Rocker, Shaker, No. 3, 3 Slats, Tape Seat, Shawl Bar, Mt. Lebanon, 33 In. 230.00
Rocker, Shaker, No. 3, Ladder Back, Tape Seat, Arms 250.00
Rocker, Shaker, No. 4, Upholstered Seat, 3 Slats, Shawl Bar, 33 3/4 x 16 In. 259.00
Rocker, Shaker, No. 6, Tape Seat, 4 Slats, Acorn Finials, Arms, Mt. Lebanon, 42 In. 635.00
Rocker, Shaker, No. 7, Ladder Back, Tape Seat, Arms, Mt. Lebanon ....385.00 to 715.00
Rocker, Shaker, No. 7, Tape Seat, 4 Slats, Shawl Bar, Arms, Mt. Lebanon, 41 x 14 1/2 In. 980.00
Rocker, Shaker, Tiger Maple, Taped Seat, New Lebanon, N.Y., c.1830-40, 46 In. .... *ILLUS* 8625.00
Rocker, Stickley Bros., Oak, Yellow & Brown Floral Upholstery, 1912-18, 29 In. 1560.00
Rocker, Teak, Upholstered, Frimann Skeie & Co., Norway, c.1970 .... 190.00
Rocker, Victorian, Oak, Pressed Back, Scrolled Arms, 41 x 25 x 32 In. 145.00
Rocker, Victorian, Oak, Swing-Out Footrest, c.1900, 42 In. .... *ILLUS* 206.00
Rocker, Victorian, Walnut, Carved Supports, Velvet Upholstery, Open Arms, 46 x 25 In. 170.00
Rocker, William IV, Mahogany, Leather, Slung Back, Scrolling Arms, c.1850, 36 In. 1530.00
Rocker, Windsor, Bow Back, Red Paint, Saddle Seat, Late 1700s, 35 In. 1060.00
Rocker, Windsor, Comb Back, Arrow Back, Arms, 41 x 14 3/4 In. 145.00
Rocker, Windsor, Comb Back, Ash, Maple, Continuous Arm, c.1810, 41 In. 295.00
Rocker, Windsor, Comb Back, Fruit Design, Mustard Paint, Grain Painted Seat, 1800s 220.00
Rocker, Windsor, Comb Back, Green, Yellow Stripes, c.1825, 40 1/2 x 16 In. 1175.00
Rocker, Windsor, Comb Back, Poplar, Saddle Seat, 41 1/2 x 25 x 24 In. 460.00
Rocker, Windsor, Fanback, 7 Spindles, Serpentine Crest, Arms, c.1810, 46 In. 410.00
Rocker, Windsor, Fanback, Carved Ears, 44 In. 2875.00
Rocker, Wing, Queen Anne, Painted, Woven Tape Seat, 17 1/2 x 46 In. 550.00
Rocker & Ottoman, V. Kagan, Cherry Frame, Boris Kroll Fabric, 1960s, 36 x 30 In. 10620.00
Safe, Perry Fire Vault, Oak, Round, Concrete Inside, Key, 14 x 7 In. 200.00
Screen, 2-Panel, Birds, Flowers, Ivory & Bone Inlay, Japan, 1868-1911, 72 x 67 In. 1530.00
Screen, 2-Panel, Bone, Mother-Of-Pearl, Lacquer, Flowers, Japan, c.1890, 70 x 64 In. 175.00
Screen, 2-Panel, Geese, Snowy Marsh, Japan, 1800s, 49 x 47 In. 1035.00
Screen, 2-Panel, Overlaid, Birds, Flowers, Japan, c.1900, 72 x 70 In. 470.00
Screen, 2-Panel, Pine, Bamboo, Winter Scene, Japan, 1800s, 67 x 63 In. 2350.00
Screen, 3-Panel, Arts & Crafts, Shaped Bottom, Carved Flowers, 71 In. 1560.00
Screen, 3-Panel, Black Lacquer, Zodiac Animals, Birds, Insects, Flowers, 70 x 51 In. 205.00
Screen, 3-Panel, Carved Leaves, Indo-Persian, Late 1800s, 42 x 46 1/2 In. 325.00
Screen, 3-Panel, Cast Bronze, Copper Panels, Inset Clock, Key Wind, 13 x 17 In. 1100.00
Screen, 3-Panel, Chinoiserie Squares, Birds, Trees, Nailhead Trim, France, c.1920, 74 In. 2350.00

Screen, 3-Panel, Contemporary, Maple, Walnut Stained, Gothic Top, 85 x 51 In. 165.00
Screen, 3-Panel, Directoire Style, Wood, Polychromed, Decoupage, 66 1/2 x 55 In. 705.00
Screen, 3-Panel, Eastlake, Ebonized, Chinese-Style Fabric, 70 x 60 In. 558.00
Screen, 3-Panel, G. Stickley, Paneled Bottom, Leather-Paned Top, 68 x 66 In. 4406.00
Screen, 3-Panel, Louis XV Style, Walnut, Carved, Chinoiserie Panel, 56 x 70 In. 1020.00
Screen, 3-Panel, Louis XVI Style, Gilt, Mirror, Lattice Panel, Casters, 72 x 74 In. 1650.00
Screen, 3-Panel, Mahogany, Oriental Cloth Inserts, Spindles, 80 1/4 In. 230.00
Screen, 3-Panel, Painted, Flowers, Scrolls, Folding, Early 1900s, 69 x 54 In. 650.00
Screen, 3-Panel, Rococo Style, Gilt, Silk, Glass, Continental, 64 x 61 1/2 In. 1180.00
Screen, 3-Panel, Rococo Style, Painted, Parcel Gilt, Mirrors, Italy, c.1910, 69 x 60 In. 1120.00
Screen, 3-Panel, Tooled Leather, Arched, Early 20th Century, 72 x 67 1/2 In. 415.00
Screen, 3-Panel, Victorian, Decoupage, Ebonized, Gilt, c.1890, 68 x 66 In. 1116.00
Screen, 4-Panel, Art Nouveau, Mahogany, Oil On Canvas, 4 Seasons, 1905, 62 In. 1410.00
Screen, 4-Panel, Black Lacquer, Soapstone, Vase With Flowers, Chinese, 72 x 72 In. 500.00
Screen, 4-Panel, Carved, Pierced, Rosettes, Leaves, India, c.1970, 73 x 80 In. 415.00
Screen, 4-Panel, Coromandel Style, Painted Figures, Brass Hinges, 72 x 64 In. 575.00
Screen, 4-Panel, Figures Relaxing, Ink On Gold Paper, Black Lacquer Frame, 36 x 74 In. 550.00
Screen, 4-Panel, Gothic Revival, Oak, Fabric Lined, G. Gilbert Scott, c.1870, 78 x 100 In. 7200.00
Screen, 4-Panel, Mahogany, Incised, Polychrome, Chinese, c.1910, 72 x 76 In. 880.00
Screen, 4-Panel, Oak, Glass, Carved Flowers, Brass Hinges, 52 x 46 In. 175.00
Screen, 4-Panel, Oil Paint, Haystacking Scene, Leather Edges, 71 3/4 In. 6168.00
Screen, 4-Panel, Oriental, Carved, Mother-Of-Pearl, Black Lacquer, 72 In. 325.00
Screen, 4-Panel, Paper, Green, Grape Harvesting Scene, Bernard Et Cie, 72 x 80 In. 4400.00
Screen, 4-Panel, Silk Stitched Peacocks, Black Ground, Oriental, c.1950, 67 x 92 In. 60.00
Screen, 4-Panel, Wood, Mythical Animals, Figures, Chinese, Late 1800s, 75 x 85 In. 2230.00
Screen, 5-Panel, Oil On Canvas, Napoleon On Elba, Folding, Continental, 59 x 100 In. 590.00
Screen, 6-Panel, Ash Plywood, Canvas, Red, Folding, 1956, 67 5/8 x 54 6/8 In. 12000.00
Screen, 6-Panel, Black Lacquer, Soapstone, Birds, Flowers, Chinese, 72 x 96 In. . . . . .590.00 to 825.00
Screen, 6-Panel, Black Lacquer, Soapstone, Figures, Chinese, 72 x 96 In. 530.00
Screen, 6-Panel, Cinnabar Lacquer, Court Life, Dragons, Flowers, c.1910, 72 x 96 In. 470.00
Screen, 6-Panel, Coromandel, Birds, Flowers, Folding, Chinese, Late 1800s, 72 x 96 In. 529.00
Screen, 6-Panel, Paper, Polychrome, Warriors Hunting Wild Boar, Leopards, 71 x 106 In. 645.00
Screen, 6-Panel, Peacocks, Peonies, Leaf Scroll Border, Chinese, 72 x 96 In. 235.00
Screen, 6-Panel, Portuguese Style, Leather, Arched Crests, 96 x 117 In. 1410.00
Screen, 6-Panel, Poul Kjaerholm, Pine, Denmark, c.1956, 55 x 78 In. 4150.00
Screen, 7-Panel, Victorian, Wood, Glass, Decoupage Flowers, 17 1/2 x 32 In. 2400.00
Screen, 8-Panel, Coromandel, Overall Flowers, Birds, Chinese, 84 x 128 In. 1989.00
Screen, 8-Panel, Lacquer, Hundred Boys, Chinese, 1820-50, 111 x 156 In. 15860.00
Screen, 8-Panel, Lacquer, Inlay, Chinese, c.1800, 85 x 174 In. 3290.00
Screen, 8-Panel, Paper On Wood, Watercolor, Ink, Folding, France, c.1935, 84 x 93 In. 1645.00
Screen, Bone, Mother-Of-Pearl, Lacquer, Birds, Branches, Japan, 42 x 20 In., Pair 470.00
Screen, Openwork, Scattered H's Design, Iron, 108 x 48 In. 604.00
Screen, P. Evans, Painted, Steel, 1967, 72 3/4 x 96 x 4 In. . . . . ***ILLUS*** 90000.00
Screen, Poul Kjaerholm, PK111, Oregon Pine, Laminated, E.K. Christensen, c.1956 . . . . 9000.00
Screen, Rosewood, Gold Lacquer Plaques, Baskets, Japan, c.1890, 73 x 57 In. 2470.00
Screen, Slate, Carved, Palace Scene, Chinese, 1800s, 20 x 12 In. 2235.00
Screen, Table Top, Rosewood, Marble, Court Scene, Calligraphy, Chinese, 1800s, 20 x 15 In. 355.00
Screen, Victorian, Cherry, Black Lacquer, Hollyhocks, Flowers, Folding, 66 In. 1540.00
Secretary, Chippendale Style, Block Front, 20th Century, 102 x 45 x 21 In. 165.00
Secretary, Chippendale Style, Drop Front, Mahogany, Drawers, Mid 1900s, 86 x 38 In. 765.00
Secretary, Chippendale, Slant Front, Cherry, Dovetailed, 4 Drawers, 2 Parts, 36 x 44 In. 6900.00
Secretary, Chippendale, Slant Front, Maple, Bonnet Top, 2 Parts, 87 x 36 x 19 In. 8050.00
Secretary, Drop Front, Birch, Stepped Cornice, Berry, Leaf Carved, 60 x 60 1/2 In. 3335.00
Secretary, Drop Front, Fruitwood, Painted, Continental, 1800s, 56 x 37 x 17 In. 2705.00
Secretary, Drop Front, Kingwood, Tulipwood, Marquetry, Gilt Brass, 56 x 31 x 19 In. 3760.00
Secretary, Drop Front, Mahogany Veneer, Bookcase, Shelves, 2 Doors, 88 In. 1430.00
Secretary, Drop Front, Mahogany, Brass Mounted, Marble, France, c.1815, 55 x 29 In. 2820.00
Secretary, Drop Front, Mahogany, Marble, Leather, France, 44 x 40 x 23 In. 3740.00
Secretary, Drop Front, Marble Top, Bombe, Marquetry, 3 Drawers, 52 x 29 In. 1265.00
Secretary, Drop Front, Oak, 2-Door Bookcase, c.1900, 66 x 33 1/2 In. 600.00
Secretary, Drop Front, Painted, Serpentine, 3 Drawers, Venice, 39 3/4 x 37 In. 2820.00

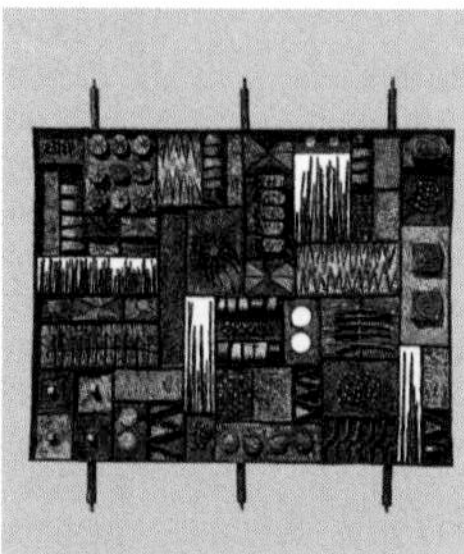
Furniture, Screen, P. Evans, Painted, Steel, 1967, 72 3/4 x 96 x 4 In.

Furniture, Secretary, Oak, Drop Front Desk, Curved Mirror, Early 20th Century, 70 x 36 In.

Furniture, Server, Oak, Ebonized, Putti, Velvet Pads, W.B. Moses & Sons, 51 1/2 x 44 x 21 In.

Secretary, Drop Front, Walnut, Molded Crest, Sunken Panels, 80 1/4 x 29 x 15 1/2 In. 2090.00
Secretary, Empire, Mahogany, Panel Doors, Shelves, Bun Feet, 76 1/2 x 37 x 22 1/2 In. 2006.00
Secretary, Federal, Birch, 6 Drawers, 2 Doors, 2 Parts, N.H., 57 x 41 x 20 In. 2300.00
Secretary, Federal, Drop Front, Mahogany, c.1820, 92 x 45 In. 940.00
Secretary, George I Style, Slant Front, Walnut, 1700s, 39 3/4 x 37 1/2 x 20 1/2 In. 1415.00
Secretary, George II, Chinoiserie, Red Lacquer, 1700s, 40 x 22 x 81 In. 4680.00
Secretary, George II, Mahogany, Arched Astragal Glazed Doors, 89 x 41 In. 7640.00
Secretary, George III Style, Mahogany, Slant Front, 97 x 42 x 23 In. 2940.00
Secretary, George III, Drop Front, Mahogany, 2 Short Drawers, 5 Drawers, 60 x 27 In. 4995.00
Secretary, George III, Drop Front, Mahogany, 2 Short Over 2 Long Drawers, 43 x 27 In. 1175.00
Secretary, George III, Drop Front, Mahogany, 4 Drawers, c.1785, 89 x 40 In. 5405.00
Secretary, George III, Drop Front, Mahogany, Drawers, Cubbyholes, 90 x 48 x 21 In. 4255.00
Secretary, George III, Mahogany, Hinged Front, 3 Drawers, 2 Doors, 88 x 39 In. 3600.00
Secretary, George III, Slant Front, Mahogany, c.1785, 88 x 42 In. 6460.00
Secretary, George III, Slant Front, Mahogany, c.1785, 94 x 46 In. 6756.00
Secretary, Georgian Style, Painted, Chinese Scenes, Drawers, Cubbyholes, 78 x 26 In. 1495.00
Secretary, Hepplewhite, Mahogany, String, Banded Inlay, Pigeonholes, 43 x 38 x 21 In. 546.00
Secretary, Hepplewhite, Mahogany, Tambour Section, 2 Doors, Flat Front, 42 x 38 In. 2530.00
Secretary, Jules Leleu, Drop Front, 2 Drawers, 2 Cabinets, 54 x 55 x 18 In. 5605.00
Secretary, Napoleon III, Drop Front, Ebonized, Ivory Inlay, 4 Drawers, 56 x 29 In. 3760.00
Secretary, Neoclassical, Bird's-Eye Maple, Cherry, Canted Cornice, Paneled Doors, 73 In. 825.00
Secretary, Neoclassical, Mahogany, Arched Glazed Doors, 4 Drawers, 87 x 45 In. 4995.00
Secretary, Neoclassical, Mahogany, Baltimore, c.1815, 104 x 47 x 24 In. 6465.00
Secretary, Oak, Carved, Lion's Head, Acanthus, Curved Glass Door, Mirror, 75 x 41 In. 940.00
Secretary, Oak, Drop Front Desk, Curved Mirror, Early 20th Century, 70 x 36 In. .... *ILLUS* 558.00
Secretary, Regency, Mahogany, Dentillated Cornice, 96 x 46 x 23 In. 7930.00
Secretary, Restauration, Drop Front, Mahogany, Marble, Paneled, 56 x 38 In. 3055.00
Secretary, Rosewood, Molded Edge, Drawers, 19th Century, 44 x 17 x 41 In. 905.00
Secretary, Sheraton, 2 Glass Doors, 3 Drawers, 72 x 40 x 18 In. 1150.00
Secretary, Sheraton, Drop Front, Walnut, Peaked Crest, 80 x 29 In. 2090.00
Secretary, Sheraton, Glass Doors, Drawers, Maine, c.1815, 86 x 54 x 24 In. 4600.00
Secretary, Sheraton, Panel Doors, 3 Drawers, Foldover Top, Maine, 57 x 39 In. 1380.00
Secretary, Victorian, Drop Front, Mahogany, Glazed Doors, 1800s, 87 x 48 In. 735.00
Secretary, Victorian, Drop Front, Oak, Intaglio-Carved Crest, c.1900, 19 x 38 In. 410.00
Secretary, Victorian, Walnut, 7 Drawers, c.1870, 87 x 72 In. 1060.00
Secretary, William & Mary, English Oak, Cornice, Astragal Glazed Doors, 74 x 30 In. 1645.00
Secretary, William IV, Mahogany, Gothic Carved, c.1850, 101 x 49 In. 8225.00
Semainier, Directoire, Mahogany, Marble Top, 7 Drawers, 1800s, 54 x 31 x 17 In. 940.00
Semainier, Marble Top, 7 Drawers, Parquetry, France, 48 x 17 In., Pair 1770.00
Sercretary, George Jack, Mahogany, England, c.1905, 79 x 50 In. 6550.00
Server, Eastlake, Mixed Wood, 2 Paneled Doors, Drawers, Shelf, 59 x 43 1/2 x 16 In. 415.00
Server, Federal, Mahogany, Spiral Carving, 2 Short Over 1 Long Drawer, 35 x 42 In. 4406.00
Server, G. Stickley, Arched Rail, Iron Hardware, 2 Drawers, 42 x 18 x 38 In. 3175.00
Server, G. Stickley, Backsplash, Arched Apron, Drawer, Copper Pull, 39 x 42 In. 4800.00

Server, Hepplewhite Style, Mahogany, Pine, Veneer, Bellflowers, 41 x 21 x 42 In. 3105.00
Server, Linen Drawer, 3 Small Drawers, Open Shelf, Arched Apron, 40 x 48 x 18 In. 17625.00
Server, Louis XVI Style, Mahogany, Marble Top, 3 Drawers, Doors, 40 x 63 x 19 In. 4935.00
Server, Mahogany, Oak, 2 Drawers, Doors, Kittinger, Buffalo, 31 x 42 x 18 In. 200.00
Server, Mahogany, Serpentine, Arched Backsplash, Continental, 34 x 48 x 20 1/2 In. 385.00
Server, Napoleon III, Kingwood, Inlaid, Marble Top, Late 1800s, 40 x 66 In. 2596.00
Server, Neoclassical, Mahogany, Marble Top, Scrolls, Baltimore, c.1830, 39 x 43 In. 6169.00
Server, Oak, Arched Backsplash, Leaf Edge, Acanthus Frieze, England, c.1850, 35 x 49 In. 1645.00
Server, Oak, Ebonized, Putti, Velvet Pads, W.B. Moses & Sons, 51 1/2 x 44 x 21 In. .... *ILLUS* 1035.00
Server, Onondaga Shops, 3 Drawers, Hammered Copper Ring Pulls, Backsplash, 39 x 44 In. 1410.00
Server, Onondaga Shops, Panel Sides, Shelf, 5 Drawers, Pyramid Knobs, 45 x 48 In. 8225.00
Server, Sheraton, Mahogany, 3 Drawers, Acanthus-Carved Legs, Shelf, 33 x 33 x 20 In. 1210.00
Server, Sheraton, Mahogany, Cupboard, 3 Drawers, 34 x 45 x 49 In. 1955.00
Server, William IV, Rosewood, Broken Triangular Pediment, c.1850, 42 x 53 In. 1290.00
Settee, Aesthetic Revival, Ebonized, Angular Backrest, Upholstered, 40 In. 825.00
Settee, Aesthetic Revival, Ebonized, Rectangular Backrest, Circular Arms, 48 In. 1175.00
Settee, Aesthetic Revival, Parcel Gilt, Ebonized, Angular Designs, c.1875, 63 In. 560.00
Settee, Arts & Crafts, 9 Vertical Slats, Leather Cushion, Arched Rail, 60 x 27 x 38 In. 1175.00
Settee, Arts & Crafts, Fruitwood, Spindle Back, England, c.1900, 32 x 50 x 18 In. 470.00
Settee, Baker, Curved Back, Gold Silk, Short Legs, 26 x 67 x 30 In. 2125.00
Settee, Belter, Rococo Revival, Rosewood, Carved, c.1860, 52 x 64 In. 31200.00
Settee, Black Forest, Carved, Scrolling, Standing Bears Support Seat, 52 x 13 x 39 In. 4890.00
Settee, Charles X, Mahogany, Padded, Bellflower Crest, c.1815, 39 x 60 In. 940.00
Settee, Chinese Chippendale, Camelback, Mahogany, Upholstered, 72 In. 295.00
Settee, Chippendale Style, Mahogany, Camelback, Beaded Legs, Upholstered, 57 In. 375.00
Settee, Chippendale Style, Mahogany, Camelback, Upholstered, c.1950, 34 x 31 In. 575.00
Settee, Chippendale Style, Mahogany, Chairback, Serpentine Crest Rail, 40 x 50 In. 4900.00
Settee, Chippendale, Walnut, Scrolled Crest, Needlepoint, Arms, England, 40 x 59 In. 6900.00
Settee, Double Chairback, Open Arm, Rush Seat, 49 In. 295.00
Settee, Dutch Colonial, Hardwood, Cane, Arched Backrest, Scrolled Arms, 1800s, 77 In. 2235.00
Settee, Eero Saarinen, Womb, Upholstered, Knoll, 36 x 62 x 33 In. ....1920.00 to 3186.00
Settee, Elk Antlers, Upholstered, Brass Tacks, 42 x 69 x 28 In. 460.00
Settee, Empire, Scrolled Arms, Shaped Back, Regency Stripe Upholstery, 76 In. 760.00
Settee, Federal, Straight Back, Curved Arms, Early 1800s, 33 x 59 In. 1528.00
Settee, French Provincial, Fruitwood, Silk Upholstery, 78 In. 645.00
Settee, G. Nakashima, Slatted Back, Armless, Upholstered, Dowel Legs, 31 x 48 x 32 In. 7080.00
Settee, G. Nakashima, Walnut, Spindle Back, Cushion, 48 In. 4185.00
Settee, Georgian Style, Walnut, Triple Chairback, Slip Seat, Openwork Splats, Arms, 50 In. 880.00
Settee, John Saladino, Leather, 31 x 46 In. 1540.00
Settee, Leather, Button Back, Roll Over Arms, Turned Legs, c.1940, 32 x 61 x 34 In. 235.00
Settee, Louis XIII Style, Walnut, Carved, 19th Century, 45 x 58 x 26 In. 770.00
Settee, Louis XV Style, Fruitwood, Carved Crest, Domed, Padded Back, 36 x 43 In. 940.00
Settee, Louis XV Style, Fruitwood, Carved, 1900s, 33 3/4 x 49 3/4 x 20 1/2 In., Pair 770.00
Settee, Louis XV Style, Gilt, Shell & Flower Crest, Padded, c.1890, 43 x 23 In. 3525.00
Settee, Louis XVI Style, Beech, Cushion, Fluted Legs, 1800s, 32 In. 825.00
Settee, Louis XVI Style, Polychrome, Padded Seat, Back, Arms, c.1890, 42 x 58 In. 1645.00
Settee, Louis XVI Style, Walnut, Carved, Antiqued Finish, Mid 20th Century, 42 x 68 In. 150.00
Settee, Louis XVI, Carved, Regency Stripe Upholstery, 80 In. 815.00
Settee, Mahogany, Molded Seat & Back Rail, Slip Seat, Ogee Bracket Feet, 28 x 40 In. 1765.00
Settee, Mahogany, Serpentine Back, Floral Tapestry Upholstery 459.00
Settee, Napoleon III, Walnut, Padded, Cabriole Legs, Arms, c.1850, 29 x 90 In. 2350.00
Settee, Painted, Scalloped Back, Turned Spindles, Scrolled Arms, c.1820, 36 x 75 In. 935.00
Settee, Queen Anne Style, Mahogany, Triple Chairback, Slip Seat, Early 1900s, 45 x 56 In. 560.00
Settee, Queen Anne Style, Upholstered, Cabriole Legs, Scrolled Arms, 34 x 53 x 31 In. 295.00
Settee, Regency Style, Mahogany, Serpentine, Late 1800s, 51 1/2 In., Pair 3408.00
Settee, Regency, Quadruple Chairback, Painted, Parcel Gilt, Cane, c.1810, 73 In. 4200.00
Settee, Restauration, Mahogany, Dolphin Uprights, Closed Arms, c.1815, 36 x 47 In. 1530.00
Settee, Rococo Revival, Laminated Rosewood, Henry Ford Pattern, 59 In. 8910.00
Settee, Rococo Revival, Mahogany, Serpentine Seat, Upholstered, c.1850, 34 x 62 In. 150.00
Settee, Shaker, Birch & Pine, Canted Crest Rail, 16-Spoke Back, Enfield, N.H., 30 x 50 x 13 In. 31050.00
Settee, Shaker, Maple, Cherry, Dark Varnish, 2 Slats, Rail Back, Early 1800s, 32 x 71 x 32 In. 6650.00

Furniture, Settee, Shaker, Maple, Taped Seat, Mt. Lebanon, N.Y., c.1880-1900

Furniture, Sideboard, Burl Walnut, Marble Top, Carved Animals, 101 x 80 x 28 In.

Settee, Shaker, Maple, Taped Seat, Mt. Lebanon, N.Y., c.1880-1900 .... *ILLUS* 10350.00
Settee, Triple Chairback, Half Spindles, Gilt Stenciled Crest, Pennsylvania, 75 In. 9900.00
Settee, Victorian, Walnut, Open Back, Upholstered, S-Shaped Side Supports, 30 x 53 In. 390.00
Settee, Victorian, Walnut, Upholstered, Finger Mold Decoration, 34 x 55 x 28 In. 200.00
Settee, Wicker, Wood, Flat Arms, c.1900, 35 x 47 In. 545.00
Settee, William IV Style, Mahogany, Leather Seat, Downswept Arms, 37 x 60 In. 2820.00
Settee, Windsor, Arrow Back, Arms, 37 3/4 In. 6500.00
Settee, Windsor, Double Chairback, Flat Spindles, Painted, Plank Seat, 36 x 41 x 14 In. 95225.00
Settee, Windsor, Low Back, Flattened Arms, Pa., Late 1700s, 28 x 83 In., Pair 8965.00
Settee, Windsor, Low Back, Plank Seat, 8 Legs, Pa., Early 1800s, 29 x 81 In. 3230.00
Settee, Windsor, Mahogany, Rush Seat, Ring Turned Legs, 47 x 20 1/2 x 39 In. 1095.00
Settee, Wing, Louis XV Style, Gold Finish, c.1950, 45 x 55 x 30 In. 115.00
Settle, Arrow Back, Red & Black Graining, Stenciling, Fruit Baskets, 17 x 77 1/2 In. 2185.00
Settle, Beaded Backboards, Plank Seat, England, 63 1/2 x 68 x 22 In. 1380.00
Settle, G. Stickley, Back Slats, Beveled Front Stretcher, Spring Cushion, 28 x 72 In. 3290.00
Settle, G. Stickley, Vertical Slats, Tapered Posts, Leather Seat, Even Arm, 39 x 76 In. 8225.00
Settle, L. & J.G. Stickley, Oak, Wide Slat Back, Sides, Cushion, 36 x 72 In. 2530.00
Settle, Nutting, No. 389, Maple, Pine, Triple Chairback, 51 x 59 x 22 In. 1045.00
Settle, Pine, Painted, Stenciled Fruit, Shaped Crest, Scrolled Arms, 36 x 82 x 20 In. 770.00
Shelf, Aalto, Model 111, Laminated Birch, Artek, Finland, c.1933, 33 x 21 In. 7645.00
Shelf, Chippendale Style, Mahogany, Mirror, Chinese, Early 1900s, 28 x 28 In., Pair 1115.00
Shelf, Corner, Hanging, Poplar, Red Paint, 3 Shaped Backboards, 4 Shelves, 46 1/2 In. 2015.00
Shelf, Corner, Hanging, Rococo Style, Gilt, Carved, Dresden, 38 x 25 x 17 In. 1410.00
Shelf, Corner, Walnut, Graduated, 4 Tiers, Victorian, 47 x 24 x 17 1/2 In. 138.00
Shelf, Fruitwood, Figural, Bearded Pirates, Smoking Pipes, 6 In., Pair 400.00
Shelf, G. Nakashima, Corner, Walnut, Free Front Edge, L-Bracket, 11 x 30 x 19 In. 4130.00
Shelf, George III, Mahogany, 3 Drawers, Bowfront, Early 1800s, 30 x 19 x 8 In. 880.00
Shelf, Gilt, Acanthus Leaf Spray, Celadon Paint, 14 x 14 In. 1292.00
Shelf, Giltwood, Carved, Polychrome, Draped, Tasseled Proscenium, 34 x 18 In. 2585.00
Shelf, Hanging, Eastlake, Ebonized, 4 Mirrored Portals, Spindle-Front Door, 21 In. 705.00
Shelf, Hanging, George V, Mahogany, Plate Grooves, Scroll, 2 Doors, c.1915, 26 x 36 In. 998.00
Shelf, Hanging, Maple, 3 Tiers, Scrolled Ends, 19th Century, 28 x 23 x 8 In. 765.00
Shelf, Hanging, Nutting, No. 906, Pine, 19 x 30 In. 770.00
Shelf, Hanging, P. Evans, Glass, 2 Wave-Design Brackets, c.1973, 15 x 96 In. 2240.00
Shelf, Hanging, Pine, 2 Tiers, Lollipop Handle, Late 19th Century, 17 1/2 In. 165.00
Shelf, Hanging, Pine, 3 Graduated Shelves, Plate Rails, Scalloped Ends, 33 x 38 In. 315.00
Shelf, Hanging, Pine, 4 Shelves, Plate Grooves, 1900s, 48 x 39 In. 266.00
Shelf, Hanging, Pine, Brown Stain, Wire Nails, Drawer, Curved Ends, 15 3/4 x 14 In. 345.00
Shelf, Hanging, Pine, Red Graining, 4 Drawers, Shaped Gallery, 19 x 15 x 25 In. 460.00
Shelf, Hanging, Pine, Red Paint, Shaped Sides, Beaded Edges, 1800s, 12 1/2 x 16 In. 380.00
Shelf, Hanging, Pine, Red Wash, Relief Carved, Scrolled Supports, 39 x 12 In. 460.00
Shelf, Hanging, Poplar, 2 Shelves, Shaped Side Panels, 19th Century, 25 x 37 In. 118.00
Shelf, Hanging, Porcelain, Mirrored, Fluted Columns, Scroll, Basket Shape, 26 In., Pair 1765.00

A fresh ink stain on wood can be removed by washing with water and then applying lemon juice.

Furniture, Sideboard, Regency, Mahogany, Leaf Carved, c.1820-25, 48 x 86 x 25 In.

Shelf, Hanging, Red & Yellow Paint, Mirrored, 23 x 11 In. 316.00
Shelf, Hanging, Regency, Mahogany, Diamond Inlay, 16 x 26 1/2 In. 2006.00
Shelf, Hanging, Walnut, 4 Shelves, Scalloped Base, Crest, Pierced Stars, 20 x 6 x 40 In. 805.00
Shelf, Hanging, Walnut, Whale Ends, 2 Drawers, 1800s 605.00
Shelf, Mahogany, Whale Ends, 4 Graduated Shelves, Early 1800s, 33 x 27 In. 1528.00
Shelf, Milk, Rectangular Back, Sloping Sides, Demilune Cutouts, 2 Shelves, 35 x 36 In. 840.00
Shelf, Renaissance Revival, Onyx, Brass, Beveled Glass, c.1880, 51 x 40 In. 765.00
Shlef, Hanging, Pewter, Pine, Shaped Sides, Dovetailed, 26 1/2 x 32 1/4 In. 345.00
Sideboard, Adam Style, Mahogany, Satinwood Banding, D-Shape, 1800s, 37 x 89 In. 3305.00
Sideboard, Aesthetic Revival, Ebonized, Drop Center, Glass Doors, 41 x 61 In. 118.00
Sideboard, Aesthetic Revival, Oak, 2 Drawers, 4 Doors, England, Late 1800s, 78 x 72 In. 1765.00
Sideboard, Aesthetic Revival, Walnut, Brass Mount, 5-Sided, Carvings, c.1885, 33 x 58 In. 1116.00
Sideboard, Art Deco, Linen Carving, 3 Drawers, 2 Lower Doors, 36 x 54 In. 106.00
Sideboard, Art Deco, Satinwood, Sliding Glass Doors, Mirrored Back, 62 x 43 In. 325.00
Sideboard, Arts & Crafts, Oak, Beveled Mirror, Paneled Doors, 56 x 54 x 23 In. 345.00
Sideboard, Biedermeier, Walnut, 2 Drawers, Paneled Doors, 40 x 54 In. 1265.00
Sideboard, Brown Saltman, 3 Drawers, 2 Side Cabinets, 37 x 74 x 20 In. 530.00
Sideboard, Burl Walnut, Marble Top, Carved Animals, 101 x 80 x 28 In. . . . . *ILLUS* 6613.00
Sideboard, Carved, Fluted Frieze, 5 Drawers, Doors, Continental, 49 x 63 x 21 In. 4830.00
Sideboard, Cherry, Mahogany, Drawers, Doors, Rope-Turned Columns, 55 x 62 x 22 In. 805.00
Sideboard, Chippendale, Drawers, 4 Square Legs, England, 27 3/4 x 30 x 16 In. 1955.00
Sideboard, Edwardian, Mahogany, Drawers, Cupboards, 37 x 25 x 65 1/2 In. 380.00
Sideboard, Empire, Mahogany, Flame Veneer, Pine, Panel Doors, Drawers, 73 x 24 In. 1208.00
Sideboard, Federal Style, Mahogany, 2 Drawers, Faux Drawer, Doors, 37 x 71 x 24 In. 2415.00
Sideboard, Federal, Cherry Inlay, Crossbanded Border, Frieze, c.1800, 44 x 43 In. 4406.00
Sideboard, Federal, Mahogany, Inlaid, Bowfront, Curved Ends, c.1795, 43 x 74 In. 7768.00
Sideboard, Federal, Mahogany, Inlaid, Serpentine, Bowfront, 39 1/4 x 73 x 26 In. 2590.00
Sideboard, Federal, Mahogany, Inlaid, Serpentine, N.Y., c.1800, 39 x 70 x 30 In. 9400.00
Sideboard, Federal, Mahogany, Inlaid, Veneered, Mid-Atlantic, c.1800, 40 x 76 In. 7200.00
Sideboard, Federal, Mahogany, Rosewood Crossbanding, Reeded Stiles, 40 x 67 In. 2115.00
Sideboard, G. Stickley, Oak, 3 Drawers, 2 Doors, Plate Rack, 45 x 49 x 18 In. 5175.00
Sideboard, George III Style, Mahogany, 2 Drawers, Early 1900s, 36 x 61 x 19 In. 3835.00
Sideboard, George III Style, Mahogany, Drawer, Side Cupboards, 36 x 75 In. 1997.00
Sideboard, George III Style, Mahogany, Serpentine, 6 Legs, 36 x 59 1/2 x 21 In. 850.00
Sideboard, George III Style, Mahogany, Serpentine, 8 Legs, 36 x 80 1/2 x 26 In. 2470.00
Sideboard, George III Style, Mahogany, String Inlay, Serpentine Top, Doors, 31 x 48 In. 235.00
Sideboard, George III Style, Parquetry, Fluted Stiles, c.1910, 43 x 55 x 24 In. 2240.00
Sideboard, George III, Mahogany, 3 Drawers, Bowed Top, 35 3/4 x 47 x 22 In. 3995.00
Sideboard, George III, Mahogany, 36 1/4 x 65 1/4 x 23 1/4 In. 6600.00
Sideboard, George III, Mahogany, Bowfront, String Inlay, Spade Feet, 37 x 58 In. 2230.00
Sideboard, George III, Mahogany, Boxwood Inlay, Bowfront, Early 1800s, 34 x 44 In. 999.00
Sideboard, George III, Mahogany, Drawer, 2 Doors, 6 Legs, England, c.1810, 37 x 78 In. 2360.00
Sideboard, George III, Mahogany, Drawer, Shelf, c.1785, 30 x 43 x 24 In. 7200.00
Sideboard, George III, Mahogany, Inlaid, Drawer, 2 Doors, Early 1800s, 36 x 62 In. 3055.00
Sideboard, George IV, Mahogany, Ebony Stringing, 5 Drawers, c.1825, 36 x 49 In. 1765.00

Sideboard, Georgian Style, Mahogany, 3 Drawers, 4 Doors, 1900s, 38 x 49 x 20 In. 1175.00
Sideboard, Georgian Style, Mahogany, Serpentine, 1900s, 39 x 66 x 23 In. 1116.00
Sideboard, Georgian, Mahogany, Compartments, 36 x 25 x 84 In. 1335.00
Sideboard, Georgian, Mahogany, Inlaid, Bowed Front, 34 x 25 x 51 In. 1525.00
Sideboard, Georgian, Rosewood, Ebony, Serpentine Front, 2 Drawers, 35 x 40 In. 3260.00
Sideboard, Gio Ponti, Walnut, 4 Drawers, Cutlery Sections, c.1950, 37 x 70 x 19 In. 10200.00
Sideboard, Hepplewhite Style, Mahogany, Bowfront, Drawers, 36 x 60 x 25 In. 765.00
Sideboard, Hepplewhite Style, Mahogany, Bowfront, Drawers, Doors, 1900s, 39 x 74 In. 1265.00
Sideboard, Hepplewhite Style, Mahogany, Inlaid, Flame Veneer, Drawers, 66 x 24 In. 1725.00
Sideboard, Hepplewhite Style, Mahogany, Serpentine, 20th Century, 36 x 61 In. 710.00
Sideboard, Hepplewhite Style, Mahogany, Veneer, Fluted, Tapered Legs, 37 x 72 In. 1670.00
Sideboard, Italian Style, Carved, Marble Top, D-Shape, 2 Drawers, 39 x 85 In. 635.00
Sideboard, Limbert, 2 Half Drawers, Full Drawer, Doors, Plate Rail, 45 x 45 In. 2468.00
Sideboard, Limbert, Mirror, Slatted Backsplash, 2 Drawers, Doors, 52 x 36 In. 2350.00
Sideboard, Mahogany, 3 Drawers, 2 Doors, Scrolled Legs, 19th Century, 50 x 44 In. 150.00
Sideboard, Mahogany, Marble Top, Mirror, 3 Drawers, 2 Doors, Late 1800s, 88 x 53 In. 2350.00
Sideboard, Mahogany, Satinwood Inlay, D-Shape Top, Brass Gallery, 72 In. 13920.00
Sideboard, Mirrored Backsplash, Front Posts, Drawer, Cabinet Doors, 66 x 50 x 23 In. 2350.00
Sideboard, Neoclassical, Mahogany, Brass Mounts, 3 Drawers, 4 Doors, 43 x 74 In. 3525.00
Sideboard, Neoclassical, Mahogany, Marble, Mirror, Philadelphia, c.1830, 53 x 72 In. 9106.00
Sideboard, Neoclassical, Mahogany, Pedimented Gallery, 3 Drawers, c.1835, 17 x 19 In. 3230.00
Sideboard, Oak, Burl Walnut, 3 Drawers, 3-Paneled Doors, c.1885, 36 x 72 x 24 In. 635.00
Sideboard, Oak, Carved, Round Mirror, 3 Drawers Over 2 Doors, 80 x 48 In. 940.00
Sideboard, Oak, Mirror, 3 Drawers, Shelf Top, Brass Pulls, c.1910, 75 x 46 x 22 In. 385.00
Sideboard, Oak, Mirrored Back, 3 Sections, Banisters, Carved Crest, 79 x 24 x 69 In. 980.00
Sideboard, Oak, Shelves, Plate Rails, 3 Drawers, Wales, 1800s, 84 x 59 x 17 In. 2115.00
Sideboard, P. Evans, Patchwork Burl, Chrome, Cityscape, 4 Doors, 33 x 84 In. 4425.00
Sideboard, Pierre Cardin, Burl Veneer, 4 Doors, Brass, Chrome, 30 x 74 In. 3068.00
Sideboard, Pine, 3 Drawers, Turned Legs, 32 x 35 x 17 In. 520.00
Sideboard, Pine, Flared Cornice, 2 Shelves, 2 Drawers, Wales, 1800s, 72 x 41 In. 410.00
Sideboard, Regency, Mahogany, Bowfront, 5 Drawers, Early 1800s, 36 x 66 x 28 In. 8225.00
Sideboard, Regency, Mahogany, Brass Gallery, Scotland, c.1815, 56 x 93 x 32 In. 4700.00
Sideboard, Regency, Mahogany, Ebony Inlay, Backsplash, c.1800, 46 x 90 x 29 In. 5580.00
Sideboard, Regency, Mahogany, Inlaid, Bowfront, Early 1800s, 36 x 54 x 24 In. 1645.00
Sideboard, Regency, Mahogany, Inlaid, Bowfront, Early 1800s, 37 x 69 x 31 In. 5290.00
Sideboard, Regency, Mahogany, Inlaid, Pedestal Ends, c.1820, 42 x 88 x 29 In. 4406.00
Sideboard, Regency, Mahogany, Leaf Carved, c.1820-25, 48 x 86 x 25 In. .... *ILLUS* 2115.00
Sideboard, Regency, Mahogany, Pedestal, Scotland, 1810-20, 51 x 81 x 30 In. 4700.00
Sideboard, Regency, Mahogany, Serpentine Top, 2 Drawers, c.1815, 60 x 78 In. 6460.00
Sideboard, Regency, Oak, Inlaid, 2 Cabinets, 3 Beaded Drawers, Wales, 1800s, 83 x 70 In. 2350.00
Sideboard, Regency, Stage Top, Brass Gallery, Scotland, Early 1800s, 64 x 76 x 25 In. 2350.00
Sideboard, Renaissance Revival, Burl Walnut, Tall Back, Marble Top, 90 x 62 In. 2350.00
Sideboard, Renaissance Revival, Walnut, Marble Top, Shelves On Brackets, 88 x 59 In. 3760.00
Sideboard, Robsjohn-Gibbings, Walnut, 3 Doors, Flared Legs, Widdicomb, 34 x 67 In. 1005.00
Sideboard, Stickley Bros., Oak, Paneled Backsplash, 4 Drawers, 2 Doors, 46 x 55 In. 2070.00
Sideboard, Victorian, Golden Oak, 3 Drawers, 3 Doors, Late 1800s, 74 x 60 In. 1528.00
Sideboard, Victorian, Mahogany, Brass Mounted, Drawer, 2 Doors, 57 x 78 In. 1645.00
Sideboard, Victorian, Oak, Applied Scroll Carvings, 4 Drawers, 72 x 45 x 21 In. 290.00
Sideboard, Victorian, Oak, Carved Rope Decoration, 49 x 48 x 24 In. 345.00
Sideboard, Walnut, Poplar, Pine, Open Section, 2 Drawers, H. Lamond, 53 x 57 x 26 In. 4600.00
Sideboard, Wegner, Teak, 2 Pieces, 2 Glass Doors, 6 Drawers, 71 x 71 x 22 In. 2125.00
Sideboard, William IV, Beaded Edge, Pedestal Ends, c.1840, 39 x 103 x 31 In. 5580.00
Sideboard, Wormley, 3 Drawers, 3 Sliding Doors, Dunbar, 1950, 32 In. 2820.00
Sideboard, Yellow Pine, Backsplash, Drawers, 2-Board Top, 44 x 60 x 24 In. 3450.00
Silver Chest, Hepplewhite Style, Mahogany, Inlaid, Lift Top, Tray Bottom, 41 x 30 x 18 In. 635.00
Sofa, Arne Jacobsen, Swan, Wool, Aluminum Base, Fritz Hansen, 30 x 57 x 29 In. 2596.00
Sofa, Arts & Crafts, Sleeper, Oak, Upholstered, Label, Ernest J. Sultan Mfg. Co., Calif. 280.00
Sofa, Beech, Tapestry Upholstery, Continental, 86 In. 4406.00
Sofa, Biedermeier, Maple, Part Ebonized, Upholstered, Arched Back, 72 x 30 In. 1116.00
Sofa, Biedermeier, Maple, Part Ebonized, Upholstered, Sweden, 1800s, 67 In. 1765.00
Sofa, Chesterfield, Edwardian, Leather Upholstery, Tufted, c.1900, 28 x 81 In. 1290.00

Sofa, Chesterfield, Green Leather, Scrolling Arms, Hardwood Legs, 27 x 80 x 36 In. 5405.00
Sofa, Chippendale Style, Camelback, 3 Front Feet, Upholstered, 1930s, 71 In. 575.00
Sofa, Chippendale Style, Camelback, Mahogany, 8 Legs, 40 x 32 x 17 In. 1725.00
Sofa, Chippendale Style, Camelback, Mahogany, Rocaille-Carved Cabriole Legs, 75 In. 410.00
Sofa, Chippendale Style, Camelback, Mahogany, Rolled Arms, 7 Legs, 37 x 86 x 32 In. 990.00
Sofa, Chippendale Style, Camelback, Mahogany, Upholstered, 1900s, 35 x 76 x 29 In. 1239.00
Sofa, Chippendale Style, Camelback, Scrolled Arms, Early 1900s, 34 x 75 x 20 In. 1530.00
Sofa, Chippendale, Camelback, Mahogany, Floral Tapestry Upholstered, 1800, 69 In. 2990.00
Sofa, Cini Boeri, Modular, Knoll, c.1972, 20 x 90 x 33 In. ....4320.00 to 4800.00
Sofa, Curly Maple, Oak, Serpentine Arm Supports, Arched Crest, Zoar, 74 x 24 x 37 In. 2070.00
Sofa, D. Chadwick, Crescent, 4 Sections, Foam, Herman Miller, c.1972, 108 In. 189.00
Sofa, Dunbar, Upholstered, Ebonized Legs, 3 Seats, Even Arms, 27 x 84 x 26 In. 5310.00
Sofa, Edwardian, Mahogany, Satinwood Inlay, Cane, Shaped Arms, c.1890, 37 x 62 In. 1880.00
Sofa, Empire Style, Outscrolled Arms, Scrolled Stiles, Upholstered, 36 x 73 x 22 In. 2360.00
Sofa, Empire, Mahogany, Flame Veneer, Pine, Inlaid Panels, Upholstered, 83 x 25 In. 2070.00
Sofa, Empire, Mahogany, Scrolled Acanthus, Upholstered, Paw Feet, 59 x 25 In. 2415.00
Sofa, Empire, Mahogany, Square, Ogee Molded Seat, Crest Rail, Scroll Arms, 35 x 84 In. 4138.00
Sofa, Federal Style, Mahogany, Paneled Crest, Bows, Swags, Reeded Arms, 71 x 27 In. 3105.00
Sofa, Federal Style, Molded Frame, Padded, Cushion, Upholstered, 34 x 77 x 26 In. 770.00
Sofa, Federal, Mahogany Inlay, Upholstered, Arched Back, c.1815, 34 x 79 In. 11750.00
Sofa, Federal, Mahogany Inlay, Upholstered, New York, c.1810, 37 x 75 x 24 In. 4200.00
Sofa, Federal, Mahogany, Reeded Arms & Legs, Button Feet, Philadelphia, 35 x 75 In. 7930.00
Sofa, Finn Juhl, No. 53, Teak, Upholstered, Niels Vodder, c.1953, 30 x 51 x 30 In. 7200.00
Sofa, G. Nakashima, Cane Back, Upholstered, Plank Legs, Widdicomb, 31 x 102 In. 7670.00
Sofa, G. Nelson, Hinged Back, Sleeper, Herman Miller, 1960s, 82 x 36 x 28 In. 3620.00
Sofa, George III Style, Mahogany, Upholstered, Scroll Carving, c.1900, 37 x 70 In. 1880.00
Sofa, George III, Hepplewhite, Mahogany, Serpentine Crest, Tapered Legs, 1785, 83 In. 4995.00
Sofa, Gothic Revival, Oak, Paneled Seat Rail, Arched Panels, c.1850, 41 x 62 In. 1175.00
Sofa, Hans Olsen, Dansk, 3 Cushions, Leather, C.S. Mobler, 74 In. 430.00
Sofa, Henredon, William & Mary Style, 3 Humpback, Upholstered, 40 x 78 x 34 In. 1890.00
Sofa, J. Hoffmann, Chrome, Cowhide, 3 Sections, Howell, c.1936, 31 x 80 In. 3540.00
Sofa, Jules Leleu, Oak, Upholstered, c.1940, 30 1/4 x 61 1/2 x 43 1/2 In. 6600.00
Sofa, Kidney Shape, Rolled Back Chenille Upholstery, Brass Base, 1970s, 31 x 75 In. 2596.00
Sofa, Kittinger, George II Style, Camelback, Outscrolled Arms, 39 x 74 x 32 In. 1535.00
Sofa, Louis XV Style, Giltwood, 19th Century, 39 x 55 x 29 In. 885.00
Sofa, Louis XV, Beech, Carved, Stained, 3 Seats, Serpentine Front, 40 x 74 In. 5405.00
Sofa, Louis XVI Style, Gilt, Flowers, Upholstered, 1900s, 40 1/2 x 56 In. 885.00
Sofa, Mahogany, Molded Crest Rail, Scrolled Arms, Philadelphia, c.1820, 31 x 88 In. 1765.00
Sofa, Mahogany, Veneered, Carved, Upholstered, c.1820, 38 1/4 x 27 1/2 x 102 In. 5700.00
Sofa, Maurizio Tempestini, Cushions, J.B. Salterini, c.1950, 39 x 80 x 29 In. 900.00
Sofa, Neoclassical Style, Mahogany, Rolled Arms, Carved, Splayed Feet, 32 x 88 In. 1410.00
Sofa, Neoclassical, Mahogany Veneer, Upholstered, New England, c.1825, 17 x 33 In. 705.00
Sofa, Neoclassical, Mahogany, Carved Scrolled Crest Rail & Arms, Paw Feet, c.1830 .... 600.00
Sofa, Neoclassical, Mahogany, Closed Scroll Arms, c.1835, 34 x 81 In. 2585.00
Sofa, Neoclassical, Mahogany, Ogee Crest Rail, Straight Arms, c.1840, 38 x 84 In. 470.00
Sofa, Neoclassical, Mahogany, Scrolled Crest Rail, Arms, c.1830, 34 x 77 x 25 In. 2820.00
Sofa, Neoclassical, Mahogany, Scrolled Crest, Arms, Carved Cornucopiae, Velvet, 36 In. 660.00
Sofa, Neoclassical, Mahogany, Serpentine Back, Scroll Arms, c.1835, 32 x 79 In. 1175.00
Sofa, Padouk, Carved, Chinese Export, c.1830, 33 1/2 x 81 1/2 In. 6000.00
Sofa, Regency, Mahogany, Painted, Tapered, Splayed Legs, Casters, 36 x 77 x 36 In. 1415.00
Sofa, Richard Schultz, No. 704, Sleeper, Knoll, c.1960, 29 x 33 x 83 In. 2520.00
Sofa, Robert Venturi, Grandmother, Leather, Knoll, c.1984, 32 x 84 x 38 In. 19200.00
Sofa, Robsjohn-Gibbings, Blond Wood, 3 Seats, Upholstered, Widdicomb, 31 x 92 In. 1770.00
Sofa, Rococo Revival, Rosewood, Laminated, 3-Part Back, c.1850, 42 x 69 In. 4230.00
Sofa, Rococo Revival, Rosewood, Laminated, Carved Crest, Tufted, 54 x 77 In. 10575.00
Sofa, Rococo Revival, Walnut, Fruit, Leaf, Flower Crests, Upholstered, c.1850, 90 In. 1795.00
Sofa, Rococo Style, Mahogany, Veneer, Upholstered, Scrolled Stiles, 31 x 73 x 29 In. 295.00
Sofa, Rococo, Walnut, Scalloped Crest, Scrolled Arms, Continental, 1700s, 39 x 90 In. 2644.00
Sofa, Rosewood, Archaic Designs, Chinese, 1800s, 36 x 23 x 74 In. 499.00
Sofa, Sheraton Style, Double Scallop Back, Upholstered, 36 1/2 x 76 1/2 x 28 In. 345.00
Sofa, Sheraton Style, Mahogany, Maple Arms, Upholstered, 32 1/4 x 67 In. 978.00

Sofa, Sheraton Style, Upholstered, Nail-Head Trim, 3 Cushions, 34 x 77 1/2 x 25 In. 200.00
Sofa, Sheraton, Mahogany, Curved Crest Rail, Upholstered, Reeded Legs, c.1820, 73 In. 9560.00
Sofa, Sheraton, Mahogany, Inlaid, Upholstered, 4 Reed-Front Legs, 38 x 72 In. 1265.00
Sofa, Sheraton, Mahogany, Reeded Top Rail, Upholstered, Turned Front Legs, 33 x 74 In. 980.00
Sofa, Sheraton, Mahogany, Scroll Back Crest, Upholstered, 37 x 76 x 24 In. 2300.00
Sofa, Sheraton, Mahogany, Scrolled Arms, Reeded Legs, 73 In. 1610.00
Sofa, Tete-A-Tete, Chromed Steel, Removable Vinyl Cushions, 43 x 20 x 30 In. 1175.00
Sofa, Thema, Upholstered, Enameled Steel Frame, Italy, 29 x 73 x 36 In. 3835.00
Sofa, Tufted, Buttoned, Velvet, Loose Seat Cushions, Pleated Skirt, 28 x 86 x 28 In. 236.00
Sofa, Victorian, Mahogany, Curved Back, Serpentine, N.Y., c.1850, 41 x 80 In. 880.00
Sofa, Victorian, Rosewood, Serpentine, Leaves, Cabriole Legs, c.1865, 79 In. 1295.00
Sofa, Victorian, Walnut, Grape Carved, Shaped Crest, Upholstered, 38 x 68 In. 150.00
Sofa, Wegner, Rosewood, Upholstered, Even Arms, 26 x 75 x 31 In. 3835.00
Sofa, Wormley, Upholstered, Down-Filled Cushions, Wood Legs, 87 x 34 x 28 In. 1058.00
Spool Stand, Shaker, Cherry, Enfield, Conn., c.1885, 9 1/2 x 5 In. 250.00
Stand, Aesthetic Revival, Moorish Style, Gilt, Scrolled, c.1880, 41 x 20 In. 380.00
Stand, Beech, Mixed Hardwood, Frame, Panel Friezes, Italy, 20 x 16 x 12 In., Pair 2185.00
Stand, Biedermeier, Drawer, Oval, 4 Tapered Legs, 28 x 19 In. 920.00
Stand, Birch, Maple, Threaded Shaft Supports, Adjustable, Tripod Base, 42 x 14 In. 880.00
Stand, Birch, Pine, Scalloped Shelf, Drawer, Cut Corner Top, Stretchers, 17 x 16 1/2 In. 575.00
Stand, Black Forest, Dog, Shih-Tzu, c.1890, 41 x 11 1/2 x 16 1/2 In. 3360.00
Stand, Black Lacquer, Mother-Of-Pearl Inlay, Chinese, 9 x 13 x 8 3/4 In. 530.00
Stand, Blackamoor, Parcel Gilt, Carved, Polychrome, Italy, Late 1800s, 25 In., Pair 3525.00
Stand, Cherry, Curly Maple, Maple Veneer, Burl Inlay, Dovetailed Drawers, 22 x 20 In. 661.00
Stand, Cherry, Poplar, Inlaid, 2-Board Top, Dovetailed Drawer, 28 x 24 x 19 In. 316.00
Stand, Chippendale Style, Mahogany, Scalloped Galleried Top, 1900s, 27 x 17 In. 265.00
Stand, Corner, Fruitwood, Carved Flowers, Leaves, Bowed Front, 3 Sides, 32 x 23 In. 470.00
Stand, Eliel Saarinen, 4 Drawers, John Stuart, 1940s, 30 x 21 x 18 In., Pair 3900.00
Stand, Elm, Octagonal, Silver Mounted, 24 x 25 x 15 In. 800.00
Stand, Empire, Mahogany Veneer, Bronze, Drawer, 29 x 24 x 18 In. 360.00
Stand, Federal, Black, Ring Pulls, Cookie Corner Top, Stencil, Drawer, 29 x 21 In. 316.00
Stand, Federal, Cherry, Bird's-Eye Maple, String Inlay, Drawer, 1800s, 25 x 16 In. 499.00
Stand, Federal, Cherry, Drawer, New England, c.1800, 28 3/4 x 17 x 17 In. 1440.00
Stand, Federal, Cherry, Overhang Top, Drawer, New England, c.1810, 28 x 18 In. 355.00
Stand, Federal, Cherry, Overhang Top, Drawer, Straight Skirt, c.1810, 28 x 16 In. 825.00
Stand, Federal, Green Paint, Trapezoid Apron, Drawer, Turned Legs, 26 In. 2150.00
Stand, Federal, Mahogany Top, Maple Drawer, Brass Knob, 26 x 17 x 15 In. 690.00
Stand, Federal, Mahogany, 2 Drawers, Ring Handles, 30 x 22 In. 750.00
Stand, Federal, Mahogany, Inlay, Checkered Banding, Drawer, c.1800, 28 x 18 x 17 In. 380.00
Stand, Federal, Maple, Mahogany, Drawer, c.1800, 29 1/2 x 20 x 16 1/2 In. 2700.00
Stand, Federal, Pine, Drawer, Overhang Top, Ivory Inlaid Diamond, 30 x 21 In. 470.00
Stand, Federal, Red Paint, Drawer, Early 19th Century, 27 3/8 x 18 3/4 x 18 In. 295.00
Stand, Federal, Tiger Maple, Overhang Top, Drawer, Straight Skirt, c.1810, 30 x 18 In. 7638.00
Stand, Fern, Art Nouveau, Mahogany, Pierced Brass Apron Trim, Curved Legs, 44 In. 575.00
Stand, Fern, Arts & Crafts, Oak, Golden, Square Base, Top, Tapered Column, 32 x 13 In. 58.00
Stand, Fern, Brass, Onyx, Scrolling Leaves, Shelf, Curved Legs, Early 1900s, 30 x 13 In. 180.00
Stand, Fern, Carved, Octagon Stone Inlay, Chinese, 37 x 12 In. 80.00
Stand, Fern, Cast Brass, Green Marble, Iron Crosspieces, Tripod Base, 19 x 29 In. 200.00
Stand, Fern, Georgian Style, Mahogany, Dish Top, Reeded Pedestal, c.1890, 46 x 12 In. 235.00
Stand, Fern, Mahogany, Inlay, Splayed Legs, 37 x 12 In. 345.00
Stand, Fern, Oak, c.1890, 12 x 12 x 38 In. 95.00
Stand, Fern, Teak, Grapevines, Dragon, Soapstone Insert, Quatrefoil Top, 36 x 20 In. 316.00
Stand, Fern, Victorian, Carved Flower Top, Shelf, Bamboo-Style Legs, 23 x 17 In. 175.00
Stand, Fern, Walnut, Brass Lion Feet, 32 x 14 In. 300.00
Stand, Fishbowl, Cast Iron Base, Clear Glass Bowl, 34 In. 554.00
Stand, Fishbowl, Wrought Iron, Base, Scroll Feet, Clear Glass Bowl, 7 1/2 In. 55.00
Stand, G. Nelson, Birch, Laminate Tops, Shelf, Ebonized Wood Legs, 24 x 18 In., Pair 900.00
Stand, George III, Mahogany, Reticulated Apron, X-Stretcher, Spade Feet, 27 x 14 In. 825.00
Stand, Girl, Kneeling, Holding Dish Top, Wood, Turned Base, Italy, 20 x 9 In. 1295.00
Stand, Gothic Revival, Walnut, 6-Sided Top, 3-Column Base, 29 x 23 In. 805.00
Stand, Hepplewhite, Birch, Drawer, Overhang Top, Brass Pull, c.1815, 28 x 20 In. 430.00

Stand, Hepplewhite, Cherry, 1-Board Top, Drawer, Square Legs, c.1825, 28 x 20 x 17 In. 288.00
Stand, Hepplewhite, Cherry, Drawer, Brass Knob, Tapered Square Legs, 29 x 18 In. 200.00
Stand, Hepplewhite, Cherry, Drawer, Overhang Top, Square Tapered Legs, 28 x 18 x 22 In. 220.00
Stand, Hepplewhite, Cherry, Poplar, Chestnut, Drawer, 1-Board Top, 18 x 17 x 29 In. 690.00
Stand, Hepplewhite, Cherry, Rosette Knob, 26 x 19 x 19 In. 290.00
Stand, Hepplewhite, Curly Maple, Cherry Legs, Drawer, 22 x 25 In. 1150.00
Stand, Hepplewhite, Mahogany, 2 Drawers, Glass Pulls, Mass., c.1800, 28 x 15 1/2 In. 750.00
Stand, Hepplewhite, Pine, Drawer, Overhang Top, 28 x 18 x 20 In. 250.00
Stand, Hepplewhite, Red Wash, 2 Drawers, Sandwich Glass Pulls, Maine, c.1810, 29 x 17 In. 290.00
Stand, Hepplewhite, Shaped Top, Drawer, Brass Pull, 27 x 19 x 16 In. 405.00
Stand, Hepplewhite, Walnut, 2-Board Top, Mortise & Pin, Drawer, 28 x 23 x 19 In. 375.00
Stand, Huang Huali, Paneled Center, Molded Frieze, 4 Legs, Chinese, 30 x 14 1/2 In. 1020.00
Stand, Liberty & Co., Arts & Crafts, Mahogany, 2 Tiers, Heart Cutouts, c.1905, 28 x 25 In. 175.00
Stand, Louis XV Style, Beech, Marble Top, Drawer, Door, Early 1900s, 33 In. 295.00
Stand, Louis XV Style, Beech, Marble Top, Serpentine, Drawer, 34 x 15 x 15 In. 440.00
Stand, Louis XV, Fruitwood, Burl, Bowfront, 2 Doors, Porcelain Scenes, 20 x 32 In. 546.00
Stand, Louis XVI Style, Mahogany, Marble Top, Fluted Legs, 1800s, 34 x 16 In. 82.00
Stand, Magazine, G. Stickley, 4 Shelves, Tacked Leather Strips, 44 x 15 In. 7920.00
Stand, Magazine, L. & J.G. Stickley, 4 Shelves, Stretchers, Chamfered Back, 45 In. 2115.00
Stand, Magazine, Michigan Chair Co., Overhang Top, Side Slats, 33 x 16 1/2 In. 1060.00
Stand, Magazine, Roycroft, 5 Shelves, Mortised, Flaring Sides, Orb, Cross, 64 x 24 x 18 In. 5875.00
Stand, Magazine, Victorian, Bamboo, Pine, Pyrography, c.1885, 44 x 21 In. 234.00
Stand, Mahogany, Banded Burl Top, Beaded, Ivory Pulls, Brass Handles, 29 x 18 In. 660.00
Stand, Mahogany, Dark Stain, Overhang Top, Drawer, Early 1800s, 29 x 19 In. 1115.00
Stand, Mahogany, Ebonized, Square Top, 2 Drawers, 30 x 14 x 14 In. 177.00
Stand, Mahogany, Round, 3 Scrolled Supports, Triangular Plinth Base, 29 x 15 In. 1880.00
Stand, Mahogany, Shaped Top, Turned Legs, Drawer, Early 1800s, 29 x 20 In. 290.00
Stand, Maple, Drawer, Bulbous Legs, Peg Feet, Early 1800s, 29 x 24 x 22 In. 205.00
Stand, Music, Cast Iron, Ornate Tripod Foot, Oak Music Tray, 42 In. 99.00
Stand, Music, George III Style, Mahogany, Double, Pierced Lyre Design, 50 x 18 In. 499.00
Stand, Music, Iron, Wavy Back Stretchers, Leaf Cartouche Crest, 3 Feet, 1700s, 58 x 17 In. 2478.00
Stand, Music, Louis XVI Style, Gilt Wood, Brass Sconces, Late 1800s, 53 3/4 x 14 1/4 In. 1534.00
Stand, Music, Marquetry, Flowers, Mahogany Base, 1800s, 24 x 18 x 12 In. 69.00
Stand, Music, Marquetry, Mahogany, Satin Wood, 3 Shelves, c.1850, 25 x 18 In. 441.00
Stand, Music, Regency Style, Mahogany, Pierced Lyre Shelf, c.1900, 59 1/4 x 17 x 13 In. 1298.00
Stand, Music, Regency, Mahogany, Brass Inlay, Lattice Work, Early 1800s, 53 1/2 x 17 x 10 In. ... 2006.00
Stand, Music, Victorian, Bamboo, Oak, 5 Shelves, Ball Tops, Feet, c.1890, 38 1/2 x 18 In. 248.00
Stand, Neoclassical, Cherry, Rectangular Top, Shaped Corners, Drawer, c.1825, 29 x 21 In. 380.00
Stand, Neoclassical, Green Stone Top, Round, 33 x 12 In., Pair 215.00
Stand, Neoclassical, Maple, Drop Leaf, 2 Drawers, Glass Pulls, Ball Feet, c.1825, 27 In. 420.00
Stand, Neoclassical, Marble Top, Tambour Cupboard, Russia, 31 x 13 x 12 In. 470.00
Stand, Oak, 2 Drawers, 1800s, 31 x 18 x 20 In. 220.00
Stand, Painted, Checkerboard Top, Faux Marble Border, Drawer, 30 x 17 In. 2938.00
Stand, Painted, Hexagonal Top, Eye & Dash Decoration, Faux Drawer, 29 x 22 In. 220.00
Stand, Pine Top, 1-Board, Grooved Molding, Stretcher Base, Turned Legs, 20 1/2 x 16 In. 259.00
Stand, Pine, Gray Paint, 2 Mortised Shelves, Square Nails, 31 x 41 x 12 In. 775.00
Stand, Plant, Arts & Crafts, Oak, 27 1/2 x 13 In. 175.00
Stand, Plant, Eastlake, Ebonized, 3 Tiers, Turned, Reeded Supports, 30 x 14 In. 90.00
Stand, Plant, Eastlake, Ebonized, Marble Top, Pedestal, Leaves, 32 x 15 1/2 In. 176.00
Stand, Plant, G. Stickley, Clipped Corners, Lower Shelf, Tapered Stretchers, 29 x 18 In. 1645.00
Stand, Plant, G. Stickley, No. 48, Oak, 26 x 14 x 14 In. 3120.00
Stand, Plant, G. Stickley, Square Top, Notched Apron, Signed, 14 x 14 x 28 In. 1880.00
Stand, Plant, Limbert, Hexagonal Top, Tapered Hexagonal Base, 13 x 13 x 37 In. 1528.00
Stand, Plant, Louis XVI Style, Beech, Gilt Metal, Marble Top, Shelf, 40 x 12 In. 646.00
Stand, Plant, Old Hickory, Paine Furniture Co., 30 x 13 x 13 In. 825.00
Stand, Plant, Stickley Bros., Square Overhang Top, Cloud Lift Apron, 34 x 14 In. 1528.00
Stand, Plant, Stickley, Square Top, Curved Aprons, Stretchers, 22 x 15 1/2 In. 1880.00
Stand, Plant, Victorian, Oak, Spool Turned, 4-Footed, 28 x 20 In. .... *ILLUS* 264.00
Stand, Plant, W. McArthur, Anodized Aluminum, c.1932, 30 3/8 x 16 In. 3600.00
Stand, Plant, White Pine, Green Paint, Block & Ring Turned Legs, 35 x 45 x 24 In. 470.00
Stand, Poplar, Cherry, 2-Board Top, Mortise & Tenon, Drawer, Cut Nails, 29 x 23 x 25 In. 290.00

Furniture, Stand, Plant, Victorian, Oak, Spool Turned, 4-Footed, 28 x 20 In.

Furniture, Stand, Walnut, 6-Sided Top, Lacquer, Shanxi Province, 1800s, 29 1/2 x 13 1/2 In., Pair

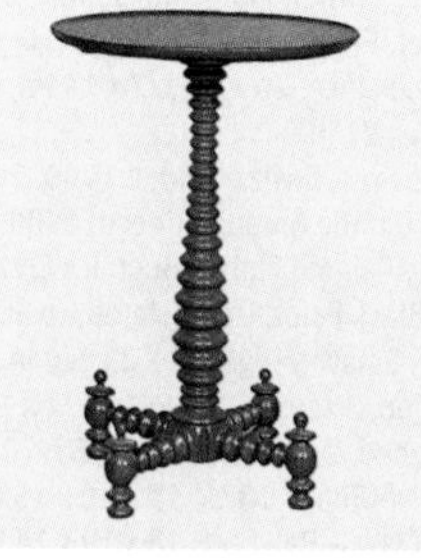

Stand, Queen Anne, Maple, Tilt Top, 17 x 17 x 29 In. 520.00
Stand, Regency Style, Steel, Gilt, Hipped Baluster, Flared Legs, 42 x 14 In. 180.00
Stand, Renaissance Revival, Brass, Onyx, Scrolled Handles, c.1880, 33 x 21 x 15 In. 235.00
Stand, Renaissance Revival, Moorish Style, Gilt, Metal, Onyx, c.1880, 31 x 12 In. 150.00
Stand, Renaissance Revival, Walnut, Marble Top, Barley Twist Legs, c.1890, 38 x 19 In. 147.00
Stand, Rosewood, Marble Top, 2 Tiers, Pierced Skirt, 5-Footed, Asia, 32 x 22 In. 1325.00
Stand, Rosewood, Marble Top, Pierced Skirt, 4 Cabriole Legs, Asia, 33 x 13 In. 1150.00
Stand, Rosewood, Marble, 2 Tiers, Rectangular Top, Carved Skirt, 34 x 17 x 13 In. 770.00
Stand, Rosewood, Marble, Chinese, 19 x 14 x 10 In. 180.00
Stand, Shaker, Birch, Cherry Base, Natural Finish, Drawer, Canterbury, c.1850, 28 x 19 In. 2800.00
Stand, Shaker, Maple, Bird's-Eye & Tiger Maple, 1 Board Top, Drawer, Cherry Pull, 26 x 19 In. 9945.00
Stand, Shaving, Neoclassical, Mahogany, Mirror, Drawers, Boston, c.1825, 23 x 23 In. 1880.00
Stand, Shaving, Sheraton, Mahogany, Boxwood Inlay, 5 Drawers, Mirror, 24 In. 316.00
Stand, Sheraton, Cherry, Curly Maple Drawer Front, 21 3/8 x 20 7/8 x 29 In. 403.00
Stand, Sheraton, Cherry, Drawer, 29 x 22 x 18 In. 460.00
Stand, Sheraton, Cherry, Drawer, Red Paint, Overhang Top, 28 1/2 x 16 1/2 In. 550.00
Stand, Sheraton, Cherry, Mahogany Finish, Drawer, Overhang Top, 28 x 20 x 18 In. 302.00
Stand, Sheraton, Cherry, Maple Drawer Front, Glass Knobs, Turned Legs, 29 x 22 x 18 In. 431.00
Stand, Sheraton, Cherry, Walnut, Drawer, Turned Legs, 23 x 19 x 30 In. 230.00
Stand, Sheraton, Curly Maple, 2 Drawers, Spiral-Carved Legs, c.1815, 29 x 21 x 17 In. 1380.00
Stand, Sheraton, Mahogany, Drop Leaf, 2 Drawers, New England, c.1815, 29 x 18 In. 834.00
Stand, Sheraton, Maple Top, 2 Walnut Drawers, Spiral Legs, 29 x 18 x 21 In. 450.00
Stand, Sheraton, Maple, Curly Maple, Drawer, Turned Legs, c.1825, 29 x 18 x 21 In. 431.00
Stand, Sheraton, Pine, Curly Maple, Drawer, 27 3/4 x 19 x 19 In. 546.00
Stand, Sheraton, Poplar, Pine, Red Paint, Drawer, Turned Ball Feet, 21 x 19 In. 259.00
Stand, Sheraton, Rosewood Edge, Mahogany Veneer, Drawers, Brass Knobs, 29 x 19 In. 460.00
Stand, Sheraton, Round, 2-Board Top, Drawer, Turned Legs, 31 x 27 In. 230.00
Stand, Smoking, Airplane, Chrome, American, c.1935, 34 In. 207.00
Stand, Smoking, Alabaster Pedestal & Base, Top Handle, Lighter, 2 Ashtrays, 28 1/2 In. 240.00
Stand, Smoking, Arts & Crafts, Oak, Tapered Square, Lakeside Craft Shops, 28 x 12 In. 230.00
Stand, Smoking, Black Forest, Walnut, Bear Support, Lift Top, c.1800, 30 x 20 In. 5515.00
Stand, Smoking, Green Alabaster, Brass Frame & Handle, 30 In. 100.00
Stand, Smoking, Nickel Finish, Light-Up, c.1930, 29 x 10 In. 205.00
Stand, Smoking, Painted Design, Copper Lined, c.1930, 26 x 22 In. 95.00
Stand, Softwood, Yellow Graining, Drawer, Turned Legs, Ball Feet, 30 x 19 x 19 In. 300.00
Stand, Stickley Bros., No. 141, Wide Arched Apron, Splayed Legs, X-Shaped Base, 34 In. 900.00
Stand, Teakwood, Carved, Inset Lacquer Top, Trees, Birds, Chinese Export, 31 x 19 In. 460.00
Stand, Telephone, Arts & Crafts, Oak, 3 Flat Legs, Arrow, Spade Cutouts, 28 x 14 In. 145.00
Stand, Telephone, Teak, Black Formica Top, 2 Sliding Trays, Drawer, 1958, 22 In. 635.00
Stand, Tray, Double, Rosewood, Brass Dragon Heads, Chinese Export, 1800s, 28 x 21 In. 470.00
Stand, Twig, Painted, Primary Colors, Panel Top, Canvas Cover, Tripod Base, 13 x 18 In. 230.00
Stand, Victorian, Cherry, Leaf Carved, Reticulated, Barley Twist Posts, c.1890, 35 x 14 In. 385.00
Stand, Victorian, Oak, Paneled, 39 x 27 x 18 In. 115.00
Stand, Walnut, 2-Board Top, Beveled Drawer, 19th Century, 28 x 23 3/4 x 24 In. 460.00
Stand, Walnut, 6-Sided Top, Lacquer, Shanxi Province, 29 1/2 x 13 1/2 In., Pair . . . . . ***ILLUS*** 472.00
Stand, Walnut, Applied Molded Top, Turned Legs, Drawer, Square, c.1830, 29 x 17 In. 430.00
Stand, Walnut, Lacquer, Hexagonal Top, Openwork, Cabriole Legs, Chinese, 29 x 13 In. 472.00

Stand, Walnut, Molded Top, Fluted Frieze, Drawer, Plank Sides, Italy, 21 x 23 x 18 In. 920.00
Stand, Walnut, Pine, 1-Board Top, Drawer, Pegged, Nailed, Tapered Legs, 29 x 22 x 19 In. 230.00
Stand, Walnut, Plant Top, Tapered Frieze, France, 20 x 16 1/2 x 14 In., Pair 2300.00
Stand, Wicker, White Paint, Birdcage, 74 x 21 In. 118.00
Stand, Wood, Bear, Trays On Paws, Glass Eyes, Switzerland, c.1900, 20 1/2 In. 2530.00
Stand, Wood, Lacquer, Rectangular Top, Bombe Apron, Chinese, 1900s, 11 x 20 x 14 In. 266.00
Step, Sewing, Shaker, Double, Pine, Blue Painted Finish, Bootjack End, 9 1/2 x 9 1/2 x 9 3/4 In. .. 700.00
Stool, Aesthetic Revival, Faux Bamboo, Black Paint, Upholstered, Oval, c.1890, 7 x 13 x 11 In. ... 235.00
Stool, Biedermeier, Blond, Padded Seat, Splayed Legs, 22 x 23 1/4 In., Pair 880.00
Stool, Biedermeier, Fruitwood, Padded Top, 3 Legs, c.1815, 16 1/2 x 13 In., Pair 1175.00
Stool, Camp, Folding, Hunter & Deer, Signed, Dated June 19th 1892, 18 x 26 In. 4715.00
Stool, Cherry, Black Lacquer, Maroon Velvet Top, c.1871, 19 x 20 x 15 In. 330.00
Stool, Chippendale Style, Needlepoint, Claw & Ball Feet, 18 x 19 x 15 In. 259.00
Stool, Eames, Time-Life, Walnut, Turned Form, Herman Miller, 15 x 13 In. 1080.00
Stool, Eero Saarinen, Tulip, Knoll, c.1956, 16 x 15 In., Pair 1440.00
Stool, Eric Buck, Teak, Rosewood, Vinyl, 33 x 15 x 17 In., Pair 1020.00
Stool, G. Nakashima, Greenrock, Upholstered, 11 x 18 In., Pair 14160.00
Stool, George II Style, Giltwood, Lacquer, Padded, Gilt Accents, Frieze, 20 x 27 In. 1645.00
Stool, George II, Walnut, 17 x 21 x 19 In. 4200.00
Stool, George III Style, Mahogany, Cabriole Legs, c.1900, 18 x 26 x 19 In. 590.00
Stool, George III Style, Mahogany, Padded Top, Cabriole Legs, Late 1800s, 22 x 20 In. 175.00
Stool, George III Style, Mahogany, Padded, Cabriole Legs, 18 x 25 In., Pair 940.00
Stool, George III, Mahogany, c.1765, 18 x 20 1/2 x 15 In. 960.00
Stool, Green Paint, Splayed Legs, 23 In. 315.00
Stool, Hardwood, Mother-Of-Pearl Inlay, Latticed, Morocco, 20 x 18 In., Pair 765.00
Stool, I. Noguchi, Rocker, Ebonized Seat, Base, Chrome, Corseted, 16 x 14 In. 3540.00
Stool, Jacobean Style, Oak, Elm, Rectangular Seat, Shaped Apron, 1800s, 23 x 18 In. 1295.00
Stool, Jere Osgood, Walnut, Low Back, 25 x 15 x 15 In. 2125.00
Stool, Limbert, No. 213, Oak, Rectangular, Arched Apron, 19 x 20 x 14 In. 600.00
Stool, Louis XVI Style, Gilt, Upholstered, Needlepoint Seat, 16 x 19 x 18 In. 498.00
Stool, Mahogany, Gilt Feet & Skirt, Needlepoint Top, Beaded Bird, Round, 7 x 15 In. 375.00
Stool, Marcel Breuer, No. B9, Steel, Wood, c.1927, 18 x 17 3/4 x 15 In. 3900.00
Stool, Neoclassical, Mahogany, Concave Upholstered Seat, C-Scroll Base, 17 x 23 In. 940.00
Stool, Neoclassical, Mahogany, Upholstered, Scroll Sides, 18 x 24 In. 635.00
Stool, Nutting, No. 153, Windsor, Oval, 8 In. 305.00
Stool, Nutting, No. 165, Maple, Low Joints, 15 x 20 x 12 In. 605.00
Stool, Organ, Cast Iron, Curved, 8-Sided, Swivels, Vase Support, 22 x 17 In. 85.00
Stool, Piano, Gilt, Carved Lyre, Scroll Back, Adjustable Swivel Seat, 38 x 18 In. 546.00
Stool, Piano, Mahogany, 4-Footed, High Edwardian-Heeled Lady's Boots, 19 x 22 In. 998.00
Stool, Piano, Regency, Mahogany, Needlepoint, Tapered Legs, Early 1800s, 21 x 15 In. 295.00
Stool, Piano, Restauration, Rosewood, Scalloped, Adjustable, Early 1800s, 20 x 15 In. 325.00
Stool, Piano, Schoenhut, Wood, 21 x 21 In., Child's 168.00
Stool, Piano, Sheraton, Birch, Pine, Turned, Flame Stitch Upholstery, c.1832, 13 x 16 In. 200.00
Stool, Piano, Victorian, Mahogany, Adjustable, 19th Century, 18 x 20 1/2 x 14 In. 445.00
Stool, Regency, Mahogany, Padded, Pineapple Feet, c.1850, 15 1/2 x 50 In., Pair 2585.00
Stool, Regency, Mahogany, Tapered Legs, Canted Feet, Needlework Cushion, 20 x 16 In. 375.00
Stool, Robsjohn-Gibbings, No. 1, Saridis, Athens, c.1961, 18 x 22 x 22 In., Pair 9600.00
Stool, Ruhlmann, Black Lacquer, Cork Top, Bronze Feet, 20 x 13 In. 1420.00
Stool, Shaker, Maple, Ebony Finish, Black Ash Splint, Turned Legs, c.1880, 16 x 15 In. 1110.00
Stool, Shaker, Maple, Natural Finish, Pine, Square, Chamfered Seat, Box Stretchers, 33 x 13 In. .. 380.00
Stool, Sheraton, Mahogany, Upholstered, Molded Apron, Tapered Turned Legs 175.00
Stool, Sori Yanagi, Butterfly, Tendo-Mokko, c.1954, 15 x 17 x 12 In. 5040.00
Stool, Square, Curved Skirt & Stretchers, Through Tenon, 22 x 14 In., Pair 8225.00
Stool, Teak, Rectangular Top, Square Fluted Legs, Chinese, Early 1900s, 9 x 15 x 11 In. 59.00
Stool, Walnut, Burl Walnut, Plank Lift Top, Curule Base, Late Victorian, 17 x 20 In. 470.00
Stool, Walnut, Green Marble, Square Inset Top, Chinese, 19 x 18 1/2 In. 385.00
Stool, Windsor, Birch, Pine, Dark Brown Finish, Bamboo Turned Legs, 11 1/2 x 10 In. 345.00
Stool, Windsor, Brown Paint, Yellow Stripes, Round Top, Splayed Legs, 19 x 13 In. 590.00
Stool Set, Primavera Wood, Bamboo, Patent Leather, 41 x 20 x 20 In., 6 Piece 8965.00
Storage Unit, Eames, ESU, Herman Miller, Birch, c.1952, 58 1/2 x 47 x 17 In. .... ***ILLUS*** 11750.00
Table, Aalto, Linoleum Top, Round, Finmar, c.1930 .... 1920.00

Table, Abolitionist, Wood Top, Cast Iron, Slavery Abolished Shield, c.1850, 30 x 24 In. 2000.00
Table, Adirondack, Painted, Round, Pinwheel Design, Sapling Border, 28 3/4 x 25 In. 645.00
Table, Altar, Elm, Lacquer, Dragons, Chinese, c.1850, 34 1/2 x 76 x 16 In. 355.00
Table, Altar, Elm, Shaped Apron, Square Legs, Chinese, 72 x 31 1/2 In. 575.00
Table, Altar, Huang Huali, Rectangular, Molded Edge, Turned Legs, Chinese, 1735-96, Pair 4200.00
Table, Altar, Mahogany, Fretwork Apron, Block Legs, Chinese, 42 x 96 In. 1000.00
Table, Altar, Padouk, Carved Frieze, Inlaid Nephrite, Chinese, 35 x 51 In. 10869.00
Table, Altar, Painted, Honeycomb Splat, Flowers, Tibet, 25 x 34 x 15 In. 470.00
Table, Andre Arbus, Sycamore, Brass, 1940s, 23 3/4 x 23 1/2 x 16 In. 7800.00
Table, Arrebo, Rosewood, Rectangular Top, Dowel Legs, Denmark, 20 x 60 x 20 In. 355.00
Table, Art Deco, Ebonized, Shells, Feathers, Flowers, 3 Peacock Legs, France, 27 x 31 In. 470.00
Table, Art Deco, Iron, Leather Top, Painted Rooster, 29 x 18 x 18 In., Pair 720.00
Table, Art Deco, Mahogany, Brass, Foldover, 8-Sided, France, c.1920, 32 x 34 In. 3290.00
Table, Art Deco, Round Top, Cruciform Base, 26 x 28 In., Pair 3540.00
Table, Arts & Crafts, Oak, 30 x 26 In. 175.00
Table, Arts & Crafts, Tile Top, Hispano Moresque Medallion, 25 x 20 1/2 In. 325.00
Table, Arts & Crafts, Wood, Polychrome Flower Tile Top, Calif., 18 x 24 x 16 In. 325.00
Table, Baker's, Double Possum Belly, Sheet Metal Drawers, Cutting Board, Pine, 1880 .... 755.00
Table, Bamboo, Lacquer, Drawer, Anglo-Indian, c.1900, 28 x 25 x 17 In. 1115.00
Table, Bamboo, Lacquered, Tiers, Anglo-Indian, 30 3/4 x 16 x 16 In., Pair 705.00
Table, Baroque, Blackamoor, Shaped Top, Putto Standard, Italy, 1900s, 37 In., Pair 1528.00
Table, Beaux Arts, Slate Top, Flowers, 3 Graces Support, Granite & Bronze Base, 30 In. 9106.00
Table, Belle Epoque, Giltwood, Marble Top, Oval, Late 1800s, 31 x 27 In. 340.00
Table, Belle Epoque, Wrought Iron, Green Marble Top, Round, Shaped Legs, France, 31 x 49 In. 1765.00
Table, Biedermeier, Burl Maple, Drawer, Dark Wood Legs, 29 x 18 In., Pair 858.00
Table, Biedermeier, Fruitwood, Ebonized, Round, 3-Sided Base, 1800s, 29 x 30 In. 1410.00
Table, Biedermeier, Fruitwood, Oval, Expanding, Bead Molded, 1800s, 30 x 49 x 41 In. 4115.00
Table, Biedermeier, Mahogany, Blackamoor Heads, Drawer, Concave Shelf, 30 x 23 In. 1760.00
Table, Biedermeier, Maple, Inlaid, Oval, Scalloped Apron, Plinth Base, 30 x 47 In. 1880.00
Table, Birch Plywood Top, Folding Chromed-Steel Legs, 34 x 34 x 28 1/2 In. 1765.00
Table, Black Lacquer, Chinese, 18 1/2 x 50 x 21 In. 4200.00
Table, Black Marble Top, Silvered Bronze, Winged Seminude Figural Legs, 32 x 18 In. 770.00
Table, Black, Red Lacquer, 3-Stepped Top, Shaped Skirt, Chinese, 32 x 24 x 14 In. 355.00
Table, Bronze, Dolphin Base, 20th Century, 30 x 34 x 15 In. 415.00
Table, Bronze, Patinated, 3 Crossed Sword Legs, 28 x 27 In. 1060.00
Table, Bugatti, Wood, 2 Tiers, Ebonized, Pewter & Bone Inlay, 52 3/8 x 14 3/8 In. 9315.00
Table, Burl Top, Banded Inlay, Frieze Drawer, Carved Cabriole Legs, 30 x 43 x 22 In. 4830.00
Table, Burl Veneer Top, Sculptural Base, 3 Legs, Sweden, 22 x 36 In. 649.00
Table, Burl Walnut, Rosewood Banding, Gilt, England, 37 x 74 x 17 In., Pair 6756.00
Table, Burl, 3 Root Legs, Chinese, c.1850, 29 x 20 In. 2470.00
Table, Butcher Block, 30 x 40 In. 695.00
Table, Butcher Block, Pine Base, 20th Century, 34 x 24 x 18 In. 295.00
Table, Butterfly, Quebec, 1800s, 30 x 44 x 48 In. 990.00
Table, Campaign, Empire, Mahogany, Flip Leaves, Folding Legs, c.1810, 26 x 29 In. 2585.00
Table, Card, Eames, DTW-40, Square, Herman Miller, c.1950, 29 x 34 In. 3300.00
Table, Card, Empire, Flap Leaf, Mahogany Veneer, Square Pedestal, 29 x 36 x 18 In. 175.00
Table, Card, Federal, Cherry, Red Stain, Folding Overhang Top, c.1800, 29 x 36 In. 470.00
Table, Card, Federal, Demilune, Tilt Top, 29 x 41 x 18 In. 410.00
Table, Card, Federal, Folding, Bow-Shape Top, New England, Early 1800s, 36 In. 7768.00
Table, Card, Federal, Mahogany, Folding Top, Cock-Beaded Skirt, 29 x 32 x 16 In. 1645.00
Table, Card, Federal, Mahogany, Folding Top, New England, Early 1800s, 36 In. 6575.00
Table, Card, Federal, Mahogany, Inlaid, Beaded Skirt, Tapered Legs, 29 x 36 x 17 In. 2705.00
Table, Card, Federal, Mahogany, Inlaid, Demilune, Foldover Top, c.1790, 30 x 37 In. 3408.00
Table, Card, Federal, Mahogany, Inlaid, Double-Hinged Top, c.1790, 29 x 36 x 17 In. 999.00
Table, Card, Federal, Mahogany, Inlaid, Hinged Top, 31 x 36 x 18 In. 10925.00
Table, Card, Federal, Mahogany, Pine, Inlaid, Serpentine Apron, 36 x 18 x 28 In. 865.00
Table, Card, Federal, Mahogany, Veneer Inlay, Oval Corners, c.1800, 29 x 34 3/4 In. 2115.00
Table, Card, Federal, Mahogany, Veneer, Folding Top, Beaded Skirt, c.1800, 30 x 34 In. 880.00
Table, Card, Federal, Maple, Mahogany Inlay, Band Accents, 36 x 28 In. 2185.00
Table, Card, Federal, Reeded Edge, Tapered Reeded Legs, 29 x 45 3/4 x 23 In. 4995.00
Table, Card, George II, Mahogany, Serpentine Front, Foldover Top, 29 x 38 In. 3450.00

Furniture, Storage Unit, Eames, ESU, Herman Miller, Birch, c.1952, 58 1/2 x 47 x 17 In.

Furniture, Table, Center, Renaissance Revival, Walnut, Marquetry Inlaid, Gilt, Rosewood, Flowers

Table, Card, George III, Mahogany, Foldover Top, Drawer, Tapered Legs, 29 x 28 In. 3910.00
Table, Card, Hepplewhite, Mahogany, Bowfront, Mass., c.1785, 28 x 36 x 17 In. 4025.00
Table, Card, Hepplewhite, Mahogany, Line, Oval Inlay, 35 In. 750.00
Table, Card, Hepplewhite, Mahogany, Serpentine, Late 1700s, 31 x 37 x 17 In. 1955.00
Table, Card, Hepplewhite, Veneered, Inlaid, Charleston, c.1790, 29 x 36 In. 9000.00
Table, Card, Mahogany, Flame Birch, Bird's-Eye Maple, Foldover, c.1810, 29 x 37 In. 2880.00
Table, Card, Maple, Brass Inlay, Pedestal Base, Brass Casters, England, 21 x 36 x 16 In. 605.00
Table, Card, Neoclassical, Mahogany, Foldover Top, c.1825, 29 x 36 x 19 In. 1645.00
Table, Card, Neoclassical, Mahogany, Spiral Turned Pedestal, Paw Feet, 29 x 37 In. 2940.00
Table, Card, Queen Anne, Mahogany, Frieze Drawer, Lappet Legs, 1700s, 29 x 33 In. 3175.00
Table, Card, Rosewood, Felt Surface, Turned Stem, Paw Feet, 29 x 36 x 18 In. 410.00
Table, Card, Sheraton, Mahogany, Boston, 1800-15, 30 x 36 x 18 In. 4025.00
Table, Card, Sheraton, Mahogany, Cherry, Foldover, c.1820, 29 x 36 x 17 In., Pair 3738.00
Table, Card, Sheraton, Mahogany, Serpentine Front, Ribbed Edge, 30 x 36 x 18 In. 690.00
Table, Card, Sheraton, Mahogany, Serpentine, R. Jordan, Mass., c.1790, 30 x 37 In. 9430.00
Table, Card, Sheraton, Mahogany, Shaped Top, Reeded Edge, 29 x 36 In. 460.00
Table, Card, W. McArthur, Oilcloth Top, Tubular Aluminum, Square, 29 x 32 In. 1298.00
Table, Castelli, Plastic Top, Pedestal, Chrome Base, Folding, Round, 27 x 38 In. 649.00
Table, Center, Aesthetic Revival, Ebonized, Polychrome, Marble Top, 30 x 27 In. 765.00
Table, Center, Aesthetic Revival, Mahogany, Trestle Base, c.1875, 30 x 40 In. 1175.00
Table, Center, Argente & Specimen Marble Top, 3 Putti Legs, Italy, 26 x 32 In. 1410.00
Table, Center, Biedermeier, Mahogany, Oval Top, Baltic, c.1850, 31 x 78 x 50 In. 1880.00
Table, Center, Ch'ien Lung Style, Bamboo, Elm, Patinated, Chinese, 1900s, 34 x 37 In. 380.00
Table, Center, Charles X, Mahogany, Marble Top, 3-Footed, c.1815, 30 x 39 In. 1060.00
Table, Center, Eastlake, Ebonized, Parcel Gilt, 8-Sided, 31 x 32 x 28 In. 765.00
Table, Center, Edwardian, Mahogany, Polychrome, c.1900, 27 x 33 In. 3290.00
Table, Center, Empire Revival, Mahogany, Leather Top, Zangerle, Mid 1900s, 30 x 28 In. 90.00
Table, Center, Louis XVI Style, Beech, Marble, Multicolored, Early 1900s, 31 x 48 In. 2230.00
Table, Center, Louis XVI Style, Mahogany, Parcel Gilt, Brass Inlay, c.1890, 31 x 30 In. 2585.00
Table, Center, Mahogany, Inlaid, Oval, Music Symbols, Shelf, Casters, 29 x 31 x 21 In. 1095.00
Table, Center, Marble Top, Gilt, Composition, Stone, Italy, c.1850, 32 x 86 In. 5170.00
Table, Center, Napoleon III, Black Lacquer, Ormolu Mounted, c.1865, 31 x 59 x 36 In. 588.00
Table, Center, Neoclassical, Mahogany, Bulbous Stem, 3 Paw Feet, c.1825, 30 x 42 In. 7875.00
Table, Center, Neoclassical, Mahogany, Ebonized, Bronze, 1800s, 30 x 41 In. 5875.00
Table, Center, Neoclassical, Mahogany, Marble Top, Pedestal, c.1830, 30 x 36 In. 2328.00
Table, Center, Neoclassical, Mahogany, Marble Top, Plinth Base, Scroll Feet, 29 x 36 In. 2938.00
Table, Center, Neoclassical, Mahogany, Marble, Round, 1820-30, 30 x 36 In. 8815.00
Table, Center, Neoclassical, Molded Skirt, Pedestal, Scrolled Legs, c.1840, 29 x 31 In. 1116.00
Table, Center, Oak, Octagonal Top, Compass Points, England, 1800s, 29 x 51 In. 2233.00
Table, Center, Oak, Turned Legs, c.1900, 29 x 24 In. 92.00
Table, Center, Regency Style, Mahogany, Marble, Dolphins, Tripod, England, 28 x 40 In. 2820.00
Table, Center, Regency, Rosewood, Calamander Banding, String Inlay, 28 x 47 In. 12925.00
Table, Center, Renaissance Revival, Rosewood, Marquetry Flower Basket, 29 x 39 In. 6465.00
Table, Center, Renaissance Revival, Walnut, Marquetry Inlaid, Gilt, Rosewood, Flowers ..... *ILLUS* 4600.00
Table, Center, Rococo Revival, Rosewood, Quatrefoil Marble Top, c.1850, 30 x 37 In. 1800.00
Table, Center, Rosewood, White Marble Top, Curved Plinth Base, Bun Feet, 29 x 37 In. 1763.00
Table, Center, Scalloped Top, Carved Cabriole Legs, Mid 20th Century, 28 x 28 In. 176.00

Table, Center, Sunburst Parquetry, Round, Stretcher Shelf, Cabriole Legs, 29 x 36 In. 2350.00
Table, Center, William & Mary, Drawer, England, c.1700, 26 x 22 x 35 In. 7475.00
Table, Charles II, Walnut, 2 End Drawers, Gateleg, c.1680, 30 x 21 x 56 In. 10200.00
Table, Cherry, Grain Painted, Overhang Top, Drawer, Ring Turned Legs, 29 x 30 In. 411.00
Table, Chinese Chippendale, Mahogany, Fret-Carved Frieze, X-Stretcher, 28 x 33 In. 705.00
Table, Chippendale Style, Mahogany, Bar & Dot, 3 Tiers, Tripod Base, 45 x 25 In. 201.00
Table, Chippendale Style, Mahogany, Guilloche-Carved Frieze, c.1900, 30 x 37 In. 1175.00
Table, Chippendale, Mahogany, Carved Backsplash, 3-Drawer Frieze, 44 x 58 In., Pair 3819.00
Table, Chippendale, Mahogany, Drop Front, Hinges, Cabriole Legs, 28 x 15 x 44 In. 2300.00
Table, Coffee, Art Deco, Black Glass Top, Wrought Iron Base, France, 17 x 29 x 15 In. 443.00
Table, Coffee, Art Deco, Gilt Metal, Lucite, 1900s, 20 x 41 x 21 In. 1888.00
Table, Coffee, Art Deco, Mahogany, 4 Ebonized Scroll Supports, c.1920, 24 x 27 In. 1760.00
Table, Coffee, Art Deco, Mahogany, Chrome Mounted, France, c.1920, 24 x 36 In. 1997.00
Table, Coffee, Art Deco, Oval Top, Double Pedestal, France, 19 x 45 x 23 In. 885.00
Table, Coffee, Birch, Glass Top, Aluminum Connector, 50 x 36 x 15 1/2 In. 3055.00
Table, Coffee, Book Form, Drawer, 17 1/2 x 37 1/4 x 23 1/2 In. 230.00
Table, Coffee, Ceramic Tile, Pomona Tile Co., c.1955, 17 x 20 x 44 In. 600.00
Table, Coffee, Checkerboard Top, Stars, 20 x 44 x 24 In. 550.00
Table, Coffee, Chinoiserie, Ebonized Wood, 15 1/2 x 47 x 23 1/2 In. 2040.00
Table, Coffee, Directoire Style, Brass, Marble Top, H-Stretcher, Early 1900s, 17 x 36 In. 1527.00
Table, Coffee, Ebonized Wood, Silver Leaf Under Glass, 32 x 32 x 15 1/2 In. 470.00
Table, Coffee, Edwardian, Lacquer, Brass, Cranes, Mountains, Early 1900s, 19 x 37 In. 1645.00
Table, Coffee, Frank Lloyd Wright, Green Top, Cruciform Base, Henredon, 16 x 36 In. 4500.00
Table, Coffee, Frankl, Cork, Johnson Furniture Co., c.1950, 14 x 46 x 44 In. 4200.00
Table, Coffee, G. Nakashima, Butterfly Cross Base, Widdicomb, c.1958, 13 x 36 In. 2950.00
Table, Coffee, G. Nelson, No. 5452, Swag Leg, Herman Miller, c.1955, 16 x 29 In. 330.00
Table, Coffee, George II Style, Mahogany, Glass Top, Shell & Leaf Edge, 20 x 41 In. 295.00
Table, Coffee, Glass, Round, Stepped Metal Base, 16 x 42 In. 385.00
Table, Coffee, I. Noguchi, Boomerang, Walnut, Glass, 16 x 51 x 36 In. 3068.00
Table, Coffee, I. Noguchi, Ebonized Birch, Green Glass, 1957, 15 x 50 1/2 x 36 In. 2150.00
Table, Coffee, I. Noguchi, Ebonized Wood, Glass, 1944, 15 5/8 x 35 7/8 x 50 3/8 In. 9000.00
Table, Coffee, I. Noguchi, IN50, Glass, Herman Miller, c.1947, 15 x 51 x 36 In. 3300.00
Table, Coffee, J. Adnet, Leather, Iron, Brass, Glass, c.1950, 17 x 37 x 17 In. 4800.00
Table, Coffee, John Keal, Brown Saltman, c.1958, 16 x 25 x 60 In. 960.00
Table, Coffee, Joseph D'Urso, Steel, Glass, Knoll, c.1980, 15 x 22 x 22 In. 4800.00
Table, Coffee, Karl Springer, Lacquered Patchwork, L Extension, Pivoting, 17 x 53 In. 826.00
Table, Coffee, Karl Springer, Lucite, Plate Glass, Brass, 16 x 38 x 22 In. 1298.00
Table, Coffee, Katavolos Littell & Kelley, Dowel Top, Iron Frame, 12 x 62 x 17 In. 415.00
Table, Coffee, Lacquer, Cloisonne, 3 Butterfly & Lotus Panels, Chinese, 17 x 50 x 18 In. 590.00
Table, Coffee, Louis XV Style, Marble Top, Italy, 20th Century, 16 x 40 In. 189.00
Table, Coffee, Louis XVI Style, Gilt, Onyx, Early 1900s, 23 x 28 In. 940.00
Table, Coffee, Louis XVI, Wrought Steel, Brass, Marble, 18 x 51 x 19 In. 1175.00
Table, Coffee, Mahogany, Shelf, Round Top, Inset Cork, 42 x 22 In. 940.00
Table, Coffee, McCobb, Laminate Top, Drawer, Shelf, 14 x 54 x 32 In. 470.00
Table, Coffee, Mies Van Der Rohe, Barcelona, Glass, Chrome, Knoll, 17 x 40 In. 590.00
Table, Coffee, Neoclassical Form, Chrome, Brass, Beveled Glass Top, 17 1/2 x 36 In. 330.00
Table, Coffee, P. Evans, Glass Top, Round, Stalagmite Base, 1972, 16 x 36 In. 3425.00
Table, Coffee, P. Evans, Glass, Random Height Bronze Panels, 1972, 16 x 60 x 34 In. 2360.00
Table, Coffee, P. Evans, Sculpted Steel, Glass Top, Butterfly Base, 16 x 48 In. 2478.00
Table, Coffee, Pewter, Bronze, Brass Top, Asian Design, Octagonal Base, 47 x 17 In. 4415.00
Table, Coffee, Philip & Kelvin LaVerne, Bronze, Chinese Palace Gate, 18 x 42 In. 4425.00
Table, Coffee, Philip & Kelvin LaVerne, Bronze, Flowers, Vines, 21 x 39 In. 2950.00
Table, Coffee, Philip & Kelvin LaVerne, Pewter, Brass & Bronze Top, 1960s, 17 x 47 In. ..... *ILLUS* 4406.00
Table, Coffee, Pink Mirrored Glass, Beveled Edge, Hexagonal, 17 x 36 In. 470.00
Table, Coffee, Poul Kjaerholm, PK61, Chromium-Plated Steel, Slate, 13 x 34 In. 8400.00
Table, Coffee, Rectangular, Gilt, Smoked Mirror Top, 19 x 37 x 25 In. 590.00
Table, Coffee, Richard Schultz, Petal, Knoll, c.1960, 15 x 43 In. 1200.00
Table, Coffee, Robsjohn-Gibbings, Maple, Glass, Widdicomb, 1950s, 17 x 50 x 34 In. 7200.00
Table, Coffee, Stainless Steel Base, Rectangular Glass Top, c.1970, 60 x 26 x 19 In. 940.00
Table, Coffee, Stefan Siwinski, Fiberglass, Korina Designs, c.1975, 15 x 30 x 60 In. 2260.00
Table, Coffee, Surfboard Top, Denmark, c.1960, 15 x 66 x 18 In. 205.00

Furniture, Table, Coffee, Philip & Kelvin LaVerne, Pewter, Brass & Bronze Top, 1960s, 17 x 47 In.

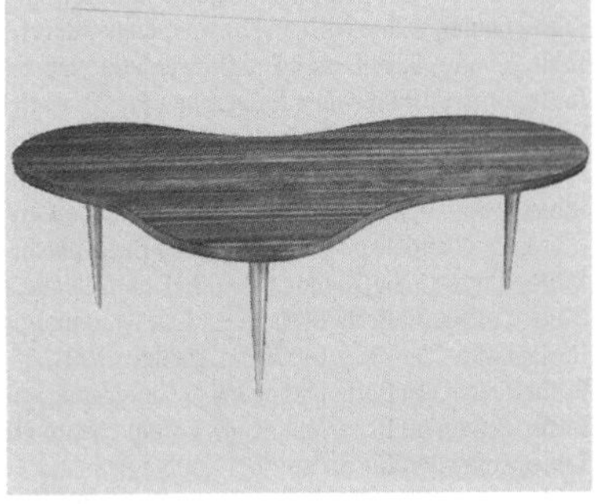

Furniture, Table, Coffee, Widdicomb, Cherry, Biomorphic, Marked, 19 1/2 x 71 x 44 In.

Table, Coffee, V. Kagan, Marble, L-Shaped Ends, 17 x 84 x 28 In. 590.00
Table, Coffee, V. Kagan, Snail, Dux, c.1960, 15 x 42 x 37 In. 3300.00
Table, Coffee, V. Kagan, Tri-Symmetric, Kagan-Dreyfus, c.1955, 19 x 30 x 25 In. 1320.00
Table, Coffee, W. McArthur, Anodized Aluminum, Glass, 1930s, 16 x 26 In. 10800.00
Table, Coffee, W. Platner, Rosewood Top, Overhang, Knoll, 16 x 42 In. 1440.00
Table, Coffee, W. Platner, Walnut, Round, Corseted Wire Base, Knoll, 16 x 36 In. 1415.00
Table, Coffee, Walnut, Oak Veneer, 21 x 30 x 30 In. 269.00
Table, Coffee, Widdicomb, Cherry, Biomorphic, Marked, 19 1/2 x 71 x 44 In. .... *ILLUS* 3055.00
Table, Coffee, Wormley, Mahogany, Inset Cork Top, 50 1/2 x 15 x 15 1/2 In. 590.00
Table, Console, Art Deco, Brass, Iron, Parcel Gilt, Lattice Cut, France, c.1915, 48 x 24 In. 1530.00
Table, Console, Art Deco, Oak, Demilune, France, c.1920, 30 x 39 x 15 In. 936.00
Table, Console, Baroque, Gilt, Marble, Wall Mount, 30 x 17 In. 2115.00
Table, Console, Baroque, Parcel Gilt, Mahogany, Marble Top, 34 x 53 In. 3175.00
Table, Console, Black, Green Faux Marble, Greek Key Frieze, 36 x 37 x 21 In., 2 Piece 4830.00
Table, Console, Empire Style, Mahogany, Marble Top, c.1900, 29 1/2 x 48 x 22 In. 705.00
Table, Console, Empire Style, Mahogany, Rectangular Top, Inset Marble, 34 x 36 In. 1410.00
Table, Console, Federal Style, Mahogany, Octagonal, Flip Flop, 28 x 36 x 35 In. 445.00
Table, Console, Federal, Mahogany, Veneer, Veined Marble Top, 29 x 37 x 18 In. 7050.00
Table, Console, G. Stickley, 2 Drawers, Hammered Copper Pulls, 29 x 40 x 19 In. 1880.00
Table, Console, George III Style, Mahogany, Bowed Top, Concave Sides, 33 x 60 In. 1765.00
Table, Console, George III Style, Mahogany, Burl Paneled Frieze, 33 x 45 In., Pair 2230.00
Table, Console, George III Style, Mahogany, Demilune, Banded, 34 x 45 In., Pair 2000.00
Table, Console, George III Style, Mahogany, Demilune, Late 1800s, 30 x 43 x 24 In. 380.00
Table, Console, George III Style, Mahogany, Demilune, Pierced Frieze, 33 x 48 In., Pair 940.00
Table, Console, George III Style, Mahogany, Gilt, Carved Garland, 33 x 56 x 26 In. 2000.00
Table, Console, George III, Mahogany, Banded, Demilune Top, 33 1/2 x 45 In., Pair 2230.00
Table, Console, George IV, Mahogany, Parcel Ebonized, Gilt, Lions, c.1815, 36 x 42 In. 1645.00
Table, Console, Gilt, Carved, Marble Top, 20th Century, 32 3/4 x 51 x 21 In. 710.00
Table, Console, Gilt, Crackle Glass Top, Demilune, Drawer, Square Legs, 35 x 59 In. 3290.00
Table, Console, Gilt, Crackled Glass, 3 Drawers, Square Legs, Italy, 36 x 73 In. 1760.00
Table, Console, Hong-Mu, Marble, Openwork Scrolls, Chinese Export, 34 x 30 In., Pair 646.00
Table, Console, Iron, Bombe Front, Faux Marble, France, c.1915, 39 x 53 In., Pair 880.00
Table, Console, Joubert & Petit, Oak, Marble Top, 31 x 71 x 47 1/4 In. 9315.00
Table, Console, Late Regency, Walnut, Mahogany, Ormolu, c.1890, 39 x 48 In., Pair 2585.00
Table, Console, Louis XV Style, Gilt, Marble Top, 39 1/2 x 53 1/2 x 22 3/4 In. 6000.00
Table, Console, Louis XV Style, Gilt, Marble, Garland Pendants, 34 x 38 In. 325.00
Table, Console, Louis XV Style, Gilt, Marble, Serpentine, c.1910, 35 x 72 In. 2235.00
Table, Console, Louis XV Style, Painted, Parcel Gilt, Marble Top, c.1880, 33 x 17 x 11 In. 529.00
Table, Console, Louis XV Style, Walnut, Serpentine Top, Rocaille Apron, 32 x 41 In. 1998.00
Table, Console, Louis XV, Oak, Shaped Apron, Cabriole Legs, 31 1/2 x 32 x 19 In. 885.00
Table, Console, Louis XVI Style, Gilt Bronze, 2 Frieze Drawers, 38 x 66 3/4 x 20 In. 9000.00
Table, Console, Louis XVI Style, Gilt, Marble Top, Lyre, 38 x 50 In. 2820.00
Table, Console, Louis XVI Style, Mahogany, Gilt Bronze, c.1900, 39 x 57 x 20 In. 7200.00

Table, Console, Louis XVI Style, Mahogany, Gilt, Carved Frieze, 6 Legs, 35 x 54 In. 1760.00
Table, Console, Louis XVI Style, Parcel Gilt, Iron, Scrolls, France, 29 x 71 In. 3055.00
Table, Console, Louis XVI Style, Parcel Gilt, Wrought Iron, Marble Top, 35 1/2 x 69 In. 2000.00
Table, Console, Mahogany, Dolphin Supports, Plinth Base, 32 x 54 In. 2350.00
Table, Console, Oak, 4 Drawers, Griffin Supports, Late 1800s, 32 x 58 x 33 In. ....620.00 to 1000.00
Table, Console, Opaline Top, Chrome Legs, France, 1930s, 23 x 32 x 14 In.................... 4248.00
Table, Console, P. Evans, Directional, Burl Patchwork, Chrome, 29 x 56 In. 530.00
Table, Console, Painted Flowers, Serpentine Green Marble Top, 34 x 47 In., Pair 3525.00
Table, Console, Polychrome, Gilt, Faux Marble, Scrolling Garland, 31 x 48 In. 2820.00
Table, Console, Polychrome, Marble Top, Cabriole Legs, Italy, Late 1800s, 31 x 40 In. 2820.00
Table, Console, Regency Style, Cast Iron, Demilune, Spray Of Flowers, 31 x 50 In. 2115.00
Table, Console, Regency, Mahogany, Inlaid, Drop Leaf, 2 Drawers, c.1820, 27 x 48 In............ 825.00
Table, Console, Rococo Revival, Rosewood, Laminated, Serpentine Top, 35 x 59 x 21 In. 8518.00
Table, Console, Rococo Revival, Walnut, Marble Top, Austria, 1800s, 35 x 56 In. 1260.00
Table, Console, Sheraton Style, Serpentine, Flip Top, 19th Century, 29 x 35 x 17 In............. 1005.00
Table, Console, Venetian Style, Gilt, Specimen Marble Top, Trestle Base, 36 x 63 In. 5290.00
Table, Console, Walnut, Marble Top, Demilune, Fluted Frieze, England, 1800s, 33 x 63 In. 620.00
Table, Console, Walnut, Serpentine Marble Top, Carved, Cherubs, Swags, 31 x 34 In. 3820.00
Table, Console, Wendell Castle, Inverted V Legs, Caligari, 1987, 41 x 68 In. 6490.00
Table, Console, Wormley, Shell, Pine, Carved Wave Edges, Dunbar, 30 x 32 In. 3600.00
Table, Console, Wrought Iron, Charcoal Marble Top, Bombe Base, 33 x 79 x 36 In. 2585.00
Table, Corner, H. Probber, 2 Tiers, Drawer, Brass Legs, 26 x 32 In. 85.00
Table, Cypress, 2-Board Top, Drawer, Molded Square Legs, 32 x 43 x 32 In. 3525.00
Table, Cypress, Pegged Construction, Drawer, Square Tapered Legs, 29 x 34 x 19 In. 705.00
Table, Dinette, Drop Leaf, Oak, Turned Legs, c.1930, 30 x 36 In. 405.00
Table, Dinette, Osvaldo Borsani, Round Leather Top, Steel Legs, 25 x 40 In. 470.00
Table, Dinette, Plate Glass Top, 3 Columns, Lucite, Brass, 29 x 36 In.......................... 470.00
Table, Dining, Art Deco, Glass, 20th Century 30 x 72 x 40 In. 945.00
Table, Dining, Biedermeier, Bird's-Eye Maple, Square Leg, 3 Leaves, 31 x 50 In................ 2940.00
Table, Dining, Biedermeier, Oval, 3-Part Base, Ball Feet, 30 x 75 x 48 In. 1180.00
Table, Dining, Carl Hansen & Sons, c.1950, 30 x 39 x 71 In.................................. 5100.00
Table, Dining, Cherry, 5-Board Top, Breadboard, Extensions, 30 x 74 x 35 In. 2420.00
Table, Dining, Chippendale Style, Mahogany, Gateleg, Oval, 1800s, 28 x 65 In. 410.00
Table, Dining, Drop Leaf, 18th-Century Style, Oak, Tapered Support, Pad Feet, 84 x 22 In. 1240.00
Table, Dining, Drop Leaf, 6 Turned Spiral-Carved Legs, c.1825, 29 x 52 In. 558.00
Table, Dining, Drop Leaf, Aalto, Birch, Bentwood, Laminate Top, 28 x 30 In. 1416.00
Table, Dining, Drop Leaf, Cherry, Turned Legs, Ball Feet, c.1825, 46 x 44 In. 215.00
Table, Dining, Drop Leaf, Chippendale, Arched Apron, Pa., c.1770, 28 x 55 x 48 In. 13145.00
Table, Dining, Drop Leaf, Chippendale, Mahogany, Claw & Ball Feet, c.1785, 61 x 53 In. 2390.00
Table, Dining, Drop Leaf, Empire, Mahogany, Center Column, Quatrefoil Base, 29 x 42 In. 290.00
Table, Dining, Drop Leaf, Federal, Cherry, Overhang Top, c.1790, 28 x 47 x 47 In. 560.00
Table, Dining, Drop Leaf, Federal, Cherry, Turned Legs, c.1815, 60 x 46 In. 390.00
Table, Dining, Drop Leaf, Federal, Maple, Square Tapered Legs, c.1800, 29 x 46 In. 2000.00
Table, Dining, Drop Leaf, Federal, Walnut, Southern U.S., Early 1800s, 29 x 46 In. 470.00
Table, Dining, Drop Leaf, G. Stickley, Cherry, Spoon Feet, c.1950, 30 x 40 x 29 In. 345.00
Table, Dining, Drop Leaf, George III, Mahogany, Demilune, c.1800, 30 x 16 x 48 In. 1000.00
Table, Dining, Drop Leaf, Hepplewhite Style, Mahogany, Late 1800s, 30 x 23 In. Closed 385.00
Table, Dining, Drop Leaf, Hepplewhite, Hardwood, Square Legs, 29 x 40 In. 175.00
Table, Dining, Drop Leaf, Hepplewhite, Swing-Out Leg Supports, 28 x 16 x 47 In. 115.00
Table, Dining, Drop Leaf, Mahogany, Pedestal, Splayed Legs, Paw Feet, 29 x 52 In. 1765.00
Table, Dining, Drop Leaf, Neoclassical, 2 Faux Drawers, Pedestal, Claw Feet, 29 x 40 In. 1035.00
Table, Dining, Drop Leaf, Neoclassical, Mahogany, S-Scroll Legs, Paw Feet, 29 x 25 In. 1469.00
Table, Dining, Drop Leaf, Oak, England, Late 18th Century, 28 x 64 x 54 In.................... 355.00
Table, Dining, Drop Leaf, Queen Anne, Cherry, Valanced Skirt, c.1760, 28 x 42 In. 2705.00
Table, Dining, Drop Leaf, Queen Anne, Mahogany, Cabriole Legs, 1700s, 28 x 49 x 19 In. 1725.00
Table, Dining, Drop Leaf, Queen Anne, Mahogany, Oval, Brunswick, Maine, 69 x 52 In. 865.00
Table, Dining, Drop Leaf, Queen Anne, Maple, Rounded Ends, 28 x 36 In. 375.00
Table, Dining, Drop Leaf, Sheraton, Cherry, 28 1/4 x 47 x 21 In. 605.00
Table, Dining, Drop Leaf, Sheraton, Cherry, 31 x 48 x 23 In. 690.00
Table, Dining, Drop Leaf, Sheraton, Mahogany, Reeded Legs, c.1810, 30 x 93 In. 1495.00
Table, Dining, Drop Leaf, Sheraton, Mahogany, Turned Legs, 29 x 48 x 17 In. 290.00

Table, Dining, Drop Leaf, Turned Legs, Ball Feet, Early 1800s, 30 x 54 In. 300.00
Table, Dining, Drop Leaf, Walnut, Trestle, c.1960, 28 3/4 x 66 1/6 x 62 In. 9000.00
Table, Dining, Federal Style, Mahogany, Double Pedestal, 3 Leaves, 29 x 45 x 72 In. 1898.00
Table, Dining, Federal Style, Mahogany, Rounded Corners, 1900s, 31 x 64 x 43 In. 2240.00
Table, Dining, Federal, Mahogany, Carved, D-Shape, Swing Supports, c.1810, 50 x 96 In. 4900.00
Table, Dining, Federal, Mahogany, Cherry, D-Shape, 9 Turned & Reeded Legs 2160.00
Table, Dining, Finn Juhl, 2 Leaves, France & Sons, c.1952, 29 x 73 x 40 In. 3600.00
Table, Dining, Finn Juhl, Teak, Boat Top, Tapered Dowel Legs, Baker, 29 x 68 x 47 In. 710.00
Table, Dining, Frank Lloyd Wright, Heritage Hendredon, c.1956, 29 x 42 x 64 In. 1200.00
Table, Dining, Frankl, Cork, 2 Leaves, Johnson Furniture Co., c.1950, 29 x 42 x 72 In. 1680.00
Table, Dining, Frankl, Mahogany, Cork Top, Grooved Edges, Leaves, 29 x 72 In. 1800.00
Table, Dining, French Provincial, Oak, Draw Leaf, 20th Century, 30 x 59 In. 590.00
Table, Dining, French Provincial, Walnut, Extension, 28 x 43 x 74 In. 1530.00
Table, Dining, G. Nakashima, Round Top, Flared Dowel Legs, 29 x 54 In. 8850.00
Table, Dining, G. Nakashima, Sundra, Boat Top, Plank Legs, Widdicomb, 29 x 72 In. 3185.00
Table, Dining, G. Nakashima, Walnut, Round, Flared & Tapered Legs, 29 x 48 In. 4425.00
Table, Dining, G. Nelson, Laminate Top, Chrome Base, Herman Miller, 30 x 72 In. 1770.00
Table, Dining, G. Stickley, Round Top, Tapered Legs, Signed, 54 x 28 In. 1880.00
Table, Dining, George III Style, Mahogany, 2 Pedestals, 28 1/2 x 54 In. 1765.00
Table, Dining, George III Style, Mahogany, 3 Pedestals, 1900s, 29 x 40 In. 1880.00
Table, Dining, George III Style, Mahogany, Inlay, 20th Century, 65 3/4 In. 1298.00
Table, Dining, George III Style, Mahogany, Inlay, Round, Pedestal, 1900s, 29 x 66 In. 1300.00
Table, Dining, George III, Mahogany, 2 Pedestals, Early 1800s, 29 x 95 In. 5875.00
Table, Dining, George III, Mahogany, 3 4-Footed Pedestals, 28 x 46 x 103 In. 3600.00
Table, Dining, George III, Mahogany, 3 Pedestals, Leaf Carved, 2 Leaves, 29 x 120 In. 3290.00
Table, Dining, Georgian Style, Mahogany, 3 Pedestals, 1900s, 30 x 111 x 46 In. 1180.00
Table, Dining, Georgian, Mahogany, Extension, Square Tapered Supports, 89 In. 615.00
Table, Dining, Henredon, Walnut, Oval, Antiqued Base, 2 Leaves, c.1965, 30 x 45 In. 70.00
Table, Dining, Hepplewhite Style, Mahogany, Round, Banded Inlay, 6 Legs, 30 x 24 In. 550.00
Table, Dining, Herman Miller, Walnut Veneer, Chrome, Rectangular, 30 x 78 x 36 In. 1060.00
Table, Dining, Karl Springer, Double Pedestal, Lacquered Goatskin, 29 x 72 x 48 In. 3420.00
Table, Dining, Louis XVI Style, Walnut Top, Cream Painted Skirt & Legs, 29 x 72 In. 590.00
Table, Dining, Mahogany Veneer, Diamond Inlay, 31 x 70 x 44 In. 1180.00
Table, Dining, Mahogany, Extension, Crank, Maple & Co., 30 x 85 x 60 In. 6000.00
Table, Dining, Mahogany, Faux Marquetry, Flowers, Scrollwork, Dutch, 31 x 45 In. 1595.00
Table, Dining, Mahogany, Round, Turned Split Column, Claw Feet, 3 Leaves, 30 x 48 In. 300.00
Table, Dining, Mahogany, Veneers, Oval, Duck Feet, 29 1/2 x 55 1/2 x 40 In. 345.00
Table, Dining, Milo Baughman, Parson Style, Burl Veneer, 29 x 78 In. 2880.00
Table, Dining, Neoclassical, Mahogany, 4-Column Pedestal, c.1830, 29 x 52 x 90 In. 4406.00
Table, Dining, Neoclassical, Mahogany, Pedestal, D-Shape, c.1840, 29 x 44 x 65 In. 4700.00
Table, Dining, Old Hickory, Refectory Style, Splayed Stretcher Base, 30 x 54 In. 3900.00
Table, Dining, P. Evans, Sculpted Bronze, Glass Top, Stalagmite Base, 1973, 30 x 84 In. 5605.00
Table, Dining, Paul Mayen, Glass Top, Chrome Base, Habitat, c.1970, 29 x 54 In. 360.00
Table, Dining, Pine, Plank Top, Breadboard Ends, Tapered Legs, 1900s, 30 x 97 x 49 In. 445.00
Table, Dining, Regency Style, Burl Walnut, Oval, Splayed Horseshoe Base, 30 x 75 In. 2585.00
Table, Dining, Regency Style, Mahogany, 2 3-Leg Pedestals, 3 Leaves, 30 x 46 x 64 In. 9000.00
Table, Dining, Regency Style, Mahogany, 2 Pedestals, Splayed Legs, 29 x 70 x 42 In. 945.00
Table, Dining, Regency Style, Mahogany, Banded, 2 Pedestals, 3-Part Base, 29 x 126 In. 1059.00
Table, Dining, Regency Style, Mahogany, Extension, Round Top, 31 x 61 In. 11750.00
Table, Dining, Regency Style, Mahogany, Greek Key Border, Oval, Splayed Legs, 70 In. 2115.00
Table, Dining, Regency Style, Mahogany, Parcel Gilt, 3 Dolphins, Paw Feet, 28 x 58 In. 2940.00
Table, Dining, Regency, Mahogany, 2 Pedestals, 28 x 49 x 75 In. 10800.00
Table, Dining, Robsjohn-Gibbings, Bleached Mahogany, Dowel Legs, 29 x 88 In. 3600.00
Table, Dining, Rosewood, Hand Crafted, East India, 28 x 96 x 44 In. 8965.00
Table, Dining, Russel Wright, Maple, Hinged Top, Heywood-Wakefield Co., 29 x 50 In. 1300.00
Table, Dining, Sheraton Style, Mahogany, Double Pedestal, 1900s, 30 x 96 x 46 In. 2360.00
Table, Dining, Split Pedestal, Round Top, Curved Feet, 4 Leaves, 29 1/2 x 54 In. 8225.00
Table, Dining, Split Pedestal, Round Top, Tapered Base, Shoe Feet, 4 Leaves, 30 x 54 In. 2235.00
Table, Dining, Stefan Siwinski, Wood, Steel, Korina Designs, c.1970, 29 x 42 In. 550.00
Table, Dining, Stickley Bros., No. 2404, Mahogany, 5 Legs, 54 x 29 In. 3850.00
Table, Dining, Teak, Oval, Tapered Legs, Denmark, c.1965, 29 x 35 x 68 In. 50.00

Table, Dining, Tommi Parzinger, Parquetry Top, Fluted Legs, 30 x 68 x 39 In. 2596.00
Table, Dining, V. Kagan, Cubist, Zebrawood, Glass Top, 29 x 74 x 44 In. 7080.00
Table, Dining, Victorian, Oak, Baluster & Flute-Carved Legs, Square, 29 x 47 x 47 In. 405.00
Table, Dining, Victorian, Oak, Square, 5 Flute-Carved Legs, 30 x 44 x 44 In. 200.00
Table, Dining, Walnut, Burl Walnut Veneer, Glass Top, Flared Legs, Oval, Italy, 31 x 78 In. 885.00
Table, Dining, William IV Style, Mahogany, 3 Pedestals, Paw Casters, 30 x 52 In. 6460.00
Table, Dining, William IV Style, Mahogany, Patera Carving, 30 x 52 In. 8225.00
Table, Directoire Style, Mahogany, 2 Drawers, Early 1900s, 26 x 24 In., Pair 880.00
Table, Directoire Style, Mahogany, Round Marble Top, 3 Gilt Columns, 61 x 61 In. 815.00
Table, Directoire, Mahogany, Drawers, Extending Surface, 37 x 22 x 44 In. 760.00
Table, Drafting, Oak, Adjustable, c.1915, 32 1/4 x 42 x 31 In. 375.00
Table, Dragons, 3 Drawers, Brass Pulls, Mortised Joints, Spade Feet, Chinese, 34 x 64 In. 920.00
Table, Dressing, Basswood, Pine, Drawer, 2-Board Top, 30 x 15 3/4 x 26 1/2 In. 460.00
Table, Dressing, Empire Style, Mahogany, Ormolu, Mirror, Round, c.1850, 67 In. 7050.00
Table, Dressing, Federal, Mahogany, Philadelphia, Early 1800s, 32 x 24 x 21 In. 6169.00
Table, Dressing, George II Style, Mahogany, Kneehole, 3 Drawers, c.1850, 31 x 37 In. 590.00
Table, Dressing, Louis Phillipe, Rosewood, Lift Top, Mirror, Cabriole Legs, 32 x 39 In. 355.00
Table, Dressing, Louis XV Style, Walnut, Serpentine Top, 3 Drawers, 30 x 45 In. 295.00
Table, Dressing, M.F. Cahoon, Pine, 3 Drawers, Morning Glories, 34 x 36 x 20 In. 405.00
Table, Dressing, Mahogany, 5 Drawers, Gallery, England, c.1850, 32 x 42 x 22 In. 1410.00
Table, Dressing, Mahogany, Veneer, Inlaid Mirror, Dovetailed Drawers, 27 x 26 x 9 In. 460.00
Table, Dressing, Mahogany, Veneer, Marquetry, Floral, 39 x 20 x 57 In. 1150.00
Table, Dressing, Neoclassical, Painted, Parcel Gilt, Faux Green Marble, 29 x 45 In. 940.00
Table, Dressing, Pine, Yellow Paint, Gold, Black Stencil, Drawer, 31 1/2 x 16 In. 2990.00
Table, Dressing, Queen Anne Style, Walnut, 4 Drawers, 1800s, 33 x 36 x 22 In. 4780.00
Table, Dressing, Queen Anne Style, Yew, 20th Century, 30 x 44 x 22 In. 355.00
Table, Dressing, Queen Anne, 3 Drawers, 18th Century, 27 x 30 x 18 1/2 In. 710.00
Table, Dressing, Queen Anne, Walnut Herringbone Veneer, 3 Drawers, 30 x 34 In. 5580.00
Table, Dressing, Queen Anne, Walnut, Inlaid Fan, 5 Drawers, 1700s, 30 x 30 x 19 In. 2115.00
Table, Dressing, Renaissance Revival, Gilt Brass, Continental, 1800s, 23 x 15 1/2 In. 355.00
Table, Drop Leaf, Aesthetic Revival, Spindled Gallery, England, c.1885, 24 x 24 In. 235.00
Table, Drop Leaf, Cherry, Poplar, Drawer, Rope Twist Legs, Ball Feet, 36 x 19 x 29 In. 1150.00
Table, Drop Leaf, Chippendale, Cherry, Overhang, Straight Apron, Late 1700s, 28 x 19 In. 1880.00
Table, Drop Leaf, Chippendale, Maple, Block Molded Legs, c.1780, 26 x 38 x 21 In. 403.00
Table, Drop Leaf, Curly Maple, 2-Board Top, Curved Drawer Front, 29 x 40 x 21 In. 920.00
Table, Drop Leaf, Drawer, Cut Corners, Quatrefoil Base, 29 x 39 x 25 In. 4600.00
Table, Drop Leaf, English Oak, Barley Twist Legs, Oval Top, 48 x 60 In. 2995.00
Table, Drop Leaf, Federal Style, Mahogany, 19th Century, 30 x 50 x 35 In. 265.00
Table, Drop Leaf, Federal, 3 Drawers, Tapered Spiral Legs, Casters, 30 x 17 x 18 In. 1920.00
Table, Drop Leaf, Federal, Mahogany, 2 Drawers, Tapered Legs, 29 x 15 x 18 In. 530.00
Table, Drop Leaf, Federal, Mahogany, 3 Sections, Demilune Ends, c.1800, 152 x 48 In. 7170.00
Table, Drop Leaf, Federal, Mahogany, Pine, Acanthus Leaves, 6 Legs, 29 x 54 x 29 In. 748.00
Table, Drop Leaf, Federal, Red Paint, Ring Turned Legs, 27 1/2 x 55 x 29 In. 655.00
Table, Drop Leaf, G. Nakashima, Trapezoid, Half-Circle Sides, 59 x 47 x 28 In. 2940.00
Table, Drop Leaf, George III, Mahogany, Chamfered Square Supports, 72 In. 525.00
Table, Drop Leaf, George III, Mahogany, Tapered Square Legs, 29 x 43 x 36 In. 1880.00
Table, Drop Leaf, Georgian, Mahogany, 2 Short Drawers, Pedestal, 28 x 28 In. 1430.00
Table, Drop Leaf, Georgian, Mahogany, D-Shape Leaves, 1700s, 28 x 37 In. 2350.00
Table, Drop Leaf, Georgian, Mahogany, Ireland, Late 1700s, 29 x 79 x 50 In. 8225.00
Table, Drop Leaf, Henkel Harris, Queen Anne Style, Oval, 20th Century, 29 1/2 x 48 In. 445.00
Table, Drop Leaf, Hepplewhite, Birch, Round Leaves, Old Red Paint, 28 x 41 x 16 In. 165.00
Table, Drop Leaf, Hepplewhite, Burl Walnut, Pegged Mortise Joints, 42 In. 9315.00
Table, Drop Leaf, Hepplewhite, Cherry, 28 x 32 x 18 In. 290.00
Table, Drop Leaf, Hepplewhite, Cherry, Tapered Legs, New England, 1800s 385.00
Table, Drop Leaf, Hepplewhite, Maple Top, Cherry Base, 25 x 30 x 15 In. 920.00
Table, Drop Leaf, Hepplewhite, Poplar, Cypress, 2-Board Top, 51 x 30 1/4 In. 575.00
Table, Drop Leaf, Mahogany, c.1800, 29 x 48 x 49 In. 1080.00
Table, Drop Leaf, Mahogany, Pedestal, Drawer, 19th Century, 28 x 42 x 42 In. 765.00
Table, Drop Leaf, Maple, c.1820, 28 x 19 x 41 In. 900.00
Table, Drop Leaf, Napoleon III, Ebonized Fruitwood, Gilt Brass Mounted, 29 x 46 In. 3525.00
Table, Drop Leaf, Neoclassical, Mahogany, Reeded Edge, Baltimore, c.1810, 29 x 72 In. 2645.00

Table, Drop Leaf, Neoclassical, Rosewood, England, c.1840, 29 x 35 x 36 In. 1295.00
Table, Drop Leaf, Neoclassical, Tiger Maple, Drawers, Acorn Pendants, c.1830, 28 x 17 In. 765.00
Table, Drop Leaf, Oak, Gateleg, Turned Supports, Spanish Hoof Feet, 1700s, 28 x 58 In. 970.00
Table, Drop Leaf, Oak, Oval Plank Top, Gateleg, Ball Feet, 28 1/2 x 61 1/2 x 48 In. 2124.00
Table, Drop Leaf, Oak, Removable Breadboard, 17th Century, Opens To 88 In. 3155.00
Table, Drop Leaf, Old Hickory, Spindle Gatelegs, Oval Oak Top, 29 1/2 x 49 x 36 In. 2056.00
Table, Drop Leaf, Pine, Drawer, Square Legs, Peg Feet, Casters, 29 x 71 x 47 In. 445.00
Table, Drop Leaf, Queen Anne Style, Mahogany, Pad Feet, c.1850, 28 x 45 x 42 In. 998.00
Table, Drop Leaf, Queen Anne Style, Swing Leg, 29 x 36 1/2 x 35 In. 295.00
Table, Drop Leaf, Queen Anne, Mahogany, Dutch Feet, England, 28 x 42 x 13 In. 635.00
Table, Drop Leaf, Queen Anne, Maple, D-Shape Leaves, Scalloped Apron, 26 x 26 In. 646.00
Table, Drop Leaf, Queen Anne, Walnut, 6 Legs, 2 Swing Legs, 1700s, 53 x 39 In. 1135.00
Table, Drop Leaf, Queen Anne, Walnut, D-Shape Leaves, Round Legs, 1700s, 29 x 40 In. 1058.00
Table, Drop Leaf, Queen Anne, Walnut, Figured, Pa., c.1760, 28 x 18 In. 8400.00
Table, Drop Leaf, Queen Anne, Walnut, Tapered Legs, Pad Feet, 28 x 53 x 42 In. 530.00
Table, Drop Leaf, Regency Style, Mahogany, String Inlay, Late 1800s, 28 x 63 In. 1060.00
Table, Drop Leaf, Regency, Mahogany, Banded Top, Drawers, 1800s, 28 x 36 1/2 In. 5875.00
Table, Drop Leaf, Regency, Mahogany, Drawers, Columnar Legs, 28 x 37 x 18 In. 1120.00
Table, Drop Leaf, Regency, Mahogany, Ebony Inlay, 2 Drawers, Pedestal, 28 x 33 In. 3680.00
Table, Drop Leaf, Regency, Mahogany, Pedestal, 28 x 44 x 40 In. 470.00
Table, Drop Leaf, Regency, Mahogany, Pedestal, Early 1800s, 28 x 44 In. 415.00
Table, Drop Leaf, Rococo Revival, Walnut, Gadrooned, Scrolled Trestle Base, 30 x 30 In. 1410.00
Table, Drop Leaf, Satinwood, Columnar Legs, 28 1/4 x 51 x 30 1/2 In. 1890.00
Table, Drop Leaf, Sheraton, Birch, Painted, Turned Legs, Pegged Joints, 36 x 14 x 27 In. 575.00
Table, Drop Leaf, Sheraton, Cherry, 44 x 20 In. 220.00
Table, Drop Leaf, Sheraton, Cherry, Turned Legs, Castors, 29 1/2 x 47 x 16 1/2 In. 385.00
Table, Drop Leaf, Sheraton, Cherry, Turned Legs, Tapered Feet, 44 x 30 In. 400.00
Table, Drop Leaf, Sheraton, Curly Maple, Cherry, Ball & Peg Feet, Ohio, 28 x 17 In. 1325.00
Table, Drop Leaf, Sheraton, Figured Maple, Cut Corners, Turned Legs, 28 x 42 x 20 In. 865.00
Table, Drop Leaf, Sheraton, Mahogany, 2 Drawers, Portland, Maine, 17 x 20 x 29 In. 290.00
Table, Drop Leaf, Sheraton, Mahogany, 3 Sections, c.1835, 29 x 107 In. 2350.00
Table, Drop Leaf, Sheraton, Mahogany, Maple, 1800s, 40 1/2 In. 330.00
Table, Drop Leaf, Sheraton, Old Red Paint, Drawer, Turned Legs, 29 1/2 x 42 In. 165.00
Table, Drop Leaf, Sheraton, Pine, Maple, Turned Legs, Mortise & Peg, 41 x 17 In. 345.00
Table, Drop Leaf, Sutherland, Edwardian, Mahogany, Crossbanded, Tapered Legs, 22 1/2 In. 285.00
Table, Drop Leaf, Teak, Extension, c.1965, 29 x 37 x 50 In. 115.00
Table, Drop Leaf, Tiger Maple, Tapered Square Legs, 42 1/4 x 40 1/2 In. 1898.00
Table, Drop Leaf, Walnut, Arched, Carved Apron, Square Legs, Pa., c.1800, 43 x 34 In. 1135.00
Table, Drop Leaf, Walnut, Turned Legs, c.1850, 29 x 40 x 25 In. 230.00
Table, Drop Leaf, William & Mary, Maple, Sycamore, Pine Top, 27 x 43 In. 17625.00
Table, Drop Leaf, William & Mary, Oval Top, Gateleg, Early 1700s, 26 x 43 1/2 In. 6465.00
Table, Drum, Georgian Style, Mahogany, Leather Top, 8 Faux Drawers, 1900s, 30 x 52 In. 649.00
Table, Drum, Regency, 4 Frieze Drawers, 4 Hipped Saber Legs, 29 x 48 In. 4115.00
Table, Drum, Regency, Mahogany, Leather Top, Tripod Base, Early 1800s, 29 x 36 In. 3525.00
Table, Drum, William IV Style, Mahogany, String Inlay, Leather, Drawers, 31 x 49 In. 2585.00
Table, Eames, Blond Mahogany Plywood, Chrome Legs, Folding, 29 x 54 x 34 In. 60.00
Table, Eames, CTM, Round, P. Evans, c.1948, 16 x 34 In. 3240.00
Table, Eastlake Style, Walnut, Hinged Top, Late 19th Century, 28 x 19 x 16 In. 236.00
Table, Eastlake, Ebonized, Splayed Legs, Drawer, Turned Legs, 29 x 39 In. 499.00
Table, Edwardian, Boxwood, Mahogany Inlay, Raised Shelf Stretcher, 29 1/2 x 30 In. 175.00
Table, Edwardian, Mahogany, Folding, 8-Sided, c.1900, 20 x 24 In. 470.00
Table, Edwardian, Mahogany, Inlaid, Oval Tiers, Bellflower Supports, 39 x 21 1/2 In. 950.00
Table, Edwardian, Mahogany, Satinwood Inlay, 8-Sided Top, c.1890, 30 x 30 In. 410.00
Table, Edwardian, Satinwood, Marquetry, Bowfront, 29 x 10 1/2 In., Pair 1940.00
Table, Elizabethan Style, Draw Top, Hub & Block Legs, c.1700, 30 x 24 x 66 In. 7765.00
Table, Elm, Green Lacquer, Drawer, Cabriole Legs, Chinese, 33 x 33 x 17 In. 413.00
Table, Elm, Green Marble, Rectangular Top, Chinese, 33 x 38 x 16 In. 649.00
Table, Elm, Lacquer, Apron, Rectangular Legs, Chinese, 22 x 15 x 10 In., Pair 295.00
Table, Elm, Lute, Chinese, c.1850, 33 x 39 x 19 In. 325.00
Table, Empire Style, Gilt Bronze, Marble Top, Early 1900s, 27 x 17 In. 2350.00
Table, Empire Style, Gilt Bronze, Marble Top, Round, 28 x 12 In., Pair 2115.00

Furniture, Table, G. Stickley, Arched Cross Stretchers, Faceted Finial, 29 x 24 In.

Furniture, Table, G. Stickley, Mortised Legs , Stacked, Finial, 28 x 24 In.

Table, Empire Style, Mahogany, Brass Mounted, Late 1800s, 30 x 24 In. 2350.00
Table, Empire Style, Mahogany, Marble, Gilt Bronze, c.1900, 40 x 49 x 30 In. 6000.00
Table, Empire Style, Patinated Bronze, 3 Shelves, Greek Key Border, 36 x 25 In., Pair 5640.00
Table, Empire, Mahogany, Poplar, Swivel & Flip Top, Quatrefoil Base, 31 x 34 In. 115.00
Table, English Oak, Gateleg, Early 20th Century, 28 x 35 1/2 x 16 In. 470.00
Table, Farm, Cypress, Plain Skirt, Square Tapered Legs, Louisiana, 1800s, 29 x 39 In. 1765.00
Table, Farm, Pine, Plank Top, 2 Drawers, 1800s, 33 x 93 x 36 In. 1535.00
Table, Farm, Red Paint, 3-Board Top, Drawer, Shaped Apron, 30 x 75 x 41 In. 470.00
Table, Federal Style, Mahogany, 3 Parts, 1900s, 29 x 127 x 47 In. 1840.00
Table, Federal, Butternut, Pine, Overhang Top, New England, c.1800, 28 x 42 In. 999.00
Table, Federal, Figured Mahogany, Inlaid, Baltimore, c.1795, 28 1/2 x 21 In. 4500.00
Table, Federal, Mahogany Veneers, Marble Top, Pedestal, Paw Feet, 31 1/2 x 40 In. 1610.00
Table, Federal, Mahogany, Carved, Veneer, 32 1/4 x 24 x 13 1/4 In. 4995.00
Table, Federal, Mahogany, Outset Spiral Posts, Lyre Supports, Splayed Legs, 29 x 20 In. 3230.00
Table, Federal, Mahogany, String Inlay, Drawer, Straight Skirt, c.1800, 28 x 18 In. 825.00
Table, Federal, Mahogany, Veneer, 5 Turned Legs, 2 Swing Legs, 30 x 50 In. 1765.00
Table, Federal, Mixed Wood, Square Plank Top, Tapered Legs, 28 x 18 x 18 In. 355.00
Table, Federal, Tiger Maple, Drawers, Baluster Legs, Peg Feet, 27 1/2 x 24 3/4 x 19 In. 826.00
Table, Florence Knoll, Rosewood, Square, Post 1950, 17 x 27 In. 390.00
Table, Florence Knoll, Square, c.1960, 19 x 20 In., Pair 840.00
Table, Fontana Arte, Glass Top, Round, Bronze Hinges, 8-Sided Feet, 17 x 32 In. 4248.00
Table, Fontana Arte, Mahogany, Glass Top, 16 Circles, Iron Feet, 17 x 35 In. 5899.00
Table, Frank Lloyd Wright, Usonian, Hexagonal Top, 6-Slab Base, 19 1/2 x 42 In. 1140.00
Table, Frankl, Laminated Cork, Clip Corners, 22 x 32 In. 1180.00
Table, French Provincial, Cherry, Ash, 2 Drawers, c.1830, 31 x 63 In. 588.00
Table, French Provincial, Fruitwood, Rectangular Top, Drawer, 29 x 56 In. 560.00
Table, French Provincial, Fruitwood, Round, 3-Section Pedestal, 29 x 32 In. 1880.00
Table, French Provincial, Fruitwood, Square Legs, 30 x 124 In. 245.00
Table, French Provincial, Hardwood, Planked, Paneled Frieze, 14 1/2 x 60 1/2 In. 2585.00
Table, French Provincial, Oak, Carved, 2 Drawers, c.1950, 22 x 27 x 24 In. 144.00
Table, French Provincial, Painted, Round, Twig & Post, 1900s, 29 x 47 In. 530.00
Table, French Provincial, Walnut, Galleried Top, Storage Below, Early 1800s, 16 In. 345.00
Table, French Provincial, Walnut, Oval, Spindled Gallery, 5 Shelves, 31 x 30 In. 1057.00
Table, Fruitwood, Marble Top, Shaped Apron, Turned Fluted Legs, 32 x 71 In. 1290.00
Table, G. Durand, Louis XV, Rosewood, Ormolu, Marble Top, c.1810, 28 x 17 In. 3525.00
Table, G. Nakashima, Free Edge, Walnut, Rectangular, 17 x 29 x 28 In. 3585.00
Table, G. Nakashima, Free Edge, Walnut, Spindle Shelf, Dowel Legs, 21 x 28 In., Pair 9440.00
Table, G. Nakashima, Portsmouth, Rectangular Top, Plank Legs, 21 x 28 x 20 In. 8260.00
Table, G. Nakashima, Walnut, Round Top, 3 Tapered Legs, 21 x 26 In. 1800.00
Table, G. Nakashima, Walnut, Tricornered, 21 x 27 x 21 1/2 In. 2800.00
Table, G. Stickley, Arched Cross Stretchers, Faceted Finial, 29 x 24 In. *ILLUS* 1410.00
Table, G. Stickley, Cross Stretcher, Through Tenons, 30 x 40 x 28 In. 6465.00
Table, G. Stickley, Director's, Rectangular, Splayed Legs, Shoefoot, 72 x 36 x 30 In. 8815.00
Table, G. Stickley, Eastwood, Round, Mortised Legs, Crossed Stretchers, 23 x 24 In. 7640.00
Table, G. Stickley, Mortised Legs, Stacked, Finial, 28 x 24 In. . . . . *ILLUS* 12925.00
Table, G. Stickley, Overhanging Top, Upended Stretcher, Mortised, 30 x 40 x 28 In. 2235.00
Table, G. Stickley, Round Top, Arched Cross Stretcher, Central Faceted, 30 x 29 In. 2350.00

Table, G. Stickley, Square, Clipped Corners, Lower Shelf, 29 x 24 x 24 In. 1645.00
Table, Galle, Art Nouveau, Fruitwood, Dragonflies, Early 1900s, 30 x 16 x 24 In. 1885.00
Table, Galle, Mahogany, 2 Tiers, Marquetry, 1800s, 40 1/2 x 17 3/8 In. 3415.00
Table, Galle, Mahogany, 2 Tiers, Marquetry, 1800s, 44 x 16 1/2 In. 2795.00
Table, Game, Anglo-Indian, Hardwood, Flip Top, Urn Stem, Colonial, c.1830, 31 x 36 x 18 In. 1175.00
Table, Game, Black Paint, 4 Drawers, Checkerboard Top, c.1820, 29 x 18 In. 765.00
Table, Game, Chip-Carved Tree, Rounded Corners, 4 Open Compartments, 29 x 27 In. 150.00
Table, Game, Edwardian, Mahogany, Holly Inlay, Handkerchief Point, 92 x 22 In. 1880.00
Table, Game, Edwardian, Mahogany, Kingwood, Inlay Trisected Top, c.1900, 29 x 31 In. 499.00
Table, Game, Empire, Mahogany, Flip Top, Pedestal, 4-Footed, c.1850, 29 x 36 In. 385.00
Table, Game, Federal Style, Mahogany, Flip Top, D-Shape, Early 1800s, 29 x 36 In. 1770.00
Table, Game, Federal, Mahogany, Bellflower Inlay, Serpentine Top, 30 x 36 In. 390.00
Table, Game, Federal, Mahogany, Elliptical Top, Reeded Edge, Legs, Peg Feet, 29 x 37 In. 956.00
Table, Game, Federal, Mahogany, Serpentine Edge, Turned & Reeded Legs, 29 x 37 In. 1175.00
Table, Game, Federal, Mahogany, Serpentine Flip Top, 30 x 35 3/4 x 17 3/4 In. 1005.00
Table, Game, French Provincial, Scalloped Skirt, Cabriole Legs, 31 x 34 x 17 In. 176.00
Table, Game, George II Style, Mahogany, Flip Top, Leather, 28 1/2 x 35 1/2 x 17 1/2 In. 325.00
Table, Game, George II, Mahogany, Accordion Action, Early 1700s, 28 x 31 x 16 In. 1528.00
Table, Game, George III, Mahogany, Rosewood Banded, c.1800, 29 x 36 In. 1645.00
Table, Game, George III, Mahogany, Shaped Apron, Flip Top, 36 In. 571.00
Table, Game, George III, Mahogany, String Inlaid Edge, Flip Top, Late 1800s, 29 x 35 In. 820.00
Table, Game, Georgian Style, Mahogany, Flip Top, c.1850, 29 x 36 In. 470.00
Table, Game, Karl Springer, Ivory Lacquer, Grasscloth Finish, Chrome, 29 x 48 In. 2950.00
Table, Game, Louis XVI Style, Fruitwood, Marquetry, Shaped Skirt, 29 x 27 In. 305.00
Table, Game, Mah-Jongg, Black Lacquer, Drawer, Scroll Border, Folding, c.1915, 28 x 34 In. 110.00
Table, Game, Mahogany, 2-Board Top, Urn Pedestal, 4 Saber Legs, 28 x 36 x 26 In. 6325.00
Table, Game, Mahogany, Carved Frieze, Ring & Spiral Turned Legs, Peg Feet, 29 x 48 In. 1315.00
Table, Game, Mahogany, Turret Corners, Frieze, Cabriole Legs, England, 29 x 36 In. 5500.00
Table, Game, Mahogany, Walnut, Leather, Swivel Top, Continental, c.1810, 27 x 23 In. 4800.00
Table, Game, Marquetry, Dutch, Early 19th Century, 29 x 28 x 14 In. 3420.00
Table, Game, Neoclassical, Bird's-Eye Maple, 8-Sided Top, Dutch, c.1820, 29 x 42 In. 2056.00
Table, Game, Neoclassical, Mahogany, Flip Top, Swivels, Phila., c.1830, 29 x 36 In. 2115.00
Table, Game, Neoclassical, Mahogany, Molded Top & Frieze, 1800s, 29 x 34 In. 206.00
Table, Game, Neoclassical, Mahogany, Square Tapered Pedestal, 29 x 33 In. 558.00
Table, Game, Parquetry Top, Baluster Support, 1900s, 27 x 21 In. 770.00
Table, Game, Queen Anne Style, Mixed Wood, Checkerboard, Pedestal, 26 x 15 x 15 In. 236.00
Table, Game, Queen Anne, Mahogany, Cabriole Legs, England, 1700s, 29 x 32 x 31 In. 1180.00
Table, Game, Queen Anne, Mahogany, Flip Top, Felt, England, 1700s, 29 x 33 x 32 In. 1890.00
Table, Game, Reform Movement, Walnut, Demilune Top, England, c.1885, 31 x 36 In. 325.00
Table, Game, Regency, Mahogany, Leather Surface, c.1815, 29 x 36 In. 1890.00
Table, Game, Regency, Rosewood, Brass Inlay, c.1810, 29 x 36 x 18 In. 2280.00
Table, Game, Revolving, 2-Sided, American Curtain Fixture Co., 34 x 17 In. 1410.00
Table, Game, Slots, Corner Disks, Cabriole Legs, Disk Padded Feet, England, 27 x 34 In. 7500.00
Table, Game, Walnut, Mahogany, Ebony, Maple, Marquetry, Parquetry, 25 x 30 In. 290.00
Table, Game, William IV, Flip Top, Inset Surface, 29 x 35 1/2 In. 815.00
Table, George II, Mahogany, Spider Gateleg, c.1765, 29 x 12 x 24 In. 2400.00
Table, George III Style, Demilune Top, Starburst Inlay, Square Legs, 28 x 42 x 22 In. 705.00
Table, George III Style, Mahogany, Carved, X-Stretcher, 19th Century, 28 x 21 x 28 In. 2230.00
Table, George III Style, Mahogany, Columnar Pedestal, 1800s, 29 x 60 In. 1534.00
Table, George III Style, Mahogany, Fluted Frieze, Bellflowers, c.1900, 31 x 61 In. 2585.00
Table, George III Style, Mahogany, Frieze, Chamfered Legs, 34 x 64 x 25 In. 3525.00
Table, George III Style, Mahogany, Inlaid, Oval, Tapered Legs, 2 Leaves, 29 x 110 In. 1998.00
Table, George III Style, Mahogany, Reeded Edge, 2 Pedestals, 29 x 58 In. 7638.00
Table, George III, Chinoiserie, Landscape, Black Lacquer, Tripod, c.1810, 28 x 18 In. 1410.00
Table, George III, Mahogany, Round Top, Raised Edge, Pedestal, 3 Legs, 28 x 18 In. 510.00
Table, George III, Mahogany, Satinwood, 3 Pedestals, 1900s, 30 x 47 x 140 In. 4700.00
Table, George III, Mahogany, Spider Gateleg, c.1765, 28 x 30 x 40 In. 4800.00
Table, George III, Mahogany, Spider Gateleg, c.1770, 28 x 13 x 32 In. 1800.00
Table, George III, Polychrome, Gilt, Hardstone Scene, Octagonal, c.1800, 25 x 22 In. 2230.00
Table, George III, Satinwood, Hardwood Inlay, Drawer, Tapered Legs, 29 x 34 x 28 In. 1525.00
Table, George III, Yew, Mahogany, Pedestal, 2 Drawers, 3-Footed, c.1770, 30 x 20 x 15 In. 3525.00

Only use one type of furniture polish. If you switch from an oil polish to a wax polish, the surface will appear smudged.

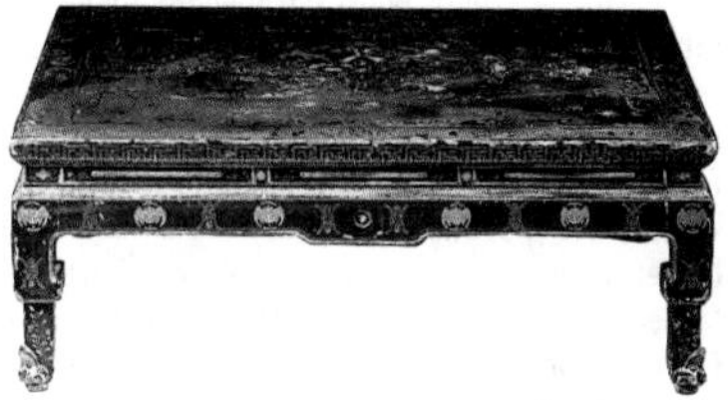

Furniture, Table, Lacquered, Gilt Design, Chinese

Table, George VI, Mahogany, Tiers, Cornucopia Supports, 27 x 27 In., Pair 1760.00
Table, Georgian Style, Burl Walnut, Pedestal Tripod Base, Early 1900s, 26 x 14 In. 265.00
Table, Georgian Style, Mahogany, Oval, Octagonal Pedestal, Splay Legs, 29 x 60 x 46 In. 415.00
Table, Georgian, Mahogany, Rectangular Top, Spider Gateleg, c.1900, 28 x 30 In. 2000.00
Table, Gilt Beech Top, Tiers, Dragon Legs, Italy, 1900, 27 1/2 In. 805.00
Table, Gilt Brass, Marble, Stretchers, France, 28 x 22 In., Pair 2585.00
Table, Guard Room, Mahogany, Plank Top, Iron Stretchers, 30 x 80 In. 1060.00
Table, Gueridon, Louis XV Style, Mahogany, Bronze Mounted, Marble, 24 x 29 In. 645.00
Table, Gueridon, Louis XV Style, Tulipwood, Kingwood, Late 1800s, 30 x 18 x 12 In. 645.00
Table, Gueridon, Neoclassical, Bronze, Marble, Scroll Legs, Ram's Head, 27 x 28 In., Pair 4995.00
Table, Gueridon, Philip & Kelvin LaVerne, Patinated Metal, 1950s, 21 x 12 In., Pair 7800.00
Table, Gueridon, Tiger Maple, Oval, 3 Scrolled Legs, Early 1800s, 27 x 22 x 19 In. 4820.00
Table, Guy Barker, Tripod, Round Top, Raymor, c.1951, 14 3/4 x 28 In. 660.00
Table, H. Van Kepple & Taylor Green, Mahogany, 1946, 14 3/4 x 34 x 66 In. 2880.00
Table, Hardwood, 1-Board Top, New England, 1700s, 27 x 34 x 24 1/2 In. 415.00
Table, Harvest, Drop Leaf, 28 x 65 x 17 In. 380.00
Table, Harvest, Hepplewhite Style, Birch, Pine, Tapered Legs, 72 x 29 1/2 In. 405.00
Table, Harvest, Maple, Pine, Dovetailed Drawer, 3-Board Top, 108 x 35 3/4 x 30 In. 2530.00
Table, Harvest, Pine Top, Cherry Legs, Aprons, 95 1/2 x 36 x 31 In. 865.00
Table, Harvest, Pine, Drop Leaf, 1800s, 31 x 72 x 23 In. 460.00
Table, Harvest, Pine, Drop Leaf, Tapered Legs, 2 Leaves, 29 x 85 In. 935.00
Table, Harvest, Softwood, Green Paint, Drop Leaf, Drawer, Turnip Feet, 1700s, 28 x 53 In. 2350.00
Table, Hepplewhite Style, George III, Mahogany, Demilune, Dentil Frieze, 33 In. 2000.00
Table, Hepplewhite, Curly Maple, Walnut, 2-Board Top, Pedestal, Spider Legs, 23 x 26 In. 230.00
Table, Hepplewhite, Mahogany, Molded Edge, Carved Design, Drawer, 10 x 6 x 7 In. 374.00
Table, Hepplewhite, Oak, Mahogany Veneer, 3 Drawers, England, 31 x 30 x 19 In. 865.00
Table, Hepplewhite, Pine, Drawer, Scallop Top, 20 x 15 1/2 In. 690.00
Table, Hepplewhite, Red Paint, Breadboard Top, Drawer, 24 x 28 x 28 In. 1840.00
Table, Hepplewhite, Wavy Birch, Tapered Legs, Maine, c.1800, 29 x 49 x 19 In. 520.00
Table, Herter Bros., Neogrecque, Inlaid, Ebonized, c.1870, 32 x 48 x 28 In. 5875.00
Table, I. Noguchi, White Formica-Covered Birch, Black Rods, Iron Base, 20 x 24 In. 1080.00
Table, Irish Regency, Mahogany, Carved Scroll Supports, Plinth Feet, 36 x 90 In. 4400.00
Table, J. Hoffmann, Beech, Laminated, Turned, Solid, c.1908, 26 x 19 1/2 In. 1600.00
Table, Jacobean Style, Oval Top, Gateleg, Spiral Twist Legs, 1900s, 25 x 24 x 18 In. 180.00
Table, John Dickinson, Tin, Galvanized, Brass, No. 107, 1970s, 24 x 27 In. 16800.00
Table, Jules Leleu, Steel, Bronze, Marble Top, Tripod Base, 19 3/4 x 35 In. 6209.00
Table, Kang, Rosewood, Flared Apron, Scrolled Cabriole Legs, Chinese, 7 x 31 In. 350.00
Table, Karl Springer, Cube, c.1975, 23 x 24 x 36 In. 600.00
Table, Karl Springer, Waterfall, Lacquered Basketweave Finish, 24 x 59 x 24 In. 1180.00
Table, Kem Weber, Mueller Furniture, c.1935, 22 x 14 x 25 In. 7200.00
Table, Kingwood, Rosewood, Drawers, Bronze Mount, France, 1800s, 32 x 79 x 40 In. 9400.00
Table, Lacquered, 3 Reserves, Landscape, Chinese, 15 1/2 x 43 x 17 3/4 In. 153.00
Table, Lacquered, Gilt Design, Chinese .... *ILLUS* 1888.00
Table, Lazy Susan, Pine, X-Stretcher, Straight Apron, 1800s, 30 x 48 In. 1320.00
Table, Lazy Susan, Yellow Pine, Oak, Spindle Axle, 32 x 55 In. 4140.00

Table, Leather Inset Top, Late 19th Century, 36 x 24 x 29 1/2 In. 410.00
Table, Library, Arts & Crafts, Oak, Dovetailed Drawer, Shelf, 31 x 42 In. 230.00
Table, Library, Baroque, Walnut, Iron Stretcher, Spain, 1800s, 33 x 61 x 39 In. 2595.00
Table, Library, Cherry, Bookcase Shelves, Spindle Galleries, c.1910, 29 x 37 x 24 In. 99.00
Table, Library, Empire Revival, Mahogany, Scrolled & Carved Pedestal, 30 x 60 x 26 In. 375.00
Table, Library, G. Stickley, 2 Drawers, Cast-Iron Oval Pulls, Corbels, 30 x 45 x 30 In. 2820.00
Table, Library, G. Stickley, Arched Apron, Lower Shelf, Tapered Legs, 29 x 50 x 29 In. 3240.00
Table, Library, G. Stickley, Round Top, Arched Aprons & Cross Stretchers, 29 x 40 In. 6465.00
Table, Library, G. Stickley, Tacked-On Leather Top, Trestle Base, 30 x 48 x 30 In. 9400.00
Table, Library, Gothic Revival, Oak, Carved Frieze, Trestle Base, 28 x 72 x 41 In. 679.00
Table, Library, Limbert, Oak, Drawer, Bookshelf Ends, 29 x 45 x 26 In. 865.00
Table, Library, Limbert, Oak, Ebony Inlay, Drawer, Shoe Foot, Cane Panels, 30 x 48 In. 3900.00
Table, Library, Mahogany, Carved, Lion's Masks, Shaped Stretcher Shelf, 28 x 46 In. 1410.00
Table, Library, Oak, 2 Drawers, Molded Top, c.1870-1880, 33 x 72 x 31 1/2 In. 2035.00
Table, Library, Oval Top, Divided Shelf, Chamfered Sides, Michigan Chair Co., 29 x 44 In. 720.00
Table, Library, Regency Style, Mahogany, Leather Inset, 30 x 49 x 27 In. 1440.00
Table, Library, Regency, Mahogany, Leather Top, 3 Drawers, Reeded Legs, 30 x 60 In. 4920.00
Table, Library, Regency, Rosewood, Leather Insert, Early 1800s, 29 x 44 x 27 In. 3055.00
Table, Library, Renaissance Revival, Mahogany, Leather, Drawers, c.1870, 31 x 59 x 30 In. 4700.00
Table, Library, Rococo Revival, Carved Apron, Griffin Supports, 1800s, 32 x 62 x 30 In. 1870.00
Table, Library, Shelf, Drawers, Lion-Carved Legs, 29 x 54 x 33 In. 1438.00
Table, Library, Spindled Sides, Blind Drawer, Shelf Stretcher, 30 x 30 x 24 In. 1060.00
Table, Library, Trestle, Molded Edge, Scroll & Shield Legs, 31 x 64 x 41 In. 1380.00
Table, Library, Victorian, Walnut, Red Leather Insert, Folding, 29 x 35 In. 200.00
Table, Library, William IV, Mahogany, Leather Top, Drawers, 30 x 53 In. 4113.00
Table, Library, William IV, Rosewood, Banded, Lyre Ends, c.1850, 27 x 42 In. 1116.00
Table, Louis XV Style, Kingwood, Faux Marquetry, Metal, Serpentine, 36 x 47 In. 1295.00
Table, Louis XV Style, Kingwood, Marquetry, Floral, Scroll Design, c.1900, 31 x 23 In. 2585.00
Table, Louis XV Style, Kingwood, Parquetry, Ormolu, c.1810, 26 In. 1760.00
Table, Louis XV Style, Leather, Drawer, Cabriole Legs, 31 x 55 x 26 In. 585.00
Table, Louis XV Style, Mahogany, Demilune, 32 x 33 x 14 In., Pair 345.00
Table, Louis XV Style, Mahogany, Drawer, 23 x 24 In. 645.00
Table, Louis XV Style, Mahogany, Ormolu, Marble Top, c.1890, 29 x 17 In. 590.00
Table, Louis XV Style, Marble Top, Round, Cabriole Legs, 32 x 24 In. 530.00
Table, Louis XV, Fruitwood, Black Marble Top, Gallery, 30 x 21 In. 765.00
Table, Louis XV, Fruitwood, Kidney Shape Top, Inlay, c.1900, 26 x 18 x 10 In., Pair 940.00
Table, Louis XV, Walnut, Fruitwood, Serpentine Frieze, Cabriole Legs, 29 x 32 x 22 In. 2905.00
Table, Louis XV, Walnut, Scalloped Skirt, Shell Cartouches, Cabriole Legs, 31 x 24 In. 1295.00
Table, Louis XVI Style, Beech, Marble Top, Gilt Metal, 1900s, 20 x 41 x 20 In. 1998.00
Table, Louis XVI Style, Bronze, Marble Top, Mahogany Skirt, Cloverleaf, 29 x 22 In. 4700.00
Table, Louis XVI Style, Cherry, Walnut, Paneled Skirt, Late 1800s, 28 x 41 In. 380.00
Table, Louis XVI Style, Gilt Bronze Mounted, 20th Century, 24 3/4 x 31 3/4 In. 590.00
Table, Louis XVI Style, Gilt, Marble Top, Pierced Frieze, 30 x 40 x 20 In. 2230.00
Table, Louis XVI Style, Mahogany, Marble Top, Brass Mount, c.1890, 26 x 15 In., Pair 1527.00
Table, Louis XVI Style, Mahogany, Marble Top, Round, Brass Gallery, 35 x 21 In. 1997.00
Table, Louis XVI Style, Mahogany, Ormolu, Marble Top, Drawer, 29 x 29 In. 1800.00
Table, Louis XVI Style, Mahogany, Satinwood, Gilt Bronze, 29 x 26 x 17 In. 6000.00
Table, Louis XVI Style, Marble Top, Polychrome, c.1910, 30 x 22 In. 1760.00
Table, Louis XVI, Brass, Smoked Glass, Tiers, Bamboo Turned, 23 x 21 x 7 In. 820.00
Table, Louis XVI, Kingwood, Rosewood, Tulipwood, Parquetry Top, 30 x 27 In. 5915.00
Table, Louis XVI, Mahogany, Brass Mounted, Gilt Tooled Surface, 29 x 21 x 33 In. 1048.00
Table, Louis XVI, Parquetry, Pullout Writing Surface, 1700s, 27 x 16 x 29 In. 3220.00
Table, Macassar Ebony, Parchment, French, c.1925, 17 1/4 x 30 In. 5760.00
Table, Mahogany Veneer, Marble Top, 2 Tiers, 29 1/4 x 18 x 14 1/2 In., Pair 430.00
Table, Mahogany, Beech, Brass Inlay, Early 1900s, 22 x 16 In., Pair 1290.00
Table, Mahogany, Brass Lattice Banding, Tapered Cuffed Legs, 29 x 30 x 19 In., Pair 2938.00
Table, Mahogany, Dutch Marquetry, Checker Band, X-Stretcher, 31 x 31 In. 3058.00
Table, Mahogany, Exotic Wood Parquetry, Scroll Feet, Continental, 28 x 31 In. 3055.00
Table, Mahogany, Flip Top, Pedestal, Turned Baluster, Scrolled Legs, 29 x 48 1/2 x 55 In. 825.00
Table, Mahogany, Gilt Tooled, Leather Top, Drawer, 1800s, 29 x 30 x 54 In. 905.00
Table, Mahogany, Marble Top, 3 Caryatid Supports, Block Feet, 30 3/4 x 36 In. 2950.00

Table, Mahogany, Marble Top, Drawer, Recessed Panel Door, 30 x 14 x 12 1/2 In. 148.00
Table, Mahogany, Marble Top, Inlaid Urn, Birds, Shells, Dolphin Supports, 31 x 46 In. 3525.00
Table, Mahogany, Marble Top, Lyre Base, Drawer, 28 1/2 x 18 x 14 In., Pair 415.00
Table, Mahogany, Marble Top, Round, Hexagonal, Baluster Pedestal, 28 x 38 In. 2950.00
Table, Mahogany, Medial Shelf, Drawer, Square, 35 x 21 In. 1415.00
Table, Mahogany, Oil-Filled Compass Inset, Brass Case, 18 1/2 x 14 x 14 In. 440.00
Table, Mahogany, Oval Dish Top, 19th Century, Trestle Supports, 19 In. 715.00
Table, Mahogany, Pedestal, Bronze Mounts, Figural, Swag, 32 x 24 In. 275.00
Table, Mahogany, Satinwood, Inlaid Ovals, Drawer, Continental, 1800s, 27 x 29 In. 2820.00
Table, Maple, Pine Top, Turned Legs, Early 1700s, 26 1/2 x 25 1/2 x 20 In. 825.00
Table, Maple, Pine, Gray Paint, Turned Legs, 29 x 23 1/2 x 48 In. 415.00
Table, Maple, Pine, Rectangular Top, Straight Skirt, Drawer, Mid 1700s, 27 x 43 In. 5875.00
Table, Marcel Kammerer, Ebonized Beech, Brass, G. Thonet, c.1904, 31 x 21 x 21 In. 7200.00
Table, Marquetry, Galleried, Drawer, Shelf, Oval, France, c.1800, 30 x 29 x 22 In. 4095.00
Table, Marquetry, Parquetry, Geometric Band, Scene, St. George, 30 x 32 In. 646.00
Table, Mies Van Der Rohe, Barcelona, Glass Top, Stainless Steel Base, Knoll, 16 x 40 In. 720.00
Table, Ministry, Shaker, Drop Leaf, Birch, Red Paint, Turned Legs, Rounded Rule Joint, 27 x 36 In. . 7605.00
Table, Mixed Wood, Cherry Stain, 1-Board Peg Top, 37 x 20 x 27 In. 660.00
Table, Mixed Wood, Star Inlay, Ring Turned Legs, 27 1/2 x 48 1/2 x 25 In. 385.00
Table, Napoleon III, Hardwood, Ebonized, Boulle, Gilt Bronze Mounted, 31 x 59 In. 9106.00
Table, Napoleon III, Hardwood, Ebonized, Gilt Bronze Mounted, 31 x 55 In., Pair 3995.00
Table, Napoleon III, Kingwood, 3 Drawers, c.1865, 28 x 14 In. 265.00
Table, Napoleon III, Kingwood, Marble Top, Brass Mounted, 28 x 18 x 14 In. 1645.00
Table, Neoclassical, Giltwood, White Paint, Marble Top, 1700s, 34 x 43 In. 1175.00
Table, Neoclassical, Mahogany, Cylindrical Pedestal, 4 Paw Feet, c.1825, 30 x 48 In. 1470.00
Table, Neoclassical, Mahogany, Mahogany Veneer, Round Top, c.1835, 32 x 36 In. 411.00
Table, Neoclassical, Marble Top, Bombe, Serpentine, Bronze C-Scrolls, 28 In., Pair 3525.00
Table, Nesting, A. Sorenson, Birch Plywood, Iron, Knoll, 1940s, 17 x 25 x 21 In., 3 Piece 1560.00
Table, Nesting, Black Lacquer, Oriental Landscape, Trestle Supports, 29 In., 4 Piece 1530.00
Table, Nesting, Blackwood, Chinese, 24 x 16 1/2 In., 4 Piece 270.00
Table, Nesting, Cast Aluminum, Italy, c.1935, 9 3/4 x 23 1/4 In. 4200.00
Table, Nesting, Ebonized, Oriental Scene, Pierced Supports, 28 x 20 In., 3 Piece 1290.00
Table, Nesting, J. Hoffmann, Beech, Stained, Austria, c.1905, 24 x 18 In., 4 Piece 8736.00
Table, Nesting, Lacquer, Chinoiserie, Dragon Feet, c.1860, 29 x 24 x 16 In., 4 Piece 330.00
Table, Nesting, Mahogany, Glass Insert Top, 22 x 15 x 12 In., 3 Piece 250.00
Table, Nesting, Mahogany, Inlaid, Turned Legs, 2-Stretcher Base, 25 x 22 In., 4 Piece 290.00
Table, Nesting, Oriental, Parcel Gilt, Black Lacquer, Victorian, 27 x 19 In., 4 Piece 1530.00
Table, Nesting, Paul Laszlo, Walnut, Ebonized, 1950s, 22 x 24 x 16 In., 3 Piece 1000.00
Table, Nesting, Regency Style, Burr Maple, 29 1/2 x 30 x 13 1/2 In., 4 Piece 1800.00
Table, North African Mahogany, Polychrome, Inlaid, Geometric, 25 x 18 In., Pair 940.00
Table, Nutting, No. 605, Round Top, 3 Legs, Early 1900s, 28 In. 206.00
Table, Nutting, No. 615, Maple, Trestle Base, 29 x 42 x 30 In. 990.00
Table, O. Bach, Marble Top, Ironwork, Curled, Dragons, Leaves, Bronze Finish, 33 In. 5400.00
Table, Oak, 2 Drawers, Turned Legs, Continental, 18th Century, 31 x 63 x 28 In. 469.00
Table, Oak, Draw Leaf, Removable Breadboard, Urn Legs, England, 29 x 49 In. 3105.00
Table, Oak, Gateleg, 28 1/2 x 48 1/24 x 20 In. 575.00
Table, Oak, Quartersawn, 2 Tiers, Square Top, Ball-Top Legs, c.1910, 30 1/2 x 26 In. 275.00
Table, Oak, Round, Split Pedestal, 4 Claw Feet, 30 x 48 In. 175.00
Table, Oriental, Elm, Red Brown Paint, Turned Legs, Shaped Returns, 90 x 17 1/2 In. 430.00
Table, P. Evans, Ash, Metal, c.1970, 29 1/4 x 44 In. 2689.00
Table, P. Evans, Bronze, Glass Top, Round, 1969, 16 x 26 In., Pair 6490.00
Table, P. Evans, Burl Veneer, Brass Patchwork, 18 x 27 x 18 In. 826.00
Table, P. Evans, Metal Patchwork Base, Plate Glass Top, Cityscape, 16 x 48 In. 2596.00
Table, Painted, Mohegan Island Images, Tapered Legs, c.1920, 24 x 22 In. 385.00
Table, Papier-Mache, Lacquer, Chinoiserie, Dish Top, 24 x 10 1/2 In. 470.00
Table, Pembroke, Cherry, Apron Drawer, Brass Bail, Square Legs, 28 x 57 x 33 In. 1315.00
Table, Pembroke, Cherry, Fluted End Apron, Turned Legs, 30 x 36 x 19 In. 470.00
Table, Pembroke, Chippendale, Cherry, Pine, 2-Board Top, Shaped Apron, 36 x 27 In. 575.00
Table, Pembroke, Chippendale, Mahogany, Chamfered Legs, X-Stretcher, c.1790 .... 1435.00
Table, Pembroke, Chippendale, Mahogany, Serpentine, c.1775, 26 x 36 x 20 In. 775.00
Table, Pembroke, Chippendale, Pegged, Scalloped End Aprons, 36 x 16 x 27 3/4 In. 460.00

Table, Pembroke, Federal Style, Mahogany Inlay, 29 1/2 x 39 1/2 x 33 1/2 In. 415.00
Table, Pembroke, Federal, Cherry, Carved, 29 x 21 x 37 1/2 In. 470.00
Table, Pembroke, Federal, Cherry, Drawer, c.1815, 29 x 24 In. 2468.00
Table, Pembroke, Federal, Cherry, Pine, Dovetail Drawer, 2-Board Top, 28 x 36 x 20 In. 1785.00
Table, Pembroke, Federal, Cherry, Plain Skirt, Square Legs, c.1800, 29 x 34 x 35 In. 499.00
Table, Pembroke, Federal, D-Shape Leaves, Tapered Legs, Early 1800s, 29 x 36 x 41 In. 380.00
Table, Pembroke, Federal, Mahogany, Double Stringing, Icicle Inlay, 27 x 31 In. 1765.00
Table, Pembroke, Federal, Mahogany, Inlaid, 28 3/4 x 34 x 21 In. 590.00
Table, Pembroke, Federal, Mahogany, Inlaid, c.1795, 29 x 20 x 32 In. 1765.00
Table, Pembroke, Federal, Mahogany, Reeded Legs, Turned Feet, 28 x 42 x 35 In. 385.00
Table, Pembroke, Federal, Mahogany, String Inlay, 1800s, 29 x 34 In. 880.00
Table, Pembroke, Federal, Mahogany, Veneer, Brass Ball Feet, c.1820, 29 x 24 In. 470.00
Table, Pembroke, Federal, Tiger Maple, Drawer, c.1800, 29 x 35 In. 2115.00
Table, Pembroke, George III Style, Mahogany, Satinwood Inlay, 1900s, 27 x 36 In. 355.00
Table, Pembroke, George III, Mahogany, Drawer, c.1800, 29 x 32 In. 1410.00
Table, Pembroke, George III, Mahogany, Rounded Corners, Late 1700s, 28 x 29 In. 880.00
Table, Pembroke, George III, Mahogany, Rounded Leaves, c.1780, 29 x 19 x 30 In. 1680.00
Table, Pembroke, George III, Mahogany, Satinwood Banding, 28 x 23 In. 1880.00
Table, Pembroke, George III, Mahogany, Serpentine Edge, Drawer, 28 x 28 x 38 In. 1225.00
Table, Pembroke, George III, Mahogany, String Inlay, Demilune Leaves, 28 x 38 In. 3525.00
Table, Pembroke, George III, Satinwood, Frieze Drawers, Square Legs, Spade Feet, 29 In. 1610.00
Table, Pembroke, George III, Satinwood, Inlaid, Frieze Drawer, c.1790, 28 x 30 In. 1765.00
Table, Pembroke, George III, Satinwood, Inlaid, Stone Knob, c.1790, 28 x 16 In. 6000.00
Table, Pembroke, George IV, Mahogany, D-Shape Leaves, c.1820, 29 x 22 In. 646.00
Table, Pembroke, Hepplewhite, Cherry, New England, 1800s, 28 x 30 x 20 In. 415.00
Table, Pembroke, Hepplewhite, Mahogany, R.I., c.1785, 28 x 20 x 34 In. 1095.00
Table, Pembroke, Hepplewhite, Mahogany, Reeded Edge, 29 x 36 x 19 In. 1610.00
Table, Pembroke, Hepplewhite, Walnut, Pine, Poplar, Inlay, Drawers, 19 x 40 x 29 In. 575.00
Table, Pembroke, Mahogany, 33 x 25 1/2 x 17 In. 2500.00
Table, Pembroke, Mahogany, Banded Inlay, Faux Drawer, 28 x 42 x 35 In. 385.00
Table, Pembroke, Mahogany, Bellflower Inlay, c.1790, 40 x 33 In. 10755.00
Table, Pembroke, Mahogany, Serpentine Top, Brass Pull, Square Legs, 29 x 36 In. 1725.00
Table, Pembroke, Mahogany, Spiral Turned Legs, 28 x 36 In. 2400.00
Table, Pembroke, Mahogany, Square, Tapered Legs, 29 x 31 In. 1095.00
Table, Pembroke, Mahogany, X-Stretcher, Marlborough Feet, 29 x 19 x 32 In. 2760.00
Table, Pembroke, Neoclassical, Mahogany, 1-Board Top, Drawer, 28 x 39 In. 1175.00
Table, Pembroke, Neoclassical, Mahogany, Mid-Atlantic, c.1815-25, 29 x 22 In. 1528.00
Table, Pembroke, Neoclassical, Mahogany, Rectangular Leaves, c.1840, 28 x 41 In. 590.00
Table, Pembroke, Sheraton, Mahogany, Brass Caster Feet, 29 x 32 x 19 In. 345.00
Table, Pembroke, Sheraton, Mahogany, Rope Turned Legs, c.1820, 29 x 38 In. 520.00
Table, Pembroke, Sheraton, Rosewood Veneer, Fluted Legs, 30 x 21 In. 575.00
Table, Pembroke, Walnut, Rectangular Leaves, Square Legs, Cross Stretcher, 37 In. 1060.00
Table, Pier, Empire Style, Mahogany, Marble Top, Base, 33 x 38 x 21 In. 660.00
Table, Pier, George III, Tulipwood, Sycamore, Satinwood, Mahogany, c.1780, 33 x 46 In. 4200.00
Table, Pier, Gilt, Marble Top, Blackamoors, Flower Urn, Continental, 35 x 58 In. 6465.00
Table, Pier, Marble Top, Carved, Gilt, Whitewash, c.1890, 32 x 37 In. 1100.00
Table, Pier, Neoclassical, Mahogany, Brass Gallery, Corinthian Columns, Shelf, 41 x 42 In. 1650.00
Table, Pier, Neoclassical, Mahogany, Gilt, Gadrooned Edge, 37 x 39 x 17 In. 2270.00
Table, Pier, Neoclassical, Mahogany, Marble Top, c.1830, 39 x 51 x 27 In. 2940.00
Table, Pier, Neoclassical, Marble Top, Ormolu Mounted, Front Columns, c.1825, 35 x 39 In. 8750.00
Table, Pier, Neoclassical, Rosewood, Marble Top, Scrolls, c.1830, 37 x 44 x 21 In. 2940.00
Table, Pier, Rococo Revival, Mahogany, Serpentine Marble Top, c.1850, 36 x 43 In. 2115.00
Table, Pier, William IV, Mahogany, Marble Top, Portrait Medallion, Adams, 33 x 40 In. 1765.00
Table, Pine, 2 Deep Drawers, Square Legs, 36 1/2 x 46 x 23 In. 645.00
Table, Pine, Demilune, 3 Tapered Square Legs, Mortise & Pinned, 35 x 32 x 18 In. 375.00
Table, Pine, Oak, Green 2-Board Top, Brown Grained Base, 33 1/4 x 25 x 30 In. 460.00
Table, Pine, Rectangular, Rounded Edge, Drawer, Cabriole Legs, 29 x 31 x 24 In. 1180.00
Table, Pine, Scrubbed, Blue Painted Sawbuck Base, 19th Century, 26 1/2 x 35 In. 440.00
Table, Pine, Yellow Chestnut, Dentil Molding, Tapered Legs, 30 x 38 x 23 In. 1150.00
Table, Polychrome, Marble Top, Gadroon-Carved Edge, Frieze, 36 x 63 In. 1645.00
Table, Provincial, Cherry, Banded Top, Frieze, Drawer, Slide, 30 x 79 In. 2820.00

Table, Queen Anne Style, Mahogany, 20th Century, 27 x 57 x 18 In. 325.00
Table, Queen Anne Style, Mahogany, Round, 20th Century, 25 3/4 x 30 In. 415.00
Table, Queen Anne Style, Mahogany, Scalloped Apron, Pad Feet, 1800s, 28 x 49 In. 264.00
Table, Queen Anne, Cherry, Maple, Overhang Top, Splayed Legs, 27 x 32 x 25 In. 3878.00
Table, Queen Anne, Mahogany, Black Marble Top, Cabriole Legs, 28 x 29 In. 3230.00
Table, Red Lacquer, Chinese, c.1900, 14 x 61 x 16 1/2 In. 945.00
Table, Red Lacquer, Chinese, c.1900, 15 x 58 x 14 1/2 In. 708.00
Table, Red Lacquer, Incised Peonies, Cabriole Legs, Chinese, 31 x 37 x 25 In. 3420.00
Table, Red Lacquer, Mother-Of-Pearl, Shaped Top, Qing Dynasty, 29 x 29 x 24 In. 2596.00
Table, Refectory, French Provincial, Fruitwood, Plank Top, Drawer, c.1890, 29 x 76 In. 2115.00
Table, Refectory, Jacobean, Oak, Carved, Cup & Cover, Stretcher, 30 x 71 In. 1116.00
Table, Refectory, Louis XIII Style, Walnut, Parquetry, Late 1800s, 30 x 25 x 65 In. 1880.00
Table, Refectory, Oak, 4-Board Top, Breadboard Ends, Stretchers, 95 x 30 In. 2820.00
Table, Refectory, Oak, Carved Apron, Turned Legs, 29 x 69 1/2 x 29 3/4 In. 770.00
Table, Refectory, Renaissance Revival, Mahogany, Continental, 1800s, 31 x 35 In. 4115.00
Table, Refectory, Renaissance Revival, Walnut, Gadrooned, Griffin Legs, 33 x 67 x 28 In. 3420.00
Table, Refectory, Spanish Baroque, Walnut, Chip Carved, Drawer, 31 x 68 In. 705.00
Table, Refectory, Spanish Colonial, Molded, Punch Work, Drawer, 1700s, 29 x 60 In. 2115.00
Table, Refectory, Walnut, Oak, 3 Parts, Paneled Pedestal, Lap-Jointed Felt, 30 x 33 1/2 In. 2185.00
Table, Refectory, Walnut, Plank Top, England, 29 1/2 x 88 1/2 In. 4700.00
Table, Regency Style, 2 Baluster Tripod Pedestals, England, 1900s, 30 x 64 In. 1060.00
Table, Regency Style, Burl Walnut, Pedestal, Casters, 27 1/2 x 53 1/2 x 38 1/2 In. 1120.00
Table, Regency Style, Gilt, Patinated Bronze, Marble, Egyptian Maidens, 32 x 45 In. 3055.00
Table, Regency Style, Mahogany, 2 Baluster Tripod Pedestals, 1900s, 30 x 64 In. 1535.00
Table, Regency Style, Parcel Gilt, Rectangular, 20th Century, 20 x 23 1/2 x 17 3/4 In. 200.00
Table, Regency, Mahogany, 3 Sections, Round Legs, Anglo-Irish, 29 x 54 In. 5290.00
Table, Restauration, Mahogany, Round Top, Round Standard, Bun Feet, 29 x 42 In. 2230.00
Table, Robsjohn-Gibbings, Square, Flared Legs, 16 x 21 In., Pair 2006.00
Table, Rococo Revival, Rosewood, Serpentine Skirt, Marble Top, 36 x 27 In., Pair 940.00
Table, Rococo Style, Marquetry, Oval, 20 x 32 x 21 1/2 In. 180.00
Table, Rosewood, Brass String Inlay, Spider Legs, Round, 28 x 28 In. 1760.00
Table, Rosewood, Brass, 2 Drawers, Chinese, 1800s, 33 x 20 x 30 In. 470.00
Table, Rosewood, Marble Top, Bombe Skirt, Chinese, 33 x 43 x 26 In. 9440.00
Table, Rosewood, Reeded Apron, Shaped Inset, Paw Feet, Chinese, 21 x 37 x 22 In. 120.00
Table, Sawbuck, Pine, Red Paint, 3-Board Top, Early 19th Century, 27 x 35 x 56 In. 330.00
Table, Sewing, 3 Tiered Drawers, Pincushion Top, Painted, Folk Art, Roanoke, 19 x 15 x 11 In. 2530.00
Table, Sewing, Arts & Crafts, Oak, 30 x 32 x 22 In. 60.00
Table, Sewing, Biedermeier, Walnut, Drawer, Arched Base, c.1835, 30 x 24 x 18 In. 620.00
Table, Sewing, Black Lacquer, Figures In Garden, Chinese, 1800s, 24 1/2 x 17 x 28 In. 1175.00
Table, Sewing, Cherry, Pine Top, Maple Drawer Fronts, Drop Leaf, 28 x 18 x 22 In. 374.00
Table, Sewing, Eastlake, Ebonized, Inlaid, Rectangular, Splayed Legs, c.1875, 30 x 26 In. 470.00
Table, Sewing, Empire, Mahogany, Drop Leaf, 2 Drawers, 28 x 17 x 16 In. 430.00
Table, Sewing, Federal, Mahogany, 2 Drawers, Cut Glass Pulls, 1800s, 29 x 23 x 16 In. 385.00
Table, Sewing, Federal, Mahogany, 2 Drawers, Early 1800s, 29 x 20 1/2 In. 2235.00
Table, Sewing, Federal, Maple Veneer, Serpentine, 2 Drawers, Boston, c.1810, 30 x 28 In. 2235.00
Table, Sewing, Federal, Pine, Plank Top, Breadboard Ends, Drawer, 1800s, 28 x 20 In. 180.00
Table, Sewing, Federal, Walnut, Inlaid, 2 Drawers, Early 1800s, 31 x 25 x 19 In. 529.00
Table, Sewing, G. Stickley, No. 630, Drop Leaf, 3 Drawers, Red Decal, 28 x 17 x 17 In. 1920.00
Table, Sewing, Hepplewhite, Birch, Pine, 2-Board, Tapered Legs, 49 1/4 x 32 x 27 3/4 In. 920.00
Table, Sewing, Hepplewhite, Pine, Black Paint, Square Tapered Legs, 28 x 24 In. 115.00
Table, Sewing, Heywood Bros. & Co., Wicker, Lift Top, Accessories, c.1910, 27 x 17 In. 160.00
Table, Sewing, Mahogany, Drop Leaf, 2 Drawers, Glass Knobs, 8-Sided Legs, 28 x 17 In. 167.00
Table, Sewing, Mahogany, Marquetry, Hexagonal, Drawers, Faceted Ball Stem, 3-Footed, 30 In. 765.00
Table, Sewing, Neoclassical, Mahogany, 2 Drawers, c.1820, 31 x 24 x 18 In. 1175.00
Table, Sewing, Neoclassical, Mahogany, 2 Drawers, U.S., c.1830-40, 28 x 21 In. 940.00
Table, Sewing, Neoclassical, Mahogany, Drop Leaf, c.1820, 29 In. 120.00
Table, Sewing, Neoclassical, Mahogany, Pullout Work Bag, Early 1800s, 31 x 21 In. 1530.00
Table, Sewing, Nutting, Sheraton Style, Mahogany, Drawer, Basket Slide, 28 x 17 In. 920.00
Table, Sewing, Painted, Venetian, Fold-Out Top, Scalloped Skirt, Flowers, 29 x 22 In. 1880.00
Table, Sewing, Pine Top, Deep Overhang, Oak Apron, Curly Maple Legs, 29 x 18 In. 345.00
Table, Sewing, Pine, Fruitwood, Drawer, Square Legs, Early 1800s, 28 x 42 x 30 In. 1880.00

Table, Sewing, Poplar, Dovetailed Drawer, 2 Posts, Soap Hollow, Stenciled 1872 LAY, 15 x 9 In. 4600.00
Table, Sewing, Regency Style, Mahogany, Storage Well, 31 x 18 3/4 x 14 1/2 In. 560.00
Table, Sewing, Regency, Walnut, 8-Sided, Tapered Pedestal, England, c.1850, 30 x 18 In. 945.00
Table, Sewing, Restauration, Mahogany, Scrolled Trestle Base, c.1810, 32 x 21 x 17 In. 2938.00
Table, Sewing, Rococo Revival, Lift Coffin Top, Drawer, Cabriole Legs, 31 x 24 In. 2230.00
Table, Sewing, Shaker, Cherry, Pine, Red Stain, 2 Drawers, Brass Pulls, c.1840, 26 x 22 x 19 In. 8775.00
Table, Sewing, Shaker, Pine, Cherry, Red Paint, Scrubbed Top, Drawer, 27 3/4 x 51 In. 9945.00
Table, Sewing, Shaker, Pine, Maple, Natural Varnish, Tray Top, Drawer, c.1840, 27 x 29 x 20 In. 6435.00
Table, Sewing, Sheraton, Birch, Drawer, Rope-Carved Legs, New England, 28 x 20 In. 460.00
Table, Sewing, Sheraton, Cherry, 2 Drawers, 29 x 19 x 19 In. 430.00
Table, Sewing, Sheraton, Hardwood, Drawer, Ball Feet, New England, c.1825, 29 x 24 In. 230.00
Table, Sewing, Sheraton, Mahogany, 2 Drawers, Early 1800s, 30 x 17 x 21 In. 460.00
Table, Sewing, Sheraton, Mahogany, 2 Drawers, Reeded Legs, 26 x 14 x 15 In. 415.00
Table, Sewing, Sheraton, Mahogany, Drawer, Rope Turned Legs, 28 x 19 x 19 In. 635.00
Table, Sewing, Sheraton, Mahogany, Oval Corners, Reeded Legs, 26 x 14 x 14 In. 413.00
Table, Sewing, Sheraton, Pine, 2 Drawers, Turned Legs, 30 x 18 x 16 In. 316.00
Table, Sewing, Sponge Grain Painted, Drawer, Tapered Legs, Early 1800s, 28 x 19 x 17 In. 1990.00
Table, Sewing, Stickley Bros., Drop Leaf, 3 Drawers, Square Faceted Pulls, 29 x 18 In. 1530.00
Table, Sewing, Tiger Maple, Drawer, Lower Shelf, New Hampshire, 18 x 16 x 29 In. 345.00
Table, Sewing, Victorian, Walnut, Drawer, 19th Century, 28 In. 106.00
Table, Sewing, Victorian, Walnut, Drawers, Pierced Trestle Supports, c.1890, 29 x 18 In. 235.00
Table, Sewing, Walnut, Drawer, Baluster Turned Legs, Pa., Late 1700s, 31 x 31 x 26 In. 657.00
Table, Sewing, Walnut, Drawer, Turned Legs, c.1820, 28 x 22 x 19 In. 259.00
Table, Sewing, Walnut, Oval Top, Turned Legs, c.1830, 26 x 30 x 20 In. 115.00
Table, Sewing, Walnut, Pullout Lift Top, Fold-Out Pincushion, England, 1830s 1600.00
Table, Sewing, Weaver's, Pine Top, Chamfered Pedestal, Early 1800s, 30 1/2 x 20 In. 295.00
Table, Shaker, Cherry, Poplar, Pine, Natural Varnish Finish, Drawer, c.1840, 29 x 28 x 21 1/2 In. 3510.00
Table, Sheraton Style, Curly Maple, Red Brown, 4-Board Top, Drawers, 59 x 31 In. 405.00
Table, Sheraton, Red Paint, Scrub Top, Breadboard Ends, 25 x 43 1/2 x 32 1/2 In. 500.00
Table, Sheraton, Walnut, Drawer, Tapered Legs, Pegged Tenons, c.1800, 29 x 16 In. 265.00
Table, Sheraton, Walnut, Rectangular, Drawer, Diamond Inlay, Turned Legs, 29 In. 480.00
Table, Sheraton, Walnut, Tapered Legs, Turned Feet, Drawer, c.1800, 29 x 20 In. 325.00
Table, Side, Biedermeier, Birch, Ash, Drawer, Trestle Base, Lyre Ends, 30 x 38 In. 940.00
Table, Side, Biedermeier, Maple, Mahogany, Scalloped Skirt, Drawer, 29 x 18 In., Pair 1410.00
Table, Side, Charles II Style, Doors, 26 3/4 x 18 1/4 x 26 1/4 In. 1080.00
Table, Side, Cherry, 2 Drawers, Cabriole Legs, Louisiana, Late 1700s, 31 x 21 x 18 In. 4700.00
Table, Side, Edwardian, Glass Top, Lacquered Shelf, Flowers, c.1910, 25 x 26 In., Pair 1880.00
Table, Side, Edwardian, Mahogany, Inlaid Banding, Drawer, c.1900, 31 x 34 In. 646.00
Table, Side, Eero Saarinen, Teak, Round, Knoll, c.1956, 15 x 36 In. 900.00
Table, Side, Empire Style, Mahogany, Ormolu, Marble Top, c.1850, 38 x 37 In., Pair 1880.00
Table, Side, Federal Style, Cherry, Cypress, Gallery, La., c.1830, 32 x 19 x 16 In. 6756.00
Table, Side, Fontana Arte, Wedge Shaped Top, Glass, Brass Base, 20 x 13 x 16 In. 1770.00
Table, Side, George II, Mahogany, Drawer, 27 1/2 x 30 x 16 In. 4500.00
Table, Side, George III Style, Burl Walnut, Inlay, Gilt Bronze, Oval Top, 30 x 32 In. 1528.00
Table, Side, George III Style, Mahogany, Shelf, 29 x 25 1/2 x 16 1/2 In. 1440.00
Table, Side, George III, Mahogany, 27 1/4 x 24 x 16 3/4 In. 450.00
Table, Side, George III, Mahogany, c.1770, 33 x 24 x 19 In. 3000.00
Table, Side, George III, Satinwood, Ebony Stringing, Square Legs, Oval, 29 x 26 x 19 In. 3525.00
Table, Side, Georgian Style, Walnut, Inlaid, Demilune, 1900s, 32 x 45 x 19 In. 765.00
Table, Side, Georgian, Mahogany, String Inlay, Square Legs, Drawer, 1800s, 28 x 28 In. 295.00
Table, Side, I. Noguchi, Round, Knoll, c.1954, 20 x 24 In. 1560.00
Table, Side, Ico Parisi, Walnut Veneer, M. Singer & Sons, 1950s, 26 x 24 x 18 In. 5100.00
Table, Side, Jean Prouve, Lacquered Steel, Oak, Aluminum, c.1933, 32 x 16 x 13 In. 7200.00
Table, Side, Kittinger, Pedestal, Black Lacquer, Ball Feet, Arrow Shaft, 26 x 16 In. 415.00
Table, Side, L. Pontoppidan, Teak, Denmark, c.1970, 22 x 15 x 23 In. 125.00
Table, Side, Louis XV Style, Walnut, Serpentine Top, Cabriole Legs, 29 x 36 In. 325.00
Table, Side, Louis XVI Style, Mahogany, Drawer, Inlaid, Oval, 29 x 24 x 18 In., Pair 705.00
Table, Side, Maple, 2 Drawers, Wood Knobs, 1800s, 32 x 19 x 19 In. 1440.00
Table, Side, Max Kuehne, Silver Leaf Top, Ivory Flowers, 18 3/4 x 24 In. 2006.00
Table, Side, Mirrored, Tapered Pedestal, James Clark Ltd., England, 24 x 24 In., Pair 2950.00
Table, Side, Neoclassical, Walnut, 2 Drawers, Drop Leaf, 29 x 19 In. 540.00

Table, Side, Oak, Drawer, Bobbin Turned Legs, England, Late 1700s, 30 x 35 In. 645.00
Table, Side, Oak, Limed, France, c.1930, 20 x 18 x 14 In., Pair 8400.00
Table, Side, Oak, Rose Marble Top, England, Early 1900s, 33 x 17 x 15 In. 175.00
Table, Side, Oak, Walnut, 2 Doors, Box Stretcher, England, Late 1700s, 32 x 42 In. 1760.00
Table, Side, Pine, Marble Top, Carved Designs, England, 1800s, 31 x 17 x 15 In. 69.00
Table, Side, Pine, Marble Top, England, 1800s, 30 x 17 x 15 In. 92.00
Table, Side, Pine, Marble Top, England, 1800s, 31 x 17 x 16 In. 80.00
Table, Side, Polychromed, Scalloped Top, Leaf Border, Italy, c.1850, 34 x 40 In. 1527.00
Table, Side, Queen Anne Style, Walnut, Crossbanded, Drawer, 1800s, 28 x 20 In. 940.00
Table, Side, Queen Anne, Birch, Drawer, Square Top, Cabriole Legs, Pad Feet, 27 x 20 In. 175.00
Table, Side, R. Subes, Wrought Iron, Glass, Parcel Gilt, c.1940, 20 1/2 In., Pair 7800.00
Table, Side, Regency, Rosewood, Burr Elm, c.1810, 27 3/4 x 18 x 18 In. 3000.00
Table, Side, Risom, No. T-421, c.1955, 25 x 21 x 17 In. 540.00
Table, Side, Rosewood, Marble Top, Round, Chinese, 1800s, 22 x 22 In. 1415.00
Table, Side, Sheraton Style, Mahogany, Drop Leaf, Brass Pulls, 29 x 19 x 16 In., Pair 605.00
Table, Side, Sheraton, Mahogany, Ball Feet, England, Early 1800s, 30 x 53 In., Pair 2230.00
Table, Side, Stefan Siwinski, Fiberglass, Korina Designs, c.1972, 16 x 30 In., Pair 1040.00
Table, Side, Stefan Siwinski, Wood, Laminated, Korina Designs, c.1970, 18 x 24 In. 210.00
Table, Side, Teak, Triangular Top, Splayed Legs, Imperial Furn., Ontario, c.1960, 18 x 21 In. 85.00
Table, Side, V. Kagan, Oak, Round Top, Sculptural Cross Base, 23 x 30 In. 2125.00
Table, Side, W. Platner, Teak Top, Inset, Round, Knoll, c.1966, 18 x 15 1/2 In. 900.00
Table, Side, Walnut, Arched Trestle Base, Continental, Late 1700s, 28 x 39 x 20 In. 2235.00
Table, Side, William & Mary Style, Walnut, Demilune, 2 Drawers, 28 x 28 x 14 In. 940.00
Table, Step, Art Deco, Tubular Chrome, 2 Shelves, 22 x 27 In. 145.00
Table, Step, Heywood-Wakefield Co., c.1950, 23 x 30 x 16 In., Pair 316.00
Table, Tapio Wirkkala, Blond Mahogany, Steel, Asko, c.1958, 23 x 47 x 23 In. 3600.00
Table, Tapiovaara, Concave Triangular Top, Tapered Dowel Legs, 16 x 25 In. 1650.00
Table, Tavern, Curly Maple, Oval 2-Board Top, Stretcher, Turned Legs, 22 x 28 x 24 In. 1208.00
Table, Tavern, Federal, Maple, Pine, Overhang Top, Beaded Legs, Early 1800s, 26 x 40 In. 940.00
Table, Tavern, Federal, Maple, Pine, Red Paint, Skirt, Drawer, 28 x 42 x 26 In. 2705.00
Table, Tavern, Maple Top, Splayed Legs, Oval, 26 1/2 x 31 3/4 x 23 1/4 In. 345.00
Table, Tavern, Maple, Pine, Overhang Top, Drawer, Turned Legs, 26 x 39 1/2 In. 3175.00
Table, Tavern, Maple, Pine, Overhang Top, New England, 1700s, 27 x 42 x 28 In. 1645.00
Table, Tavern, Nutting, No. 660, Pine Top, Tiger Maple Sides, 36 x 24 x 26 3/4 In. 935.00
Table, Tavern, Oak, Overhang Top, Straight Skirt, Ring Turned Legs, 1700s, 27 x 47 In. 355.00
Table, Tavern, Painted Faux Tortoiseshell Top, c.1780, 30 x 42 In. 4700.00
Table, Tavern, Pine, Maple, Gray & Blue Paint, c.1790, 29 x 46 1/2 x 29 In. 1765.00
Table, Tavern, Pine, Maple, Oak, Oval Top, Box Stretcher, 18th Century, 28 x 25 x 35 In. 1165.00
Table, Tavern, Queen Anne, Mahogany, Figured, 3 Legs, R.I., c.1760, 29 x 28 In. 4500.00
Table, Tavern, Queen Anne, Maple, Oval Top, Tapered Legs, Pad Feet, 34 x 25 x 26 In. 3220.00
Table, Tavern, Queen Anne, Maple, Pine, Shaped Apron, c.1775, 26 x 24 x 34 In. 920.00
Table, Tavern, Queen Anne, Maple, Pine, Turned Feet, 43 1/2 x 24 1/2 x 26 3/4 In. 1265.00
Table, Tavern, Queen Anne, Pine Top, Drawer, 45 x 26 x 26 In. 1725.00
Table, Tavern, Red Paint, Scrub Top, Drawer, Stretcher Base, 27 x 26 x 26 In. 8050.00
Table, Tavern, Red Wash, Stretcher Base, 53 x 34 x 29 In. 1265.00
Table, Tavern, Removable Top, 2 Drawers, Stretcher Base, 1700s, 30 x 56 x 33 In. 345.00
Table, Tavern, Scallop Top, Stretcher Base, T-Head Nails, 18th Century, 32 x 18 x 29 In. 2590.00
Table, Tavern, Walnut, Breadboard Top, 2 Drawers, Tapered Legs, Pad Feet, 30 x 52 In. 5520.00
Table, Tavern, White & Green Paint, Pegged, Turned Legs, Early 1800s, 18 x 36 x 27 In. 635.00
Table, Tea, Chippendale, Mahogany, 8-Sided, Openwork Gallery, 3 Claw Feet, 28 x 28 In. 575.00
Table, Tea, Chippendale, Mahogany, Gallery Top, Shelf, Brass Pull, 29 x 23 In. 920.00
Table, Tea, Chippendale, Mahogany, Piecrust Top, Tripod, England, 1700s, 29 x 34 In. 2000.00
Table, Tea, Drop Leaf, Queen Anne, Mahogany, Oval, Scalloped, c.1750, 28 x 33 In. 1530.00
Table, Tea, Drop Leaf, Queen Anne, Mahogany, Scalloped Skirts, 28 x 24 In. 2115.00
Table, Tea, George II, Mahogany, Dish Top, c.1735, 29 x 33 x 20 In. 4406.00
Table, Tea, George II, Mahogany, Frieze Drawer, Ireland, c.1750, 30 x 31 x 21 In. 8400.00
Table, Tea, George III Style, Mahogany, Round, Baluster Pedestal, 30 x 29 In. 355.00
Table, Tea, Georgian, Mahogany, Birdcage, 1700s, 28 x 36 In. 440.00
Table, Tea, L. & J.G. Stickley, No. 508, Round, Lower Shelf, Handcraft Decal, 24 x 24 In. 1440.00
Table, Tea, Maple, Pine, Oval Overhang Top, Turned Feet, 27 x 19 x 29 In. 3820.00
Table, Tea, Marquetry, Petal Design, Circles, Pedestal Base, Scroll Legs, 28 In. 460.00

Table, Tea, Painted, Oval Overhang, Block Turned Tapered Legs, Mid 1700s, 27 x 37 In. 6465.00
Table, Tea, Queen Anne Style, Cherry, Porringer Top, Pad Feet, Eldred Wheeler, 33 In. 400.00
Table, Tea, Queen Anne, Cherry, Maple, Oval Top, Shaped Skirt, Duck Feet, 26 x 23 x 32 In. 770.00
Table, Tea, Queen Anne, Cherry, New Hampshire, 27 1/2 x 27 x 36 In. 660.00
Table, Tea, Queen Anne, Mahogany, Cabriole Legs, Pad Feet, 28 x 18 1/4 x 25 In. 430.00
Table, Tea, Queen Anne, Mahogany, Porringer Top, Nantucket, 32 x 24 x 27 In. 5750.00
Table, Tea, Queen Anne, Maple, Red Paint, Overhang Top, Late 1700s, 26 x 22 In. 1410.00
Table, Tea, Queen Anne, Red Paint, Porringer Top, Late 1700s, 26 x 22 In. 3819.00
Table, Tea, Queen Anne, Walnut, Dish Top, Turned Shaft, Tripod, 1700s, 28 x 31 In. 715.00
Table, Tea, Softwood, Brown Paint, Molded Skirt, Concave Drawer, 29 x 34 In. 250.00
Table, Tea, Tilt Top, Cherry, Birdcage Support, Cabriole Legs, Slipper Feet, 27 x 29 In. 530.00
Table, Tea, Tilt Top, Chippendale Style, Mahogany, Piecrust Top, Birdcage Support, 34 In. 480.00
Table, Tea, Tilt Top, Chippendale, Mahogany, Cabriole Legs, Claw & Ball Feet, 32 1/2 x 28 In. 1150.00
Table, Tea, Tilt Top, Chippendale, Mahogany, Carved, Figured, Phila., c.1770, 29 x 36 In. 3600.00
Table, Tea, Tilt Top, Chippendale, Mahogany, Dish Top, Turned Pedestal, 29 x 29 In. 1725.00
Table, Tea, Tilt Top, Chippendale, Mahogany, Pedestal, Arched Legs, R.I., 1700s, 29 x 33 In. 1095.00
Table, Tea, Tilt Top, George II, Turned Standard, Tripod Base, Snake Feet, 24 x 27 In. 410.00
Table, Tea, Tilt Top, George III, Mahogany, Piecrust Top, Late 1700s, 27 x 30 In. 3525.00
Table, Tea, Tilt Top, George III, Mahogany, Piecrust Top, Tripod Base, c.1750, 28 x 32 In. 880.00
Table, Tea, Tilt Top, Georgian, Piecrust, Ball Turned Shaft, 3 Snake Feet, 29 x 33 In. 2300.00
Table, Tea, Tilt Top, Mahogany, Round Top, Brass Latch, 3-Footed, 28 x 21 1/2 In. 880.00
Table, Tea, Tilt Top, Mahogany, Turned Pedestal, Snake Feet, 27 x 31 In. 520.00
Table, Tea, Tilt Top, Queen Anne Style, Mahogany, Veneer, Scalloped Base, 1900s, 27 In. 345.00
Table, Tea, Tilt Top, Queen Anne, 1-Board Top, Urn Pedestal, 1750-1800, 28 x 30 In. 880.00
Table, Tea, Tilt Top, Queen Anne, Birdcage, Round, 3 Snake Feet, 28 x 32 x 33 In. 1670.00
Table, Tea, Tilt Top, Queen Anne, Curly Maple, Round, 3 Snake Feet, 27 x 31 In. 920.00
Table, Tea, Tilt Top, Queen Anne, Mahogany, Birdcage Platform, Tripod, 27 x 26 In. 560.00
Table, Tea, Tilt Top, Queen Anne, Mahogany, Serpentine, Mass., c.1780, 28 3/4 x 42 In. 1080.00
Table, Tea, Tilt Top, Queen Anne, Maple, Notched Corners, 28 x 28 x 27 In. 575.00
Table, Tea, Tilt Top, Rectangular, Turned Pedestal, 3-Footed, 19th Century, 29 x 26 In. 265.00
Table, Tea, Tilt Top, Rosewood, Acanthus-Carved Stem, Cabriole Dragon Legs, 28 x 23 In. 675.00
Table, Tea, Tilt Top, Walnut, Scrolled Legs, Turned Pedestal, c.1865, 30 x 34 In. 265.00
Table, Tea, Walnut, 3-Board Top, Shaped Apron, Cabriole Legs, 26 x 28 3/4 x 19 In. 660.00
Table, Teak, Embossed Gray Leather Top, 15 x 24 x 24 In. 5079.00
Table, Teak, Leather, Inset Magazine Holder, c.1970, 18 x 18 In. 95.00
Table, Tiger Maple, Bird's-Eye Maple Veneer, Drawers, 29 x 21 x 17 In. 3290.00
Table, Tiger Maple, Drawer, Turned Spool Legs, Ball Feet, 31 x 25 3/4 x 24 In. 236.00
Table, Tilt Top, Black Lacquer, Polychrome & Gilt Oriental Figures, 30 x 24 x 18 In. 1116.00
Table, Tilt Top, Black Paint, Polychrome Flowers, Round, 3 Turned Legs, 50 x 30 In. 940.00
Table, Tilt Top, Chippendale Style, Mahogany, Piecrust Top, Cabriole Legs, 23 x 23 In. 1610.00
Table, Tilt Top, Colonial, Teak, Baluster Support, Early 1800s, 32 x 55 In. 1300.00
Table, Tilt Top, Fruitwood, Double Baluster Base, Round Plinth, 29 x 42 x 30 In. 944.00
Table, Tilt Top, George III Style, Mahogany, Piecrust Top, Tripod, 1800s, 28 x 20 In. 765.00
Table, Tilt Top, George III Style, Mahogany, Piecrust, Tripod, c.1850, 27 x 29 In. 590.00
Table, Tilt Top, George III Style, Mahogany, Piecrust, Tripod, c.1890, 30 x 25 In., Pair 1175.00
Table, Tilt Top, George III Style, Mahogany, Piecrust, Tripod, Late 1800s, 32 x 37 In. 940.00
Table, Tilt Top, George III Style, Mahogany, Round, Tripod, Cabriole Legs, 27 x 25 In. 880.00
Table, Tilt Top, George III Style, Tripod, Birdcage Support, c.1900, 28 In., Pr. 998.00
Table, Tilt Top, George III, Mahogany, Lobed Edge, 3 Legs, 28 x 30 In. 765.00
Table, Tilt Top, George III, Mahogany, Piecrust Edge, Tripod, 30 x 35 1/4 In. 4700.00
Table, Tilt Top, George III, Mahogany, Piecrust Edges, Tripod, 20 x 26 In. 765.00
Table, Tilt Top, George III, Mahogany, Round Top, 3-Part Base, 27 x 22 In. 180.00
Table, Tilt Top, George III, Mahogany, Round Top, Baluster Base, 27 x 31 1/2 x 32 In. 770.00
Table, Tilt Top, George III, Oak, Pedestal, Tripod Supports, 32 In. 449.00
Table, Tilt Top, Georgian, Mahogany, Yew Banding, Round, 1700s, 29 x 29 1/4 In. 445.00
Table, Tilt Top, Mahogany, Birdcage Claw & Ball Feet, Round, c.1775, 27 1/2 In. 1250.00
Table, Tilt Top, Mahogany, Birdcage, Acanthus Leaves On Legs, Claw & Ball Feet, 33 In. 1850.00
Table, Tilt Top, Mahogany, Canted Corners, Pedestal, Early 1800s, 26 x 15 x 22 In. 285.00
Table, Tilt Top, Mahogany, Dutch Marquetry, Pedestal, Early 1800s, 29 x 28 In. 2039.00
Table, Tilt Top, Mahogany, Piecrust Top, Birdcage, Baluster Pedestal, 26 x 28 1/2 In. 560.00
Table, Tilt Top, Neoclassical, Flame Veneer Bands, Acanthus Paw Feet, 28 x 42 In. 8813.00

Table, Tilt Top, Neoclassical, Mahogany, 3-Footed, Denmark, c.1830, 30 x 38 In. 1880.00
Table, Tilt Top, Neoclassical, Mahogany, Tapered Shaft, 3-Footed, c.1825, 28 x 35 In. 2409.00
Table, Tilt Top, Neoclassical, Mahogany, Tri-Form Base, 29 x 24 In. 1265.00
Table, Tilt Top, Papier-Mache, Mother-Of-Pearl Decoration 4500.00
Table, Tilt Top, Pine, Scrubbed, Drawer, Shoe Feet, 29 x 47 x 23 In. 9560.00
Table, Tilt Top, Queen Anne, Curly Maple, Vase-Turned Pedestal, Tripod, 29 x 36 In. 1094.00
Table, Tilt Top, Regency, Mahogany, Ireland, c.1815, 30 x 65 In. 3525.00
Table, Tilt Top, Regency, Mahogany, Oval, Pedestal, Reeded Legs, 30 x 53 In. 1528.00
Table, Tilt Top, Regency, Mahogany, Pedestal, c.1835, 28 x 47 1/2 In. 1295.00
Table, Tilt Top, Regency, Mahogany, Turned Pedestal, 3-Footed, c.1815 .... 2875.00
Table, Tilt Top, Rosemaling, Scalloped Top, Gateleg, Scandinavia, Mid 1900s, 24 x 29 In. 765.00
Table, Tilt Top, Walnut, Birdcage, Ring & Vase Turnings, 1700s, 28 1/4 x 27 In. 550.00
Table, Tilt Top, William IV, Mahogany, Round, Columnar Standard, 29 x 47 In. 2230.00
Table, Tilt Top, Wrought Iron, Ceramic Tiles, Hand Painted, 18 1/4 In. Square 120.00
Table, Tony Paul, Adjustable, 3-Footed, c.1958, 22 x 18 In. 660.00
Table, Tray, Ash Plywood, Molded, Chromed Steel Base, Adjustable, 15 x 15 x 20 In. 765.00
Table, Tray, Carved Wood, Indian Brass, Chased, c.1900, 21 x 23 In. 175.00
Table, Tray, Chinese Chippendale, Mahogany, Pierced Gallery, 27 x 24 In., Pair 705.00
Table, Tray, English Oak Inlay, Medallion, Garlands, Tapered Legs, 22 x 27 x 20 In. 560.00
Table, Tray, G. Nelson, No. 4950, Adjustable, Herman Miller, c.1948, 19 x 15 x 15 In. 1680.00
Table, Tray, G. Nelson, No. 4950, Not Adjustable, Herman Miller, c.1948, 19 x 15 x 15 In. 840.00
Table, Tray, Hardwood, Pierce Carved, Brass Inlay, 8 Panels, Middle East 235.00
Table, Tray, Mahogany, Folding Stand, 31 x 33 1/2 x 20 In. 180.00
Table, Tray, Mahogany, Raised Gallery, 21 1/2 x 3 1/2 x 20 In. 495.00
Table, Tray, On Stand, Mahogany, 35 1/2 x 21 x 27 In. 300.00
Table, Tray, Queen Anne Style, Papier-Mache, Lacquer, Gilt, England, 21 x 23 In. 1175.00
Table, Tray, Regency, Mahogany, Pierced Handles, Later Stand, c.1820, 33 x 28 In. 570.00
Table, Tray, Victorian, Mahogany, Heart-Shape Handles, 1800s, 23 x 21 In. 1120.00
Table, Tray, Victorian, Mahogany, Pierced Serpentine Gallery, 1800s, 31 x 29 In. 5288.00
Table, Tray, Victorian, Papier-Mache, Roses, Ebonized Bamboo, 27 x 24 In. 645.00
Table, Tray, Walnut, Scrolling Gallery, Tapered Legs, 1900s, 9 3/4 x 24 x 15 In. 189.00
Table, Trestle, Burl Elm, Planks, Square Legs, England, 31 1/2 x 74 x 35 1/2 In. 1469.00
Table, Trestle, Coutellier, Walnut, Vase Shaped Legs, Shoe Feet, 1969, 30 x 80 In. 145.00
Table, Trestle, G. Stickley, Leather Top, Lower Shelf, Keyed Through Tenons, 29 x 48 In. 3819.00
Table, Trestle, G. Stickley, Mouse Hole, Upended Stretchers, Plank Sides, 29 x 84 x 42 In. 7050.00
Table, Trestle, Napoleon III, Fruitwood, Crossband, Drawer, 30 x 27 1/2 x 17 1/2 In. 765.00
Table, Trestle, Oak, Parquet Top, Baluster Legs, England, 1900s, 30 x 87 x 35 In. 1650.00
Table, Trestle, Pine, Washed Top, Red Wash Base, Shoe Foot, 27 x 55 x 29 In. 1495.00
Table, Tudor Style, Oak, Turned, Stretcher, Legs, 37 x 24 3/4 x 28 1/2 In. 530.00
Table, V. Kagan, Capricorn Line, Wire, Mesh, 2 Tiers, 1950s, 29 x 30 In. 945.00
Table, Victorian, Mahogany, Inlaid, Cabriole Legs, Brass Casters, 30 x 67 In. 1528.00
Table, Victorian, Mahogany, Marquetry, Turtle Top, Drawer, 1800s, 30 x 39 In. 410.00
Table, Victorian, Mahogany, Serpentine Top, c.1850, 29 x 51 x 39 In. 353.00
Table, Victorian, Marble Top, Apron Medallions, Bun Feet, Oval, 1800s, 37 x 26 In. 645.00
Table, Victorian, Marble Top, Wrought Iron, Scrolled Rope-Twist Frame, 19 x 41 In. 440.00
Table, Victorian, Oak, Turned Legs, 29 x 24 In. 104.00
Table, Victorian, Polychromed, Parcel Gilt, Black Lacquer, c.1850, 28 x 45 In. 2115.00
Table, Victorian, Walnut, Marble Top, 29 x 30 In. 750.00
Table, Victorian, Walnut, Marble Top, Turned Shaft, Late 1800s, 29 x 27 In. 276.00
Table, Victorian, Walnut, Marble Turtle Top, 29 x 37 In. 750.00
Table, W. McArthur, Anodized Aluminum, Rubber, Glass, 1930s, 21 x 18 In. 6000.00
Table, W. McArthur, Black Top, Round, Tubular Aluminum Base, 30 x 36 In. 2240.00
Table, W. Platner, Mahogany Top, Overhang, Knoll, c.1966, 18 1/2 x 24 In. 1020.00
Table, W. Platner, Marble Top, Gray, Inset, Knoll, c.1966, 18 x 15 1/2 In. 1680.00
Table, W. Platner, Marble Top, White, Inset, Knoll, c.1966, 18 x 15 1/2 In. 1140.00
Table, W. Platner, Rosewood Top, Overhang, Knoll, c.1966, 18 1/2 x 24 In. 1200.00
Table, W. Platner, Teak Top, Overhang, Knoll, c.1966, 19 x 24 In. 1020.00
Table, Walnut, 2-Board Top, 2 Drawers, Stretcher, Pa., c.1800, 54 x 35 In. 598.00
Table, Walnut, 3-Plank Top, 2 Drawers, Cabriole Legs, Pa., c.1770, 67 x 33 In. 3585.00
Table, Walnut, Birch, Marquetry, Scrolling Vines & Flowers, Square Legs, 29 x 23 In. 2115.00
Table, Walnut, Fruitwood Marquetry, Armorial, Continental, c.1745, 31 x 35 In. 1175.00

Table, Walnut, Gateleg, c.1850, 29 x 42 x 19 In. 259.00
Table, Walnut, Lacquered, Rectangular, Chinese, 33 x 37 x 18 1/4 In. 710.00
Table, Walnut, Maple Finish, Magazine Rack, 36 1/2 x 54 x 16 1/2 In. 6870.00
Table, Walnut, Marble Top, Carved Nude & Dolphin Legs, 31 x 24 In. 259.00
Table, Walnut, Marble Top, Continental, Late 1800s, 31 x 51 In. 1645.00
Table, Walnut, Marquetry, Apron, Cabriole Legs, Mongolia, 10 x 26 In. 560.00
Table, Walnut, Pedestal, Free Edge, James Martin, 26 x 22 x 21 In. 2360.00
Table, Walnut, Pine, Drawer, Medallions, Stretcher Base, Lyre Shape Legs, 40 x 26 In. 690.00
Table, Walnut, Plank Top, Turned Legs, Wrought Iron Braces, Spain, 30 x 62 x 45 In. 2360.00
Table, Walnut, Scalloped Skirt, Acanthus-Carved Legs, England, c.1700, 33 x 63 In. 5580.00
Table, Walnut, Starburst Inlay, Raised Scalloped Edge, 3 Carved Splayed Legs, 21 In. 1290.00
Table, Walter Lamb, Patio, Glass, Tubular Bronze, 17 x 49 In. 2360.00
Table, Wicker, Wood Top, Round, Pierced Scrolling, Cabriole Legs, 30 1/2 x 21 3/4 In. 150.00
Table, Wicker, Wood Top, White, Tapered Legs, Shelf With Braided Edge, c.1890, 30 x 30 x 22 In. ... 125.00
Table, William & Mary, Maple, Round Overhang Top, 1700s, 24 x 24 In. 5580.00
Table, William & Mary, Oval, Gateleg, Button Feet, Early 1700s, 27 x 39 In. 240.00
Table, William IV, Mahogany, Pedestal, 4-Footed, c.1850, 30 x 53 In. 1530.00
Table, William IV, Oak, Carved, 2 Tiers, Ebonized Beading, Trestle Supports, 37 x 54 In. 4935.00
Table, Wine, Elm & Puddingstone, Chinese, 33 x 42 1/4 x 19 1/2 In. 1120.00
Table, Wine, Elm, Marble Top, Chinese, Ming Dynasty, 31 1/2 x 40 x 18 In. 649.00
Table, Wine, French Provincial, Fruitwood, Tilt-Top, 1890s, 29 1/2 In. 1340.00
Table, Wine, Mahogany, Brass Mounted, Semicircle Top, Late 1800s, 32 x 54 x 30 In. 1175.00
Table, Wine, Oak, 3-Board Tilt Top, Shoe Feet, Continental, 27 x 24 In. 345.00
Table, Wine, Queen Anne, Cherry, Urn-Turned Pedestal, 3 Arched Legs, c.1750, 26 x 17 In. 405.00
Table, Wood, Black Lacquer, Low, 3 Spherical Feet, Screw Turned Pedestal, 19 x 24 In. 960.00
Table, Wood, Polychrome, Flowers, Scroll, Drawer, Tibet, 1800s, 17 x 33 x 17 In. 180.00
Table, Wormley, Burl, Faceted Round Cabinet, Door, Glass Top, 22 x 21 In. 2800.00
Table, Wormley, Magazine, Walnut Top, Mahogany Frame, Holders, 25 x 25 x 22 In. 1293.00
Table, Wormley, Mahogany, 2 Tiers, 3 Tapered Flared Legs, 22 x 28 In. 1880.00
Table, Wormley, Mahogany, 2 Tiers, 48 x 18 x 28 1/2 In. 880.00
Table, Wormley, No. 4856, Walnut, Birch, Round, Dunbar, 27 x 25 In. 2715.00
Table, Wormley, Sheaf Of Wheat, Round Travertine Top, Ash Slat Base, 20 x 29 In. 920.00
Table, Wormley, Trapezoid, Mosaic Top, Tripod Base, Dunbar, 22 x 16 x 14 In. 6490.00
Table, Wormley, Wedge Shape, Dunbar, c.1948, 32 x 22 x 25 In. 720.00
Table, Writing, Chinoiserie, Lacquer, Gilt, 2 Drawers, England, c.1900, 36 x 41 In. 2645.00
Table, Writing, Colonial Style, Mahogany, Leather, 3 Drawers, 1900s, 30 x 49 In. 735.00
Table, Writing, French Provincial, Fruitwood, Inset Leather Surface, Drawer, 27 x 30 In. 1175.00
Table, Writing, George III Style, Mahogany, 3 Drawers, 31 x 49 x 27 In. 9600.00
Table, Writing, George III Style, Mahogany, Leather Inset, 30 x 48 x 23 In. 2700.00
Table, Writing, George III, Mahogany, Hinged Top, Leather, c.1790, 36 x 36 x 25 In. 5400.00
Table, Writing, Louis XV Style, 19th Century, 38 1/2 x 39 x 25 In. 415.00
Table, Writing, Louis XVI Style, Beech, Frieze Drawers, Tapered Legs, 30 x 51 In. 940.00
Table, Writing, Regency Style, Blond Mahogany, 20th Century, 30 x 53 3/4 x 29 In. 1120.00
Table, Writing, Regency, Mahogany, Oak, Crossbanded, Ebony Inlay, c.1820, 29 x 52 In. 4995.00
Table, Writing, Victorian, Kidney Shape, Fitted Drawers, Late 1800s, 31 x 42 In. 1528.00
Table, Writing, William IV, Mahogany, Leather Surface, 3 Drawers, c.1850, 30 x 74 In. 1997.00
Table, Writing, William IV, Mahogany, Leather Top, Turned Legs, c.1845, 29 x 46 In. 1175.00
Table, Wrought Iron, Glass Top, Hourglass Form, Spain, 96 In. 455.00
Table Support, Bronze, Figural, Mermaid, Extended Arms, Trailing Hair, 31 x 32 x 25 In. 1298.00
Tabouret, G. Stickley, Round Top, Arched Cross Stretchers, c.1904, 15 x 14 In. 1765.00
Tabouret, L. & G. Stickley, Octagonal Top, Arched Cross Stretchers, 20 x 18 In. 1410.00
Tabouret, Limbert, No. 210, Round Top, Arched Apron, Flared Legs, 16 x 13 In. 360.00
Tabouret, Rosewood, Marble Plaque Inset, Chinese, Late 1800s, 32 In. 295.00
Tabouret, Rosewood, Marble Top, High Relief Carving, 26 x 15 x 14 In., Pair 820.00
Tabouret, Silvered Wood, Lacquered, c.1930, 21 In. 8400.00
Tea Cart, Art Deco, Wicker, c.1930, 30 x 35 In. 206.00
Tea Cart, Brass, Glass, 2 Tiers, Spoked Wheels, 36 1/2 x 38 x 22 In. 520.00
Tea Cart, Cees Braakman, Pastoe, 27 x 31 x 18 In. 660.00
Tea Cart, Heywood-Wakefield Co., Drop Leaf, Shelf, 28 x 49 x 38 In. 120.00
Tea Cart, Oak, Spoked Wheels, c.1900, 34 x 31 x 17 In. 46.00
Tray, Mahogany, Kidney Shape, Contrasting Inlays, Brass Handles, 15 x 24 In. 147.00

Trolley, Burl Walnut, Ebony Inlay, 3 Tiers, Drawer, England, 1800s, 52 x 54 In. 3290.00
Trolley, William IV, Mahogany, 2 Tiers, 2 Lower Drawers, Reeded Supports, 60 x 45 In. 2115.00
Trolley, William IV, Mahogany, 3 Tiers, Finials, Turned Legs, c.1840, 56 x 54 In. 1528.00
Trolley, William IV, Mahogany, 3 Tiers, Middle Drawer, c.1840, 43 x 53 In. 2820.00
Trolley, William IV, Mahogany, 3 Tiers, Reeded Posts, Melon Feet, 41 x 47 x 18 In. 3175.00
Umbrella Stand, Brass, Repousse, Figures In Relief, Paw Feet, 29 In. 750.00
Umbrella Stand, Cast Iron, 16 Slots, c.1850, 26 1/4 x 34 x 12 In. 145.00
Umbrella Stand, G. Stickley, No. 100, Slats, Riveted Rings, 24 x 11 1/2 In. 2468.00
Umbrella Stand, Gucci, Brass, Metal, Wood, Leather, Leatherette, 10 3/4 In., c.1972 .... 6600.00
Umbrella Stand, Iron, Football Player, Early 1900s, 33 x 20 x 11 In. 470.00
Umbrella Stand, Maddock, Royal Porcelain, Flowers, Transfer, Late 1800s, 19 3/4 In. 90.00
Umbrella Stand, Regency Style, Mahogany, Brass Strapwork, Lion's-Head Handles, 24 In. 1527.00
Umbrella Stand, Regency Style, Wrought Iron, 20th Century, 25 1/2 x 16 1/4 In. 118.00
Umbrella Stand, W. McArthur, Copper-Plated Aluminum, 1930s, 22 1/2 x 12 In. 3600.00
Vanity, Art Deco, Mirror, c.1935, 70 x 48 x 17 In. 120.00
Vanity, Bird's-Eye Maple, Beveled Glass Mirror, Austria, c.1900, 58 x 39 x 15 In. 1520.00
Vanity, Federal, Mahogany, String Inlay, Door, Drawers, 32 x 17 3/4 x 17 3/4 In. 345.00
Vanity, G. Nelson, No. 4609, Herman Miller, c.1948, 58 x 35 x 20 In. 1080.00
Vanity, Poudreuse, Mahogany, Lift Top, Drawer, Hepplewhite Style Legs, 30 x 22 In. 220.00
Vitrine, Art Nouveau, Mahogany, Mirror Back, 6 Shelves, c.1900, 59 x 32 In. 380.00
Vitrine, Biedermeier, Walnut, Framed Door, Mirrored Shelves, 66 1/2 x 40 x 22 In. 708.00
Vitrine, Biedermeier, Walnut, Glazed Doors, Oval Panels, Tapered Bars, 77 x 48 In. 2820.00
Vitrine, Chippendale Style, Mahogany Shelves, Doors, Edwardian, 50 x 18 In. 998.00
Vitrine, Chippendale Style, Mahogany, Glazed Top, Panels, Chinese, 29 x 17 x 17 In. 635.00
Vitrine, Edwardian, Mahogany, Inlaid Frieze, Vine Garland, Masque Center, 57 x 36 In. 587.00
Vitrine, G. Stickley, Oak, Slat Stretchers, Tapered Legs, 30 x 20 In. 1265.00
Vitrine, George III Style, Mahogany, Beveled Glass, 1900s, 29 x 32 x 22 In. 470.00
Vitrine, George III Style, Walnut Veneer, 6 Glazed Panels, Door, 1900s, 29 x 15 In., Pair 826.00
Vitrine, Louis XV Style, Gilt, Serpentine Case, Shelf Stretcher, 55 x 25 In. 147.00
Vitrine, Louis XVI Style, Gilt, Leaf-Pierced Cornice, 1800s, 41 x 32 In. 3055.00
Vitrine, Louis XVI Style, Mahogany, Gilt Bronze, Demilune, c.1885, 64 x 32 x 15 In. 9600.00
Vitrine, Louis XVI Style, Mahogany, Ormolu Mounted, Glazed, c.1900, 29 x 32 In. 3525.00
Vitrine, Mahogany, Pierced Galleries, Mirror Back, 3 Sections, c.1885, 85 x 51 In. 2820.00
Vitrine, Napoleon III, Plum Pudding Mahogany, Glass Shelves, 91 x 46 In. 3290.00
Vitrine, Neoclassical, Gilt Metal, Ebonized, Early 1900s, 55 x 25 In. 470.00
Vitrine, Renaissance Revival, Oak, Glazed Doors, Continental, c.1885, 87 x 56 In. 7200.00
Vitrine, Renaissance Revival, Walnut, Mirrored Back, Pedestal, c.1890, 45 x 14 In. 1235.00
Vitrine, Rococo Revival, Giltwood, Trapezoidal, Flowers, Italy, 1800s, 60 x 34 x 10 In. 3305.00
Vitrine, Rococo Style, Painted, Mirrored Cabinet, Curved Glass, France, 54 x 25 In. 1120.00
Vitrine, Vernis Martin, Gilt, Composition, c.1900, 56 x 28 In. 1295.00
Vitrine, Vernis Martin, Glass Sides, Metal, 1900s, 60 x 26 x 16 In. 440.00
Vitrine, Walnut, Flat Top, Ormolu Mounts, 29 1/4 x 24 x 16 1/2 In. 430.00
Vitrine, Walnut, Flat Top, Ormolu Mounts, 29 1/4 x 39 3/4 x 24 1/2 In. 345.00
Wagon Seat, Maple, Hickory, Double Ladder Back, 31 1/2 x 33 x 15 In. 375.00
Wall Unit, Eames, ESU-100N, Laminated Wood, Masonite, Steel, c.1950, 20 x 47 In. 3930.00
Wardrobe, Empire, Mahogany, Flame Veneer, Breakdown, 64 x 28 x 93 In. 3450.00
Wardrobe, George III, Mahogany, 2-Paneled Doors Over 5 Drawers, 88 x 48 In. 5290.00
Wardrobe, George III, Mahogany, Swan's-Neck Pediment, Late 1700s, 91 x 58 x 24 In. 3055.00
Wardrobe, H. Probber, Cane, Sliding Doors, Plinth Base, 75 x 47 In. 1534.00
Wardrobe, Mahogany, 2 Doors, Lower Drawer, Mirrors, Carved Center Crest, 80 x 51 In. 529.00
Wardrobe, Painted Flowers, Cream, Green, Gilt, Domed Cornice, 2 Doors, Italy, 85 In. 2115.00
Wardrobe, Pine, Grain Painted, 2 Doors, Molded Top, Ball Feet, 19th Century, 68 x 47 In. 660.00
Wardrobe, Pine, Red Brown Paint, Stepped Cornice, 2 Doors, 76 x 50 In. 489.00
Wardrobe, Poplar, Blue Green Paint, Raised Panel Door, Wooden Latch, 52 x 21 x 79 In. 374.00
Wardrobe, Rococo Revival, Mahogany, 2 Doors, 3 Drawers, England, 99 x 88 x 24 In. 3510.00
Wardrobe, Walnut, Banded Inlay, 2 Doors, 59 x 51 x 25 In. 660.00
Wardrobe, Walnut, Mahogany, 2-Paneled Doors, 3 Banded Drawers, 86 x 69 In. 2937.00
Wardrobe, William IV, Breakfront, Paneled Doors, Fitted Interior, 80 x 26 In. 3290.00
Wardrobe, William IV, Mahogany, 2-Paneled Doors, 2 Over 3 Drawers, 81 x 83 In. 4113.00
Washstand, Bamboo, Yellow Paint, Carved Marble Top, Drawer, England, 1800s, 29 In. 467.00
Washstand, Corner, Federal, Figured Maple, Bowfront, Shelf, Early 1800s, 37 x 24 In. 1554.00

Washstand, Federal, Mahogany, Bird's-Eye Maple, Splashboard, c.1815, 39 x 23 In. 705.00
Washstand, George II Style, Mahogany, 2 Tiers, Square Top, Legs, 32 x 14 x 15 In. 59.00
Washstand, George III Style, Mahogany, Shelf, 3 Snake Feet, 32 x 12 3/4 In. 115.00
Washstand, George III, Mahogany, Inlaid, Cutouts, Tambour Door, Drawer, 40 x 20 In. 476.00
Washstand, George III, Mahogany, Inlaid, Tall Backsplash, c.1800, 45 x 25 In. 940.00
Washstand, Lacquered, Carved, Gilt Washbowl, Chinese, Early 1900s, 66 x 14 In. 411.00
Washstand, Mahogany, 3 Tiers, Molded Edge, Drawer, England, 32 x 18 x 15 In. 316.00
Washstand, Mahogany, Grained, 3/4 Splashboard, Drawer, Victorian, 1800s, 33 x 18 In. 147.00
Washstand, Mahogany, Inlaid, Pierced Piecrust Top, c.1810, 40 x 23 In. 120.00
Washstand, Neoclassical, Mahogany, Drawer, Mid-Atlantic, c.1825, 33 1/2 x 26 In. 646.00
Washstand, Painted, Soap Hollow, Stenciled, Oversized Top, Drawer, 22 x 21 7/8 In. 7170.00
Washstand, Renaissance Revival, Walnut, Marble Top, Doors, 37 3/4 x 31 1/4 x 17 In. 500.00
Washstand, Sheraton Style, Drawer, John Hill, Maine, 1800s, 34 x 32 x 19 In. 460.00
Washstand, Sheraton, Faux Tiger Maple Finish, Drawer, Shelf, 29 x 34 x 17 In. 1265.00
Washstand, Sheraton, Mahogany, Nantucket, c.1815, 44 x 24 x 18 In. 920.00
Washstand, Sheraton, Scrolled Splashboard, 2 Drawers, 28 x 31 x 14 In. 400.00
Washstand, Softwood, Flowers, Gallery Back, New England, 39 x 19 x 16 In. 495.00
Washstand, Softwood, Gallery, Step-Down Sides, Drawers, Open Shelf, 38 In. 275.00
Washstand, Softwood, Shaped Gallery, Drawers, Shelf, New England, 38 In. 275.00
Washstand, Stylized Flowers, Scrolled Sides, Basin Cutout, Shelf, 39 x 19 x 16 In. 495.00
Washstand, Victorian, Mahogany, Drawer, Middle Shelf, c.1850, 37 x 19 x 18 In. 235.00
Washstand, Victorian, Walnut, Ebony, Teardrop Pulls, 37 x 29 In. 250.00
Washstand, Walnut, Red Lacquer, Foo Dog, Flower Sprays, 2 Doors, 66 x 18 x 20 In. 740.00
Washstand, Yellow Paint, Gold Stencil, Drawer, Splashboard, 29 x 32 x 15 In. 518.00
Washstand, Yellow Paint, Scrolled Splashboard, Shelves, c.1840, 32 x 19 In. 470.00
Wastebasket, Gucci, Calf Leather, Silver Trim, 1970s, 10 In. 720.00
Wastebasket, Leather, Over Wood, Octagonal, J. Adnet For Hermes, 1950s, 14 x 12 In. 1900.00
Wastebasket, Stickley Bros., Flared Slatted Sides, Cutout Handles, 18 x 14 In. 825.00
Whatnot Shelf, Faux Rosewood Grain, 4 Tiers, Victorian, 1800s, 46 x 20 In. 1175.00
Whatnot Shelf, Victorian, Walnut, 3 Tiers, Leaf-Carved Supports, 40 x 45 x 6 In. 325.00
Window Seat, Biedermeier, Mahogany, Mortise & Tenon, Ebonized Finials, 23 x 24 In. 546.00
Window Seat, Louis XVI Style, Gilt, Padded, Outscrolled, Late 1800s, 28 x 45 In. 940.00
Window Seat, Neoclassical, Mahogany, Green Floral Upholstery, 27 x 4 x 18 In. 120.00
Window Seat, Painted, Upholstered, Flowers, Italy, 19th Century, 17 x 37 x 12 In. 1380.00
Window Seat, Regency Style, Padded Seat, Tapered Legs, 22 x 47 In., Pair 1997.00
Window Seat, Regency, Parcel Gilt, Faux Rosewood, Padded Arms, 25 x 55 In., Pair 3055.00
Window Seat, Restauration, Mahogany, Fan Splat Ends, Early 1900s, 31 x 76 In. 1997.00
Wine Cooler, George III Style, Mahogany, Carved, Liner, c.1900, 32 x 15 In. 3300.00
Wine Cooler, George III, Mahogany, Brass, Zinc Liner, Oval, c.1800, 25 x 24 x 17 In. 3525.00
Wine Cooler, Georgian, Slatted Wood, 2 Brass Bands, Oval, 1800s, 8 x 23 1/2 x 17 In. 1495.00
Wine Cooler, Hammered Copper, Brass Handles, Stainless Steel Insert, 8 x 13 In. 195.00
Wine Rack, Wrought Iron, Hinged Door, Green Paint, 50-Bottle Capacity, 46 x 23 In. 645.00

G. ARGY-ROUSSEAU is the impressed mark used on a variety of objects in the Art Deco style. Gabriel Argy-Rousseau, born in 1885, was a French glass artist. In 1921, he formed a partnership that made pate-de-verre and other glass. He worked until 1952 and died in 1953.

G-ARGY-
ROUSSEAU

Frame, Flowers, Red, White, Blue, Pate-De-Verre, 4 x 4 3/4 In. 3278.00
Night-Light, Red Roses, Green Leaves, Mottled Maize Ground, Pate-De-Verre, 7 In. 4690.00
Night-Light, Roses, Stems, Leaves Band, Red Rose Petals, Pate-De-Verre, 7 In. 1208.00
Paperweight, Cube, Amber, Brown, Butterflies, Pate-De-Verre, 1 3/4 In. 3000.00
Paperweight, Lime Green Cube, Brown Swirls, 2 Moths On Top, Pate-De-Verre, 2 3/4 In. 2185.00
Pendant, Butterfly, Amber Wings, Brown, Clear Ground, Pate-De-Verre, 2 1/8 In. 1265.00
Pendant, Green Leaves, Red Berries, Green Chord, c.1920, 2 3/4 x 2 In. 1315.00
Pendant, Rectangular, Pinecone, Pine Needles, Pate-De-Verre, Signed, 2 3/4 In. 1035.00
Pendant, White Blossoms, Yellow Stamens, Clear Ground, Pate-De-Verre, 2 1/4 In. 1150.00
Vase, Brown Shading To Red, Incised, Solid Handles, Pate-De-Verre, Signed, 6 1/4 In. 4800.00
Vase, Bud, Ribbed, 2 Eagles, Raspberry Ribbons, Purple Border, Signed, 5 1/4 In. 7560.00
Vase, Magenta, Vertical Molded Lines, Solid Scroll Handle, Pate-De-Verre, 6 In. 4920.00
Vase, Musiciennes Grecs, Gray, Pate-De-Verre, c.1928, 9 3/4 In. 14950.00

GALLE was a designer who made glass, pottery, furniture, and other Art Nouveau items. Emile Galle founded his factory in France in 1874. After Galle's death in 1904, the firm continued to make glass and furniture until 1931. The name *Galle* was used as a mark, but it was often hidden in the design of the object. Galle glass is listed here. Pottery is in the next section. His furniture is listed in the Furniture category.

Basket, Scrolls, Sail Boat, Sunset, Gold Enameled, Oblong, c.1900, 6 1/4 In. 896.00
Bowl, Scenic, Trees, Water, Mottled Yellow, Frosted Ground, Signed, 11 x 6 1/2 In. 3450.00
Box, Cover, Maroon Leaves, Berries, Frosted Ground, Cameo, Signed, 6 1/2 In. 403.00
Box, Cover, Ruby Overlay, Flower, Leaves, Tapered Cylinder, c.1900, 3 1/2 In. 956.00
Condiment Set, Decanters, Jar, Cover, Tray, Enameled Flowers, Leaves, Multicolored, 12 1/2 In. .. 1955.00
Ewer, Enameled, Man Playing Bag Pipe, Peasants, Handle, 8 x 6 In. 900.00
Flask, Flowers, Multilayered, Silver Sheet Inclusions, Flame Stopper, 8 1/2 In. ......13200.00 to 14000.00
Flask, Verrerie Parlant, Rien Sans Amour, Applied Hearts, Cover, 10 1/2 In. 7140.00
Jar, Cover, Lake, Boats, Swallows, Trees, Oval, c.1890, 3 1/2 x 7 In. 1912.00
Jar, Cover, Orange Overlay, Flowers, Leaves, Oval, Cameo, c.1900, 4 In. 1076.00
Lamp, Chandelier, 3-Light, Red Flower Clusters, Leaves, Cream Ground, Chains, 19 1/2 In. 5400.00
Lamp, Roses, Orange, Brown, Cameo, Patinated Bronze Mount, 20 1/2 In. 10620.00
Lamp Base, Blue, Purple Clematis Flowers, Yellow Ground, Mold-Blown Cameo, 6 1/2 In. 2015.00
Perfume Bottle, Atomizer, Red, Brown Glass, Flowering Shrub, 8 In. 1840.00
Scent Bottle, Flowers, Leaves, Peach, Silver Foot, Hinged Lid, Glass Stopper, 5 1/2 In. 1438.00
Tumbler, Amethyst Leaves, Branches, Green, White Frosted Ground, Cameo, Signed, 2 1/8 In. 300.00
Tumbler, Enameled Leaves, Stems, Flying Insects, Clear, Etched Veining, Applied Handle, 1 1/4 In. 430.00
Tumbler, Flower Blossoms, Leaves, Orange, Frosted Ground, Cameo, Signed, 2 1/2 In. 240.00
Vase, Amber, Ribbed, Enameled Mums, Leafy Stems, Bucket Shape, Ruffled Rim, Signed, 5 1/4 In. 1236.00
Vase, Amethyst Flower Blossoms, Leaves, Butterfly, Frosted Ground, Cameo, Signed, 3 3/4 In. 430.00
Vase, Amethyst Flower Blossoms, Leaves, Clear, Applied Handles, Cameo, 11 x 9 1/2 In. 4140.00
Vase, Amethyst, Morning Glories, Leaves, Flared Rim, Pedestal Foot, Cameo, Signed, 6 1/2 In. 3910.00
Vase, Anemone Flowers, Leaves, Etched, Short Neck, Oval, c.1900, 8 In. 2150.00
Vase, Banjo, Dragonfly, Lily Pads, Orange Overlay, c.1890, 6 1/2 In. 2629.00
Vase, Banjo, Flowers, Green Overlay, Pink Ground, c.1890, 6 1/2 In. 780.00
Vase, Banjo, Grasses, Trees, Yellow, c.1890, 6 1/2 In. 840.00
Vase, Banjo, Green Leaves, Vines, Hanging Seedpods, Frosted Ground, 6 3/4 In. 690.00
Vase, Banjo, Leaves, Pod, Brown, Green, Pink, White Frosted Ground, Cameo, Signed, 6 1/2 In. ... 920.00
Vase, Banjo, Purple Flower, Leaves, Frosted Ground, 6 3/4 In. 1265.00
Vase, Bleeding Heart Blossoms, Leaves, Translucent Green, Enameled, Cameo, Signed, 11 In. 3740.00
Vase, Blossoms, Leaves, Orange, Cameo, 4 1/2 In. 520.00
Vase, Chrysanthemums, Orange, Red, Yellow, Frosted, Green Ground, Bulbous, Cameo, 29 1/2 In. 3528.00
Vase, Columbines, Amethyst Overlay, Bulbous Base, Cameo, c.1900, 2 1/4 In. 478.00
Vase, Crocus, Purple, White Ground, Baluster, 3 1/4 In. 316.00
Vase, Cross Of Lorraine, Amber, Optic Ribbed, Scissored Rim, Thistle, Enameled, Signed, 5 In. 805.00
Vase, Daisies, Leaves, Red & Brown Overlay, Oval, c.1900, 16 3/4 In. 3100.00
Vase, Ducks, French Horn, Orange Overlay, Oval, Cameo, c.1900, 4 In. 1195.00
Vase, Enameled Bird On Branch, Blossoms, Leaves, Berries, Translucent Ground, Cameo, 10 In. .. 6038.00
Vase, Enameled Flowers, Applied Beads, Green Mottled Ground, Cameo, Signed, 13 3/4 In. 570.00
Vase, Enameled Flowers, Leaves, Applied Clear Cabochon, Signed, 11 In. 4140.00
Vase, Enameled Flowers, Leaves, Green, Gold, Molded Handles, c.1890, 11 3/8 In. 3120.00
Vase, Enameled Flowers, Scalloped Rim, Bulbous Base, 1900, 3 In. 265.00
Vase, Fern, Meadow Grasses, Olive Green, Chocolate Brown, Cameo, 9 5/8 In. 1840.00
Vase, Flower Blossoms, Leaves, Orange, Frosted Ground, Cameo, Signed, 3 7/8 In. 240.00
Vase, Flowers, Blue, Stylized Leaves, Applied Frosted Foot, Cameo, Signed, 15 3/4 In. 1080.00
Vase, Flowers, Green, Amethyst, White, Pink Ground, Cameo, Signed, 3 1/2 In. 750.00
Vase, Flowers, Hanging, Lavender, Vines, Green Leaves, Cameo, 12 In. 1380.00
Vase, Flowers, Lavender, Hanging From Vine, Windowpane, Frosted Ground, Cameo, 16 In. 2933.00
Vase, Flowers, Leaves, Purple Overlay, Yellow Ground, Oval, Cameo, c.1890, 10 In. 720.00
Vase, Flowers, Leaves, Stems, Brown, Green, Slender Neck, Bulbous Foot, Cameo, 29 1/2 In. 6615.00
Vase, Flowers, Purple, Stems, Leaves, Cream Ground, Cameo, Signed, 12 In. 1495.00
Vase, Flowers, Red, Frosted Shaded Peach Ground, Cameo, 3 3/4 In. 920.00
Vase, Flowers, Red, Yellow, Frosted Ground, Bulbous, Footed, Cameo, 20 In. 7050.00

A hair dryer set for cool can be used to blow the dust off very ornate pieces of porcelain.

Galle Pottery, Pitcher, Brown, Poppies, Earthenware, Signed, Croix De Lorraine, 7 3/4 In.

Vase, Flowers, Smoky Purple, Leaves, Stems, Green To Clear Ground, Cameo, 6 In. 4560.00
Vase, Fruit, Leaves, Oval, Mold-Blown, Cameo, c.1900, 15 1/2 In. 12725.00
Vase, Hillside Forest, Mountains, Blue, Amber Sky, Enameled, 7 In. 1730.00
Vase, Hydrangeas, Blue, Woody Branches, Olive Green Leaves, Square, Cameo, 5 7/8 In. 1610.00
Vase, Iris, Green, Lavender, White, Frosted To Orange Ground, Corseted, 22 In. 3968.00
Vase, Iris, Leaves, Amethyst Overlay, Baluster, c.1900, 7 3/4 In. 685.00
Vase, Iris, Leaves, Etched, Flared, Amethyst Foot, Knopped Stem, c.1900, 13 1/4 In. 1555.00
Vase, Irises, Leaves, Gray, Yellow, Red Overlay, Tapered, Cameo, 1920, 12 1/2 In. 2357.00
Vase, Irises, Leaves, Orange, Green, Amethyst Overlay, Frosted Ground, Cameo, c.1900, 16 3/4 In. 8100.00
Vase, Landscape, Brown, Green, Pink, Frosted Ground, Cameo, Signed, 18 In. 7638.00
Vase, Landscape, Forest, River, Boats, Olive Green, Frosted Shaded To Tangerine Ground, 13 In. .. 3360.00
Vase, Leaves, Berries, Amethyst, Green, Clear Frosted Ground, Cameo, Signed, 5 In. 520.00
Vase, Leaves, Pink, Green, Yellow, Frosted Ground, Oval, Cameo, 4 1/8 In. 800.00
Vase, Lilac, Green, White, Flowers, Peach Shaded To Frosted Ground, Cameo, Signed, 6 1/2 In. ... 2530.00
Vase, Olives, Leaves, Amber To Peach Ground, Cameo, Signed, 6 1/4 In. 1080.00
Vase, Orange Transparent Leaves, Stems, Berries, Frosted Ground, Cameo, Signed, 5 1/2 In. 805.00
Vase, Orange Transparent Leaves, Stems, Berries, Frosted Ground, Fire Polished, Cameo, 10 In. 1200.00
Vase, Orchids, Green, Forest, Pink, Oval, Cameo, Signed, 5 In. 1438.00
Vase, Persian Riders On Horses, Arabesque Flowers, Enameled, Oval, c.1890, 4 1/2 x 8 3/4 In. 5080.00
Vase, Pilgrim, Landscape, Blue Mountains & Lake, 8 1/2 In. 5175.00
Vase, Plums, Leaves, Etched, Cranberry On Yellow, Green, Bulbous Middle, Cameo, c.1900, 4 In. .. 1675.00
Vase, Pond, Lily Pads, Dragonflies, Amber Overlay, Etched, Flared, Cameo, 18 In. 8050.00
Vase, Poppies, Etched, Pink Ground, Cupped Rim, Oval, c.1890, 5 In. 660.00
Vase, Poppies, Orange, Long Stems, Frosted Ground, Cameo, 4 5/8 In. 430.00
Vase, Poppies, Pink, Olive Green Leaves, Frosted Ground, Cameo, 7 1/2 In. 1610.00
Vase, Roses, Amber Ground, Windowpane, Flared Rim, Footed, Cameo, Signed, 16 In. 4600.00
Vase, Seminude Woman, Transparent Gown, Intaglio Carved, Signed, 9 1/2 In. 1725.00
Vase, Stick, Alabaster, Butterscotch, Mums, Fire Polished, Bulbous Base, Cameo, 16 In. 3450.00
Vase, Stick, Flowers, Leaves, Pink To Clear, Bulbous Base, Cameo, c.1890, 8 1/4 In. 685.00
Vase, Stick, Lavender, Green, White Flowers, Leaves, Vines, Pink Ground, Cameo, 11 In. 1900.00
Vase, Stick, Mottled, Blue, Orange Leaves, Flowers, Cameo, 9 In. 865.00
Vase, Stick, Phlox, Purple Overlay, Bulbous Base, Cameo, c.1900, 12 In. 1195.00
Vase, Stick, Red Overlay, Leaves, Berries, Bulbous Base, Cameo, c.1890, 8 In. 478.00
Vase, Stick, Wisteria Vine, Amethyst, Pink, Frosted Ground, Cameo, 8 1/8 In. 750.00
Vase, Thistle, Green, Frosted Cream Ground, Cameo, Signed, 3 3/4 In. 420.00
Vase, Thistles, Green, Peach Ground, Frosted, Footed, Cameo, 16 1/2 In. 1725.00
Vase, Trees, Pond, Brown Overlay, Flattened Oval, Cupped Rim, c.1900, 5 1/2 In. 1315.00
Vase, Verrerie Parlante, Carved Verse, Gold Enamled, 4 1/2 In. 6800.00

GALLE POTTERY was made by Emile Galle, the famous French designer, after 1874. The pieces were marked with the initials *E. G.* impressed, *Em. Galle Faiencerie de Nancy*, or a version of his signature. Galle is best known for his glass, listed above.

Candelabrum, 4-Light, Lions, Heraldic, Parcel Gilt, Blue & Gray, Faience, 22 1/4 In. 3760.00
Clock, Blue & White, Tower, Lion, Scrolled Foliage, Faience, 19 In. 12500.00

Figure, Lion, Rampant, Blue, White, Faience, c.1880, 16 1/4 In., Pair 7200.00
Pitcher, Brown, Poppies, Earthenware, Signed, Croix De Lorraine, 7 3/4 In. .... *ILLUS* 1728.00
Pitcher, Purple Glaze, Praying Mantis, Spider Mums, Branches, 7 1/4 In. 1725.00
Pitcher, Water, Brown, Blue Glaze, Gold Spatters, Insects, Leaves, Bulbous, Faience, 7 1/2 In. 3760.00

GAME collectors like all types of games. Of special interest are any board games or card games. Transogram and other company names are included in the description when known. Other games may be found listed under Card, Toy, or the name of the character or celebrity featured in the game.

Adams' Real Magic, S.S. Adams, Asbury Park, N.J., Box, 1920s 410.00
Addams Family, Ideal, Board, 1964 .... 80.00
Addams Family, Milton Bradley, Card, 1965, 6 x 7 1/2 In. 25.00
Bagatelle, Spring Action, Lithograph, Red Frame, Souvenir From Universal Theatres, Levy 275.00
Baker's Ball Game For Men & Boys, W.J. Baker Company, 1920, 27 x 27 In. 2320.00
Barney Google & Spark Plug, Milton Bradley, Board, 1923 .... 355.00
Big League Table Base Ball, Edwards Manufacturing Co., 27 x 27 In. 6960.00
Bo Peep, McLoughlin, 13 x 15 In. 350.00
Board, Checkers & Backgammon, Book Shape, Drawer, Grain Painted, WB, MB, 18 x 17 3/4 In. ... 1320.00
Board, Checkers & Backgammon, Painted 165.00
Board, Checkers & Backgammon, Wood Frame, 18 3/4 x 19 In. 1840.00
Board, Checkers & Parcheesi, Painted, 20th Century, 21 x 21 In. 80.00
Board, Checkers & Parcheesi, Pine, Painted, Orange, Red, Black, 27 x 18 1/2 In. 575.00
Board, Checkers & Parcheesi, Red, Yellow, White, c.1870, 18 1/4 x 26 1/4 In. 880.00
Board, Checkers, 2-Sided, Hinged Lid, Framed Edge, 16 3/4 x 26 In. 748.00
Board, Checkers, Black & Amber Painted Squares, Raised Edge, A.C. Abear, 1929, 17 In. 220.00
Board, Checkers, Black, Red, Green Paint, 2-Tone Gilding, Beveled Edges, Metal Trim, 20 x 20 In. .. 5750.00
Board, Checkers, Breadboard End, Orange & Salmon Paint, 14 3/4 x 16 1/2 In. 175.00
Board, Checkers, Globe & Rutgers Fire Insurance Co., N.Y., 1800s, 17 x 25 In. 660.00
Board, Checkers, Green & Mustard Squares, RM Monogram, P. Fafard, 18 3/4 x 30 3/4 In. 1560.00
Board, Checkers, Green, Red, Yellow, Square Nails, New England, Mid 1800s, 16 x 16 In. 3950.00
Board, Checkers, JLT, Red, Black, c.1870, 20 x 30 1/4 In. 550.00
Board, Checkers, Mustard & Black, Painted, Wood, Pine Panel, 19 x 30 In. 588.00
Board, Checkers, Painted, Green, Yellow, Black, Quebec, 21 x 31 In. 570.00
Board, Checkers, Pine, 2-Sided, Painted, Square Nails, c.1875, 16 x 12 In. 2850.00
Board, Checkers, Pine, 3 Colors, New England, c.1860, 12 x 12 1/2 In. 2350.00
Board, Checkers, Red & Black, Reverse On Glass, Frame 55.00
Board, Checkers, Red & Black, Yellow Line Divider, 19th Century, 28 x 17 1/2 In. 155.00
Board, Checkers, Red & Natural Squares, Black Border, Wood, Folding, 14 1/2 In. 80.00
Board, Checkers, Walnut, 4 Colors, Brass Hinges, Late 1800s, 14 x 14 In. 1650.00
Board, Checkers, Wood, Inlaid, Drawer, Dovetailed, 2 1/2 x 15 x 12 1/2 In. 230.00
Board, Cribbage, Ivory, 3 Ball Feet, 2 Pegs, 22 3/4 In. 115.00
Board, Cribbage, Ivory, Inuit, Carved, Water Monster Attacking Walrus, Engraved Kayak, 25 In. 5580.00
Board, Cribbage, Ivory, Scrolling Flowers, Figures In Garden, Chinese, Late 1800s, 9 1/2 In. 175.00
Board, Cribbage, Walnut, Inlaid, 5-Point Stars, Spreadwing Eagles, 14 x 3 In. 323.00
Board, Iron, 2-Sided, On Wood Stand, Ditty Box, 1873 Patent, 35 x 17 x 15 In. 1035.00
Board, Lacquer, Folding, Bone Figures, 19 1/2 In. 230.00
Board, Leather, Wood, Decorated, Hinged Mahogany Case, Late 1800s, 23 x 23 In. 720.00
Board, Nosey, McLoughlin Brothers., N.Y., Card, 1905 .... 168.00
Board, Painted Wood, Iron Starburst Center, Numbered Outer Ring, Iron Posts, 19 3/4 In. 303.00
Board, Painted, Red & Black, Gold Stripes, Monkey & Lion At Ends, c.1880, 31 x 19 In. 990.00
Board, Parcheesi, 2 Pine Boards, Breadboard Ends, Yellow, Green, 19 x 21 In. 460.00
Board, Parcheesi, 2-Sided, Breadboard End, 23 x 29 In. 1150.00
Board, Parcheesi, On Breadboard, Painted, Folk Art, 30 x 16 In. 1140.00
Board, Parcheesi, Painted Green, Red, White, J.A.B., Lowell, Mass., 24 1/2 x 24 1/2 In. 657.00
Board, Parcheesi, Painted, 3 Boards, Molded Edge, 20 1/2 x 21 In. 660.00
Board, Slate, Simulates Marble, Green, Yellow, Red, Black & Brown Squares, 20 x 20 In. 290.00
Board, Square, Painted Coiled Snake, 63 Holes, 16 x 15 1/2 In. 1725.00
Board, Walnut, Swivel Out Compartment, 32 Sandwich Glass Marbles, Round, 1800s 330.00
Bowling, King Pin, Baldwin Company, 1930s, 29 1/2 In. 125.00
Bullwinkle Ring Toss, Whitman, Box, Unopened, 1972, 8 x 15 In. 90.00

Card Holdout, Wizard, Nickel Plated, c.1906 .... 58.00
Champion Game Of Base Ball, Brouthers, Clarkson, Schutz Copyright, 1889, 7 5/8 x 4 In. 2610.00
Chess Pieces, Ivory, 16 Ivory Color, 16 Red Dyed, 7 In., 32 Piece 870.00
Chess Set, Ivory Pieces, Teak Board, Chinese, 1960, 7-In King, 26-In. Board, 32 Piece 2050.00
Chess Set, Ivory, Figures, Folding Board, Maple, Rosewood Squares, 12 3/8 x 12 1/2 In. 375.00
Chess Set, Ivory, Red & White Stained, Chinese, 4 In. 115.00
Chess Set, Pottery, Gladys Eleanor Montgomery, 1930s, 5 1/2 To 8 In., 32 Piece 285.00
Chess Set, Turned Wood, Pine Box, Slide Lid, c.1925 .... 55.00
Chinese Checkers, 60 Marbles, No. 00, Box 50.00
Clown Ball Toss, Papier-Mache, Numbered Wood Box, 22 In. 100.00
Conjuring Tricks, Spears Games, J.W.S. & S. Of Bavaria, Box, Germany, 1920s 569.00
Dart Board, Pine, Painted, Breadboard Ends, Round, New York, c.1895, 21 x 21 In. 1850.00
Dexterity Puzzle, Bomb Over Hiroshima, A.C. Gilbert, 4 1/2 In. 80.00
Dexterity Puzzle, Capture The Cooties, Irving Smith, 5 In. 35.00
Dexterity Puzzle, Dumb-Bells Puzzle, R. Journet, 5 In. 20.00
Dexterity Puzzle, Hungry Pup, A.C. Gilbert, 4 1/2 In. 39.00
Dexterity Puzzle, Phlipemin, R. Journet, 4 1/4 In. 20.00
Dexterity Puzzle, Rin Tin Tin Rusty, Tin, Paper, Celluloid, Nabisco, 1950s, 1 3/8 In. 45.00
Dice, Soldier's, Hand Made, Bone, Revolutionary War, Pair 75.00
Dice Game, Birdcage, Chuck-A-Luck, E.S. Lowe, Box, 1941, 5 In. 125.00
Dominoes, Bone & Ebony, Box, Slide Lid, 19th Century 250.00
Dominoes, Bone, Box, 28 Piece 99.00
Fantasy Island, Island On Box, Columbia Pictures Television, Ideal, Board, 1978 .... 30.00
Fibber McGee & Wistful Vista Mystery, Milton Bradley, Board, 1940 .... 65.00
Fish Pond, Paper, Bradley, Box, 18 1/2 In. 65.00
Game Of Base Ball, Selchow & Richter, N.Y., Box, 5 1/8 x 5 1/8 In. 715.00
Game Of Base-Ball, Metal Players, McLoughlin Brothers, Board, 1886, 17 x 9 1/2 In. 1625.00
Gaming Pin, Turned Wood, Carnival, Painted Face, Brown, White, 15 x 3 1/4 In. 250.00
Gee-Wiz Horse Race, Wolverine, Box, 1930s .... 155.00 to 160.00
Gilbert's Mysto Magic, Box, 1920s 1455.00
Great American Baseball, Metal Board, Wooden Pegs, Hustler, 1920s 235.00
Green Ghost, Glows In The Dark, Transogram, Board, Box, 1965 .... 170.00
Grid-Craft, Football, Box, 1926 .... 140.00
Haunted House, Hidden Doors, Ideal, 3-D Board, 1962 .... 310.00
Hold-Out Device, Kepplinger, Shadowbox Frame, c.1890, 17 1/4 x 30 3/8 In. 1390.00
Honey West, Girl Private Eye, Ideal, Board, 1965, 10 x 18 In. 210.00
Hoop Toss, Wood, Painted, Late 1800s 110.00
Jigsaw Puzzle, Girl, Chalkboard, Cat, Jessie Willcox Smith, c.1923, 8 x 8 1/2 In. 100.00
Jigsaw Puzzle, Girl, Doll, In Bed, Woman, Wood, Jessie Willcox Smith, c.1923, 8 x 8 In. 100.00
Jigsaw Puzzle, Night Before Christmas, Milton Bradley, Boxed Set Of 3 .... 355.00
Jigsaw Puzzle, Raggedy Ann, Milton Bradley, Complete Box Of 3, 1944 .... 95.00
Jigsaw Puzzle, Santa Claus Puzzle Box, 3 Cardboards, Milton Bradley, Box, 9 1/4 x 13 In. 470.00
Juega De Magic, Borras, Spain, 1920s, 4 1/2 x 18 1/2 x 14 1/2 In. 355.00
Junior Bicycle Game, Parker Brothers, 2 Spinners, Board, c.1897, 11 1/2 x 17 In. 220.00
Kentucky Derby Race Game, Spinning Arrow, Tin, Box, Chein 35.00
L'Habit Fait L'Homme, Optical Transformation, Case, Dutch, 1700s, 2 1/4 x 3 1/4 In. 24675.00
Lotto, Wood, McLaughlin, Box, 9 1/2 In. 6.00
Major League Indoor Base Ball, Philadelphia Game Co., Board, 1910, 19 3/8 x 13 1/4 In. 3190.00
Messenger Boy, Milton Bradley Co., Spinner, Board, Box, c.1910 .... 138.00
Mickey Mantle's Big League Baseball, Gardner, Board, Box, 1960 .... 212.00
Mister Ed The Talking Horse, Parker Brothers, Board, 1962 .... 75.00
Mystery Gun, Tin, Lithograph, McDowell Mfg., No. 55, Marble, 1920s 125.00
Nodding Nancy, Mammy With Bandanna, Pipe, Ring Toss, Parker Brothers 230.00
Old Maid, Milton Bradley, Card, Box 39.00
Ozark Ike's, Little League Baseball, Built-Rite, 1956 .... 95.00
Parlor Football, McLoughlin Brothers, Board, Box, 1890s 555.00
Peter Rabbit's Race Game, Frederick Warne, England, Board, Box, 11 1/2 x 20 1/4 In. 1000.00
Pilgrim's Progress, Folding Board, Box, McLoughlin Brothers, 1875, 19 In. 95.00
Pinball, Aces High, Tin Lithograph, Durable Toys, 1920s 225.00
Pinhead, Hide & Seek, Remco, Board, 1959 .... 9.00
Poker, Chips, Holder, Victoria, Wood Holder, Ivory Chips 198.00

Pop-A-Bird, Shooting, Marks, Box 17.00
Puzzle, Blocks, Paper Lithograph, Continents, Countries, Geographic Educator Corp., 8 x 10 In. 138.00
Railroad, Cross Country Route, George Thistleton, Board, 1872, 19 x 22 In. 880.00
Ring Ball Toss, Clown, Pine, Painted, c.1900, 35 x 18 In. 2200.00
Rip Van Winkle, Paper, Edgar O. Clarke, Board, Box, 19 1/2 In. 250.00
Rudolph The Red-Nosed Reindeer, Parker Brothers, Board, 1948 .... 365.00
Scarlett O'Hara, Box, 1939 .... 195.00
Six Day Bike Race, 2-Sided, Lindstrom Tool & Toy Co., Tin, Board, 15 x 19 1/2 In. 120.00
Slalom, Tin, Battery, Japan, Box, 1950s, 15 1/4 In. 145.00
Snow White & Seven Dwarfs, Parker Brothers, Board, 1938 .... 350.00
Sweepstakes, Dice, Pre 1910, 10 1/4 x 11 3/4 In. 280.00
Target, Black, Tin, 3 Targets, A.J.J. Co., 9 In. 336.00
Target, Mighty Kong Big Mouth Tin, Battery Operated, Marx, Box, 13 In. 385.00
Time Bomb, Box, Milton Bradley, 1965 .... 90.00
Transogram Johnny Quest, Hanna-Barbera, Board, Box, 1964, 10 x 20 In. 390.00
Walter Johnson Baseball Game, Next Best To Real Game, Board, 1920s, 14 x 10 In. 430.00
Wheel, Gambling, 8 Panels, Horses, Numbers, Mirrored Center, Pedestal, 45 In. 358.00
Wheel, Gambling, Big 6, Mirrored Starburst, Iron Legs, H.C. Evans, Chicago, 89 1/2 x 60 In. 3190.00
Wheel, Gambling, Center Spokes, Multicolored, Iron Posts, 30 In. 300.00
Wheel, Gambling, Mirrored Starburst, Star Terminals, Cabriole Legs, 60 x 89 1/2 In. 3190.00
Wheel, Gambling, Mt. Carmel, Wood, Polychrome, Pinwheel, Spokes, Iron Posts, 30 In. 305.00
Wheel, Gambling, Painted, Wood, Solid Hub, Birds, Outer Number Ring, Iron Post, 23 In. 140.00
Wheel, Gambling, Painted, Wood, Spokes, Bird, Outer Number Ring, Iron Posts, 30 In. 385.00
Wheel, Gambling, Painted, Wood, Spokes, Outer Number Ring, Iron Posts, 23 In. 155.00
Wheel, Gambling, Painted, Wood, Starburst, Outer Number Ring, Iron Posts, 20 1/4 In. 240.00
Wheel, Roulette, Wood, Painted, 25 In. 495.00
Who's Afraid Of The Big Bad Wolf, Parker Brothers, Board, 1933 .... 190.00
Wild Bill Hickok, Cavalry & Indians, Guy Madison, Built-Rite, Board, 1950s 95.00
Winner Takes All, Country Fair, Red, Silver, Blue, Spinning Arrow, Square, Board, 30 3/4 In. 330.00
Wizard Of Oz, 1st Edition, Parker Brothers, Copyright 1922 .... 1700.00
Wonderful Game Of Oz, Paperboard, Pewter Pieces, Parker Bros., Box, 1921, 18 In. ....550.00 to 2000.00
World's Educator, W.S. Reed, Leominster, Mass., Wood Box, 1889, 15 1/2 x 5 In. 120.00
Yacht Race, Picture Of Sailboat Racing, Clark & Snowdon Co., Board, c.1895 .... 120.00
Zimmer's Base Ball, Zimmer, Board, 1885, 21 1/4 x 21 1/4 In. 10440.00
Zippy Zepps Air, Zeppelin Illustration, All Fair Toys & Games, 1920s, 9 x 18 x 1 In. 660.00

GAME PLATES are plates of any make decorated with pictures of birds, animals, or fish. The game plates usually came in sets consisting of twelve dishes and a serving platter. These sets were most popular during the 1880s.

Game Bird, Ivory Luster, Beaded Rim, OG Germany, 9 In. 30.00
Game Birds, Scalloped Rims, Limoges, c.1910, 17 1/2-In. Platter, 9-In. Plate, 6 Piece 210.00
Grouse, Gold Rim, Rydalia Ware, Hancock, England, c.1930, 4 1/2 In. 19.60
Grouse, Transfer, Orange Border, Daudin, c.1900, 8 In. 25.00
Mountain Quail, Transfer, Pink & Gold Edge, Sterling China, 7 3/4 In. 14.00
Pheasant, Borgfeldt, Coronet, 1906-20, 9 3/4 In. 65.00
Pheasant, R.K. Beck, Taylor Smith & Taylor, c.1915, 9 1/2 In. 72.00
Retailed By Ovington Bros., N.Y., Limoges, 9 3/4-In. Platter, 13 Piece 472.00
Ruffed Grouse, Centura, Corning, 10 In. 50.00
Snipe, Red Border, Gold Lacey Leaf, Scalloped, Haviland, Limoges, 1903-10, 9 In. 195.00
Turkey, Hand Painted, Leonard, Limoges, c.1900, 18 1/2 In., 9 Piece 295.00
Turkey Set, Platter, Plates, Wild Turkeys, Johnson Brothers, 13 Piece 316.00

GARDEN FURNISHINGS have been popular for centuries. The stone or metal statues, wire, iron, or rustic furniture, urns and fountains, sundials, and small figurines are included in this category. Many of the metal pieces have been made continuously for years.

Basin, Marble, Eagle, Shallow, Egg & Dart Molding, 36 x 16 In., Pair 5288.00
Basket, Hoop Handle, Cement, c.1920, 34 In. 2400.00
Bench, Arched Pierced Back, Relief Plaque, Rounded Arms, Black, Cast Iron, 43 x 71 In. 350.00
Bench, Fern & Blackberry Pattern, Cast Iron, c.1850, 33 1/2 x 55 In. 3290.00
Bench, Fern Pattern, Cast Iron, Kramer Foundry, Leavenworth, Kansas, 33 x 55 In. 2350.00

Bench, Fern Pattern, Curved Scalloped Back, Winged Legs, Paw Feet, Cast Iron, 30 x 14 In. 2480.00
Bench, Green, Strapwork Back, Scrolls, Slat Seat, Wrought Iron, 37 x 63 In., Pair 5580.00
Bench, Laurel Pattern Back, Gryphon Armrests, Claw Feet, Cast Iron, 30 x 43 In. 2115.00
Bench, Laurel Pattern, Black Paint, Cast Iron, 33 1/2 x 39 x 32 In. 1076.00
Bench, Neoclassical, Strapwork Seat, Diamond Back, Iron, Arms, 22 x 30 In., Pair 646.00
Bench, Passion Flower, Leaves, Vines, Bird Heads, Cast Iron, 35 x 42 In. 4325.00
Bench, Planks, Branchwork Arms, Legs, Patinated Bronze, 1900s, 31 x 61 x 12 In., Pair 5580.00
Bench, Renaissance Scroll Pattern, Cast Aluminum, c.1950, 33 x 42 In. 560.00
Bench, Tree Stump, Textured Oval Tops, Terra-Cotta, 18 x 17 In., Pair 1150.00
Bench, Vining Scrolls, Hoof Feet, Scroll Arms, Cast Iron, 37 x 43 x 16 In., Pair 2328.00
Birdbath, Flower Petal Flared Rim, Triple Cherub Base, Cast Stone, 36 x 28 In. 95.00
Birdbath, Neoclassical Style, Cherub, Fish, Griffins, Rams, Metal, 1900s, 57 x 24 In. 1175.00
Birdbath, Scallop Shell, Putti, Black Paint, Cast Iron, 14 In. 80.00
Birdhouse, 3 Onion Shape Spires, Painted, Salmon, Yellow, Wood, 12 x 20 x 26 In. 920.00
Bootscraper, Boxer Dog Finial, Cast Iron, Attached Brushes, Molded Base, 19 x 15 In. 115.00
Bootscraper, Crosscut Saw, 2 Men Sawing Log, Gray Paint, 6 x 2 x 16 In. 560.00
Bootscraper, Dachshund, Iron, Black, 19th Century, 7 1/4 x 20 1/2 In. 175.00
Bootscraper, Duck, Iron, Black Paint, 15 In. 275.00
Bootscraper, Irish Setter, Iron, White & Black Paint, 15 x 18 In. 192.00
Bootscraper, Lyre Form, Iron, c.1865, 6 1/2 x 13 1/4 In. 587.00
Chair, Fern & Blackberry Pattern, Cast Iron, 1800s, 32 1/2 x 19 In. 3290.00
Chair, Laurel Pattern Back, Gryphon Armrests, Cast Iron, Marked Hart, 27 x 27 In., Pair 2235.00
Chair, Laurel Pattern, Curved Back, Black Paint, Cast Iron, 32 In. 956.00
Chair, Morning Glory Pattern, Cast Iron, 32 1/2 In., Pair 1175.00
Chair, Oval Pierced Back, Round Seat, Pierced, Leaves, Cast Iron, 35 x 16 In., Pair 470.00
Chair, Quarter Moon Cutouts, Iron, Verdigris, c.1920, 30 x 23 In., Pair 2124.00
Chair, Renaissance Scroll Pattern, Arms, Cast Aluminum, c.1950, 31 1/2 In., Pair 499.00
Chair, Rococo Revival Style, Pierced, Aluminum, 1900s, 34 x 27 In., Pair 295.00
Chair Set, Openwork Back & Seat, Cross Stretcher, Claw Feet, Cast Aluminum, 32 In., 4 Piece 550.00
Figure, Boy Holding Lamp, Bronze, Verdigris Patina, 20th Century, 34 x 24 x 6 In. 550.00
Figure, Dog, Whippet, Seated, Free-Form Base, Lead, 16 1/2 In., Pair 1058.00
Figure, Owl, Molded 1/2 Round, Perched On Branch, Zinc, Glass Eyes, 21 1/4 In. 1293.00
Figure, Putto, Holding Bow & Heart, Arrows In Quiver, Rectangular Base, Lead, 30 In. 1265.00
Figure, Rooster, White Paint, Cast Iron, 15 In. 65.00
Figure, Seated Hound Holding Fruit Basket, Patinated Cement, 23 1/2 x 14 In. 450.00
Figure, St. Francis Of Assisi, Robe, Bird On Each Arm, Cast Stone, 34 x 14 x 7 In. 325.00
Figure, Turtle, Bronze, Fitted For Fountain, 8 x 18 1/2 In. 1060.00
Figure, Whippet, Laying Down, Cast Cement, Early 1900s, 17 x 27 In. 115.00
Figure, Young Man, Woman, Peasant Clothing, Cast Lead, 31 1/2 x 33 1/2 In., Pair 765.00
Fountain, 2 Tiers Basins, Muses, Mermaids, Dolphins, Bronze, Patinated, 96 x 44 In. . . .6169.00 to 7345.00
Fountain, 2 Tiers, 3 Swans, Baluster Pedestal, Cast Iron, 54 x 23 In. 587.00
Fountain, 2 Tiers, Boy Holding Fish Spigot, Dolphin Base, 3 Paw Feet, Cast Bronze, 62 In. 1880.00
Fountain, 3 Tiers, 3 Swans, Center Pedestal, Cast Zinc, 56 x 56 In. 2300.00
Fountain, Baroque Style, Putto, Urn, Musicians, Dolphins, Rocaille Base, 105 x 75 In. 14100.00
Fountain, Boy Holding Fish, Bronze, Water Sprays, Fish's Mouth, 26 x 14 In. 2400.00
Fountain, Boy On Turtle, Bronze, Green Patina, Tiffany & Co., 32 1/2 x 21 1/2 x 16 In. 12650.00
Fountain, Bronze, Boy Playing Flute, 52 x 16 In. 2457.00
Fountain, Bronze, Leaping Carp, 11 In. 46.00
Fountain, Carved, Cherub, Scallop Shell Basin, White Marble, 36 In. 1880.00
Fountain, Girl In Frog Pool, Frog Water Spouts, Bronze, Early 20th Century, 39 3/4 In. 3408.00
Fountain, Herons, 1 Head Up, 1 Head Down, Bronze, Verdigris Patina, 79 & 60 In., Pair 2056.00
Fountain, Lion Head, Lead, 40 x 36 In. 3510.00
Fountain, Play Days, Nude Woman, Frogs, Bronze, Patina, 20th Century, 41 1/2 x 14 In. 3250.00
Fountain, Victorian Style, 2 Tiers, Cattails, Egrets, Bulbous Pedestal, Aluminum, 65 x 35 In. 499.00
Fountain, Wall, Lion, Silvered, Brass Plate, 9 1/2 x 7 3/4 In. 430.00
Gnome, Painted, Red Hat, Green Pants, Gray Beard, Rosy Cheeks, Cast Iron, 11 In. 230.00
Hitching Post, Black Boy, On Bale Of Cotton, Iron, 44 x 15 In. 3600.00
Hitching Post, Black Man, On Bale Of Cotton, Iron, 44 1/2 In. 690.00
Hitching Post, Horse Head Finial, Black Paint Trace, Cast Iron, 19th Century, 14 1/2 In. 558.00
Hitching Post, Horse Head Finial, Iron, 44 In., Pair . . . . .748.00 to 1080.00
Hitching Post, Horse Head Finial, Iron, 48 In., Pair 690.00

Hitching Post, Horse Head Finial, Iron, 67 In. 546.00
Hitching Post, Jockey, Black Boots, White Pants, Red Shirt, Hand On Hip, Iron, 48 x 31 In. 960.00
Hitching Post, Jockey, Black Man, Hat, Ho Dar, New Bremen, Cast Iron, 23 1/2 x 10 In. 865.00
Hitching Post, Jockey, Black, Polychrome, Cast Iron, Early 20th Century, 37 In., Pair 295.00
Hitching Post, Jockey, Painted, Black, Blue Vest, Red Pants, Hat, Cast Iron, 38 In. 489.00
Hitching Post, Jockey, Painted, Blue Shirt, Iron, Square Base, c.1850, 46 x 16 In. 3819.00
Hitching Post Finial, Seated Spaniel, Ring At Neck, Cast Iron, 5 1/4 x 11 1/2 In. 520.00
Jardiniere, 4 Lobes With Lion's Mask, Molded Rim & Base, Cast Iron, 10 x 16 In., Pair 382.00
Jardiniere, Empire Style, Ormolu, Gold Wreath, Ball Finials & Feet, Iron, 23 x 18 In., Pair 1762.00
Jardiniere, Georgian Style, Rectangular, Rosettes, Drapery, Iron, 1900s, 15 x 25 In., Pair 294.00
Lavabo, Wall Mounted, Lion Head, Aluminum, 34 x 18 In. 85.00
Lawn Sprinkler, Alligator, Red Paint, Cast Iron, 10 In. 165.00
Lawn Sprinkler, Frog, Seated, On Ball, Red & Brown Paint, Cast Iron, 9 In. 165.00
Ornament, Figural, Bull's Head, Cast Iron, Scrolled Plaque, Ribbons, Swags, 23 x 16 In. 1998.00
Ornament, Sea Nymph On Dolphin, Terra-Cotta Glazed, Cast Stone, 26 x 23 In. 940.00
Plant Stand, see Furniture, Stand, Plant
Planter, Terra-Cotta, Cast Stone, Beaux Arts Revival Style, 42 x 46 In., Pair 3290.00
Planter, Urn Shape, Scroll Handles, Square Pedestal Base, Cast Iron, 36 In., Pair 1016.00
Planter, Urn Shape, Square Base, Floral Panels, Cast Iron, 42 In. 840.00
Planter, Urn, 2 Handles, White Paint, Cast Iron, c.1875, 30 x 12 x 13 In. 2950.00
Sculpture, Barbedienne, Woman, Child, Bronze, 1800s, 39 x 27 In. 9360.00
Seat, Aesthetic Movement, Earthenware, Barrel, Blossoms, England, Late 1800s, 19 In. 440.00
Seat, Barrel Shape, Famille Jeune, Phoenix, Chinese, 1800s, 19 In., Pair 1765.00
Seat, Blue, White, Hexagonal Barrel, Porcelain, Chain, 19th Century, 19 1/4 In., Pair 2235.00
Seat, Cabbage Leaf, Porcelain, Chinese, 20th Century, 18 1/2 In., Pair 710.00
Seat, Celadon, Molded Birds, Flowering Branches, 2 Bands Chinese Export, 16 1/2 In. 1195.00
Seat, Dragon, Phoenix, Flower, Famille Rose, Chinese Export, 19 In. 1672.00
Seat, Drum Shape, Bowed Supports, Rosewood, Chinese, 18 x 16 In. 175.00
Seat, Famille Jeune, Square, Bulging Sides, Dragons, Flowers, Yellow, Canton, 1800s, 19 In. 1880.00
Seat, Famille Rose, Chinese Export, Early 20th Century, 18 1/4 In. 840.00
Seat, Fitzhugh, Green, White, Chinese Export, 20 In., Pair 1060.00
Seat, Flowers, Cutout Design, Protruding Dots, Famille Rose, Chinese Export, 1800s, 18 In. 425.00
Seat, Hexagonal, Bamboo Molding, Celadon Glaze, Quatrefoil Panels, 13 x 18 3/4 In. 750.00
Seat, Laurel Pattern, Openwork, Curved Back, White Paint, Cast Iron, 19th Century, 33 In. 1795.00
Seat, Multicolored, Flowers, Leaf Border, Courtyard, Chinese Export, 1800s, 18 In., Pair 1410.00
Seat, Pierced, Celadon, Pate-Sur-Pate, Hexagonal, Porcelain, Chinese, Late 1800s, 19 In. 650.00
Sprinkler, Sprinkling Sambo, Wood, Painted, Articulated Arm, Rubber Hose, 40 x 11 In. 355.00
Sundial, 8-Sided, England, Brass, 8 1/2 In. 220.00
Sundial, Globe, Bronze, Oak Base, 8 1/2 In. 90.00
Sundial, Neoclassical Style, Patinated Brass, Terra-Cotta Pedestal, Cast Stone, 39 x 22 In. 590.00
Sundial, Round, I Tell Hours Amidst Flowers, Brass, W. Bond, 1795, 9 1/2 In. 60.00
Sundial, Slate, Horizontal, Rich Melvin, Dublin, Bronze, c.1772, 8 x 8 In. 95.00
Table, Elephant Shape, 8-Sided Top, Ceramic, 19 1/2 x 18 In. 175.00
Table, Marble Top, 6-Sided Top, Tripod Base, Iron, Victorian, 30 In. 560.00
Table, Masks & Leaf Base, White Paint, Turned Wood Top, Iron, 1800s, 28 x 24 In., Pair 470.00
Urn, 3 Sections, Green Paint, Relief Cast Designs, Swallows, Flowers, Cast Iron, 34 In. 290.00
Urn, Bacchus Masks, Grapes, Vines, Bronze, Gilt, France, 14 x 5 In., Pair 3230.00
Urn, Campagna, Cover, Neoclassical, Grapes, Bacchante, Cone Finial, Bronze, 32 x 15 In., Pair 2115.00
Urn, Campana Shape, Lobed Body, Iron, c.1850, 26 x 30 In., Pair 7640.00
Urn, Campana, Square Base, Bronze, Gilt, France, c.1850, 13 1/2 In., Pair 978.00
Urn, Classical Revival, Squat, Egg Shape, Grapevine, Satyr, Bronze, 20 In., Pair 2938.00
Urn, Classical Shape, Cast Iron, Early 1900s, 25 x 19 In., Pair 315.00
Urn, Classical Style, Bronze, Ormolu Mounted, White Crackle Glaze, 1900s, 15 1/2 x 8 In. 248.00
Urn, Classical Style, Bronze, Silvered, Gilded, Greek Key, Swag, 18 x 20 In. 170.00
Urn, Cover, Classical Style, Fruit, Flower Swags, Ram's Head Handles, Fruit Finial, 87 x 24 In. 2070.00
Urn, Cover, Fluted Oval, Flower Garlands, Masks, Trumpet Foot, Lead, 30 In., Pair 940.00
Urn, French Provincial, Swags, Footed, Green Glaze, Terra-Cotta, 16 1/2 x 13 In., Pair 380.00
Urn, Neoclassical Style, Campana Shape, Egg & Dart Molding, Cast Iron, 35 x 19 In., Pair 470.00
Urn, Neoclassical Style, Campana Shape, Egg & Dart Molding, Cast Iron, 43 x 22 In., Pair 820.00
Urn, Neoclassical Style, Terra-Cotta Glaze, Pedestal, Cast Stone, 42 x 19 In., Pair 1530.00
Urn, Neoclassical Style, Terra-Cotta Glaze, Rams, Putti, Dolphins, Cast Stone, 42 x 32 In., Pair 1175.00

Urn, Phoenix Birds, Leaves, Scrolled Handles, Pedestal, Cast Iron, 27 x 21 In. 615.00
Urn, Renaissance Style, Campagna, Boar's Head, Patinated Bronze, 41 x 26 In., Pair 2468.00
Urn, Tazza Shape Bowl, Leaf Molded Rim, Tripod Base, Cast Metal, 31 x 21 In., Pair 2350.00
Urn, Victorian, Scrolled Handles, White Paint, Cast Iron, 1800s, 27 1/2 x 29 In., Pair 1058.00

GARDNER Porcelain Works was founded in Verbiki, outside Moscow, by the English-born Francis Gardner in 1766. The Gardner family retained ownership of the factory until 1891 and produced porcelain tablewares, figurines, and faience.

ΓΑΡΔΗΕΡΖ

Figurine, Blind Beggar, c.1870, 5 3/4 In. 1998.00
Figurine, Boxer, Rococo Trimmed Base, Russia, c.1840, 7 1/2 In. 5875.00
Figurine, Cat, Lying Down, c.1860, 4 In. 999.00
Figurine, Coachman, Hands On Hips, c.1845, 7 3/8 In. 4700.00
Figurine, Dog, Seated, By Tree Trunk, Early 1800s, 2 1/2 In. 1295.00
Figurine, Girl, Holding Flower Basket, Early 1800s, 5 1/4 In. 3819.00
Figurine, Lady, Fashionably Dressed, Russia, c.1820, 8 1/4 In. 5580.00
Figurine, Man, Carrying Bow, Arrow, Dead Animal, c.1840, 6 1/2 In. 3819.00
Figurine, Man, Holding Tree Branch, c.1850, 4 In. 2820.00
Figurine, Man, Standing, c.1850, 3 1/4 In. 1645.00
Figurine, Nude Woman, Dressing, c.1850, 7 1/2 In. 11750.00
Figurine, Nude Woman, Pink Bonnet, c.1845, 7 3/4 In. 11165.00
Figurine, Old Man, Hands In Pockets, Russia, c.1850, 9 In. 3290.00
Figurine, Peasant Eating, Seated, Russia, c.1860, 4 3/4 In. 1880.00
Figurine, Peasant Girl, Left Hand Shielding Eyes, Sheaf Of Corn, Russia, c.1870, 8 1/2 In. 1880.00
Figurine, Peasant Girl, Picking Mushrooms, c.1800, 4 1/2 In. 4115.00
Figurine, Peasant Woman, Seated On Bench, Russia, c.1850, 5 1/2 In. 2115.00
Figurine, Peasant, Drinking From Kovsh, c.1860, 5 1/2 In. 1998.00
Figurine, Spaniard, c.1820, 7 3/4 In. 8225.00
Group, Woman, On Sofa, Boy, Kneeling, c.1840, 2 1/4 In. 5580.00

GAUDY DUTCH pottery was made in England for America from about 1810 to 1820. It is a white earthenware with Imari-style decorations of red, blue, green, yellow, and black. Only sixteen patterns of Gaudy Dutch were made: Butterfly, Carnation, Dahlia, Double Rose, Dove, Grape, Leaf, Oyster, Primrose, Single Rose, Strawflower, Sunflower, Urn, War Bonnet, Zinnia, and No Name. Other similar wares are called *Gaudy Ironstone* and *Gaudy Welsh*.

Bowl, Carnation, 5 5/8 x 2 3/4 In. 730.00
Bowl, War Bonnet, Fluted Sides, 6 x 3 In. 60.00
Creamer, War Bonnet, Staffordshire, Early 1800s, 4 3/8 In. 837.00
Cup & Saucer, Dove, Handeless 978.00
Cup & Saucer, Handleless, Oyster 431.00
Cup & Saucer, Handleless, Single Rose, Blue Rim 230.00
Cup & Saucer, Oyster 209.00
Cup Plate, Carnation, Narrow Border, Staffordshire, Early 1800s, 3 3/4 In. 1554.00
Cup Plate, Single Rose, Double Line Border, Staffordshire, Early 1800s, 4 In. 598.00
Cup Plate, War Bonnet, Staffordshire, Early 1800s, 3 1/4 In. 1434.00
Pitcher, Grape, Staffordshire, Early 1800s, 6 In. 2510.00
Pitcher, Water, Grape, Flaring Foot, Staffordshire, Early 1800s, 9 1/2 x 8 1/2 In. 9560.00
Plate, Bread & Butter, Grape, Staffordshire, Early 1800s, 5 1/4 In., 6 Piece 956.00
Plate, Bread & Butter, Rose, Double Line Border, Staffordshire, 1800s, 5 5/8 In. 254.00
Plate, Bread & Butter, Urn, Staffordshire, Early 1800s, 6 1/4 In. 254.00
Plate, Butterfly, Staffordshire, Early 1800s, 7 3/8 In. 777.00
Plate, Butterfly, Staffordshire, Early 1800s, 8 3/4 In. .... 2032.00 to 3107.00
Plate, Carnation, Blue & Yellow Border, 8 3/8 In. 546.00
Plate, Carnation, Stem Border, Staffordshire, Early 1800s, 9 3/4 In. 388.00
Plate, Dahlia, Staffordshire, Early 1800s, 8 In. 6573.00
Plate, Deep Dish, Sunflower, Staffordshire, Early 1800s, 9 3/4 In. 1793.00
Plate, Dinner, Double Rose, Staffordshire, Early 1800s, 10 In. .... 897.00 to 1135.00
Plate, Dove, 8 1/4 In. 275.00
Plate, Rose, 7 1/4 In. 358.00

Plate, Single Rose, 9 3/4 In. 495.00
Plate, Single Rose, Blue Border, 8 1/4 In. .... 173.00 to 489.00
Plate, Toddy, War Bonnet, Staffordshire, Early 1800s, 5 In. 328.00
Plate, Urn, 8 1/4 In. 770.00
Plate, Urn, Staffordshire, Early 1800s, 8 1/4 In., Pair 598.00
Plate, Urn, Staffordshire, Early 1800s, 10 In., 10 Piece 2032.00
Plate, War Bonnet, Shaped Edge, Staffordshire, Early 1800s, 9 3/4 In. 598.00
Plate, War Bonnet, Staffordshire, Early 1800s, 9 3/4 In. .... 538.00 to 717.00
Saucer, Single Rose, 5 5/8 In. 138.00
Soup, Dish, Cream, Grape, 9 7/8 In. 550.00
Soup, Dish, Double Rose, Staffordshire, Early 1800s, 9 In. 254.00
Soup, Dish, Grape, Early 1800s, 7 1/8 In., Pair 538.00
Soup, Dish, War Bonnet, Shaped Edge, Staffordshire, Early 1800s, 8 1/4 In. .... 448.00 to 508.00
Soup, Dish, War Bonnet, Staffordshire, Early 1800s, 7 In. 538.00
Soup, Dish, War Bonnet, Staffordshire, Early 1800s, 8 In. .... 224.00 to 284.00
Sugar, Cover, Carnation, Shell Handles, 5 3/4 x 5 1/4 In. 748.00
Tea Bowl & Saucer, Butterfly, Staffordshire, Early 1800s .... 598.00 to 1016.00
Tea Bowl & Saucer, Double Rose, Staffordshire, Early 1800s 278.00
Tea Bowl & Saucer, Oyster, Orange, Staffordshire, Early 1800s .... 418.00 to 568.00
Tea Bowl & Saucer, Single Rose, Staffordshire, Single Border, Early 1800s 166.00
Tea Bowl & Saucer, Sunflower, Staffordshire, Early 1800s .... 135.00 to 195.00
Tea Bowl & Saucer, Urn, Staffordshire, Early 1800s .... 308.00 to 328.00
Tea Bowl & Saucer, War Bonnet, Staffordshire, Early 1800s 388.00
Tea Set, Grape, Staffordshire, Early 1800s, 7-In. Teapot, 3 Piece 757.00
Toddy Plate, Grape, 4 1/2 In. 385.00
Waste Bowl, Butterfly, Staffordshire, Early 1800s, 3 1/2 x 6 3/8 In. 1434.00
Waste Bowl, Carnation, 3 x 5 3/8 In. 385.00
Waste Bowl, Grape, Staffordshire, Early 1900s 388.00
Waste Bowl, Urn, Staffordshire, Early 1800s, 5 1/4 In. 598.00

GAUDY IRONSTONE is the collector's name for the ironstone wares with the bright patterns similar to Gaudy Dutch. It was made in England for the American market after 1850. There may be other examples found in the listing for Ironstone or under the name of the ceramic factory.

Bowl, Vegetable, Fern & Flower, Octagonal, 9 x 7 In. 116.00
Creamer, Flower, Hand Painted, c.1840, 5 3/4 x 5 In. 85.00
Cup & Saucer, Morning Glory & Strawberry 300.00
Cup & Saucer, Strawberry, Paneled, 3 In., 5 7/8-In. Saucer 165.00
Pitcher, 8 1/4 x 6 In. 350.00
Pitcher, Rabbits, Playing Tennis, Spatter Flower Border, 12 1/2 In. 805.00
Plate, Blackberry, Impressed Mark, Paris White Ironstone China, 8 1/2 In. 94.00
Plate, Flow Blue, Hand Painted, c.1850, 8 1/4 In. 150.00
Plate, Hand Painted, Copper Luster, Pink Luster Border, 8 1/4 In. 150.00
Plate, Morning Glory & Strawberry, 8 3/4 In. 350.00
Plate, Primrose, 8 1/4 In. 350.00
Plate, Seeing Eye, 8 1/4 In. 350.00
Plate, Strawberry, Paneled, 8 In. 195.00
Platter, Adams' Rose, Green & Blue Leaves, Rabbit Border, 10 1/2 x 15 In. 230.00
Sugar, Cover, Floral, Hand Painted, c.1840, 7 1/2 In. 150.00
Waste Bowl, Seeing Eye, 3 1/2 x 5 In. 280.00

GAUDY WELSH is an Imari-decorated earthenware with red, blue, green, and gold decorations. Most Gaudy Welsh was made in England for the American market. It was made from 1820 to about 1860.

Bowl, Strawberries, Cobalt Blue Flourishes, Copper Luster, 2 3/4 x 14 1/4 In. 374.00
Bowl, Tulip, 3 1/2 x 6 5/8 In. 85.00
Bowl, Tulip, 3 1/4 x 5 3/4 In. 60.00
Bowl, Tulip, 3 x 6 1/8 In. 60.00
Cake Server, Flower, Leaf, Butterfly, Old Derby, Ridgeway, 9 1/2 x 13 In. 248.00
Creamer, Oyster, 4 In. 250.00
Creamer, Tulip, 5 In. 20.00

Creamer, Tulip, Octopus Foot, 5 In. 60.00
Cup & Saucer, Grape Variant 500.00
Cup & Saucer, Grapevine 22.00
Cup Plate, Urn 125.00
Mini Bowl & Pitcher, Grape, 3 1/4 In. 450.00
Mug, Chinoiserie, 3 In. 135.00
Mug, Cider, Grape, 5 In. 550.00
Mug, Grape, Miniature, 2 In. 145.00
Pitcher, Conwy, 7 In. 425.00
Pitcher, Cream, Oyster, 4 In. 105.00
Pitcher, Cream, Sunflower, Paneled, Snake Handle, Allertons Est. 1831, 5 1/2 In. 116.00
Plate, Grapevine, 8 In. 22.00
Plate, Tulip, Pierced Handle, 9 1/2 In. 110.00
Sugar, Tulip, 7 1/2 In. 66.00
Sugar, Tulip, Octopus Foot, 7 1/2 In. 105.00

GEISHA GIRL porcelain was made for export in the late nineteenth century in Japan. It was an inexpensive porcelain often sold in dime stores or used as free premiums. Pieces are sometimes marked with the name of a store. Japanese ladies in kimonos are pictured on the dishes. There are over 125 recorded patterns. Borders of red, blue, green, gold, brown, or several of these colors were used. Modern reproductions are being made.

Chocolate Cup & Saucer, 3-In. Cup, 5-In. Saucer 12.00
Chocolate Pot, Cobalt Blue, Gold, Red Mark, 1940s, 10 In. 75.00
Cocoa Cup, Geisha Girls, Flower Garden, c.1940, 3 In. 25.00
Demitasse Cup & Saucer, Red, 2 1/4-In. Cup, 4 3/8-In. Saucer 10.00
Pitcher, 3 In. 24.00
Plate, Gold Trim, 7 1/4 In. .... 19.00 to 25.00
Plate, Oval, Green Stamp, 12 1/2 x 6 In. 27.00
Salt, Master, 3-Footed, Blue Trim, Scalloped 20.00
Saucer, Silk Screen, Hand Painted, Red Mark, 5 1/2 In. 3.00
Shaker, 2 1/4 In. 5.00
Toothpick, 2 1/2 In. 20.00
Vase, Geisha Girls, Wisteria Flowers, 3 3/4 In. 20.00

GENE AUTRY was born in 1907. He began his career as the "Singing Cowboy" in 1928. His first movie appearance was in 1934, his last in 1958. His likeness and that of the Wonder Horse, Champion, were used on toys, books, lunch boxes, and advertisements.

Bicycle, Gun, Holster, 34 In. 4760.00
Book, Cut Out, Perforated, Merrill Publishing Co., c.1940, 10 1/2 x 15 In., 12 Pages 800.00
Cap Gun, Cast Iron, Pearl Colored Grips, Kenton, 7 In. 90.00
Cap Gun, Champion, Black Grips, Hubley, 7 1/2 In. 138.00
Cap Gun, Red Handles, Cast Signature, Kenton, 6 In. 80.00
Guitar, Automatic Chord Player, Embossed Images, Plastic, Emenee, 1950s, 33 In. 329.00
Guitar, Plastic, Embossed Western Scene, Emenee, 1950s, 32 In. 135.00
Gun & Holster Set, Double, Revolving Cylinder, Studded Holster, Leslie Henry 285.00
Gun & Holster Set, Official Ranch Outfit, Leslie-Henry, Box, 9 1/2-In. Guns 450.00
Lunch Box, Universal, Box, 1954 .... 1552.00
Writing Tablet, Gene Playing Guitar, 1940s, 10 x 8 In. 45.00

GIBSON GIRL black-and-blue decorated plates were made in the early 1900s. Twenty-four different 10 1/2-inch plates were made by the Royal Doulton pottery at Lambeth, England. These pictured scenes from the book *A Widow and Her Friends* by Charles Dana Gibson. Another set of twelve 9-inch plates featuring pictures of the heads of Gibson Girls had all-blue decoration. Many other items also pictured the famous Gibson Girl.

Plate, Failing To Find Rest & Quiet In The Country She Decides To Return Home, 10 1/2 In. 65.00
Plate, Message From The Outside World, Flow Blue Border, 10 1/2 In. 40.00

If you use plate hangers to display your plates, be sure they are not too tight. Clips should be covered with a soft material so they don't scratch the plate.

Gibson Girl, Plate, They Take A Morning Run, 1901, 10 1/2 In.

Plate, Mr. Waddles Arrives Late & Finds Her Card Filled, c.1900, 10 1/2 In. 310.00
Plate, She Becomes A Trained Nurse, Flow Blue Border, 10 1/2 In. 84.00
Plate, She Contemplates The Cloister, Flow Blue Border, 10 1/2 In. 65.00
Plate, She Finds Some Consolation In Her Mirror, 10 1/2 In. 83.00
Plate, She Is The Subject Of More Hostile Criticism, 10 1/2 In. 225.00
Plate, Some Think She Has Remained In Retirement Too Long, 10 1/2 In. 65.00
Plate, They All Go Skating, 10 1/2 In. 73.00
Plate, They Take A Morning Run, 1901, 10 1/2 In. .... *ILLUS* 96.00
Print, Gibson Girl No. 8, Page From Collected Works Of Gibson, Scribner, 1906 .... 5.00
Print, Gibson Girl No. 9, Page From Collected Works Of Gibson, Scribner, 1906 .... 12.00

GIRL SCOUT collectors search for anything pertaining to the Girl Scouts, including uniforms, publications, and old cookie boxes. The Girl Scout movement started in 1912, two years after the Boy Scouts. It began under Juliette Gordon Low of Savannah, Georgia. The first Girl Scout cookies were sold in 1928.

Book, Brown Book For Brown Owls, 3rd Edition, 1926 .... 76.00
Camera, Jem Jr. 120, Aluminum, Art Deco Design, 1940s, 4 1/2 x 4 1/2 In. 25.00
Camera Kit, Official Girls Scout Instant-Load 900, Flashcube, Box, c.1968 .... 60.00
Catalog, Girl Scout Equipment, Fall, 1931, 10 x 7 1/2 In. 67.00
Doll, Brownie Uniform, Effanbee, c.1966 .... 62.00
Handbook, Brownie Scout, N.Y., 1959, 95 Pages 8.00
Handbook, Girl Scout, N.Y., 1951, 527 Pages 11.00
Hatchet, Oak Handle, Girl Scout Emblem, Plumb, 10 1/2 In. 76.00
Lunch Pail, Tin, Green, Scout, Leader, Girls Playing Sports, Bail Handles, c.1930 .... 59.00
Pin, Well-Behaved Women Rarely Make History, Goldtone Metal, Enamel, Oval, 1 1/2 In. 42.00
Ring, Girl Scout U.S.A., Girl Scout Emblem, Gold Filled, Green Stone, Size 9 .... 190.00
Scarf, Cotton, 4 Trefoils, Girl Scouts, 1960s, 16 x 22 In. 40.00
Whiskbroom, Retractable Bristles, Green Plastic Handle, c.1950, 4 x 2 In. 28.00
Wristwatch, Windup, Silvertone Stretch Band, Medana, 1940s 140.00

GLASS-ART. Art glass means any of the many forms of glassware made during the late nineteenth or early twentieth century. These wares were expensive and production was limited. Art glass is not the typical commercial glass that was made in large quantities, and most of the art glass was produced by hand methods. Later twentieth-century glass is listed under Glass-Contemporary, Glass-Midcentury, or Glass-Venetian. Even more art glass may be found in categories such as Burmese, Cameo Glass, Tiffany, and other factory names.

Biscuit Jar, Cover, Overshot, Applied Green Serpent, Gold Enameled, 1870-90, 7 1/2 In. 358.00
Bowl, Blue, Green, Mottled, Clear Cased, Irregular Bubbles, France, 7 1/2 In. 115.00
Bowl, Gold, Brown, White Waves, Shaped Edge, 8 3/8 In. 200.00
Bowl, Iridescent Gold, Purple Ruffled Edge, 8 1/2 In. 150.00
Bowl, Leaf Shape, Cranberry, Overshot, Gold Enameled, 1870-90, 2 3/4 x 8 x 11 In. 99.00
Bowl, Multicolored Iridescent, Thumbprint, 9 In. 180.00

Glass-Art, Finger Bowl, Overshot, Green, Plain Rim, 1870-90, 3 1/4 x 4 1/2 In.

Glass-Art, Pitcher, Overshot, Blue, Bulbous, Amber Handle, 1870-87, 7 x 3 In.

Glass-Blown, Cruet, 3-Piece Mold, Cobalt Blue, 16 Ribs, Stopper, c.1830, 9 1/2 In.

Bowl, Yellow Cased, Tricornered, Folded Rim, 10 In. 170.00
Box, White Opaque, Hinged, 4 x 5 In. 110.00
Creamer, Green Agata, Optic Ribbed, Mottled, Gold Trim, 4 3/4 In. 259.00
Dish, Cover, Green Agata, Amethyst Staining, Applied Finial, 6 In. 920.00
Epergne, 1 Lily, 3 Canes, Hanging, Baskets, Opalescent, Ruffled Base, Rigaree, 21 In. 690.00
Epergne, 1 Lily, Compote Shape, Overshot, Applied Serpent, Gold Scalloped Rim, 1870-90, 9 In. .. 358.00
Epergne, 4 Lilies, Blue, Clear, Opalescent, Ruffled Edge, c.1885, 17 In. 558.00
Figurine, Bird, Frosted, Clear Base, Jean & Jann Martel, France, 1920s, 4 1/2 In. 66.00
Figurine, Pear, Raspberry Pink Shading To Pale Pink, Applied Crystal Stem, 4 1/4 In. 330.00
Finger Bowl, Overshot, Green, Plain Rim, 1870-90, 3 1/4 x 4 1/2 In. .... *ILLUS* 120.00
Florentine, Cameo, Rose, Vase, Pink, Enameled, White Lace, 8 1/2 In. 230.00
Goblet, Gold Enameled, 8-Lobe Bowl, Overshot, 1870-90, 7 x 2 3/4 In. 50.00
Goblet, Overshot, Applied Ruby Serpent, Gold Trim, 1870-90, 7 1/2 In., Pair 440.00
Goblet, Overshot, Applied Ruby Serpent, Gold Trim, 1870-90, 8 x 3 1/8 In. ....190.00 to 231.00
Gold Iridescent, Oil Spot, Applied 4-Legged Stand, Green Iridescent, Continental, 7 1/2 In. 690.00
Pitcher, Enameled, Multicolored Flowers, Bulbous, Ruffled Edge, Victorian, 9 1/2 In. 104.00
Pitcher, Opaque Blue, Reeded Handle, 8 3/4 In. 200.00
Pitcher, Opaque Pink Swirled Ribs, Clear Reeded Handle, 8 3/4 In. 100.00
Pitcher, Overshot, Blue, Bulbous, Amber Handle, 1870-87, 7 x 3 In. .... *ILLUS* 230.00
Pitcher, Pink & White, Star Crimped Rim, 8 1/2 In. 140.00
Pitcher, Tortoiseshell, Star Crimped Rim, 8 1/2 In. 150.00
Powder Box, Cover, Overshot, Gold Applied Green Serpent, 1870-90, 3 3/4 x 3 1/4 In. 176.00
Powder Box, Cover, Overshot, Gold Applied Ruby Serpent Cover, 1870-90, 4 1/2 x 4 In. 265.00
Salt, Pink Opalescent, Ribs, Gold Iridescent Interior, 2 1/2 In., 3 Piece 240.00
Salt, White Opalescent, Green Iridescent, Shaped Rim, 3 In. 86.00
Sculpture, Secuso Glass, Pulled Crystal Wing Shape, Footed Marble Base, 38 In. 765.00
Sculpture, Woman's Head, Smiling, Art Deco, Henri Navarre, 21 1/4 In. 4657.00
Shade, Iridescent, Gold Zipper Pattern, 5 1/4 In. 460.00
Shade, White Ground, Gold Iridescent, Pulled Feather, 7 x 5 x 4 In. 660.00
Sherbet, Rosaline, Amethyst Stem, 3 In., 4 Piece 115.00
Spooner, Dew Drop, Canary, Hobbs Brockunier, 4 x 4 In. 99.00
Spooner, Dew Drop, Sapphire, Hobbs Brockunier, 4 In. ....39.00 to 50.00
Stand, Griffin Holder, Amber, Satin, Hobbs Brockunier, 3 1/8 In. 1265.00
Sugar, Green Agata, Optic Ribbed, Mineral Staining, Applied Handles, 5 1/2 In. 920.00
Sugar Shaker, Blue, Inverted Thumbprint, c.1900, 4 1/2 In. 115.00
Syrup, Inverted Thumbprint, Blue, Hobbs, c.1883, 8 In. 200.00
Tumbler, Green Agata, Amethyst & Gold Staining, 3 3/4 In. 403.00
Tumbler, Overshot, Cranberry, Gold, Cut Stars, Punties, Footed, 1870-90, 6 1/4 In. 90.00
Tumbler, White Ribs, Applied Ruby Rim, Victorian, 3 1/2 In. 46.00
Vase, Amber, Pink Flowers, Green Stems, Continental, Optic Ribbed, 15 In., Pair 805.00
Vase, Birds, Blackberry Branches, Bulbous, Scalloped Rim, c.1900, 18 3/4 In. 1673.00
Vase, Dionysian Cherub, Butterflies, Enameled, Oval, Signed, Ahne, France, 8 3/4 In. 206.00
Vase, Egg Shape, Optic Ribbed, Scalloped Rim, Amber, Pink Flowers, Continental, 7 In. 460.00
Vase, Flower Form, Combed, Pulled Leaves, Ruffled Edge, Bronze Holder, 14 1/2 In. 1610.00

Vase, Gold Iridescent, Pulled Feathers, Cream Ground, Flared Rim, Applied Foot, 11 In. 330.00
Vase, Green, Amphora Shape, Joep Nicolas, Leerdam, 1930s, 15 3/4 In. 396.00
Vase, Green, Mottled, Gold Enameled, Tapered, Pinched & Ruffled Rim, Continental, 12 In. 28.00
Vase, Maroon Cased, Enameled Stork, 6 3/4 In., Pair 125.00
Vase, Opaque Green, Enameled Flowers, 5 1/2 In. 25.00
Vase, Orange, Yellow, Mottled, Brown Rim, Urn Shape, Footed, Monart, 8 1/4 In. 145.00
Vase, Pink, Amethyst, Mottled, Gold Flecks, Squat, Bulbous, Monart, 8 In. 145.00
Vase, Pink, Blue & Yellow Spatter, Urn Shape, Monart, 7 1/2 In. 200.00
Vase, Pink, White, Blue Flowers, Leaves, Vines, Aventurine Green, Ball Shape, 8 3/8 In. 1610.00
Vase, Pulled Feather, Blue Iridescent Ground, Bronze Iridescent Threading, Footed, 7 In. 115.00
Vase, Purple, Brown Iridescent, Gold, Blue Iridescent Arches, Cobalt Blue Base, 7 1/2 In. 431.00
Vase, Red, Bubbly, Iridescent Ground, Blue Stylized Leaves, Vines, 11 In. 460.00
Vase, Rose, Iridescent Speckle, 10 1/4 In. 29.00
Vase, Trumpet, Green, Iridescent, Gilt, Polychrome, Art Nouveau, Continental, 6 1/4 In. 86.00
Vase, Vines, Heart Shape Leaves, Brown, Golden, Pillow Form, Craig Zweifel, 9 5/8 In. 290.00

GLASS-BLOWN was formed by forcing air through a rod into molten glass. Early glass and some forms of art glass were hand blown. Other types of glass were molded or pressed.

Ale Glass, Pattern Molded, 8 Vertical Ribs, Pontil, Conical Bowl, c.1825, 5 x 2 1/4 In. 176.00
Bowl, 20 Diamonds, Funnel Foot, Cupped Rim, Pontil, c.1775-1810, 3 1/2 In. 275.00
Bowl, Amber, Tooled, Folded Rim, Pontil, 1830-55, 5 x 7 In. 660.00
Bowl, Aqua, 14 Ribs, Flared Rim, New Jersey, Pontil, 4 x 7 In. 1540.00
Bowl, Aqua, Flared, Folded Rim, c.1850-70, 7 x 12 1/2 In. 440.00
Bowl, Aqua, Flared, Rolled Rim, Pontil, 3 7/8 x 10 In. 825.00
Bowl, Black Amber, Punched Sides, Dome Base, c.1825, 4 1/4 x 7 In. 770.00
Bowl, Blue, Flared Rim, 3 1/2 x 7 3/4 In. 22.00
Bowl, Cobalt Blue, 18 Ribs, Swirled To Right, Footed, 3 5/8 In. 785.00
Bowl, Cobalt Blue, Applied Threading, Tooled Rim, Pontil, 5 x 9 1/8 In. 235.00
Bowl, Cranberry, Cupped Rim, Pontil, c.1860-80, 3 3/4 In. 255.00
Bowl, Egg Shape, Inverted Baluster Stem, High Dome Foot, c.1875, 5 3/4 In. 525.00
Bowl, Folded Rim, Flat Base, Pontil, c.1875, 5 1/2 x 8 1/4 In. 70.00
Bowl, Green Aqua, Folded Rim, South Jersey, Pontil, 1830, 3 1/4 In. 130.00
Bowl, Green Aqua, Footed, Pontil, 1820-40, 4 In. 1350.00
Bowl, Green Tint, Applied Blue Rim, Footed, c.1785, 4 x 6 1/2 In. 3960.00
Bowl, Green, Deep, Folded & Tooled Rim, Pontil, c.1840, 4 1/4 In. 880.00
Bowl, Green, Folded Rim, Pontil, 1840-65, 5 x 6 In. 358.00
Bowl, Lavender, Amethyst, Folded Rim, Pontil, c.1840-70, 4 1/4 x 8 3/4 In. 470.00
Bowl, Molded, Green, Scalloped Rim, Footed Sides, 4 x 6 In. 80.00
Bowl, Witch's Ball Cover, Cobalt Blue, Folded Rim, Pontil, 1835-50, 7 In. 330.00
Bowl, Yellow Amber, Tooled Rim, Pontil, 5 1/8 x 7 1/2 In. 1008.00
Cake Stand, Cupped Rim, Dome Base, Hollow 3-Part Column, 12 x 8 3/4 In. 430.00
Celery Vase, 3-Piece Mold, Tooled Rim, Ground Pontil, Footed, 8 3/4 In. 418.00
Champagne, Wafer Base, 18th Century, 6 1/4 x 3 In. 358.00
Compote, Pillar Mold, Clear, Flared Rim, Baluster Stem, Pontil, c.1840-60, 10 In. 231.00
Compote, Scalloped Rims, 8-Pillar Base, Ball Knops, Applied Feet, c.1860, 5 1/2 In. 715.00
Creamer, 28 Panels, Puce Amethyst, Arching Handle, Rigaree, Pontil, 3 1/2 In. 2310.00
Creamer, Amethyst, 16 Ribs, Applied Handle, Pontil, c.1825, 4 In. 1650.00
Creamer, Amethyst, Flared Rim, Applied Handle, Footed, 3 3/4 x 2 In. 25.00
Creamer, Amethyst, Raised Bands, Applied Scrolled Handle, 4 1/2 x 6 x 3 3/4 In. 250.00
Creamer, Amethyst, Rigaree, Applied Handle, Drawn Foot, c.1840, 4 1/2 In. 550.00
Creamer, Amethyst, Scrolled Rim, C-Scroll Handle, Footed, 4 1/2 x 6 In. 248.00
Creamer, Aqua, Rigaree, Tooled Neck, Spout, Applied Handle, Pontil, 5 1/2 In. 330.00
Creamer, Aqua, Threaded Neck, Applied Handle, Footed, Pontil, c.1835, 4 1/2 In. 330.00
Creamer, Blue, Ribbed Base, Arched Handle, Pontil, 3 1/4 In. 385.00
Creamer, Blue, Thumbprint Panel, Handle, Footed, 3 3/4 x 4 1/4 x 2 1/2 In. 195.00
Creamer, Clear, 3-Piece Mold, Loop Handle, Flared Rim, 1835, 3 1/2 In. 330.00
Creamer, Clear, 12 Panels, Applied Lavender Rim, Curled Handle, 1840-60, 4 In. 358.00
Creamer, Clear, Applied Blue Band, Rigaree, Handle, Pontil, c.1840, 3 1/2 In. 190.00
Creamer, Clear, Cut Body, Spout, Applied Handle, Pontil, 1840-60, 4 3/4 In. 190.00
Creamer, Cobalt Blue, Applied Solid Handle, Rigaree, Pontil, 1825-45, 4 1/2 In. 550.00

Creamer, Cobalt Blue, Applied White Banding, Handle, Foot, 1830-45, 4 1/2 In. 550.00
Creamer, Cobalt Blue, Arched Handle, Drawn Foot, Pontil, N.J., c.1845, 5 1/2 In. 1045.00
Creamer, Cobalt Blue, Baluster, Applied Handle, Footed, c.1900, 3 3/4 In. 120.00
Creamer, Cobalt Blue, Handle, Funnel Foot, c.1830, 5 1/2 In. 1760.00
Creamer, Cobalt Blue, Oval, Applied, Curled Handle, Pontil, 1830-50, 3 In. 265.00
Creamer, Cobalt Blue, Tooled, Flared Rim, Applied Curled Handle, 1830-50, 5 1/2 In. 190.00
Creamer, Geometric, Clear, Diamonds, 16 Ribs, Flint, Cobalt Rim, 1780-1810, 3 1/2 In. 330.00
Creamer, Geometric, Cobalt Blue, 6 Rows, Of 12 Diamonds, Paneled, Handle, 1825, 3 1/2 In. 230.00
Creamer, Geometric, Sapphire Blue, 11 Diamonds, Ear Shaped Handle, 1815, 4 1/4 In. 1870.00
Creamer, Geometric, Sapphire Blue, Diamond Rows, Paneled, Handle, c.1825, 3 1/4 In. 210.00
Creamer, Green, Applied Handle, Footed, 5 x 2 3/4 In. 35.00
Creamer, Pattern Molded, 16 Ribs, Swirled To Right, Cobalt Blue, Folded Rim, 3 1/4 In. 90.00
Creamer, Pillar Mold, Clear, 8 Panels, Base, Rigaree, Applied Handle, Pontil, 1830-50, 5 1/4 In. .. 330.00
Creamer, Thumbprint Panel, Footed, Blue, Handle, 3 3/4 x 4 1/4 x 2 1/2 In. 195.00
Creamer, Yellow Olive Green, White Trailing, Pontil, 1800-40, 2 1/2 In. 495.00
Cruet, 3-Piece Mold, Cobalt Blue, 16 Ribs, Stopper, c.1830, 9 1/2 In. .... ***ILLUS*** 2640.00
Cruet, Paneled, 15 Ribs, Hollow Handle, Stopper, c.1825, 9 1/4 In. 165.00
Custard, Pillar Mold, 8 Panels, Sapphire Blue, Flared Rim, Baluster Stem, Ball Knop, Foot, 4 In. 358.00
Decanter, 3-Piece Mold, Baroque, Cobalt Blue, Flared Rim, Annulated Rings, Pontil, 6 3/4 In. 110.00
Decanter, 3-Piece Mold, Beehive, Aqua, Flared Rim, Pontil, 7 1/4 In. 780.00
Decanter, 3-Piece Mold, Golden Yellow Amber, Sheared Mouth, Pontil, Pt. 770.00
Decanter, 3-Piece Mold, Horn Of Plenty, Clear, Stopper, Pontil, c.1830, 12 In. 330.00
Decanter, 3-Piece Mold, Leaf, Daisy, Clear, Neck Rings, Stopper, 1825-40, 9 1/2 In. 440.00
Decanter, 8 Panels, Yellow, Applied Bar Lip, Pontil Base, c.1855-65, 10 In. 1760.00
Decanter, Case, Cut, Flowers, Applied Lip, Disk Stopper, c.1775, 9 1/4 In. 175.00
Decanter, Clear, Flint, Pittsburgh, 1840-60, 10 In., Pair 234.00
Decanter, Cobalt Blue, Teardrop Stopper, Gold Shield Label, 9 1/2 x 3 1/2 In. 28.00
Decanter, Cobalt Blue, Threading, Plain Lip, Pontil, c.1800, Qt., 9 In. 525.00
Decanter, Gray Green, Sandwich Star, Bulbous, Inward Rolled, Flared Rim, Pontil, Qt. 830.00
Decanter, Pillar Mold, 8 Panels, Cobalt Blue Stripes, Applied Bar Lip, Pontil, c.1840, 12 In. 770.00
Decanter, Pillar Mold, 8 Panels, Cobalt Blue, Applied Lip, Pontil, 1840s, 10 3/4 In., Pair 6600.00
Decanter, Pillar Mold, Drape, Clear, Applied Ring, Bar Lip, 1850-60, 12 1/4 In., Pair 358.00
Decanter, Plain Lip, Disk Stopper, England, Late 1700s, Qt., 11 1/2 In. 110.00
Decanter, Tapered, Plain Lip, Cross Hatched Disk Stopper, Pontil, c.1800, 1/2 Pt., 8 1/2 In. 275.00
Decanter, Tapered, Plain Lip, Disk Stopper, Pontil, c.1800, Pt., 9 In. 185.00
Dish, Gray Tint, Wide Flared Rim, c.1800, 1 1/2 x 6 1/2 In. 220.00
Dispenser, Cobalt Blue, Oval Reservoir, Metal Spout, Thumb Print, 30 x 9 1/4 In. 990.00
Eggcup, Cobalt Blue, Flared Rim, Disc Type Base, White Loop Pontil, 4 In. 165.00
Eggcup, Opaque White, Blue Rim, Circular Foot, Pontil, c.1825, 3 1/2 x 2 1/4 In. 22.00
Ewer, Centennial, Scrolling Leaf Wreath, La Grave, c.1876, 12 1/8 In. 143.00
Fishbowl, Aqua, 13 In. 110.00
Flycatcher, Green, 3 Applied Feet, Ground Stopper, 9 1/2 x 6 In. 175.00
Flycatcher, Lavender, Squat, Cork, Wire Hanger, Arjona, 6 1/2 In. 145.00
Goblet, 6 Broad Panels, Baluster Stem, c.1850, 6 1/4 In. 66.00
Goblet, 8 Broad Panels, Baluster Stem, c.1850, 5 3/4 x 3 3/8 In. 35.00
Goblet, Clear, Opaque White Rim, Baluster Stem, Flared Foot, Flint, 8 1/4 x 5 1/2 In. 130.00
Goblet, Cover, Arms Of King George II, Lauenstein, c.1750, 13 1/2 In. 5080.00
Goblet, Cover, Arms Of King George III, Lauenstein, c.1760, 12 1/2 In. 4356.00
Goblet, Olive Amber, Knopped Baluster Stem, Pontil, 1850-65, 7 3/4 In. 230.00
Hat, Aqua, Folded Brim, Pontil, 1850-65, 6 In. 415.00
Hat, Aqua, Turned Down Sides, c.1850, 1 1/2 x 2 3/4 In. 198.00
Hat, Cobalt Blue, 18 Ribs, Upward Folded Rim, 3-Piece Mold, Pontil, 3 In. 1100.00
Hat, Cobalt Blue, Upward Folded Rim, 3 Mold, Pontil, c.1825, 2 1/4 In. 605.00
Jar, Amethyst, Flared Rim, Pontil, 8 3/4 x 5 3/8 In. 550.00
Jar, Cover, Amethyst, Tooled Rim, Ball Finial, 1830-50, 10 1/2 In. 176.00
Jar, Dome Cover, Gray, Blue Rim & Finial Tip, c.1800, 4 1/4 In. 305.00
Jar, Pink, Amethyst, Flared Rim, Pontil, c.1825, 8 In. 55.00
Jug, Amethyst, Paneled, 18 Vertical Ribs, Handle, Crimped Foot, c.1875, 5 1/2 In. 99.00
Jug, Engraved, Flowers, Pear Shape, Angular Spout, Kick-Up Base, c.1815, 7 1/2 In. 2090.00
Jug, Olive Amber, Applied Curled Handle, Flared Rim, Pontil, 1800-30, 2 3/4 In. 3025.00

Lamp, Hurricane, Emerald Green, Flared Rim, Upward Folded Base, 1810-30, 22 In. 1320.00
Milk Pan, Aqua, Flared Sides, Folded Rim, c.1825, 3 x 10 3/4 In. 550.00
Milk Pan, Cobalt Blue, Folded Rim, Pontil, 1820-40, 2 1/4 In. 468.00
Milk Pan, Cobalt Blue, Folded Rim, Pontil, c.1830, 2 3/4 x 9 1/2 In. 880.00
Milk Pan, Cobalt Blue, Rolled Rim, Pontil, 2 1/2 x 7 1/8 In. 560.00
Milk Pan, Cobalt Blue, Tooled Rim, Pontil, 1 3/4 x 5 3/4 In. 179.00
Milk Pan, Honey Amber Puce, Flared, Folded Rim, Pontil, c.1835, 4 x 10 1/4 In. 1045.00
Milk Pan, Teal Green, Folded Rim, Pontil, c.1850, 2 1/2 x 7 In. 231.00
Milk Pan, Yellow Amber, Folded Rim, Pontil, 4 x 8 1/2 In. 825.00
Milk Pan, Yellow Olive, Folded Rim, Pontil, c.1840, 3 In. 440.00
Mug, Amethyst, 16 Ribs, Broken Swirl, Applied Handle, 1820-35, 2 1/2 In. 550.00
Mug, Amethyst, Enameled, Remember Me, Handle, 3 3/4 In. 45.00
Mug, Cobalt Blue, Folded, Tooled Rim, Applied Curled Handle, Pontil, 1835-55, 3 In. 242.00
Mug, Gold Enameled, Flowers, Stars, Barrel Shape, Applied Handle, c.1800, 5 3/4 In. 155.00
Mug, Opaque, Enameled, Gold Trim, Flowers, Barrel Shaped, C-Scroll Handle, 3 1/4 In. 35.00
Mug, Pillar Molded, Blue, Striations, Tooled Rim, Applied Curled Handle, 3 1/4 In. 358.00
Mug, Remember Me, Opaque White, C-Scroll Handle, Flared Base, 4 x 2 3/4 In. 17.00
Mug, Sapphire Blue, Paneled, 16 Ribs, Swirled To Right, c.1830, 3 In. 1595.00
Pitcher, 3-Piece Mold, Bulbous, Tooled Rim, Reeded Handle, Footed, Pontil, 7 1/4 In. 560.00
Pitcher, Amber, Lily Pad Swag, Applied Handle, Base, 1865-75, 7 3/4 In. 413.00
Pitcher, Aqua Ball, Flared Rim, Applied Handle, Pontil, 1830-50, 4 In. 1100.00
Pitcher, Aqua, Applied Lily Pad, Ridge Handle, Circular Base, 1830-55, 6 3/4 In. 2750.00
Pitcher, Aqua, Arched Handle, Applied Foot, Pontil, 1860-75, 8 In. 1320.00
Pitcher, Aqua, Bulbous, Applied Handle, Crimped Foot, Pontil, c.1850, 7 1/2 In. 1760.00
Pitcher, Aqua, Bulbous, Looping Handle, Applied Base, Pontil, New Jersey, 7 1/2 In. 1760.00
Pitcher, Aqua, Lily Pad Swag, Threading, C-Scroll Handle, N.Y., 7 3/4 In. .... *ILLUS* 11000.00
Pitcher, Aqua, White Looping, Applied Curled Handle, Pontil, 1830-45, 6 In. 2695.00
Pitcher, Clear Multicolored, Lily Pad Swag, Applied Hollow Handle, Foot, 7 In. 440.00
Pitcher, Cobalt Blue, 16 Ribs, Applied Handle, Iron Pontil, 1820-40, 3 In. 525.00
Pitcher, Cobalt Blue, Applied Loop Handle, Pontil, c.1830-50, 1 1/2 In. 440.00
Pitcher, Gray Clear, Baluster, Arched Handle, Disc Foot, 1818-40, 9 1/2 In. 3300.00
Pitcher, Scrolling, Medial Bands, Folded Rim, Applied Handle, c.1830, 6 3/4 In. 940.00
Pokal, Cover, Amber, Enameled, Cavalier Holding Stein Upside-Down, Finial, 17 In. 154.00
Punch Bowl, Pattern Molded, Expanded Diamond, Folded Rim, Footed, 7 3/8 x 8 1/2 In. 303.00
Punch Bowl, Straight Rim, Honeycomb, Pedestal, Flint, c.1840, 10 3/4 x 15 3/4 In. 765.00
Punch Cup, Sprig & Oval Band, Barrel Shape, Applied Handle, c.1800, 2 1/2 In. 99.00
Rolling Pin, Fiery Opalescent, Pontil, c.1825, 16 1/2 x 2 3/8 In. 39.00
Rummer, 11 Panels, Swirled To Right, Deep Bowl, Stem, Footed, c.1800, 4 1/2 In. 45.00
Rummer, 12 Panels, Deep Bowl, Drawn Stem, Footed, Pontil, c.1800, 5 x 3 1/4 In. 55.00
Salt, 3-Piece Mold, Clear, Beaded Arches, Scalloped Rib Foot, Handle, c.1875, 4 1/8 In. 65.00
Salt, 3-Piece Mold, Ruby Stained, Flared Rim, c.1875, 2 1/4 x 3 In. 358.00
Salt, 10 Ribs, Cobalt Blue, Folded Rim, Applied Foot, 2 x 3 3/4 In. 209.00
Salt, 12 Ribs, Ogee, Aqua, Applied Base, Pontil, 1820-40, 2 1/2 In. 385.00
Salt, 20 Diamonds, Citron, Footed, Pontil, 1820-50, 2 3/4 In. 330.00
Salt, Amethyst, Hexagonal, Footed, 2 1/2 In. 45.00
Salt, Blue, Flared, Ribbed, Folded Rim, c.1840, 2 1/2 x 4 1/2 In. 240.00
Salt, Blue, Hexagonal, Urn, 3 3/8 x 3 1/2 In. 90.00
Salt, Clear, Oval, Bands, Thumbprint, Octagonal Stem, 3 1/2 x 4 x 2 1/2 In., Pair 33.00
Salt, Clear, White Loop, Applied Base, Pontil, 1830-60, 2 1/4 In. 275.00
Salt, Cobalt Blue, Checkered Diamond, Applied Foot, c.1790, 2 1/2 In. 880.00
Salt, Cobalt Blue, Flared Rim, Applied Baluster Stem, Footed, c.1830, 2 In. 209.00
Salt, Cobalt Blue, Flared Rim, Drawn Foot, Pontil, 1840-60, 3 In. 220.00
Salt, Cobalt Blue, White Rim, Funnel Foot, Pontil, 1780-1830, 2 In. 165.00
Salt, Laurel Leaf Rim Band, c.1800, 1 3/4 x 2 3/4 In. 88.00
Salt, Pattern Molded, 7 Rows, 16 Diamonds, Ribbed Stem, Footed, c.1800, 2 3/4 In. 110.00
Salt, Pattern Molded, 7 Rows, 20 Diamonds, Cobalt Blue, Footed, c.1800, 3 3/8 In. 248.00
Salt, Pattern Molded, 12 Ribs, Swirled Right, Cobalt Blue, Footed, c.1800, 2 3/4 In. 303.00
Salt, Pattern Molded, 26 Ribs, Swirled Right, Cobalt Blue, Pontil, c.1830, 3 In. 685.00
Salt, Pattern Molded, Checkered Diamond, Cobalt Blue, Ogee, 1785, 3 In. .... *ILLUS* 4620.00
Salt, Pattern Molded, Cobalt Blue, 12 Ribs, Footed, c.1810, 3 1/2 In. 165.00

Glass-Blown, Pitcher, Aqua, Lily Pad Swag, Threading, C-Scroll Handle, N.Y., 7 3/4 In.

Glass-Blown, Salt, Pattern Molded, Checkered Diamond, Cobalt Blue, Ogee, 1785, 3 In.

Glass-Blown, Tumbler, Jelly, Green, Paneled, Bell, 18 Ribs, Swirled Right, c.1800, 3 3/4 In.

Salt, Pattern Molded, Expanded Diamond, Ribbed Stem, Footed, 2 3/4 x 2 1/4 In. 99.00
Salt, Pattern Molded, Paneled, Olive Yellow, Tooled Flared, Baluster, Foot, 1 3/4 In. 77.00
Salt, Sapphire Blue, 21 Swirled Ribs, Wafer Baluster, Footed, Pontil, c.1855, 2 1/2 In. 330.00
Salver, Upward Folded Rim, Baluster Stem, Mid 1800s, 6 1/2 x 11 3/4 In. 353.00
Sugar, Amethyst, Conical Foot, Pontil, 4 In. 330.00
Sugar, Amethyst, Hollow Baluster Stem, Upward Folded Foot, 1790-1815, 4 1/4 In. 275.00
Sugar, Ashburton, Opalescent White, 4 1/2 x 4 1/2 In. 50.00
Sugar, Cobalt Blue, Flattened Cover, Knop Finial, Tapered Foot, 6 In. 1790.00
Sugar, Cobalt Blue, White, Knopped Baluster Stem, Footed, Pontil, c.1840s, 6 In. 275.00
Sugar, Cover, Aqua Blue, Galleried Rim, Spool Finial, 9 1/4 In. 3300.00
Sugar, Cover, Aqua, Rolled Rim, Globular Bowl, Knopped Foot, 9 In. 6463.00
Sugar, Cover, Canary, Gothic Arch Panels, Round Base, 5 1/4 x 4 3/4 In. 468.00
Sugar, Cover, Clear, Galleried Rim, Applied Conical Base, Pontil, 1835-50, 6 1/4 In. 715.00
Sugar, Cover, Clear, White Loop, Galleried Rim, Spool Finial, Baluster Stem, Foot, 9 In. 3300.00
Sugar, Cover, Cobalt Blue, Applied Finial, Pontil, 1790-1820, 5 1/2 In. 440.00
Sugar, Cover, Cobalt Blue, Lead Glass, Knopped Baluster, Flint, c.1800, 7 1/2 In. 1210.00
Sugar, Cover, Green, Panels, Applied Finial, Baluster Stem, Footed, 10 1/4 In. 2420.00
Sugar, Cover, Opal, Applied Blue Rim, Cobalt Blue Finial, Wafer Baluster, c.1790, 6 In. 1045.00
Sugar, Cover, Opaque White, Gothic Arches, Tapered Round Base, 5 1/2 x 4 3/4 In. 60.00
Sugar, Dome Cover, Cobalt Blue, Wide Sheared Rim, Applied Stem, Base, Pontil, 7 In. 1650.00
Sugar, Emerald Green, Folded Rim, Applied Foot, Pontil, Continental, 5 3/4 In. 56.00
Sugar, Pattern Molded, Diamonds, Cobalt Blue, Early 1800s, 4 In. 450.00
Sugar, Pillar Molded, 8 Panels, Folded Rim, Blade Knopped Base, Pontil, 4 1/2 In. 165.00
Sugar, Pillar Molded, 8 Panels, Lavender, Flared Rim, Footed, Pontil, c.1790, 3 In. 415.00
Sweetmeat Stand, 8 Vertical Ribs, Turned Over Rim, Knop Stem, Foot, c.1825, 4 In. 230.00
Sweetmeat Stand, 10 Ribs, Pillar Molded, Cobalt Blue, c.1825, 4 1/4 In. 525.00
Syrup, Cobalt Blue, 16 Vertical Ribs, Twisted Neck, Blob Stopper, 6 3/4 In. 420.00
Tumbler, Ale, Gray Tint, Conical Bowl, Thick Base, Squat Knop, c.1775, 5 x 3 In. 303.00
Tumbler, Ale, Pattern Molded, 8 Flutes, Fiery Opalescent, 1850-90, 5 1/4 In. 825.00
Tumbler, Amber, 3 3/4 In. 45.00
Tumbler, Blue, Pontil, 4 1/4 In. 385.00
Tumbler, Clear, 8 Panels, Flared Rim, c.1800, 3 1/2 x 2 3/4 In. 330.00
Tumbler, Clear, Red Amber, Pontil, 1847-57, 3 1/2 In. 468.00
Tumbler, Cobalt Blue, Half Thumbprint, Oval, Hexagonal Base, 3 1/2 x 2 3/4 In. 30.00
Tumbler, Enameled Flower Band, Straight Sides, Flint, 3 x 2 3/8 In. 55.00
Tumbler, Enameled Flowers, Orange, Green, White, Blue, Flint, Straight Sides, 3 In. 55.00
Tumbler, Firing Glass, Gray Green, Conical Bowl, Thick Waisted Base, c.1825, 5 x 2 In. 165.00
Tumbler, Flip, Aqua, Engraved Flower Basket, 8 1/4 In. 165.00
Tumbler, Flip, Cobalt Blue, Ribbed, Paneled, 5 1/2 x 4 1/2 In. 165.00
Tumbler, Flip, Cobalt Blue, Thumbprint Panels, 3 1/4 x 3 1/4 In. 55.00
Tumbler, Flip, Engraved, Wheat Sprays, Hops, Leaves, W. Davis, c.1800, 5 3/4 In. 605.00
Tumbler, Flip, Pattern Molded, Cobalt Blue, Mold, Ribbed Panels, 5 1/2 x 4 1/2 In. 165.00
Tumbler, Flip, Pattern Molded, Stylized Flower, Pontil, Continental, 1800, 6 x 4 1/2 In. 165.00
Tumbler, Flip, Purple, Cobalt Blue, 2 Panels, Pontil Base, c.1870-80, 3 3/4 In. 88.00

Tumbler, Flip, Sailboat, Sawtooth Rim, 8 x 6 In. 300.00
Tumbler, Green, Applied Amber Rim, Pontil, 1840-60, 3 1/2 In. 385.00
Tumbler, Jelly, Green, Paneled, Bell, 18 Ribs, Swirled Right, c.1800, 3 3/4 In. .... *ILLUS* 4620.00
Tumbler, Lemonade, 7-Arches, Applied Handle, Pontil, Flint, 3 x 3 In. 39.00
Tumbler, Opaque White, Enameled Flower, Line Banding, Tapered, 3 1/4 In. 33.00
Tumbler, Toddy, Cobalt Blue, Handle, Tooled Baluster, Disc Base, c.1850, 3 1/4 In., Pair 190.00
Urn, Cover, Corseted, Cut Panels, Footed, c.1850, 13 x 6 1/2 In. 155.00
Vase, Cobalt Blue, Bulbous, Flared, Squared Rim, Applied Clear, Cobalt Base, 7 1/2 In. 165.00
Vase, Cobalt Blue, Rolled Rim, Baluster, c.1865, 8 1/4 x 5 In. 165.00
Vase, Cobalt Blue, Rolled Rim, Pontil, 8 1/4 In., Pair 220.00
Vase, Hyacinth, Cobalt Blue, Sheared & Tooled Rim, Pontil, 6 3/4 In. 160.00
Vase, Hyacinth, Purple Amethyst, Tooled Lip, Pontil, 7 In. 150.00
Vase, Pattern Molded, 26 Ribs, Swirled, Green, 1840-70, 6 1/4 In. 120.00
Vase, Pattern Molded, Blue, Oblong Thumbprint Panels, Band, Flared, 10 7/8 x 3 In. 195.00
Vase, Pattern Molded, Diamond & Fan, Ribbed Band, Flared Base, Gold Leaves, 9 3/4 x 4 In. 209.00
Vase, Sapphire Blue, Flared Rim, Applied Annulated Ring, Drawn Foot, Pontil, 6 1/2 In. 220.00
Vase, Smokey Clear, Yellow Looping, Pontil Base, 1865-75, 6 1/2 In. 220.00
Vase, Trumpet, 3-Piece Mold, Daisy & Scroll, Stippled, Opalescent, c.1850, 5 1/2 In. 155.00
Vase, Trumpet, Amethyst, Dome Foot, c.1815, 7 1/2 x 3 3/8 In. 1980.00
Vase, Trumpet, Olive Amber, White Flecks, Footed, Tooled Flared Mouth, Pontil, 1840-60, 6 3/8 In. 2200.00
Vase, Witch's Ball Cover, Amethyst, Flared Rim, Base, Open Pontil, 1840-60, 4 In. 715.00
Vase, Witch's Ball Cover, Clear, White Loop, Bulbous, Flared Rim, Wafer, c.1840, 13 In. 990.00
Whimsey, Billy Club, Marbrie, White Loopings, 3 Rings, Pontil, c.1875, 9 1/4 In. 110.00
Wine, Clear Funnel Bowl, White Air Twist Stem, Pontil, c.1785, 4 5/8 In. 525.00
Wine, Conical Bowl, Drawn Stem, Folded Rim, c.1775, 4 1/4 In. .... 65.00 to 88.00
Wine, Cupped Bowl, Engraved, Leaves, Grapes, 7 Bubble Base, c.1775, 6 3/4 In. 495.00
Wine, Cupped Bowl, Flower, Leaves, Circular Foot, c.1800, 5 x 2 1/4 In. 120.00
Wine, Engraved, Saxon, 1720, 6 1/2 In. 3195.00
Wine, Ogee Bowl, Opaque White Air Twist Stem, c.1785, 5 x 2 In. 550.00
Wine, Opaque White Air Twist Stem, Funnel Bowl, Conical Foot, 6 In. 185.00
Wine, Pink, White, Air Twist Stem, 1700s, 4 1/2 In. 360.00
Wine, White Air Twist Stem, 1700s, 6 In. 385.00
Wine Rinser, Pattern Molded, 7 Rows Of 10 Diamonds, 2 Spouts, c.1875, 4 x 4 1/4 In. 66.00
Witch's Ball, Clear, White Looping, Open Pontil, 1850-70, 4 1/2 In. 240.00
Witch's Ball, Trumpet Stand, White Loopings, 14 In. 660.00

GLASS-BOHEMIAN Bohemian glass is an ornate overlay or flashed glass made during the Victorian era. It has been reproduced in Bohemia, which is now a part of the Czech Republic. Glass made from 1875 to 1900 is preferred by collectors.

Beaker, Ruby Stain, Wheel-Cut, Castle Bornholen, Faceted Body, 5 In. 88.00
Bottle, Stopper, Blue Cut To White, Gold Enameled, Moorish Style, 8 1/2 In., Pair 575.00
Bowl, Ruby, Blue Iridescent, Art Nouveau, Pallme-Konig & Habel, 4 3/4 In. 3055.00
Cordial Set, Ruby Cut To Clear, Grapevine, Decanter, 6 Cordials 260.00
Decanter, Amber Cut To Clear, Optic Pattern, Stopper, c.1900, 15 1/2 In., Pair 94.00
Decanter, Amber, Stopper, 9 In. 265.00
Decanter, Cut Glass, Blue Overlay, Applied Interior Figure, 11 1/2 In. 145.00
Decanter Set, Ruby Cut To Clear, Castle, Stag, Rounded Square Decanter, 6 Piece 200.00
Decanter Set, Ruby Flashed, 8 Glasses, 8 1/2 In. 200.00
Dresser Box, Green, Gilt Bronze Frame, 1900, 4 1/2 In. 290.00
Ewer, Green, Enameled Ferns, Gold Trim, Square, c.1890, 7 x 3 3/4 In. 350.00
Goblet, Burgundy, Yellow, Burgundy, Cut To Clear Checkered, Stem, Otto Prutscher, 8 In. 2040.00
Jar, Cover, Amber Cut To Clear, Enameled Pink Rose Medallion, 9 In. 150.00
Lamp Base, Ruby Flashed, White Case, Ormolu Mounted, Electrified, c.1890, 23 In. 558.00
Newel Post, Cobalt Blue, Cut To Clear, Oval, Oculus Pattern, 13 1/2 In. 1762.00
Perfume Bottle, Art Deco, Pink, Cherubs, Reclining Maidens, Halama, 8 x 6 1/2 In. 125.00
Perfume Bottle, Vaseline Glass, Stopper, 8 Ridges, 7 1/2 In. 104.00
Pitcher, Melon Lobed, Smoke Body, Blue Feet, Flowers, Handle, Graf Harrach, 4 1/2 In. 115.00
Spooner, Cobalt Cut To Clear, Gold Enameled, 5 3/8 In. 165.00
Trinket Box, Blue & White, Cut To Clear, Early 1900s, 4 1/4 x 5 1/4 In. 470.00
Urn, Cover, Amber, Cut To Clear, c.1900, 7 3/4 In. 53.00

Vase, Amber Cut To Clear, 8 In., Pair 410.00
Vase, Amber Flashed, Enameled, Mythical Figures, R. Wurtig, c.1900, 12 1/2 In. 176.00
Vase, Amber Glass, c.1930, 11 In. 176.00
Vase, Amber Shaded To Cranberry, Oil Spots, Fan Shape, 9 1/2 In. 259.00
Vase, Black Iridescent, Rolled Rim, Art Nouveau, Pallme-Konig & Habel, c.1900, 10 In. 352.00
Vase, Blue, Green Iridescent, Threading, Pinched Rim, Austria, 8 3/4 In. 405.00
Vase, Blue, Lead Crystal, 1850, 13 In. 1989.00
Vase, Cased Cranberry Spatter, Gold Enameled Flowers, c.1920, 6 In. 80.00
Vase, Chestnut, Magnum Thumbprint Cut, Rolled Rim, Dome Cover, 15 In., Pair 1116.00
Vase, Clear, Red, Green, Black Enameled Design, Weiner Werkstatte, 6 1/2 In. 360.00
Vase, Clear, Satin, Applied Green Tadpoles, Pallme-Konig, c.1910, 5 3/4 In. 175.00
Vase, Egg Shape, Crimson, Green, Mottled, Orange, Blue Highlights, Kralik, 6 1/2 In. 374.00
Vase, Enameled, Blood Red, c.1880, 10 1/2 In., Pair 295.00
Vase, Enameled, Peacock, Mountain Village, Tapered, Flared Base, 3-Footed, 11 In. 863.00
Vase, Frosted, Clear, Molded, Bacchus, Grapes, c.1930, 11 1/4 In. 145.00
Vase, Gold, Textured Ground, Applied Green Coil, 13 3/4 In. 230.00
Vase, Green Iridescent, Amethyst, Red, Spatter, Squat, Lobed, 3 In. 690.00
Vase, Green Iridescent, Blue Iridescent Pattern, Kralik, 12 In. 200.00
Vase, Green Iridescent, Gilt, Brass Holder, Art Nouveau, c.1915, 14 1/4 In. 1762.00
Vase, Green Iridescent, Rosewater Bottle Shape, Austrian, 7 3/4 In. 230.00
Vase, Green, Applied Lattice, Pallme-Konig, c.1910, 6 1/4 In. 145.00
Vase, Marquetry, Bulbous, Amber Marbelized, Flowers, Bamboo Stems, 14 1/2 In. 2013.00
Vase, Mottled Pink, Brown Threading, Baluster, Metal Rim, 7 In. 206.00
Vase, Purple Iridescent, Scalloped Rim, Threading, Bronze Base, 10 In. 403.00
Vase, Red Shaded To Clear, Iris, Gold & Multicolor Enamel, 11 1/2 In. 748.00
Vase, Silveria, Shell Shape, Leaf Feet, Pink, Silver, Green Threading, 4 1/2 In., Pair 259.00
Wedding Beaker, Cut & Enameled Design, Brass Torso, Fritz Heckert, 4 1/4 In. 965.00

GLASS-CONTEMPORARY includes pieces by glass artists working after 1975. Many of these pieces are free-form, one-of-a-kind sculptures. Paperweights by contemporary artists are listed in the Paperweight category. Earlier studio glass may be found in Glass-Venetian.

Bowl, Free-Form, Random Pattern, Stephen Rich Nelson, 1989, 19 1/4 In. 118.00
Bowl, Pink, Feather, Pedestal Base, Signed, Marc S. Boutte, 1998, 4 1/2 x 5 In. 80.00
Bowl, Smoke Tree, Textured, Green, Pink Shading, Glen Lukens, 10 In. 175.00
Decanter, Stopper, Bulbous, Translucent Aqua, Cabochons, Signed, Labino, 1969, 10 In. 230.00
Figurine, Swan, Clear, Lilac Veil, Pulled Loops, John Lotton, 10 1/2 In. 575.00
Mug, Applied Amber Handle, Signed, Dominick Labino, c.1969, 5 In. 94.00
Pitcher, Blue, Free-Form, Signed, Labino, 1968, 6 In. 230.00
Sculpture, Macchia, Signed, Dale Chihuly, c.1983, 14 In. 16800.00
Sculpture, Pyramid, Green, Gold, Lavender, Satin Finish, Ivo Lill, 5 1/2 In. 705.00
Vase, Amber, White, Peach, Mottled, Free-Form, Kent Ipsen, 12 x 9 In. 1534.00
Vase, Ariel, Green, Bubbles, Round, Labino, 3 1/4 In. 290.00
Vase, Blue Iridescent, Hawthorne Branches, Millefiori, 7 1/4 In. 690.00
Vase, Blue, Amethyst, Cream, Leaves, Vines, Oval, Lotton, 1976, 3 1/2 In. 460.00
Vase, Clear, Iris, Footed, Ed Alexander, Orient & Flume, 9 1/2 In. 290.00
Vase, Clear, Maroon Flowers, Leaves, Steven Lundberg, 5 1/8 In. 690.00
Vase, Cobalt Blue, Red, Green & Opal Pulled Feathers, Orient & Flume, 10 In. 60.00
Vase, Dripping Blue Lava, Cypriot Caramel, Lotton, 1979, 4 In. 430.00
Vase, Feather, Green Iridescent Purple, Blue, Matte Ivory, C. Lotton, 10 1/4 In. 1095.00
Vase, Feathered Trails, Oval, Shouldered, Donald Carlson, 1976, 7 In. 66.00
Vase, Gold Iridescent, Flowers, Millefiori, Shouldered, Orient & Flume, 1982, 9 In. 315.00
Vase, Gold Iridescent, Millefiori, Hawthorne, Orient & Flume, 1972, 11 In. 400.00
Vase, Gold, Red Feather, Peacock Eye, White Ground, 9 1/2 In. 200.00
Vase, Green Iridescent, Blue Pulled Feathers, Shouldered, R. Held, 10 In. 100.00
Vase, Green Iridescent, Gold Flowers, Pale Amber Ground, C. Lotton, 1988, 5 1/2 In. 460.00
Vase, Green, Blue, Textured, Cut Circles, Vladimir Jelinek, 1969, 10 1/4 In. 518.00
Vase, Green, Interior Red Striations, Blue Dots, Footed, 20th Century, 12 In. 150.00
Vase, Iridescent, Flattened, Oval, Robert Held, c.1980, 13 3/4 In. 94.00
Vase, Lava, Pink Spatter, Dark Veins, Blue Iridescent, Lotton, 10 3/8 In. 690.00
Vase, Nanae, Umeda, Screened Dots, Burgundy, Blue, Square, Sottsass, 12 x 4 1/2 In. 470.00

Vase, Opal, Blue Hooked Feather, Mark Peiser, 1972, 3 1/2 In. 230.00
Vase, Paperweight, Clear, Green Leaves, Red Flower, Orient & Flume, 6 In. 146.00
Vase, Paperweight, Daffodils, Green Stem, Translucent, Signed, Lundberg, 1988, 8 In. 690.00
Vase, Paperweight, Millefiori Flowers, Cream Ground, Messenger, 6 1/2 In. 300.00
Vase, Paperweight, Spring Garden Wisteria, Oval, Chris Heilman, 6 1/2 In. 400.00
Vase, Peacock Feather, Green, Gold Iridescent, Blue Ground, C. Lotton, 1993, 12 In. 1265.00
Vase, Pink, White Blossoms, Leaves, Vines, Transparent Amber, Lotton, 11 5/8 In. 1840.00
Vase, Purple & Green, Large Bubbles, Pinched Teardrop Shape, Labino, 6 In. 430.00
Vase, Purple Iridescent, Blue, Green Combed Trail, Orient & Flume, 13 In. 295.00
Vase, Purple Iridescent, Green, Gold, Blue, C. Lotton, 1993, 11 1/2 In. 978.00
Vase, Red, Blue Translucent Stripes, Elongated Teardrop Shape, Labino, 12 In. 460.00
Vase, Swirled Feathers, Green, Yellow Ocher, Cranberry Field, C. Lotton, 1991, 11 In. 690.00
Vase, Swirled Leaf, Gold, Texture, Red Iridescent, Orange Field, C. Lotton, 1993, 6 1/2 In. 920.00
Vase, Yellow Hearts, Vines, Gold Lustre Ground, Shouldered, Carlson, 5 1/2 In. 90.00

GLASS-CUT, see Cut Glass category.

GLASS-DEPRESSION, see Depression Glass category.

GLASS-MIDCENTURY refers to art glass made from the 1940s to the early 1970s. Some glass factories, such as Baccarat or Orrefors, are listed under their own categories. Earlier glass may be listed in the Glass-Art and Glass-Contemporary categories. Italian glass may be found in Glass-Venetian.

Bottle, Figural, Bird, Smoke Brown, Tapered Spout, Scandinavia, 5 3/4 In. 85.00
Bottle, Mottled Orange, Brown, Clear, Free-Form, Cut, Acid Textured, 8 1/2 In. 7188.00
Bowl, Coquille, Orange Over White, Abstract Shape, Flygfors, Sweden, 14 1/2 In. 250.00
Bowl, Floral, Underplate, Classic Line, Gold Concentric Tracery, Higgins, 12 1/2 In. 400.00
Candlestick, Blue Cased, Flared Base, Tapered, Bucka Nissen, Copenhagen, 4 1/2 In., Pair 150.00
Charger, Blue & Green Tongue-Shaped Decoration, 16 3/4 In. 385.00
Cocktail Set, Ultima Thule, Tapio Wirkkala, Finland, 9-In. Carafe, 11 Piece 225.00
Compote, Olive Green, Raised Circles At Rim, Hadeland, Norway, 5 1/2 x 10 3/4 In. 400.00
Decanter, Green, Bulbous, Beaked Spout, Kjell Blomberg, Gullaskruf, Sweden, 6 1/2 .... 225.00
Decanter, Turquoise Over White, Lacquered Wood Stopper, Kastrup, Denmark, 18 In. 325.00
Dish, Abstract, Orange Ground, Square, Michael & Frances Higgins, 1950s, 10 In. 95.00
Dish, Clear & Turquoise, Silver Silkscreened Decoration, Square, Higgins, 10 In. 125.00
Dish, Iceberg, Mold Blown, Cased, Timo Sarpaneva, Finland, c.1953, 9 1/4 In. 1090.00
Plaque, After The Rain, Colored Silverleaf, Frame, Edris Eckhardt, 8 x 9 In. 780.00
Plaque, Bowl Of Flowers, Fused, Gold Decoration, Frame, Higgins, 21 x 11 In. 510.00
Plaque, Midnight Bouquet, Colored Silver, Gold Leaf, Edris Eckhardt, 11 x 8 In. 840.00
Plate, Flip Art, Blue, Stylized Leaves & Flowers, Higgins, 13 In. 360.00
Plate, Tyrannus Rex, Mosaic Design, Gold Leaf Trim, Higgins, 11 1/4 In. 780.00
Platter, Orgy, Red Orange, Gray, Fused, Round, Higgins, 13 1/2 In. 1560.00
Salt & Pepper, Carnaby, Blue Cased, Mushroom Shape, Holmegaard, 4 In. 95.00
Tray, Mandarin, Red, Orange, Mauve Raditing Triangles, Slumped, Higgins, 7 x 10 In. 180.00
Tumbler, Iced Tea, El Rancho, Bryce, Amethyst, 5 1/2 In. 10.00
Vase, Amethyst, Protruding Bubbles, Nanny Still, Riihimaki, Finland, 11 In. 150.00
Vase, Bud, Target, Clear, Red & Green Design, Pukeberg, Sweden, 4 1/2 In. 125.00
Vase, Carnaby, Orange Cased, Flattened, Flared Rim, Kastrup, Denmark, 6 1/2 In., Pair 345.00
Vase, Crackle, Ruffled Rim, Amethyst, Bischoff, 1940-63, 8 1/2 In. 145.00
Vase, Green Streaks, Pulled Designs, White Friars, England, c.1950, 6 3/4 In. 69.00
Vase, Green, Orange, Textured Surface, Cut Circles, Vladimir Jelinek, 1969, 12 In. 707.00
Vase, Kalvolan Kanto, Tree Stump, Clear, Tapio Wirkkala, Finland, c.1948, 7 1/4 In. 2075.00
Vase, Ogee Arched Form, Green, Floris Meydam, Leerdam Unica, 1960s, 9 In. 245.00
Vase, Orange, Wood Grain Texture, Cylindrical, Scandinavia, 10 In. 85.00
Vase, Tribal, Smoke Brown, Extruded Glass, Buttons, Viktor Berndt, Sweden, 7 x 5 In. 285.00

GLASS-VENETIAN. Venetian glass has been made near Venice, Italy, since the thirteenth century. Thin, colored glass with applied decoration is favored, although many other types have been made. Collectors have recently become interested in the Art Deco and 1950s designs. Glass was made on the Venetian island of Murano from 1291. The output dwindled in the late seventeenth century but began to flourish again in the 1850s. Some of the old techniques of glassmaking were revived, and firms today make traditional designs and original modern glass. Since 1981, the name *Murano* may only be used on glass made on Murano Island. Other pieces of Italian glass may be found in the Glass-Contemporary and Glass-Midcentury categories of this book.

Bottle, Clear, Green Interior, Stopper, Paolo Venini, 1950s, 7 1/2 In. 755.00
Bottle, Pink, Murrines, Ribbon, Narrow Neck, Ansolo Fuga, Avem, 17 x 8 1/2 In. 7080.00
Bowl, Caccia, Clear, Gray, White, Black Bull's-Eye Murrhina, Barovier & Toso, 4 x 7 In. 2040.00
Bowl, Footed, Alternating Colored Band, Latticinio Ribbons, 5 1/2 In. 150.00
Bowl, Inciso, Sommerso, Olive Green, Flared, Venini, 6 1/4 x 12 In. 1535.00
Bowl, Intarsia, Hemispherical, Red Triangles, Barovier & Toso, 4 x 9 3/4 In. 1534.00
Bowl, Patchwork, Opalescent Rectangles, Barovier & Toso, c.1957, 5 In. 990.00
Bowl, Reticello, Flared, Venini, 1981, 6 1/2 x 11 1/4 In. 265.00
Centerpiece, Rainbow, 4-Footed, Hand Blown, 6 x 14 x 16 In. 120.00
Charger, Enameled, Commedia Dell'Arte Figures, 20 In. 425.00
Compote, Clear, Impressed Gold Flowers, c.1900, 10 x 6 1/2 In. 90.00
Dish, Dessert, Cranberry, Flower-Footed, Gold Leaf Inclusion, Murano, 5 In., 9 Piece 470.00
Figurine, Arlecchino, Pezzato, Lattimo Details, Fulvio Bianconi, 12 1/2 In. 4425.00
Figurine, Dancing Woman, White, Orange Dress, Lattimo, Ercole Barovier, 11 In. 3068.00
Figurine, Duck, Clear, Embedded Silver Leaf, Applied Yellow Beak, Eyes, 14 1/2 In. 345.00
Figurine, Duck, Signed, Nason & Murano, Italy, 7 1/2 In. 175.00
Figurine, Rooster, Lattimo Multicolored, Black Base, Fulvio Bianconi, 8 In. 3186.00
Figurine, Woman, Dress, Applied Features, Barovier & Toso, 7 1/4 x 4 3/4 In. 118.00
Urn, Rosso Corallo, Red, Opaque, Buttressed Handles, Martinuzzi, 7 x 5 3/4 In. 1180.00
Vase, Athena Catterdrale, Tesserae, Bulbous, Barovier & Toso, 11 x 7 In. 10030.00
Vase, Aventurine, Orange Bands, Pillow, Flared, Fratelli Toso, 11 x 10 In. 885.00
Vase, Aventurine, Orange Inclusions, Black Ground, Globular, 1950s, 8 3/4 In. 165.00
Vase, Black, Gold Foil, Corseted, Scalloped Base, Zecchin-Martinuzzi, 10 1/2 x 4 In. 885.00
Vase, Calla, White Fenicio, Tyra Lundgren, Venini, 12 1/2 x 8 1/2 In. 1298.00
Vase, Clear, 4 Scroll Handles, M.V.M. Capellin, Vittorio Zecchin, 1920s, 6 3/4 In. 245.00
Vase, Clear, Mica, Blue Rim, Grape Handles, Barovier & Toso, Murano, 1930s, 7 3/4 In. 825.00
Vase, Clear, Pink Cased, Bulbous, Gold Trim, Salviati, 14 1/2 In. 600.00
Vase, Corseted, Black & White Candies, Venini, 16 1/4 In. 3835.00
Vase, Dove Shape, Pink, Mottled, Flavio Poli, 4 1/2 x 7 1/4 In. 236.00
Vase, Fish Shape, Murrine Features, Cenedese, 8 3/4 x 14 3/4 In. 1060.00
Vase, Graffito Barbarico, Festoon, Teal, Oval, Barovier & Toso, 11 1/2 x 9 1/4 In. 1770.00
Vase, Inciso, Amber Sommerso, Flared, Venini, 6 1/2 x 5 1/2 In. 1062.00
Vase, Inciso, Blue, Cased In Clear, Wheel Cut, Paolo Venini, c.1955, 19 In. 8299.00
Vase, Occhi, Tobia Scarpa, Venini Italia, 1960s, 9 In. 1680.00
Vase, Patchwork, Lattimo Ground, Elongated Gourd, Ansolo Fuga, Avem, 16 3/4 In. 5015.00
Vase, Pezzato, Red, Blue, Green, Patchwork, Fulvio Bianconi, 9 1/4 x 6 1/4 In. 4425.00
Vase, Pink Aventurine, Flecked Gold, Diamond Optic, Bulbous, Flared Rim, 5 In. 403.00
Vase, Ruby, Silver Foil, 2 Openings, Asymmetrical, Giulio Radi, A.Ve.M., 7 1/4 x 5 1/2 In. 2950.00
Vase, Sassi, Small Opening, Bands, Luciano Gaspari, Salviati, 10 1/2 x 5 1/2 In. 1180.00
Vase, Spicchi, Pear Shape, Paneled, Fulvio Bianconi, Venini, 8 3/4 x 5 1/2 In. 2950.00
Vase, Spiral, Red, Red Orange, Black, T. Stearns, Murano, 11 x 3 3/4 In. 5600.00
Vase, Spirals, Iridescent, Corroso, Carlo Scarpa, Venini, c.1936, 12 1/2 In. 9898.00
Vase, Trumpet, Clear, White, Red & Gold Internal Swirls, Toso, 10 In. 58.00
Vase, Zanfirico, Clear Handles, Oval, Elongated, 1960s, 16 1/4 In. 75.00

GLASSES for the eyes, or spectacles, were mentioned in a manuscript in 1289 and have been used ever since. The first eyeglasses with rigid side pieces were made in London in 1727. Bifocals were invented by Benjamin Franklin in 1785. Lorgnettes were popular in late Victorian times. Opera Glasses are listed in their own category.

Cat's-Eye, Aluminum, Copper Tone, Bagette Rhinestones, Art Craft 15.00
Cat's-Eye, Bakelite, Butterscotch, Carved Lines, Vogue, 1950s 32.00
Cat's-Eye, Brown Translucent Plastic, Topaz Rhinestones, Gold Accents, 1950s 22.00
Cat's-Eye, Pearlized Amethyst, France, 1950s 49.00

Cat's-Eye, Silver, Polished, Marcasite Rhinestones, 1950s 50.00
Lorgnette, 14K Gold, Etched Design, Applied Salamander, Link Chain, 1920 .... 1200.00
Lorgnette, Pearls, Filigree Chain, 14K & 18K White Gold, Art Deco, 1917 .... 205.00
Lorgnette, Tortoiseshell, Elaborately Carved Handle, 1890s, 10 1/2-In. Handle 395.00
Monocular, Gilt Brass, Ivory, Screw Barrel Focusing, 2 In. 118.00
Pince-Nez, Gilt Metal Frames, Oval Lenses, Engraved Adjustment Lever, c.1890 .... 188.00
Pince-Nez, Gold Tone Metal, Nose Piece, Attached Chain, Hairpin, c.1900 .... 90.00
Round Lenses, Ribbon Loops, Steel Case, c.1750, Pair 250.00
Spectacles, 14K Gold, Octagonal Lenses, c.1890 .... 115.00
Sun, Aviator, Gold Rim, Green Glass, Ray-Ban, Bausch & Lomb, Leather Case, 1950s 32.00
Sun, Folding, Metal Frame, Black & White Enamelled Art Deco Case, Link Chain 150.00

GLIDDEN Pottery worked in Alfred, New York, from 1940 to 1957. The pottery made stoneware, dinnerware, and art objects.

Bowl, No. 22, Turquoise Matrix Glaze, 11 x 9 In. 25.00
Casserole, Cover, No. 165, Oven Proof, Mottled Green Teal 28.00
Planter, No. 104, Turquoise Matrix, 2 x 4 1/4 x 2 3/8 In. 21.00
Planter, No. 106, Rectangular, Mottled Turquoise, 1950s, 3 1/2 x 8 1/4 x 4 In. 13.00
Tray, No. 35, Poodle, Cream Ground, Yellow Rim, Square, 5 1/2 In. 15.00
Vase, Ball, No. 49, Turquoise Matrix Glaze, 6 1/2 In. 55.00
Vase, No. 86, Rolled Rim, Mottled, Turquoise Matrix Glaze, 7 1/2 In. 45.00
Vase, No. 87, Turquoise Rose, 8 In. 45.00

GOEBEL is the mark used by W. Goebel Porzellanfabrik of Oeslau, Germany, now Rodental, Germany. Many types of figurines and dishes have been made. The firm is still working. The pieces marked *Goebel Hummel* are listed under Hummel in this book.

Bank, 2 Cats On Doghouse, Sleeping Dog, 6 x 3 3/4 x 3 In. .... 45.00 to 125.00
Figurine, Bird, Cardinal, Male, 1972-79, 2 3/4 x 4 1/4 In. 115.00
Figurine, Blumenkinder, Chick Boy, 8 In. 140.00
Figurine, Blumenkinder, Courting Country Style, 1970, 8 x 6 In. 180.00
Figurine, Blumenkinder, First Date, 1970, 9 x 4 In. 175.00
Figurine, Book Worm, Girl, Sitting, Dress, Red Polka Dots, c.1960, 4 x 3 1/2 In. 249.00
Figurine, Cat, Sleeping, 9 1/2 In. 58.00
Figurine, Co-Boy, Tom, Honey Jar, 1970, 8 In. 95.00
Figurine, Courting Couple, 1924-49, 3 In. 59.00
Figurine, Dog, Boxer, Sitting, Full Bee, 1940-58, 5 In. 90.00
Figurine, Dog, Dachshund, Tag, Label, Box, 1972-79, 5 1/2 In. 250.00
Figurine, Girl, Sitting Pretty, Charlot Byj, 1972-79, 5 In. 105.00
Figurine, Strike Bowler Boy, Redhead, Charlot Byj, 1957, 3 3/4 x 2 1/8 x 4 1/2 In. 130.00
Mug, Clown, 4 1/2 In. 50.00
Mug, Friar Tuck, Full Bee, 1950s, 5 1/4 In. 80.00
Pitcher, Harlequin, 8 In. 75.00
Planter, Swan, 4 x 5 In. 55.00
Plate, Twelve Tribes Of Israel, Old Testament Series, Laszlo Ispanky, 1978, 12 In. 98.00
Salt & Pepper, Bashful Tyroleans, Full Bee, 1950-54, 3 In. 55.00
Salt & Pepper, Chimney Sweep, In Basket, 3 1/2 In. 40.00
Sugar & Creamer, Tray, Friars, 6 3/4-In. Tray .... 100.00 to 120.00
Vase, Swan, Upspread Wings, Curved Neck, 9 x 5 In. 79.00

GOLDSCHEIDER has made porcelains in three places. The family left Vienna in 1938 and started factories in England and in Trenton, New Jersey. The New Jersey factory started in 1940 as Goldscheider-U.S.A. In 1941 it became Goldscheider-Everlast Corporation. From 1947 to 1953 it was Goldcrest Ceramics Corporation. In 1950 the Vienna plant was returned to Mr. Goldscheider, and the company continues in business. The Trenton, New Jersey, business, now called *Goldscheider of Vienna*, imports all of the pieces.

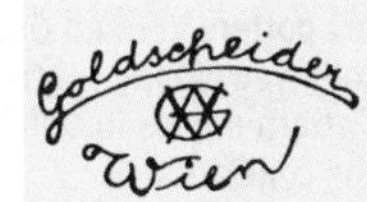

Figurine, Country Girl, Pre World War I, 14 x 11 1/2 x 8 In. 1350.00
Figurine, Deco Dancers, Katzenhutte, 20 x 14 x 6 In. 2250.00
Figurine, Diana With Borzoi, c.1912, 24 x 8 In. 3500.00
Figurine, Dog, Springer Spaniel Puppy, 4 1/2 In. 65.00

Figurine, Faust, Lorenzl, c.1927, 15 x 8 x 5 In. 2200.00
Figurine, Flamenco Dancer, Art Nouveau, 19 x 13 1/2 x 8 1/2 In. 2500.00
Figurine, Madonna, 5 x 4 In. 295.00
Figurine, Nude Woman, Standing, Draped, c.1897, 29 x 7 In. 95.00
Figurine, Prince Of Wales, Peggy Porschner, 7 1/8 In. 125.00
Figurine, Putto, With Stubborn Ram, c.1915, 9 1/2 x 10 x 4 In. 1500.00
Figurine, Woman, Holding Hat On Her Head, 6 3/4 In. 85.00
Figurine, Woman, Holding Straw Hat, Goldstar Everlast, 11 In. 185.00
Lamp, Boudoir, Nude Woman Under Tree, 12 x 9 In. 2500.00
Vase, 6 Heads, 5 Women, Devil, Flowers, 17 1/2 x 21 In. 3740.00

GOLF, see Sports category.

GOOFUS GLASS was made from about 1900 to 1920 by many American factories. It was originally painted gold, red, green, bronze, pink, purple, or other bright colors. Many pieces are found today with flaking paint, and this lowers the value.

Bonbon, La Belle Rose, 6 In. 17.00
Bowl, Intaglio, Peach, Pattern, Opalescent Edge, c.1930, 3 1/2 x 11 3/4 In. 145.00
Bowl, Roses In The Snow, Scalloped & Ruffled Edge, 2 1/2 x 9 1/4 In. 43.00
Bowl, Thistle, Shallow, 6 3/4 In. 12.00
Plate, Carnation, c.1930, 11 In. 45.00
Plate, Pinecones & Panels, 6 1/2 In. 70.00
Plate, Roses, 8 1/2 In. 50.00
Plate, Roses, 11 In. 65.00
Platter, La Belle Rose, 10 3/4 In. 60.00
Vase, Bird & Grape, 9 In. 90.00
Vase, Grape, Cracked Ice, 7 3/4 In. 21.00
Vase, Red Rose, Cracked Ice, 14 In., Pair 95.00

GOSS china has been made since 1858. English potter William Henry Goss first made it at the Falcon Pottery in Stoke-on-Trent. The factory name was changed to Goss China Company in 1934 when it was taken over by Cauldon Potteries. Production ceased in 1940. Goss china resembles Irish Belleek in both body and glaze. The company also made popular souvenir china, usually marked with local crests and names.

Berry Bowl, Fruit, Beige Ground, Staffordshire, 6 Piece 20.00
Casserole, Fruit, Hand Painted, Staffordshire, 3 x 8 1/2 In. 20.00
Cup & Saucer, Tintagel Crest, 1 1/2 x 4-In. Cup, 4 3/4-In. Saucer 28.00
Dish, Jubilee, 1897, 4 In. 55.00
Jug, St. Ives Crest, 2 x 2 5/8 In. 30.00
Mug, Sir William Wallace Crest, Sir W. Scott Arms, Dunoon Badge, 1 1/2 x 2 In. 30.00
Pot, Arms At Abbotsford, Watch Weel, Gilded Rim, 1 3/4 x 2 In. 17.00
Pot, Cover, Weymouth Arms, 3-Masted Ship, Gilded Rims, Souvenir, 2 3/4 x 2 In. 32.00
Pot, Pipkin, Okehampton Crest, Gilded Rim, 2 1/4 x 2 1/4 In. 38.00
Vase, Torquay Crest, Souvenir, 2 1/4 x 1 3/4 In. 27.00
Vase, Windsor Crest, Gilded Rim, Souvenir, 2 1/4 In. 31.00

GOUDA, Holland, has been a pottery center since the seventeenth century. Two firms, the Zenith pottery, established in the eighteenth century, and the Zuid-Hollandsche pottery made the brightly colored art pottery marked *Gouda* from 1898 to about 1964. Other factories followed. Many pieces featured Art Nouveau or Art Deco designs. Pattern names in Dutch, listed here, seem strange to English speaking collectors.

Ashtray, Black, White Dots, Hand Painted, Gold Gilt, Roma Royal Zuid, 4 In. 22.00
Bell, Dutch Girl's Head, Blue Delft Style, Royal Z. Holland, Signed, 2 3/4 In. 35.00
Bowl, Centerpiece, Stylized Pansies, Abstracts, Brown Ground, 1900, 4 x 11 1/2 In. 175.00
Bowl, Flowers, Petals, Mauve, Magenta, Leaf Ground, 2 x 9 3/4 In. 316.00
Bowl, Multicolored Patterns, 6 x 8 3/4 In. 525.00
Bowl, Pansy, Leaves, Bud, Flat Style, Curved In Rim, Arch, Dot, 1920, 3 x 13 1/2 In. 115.00

Bowl, Stylized Leaf, Rust, Yellow, Brown Ground, Liberty Of London, 3 1/4 x 8 1/4 In. 259.00
Cake Plate, Priza, Flower, 3-Footed, Hand Painted, Plateelbakkery Zuid, c.1915, 2 x 8 In. 170.00
Candlestick, Dot & Triangular, Moat Style Rim, Ribbed Neck, Orange, Blue, 9 x 4 1/2 In., Pair 259.00
Candlestick, Double Gourd Mouth, Moat Style, Scalloped Rim, 1920, 16 x 5 1/2 In. 200.00
Candlestick, Rhodian, Abstracts, Cobalt Blue, Rust, Turquoise, Brown, 1922, 14 1/2 x 6 1/2 In. .. 200.00
Candlestick, Tulip, Diagonal, Ribbed, Moat Style Pedestal, 1925, 7 3/4 x 5 1/2 In., Pair 375.00
Chamberstick, Sambesi, c.1924, 3 1/4 x 6 1/2 In. 225.00
Chamberstick, Suled, 1910-20, 3 1/4 x 4 3/4 In. 250.00
Compote, Rhodian, Rust, Green, Blue, Chartreuse, 2 Handles, 3 1/2 x 10 In. 230.00
Ewer, Modern Dutch, Polychrome, Goedewaagen, 5 3/8 In. 30.00
Ginger Jar, Abstracts, Yellow, Cobalt Blue, Teal, Brown, Regina, 21 x 11 In. 259.00
Humidor, Tobacco, Men, Pipes, Goedewaagen, 1977 .... 55.00
Incense Burner, Palace Style, Stripes, Palace Style, Circular Base, 5 1/2 x 7 In. 200.00
Jardiniere, Bertino, Flowers, Glossy, Royal Zuid, Signed, 6 x 6 1/2 In. 199.00
Jardiniere, Bird On Branch, Brown, Cobalt Blue, Teal, Swirls, 7 3/4 x 10 In. 460.00
Jardiniere, Peacock, Canoe Shape, Polychrome, Handles, 8 x 15 In. 405.00
Lamp Base, Electric, Tulip, Magenta, Petals, Purple, Leaves, Bulbous, 2 Handles, 1920, 12 In. ... 144.00
Pipe, Clay, Exaggerated Thick Lipped Black Man's Face, 7 1/4 In. 95.00
Pitcher, Cora, Hand Painted, Royal Goedewaagen, 8 In. 35.00
Pitcher, Grety, Ribbed Neck, Rust Flowers, Turquoise Panel, 1925, 9 1/2 x 5 1/2 In. 144.00
Pitcher, Peapod Leaves, Flowers, Dots, Points, Mocha Ground, 1918, 10 1/2 x 4 1/2 In. 430.00
Pitcher, Stylized Flowers, Swollen, Marked, 11 In. 210.00
Pitcher, Zenith Plateelbakkery, Floral, c.1930, 5 x 4 In. 230.00
Plate, Unique Metalique Glaze, Scalloped Edge, c.1950, 8 1/4 In. 350.00
Tobacco Jar, Cover, Marked, Arnhem Holland, 6 1/2 In. 115.00
Tray, Beek, Rust, Ocher, Abstracts, Cobalt Blue, Flared Rim, Swirl, Dot, 12 In. 200.00
Tray, Rockets, Purple, Cobalt Blue, Rust, Black Lined, Dotted Center, 1925, 11 1/2 In. 489.00
Vase, Abstract, Turquoise, Sage, Chartreuse, Black, Matte Glaze, 1921, 9 3/4 x 4 In. 546.00
Vase, Abstract, White, Yellow, Green, Sage, Cobalt Blue, Rust, 1912, 13 x 5 1/2 In. 430.00
Vase, Art Deco, Blue Swirl, Flared Mouth, Rust Dots, 16 1/4 x 9 In. 200.00
Vase, Arts & Crafts, Green Matte Glaze, 4 Twisted Handles, Recessed Panels, 10 x 4 1/2 In. 489.00
Vase, Bertino, Hand Painted, No. 2842, Signed, 5 1/4 In. 70.00
Vase, Bird Peering Upwards, Standing On Yellow, Chartreuse Rows, 7 1/2 x 3 1/2 In. 145.00
Vase, Blue, Regina, No. 1170, 6 1/4 In. 55.00
Vase, Butterfly, Winged, Lavender Swirls, 1929, 10 3/4 x 6 3/4 In. 475.00
Vase, Candia, Yellow Dots, Stylized Abstracts, Rust, Cobalt Blue, Green, 8 1/4 x 6 In. 175.00
Vase, Ewer, Purple, Magenta Pansy, Green Leaf, Bud Form Style, Handle, 1906, 3 3/4 x 5 In. 175.00
Vase, Flattened Ball Shape, Flowers, Everted Rim, c.1930, 6 In. 55.00
Vase, Flower, Teal, Sage, Pumpkins, 9 3/4 x 5 In. 144.00
Vase, Flowers, Heart Shape Petals, Leaves, Magenta, Purple, Green, 10 x 6 In. 375.00
Vase, Flowers, Lavender, Green, Navy, Ivory Ground, Handles, Tapered, Pedestal, 10 3/4 x 4 In. ... 1725.00
Vase, Flowers, Magenta, Purple, Violet, Double Handle, 13 1/2 x 10 In. 865.00
Vase, Flowers, Purple, Stylized Leaves, Yellow Ground, Handles, 18 x 17 In. 306.00
Vase, Geometric Flowers, Early 1900s, 6 1/2 x 4 1/2 In. 185.00
Vase, Golenette, Bird Perched On Branch, Peering Upwards, Polychrome, 7 1/2 x 4 In. 316.00
Vase, Hand Painted, Regina, 6 5/8 x 3 3/4 In. 275.00
Vase, Hand Painted, Roos, No. 269, Goedewaagen, c.1935, 10 In. 175.00
Vase, Hollandia, Abstract Panels, Gray, Blue, Cobalt Blue, Yellow, Sage, 1918, 10 1/4 x 7 In. 259.00
Vase, Juliana, Ivora, c.1920, 10 1/4 x 5 1/2 In., Pair 1200.00
Vase, Kantjes, Burgundy, Green, Globular Base, Yellow, Gray, White Ground, 6 3/4 x 5 In. 375.00
Vase, Kelat, Flowers, Protruding Lip, Pointed Handles, Bulbous, 1922, 8 x 6 1/2 In. 316.00
Vase, Lady, Stylized Turquoise Leaves, Rust Flowers, Cobalt Blue, Brown, 1926, 7 1/2 x 5 In. 805.00
Vase, Lavender, Teal, Cobalt Blue, 1923, 7 1/2 x 4 In. 345.00
Vase, Leaves, Brown, Rust, Mahogany, Green, Blue, Trophy Style, Ribbed Pedestal, 15 x 10 In. 230.00
Vase, Oriental, Spherical Mouth, Arches, Dots, Ribbed Neck, 11 x 4 1/2 In. 460.00
Vase, Peacock On Branch, Abstracts, Ivory Ground, 1910, 9 1/2 x 3 In. 865.00
Vase, Rhodian, 1924, 7 1/2 In. 325.00
Vase, Stylized Flower, Dotted, Triangular Petals, Sun Yellow, Blue, Lavender, 14 x 6 In. 316.00
Vase, Stylized Flowers, Leaves, Green, Purple, Brown, Black, Handle, 1908, 6 1/2 x 3 1/2 In. 430.00
Vase, Stylized Leaves, Cobalt Blue Glaze, Turquoise, Green, Rust, Handle, 12 1/4 x 8 3/4 In. 288.00
Vase, Tulip, Flowers, Magenta, Purple, Lavender, Turquoise, Sage Fields, 11 1/4 x 9 1/4 In. 115.00

Vase, Tulips, Blue, Teardrop, Dots, Bottle Neck, Leaf Ground, Yellow, Green, Blue, 9 3/4 x 4 1/2 In. 635.00
Vase, Tulips, Cobalt Blue, Jade Green Ground, Double Gourd, High Glaze, 9 1/2 x 10 In. 345.00
Vase, Woman Portrait, Stylized Purple Tulip, Cascading Tendrils, Leaves, 11 3/4 x 7 In. 430.00
Wall Plaque, Blue Bird, White, Violet, Ocher, 14 1/2 In. 1150.00
Wall Plaque, Eland, Gazelle Jumping Through Stylized Shrubbery, 12 x 9 In. 290.00
Wall Plaque, Peacock, Abstract Borders, Feathers, Cobalt Blue, 12 In. 230.00
Wall Plaque, Persian, Flowers, Footed, 14 1/2 In. 230.00
Wall Plaque, Sourac, Stylized Fruit, Turquoise, Lavender, Rust, Mahogany, 12 1/2 In. 345.00
Wall Plaque Set, Madro, Brown Flowers, Yellow Stamen, Abstracts, 1 1/2 x 9 In., 3 Piece 375.00

GRANITEWARE is an enameled tinware that has been used in the kitchen from the late nineteenth century to the present. Earlier graniteware was green or turquoise blue, with white spatters. The later ware was gray with white spatters. Reproductions are being made in all colors.

Baking Pan, Chrysolite, 8 x 11 In. 185.00
Bed Pan, Cobalt Blue, White, Speckled, 4 x 11 1/2 x 13 3/4 In. 15.00
Berry Bucket, 3 1/2 In. 25.00
Berry Bucket, Flat Lid, Western Electric Paper Label, 4 In. 145.00
Bowl, Blue & White Splashed, 2 1/2 x 10 1/2 In. 50.00
Bowl, Blue & White Swirl, Black Trim, 1960s, 2 1/2 x 6 1/8 In. 35.00
Bowl, Blue & White, 3 x 7 1/2 In. 6.00
Bowl, Gray & White Swirl, Stamped Columbia, 3 3/4 In. 20.00
Bowl, Gray, 2 x 5 In. 65.00
Bowl, Red & White Swirl, 6 1/2 In. 4.00
Bowl, Vegetable, Aqua Swirl, Rectangular, 1950s 10.00
Broiler, Cover, Gray, White, Mottled, 5 x 13 x 8 In. 43.00
Butter, Cream, Gold, France, 4 x 7 1/2 In. 125.00
Canner, Cover, Marked No. 5, c.1950, 14 1/4 In. 45.00
Coffee Biggin, Red, White, France, 1930s, 11 1/2 In. 225.00
Coffee Boiler, Blue & White Swirl, Pit Bottom, Granite Lid 90.00
Coffeepot, Blue & White, Mottled, 10 1/2 In. 129.00
Coffeepot, Blue Speckled, Pewter Trim, 11 In. 85.00
Coffeepot, Brown, Mottled, 7 In. 150.00
Coffeepot, Cobalt & White Swirl, Granite Lid, 9 In. 95.00
Coffeepot, Cover, Blue, Mottled, Child's, 6 1/2 x 3 5/8 In. 165.00
Coffeepot, Granite Lid, 9 In. 20.00
Coffeepot, Granite Lid, Gray, Bottom Stamped L & G Extra Agate, 5 1/2 In. 145.00
Coffeepot, Hinged Lid, Brown, Mottled, Black Trim, 9 3/4 x 6 1/4 In. 150.00
Coffeepot, Insert, Blue, Speckled, 9 In. 25.00
Coffeepot, Primo Paper Label, 8 1/4 In. 50.00
Coffeepot, Tin Cover, Acorn Finial, Gray, c.1900, 8 In. 75.00
Coffeepot, Turquoise Speckled, c.1970, 8 1/2 In. 25.00
Coffeepot, Wire Bail Handle, Black, Speckled, 8 In. 139.00
Colander, Blue & White, Speckled, 10 1/4 In. 10.00
Colander, Gray, Handles, 1870-1900 195.00
Colander, Gray, Mottled, Netherlands, 5 x 9 In. 65.00
Cup, Blue & White Swirl, 2 x 4 In. 30.00
Cup, Brown, Gray, Speckled, 3 x 3 1/4 In. 35.00
Cup, Gray, Mottled, 4 x 2 1/4 In. 9.00
Dishpan, Blue Swirl, 3 x 12 In. 25.00
Drainer Pan, Brown, White, Spatter, 3 x 11 In. 35.00
Funnel, Cobalt Blue & White Swirl, 5 1/2 In. 75.00
Funnel, Gray, Mottled, 9 x 7 3/4 In. 50.00
Funnel, White, Cobalt Blue Trim, Miniature 20.00
Funnel Cake Pan, Splotchy Blue, 3 1/4 x 9 3/4 In. 185.00
Griddle, Round, Handle, Embossed National 45.00
Kettle, Berlin, Chrysolite, Granite Lid, 9 1/2 In. 85.00
Kettle, Preserve, Chrysolite, 8 In. 85.00
Ladle, Blue, 12 In. 7.00
Ladle, Brown & White Swirl 40.00 to 75.00

Ladle, Soup, Pewter Trim, Wooden Handle 375.00
Lunch Box, Brown, White, Speckled, Insert, France, 5 1/2 x 6 1/4 In. 95.00
Measure, Riveted Handle, Spout, Stamped L & G Extra Agate, 4 3/4 In. 25.00
Measure, Seamless, 3 1/8 In. 55.00
Milk Can, Blue & White Swirl, 8 1/2 In. 375.00
Milk Can, Cover, Onyx, Wood Bail Handle, Seamed Body, 8 x 4 In. 85.00
Mixing Bowl, Blue, White, Spatter, Blue Rim, 4 x 10 In. 22.00
Mixing Spoon, Blue, Speckled, 14 In. 45.00
Mold, Corn, 6 In. 195.00
Mold, Rabbit, 3 1/2 In. 85.00
Mold, Strawberry, 5 In. 105.00
Mold, Wheat, 7 In. 105.00
Muffin Pan, Gray, Mottled, 8 Cup, 15 1/4 x 8 1/4 In. 65.00
Muffin Pan, Gray, Mottled, Square, 9 Cup, 11 1/2 In. 65.00
Muffin Pan, Individual, 3 1/4 In., 3 Piece 40.00
Mug, Blue, White, Mottled, 3 1/8 x 3 1/2 In. 25.00
Napkin Ring, Blue, White, 1 1/3 x 1 3/4 In., 6 Piece 15.00
Pail, Water, White, Red Trim, Kanawha Paper Label, 5 In. 28.00
Pan, Blue, White Specks, 2 Spouts, Handle, 2 x 8 1/2 In. 10.00
Pan, Blue, White, 5 x 16 In. 32.00
Pan, Blue, White, Speckled, 7-In. Handle, 4 1/4 x 10 1/4 In. 60.00
Pan, Brown, White Specks, 2 x 7 3/4 In. 11.00
Pan, Corn Stick, Iron, Enamel, Griswold, No. 830, c.1950, 13 x 5 3/4 In. 165.00
Pan, Cover, Blue, White Specks, 6 Cup, 3 1/2 x 12 1/2 In. 11.00
Pan, Frying, Brown & White Swirl, 10 In. 65.00
Pan, Jelly Roll, 11 In. 23.00
Pie Pan, Blue, White, Swirl, 8 3/4 In. 35.00
Pie Pan, Cobalt Blue, Swirl, White Interior, 9 3/4 In. 40.00
Pie Pan, Gray, Mottled, 1930s, 7 3/4 In. 15.00
Pie Pan, Navy, White, Small Speckles, 1 x 9 1/4 In. 35.00
Pie Plate, Chrysolite, 8 3/4 In. 50.00
Pie Plate, Cobalt Blue & White Swirl, 9 In. 30.00
Pitcher, Green & Red, White Ground, c.1940, 14 In. 190.00
Pitcher, Water, Bulbous, 6 3/4 In. 100.00
Pitcher, White, Blue, France, 14 3/4 In. 110.00
Pitcher, White, Red, France, 1930s, 14 In. 145.00
Plate, Blue & White Swirl, Black Trim, 1960s, 10 1/4 In. 35.00
Platter, Turkey, Oval, 22 In. 65.00
Pot, Cover, Blue, White Specks, Wooden Bail Handle, 8 1/2 x 9 3/4 In. 40.00
Pot, Cover, Gray, White, Mottled, 4 1/2 x 7 In. 15.00
Pus Pan, Kidney Shape, Gray, White, Mottled, 2 x 11 x 5 1/2 In. 27.50
Roaster, Blue, White Specks, 16 1/4 x 12 1/4 In. 20.00
Roaster, Cover, Gray, Mottled, Rack Insert, 13 x 17 x 7 1/2 In. 27.50
Roaster, Cream City Juicy Krisp, Oval, 3 Piece 33.00
Roaster, Oval, 20 In. 10.00
Saucepan, Lid, Aqua Swirl, 1950s 13.00
Saucepan, Red & White Swirl, Cover, 6 3/4 In. 5.00
Scoop, Grocer's, Tube Handle 55.00
Soap Dish, Blue Swirl, Scalloped Edge, Hanging, 4 1/4 x 6 In. 95.00
Soap Dish, Shell Shape, Primo Paper Label 115.00
Suds Dipper, Gray, Mottled, 2 1/4 x 4 3/4 x 12 1/2 In. 89.00
Syrup, Pewter Trim, Lady Head Finial 850.00
Tea Steeper, Granite Lid, Iris Ware 215.00
Teakettle, Orange Brown, White Swirls, Black Inside, Bottom, 9 x 32 In. 299.00
Teapot, Blue Speckled, Pewter Trim, Wood Handle 90.00
Teapot, Flowers, Wood Handle 13.00
Teapot, Granite Lid, Red & White Swirl, 8 In. 15.00
Teapot, Hinged Cover, Cobalt Blue & White, Wood Finial, 8 In. 160.00
Teapot, Pewter Trim, Egg Shape, 2 Cup, 5 3/4 In. 225.00
Teapot, Pewter Trim, Scalloped, 9 1/2 In. 90.00
Teapot, Tin Lid, Stamped L & G, 6 1/2 In. 50.00

Tray, Grooved, 10 In. 85.00
Tray, Pewter Trim, Handles, Stamped Manning & Bowman & Co., 15 1/2 x 12 In. 1400.00
Tray, Round, 14 In. 48.00
Washbasin, Blue & White Columbian Swirl, Salesman Sample 35.00

GREENTOWN glass was made by the Indiana Tumbler and Goblet Company of Greentown, Indiana, from 1894 to 1903. In 1899, the factory became part of National Glass Company. A variety of pressed glass was made. Additional pieces may be found in other categories, such as Chocolate Glass, Holly Amber, Milk Glass, and Pressed Glass.

Austrian, Tumbler, 3 5/8 In. 45.00
Austrian, Vase, 6 In. 45.00
Cord Drapery, Dish, Cobalt Blue, 6 1/2 In. 110.00
Cord Drapery, Spooner, 4 x 4 1/2 In. 45.00
Holly Amber, Tumbler, 4 In. 40.00
Pleat Band, Cake Stand, 4 x 6 1/2 In. 75.00
Shuttle, Punch Cup 8.00
Shuttle, Wine 18.00
Teardrop & Tassel, Butter, No Cover, 1 3/4 x 6 3/8 In. 48.00

GRUEBY Faience Company of Boston, Massachusetts, was incorporated in 1897 by William H. Grueby. Garden statuary, art pottery, and architectural tiles were made until 1920. The company developed a green matte glaze that was so popular it was copied by many other factories making a less expensive type of pottery. This eventually led to the financial problems of the pottery.

Bowl, Green Glaze, Closed Mouth, 2 1/4 x 5 1/4 In. 1150.00
Bowl, Green Glaze, Ribbed Panels, Textured, 2 3/4 x 8 In. 475.00
Paperweight, Scarab, Blue Glaze, 4 In. 690.00
Paperweight, Scarab, Green Matte Glaze, 4 x 2 3/4 In. 705.00
Paperweight, Scarab, Mottled Blue Green Glaze, 1 1/2 x 4 In. 325.00
Tile, Boy & Dog, 7 1/2 x 12 1/4 In. 690.00
Tile, Rabbit, Square, Arts & Crafts Oak Frame, 4 In. 2880.00
Tile, Seagulls Flying Over Green Waves, Cuenca, Hammered Copper, Footed Trivet, 4 In. 999.00
Tile, Ship, Curly Waves, Cuenca, Indigo, Ivory, Blue Gray Ground, Signed, AS, 6 In. 1295.00
Tile, Water Lily, Buds, Pads, Blue Matte Glaze, 6 x 6 In. 3335.00
Vase, Apple Green Semimatte Glaze, Bisque Body, Spherical, 3 1/2 In. 295.00
Vase, Bulbous, Flared Lip, Recessed Neck, 4 1/2 x 5 1/2 In. 865.00
Vase, Crown Over Dragon, Horse, Green High Glaze, Embossed, Handle, 16 x 9 1/2 In. 4900.00
Vase, Green Matte Glaze, Bulbous, Impressed Mark, 5 In. 960.00
Vase, Green Matte Glaze, Carved, Applied Leaves, Bugs, Feathered, 11 1/2 x 5 1/2 In. 3290.00
Vase, Green Matte Glaze, Carved, Applied Vertical Leaves, Impressed Mark, 4 3/4 In. 3100.00
Vase, Green Matte Glaze, Feathered, Gourd Shape, 18 1/2 x 8 1/2 In. 7600.00
Vase, Green Matte Glaze, Trefoil, Buds, Leaves, Feathered, 7 1/2 x 4 1/2 In. 1880.00
Vase, Green Matte Glaze, Veined Spherical Ribs, Flared Rim, 6 x 7 In. 2350.00

GUNDERSEN glass was made at the Gundersen-Pairpoint Glass Works of New Bedford, Massachusetts, from 1952 to 1957. Gundersen Peachblow is especially famous.

Bowl, Peachblow, Handles, 6 In. 206.00
Decanter, Peachblow, Bulbous, Footed, Stopper, 12 In. 288.00
Pitcher, Milk, Peachblow, Matte, Applied White Handle, 4 3/4 In. 288.00
Tazza, Peachblow, Matte, Melon Ribbed Knop, Ruffled Rim, 6 3/4 x 7 1/4 In. 288.00
Vase, Lily, Peachblow, 9 In. 173.00

GUNS that may be classed as toys, such as BB guns, air rifles, and cap guns, are listed in the Toy category.

GUSTAVSBERG ceramics factory was founded in 1827 near Stockholm, Sweden. It is best known to collectors for its twentieth-century artwares, especially a green stoneware with silver inlay called *Argenta*.

Gustafsberg

Cup, Brown, Green, Vertical Lines, Wilhelm Kage, 3 5/8 In. 2640.00

Dish, Squares, Rounded Corners, Wilhelm Kage, 1940s, 2 x 11 1/4 In. 2280.00
Jardiniere, 4-Footed, Glazed, Yellow, Brown, Wilhelm Kage, 1940s, 6 x 8 1/2 x 6 In. 3600.00
Sculpture, Fish, Wilhelm Kage, 1940s, 24 1/4 In. 5400.00
Vase, 4-Footed, Inverted Cone Insert, Wilhelm Kage, 1940s, 8 In. 7200.00
Vase, 10 Bands, Turquoise Drip, Wilhelm Kage, 1940s, 14 3/4 In. 5040.00
Vase, Cylindrical, 4 Raised Bands, Turquoise Drip, Wilhelm Kage, 1940s, 5 In. 2880.00
Vase, Cylindrical, Cutout Feet, Lines, Red, Brown, Wilhelm Kage, 1940s, 9 1/2 In. 7200.00
Vase, Cylindrical, Multiple Raised Bands, Blue, Wilhelm Kage, 1940s, 16 In. 10200.00
Vase, Cylindrical, Small Opening, Squares, Rectangles, Wilhelm Kage, 1940s, 5 1/2 In. 6600.00
Vase, Flowers, Leaves, Mottled Turquoise Ground, Josef Ekberg, 1922, 5 In. 265.00
Vase, Footed, Nude Woman, Silver Decoration, Argenta, 1930s, 4 1/4 In. 358.00
Vase, Long Smooth Neck, Geometrics, Blue, Wilhelm Kage, 1940s, 16 3/4 In. 5040.00
Vase, Onion Shape, Berndt Friberg, 1950s, 4 1/4 In. 1040.00
Vase, Spherical, Small Mouth, Berndt Friberg, c.1960, 4 x 4 In. 420.00

GUTTA-PERCHA was one of the first plastic materials. It was made from a mixture of resins from Malaysian trees. It was molded and used for daguerreotype cases, toilet articles, and picture frames in the nineteenth century.

Bracelet, Hinged 45.00
Brush & Mirror, Birds, Branches, Berries, Flowers, Florence, Patented 1866, 10 In. 250.00
Frame, Beaded, Gold Painted Liner, Convex Glass, Oval, c.1865, 6 1/4 x 5 1/2 In. 84.00
Frame, Oval Mirror, c.1880, 19 x 14 In. 650.00
Locket, Chain, Sterling Silver 4-Leaf Clover, Oval Locket, 25 In. 185.00
Mirror, Hand, Black, Flower, Violet, Diatite, Patent 1868 & 1872, 10 1/2 x 4 In. 155.00
Mirror, Patented March, 1878, 12 x 5 3/8 In. 85.00
Picture Frame, Cameo, Classical Head, In Profile, 3 3/4 x 3 3/8 In. 200.00
Pin, Bar, Flowers, Leaves, 5/8 x 2 1/2 In. 65.00
Pin, Mourning, Acorns, Leaves, Victorian, 2 x 2 1/2 In. 110.00

HAEGER Potteries, Inc., Dundee, Illinois, started making commercial artwares in 1914. Early pieces were marked with the name *Haeger* written over an *H*. About 1938, the mark *Royal Haeger* was used in honor of Royal Hickman, a designer at the factory. The firm is still making florist wares and lamp bases. See also the Royal Hickman category.

Haeger

Ashtray, Boomerang, Lavender Agate Glaze, 5 Rests, No. 107, 10 1/4 In. 38.00
Ashtray, Daisy Rim, Gold Glaze, No. 2021S 20.00
Ashtray, Free-Form, Turquoise Interior, Black Exterior, 12 1/4 x 9 In. 40.00
Ashtray, Haeger 100th Anniversary, 1971, 4 1/2 x 4 1/2 In. 35.00
Ashtray, Leather Wrap, 3 Holders, Brown & Orange, Green Ground, No. 2069, 1970s, 8 In. 55.00
Bank, Frog, 5 In. 95.00
Bank, Monkey, 7 In. 95.00
Bookends, Horse, 5 x 9 In. 90.00
Box, Biomorphic, Chartreuse Agate Glaze, Pinch Handle, No. R1166, 3 x 10 x 6 In. 35.00
Candleholder, 2 Leaves, 2 Sticks, 5 1/4 x 4 1/2 x 3 1/2 In. 25.00
Candleholder, Finger Loop, Orange, 9 x 7 x 6 In. 25.00
Console, Leaf, Blue Matte Interior, White Exterior 22.00
Figurine, Cat, Egyptian, Green Eye, 20 In. 165.00
Figurine, Cat, Orange, 15 In. 95.00
Figurine, Deer Head, 16 In. 275.00
Figurine, Dog, Poodle, 9 1/2 In. 65.00
Figurine, Donkey, 9 1/2 In. 55.00
Figurine, Prospector, 12 x 7 In. 185.00
Figurine, Ram, Rearing, 19 x 16 In. 75.00
Figurine, Swan, Black, 19 1/4 x 9 1/4 x 7 In. 125.00
Flower Frog, Nude Woman, Sitting 59.00
Lamp, Dog, Irish Setter, 1950s, 9 x 10 x 6 In. 149.00
Lamp, Etruscan, Blue, 22 In. 125.00
Planter, Dog, Basset Hound, 4 In. 38.00
Planter, Fawn, Blue Green, 8 x 10 In. 24.00

Planter, Madonna & Child, 11 1/4 In. 48.00
Planter, Raccoon, 5 x 9 In. 75.00
Planter, Ribbed, Green, No. 225, 5 x 7 In. 25.00
Planter, Tiger, Green, 1950s, 5 3/4 x 10 In. 48.00
Vase, Cobra, Red, 16 In. 135.00
Vase, Double Leaf, Hickman, 13 x 16 In. 49.00
Vase, Graphic Wrap, 11 In. 38.00
Vase, Green Sponge, 12 Faceted Sides, Arts & Crafts Style, 10 1/4 x 7 3/4 In. 113.00
Vase, Peacock Glaze, Baluster Shape, 1960s, 12 In. 95.00
Vase, Sailfish, Green, No. 271, 9 x 13 In. 42.00

HALF-DOLL, see Pincushion Doll category.

HALL CHINA Company started in East Liverpool, Ohio, in 1903. The firm made many types of wares. Collectors search for the Hall teapots made from the 1920s to the 1950s. The dinnerwares of the same period, especially Autumn Leaf pattern, are also popular. The Hall China Company is still working. For more information, see *Kovels' Depression Glass & Dinnerware Price List*. Autumn Leaf pattern dishes are listed in their own category in this book.

Bean Pot, Cover, 5 x 6 In. 250.00
Casserole, Cover Only, Radiance, 7 1/2 In. 19.00
Crocus, Bowl, Vegetable, Round, 9 1/4 In. 38.00
Floral Lattice, Casserole, Cover, 8 1/4 In. 35.00
Heather Rose, Bowl, Dessert, 5 1/4 In. 7.00
Heather Rose, Mixing Bowl, Platinum Trim, 9 In. 17.00
Poppy, Platter, 13 1/2 In. 43.00
Quartermaster, Sauceboat, White, 10 In. 35.00
Red Poppy, Salt & Pepper, Handles 38.00
Taverne, Coffeepot, Cover, 9 In. 85.00
Wildfire, Bowl, Fruit, 5 1/2 In. 7.25
Wildfire, Bowl, Vegetable, 9 In. 8.00 to 15.00
Wildfire, Cup 14.00
Wildfire, Plate, Dinner, 10 In. 10.00
Wildfire, Saucer 3.00
Wildfire, Soup, Dish, 8 1/2 In. 13.00

HALLOWEEN is an ancient holiday that has changed in the last 200 years. The jack-o'-lantern, witches on broomsticks, and orange decorations seem to be twentieth-century creations. Collectors started to become serious about collecting Halloween-related items in the late 1970s. The papier-mache decorations, now replaced by plastic, and old costumes are in demand.

Bridge Tally Card, Witch, Moon, Cat, Jack-O'-Lantern, Samuel L. Schmucker 403.00
Bulb, Ghost Light, 1940s, 4 In. 280.00
Costume, Blondie, Collegeville, Medium, Box, 1950s 45.00
Costume, Felix, Bland Charnas Co., Box 138.00
Costume, Wonder Woman, Mask, Red, Blue & Yellow, Boxed, Ben Cooper, 1987, Small 45.00
Jack-O'-Lantern, Black Cat On Fence, Papier-Mache, Inserts, 1930s 338.00
Jack-O'-Lantern, Molded Cardboard, Hanging, Candleholder, 1920s, 7 In. 224.00
Jack-O'-Lantern, Molded Cardboard, Inserts, 1920s, 3 1/2 In. 448.00
Jack-O'-Lantern, Molded Cardboard, Inserts, 1920s, 7 x 6 In. 505.00
Jack-O'-Lantern, Molded Cardboard, Moustache, Beard, Eyebrows, 1920s, 5 1/2 In. 225.00
Jack-O'-Lantern, Papier-Mache, 1930s, 9 x 7 In. 140.00
Jack-O'-Lantern, Papier-Mache, 2-Faced, 1930s, 5 1/2 In. 390.00
Jack-O'-Lantern, Papier-Mache, 5 In. 65.00
Jack-O'-Lantern, Papier-Mache, 6 In. 75.00 to 127.00
Jack-O'-Lantern, Papier-Mache, Germany, 1920s 140.00
Jack-O'-Lantern, Papier-Mache, Original Insert, Bail, Germany, c.1920 200.00
Jack-O'-Lantern, Scary Cat, Papier-Mache, 1930s, 8 x 6 In. 280.00
Jack-O'-Lantern, Scary Cat, Papier-Mache, Inserts, 1930s, 8 x 6 In. 560.00
Nodder, Pumpkin Head, Germany, 1890-1910, 7 In. 952.00

When framing a charcoal or pastel drawing, use real glass. Plastic will pick up static electricity and actually pull the charcoal or pastel dust off the paper.

Halloween, Toy, Witch, Riding Motorcycle, 1940s, 7 In.

Postcard, Best Hallowe'en Wishes, Schmucker, Winsch 173.00
Postcard, Hallowe'en Greetings, Boy, Puppy, Cat, Jack-O'-Lanterns, Winsch 230.00
Postcard, Jack-O'-Lantern, Black Devil, H.B. Griggs 145.00
Postcard, Jolly Halloween, Children, Jack-O'-Lantern, Winsch 230.00
Postcard, Merry Halloween, Girl, Jack-O'-Lantern, Mechanical, Clapsaddle 259.00
Postcard, Starry Halloween, Schmucker, Frexias, Winsch 405.00
Toy, Man, Holding Pumpkin, Chalk, 16 x 7 In. 5040.00
Toy, Mechanical, Plays Drums, Cardboard Head, Cloth, Wood, Germany, 8 In. 670.00
Toy, Pumpkin Man, Papier-Mache, 1930s, 7 In. 280.00
Toy, Squeak, Cat, Mechanical, Papier-Mache Head, Cloth Body, Germany, 7 In. 3080.00
Toy, Veggie Man, Composition, Mouth Open, Closes, Mechanical, Germany, 4 1/2 In. 448.00
Toy, Veggie Man, Top Hat, Cardboard, Composition, Painted Features, Pre 1920, 4 In. 168.00
Toy, Witch, Riding Bike, Plastic, 1940s, 7 x 5 In. 448.00
Toy, Witch, Riding Motorcycle, 1940s, 7 In. .... *ILLUS* 715.00
Toy, Witch, Riding Rocket, Plastic, Black, Orange Wheels, Rosbro, 1940s, 6 In. 615.00
Toy, Witch, Riding Rocket, Plastic, Clear, Orange Wheels, Kokomold, 1940s, 8 In. 615.00
Toy, Witch, Riding Rocket, Plastic, Orange, Black Wheels, Kokomold, 1940s, 8 In. 670.00
Toy, Witch, Riding Rocket, Plastic, Orange, Black Wheels, Rosbro, 1940s, 6 In. 448.00

HAMPSHIRE pottery was made in Keene, New Hampshire, between 1871 and 1923. Hampshire developed a line of colored glazed wares as early as 1883, including a Royal Worcester-type pink, olive green, blue, and mahogany. Pieces are marked with the printed mark or the impressed name *Hampshire Pottery* or *J.S.T. & Co., Keene, N.H.* Many pieces were marked with city names and sold as souvenirs.

Bowl, Flowers, Green Matte Glaze, Gray Streaks, Incised, 4 1/4 x 11 In. 430.00
Bowl, Landscape, Green Matte Glaze, Chartreuse Speckling, Spherical, 2 3/4 x 5 1/2 In. 175.00
Bowl, Leaf Form, Blue, Green Semimatte Glaze, 2 3/4 In. 635.00
Bowl, Lily Blossoms, Pads, Embossed, Green Matte Glaze, 3 x 9 1/2 In. 460.00
Bowl, White Mottled, Streaked Glaze, Navy Blue Ground, Incised, Squat, 3 1/4 x 6 In. 1265.00
Candleholder, Mottled Green Glaze, Black, Gray Stripes, 6 1/2 x 4 1/2 In. 518.00
Creamer, Green Matte Glaze, Side Handle, Protruding Spout, 4 x 5 In. 145.00
Fairy Lamp, Leaves, Green Matte Glaze, Rolled Lip, Branch Handles, 5 3/4 x 7 3/4 In. 405.00
Lamp Base, Green Matte Glaze, Electrified, Onion Shape, Recessed Panels, 12 x 11 In. 920.00
Lamp Base, Green Matte Glaze, Embossed Flowers, Buds, Spherical, 10 1/2 x 8 In. 980.00
Lamp Base, Mottled Green, Brown Matte Glaze, Bulbous, 20 In. 1060.00
Lamp Base, Oil, Green Matte Glaze, Water Lily, Raised Veins, Cylindrical, Shade, 7 x 6 In. 1725.00
Lamp Base, Oil, Tulip, Spherical, 5 3/4 x 12 In. 2070.00
Pitcher, Organic Design At Top, Green Matte Glaze, Marked, 7 1/2 In. 430.00
Stein, Green Matte Glaze, Embossed, Handle, 5 1/2 x 4 1/2 In. 58.00
Vase, Art Deco, Ribbed Neck, Bands, Recessed Panels, Pinched Design, 7 x 5 1/4 In. 575.00
Vase, Blue Mottled Glaze, Speckles, Embossed, 8 x 4 In. 1150.00
Vase, Buds, Leaves, Green High Glaze, Incised, 7 x 4 In. 430.00
Vase, Cattail, Embossed, Green Matte Glaze Ground, Globular, Veining, 4 1/2 x 6 1/2 In. 805.00
Vase, Double Leaf, Green Matte Glaze, Veining, 8 1/2 x 6 1/2 In. 1150.00

Handel, Lamp, 8 Panels, Cattails, Filigree Overlay, Acorn Pulls, 23 In.

Handel, Lamp, 9 Panels, Hawaiian Tropic, Filigree Overlay, Palm Tree, Acorn Pulls, 24 In.

Handel, Lamp, Domed Shade, Daffodil, Signed, Palme, 18 In.

Vase, Flowers, Buds, Green Matte Glaze, 6 3/4 x 4 1/4 In. 805.00
Vase, Green Matte Glaze Ground, Trumpet, Bulbous, Incised, 9 1/4 x 6 1/2 In. 546.00
Vase, Molded, Buds, Leaves, Green, Teal Blue Mottled Matte Glaze, 6 3/4 x 4 In. 765.00
Vase, Mottled Blue, Green Matte Glaze, 5 1/4 In. 690.00
Vase, Mottled Green Matte Glaze, Swollen Form, 8 1/2 In. 529.00
Vase, Mottled, Textured Glaze, Cobalt Blue Veining, Squat, 3 1/4 x 5 1/2 In. 865.00
Vase, Panels, Blue Matte Glaze, Veined, Green Glaze On Shoulder, 6 x 6 3/4 In. 460.00
Vase, Panels, Caramel, Ocher Glaze, Mottled, Gourd Shape, 3 3/4 x 3 1/2 In. 920.00
Vase, Panels, Green Matte Glaze, Cobalt Blue Veining, Blue Matte Ground, 7 x 4 In. 430.00
Vase, Pansy, Green Matte Glaze, Embossed, Cascading Stems, 11 3/4 x 3 1/2 In. 2415.00
Vase, Trumpet, Blue, White Mottled, Bulbous, Raised Panels, 9 1/4 x 6 1/2 In. 920.00
Vase, Trumpet, Navy Blue Glaze, Gray Accents, Flared Lip, Bulbous, 9 1/2 x 6 1/2 In. 978.00
Vase, Tulip, Double Stems, Stylized Leaves, Green Matte Ground, 8 3/4 x 5 1/2 In. 1600.00
Vase, Yellow Oatmeal Matte Glaze, Incised Panels, Mottled, 7 1/2 x 4 In. 375.00

HANDEL glass was made by Philip Handel working in Meriden, Connecticut, from 1885 and in New York City from 1893 to 1933. The firm made art glass and other types of lamps. Handel shades were made not only of leaded glass in a style reminiscent of Tiffany but also of reverse painted glass. Handel also made vases and other glass objects.

HANDEL

Candle Sconce, Copper, Hammered, Mushroom Socket, 10 x 6 1/4 In. 431.00
Lamp, 6 Panels, Bent Caramel Slag Glass, Copper Tone Metal, Arts & Crafts Frame, 24 In. 4025.00
Lamp, 6 Panels, Metal Overlay, Flowers, Amber & Purple Slag Glass, White, 13 1/2 In. 1725.00
Lamp, 8 Panels, Cattails, Filigree Overlay, Acorn Pulls, 23 In. .... *ILLUS* 40250.00
Lamp, 8 Panels, Metal Overlay, Bronze Patina, 4-Lyre Base, 30 3/4 In. 1955.00
Lamp, 9 Panels, Hawaiian Tropic, Filigree Overlay, Palm Tree, Acorn Pulls, 24 In. .... *ILLUS* 5570.00
Lamp, Brown Shade, Etched, Bell-Shaped Base, No. 6068, 54 In. 4200.00
Lamp, Chipped Ice, Opal Glass Shade, 18 x 23 In. 1890.00
Lamp, Chipped Ice, Roses, Butterflies, Tree Trunks, 15 x 7 In. 1438.00
Lamp, Desert Scene, Figures, Palm Tree, 8 x 17 In. 4140.00
Lamp, Desk, 4 Panels, Metal Overlay, Caramel Slag Glass, 15 In. 978.00
Lamp, Domed Shade, Daffodil, Signed, Palme, 18 In. .... *ILLUS* 9520.00
Lamp, Domed Shade, Desert Scene, Figures, Palm Trees, Ruins, 8 x 17 3/4 In. 4140.00
Lamp, Domed Shade, Sunset, Signed, 16 In. .... *ILLUS* 3640.00
Lamp, Dropped Apron Shade, Berries, Flowers, Signed, 15 In. .... *ILLUS* 3360.00
Lamp, Jungle Bird, Macaws On Branch, Flying, Leaves, Pierced Foot, 23 In. .... *ILLUS* 17825.00
Lamp, Piano, Adjustable, Paneled Shade, Textured, Maidenhair Fern, 13 x 7 1/2 x 4 In. 1380.00
Lamp, Wooded Landscape, Patinated Metal, Baluster Base, 24 x 18 In. 585.00
Night-Light, Domed Shade, Parrots, Flowers, Yellow Chipped Ice Ground, 8 In. 1035.00
Shade, Globe, Flowers, Stems, Leaves, Exotic Birds, 9 1/2 In. 4025.00
Vase, Teroma, Yellow Flower, Leaves, Oval, Ruffled Edge, c.1910, 10 1/2 In. 613.00

HARDWARE, see Architectural category.

Handel, Lamp, Domed Shade, Sunset, Signed, 16 In.

Handel, Lamp, Dropped Apron Shade, Berries, Flowers, Signed, 15 In.

Handel, Lamp, Jungle Bird, Macaws On Branch, Flying, Leaves, Pierced Foot, 23 In.

HARKER Pottery Company was incorporated in 1890 in East Liverpool, Ohio. The Harker family had been making pottery in the area since 1840. The company made many types of pottery but by the Civil War was making quantities of yellowware from native clays. They also made Rockingham-type brown-glazed pottery and whiteware. The plant was moved to Chester, West Virginia, in 1931. Dinnerwares were made and sold nationally. In 1971 the company was sold to Jeannette Glass Company and all operations ceased in 1972. For more information, see *Kovels' Depression Glass & Dinnerware Price List*.

Amy, Salad Server 39.00
Cameoware, Cup, Blue 10.00
Cameoware, Plate, Blue, 10 1/4 In. 23.00
Cameoware, Saucer, Blue 4.00
Chesterton, Bowl, Vegetable, Gray, 9 In. 25.00
Chesterton, Cup & Saucer, Gray 9.00
Chesterton, Plate, Gray, 6 1/4 In. 4.00
Chesterton, Platter, Oval, Gray, 12 In. 19.00
Fruits, Cake Lifter & Salad Fork, Pair 55.00
Heritance, Dish, Cover, 2-Part, Oval 50.00
Ivy Vine, Bowl, Dessert, 5 1/2 In. 6.25
Ivy Vine, Creamer 14.50
Ivy Vine, Cup 10.00
Ivy Vine, Gravy Boat .... 16.00 to 19.00
Ivy Vine, Plate, Dinner, 10 1/4 In. 14.00
Ivy Vine, Range Drip Jar, Cover 48.00
Ivy Vine, Range Salt Shaker 18.00
Ivy Vine, Saucer 3.00
Ivy Vine, Soup, Dish, 8 3/8 In. 14.00
Ivy Vine, Sugar & Cover 18.00
Modern Tulip, Bowl, Cereal, 6 1/8 In. 9.00
Modern Tulip, Bowl, Vegetable, 8 1/4 In. 19.50
Modern Tulip, Casserole, Cover, 8 5/8 In. 45.00
Modern Tulip, Cookie Jar, Cover, Oval 85.00
Modern Tulip, Custard Cup, Modern Age Shape 6.00
Modern Tulip, Pie Baker, 10 In. .... 22.00 to 30.00
Modern Tulip, Plate, Bread & Butter, 6 1/8 In. 5.00
Modern Tulip, Plate, Dinner, 9 1/2 In. 9.00
Modern Tulip, Plate, Square, 6 5/8 In. 8.00
Modern Tulip, Platter, 13 3/4 In. 38.00
Modern Tulip, Soup, Dish, 7 1/2 In. 12.00
Modern Tulip, Utility Plate, 11 In. 27.00
Petit Point Rose, Casserole, Cover, 8 1/2 In. 50.00
Petit Point Rose, Cheese Plate, 11 In. 40.00

Petit Point Rose, Mixing Bowl, 7 In. 16.00
Petit Point Rose, Mixing Bowl, 8 In. 23.00
Petit Point Rose, Mixing Bowl, 9 In. 27.00
Petit Point Rose, Pie Baker, 9 In. 30.00
Petit Point Rose, Plate, Dinner, 10 In. 27.00
Petit Point Rose, Utility Plate, 11 In. 28.50
Red Apple, Bowl, Swirled, 9 In. 38.00
Red Apple, Cheese Plate, 11 In. 50.00

HARLEQUIN dinnerware was produced by the Homer Laughlin Company from 1938 to 1964, and sold without trademark by the F. W. Woolworth Co. It has a concentric ring design like Fiesta, but the rings are separated from the rim by a plain margin. Cup handles are triangular in shape. Seven different novelty animal figurines were introduced in 1939. For more information on Harlequin dinnerware, see *Kovels' Depression Glass & Dinnerware Price List*.

Chartreuse, Creamer, 4 In. 20.00
Gray, Eggcup, Double, 3 In. 43.00
Gray, Saucer 5.00
Green, Eggcup, Double, 3 In. 28.00
Light Green, Bowl, Fruit, 5 1/8 In. 32.00
Light Green, Bowl, Oatmeal, 36s 28.00
Light Green, Pitcher, 22 Oz. 125.00
Mauve Blue, Bowl, Oatmeal, 36s 25.00
Mauve Blue, Platter, 11 In. 17.50
Mauve Blue, Salt & Pepper, 3 1/2 In. 28.00
Medium Green, Bowl, Salad, 7 1/2 In. 26.00
Medium Green, Plate, Dinner, 10 In. 80.00
Red, Eggcup, Double, 3 In. 25.00
Red, Pitcher, 6 3/8 In. 95.00
Red, Syrup, Dripcut Top, 5 7/8 In. 490.00
Rose, Pitcher, Water, Ice Lip 100.00
Rose, Plate, 7 In. 10.00
Rose, Soup, Dish, 8 1/2 In. 18.00
Rose, Sugar, Cover 25.00
Rose, Tumbler, 4 3/8 In. 80.00
Turquoise, Cup .... 8.00 to 15.00
Turquoise, Plate, Luncheon, 9 In. 8.00
Turquoise, Saucer 4.00
Yellow, Bowl, Cereal, Oatmeal, 36s 18.00
Yellow, Bowl, Fruit, 5 1/8 In. 30.00
Yellow, Bowl, Salad, Individual, 7 1/4 In. 24.00
Yellow, Gravy Boat, 8 1/2 In. 15.00
Yellow, Pitcher, Round, 22 Oz. 150.00
Yellow, Plate, Luncheon, 9 1/4 In. 8.00
Yellow, Platter, 11 1/4 x 9 In. 10.00
Yellow, Sugar 9.00
Yellow, Teacup 7.00
Yellow, Tumbler, 4 3/8 In. 45.00

HATPIN collectors search for pins popular from 1860 to 1920. The long pin, often over four inches, was used to hold the hat in place on the hair. The tops of the pins were made of all materials, from solid gold and real gemstones to ceramics and glass. Be careful to buy original hatpins and not recent pieces made by altering old buttons.

Amber Stone, Filigree, Victorian, 12 In. 51.00
Carnival Glass, Bee On Honeycomb, 1 1/4 x 8 1/4 In. 63.00
Carnival Glass, Butterfly, Brass Stem, 1 3/4 x 1 1/4 x 8 1/2 In. 51.00
Carnival Glass, Iridescent, 6 Plums, Cattails, 1 5/8 x 5 3/4 In. 45.00
Carnival Glass, Strawberry, Amber 350.00
Carnival Glass, Strawberry, Green 275.00

Carnival Glass, Top O' The Morning, 1 1/2 x 9 3/4 In. 50.00
Cloisonne, Fleur-De-Lis, Flower, 10 In. 43.00
Colored Stones, Amethyst, Triangular Top, c.1895, 2 x 10 1/2 In. 500.00
Enamel, Violet, Seed Pearl, Victorian, 2 1/2-In. Top 21.00
Faceted Citrine Crystal, 12 1/4 In. 38.00
Glass, Black, Colored Petals, Oval, 11 In. 21.00
Glass, Blue, Prong Set Rhinestones, Round Top, c.1908, 1 1/8 x 11 1/2 In. 87.00
Glass, Grape Cluster, Brass Leaves, 1 1/2 x 9 1/2 In. 35.00
Glass, Green, Swirl, Silver Stem, 3/4 x 10 In. 15.50
Micro Mosaic, Hat Shape, Daisies, Roses, 1 1/4 x 11 In. 69.00
Mourning, Black Flower, Victorian, 2 1/2-In. Flower 23.25
Porcelain, Flower, Painted, Gold Color Metal Stem, 11 In. 37.00
Rhinestone, Purple, Four Drop Corners, 9 1/3 In. 128.00
Rhinestone, Star Shape, Curled Points, Victorian, 1 3/4 x 10 In. 49.00
Rhinestones, Coral Color Stones, c.1908, 1 1/4 x 10 3/8 In. 119.00
Rhinestones, Flower, Brass Stem, 1 1/2 x 9 1/2 In. 69.00
Stanhope, Crystal Star, Gold Color Metal, 6 In. 18.00
Topaz Colored Stone, Art Nouveau, c.1905, 13 3/4 In. 122.00
Turquoise Ball, Gold Metal Cover, 8 1/4 In. 85.00

HATPIN HOLDERS were needed when hatpins were fashionable from 1860 to 1920. The large, heavy hat required special long-shanked pins to hold it in place. The hatpin holder resembles a large saltshaker, but it often has no opening at the bottom as a shaker does. Hatpin holders were made of all types of ceramics and metal. Look for other pieces under the names of specific manufacturers.

Carnival Glass, Grape & Cable, Northwood, Unmarked, 7 In. 29.00
Carnival Glass, Grape & Cable, Ribbed Feet, Red, 7 1/2 In. 15.50
Glass, Cut, Vienna Pattern, Fry, Pa., 1874-1933, 6 3/4 x 2 3/4 In. 780.00
Glass, Jadeite Type, Rhinestones, 6 3/4 x 1 5/8 In. 135.00
Glass, Pink, Grapes, Footed, 6 In. 9.00
Metal, 24 Holes, Robed Chinese Man, Pierced Dish, c.1820, 6 1/4 In. 136.00
Porcelain, 7 Holes, Flower Transfer, Wreath Gilding, Austria, 5 1/4 x 2 3/4 In. 34.00
Porcelain, Calla Lilies, 13 Holes, RS Germany, 4 1/2 x 3 In. 30.00
Porcelain, Couple Of Nuts, Men In Top Hats, Schafer & Vater, 3 1/4 x 4 In. 159.00
Porcelain, Desert Scene, Noritake, 1920s, 4 3/4 x 2 3/4 In. 88.00
Porcelain, Flower Bouquet, White, Turquoise, Gilt Trim, Nippon, 5 1/4 x 4 1/4 In. 11.00
Porcelain, Flowers, Gilt Filigree, Nippon Style, Unmarked, 4 3/4 x 2 1/2 In. 17.00
Porcelain, Flowers, Gold Trim, Hand Painted, Nippon, 4 In. 11.00
Porcelain, Forget-Me-Nots, Hand Painted, Candlewicking Design, 5 In. 16.00
Porcelain, Forget-Me-Nots, Hand Painted, Victorian, 5 x 2 1/2 In. 28.00
Porcelain, Pink Roses, Wilkinson Ltd., England, 4 1/2 In. 23.00
Porcelain, Swallows, Sky, 11 Holes, 5 x 3 In. 35.00
Porcelain, Swans, 5 x 3 In. 10.00

HAVILAND china has been made in Limoges, France, since 1842. The factory was started by the Haviland Brothers of New York City. Pieces are marked *H & Co.*, *Haviland & Co.*, or *Theodore Haviland*. It is possible to match existing sets of dishes through dealers who specialize in Haviland china. Other factories worked in the town of Limoges making a similar chinaware. These porcelains are listed in this book under Limoges.

HAVILAND & CO.

Bowl, Footed, Roses, Leaves, Gilt Rim, 1876-1930, 2 1/4 x 5 In. 89.00
Bowl, Vegetable, Flowers, Leaves, Scalloped Rim, 1893-1930, 2 x 9 1/4 In. 70.00
Butter Chip, Pink Flowers, Gold Trim, Theodore Haviland, c.1893, 3 1/4 In. 30.00
Casserole, Cover, Flowers, Gold Trim, 1893-1930, 4 1/2 x 8 1/2 In. 75.00
Charger, Roses, Hand Painted, Gold Enamel, 1876-86, 11 1/4 In. 245.00
Coffeepot, Apple Blossom, Theodore Haviland 285.00
Cup & Saucer, Roses, Gilded Rims, Handle, 1893-1930 .... 55.00
Dresser Tray, Wisteria, Charles Field Haviland, 1891-1900, 12 3/4 x 9 In. 225.00
Fish Set, Fish In Landscape, Gilt Rim, Platter, 10 Lobed Plates, T. Haviland, 11 Piece 2085.00

Gravy Boat, Attached Underplate, Folded Edges, Flowers, Animals, 8 x 5 1/2 In. 150.00
Pin Tray, Roses, Yellow Ground, 1893-1930, 8 1/2 x 7 1/4 In. 90.00
Pitcher, Painted Flowers, Applied Ribbons, Brown, Marked, A.D., 12 In. 2510.00
Plate, Dinner, Roses, Scalloped Edge, Hand Painted, 1876-1930, 9 1/2 In. 15.00
Plate, Drop Rose, 7 In. 110.00
Plate, Green & Red Pattern, Gold Rim, Theodore Haviland, 1920s, 7 1/2 In. 12.00
Plate, Luncheon, Rose Colored Rim, 9 1/2 In., 12 Piece 234.00
Plate, Salad, Trellis, 7 3/4 In. 25.00
Plate, White, Cobalt Blue Rim, Rococo Designs, Gold Band, 10 1/4 In., 12 Piece 705.00
Plate Set, Oyster, Underglaze Green H & Co. Mark, 8 1/2 In., 8 Piece 1888.00
Platter, Narcissus, Gold Rim, Oval, 14 In. 75.00
Platter, Scalloped Edge, c.1910, 13 x 20 In. 35.00
Serving Bowl, Folded Edge, Flowers, Deer, Lions, Gold Rim, 9 x 7 In. 150.00
Serving Bowl, Folded Edges, Square, Flowers, Deer, Lions, Gold Rim, 9 1/2 x 9 1/2 In. 175.00
Serving Bowl, Narcissus, Gold Rim, 9 1/4 In. 50.00
Trinket Box, Cover, Flowers, Gold Trim, Scrolling, Oval, 2 1/2 x 5 In. 125.00
Tureen, Soup, Cover, Folded Edge, Flowers, Deer, Lions, Gold Rim, Shell Handles 350.00
Vase, Pastoral Scene, Cows, Trees, c.1876, 14 1/4 In. 2629.00

HAWKES cut glass was made by T. G. Hawkes & Company of Corning, New York, founded in 1880. The firm cut glass blanks made at other glassworks until 1962. Many pieces are marked with the trademark, a trefoil ring enclosing a fleur-de-lis and two hawks. Cut glass by other manufacturers is listed under either the factory name or in the general Cut Glass category.

Ashtray, Millicent Stripes, Engraved Spanish Galleon Scene, Signed, 5 In. 39.00
Bowl, Grecian Pattern, Wood Wheel Finish, 4 x 10 In. 2875.00
Bowl, Hobstar & Boxed Diamond, Shallow, Signed, 2 x 9 In. 460.00
Bowl, Hobstar Chain, Intaglio Flowers, 4 x 8 In. 125.00
Bowl, Holland Pattern, 9 1/2 In. 250.00
Bowl, Kensington Pattern, 2 3/4 x 9 3/8 In. 1275.00
Bowl, North Star Pattern, Signed, 4 1/2 x 9 In. 450.00
Bowl, Poppies, Gravic, Double Signed, 4 x 9 In. 220.00
Bowl, Queens Pattern, 3 3/4 x 7 3/4 In. 468.00
Box, Cover, Millicent Pattern, Round, Sterling Finial, Signed, 4 x 6 In. 80.00
Celery Dish, Millicent Pattern, Signed, 11 1/2 x 6 In. 60.00
Celery Tray, Brazilian Pattern, 13 In. 85.00
Cocktail Set, Martini, Millicent Pattern, 5 Piece 150.00
Decanter, Oval Panels, Rings, Stopper, 12 x 5 1/2 In., Pair 200.00
Decanter, Venetian Pattern, Hobstar Wafer Base, Handle, 11 In. 385.00
Dish, Diamond Pattern, Round, Silver Pedestal Base, 4 1/2 x 5 1/2 In. 145.00
Ice Bucket, Millicent Pattern, Sterling Silver Rim, Bail, Signed, 6 In. 120.00
Pin Tray, Millicent Pattern, Signed, 3 3/4 In. 40.00
Pitcher, Cider, Flower Blossoms & Leaves, Gravic, Signed, 7 1/2 In. 360.00
Plate, 6 Hobstars, Engraved Bands, Rayed Center, Signed, 10 In. 125.00
Plate, Festoon Pattern, 7 In. 660.00
Punch Bowl, Albion Pattern, Scalloped Rim, 7 1/4 x 15 In. 1100.00
Punch Bowl, Hobstar, Strawberry Diamond, Fan, Signed, 14 In. 690.00
Punch Bowl, Stand, Queens Pattern, Signed, 12 x 12 In. 3410.00
Rose Bowl, Gladys Pattern, 6 In. 580.00
Sherbet Set, Millicent Pattern, Signed, 12 Piece 200.00
Sugar & Creamer, Millicent Pattern, Sterling Silver Pedestal Base, Signed 100.00
Tazza, Carnations, Gravic, Signed, 6 x 9 1/2 In. 415.00
Tray, North Star Pattern, Signed, 15 In. 2645.00
Vase, Blue Cut To Clear, Bird, Flowers, Gravic Gold Enameled Rim, c.1900s, 10 In. 190.00
Vase, Brunswick Pattern, Corseted, 11 In. 1320.00
Vase, Delft Diamond Pattern, c.1920, 13 In. 145.00
Vase, Flowers, Intaglio, Flared Rim, Pedestal Base, Signed, 12 In. 165.00
Vase, Hobstar Chain, Engraved Floral, Pinched Waist, Signed, 8 1/4 x 5 1/2 In. 100.00
Vase, Hobstar Chain, Step-Cut Neck, Teardrop Stem, 32-Point Hobstar Base, Footed, 12 3/4 In. ... 825.00
Vase, Iris, Gravic, Flared, Pedestal Base, Signed, 23 In. 2420.00

Vase, Millicent Pattern, Cornucopia Medallions, Basket & Urn, Footed, 12 In. 375.00
Vase, Trumpet, Brunswick Pattern, 12 In. 440.00
Vase, Trumpet, Brunswick Pattern, Signed, 16 In. 2310.00
Vase, Trumpet, Navarre Pattern, Hobstar Base, 13 3/4 In. 440.00
Vase, Trumpet, Queens Pattern, Flared, Footed, 14 In. 880.00
Vase, Yellow To Clear, Engraved Plumed Bird, Blossom Branch, 8 1/4 In. 150.00
Water Set, Millicent Pattern, Signed, 8 1/4-In. Pitcher, 5 Piece 350.00

HEAD VASES, generally showing a woman from the shoulders up, were used by florists primarily in the 1950s and 1960s. Made in a variety of sizes and often decorated with imitation jewelry and other lifelike accessories, the vases were manufactured in Japan and the U.S.A. Less elaborate examples were made as early as the 1930s. Religious themes, babies, and animals are also common subjects. Other head vases are listed under manufacturers' names and can be located through the index at the back of this book.

Abigail, Heads Up, 10th Annual Head Vase Convention, Box, 6 1/2 In. 499.00
Dog, Boxer, Brown, Inarco, Japan, 6 In. 23.00
Doris Day, Blond, Blue Hair Bow, c.1960 .... 495.00
Eve Grand Entrance, Box, 1987, 6 In. 399.00
Girl, Blond, Green Hat, Holding Bud Vase, Sealy, Japan, c.1950, 4 1/2 In. 35.00
Girl, Brown Hair, Bandanna, Pursed Lips, Yellow Dress, White Sleeves, Velco, 5 1/2 In. 195.00
Girl, Umbrella, Blue Dress, White Hat, Light Blue Bow, 4 3/8 In. 215.00
Girl, Umbrella, Green Bow, Stripes, 3 1/2 In. 250.00
Jackie Kennedy, Inarco, c.1964, 6 In. 985.00
Teen, Blond Bouffant Hair, Black Jacket, Inarco, 8 In. 325.00
Woman, Ash Blond, White Flowers In Hair, Aqua Eye Shadow, Pearl Earrings, 6 1/2 In. 59.00
Woman, Blond Curls, Green Bonnet & Bow, 6 x 4 In. 59.00
Woman, Blond, Black Glove, Pearl Bracelet, Napco, 1956, 5 1/2 In. 245.00
Woman, Blond, Black Hat, White Bow With Polka Dots, Pearl Earrings, Napco, 1956, 5 1/2 In. 85.00
Woman, Blond, Blue Dress & Earrings, Pearl Necklace, Bisque, 4 In. 45.00
Woman, Blond, Pearl Earrings, Red Nail Polish, Ardco, 6 In. 215.00
Woman, Blond, Pearl Earrings, White Hat, Rubens, 1959, 6 In. 245.00
Woman, Blond, Pearl Necklace, Earrings, Rosy Cheeks, Ardco, 7 1/2 In. 325.00
Woman, Blond, Upswept Hair, Green Flowers, Green Dress, Gold Trim, 5 x 3 In. 32.00
Woman, Blond, Yellow Hair Bows, Green Dress, White Ruffle, Inarco, 7 In. 395.00
Woman, Brown Hair, Blue Eyes, Yellow Sweater, Pearl Earrings, Relpo, 5 1/2 In. 230.00
Woman, Brunette, Earrings, Necklace, Green Dress, Napcoware, 10 1/2 In. 930.00
Woman, Flowered Hat, Pearl Earrings, Necklace, Turquoise Colored Ring, Relpo, 7 In. 445.00
Woman, Frosted Hair, Blue Glove, 3 Neck Flowers, Pearl Earrings, Napcoware, 7 1/2 In. 290.00
Woman, Green Hat, Dress, Napcoware, 10 1/2 In. 864.00
Woman, Pearl Earrings, Necklace, Pink Dress, Inarco, c.1963, 6 In. 245.00
Woman, Pearl Necklace, Green Dress, White Glove, Relpo, Japan, 7 1/4 In. 319.00

HEDI SCHOOP Art Creations, North Hollywood, California, started about 1945 and was working until 1954. Schoop made ceramic figurines, lamps, planters, and tablewares.

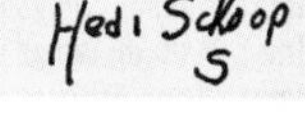

Ashtray, Duck, Turquoise, Gold, 5 1/2 x 8 In. 40.00
Box, Butterfly, Yellow, White, 3 1/2 x 6 x 3 1/2 In. 55.00
Figurine, Book Woman, 9 In. 58.00
Figurine, Exotic Woman, Green & Black Dress, Pink & Gold Accents, 12 1/2 In. ....95.00 to 125.00
Figurine, Girl, Holding Bouquet, Pleated Skirt, 9 1/4 x 7 In. 75.00
Figurine, Marguerita, 12 1/2 In. 125.00
Figurine, Oriental Man, 12 1/2 In. 58.00
Figurine, Rooster, Green, Brown, 13 In. 125.00
Figurine, Woman, Black & Gold Dress, Billowing, 9 In. 110.00
Figurine, Woman, Dancing, Pink, Gold, 9 1/2 In. 110.00
Figurine, Woman, With Buckets, White Dress, 13 1/2 In. 125.00
Planter, Horse, Pink, White, Green Saddle, 9 3/4 x 10 1/2 In. 75.00
Planter, Tyrolean Girl, 11 In. 75.00
Wall Pocket, Sponge Interior, Matte Exterior, Abstract Design, 4 1/2 x 4 In. 85.00

HEINTZ ART Metal Shop used the letters *HAMS* in a diamond as a mark. Otto Heintz took over the Arts & Crafts Company in Buffalo, New York, in 1903. By 1906 it had become the Heintz Art Metal Shop. It remained in business until 1930. The company made ashtrays, bookends, boxes, bowls, desk sets, vases, trophies, and smoking sets. The best-known pieces are made of copper, brass, and bronze with silver overlay. Similar pieces were made by Smith Metal Arts and were marked *Silver Crest*. Some pieces by both companies are unmarked.

Bookends, Bronze, Silver Overlay Gulls, 5 1/8 x 5 1/2 In. 115.00
Bowl, Bronze, Applied Sterling Silver, Patina, 10 1/2 In. 264.00
Bowl, Shallow, Bronze, Silver Leaves & Branch Overlay, 2 x 6 1/2 In. 230.00
Bowl, Sterling On Bronze, Inlaid Art Deco Flowers, Vine, Flared, 7 3/4 In. 290.00
Candleholder, Bronze, Sterling Silver Applied Flowers, Footed, 5 x 5 1/2 In., Pair 120.00
Desk Set, Covered Box, Art Deco Silver Design, Monogram, Early 1900s, 10 Piece 880.00
Lamp, Boudoir, Mottled Green, Silver Overlay, Flower, Cutout Shade, 9 1/2 In. 690.00
Lamp, Virginia Creeper Pattern, Sterling On Bronze, 3-Socket Base, 20 x 16 1/2 In. 5290.00
Plate, Bronze, Silver Overlay Trees, 5 3/4 In. 230.00
Vase, Bronze, Applied Silver Daffodil, Cylindrical, 12 In. 1058.00
Vase, Bronze, Sterling Silver Flowers, Tapered, Folded-In Rim, 7 In. 2400.00
Vase, Daffodils, Green Ground, Sterling On Bronze, Cylindrical, 8 x 3 3/4 In. 380.00
Vase, Poppies, Verdigris Ground, Sterling On Bronze, Overlaid, Stamp HAMS, 12 1/2 In. 470.00
Vase, Silver Daffodils, Verdigris Patinated Ground, Sterling On Bronze, 14 3/4 x 4 In. 1115.00

HEISEY glass was made from 1896 to 1957 in Newark, Ohio, by A. H. Heisey and Co., Inc. The Imperial Glass Company of Bellaire, Ohio, bought some of the molds and the rights to the trademark. Some Heisey patterns have been made by Imperial since 1960. After 1968, they stopped using the *H* trademark. Heisey used romantic names for colors, such as *Sahara*. Do not confuse color and pattern names. The Custard Glass and Ruby Glass categories may also include some Heisey pieces.

Alexandrite, Relish, 1 1/4 x 7 1/2 In. 475.00
Alibi, Cocktail, Footed, Tally Ho Etch 110.00
Animal, Asiatic Pheasant 115.00
Animal, Baby Elephant, Amber 1300.00
Animal, Colt, Kicking, Cobalt Blue, 4 In. 65.00
Animal, Colt, Standing .... 60.00 to 130.00
Animal, Duckling, Standing 110.00
Animal, Elephant .... 170.00 to 180.00
Animal, Giraffe, Head Back 110.00
Animal, Goose, Wings Half .... 50.00 to 125.00
Animal, Goose, Wings Up .... 50.00 to 113.00
Animal, Mallard, Wings Down 300.00
Animal, Mallard, Wings Half 275.00
Animal, Piglet, Sitting 115.00
Animal, Plug Horse 45.00
Animal, Ringneck Pheasant 95.00
Animal, Scottie Dog .... 75.00 to 125.00
Animal, Sow, Paper Label 450.00
Animal, Sparrow .... 45.00 to 60.00
Aqua Caliente, Cocktail, Fox Chase Etch, 4 Piece 110.00
Aristocrat, Candlestick, Pair, 7 In. 75.00
Aristocrat, Candy Jar, Cover, Cobalt Blue 550.00
Aristocrat, Lamp, 19 1/2 x 8 3/4 In. 1050.00
Banded Flute, Jar, Horseradish 25.00
Barcelona, Bowl, Footed, 4 x 10 1/2 In. 165.00
Beaded Panel & Sunburst, Biscuit Jar, Cover 180.00
Beaded Panel & Sunburst, Salt & Pepper 15.00
Beaded Panel & Sunburst, Sugar & Creamer 70.00

Beaded Panel & Sunburst, Tumbler 20.00
Beaded Swag, Mug, Ruby Stain, Souvenir, Mamie Davis, 1907, 3 1/2 In. 25.00
Beaded Swag, Nappy, Opal, Metal Base, 5 In. 10.00
Beaded Swag, Wine, Ivorina Verde 25.00
Beaded Swag, Wine, Ivorina Verde, Souvenir, Bay City, Mich., 3 3/4 In. 50.00
Beaded Swag, Wine, Ruby Stain 35.00
Cabochon, Candleblock, Jungle Flower Cutting, Silver Rims, Pair 40.00
Cabochon, Goblet 5.00
Carcassone, Tumbler, Flagon, Alexandrite, Clear Foot, 12 Oz. 250.00
Carcassone, Tumbler, Wine, Footed, Cobalt Blue, 3 In. 130.00
Carnation, Vase, 9 In. 15.00
Charter Oak, Compote, Flamingo, 7 In. 30.00
Chintz, Champagne, Sahara, 5 3/4 In. 42.00
Chintz, Cordial, Sahara, 1 Oz., 3 3/4 In. 225.00
Coarse Rib, Cruet, Stopper, 6 In. 23.00
Cobel, Cocktail Shaker 150.00
Coleport, Ice Bucket, Metal Tongs 65.00
Colonial, Finger Bowl, 4 1/2 In. 20.00
Colonial, Punch Set, Bowl, 12 1/2-In. Bowl, 9 Piece 92.00
Colonial, Vase, Sweet Pea, Carnation, Swung, 14 1/2 x 7 1/2 In. 185.00
Colonial, Whiskey, 2 1/4 In. 17.50
Colonial Panel, Pitcher, Pt. 60.00
Colonial Star, Candy Dish, Footed, 2 1/2 x 5 1/2 In. 25.00
Continental, Dish, Jelly, Footed 30.00
Country Club, Cocktail Shaker, Strainer, Stopper, Qt. 75.00
Creole, Cordial, Alexandrite, 3 3/4 In. 385.00
Cross Lined Flute, Cruet, Stopper 20.00
Crystolite, Bowl, Cover, Preserve, 2 Handles, 4 x 6 In. 70.00
Crystolite, Bowl, Gardenia, Shallow, 10 1/2 In. 65.00
Crystolite, Cake Stand, 11 In. 450.00
Crystolite, Candleblock, Pair 20.00
Crystolite, Candlestick, Banded, 3 x 3 1/4 In., Pair 95.00
Crystolite, Candy Dish, Cover, Handle 25.00
Crystolite, Cigarette Box, Cover, 3 1/2 x 4 1/2 In. 40.00
Crystolite, Cocktail Shaker, Qt. 240.00
Crystolite, Compote, Cheese, 2 3/4 x 5 1/2 In. ....29.00 to 33.00
Crystolite, Cruet, 3 Oz. 20.00
Crystolite, Dish, Jelly, 2 Handles, 6 In. 25.00
Crystolite, Dish, Praline, Shell, 7 In. 28.00
Crystolite, Goblet, 10 Oz., 6 In. 18.00
Crystolite, Ice Bucket, Metal Handle & Tongs 75.00
Crystolite, Mustard Jar, Slotted Lid, 2 1/2 In. 28.00
Crystolite, Nut Dish, Footed, Oval 35.00
Crystolite, Nut Dish, Shell, 4 Piece 50.00
Crystolite, Oyster Cocktail, 3 1/2 In. 23.00
Crystolite, Pitcher, Ice Lip, 1/2 Gal. 70.00
Crystolite, Plate, 7 1/2 In. ....16.00 to 20.00
Crystolite, Plate, Snack, 8 In. 35.00
Crystolite, Relish, 3 Sections, 9 1/2 x 7 1/2 In. ....20.00 to 40.00
Crystolite, Relish, 4 Sections, Clover Leaf, 9 In. 40.00
Crystolite, Relish, 5 Sections, 10 In. 25.00
Crystolite, Saltshaker, Glass Top 15.00
Crystolite, Sherbet, 3 3/4 In. ....14.00 to 18.00
Crystolite, Sugar & Creamer, Oval ....10.00 to 15.00
Crystolite, Sugar & Creamer, Oval, Tray ....35.00 to 68.00
Crystolite, Sugar & Creamer, Round 90.00
Crystolite, Torte Plate, Shell, 13 In. ....25.00 to 30.00
Crystolite, Tray, Oval, 13 In. 30.00
Crystolite, Tray, Sugar & Creamer 20.00
Crystolite, Tumbler, Blown, 4 1/4 In. 38.00
Crystolite, Tumbler, Pressed, 10 Oz. 30.00

Crystolite, Vase, 3 x 3 1/4 In. 30.00
Diamond Band, Sherbet, 4 Oz. 110.00
Diamond Point, Ashtray 5.00
Dolly Madison, Wine, 6 x 2 3/4 In. 95.00
Dolphin, Candlestick, 5 x 4 In., Pair 430.00
Double Rib & Panel, Basket, Flamingo, 8 1/4 x 6 In. 225.00
Double Rib & Panel, Cruet, 3 Oz. 5.00
Double Rib & Panel, Sugar & Creamer 25.00
Duquesne, Parfait, Sahara, 5 Oz., 6 In. 55.00
Eagle, Plate, Moongleam, 8 In. 60.00
Empress, Ashtray, Cobalt Blue, 1 x 7 x 4 In. 250.00
Empress, Ashtray, Flamingo, 1 x 7 x 4 In. 215.00
Empress, Ashtray, Moongleam 140.00
Empress, Bowl, Dolphin Footed, Alexandrite, 4 1/4 x 10 3/4 In. 735.00
Empress, Bowl, Floral, Alexandrite, 3 1/4 x 12 In. 875.00
Empress, Bowl, Floral, Sahara, 8 1/2 In. 30.00
Empress, Candlestick, Dolphin Footed, Sahara, 6 In. .... 130.00 to 190.00
Empress, Celery Dish, Alexandrite, 13 1/2 x 3 3/4 In. 275.00
Empress, Compote, Flamingo, 6 In. 40.00
Empress, Cruet, Stopper, Flamingo, 4 Oz. 50.00
Empress, Cup & Saucer, Alexandrite 165.00
Empress, Dish, Mint, Alexandrite, 2 x 5 1/2 In. 375.00
Empress, Ice Bucket, Dolphin Footed, Sterling Silver Fruit Overlay, 6 3/4 x 6 In. 200.00
Empress, Nut Dish, Moongleam .... 25.00 to 45.00
Empress, Nut Dish, Sahara .... 15.00 to 20.00
Empress, Pitcher, Flamingo, 3 Pt. 110.00
Empress, Plate, Salad, Sahara, 8 1/8 In. 42.00
Empress, Plate, Square, Alexandrite, 8 1/2 In. 25.00
Empress, Plate, Square, Moongleam, 6 In. .... 30.00 to 35.00
Empress, Relish, 4 Sections, Sahara, 9 In. 40.00
Empress, Relish, Center Handle, Triplex, Moongleam, 10 In. 50.00
Empress, Relish, Triplex, Sahara, 7 In. 20.00
Empress, Relish, Triplex, Sahara, 10 In. 25.00
Empress, Sherbet, Sahara, 4 Oz. 20.00
Empress, Sugar & Creamer, Dolphin Footed, Alexandrite, 3 1/4 In. 595.00
Empress, Sugar & Creamer, Flamingo 50.00
Empress, Sugar & Creamer, Moongleam 85.00
Empress, Sugar & Creamer, Sahara 30.00
Empress, Tumbler, Flamingo, 8 Oz. 45.00
Fancy Loop, Berry Bowl, 8 In. 55.00
Fancy Loop, Bowl, Square, Gold Trim, 4 In. 85.00
Fancy Loop, Celery Tray, 11 1/2 In. 55.00
Fancy Loop, Creamer, Emerald, Gold Trim 80.00
Fancy Loop, Sugar & Creamer .... 30.00 to 45.00
Fancy Loop, Wine, 3 Oz. .... 25.00 to 35.00
Fandango, Cruet, Stopper, 4 Oz. 50.00
Fandango, Custard Cup 10.00
Fandango, Nappy, 4 In. 10.00
Fandango, Nappy, Crimped, 8 In. 25.00
Fandango, Sugar & Creamer 40.00
Fish, Bookends 70.00
Flat Panel, Bottle, Water, 8 1/4 In. 60.00
Flat Panel, Jar, Horseradish, Cover .... 30.00 to 40.00
Flat Panel, Toothpick 35.00
Foxchase, Tumbler, 10 Oz. 63.00
Galaxy, Sherbet, Flamingo, 4 3/4 In. 35.00
Gascony, Tumbler, Wine, Tangerine, 2 3/4 In. 375.00
Georgian, Candlestick, 9 In. 30.00
Greek Key, Celery Dish 130.00
Greek Key, Dish, Banana Split, Footed, 7 1/2 In. 35.00
Greek Key, Goblet 155.00

Greek Key, Jar, Cherry, Cover 80.00
Greek Key, Nappy, 5 In. 20.00
Greek Key, Nut Dish, Footed 25.00
Greek Key, Plate, Metal Frame, 10 In. .... 95.00 to 115.00
Greek Key, Sherbet, 4 1/2 In. 23.00
Greek Key, Tray, Pastry 100.00
Groove & Slash, Cruet, 6 Oz. 65.00
Half Circle, Sugar & Creamer, Flamingo .... 95.00 to 100.00
Half Circle, Sugar & Creamer, Sahara 90.00
Hartman, Plate, 6 1/2 In. 10.00
Ipswich, Champagne, 5 Oz. .... 20.00 to 25.00
Ipswich, Finger Bowl Liner, 5 3/4 In. 25.00
Ipswich, Goblet, 5 3/4 In. 35.00
Ipswich, Goblet, Sahara, Skirted, 5 3/4 In. 65.00
Ipswich, Oyster Cocktail, 4 Oz., 3 1/4 In. 15.00
Ipswich, Plate, Luncheon, Square, 8 In. 35.00
Ipswich, Plate, Salad, 7 In. 30.00
Ipswich, Sherbet, 4 Oz., 3 1/4 In. 15.00
Ipswich, Tumbler, Juice, 5 Oz. 30.00
Ipswich, Tumbler, Schoppen, 12 Oz., 5 1/2 In. 80.00
Ipswich, Tumbler, Soda, Footed, 8 Oz., 5 3/4 In. .... 25.00 to 40.00
Ivy, Relish, Sections, 11 1/4 In. 90.00
Jacobean, Candlestick, Pair, 9 In. 575.00
King Arthur, Sherbet, Stem, Diamond Optic, Moongleam, 5 Oz., 3 3/4 In. 20.00
Lariat, Basket, 5 1/2 x 8 1/2 x 5 3/4 In. 150.00
Lariat, Candlestick Holder, 3-Light, Pair 45.00
Lariat, Candlestick, 2-Light .... 25.00 to 30.00
Lariat, Candy Box, Cover, 6 x 6 In. 85.00
Lariat, Candy Dish, Loop & Leaf Cover, 7 1/4 In. 80.00
Lariat, Candy Jar, Cover, 9 1/2 x 7 In. 200.00
Lariat, Cigarette Box, 4 1/4 In. 80.00
Lariat, Cocktail, Moonglo Cutting, 3 1/2 Oz., 4 In. 2.00
Lariat, Cordial, Moonglo Cutting 55.00
Lariat, Egg Plate, 13 In. 130.00
Lariat, Nut Dish, 4 In. 36.00
Lariat, Plate, 9 In. 50.00
Lariat, Plate, Cabaret, 14 In. 35.00
Lariat, Relish, 3 Sections, 12 x 8 In. 75.00
Lariat, Relish, Handles, 12 1/2 x 5 In. 30.00
Lariat, Relish, Sections, 1 1/2 x 12 1/4 In. 20.00
Lariat, Sandwich Server, 4 x 14 1/2 In. 190.00
Lariat, Sugar & Creamer 35.00
Lariat, Torte Plate, 14 3/4 In. 65.00
Lariat, Tray, Center, Round, 13 In. 20.00
Lariat, Tumbler, Iced Tea, 12 Oz., 5 5/8 In. 32.00
Laverne, Bowl, Footed, Green, 3 1/2 x 11 1/4 In. 135.00
Little Squatter, Candlestick, Flamingo, Pair 20.00
Little Squatter, Candlestick, Moongleam, Pair 50.00
Locket On Chain, Nappy, 5 In. 10.00
Locket On Chain, Spooner, 4 x 3 1/2 In. 121.00
Locket On Chain, Toothpick 500.00
Lodestar, Pitcher, Dawn, 5 x 6 1/2 In. 160.00
Mayflower, Cocktail, Wabash, 3 Oz., 5 In. 20.00
McGrady, Syrup, Flamingo, 5 Oz. 15.00
Mercury, Candlestick, 3 3/4 x 4 3/4 In. 25.00
Mercury, Candlestick, Flamingo, 9 In. 160.00
Mercury, Candlestick, Moongleam, 3 In., Pair 35.00
Minuet, Dish, Dressing, Queen Ann, 2 3/8 x 8 1/4 x 5 In. 85.00
Minuet, Goblet, Symphone, 9 Oz., 8 1/4 In. 35.00
Minuet, Plate, Salad, 7 In. 15.00
Minuet, Relish, Sections, 11 1/4 x 6 3/4 In. 150.00

Minuet, Sugar & Creamer, 3 1/4 x 5 In. 130.00
Minuet, Tray, Queen Ann, 15 In. 25.00
Miss Muffet, Candlestick, Flamingo, Pair 20.00
Narrow Flute, Cruet, 4 Oz. 35.00
Narrow Flute, Dish, Jelly, Handles 20.00
Narrow Flute, Pickle Tray, 6 3/4 In. 55.00
Narrow Flute, Pitcher, Pt. 40.00
Narrow Flute, Plate, 5 In. 5.00
Narrow Flute, Relish, 4 Sections, 8 In. 25.00
Narrow Flute, Sugar & Creamer 25.00
Narrow Flute, Sugar & Creamer, Flamingo 55.00
Narrow Flutes, Sugar Cube Holder, Domino, 8 1/4 x 2 In. 50.00
No. 1401 Pattern, Platter, Oval, 1930-38, 14 In. 45.00
Oakwood, Soda, Nimrod Carving, 8 Oz. 60.00
Oakwood, Soda, Nimrod Carving, 10 Oz. 40.00
Oakwood, Whiskey, Fox Chase Cut, 8 Oz., 4 Piece 120.00
Octagon, Bonbon, Marigold, 6 In. 25.00
Octagon, Cheese Plate, Marigold, Handles, 6 In. 15.00
Octagon, Dessert, Moongleam 20.00
Octagon, Dish, Mayonnaise, Moongleam, 5 1/2 In. 30.00
Octagon, Ice Bucket, Moongleam, Metal Handle, Tongs 90.00
Octagon, Ice Bucket, Tongs, Wheel Cut, 4 1/4 x 8 1/2 In. 325.00
Octagon, Nut Dish, Flamingo 35.00
Octagon, Nut Dish, Moongleam 20.00
Old Colony, Bowl, Empress, Oval, Sahara, 10 In. 70.00
Old Colony, Cocktail, Sahara, Carcassone, 2 1/4 In. 23.00
Old Colony, Pitcher, Sahara, Empress, 3 Pt. 190.00
Old Colony, Plate, Sahara, Empress, 8 In. 10.00
Old Colony, Relish, Sahara, 7 1/4 In. 38.00
Old Colony, Sandwich Server, Center Handle, Empress, Sahara, 12 In. 25.00
Old Colony, Sugar & Creamer, Empress 25.00
Old Dominion, Goblet, Alexandrite, 8 In. 235.00
Old Queen Ann, Bowl, Crimped, 8 In. 45.00
Old Queen Ann, Celery Dish, 13 In. 45.00
Old Sandwich, Bottle, Oil, 8 1/2 x 3 In. 130.00
Old Sandwich, Bowl, Floral, Oval, Sahara, 12 In. 50.00
Old Sandwich, Bowl, Sahara, 11 In. 100.00
Old Sandwich, Candlestick, 6 1/8 x 4 In. 73.00
Old Sandwich, Cruet, 2 Oz. 50.00
Old Williamsburg, Candlestick, 7 1/2 In. 39.00
Old Williamsburg, Oyster Cocktail, 4 1/2 x 3 1/4 In. 40.00
Old Williamsburg, Sugar & Creamer, Sterling Silver Base 15.00
Orchid Etch, Bell, Dinner, Tyrolean 70.00
Orchid Etch, Bowl, Crimped, Waverly, 12 In. 90.00
Orchid Etch, Bowl, Dolphin Footed, 3 x 7 1/2 In. 113.00
Orchid Etch, Candlestick, 2-Light, Flame, 6 1/2 x 6 3/8 In. 125.00
Orchid Etch, Candlestick, 2-Light, Trident, 5 1/2 In. 55.00
Orchid Etch, Candy Jar, Cover, Waverly, Seahorse Finial 110.00
Orchid Etch, Celery Dish, 12 x 4 1/2 In. 80.00
Orchid Etch, Champagne, Tyrolean, 6 Oz. 10.00
Orchid Etch, Compote, 3 x 5 1/2 In. ....55.00 to 65.00
Orchid Etch, Compote, 5 x 7 1/4 In. 155.00
Orchid Etch, Creamer, 3 In. 35.00
Orchid Etch, Dish, Jelly, Handles, 4-Footed, 7 In. 95.00
Orchid Etch, Dish, Mint, Queen Ann, 5 1/2 x 2 1/4 In. 45.00
Orchid Etch, Goblet, 10 Oz., 6 In. 42.00
Orchid Etch, Goblet, Graceful 45.00
Orchid Etch, Plate, Salad, 7 In. 20.00
Orchid Etch, Plate, Salad, 8 In. 43.00
Orchid Etch, Platter, 15 In. 80.00
Orchid Etch, Relish, 3 Sections, 7 1/4 In. 115.00

Orchid Etch, Relish, 3 Sections, Waverly, Oval, 12 In. 25.00
Orchid Etch, Sherbet, Low, 4 In. 30.00
Orchid Etch, Sugar & Creamer, 4 x 4 In. 60.00
Orchid Etch, Sugar & Creamer, Tray, 4 In. 140.00
Orchid Etch, Sugar, 3 In. 35.00
Orchid Etch, Torte Plate, 14 In. .... 80.00 to 85.00
Orchid Etch, Torte Plate, Handles, 12 In. 125.00
Orchid Etch, Vase, Fan, Lariat, 7 1/2 x 6 1/4 In. 165.00
Orchid Etch, Vase, Violet, Waverly, Footed, 4 In. 70.00
Orchid Etch, Wine, 3 Oz., 5 1/8 In. 111.00
Orchid Waverly, Compote, 3 x 6 In. 48.00
Peerless, Butter, Cover 45.00
Peerless, Cordial 20.00
Peerless, Goblet, 5 Oz., 3 3/4 In. 20.00
Peerless, Sugar & Creamer 45.00
Peerless, Sugar & Creamer, Individual .... 10.00 to 15.00
Peerless, Toothpick 40.00
Penguin, Decanter, Sherry, Pt., 8 1/2 x 4 1/8 In. 535.00
Petal, Creamer, Sahara 15.00
Petal, Sugar & Creamer, Flamingo 55.00
Petal, Sugar & Creamer, Moongleam 60.00
Petticoat Dolphin, Candlestick, Flamingo, 6 In. 400.00
Picket, Basket, Wheel Cut, 10 1/2 x 8 1/4 x 5 3/8 In. 245.00
Pillows, Jug, Molasses, Metal Top, 7 Oz. 160.00
Pillows, Vase, Ball, 4 1/2 In. 80.00
Pineapple & Fan, Creamer, 4 In. 155.00
Pineapple & Fan, Mug 25.00
Pineapple & Fan, Salt & Pepper 20.00
Pinwheel & Fan, Bowl, 3 1/2 x 8 1/2 In. 95.00
Pinwheel & Fan, Pitcher 65.00
Pinwheel & Fan, Powder Jar, Metal Cover 25.00
Pinwheel & Fan, Punch Cup, Moongleam 45.00
Plain Band, Salt 20.00
Plain Band, Wine, Ruby Stain 10.00
Plantation, Butter, Cover, 1/4 Lb., 7 x 2 3/4 In. 175.00
Plantation, Cake Stand, 4 1/2 x 14 In. 239.00
Plantation, Candleblock, Pineapple Shape, Pair 180.00
Plantation, Candlestick, 2-Light, 5 3/4 x 8 3/4 In. 130.00
Plantation, Candy Box, Cover, 7 In. 75.00
Plantation, Candy Jar, Cover, Footed, 8 1/2 In. .... 200.00 to 240.00
Plantation, Cheese Dish, Cover, Footed, 6 x 4 3/4 In. 98.00
Plantation, Claret, 4 1/2 Oz., 5 1/8 x 2 3/4 In. 50.00
Plantation, Compote, Shallow, 7 In. .... 35.00 to 45.00
Plantation, Dish, Jelly, Handles, Plantation Ivy Etch, 6 1/2 In. 50.00
Plantation, Dish, Jelly, Handles, Silver Overlay Leaves, 6 1/2 In. 65.00
Plantation, Dish, Salad Dressing, Sections, Ladles 45.00
Plantation, Goblet, Plantation Ivy Etch, 10 Oz., 6 x 3 1/2 In. 50.00
Plantation, Jam Jar, Spoon, Pineapple Shape .... 175.00 to 210.00
Plantation, Pitcher, Ice Lip, 1/2 Gal., 8 1/4 In. 425.00
Plantation, Plate, Salad, 8 In. 15.00
Plantation, Sherbet, 6 1/2 Oz., 4 1/4 In. .... 35.00 to 40.00
Plantation, Syrup, Metal Cover, Bakelite Handle, 4 3/4 In. .... 179.00 to 190.00
Plantation, Tumbler, Iced Tea, Footed, 12 Oz., 6 3/4 In. 125.00
Plantation, Vase, Bud, Plantation Ivy Etch, 5 1/2 In. 150.00
Plantation, Wine, 3 Oz., 5 1/4 In. 50.00
Plantation Rose, Dish, Mayonnaise, 4 1/4 In. 700.00
Pleat & Panel, Bowl, Moongleam, Wheel Cut, 9 In. 60.00
Pleat & Panel, Cruet, Stopper, Amber 900.00
Pleat & Panel, Jam Jar, Footed, Flamingo 25.00
Pleat & Panel, Pitcher, Flamingo, 3 Pt. 65.00
Pressed Diamond Flamingo, Bowl, 6 In., 2 Piece 35.00

Prince Of Wales Plumes, Bottle, Water 130.00
Prince Of Wales Plumes, Celery Dish 60.00
Prince Of Wales Plumes, Toothpick 110.00
Priscilla, Cruet, Stopper, 4 Oz. 30.00
Priscilla, Toothpick 20.00
Priscilla, Vase, Rose, 7 In. 35.00
Prism Band, Decanter, Moongleam 235.00
Prison Band, Decanter, Stopper 45.00
Provincial, Candlestick, 3-Light, Pair 70.00
Provincial, Candy Jar, Cover, Limelight, 8 1/2 x 5 In. 585.00
Provincial, Sugar & Creamer 15.00
Provincial, Tumbler, Juice, Footed, 5 Oz. 14.00
Punty & Diamond Point, Celery Dish 160.00
Punty Band, Mug, Ivorina Verde, 8 Oz. 35.00
Punty Band, Wine, Ruby Stain 10.00
Puritan, Bonbon, 7 In. 35.00
Puritan, Bowl, 8 In. 15.00
Puritan, Cigarette Box, Cover, Horse's Head Finial, 4 x 6 x 4 In. 225.00
Puritan, Cigarette Box, Cover, Horse's Head, 3 3/4 x 4 1/4 x 3 3/4 In. 125.00
Puritan, Cordial 10.00
Puritan, Nappy, 8 1/2 In. 10.00
Puritan, Pitcher, Squat, 1/2 Pt 70.00
Puritan, Pitcher, Tankard, Qt. 10.00
Puritan, Sherbet, Ruffled Edge 15.00
Puritan, Spooner, Footed 25.00
Quator, Sugar & Creamer, 3 3/4 x 6 In. 65.00
Queen Ann, Bowl, Dolphin Footed 35.00
Queen Ann, Candlestick, 2-Light, Pair 120.00
Queen Ann, Oil Cruet, Belle Le Rose Etch, 6 Oz. 45.00
Quilt, Ashtray, 3 In., 4 Piece 45.00
Quilt, Cigarette Box, Lid, 5 In. 50.00
Recessed Panel, Candy Jar, Cover, 15 1/2 x 6 3/4 In. 995.00
Recessed Panel, Candy Jar, Green Stain, Gold Enameled, Scrolls, 9 3/4 In. 195.00
Regency, Candy Dish, Cover, 2 Sections 210.00
Revere, Dish, Lemon, 2 Handles 20.00
Revere, Dish, Mayonnaise, Underplate, 2 Sections 10.00
Ridge & Star, Plate, Hawthorne, 7 1/2 In. 5.00
Ridge & Star, Plate, Hawthorne, 8 1/2 In. 45.00
Ridgeleigh, Ashtray Set, Bridge, 4 Piece 180.00
Ridgeleigh, Ashtray, Diamond, Sahara, 1 x 4 1/8 In. 145.00
Ridgeleigh, Ashtray, Spade 5.00
Ridgeleigh, Bowl, 9 In. 20.00
Ridgeleigh, Bowl, Floral, 10 In. 15.00
Ridgeleigh, Cheese Dish, 6 In. 25.00
Ridgeleigh, Coaster, 3 3/4 In., 4 Piece 45.00
Ridgeleigh, Coaster, Sahara, 3 3/4 In. 25.00
Ridgeleigh, Cocktail Shaker, Qt. 163.00
Ridgeleigh, Creamer 20.00
Ridgeleigh, Cruet, 4 In. 100.00
Ridgeleigh, Dish, Jelly, Sections, 6 In. ....10.00 to 25.00
Ridgeleigh, Jam Jar, Cover, 5 x 4 In. 125.00
Ridgeleigh, Mustard Jar, Cover 20.00
Ridgeleigh, Nut Dish, 7 x 4 1/2 In. 25.00
Ridgeleigh, Pitcher, 1/2 Gal. 240.00
Ridgeleigh, Plate, 6 1/2 In. 20.00
Ridgeleigh, Relish, Star Shape, 5 Sections, 10 In. ....25.00 to 50.00
Ridgeleigh, Salt & Pepper, 3 In. 90.00
Ridgeleigh, Sugar & Creamer 33.00
Ridgeleigh, Torte Plate, 11 In. ....20.00 to 30.00
Ridgeleigh, Tray, 4 1/2 x 8 1/2 In. 20.00
Ridgeleigh, Tray, Celery & Olive, Sections, 12 In. 50.00

Ridgeleigh, Vase, 6 In. 40.00
Ridgeleigh, Vase, Sahara, 4 3/4 x 5 In. 180.00
Ring Band, Cruet, Ivorina Verde, Clear Faceted Stopper 65.00
Rooster, Cocktail Shaker, Stopper, Strainer, Qt., 14 1/2 In. .... 125.00 to 250.00
Rooster, Cocktail, 3 1/2 Oz., 5 1/2 In. 69.00
Rosalie, Sugar & Creamer, Tray, Queen Ann 65.00
Rose Etch, Ashtray, Square, 3/4 x 3 In. 50.00
Rose Etch, Bowl, Footed, Waverly, 3 x 5 1/2 In. 65.00
Rose Etch, Bowl, Gardenia, Waverly, 12 1/2 In. 45.00
Rose Etch, Cake Plate, Pedestal, 2 x 14 In. 150.00
Rose Etch, Candlestick, 2-Light, 6 x 5 1/4 In. 66.00
Rose Etch, Celery Dish, 12 In. 65.00
Rose Etch, Champagne, 6 Oz., 4 1/2 In. 43.00
Rose Etch, Cordial, Oz., 4 1/4 In. 165.00
Rose Etch, Epernette, 3 1/2 x 6 In., Pair 2000.00
Rose Etch, Saltshaker, Footed, Waverly, 4 1/2 In. 29.00
Rose Etch, Sandwich Server, Center Handle, 14 1/2 In. .... 200.00 to 230.00
Rose Etch, Sugar & Creamer, 8-Sided Foot, Waverly Blank 84.00
Satellite, Candleblock 50.00
Saturn, Cruet, 2 Oz. 25.00
Saturn, Mustard, Cover, Silver Overlay Finial, 3 3/4 x 2 1/4 In. 93.00
Sesquicentennial, Ashtray 20.00
Skirted Panel, Candlestick, Toy, 3 1/2 In. 30.00
Spanish, Goblet, Cobalt Blue, 10 Oz., 7 1/2 In. 130.00
Spanish, Wine, Etched, 2 Oz., 4 3/4 In. 72.00
Stanhope, Goblet, 10 Oz., 6 In. 29.00
Sunburst, Bowl, Cereal, 4 1/2 In. 30.00
Sunburst, Butter, Cover 35.00
Sunburst, Dish, Jelly, Footed, 5 In. 55.00
Sunburst, Dish, Pickle, Oval, 7 In. 30.00
Sunburst, Eggcup, 4 Piece 190.00
Sunburst, Nappy, 5 In. 5.00
Sunburst, Plate, 6 In. 10.00
Sunburst, Sugar & Creamer, Oval 35.00
Sunflower, Candlestick, Pair 25.00
Sunflower, Tumbler, 8 Oz. 10.00
Thumbprint & Panel, Candlestick, Pair 65.00
Tom Thumb, Candlestick, Pair, Toy 110.00
Toujours, Dish, Mayonnaise, Footed 10.00
Touraine, Cruet, 6 Oz. 15.00
Touraine, Tumbler, Amber, Fred Harvey, 5 Oz. 85.00
Tricorne, Candlestick, 3-Light, Moongleam 80.00
Trident, Candlestick, 2-Light, 6 1/2 In., Pair 165.00
Trident, Candlestick, 2-Light, Alexandrite 230.00
Trident, Candlestick, Sahara, 2-Light, 6 1/2 In., Pair 250.00
Tudor, Celery Dish, Oval, 12 In. 18.00
Tudor, Cruet, 6 Oz. 15.00
Tudor, Pitcher, Pt. 70.00
Twist, Bonbon, Flamingo 35.00
Twist, Bowl, Moongleam, 4-Footed, Oval, 12 x 9 1/2 In. 125.00
Twist, Bowl, Nasturtium, Alexandrite, 5 x 8 In. 850.00
Twist, Celery Dish, Marigold, 13 In. 20.00
Twist, Compote, Flamingo, 7 In. 135.00
Twist, Compote, Moongleam, 7 In. 125.00
Twist, Cruet, 4 Oz. 20.00
Twist, Nappy, Moongleam, 4 In. 35.00
Twist, Nut Dish, Marigold 35.00
Twist, Nut Dish, Moongleam 40.00
Twist, Plate, Flamingo, 8 In. 45.00
Twist, Plate, Marigold, 6 In. 20.00
Twist, Relish, Marigold, 10 In. 25.00

Victorian, Cheese Dish, Footed 30.00
Victorian, Goblet, 2-Ball Stem, 9 Oz. 30.00
Victorian, Sugar & Creamer 25.00
Victorian, Vase, 4 In. 25.00
Wabash, Cordial, Oz., 3 1/2 In. 45.00
Waldorf Astoria, Toothpick 60.00
Wampum, Bowl, Salad, 10 In. 70.00
Wampum, Candlestick, Pair 25.00
Warwick, Candleholder, Cobalt Blue 100.00
Warwick, Candleholder, Pair 25.00
Warwick, Vase, 5 In. 40.00
Warwick, Vase, 7 In. 55.00
Warwick, Vase, 9 In. 35.00
Warwick, Vase, Sahara, 7 In. 65.00
Waverly, Bowl, Footed, 7 1/2 In. 37.00
Waverly, Epergnette, Pair 10.00
Waverly, Plate, Salad, 8 1/2 In. 25.00
Waverly, Relish, 3 Sections, 7 1/4 In. 28.00
Waverly, Relish, 3 Sections, 11 1/2 x 8 In. 22.00
Waverly, Salt & Pepper, Metal Lids, Silver Overlay 15.00
Waverly, Sugar & Creamer, 2 1/2 x 2 1/2 In. 38.00
Whaley, Tankard, Monticello Etch, 54 Oz. 50.00
Wide Panel, Creamer, Sahara, 4 In. 35.00
Williamsburg, Candelabrum, 4-Light, Prisms, 20 1/2 x 12 In., Pair 468.00
Williamsburg, Candlestick, 3-Light 40.00
Winged Scroll, Celery Dish 140.00
Winged Scroll, Cigarette Holder 140.00
Winged Scroll, Nappy, Emerald, 7 1/2 In. 95.00
Winged Scroll, Pin Tray, Ivorina Verde 210.00
Winged Scroll, Spooner, Ivorina Verde, Enameled Flowers, 3 1/2 In. 66.00
Winged Scroll, Toothpick, Ivorina Verde 79.00
Yeoman, Ashtray, Bowtie, Flamingo, Handle, 4 In. 50.00
Yeoman, Ashtray, Bowtie, Moongleam, 4 In. . . . . . 55.00 to 63.00
Yeoman, Bowl, Floral, Flamingo, 12 In. 70.00
Yeoman, Bowl, Floral, Hawthorne, 12 In. 15.00
Yeoman, Compote, Moongleam 50.00
Yeoman, Creamer, Marigold, Hotel 20.00
Yeoman, Cruet, Stopper, Sahara, 4 Oz. 60.00
Yeoman, Goblet, Sahara, 5 3/8 In. 35.00
Yeoman, Mustard Jar, Cover, Sahara, Handle 130.00
Yeoman, Relish, 3 Sections, Moongleam, 13 In. 78.00

HEREND, see Fischer category.

HEUBACH is the collector's name for Gebruder Heubach, a firm working in Lichten, Germany, from 1840 to 1925. It is best known for bisque dolls and doll heads, their principal products. They also manufactured bisque figurines, including piano babies, beginning in the 1880s, and glazed figurines in the 1900s. Piano Babies are listed in their own category. Dolls are included in the Doll category under Gebruder Heubach and Heubach. Another factory, Ernst Heubach, working in Koppelsdorf, Germany, also made porcelain and dolls. These will also be found in the Doll category under Heubach Koppelsdorf.

Candy Container, Girl On Snowball, Bisque Head, Cardboard Ball, 1920s 365.00
Figurine, Baby, Sitting, Smiling, Finger On Lips, 1900s, 3 3/4 x 2 1/2 In. 229.00
Figurine, Child, Sitting On Stone, Holding Towel, Blue Eyes, Curly Blond Hair, Cap, 12 In. 275.00
Figurine, Dancing Girl, 1900s, 12 In. 499.00
Figurine, Dog, Bisque, White, Shaggy, Begging, 6 In. 358.00
Figurine, Girl, Pleated Dress, Blond, Blue Eyes, Rosy Cheeks, 1900s, 6 1/2 In. . . . . . 139.00 to 149.00
Vase, Bud, Dutch Girl, 5 In. 69.00

HISTORIC BLUE, see factory names, such as Adams, Ridgway, and Staffordshire.

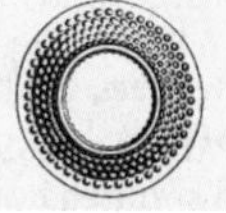

HOBNAIL glass is a style of glass with bumps all over. Dozens of hobnail patterns and variants have been made. Clear, colored, and opalescent hobnail have been made and are being reproduced. Other pieces of hobnail may also be listed in the Duncan & Miller and Fenton categories.

Basket, Blue, Star Base, 5 1/2 x 6 In. 25.00
Basket, Cobalt Blue, 4-Piece Mold, Ruffled Edge, Clear Handle, 5 1/2 x 4 In. 45.00
Basket, Green, Fluted Edge, Twisted Handle, 8 x 7 In. 34.00
Candy Dish, Fan Shape, 1 3/4 x 6 In. 45.00
Cookie Jar, Cover, Milk Glass, Handles, 8 1/2 x 6 In. 65.00
Cup & Saucer, Pink, 2 1/4 x 3 3/4 In. 17.00
Decanter, Square, 9 1/2 x 3 1/2 x 3 1/2 In. 22.00
Egg Plate, 11 1/4 In. .... 35.00 to 38.00
Mug, Blue, 3 1/8 x 3 3/4 In. 19.00
Relish, Sections, Handles, 10 In. 20.00
Sugar & Creamer, Opalescent, Milk Glass, 2 3/4 In. 48.00
Syrup, Opalescent, Crimped Opening, 6 In. 125.00
Top Hat, Blue, 3 x 3 x 3 In. 68.00
Vase, Bud, Opalescent, 6 In. 19.00

HOCHST, or Hoechst, porcelain was made in Germany from 1746 to 1796. It was marked with a six-spoke wheel. Be careful when buying Hochst; many other firms have used a very similar wheel-shaped mark.

Plate, Prince Electoral, Hand Painted, Flowers, c.1776, 9 1/4 In., 12 Piece 2225.00
Tea & Coffee Set, Purple, Red & Green Flowers, Gilt Rim, c.1765, 25 Piece 8659.00

HOLLY AMBER, or golden agate, glass was made by the Indiana Tumbler and Goblet Company of Greentown, Indiana, from January 1, 1903, to June 13, 1903. It is a pressed glass pattern featuring holly leaves in the amber-shaded glass. The glass was made with shadings that range from creamy opalescent to brown-amber.

Dish, Pickle, Oval, 9 In. 305.00
Nappy, 4 1/4 In. .... 75.00 to 130.00
Toothpick Holder 15.00

HOLT-HOWARD was an importer who started working in 1949 in Stamford, Connecticut. The company sold many types of table accessories, such as condiment jars, decanters, spoon holders, and saltshakers. The figures shown on some of his pieces had a cartoon-like quality. The company was bought out by General Housewares Corporation in 1969. Holt-Howard pieces are often marked with the name and the year or *HH* and the year stamped in black. The *HH* mark was used until 1974. There was also a black and silver label. Production of Holt-Howard ceased in 1990. Similar pieces by the same Holt-Howard designer are being made today and are marked *GHA*.

Ashtray, Cozy Kitten, c.1958, 4 3/4 x 4 3/4 In. .... 85.00 to 95.00
Bank, Coin Kitty, Bobbing, Pink, 1958, 5 1/2 x 4 1/4 In. 290.00
Candleholder, Candle Miss, Blue, c.1958, 4 3/4 In. 28.00
Candy Jar, Cover, Santa, Pop-Up, Just Take 1, c.1960, 6 x 5 In. 285.00
Cherries Jar, Pixie Ware, 1958, 5 1/2 In. 265.00
Cruet, Pixie Ware, Italian Dressing, c.1959, 7 1/2 x 3 1/4 In. 299.00
Cruet, Pixie Ware, Russian Dressing, c.1959, 7 1/2 x 3 1/4 In. 299.00
Honey Jar, Pixie Ware, 1959, 5 1/2 In. 950.00
Jam 'n Jelly Jar, Pixie Ware, 1958, 5 1/2 In. 135.00
Ketchup Jar, Pixie Ware, 1958, 5 1/2 In. 135.00
Mayonnaise Jar, Pixie Ware, 1959, 5 1/2 In. 335.00
Memo Minder, Cozy Kitten, c.1960, 7 x 4 3/8 In. 190.00
Olive Jar, Pixie Ware, 1958, 5 1/2 In. 220.00
Onion Jar, Jeeves, Onions If You Please, 1960, 5 1/2 x 4 In. 135.00

Onion Jar, Pixie Ware, 1958, 5 1/2 In. ....160.00 to 335.00
Pitcher, Coq Rouge, Rooster, 8 In. 70.00
Salt & Pepper, Cozy Kitten, 1959, 4 1/4 In. 65.00
Stringholder, Cozy Kitten, 1958, 4 1/2 x 5 1/2 In. ....85.00 to 135.00

HOPALONG CASSIDY was a character in a series of twenty-eight books written by Clarence E. Milford, first published in 1907. Movies and television shows were made based on the character. The best-known actor playing Hopalong Cassidy was William Lawrence Boyd. His first movie appearance was in 1919, but the first Hopalong Cassidy film was not until 1934. Sixty-six films were made. In 1948, William Boyd purchased the television rights to the movies, then later made fifty-two new programs. In the 1950s, Hopalong Cassidy and his horse, named Topper, were seen in comics, records, toys, and other products. Boyd died in 1972.

Button, I Follow Hoppy, Herald American, Lithograph, Round 14.00
Clock, Alarm, Hoppy On Topper, Black, Metal, Round, U.S. Time, 5 1/2 In. 280.00
Cup, Milk Glass, Blue Graphics, 3 In. 27.00
Cup Set, Milk Glass, 1 Each Red, Blue, Black, Green Graphics, 3 In., 4 Piece 127.00
Decal Sheet, Multicolored, 1950s, 30 x 22 In. 110.00
Display, Wristwatch, Shock Resistant, Timex, 1950s, 3 1/2 x 4 x 15 In. 7150.00
Figure, Chalk, Hand Painted, Red & Silver Sparkles, Pa., 15 In. 110.00
Figurine, Hoppy On Topper, Plastic, Painted, Ideal, Box, 1950, 5 3/4 In. 190.00
Gun & Holster Set, Double, 4 Bullets, 7 1/2-In. Guns 249.00
Lamp, Motion, Red, Rotolamp Junior Econolite Corp., c.1949, 10 In. 230.00
Lunch Box, Metal, Blue, Bottle, Aladdin, 1950-51, 3 3/4 x 7 x 8 In. 545.00
Milk Bottle, Cloverdale Milk, Black & Red Pyro, Square, Pt. 10.00
Milk Bottle, Hoppy's Favorite, O'Fallon Milk Is A Winner, Qt., 9 In. 22.00
Pin, Gun & Holster, Gold, Gun Hooked To Holster By Chain 70.00
Radio, Hoppy Riding Topper, Steel, Embossed, Arvin, c.1950, 5 x 8 x 4 In. 450.00
Soap, Cowboy, Factory Sealed, Colgate-Palmolive-Peet Co., 1940s, 3 3/4 In. 52.00
Thermos Bottle, Steel, Lithograph, Yellow, Red Cup, Aladdin, 1950s, 6 1/2 In. 76.00
Thermos Bottle, Steel, Lithograph, Yellow, Red Cup, Aladdin, Box, 1950s, 6 1/2 In. 105.00
Toy, Range Rider, Tin, Windup, Marx, 1940s, 9 1/2 In. 605.00
Toy, Shooting Gallery, 5 Targets, 2 Balls, Tin, Windup, Automatic Toy Co., Box, 18 In. 340.00
Tumbler, Milk Glass, Black Graphics, 5 In. 27.00
View-Master, Hopalong & Topper, No. 955, 1950s 13.00
Wristwatch, Plastic Case, Saddle Display, U.S. Time, Box, 1955 ....385.00 to 543.00

HORN was used to make many types of boxes, furniture inlays, jewelry, and whimsies.

Box, Carved, Hinged, Painted, c.1800, 7/8 x 2 1/2 x 3 3/8 In. 146.00
Cup, Carved, Polychromed, Red, Yellow, Green, Spanish Colonial, 1600s, 4 1/2 x 3 x 2 1/2 In. 935.00
Cup, Engraved, Hunters, Dogs, Birds, England, 1800s 350.00
Flask, Yak, Black, Recurved Body, 4 Brass Bands, Leather Strap, Tibet, 20th Century, 18 In. 246.00
Pokal, Animal Face At Tip, Brass Mount, Lid, 14 In. 483.00
Snuff Bottle, Banded, Screw Lid, 1800s, 1 3/4 x 3/4 In. 78.00
Snuffbox, Oval, Brass Tacks, Hinge, 3 In. 201.00
Stag, Carved, Frog On Lotus Pod, On Stand, Japan, Late 19th Century 1150.00
Steer, Carved, Fish Shape, Expociason De Arte Mexicano, American Federation Of Arts, 13 In. 40.00
Tusk, Carved, Oval, Fitted Cover, Inuit, 2 1/4 x 2 1/4 In. 176.00

HOWARD PIERCE began working in Southern California in 1936. In 1945, he opened a pottery in Claremont. He moved to Joshua Tree in 1968 and continued making pottery until 1991. His contemporary-looking figurines are popular with collectors. Though most pieces are marked with his name, smaller items from his sets often were not marked.

Figurine, Bird, Head Down, Ring Around Eye, Brown, 2 3/4 In. 25.00
Figurine, Bird, Head Up, Ring Around Eye, Brown, 2 3/4 In. 25.00
Figurine, Cotton Tail Bunny Rabbit, Blue Glaze, Signed, 1990 .... 45.00

Rub linseed oil on dull deer antlers, but use floor wax on African antelope or wild sheep horns.

Howdy Doody, Puppet, Push Button, Wood, Kohner Bros., 6 In.

Figurine, Deer, Resting, 5 1/2 In. 70.00
Figurine, Goose, 7 1/2 x 5 1/2 In. 40.00
Figurine, Heron, Brown, Beige, Blue, 10 In. 415.00
Figurine, Native Girl, 7 1/4 In. 89.00
Figurine, Pelican, Mottled Green, Blue Undertone, 7 In. 115.00
Figurine, Quail, 5 1/2 In. 75.00
Figurine, Raccoon, 8 1/2 In. 115.00
Figurine Set, Quail Family, Mother, 2 Chicks, 6 In., 4 In., 2 1/2 In., 3 Piece .... 40.00 to 69.00
Planter, Owl, Gold Line, 1950s, 6 x 6 3/4 In. 40.00

HOWDY DOODY and Buffalo Bob were the main characters in a children's series televised from 1947 to 1960. Howdy was a redheaded puppet. The series became popular with college students in the late 1970s when Buffalo Bob began to lecture on campuses.

Band, Clarabell Plays Piano, Howdy Doody, Tin Lithograph, Linemar, 1950s, 6 In. 1760.00
Bank, Shawnee, 7 In. 675.00
Cookie Jar, Purinton, Early 1950s, 9 3/4 In. 900.00
Doll, Moving Glass Eyes, Composition, Painted Hair, Box, Effanbee, 1950s, 23 In. 367.00
Doll, Plastic, Cloth, Ideal, Kagran, Box, 1952, 19 In. 275.00
Doll, Vinyl, Sheriff Badge, Stahlwood, Kagran, Package, c.1950, 13 In. 138.00
Doodler, Battery Operated, Harrett-Gilmar, Box, 1950s, 8 1/2 x 13 1/2 In. 120.00
Figure, Wood, Jointed, 12 In. 220.00
Game, Electric Carnival, Battery Operated, Harrett-Gilmar, Box, 8 1/2 x 13 1/2 In. 110.00
Marionette, Clarabell, Composition Head, Wood, Peter Puppet, Kagran, 1950, 15 In. 385.00
Marionette, Composition Head, Peter Puppet, Kagran, Box, c.1950, 15 In. .... 300.00 to 410.00
Marionette, Flub-A-Dub, Composition Head, Peter Puppet, Kagran, 1950, 14 1/2 In. 908.00
Marionette, Princess Summerfall-Winterspring, Peter Puppet, Kagran, 1950, 13 In. 415.00
Puppet, Push Button, Clarabell, Wood, Kohner, 6 In. 145.00
Puppet, Push Button, Howdy Doody, Wood, Plastic, Kohner, Box, c.1950, 6 In. 165.00
Puppet, Push Button, Wood, Kohner Bros., 6 In. .... *ILLUS* 77.00
Toy, Band, Bob Plays Piano, Tin, Windup, Unique Art, Box, 1950s, 7 In. 2130.00
Toy, Band, Buffalo Bob Plays Piano, Tin, Windup, Unique Art, 1950s, 8 In. 908.00
Toy, Figure Set, Plastic, Kagran, Box, 1948-50, 4 In., 5 Piece 110.00
Toy, Pump Mobile, Tin, Windup, Nylint, Box, 9 In. 415.00
Tumbler, Welch's Sure Helps Make You Strong, 1953, 4 1/8 In. 9.00

HULL pottery was made in Crooksville, Ohio, from 1905. Addis E. Hull bought the Acme Pottery Company and started making ceramic wares. In 1917, A. E. Hull Pottery began making art pottery as well as the commercial wares. For a short time, 1921 to 1929, the firm also sold pottery imported from Europe. The dinnerwares of the 1940s, including the Little Red Riding Hood line, the high gloss artwares of the 1950s, and the matte wares of the 1940s, are all popular with collectors. The firm officially closed in March 1986.

Bank, Corky Pig, Pink, White, Blue, c.1950s, 4 1/2 x 5 x 6 3/4 In. .... 130.00 to 200.00

Blossom Flite, Basket, 6 In. 75.00
Blossom Flite, Console, Pink, 16 1/2 In. 195.00
Blossom Flite, Pitcher, 6 In. 75.00
Bouquet, Pitcher, Cinderella, Kitchenware, c.1949, 64 Oz. 120.00
Bow Knot, Basket, Pink, Blue, 6 1/2 x 5 1/2 In. 290.00
Bow Knot, Candlestick, 5 1/2 x 4 x 3 In. 125.00
Bow Knot, Ewer, c.1949, 13 1/2 In. 1250.00
Bow Knot, Jardiniere, Pink, Green, Late 1940s, 9 3/8 In. 850.00
Bow Knot, Sugar, Cover, 4 3/4 x 5 1/2 In. 180.00
Bow Knot, Vase, 8 1/2 In. ....310.00 to 395.00
Calla Lily, Vase, 7 x 5 3/4 In. 100.00
Continental, Vase, Mountain Blue, 13 3/4 In. 175.00
Cookie Jar, Bean Pot, Cookies, Brown, 8 1/4 In. 12.00
Cookie Jar, Gingerbread Man, 11 3/4 x 9 1/2 In. 385.00
Dogwood, Vase, c.1943, 4 3/4 x 3 3/8 In. 75.00
Floral, Basket, Gold Trim, 1950s, 6 1/2 In. 95.00
Iris, Basket, Matte, 1940s, 7 x 7 1/2 x 5 In. 375.00
Magnolia, Ewer, 7 1/4 x 5 1/2 In. 165.00
Magnolia, Vase, 2 Handles, 15 In. 395.00
Magnolia, Vase, 8 1/2 In. 295.00
Magnolia, Vase, Yellow To Brown, c.1946, 8 1/2 In. 135.00
Magnolia Gloss, Vase, 2 Handles, c.1948, 8 1/2 In. 85.00
Magnolia Matte, Pitcher, Pastel, Pink, Green, 1940s, 13 1/2 In. 425.00
Magnolia Matte, Vase, Dusty Rose, Yellow, c.1946, 10 1/2 In. 210.00
Magnolia Matte, Vase, Pink, Blue, 8 1/2 In. ....165.00 to 225.00
Magnolia Matte, Vase, Yellow, c.1947, 4 3/4 In. 65.00
Open Rose, Vase, 2 Offset Handles, 4 3/4 In. 150.00
Open Rose, Vase, 8 1/2 In. 245.00
Parchment & Pine, Teapot, 6 x 11 1/2 In. 130.00
Poppy, Planter, 6 1/2 In. 225.00
Poppy, Vase, c.1940, 5 In. 150.00
Red Riding Hood, Canister, Cover, Salt, 9 3/4 x 7 x 5 1/8 In. 900.00
Red Riding Hood, Cookie Jar, 12 In. 350.00
Rosella, Ewer, c.1946, 6 1/2 In. 95.00
Rosella, Vase, 8 1/2 In. 80.00
Serenade, Ashtray, c.1957, 13 x 10 1/2 In. 85.00
Serenade, Pitcher, Yellow, Matte, Stippled Texture, 1957, 6 1/2 In. 95.00
Serenade, Vase, Pink, 10 3/4 x 5 1/2 In. 135.00
Sueno Tulip, Vase, c.1938, 6 In. ....135.00 to 225.00
Sunglow, Wall Pocket, Iron Shape, Pansy, Butterfly, Early 1950s 125.00
Sunglow, Wall Pocket, Whisk Broom Shape, 8 1/4 In. 125.00
Tokay, Basket, 1950s, 8 In. 40.00
Tokay, Vase, 1958, 5 1/2 x 6 In. 40.00
Water Lily, Candleholder, c.1948, 4 1/2 In. 85.00
Water Lily, Console Bowl, c.1948, 13 1/2 In. 185.00
Water Lily, Flowerpot, Pink, Yellow, Green, 5 3/4 x 5 3/4 In. 155.00
Water Lily, Vase, 8 1/2 In. 200.00
Water Lily, Vase, 10 1/2 In. 275.00
Water Lily, Vase, c.1948, 5 1/2 In. ....60.00 to 95.00
Water Lily, Vase, c.1948, 6 1/2 In. ....89.00 to 150.00
Water Lily, Vase, c.1948, 9 1/2 x 6 1/2 In. 125.00
Wild Flower, Cornucopia, Early 1950s, 8 1/2 In. 185.00
Wild Flower, Vase, 9 1/2 In. ....250.00 to 340.00
Wild Flower, Vase, Matte, 1940s, 10 1/2 In. 225.00
Wild Flower, Vase, Pastel, Matte, 12 1/4 In. 689.00
Woodland, Basket, 9 1/2 x 6 x 3 1/2 In. 135.00
Woodland, Basket, 9 3/4 In. ....135.00 to 165.00
Woodland, Cornucopia, Glossy, 1950s, 11 In. 115.00
Woodland, Ewer, Glossy, 5 1/2 In. 50.00
Woodland, Jardiniere, Matte, 1949-54, 5 1/2 In. 115.00

HUMMEL figurines, based on the drawings of the nun M.I. Hummel (Berta Hummel), are made by the W. Goebel Porzellanfabrik of Oeslau, Germany, now Rodenthal, Germany. They were first made in 1935. The *Crown* mark was used from 1935 to 1949. The company added the *bee* marks in 1950. The *full bee* with variations, was used from 1950 to 1959; *stylized bee*, 1957 to 1972; *three line mark*, 1964 to 1972; *last bee*, sometimes called *vee over gee*, 1972 to 1979. In 1979 the V bee symbol was removed from the mark. *U.S. Zone* was part of the mark from 1946 to 1948; *W. Germany* was part of the mark from 1960 to 1990; The *Goebel, W. Germany* mark, called the *missing bee* mark, was used from 1979 to 1990; *Goebel, Germany* with the crown and *WG*, originally called the *new mark*, was used from 1991 through part of 1999. The newest version of the bee mark with the word *Goebel*, the *current mark* or *Goebel with full bee*, was adopted in 2000. A special *Year 2000* backstamp was also introduced. Porcelain figures inspired by Berta Hummel's drawings were introduced in 1997. These are marked *BH* followed by a number. They are made in the Far East, not Germany. Other decorative items and plates that feature Hummel drawings have been made by Schmid Brothers, Inc., since 1971.

Figurine, No. 10/1, Flower Madonna, Vee Over Gee 148.00
Figurine, No. 11/0, Merry Wanderer, New Mark 70.00
Figurine, No. 56, Culprits, Stylized Bee 136.00
Figurine, No. 66, Farm Boy, Millennium Bee 115.00
Figurine, No. 67, Doll Mother, Vee Over Gee 125.00
Figurine, No. 69, Happy Pastime, New Mark, 3 1/2 In. 80.00
Figurine, No. 71, Stormy Weather, Missing Bee 117.00
Figurine, No. 89/1, Little Cellist, Stylized Bee 175.00
Figurine, No. 94/1, Surprise, New Mark 136.00
Figurine, No. 98/2/0, Sister, Vee Over Gee 125.00
Figurine, No. 119, Postman, Stylized Bee 125.00
Figurine, No. 142/X, Apple Tree Boy, Vee Over Gee 5000.00
Figurine, No. 173/0, Festival Harmony, Vee Over Gee 230.00
Figurine, No. 179, Coquettes, Vee Over Gee 115.00
Figurine, No. 195, Barnyard Hero, Stylized Bee 115.00
Figurine, No. 200/0, Little Goat Herder, Full Bee 136.00
Figurine, No. 224/1, Wayside Harmony, Stylized Bee 230.00
Figurine, No. 306, Little Bookkeeper, Vee Over Gee 125.00
Figurine, No. 321, Wash Day, New Mark 66.00
Figurine, No. 333, Blessed Event, Missing Bee 170.00
Figurine, No. 337, Cinderella, Vee Over Gee 125.00
Figurine, No. 348, Ring Around The Rosie, New Mark 795.00
Figurine, No. 373, Just Fishing, Missing Bee 114.00
Figurine, No. 406, Pleasant Journey, Missing Bee 110.00
Lamp Base, No. 232, Happy Days, Last Bee Mark 90.00
Plaque, No. 187, Hummel Figurines, Last Bee Mark 55.00

HUTSCHENREUTHER Porcelain Company of Selb, Germany, was established in 1814 and is still working. The company makes fine quality porcelain dinnerwares and figurines. The mark has changed through the years, but the name and the lion insignia appear in most versions.

Bell, 1981, Bell Of The Year, Fuchsia Flowers, Box, 5 1/2 In. 36.00
Bowl, Blue Onion, 1925-39, 1 1/4 x 5 5/8 In. 15.00
Bowl, Pink Apple Blossoms, Gold Trim, Hand Painted, Signed, 9 In. 125.00
Celery Dish, Josephine Favorite, Luster, 1890-1910, 1 3/4 x 5 1/4 x 12 1/2 In. 30.00
Coffeepot, Savona, Green & Cobalt Blue Design, White Body, 5 Cup 200.00
Cup & Saucer, Cherrywood, Platinum Trim, 3-In. Cup, 6-In. Saucer 20.00
Figurine, Hippopotamus, 1 3/4 x 4 In. 125.00
Figurine, Nude Maiden, Flower Hair Piece, Dolphin, Green Mark, 12 1/2 In. 360.00

Figurine, Nude Nymphette, Feeding Fawn, Pre WWII, 4 1/2 x 10 x 13 In. 950.00
Figurine, Woman Volleyball Player, Outstretched Arms, Ball, Marked, 9 In. 960.00
Gravy Boat, Attached Underplate, 2 Handles, Flowers, 3 1/2 x 5 3/4 x 9 1/2 In. 50.00
Gravy Boat, Attached Underplate, Maple Leaf Pattern, Gold Trim 25.00
Ornament, Egg, Flowers, Butterflies, No. 3, 1987, 1 3/4 In. 15.00
Plate, Christmas Angel, Etienne Boyer, 1998, 8 1/2 In. 55.00
Plate, Joyous Meeting, 2 Wrens, Gunther Granget Series, 1976, 10 1/8 In. 75.00
Plate, Nasturtium, Red Orange, Yellow, Gold Trim, Selb Bavaria, 6 In. 45.00
Plate, October Plate Of The Month Series, Pigeon, Ole Winther, 1978, 6 1/4 In. 30.00
Plate, Souvenir, Italy, Pope & Kennedys, Gold Rim 35.00
Plate Set, Gold Embossed Border, Flowers, Royal Bavarian, 10 3/4 In., 12 Piece 2015.00
Platter, Wild Rose, Scalloped Edge, Flowers, Gold Trim, 1925-41, 14 x 10 In. 285.00
Serving Bowl, Dundee, 1939-64, 2 1/4 x 7 5/8 x 10 1/8 In. 65.00
Sugar, Dundee, 1939-64, 4 1/8 In. 65.00
Sugar, Gold Trim, Marked Margarete 1814, 1930s, 4 In. 20.00
Trinket Box, Cover, Flowers, Transfer, Flower Bud Finial 125.00

ICONS, special, revered pictures of Jesus, Mary, or a saint, are usually Russian or Byzantine. The small icons collected today are made of wood and tin or precious metals. Many modern copies have been made in the old style and are being sold to tourists in Russia and Europe and at shops in the United States. Rare, old icons have sold for over $50,000.

Annunciation, Burial Of Christ, Enamel, 2-Sided, France, 1700s, 3 x 2 3/8 In. 880.00
Apostle St. John, Contemplating His Gospel, Angel, Russia, 18th Century, 12 x 10 In. 1645.00
Archangel Conquering Demon, Continental, Wood, Carved, Painted, 18th Century, 29 1/2 In. 800.00
Assembly Of The Archangel Michael, Gold Leaf Ground, Angels, Disk, Russia, 14 x 12 In. 2585.00
Christ Enthroned, Russia, Contemporary, 41 x 25 1/2 In. 2700.00
Christ Pantocrator, Wood, Polychrome, Embossed Brass Riza, Russia, 9 x 7 In. 440.00
Coronation Of The Mother Of God, Gold Leaf Field, Russia, c.1890, 14 1/2 x 12 1/2 In. 4465.00
Eight Saints, Protectors Of The Horses, Polychrome, Repousse Gilt Brass Riza, 12 x 10 In. 590.00
Holy John The Forerunner, Holding Diskos, Lamb Of God, Russia, 1700s, 12 x 10 In. 1410.00
Holy Napkin, Face Of Christ, Russia, 19th Century, 21 x 17 In. 940.00
Jesus, Seated, Crown Of Thorns, Continental, Wood, Carved, Painted, 18th Century, 40 In. 750.00
Lord Almighty, Christ Delivers Blessing, Gold Leaf, Russia, 19th Century, 12 x 10 In. 645.00
Lord Almighty, Painted, Overlaid, Repousse, Chased Riza, Russia, 8 3/4 x 7 3/4 In. 295.00
Madonna & Child, Byzantine Style, Brass Argente, Enameled, Parcel Gilt Riza, 12 x 10 In. 410.00
Madonna & Child, Multicolored, Carved, Europe, 17th Century, 28 In. 3738.00
Madonna & Child, Tempera On Wood, Russia, 12 x 10 1/2 x 1 1/4 In. 375.00
Our Lady Of The Angels, Wood, Painted, Spanish Colonial, Peru, Early 1800s, 11 x 8 In. 260.00
Selected Saints, Martha, Ephraim Bishop, Anthysa, Russia, c.1890, 12 1/4 x 10 1/2 In. 1060.00
St. George, Slaying Dragon, Tempera On Wood Panel, 9 3/4 x 8 x 1 In. 750.00
Triptych, Folding, Christ In Glory, Gilt Bronze Argente, Cross Finial, Closed 17 x 5 In. 1880.00
Virgin Of Kazan, Strapwork, Engraved, Sterling Silver Riza, Russia, c.1809, 7 x 5 3/4 In. 470.00

IMARI porcelain was made in Japan and China beginning in the 17th century. In the 18th century and later, it was copied by porcelain factories in Germany, France, England, and the United States. It was especially popular in the 19th century and is still being made. Imari is characteristically decorated with stylized bamboo, floral, and geometric designs in orange, red, green, and blue. The name comes from the Japanese port of Imari, which exported the ware made nearby in a factory at Arita. *Imari* is now a general term for any pattern of this type.

Basin, Brocade, Gilt Brass Mounts, Louis XVI, Leaf Scroll Handles, Meiji, 14 x 22 x 13 In. 5170.00
Bowl, Black Ships, Portuguese Figures, Eagle Center, Japan, 1800s, 3 1/2 x 9 1/2 In. 825.00
Bowl, Blue Scrolls, Orange Peonies, 8-Sided, Hardwood Stand, 1800s, 2 3/4 x 9 In. 265.00
Bowl, Blue, White, Leaves, Flowers, Karakusa Design, Early 1800s, 6 In. 45.00
Bowl, Flared Sides, Scalloped Rim, Flowers, Gold Trim, 1800s, 14 1/8 In. 2350.00
Bowl, Flat Rim, Double Foot Ring, Rabbit, Waves, 3 Friends Border, 3 x 9 In. 230.00
Bowl, Flowers, Brocade, Pagoda, 16 In. 325.00

Imari, Bowl, Scalloped Border, Cobalt Blue & Iron Red Flowers, 2 1/2 x 13 3/4 In.

Imari, Jar, Cover, Phoenix, Late 19th Century, 8 1/2 x 6 1/2 In., Pair

Bowl, Flowers, Fukugawa, Japan, Late 19th Century, 9 3/4 In. 470.00
Bowl, Flowers, Japan, Late 19th Century, 3 1/4 x 11 In. 500.00
Bowl, Footed, Flat, Inverted Rim, Trellis, Fence, Birds, Prunus, Ruyi Head Border, 3 x 12 In. 58.00
Bowl, Footed, Flower Vase, Paneled Sides, 4 x 10 In. 230.00
Bowl, Oval, Footed, Ribbed, Scalloped Border, Phoenix, Vine, 2 7/8 x 13 1/2 x 9 7/8 In. 230.00
Bowl, Reserve Decoration, Japan, 19th Century, 3 1/4 x 8 3/4 In. 176.00
Bowl, Ribbed, Oval, Scalloped Edge, Central Flowers, Vines, 2 1/2 x 8 7/8 In. 340.00
Bowl, Scalloped Border, Cobalt Blue & Iron Red Flowers, 2 1/2 x 13 3/4 In. .... *ILLUS* 460.00
Bowl, Scalloped Everted Rim, Shishi, Peony, Scrolling Vine, Insect, Flower, 2 3/4 x 8 1/2 In. 180.00
Centerpiece, Dore Bronze, Bowl Supported By 3 Female Figures, 20 x 16 In. 1170.00
Charger, 6 Panels, Multicolored, 15 1/2 In. 460.00
Charger, Bamboo, Pine, Prunus, Brocades, Shishi, Peonies, Japan, Late 1800s, 18 In. 235.00
Charger, Bird, Flower, Brocade, Japan, Late 19th Century, 18 1/2 In. 500.00
Charger, Birds, Landscapes, Red Ground, 1850-90, 2 3/4 x 15 5/8 In. 410.00
Charger, Birds, Trees, Multicolored, Early 1900s, 18 In. 590.00
Charger, Brocade, Flower Lotus Petals, Panels, Center Phoenix Medallion, 12 3/4 In. 140.00
Charger, Carp, Relief, Waves, Japan, 19th Century, 18 1/2 In. 1175.00
Charger, Central Medallion, Pagoda, Birds, Flowers, Flying Crane, 19 In. 920.00
Charger, Chrysanthemums, Tree, Bird, Flowers, 1800s, 15 3/4 In. 645.00
Charger, Dragon & Banner Center, 3 Friends Border, Japan, 1800s, 15 1/2 In. 460.00
Charger, Dragon, Palace Lions, Lotus Blossoms, 1800s, 13 1/2 In. 720.00
Charger, Fans, Multicolored, Japan, 1800s, 18 In. 765.00
Charger, Flower Basket, Passion Flower Border, Japan, Late 1700s, 17 1/4 In. 1090.00
Charger, Flower Reserves, Leaf Edge, Brocade Borders, 17 In. 295.00
Charger, Flower Shape, Bird, Flower, Japan, Late 19th Century, 12 1/2 In. 185.00
Charger, Flower Shape, Juemrous Bat, Chrysanthemum Center, Japan, Late 1800s, 16 In. 460.00
Charger, Flowers, Landscape, Peony, Wisteria Bonsai, Late 1800s, 22 In. 645.00
Charger, Geometrics, Blue, White, 18 1/2 In. 145.00
Charger, Medallion, Stylized Flower, Shaped Cartouches, Leaf, Vine, 3 x 21 3/4 In. 805.00
Charger, Peonies, Shishi Over Waves Cartouches, Leaves, Green, Lavender, 1 1/2 x 12 1/2 In. 460.00
Charger, Ribbed, 3 Central Flowers, Flower Ground, 1 7/8 x 12 In. 400.00
Charger, Scalloped Rim, Reticulated Cavetto, Flowers, Japan, 18 1/4 In., Pair 1060.00
Charger, Swirling Brocade, Center Flower Roundel, Japan, 1800s, 14 3/4 In. 880.00
Charger, Underglaze Blue, Multicolored Enamels, Gilt, Floral Panels, Ground, 24 In. 2230.00
Coffeepot, Dome Cover, Hinged, Silver Mounted, Early 1700s, 9 1/4 In. 1200.00
Dish, 3 Friends, Cranes, Karako, Rectangular, Japan, Late 19th Century, 7 1/4 In., Pair 100.00
Dish, Fish, Nesting, Japan, 18 1/2 & 16 1/2 In. 200.00
Dish, Kirin, Cherry Tree, Rectangular, Japan, 1800s, 10 x 8 In. 185.00
Dish, Shrimp, Boat Shape, 13 In. 460.00
Dish Set, 3 Friends, Flower Border, Karakusa Exterior, Blue, White, c.1850, 7 In., 8 Piece 1150.00
Ginger Jar, Finial Cover, 6 In. .... 145.00 to 230.00
Jar, 8-Sided, Peony, Fruit Tree, Figural & Iris Band, Japan, Early 1700s, 22 In. 3220.00
Jar, Cover, Animals, Birds, Flowers, Blue Ground, Gilt Accents, Japan, 18th Century, 17 1/2 In. 705.00

Jar, Cover, Dragon, Brocade Bands, 19th Century, 18 1/2 In. 705.00
Jar, Cover, Phoenix, Late 19th Century, 8 1/2 x 6 1/2 In., Pair .... *ILLUS* 1495.00
Jardiniere, Flowers, Geometrics, Winged Horses, Clouds, 3 Scalloped Feet, 15 x 21 In. 1175.00
Jug, Inverted Pear Shape, Melon Ribbed Body, Dome Cover, Lion Finial, 1800s, 27 In., Pair 4315.00
Planter, Tapered, Potted Flowers, Birds, 11 1/2 x 15 In. 1208.00
Plate, Fish, Cobalt Blue, Iron Red, Green Highlights, Late 19th Century, 9 1/4 x 7 1/2 In. .... *ILLUS* 1265.00
Plate, Hunting Scene, Chinese, 17th Century, 8 3/4 In. 413.00
Plate, Painted, Blue Flowers, Chinese, 18th Century, 9 1/4 In., Pair 350.00
Plate Set, Birds, Flowers, 9 In., 6 Piece 390.00
Plate Set, Flowers, Scalloped Edge, 9 5/8 In., 6 Piece 269.00
Plate Set, Shishi, Birds, Flowers, Japan, Late 19th Century, 9 In., 6 Piece 445.00
Platter, 8-Sided, Gilt Chrysanthemum, Flowers, 15 1/4 x 11 1/4 In. 440.00
Platter, Meat, Footed, Blue, Orange, Gold, Green, 20 1/2 x 17 In. 1250.00
Platter, Multicolored, Ring Decorated Border, Oval, Japan, 11 1/2 x 13 3/4 In. 259.00
Sake Bottle, 3 Chinese Characters, 1800s, 11 In. 118.00
Sake Bottle, Birds, Flowers, Square Shape, 1700s, 9 1/2 In. 1410.00
Sake Bottle, Enameled Leafy Vines, Kiyomizu Ware, 1800s, 9 1/4 In. 529.00
Sake Bottle, Flowers, Floating In Stream, Kakiemon Decoration, Japan, 1800s, 6 1/2 In. 410.00
Sake Bottle, Gourd Shape, Leaves, Kakiemon Style Design, 1700s, 8 3/4 In. 1530.00
Sake Bottle, Hotei & Bag Of Wealth Shape, 1700s, 8 In. 880.00
Serving Bowl, Oval, 11 x 7 1/2 In. 460.00
Serving Dish, Bird, Garden, Flower Border, Rectangular, Late 1800s, 11 1/2 x 13 1/4 In. 489.00
Serving Dish, Cover, 8 In. 400.00
Serving Dish, Lobed, 10 In. 85.00
Temple Jar, Cover, 6-Sided, Polychrome, Japan, 15 In. 805.00
Tray, Multicolored, Flowers, Bow Handles, Japan, 16 In. 350.00
Tureen, Flowers, Rocks, Green, Blue, Yellow, Red, Gold, Japan, 1700s, 12 1/2 In. 6600.00
Vase, Baluster Shape, Geisha Under Cherry Trees, Birds, 18 5/8 In., Pair 3645.00
Vase, Brocade Pattern, Globular, Slender Neck, 19th Century, 10 In. 205.00
Vase, Cover, Baluster, Japan, c.1700, 24 3/4 In., Pair 17425.00
Vase, Egg Shape, Cylindrical Neck, Maple Leaf, Flowers, Ho Birds, c.1850, 17 1/2 In., Pair 1955.00
Vase, Flowers, Leaves, Japan, 1800s, 9 3/4 In., Pair 825.00
Vase, Hand Painted Designs, 7 1/2 In., Pair 105.00
Vase, Hand Painted, Mounted As Lamp, Japan, 20th Century, 15 In. 118.00
Vase, Ho Bird, Urn, Maple, Chrysanthemum, c.1860, 24 1/2 In., Pair 3450.00
Vase, Molded Flower Sprig, Multicolored, Hexagonal, Japan, 1800s, 7 In., Pair 205.00
Vase, Square, Embossed Geisha, 9 In. 345.00
Vase, Trumpet Mouth, Dragon, Flower Ground, Late 1800s, 18 1/2 In. 315.00
Vase, Trumpet Shape, Melon Ribbing, Lions, Peonies, Japan, Early 1800s, 14 In, Pair 1840.00

IMPERIAL GLASS Corporation was founded in Bellaire, Ohio, in 1901. It became a subsidiary of Lenox, Inc., in 1973 and was sold to Arthur R. Lorch in 1981. It was sold again in 1982, and went bankrupt in 1984. In 1985, the molds and some assets were sold. The Imperial glass preferred by the collector is freehand art glass, carnival glass, slag glass, stretch glass, and other top-quality tablewares. Tablewares and animals are listed here. The others may be found in the appropriate sections.

IMPE RIAL

Art Glass, Vase, Blue Iridescent, Green, Highlights, Flared Lip, 11 1/2 In. 288.00
Art Glass, Vase, Heart & Vine, Trifold Loop Handles, Cobalt Blue, Footed, 11 In. 1260.00
Art Glass, Vase, Orange Iridescent, Blue Pulled Feathers, Flared & Flattened Rim, 9 In. 920.00
Art Glass, Vase, White Ground, Blue Decoration, 7 1/4 In. 315.00
Beaded Block, Rose Bowl, Blue Opalescent, 4 1/2 In. 119.00
Beaded Block, Vase, Footed, Blue, 5 1/4 In. 45.00
Candlewick, Ashtray, Extended Cigarette Rest, 4 7/8 In. 10.00
Candlewick, Bowl, Flared, 10 1/2 In. 60.00
Candlewick, Bowl, Handles, 8 1/2 In. 35.00
Candlewick, Candlestick, 3 1/2 In. 20.00
Candlewick, Cocktail, 4-Bead Stem, 4 Oz. 17.00
Candlewick, Creamer 8.00
Candlewick, Dish, Baked Apple, Blue, 6 1/2 In. 150.00

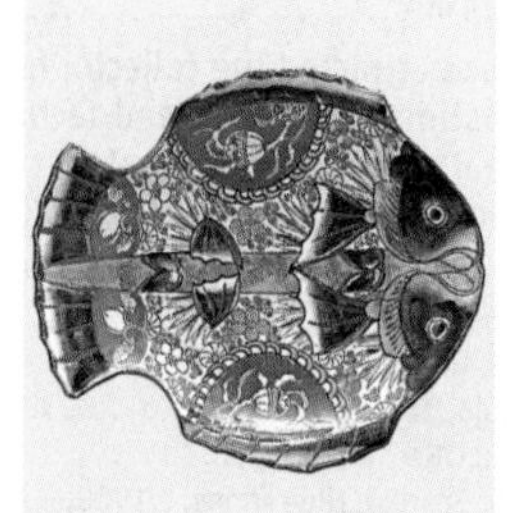

Imari, Plate, Fish, Cobalt Blue, Iron Red, Green Highlights, Late 19th Century, 9 1/4 x 7 1/2 In.

Imperial, Vase, Art Glass, Lead Luster, Marigold, Green Trailing, 5 3/4 In.

Candlewick, Dish, Mayonnaise, Underplate 50.00
Candlewick, Egg Plate, Heart-Shaped Center Handle, 11 1/2 In. .... 83.00 to 150.00
Candlewick, Goblet, Ritz Blue, Clear 2-Bead Stem, 9 Oz. 225.00
Candlewick, Goblet, Ruby, Clear 2-Bead Stem, 9 Oz. 145.00
Candlewick, Hurricane Lamp, 10 1/4 In. 135.00
Candlewick, Plate, Dinner, 10 In. 45.00
Candlewick, Plate, Salad, 8 In. 20.00
Candlewick, Relish, 4 Sections, 4 Handles, Round, 8 1/2 In. 35.00
Candlewick, Relish, 5 Sections, Round, 13 In. 110.00
Candlewick, Relish, Sections, 6 1/2 In. 15.00
Candlewick, Salt & Pepper 25.00
Candlewick, Tumbler, 10 Oz., 4 3/4 In. .... 12.00 to 19.00
Candlewick, Tumbler, Iced Tea, Footed, 12 Oz., 6 1/4 In. .... 20.00 to 28.00
Candlewick, Tumbler, Juice, Footed, 5 Oz., 4 1/4 In. 18.00
Cape Cod, Cake Plate, 4-Footed, Square, 10 In. 90.00
Cape Cod, Candlestick, 4 In., Pair 55.00
Cape Cod, Candy Dish, Cover, Square Pedestal Base, 10 x 6 In. 85.00
Cape Cod, Dish, Pickle, 7 In. 15.00
Cape Cod, Jam Jar, Cover, Underplate 40.00
Cape Cod, Parfait, 5 3/4 In. 8.00
Cape Cod, Pitcher, Ice Lip, 4 Oz., 5 3/4 In. 55.00
Cape Cod, Relish, 3 Sections, 9 1/4 x 8 1/2 In. 25.00
Cape Cod, Salt & Pepper, Yellow 45.00
Cape Cod, Sugar & Creamer 30.00
Cape Cod, Torte Plate, 14 1/2 In. 50.00
Cape Cod, Tumbler, Juice, Footed, 5 Oz., 5 1/4 In. 8.00
Cape Cod, Tumbler, Whiskey, 2 Oz. 15.00
Cut Glass, Vase, Blue Iridescent, Rolled Rim, 11 In. 200.00
Cut Glass, Vase, Cylindrical, Orange Iridescent, Blue Draped Loops, 10 In. 345.00
Cut Glass, Vase, Royal Blue Ground, Opal Heart, Vine, Marigold, 10 1/4 In. 1150.00
Grape, Bowl, Milk Glass, Crimped Edge, 9 In. 34.00
Grape, Pitcher, Milk, Milk Glass, 11 In. 50.00
Grape, Tumbler, Iced Tea, Milk Glass, 6 In. 25.00
Grape, Vase, Milk Glass, Flared, Footed, 10 In. 20.00
Lace Edge, Candlestick, Domed Foot, 4 1/2 In. 25.00
Lariat, Bowl, Loop & Leaf Cover, Caramel Slag, 4 1/2 x 7 1/4 In. 75.00
Molly, Sandwich Server, Octagonal, Handles, 12 1/2 In. 45.00
Nu-Cut, Compote, Milk Glass, 7 1/2 x 6 In. 45.00
Nu-Cut, Creamer 25.00
Nu-Cut, Sugar 25.00
Old Williamsburg, Sherbet, Azalea, 4 3/4 In. 15.00
Old Williamsburg, Wine, Azalea, 3 1/2 Oz., 5 1/4 In. 17.00
Paperweight, Tiger, Black, 2 3/4 x 8 In. 175.00
Pillar Flute, Bowl, Blue Glo, Flared, 10 1/4 In. 40.00
Pillar Flute, Sugar & Creamer, Blue Glo 50.00
Twisted Optic, Pitcher, Mulberry, 76 Oz. 75.00
Vase, Art Glass, Lead Luster, Marigold, Green Trailing, 5 3/4 In. .... *ILLUS* 115.00

Windmill, Bowl, Footed, Marigold, 8 3/4 In. . . . 80.00

INDIAN art from North America has attracted the collector for many years. Each tribe has its own distinctive designs and techniques. Baskets, jewelry, pottery, and leatherwork are of greatest collector interest. Eskimo art is listed in another category in this book.

Awl Case, Lakota, Rawhide, Multicolored Bands, Beaded Drops, Tin Cone Danglers, 13 In. . . . 200.00
Awl Case, Sioux, Beaded, Tapered, Drops, Thongs, 1930s, 11 In. . . . 345.00
Bag, Apache, Strike-A-Lite, Cone Drops, Dangles, 1880s, 10 In. . . . 1925.00
Bag, Blackfoot, Tobacco, Beaded, Buffalo, 1880s, 39 1/2 In. . . . 1760.00
Bag, Charm, Great Lakes, Wool, Beaded Otter Tail, 6 1/2 In. . . . 1765.00
Bag, Cheyenne, Bandolier, Geometrics, Beaded, Hide Fringe, c.1900, 8 x 14 In. . . . 1840.00
Bag, Crow, Tobacco, Beaded, Fringe, 1880s, 25 In. . . . 3850.00
Bag, Iroquois, Flap, Niagara Style, Beaded Flowers, Early 1900s, 6 x 6 1/2 In. . . . 160.00
Bag, Kiowa, Strike-A-Lite, Long Fringe, 1870s, 19 In. . . . 2420.00
Bag, Menominee, Bandolier, Abstract Flowers, Beaded Tabs, Wool Tassels, 40 In. . . . 2468.00
Bag, Nez Perce, Beaded, Elk, Flowers, Leaves, c.1900, 11 x 13 In. . . . 748.00
Bag, Nez Perce, Cornhusk, 8-Point Stars, 9 3/4 x 9 3/4 In. . . . 275.00
Bag, Nez Perce, Cornhusk, Applied Fabric, 10 3/4 x 9 1/2 In. . . . 545.00
Bag, Nez Perce, Cornhusk, Geometrics, c.1900, 11 x 9 In. . . . 315.00
Bag, Nez Perce, Cornhusk, Jute, Red & Black Zigzags, c.1920, 14 1/2 x 8 In. . . . 315.00
Bag, Nez Perce, Cornhusk, Pine Trees, Flowers, Arrowheads, c.1860, 11 x 11 In. . . . 805.00
Bag, Nez Perce, Cornhusk, Polychrome, Flat, c.1900, 14 x 17 In. . . . 920.00
Bag, Nez Perce, Cornhusk, Triangles, 9 1/2 x 9 In. . . . 550.00
Bag, Nez Perce, Cornhusk, Woven, Geometrics, c.1940, 18 x 13 In. . . . 375.00
Bag, Northern Plains, Beaded, Geometrics, Lavender Ground, 10 x 17 In. . . . 3450.00
Bag, Northern Plains, Beaded, Thread Sewn, Flat, Flowers, 8 x 8 1/2 In. . . . 290.00
Bag, Northern Plains, Scalloped Edge, Fringe, Elk Tooth Button, Beads, 1900s, 5 1/2 x 6 1/4 In. . . 288.00
Bag, Ojibwa, Bandolier, Cloth, Beaded Flowers, White Ground, Bead & Yarn Danglers, 47 In. . . . 1763.00
Bag, Ojibwa, Bandolier, Cloth, Beaded Geometric Designs, Red Tassels, 35 In. . . . 2703.00
Bag, Plains, Slat, Quilled, White Buckskin, Beaded Handle, 8 1/2 x 9 In. . . . 489.00
Bag, Plateau, Beaded, Eagle Feeding Nest, Fringe, 14 x 13 In. . . . 690.00
Bag, Plateau, Beaded, Flat, Rose, Blue Ground, Hide Covered, 8 1/2 x 9 1/2 In. . . . 160.00
Bag, Plateau, Elk Hide, Beaded Panel, Drawstring, Long Fringe, c.1950, 14 x 6 In. . . . 430.00
Bag, Plateau, Fully Beaded, Flower, Sinew Sewn, Early 1900s, 10 x 8 In. . . . 259.00
Bag, Plateau, Fully Beaded, Flowers, Geometrics, Early 1900s, 9 1/2 x 8 In. . . . 489.00
Bag, Potawatomi, Bandolier, Great Lakes, 1880s, 39 1/2 In. . . . 3575.00
Bag, Sioux, Buckskin, Sinew Sewn, Lazy Stitch, Beaded, Drawstring Holes, Fringe, 7 x 4 In. . . . 230.00
Bag, Sioux, Doctor's, Buckskin, Sinew Sewn, Lazy Stitch, Early 1900s, 8 x 11 x 6 In. . . . 2300.00
Bag, Ute, Strike-A-Lite, Harness Leather, Beaded, 1890s, 6 In. . . . 580.00
Bag, Ute, Tobacco, Beaded, Flap, Fringe, 19 In. . . . 4675.00
Bag, Wasco, Bandolier, Octopus, Skeletal Figures, Pony Beads, c.1850, 39 x 7 1/2 In. . . . 11500.00
Bag, Winnebago, Bandolier, Loom Beaded, Tassels, Trade Beads, Stroud, Muslin, 36 x 15 1/2 In. . 4025.00
Bag, Yakima, Beaded Flap, Elk, Poppies, c.1920, 14 x 14 In. . . . 635.00
Bag, Zuni, Suede, Seed Beads . . . 415.00
Bandolier, Menominee, Beaded, Flowers, Blue Ground, Tassels, 1875-1900, 40 In. . . . *ILLUS* 2468.00
Bandolier, Ojibwa, Beaded, Geometrics, Flowers, Late 19th Century, 35 In. . . . *ILLUS* 2703.00
Basket, Algonquin, Wall, Hanging, Porcupine Fancy Weaving, Hanging Bell . . . 259.00
Basket, Apache, Coiled, Geometrics, 13 1/2 In. . . . 468.00
Basket, Apache, Human Figures, Crosses, Wide Mouth, Early 1900s, 8 1/2 x 13 In. . . . 2070.00
Basket, Attu, Openwork Roped Edge, Applied Decorations, Early 1900s, 9 x 10 In. . . . 518.00
Basket, Cherokee, Coil, Laced Edge, Triangles, c.1870-80, 11 1/4 In. . . . 275.00
Basket, Cherokee, River Cane, Bentwood Handle, 1920s, 7 1/2 x 6 1/2 In. . . . 405.00
Basket, Cherokee, River Cane, Bentwood Handles, Hinges, 12 x 11 x 6 In. . . . 260.00
Basket, Cherokee, River Cane, Double Diamond Band, 11 1/2 x 12 x 7 1/4 In. . . . 750.00
Basket, Cherokee, River Cane, Double Woven, Bentwood Oak Handle, 14 x 12 x 7 In. . . . 3910.00
Basket, Cherokee, River Cane, Double Woven, Brown, Geometrics, 6 x 8 1/2 x 8 1/2 In. . . . 403.00
Basket, Cherokee, River Cane, Double Woven, Cylindrical, Flared Rim, 16 x 11 3/4 In. . . . 1093.00
Basket, Cherokee, River Cane, Double Woven, Square To Round, 13 x 11 In. . . . 1840.00
Basket, Cherokee, River Cane, Double Woven, Square To Round, Butternut, Bloodroot, 10 x 9 In. . . 920.00
Basket, Cherokee, River Cane, Double Woven, Square To Round, Flared Rim, 13 x 13 In. . . . 1035.00

Indian, Bandolier, Menominee, Beaded, Flowers, Blue Ground, Tassels, 1875-1900, 40 In.

Indian, Bandolier, Ojibwa, Beaded, Geometrics, Flowers, Late 19th Century, 35 In.

Basket, Cherokee, River Cane, Double Woven, Square To Round, Flared Rim, 14 x 13 3/4 In. 2185.00
Basket, Cherokee, River Cane, Double Woven, Tapered, Flared Rim, 14 x 10 1/4 x 9 In. 3910.00
Basket, Cherokee, River Cane, Double Wrapped, Oak Split Rim, 12 1/2 x 12 1/2 In. 460.00
Basket, Cherokee, River Cane, Lid, Double Woven Bands, Geometrics, Brown, Orange, 10 x 9 In. .. 1955.00
Basket, Cherokee, River Cane, Notched Bentwood, Oak Handle, 1930s, 11 x 9 In. 375.00
Basket, Cherokee, River Cane, Shopping, Hinges, Bentwood Handles, 13 1/2 x 11 x 8 In. 230.00
Basket, Cherokee, River Cane, Shopping, Wood Handles, Hinges, Split Rim, Leather, 15 x 14 In. .. 175.00
Basket, Cherokee, Storage, Cane, Soft Dyed, Interlocking Diamond, 19 x 17 In. 920.00
Basket, Chitimacha, Cane, Diamond, Circular Medallions, Black, Red Interior, 2 3/4 x 9 In. 550.00
Basket, Chitimacha, Cane, Double Woven, Geometrics, Squares In Squares, 4 3/4 x 4 3/4 In. 180.00
Basket, Chitimacha, Cane, Orange, Brown Bands, Stylized Star Center, 1 1/2 x 5 1/2 In. 259.00
Basket, Chitimacha, Cane, Square To Round, 5 x 9 3/4 In. 259.00
Basket, Chitimacha, Cane, Yellow, Black, Red Geometric Bands, 3 1/2 x 5 1/2 In. 801.00
Basket, Chitimacha, Cover, Swamp Cane, Double Woven, Geometrics, 6 1/2 x 6 1/2 In. 2530.00
Basket, Chitimacha, Double Woven, c.1910, 6 1/2 x 5 1/2 In. 2115.00
Basket, Chitimacha, Flying Geese, Natural, Red, Black, Yellow, 5 1/2 x 9 1/2 x 9 1/4 In. 720.00
Basket, Chitimacha, River Cane, Black, Red Interior Bands, 1 3/4 x 6 7/8 In. 230.00
Basket, Chitimacha, River Cane, Cover, Double Woven, 3 1/4 x 1 1/2 x 1 1/2 In. 259.00
Basket, Chitimacha, River Cane, Double Woven, Square To Round, 3 x 3 3/4 In. 35.00
Basket, Chitimacha, River Cane, Geometrics, Black, Red, 2 x 7 3/4 In. 315.00
Basket, Chitimacha, River Cane, Multicolored, Square To Round, 5 1/2 x 12 1/2 In. 1265.00
Basket, Chitimacha, River Cane, Red, Yellow, Black Geometric Bands, 1 1/4 x 3 3/4 In., Pair 805.00
Basket, Chitimacha, River Cane, Wrapped Rim, Interior Bands, Medallion, 2 1/2 x 9 3/4 In. 200.00
Basket, Chitimacha, Trinket, Double Woven, Blackbird's Eye, 4 x 2 1/4 x 2 1/4 In. 350.00
Basket, Choctaw, Cane, Square Base, Wrapped Rim, Flared, 17 1/2 x 21 In. 259.00
Basket, Choctaw, Cover, Handle, Palmetto Stem, Natural Dye, c.1900, 17 1/2 x 12 x 11 In. 1880.00
Basket, Choctaw, River Cane, Flower, Wrapped Handles, Rim, Foot Ring, 15 1/2 x 23 x 19 In. 259.00
Basket, Choctaw, Utility, Split Cane, Geometrics, 6 1/2 x 13 1/2 In. 2350.00
Basket, Coiled, Geometrics, Oval, 7 1/2 x 5 1/2 In. 374.00
Basket, Coiled, Geometrics, Round, 8 1/2 x 5 In. 290.00
Basket, Coiled, Shallow Bowl, Geometrics, 10 1/2 In. 190.00
Basket, Coushatta, River Cane, Square To Round, Double Wrapped Rim, Handle, 8 x 8 In. 489.00
Basket, Cover, Boot Shape, Figures, Geometrics, c.1960, 9 x 11 x 7 In. 345.00
Basket, Cover, Oval, Hinge, Braided Oak Handle, 14 1/2 x 19 x 14 In. 315.00
Basket, Cowlitz, Hard Sided, Imbricated, Geometrics, c.1900, 6 1/2 x 7 1/4 In. 1150.00
Basket, Great Lakes, Cover, Storage, Angled Middle Divider, Shoulder, c.1800, 6 1/2 In. 185.00
Basket, Hinged Cover, Sweet Grass, Round, 5 1/2 In. 65.00
Basket, Hopi, Coiled, Zigzags, 1940s, 7 1/4 x 8 1/4 In. 316.00
Basket, Hupa, Cover, Fine Weave, Geometrics, Top Knot Handle, c.1910, 10 x 9 1/2 In. 2300.00
Basket, Hupa, Rhomboid Designs, Early 1900s, 5 x 7 1/4 In. 633.00
Basket, Iroquois, Cover, Birch Bark, Quilled Flowers, 1900s, 6 1/2 x 10 In. 178.00
Basket, Klickitat, 2 Zigzag Bands, Rim Loops, c.1930, 13 1/2 x 12 1/4 In. 2300.00
Basket, Lilooet, Geometrics, Early 1900s, 14 3/4 x 13 1/4 x 16 In. 1150.00
Basket, Mission, 4 Human Figures, Holding Hands, c.1900, 3 x 5 In. 635.00
Basket, Navajo, Red, Black Sheep, Human, Geometric Figures, c.1980, 24 In. 518.00
Basket, Navajo, Wedding, 1900s, 9 1/4 x 1 1/2 In. 115.00
Basket, Nez Perce, Cornhusk, Overlaid Geometric Fabric, Straight-Sided, 7 x 9 1/4 In. 690.00

Basket, Nootka, Cover, Star, Wave, Polychrome, c.1910, 4 In. 130.00
Basket, Nootka, Cover, Whaler, Bird, c.1910, 2 x 4 In. 259.00
Basket, Nootka, Makah, Bottle, Cover, Basketry, Whale, Bird, Whalers On Boat, 1900s, 8 1/2 In. 315.00
Basket, Northern California, Chevron & Quail Feather Pattern, Cone Shape, 13 In. 1116.00
Basket, Paiute, Beaded, Single Rod, Arrow, Flower, Diamond, 1930s, 3 1/4 x 5 1/2 In. 690.00
Basket, Paiute, Bottle, Twined, 2 Geometric Bands, Tapered, 2 Fiber Lug Handles, 22 x 15 In. 2350.00
Basket, Panamint, Flared, Bowl, Eagles, Owls, Early 1900s, 3 x 2 In. 1610.00
Basket, Papago, Cover, Wheat Stitch, c.1970, 8 x 10 x 13 In. 150.00
Basket, Papago, Handles, Multicolored Serpent, c.1970, 6 x 12 x 16 In. 138.00
Basket, Papago, Multicolored, Saguaro Cactus, Birds, c.1970, 13 1/2 x 12 1/2 In. 430.00
Basket, Passamaquoddy, Woven Split Ash, Bentwood Handles, 9 1/2 x 9 1/2 In. 175.00
Basket, Pima, Bowl, Round, Willow & Devil's Claw Design, Early 1900s, 3 3/4 x 14 In. 590.00
Basket, Pima, Coiled, Braided Rim, Bands, Stepped Geometrics, 3 3/4 x 14 1/2 In. 805.00
Basket, Pima, Figures, Dogs, In Martynia, Willow, Woven, 2 1/4 x 5 In. 115.00
Basket, Pima, Flying Geese, c.1900, 5 x 9 In. 138.00
Basket, Pocket, Hanging Tear Drop, Hemlock, Pinecone Decoration, 8 1/2 In. 230.00
Basket, Pomo, Lightning Design, c.1900, 4 In. 345.00
Basket, Pomo, Topknot Chevron Designs, Ealruy 1900s, 3 x 5 In. 1840.00
Basket, Salishan, Cover, Geometrics, Pedestal Base, c.1900, 8 x 11 x 11 In. 1093.00
Basket, Seneca, Woodlands, Cover, Carrying, Handle, Red Band, 1900s, 21 x 18 In. 127.00
Basket, Skokomish, Storage, Dogs Encircling Rim, c.1900, 13 x 13 In. 3450.00
Basket, Southwest, Coiled, Tumbling Logs, 4 7/8 x 9 3/4 In. 200.00
Basket, Tlingit, Bottle, Cover, Multicolored Geometric Bands, Brown Ground, 10 In. 999.00
Basket, Tlingit, Bottle, Cover, Twined, Woven, Fret & Chevron Bands, 12 1/2 In. 470.00
Basket, Woodland, Splint, Woven, Round Over Square, Red Circle, Green Sprig, 6 x 13 In. 295.00
Basket, Woodland, Splint, Yellow, Green, Salmon, Black, Cover, Late 1800s, 15 x 11 In. 2450.00
Basket, Woven, Cover, Glass Ball Finial, 6 3/4 In. 430.00
Basket, Yokuts, Diamond Bands, 4 1/2 x 9 1/8 In. 2750.00
Bell, Navajo, Silver, Turquoise Cabochon, Stamped, 2 3/4 In. 219.00
Belt, Chain, 14 Conchas, Sterling Silver, Signed, L.L., Wriggling Snake 770.00
Belt, Comanche, 9 Conchas, Harness Leather, Green Rattlesnake Skin, 19th Century, 39 x 2 1/2 In. 1095.00
Belt, Crow, Beaded Panels, Brass Tacks, Harness Buckle, c.1900, 44 In. 880.00
Belt, Navajo, 12 Conchas, Buckle, Leather, c.1940 1295.00
Belt, Navajo, Conchas, Butterflies, c.1935 2750.00
Belt, Navajo, Link Conchas, Stamp Work, Green Turquoise, c.1935 595.00
Belt, Navajo, Silver, 6 Conchas, Winged Buckle, 20th Century, 4 1/2 In. ***ILLUS*** 881.00
Belt Buckle, Navajo, Silver, Turquoise Stones, Carved Bone Ram, c.1970, 3 x 4 In. 259.00
Blanket, Chimayo, Stylized Medallions, Red Ground, Fringe, 75 1/2 x 51 In. 2100.00
Blanket, Navajo, Double Saddle, Serrated Bands, Red, Gray, Corner Fringe, 55 x 45 In. 460.00
Blanket, Navajo, Eye Dazzler, Triangles, Orange, Red, Black, Tan, Fret Border, 29 x 36 In. 750.00
Blanket, Navajo, Friendship Sign, Gray, Red, 84 x 52 In. 345.00
Blanket, Navajo, Saddle, Red, Floating Diamonds, Fret Border, Black Fringe, 29 x 32 In. 5875.00
Blanket, Navajo, Woven, Zigzag Lines, Straight Bands, Transitional, Child's, 51 x 30 In. 9600.00
Bolo, Zuni, Horse, Inlay, c.1955, 1 1/2 x 1 5/8 In. 295.00
Bolo, Zuni, Raised Channel Inlay, Matching Tips, c.1940, 2 7/8 In. 1595.00
Bolo, Zuni, Stick Indian Figure, Full Headdress, c.1945, 2 1/8 In. 495.00
Bow, Apache, Quiver, 6 Arrows, 19th Century, 42-In. Bow 944.00
Bow, Cheyenne, Hardwood, Patina, Wyoming, 19th Century, 44 In. 345.00
Bow, Plains, Sinew Wrapped, 1870s, 42 In. 688.00
Bow & Arrows, Apache, 3 Arrows, 1922, 24 & 17 In. 316.00
Bowl, Acoma, Pottery, Incised, Black, White Scroll, Step Motif, 1900s, 7 1/2 x 9 In. 184.00
Bowl, Anasazi, Pottery, Black On White, Interior Designs, Prehistoric, 8 1/2 x 4 In. 259.00
Bowl, Anasazi, Pottery, Black On White, Puerco, Interior Geometrics, 8 x 3 In. 345.00
Bowl, Anasazi, Pottery, Multicolored, Interior, Exterior Designs, 6 1/2 x 3 In. 259.00
Bowl, Apache, Basket, Coiled, Multicolored 7-Petal Flower, Dogs, 2 1/2 x 11 In. 940.00
Bowl, Apache, Basket, Coiled, Row Of Figures, Dogs, Geometrics, 6 x 7 3/4 In. 11740.00
Bowl, Hopi, Disk Shape, Multicolored Bird, Geometrics, S. Yessuth, 5 x 10 1/2 In. 431.00
Bowl, Hopi, Pottery, Stylized Bird, Black On Buff, Early 1900s, 3 x 9 1/2 In. 374.00
Bowl, Hupa, Basket, Acorn Shape, Geometrics, c.1930, 8 x 12 In. 341.00
Bowl, Northwest Coast, Wood, Carved, Seal Shape, Incised Features, Brass Eyes, 19 In. 705.00
Bowl, Pima, Basket, Slanted Sides, Geometrics, Martynia, Willow Ground, 7 1/2 x 3 7/8 In. 518.00

Bowl, Pima, Coiled, Geometrics, Flaring, Willow, Devil's Claw, 16 In. 2040.00
Bowl, Pima, Coiled, Willow, Devil's Claw, Whirling Devices, 7 3/4 In. 480.00
Bowl, Pomo, Basket, Coiled, Flared, Shells, Beaded Danglers, 4 x 10 In. 6463.00
Bowl, Pomo, Basket, Stepped Diagonal Devices, Oval, Flat Bottom, 2 1/2 x 7 In. 705.00
Bowl, San Ildefonso, Black, Serpent Design, Round, 8 In. 450.00
Bowl, San Ildefonso, Blackware, Bulbous, Tapered Neck, Feather Devices, 4 In. 588.00
Bowl, San Ildefonso, Blackware, Polished, Bulbous, Maria Poveka, 3 x 3 3/4 In. 881.00
Bowl, San Luis, Pottery, Multicolored Flowers, c.1920, 8 x 12 In. 69.00
Bowl, Santa Clara, Blackware, Carved Avanu Pattern, Betty Naranjo, 5 x 5 1/2 In. 353.00
Bowl, Santa Clara, Blackware, Signed, Peggy Tafoya, 2 3/4 x 4 In. 110.00
Bowl, Santa Clara, Redware, Incised Decoration, Margaret Tafoya, 4 1/2 x 5 1/2 In. 550.00
Bowl, Southwest, Basket, 8-Point Star, Stepped Devices, Braided Rim, Flared, 15 In. 1645.00
Bowl, Southwest, Coil, Textured Base, Birds, Yucca, Corn, 7 1/2 x 16 1/2 In. 805.00
Bowl, Tlingit, Basket, Twined, Diamonds, Crosses, Zigzags, Flat Bottom, 5 x 6 1/2 In. 881.00
Bowl, Yokuts, Basket, Band Of Humans Holding Hands, Rattlesnake Design, 7 x 17 In. 14100.00
Bowl, Yokuts, Basket, Coiled, 2 Bands Of Rattlesnake Pattern, Flared, 10 1/2 x 21 In. 5581.00
Bowl, Zuni, Pottery, Bird, Flowers, 1900s, 5 x 14 In. 207.00
Box, Navajo, Sterling Silver, Cover, Stamped, 1 1/2 x 3 x 5 In. 316.00
Bracelet, Cuff, Silver, Turquoise, Pierced Design, 3 Turquoise Stones, Signed, Lomay 303.00
Bracelet, Eagle, Cuff, Turquoise, Signed Black Goat 460.00
Bracelet, Hopi, Silver, Inlaid Mudhead Kachina, Coral, Turquoise, Shell, Jet, Tortoise, 6 x 2 In. 288.00
Bracelet, Navajo, 5 Oval Turquoise Cabochons, Hand Stamped Arrows, 5 5/8 In. 259.00
Bracelet, Navajo, Hand Wrought Silver, Turquoise Cluster, 7 x 1 3/4 x 2 In. 127.00
Bracelet, Navajo, Silver, 7 Spider Webs, Turquoise Cabochons, c.1950, 4 1/2 In. 690.00
Bracelet, Navajo, Square Turquoise Cabochons, 2 Wire Spun Bands, 1930s, 6 1/4 In. 259.00
Bracelet, Navajo, Turquoise, Silver, Signed, Kayo 502.00
Bracelet, Zuni, Cuff, Stone-To-Stone, Rain Dancer 460.00
Bracelet, Zuni, Petit Point Turquoise Stones, 3 Silver Bands, c.1950, 5 1/2 In. 259.00
Bracelet, Zuni, Stone-To-Stone Butterfly, Jet, Oyster, Twist Wire, c.1940, 5 1/2 x 1 3/4 In. 403.00
Breastplate, Crow, Hair-Pipe Bone, Beaded, Ribbon, Fringe, c.1950, 11 x 11 In. 173.00
Breastplate, Sioux, Hair-Pipe Bone, Brass Beads, c.1930, 11 1/2 x 14 In. 1035.00
Bridle, Navajo, Silver, Naja, Iron, c.1900, 10 x 20 In. 2185.00
Buckle, Hopi, Bird, Overlay, Silver, c.1960, 2 x 1 3/8 In. 495.00
Buckle, Hopi, Overlay, Sterling Silver, Priest Praying For Rain, 3 3/4 x 2 1/2 In. 150.00
Buckle, Laguna, Spider Web Turquoise, Coral, Ironwood, Mid 1900s, 2 x 3 In. 259.00
Buckle, Navajo, Ingot Silver, Scalloped Design, Round, c.1930, 3 In. 495.00
Buckle, Navajo, Silver, Oxblood Coral, 2 Keepers, Hand Stamped, 2 1/2 x 6 In. 230.00
Buckle, Navajo, Sterling Silver, Thunderbird Overlay, c.1930, 2 x 3 In. 403.00
Buckle, Zuni, Stone-To-Stone, Jet, Shell, Spiny Oyster, c.1940, 2 3/4 In. 316.00
Canoe, Iroquois, Birch Bark, Quilled Flowers, c.1910, 9 x 11 x 40 In. 316.00
Canteen, Hopi, Pottery, Birds, Polychrome, Lugs, 1940s, 6 3/4 x 9 1/4 In. 10350.00
Canteen, Hopi, Pottery, Flattened, Multicolored, Curved Lines, c.1910, 3 1/2 x 11 In. 1955.00
Canteen, Hopi, Pottery, Stylized Kachina Face, Cream Orange Slip, 2 Lugs, Spout, 6 In. 1175.00
Case, Feather, Plateau, Painted Cylindrical Rawhide, Buckskin Drawstring, 1900s, 14 x 5 In. 288.00
Case, Knife, Cree, Moosehide, Leaf Beadwork, Hide Fringe, 1920s, 39 x 7 In. 920.00
Case, Rifle, Northern Plains, Buffalo Hide, Beaded Hourglass Ends, Fringe, 44 In. 12925.00
Coat, Plains, Hide, Stand-Up Collar, Fringe At Seams & Edges, Thread-Sewn, 44 In. 2820.00
Coat, Seminole, Satin, Cloth, c.1980, Man's, Size L-XL, 31 x 29 In. 140.00
Corn Sifter, Choctaw, Woven Basket, Plaited, c.1890, 20 1/2 x 15 In. 405.00
Cradle, Blackfoot, Beaded, Coin Drops, Rawhide Fringe, 26 In. 3025.00
Cradle, Plateau, Bentwood, Buckskin Trim, Beaded, Sunshade, Doll, c.1910, 7 x 15 1/4 In. 748.00
Cradle, Salish, Basket, Coiled, Carved Head Bar, Woven Straps, 28 In. 529.00
Cradle, Salish, Basket, Imbricated Geometrics, Early 1900s, 4 x 10 x 25 In. 690.00
Cradle, Sioux, Beaded, 1880s, 13 In. 3630.00
Cradle, Ute, Wood, Round Top, Tapered, Hide Covering, Beaded, Cross, Horse Track, 21 In. 8815.00
Cradle Cover, Plains, Quilled, Rawhide Dangle, 10 x 9 In. 7700.00
Cradleboard, Apache, Cloth, Carved, Bentwood, Sunshade, c.1970, 34 x 14 x 14 In. 138.00
Cradleboard, Nez Perce, Pine Slats, Brass Tacks, Cover, Cowry Shells, c.1970, 40 x 9 x 10 In. 259.00
Cradleboard, Plateau, Carved Lace, Cedar Slat, 1900s, 26 x 8 In. 45.00
Cradleboard, Shoshone, Papoose, Beaded, 1880s, 20 In. 3850.00
Cradleboard, Sioux, Beaded, 1880s, 28 1/2 In. 6600.00

Cuffs, Plains, Buckskin, Fully Quilled, Geometrics, Early 1900s, Child's, 6 1/2 x 5 3/4 In. 920.00
Doll, Eastern Woodlands, Cornhusk, Full Regalia, Beaded Trim, Early 1900s, 9 In. 127.00
Doll, Lakota, Cloth, Beaded Dress, Applied Hair, Drawn Features, Necklace, 20 In. 3525.00
Doll, Leather, Wearing Skirt & Shawl, Quiver At Waist, Beaded, 17 1/2 x 9 In. 575.00
Doll, Mojave, Clay, Cloth Skirt, Beaded Earrings & Necklace, Horsehair Hair, 7 In. 499.00
Doll, Navajo, Hand Painted Face, Sequin, Bead Jewelry, Velvet Dress, c.1960, 17 In. 45.00
Doll, Navajo, Muslin, Metal Concha, Earrings, Skirt, Beaded Necklace, Early 1900s, 15 In. 185.00
Doll, Plains, Kidskin, Beaded Features, Painted Costume, Flannel Blanket, Cradleboard, 14 In. ... 935.00
Doll, Plains, Kidskin, Flat Dimensional Face, Yarn Hair, Beaded Facial Features, Muslin Body, 14 In. 880.00
Doll, Plains, Male, Beaded, Bone Breastplate, Black Braids, c.1890, 14 In. 1265.00
Doll, Sienna Bisque Socket Head, Glass Eyes, Human Hair, Composition, Wood, Ball Jointed, 15 In. 3190.00
Doll, Sienna Bisque Socket Head, Glass Eyes, Sculpted Details, Mohair, Composition, 11 In. 990.00
Doll, Skookum, Brave, Label, Box, 12 In. 288.00
Dress, Apache, Blue Velvet, Jangle Style, McPherson Tobacco Can Lids, c.1950, 47 In. 115.00
Dress, Blackfoot, Hide, Fringe, Beaded Yoke, Trade Bead Drops, Early 1900s, 52 x 50 In. 2070.00
Dress, Pueblo, Spun Wool, Woven, c.1950, 37 x 18 In., 2 Piece 130.00
Drum, Apache, Long Style, Bent, Stretched Rawhide Skins, 1900s, 18 1/4 x 11 1/2 In. 150.00
Drum, Arapaho, Gaming, Cottonwood, Rawhide, Painted, 2 Beaters, Early 1900s, 10 x 6 In. 345.00
Drum, Great Lakes, Double Headed, Human, Animal Celestial Images, c.1900, 2 x 19 In. 1095.00
Drum, Hopi, Cottonwood, Rawhide Heads, Early 1900s, 6 1/2 In. 345.00
Drum, Hopi, Cottonwood, Rawhide, 1900s, Child's, 5 x 8 In. 518.00
Drum, Hopi, Rawhide, Wrapped, Carved Cottonwood, Blue, Green, Child's, 3 3/4 x 5 1/4 In. 259.00
Drum, Kwakiutl, Double Headed, Hide, Painted Images, Wool Edge, Lacing, 13 In. 405.00
Drum, Northwest Coast, Wood, Rawhide, Painted, Killer Whale Imagery, 9 3/4 In. 646.00
Drum, Taos, Dance, Cottonwood, Rawhide Skins, Red, White, Blue, 1900s, 17 x 13 1/2 In. 345.00
Earrings, Zuni, Hand Wrought Silver, Turquoise Cluster, Drop, 3 In. 138.00
Fetish, Blackfoot, Sinew Sewn, Umbilical, Tin Cones, Horsehair, Early 1900s, 5 3/4 In. 460.00
Fetish, Cheyenne, Lizard Shape, Buckskin, Fully Beaded, Early 1900s, 7 x 2 In. 430.00
Fetish, Plains, Beaded, Tin Drops, 1880s, 6 In. 550.00
Fetish, Sioux, Beaded, Umbilical Cord, 8 In. 935.00
Fetish, Zuni, Bear, Carved, Turquoise, Stone Mounted, Shells, Coral, 1 3/4 x 2 1/2 In. 1210.00
Fetish, Zuni, Snake, Carved Antler, Turquoise Dots, 1950s, 12 In. 130.00
Figurine, Bird, Acoma, Pottery, Painted Birds, Leaves, Cream Ground, Open Beak, 4 In. 825.00
Figurine, Canoe, 5 Spirit Figures, Yellow Cedar, 37 In. 980.00
Figurine, Owl, Acoma, Pottery, Black, Red, White, Protruding Ears, c.1930, 7 x 6 In. 805.00
Firebag, Crow, Sinew Sewn, Beaded, Striker, Flint, c.1870, 3 1/2 x 6 1/4 In. 2300.00
Fish Trap, Northwest Coast, Split Rush, Rectangular, Woven Slats, Flared, c.1880, 15 1/4 In. 220.00
Gauntlets, Assiniboin, Beaded, Flowers, Fringed Top, Early 1900s, Woman's, 12 In. 430.00
Gauntlets, Blackfoot, Hide, Beaded, Flowers, Fringe, Montana, Early 1900s, 13 x 8 In. 316.00
Gauntlets, Buckskin, Beaded, Red Rose, Fringe, c.1950, 14 1/4 x 8 In. 518.00
Gauntlets, Buckskin, Flower Beaded Uppers, Fringe, Gloves, 1900s, Man's, 12 x 7 1/2 In. 185.00
Gloves, Plateau, Buckskin, Beaded Spiders, Black Tick Outline, 1940s, 9 In. 90.00
Hair Binder, Winnebago, Canadian Coins, Early 1900s 980.00
Hair Drop, Plains, Buckskin, Quilled Panel, Brass Bells, Scalp Locks, Fringe, 11 x 1 1/2 In. 520.00
Hair Tie, Sioux, Sinew Sewn, Beaded, Lazy Stitch, Fringe, 4 1/2 x 2 In., Pair 1840.00
Hat, Nootka, Twined Cedar Bark, Cone Shape, Painted Stylized Animals, 4 x 13 In. 6465.00
Hat, Northern California, Basketry, Brown Quail Feather Pattern, 3 x 7 In. 705.00
Headdress, Apache, Devil Dancer's, Ceremonial, Wood Slats, Cloth Cowl, c.1950, 24 x 31 In. 430.00
Headdress, Kayapo, Feather, Hyacinth Macaw, Blue, Fiber Bound, Red, Brazil, 29 1/2 In. 330.00
Hide Scraper, Plains, Hand Carved Handle, Buffalo Hide Wrap, Iron Blade, c.1870, 12 x 5 In. 545.00
Jar, Hopi, Pottery, Diagonal Abstract Feathers, Red, Brown, Buff Ground, 6 1/2 In. 880.00
Jar, San Ildefonso, Blackware, Marie & Santana, 3 1/2 In. 1058.00
Jar, San Ildefonso, Blackware, Squat, Feather, Geometrics, Marie & Santana, 5 1/2 In. 10200.00
Jar, San Ildefonso, Blackware, Squat, Feather, Geometrics, Santana/Adam, 5 1/4 In. 8400.00
Jar, Santa Clara, Melon, Redware, Signed, Helen Shupla, 6 1/4 x 9 In. 2860.00
Jar, Wedding, Santa Clara, Blackware, Incised Geometrics, Margaret Tafoya, 11 In. 3575.00
Jar, Zuni, Pottery, Deer, Geometrics, Cream Ground, Tapered Neck, 5 x 7 In. 529.00
Jigging Stick, Ojibwa, Wood, Fish Head End, Black, White Spots, Red Gills 115.00
Kachina, Hopi, Aholi, Chief's Lieutenant, Jimmy Kewonwytewa, c.1950, 19 In. 3450.00
Kachina, Hopi, Antelope, Cottonwood Root, H. Tanakhongwa, Tag, c.1971, 10 3/4 In. 315.00

Kachina, Hopi, Cottonwood Root, Buckskin Moccasins, Muslin, c.1950, 12 In. 635.00
Kachina, Hopi, Cottonwood Root, Carved, Painted, Jimmy Kewonwytewa, c.1950, 10 In. 750.00
Kachina, Hopi, Cottonwood, Mudhead Case Mask, Painted Clothing, c.1900, 9 1/2 In. 7640.00
Kachina, Hopi, Crow Mother, Headdress, 9 3/4 In. 1610.00
Kachina, Hopi, Cumulus Cloud Girl, Wood, Feather Decoration, Holds Bowl, 10 In. 1380.00
Kachina, Hopi, Fox Dancer, Early 1900s, 9 In. 1380.00
Kachina, Hopi, Left Handed, Cottonwood, c.1950, 10 1/2 In. 259.00
Kachina, Hopi, Masked Duck, Cottonwood Root, Early 1900s, 10 1/4 In. 750.00
Kachina, Hopi, Palolokong, Water Serpent, Henry Shelton, c.1970, 13 In. 635.00
Kachina, Hopi, Shalako Mana, Striped Outfit, Headdress, 11 In. 1955.00
Kachina, Hopi, Shalako Mana, Striped Outfit, Headdress, 9 3/4 In. 1725.00
Kachina, Hopi, Wood, Carved, Wearing Mask, Tablita, Kilt, Fancy Sash, 11 1/2 In. 3525.00
Kachina, Zuni, Early 1900s, 7 1/4 In. 635.00
Knife & Sheath, Cheyenne, Buckskin, Sinew Sewn, Beaded, Lazy Stitch, 9 x 7 x 1 1/2 In. 489.00
Knife & Sheath, Chippewa, Beaded, Flowers, Blue Ground, 16 In. 1100.00
Knife & Sheath, Plains, Skinning, Buckskin, Sinew Sewn, Beaded, Lazy Stitch, c.1910, 7 In. 545.00
Knife & Sheath, Sioux, Antler Handle, Beaded, Tin Cone Drops, 1880s, 14 In. 1375.00
Knife & Sheath, Sioux, Beaded, 1880s, 12 5/8 In. 1100.00
Knife & Sheath, Sioux, Buckskin, Sinew Sewn, Beaded, Lazy Stitch, Bone Handle, 10 x 3 In. 405.00
Knife & Sheath, Sioux, Leaf Shape Blade, Buffalo Bone Grip, Beaded, c.1860, 5 1/8 In. 1250.00
Knife Sheath, Blackfoot, Buffalo Hide, Sinew Sewn, Beaded, c.1890, 12 In. 400.00
Knife Sheath, Sioux, Leather, Beaded, Lazy Stitch, Early 1880s, 9 x 3 In. 220.00
Knife Sheath, Southern Plains, Beaded, Red, Blue, Green, Fringe, Tin Cones, Tassels, 9 In. 690.00
Knife Sling, Dagger, Beaded, Leather, c.1886, 10 3/4 In. 500.00
Ladle, Mesa Verde, Anasazi Pottery, 2 Roll Handle, Prehistoric, 2 1/2 x 8 In. 230.00
Lantern, Nootka, Makah, Basket, Animals, Birds, Whales, Whalers, Green Whirling, 16 1/2 In. 920.00
Ledger, Drawing, Mounted Indian, Trading Rifle With White Man, Teepee, 11 x 7 1/2 In. 90.00
Leggings, Blackfoot, Mountain Sheep Hide, Fringe, Beaded Strips, c.1880, 30 x 9 In. 3738.00
Leggings, Cheyenne, Elk Hide, Beaded, Yellow Ocher, Brass Buttons, c.1870, 12 x 30 In. 3738.00
Leggings, Sioux, Beaded, 1890s, 15 1/2 In. 1375.00
Leggings, Southern Plains, Kiowa, Netted, Brick, Overlay Stitch, 14 3/4 x 7 1/4 In. 2300.00
Lodge Pole, Penobscot, Bear, Indian, Beaver, Leo Francis, Maine 720.00
Martingale, Crow, Buckskin, Beaded, Tradecloth Trim, Canvas, Bells, Tassels, c.1910, 31 x 15 In. 4315.00
Mask, Iroquois, Cornhusk, Hand Woven, Protruding Nose, Early 1900s, 10 x 12 In. 400.00
Mask, Iroquois, False Face, Medicine, Horse Hair, Teeth, Eyes, 1900s, 4 x 10 1/2 In. 185.00
Mask, Iroquois, Seneca, False Face Devil, Horns, Cutout Eyes, Hand Carved, c.1950, 12 x 8 In. 160.00
Mask, Iroquois, Seneca, False Face Society, Hand Carved, c.1920, 8 x 11 In. 518.00
Medicine Horn, Sioux, Buffalo, Quilled Fringe, Tin Cones, c.1880, 15 In. 2070.00
Moccasin, Beaded, Sinew Sewn Soles, 3 1/2 x 10 x 3 1/2 In., Pair 230.00
Moccasins, Apache, Buckskin, Beaded, Symbols & Chevrons, High Top, Girl's, 12 x 9 In. 2000.00
Moccasins, Apache, Ceremonial, High Top, Toe Tab, Yellow Ocher, Early 1900s, 10 x 30 In. 550.00
Moccasins, Apache, High Top, Beaded, Yellow Ocher, 1880s, 8 1/2 x 16 In. 715.00
Moccasins, Arapaho, Beaded, Geometrics, High Top, Fringe, Yellow Ocher, Woman's, 9 In. 4115.00
Moccasins, Arapaho, High Top, Beaded, Antelope Hide, Yellow Ocher, c.1880, 5 1/2 x 10 In. 3738.00
Moccasins, Blackfoot, Buffalo Hide, Beaded, c.1880, 11 In. 1840.00
Moccasins, Cheyenne, Beaded, 1880s, Woman's, 9 3/4 In. 1100.00
Moccasins, Cheyenne, Sinew, Beaded, Lazy Stitch, Geometrics, 11 3/4 In. 690.00
Moccasins, Chippewa, Puckered Toe, Beaded Flowers, c.1900s, 9 In. 315.00
Moccasins, Cree, Elk Hide, Flower Beaded Ankle Straps, Pinched Toe, c.1950, 10 In. 345.00
Moccasins, Crow, Beaded, Flowers, 1880s, 10 In. 770.00
Moccasins, Dakota, Beaded Abstract Flowers, Cloth Ankle Trim, Hard Sole, 8 1/2 In. 323.00
Moccasins, Gros Ventre, Rawhide Soles, Beaded, Lazy Stitch, c.1900, 10 In. 920.00
Moccasins, Huron, Buckskin, Pinched Toe, Embroidered, Beaded, c.1900, 4 1/2 In. 185.00
Moccasins, Huron, Green Beaded Lines, Ankle Flaps, c.1800, 5 In. 2875.00
Moccasins, Iroquois, Buckskin, Blue Cloth, White Beads, c.1900, 5 In. 195.00
Moccasins, Iroquois, Deerskin, Felt, Beaded, 1890s, 10 1/2 In. 275.00
Moccasins, Kiowa, Beaded, Tassels, Bone Drops, 10 In. 2035.00
Moccasins, Kiowa, Buffalo Hide, Red Cloth Inset, Beaded Geometrics, Fringe, 10 1/2 In. 15275.00
Moccasins, Lakota, Blue Buffalo Tracks, Geometrics, White Ground, 10 1/2 In. 999.00
Moccasins, Lakota, Green Buffalo Tracks, Geometrics, Light Blue Ground, 10 In. 1410.00

Indian, Belt, Navajo, Silver, 6 Conchas, Winged Buckle, 20th Century, 4 1/2 In.

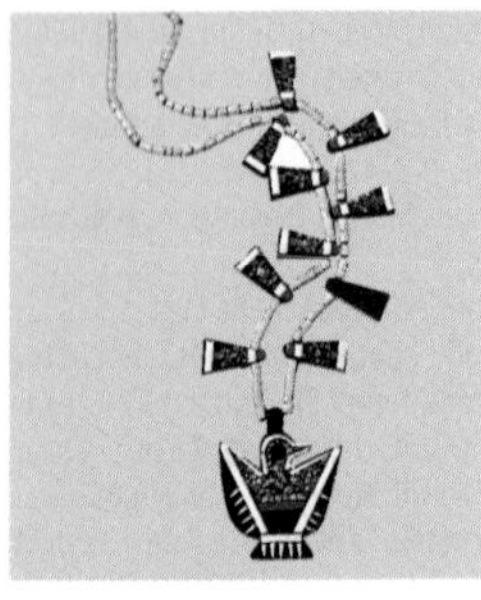

Indian, Necklace, Coral, Silver, 20th Century, 12 In.

Indian, Necklace, Navajo, Squash Blossom, Silver, Turquoise, c.1950, 13 1/3 In.

Moccasins, Lakota, Multicolored Geometrics, White Ground, Blue Vamp, Crosses, 10 In. 940.00
Moccasins, Plains, Sinew, Beaded, Lazy Stitch, Hard Soles, 1800s, Size 12 .... 920.00
Moccasins, Plateau, High Top, Flower Beadwork, Hard Soles, 1900s, 6 1/2 x 6 1/2 In. 400.00
Moccasins, Sioux, Beaded, 1880s, Men's, 10 3/4 In. 963.00
Moccasins, Sioux, Beaded, Antelope Hide, Buffalo Soles, c.1920, Child's, 5 In. 315.00
Moccasins, Sioux, Beaded, Lazy Stitch, Crosses, Chevrons, c.1880, Size 10 .... 978.00
Moccasins, Sioux, Beaded, Sinew Sewn, Buffalo Hide, Soles, c.1880, Baby's, 5 In. 1495.00
Moccasins, Sioux, Beaded, Sinew Sewn, Lazy Stitch, Hard Sole, c.1900, 10 In. 1840.00
Moccasins, Tlingit, Moose Hide, Pinched Toes, Rabbit Fur Trim, Beaded, c.1910, 10 In. 375.00
Moccasins, Winnebago, Beaded, 1890s, 10 1/2 In. 550.00
Necklace, Coral, Silver, 20th Century, 12 In. .... *ILLUS* 411.00
Necklace, Crow, Felt, Brass, Beads, Brass Ball, c.1865, 7 In. 1760.00
Necklace, Earrings, Zuni, Stone-On-Stone, Coral, Turquoise Inlay, Earrings, 26 In. 430.00
Necklace, Navajo, 4 Strands, Clamshell, Turquoise, c.1940, 22 In. 185.00
Necklace, Navajo, 5 Squash Blossoms, Naja, Silver Bead, 12 1/2 In. 259.00
Necklace, Navajo, Hand Wrought Silver, Turquoise, 7 1/2 x 2 x 2 In. 140.00
Necklace, Navajo, Oxblood Red Coral, c.1970, 21 In. 180.00
Necklace, Navajo, Shadow Box, Turquoise On Side, Naja, 1970, 13 x 4 1/2 In. 259.00
Necklace, Navajo, Silver, 8 Claw, 15 Jade, Gemstone Cabochons, Beads, 1970s, 31 In. 259.00
Necklace, Navajo, Silver, Squash Blossom, 6 Blossoms, Double Rows, Naja, 10 In. 441.00
Necklace, Navajo, Squash Blossom, Handmade Beads, c.1920, 32 In. 460.00
Necklace, Navajo, Squash Blossom, Handmade Beads, Turquoise, c.1930, 32 In. 546.00
Necklace, Navajo, Squash Blossom, Peyote Bird, c.1970, 4 1/2 x 3 In. 259.00
Necklace, Navajo, Squash Blossom, Silver, Turquoise, c.1950, 13 1/3 In. .... *ILLUS* 470.00
Necklace, Navajo, Squash Blossom, Sterling Silver, 17 Turquoise Stones, c.1970, 3 x 26 In. 316.00
Necklace, Pueblo, 4 Strands, Oxblood Coral, Turquoise, c.1970, 28 In. 178.00
Necklace, Pueblo, Gemstone Fetish, c.1990, 26 In. 259.00
Necklace, Pueblo, Jocla Corns, Turquoise Beads, 30 In. 127.00
Necklace, Pueblo, Turquoise Disc Beads, Hand Knotted, Sterling Cones, c.1980, 24 In. 92.00
Necklace, Santo Domingo, 7 Strands, Italian Coral, Shell Heishi, Silver Cones, c.1960, 25 In. 546.00
Necklace, Santo Domingo, Turquoise Chip Inlay, Thunderbird Pendant, Bone Heishi, 1920s, 24 In. 288.00
Necklace, Squash Blossom, Hollow Beaded Chain, Pendant, Turquoise, Pear Shape 165.00
Necklace, Turquoise, 2 Strands, Shell, Green Turquoise, Heishi, 30 In. 138.00
Necklace, Zuni, 3 Part Silver, Blossom Beads, Devil Dance, Inlaid, Mother-Of-Pearl, 16 In. 374.00
Necklace, Zuni, Squash Blossom, Naja, Turquoise, Mother-Of-Pearl, Coral, Sunface, 14 In. 403.00
Olla, Acoma, Geometrics, Black, Rust, White Ground, c.1900, 10 x 12 In. 2588.00
Olla, Acoma, Pottery, Orange & Black Triangles, Cream Ground, High Shoulder, 7 x 10 In. 1528.00
Olla, San Ildefonso, Pottery, Black & Red Geometrics, Abstract Flowers, 10 x 12 In. 2350.00
Olla, Santa Clara, Blackware, Incised Avanyu Design, Signed, 6 1/2 x 8 1/2 In. 660.00
Olla, Sierra Madre, Pottery, c.1880, 15 x 16 1/2 In. 161.00
Olla, Zia, Pottery, Black & Red, Abstract Flowers & Birds, Tapered Neck, 15 x 16 In. 11163.00
Olla, Zuni, Horned Animals, Birds, Black, Rust, White Ground, c.1880, 11 x 15 In. 18400.00
Parfleche, Case, Hide Bound, Blue Stroud Edge, Early 1900s, 14 x 10 In. 315.00

Parfleche, Case, Plains, Rawhide, American Flags, Fringe, Early 1900s, 10 x 15 x 8 In. 2875.00
Parfleche, Crow, Bonnet Case, Rawhide, Mineral Painted, Early 1900s, 14 x 28 In. 2590.00
Parfleche, Crow, Elk Hide, Mineral Painted, c.1860, 11 x 18 In. 635.00
Parfleche, Crow, Elk Hide, Mineral Painted, c.1870, 14 x 28 In. 805.00
Parfleche, Envelope, Crow, Hide, Painted, Geometrics, 27 In. 2700.00
Parfleche, Sioux, Envelope, Rawhide, Painted, Folding, 1900s, 11 x 19 In. 635.00
Parfleche, Southern Plains, Envelope, Painted, Late 1900s, 14 x 26 In. 520.00
Pendant, Zuni, Hummingbird, Turquoise, Coral, Mother-Of-Pearl, Shell, Sterling, 1975, 3 In. 160.00
Pendant, Zuni, Inlaid Bear, Turquoise, Shell, Coral, Late 1900s, 1 3/4 x 2 1/2 In. 115.00
Pillow, Beadwork, Tourist, Bird, Leaf Border, Purple Velvet, 10 x 8 In. 80.00
Pin, Navajo, Central Turquoise, 30 Smaller Stones, Silverwork, c.1940, 3 1/2 x 2 3/8 In. 1295.00
Pin, Navajo, Western Boot, Brass, Silver, Copper, Turquoise, UITA 22, c.1935, 1 1/2 In. 195.00
Pin, Thunderbird, Sterling Silver, Turquoise, Signed, Stylized A In Circle 85.00
Pin, Zuni, Bug, Wings Open, Mosaic Inlay, Black & White, c.1935, 2 1/2 x 2 In. 795.00
Pin, Zuni, Butterfly, Mosaic Inlay, c.1945, 1 7/8 x 1 3/4 In. 695.00
Pin, Zuni, Rainbow God, Stone-To-Stone, Turquoise, Spiny Oyster, Shell, c.1940, 4 x 2 1/4 In. 430.00
Pin, Zuni, Shalako, Kachina, Channel Inlay, c.1945, 2 1/8 x 1 1/8 In. 695.00
Pin, Zuni, Thunderbird, Stone-To-Stone, Jet, Turquoise, Shell, Silver, 2 1/4 x 2 1/8 In. 210.00
Pipe, Eastern Sioux, Catlinite, Inlaid Snake, Carved Stem, 32 1/2 In. 4675.00
Pipe, Eastern Sioux, Catlinite, Original Stem, 1860s, 25 In. 1430.00
Pipe, Northwest Coast, Figure, Face, Hat, Walnut, Ivory, Abalone Ears, 3 x 5 x 2 In. 3335.00
Pipe, Plains, 2 Parts, Wooden Joints, 5 x 24 In. 600.00
Pipe, Plains, Catlinite Bowl, Carved, Quilled Center, 4 Brass Tacks, 8 x 4 x 1 1/4 In. 489.00
Pipe, Sioux, Catlinite, Carved, Tacks, Painted Stem, Mid 1900s, 22 In. 259.00
Pipe, Sioux, Catlinite, Polychrome Bowl, Deer Hide Covered Stem, Copper Trim, 1800s, 24 In. 320.00
Pipe, Sioux, Stone, Black, Wood Stem, c.1860, 16 1/2 x 2 1/2 In. 750.00
Pipe & Bowl, Sioux, Trade Cloth & Quill Braided, Ermine Drop, c.1870, 27 In. 870.00
Pipe Ax, Sioux, Pewter Head, File Burned & Inlaid Haft, Beaded Drop, 7 x 19 In. 1095.00
Pipe Bag, Assiniboin, Hide, Beaded, Quilled, Tin Cone & Feather Drops, 1890s, 34 x 5 In. 3165.00
Pipe Bag, Central Plains, Buffalo Hide, Beaded, Quilled Pipes, Horse Tracks, Fringe, 30 In. 3290.00
Pipe Bag, Cree, Multicolored Beads, White Ground, Tab Top, Fringed Bottom, 27 In. 499.00
Pipe Bag, Lakota, Beaded Warrior On Horse, Quilled, Horsehair & Cone Danglers, 35 In. 7638.00
Pipe Bag, Lakota, Beaded, Quill-Wrapped Drops, Fringe, 33 In. 4406.00
Pipe Bag, Piegan, Tab Top, Sinew & Thread Sewn, Mountain Sheep Hide, Bead Trim, 21 x 5 In. 3738.00
Pipe Bag, Shoshone, Sinew, Beaded, Crosses, Geometrics, Bugle Bead, Fringe, 22 x 6 In. 1495.00
Pipe Bag, Sioux, Beaded, Fringe, 1880s, 19 1/2 In. 1375.00
Pipe Bag, Sioux, Buckskin, Beaded, Lazy Stitch, Fringe, Late 1900s, 7 1/4 x 18 In. 290.00
Pipe Bowl & Stem, Sioux, Quilled, 1870s, 31 1/2 In. 2200.00
Pipe Stem, Hardware, Carved, Painted, Deer, Buffalo, Dragonfly, Bear, Ram, Turtle, 38 In. 865.00
Pitcher, Cochiti, Pottery, Black-On-Cream Decoration, Round, Bird Effigy Head Spout, Handle, 8 In. 705.00
Pot, Acoma, Pottery, Stylized Figures, 12 x 11 In. 13225.00
Pouch, Apache, Hide, 2 Beaded Figures, Cross, Circle, U-Shape, Fringe, 9 In. 2000.00
Pouch, Iroquois, Wool, Beaded, Flowers, Flaps, 6 1/4 In. 325.00
Pouch, Plains, Buckskin, Yellow Ocher, Sinew Seam, Beaded, Lazy Stitch, 1930s, 5 x 4 1/4 In. 345.00
Pouch, Plains, Sioux, Buckskin, Beaded Flap, Lazy Stitch, c.1970, 8 x 7 In. 219.00
Pouch, Plateau, Beaded Eagle & Elk On Flap, Blue Ground, U-Shape, Belt Loops, 8 In. 825.00
Pouch, Plateau, Hide, Beaded Front, Red Trade Cloth Back, Calico Lining, Strap, 12 x 11 In. 294.00
Pouch, Sioux, Buckskin, Morning Stars, American Flags, Beaded, Sinew, c.1910, 6 x 5 In. 430.00
Pouch, Sioux, Fully Beaded, No. 16 Seed Beads, c.1900, 6 x 4 1/2 In. 1840.00
Pouch, Sioux, Medicine, Sundance, Tobacco Plant, Beaded, Sinew, c.1890, 3 1/2 x 5 In. 460.00
Pouch, Southern Plains, Beaded, Trapezoidal, Hide, Cross, Diamond, Multicolored, 8 1/2 In. 2300.00
Powder Horn, Great Lakes, Woven Strap, c.1880, 13-In. Horn, 70-In. Strap 430.00
Rattle, Blackfoot, Rawhide, Horsetail Drop, Early 1900s, 4 x 20 In. 315.00
Rattle, Hopi, Dance, Gourd, Painted, c.1920, 5 x 10 1/2 In. 290.00
Rattle, Hopi, Gourd, Carved, Painted, Morning Star, 1900s, 14 In. 150.00
Rattle, Hopi, Gourd, Polychrome, 1900s 185.00
Rattle, Mandan Sioux, Dew Claw, Beaded, 25 In. 1100.00
Rattle, Northern Plains, Warrior, 2 Buffalo Horns, Cloth, Beaded Rosette, c.1910, 10 3/4 In. 330.00
Rattle, Northwest Coast, Whale Effigy, Carved, Painted, 12 x 5 In. 230.00
Rattle, Northwest Coast, Whale Effigy, Wood, Carved, Painted, 12 1/4 In. 410.00

Rattle, Tlingit, Dance, Human Head, Open Mouth, Painted Features, 10 1/2 x 5 In. 2070.00
Ring, Navajo, 2 Round Turquoise, Ingot Plate Mounting, Hand-Drawn Wire, c.1915, Size 10 1/2 ... 595.00
Ring, Navajo, 3 Turquoise, Filed Setting, c.1925, Size 6 1/2 .... 395.00
Ring, Navajo, Blue Gem Turquoise, Center Oval, 2 Rows Of Balls, c.1945, Size 8 1/4 .... 225.00
Ring, Zuni, 7 Row, Petit Point Turquoise, Sterling Silver, c.1974, Size 10 .... 150.00
Ring, Zuni, Turquoise, Channel Set, c.1935, Size 7 1/2 .... 195.00
Rug, Chimayo, Central Panel, Feather, New Mexico, 77 x 52 In. 345.00
Rug, Chimayo, Elongated Diamond, Natural, Black, Gray, Wool, Mexico, 79 x 52 In. 259.00
Rug, Navajo, 2 Diamond Medallions, Serrated, Gray Field, 48 x 75 In. 1035.00
Rug, Navajo, 2 Gray Hills, 2 Stepped Center Diamonds, Banded Border, 74 x 53 In. 6600.00
Rug, Navajo, 2 Gray Hills, Black Border, 1900s, 41 x 28 In. 288.00
Rug, Navajo, 2 Gray Hills, Box Medallion Corners, Stepped Diamond, 81 x 47 1/2 In. 3300.00
Rug, Navajo, 2 Gray Hills, c.1970, 15 x 16 In. 40.00
Rug, Navajo, 2 Gray Hills, Central Lozenge, c.1970, 44 x 32 In. 575.00
Rug, Navajo, 2 Gray Hills, Central Medallion, Crenulated Edge Band, 72 x 42 In. 3600.00
Rug, Navajo, 2 Gray Hills, Central Stepped Diamond, Geometrics, 74 x 50 In. 3000.00
Rug, Navajo, 2 Gray Hills, Ivory, Brown, Tan, Stepped Border, 73 1/2 x 46 In. 4200.00
Rug, Navajo, 3 Yei Women, c.1940, 36 x 72 In. 115.00
Rug, Navajo, 4 Yei Figures, Dancing, Playing Flute, c.1970, 17 x 15 In. 130.00
Rug, Navajo, 6 Yei Figures, Brown Ground, c.1965, 59 x 44 In. 1380.00
Rug, Navajo, Black & Green Diamonds, Whirling Logs, Crosses, Zigzag Border, 52 x 75 In. 4406.00
Rug, Navajo, Central Diamond, Black, White, Gray, Tan & Cream, 1940, 45 x 69 In. 670.00
Rug, Navajo, Cornstalk Yei Figures, c.1970, 23 x 31 In. 180.00
Rug, Navajo, Cornstalk, Birds, Feathers, Serrated Triangle Border, 43 x 53 In. 2115.00
Rug, Navajo, Crosses, Arrows, Geometrics, 82 x 43 In. 2590.00
Rug, Navajo, Crystal, Crosses, Hooks, Line, Box Border, Early 1900s, 90 x 47 In. 865.00
Rug, Navajo, Crystal, Multicolored Figures, Dark Ground, c.1925, 67 x 43 In. 1380.00
Rug, Navajo, Crystal, Red, Black, Cream, Gray Ground, 86 x 57 In. 1300.00
Rug, Navajo, Crystal, Whirling Logs, Feathers, Water Bugs, c.1900, 62 x 120 In. 4315.00
Rug, Navajo, Diamond Blocks, Stepped, Blue, Red, Orange, Brown, White, 34 x 46 In. 290.00
Rug, Navajo, Diamond, Red, Black, White, Gray Ground, Black, White Border, 39 x 64 In. 520.00
Rug, Navajo, Diamonds, Red, Orange, Tan, Black, Cross, Serrated Border, 62 x 32 1/2 In. 290.00
Rug, Navajo, Dual Whirling Log, Serrated Border, 64 x 48 In. 805.00
Rug, Navajo, Eye Dazzler, Multicolored, 2 Diamonds, Crosses, Fringe, 36 x 54 In. 4406.00
Rug, Navajo, Eye Dazzler, Transitional, Serrated Concentric Diamonds, 80 x 55 In. 6600.00
Rug, Navajo, Friendship Sign, Arrows, Feathers, 86 x 60 In. 1335.00
Rug, Navajo, Ganado, Serrated Diamond, Central Cross Motifs, 73 x 55 In. 635.00
Rug, Navajo, Ganado, Stepped Diamond, Red, Gray, Brown, Black, c.1950, 52 x 63 In. 430.00
Rug, Navajo, Geometric Border, Orange, Cream, Gray, Brown, c.1960, 36 x 31 1/4 In. 185.00
Rug, Navajo, Geometric Medallion, Gray Ground, Brown, Off-White Borders, 49 x 67 In. 700.00
Rug, Navajo, Geometric, Red, Black, White, Brown Ground, 42 x 39 In. 999.00
Rug, Navajo, Geometric, Red, Cream, Brown Field, c.1920, 51 x 71 In. 2115.00
Rug, Navajo, Geometrics, Arrows, Hooks, Red, Gray Field, 29 x 50 In. 115.00
Rug, Navajo, Geometrics, Central, Star Corners, Beige Field, 55 x 73 In. 1265.00
Rug, Navajo, Germantown, Red, Gold, Brown, Green, Late 1800s, 45 x 30 In. 2590.00
Rug, Navajo, Klagetoh, Geometrics, Brown Ground, c.1925, 55 x 34 1/2 In. 1265.00
Rug, Navajo, Multiple Borders, Black, Black & White Fret, Tan Ground, 55 x 36 In. 460.00
Rug, Navajo, Pictorial, 6 Yei Figures, Ivory, Gray, Brown, Red, Green, 55 x 36 In. 4800.00
Rug, Navajo, Red, Brown Square, Tan Ground, 78 x 44 In. 2015.00
Rug, Navajo, Red, Brown, Brown & Ivory, Corner Tassels, 120 x 82 In. 7425.00
Rug, Navajo, Red, Natural, Dark, Brown, 30 x 62 In. 259.00
Rug, Navajo, Regional, Chief's Third Phase, Stripes, Stepped Diamonds, 54 x 51 In. 3900.00
Rug, Navajo, Rust Field, Yellow, Gray, White, Corner Tassels, c.1910, 68 x 52 In. 6005.00
Rug, Navajo, Serrated Center Bands, Stepped Border, c.1950, 62 x 30 In. 750.00
Rug, Navajo, Serrated Diamonds, Gray Terraced, Banded Ends, Red, Black, 39 x 58 In. 290.00
Rug, Navajo, Serrated Diamonds, Mirror Design, Orange, Red, Gray, Black, 48 x 30 1/2 In. 405.00
Rug, Navajo, Serrated Diamonds, Red Ground, Fringed Ends, 34 x 50 In. 6463.00
Rug, Navajo, Stepped Diamond & Feather, Gray Ground, Fret Border, 68 x 41 In. 2820.00
Rug, Navajo, Stepped Terrace Border, White, Red, Black Border, Lattice Panel, 34 x 57 In. 290.00
Rug, Navajo, Storm Pattern, Brown, Natural Borders, 52 x 83 In. 460.00

Rug, Navajo, Storm Pattern, Sawtooth Borders, 51 x 81 In. 1035.00
Rug, Navajo, Tree Of Life, Bird, Nest, c.1960, 32 x 20 In. 207.00
Rug, Navajo, Tree Of Life, Birds, Rabbits, c.1980, 18 1/2 x 18 In. 196.00
Rug, Navajo, Vegetal Dye, Terraced Bands, Brown, Green, Tan, 62 x 37 In. 230.00
Rug, Navajo, Yei Figures, Geometric Border, c.1925, 59 x 46 In. 1840.00
Rug, Navajo, Yei, Double Row Of Figures, c.1925, 69 x 40 In. 1380.00
Rug, Navajo, Zigzags, Rectangles, Diamonds, 166 x 108 In. 13800.00
Rug, Zapotec, Mexico, Whirling Logs, Black Ground, c.1950, 51 x 80 In. 69.00
Scalp Lock, Mounted On Bead & Fabric Panel, Early 20th Century, 19 In. 1229.00
Seed Pot, Acoma, Pottery, Cindy Santiago, 5 x 6 1/2 In. 380.00
Seed Pot, Pottery, Edwina Tortalia, 5 x 5 In. 265.00
Seed Pot, Pottery, Gloria Guchupin, 6 x 6 In. 350.00
Serape, Navajo, Red, Green, Blue Vertical Lightning Pattern, Red Ground, 69 x 48 In. 7050.00
Sewing Tool, Northwest Coast, Carved Bone, Copper Pins, Bird In Flight, 7 1/2 In. 920.00
Shirt, Blackfoot, Warrior's, Beaded Hide, Fringe, Ermine Drops, Leggings, 1900s, 60 x 46 In. 7480.00
Shirt, Cotton, Painted, Yellow Ground, Black Necklace, Crosses, Green Border, Fringe 2530.00
Shirt, War, Beaded Strips, Buckskin, Horse Hair Drops, Twist Fringe, Early 1900s, 37 x 19 In. 375.00
Skirt, Flathead, Tradecloth, Flowers, Glass Tube Beads, Early 1900s, 36 x 32 In. 1150.00
Strike-A-Lite, Sioux, 2 Beaded Cone Drops, 7 1/2 In. 880.00
Teepee, Lakota, Wood, Hide, Painted Warriors, Buffalo, Beaded Flap, Miniature, 20 x 14 In. 8815.00
Telescope, Blackfoot, Brass, Beadwork Cover, Alberta, Canada, 1800s, 9 x 2 In. 575.00
Tomahawk, Brass Head, Oak Handle, Husk Wrapped, Late 1900s, 18 1/2 x 7 In. 375.00
Tomahawk, Plains, Beaded, File Branded Handle, 1870s, 12 1/2 In. 1925.00
Tomahawk, Plains, Maple Shaft, Iron Blade, Hand Wrought, c.1850, 22 x 8 In. 520.00
Tomahawk, Plains, Pipe, Iron Spontoon Head, Pierced, File Burned Shaft, 1800s, 11 1/2 x 25 In. 1265.00
Totem, Argilite, Raven, 2 Spirit Animal Figures, 19 1/4 x 3 1/2 x 3 1/2 In. 2300.00
Totem, Bird Figure With Outstretched Wings At Top, Hand Carved, Painted, 22 1/2 In. 115.00
Totem Pole, Northwest Coast, 3 Figures, Cedar, Hand Carved, White, c.1935, 13 In. 290.00
Totem Pole, Northwest Coast, 3 Figures, Cedar, Relief Carved, Early 1900s, 11 1/4 In. 290.00
Totem Pole, Northwest Coast, 4 Figures, Relief Carved, Black, Green, Early 1900s, 15 In. 185.00
Totem Pole, Northwest Coast, 7 Figures, Hand Carved, Ram, Eagles, Thunderbirds, c.1937, 28 In. 430.00
Totem Pole, Northwest Coast, Bird, Outstretched Wings, Whale, 13 x 8 In. 375.00
Totem Pole, Northwest Coast, Painted, Abstract Faces, Totemic Animals, 59 In. 8225.00
Trade Beads, 2 Strands, Bohemian Red Glass, Faceted, 1900s, 27 In. 130.00
Tray, Hopi, Basket, Butterfly Pattern, Polychrome, c.1950, 12 In. 195.00
Tray, Klamath, Basket, Arrows, Birds, Red Accents, Early 1900s, 12 In. 489.00
Tray, Pima, Basket, Coiled, Flared, Geometrics, Willow, Devil's Claw, 12 3/4 In. 1800.00
Tray, Pima, Basket, Woven, Modified Squash Blossom, Early 1900s, 2 1/2 x 13 1/2 In. 259.00
Tray, Winnowing Basket, Yokuts, Twined, Bands Of Geometrics, Fan Shape, 22 x 21 In. 705.00
Tray, Yavapai, Basket, Boxed Checks, Whirlwind Pattern, Early 1900s, 14 x 2 1/2 In. 3450.00
Tray, Yokuts, Basket, Whirlwind Design, Early 1900s, 16 1/2 In. 750.00
Trunk, Painted, Tin, Wood Grain, Oak Rim, c.1895, 19 x 30 x 17 In. 230.00
Vase, Acoma, Pottery, Polychrome Painted, Geometrics, c.1950, 8 1/4 x 9 1/2 In. 1150.00
Vase, Santa Clara, Pottery, Blackware, Ribbed Shoulder, 4 Bear Paws, Flared Rim, 16 In. 19975.00
Vest, Lakota, Beaded, Warriors On Horseback, Teepees, Stars, Ribbon Trim, 22 x 18 In. 14100.00
Vest, Lakota, Hide, Beaded Geometrics, White Ground, Cloth Trim, Child's, 19 In. 2115.00
Vest, Plains, Beaded, Lazy Stitch, Geometrics, Early 1900s, Child's, 12 1/4 x 11 In. 3165.00
Vest, Potowatomi, Beaded, 1880s, Child's, 25 x 14 1/2 In. 4400.00
Vest, Sioux, Beaded, Buffalo Hide, Geometrics, c.1880, 18 x 20 In. 7475.00
Vest, Sioux, Beaded, Deer, Indians On Horses, Sinew Sewn, Fringe, 24 In. 10800.00
Wampum, Nez Perce, 2 Strands, Clamshell, Mid 1900s, 54 In. 185.00
War Club, Great Lakes, Carved, Wrought Iron Spike, 1800s, 23 In. 545.00
War Club, Great Lakes, Figural, Wood Shaft, Bird Shape Head, Spike, 1800s, 24 1/4 In. 529.00
War Club, Penobscot, Painted, Warrior Face, Chip Carved Handle, BE, 24 1/2 In. 345.00
War Club, Plains, Ball, Bird Effigy, Brass Tack Eyes, Horsehair Drop, c.1900, 24 x 5 In. 920.00
War Club, Plains, Beaded, Rawhide Cover, Tin Drops, Fringe, 1890, 21 In. 275.00
War Club, Sioux, Oval Stone Head, Beaded Handle, Hide Fringe, 1890, 23 x 5 In. 460.00
War Club, Sioux, Oval, Grooved Dolomite, Rawhide Binding, Horse Scalp, 1860s, 16 x 6 In. 920.00
War Club, Woodlands, Burl & Branch, Bird Beak Head, Early 1900s, 24 1/2 x 7 1/2 In. 259.00
War Lance, Plains, Leaf Shape, c.1870, 10 3/4 In. 650.00
Watchband, Zuni, Hand Stamped, 10 Coral Cabochons, c.1964, 5 x 1 1/4 x 1/2 In. 50.00

INDIAN TREE is a china pattern that was popular during the last half of the nineteenth century. It was copied from earlier Indian textile patterns that were very similar. The pattern includes the crooked branch of a tree and a partial landscape with exotic flowers and leaves. Green, blue, pink, and orange were the favored colors used in the design.

Bowl, Oval, Fluted Edge, Coalport, 6 x 5 In. 29.00
Bowl, Vegetable, Oval, Handles, Cover, Maddock & Sons, 12 x 7 1/4 In. 65.00
Cup & Saucer, After Dinner, Coalport, c.1910, 2 Sets 75.00
Cup & Saucer, Copeland Spode, c.1920 .... 35.00
Cup & Saucer, S. Hancock & Sons 11.00
Cup & Saucer, Shelley, China, England 128.00
Pitcher, Milk, New York, New Haven & Hartford Railroad, Shenango China, c.1915, Pt. 300.00
Plate, Dessert, Coalport, 6 1/2 In. 14.00
Platter, Oval, Copeland Spode, 18 x 14 1/2 In. 225.00
Platter, Oval, Shaped Rim, Minton, c.1845, 14 1/2 In. 550.00
Sponge Bowl, Mason's Ironstone 39.00
Teapot, Maddock & Sons, 4 Cup 60.00

INKSTANDS were made to be placed on a desk. They held some type of container for ink, and possibly a sander, a pen tray, a pen, a holder for pounce, and even a candle to melt the sealing wax. Inkstands date to the eighteenth century and have been made of silver, copper, ceramics, and glass. Additional inkstands may be found in these and other related categories.

Brass, Lily Pad Shape, 2 Iridescent Green Glass Wells, Austria, c.1900, 10 1/4 In. 245.00
Bronze, Classical Revival, Dante, 2 Inkwells, Paw Feet, Late 1800s, 15 1/4 In. 353.00
Bronze, Cover, 2 Wells, Pen Trough, Applied Cityscape, Art Deco, c.1920, 16 x 9 x 7 In. 775.00
Bronze, Empire Style, Gilt, Patinated, Green Marble, Paw Feet, Late 1800s, 13 In. 588.00
Bronze, Man & Woman In Car, Germany, Early 1900s, 4 3/4 x 2 3/4 x 9 In. 690.00
Bronze, Motorist, Sitting On Stump, Inspecting Tire, Early 1900s, 9 x 5 In. 427.00
Cast Iron, Reticulated, Glass Well, Eastlake Design, 19th Century, 5 1/4 In. 106.00
Gilt Bronze, Roman Warrior, 2 Pots, Polished Slate Base, 10 x 15 x 7 In. 345.00
Metal, Car, 2 Drivers, Helmets, Goggles, Copper Color, Early 1900s, 3 1/4 x 8 3/4 In. 1799.00
Metal, Hobo & Scottie Dog, Bronze Wash, 1920s, 9 1/2 x 5 x 4 3/4 In. 150.00
Nickel Silver, Dirigible, 2 Glass Wells, France, Early 1900s, 7 x 16 In. 3614.00
Pewter, Hinged Top, Pens & Pencils Compartment, England, c.1800 .... 795.00
Porcelain, Carriage Shape, Gilt Bronze Mounts, Samson, France, 19th Century, 8 In. 764.00
Porcelain, Tray, Inkwell, Shaker, Blue Scepter, KPM, c.1900, 10 1/4 In. 24.00
Pressed Glass, Lacy, Arch & Diamond, Hinged Lid, Brass Mounts, France, 1835-45, 2 1/2 x 8 In. 303.00
Silver, Dragon, Circular, Hinged Cover, 4 Scroll-Leaf Legs, Wang Hing, c.1890, 2 x 3 3/8 In. 950.00
Silver, Edwardian Style, Gadrooned Border, Openwork Legs, 4 x 12 In. 1763.00

INKWELLS, of course, held ink. Ready-made ink was first made about 1836 and was sold in bottles. The desk inkwell had a narrow hole so the pen would not slip inside. Inkwells were made of many materials, such as pottery, glass, pewter, and silver. Look in these categories for more listings of inkwells.

3 Geese, Staffordshire, 1800s, 4 3/4 In. 60.00
Archibald Knox, Tudric, Flattened Circular Shape, Pewter, England, Early 1900s, 5 In. 396.00
Archibald Knox, Tudric, Spreading Circular Shape, Pewter, England, Early 1900s, 4 In. 470.00
Blackamoor, On Camel, Torso Opens, Austria, 1890s, 4 In. 120.00
Brass, Fisherman With Spear In Boat, 6 x 8 1/2 In. 316.00
Brass, Raised Relief, Pierced Design, England, 12 x 8 In. 70.00
Bronze, Bear Seated Atop Basket, Patinated, Glass Bottle, Russia, Late 1800s, 4 1/4 In. 205.00
Bronze, Gray Jade, Rosewood Hinged Lid, Chinese, 4 x 3 3/4 In. 556.00
Cast Iron, Elk, Cover, Glass Insert, 5 x 6 In. 225.00
Cowrie Shell, Hinged Mother-Of-Pearl Lid, Glass Insert, 2 x 3 1/2 In. 290.00
Crystal, Silver Plate, 2 1/2 In., Pair 71.00
Crystal, Sterling Flip Lid, Square, 4 3/4 x 5 In. 325.00

Cut Glass, Art Nouveau, Square, Open Rest, Gilded Metal Base, c.1902, 4 1/2 x 6 In. 165.00
Cut Glass, Intaglio Cut, Flower Sprays, Square, Silver Lid, 3 1/2 x 4 In. 470.00
Cut Glass, Square, Prism Body, Signed, Shreve, Silver Lid, 4 In. 750.00
Double, Organic Shape, Liners, Pewter, Kayserzinn, 4 1/2 x 12 In. 708.00
Glass, Blown, Amethyst, Funnel Shape, Spool Baluster, Cover, Foot, 1770-1810, 3 In. 440.00
Glass, Blown, Green, 6-Sided, Rolled Lip, Embossed, Open Pontil, 2 1/2 In. 935.00
Glass, Blown, Green, 8-Sided, Rolled Lip, Open Pontil, c.1850-60, 2 1/2 In. 358.00
Glass, Blown, Leaf Cap, Iridescent Purple Ground, Threading, Glass Insert, Palme-Lonig, 4 x 2 In. .. 520.00
Glass, Blown, Olive Amber, 3-Piece Mold, Cylindrical, Pontil, 1830, 1 3/4 x 2 1/4 In. 190.00
Glass, Blown, Olive Green, 3-Piece Mold, Applied Disk Opening, Pontil, c.1825, 1 1/2 x 2 1/4 In. . 176.00
Glass, Blown, Olive Green, 3-Piece Mold, Applied Disk Opening, Pontil, c.1825, 2 x 2 1/2 In. 230.00
Glass, Blown, Olive Green, 3-Piece Mold, Keene Marlboro St. Glassworks, c.1830, 2 x 1 1/2 In. ... 200.00
Glass, Blown, Stopper, Clear, Cobalt Blue Funnel, Applied Base, Pontil, 1865-75, 9 In. 1540.00
Glass, Clear, Air Trap, Silver Plated Top, Pairpoint, 4 1/4 In. 150.00
Glass, Green, Applied Corner Rigaree, Flared Lip, Open Pontil Base, c.1850-70, 1 3/4 In. 523.00
Glass, Green, Pattern Molded, 26 Vertical Ribs, Applied Handle, Kick-Up Base, 2 x 2 In. 440.00
Glass, Peachblow, Spherical, Cast Brass Cover, England, c.1885, 4 In. 1095.00
Glass, Pyramid, Iridescent, Pulled Thread Decoration, Pallme Konig & Habel, c.1900, 2 1/2 In. ... 380.00
Glass, Umbrella Shape, Iridescent Blue, Applied Threading, Metal Cover, Loetz, 4 In. 420.00
Hinged Lid, Black Cherubs, Embossed, Flowers, Spelter, Raised Filigree, c.1900, 4 1/2 In. 165.00
Lacy Glass, Diamond Pattern, 3 Wells For Ink, Stand, 5 1/4 x 8 1/4 In. 105.00
Marble, Art Deco, Green, Double, Hinged Lid, Pen Tray, Brass Mount Hinges, 3 1/2 x 16 In. 248.00
Metal, 2 Baseball Batters, Crystal Ink Jar, 1880s, 4 x 6 1/4 x 3 1/2 In. 5510.00
Metal, Dog Head, Glass Insert, 4 x 6 In. 300.00
Metal, Musical, Woman, Leaves, Bronze Finish, 2 Tunes, Art Nouveau, France, c.1890, 11 In. 1120.00
Metal, Race Car, 2 Drivers, WMF, Germany, c.1900, 9 1/2 x 14 1/2 x 5 In. 1799.00
Minstrel, Fiddle Player, Porcelain, Painted, France, 1850s, 5 In. 150.00
Mixed Metal, Naturalistic Lava Rock Shape, Red, Brown, Hammered Button Lid, 3 x 4 In. 410.00
Opalescent, Pressed Pattern, 2 Pots, Lids, c.1830-50, 3 x 8 1/2 In. 605.00
Paperweight, Green Aqua, 3 Doughnut Form Segments, Flared Mouth, Pontil, Stopper, 6 3/4 In. .. 1450.00
Porcelain, Thomas Black Ink, Paper, LH Thomas Co., 1800s, 1 5/8 In. 112.00
Pottery, Pomegranate Pattern, Metal Hinged Lid, Moorcroft, 2 In. 645.00
Pressed Glass, Early Thumbprint, Britannia Lid, 20 Rays Under Base, Flint, 2 3/4 x 3 3/8 In. 360.00
Purple Amethyst, Galleried Type Rim, Funnel Opening, Pontil Base, 1820-40, 2 In. 110.00
Quartz, Smokey, Dragon, Emerald Eyes, Jade, Coral, Gold, c.1925, 4 3/4 x 5 In. 9600.00
Satsuma, Flowers, 4 1/2 In. 710.00
Shell Shape, Cover, Flowers, Gilding, Swansea, 1816-26, 4 In. 5765.00
Silver, Copper, Enamel, Glass, Cymric, Archibald Knox, England, c.1900, 7 1/4 In. 12010.00
Silver, Enamel, Glass Liner, Cymric, Archibald Knox, England, 1904, 8 3/4 In. 9828.00
Silver, Sloping Sides, Inlaid Lid, Bronze Base, String & Quatrefoil Inlay, Arts & Crafts, 3 x 7 In. 295.00
Silver, Turquoise Cabochons, Glass Liner, Archibald Knox, England, 1906, 4 3/4 In. 20748.00
Silver Plate, Baseball Player, Glass Jar, Simpson Hall Miller & Co., c.1880, 3 3/4 x 2 1/2 In. 4060.00
Squiggles, Crude, Redware, c.1850, 2 x 4 1/2 In. 110.00
Standish, Regency, Cobalt, Urn Shaped Pounce Pot, Sheffield, 1800s, 3 1/4 x 7 1/2 In. 411.00
Stoneware, 3 Flower Sprays, 3 Quill Holes, 1 3/4 x 3 In. 550.00
Stoneware, Tan, Mottled, c.1850, 3 3/4 In. 175.00
Teakettle, Starch Blue, 3-Piece Mold, 6-Double Lobe & Rib Panels, c.1875, 2 3/4 In. 360.00
Wood, Carved, Pear Shape, Leaf Base, Painted, Glass Inkwell, 8 3/4 In. 230.00

INSULATORS of glass or pottery have been made for use on telegraph or telephone poles since 1844. Thousands of different styles of insulators have been made. Most common are those of clear or aqua glass; most desirable are the threadless types made from 1850 to 1870.

Armstrong, No. 512U, Saddle Wire Groove, Double Petticoat, Smooth Base, Clear 5.00
Armstrong, Pedestal Base, Salesman Sample, Clear 375.00
Brookfield, No. 31, Side Wire Groove, Single Petticoat, Aqua 1.00
Brookfield, Side Wire Groove, Single Petticoat, Green Aqua, Amber Swirls 3.00
Brookfield, W.U.T., Side Wire Groove, Single Petticoat, Amber Swirls 275.00
California, Side Wire Groove, Double Petticoat, Smooth Base, Smoky Light Purple 40.00

Castle, Saddle Wire Groove, Double Petticoat, Strawberry 825.00
Diamond, Side Wire Groove, Single Petticoat, Royal Purple 30.00
Diamond, Side Wire Groove, Single Petticoat, Smooth Base, Peach 180.00
Foster Brothers, Side Wire Groove, Pilgrim Hat, Rounded Dome, Olive Black 455.00
Good, No. 16, Side Wire Groove, Single Petticoat, Smooth Base, Aqua 10.00
H.B.R., Side Wire Groove, Double Petticoat, Smooth Base, Ice Blue 30.00
H.G. Co., N.A.T.CO., Side Wire Groove, Double Petticoat, Peacock Blue 1430.00
Hemingray, No. 8, Side Wire Groove, Single Petticoat, Smooth Base, Ice Green 100.00
Hemingray, No. 62, Saddle Wire Groove, Ice 15.00
Hemingray, No. 95, Mine, Pinhole Goes All The Way Through, Aqua 140.00
Hemingray, No. E-3, Saddle Wire Groove, Double Petticoat, Light Lemon 120.00
Hemingray, Side Wire Groove, Single Petticoat, Purple, 2-Tone 577.00
Kerr, No. DP1, Side Wire Groove, Double Petticoat, Clear 2.00
Locke, No. 16, Saddle Wire Groove, Triple Petticoat, Dark Yellow Green 155.00
Maydwell, No. 42, Side Wire Groove, Double Petticoat, Ice 5.00
McLaughlin, No. 20, Side Wire Groove, Double Petticoat, Green 34.00
McLaughlin, No. 42, Side Wire Groove, Double Petticoat, Dark Aqua 5.00
McLaughlin, No. 62, Cable, Ears, Emerald Green 412.00
McLaughlin, No. 64, 7-Up 28.00
No Name, Side Wire Groove Signal, Concave Skirt, Blue Aqua, Some Milk 275.00
No Name, Side Wire Groove, Beehive, Threadless, Light Aqua 495.00
Pat App For, No. 3, Side Wire Groove, Single Petticoat, Smooth Base, Junky Blue Aqua 45.00
Postal, Saddle Wire Groove, Double Petticoat, Emerald Green, Amber Swirling 75.00
Postal, Side Wire Groove, Double Petticoat, Smooth Base, Blue Aqua 5.00
Pyrex, No. 63, Saddle Wire Groove, Double Petticoat, Smooth Base, Carnival 40.00
S.S. & Co. Mfg's, Chicago, Side Wire Groove, Double Petticoat, Lime Green 440.00
Star, Cable, 2 Ears, Aqua 330.00
Star, Side Wire Groove, Double Petticoat, Smooth Base, Yellow Green 20.00
Star, Side Wire Groove, Single Petticoat, Smooth Base, Aqua 9.00
Texcoco, Side Wire Groove, Double Petticoat, Emerald Green 292.00
W.F.G. Co., No. 16, Side Wire Groove, Single Petticoat, Smooth Base, Light Purple 75.00
Wade, Pin Type, Wood Cover, Aqua 960.00
Whitall Tatum, No. 1, Side Wire Groove, Double Petticoat, Smooth Base, Amethyst 25.00
Whitall Tatum, No. 1, Side Wire Groove, Double Petticoat, Smooth Base, Purple 30.00

IRISH BELLEEK, see Belleek category.

IRON is a metal that has been used by man since prehistoric times. It is a popular metal for tools and decorative items like doorstops that need as much weight as possible. Items are listed here or under other appropriate headings, such as Bookends, Doorstop, Kitchen, Match Holder, or Tool. The tool that is used for ironing clothes, an iron, is listed in the Kitchen category under Iron and Sadiron.

Book Press, Platens, Single Screw Compression, 1820s, 8 x 12 In. 250.00
Bootjack, Compass Flower Decoration, 1800s, 14 3/4 In. 242.00
Bootjack, Gun Splits To Reveal Boot Jack, Hinged, 2 x 8 1/2 In. 100.00
Brackets, Shelf, Cast, Arm Shape, Grasping Doorknob, 19th Century, 5 x 17 In. 1000.00
Bust, African Man, Iron, Black Paint, 8 1/2 In. 518.00
Ceiling Fixture, Mica, Samuel Yellin, c.1920, 10 1/2 x 16 In. 9600.00
Censer, Boat Shape, Handles, 4 Legs, Doves, Flowers, Carp, c.1900, 6 1/4 x 7 In. 11500.00
Cigar Cutter, Wood Base, 22 In. 55.00
Cuspidor, Turtle, Bronze Wash, Royal Novelty, Chicago, c.1900, 13 1/2 In. 1045.00
Cuspidor, Turtle, Cast, Tin Shell, 14 In. 196.00
Dish, Cast, Leaf Shape, 12 1/2 In. 47.00
Ewer, Engraved Flowers, Gold Inlay, Persia, 1800s, 10 1/4 In. 1175.00
Figure, Cat, Facing Dog, Silhouette, Mounted On Stand, Sheet Iron, 24 In. 720.00
Figure, Cavalier, Renaissance Dress, Black Paint, Victorian, Oval Base, 66 In. 1528.00
Figure, Dog, Hound, Reclining, Head Up, Cast, Plinth Base, 15 x 21 In., Pair 2820.00
Figure, Dog, Terrier, Ivory Paint, 14 In. 75.00
Figure, Dog, Whippet, Seated, Cast, Oval Base, 12 3/4 x 7 1/4 In. 259.00
Figure, Dragon, Gold Inlaid Eyes, Tail, Japan, 19th Century, 21 In. 5290.00

Figure, Eagle, On Globe, Spread Wings, Gold Paint, 9 In. 140.00
Figure, Eagle, Spread Wings, Cast, 10 1/2 In. 55.00
Figure, Eagle, Spread Wings, Late 1800s, 30 In. 330.00
Figure, Eagle, Spread Wings, Silver Paint, 11 1/2 In. 65.00
Figure, Frog, Cast, Glass Eyes, Signed, RH Rich, East Hampton, 7 In. 400.00
Figure, Frog, Cast, Green & White Paint, 9 1/2 In. 230.00
Figure, Horse, Running, Full Body, Horsehair Tail, Cast, Carved, Painted Wood, 21 x 23 In. 765.00
Figure, Lion, Buddhist, Korea, 1700s, 12 In., Pair 1175.00
Figure, Lion, Lying Down, Canova Style, c.1850, 22 x 36 In., Pair 8519.00
Figure, Pig, Black Paint, 8 1/2 In. 60.00
Figure, Shooting Gallery Squirrel, Weirs Beach, 10 In. 58.00
Match Striker, Shoe Shape, Victorian, 4 In., Pair 66.00
Paperweight, Dog, Terrier, Hubley, 1930s 150.00
Plaque, Goddess Kannon, Japan, 1800s, 13 1/2 In. 350.00
Plaque, Last Supper, Bronze Wash, Early 1900s, 14 1/2 x 26 1/2 In. 248.00
Road Sign, Canterbury, Black & White Paint, 8 x 50 In. 165.00
Shackles, Alcatraz, Marked 250.00
Statue, Classical Woman, Holding Bouquet, Flowers, 71 x 24 In. 1265.00
Thermo Barrel, Cast, Early 20th Century, 3 In. 35.00
Votive Stand, 4 Stepped Rows Of Holders, Twist Supports, Continental, 39 x 36 In. 205.00
Wax Jack, Spring Activated Pincers, Slender Shaft, Tripod Feet, 7 In. 825.00
Wheel, Cider Press, Red, Gold Over Black Paint, 25 1/2 In. 675.00
Windmill Weight, Bull, Wood Base, c.1900, 24 x 17 1/2 In. 1035.00
Windmill Weight, Rooster, Cast, Painted, 19 In. 863.00
Windmill Weight, Rooster, Marked Hummer E184, Elgin Wind Power & Pump Co., 11 In. 575.00

IRONSTONE china was first made in 1813. It gained its greatest popularity during the mid-nineteenth century. The heavy, durable, off-white pottery was made in white or was decorated with any of hundreds of patterns. Much flow blue pottery was made of ironstone. Some of the decorations were raised. Many pieces of ironstone are unmarked, but some English and American factories included the word *Ironstone* in their marks. Additional pieces may be listed in other categories, such as Chelsea Grape, Chelsea Sprig, Flow Blue, Gaudy Ironstone, Mason's Ironstone, Moss Rose, Staffordshire, and Tea Leaf Ironstone.

Chamber Set, Brown Foliage Pattern, Marked Franklin, 7 Piece 168.00
Chamber Set, Pitchers, Basket Weave, Lion Head Handles, 8 Piece 195.00
Coffeepot, Cover, Tulip, Blue, Paneled, Gooseneck Spout, Square Handle, 9 1/4 In. 550.00
Creamer & Sugar, Cobalt Blue Marbleized, Applied Handle, 3 3/4 x 2 1/2 In. 115.00
Footbath, Oval, Snake Handles, Enamel Flowers, England, 1800s, 17 3/4 In. 1645.00
Pitcher, Clobber Ware, c.1820, 6 In. 146.00
Pitcher, St. Johns, Blue, Molded Leaf Decoration, 7 1/2 In. 190.00
Plate, Armorial, Center Initials EML, Maple Leaves, Beaver, Dog, England, 1800s 150.00
Plate, Dinner, Ashworth, Imari Style, 10 1/2 In., 12 Piece 374.00
Plate, Fish, Underwater Scenes, Maroon Border, Gold Trim, Fonteville, 9 In., 12 Piece 382.00
Plate, Luster, 8 3/8 In. 33.00
Plate, Soup, Flower Urn Center, Flower Cartouche Border, 10 In., 10 Piece 325.00
Plate, Tulip, Blue, Paneled, 8 1/2 In. 83.00
Plate Set, Sydeham, 10 1/2 In., 10 Piece 518.00
Platter, Canova, Blue, White, T. Mayer, Longport, 15 1/2 In. 115.00
Platter, Geometric Flower, Blue, England, 17 1/2 In. 52.00
Platter, Pagodas, Garden, Scroll, Geometrics, Transfer Printed, England, c.1850, 20 x 16 In. 141.00
Platter, Well & Tree, Teutonic, Blue, White, England, c.1890 .... 263.00
Service, Ashworth Brothers, Birds, Architectural Landscape, Oriental Temples, 16 Piece 726.00
Sugar, Tulip, Blue, Shell Form Handles, 8 1/2 In. 605.00
Syrup, Paneled Flow Blue & Red Flowers, Acanthus Leaf Handle, Pewter Lid, 10 In. 515.00
Tureen, Cover, J. & G. Meakin, c.1860, 7 x 11 1/2 In. 70.00
Tureen, Cover, Undertray, Brown, White, 8 1/4 x 13 1/2 In. 58.00
Tureen, Lozenge Shape, Kyoto Pattern, 8 x 14 3/4 In. 69.00
Tureen, Sauce, Cover, Lake Pattern, Transfer, Gray, Indian Scene, St. Lawrence, 6 1/2 In. 210.00

IVORY from the tusk of an elephant is thought by many to be the only true ivory. To most collectors, the term *ivory* also includes such natural materials as walrus, hippopotamus, or whale teeth or tusks, and some of the vegetable materials that are of similar texture and density. Other ivory items may be found in the Scrimshaw and Netsuke categories. Collectors should be aware of the recent laws limiting the buying and selling of elephant ivory and scrimshaw.

Birdcage, 4 Birds, 9 In. 863.00
Boat, Mythical Figures, Chinese, c.1900, 10 In. 270.00
Box, Cover, Lotus Blossom, Insect, Branches, Wood Base, Chinese, 4 In. 1645.00
Box, Cover, Mask Carvings, Japan, 1800s, 2 1/4 In. 355.00
Box, Figures & Flower Panels, Chinese, 1800s, 7 In. 1528.00
Box, Knife, Doctor's Lady, Carved, Nude, Reclining Lady, Wooden Couch, Chinese, 9 In. 820.00
Box, Money Bag, Mice, Inlaid Eyes, Horn, Coral, Japan, 1800s, 4 In. 4115.00
Box, Mother-Of-Pearl, Carved, Hinged, Late 18th Century, 5/8 x 2 1/4 x 3 1/4 In. 235.00
Box, Smiling Buddhas, Carved, Chinese, 1900-20, 5 x 4 In. 320.00
Box, Trees, Elephants, Relief, India, 4 x 3 In. 176.00
Box, Work, Hinged Top, Interior Wells, Anglo-Indian, c.1850, 7 x 13 In. 4500.00
Brush Holder, Figures In Garden, Carved, Pierced, Chinese, 1800s, 4 In. 529.00
Brush Holder, Figures In Landscape, Chinese, 1700s, 4 1/2 In. 12925.00
Brush Holder, Flowers, Chinese, 1800s, 8 In. 265.00
Brush Holder, Taoist Divinities, Chinese, 19th Century, 4 3/4 In. 1528.00
Brush Pot, Landscape, Poem, Chinese, 1700s, 5 In. 2938.00
Brush Pot, Opera Actors, Chinese, 19th Century, 4 1/2 In. 1058.00
Brush Pot, Squirrels, Grapevines, Crosshatched Ground, Chinese, 1800s, 5 In. 1410.00
Case, Carte De Visite, Flowers, Chinese, 1800s, 5 x 3 In. 470.00
Container, Cover, Buddha, Lotus Throne, Women At Altar, Figures, Pine Tree, Oriental, 17 In. 635.00
Cricket Cage, Cover, Flowers, Pierced, Cylindrical, Horn, 4 In. 127.00
Cricket Cage, Cover, Pierced, Dragon, Phoenix, Molded Fret, 6 In. 258.00
Crucifix, Carved, Christ Figure, Patina, Continental, 1800s, 7 In. 705.00
Elephant Tusk, Flowers, Silver Repousse Stand, Chinese, 19th Century, 33 1/2 In. 4700.00
Ewer, Dragon, Rooster Spout, Dragon Handles, Temple Jar Shape, 14 1/4 In. 80.00
Figurine, 18 Arms, Lotus Throne, Blossomed Aureole, Attributes, 1900s, 10 In. 1950.00
Figurine, 8 Immortals, Clouds, Bats, Wire Wood Base, Oriental, 9 1/4 In. 546.00
Figurine, Bearded Jolly Man, Rotund Stomach, Carrying Fan, Oriental, 11 3/4 In. 460.00
Figurine, Birds On Peony, Exotic Plumage, 12 In. 1265.00
Figurine, Buddha, Chinese, 18th Century, 7 1/2 In. 1293.00
Figurine, Buddha, Holding Buddha, 17 1/2 In. 1140.00
Figurine, Bullfighters, Wood Frame, Spain, 6 1/4 x 6 1/4 In., Pair 120.00
Figurine, Deity, Parasol, Bough Of Fruit, Japan, 1800s, 6 In. 1116.00
Figurine, Dragon, Fire Breathing, Wood Base, 10 1/4 x 5 3/8 In. 115.00
Figurine, Duck, Lying Down, Incised Feathers, Signed, Japan, 3 In. 176.00
Figurine, Elder, Teakwood Base, 5 In., Pair 235.00
Figurine, Emperor Holding Peony Blossoms, 17 3/4 In. 1080.00
Figurine, Emperor, Empress, Chinese, 10 In., Pair 410.00
Figurine, Emperor, Empress, Seated On Dragon, Phoenix Thrones, Chinese, 11 In., Pair 3055.00
Figurine, Emperor, Empress, Sitting, Chinese, 1900s, 5 1/4 In., Pair 325.00
Figurine, Emperor, Empress, Stand, 4 In., Pair 265.00
Figurine, Emperor, Empress, Standing, Chinese, 1900s, 8 1/4 In., Pair 560.00
Figurine, Exotic Birds, Perched On Flowering Branches, Oriental, 11 3/8 In., Pair 635.00
Figurine, Farmer, Shovel, Basket Of Melons, Lacquer-On-Wood, Signed, Japan, 7 1/4 In. 575.00
Figurine, Female Bather Surprised, Standing Seminude, Clasping Sheet, 10 In. 2115.00
Figurine, Fisherman, Japan, c.1900, 5 x 5 In. 265.00
Figurine, Frog, 3-Legged, Rising Moon, Chinese, 1800s, 5 In. 440.00
Figurine, Gama Sennin, Leaf Apron, Frogs, Japan, Late 19th Century, 11 1/4 In. 6900.00
Figurine, Geisha, Elaborate Hair, Kimono Incised, Phoenix On Back, 10 In. 520.00
Figurine, Geisha, Holding Biwa, Adjusting Hair, Japan, Early 1900s, 10 In. 575.00
Figurine, Geisha, Holding Lantern, Box, Stained Details, Wood Stand, Japan, 9 In. 646.00
Figurine, Girl, Holding Flower Vase, Chinese, 1800s, 5 1/2 In. 295.00
Figurine, Gods Of Longevity Under Flowering Tree, Japan, 1800s, 2 x 2 In. 705.00

Figurine, Heads Carrying Baskets, Wood Base, Africa, 4 7/8 In., Pair 120.00
Figurine, Horse & Rider, Japan, 8 In. 470.00
Figurine, Hotei, Carrying Sack, Japan, Early 1900s, 4 1/4 In. 315.00
Figurine, Imperial Couple, Emperor, Dragon Throne, Empress, Phoenix Throne, 12 In. 2286.00
Figurine, Jurojin, Child, Pet Deer, Japan, 1800s, 6 In. 1530.00
Figurine, Lama Seated On Lotus Throne, Chinese, 19th Century, 6 1/2 In. 1645.00
Figurine, Lions, Carved, Rosewood Base, Chinese, 2 1/2 x 5 In., Pair 350.00
Figurine, Lobster, Japan, 16 In. 8775.00
Figurine, Madonna & Child, Leafy Crown, Smiling, Germany, 8 3/4 x 2 1/2 x 2 In. 4830.00
Figurine, Maitreya, 22 Arms, Holding Ritual Items, 1800s, 24 1/2 In. 7638.00
Figurine, Man, Carrying Boy With Parasol, Stork In Hand, Red, Brown, Green Ink, 10 1/2 In. 520.00
Figurine, Man, Cleaning His Ear, Chinese, 1800s, 9 1/2 In. 1290.00
Figurine, Man, With Parasol, Mother-Of-Pearl Fan, Head, Feet, Hands, Belts, Inlaid Wood, 11 In. .. 259.00
Figurine, Mary Queen Of Scots, Skirt Hinged, Carved Triptych, 1800s, 5 3/4 In. 825.00
Figurine, Monk, Patina, Sitting, Standing, Beads, Bell, Leaf, Chinese, 8 x 2 1/2 x 2 In., Pair 2990.00
Figurine, Monkey Trainer, Japan, 1800s, 5 In. 499.00
Figurine, Oni Demon, Monkey, Japan, 1800s, 5 In. 1116.00
Figurine, Pleasure Boat, Chinese, 1800s, 11 In. 1645.00
Figurine, Rhinoceros, 6 1/4 In. 260.00
Figurine, Scholar Carrying Staff, Flower, Oriental, 14 In. 400.00
Figurine, Scholar With Scroll, Dragon Headed Staff, Signed, 10 7/8 In. 400.00
Figurine, Scholar, Bearded, Holding Ball, 8 In. 145.00
Figurine, Seated Figure, Crosshatched Hair, Holding Fly Whisk, Brown Stain, 6 In. 115.00
Figurine, Seated Figure, Elaborate Headdress, Brown Stain, Africa, 8 In. 145.00
Figurine, Seated Tribal Chieftain, Bound Captive, Brown, Africa, 16 In. 145.00
Figurine, Ship, Gods Of Luck, Japan, 19th Century, 22 In. 3055.00
Figurine, Shojo Maker, Japan, 1800s, 2 1/2 x 3 1/2 In. 2470.00
Figurine, Tall Terraced Garden, Wooden Plinth, Oriental, 8 In. 200.00
Figurine, Warrior With Spear, Sword, Oriental, 10 3/4 In. 400.00
Figurine, Woman, Butterfly Pendant, Beaded Headdress, Flower Basket, Fan, Oriental, 14 In. 575.00
Figurine, Woman, Carrying Child On Back, Stained Red, Brown, Africa, 13 1/2 In. 230.00
Figurine, Woman, Chinese Costume, Holding Child, Japan, Late 1800s, 8 1/4 In. 440.00
Figurine, Woman, Court Lady, Bird Headdress, 19th Century, 9 1/2 In. 500.00
Figurine, Woman, Dancer, Box, Japan, 1800s, 9 In. 825.00
Figurine, Woman, Holding Fan, Rose, Black Ink Details, Oriental, Wood Stand, 13 1/4 In. 489.00
Figurine, Woman, Holding Flowers, Oriental, 15 1/2 In. 489.00
Figurine, Woman, Holding Water Lily, Wood Stand, 11 1/4 In. 430.00
Figurine, Woman, Kneeling Wearing Beaded Jewelry, Brown Stain, Africa, 8 5/8 In. 145.00
Figurine, Woman, Long Robe, High Chignon, Chinese, 24 1/2 In. 2596.00
Figurine, Woman, Looking In Mirror, c.1885, 9 1/4 In. 8400.00
Figurine, Woman, Nude, Wood Plinth, 8 x 10 3/4 In. 405.00
Figurine, Woman, Nursing Baby, Brown Stain, Africa, 13 3/4 In. 290.00
Figurine, Woman, Nursing Child, Red, Amber Stain, 10 In. 115.00
Figurine, Woman, Parasol, Box, Japan, 1800s, 6 In. 825.00
Figurine, Woman, Stylishly Dressed, Rococo Style Base, Germany, 7 1/2 x 2 1/2 In. 1725.00
Figurine, Woman, With Flowers, Elaborate Hair, Oriental, 13 1/2 In. 489.00
Group, 2 Dogs, Spaniels, Running Across A Bridge, Japan, 1800s, 11 In. 3819.00
Group, 2 Elephants, Mother, Calf, Japan, 4 1/2 In. 118.00
Group, 3 Chinese Generals, At Table, Masanobu, Japan, Late 1800s, 4 3/4 In. 1955.00
Group, 5 Dancers In Lion's Mask, Japan, 1800s, 3 1/2 In. 765.00
Group, Buildings, People, Wooded Area, Temple, Horse, Rider, Boat, Wood Base, 18 In. 546.00
Group, Carpenter, On Barrel, Japan, Late 19th Century, 6 In. 150.00
Group, Elephant & Travelers, Signed, Japan, 2 In. 645.00
Group, Fishing Boat, 2 Men Casting Net, Woman Cooking Fish, Water Lilies, 12 3/4 x 3 3/4 In. 489.00
Group, Horse, 4 Men, Rickshaw, Oriental, 12 1/2 x 17 x 8 1/2 In. 2160.00
Group, Horses, Carved, Stained, 8 Horses Of Wang Mu, 8 Piece 2585.00
Group, Impalas, Elephants, Men In Boat, Women With Mortar, Pestle, Africa, 13 1/2 In. 115.00
Group, Kwannon, On Foo Dogs, Lotus Throne, Wood, Japan, 1868-1912, 10 In. 4200.00
Group, Mahut, Riding An Elephant, Japan, Late 19th Century, 4 In. 635.00
Group, Man, Startled By Painting Of Screen Coming To Life, Japan, 1800s, 7 x 5 In. 1530.00
Group, Warrior On Foo Dog, Stepped Base, Oriental, 15 1/4 x 10 x 5 1/2 In. 2185.00

Group, Witch, Trapping Anchin In Temple Bell, Japan, 1900s, 4 1/2 In. 230.00
Jar, 2 Piece, 3 Ball & Claw Feet, Oval, Handles, Wood Base, Oriental, 17 1/2 x 17 In. 1320.00
Landscape, Curved Tusk Shape, Wood Stand, Box, Chinese, 17 1/2 In. 1760.00
Magnifying Glass, Ivory Handle, Dragon, Brass, Semiprecious Stones, Tassel, Silk Case, 10 In. 115.00
Medicine Container, Human, Animal, Indonesian, Batak, c.1900, 20 In. 999.00
Mirror, Frame, Shield Crests, Grapes, Easel Back, 15 In. 430.00
Model, House, 2 Villagers, Trees, River, Japan, 1800s, 2 1/2 x 2 In. 499.00
Okimono, 2 Sumo Wrestlers, Oval Platform, Japan, 1900s, 3 In. 920.00
Okimono, Deity Holding Plant Stems, Basket Of Fish, Dragon, Japan, 6 1/2 x 3 x 2 In. 1265.00
Okimono, Gama Sennin, Balancing Large Frog On Shoulders, Japan, 1800s, 3 1/2 In. 1725.00
Okimono, Goose, Inlaid Eyes, Japan, Late 19th Century, 4 1/4 In. 575.00
Okimono, Man, Child On Back, Child On Thigh, Japan, 10 3/4 x 3 1/2 x 12 1/2 In. 1178.00
Okimono, Monkey Trainer, One On His Head, Boy Playing Flute, Japan, c.1900, 6 1/2 In. 619.00
Okimono, Pomegranate, Orange, Green, Japan, 1 3/4 x 2 x 1 7/8 In. 115.00
Okimono, Samurai, Holding Books, Scrolls, Japan, 6 1/2 x 2 1/4 x 2 3/4 In. 1380.00
Okimono, Sandal Maker With Cat, Japan, 1800s, 2 1/4 In. 489.00
Page Turner, Curved Blade, Tree Trunk Grip, Sennin Figure, Daruma Terminal, 16 In. 160.00
Page Turner, Elephants, Japan, Late 19th Century, 15 1/2 In. 330.00
Page Turner, Flowers, Chinese, 1800s, 4 In. 265.00
Page Turner, Shibayama, Flowers, Birds, Insects, Color Inlay, Japan, Late 1800s, 13 In. 305.00
Parasol Handle, Dragons, Japan, 1800s, 12 In. 529.00
Parasol Handle, Flowers, Thunder God, Traveler, Japan, 1800s, 15 In. 765.00
Parasol Handle, Hawk, On Tree, With Snake, Mother-Of-Pearl Eyes, 5 1/2 In. 86.00
Parasol Handle, Masks, Japan, 1800s, 10 1/2 In. 325.00
Pendant, Crucifix, Cylindrical Cross Pieces, Carved, Winged Putto Masque Center, 6 x 3 In. 205.00
Pie Crimper, Whale, Carved, Reticulated End, Scalloped Edge, 7 1/2 In. 460.00
Puzzle Ball, Chinese, 19th Century, 2 In. 235.00
Puzzle Ball, Chinese, 19th Century, 15 x 5 In. 805.00
Puzzle Ball, Flowers, Chinese, 1800s, 4 In. 1058.00
Puzzle Ball, Stand, 19th Century, 3 1/2 x 14 In. 3450.00
Puzzle Ball, Wood Stand, Dragons, Clouds, Pierced Balls, Coins, Stars, Chinese, 16 x 4 In. 489.00
Ring Box, Brass, Hand Painted, 18th Century Woman, France, c.1900, 1 3/8 x 1 1/2 In. 235.00
Seal, Crane, Lotus Finial, Seed Pods, Dragon, Cloud, Rectangular, Chinese, 5 1/2 In. 2300.00
Seal, Lion, Stylized Calligraphy, Rectangular, 1 3/4 In. 430.00
Statue, Hsi Wang Mu, Holding Flower Bough, Phoenix, Chinese, Late 1800s, 28 In. 2468.00
Stringed Instrument Pick, Japan, Signed, 7 3/4 In. 355.00
Tableau, Traveler, Seated On Bench, Tea Utensils, Japan, c.1900, 8 1/2 In. 3240.00
Tankard, Bacchanal, Silver Mounts, Figural Finial, Hallmark, Germany, 18 1/2 In. 23400.00
Teapot, Domed Cover, Carved, Chinese, 19th Century, 5 1/2 x 5 1/2 In. 295.00
Toothbrush, Pig Bristles, Victorian, 6 In. 27.00
Tray, Bats, Pine Trees, Chinese, 1700s, 7 In. 3525.00
Tusk, Carved, Rhinos, Elephants, Hippo, 18 1/2 In. 115.00
Vase, Elephant Head, Loose Ring Handles, Shou, Lattice Design, Hu Form, 8 3/4 In., Pair 840.00
Wall Plaques, Native Holding Urn, Trees, Scalloped Rims, Oak Plaques, Africa, 31 1/2 In., Pair ... 259.00
Wrist Rest, Attendants Walking Up Mountain, Boat, Inscription, Chinese, 9 3/4 x 2 3/8 In. 2415.00
Wrist Rest, Erotic Scene, Lotus Leaf, 2 x 3 1/4 In. 1265.00
Wrist Rest, High Relief, Boys Playing, Pine Tree, Chinese, c.1900, 7 1/2 In. 570.00
Wrist Rest, Riders Ascending To Mountain Retreat, 9 1/2 In., Pair 1905.00
Zushi, Kwannon, On Lotus Base, Japan, c.1900, 4 1/2 In. 900.00

JACK ARMSTRONG, the all-American boy, was the hero of a radio serial from 1933 to 1951. Premiums were offered to the listeners until the mid-1940s. Jack Armstrong's best-known endorsement is for Wheaties.

Better Little Book, Jack Armstrong & Mystery Of Iron Key, Whitman, 1939 .... 20.00 to 31.00
Film Viewer, Bakelite, Brown, Film Roll, Pamphlets, Box, 4 In. 23.00
Flashlight, 4 1/2 x 1 1/2 In. 85.00
Hike-O-Meter, 1930s, 2 3/4 In. 9.00
Kit, Write A Fighter Corps, 1942 .... 34.00
Magic Answer Box, Tin, Wheaties, 1938, 3 3/4 In. 156.00
Phonograph Album, Wheaties Presents, All American Boy, General Mills, 1973 .... 3.00 to 7.50

Ring, Dragon's Eye, Glow In Dark, Premium 275.00
Ring, Secret Egyptian Whistle 28.45
Secret Bombsight, Wood, Lithograph Paper Labels, Wheaties, 1942, 3 x 2 1/2 In. 48.00
Shooting Plane, Gun, Round Disk, Mailing Box, 1930s 24.00
Sun Watch Decoder, Premium, 1940s 34.00
Wheaties, Box Back, Flying Fortress Escape, 1939, 6 x 8 1/4 In. 42.00
Wheaties, Box Back, Rescues Cast Away Crew, 1939, 6 x 8 1/8 In. 44.00

JACK-IN-THE-PULPIT vases, oddly shaped like trumpets, resemble the wild plant called jack-in-the-pulpit. The design originated in the late Victorian years. Vases in the jack-in-the-pulpit shape were made of ceramic or glass, and the complete list of page references can be found in the index.

Vase, Amethyst, Ribbed, Gold Flowers & Swags, 13 1/2 In. 165.00
Vase, Blue Opalescent Swags, Bulbous Bottom, 4 1/2 In. 225.00
Vase, Clear, Faded Opaque Edges, 1920s, 6 1/4 In. 100.00
Vase, Frosted, Yellow & Gold Enamel Flowers, White Leaves, Rust Rim, c.1910, 8 In. 100.00
Vase, Glass, Blue Iridescent, Cobalt Pulled Feather, Lundberg, 1978, 5 1/4 In. 115.00
Vase, Glass, Blue Iridescent, Green Pulled Feather, Gabriel Pattern, Lundberg, 13 1/2 In. 230.00
Vase, Glass, Green, Opalescent, 6 In. 90.00
Vase, Glass, Iridescent Blue, Ribbed Body, Signed Lundberg, 13 1/4 In. 604.00
Vase, Glass, Orient & Flume, Turquoise, Pulled Feather, Iridescent Gold, 1978, 14 In. 690.00
Vase, Iridescent Blue, Ribbed, Gold Interior, Signed, Lundberg Studios, 1915, 13 1/4 In. ... *ILLUS* 578.00
Vase, Light Blue Opalescent, 7 x 6 In. 55.00
Vase, Opaline Glass, Red Shaded To Deep Cranberry Crimped Edges, 9 In. 279.00
Vase, Robin's-Egg Blue Cased, Swirled, Cranberry Flowers, Clear Rigaree Handle, 9 In. 175.00
Vase, Vaseline Glass, Green Spatter Decoration, 5-Petal Feet, 8 3/4 In. 350.00
Vase, Vaseline Glass, Opalescent, Yellow & White Enamel Flowers, c.1900, 15 1/2 In. 395.00

JADE is the name for two different minerals, nephrite and jadeite. Nephrite is the mineral used for most early Oriental carvings. Jade is a very tough stone that is found in many colors from dark green to pale lavender. Jade carvings are still being made in the old styles, so collectors must be careful not to be fooled by recent pieces. Jade jewelry is found in this book under Jewelry.

Archer's Ring, Incised Flowers, Green White, Chinese, 1900s, 1 3/4 In. 95.00
Archer's Ring, Muttonfat, Brown, Black, Tan Shading, Chinese 58.00
Archer's Ring, Muttonfat, Concentric Design, Chinese 80.00
Archer's Ring, Spinach Green, Cylindrical, Chinese 105.00
Belt Hook, Phoenix, Insect, White, Chinese, 4 1/4 In. 105.00
Bowl, Cover, Light Green, Foot Ring, Flared Sides, Beveled Lip, Hardstone, Chinese, 2 x 5 In., Pair . 978.00
Bowl, Mottled Green, Bell Shape, Chinese, 5 1/2 In. 780.00
Box, Cover, Scallop Shape, Carved, Decorations, Chinese, 4 1/2 x 5 1/4 x 1 3/8 In. 645.00
Brush Rest, Mountain, Celadon Color, Yellow Marking, Chinese, 1800s, 5 In. 470.00
Brush Washer, Nephrite, 2 Conjoined Bowls, Relief Fungi, Vines, 1700s, 3 In. 535.00
Brushpot, Gray, Figural Landscape, Cylindrical, White, Chinese, 4 In. 4200.00
Censer, Masks, Lion Mask Handles, Celadon Stone, Chinese, 1800s, 5 1/2 x 6 In. 1645.00
Centerpiece, Carved, Bowl, Dragon, Chinese, 19th Century, 3 1/2 x 9 x 12 1/2 In. 2225.00
Cricket Cage, Tubular, Dragon, Leaves, Flowers, Wood Stand, Chinese, Late 1800s, 9 1/2 In. 4700.00
Figurine, 2 Dragons, Bats, Chinese, 19th Century, 5 1/2 In. 999.00
Figurine, Bear, Celadon, Chinese, 19th Century, 5 In. 940.00
Figurine, Cabbage, Green, Chinese, 1900s, 4 1/2 In. 380.00
Figurine, Camel, Chinese, 5 In. 266.00
Figurine, Camel, Reclining, Celadon, Chinese, 19th Century, 8 In. 2235.00
Figurine, Caparisoned Horse, Silver Inlaid Stand, Box, Chinese, 1900s, 8 1/2 In. 265.00
Figurine, Carved, Dragons Carrying Urns, Teakwood Base, Cover, 9 In. 175.00
Figurine, Dog, Seated, Celadon, Chinese, 4 In. 236.00
Figurine, Egrets, Celadon, Chinese, 5 5/8 x 3 x 1 3/4 In., Pair 750.00
Figurine, Fish Set, Carved, Serpentine, Teakwood Bases, Chinese, 3 In., 5 Piece 176.00
Figurine, Foo Dog, Celadon, Chinese, 8 In. 295.00
Figurine, Foo Dog, Winged, Teakwood Base, 5 1/2 In., Pair 145.00

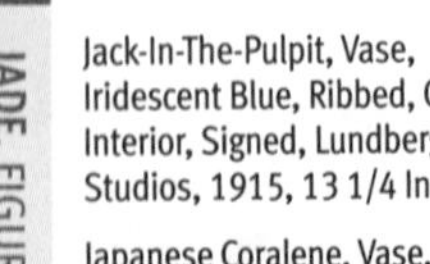

Jack-In-The-Pulpit, Vase, Iridescent Blue, Ribbed, Gold Interior, Signed, Lundberg Studios, 1915, 13 1/4 In.

Japanese Coralene, Vase, 35 Butterflies, Glass Beads, Satin Ground, c.1909, 9 1/2 In.

Figurine, Foo Dog, With Ball, Teakwood Base, 4 In. 115.00
Figurine, God Of Longevity, In Reverie, Boy On Back, Nephrite, 2 In. 267.00
Figurine, Meijin Holding Branch, Flowers, Lavender, Green, Chinese, 11 1/2 In. 4025.00
Figurine, Meijin Holding Prunus Branch, Red, Green Jadeite, Chinese, 7 1/4 In. 430.00
Figurine, Oriental Woman, Standing, Carved, 12 1/4 In. 235.00
Figurine, Plants, Bird, Celadon, China, 6 1/2 In. 235.00
Figurine, Quan Yin Seated, Flower, Bamboo Robe, White, Chinese, 6 1/2 In. 3600.00
Figurine, Twins, Laughing, Holding Flower, Animal, Hardstone, Chinese, 9 3/4 x 6 x 2 1/2 In. 4830.00
Figurine, Xi Wang Mu, Holding Peach, Phoenix, Attendant, Hardstone, Chinese, 11 x 6 x 2 1/2 In. .. 2990.00
Fruit, Grape Bunches, Amethyst, Quartz, Carved, 3 Sets 120.00
Group, Ram, 2 Ewes, White, Chinese, 6 In. 8050.00
Group, White, Apple Green, 3 Meiren, Flowering Branches, Chinese, 6 1/4 In. 531.00
Hairpin, Celadon, Translucent, Chinese, 19th Century, 12 x 1 1/4 In. 355.00
Jar, Cover, Leaf, Flowers, Grasshopper, 6 1/4 In. 310.00
Jar, Leaves, Flowers, Grasshopper, Raised, Carved, 6 1/4 In. 310.00
Kovash, Boat Shape, Nephrite, Silver Stern, Man, Cyrillic Inscription, c.1909, 9 1/2 x 15 3/4 In. .. 8965.00
Plaque, Nephrite, Monkeys, Holding Drum, Long Life Emblem, Chinese, c.1800, 2 1/2 In. 285.00
Screen, Palace Scene, Spinach Green, Rosewood Frame, 10 1/4 x 5 3/4 In. 580.00
Screen, Pavilions By Lakeside, Celadon, Rosewood Frame, 8 1/2 x 6 In. 3820.00
Seal, Dragon, Cloud, Apple Green, Chinese, 1800s, 2 x 2 In. 825.00
Teapot, Cover, 3-Lobed, Fruit Form, Bamboo Handle, Branch Finial, White, Chinese, 6 In. 7475.00
Urn, Cover, 3 Lion Paw Feet, Applied Bird Handles, Lion, Teakwood Base, 7 In. 175.00
Urn, Cover, Carved, Baluster Shape, Lotus Flowers, Vines, Twisted Flame Knobs, 10 1/2 In. 6168.00
Urn, Foo Dog Cover, Carved, Spinach Colored, Handles, Chinese, 14 In. 1170.00
Vase, Bird, Flower, Relief, Flower Form, Celadon, Yellow, Gilt Wood Stand, Chinese, 5 In. 920.00
Vase, Cover, Celadon, Chinese, 6 1/2 In. 265.00
Vase, Cover, Green, Foo Dog, Chain, Chinese, 7 In. 235.00
Vase, Cover, Relief Fruit, Dragon Handles, Green, White Jadeite, Oval, Chinese, 4 1/4 In. 1840.00
Vase, Dome Cover, Passion Flower, Ball Finial, Carved Mogul Style, Chinese, 7 1/2 In. 4025.00
Vase, Peach Branch, Tree Stump, Jadeite, Green, Chinese, 3 1/4 In. 920.00
Vase, Pine Tree Shape, Chinese, 1800s, 6 1/4 In. 765.00

JAPANESE CORALENE is a ceramic decorated with small raised beads and dots. It was first made in the nineteenth century. Later wares made to imitate coralene had dots of enamel. There is also another type of coralene that is made with small glass beads on glass containers.

Vase, 35 Butterflies, Glass Beads, Satin Ground, c.1909, 9 1/2 In. .... ***ILLUS*** 1292.00

JAPANESE WOODBLOCK PRINTS are listed in this book in the Print category under Japanese.

JASPERWARE can be made in different ways. Some pieces are made from a solid colored clay with applied raised designs of a contrasting colored clay. Other pieces are made entirely of one color clay with raised decorations that are glazed with a contrasting color. Additional pieces of jasperware may also be listed in the Wedgwood category or under various art potteries.

Jar, Cover, Blue, Classical Female Figures, 4 Seasons, Impressed, Adams, 6 x 6 1/2 In. 115.00

Plaque, Wall, 3-Dimensional, 12 x 9 1/2 In. 300.00
Plaque, Wall, Germany, 13 x 11 In. 275.00
Teapot, Lavender Ground, 3 3/4 x 4 1/2 In. 610.00

JEWELRY, whether made from gold and precious gems or plastic and colored glass, is popular with collectors. Values are determined by the intrinsic value of the stones and metal and by the skill of the craftsmen and designers. Victorian and older jewelry have been collected since the 1950s. More recent interests are Art Deco and Edwardian styles, Mexican and Danish silver jewelry, and beads of all kinds. Copies of almost all styles are being made. American Indian jewelry is listed in the Indian category. Tiffany jewelry is listed here.

Belt, Silver, Niello, Mideastern, 22 In. 185.00
Belt Buckle, Gilt Brass, Repousse, Flowers, Leaves, Palm Fronds, c.1830, 3 1/2 x 1 3/4 In. 95.00
Bracelet, 5 Amethyst, Green Enamel, Ribbed Links, 18K Gold, De Vroomen, 7 In. 3175.00
Bracelet, Bakelite, Bangle, 3 Raised Sections, Gold Metal Frame, Hinged, 6 1/4 In. 2235.00
Bracelet, Bakelite, Bangle, Apple Juice, Reverse Carved, Painted, Basket Weave, 7 3/4 In. 1528.00
Bracelet, Bakelite, Bangle, Apple Juice, Reverse Carved, Polka Dot, 7 1/2 In. 1116.00
Bracelet, Bakelite, Bangle, Butterscotch, 2 Licorice Strips, Hinged, 6 1/4 In. 499.00
Bracelet, Bakelite, Bangle, Butterscotch, Fish, Hinged, 6 1/4 In. 1175.00
Bracelet, Bakelite, Bangle, Butterscotch, Flowers, 7 3/4 In. 588.00
Bracelet, Bakelite, Bangle, Butterscotch, Leaves, 7 3/4 In. ....705.00 to 765.00
Bracelet, Bakelite, Bangle, Butterscotch, Peacock Feather, Carved, Wide, 8 In. 1116.00
Bracelet, Bakelite, Bangle, Green, Carved Leaves, 3/4 x 2 1/2 In. 85.00
Bracelet, Bakelite, Bangle, Green, Carved, 7 3/4 In. 646.00
Bracelet, Bakelite, Bangle, Palm Trees, Flowers, Carved, Wide, 7 3/4 In. 6756.00
Bracelet, Bakelite, Bangle, Reverse Carved, Painted Polka Dots, Yellow, Blue, Red, 7 3/4 In. 2465.00
Bracelet, Bakelite, Bangle, Reverse Carved, Polka Dots, Painted, Wide, 7 3/4 In. 2468.00
Bracelet, Bakelite, Bangle, Sailboat, Anchors, Hinged, 6 7/8 In. 3408.00
Bracelet, Bakelite, Bangle, Yellow, Licorice Dots, Hinged, 6 1/4 In. 590.00
Bracelet, Bakelite, Buckle, Stretch, Translucent Red & Brown, Gold Tone Accents 1880.00
Bracelet, Bakelite, Reverse Carved, Polka Dots, Corinne Davidov 2468.00
Bracelet, Bangle, Diamond, Beaded Wirework, 14K Gold, Faberge, 6 1/4 In. 3525.00
Bracelet, Bangle, Enamel, Diamonds, Seed Pearls, Locket, Hinged, 15K Gold, Victorian 765.00
Bracelet, Bangle, Hinged, Beast, Eating Tail, Wood, Ruby Eyes, 18K Gold, Buccellati 4350.00
Bracelet, Bangle, Hinged, Diamond, 18K Gold, Tiffany, c.1970, 6 1/2 In. 2938.00
Bracelet, Bangle, Hinged, Faux Screwheads, 18K Yellow Gold, Cartiere 580.00
Bracelet, Bangle, Hinged, Turquoise, Diamond, 18K Gold, Mauboussin, 6 1/2 In. 1410.00
Bracelet, Bangle, Interlocking Ball Terminals, 18K Gold, Cartier, 6 1/2 In. 205.00
Bracelet, Bangle, Lapis, Mother-Of-Pearl, Arched Panels, 18K Gold, Tiffany, 6 3/4 In. 3645.00
Bracelet, Bangle, Plastic, Flowers Carved, c.1960, 2 1/2 In. 75.00
Bracelet, Bangle, Ram's Heads, Sapphire, 22K Gold, Zolotas, 5 1/2 In. 1175.00
Bracelet, Bangle, Rope Twist Ball Terminals, Wire Twist, Etruscan Revival, 14K Gold 499.00
Bracelet, Bangle, Twisted Nail, 14K Gold, Fritzsche & Co., Newark, Edwardian, 1908, 7 In. 646.00
Bracelet, Butterfly, Opal, Diamond, Amethyst, Art Nouveau, Riker Bros., c.1918, 7 1/2 In. 8225.00
Bracelet, Carnelian, 3 Carved Disks, Enamel, 14K Gold Links, Art Deco, 7 In. 765.00
Bracelet, Charm, Platinum, Seed Pearls, 8 Charms, Art Deco, 6 1/2 In. 5875.00
Bracelet, Cuff, Brass, Art Smith, 1948, 1 3/4 x 2 3/4 x 2 1/4 In. 3840.00
Bracelet, Cuff, Flexible, Rope Twist, 18K Bicolor Gold, Parentesi, Bulgari 1175.00
Bracelet, Cuff, Link, Flexible, 18K Gold, Cartier 3525.00
Bracelet, Diamonds, Oval Knot Links, 14K Gold, Art Nouveau, 6 1/2 In. 295.00
Bracelet, Diamonds, Rectangular Links, Platinum, Art Deco, 7 1/2 In. 3290.00
Bracelet, Diamonds, Single Cut, Bead Set, 14K White Gold, Art Deco, 7 In. 2940.00
Bracelet, Emerald, Diamond, Onyx, Arched Links, 18K Gold, Art Deco, 6 1/4 In. 1410.00
Bracelet, Emerald, Single Cut Diamonds, Art Deco, 7 3/8 In. 7050.00
Bracelet, Enamel, Geometric Design, 14K Gold, c.1915, 7 In. 235.00
Bracelet, Flexible, Curved & D Shaped Link, 18K Gold, Cartier, 7 1/8 In. 1528.00
Bracelet, Glass, Cerisier, Cherries, Black, White Patina, Elasticized Elements, Lalique, c.1928 .... 3819.00
Bracelet, Hinged, European Cut Diamond, Coiled Nail, 14K Gold, c.1908, 7 In. 1765.00
Bracelet, Link, Curb, 2 Rows, 14K Gold, Tiffany, 7 In. 1175.00

Bracelet, Link, Curb, Flattened, Silver, 18K Gold, Hermes, 8 In. 1295.00
Bracelet, Link, Curb, Heart Padlock, 9K Gold, 7 In. 175.00
Bracelet, Link, Curb, Solid, Fluted, 14K Gold, Tiffany, c.1950, 7 1/2 In. 705.00
Bracelet, Link, Curb, Twisted, Padlock Closure, 9K Rose Gold, B&S, Victorian, 7 3/4 In. 235.00
Bracelet, Link, Diamonds, Pearls, Chryoprase, 19K Gold, 1940s, 8 x 3/4 In. 705.00
Bracelet, Link, Double Curb, 18K Yellow, Gold, France 540.00
Bracelet, Link, Heart Shape, Silver, N. Giles, Mexico 179.00
Bracelet, Link, Looping, 18K Gold, Ventrella, Rome, 8 In. 999.00
Bracelet, Link, Navette Shape, Rudy, Diamond, Platinum, France, Art Deco, 7 1/4 In. 7050.00
Bracelet, Links, Arched, 18K Gold, Tiffany, 7 In. 410.00
Bracelet, Mesh, Braided, European Cut Diamond In Clasp, 14K Yellow Gold, Victorian 635.00
Bracelet, Mourning, Woven Hair, Gold, Floral & Scroll Clasp, c.1850, 8 x 7 In. 265.00
Bracelet, Oyster Shells, Cultured Pearls, 14K Gold, Ruser, 7 In. 1175.00
Bracelet, Panther, Diamonds, Ruby Spots, Emerald Eyes, Flexible, 18K Gold, Lavianne, 7 1/2 In. .. 4700.00
Bracelet, Platinum, Coral, Diamond, Emerald, Art Deco, 6 1/2 In. 6465.00
Bracelet, Platinum, Diamond, Beaded Edge, Art Deco, 7 1/2 In. 12925.00
Bracelet, Platinum, Diamond, Geometric Links, Art Deco, 6 1/2 In. 2585.00
Bracelet, Platinum, Diamond, Open Gallery, Beaded Edge, Art Deco, 7 1/2 In. 8225.00
Bracelet, Platinum, Diamond, Sapphire, Beaded Edge, Art Deco, 7 In. 5580.00
Bracelet, Platinum, Diamond, Straight Line, Engraved Box Links, Art Deco 2350.00
Bracelet, Scarab, Carnelian, Brickwork Link, 18K Gold, France, Retro, 8 In. 825.00
Bracelet, Scarab, Lapis Lazuli, Pearl, Gold Carved, Egyptian Revival 4500.00
Bracelet, Sterling Silver, Curb Links, Buckle Clasp, Hermes, Paris, 8 In. 765.00
Bracelet, Sterling Silver, Enamel, Rectangular Panels, Raised Waves, D. Andersen, Norway 210.00
Bracelet, Sterling Silver, Flower Plaques, Tiffany, 1950s, 7 In. 440.00
Bracelet, Sterling Silver, Hammered Links, Blue Agate Cabochons, Bjarne, 6 1/2 In. 575.00
Bracelet, Sterling Silver, Leaf Links, Flowers, Georg Jensen, 6 3/4 In. 646.00
Bracelet, Sterling Silver, Leaf Links, Georg Jensen, 7 1/4 In. 999.00
Bracelet, Stylized Greek Key, 2 Rows, 18K Gold, Zolotas, 7 1/8 In. 880.00
Bracelet, Vermeil, Celadon, Peking Enamel, Jade, Petal Border, Filigree, Chinese 500.00
Bracelet & Earrings, Amethyst Grapes, Seed Pearl, 14K Gold, Victorian, 16 In. 999.00
Buckle, Amethyst, Silver, Pear Shape, Flowerhead, Art Nouveau, c.1910, 3 x 2 1/8 In. 1535.00
Buckle, Bakelite, Parrot, Orange Head, Black Frame, 4 In. 295.00
Buckle, White Jade, Pierced, Relief Dragon, 2 Piece, 3 3/4 In. 1920.00
Chatelaine, 5-Chain, Cherub, Griffin, Heart, Embossed, Sterling Silver .... ***ILLUS*** 2000.00
Chatelaine, Watch, Mixed Metal, Morning Glories, Jeweled Movement, c.1882, 6 In. 470.00
Cigarette Case, 18K Yellow Gold, Engine Turned Decoration, c.1948, 3 1/4 In. 1355.00
Cigarette Case, Incised Lines, 14K Gold, Tiffany, 4 1/2 x 3 1/8 In. 1175.00
Cigarette Case, Silver Plate, Bi-Plane, 1916, 3 1/2 x 4 1/4 In. 1095.00
Cigarette Case, Silver, Camille Jenatzy, Race Car Driver, c.1900, 3 x 4 x 1/2 In. 835.00
Cigarette Case, Silver, Graf & Stift Automobile Grille Shape, 1923, 3 x 4 x 3/8 In. 1115.00
Cigarette Case, Tortoiseshell, Platinum, Diamond, Art Deco, France, 5 1/2 In. 150.00
Cuff Links, Abstract Lines, Sterling Silver, Enamel, Cellini, 1950s, 1 x 3/4 In. 175.00
Cuff Links, Deck Of Cards, Spread Out, Enameled Suits, Gold, Anson, 1 x 5/8 In. 65.00
Cuff Links, Delft Portrait, Cavalier, Silver Mesh, Wrap Style, Swank, 1960s, 1 In. 125.00
Cuff Links, Diamond, Emerald Edge, Diamond Shape, Open Gallery, Art Deco 2000.00
Cuff Links, Double Link, Diamond Melee, Platinum Top, Round, 14K Gold, Edwardian 380.00
Cuff Links, Double Link, Geometric Scrolls, 14K Gold, Art Deco, H.A. Spoehr 235.00
Cuff Links, Double Link, Steeplechase, Horse, Jockey, 14K Gold, Continental, c.1910 .... 1645.00
Cuff Links, Geometric Scrolls, Garland, 14K Gold, Art Nouveau, Brassler Co., Newark 235.00
Cuff Links, Golf Ball & Club, 14K Gold, Larter & Sons 645.00
Cuff Links, Golfer In Relief, Sterling Silver, Round, Fenwick & Sailors, c.1950, 7/8 In. 125.00
Cuff Links, Japanese Scholar, Porcelain, Painted, Gold, Toshikane For Swank, c.1960, 3/4 In. 175.00
Cuff Links, Mother-Of-Pearl, Reverse Painted, Fishing Fly, Gold Ship's Wheel, Swank, 3/4 In. 65.00
Cuff Links, Onyx Bar, Rope Twist Mount, 14K Gold, Larter 395.00
Cuff Links, Oval Blue Rhinestone, Silver Mesh, Wrap Style, Swank, 1960s, 1 x 3/4 In. 110.00
Cuff Links, Oval Red Agate, Silver Mesh, Wrap Style, Hickock, 1960s, 1 x 3/4 In. 110.00
Cuff Links, Pearl, Arched Sterling Silver Mount, Mikimoto, 1 In. 120.00
Cuff Links, Remington Typewriters, Sterling Silver, c.1950, 3/4 x 3/4 In. 125.00
Cuff Links, Sapphire, Textured Round, 14K Yellow Gold, Tiffany 1065.00
Cuff Links, Scottie Dog, Gold Tone, Swank, c.1960, 3/4 x 5/8 In. 115.00

Jewelry, Chatelaine, 5-Chain, Cherub, Griffin, Heart, Embossed, Sterling Silver

Jewelry, Pin, Bakelite, Dog, Hat, Bowtie, Movable Eyes, Painted, 3 In.

Cuff Links, Square Blue Cat's-Eye Stone, Silver Mesh, Wrap Style, 1960s, 1 In. 110.00
Cuff Links, Vintage Cars, Sterling Silver, Fenwick & Sailors, 1950s, 1 1/4 x 1/2 In. 140.00
Cuff Links, Woman, Veil, 18K Gold, Art Nouveau, Box 235.00
Earrings, 12 Loop, Suspended Abstract Shape, 18K Gold, Polished, Clip-On, Bulgari 2000.00
Earrings, Coral Cabochon, Rope Twist Frame, 18K Gold, Clip-On, Tiffany 880.00
Earrings, Diamond, Emerald, Pave Set, 18K Gold, Studs, Cartier 1765.00
Earrings, Diamond, Gold, Paloma Picasso, Tiffany 1850.00
Earrings, Diamonds, 18K Gold, Spiga, Bulgari 1998.00
Earrings, Diamonds, Full Cut, Platinum, 14K Gold, Ruser 4406.00
Earrings, Diamonds, Rubies, Sapphires, Emeralds, Platinum, Art Deco, 3/4 x 1/2 In. 1528.00
Earrings, Fan Shape, Full Cut Diamonds, 18K Gold, Kurt Wayne 2585.00
Earrings, Flower Basket, Diamonds, Platinum, Gold, Screw Back, Edwardian, 3/4 x 1/2 In. 765.00
Earrings, Flowers, Diamonds, 18K Gold, Schlumberger, Tiffany Box, 3/4 In. 5580.00
Earrings, Garnet, Rose Cut Diamond, Gold, Silver, Georgian 4500.00
Earrings, Half Hoop, Diamond Melee, 18K Gold, Marina B. 1058.00
Earrings, Half Hoop, Ribbed, Channel Set Rubies, 18K Gold, David Yurman 1410.00
Earrings, Hoop, Diamond Melee, 18K White Gold, Cartier 6465.00
Earrings, Hoop, Hammered, 18K Gold, Clip-On, 1 1/2 x 1 5/8 In. 605.00
Earrings, Hoop, Ribbed, Diamond Melee, 18K Gold, Cartier, 5/8 In. 590.00
Earrings, Hoop, Wirework, 18K Gold, Etruscan Revival 295.00
Earrings, Horses, Bridled, Horseshoe Shaped Frame, Quartz, Crystal, 14K Gold, c.1945 .... 705.00
Earrings, Keshi Pearl, Pink Tourmaline, 18K White Gold, Clip-On, Donna Vock 1880.00
Earrings, Kyanite, Diamond Set Leaf, 18K White Gold 385.00
Earrings, Love, Screw Heads, 18K White Gold, Cartier, Box 999.00
Earrings, Onyx, Diamond, Jadeite Disk, Detachable Drops, Art Deco 6345.00
Earrings, Pendant, Beaded Wirework, Sphere Shape, 14K Gold, Etruscan Revival 999.00
Earrings, Pendant, Cameo, Cherub, Beads, Wirework Flowers, Coral, 18K Gold, Victorian 206.00
Earrings, Pendant, Chalcedony, Diamond, Demantoid Garnet, Victorian, c.1870 .... 1880.00
Earrings, Pendant, Diamond, Platinum, Beaded Edge, Art Deco 3645.00
Earrings, Pendant, Pearl, Flower & Leaf, 18K Gold, 1900, 2 5/8 In. 4995.00
Earrings, Rock Crystal, Pearls, Cabochon Sapphire, Gold, Annabel Jones, London 1850.00
Earrings, Rope Twist, Asymmetrical, Diamond Melee, 18K Gold, Clip-On, Stele, Paris 3525.00
Earrings, Sterling Silver, Cherry Cluster, Pierced, Chased, Kalo Shop, 1 In. 245.00
Earrings, Sterling Silver, Dome Shape, Studs, Georg Jensen, Box 130.00
Earrings, Sterling Silver, Half Sphere Shape, Screwback, Kalo Shop, 5/8 In. 215.00
Earrings, Sterling Silver, Organic Asymmetrical Shape, Clip-On, No. 119, Georg Jensen 235.00
Earrings, Sterling Silver, Stylized Flower, Clip-On, Signed La Paglia, 1940s 235.00
Earrings, Wheat Sheaves, Clip-On, No. 106, Gundorph Albertus, Georg Jensen, Denmark 165.00
Earrings, X Shape, 18K Gold, Paloma Picasso, Tiffany ....765.00 to 825.00
Glass, Ring, Marguerites, Opalescent, Gray Patina, Gold Mount, Lalique, c.1919, 1/2 In. 3120.00
Hair Comb, Micro, Mosaic, Silver Filigree, Doves, Leaves, 1880s, 4 x 4 In. 588.00
Hatpins are listed in this book in the Hatpin category.
Lavaliere, Diamond, Pearls, Platinum, Trace Link Chain, Edwardian, 17 1/2 In. 765.00
Lavaliere, Peridot, Cushion Cut Tourmaline, Pearls, 15K Yellow Gold, 16 In. 1638.00
Locket, Black Enamel, Pearls, Flowers, Oval, 14K Yellow Gold 155.00
Locket, Flower, Enamel, Seed Pearls, 18K Gold, Art Nouveau, 1894 .... 588.00
Necessaire, Diamond Flowers, Mirror Inside, 18K Gold, Cartier, c.1955 .... 7638.00

Necklace, 88 Pearls, Graduated, Diamond Trefoil Clasp, Tiffany, c.1910, 16 In. 2938.00
Necklace, Agate, Trace Link Chain, 18K Gold, Helen Woodhall, Box, 15 3/4 In. 410.00
Necklace, Angel Skin Coral, 3 Strands, 14K Gold Clasp, 1960s, 21 In. 295.00
Necklace, Bakelite, 21 Beads, Carved Flowers, Butterscotch, 30 In. 825.00
Necklace, Bakelite, 4 Knight Charms, Goldtone Metal Links, 16 1/2 In. 560.00
Necklace, Bakelite, Beads, Blue Glass Disks, c.1930, 38 In. 205.00
Necklace, Bakelite, Butterscotch Swirl Beads, Graduated, 31 1/2 In. 80.00
Necklace, Bakelite, Pear & Leaf Drops, Yellow Trace Links, 16 1/2 In. 1058.00
Necklace, Chain, Double Rope Twist, 14K Gold, Tiffany, 16 3/4 In. 940.00
Necklace, Chain, Wirework Links, 14K Gold, Art Nouveau, 59 1/2 In. 940.00
Necklace, Coral, Red, 2 Strands, Rose Gold Clasp, 1960s, 20 In. 1765.00
Necklace, Diamond, Enamel, Seed Pearls, Silk Cord, Mogul Style 9200.00
Necklace, Faux Pearl, Swirled Glass Beads, Coco Chanel, 1930s, 28 In. 825.00
Necklace, Festoon, Amethysts, Diamond Melee, 14K Gold, Art Nouveau, 16 In. 2470.00
Necklace, Festoon, Amethysts, Trace Link Chain, 14K Gold, c.1910, 18 1/2 In. 764.00
Necklace, Filigree, Graduated Quatrefoils, Flower Accents, 18K Gold, Late 1800s, 16 In. 2235.00
Necklace, Fringe, Cylindrical Links, Plaques, 18K Gold, Etruscan Revival, 16 3/4 In. 7930.00
Necklace, Link, Tubular, Graduated, Silver, Mexico, 16 In. 285.00
Necklace, Mandarin Garnet, Blue Cut Glass, Coral, Peach Pit Beads, 1900s 600.00
Necklace, Mesh, Sterling Silver, Elsa Peretti, Tiffany & Co., 48 In. 380.00
Necklace, Opals, Amethysts, Gilt Silver Wirework Links, c.1960, 18 1/2 In. 175.00
Necklace, Oval, 3 Ladybugs, Swirls, Red Cotton String, G.Argy-Rousseau, c.1920, 2 1/2 x 18 In. .. 1435.00
Necklace, Pendant, 43 Diamonds, Trace Link Chain, Platinum, c.1915, 16 1/2 In. 3408.00
Necklace, Pendant, Black Mother-Of-Pearl, Lace-Covered Rubber, Sylvia Gottwald 355.00
Necklace, Pendant, Emerald, Diamonds, Fetter Link Chain, 14K White Gold, 1960s, 17-In. Chain .. 530.00
Necklace, Pendant, Glass, Vase Of Flowers, Rope Chain, 16 1/2 In. 265.00
Necklace, Pendant, Heart Shape, Link Chain, 18K Gold, Paloma Picasso, Tiffany, 19 1/4 In. 645.00
Necklace, Pendant, Locket, Dove, Branch, Diamond, 14K Gold, Victorian 1295.00
Necklace, Pendant, Plique-A-Jour Enamel, Wings, Berries, Amethyst, Silver, Art Nouveau 1880.00
Necklace, Pendant, Plique-A-Jour, Amethyst, Pearl, Art Nouveau, 21 3/4 In. 1880.00
Necklace, Pendant, Silver, Organic Design, Scandinavia, 14 1/2 In. 120.00
Necklace, Rope Twist, Florentine, 18K Gold, Italian Hallmark, 16 In. 750.00
Necklace, Sterling Silver, Flower Heads, Georg Jensen, Denmark, 14 In. 1229.00
Necklace, Sterling Silver, Flower Links, Georg Jensen, Denmark, 16 In. 895.00
Necklace, Sterling Silver, Fringe, Antonio Pineda, Mexico, 16 In. 800.00
Necklace, Sterling Silver, Green Onyx, Leaf Designs, Georg Jensen, 35 In. 2938.00
Necklace, Sterling Silver, Moonstone, Leaf Links, Georg Jensen, 16 3/4 In. 4230.00
Necklace, Tourmaline, Aquamarine, Peridot, Trace Link Chain, 9K Gold, c.1910, 15 3/4 In. 1645.00
Necklace, Turquoise Beads, Seed Pearls, 2 Strands, Art Nouveau, 15 In. 120.00
Necklace & Earrings, Pearls, Crystals, 3 Strands, Originals By Robert, Late 1940s 59.00
Necklace Set, Cuff Bracelet, Earrings, Leaves, Sterling Silver, Los Castillo, Mexico, 1950s 1180.00
Pendant, Agate, Dragonfly, Bat, Fruit, Jui, Red, Brown Flower Blossom, 2 In. 1955.00
Pendant, Amber, Teardrop, c.1900, 2 In. 8050.00
Pendant, Bird, Rock Crystal, Reverse Painted, Intaglio, Gold, Etruscan Style, England 4500.00
Pendant, Black Opal, Diamond, Enamel, Marquise Gold Mount, Arts & Crafts, 1 In. 1210.00
Pendant, Citrine, Oval, Faceted, Applied Beetle, 2 1/2 x 2 In. 550.00
Pendant, Cross, 11 Brilliant Cut Diamonds, Platinum Chain, Tiffany & Co. 1550.00
Pendant, Glass, Figurine Ailee, Winged Figure, Clear, Frosted, Lalique, c.1919, 2 1/2 In. 2400.00
Pendant, Glass, Grain, Berries, Vines, Green, 3-Sided, Rounded Corners, Lalique, 1920s, 1 3/4 In. 566.00
Pendant, Glass, Guepes, Wasps, Electric Blue, Lalique, c.1920, 2 1/4 In. 1175.00
Pendant, Glass, Lys, Lilies, Blue, Triangular, Rounded Corners, Lalique, 1920s, 2 In. 490.00
Pendant, Glass, Plumes, Wreath, Feathers, Red, Lalique, Post 1945, 1 3/4 In. 226.00
Pendant, Glass, Sorbier, Rowan Tree, Electric Blue, Silk Cord, Lalique, c.1920, 2 In. 600.00
Pendant, Heart Shape, Seed Pearls, 14K Gold, Krementz & Co., Edwardian, 7/8 In. 825.00
Pendant, Jade, Squirrel, Grapes, Silk Cord, Coral Bead, 2 In. 1440.00
Pendant, Jadeite, Green, Pierced Leaf, 2 1/4 In. 980.00
Pendant, Loyalty, Brass, Oval, Suspension Hole, c.1705, 2 In. 325.00
Pendant, Mirror, Psyche, Clear, Frosted, Gray Patina, Lalique, c.1919, 3 1/4 In. 3600.00
Pendant, Relief Carved Bamboo & Leaves, Silk Cord, Jadeite, Seed Pearl, Red Coral, 2 In. 1150.00
Pendant, Sterling Silver, Labradorite, Robert R. Jarvie, c.1915, 1 3/8 x 3/4 In. 7200.00
Pin, 2 Elephants, Emerald Eye, 18K Gold, Cartier, 1 1/4 x 3/4 In. 1116.00

Jewelry, Pin, Bakelite, Frog, Playing Mandolin, Movable Arm, 2 7/8 In.

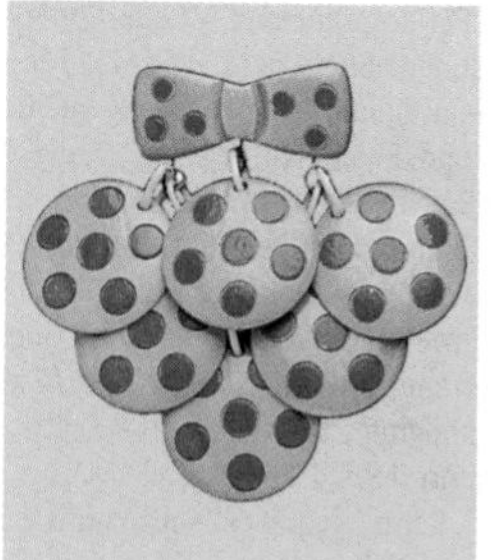

Jewelry, Pin, Bakelite, Polka Dot, Yellow, Red Dots, 6-Disks, 3 3/4 In.

Jewelry, Pin, Bakelite, Shield, Raised Star, Red, White, Blue, 2 1/2 In.

Pin, 3 Swallows, Diamonds, Ruby Eyes, Platinum, J.E. Caldwell, c.1900, 1 1/2 In. 1410.00
Pin, Abstract Shape, Carved Bead, Claire Falkenstein, 1948, 4 1/2 x 2 1/2 In. 4080.00
Pin, Abstract Shape, Sterling Silver, No. 368, Georg Jensen, Box, 1960s, 1 3/4 In. 295.00
Pin, Abstract Shape, Sterling Silver, Round, No. 15, Georg Jensen 440.00
Pin, Amazonite, Bezel Set, Sterling Silver, Leaves, Berries, No. 68, Georg Jensen 440.00
Pin, Amethyst, Pearls, 14K Gold, Edwardian, 1 x 5/8 In., Pair 220.00
Pin, Amethyst, Seed Pearls, 14K Gold, Allsopp & Allsopp, Edwardian, 1 In. 295.00
Pin, Angel, Diamonds, Pearl Wings, Cloud, Halo, 14K Gold, Platinum, Ruser, 2 1/2 In. 2468.00
Pin, Angel, Pearl Wings, Clouds, 14K Gold, Ruser 529.00
Pin, Aquamarine, Diamond, Pearls, Art Nouveau, Whiteside & Blank, c.1895, 1 1/8 x 1 In. 1116.00
Pin, Bakelite, Bar, Long Stem, Dangling Cherries, 4 In. 500.00
Pin, Bakelite, Bow, 6 Hanging Disks, Red Polka Dots, 3 3/4 In. 3760.00
Pin, Bakelite, Cigarette, In Holder, 9 Matches, Painted 3760.00
Pin, Bakelite, Cigarette, Matches, Dangling Matches, 3 In. 3760.00
Pin, Bakelite, Dog, Hat, Bowtie, Movable Eyes, Painted, 3 In. .... *ILLUS* 558.00
Pin, Bakelite, Fish, Tropical, Reverse Carved, Painted, 3 In. 825.00
Pin, Bakelite, Frog, Playing Mandolin, Movable Arm, 2 7/8 In. .... *ILLUS* 1058.00
Pin, Bakelite, Hat, Marbled Yellow, Brown Lines, 4 Cherries, 2 3/4 In. 1175.00
Pin, Bakelite, Hat, Pears, 3 In. 999.00
Pin, Bakelite, Hat, Wide Brim, 4 Cherries, 2 3/4 In. 1175.00
Pin, Bakelite, Key, Dangling Heart, Red, 4 In. 1060.00
Pin, Bakelite, Log, Dangling Fruit, 3 1/2 In. .... 590.00 to 880.00
Pin, Bakelite, Man Riding Donkey, Wooden Sombrero, 2 1/4 In. 295.00
Pin, Bakelite, Moon & Palm Tree, Butterscotch, Painted, 2 1/2 In. 1400.00
Pin, Bakelite, Nurse, Jointed, Yellow, Green, Painted, 2 3/4 In. .... 825.00 to 880.00
Pin, Bakelite, Polka Dot, Yellow, Red Dots, 6-Disks, 3 3/4 In. .... *ILLUS* 3760.00
Pin, Bakelite, Shield, Raised Star, Red, White, Blue, 2 1/2 In. .... *ILLUS* 1410.00
Pin, Bakelite, Ship In Bottle, Reverse Carved, Painted, 2 3/4 In. 1175.00
Pin, Bakelite, Soldier, Yellow, Brown, Jointed, Painted, 3 1/2 In. .... *ILLUS* 823.00
Pin, Bar, 2 Flowers, Seed Pearls, Garnet, Rectangular, Stepped, 14K Gold, 1 5/8 In. 575.00
Pin, Bar, Amazonite Cabochon, Grape Leaves, Oval, 14K Gold, 1 3/16 In. 395.00
Pin, Bar, Diamond, Pearls, Platinum, Openwork Frame, Art Deco, c.1920 .... 1525.00
Pin, Bar, Diamond, Star Shaped, Rope Twist Frame, 14K Gold, Victorian, 2 3/8 In. 138.00
Pin, Bar, Diamonds, Platinum Openwork Mount, Beaded Edge, Art Deco 176.00
Pin, Bee, Brilliant Cut Diamonds, Ruby Eyes, 18K Gold 440.00
Pin, Bee, Diamond, Ruby, 18K Gold, 3/4 In. 920.00
Pin, Beetle, Platinum & Gold, Demantoid Garnet, Diamonds, Rubies 17500.00
Pin, Bird, Diamond, Turquoise, Engraved Feathers, 18K Gold, Cartier, 2 In. 3055.00
Pin, Branch Shape, Hanging Fruit, Silver, Dyed Onyx, Mexico, c.1950 .... 226.00
Pin, Brass, Copper, Art Smith, 1950s, 3 1/4 x 2 3/4 In. 1200.00
Pin, Butterfly, 87 Brilliant Cut Diamonds, 14K White Gold 685.00
Pin, Butterfly, Pearls, Diamonds, 14K Gold, Ruser, 1 x 1 1/4 In. 1765.00
Pin, Butterfly, Seed Pearls, Diamonds, 14K Gold, American Hallmark, Edwardian 380.00
Pin, Butterfly, Silver, Amber, Moonstone, Skonvirke, Marius Hammer, c.1910, 3 x 2 In. 380.00

Pin, Cabochon Tourmaline, Cabochon Peridot, Diamond & Gold Hippopotamus 3500.00
Pin, Cameo, Bacchante Maiden, Carved Pink Shell, Oval, Gold Filled Frame, Victorian 870.00
Pin, Cameo, Blackamoor, Agate, Rose-Cut Diamond, Pearl, Ruby, 18K Gold 18500.00
Pin, Cameo, Carved Moonstone, Diamond, Enamel Jockey 7500.00
Pin, Cameo, Classical Female, Flower Basket, Shell, 14K Gold Frame, c.1890, 1 1/2 In. 250.00
Pin, Cameo, Classical Maiden, Coral, Diamond Border, Gold, Platinum, Edwardian, 1 3/4 In. 1115.00
Pin, Cameo, Dove, Birdbath, Shell, Carved, Oval, Gold Rope Twist Mount, 2 3/8 x 2 In. 250.00
Pin, Cameo, Woman Surrounded By Flower Garlands, Carved Coral, Gold Mount 2750.00
Pin, Cameo, Woman, Shell, 14K Gold Frame, Engraved, c.1930, 1 1/2 x 1 1/4 In. 193.00
Pin, Carnelian, Leaf & Berry Frame, Monogram, 14K Gold, Arts & Crafts, 1 1/4 In. 765.00
Pin, Circle, Bow, Diamonds, Platinum, Art Deco, 2 1/4 In. 5290.00
Pin, Citrine Flowers, Ribbon, 14K Gold, Retro, Wordley Allsopp & Bliss, 3 In. 590.00
Pin, Citrine, Diamond, Platinum Topped 18K Gold Mount, Edwardian, Box 705.00
Pin, Citrine, Seed Pearls, 14K Gold, Edwardian, 1 1/4 In. 880.00
Pin, Clown, Jointed Legs & Arms, Rubies, Diamonds, Sapphires, 18K Gold, 2 1/4 In. 295.00
Pin, Crab, Platinum, Diamond, 18K Gold, Hammered, David Webb, 2 5/8 In. 4348.00
Pin, Crescent & Circle, Sapphire, Seed Pearls, 14K Gold, Edwardian 380.00
Pin, Diamond Melee, 14K Bicolor Gold, American Hallmark, Retro 499.00
Pin, Diamond, Emerald, Platinum, Rectangular, Art Deco, Tiffany, 1 5/8 In. 7638.00
Pin, Diamonds, Sapphires, Wing Shape, 14K White Gold, Diamond Drop, Art Deco, 2 In. 6500.00
Pin, Dolphin, Diamond, Ruby, Gold, Silver Chimerical 6800.00
Pin, Dorothy, Wizard Of Oz, Celluloid, Promotional Pin, 1939, 1 1/4 In. 500.00
Pin, Dragon, Fairyland Luster, Opal Luster Ground, Round, Gold Mount, 1920, 2 In. 460.00
Pin, Dragonfly, Gold, Platinum, Rose Cut Diamond, Emerald, Ruby 3200.00
Pin, Enamel, Ruby, Diamonds, 18K Gold, Renaissance Revival, Carlo Giuliano, 1 In. 7050.00
Pin, Face, Turban, Sunstone Feldspar, 18K Gold, Luis Sanz, 1 1/2 In. 705.00
Pin, Feather, 7 Sapphires, 18K Yellow Gold, Italian Hallmark FRL, 2 In. 460.00
Pin, Flower Basket, Gems, Pearls, Platinum, 18K Gold, Edwardian, 1 1/4 x 1 1/2 In. 3400.00
Pin, Flower Bouquet, Diamond, Platinum, Art Deco, 1 3/4 In. 5290.00
Pin, Flower, Rose Cut Diamond, Art Nouveau, 14K Gold 195.00
Pin, Flower, Ruby, Diamond, Enamel, 14K Yellow Gold, c.1920 .... 2820.00
Pin, Flower, Ruby, Diamond, Millegrain Accents, Round, Edwardian, 1 1/2 In. 4700.00
Pin, Flower, Stylized, Turquoise, 18K Gold, Tiffany, 2 In. 1058.00
Pin, Flowers, 4 Petals, Sapphire, Diamond, 14K Gold, L.E. Garrigus & Co., c.1950 .... 530.00
Pin, Flowers, Nickel Plated Silver, Acid Etched, Carence Crafters, 1 3/8 x 2 1/2 In. 325.00
Pin, Glass, Feuilles De Lierre, Ivy Green, Metal Backing, Lalique, c.1912, 1 1/8 In. 1320.00
Pin, Grape Cluster, Leaf, Cultured Pearls, Diamonds, 18K Gold, Van Cleef & Arpels 3055.00
Pin, Grapevines, Wirework, Applied Beads, 18K Gold, Etruscan Revival, 1870 .... 380.00
Pin, Griffin, Ruby Eye, 14K Gold, Art Nouveau, 1 1/2 In. 410.00
Pin, Horse's Head, Silver, Gold Mount, 1960s, Gucci 375.00
Pin, Horse, Galloping, Textured Gold Fur, Diamond Mane, 18K Gold, 1 1/2 In. 354.00
Pin, Hummingbird, Enamel, 14K Yellow Gold 350.00
Pin, Leaf, Nephrite, 14K Yellow Gold, Carved, Gump's 565.00
Pin, Leaves, Scrolling Vines, 14K Gold, FSH, Arts & Crafts 499.00
Pin, Lobster, Diamonds, Emeralds, 18K Gold, Lavianne, 2 1/2 In. 1645.00
Pin, Medallion, Soldier, Axe, Roma, Silver, Etruscan Style, Shiebler, N.Y., Late 1800s, 3 In. 895.00
Pin, Micro Mosaic, Swans Among Flowers, Black Ground, Geometric Frame, 2 1/2 In. 1765.00
Pin, Monkey, On Branch, Ruby Melee Eyes, 14K Gold, Ruser, 1 1/2 In. 1175.00
Pin, Mourning, Rose Gold, Vellum, Lock Of Hair, 1800s, 2 3/4 x 2 1/4 In. 150.00
Pin, Mule, 3 Turquoise Cabochons, Ruby Eye, 18K Yellow Gold, Signed Cherny 230.00
Pin, Owl, Turquoise, Diamonds, Rubies, 18K Gold, Cartier 4995.00
Pin, Pendant, Crab, 36 Brilliant Cut Diamonds, Coral Cabochon, 18K Yellow Gold 1741.00
Pin, Penguin With Parasol, Carved Lapis Lazuli, Gold, Tiffany 1850.00
Pin, Peridot, Heart Shape Enamel Leaves, Seed Pearls, Art Nouveau, Krementz & Co. 700.00
Pin, Pink Tourmaline, Rope Work Frame, Tassels, 14K Gold, J. Schlumberger, c.1950 .... 8813.00
Pin, Pinwheel, 18K Gold, Tiffany, 1 1/4 In. 646.00
Pin, Plaque, Woman, Porcelain, Enamel & Leaf Frame, 14K Gold, c.1910 .... 176.00
Pin, Plume & Ribbon, Diamond, Pearls, 1950s, 2 1/2 x 2 In. 1765.00
Pin, Poodle, 14K Gold, Rubies, Emeralds, Diamonds, Robert Altman ....*ILLUS* 470.00
Pin, Sailboat, Platinum, Diamonds, Baguettes, Pave Set, Ruby, Onyx, Art Deco 16500.00
Pin, Sapphire, Diamond, Scrolled Openwork Mount, 14K Gold, Art Nouveau, Box, 1 3/4 In. 165.00

Pin, Sapphires, Rubies, Diamonds, Pearls, Emerald, Stylized Tube Hinge, India, 2 1/2 x 4 In. 1416.00
Pin, Scarab, Champleve Enamel, Polychrome Snakes, 14K Gold, Art Nouveau 705.00
Pin, Scrolls, Ribbed, 14K Gold, Retro, Tiffany & Co. 355.00
Pin, Snail, Lapis Shell, 18K Gold, Hermes, Paris, 1 1/2 In. 999.00
Pin, Snail, Sapphire, Diamond, 18K Gold, Cartier, 1 1/2 In. 1765.00
Pin, Star, Stylized, 4 Points, 2 Balls, Brass, Art Smith, 1950s, 2 1/2 x 4 In. 1320.00
Pin, Sterling Silver, 2 Oval Blue Rhinestones, Applied Flowers, Drop Pendant, Hobe, 2 In. 175.00
Pin, Sterling Silver, 2 Tulips, Swirled, Georg Jensen, 1 1/4 In. 245.00
Pin, Sterling Silver, 5-Sided, Pierced, Brown Agate, Celtic, Carence Crafters, 1 3/8 In. 1600.00
Pin, Sterling Silver, Central Rose Blossom, Chased, Oval, Peer Smed, 1 1/4 x 2 In. 495.00
Pin, Sterling Silver, Lapis, Flower, Leaves, No. 193, Georg Jensen, 1 3/4 In. 2000.00
Pin, Sterling Silver, Leaves, Berries, No. 82A, Georg Jensen 235.00
Pin, Sterling Silver, Stylized Leaves, Round, No. 20, Georg Jensen 825.00
Pin, Sterling Silver, Swans In Flight, White Enamel, Erik Magnussen, 2 1/4 In. 185.00
Pin, Sterling Silver, Swirled Blossom, Bead, Leaf, Oval, C.P. Petterson, 1 3/4 x 2 1/2 In. 425.00
Pin, Sterling Silver, Thistle, Oval, Pierced, Chased, 1 5/8 x 2 1/8 In. 475.00
Pin, Tourmaline, Pear Shaped, Tassels, 14K Gold, Jean Schlumberger, c.1950 .... 8815.00
Pin, Woman With Flowing Hair, Flower Garland, Sterling Silver, Art Nouveau 265.00
Pin & Bracelet, Dove & Wreath, Silver Sterling, Georg Jensen, c.1944 .... 990.00
Ring, 3 Diamonds, Platinum, Openwork, Beaded Edge, Art Deco, Size 6 .... 1998.00
Ring, 13 Diamonds, White Enamel, Platinum, David Webb, 1970 .... 3360.00
Ring, Amethyst, Tourmalines, Iolites, 18K White Gold, Chanel, Size 7 .... 3525.00
Ring, Aquamarine, Citrine, Tourmaline, 18K Gold, Bulgari, Size 5 1/2 In. 2235.00
Ring, Black Opal, 83 Diamonds, Platinum, 18K Gold Mount, c.1905 .... 5460.00
Ring, Bypass, Diamond, Platinum, Jabel, Size 5 1/2 .... 1295.00
Ring, Citrine, Diamond Melee, 18K Gold, Chaumet, Paris, Size 6 1/2 .... 940.00
Ring, Coral, Scrolling Mount, 14K Gold, Art Nouveau, Size 4 .... 235.00
Ring, Demantoid Garnet, 5 Stones, 14K Gold, c.1940, Size 6 1/2 .... 7640.00
Ring, Diamond Solitaire, 6-Prong Set, Platinum On Gold, Tiffany, Box, Size 4 1/2 .... 2235.00
Ring, Diamond, Acanthus Leaf, Platinum, 14K Gold, Neoclassical, Kind & Sons, Size 7 1/2 .... 4110.00
Ring, Diamond, Platinum, Openwork, Beaded Edge, Art Deco, Size 3 3/4 .... 999.00
Ring, Diamond, Star Sapphire, Platinum, Diamond, Art Deco, Size 8 .... 1770.00
Ring, Diamonds, Flexible Band, Hearts, 18K Gold, Cartier, Size 6 .... 2115.00
Ring, Dinner, Smoky Topaz, Oval, 10K Gold Mount, Retro 206.00
Ring, Dragonfly, Blue Topaz, Emerald Cut Sapphire, 18K White Gold, Size 8 .... 1150.00
Ring, Emerald, Diamond Melee, Open Gallery, 18K Gold, Oscar Heyman, Size 5 1/2 .... 2000.00
Ring, Emerald, Diamond, 18K Gold, Platinum, Oscar Heyman, Size 5 1/2 .... 2700.00
Ring, Emerald, Diamonds, Beaded Edge, Art Deco, Size 2 1/4 .... 470.00
Ring, Eternity Band, Platinum, Sapphire, Diamond, Tiffany & Co., Size 5 3/4 .... 1410.00
Ring, Knot, 18K Gold, Hermes, Paris, Box, Size 6 .... 940.00
Ring, Memorial, Geo. Washington's Hair, Octagonal Bezel, Pink Gold, Inscribed, c.1799 .... 4800.00
Ring, Mother-Of-Pearl, Man Holding Flower, Octagonal, Victorian, c.1825, Size 8 1/2 .... 470.00
Ring, Opal, European Cut Diamonds, Flower, 14K Gold, Victorian, Size 5 1/2 .... 325.00
Ring, Opal, Square, Prong Set, Diamonds, Art Deco, Tiffany & Co., Size 8 1/2 .... 9400.00
Ring, Panther, Emerald Eyes, Onyx Nose, 18K Gold, Cartier, Size 6 1/2 .... 1295.00
Ring, Platinum, 2 Jadeite Cabochons, Baguette & Marquise Diamonds, Gumps, Size 5 .... 3290.00
Ring, Platinum, Diamond Solitaire, Diamond Melee Border, Art Deco, Size 6 .... 3175.00
Ring, Platinum, Diamond, Scrolling Leaf Mount, 14K Gold, Art Deco, Size 8 3/4 .... 940.00
Ring, Platinum, Old European Cut Diamond, Bead Set, Art Deco, Size 7 1/4 .... 999.00
Ring, Rolling, 3 Interlocking Bands, 18K Tricolor Gold, Cartier 470.00
Ring, Rubies, Channel Set, 18K Gold, Mauboussin, France, Size 6 1/2 .... 1175.00
Ring, Ruby, Diamond Melee, 14K Bicolor Gold, Retro 325.00
Ring, Sapphire, Diamond, 18K Gold, Kurt Wayne 1765.00
Ring, Sapphire, Diamond, Art Deco, France, Size 6 .... 3525.00
Ring, Sapphire, Gypsy Set, Etoile, 18K Gold, Tiffany, Size 5 3/4 .... 325.00
Ring, Sapphire, Pear Cut, 6 Baguette Diamonds, 18K White, Secrett 1597.00
Ring, Sapphires, Diamond Melee, Platinum Topped 14K Gold, Edwardian, Size 4 1/2 .... 1295.00
Ring, Serpent, Coiled, Emerald Eyes, 18K Gold, Size 5 1/4 .... 220.00
Ring, Stainless Steel, 18K Gold, Parentesi, Bulgari, Size 6 1/4 .... 499.00
Ring, Sterling Silver, Asymmetric, Stylized Leaf, Oval Carnelian Cabochon, Brandt, 4 1/2 .... 495.00
Ring, Sterling Silver, Onyx, Green, Flowers, Leaves, Size 6 1/2 .... 525.00

Jewelry, Pin, Bakelite, Soldier, Yellow, Brown, Jointed, Painted, 3 1/2 In.

Jewelry, Pin, Poodle, 14K Gold, Rubies, Emeralds, Diamonds, Robert Altman

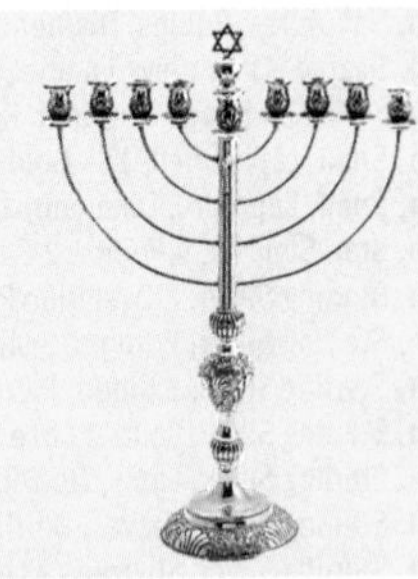
Judaica, Menorah, Silver, Shells, Star Of David, London, England, c.1929, 19 In.

Ring, Sterling Silver, Stepped Shank, Red Coral Cabochon, Art Deco, Kalo Shop, 11 In. 875.00
Ring, Tanzanite, Baguette Diamond, Platinum, Tiffany & Co. 12500.00
Ring, Topaz, Baguette Cut, 14K Gold, Size 7 1/4 .... 210.00
Ring, Topaz, Blue, Emerald Cut, Calf's-Head Cut Sapphire, Platinum, Oscar Heyman Bros. 7500.00
Ring, Turquoise, Diamond, 14K Gold, Shreve Crump & Low, Size 8 .... 825.00
Seal Fob, Geometric Scroll, Ruffle, Laurel, Grosgrain Band, 14K Gold, Art Nouveau 235.00
Stickpin, Diamonds, Platinum, 18K Gold Mount, Round Top, Edwardian 765.00
Stickpin, Horse's Head, Riding Crop, Seed Pearls, Platinum, 14K Gold, Edwardian 265.00
Watches are listed in their own category.
Watch Chain, Gilt Silver, Gem Set, Diamonds, Opals, Pearls, Enamel, Art Deco, 32 1/4 In. 470.00
Watch Pin, Pharaoh's Head, Demantoid Garnet, Seed Pearls, Art Deco, Carter, Howe & Co. 1765.00
Wristwatches are listed in their own category.

JOHN ROGERS statues were made from 1859 to 1892. The originals were bronze, but the thousands of copies made by the Rogers factory were of painted plaster. Eighty different figures were created. Similar painted plaster figures were produced by some other factories. Rights to the figures were sold in 1893 and they were manufactured for several more years by the Rogers Statuette Co. Never repaint a Rogers figure because this lowers the value to collectors.

Group, Coming To The Parson, 1870, 22 In. 230.00
Group, Courtship Of Sleepy Hollow, 1868, 17 x 14 x 10 In. 210.00
Group, Football, c.1891, 16 x 10 x 11 In. 4375.00
Group, Rip Van Winkle At Home, 1871, 19 x 11 x 12 In. 379.00
Group, Watch On The Santa Maria, 1893, 15 x 13 In. 785.00
Group, Weighing The Baby, 1876, 21 In. 489.00

JOSEF ORIGINALS ceramics were designed by Muriel Joseph George. The first pieces were made in California from 1945 to 1962. They were then manufactured in Japan. The company was sold to George Good in 1982 and he continued to make Josef Originals until 1985. The company was then sold to Southland Corporation. The name is now owned by Applause, and the Birthday Girl series is still being made.

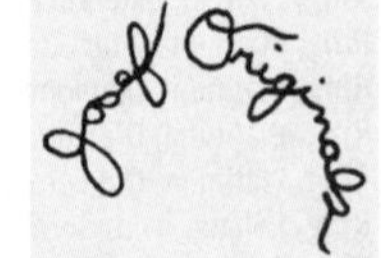

Figurine, Baby In Bassinet, c.1960, 3 x 4 In. 52.00
Figurine, Ballerina, Little Tutu, Aquamarine Dress, 3 Rhinestones, c.1960, 4 In. 33.00
Figurine, Belle, Green Dress, High Heels, 8 In. 106.00
Figurine, Cat, Puff, 1945-62, 3 x 3 In. 50.00
Figurine, Little Internationals, India, Girl, Sari, c.1960, 3 1/2 In. 103.00
Figurine, Little Internationals, Russia, Girl, Russian Clothes, 1960s, 3 1/2 In. 40.00
Figurine, Mary Ann, Holding Baby, 3 1/2 In. 55.00
Figurine, Small World, America, Girl, Flower Basket, c.1985, 4 1/2 In. 62.00
Figurine, Woman, Blue Dress, Holding Box Of Roses, 8 In. 65.00
Figurine, Woman, Colonial, Mirror, Green Dress, 7 1/2 In. 105.00

Music Box, Impossible Dream, Girl & Dog, 1950s, 5 x 3 In. 36.00
Music Box, Mother & Child, Lullaby, 6 1/2 In. 49.00
Music Box, Raindrops Keep Falling, Boy & Girl, Under Umbrella, 6 1/2 In. 25.00
Pie Vent, Bird, Canary Yellow, 3 In. 45.00
Planter, Figure, Girl, Holding Cat, 8 In. 15.00
Vase, Bud, Woman, 9 1/2 In. 5.00

JUDAICA is any memorabilia that refers to the Jews or the Jewish religion. Interests range from newspaper clippings that mention eighteenth- and nineteenth-century Jewish Americans to religious objects, such as menorahs or spice boxes. Age, condition, and the intrinsic value of the material, as well as the historic and artistic importance, determine the value.

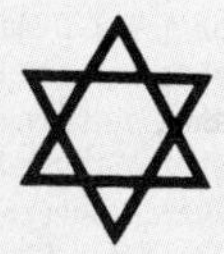

Altar Mount, Wood, Cloud Form, Inscribed, Triangle Panel, Gesso, 1700s, 19 1/4 In. 300.00
Charity Box, House Shape, Inlaid, 12 1/2 x 7 1/2 x 6 In. 995.00
Charity Box, Wooden, Painted, Arched Roof, Galleried Tray, 1900s, 15 In. 1580.00
Cup, Kiddush, Cased Glass, Panels, Flowers, Star Of David, Inscriptions, 4 3/4 In. 335.00
Lamp, Hanukkah, Silver, Fluted Column, Flared Base, Star Of David, c.1890, 13 3/4 In. 2410.00
Lamp, Hanukkah, Silver, Oblong Plinth, Floral Scroll Feet, Continental, c.1875, 12 1/2 In. 3340.00
Marriage Contract, North Africa, 20th Century, 22 3/4 x 17 1/4 In. 325.00
Megillah, On Parchment, 16th Century, 12 1/2 In. 395.00
Menorah, Hanukkah, Silver, Continental, c.1900, 11 x 9 1/2 In. 878.00
Menorah, Silver, 9-Light, Shell Pattern Foot, Star Of David Top, London, c.1929, 19 In. 1745.00
Menorah, Silver, Hazorfim, 8 Sockets, Angular Arms, Lion Finial, 1900s, 18 1/2 In. 240.00
Menorah, Silver, Shells, Star Of David, London, England, c.1929, 19 In. .... *ILLUS* 1743.00
Plate, Seder, Porcelain, Karlsbad, 6 Shells, Star Of David, 20th Century, 10 1/2 In. 223.00
Plate, Seder, Porcelain, Sabbath Scene, Inscriptions, Inlet Handles, 1900s, 15 In. 240.00
Plate, Seder, Rose Ground, Yellow & Brown Design, Aqua Border, Flower In Center, 1900 .... 585.00
Scribe's Set, Brass, Inscribed, Geometric, Stylized Floral Bands, North Africa, 9 1/2 In. 260.00
Spice Box, Silver, Fish Shape, Articulated Scales, Turquoise Stone Eyes, Middle East, 9 In. 205.00
Spice Container, Bronze, Footed, Hinged Cover, Repousse, Shell Design, Dutch, 5 x 7 1/2 In. 165.00
Spice Tower, Silver, Openwork Body, 4 Flags, Knopped Column, Dome Base, 9 1/4 In. 300.00
Torah Scroll Pointer, Silver, Plate, 10 1/4 To 11 3/4 In., Europe, North Africa, 5 Piece 390.00

JUGTOWN Pottery refers to pottery made in North Carolina as far back as the 1750s. In 1915, Juliana and Jacques Busbee set up a training and sales organization for what they named *Jugtown Pottery*. In 1921, they built a shop at Jugtown, North Carolina, and hired Ben Owen as a potter in 1923. The Busbees moved the village store where the pottery was sold to New York City. Juliana Busbee sold the New York store in 1926 and moved into a log cabin near the Jugtown Pottery. The pottery closed in 1959. It reopened in 1960 and is still working near Seagrove, North Carolina.

Bowl, Flat Rim, Footed, Blue Glaze, Ben Owen I, 1930s, 4 1/2 x 7 In. 1045.00
Bowl, Oriental White Glaze, Ben Owen, 1930s, 4 x 11 In. 120.00
Bowl, Pie Crust Shoulder, Frothy White Matte Glaze, Red, Turquoise Accents, 6 x 12 In. 529.00
Pitcher, Lead Glaze, Orange, c.1925, 9 In. 120.00
Platter, Lead Glaze, Orange, Ben Owen I, c.1930, 14 3/4 In. 143.00
Tray, Bent, Lead Glaze, Orange, Ben Owen I, 10 1/2 x 12 1/4 In. 220.00
Urn, Bulbous, Rolled Rim, 2 Looped Handles, Glossy Black Glaze, 12 x 10 1/2 In. 1150.00
Vase, Shouldered, Mottled Green & Red Glaze, Impressed Mark, 5 In. 390.00
Vase, Tapered, Blue & Red Glaze, Impressed Mark, 6 1/4 In. 390.00

JUKEBOXES play records. The first coin-operated phonograph was demonstrated in 1889. In 1906 the Automatic Entertainer appeared, the first coin-operated phonograph to offer several different selections of music. The first electrically powered jukebox was introduced in 1927. Collectors search for jukeboxes of all ages, especially those with flashing lights and unusual design and graphics.

AMI, Model 201, Singing Towers, Mahogany Case, 78 RPM, c.1940, 70 x 36 x 25 In. 2640.00

AMI, Model A, Mother Of Plastic, 40 Selections, 78 RPM, 1946, 72 x 38 x 26 In. ....2520.00 to 3850.00
Mills, Empress, 20 Selections, 78 RPM, 1940-41, 57 x 34 x 23 In. 1760.00
NSM, Prestige, Wood, Chrome Case, 51 1/2 In. 110.00
Ristaucrat, 45 Music Box, Plastic Dome, Marquee, 45 RPM, c.1950, 16 x 12 In. 2016.00
Scopitone, Model SX 36, Video, France, 1965 .... 1469.00
Seeburg, Consolette, Chrome, Glass, 160 Selections, 1960s, 15 In. 22.00
Seeburg, Model V-3WA, Wall-O-Matic 200, 200 Selections, Chrome, Glass, 1955, 15 x 13 In. 120.00
Seeburg, Wall-O-Matic, Chrome, Glass, 1950s, 14 1/2 In. 99.00
Speaker, Wurlitzer, Model 4000, Silver Star, Metal, Chrome Finish, 1946-50, 24 In. 880.00
Speaker, Wurlitzer, Model 4002, Plastic Star, Pressed Steel, 1946-48, 24 In. 550.00
Speaker, Wurlitzer, Model 4004, Musical Note, Wall Mount, Mahogany, 1946-47, 16 1/2 In. 520.00
Wurlitzer, Model 750, 24 Selections, 78 RPM, 1941, 56 x 32 x 29 In. 3105.00
Wurlitzer, Model 1015, Bubbler, 24 Selections, 78 RPM, 1946-1947, 60 x 33 x 25 In. ..5225.00 to 7840.00
Wurlitzer, Model 1100, Cathedral Front, 24 Selections, 78 RPM, 1948, 58 x 31 x 27 In. .6600.00 to 6720.00
Wurlitzer, Model 1700, Curved Glass Top, 104 Selections, 45 RPM, 1954, 56 x 32 In. 2240.00
Wurlitzer, Model 2204, Art Deco, Console, 104 Selections, 45 RPM, 1958, 55 x 36 In. 130.00
Wurlitzer, Model 2900, Art Deco, 200 Selections, 45 & 33 RPM, 1965, 51 x 34 In. 55.00

KATE GREENAWAY, who was a famous illustrator of children's books, drew pictures of children in high-waisted Empire dresses. She lived from 1846 to 1901. Her designs appear on china, glass, and other pieces.

Book, Apple Pie, Routledge, London, 1886 .... 950.00
Book, Kate Greenaway's Book Of Games, Routledge, London, 1889 .... 600.00
Book, Kate Greenway's Alphabet, 1st Edition, Routledge, 1885 .... 250.00
Book, Little Wide-Awake, Mrs. Sale Barker, Routledge, London, 1880 .... 225.00
Calendar, George Routledge, London, 1884, 6 1/4 x 9 In. 600.00

KAY FINCH Ceramics were made in Corona Del Mar, California, from 1935 to 1963. The hand-decorated pieces often depicted whimsical animals and people. Pastel colors were used.

Kay Finch
CALIFORNIA

Figurine, Duck, Marching, Blue Feet, 1940s, 1 1/2 In. ....41.00 to 55.00
Figurine, Elephant, Violets & Leaves On Ears, Purple Toenails, 4 1/2 In. 114.00
Figurine, Monkey, Happy, Brown, Sitting, Hand By Ear, 11 x 9 In. 294.00
Figurine, Monkey, Monkeyshines, White, Standing, Waving, 9 1/2 x 7 1/2 In. 183.00
Figurine, Pig, Blue Ears, Nose, 3 In. 104.00
Figurine Set, Rabbits, Mother, 2 Babies, 8-In. Mother, 2 1/2 x 4-In. Babies, 3 Piece 188.00
Stein, Afghan Hound, Apricot, Black, 7 1/2 x 6 1/2 In. 700.00

KAYSERZINN, see Pewter category.

KELVA glassware was made by the C. F. Monroe Company of Meriden, Connecticut, about 1904. It is a pale, pastel-painted glass decorated with flowers, designs, or scenes. Kelva resembles Nakara and Wave Crest, two other glasswares made by the same company.

KELVA

Box, Hinged Cover, Rose Ground, Lilies, 1890s, 3 1/2 x 6 In. 750.00
Pin Box, Red, White Flowers, Metal Neck, No Cover, 4 In. 120.00

KEMPLE glass was made by John Kemple of East Palestine, Ohio, and Kenova, West Virginia, from 1945 to 1970. The glass was made from old molds. Many designs and colors were made. Kemple pieces are usually marked with a *K* on the bottom. Many milk glass pieces were made with or without the mark.

Bonbon, Sunburst Pattern, Milk Glass, Handles 25.00
Bowl, Jelly, Footed, Martec Pattern, Honey Amber, 5 x 4 In. 20.00
Bowl, Quintec Pattern, Amber Marigold, 3 1/4 x 7 1/2 In. 25.00
Candlestick, Bull's-Eye, Wheatonware, Amber, 4 3/4 x 2 In. 6.00
Compote, Martec Pattern, Honey Amber, 1970s 15.00
Goblet, Lace & Dewdrop, Amber, 6 x 3 1/8 In. 15.00
Plate, Milk Glass, Cabin, Snow, Woods, Hand Painted, Lacey Heart Edge, 7 1/4 In. 25.00
Plate, Milk Glass, Sheaf Of Wheat Border, 7 1/2 In. 25.00
Plate, Windmill, Hand Painted, Lacey Heart Edge, 7 1/4 In. 20.00

KENTON HILLS Pottery in Erlanger, Kentucky, made artwares, including vases and figurines that resembled Rookwood, probably because so many of the original artists and workmen had worked at the Rookwood plant. Kenton Hills opened in 1939 and closed during World War II.

Figurine, Mother & Child, Brown Glaze, Impressed Mark, Signed, David Seyler, 13 1/2 In. 896.00

KEW BLAS is the name used by the Union Glass Company of Somerville, Massachusetts. The name refers to an iridescent golden glass made from the 1890s to 1924. The iridescent glass was reminiscent of the Tiffany glass of the period.

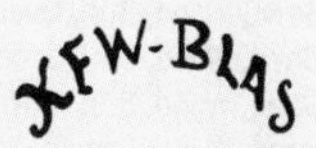

Candlestick, Gold Iridescent, Optic Ribbed, Scalloped Rim, 8 1/4 In., Pair 489.00
Vase, Flower Form, Gold Iridescent, Pink, Blue, Purple, Footed, Signed, 8 1/4 In. 400.00
Vase, Gold & Green Iridescent Pulled Feathers, Opal Ground, Oval, 5 In. 430.00
Vase, Gold Iridescent Pulled Feathers, Opal Ground, Signed, 9 1/2 In. 748.00
Vase, Gold Pulled Feather, Peach Ground, Signed, 4 3/4 In. 489.00
Vase, Gold, Green Pulled Feather, White Ground, Gold Interior, Signed, 8 3/4 In. 748.00
Vase, Green Pulled Feathers, White Ground, Gold Interior, 5 In. 800.00
Vase, Platinum Iridescent Wave, Gold Iridescent Ground, Green, Ruffled Edge, 7 1/4 In. 575.00
Vase, White, Green, Gold Interior, Shaped Rim, 10 In. 575.00

KEWPIES, designed by Rose O'Neill, were first pictured in the *Ladies' Home Journal.* The figures, which are similar to pixies, were a success, and Kewpie dolls and figurines started appearing in 1911. Kewpie pictures and other items soon followed. Collectors search for all items that picture the little winged people.

Bisque, Bride & Groom, Crepe Paper Tux, Hat & Veil, Sticker, 4 1/2 In., Pair 105.00
Bisque, Half Doll, Left-Glancing Eyes, Jointed Bisque Arms, Elephant Pincushion, 3 1/2 In. 1065.00
Bisque, Heart Sticker On Front, Rose O'Neill Sticker On Back, Japan, 1913, 7 In. 151.00
Bisque, Left-Glancing Eyes, Blue Wings, Jointed Shoulders & Hips, 8 In. 195.00
Bisque, Left-Glancing Eyes, Seated At Table, Bisque Wicker Chair, Germany, 4 1/2 In. 5390.00
Bisque, Right-Glancing Eyes, On Chair, Folded Arms, Germany, c.1915, 4 In. 440.00
Bisque, Right-Glancing Eyes, On Swing, Book On Lap, Germany, 1912, 2 1/2 In. 2420.00
Bisque, Right-Glancing Eyes, Seated With Book, Germany, c.1912, 3 1/2 In. 580.00
Bisque, Right-Glancing Eyes, Standing, Jointed, Uncle Sam, 4 In. 644.00
Bisque, Soldier Bursting From Eggshell, Helmet, Rifle, Germany, c.1914, 3 1/2 In. 3300.00
Bisque, Standing, Clasping Candy Sack, Self Base, 4 1/2 In. 950.00
Book, The Kewpies, Their Book, Rose O'Neill, Stokes, N.Y., 1913 .... 1500.00
Bulb, Glass, Figural, Christmas, 2 1/4 In. 18.00
Candy Container, Kewpie By Barrel, Partial Paint, Replacement Closure 50.00
Huggers, For Wedding Cake, Crepe Paper Wedding Costumes, 1935, 2 In. 475.00
Perfume Bottle, Sitting, Hand On Chin, Germany, 2 1/4 In. 85.00

KING'S ROSE, see Soft Paste category.

KITCHEN utensils of all types, from eggbeaters to bowls, are collected today. Handmade wooden and metal items, like ladles and apple peelers, were made in the early nineteenth century. Mass-produced pieces, like iron apple peelers and graniteware, were made in the nineteenth century. Also included in this category are utensils used for other household chores, such as laundry and cleaning. Other kitchen wares are listed under manufacturers' names or under Advertising, Iron, Tool, or Wooden.

Board, Cutting, Painted, Bird, 17 3/8 x 10 1/8 In. 165.00
Board, Springerle, 6 Geometric Designs, Nail, 4 1/4 x 15 In. 90.00
Bowl, Dough, Pine, Carved Ends, Finger Holds, Old Green Paint, 37 x 20 In. 259.00
Bowl, Dough, Wood, Waxed Finish, Elliptical, French Provincial, 7 x 32 In. 325.00
Bowl, Hardwood, Burl, Carved, Angels, Deer, Flowers, Hunters On Horseback, 4 1/2 x 2 In. 115.00
Bowl, Norfolk Pine, Thin Sides, Flared, Footed, Ron Kent, 4 x 5 In. 660.00
Bowl, Salad, Bird's-Eye Maple, c.1920, 15 & 19 In., 2 Piece 700.00
Bowl, White Pine, Turned, Ed Mouthrop, 5 x 11 1/2 In. 3304.00
Bowl, Wood, Ash, Red Paint, 19th Century, 6 x 17 In. 382.00

Bowl, Wood, Blue Paint, Turned, 10 1/2 x 3 In. 430.00
Bowl, Wood, Blue Paint, Turned, 13 In. 99.00
Bowl, Wood, Blue Paint, Turned, 16 1/2 In. 250.00
Bowl, Wood, Burl, Carved, Handles, Pierced, Early 19th Century, 8 x 21 1/2 In. 4406.00
Bowl, Wood, Burl, Carved, Round, Early 19th Century, 4 1/2 x 15 1/4 In. 881.00
Bowl, Wood, Burl, Irregular Rim, 7 x 16 In. 657.00
Bowl, Wood, Burl, Maple, Turned, Lip, Footed, New England, 1800s, 20 x 6 In. 9500.00
Bowl, Wood, Burl, Oval, Cutout Handles, Great Lakes, 19th Century, 9 1/2 In. 6325.00
Bowl, Wood, Burl, Scoop, Wide Collar, Notched Handle, 5 3/8 x 15 3/4 In. 2350.00
Bowl, Wood, Burl, Turned Collar, Early 19th Century, 3 3/8 x 9 1/4 In. 411.00
Bowl, Wood, Carved, Leaves, Handle, Spout, Carved Base, Early 1900s, 15 x 19 x 14 In. 235.00
Bowl, Wood, Chopping, Blue Paint, Oval, 22 In. 247.00
Bowl, Wood, Chopping, Maple, Oblong, Green Paint, Early 19th Century, 3 3/4 x 11 In. 353.00
Bowl, Wood, Chopping, Maple, Oval, Painted, Old Splint Composition, 1800s, 26 1/2 In. 192.00
Bowl, Wood, Chopping, Red Paint, 22 1/2 In. 1150.00
Bowl, Wood, Chopping, Round, Old Red Paint, 16 In. 85.00
Bowl, Wood, Chopping, Turned, 23 In. 460.00
Bowl, Wood, Incised Band, Turned, Footed, Scrubbed Interior, 15 1/2 x 3 1/2 In. 115.00
Bowl, Wood, Maple, Blue Paint, Turned, 18th Century, 5 1/2 x 16 1/2 In. 605.00
Bowl, Wood, Red Paint, Scrubbed Interior, Notched Handholds, Tool Marks, 22 In. 690.00
Bowl, Wood, Walnut, Irregular Round Shape, 1 3/4 x 12 In. 520.00
Bucket, Gourd, Iron Feet, Bail Handle, 6 In. 288.00
Bucket, Wood, Wire, Pinstripe Band, Bail Handle, Hand Grip, 2 3/8 In. 330.00
Bundt Pan, Aluminum, West Bend Co., 4 x 10 1/4 In. 38.00
Butter Mold, look under Mold, Butter in this category.
Butter Paddle, 4 6-Petal Stars, Handle, 9 x 3 1/2 In. 115.00
Butter Paddle, Burl, 5 1/2 x 6 1/2 In. 431.00
Butter Paddle, Burl, Dark Patina, 6 3/4 In. 431.00
Butter Paddle, Curved Handle, 8 1/2 x 3 3/4 In. 11.00
Butter Paddle, Stamp Handle, Star, Zigzag Border, 9 x 5 In. 690.00
Butter Scoop, Softwood, Tapered, Curved Handle, 8 1/2 x 5 1/2 In. 35.00
Butter Stamp, 2 Flowers, Leaf, Banded Border, Hexagonal, 4 3/4 x 4 In. 35.00
Butter Stamp, 2 Leaves, Chip Carved Center, Zigzag Border, Wood, Lollipop, 2 x 4 3/4 In. 575.00
Butter Stamp, 2-Part, 4 Prints, Square, Wood, Kinerson Type, 3 3/4 x 6 In. 69.00
Butter Stamp, 3 Leaves, 2 Stars, Serrated Banded Border, 2 1/2 x 3 3/8 In. 121.00
Butter Stamp, 3-Part, 8 Decorations, Rectangular, Wood, Kinerson Type, 7 x 6 In. 69.00
Butter Stamp, 4 Prints, Wood, Rectangular, Kinerson Type, 3 1/2 x 11 In. 104.00
Butter Stamp, 6-Point Star, Feather, Button Hook, Leaf, 2-Sided, Lollipop, 3 x 8 1/2 In. 400.00
Butter Stamp, 6-Point Star, Geometrics, Wood, Elliptical, Handle, 2 1/4 x 9 x 4 In. 144.00
Butter Stamp, Acorns On Branch, Oak Leaves, 3 3/4 In. 94.00
Butter Stamp, Carved Cow, Scalloped Edge, Handle, 4 3/4 In. 109.00
Butter Stamp, Cow, Branches, Serrated Edge, 4 5/8 In. 150.00
Butter Stamp, Cow, Metal Bound, Roll Type, 3-Part, 6-Sided, 4 1/2 x 2 3/4 In. 120.00
Butter Stamp, Cow, Standing By Tree, Branch Above, Serrated Edge, 3 1/2 In. 165.00
Butter Stamp, Cow, Standing By Tree, Branch, Serrated Edge, 4 1/4 In. 165.00
Butter Stamp, Cow, Tree, Leaves, Gadrooned Border, 1/2 Round, 3 3/8 x 7 In. 671.00
Butter Stamp, Double Sheaf Of Wheat, Gouge Border, Metal Handle, 6 1/2 x 3 1/2 In. 45.00
Butter Stamp, Dove, Flying, Feather Edge, Wood, 4 1/4 x 2 3/4 In. 345.00
Butter Stamp, Eagle, On Branch, Star, Serrated Edge, 3 1/2 In. 248.00
Butter Stamp, Eagle, On Branch, Star, Serrated Edge, 4 3/8 In. 303.00
Butter Stamp, Eagle, Shield Chest, Flower Sprays, Band Border, Round Handle, 2 3/4 x 4 In. 50.00
Butter Stamp, Eagle, Spread Wings, Leaves, 8-Sided, Carved, 3 3/4 In. 175.00
Butter Stamp, Eagle, Star, Handle, 4 In. 230.00
Butter Stamp, Eagle, Star, Serrated Border, Round, 4 x 2 1/2 In. 85.00
Butter Stamp, Fish, 2 Leaves, Serrated Band, 5 1/4 x 2 3/4 In. 275.00
Butter Stamp, Flower, Bell Shaped Case, Serrated Band Border, 6 x 3 1/2 In. 20.00
Butter Stamp, Flower, Hatch Mark Banding, Diamond Shape Handle, Round, 4 1/4 In. 60.00
Butter Stamp, Flower, Heart, Fan Corners, Mortised, Rectangular, Case, 2 x 8 3/4 In. 225.00
Butter Stamp, Flower, Incised, Carved, Stems, Serrated Edge, 4 In. 44.00
Butter Stamp, Flowers, Crescent Leaf, Leaves, Serrated Edge, 2 In. 248.00
Butter Stamp, Flowers, Leaves, Banded Border, Barrel Case, Hexagonal, 4 3/4 x 4 In. 33.00

Kitchen, Flue Cover, Bowl Of Cherries, Crimped Frame, Germany, 9 1/2 In. Diam.

Kitchen, Flue Cover, Boy In Wagon, Pulled By Dog, 9 1/2 In. Diam.

Kitchen, Flue Cover, Cowgirl, Gun & Lasso, Crimped Frame, Oval, Germany, 9 1/4 x 8 In.

Butter Stamp, Flowers, Leaves, Serrated Band Border, Round, 3 1/2 x 2 3/4 In. 45.00
Butter Stamp, Flowers, Serrated Banded Border, Bell Shape Case, 6 x 3 1/2 In. 20.00
Butter Stamp, Greek Letters, Geometric, Rectangular Handle, 1945, 1 3/4 x 4 1/4 In. 11.00
Butter Stamp, Leaf, Rising Sun, Wood, Lollipop, 2 1/4 x 4 1/2 In. 315.00
Butter Stamp, Leaves, Initials, Banded Border, Mushroom Handle, Round, 3 1/2 x 3 3/4 In. 176.00
Butter Stamp, Lollipop Shape, Snowflake, Incised, Carved, 4 3/8 x 10 3/4 In. 248.00
Butter Stamp, Pear, 3 Leaves, Round, 2 x 2 In. 50.00
Butter Stamp, Pineapple, Leaves, Stars, 2 Piece, 7 x 5 In. 1495.00
Butter Stamp, Rabbit, Running, Plunger Type, 7 1/2 x 3 In. 230.00
Butter Stamp, Rooster, Crowing, Plunger Type, Round, 5 1/2 x 4 1/4 In. 330.00
Butter Stamp, Rooster, Foliage, Fern Stems, Serrated Edge, 4 1/2 In. 825.00
Butter Stamp, Scallop Shell, Round Dome Shape, 3 x 5 In. 66.00
Butter Stamp, Sheaf Of Wheat, Leaves, Incised Band Border, 2 3/4 x 3 5/8 In. 35.00
Butter Stamp, Sheaf Of Wheat, Stars, Vine, 2 In. 40.00
Butter Stamp, Snowflake, Geometric, Round, 2 x 5 In. 55.00
Butter Stamp, Snowflake, Oval, 1 1/2 x 3 3/4 In. 35.00
Butter Stamp, Squirrel, Carved, Turned Handle, Round, 2 1/4 x 1 3/4 In. 316.00
Butter Stamp, Star, Triangular Chipped Decoration, Wood, Lollipop, 4 3/4 x 8 In. 405.00
Butter Stamp, Strawberry, Hatch Carved, Incised Foliage, 3 In. 44.00
Butter Stamp, Stylized Tulip, Coggled Rim, Handle, 3 5/8 In. 485.00
Butter Stamp, Stylized Tulip, Incised Lattice Panels, Stepped Sawtooth Border, 4 1/4 In. 545.00
Butter Stamp, Sunburst, Round, 2 3/4 x 3 In. 35.00
Butter Stamp, Swan, Serrated Border, Plunger Type, Wood, Round, 8 1/4 x 5 In. 80.00
Butter Stamp, Thistle & Leaves, Vine Border, 4 1/2 In. 180.00
Butter Stamp, Thistle, Leaf Wreath, Round, Bell Shape Case, 7 3/4 x 4 3/8 In. 35.00
Butter Stamp, Thistle, Leaves, Band Border, Round, 2 1/2 x 3 3/4 In. 35.00
Butter Stamp, Tulip & Stars, 1800s, 4 3/8 In. 440.00
Butter Stamp, Tulip, Chip Carved, Heart Handle, Oval, Penn., 7 In. 1150.00
Butter Stamp, Tulip, Closed, Carved, Shaped Leaves, Serrated Edge, 4 1/8 In. 75.00
Butter Stamp, Urn Of Flowers, Stems, Deep Hatch, Serrated Edge, 4 1/2 In. 550.00
Butter Stamp, Wood, Fish, Plunger Type, Round, 7 x 3 3/4 In. 200.00
Cabbage Cutter, Walnut, Heart Cutout Handle, Cherry, Half Spindles, 25 x 8 1/2 In. 460.00
Cake Board, Mahogany, George Washington, Liberty, Justice, Eagle, c.1830, 15 x 24 In. 4200.00
Cake Board, Wood, Man On Horse, Blowing Trumpet, Round, c.1800, 15 In. 575.00
Caldron, Bronze, 3-Footed, Handle, Flemish, Early 17th Century 750.00
Caldron, Bronze, Flared Handles, Mounts, Spout, Tripod Feet, Syria, 11 x 17 x 16 1/2 In. 3450.00
Cherry Pitter, Table Model, Cast Iron, Pat'd. Nov. 17, 1863, 19th Century, 11 In. 55.00
Churn, Cobalt Blue Tulip, M. Woodruff & Co., Cortland, 4 Gal., 17 In. 2300.00
Churn, Cypress, Tapered Body, Paddle Plunger, 1800s, 38 x 11 In. 353.00
Churn, Dasher, Slat Side, 3 Metal Bands, Blue Paint, 20 x 8 1/2 In. 270.00
Churn, Embossed Glass, Dazey, No. 40, St. Louis, Patented Feb 4 22, 14 x 6 In. 160.00
Coffee Grinders are listed in the Coffee Mill category.
Colander, Tin, Punched, Compass Flower, 2 Handles, 1800s, 10 In. 95.00
Cookie Board, Springerle, Hearts, Flowers, 2-Sided, 1810, 13 x 10 1/4 In. 715.00

Cookie Cutter, Belsnickle, Long Beard, Tin, c.1900, 6 In. 210.00
Cookie Cutter, Bird, Flared Tail, Tin, 5/8 x 6 3/8 In. 375.00
Cookie Cutter, Church Shape, Tin, 1940s, 4 x 3 3/4 In. 12.00
Cookie Cutter, Family, Man, Woman, 3 Girls, Tin, 4 To 5 In., 5 Piece 115.00
Cookie Cutter, Indian, Holding Tomahawk, Mounted, Tin, 1 x 4 1/4 x 7 3/4 In. 578.00
Cookie Cutter, Man On Horseback, Loop Handle, Flat Plate, 8 x 8 In. 110.00
Cookie Cutter, Man, 10 In. 4800.00
Cookie Cutter, Poodle Dog, Aluminum, 2 3/4 x 3 1/4 In. 4.00
Cookie Cutter, Rooster, Flat Plate, Loop Handle, 6 3/8 x 7 1/2 In., Pair 230.00
Cookie Cutter, Santa Claus, Pack On Back, Mounted, Tin, 10 1/4 x 6 1/4 In. 430.00
Cream Separator, McCormick-Deering, Cast Iron, Painted, Black, Scale, Arcade, 4 7/8 In. 385.00
Dough Box, Cover, Dovetailed, Splayed Legs, Early 1800s, 28 x 42 x 26 In. 403.00
Dough Box, Cover, Walnut, Breadboard Ends, Dovetailed, Penn., c.1815, 29 x 66 x 29 In. 1610.00
Dough Box, On Stand, French Provincial, Fruitwood, Carved, Turned Legs, 39 x 51 In. 1880.00
Dough Box, Yellow Paint, Canted, Splayed Legs, Early 1800s, 19 1/2 x 19 1/4 x 15 1/2 In. 294.00
Dough Scraper, Heart Shape, Cutout, Handle, Diamond Faceted, Iron, 3 3/4 x 4 In. 990.00
Dough Scraper, Whitesmithed, 1891 Indian Head Penny Handle, 5 In. 110.00
Dough Scraper, Wrought Iron, Cutout Heart, Round Handle, 3 x 3 3/4 In. 990.00
Dough Trough, Cover, Pine, Nailed Construction, Tapered Sides, 1800s, 11 x 32 In. 55.00
Flour Bin, Pine, Double, Fold-Out Bread Board Top, 37 x 35 x 19 In. 375.00
Flour Sifter, Angled Bin, Turn Crank, Wood Dowels, Trestle Legs, Gray Paint, 12 x 10 In. 125.00
Flue Cover, Bowl Of Cherries, Crimped Frame, Germany, 9 1/2 In. Diam. .... *ILLUS* 143.00
Flue Cover, Boy In Wagon, Pulled By Dog, 9 1/2 In. Diam. .... *ILLUS* 193.00
Flue Cover, Cardboard, Girl, Flowers, Ostrich Plumes In Hat, Pink Bow, Victorian, 14 In. 260.00
Flue Cover, Cowgirl, Gun & Lasso, Crimped Frame, Oval, Germany, 9 1/4 x 8 In. .... *ILLUS* 546.00
Flue Cover, Victorian Boy & Girl, Crossing Stream, 9 1/2 In. Diam. 55.00
Flue Cover, Woman, Early Automobile, Ocean, c.1905, 9 1/2 In. 330.00
Food Chopper, Turned Handle, 1800s, 8 1/2 In. 75.00
Fork, 2-Tine, Rattail Handle, Whitesmithed, Pa., 22 In. 39.00
Fork, Flesh, 2-Tine, Rattail Handle, Whitesmithed, c.1800, 18 1/2 In. 35.00
Fork, Heart Handle, Forged, Iron, 17 In. 98.00
Fork, Meat, 2-Tine, Wrought Iron, Flat Handle, Hook Hanger, Stamped, 11 1/2 x 1 1/4 In. 220.00
Fork, Presentation, 2-Tine, Pennsylvania, Iron, 1804, 17 3/4 In. 800.00
Fork, Wrought Iron, Loop Hanger, Stamped J. Schmidt 1845, 18 In. 415.00
Fork, Wrought Iron, Ring Hanger, J.W. Snyder, 21 In. 45.00
Grater, Nutmeg, Bellows Shape, Cast Iron, J.M. Smith, Patented June 7, 1870, 4 In. 275.00
Griddle, Bail Handle, Wagner Ware, 5 3/8 In. 60.00
Ice Chest, Pine, Double Lift Top, Zinc Lining, Ball Feet, White Paint, 1800s, 29 x 40 x 24 In. 220.00
Ice Cream Maker, Acme Jr., 5 Minute Freezer, Acme Can Co. Inc., Philadelphia 56.00
Ice Cream Sandwich Maker, Bronze, Wood Handle, Springless Plunger, 8 1/2 In. 935.00
Ice Cream Sandwich Maker, Dan Dee, Nickel Plated, c.1920, 11 1/2 In. 2320.00
Ice Cream Sandwich Maker, German Silver Handle, Cake Cone Co., St. Louis, Mo., 9 In. 210.00
Ice Cream Sandwich Maker, Plunger, Brass, Nickel Plated Handle, 10 1/4 In. 4400.00
Ice Cream Scoop, Wood Handle, Mechanical, Square, Fills Icypi Sandwichs, 1920s 200.00
Ice Cream Slicer, Dover Round Bowl Thumb Lever, Nickel Plated, Handle, Pat. 1928, 11 In. 522.00
Icebox, Oak, Paneled Doors, c.1900, 46 x 31 x 17 In. 403.00
Icebox, Wood, 3 Doors, 48 x 38 In. 440.00
Iron, Gem, Wood Handle, Silver Paint, 4 In. 170.00
Iron, Goffering, Tripod Base, Penny Feet, 1850 .... 1380.00
Iron, No. W110, Winchester, Electric 173.00
Iron, Our Pet, J.E. Stevens Co., 3 9/16 In. 165.00
Iron, Polisher, Orion, No. 2, Cast Iron, Black Paint, 3 In. 157.00
Iron, Polisher, Savery Co., No. 2, New York, 3 3/8 In. 46.00
Iron, Pressing, Wapak, No. 1, Silver Paint, 3 5/8 In. 100.00
Iron, Sailmaker's, The John Carbery Co., Cincinnati, Ohio, Sailors, 3 7/8 In. 720.00
Iron, Swan, Cast Iron, Yellow Over Blue Paint, Child's, 2 In. 67.00
Iron, Swan, Cast Iron, Yellow Paint, Child's, 1 1/2 In. 452.00
Iron, Swan, Open Curl, 2 1/8 In. 60.00
Iron, Swan, Open Curl, 2 7/8 In. 55.00
Iron, Swan, Rara Avis, 3 3/8 In. 3630.00
Iron, Swan, White, Red, Yellow Paint, Child's, 2 In. 300.00

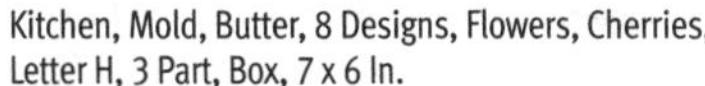

Kitchen, Mold, Butter, 8 Designs, Flowers, Cherries, Letter H, 3 Part, Box, 7 x 6 In.

Mold, Butter, Cow Under Tree, Notched Border, Turned Handle, 4 1/2 In.

Keg, Rum, Round, Painted, Wood, Riveted Joints, Leather Handle Remnants, 1860s, 6 In. 264.00
Kettle, Apple Butter, Copper, Iron Bail Handle, 19 x 29 In. 191.00
Kettle, Cast Iron, Archaic Designs, Bronze Top, Japan, c.1900, 7 1/2 In. 147.00
Kettle, Cast Iron, Birds, Flowers, 19th Century, Japan, 11 In. 1880.00
Kettle, Cast Iron, Fan, Double Gourd, Man, Duck, Copper Lid, Inlaid Gold, Silver, Japan, 5 In. 1998.00
Kettle, Cast Iron, Lotus Plants, Gold, Silver Inlay, Japan, 19th Century, 8 1/2 In. 705.00
Kettle, Iron, Lazy-Arm, J.K., Bail, Feet, Shaped Lid, 1700s, 10 1/2 In. 578.00
Kettle, Sugar, Cast Iron, Bowl Shape, Chattanooga Iron Works, 50 Gal., 48 1/2 In. 2232.00
Kettle, Sugar, Cast Iron, Flared Rim, Dished Basin, 19th Century, 55 In. 5170.00
Kettle, Sugar, Cast Iron, Shallow Bowl, Wide Rim, 13 x 48 In. 3819.00
Kettle, Sugar, Iron, Basin Shape, Olden's M. Co., Columbus, c.1850, 15 x 40 In. 3819.00
Kettle, Sugar, Iron, Flared Rim, Leeds & Co., New Orleans, 22 1/2 x 55 1/2 In. 2585.00
Ladle, Openwork Handle, Peacock In Relief, Fruitwood, 15 x 4 x 2 In. 81.00
Ladle, Wrought Iron, Brass Bowl, Hook Hanger, J. Schmidt, 19 1/4 In. 358.00
Ladle, Wrought Iron, Flat Handle, Hook Hanger, J. Schmidt, 11 x 2 In. 358.00
Ladle, Wrought Iron, Hook Hanger, J. Schmidt, 1847, 15 In. 363.00
Ladle, Wrought Iron, Stamped, Rattail End, J. Schmidt, 10 1/2 In. 248.00
Lazy Susan, Mahogany, 2 Sections, Round Top, Molded Edge, 10 1/2 x 25 1/2 In. 330.00
Match Holders can be found in their own category.
Match Safes can be found in their own category.
Meat Grinder, Wood Handle, Winchester Repeating Arms Co., New Haven, 11 In. 80.00
Mixer, Milk Shake, Green, Stainless Steel Cup, Model No. 25, Gilchrist Co., 17 1/2 In. 180.00
Mold, Ice Cream, see also Pewter category.
Molds may also be found in the Pewter and Tinware categories.
Mold, Butter, 8 Designs, Flowers, Cherries, Letter H, 3 Part, Box, 7 x 6 In. . . . . ***ILLUS*** 69.00
Mold, Butter, Cow Under Tree, Notched Border, Turned Handle, 4 1/2 In. . . . . ***ILLUS*** 270.00
Mold, Butter, Eagle, Spread Wing, Leaves, 8-Sided, 3 3/4 In. . . . . ***ILLUS*** 173.00
Mold, Butter, Lollipop, 6-Point Star, Triangular Chipped Border, 4 3/4 In. . . . . ***ILLUS*** 403.00
Mold, Butter, Pineapple, Leaves, Stars, Handle, 5 In., 2 Piece . . . . ***ILLUS*** 1495.00
Mold, Butter, Wood, Steel Top & Handle, 10 1/4 x 5 3/4 In. 120.00
Mold, Cake, Blanket Wrapped Baby, Bow, Oval, Redware, Incised, Handle, 2 1/2 x 16 In. 303.00
Mold, Candle, see Tinware category.
Mold, Chocolate, Turkey, Tin, 3-Piece, Anton Reiche, No. 14783, Germany, 4 x 3 3/4 In. 138.00
Mold, Fluted, 3 Berries, Sponged Brown Glaze, Redware, 2 x 4 3/8 In. 105.00
Mold, Food, Center Tube, Lead Glaze, Scalloped Rim, Redware, 19th Century, 3 x 8 1/4 In. 39.00
Mold, Food, Lead, Manganese Glaze, Signed, John Bell, 2 1/4 x 4 1/4 In. 1870.00
Mold, Food, Lion Reclining, Ironstone, Oval, 19th Century, 6 7/8 In. 28.00
Mold, Food, Santa, Hello Kiddies, Cast Iron, Griswold, 1930s, 12 In. 160.00
Mold, Food, Swirled, Redware, 1800s, 7 In. 35.00
Mold, Food, Turk's Head, Green & Brown Accents, Redware, c.1840, 7 1/2 In. 90.00
Mold, Food, Turk's Head, Redware, Salt Glazed, 3 x 8 1/2 In. 195.00
Mold, Food, Turk's Head, Sponged Manganese, Overglaze, Redware, c.1850, 4 1/4 x 8 1/2 In. 415.00
Mold, Jelly, Redware, Brown Glazed Interior, 2 1/4 x 5 In. 45.00
Mold, Pudding, Blue Glass, Round, Embossed, Tin Mount, Ring Hanger, 9 1/2 In. 99.00

Kitchen, Mold, Butter, Eagle, Spread Wing, Leaves, 8-Sided, 3 3/4 In.

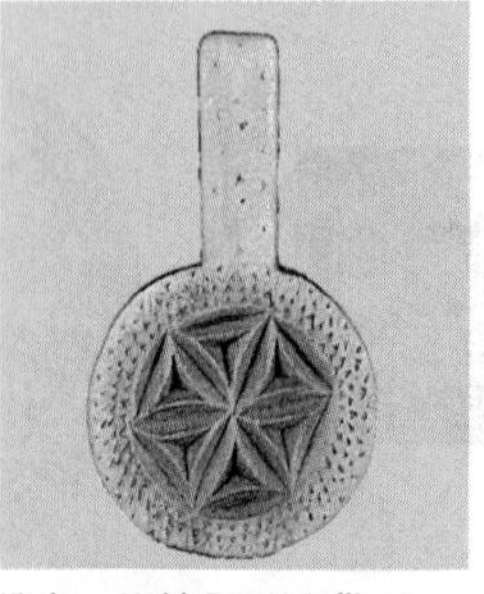
Kitchen, Mold, Butter, Lollipop, 6-Point Star, Triangular Chipped Border, 4 3/4 In.

Kitchen, Mold, Butter, Pineapple, Leaves, Stars, Handle, 5 In., 2 Piece

Mold, Pudding, Grape Cluster, Gold Glass, Brass Mount, Ring Hanger, 4 x 2 3/4 In. 88.00
Mold, Pudding, Grape Cluster, Gold, Brass Mount, Ring Hanger, 4 x 2 3/4 In. 110.00
Mold, Pudding, Grape Cluster, Silver, Brass Mount, Ring Hanger, 4 x 2 3/4 In. 83.00
Mold, Pudding, Green Glass, Oval, Brass Mount, Ring Hanger, 3 3/4 x 2 1/2 In. 6.00
Mold, Pudding, Green Glass, Oval, Brass Mount, Ring Hanger, 7 x 5 In. 99.00
Mortar, Burl, Footed, Incised Band, Round, 6 1/2 x 5 3/4 In. 308.00
Mortar & Pestle, Acadian Cypress, Footed, Louisiana, 1700s, 28 x 14 In. 1765.00
Mortar & Pestle, Burl, 8 x 8 In. 748.00
Mortar & Pestle, Cast Iron, Tapered Mortar, 1700s, 5 x 10 In. 118.00
Mortar & Pestle, Lignum Vitae, c.1825, 12 In. 115.00
Mortar & Pestle, Wood, 1800s, 11 3/4 In. 46.00
Nut Pick Set, Quackenbush, Wood Box, Cloth Lining, 6 Picks, Cracker 18.00
Olive Oil Dispensing Tin, Phenix Dispensing Tank, Whitall Tatum Co., 13 In. 56.00
Pan, Popover, Griswold No. 10, Pattern No. 948 .... 75.00
Pan, Sauce, Iron, Kenton, 5 3/4 x 3 1/2 In. 72.00
Peel, Wrought Iron, Heart Handle Hanger, c.1800, 38 In. 154.00
Peel, Wrought Iron, Tapered Blade, Faceted Hanger, 26 1/2 In. 45.00
Peeler, Apple, Rope, Wood Pins, Painted, 1800s, 26 x 8 x 10 1/2 In. 440.00
Peeler, Apple, Table Top, Wood Handle, Screw Adjustments, Iron Apple Holder, 10 x 26 In. 330.00
Pepper Mill, Ivory, Silver, England, 3 1/4 In. 235.00
Pie Crimper, Bone, Tuned Handle, 3-Tine Fork, 6 1/2 In. 345.00
Pie Crimper, Brass, Wrought Iron, Square Shaft, Wood Handle, 9 x 1 1/4 In. 248.00
Pie Lifter, Fruitwood Handle, Rattails, Whitesmithed, 1800s, 35 In. 60.00
Pie Safe, Cypress, Drawers, Screen Doors, Louisiana, Late 1800s, 74 x 37 x 15 In. 880.00
Pot, Copper, Wrought Iron, Long Turned Wood Handle, J. Moyer, 22 1/2 In. 39.00
Pot, Cover, Iron, 3-Footed, A. Baldwin Co., New Orleans, 1800s, 5 1/4 x 9 1/4 In. 235.00
Rack, Butcher's, Scrolls, 3 Hooks, Iron, France, 36 x 32 In. 767.00
Rack, Drying, Pine, Mortise Crossbars, Square Nails, Brown Paint, 54 x 31 1/2 In. 86.00
Rack, Herb Drying, 4 Horizontal Slats, Shaped Double Foot, Late 1800s, 41 x 33 In. 210.00
Rack, Spice Drying, 2 Tier, Natural Finish, 1800s 66.00
Rack, Spoon, Pine, Blue Paint, Mortised Construction, Scalloped, c.1800, 22 x 20 1/2 In. 385.00
Rack, Utensil, Pine, Iron Hooks, Hangers, Tulip, Hex Designs, Beaded, Scalloped, 9 x 33 In. 94.00
Reamers are listed in their own category.
Roaster, Drip Pan, Wrought Iron, Tilting Fork, Penny Feet, 18 1/2 In. 275.00
Rolling Pin, Milk Glass, Blown, Pale Blue Opalescent, Sheared Pontil, 27 1/4 In. 168.00
Rolling Pin, Pastry, Turned Wood, Flower, Hatch Carved Border, 13 1/2 x 2 3/4 In. 240.00
Rolling Pin, Wildflower, Stoneware 200.00
Rolling Pin, Wood, Flower, Hatch Carved Border, Incised Handle, 13 1/2 x 2 3/4 In. 242.00
Rolling Pin, Wood, Painted, Red, Black, 18 In. 90.00
Sadiron, Spiral Handle, Salesman Sample, 1 Lb., 1 3/4 x 2 3/4 In. 50.00
Salt & Pepper Shakers are listed in their own category.
Scoop, Ice Cream, Clipper, Disher, Double Scraper, Gear, Nickel Plated, Pat. 1905, 9 1/4 In. 140.00
Scoop, Ice Cream, Clipper, Double Scraper, Giles & Nielsen, Nickel Plated, Pat. Feb. 7, 1905, 9 In. . 176.00
Scoop, Ice Cream, Conical, Nickel Plated, Brass Handle, Patd. Oct. 16, 1906, 9 In. 385.00

Scoop, Ice Cream, Conical, Squeeze Type, Nickel Plated Metal, Pat. 1894, 8 1/2 In. 275.00
Scoop, Ice Cream, Cylindrical, Nickel Plated, Wood Handle, Plunger, Pat. 1931, 9 In. 2530.00
Scoop, Ice Cream, Cylindrical, Trigger Grip Handle, Plunger, Nickel Plated, 9 1/2 In. 412.00
Scoop, Ice Cream, Heart Shape, Marcos Novelty Co., 1925, 11 x 2 7/8 In. ....2970.00 to 7825.00
Scoop, Ice Cream, New Sundae, Original Box, Metal, Size 20, 9 1/2 In. 1680.00
Scoop, Ice Cream, Rectangular Bowl, Nickel Plated, Wood Handle, Thumb Lever, 10 In. 4540.00
Scoop, Ice Cream, Round Bowl, Point Outside, Nickel Plated Brass, 11 1/4 In. 1980.00
Skillet, Griswold, No. 0-562, Child's 60.00
Skillet, Griswold, No. 2, Aluminum, 3 x 4 1/16 In. 209.00
Skillet, Griswold, Square, No. 1, 775, Child's 145.00
Skillet, Single Spout, Iron, Kenton, 6 x 3 In. 55.00
Skillet, Wagner, Iron, Sidney, Oh., 6 7/8 x 4 7/8 In. 48.00
Skillet, Wrought Iron Range Co. Home Comfort, Salesman Sample, St. Louis Mo., 3 x 4 In. 150.00
Skillet, Wrought Iron, 12-In. Handle, 1800s, 11 1/2 In. 55.00
Skimmer, Wrought Iron, Brass Bowl, Stamped, J. Schmidt, 1848, 19 3/4 In. 415.00
Spatula, Iron, Punch Decorated, Heart On Handle, Whitesmithed, 1800s, 14 1/2 In. 50.00
Spatula, Thistle, Long Handle, Whitesmithed, 1800s, 19 1/4 In. 66.00
Spatula, Wrought Iron, Flat Handle, Scalloped Edge, Heart Hanger, H.R. Eby, 10 1/2 In. 55.00
Spatula, Wrought Iron, Rattail Handle, 1800s, 13 In. 39.00
Spice Box, Pine, 4 Drawers, Grain Painted, New England, c.1840, 10 x 9 In. 1650.00
Spice Box, Pine, Painted, Porcelain Knobs, 9 Drawers, Metal Handle, 10 3/4 x 5 1/4 x 7 3/4 In. 345.00
Spice Box, Tin, Punched, Ovals, Hearts, Ring Feet, Handle, 8 Compartments, 3 x 9 In. 200.00
Spice Box, Traveling, Pine, 15 Drawers, Ivory Pulls, c.1875, 20 x 12 x 6 In. 825.00
Spice Box, Walnut, 9 Drawers, c.1875, 16 1/4 x 11 In. 200.00
Spice Rack, Hanging, Plastic, Griffith, 10 Bottles, 5 x 9 1/8 In. 85.00
Spoon, Heart Shape Bowl, Whitesmithed, Rattail Handle, c.1800, 15 1/2 In. ....44.00 to 55.00
Spoon, Serving, Brass, Wrought Iron, Flat Handle, Pierced End, Shaped Bowl, 11 In. 28.00
Spoon Rack, Pine, 2 Tiers, Shaped Pierced Backboard, Early 1800s, 21 x 15 In. 323.00
Spoon Rest, Black Mammy & Chef, Cast Iron, Toledo Stove & Range Co., 7 3/4 & 8 In., Pair 255.00
Sprinkler Bottle, Chinaman, Porcelain, Hand Painted, Metal Cap, 8 1/2 In. 125.00
Sprinkler Bottle, Dutch Boy, Ceramic, Souvenir Of Lake George, N.Y., 8 1/4 x 2 5/8 In. 250.00
Sprinkler Bottle, Merry Maid, 6 3/4 In. 85.00
Sprinkler Bottle, Siamese Cat, Ceramic, 8 1/4 In. 195.00
Sprinkler Bottle, Sprinkle Plenty, Chinese Boy, Gothamware, 8 3/4 x 3 In. 130.00
Stringholder, Round, 2 Sections, Figured Wood, Burl, Round Base, 6 In. 345.00
Stringholder, Wood, Bee Skep Shape, Turned, Domed, Covered, 7 x 7 5/8 In. 825.00
Tetsubin, Iron, Square, Willow Tree, Moon, Bronze Cover, Japan, Early 1800s, 6 3/4 In. 330.00
Toaster, Push Button, Drop Handles, Nickel Body, Universal, c.1929, 9 In. 410.00
Toaster, Turnover, Chrome, Westinghouse, Patented July 28, 1914, 7 1/2 In. 70.00
Toaster, Wrought Iron, Band, Splayed Sides, Arched Feet, Pivoting Handle, 7 x 17 x 22 In. 178.00
Toaster, Wrought Iron, T-Shaped, Handle, Swivel, 6 x 24 1/2 x 12 1/2 In. 374.00
Tongs, Wrought Iron, Square Handle, Scrolled Hanger, Incised, 14 1/4 In. 33.00
Trivet, see Trivet category.
Utensils, Ladle, Skimmer, Wrought, Iron, Brass Inlaid Squares, Initials TL, 1823, 18 1/2 In. 1610.00
Wafer Iron, Iron, Dutch Flat Hearts, c.1800, 33 In. 231.00
Waffle Iron, Cast Iron, 4 In. 245.00
Waffle Iron, Cast Iron, Wagner, Pat'd Feb. 22nd 1910, Sidney, Ohio, 7 In. 121.00
Waffle Iron, Griswold, Wood Handles, Round 2600.00
Waffle Iron, Walton Foundry, 4 In. 55.00
Wash Stick, Hardwood, Chip Carving, Star, 1800s, 28 3/4 In. 105.00
Washboard, Poplar, Redware, Brown Mottled Glaze, 7 x 14 In. 403.00
Washing Machine, Softwood, J.T. King Builder, York, Pa., 1870s, 36 x 40 In. 220.00

KNIFE collectors usually specialize in a single type. In the 1960s, the United States government passed a law that required knife manufacturers to mark their knives with the country of origin. This seemed to encourage the collectors, and knife collecting became an interest of a large group of people. All types of knives are collected, from top quality twentieth-century examples to old bone- or pearl-handled knives in excellent condition.

Antler Handle, Hand Forged Blade, 1860s, 16 1/2 In. 525.00

Arkansas Toothpick Fighting, Double Edge, White Metal Grip, 1850-60, 11 1/2 In. 650.00
Bone Handle, Miller Brothers Blade, C.C. Crain Hardware, MBC Corn, 5 1/4 In. 27.00
Bowie, 2-Piece Horn Handle, 1861, 11 1/2-In. Blade 508.00
Bowie, 8-Sided Bone Handle, Thomas Lamb, Washington, D.C., c.1840, 16 1/4 In. 5500.00
Bowie, Clip Point, Bone Handle, Pre 1900, 8 3/4-In. Blade, 13 3/4 In. 205.00
Bowie, Frontiersman, Stag Handles, Snake, H.C. Initials, S&J Kitchen, Sheffield, 14 1/8 In. 1650.00
Bowie, Mother-Of-Pearl, I*XL, G. Wostenholm & Son, Sheffield, c.1900, 11 1/4 In. 805.00
Bowie, Rosewood Handle, Mother-Of-Pearl Inlay Circle, 15 3/4 x 2 3/4 In. 935.00
Bowie, Single Edge, Steel, Silver Handle, Leather Sheath, c.1883, 15 1/4 In. 1227.00
Bowie, Wood Grip, Clipped Point Blade, Pewter Studs, c.1850, 11 1/2 In. 1350.00
Corn Razor, 3 Pin, Bone Handles, Leather Sheath, J.R. Torrey, Mass., 1800s, 5 1/2 In. 60.00
Crooked, Carved Clover & Star, 9 1/2 In. 375.00
Crooked, Carved Heart, 8 1/2 In. 290.00
Crooked, Carved Wood, Hearts, Maple Handle, Pierced Ball Finial, Initials, 8 1/2 In. 940.00
Crooked, Carved, Painted Handle, 9 1/2 In. 520.00
Crooked, Chip Carved Handle, 11 In. 230.00
Dagger, Belt, Beveled Edge, Snakeskin Grip, Leather Scabbard, Sudan, 7 In. 135.00
Dagger, Belt, Horn Tip, Bone Grip, Inscribed, Mahdist War, Sudan 185.00
Dagger, Indo Persian, Recurve, 2 Piece Antler Grips, Brass Rivets, c.1800, 11 1/2 In. 375.00
Dagger, Kodzuka, Steel Blade, Japan, 19th Century, 8 1/4 In. 295.00
Dagger, Nazi Hitler Youth, Scabbard, 6-In. Blade 173.00
Dagger, Nazi R.A.D. Officer, Scabbard, 10-In. Blade 345.00
Dagger, Nazi S.S., Scabbard, 8 1/2-In. Blade 750.00
Dagger, Officer's, Concealed, Swagger Stick, Cylindrical, Leather, Continental, c.1880, 21 In. 265.00
Dagger, Ottoman, Jambiya Shape, Walrus Ivory Hilt, Steel Blade, c.1800, 18 3/4 In. 705.00
Dagger, Persian, T-Back Blade, Etched, 2 Piece Bone Grip, 2 Piece Ivory Pommel, 7 3/4 In. 425.00
Dagger, Robe, Skull Crusher Pommel, Reptile Skin Grip, Leather Wrist Loop, Sudan, 8 1/4 In. 128.00
Dagger, Sheath, Nazi, 17 In. 170.00
Dagger, Single Edge, Watered Steel Blade, Wood Hilt & Scabbard, Java, 1800s, 17 In. 120.00
Dagger, Steel Blade, Silver Ferrule, Stylized Garuda, Indonesia, 19th Century, 17 In. 118.00
Dagger Set, Curved, Straight Blades, Inscribed, Bone, Horn Tips, Scabbard, Sudan, 6 1/2 In., 3 .. 445.00
Dirk, Hollow, Triangular Section, Staghorn Grip, Scotland, c.1815, 11-In. Blade 1350.00
Dirk, Presentation, Knights, Arches, Cabochon, Sheath, Scotland, Early 1900s, 21 1/4 In. 2115.00
Doctor's, Hornet, Ivory Handles, Simmons Hardware, Germany, 3 5/8-In. Blade 150.00
Folding, Stag Handles, McIntee, Shaw, Sheffield, 10 3/4 In. 176.00
Hunting, Bone Handle, Metal Tipped Scabbard, Wilbert Cutlery Co., 8 1/4 In. 155.00
Hunting, Trailmaker, Leather Washer Handle, Marbles, 1940s, 14 3/8 In. 790.00
Kris, Steel Blade, Horn Hilt, Wood Scabbard, Silver Mounts, Sumatra, 1800s, 24 1/2 In. 265.00
Kris, Watered Steel Blade, Straight, Wood Hilt, Nude Figure, Bali, 1800s, 26 In. 646.00
Mess Kit, Cast Aluminum, Stainless Steel Blade, U.S. Army, World War I 8.00
Pen, Woman's Leg, Art Nouveau, Syracuse, Late Victorian 35.00
Pocket, Bulldog Brand, 3 Blades, 1984 Kentucky Derby, Germany, 3 3/8 In. 60.00
Pocket, Bulldog Brand, Lady Leg, Celluloid Handles, Cranberry Burl, Germany, 3 1/4 In. 30.00
Pocket, Bulldog Brand, Lady Leg, Celluloid Handles, Walnut Burl, Germany, 3 1/4 In. 25.00
Pocket, Figural, Gun, 7 In. 60.00
Pocket, Joseph Rodgers, Stag Handle, To Strike Fire, No. 6, Sheffield, England, 7 1/4-In. Blade ... 385.00
Pocket, Marble's, No. 83, Safety, Stag Handle, Gladstone, Mich., 1920s, 4 1/4 In. 606.00
Pocket, Robeson, No. 622382, Stag Handle, 2 Blades, 4 1/8 In. 290.00
Pocket, Winchester, No. 2087, Pen & Spear Blades, Celluloid Handles, 3 In. 135.00
Pocket, Winchester, No. 3353, Mother-Of-Pearl Handles, 2 5/8 In. 157.00
Pommel, La Tene, Celtic, Ring, Recurve, c.200 B.C., 8 In. 465.00
Pommel, La Tene, Celtic, Ring, Recurve, c.200 B.C., 14 1/4 In. 750.00
Pommel, La Tene, Celtic, Ring, Recurve, c.400 B.C., 10 1/2 In. 475.00
Sheath, Great Plains, Sioux, Multicolored, Geometric Pattern, Beaded, c.1890 .... 4125.00
Simmons Hardware, Hornet, 2 Blades, Mother-Of-Pearl Handles 63.00
Stag Handle, Marked, G. Naack, 10 In. 140.00
Throwing, Azande, Hide-Wrapped Grip, Pierced Center, Chiseled Lattice, c.1850, 16 3/4 In. 565.00
Throwing, Banza, Hide-Wrapped Grip, Iron Head, c.1850, 16 In. 585.00

KNOWLES, TAYLOR & KNOWLES items may be found in the Lotus Ware category.

KOREAN WARE, see Sumida.

KOSTA, the oldest Swedish glass factory, was founded in 1742. During the 1920s through the 1950s, many pieces of original design were made at the factory. Kosta and Boda merged with Afors in 1964 and created the Afors Group in 1971. In 1976, the name *Kosta Boda* was adopted. The company merged with Orrefors in 1990 and is still working.

Chandelier, Erik Hoglund, Glass, Iron, Stromberg Ironworks, c.1957, 43 x 19 1/2 In. 4500.00
Vase, Cylindrical, Tapers, Birds, Speckled Ground, Ulrica Hydman, 1980s, 9 In. 300.00
Vase, Domed, 3 Red Medallions, Horizontal Stripes, Bertil Vallien, 1980s, 7 3/4 In. 150.00
Vase, Flattened, Fish, Bubbles, Ulrica Hydman, Boda, 10 1/2 x 5 1/4 In. 885.00
Vase, Shades Of Green, Trees, Birds, Cylindrical, Signed, 1980s, 6 In. 288.00

KPM refers to Berlin porcelain, but the same initials were used alone and in combination with other symbols by several German porcelain makers. They include the Konigliche Porzellan Manufaktur of Berlin, initials used in mark, 1823–1847; Meissen, 1723–1724 only; Krister Porzellan Manufaktur in Waldenburg, after 1831; Kranichfelder Porzellan Manufaktur in Kranichfeld, after 1903; and the Kister Porzellan Manufaktur in Scheibe, after 1838.

K.P.M

Bowl, Boat Shape, Rocaille Rim, Enamel, Fruit, Flowers, Late 1800s, 15 In. 265.00
Candleholder, Bisque, Lithophane, Landscape, Castle, Iron Stem, Late 1800s, 7 x 6 In. 765.00
Compote, Bird Game Reserves, Dresden, 1800s, 6 3/4 x 7 1/4 In. 205.00
Cup & Saucer, Demitasse, Gilt, Lavender Ground, Blue Scepter, Late 1800, 3 3/4 In. 25.00
Cup & Saucer, Iron Cross & Oak Leaf 175.00
Jar, Cover, Cobalt Blue Ground, Enamel Decorated, Flowers, Oblong, Tapered, 12 In. 2585.00
Plaque, 3 Women, Various Stages Of Dress & Life, Scepter Mark, Gilt Frame, 14 1/2 x 11 1/2 In. .. 6040.00
Plaque, Berlin, Painted, Man Painted Greek Pottery, c.1900, 10 x 7 1/2 In. 5290.00
Plaque, Children In Garden, Scepter Mark, Late 1800s, 8 3/8 x 6 1/4 In. 7050.00
Plaque, Frederick The Great, Gilt, Beaded Enamel, Porcelain, 14 In. 265.00
Plaque, Good Night, Woman, Holding Candle, Late 1800s, 9 1/4 x 6 3/8 In. 3400.00
Plaque, Joyeux Toast, Malty, 13 1/4 x 11 1/4 In. 7605.00
Plaque, Le Soir, Women, Nude, River, Giltwood Frame, Early 1900s, 10 x 7 1/2 In. 7638.00
Plaque, Man, Kissing Woman, On Sofa, Painted, E. Volk, Late 1800s, 8 1/2 x 12 1/2 In. 10638.00
Plaque, Man, Women, Dog, Garden, Early 1900s, 19 1/4 x 15 1/4 In. 6000.00
Plaque, Mary Magdalene, Hand Painted, 1800s, 10 1/2 x 8 1/2 In. 7605.00
Plaque, Monk, Kissing Baby, c.1900, 11 1/8 x 8 3/4 In. 3300.00
Plaque, Princess Louise, Descending Staircase, In Gown & Cloak, Berlin, 13 x 8 In. 6465.00
Plaque, Saint Jerome In The Desert, Seated, Black Robe, Marked, 13 x 11 1/4 In. 2400.00
Plaque, Seminude Woman, Long Flowing Hair, Lavender Drape, Gold Frame, 5 x 4 In. 1440.00
Plaque, Seminude Woman, Long Hair, Oval, Gesso Frame, 13 x 11 In. 12075.00
Plaque, Sistine Madonna, c.1900, 16 1/8 x 12 1/2 In. 11400.00
Plaque, Slave, Woman, c.1900, 9 3/8 x 6 3/8 In. 4200.00
Plaque, St. Jerome Kneeling Before Altar, Book, Scepter Mark, Frame, 9 x 11 In. 4025.00
Plaque, Woman, Flowing Hair, Red Flower, Ornate Gilt Frame, 10 1/2 x 8 1/2 In. 11155.00
Plaque, Woman, Musical Instrument, Oval, Scepter Mark, Frame, 10 1/2 x 8 3/4 In. 1900.00
Plate, Frederick The Great, 9 1/2 In. 715.00
Punchbowl, Pedestal, 8 Mugs, 6 x 12 1/2 In. 150.00
Salt Cellars, Open, Rococo Revival, Figural, Cherub, 5 1/2 x 5 In., 4 Piece 470.00
Tea & Coffee Service, Blue Tulips, Gilt Stems, Gilt Edge, Mid 19th Century, 27 In. 825.00
Tureen, Soup, Egg Shape, Crabstock Handles, Flowers, Gilt Enamel, Late 1800s, 16 In. 235.00
Urn, Roman Scenes, Damascene Accents, Swan Handles, Gold Pedestal Base, 27 In., Pair 1645.00
Vase, Figural, Stork, Baby In Rushes, Late 19th Century, 9 In. 235.00

KU KLUX KLAN items are now collected because of their historic importance. Literature, robes, and memorabilia are seen at shows and auctions. Laws passed in 1870 and 1871 caused the decline of the Klan. A second group calling itself the Ku Klux Klan emerged in 1915. There are still local groups using the name.

Belt Buckle, Metal, Hooded Klansman, Flag, Burning Cross, 4 x 2 1/2 In. 45.00
Book, Ku Klux Klan In Prophecy, Bishop Alma White, 2nd Edition, 1925, 144 Pages 50.00

Broadside, Klorero, Knight Rider, Fiery Cross, Long Island, N.Y., 1926, 10 In. 25.00
Broadside, Propaganda, Klansman At Helm, Bible In Public School Boat, 7 1/2 In. 35.00
Brochure, N.Y. Klan Observations, Al Smith Kissing Ring Of Cardinal Bonzano, 6 In. 50.00
Business Card, White Supremacist, Race Mixing Is Wrong, Pastor E.S. Hall, 3 1/2 In. 10.00
Coin, Silver, Nickel, Stone Mtn. Ga., Thanksgiving Nig, Fiery Cross, 1915, 1 1/4 In. 80.00
Door Mount, Pewter, Hooded Klansman, Oversize Cross On Chest, 4 In. 45.00
Flyer, Patriotic Lecture, Lighted Cross, Victorville Ca., 1920s, 6 1/2 In. 70.00
Magazine, The Dawn, Paper Lithograph, KKK Ads, Articles, Photos, Sept. 1929, 12 In. 80.00
Mirror, Ku Klux Klan In Prophecy, Procession, Washington D.C., 1960s, 3 1/2 x 2 1/2 In. 50.00
Paperweight, Glass, Klansman, 1 Country, 1 School, 1 Flag, 3 x 3 1/2 In. 114.00
Plate, One School, Klansmen March Into Schoolhouse, 1925, 6 1/4 In. 95.00
Robe, Hood, Cotton, Red Sash, 2nd Degree Knight, Bullion Tassel, c.1930 .... 400.00
Sheet Music, Face Behind The Mask, Wm. L. Thompson, 1934 .... 52.00
Statue, Red Blood Drop Patch On Chest, Porcelain, 21 1/2 In. 394.00

KUTANI porcelain was made in Japan after the mid-seventeenth century. Most of the pieces found today are nineteenth-century. Collectors often use the term *Kutani* to refer to just the later, colorful pieces decorated with red, gold, and black pictures of warriors, animals, and birds.

Bowl, Boys Playing, Scrolling Leaves, Blue Green, 4 1/2 x 9 3/4 In. 354.00
Bowl, Children Playing, 1800s, 12 In. 380.00
Bowl, Flowers, Ruffled Rim, Blue Ground, Late 1800s, 18 In. Diam. 325.00
Bowl, Man, Trees, Blue Green, 7 1/4 In. 470.00
Dish, Lozenge Shape, Landscape, Blue Green, 1800s, 6 3/4 In., Pair 69.00
Jar, Cover, Baluster, Flower Rondels, Borders, Red, Green, Blue, 19th Century, 23 In. 880.00
Plate, Flying Bird Above Heads, Leaves, Flowering Branches, 10 1/2 In., 8 Piece 649.00
Plate & Jug, Birds, Lotus Blossoms, c.1900, 8 1/2 In. 118.00
Sake Bottle, Coiled Dragon, 1800s, 7 1/2 In. 765.00
Vase, 100 Flowers, Nashiji Ground, Metal Flakes, Clear Lacquer, Late 1800s, 9 3/4 In. 750.00
Vase, Baluster, Flowers, Scrolling Tendrils, Red Ground, 1900s, Pair 530.00
Vase, Cover, Stand, Birds, Flowers, Red, 1800s, 27 In. 1880.00
Vase, Figures On Veranda, Brocade, Red, Lamp Mount, 1800s, 17 In., Pair 940.00
Vase, Floral Reserves, Handles, 9 1/2 In. 235.00
Vase, Peony, Butterfly, c.1890 .... 385.00
Vase, Women, Children, Late 1800s, 18 In. 440.00

L.G. WRIGHT Glass Company of New Martinsville, West Virginia, started selling glassware in 1937. Founder "Si" Wright contracted with Ohio and West Virginia glass factories to reproduce popular pressed glass patterns, like Rose & Snow, Baltimore Pear, and Three Face, and opalescent patterns, like Daisy & Fern and Swirl. Collectors can tell the difference between the original glasswares and L.G. Wright reproductions because of colors and differences in production techniques. Some L.G. Wright items are marked with an underlined W in a circle. Items that were made from old Northwood molds have an altered Northwood mark—an angled line was added to the N to make it look like a W. Collectors refer to this mark as "the wobbly W."

Daisy & Button, Hat, 2 1/2 x 3 In. 9.00
Daisy & Button, Pin Box, 2 x 3 3/4 In. 15.00
Daisy & Fern, Barber Bottle, Squat, Melon-Ribbed, Rolled Rim, Canary, Opalescent, 7 In. 115.00
Daisy & Fern, Cruet, Vaseline Opalescent, 7 x 4 In. 250.00
Daisy & Fern, Tumbler, Opalescent, Cranberry, 3 1/2 In. 80.00
Fern, Creamer, Vaseline Opalescent, Tall 65.00
Fern, Lamp, Vaseline Opalescent, 21 In. 700.00
Fern, Rose Bowl, Vaseline Opalescent, Small 65.00
Honeycomb, Creamer, Blue, 5 1/4 x 4 1/2 In. 55.00
Inverted Thumbprint, Pitcher, Blue, c.1950, 8 x 6 1/2 In. 90.00
Maize, Candy Dish, Cover, Amber Overlay, Corn Finial 300.00
Moon & Star, Ashtray, Ruby, 6-Sided, 1 1/8 x 5 1/2 In. 75.00
Moon & Star, Compote, Scalloped Edge, Amberina, 3 1/2 x 4 1/2 In. 20.00

Moon & Star, Console, Blue, c.1970, 4 x 7 1/2 In. 49.00
Moon & Star, Decanter, Stopper, Ruby, 11 3/4 In. 125.00
Moon & Star, Toothpick, Scalloped Rim, Flat Base, 2 1/2 x 2 In. 25.00
Moss Rose, Creamer, Custard Glass, Applied Handle, 5 1/2 In. 125.00
Moss Rose, Cruet, White Satin, 7 1/2 x 3 1/4 In. 135.00
Moss Rose, Pitcher, Milk, Custard Glass, Crimped Rim, 6 1/2 In. 135.00
Paneled Grape, Goblet, Blue Opalescent, 8 Oz., 5 3/4 In. 38.00
Paneled Grape, Plate, Ruby, 9 1/2 In. 40.00
Paneled Grape, Punch Bowl Set, Ruby, 9 1/2 x 15 In., 11 Piece 650.00
Swirl, Cruet, Stopper, Aqua Opalescent, 7 In. 95.00
Wedding Ring, Sherbet, Low, Amber, 4 1/2 In. 17.00
Wild Rose, Compote, Green, c.1950 .... 28.00

LACQUER is a type of varnish. Collectors are most interested in the Chinese and Japanese lacquer wares made from the Japanese varnish tree. Lacquer wares are made from wood with many coats of lacquer. Sometimes the piece is carved or decorated with ivory or metal inlay.

Altar, Black, Kwannon Figure, On Lotus Throne, Japan, 1800s, 10 In. 1035.00
Box, Black, Coastal Scene, Mountains, Japan, 1800s, 6 1/2 x 5 In. 765.00
Box, Black, Gold, 2 Sections, Rectangular, Flower Garden, Japan, 1800s, 6 x 9 1/2 x 7 In. 575.00
Box, Black, Gold, 5 Sections, Temple, Landscape, Japan, 1800s, 17 1/2 In. 2875.00
Box, Black, Mother-Of-Pearl, Prunus, Early 1900s, 2 1/2 x 5 3/4 In. 1495.00
Box, Brown, Mother-Of-Pearl & Wire Inlay, Korea, 1700s, 6 x 4 x 4 In. 325.00
Box, Cover, Gold, Brocade, Bonsai, 3 Compartments, Japan, 1800s, 2 1/2 In. 560.00
Box, Game, Black, Celestial Dragons, Chinese Pavilions, Fitted, 6 x 15 x 13 In. 2350.00
Box, Gold, Brown, Woman On Veranda, Japan, 1800s, 8 1/2 x 9 In. 825.00
Box, Gold, Flowers, Silver, Red, Green, Japan, Early 1900s, 5 x 3 1/2 In. 380.00
Box, Gold, Hiramakie Shrine, Silver Rim, Japan, Early 1800s, 2 1/2 x 5 1/2 x 4 1/4 In. 2990.00
Box, Gold, Inlaid, 2 Sages, Ivory Faces, Playing Karako, Japan, Early 1800s, 5 x 10 x 8 In. 750.00
Box, Letter, Dragon, Cloud, Japan, Late 1800s, 11 In. 69.00
Box, Metal Inlay, Lotus, Butterflies, Japan, 1800s, 5 3/4 x 12 3/4 x 9 In. 1495.00
Box, Peony, Japan, Late 1800s, 6 x 13 x 11 In. 520.00
Box, Sewing, Gold, Black, Ivory Accessories, Chinese, 1800s, 12 x 10 x 5 In. 235.00
Box, Writing, Sunset, Waves, Instruments, Japan, 9 1/4 x 8 3/4 In. 4425.00
Cabinet, Black, Gold, Hinged Doors, 5 Drawers, Japan, Meiji Period, 7 1/2 x 6 3/4 In. 780.00
Card Case, Brown, Gold Lacquer Vine, Flowering Gourds, Grasshopper, 4 1/2 x 2 3/4 In. 410.00
Card Case, Relief, Water Pavilion, Mountains, Japan, 1900s, 4 In. 950.00
Cigar Case, Hand Painted, Woman's Portrait, Papier-Mache, Side Leather, 5 1/2 x 2 3/4 In. 60.00
Curio Shelf, Oriental Style, Black, Mirrored, c.1900, 17 3/4 x 12 In. 380.00
Dumbwaiter, 2 Tiers, 8-Sided, Pagoda, Landscape, Occupied Japan, c.1950, 19 x 17 In. 235.00
Figurine, Buddha, Seated On Lotus Throne, Japan, Edo Period, 7 1/2 In. 330.00
Figurine, Buddha, Seated On Lotus Throne, Japan, Edo Period, 15 In. 2640.00
Jubako, 4 Boxes, Trays, Pheasant, Drawer, Sake Bottles, Japan, 1800s, 10 1/2 x 10 1/4 In. 805.00
Mask, Gold, Japan, Box, Early 1900s 206.00
Mask, On Wood, Okame, Japan, Early 1900s, 8 1/4 In. 150.00
Mask, On Wood, Young Woman, Japan, 1900s, 8 1/4 In. 115.00
Okimono, On Wood, Oni, Seated, Ivory Teeth, Inlaid Eyes, 1800s, 3 In. 635.00
Plaque, Multiple Figures, Black Border, Signed, LR, Russia, 18 x 13 In. 110.00
Sake Cup, Red, Gold, Calligraphy, Chrysanthemum, Japan, 1800s, 3 1/2 In. 45.00
Sake Cup, Red, Gold, Calligraphy, Japan, Late 1800s, 4 1/4 In. 115.00
Sake Cup, Red, Gold, Karako, Watching Cockfight, Japan, 1800s, 4 In. 144.00
Sake Cup, Red, Gold, Man, In Stream, Landscape, Birds, Trees, Japan, 1800s, 5 In. 175.00
Sake Cup, Red, Gold, Tortoise, Castle, Mount Fuji, Japan, 1800s, 4 In. 108.00
Shrine, Black, Gold, Hinged Doors, Latticed, Japan, Late 19th Century, 49 x 21 In. 431.00
Shrine Carving, Gold, Carved Wood, Bowl Shape, Buddha, 17 Deities, Edo Period, 26 In. 2160.00
Smoking Set, Black & Gold, 3 Drawers, Inset Copper Koro, 11 x 8 x 8 In. 316.00
Stand, Flowers, Phoenixes, Carved Wood, Black, Red, Japan, c.1900, 15 1/2 x 12 x 7 In. 88.00
Tray, Painted, Flower Bouquet, Oblong, Scalloped Border, England, 23 1/4 x 31 In. 264.00
Tray, Scenic Landscape, Chinese, 19th Century, 13 x 20 In. 146.00

LADY HEAD VASE, see Head Vase.

LALIQUE glass was made by Rene Lalique in Paris, France, between the 1890s and his death in 1945. The glass was molded, pressed, and engraved in Art Nouveau and Art Deco styles. Pieces were marked with the signature *R. Lalique*. Lalique glass is still being made. Pieces made after 1945 bear the mark *Lalique*. Jewelry made by Rene Lalique is listed in the Jewelry category.

R.LALIQUE

Architectural Panel, Jeune Faune Et Vigne, Faun & Vine, Clear, Frosted, c.1929, 12 In. 1058.00
Ashtray, Alaska, Opalescent, Blue Patina, c.1931, 3 In. 1680.00
Ashtray, Alice, Clear, Gray Patina, Octagonal, c.1924, 4 1/2 In. 705.00
Ashtray, Archers, Clear & Frosted, Gray Patina, Round, c.1922, 4 1/2 In. 823.00
Ashtray, Canard, Duck, Figural, Opalescent, Jade Green, c.1925, 2 3/4 In. 900.00
Ashtray, Dahlia Et Papillon, Dahlia & Butterfly, Clear, Frosted, Blue Patina, c.1931, 6 1/4 In. 2400.00
Ashtray, Feuilles, Leaves, Electric Blue, Oval, c.1924, 6 7/8 In. 626.00
Ashtray, Medicis, Electric Blue, Oval, c.1924, 5 7/8 In. 1043.00
Ashtray, Moineau, Sparrow, Figural, Clear, Frosted, c.1925, 4 1/2 In. 495.00
Ashtray, Pinson, Finch, Figural, Electric Blue, c.1930, 3 1/2 In. 1800.00
Ashtray, Serpent, Blue, Round, c.1920, 5 7/8 In. 1680.00
Ashtray, Sirenes, Mermaids, Opalescent, Aqua Patina, Round, c.1920, 2 x 4 1/2 In. 2115.00
Ashtray, Sumatra, Frosted, Green Patina, Round, c.1929, 5 1/2 In. 600.00
Ashtray, Vezelay, Grape Leaves, Amber, Square, c.1924, 4 1/2 In. 881.00
Blotter, Deux Sirenes Couchees, Mermaids Facing, Clear, Frosted, Gray Patina, c.1920, 6 1/2 In. .. 1880.00
Bowl, Anvers, Fish & Seaweed, Frosted Blue, c.1930, 15 1/2 In. 6600.00
Bowl, Calypso, Swirling Sirens, Clear, Opalescent, c.1930, 2 3/8 x 14 1/4 In. 5040.00
Bowl, Chantilly, Clear, Frosted, Sepia Patina, Octagonal, c.1942, 11 1/4 In. 360.00
Bowl, Chene, Oak Leaves, Clear, Frosted, Oval, c.1975, 24 1/2 In. 470.00
Bowl, Chiens No. 1, Greyhounds, Clear, Frosted, Gray Patina, c.1921, 9 1/4 In. 840.00
Bowl, Gui No. 1, Mistletoe, Opalescent Mint Green, c.1921, 9 1/4 In. 3000.00
Bowl, Madagascar, Monkey Heads, Clear, Frosted, Sepia Patina, c.1928, 13 In. 9400.00
Bowl, Muguet, Lily Of The Valley, Opalescent, Flared Rim, c.1931, 12 5/8 In. 4700.00
Bowl, Nemours, Flower Heads, Clear, Frosted, Sepia Patina, Brown Enamel, c.1929, 10 In. 840.00
Bowl, Nemours, Flower Heads, Enameled Black Centers, Clear, Frosted, Post 1945, 10 In. 452.00
Bowl, Nonnettes, Birds, Opalescent, c.1928, 8 5/8 In. ....1058.00 to 1320.00
Bowl, Ondines, Water Nymphs, Opalescent, Flared Rim, c.1921, 8 1/4 In. 1920.00
Bowl, Perruches, Parakeets, Frosted Opalescent, c.1931, 9 3/4 In. ....3840.00 to 4922.00
Bowl, Pinsons, Finches, Serrated Leaves, Amber, c.1933, 9 In. 2160.00
Bowl, Pinsons, Finches, Serrated Leaves, Clear, Frosted, Post 1945, 9 1/4 In. 330.00
Bowl, Poissons, Fish, Opalescent, c.1931, 11 1/2 In. 900.00
Bowl, Rosace, Radiating Triangles, Blue, c.1930, 11 3/4 In. 2400.00
Bowl, Rosace, Radiating Triangles, Opalescent, c.1930, 11 3/4 In. 540.00
Bowl, Roscoff, Fish, Bubbles, Clear, Frosted, c.1932, 13 3/4 In. 600.00
Bowl, Sirene, Mermaid, Opalescent, 3-Footed, c.1920, 14 1/4 In. 7200.00
Bowl, Volubilis, 3 Morning Glories, Opalescent, Yellow, c.1921, 8 1/2 In. ....720.00 to 881.00
Box, Cover, Amour Assis, Seated Cupid, Clear, Frosted, Blue Patina, c.1919, 5 1/2 In. 4113.00
Box, Cover, Chantilly, Does, Clear, Frosted, Sepia Patina, c.1924, 3 1/2 In. 1175.00
Box, Cover, Cheveux De Venus, Nigella Flower, Clear, Sepia Patina, c.1910, 2 3/4 In. 2160.00
Box, Cover, Cigales, Cicadas, Opalescent, c.1921, 10 In. 840.00
Box, Cover, Cigarette, Abduhla, Clear, c.1934, 10 1/4 In. 881.00
Box, Cover, Cigarette, Hirondelles, Swallows, Clear, Frosted, Blue Patina, c.1923, 4 In. 1528.00
Box, Cover, Coquilles, Shells, Opalescent, Gray Patina, c.1920, 2 3/4 In. 780.00
Box, Cover, Cyprins, Carp, Opalescent, c.1921, 10 In. 2400.00
Box, Cover, D'Orsay, Deux Sirenes, 2 Mermaids, Opalescent, Carved Base, 3 1/4 In. 1920.00
Box, Cover, D'Orsay, Le Lys, Clear, Frosted, Sepia Patina, c.1922, 4 In. 450.00
Box, Cover, Deux Figurines, 2 Nudes, Clear, Gray Patina, c.1919, 2 3/4 In. 1763.00
Box, Cover, Deux Pigeons, 2 Pigeons, Clear, Frosted, Sepia Patina, c.1919, 2 3/4 In. 1140.00
Box, Cover, Deux Sirenes, 2 Sirens, Yellow Glass, c.1921, 10 1/8 In. 3840.00
Box, Cover, Enfants, Babies Circle Base, Clear, Frosted, Sepia Patina, c.1931, 3 3/4 In. 1175.00
Box, Cover, Fontainebleau, Rabbits & Birds, Clear, Frosted, Blue Patina, c.1924, 3 1/4 In. 720.00
Box, Cover, Hirondelles, Swallows, Gray Patina, Signed, R. Lalique, 3 1/8 x 4 In. 1080.00
Box, Cover, Libellules, Dragonflies, Amber, 6 1/2 In. 1763.00
Box, Cover, Monnaie Du Pape, Honesty Leaves, Glass, Wood, Foil, Key, 1920, 12 1/4 In. 6933.00

Box, Cover, Panier De Roses, Basket Of Roses, Clear, Frosted, Blue Patina, c.1919, 3 1/4 In. 2160.00
Box, Cover, Pommier Du Japon, Arys, Flowering Branches, Black, Gray Patina, c.1919, 3 1/4 In. ... 1410.00
Box, Cover, Quatre Papillons, 4 Butterflies, Clear, Frosted, Blue Patina, c.1911, 3 In. 1320.00
Box, Cover, Quatre Papillons, 4 Butterflies, Opalescent, Round, 1911, 3 1/8 In. 2468.00
Box, Cover, Quatre Scarabees, 4 Scarabs, Electric Blue, c.1911, 3 1/4 In. 2640.00
Box, Cover, Rambouillet, Herons, Clear, Frosted, Gray Patina, c.1924, 3 1/4 In. 720.00
Box, Cover, Roger Et Gallet, Cigalia, Clear, Frosted, Green Patina, 3 In. 1200.00
Box, Cover, Roses En Relief, Garlands Of Roses, Clear, Frosted, Sepia Patina, c.1913, 6 3/4 In. 10200.00
Box, Cover, Sultane, Clear, Frosted, Geometric Designs, Nude Figure Finial, 5 1/2 In. 1414.00
Box, Cover, Tokio, Chrysanthemum, Yellow Amber, c.1921, 6 5/8 In. 1440.00
Box, Cover, Victoire, Winged Victory, Clear, Frosted, Gray Patina, c.1919, 2 3/4 In. 3900.00
Box, Cover, Worth Dans La Nuit, Clear, Blue Enamel, c.1926, 4 3/4 In. 2585.00
Candlestick, Saint-Gall, Overall Bubbles, Clear, c.1934, 5 1/4 In., Pair 780.00
Carafe, Sirenes Et Grenouilles, Mermaids & Frogs, Clear, Gray Patina, c.1911, 15 1/2 In. 10560.00
Carafe, Six Figurines, Clear, Frosted, Sepia Patina, c.1914, 14 In. 4113.00
Carafe, Stopper, Six Tetes, 6 Heads, Clear, Frosted, Gray Patina, c.1914, 14 In. 12000.00
Ceiling Light, Coquilles, Shells, Opalescent, Metal Fittings, Silk Cord, c.1921, 11 3/4 In. 1880.00
Ceiling Light, Dahlias, Clear, Frosted, Domed Shade, Flowers, c.1930, 12 In. 2639.00
Centerpiece, Charme, Square, 1933, 9 1/4 In. 800.00
Champagne, Rapace, Clear, Violet Blue Bird Stem, c.1929, 4 1/2 In. 1293.00
Clock, Cinq Hirondelles, 5 Swallows, Clear, Frosted, Blue Enamel, Windup, c.1920, 5 7/8 In. 4800.00
Clock, Deux Figurines, Classical Maidens, Wreath, Original Movement, Light-Up, c.1926, 15 In. .. 22800.00
Clock, Moineaux, Sparrows, Clear, Frosted, Sepia Patina, Art Deco Metal Face, c.1924, 8 1/2 In. .. 6000.00
Clock, Naiades, Water Nymphs, Goldtone Dial, Greek Key, c.1924, 4 1/2 In. 2585.00
Clock, Pierrots, Birds, Clear, Blue Patina, c.1931, 5 In. 1920.00
Clock, Sirenes, Mermaids, Frosted, c.1928, 10 1/4 In. 14400.00
Clock, Six Hirondelles Perchees, 6 Perching Swallows, Clear, Frosted, Windup, c.1920, 5 5/8 In. .. 3000.00
Cocktail Shaker, Thomery, Grapevines, Clear, Frosted, Sepia Patina, c.1928, 9 In. 6600.00
Crucifix, Christ, Clear, Frosted, Wood Base, c.1935, 7 1/8 In. 960.00
Door Handle, Fauns, Vine, Molded, Double, 16 3/4 x 10 1/4 In. 10866.00
Drinking Service, Jaffa, Arched Vertical Bands, Art Deco, Amber, c.1931, 9 1/8 In., 6 Piece 1998.00
Figurine, Avec Guirlande De Fruits, Nude, Garland, Clear, Frosted, Sepia, c.1912, 8 1/4 In. 9000.00
Figurine, Coq De Jongle, Rooster, Clear, Frosted, c.1936, 17 In. 3525.00
Figurine, Floreal, Kneeling Nude, Flowers, Clear, Frosted, Black Glass Foot, c.1950, 3 1/2 In. 180.00
Figurine, Moyenne Voilee, Veiled Woman, Clear, Frosted, Gray Patina, c.1912, 5 1/2 In. 2585.00
Figurine, Naiade, Water Nymph, Clear, Sepia Patina, c.1920, 5 1/4 In. 2400.00
Figurine, Panthere, Panther, Clear, Frosted, c.1990, 14 1/2 In. 780.00
Figurine, Sanglier, Warthog, Smoky Quartz, Carved, Round Base, Signed, 2 1/2 x 3 1/2 In. 450.00
Figurine, Suzanne, Opalescent, 1925, 10 3/4 In. 20786.00
Figurine, Vierge A L'Enfant, Virgin & Child, Clear, Frosted, c.1934, 15 3/4 In. 1920.00
Figurine, Voilee Mains Jointes, Veiled Woman, Opalescent, c.1919, 11 In. 11400.00
Finger Bowl, Underplate, Lotus, Clear, Brown Enamel, c.1923, 7 1/8 In., Pair 382.00
Frame, Quatre Perruches, 4 Parakeets, Clear, Frosted, c.1926, 4 x 4 In. 1320.00
Glass, Bague Lezards, Ring Of Lizards, Clear, Frosted, Sepia Patina, c.1912, 5 1/4 In. 1410.00
Goblet, Hesperides, Swirling Leaves, Clear, Frosted, c.1931, 5 In., Pair 540.00
Goblet, Normandie, Art Deco Foot, CGT Monogram, c.1934, 3 1/8 In., Pair 1320.00
Goblet, Quatre Grenouilles, 4 Frogs, Clear, Frosted, Green Patina, c.1912, 5 1/2 In. 2640.00
Goblet, Wine, Rapace, Clear, Violet Glass Bird Stem, Base, c.1929, 4 5/8 In. 1320.00
Goblet, Wine, Vigne, Grapevine, Clear, Frosted, Sepia Patina, c.1912, 7 In. 4500.00
Hand Mirror, Deux Chevres, 2 Goats, Clear, Frosted, Blue Patina, c.1919, 6 1/4 In. 2160.00
Hood Ornament, Archer, Clear, Frosted, c.1926, 7 3/4 In. 2400.00
Hood Ornament, Chrysis, Kneeling Female Nude, Clear, Frosted, Gray Patina, c.1931, 5 3/8 In. ... 3900.00
Hood Ornament, Coq Nain, Dwarf Cockerel, Smoked Glass, 1928, 8 In. 3300.00
Hood Ornament, Faucon, Falcon, Chrome Collar, c.1925, 7 1/4 In. 5414.00
Hood Ornament, Faucon, Falcon, Clear, c.1925, 6 In. 2640.00
Hood Ornament, Grande Libellule, Large Dragonfly, c.1928, 8 1/4 In. 8813.00
Hood Ornament, Grenouille, Frog, Partially Frosted, Chrome Base, c.1928, 5 In. 15244.00
Hood Ornament, Hirondelle, Swallow, Clear, Frosted, Amethyst Tint, c.1928, 5 7/8 In. 2880.00
Hood Ornament, Levrier, Greyhound, Clear, Frosted, c.1928, 7 3/4 In. 9600.00
Hood Ornament, Longchamp B, Race Horse, c.1929, 6 3/8 In. 11166.00
Hood Ornament, Naiade, Water Nymph, Opalescent, c.1920, 5 1/4 In. 11166.00

Hood Ornament, Perche, Freshwater Perch, Yellow, c.1929, 6 1/4 In. 6552.00
Hood Ornament, Pintade, Guinea Fowl, Clear, Frosted, On Base, c.1929, 6 In. 7200.00
Hood Ornament, Sanglier, Wild Boar, Topaz, c.1929, 3 1/2 In. 1800.00
Hood Ornament, Sirene, Little Mermaid, Opalescent, c.1920, 4 1/8 In. 4113.00
Hood Ornament, Tete D'Aigle, Eagle Head, c.1928, 4 1/2 In. 3697.00
Hood Ornament, Tete D'Epervier, Sparrow Hawk Head, Clear, Frosted, c.1928, 2 1/2 In. 2640.00
Hood Ornament, Tete D'Epervier, Sparrow Hawk Head, Opalescent, c.1928, 2 3/8 In. 5414.00
Hood Ornament, Tete De Belier, Ram's Head, Frosted, Polished, c.1928, 4 1/2 In. .....8225.00 to 9227.00
Hood Ornament, Tete De Coq, Rooster Head, Clear, Frosted, Bookend Base, c.1928, 8 In. 1560.00
Hood Ornament, Tete De Paon, Peacock Head, c.1928, 8 1/4 In. 10151.00
Hood Ornament, Victoire, Spirit Of Wind, Chrome Collar, c.1928, 10 1/4 In. 25151.00
Hood Ornament, Vitesse, Kneeling Nude Female, Frosted, c.1929, 7 1/4 In. 16800.00
Ice Bucket, Reimes, Clear, Frosted, c.1938, 7 1/4 In. 1320.00
Inkwell, Biches, Does, Clear, Frosted, Sepia Patina, c.1912, 4 1/2 In. 1740.00
Inkwell, Quatre Sirenes, 4 Mermaids, Opalescent, Blue Patina, c.1920, 6 1/4 In. 4113.00
Inkwell, Trois Papillons, 3 Butterflies, Clear, Frosted, Sepia Patina, c.1912, 3 1/2 In. 2760.00
Jardiniere, Oeillets, Carnations, Clear, Frosted, Sepia Patina, Oval, c.1936, 14 3/4 In. 1800.00
Jardiniere, Papillons, Butterfly Handles, Clear, Frosted, Blue Enamel, Square, c.1935, 10 7/8 In. . . 6600.00
Lamp, Cariatides, Glass, Molded, Frosted, c.1920, 12 1/2 In. 14400.00
Menu Holder, Faune, Faun Head, Clear, Frosted, Sepia Patina, c.1928, 5 1/2 In. ....1200.00 to 1293.00
Paperweight, Barbillon, Fish, Clear, Frosted, Green Patina, 3 x 3 1/2 In. 1645.00
Paperweight, Bison, Clear, Frosted, c.1931, 4 x 4 1/4 In. 999.00
Perfume Bottle, Amelie, Overlapping Leaves Or Feathers, Signed, 3 In. 805.00
Perfume Bottle, Amphytrite, Glass, Molded Shell, Woman On Stopper, 3 In. 1380.00
Perfume Bottle, Arys, Faisons Un Reve, Clear, 8 Panels Divided By Beaded Line, 5 In. 690.00
Perfume Bottle, Camille, Clear, Frosted, Blue Patina, c.1927, 2 1/2 In. 720.00
Perfume Bottle, Coty, Cyclamen, Clear, Frosted, c.1920, 6 In. 823.00
Perfume Bottle, D'Orsay, Ambre D'Orsay, Black, Women In Gowns, Flowers, Signed, 5 In. 1495.00
Perfume Bottle, D'Orsay, L'Elegance, Clear, Frosted, Sepia, 2 Women In Gowns, 3 In. 375.00
Perfume Bottle, D'Orsay, Le Lys, Clear, Sepia Patina, c.1922, 4 In. ....480.00 to 720.00
Perfume Bottle, D'Orsay, Mystere D'Orsay, Black Glass, Silk Lined Leather Box, c.1912, 3 3/4 In. . . 1200.00
Perfume Bottle, Dahlia, Clear, Frosted, Black Enamel, c.1931, 3 1/2 In. 330.00
Perfume Bottle, Deux Fleurs, Clear, Stopper, Shaped Like 2 Flowers, 3 1/2 In. 185.00
Perfume Bottle, Duncan, Flacon No. 4, Clear, Frosted, Sepia Patina, c.1947, 7 1/2 In. 1410.00
Perfume Bottle, Gabilla, La Violette, Clear, Frosted, Violet Enamel, c.1925, 3 1/4 In. 4406.00
Perfume Bottle, Lengyal, Imperial, Clear, Frosted, Label, c.1936, 2 5/8 In. 480.00
Perfume Bottle, Lentille, Clear, Frosted, Gray Patina, c.1912, 3 In. 1410.00
Perfume Bottle, Marquita, Clear, Frosted, Blue Patina, c.1927, 3 1/4 In. 1440.00
Perfume Bottle, Nina Ricci, Coeur Joie, Clear, Frosted, Heart, Leaves, Flowers, 5 3/4 In. 690.00
Perfume Bottle, Nina Ricci, L'Air Du Temps, Double Doves, Display, 12 1/4 In. 900.00
Perfume Bottle, Nina Ricci, L'Air Du Temps, Doves, 4 x 3 1/2 In. 75.00
Perfume Bottle, Olives, Clear, Frosted, Sepia Patina, c.1912, 4 1/4 In. 1020.00
Perfume Bottle, Perles, Clear, Flacon No. 2, c.1926, 6 3/4 In. 570.00
Perfume Bottle, Rosace Figurines, Frosted Glass Stopper, c.1932, 5 In. 1560.00
Perfume Bottle, Telline, Semiopaque, Stopper, Shell Shape, Blue Stain, c.1932, 4 In. 1265.00
Perfume Bottle, Veolay, Niobe Violet, Clear, Frosted, c.1928, 4 1/4 In. 480.00
Perfume Bottle, Worth, Dans La Nuit, Cobalt Blue, Sealed, Box, c.1925, 4 In. 240.00
Perfume Bottle, Worth, Imprudence, Clear, c.1938, 3 In. 360.00
Perfume Bottle, Worth, Rose, Clear, Molded Flowers, c.1937, 5 1/4 In. 420.00
Perfume Bottle, Worth, Sans Adieu, Green, c.1929, 5 3/4 In. 720.00
Perfume Bottle, Worth, Vers Le Jour, Shaded Amber, c.1926, 4 1/4 In. 1293.00
Perfume Burner, Carrousel, Birds In Circle, Clear, Frosted, Sepia Patina, c.1930, 5 1/4 In. 8400.00
Perfume Burner, Papillons, Butterflies, Amber, White Patina, c.1920, 7 1/2 In. 6600.00
Perfume Burner, Papillons, Butterflies, Opalescent, Blue Green Patina, c.1920, 7 1/2 In. 4200.00
Perfume Burner, Sirenes, Mermaids, Clear, Frosted, Blue Patina, c.1920, 6 3/4 In. 5100.00
Perfume Burner, Sirenes, Mermaids, Opalescent, c.1920, 6 3/4 In. 5700.00
Pin, Barrette Aubepines, Clear, Amethyst Foil, Gilt Metal Back, c.1912, 2 3/8 In. 1080.00
Plaque, Exhibition, Clear, Frosted, Musee Des Arts Decoratifs, c.1931, 3 7/8 x 5 3/8 In. 1880.00
Plaque, Hirondelles, Swallows, Clear, Frosted Glass, Bronze Base, c.1922, 13 5/8 x 10 1/2 In. . . . 9600.00
Plate, Coquilles, 4 Scallop Shells, Opalescent, c.1924, 11 3/4 In. 720.00
Plate, Marienthal, Opalescent, c.1931, 7 In. 360.00

Plate, Ondines, Water Nymphs, Opalescent, c.1921, 10 3/4 In. 1680.00
Powder Box, Petalia, Tokalon, Printed Paper, Sealed, Contents, c.1925, 3 1/4 In. 210.00
Powder Jar, Semis De Fleurs, D'Heraud, Clear, Glass, Metal Cover, c.1926, 4 1/2 In. 360.00
Seal, Anneau Lezards, Lizard Ring, Clear, Frosted, Gray Patina, c.1912, 1 3/4 In. 3240.00
Seal, Bleuets, Cornflowers, Clear, Frosted, Gray Patina, c.1912, 1 3/4 In. 2640.00
Seal, Canard, Duck, Clear, Frosted, Sepia Patina, c.1925, 2 1/2 In. 1116.00
Seal, Dindon, Turkey, Topaz, c.1925, 2 1/8 In. 960.00
Seal, Double Fleur, Double Flower, Clear, Frosted, Sepia Patina, c.1919, 1 1/2 In. 823.00
Seal, Ecureuil, Squirrel, Opalescent, c.1931, 4 1/4 In. 1293.00
Seal, Hirondelles, Swallows, Clear, Frosted, Fitted Box, c.1919, 2 In. 1440.00
Seal, Pinson, Finch, Clear, Frosted, Green Patina, c.1930, 1 3/4 In. 3120.00
Seal, Renard, Fox, Topaz, c.1913, 1 3/4 In. 646.00
Seal, Soucis, Marigolds, Clear, Frosted, Sepia Patina, c.1931, 3 1/4 In. 2115.00
Seal, Statuette Drapee, Draped Nude, Opalescent, c.1912, 2 1/2 In. ....2640.00 to 4113.00
Seal, Tete D'aigle, Eagle Head, Clear, Gray Patina, c.1911, 3 1/8 In. 1200.00
Seal, Vase De Fleurs, Vase Of Flowers, Clear, Frosted, Gray Patina, c.1919, 2 3/8 In. 3525.00
Sign, Lalique Cristallerie France, c.1950, 5 In. 390.00
Vase, Ajaccio, Sleeping Gazelles, Starlit Sky, Blue Patina, Flared, R. Lalique, 8 In. ......2300.00 to 2588.00
Vase, Aras, Birds, Fruit, Leaves, Wintergreen, c.1930, 9 1/2 In. 18852.00
Vase, Archers, Nude Male Archers, Swooping Birds, Topaz, c.1921, 10 1/2 In. 6600.00
Vase, Avallon, Birds & Grapes, Branches, Fruit, Blue Patina, Signed, R. Lalique, 5 1/2 In. 2070.00
Vase, Bacchantes, Frieze Of Female Nudes, Flaring, Molded, Frosted, 9 1/2 In. ....1548.00 to 3105.00
Vase, Bacchantes, Frieze Of Female Nudes, Frosted, Gray, c.1930, 9 1/2 In. 18852.00
Vase, Bacchantes, Frieze Of Female Nudes, Textured, Amber Patina, Signed, R. Lalique, 9 1/2 In. ... 8338.00
Vase, Bacchantes, Frieze Of Female Nudes, Topaz, Wheel Cut, c.1927, 9 1/2 In. 3819.00
Vase, Bagatelle, 12 Molded Birds, Leaves, Clear, Frosted, c.1919, 6 3/4 In. 1250.00
Vase, Beaulieu, Band Of Intaglio Leaves, Vines, Turquoise Patina, 6 In. 1150.00
Vase, Beliers, Ram Handles, Opalescent, Wheel Cut, c.1925, 7 1/2 In. 3290.00
Vase, Beliers, Ram Handles, Topaz, c.1925., 7 1/8 In. 1800.00
Vase, Bellis, Ribbed Leaves, Opalescent, c.1926, 5 3/4 In. 1763.00
Vase, Biskra, 8 Long, Narrow Leaves, Honey Amber, c.1932, 11 1/4 In. 10800.00
Vase, Biskra, 8 Long, Narrow Leaves, Melon Form, Clear, Frosted Green, c.1932, 11 1/4 In. 4200.00
Vase, Borneo, Birds & Leaves, Clear, Frosted, Blue Enamel, c.1930, 9 1/4 In. 2820.00
Vase, Bresse, Swirling Feathers, Cased Jade Green, c.1931, 4 1/8 In. 3525.00
Vase, Camaret, 4 Bands Of Fish, Clear, Frosted, c.1928, 5 1/2 In. 1140.00
Vase, Camaret, 4 Bands Of Fish, Topaz, c.1928, 5 1/2 In. 1920.00
Vase, Camargue, 4 Cartouches, Horses Rearing, Clear, Frosted, Sepia Patina, c.1942, 11 1/4 In. .. 6600.00
Vase, Ceylan, 4 Pairs Of Parakeets, Perched On Branches, Opalescent, c.1924, 10 1/2 In. 6702.00
Vase, Ceylan, 4 Pairs Of Parakeets, Perched On Branches, Yellow Amber, c.1924, 9 1/4 In. 8400.00
Vase, Chamois, Stylized Antelopes, 2 Tiers Overlap, Amber, White Patina, c.1931, 4 3/4 In. 3900.00
Vase, Chamonix, Vertical Bands, Opalescent, c.1933, 6 In. 1020.00
Vase, Coqs Et Plumes, 12 Strutting Cock Roosters, Clear, Frosted, Sepia Patina, c.1928, 5 7/8 In. ... 1440.00
Vase, Dahlias, Overlapping Flower Heads, Clear, Frosted, Green Patina, Black, c.1923, 7 In. 2520.00
Vase, Danaides, Female Nudes, Pour Water From Urn, Blue Patina, R. Lalique, 7 1/4 In. .4140.00 to 5463.00
Vase, Dauphins, Fish In Waves, Clear, Frosted, Blue Patina, c.1932, 5 1/2 In. 1680.00
Vase, Domremy, Thistles, Cased Opalescent, c.1926, 8 3/8 In. 1293.00
Vase, Druide, Overlapping Mistletoe Branches, Opalescent, c.1924, 7 1/8 In. 420.00
Vase, Ecailles, Overlapping Scales, Red Amber, c.1932, 9 3/4 In. 5875.00
Vase, Escargot, Snail Shell Form, Clear, Frosted, c.1920, 8 1/8 In. 2640.00
Vase, Espalion, Allover Ferns, Opalescent, c.1927, 7 In. 940.00
Vase, Eucalyptus, Leaves, Overlap, Bud Feet, Opalescent, Blue Green Patina, c.1925, 6 3/8 In. 2760.00
Vase, Feuilles, 3 Rows Of Vertical Leaves, Clear, Frosted, Sepia Patina, c.1934, 7 1/8 In. 1680.00
Vase, Formose, Swirling Carp, Opalescent, c.1924, 6 5/8 In. ....2400.00 to 2585.00
Vase, Formose, Swirling Carp, Red, c.1924, 6 1/2 In. 7200.00
Vase, Fougeres, 4 Rows Of Molded Leaves, Clear, Frosted, Gray Patina, c.1912, 6 1/4 In. 1058.00
Vase, Grape Bath, Muscat, Stylized Grapevines, Opalescent, c.1938, 6 1/4 In. ....1080.00 to 1200.00
Vase, Gui, Mistletoe & Berries, Opalescent, Pea Green Patina, c.1920, 6 3/4 In. 1998.00
Vase, Guirlande De Roses, Rose Garlands, Oval, Clear, Frosted, Blue Patina, c.1914, 5 1/8 In. 960.00
Vase, Hirondelles, Swooping Swallows, Clear, Frosted, Blue Patina, c.1919, 9 In. 19975.00
Vase, Honfleur, Flowing Leaf, Handles, Brown Patina, Signed, R. Lalique, 5 1/2 In. 1553.00
Vase, Laiterons, Overall Arched Serrated Leaves, Amber, White Patina, c.1931, 3 1/8 In. 3120.00

Vase, Le Mans, Overall Roosters, Cased Opalescent Turquoise, c.1931, 4 1/8 In. 3480.00
Vase, Lievres, Band Of Rabbits, Spiraling Vine, Opalescent, Bluish Patina, c.1923, 6 1/2 In. 1175.00
Vase, Lutteurs, Wrestlers, Opalescent, Gray Patina, c.1914, 5 3/8 In. 4700.00
Vase, Malines, Pointed Leaves, Opalescent, Blue Green Patina, c.1924, 5 In. 823.00
Vase, Marguerites, Daisies, Pressed, Translucent, Gold Washed, Pre 1947, 8 1/4 In. 1880.00
Vase, Meandres, Wavy Bands, Clear, Frosted, c.1934, 6 1/2 In. 881.00
Vase, Meduse, Spiraling Tentacles, Clear, Frosted, c.1921, 6 1/4 In. 1175.00
Vase, Moissac, Overlapping Raised Leaves, Topaz, c.1927, 5 1/8 In. 960.00
Vase, Monnaie Du Pape, Money Plant, Coin-Shaped Flowers, Plum, c.1914, 7 1/8 In. 9400.00
Vase, Montargis, Spiraling Ferns, Black, Amethyst, Frosted, 1930s, 7 3/4 In. 5656.00
Vase, Montmorency, 4 Bands Of Cherries, Raised, Opalescent, c.1930, 7 7/8 In. 8225.00
Vase, Nefliers, Flowers, Leaves, Vase, Clear, Frosted, Gray Patina, c.1923, 5 1/2 In. 940.00
Vase, Oleron, Little Fish, Opalescent, Silver Metal Collar, c.1927, 3 1/2 In. ....780.00 to 822.00
Vase, Ormeaux, Overlapping Elm Leaves, Amber, c.1926, 5/8 In. 3525.00
Vase, Ormeaux, Overlapping Elm Leaves, Cased Jade Green, c.1926, 6 1/2 In. ....2747.00 to 3600.00
Vase, Ormeaux, Overlapping Elm Leaves, Cased Opalescent, Blue Patina, c.1926, 6 1/2 In. 1440.00
Vase, Ormeaux, Overlapping Elm Leaves, White, Signed, R. Lalique, c.1926, 6 1/2 In. 978.00
Vase, Ornis, Bird Handles, Chalice Form, Opalescent, c.1926, 7 1/8 In. 4500.00
Vase, Oursin, Sea Urchin, Clear, Frosted, Blue Patina, c.1935, 7 In. 1320.00
Vase, Palmes, Overlapping Palm Leaves, Green, White Patina, c.1923, 4 1/2 In. 2640.00
Vase, Pan, Pan Pipes, Portrait, Clear, Frosted, c.1937, 12 1/2 In. 5875.00
Vase, Paquerettes, Daisies, Opalescent, Blue Green Patina, c.1934, 7 In. 2468.00
Vase, Pensees, Overlapping Pansies, Clear, Frosted, Sepia Patina, Blue Enamel, c.1920, 5 In. 5400.00
Vase, Penthievre, Stylized Fish, Angular Bands, Clear, Frosted, Blue Patina, c.1928, 10 1/2 In. ... 4113.00
Vase, Perles, Garlands Of Pearls, Opalescent, c.1925, 5 In. 1645.00
Vase, Perruches, Pairs Of Parakeets On Branches, Clear, Sepia Patina, c.1919, 10 1/8 In. 5040.00
Vase, Perruches, Pairs Of Parakeets On Branches, Electric Blue, c.1919, 10 In. 19975.00
Vase, Plumes, Ostrich Feathers, Reddish Brown, Signed, R. Lalique, c.1920, 8 In. 2160.00
Vase, Raisins, Grapes & Vines, Amber Patina, 6 1/4 In. 920.00
Vase, Raisins, Grapes & Vines, Opalescent, Blue Patina, c.1928, 6 1/8 In. 1320.00
Vase, Rampillon, Cabachons & Flowers, Gray, c.1927, 5 In. 1200.00
Vase, Rampillon, Cabachons & Flowers, Topaz, c.1927, 5 In. 2640.00
Vase, Renoncules, Buttercups On Base, Flared Top, Opalescent c.1930, 5 3/4 x 6 1/2 In. 1500.00
Vase, Ronsard, Female Figures Within Rose Wreath Handles, c.1926, 8 1/4 In. 3910.00
Vase, Royat, Vertical Molded Ridges, Tapered Form, Clear, Frosted, Post 1945, 6 1/4 In. 377.00
Vase, Saint-Francois, Finches On Branches, Clear, Frosted, c.1930, 6 5/8 In. 1200.00
Vase, Sauge, Sage Leaves, Cased Yellow, Sepia Patina, c.1923, 10 In. 2350.00
Vase, Senart, Squirrels On Branches, Trumpet Shape, Ruby, c.1940, 8 In. 16100.00
Vase, Soleils, Sunbursts, Clear, Frosted, c.1936, 9 In. 2233.00
Vase, Soudan, 3 Bands Of Running Gazelles, Signed, R. Lalique, c.1928, 7 In. 2070.00
Vase, Sylvie, 2 Birds, Clear, Frosted, Flower Frog, 1970s, 8 1/4 In. 360.00
Vase, Thibet, Ibex Handles, Cylindrical Form, Frosted, c.1931, 8 1/8 In. 4800.00
Vase, Tournesols, Sunflowers, Raised Centers, Opalescent, Blue Green Patina, c.1927, 4 3/4 In. .. 960.00
Vase, Tournesols, Sunflowers, Raised Centers, Opalescent, Green Patina, c.1927, 4 1/2 In. 1800.00
Vase, Tourterelles, Turtle Doves, Figural Cover, c.1925, 11 1/8 In. 7626.00
Vase, Tristan, Flared Leaf Handles, Clear, Frosted, Green, c.1928, 8 1/8 In. 4113.00
Wine Cooler, Clos Sainte-Odile, Portrait & Grapevines, Letters, Clear, Frosted, Sepia, c.1922, 9 In. 3240.00
Wine Cooler, Ganymede, Entwined Nudes, Clear, Frosted, c.1945, 9 In. 2040.00
Wine Cooler, Ganymede, Entwined Nudes, Clear, Frosted, c.1990, 9 In. 1020.00

LAMPS of every type, from the early oil-burning Betty and Phoebe lamps to the recent electric lamps with glass or beaded shades, interest collectors. Fuels used in lamps changed through the years; whale oil (1800–40), camphene (1828), Argand (1830), lard (1833–63), turpentine and alcohol (1840s), gas (1850–79), kerosene (1860), and electricity (1879) are the most common. Other lamps are listed by manufacturer or type of material.

Advertising, Pabst Blue Ribbon, Boxer, Ring, Bottle, 1950s-60s 495.00
Advertising, Schlitz, Light-Up, Blue Globe, 1958, 22 In. 60.00
Aladdin, A-1243, Venetian Vase, Green 310.00
Aladdin, A-1246, Venetian Vase, Orange 525.00

Aladdin, B-25, Victoria, Decorated China 380.00
Aladdin, B-26, Simplicity, Alacite, Decalmania 395.00
Aladdin, B-30, Simplicity, White, Flying Ducks Shade 130.00
Aladdin, B-47, Washington Drape, Bell Stem, Clear 115.00
Aladdin, B-53, Washington Drape, Clear 65.00
Aladdin, B-54E, Washington Drape, Emerald Green 490.00
Aladdin, B-62, Short Lincoln Drape, Ruby 700.00
Aladdin, B-70, Solitaire, White Moonstone 1700.00
Aladdin, B-75, Tall Lincoln Drape, Alacite ....75.00 to 105.00
Aladdin, B-75, Tall Lincoln Drape, Alacite, Scalloped Foot 375.00
Aladdin, B-76, Tall Lincoln Drape, Cobalt Blue 950.00
Aladdin, B-76, Tall Lincoln Drape, Cobalt Blue, Plain Foot 865.00
Aladdin, B-76, Tall Lincoln Drape, Cobalt Blue, Scalloped Foot ....950.00 to 1350.00
Aladdin, B-77, Tall Lincoln Drape, Ruby, Burner ....500.00 to 610.00
Aladdin, B-83, Beehive, Ruby, Burner 675.00
Aladdin, B-87, Vertique, Rose Moonstone 345.00
Aladdin, B-87, Vertique, Rose Moonstone, Burner 380.00
Aladdin, B-91, Quilt, White Moonstone, Pink Moonstone Foot 315.00
Aladdin, B-92, Vertique, Green Moonstone 340.00
Aladdin, B-101, Corinthian, Amber 55.00
Aladdin, B-102, Corinthian, Green 75.00
Aladdin, B-104, Colonial, Clear ....75.00 to 105.00
Aladdin, B-108, Cathedral, Green 75.00
Aladdin, B-111, Cathedral, Green Moonstone 230.00
Aladdin, B-112, Rose Moonstone 295.00
Aladdin, B-120, Majestic, White Moonstone 230.00
Aladdin, Brass, Classical Engraving, Cranberry Shade, Caesar, Chariot, Kerosene, 21 x 10 In. 305.00
Aladdin, Frosted Shade, Cottage By Lake, White Enamel Base, 9 3/4 In. 210.00
Aladdin, G-124, Velvex, Painted Metal 410.00
Aladdin, G-166, Peach Moonstone 45.00
Aladdin, G-243, Alacite, No. 909H Fluted Shade 60.00
Aladdin, G-294D, Gold Lustre, Alacite, Wheatstaff 45.00
Argand, 1-Light, Bronze, Urn Font, Prisms, Glass Shade, c.1840, 11 1/2 In., Pair 3525.00
Argand, Bronze, Patinated, Fluted, Tapered, Electrified, England, c.1850, 18 In., Pair 1293.00
Argand, J. B. Wilbor, Single Arm, Brass, New York, 15 1/2 In., Pair 1035.00
Astral, Cornelius & Co., Cut Glass Shade, Cast, Gilded, Trefoil Base, Gothic Designs, 29 In. 1380.00
Astral, Gilt Brass Stem, Marble Base, Frosted Flower Cut Shade, 1800s, 22 1/4 In. 748.00
Astral, Gilt Brass, Cut Glass Shade, Prisms, Columnar, Wheel-Cut Flowers, 27 1/2 In. 2115.00
Astral, Sinumbra, Applied Decorations, Cut Overlay Column, Roses, Gilded Brass Base, 32 In. 1955.00
Astral, Sinumbra, Glass, Cut, Etched, Flowers, Leaves, c.1850, 9 1/2 x 14 1/2 In. 765.00
Astral, Sinumbra, Tole, Cylindrical Standard, 8-Sided Plinth, Electrified, 25 In., Pair 1530.00
Astral, Solar, Blown & Etched Glass, Brass, Danby Marble, Gilt Lacquer, Electrified, c.1835, 10 In. 530.00
Betty, Brass, 22 In. 590.00
Betty, Brass, Copper, Dutch, 19th Century 29.00
Betty, Colonial, c.1800, 8-In. Hook, 5 1/2 x 4 3/4 In. 266.00
Betty, Iron, c.1750, 5 x 4 1/2 In. 290.00
Betty, Tin, Single Wick Support, Strap Handle, Tidy Stand, Saucer Base, Early 1800s, 12 1/4 In. .. 264.00
Betty, Tin, Wire Hanger, Cylindrical Font, Cover, 2 Spouts, Dish Base, 19th Century, 8 In. 206.00
Betty, Wrought Iron 77.00
Bouillotte, 2-Light, Empire Style, Tole Shade, Gilt Bronze, Acanthus Scroll Arms, 25 In., Pair 705.00
Bouillotte, 2-Light, Restauration Style, Tole Shade, Engine Turned Brass, France, 28 In. 499.00
Bouillotte, 3-Light, Brass, Tin Shade, Cream Paint, Electrified, 1800s, 25 In. 558.00
Bouillotte, 3-Light, Louis XV Style, Gilt Bronze, Electrified, France, c.1900, 24 1/2 In. 2115.00
Bouillotte, 3-Light, Neoclassical, Green Tole Shade, 25 x 16 In., Pair 1410.00
Bouillotte, 4-Light, Brass, Tole Shades, Swan Arms, Dolphin, Continental, 1900s, 29 1/4 In., Pair 345.00
Bradley & Hubbard lamps are included in the Bradley & Hubbard category.
Candle, Regency, Reverse Painted Shade, Silver Plate, M. Boulton, Sheffield, 1800s, 6 3/4 In., Pair 1700.00
Ceiling, Delatte, Mottled, Red, Blue & Yellow Glass Shade, 3 Chain Cap, France, 14 In. 748.00
Ceiling, Etched, Frosted Glass, Beaded, 20th Century, 16 x 15 In. 265.00
Chamber, Embossed, Metal Handles, 6 1/2 In. 125.00
Chandelier, 1-Light, Crystal, Gilt Bronze, 20th Century, 11 x 7 3/4 In. 470.00

Chandelier, 2-Light, Neoclassical, Tole, France, 1900s, 46 x 12 In. 590.00
Chandelier, 3-Light, Brass, Grapevines, Leaves, Clusters, 12 x 9 In. 175.00
Chandelier, 3-Light, Gilt Metal, 20th Century, 32 x 22 In. 140.00
Chandelier, 3-Light, Loop Bow, Stylized Flower Shade Holders, 23 In. 345.00
Chandelier, 3-Light, Napoleon III, Gilt Brass, Ruby, White Opaline Glass, 21 x 13 1/2 In. 820.00
Chandelier, 3-Light, Prairie School, Bronze, Cut Out Design, Slag Glass, Chains, 36 x 30 In. 3400.00
Chandelier, 4-Light, Electric, Iron Band, 4 Chains, 44 x 23 1/2 In. 220.00
Chandelier, 4-Light, Empire Style, Brass, Black Patinated Metal, Saucer Shape Tier, 10 x 19 In. 382.00
Chandelier, 4-Light, Gilt Metal, Grapevine Standard, Scrolled Arms, Victorian, 32 In. 2235.00
Chandelier, 4-Light, Hoffman Style, Brass, Glass, 20th Century, 41 x 12 In. 236.00
Chandelier, 4-Light, Neoclassical, Gilt Sphere Finial, Fleur-De-Lis, Lyre, Shades, 22 x 16 In. 2705.00
Chandelier, 5-Light, Bronze, Winged Dragons, Shade Holders, Leaves, Swirls, 26 x 29 In. 4315.00
Chandelier, 5-Light, Continental Style, Tole, 20th Century, 24 x 21 In. 295.00
Chandelier, 5-Light, Georgian Style, Inverted Bowl Shape, Crystal, 24 1/2 x 18 In. 415.00
Chandelier, 5-Light, Gilt Bronze, Cut Glass, Dolphins, Pinecone Pendant, France, 26 In. 1645.00
Chandelier, 5-Light, Neoclassical, Gilt Metal, Cage Shape, 20th Century, 18 x 11 In. 384.00
Chandelier, 5-Light, Prisms, Scrolled, Swirled Glass, Bobeches, 20th Century, 36 x 35 In. 2875.00
Chandelier, 5-Light, Tommi Parzinger, Iron, Candlestick Fixtures, Silk Shades, 1950s, 42 x 44 In. 2950.00
Chandelier, 6 Light, Meissen Style, Polychrome, Flower Pendant Drops, 1900s, 36 x 20 In. 236.00
Chandelier, 6-Light, Art Deco, Silvered Nickel, Facet-Cut Spears, Faux Candles, 33 x 26 In. 5405.00
Chandelier, 6-Light, Brass, Scrolled Arms, Eagles, Russia, c.1900, 31 1/2 In. 1410.00
Chandelier, 6-Light, Carved Giltwood, Melon Rib Bulb, Scrolling Bracket, 29 x 42 In. 1850.00
Chandelier, 6-Light, Crystal, Brass, Copper, Gas Style, 1900s, 40 x 36 In. 1535.00
Chandelier, 6-Light, Empire Revival, Bronze, Drapery, Tassels, Palm Fronds, c.1900, 25 In. 1765.00
Chandelier, 6-Light, Empire Style, Gilt Bronze, Tole, Acanthus Pendants, 33 x 25 In. 1765.00
Chandelier, 6-Light, Empire Style, Scrolling Arms, Candles, France, 1900s, 49 x 31 In. 825.00
Chandelier, 6-Light, Iron, Glass Dome, Frosted, Mottled, Muller Freres, 35 x 24 In. 1210.00
Chandelier, 6-Light, Louis XIV Style, Giltwood, Ivory Faux Candles, c.1900, 36 x 30 In. 3290.00
Chandelier, 6-Light, Louis XV Style, Crystal, Teardrop Pendants, 1900s, 27 x 17 In. 472.00
Chandelier, 6-Light, Louis XVI Style, Gilt Brass, Quiver, Leaf Arms, 40 1/2 x 24 1/2 In. 940.00
Chandelier, 6-Light, Neoclassical, Glass Chains, Pendants, Ruby Glass Plate, 42 x 27 In. 3055.00
Chandelier, 6-Light, Painted Wood, Metal, Prisms, Swags, 36 x 24 In. 825.00
Chandelier, 6-Light, Parcel Gilt, Crimson Tole, Hexagonal, France, 1900s, 40 In. 17625.00
Chandelier, 6-Light, Restauration Style, Gilt Brass, Cut & Pressed Glass, France, 24 x 19 In. 1290.00
Chandelier, 6-Light, Tin, Candlearms, Drip Pans, Crimped Edge, Drop Loop Finial, 17 x 26 In. 880.00
Chandelier, 6-Light, Tin, Punched Decoration, Cone Shape, Scrolled Candle Arms, 17 x 26 In. 880.00
Chandelier, 6-Light, Wood, Iron, Carved, Continental, 20th Century, 28 x 30 In. 708.00
Chandelier, 6-Light, Wrought Iron, Link Chains, Carved Leaf, Scroll, 15 x 31 x 15 1/2 In. 354.00
Chandelier, 7-Light, Baroque Style, Brass, Serpentine Arms, Multi Knopped Standard, 17 In. 705.00
Chandelier, 8-Light, Brass, Scrolled Serpentine, Ring-Turned Column, Ball Finial, 24 x 16 In. 635.00
Chandelier, 8-Light, Crystal, Twisted Arms, Faceted Balls, Pendants, Czechoslovakia, 33 x 33 In. 410.00
Chandelier, 8-Light, Empire Style, Bronze, Gilt, Winged Figures, Continental, 1900s, 34 x 28 In. 2596.00
Chandelier, 8-Light, Empire Style, Gilt Bronze, Tole, Cherub, Electrified, 44 x 19 In. 4700.00
Chandelier, 8-Light, Gilt Brass, Mythological Beasts, Putti, Leafy Arms, 1700s, 37 x 28 In. 857.00
Chandelier, 8-Light, Italian Style, Giltwood, Iron, 20th Century, 25 x 30 In. 500.00
Chandelier, 8-Light, Louis XV Style, Gilt Metal, Glass, 4 Scrolling Straps, 29 x 19 In. 2235.00
Chandelier, 8-Light, Louis XV Style, Iron, Cage Shape, Acanthus Leaf, France, 40 x 35 In. 820.00
Chandelier, 8-Light, Louis XVI Style, Giltwood, Carved, France, 20th Century, 32 x 28 In. 1292.00
Chandelier, 8-Light, Regency Style, Gilt Bronze, c.1900, 50 x 33 In. 6000.00
Chandelier, 8-Light, Rococo Style, Brass, Glass Chains & Pendants, Cage Form, 35 x 24 In. 3055.00
Chandelier, 8-Light, Verner Panton, Chrome, Brass, Spheres, Tiered Strands, 39 x 16 In. 10030.00
Chandelier, 10-Light, Brass, Cut Crystal, Prisms, White Wax Candle Sleeves, 30 x 25 In. 660.00
Chandelier, 10-Light, Classical Revival, Cut Glass, Baluster Stem, Electrified, Early 1900s, 20 In. 590.00
Chandelier, 10-Light, Louis XV Style, Bronze, Crystal, 5 Arms, Early 1900s, 36 x 26 In. 1003.00
Chandelier, 10-Light, Louis XV Style, Wrought Iron, Flowerhead Candle Sockets, 41 x 30 In. 590.00
Chandelier, 10-Light, Metal, Scrolling Branches, Crystal Drops, 1900s, 28 x 32 In. 590.00
Chandelier, 12-Light, Baroque Style, Brass, 2 Tiers, 20th Century, 27 x 24 In. 2400.00
Chandelier, 12-Light, Baroque Style, Brass, 2 Tiers, 20th Century, 32 x 30 In. 1180.00
Chandelier, 12-Light, Baroque Style, Brass, Baluster Stem, Serpentine Scrolled Arms, 33 In. 3645.00
Chandelier, 12-Light, Bronze Dore, 3 Linked Chains, Porcelain Cups, Ormolu, Sevres, 27 x 24 In. 690.00
Chandelier, 12-Light, Cut Glass, 6 Gooseneck Arms, Prisms, 41 x 30 In. 1840.00

Lamp, Electric, Bust, John Wayne, Glazed Pottery, 24 In.

Lamp, Electric, Duffner & Kimberly, 4 Panels, Fleur-De-Lis, Cast Bronze Base, 23 x 19 In.

Chandelier, 12-Light, Gilt Bronze, Cut Glass, Electrified, France, c.1885, 42 x 27 In. 2585.00
Chandelier, 12-Light, Glass, Cranberry Cut To Clear, Pierced Bronze Supports, 45 In. 7050.00
Chandelier, 12-Light, Iron, Gilt, Cut Glass, Bead Strands, Italy, 48 x 45 In. 3760.00
Chandelier, 12-Light, Louis XV Style, Gilt Bronze, Third Republic, Late 1800s, 37 x 31 In. 2820.00
Chandelier, 12-Light, Louis XVI Style, Gilt Bronze, Cut Glass, Scrolling Arms, 32 x 26 In. 2235.00
Chandelier, 12-Light, Napoleon III, Gilt Bronze, Rock Crystal, c.1870, 41 x 33 In. 9989.00
Chandelier, 12-Light, Openwork Baluster, Beads, Chains, Topaz & Clear Pendants, 45 In. 7050.00
Chandelier, 12-Light, Steel, Frosted Glass Shades, Circular, 43 x 27 In. 450.00
Chandelier, 16-Light, Bronze Dore, Scrolled, Branched Arms, 3 Tiers, Sevres, 35 x 29 In. 3680.00
Chandelier, 18-Light, Neoclassical, Brass, Cut Glass, 42 In. 6000.00
Chandelier, 18-Light, Swags, Prisms, Bell-Shaped Hood, 2 Tiers, 6 Above 12 Arms, 44 x 41 In. 3335.00
Chandelier, 23-Light, Iron, Painted, Cascading Scroll, Leaves, Flower Sockets, 60 x 42 In. 1595.00
Chandelier, 30-Light, Louis XVI Style, Gilt Bronze, Leaf-Shape Corona, 36 x 38 In. 2115.00
Chandelier, Baroque Style, Brass, Iron, Dutch, Electrified, Mid 19th Century 2160.00
Chandelier, Empire Style, Gilt Bronze, Patinated, Winged Women, c.1900, 38 1/2 In. 7200.00
Chandelier, Gilt Metal, Flower Form, Drop Prisms, 14 1/2 x 16 In. 645.00
Chandelier, Louis XV Style, Colored Crystal, 20th Century, 30 x 20 In. 708.00
Chandelier, Louis XV Style, Gilt Bronze, Glass Paneled, Putto, France, c.1915, 27 x 17 In. 2350.00
Chandelier, Louis XVI Style, Gilt Bronze, 20th Century, 37 x 19 1/2 In. 472.00
Chandelier, Venini, Glass Bar Prisms, Metal Frame, 1960s, 18 x 18 In. 3420.00
Chandelier, Vistosi, Blown Glass Disks, Tiered Frame, 1960s, 22 x 18 In. 2595.00
Clear, Bull's-Eye & Fleur-De-Lis, Brass Stem, Marble Base, 9 1/2 In. 110.00
Electric, 2-Light, Bronze, 6-Sided, Wooden Top, Tapered Base, Chinese, 30 x 10 1/2 x 5 In. 138.00
Electric, 2-Light, Bronze, Tapered Oval, Carved Wooden Base, 33 x 8 1/2 x 6 In. 140.00
Electric, 2-Light, Edwardian, Pendant Sockets, Mahogany, Parcel Gilt, Tripod, c.1900, 57 In., Pair . 1057.00
Electric, 2-Light, Neoclassical, Carved Bust, Oval Black Tole Shade, Wood Base, 20 In., Pair 1275.00
Electric, 8-Panel Shade, Yellow Slag Glass, Gilt Metal Base, Late 1800s, 23 x 21 In. 708.00
Electric, 12-Light, Atomic, Chrome, c.1970, 62 In. 207.00
Electric, Amelia Earhart & Parachute, North America Map, c.1930, 18 1/2 In. 431.00
Electric, Angelo Lelli, Lever Adjustment, Arredoluce, c.1955, 14 In. 2040.00
Electric, Angelo Lelli, Spotlight, Contrast, c.1962, 9 3/4 In. 1680.00
Electric, Arredoluce, Single Arm, Flared Shade, Enameled, Chrome Shaft, Marble Base, Italy, 58 In. 1005.00
Electric, Art Deco, Caramel & Green Slag Glass Panels, Cast Bronze, Incised Base 440.00
Electric, Art Deco, Chrome, Semicircular Glass Panels, Balls, Bakelite Shaft, 11 x 8 In. 325.00
Electric, Art Deco, Elephant, Bronze, Glass Globe, 10 1/2 x 10 3/4 x 3 1/4 In. 590.00
Electric, Art Deco, Green Dome, Brass, Patinated, Lacquered, c.1930, 20 1/2 In. 160.00
Electric, Art Glass, Pulled Leaf, Multicolor Iridescent Ground, Helmet Shade, 12 In. 920.00
Electric, Art Nouveau, Female Figure, Gold, Ivory, Floral Accents, 3-Footed Base, 24 x 6 In. 61.00
Electric, Arteluce, Brass Column, 3 Adjustable Arms, Metal Shades, Tripod Base, 61 In. 4200.00
Electric, Arteluce, Chrome, Adjustable Arm, White Enameled Shade, Marble Base, 68 x 24 In. 1800.00
Electric, Arteluce, Enameled Metal, 3 Chrome Fixtures, Pierced, Magnetic Mounts, Tripod, 77 In. .. 768.00
Electric, Arteluce, Metal, Spherical Fixtures, Magnetic Mount, Chrome, Greek Key, 79 In. 2596.00
Electric, Arteluce, Triennale, Chrome, Black Shades, c.1953, 84 In. 4800.00
Electric, Artistic Lamp Mfg., Brass & Marble Base, Crystal Stem, N.Y.C., 23 In. 90.00
Electric, Arts & Crafts, Green Slag Glass Panels, Fringed Shade, 69 1/2 x 27 In. 2235.00
Electric, Arts & Crafts, Slag Glass, Green Bronzed Metal Base, 25 1/2 x 18 3/4 In. 658.00
Electric, Benedict, Copper, Hammered, Adjustable, 3 Panel Mica Shade, 23 x 8 1/2 x 13 1/2 In. .. 1410.00

Lamp, Electric, Duffner & Kimberly, Leaded Glass, 8 Amber Jewels, Heart Cutout Base, 22 x 18 In.

Lamp, Electric, Jefferson, Landscape, Road, Trees, Bronze Base, Signed, 16 In.

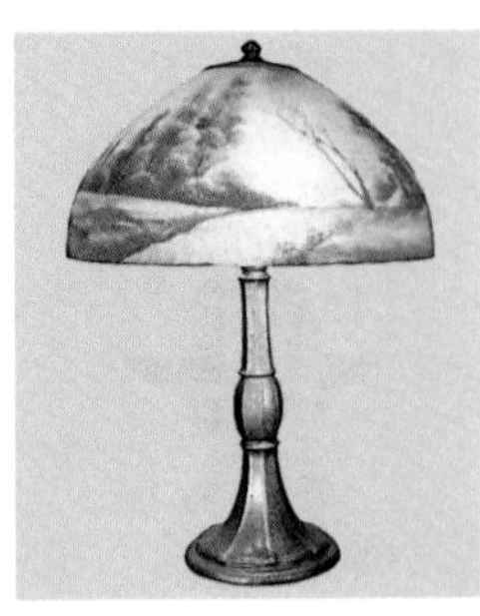

Electric, Blackamoor, Polychrome, Molded Plaster, Mid 20th Century, 30 In., Pair 1058.00
Electric, Brass, 3 Enameled Shades, Red, Green, Yellow, 75 x 26 In. 2240.00
Electric, Brass, Double-Ring Pedestal, Pull Chain Switch, 3-Footed, 20th Century, 16 x 7 In. 305.00
Electric, Brass, Gilt Metal, Marble, 3-Arrow Standard, France, 1940s, 72 In. 5100.00
Electric, Brass, Reticulated, Multiple Colored Inset Jewels, 7 1/2 In. 375.00
Electric, Bronze, Domed Shade, Scroll Designs, Pierced, Marble Base, Continental, c.1920, 18 In. . 265.00
Electric, Bronze, Dragon & Ring Handles, Double Fixture, Chinese, 26 1/2 x 8 x 6 In. 110.00
Electric, Bronze, Egg Shape, Double Fixture, Chinese, 28 x 6 1/2 In., Pair 415.00
Electric, Bronze, Multicolored Cloisonne Band, Bulbous, Tapered, c.1900, 18 x 4 In. 235.00
Electric, Bronze, Nymph Holding Satyr, Grapevine-Covered Tree Trunk, 30 In., Pair 4115.00
Electric, Bronze, Woman, Brown & Gold Patina, Louis Chalon, c.1900, 15 3/4 In. 9315.00
Electric, Bust, John Wayne, Glazed Pottery, 24 In. .... *ILLUS* 55.00
Electric, Cast Iron, Beaver, Maple Leaves, Over Log, Patinated Copper Finish 150.00
Electric, Ceiling, C.F. Otto Mueller, Milk Glass, Nickel Plated, Sistrah-Licht, c.1932, 38 x 15 In. 1180.00
Electric, Chocolate Art Glass & Metal Shade, Spelter, c.1930, 16 x 14 In. 90.00
Electric, Christian Dell, Desk, Adjustable, Kaiser & Co., c.1934 .... 330.00
Electric, Christian Dell, Scissor, Black Enameled Metal, Kaiser & Co., 1940s 885.00
Electric, Chrome, Beehive Shape, 1930s, 12 1/2 In., Pair 300.00
Electric, Chrome, Plexiglas, Monofilament, c.1970, 26 In. 45.00
Electric, Classique, Reverse Painted, Bell-Shape Shade, Chipped Ice Texture, Sunset Scene, 23 In. 1469.00
Electric, Clewell, Hammered Brass, Blue, Green, Electroplated Copper, 15 3/4 In. 978.00
Electric, Contemporary, Chrome, Crystal, Spiked Sphere, 20th Century, 13 x 24 In. 945.00
Electric, Curtis Jere, 2-Light, Black Shades, c.1972, 22 1/2 In., Pair 1560.00
Electric, Curtis Jere, Crane, Adjustable, c.1972, 114 In. 1680.00
Electric, Cut Glass, Dome Top, Teardrop Prism, 12 x 24 1/2 In. 1287.00
Electric, Cut Glass, Hobstar, File & Fan Pattern, Mushroom Shade, Pendants, 17 In. 1650.00
Electric, Cut Glass, Teardrop Stem, Mushroom Shade, Flowers, Butterflies, Pendants, 19 In. 550.00
Electric, Danish Modern, Cylindrical Linen Shade, c.1916, 27 In. 80.00
Electric, David Cressey, Pro Artisan, Stoneware, Glazed, c.1970, 35 In. 840.00
Electric, Desk, Chromed, Lacquered Metal, 19 x 37 In. 7800.00
Electric, Directoire Style, Brass, Single Fixture, Early 20th Century, 29 x 10 In. 355.00
Electric, Dominique, 8-Sided, Bronze, Gilt, Parchment Leather, 8 1/4 x 5 3/4 In. 4657.00
Electric, Drop Head, Dragonflies, Blue Ground, Mottled Glass, 22 x 31 In. 4888.00
Electric, Duffner & Kimberly, 4 Panels, Fleur-De-Lis, Cast Bronze Base, 23 x 19 In. .... *ILLUS* 43700.00
Electric, Duffner & Kimberly, Leaded Glass, 8 Amber Jewels, Heart Cutout Base, 22 x 18 In. . *ILLUS* 4312.00
Electric, Edgar Brandt, Wrought Iron, Hammered, 11 3/4 x 3 1/2 In. 7760.00
Electric, Eduard-Wilfred Buquet, Steel, Nickel Plated, Ebonized Wood, France, c.1927, 39 3/4 In. . 6550.00
Electric, Empire Style, Brass, Smoked Glass, 20th Century, 38 In. 225.00
Electric, Empire Style, Gilt Metal Mounted, Toleware, Columns, Spiraling Leaves, 26 In., Pair 1450.00
Electric, Ernesto Gismondi, Sinesti Terra, Enameled, Artemide, 56 x 8 3/4 In. 355.00
Electric, Figurine, Woman, Adjusting Shawl, Flower Vine, Blossom, 13 x 10 In. 460.00
Electric, Fontana Arte, Brass, Enamel, Adjustable Shaft, Plate Glass Base, 19 x 10 In. 1890.00
Electric, Franz Hagenauer, Wood, 2 Figures, Arms Raised, c.1930, 36 In. 3900.00
Electric, G. Nakashima, Burlwood, Paper Shade, 2 Columns, Free-Form Base, c.1956, 33 x 16 In. . 8850.00
Electric, G. Nelson, Bubble, Elliptical, Howard Miller, c.1952 .... 780.00
Electric, G. Nelson, Bubble, Spherical, Howard Miller, c.1952, 17 1/2 In. 216.00
Electric, G. Nelson, Half Nelson, Enamel, Chrome, Disc Shade, Koch & Lowy, 18 x 16 In. 1650.00

Lamp, Electric, Miller, Metal Overlay, Tree & House Silhouette, Slag Glass, 20 In.

Lamp, Electric, Moe Bridges, Landscape, Pond, Trees, Signed Shade & Base, 15 In.

Electric, G. Stickley, 6-Sided Mica Shade, Hammered Copper Base, 3 Handles, 14 In. 2400.00
Electric, Gaetano Sciolari, Brass, 9 Sockets, Lucite Accents, Chain, 22 1/4 x 25 1/4 In. 1060.00
Electric, Gilt & Bronze Patinated, Flower & Turned Column, Masks, Footed, c.1920, 68 In. 245.00
Electric, Gilt Goat's Mask, Flower Panels, Gilt Borders, Sevres, c.1900, 25 In., Pair 1019.00
Electric, Giltwood, Crystal Finial, Reeded Standard, Acanthine Carved Base, Italy, c.1900, 74 In. .. 765.00
Electric, Gino Sarfatti, Desk, 3 Bent Brass Stems, 3 Enameled Metal Shades, Knoll, 11 x 12 In. ... 1200.00
Electric, Gooseneck, Brass Twist Stem, Ball Insert, Silk Shade, Iron Base, c.1915, 56 x 10 In...... 138.00
Electric, Greta Grossman, Grasshopper, Black Enamel, Tubular Metal, Cone-Shape Shade, 51 In. .. 1120.00
Electric, Greta Magnusson Grossman, Tripod, No. 831, White, Ralph O. Smith, c.1949, 49 In. 4500.00
Electric, Hanging, 3-Light, Brass, Glass, 6 Glass Panels, c.1935, 19 x 9 In. 110.00
Electric, Hanging, 3-Light, Federal Style, Blown, Cut Glass, Brass Stem, 24 x 14 In. 495.00
Electric, Hanging, 6-Light, Stained Glass, 12 Panels, Link Chain, Lion's-Head Mount, 22 In. 2760.00
Electric, Hanging, Leaded Glass, Swag Border, Gilt Metal, Onyx Base, Early 1900s, 20 In. 176.00
Electric, Hanging, Paul Evans, Steel, T-Shape, 4 Sockets, Square Ceiling Plate, 36 x 30 In......... 1535.00
Electric, Hanging, Poul Henningsen, Artichoke, Louis Poulsen, c.1957, 15 x 19 In. 3600.00
Electric, Hanging, V. Panton, Fun 6 DM, Luber, c.1964, 26 In.. 1200.00
Electric, Hanging, V. Panton, Spiral, SP1, Luber, c.1969, 42 In. 1560.00
Electric, Heifetz Co., Brass, Enameled Metal, Wood, c.1950, 36 12 In. 9600.00
Electric, I. Noguchi, Bamboo, No. BB3, Akari, c.1951, 68 In. 960.00
Electric, I. Noguchi, No. UF4, Paper, Akari, c.1951, 84 In.. 1140.00
Electric, Ingo Maurer, Light Bulb Shape, Injection Molded, Design M, Late 1960s, 24 x 13 In. 770.00
Electric, J. Adnet, Clear Glass, Nickeled Bronze, 8 1/4 x 6 In. 3540.00
Electric, J. Adnet, Leather, Brass, 3-Footed, c.1950, 29 In. 3000.00
Electric, J. Adnet, Leather, Brass, c.1950, 24 1/2 In. 3600.00
Electric, Jean Boris Lacroix, Nickel-Plated Bronze, Frosted Glass, c.1928, 11 1/2 In. 8400.00
Electric, Jean Royere, Iron, Painted, Oblong Shade, 2 Standards, 4-Footed, 1948, 13 x 13 x 4 In. .. 4200.00
Electric, Jefferson, Landscape, Road, Trees, Bronze Base, Signed, 16 In. .... *ILLUS* 840.00
Electric, Jefferson, Reverse Painted Shade, Red & Blue Flowers, Bronzed Metal Base, 21 x 16 In. .. 1140.00
Electric, Jefferson, Reverse Painted, Domed Shade, Chipped Ice, Landscape, 2 Sockets, 16 x 22 In. 1265.00
Electric, Keramos, Glazed Ceramic, White, Brown Band, c.1950, 8-In. Base 900.00
Electric, Keramos, Glazed Ceramic, White, Brown Lines, Oak Foot, c.1950, 10-In. Base 2880.00
Electric, Kiddy Lite, Dopey, Micro Lite, 1938 .... 475.00
Electric, Kurt Versen, Aluminum, Double Shaft, Egg-Shape Shade, Stepped Strips, 59 x 18 In. 1888.00
Electric, Laurel, White Frosted Glass Shade, Enameled Tubular Base, 57 x 12 In., Pair 945.00
Electric, Le Verrier, Nude, Arched Back, Outstretched Arms, Globular Shade, Bronze, 15 1/4 In. ... 1508.00
Electric, Leaded Glass, Metal, Domed Shade, Carmel, Green Glass, Vase Standard, 20 x 26 In. 375.00
Electric, Leaded Glass, Overlay, Caramel Slag, 6 Panels, Flower, Leaf Base, c.1905, 25 x 20 1/2 In. 440.00
Electric, Lipstick, Cylinder, Polished Chrome, 4 Sockets, Plastic Shade, 64 x 10 In. 1416.00
Electric, Louis XVI Style, Porcelain, Ormolu Mounted, France, Late 1800s, 19 In., Pair 1765.00
Electric, M. Nakashima, Walnut, Maple, Natural Woodblock Base, Cylindrical, 19 1/2 In., Pair 3600.00
Electric, M. Wanders, Big Shadow, Orange Cloth, Internally Lit, Cappellini, c.1968, 38 In......... 1440.00
Electric, Mahogany, Carved, Column, Punched Stars Base, Leaves, Beads, Turned Feet, 70 In. 259.00
Electric, Marble, Flower Carved, Urn Shape, Square Base, c.1930, 21 x 4 In., Pair 245.00
Electric, Marble, Urn Shape, Gilt Mounted, Bacchus Mask Handles, Garlands, 1900s, 22 In., Pair . 1935.00
Electric, Metal, Patinated, Domed Shade, Tapered Stem, Greek Key, c.1910, 10 In. 245.00
Electric, Miller, Metal Overlay, Tree & House Silhouette, Slag Glass, 20 In. .... *ILLUS* 840.00
Electric, Moe Bridges, Landscape, Pond, Trees, Signed Shade & Base, 15 In. .... *ILLUS* 952.00

Lamp, Electric, Pittsburgh, Swan Scene, Dark Green, Purple, Bronze Base, 16 In.

Lamp, Electric, TV, Mallard In Cattails, Ceramic, Planter Base, Lane & Co., 14 In.

Electric, Muller Freres Cameo Glass Shade, Landscape, Iron, Early 1900s, 12 1/2 In. 800.00
Electric, Neal Small, Plastic, Molded, White, Chrome Connectors, Book Matched, 18 x 12 In. 530.00
Electric, Neoclassical Style, Continental, Early 20th Century, 6 1/2 x 14 1/4 In., Pair 470.00
Electric, Nude Woman, Kneeling, Holding Urn, Bronze, Marble, Continental, 1900s, 18 In. 265.00
Electric, Oscar Bach, Art Deco, Bronze, Patinated, Signed, 68 In. 1586.00
Electric, Parchment Shade, Leather, Metal, 1950s, 28 1/4 In. 7800.00
Electric, Piano, Bronze, Brown Patina, Mosserine Shade, 15 In. 920.00
Electric, Pipistrello, Enamel, White, Steel, Gae Aulenti, Martinelli Luce, 1960s, 32 x 21 In., Pair .. 1319.00
Electric, Pittsburgh, Art Nouveau, Lake, Trees, Reverse Painted, c.1910, 12 1/4 In. 1315.00
Electric, Pittsburgh, Reverse Painted, Winter Scene, Cabin In Woods, Art Nouveau Base, 21 In. ... 1495.00
Electric, Pittsburgh, Swan Scene, Dark Green, Purple, Bronze Base, 16 In. .... *ILLUS* 1568.00
Electric, Plastic, Molded, Rougier, c.1986, 70 In. 396.00
Electric, Polychrome, Giltwood, Leaf-Carved Standard, Pleated Shade, Italy, Early 1900s, 64 In. ... 1292.00
Electric, Porcelain, Baluster Vase Shape, Blue, Hundred Antiques Design, c.1900, 30 In. 645.00
Electric, Porcelain, Black Lacquered Pedestal, Hand Woven Shades, 37 1/2 In., Pair 3780.00
Electric, Porcelain, Vase Shape, Overall Gilt, Landscape, Figural Decoration, Chinese, 25 1/2 In. .. 760.00
Electric, Poul Henningsen, Glass, Brass, L. Poulsen & Co., 1928-33, 21 1/2 In. 9600.00
Electric, Prairie School, Leaded Glass, Patinated Bronze, 23 1/8 In. 36000.00
Electric, Red Iridescent Shade, Blue Zipper Design, Tree Trunk Base, 14 In. 518.00
Electric, Revere Chrome, Woman's Head, 10 x 4 In., Pair 445.00
Electric, Reverse Painted, Rose, Green Ground, Chipped Ice, Cast Base, 3 Sockets, 21 1/2 In. 1150.00
Electric, Robert Sonneman, Metal, Bent, Riveted, Chrome, 4 Sockets, 32 x 16 1/4 In., Pair 1770.00
Electric, Robot, Polished Chrome, Torino, Italy, 31 In. 1120.00
Electric, Rock Crystal, Brass Mounted, Baluster Shape, Spiral Turning, 6-Sided Foot, 21 In. 3819.00
Electric, Roland Smith, Metal, Wood, Painted, Victor, c.1948, 72 1/2 In. 2185.00
Electric, Rose Dodds, Ceramic, Glazed, c.1955, 22 1/2 In., Pair 1200.00
Electric, Ruba Rombic 625.00
Electric, Salviati & Co., Glass, Baluster Shape, Circular Base, 1960s, 30 1/4 In., Pair 2260.00
Electric, Sandwich Cut Overlay, White, Blue, Stepped Marble Base, 19 1/2 In. 495.00
Electric, Singleton, Stone, Plastic, Italy, c.1975, 23 x 24 In. 160.00
Electric, Slag Glass Shade, Owl, Metal, Patinated, Early 1900s, 15 1/2 In. 285.00
Electric, Slag Panel, Iron Base, Onyx Knop, Embossed Metal Frame, 22 1/2 In. 440.00
Electric, Stained Glass, Dome, Flowers, Leaves, Brass Base, 23 x 18 In. 210.00
Electric, Tiffany Style, Leaded Dragonfly Shade, Jeweled Glass Base, Bronzed Mounts, 25 In., Pair . 355.00
Electric, Tin, Repousse, Jeweled Shade, Iznik-Style Pottery Base, Middle East, c.1950, 36 In. 105.00
Electric, Tommi Parzinger, 8 Candlestick Fixtures, Iron, Tripod Base, 72 x 18 In. 2006.00
Electric, Touring Automobile Shade, Slag Panel, Cast Base, Reticulated, 1920s, 18 In. 470.00
Electric, TV, Mallard In Cattails, Ceramic, Planter Base, Lane & Co., 14 In. .... *ILLUS* 65.00
Electric, V. Panton Chrome, Brass, 6 Sockets, Spokes, Spheres, 8 1/2 x 28 In., Pair .....2480.00 to 3186.00
Electric, Verre Lumiere, 1 Socket, Frosted Glass, Bulbous Base, 10 1/2 x 8 3/4 In. 236.00
Electric, Wendell Castle, Above Thy Fruited Plain, Lantern Shape, Carved Pears, 64 x 20 In. 3835.00
Electric, Western Boots, Leather, Canvas, Brass, Horseshoe, Shade, Gucci, 1960s 5100.00
Electric, Wheel-Cut Glass, Bronze, Dogwood Blossoms, Purple Ground, 13 x 6 1/2 In. 823.00
Electric, Wicker, Domed Shade, c.1910, 69 x 28 In. 590.00
Electric, William Wyman, Ceramic, Earth-Tone Bands, Brown, 1968, 16 1/2 x 5 x 4 In. 2125.00
Electric, Zahara Schatz, Heifetz, c.1951, 38 x 13 1/2 x 10 In. 4800.00

Fairy, Blue Satin, 3-Piece Mold, Domed Shade, Ruffled Rim Base, Clarke Insert, 6 1/2 In. 635.00
Fairy, Blue Satin, Diamond Quilted, Clarke Base, 3 1/2 In. 100.00
Fairy, Cranberry Overshot, Swirled Shade, Ruffled Base, 6 In. 405.00
Fairy, Hobbs Brockunier, Blue Satin, Ruffled Rim Bowl, Clarke Base, 5 In. 805.00
Fat, Hammered Bronze, Molded Body, Nepal, 18th Century, 21 x 9 In. 440.00
Fluid, Art Nouveau, Brass, c.1900, 60 In. 710.00
Fluid, Blue Font, Raised Decoration, Milk Glass Base, 10 In., Pair 546.00
Fluid, Cut Glass, Wheel-Cut Font, Standard, Shield, Thistle, Star, Punty Motifs, 16 1/2 In. 1293.00
Fluid, Ormolu, Multi-Section, Glass Body, Decorated, Foliate Mounts, Continental, 62 In. 1120.00
Fluid, Powder Blue Milk Glass Font, Arch Pattern, Milk Glass Base, c.1850, 9 1/2 In., Pair 460.00
Fluid, R.S. Merrill Burner, Applied Handle, Brass Collar, Finger, 1865-70, 4 1/4 x 3 1/2 In. 200.00
Gas, Coleman Style, Green Slag Glass Paneled Shade, 20 In. 147.00
Gas, Gasolier, 7-Light, Rococo, Leaf Scroll Arms, Gilt Bronze, Brass, Electrified, 27 In., Pair 2235.00
Grease, 4 Spouts, Hanger, c.1680, 5 1/2 x 4 In. 355.00
Handel lamps are included in the Handel category.
Hanging, Brass, Jewels, Beveled Glass, 30 x 10 1/2 In. .... *ILLUS* 225.00
Hanging, Pink Roses, Green Leaves, Prisms, 14 In. .... *ILLUS* 1300.00
Hanging, Pink Satin, Cottage Scene, Embossed Flowers, 10 1/2 In. .... *ILLUS* 1000.00
Kerosene, Adlams Burner, Ribbed, Lip Chimney, Finger, 1863-75, 2 3/4 x 4 3/4 In. 240.00
Kerosene, Adlams, String Burner, Chimney, No Base, 1861-70, 5 3/4 In. 605.00
Kerosene, Aesthetic Style, Cranberry Shade, Magnum Hobnail, Brass Mounted, 32 x 18 In. 1997.00
Kerosene, Amethyst, Twinkle, Chimney, 6 3/4 In. 88.00
Kerosene, Ball & Broad Flute, 3-Piece Mold Font, 6-Sided Stem, Brass Collar, c.1870, 6 1/2 In. 495.00
Kerosene, Banquet, Silver Plate, Meriden, 17 In. 100.00
Kerosene, Banquet, White Opaque, Glass, Enameled Flowers, Victorian, Late 1800s, 28 In. 144.00
Kerosene, Blue Art Glass, Swirl, 6 In. 80.00
Kerosene, Blue Satin Glass, Round Shade, Spiral Ribs, Drape Pattern Chimney, 29 In. 295.00
Kerosene, Brass, Cupids Among Flowers, Stylized Shell, Duplex Burner, Brass Feet, 20 In. 290.00
Kerosene, Bull's-Eye, Fleur-De-Lis, Heart, 8-Sided Stem, 16-Scallop Foot, 1850-70, 8 3/4 In. 470.00
Kerosene, Cahoon Burner, Ribbed, Lip Chimney, Finger, 1860-75, 2 3/4 x 3 1/2 In. 825.00
Kerosene, Carnival Glass, Zipper Loop, 8 In. 800.00
Kerosene, Carriage, Brass, Beveled Glass, c.1870, 28 1/2 In., Pair 1058.00
Kerosene, Carriage, Silver Plate, Brass, Scrolls, Scalloped Edges, c.1890, 37 In., Pair 646.00
Kerosene, Cobalt Blue, Stripe, Opaque, Swirled, 1870-87 .... 3410.00
Kerosene, Corinthian Column, Brass, Cut Glass, Double Burner, England, c.1875, 34 x 7 1/2 In. 410.00
Kerosene, Cranberry Stain, Engraved Flowers, Frosted Round Shade, Brass Base, 28 In., Pair 410.00
Kerosene, Dietz, No. 866, Finger, Sunburst, 1860-75, 2 1/4 x 2 1/4 In. 305.00
Kerosene, Dietz, No. 874, Cahoon Burner, Swirled Rib, Finger, Lip Chimney, 1861-75, 3 1/2 In. 660.00
Kerosene, Flow Blue, Cased Light Blue Shade, 17 In. 125.00
Kerosene, Frosted Shade, Duplex, England, Victorian, c.1890, 35 x 17 In. 235.00
Kerosene, Gagneau, Louis XVI Style, Bronze, Marble, Paris, c.1865, 33 In., Pair 3525.00
Kerosene, Glass, Cranberry Cut To Clear, Brass Plinth, Marble Base, 1800s, 12 In. 175.00
Kerosene, Gone With The Wind, Hyacinth, Marigold 750.00
Kerosene, Gone With The Wind, Pink Satin, Floral Mold, 24 In. 1100.00
Kerosene, Gone With The Wind, Red Satin, 25 In. 550.00
Kerosene, Gray String Burner, Lip Chimney, 1865-80, 2 1/2 x 3 1/4 In. 220.00
Kerosene, Hanging, Arts & Crafts, 4-Light, Gilt Leaded Pendants, Bronze Base, c.1910, 25 In. 4700.00
Kerosene, Hanging, Blown Glass Bowl, Wafer Base, Brass Collar, Embossed Ivy, Birds, 23 In. 400.00
Kerosene, Hanging, Blue Melon Rib, Diamond Quilted, Fittings, 9 In. 300.00
Kerosene, Hanging, Brass, Multiple Jewels, Beveled Glass, 30 x 10 1/2 In. 225.00
Kerosene, Hanging, Grape & Lattice, Consolidated, Pat. May 31 1910, 13 In. 940.00
Kerosene, Hitchcock, Mechanical Draft, Brass, Nickel Plated, c.1868, 12 1/4 In. 588.00
Kerosene, Jones Burner, Honeycomb Stand, Blue Square Base, 1859-70, 10 1/4 In. 468.00
Kerosene, Jones No. 2 Burner, Lip Chimney, No Base, 1859-65, 12 In. 130.00
Kerosene, Louis XVI Style, Glass, Gilt Brass Mounted, Porcelain, Sevres Style, 22 In. 470.00
Kerosene, Milk Glass, Light Green, 3 1/2 In. 20.00
Kerosene, Milk Glass, Pink & White, 7 1/2 In. 260.00
Kerosene, No. 2 P & A Unique Burner, Lip Chimney, 4-In. Shade Ring, 1870-85, 12 In. 120.00
Kerosene, Peg, Opalescent White Glass, Corinthian Column, Beaded Socket, 9 In. 145.00
Kerosene, Pink Satin, Frosted Shade, 14 1/2 In. 100.00

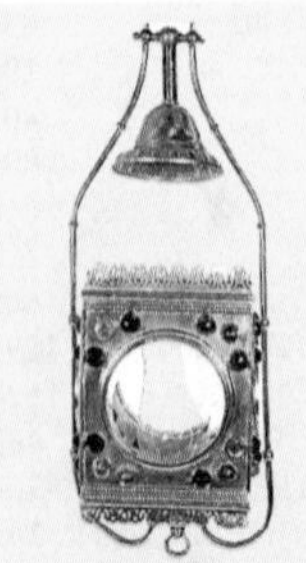

Lamp, Hanging, Brass, Jewels, Beveled Glass, 30 x 10 1/2 In.

Lamp, Hanging, Pink Roses, Green Leaves, Prisms, 14 In.

Lamp, Hanging, Pink Satin, Cottage Scene, Embossed Flowers, 10 1/2 In.

Kerosene, Pink Satin, Melon Rib, Metal Filigree Overlay, 4 1/2 In. 150.00
Kerosene, Pressed Glass, Bellflower Single Vine, Right Facing Vines, Brass Collar, 7 1/2 In. 130.00
Kerosene, Pressed Glass, Periwinkle, Brass Collar, Flint, 7 1/8 x 4 1/4 In. 155.00
Kerosene, Putto, Etched Shade, c.1898, 18 In. 316.00
Kerosene, Pyriform, Opal Font, Alabaster Clambroth Base, Brass Collar, 1870-87, 10 In. 120.00
Kerosene, Red Satin Glass, 7 1/2 In. 450.00
Kerosene, Ribbed Beehive, Applied Handle, Brass Collar, Finger, 1860-80, 2 1/8 x 2 1/2 In. 12.00
Kerosene, Ribbed, Rayed Base, Fine Line Collar, No. 1 Burner, Chimney, Finger, 1865-75, 3 In. 165.00
Kerosene, Ridges Burner, Lip Chimney, Dotted Band, Finger, 1862-70, 2 3/4 x 3 3/4 In. 415.00
Kerosene, Ripley Marriage Stand, Starch Blue Fonts, White Base, c.1875, 12 1/2 In. 715.00
Kerosene, Rococo Style, Slag Glass Shade, Gilt, Brass, Onyx, Bronze Patinated, 33 x 13 In. 1175.00
Kerosene, Ruby Flash, Miniature, 6 1/4 In. 40.00
Kerosene, Skater's, Cobalt Blue Globe, Brass Cap, Bail Handle, W.B.G. Corp., 1875-1900, 7 In. 385.00
Kerosene, Skater's, Green Globe, Brass Cap, Bail Handle, 1875-1900, 7 x 3 1/8 In. 360.00
Kerosene, Skater's, Jewel, Amethyst Globe, Tin Cap, Bail Handle, 1875-1900, 7 x 3 In. 825.00
Kerosene, Student, Brass Harvard Base, 2 Ruby-Cased Red Shades, 22 1/2 In. 1955.00
Kerosene, Student, Brass, Double, Cased Green Shades, 1800s, 24 x 27 In. 460.00
Kerosene, Student, Brass, Green Case, Ribbed Shade, 22 1/2 x 6 In. 275.00
Kerosene, White Satin, Beaded Drape, 11 In. 60.00
Lard, Berkshire Variant, Brass Collar, Finger, 1855-70, 2 3/4 x 3 3/4 In. 275.00
Oil, Air Twist, Clear, Cut Font, 1800s, 12 1/2 In. 605.00
Oil, Amethyst Font, Brass Stem, Marble Base, 10 In. 605.00
Oil, Amethyst Font, To Clear Font, Brass Stem, Stepped Marble Base, 16 1/2 In. 220.00
Oil, Amethyst, Glass, Hexagonal Sides, Base, Metal Screw Top, 8 3/4 x 3 1/2 In. 155.00
Oil, Aqua, Clear, Petal Pattern Reservoir, Dome & Scroll Base, Brass Burner, 8 1/4 In. 165.00
Oil, Art Nouveau, Gimbal, Copper Tray, Sterling Rim, AL Monogram, Shreve & Co., 10 x 5 1/2 In. 865.00
Oil, Arts & Crafts, Hammered Copper, 4-Arm Spider Supports, Metal Shade, 14 1/2 In. 3565.00
Oil, Blown Font, Wafer Stem, Stepped Pressed Glass Base, 12 1/4 In., Pair 345.00
Oil, Blown Glass, Amber Font, Clear Stem, Base, 7 3/4 In. 715.00
Oil, Blown Pear-Shape Font, Ringed Wafer, Pressed Lacy Glass Base, 8 1/2 In. 290.00
Oil, Blue Opalescent Swirl, Finger, Victorian, 5 1/4 In. 305.00
Oil, Blue Opalescent, Clear Base, Finger, 5 1/2 In. 305.00
Oil, Blue, Opaque White, Thumbprint, Oval, Diamond, Brass Screw Top, 7 3/4 x 4 x 4 In. 90.00
Oil, Blue, Pressed Tulip, Marble Base, 11 3/4 In. 385.00
Oil, Blue, Thumbprint Sides, Acanthus Stem, Cast Metal, Pewter Screw Top, 10 3/4 In. 155.00
Oil, Blue, Thumbprint, Round Reservoir, Acanthus Stem, Flower, Metal, 10 3/4 x 3 In. 155.00
Oil, Blue, White, Egg-Shape Reservoir, Thumbprint, Diamond, Brass Top, 7 3/4 x 4 In. 90.00
Oil, Blue, White, Opaque, Brass Wick Holder, Ribbed Font, Banner P & A, 13 x 4 In. 240.00
Oil, Brass, Etched Hurricane Globe, 27 In., Pair 1170.00
Oil, Bristol, White Opaline, Urn Shape, Gold-Lined Blue Flowers, Rust Ground, 22 In., Pair 295.00
Oil, Bronze, Figural Handle Depicting Ganesha, Shiva In Flaming Aureole, Nepal, 6 In. 325.00
Oil, Canary Yellow, Egg-Shape Reservoir, Clear Stem, Brass Screw Top, 10 1/2 In. 155.00
Oil, Carcel, Napoleon III, Gilt Brass Mounted, Matte Teal Enameled, Late 1800s, 18 In., Pair 646.00
Oil, Clambroth Font, Gold Highlights, Brass Connector, Opaline Base, Gold Highlights, 9 In. 90.00

Oil, Clear, Aqua, Petal Reservoir, Domed, Scrolled Base, Brass Screw Burner, 8 1/4 x 4 In. 165.00
Oil, Clear, Embossed Painted Grapevine, 9 1/2 In. 90.00
Oil, Clear, Opaque White, Hexagonal, Flowers, Brass Screw Top, 4 x 2 1/4 In. 187.00
Oil, Clear, Reservoir, Octagon Stem, Square Base, Brass Screw Burner, 9 x 3 1/2 In. 45.00
Oil, Cranberry Flash, Leaf & Berry, Brass Stem, Electrified, England, Late 1800s, 14 In., Pair 206.00
Oil, Cranberry Opalescent Top, Clear Base, Victorian, 7 1/4 In. 248.00
Oil, Cranberry Opalescent, Coin Spot Font, Victorian, 7 1/4 In. 385.00
Oil, Cranberry, Grape, Leaves, Cameo, Cylindrical Shade, 6 3/4 & 2 In. 345.00
Oil, Cut Overlay Font, White Cut To Cranberry, Clambroth Column, Brass, Marble, 15 In. 978.00
Oil, Etched Flower Font, Figure Pedestal, 1800s, 13 In. 115.00
Oil, Frosted Bulb Font, Cut Designs, Pressed Square Base, Wafers, Brass Collar, 11 In. 259.00
Oil, Globe Font, Hollow Knop & Wafer Stem, Pressed Base, Columns, Baskets, 9 1/2 In. 489.00
Oil, Green Glass, Diamond Point, 1800s, 9 In., Pair 230.00
Oil, Heart Font, Paneled Baluster Stem, Hexagonal Base, Brass Collar, 7 3/4 In. 86.00
Oil, Milk Glass, Flowers, Clambroth Base, 9 In. 110.00
Oil, Napoleon III, Ebonized, Gilt, Chinoiserie, Brass, Pierced Gallery, Adjustable Arm, 63 In. 998.00
Oil, Owl, Green Painted, Raspberry Eyes, 8 In. 460.00
Oil, Pattern Molded, Acanthus Leaf Font, Stem, Square, Stepped Base, Copper Collar, 11 1/8 In. .. 460.00
Oil, Pattern Molded, Emerald Green, Neck Rings, Baluster Stem, Footed, c.1860, 7 1/2 In. 450.00
Oil, Pattern Molded, Green Font, Flower Petal Band, Domed Top, Marble Base, 13 1/4 In. 230.00
Oil, Pink & White, Swirled Case, Clear Applied Feet, 5 In. 110.00
Oil, Porcelain, Blue & White, Hand Painted, Medallions, Japan, 1800s, 10 In. 176.00
Oil, Porcelain, Gilt Bronze, France, c.1860, 29 In., Pair 189.00
Oil, Porcelain, Polychrome, Bronze Mounted, England, c.1865, 6 1/2 x 8 1/2 In., Pair 370.00
Oil, S.P.B. & P.F. Co., Clear, Applied Handle, Finger, 2 3/4 In. 55.00
Oil, Tapered Side Reservoir, Octagon Stem, Square Base, Brass Burner, 9 x 3 1/2 In. 45.00
Oil, Vaseline Glass, Daisy & Band, Cut Crystal Pendants, Bronze, c.1890, 9 In. 230.00
Oil, Whale Oil, Clear, 8 Panels, Pewter Fitting, Applied Handle, Finger, 5 In. 165.00
Oil, White Cut To Clear Font, Flowers, Brass Stem, Cast Roses & Grapes, Marble, 15 1/2 In. 405.00
Oil, White Cut To Cranberry, Brass Frame, Grape, Leaf, Cut Prisms, 16 In. 1725.00
Oil, White, c.1840, 8 1/2 In., Pair 190.00
Oil, Yellow, Clear, Oval Reservoir, Brass Screw Top, 10 1/2 x 4 5/8 In. 155.00
Pairpoint lamps are in the Pairpoint category.
Perfume, Art Deco, Pink Porcelain, Lady With Gold Cup, Yellow Glass Ball, 7 In. 160.00
Perfume, Clear Glass, Black Over Milk Glass Top, Horse's Head, 3 3/4 In. 115.00
Perfume, Llasa Apso Shape, Black, White, Blue Eyes, Germany, 5 1/2 In. 46.00
Rush, Candleholder, Hardwood Base, 1700s, 10 In. 440.00
Rush Holder, Wrought Iron, Hinged, Round Counterweight, Wood Base, 18 In. 316.00
Rush Holder, Wrought Iron, Wood, Spring Gripper, Side Curved, Continental, 1700s, 31 In. 646.00
Sconce, 1-Light, Fontana Arte, Glass, Carved Leaf Design, 29 1/2 x 6 7/8 In., Pair 11642.00
Sconce, 1-Light, Oval Mirrored Back, Crimped Candle Cup, 12 1/2 In., Pair 3884.00
Sconce, 2-Light, Black Tole, Brass, Eagles, 14 1/2 In., Pair 176.00
Sconce, 2-Light, Bronze, Tapered Plinth, Cherubs, Wreath, Acanthus Leaf Arms, 16 x 11 1/2 In. ... 220.00
Sconce, 2-Light, Candle, Tin, Mirrored, Crimped Top, Line Decoration, 15 In. 415.00
Sconce, 2-Light, Cornucopia, Leaf, Fruit, c.1920-30, 20 x 14 x 9 In., Pair 248.00
Sconce, 2-Light, Gilt Brass, Regency Style, Crabstock Candlearms, 14 x 10 1/2 In. 881.00
Sconce, 2-Light, Louis XV Style, Gilt Bronze, Ram Horns, Electrified, 1900s, 14 1/2 In., Pair 1645.00
Sconce, 2-Light, Louis XV Style, Gilt Metal, Rocaille Acanthus Arms, 1900s, 16 In., Pair 2350.00
Sconce, 2-Light, Louis XVI Style, c.1885, 26 In., Pair 7800.00
Sconce, 2-Light, Louis XVI Style, Gilt Bronze, Flowers, 1800s, 14 x 8 In., Pair 1560.00
Sconce, 2-Light, Louis XVI Style, Ormolu, Late 19th Century, 17 x 8 In., Pair 415.00
Sconce, 2-Light, Neoclassical, Carved, Gilded, Eagle, Late 1800s, 26 In. 1765.00
Sconce, 2-Light, Rock Crystal, 12 1/2 In. 9600.00
Sconce, 2-Light, Rococo, Gilt Bronze, Mirrored, England, c.1850, 17 x 10 1/2 In., Pair 1528.00
Sconce, 2-Light, Tommi Parzinger, Brass, Starburst, Glass Beads, 19 x 14 In. 3835.00
Sconce, 2-Light, Tommi Parzinger, Chrome, Starburst, Glass Beads, 19 x 14 In. 3835.00
Sconce, 3-Light, Aesthetic Movement, Gilt Brass, Serpentine Arms, 12 x 10 x 12 In. 146.00
Sconce, 3-Light, Art Nouveau, Pulled Feather Lily Shades, Brown, Green Patina, 12 1/2 x 4 3/4 In. 345.00
Sconce, 3-Light, Brass, Baluster Backplate, Scrolling Arms, 15 1/4 In., 4 Piece 500.00
Sconce, 3-Light, Brass, Repousse, Northern Europe, Early 1800s, 32 In., Pair 3200.00
Sconce, 3-Light, French Provincial, Flower, Wheat Stocks, Gilt, 1900s, 26 x 13 In., Pair 1150.00

Sconce, 3-Light, Giltwood, Scrolled Metal Arms, 39 x 12 x 10 In. 1610.00
Sconce, 3-Light, Giltwood, Tassels & Garland Backplate, Continental, 26 x 14 In., Pair 1998.00
Sconce, 3-Light, Iron, Fleur-De-Lis Backplate, Scrolled Arms, Leaves, 24 x 16 In., 4 Piece 355.00
Sconce, 3-Light, Louis XIV Style, Gilt Metal, Late 19th Century, 14 In., Pair 649.00
Sconce, 3-Light, Louis XV Style, Gilt Bronze, Rocaille Backplate, Scrolled Arms, 13 3/4 In., Pair ... 235.00
Sconce, 3-Light, Louis XV Style, Gilt Bronze, Scrolled Backplate, Late 1800s, 24 1/2 In., Pair 1058.00
Sconce, 3-Light, Louis XV, Gilt Bronze, Leaf Scrolls, 25 1/2 x 14 1/2 In., 2 Pairs 2820.00
Sconce, 3-Light, Louis XVI Style, Bronze, 20 1/2 x 11 1/2 In., 4 Piece 649.00
Sconce, 3-Light, Louis XVI Style, Bronze, Gilt, Electrified, Early 1900s, 23 1/2 In., Pair 1058.00
Sconce, 3-Light, Rococo Style, Metal, Scrolling Arms, Leaves, 26 x 15 In., Pair 353.00
Sconce, 4-Light, Restauration Style, Cast Brass, Cut Glass, France, c.1915, 34 x 24 In., Pair 1880.00
Sconce, 4-Light, Winged Dragon, Bronze, On Shaped Board, 34 1/2 x 16 In. 2933.00
Sconce, 5-Light, Gilt Bronze, Louis XVI Style, Pendant Fruited Vine, 20 x 12 In., Pair 1410.00
Sconce, 5-Light, Giltwood, Swans, Baltic, Early 1800s, 23 1/2 x 17 In., Pair 10280.00
Sconce, 5-Light, Neoclassical, Patinated Metal, 18 1/2 x 34 In. 1170.00
Sconce, 7-Light, Brass, Scrolled Arms, Women Heads, Urn Finial, Electrified, 33 x 27 x 13 In. 546.00
Sconce, 7-Light, Gilt Brass, Louis XVI, Teardrops Prisms, 21 1/2 In., Pair 3525.00
Sconce, A.V. Mazzega, Cased Glass, Black, White, Italy, 9 1/2 x 14 x 4 1/2 In., Pair 885.00
Sconce, Art Deco, Wood, Painted, Frosted Glass Strips, 48 x 12 1/2 In. 3850.00
Sconce, Benedict Studios, Copper, Lantern, Heart Cutouts, Vaseline Glass, 17 x 19 In., Pair 4800.00
Sconce, Bronze, Patinated, Parcel Gilt Brass, Flambeau Shape, 10 1/2 x 5 1/4 In., 4 Piece 1880.00
Sconce, Candle, Brass, Swivel Arm, Ornate Back Plate, Victorian, 4 x 8 In., Pair 165.00
Sconce, Candle, Matte Green & Blue Drip, Rose Glaze 950.00
Sconce, Cast Bronze, Flowering Plum Tree, Gnarled Branches, Chinese, 38 x 16 In., Pair 2585.00
Sconce, Cast Iron, Bronze-Colored Plating, Jeweled Inserts, Flowers, 21 x 8 1/2 In., Pair 276.00
Sconce, Claycraft, Mission Scene, Matte Polychrome, Stamped, 15 x 5 1/2 In., Pair 1528.00
Sconce, Empire, Gilt, Ebonized, Mirror Backed, Flowers, France, 1800s, 17 3/4 x 10 1/4 In. 1234.00
Sconce, Louis XV Style, Gilt, c.1940, 22 x 11 x 6 1/2 In, Pair 1170.00
Sconce, Louis XVI Style, Bronze Dore, Ribbon, Flowers, Grapevine, 23 1/2 x 11 x 8 In., Pair 1725.00
Sconce, Lundberg, Glass, Hooked Feather Glass Shade, Green, Opal, Bronze, 5 3/4-In. Shade 115.00
Sconce, Neoclassical, Brass, Flower Form, Prisms, Russia, 1800, 23 1/4 In., Pair 940.00
Sconce, Serge Mouille, Aluminum, Enameled, Steel, Brass, France, 9 x 11 1/2 In., Pair 5460.00
Sconce, Tin, Circular Crest, Crimped Edges, Half-Moon Base, 7 1/4 x 2 1/8 In., Pair 138.00
Sconce, Tin, Crimped Circle Crest, Half-Moon Base, Electrified, 13 3/4 x 5 1/4 In. 55.00
Sconce, Tin, Crimped Top, Old Paint, 19th Century, 14 In. 200.00
Sconce, Tin, Diamond Shape, Painted, Crimped Back, 19th Century, 6 In. 300.00
Sconce, Tin, Embossed Flower Border, 19th Century, 16 In. 412.00
Sconce, Tin, Fan Crest, Punched, Reeded, Half-Moon Base, Black Paint, Electrified, 14 x 5 In. 110.00
Sconce, Tin, Mirror Back, 1800s, 10 In., Pair 259.00
Sconce, Tin, Punched, Round Candleholder, Drip Pan, 8 x 8 x 4 1/2 In. 28.00
Sconce, Tin, Scalloped Edges, Yellow Paint, Mirror Back, 24 1/2 In., Pair 478.00
Tiffany lamps are listed in the Tiffany category.
Torchere, Art Nouveau, Bronze, 20th Century, 51 x 18 x 18 In., Pair 1120.00
Torchere, Bronze Trumpet Shade, Wrought Iron, 3 Shaped & Scrolled Legs, 77 In., Pair 4995.00
Torchere, Bronze, Flaring Alabaster Shade, Scroll Foot Base, 71 x 19 In. 3070.00
Torchere, George II, Mahogany, Parcel Gilt, 31 x 11 3/4 In. 1800.00
Torchere, Giltwood, Tapered, Stop Fluted Standard, Leaf Carved Accent, 66 x 19 In. 940.00
Torchere, Roman Style, Bronze, Patinated, Paw Feet, Palmettes, Grand Tour, 61 x 16 In., Pair 12925.00
Whale Oil, Blown Font, Bulbous, Pressed Stepped Base, 1830-45, 7 In. 90.00
Whale Oil, Blown Font, Conical Shape, Applied Handle, 2-Tube Burner, Finger, 1820-40, 3 In. 358.00
Whale Oil, Blown Glass, Blue, White Opaque, Brass Wick Holder, Ribbed, Flared, 13 In. 242.00
Whale Oil, Blown Glass, Cone, Double Knop Stem, Ear Handle, c.1825, 5 1/2 In. 415.00
Whale Oil, Blown Glass, Frosted, Flower Bands, Cylindrical, Pewter Wick Holder, 6 7/8 In. 110.00
Whale Oil, Blown Glass, Oval, Pewter Screw Top, Square Base, 6 7/8 x 2 1/2 In. 60.00
Whale Oil, Blown, Compressed Ball Font, 4-Tube Burner, 1840-60, 6 1/2 In. 415.00
Whale Oil, Blown, Cone Font, Pressed Base, Circular Steps, 1828-35, 10 1/4 In. 230.00
Whale Oil, Blown, Squat Ball Font, Solid Stem, Brass Collar, 1840-60, 6 1/2 In. 65.00
Whale Oil, Blown, Squat Ball Font, Solid Stem, Pewter Collar, 1840-60, 5 3/4 In. 90.00
Whale Oil, Brass, Bell-Shape Font, Ribbed, Dolphin Handle, Saucer Base, 1800, 8 In., Pair 520.00
Whale Oil, Brass, Belted Ball-Shape Font, Baluster Shaft, Domed Base, c.1820, 8 1/2 In., Pair ... 1528.00

Whale Oil, Bulbous Pressed Glass Font, 4-Lobe Base, Interior Prisms, 1830-45, 6 3/4 In. 120.00
Whale Oil, Canary Yellow, Paneled, 1800s, 9 1/4 In. 430.00
Whale Oil, Clambroth, Fluted Column, Ribbed Font, Tube Burner, 2-Tiered Foot, 13 In. 460.00
Whale Oil, Clear Bulbous Font, Applied Knop Baluster, Pressed Base, c.1825, 6 In., Pair 275.00
Whale Oil, Clear, Cut Fonts, Drop Prisms, 1800s, 15 1/2 In., Pair 230.00
Whale Oil, Clear, Etched Globe, Engraved Reservoir, Hollow Baluster, 1825-35, 20 1/4 In. 468.00
Whale Oil, Cylindrical, Frosted, Flower Band, Square Base, Pewter Wick Holder, 6 1/2 x 2 3/4 In. ... 110.00
Whale Oil, Diamond Point & Fine Rib Panel, Brass Collar, 1850-70, 4 1/4 x 3 1/4 In. 90.00
Whale Oil, Diamond Point & Fine Rib, E.F. Jones Burner, Finger, 1850-70, 4 1/4 In. 468.00
Whale Oil, Egg Shape, Pewter Screw Top, Square Base, 6 7/8 x 2 1/2 In. 60.00
Whale Oil, Egg-Shaped Font, Brass, Cast, Turned, Portland, Me., 8 1/4 In. 1438.00
Whale Oil, Ellipse & Oval, 6-Sided Font, Pewter Collar, 2-Tube Burner, 1840-60, 6 1/2 In., Pair ... 308.00
Whale Oil, Flint Glass, Blown, Pressed, Stepped Base, 1800s, 7 1/2 In. 165.00
Whale Oil, Flint Glass, Pressed Sawtooth Pattern, 10 In. 138.00
Whale Oil, Glass Font, Funnel Foot, Triple Applied & Tooled Baluster, c.1825, 9 1/2 In. 1870.00
Whale Oil, Heart, Flowers, Thumbprints, Gilt, 2-Tube Burner, 1845-60, 8 1/4 In. 176.00
Whale Oil, Lined Panels, 6-Sided Font, Stem, 2-Tube Burner, 1840-50, 6 1/4 In. 99.00
Whale Oil, Lyre & Harp, Finger, Applied Handle, Brass Collar, 1840-70, 5 x 4 In. 415.00
Whale Oil, Moon & Star, Applied Handle, 6 In. 259.00
Whale Oil, Moon & Star, Brass Stem, Marble Base, 2-Tube Burner, 1850-60, 10 1/4 In. 230.00
Whale Oil, Moon & Star, Finger, Brass Collar, 1-Tube Burner, 1850-70, 3 1/8 In. 415.00
Whale Oil, Moon & Star, Finger, Brass Collar, Molded Handle, 1850-70, 4 3/8 x 3 3/8 In. 145.00
Whale Oil, Peg, Blown, Inverted Pyriform, Brass Collar, 2-Tube Burner, 1860-75, 9 In. 176.00
Whale Oil, Peg, Pattern Molded, Aquamarine, Compressed Globe, 1840-60, 3 1/2 x 2 3/4 In. 308.00
Whale Oil, Pressed Glass, Bigler, 8-Sided Stem, Pewter Collar, 2-Tube Burner, 11 5/8 In. 200.00
Whale Oil, Prism & Flattened Sawtooth, 6-Sided Base, Brass Collar, 2-Tube Burner, c.1850, 9 In. .. 209.00
Whale Oil, Prism Base, Brass Collar, Noyes Brass Burner, 1855-65, 6 1/4 In. 330.00
Whale Oil, Ring Punty, Black Base, Brass, 2-Tube Burner, 1860-75, 9 x 4 In. 165.00
Whale Oil, Sunken Circles, 3-Piece Mold Font, 2-Tube Burner, 1855-70, 6 1/2 In. 145.00
Whale Oil, Thomas Cains, Pressed Glass Base, Bulb Shape, c.1830, 8 In. 825.00
LAMPSHADE, Amber, Diamond Quilted, Fittings, 10 In. 150.00
Bull's-Eye, Red Satin 300.00
Consolidated, Reverse Painted, Blown, Oval, Grapes & Leaves, c.1910, 5 1/2 In. 59.00
Cranberry, Diamond Quilted, Fittings, 9 In. 500.00
Cranberry, Fittings, 8 1/2 In. 550.00
Leaded, Domed, Carmel Slag, Green Leaves, Red Grape Clusters, c.1905, 11 x 19 In. 550.00
Mother-Of-Pearl, Melon-Ribbed Green Glass, White Cased, Herringbone, 5 1/2 In. 24.00
Pink Satin, Fittings, 8 1/2 In. 500.00
Pink Satin, Fittings, 10 1/2 In. 1000.00
Stained Glass, Leaded, Irises, White & Caramel Ground, Lyn Hovey Studios, Mass., 7 x 15 In. 110.00
Vaseline, Opalescent, 8 x 6 3/4 In. 100.00

LANTERNS are a special type of lighting device. They have a light source, usually a candle, totally hidden inside the walls of the lantern. Light is seen through holes or glass sections.

Barn, Glass Reflectory, 1800s, 21 In. 104.00
Bicycle, Tin, Jos. Lucas & Son's, King Of The Road, Patented U.S.A., July 23rd 1889 .... 58.00
Bicycle, Tin, W.B. Brown's Rob Roy Safety Lamp 58.00
Candle, Pine & Birch, Mortised, Glass Panes, Hinged Door, Wire Handle, 14 1/4 In. 288.00
Carriage, Copper, Brass, Black Paint, Glass, Reflectors, Belgium, 1800s, 24 x 8 x 8 In., Pair 2350.00
Carriage, Kerosene, Glass, Davey & Co., England, Early 1900s, 14 1/4 x 7 1/2 In., Pair 295.00
Carriage, Tin, Glass, Painted Black, Triangular, Pierced Chimneys, Hinged, 12 In., Pair 382.00
Copper, Hammered, 6 Square Cutouts, Amber Glass, G. Stickley, 6 x 6 x 11 In. ....2115.00 to 2350.00
Copper, Hammered, Riveted Trellis Top, Overhand Cap, Yellow Glass, Stickley, 10 x 6 In. 2585.00
Dutch Indies Style, Glass Bell, 20th Century, 21 x 12 3/4 In. 470.00
Hall, 6-Light, Regency, Gilt Metal, 24 1/2 x 16 1/2 In. 7800.00
Hall, Blue Opaline Glass, Brass, Bell Shape, England, 1800s, 12 In. 765.00
Hall, French Provincial, Iron Strap Cage, Amber Glass Lining, Twist Chains, 49 x 19 In. 1762.00
Hall, Glass, Faceted Pendant, Gilding, France, c.1800, 34 x 14 In. 3290.00
Kerosene, Red Glass, Star, Brass Label, 11 1/2 x 19 In. 550.00

Oil, Brass, 20th Century, 12 x 5 x 5 In., Pair 47.00
Pewter, Tabletop, Magnifiers, 10 1/2 In. 468.00
Pierced Copper Cage, Green Glass Globe, Electrified, Helvic, N.Y., Pair 660.00
Skater's, Brass Frame, Clear Globe, 6 1/2 In. 90.00
Skater's, Brass, Chain, Ray Holder, 11 In. 235.00
Tin, 3 Spout Wick Tubes, Loop Lift-On Lid, Copper Swing Handle, 6 x 6 3/4 In. 145.00
Tin, Candle, Semicircular, Glass Pane Front, Hinged Door, Hanging Loop, 17 In. 175.00
Tin, Onion, Oil Burner, Pierced Top, Flared Base, Clear Globe, Swing Carry Handle, 11 In. 195.00
Tin, Pierced, Double Whale Oil Burner, Shaped Globe, Wire Glass Frame, 19th Century, 12 In. 255.00
Tin, Punched, Conical Top, Looped Handle, Hinged Door, Gold Paint, 8 1/2 x 3 3/4 In. 195.00
Tin, Semicircular, Candle Socket, Glass Pane Front, Hinged Door, Wire Handle, 12 In. 175.00
Wall, Wrought Iron, Painted, 6-Sided, Scrollwork Cage, Fleur-De-Lis, 45 x 14 In., Pair 1175.00

LE VERRE FRANCAIS is one of the many types of cameo glass made in France. The glass was made by the C. Schneider factory in Epinay-sur-Seine from 1918 to 1933. It is a mottled glass, usually decorated with floral designs, and bears the incised signature *Le Verre Francais*.

Atomizer, Stylized Flowers, Leaves, Tortoiseshell Glass, Frosted Yellow Ground, 6 1/2 In. 920.00
Lamp, Glass, Pomegranate Shade, Red Over Mottled Orange, Bronze Base, 11 1/2 In. 2235.00
Lamp, Orange, Marbleized Brown, Flowers, 19 3/4 In. 2830.00
Lamp, Stylized Leaves, Vines, Tortoiseshell Marbling, Orange Ground, 16 In. 3395.00
Lamp Base, Mottled, Yellow, Orange Trees, 5 1/4 In. 345.00
Vase, Art Deco Flower, Orange Ground, Footed, Flared Rim, 11 1/2 In. 1785.00
Vase, Blooms, Vines, Berries, Orange, Red, Brown, Yellow Ground, 13 5/8 In. 1955.00
Vase, Brown, Orange Flowers, Citron Mottled Ground, Art Deco, Signed, 12 3/4 In. 2245.00
Vase, Chestnuts, Dark Purple On Orange, Handles, Art Nouveau, 13 1/2 In. 1495.00
Vase, Decor Epinette, Ruby, Flowers, Mottled, Art Deco, 16 In. 2185.00
Vase, Decor Patura, Mottled Yellow & Orange, Brown, 15 3/4 In. 3105.00
Vase, Flowers, Branches, Orange, 1930, 19 In. 3020.00
Vase, Flowers, Stylized, Orange, Tortoiseshell Marbling, Yellow Mottled Ground, 17 3/4 In. 3395.00
Vase, Flowers, Vertical Bands, Orange, Mottled, c.1925, 17 1/4 In. 1508.00
Vase, Frosted To Yellow, Stylized Purple Flowers, Chalice Shape, 14 In. 2875.00
Vase, Fuchsia, Red Neck Shaded To Cobalt Blue Foot, 12 1/4 In. 3335.00
Vase, Globular, Art Deco Elements, Piarder, Acid Etched, c.1920, 4 1/2 In. 310.00
Vase, Money Plant, Mottled Orange, Peach Ground, Tapered, 15 In. 2760.00
Vase, Mottled Lavender & White, Amethyst Art Deco Flowers, Bulbous, 12 In. 2760.00
Vase, Mottled Maize, Orange Fuchsia, Bulbous, Purple Handles, 12 In. 3960.00
Vase, Mottled Peach, Peacock, Orange & Blue, Signed, 16 In. 3120.00
Vase, Mottled Rose, Flowers, Footed, Signed, 11 In. 2128.00
Vase, Mottled Yellow, Hollyhocks, Cobalt Blue, Orange, Bulbous Middle, Footed, 14 In. 2645.00
Vase, Mottled Yellow, Roses, Rectangular, 7 1/2 In. 805.00
Vase, Palm Tree, Yellow & Orange, Frosted Ground, Bulbous, 7 1/2 In. 3105.00
Vase, Red Freesia Fading Into Blue Foot, Chalice Shape, Art Deco, 15 1/4 In. 3335.00
Vase, Snails, Orange, Brown, Yellow Ground, Footed, 8 In. 1645.00
Vase, Trees, Stylized, Red & Orange, Peach & Yellow Ground, Bulbous, 11 In. 3360.00

LEATHER is tanned animal hide and it has been used to make decorative and useful objects for centuries. Leather objects must be carefully preserved with proper humidity and oiling or the leather will deteriorate and crack. This damage cannot be repaired.

Bucket, Armorial Design On Side, 10 x 14 x 12 In. 410.00
Carrying Case, Wells Fargo Express SF Cal., Double Loci 495.00
Cartridge Box, Brockton, Brass Letters, 1800s 495.00
Cartridge Case, 69 Caliber, Wood Interior, 24 Holes, c.1812, 2 1/2 x 7 1/2 x 4 1/2 In. 414.00
Child's Outfit, Pants, Jacket, Vest, Applied Scrolls, Bohemia, Early 1900s 25.00
Mail Pouch, Brass Studs, White Paint, Revolutionary War, 1776, 4 3/4 x 13 3/4 In. 708.00
Vessel, Incised, Fighting Scenes, Couple, Men, Oblong, Continental, 1800s, 8 1/2 x 9 In. 118.00
Wastebasket, 8-Sided, J. Adnet For Hermes, 1950s, 14 x 12 In. 1900.00

LEEDS pottery was made at Leeds, Yorkshire, England, from 1774 to 1878. Most Leeds ware was not marked. Early Leeds pieces had distinctive twisted handles with a greenish glaze on part of the creamy ware. Later ware often had blue borders on the creamy pottery. A Chicago company named Leeds made many Disney-inspired figurines. They are listed in the Disneyana category.

LEEDS POTTERY.

Creamer, Flowers, 4 Colors, 3 1/4 x 2 1/2 In. 193.00
Cup & Saucer, Flowers, Leaves, 3 Colors, Handleless, Pearlware 220.00
Cup & Saucer, Flowers, Leaves, 4 Colors, Handleless, Pearlware 110.00
Cup & Saucer, Yellow & Brown Flowers, Blue Rim, Soft Paste, 2 1/4-In. Cup, 5-In. Saucer 55.00
Cup Plate, Blue Edge, 4 1/2 In. 52.00
Cuspidor, Ladies, Blue Flowers, Funneled Top, Oversized Spout, Handle, Soft Paste, 4 In. 440.00
Match Holder, Green, 3 In. 86.00
Plate, Eagle, Spread Wings, Green Edge, Arrows, Olive Branch, Stars, Soft Paste, 8 In. 1100.00
Soup, Cream, Eagle, Shield Breast, Red, Blue Feather Edge, Soft Paste, 8 In. 825.00
Sugar, Leaves, Blue Band, Molded Lion & Ring Handles, Pearlware, 4 1/2 In. 248.00
Tray, Green, Oval, 11 1/2 In. 237.00

LEFTON is a mark found on pottery, porcelain, glass, and other wares imported by the Geo. Zoltan Lefton Company. The company began in 1941 and is still in business. It was restructured in 2002 and is now called the Lefton Company. The company mark has changed through the years; but because marks have been used for long periods of time, they are of little help in dating an object.

Ashtray, Candy Cane & Holly, 2 Holders, Marked, Foil Label, 3 3/4 In. 7.50
Ashtray, Hat, Red Sticker, 2 1/2 x 5 x 6 In. 55.00
Ashtray, White Holly, Christmas, 7 1/4 In. 30.00
Bank, Baby, 1950s, 7 1/4 In. 145.00
Bone Dish, Roses, Pink, Pastel Green Ground, Gold Trim, 6 1/2 In. 10.00
Bookends, White Poodles, Sitting On Books, 6 In. 59.00
Candleholder, Mr. & Mrs. Snowman, 4 1/8 In., Pair 25.00
Canister Set, Americana, 8 Piece 245.00
Coffeepot, Green Heritage, Rose, Gold Handle, 2 Piece 140.00
Compote, Holly, Berries, Footed, Gold Accents, 4 In. 25.00
Cookie Jar, Americana, Rose Finial, Handles, 7 x 6 3/8 In. 85.00
Cookie Jar, Miss Priss, Late 1960s, 7 1/4 In. 148.00
Figurine, Angel Girl, Holding 2 Red Hearts, Red Ribbon In Hair, 3 1/4 In. 18.00
Figurine, Goldfinch, 6 3/4 In. 26.00
Figurine, Rabbit, White, Marked Lefton & Japan, 4 x 4 1/2 In. 18.00
Figurine, Woman, Pink Dress, Bonnet, Spaghetti Decorations, Gold Trim, 6 In. 18.00
Gravy Boat, Attached Underplate, White Christmas, 9 In. 55.00
Head Vase, Woman, Hand To Face, Hat With Feather, Pink Rose At Neck, 7 1/2 In. 325.00
Jam Jar, Americana Regal Rose, Cover, Rosebud Finial, Spoon 20.00
Salad Set, Americana, Fork, Spoon, 9 1/2 In. 35.00
Salt & Pepper, Americana, Roses, 3 3/4 In. 75.00
Teapot, Stacking, Rose Chintz, Teapot, Creamer, Sugar, Cover, Strainer, Catch Basin, 6 Piece 250.00
Tidbit, 2 Tiers, Violet Chintz, 9 1/4 In. 125.00
Vase, Santa, In Chair, Bag, No. 2248 .... 15.00
Violet, Sugar & Creamer, Chintz, Serrated Gold Covers 85.00

LEGRAS was founded in 1864 by Auguste Legras at St. Denis, France. It is best known for cameo glass and enamel-decorated glass with Art Nouveau designs. Legras merged with Pantin in 1920 and became the Verreries et Cristalleries de St. Denis et de Pantin Reunies.

Vase, Amethyst Leaves, Vines, Chipped Ice Ground, Cameo, Signed, 10 In. 230.00
Vase, Blue & Gold Peacock, Green Oak Leaves, Acorns, Cameo, 8 In. 1438.00
Vase, Blue Peacock, Tricornered Rim, Cushion Foot, Cameo, c.1900, 16 1/4 In. 1315.00
Vase, Blue, Cranberry, Pheasants, Trees, Grass, Shouldered, Cameo, 7 In. 978.00
Vase, Enameled Cabin In Meadow, Woods, Orange, 14 3/4 In. 431.00
Vase, Enameled Lake Scene, Mountains, Trees, Clear, Pink Frosted, Cameo, 6 In. 489.00
Vase, Enameled Sheep On Hillside, Trees, Leaves, Signed, 10 In. 374.00
Vase, Enameled, Trees, Lake, Sailboats, Amber Ground, Signed, 16 In. 518.00
Vase, Fog Over River Valley, Tree, Marmalade Sky, Cameo, 5 7/8 In. 635.00
Vase, Mottled Blue, Yellow, Orange, Floral Medallions, Enameled, c.1920, 5 3/4 In. 411.00

Vase, Path, Trees, Pond, Cameo, c.1920, 11 In. 570.00
Vase, Wintery Landscape, Village, Mountain, Trees, Cameo, 4 1/4 In. 865.00

LENOX is the name of a porcelain maker. Walter Scott Lenox and Jonathan Cox founded the Ceramic Art Company in Trenton, New Jersey, in 1889. In 1906, Lenox left and started his own company called *Lenox*. The company makes a porcelain that is similar to Irish Belleek. Lenox was bought by Department 56 in 2005. The marks used by the firm have changed through the years and collectors prefer the earlier examples. Related pieces may also be listed in the Ceramic Art Co. category.

Bell, Holiday Gold, Holly, Berries, Gold Bands, Sculpted Handle, 5 1/2 x 3 1/4 In. 48.00
Bowl, Leaf Shape, Gold Rim, Green Lenox Mark, 1930s, 9 1/4 In. 130.00
Bowl, Serenade, Ivory, Flowers, Birds, 24K Gold Trim, 3 1/2 x 8 3/4 In. 85.00
Bowl, Vegetable, Plum Blossoms, Oval 180.00
Cake Plate, Footed, Holiday Gold, Holly, Berries, Gold Band, Scalloped, c.1974, 3 3/4 x 10 1/2 In. 175.00
Cup & Saucer, Footed, Lafayette 40.00
Demitasse Set, Vase Shape Coffeepot, Cerulean Blue, Gilt Trim, Belleek, 3 Piece 1645.00
Drink Set, Cylindrical Pitcher, Dragon-Form Handles, Gilt Trim, Belleek, 7 Piece 645.00
Mantel Clock, Quartz, Battery Operated, Fruits Of Life, 24K Gold Trim, 5 x 8 3/4 In. 30.00
Pitcher, Carolina, 24K Gold Trim, 7 1/2 In. 36.00
Plate, Dinner, Autumn, 10 1/2 In. 35.00
Plate, Salad, Priscilla, Blue Wreath Mark, 8 1/2 In. 12.00
Platter, Fairfield, Yellow Band, Blue & Pink Flowers, Platinum Rim, Gold Mark, 16 In. 85.00
Soup, Cream, Handles, Castle Garden, Gold Trim, 2 1/4 x 4 3/4 In. 60.00
Stein, Monk, Seated, Holding Up Glass, Painted, Green, Sterling Silver Lid Mounts, 1/2 Liter 350.00
Tea Strainer, Drip Stand, Porcelain, Handle, Hand Painted Violets, Gilding, 4 x 6 In. 250.00
Vase, Bud, Gourd Shape, Sterling Overlay Flowers, 6 1/2 In. 81.00
Vase, Bud, Ivory, Rose, Leaves, Gold Bands, Bulbous, Flared Neck, Green Mark, c.1930, 8 In. 49.00
Vase, Cylindrical, Blue Ground, Oriental Design, 9 1/2 x 4 3/4 In. 468.00

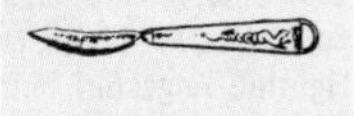

LETTER OPENERS have been used since the eighteenth century. Ivory and silver were favored by the well-to-do. In the late nineteenth century, the letter opener was popular as an advertising giveaway and many were made of metal or celluloid. Brass openers with figural handles were also popular.

African Face Handle, Ebony, 8 3/4 In. 4.00
Anaconda Mine, Butte, Montana, Copper 11.50
Eagle, Plane, Mountains, Gilded, Inscription, Leatherette Case, c.1918, 11 1/2 In. 1945.00
Elk Finial, Bear, Adirondack Mountains, Brass, 7 In. 20.00
Feather Shape Blade, Bird Handle, Silver, Gorham Attribution, c.1880, 6 1/2 In. 837.00
Fox Head Handle, Bronze, Austria, c.1900, 10 1/4 In. 130.00
Frog, Bronze, Kobe, Japan, 1900-20 .... 28.00
Indian, Headdress, Silver, Hammered Blade, Shepard Mfg., c.1900, 7 1/2 In. 448.00
Israel, Wailing Wall, Men Praying, Brass, 7 1/2 In. 13.00
Ivory Blade, Jasper Handle, Silver Mounts, Box, Austria-Hungary, c.1900, 11 1/2 In. 529.00
Montana, Treasure State, Helena, Butte, Metal, 6 1/4 In. 8.00
Mother-Of-Pearl Blade, Sterling Handle, F&B Mark, c.1900, 3 3/4 In. 50.00
Nude Woman Handle, Brass, 9 In. 103.00
Parrot, Metal, France, 8 In. 9.00
Rifle Shape, Iron, Gettysburg, 7 5/8 In. 10.00
Salesian Missions, Can You Take My Little Brother?, Elephants, On Card 11.00
Silver, Enamel, Ivory, Palmettes, Continental, 1830-40, 8 1/2 In. 176.00
Silver, Georg Jensen, Blossom Pattern, Box 190.00
Silver, Mother-Of-Pearl Handle, Art Nouveau, Victorian, 5 3/4 In. 82.00
Silver, Repousse Handle, S. Kirk & Son, 6 In. 50.00
Sword Shape, Norwich University, Scabbard, 9 1/2 In. 128.00
Sword Shape, Scrolls, Woman, Silver, Mixed Metal, R. Blackinton, c.1910, 8 In. 299.00
Sword Shape, Souvenir Of Havana, Cobra Head Handle, 7 1/2 In. 13.00
Thistle, Brass, Scotland, Art Nouveau, 1920s, 9 In. 57.00
Woman's Leg, Rhinestone Accents, Remembrance On Back, Plastic, 8 1/2 x 2 In. 68.00

LIBBEY Glass Company has made many types of glass since 1888, including the cut glass and tablewares that are collected today. The stemwares of the 1930s and 1940s are once again in style. The Toledo, Ohio, firm was purchased by Owens-Illinois in 1935 and is still working under the name Libbey Incorporated. Maize is listed in its own category.

Basket, Bull's-Eye Cutting, Engraved Flowers, Cut Handle, Signed, 12 x 9 3/4 In. 935.00
Basket, Engraved Floral & Bull's-Eye, Pattern Cut Handle, 12 1/2 x 10 In. 700.00
Bowl, Alternating Cut Starbursts & Ovals, 4 x 8 x 8 In. 147.00
Bowl, Amberina, Optic Ribbed, Flared, Scalloped Rim, Signed, 4 1/2 In. 805.00
Bowl, Ellsmere Cutting, 8 In. .... 375.00 to 715.00
Bowl, Flowers, Waffle Diamond Cutting, 3 1/2 x 8 1/4 In. 58.00
Candlestick, Teardrop Stem, Rayed Base, Signed, 10 1/2 In., Pair 415.00
Celery Dish, Ellsmere Cutting Variation, Rolled Rim, 2 3/4 x 11 3/4 x 5 1/2 In. 490.00
Champagne, Clear Bowl & Stem, Cranberry Egg Shape Knop, Nash, 1931, 5 1/2 In. 200.00
Compote, Amberina, Diamond Quilted, 8 In. 690.00
Compote, Hobstar, Prism, Strawberry Diamond & Fan Cutting, Teardrop Stem, 10 In. 660.00
Dish, Jelly, Hobstars, Prism Cutting, Reverse Sunburst Footed, 11 In. 460.00
Pitcher, Harvard Cutting, 5 1/2 In. 220.00
Punch Bowl, Ellsmere Cutting Variation, Center Hobnails, Notched, Signed, 9 x 14 In. 6050.00
Punch Bowl, Small & Large Hobstars Cutting, Notched Scalloped Edge, 7 x 14 In. 10450.00
Rose Bowl, Amberina, Coin Spot, Draped Rigaree, 3 Reeded Feet, 4 In. 1610.00
Tankard, Water, Hobstars, Fans Cutting, 9 x 6 In. 295.00
Tazza, Ozella Cutting, 5 1/2 x 8 In. 460.00
Tray, Ice Cream, Gloria Cutting, 7 1/2 x 14 In. 345.00
Tray, Thistle Cutting, Round, Scalloped Edge, Signed, 12 In. 770.00
Vase, Bud, Amberina, Optic Ribbed, Bottle Shape, Footed, 9 In. 720.00
Vase, Jack-In-The-Pulpit, Amberina, 7 1/4 In. 345.00
Vase, Stick, Amberina, Tapered, Signed, 8 3/4 In. 980.00
Vase, Trumpet, Colonna Cutting, 24-Point Hobstar Base, 24 In. 1540.00

LIGHTERS for cigarettes and cigars are collectible. Cigarettes became popular in the late nineteenth century, and with the cigarette came matches and cigarette lighters. All types of lighters are collected, from solid gold to the first of the recent disposable lighters. Most examples found were made after 1940. Some lighters may be found in the Jewelry category in this book.

Airplane, High Wing, Art Deco, Mono, 6 In. 66.00
Aluminum Crown Lighter Corp., Milwaukee, Wis. 40.00
Candle, Gas, Grapes, Leaves, Brass, c.1900, 14 x 6 In. 428.00
Cigar, Bradley & Hubbard, Oil Lamp, Cobalt Blue Shade, Glass Column, Victorian, Countertop 245.00
Cigar, Dominick & Haff, Silver, Hammered, Round Base, Sweeping Handle, c.1890, 3 In. 598.00
Cigar, Figural, Bulldog, Cast Iron, c.1930, 6 In. 325.00
Cigar, Gorham, Mixed Metal, Roman Lantern, Lion Mask Handle, c.1883, 2 x 4 3/4 x 3 In. 155.00
Cigar, Lamp Post, Hinged Lid, Cast Iron, Brass, 9 In. 120.00
Cigar, Teak, Welded Steel Wire, c.1970, 46 In. 65.00
Dunhill, Aquarium, Painted Scene, Glass Exterior, Silvered Mechanism, c.1930, 4 In. 1602.00
Landshut Bayern, Keg Shape, Germany, 2 x 1 5/8 In. 35.00
Ronson, Black Bartender, Bar, Touch Tip, 7 In. 2970.00
Ronson, Woman Bartender, Silver, Bar, Touch Tip, 7 1/2 In. 2970.00
Rouleet, Butane, Roulette Wheel In Front, Box, 1950s, 2 x 5/8 In. 50.00
Silver, Automobile Wheel, Fabric Wick, 1910, 4 1/2 In. 419.00

LIGHTNING ROD and lightning rod balls are collected. The glass balls were at the center of the rod that was attached to the roof of a house or barn to avoid lightning damage.

Arrow, Brass, Cast Iron, Blue Glass Ball, Early 1900s, 17-In. Arrow, 66 In. 105.00
Arrow, Green Glass, 4 In. 48.00
Arrow, Purple Glass Insert, Wavy Pattern, 19 In. 76.00
Brass, Spike, Roof Ridge Mount, 18 In. 41.00
Copper, Amethyst Glass Ball, Tripod Base, 70 In. 26.00

Finial, Twig Branch, 10 In. 49.00

Spear Finial, Spiral, Milk Glass Ball, 64 In. 90.00

Spear Finial, Tripod Base, 3-Footed, White Balls, 40 In. 27.00

Starburst Pattern, 6 1/2-In. Starburst, 14 In. 19.00

Tree Branch Finial, Tripod Base, 3-Footed, 70 1/2 In. 66.00

LIGHTING ROD BALL, 8-Sided, Light Green Glass, Aluminum Caps, 4 1/4 x 4 In. 76.00

Amethyst Glass, Moon & Star, Goshen Lightning Rod Co., c.1900, 5 In. ....55.00 to 69.00

Blue, Milk Glass, Round, Late 1800s, 5 In. 60.00

Blue Glass, Moon & Star, 5 In. 49.00

Blue Glass, Moon & Star, Goshen Design, 4 3/4 In. 75.00

Cobalt Blue, 4 7/8 In. 82.00

Diddie Blitzen, Cherry Red 179.00

Milk Glass, Round, 5 In. 55.00

Milk Glass, Starburst, Hawkeye, 5 x 4 1/2 In. 32.00

Milk Glass, White, 4 1/2 In. 26.00

Raised Quilt Design, Red, Kretzer, 5 3/4 x 16 In. 275.00

LIMOGES porcelain has been made in Limoges, France, since the mid-nineteenth century. Fine porcelains were made by many factories, including Haviland, Ahrenfeldt, Guerin, Pouyat, Elite, and others. Modern porcelains are being made at Limoges and the word *Limoges* as part of the mark is not an indication of age. Haviland, one of the Limoges factories, is listed as a separate category in this book.

Airplane, U.S. Navy, Hand Painted, Rochard, Box, 5 x 3 3/4 In. 88.00

Box, Eros, Flowers, Blue Celeste, Parcel Gilt, 2 x 4 x 4 In. 146.00

Bust, Boy, Girl, After Houdon, Bisque, C. Tharaud, France, 12 In., Pair 234.00

Drinking Set, Rabbits, Landscapes, Painted, Enamel Decorated, c.1900, 14 In. 1410.00

Ewer, Pinecone, Lavender Glaze, Shading To Blue, Gilded Handle, Spout, 10 In. 225.00

Figurine, Golfer, Yellow, 1920s, 10 1/2 In. 419.00

Jardiniere, Flowers, Lion Mask Handles, Footed, c.1900, 14 In. 205.00

Jewelry Box, Russian Egg Style, Cover, Brass Feet, 6 x 4 In. 99.00

Letter Press, Book Shape, Metal Frame, Painted, Putti, Flowers, 11 1/2 x 9 1/2 In. 140.00

Mug, Occupational, Fireman, Hand Painted, Horse Drawn Fire Wagon, 3 1/2 x 3 5/8 In. 605.00

Pitcher, Cider, T & V, Signed, 8 In. 525.00

Pitcher, Hand Painted, T & V, Signed, Josephine A. Worcester, c.1897, 14 3/4 In. 410.00

Plaque, Diana, Nude, Bow, Arrow, Enamel, Frame, Late 1800s, 11 x 8 1/4 In. 7200.00

Plaque, Mary & Baby Jesus, Hand Painted, Arts & Crafts, 1913, 18 In. 4406.00

Plaque, Nude Woman, Entering Pool, Hand Painted, Gilt Frame, c.1890, 14 3/4 x 12 In. 2629.00

Plaque, Woman In Red Dress, Enamel, 1900, 5 1/2 x 4 In. 374.00

Plate, Cherry, 8 In., Pair 110.00

Plate, Dinner, Lafayette, 18 Piece 878.00

Platter, JPL, 21 x 14 1/2 In. 400.00

Platter, Oval, 17 1/2 x 11 In. 70.00

Punch Bowl Set, Pedestal, Marked T & V, 6 Cups, 6 1/2 x 14 In. 1100.00

Service Plate Set, Floral Decorated Rim, Center, 11 In., 12 Piece 585.00

Sugar, A. Lanternier & Co., Hand Painted, c.1890, 5 3/4 x 8 In. 35.00

Tray, Game Bird Decoration, Hand Painted, Marked T & V, c.1900, 16 In. 82.00

Vase, 2 Women At Garden Staircase, Hand Painted, c.1900, 12 1/2 In. 322.00

Vase, Bee, Flowers, c.1900, 6 x 8 In. 176.00

Vase, Gilt Bronze Mounted, Parcel Gilt Mirror Back, Chinese Style, 26 x 12 In. 323.00

LINDBERGH was a national hero. In 1927, Charles Lindbergh, the aviator, became the first man to make a nonstop solo flight across the Atlantic Ocean. In 1932, his son was kidnapped and murdered, and Lindbergh was again the center of public interest. He died in 1974. All types of Lindbergh memorabilia are collected.

Ashtray, Ceramic, Our National Hero, Ceramic, Yellow 45.00

Banner, Welcome Capt. Lindbergh, Spirit Of St. Louis, Embroidered, 1927, 9 x 5 In. 776.00

Banner, Welcome Lindbergh, Orange Ground, Sackcloth, Frame, Late 1920s, 18 1/4 x 23 1/2 In... 1013.00

Bookends, Aviator, Iron, Connecticut Mfg. Co., 5 1/2 In. 92.00

Bookends, Cast Iron, 1930s 225.00

Bookends, Charles Lindbergh Bust, Aviator, Brass, Foundry Mark, 6 In. 63.00

Bust, King Of Air, Gold Color, 1927, 26 1/2 In. 353.00

Button, Colonel Chas. Plucky Lindbergh, Celluloid, 1 In. 30.00

Button, New York To Paris, American Flags, Spirit Of St. Louis, Celluloid, 1 3/4 In. 265.00

Button, Our Hero, Capt. Chas. A. Lindbergh, Celluloid, 1 In. 37.00

Button, Spirit Of St. Louis, Capt. Lindbergh, Celluloid, 1 1/4 In. 309.00

Candy Container, Airplane, Spirit Of St. Louis, Amber Glass, Original Closure 413.00

Clock, Sepia Ground, Germany, Late 1920s, 5 x 5 In. 419.00

Clock, Spirit Of St. Louis, Bakelite, Late 1920s, 3 1/4 x 10 1/4 In. 920.00

Decanter, Spirit Of St. Louis, Late 1920s, 14 x 13 1/4 In. 759.00

Hood Ornament, Head, Wings, Aluminum, c.1928, 8 1/2 x 5 1/2 In. 1767.00

Photograph, Autograph, Inscription, Underwood, Matte, Frame, 1927, 22 1/4 x 20 In. 4375.00

Plate, Portrait, Spirit Of St. Louis, Yellow Glaze, Sebring, Ohio, 1927, 9 In. 196.00

Postcard, Lindy In Plane, First Airmail To Panama, February, 1929 374.00

Radiator Neck Ornament, Spirit Of St. Louis, 5 48-Star Flags, c.1927 750.00

Sheet Music, He Said That He Would Do It & He Did!, 1927 18.00

Statue, Aviation, Athletic Man, Spirit Of St. Louis, Spelter, E. Jallet, 19 1/2 In. 1980.00

Stickpin, Spirit Of St. Louis, Silver Color 59.00

Tapestry, Portrait, Nose Of Plane, France, c.1927, 19 1/2 x 56 1/2 In. 949.00

Textile, Journey Scenes, Cotton, Burgundy, c.1927, 16 1/4 x 16 3/4 In. 255.00

Toy, Airplane, Lindy, Monoplane, Aluminum, Hubley, 4 1/2 In. 250.00

Vase, Spirit Of St. Louis, Glass, Pink, Etched, c.1927, 3 3/4 x 2 In. 427.00

Wagon, Lindy Flyer, Wood, Late 1920s, 36 1/4 x 15 1/2 x 15 1/4 In. 1058.00

LITHOPHANES are porcelain pictures made by casting clay in layers of various thicknesses. When a piece is held to the light, a picture of light and shadow is seen through it. Most lithophanes date from the 1825–1875 period. A few are still being made. Many lithophanes sold today were originally panels for lampshades.

Candle Light, 2-Panel, Children, Angel & Child, Cranberry Glass, Victorian, 3 1/2 x 3 In. 150.00

Candleholder, Bisque, Shepherd, Metal Stem, Germany, 7 1/2 x 6 1/8 In. 353.00

Lamp, Ecstasy, Maxfield Parrish, Metal Base, Post 1929, 9 1/2 x 5 In. 48.00

Lamp, Von Schierholz, Germany, 1817, 4 3 x 2 1/2-In. Panels, 17 1/2-In. Lamp 170.00

Lampshade, Nude Maidens, Mythological Figures, Dresden, 5 In. 27.00

Panel, Cottage, Hillside, Parian, ADC & Crown Mark, 6 x 4 In. 50.00

LIVERPOOL, England, has been the site of many pottery and porcelain factories since the eighteenth century. Color-decorated porcelains, transfer-printed earthenware, stoneware, basalt, figurines, and other wares were made. Sadler and Green made print-decorated wares from 1756. Many of the pieces were made for the American market and feature patriotic emblems, such as eagles, flags, and other special-interest motifs. Liverpool pitchers are always called Liverpool jugs by collectors.

Bottle, Flower & Leaf, Blue, White, Delftware, c.1750, 8 3/4 In. 764.00

Creamer, Washington, Lafayette, Verses, Eagle, Spread Wings, Square Handle, 5 In. 415.00

Jug, Bridge Cathedral, House, Fisherman, Black Transfer, Pearlware, 9 In. 805.00

Jug, Cream, Washington, His Country's Father, Verse, Transfer, 5 In. 415.00

Jug, George Washington, Union To People Of America, c.1790, 9 In. 7929.00

Jug, Hepsabeth Mannanship, Apotheosis Of Washington, Creamware, Early 1800s, 8 In. 2629.00

Jug, John Adams, Success To America, 1800s, 11 x 9 In. 12285.00

Jug, Joseph Babson, Peace Commerce & Friendship, Creamware, Early 1800s, 13 In. 3885.00

Jug, Masonic Emblem, Verse, Creamware, Early 1800s, 9 In. 717.00

Jug, Robert Fowler, Ship, 3 Transfers, 8 In. 4000.00

Jug, Ship Caroline, James Leech, Eagle, Shipwright's Arms, Black Transfers, 8 3/4 In. 290.00

Jug, Ship, Scene, Multicolored Enamel, Transfer Printed, Creamware, 1800s, 12 In. 5288.00

Jug, Success To America, Polychrome, Black Transfer, Oval, c.1802, 10 1/8 In. 3055.00

Jug, Thomas Jefferson, President Of United States, c.1807, 8 In. 12329.00

Jug, Washington & Independence, Ship, Presentation, c.1800, 10 1/2 In. 10925.00

Jug, Washington Being Lifted Into Heaven, Lady Liberty, Eagle, 10 3/4 In. 2010.00

Jug, Washington Being Lifted To Heaven, Apotheosis, 3 Black Transfers, 10 3/4 In. 2015.00

Jug, Washington In Glory, America In Tears, Creamware, Early 1800s, 10 In. .... 1910.00 to 2030.00
Jug, Washington Monument, Creamware, Early 1800s, 9 In. 1795.00
Jug, Washington Monument, Creamware, Early 1800s, 10 In. 1910.00
Mug, Peace Commerce & Honest Friendship, Creamware, Early 1800s, 4 3/4 In. 2868.00
Mug, Washington, Lady Liberty, Bring Freedom To America, Late 1700s, 5 3/4 In. 4427.00
Tankard, George Washington, Long Live The President Of The United States 6572.00

LLADRO is a Spanish porcelain. Juan, Jose, and Vicente Lladro opened a ceramics workshop in Almacera in 1951. They soon began making figurines in a distinctive, elongated style. In 1958 the factory moved to Tabernes Blanques, Spain. The company makes stoneware and porcelain figurines and vases in limited and unlimited editions. Dates given are first and last years of production.

LLADRÓ®

Figurine, Anniversary Waltz, Dancing Couple, No. 1372, 12 1/4 In. 176.00
Figurine, Chit Chat, Girl On Phone, No. 5466, 7 3/4 In. 70.00
Figurine, Courting Couple, 15 In. 293.00
Figurine, Don Quixote, Standing, No. 4854, 11 3/4 In. 140.00
Figurine, Dressing For Ballet, No. 5865, 9 1/2 In. 263.00
Figurine, Ducks Flapping, No. 4759 .... 242.00
Figurine, Familiar Rallye, Antique Car, Passengers, Dogs, Driver, No. 1146, 13 1/4 In. 2269.00
Figurine, Garden Breeze, No. 3583 .... 102.00
Figurine, Girl With Doll, No. 1083, 9 In. 205.00
Figurine, Japanese Girl Flower Decorating, No. 4840, 7 1/2 In. 117.00
Figurine, Jolie, No. 5210, 7 1/2 In. 82.00
Figurine, Little Pals, No. 7600, 8 3/4 In. 978.00
Figurine, Little Traveller, No. 7602, 8 1/2 In. 299.00
Figurine, Love In Bloom, No. 2304, 9 3/4 In. 176.00
Figurine, Mommy, It's Cold, No. 5715, 8 In. 176.00
Figurine, Phyllis, Seated Ballerina, No. 1356, 6 In. 140.00
Figurine, Rickshaw Ride, Stand, No. 1383, 12 In. 761.00
Figurine, School Days, No. 7604, 8 1/4 In. 140.00
Figurine, Seated Girl With Lamb & Dog, 9 In. 176.00
Figurine, Spring Bouquets, No. 7603, 8 1/4 In. 47.00
Figurine, Woman With Umbrella, No. 4805, 19 1/4 In. 380.00

LOETZ glass was made in many varieties. Johann Loetz bought a glassworks in Austria in 1840. He died in 1848 and his widow ran the company; then in 1879, his grandson took over. Most collectors recognize the iridescent gold glass similar to Tiffany, but many other types were made. The firm closed during World War II.

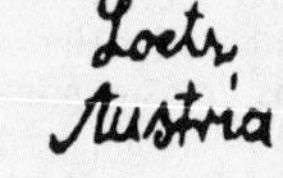

Bowl, Crackle, Blue Iridescent, Green, Cobalt Blue Ground, Ruffled Edge, 3 1/2 In. 115.00
Bowl, Crackle, Translucent, Applied Amber Handles, 13 x 5 1/4 In. 460.00
Bowl, Oil Spot, Gold Iridescent, Ruffled Edge, 2 Reeded Handles, 4 1/2 In. 510.00
Bowl, Oil Spot, Green, 4 1/4 x 6 1/4 In. 225.00
Bowl, Oil Spot, Purple Iridescent, Ruffled Edge, 9 In. 230.00
Box, Cover, Flowers, Leaves, 3 Applied Glass Feet, Cameo, Signed, 5 In. 546.00
Box, Cover, Oil Spot, Enameled, Leaves, Peacock, Poppies, c.1900, 2 3/4 x 5 1/2 In. 956.00
Box, Cover, Yellow Iridescent, Round, Brass Mount, Fire-Polished, c.1900, 5 In. 239.00
Compote, Oil Spot, Cranberry, Bronze Figural Woman Base, 19 In. 690.00
Console, Green Iridescent, Ribbed, Swirled, Ruffled Edge, Brass Footed Base, 12 In. 360.00
Inkwell, Bulbous, Green & Red Threading, Brass Cover, c.1900, 3 1/4 In. 390.00
Inkwell, Quatrefoil, Iridescent, Threading, Square Foot, Bronze Cover, c.1900, 3 1/2 In. 715.00
Lamp, Beehive, Orange Spiral Glass Shade, Arts & Crafts Metal Base, c.1900, 15 In. 598.00
Lamp, Silver Plated Brass Base, Dome Glass Shade, Dimples, Green Threads, c.1900, 15 3/4 In. .. 568.00
Shade, Pulled Feather, Ruby Threading, Ruffled Edge, c.1900, 5 In. 114.00
Shade, Pulled Hearts & Vine, Red Pulled Feather, Ruffled Edge, c.1900, 5 1/2 In. 265.00
Vase, Amber Iridescent Waves, Opalescent, c.1900, 6 1/4 In. 754.00
Vase, Amber Iridescent, Blue Trails, Red & Silver Tendrils, c.1900, 4 In. 3959.00
Vase, Amber Iridescent, Silver Overlay, Orchids, Leaves, c.1900, 4 1/4 In. 320.00
Vase, Amber, Applied Iridescent Gold Loopings & Dots, Tapered, Ruffled Edge, 9 In. 660.00

Vase, Amber, Gold Iridescent, Purple Highlights, Squat, Dimpled, 3 1/2 In. 805.00
Vase, Amber, Undulating Trails, Flared & Rolled Rim, Baluster, c.1900, 6 1/4 In. 1795.00
Vase, Amethyst Iridescent, Pulled Feather, 3 1/2 In. 935.00
Vase, Astra, Gold Iridescent, Pinched Sides, Bottle Shape, 4 3/4 In. 175.00
Vase, Black Amethyst, Pulled Loops, Handles, 10 1/2 In. 690.00
Vase, Blue Iridescent, Amber Ground, Silver Overlay, Leaves, Stems, 6 In. 3450.00
Vase, Blue Iridescent, Draped Loops, Copper Iridescent Ground, 5 1/8 In. 1495.00
Vase, Blue Iridescent, Platinum Waves, Red, Amber Foot, 12 1/4 In. 2875.00
Vase, Candia Phanomen, Amber Iridescent, Blue Green, Cylindrical, 6 In. 1725.00
Vase, Clambroth Iridescent, Ribbed, Applied Glass Base, 5 Pulled Feet, 5 In. 570.00
Vase, Clear, Bubbles, Applied Iridescent Blue Cattail, Leaves & Ruffled Foot, 6 3/4 x 8 3/4 In. 660.00
Vase, Cobalt Blue Iridescent, Textured, Medallion, Blue Stylized Flowers, Stems, 5 In. 86.00
Vase, Cobalt Blue, Applied Tendrils, Tapered, Flared, 8 1/2 In. 1295.00
Vase, Fan, Oil Spot, 7 Finger, Blue Iridescent, Papillon, c.1899, 9 1/4 In. 2015.00
Vase, Federzeichnung, Brown, Ivory Swirls, Gilt Curl Pattern, Baluster, c.1900, 9 1/2 In. 2365.00
Vase, Gold Iridescent Waves, Platinum, Egg Shape, Petal Top, Rolled Rim, 8 1/2 In. 480.00
Vase, Gold Iridescent Waves, Silver Overlay Flowers, Vines, Signed, 6 In. 3450.00
Vase, Gold Iridescent, Bulbous Top, Dimpled, Cylindrical Base, c.1900, 9 1/2 In. 1135.00
Vase, Gold Iridescent, Egg Shape, Rolled Rim, c.1900, 5 1/2 In. 179.00
Vase, Gold Iridescent, Engraved, Poppies, Stems, Silver Overlay, 4 In. 2185.00
Vase, Gold Iridescent, Figural Pig, Applied Ear, Legs, 5 1/4 x 9 1/2 In. 1150.00
Vase, Gold Iridescent, Figural, Fish Head, Blue & Magenta Highlights, c.1900, 5 1/4 In. 657.00
Vase, Gold Iridescent, Tricornered, Rolled Rim, 3 Flower Medallions, 8 3/4 In. 518.00
Vase, Green Iridescent, Blue Diaspora, Pinched Side, 4 In. 175.00
Vase, Green Iridescent, Blue, Blown Into Metal Frame, Art Nouveau, 14 1/2 In. 960.00
Vase, Green Iridescent, Diamond Quilted, Applied Metal Collar, 7 In. 175.00
Vase, Green Iridescent, Fish Scale, Embossed Bronze Frame, Grapes, Leaves, 6 1/2 In. 230.00
Vase, Green Iridescent, Folded Sides, Clear Handle, 19 1/2 In. 59.00
Vase, Green Iridescent, Rust & Cream Waves, Flared Rim, Footed, 10 In. 1495.00
Vase, Green Stylized Venus Flytrap, Gold Iridescent Silver, Free-Form Foot, Stem, 8 In. 1095.00
Vase, Green, Purple & Blue Swirling Iridescent, Silver Overlay, Iris, 6 In. 2645.00
Vase, Green, Red, White, Iridescent, Bulbous, Cylindrical Neck, Flared Rim, c.1900, 10 In. 325.00
Vase, Marmorierte, Red, Gray, Brass 3-Footed Stand, 9 In. 405.00
Vase, Medici, Oil Spot, Amethyst Iridescent, Tricornered Rim, 8 In. 805.00
Vase, Multicolored Iridescent Ribbons, Triangular, Pinched Corners, 10 In. 115.00
Vase, Oil Spot, Amber Iridescent, Blue Undulating Band, Bulbous, Flaring Rim, c.1900, 6 1/2 In. ... 1555.00
Vase, Oil Spot, Blue Over Bronze Iridescent, Bulbous, 6 1/4 In. 400.00
Vase, Oil Spot, Blue, Applied Iridescent Handles, Art Nouveau, 7 1/2 In. 1058.00
Vase, Oil Spot, Blue, Gold Iridescent, Handles, Squat, 2 In. 200.00
Vase, Oil Spot, Blue, Green Iridescent, Ruffled Edge, Metal Dolphin Base, 3-Footed, 7 1/2 In. 115.00
Vase, Oil Spot, Gold, Amber Iridescent, Blue Highlights, Cylindrical, 9 1/2 In. 230.00
Vase, Oil Spot, Platinum, Gold Iridescent, Tree Trunk Shape, 5 1/2 x 6 1/2 In. 690.00
Vase, Opalescent, Green Tint, Wide Ruffled Edge, 2 1/2 x 5 1/2 In. 60.00
Vase, Pampas, Applied Sterling Silver Overlay, Art Nouveau, 4 In. 1680.00
Vase, Pearl Iridescent, Pulled Salmon, Silvery Blue Trails, Silver Overlay, 4 5/8 In. 2070.00
Vase, Phanomen, Gold Iridescent, Short Neck, Cylindrical Body, Flared Rim, c.1900, 6 In. 1076.00
Vase, Phanomen, Orange Iridescent, Bulbous Base, Tapered Top, 11 1/2 In. 1320.00
Vase, Phanomen, Scalloped Edge, Blue Iridescent, Green, Baluster, c.1900, 11 3/4 In. 1135.00
Vase, Platinum Iridescent Waves, Green Transparent Ground, 9 In. 230.00
Vase, Purple Flowers, Custard Ground, Cameo, 5 3/8 In. 489.00
Vase, Red Over Amber, Enameled Stylized Flowers, Stems, Leaves, Cameo, 9 1/2 In. 690.00
Vase, Rusticana, Green Iridescent, Pinched Sides, Tricornered, 5 In. 86.00
Vase, Salmon Iridescent, Blue, Green, Magenta, Pulled Feather, Double Gourd, c.1900, 4 1/4 In. . 1315.00
Vase, Seafoam, Waves, Green Iridescent, Rolled Rim, Egg Shape, c.1900, 8 1/4 In. 1435.00
Vase, Silver Flower Overlay, Quatrefoil Ruffled Edge, Baluster, c.1900, 11 1/4 In. 1315.00
Vase, Silver, Green Iridescent, Luminescent Red, Flame Shaped Fingers, 5 1/2 In. 2475.00
Vase, Titania, Green Ground, Paperweight, 6 3/4 In. 2070.00
Vase, Translucent Iridescent, Applied Amber Drips, Pads, Chipped Ice, Applied Rim, 7 1/4 x 8 In. ... 460.00
Vase, Trumpet, Enameled Flowers, Orange Ground, Brown, 6-Sided, c.1900, 9 1/4 In. 657.00
Vase, Trumpet, Gold Iridescent, Hooked & Pulled Design, Bulbous, c.1900, 6 3/4 In. 996.00
Vase, White Iridescent, Lily Shape, c.1900, 9 1/4 In. 259.00

Lone Ranger, Display, Merita Bread, Lone Ranger Safety Club, Cardboard, 25 1/2 x 16 In.

Lone Ranger, Doll, Composition Head, Stuffed Body, Dollcraft Novelty Co., 1938, 15 1/2 In.

Lone Ranger, Toy, Bat-O-Ball, Pure Oil Co., 1939, 9 3/4 x 4 3/4 In.

LONE RANGER, a fictional character, was introduced on the radio in 1932. Over three thousand shows were produced before the series ended in 1954. In 1938, the first Lone Ranger movie was made. Television shows were started in 1949 and are still seen on some stations. The Lone Ranger appears on many products and was even the name of a restaurant chain for several years.

Bullet, Silver, Secret Compartment, Kix, 1940s, 1 1/4 In. 40.00
Button, Ad, May Co., Horseshoe Rim, 1 1/4 In. 28.00
Cap Gun, Hi-Yo Silver, Cast Iron, Nickel Finish, Plastic Grip, Kilgore, 1938, 8 1/4 In. 207.00
Display, Merita Bread, Lone Ranger Safety Club, Cardboard, 25 1/2 x 16 In. .... *ILLUS* 1000.00
Doll, Composition Head, Stuffed Body, Dollcraft Novelty Co., 1938, 15 1/2 In. .... *ILLUS* 818.00
Doll, Composition, Mask, Removable Hat, Dollcraft Novelty Co., 10 1/2 In. .... 750.00 to 1667.00
Doll, Lone Ranger, Composition, Dollcraft Novelty Co., Box, 1938, 20 In. 800.00
Doll, Tonto, Composition, Dollcraft Novelty Co., Box, 1938, 20 In. 800.00
Figurine, Lone Ranger On Silver, Chalkware, 11 In. 100.00
First Aid Kit, American White Cross Labs Inc., 24 Page Guide, 1938, 4 x 4 In. 155.00
Game, Lone Ranger Chase, Instructions, Peter Pan, Box, England, 1950s, 10 x 19 In. 230.00
Game, Ludo, Peter Pan, England, 1959, 7 1/2 x 16 In. 110.00
Game, Target, Gun, Marx, Box, 1946, 17 1/2 In. 504.00
Headband, Tonto, Hi-Yo Silver, Fabric, Feather, 1939, 1 3/4 x 16 In. 110.00
Pencil Box, American Lead Pencil Co., 1930s, 4 x 9 In. 110.00
Poster, Masked Idol Of Millions, Chicago Herald, Sept. 11, 1938, 21 1/2 x 16 1/2 In. 661.00
Radio, Lone Ranger On Silver, White, Red, Black, Lights Up, Plastic, Airline, c.1940, 6 x 7 x 5 In. .. 9620.00
Rifle, Click, Telescopic Sight, Plastic, Marx, Box, 1950s, 5 1/4 x 25 In. 405.00
Ring, Kix Atomic Bomb, Kix, Instructions, Box, 1947, 2 1/2 x 1 1/4 In. 246.00
Ring, Movie Film, 1949, 1 1/4 Opens To 2 In. 69.00
Ring, Six Gun, General Mills, Box, Insert, 1947, 2 1/4 In. 640.00
Ring, Weather Forecasting, Brass, Plastic, Mailer, 1946, 4 x 5 1/2 In. 168.00
Sign, Merita Bread, Tin Lithograph, Embossed, 1940s, 36 In. 550.00
Toy, Bat-O-Ball, Pure Oil Co., 1939, 9 3/4 x 4 3/4 In. .... *ILLUS* 333.00
Toy, Hi-Yo Silver, Ranger On Rearing Horse, Lasso, Marx, Box, 1938, 7 1/2 In. 495.00
Toy, Range Rider, Tin, Windup, Marx, 1938, 9 1/2 In. 275.00

LONGWY Workshop of Longwy, France, first made ceramic wares in 1798. The workshop is still in business. Most of the ceramic pieces found today are glazed with many colors to resemble cloisonne or other enameled metal. Many pieces were made with stylized figures and Art Deco designs. The factory used a variety of marks.

Bowl, Flower & Leaf Bands, 3 Stepped Feet, c.1930, 8 1/2 In. 226.00
Bowl, Flowers, Leaves, Berries, Footed, c.1930, 8 In. 150.00
Bowl, Woman Picking Fruit, Yellow Border, Art Deco, Pomone Bon Marche, 1925, 8 In. 1100.00
Charger, Primavera, 2 Ladies, Deer, Marked, 15 In. 1555.00
Charger, Renaissance, Triangular, Turquoise, Crackled, M.P. Chevallier, 1951-62, 10 1/2 In. 395.00

Tile, Large Cartouche, Birds Over Pond Flower Border, Turquoise Ground, Square, 8 In. 150.00
Trivet, Bird, Flowers, Blue Ground, Enameled, Padded Feet, 8-Sided, 10 In. 395.00
Trivet, Brass, Tile, Serpent Handles, Mosaic Style, 8 1/2 x 11 In. 280.00
Vase, Pink & Green Flowers, White Ground, Bulbous Base, 1880s, 10 In., Pair 3500.00
Vase, Swirled Stripes Of Flowers, Blue, White, 9 3/4 In. 295.00

LOTUS WARE was made by the Knowles, Taylor & Knowles Company of East Liverpool, Ohio, from 1890 to 1900. Lotus Ware, a thin porcelain that resembles Belleek, was sometimes decorated outside the factory.

Bowl, Columbia, Purple Applied Flowers, Beaded & Ruffled Rim, 1891-96, 4 1/2 x 5 In. 525.00
Jar, White, Diagonal Leaf Like Pattern, c.1890, 5 1/4 x 5 1/4 In. 449.00
Tray, Shell Shape, Berries, Leaves, Thorny Stems, Signed, W.W., 8 1/2 x 8 3/4 In. 500.00
Tray, Shell Shape, Hand Painted Flowers, Marked, 8 3/4 In. 500.00
Vase, Columbia, Applied Flowers, Pink, Yellow, Blue, White Ground, 4 1/2 In. 400.00

LOW art tiles were made by the J. and J. G. Low Art Tile Works of Chelsea, Massachusetts, from 1877 to 1902. A variety of art and other tiles were made. Some of the tiles were made by a process called *natural*, some were hand modeled, and some were made mechanically.

J.&J.G.LOW

Tile, Autumn, Woman With Flowing Hair, Teal Green, 6 1/4 x 4 1/2 In. 158.00
Tile, Colonial Man, Golden Yellow Glaze, Dated, 1885, 7 x 5 In. 200.00
Tile, Cordelia, Classical Woman, Verse, Teal Blue, 8 1/4 x 4 3/4 In. 100.00
Tile, Flowers, Light & Dark Brown, 6 x 2 1/8 In. 76.00
Tile, Flowers, Maroon, Square, c.1883, 4 3/8 In. 25.00
Tile, Man Wearing Cape, Holding Staff, Carrying Bundle Of Sticks On Back, 8 1/4 x 4 3/4 In. 400.00
Tile, Summer, Grecian Man, Turquoise, 6 x 4 In. 260.00
Tile, Victorian Woman, Blue Glaze, Dated, 1885, 7 x 5 In. 200.00

LUNCH BOXES and lunch pails have been used to carry lunches to school or work since the nineteenth century. Today, most collectors want either early tobacco advertising boxes or children's lunch boxes made since the 1930s. These boxes are made of metal or plastic. Boxes listed here include the original Thermos bottle inside the box unless otherwise indicated. Movie, television, and cartoon characters may be found in their own categories. Tobacco tin pails and lunch boxes are listed in the Advertising category.

LUNCH BOX, Alvin & Chipmunks, Vinyl, King Seeley Thermos Co., 1963, 4 x 7 x 9 In. 336.00
Animal Crackers, Iten Biscuit Co., Tindeco, 2 3/8 x 4 5/8 In. 330.00
Battle Kit, Metal, King Seeley Thermos Co., 1965-66 .... 125.00
Bobby Sherman, Metal, No Thermos, King Seeley Thermos Co., 1972 .... 28.00
Bozo The Clown, Dome Top, Metal, Aladdin, 1963 .... 28.00 to 81.00
Bugaloos, Metal, No Thermos, Aladdin, 1971 .... 39.00
Bullwinkle & Rocky, Universal, 1962 .... 760.00
Casey Jones, Dome Top, Metal, Universal, 1960 .... 190.00
Charlie's Angels, Brunchbag, Blue, Zipper, Tag, Unused, Aladdin, 1978 .... 80.00
Chinese Pandas, Hsing-Hsing & Ling-Ling, Vinyl, Travel Toy, 1972, 7 x 9 In. .... *ILLUS* 1000.00
Chuck Wagon, Cowboy Making Breakfast, Vinyl, Mattel, No Thermos, 1967, 7 x 8 3/4 x 4 In. 2645.00
Doctor Doolittle, Metal, Aladdin, 1968 .... 340.00
Dr. Seuss, Cat In Hat, Vinyl, Blue, Aladdin, 1970 .... 128.00
Dudley Do-Right, Metal, Universal, 1962 .... 760.00
Dukes Of Hazzard, Metal, Aladdin, 1980, 3 3/4 x 8 x 7 In. .... 24.00 to 40.00
Dutch Cottage, Dome Top, Steel, American Thermos Bottle Co., c.1958 .... 224.00
Emergency, Metal, No Thermos, Aladdin, 1973 .... 57.00
Family Affair, Metal, King Seeley Thermos Co., 1969-70 .... 40.00
Green Hornet, Metal, King Seeley Thermos Co., c.1967 .... 285.00
Gremlins, Metal, Aladdin, 1984 .... 30.00
Grizzly Adams, Dome Top, Metal, No Thermos, Aladdin, 1977 .... 40.00
Hair Bear Bunch, King Seeley Thermos Co., 1972-73 .... 95.00
Hogan's Heroes, Prisoner Barracks, Metal, Dome, Aladdin, 1966, 7 x 9 In. .... *ILLUS* 400.00
Holly Hobbie, Metal, American Greetings Corporation, Aladdin, c.1979 .... 30.00

Lunch Box, Chinese Pandas, Hsing-Hsing & Ling-Ling, Vinyl, Travel Toy, 1972, 7 x 9 In.

Lunch Box, Hogan's Heroes, Prisoner Barracks, Metal, Dome, Aladdin, 1966, 7 x 9 In.

Lunch Box, Nancy Drew Mysteries, Plastic, King Seeley, Universal, 1977, 7 1/2 x 8 3/4 In.

Huckleberry Hound, Metal, Aladdin, 1961 .... 180.00
Jetsons, Dome Top, Metal, Aladdin, 1963 .... 1830.00
Joe Palooka, Tin, Removable Lid, Continental Can, 7 x 4 In. .... 115.00 to 196.00
King Kong, Metal, Tag, King Seeley Thermos Co., 1977 .... 100.00
KISS, Metal, No Thermos, King Seeley Thermos Co., 1977 .... 75.00
Knight Rider, Universal City Studios, King Seeley Thermos Co., 1984-85 .... 55.00
Kung Fu, Metal, King Seeley Thermos Co., 1974 .... 26.00
Liddle Kiddles, Vinyl, King Seeley Thermos Co., c.1969, 4 x 7 x 9 In. 196.00
Lidsville, Metal, Aladdin, 1971, 4 x 7 x 8 In. 196.00
Lost In Space, Dome Top, Steel, King Seeley Thermos Co., 1967 .... 225.00
Mam'zelle, Vinyl, Aladdin, 1970-71 .... 105.00
Mike Mercury's Supercar Orbital Food Container, Metal, Universal, 1962 .... 475.00
Miss America, Metal, No Thermos, Aladdin, 1972 .... 24.00
Monkees, Vinyl, King Seeley Thermos Co., 1967 .... 615.00
Munsters, Munstermobile, King Seeley Thermos Co., 1965 .... 112.00 to 535.00
Nancy Drew Mysteries, Plastic, King Seeley, Universal, 1977, 7 1/2 x 8 3/4 In. .... *ILLUS* 131.00
New Zoo Revue, Vinyl, Aladdin, 1970s, 4 x 7 x 8 3/4 In. 420.00
Paladin, Have Gun Will Travel, Metal, Aladdin, 1960 .... 115.00
Peanuts, Vinyl, Comic Strip, King Seeley Thermos Co., Red, 1967-68 .... 120.00
Pebbles & Bamm-Bamm, Vinyl, Gary, 1978, 3 1/2 x 7 1/4 x 8 3/4 In. 225.00
Plaid, Metal, American Thermos Bottle Co., 1960 .... 95.00
Polly's Picture Party, Children, Flicker Image, Blue, Vinyl, No Thermos, 1960, 7 x 9 x 3 In. 2300.00
Psychedelic, Dome Top, Steel, Aladdin, c.1969 .... 170.00
Rifleman, Metal, Aladdin, 1961, 4 x 7 x 8 In. 430.00
Rifleman, No Thermos, Aladdin, 1960 .... 76.00 to 128.00
Road Runner, Metal, No Thermos, King Seeley Thermos Co., 1970 .... 40.00
Sabrina, Vinyl, Yellow, No Thermos, 1972 .... 70.00
Scooby Doo, Metal, King Seeley Thermos Co., 1973-76 .... 148.00
Secret Of NIMH, Metal, Aladdin, 1982 .... 50.00
Service Station, Dome, Vinyl, Gas Pumps, Mechanic, Cars, 1960s, 7 x 9 In. 450.00
Sesame Street, Green Rim, Tag, Unused, Aladdin, 1979 .... 50.00
Smokey The Bear, Vinyl, King Seeley Thermos Co., 1965-66 .... 400.00
Strawberry Shortcake, Metal, Aladdin, 1980 .... 25.00
Tarzan, Metal, No Thermos, Aladdin, 1966 .... 40.00
Tom Corbett Space Cadet, Metal, Aladdin, 1954 .... 128.00
Underdog, Metal, Okay Industries, 1974 .... 610.00
VW Bus, Dome Top, Tin, Plastic, Omni Graphics, 1960s, 10 In. 500.00
Wagon Train, Metal, No Thermos, King Seeley Thermos Co., 1964 .... 158.00
Wonder Woman, Vinyl, Yellow, No Thermos, Aladdin, 1978, 9 In. 40.00
LUNCH BOX THERMOS, Alvin & Chipmunks, Red Cup, King Seeley Thermos Co., 1963, 10 Oz., 8 In. 19.50
Barbie, Campus Queen, King Seeley Thermos Co., 1967 .... 65.00
Blondie, Blue Cup, King Seeley Thermos Co., 1969, 8 Oz., 6 1/2 In. 12.86
Flintstones, Black Cup, Aladdin, 1/2 Pt., 6 1/2 In. 9.00

Fonz, Red Cup, Paramount, 1976, 9 3/4 x 3 1/8 In. 39.00
Globe Trotter, Red Cup, Big Ben, Pyramids, Taj Mahal, Aladdin, 1959, 6 1/2 In. 20.60
Hot Wheels, Metal, King Seeley Thermos Co., 1968 .... 7.16
Munsters, Red Cup, King Seeley Thermos Co., 1965, 7 1/2 In. 33.00
Partridge Family, King Seeley Thermos Co., 1971, 1/2 Pt., 6 1/2 In. 13.50
Treasure Chest Map, Yellow Cup, Aladdin, 1961, 1/2 Pt., 6 1/2 In. 15.50

LUNEVILLE, a French faience factory, was established about 1730 by Jacques Chambrette. It is best known for its fine biscuit figures and groups and for large faience dogs and lions. The early pieces were unmarked. The firm was acquired by Keller and Guerin and is still working.

Charger, Flower Bouquet, Butterfly, Insects, 13 In. 2750.00
Soup, Dish, Flowers & Leaves, Blue & Yellow Bands, Flow Blue Mark, 1 3/4 x 9 In., 6 Piece 175.00
Vase, Cover, Lion, Fleur-De-Lis, Blue Ground, c.1900, 29 1/4 In. 2700.00
Vase, Landscape, Dancing Women, Purple & Brown On Orange Ground, 11 In. 1650.00
Vase, Marbleized Blue & Red Top, White Base, Satin, Bulbous, 8 1/4 In. 300.00

LUSTER glaze was meant to resemble copper, silver, or gold. The term *luster* includes any piece with some luster trim. It has been used since the sixteenth century. Some of the luster found today was made during the nineteenth century. The metallic glazes are applied on pottery. The finished color depends on the combination of the clay color and the glaze. Blue, orange, gold, and pearlized luster decorations were used by Japanese and German firms in the early 1900s. Tea Leaf pieces have their own category.

Canary, Mug, Present For A Good Girl, Red Transfer, 2 In., Child's 525.00
Copper, Bowl, Bird Among Leaves, Flowers, Leaves, Spain, 5 1/4 x 10 In. 635.00
Copper, Candlestick, Painted, Cobalt Bands, Raised Images, Seated Woman, 7 3/4 In., Pair 115.00
Copper, Charger, 5 Radiating Lines, Leaves, Circles, 2 Holes, 3 1/8 x 15 3/8 In. 3680.00
Copper, Charger, Figure, Holding Bird, On Horse, 5 Concentric Circles, Spain, 1 5/8 x 14 In. 546.00
Copper, Charger, Leaves, Hole, 5 Petals, Arabesques, Circles, Spain, 2 3/4 x 15 1/2 In. 2990.00
Copper, Charger, Moorish Style, Pierced Hole, Cat, Vines, Fruit, Spain, 3 x 15 In. 8625.00
Copper, Creamer, Canary Band, White Reserves, Transfers, Lafayette, Scroll Handle, 4 In. 575.00
Copper, Jug, Transfer, Painted Scene, Charity, Mid 19th Century, 5 1/2 In. 35.00
Copper, Mug, Transfer, Little Jockey, 2 1/4 In., Child's 220.00
Copper, Pitcher, Andrew Jackson, Yellow Band, 1828-32, 8 1/2 In. 8735.00
Copper, Pitcher, Creamer, Embossed Body, Multicolored Oriental Man, Clock Face, 6 In. 72.00
Copper, Pitcher, Green Banding, 1800s, 7 1/4 In. 138.00
Copper, Pitcher, Harrison & Reform, 1840, 8 x 6 1/4 In. 8536.00
Copper, Pitcher, Harrison & Reform, Log Cabin, 1840, 9 1/2 In. 6485.00
Copper, Pitcher, Pink Luster Trim, 1800s, 8 3/4 In. 196.00
Copper, Pitcher, Transfer, Harrison & Reform, Tippecanoe, Staffordshire, c.1840, 8 In. 4780.00
Copper, Pitcher, Transfer, Harrison, Our Country's Hope, Staffordshire, c.1840, 8 1/2 In. 7170.00
Fairyland luster is included in the Wedgwood category.
Pink, Mug, For My Dear Boy, 2 1/4 In. 275.00
Pink, Pitcher, Clipper Ship, North Umberland 74, Staffordshire, c.1820, 8 1/2 In. 556.00
Pink, Pitcher, West Bridge, Sunderland, Staffordshire, c.1830, 9 In. 760.00
Pink, Plate, General Jackson, Hero Of New Orleans, Staffordshire, c.1830, 8 1/2 In., Pair 1912.00
Sunderland luster pieces are listed in the Sunderland category.
Tea Leaf luster pieces are listed in the Tea Leaf Ironstone category.

LUSTRE ART GLASS Company was founded in Long Island, New York, in 1920 by Conrad Vahlsing and Paul Frank. The company made lampshades and globes that are almost indistinguishable from those made by Quezal. Most of the shades made by the company were unmarked.

Lamp, Electric, White Cased Cut To Cranberry, Thistle Shaped Body, c.1900, 14 1/2 In., Pair 705.00
Lamp, Electric, Woman, White Metal, Iridescent Shades, Pulled Feathers, Art Nouveau, 16 In. 345.00
Lamp, Red Cased, Enameled, Back Cut Albert Prisms, Late 1800s, 13 1/2 x 6 1/2 In., Pair 940.00
Shade, Cream, Gold Threading, Heart & Vine, Notched Rim, 5 1/2 In., Pair 345.00

LUSTRES are mantel decorations or pedestal vases with many hanging glass prisms. The name really refers to the prisms, and it is proper to refer to a single glass prism as a lustre. Either spelling, luster or lustre, is correct.

Clear, Trumpet, Faceted Drops, Prisms, Footed, Bohemian, 10 In., Pair 1548.00
Cobalt Blue, Enameled Flowers, 5 3/4 & 7 1/4-In. Prisms, 14 1/2 x 7 In. 690.00
Cranberry Glass, 11 1/2 In., Pair 750.00
Cut Glass, Honeycomb, Pineapple-End Cut Prisms, 11 In., Pair 690.00
Cut Glass, Opaque White To Cranberry, Gold, Enameled Flowers, 11 1/2 In. 345.00
Enameled Glass, Bohemian Style, 1900s, 16 In., Pair 263.00
Opaline, Enameled Flowers, 2 Tiers Of Albert Spears, Brass Base, 30 In. 470.00
Ruby, Enameled Flowers, Gilt Scalloped Edges, Albert Prisms, Bohemian, 31 In., Pair 1292.00
Ruby Stain, Cut Glass, Engraved, Bohemian, Egermann, 12 In., Pair 822.00
Vieux Rose, Enameled Flowers, Gold Trim, Round Frosted Shape, Albert Spears, 27 In., Pair 528.00

LUTZ glass was made by Nicolas Lutz working at the Boston and Sandwich Glass Company from 1870 to 1888. He made delicate and intricate threaded glass of several colors. Other similar wares made by other makers are now known by the generic name *Lutz*.

Finger Bowl, Threaded Opal, Blue, Late 1800s, 5 In. 144.00

MAASTRICHT, Holland, was the city where Petrus Regout established the De Sphinx pottery in 1836. The firm was noted for its transfer-printed earthenware. Many factories in Maastricht are still making ceramics.

Charger, Nour Du Chattel, Windmill Scene, Delft Blue, 15 1/2 In. 55.00
Gravy Boat, Underplate, Blue Willow Transfer, 9 1/4 In. 45.00
Plate, Yellow Flowers, Blue Sponged Border, 6 1/2 In. 25.00

MACINTYRE, see Moorcroft category.

MAIZE glass was made by W.L. Libbey & Son Company of Toledo, Ohio, after 1889. The glass resembled an ear of corn. The leaves were usually green, but some pieces were made with blue or red leaves. The kernels of corn were light yellow, white, or light green.

Celery Vase, Amber, Blue Leaves, 6 1/2 In. 175.00
Shaker, Gold Husks, 4 In. 180.00
Sugar Shaker, Gold Enameled Husks, 5 1/2 In. 375.00

MAJOLICA is a general term for any pottery glazed with an opaque tin enamel that conceals the color of the clay body. It has been made since the fourteenth century. Today's collector is most likely to find Victorian majolica. The heavy, colorful ware is rarely marked. Some famous makers include Wedgwood; Minton; Griffen, Smith and Hill (marked *Etruscan*); and Chesapeake Pottery (marked *Avalon* or *Clifton*). Majolica made by Wedgwood is listed in the Wedgwood category.

Ashtray, Fox, Figural, George Jones, 4 In. 546.00
Basket, Basket Weave, White Ground, Pink Interior, 6 1/2 In. 100.00
Basket, Begonia Leaf, Wicker Vine Handle, Etruscan, 12 In. 690.00
Basket, Blackberry, Basket Weave, Round, Vine Handle, 4 1/2 In. 168.00
Basket, Cover, Chicks & Eggs, Continental, 8 In. 645.00
Basket, Fish Shape, 15 In. 316.00
Basket, Flower, Twig Footed, T.C. Brown Westhead Moore & Co., 8 1/2 x 7 In. 1456.00
Basket, Maple Leaf, Etruscan, 9 In. 125.00
Basket, Mottled, Vine Handle, Applied Flowers, Thomas Forester & Sons 175.00
Basket, Rose, Open Cut Sides, Plums, Applied Flowers, Gold Trim, Scrolled Handle, 10 x 9 In. 145.00
Basket, Seafood, Cover, Lobster, Figural, Sprigs Of Seaweed, George Jones, 9 In. 5175.00
Basket, Strawberry, Yellow Basket Weave, Pink Ribbon, George Jones, 11 1/2 x 9 In. 6038.00
Basket, Turquoise, Pink Rope Handle, 5 1/2 In. 405.00
Basket, Water Lily, Strawberry, Sugar & Creamer, 2 Spoons, George Jones, 13 1/2 x 7 In. 9775.00
Bottle, Krause Continental Avian, Gentleman, Top Hat, Glasses, Umbrella, Figural, 15 In. 6440.00

Bowl, Diamond Shape, Floral & Basket Weave, Footed, 15 In., Pair 224.00
Bowl, Fish, Mottled, Everted Rim, Oval, Continental, 1800s, 14 In. 500.00
Bowl, Multicolored, Vine & Flower Rim, Center Scene, Angel Riding Lion, Etruscan, 9 3/4 In. 316.00
Bowl, Putti Handles, Oak Leaf Garlands, Acorns, Satyr Masks, Minton, 18 In. 1035.00
Bowl, Shell & Seaweed, Etruscan, 7 3/4 In. 112.00
Bowl, Shell & Seaweed, Shells Around Rim, Etruscan, 8 1/4 In. 127.00
Bowl, Shell Shape, 2 Naiads, Aquatic Leaves, Minton, 1866, 17 1/2 In. 3819.00
Bowl, Shell Shape, Shell Feet, Holdcroft, 11 In. 50.00
Bowl Set, Grape Leaf, 7 In., 5 Piece 252.00
Box, Cover, Bunny, In Crate, T.C. Brown Westhead Moore & Co., 7 In. 6720.00
Box, Sardine, Albino, Pink Accents 110.00
Box, Sardine, Basket Weave Base, Fish On Lily Pad Bed, Victoria Pottery Co., 8 In. 546.00
Box, Sardine, Bird, Dragonflies On Cover, Lily Pads, Water Lilies 1150.00
Box, Sardine, Cobalt Blue Leaves, Overlapping Fish, Seaweed Bed, Etruscan 690.00
Box, Sardine, Fish At Base, Lid 560.00
Box, Sardine, Seaweed & Fish, Cobalt Blue, Attached Undertray, Minton 1230.00
Box, Sardine, Turquoise, Basket Weave, Shell Finial 560.00
Bread Tray, Leaf, Fern, Cobalt Blue Border, Mottled Center, 14 1/2 In. 633.00
Bread Tray, Rustic Berry, Wheat, 14 1/2 In. 460.00
Bread Tray, Wardle, Bamboo, Fern, Cobalt Blue Center, 13 1/2 In. 185.00
Bread Tray, Waste Not Want Not, Butterflies, 13 1/2 In. 230.00
Bread Tray, Wheat, Cobalt Blue Center, 13 In. 460.00
Butter, Cover, Bird & Artichoke, Attached Undertray 225.00
Butter, Insert, Shell & Seaweed, Etruscan 690.00
Butter Pat, Basket, Begonia Leaf, Turquoise 110.00
Butter Pat, Fan Shape, Pink Ground, Eureka 80.00
Butter Pat, Floral & Leaf, Yellow Rim 28.00
Butter Pat, Floral Rim, George Jones 728.00
Butter Pat, Flower, On Basket, Floral Relief Rim 34.00
Butter Pat, Geranium Leaf, Yellow Rim, Etruscan, Pair 67.00
Butter Pat, Geranium, Etruscan 10.00
Butter Pat, Honey Comb & Fern, Holdcroft 288.00
Butter Pat, Leaf & Basket, Lavender Ground, Handle, Continental 127.00
Butter Pat, Leaf Shape, Twig Handle 105.00
Butter Pat, Maple Leaf, Etruscan 67.00
Butter Pat, Maple Leaf, Pink Ground, Etruscan 127.00
Butter Pat, Morning Glory, On Napkin, Continental 127.00
Butter Pat, Pansy, Multicolored, Etruscan 67.00
Butter Pat, Pond Lily, Etruscan 40.00
Butter Pat, Shell & Seaweed, 3 Piece 70.00
Butter Pat, Shell & Seaweed, Etruscan .... 104.00 to 184.00
Butter Pat, Turquoise Floral, Holdcroft 112.00
Butter Tub, Cobalt Blue, Round, Bird, Butterflies, Dragonflies, Water Lilies 1333.00
Butter Tub, Underplate, Attached, Cover, Cow, Pineapple 365.00
Cachepot, Stand, Bamboo, Ribbon & Bow, Mottled Yellow & Brown, Minton, 8 In. 560.00
Cachepot, Stand, Pond Lily, Brown Ground, Holdcroft, 6 3/4 In. 1035.00
Cake Stand, Maple Leaves, Pink Ground, Etruscan 140.00
Cake Stand, Merry Xmas, Happy New Year, Turquoise, Eureka Pottery Co., 9 1/2 In. 546.00
Cake Stand, Pond Lily, Stork On Base, 9 3/4 In. 157.00
Cake Stand, Ribbon & Bow, Basket Ground, Fielding, 9 1/4 In. 448.00
Cake Stand, Shell, Fishnet, Fielding, Low 336.00
Candleholder, Lady Frog, Figural, Continental, 8 In. 316.00
Candleholder, Palissy Style, Shell & Seaweed, Portugal, 6 1/2 In. 34.00
Candlestick, Palissy, Lion Face Rim, Snake, Frog, Snail, Shells, Ferns, 17 In. 2990.00
Card Holder, Palissy, Fish, On Waves, 5 In. 633.00
Centerpiece, Galleon Shape, W. Schiller & Sons, Germany, Late 1800s, 15 1/2 In. 1293.00
Chamberstick, Handles, Etruscan, 4 1/2 In., Pair 184.00
Charger, Dragon, Coat Of Arms, Scrolling Leaves, Ivory Ground, 15 1/2 In. 150.00
Charger, Finding Moses In Bulrushes, Renaissance Revival Border, Italy, 1800s, 25 In. 1998.00
Charger, Palissy Ware, Fish, Snake, Lizard, Shells, Ferns, c.1880, 16 In. 2700.00
Charger, Tin Glazed Earthenware, Allegorical Scene, Judgment Of Solomon, 25 In. 1175.00

Clean the feathers on a stuffed bird with chunks of fresh white bread. After cleaning, spray lightly with hair spray.

Majolica, Cheese Keeper, Calla Lily, Turquoise, Cow Finial, George Jones, 11 1/4 In.

Cheese Keeper, Apple Blossom, Basket Weave Cover, George Jones, 11 In. 460.00
Cheese Keeper, Calla Lily, Turquoise, Cow Finial, George Jones, 11 1/4 In. .... *ILLUS* 17250.00
Cheese Keeper, Castle, Ivy, Leaves, George Jones, 12 1/2 In. 2300.00
Cheese Keeper, Cobalt Blue, Dragonfly, Water Lily, Floral Finial, George Jones, 13 x 11 In. 8915.00
Cheese Keeper, Cobalt Blue, Rope & Fern, Floral Top, Base Rim, Forester, 11 x 12 1/2 In. 1610.00
Cheese Keeper, Pickets, George Jones, Late 1800s, 9 x 9 In. 635.00
Cheese Keeper, Stork, In Marsh, Ivory Ground, Thomas Forester & Sons, 12 In. 635.00
Cheese Keeper, Swan & Water Lily, Etruscan, 7 1/2 In. 1065.00
Cheese Keeper, Turquoise, Picket Fence, George Jones, 10 x 7 1/2 In. 1725.00
Cheese Keeper, Turquoise, Wild Rose, Twig Handle, George Jones, 11 x 11 1/2 In. 2300.00
Clock, Plate, Avalon Beetle, 8 1/4 In. 316.00
Clock, Shelf, France, 7 1/4 In. 110.00
Compote, Begonia Leaf, Overlapping, Pink Rim, 10 1/4 x 6 In. 336.00
Compote, Daisy, Wheat, Ribbon & Bow, Footed, Fielding, 9 In. 185.00
Compote, Flying Crane, Turquoise Pebble Ground, Holdcroft, 9 3/4 In. 196.00
Compote, Fox & Rabbit, Oval Bowl, Oak Tree Support, George Jones, 8 In. 7188.00
Compote, Leaf Shape Plate, Trumpet Stem, Pink, Brown, Green, 6 1/8 In., 2 Piece 558.00
Compote, Lily Of The Valley, Continental, Pair 100.00
Compote, Shell & Seaweed, Pointed Shell Bowl, Etruscan, 9 3/4 x 6 In. 748.00
Creamer, Butter Churn, Brownfield, 3 In. 45.00
Creamer, Coral, Etruscan, 4 In. 219.00
Creamer, Corn, Mounted Pewter Top, Etruscan, 5 In. 345.00
Creamer, Ribbon & Bow, Fielding 123.00
Creamer, Rustic Floral, Tree Bark, George Jones, 3 In. 259.00
Creamer, Shell & Fishnet, Coral Handle, Fielding, 4 In. 504.00
Creamer, Shell & Seaweed, Etruscan, 3 1/2 In. 134.00
Creamer, Sunflower, Etruscan, 3 3/4 In. 90.00
Creamer, Wild Rose, Butterfly Spout, 4 In. 104.00
Creamer, Wild Rose, Butterfly Spout, Etruscan, 4 1/2 In. 69.00
Creamer, Wild Rose, Cobalt Blue, 3 1/4 In. 190.00
Cup & Saucer, Bird & Fan, Wardle .... 45.00 to 67.00
Cup & Saucer, Demitasse, Morning Glory, Napkin 56.00
Cup & Saucer, Fan & Scroll, Fielding 100.00
Cup & Saucer, Shell & Seaweed, Etruscan .... 63.00 to 93.00
Cup & Saucer, Wild Rose & Rope, Yellow 112.00
Cuspidor, Cobalt Blue Shell & Seaweed, 6-Sided, 6 In. 161.00
Cuspidor, Floral, Cobalt Blue Accent, Square 123.00
Cuspidor, Water Lily, Etruscan, 7 In. 127.00
Cuspidor, Wild Rose, Trellis, Cobalt Blue 672.00
Decanter, Figural, Parrot, France, 12 In. 34.00
Dish, Begonia, Etruscan, 5 Piece 364.00
Dish, Bird, Mounted, Holly, Berry, Twig Feet, George Jones, 8 In. 644.00
Dish, Carp, On Ferns, Trompe L'Oeil, In Oval Basket, Longchamp, c.1870, 18 In. 588.00
Dish, Clam Shell Shape, 4 Divided Parts, Late 1800s, 9 In. 230.00
Dish, Game, Fox, Bed Of Ferns, Dead Game, Turquoise Base, George Jones, 11 In. 4485.00

Dish, Game, Hunting Dog, Gun, Rabbit & Pheasant, Paw Feet, Minton, 13 1/2 In. 7190.00
Dish, Game, Turquoise Ground, Quail Lid, George Jones, 13 1/2 In. .... *ILLUS* 57500.00
Dish, Muffin, Cover, Turquoise, Apple Blossom, Twig Handle, George Jones 1904.00
Egg Holder, Center Handle, Brown Ground, Turquoise Wells, Wheat, 8 1/4 In. 460.00
Ewer, Palissy Style, Shell Motif, Mermaid, Spout, Cobalt Blue Ground, Minton, 14 In. 1955.00
Figurine, Black Boy, Lying Down, Basket, Eating Watermelon, 5 1/2 In. 224.00
Figurine, Kitten, On Shoe, Continental, 5 In. 112.00
Figurine, Monkey, Backpack, Cobalt Blue Bucket, 8 1/2 In. 420.00
Fish Service Set, Fish, Seaweed, Waves, Flower Handles, Tray, 4 Sauce Dishes, 15 In. 805.00
Flower Holder, Cobalt, Lily Of The Valley, 5 Finger, Minton, 7 1/2 In. 3910.00
Flower Holder, Swan & Boat, Adams, 8 1/4 In. 259.00
Garden Seat, Cobalt Blue, Dragonfly, Swallow, Water Lily, Cattail, George Jones, 19 In. 4025.00
Garden Seat, Hexagonal, Turquoise Ground, Bamboo Corners, Holdcroft, 18 1/2 In. 4715.00
Garden Seat, Openwork, Porcelain, 18 1/2 x 13 1/2 In. 2800.00
Garden Seat, Passion Flower, Cobalt Blue, Minton, 18 In. 4480.00
Garden Seat, Turquoise, Calla Lily, George Jones, 19 In. 9490.00
Honey Pot, Choisy-Le-Roi, Shell Shape, Bee On Cover, France 448.00
Humidor, Black Jockey Head, 5 In. 78.00
Humidor, Bulldog Head, Figural 123.00
Humidor, Elephant, Pipe, Red Smoking Jacket, Continental, 8 In. 978.00
Humidor, Fox, In Hole, Figural 224.00
Humidor, Frog, Figural, Mandolin, Blue Cap, Continental, 8 In. 690.00
Humidor, Frog, Figural, Red Smoking Jacket, 7 1/2 In. 196.00
Humidor, Indian Chief, 5 In. 90.00
Humidor, Lady, Red Scarf In Hair, 5 In. 56.00
Humidor, Man, Blue Hat, Pipe, 6 In. 45.00
Humidor, Man, Cap, Large Cigar, 5 In. 56.00
Humidor, Match Striker, Cigar Holder, Beehive, 5 3/4 In. 112.00
Humidor, Monkey Head, Figural, Mafra, 6 In. 168.00
Humidor, Pig, Figural, Purple Vest, 5 1/2 In. 140.00
Humidor, Skull, Pink Blue & White Cap, 7 In. 67.00
Humidor, Tiger Head, Hat, 5 In. 112.00
Humidor, Tray, Tiger On Leaf, Continental 78.00
Inkwell, Hens, Figural, Glass Insert, Portugal, 4 1/4 In. 224.00
Jardiniere, Art Nouveau Style, 9 In., Pair 354.00
Jardiniere, Cobalt Blue, Oval, Lady's Head Handles, Flower, Leaf Garlands, Holdcroft, 22 In. 2300.00
Jardiniere, Cobalt Blue, Oval, Leaf Handles, Scenic Panels, Putti, Minton, 17 1/2 x 8 In. 1150.00
Jardiniere, Cobalt Blue, Swan, On Waves, Cattails, Holdcroft, 16 x 15 In. 748.00
Jardiniere, Leaf, Trellis, Flower Garlands, Minton, 12 x 14 In. 2645.00
Jardiniere, Lion's Head, Malachite, Paw Feet, Minton, 20 x 18 In. 1120.00
Jardiniere, Oval, Footed, Cobalt Blue Accents, 15 In. 280.00
Jardiniere, Pansy, France, 9 x 9 In., Pair 530.00
Jardiniere, Ram's Head, Floral & Fruit, Garland Drapes, Minton, 10 x 20 In. 2355.00
Jardiniere, Roses & Lattice, Early 20th Century, 8 3/4 In. 29.00
Jardiniere, Stand, Fern, Floral, John Adams, 17 In. 1380.00
Jardiniere, Tree Trunk, Hawk, Dead Bird, Oak Leaves, Acorn, Thomas Sergeant, 14 x 10 In. 2875.00
Jardiniere, Turquoise, Swan, Water Lily, Cattail, George Jones, 11 1/2 x 14 In. 978.00
Jug, Baseball & Soccer, Monochrome, Green, Etruscan, 8 In. 185.00
Jug, Palissy Style, Tree Trunk, Oak Leaves, Acorns, Snake & Frog On Spout, 10 In. 748.00
Kettle, Twig, Sanded, Floral, 3-Footed, 9 In. 308.00
Ladle, Tureen, Cabbage, Portugal, 9 In. 11.00
Marmalade Pot, Strawberry, Bird Finial, Twig Feet, 6 1/2 In. 4600.00
Match Striker, 2 Birds, On Bench, With Basket, 5 1/2 In. 748.00
Match Striker, Boy & Girl, Under Umbrella, Shock Of Wheat, 5 In. 100.00
Match Striker, Frog, Mandolin, Flowers, Continental, 6 In. 58.00
Match Striker, Owl, On Log 100.00
Mirror, Dresser, Art Nouveau, Winged Lady, Overlooking Pond, Water Lilies, 24 In. 920.00
Mug, Bamboo, 2 Frogs Inside 146.00
Mug, Rabbit, Rabbit Handle, France, 3 1/2 In. 308.00
Mug, Scenic, Frog Inside 56.00
Mug, Shaving, Wheat, Daisy, Ribbon & Bow, Fielding 34.00

Mug, Strawberry, Basket Weave 84.00
Mug, Turquoise, Pond Lily, Holdcroft 207.00
Mug, Water Lily, Cobalt Blue Rim, Etruscan 175.00
Mustache Cup, Butterfly, Fielding 112.00
Napkin Ring, Lily Of The Valley, Pink Ribbon, Bow, George Jones, 6 In. 1955.00
Oyster Plate, 6 Wells, Cobalt Blue, Alternating Pink & Green, Yellow Center, 10 In. 259.00
Oyster Plate, Alternating Pink & White Wells, 9 In. 196.00
Oyster Plate, Crescent Shape, Cobalt Blue Ground, Seaweed Sprig, 9 In. 1150.00
Oyster Plate, Fish, Germany, 13 1/4 In. 22.00
Oyster Plate, Pink, Raised Center Shell, George Jones, 10 1/2 In. 2760.00
Oyster Plate, Seaweed, Coral Between Wells, Cobalt Blue Center, 10 In. 460.00
Paperweight, Justice, Eagle, Young In Nest, Trenton Pottery, 3 3/4 In. 175.00
Pedestal, Lion, Winged, Seated, 8-Sided Top, Gold, Green, Continental, c.1885, 45 x 15 In. 820.00
Pitcher, Asparagus, France, 8 In. 1035.00
Pitcher, Barrel, Ram's Head Spout, Brownfield, 8 In. 123.00
Pitcher, Bear, With Drum, Figural, Holdcroft, 8 1/2 In. 672.00
Pitcher, Bear, With Spoon, Figural, Holdcroft, 9 3/4 In. 748.00
Pitcher, Bird & Fan, Cobalt Blue, Wardle, 9 In. 230.00
Pitcher, Blackberry, Yellow Bark Ground, 5 In. 45.00
Pitcher, Butterfly, Bird, Hawthorn, 8 3/4 In. 115.00
Pitcher, Calla Lily, Flowers, Cobalt Blue, 10 In. 616.00
Pitcher, Cat, With Fiddle, Figural, France, 9 1/4 In. 476.00
Pitcher, Chickens In Barnyard, 6 1/2 In. 168.00
Pitcher, Chickens In Barnyard, 9 In. 168.00
Pitcher, Corn, 7 1/2 In. 134.00
Pitcher, Cottage, Figural, Warrilow & Cope, 5 In. 430.00
Pitcher, Duck, Figural, Frie Onnaing, 9 In. 28.00
Pitcher, English Corn, 9 1/2 In. 230.00
Pitcher, Fan & Scroll, Fielding, 6 1/2 In. 196.00
Pitcher, Fan & Scroll, Fielding, 7 1/2 In. 364.00
Pitcher, Feed Sack, T.C. Brown Westhead Moore & Co., 7 In. 179.00
Pitcher, Fern & Lily Of The Valley, Cobalt Blue, T.C. Brown Westhead Moore & Co., 6 In. 1495.00
Pitcher, Fern, Etruscan, 8 In. 336.00
Pitcher, Fish, Figural, 9 1/4 In. 146.00
Pitcher, Fish, Figural, 13 In. . . . . . .100.00 to 207.00
Pitcher, Fish, Figural, England, c.1880, 9 In. 234.00
Pitcher, Fish, Figural, Fish Handle, 8 In. 259.00
Pitcher, Floral & Leaf Spout, 6 In. 78.00
Pitcher, Floral & Rope, 5 3/4 In. 56.00
Pitcher, Flower, Turquoise, Pewter Lid, 7 In. 190.00
Pitcher, Flower, Vine Handle, Turquoise, 9 In. 168.00
Pitcher, Flowers, Frie Onnaing, 8 In. 235.00
Pitcher, Flowers, Leaves, 3-Color Glaze, 7 1/4 In. 35.00
Pitcher, Flowers, Tin Top, Morely & Co., Late 1800s, 7 1/2 In. 200.00
Pitcher, Fox & Grape, Cobalt Blue, 10 In. 1120.00
Pitcher, Frog, Figural, On Lily Pad, Edward Steele, 12 1/2 In. 1495.00
Pitcher, Frog, Smoking Pipe, Figural, 5 Lilies, Brown Coat, 10 In. 784.00
Pitcher, Game, Lavender Ground, Holdcroft, 11 In. 390.00
Pitcher, Goat, Yellow Ground, 8 In. 140.00
Pitcher, Grape & Bark, Pewter Lid, 7 In. 67.00
Pitcher, Grape & Fern, Treebark, Brownfield, 9 In. 67.00
Pitcher, Hummingbird & Basket Weave, Fielding, 8 1/2 In. 365.00
Pitcher, Lavender, Basket Weave & Flower, 11 In. 336.00
Pitcher, Lily Of The Valley & Rope, Lavender Lid, Samuel Lear, 12 1/2 In. 489.00
Pitcher, Lily Of The Valley & Rope, Rope Handle, Samuel Lear, 8 In. 616.00
Pitcher, Maple Leaf & Picket Fence, Turquoise, 7 In. 112.00
Pitcher, Milk, Flowers, Leaves, 5 1/2 In. 115.00
Pitcher, Monkey, Figural, Multicolored, France, 11 1/2 In. 1064.00
Pitcher, Morning Glory & Ribbon, Fielding, 6 In. 78.00
Pitcher, Mottled Brick & Ivy, Pewter Lid, 7 1/2 In. 78.00
Pitcher, New England Aster, 7 1/4 In. 160.00

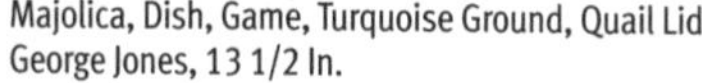

Majolica, Dish, Game, Turquoise Ground, Quail Lid, George Jones, 13 1/2 In.

Majolica, Platter, 5 Overlapping Fish, Snake, Frog, Barbizet, Palissy, c.1865, 17 1/2 In.

Pitcher, Owl, Figural, 6 1/2 In. 78.00
Pitcher, Owl, Figural, 7 1/4 In. 280.00
Pitcher, Owl, Figural, 11 In. 56.00
Pitcher, Parrot, Figural, 9 1/2 In. 336.00
Pitcher, Picket Fence, Basket Weave, Leaf, Pewter Lid, 5 In. 112.00
Pitcher, Picket Fence, Leaf, Basket Weave, Cobalt Blue, Pewter Lid, 4 1/2 In. 168.00
Pitcher, Pineapple, 6 1/2 In. 190.00
Pitcher, Pineapple, 7 3/4 In. 190.00
Pitcher, Pineapple, 9 In. 280.00
Pitcher, Pineapple, Pewter Lid, 5 1/2 In. 179.00
Pitcher, Pineapple, Pewter Lid, 6 In. 168.00
Pitcher, Rat, With Umbrella, Figural, France, 7 3/4 In. 1265.00
Pitcher, Robin, On Branch, Green Leaves, Vine, Cobalt Blue, George Jones, 6 1/4 In. 2128.00
Pitcher, Rustic Tree Trunk, Frog, Flowers, Fern, George Jones, 5 In. 390.00
Pitcher, Shell & Seaweed, Coral, 8 In. 308.00
Pitcher, Shell & Seaweed, Etruscan, 4 1/2 In. 495.00
Pitcher, Shell & Seaweed, Etruscan, 5 3/4 In. 225.00
Pitcher, Shell & Seaweed, Etruscan, 6 In. 173.00
Pitcher, Shell, Coral, Seaweed, Waves, Wardle, 8 In. 1035.00
Pitcher, Shell, Figural, Fielding, 8 1/2 In. 448.00
Pitcher, Shell, Figural, Fielding, 10 In. 392.00
Pitcher, Shell, Fishnet, Carol Handle, Fielding, 6 1/2 In. 805.00
Pitcher, Squat, Flower, Turquoise, 6 In. 224.00
Pitcher, Stork, In Marsh, Cobalt Blue, Pewter Top, Goose Head Handle, 11 In. 633.00
Pitcher, Sunflower, Dragon Handles, 8 1/2 In. 90.00
Pitcher, Sunflower, Lavender Ground, Etruscan, 4 1/2 In. 448.00
Pitcher, Tree Trunk, Chocolate Glaze, Vine & Flower Handle, c.1900, 10 In. 455.00
Pitcher, Turquoise, 6-Sided, Floral, Wheat, 9 1/2 In. 375.00
Pitcher, U.S. Grant, 10 In. 196.00
Pitcher, Water Lily, Samuel Lear, 5 1/2 In. 179.00
Pitcher, Wild Rose, Pebble Ground, Cobalt Blue, Handle, 7 In. 173.00
Pitcher, Wild Rose, Treebark, George Jones, 8 1/4 In. 978.00
Pitcher Set, Hawthorne Pattern, Etruscan, 4 Graduated Sizes, 5 To 8 In. 575.00
Planter, Frog, Mandolin Vases, Continental, Pair 225.00
Plaque, Crab, Palissy Style, 11 1/2 In. 100.00
Plaque, Fish, On Sandbar In Center, Lizard, Butterfly, Shells, Oval, Palissy, 10 1/2 In. 2013.00
Plaque, Parakeets, On Branch, High Relief, France, 16 In. 336.00
Plaque, Snails, Sea Creatures, Grass Ground, Palissy, Portugal, 5 In. 168.00
Plaque, Snake, Lizards, Grass Ground, Palissy, Portugal, 12 In. 670.00
Plate, Asparagus, France, 9 1/2 In. 106.00
Plate, Begonia Leaf, Overlapping, 8 1/2 In. 85.00
Plate, Boy, On Bicycle, France, 7 1/2 In. 146.00
Plate, Cauliflower, Etruscan, 8 In. 157.00

Plate, Cauliflower, Etruscan, 9 In. .... 135.00 to 184.00
Plate, Fan, Butterfly, Pebble Ground, Fielding, 8 1/2 In. 127.00
Plate, Fern, Leaf, Pink Ground, George Jones, 8 1/4 In. 604.00
Plate, Fish, Eels, Shells, Seaweed, Mottled Brown Ground, Palissy Style, 2 1/2 x 9 1/2 In. 1495.00
Plate, Fish, On Island, Snake, Butterfly, Ferns, Barbizet, Palissy, c.1865, 10 1/2 In. 2520.00
Plate, Maple Leaf, On Basket, Etruscan, 9 In. 134.00
Plate, Maple Leaf, On Basket, Yellow Rim, Etruscan, 9 In. 110.00
Plate, Maple Leaf, Pink Wicker Ground, 8 1/2 In. 196.00
Plate, Oyster, Turquoise, Raised Center Shell, George Jones, 8 In. 1345.00
Plate, Pond Lily, Cobalt Blue Center, Etruscan, 8 In. 90.00
Plate, Pond Lily, George Jones, 9 In. .... 448.00 to 560.00
Plate, Pond Lily, Holdcroft, 8 1/2 In. 196.00
Plate, Roman Ruin, Scroll Border, 2 Portrait Reserves, Continental, 1800s, 10 1/4 In. 118.00
Plate, Shell & Seaweed, Etruscan, 7 In., Pair 250.00
Plate, Shell & Seaweed, Etruscan, 9 1/4 In. 207.00
Plate, Shrimping, Shells & Seaweed, Lady Netting Shrimp, George Jones, 9 1/2 In. 2990.00
Plate, Stork, In Marsh, Wire Basket Frame, France, 9 In. 196.00
Plate, Strawberry & Apple, Cobalt Blue Basket Weave Ground, Etruscan, 9 In. 489.00
Plate, Strawberry & Apple, Etruscan, 9 In. 168.00
Plate, Swan, Water Lily, France, 10 In. 105.00
Plate, Turquoise, Fish & Daisy, Holdcroft, 8 1/2 In. 390.00
Plate Set, Dessert, Dark Green, Daisy, Wheat, Ribbon & Bow, Fielding, 9 Piece 430.00
Plate Set, Overlapping Begonia Leaf, 8 3/4 In., 4 Piece 460.00
Plate Set, Shell & Seaweed, Etruscan, 7 In., 6 Piece 405.00
Platter, 5 Overlapping Fish, Snake, Frog, Barbizet, Palissy, c.1865, 17 1/2 In. .... *ILLUS* 6050.00
Platter, Bamboo & Fern, Cobalt Blue Center, Wardle, 13 1/2 In. 390.00
Platter, Begonia Leaf, On Basket, 13 1/2 In. 420.00
Platter, Cattail & Pond Lily, Minton, c.1870, 24 x 15 In. 7280.00
Platter, Cobalt Blue Wild Rose, 13 1/2 In. 430.00
Platter, Crab, Cover, Minton, 16 In. 6038.00
Platter, Dog, Doghouse, 11 In. 125.00
Platter, Dog, Doghouse, Leaves & Fern Border, 11 In. 316.00
Platter, Eat Thy Bread With Thankfulness, Begonia Leaf, 12 1/2 In. 336.00
Platter, Fruit, Octagonal, Forrester, 11 3/4 In. 140.00
Platter, Geranium, Etruscan, 12 In. 225.00
Platter, Leaf & Fern, Cobalt Blue Rim, Mottled Center, 14 1/2 In. 336.00
Platter, Mottled Center, Turquoise Border, Leaves, Berries, George Jones, 13 In. 3680.00
Platter, Palissy Style, Oval, Mythological Figure Border, Minton, 4 Wells, 14 1/2 In. 1725.00
Platter, Pear & Apple, 13 In. 420.00
Platter, Shell & Seaweed, Etruscan, 13 3/4 In. 575.00
Platter, Snake, On Island, Fish, Shells Frog, Salamander, Insects, Oval, Palissy, 21 In. 896.00
Platter, Sunflower & Classical Urn, Samuel Lear, 14 1/2 In. 280.00
Platter, Waste Not Want Not, Mottled, Floral, 13 1/2 In. 358.00
Punch Bowl, Lily, Cobalt Blue, Etruscan, 9 1/4 In. 728.00
Sauce, Undertray, Pink Sunflower, Etruscan, 5 In. 316.00
Server, Strawberry, Napkin, Pink Ground, Sugar & Creamer, George Jones, 15 In. 920.00
Server, Strawberry, Vine Handle, Cobalt Blue, 2 Sections, 10 1/2 In. 336.00
Server, Sugar & Creamer, Strawberry, Turquoise Napkin, George Jones, 14 1/2 In. 1065.00
Server, Yellow Basket Weave Strawberry, Vine Handle, Attached Sugar & Creamer 365.00
Stand, Pink, Pointed Leaves, Round, George Jones, 7 1/2 In. 250.00
Stein, Square, Green Glaze, Relief, Inlaid Lid, 1 1/4 Liter 297.00
Sugar, Pink Strawberry, Twig Feet, Minton, 2 1/2 In. 85.00
Sugar & Creamer, Cover, Wild Rose, Etruscan 90.00
Sugar & Creamer, Oriental, Bird & Prunus, Flat Sides 168.00
Sugar & Creamer, Pear & Apple 84.00
Sugar & Creamer, Wild Rose & Rope, Turquoise 120.00
Syrup, Bamboo & Blackberry, Pewter Lid, 6 In. 45.00
Syrup, Bamboo With Iris, Etruscan, c.1875, 8 In. 345.00
Syrup, Bamboo, Etruscan, Pewter Lid 308.00
Syrup, Blue Sunflower, Etruscan, c.1875, 8 1/2 In. 489.00
Syrup, Cobalt Blue Sunflower, Pewter Lid, Etruscan, 8 In. 805.00

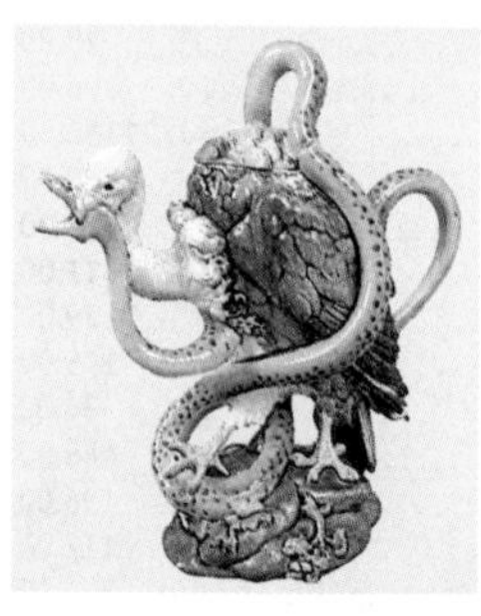

Majolica, Teapot, Vulture & Serpent, Minton, 9 In.

Majolica, Tray, Fish, Frog, Butterfly, Sea Creatures, Palissy, 12 1/2 In.

Syrup, Coral, Pewter Lid, Late 1800s, Etruscan, 4 1/4 In. 430.00
Syrup, Dragonfly, Fan, Cobalt Blue, 6 In. 460.00
Syrup, Fish, Fish Handle, Cobalt Blue, Pewter Lid, 8 In. 476.00
Tankard, Fox Hunt, Pewter Mounted Lid, Dog With Quail, Rabbit, George Jones, 12 In. 2875.00
Tankard, Fox, Cobalt Blue Ground, Hinged Pewter Lid, George Jones, 11 3/4 In. 2576.00
Tea Service, Tray, Fan, Scroll, Insect, Turquoise, Fielding, 8 Piece 4025.00
Tea Set, Albino Shell & Seaweed, Teapot, Sugar, Creamer, Saucer, Etruscan, 3 Plates 430.00
Tea Set, Apple Blossom, Basket Weave, George Jones, 19 1/2 In. 6900.00
Tea Set, Bird & Fan, Coffeepot, Teapot, Creamer, Sugar, Wardle 365.00
Tea Set, Bird & Fan, Pebble Ground, 3 Piece 250.00
Tea Set, Shell & Seaweed, Crooked Spout, Sugar, Creamer, Spooner, Etruscan, 4 Piece 633.00
Tea Set, Shell & Seaweed, Etruscan, Teapot, Creamer, Sugar, Spooner 560.00
Tea Set, Turquoise, Drum Shape, Fielding, 3 Piece 1035.00
Tea Set, Yellow Pinecone, Floral, Cobalt Blue Accent 250.00
Teapot, Bird & Fan, Butterfly Finial, 9 In. 78.00
Teapot, Bird & Fan, Wardle, 6 In. 110.00
Teapot, Blackberry & Bark, Holdcroft, 4 1/2 In. 530.00
Teapot, Cauliflower, Etruscan 78.00
Teapot, Cobalt Blue, Monkey Handle, Floral, George Jones, 9 1/2 In. 2875.00
Teapot, Cobalt Blue, Oval, Bird & Fan, Butterfly Finial, 9 1/2 In. 430.00
Teapot, Figural, Monkey & Coconut, Minton, 8 1/2 In. ....3640.00 to 4600.00
Teapot, Figural, Spikey Fish, Minton, c.1878, 7 1/4 In. 8625.00
Teapot, Fish, Swallowing Fish 250.00
Teapot, Isle Of Man, Union Jack, Flag, Brownfield, 7 3/4 In. 1150.00
Teapot, Parrots, On Branch, Yellow Ground, Fielding, 8 1/2 In. 448.00
Teapot, Shells, Waves, Coral, Seaweed, Mounted Pewter Lid, 6 1/2 In. 400.00
Teapot, Turquoise Honeycomb, Holdcroft, 5 In. 345.00
Teapot, Vulture & Serpent, Minton, 9 In. .... *ILLUS* 71875.00
Tile, Cobalt Blue Flower, Square, England, 8 In. 748.00
Tile, Cobalt Blue Swan In Water, Square, George Jones, 8 In. 2300.00
Tile, Cobalt Blue Water Lily, Square, George Jones, 8 In. 518.00
Tile, Wire Trivet Frame, Hen With Chicks, 6 In. 225.00
Tobacco Jar, Coil Of Rope, Figural, Isle Of Man, Holdcroft, 9 1/2 In. 1668.00
Tray, Bird, On Branch, Floral & Wheat, 13 In. 336.00
Tray, Fan & Butterfly, Turquoise Pebble Ground, 2 Handles, Fielding, 10 3/4 In. 280.00
Tray, Fish, 3 Fish Dishes, Portugal 28.00
Tray, Fish, Frog, Butterfly, Sea Creatures, Palissy, 12 1/2 In. .... *ILLUS* 1980.00
Tray, Fish, On Bed Of Leaves, Cobalt Blue, 12 In. 308.00
Tray, Fox, Pink Ground, George Jones, 11 In. 1095.00
Tray, Lady In High Relief, Building Scene, Oval, Palissy, 14 In. 1265.00
Tray, Lady On Ladder Picking Apples, Cobalt Blue Ground, Naughty, 6 3/4 In. 168.00
Tray, Lobsters, Crabs, Lemons, Seaweed Border, Shell & Seaweed Center, Minton, 24 In. 9200.00
Tray, Pink, Crescent Shape, George Jones, 9 3/4 In. 575.00
Tray, Revolving, Augustus Welby Northmore Pugin, Fleur-De-Lis, Minton, 18 In. 2185.00
Tray, Sunflower & Begonia Leaf, Cobalt Blue, 11 In. 365.00
Tray, Turquoise, Butterfly, Dragonfly, Bee, Wheat, Bamboo, George Jones, 13 In. 3220.00
Tree Tub, Flowers, Birds, Everted Rim, 2 Masque Handles, c.1915, 16 x 24 3/4 In. 998.00

Tureen, Vegetable, Vegetable Feet, Handles, Portugal, 8 1/2 In. 28.00
Umbrella Stand, Cobalt Blue, Scenic Panel 196.00
Umbrella Stand, Fielding, Cobalt Blue, Stork, Cattail, 19 3/4 In. 1150.00
Urn, Multicolored Harvest Scenes, Coiled Snake & Mask Handles, Footed, 37 1/2 In. 1880.00
Vase, Alligator Handles, Applied Leaves, Sea Creatures, Cobalt Blue, Palissy, 14 1/2 In. 224.00
Vase, Art Nouveau, Continental, 15 1/2 In., Pair 11.00
Vase, Bird In Flight, 2 Handles, 9 3/4 In. 129.00
Vase, Birds Nest, Applied Bird, 1900s, 8 In. 115.00
Vase, Blackamoor Woman, Carrying Tray, 11 1/2 In. 34.00
Vase, Boy, Climbing Tree, Holdcroft, 7 In. 448.00
Vase, Bud, Parrot, On Branch, Delphin Massier, 11 In. 196.00
Vase, Bud, Swan, Figural, Cornucopia, 4 1/2 In. 112.00
Vase, Campana, Bacchic Masks, Grapevine, Garland Drapes, Palissy, 11 1/4 In. 224.00
Vase, Cat, With Basket, 5 In. 392.00
Vase, Floor, Hand Painted, Scenic, Scrolled Twin Snake Handles, 20th Century, 24 In. 118.00
Vase, Heron, c.1900, 35 In., Pair 7200.00
Vase, Queen's, Baluster, Cobalt Blue, Grapevines, Ram's Head Handles, Minton, 27 In. 4600.00
Vase, Sea Life, Sea Creatures, Massier, 11 In. 336.00
Vase, Spill, Dog, Massier, France, 15 In. 896.00
Vase, Turquoise, Basket Weave, Square Base, Applied Flowers, Minton, 6 3/4 In., Pair 1265.00
Wall Pocket, Daisy, Figural, Jerome Massier, 8 In. 840.00
Wall Pocket, Monkey, On Bark, Coconut, Palissy, 18 1/2 In. 1008.00
Wall Pocket, Rooster Head, Delphin Massier, 6 1/2 In. 784.00
Waste Bowl, Basket Weave, Flower, Fielding, 4 1/2 In. 45.00
Waste Bowl, Wild Rose, Rope, 5 1/2 In. 112.00
Wine Cooler, Shell, On Rock, Crayfish, Lizard, Beetles, Palissy, Francois Maurice, 17 In. 3920.00

MALACHITE is a green stone with unusual layers or rings of darker green shades. It is often polished and used for decorative objects. Most malachite comes from Siberia or Australia.

Box, 2 Nude Women On Cover, 2 Nude Women Swimming, 4 In. 430.00
Box, Cover, Woman, 3 1/2 In. 518.00
Box, Molded 3 Muses Playing Instruments, 4 1/2 In. 1035.00
Cameo, Man, Beard, Frame, 1 1/4 x 1 1/4 In. 468.00
Figurine, Female Immortal, Flowing Robes, Flower Bowl, Stand, Chinese, 8 1/2 In. 470.00
Group, Meiren & Scholar, Robes, Branches, Chinese, 13 3/4 In. 1180.00
Perfume Bottle, Birth Of Venus, Stopper As Shell, Fish In Relief, Dabber, 7 In. 1955.00
Perfume Bottle, Stopper, Molded Cupids, Flower Bouquet, 6 1/2 In. 150.00
Vase, Cover, Flattened Oval, Stylized Dragons, Ring Handles, Chinese, 7 1/4 In. 561.00

MAPS of all types have been collected for centuries. The earliest known printed maps were made in 1478. The first printed street map showed London in 1559. The first road maps for use by drivers of automobiles were made in 1901. Collectors buy maps that were pages of old books, as well as the multifolded road maps popular in this century.

Americae, Mappa Generalis, Homann Heirs, Mat, Frame, 1746, 22 1/2 x 23 In. 1980.00
Americas, Ships, Hand Colored, Mat, Frame, 1631, 16 x 20 1/2 In. 2039.00
Amerique, Le Rouge, Frame, France, 1746, 34 1/2 In. 3215.00
Atlas, World Geographic Atlas, Composite Of Man's Environment, c.1953, 368 Pages 11.00
Boston Inner Harbor, June 1897, Frame, 34 3/4 x 42 3/4 In. 147.00
Buffalo-Niagara Region Road Map, Mileage Chart, Folded, Socony, Folio, 1937 .... 12.00
Canada, Louisiane, Possessions Angl, Hand Colored, Robert De Vaugondy, Paris, 1762, 10 x 12 In. 440.00
Carolina, Herman Moll, England, c.1729, 9 x 12 In. 1725.00
Carte De La Californie, Robert De Vaudondy, Didier, Livourne, Mat, 1779, 16 x 19 3/4 In. 600.00
Celestial, Orrery, Brass, Collapsible, 8 Disks, Fellipo Lelli, Italy, 13 In. 2585.00
Celestial, Orrery, Revolving, Star Chart, Brass Hands, Philips', 10 In. 235.00
Celestial, Planisphere, Henry Whitall, N.J., c.1883, 15 In. 410.00
Celestial, Star & Planet Finder, Constellations, Calendars, Suspension Loop, Barritt Serviss, 1906 118.00
Delaware, Maryland, Virginia & West Virginia, Amoco, 2 Panels, 1920, 9 x 4 In. 70.00
Fort Benning, Georgia, Fire Control, Sheet 1, Engineer Dept., U.S. Army, 1921 .... 12.00

Gettysburg, Antietam, Emmitsburg Sheet, Topographical, U.S. Army, 1925 .... 10.00
Globe, 12 Gores, Fruitwood Stand, Glass Display Case, 6 1/2 In. 325.00
Globe, Base, Turned Mahogany Legs, Reeding, Revolving Ring, Interior Light, 39 In. 489.00
Globe, Celestial, Newton's, 12 Gores, Walnut Stand, London, 7 1/2 x 4 1/4 In. 2938.00
Globe, Celestial, Papier-Mache, Chrome Base, Rand McNally, 16 x 12 In. 118.00
Globe, Celestial, Pocket Planetarium, Brass Sun, Ivory Planets, Newton, 3 In. 9988.00
Globe, Terrestrial, 12 Engraved Gores, Walnut Stand, Gilman & Joslin, 21 x 12 In. 1410.00
Globe, Terrestrial, 12 Hand Colored Gores, Wilson's New American, c.1835, 18 x 13 In. 4995.00
Globe, Terrestrial, C.S. Hammond & Co., Brass Hour Ring, Copper Base, Boston, 9 x 6 In. 176.00
Globe, Terrestrial, C.W. Bacon, London, Mahogany Pillar & Scroll Stand, Hammond, 47 In. 9988.00
Globe, Terrestrial, Copley Joslin Improved, Iron Stand, Gilman Joslin, c.1885, 23 x 16 In. 4700.00
Globe, Terrestrial, Cosmopolitan, Illuminated, Tripod, Dunbar, Rand McNally, 33 x 20 In. 708.00
Globe, Terrestrial, Cyrillic Printing, Ebonized Stand, Russia, 1800s, 9 1/2 x 20 In. 880.00
Globe, Terrestrial, G.W. Bacon & Co., Milton Bradley, London, c.1930, 13 1/2 In. 325.00
Globe, Terrestrial, Gilman Joslin, Boston, Floor Model, 1870-90, 16 In. 3290.00
Globe, Terrestrial, Hammond, 12 Colored Gores, Plastic Cover, Nickel Plated Tripod, 12 In. 235.00
Globe, Terrestrial, London Geographical Institute, G. Philip & Son, 12 x 6 In. 176.00
Globe, Terrestrial, New & Improved Terrestrial Pocket Globe, Newton, Early 1800s, 3 In. 9990.00
Globe, Terrestrial, New Globe Of Earth, Nicholas Lane, London, 2 3/4 In. 9990.00
Globe, Terrestrial, Wood Stand, W.&A.K. Johnston, Edinburgh, 1886, 15 x 10 1/2 In. 350.00
Globe & Starfinder, Celestial, Brass Base, Rand McNally, c.1930, 16 x 8 In. 590.00
Louisiana, Mississippi, Arkansas, Counties, Johnson's Atlas, Frame, c.1900, 24 x 18 In. 646.00
Louisiana & River Mississippi, John Senex, Mat, Frame, 1721, 34 x 37 In. 1685.00
Maine, Province, Samuel Lewis, 1794, 15 x 10 In. 1095.00
Mississippi & Ohio Rivers, Indian Nations, 1784, 14 x 20 In., 2 Pages 1780.00
Nantucket, Frame, c.1869, 41 x 26 In. 1725.00
New Hampshire, Philip Carrigan, Concord, N.H., 1816, 61 x 47 In. 12500.00
New York, Engraved, Laid Paper, Hand Colored, Frame, J. Reid, N.Y., 1796, 23 x 25 In. 1898.00
New York, Westchester & Putman Cos., Mileage Chart, Folded, Socony, 1937, Folio 12.00
North America, Panama To Greenland, J. Rapkin, J&F Tallis, c.1850, 14 x 10 1/4 In. 325.00
Sicily, Hand Colored, Wood Frame, Nicolaum Visscher, c.1680, 18 1/2 x 22 1/2 In. 316.00
Terrestrial, Orbis Vetus, World, Robert De Vaugondy, Mat, Frame, 1752, 20 1/2 x 30 In. 1115.00
United States, 50 State, Roll Up, Canvas Material, 57 3/8 x 67 1/2 In. 85.00
United States, Engraved, Hand Colored, J. Rapkin, J&F Tallis, c.1850, 10 1/4 x 14 In. .....245.00 to 276.00
Virginiae & Floridae, Mid-Atlantic Coast, Mat, Frame, Willem Jansz Blaeu, 1640, 17 x 22 In. 1685.00
Virginiae Partis Australis, Et Floridae Partis, Blaeu, Amsterdam, c.1640, 15 1/4 x 20 In. 1610.00
Western Hemisphere, Copper Engraved, Hand Colored, S. Neele, c.1804, 20 1/4 x 16 1/4 In. 375.00
World, 2 Hemispheres, Embroidered, Silk On Silk, Frame, 1819, 9 5/8 x 17 1/2 In. 3910.00
World, 2 Hemispheres, Matted, Frame, Daniel Stoopendaal, Late 1600s, 12 1/2 x 18 In. 1800.00

MARBLE collectors pay highest prices for glass and sulphide marbles. The game of marbles has been popular since the days of the ancient Romans. American children were able to buy marbles by the mid-eighteenth century. Dutch glazed clay marbles were least expensive. Glazed pottery marbles, attributed to the Bennington potteries in Vermont, were of a better quality. Marbles made of pink marble were also available by the 1830s. Glass marbles seem to have been made later. By 1880, Samuel C. Dyke of South Akron, Ohio, was making clay marbles and The National Onyx Marble Company was making marbles of onyx. The Navarre Glass Marble Company of Navarre, Ohio, and M. B. Mishler of Ravenna, Ohio, made the glass marbles. Ohio remained the center of the marble industry, and the Akron-made Akro Agate brand became nationally known. Other pieces made by Akro Agate are listed in this book in the Akro Agate category. Sulphides are glass marbles with frosted white figures in the center.

Akro Agate, Blue Oxblood, Corkscrew, 3/4 In. 56.00
Akro Agate, Corkscrew, 5/8 In. 5.00
Akro Agate, Lemonade Oxblood, 5/8 In. 85.00
Akro Agate, Limeade Oxblood, 3/4 In. 504.00
Akro Agate, Moss, 5/8 In. 5.00

Akro Agate, Swirl, Blue, White, 5/8 In. 5.00
Christensen, Cobra, Yellow, Purple, 21/32 In. 896.00
Christensen Flame, White, Tan, Red, 19/32 In. 168.00
Glass, End Of Day, Segmented Onion Skin, Early 20th Century, 2 In. 265.00
Latticinio, Core Swirl, 3 Stage, Red, Blue, Green, Yellow, White, 29/32 In. 140.00
Lutz, Coal Swirl, 1 5/8 In. 288.00
Lutz, Type 1, Yellow Bands, 1 3/8 In. 495.00
Onionskin, 4 Lobes, White, Red, Teal, Yellow, Shrunken Core, 2 1/4 In. 504.00
Onionskin, 12 Lobes, Red On White, 1 29/32 In. 1345.00
Onionskin, Blue, Red On White, Mica, Hazy, 2 11/32 In. 250.00
Onionskin, Green, Yellow, Pink On White, 1 3/4 In. 250.00
Onionskin, Mica, Pink, White, 2 1/4 In. 1792.00
Onionskin, Pink, Green, Yellow On White, 1 3/4 In. 840.00
Onionskin Lutz, Blue, White, Green, Pink Streaks, 2 1/16 In. 728.00
Onionskin Lutz, Yellow, Black, White, Blue, Green, Orange Lines, 17 Lutz Lines, 13/16 In. 135.00
Picture, Cartoon Characters, Smitty, Herbie, Skeezix, Sandy, Ko Ko, Bimbo, 12 Piece 1650.00
Slag, Brown, 1 7/8 In. 448.00
Slag, Green, Glass, Pontil, 1 15/32 In. 140.00
Sulphide, Bear, 1 3/8 In. 40.00
Sulphide, Clear White Love Birds Center, 1 7/8 In. 355.00
Sulphide, Cow, 1 1/2 In. 116.00
Sulphide, Dog, 2 In. 30.00
Sulphide, Goat, 1 1/2 In. 110.00
Sulphide, Horse, 1 3/4 In. 30.00
Swirl, Red, Blue, White, Green & Yellow, White Latticinio Exterior, Sandwich Glass, 2 In. 85.00
Swirl, Red, White, Blue, Sandwich Glass, 2 1/4 In. 220.00
Swirl, Red, White, Blue, Yellow, Sandwich Glass, 2 1/4 In. 165.00
Swirl, Solid Core, 2 1/4 In. 165.00
Swirl, Yellow, Green, Red, 3/4 In. 56.00

MARBLE CARVINGS, such as large or small figurines, groups of people or animals, and architectural decorations, have been a special art form since the time of the ancient Greeks. Reproductions, especially of large Victorian groups, are being made of a mixture using marble dust. These are very difficult to detect and collectors should be careful. Other carvings are listed under Alabaster.

Bowl, Footed, Angelo Mangiarotti, Knoll, 1970s, 7 x 6 In. 900.00
Bust, Antinous, Waisted Socle Base, After The Antique, Italy, 1800s, 21 1/2 In. 4065.00
Bust, Aphrodite, Downward Looking, Turned Socle, 16 1/2 x 13 1/2 In. 590.00
Bust, Apollo, Low Socle, F. Vichi, Italy, c.1900, 19 In. 1530.00
Bust, Ernst August, King Of Hanover, William Behnes, London, 1829, 30 In. 4356.00
Bust, Felix Mendelssohn, Swiveling Socle, 15 1/2 x 8 In. 176.00
Bust, Henry Ward Beecher, Incised Signature, Thomas Ball, c.1860, 23 In. 8815.00
Bust, Hermes, Turned Socle, 24 x 24 In. 4400.00
Bust, Julius Caesar, 2-Tone, 24 1/2 x 15 In. 1290.00
Bust, La Dame Aux Perles, G. Petrilli, Florence, Italy, c.1885, 23 x 17 In. 3760.00
Bust, Man, Bearded, Classically Draped, J.A. Jackson, 25 1/2 In. 2350.00
Bust, Man, Victorian, 1884, 31 1/2 In. 5875.00
Bust, Nymph, Wearing Chiton, Waterlily Bands, Europe, c.1900, 14 3/4 In. 1295.00
Bust, Vestal Virgin, Neoclassical, Turned Socle, 24 x 11 In. 1350.00
Bust, Woman, Battelli, Italy, c.1880, 24 In. 936.00
Bust, Woman, Elegant, Chignon With Beaded Comb, Turned Socle, 29 In. 5580.00
Bust, Woman, Laurel Crown, E. Fiaschi, Italy, Early 1800s, 16 1/2 x 16 In. 1998.00
Bust, Woman, Neoclassical, Elegantly Draped, Turned Socle, 30 x 19 In. 4400.00
Group, Boy Holding Chicks, Girl Holding Puppies, Late 1800s, 23 In., Pair 3055.00
Group, Eagle, Wings Slightly Open, Perched On Rock, 12 1/4 In. 345.00
Panel, Mount Purgatory, Continental, 21 1/2 x 53 1/4 In. 8400.00
Pedestal, Circular Base, Red, Gray, Jasper, c.1900, 9 In., Pair 205.00
Pedestal, Ionic Column, Green, Variegated, Fluted, Plinth Base, 17 1/2 In., Pair 3525.00
Pedestal, Neoclassical, Bronze Mounted, Green, Garland, Bouquet, 46 x 13 1/4 In., Pair 4995.00
Pedestal, Renaissance, Domed Octagonal Base, c.1900, 51 x 9 In. 1175.00

Pedestal, Tapered, Fluted, Square Top, Verde Antico, 1800s, 38 1/2 x 10 In. 370.00
Statue, Buddha, Chinese, c.1850, 22 In. 560.00
Statue, Buddha, Head, Chinese, c.1800, 11 In. 945.00
Statue, Female Nude, Flowers, White, Arch Ground, Brown Base, Art Nouveau, 10 In. 240.00
Statue, Flora, Holding Flower, 51 x 18 In. 2645.00
Statue, Foo Dog, Seated, Freestanding Front Legs, Oriental, 24 In., Pair 690.00
Statue, Goddess, Chinese, 20th Century, 19 In. 1645.00
Statue, Lion, Paw Resting On Sphere, Rectangular Base, 10 x 13 In., Pair 205.00
Statue, Roman Soldier, Wood Base, Italy, 12 1/2 x 5 1/2 In. 1610.00
Statue, Torso, Male Nude, After The Antique, Carrara Base, Italy, 18 In. 470.00
Statue, Torso, Male Nude, Square Plinth Base, 34 x 16 In. 4115.00
Statue, Venus, Crouching, After Antique, Green Marble Column, 1800s, 75 In. 11165.00
Urn, Bronze Ormolu Mounted, 19th Century, France, 21 In., Pair 2340.00
Urn, Campana, Gilt Swags & Trim, Bronze Cherub Handles, Plinth Base, 17 In., Pair 1645.00
Urn, Classical, Carrara Marble, 15 In., 3 Piece 1645.00
Urn, Classical, Flared Rim, Narrow Neck, Variegated, 19 1/2 x 15 In. 250.00
Urn, Cover, Classical, Spiral Flutes, Acorn Finial, 26 x 16 In., Pair 2645.00
Vase, Cubist Handles, M. De Baiser Gratery, 11 x 7 7/8 In. 4967.00
Woman Playing Pipes, Continental, 19th Century, 35 In. 3600.00

MARBLEHEAD Pottery was founded in 1905 by Dr. J. Hall as a rehabilitative program for the patients of a Marblehead, Massachusetts, sanitarium. Two years later it was separated from the sanitarium and it continued operations until 1936. Many of the pieces were decorated with marine motifs.

Berry Bowl, Midnight Blue Glaze, Blue Interior, 3 1/4 x 5 3/4 In. 1840.00
Bowl, Flecked Caramel Matte Glaze Over Ocher, Speckled Interior, 3 1/2 x 5 In. 405.00
Bowl, Plum, Lavender Matte Glaze, Frothy White, Lavender Glaze Interior, 9 In. 345.00
Hanging Basket, Lavender Matte Glaze, 4 1/2 In. 120.00
Plant Hanger, Beehive Shape, Blue Glaze, Ruffled Style Mouth, 5 3/4 x 5 1/4 In. 316.00
Plant Hanger, Torpedo Style, Plum, Lavender Matte Glaze, 3 Handles, 3 3/4 x 5 1/4 In. 201.00
Tile, Duck, Blue Ground, Incised Mark, 1900s, 5 3/4 x 5 3/4 In. 440.00
Vase, Blue Matte Glaze, 5 In. 345.00
Vase, Blue Matte Glaze, 6 1/4 x 5 1/2 In. 18.00
Vase, Blue Matte Glaze, Squat, Impressed Mark, 3 1/4 In. 300.00
Vase, Brown Matte Glaze, Tapered, Impressed Mark, 3 1/2 In. 210.00
Vase, Bud, Ocher Brown Matte Glaze, 6 x 2 3/4 In. 375.00
Vase, Gray Matte Glaze, Cylindrical, Impressed Mark, 8 1/2 In. 1140.00
Vase, Gray Purple Matte Glaze, Tapered, 3 1/2 In. 265.00
Vase, Green Matte Glaze, Brown Geometric Design, Tapered, Broad, M.T., 4 In. 500.00
Vase, Green Matte Glaze, Round, Impressed Mark, 3 1/4 In. 360.00
Vase, Pink Matte Glaze, Low Form, Impressed Mark, 3 1/2 In. 240.00
Vase, Purple Matte Glaze, Round, Impressed Mark, 3 1/2 In. 510.00
Vase, Purple Matte Glaze, Tapered, Impressed Mark, 3 1/2 In. 210.00
Vase, Yellow Matte Glaze, Flared, Impressed Mark, 4 1/4 In. 600.00
Vase, Yellow Matte Glaze, Tapered, Impressed Mark, 6 1/4 In. 840.00
Wall Pocket, Carved, Painted Flowers, Pink, Blue, Gray Ground, 7 x 5 In. 1880.00

MARTIN BROTHERS of Middlesex, England, made Martinware, a salt-glazed stoneware, between 1873 and 1915. Many figural jugs and vases were made by the three brothers. Of special interest are the fanciful birds, usually made with removable heads.

Martin Bros
London

Figurine, Undersea, Grotesque, 1898, 6 3/4 In. 9600.00
Jug, Earthenware, Face 5063.00
Jug, Face, 2-Sided, Barrister, c.1900, 6 3/4 In. 7800.00
Jug, Face, Glazed, 1891, 8 3/4 In. 5400.00
Jug, Face, Glazed, 1901, 7 7/8 In. 4200.00
Jug, Leaves, Blue, Green, Incised, Painted, Stoneware, c.1890, 7 In. 615.00
Spoon Warmer, Glazed, Grotesque, Gaping Mouth, 1898, 5 1/2 In. 8400.00
Vase, Scrolling Leaves, Waves, Egg Shape, 4 Handles, 1894, 15 1/2 In. 3600.00

MARY GREGORY is the name used for a type of glass that is easily

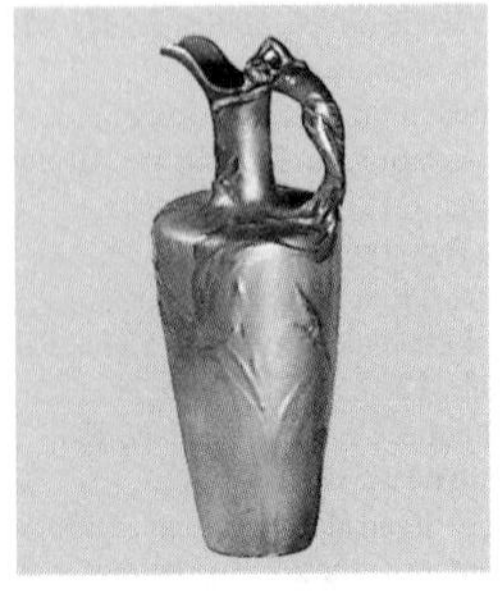

Mary Gregory, Bottle, Barber, Amethyst, Victorian, Boy

Massier, Pitcher, Iris Design, Iridescent Glaze, Handle In Form Of Woman, Signed, 27 In.

identified. White figures were painted on clear or colored glass as the decoration. The figures chosen were usually children at play. The first glass known as Mary Gregory was made about 1870. Similar glass is made even today. The traditional story has been that the glass was made at the Sandwich Glass works in Boston by a woman named Mary Gregory. Recent research suggests that it is possible that none was made at Sandwich. In general, all-white figures were used in the United States, tinted faces were probably used in Bohemia, France, Italy, Germany, Switzerland, and England. Children standing, not playing, were pictured after the 1950s.

Bottle, Barber, Amethyst, Victorian, Boy .... *ILLUS* 252.00
Bottle, Barber, Girl, Flowers, Green, 9 In. 220.00
Bowl, Green, Cherub, Leaves, Paneled Sides, 5 x 2 3/4 In. 45.00
Box, Hinged Cover, Blue, Girl With Bird, Brass Feet, 4 x 3 1/4 In. 250.00
Cruet, Ruby Flashed, Girl, Reaching For Flowers, Leaves, Stopper, Clear Handle 65.00
Cup, Cranberry, Girl, Landscape, Gold Rim, 8-Sided, Clear Handle 70.00
Dresser Box, Hinged Cover, Black Amethyst, Girl, Round, 1880s, 2 1/2 x 2 1/2 In. 280.00
Dresser Box, Hinged Cover, Blue, Girl, Butterfly, Tree, Grass, Square, 4 1/4 x 4 1/4 In. 435.00
Ewer, Green, Bicycle Racer, Pewter Lid & Thumb Latch, c.1896, 15 In. 220.00
Lamp, Oil, Black Amethyst Base, Bird, Branch, Flowers, Twin Burner, 22 In. 135.00
Loving Cup, Cranberry, Boy With Sword, Gold Enameled Flowers, Handles, 4 3/4 In. 250.00
Mug, Blue Coin Spot, Girl Holding Flowers, 5 In. 100.00
Mug, Blue, Knight, 4 1/2 In. 10.00
Pickle Castor, Cranberry, Boy, Pushing Girl On Swing, Metal Frame, 10 1/2 In. 90.00
Pitcher, Blue, Oriental Woman Holding Fan, 9 In. 80.00
Pitcher, Cobalt Blue, Boy Chasing Bird, 9 1/2 In. 50.00
Pitcher, Green Translucent, Lady Picking Flower, Late 1800s, 11 In. 118.00
Pitcher, Green, Cherubs, Flowers, Applied Clear Handle 112.00
Pitcher, Tankard, Green, Girl, 10 1/2 In. 105.00
Pitcher, Water, Cranberry, Gnomes, Clear Reeded Handle, 8 1/2 In. 50.00
Stein, Amber, Girl, Trees, Pewter Lid, 12 1/2 x 5 In. 128.00
Tumble Up, Blue, Boy, Pushing Girl On Swing, 8 In., 2 Piece 35.00
Tumble Up, Cobalt Blue, Girl Holding Bird, 7 In., 2 Piece 225.00
Tumbler, Blue, Girl, 4 In. 20.00
Tumbler, Cranberry, Boy, Holding Flower, 1890s, 4 1/2 In. 115.00
Tumbler, Cranberry, Girl, Holding Flower, Corseted, c.1900, 4 1/2 In. 80.00
Tumbler, Green, Girl, 3 1/2 In. 25.00
Tumbler, Jelly, Cranberry, Boy, Bird, Tree, Pedestal Base, c.1920, 3 1/4 In. 40.00
Urn, Cover, Blue, 2 Cherubs Smelling Flowers, Applied Amber Ridges, 20 In. 300.00
Vase, Blue, Man & Boy In Field, 9 In., Pair 110.00
Vase, Cobalt Blue, Boy Catching Fish, 10 In. 80.00
Vase, Cranberry, Boy Chasing Bird, 6 In. 25.00
Vase, Cranberry, Girl, Holding Flower, 3 1/4 x 1 1/2 In. 125.00
Vase, Cranberry, Girl, On Fence, Tree, Ribbed, Ruffled Edge, 11 In. 102.00
Vase, Cranberry, Girl, Playing With Bubbles, 7 1/2 In. 50.00

Vase, Cranberry, Man & Woman Courting, 10 In., Pair 175.00
Vase, Emerald Green, Boy With Trumpet, 8 1/4 In. 50.00
Vase, Emerald Green, Man & Woman Leaning On Fence, Applied Clear Rigaree, 11 In., Pair 300.00
Vase, Translucent Blue, Boy, Catching Butterfly, White Enameling, 7 1/4 In. 60.00
Vase, Trumpet, Cranberry, Boy, Holding Flower, 8 In. 100.00

MASON'S IRONSTONE was made by the English pottery of Charles J. Mason after 1813. Mason, of Lane Delph, was given a patent for this improved earthenware. He usually called it "Mason's Patent Ironstone China." It resisted chipping and breaking so it became popular for dinnerwares and other table service dishes. Vases and other decorative pieces were also made. The ironstone was decorated with orange, blue, gold, and other colors, often in Japanese inspired designs. The firm had financial difficulties but the molds and the name Mason were used by many owners through the years, including Francis Morley, Taylor Ashworth, George L. Ashworth, and John Shaw. Mason's joined the Wedgwood group in 1973 and the name is still found on dinnerwares.

Bowl, Cobalt Blue, White, Paneled, Leaves, Flowers, 10 In. 31.00
Bowl, Manchu Pattern, Flowers, Buterflies, Yellow, Green, Scalloped Rim, 9 In. 25.00
Cake Plate, Blue & White Decoration, Square, Handles, c.1910, 12 In., Pair 1500.00
Cake Plate, Vista, Red & White, Square, Pierced Handles, 9 1/2 In. 51.00
Cup & Saucer, Strathmore 40.00
Dish, Flowers, Raised Decoration, 9 1/2 In. 138.00
Dish, Leaf Shape, c.1820, 11 x 7 1/2 In. 295.00
Ginger Jar, Formosa Pattern, Birds, Flowers, Yellow, Green, Brown, Turquoise, 9 In. 39.00
Jug, Brown Transfer, Couples On Lawn, Lake, Building, Scalloped Rim, 6 1/8 In. 69.00
Jug, Hydra, Octagonal, Serpent Handle, Japan Palette, c.1825, 7 1/2 In. 306.00
Jug, Imari Decoration, Blue, Rust, Serpent Handle, 4 1/2 In. 295.00
Mustard Pot, Chartreuse Pattern, 1880s, 4 1/4 In. 60.00
Pitcher, Cupid, c.1870, 6 1/4 In. 45.00
Pitcher, Vista, Purple, Green, 1925-30, 5 1/2 In. 125.00
Pitcher, Vista, White, Pink Design, 32 Oz., 6 In. 60.00
Plate, Brocade, Ivory Ground, Gilt Edge, 1900-40, 6 In. 75.00
Plate, Divided, South Seas Series, Palm Tree, Shell, Starfish, 3 Sections, 10 1/2 In. 12.00
Plate, Garden, Pagoda, Flowers, Square, Rounded Corners, Pierced Handles, 9 In. 194.00
Plate, Salad, Persiana, Flowers, Orange, Yellow, Blue, 7 In. 28.00
Platter, Birds, On Flowering Branches, 9 x 6 1/4 In. 495.00
Platter, Chinoiserie Decoration, Gold Trim, c.1845, 13 x 10 1/4 In. 550.00
Sauceboat, Cover, Underplate, Ladle, Vista, Red & White 188.00
Tea Caddy, Strathmore, 6-Sided, 6 In. 97.00
Tea Set, Polychrome, Teapot, Plate, Pitcher, Creamer, Sugar, 6 Cups, Saucers 105.00
Teapot, Cover, Watteau, Red Transfer, 8 3/4 In. 250.00
Teapot, Vista, Red & White, 7 In. 58.00
Toast Holder, Vista, Red & White, 3 x 5 x 2 In. 103.00
Vase, Paisley, c.1840, 19 In. 439.00

MASONIC, see Fraternal category.

MASSIER, a French art pottery, was made by brothers Jerome, Delphin, and Clement Massier in Vallauris and Golfe-Juan, France, in the late nineteenth and early twentieth centuries. It has an iridescent metallic luster glaze that resembles the Weller Sicardo pottery glaze. Most pieces are marked *J. Massier*. Massier may also be listed in the Majolica category.

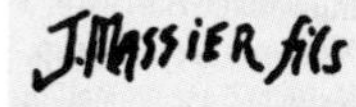

Charger, Woman, Brunette, Garlands, Irises, Leaves, Art Nouveau, 12 In. 4500.00
Knife Rest, Flowers, Leaves, Triangular Shape, Signed, 1 1/4 x 3 3/4 In. 68.00
Pitcher, Iris Design, Iridescent Glaze, Handle In Form Of Woman, Signed, 27 In. .... *ILLUS* 7920.00
Plate, Cat Holding Kitten, Etched, Red Iridescent Glaze, Signed, 8 In. 1920.00
Vase, Brown, Metallic, Handles, 13 3/4 In. 385.00

Vase, Brown, Metallic, Luster, Pierced Neck, Handles, Vallauris, 12 1/2 In. 389.00
Vase, Incised Flowers, Twisted Handles, Vallauris, 5 1/2 In. 185.00
Vase, Iridescent, Butterflies, 2 Shaped Cutout Handles, Signed, 11 1/2 In. 1800.00
Vase, Iridescent, Metallic Glaze, Web Design, Shouldered, Impressed Mark, 4 1/2 In. 1076.00
Vase, Iridescent, Mottled, Gourd Shape, 2 Twisted Handles, 6 1/4 In. 390.00
Vase, Ivory, Brown Bulbous Rim, Applied Nude Figure, Marked, 11 In. 1050.00
Vase, Landscape, Multicolored Metallic Glaze, Footed, Handles, Signed, 14 In. 8812.00
Vase, Leaves, Metallic Glaze, Iridescent, Handles, Footed, Signed, 8 In. 2510.00

MATCH HOLDERS were made to hold the large wooden matches that were used in the nineteenth and twentieth centuries for a variety of purposes. The kitchen stove and the fireplace or furnace had to be lit regularly. One type of match holder was made to hang on the wall, another was designed to be kept on a tabletop. Of special interest today are match holders that have advertisements as part of the design.

3 Black Babies On Log, Bisque, Hand Painted, Austria, 1890s, 3 1/2 In. 65.00
Armour Canned Meat, Tin Lithograph, 4 7/8 x 3 3/8 In. 330.00
August Flower, German Syrup, Black Man, Smoking, Cardboard, Die Cut, 8 x 5 In. 1375.00
Baseball Player, Fence, Cast Iron, 1880s 1390.00
Bennett's Brilliantshine Metal Polish, Tin Lithograph, 5 x 3 1/2 In. 770.00
Black Boy, Leaning On Barrel, Holding Box, Cigar Holder, Bisque, 8 1/2 In. 56.00
Black Boy, On Tree Stump, Yellow Jacket, Cap, Cigar Holder, Bisque, 8 In. 56.00
Black Boy Stealing Pigs, Austria, 1880s, 5 1/2 In. 120.00
Black Boy With Melon, Bisque, Hand Painted, Austria, 1890s, 4 1/2 In. 95.00
Black Boy With Newsboy Cap, Terra-Cotta, 7 In. 390.00
Black Cat Shoe Dressing, Black Kitty, Tin, 5 1/2 x 4 1/4 In. 1075.00
Black Corn Girl, Basket, Ear Of Corn, Bisque, Hand Painted, Austria, 1890s, 5 1/2 In. 116.00
Black Figure, Suit, Porcelain, Hand Painted, c.1900, 7 1/2 In. 105.00
Black Head, Exaggerated Features, Chalkware, Painted, 1920s, 4 1/4 In. 225.00
Black Man Grins, Figural, Matches In Top, Ceramic, 1880s, 3 In. 95.00
Black Man Playing Accordion, Bisque, 8 In. 85.00
Black Man Waving Hat, Bisque, 5 In. 28.00
Black Man's Head, Ruffled White Collar, Striker On Back, Ceramic, 3 1/2 In. 140.00
Blackamoor, Screaming, Bust, Porcelain, Painted, Austria, 1890s, 2 3/4 In. 80.00
Blackamoor Boy, Basket, Painted, Pedestal, Majolica, Austria, 1880s, 6 In. 165.00
Boy Carrying Basket On Back, Ashtray, Original Paint, Hubley, No. 311, c.1900, 6 1/2 In. 110.00
Boy With Crashed Bicycle, Bisque, Cigar Compartment, Germany, c.1890, 8 In. 165.00
Bucket Form, Copper, Silver Crab, Aesthetic Movement, Gorham, c.1883, 2 x 2 In. 410.00
Buffalo Brewing Co., Embossed Cowboy, Buffaloes, Celluloid, 2 3/4 x 1 1/2 In. 385.00
Chicago School, Copper, Oak, Prairie School Backplate, Wooden Tile, 8 x 8 In. 705.00
Cigarette, Black Baby In Basket, Hand Painted, Bisque, Austria, 1890s, 3 1/4 In. 150.00
Climax Horse Collars, Tin, Brown Horse Wearing Collar, 4 x 3 In. 355.00
Dead Game, Cast Iron, Brass Wash, 1870, 8 3/4 In. 100.00
DeLaval Cream Separators, Tin Lithograph, Die Cut, Box, 6 1/4 x 4 In. 495.00
Devil, Entrapped, Cast Iron, c.1900, 6 1/2 In. 470.00
Embossed Scroll Design, Silvered, Late 19th Century, 3 In. 94.00
Grotesque Face, Embossed Gothic Style Back Plate, Cast Iron, 7 1/4 In. 235.00
Lyre, Wreath, Guitar, Tambourine, Scroddleware, 5 1/2 x 6 3/4 In. 121.00
Merry War Lye, Wash Woman, Lithograph, 5 1/2 x 3 3/4 In. 468.00
Milwaukee Harvester Machines, Tin Lithograph, 5 1/2 x 3 3/4 In. 1375.00
Mother's Worm Syrup, Tin, Grandmother, Child, 6 3/4 In. 525.00
Natural Gas, Promotion, Embossed, Turn Off Burner When Not Using, c.1900, 8 In. 94.00
Rastus, Hand Painted, Bisque, Schafer & Vater, 1890s, 4 3/4 In. 265.00
Rockford Watch, E.T. Andrew Jeweler, Hand, Watch, Tin Lithograph, 4 3/4 x 2 5/8 In. 852.00
Rooster, 3 Baskets, Pottery, Impressed, 6 3/4 x 7 In. 47.00
Snapping Turtle Head, Strike, 4 1/4 In. 75.00
Vulcan Plow Co., Blacksmith, Tin, Lithograph, Die Cut, 8 x 2 3/4 In. 1320.00
What A Bust, Black Man Holding White Woman, Bisque, Prewar, Japan, 3 3/4 In. 80.00
Wrigley's, Tin Lithograph, Juicy Fruit Gum, 4 7/8 x 3 3/8 x 1 3/8 In. 300.00

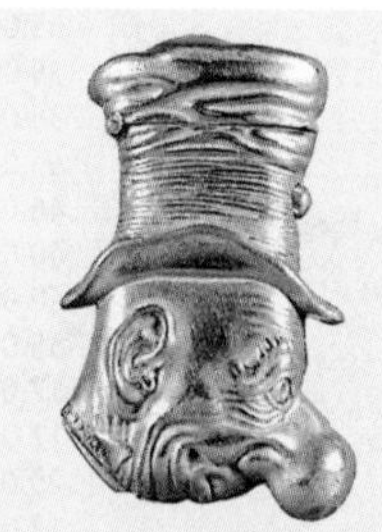
Match Safe, Alley Sloper, Nickel Plated Brass, Pushbottom Release, c.1890

Match Safe, Art Nouveau, Woman's Profile & Flowers, Sterling Silver, c.1900

Match Safe, Owl, Brass

MATCH SAFES were designed to be carried in the pocket. Early matches were made with phosphorus and could ignite unexpectedly. The matches were safely stored in the tightly closed container. Match safes were made in sterling silver, plated silver, or other metals. The English call these *vesta boxes*.

Alley Sloper, Nickel Plated Brass, Pushbottom Release, c.1890 .... *ILLUS* 330.00
American Manure Spreader, Farmer, Tin Lithograph, 4 7/8 x 3 3/8 In. 740.00
Arm & Hammer, Compliments Of Church & Co., Gutta-Percha, 3 x 1 1/4 In. 350.00
Art Nouveau, Woman's Profile & Flowers, Sterling Silver, c.1900 .... *ILLUS* 275.00
Automobile, Art Nouveau Border 1650.00
Automobile, Fence, Tree, Clouds 1100.00
Baseball Players, Silver Plate, 1880s, 2 3/4 x 1 1/2 In. 1276.00
Bryant & Mays Wax Vistas, 3 Racing Cyclists, Tin, Brass Finish, 1 3/4 x 1 1/2 In. 77.00
Diamond Matches, Man, Under Umbrella, Fishing, Tin Lithograph, 1 5/8 x 2 3/8 In. 220.00
Dr. Shoop's, Health Coffee Imitation, W.W. Stalker, Halfway, Ore., Tin Lithograph, 5 x 3 In. 275.00
Dr. Shoop's, Lax-Ets, A Candy Bowel Laxative, Only 5 Cents A Box, Tin Lithograph, 5 x 3 1/2 In. ... 187.00
Floral Border, Engraved Monogram, Sterling Silver, Simons Bros., Philadelphia, c.1895 .... 28.00
Garfield Memorial, Embossed, Brass 85.00
General Arthur's Cigars, Suit All Mankind, Tin, 1 x 1 3/4 x 1/2 In. 145.00
Hoffmans Polish, Nude Woman, Jug, Celluloid Over Metal, 2 3/4 x 1 1/2 x 7/16 In. 632.00
Hunter Whiskey, Baltimore Rye, First Over The Bars, Celluloid Over Metal, 2 3/4 x 1 1/2 In. 358.00
International Stock Food Co., Dan Patch, Horses, Tin, 1 3/4 x 2 3/8 x 3/8 In. 580.00
Martin-Perrin Co., Wholesale Liquors, Kansas City, Mo., Stoneware, 4 1/2 In. 798.00
Molassine Horse & Cattle Food, Nude Woman, Celluloid, Whitehead & Hoag, 1905 Patent 405.00
Owl, Brass .... *ILLUS* 110.00
Primley's Pepsin Gum, Aluminum, 2 7/8 x 1 5/8 x 7/16 In. 265.00
San Felice Cigars, Metal, Pocket, Celluloid, 2 3/8 x 1 3/4 x 3/8 In. 255.00
Snake, Brass, Glass Eyes 660.00
Sock, Nickel Plated Brass, Ribs, Tassels, c.1890 .... 525.00
Vacuum Oil Co., Lighthouse, Floating Barrel, Celluloid, Metal, Rochester, N.Y., 2 1/4 In. 578.00
Wyoming Clothier, Woman, Celluloid Over Metal, 2 1/2 x 1 1/2 In. 523.00

MCCOY pottery was made in Roseville, Ohio. Nelson McCoy and J.W. McCoy established the Nelson McCoy Sanitary and Stoneware Company in Roseville, Ohio, in 1910. The firm made art pottery after 1926. In 1933 it became the Nelson McCoy Pottery Company. Pieces marked *McCoy* were made by the Nelson McCoy Pottery Company. Cookie jars were made from about 1940 until December 1990, when the McCoy factory closed. Since 1991 pottery with the McCoy mark has been made by firms unrelated to the original company. Because there was a company named Brush-McCoy, there is great confusion between Brush and Nelson McCoy pieces. See Brush category for more information.

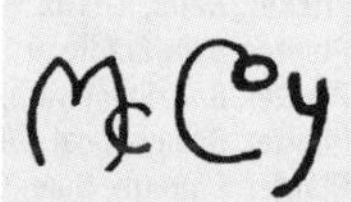

Bank, Williamsburg, Savings, 7 In. 55.00
Basket, Hanging, Butterfly, White, 6 1/2 In. 50.00

Bookends, Lily Bud, 5 3/4 In. 65.00
Bookends, Lily, Yellow, Green, 5 1/2 In. 75.00
Bowl, Blue Butterflies, Inward Folded Green Rim, 2 1/2 x 9 1/2 In. 235.00
Coffee Server, El Rancho, 14 Cup 45.00
Cookie Jar, Bear, Upside Down, Black, White, 12 In. 46.00
Cookie Jar, Chef, 11 In. 40.00
Cookie Jar, Circus Horse, 10 1/2 In. 40.00
Cookie Jar, Clown, Bust, 11 In. 35.00
Cookie Jar, Coffee Grinder, 10 In. 17.00
Cookie Jar, Coffee Mug, 9 In. 17.00
Cookie Jar, Cookie Wagon, 9 1/2 In. 29.00
Cookie Jar, Cookstove, Black, 9 In. 17.00
Cookie Jar, Covered Wagon, 7 1/4 In. 40.00
Cookie Jar, Dog On Basketweave, 10 1/4 In. 40.00
Cookie Jar, Duck On Basketweave, 10 In. 20.00
Cookie Jar, Hamm's Bear, 13 In. 154.00
Cookie Jar, Have A Happy Day, Yellow, 11 In. 12.00
Cookie Jar, Hobbyhorse, White, 10 1/2 In. 58.00
Cookie Jar, Hobnail, Round, Green, 8 1/4 In. 29.00
Cookie Jar, Honey Bear, 8 1/2 In. 35.00
Cookie Jar, Indian, Cookies, 11 3/4 In. 105.00
Cookie Jar, Keebler Elf, 10 In. 25.00
Cookie Jar, Kittens On Ball Of Yarn, Green, 8 1/2 In. 40.00
Cookie Jar, Lamb On Basketweave, 10 1/4 In. 25.00
Cookie Jar, Mr. & Mrs. Owl, 10 3/4 In. 60.00
Cookie Jar, Nabisco, 9 1/2 In. 29.00
Cookie Jar, Owl, Brown, 10 In. 75.00
Cookie Jar, Pinecones On Basketweave, 10 In. 20.00
Cookie Jar, Polar Bear, 10 1/2 In. 17.00
Cookie Jar, Puppy, Holding Sign, 9 1/2 In. 29.00
Cookie Jar, Thinking Puppy, 11 In. 20.00
Cookie Jar, Touring Car, 6 1/2 In. 29.00
Cookie Jar, Train Engine, Yellow, 11 1/2 In. 75.00
Cookie Jar, World Globe, Airplane, 10 In. 253.00
Cookie Jar, Wren House, Brown Bird, Green Trim, 10 In. 29.00
Dresser Caddy, Buffalo, 9 1/2 In. 15.00
Fernery, Window Box, Hobnail, 6 3/4 x 4 1/2 In. 15.00
Figurine, Fawn, Chartreuse, 5 In. 45.00
Flower Bowl Ornament, Peacock, White 75.00
Flower Pot, Stoneware, White, Berry, Leaf, 6 In. 45.00
Grease Jar, Cabbage, 7 In. 30.00
Jardiniere, Butterfly, 4 In. 25.00
Jardiniere, Butterfly, Square, 3 In. 40.00
Jardiniere, Rustic Pinecone, 4 In. 10.00
Mixing Bowl Set, Pink, Blue Bands, 6, 8, 10 & 12 In. 75.00
Mug, Nixon, 5 In. 175.00
Pitcher, Chicken, 6 In. 40.00
Pitcher, Elephant, Can't Do It Alone, 5 3/4 In. 65.00
Pitcher, Indian, Gloss Brown, 8 1/2 In. 15.00
Pitcher, Parrot, 7 In. 80.00
Pitcher, Water, Gloss Brown, 5 In. 15.00
Pitcher, Water, Ice Lip, Maroon, 7 In. 20.00
Planter, Baby Cradle, 9 1/2 In. 20.00
Planter, Ball, Stoneware, 6 In. 55.00
Planter, Banana Boat, Calypso, 11 In. 45.00
Planter, Butterfly, Blue, 5 1/2 In. 35.00
Planter, Butterfly, White, 5 1/2 In. 25.00
Planter, Calypso, Fish Net, 11 In. 245.00
Planter, Cowboy Boots, 7 In. 5.00
Planter, Cowboy Hat, 8 In. 20.00
Planter, Dog, Bird, Green, Brown 325.00

Planter, Dog, Dachshund, Stretch, Blue, 7 1/4 In. 150.00
Planter, Dog, Scottie, 8 In. 45.00
Planter, Fawn, 5 1/2 In. .... 20.00 to 50.00
Planter, Football, 7 In. 50.00
Planter, Goat, Stretch, Aqua, 5 3/4 In. 55.00
Planter, Grass Growing Gleep, 8 In. 30.00
Planter, Hobnail, Yellow, 3 3/4 In. 13.00
Planter, Lamb, Blue Bow, 6 1/2 In. 20.00
Planter, Liberty Bell, 10 In. 145.00
Planter, Log, Brown, 8 3/4 In. 5.00
Planter, Madonna, Floraline Version, 6 In. 175.00
Planter, Parrot, 7 1/2 In. 15.00
Planter, Pelican, 5 1/4 In. 15.00
Planter, Pheasant, 7 1/2 In. 45.00
Planter, Piggy, 6 In. 10.00
Planter, Pony, 7 In. 45.00
Planter, Quails, 9 In. 30.00
Planter, Rocking Horse, 7 1/2 In. 25.00
Planter, Snowman, 6 1/4 In. 70.00
Planter, Swan, White, 6 3/4 In. 12.50
Planter, Teal, 3 x 6 In. 10.00
Planter, Turtle, 12 In. 25.00
Planter, Turtle, Yellow, 5 In. 55.00
Planter, Uncle Sam, 7 3/4 In. 35.00
Planter, Window Box, Blossomtime 30.00
Pot, Stoneware, 7 In. 160.00
Salt & Pepper, Pepper, Cucumber, 5 1/4 In. 50.00
Vase, Arrowhead, Yellow, 8 In. 20.00
Vase, Blossomtime, 6 1/2 In. 25.00
Vase, Bud, Double, Burgundy, 6 In. 35.00
Vase, Bud, Lily, Yellow, 8 In. 25.00
Vase, Bud, Lily, Yellow, 10 In. 30.00
Vase, Butterfly, 2 Handles, Blue, 10 In. 120.00
Vase, Butterfly, Cylindrical, Blue, 8 In. 50.00
Vase, Butterfly, Cylindrical, Pink, 9 In. 45.00
Vase, Butterfly, Cylindrical, Yellow, 8 In. 20.00
Vase, Castlegate, Butterfly, Blue, 7 In. 50.00
Vase, Castlegate, Hobnail, Blue, 7 In. 105.00
Vase, Cobalt Blue, Stoneware, 7 In. 55.00
Vase, Double Handles, Floor, 12 In. 75.00
Vase, Double Tulip, 6 1/2 In. 45.00
Vase, Fan, Blue, 15 In. 40.00
Vase, Fan, Yellow, 6 1/2 In. 30.00
Vase, Hand, White, 8 In. 40.00
Vase, Lily, Yellow, 8 In. 25.00
Vase, Triple Hyacinth, 8 In. 60.00
Vase, White, Black, Pedestal, 10 In. 30.00
Wall Pocket, Lily, White, 8 In. 20.00
Wall Pocket, Owls, 8 In. 40.00
Wall Pocket, Pear, 7 In. 40.00

MCKEE is a name associated with various glass enterprises in the United States since 1836, including J. & F. McKee (1850), Bryce, McKee & Co. (1850 to 1854), McKee and Brothers (1865), and National Glass Co. (1899). In 1903, the McKee Glass Company was formed in Jeannette, Pennsylvania. It became McKee Division of the Thatcher Glass Co. in 1951 and was bought out by the Jeannette Corporation in 1961. Pressed glass, kitchenwares, and tablewares were produced. Jeannette Corporation closed in the early 1980s. Additional pieces may be included in the Custard Glass category.

Bowl, Wiltec, Pres Cut, Square, 9 3/4 In. 50.00

Celery Dish, Innovation, Pres Cut, 12 In. 10.00
Compote, Aztec, Pres Cut, 4 1/2 In. 12.00
Mixing Bowl, Jadite, Vertical Ribs, 9 In. 53.00
Punch Bowl, Stand, Aztec, Pres Cut, 13 x 7 1/2 In. 100.00
Salt & Pepper, Beehive, Jade Green, 4 In. 20.00
Salt & Pepper, Small Black Letters, Jade Green, 5 In. 90.00
Saltshaker, Black Letters, Stripes, Milk Glass, 4 1/2 In. 45.00
Spice Set, Roman Arches, Jade Green, 4 In., 14 Piece 115.00
Spooner, Ultec, Pres Cut, 3 1/2 In. 20.00

MECHANICAL BANKS are listed in the Bank category.

MEDICAL office furniture, operating tools, microscopes, thermometers, and other paraphernalia used by doctors are included in this category. Veterinary collectibles are also included here. Medicine bottles are listed in the Bottle category. There are related collectibles listed under Dental.

Amputation Set, Saws, Ebony Handles, Knives, Mahogany Case, 16 In. 2468.00
Apothecary Cupboard, 2 Part, Step Back, 26 Drawers, 14 Cubby Holes, 54 x 66 In. 3300.00
Bags, Doctor's, Cowhide Leather, Fitted 145.00
Bleeder, 1 Blade, Buffalo Horn Handle, W. Pepys, 1860s, 3 3/4 x 1 1/2 In. 105.00
Bleeder, 1 Blade, Tortoiseshell Thumb, W. Pepys, 3 In. 95.00
Bleeder, 3 Blades, Brass Handle, 3 1/4 In. 88.00
Bleeder, 3 Blades, Brass Handles, Cardboard Case, 1860s, 1 In. 98.00
Bleeder, 3 Blades, Brass, Borwick .... 50.00 to 55.00
Bleeder, 3 Blades, Brass, Island Works Jackson Co. 45.00
Bleeder, 3 Blades, Horn Handles, Broom Logo, D. Miller & Sons, 1860s, 3 1/4 In. 125.00
Bleeder, 3 Blades, Horn Handles, Metal Blades, G. Gregory, 1860s, 3 In. 115.00
Bleeder, 3 Blades, Iron, Brass Handle, Borwick, 1860s, 2 7/8 In. 60.00
Bleeder, 3 Blades, Jackson & Co. AF Island Works, Brass Case, 1860s, 3 1/8 In. 107.00
Cabinet, Apothecary, Mahogany, Sliding Compartments, 12 x 11 1/2 x 11 3/4 In. 1355.00
Cabinet, Apothecary, Powder Blue Paint, American, 19th Century, 46 x 59 In. 10800.00
Cabinet, Veterinary, Dr. Lesure's, 27 In. 3640.00
Chest, Apothecary, 6 Drawers, Paper Labels, Dovetailed, 19th Century, 12 x 20 1/2 In. 220.00
Chest, Apothecary, 27 Drawers, Black Paint, Bracket Feet, 65 x 37 x 14 In. 1760.00
Chest, Apothecary, 30 Drawers, Molded Base, White Paint, 41 x 54 x 9 In. 990.00
Chest, Apothecary, 55 Drawers, Green Paint, 54 x 35 x 13 In. 990.00
Chest, Apothecary, Bottles, Canisters, Drawers, Doors, 1700s, 6 1/4 In. 2115.00
Chest, Domestic, Drop Front, Mahogany, Silk Lining, Bottles, Canisters, 8 1/2 In. 235.00
Corn Raiser, Case, F.B. Trademark 16.50
Cupping Set, 6 Glasses, Brass Valves, Milikin Patent Scarificator, Case, 9 In. 825.00
Cupping Set, 10 Blade Lacquered Brass Scarificator, Pump, 5 Cups, Case, 7 1/2 In. 1528.00
Drug Jar, Wet, Blue & White, Glazed, Baluster Shape, Handle, Spout, Painted, 7 In. 265.00
Electro Device, Leatherette Cover, Wood Case, Marble Control Panel, Aloe Co., Early 1905s, 17 In. 25.00
Electro Therapeutic Machine, G.A. Supplee, Rosewood Handle, Oak Case, 8 In. 118.00
Enema, Bigg, Double Action, Brass Pump, Bone Handle, Mahogany Case, 10 1/2 In. 355.00
Etui, Shagreen, Silver Mounted, Tortoiseshell Guards, 4 Lancets, 2 3/4 In. 646.00
Etui, Silver Mounted, Fish-Skin Cover, Instruments, Compartments, 3 3/4 In. 880.00
Jar, Peruv-Bark, Hand Blown, Gold Color Cover, York Glass, England, c.1845, 33 x 14 In. 569.00
Kit, Surgical, Field, Amputee, Saws, Knives, Cargill, Box, c.1770, 18 x 8 x 3 In. 8625.00
Leech Jar, Ceramic, White, c.1800, 8 In. 4680.00
Mortar & Pestle, Cast Iron, Flared Rim, Late 1880s, 6 1/2 x 6 1/2 In. 190.00
Sign, Eyeglass Frame Shape, Painted Eyes, 6 x 24 1/8 In. 588.00
Skull, Model, Flexible Lower Jaw, Plastic Teeth, 1950s, 3 In. 95.00
Sphygmograph, Millikin & Downe, Clockwork, Leather Case, 3 In. 176.00
Tool, Operating, Amputation Saw & Knife, Wooden Handle, 1861, 17 In. 270.00
Trephine Set, Peter Rose, Instruments, Rosewood Veneer, Mahogany Case 2585.00

MEISSEN is a town in Germany where porcelain has been made since 1710. Any china made in the town can be called Meissen, although the famous Meissen factory made the finest porcelains of the area. The crossed swords mark of the great Meissen factory has been copied by many other firms in Germany and other parts of the world. Pieces of Meissen dinnerware in the Onion pattern are listed in their own category in this book.

Bowl, Centerpiece, Fired Gold, Crossed Swords, 2 x 12 In. 146.00
Bowl, Fruit, Parcel Gilt, Blue & Gilt Enamel, Molded Cartouches, 10 1/4 In. 90.00
Box, Cover, Lemon Shape, 1755-60, 4 In. 5100.00
Candelabrum, 4-Light, Scrolling Arms, 2 Allegorical Putti, Relief Flowers, 20 In., Pair 1997.00
Caudle Cup, Cover, Stand, Yellow Ground, Watteau Figures, Landscape, 1740-45, 6 3/4 In., Pair .. 6000.00
Centerpiece, Arab Figures, 2-Part, Circular, White, E. Marcel Sandoz, 6 3/4 x 19 3/4 In. 10620.00
Centerpiece Stand, Nereid, Kneeling, Supporting Shell Shape Dish, 24 1/2 In. 6756.00
Cheese Dish, Insects, Flowers, Pierced, 3 Scroll Handles & Feet, Attached Underplate, 8 In. 6926.00
Coffee Set, Cups, Stands, Pot, 7 1/2 In. 295.00
Compote, Amorous Couple, Pierced Cavetto, Flowers, Footed, Gilt, Crossed Swords, 9 x 5 1/2 In. .. 900.00
Crucifix, Bronze Figure, Enamel, Max Esser Design, c.1930, 33 3/8 In. 7200.00
Cup, Leipzig View, 1815-25, 3 1/2 In. 700.00
Cup, View Of Dresden, 1840-60, 3 In. 1285.00
Cup, Wesenstein, View, 1820-40, 2 1/4 In. 675.00
Cup & Saucer, Berlin Museum, Borse Berlin, Opera House, Theater 1550.00
Cup & Saucer, Marcolini, Painted, Figure Panels, Mountain Landscape, 1700s 677.00
Cup & Saucer, Yellow Ground, Enamel Decorated, Flowers, Figures, Landscapes 1880.00
Ewer, Allegorical, Pan, Diana, Hunting Scene, Wheatsheaf Handle, c.1875, 26 1/4 In. 4200.00
Figurine, Africa, Allegorical, Continents, After Johann Joachim Kaendler, c.1745, 11 1/2 In. 4700.00
Figurine, Allegorical, Wind, Putto, Birdcage, Bird In Each Hand, 19th Century, 5 In. 825.00
Figurine, Angels, Winged, Depicting Victory, Making Porridge, Grinding Coffee, 5 In., Pair 2115.00
Figurine, Boy, On Hobbyhorse, Newsprint Hat, 20th Century, 7 In. 1175.00
Figurine, Dog, Empress Catherine Of Russia's Favorite, On Flowered Cushion, 17 In. 11255.00
Figurine, Dog, Pug, Male, Female & Pup, Late 1800s, 9 1/2 In., Pair 6463.00
Figurine, Dog, Pug, Seated, Brown, Black, Germany, Late 1800s, 5 1/4 In. 1175.00
Figurine, Equestrian, Poland & Saxony Arms, c.1850, 20 1/2 In. 6000.00
Figurine, Harlequin, Costumed, Seated On Stump, Holding Jug, Hat, 1900s, 6 In. 1330.00
Figurine, Polar Bear, Early 1900s, 21 1/4 In. 10200.00
Figurine, Sower, Seed Sack, Crossed Swords, c.1745, 8 3/8 In. 7200.00
Figurine, Thrush, Gray, White, Rocky Base, Green Leaves, c.1750, 8 In. 4200.00
Figurine, Woman, With Basin, Incised 2875, Late 18th Century, 7 In. 765.00
Figurine, Young Woman, At Table, Bread, Wine, Fruit, Painted, Gilt, Late 1800s, 5 In. 1355.00
Group, 2 Female Figures, Male En Bocage, Late 19th Century, 5 1/2 x 10 In. 585.00
Group, 4 Figures, Ring-Around-The-Rosy, Enamel, Gilt, Late 1800s, 5 3/4 In. 2585.00
Group, Allegorical, Enamel, Satyr, Wrestling Goat, Rocky Base, 1800s, 6 In. 1295.00
Group, Aphrodite & Ares, Multicolored, c.1850, 18 x 10 1/2 In. 3525.00
Group, Augustus The Strong, Dancing With Wife, Black Gown, Flowers, 8 In. 880.00
Group, Courting Couple, Woman Taking Pinch Of Snuff, Applied Flowers, 5 1/4 In. 12988.00
Group, Drunken Silenus On Donkey, Incised 2724, Crossed Swords Mark, c.1875, 9 x 7 3/4 In. ... 950.00
Group, Europa & The Bull, Incised 2697, Crossed Swords Mark, c.1875, 9 x 7 1/4 In. 1900.00
Group, Flirtatious Couple, 18th Century Costume, Late 1800s, 12 1/2 In. 2516.00
Group, Goddess, 2 Gods, Nyx, Hypos, Thanatos, Multicolored, c.1870, 14 x 10 1/4 In. 4406.00
Group, Musicians, Man, Woman, On Sofa, c.1875, 5 3/4 In. 2400.00
Group, Mythological, 3 Fates, Saturn, c.1875, 14 1/4 In. 5100.00
Group, Pugs, Grassy Base, c.1900, 2 5/8 In. 999.00
Group, Shepherd, Sheep, Tree, Dog, c.1755, 7 In. 3500.00
Group, Triumph Of Venus, Late 1800s, 11 x 17 1/4 In. 9269.00
Plaque, Feldartillerie, Regimental, General Feld Zeugmeister, 1 Brandbg, Nr. 3, 10 In. 195.00
Plaque, Garde, Dragoner, Regiment 1, Grossh, Hessisches, Nr. 23, 10 In. 195.00
Plaque, Garden Of Love, c.1850, 10 1/4 x 12 3/4 In. 8650.00
Plate, Alliance Of 1914-1916, 9 1/2 In. 305.00
Plate, Dessert, Flower Center, Flower Border, 6 In., 12 Piece 265.00
Plate, Franke'sche Stiftung, 1840-60, 7 1/2 In. 1930.00

Plate, Marbach View, 1860-70, 9 3/4 In. 1415.00
Plate, Tavern Scene, Pierced Rim, Enamel Border, Wood Frame, Germany, 1800s, 8 1/2 In. 4115.00
Plate, Wesenstein View, 1860-70, 9 3/4 In. 1415.00
Platter, Fish, Burgundy Border, Gilt Quatrefoils, Flowers, 1900s, 21 1/2 In. 118.00
Platter, Oval, Red Poppy Center, Early 20th Century, 15 3/4 In. 176.00
Potpourri, Cover, Pear Shape, Flowers, Putti, Courting Couple, c.1900, 20 3/4 In. 3055.00
Soup, Dish, Spring Flowers Pattern, Gold Rim, Marked, 10 In., 12 Piece 499.00
Table, Tripod, Painted, Backgammon Players, c.1860, 30 1/4 In. 11616.00
Tazza, Boy Holding Wreath, Reticulated Border, 2 Tiers, Blue, White, 15 x 9 In., Pair 1495.00
Teapot, Bulbous, Grape Leaves, Gilt Highlights, Bird Handle, c.1818, 7 1/2 In. 405.00
Teapot, Cover, Cockerel, c.1750, 9 In. 5700.00
Tureen, Cover, Circular, 2 Handles, Flowers, Crossed Swords Mark, c.1750, 12 3/4 In. 1800.00
Tureen, Sauce, Cover, Melon Shape Loop Handle, Pink & Turquoise, 9 In. 410.00
Tureen, Underplate, Mermaids, Swans, Butterflies, 6 1/2 x 16 1/4 x 11 1/2 In. 1380.00
Urn, Baluster, Ribbed Foot, 2 Snake Handles, 10 1/2 In., Pair 1495.00
Urn, Loop Handles, Snake Terminals, Crossed Swords, 15 1/4 x 10 x 6 1/2 In., Pair 1495.00
Vase, Cover, Stand, 2 Handles, Flowers, 1840-60, 34 1/2 In. 8239.00
Vase, Egg Shape, Gilt Rim, Snake Handle, Trumpet Foot, 15 In., Pair 3750.00
Vase, Mantel, Amphora Shape, Loop Handles, Trumpet Base, 12 In., Pair 765.00
Vase, Venus & Amor, Amorous Shepherd, Urn Shape, 2 Handles, Blue Ground, c.1860, 15 In. 8239.00

MERCURY GLASS, or silvered glass, was first made in the 1850s. It lost favor for a while but became popular again about 1910. It looks like a piece of silver.

Bottle, Flask, Fluted, Rectangular Base 1475.00
Candlestick, Baluster Stem, Footed, 11 In. 64.00
Perfume Bottle, Teardrop Shape, Black & White Swirls, Stopper, Laydown, Art Deco 135.00
• **Tieback,** Round, Original Screw, 3 In., c.1890, Pair 175.00
Vase, Blue Crackle Overlay, Painted Flowers, Squat, Tapered, Footed, c.1890, 5 In. 240.00
Vase, Cylindrical, Fluted, Flared Rim, 18 1/2 x 9 In. 1400.00
Vase, Peacock Blue, Frosted, Painted Fuchsias, Turned Sections, Footed, 8 In. 245.00
Vase, Prussian Blue Paint, Band Of Flowers, Flared, Footed, 8 1/2 In. 285.00
Witch's Ball, Cone-Shaped Pedestal Base, c.1850, 10 x 6 1/2 In. 495.00

MERRIMAC POTTERY Company was founded by Thomas Nickerson in Newburyport, Massachusetts, in 1902. The company made art pottery, garden pottery, and reproductions of Roman pottery. The pottery burned to the ground in 1908.

MERRIMAC CERAMIC COMPANY

Vase, Ridged, Dimpled, Bulbous, Green Matte Glaze, 4 1/2 x 4 1/2 In. 588.00

METLOX POTTERIES was founded in 1927 in Manhattan Beach, California. Dinnerware was made beginning in 1931. Evan K. Shaw purchased the company in 1946 and expanded the number of patterns. Poppytrail (1946-1989) and Vernonware (1958-1980) were divisions of Metlox under E.K. Shaw's direction. The factory closed in 1989.

Poppytrail METLOX

Antiqua, Cup & Saucer 7.50
Antique Grape, Butter 48.00
Antique Grape, Cup & Saucer 12.00
Blue Dahlia, Plate, Dinner, 10 1/4 In. 15.00
California Ivy, Plate, Luncheon, 9 1/4 In. 10.00
California Ivy, Salt & Pepper, 3 In. 23.00
California Peach Blossom, Celery Dish, 12 3/4 In. 55.00
California Peach Blossom, Gravy Boat 80.00
California Provincial, Plate, Bread & Butter, 6 3/8 In. 6.00
California Provincial, Sugar & Creamer 38.00
California Strawberry, Bowl, Cereal, 5 5/8 In. 18.00
California Tiempo, Platter, Oval, Walnut, Sky Blue, 13 1/4 In. 25.00
Colonial Heritage, Bowl, Vegetable, Divided, 2 1//2 x 12 x 5 1/2 In. 25.00
Colonial Heritage, Butter, Cover Only 25.00
Colorstax, Plate, Dinner, Aqua, 10 1/2 In. 12.00
Cookie Jar, Corn, Vegetable Line, 1960s, 10 1/2 In. 175.00
Cookie Jar, Mammy, Cook, Yellow, 13 1/2 In. .... 161.00 to 440.00

Cookie Jar, Mouse, Chef Pierre, 13 In. . . . 12.00
Cookie Jar, Pig, Slenderella, 13 In. . . . 200.00
Cookie Jar, Santa, Black, 14 In. . . . 115.00
Cookie Jar, Squirrel On Pinecone, 12 In. . . . 160.00
Cookie Jar, Teddy Bear, Holding Cookie, Blue Sweater, 11 1/2 In. . . . 11.50
Cookie Jar, Topsy, 9 1/2 In. . . . 595.00
Della Robbia, Cup & Saucer . . . 9.00
Golden Fruit, Carafe, Cover, 6 Cup . . . 60.00
Homestead Provincial, Bean Pot, Handle, 9 1/2 x 7 3/4 In. . . . 150.00
Homestead Provincial, Bowl, Fruit, 6 In. . . . 12.00
Homestead Provincial, Chop Plate, 12 1/4 In. . . . 25.00
Homestead Provincial, Jam Jar, 4 3/4 x 3 In. . . . 60.00
Homestead Provincial, Soup, Dish, 8 In. . . . 12.00
Lotus, Plate, Salad, Yellow, 8 1/2 In. . . . 18.00
Mixing Bowl, Midnight Blue . . . 150.00
Navajo, Platter, 9 3/8 x 14 5/8 In. . . . 24.00
Navajo, Soup, Dish, 8 In. . . . 15.00
Oh Susanna, Cup & Saucer . . . 10.00
Provincial Fruit, Bowl, Vegetable, Round, Hand Painted, Green Rim, 10 In. . . . 20.00
Provincial Fruit, Cup & Saucer . . . 15.00
Provincial Fruit, Plate, Dinner, 10 1/2 In. . . . 5.00
Provincial Fruit, Platter, Oval, 16 In. . . . 70.00
Provincial Fruit, Sugar & Creamer . . . 55.00
Red Rooster, Ashtray, Square, 6 3/8 In. . . . 20.00
Red Rooster, Bowl, Salad, 11 1/8 In. . . . 95.00
Red Rooster, Bowl, Vegetable, Divided, 12 In. . . . 60.00
Red Rooster, Bread Server, 9 1/2 In. . . . 100.00
Red Rooster, Canister Set, 4 Piece . . . 250.00
Red Rooster, Plate, Salad, 7 1/2 In. . . . 10.00
Red Rooster, Saucer, 6 In. . . . 2.50
Rose-A-Day, Plate, Dinner, 10 In. . . . 18.00
San Fernando, Bowl, Cereal, 6 7/8 In. . . . 8.00
Sculptured Daisy, Platter, Oval, 14 1/4 In. . . . 58.00
Sculptured Daisy, Saucer, 6 1/4 In. . . . 10.00
Sculptured Grape, Bowl, Fruit, 6 In. . . . 6.50
Sculptured Grape, Cup & Saucer . . . 7.50 to 9.00
Sculptured Grape, Plate, Salad, 7 1/2 In. . . . 6.00
Sculptured Grape, Platter, Oval, 12 1/2 x 9 In. . . . 20.00
Sculptured Zinnia, Gravy Boat, Attached Underplate . . . 25.00
Tickled Pink, Creamer . . . 25.00
Tickled Pink, Gravy Boat . . . 35.00
Tickled Pink, Salt & Pepper, Wood Stoppers . . . 40.00
True Blue, Bowl, Vegetable, Round, 9 1/4 In. . . . 12.00
Vineyard, Plate, Dinner, 10 3/4 In. . . . 12.50
Vineyard, Sugar & Creamer . . . 36.00
Wild Poppy, Bowl, Cereal, 6 1/2 In. . . . 10.00
Woodland Gold, Creamer . . . 20.00
Woodland Gold, Saucer . . . 3.00
Woodland Gold, Sugar, Cover . . . 25.00

METTLACH, Germany, is a city where the Villeroy and Boch factories worked. Steins from the firm are marked with the word *Mettlach* or the castle mark. They date from about 1842. Pieces marked *Mettlach* are still being made. *PUG* means painted under glaze. The steins can be dated from the marks on the bottom, which include a date-number code. Other pieces may be listed in the Villeroy & Boch category.

Beaker, No. 2327-1024, 1/4 Liter, Flute Player, PUG . . . 55.00
Beaker, No. 2327-1290a, 1/4 Liter, State Crest Of Prussia, PUG . . . 150.00
Beaker, No. 2327-1302, 1/4 Liter, American Eagle, PUG . . . 155.00
Beaker, No. 2368, 1/4 Liter, Banff, PUG . . . 345.00
Beaker, No. 2368-1014, 1/4 Liter, Munich Child, PUG, H. Schlitt . . . 85.00

Beaker, No. 2842-1172, 1/4 Liter, Gnome Drinking, PUG 145.00
Beaker, No. 2842-1173, 1/4 Liter, Gnome Drinking, PUG 66.00
Beaker, No. 2904-983, 1/4 Liter, Falstaff, PUG 485.00
Beaker, No. 3012, 1/4 Liter, Hires Root Beer, PUG 202.00
Cake Plate, No. 3471, Etched, 6 x 8 In. 190.00
Candy Dish, No. 3470, Etched, 4 1/2 x 5 1/2 In. 138.00
Ice Bucket, No. 1310, Flower, Etched, Glazed, Silver Plated Rim & Handle, Lid, 6 x 8 In. 360.00
Mug, Drink Hires Root Beer, Boy, Bib, Pointing, No. 3095 IV 24 06 .... 189.00
Mug, Fraternal Student Shield, Cream, Brown, Black, White, POG, 2 In. 110.00
Mug, Hires For Mine, Boy, Bib, Pointing, No. 3175 IV 26 07 .... 300.00
Mug, Hires Root Beer, Boy, Mug, Join Health & Cheer, 5 In. 495.00
Mug, Hires Root Beer, Health & Cheer, Boy, Bowtie, Stoneware, 5 In. 209.00
Mug, No. 3095, 1/2 Liter, Hires Root Beer, PUG 242.00
Mug, No. 3175, 1/3 Liter, Verse, Bier Her, Bier Her, Oder Ich Fall Um, PUG 116.00
Planter, No. 3075, Art Deco, Etched, 3 1/2 x 10 1/2 In. 288.00
Plaque, American Soldier Holding Flag, May 8, 1945, PUG, 11 In. 120.00
Plaque, Harvesting Scenes, Phanolith, c.1905, 18 In., Pair 3600.00
Plaque, No. 167a, Castle, PUG, 15 In. 300.00
Plaque, No. 895, Cherub & Griffin, Etched, 12 1/2 In. 580.00
Plaque, No. 1044, Faenza B., PUG, 10 1/2 In. 240.00
Plaque, No. 1044, Hamburg, PUG, 12 In. 195.00
Plaque, No. 1044, Mannheim Paradeplatz & Krauthaus, PUG, 12 In. 180.00
Plaque, No. 1044, Munich, Das Maximilianeum, PUG, 12 In. 215.00
Plaque, No. 1044, Trier Dom, PUG, 10 1/2 In. 248.00
Plaque, No. 1044-92, Stadthaus In Berncastel, PUG, 14 In. 120.00
Plaque, No. 1044-93, Burghaus Kurbisch, PUG, 14 In. 138.00
Plaque, No. 1044-94, Altes Stadtthor Cochem, PUG, 12 In. 145.00
Plaque, No. 1044-95, Burg Eltz, PUG, 12 In. 330.00
Plaque, No. 1044-97, Ruine Bischofstein, PUG, 12 In. 240.00
Plaque, No. 1044-121, 2 York Minster Cathedral, PUG, 14 In. 260.00
Plaque, No. 1044-129, Nurnberg, Henkersteg, PUG, 12 In. 228.00
Plaque, No. 1044-148, Neuschwanstein, PUG, 14 In. 299.00
Plaque, No. 1044-159, Kaub On Rhine, PUG, 12 In. 240.00
Plaque, No. 1044-160, Rolandseck, Siebengebirge, PUG, 12 In. 195.00
Plaque, No. 1044-169, Dresden Altstadt, PUG, 12 In. 248.00
Plaque, No. 1044-172, Die Wartburg, PUG, 12 In. 265.00
Plaque, No. 1044-190, Stuttgart, Schlossplatz, PUG, 12 In. 240.00
Plaque, No. 1044-202, Kidrich On The Rhine, PUG, 12 In. 215.00
Plaque, No. 1044-217, Schlosshof Heidelberg, PUG, 12 In. 240.00
Plaque, No. 1044-353, Chinese Boat Scene, PUG, 14 In. 145.00
Plaque, No. 1044-483, Ehrenburg, PUG, 12 In. 287.00
Plaque, No. 1044-938, Flowers, PUG, 17 In. 265.00
Plaque, No. 1044-1099, Young Girl & 2 Young Boys, PUG, 17 In. 575.00
Plaque, No. 1044-1100, Young Girl & Boy, PUG, 17 1/2 In. 725.00
Plaque, No. 1044-1104, Farm, Woman, Geese, PUG, 17 In. 600.00
Plaque, No. 1044-5087, Sailboats, Delft, 12 In. 195.00
Plaque, No. 1044-5090, Windmill Scene, Delft, 14 In. 242.00
Plaque, No. 1044-5154, Windmill Scene, Delft, PUG, 12 In. 97.00
Plaque, No. 1044-5178, Windmill At Seashore Scene, Delft, 17 In. 395.00
Plaque, No. 1044-5182C, Man's Portrait, Delft, 13 1/2 In. 190.00
Plaque, No. 1044-5196, Mountain Scene, Delft, 17 In. 395.00
Plaque, No. 1044-9025, Fish & Lobster, PUG, 14 In. 217.00
Plaque, No. 1044-9030, Ducks, PUG, 14 In. ....138.00 to 145.00
Plaque, No. 1048-3036I, Baptism, Etched, 16 In. 390.00
Plaque, No. 1048-3036V, Crowning Of Carl The Great By Pope Leo III, Etched, 16 In. 485.00
Plaque, No. 1048-3036VI, Building The Aachen Munsters, Etched, 16 In. 277.00
Plaque, No. 1387, Knight, Etched, 11 In. 385.00
Plaque, No. 1473, Woman, With Basket Of Fruit, Etched, C. Warth, 11 x 17 In. 1569.00
Plaque, No. 2022, Young Man Playing Lute, Etched & Relief, 20 In. 690.00
Plaque, No. 2041, Man & Woman On Horseback, Etched, Stocke, 15 In. 485.00
Plaque, No. 2071, 3 Dogs Attacking Boar, PUG, Stocke, 15 1/2 In. 485.00

Plaque, No. 2078, 2 Ulanens On Horseback, Snow Covered Field, Etched, Stocke, 15 In. 1208.00
Plaque, No. 2079, 4 Dragoners On Horseback, Etched, 15 In. 1449.00
Plaque, No. 2112, Gnome In Tree, Holding 2 Bottles, 16 In. 930.00
Plaque, No. 2148, Snow White & Seven Dwarfs, Etched, 16 In. 615.00
Plaque, No. 2187, Knight On Horseback, House Of Hohenzollern, 17 1/2 In. 1210.00
Plaque, No. 2443, Trojan Lady & Her Servants, Cameo, 19 In. 380.00
Plaque, No. 2484, Knight On White Horse, Etched, 12 In. 330.00
Plaque, No. 2517, Town Scene Of Konigstein, Eched, 17 1/2 In. 605.00
Plaque, No. 2518, Town Scene Of Meissen, Etched, 17 1/2 In. 1210.00
Plaque, No. 2621, Cavalier Pouring Wine, Etched, 7 1/2 In. 195.00
Plaque, No. 2795, Words Of Love, Cameo, Green Ground, Marked, 17 1/2 In. 875.00
Plaque, No. 2875, Woman Holding Banner, 2 Other Figures, Cameo, 18 In. 425.00
Plaque, No. 3161, 2 Cavaliers Drinking, Etched, 17 1/2 In. 605.00
Plaque, No. 3162, 2 Cavaliers Toasting, 17 1/2 In. 550.00
Plaque, No. 3225-1290, Berlin, Shield, PUG, 11 x 13 1/4 In. 660.00
Plaque, No. 3225-1290, Dresden, Shield, PUG, 11 x 13 1/4 In. 475.00
Plaque, No. 3225-1290, Elks Club, Shield, PUG, 11 x 13 1/4 In. 468.00
Plaque, No. 3225-1290, England, Shield, PUG, 11 x 13 1/4 In. ....400.00 to 600.00
Plaque, No. 3225-1290, Frankfurt, Shield, PUG, 11 x 13 1/4 In. 415.00
Plaque, No. 3225-1290, French Republic, Shield, PUG, 11 x 13 1/4 In. 725.00
Plaque, No. 3225-1290, Munich, Shield, PUG, 11 x 13 1/4 In. 715.00
Plaque, No. 3225-1290, Prussian Eagle, Shield, PUG, 11 x 13 1/4 In. 625.00
Plaque, No. 3225-1290E, Hessen Shield, PUG, 13 1/4 x 11 In. 725.00
Plaque, No. 5130-225, House In Mountains, Delft, 14 In. 95.00
Plaque, No. 5279, Card Game, Delft, 15 1/2 In. 360.00
Punch Bowl, No. 2087, 8 Liter, Underplate, Cover, Dancing Scene, Relief 360.00
Punch Bowl, No. 2234, 6 Liter, Cover, Leaves On Vines, Dwarf Finial, Birds, Grapes, Relief 345.00
Punch Bowl, No. 2595-1072, 2 Liter, Cover, Children Eating & Drinking, PUG 360.00
Stein, No. 202, 1/2 Liter, Men Singing, Relief 176.00
Stein, No. 406, 1/2 Liter, Cavaliers Bowling, Painted Pewter Lid 360.00
Stein, No. 485, 1/2 Liter, Musicians, Dancers, Relief, Inlaid Lid 185.00
Stein, No. 783, 1/2 Liter, Children On Beer Bock, Bock Bier, Relief, Inlaid Lid 185.00
Stein, No. 1005, 1 Liter, Tavern Scene, Relief, Inlaid Lid 600.00
Stein, No. 1028, 1/2 Liter, Man, Carrying Hay, Woman, Relief, Inlaid Lid 95.00
Stein, No. 1028, 2 1/3 Liter, Man Carrying Hay, Woman, No Lid 75.00
Stein, No. 1028, 2 1/3 Liter, Man Carrying Hay, Woman, Relief, Inlaid Lid 230.00
Stein, No. 1146, 1/2 Liter, Students Drinking In Tavern, Etched, Pewter Lid 260.00
Stein, No. 1157, 1 Liter, Cavaliers, 4 Panels, Relief, Inlaid Lid 475.00
Stein, No. 1161, 7 Liter, 2 Ladies, Verse, Etched, Inlaid Lid 2200.00
Stein, No. 1164, 1/2 Liter, Musician & Girl, Etched, Inlaid Lid, Warth 440.00
Stein, No. 1184, 1/3 Liter, Floral Design, Relief, Inlaid Lid 132.00
Stein, No. 1396, 1/2 Liter, Nymph Drinking, Etched, Inlaid Lid 280.00
Stein, No. 1467, 1/2 Liter, Harvest Scenes, Relief, Inlaid Lid 140.00
Stein, No. 1508, 1/2 Liter, Tavern Scene, Etched, Inlaid Lid, Gorig 445.00
Stein, No. 1520, 1/2 Liter, Cavaliers & Eagle, Etched, Inlaid Lid, Gorig 165.00
Stein, No. 1526, 1 Liter, Scene Of Arts & Trades, Relief, Pewter Lid With Harp Thumblift 310.00
Stein, No. 1526, 1 Liter, Student Society, Transfer, Enameled, Pewter Lid 545.00
Stein, No. 1526, 1/2 Liter, Companhia Antarctica Paulista Sao Paulo, PUG, Pewter Lid 330.00
Stein, No. 1526, 1/2 Liter, New York Beer Brewer, PUG, Inlaid Lid ....176.00 to 215.00
Stein, No. 1526, 1/2 Liter, Night Watchman, Adjusting Clock, PUG, Pewter Lid 169.00
Stein, No. 1526, 1/2 Liter, Student Shield, Painted, Engraved, Zirkel, Pewter Lid 130.00
Stein, No. 1526, 1/2 Liter, Student Society, Salingia Sei's Panier, Transfer, Enamel, Pewter Lid ... 215.00
Stein, No. 1526, 1/2 Liter, Student Society, Uttenruthia Sei's Panier, PUG, Pewter Lid .....190.00 to 240.00
Stein, No. 1526-589, 1/2 Liter, Men Drinking, PUG, Pewter Lid ....93.00 to 150.00
Stein, No. 1526-592, 1/2 Liter, Man & Barmaid, PUG, Pewter Lid 135.00
Stein, No. 1526-598, 1 Liter, Man Holding Rifle, PUG, Pewter Lid 219.00
Stein, No. 1526-625, 1 Liter, Musician & Verse, PUG, Pewter Lid 330.00
Stein, No. 1526-661, 1/2 Liter, Cavalier & Verse, PUG 248.00
Stein, No. 1526-662, 1/2 Liter, Athletic Design, PUG, Pewter Lid 240.00
Stein, No. 1526-702, 3 Liter, Beer Parade, PUG, Pewter Lid 375.00
Stein, No. 1526-983, 3 Liter, Falstaff, PUG, Pewter Lid 635.00

Stein, No. 1526-1009, 1/2 Liter, Dwarfs Turning Wine Press, Pewter Lid, PUG 324.00
Stein, No. 1526-1074, 1 Liter, Man Smoking, PUG, Pewter Lid, H. Schlitt 477.00
Stein, No. 1526-1078, 1/2 Liter, Man Drinking, PUG, Pewter Lid, H. Schlitt 575.00
Stein, No. 1526-1109, 1 Liter, Musicians, PUG, Pewter Lid, Schlitt 358.00
Stein, No. 1526-1109, 1 Liter, Musicians, Relief, Pewter Lid With Lyre, H. Schlitt 550.00
Stein, No. 1526-1145, 1/2 Liter, Man Drinking, Pewter Lid With Barmaid, H. Schlitt ....175.00 to 242.00
Stein, No. 1526-1383, 1/2 Liter, Man Rowing, PUG, Pewter Lid 725.00
Stein, No. 1526-1502, 1/2 Liter, Military, PUG, Inlaid Lid 390.00
Stein, No. 1526-1508, 1/2 Liter, Military Man, PUG, Pewter Lid, Strap 180.00
Stein, No. 1527, 1/2 Liter, Cavaliers Drinking, Etched, Inlaid Lid 600.00
Stein, No. 1562, 5 3/4 Liter, Trumpeter Of Sackingen, Etched, Pewter Lid 1520.00
Stein, No. 1695, 1/2 Liter, Scenes Of Hunters, Etched, Inlid Lid 358.00
Stein, No. 1733, 1/2 Liter, Jockeys, Horses, Inlaid Jockey Cap Lid 1073.00
Stein, No. 1737, 2 Liter, Wheat Design, Relief, Inlaid Lid ....70.00 to 308.00
Stein, No. 1742, 1/2 Liter, Scene Of Gottingen, Etched, Inlaid Lid 220.00
Stein, No. 1744, 1/3 Liter, Wheat Design, Mosaic, Inlaid Lid 266.00
Stein, No. 1756, 1 Liter, Man Drinking, Relief & Tapestry, Inlaid Lid 358.00
Stein, No. 1771, 3 Liter, Mosaic, Geometric, Inlaid Lid 523.00
Stein, No. 1786, 1/2 Liter, St. Florian Extinguishing Fire, Etched, Pewter Lid 461.00
Stein, No. 1796, 1/2 Liter, Cavalier Drinking, Etched, Inlaid Lid, C. Warth 431.00
Stein, No. 1816, 1/3 Liter, Floral Design, Mosaic & Relief, Inlaid Lid 202.00
Stein, No. 1861-1048, 1/2 Liter, Gambrinus Rex, Etched & PUG, Pewter Lid 230.00
Stein, No. 1863, 1/2 Liter, Scene Of Stuttgart, Etched, Inlaid Lid 550.00
Stein, No. 1909, 1/2 Liter, Yale University, PUG, Pewter Lid 610.00
Stein, No. 1909-727, 1/2 Liter, Dwarves Bowling, PUG, Pewter Lid ....190.00 to 309.00
Stein, No. 1909-727, 1/3 Liter, Dwarf Bowling, PUG, Pewter Lid 190.00
Stein, No. 1909-732, 1/2 Liter, Drunken Man Sleeping, PUG, Pewter Lid, H. Schlitt 330.00
Stein, No. 1909-943, 1/2 Liter, 3 Men & Beer Barrel, PUG, Pewter Lid 355.00
Stein, No. 1909-979, 1/2 Liter, Frog Choir, PUG, Pewter Lid 705.00
Stein, No. 1909-983, 1/2 Liter, Falstaff, PUG, Pewter Lid 265.00
Stein, No. 1909-1038, 1/2 Liter, Frogs Drinking In Pond, PUG, Pewter Lid 357.00
Stein, No. 1909-1143, 1/2 Liter, Cavaliers Drinking, PUG, Pewter Lid, H. Schlitt ....200.00 to 362.00
Stein, No. 1909-1176, 1/2 Liter, Spiel, PUG, Pewter Lid 348.00
Stein, No. 1909-1212, 1/2 Liter, Dwarf Bowling, PUG, Pewter Lid, Boy & Bowling Pin 150.00
Stein, No. 1909-1278, 1/2 Liter, 2 Children & Cat, PUG, Pewter Lid 445.00
Stein, No. 1909-1293, 1/2 Liter, Mountain Climbing Equipment, PUG, Pewter Lid 1310.00
Stein, No. 1909-1351, 1/2 Liter, Crossed Flags, Weapons, PUG, Pewter Lid 390.00
Stein, No. 1932, 1 Liter, Cavaliers Toasting, Etched, Inlaid Lid, C. Warth 520.00
Stein, No. 1938, 1/4 Liter, Geometric Design, Mosaic, Inlaid Lid 215.00
Stein, No. 1939, 1/4 Liter, Etched, Glazed, Pewter Lid ....190.00 to 217.00
Stein, No. 1968, 1/2 Liter, Lovers, Etched, Inlaid Lid 285.00
Stein, No. 1972, 1/4 Liter, 4 Scenes, Etched, Inlaid Lid 350.00
Stein, No. 2001A, 1/2 Liter, Law, Etched, Glazed, Inlaid Lid 598.00
Stein, No. 2001B, 1/2 Liter, Medicine, Etched, Glazed, Inlaid Lid ....429.00 to 550.00
Stein, No. 2001F, 1/2 Liter, Architecture, Etched, Glazed, Inlaid Lid 665.00
Stein, No. 2001K, 1/2 Liter, Commerce, Etched, Glazed, Inlaid Lid 425.00
Stein, No. 2005, 1/2 Liter, 4 People Having Dinner, Etched, Inlaid Lid, H. D. Gasthaus 330.00
Stein, No. 2007, 1/2 Liter, Black Cat, Hiddigeigei, Etched, Inlaid Lid, F. Stuck 605.00
Stein, No. 2009, 1/2 Liter, Man & Woman Dancing, Etched, Inlaid Lid, F. Stuck 605.00
Stein, No. 2024, 1/2 Liter, Berlin, Etched, Glazed, Inlaid Lid ....430.00 to 550.00
Stein, No. 2025, 1/2 Liter, Festive Scene With Cherubs, Etched, Inlaid Lid 159.00
Stein, No. 2028, 1/2 Liter, Men In Tavern, Etched, Inlaid Lid ....303.00 to 389.00
Stein, No. 2029, 1/2 Liter, Military, Etched, Inlaid Lid 745.00
Stein, No. 2031, 1/2 Liter, Officers & Soldiers, Etched, Inlaid Lid 908.00
Stein, No. 2035, 1/2 Liter, Bacchus Carousing, Etched ....275.00 to 285.00
Stein, No. 2038, 3 4/5 Liter, Rodenstein, Relief, Inlaid Castle Lid 3165.00
Stein, No. 2040, 4 Liter, German Soldiers, Etched, Inlaid Lid 5940.00
Stein, No. 2050, 1/2 Liter, Man & Woman, Verse, Etched, Inlaid Slipper Lid 1610.00
Stein, No. 2051, 1/2 Liter, 7 Students Drinking, Etched, Inlaid Lid 445.00
Stein, No. 2057, 1/3 Liter, Peasants Dancing, Etched, Inlaid Lid ....159.00 to 440.00

Stein, No. 2065, 2 1/2 Liter, Man & Barmaid, Etched, Inlaid Lid, H. Schlitt 855.00
Stein, No. 2077, 1/3 Liter, Coat Of Arms, Relief, Inlaid Lid ....92.00 to 100.00
Stein, No. 2082, 1 Liter, William Tell, Son, Apple, Etched, Inlaid Lid 1810.00
Stein, No. 2083, 1 Liter, Boar Hunt, Etched, Inlaid Lid 575.00
Stein, No. 2089, 1/2 Liter, Angel Serving Dinner & Beer, Etched, Inlaid Lid, Schlitt ....550.00 to 665.00
Stein, No. 2090, 1/2 Liter, Man Smoking, Etched, Inlaid Lid, H. Schlitt ....466.00 to 485.00
Stein, No. 2090, 1 Liter, Man Smoking At Table, Etched, Inlaid Lid, H. Schlitt 725.00
Stein, No. 2091, 1/2 Liter, St. Florian Pouring Water, Etched, Inlaid Lid, H. Schlitt 667.00
Stein, No. 2092, 1/2 Liter, Dwarf Adjusting Clock, Etched, Inlaid Lid 330.00
Stein, No. 2093, 1/2 Liter, 4 Cards, Etched, Inlaid Lid ....260.00 to 635.00
Stein, No. 2097, 1/2 Liter, Music, Etched, Inlaid Lid ....160.00 to 375.00
Stein, No. 2099, 1/3 Liter, Flowers, Art Nouveau, Mosaic, Inlaid Lid 266.00
Stein, No. 2100, 1/3 Liter, Germans Meeting Romans, Inlaid Lid 485.00
Stein, No. 2107, 2 1/4 Liter, Gambrinus On Throne, Etched, Inlaid Lid, H. Schlitt 1086.00
Stein, No. 2131, 1/2 Liter, Barroom Scenes, Relief, Inlaid Lid 270.00
Stein, No. 2134, 1/2 Liter, Gnome In Nest, Etched, Inlaid Lid, H. Schlitt 925.00
Stein, No. 2134, 1/3 Liter, Gnome In Nest, Etched, Inlaid Lid 625.00
Stein, No. 2136, 1/2 Liter, Adolphus Busch Brewery, Etched, PUG, Inlaid Lid 3105.00
Stein, No. 2140-754, 1/2 Liter, 1st Garde Regiment Zu Fuss, PUG, Pewter Lid 330.00
Stein, No. 2140-941, 1/2 Liter, Bier Barometer, PUG, Pewter Lid 280.00
Stein, No. 2140-1047, 1/2 Liter, Dwarves Smoking, PUG, Pewter Lid ....185.00 to 358.00
Stein, No. 2176-954, 2 3/4 Liter, Drinking Scenes, PUG, Pewter Lid, H. Schlitt 530.00
Stein, No. 2179-961, 1/4 Liter, Prosit, PUG, Pewter Lid 170.00
Stein, No. 2182, 1/2 Liter, Bowling Scene, Relief, Inlaid Lid ....300.00 to 780.00
Stein, No. 2183-953, 3 1/4 Liter, Dwaves, PUG, Inlaid Lid 460.00
Stein, No. 2191, 1/2 Liter, Military Joke, Etruscan, Etched, Inlaid Lid, H. Schlitt ....627.00 to 845.00
Stein, No. 2194, 3 1/3 Liter, Whale At Ascalon, Relief, Inlaid Lid 578.00
Stein, No. 2210, 3 1/4 Liter, Bowling Scene, Cameo, Inlaid Lid 240.00
Stein, No. 2220, 3 3/4 Liter, Peacock, Flowers, Inlaid Lid, Relief 275.00
Stein, No. 2221-901, 1/2 Liter, Wurttemberg Military Commemorative, PUG, Relief Pewter Lid 465.00
Stein, No. 2227, 4 1/3 Liter, Imperial German Military, PUG, Inlaid Lid With Eagle 6600.00
Stein, No. 2230, 1/2 Liter, Man & Barmaid, Etched 523.00
Stein, No. 2231, 1/2 Liter, Tavern Scene, Etched, Inlaid Lid 424.00
Stein, No. 2235, 1/2 Liter, Barmaid Holding Steins, Etched, Inlaid Lid ....500.00 to 725.00
Stein, No. 2261-1012, 2 1/4 Liter, German Warriors, Schlitt, PUG, Pewter Lid, H. Schlitt 635.00
Stein, No. 2262-1041, 4 1/4 Liter, Drunken Judges, PUG, Pewter Lid 1280.00
Stein, No. 2270-994, 3 1/3 Liter, Cavalier & Barmaid, PUG, Pewter Lid 485.00
Stein, No. 2270-994, 3 1/3 Liter, Soldiers Drinking, PUG, Pewter Lid 754.00
Stein, No. 2276, 1/2 Liter, Nurnberg Goose Boy, Etched, Relief, Pewter Lid, Strap 200.00
Stein, No. 2277, 1/4 Liter, Nurnberg, Etched, Inlaid Lid 219.00
Stein, No. 2285, 1/2 Liter, Guitar Player & Young Couple, Etched, Inlaid Lid 485.00
Stein, No. 2303, Bartholomay's Brewing Co., PUG, Pewter Lid, 3 In. 275.00
Stein, No. 2324, 1/4 Liter, Football Game, Etched, Pewter Lid 965.00
Stein, No. 2333-1032, 1/3 Liter, Dwarves, PUG, Pewter Lid 135.00
Stein, No. 2333-1033, 1/3 Liter, Dwarves, PUG, Pewter Lid 127.00
Stein, No. 2348-1022, 3 Liter, Musicians & Dancers, PUG, Pewter Lid 260.00
Stein, No. 2349-1023, 1/4 Liter, Man Playing Violin, PUG, Pewter Lid 154.00
Stein, No. 2358, 1/2 Liter, People Dining, Relief, Lid With Inlaid Corn Cob 230.00
Stein, No. 2373, 1/2 Liter, St. Augustine, Florida, Etched, Inlaid Lid 525.00
Stein, No. 2382, 1/2 Liter, Thirsty Rider, Etched, Inlaid Lid, Schlitt ....265.00 to 552.00
Stein, No. 2384-1143, 2 1/4 Liter, Cavaliers Drinking, PUG, Pewter Lid, H. Schlitt 725.00
Stein, No. 2388, 1/2 Liter, Stacked Pretzels, Character, Inlaid Lid, Pretzel Handle ....345.00 to 392.00
Stein, No. 2393-1197, 3 1/4 Liter, Couple Walking At Seashore, PUG, Pewter Lid 200.00
Stein, No. 2401, 1/2 Liter, Tannheuser In Venusberg, Etched, Inlaid Lid 755.00
Stein, No. 2441, 1/2 Liter, Gambling Scene, Etched, Inlaid Lid ....518.00 to 635.00
Stein, No. 2501, 1/2 Liter, Drinking Scene, Etched, Pewter Lid, Quidenus 350.00
Stein, No. 2524, 4 1/4 Liter, Knight On Horse, Die Kannenburg, Etched, Inlaid Lid, H. Schlitt 2313.00
Stein, No. 2526, 1/2 Liter, Hunt Scene, Creussen, Relief, Pewter Lid 759.00
Stein, No. 2530, 1/3 Liter, Boar Hunt, Cameo, Inlaid Lid 475.00
Stein, No. 2531, 1/2 Liter, Monk With Jug Of Beer, Etched, Inlaid Lid 160.00

Stein, No. 2532, 1/2 Liter, Drunken Scene, Etched, Inlaid Lid, F. Quidenus 250.00
Stein, No. 2557, 1/2 Liter, Drinking Scene, Relief, Inlaid Lid 390.00
Stein, No. 2580, 1/2 Liter, Knight In Castle, Die Kannenburg, Etched, Inlaid Lid, H. Schlitt 875.00
Stein, No. 2581, 1/2 Liter, Choir, Etched, Inlaid Lid, F. Quidenus ....358.00 to 605.00
Stein, No. 2582, 1 Liter, Jester On Table, Etched, Inlaid Lid With Jester, F. Quidenus 795.00
Stein, No. 2585, 1/2 Liter, Munich Child Standing On Globe, Relief, Etched, Inlaid Lid 460.00
Stein, No. 2608, 1/3 Liter, Drinking, Courting & Music, Cameo, Inlaid Lid 360.00
Stein, No. 2621, Cavalier Pouring Wine, Etched, 7 1/2 In. 195.00
Stein, No. 2628, 1/2 Liter, Bowling & Tavern Scenes, Cameo, Inlaid Lid 275.00
Stein, No. 2639, 1/2 Liter, Blacksmith & Cavalier, Etched, Inlaid Lid 585.00
Stein, No. 2693, 1/2 Liter, Tavern Scene, Etched, Inlaid Lid 485.00
Stein, No. 2716, 1 Liter, Waitress, Men, Etched, Inlaid Lid, F. Quidenus 580.00
Stein, No. 2718, 1/2 Liter, David & Goliath, Etched, Glazed, Inlaid Lid 1995.00
Stein, No. 2752, 1/2 Liter, Men Drinking At Table, Etched, Inlaid Lid, H. Schlitt 330.00
Stein, No. 2755, 1/2 Liter, Man & Woman Drinking, Cameo, Inlaid Lid, Stahl 845.00
Stein, No. 2757, 2 1/3 Liter, Dancing & Drinking Scenes, Cameo, Inlaid Lid, Stahl 2259.00
Stein, No. 2766, 1/2 Liter, Man Drinking, Etched, Inlaid Lid 725.00
Stein, No. 2772, 1/2 Liter, Brown University, Relief, Pewter Lid 275.00
Stein, No. 2776, 1/2 Liter, Man In Wine Cellar, Etched, Inlaid Lid 665.00
Stein, No. 2780, 1 Liter, Man Serenading Woman, Etched, Inlaid Lid 620.00
Stein, No. 2783-6128, 4 3/4 Liter, Man Drinking, Rookwood, Pewter Lid 725.00
Stein, No. 2787-6132, 2 1/4 Liter, Man Smoking, Rookwood, Pewter Lid 560.00
Stein, No. 2788-6133, 1/2 Liter, Cavalier, Rookwood, Pewter Lid 290.00
Stein, No. 2788-6143, 1/2 Liter, Man Drinking, Rookwood, Pewter Lid 156.00
Stein, No. 2789-6134, 1/2 Liter, Man With Pipe, Rookwood, Pewter Lid 330.00
Stein, No. 2790-6135, 1/2 Liter, Man Drinking, Rookwood, Pewter Lid 468.00
Stein, No. 2796, 3 Liter, Heidelberg, Etched, Inlaid Lid 715.00
Stein, No. 2800, 1/2 Liter, Art Nouveau, Etched, Inlaid Lid 360.00
Stein, No. 2802, 1/2 Liter, Art Nouveau, Etched, Inlaid Lid 330.00
Stein, No. 2828, 1 Liter, Wartburg, Houses, Tower, Relief, Etched, Inlaid Lid 1449.00
Stein, No. 2833B, 1/2 Liter, Hunters In Forest, Etched, Inlaid Lid 375.00
Stein, No. 2833C, 1/2 Liter, Lorley River, Etched, Inlaid Lid 450.00
Stein, No. 2833D, 1/2 Liter, Man & Woman Holding Hands, Etched, Inlaid Lid 406.00
Stein, No. 2833E, 1/2 Liter, Soldiers In Forest In Winter, Etched, Inlaid Lid 240.00
Stein, No. 2833E, 1/3 Liter, Soldiers In Forest In Winter, Etched, Inlaid Lid 265.00
Stein, No. 2833F, 1/2 Liter, Students Drinking, Etched, Inlaid Lid ....335.00 to 368.00
Stein, No. 2872, 1/2 Liter, Cornell University, Etched, Inlaid Lid 635.00
Stein, No. 2880, 1/2 Liter, Tavern Scene, Etched, Inlaid Lid, F. Quidenus 455.00
Stein, No. 2880, 1 Liter, Tavern Scene, Etched, Inlaid Lid, F. Quidenus 710.00
Stein, No. 2893-129, 3 Liter, Prussian Eagle, PUG 280.00
Stein, No. 2893-1197, 2 1/2 Liter, Fisherman & Woman, PUG, Pewter Lid ....115.00 to 255.00
Stein, No. 2917, 1/2 Liter, Munchen Child, Inlaid Lid With Lion & Shield, Etched 3140.00
Stein, No. 2930, 3 1/2 Liter, Man & Woman, Verse, Relief, Inlaid Lid 185.00
Stein, No. 2936, 1/2 Liter, Elk's Club, Art Nouveau, Etched, Inlaid Lid ....165.00 to 466.00
Stein, No. 2937, 1/2 Liter, Nightwatchman, Etched, Inlaid Lid 830.00
Stein, No. 2957, 1/2 Liter, Bowling Scene, Etched, Inlaid Lid 335.00
Stein, No. 2959, 1/2 Liter, Boy Bowling, Etched, Inlaid Lid, F. Quidenus 378.00
Stein, No. 3000, 1/2 Liter, Women, 3 Panels, Etched, Pewter Lid, F. Ringer 485.00
Stein, No. 3135, 1/2 Liter, American Flag & Eagles, Etched, Inlaid Lid 305.00
Stein, No. 3143, 1/2 Liter, Tyrolean Scene, Etched, Inlaid Lid 336.00
Stein, No. 3144, 1/2 Liter, Black Forest Scene, Etched, Inlaid Lid, F. Quidenus 798.00
Stein, No. 3185-1360, 1/2 Liter, Fox Hunt Scene, PUG, Inlaid Lid 725.00
Stein, No. 3321, 1/2 Liter, Art Nouveau, Etched, Inlaid Lid 130.00
Stein, No. 3328-542, 1/2 Liter, Man Drinking, Transfer, Enamel, Inlaid Lid, Bavaria 355.00
Stein, No. 3342-546, 1/2 Liter, Suits Of Cards, 4 Sides, Bavaria, Inlaid Lid 3625.00
Stein, No. 3344-551, 1/2 Liter, Students Drinking, 6 Sides, Bavaria, Inlaid Lid 605.00
Stein, No. 5002, 4 1/2 Liter, 3 Scenes, People, Faience, Pewter Lid 1159.00
Stein, No. 5005, 1/2 Liter, Man & Trees, Pewter Lid, Faience ....190.00 to 417.00
Stein, No. 5013-965, 1/2 Liter, Crest, Faience, Pewter Lid 218.00
Stein, No. 5019, 1 Liter, Flower, Faience, Pewter Lid 965.00

Stein, No. 5024, 1 Liter, Flowers, Faience, Pewter Lid 645.00
Stein, No. 5190, 1/2 Liter, Man Drinking, Faience, Pewter Lid 360.00
Stein, No. 5395, 1/2 Liter, Dancing Couple, Faience, Pewter Lid 500.00
Stein Set, No. 2210, 3 1/4 Liter, Tavern & Bowling Scene, Relief, Inlaid Lid, 6 Piece 1090.00
Tobacco Jar, No. 2268-1058, Dwarves, PUG, 7 1/4 In. 345.00
Vase, No. 1409, Geometric Design, Snake Handles, Mosaic, 11 In., Pair 385.00
Vase, No. 1462, Women, 4 Panels, Etched, C. Warth, 13 In. 240.00
Vase, No. 1591, Boy, Etched, 13 In. 320.00
Vase, No. 1596, Geometric Design, Mosaic, 8 In. 210.00
Vase, No. 1988, Flowers, Gold Trim, Mosaic, 12 In., Pair 385.00
Vase, No. 2414, Flowers, Art Nouveau, Handles, Etched, 13 1/2 In. 430.00
Vase, No. 2416, Flowers, Art Nouveau, 6 Looped Handles, Etched, 16 In. 1800.00
Vase, No. 2613-276, Black Forest Woman, PUG, 10 3/4 In. 485.00
Vase, No. 3040, Girls, 4 Panels, Cameo, 12 In. 330.00

MILK GLASS was named for its milky white color. It was first made in England during the 1700s. The height of its popularity in the United States was from 1870 to 1880. It is now correct to refer to some colored glass as blue milk glass, black milk glass, etc. Reproductions of milk glass are being made and sold in many stores. Related pieces may be listed in the Cosmos and Westmoreland categories.

Bottle, Barber, Cluster Of Purple Violets, Green Leaves, Hair Tonic, 8 3/4 In. 125.00
Bowl, Daisy Pattern, Openwork Border, Challinor & Taylor, 4 1/4 x 8 1/2 In. 95.00
Bowl, Dancing Sailor Border, Atterbury, 3 x 5 x 8 In. 31.00
Bowl, Turquoise, Ribbed, Scalloped Rim, Vallerysthal, France, 8 1/2 x 4 3/4 In. 65.00
Box, Cover, Figural, Battleship, Admiral Dewey, 5 1/2 In. 40.00
Box, Cover, Scrolled Edges, 4 Scroll Feet, 1890s, 4 x 2 1/2 In. 20.00
Cake Stand, Painted Apple Blossoms, Gold Trim, Pedestal Base, Challinor, 6 x 9 In. 55.00
Candlestick, Ruffled Lace Edge Border, 2 x 6 In. 20.00
Candy Dish, Cover, Lacy Dewdrop, Round Ribbed Finial, 3 3/4 x 3 3/4 In. 24.00
Card Holder, Grapevines & Leaves, 4-Footed, 2 1/2 x 3 x 1 1/2 In. 20.00
Celery Vase, Monkey, Opalescent, Rayed Base, 6 3/4 x 3 3/4 In. 1045.00
Compote, Atlas Stem, Holding Flared Bowl, Scalloped Rim, Ribbed Foot, Atterbury, 8 x 9 In. 7.00
Creamer, Figural, Owl, Gold Glass Eyes, Challinor & Taylor, 3 1/2 x 3 1/2 In. 141.00
Creamer, Louis XV, Blue, Footed, Vallerysthal 45.00
Cruet, Tree Of Life, Stopper, Challinor & Taylor, 5 In. 65.00
Dish, Cat On Drum Cover, 4 5/8 In. 20.00
Dish, Cover, Figural Squirrel On Acorn, 6 3/4 In. 25.00
Dish, Crawfish, Cover, Beaded, Tab Handles, 4 1/4 x 7 1/2 x 3 1/4 In. 95.00
Dish, Duck Cover, Amethyst Head, Atterbury, 5 x 4 x 9 In. 110.00
Dish, Figural, Fish, Atterbury, 9 1/2 In. 40.00
Dish, Hen On Nest Cover, Red Glass Eyes, Challinor & Taylor, 7 1/4 In. 45.00
Dish, Mother Eagle Cover, 3 Baby Eagles Under Wings, Challinor & Taylor, 7 1/8 In. 263.00
Dish, Pickle, Sections, Fish Scale Pattern, Center Disc Handle, Atterbury, 8 x 5 1/2 In. 45.00
Dish, Rabbit, Cover, Atterbury, 4 In. 225.00
Dish, Swan On Water Cover, Swimming Fish, Blue Grass Eye, Challinor & Taylor, 7 1/8 In. 243.00
Egg, 5 In. 40.00
Jar, Owl Cover, Atterbury, 6 3/4 x 3 1/2 In. 66.00
Mug, Bird & Wheat, Atterbury, 3 1/4 In. 22.00
Pitcher, Figural, Owl, Gold Glass Eyes, Challinor & Taylor, 7 1/4 In. 150.00
Plate, Angel & Harp, 8 In. 5.00
Plate, Blue, Basketweave, Lattice Openwork Edge, Sowerbury & Gateshead, 8 In. 110.00
Plate, Forget-Me-Not, Lattice Border, Tiny Flowers, c.1900, 7 1/4 In. 32.00
Plate, Scroll & Eye Border, Atterbury, 8 In. 35.00
Platter, Openwork Border, Circles & Ovals, Round, Atterbury, 11 1/4 In. 65.00
Shaker, Johnny Bull, Atterbury, 6 1/4 In. 62.00
Spooner, Blackberry Bramble, Blackberry Handles, 4 1/2 x 3 3/4 In. 40.00
Syrup, Fishnet & Poppies, Enameled, 7 In. 92.00
Syrup, French Primrose, Pewter Lid, c.1872, 8 In. 69.00
Syrup, Tree Of Life, Green Leaf, Hinged Metal Cover, Challinor 235.00
Tray, Dresser, Summer Flowers, Scrolled Edges, Footed, Butler Bros., 12 1/2 x 8 In. 40.00

MILLEFIORI means, literally, a thousand flowers. Many small pieces of glass resembling flowers are grouped together to form a design. It is a type of glasswork popular in paperweights and some are listed in that category.

Bell, Gold Aventurine Handle, Murano, 5 In. 25.00
Cigarette Holder, Ruffled Edge, Murano, 3 1/2 In. 35.00
Vase, Urn Shape, Murano, 3 1/3 In. 45.00

MINTON china has been made in the Staffordshire region of England from 1793 to the present. The firm became part of the Royal Doulton Tableware Group in 1968, but the wares continued to be marked *Minton*. The word *England* was added in 1891. Minton majolica is listed in this book in the Majolica category.

Bough Pot, Cover, Painted, Continuous Scene, Grazing Goats, 6 1/2 In. 2185.00
Centerpiece, Oval Basket, Parian Kneeling Nereids, c.1861, 13 In. 2446.00
Charger, Earthenware, Enamel & Gilt Design, Elizabethan Minstrel Scene, 19 In. 4700.00
Charger, Enamel, Gilt, Elizabethan Minstrel Scene, England, 1800s, 19 1/4 In. 4700.00
Charger, White Cockatoo, Perched On Branch, Orchids, Red Ground, c.1873, 21 In., Pair 8656.00
Dish, Sweetmeat, Double Dolphin, Conch Shell, 9 1/4 In. 2300.00
Figurine, Harvest Girl, With Basket, 8 1/2 In. 896.00
Flower Holder, Picket Fence, Floral, Curved, No. 1575 .... 110.00
Jardiniere, Pedestal, 3 Men Supporting, 3 Lion's Heads, Fruit Garlands, 20 1/2 In. 2990.00
Jug, Wine, Celadon, Parian Body, Female Figure Handle, Cherubs, 1876, 7 In. 825.00
Match Holder, Hogarth Figural, Boy & Girl, 7 1/2 In., Pair 1035.00
Oyster Plate, 6 Wells, Green, 9 In. 805.00
Oyster Plate, 6 Wells, Monogram, Pink, 9 In. 1265.00
Oyster Plate, 6 Wells, Turquoise, 9 1/4 In. 112.00
Oyster Plate, 6 Wells, Yellow, 9 In. 2990.00
Oyster Plate, 9 Wells, Turquoise, 9 3/4 In. 1095.00
Oyster Stand, 4 Tiers, Revolving, Fish Handle, 10 In. 9775.00
Pitcher, Blue & White Transfer, c.1891 .... 215.00
Pitcher, Diana, Bearded Man Below Spout, 11 1/2 In. 400.00
Pitcher, Lily, Flowers, Pewter Top, 8 In. 2300.00
Plaque, Scenic, Round, Cupid, Girl On Shore, Using Telescope, Sailor, 13 In., Pair 3565.00
Plate, Hand Painted, Reticulated Rim, 2 Young Girls Waving, Greek Key, 10 In. 470.00
Plate, Youth, Red Hat, Hand Painted, Earthenware, Ellen Welby, 1877, 9 3/4 In. 705.00
Plate Set, Creamware, Green Transfer, Branch Design, 20th Century, 10 1/4 In., 12 Piece 765.00
Potpourri Vase, Cover, Ship, Scrolled Leaf Borders, 1878, 17 In. 3819.00
Server, Water Lily Center, 13 In. 1064.00
Vase, Birds, Insects, Flowering Branches, Blue Ground, Enamel, c.1875, 7 1/4 In. 705.00
Vase, Cover, Pate-Sur-Pate, Children, Wreath, Ribbon Handles, Blue Ground, 15 In. 7638.00
Vase, Cover, Pate-Sur-Pate, Woman, Wreath, Ribbon Handles, Cream Ground, 15 1/2 In. 5580.00
Vase, Pate-Sur-Pate, Diana, Cherubs, Green Cartouche, Gold, Cream Ground, 8 1/2 In., Pair 4600.00
Vase, Pate-Sur-Pate, White Putti, Butterflies, Black Ground, 2 Handles, Gilt Trim, 13 In., Pair 940.00

MIRRORS are listed in the Furniture category under Mirror.

MOCHA pottery is an English-made product that was sold in America during the early 1800s. It is a heavy pottery with pale coffee-and-cream coloring. Designs of blue, brown, green, orange, black, or white were added to the pottery and given fanciful names, such as *Tree*, *Snail Trail*, or *Moss*. Mocha designs are sometimes found in pearlware. A few pieces of mocha ware were made in France, the United States, and other countries.

Bowl, Earthworm, Blue & Brown, Blue Bands, 6 1/4 In. 330.00
Bowl, Earthworm, Blue & Brown, Brown Bands, 6 1/4 In. 385.00
Bowl, Earthworm, Blue, Brown Bands, 5 1/2 In. 165.00
Bowl, Earthworm, Blue, Tan, Bands, Green Lattice, 3 3/4 x 7 1/2 In. 1870.00
Bowl, Earthworm, Coggle, 4 x 7 1/4 In. 520.00
Bowl, Earthworm, Green Band, Brown Pinstripes, 3 x 5 1/2 In. 195.00
Bowl, Earthworm, Yellow Band, Brown Pinstripes, Dimpled Green Rim, 4 x 8 3/4 In. 770.00
Bowl, Seaweed, Blue, White Band, Yellowware, 3 x 4 1/2 In. 110.00

Mocha, Jug, Cat's-Eye, Brown, Blue, Ocher Bands, Pearlware, c.1820, 9 In.

Mocha, Mug, Dipped Fan, Orange Ground, Checkerboard Border, c.1800, 2 1/2 In.

Bowl, Seaweed, Red, White Band, Black Pinstripes, Yellowware, 2 3/4 x 4 1/2 In. 440.00
Bowl, Tooled Band, Lines, Brown, Blue, Rust, Green Stripes, 7 3/8 x 3 3/8 In. 290.00
Castor, Cat's-Eye, Blue, Brown & Bittersweet Banding, England, 1800s, 4 1/2 In. 2990.00
Chamber Pot, Blue & White Seaweed Band, Yellowware, 5 1/4 x 8 1/2 In. 690.00
Creamer, Brown & Green Bands, Green Tooled Design, 3 1/2 In. 220.00
Creamer, Seaweed, Black, Light Gray Ground, Tooled Green Band, 4 1/2 In. 300.00
Jug, Cat's-Eye, Brown, Blue, Ocher Bands, Pearlware, c.1820, 9 In. .... *ILLUS* 4560.00
Jug, Earthworm, Cat's-Eye, Leaf Handle, 1800s, 6 3/4 In. 1955.00
Jug, Extruded Strap Handle, Bands, Leaf Terminals, Wavy Lines, c.1830, 6 In. 3760.00
Jug, Geometrics, Beaded, Seaweed, Leaf Handle, 6 1/4 In. 1840.00
Jug, Seaweed, Leaf Handle, Brown, Blue, Orange, 1800s, 7 In. 1955.00
Muffineer, Earthworm, 4 1/4 In. 2300.00
Mug, Cat's-Eye, 3 In. 460.00
Mug, Dipped Fan, Orange Ground, Checkerboard Border, c.1800, 2 1/2 In. .... *ILLUS* 4200.00
Mug, Earthworm, 5 3/4 In. 1035.00
Mug, Earthworm, Band, Black Pinstripes, Latticework, Green Glaze, Scrolled Handle, 3 In. 495.00
Mug, Earthworm, Banded, Pearlware, Strap Handle, 1805-20, 6 1/4 In. .... *ILLUS* 1920.00
Mug, Earthworm, Blue Ground, Squiggles, Chain Link Top Band, 1800s, 6 In. 1610.00
Mug, Earthworm, Polka Dot, Black Band, Applied Loop Handles, 5 3/4 In. 7700.00
Mug, Earthworm, Tricolor, Brown Stripes, Green Tooled Band, Orange Band, Handle, 5 In. 2130.00
Mug, Marbleized, Green Incised Top Band, 1800s, 2 1/4 In. 805.00
Mug, Pearlware, Dipped In Ocher Slip, Brown Rim Band, Early 1800s, 5 3/4 In. 880.00
Mug, Seaweed, 3 1/2 In. 635.00
Mug, Seaweed, 4 1/2 In. 489.00
Mug, Seaweed, Band, Black Pinstripes, Scrolled Handle, Child's, 2 In. 330.00
Mug, Seaweed, Bands, Blue, Tan, Black Pinstripes, Scrolled Handle, 5 In. 110.00
Mug, Seaweed, Blue, Band, Scrolled Handle, Yellowware, 3 1/2 In. 550.00
Mug, Seaweed, Blue, Black Bands, Scrolled Handle, 6 In. 385.00
Mug, Seaweed, Blue, White Band, Scrolled Handle, Yellowware, 3 1/2 In. 550.00
Mug, Seaweed, Leaf Handle, Brown & Sienna Bands, 4 3/4 x 5 1/4 In. 635.00
Mug, Seaweed, Pinstripes, Sand Colored Band, Scrolled Handle, Child's, 2 In. 330.00
Mug, Seaweed, Sienna Ground, Basket Weave Band, Leaf Handle, 4 3/4 In. 690.00
Pepper Pot, Cat's-Eye, Bands, Blue Ground, Bulbous, 4 1/2 In. 5170.00
Pepper Pot, Dome Top, Cat's-Eye, Blue Ground, Rust & Brown Bands, Bulbous, 4 1/4 In. 275.00
Pepper Pot, Dome Top, Cat's-Eye, Multicolored Bands, Blue Ground, 4 1/2 In. 5170.00
Pepper Pot, Dome Top, Seaweed, White Band, Blue Stripes, Yellowware, Bulbous, 4 In. 385.00
Pepper Pot, Dome Top, Vertical Bands, White Lid, Blue Bands, 4 In. 358.00
Pepper Pot, Earthworm, Blue, Orange Bands, 4 1/4 In. 2530.00
Pepper Pot, Earthworm, Polychrome, Gray Ground, Tooled Green Band, 4 3/4 In. 2300.00
Pepper Pot, Footed Baluster Shape, Brown, Gold Bands, Early 1800s, 4 1/4 In. 3290.00
Pepper Pot, Geometric, 1800s, 4 In. 290.00
Pepper Pot, Seaweed, Cinnamon Ground, Blue Band, 1800s, 4 3/4 In. 460.00
Pitcher, Cat's-Eye, Brown & Blue, Gray Band, 6 3/4 In. 475.00
Pitcher, Earthworm, Blue Bands, Brown Pinstripes, Scrolled Handle, Bulbous, 6 In. 330.00
Pitcher, Earthworm, Rust & White, Green, Bands, Brown & Blue, Barrel Form, 5 3/4 In. 1100.00
Pitcher, Marbleized Splotches, Brown, Blue, Cream, Pearlware, c.1790, 8 In. .... *ILLUS* 2880.00
Pitcher, Seaweed, Applied Extruded Strap Handle, c.1871, 1 Gal., 9 1/2 In. 705.00
Pitcher, Tooled Green Band, Brown Stripes, Tricolor Earthworm, Yellow, Handle, 6 In. 690.00

Mocha, Mug, Earthworm, Banded, Pearlware, Strap Handle, 1805-20, 6 1/4 In.

Mocha, Pitcher, Marbleized Splotches, Brown, Blue, Cream, Pearlware, c.1790, 8 In.

Tankard, Geometric Bands, Blue Bands, Chain Link, Leaf Handle, Step Base, 1800s, 5 3/4 x 4 In. . . 920.00
Tub, Cover, Seaweed Green, Cream Bands, Yellowware, 5 x 7 In. 546.00
Water Closet Pull, Impressed 6200.00

MONMOUTH Pottery Company started working in Monmouth, Illinois, in 1892. The pottery made a variety of utilitarian wares. It became part of Western Stoneware Company in 1906. The maple leaf mark was used until 1930. If *Co.* appears as part of the mark, the piece was made before 1906.

Bowl, Golden Tan Matte, Speckles, Mojave Line, 2 3/4 x 8 3/4 In. 10.00
Casserole, Cover, Handle, Blue, Individual 10.00
Casserole, Spatterware, Dark Tan, Burgundy Spatter, 6 x 8 1/2 In. 80.00
Cookie Jar, Cookie Jug, 10 x 7 In. 35.00
Cookie Jar, Maple Leaf Bottom, c.1940, 7 x 5 3/4 In. 95.00
Dish, Curved Divider, Olive Green, Maple Leaf Mark, 2 1/2 x 9 3/8 x 7 1/4 In. 21.00
Figurine, Cow, Calf, Brown Glaze, 6 1/2 x 4 1/2 In. 2415.00
Jug, Stoneware, Maple Leaf, Blue, 4 Gal., 17 In. 35.00
Mixing Bowl, Turquoise, Ridged Base, Rim, 3 x 5 In. 68.00
Vase, Floor, Green Matte, Ribbed, 14 x 7 3/4 In. 137.50
Vase, Floor, Green Matte, Ribbed, 1940s, 18 x 10 In. 163.00

MONT JOYE, see Mt. Joye category.

MOORCROFT pottery was first made in Burslem, England, in 1913. William Moorcroft had managed the art pottery department for James Macintyre & Company of England from 1898 to 1913. The Moorcroft pottery continues today, although William Moorcroft died in 1945. The earlier wares are similar to the modern ones, but color and marking will help indicate the age.

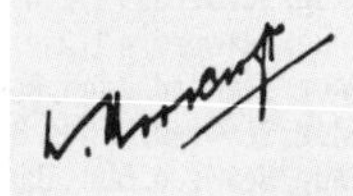

Ashtray, Fish, Flambe Glaze, Red, Blue Green Ground, Rounded Sides, 5 1/2 In. 295.00
Biscuit Box, Pomegranate, Blue Ground, Cover, Handles, Signed, 7 In. 1440.00
Biscuit Jar, Cover, Flamminian, Green, Square, Macintyre, 6 In. 315.00
Biscuit Jar, Floral Spray, Cover, Handle, Marked, Macintyre, c.1908, 7 1/4 In. 300.00
Biscuit Jar, Pomegranate, Bulbous Top, Metal Rim, Cover & Handle, 8 3/4 In. 1196.00
Bowl, Bermuda Lily, White Flowers, Green Ground, Flared, Impressed Mark, 9 3/4 In. 185.00
Bowl, Clematis, White Ground, Flared, 7 1/2 In. 139.00
Bowl, Columbine, Green Ground, Flared Sides, 10 In. 276.00
Bowl, Cornflower, 2 Handles, 10 3/4 In. 1565.00
Bowl, Cover, African Lily, Green Ground, Blue Foot & Knob Finial, Marked, 5 3/4 In. 276.00
Bowl, Cover, Attached Underplate, Red Flowers, Green Stems, Signed, Impressed, 5 1/2 In. 420.00
Bowl, Cover, Flowers, Green, Yellow, Red, Blue, 3 1/2 In. 835.00
Bowl, Cover, Grape & Leaf, Rounded Sides, 6 1/2 In. 460.00
Bowl, Dawn, Blue, 12 In. 735.00
Bowl, Eventide Landscape, Red, Peach, Green, 1 1/2 x 4 1/4 In. 115.00
Bowl, Eventide, Metal Rim, Impressed Mark, c.1925, 4 In. 690.00
Bowl, Flamminian, Pink, Handles, Signed, c.1915, 11 3/4 In. 240.00
Bowl, Florian, 2 Wide Squared Handles, Macintyre, 12 1/4 In. 1656.00
Bowl, Fruit, Cobalt Blue Ground, 2 Handles, 11 In. 390.00
Bowl, Moonlit Blue, Landscape, Footed, Signed, Impressed Mark, 5 1/2 x 7 In. 2630.00

Bowl, Moonlit Blue, Metal Stand-Up Rim, Impressed Mark, c.1925, 8 3/4 In. 460.00
Bowl, Pansy, Blue Ground, Signed, Impressed Mark, 4 x 10 1/2 In. 420.00
Bowl, Pansy, Burslem Mark, c.1915, 7 In. 2576.00
Bowl, Pansy, Flared Sides, Macintyre, 1912, 7 In. 5060.00
Bowl, Pomegranate, 2 Handles, 10 3/4 In. 276.00
Bowl, Pomegranate, 3-Footed, Burslem Mark, 7 In. 405.00
Bowl, Pomegranate, Red, Mottled Brown & Green Ground, Signed, Impressed Mark, 5 In. 920.00
Bowl, Wheat Panels, 8-Sided, Impressed Mark, 1930s, 10 3/4 In. 350.00
Box, Cover, Flamminian, Red, Rectangular, Concave Sides, 7 3/4 In. 368.00
Box, Cover, Orchids, Flambe Glaze, Rectangular, Impressed Mark, 5 In. 165.00
Candlestick, Grape & Leaf, Flambe Glaze, Ball Shape, Disc Foot, c.1930, 4 In. 506.00
Candlestick, Wisteria, Neck Rings, Flared Cup & Foot, 7 1/4 In., Pair 830.00
Coffee Set, Spring Flowers, Blue Foot & Handle, 8-In. Pot, 3 Piece 460.00
Compote, Moonlit Blue, Tudric Pewter, Pedestal Base, 4 1/2 In. 460.00
Compote, Pomegranate, 7 3/4 In. 350.00
Compote, Poppies, Tudric Pewter Pedestal Base, For Liberty & Co., 4 1/2 In. 1196.00
Creamer, Floral Spray, Impressed Mark, Macintyre, c.1900, 2 3/4 In. 90.00
Creamer, Gesso Faience, Marked, Macintyre, c.1905, 2 1/2 In. 90.00
Cup & Saucer, Dawn, Straight-Sided Cup, Impressed Mark 1656.00
Cup & Saucer, Dura Ware, Blue & Gold Border Design, Green Ground, Flared Cup 460.00
Cup & Saucer, Florian Ware, Poppies, Blue, Green, Flared Cup, Macintyre 1105.00
Cup & Saucer, Grape & Leaf, Red Flambe Glaze, Straight-Sided Cup 645.00
Cup & Saucer, Seaweed, Blue, White, Macintyre, c.1904 .... 645.00
Cup & Saucer, White, Blue Stylized Flowers & Swags, Gold Scalloped Border 875.00
Cup & Saucer, Wisteria, Straight-Sided Cup, Impressed Mark 386.00
Ginger, Cover, Moonlit Blue, Impressed Mark, c.1925, 9 1/2 In. 6624.00
Goblet, Alhambra, Dahlia, Cobalt Blue, Orange, Red, Gold Trim, Macintyre, 5 3/4 In. 645.00
Inkwell, Tray, Wisteria, Blue Ground, Signed, Impressed Mark, 3 x 9 In. 570.00
Jar, Cover, Eventide, 2 Handles, Impressed Mark, 7 In. 2390.00
Jar, Cover, Grape & Leaf, Cylindrical, Impressed Mark, 3 1/2 In. 239.00
Jar, Cover, Moonlit Blue Landscape, Green, 1924, 15 In. 9600.00
Jar, Cover, Pomegranate, Blue Ground, Signed, Impressed Mark, 4 1/4 In. 840.00
Jar, Cover, Pomegranate, Blue Ground, Signed, Impressed Mark, Paper Label, 6 1/2 In. Diam. 780.00
Jar, Cover, Spring Flowers, Cylindrical, Impressed Mark, c.1940, 3 3/4 In. 258.00
Jardiniere, Flamminian, Green, Signed, Marked, c.1918, 9 In. 510.00
Jardiniere, Pomegranate, 11 1/2 In. 1748.00
Jug, Aurelian, Cobalt Blue, Gold Design, Shaped Handle, Macintyre, 12 In. 276.00
Jug, Buttercup, Yellow & Blue Flowers, Dark Blue Ground, c.1991, 5 3/4 In. 220.00
Jug, Dura Ware, Stand-Up Rim, Blue Handle, Macintyre, 4 1/2 In. 295.00
Jug, Fish, Blue, Incised Stripes On Base & Foot, Green Handle, Impressed Mark, 6 In. 875.00
Jug, Grape & Leaf, Impressed Mark, 7 3/4 In. 368.00
Jug, Oranges, Yellow Ground, Black Dots On Rim, Impressed Mark, 6 In. 220.00
Jug, Pansy, Stand-Up Rim, 1913, 4 3/4 In. 2390.00
Jug, Poppies, White, Blue & Green Flowers, Blue Handle, 5 3/4 In. 460.00
Pitcher, Blue Poppy, Ivory Ground, Pewter Lid, Marked, Numbered, Macintyre, 6 In. 540.00
Pitcher, Claremont Toadstool, Signed, 5 x 6 1/2 In. 540.00
Pitcher, Florian, Blue Flowers, Green Ground, Marked, Macintyre, c.1900, 6 1/2 In. 420.00
Pitcher, Gesso Faience Anemone, Marked, Macintyre, c.1900, 7 In. 270.00
Planter, Columbine, Blue Ground, Impressed Mark, c.1980, 6 3/4 In. 330.00
Plate, Bougainvillea, White Ground, 10 1/2 In. 175.00
Plate, Fern, Blue, White, 7 1/2 In. 294.00
Plate, Fish, Green, Impressed Mark, c.1930, 8 1/4 In. 1380.00
Plate, Gingko Leaves, Marked, Macintyre, c.1905, 7 1/2 In. 450.00
Plate, Grape & Leaf, Blue, Green, Impressed Mark, 1930s, 7 1/2 In. 350.00
Plate, Moonlit Blue, Signed, Impressed Mark, 7 1/2 In. 520.00
Plate, Pomegranate, 7 1/4 In. 1012.00
Plate, Poppy, Impressed Mark, c.1925, 7 1/2 In. 1012.00
Plate, Wild Rose, Pink Flowers, Yellow Ground, c.1980, 10 1/4 In. 690.00
Plate, Wisteria, 7 1/2 In. 736.00
Preserve Pot, Yellow Luster, Metal Mounts, Handle, & Spoon, 5 In. 185.00
Salt & Pepper, Wisteria, Paper Label, 3 1/2 In. 386.00

Tea Set, Orchids, Dark Blue Ground, Green Inside, 1940s, 6-In. Pot, 3 Piece 460.00
Teapot, Blue Forget-Me-Nots, Ivory Ground, Gold Trim, Signed, 4 x 6 1/2 In. 450.00
Teapot, Cover, Floral Swag, Green, Blue, Marked, Macintyre, 4 1/2 In. 240.00
Tobacco Jar, Cover, Pomegranate, 5 3/4 In. 1010.00
Tobacco Jar, Florian, Blue Ground, Signed, Stamp Mark, 6 In. 660.00
Tray, Lilac, Blue & Yellow Floral Border, White Ground, Rectangular, 13 1/4 In. 1472.00
Vase, Anemone, Flambe Glaze, Signed, Marked, c.1935, 9 In. 570.00
Vase, Anemone, Green Ground, Bulbous, Signed, Impressed Mark, 10 1/4 In. 330.00
Vase, Anemone, Green Shaded To Blue Glaze, Bulbous, 6 In. 295.00
Vase, Anemone, White Ground, Bulbous, Signed, Impressed Mark, 6 In. 540.00
Vase, Apple Blossom, Green, Bulbous, Slender Neck, Tapered, Signed, Impressed Mark, 12 In. ... 1435.00
Vase, Art Pottery, Flowers, Cobalt Blue Ground, Mid 20th Century, 6 In. 265.00
Vase, Arum Lily, Yellow Green Ground, Baluster, c.1960, 10 3/4 In. 645.00
Vase, Baluster, Pomegranate, Cobalt Blue Ground, 12 1/2 x 6 1/2 In. 1058.00
Vase, Birds, Yellow Ground, Bulbous, Signed, Impressed Mark, 8 In. 900.00
Vase, Blackberry & Leaf, Flambe Glaze, Bulbous Top, 1930s, 9 In. 1014.00
Vase, Blue Streaks Over White, Hand Thrown, Impressed Mark, c.1935, 7 1/2 In. 270.00
Vase, Bowl, Anemone, Dark Blue Ground, Impressed Mark, 8 3/4 In. 440.00
Vase, Chestnut Leaves, Brown Ground, M. Nash, 1987, 14 1/2 In. 506.00
Vase, Claremont, Green Ground, Burslem, c.1918, 14 1/4 In. 6070.00
Vase, Claremont, Green, Bulbous Neck, 5 3/4 In. 1656.00
Vase, Claremont, Red Flambe, Bulbous, Squat, 2 Handles, c.1920, 4 3/4 In. 2760.00
Vase, Claremont, Squat, Flattened Loop Handles, Footed, 4 In. 1748.00
Vase, Claremont, Toadstools, Green Ground, Red, Yellow, Signed, Impressed Mark, 7 In. 1200.00
Vase, Clematis, Bulbous, Cylindrical Neck, 6 3/4 In. 330.00
Vase, Columbine, Blue Ground, Dark Blue Foot, 11 1/4 In. 506.00
Vase, Cornflower, Powder Blue, Flared Base & Rim, c.1925, 10 In. 550.00
Vase, Cornflower, Powder Blue, Flared, Impressed Marks, 6 1/4 In. 690.00
Vase, Cover, Pomegranate, Urn Shape, 2 Handles, Macintyre, 12 1/2 In. 9200.00
Vase, Dianthus, Green Ground, Tapered, Impressed Mark, 4 In. 240.00
Vase, Dianthus, Red Ground, Tapered, Impressed Mark, 4 In. 240.00
Vase, Eventide, Tan, Red, Tapered, Signed, Impressed Mark, 6 In. 2150.00
Vase, Eventide, Wide Mouth, Folded-In Rim, Impressed Mark, 6 1/2 In. 1472.00
Vase, Finches, Blue Ground, Bulbous, Mary Etheridge, Initials WM, c.1988, 11 3/4 In. 690.00
Vase, Flamminian, Bulbous Bottom, Flared Rim, Macintyre, 6 3/4 In. 500.00
Vase, Flamminian, Carafe Shape, Red Glaze, Flower Discs, c.1914, 10 1/2 In. 368.00
Vase, Flamminian, Green Ground, Tapered, Signed, Impressed Mark, 12 In. 480.00
Vase, Flamminian, Red, Squat Bottom, Elongated Neck, Flared Rim, Macintyre, 19 1/4 In. 875.00
Vase, Florian, Cornflower, Blue, White, Bulbous, Squat, Macintyre, 3 1/2 In. 315.00
Vase, Florian, Cornflower, White, Blue & Green Flowers, Footed, Macintyre, 6 1/2 In. 2390.00
Vase, Florian, Flambe, Swollen Form, Signed, Impressed Mark, 7 In. 300.00
Vase, Florian, Freesia, Bulbous Bottom, 2 Handles, Macintyre, 8 1/2 In. 828.00
Vase, Florian, Hazeldene, White, Blue Green Trees, Macintyre, 7 In. 6900.00
Vase, Florian, Peacock Feather, White Ground, Footed, Signed, Impressed Mark, 6 In. 1200.00
Vase, Florian, Poppies, White, Blue, Green, Corseted, Wide Rim, 4 3/4 In. 644.00
Vase, Florian, Slender Form, Blue, White, Signed, Stamped Mark, 10 In. 360.00
Vase, Florian, Violets, Blue, White, Flared & Scalloped Rim, Macintyre, 10 In. 552.00
Vase, Flowers, Red Tulips, Flared, Signed, Marked, Macintyre, c.1910, 9 In. 2280.00
Vase, Flowers, Red Tulips, Forget-Me-Nots, Ivory Ground, Signed, Marked, Macintyre, 5 3/4 In. ... 1434.00
Vase, Flowers, Spring, White, Blue, Red, Impressed Mark, c.1940, 2 3/4 In. 505.00
Vase, Flowers, Yellow, Green, Blue, 7 1/2 In. 1610.00
Vase, Freesia, Red Flambe Glaze, Impressed Mark, c.1934, 9 1/4 In. 2208.00
Vase, Freesia, Red Ground, Bulbous, Signed, Impressed Mark, 5 In. 900.00
Vase, Grape & Leaf, Brown Ground, Shouldered, Signed, Impressed Mark, 8 1/2 In. 780.00
Vase, Grape & Leaf, Dark Blue Ground, Baluster Shape, 6 1/4 In. 350.00
Vase, Grape & Leaf, Flambe Glaze, Signed, Marked, c.1933, 10 1/2 In. 390.00
Vase, Grape & Leaf, Red Flambe Glaze, 7 In. 782.00
Vase, Grape & Leaf, Shouldered, Flared Rim, Impressed Mark, 6 In. 552.00
Vase, Grape & Leaf, Swollen, Signed, Impressed Mark, 6 1/2 In. 450.00
Vase, Grape, Yellow Ground, Shouldered, Signed, Marked, Made For Liberty & Co., 5 In. 1135.00
Vase, Hazeldene, Yellow Green, Blue & Green Trees, Bulbous, Corseted, 6 In. 2208.00

Moriage, Vase, Snow Geese, Flying Over Flowers, Oriental China Nippon Mark, c.1915, 9 In.

Moser, Mug, Queen Louise, Gold Scrolls & Frame, Medallion, 5 In.

Moser, Tankard, Translucent Green, Peacock Feathers, Acanthus Bands, Cabachons, 11 1/2 In.

Vase, Honesty, White Ground, Blue, Flared, Shouldered, Signed, Impressed Mark, 7 In. 640.00
Vase, Iris, Bulbous, Signed, c.1905, 9 3/4 In. 780.00
Vase, Lilies, Iris, WM Initials, 6 1/2 In. 259.00
Vase, Magnolias, Pink, Deep Cobalt Blue Ground, Signed, Paper Label, 1976, 10 In. 360.00
Vase, Moonlit Blue, Blue & Green Trees, Impressed Mark, c.1925, 8 1/4 In. 4048.00
Vase, Moonlit Blue, Landscape, Bulbous, Signed, Impressed Mark, 6 1/4 In. 1912.00
Vase, Moonlit Blue, Tudric Pewter Mounted Base & Spread Foot, c.1925, 7 In. 1748.00
Vase, Mount Fuji Spring Blossom, c.1990, 14 1/4 In. 920.00
Vase, Orchid, Flambe Glaze, Bulbous, Folded-Over Rim, Impressed Mark, 11 1/2 In. 6440.00
Vase, Orchids, Flambe Glaze, Ball Shape, Impressed Mark, c.1930s, 6 In. 1010.00
Vase, Pansy, Bulbous, Cylindrical Neck, 4 3/4 In. 5520.00
Vase, Peacock Feather, White, Blue, Impressed Mark, c.1925, 8 1/4 In. 2390.00
Vase, Peacock Feathers, Brown, Tan, Signed, Impressed, c.1935, 7 In. 450.00
Vase, Pink Anemones, Blue, Green, Blue Ground, Globular, 8 In. 430.00
Vase, Polar Bear, Ball Shape, White Ground, Sue Gibbs, c.1988, 6 1/2 In. 1010.00
Vase, Pomegranate, Bands, Flambe Glaze, Dark Blue Ground, Impressed Mark, 13 In. 2392.00
Vase, Pomegranate, Blue Ground, Hammered Pewter Top, Signed, Impressed, 7 In. 960.00
Vase, Pomegranate, Bulbous Neck, Flared Foot, 2 Loop Handles, 8 3/4 In. 4600.00
Vase, Pomegranate, Green Ground, Flared, Signed, 13 In. 1675.00
Vase, Pomegranate, Pewter Neck & Rim, 4 1/2 In. 460.00
Vase, Pomegranate, Slender Gourd, Flared Lip, Blue Ground, c.1915, 11 1/2 In. 160.00
Vase, Pomegranate, Tan Ground, Bulbous, Signed, 1914, 5 In. 1435.00
Vase, Pomegranates, Red, Black Matte Glaze, 5 5/8 In. 490.00
Vase, Poppy, 8 1/2 In. 1110.00
Vase, Poppy, Blue Ground, Shouldered Form, Signed, Impressed Mark, 10 1/4 In. 1800.00
Vase, Poppy, Dark Blue, Red Flambe Glaze, Impressed Mark, 7 In. 3680.00
Vase, Poppy, White Ground, Blue, Green, Bulbous, Signed, Impressed Mark, 7 In. 840.00
Vase, Rain Forest, Green, Purple & Orange Flowers, Bulbous Top, 1993, 16 In. 1750.00
Vase, Spanish, Flared Rim, Footed, 9 In. 4785.00
Vase, Waratah, Bulbous, Stand-Up Rim, Impressed Mark, c.1932, 4 In. 7545.00
Vase, Waving Corn, Inverted Baluster Shape, Impressed Mark, 12 In. 920.00
Vase, Waving Corn, White Ground, Pink & Green Sheaves, Footed, 6 In. 875.00
Vase, Wisteria Panels, Red Flambe, Dark Blue Ground, Bulbous, 14 1/2 In. 3680.00
Vase, Wisteria, Bands, Bulbous, 9 1/4 In. 1840.00
Vase, Wisteria, Bands, Washed Blue, Marked, 1930, 6 1/4 In. 990.00
Vase, Wisteria, Bulbous Top, 1913, 12 In., Pair 7820.00
Vase, Wisteria, Bulbous, Impressed Mark, c.1925, 6 In. 370.00
Vase, Zipper, Squat, Baluster, Green To Flambe Glaze, c.1934, 8 1/2 In. 150.00

MORIAGE is a special type of raised decoration used on some Japanese pottery. Sometimes pieces of clay were shaped by hand and applied to the item; sometimes the clay was squeezed from a tube in the way we apply cake frosting. One type of moriage is called *Dragonware* and is listed under that name.

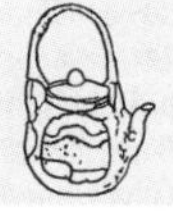

Basket, Snow Geese, Flying, Handle, Unmarked, c.1915, 8 3/4 In. 1528.00

Cup & Saucer, Brown Ground, Oriental Man & Woman, Gold Trim, 1 3/4-In. Cup, 5-In. Saucer 22.50
Ewer, Hawaii Photographs, Women, Grass Skirts 780.00
Humidor, Cigar & Matches, 3 Handles, Blue Maple Leaf, c.1910, 6 1/2 In. 705.00
Humidor, Grape Leaves, Wild Flowers, Unmarked, c.1915, 6 1/2 In. 500.00
Humidor, Hunt Scene, Blue Maple Leaf, c.1900, 5 1/2 In. 999.00
Humidor, Indian, Chief Sitting Bull, Blue Maple Leaf, c.1900, 7 1/2 In. 3760.00
Mustard Pot, Attached Base, Scalloped, 3 1/2 x 4 1/2 In. 125.00
Plaque, Children In Wheat, Blue Maple Leaf, c.1920, 10 In. 355.00
Plaque, Indian, Chief Sitting Bull, Blue Maple Leaf, c.1900, 10 In. 2470.00
Plaque, White Woodland, Trees, Mountains, c.1915, 10 In. 1410.00
Stein, Stylized Flowers, Green M In Wreath, c.1910, 7 In. 295.00
Tea Set, Teapot, 6 Cups, Saucers, 7 x 7-In. Teapot, 2-In. Cup, 4-In. Saucer 60.00
Tea Strainer, White Cover, Roses, Gold Beaded Rim, 2 x 4 x 6 In. 95.00
Urn, Cover, Snow Geese, Blue Royal Moriye Mark, c.1915, 9 1/2 In. 705.00
Vase, Birds In Flight, Countryside, Blue Maple Leaf, c.1915, 10 1/4 In. 1175.00
Vase, Birds In Flight, Handles, Green Maple Leaf, c.1915, 6 In. 825.00
Vase, Birds, Handles, Blue Maple Leaf, c.1915, 8 In. 2233.00
Vase, Flat, Geisha, Seated, Cream Base, 5 1/4 x 7 In. 175.00
Vase, Portrait, Queen Louise, Handles, Blue Maple Leaf, c.1900, 10 1/4 In. 4465.00
Vase, Seagulls, Waves, Handles, Blue Maple Leaf, c.1915, 10 In. 1765.00
Vase, Snow Geese, Flying Over Flowers, Oriental China Nippon Mark, c.1915, 9 In. .... *ILLUS* 3055.00
Vase, Snow Geese, Handles, Blue Maple Leaf, c.1915, 9 In. 2585.00
Vase, Snow Geese, Handles, Blue Maple Leaf, c.1915, 11 1/2 In. 3055.00
Wall Pocket, Dragon, Lusterware, Carmel, Brass Rim Glaze 100.00

MOSAIC TILE COMPANY of Zanesville, Ohio, was started by Karl Langerbeck and Herman Mueller in 1894. Many types of plain and ornamental tiles were made until 1959. The company closed in 1967. The company also made some ashtrays, bookends, and related giftwares. Most pieces are marked with the entwined *MTC* monogram.

Figure, Dog, Lying Down, Head On Paws, 3 x 8 3/8 x 3 3/4 In. 315.00
Fortune & Boy, Nursery Rhyme Series, Walter Crane, Square, 6 In. 65.00
Tile, Daffodils, Yellow, Teal Leaves, Band Border, Holder, Signed, 6 x 6 In. 90.00
Trivet, Gemini Zodiac, Square, c.1950, 6 In. 20.00
Trivet, Little Bo Peep, Nursery Rhyme Series, Molded Round Feet, Square, c.1930, 6 In. 95.00
Turtle, Whimsy, Removable Shell Cover, Terra-Cotta Glaze, 4 x 3 In. 90.00
Woodpecker, Cuerda Seca, Square, 4 1/4 In. 245.00

MOSER glass is made by Ludwig Moser und Sohne, a Bohemian (Czech) glasshouse founded in 1857. Art Nouveau-type glassware and iridescent glassware were made. The most famous Moser glass is decorated with heavy enameling in gold and bright colors. The firm, Moser Glassworks, is still working in Karlsbad, West Czech Republic. Few pieces of Moser glass are marked.

Barber Bottle, Portrait, Gold Stenciling, c.1885, 7 1/4 In. 575.00
Bowl, Cranberry Cut To Clear, Engraved Leaves & Scrolls, Lobed, Cabochons, Bouquets, 5 In. 323.00
Box, Hinged Cover, Casket Shape, Amethyst Cut To Clear, Gold Swags & Beading, 2 x 8 x 3 In. 590.00
Candlestick, Amber, Optic Ribbed, Gold Band, Warriors, Column Shape, Signed, 7 In., Pair 259.00
Chalice, Cover, Urn Shape, Prussian Blue, Peacock Eyes, Acanthus Scrolling, 14 In. 1440.00
Champagne, Intaglio Carved, Birds, Trees, Multicolored, 5 1/2 In., 6 Piece 518.00
Compote, Cranberry Cut To Clear, Deer Running In Forest, Star-Cut Base, 9 x 7 In. 518.00
Compote, Peacocks, Roses, Enameled, Bubble Stem, Footed, Scalloped Rim, 11 In. 1555.00
Cordial, Faceted, Leaves, Gold Encrusted Rim, Foot, Pair, 3 1/2 In. 460.00
Cruet, Cranberry, Leaves, Acorns, Clear Reeded Handle, Faceted Stopper, 8 In. 460.00
Cup, Cranberry Gold, Acanthus Scrolling, Applied Handles, Scrolled Rim, 3 1/2 In., 4 Piece 460.00
Cup, Prussian Blue, Coin Spot, Oak Leaves, Applied Acorn Jewels, Insect, 2 1/4 In. 145.00
Decanter, Lavender, Etched, Pear Shape, Early 1900s, 17 1/2 In. 499.00
Eggcup, Thumbprint, Red, Blue, Yellow, Green, Leaves, Vines, 4 1/4 In. .... 375.00 to 430.00
Ewer, Blue Flowers, Green Leaves, Corseted, Optic Ribbed, 13 1/2 In. 315.00
Ewer, Cobalt Blue, Applied Bird, Acorns, Branches, Pedestal Foot, Amber Handle, 18 In. 3565.00
Finger Bowl, Underplate, Gold Leaves & Flowers, Scalloped Rim, Applied Feet, 7 In. 290.00

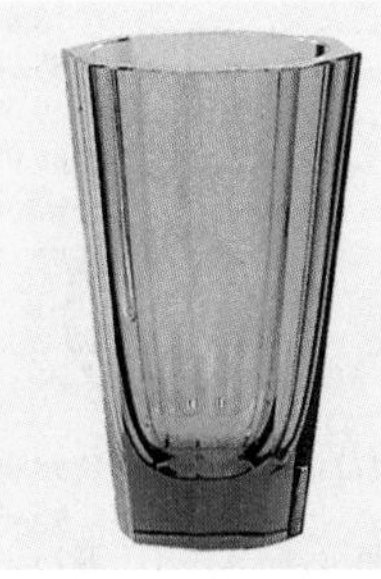

Moser, Vase, Amber, Faceted, Signed, Moser Carlsbad, 7 1/4 In.

Moser, Vase, Enameled Scene, Multicolored, Signed, Royo, 14 In.

Garniture Set, Compote, Urns, Cranberry, Victorian Lady Medallion, 13 1/2-In. Urn, 3 Piece 1955.00
Goblet, Enameled Scrolling, Internal Twisted Ruby Ribbon, Faceted Stem, 6 In., Pair 175.00
Goblet, Exotic Flowers, Vines, Enameled, Silver, Lilac Luster, 7 1/4 In., 10 Piece 2645.00
Goblet, Gold Encrusted, Gold Cabochons, Enameled Branches, Baluster, 7 1/4 In., Pair 635.00
Goblet, Gold Flowers, Scrolls, Blue, Pink, 3-Lobed Bowl, Spreading Foot, 6 1/4 In., Pair 978.00
Goblet, Green Bowl, Multicolored Leaves, Raspberry Cabochons, Jewels, 8 3/4 In. 575.00
Goblet, Green, Gold Encrusted, Multicolored Scrolling Leaves, Faceted, 8 1/4 In. 288.00
Goblet, Leaves, Swirls, Lady In Flowing Gown, 4 Medallions, Rippled, 5 3/4 In., 8 Piece 978.00
Letter Holder, Clear, Intaglio-Carved, Stemmed Flowers, Satin, 9 In. 660.00
Mug, Queen Louise, Gold Scrolls & Frame, Medallion, 5 In. .... *ILLUS* 115.00
Napkin Ring, Cranberry, Flowers, Gold, Enamel, 2 In. 150.00
Perfume Bottle, Atomizer, Green Satin Glass, Gold Band Women Warriors, Footed, 12 In. 290.00
Pitcher, Marquetry, Clear, Red Cherries, Green Branches, Intaglio Cut Leaves, 10 In. 750.00
Plaque, Amber, Enamel, Austrian, German, Italian Shields, Angel, Oak Leaf, Acorn Necklace, 14 In. 770.00
Tankard, Prussian Blue, Gold Insects, Variegated Leaves, 11 1/4 In. 1208.00
Tankard, Translucent Green, Peacock Feathers, Acanthus Bands, Cabachons, 11 1/2 In. .... *ILLUS* 1265.00
Tumbler, Cranberry, Gold Coralene Leaves, Winter Tree Scene, Shouldered, 6 In. 345.00
Tumbler, Green, Grape Leaves, Insects, Multicolored, Satin, 4 1/2 In. 230.00
Tumbler, Green, Oak Leaves, Applied Insects, Jeweled Acorns, Satin, 4 1/2 In. 520.00
Vase, Allover Gold Tracery, Birds, Flowers, Footed, Bulbous, Handles, 10 In. 1610.00
Vase, Amber, Faceted, Signed, Moser Carlsbad, 7 1/4 In. .... *ILLUS* 115.00
Vase, Amber, Gold Enameled Warrior Band, c.1915, 4 3/4 In. 300.00
Vase, Blue, Alexandrite, Footed, Cylindrical, 10 1/2 In. 490.00
Vase, Clear, Allover Floral Engraving, Ruby Flashed Medallions, Gold Trim, Bulbous, 4 3/4 In. 420.00
Vase, Clear, Gold Scrolling, Oval Lady's Portrait, Urn Shape, Handles, 10 1/2 In. 460.00
Vase, Clear, Intaglio Carved Flowers, Leaves, Red Marquetry Base, 8 3/4 In. 2300.00
Vase, Clear, Morning Glory, Vine, Gold Enameled, Tapered, c.1890, 7 In. 840.00
Vase, Clear, Optic Ribbed, Ruby Flashed Collar, Flowers, 3 Applied Rope Twist Handles, 7 1/2 In. .. 200.00
Vase, Enameled Scene, Multicolored, Signed, Royo, 14 In. .... *ILLUS* 288.00
Vase, Fan, Dark Amber, Enameled Leaf, Beetle & Applied Grapes, Footed, 5 1/2 In. 1800.00
Vase, Fan, Orange Amber, Enameled Flowers, Applied Clear Rigaree Feet, Rim, 7 1/2 x 12 In. 358.00
Vase, Green, Enameled Flowers, Leaves, Stems, Butterfly, 8 1/2 In. 575.00
Vase, Marquetry, Cranberry, Gold Enameled, Flowers, Pedestal Base, 5 In. 300.00
Vase, Stick, Cranberry, Insects, Enameled Leaves, 9 In. 1150.00
Vase, Stick, Plants, Vines, Beetles, Butterflies, Bulbous Body, c.1900, 12 1/2 In. 508.00
Vase, Trumpet, Apricot Shaded To Clear, Gold Enamel Design, 17 1/2 In. 300.00
Vase, Trumpet, Flowers, Blossoms, Cranberry Cut To Clear, Gold Enameled, 16 1/2 In. 350.00
Vase, Yellow Shaded To White, Fern Leaves, Enameled, Ribbed, Applied Hooks, 7 1/4 In. 489.00
Wine, Clear, Gold Enameled, Cut, Faceted Body, Gold Encrusted, Leaves, 4 3/4 In. 175.00
Wine Set, Decanter, Goblets, Jeweled Cobalt Blue Panes, Gilt Metal Frame, 12 & 5 In., 7 Piece 575.00

MOSS ROSE china was made by many firms from 1808 to 1900. It has a typical moss rose pictured as the design. The plant is not as popular now as it was in Victorian gardens, so the fuzz-covered bud is unfamiliar to most collectors. The dishes were usually decorated with pink and green flowers.

Cup & Saucer, Gold Trim, Collingwoods, England 22.00

Dish, Platinum Trim, Fujiyama, Japan, 4 1/4 x 3 In. 18.00
Eggcup, Scalloped Top, Gold Trim, 2 1/8 x 1 7/8 In., 6 Piece 55.00
Platter, UCAGCO China Co., Japan, 14 1/4 x 10 1/4 In. 49.00
Teapot, George Jones & Sons, Staffordshire, England, Late 1800s, 7 1/2 x 10 In. 65.00

MOTHER-OF-PEARL GLASS, or pearl satin glass, was first made in the 1850s in England and in Massachusetts. It was a special type of mold-blown satin glass with air bubbles in the glass, giving it a pearlized color. It has been reproduced. Mother-of-pearl shell objects are listed under Pearl.

Bowl, Rainbow, Diamond-Quilted Tricornered Rim, Vaseline Rigaree, 3-Footed, 8 1/2 In. 1898.00
Bride's Bowl, Diamond-Quilted, Salmon, 8 1/2 In. 345.00
Compote, Rainbow, Diamond-Quilted Foot, Scalloped Rim, Baluster Stem, 9 1/2 In. 2415.00
Ewer, Diamond-Quilted, Peach, Applied Clear Satin Handle, 8 In. 80.00
Jam Jar, Raindrop, Butterscotch, Silver Plated Caddy, Spoon, 7 In. 248.00
Nappy, Jack-In-The-Pulpit, Rainbow, Diamond-Quilted, Ruffled Edge, 4 1/4 In. 1553.00
Sugar & Creamer, Diamond-Quilted, Pink, 4 1/2 In. 495.00
Vase, Blue, Diamond-Quilted, Geometric, Butterflies, Shouldered, Handles, 5 In. 230.00
Vase, Diamond-Quilted, Blue, Applied Enameled Stems, 8 In. 525.00
Vase, Stick, Blue, Camphor Handles, Bulbous Base, Leaves, Thorny Feet, England, 9 In. 1380.00

MOTORCYCLES and motorcycle accessories of all types are being collected today. Examples can be found that date back to the early years of the twentieth century. Toy motorcycles are listed in the Toy category.

Broadside, Indian Service Car, Motorcycle, Sidecar, c.1915, 21 x 30 In. 560.00
Helmet, Leather, Goggles, 1939 .... 610.00
Motorcycle, Monark Silver King, Super Twin, Kegel's Rent-A-Bike, 1950 .... 4475.00
Postcard, Greatest Innovation In Scott History, 300 C.C. Squirrel 210.00
Postcard, Harley-Davidson, Man Driving, Woman In Side Car, Real Photo 259.00
Postcard, Indian Motorcycle, Real Photo 259.00
Poster, Griffon, Man, Riding Motorcycle, Sea, Mountains, France, 1904, 56 x 40 In. 2500.00
Poster, NSU Motorrader, Touren U. Sportmodelle, Germany, 1946, 36 x 26 3/4 In. 1485.00
Side Car, Pal, Pneumatic Safety, 3-Wheel, Indian Motorcycle Co., Springfield, Mass., 1926 .... 5720.00

MOUNT WASHINGTON, see Mt. Washington category.

MOVIE memorabilia of all types is collected. Animation Art, Games, Sheet Music, Toys, and some celebrity items are listed in their own sections. A lobby card is 11 by 14 inches. A set of lobby cards includes seven scene cards and one title card. A one sheet, the standard movie poster, is 27 by 41 inches. A three sheet is 81 by 40 inches. A half sheet is 22 by 28 inches. A window card, made of cardboard, is 14 by 22 inches. An insert is 14 by 36 inches. A herald is a promotional item handed out to patrons. Press books, which contain many ad slicks, are sent to film exhibitors to aid in advertising the film. Press books and/or press kits (with photos) are sent to the media to promote a movie.

Brassiere, Marilyn Monroe, Hollywood Vassarette, V-Ette, Debutante, Size 36C 4024.00
Button, Billy Jack For President, Celluloid, Round, 1971 .... 14.00
Button, Don't Miss Wizard Of Oz At Loew's Palace, Scarecrow, Yellow, 1939, 1 1/4 In. 452.00
Button, I'm Your Manchurian Candidate, Celluloid, 1962, 2 1/4 In. 73.00
Button, Wizard Of Oz, Judy Garland, Orange Border, 1939, 1 1/4 In. 498.00
Detroit Tigers Uniform, Tommy Lee Jones As Ty Cobb, 1994 .... 458.00
Insert, Niagara, Marilyn Monroe, 1953 .... 708.00
Lobby Card, All The World's A Stooge, Columbia, 1941 .... 1298.00
Lobby Card, Another Thin Man, MGM, 1939 .... 384.00
Lobby Card, At The Circus, Marx Bros., 1939, Title Card 1799.00
Lobby Card, At The Circus, Marx Bros., MGM, 1939 .... 177.00
Lobby Card, Gilda, Rita Hayworth, Columbia, 1946 .... 413.00
Lobby Card, Son Of Kong, RKO, 1933 .... 2360.00
Lobby Card, The Idle Class, Charlie Chaplin, 1st National Studios, 1920 .... 187.00

Lobby Card, Treasure Of Sierra Madre, Humphrey Bogart, Warner Bros., 1948 .... 419.00
Poster, 3 Stooges, Rumpus In Harem, 1956, 1 Sheet 509.00
Poster, Abe Lincoln In Illinois, Raymond Massey, 1940, 1 Sheet 679.00
Poster, Ace Of Cactus Range, Art Mix, Otis Stone Lithograph, 1924, 1 Sheet 415.00
Poster, Adventures Of Robin Hood, Re-release, Warner Bros., 1950s, 1 Sheet 177.00
Poster, Alamo, United Artists, 1960, 1 Sheet 236.00
Poster, Ali Baba & 40 Thieves, Linen Back, Universal, 1943, 1 Sheet 236.00
Poster, American Graffiti, 1973, Linen Back, 1 Sheet 200.00
Poster, An American In Paris, MGM, 1951, 1 Sheet 295.00
Poster, Annie Get Your Gun, Betty Hutton, Linen Back, 1950, 3 Sheet 265.00
Poster, Arsenic & Old Lace, Cary Grant, 1944, 1 Sheet 1760.00
Poster, Attack Of The Crab Monsters, Linen Back, 1957, 1 Sheet 1770.00
Poster, Big Jake, John Wayne, 1971 .... 118.00
Poster, Bowery Boys Meet The Monsters, 1954, Insert 118.00
Poster, Cash & Hash, 3 Stooges, 1955, 1 Sheet 860.00
Poster, Confessions Of A Nazi Spy, Linen Back, Warner Bros., 1939, Insert 266.00
Poster, Cowboy & The Lady, Gary Cooper, 1938, 1 Sheet 325.00
Poster, Dakota, John Wayne, Linen Back, Republic, 1945, Insert 236.00
Poster, Drums Along The Mohawk, Claudette Colbert & Henry Fonda, 1939, 1 Sheet 520.00
Poster, E.T. The Extra-Terrestrial, Steven Spielberg, 1982, 1 Sheet 750.00
Poster, Excitement, Laura La Plante, c.1924, 1 Sheet 385.00
Poster, Fish Called Wanda, 1988, 1 Sheet 21.00
Poster, Flying Disc Man From Mars, Linen Back, 1950, 1 Sheet 295.00
Poster, Forbidden Planet, 1956, Insert 2221.00
Poster, Forever Darling, 1956, 1 Sheet 153.00
Poster, Frankenstein, Boris Karloff, Reissue, 1950s, 1 Sheet 1485.00
Poster, From Russia With Love, James Bond, Sean Connery, 1964, 1 Sheet 679.00
Poster, Full Metal Jacket, Stanley Kubrick, 1987, 1 Sheet 81.00
Poster, Gentlemen Prefer Blonds, Marilyn Monroe, 1953, 1 Sheet 665.00
Poster, Gilda, Rita Hayworth, Linen Back, 1946, 1 Sheet 1125.00
Poster, Gone With The Wind, Clark Gable, Linen Back, Frame, 1939, Insert 7638.00
Poster, Great Escape, Steve McQueen, 1963, 1 Sheet 236.00
Poster, Harvey, James Stewart & Rabbit, 1950, Insert 600.00
Poster, Hell's Kitchen, Ronald Reagan, Dead End Kids, 1939, 1 Sheet 1090.00
Poster, Honky Tonk, Gable & Turner, Restored, 1941, Half Sheet 354.00
Poster, Incredible Shrinking Man, 1957, Half Sheet 560.00
Poster, It Came From Outer Space, Richard Carlson & Barbara Rush, 1953, 1 Sheet 870.00
Poster, It, Clara Bow, Linen Back, Restored, 1927, 1 Sheet 24780.00
Poster, Key Largo, Bogart, Robinson, Bacall, Linen Back, 1948, 1 Sheet 1770.00
Poster, Laura, Gene Tierney, Linen Back, Frame, 1944, 1 Sheet 6465.00
Poster, Man For All Seasons, Linen Back, 1966, 1 Sheet 325.00
Poster, Merrie Melodies, Old Gray Hare, Warner Bros., Cartoon, 1952, 1 Sheet 900.00
Poster, Pardon Us, Stan Laurel, Oliver Hardy, Linen Back, Frame, 1931, 1 Sheet 5290.00
Poster, Prince & Showgirl, Marilyn Monroe, Laurence Olivier, 1957, 1 Sheet 730.00
Poster, Rebel Without A Cause, James Dean, Warner Bros., 1955, Window Card 500.00
Poster, Rocky, Sylvester Stallone, 1976, 1 Sheet 118.00
Poster, Sabrina, Audrey Hepburn, Linen Back, 1954, 1 Sheet 355.00
Poster, Shootist, John Wayne, Linen Back, 1976, 1 Sheet 135.00
Poster, Some Like It Hot, Monroe, Curtis, Lemmon, United Artists, 1959, Insert 826.00
Poster, Son Of Kong, Restored, 1933, Window Card 5900.00
Poster, Spy Smasher Serial, Chapter 6, 1942, 1 Sheet 458.00
Poster, Stage Door, Katherine Hepburn & Ginger Rogers, Restored, 1927, Window Card 354.00
Poster, Sting, Newman & Redford, Linen Back, 1974, 1 Sheet 266.00
Poster, Stolen Life, Bette Davis, Linen Back, 1946, 1 Sheet 405.00
Poster, Suez, Tyrone Power, 1938, 1 Sheet 6465.00
Poster, Taxi Driver, Robert DeNiro, 1976, Linen Back, 1 Sheet 280.00
Poster, The Day The Earth Stood Still, Patricia Neal, 1951, 1 Sheet 10925.00
Poster, The Dolly Sisters, Betty Grable, June Haver, Linen Back, 1945, 3 Sheet 385.00
Poster, The Godfather, Linen Back, 1972, 2 Sheet 266.00
Poster, The Lady Eve, Barbara Stanwick & Henry Fonda, 1941, 1 Sheet 5290.00
Poster, The Little Colonel, Shirley Temple, 1935, Half Sheet 305.00

To remove stains from a glass vase, fill it with a mixture of ammonia and water and let it stand for a few hours.

Mt. Washington, Vase, Jack-In-The-Pulpit, Light Blue To Deep Pink, Acid Finish, Peachblow, 12 1/2 In.

Poster, Them, James Whitmore, 1954, 3 Sheet 1150.00
Poster, West Side Story, Natalie Wood, 1961, 1 Sheet 354.00
Poster, Zulu, Michael Caine, Linen Back, 1964, 41 x 27 In. 295.00
Puzzle, King Kong, Mailer, 1933, 21 3/4 x 10 1/2 In. 1635.00
Skirt, Marilyn Monroe, Wool, Straight Cut, Black, Forstmann, 30 x 12 1/2 In. 1350.00
Trenchcoat, Humphrey Bogart, Casablanca, 1942, Size 39 .... 6550.00

MT. JOYE is an enameled cameo glass made in the late nineteenth and twentieth centuries by Saint-Hilaire Touvier de Varraux and Co. of Pantin, France. This same company made De Vez glass. Pieces were usually decorated with enameling. Most pieces are not marked.

Vase, Acorns, Leaves, Textured Green Ground, 6 In. 115.00
Vase, Green Ground, Enameled Flowers, Baluster, Quatrefoil Rim, c.1900, 11 3/4 In. 660.00
Vase, Green, Acorn, Gold, Enameled, Cupped Rim, Baluster Stem, Footed, c.1915, 17 In. 775.00
Vase, Purple Iris, Gold Leaves, Icicle Border, Textured Clear Ground, Rectangular, 12 In. 690.00

MT. WASHINGTON Glass Works started in 1837 in South Boston, Massachusetts. In 1870 the company moved to New Bedford, Massachusetts. Many types of art glass were made there until 1894, when the company merged with Pairpoint Manufacturing Co. Amberina, Burmese, Crown Milano, Cut Glass, Peachblow, and Royal Flemish are each listed in their own category.

Basket, Shaded Pink, Green Interior, Pearl Satin Thorn Handle, Ruffled Edge, 11 In. 570.00
Biscuit Jar, Blue Flowers, Melon Ribbed, Double Rope Twist Handle, 6 In. 175.00
Biscuit Jar, Gold Enameled Apple Blossoms, Colonial White, c.1885, 8 In. 259.00
Biscuit Jar, Mauve Shaded To Cream, Leaves, Flowers, 7 1/2 In. 430.00
Biscuit Jar, Opaque Green, Melon Ribbed, Silver Plate Cover & Overlay, Bail Handle, 7 In. 150.00
Bride's Bowl, Griffins, Holding Urn, Leaves, Alabaster Body, Cameo, 9 In. 545.00
Compote, Napoli, 10 Roses, Gold Enameled, 9 1/2 x 6 In. 575.00
Cruet, Colonial White, Satin, Faceted Stopper, 6 1/4 In. 145.00
Cruet, Stopper, Enameled Chrysanthemum, Ribbed, Red Trim, 6 3/4 In. 2185.00
Dish, Sweetmeat, Colonial White, Ribbed, Gold Enameled, 4 x 5 1/2 In. 460.00
Ewer, Cover, Cream, Opal, Cherubs, Gold Medallions, Rope Handle, Footed, 15 In. 13800.00
Lemonade Set, Rose Amber, 8 1/2-In. Pitcher, 5 Piece 1725.00
Mustard Jar, Opal, Ribbed, Blue Flowers, Metal Flip Lid, 3 In. 315.00
Pitcher, Blossom & Leaf, Colonial White, Square Mouth, 8 In. 160.00
Pitcher, Blossom & Leaf, Square Mouth, White Satin, 8 In. 160.00
Pitcher, Flower Medallion, Gold Scrolling, Colonial White, Handle, Squat 635.00
Punch Bowl, Base, Tulip Pattern, 10 1/2 x 11 1/2 In. 3575.00
Rose Bowl, Napoli, Clear, Ribbed, Crimped, Applied Internal Flower, Signed, 4 1/2 In. 175.00
Salt, Barrel Shape, Deep Red, Textured Bark Body, Yellow & White Mums, 3 In. 710.00
Salt & Pepper, Tomato Shape, Enameled, Late 1800s, 2 1/2 In. 175.00
Shaker, Cockle Shell, Clear, Satin, Purple Flowers, Green Stems, 3 In. 575.00
Spill, Flowers, Blue Shaded To Clear, Satin, 6 1/2 In. 200.00
Sugar Shaker, Egg Shape, Enameled Forget-Me-Nots, Satin Ground, Late 1800s, 4 1/4 In. 230.00

Sugar Shaker, Egg Shape, Maiden Hair Fern, Enameled, Late 1800s, 4 1/4 In. 230.00
Sugar Shaker, Tomato Shape, Enameled Leaves, Satin Ground, c.1890, 2 1/4 In. 259.00
Sugar Shaker, Tomato Shape, Flowers, Satin Ground, c.1890, 2 1/2 In. 175.00
Syrup, Rose Amber, Egg Shape Body, Coin Spot, Silver Plate Lid, Handle, 5 1/2 In. 1610.00
Toothpick, Green Opalescent, Flowers, Finger Cut Rim, 2 1/4 In. 2760.00
Vase, Colonial Ware, Pansies, Gilt, Gold Strap Handles, 9 1/4 In. 1265.00
Vase, Jack-In-The-Pulpit, Blue Shaded To Pink, 12 1/4 In. 1778.00
Vase, Jack-In-The-Pulpit, Light Blue To Deep Pink, Acid Finish, Peachblow, 12 1/2 In. .... *ILLUS* 3450.00
Vase, Jack-In-The-Pulpit, White, Ruffled Rim, 13 1/2 In. 200.00
Vase, Trumpet, Napoli, Enameled Gold Flowers, Bulbous Base, 16 In. 920.00
Vase, Verona, Flowers, Pink, Opalescent Yellow, Ribbed 1035.00

MULLER FRERES, French for Muller Brothers, made cameo and other glass from about 1895 to 1933. Their factory was first located in Luneville, then in nearby Croismare, France. Pieces were usually marked with the company name.

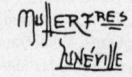

Lamp, 3-Light, Mottled Orange Shades, Brass Art Nouveau Base, Signed, 15 In. 510.00
Lamp, Bell Shade, Mottled Red, Blue, Leafy Branch Swirls, Cameo, 19 In. 575.00
Lamp, Metal Base, Tooled Foot, Surrounding Curlicues, Shade, Art Deco, 11 1/2 In. 1610.00
Lamp, Mottled Pink Glass Shade, Wrought Iron Base, Round, Curled, 11 In. 290.00
Lamp, Poppies, Leaves, Glass Base, Round Foot, Domed Shade, Cameo, c.1900, 20 In. 10158.00
Rose Bowl, Clear, Satin, High Relief Art Deco Design, Signed, 6 In. 58.00
Vase, Arabs, Camels, Oasis, Greens, Black, Red, White Ground, Cameo, 9 1/2 In. 1265.00
Vase, Butterflies, Forest, Orange, Cream, Cameo, 8 3/4 In. 575.00
Vase, Flowering Branches, Purple Shaded To Cream Ground, Enameled, 5 1/2 In. 1150.00
Vase, Gloire Aviation, Strasbourg Cathedral, 1906, 6 3/4 x 4 1/2 In. 690.00
Vase, Interior Decorated, Mottled Blue Top, Bottom, Pink, Yellow, White, 1900s, 10 1/2 In. 145.00
Vase, Leaves, Stems, Flowers, Frosted Ground, Landscape Scene, Applied Handles, 11 In. 1610.00
Vase, Mottled Sunset Colors, Gold Flecks, Paperweight Style, Bulbous, Tapered Rim, 12 In. 1020.00
Vase, Orange, Mottled, Blue Rim, Silver Inclusions, Footed, 12 1/2 In. 489.00
Vase, Orange, Trees, Deer, Oval, Cameo, 6 1/2 In. 748.00
Vase, Pine Trees, Rocks, Lake, Mountains, Enameled, 12 1/2 In. 3278.00
Vase, Stick, Flowers, Cranberry Overlay, Bulbous Base, Cameo, c.1900, 16 In. 1370.00
Vase, Stick, Mottled Blue, Ocher, Rose, Bulbous Base, Cameo, c.1920, 15 1/2 In. 265.00
Vase, Tibetan Scene, Man In Fur Coat, Tree, Green Ground, Cameo, Signed, 9 3/4 In. 5175.00
Vase, Windswept Trees, Rain, Frosted, Orange Ground, Enameled, Cameo, 14 In. 1115.00
Vase, Yellow & Orange Chevron Design, Mica Flecks, Flared, 12 In. 960.00

MUNCIE Clay Products Company was established by Charles Benham in Muncie, Indiana, in 1922. The company made pottery for the florist and giftshop trade. The company closed by 1939. Pieces are marked with the name *Muncie* or just with a system of numbers and letters, like *1A*.

Ashtray, Green Matte Drip Over Rose Glaze, Pair 425.00
Pitcher, Water, Green Drip Over Lavender Matte, 7 1/2 In. 89.00
Vase, Airbrushed Rose Matte Over Blue, c.1925, 4 1/8 x 2 1/2 In. 48.00
Vase, Flaring, Orange Peel, 7 1/2 In. 200.00
Vase, Gloss Green Glaze, 6 1/2 x 6 1/2 In. 350.00
Vase, Orange Peel Glaze, 6 x 5 In. 75.00
Vase, Ruba Rombic, Blue Matte Over Green, No. 312, Marked, 5 In. ....450.00 to 540.00
Vase, Ruba Rombic, White Matte Drip Over Blue Glaze, 5 In. 350.00
Wall Pocket, Shape No. 266, Gloss Brown Glaze 400.00

MURANO, see Glass-Venetian category.

MUSIC boxes and musical instruments are listed here. Phonograph records, jukeboxes, phonographs, and sheet music are listed in other categories in this book.

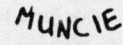

Accordion, Case, Salesman's Sample, Case, Late 1920s 282.00
Accordion, Tanzbaer, Mechanical, 16-Note Roll, Walnut Case, 11 In. 646.00
Banjo, Ivory Inlay, Mother-Of-Pearl Peghead, Turned Ivory Pegs, Carved Neck Head, 36 In. 598.00
Banjo, Tenor, Slingerland Troubadour, Rosewood, Mother-Of-Pearl, Case, 36 x 10 3/4 In. 1220.00

Banjo, Windsor Artiste, Model No. 2, Hollow Neck Zither, Rosewood, c.1920, 38 x 14 In. 770.00
Banjo Mandolin, 8 Strings, Cherry, Nickel Plate Brass Head, Mother-Of-Pearl Fret, 23 x 8 In. 303.00
Bass, Double, Ply Construction, Czechoslovakia, 42 In. 438.00
Baton, Director's, Original Case, 17 In. 275.00
Box, Band Organ, Wurlitzer, Artizan 46-Key Action, Flywheel, Wood Pipes, 38 x 47 In. 7345.00
Box, BB&Cie, Cylinder, Walnut Case, 6 Tunes, c.1840, 4 x 17 x 6 In. 2800.00
Box, Bremond, Bells Exposed, Winding Lever, 10 Tunes, 22 1/2-In. Cylinder, 13 In. 2115.00
Box, Bremond, Mandoline, Rosewood Veneer, Lever Wind, 6 Tunes, 13-In. Cylinder, 20 In. 2585.00
Box, Bremond, Organocleide, Burl Walnut Veneer Case, 6 Tunes, 17-In. Cylinder, 29 In. 12925.00
Box, Bremond, Part Mandoline, Burl Walnut Veneer Case, 4 Tunes, 13-In. Cylinder, 26 In. 11515.00
Box, Chocolat Menier, Wood, Shipping Crate Shape, France, c.1900, 5 x 2 In. 280.00
Box, Crank, Cherry, Children, Dressing Dog, 4 Tunes, France, c.1885, 5 1/2 x 4 In. 505.00
Box, Crank, Lacquered, Forest, 2 Tunes, France, c.1850, 3 1/4 x 2 1/2 In. 308.00
Box, Crank, Metal Frame, Porcelain Knob, Children, Beach, 3 Tunes, Swiss, c.1900, 2 1/4 In. 365.00
Box, Criterion, Mahogany Case, On Paneled Case, 20 1/2-In. Disc, 44 x 33 In. 19975.00
Box, Criterion, Oak Case, Double Comb, 20 11 1/2-In. Discs, c.1900, 16 1/2 In. 3920.00
Box, Criterion, Walnut, Disc, 8 1/2 x 15 1/2 x 15 In. 690.00
Box, Cylinder, 8 Tunes, Cased, Swiss, c.1885, 5 x 16 x 8 In. 820.00
Box, Cylinder, Carved, Inlaid, Boxwood, Ebony, 3 Tunes, Black Forest, 38 In. 1645.00
Box, Cylinder, Drum, Castanet, Bell, Mahogany, 12 Tunes, 10 3/4 x 30 x 14 1/2 In. 1955.00
Box, Cylinder, Ideal Sublime Harmonie, Oak Case, Swiss, 1880-90, 11 x 29 x 15 In. 4115.00
Box, Cylinder, Jacot & Son, Ideal Piccolo, Oak Case, Carved, c.1886, 8 1/2 x 27 x 12 In. 1880.00
Box, Cylinder, Rosewood Case, Floral Inlay, Swiss, 1800s, 26 In. 590.00
Box, Cylinder, Rosewood Case, Marquetry Lid, Swiss, c.1885, 5 1/4 x 17 In. 820.00
Box, Cylinder, Sectional Comb, Fusee Drive, Fruitwood Box, Swiss, c.1820, 9 x 3 x 4 In. 8960.00
Box, Cylinder, Visible Bells, 12 Tunes, Swiss, 1892, 12 x 22 x 13 In. 3696.00
Box, Drum, Bells, Castanet, Wood Case, 8 Tunes, France, 10 1/2 x 23 x 11 In. 5600.00
Box, Ducommun Girod, Visible Bell, Rosewood Veneer, 12 Tunes, 13-In. Cylinder, 23 In. 2115.00
Box, Euphonia, Model 55, Mahogany, Ormolu, Double Comb, 5 15 1/2-In. Discs, 21 x 12 In. 2800.00
Box, George Baker, Interchangeable Cylinder, Rosewood Veneer, 13-In. Cylinder, 34 In. 30550.00
Box, Heller, Expressive, Hidden Bells, Grained Case, 8 Tunes, 13-In. Cylinder, 23 In. 2585.00
Box, Kalliope, Disc, Saucer Bells, Single Comb, 11 1/2 In. 499.00
Box, Kalliope, Fruitwood Case, 21 Discs, Table Top, 15 x 15 5/8 In. 675.00
Box, Kalliope, Leipzig, No. 50G, Disc, 6 Bells, c.1902, 11 1/2 x 10 1/2 In. 670.00
Box, Kalliope, Stained Case, Motor Wind, 7-In. Disc, 10 1/4 In. 590.00
Box, L'Epee, Grained Case, Key Wind, 6 Tunes, 10 3/4-In. Cylinder, 18 In. 1116.00
Box, LeCoultre & Brechet, Walnut Case, 8 Tunes, 14 1/2-In. Cylinder, 23 In. 6465.00
Box, LeCoultre, Walnut Case, No. 3816, 4 Overture, 21 3/4-In. Cylinder, 12 x 3 1/4 In. 15275.00
Box, Mermod Freres, Forte-Piccolo, Cylinder, Satinwood, 36 Tunes, c.1890, 13 x 23 x 18 In. 7840.00
Box, Mermod Freres, Harmony Piccolo, 8 Tunes, Winding Lever, 23 1/2-In. Cylinder, 13 In. 1998.00
Box, Mermod Freres, Piccolo Zither, Tulipwood Banded Rosewood, 12 Tunes, 16 In. 1116.00
Box, Nicole Freres, 12 Tunes, Cylinder, Rosewood Case, c.1865, 21 x 8 1/2 x 6 In. 4480.00
Box, Nicole Freres, Cylinder, Marquetry Sphinxes, 10 Tunes, c.1865, 8 x 18 x 5 In. 4200.00
Box, Nicole Freres, Forte-Piano, Cylinder, 6 Tunes, Swiss, c.1850, 20 In. 7000.00
Box, Nicole Freres, Forte-Piano, Grained Case, Lever Wind, 8 Tunes, 21 3/4-In Cylinder, 33 In. 8225.00
Box, Nicole Freres, No. 26639, Walnut Case, Key Wind, 6-In. Cylinder, 11 1/2 In. 1765.00
Box, Nicole Freres, No. 44988, Grained Case, 6 Tunes, 11-In. Cylinder, 18 1/2 In. 764.00
Box, Nicole Freres, Overture, Rosewood Case, Lever Wind, 4 Tunes, 16 1/2-In. Cylinder 8815.00
Box, Nicole Freres, Rosewood Veneer Case, 12 Tunes, 18-In. Cylinder, 29 1/2 In. 1116.00
Box, Paillard, Amobean, Cylinder, Rosewood Case, 3 Extra Cylinders, c.1880, 9 1/2 x 22 x 7 In. ... 710.00
Box, Paillard, Columbia, Cylinder, Wood Case, 10 Tunes, c.1895, 5 x 17 x 8 In. 1568.00
Box, Paillard, Cylinder, Mandolin Teeth, Zither, Selector, Lever Wind, 8 Tunes, 17 1/2 x 3 1/4 In. .. 5875.00
Box, Paillard, Cylinder, Nickel Plated, Zither, Indicator, Selector, Handles, 12 Tunes, 28 In. 1528.00
Box, Paillard, No. 4471, Mandoline Expressive Zither, 17 1/2-In. Cylinder, 36 In. 5875.00
Box, Paillard, No. 4821, Rosewood Case, Zither, 12 Tunes, 17-In. Cylinder, 35 In. 9988.00
Box, Paillard, Sublime Harmony, Cylinder, Walnut Veneer, 12 Tunes, c.1886, 9 x 30 x 12 In. 4145.00
Box, Picolo Cithare, Gamme, Rosewood Veneer, 10 Tunes, 14 1/4-In. Cylinder, 25 In. 2115.00
Box, Polyphon, Disc, Walnut Case, 12 Bells, Germany, 7 14-In. Discs, c.1900, 10 x 19 In. 3878.00
Box, Regina, Disc, Mahogany Case, Late 1800s, 19 15 1/2-In. Discs, 21 x 19 x 10 In. 3910.00
Box, Regina, Double Comb, Queen, Cherubs, Mahogany Cabinet, 75 Discs, c.1899, 27 x 21 In. ... 7840.00
Box, Regina, Dragon Front, Autochange, 13 Discs, 27 In. 27025.00

Box, Regina, Mahogany Case, Double Comb, c.1897, 8 15 1/2-In. Disc, 21 In. 3819.00
Box, Regina, Single Comb, Oak Case, Polychrome Print, 8 1/4-In. Disc, 12 1/2 In. 940.00
Box, Regina, Table Model, 1 Disc, c.1900, 11 1/2-In. Disc 4780.00
Box, Regina, Upright Disc, Quartersawn Oak Case, 12 27-In. Discs, 64 In. 17600.00
Box, Reymond Nicole, Cylinder, Fruitwood, Wood Handle, Key Wind, 11 1/2 & 7 1/2 In. 1530.00
Box, Samuel Troll Fils, Cylinder, Burl Walnut Case, 8 Tunes, c.1870, 12 x 25 x 13 1/2 In. 7000.00
Box, Singing Bird, Barrel Movement, Domed Brass Cage, Germany, 1900s, 9 In. 646.00
Box, Singing Bird, Bontems, 4 Birds, Bush, Butterfly, Waterfall, Clock, c.1890, 27 x 18 In. 10920.00
Box, Singing Bird, Bontems, Cage, 3 Movements, Wood Base, c.1885, 19 In. 3360.00
Box, Singing Bird, Bontems, Tortoiseshell, 2 Movements, c.1900, 3 3/4 x 3 In. 2465.00
Box, Singing Bird, Cage, Animated, France, c.1920, 6 x 11 In. 660.00
Box, Singing Bird, Cage, Brass, Circular Repousse Base, Barrel Movement, 1900s, 12 In. 529.00
Box, Singing Bird, Cage, Bronze Dore, Drawer, Feathers, France, c.1925, 6 x 4 In. 1680.00
Box, Singing Bird, Cage, Real Feathers, Glass Eyes, Brass Perch, Key Wind, 12 1/2 In. 1050.00
Box, Singing Bird, Charles Bruguier, Enamel, Silver, c.1850, 3 1/2 x 2 1/4 In. 12320.00
Box, Singing Bird, Griesbaum, 3 Movements, Silver Plated Box, c.1950, 4 x 2 1/2 In. 2130.00
Box, Singing Bird, Griesbaum, Barrel Movement, Domed Brass Cage, 1900s, 12 In. 325.00
Box, Singing Bird, No. 3077, Moving Beak, Wings, Perch, Reuge, 4 1/2 In. 2468.00
Box, Singing Bird, Silver, Embossed, Round Center Lid, Bird Pops Up, Swiss, c.1930, 4 x 2 In. 2688.00
Box, Singing Bird, Sterling Silver, Key Wind, Swiss, c.1920, 2 1/2 x 4 In. 2016.00
Box, Singing Bird, Wood Box, Painted, Man, Trees, Statue, Swiss, c.1860, 4 x 2 1/2 In. 2350.00
Box, Spoutnik I, Clock, Plastic, C. Felder, Box, 1957, 6 In. 427.00
Box, Stella, Mahogany, 40 17 1/2-In. Discs, c.1899, 13 x 30 x 22 In. 7560.00
Box, Symphonion, Diametric Combs, Walnut Case, 14 10 3/4-In. Discs, 17 In. 1175.00
Box, Symphonion, Disc, Spanish Dancer, Guitarist, No. 10, Germany, c.1900, 11 x 5 x 9 In. 1290.00
Box, Symphonion, Duplex, Walnut Case, 2 13 1/2-In. Discs, 35 In. 4115.00
Box, Symphonion, Mahogany Case, Double Comb, c.1900, 15 3/4-In. Disc, 25 In. 4200.00
Box, Symphonion, No. 30A, Mahogany, Marquetry, Disc, Single Comb, 22 x 11 In. 3585.00
Box, Symphonion, No. 48, Walnut Case, Cherubs, Instruments, c.1900, 6 1/2 x 11 x 13 In. 2240.00
Box, Thorens, Wood Case, Top Wind, 40 4 1/2-In. Discs, 10 In. 175.00
Bugle, Steer Horn, Green, Silver Mouth Piece, Silver Mounted, Continental, 21 In. 275.00
Chair, Walnut, Cylinder, Lyre Form Back, Carved Wreath, Boxwood Inlaid, 3 Tunes, 37 In. 1410.00
Cimbalom, 2 Wood Handled Hammers, Case, 37 x 17 1/2 In. 295.00
Clarinet, Selmer, Case, 20 In. 649.00
Clarinet, Selmer, Case, 24 In. 443.00
Concertina, Tanzbaer, Mechanical, 28-Note Roll, Flywheel, Veneered Case, 15 In. 410.00
Drum, Marching, Hickory, Hemp Rope, Leather Tensioners, c.1850, 11 In. 59.00
Drum, Snare, Applied Engraving, Eagle, Red, Yellow, Blue, White, Green, 8 1/2 In., Child's 2875.00
Drum, Windsors Makers, Wood Case, Birmingham, England, 15 x 27 In. 265.00
Drumstick, American Revolution, Late 1700s, Pair 150.00
Dulcimer, Walnut, Wood Case, 7 1/2 x 35 In. 55.00
Flute, Silver, Yamaha, Model YFL61, Case 665.00
Grand Harmonicon, Mahogany, Walnut, Glass, c.1825, 31 x 26 1/2 x 24 1/2 In. 2590.00
Guitar, C.F. Martin, Model D-28, Acoustic, 41 In. 12870.00
Guitar, Framus, Model 5170, Arch Back, Vinyl Cover, 19 In. 65.00
Guitar, Luigi Filano, Spruce Top, Scroll Peg Head, Flower Applique, Case, Naples, 1842 .... 3335.00
Guitar, Rickenbacker, Model 325DD, Rose Morris, Fireglo, British Model, Case, 1964 .... 8600.00
Guitar, Rickenbacker, Model 325DF, Jetglo Finish, American Model, Case, 1964, 38 In. 6700.00
Harmonica, Rolmonica, $1.00 Price, Montgomery Ward, Baltimore, Md., 1928, 5 In. 28.00
Harmonica, Rolmonica, $1.00 Price, Montgomery Ward, Baltimore, Md., Box, 1928, 5 In. 66.00
Harp, Lyon & Healy, Neoclassical, Bird's Eye Maple, Parcel Gilt, c.1900, 64 3/4 x 36 In. 1890.00
Harp, Wood, Bronze Painted Soundboard, c.1874, 30 1/2 x 21 1/2 In., Child's 1060.00
Mandolin, Ditson Co., Empire, Victory, Rosewood, Melon Style Back, c.1910 .... 105.00
Organ, Band, Wurlitzer, Artizan 46-Key Action, 54 Pipes, Oak Case, 47 x 38 x 22 In. 7344.00
Organ, Barrel, Frati & Co., Rosewood Case, 8-Tune Barrel, Portable, 24 In. 5580.00
Organ, Barrel, Mahogany Cabinet, 8 Tunes, France, c.1880, 38 x 31 x 25 In. 2912.00
Organ, Crown, Geo. P. Bent Mfg., Oak, Carved, Oil Lamp Holders, Chicago, U.S.A., 72 x 47 In. 850.00
Organ, Parlor, Antoine Henry, 10 Tunes, Charles X. Wood Case, France, c.1830, 20 x 19 x 16 In. 4200.00
Organ, Parlor, Beckwith, Oak, Shelves, Carvings, c.1900, 80 In. 230.00
Organ, Player, Aeolian Orchestrelle, Mahogany, Carved, 19 Stops, 58 Notes, 66 x 180 In. 1175.00
Organ, Pump, Crown Organ Co., Oak, Carved, Mirrored Back, Stool, 78 x 46 x 22 In. 118.00

Organ, Roller, Concert, Walnut Case, 20 Notes, 6 Cobs, 18 In. 380.00
Organ, Roller, Melodia Mechanical Orguinette Co., Walnut Case, 24 Rolls, N.Y., 12 x 13 In. 575.00
Organ, Table, Slant Front, 30 Pipes, Walnut, Cylinder, France, Early 1800s, 16 x 17 x 14 In. 1680.00
Organette, Mechanical Orguinette Co., Celestina, Walnut Case, 20 Notes, Gilt Stencil, 14 In. 470.00
Photograph Album, Ami Rivenc, Windmill & Ship Automated Scene, 12 x 10 In. 1880.00
Piano, Baby Grand, A.B. Chase, Artistano Player, Mahogany, c.1925, 40 x 60 In. 1765.00
Piano, Baby Grand, Baldwin, Art Deco, Ebonized, Burr, 1931-40, 37 x 56 x 65 In. 14400.00
Piano, Concert Grand, Steinway, Ebonized, Circular Stool, 39 x 60 x 108 In. 72000.00
Piano, G. Huppman, Mahogany, Rosewood Inlay, Classical Style, Baltimore, c.1830, 35 x 67 In. 4406.00
Piano, Grand, Steinway & Sons, Model L, Ebonized Mahogany, c.1925, 70 1/2 In. 7475.00
Piano, Grand, Steinway & Sons, Model O, c.1925, 60 3/4 In. 8625.00
Piano, Grand, Steinway, Model M, No. 476235, Mahogany, Bench, Signed, 1985, 67 In. 16100.00
Piano, Orchestrion, Phillips, Walnut Case, 88-Note Roll Mechanism, 86 x 67 x 23 In. 11750.00
Piano, Upright, Spard, Louis XVI Style, Gilt Mountings, Paris, Early 1900s, 50 x 58 x 25 In. 1298.00
Piano, Upright, Steinway & Sons, Mahogany, Recessed Panels, Ivory Keys, 54 x 62 x 28 In. 1210.00
Saxophone, Tenor, Selmer, Super, Gold Plated, Case, 1932 .... 2990.00
Serinette, Laberte-Humbert, Fruitwood Case, 8 Tunes, c.1850, 11 x 9 In. 1344.00
Serinette, Mirecourt, Walnut Case, Bird Sounds, Turn Crank, France, c.1850, 12 x 9 In. 1344.00
Snuffbox, F. Nicole, Tortoiseshell Case, Reverse Painted Lid, 2 Tunes, 2 1/2-In. Cylinder 4700.00
Snuffbox, No. 284, Composition Case, 2 Tunes, 3 3/4 In. 705.00
Trumpet, Abbott, Brass, 8-Sided Bell, Case, Mouthpiece 46.00
Violin, J. Didelot, Bow, Wood Case, France, Early 1900s, 23 1/2 In. 531.00
Violin, Jacobi Label, Case, Bow, LOB, Germany 68.00
Violin, Nicolus Lupot, Curly Maple, Spruce, 2-Piece Back, Bow, Cremona, 1857, 14 In. 2115.00
Violin, Stradivarius Copy, 2-Piece Back, Medium Curl, Red Orange, Czechoslovakia, 14 In. 191.00
Violin, Stradivarius Copy, Case, Bow, Czechoslovakia, Child's, 13 In. 152.00
Violin Case, Bird's-Eye Maple, Dovetailed, Cast Iron Bail Handle, 30 x 5 In. 173.00

MUSTACHE CUPS were popular from 1850 to 1900 when the large, flowing mustache was in style. A ledge of china or silver held the hair out of the liquid in the cup. This kept the mustache tidy and also kept the mustache wax from melting. Left-handed mustache cups are rare but are being reproduced.

1895 Duryea Motor Wagon, Lord Nelson Pottery, 3 3/4 In. 12.00
2-Tone Daisies, Pink & Yellow, White Ground, Fluted Swirls, Porcelain, 3 1/4 In. 50.00
Fire Engine, Pulled By Horses, Firemen, Gold Trim, Porcelain, 4 x 4 1/2 In. 25.00
Flowers, Kettle Shape, Heavy Gold Trim, Twig Handle, 4-Footed, Saucer 155.00
Horse's Head, Gilt Trim Forming Frame, Ruffled Sides & Rim, Side Spout, 4 In. 34.00
Puppy's Head, Flowers, Pink Luster, Gold Letters, A Present, 6 1/4-In. Saucer 95.00
Roses, Gold Leaves & Fleur-De-Lis, 6-Sided, RS Prussia, 4 In. 50.00
Shell & Seaweed Pattern, Majolica, Griffen, Smith & Hill, c.1885, 6 1/8-In. Saucer 250.00
Snow Scene, Twigs, Pink Border, Saucer 125.00
Violets, Light Green Ground, Gold Trim, Shaped Rim, Porcelain, Brandenburg 85.00
Your Father's Mustache, Man With Handlebar Mustache, Ceramic, 3 1/2 In. 35.00

MZ AUSTRIA is the wording on a mark used by Moritz Zdekauer on porcelains made at his works in Altrolau, Austria, from 1884 to 1909. The mark was changed to *MZ Altrolau* in 1909, when the firm was purchased by C.M. Hutschenreuther. The firm operated under the name Altrolau Porcelain Factories from 1909 to 1945. It was nationalized after World War II. The pieces were decorated with lavish floral patterns and overglaze gold decoration. Full sets of dishes were made as well as vases, toilet sets, and other wares.

MZ Austria

Bone Dish, Floral Border, Pink & Green, Gold Stripe Trim, 6 3/4 In. 8.00
Candy Dish, Violets, Green Border, Leaf Shape, Ruffled Rim, Yellow Loop Handle, 6 x 6 1/2 In. 18.00
Chocolate Pot, Pink Roses, Green Shaded Ground, Gold Trim, Scroll Handle 60.00
Hair Receiver, Pink Roses, Ferns, Flower Shape, 2 1/2 x 4 In. 80.00
Mustard Pot, Bridal Rose, Shaped Finial & Handle, Spoon, 4 In. 130.00
Plate, Pink & Red Roses, Pastel Blue Border, Scalloped Edge, 6 In. 45.00
Plate, Red & Yellow Poppies, Green Ground, Gold Trim, Scalloped Edge, 8 3/4 In. 20.00
Salt & Pepper, Bridal Rose, Shaped Edges, 3 In. 82.00

NAILSEA glass was made in the Bristol district in England from 1788 to 1873. It was made by many different factories, not just the Nailsea Glass House. Many pieces were made with loopings of either white or colored glass as decoration.

Bowl, Olive Green, White, Red Flecks, Outward Rolled Lip, Pontil, c.1820, 3 x 6 1/4 In. 825.00
Bride's Bowl, Blue, Folded Rim, Silver Plated Frame, Simpson, Hall & Miller, 10 In. 850.00
Creamer, Olive Amber, White Mottled, Applied Solid Handle, Curl, Base, Pontil, 5 In. 825.00
Decanter, Aqua, Red, White, Blue Splotches, Flared Lip, Pontil, c.1830-50, 9 1/2 In. 330.00
Fairy Lamp, Hanging, Citron Shade, White Draped Looping, Clarke Burner, Tricornered Base, 8 In. . 920.00
Fairy Lamp, Red, Dome, White Draped Looping, Clarke Burner, 5 In. 230.00
Flask, Pink & White Looping, 8 In. 220.00
Jug, Olive Green, Applied Handle, Pontil, c.1820-40, 10 1/2 In. 770.00
Powder Horn, Clear, White Opalescent Loopings, Applied Neck Rings, 10 1/2 In. 100.00
Rolling Pin, Marbrie, Aqua, Red Loopings, Pontil, c.1850, 15 x 2 3/8 In. 155.00
Stirrup Cup, Boot Shape, Marbrie, White Loops, Pontil, c.1875, 7 1/4 x 2 3/8 In. 240.00
Vase, Clear, Red, White Drag Loop, Applied White Rim, 1830-50, 9 In. 825.00
Vase, Red & Blue Spiral Looping, Fluted Rim, Funnel Foot, Flint, c.1850, 12 In. 468.00
Vase, Witch's Ball Cover, White, Pink, Red Looping, 1830-50, 10 In. 1870.00
Whimsy, Pipe, Cranberry Opalescent, Cobalt Stem, White Looping, 26 In. 520.00
Witch's Ball, Cranberry, Clear, White Loop, Pontil, 1850-75, 4 1/2 In. 468.00
Witch's Ball, Marbrie Decoration, Cased Opaque, Red Loopings, Pontil, 1860-80, 5 1/4 In. 525.00
Witch's Ball, Marbrie Decoration, White Loops, Pontil, c.1875, 6 1/4 In. 155.00
Witch's Ball, Red, White & Blue Looping, Pontil, 1840-70, 4 3/4 In. 990.00

NANKING is a type of blue-and-white porcelain made in Canton, China, since the late eighteenth century. It is very similar to Canton, which is listed under its own name in this book. Both Nanking and Canton are part of a larger group now called *Chinese export* porcelain. Nanking has a spear-and-post border and may have gold decoration.

Bowl, Blue & White, 2 Bird, Cut Corner, 19th Century, 5 1/2 x 10 In. 575.00
Bowl, Vegetable, Man On Bridge, Diamond Shaped, Scalloped Edges, 7 x 9 In., Pair 230.00
Bowl Set, Blue & White, 2 Bird, 4 Bowls 6 1/2 In., 3 Bowls 4 1/2 In. 105.00
Plate, Salad, Blue & White, 2 Bird, 19th Century, 7 3/4 In., 9 Piece 345.00
Plate, Warming, 2 Bird, 9 3/4 In., Pair 546.00
Platter, Blue & White, 2 Bird, 19th Century, 12 1/2 & 13 In. 430.00
Sauceboat, Blue & White, 2 Bird, 19th Century, 7 1/2 In., Pair 259.00
Tea Caddy, Blue & White, Gilt Trim, Sloping Shoulder, 4 5/8 In. 345.00
Tea Caddy, Blue & White, Riverscape, 18th Century, 11 In. 1120.00
Vase, Cover, Flat Sides, Coastal Village, Serpent Handles, Late 1700s, 22 1/4 In., Pair 7638.00

NAPKIN RINGS were in fashion from 1869 to about 1900. They were made of silver, porcelain, wood, and other materials. They are still being made today. The most popular rings with collectors are the silver plated figural examples. Small, realistic figures were made to hold the ring. Good and poor reproductions of the more expensive rings are now being made and collectors must be very careful.

Bakelite, Figural, Bird, Red, Black Beak 95.00
Bakelite, Figural, Duck, Yellow, Pointed Orange Beak, 2 1/2 In. 51.00
Bakelite, Figural, Rabbit, Butterscotch, Red Glass Eye, 2 In. 78.00
Bakelite, Figural, Red Rooster, Blue Wheels, 3 In. 175.00
Bakelite, Figural, Scottie Dog, Red, 3 In. 45.00
Horn, Black, Sterling Silver Shield, c.1900 .... 75.00
Metal, Filigree, Cloisonne Panel, 1 3/4 x 1 1/2 In. 175.00
Silver, Acid Etched, Children Playing In Garden, Verse, c.1900, Child's, 1 In. 150.00
Silver, Niello, Flowers, c.1920, 1 7/8 In. 75.00
Silver Plate, Figural, Baseball Boy, Kate Greenaway .... *ILLUS* 770.00
Silver Plate, Figural, Boy Feeding Dog, Meriden, Victorian, 3 1/4 In. 895.00
Silver Plate, Figural, Bulldog, Grapevine Wreath, 2 3/4 x 3 In. 359.00
Silver Plate, Figural, Cherub With Large Wings, Seated .... *ILLUS* 2475.00

Napkin Ring, Silver Plate, Figural, Baseball Boy, Kate Greenaway

Napkin Ring, Silver Plate, Figural, Cherub With Large Wings, Seated

Napkin Ring, Silver Plate, Figural, Fan, In Front Of Ring

Silver Plate, Figural, Fan, In Front Of Ring .... *ILLUS* 55.00
Silver Plate, Figural, Girl Carrying Flower Basket, 2 1/2 In. 750.00
Sterling Silver, Concave Sides, Monogram, Birks Sterling, c.1930, 7/8 x 1 3/4 In. 55.00
Sterling Silver, Cutout Pied Piper, Monogram, 1956 .... 65.00
Sterling Silver, Engine Turned Decoration, Bakelite Interior, Birmingham, 1939 .... 85.00
Sterling Silver, Figural, Mouse, Embossed Flowers, James W. Tufts, 1800s 595.00
Sterling Silver, Hinge Style Decoration, Shreve & Co., San Francisco, 1 3/4 x 1 3/4 In. 425.00
Sterling Silver, Pierced Decoration, 5/8 x 1 3/4 In. 34.00
Sterling Silver, Raised Japanese Characters, Bamboo Border, 1 1/4 x 1 3/4 In. 179.00

NASH glass was made in Corona, New York, from about 1928 to 1931. A. Douglas Nash bought the Corona glassworks from Louis C. Tiffany in 1928 and founded the A. Douglas Nash Corporation with support from his father, Arthur J. Nash. Arthur had worked at the Webb factory in England and for the Tiffany Glassworks in Corona.

NASH

Vase, Amber, Olive Green Vertical Zipper, Mottled Blue, Green Iridescent Ground, 8 1/4 In. 834.00
Vase, Gold Iridescent, Purple, Pedestal Foot, Ribbed, 4 1/4 In. 230.00
Vase, Green, Brown Chintz Decoration, Bulbous, Flared Rim, Applied Crystal Foot, 7 1/2 In. 865.00

NAUTICAL antiques are listed in this category. Any of the many objects that were made or used by the seafaring trade, including ship parts, models, and tools, are included. Other pieces may be found listed under Scrimshaw.

Alarm Rattle, U.S. Navy, Oak, Ratchet Handle, 8 x 10 In. 239.00
Bag, Sailmaker's, Canvas, 4 Iron Fids, 2 Wooden Fids, Half-Model 375.00
Barographs, Wooden Case, 9 & 11 In. 375.00
Bell, U.S. Navy, Cast Iron, Marked, U.S.N., 10 In. 90.00
Canoe, Birch Bark, Indian Chief Decoration, 70 In. 495.00
Canoe, Fiberglass, Cedar Strip, Oak Gunnels, Mahogany, Cane Seats, c.1970, 18 x 39 In. 660.00
Chart Case, Sailor Made, Dovetailed, Paneled Top, 3 3/4 x 34 x 9 1/4 In. 230.00
Chest, Captain's, Camphorwood, Brass Bound, Chinese, c.1850, 21 3/4 x 42 1/2 In. 1380.00
Chest, Pine, 6-Board, Lift Top, Blue Paint, 17 x 37 x 18 1/2 In. 550.00
Chest, Seaman's, 6-Board, Dovetailed, Flower & Vine Inlay, Lidded Till, Bail Handles, 18 x 31 In. ... 1035.00
Chest, Seaman's, Camphorwood, Leather, Chinese, 1830-50, 10 1/2 x 25 x 12 1/2 In. 460.00
Chest, Seaman's, Painted, Metal Bound Edges, 3 Trays, A.W. Kelley, 17 1/2 x 36 x 18 In. 150.00
Chest, Seaman's, Pine, 6-Board, Dovetailed, Till, Early 1800s, 16 1/2 x 43 1/2 In. 145.00
Chest, Seaman's, Pine, Canted, Dovetailed, Ditty Box, Gray, 18 1/2 x 43 x 18 1/2 In. 605.00
Chest, Seaman's, Pine, Green Paint, Strap Hinges, Rope Handles, 18 x 33 x 19 In. 259.00
Chest, Seaman's, Teak, Dovetailed, Inlaid Stars & Vines, Lidded Till, 15 x 30 x 15 In. 750.00
Chest, Seaman's, Teak, Ivory Inlay, Flowers, Dovetailed, Till, 18 1/2 x 37 1/4 x 17 In. 2015.00
Chronometer, 2-Day, Heath & Co. Ltd., Fusee Movement, Mahogany Case, 7 In. 1295.00
Chronometer, 2-Day, Ulysse Nardin, 3-In. Roman Dial, Brass Gimbal, Mahogany Case, 6 In. 1410.00
Chronometer, Mahogany Case, 56-Hour, Charles Frodsham, c.1885, 6 3/4 In. 4200.00
Clinometer, Mahogany Frame, Brass Arm, Scale, 9 1/4 In. 380.00
Clock, Barometer, Carrington England, Brass, Oak Mounted, 12 x 21 In., 2 Piece 265.00

Clock, Deck, Seth Thomas, Mark I, Stainless Steel Case, Black Dial, c.1939, 8 In. 336.00
Clock, Ship's Bell, Seth Thomas, 24-Hour, Time & Strike, Nickel-Plated Case, c.1930, 7 In. 250.00
Clock, Ship's Bell, Seth Thomas, 30-Hour, Wall, Wardroom, Oak Case, c.1910, 8 1/2 In. 728.00
Clock, Ship's Bell, Seth Thomas, Mayflower 3, 8-Day, Time & Strike, c.1950, 8 1/2 In. 390.00
Clock, Ship's Bell, Seth Thomas, Yacht, 30-Hour, Time & Strike, c.1913, 10 1/2 In. 1625.00
Clock, Ship's Bell, Waterbury, No. 10, 8-Day, Time & Strike, Brass Case, 8 In. 336.00
Clock, Ship's Bell, Waterbury, Spokes, Wood Base, 4-In. Dial, 18 In. 130.00
Clock, Waterbury, 8-Day, Motor Boat No. 2, Brass Case, c.1929, 5 In. 365.00
Clock & Barometer, Chelsea, Wood Stand, Brass, 6 1/2 x 8 x 4 In., 2 Piece 805.00
Compass, Brass, John E. Hand & Son, Hinged Lid, Copper, c.1940, 7 x 7 x 7 In. 146.00
Compass, Danforth, Constellation, Brass, c.1950, 9 x 9 In. 175.00
Compass, F.W. Lincoln Jr., Floating Card, Green Bowl, Boston, Red Case, 10 In. 999.00
Compass, Ritchie, Liquid, Gimbaled Mount, Mahogany Case, Boston, 1870 Patent, 7 In. 155.00
Compass, Ship's, R.W. Lincoln, Jr. & Co., 10 1/2 In. 999.00
Compass, Ship's, S. Thaxter & Son, Pine Case, 10 In. 295.00
Compass, Side Mounted Oil Lanterns, 19th Century, 10 x 12 In. 530.00
Desk, Captain's, Sheraton, Mahogany, Drawer, Writing Slide, Shelf, 30 x 27 In. 1095.00
Desk Watch, Silvered Dial, Model 3, U.S.S.R., Box, c.1956, 2 1/2 In. 505.00
Diorama, 3-Masted Sailing Ship, Simulated Waves, New England Village, 42 x 31 In. 2015.00
Diorama, Clipper Ship, Sovereign Of The Seas, Half-Model, 20th Century, 27 x 36 In. 499.00
Diorama, Ship, 2-Masted, En Accion De Gracias, 15 x 19 3/4 In. 430.00
Figurehead, Woman, Arm To Forehead, Full Bodied, Multicolored, 24 x 7 x 9 In. 2750.00
Half-Model, Baby Bootlegger, 1925 Gold Cup Trophy Winner, Mahogany, Case, 14 x 45 In. 1380.00
Half-Model, Bequia B.V.I., Gaff Rigged Sloop, Wood, Carved, 36 x 36 In. 410.00
Half-Model, Brig, Fair America, Wood, Carved, 24 x 40 In. 405.00
Half-Model, Brigantine, Newsboy, Carved, Painted, Harry Connell, 20th Century, 17 x 21 In. 705.00
Half-Model, Canadian Clipper Ship, Rita, Pat Lewis, N.F, Case, c.1920, 27 x 42 x 13 In. 1150.00
Half-Model, Canoes, Wood, Enamel, Hand Made, 28 & 32 In. 175.00
Half-Model, Clipper Ship, Young America, Harry Connell, 20th Century, 14 1/2 x 20 In. 940.00
Half-Model, Corinnas, Iron Ship, Bone, Wood, Scott & Parker, c.1861, 11 x 48 In. 995.00
Half-Model, Huron, U.S. Coast Guard, Light Ship, Wood, 20th Century, 14 x 20 In. 295.00
Half-Model, Laminated Wood, Early 20th Century, 7 x 47 In. 2705.00
Half-Model, Laminated Wood, Wood Panel Mount, Early 1900s, 7 x 41 In. 1645.00
Half-Model, Light & Dark Stripes, Laminated, Varnish, Maine, 1870s, 15 1/2 x 68 In. 5175.00
Half-Model, Nantucket Whale Ship, Criterion, Carved, Painted, 16 x 61 In. 805.00
Half-Model, Painted, White, Green, Walnut Backboard, c.1925, 16 x 51 In. 1610.00
Half-Model, Sailboat, Wood, Carved, Cutter Rig 265.00
Half-Model, Sailing Ship, Santa Maria, Hand Carved, c.1880, 37 x 42 In. 265.00
Half-Model, Schooner, Wood, Canvas Sail, Lifeboat, Metal Keel, Rudder, 1900s, 46 x 44 In. 165.00
Half-Model, Ship, Arizona, 3-Masted, Full Sail & Rigging, Wood, Painted, 44 In. 165.00
Half-Model, Ship, Mary, Plank Frame, Case, 38 x 48 x 17 In. 978.00
Half-Model, Ship, Single Mast, Triple Plank, Cannon, Eddie Orluk, c.1985, 19 3/4 x 24 In. 355.00
Half-Model, Shipwright's, Scribed Grids, Cherry Wood, 1800s, 7 x 36 In. 530.00
Half-Model, Sovereign Of The Seas, 3-Masted, Full Rigging, Carved, Painted, 18 x 25 1/2 In. 705.00
Half-Model, Steam Trawler, Carved, Inlaid, Painted, Early 20th Century, 6 x 14 1/4 In. 940.00
Half-Model, Wood, On Walnut Board, 41 1/2 x 9 1/2 In. 230.00
Harpoon Head, Whaling, Iron, Hand Forged, c.1850, 35 1/4 In. 380.00
Lamp, Navigation, 90 Degree, Corner, Tin, Red & Blue Lenses, 12 x 5 In., Pair 105.00
Lamp, Whale Oil, Pewter, Gimball Mounted, Bulbous, Saucer Base, 5 1/4 x 5 In. 525.00
Lamp, William Harvie & Co., Birmingham, Copper, Brass, Glass Globe, Electrified, 18 In. 80.00
Lantern, Copper, Brass, 360 Degree Lens, Clear, Bail Handle, Electrified, Anchor, 16 x 7 In. 195.00
Lantern, Marine, Copper, Green Lens, Marked Bow Starboard, 16 1/2 In. 175.00
Lantern, Masthead, Maker Badge Meteorite, Copper, Brass, Fresnel Glass Lens, 25 In. 290.00
Lantern, Ship's Masthead, Clear Lens, Nickel Over Brass, 27 x 13 In. 920.00
Lantern, Ship's, Marked Toplicht, Germany, Copper & Brass, 24 1/2 In. 200.00
Light, Deck, Copper, Brass, 20th Century, 11 1/2 In., Pair 230.00
Light, Masthead, Copper, Handle, 21 In. 115.00
Model, Prisoner Of War Ship, 3-Masted, Wood Stand, Case, France, 1800s, 13 In. 499.00
Model, Ship Hull, Hand Made, Sheet Copper, 9 1/2 x 9 1/2 x 86 In. 575.00
Model, Ship, 3-Masted, Full Rigging, Case, E. Orluk, 1990, 62 1/2 x 49 x 20 1/2 In. 2000.00
Octant, Brass, Ebony, Carved Walnut Case, Oak Box, Germany, 19th Century 489.00

Octant, Nairne & Blunt, London, Vernier, Mahogany, Brass Carrier, 17-In. Radius ... 1765.00
Octant, Spencer, Browning & Co., Ebony, Bone Arc, Brass Arm, Case, 13-In. Radius ... 380.00
Octant, Spencer, Browning & Co., London, Brass, Lattice Frame, Silvered Scale, 8-In. Radius ... 765.00
Outboard Motor, Seagull, Best Outboard Motor For World, Decal, England ... 635.00
Pond Boat, Mixed Wood, Full Sail, Metal Keel, Painted, 20 In. ... 110.00
Pond Boat, Wood, Canvas Sail, Metal Keel, Painted, 30 In. ... 165.00
Pond Boat, Wood, Full Canvas Sail, Metal Keel, Pine Stand, 27 In. ... 330.00
Pond Boat, Wood, Windup, Kellerman, Box, 26 In. ... 990.00
Port Light, Round, Brass, Glass, c.1900, 12 In., Pair ... 105.00
Quadrant, Dolland, London, Ebony, Brass, Ivory Scales, Pine Case, Harwich, 19th Century ... 690.00
Sailor's, Valentine, Anchor, Shells, Green Velvet Ground, Heart Pincushion, 9 In. ... 140.00
Sailor's Valentine, Shells, Home Again, Heart, 2 Octagonal Boxes Hinged Together ... 1005.00
Sector, G. Adams, London, Ivory, Brass Hinge, Latitude & Hour Calibrations, 6 In. ... 940.00
Sextant, Brass, 19th Century, 12 In. ... 375.00
Sextant, John Bruce & Sons, Liverpool, Mirrors, Filters, Scopes, Oak Box, c.1918 ... 499.00
Sextant, Kriegsmarine, Case, Plath, German, World War II Vintage ... 316.00
Sextant, Robert King, New York, Wood Frame, Ivory Scale, Box, 11 In. ... 207.00
Sextant, Spencer Browning & Co., Ebony, Ivory, Brass, Wood Case, 12 x 10 In. ... 720.00
Sextant, Spencer, Browning & Co., London, Brass, Mahogany Case ... 805.00
Sextant, Stanley, London, Lacquered Brass Box, Magnifier, Telescope, 1917 ... 70.00
Sextant, Thos. Jones, Vernier, Ebony, Bone Scale, Brass Arm, Mahogany Case, 10-In. Radius ... 825.00
Sextant, Troughton & Simms, London, Silver Scale, Vernier, Case, Brass Box, 3 In. ... 265.00
Sextant, Troughton & Simms, Presentation Engraving, Lacquered Brass Box, 2 3/4 In. ... 440.00
Ship In A Bottle, Coast Guard Bark, Eagle, 12 In. ... 80.00
Ship Model, see Nautical, Model.
Spectrometer, Wm. Gaertner & Co., Optical, Bench Mounted, 1920 ... 675.00
Steam Whistle, SS Normandie, Bronze, c.1942 ... 460.00
Trouble Lights, 2 Additional Lights, Oceanic, Hand Held, c.1920, 12 In. ... 205.00
Valentine, Sailor's, Letter Holder, Shells, Woman's Portrait, Green & Red Plaid Trim, 8 In. ... 275.00
Wheel, Ship, Wood, Brass Hub, 40 In. ... 690.00
Work Bag, Leather, Rope, Stitched Decoration ... 518.00
Wreckwood, Titanic's Grand Staircase, Wood, 1912, 2 1/2 x 5 In., 2 Piece ... 1015.00

NETSUKES are small ivory, wood, metal, or porcelain pieces used as toggles on the end of the cord that held a Japanese money pouch or inro. The earliest date from the sixteenth century. Many are miniature, carved works of art. This category also includes the ojime, the slide or string fastener that was used on the inro cord.

Bone, Kwanyu, Chinese General, Holding Bear, 1700s, 4 In. ... 2185.00
Bone, Peasant, Holding Wooden Staff, 1800s ... 58.00
Bone, Rat, Inlaid Eyes, On Leaf, Chestnut, Early 1800s ... 230.00
Bone, Samurai, Warrior, Full Armor, Playing Flute, c.1800 ... 431.00
Brass, Gourd, Removable Cover, 1800s ... 115.00
Copper-Zinc-Tin Alloy, Water Imp Leading Blind Man Across Stream, 1800s ... 290.00
Ebony, Foo Dog, Seated, On Rectangular Platform, 1800s ... 460.00
Ebony, Gold Lacquer, Young Dragon, Gilt Details, Early 1800s ... 431.00
Ebony, Okame, Goddess Of Mirth, Goblin Mask, Long Nose, Signed, Gyokusai, 1800s ... 1610.00
Ebony, Warrior, Subduing Foo Dog, Hollow Eyes, Signed, Miwa, Late 1700s ... 4313.00
Ebony, Water Buffalo, Lying Down, 1800s ... 230.00
Ebony & Coral, Bird, Eating Fruit, Signed, Kogyoku, 1900s ... 1265.00
Ebony & Ivory, Man Holding Vase, Book With Child, Chinese, 2 1/2 In. ... 120.00
Ebony & Ivory, Man Playing Drum, With Child, Chinese, 2 1/2 In. ... 120.00
Ebony & Ivory, Man With Cup, Man With Pitcher, Chinese, 2 1/2 In. ... 293.00
Fruit Pit, Benkei On Horseback, 19th Century, 1 1/4 In. ... 176.00
Inro, Black & Gold Lacquer, 5 Compartments, Dragon, Cloud, Nashiji Interior, 1700s ... 1495.00
Inro, Black Lacquer, 3 Compartments, Pewter Horse, Signed, Toshida Soetsu, 1700s ... 575.00
Inro, Burgaute Lacquer, 3 Compartments, Glass Ojime, Ebony Netsuke, Calligraphic, Fret, 1800s ... 575.00
Inro, Coral, Malachite, Black, Gold, 2 Compartments, Shrubs, Berries, Signed, Toji, 1800s ... 3105.00
Inro, Ebony, 4 Compartments, Landscape, Signed, 1800s ... 430.00
Inro, Gold Lacquer, 4 Compartments, Copper Ojime, Bone Netsuke, Landscape, c.1800 ... 865.00
Inro, Gold Lacquer, 4 Compartments, Takamakie, Lohan God, Dragon, Yoyusai, Early 1800s ... 4315.00

Inro, Gold Lacquer, 5 Compartments, Silver Narcissus, 1700s 1610.00
Inro, Lacquer, 4 Compartments, Leaves, Japan, Late 19th Century, 3 1/4 In. 825.00
Inro, Lacquer, Dragon, On Cloud, Wave, Metal Flakes In Lacquer, Interior, Early 1800s 1265.00
Inro, Pottery, Lacquer On Wood, 2 Compartments, Puppies, Signed, Jokasai, Early1800s 2875.00
Ivory, 2 Fish, Lying On Bamboo, Signed, Kosen, 1800s 1095.00
Ivory, 2 People, Kneeling, Washing Clothes, Wood Base, 1 1/4 x 2 x 1 In. 85.00
Ivory, 2 Puppies, Inlaid Eyes, 1 1/4 In. 825.00
Ivory, 2 Turtles, Lotus Blossom, 2 x 1 1/2 In. 170.00
Ivory, 3 Beetles, Fly, Climbing Decaying Tree Stump, Late 19th Century 1380.00
Ivory, 3 Children, Playing Drum, Fan, Mask, Signed, Shomin, 1800s 460.00
Ivory, 3 Shells, Interior Village Scene, 1800s, 2 In. 325.00
Ivory, 4 Men, Carrying Man In Cart, 2 In. 560.00
Ivory, 11 Blind Men, Climbing On Elephant, Signed, Masatsugu, Late 19th Century 2070.00
Ivory, Ashinaga, Long Legged God, Tenaga, Octopus, Late 1800s 690.00
Ivory, Basket, Peony Flowers, 18th Century 765.00
Ivory, Daikoku, God Of Prosperity, Holding Hammer, Rate, Signed, Mitsuhiro, 1800s 1095.00
Ivory, Daruma, Fat Old Man, Seated, 19th Century 590.00
Ivory, Dutchman, Holding Trumpet, Inlaid Horn Eyes, 1700s 2070.00
Ivory, Ferry, 5 People, 1800s, 4 1/2 In. 765.00
Ivory, Fisher Woman, Octopus, Clamshell Shape, 19th Century, 1 1/2 In. 940.00
Ivory, Foo Dog Mask, Movable Jaw, Ears, 19th Century 646.00
Ivory, Foo Dog, 2 x 2 1/8 In. 95.00
Ivory, Foo Dog, Curly Hair, Guarding Ball, 1700s 518.00
Ivory, Foo Dog, Guarding Large Ball, Late 1700s 805.00
Ivory, Foo Dog, On Brocade Ball, 19th Century, 2 In. 1763.00
Ivory, Horse, Grazing, Inlaid Eyes, Kyoto School, 1700s 6325.00
Ivory, Hotei, God Of Happiness, Bag Of Wealth, 2 In. 1058.00
Ivory, Jurojin, God Of Longevity, Leaning On Mokugyo Bell, Masayuki, Early 1900s 259.00
Ivory, Kirin, Mythical Beast, Seated, Inlaid Eyes, Early 1800s 1035.00
Ivory, Man & Skeleton, Chinese, 2 In. 235.00
Ivory, Man, Dancing, Holding Peach, Fan, 1700s 1495.00
Ivory, Man, Hiding In Okame, Goddess Of Mirth Mask, Signed, Mitsumasa, 1900s 230.00
Ivory, Man, Holding Agate Fish, Chinese, 1 1/4 In. 295.00
Ivory, Man, Holding Lapis Mask, Chinese, 2 In. 176.00
Ivory, Man, Holding Wooden Box 880.00
Ivory, Man, On Hollowed Log, 19th Century, 2 1/4 In. 1060.00
Ivory, Man, Seated, Dragon, 2 In. 95.00
Ivory, Man, Seated, Tiger, Dragon, Signed, Masayuki, 1800s 375.00
Ivory, Monkey, Watching Beetle, On Melon, Masamin, Late 19th Century 690.00
Ivory, Octopus & Woman, Erotic, Chinese, 2 1/2 In. 293.00
Ivory, Octopus, 19th Century 380.00
Ivory, Oni Tying Fish, Horn Inlays, 19th Century, 2 In. 529.00
Ivory, Puppy, Pearl, On Treasure Sack, 1700s 260.00
Ivory, Sage, Carrying Cauldron With Dragon, Inlaid Eyes, 1700s 750.00
Ivory, Sage, Mugwart Cape, Holding Peach Branch, 1700s 1380.00
Ivory, Seated Man, With Flowers In Lapis Pot, Chinese, 1 1/2 In. 295.00
Ivory, Sennin, Hermit Sage, Dragon Emerging From Begging Bowl, 19th Century 1410.00
Ivory, Sennin, Hermit Sage, Reading On Scroll, Riding Carp, Signed, Ikkosai, Late 19th Century ... 865.00
Ivory, Shojo, Drunken Sprite, Sleeping, Flower Kimono, 1700s 2070.00
Ivory, Shoki, Demon, Catching Demon In Bucket, Silver & Coral Inlay, 1800s 880.00
Ivory, Tiger, Inlaid Eyes, Signed, Ransen, 1800s 3105.00
Ivory, Water Buffalo, Lying Down, Inlaid Eyes, Signed, Hakuryu, Early 1800s 4888.00
Ivory, Woman Warrior, On Carp, Stabbing It With Knife, Signed, Toshimune, Late 1800s 1380.00
Kagamibuta, Mixed Metal, Nio, Temple Guardian Uprooting Tree, 1800s 635.00
Lacquer, Manju, Red, Leaf 7 Scroll, Japan, Early 1900s 150.00
Lacquer, Red, Peasant, Holding Straw Hat, 1800s 150.00
Nut, Castle, Moat, Water Wheel, Figures, Hauling Boat, Mother-Of-Pearl Moon, 2 In. 190.00
Ojime, Bronze, Bird, Fruit Branch, Silver & Gold Relief, Signed, Komin, 1800s 863.00
Ojime, Composition, Daruma, Fat Old Man, Kwannon, Goddess Of Mercy, Seated, Late 1800s 104.00
Ojime, Copper, Clamshell, Gilt Details, Signed, 1800s 690.00
Ojime, Copper-Zinc-Tin Alloy, Gilt Silver, Seed Form, Peony, Late 19th Century 374.00

Ojime, Gold, Ball, Pierced Leaves, 1800s 1035.00
Ojime, Ivory, Ball, Procession, Nobleman, Palanquin, Late 19th Century 405.00
Ojime, Ivory, Ball, Samurai, Warrior, Bird, Dog, Monkey, Signed, Late 19th Century 518.00
Ojime, Ivory, Ball, Warrior Battling A Tengu, Late 19th Century 405.00
Ojime, Ivory, Child, Kneeling, Holding Mask, c.1800 .... 375.00
Ojime, Ivory, Shibayama Inlay Decoration, Seed Form, Plant, Berry, Late 19th Century 316.00
Ojime, Lacquer On Ivory, Ho Bird, Cylindrical, Mother-Of-Pearl Inlay, 1800s 3105.00
Ojime, Silver, Ball, Ho Bird, Pierced, 1800s 865.00
Ojime, Silver, Ball, Pierced Flowers, 1800s 518.00
Ojime, Silver, Copper, Gold, Yin-Yang Symbol, Cylindrical, Late 19th Century 460.00
Oxherd, Smiling Boy Riding Back Of Beast, Wood, Inscribed, Shosai, 2 In. 270.00
Peach Pit, Lion, Peony, 1800s 140.00
Porcelain, Hirado, Foo Dog, Loose Ball In Mouth, 1700s 127.00
Porcelain, Hotei, God Of Happiness, Playing With A Small Boy, c.1850 .... 127.00
Porcelain, Rabbit, On Treasure Sack, 1800s 375.00
Stag Antler, Woman Sea Diver, 18th Century, 3 1/2 In. 650.00
Staghorn, Stone Cottage, Pine Tree, 1800s 140.00
Staghorn, Stone Sage, Holding Inro, 1700s 400.00
Umimatsu, Frog, On Stump, Iwami School, 1 1/4 In. 650.00
Wood, 2 Eggplants, Lying On Leaf, 1800s 230.00
Wood, 2 Peanuts, 1800 .... 115.00
Wood, 2 Small Turtles Climbing On Large Turtle, Signed, Masatami To, c.1850 .... 8625.00
Wood, 2 Temple Guardians, Wrestling, Inlaid Eyes, 1800s 6325.00
Wood, 3 Monkeys, Inlaid Eyes, Masakazu, 1800s 3220.00
Wood, 5 Frogs On Lily Pad, 1800s 230.00
Wood, 6 Masks, 1800s 390.00
Wood, Ashinaga, Long Armed God, Standing, Holding Octopus, Inlaid Eyes, 1800s, 5 In. 1150.00
Wood, Badger, Disguised As Priest, 1700s 1380.00
Wood, Broom Seller, Beating Gourd, Signed, Late 19th Century 1150.00
Wood, Demon Mask, 19th Century, 2 In. 1060.00
Wood, Dragon, Coiled, Holding Pearl, Signed, Yoshihisa, Early 1800s 1380.00
Wood, Gourd, Leaf, Vine, 1800s 115.00
Wood, Horned Frog, Inlaid Eyes, 1700s 2415.00
Wood, Ivory, Inlaid, Daruma, Fat Old Man, Mouth & Eye Open, Takoku, Late 1800s, 1 1/4 In. 5000.00
Wood, Man Lifting Stone, Ivory Inlaid Eye, Mother-Of-Pearl Plaque, 19th Century 765.00
Wood, Monkey, Peach Branch, Inlaid Eyes, Mitsuhide, 1800s 2300.00
Wood, Mushrooms, 19th Century, 1 1/4 In. 295.00
Wood, Rat Catcher, 19th Century, 1 1/2 In. 529.00
Wood, Reclining Horse, 19th Century 1880.00
Wood, Shojo, Drunken Sprite, Sleeping, Brocade Kimono, Signed, Hidari Issan, 1800s 920.00
Wood, Shoki, Oni, Demon, 1800s 259.00
Wood, Silver, Fruit, Branch, Leaves, Silver Leaf, 1800s 259.00

NEWCOMB Pottery was founded by Ellsworth and William Woodward at Sophie Newcomb College, New Orleans, Louisiana, in 1895. The work continued through the 1940s. Pieces of this art pottery are marked with the printed letters *NC* and often have the incised initials of the artist as well. Most pieces have a matte glaze and incised decoration.

Bowl, Flowers, Blue Ground, Cobalt Blue Glaze, L. Nicholson & J. Meyer, 2 1/2 x 7 In. 805.00
Bowl, Forget-Me-Nots, Blue Matte Ground, Sadie Irvine & Joseph Meyer, 3 1/8 x 5 3/4 In. 1955.00
Bowl, Gardenias, Blue, Green, Yellow, Matte Glaze, Sloped Rim, A.F. Simpson, 4 x 8 In. 1470.00
Creamer, Cover, 1908, 5 In. 1955.00
Dish, Elongated Leaf Shape, Blue Green, High Glaze, Leona Nicholson, 1949, 14 In. 325.00
Pitcher, Daffodils, Rose & Blue Underglaze, Sadie Irvine, 1919, 5 7/8 In. 1175.00
Tankard, Flowers, Ada Lonnegan, J. Meyer, 1903, 5 3/4 x 4 1/2 In. 2350.00
Tile, Painted Flower, High Glaze, S. Irvine, 4 1/2 In. 4113.00
Trivet, Flowers, Relief, Blue Matte Ground, Anna Frances Simpson, 5 1/2 In. 1610.00
Tyg, Grapevine, Inscription, Amelie Roman, c.1901, 6 1/4 x 6 In. 22325.00
Vase, Aqua Drip Glaze, Cobalt Blue Flecks, Brown Flambe Rim, Flared, 6 x 5 1/4 In. 375.00
Vase, Blossoms, Blue, Green, Yellow, Semimatte Glaze, Cylindrical, Flared Rim, J. Meyer, 5 In. 1470.00
Vase, Blue Glaze, Cylindrical, Closed-In Rim, 5 3/4 x 3 In. 470.00

Vase, Blue, Purple, Organic Design, 6 In. 2468.00
Vase, Flowers, Blue Matte Ground, Globular, Anna Frances Simpson, 5 x 6 In. 3105.00
Vase, Flowers, Ocher, Yellow, Blue Glaze Ground, Sadie Irvine, 6 1/3 x 3 1/2 In. 1610.00
Vase, Flowers, Pink & Blue, Blue Ground, Shouldered, Henrietta Bailey, 8 1/4 In. 3900.00
Vase, Gulf Stream Glaze, Baluster, c.1945, 5 3/4 x 5 1/4 In. 470.00
Vase, Honeysuckle, Anna Frances Simpson, 1919, 6 1/4 x 3 1/2 In. 1880.00
Vase, Irises, Marie De Hoa LeBlanc, 1898-1914, 16 1/2 In. 22325.00
Vase, Leaves, Blue, Green, Irene Borden Keep, c.1902, 3 x 5 In. 1880.00
Vase, Moon & Moss, Baluster, F.A. Ford & A.C. Arbo, 6 1/2 In. 2585.00
Vase, Moon & Moss, Blue & Green, Semimatte Glaze, S. Irvine, 1931, 4 1/2 In. 2818.00
Vase, Morning Glories, Blue, Pink & Green Underglaze, Sadie Irvine, 1924, 11 In. 3230.00
Vase, Painted Swamp Lilies, Blue, Purple, H. Bailey, 6 In. 3819.00
Vase, Scenic Landscape, Moss-Laden Trees, Moon, S. Levine, 7 In. 5288.00
Vase, Triangles, Blue Matte Ground, Art Deco, Sadie Irvine, 3 1/4 x 3 3/4 In. 1380.00
Vase, White, Yellow Daffodils, Green Ground, Sadie Irvine, 1913, 4 In. 2350.00
Vase, Wood, Brass Inlay, Leaves, Arts & Crafts, Cylindrical, 3-Footed, 3 1/2 x 4 In. 825.00
Vase, Wreath, White Buds, Leaves, Blue Ground, Bulbous, May Morel, 5 1/2 In. 2820.00
Vase, Yellow, Blue Blossoms, Cobalt Blue, Green Ground, Leona Nicholson, 13 In. 26438.00

NILOAK Pottery (Kaolin spelled backward) was made at the Hyten Brothers Pottery in Benton, Arkansas, between 1909 and 1947. Although the factory did make cast and molded wares, collectors are most interested in the marbleized art pottery line made of colored swirls of clay. It was called *Mission Ware*. By 1931 the company made castware, and many of these pieces were marked with the name *Hywood*.

NILOAK

Ashtray, Crow-Burlingame Co. 20.00
Candleholder, Marbleized, Flared Base, Handle, Teal, Brown, Cream, 4 1/2 x 5 1/2 In. 267.00
Ewer, Flower, Ozark Dawn II, 10 3/4 In. 60.00
Ewer, Silhouettes, White Matte, 10 In. 25.00
Flower Frog, Ozark Blue, 5 In. 30.00
Pitcher, Ozark Dawn II, 8 3/4 In. 40.00
Pitcher, Texas, Red Fox Glaze, 3 1/2 In. 50.00
Planter, Deer, Ozark Dawn II, 8 1/2 In. 25.00
Planter, Duck, Pink Matte, 3 1/2 In. 5.00
Planter, Elephant, Glossy Light Blue, 6 In. 22.50
Planter, Frog, Glass Light Blue, 5 In. 17.50
Planter, Southern Belle, Standing, Ozark Dawn II, 10 In. 75.00
Planter, Swan, Glossy Blue, 7 1/2 In. 25.00
Sugar & Creamer, Peacock Blue 30.00
Vase, 2 Handles, Ozark Dawn II, 7 In. 35.00
Vase, Bud, Ozark Dawn, 7 In. 35.00
Vase, Egg Shape, Marbleized, 12 x 6 1/2 In. 518.00
Vase, Marbleized, Baluster, Teal, Tan, Brown, Ivory, c.1927, 6 1/2 x 3 1/4 In. 132.00
Vase, Marbleized, Bulbous, Brown, Green, Cream, 5 x 6 In. 275.00
Vase, Marbleized, Classical Shape, Rolled Rim, Brown, Tan, Blue, 6 1/2 x 3 1/2 In. 200.00
Vase, Marbleized, Corseted Neck, Brown, Blue, Tan, 5 x 3 In. 175.00
Vase, Marbleized, Corseted, Blue, Tan, Rust, 10 In. 250.00
Vase, Marbleized, Round, Rolled Rim, Squat, Cream, Brown, Blue, Rust, 3 1/4 x 5 1/4 In. 100.00
Vase, Marbleized, Shouldered, Flared Rim, Blue, Tan, Ivory, 4 3/4 x 3 In. 150.00
Vase, Ozark Dawn II, 7 In. 50.00
Vase, Tulip, Light Gloss Blue, 7 In. 17.50
Wishing Well, Covered, Ozark Blue, 8 In. 30.00

NIPPON porcelain was made in Japan from 1891 to 1921. *Nippon* is the Japanese word for *Japan*. A few firms continued to use the word *Nippon* on ceramics after 1921 as a part of the company name more than as an identification of the country of origin. More pieces marked Nippon will be found in the Dragonware, Moriage, and Noritake categories.

Ashtray, Dog, Enameled Scrolling, Blue Maple Leaf Mark, c.1910, 5 1/2 In. 765.00

Berry Set, Swans, Lake, Reticulated, Handle, Red TN In Wreath, c.1920, 10 1/4 In., 7 Piece 560.00
Bowl, Flowers, Blown Out Panels, c.1900, 10 1/2 In. 175.00
Bowl, Porcelain, Early 20th Century, 3 3/4 x 9 1/2 In. 35.00
Bowl, Woodland, Enamel, Handles, Blue Maple Leaf, c.1900, 7 1/8 In. 200.00
Charger, Indian On Horseback, Firing Rifle, Molded, 1911-21, 14 In. 1765.00
Chocolate Set, Butterflies, Green Mark 235.00
Chocolate Set, Flowers, Gilt Scrolls, c.1910, 7 Piece 1880.00
Chocolate Set, Swan Lake, Enameled Jewels, c.1910, 9 In., 7 Piece 1295.00
Cracker Jar, Cover, Peacocks, Coralene, c.1909, 7 1/2 In. 999.00
Cracker Jar, Cover, Water Lily, Gilt Border, Blue Maple Leaf, c.1900, 9 In. 70.00
Cracker Jar, Cover, Woodland, Griffin Border, Enamel, Blue M In Wreath, c.1900, 8 1/4 In. 1115.00
Dresser Box, Flowers, Pink & White Ground, Coralene, c.1909, 4 1/8 In. 560.00
Dresser Set, Stork Delivering Baby, Blue M In Wreath, c.1920, 11-In. Tray, 5 Piece 999.00
Ewer, Calla Lily, Dragonfly, Green, Yellow, Cobalt Blue Trim, Coralene, c.1909, 5 1/4 In. 705.00
Ewer, Portrait, 4 Seasons, Woman, Flowers, Cobalt Blue, Unmarked, c.1900, 6 1/4 In. 645.00
Ewer, Stylized Flowers, Blue To Green Ground, Coralene, c.1909, 10 In. 880.00
Ferner, Woodland, Enamel, Footed, Blue Maple Leaf, c.1900, 5 1/2 In. 825.00
Ferner, Woodland, Footed, Handles, Blue M In Wreath, c.1900, c.1900, 8 In. 590.00
Game Service, Game Birds, Wild Roses, Lattice Border, Blue Maple Leaf, c.1910, 7 Piece 2820.00
Humidor, Boy Stealing Goose, Green I&E Japan, c.1915, 6 In. 1058.00
Humidor, Coaching Days, Blue Maple Leaf, c.1915, 6 In. 500.00
Humidor, Cover, Woodland, Enamel, Griffin Border, Blue M In Wreath, c.1900, 6 1/4 In. 1765.00
Humidor, Lion & Lioness, Molded, Relief, Moriage Design, M In Wreath, 1911-21, 7 In. 764.00
Humidor, Moose Head, Transfer, c.1915, 6 1/2 In. 440.00
Humidor, Skull & Bones, Green Maple Leaf, c.1900, 5 1/2 In. 1293.00
Humidor, Stone Bridge Over Stream, Blue M In Wreath, c.1915, 6 In. 265.00
Inkwell, Cover, Geese, Square Base, Insert, Blue M In Wreath, c.1915, 2 3/4 In. 150.00
Jar, Cover, Butterflies, Cobalt Blue Trim, Coralene, c.1909, 4 In. 410.00
Jug, Carnations, Blue Ground, Coralene, c.1909, 11 In. 2585.00
Jug, Morning Glory, Green Ground, Cobalt Blue Trim, Coralene, c.1909, 4 1/4 In. 295.00
Jug, Whiskey, Hunt Scene, Moriage Border, Blue Maple Leaf, c.1900, 7 In. 530.00
Jug, Whiskey, Russian Scene, Woman, Boy, Dog, Blue M In Wreath, c.1915, 5 3/4 In. 645.00
Jug, Wine, Monk Playing Violin, Green Maple Leaf, c.1900, 9 1/4 In. 1880.00
Jug, Wine, Mountain Scene, Lattice, Petit Point Jewels, Blue Maple Leaf, c.1900, 9 1/4 In. 590.00
Jug, Wine, Woodland, Enamel, Handle, Blue Maple Leaf, c.1900, 9 1/2 In. 1058.00
Plaque, Fisherman Lighting Pipe, Brown Sea, Self-Framed, 1911-21, 12 x 9 In. 15275.00
Plaque, Full Face Lion, Unmarked, 1911-21, 10 1/2 In. 1410.00
Plaque, Geese, Walking, Enameled Accents, Blue Maple Leaf, c.1910, 11 In. 590.00
Plaque, Mountains, Flower, Blue M In Wreath, c.1910, 10 3/4 In. 2585.00
Plaque, Russian Scene, Woman, Boy, Dog, Blue M In Wreath, c.1915, 9 In. 410.00
Plaque, Seagulls & Waves, Enameled Accents, Blue Maple Leaf, c.1910, 11 In. 750.00
Plate, 4 Seasons, Woman, Gilt Rim, Enamel Jeweled, Blue Maple Leaf, c.1900, 10 1/4 In. 1998.00
Plate, Blown Out, Bulldog, Studded Collar, Shaded Ground, Greek Key, 10 1/2 In. 575.00
Plate, Portrait, Countess Anna Potocka, Blue Maple Leaf, c.1900, 10 1/4 In. 881.00
Plate, Portrait, Woman, Enameled Jewels, Unmarked, c.1910, 10 In. 558.00
Sauceboat, Woodland, Enamel, Griffin Border, Blue Maple Leaf, c.1900, 8 In. 265.00
Shaving Mug, Woodland, Enamel, Handle, Blue Maple Leaf, c.1900, 3 1/2 In. 529.00
Smoking Set, Country Windmill, Blue Maple Leaf, c.1915, 11-In. Tray, 5 Piece 998.00
Stein, Cottage, Lake, Enamel, Blue Maple Leaf, c.1900, 7 In. 380.00
Stein, Hunt Scene, Blue Maple Leaf, c.1900, 7 In. 355.00
Stein, Woodland, Enamel, Blue Maple Leaf, c.1900, 7 In. 825.00
Sugar & Creamer, Pedestal 80.00
Tea Set, Flying Geese, Gold Leaves, Turquoise Ground, Jeweled Border, 9 Piece 345.00
Tray, Woodland, Enamel, Trefoil, Blue Maple Leaf, c.1900, 5 In. 505.00
Urn, Cover, Wild Roses, Coralene, 2 Handles, c.1909, 15 In. 2115.00
Urn, Cover, Wild Roses, Green Ground, Coralene, Handles, c.1909, 9 1/4 In. 765.00
Urn, Flowers, Raised Gold Dots, Hand Applied, Maple Leaf Mark, 13 In. 288.00
Urn, Indian & Goose, Marsh, Gilt & Geometrics, M In Wreath, 21 In. ...... *ILLUS* 20563.00
Urn, Pastoral Scene, Bolted, Blue M In Wreath, c.1900, 15 1/4 In. 1410.00
Vase, Autumn Countryside, Cobalt Blue, Jeweled, Blue Maple Leaf, c.1910, 10 1/4 In. 1175.00
Vase, Autumn Countryside, Gilt Scrolls, Cobalt Blue, Jeweled, Unmarked, c.1900, 7 In. 355.00

Nippon, Urn, Indian & Goose, Marsh, Gilt & Geometrics, M In Wreath, 21 In.

Nippon, Vase, Queen Louise, Transfer Portrait, Jeweled Ground, Mark, c.1900, 10 1/4 In.

Nippon, Vase, Woodland Scene, Raised Enamel, Griffin Border, 3 Handles, c.1900, 8 In.

Vase, Bird, Cherry Blossoms, Coralene, c.1909, 9 3/4 In. 825.00
Vase, Bird, Fruit Blossoms, Purple Ground, Coralene, Handles, c.1909, 12 In. 1116.00
Vase, Bleeding Hearts, Coralene, 2 Handles, c.1909, 13 1/2 In. 2233.00
Vase, Bleeding Hearts, Coralene, c.1909, 6 3/4 In. 765.00
Vase, Carnations, Amber To Green Ground, Coralene, 3-Footed, c.1909, 8 1/4 In. 940.00
Vase, Coaching Days, 2 Handles, Unmarked, c.1910, 7 In. 825.00
Vase, Daffodils, Green & Pink Ground, Coralene, Handles, c.1909, 10 3/4 In. 558.00
Vase, Daffodils, Purple, Coralene, 2 Handles, c.1909, 7 In. 705.00
Vase, Dahlias, Amethyst Ground, Coralene, c.1909, 4 3/4 In. 645.00
Vase, Flowers, Amber & Blue Satin Ground, Coralene, Handles, c.1909, 8 1/4 In. 705.00
Vase, Flowers, Amber & Green Ground, Cobalt Blue Trim, Coralene, c.1909, 5 In. 765.00
Vase, Flowers, Brown & Orange, Coralene, c.1909, 8 1/8 In. 646.00
Vase, Flowers, Brown Ground, Blue Trim, Coralene, Handles, Footed, c.1909, 6 3/4 In. 1116.00
Vase, Flowers, Coralene, 2 Handles, c.1909, 12 In. 1645.00
Vase, Flowers, Green & Purple Ground, Cobalt Blue Trim, Coralene, Handles, c.1909, 8 In. 705.00
Vase, Flowers, Mottled Amber To Green Ground, Coralene, Handles, c.1909, 5 In. 355.00
Vase, Flowers, Purple Satin Ground, Coralene, Handles, c.1909, 9 1/8 In. 1060.00
Vase, Foxglove, Green & Pink Ground, Coralene, Handles, c.1909, 8 3/4 In. 470.00
Vase, Foxglove, Pink & Green Ground, Coralene, Handles, c.1909, 7 In. 500.00
Vase, Galle Scene, Leafless Trees, Autumn, Blue Maple Leaf, c.1915, 8 1/2 In. 1645.00
Vase, Game Birds, Quail, Gilt Rim, Blue Maple Leaf, c.1900, 15 In. 1705.00
Vase, Grapes, Green & Amber Ground, Coralene, Handles, c.1909, 6 1/2 In. 588.00
Vase, Iris, Enameled & Gilt Flowers, Coralene, 2 Handles, c.1909, 9 3/4 In. 1469.00
Vase, Iris, Flower Shape Rim, Coralene, c.1909, 8 In. 645.00
Vase, Iris, Leaves, Coralene, 2 Handles, c.1909, 13 1/4 In. 1645.00
Vase, Lilies, Brown Ground, Coralene, Footed, c.1909, 5 In. 265.00
Vase, Lilies, Cobalt Blue Trim, Coralene, c.1909, 7 In. 590.00
Vase, Lilies, Pink & Green Ground, Coralene, Handles, c.1909, 10 1/4 In. 705.00
Vase, Lily, Gold Trim, Baluster, 2 Angular Handles, 13 1/2 In. 205.00
Vase, Monastery, Snow, Enameled Jewels, Blue Maple Leaf, c.1915, 12 1/2 In. 1645.00
Vase, Mums, Amber To Green Ground, Coralene, c.1909, 10 1/2 In. 999.00
Vase, Oval, All Over Gilt, Enameled Flowers, Maple Leaf, c.1910, 10 1/2 In. 265.00
Vase, Pansies, Amber To Green & Purple Ground, Coralene, c.1909, 9 In. 565.00
Vase, Pansies, Amber-Green To Purple Ground, Coralene, c.1909, 10 1/2 In. 940.00
Vase, Peonies, Blue & Pink Ground, Coralene, Handles, Footed, c.1909, 6 3/4 In. 1175.00
Vase, Polar Bears In Snow, Footed, Y. Gotos, Green Maple Leaf, c.1915, 9 1/2 In. 3290.00
Vase, Portrait, Lady With Peacock, Enameled Jewels, Blue Maple Leaf, c.1900, 12 In. 3290.00
Vase, Portrait, Queen Louise, Enameled, Gilt, Handles, Blue Maple Leaf, c.1900, 11 1/2 In. 5640.00
Vase, Portrait, Woman, Peacock, Maple Leaf, 5 3/4 In. 430.00
Vase, Pussy Willows, Blue Ground, Cobalt Blue Trim, Coralene, Handles, c.1909, 4 1/8 In. 353.00
Vase, Queen Louise, Transfer Portrait, Jeweled Ground, Mark, c.1900, 10 1/4 In. .... *ILLUS* 4465.00
Vase, Roses, Coralene, c.1909, 8 In. 765.00
Vase, Roses, Scrolls, Amber Ground, Cobalt Blue Panels, Coralene, c.1909, 7 1/2 In. 588.00
Vase, Rural Landscape, c.1910, 10 x 5 In. 95.00

Vase, Stylized Flower, Green Ground, Cobalt Blue Trim, Coralene, Handles, c.1909, 8 1/2 In. 500.00
Vase, Stylized Flowers, Gilt Medallions, Coralene, c.1909, 7 In. 410.00
Vase, Stylized Flowers, Pink & Green Ground, Coralene, c.1909, 7 1/8 In. 410.00
Vase, Stylized Flowers, Purple, Blue & Green Ground, Coralene, Handles, c.1909, 7 1/4 In. 499.00
Vase, Sweet Peas, Purple & Green Ground, Coralene, Handles, c.1909, 9 1/8 In. 765.00
Vase, Tapestry, Fired Gold, Faux Jewels, Blue Maple Leaf, 9 1/2 In. 1150.00
Vase, Thistle Blossoms, Leaves, Amber Ground, Coralene, c.1909, 12 3/4 In. 1645.00
Vase, Trees, Green Ground, Coralene, c.1909, 10 In. 590.00
Vase, Trees, Small Houses, Gold Handles, 7 1/8 In. 230.00
Vase, Trumpet Vines, Coralene, 2 Handles, c.1909, 9 1/2 In. 705.00
Vase, Water Lilies, Blue Ground, Coralene, 2 Handles, c.1909, 5 1/4 In. 645.00
Vase, Wild Rose, Blue Ground, Coralene, Handles, c.1909, 4 In. 295.00
Vase, Wild Roses, Coralene, Reticulated Rim, Handles, c.1909, 9 3/4 In. 880.00
Vase, Wild Roses, Lime-Blue Ground, Coralene, c.1909, 12 In. 1175.00
Vase, Windmill, 6 Panels, Moriage Scrolls, Enameled Jewels, c.1910, 13 3/4 In. 999.00
Vase, Wisteria, Enameled Jewels, Blue Maple Leaf, c.1900, 18 In. 2585.00
Vase, Wisteria, Purple, Coralene, 2 Handles, c.1909, 11 3/4 In. 1058.00
Vase, Woodland Scene, Raised Enamel, Griffin Border, 3 Handles, c.1900, 8 In. ..... *ILLUS* 823.00
Vase, Woodland, Enamel, Griffin Border, Blue Maple Leaf, c.1900, 11 3/4 In. 1175.00
Vase, Woodland, Enamel, Griffin Border, Handles, Blue Maple Leaf, c.1900, 12 1/2 In. 1295.00

NODDERS, also called nodding figures or pagods, are figures with heads and hands that are attached to wires. Any slight movement causes the parts to move up and down. They were made in many countries during the eighteenth, nineteenth, and twentieth centuries. A few Art Deco designs are also known. Copies are being made. A more recent type of nodder is made of papier-mache or plastic. These often represent sports figures or comic characters. Sports nodders are listed in the Sports category.

Alfonse, Open Bench Seat, Cast Iron, Embossed Blanket, Hubley, 6 1/2 In. 138.00
Andy Gump, Bisque, 4 In. 110.00
Beetle Bailey, King Features Syndicate, 7 1/2 In. 56.00
Bulldog, Patent 63R2008, 13 1/4 x 17 In. 128.00
Drunk, Standing Near Lamp Post, Composition, c.1960, 6 In. 39.00
Hula Girl, Silk Grass Skirt, Tiki, Box, 1950s, 8 1/2 In. 82.00
Lt. Fuzz, King Features Syndicate, 7 1/2 In. 76.00
Man, Woman, Kissing, Plastic Car Dash Dolls, Magneto GBM, W. Germany, 4 In. 20.00
NY Mets, Composition, Marked, Japan, 1960s, 6 1/2 In. 210.00
Our Gang, Bisque, Hollow, Germany, Box, 1930, 2 To 3 1/2-In. Figures, 6 Piece 1343.00
Pig, Celluloid, Cheyney Co. Tag, Made In Germany, 1 1/2 x 4 1/4 In. 13.50
Salt & Pepper shakers are listed in the Salt & Pepper category.
Skeezix, Bisque, 3 In. 110.00
Surf's Up, Blond Surfer, Orange Board, Japan, 6 In. 25.00
Troll, Viking, Vinyl, Heico, 10 In. 40.00
Witch, Blue Skirt, Red Cape, Black Hat, Papier-Mache, Composition, Germany, 9 3/4 In. 1200.00
Woman, Persian Dress, Enamel, Orange, Black, Porcelain, Germany, Early 1900s, 7 1/2 In. 500.00

NORITAKE porcelain was made in Japan after 1904 by Nippon Toki Kaisha. The best-known Noritake pieces are marked with the M in a wreath for the Morimura Brothers, a New York City distributing company. This mark was used until the early 1950s. There may be some helpful price information in the Nippon category, since prices are comparable. Noritake Azalea is listed in the Azalea category in this book.

Ashtray, Antler, Green M In Wreath, c.1920, 6 1/2 In. 265.00
Ashtray, Dog, Lying Down, Tree, Grass, Green M In Wreath, 1911-21, 6 In. 295.00
Ashtray, Dogs, 3 Cigar Rests, Green M In Wreath, c.1921, 5 3/4 In. 295.00
Ashtray, Great Dane, Oval Tray, Green M In Wreath, 1911-21, 7 In. 470.00
Ashtray, Indian Profile, Green M In Wreath, 1911-21, 6 In. 1116.00
Ashtray, Indian, Chief Joseph, Stitched Lace Border, Green M In Wreath, c.1900, 5 1/4 In. 1058.00
Ashtray, Indian, In Headdress, Green M In Wreath, 1911-21, 6 1/2 In. 1295.00
Ashtray, Indian, Profile, In Headdress, Green M In Wreath, 1911-21, 6 1/4 x 4 3/4 In. 1410.00

If you wash vintage dishes in a dishwasher, use a no- or low-phosphate (under 1.7%) dishwashing product. Also remember that lemon-oil products are not good for silverware.

Noritake, Humidor, Indian Head, Molded, Green M In Wreath Mark, c.1911-21, 7 In.

Ashtray, Pelican, Cottage, Green M In Wreath, c.1925, 5 In. 150.00
Ashtray, Raccoon, Green M In Wreath, 1911-21, 5 In. 325.00
Ashtray, Skull Smoking, Green M In Wreath, c.1900, 5 1/2 In. 825.00
Biscuit Jar, Christmas Deer, Green M In Wreath, c.1904, 6 1/2 In. 1530.00
Bookends, 3 Horsehead, Green M In Wreath, 1911-21, 5 3/4 In. 1116.00
Bowl, Squirrel, Green M In Wreath, 1911-21, 9 In. 440.00
Box, Cover, Egyptian Playing Harp, Green M In Wreath, 1911-21, 3 x 5 3/4 In. 1528.00
Box, Cover, Swans, Lake, Autumn, Green M In Wreath, c.1910, 4 1/2 In. 295.00
Cake Set, Woodland, Enamel, Griffin Border, Green M In Wreath, c.1900, 7 Piece 765.00
Candlestick, Russian Scene, Woman, Boy, Dog, Green M In Wreath, c.1915, 8 In. 295.00
Candlestick, Woodland, Enamel, Chamber, Green M In Wreath, c.1900, 7 In. 650.00
Celery Set, Swans, Lake, Green M In Wreath, c.1920, 8 1/2-In. Bowl, 7 Piece 265.00
Chocolate Set, Art Deco, Swan, Lake, Red M In Wreath, c.1925, 10-In. Pot, 14 Piece 1530.00
Cigarette Box, Dancing Peasants, Jeweled, Green M In Wreath, c.1915, 4 1/2 In. 235.00
Cigarette Jar, Hunt Scene, Green M In Wreath, c.1900, 4 1/2 In. 295.00
Condensed Milk, Woodland, Geometrics, Green M In Wreath, c.1900 .... 176.00
Condiment Set, Harlequin, Red M In Wreath, c.1925, 5-In. Tray, 4 Piece 1175.00
Condiment Set, Woman, c.1925, 7-In. Tray, 4 Piece 295.00
Creamer, Woodland, Enamel, Griffin Border, Green M In Wreath, c.1900, 3 3/4 In. 120.00
Demitasse Set, Wildflowers, Flower Handle, Red M In Wreath, c.1925, 7 1/2-In. Pot, 13 Piece 999.00
Dessert Set, Art Deco, Woman, Red Dress, Castle, Red M In Wreath, c.1925, 22 Piece 9988.00
Dinnerware, Hand Painted No. 16234, 1920s, Service For 12 .... 1200.00
Figurine, Bird, Blue, Green M In Wreath, c.1920, 4 In. 150.00
Figurine, Bird, Yellow, Blue Head, Green M In Wreath, c.1920, 5 3/4 In. 325.00
Hair Receiver, Woodland, Enamel, Footed, Green M In Wreath, c.1900, 3 1/4 In. 235.00
Hairpin Box, Woman, Art Deco, Blue Luster, Red Made In Japan Mark, c.1925, 4 1/4 In. 206.00
Hatpin Holder, Woodland, Enamel, Green M In Wreath, c.1900, 5 In. 150.00
Humidor, 3 Horsehead, Horseshoes, Green M In Wreath, 1911-21, 7 In. 999.00
Humidor, Apollo & Rearing Dogs, Green M In Wreath, 1911-21, 6 In. 3055.00
Humidor, Children Under Tree, Green M In Wreath, 1911-21, 7 1/2 In. 8815.00
Humidor, Egyptian Scene, 6 Panels, Moriage, Green M In Wreath, c.1915, 4 1/4 In. 150.00
Humidor, Fishing Boats, Enamel Borders, Green M In Wreath, c.1915, 6 3/4 In. 470.00
Humidor, Flying Eagle, Green M In Wreath, 1911-21, 6 1/2 In. ....3290.00 to 5875.00
Humidor, Gypsy Woman, Aces, Green M In Wreath, c.1910, 5 1/4 In. 355.00
Humidor, Horse Portrait, Moriage Scrolls, Green M In Wreath, c.1900, 6 In. 1060.00
Humidor, Hunting Dog, Square, Bulbous Base, Green M In Wreath, c.1915, 5 In. 1175.00
Humidor, Indian & Bear, Green M In Wreath, 1911-21 .... 4935.00
Humidor, Indian Head, Molded, Green M In Wreath Mark, c.1911-21, 7 In. .... *ILLUS* 7050.00
Humidor, Indian On Horseback, Green M In Wreath, 1911-21, 6 1/4 In. 2350.00
Humidor, Indian Shooting, Green M In Wreath, c.1910, 7 In. 2235.00
Humidor, Kentucky Derby, Green M In Wreath, c.1910, 7 In. 590.00
Humidor, Lamp Lighter, Green M In Wreath, c.1921, 6 3/4 In. 1175.00
Humidor, Lion & Lioness, Partial Green M In Wreath, c.1911-21, 7 In. 765.00
Humidor, Owl On Branch, Green M In Wreath, 1911-21, 7 In. 1645.00
Humidor, Owl, Moriage Leaves, Green M In Wreath, c.1915, 6 1/2 In. 440.00

Humidor, Raccoon, 2 Handles, Green M In Wreath, 1911-21, 6 1/4 In. 1058.00
Humidor, Stag & Hounds, Green M In Wreath, 1911-21, 7 In. 1528.00
Humidor, Terrier, Sitting In Grassy Field, Green M In Wreath, 1911-21, 7 In. 1410.00
Humidor, Touring Automobile, Green M In Wreath, c.1915, 6 1/2 In. 880.00
Humidor, Winter Scene, Grape Vines, Green M In Wreath, c.1915, 4 1/2 In. 235.00
Inkwell, Chinese Man, Art Deco, 2 Parts, Red M In Wreath, c.1925, 4 1/2 In. 440.00
Inkwell, Harlequin Bust, 2 Parts, Ruffled Base, Red M In Wreath, c.1925, 4 In. 3760.00
Inkwell, Woman, Art Deco, 2 Parts, Green M In Wreath, c.1925, 4 3/4 In. 265.00
Inkwell, Woman, Blue Rosettes, 2 Parts, Green M In Wreath, c.1925, 4 1/2 In. 323.00
Jug, Wine, Christmas Deer, Green M In Wreath, c.1904, 7 3/4 In. 1058.00
Jug, Wine, Country Cottage, Enamel, Green M In Wreath, c.1915, 6 3/4 In. 380.00
Jug, Wine, Wine Taster, Green M In Wreath, c.1904, 9 1/4 In. 1410.00
Match Holder, Woman Golfer, Art Deco, Red M In Wreath, c.1925, 2 1/2 In. 150.00
Mug, Fisherman, Green M In Wreath, 1911-21, 5 1/2 In. 2350.00
Napkin Ring, Man, Woman, Art Deco, Red M In Wreath, c.1925, 1 1/2 In., 2 Piece 205.00
Night-Light, Owl, Electric, Green M In Wreath, c.1911-21, 7 1/2 In. 1410.00
Night-Light, Rabbit, Electric, Green M In Wreath, c.1911-21, 6 3/4 In. 3290.00
Pin Tray, Woodland, Enamel, Griffin Border, Green M In Wreath, c.1900, 2 1/2 In. 175.00
Plaque, 3 Dogs, Green M In Wreath, 1911-21, 10 1/2 In. 1880.00
Plaque, 3 Ponies, Green M In Wreath, 1911-21, 10 1/2 In. 765.00
Plaque, Apollo & Rearing Dogs, Green M In Wreath, 1911-21, 12 In. 1765.00
Plaque, Arab By Campfire, Palm Trees, Mountain, Green M In Wreath, c.1915, 8 x 10 1/2 In. 880.00
Plaque, Bedouins On Horseback, Green M In Wreath, c.1911-21, 13 3/4 In. 3995.00
Plaque, Beer & Card, Enameled Accents, Green M In Wreath, c.1910, 11 In. 380.00
Plaque, Bellowing Moose, Green M In Wreath, 1911-21, 10 3/4 In. 645.00
Plaque, Buffalo, Green M In Wreath, 1911-21, 10 1/4 In. 499.00
Plaque, Bulldog, Green M In Wreath, 1911-21, 10 1/2 In. ....1116.00 to 1645.00
Plaque, Coaching Days, Green M In Wreath, c.1910, 11 In. 940.00
Plaque, Collie & Terrier, Green M In Wreath, 1911-21 .... 940.00
Plaque, Cows Grazing By Stream, Jeweled Rim, Green M In Wreath, c.1915, 8 x 10 1/2 In. 1058.00
Plaque, Dog, St. Bernard, Moriage Rim, Green M In Wreath, c.1910, 11 In. 765.00
Plaque, Eagle, Sitting, Green M In Wreath, 1911-21, 10 1/4 In. 2585.00
Plaque, Elk, Mountain Stream, Green M In Wreath, 1911-21, 10 3/4 In. 470.00
Plaque, Elk, Standing, Dusk, Green M In Wreath, c.1910, 10 1/2 In. 259.00
Plaque, Fisherman, Green M In Wreath, 1911-21, 9 x 12 1/4 In. 15275.00
Plaque, Fishing Boats, Green M In Wreath, c.1915, 8 x 10 1/2 In. 752.00
Plaque, Full Face Lion, Green M In Wreath, 1911-21, 10 1/2 In. 1410.00
Plaque, Horsehead, Green M In Wreath, 1911-21, 10 1/2 In. 765.00
Plaque, Hunt Scene, Rectangular, Green M In Wreath, Self-Framed, c.1900, 10 1/4 x 8 In. 1293.00
Plaque, Indian & Goose, Green M In Wreath, 1911-21, 10 1/2 In. 940.00
Plaque, Indian & Goose, Under Tree, Green M In Wreath, 1911-21, 10 3/4 In. 1410.00
Plaque, Indian On Horseback, Firing Rifle, Green M In Wreath, 1911-21, 10 1/2 In. 825.00
Plaque, Indian Shooting, Horse, Green M In Wreath, c.1910, 10 1/4 In. 2350.00
Plaque, Man On Camel, Enameled Accents, Green M In Wreath, c.1910, 10 In. 325.00
Plaque, Nile River, Sailboat, Enameled Rim, Green M In Wreath, c.1910, 10 1/4 In. 265.00
Plaque, Squirrel Eating, Autumn Leaves, Green M In Wreath, 1911-21, 10 3/4 In. 440.00
Plaque, Twin Indian Profile, Green M In Wreath, 1911-21, 10 3/4 In. 1000.00
Plaque, Woman Equestrian, Green M In Wreath, c.1915, 10 1/4 In. 470.00
Plate, Portrait, Woman, Bouquet, Mother-Of-Pearl, Art Deco, Red M In Wreath, c.1925, 8 1/2 In. .. 940.00
Powder Box, Flower Finial, Art Deco, Red M In Wreath, c.1925, 4 In. 175.00
Powder Box, Jester, Bubbles, Green M In Wreath, c.1925, 4 In. 825.00
Powder Box, Lily Of The Valley, Art Deco, Green M In Wreath, c.1925, 3 3/4 In. 325.00
Powder Box, Pheasant Finial, Art Deco, Red M In Wreath, c.1925, 4 In. 120.00
Powder Box, Woman, Flower Dress, Art Deco, Red M In Wreath, c.1925, 4 In. 355.00
Powder Box, Woman, Holding Fan, Green M In Wreath, c.1925, 4 In. 440.00
Shaving Mug, Standing Elk, Enameled Jewels, Green M In Wreath, c.1915, 3 1/2 In. 355.00
Smoking Set, Man On Camel, Green M In Wreath, c.1910, 10 3/4-In. Tray, 4 Piece 1998.00
Stein, Stylized Flowers, Enamel Accents, Green M In Wreath, c.1910, 7 In. 150.00
Stein, Wine Taster, Green M In Wreath, c.1900s, 6 3/4 In. 765.00
Stein, Woodland, Enamel, Green M In Wreath, c.1904, 5 1/2 In. 765.00
Sugar & Creamer, Woodland, Enamel, Griffin Border, Green M In Wreath, c.1904, 5 In. 353.00

Tray, Harlequin, Bubbles, Red M In Wreath, c.1925, 7 In. 590.00
Tray, Kingfisher, Round, Green M In Wreath, 1911-21, 7 1/4 In. 1410.00
Tray, Suzie Skier, Art Deco, Oval, Red M In Wreath, c.1925, 8 1/2 In. 1058.00
Tray, Woman, Ball Gown, Art Deco, Oval, Green M In Wreath, c.1925, 8 1/2 In. 410.00
Tray, Woodland, Scalloped, Green M In Wreath, c.1904, 11 3/4 In. 380.00
Urn, Cows Grazing By Stream, Bolted, Green M In Wreath, c.1915, 16 In. 2235.00
Urn, Indian & Goose, Bolted, Green M In Wreath, c.1900, 21 In. 20565.00
Urn, Pastoral Cottage, Enameled Jewels, Cobalt Blue, Bolted, Green M In Wreath, c.1900, 16 In. 2585.00
Vase, Beggar Man, Desert, Green M In Wreath, 1911-21, 6 1/2 In. 2585.00
Vase, Beggar Man, Seashore, Green M In Wreath, 1911-21, 10 In. 2820.00
Vase, Game Birds, Quail, Green M In Wreath, c.1915, 13 In. 1175.00
Vase, Hunt Scene, Handles, Green M In Wreath, c.1900, 9 In. 765.00
Vase, Johnny Appleseed, The Sower, Green M In Wreath, 1911-21, 10 1/2 In. 4935.00
Vase, Man On Camel, 4 Panels, Green M In Wreath, c.1910, 7 3/4 In. 645.00
Vase, Man On Camel, 6 Panels, Green M In Wreath, c.1910, 9 In. .... 235.00 to 380.00
Vase, Man On Camel, Geometric Borders, Handles, Green M In Wreath, c.1910, 10 1/2 In. 825.00
Vase, Moose, Bellowing, Green M In Wreath, 1911-21, 13 1/2 In. 2350.00
Vase, Ostrich, Cobalt Blue, Green M In Wreath, c.1910, 8 In. 825.00
Vase, Owl & Tree Trunk, Green M In Wreath, 1911-21, 9 1/4 In. 940.00
Vase, Stone Bridge, Jeweled, Cobalt Blue, Handles, Green M In Wreath, c.1904, 8 1/2 In. 1295.00
Vase, Village Sunset, 4 Panels, Gilt Scrolls, Green M In Wreath, c.1920, 12 3/4 In. 1295.00

NORSE Pottery Company started in Edgerton, Wisconsin, in 1903. In 1904 the company moved to Rockford, Illinois. The company made a black pottery, which resembled early bronze relics of the Scandinavian countries. The firm went out of business in 1913.

Vase, 2 Bands Of Incised Repeating Wave-Like Decoration, Round, Squat, 4 x 6 In. 345.00
Vase, Applied Lizard, Bulbous Base, Elongated Flared Neck, 12 In. 1100.00
Vase, Incised Geometric Bands At Base, Tapered, 9 x 3 1/4 In. 365.00
Vase, Incised Serpents, Chains, Squat, 3-Footed, 5 1/2 x 7 1/2 In. 595.00

NORTH DAKOTA SCHOOL OF MINES was established in 1892 at the University of North Dakota. A ceramic course was included and pieces were made from the clays found in the region. Students at the university made pieces from 1909 to 1949. Although very early pieces were marked *U.N.D.*, most pieces were stamped with the full name of the university.

Bowl, Wine, 3 1/2 In. 270.00
Medallion, Buffalo, Turquoise Glaze, Round, 2 In. 225.00
Paperweight, OES, Star, 5-Sided, Red Glaze, 1916-63, 1 1/4 x 2 In. 115.00
Paperweight, Rebekah Assemblies, Blue, 3-Link Chain, Round, 3 1/2 In. 120.00
Vase, Blue Exterior, Green Interior, Arts & Crafts, 3 1/4 x 4 In. 450.00
Vase, Flowers, Embossed, Rose Matte Ground, 3 1/8 x 3 In. 460.00
Vase, Flowers, Leaves, Branch, Green Matte Ground, 4 x 4 3/4 In. 635.00
Vase, Red Glaze, Black, Brown & Red Geometric, Flared Bottom, Cable, 1948, 4 1/2 In. 570.00
Vase, Ribbed, Bulbous, Raised Panels, Blue High Glaze, 5 1/2 x 4 1/2 In. 145.00

NORTHWOOD Glass Company was founded by Harry Northwood, a glassmaker who worked for Hobbs, Brockunier and Company, La Belle Glass Company, and Buckeye Glass Company before founding his own firm. He opened one factory in Indiana, Pennsylvania, in 1896, and another in Wheeling, West Virginia, in 1902. Northwood closed when Mr. Northwood died in 1923. Many types of glass were made, including carnival, custard, goofus, and pressed. The underlined N mark was used on some pieces.

Dandelion, Water Set, Emerald Green 1008.00
Florentine, Candlestick, Ice Green, No. 349, 10 In., Pair 195.00
Leaf Umbrella, Spooner, Opal Cased Blue, 4 x 2 3/4 In. 578.00
Leaf Umbrella, Sugar Shaker, Blue, Cased To White, 4 1/2 In. 230.00
Quilted Phlox, Sugar Shaker, Blue, Cut Panel, 4 1/2 In. 175.00
Rainbow Spatter, Biscuit Jar, Red, White, Orange, Yellow, Silver Plate Handle, 11 In. 345.00

Royal Ivy, Pitcher, Embossed Leaves, Rubina, Late 1800s, 8 1/4 In. 200.00

NU-ART see Imperial category.

NUTCRACKERS of many types have been used through the centuries. At first the nutcracker was probably strong teeth or a hammer. But by the nineteenth century, many elaborate and ingenious types were made. Levers, screws, and hammer adaptations were the most popular. Because nutcrackers are still useful, they are still being made, some in the old styles.

Alligator, Iron, Monon Route, Florida Tail, Chicago Head, 8 1/2 In. 30.00
Alligator, Iron, Table Style, Eastlake Design, c.1880, 5 x 10 3/4 x 4 3/4 In. 65.00
Brass, Screw Type, 1800s, 2 x 1 7/8 In. 285.00
Brown Bear, Wood, Glass Eyes, Switzerland, 1910, 10 In. 225.00
Chamois, Wood, Glass Eyes, Hand Carved, Black Forest, Germany, 1880-1900, 7 In. 260.00
Chimpanzee, Wood, Amber Eyes, Hand Carved, 1920s, 5 x 7 1/2 In. 430.00
Dog, Cast Iron, 5 x 7 3/4 In. 35.00
Dog, Cast Iron, Nickel Plated, Raise Tail To Open Mouth, L.A. Althoff Mfg., 6 x 10 1/2 In. 55.00
Dog, Painted, Iron, 1918, 5 1/2 x 11 In. 176.00
Dragon, Cast Iron, Painted Black, Red, 9 In. 66.00
Fish, Cast Iron, c.1930, 5 In. 76.00
Man, Wood, Square Nail, Hand Carved, 1850-1900, 8 In. 250.00
Owl, Brass, Glass Eyes, Screw Type, Italy, 6 1/2 In. 68.00
Pirate's Head, Wood, Carved, c.1900, 8 In. 103.00
Squirrel, Cast Iron, Leaf Base, 7 1/2 x 11 x 8 1/2 In. 35.00
Squirrel, Cast Iron, Mounted On Wooden Bowl, 8 In. 55.00
Squirrel, Cast Iron, Press Tail, Crack Nut, 6 x 6 In. 15.00
Squirrel, On Tree Limbs, Bronze, England, Victorian, 6 1/8 In. 80.00
Wolf Head, Cast Iron, Nickel Plated, Wood Base, Pat'd 1880, 5 x 9 1/2 In. 66.00

OCCUPIED JAPAN was printed on pottery, porcelain, toys, and other goods made during the American occupation of Japan after World War II, from 1945 to 1952. Collectors now search for these pieces. The items were made for export. Ceramic items are listed here. Toys are listed in the Toy category.

Ashtray, Brass, Butterfly Under Glass, Dome In Center 90.00
Clock, Oriental Girl On Swing, Glass Dome, Red Base, 7 1/2 In. 145.00
Dinnerware, Fuji Victoria, Service For 12 .... 800.00
Figurine, Bird, Tail Up, Marked M10J, 5 1/4 In. 12.00
Figurine, Colonial Man Playing Violin, 9 1/2 In. 120.00
Figurine, Man & Woman, Victorian, Cream, Gold Highlights, 10 & 10 1/8 In. 58.00
Figurine, Owl, Brown Highlights, Marked Arch No. 94, UCAGCO, 5 3/8 In. 15.00
Jewel Casket, Silver Plate, 2 Tiers Inside, Key, Marked, Rosswell, 6 x 3 x 2 In. 55.00
Lemon Dish, Rose, Yellow, Pink, HP MIOJ Elephant Mark, No. 21, 5 1/2 In. 15.00
Planter, Boy, Girl, Red Paulux MIOJ Mark, 5 x 4 1/4 In., Pair 40.00
Tea Set, Cottage Shape, Teapot, Sugar & Creamer 125.00
Tea Set, Flower, Gold Lusterware Border, Box, 21 Piece 100.00
Vase, Attached Ballerina, White & Burgundy, 8 In. 125.00
Vase, Flared, Red Ground, Yellow & Green Foliage, 12 x 8 1/2 In. 200.00

OFFICE TECHNOLOGY includes office equipment and related products, such as adding machines, calculators, and check-writing machines. Typewriters are in their own category in this book.

Adding Machine, Addiator Universal, Standard Model, West Germany, Pocket 13.00
Adding Machine, Bakelite, Lightning Adding Machine Co., 13 In. 26.00
Adding Machine, Gem DeLux, Model 307, Stand, Box, c.1915, 6 1/2 x 6 In. 105.00
Adding Machine, Metal Frame, Glass Sides, Side Crank, 72 Keys, Burroughs 51.00
Adding Machine, Pocket Arithmometer, Metal, Tasco, Box, c.1940, 6 x 3 3/4 In. 14.00
Adding Machine, The Adder, Figure 8, Nickel Plated, C H Webb, Pat'd 1889 .... 228.00
Adding Machine Calculator, Model No LA7-180, Monroe, 1965, 7 x 10 x 11 In. 40.00
Calculator, Calculateur, Echelle & Curseur Dials, Roplex, France 130.00
Calculator, Facit, Mechanical, Sweden, 1970s 155.00

Calculator, Hewlett Packard, 19C, Programmable, Printing, Case, Booklets, 1970s 297.00
Calculator, Hewlett Packard, HP 12C, Scientific, Booklet, Case, 1980s 70.00
Calculator, Hewlett Packard, HP 9825A, Box 610.00
Calculator, Millionaire, Hans W. Egli, Mahogany Case, Swiss, 26 1/2 In. 1880.00
Coin Changer, Brass, 6 Levers, Lamson, 1891 Patent, 7 x 11 x 9 In. 1595.00
Dictaphone, Ediphone Voicewriter, Thomas Edison 470.00
Label Maker, Dymo, Executive 3, Chrome, Black, 3 Wheels, Instructions, Box 26.00
Label Maker, Dymo, Model 1610, 3 Print Wheels, 2 Tape Rolls, Box 67.00
Printing Press, Excelsior, Mercury, Model 3 x 5, Early 1900s, 13 1/2 In. 115.00
Rolodex, Single, Zephyr American Corp., New York, 7 1/2 x 5 1/2 x 7 In. 16.00
Stock Ticker, Metal, Oak Clipboard, Dow-Jones Ltd., Canada, c.1930, 49 In. 140.00
Stock Ticker, Self-Winding, Edison, c.1870, 9 x 7 In. 4300.00

OHR pottery was made in Biloxi, Mississippi, from 1883 to 1906 by George E. Ohr, a true eccentric. The pottery was made of very thin clay that was twisted, folded, and dented into odd, graceful shapes. Some pieces were lifelike models of hats, animal heads, or even a potato. Others were decorated with folded clay *snakes*. Reproductions and reworked pieces are appearing on the market. These have been reglazed, or snakes and other embellishments have been added.

Bowl, Green Mirrored Interior, Brown Mottled Exterior, Glaze Bubbles, 1 1/2 x 5 1/2 In. 1765.00
Bowl, Red & Blue Matte Glaze, Folded-In Shape, 4 1/2 In. 2640.00
Bowl, Spherical, Black Speckling, Gray Ground, Orange Interior, 2 1/2 x 4 1/2 In. 490.00
Inkwell, Cabin, Chimney, Doors, Roof, Logs, Quill Hole, Green & Tan Glaze, 2 1/8 x 3 3/8 In. 6050.00
Mug, Puzzle, Brown Mottled Glaze, Green Interior, Pierced Body & Rim, Rabbit Head, 3 1/2 In. 1870.00
Mug, Puzzle, Brown Mottled Glaze, Pierced Body, Rim, Rabbit-Mask Handle, 3 1/2 In. 1870.00
Pitcher, Semi-Bulbous, Pinched Panels, Black Glaze, 3 1/2 x 3 3/4 In. 6900.00
Teapot, Mottled Green, Brown & Black Glaze, Sculpted Serpent Top & Spout, 8 In. 2280.00
Vase, Brown Glaze, Hole To Center, Applied Branch, 2 1/4 In. 2350.00
Vase, Bud, Column Shape, Mottled Green, Lustered Glaze, 5 x 2 1/4 In. 1765.00
Vase, Buff Shaded To Russet To Brown, Corset Shape, Crimped Rim, 4 1/2 In. 1140.00
Vase, Bulbous, Textured, Jagged Style, Black Glaze, 4 1/2 x 5 In. 980.00
Vase, Cornucopia, Circular Foot, Terra-Cotta, 1900, 4 In. 1150.00
Vase, Gunmetal Matte Glaze, Pinched Form, 3 1/2 In. 2468.00
Vase, Red Clay, Painted, Squat, Signed, 3 In. 1530.00
Vase, Squat, Asymmetrical Collapsed Rim, Speckled Amber Glaze, 3 x 5 In. 4400.00

OLD PARIS, see Paris category.

OLD SLEEPY EYE, see Sleepy Eye category.

OLYMPIC, see Souvenir category.

ONION PATTERN, originally named *bulb pattern*, is a white ware decorated with cobalt blue or pink. Although it is commonly associated with Meissen, other companies made the pattern in the late nineteenth and the twentieth centuries. A rare type is called *red bud* because there are added red accents on the blue-and-white dishes.

Bowl, Open Pierced Rim, 9 x 5 In. 298.00
Cheese Slicer, Stainless Steel, Ceramic Handle, Blue, Meissen, 8 1/2 In. 28.00
Compote, Figural, Blue, 2 Tiers, Boy, Holding Wreath, Pierced, Meissen, Late 1800s, 13 1/2 In. 940.00
Cup, Oval Mark, Meissen, 1882-1930, 2 1/2 In. 29.00
Cup & Saucer, Scalloped Rim, Deep Saucer, Meissen, Germany 45.00
Dessert Set, Blue Plates, Sweetmeat Stands, Bowls, Meissen, 16 Piece 1290.00
Dinnerware Set, Blue, 90 Piece 3525.00
Dish, Leaf Shape, Branch Handle, Meissen, 2 1/2 x 8 1/4 x 7 1/2 In. 65.00
Funnel, 4 1/4 x 5 3/4 In. 78.00
Gallery Tray, Metal Gallery Rail, Oval, 18 x 14 In. 390.00
Gravy Bowl, Cover, Attached Underplate, Ernst Teichert GMBH, 6 1/2 x 9 x 6 1/2 In. 250.00
Pincushion, Shoe, 7 1/4 x 2 1/4 x 2 1/4 In. 30.00
Plate, 3 Quatrefoils, Blue Trimmed Lattice Work, Meissen, 7 1/4 In. 150.00
Plate, Dinner, Cauldon, England, 1895-1904, 9 1/2 In. 65.00
Plate, Salad, Reticulated Border, Meissen, 8 In., 8 Piece 470.00

Opalescent, Circled Scroll, Spooner, Blue, 4 1/4 x 4 In.

Opalescent, Paneled Holly, Spooner, Blue, 4 x 3 3/4 In.

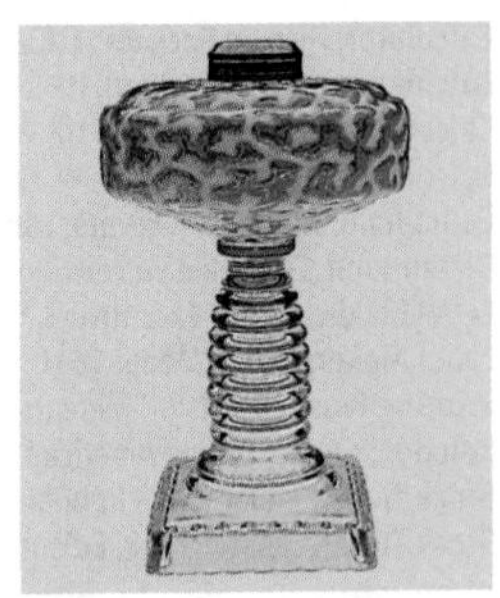
Opalescent, Seaweed, Lamp, Kerosene, Cranberry, Beehive Stem, 9 x 4 1/2 In.

Platter, 13 1/2 x 11 In. 100.00
Platter, Ernst Teichert GMBH, 18 1/2 x 13 1/2 In. 400.00
Platter, Nickel Mounted, Domed Cover, Handle, Bun Feet, Meissen, 10 1/2 x 18 In. 115.00
Rolling Pin, Stoneware, Wood Handles, 14 1/2 In. 425.00
Salt & Pepper, Cork Stoppers, 3 1/4 In. 20.00
Serving Dish, 3 Sections, Ruffled, Crimped Edge, Handle, 11 In. 235.00
Serving Dish, Scalloped Edge, Gold Trim, 2 x 9 x 6 In. 150.00
Sweetmeat Stand, Blue, Male, Female Figures Lounging, 8 x 11 In., Pair 1150.00
Teacup & Saucer, JG Meakin, England, Classic White Nordic 22.00
Teakettle, 6 x 6 3/4 In. 30.00
Teapot, Molded Scroll Spout & Handle, Dome Lid, Rose, Meissen, 10 1/4 In. 230.00
Toothbrush Holder, Vienna Woods, 3 3/4 x 3 1/4 In. 24.00
Tray, Self Handles, Detailed Shaping Surround The Rim, Square, 10 1/2 In. 125.00
Tureen, Cover, Rococo Leaf Handles, Dome Lid, Scroll Finial, Meissen, 14 1/2 x 10 In. 489.00
Urn, Cover, Lamp Mounted, Meissen, 11 1/4 In. 826.00

OPALESCENT GLASS is translucent glass that has the tones of the opal gemstone. It originated in England in the 1870s and is often found in pressed glassware made in Victorian times. Opalescent glass was first made in America in 1897 at the Northwood glassworks in Indiana, Pennsylvania. Some dealers use the terms *opaline* and *opalescent* for any of these translucent wares. More opalescent pieces may be listed in Hobnail, Northwood, Pressed Glass, and other glass categories.

Admiral Flora, Spooner, Blue, 4 1/4 In. 99.00
Adonis Swirl, Spooner, White, Amber Rim, 4 1/8 x 4 In. 176.00
Alaska, Spooner, Blue Enameled, Gold Trim, 3 1/2 x 4 In. 39.00
Alaska, Spooner, Vaseline, 3 1/2 x 4 In. 88.00
Ashburton, Sugar, White, Round Base, 4 1/2 x 4 1/2 In. 50.00
Beatty Swirl, Syrup, Blue, Molded Handle, 6 1/2 In. 345.00
Carnelian, Spooner, Blue, Gold Trim, 4 1/2 x 3 3/4 In. 55.00
Circled Scroll, Spooner, Blue, 4 1/4 x 4 In. .... *ILLUS* 77.00
Coinspot, Sugar Shaker, Blue, 4 1/2 In. 145.00
Coinspot & Swirl, Syrup, Blue, 6 In. 200.00
Daisy & Fern, Syrup, Blue, 5 In. 259.00
Daisy In Criss-Cross, Tumbler, White, c.1897, 3 1/2 In. 58.00
Dew Drop, Spooner, Ruby, 4 x 4 In. 99.00
Drapery, Spooner, Blue, 4 x 4 In. 66.00
Everglades, Cruet, Blue 425.00
Holly With Cord & Tassel, Butter, Cover, White, 6 x 4 3/4 In. 300.00
Klondyke, Spooner, Vaseline, 4 1/2 x 4 1/4 In. 55.00
Lattice, Tumbler, Ribbed, Blue, 3 1/2 In. 46.00
Opaline Brocade, Sugar Shaker, Blue, 5 In. 230.00

Paneled Holly, Spooner, Blue, 4 x 3 3/4 In. .... *ILLUS* 110.00
Ribbed Spiral, Spooner, Blue, 4 x 3 1/4 In. 77.00
Scroll With Acanthus, Spooner, Blue, 4 1/4 x 3 3/4 In. 66.00
Seaweed, Lamp, Kerosene, Cranberry, Beehive Stem, 9 x 4 1/2 In. .... *ILLUS* 1870.00
Stripe, Sugar Shaker, 5 In. 115.00
Swirl, Sugar Shaker, 9 Panel, Cranberry, 5 In. 145.00
Syrup, White, Reverse Swirl, 7 1/4 In. 200.00
Toothpicks are listed in the Toothpick category.

OPALINE, or opal glass, was made in white, green, and other colors. The glass had a matte surface and a lack of transparency. It was often gilded or painted. It was a popular mid-nineteenth-century European glassware.

Pastry Stand, Enameled, Butterfly & Berry, Silver Frame, France, c.1885, 11 x 10 3/4 In. 528.00
Vase, Aqua, Enameled Flower, Butterfly, Bee, France, 9 3/4 In., Pair 185.00
Vase, Campana Shape, Cut, Parcel Gilt, Drum Base, Brass Liner, England, c.1835, 19 In., Pair 880.00
Vase, Enameled Flowers, Cut, Parcel Gilt, Baluster, Bohemia, c.1885, 18 5/8 In., Pair 705.00
Vase, Enameled Flowers, Late 1800s, 11 1/2 In., Pair 58.00

OPERA GLASSES are needed because the stage is a long way from some of the seats at a play or an opera. Mother-of-pearl was a popular decoration on many French glasses.

Hazbroucq, Cobalt Blue Enamel, Fairies, Flowers, France, Early 1900s, 4 In. 440.00
Klein, Dezso, Mother-Of-Pearl, Gold-Plated Eye-Piece, Paintings, Budapest, c.1900 .... 410.00
Mother-Of-Pearl Casing, France 40.00
Porcelain, Cherub Decoration, 6 In. 546.00
Voigtlander, Bone, Gold Plated, Vienna, Case, Patent 1823, 4 In. 955.00

ORPHAN ANNIE first appeared in the comics in 1924. The redheaded girl and her friends have been on the radio and are still on the comic pages. A Broadway musical show and a movie in the 1980s made Annie popular again and many toys, dishes, and other memorabilia are being made.

Badge, Decoder, Brass, Telematic, 5-Point Star, Circle, 1938 .... 28.00 to 76.00
Badge, Decoder, Rotating Wheel, 26 Letters, 26 Numbers, 1937, 2 In. .... 37.00 to 44.00
Badge, Decoder, Secret Compartment, Robbins Co., 1936, 4 1/4 In. .... 13.00 to 16.00
Badge, Decoder, Secret Society, 1935, 1 1/4 In. 61.00
Badge, Secret Guard, Glow-In-The-Dark Plastic, Quaker Oats, 1941 .... *ILLUS* 84.00
Bank, Dime Register, Tin Lithograph, Round, c.1936, 3 In. 220.00
Belt, Code Captain, 1940, 29 In. 84.00
Big Little Book, Little Orphan Annie With Circus Whitman, 1934, No. 1103, 318 Pages 51.00
Bracelet, Cuff, Chicago Expo, Green Enamel, 1933, 5 In. 273.00
Collector Plate, Annie & Sandy, Knowles, 8 1/2 In. 25.00
Doll, Knickerbocker, Proctor & Gamble, Box, 1982, 15 In. .... 25.00 to 35.00
Game, Little Orphan Annie Game, Milton Bradley, 1930s, 1 1/2 x 8 1/2 x 17 In. 144.00
Game, Orphan Annie To The Rescue, Milton Bradley, 1930s, 1 x 7 3/4 x 14 In. 101.00
Lunchbox, Metal, Thermos Bottle, Aladdin, 1981 .... 18.00
Mug, Shake-Up, Green, Red Cover, Ovaltine, Beetleware, 5 x 3 In. 18.00
Mug, Shake-Up, Ovaltine Premium, Orange Top, Beetleware, 1940s, 5 In. 182.00
Mug, Shake-Up, White, Orange Cover, Ovaltine, Beetleware, 4 3/4 x 2 In. 27.00
Nodder, Bisque, 3 1/2 In. 110.00
PEZ Dispenser, Austria 85.00
PEZ Dispenser, Red Stem, 1982 .... 76.00
Pin, Annie & Sandy In Rowboat, Enamel, On Brass, 1 5/8 In. 339.00
Pin, Color Portrait, c.1928, 1 1/4 In. 339.00
Ring, Altascope, Quaker Cereals, Brass, Adjustable, Bombing & Pursuit Planes 10000.00
Ring, Annie's Face, Gold Color, 1934 .... 16.00
Ring, Silver Star Member, Secret Message, 1937 .... 88.00
Ring, Silver Star, 5-Point Star, Silver Color, 1930s 51.00
Ring, Silver Star, Triple Mystery, Secret Compartment, Silver Luster, 1938 .... 1574.00
Tea Set, Japan, Box, 1940s, 17 Piece 149.00

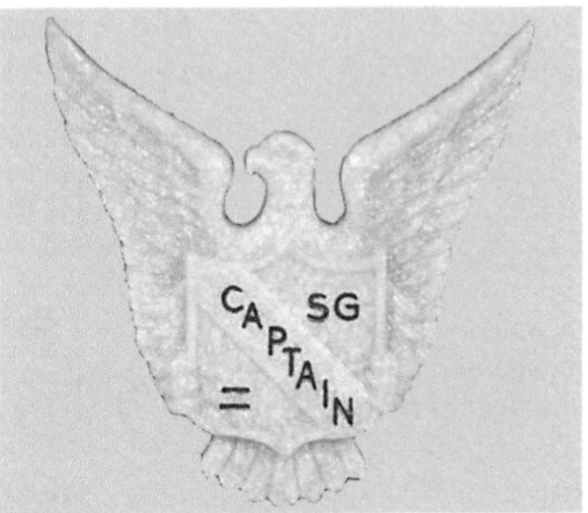

Orphan Annie, Badge, Secret Guard, Glow-In-The-Dark Plastic, Quaker Oats, 1941

Orphan Annie, Wristwatch, Chrome, Leather Band, Paul R. Gruen Inc., Box

Toothbrush Holder, Orphan Annie & Sandy, On Sofa, Bisque, Japan, 1930s, 3 1/2 In. 115.00
Wristwatch, Annie On Face, New Haven, Box, 1948 .... 525.00
Wristwatch, Chrome, Leather Band, Paul R. Gruen Inc., Box .... *ILLUS* 196.00

ORREFORS Glassworks, located in the Swedish province of Smaaland, was established in 1898. The company is still making glass for use on the table or as decorations. There is renewed interest in the glass made in the modern styles of the 1940s and 1950s. In 1990, the company merged with Kosta Boda. Most vases and decorative pieces are signed with the etched name *Orrefors.*

Orrefors

Lamp, Glass, Tapered Triangular Column, No. 1314, 17 In., Pair 2400.00
Vase, Ariel, Geometric Forms, Ingeborg Lundin, 8 1/2 x 4 1/4 In. 1115.00
Vase, Clear, Textured, Abstract, Ingeborg Lundin, 1960s, 9 3/4 In. 285.00
Vase, Engraved Pearl Divers, Black Base, Vicke Lindstrand, 1950s, 4 1/4 In. 140.00
Vase, Fish, Graal, Leaves, Oval, Edward Hald, 1940s, 5 1/2 In. .... 775.00 to 1084.00
Vase, Smoky Interior, Engraved, 10 In. 480.00

OTT & BREWER Company operated the Etruria Pottery at Trenton, New Jersey, from 1863 to 1893. They started making belleek in 1882. The firm used a variety of marks that incorporated the initials *O & B.*

O&B

Cup & Saucer, Applied Twig Handle, 2 1/4 x 3 1/4-In. Cup, 5 3/4-In. Saucer 395.00
Cup & Saucer, Limpet Shape, Lavender Glazed Interior, Belleek 70.00
Dish, 2 Handles, Fluted, Oval, Nautilus Shell Handle Terminal, 2 x 6 1/2 x 3 1/4 In. 195.00
Pitcher, Sepia Line Flower, Blue Ribbed Neck & Base, 8 1/2 In. 35.00
Vase, Posy, Leaves, Butterfly, Gilt, 5 1/2 In. 175.00

OVERBECK pottery was made by four sisters named Overbeck at a pottery in Cambridge City, Indiana. They started in 1911. They made all types of vases, each one-of-a-kind. Small, hand-modeled figurines are the most popular pieces with today's collectors. The factory continued until 1955, when the last of the four sisters died.

Figurine, Bird, Blue, Standing On Mound Of Flowers, Marked, 4 1/4 In. 345.00
Figurine, Cat, Frenzied, Incised, 4 1/4 In. 1495.00
Figurine, Dog, Barking, Incised, 2 3/4 In. 575.00
Figurine, Dog, Cocker Spaniel, Incised, 1 1/4 In. 489.00
Figurine, Ducks, Panic, Squawking, Incised, 2 In. 520.00
Figurine, Horses, Running Side By Side, Incised, 2 3/8 In. 575.00
Figurine, Kenneth Caldwell On Bicycle, Incised, 6 1/4 In. 3565.00
Figurine, Rabbit, Incised, 2 1/4 In. 400.00
Figurine, Raccoon, 1 1/2 In. 489.00
Figurine, Southern Belle, Blue Dress, Bouquet, Marked, 4 1/2 In. 290.00
Figurine, Southern Belle, Polka Dot Dress, Flowers, Bouquet, Incised, 3 7/8 In. 290.00
Figurine, Squirrel, Eating, Incised, 2 3/8 In. 489.00
Figurine, Turtle, On Spindly Legs, Incised, 1 5/8 In. 520.00

Pin, Bluebird, Flowers, 2 In. 345.00
Pin, Rose, Incised, 1 1/2 In. 196.00
Vase, Pine Trees, Flowering Bushes, Birds, 9 1/8 In. 6325.00
Vase, Tapered, Maple Leaves, Pods, Purple, Green, Buff Ground, 7 x 4 1/2 In. 4113.00

OWENS Pottery was made in Zanesville, Ohio, from 1891 to 1928. The first art pottery was made after 1896. Utopian Ware, Cyrano, Navarre, Feroza, and Henri Deux were made. Pieces were usually marked with a form of the name *Owens*. About 1907, the firm began to make tile and discontinued the art pottery wares.

Vase, Aborigine, Native American Design, 6 7/8 In. 185.00
Vase, Embossed Trees, Copper Overlay, Marked Owens Lotus, 13 1/2 x 3 3/4 In. 3175.00
Vase, Incised & Cutout Design, Green Matte Glaze, Swollen Form, 12 In. 360.00
Vase, Lotus, Green On Gray, Tan & Brown Ground, Marked, No. 225, 7 In. 600.00
Vase, Mission, Red & Green Drip Glaze, Blue Ground, Bottle Shape, Oak Stand, 15 In. 1763.00
Vase, Sunburst, Yellow Roses, Impressed, 13 5/8 In. 290.00
Vase, Utopian, 13 In. 125.00
Vase, Utopian, Clovers, Brown Glaze, Bulbous, Flared, Marked, 3 1/4 In. 180.00
Vase, Utopian, Flower, 7 1/4 In. 95.00
Vase, Utopian, Pansies, 2 Handles, 5 3/4 In. 81.00
Vase, Utopian, Wild Rose, 3 Handles, 6 7/8 In. 138.00
Vase, White Flowers, Brown & Green Glaze, Triangular, Initialed, B.M., Marked, 3 1/4 In. 210.00

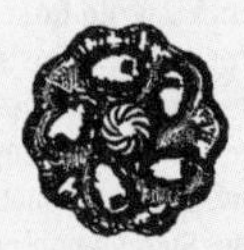

OYSTER PLATES were popular from the 1880s. Each course at dinner was served in a special dish. The oyster plate had indentations shaped like oysters. Usually six oysters were held on a plate. There is no greater value to a plate with more oysters, although that myth continues to haunt antiques dealers. There are other plates for shellfish, including cockle plates and whelk plates. The appropriately shaped indentations are part of the design of these dishes.

4 Wells, Gold Trim, H & Co Depose, Haviland Limoges, 8 In. 130.00
5 Wells, Flowers, Gold Gilt, Haviland, Limoges, 7 3/4 In. 180.00
5 Wells, Flowers, Gold Trim, Theodore Haviland, Limoges, 1900-40, 8 1/2 In. 65.00
5 Wells, Flowers, Green Leaves, H & C L France, Haviland & Co., Limoges, 9 In. 55.00
5 Wells, Flowers, Ivory Rim, Gold Outline, Germany, 1800s, 10 x 8 3/4 In. 140.00
5 Wells, Gold Trim, Limoges TV, France, 1900-40, 8 1/2 In. 80.00
5 Wells, Oriental Scene, Blue Transfer, German Weimar, 1918-45, 8 1/2 In. 75.00
5 Wells, Turkey, Sea Creatures, Haviland, Victorian, c.1885, 8 1/2 In. 189.00
5 Wells, White, Gold Outline, Siena, Gold Leaf Edge, Haviland & Co., 7 1/2 In. 180.00
6 Wells, Butterfly Center, Flowers, Fishing Scenes, Wildflowers, 9 3/4 In. 228.00
6 Wells, Deruta Majolica, Italy, 9 3/4 In. 60.00
6 Wells, Majolica, Enamel, Orchies Factory, c.1870, 10 In. 400.00
6 Wells, Majolica, Longchamp, 1890s, 9 1/2 In. 76.00
6 Wells, Majolica, St. Clement, 1850-1900, 10 In. 86.00
6 Wells, Pink Glaze, Gold Gilding, 8-Sided, JS Mark, 8 1/4 In. 50.00
6 Wells, Pottery, Sea Life, Kyoto, Japan, Late 19th Century, 9 1/2 In. 635.00
6 Wells, Sea Grass, Berries, Leaves, Gold Accents, Hand Painted 135.00
6 Wells, Turquoise, Brown, Pink, Minton, Victorian, 9 In. 375.00
Black Band, Flowers, Porcelain, Austria, 8 1/2 In. 45.00
Blue, Pink, Brown, White Ground, Porcelain, France, 10 In., Pair 115.00
Brown Seaweed, Porcelain, 9 1/4 In., 12 Piece 805.00
Gray, Pink, Brown, Porcelain, France, 9 In. 130.00
Pink, Turquoise Ground, Underglaze Blue, Altwasser, 9 1/8 In., 4 Piece 600.00

PADEN CITY Glass Manufacturing Company was established in 1916 at Paden City, West Virginia. The company made more than seventy different colors of glass. The firm closed in 1951. Paden City Pottery is not listed here.

Ardith, Candlestick, 2-Light, 5 In. 50.00
Ardith, Console, 13 In. 75.00
Black Forest, Dish, Mayonnaise, Pink 145.00
Black Forest, Plate, Cheese & Cracker, Green, 10 In. 95.00

Crow's Foot, Bowl, Vegetable, Amber, 10 In. 45.00
Crow's Foot, Cup & Saucer, Yellow, Square Saucer 15.00
Crow's Foot, Tumbler, Amber, 4 1/4 In. 25.00
Cupid, Candlestick, Cheri-Glo, 5 In., Pair 250.00
Figurine, Pelican, 10 In. .... 350.00 to 395.00
Figurine, Pheasant, Blue, 12 In. 175.00
Figurine, Pigeon 90.00
Figurine, Pony, Blue 214.00
Gazebo, Bowl, Handles, 10 1/2 In. 95.00
Gazebo, Candlestick, Gold Trim, 6 In., Pair 90.00
Gazebo, Sandwich Server, Center Goose Neck Handle 90.00
Georgian, Tumbler, Ruby, 12 Oz., 5 1/2 In. 24.00
Largo, Candlestick, 2-Light, Pair 120.00
Lela Bird, Candy Dish, Cover, Footed, Green 281.00
Lela Bird, Plate, Green, 8 In. 43.00
Maya, Bowl, Blue, 3-Footed, 12 3/4 In. 45.00
Maya, Nut Dish, Center Handle, Blue, No. 221 .... 25.00
Orchid Etch, Candlestick, Ruby, Open Stem 309.00
Peacock & Wild Rose, Candlestick, Mushroom, Cheri-Glo 67.00
Peacock & Wild Rose, Compote, Cheri-Glo 128.00
Peacock & Wild Rose, Console, Cheri-Glo, 11 In. 162.00
Peacock & Wild Rose, Console, Green, 14 In. 210.00
Peacock & Wild Rose, Dish, Mayonnaise, Underplate, Cheri-Glo 148.00
Peacock & Wild Rose, Ice Tub, Cheri-Glo, 6 In. 200.00
Penny, Creamer, Amethyst 11.00
Penny, Decanter, Ruby, 22 Oz., 11 In. 170.00
Penny, Sherbet, Amethyst, Footed 9.00
Penny, Sugar, Amethyst 11.00
Popeye & Olive, Tumbler, Ruby, 9 Oz. 30.00
Utopia, Vase, Flared, Footed, 10 1/4 In. 95.00

PAINTINGS listed in this book are not works by major artists but rather decorative paintings on ivory, board, or glass that would be of interest to the average collector. Watercolors on paper are listed under Picture. To learn the value of an oil painting by a listed artist you must contact an expert in that area.

Acrylic, On Canvas, Janua, Jim Bird, Wooden Frame, c.1989, 36 x 32 In. 4230.00
Ink & Color On Paper, Raja & Attendants, Indian Deccan School, Miniature, 11 x 8 In. 82.00
Mandarin On Horseback, Attendant, Mountain Landscape, Chinese, 33 1/2 In. 1645.00
Miniature, Portrait, Oval, King Louis XVI, Queen Marie-Antoinette, Signed, 6 x 4 In., Pair 705.00
Nautical, Mermaid, 3-Masted Ship, Hot Air Balloon, Ralph Eugene Cahoon Jr., 10 x 14 In. 15275.00
Oil On Board, Landscape, Cottage, River, Sailboat, Rockland, Maine, c.1870, 16 x 22 In. 375.00
Oil On Board, Saint Sebastian, After Giovanni Antonia, Frame, 1800s, 17 1/2 In. 940.00
Oil On Board, Toran, Pink Flamingos, At Water's Edge, Palm Trees, Frame, 14 x 12 In. 460.00
Oil On Board, Young Lady, Black Curls, Black Dress, By Open Window, 14 x 10 In. 4185.00
Oil On Canvas, 2 Kittens At Play, Brunel Neuville, Giltwood Frame, 18 x 22 In. 3055.00
Oil On Canvas, Boy Holding Red Book, American, c.1835, 24 x 20 In. 8815.00
Oil On Canvas, Country Squire, Wig, Brass Buttoned Coat, Frame, 39 x 35 In. 1035.00
Oil On Canvas, French Countryside With Herd Of Cows Grazing, Late 19th Century, 42 x 59 In. 5405.00
Oil On Canvas, Gentleman, Brown Eyes, Black Hair, Gilt Frame, 33 x 29 In. 2760.00
Oil On Canvas, Hunting Scene, British School, Giltwood Frame, Early 1800s, 19 x 25 In. 1760.00
Oil On Canvas, Landscape, Beer Garden, Ivy Covered Pavilion, Frame, 30 x 35 In. 1955.00
Oil On Canvas, Little Girl, Pink Dress, Holding Roses, c.1840, 26 x 22 In. 2466.00
Oil On Canvas, Ottinger Family Of Philadelphia, 9 People, Frame, 34 1/2 x 28 In. 6573.00
Oil On Canvas, St. Joseph Holding Christ Emmanuel, Giltwood Frame, 20 x 14 1/2 In. 880.00
Oil On Canvas, Venus Mourning Adonis In Landscape, Giltwood Frame, 44 x 48 In. 9990.00
Oil On Canvas, Victorian Woman Putting On Necklace, 20 x 24 In. 55.00
Oil On Panel, Hassidic Man, Signed, Central European, 10 x 8 1/4 In. 740.00
Oil On Tin, Hudson Valley Landscape, Frank Ivers, Rochester, N.Y., 1861, 14 x 20 In., Pair 248.00
On Ivory, English Officer, Oval, Gilt Frame, 1700s, 2 3/4 In. 349.00

Pairpoint, Lamp, Berkeley Shade, Reverse Painted, Forest Scene, 17 1/2 In.

Pairpoint, Lamp, Conical Flared Shade, Reverse Painted, Egypt, Signed, 18 In.

Pairpoint, Lamp, Farm Scene, Carlisle Shade, Reverse Painted, 21 x 17 1/2 In.

On Ivory, George Washington, 19th Century, 2 1/2 x 2 In. 720.00
On Ivory, Miniature, Lady Hamilton, Blue Gown, Black Lacquered Frame, Oval, 5 x 4 In. 140.00
On Ivory, Napoleon, On Horseback, Enameled, Brass Frame, 3 1/2 x 4 1/2 In. 765.00
On Ivory, Portrait, Girl & Dog, Oval, Rose Gold Frame, 2 1/4 x 1 3/4 In. 2990.00
On Ivory, Portrait, Man, Military Uniform, Epaulettes, Filigree Brass Frame, 3 x 2 3/4 In. 348.00
On Ivory, Portrait, Marquis De Lafayette, Ebonized Frame, Brass, c.1825, 6 1/4 x 5 1/4 In. 6325.00
On Ivory, Portrait, Queen Elizabeth, Dore Frame, c.1850, 6 3/4 x 4 1/2 In. 490.00
On Ivory, Portrait, Woman, Blue, Dress, Pearl Necklace, Cross Pendant, 3 In. 489.00
On Ivory, Portrait, Woman, Girl, Velvet Mat, Frame, 1800s, 7 1/4 x 5 1/2 In. 780.00
On Ivory, Portrait, Woman, Silver Frame, c.1880, 4 x 2 3/4 In. 530.00
On Ivory, Portrait, Young Brunette Woman, Blue Dress, Violet, Red Leather Case, 3 1/4 In. 290.00
On Ivory, Portrait, Young Girl, Blond Hair, Blue Eyes, Red Velvet Mat, Brass Frame, 3 In. 145.00
On Ivory, Portrait, Young Girl, Heart Shaped Pendant, Mid 1800s, 2 1/4 x 2 3/4 In. 205.00
On Ivory, Reclining Lady, 18th Century Costume, Wreath, France, 4 1/2 x 5 1/4 In. 368.00
Reverse On Glass, Justice, 19th Century, 10 x 7 1/2 In. 266.00
Reverse On Glass, Mariane, Woman, Red, Yellow Dress, Feathered Hat, Frame, 12 x 10 In. 345.00
Reverse On Glass, Napoleon, Young Emperor, Chinese, Frame, 1800s, 16 x 12 In. 1035.00
Reverse On Glass, Saint Barbara, Crowned, Flowers, White Ground, Frame, 12 x 10 In. 290.00
Reverse On Glass, Still Life, Peaches, Fly, 11 x 14 In. 575.00
Reverse On Glass, Young Seductress, Outdoors, Chinese, Frame, 1800s, 12 x 10 In. 1840.00

PAIRPOINT Manufacturing Company started in 1880 in New Bedford, Massachusetts. It soon joined with the glassworks nearby and made glass, silver-plated pieces, and lamps. Reverse-painted glass shades and molded shades known as *puffies* were part of the production until the 1930s. The company reorganized and changed its name several times but is still working today. Items listed here are glass or glass and metal. Silver-plated pieces are listed under Silver Plate.

Biscuit Jar, White Medallions, Purple Flowers, Green Ground, Metal Lid, 7 1/2 In. 400.00
Bowl, Myrtle Cutting, Corseted, 9 In. 550.00
Bowl, Silver Leaf Cutting, 8 3/4 In. 880.00
Bowl, Wamsutta Cutting, Pedestal Base, Handles, 6 1/2 x 13 1/2 In. 195.00
Box, Rectangular, Hinged, Singed, 3 1/2 x 6 1/2 In. 250.00
Candlestick, Amethyst, Grapevine, Cutting Leaves, Baluster Shape, 11 In., Pair 400.00
Compote, Amethyst, Clear Controlled Bubble Connector, Wafer Base, 4 5/8 x 8 In. 250.00
Compote, Bronze, Hammered, Gold Enameled Interior, No. G1461, 7 1/2 In. 115.00
Console, Etched, Amethyst, 4 1/4 x 9 3/4 In. 395.00
Lamp, Berkeley Shade, Reverse Painted, Forest Scene, 17 1/2 In. .... *ILLUS* 3080.00
Lamp, Bombay Shade, Reverse Painted, Landscape, Bulbous, Textured Satin, 17 1/2 In. 4600.00
Lamp, Conical Flared Shade, Reverse Painted, Egypt, Signed, 18 In. .... *ILLUS* 3360.00
Lamp, Delft Dutch Scene, Ribbed, Opal, Buildings, Trees, 11 In. 805.00
Lamp, Domed Emerald Green Cased Shade, Gilded Metal Base, 16 x 11 In. 550.00
Lamp, Farm Scene, Carlisle Shade, Reverse Painted, 21 x 17 1/2 In. .... *ILLUS* 1680.00
Lamp, Puffy, Albemarle, Butterflies & Roses, 12 In. .... *ILLUS* 4200.00

Pairpoint, Lamp, Puffy, Albemarle, Butterflies & Roses, 12 In.

Pairpoint, Lamp, Puffy, Butterfly, Rose, Blossoms, Brass Base, 20 x 14 In.

Pairpoint, Lamp, Puffy, Orange Tree, Blossoms, Butterflies, Tree Trunk Base, 24 x 14 In.

Lamp, Puffy, Azalea, Red, Pink, White, Yellow, Base No. 3035, Signed, c.1910, 22 x 12 In. 12925.00
Lamp, Puffy, Butterfly, Rose, Blossoms, Brass Base, 20 x 14 In. .... *ILLUS* 3450.00
Lamp, Puffy, Flowers, Green Field, Turned Goblet Shaped Mahogany Base, 7 3/4 In. 345.00
Lamp, Puffy, Grapes Shade, Grape Base, Signed, 20 x 14 In. 28000.00
Lamp, Puffy, Grapes, Silvered Metal Base, 20 x 14 3/4 In. 4095.00
Lamp, Puffy, Marlborough Shade, Floral Swags, c.1910, 23 x 15 In. 5875.00
Lamp, Puffy, Orange Tree, Blossoms, Butterflies, Tree Trunk Base, 24 x 14 In. .... *ILLUS* 46000.00
Lamp, Puffy, Poppy, Reverse Painted, Flower Support, Metal Base, 1905, 22 x 13 1/2 In. 5460.00
Lamp, Puffy, Roses, Buds, Leaves, Cream Ground, Applied Feet, 24 In. 5750.00
Lamp, Reverse Painted, Roses, Poppies, Textured Satin, 2 Socket Base, 22 x 16 In. 2350.00
Lamp, Reverse Painted, Seagulls, Ships, Wood Base, H. Fisher, 25 In. 15535.00
Lamp, Torino Shade, Poppies, Ferns, Metal Base, Paneled Urn, 21 1/2 In. 3680.00
Lamp, Tropical Birds, Conical Shade, 3-Footed Silver Plated Base, 22 x 17 1/2 In. 4025.00
Nappy, Engraved Poinsettia, Butterfly Center, Handle, 6 In. 99.00
Perfume Bottle, Amethyst Glass, Controlled Bubble Ball Stem, Teardrop Stopper, 9 1/2 In. 316.00
Punch Bowl, Base, Silver Leaf Overlay, 11 x 12 In. 3520.00
Tray, Baked Apple, Intaglio, Round, 10 1/2 In. 358.00
Vase, Engraved, Pendants, Flowers, Bubble Ball Stem, Chalice Shape, 11 3/4 x 6 3/8 In. 528.00
Vase, Milk Glass, Enameled, Pilgrims, 7 In. 100.00

PALMER COX, BROWNIES, see Brownies category.

PAPER collectibles, including almanacs, catalogs, children's books, some greeting cards, stock certificates, and other paper ephemera, are listed here. Paper calendars are listed separately in the Calendar category. Paper items may be found in many other sections, such as Christmas and Movie.

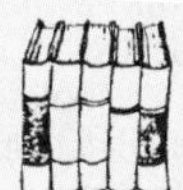

Almanac, Agricultural, J. Baer's Sons, Lancaster, Pa., 1876 .... 9.00
Almanac, Crockett, Vol. 2, No. 1, 1839, 8 x 5 In., 36 Pages 431.00
Almanac, Farmers & Mechanics Almanack, Mentz & Rovoudt, Philadelphia, 1845 .... 12.00
Almanac, Hutchin's Improved Almanack, Alexander Ming, N.Y., 1813 .... 15.00
Almanac, Poulson's Town & Country, John Bioren, 1802 .... 18.00
Billhead, New York Stoneware Pottery Fort Edward Bought Of Satterlee & Mory, c.1870 .... 176.00
Birth, Fraktur, Baptism, Printed, Hand Illuminated, Jonathon Himmelberger, 1838, 16 x 13 In. ... 83.00
Birth, Fraktur, Baptism, Printed, Hand Illuminated, Mary Ann Wisler, 1841, 20 x 17 In. 743.00
Birth, Fraktur, Baptism, Tulips, Stylized, Hand Drawn, George Wohlfart, Frame, 1812, 15 x 18 In. . 1375.00
Brochure, Empress Of Scotland Cruise, World Itinerary, 1928, 11 x 16 In., 20 Pages 24.00
Catalog, Colt Fire Arms, 1933, Blue Letters, 9 x 7 In. 55.00
Catalog, Durable Toy & Novelty Co., 5 1/2 In. 22.00
Catalog, Glen Bros., 1928, Rochester, N.Y., 24 Pages 15.00
Catalog, Iver Johnson, Bicycles, Motorcycles, Firearms, 1915, 6 3/4 x 4 3/8 In., 84 Pages 199.00
Catalog, James Purdey & Sons, 1931, Black Covers, Gold Embossing, 7 3/8 x 9 1/2 In. 80.00
Catalog, LC Smith Hunter Arms Co., 1906, 9 1/4 x 7 3/4 In. 450.00
Catalog, Marble's Arms, 1914, No. 17, Pocket, 6 1/4 x 3 1/2 In., 56 Pages 326.00
Catalog, Marble's Outing Equipment, 1929, Pocket, 6 x 3 1/4 In., 32 Pages 28.00

Catalog, Old Town Canoes & Boats, 1940, Couple In Red Canoe, 38 Pages 75.00
Catalog, Remington Firearms, 1929, Geese, Flying, Waves, Pocket, 4 x 7 In., 32 Pages 22.60
Catalog, Sherer's Teapot, 1900, November, Chicago, 10 x 14 In., 20 Pages 18.00
Catalog, Smith & Wesson, 1917, Catalog D, Photographer, Mountain Lion, 6 x 4 3/4 In. 303.00
Catalog, Stevens Rifle Telescopes, c.1910, 5 1/4 x 7 3/4 In., 32 Pages 137.00
Catalog, Wallace Nutting Pictures, 1912, 7 x 10 In., Nearly 100 Pages 176.00
Confederate Bonds, Uncut, $500, Coupons, Signed, Numbered, 1864, 27 x 16 1/2 In. 138.00
Drawing, Architectural, Elevation, Louis H. Sillivan, Schlesinger & Mayer, 1903, 20 x 33 In. 2820.00
Family Record, Leaves, Watercolor, Blue Ground, Levi Duke, Persis Chafin, c.1822, 18 x 14 In. 748.00
Family Record, Tree, Birth, Death, Watercolor, S. & A.M. Matthews, 1763-1813, 13 x 15 In. 468.00
Family Record, Watercolor, Ink, Balsbaugh, Lancaster, 19th Century, 12 1/2 x 8 In. 960.00
Fraktur, Angels, Birds, Printed, Hand Colored, D.P. Lange, Pa., Frame, c.1826, 14 x 18 In. 201.00
Fraktur, Birth & Baptism, Birds, Tulips, Northampton County, July, 1800, 7 5/8 x 7 5/8 In. 4185.00
Fraktur, Birth & Baptism, Flowers, Angels, Elsabeth Krimm, Frame, 1795, 13 1/4 x 16 In. 990.00
Fraktur, Birth & Baptism, Flowers, Figures, Birds, Georg Bikel, 1814, 12 1/2 x 15 5/8 In. 2750.00
Fraktur, Birth & Baptism, Flowers, Lea Sechler, Northampton County, Pa., 1810, 13 x 16 In. 1650.00
Fraktur, Birth, Arched Flower Wreath, Sprays, Maria Mechling, Frame, 1811, 8 1/2 x 13 1/2 In. ... 1100.00
Fraktur, Birth, Birds, Hand Drawn, Maria Moyer, Frame, 1832, 12 x 10 1/2 In. 1540.00
Fraktur, Birth, Crown, Wreath, Man In Halo, Jacob Zimmerman, Frame, 1818, 16 1/2 x 11 In. 303.00
Fraktur, Birth, Flowers, Birds, Philip Merensel, Frame, 1787, 15 1/2 x 18 1/2 In. 715.00
Fraktur, Birth, Flowers, Vine, Hand Drawn, Henrich Acker, 1775, 7 1/2 x 12 1/2 In. 1815.00
Fraktur, Birth, Hearts, Tulips, Watercolor, Pen & Ink, Laid Paper, Frame, 1797, 15 x 18 In. 1610.00
Fraktur, Birth, Shields, Flowers, Martin Brechall, Frame, 1808, 16 x 19 In. 2185.00
Fraktur, Birth, Tulip, Stylized Tree, Fern, Susannah Deeter, July 28, 1817, Frame, 8 x 6 In. 518.00
Fraktur, Heart, Birds, Tulips, Inscriptions, Pennsylvania Dutch, c.1807, 13 x 16 In. 440.00
Fraktur, Hearts, Tulips, Lambs, Inscriptions, Watercolor, Stippling, c.1834, 13 x 16 In. 1058.00
Fraktur, Kissing Birds, Illuminated, Gilt Frame, 1763, 6 1/4 x 6 1/4 In. 358.00
Fraktur, Marriage, Watercolor, Pen & Ink, Laid Paper, Spangenberg, c.1795, 15 x 10 In. 13200.00
Fraktur, Woman, In Dress, Wood Block Print, Signed, David Bixler, Frame, 3 3/4 x 3 In. 605.00
Land Grant, Aaron Dazey, 160 Acres, Signed By Abraham Lincoln, Seal, c.1862, 14 x 22 In. 230.00
Letterhead, Wells Fargo, Office General Agent, Red, White & Blue, 1900, 8 x 5 In. 50.00
Magazine, True, 25th Anniversary Issue, February, 1961 .... 15.00
Mask, Uncle Same, Sloan & Woodward, 1904, 13 In. 110.00
Menu, Hotel Cadillac, Thanksgiving '98, Embossed Letters, Detroit, 6 x 8 In., 3 Pages 140.00
Menu, Riviera Restaurant, San Francisco, 1945 .... 12.00
Menu, Sauers, Route 22, Steubenville Pike, Phone Imperial 9150, 1932 .... 12.00
Merit Reward, Bird, On Branch, Flowers, Hand Drawn, Frame, 4 1/4 x 3 1/2 In. 2090.00
Newspaper, Chicago Daily Tribune, Dewey Defeats Truman Headline, 1948 .... 1390.00
Pamphlet, Important American Game Birds, L.B. Hunt Illustrations, DuPont, 1917 .... 138.00
Receipt, Hand Scribed, Signed, Isaac Bowers, Minuteman, Boston, Sept. 20, 1811, 9 x 8 In. 185.00
Reward Of Merit, 2 Birds, Stylized Flower, Hand Drawn, Illuminated, Frame, 4 x 3 1/4 In. 745.00
Reward Of Merit, Bird, On Branch, Stylized Flowers, Hand Drawn, Ink, 4 1/4 x 3 1/2 In. 2090.00
Reward Of Merit, Stylized Flowers, Pedestal, Hand Drawn, Maple Frame, 4 3/4 x 3 1/2 In. 495.00
Stock Certificate, Delling Motors Co., Signed, Company President, Orange, Brown, 1925-26 ..... 100.00

PAPER DOLLS were probably inspired by the pantins, or jumping jacks, made in eighteenth-century Europe. By the 1880s, sheets of printed paper dolls and clothes were being made. The first paper doll books were made in the 1920s. Collectors prefer uncut sheets or books or boxed sets of paper dolls. Prices are about half as much if the pages have been cut.

Boston Lady & Her Children, 3 Dolls, 10 Outfits, Box, c.1850, 4 3/4 x 7 In. 1998.00
Box Only, Lucile Grahn, First Dancer Of London, Lithograph, 1800s, 4 3/8 x 6 3/4 In. 323.00
Fannie Gray, Blond, 5 Outfits, Hand Drawn, Second Set, Box, 1853, 6 x 8 In. 3408.00
Fanny Gray, Crosby Nichols & Co., Box, c.1854, 7 x 8 1/4 In. 5581.00
Gone With The Wind, Clark Gable, Vivien Leigh, Anne Rutherford, Merrill, 1940 .... 300.00
Judy Garland, 3 Dolls, 30 Outfits, Tom Tierney, 1982, Uncut 13.00
Le Cavalier, Figure, Hand Tinted, 7 Horses, Partial Box, 1800s, 9 x 12 1/2 In. 499.00
Psyche, 20 Outfits, 6 Hats, Journal De Modes, 1830-70, France, 8 In. 1998.00
Teddy Bear, 5 Outfits, Hats, Baseball Uniform, J. Ottmann, c.1907, 10 In., Uncut 600.00

PAPERWEIGHTS must have first appeared along with paper in ancient Egypt. Today's collectors search for every type, from the very expensive French weights of the nineteenth century to the modern artist weights or advertising pieces. The glass tops of the paperweights sometimes have been nicked or scratched, and this type of damage can be removed by polishing. Some serious collectors think this type of repair is an alteration and will not buy a repolished weight; others think it is an acceptable technique of restoration that does not change the value. Baccarat paperweights are listed separately under Baccarat.

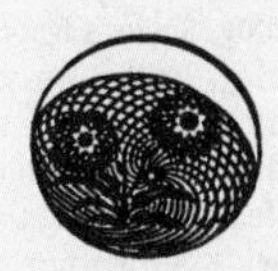

Advertising, Amherst Buffalo Cooperative Stove Co., 7/8 x 4 x 2 1/2 In. 27.50
Advertising, Big 4, Dean Chase, Columbia Counter, M C Hallett, J C F Phinney, 4 x 2 1/2 In. 55.00
Advertising, Col. Albert A Pope, Manufacture Of Bicycles, 4 1/8 x 2 5/8 In. 55.00
Advertising, Haskell, Tumblers, Fruit Jars, Jellies, Dice, c.1903, 2 3/4 In. 170.00
Advertising, John P. Lovell Arms Co., Reverse Painted, 4 x 2 1/2 In. 565.00
Advertising, Lamb Club Whiskey, Gold Leaf Border, 7/8 x 3 7/8 x 2 1/2 In. 110.00
Advertising, Maccar Truck Dealership, Celluloid, Mirror, 3 1/2 In. 231.00
Advertising, New Hampshire Bedding Co., Dice, Mirror, 7/8 x 4 1/4 x 2 3/4 In. 84.00
Amos 'n' Andy, 4 In. 303.00
Blown Glass, Clear, Devils Fire, Applied Finial, Rings, Teardrop, 1870-80, 5 1/4 In. 154.00
Boar, Karg Bros., Pigskin Leather Dealer, 3 3/4 x 5 1/2 x 2 1/4 In. 330.00
Boston & Sandwich, Fruit, Blueberry, Green Leaves, 2 x 3 In. 1100.00
Boston & Sandwich, Poinsettia, Double, Blue, Center Cane, 2 x 3 1/4 In. 330.00
Boston & Sandwich, Poinsettia, Jasper Ground, Millefiori, 2 x 3 In. 386.00
Boston & Sandwich, Poinsettia, Jasper Ground, Stippled Ground, 2 1/4 x 2 3/4 In. 770.00
Boston & Sandwich, Poinsettia, White Latticinio Ground, 2 x 3 In. 248.00
Bronze, Faubourg St. Honore, Line Vautrin, c.1950, 1/2 x 6 3/4 x 1 1/4 In. 8400.00
Bronze, Gilt, La Liberation De Paris, Line Vautrin, c.1945, 2 In. 1080.00
Crimped Petal Rose, White, Green Leaf Ground, Clear Sphere, Flared Base, 2 1/2 x 2 3/4 In. 115.00
Dog, Frosted, Scallop & Point Base, Hollow, 5 x 4 1/4 In. 198.00
Dog, Reclining, Bronze, Chinse, 19th Century, 4 In. 646.00
Figural, Elephant, Cast Iron, 3 1/2 In. 40.00
Foo Dog, Reclining, Bronze, Chinse, 18th Century, 1 1/2 In. 294.00
Funeral Car Equipment Co., Celluloid, Mirror, Round, 3 1/2 In. 209.00
Hat, Cavalry Officer's, Iron, Pre WWI, 1 x 2 1/2 In. 41.00
Hercules Gunpowder Co., Sand Filled, Label, 3 5/8 x 2 3/8 In. 231.00
John Degenhart, Amethyst Overlay, Square, 5 Oval Apertures, Orchid, 2 1/4 x 3 In. 413.00
Lucite, Encased Minnow Lure, Johnson 75th Anniversary, Box, 3 5/8 x 2 x 1 1/2 In. 26.00
Lundberg, Blue Iridescent, 3 Yellow Hooked Feathers 173.00
Metal, Bulldog, Mutual Electric & Machine Company, Detroit, Early 1900s, 5 In. 115.00
Millefiori, Spherical, Flowers, 7 Rings, 3 x 2 In. 633.00
Millville, Friendship, 2 Hearts, White Powder Pick Up, 2 1/2 x 3 1/2 In. 248.00
Millville, Friendship, Painted Dove, From A Friend, Pontil, 2 x 3 1/4 In. 1540.00
Millville, Umbrella, Trumpet Flower, Pedestal Base, Cut Top, 3 1/2 x 3 In. 220.00
Millville, Umbrella, Trumpet Flower, Pedestal Base, Cut Top, 4 x 3 1/2 In. 468.00
New England Glass Co., Amber, Whimsical, 5 Applied Glass Dots, Pontil, 3 1/2 In. 275.00
New England Glass Co., Apple, Hollow Blown, Glass Wafer Base, 3 In. 1150.00
New England Glass Co., Fruit Bouquet, Fruit, Latticinio, 2 1/4 x 3 In. 330.00
New England Glass Co., Millefiori, Nosegays, Leaf Ground, Clear Sphere, 2 x 1 3/8 In. 403.00
New England Glass Co., Mixed Fruit, Flowers, Apples, Leaves, 3 x 3 1/4 In. 1045.00
New England Glass Co., Poinsettia, Double, Purple, White Latticinio, 2 x 2 1/2 In. 220.00
New England Glass Co., Spoke Millefiori, White Latticinio Ground, 2 x 3 In. 770.00
Pear, Hollow Blown, Glass Wafer, 3 In. 604.00
Ransbottom Bros. Pottery Co., Roseville, Ohio, Picture, 4 Brothers 185.00
Snowdome, Cinderella's Midnight Magic, Standing On Steps, Carriage 167.00
Snowdome, Liberty Belle Riverboat, Steamboat Mickey As Captain 130.00
Snowdome, Mary Poppins, St. Paul's Cathedral, Plays Feed The Birds 314.00
Snowdome, Peter Pan & Tinker Bell, Flying Around Big Ben Clock Tower 168.00
St. Louis, Nosegay, Cut Diamond Base, Millefiori Flowers, 2 x 3 In. 468.00
St. Louis, Posy, Millefiori Cluster, Leaves, Garland, 1 3/4 x 3 In. 303.00

Star Shape, Sepia Picture & Our Hero-Admiral Dewey, 6 1/4 In. 75.00
Sulphide, General Burnside, End Of Day, 2 In. 192.00
Wm. McKinley, 7/8 x 4 x 2 1/2 In. 28.00

PAPIER-MACHE is made from paper mixed with glue, chalk, and other ingredients, then molded and baked. It becomes very hard and can be painted. Boxes, trays, and furniture were made of papier-mache. Some of the nineteenth-century pieces were decorated with mother-of-pearl. Papier-mache is still being used to make small toys, figures, candy containers, boxes, and other giftwares. Furniture made of papier-mache is listed in the Furniture category.

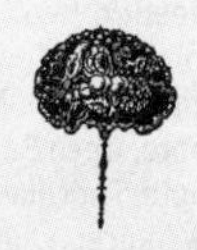

Box, Black Lacquer, Gold Scenes, Figures, In Garden, Round, 3 x 3 1/4 In. 38.00
Box, Handsome Gentleman In Top Hat, France, 12 1/2 x 5 1/2 x 1 1/2 In. 36.00
Box, Mother-Of-Pearl Decorations, 6-Sided, 1800s, 5 x 5 x 3 In. 185.00
Button, Black Mother-Of-Pearl Inlay, 3 Flowers, 2 Sets Of Leaves, 3/4 In. 10.00
Coaster, Red Roses, Leaves, Gold Ground, Papier-Mache Box, Round, Japan, 6 Piece 30.00
Desk Folio, Parcel Gilt, Black Lacquered, Eglomise, Paste Jewel Panel, 9 x 12 In. 645.00
Dresser Box, Victorian Lady, Lace Scarf, Pink Lining, 5 1/2 x 5 5/8 x 3 In. 125.00
Jewelry Box, Hand Painted, Bird, Flowers, Leaves, Black Ground, Persia, 1800s, 4 5/8 In. 200.00
Mask, Ottofuko, Japan, 1900s, 8 1/4 In. 69.00
Pin Tray, Man, Flower Border, 4 1/4 In. 45.00
Tray, Black Lacquer, Flowers, Vines, Raised Scalloped Edge, Gilt Accent, 32 x 25 In. 940.00
Tray, Cushion Shape, Multicolored, Flower & Gilt, Victorian, 26 x 26 In. 612.00
Tray, Flowers, Black Lacquer, Gilt, Multicolored, Mother-Of-Pearl, Oval, 1800s, 30 x 25 In. 1175.00
Tray, Lacquered, Irises, Butterfly, Japan, c.1900-20, 7 3/4 x 4 3/4 In. 26.00
Tray, Whiskey Bottle, Alcohol Proof, Round, Japan, 9 In. 25.00

PARASOL, see Umbrella category.

PARIAN is a fine-grained, hard-paste porcelain named for the marble it resembles. It was first made in England in 1846 and gained in favor in the United States about 1860. Figures, tea sets, vases, and other items were made of Parian at many English and American factories.

Basket, Child Pulling Doll Carriage, Late 1800s, 6 In., Pair 40.00
Bust, Abraham Lincoln, 9 In. 759.00
Bust, Charles Dickens, Staffordshire, Late 1800s, 14 1/2 In. 825.00
Bust, Classical Beauty, Early 20th Century, 8 1/2 In. 59.00
Bust, George Washington, 13 In. 748.00
Bust, John Bird Sumner, Robinson & Leadbeater, c.1880, 12 3/4 In. 1765.00
Bust, Lincoln, No Beard, Constitutional Freedom, 1860, 7 1/2 In. 4927.00
Bust, Man, Military Coat, Medal, Huttere, 1807, 14 In. 1020.00
Bust, U.S. Grant, 10 1/2 x 7 1/2 In. 995.00
Figurine, Amphitrite, With Cupid Blowing On Conch Shell, 21 x 9 In. 470.00
Figurine, Aphrodite & Eros, 23 1/4 x 11 3/4 In. 858.00
Figurine, Highland Mary, England, c.1870, 14 In. 235.00
Figurine, Le Nid, 2 Sleeping Children In Upholstered Armchair, A.O. Croisy, 15 x 14 In. 1900.00
Group, Allegorical, Eagle, Putti, Liberty Cap, Eagle's Nest, 11 In. 2000.00
Group, Woman, Seated, Dogs At Feet, Mounted As Lamp, England, 1800s, 11 3/4 In. 265.00
Pitcher, Bennington Type, Raised Flowers, White, 8 1/2 In. 330.00
Pitcher, Mount Ford, Raised Figures, c.1900, 10 In. 120.00
Syrup, Cover, Leaves, White, England, c.1857, 6 In. 145.00

PARIS, Vieux Paris, or Old Paris, is porcelain ware that is known to have been made in Paris in the eighteenth or early nineteenth century. These porcelains have no identifying mark but can be recognized by the whiteness of the porcelain and the lines and decorations. Gold decoration is often used.

Basket, Navette Form, Reticulated Sides, Satin Mulberry Bands, Marble Base, 11 x 14 In. 470.00
Basket, Reticulated, Acorns, Leaves, Gold Trim, 7 1/2 x 9 3/4 In. 575.00
Basket, Reticulated, Footed, Navette Shape, Gilded Exterior, Urn Reserve, 11 x 14 1/2 In. 705.00
Basket, Reticulated, Magenta Ground, Gildt, Multicolored Floral Reserves, 8 1/2 x 9 In. 881.00
Bottle, Scent, Figural, Woman, Hand On Hip, Multicolored, Gilt, c.1840, 13 x 5 In., Pair 529.00

Box, Cover, Jacob Petit, Schneeballen, Cartouche Shape, Flowers, 3 In. 235.00
Bulb Pot, Square, Cover, Swan Feet, Jacob Petit, Gilded Claret Ground, 8 x 5 x 5 In. 881.00
Cabaret A Deux, White & Gold, Coffeepot, Creamer, Masque Handles Sugar, Cups, Tray 763.00
Cachepot, La Courille Manufactory, Prunus Blossoms, Garland, Late 1700s, 7 3/8 In., Pair 1175.00
Candlestick, Jacob Petit, Rococo Style, White & Blue Bands, Applied Flowers, 10 In. 998.00
Chocolate Set, Cups, Swan Shape, Neck Handle, Deep Oval Saucers, Gold Trim, 6 Piece 998.00
Cologne, Cavalier, Modeled, Gothic Chapel, Troubadour Style, Early 1800s, 12 1/4 In. 380.00
Compote, Open Basket Weave, 7 x 8 In. 55.00
Compote, Reticulated, Gilt Borders, Mutlicolored Fruit Sprigs, c.1840, 7 3/4 In., Pair 600.00
Cup & Saucer, Cafe-Au-Lait, Flowers, Gilt Scrolls, Empire Blue Ground, J. Petit 150.00
Cup & Saucer, Cylindrical, Peg Footed, Bellflowers, Claret Ground, 19th Century, 4 1/8 In. 175.00
Cup & Saucer, Swan, Gilt Dagoty, Biscuit Porcelain, Early 1800s, 3 5/8 In. 881.00
Cup & Saucer, Tripodal, Swan Handle, Matte Black Ground, White Floral Garland, 3 1/4 In. 470.00
Incense Burner, Multicolored, Oriental Figure, Kneeling, c.1850, 6 x 5 In. 90.00
Lamp, Moderator, Bronze Mounted, Cylindrical, Electrified, c.1865, 22 x 6 In., Pair 940.00
Lamp Base, Gilded, Apple Green Ground, Columnar, Jacob Petit Style, 19 1/2 In. 1760.00
Plate, Denuelle, Gilded, Bearded Patriarch, Dutch Style, 9 1/8 In. 350.00
Plate, Dinner, Flower Bouquet, Gilt Scrolls, Leaves, c.1830, 10 1/8 In., 18 Piece 4800.00
Plate, Femme Mulatre St. Domingue, Woman, Landscape, Gilt Border, c.1820, 10 1/2 In. 5288.00
Plate, Gilded, Bleu Du Roi Ground, Acanthus, Flowerhead Wreath, Overglaze, 9 1/2 In. 205.00
Pot De Creme Set, 2-Tier Stand, 10 Cups, Gilt Banding, 1800s, 15 x 10-In. Stand 940.00
Tea & Coffee Service, Restauration, Neoclassical, 15 Piece 2115.00
Vase, Cornucopia, Multicolored Flowers, Gilt Leaves & Tendrils, 10 1/4 x 9 1/2 In. Pair 3055.00
Vase, Flower Shape, Red & Blue Seaweed Decoration, Gilt Trim, 5 1/2 In., Pair 173.00
Vase, Garniture, Cornucopia Galants, Rococo Style, Gilt, 13 In., Pair 1527.00
Vase, Garniture, Flower Reserves, Green Ground, 2 Handles, c.1865, 18 3/8 In., Pair 2000.00
Vase, Garniture, Handles, Footed, Painted, Figural Reserves, 13 1/2 In., Pair 1760.00
Vase, Garniture, Jacob Petit, Handles, Reticulated, Rococo Style, 17 In. 1410.00
Vase, Gilded, Amphora Shape, Italianate Landscape Reserve, 2 Handles, 10 In., Pair 1410.00
Vase, Hand Painted, Gilt Trim, Enameled Landscape, Red Ground, Gilt Foliage, 9 In., Pair 206.00
Vase, Man's Portrait, Peach, Gilt, Molded Floral Handles, Flared Leafy Rim, 15 In., Pair 940.00
Vase, Potpourri, Cover, Banded Gilding, Buff Ground, Enamel, Tavern Scene, 5 1/2 In., Pair 940.00
Vase, Romantic & Family Scenes, Green Ground, 2 Handles, c.1845, 18 1/2 x 7 1/2 In., Pair 1838.00
Vase, Spill, Castle In Landscape, Multicolored, Green Ground, J. Petit, 3 x 3 In. 410.00
Vase, Tulip Head Form, Curling Leaves, Leafy Green Base, 6 1/4 In., Pair 820.00
Vase, White, Flowers, Gilt Trim, Irregular Flared Rim, 2 Looped Handles, Footed, 10 In., Pair 69.00

PATE-DE-VERRE is an ancient technique in which glass is made by blending and refining powdered glass of different colors into molds. The process was revived by French glassmakers, especially Galle, around the end of the nineteenth century.

Mouse, Nibbling Flowers, Shaded, Frosted, Green, Amber, 2 x 5 In. 230.00
Paperweight, Mouse Sitting On Rock, Mottled Gray, Cream, DeCorchemont, 2 1/4 In. 345.00

PATE-SUR-PATE means paste on paste. The design was made by painting layers of slip on the ceramic piece until a relief decoration was formed. The method was developed at the Sevres factory in France about 1850. It became even more famous at the English Minton factory about 1870. It has since been used by many potters to make both pottery and porcelain wares.

Bowl, On Celadon, Chinese, c.1800, 20 x 8 In. 1950.00
Cup & Saucer, Camille Tharaud, Limoges, France, c.1925, 3-In. Cup, 5 1/4-In. Saucer 450.00
Humidor, Brass Tobacco Compartment, Riessler, 1800s, 5 1/2 In. 410.00
Plaque, Man, Woman, Cupid, In Cradle, Louis Solon, 1800s, 6 3/8 x 7 1/4 In. 7640.00
Plate, Woman, Eating Cherry, Art Nouveau, Flower & Swag Border, Limoges, 9 In. 495.00
Vase, Woman, Bare Breasts, Parcel Gilt, 2 Handles, Heinrich & Co., c.1885, 7 1/4 In. 295.00

PATENT MODELS were required as part of a patent application for a United States patent until 1880. In 1926 the stored patent models were sold as a group by the U.S. patent office and individual models are now appearing in the marketplace.

Animal Trap, No. 225628, John, William & Thomas Morris, 1880, 8 1/4 In. 2115.00

Apparatus For Lighting Railway Cars, No. 169658, I.F. Randolph, 1875, 11 In. 176.00
Apparatus For Warming & Ventilating Railroad Cars, No. 168426, J. Story, 1875, 8 In. 235.00
Bed Bottom Improvements, No. 201750, Clements & Decker, 1878, 10 In. 150.00
Beer Cooler, No. 9243, A. Hammer, Mahogany Box, Tin, Sept. 7, 1852, 9 1/2 In. 325.00
Blind Weaving Loom, No. 170885, Mahogany Frame, B.R. Murphy, 1875, 11 In. 295.00
Boot Jack, No. 22700, Cast Iron Frame, William W. Cansley, 1859, 11 In. 529.00
Clay Mill, No. 80008, Hand Crank, Brass, Wood, N.F. Potter, July 14, 1868, 10 In. 235.00
Compound Crank, Brass, Wood Base, Schoonover, No. 235, Nov. 30, 1880, 12 1/4 In. 276.00
Cradle, Self-Rocking, Open-Spring Motor, Seesaw Action, 13 In. 153.00
Elevating Cupboard Improvements, No. 202906, J.T. Westwood, 1878, 13 In. 499.00
Furnace, Metal Doors, Wood Case, Dome Lid, W.H. Churchman, Wisc., 6 x 10 In. 235.00
Gate Closing Device Improvements, No. 37001, L. Kolloff, 1882, 13 In. 355.00
Helicopter, Metal, No. 56057, Switzerland, 1911, 10 x 27 x 10 1/2 In. 6400.00
Improved Safety Valve For Steam Generators, No. 54716, V.D. Green, 1866, 8 In. 355.00
Printing Press, No. 77577, Mahogany Frame, W. Braidwood, 1868, 10 In. 325.00
Printing Press Improvement, No. 19672, Mahogany, Brills & Wood, 1858, 9 In. 499.00
Propelling & Steering Apparatus, No. 39936, R.H. Lecky, 1863, 11 In. 265.00
Revolving Seat Improvements, No. 140895, G.F. Dawson, 1873, 5 1/2 In. 150.00
Rotary Post Marking & Canceling Press, No. 175290, T & M Leavitt, 1875, 12 In. 999.00
Ventilator, No. 535276, Hermann Doerge, March 5, 1895, 8 In. 325.00
Washing Machine, No. 74919, Hand Cranked Agitator, Alford Lamb, 1868, 9 1/2 In. 265.00
Watchmaker's Lathe, Mahogany, Hand Cranked Shaft, 13 In. 380.00

PAUL REVERE POTTERY was made at several locations in and around Boston, Massachusetts, between 1906 and 1942. The pottery was operated as a settlement house program for teenage girls. Many pieces were signed *S.E.G.* for Saturday Evening Girls. The artists concentrated on children's dishes and tiles. Decorations were outlined in black and filled with color.

Bowl, 3 Geese, FL, 1912, 5 3/4 In., 4 Piece 1300.00
Bowl, Blue & White Band, LW, 1920, 7 In. 175.00
Bowl, Incised Hen Walking With Chick, 8 1/2 In., Pair 635.00
Bowl, Incised Rosettes, Ivory, 1911, 2 3/4 x 8 1/4 In. 1150.00
Desk Set, Cuerda Seca, Cobalt Blue, Holly, Green, Red, Blue Band, 6 Piece 9400.00
Pitcher, Band Of Rabbits, JG, 1914, 3 1/4 In. 170.00
Plate, Band Of Rabbits, JG, 1914, 6 1/4 In. 650.00
Plate, Duck Peering Upwards, Fannie Levine, 1926, 6 1/4 In. 690.00
Plate, Duck Walking In Grass, Chicory Blue Ground, Edith Brown, 1923, 7 1/2 In. 460.00
Plate, Triple Chick Chirping, Peering Upwards, White Glaze, Pink Speckling, 6 1/4 In. 1495.00
Plate Set, Lotus Flower Bands, Signed, 1910, 8 1/2 In., 12 Piece 2645.00
Vase, Landscape, Charcoal Black Glaze, Edith Brown, 1923, 10 1/2 x 5 1/2 In. 1955.00
Vase, Lotus Flower, Oval, White, Blue Glaze, Chicory Blue Glaze, 5 x 4 1/2 In. 1955.00
Vase, Twisted Panels, 1926, 8 3/4 x 7 1/2 In. 345.00

PEACHBLOW glass was made by several factories beginning in the 1880s. New England peachblow is a one-layer glass shading from red to white. Mt. Washington peachblow shades from pink to bluish-white. Hobbs, Brockunier and Company of Wheeling, West Virginia, made coral glass that they marketed as Peach Blow. It shades from yellow to peach and is lined with white glass. Reproductions of all types of peachblow have been made. Related pieces may be listed under Gunderson and Webb Peachblow.

Bowl, Hobbs, Brockunier, 2 3/4 In. 259.00
Cheese Dish, Cover, 5 1/2 x 9 In. 90.00
Creamer, 6-Crimp Rim, C-Scroll Handle, New England, 2 1/2 x 2 3/4 In. 120.00
Creamer, Amber Handle, Glossy, Hobbs, Brockunier 460.00
Creamer, Hobbs, Brockunier, 3 In. 575.00
Creamer, Wheeling Drape, Applied Clear Reeded Handle, Hobbs, Brockunier, 4 1/2 In. 345.00
Creamer, Wild Rose, Crimped, 3-Fold Rim, Alabaster Handle, New England, 4 In. 460.00
Cruet, Oil, Bulbous, Reeded Handle, Faceted Stopper, Hobbs, Brockunier, 7 1/2 In. 978.00

Cruet, Optic Ribbed, Daisies, Leaves, Gold Trim, Handle, Mt. Washington, 4 1/2 In. 3048.00
Cruet, Oval, Faceted Stopper, Applied Amber Handle, Hobbs, Brockunier, 7 1/4 In. 748.00
Cruet, Teepee Shape, Amber Handle, Glossy Faceted Stopper, Hobbs, Brockunier, 7 In. 1095.00
Decanter, Applied Reeded Handle, Amber Faceted Stopper, Hobbs, Brockunier, 9 1/2 In. 460.00
Dish, Sweetmeat, Twigs, Leaves, Flowers, Buds, Silver Plated Collar, Handle, Lid, 7 In. 520.00
Jug, Claret, Amber Reeded Handle, Rigaree Collar, Glossy, Hobbs, Brockunier, 9 1/2 In. 4600.00
Jug, Pelican, Amber Handle, Wheeling, 6 1/2 In. 2875.00
Mustard Pot, Oval, Glossy, Hinged, 2 1/2 In. 345.00
Nappy, Wild Rose, Heart Shape, Alabaster Handle, New England, 6 In. 460.00
Paperweight, Pear, New England, 5 1/2 In. 120.00
Pitcher, Applied Amber Handle, Hobbs, Brockunier, Wheeling, 4 1/2 In. 489.00
Pitcher, Square Mouth, Glossy, Hobbs, Brockunier, 8 In. 1150.00
Punch Cup, Applied Amber Handle, Hobbs, Brockunier, Wheeling, 2 1/2 In. 175.00
Punch Cup, Applied Reeded Handle, New England, 2 3/4 In. 150.00
Punch Cup, Wild Rose, Reeded Handle, New England, 2 3/4 In. 200.00
Rose Bowl, Glossy, New England, 3 3/4 In. 175.00
Rose Bowl, Worlds Fair 1893, New England, 2 3/4 In. 908.00
Saltshaker, Egg Lying Down, Columbia Exhibition 1893 Design, New England, 3 In. 120.00
Sugar, Silver Plated Holder, Hobbs, Brockunier, 7 1/2 In. 776.00
Sugar & Creamer, Optic Ribbed, Applied Loop Handles, Mt. Washington 690.00
Toothpick, Daisies, Diamond-Quilted, Bulbous, Square Mouth, Mt. Washington, 2 1/2 In. 2990.00
Toothpick, Wild Rose, Tricornered, Inverted Rim, New England, 2 In. 230.00
Tumbler, Fuchsia Shading To Amber, White Lining, Hobbs, Brockunier, 5 1/4 In. 345.00
Tumbler, Glossy, Hobbs, Brockunier, 3 3/4 In., 4 Piece 460.00
Tumbler, Opal Cased, Red To Yellow, Hobbs, Brockunier, 3 3/4 In. 200.00
Vase, Bottle Shape, Hobbs, Brockunier, 8 In. 180.00
Vase, Double Gourd, Enameled Mums, Leaves, Mt. Washington, 6 1/2 In. 4315.00
Vase, Jack-In-The-Pulpit, Blue Shaded To Pink, Mt. Washington, 12 1/4 In. 3450.00
Vase, Lily, Tricornered Rim, Mt. Washington, 8 In. 2875.00
Vase, Lily, Tricornered Rim, New England, 9 In. 605.00
Vase, Morgan, Glossy, Hobbs Brockunier, 8 In. ....635.00 to 865.00
Vase, Morgan, Griffin Base, Hobbs, Brockunier, 10 In. 1840.00
Vase, Shouldered, Glossy, Hobbs, Brockunier, 4 1/2 In. 520.00
Vase, Stick, Bulbous Base, Amber Rigaree, Glossy, Hobbs, Brockunier, 8 1/4 In. 1150.00
Vase, Stick, Bulbous Base, Glossy, Hobbs, Brockunier, 8 1/2 In. 1035.00
Vase, Stick, Bulbous Base, Glossy, Hobbs, Brockunier, 10 1/2 In. 805.00
Vase, Stick, Bulbous Base, Hobbs, Brockunier, 9 In. 863.00
Vase, Stick, Bulbous Base, Hobbs, Brockunier, 10 1/2 In. 805.00
Vase, Stick, Bulbous Base, Mt. Washington, 8 In. 2128.00
Vase, Stick, Bulbous Base, Rigaree Collar, Hobbs, Brockunier, 8 In. 635.00

PEANUTS is the title of a comic strip created by cartoonist Charles M. Schulz (1922–2000). The strip, drawn by Schulz from 1950 to 2000, features a group of children, including Charlie Brown and his sister Sally, Lucy Van Pelt and her brother Linus, Peppermint Patty, and Pig Pen, and an imaginative and independent beagle named Snoopy. The Peanuts gang has also been featured in books, television shows, and a Broadway musical.

Bowl, Spoon, Chef Snoopy, Stainless, Plastic Coated Bowl, Danara, c.1966 .... 8.00
Brunch Bag, Vinyl, Yellow, Zipper, Thermos Bottle 37.00
Bubble Bath Container, Snoopy, 8 In. 18.00
Coloring Book, Charlie Brown On Pitcher's Mound Cover, Saalfield, 1960, 32 Pages 10.00
Doll, Lucy, Flat, Rubber Like, Molded Pink Dress, 5 1/4 In. 25.00
Doll Set, Peanuts Gang, c.1960s, 5 Piece 150.00
Lunch Box, Have Lunch With Snoopy, Metal, Dome Top, c.1968 .... 23.00
Lunch Box, Red, Thermos Bottle, King Seeley, Unused, 1976 .... 39.00
Lunch Box, Wiener Roast, Peanuts Gang, Snoopy On Doghouse, Plastic, Red, Bottle, 1965 .... 65.00
Mug, Snoopy, Find A Good Spot & Everyone Else Moves In, 3 1/2 In. 12.00
Necktie, Peanuts Gang, Snoopy, No Pain No Gain 12.00
Nodder, Lego, Early 1960s, 6 In., 6 Piece 2178.00

Nodder, Snoopy Santa, Composition, c.1966, 4 In. 27.00
Ornament, Snoopy & Friends, No. 3, Panorama, Hallmark, Box 29.00
Ornament, Snoopy & Woodstock, Hockey, Hallmark, Box, 1979 .... 30.00 to 85.00
Ornament, Woodstock, On Present, Ceramic, Made In Japan, c.1965, 2 1/2 In. 26.00
Pin, Snoopy, Beagle Scout, White, Green, Metal Pin, 2 In. 10.00
Plate, Snoopy, Lying On Dog House, Christmas, Schmid, Box, 1977, 7 5/8 In. 28.00
Plate, Snoopy, Sleeping On Liberty Bell, Bicentennial, Schmid, 1976, 7 1/2 In. 32.00
Plate, Snoopy, Woodstock, Walking Tightrope, Circus, Melmac, 1965, Child's 9.00
Playset, Colorforms, Snoopy's Beagle Scouts, Stand-Up, Unused, Box, c.1965, 16 x 12 1/2 In. 85.00
Snowdome, Snoopy At School, Gang Around The Base, Musical, Peanuts Theme Song, 6 In. 40.00
Soaky, Snoopy, Camping, Red Scarf, Yellow Hat, Green Base, 9 3/4 In. 5.00
Tablecloth, Paper, Peanuts Gang, Package, 60 x 102 In. 7.50
Toy, Beanbag, Woodstock, Applause, 4 In. 8.00
Toy, Pull, Snoopy & Woodstock, Rotating Vinyl Ears, Romper Room, Hasbro, c.1972 .... 15.00
Toy, Snoopy & Woodstock, Ice Hockey, Windup, Keychain Attachment 8.00
Toy, Woodstock, Mechanical Walker, 2 3/4 In. 8.00
Tumbler, Snoopy & Woodstock, Flying Ace & His Mechanic, Welch's, No. 7 .... 2.00
Tumbler Set, Camp Snoopy, McDonald's, 1983, 6 In., 5 Piece .... 9.00 to 15.00
Wristwatch, Snoopy Playing Tennis, Denim Band, Box, 1970s 55.00

PEARL items listed here are made of the natural mother-of-pearl from shells. Such natural pearl has been used to decorate furniture and small utilitarian objects for centuries. The glassware known as mother-of-pearl is listed by that name. Opera glasses made with natural pearl shell are listed under Opera Glasses.

Box, Gold, Brass, Louis XVI Style, Round Miniature Portrait, 2 x 4 In. 325.00
Box, Hand Carved, Flower, Leaf, 5 x 3 x 2 In. 20.00
Toothpick, Abalone, Mechanical, Victorian, 2 1/2 In. 225.00

PEARLWARE is an earthenware made by Josiah Wedgwood in 1779. It was copied by other potters in England. Pearlware is only slightly different in color from creamware and for many years collectors have confused the terms. Wedgwood pieces are listed in the Wedgwood category in this book. Most pearlware with mocha designs is listed under Mocha.

Pearl

Bowl, Vegetable, Cover, Multicolored, Flowers, Flower Handle, 1800s, 10 1/2 x 7 In. 176.00
Cann, Brown Bands, Leaf Pattern, Snowflakes, Applied Handle, Early 1800s, 3 1/2 In. 595.00
Coffeepot, Dome Cover, Baluster, Leaves, Vines, Staffordshire, Early 1800s, 10 1/4 In. 660.00
Coffeepot, Dome Lid, Oriental Decoration, 1700s, 8 In. 468.00
Coffeepot, King's Rose, Baluster, Vine Border, Staffordshire, Early 1800s, 11 1/2 In. 2510.00
Creamer, Double Blue Stripes, Blue Band, Applied Handle, Leaf Terminals, 4 1/4 In. 45.00
Cup, Checkerboard, Center Dot, Multicolored, Loop Handle, Flared Base, 2 1/2 In. 250.00
Cup Plate, Flowers, Blue Edge, 4 In. 55.00
Figurine, Cat, Staffordshire, c.1800 .... 900.00
Figurine, Lion Tamer, Scroll Molded Base, Staffordshire, c.1825, 5 1/4 In. 4800.00
Figurine, Lion, Wood & Caldwell, c.1815, 5 In., Pair 4200.00
Group, Chariot, Staffordshire, c.1830, 10 In. 12000.00
Group, Royal Coat Of Arms, Earthenware, Walton, c.1820, 6 In. 4400.00
Group, Traveling Performers, Staffordshire, c.1825, 6 In. 4800.00
Jug, Portobello Type, Yellow On Brown Slip Ground, Chinoiserie Figures, 6 1/2 In. 360.00
Jug, Silver Luster, Transfer, By Plough Would Thrive, Let Wealthy & Great, c.1820, 5 1/2 In. 145.00
Mug, Blue & White, Oriental Motif, Applied Handle, 3 1/4 In. 58.00
Mug, Gunmetal Blue & Brown Bands, Applied Handle, Early 1800s, Child's, 2 In. 675.00
Pitcher, Cream3 Sets Of Double Blue Pinstripe, Blue Band, Loop Handle, 4 1/4 In. 45.00
Pitcher, Egg Shape, Flowers, Pink Border, Staffordshire, Early 1800s, 7 1/2 In. 239.00
Plate, Pheasant Sitting On Flower Branch, 4-Color, 9 3/4 In. 660.00
Plate, Soup, Flowers, Footed Bowl, Staffordshire, 10 & 6 1/2 In. 155.00
Platter, Scalloped Edge, Blue Feather, Flower Bouquets, 2 1/4 x 19 x 15 3/4 In. 259.00
Teapot, Oval Paneled, Eagle, Liberty, Staffordshire, c.1815, 7 In. 598.00
Tureen, Cover, Scalloped Blue Feather Borders, 8 1/2 x 13 1/4 x 9 In. 316.00
Vase, Spill, Bird Nesting, Staffordshire, 1815-20, 8 3/4 In. 2400.00

PEKING GLASS is a Chinese cameo glass first made popular in the eighteenth century. The Chinese have continued to make this layered glass in the old manner, and many new pieces are now available that could confuse the average buyer.

Bowl, Lotus, Green Over White, 7-Lobed Flower Form, 8 1/2 In. 230.00
Bowl, Red, c.1880, 3 1/2 In. 351.00
Bowl, White, 19th Century, 17 1/2 In. 235.00
Jar, Cobalt Blue, 4 Characters, Oval, 5 In. 1035.00
Jar, Lotus, Opalescent White, 1 3/4 x 2 3/4 In. 480.00
Jardiniere, Courtyard Scene, Enameled, Metal Mounts, 8 1/2 x 13 1/2 In. 205.00
Vase, Faceted, Cobalt Blue, 5 1/4 In. 1410.00
Vase, Lotus, Green Overlay, 9 In. 184.00
Vase, Shao Lao In Pine Grove, Baluster Shape, Green Over White, 20th Century, 9 In. 235.00

PELOTON glass is a European glass with small threads of colored glass rolled onto the surface of clear or colored glass. It is sometimes called spaghetti, or shredded coconut, glass. Most pieces found today were made in the nineteenth century.

Vase, Jack-In-The-Pulpit, Spiraling Rigaree, 13 In. 345.00

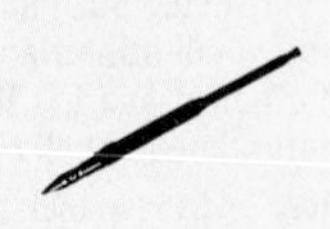

PENS replaced hand-cut quills as writing instruments in 1780 when the first steel pen point was made in England. But it was 100 years before the commercial pen was a common item. The fountain pen was invented in the 1830s but was not made in quantity until the 1880s. All types of old pens are collected. Float pens that feature small objects floating in a liquid as part of the handle are popular with collectors. Advertising pens are listed in the Advertising section of this book.

Ballpoint, Montblanc, Meisterstuck Legrand, Black, Gold Bands & Clip, 1970s 170.00
Ballpoint, Montblanc, Muller M, Burgundy, Brushed Silver, c.1950 .... 160.00
Ballpoint, Schaefer, White Dot, Sterling Silver, Diamond Crosshatch Pattern 86.00
Dip, Bakelite, Amber, No. 2 Nib, Holder, Bakelite, Black, Amber, Curled Shape, 6 1/2 In. 16.00
Dip, Mother-Of-Pearl, Gold Filled Band, Checkerboard Design, Victorian, 6 7/8 In. 95.00
Dip, Parker, Bakelite, Yellow, Art Deco Base, Black & Yellow Stripes, Square, 3 In. 70.00
Fisher Space, Apollo 7, Writes Upside Down Unused, c.1969 .... 45.00
Float, Bus Moves In Front Of World Trade Center Towers, New York Tourists, Plastic, 6 In. 8.00
Float, Eye Art, Picasso Style, Orange Plastic 2.25
Float, Johnny Quest, Climbs & Descends Rope, Snake Charmer, Plastic, Eskesen, Denmark 44.00
Float, Lady & The Tramp, Move Together & Apart, Blue Plastic 13.00
Float, Sailboat Floating Into Dock, Chicago Skyline, Orange Plastic 3.00
Float, Spy, Dark Coat, Hands In Pocket, Moves From Phone Booth, Central Intelligence Agency 13.00
Float, Woman Diving, Red Bathing Suit, Jantzen 40.00
Fountain, Alfred Dunhill, 14K, Flat Sides, Engine Turned Design, Black Clip, Germany, Box 128.00
Fountain, Chilton, No. 67R, Marbleized Brown, 14K Gold Nib 263.00
Fountain, Conklin, Endura, Cushion Point, 14K Gold, Black Plastic 57.00
Fountain, De La Rue, 18K Gold, Overall Textured Design, 1960s 900.00
Fountain, Esterbrook, Model SJ, Marbleized Blue, No. 2550 Extra-Fine Nib, c.1945 .... 30.00
Fountain, Eversharp, Dark Blue, 14K Gold Nib, Original Label 20.00
Fountain, Jaxon, Black Chased Hard Rubber, Supreme 8 Nib, 1901 Patent Date 35.00
Fountain, Koh-I-Noor, Acetograph No. 2, Box, Germany 30.00
Fountain, Parker, Blue Diamond, Vacumatic, Black, Inset Green Stripes, Gold Trim, Nib, 1940s 40.00
Fountain, Parker, Mark 1 Victory, Black, Newhaven Nib, England, c.1946 .... 72.00
Fountain, Schaeffer 1000, Brown & Yellow Stripes, Lifetime No. 79 Nib 70.00
Fountain, Swan, Blackbird, Black Hard Rubber, 14K Gold Nib, Mabie, Todd & Co., 1920s 160.00
Fountain, Swan, Mabie, Todd & Co., Gold-Filled Overlay, Engine Turned Wavy Lines, c.1920 .... 240.00
Fountain, Waterman, Ideal, 3V, Marbleized Green, Red & Mother-Of-Pearl, Gold Nib 100.00
Fountain, Waterman, Ideal, Black, Gold Latticed Filigree Overlay, c.1915 .... 250.00
Fountain, Waterman, Model 12, Eye Dropper, Clip Cap, Ideal Nib, c.1905 .... 200.00
Frank Fehr Brewing, Louisville, Ky., Floating Fehr Bottle 45.00

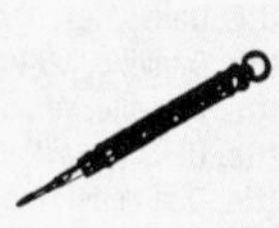

PENCILS were invented, so it is said, in 1565. The eraser was not added to the pencil until 1858. The automatic pencil was invented in 1863. Collectors today want advertising pencils or automatic pencils of unusual design. Boxes and sharpeners for pencils are also collected. Advertising pencils are listed in the Advertising category. Pencil boxes are listed in the Box category. Advertising pencils are listed in Advertising.

PENCIL, Autopoint, Truax-Traer Coal Sales Co., 5 1/2 In. 30.00
Mechanical, Aluminum, Kinsey, 5 In. 7.00
Mechanical, George W. Wentzler Mobilgas Mobiloil, Lebanon, Pa., Oil Sample 12.00
Mechanical, Sunshine Special, Mother-Of-Pearl, Missouri Pacific Railroad, QuikPoint, St. Louis ... 45.00
Set, Felix The Cat, Colored Pencils, American Lead Pencil Co., Box, 1931, 4 3/4 x 3 1/2 In. 39.00
Winchester Store, Bullet Shape, Brass Case, 1920s, 3 1/8 In. 190.00
PENCIL SHARPENER, Automatic, Automatic Pencil Sharpener Co., 1907 Patent, 4 1/2 In. 121.00
Baker's Cocoa Lady 125.00
Cowboy, Metal, Green Hat, Red Neckerchief, Blue Shirt, Japan, 1 1/2 In. ....85.00 to 110.00
Dandy, Automatic Pencil Sharpener Company, Chicago c.1919, 4 1/4 x 8 In. 150.00
Dixon Enduro No. 20, Metal, Plastic, 4 1/2 x 4 1/2 In. 40.00
Little Shaver, $1.25 Original Price, 1904 Patent, 4 In. 50.00
Metal, Violin, Bronze Color Patina, Germany, 2 1/2 In. 56.00
Roneo, Iron, Mechanical, Table Mount Clamp, N.Y., 6 3/4 In. 325.00
Timothy Mouse, Catalin Plastic, 1 3/4 In. 172.00
Wizard, 1906 Patent, 4 In. 33.00

PENNSBURY Pottery worked in Morrisville, Pennsylvania, from 1950 to 1971. Full sets of dinnerware as well as many decorative items were made. Pieces are marked with the name of the factory.

Pennsbury Pottery

Amish, Creamer, Lady & Heart, 2 1/2 In. 25.00
Amish, Pitcher, Farm Scene, 6 1/2 In. 175.00
Barbershop Quartet, Bowl, Pretzel, Oval, Signed 70.00
Dutch Talk, Bowl, Mottos, 2 1/4 x 9 In. 75.00
Plaque, B & O, Train, Inscribed, Veterans, Phil., 1955, 5 3/4 x 7 3/4 In. 65.00
Plaque, Don't Stand Up While The Room Is In Motion, 1949, 6 In. 45.00
Plaque, Pennsylvania Railroad Train, Marked, Tiger 1856, 5 3/4 x 8 In. 60.00
Plate, Angel, Holly Leaves, Candles, Marked, Yuletide Plate, Stumar, 1970, 8 In. 15.00
Plate, B & O Railroad, Lafayette, Brown, Black, Yellow, Maroon, Green Trim, 5 3/4 x 8 In. 44.00
Red Rooster, Chamberstick, 1 7/8 x 5 1/8 In. 40.00
Red Rooster, Creamer, White Ground, 4 1/2 In. 45.00
Red Rooster, Tip Tray, 6 x 8 In. 49.00
Slick Chick, Vase, Gourd, 5 In. 65.00

PEPSI-COLA, the drink and the name, was invented in 1898 but was not trademarked until 1903. The logo was changed from an elaborate script to the modern block letters in 1963. Several different logos have been used. Until 1951, the words *Pepsi* and *Cola* were separated by 2 dashes. These bottles are called *double dash*. In 1951 the modern logo with a single hyphen was introduced. All types of advertising memorabilia are collected, and reproductions are being made.

Bank, Dispenser, Tin, Plastic, Battery Operated, Linemar, Box, 9 1/2 In. 1067.00
Bottle, 70-71 Husker, Sealed, Full, 1975, 16 Oz. 10.00
Bottle, Alliance, Neb., Refreshing, Healthful, Famous For Over 30 Years, Green, 12 Oz. 44.00
Bottle, Anderson, S.C., Red & White ACL, 12 Oz. 1.70
Bottle, Burlington, N.C., Red, White & Blue Label, Double Dash 10.50
Bottle, Butte, Mont., 2 Full Glasses, Red, White & Blue Labels, Metal Cap, Unopened, 12 Oz. 28.00
Bottle, Canada Limited, Montreal, Que., Sparkling Pepsi, Contents, 1953, 10 Oz., 9 1/2 In. 1.95
Bottle, Casper, Wyoming, Double Dash, Red, White & Blue, Metal Cap, Unopened, 12 Oz. 21.00
Bottle, Clear, Red & White Pyro, Original Cap, No Deposit, No Return, Qt. 65.00
Bottle, Clemson, Undefeated Home Season, Contents, 1975, 12 Oz. 3.00
Bottle, Crystal Pepsi, Contents, Unopened, 16 Oz. ....18.00 to 25.00

Bottle, Dallas, Tex., Paper Label, Embossed Middle Label, Double Dash, 1941, 12 Oz. 22.00
Bottle, Dallas, Tex., Paper Label, Pepsi-Cola Around Middle, Original Cap, Contents, 12 Oz. 51.00
Bottle, Danville, Kentucky, 6 Oz., 8 In. 95.00
Bottle, Danville, Va., Single Dash, Red & White Painted Label, 1956, 10 Oz., 9 3/4 In. 6.00
Bottle, Diet Crystal Pepsi, Contents, Aluminum Top, 16 Oz. 12.00
Bottle, Diet Pepsi Free, Swirled, White Neck Label, Blue & Red Letters, 1/2 Liter 2.00
Bottle, Diet Pepsi, Glass, Canada, 1975, 1 1/2 Liter 3.00
Bottle, Double Dash, No Return Bottle, Short, 6 Oz. 22.00
Bottle, Durham, N.C., Double Dash, Raised Letters .... 22.00 to 36.00
Bottle, Exmore, Va., Drum, Bottle For Sale, D.O.C. 2311 .... 16.50
Bottle, Fargo, N. Dak., Double Dash, Red, White & Blue Labels, Metal Cap, Unopened, 12 Oz. 21.00
Bottle, Foil Label, Cap, 28 Oz., 11 In. 12.00
Bottle, Fountain Syrup, Blytheville, Ark., Red & White Label, Double Dash, 1940s 37.00
Bottle, Fountain Syrup, North Kansas City, Mo., Double Dash, Painted Label, Embossed, 12 Oz. 36.00
Bottle, Fountain Syrup, Pittsburgh, Pa., Double Dash, Unopened, 12 Oz. 50.00
Bottle, Greenville, S.C., Red & White ACL, 2 Full Glasses, Double Dash, 1948, 12 Oz. 22.00
Bottle, Kansas City, Missouri, Sparkling Pepsi, Double Dash, Embossed, 12 Oz. 6.00
Bottle, Los Angeles, Ca., Famous For Over 30 Years, Double Dash, Paper Labels, 12 Oz. 37.00
Bottle, Lyons, Kansas, Double Dash, ACL, Embossed Vertical Design, 1940s 12.95
Bottle, Marion, S.C., Sparkling Pepsi, Contents, 1956, 12 Oz. 20.00
Bottle, Merced, California, Double Dash, Red, White & Blue Label, 12 Oz. 10.00
Bottle, Nebraska Cornhusker Football, 1970s, 16 Oz. 8.00
Bottle, Norwich, N.Y., Double Dash, Tricolored, ACL, 12 Oz. 22.00
Bottle, Ogden, Utah, Red & White On Front, Metal Cap, Unopened, 12 Oz. 10.00
Bottle, Orlando Magic Schedule, Shaquille O'Neal, Longnecks, NBA, 1993, 6 Pack 6.00
Bottle, Pepsi Across Middle, Dispose Of Properly, Screw Top, 1978, Pt. 10.00
Bottle, Portsmouth, N.H., Single Dash, Red, White & Blue ACL, 12 Oz. 90.00
Bottle, Red & White Label, Single Dash, 12 Oz. 2.00
Bottle, Red & White Painted Labels, Etching, 1958, 12 Oz. 3.00
Bottle, Richmond, Va., Double Dash, Sparkling, ACL, Red, White, 1948, 8 Oz., 8 3/4 In. 13.00
Bottle, Roanoke, Va., Single Dash, Red & White ACL, 1959, 10 Oz., 9 3/4 In. 6.00
Bottle, Russia, Paper Label, Contents, Cap, Early 1980s 21.00
Bottle, Russia, Paper Label, Glass, 1981 .... 4.00
Bottle, San Jose Sharks, Greatest Turn In NHL, Longneck, Contents, c.1994, 12 Oz. 2.00
Bottle, Saxton, Pa., Red & White Printing, 1950s, 12 Oz. 2.00
Bottle, South Hill Virginia Bottling Company, Double Dash, c.1946, 12 Oz. 11.00
Bottle, Sparkling, Pepsi, Double Dash, Red, White & Blue Label, Cap, 1950s, 12 Oz. .... 6.00 to 11.00
Bottle, Suffolk, Va., 7 Oz. 20.00
Bottle, Tampa Bay Rowdies, Champions, Unopened, 1975, 16 Oz. .... 2.00 to 6.00
Bottle, Tarboro, N.C., Straight-Sided, Light Green, This Bottle Must Not Be Sold 10.50
Bottle, Texarkana, Texas, Single Dash, 1955 .... 10.00
Bottle, University Of Illinois, 1984 Rose Bowl, 1983 Big Ten Champs, Unopened .... 22.00 to 25.00
Bottle, Williamsport, Pa., Red, White, Blue, 12 Oz. 25.00
Bottle, World Champions Cincinnati Reds, Red & White ACL, 1975, 16 Oz., 11 In. .... 6.00 to 8.00
Bottle Cap, Cork Lined, Double Dash, Red, White, Blue, S. Carolina, 1940s 3.00
Bottle Cap, Cork Lined, Toledo, Ohio 3.00
Bottle Cap, Green Ground, White Letters, Unused, c.1910, 1 In. 31.00
Bottle Cap, Red Letters, Border, Yellow Ground, Unused, 1930s 10.00
Bottle Cap, World's Largest, Tin, 65th Anniversary, 1958, Fresno, Calif., 3 In. 10.00
Bottle Cap, Yellow Ground, Red Letters, Cork Lined, Double Dash 4.00
Bottle Carrier, Carton, Bottle Cap, For 16 Oz. Bottles, 8-Pack 3.00
Bottle Carrier, Carton, Bottle Cap, Yellow Stripes, Folding, For 12 Oz. Bottles, 6-Pack 3.00
Bottle Carrier, Drink Pepsi-Cola, Double Dash, Tin, Steel, Extending Handle, 4 x 5 x 8 In. 10.00
Bottle Carrier, Pepsi-Cola, Bigger, Better, Double Dash, Metal 20.00
Bottle Carrier, Pepsi-Cola, Double Dash, Metal, 11 x 8 1/2 x 5 In. 16.00
Bottle Carrier, Pepsi-Cola, Double Dash, Metal, Embossed, Red Paint, 4 x 8 1/4 x 5 1/2 In. 30.00
Bottle Carrier, Wood, 6-Pack, Metal Trim, Red, White & Blue Logo, 1930s 95.00
Bottle Label Set, Pepsi-Cola, Double Dash, Body & Neck Label, Salinas, Calif., c.1939 .... 10.00
Bottle Opener, Double Dash, Wall Mount, Star, c.1940 .... 31.00
Bottle Opener, Drink Pepsi-Cola, Wire Type, Long Handle, Ekco, 4 3/4 x 1 1/2 In. 3.00
Bottle Opener, Starr X, Brown Co., Wall Mount 8.00

Vintage handbags should be stored away from sunlight, heat, dust, and humidity. Store in fabric bags to prevent the accumulation of moisture, which damages Lucite and Bakelite.

Pepsi-Cola, Dispenser, Syrup, Original Spigot, Marked, Avon Co., c.1902, 19 In.

Bottle Opener, Starr X, Red Letters, Brown Co., Va., 3 1/4 x 2 3/4 In. 16.00
Calendar, Double Dash, 5 Cents, Cops, Full Pad, 1921, 18 3/4 x 9 In. 32.00
Cap, Colonial Beach Bottling Co., Colonial Beach, Va. 302.00
Cigarette Lighter, Pepsi Bottle, The Light Refreshment, KEM, 1950s, 2 3/4 In. 40.00
Clock, Drink Pepsi-Cola Ice-Cold, Double Bubble, Light-Up, Round, 1950s, 15 In. 770.00
Clock, Neon, Silver, Bottle Cap, 15 In. 43.00
Clock, Say Pepsi Please, Double Bubble, Light-Up, Round, 1950s 660.00
Cooler, Stand-Up, Metal, Pepsi Bottle Opener, 1970s, 18 x 36 x 36 In. 31.00
Crate, Pepsi, Wood, 24 Slots, Goldsboro N.C., Yellow, Metal Corners, 1976 .... 10.00
Crate, Pepsi, Wood, Yellow, Chattanooga, Tenn., For 32 Oz. Bottles, 1973 .... 2.00
Dispenser, Syrup, Original Spigot, Marked, Avon Co., c.1902, 19 In. .... *ILLUS* 31750.00
Display, Pepsi-Cola, Die Cut, Fold-Out, Bottle Holder, 13 1/2 x 6 5/8 In. 165.00
Matchbook, Pepsi-Cola, Air Squadron, 1930s-40s 8.00
Menu Board, Tin Lithograph, 19 1/2 x 30 In. 56.00
No Drip Bottle Protector, Red Letters, Waxed Paper, 1932 Patent, 7 x 4 1/2 In. 22.00
Radio, Pepsi Bottle Shape, AM, Box 11.00
Radio, Pepsi Bottle, Tube, Bakelite, 1947, 23 1/4 In. 850.00
Salt & Pepper, Swirl Bottle Shape, Glass, Plastic Cap, Box, 1958, 4 1/2 In. 10.00
Sign, A Nickel Drink, Worth A Dime, Celluloid Over Tin, 5 1/4 x 12 1/2 In. 3360.00
Sign, Bottle Cap, Metal, July, 1968, 19 In. 89.00
Sign, Bottle Cap, Red, White, Blue, 19 In. 105.00
Sign, Bottle Cap, Red, White, Blue, 1950s, 27 1/2 In. 358.00
Sign, Drink Pepsi, Frame, Embossed, Tin Lithograph, c.1910, 3 1/2 x 9 3/4 In. 224.00
Sign, Drink Pepsi-Cola Ice Cold, Bottle Cap, Metal, Double Dash, Red, White, Blue, 31 In. 510.00
Sign, Drink Pepsi-Cola, Delicious Delightful, Embossed Tin Lithograph, 4 1/2 x 11 In. 468.00
Sign, Drink Pepsi-Cola, Delicious Delightful, Red, White, Blue, Embossed, Tin Litho, 3 x 9 In. 660.00
Sign, Girl In Red Jacket, Holding Glass, Cardboard, Signed, Redmond, Frame, 30-In. Diam. 440.00
Sign, Pepsi's Best, Take No Less, Smiling Woman, Matte, Frame, 1940s, 24 x 36 In. 635.00
Sign, Pepsi-Cola, Refreshing, Healthful, Celluloid Over Tin, 5 Cents, Bottle, 1930s 3360.00
Sign, Red Letters, Plastic, Metal, 2-Sided, Rotating, Light-Up, Oval, c.1960, 10 x 20 In. 220.00
Sign, Santa Claus Holding Bottle, N. Rockwell, Cardboard, Die Cut, Easel, 1960s, 20 In. 35.00
Sign, Tin Lithograph, 17 1/2 x 48 In. 785.00
Tap Knob, Chrome, Plastic, Musical, 1940s 99.00
Thermometer, Buy Pepsi-Cola, Big Big Bottle, Tin, Wood, 27 In. 303.00
Thermometer, Buy Pepsi-Cola, Tin, 7 1/4 x 27 In. 168.00
Thermometer, Say Pepsi Please, Enamel, 7 1/4 x 28 In. 56.00
Tip Tray, Pepsi-Cola, Soda Fountain, Tin Lithograph, 6 4 3/8 In. 745.00
Vending Machine, 10 Cent, Model No. 27, Metal, 24 x 52 In. 935.00
Vending Machine, Block Letters, Bottles, 6 To 12 Oz., Free To $1, 53 x 24 x 21 In. 300.00
Vending Machine, Bottles, Old Logo, Blue, 25 Cents, La Crosse Cooler, Wisc., 60 In. 449.00

PERFUME BOTTLES are made of cut glass, pressed glass, art glass, silver, metal, enamel, and even plastic or porcelain. Although the small bottle to hold perfume was first made before the time of ancient Egypt, it is the nineteenth- and twentieth-century examples that interest today's collector. DeVilbiss Company has made atomizers of all types since 1888 but no longer makes the perfume bottle tops so popular with collectors. These were made from 1920 to 1968. The glass bottle may be by any of many manufacturers even if the atomizer is marked *DeVilbiss*. The word *factice*, which often appears in ads, refers to store display bottles. Glass or porcelain examples may be found under the appropriate name such as Lalique, Czechoslovakia, Glass-Bohemian, etc.

Alexandrite, Cut Diamond, Metal Mounts, Atomizer, Label, Germany, 3 3/4 In. 66.00
Amber Crystal, Faceted Molded Stopper, 5 1/4 In. 173.00
Amberina Glass, Optic Ribbed, Baluster, 4-Fold Rim, Footed, Libbey, 8 1/4 In. 1495.00
Amethyst, Rayed Pattern, Deco Looking, 5 x 2 1/2 x 4 3/4 In. 40.00
Atkinsons, English Lavender Water, Clear, Celluloid Cap, Basket, Box, Sealed, c.1929, 6 In. 660.00
Aureole Parfum Concentre, Pink, Stopper, Art Deco Style, 1/2 Oz., 4 1/2 In. 60.00
Black Boy, Painted, Chubby Sultan, Flower Bouquet, c.1918, 4 1/4 In. 60.00
Black Glass, Brass Encasement, Inner Glass Stopper, Dabber, Metal Cap, 2 In. 150.00
Black Glass, DeVilbiss, Chromed Metal, Black Stopper Disk, Dabber, c.1928, 6 In. 390.00
Black Glass, Enameled Detail, DeVilbiss Atomizer, Pyramid Box, c.1920, 4 1/4 In. 4800.00
Blown, Sea Horse Shape, Clear, Ribbed, Sapphire Blue Trim, 3 In. 250.00
Blue Crystal, Frosted Stopper, Women Dancing, 5 1/4 In. 690.00
Blue Crystal, Stopper, Impressed Roses, Long Dabber, 5 1/2 In. 345.00
Blue Crystal, Stopper, Star Cut, 4 1/2 In. 127.00
Blue Opaline, Brass Neck, Stopper, Intaglio Cameo, Atomizer, France, 6 3/4 In. 110.00
Boudray, Fleur Defendue, Clear, Composition Cover, Box, c.1924, 2 1/4 In. 360.00
Bourjois, Beau Belle, Clear, Metal Screw Cap, Silk Bag, c.1949, 2 In. 180.00
Boyen, Bouquet Des Allies, Clear, Glass, Black Stopper, Belgian Flags, 3 In. 140.00
Building, Clear, Domed, Pontil, Flared Out Lip, 5 1/8 In. 225.00
Building, Pontil, Rolled Lip, 6 1/4 In. 670.00
Cameo, Prussian Blue Design, Stemmed Flowers, Silver Lid, 1880, 4 In. 940.00
Cameo Glass, Citrine, Opal Overlay, Carved Flowers, Butterfly, c.1900, 4 In. 825.00
Cameo Glass, Red To Pale Pink, Gold Enameled White Flower Blossoms, 6 1/2 In. 690.00
Cameo Glass, Red, Flowers, Elongated Stems, Lay Down, Gold Flip Lid, 6 1/2 In. 3280.00
Canarina, Les Yeux Bleus, Blue Glass, Stopper, Rectangular, Overlapping Eyes, 2 In. 2645.00
Candlewick, Yellow, Imperial, Flower, DeVilbiss Atomizer, c.1953, 3 3/4 In. 195.00
Caron, Narcisse Noir, Glass, Black Glass Stopper, 3 1/2 In. 35.00
Caron, Voeu De Noel, Opalescent, Blue Bar Stopper, Molded Open Flowers, 3 1/2 In. 403.00
Carved Nut, 18K Gold Trim, Star, Handles, Foot, Round Body, 1 1/2 In. 1100.00
Cathedral, Clear, Pontil, Flared Lip, 5 3/4 In. 157.00
Cherigan, Chance, Jollivet, Glass, Green, Black, Applied Horseshoe, 1920s, 3 1/8 In. 480.00
Cherigan, Fleurs De Tabac, Jollivet, Clear, Gilding, Applied Leaves, Box, 1930s, 3 3/8 In. 660.00
Clear, Black Cap, Maiden Gathering Flowers, Red Box, 5 1/2 In. 175.00
Clear, Blue, Clear Stones Mounted, Flower Form, Dabber, Austria, 2 In. 80.00
Clear, Embossed, Pontil, Rolled Lip, 10 1/2 In. 269.00
Clear, Gray, Clear Stones, Dabber, Signed, Austria, 2 In. 58.00
Clear, Molded Butterfly, Stopper As Antenna, France, 3 In. 375.00
Clear, Silver Overlay, Flowers, Leaves, 2 1/2 In. 69.00
Clear, Stopper, Irregular Protrusions, 7 1/2 In. 35.00
Clear, Tooled Lip, Label, J. Picard, Paris, 6 7/8 In. 78.00
Clear Crystal, Gilded Pheasant, DeVilbiss Atomizer, c.1926, 9 1/4 In. 780.00
Cobalt Blue, Iridescent, White Swirl Pattern, Clear Teardrop Stopper, 1950s, 6 In. 45.00
Cobalt Blue, Stopper, Baluster, Dabber, 6 3/4 In. 175.00
Cologne, 8-Sided, Corseted, Cobalt Blue, Inward Rolled Mouth, Pontil, 6 x 2 1/4 In. 935.00
Cologne, 10 Ribs, Swirled To Right, Cobalt Blue, Pontil, Sheared, Tooled Lip, 2 3/4 In. 160.00
Cologne, 10-Sided, Corseted, Amethyst, Tooled Flared Mouth, 4 x 1 3/4 In. 358.00
Cologne, 12 Ribs, Cobalt Blue, Pontil, Sheared, Tooled Lip, 2 3/4 In. 78.00
Cologne, 12-Sided, Blue Green, Sloped Shoulders, 4 7/8 In. 258.00

Cologne, 12-Sided, Emerald Green, Tooled, Flared, 1860-80, 7 1/4 In. 1430.00
Cologne, 12-Sided, Sapphire Blue, Magenta Swirls, Tooled, Flared Mouth, Pontil, 11 1/8 In. 1210.00
Cologne, 20 Ribs, Swirled To Right, Cobalt Blue, Pontil, Sheared, Tooled Lip, Tam Stopper 448.00
Cologne, 26 Ribs, Cobalt Blue, Pontil, Sheared, Tooled Lip, 2 3/4 In. 146.00
Cologne, Blue Aqua, Bead & Flute, Tooled Mouth, 5 3/4 In. 125.00
Cologne, Christiani De Paris, Aqua, Pontil, Rolled Lip, France, 3 1/2 In. 215.00
Cologne, Clear, Dagger & Vine, Pontil, Tooled Flared Lip, 8 1/4 In. 160.00
Cologne, Clear, Embossed Ship, Pontil, Tooled Flared Lip, 4 3/4 In. 135.00
Cologne, Cobalt Blue, 8-Sided, Corseted, Rolled Lip, 6 1/8 In. 785.00
Cologne, Cobalt Blue, 8-Sided, Shaded, Corseted, Tooled Mouth, 7 In. 1345.00
Cologne, Cobalt Blue, 8-Sided, Sloped Shoulders, Applied Ringed Mouth, 7 1/2 In. 168.00
Cologne, Cobalt Blue, 12-Sided, Sloped Shoulders, Pontil, 7 3/4 In. 310.00
Cologne, Cobalt Blue, 12-Sided, Sloped Shoulders, Rolled Lip, 6 1/8 In. 258.00
Cologne, Cobalt Blue, 16 Ribs, Pontil, Tooled Mouth, 12 1/8 In. 728.00
Cologne, Cobalt Blue, Plain & Beaded Flutes, Tooled, Flared Mouth, 1860-80, 10 In. 2320.00
Cologne, Eau De Cologne, Superieure, Eagle, 12-Sided, Teal Blue, Tooled Flared Mouth, 11 In. 605.00
Cologne, Figural, Lamp Post, Clear, Ground Lip, Screw Threads, Metal Cap, 1880-1910 .... 179.00
Cologne, Lavender Purple, Molded, Bulbous Neck, Flared Rim, Panels, 5 1/4 In. 358.00
Cologne, Melon Ribbed Glass, Pink Flowers, Metal Cap, Smith Brothers, 5 In. 200.00
Cologne, Opalescent Clear, Bead & Flute, Tooled Mouth, 5 5/8 In. 179.00
Cologne, Opalescent Milk Glass, 8-Sided, Corseted, Tooled Mouth, 4 5/8 In. 560.00
Cologne, Opaque Blue, Clambroth, Gold Design, Mushroom Stopper, 7 In. 110.00
Cologne, Purple Amethyst, 8-Sided, Corseted, Rolled Lip, 4 5/8 In. 336.00
Cologne, Purple Amethyst, 12-Sided, Sloped Shoulders, Glass Stopper, 7 1/2 In. 336.00
Cologne, Purple Amethyst, Bead & Flute, Tooled Mouth, 5 7/8 In. 785.00
Cologne, Purple Lavender, 12-Sided, Sloped Shoulders, Pontil, Rolled Lip, 7 1/8 In. 308.00
Cologne, Silver, Enamel, Egg Shape, Slender Neck, Stopper, Russia, 1894, 8 3/4 In. 1410.00
Cologne, Teal Blue, 12-Sided, Tooled Mouth, 4 7/8 In. 135.00
Cologne, Trumpet, Silver, Crystal, Birmingham, England, c.1900, 6 3/4 In. 117.00
Cologne, Turquoise Blue, 10-Sided, Corseted, Tooled Lip, 6 1/2 In. 1905.00
Cologne, White Cut To Blue, Gold Highlights, Sandwich Cut Overlay, Stopper, 8 In. 148.00
Cologne, White Cut To Emerald Green, Gold Highlights, Sandwich Cut Overlay, 6 3/4 In., Pair 410.00
Corday, Femme Du Jour, Clear, Crystal, Gold Stopper, 3 1/2 In. 210.00
Corday, Orchidee Bleue, Clear, Crystal, Stopper, Flower Shaped, 2 1/2 In. 35.00
Corday, Tzigane, Frosted Glass, Impressed Zipper Design, Flat Stopper, Box, 5 1/2 In. 805.00
Coty, Cyclamen, Clear, Frosted, Stopper, Fairies, Blue Stain, Gold Label, 5 1/2 In. 2760.00
Coty, L'Aimant, Cream Skin, Black, Gold Writing, Metal Cap, Contents, 1/2 Oz. 20.00
Coty, L'Origan Eau De Toilette, Clear, Stopper, 4 1/4 In. 46.00
Crackle Glass, Peach, 3 Leaves, Hummingbird Stopper 13.00
Crystal, Amber Stopper, Flower Shape, 4 1/2 In. 46.00
Crystal, Bouquet Of Lilies Stopper, Dabber, 6 1/4 In. 219.00
Crystal, Clear, Octagonal, Steeple Form, Intaglio Cut, Pagoda Stopper, 9 1/4 In. 50.00
Crystal, Frosted, Stopper, Abstract, Multicolored, 3 3/4 In. 299.00
Crystal, Sterling Silver Cap, Inner Glass Stopper, Ribbon, Flower, 5 In. 230.00
Crystal, Stopper, Diamond Cut, 4 3/4 In. 69.00
Crystal, Stopper, Metal Fence, Flower Garlands, 6 In. 46.00
Crystal, Stopper, Molded Dancing Couple, 6-Footed, 7 1/4 In. 175.00
Cut Crystal, Hose Sprayer, 4 x 4 1/2 x 4 In. 125.00
Cut Glass, Amber To Clear, Engraved Floral, Hobstar Highlights, 5 1/4 In. 125.00
Cut Glass, Bellows Atomizer, Pat. 485015, 1 1/2 x 3 1/2 In. 100.00
Cut Glass, Blue Cut To Clear, Crosscut Diamond & Fan, Clear Stopper, 6 In. 385.00
Cut Glass, Clear, Frosted, Polished Lily-Of-The-Valley Stopper, 7 1/4 x 3 7/8 In. 44.00
Cut Glass, Cobalt To Clear, Peacock On Branch, Footed, Teardrop Stopper, Libbey, 8 In. 489.00
Cut Glass, Cranberry To Clear, Cane, 5 1/2 In. 250.00
Cut Glass, Cranberry, Circles, Ovals, Lines, Atomizer, New Bulb, 2 In. 95.00
Cut Glass, Diamonds, Teardrop Circles, Green, Stopper, 5 In. 65.00
Cut Glass, Emerald Green, Double, Brass Closures, No Stoppers, 5 In. 185.00
Cut Glass, Fan Top, 1940s, 4 3/4 x 3 1/2 In. 40.00
Cut Glass, Gilt Flip Top, c.1900, 4 In. 95.00
Cut Glass, Green, Double, Brass Closures, Clear Stoppers, 5 In. 225.00
Cut Glass, Hobstar & Lace, Blue To Clear, Stopper, C. Dorflinger & Sons, 4 1/8 In. 209.00

Cut Glass, Hobstar, Cane, Strawberry Diamond & Fan, Faceted Stopper, 5 In. 175.00
Cut Glass, Lily-Of-The-Valley Frosted Stopper, 7 In. 95.00
Cut Glass, Opaque Green, Double, Brass Closures, Clear Stoppers, 5 1/4 In. 250.00
Cut Glass, Ruby, Double, Brass Closures, Clear Stoppers, 5 In. 225.00
Cut Glass, Russian Pattern, Lay Down Shape, Embossed Sterling Silver Top, 9 In. 193.00
Cut Glass, Sterling Silver, Vial Shape, La Pierre Mfg. Co., c.1900, 4 3/4 In. 90.00
D'Orsay, Belle De Jour, Anniversary Edition, Glass, Lucite, Box, 1938, 6 3/8 In. 720.00
D'Orsay, Intoxication, Label, 3 1/2 In. 15.00
D'Orsay, Le Dandy, Black Glass, Octagonal, Stopper, 3 1/2 In. 196.00
Dabber, Peach Crystal, Long Finial, Nude Woman Covering Herself, 5 1/4 In. 127.00
Degenhart, Hand Blown, Paperweight Bottom, Stopper, John Degenhart, c.1974 .... 100.00
Dorothy Gray, Savoir Faire, Clear, Enameled Detail, Metal Screw Cap, c.1947, 1 5/8 In. 270.00
Double, Cranberry, Crystal, 10-Sided, Scrolled Silver Caps, England, Late 1800s, 4 x 1 In. 275.00
Elegant, Clear, Blue Interior, Metal Overlay, DeVilbiss Atomizer, c.1928, 7 1/2 In. 1140.00
Elizabeth Arden, Blue Grass, On Card, Easter Presentation Box, c.1934, 2 In. 240.00
Elizabeth Arden, My Love, Glass, Clear, Frosted, Sealed, Box, c.1948, 3 1/4 In. 510.00
Faberge, Tigress, Atomizer Style Top, Box, c.1960, 4 In. 85.00
Fadette, For Richard Hudnut, Clear, Frosted, Dabber, J. Viard, c.1923, 4 In. 2040.00
Filigree Brass Pedestal, Blue Rhinestones, Rose, Dabber Top, c.1950, 7 3/4 In. 95.00
Fish, Opalescent Glass, Sterling Silver Stopper, 2 1/2 In. 1265.00
Flask, Cranberry Cut To Clear, Engraved Silver Lid, Tapered, Quatrefoil Stars, 5 In. 380.00
Glass, Black, Infused Gold, Abstract, DeVilbiss Atomizer, 7 In. 374.00
Glass, Turquoise Blue, Stopper, Silver Cap, Molded Flowers, 2 1/4 In. 150.00
Goldtone Brass, Pedestal, Oval Base, Filigree Overlay, Amber Stone On Dabber 95.00
Green Crystal, Stopper, Base, Stopper Impressed With Flowers, 4 In. 92.00
Guerlain, Enameled, Opaline, Gilt Bronze Neck Mount, Stopper, c.1955, 7 1/2 In. 3480.00
Guerlain, Rose Du Moulin Azalee, Green, Glass Jar, 1907, 1 3/4 In. 127.00
Guerlain, Shalimar, Clear Crystal, Sealed, Box, 1940s, 5 1/2 In. 480.00
Hattie Carnegie, Carnegie Blue, Gilded Glass, Box, Wrapper, c.1944, 4 1/8 In. 660.00
Helena Rubenstein, Gala Performance, Glass, Clear, Sealed, Hang Tag, Box, c.1940, 6 In. 1320.00
Helena Rubenstein, Gala Performance, Stopper, Woman Dancing, 6 In. 400.00
Helena Rubenstein, Slumber Song, Clear Glass, Glass Dome, Base, c.1938, 6 1/2 In. 600.00
Hobnail, Blue, White Plastic Rose, 3 1/2 x 2 1/2 In. 32.00
Houbigant, Chantilly, Clear, Crystal, Stopper, Decanter Shape, 7 3/4 In. 255.00
House Of Tre-Jur, Stopper, Woman Dabber, Skirt, Symbols, Name, 2 1/2 In. 230.00
Imperial, Metal Overlay, Blue Jewels, DeVilbiss Atomizer, c.1926, 7 3/4 In. 10200.00
Ingrid, Ivory Crystal, Brown Graining, 1920s, 9 In. 1440.00
J.C. Boldoot, Crown Top, Porcelain, Open Car, Chauffeur, Amsterdam, 1920s, 3 3/4 In. 720.00
Lancome, Bel Automne, Clear, Frosted, Georges Delhomme, Labels, c.1947, 6 In. 720.00
Lancome, Fetes De L'Hiver, Clear, Frosted, Georges Delhomme, Labels, c.1959, 9 1/2 In. 960.00
Lancome, Limited Edition Of 1944, Frosted Glass Swirls, 4 3/4 In. 255.00
Lancome, Magie, Opalescent, Screw Cap, Georges Delhomme, Stand, Box, 1954, 5 3/4 In. 4200.00
Lanvin, Display, France, c.1930, 7 & 6 In., 2 Piece 235.00
Lanvin, My Sin, Black Glass, Gilded Black Stopper, 3 1/4 In. 90.00
Lanvin, My Sin, Black Glass, Gilding, Sealed, Box, 1930s, 3 1/4 In. 360.00
Lanvin, My Sin, Gilded Black Glass, Armand Rateau, 1930s, 2 1/8 In. 510.00
Lapis Lazuli Crystal, Molded Stylized Nude, Atomizer, 7 1/4 In. 460.00
Lavender, Gold, White Enamel, White, Coral Enamel Dots, 7 1/2 In. 58.00
Le Modern, Black Glass, DeVilbiss Atomizer, Metal Stand, c.1928, 3 1/2 In. 510.00
Le Parisien, Frosted Glass, Gold Metal Atomizer, Molded Nymphs, 6 1/4 In. 90.00
Lead Crystal, Wand Cut, Faceted, Prismatic, Western Germany, 5 1/2 x 1 3/4 In. 60.00
Legrain, Promenade A Paris, Frosted, Stopper, Woman Holding Flowers, 8 1/2 In. 196.00
Lentheric, Shanghai, Clear Glass, Stopper, Dabber, Deer Intaglio, Ball Shape, 4 1/4 In. 299.00
Lentheric Man's After Shave Powder, Brass Top, Paper Label, Partial Contents, 2 Oz., 4 In. 15.00
Les Parfum De Rosine, Arlequinade, Clear, Stopper, Enameled, Clear Panels, 6 In. 345.00
Letter Seal, Bulldog Shape, Bottle Inside, Austria, 3 1/2 In. 920.00
Lilly Dache, Dashing, Composition, Glass Interior, Silk Stand, Cover, c.1940, 7 3/8 In. 2600.00
Lionceau, Parfum Pour Blondes, Jollivet, Glass, Green, Enameled, Box, c.1930, 2 1/2 In. 300.00
Maja, Fleurys Paris, Clear, Frosted, Tiara Form Stopper, Charcoal Stained Base, 4 1/2 In. 518.00
Maja, Fleurys Paris, Frosted, Stopper, Tiara Form, 4 1/4 In. 518.00
Man's Shoe, Crystal, Round Stopper, 4 In. 140.00

Max Factor, Little Rabbit Wild Musk, Necklace, Box, 1 1/2 In. 69.00
Mennen, Hard Hat, Clear, Orange Workman's Hat, 9 1/2 In. 69.00
Milk Glass, Green, Embossed Latticework, Gold Trim, Stopper, 6 1/2 In. 35.00
Molded Glass, Opaque, White, Oval Side Panels, Scalloped & Flowered Stopper, 4 1/2 In. 35.00
Molinard, Habanita, Clear, Glass, Stopper, Cube, Raised Square Facet, 6 1/2 In. 230.00
Monkey, Red Mohair, Vial, Schuco, 1920s 975.00
Monument, Clear, Pontil, Flared-Out Lip, 6 3/8 In. 235.00
Moonstone Opalescent, Anchor Hocking, 1941-46 .... 10.00
Myon, 1000 Joies, Crystal, Metal Overcap, Inner Stopper, Perfume, Box, 3 1/2 In. 1380.00
Myon, Coeur Du Femme, Green Over White Crystal Inner Stopper, Brass Cap 2185.00
Nestly, Numero 7, Opalescent Glass, Box, 1920s, 4 1/4 In. 450.00
Niki De Saint Phalle, First Edition, Blue Glass, Metal Cap, Entwined Snakes, 3 In. 255.00
Nina Ricci, Fille D'Eve, Frosted, Stopper, Leaf Shape, Box, Label, 1 1/2 In. 115.00
Nina Ricci, L'Air Du Temps, Clear Glass, Stopper, Scalloped Edges, 6 1/2 In. 115.00
Opaque, Molded, Scalloped, Flower Stopper, Raised Oval Panels, 4 1/2 x 3 1/2 In. 35.00
Opaque Lapis Lazuli Crystal, Stopper, Chrysanthemums, Dabber, 5 1/2 In. 2185.00
Orales Freres, L'Odeur D'Amour, Black Glass Stopper, Partial Contents, 3 In. 25.00
Paperweight Glass, White Jasmine, Green Stems, Orient & Flume, 5 1/4 In. 290.00
Parfums De Paul, Nuit De Mariage, Cobalt Blue, Silver Detail, J. Viard, c.1928, 4 1/4 In. 720.00
Park & Tilford, High Heels, Clear Glass, Gold Cap, Sits In High Heel Shoe, Box, 2 1/2 In. 253.00
Porcelain, Woman Looking In Mirror Stopper, Pair, Germany, 6 3/4 In. 80.00
Potter & Moore, Mitcham Lavender, Clear, Ice Skater, Metallic Celluloid, 1920s, 4 1/4 In. 360.00
Pressed Glass, Art Deco Shape, Pink, Brass Top, DeVilbiss Atomizer, 3 1/2 In. 75.00
Pressed Glass, Frosted, Vaseline, Squat, Flower Blossom Stopper, 1 7/8 x 2 5/8 In. 77.00
Prince Matchabelli, Beloved, Blue, Golden Cross Stopper, Foil Label, Miniature 70.00
Prince Matchabelli, Duchess Of York, Amber, 5-Sided, 1924, 3 In. 785.00
Renaud, Notchenka, Black Glass, Green Patina, J. Viard, 1930s, 3 In. 1920.00
Rendes, Ting-Shang, Clear, Asian Mask, Box, c.1925, 2 3/4 In. 11400.00
Revillon, 4 Vents, Clear, Box, Labels, 1950s, 7 In. 720.00
Ricci, L'Air DuTemps, Swirls, Gold Wash Cap, 2 Greek Women Emblem, Atomizer, 5 In. 16.00
Rigaud, Fleur De Gloire, Clear, Frosted, Stopper, Molded Flowers, Center Label, 3 3/4 In. 920.00
Rosebud Perfume Co., Woodsboro, Md., Box, 2 7/8 x 1 1/2 In. 16.00
Rosine, Chez Poiret, Clear, Green, 2 Labels, c.1912, 2 1/2 In. 480.00
Rosine, Qui Es-Tu?, Clear, Black Glass, Label, c.1926, 3 In. 570.00
Ruby Glass, Vial, Engraved Silver Lid, Double End, Late 19th Century, 5 In. 176.00
Schiaparelli, Si, Glass, Enameled, Gilded, Ribbon, Faux Seal, Stand, c.1957, 4 3/4 In. 660.00
Schiaparelli, Sleeping, Candle Stick Shape, Gold Trim, 3 1/8 In. 95.00
Schiaparelli, Sleeping, Glass, Clear, Red, Box, c.1938, 5 1/4 In. 540.00
Schiaparelli, Succes Fou, Enameled White Glass, Gilded, Box, c.1953, 2 1/2 In. 1320.00
Schiaparelli, Zut, Glass, Stopper, Woman's Leg Shape, Frosted, Ribbon, 3 1/2 In. 320.00
Silver Overlay, Globular, Cranberry Glass, Stopper, Gorham, 6 1/4 x 4 In. 900.00
Sitting Cat, Frosted Glass, Stopper, 3 In. 405.00
Smarza, Oktobra Julileja, Clear Glass, Stopper, Protrusions, Red, Gold Labels, 4 In. 130.00
Steuben Glass, Alabaster, Teardrop Stopper, Rosaline, Disc Foot, 7 1/2 In. 575.00
Steuben Glass, Amethyst, Melon Ribbed, Elongated Neck, Teardrop Stopper, 7 In. 635.00
Steuben Glass, Amethyst, Melon Ribbed, Stopper, 4 1/2 In. 920.00
Steuben Glass, Gold Ruby, Elongated, Diagonally Swirled Body, Crystal Stopper, 9 1/2 In. 1095.00
Steuben Glass, Gold Ruby, Melon Ribbed, Ribbed Stopper, 5 1/4 In. 805.00
Steuben Glass, Green Jade, Urn Shape, Alabaster Foot, Teardrop Stopper, 7 In. 748.00
Steuben Glass, Ivory, Melon Ribbed, No. 1455, Celeste Blue Stopper, 4 1/2 In. 1035.00
Steuben Glass, Light Blue Jade Body, Calcite Foot & Stopper, 7 3/4 In., Pair 1708.00
Steuben Glass, Pomona Green, Cylindrical, Dabber, 7 1/2 In. 1035.00
Steuben Glass, Rosaline, Bell Shape, No. 1818, Alabaster Teardrop Stopper, 4 3/4 In. 546.00
Steuben Gold Aurene Art Glass, DeVilbiss Atomizer, c.1926, 7 1/4 In. 600.00
Tapered Square, Metal Mounts, Intaglio Cut Cameo, Atomizer, 6 7/8 x 2 3/8 In. 66.00
Vandermark, Glass, Cobalt Blue, Stopper, Fruit, Vines, 4 1/2 In. 259.00
Vantine, Frosted Glass, Stopper, Molded Seated Buddha, 4 In. 460.00
Verre De Soie Glass, Genie Bottle Shape, Etched Flowers, Steuben, 7 In. 865.00
Verre De Soie Glass, Melon Ribbed, Celeste Blue, Teardrop Stopper, Steuben, 4 1/2 In. 460.00
Verre De Soie Glass, Melon Ribbed, Rose DuBarry Stopper, Steuben, 4 1/2 In. 805.00
Victorian, Baluster, Hand Painted White Pansies, Metal Mounts, 6 In. 69.00

Victorian, Blue, Metal Stand, Metal Frieze, 4 Medallions, Parisian Scenes, 6 3/4 In. 635.00
Vigny, Golliwogg, Black Head Top, Fur Hair, Label, Paris, 1920s, 4 3/4 In. .... 475.00 to 1080.00
Volupte, Orange, Enameled, Atomizer, 6 1/2 In. 242.00
World Globe, Multicolored, Atomizer, Germany, 6 3/4 In. 138.00
Worth, Imprudence, Clear Glass, Stopper, Concentric Rings, 2 1/2 In. 127.00
Worth, Je Reviens, Clear, Stopper, Etched Muddie, 6 1/2 In. 185.00
Worth, Je Reviens, Smoky Blue Glass, Stopper, Molded Block Letters, Box, 2 1/4 In. 240.00
Worth, Requete, Clear, Stopper, Flat Round, Scalloped, Enameled, 3 In. 240.00
Yellow Crystal, Stopper, Green Rhinestones, Metal Band, Green Stones Base, 1 3/4 In. 140.00
Yellow Glass, Elongated, Egg Shape, DeVilbiss Atomizer, 6 1/2 In. 127.00

PETERS & REED Pottery Company of Zanesville, Ohio, was founded by John D. Peters and Adam Reed in 1897. Chromal, Landsun, Montene, Pereco, and Persian are some of the art lines that were made. The company, which became Zane Pottery in 1920 and Gonder Pottery in 1941, closed in 1957. Peters & Reed pottery was unmarked.

Flowerpot, Marbleized, Yellow, Blue, Green, Black, Brown, 7 1/2 In. 46.00
Jar, Cover, Shadow Ware, Black, Yellow & Blue Drip Glaze, Round, 7 x 6 In. 294.00
Jardiniere, Moss Aztec, Greek Key Rim, Squat, 10 1/2 x 16 1/2 In. 206.00
Umbrella Stand, Moss Aztec, 24 In. 558.00
Vase, Green & Brown Swirls Over Yellow Glaze, Bulbous, 6 3/4 In. 410.00
Vase, Landsun, Blue, Brown Matte, Green Ground, 8 In. 69.00
Vase, Marbleized, 9 In. 75.00
Vase, Marbleized, 12 In. 125.00
Vase, Scenic Landscape, Brown Tones, Slightly Tapered & Folded-In, 10 In. 4500.00
Vase, Shadow Ware, Yellow Green Drip Glaze, Black Ground, Handles, 21 In. 646.00
Vase, Swirling Seascape, Blue, Gold, Green, Baluster, 11 In. 470.00
Vase, Vague Landscape, Blue, Yellow Green Drip Glaze, Bulbous, Flared, 6 1/2 In. 175.00

PETRUS REGOUT, see Maastricht category.

PEWABIC POTTERY was founded by Mary Chase Perry Stratton in 1903 in Detroit, Michigan. The company made many types of art pottery, including pieces with green matte glaze and an iridescent crystalline glaze. The company continued working until the death of Mary Stratton in 1961. It was reactivated by Michigan State University in 1968.

Box, Cover, Iridescent, Figures, Animals, 2 1/2 x 3 1/2 x 3 In. 316.00
Tile, Cat, Brown, Orange & Green Matte Glaze, Impressed Mark, 1991, 7 1/2 In. 180.00
Tile, Elephant, Crackle Glaze, Square, 1994, 2 3/4 In. 35.00
Tile, Luster Glaze, Geometric, Square, c.1910, 1 1/2 In. 75.00
Vase, Copper Red Glaze, Mauve Matte, 10 5/8 In. 3220.00

PEWTER is a metal alloy of tin and lead. Some of the pewter made after 1840 has a slightly different composition and is called *Britannia metal*. This later type of pewter was worked by machine; the earlier pieces were made by hand. In the 1920s pewter came back into fashion and pieces were often marked *Genuine Pewter*. Eighteenth-, nineteenth-, and twentieth-century examples are listed here.

Basin, Gershom Jones, Eagle Touchmark, 7 7/8 x 2 In. 230.00
Beaker, Boardman & Hart, c.1828-53, 3 1/8 In. 385.00
Beaker, Reeding, Flared Base, Engraved, England, 1700s, 1/2 Pt. 118.00
Beaker, Samuel Danforth, c.1795-1814, 5 In. 1750.00
Beaker, Townsend & Compton, c.1784-1802, 2 9/16 In. 285.00
Bed Warmer, Circular, Scrolled Punch, Pierced Hinged Cover, Wooden Handle, 26 1/4 In. 558.00
Biscuit Box, Cover, Archibald Knox, Tudric, Flowers, Square, England, Early 1900s, 4 1/4 In. 1225.00
Bowl, Lovebirds, Mark, London, 8 1/2 In. 358.00
Bowl, Unmarked, American, 1700s, 8 In. 185.00
Candlestick, 4 Long Tendrils, Tapered Stem, Art Nouveau, c.1900, 8 1/4 In., Pair 300.00
Castor Stand, Elijah Braman, Taunton, Mass. 175.00
Chalice, Gleason, Mid 19th Century, 6 3/8 In. 525.00
Chalice, Trask, Cast Metal, c.1813-56, 5 5/8 In., Pair 875.00

Chamber Pot, Child's, 18th Century, England, c.1760 .... 285.00
Charger, 2 Lovebirds, X, London, Mark, Philadelphia, 13 In. 550.00
Charger, Broad Rim, Monogram, 14 3/4 In. 220.00
Charger, Engraved Metal Leg, Motto, 16 3/4 In. 172.00
Charger, Impressed London, 16 1/2 In. 259.00
Charger, Jacob Eggleston, Reeded Rim, Heraldic Eagle, Shield, Stars, Touchmarks, 1 5/8 x 13 In. .. 4600.00
Charger, Thomas D. Boardman Touchmarks, Conn., 1805-50, 13 1/8 In. 374.00
Coffee & Tea Set, Leonard Reed & Barton, Taunton, Mass., 1835-45, 4 Piece 345.00
Coffeepot, A. Griswold, Wood Wafer Finial, Eagle Touchmark, Conn., 1802-43, 10 1/4 In. 145.00
Coffeepot, A. Porter, 1800s, 12 In. 385.00
Coffeepot, Ashbil Griswold, Meriden, Ct., 9 In. 225.00
Coffeepot, Dome Lid, F. Porter, Black Handle, Bulbous, Westbrook, Me., No. 1, 11 3/8 In. 200.00
Coffeepot, Dome Lid, Scalloped Ear Handle, Marked, 11 1/4 In. 230.00
Coffeepot, Eben Smith, Lighthouse, Pinwheels, 11 In. 895.00
Coffeepot, James Putman, Malden, Ma., Marked, 10 In. 325.00
Coffeepot, Lighthouse, Dome Lid, Tapered Sides, Scrolled Handle, 1822, 11 In. 385.00
Coffeepot, Lighthouse, Engraved Leaves, c.1814-56, 11 7/8 In. 975.00
Coffeepot, Roswell Gleason, Bulbous, Tam-O-Shanter Finial, 11 1/4 In. 230.00
Coffeepot, Roswell Gleason, Lighthouse, Tapered Sides, Raised Bands, Flared Base, 11 In. 400.00
Coffeepot, William Calder, Lighthouse, Providence, R.I., 10 3/4 In. 430.00
Container, Tobacco, Tulip Design, Diamond & Block, 3 In. 1100.00
Cup, Collapsible, TH Snyder, Philadelphia, Marked 165.00
Dish, Enamel, Archibald Knox, Tudric, Scroll Handles, Hammered, Early 1900s, 11 1/2 In. 1037.00
Dish, Rimmed, George Lightner, Baltimore, Md., Eagle Touchmark, 1806-35, 11 1/4 In. 400.00
Flagon, Boardman, Lion Seated, 2 Qt., 11 1/4 In. 2950.00
Flagon, Communion, Raised Rings, Scrolled Handle, 10 1/4 In. 230.00
Flagon, Dome Foot & Lid, Sheldon & Feltman, Cylindrical, Curved Handle, N.Y., c.1847, 10 1/2 In. . 390.00
Flagon, Knight In Doorway, Pewter Cherub Feet, Lid, Inscribed, 1 1/2 Liter, 15 In. 605.00
Flagon, Taunton Britannia Mfg. Co., 1930-35, 10 3/4 In. 400.00
Flagon, William Calber, 11 1/2 In. 400.00
Hand Warmer, Ball Shape 125.00
Jug, Hinged Cover, Archibald Knox, Tudric, Cylindrical, Tapered, Enamel, c.1904, 8 In. 566.00
Jug, Hot Water, Archibald Knox, Cylindrical, Tendrils, Honesty, England, c.1903, 7 3/4 In. 707.00
Jug, Hot Water, Hinged Lid, Liberty & Co., Tapering, Leaves, England, c.1904, 6 In. 265.00
Lamp, Oil, Ships, Gimbal Mounted, Wick Covers On Chains, Bulbous, O-Ring Handle, 5 x 5 In. 165.00
Lamp, Scrolled Handle, Socket, 9 5/8 In. 345.00
Mug, Boardman, Tankard Shape, Squat, c.1828-53, Qt. 2850.00
Mug, Handle, Impressed Crown VRG, 4 1/4 In. 115.00
Mug, John Townsend, S-Scroll Handle, England, Pt., c.1755 .... 950.00
Mug, Yates, Tulip, Pt. 50.00
Pitcher, Boardman & Hart, 7 3/4 In. 236.00
Pitcher, Cover, George Richardson, Glenmore Marks, Rhode Island, 3 Qt. 1250.00
Pitcher, G. Richardson, 2 Qt., 7 In. 489.00
Pitcher, Ribbed Bands, Weighted, 14 In. 236.00
Pitcher, Rufus Dunham, Westbrook, Maine, 1837-61, 6 1/2 In. 230.00
Pitcher, Water, Boardman, Mid 19th Century, 10 1/4 In. 650.00
Plate, 2 Lovebirds, X, London, Love, Philadelphia, 6 In. 578.00
Plate, Ashbil Griswold, Touchmarks, 7 3/4 In. 200.00
Plate, August Lenck Aus Grobenhain, Woman Warrior & Wing Touchmark, 1834, 8 1/4 In. 22.00
Plate, B. Barns, Eagle, Philadelphia, 7 7/8 In. 248.00
Plate, Badger, Boston, 8 1/2 In. 275.00
Plate, Blakslee Barnes, Philadelphia, 8 In. 165.00
Plate, Boardman, Lion Touchmark, 6 3/8 In. 500.00
Plate, Gershom Jones, Providence, R.I., 8 1/4 In. 400.00
Plate, Joseph Danforth, Touchmarks, 8 In. 316.00
Plate, Konigsburg, 1810, 10 1/2 In. .... 16.00 to 39.00
Plate, Penland, Engraved & Cut Dogwood Decoration, N.C., 7 3/4 In. 46.00
Plate, Samuel Danforth, Molded Rim, Hartford, Conn., 7 7/8 In. 316.00
Plate, Samuel Hamlin, Smooth Rim, Hard Metal Mark, Providence, RI, 9 1/4 In. 1400.00
Plate, Soup, I.S. Semper Eadem, Smooth Rim, Hammered Bouge, c.1775, 9 1/2 In. 1380.00
Plate, Temple Bar, Browne Touchmark, IEW Monogram, 9 In. 60.00

Plate, Williams Billings, Providence, R.I., 7 7/8 In. 550.00
Porringer, Crown Handle, Initials WN, New England, c.1880 .... 295.00
Porringer, Flower Handle, Marked, Calber, Eagle Mark, 5 3/8 In. 475.00
Porringer, Heart, Crescent, 3 1/2 In. 150.00
Porringer, Impressed, IC, 4 1/4 In. 175.00
Porringer, Old English Ear, Marked, EC, 4 1/2 In. 450.00
Porringer, Richard King, Geometric Handle, 4 7/8 In. 785.00
Porringer, Roswell Gleason, Backward R, Mass., 1822-71, 3 1/4 In. 86.00
Porringer, Townsend, Geometric Handle, 5 3/8 In. 795.00
Pot, H.B. Ward & Co., Tall, Banded Body, Paneled Spout, 11 1/2 In. 175.00
Pot, Incised Rings, Wooden Wafer Finial, Scroll Handle, 11 3/4 In. 175.00
Pot, Ingram & Hart, Welsh Hat Type, Flat Rim, Flared Foot, Incised Rings, 12 x 8 In. 230.00
Pot, Lyman Touchmark, Conn., 1844-52, 11 1/4 In. 230.00
Rose Bowl, Archibald Knox, Tudric, Scrolling Tendrils, Leaves, c.1903, 11 3/4 In. 1697.00
Salt, Leaf Embossed Design, 2 1/4 In. 98.00
Salt & Pepper, Kem Weber, c.1930, 2 7/8 & 2 In. 3000.00
Salver, J. Danforth, Ring Handle, 6 In. 138.00
Standish, George III, Double Flapped, Rectangular, Ireland, Late 1700s, 7 1/8 In. 70.00
Sugar, Cover, Boardman, 6 3/4 In. 425.00
Sugar, Townsend, 4 3/8 x 4 3/4 In. 3650.00
Syrup, Colonial Style, c.1900, 5 1/4 In. 69.00
Tablespoon, 18th Century, c.1760, 6 Piece 250.00
Tankard, Bailey & Brainard, Conn., c.1840, 15 3/8 In. 200.00
Tankard, Townsend, Side Handle, Spout, Engraved, England, 5 3/4 x 9 1/4 In. 58.00
Teapot, Albertus Bruges, Pear Shape, Belgium, c.1764-1800 .... 1000.00
Teapot, Babbitt & Crossman, Taunton, Mass., 10 In. 175.00
Teapot, Boardman & Hart, Pear Shape, 12 In. 290.00
Teapot, Calder-Providence, Pigeon Breasted, Marked, 10, 9 1/2 In. 350.00
Teapot, Cover, Baluster Form, 19th Century, 11 1/4 In. 266.00
Teapot, Crane & Stinson, Pear Shape, Bone Finial Button, c.1810, 7 1/4 In. 1395.00
Teapot, Dixon & Son, Pear Shape, Signed, 10 In. 145.00
Teapot, George Richardson, c.1828-45, 7 1/2 In. 495.00
Teapot, H.B. Ward, Conical Lid, Paneled Spout, Pewter Handle, Touchmark, 8 1/2 In. 316.00
Teapot, I. Trask, Oval, Engraved, Wood Handle, 4 Ball Feet, Mass., 1825-56, 7 x 10 1/2 In. 1320.00
Teapot, I. Vickers, 8 In. 358.00
Teapot, John Townsend, Pear Shape, c.1748-67, 6 3/8 In. 4200.00
Teapot, McQuilin, Philadelphia, 1845-53, 8 5/8 In. 175.00
Teapot, R. Bush, Pear Shape, 8 1/2 In. 650.00
Teapot, Reed & Barton, Panels, 10 1/2 In. 365.00
Teapot, Sheldon & Feltman, Albany, 7 1/2 In. 140.00
Teapot, Smith & Co., Boston, 8 In. 150.00
Tobacco Jar, Cover, Person's Head With Cap, Interior Cover, Rosette, Circle, 4 1/2 x 5 1/2 In. 86.00
Tray, Archibald Knox, 2 Handles, Rounded Rectangular Shape, England, Early 1900s, 18 In. 470.00
Tray, Kayserzinn, Oval, Raised Iris & Shells, 20 1/2 In. 180.00
Vase, Archibald Knox, Bullet Shape, 3 Angular Handles, Leaves, c.1902, 7 1/4 In., Pair 1037.00
Vase, Archibald Knox, Bullet Shape, 3 Loop Feet, Tendrils, Leaves, England, Early 1900s, 4 In. 1225.00
Vase, Archibald Knox, Enamel, England, 1902-05, 11 1/2 In. 3276.00
Wine Pot, Nephrite Jade Finial, Handle, Spout, Flowering Tree, Chinese, 19th Century, 4 1/2 In. 499.00

PHOENIX BIRD, or Flying Phoenix, is the name given to a blue-and-white kitchenware popular between 1900 and World War II. A variant is known as Flying Turkey. Most of this dinnerware was made in Japan for sale in the dime stores in America. It is still being made.

Bowl, Fruit, Crossed Stems Mark, 5 In. 15.00
Butter Chip, Blue, 3/8 In., 4 Piece 76.00
Cup & Saucer, Flying Turkey, Demitasse, Blue, White, 2 1/4-In. Cup, 4 1/4-In. Saucer 35.00
Custard Cup, Flying Turkey, Wreath Mark, 2 5/8 In. 15.00
Salt & Pepper, Flying Turkey Pattern, No Stoppers, Japan 35.00

PHOENIX GLASS Company was founded in 1880 in Pennsylvania. The firm made commercial products, such as lampshades, bottles, and glassware. Collectors today are interested in the "Sculptured Artware" made by the company from the 1930s until the mid-1950s. Some pieces of Phoenix glass are very similar to those made by the Consolidated Lamp and Glass Company. Phoenix made Reuben Blue, lavender, and yellow pieces. These colors were not used by Consolidated. In 1970 Phoenix became a division of Anchor Hocking, then was sold to the Newell Group in 1987. The company is still working.

Vase, Ferns, White, Blue Ground, Oval, Label, 7 In. 137.00
Vase, Opal Dancing Nymphs, Cream Matte Ground, Sculptured Artware Label, 11 1/2 In. 316.00
Vase, Wild Geese, White, Pink Ground, 9 x 12 In. 100.00
Vase, Wild Geese, Yellow Pearlized, Yellow Ground, 9 x 12 In. 110.00

PHONOGRAPHS, invented by Thomas Edison in 1877, have been made by many firms. This category also includes other items associated with the phonograph. Jukeboxes and Records are listed in their own categories.

Boston Talking Machine, Little Wonder, Mica Soundbox, 6-Sided Horn, 8 Discs, c.1910, 11 In. 823.00
Columbia, Graphophone, Nickel Plated Openworks, Floating Reproducer, Oak Case, 10 In. 353.00
Columbia, Graphophone, Oak Case, Nickel Horn, 19 In. 3575.00
Edison, Amberola 30, Cylinder, c.1915, 12 3/4 x 12 1/2 x 16 In. 695.00
Edison, Amberola, V, Cylinder Mahogany Case, 4 Drawers, Cylinders, c.1913, 52 In. 343.00
Edison, Diamond Disc A-250, Mahogany Case, Drawer, c.1915, 50 In. 345.00
Edison, Home A, Cylinder, B Reproducer, Oak Case, Morning Glory Horn, c.1900, 19 In. 880.00
Edison, Home A, Cylinder, H Reproducer, Oak Case, Mega Horn, Cylinders, c.1900, 23 In. 470.00
Edison, Standard A, C Reproducer, Oak Case, Brass Horn, Dome Lid, c.1898, 12 In. 440.00
Edison, Standard B, H Reproducer, Oak Case, Witch's Hat Horn, c.1905, 11 3/4 In. 350.00
Edison, Standard C, C Reproducer, Oak Case, 2 Horns, Morning Glory, c.1908, 11 3/4 In. 410.00
Edison, Standard D, H Reproducer, Polychrome Horn, Early 1900s 865.00
Edison Gem B, C Reproducer, Oak Case, Octa8-Sided Horn, c.1903, 8 x 10 x 8 In. 765.00
Mikky Phone, Fold-Up, Steel, Occupied Japan, Case, 78 RPM Record, 4 x 6 In. 226.00
Paillard, Gramophone, Mahogany Case, Double Doors, 18 1/2 x 15 In. 190.00
Pathe Freres, Coq, Rooster, Cylinder, c.1903, 13 x 9 In. 250.00
Victor II, Oak Case, Brass Horn, c.1900, 20 In. 2800.00
Victor III, Quartersawn Oak, Horn, 28 In. 2530.00
Victor Victrola, VV-IV, Exhibition Sound Box, Oak Case, 2 Doors, 11 In. 80.00
Victor Victrola VV-XVII-1100, Disc, Gold, Courting Couple, c.1916, 22 x 24 x 47 In. 16380.00
Victrola, VV-IX, Early 1900s, 15 In. 150.00
PHONOGRAPH NEEDLE CASE, Bragshaw's Brilliantone, Medium, Contents 8.00
Brilliantone, Full Tone, 1/2 x 1 1/4 x 1/2 In. 21.00
Columbia, For Disc Graphophone, 5/8 x 1 1/4 x 1 5/8 In. 41.00
Gramophone Company, His Master's Voice, Germany, 1 1/2 x 1 1/2 In. 16.00
Marschall, Dog, Baby, 1 5/8 x 1 1/4 In. 15.00
Nobility Brand, Knight On Horse, Japan, 3/8 x 1 3/8 x 2 1/4 In. 43.00
Songster, Medium Tone, J Stead & Co., Sheffield, 1 3/4 In. 7.00
Victor, His Master's Voice, Red Ground, 2 x 1 3/8 x 1/2 In. 13.00
Victrola, Tungs-Tone Stylus, Nipper, c.1921, 1/4 x 1 x 2 In. 15.00

PHOTOGRAPHY items are listed here. The first photograph was a view from a window in France taken in 1826. The commercially successful photograph started with the daguerreotype introduced in 1839. Today all sorts of photographs and photographic equipment are collected. Albums were popular in Victorian times. Cartes de visite, popular after 1854, were mounted on 2 1/2-by-4-inch cardboard. Cabinet cards were introduced in 1866. These were mounted on 4 1/4-by-6 1/2-inch cards. Stereo views are listed under Stereo Card. The cases for daguerreotypes are listed in the Gutta-Percha category. Stereoscopes are listed in their own section.

Album, Musical, Lithographed Pages, Celluloid Cover, Edwardian, 13 In. 323.00
Albumen Print, Ruins Of Great Fire In Boston, J.P. Soule, Frame, 12 x 39 In. 470.00
Ambrotype, 2 Boys With Sticks, 1/6 Plate 80.00
Ambrotype, Boy With Book, Williard, Penn, 1/6 Plate 85.00
Ambrotype, Boy, Civil War Uniform, 1/2 Plate 300.00

Ambrotype, Boy, Holding Musket, Gutta-Percha Case, 3 3/4 x 3 1/2 In. 230.00
Ambrotype, Daguerreotypist, Camera, Tripod, Ruby Glass, Thermoplastic Case, 1/4 Plate 4600.00
Ambrotype, English Couple, Bakers, Calcutta, 1/2 Plate 60.00
Ambrotype, Man Holding Case, 1/6 Plate 20.00
Ambrotype, Men On Horses, Horizontal, Thermoplastic Case, c.1859, 1/6 Plate 1840.00
Ambrotype, Sulky In Village Street, Oval Mat, Case, 1/4 Plate 978.00
Ambrotype, Tinted, Man On Horseback, Gilt Mount, Folding Case, 1/2 Plate 294.00
Ambrotype, Workman, 1 Suspender, Ruby Glass, Oval Mat, 1/2 Case, 1/6 Plate 115.00
Cabinet Card, Apache With Cigar, Henry Buehman, Arizona 300.00
Cabinet Card, Child Drinking From Milk Bottle, Griffith's Elite, 4 1/4 x 6 1/2 In. 95.00
Cabinet Card, Walt Whitman, Pendleton, c.1872 .... 2875.00
Cabinet Card, Walt Whitman, Sarony, 1878 .... 863.00
Camera, Alpa-Reflex, Luxury, Blue Leather, 1944 .... 2645.00
Camera, American Camera Co., Demon, Detective, London, 1890, 2 1/4 In. 1945.00
Camera, Bland & Co., Sliding Box, Mahogany Body, London, 7 1/2 x 7 1/2 In. 2115.00
Camera, Cannon, AE-1, SLR, 35 mm, Case, Flash 70.00
Camera, Canon, Model 7, Fast Canon Lens, Case, 1961 .... 1320.00
Camera, Daguerrean, Rosewood Veneer, C.C. Harrison, N.Y., 11 In., 1/4 Plate 12925.00
Camera, Eastman Kodak, No. 1, Panoram-Kodak, Goetz Lens, 1900 .... 375.00
Camera, Ernemann, Ernoflex Simplex, Stereo, For 45 x 107 mm, c.1929 .... 808.00
Camera, Franke & Heidecke, Rolleiflex 4 x 4, First Model, Accessories, Box, 1931 .... 955.00
Camera, Franke & Heidecke, Rolleiflex T, First Model, Gray, Case, 1958 .... 558.00
Camera, Gandolfi, Stereo Tailboard, Mahogany Body, London, 1/2 Plate 2115.00
Camera, Hensoldt Wetzlar, Henso Reporter, 1953 .... 3819.00
Camera, Kodak, Bantam Special, 1936 .... 323.00
Camera, Kodak, Daylight B, No. 2811, 1891, 3 1/2 x 4 In. 1320.00
Camera, Kodak, Petite Lavender Step Pattern, Walter Dorwin Teague, c.1930, 5 In. 189.00
Camera, Krugener, Stereo, Panoramic, Tropical Wood, Bellows, c.1900, 4 1/2 x 6 1/2 In. 1616.00
Camera, Lechner, Carte De Visite, Gasc & Charcounet Lens, Vienna 1909.00
Camera, Leica R3, Black, Instructions, Box, Germany, 1976 .... 410.00
Camera, Leica, I, Model A, Case, 1931 .... 590.00
Camera, Leica, II, Accessories, Case, 1933 .... 590.00
Camera, Leica, IIIf No. 582560, Chrome, Summitar Lens, Case 235.00
Camera, Leicaflex SL, Black Paint, Red Plastic Button, 1969 .... 560.00
Camera, Mahogany Box, Lancaster's Patent, England, c.1885, 3 3/4 x 4 3/4 In. 2937.00
Camera, Minox IIIs, Wetzlar, No. 135568, Black Case, 1957 .... 220.00
Camera, Nikon, F3/T Champagne, Accessories, Case, 1983 .... 1028.00
Camera, Paillard Bolex, Movie, 16 mm 165.00
Camera, Robot Star 50, Silent Version, Mini Shutter Release, 1969 .... 220.00
Camera, Rochester Camera Ca., No. 1536, Mahogany, Brass, Leather, 1/2 Plate 323.00
Camera, Rolleiflex, 3.5, Green Leather Case, 1931 .... 175.00
Camera, Voigtlander, Prominent II, Germany, Box, 1959 .... 734.00
Camera, Zeiss Ikon, Contax IIIa, Case, 1956 .... 440.00
Camera, Zeiss Ikon, Super Ikonta 533/16, 1957 .... 294.00
Camera Obscura, Reflex, Tapering Stained Wood Body, Glass Screen, 16 1/2 In. 705.00
Carte De Visite, Admiral Franklin Buchannan, E. Anthony, c.1860, 4 x 2 1/4 In. 385.00
Carte De Visite, Brig. Gen. Robt. Anderson, Profile, D. Appleton, 1861, 4 x 2 1/2 In. 445.00
Carte De Visite, Brigham Young & 4 Brothers, Savage & Ottinger, Salt Lake City 598.00
Carte De Visite, Carriage Maker, Waltham, Mass., H.F. Warren 259.00
Carte De Visite, General Custer, Philadelphia Photographic Co., c.1865, 4 x 2 1/2 In. 1180.00
Carte De Visite, General W.T. Sherman, Black, White, Civil War, 4 x 2 1/2 In. 165.00
Carte De Visite, Gould & Curry Mine, Tunnel, Nevada, No. 722, Lawrence & Houseworth 966.00
Carte De Visite, Harriet Beecher Stowe, Fredericks, 1800s 173.00
Carte De Visite, Hon. Edward Everett, Philadelphia Photographic Co., c.1860, 4 x 2 1/2 In. 354.00
Carte De Visite, Kit Carson & Edwin Perrin, 1862 .... 2530.00
Carte De Visite, Lieut. Gen. U.S. Grant, J. Chapman, Frame, 1865, 5 1/2 x 4 In. 127.00
Carte De Visite, Major Anderson, Sepia Tone, E. Anthony, Civil War, 4 x 2 1/2 In. 350.00
Carte De Visite, Major W.T. Sherman, Civil War 35.00
Carte De Visite, Mount Davidson, Nevada, No. 718, Lawrence & Houseworth 690.00
Carte De Visite, Peter Cooper, Fredericks, 1800s 184.00
Carte De Visite, Victoria Woodhull, 4 x 2 1/4 In. 198.00

Photography, Magic Lantern, Buddha, No Burner, Louis Aubert, Paris, c.1879, 17 1/3 In.

Photography, Magic Lantern, Riche Model, Burner Replaced, Lapierre, Paris, c.1880, 10 In.

Daguerreotype, 2 Children, 1/6 Plate . . . 110.00
Daguerreotype, 2 Sisters Holding Hands, 1/6 Plate . . . 50.00
Daguerreotype, 3 Women With Interlocking Arms . . . 225.00
Daguerreotype, Baby In Chair, 1/6 Plate . . . 135.00
Daguerreotype, Boy In Tinted Shirt, 1/6 Plate . . . 125.00
Daguerreotype, Boy With Hoop, 1/6 Plate . . . 650.00
Daguerreotype, Child, Postmortem, 1/6 Plate . . . 600.00
Daguerreotype, Children Posed By Chair, 1/4 Plate . . . 300.00
Daguerreotype, Couple Posing, 1/2 Plate . . . 300.00
Daguerreotype, Daniel Drake, M.D., 1/6 Plate . . . 250.00
Daguerreotype, Elderly Woman In Shawl, 1/6 Plate . . . 35.00
Daguerreotype, Elderly Woman, 1/6 Plate . . . 15.00
Daguerreotype, Family Group In Garden, Glass Raised, 1/4 Plate . . . 2400.00
Daguerreotype, Father & Son, 1/6 Plate . . . 65.00
Daguerreotype, Gentleman In Top Hat, Mid 1800s, Full Plate, 8 1/2 x 6 1/2 In. . . . 1410.00
Daguerreotype, Girl In Pink Dress, 1/9 Plate . . . 90.00
Daguerreotype, Girl Sitting In Chair . . . 30.00
Daguerreotype, Grandfather & Child, 1/6 Plate . . . 50.00
Daguerreotype, Grandmother & Child, 1/6 Plate . . . 100.00
Daguerreotype, Lady In Paisley Dress, 1/6 Plate . . . 16.00
Daguerreotype, Man In Oval Fame, 1/2 Plate . . . 140.00
Daguerreotype, Man Wearing Glasses, 1/6 Plate . . . 55.00
Daguerreotype, Man With Chin Beard, S. Root, Broadway, 1/4 Plate . . . 275.00
Daguerreotype, Man With Hand On Books, 1/6 Plate . . . 55.00
Daguerreotype, Man, Bearded, 1/2 Plate . . . 270.00
Daguerreotype, Man, Bearded, Cape, Hat, 1/6 Plate . . . 85.00
Daguerreotype, Man, Seated, On Roof, Stippled Mat, Ogee Frame, 1/4 Plate . . . 1035.00
Daguerreotype, Man, Wild Hair, 1/9 Plate . . . 270.00
Daguerreotype, Midday In Garden Of Good & Evil, M. Robinson, 1/2 Plate . . . 900.00
Daguerreotype, Mother & Deceased Child, 1/6 Plate . . . 250.00
Daguerreotype, Tinsmith, F. Mott Fayetteville, 1854, 1/6 Plate . . . 6325.00
Daguerreotype, Woman & Child, 1/6 Plate . . . 55.00
Daguerreotype, Woman By Column, 1/6 Plate . . . 1800.00
Daguerreotype, Woman In Gold Frame, 1/4 Plate . . . 100.00
Daguerreotype, Woman In Gothic Chair, Velvet Case, 1/6 Plate . . . 50.00
Daguerreotype, Woman Wearing Brooch, 1/9 Plate . . . 80.00
Daguerreotype, Woman With Lace Gloves . . . 20.00
Daguerreotype, Woman With Pleated Bodice, 1/6 Plate . . . 45.00
Daguerreotype, Woman, Knitting, Reading Bible, Arched Mat, Full Case, 1/6 Plate . . . 690.00
Daguerreotype, Young Boy, B.D. Maxham, 1/9 Plate . . . 35.00
Daguerreotype, Young Woman, 1/6 Plate . . . 60.00
Exposure Meter, Adams & Co., Watch Form, Enameled Face, 60 Second Timer . . . 235.00
Kinetoscope, Peep Show Viewer, Edison, 1897, 35 mm . . . 6462.00
Kinora Reel, Magician, No. 4393, Kinora Ltd., London, Carton . . . 529.00
Lumiere Still, Bain Plangeons, Male Divers, In Sleeve, Late 1800s . . . 90.00
Lumiere Still, Lutteurs, 2 Wrestlers, No. 832, Late 1800s . . . 95.00
Magic Lantern, Buddha, No Burner, Louis Aubert, Paris, c.1879, 17 1/3 In. . . . *ILLUS* 19827.00

Magic Lantern, Ernst Plank, 12 Slides, Nuremberg, c.1902, 9 In. 485.00
Magic Lantern, Gem, 1882 Patent 265.00
Magic Lantern, Jean Schoenner, Brass Lamphouse, Steel Box, Slides, Nuremberg, 12 In. 118.00
Magic Lantern, Lapierre, Boule, 18 Slides, c.1870, 25 1/2 In. 955.00
Magic Lantern, Lapierre, Carree, 12 2 1/2-In. Slides, Paris, c.1870, 11 In. 440.00
Magic Lantern, Lapierre, Lampascope, Boule, 35 2-In. Slides, c.1870, 19 In. 558.00
Magic Lantern, Lapierre, Medallion, Candlelight, c.1880, 12 In. 440.00
Magic Lantern, Lapierre, Riche, c.1880, 10 In. 440.00
Magic Lantern, Lapierre, Salon, c.1870, 7 In. 440.00
Magic Lantern, Lumiere Freres, Carree, No. 84-4, Replaced Lens, 1880, 17 2/3 In. 2056.00
Magic Lantern, Riche Model, Burner Replaced, Lapierre, Paris, c.1880, 10 In. .... *ILLUS* 441.00
Movie Camera, Bell & Howell, 16 mm, Filmo Field Model, Case, c.1930 .... 440.00
Movie Camera, Bell & Howell, 35 mm, Model D, 1920-35 .... 3745.00
Movie Camera, Super 8 mm, Flaming Guns, Rory Calhoun, Box, Black & White 9.00
Movie Camera, Universal Camera Co., Univex 8, Art Deco Case, c.1939 .... 110.00
Mutoscope Reel, No. 2969, Electric Locomotive Tests & Races, 1905 .... 808.00
Mutoscope Reel, No. 3200, Swimming Moose, Canadian Canoeists 404.00
Mutoscope Reel, No. 7001, Artist & His Model 514.00
Orotone, Acoma, Old Well, E.S. Curtis, Gilt Frame, 2 7/8 x 3 7/8 In. 828.00
Orotone, Imageon Glass, Gold Foil Back, 3 Chiefs, Piegan, E.S. Curtis, Frame, 10 1/2 x 13 1/2 In. .. 7475.00
Orotone, Navajo, E.S. Curtis, Frame, 1904, 10 1/2 x 13 1/2 In. 8625.00
Photograph, 4 Friends, Birches, Hand Colored, D. Davidson, Mat, Frame, c.1930, 6 x 8 In. 100.00
Photograph, At Fountain, Hand Colored, May Farini, Frame, 1920-30, 14 x 11 In. 75.00
Photograph, Autumn Birches, Hand Colored, F. Thompson, Frame, 5 x 7 In. 28.00
Photograph, Bermuda, Hand Colored, H.M. Gardiner, Frame, 1915-25, 14 x 12 In. 66.00
Photograph, Black Laborers Picking Cotton, Black & White, Late 1800s, 14 x 19 In. 380.00
Photograph, Blossom Bower, D. Davidson, Signed, Mat, Frame, c.1920, 16 x 13 In. 132.00
Photograph, Canterbury Bells, Hand Colored, D. Davidson, 1910-20, 7 x 9 In. 17.00
Photograph, Cedar River Bathing Beach, Waterloo, Iowa, c.1914, 7 1/2 x 28 In. 59.00
Photograph, Coconut Palms, Bermuda, M.A. Trott, Mat, Frame, c.1915, 8 x 14 In. 28.00
Photograph, Colorado Rocky Mountains, H.L. Standley, Frame, c.1920, 14 x 12 In. 39.00
Photograph, Consultation, Hand Colored, M.H. Northend, 1910-20, 16 x 14 In. 99.00
Photograph, Drifting, Schooner, Hand Colored, Fred Thompson, 1910-20, 7 x 9 In. 80.00
Photograph, Echo Lake, Charles Sawyer, Mat, Frame, c.1920, 9 x 7 In. 39.00
Photograph, Echo Lake, Hand Colored, C. Sawyer, Mat, Frame, c.1920, 16 x 13 In. 35.00
Photograph, Falling Leaves, Fred Thompson, Mat, Frame, c.1910, 7 x 14 In. 88.00
Photograph, Feeding, Sheep, Hand Colored, Lamson Studios, c.1915, 5 x 7 In. 66.00
Photograph, Girl In Doorway, Hand Colored, C.R. Higgins, Frame, c.1910, 3 x 9 In. 39.00
Photograph, Harvey Lake, Hand Colored, C. Sawyer, Frame, 1930-35, 14 x 7 In. 176.00
Photograph, Her House In Order, D. Davidson, Mat, Frame, c.1920, 14 x 9 In. 45.00
Photograph, Historic Hallway, Hand Colored, Mary Northend, c.1915, 13 x 16 In. 88.00
Photograph, Jersey Sand Dunes, Hand Colored, A.P. Gamon, Frame, c.1915, 14 x 11 In. 35.00
Photograph, Lake George, Charles Sawyer, Mat, Frame, c.1920, 20 x 16 In. 209.00
Photograph, Lone Palm, Bermuda, P. Dowle, Frame, 1915-25, 10 x 12 In. 16.00
Photograph, Moss Island, Florida, W.J. Jarris, Mat, Frame, c.1920, 20 x 12 In. 154.00
Photograph, Mt. Lafayette & Gale River, C. Sawyer, Frame, c.1933, 10 x 6 In. 99.00
Photograph, Narrows, J. Carelton Bicknell, Mat, Frame, 1915-25, 9 x 7 In. 66.00
Photograph, National Cartoonist's Society Meeting, N.Y.C., 1967, 9 x 20 In. 110.00
Photograph, Old Garden, Bermuda, M.A. Trott, Mat, Frame, c.1920, 10 x 12 In. 39.00
Photograph, Palmetto Palms, Bermuda, Hand Colored, P. Dowle, c.1920, 7 1/2 x 7 In. 17.00
Photograph, Path To Mt. Surprise, Hand Colored, C. Sawyer, Mat, c.1910, 6 x 8 In. 50.00
Photograph, Pike's Peak, Manitou, Co., W.H. Jackson, Frame, c.1879, 11 1/2 x 15 In. 345.00
Photograph, Portrait, Afraid Of Eagle, Sioux, F.A. Rinehart, Sepiatone, 1898, 7 x 9 In. 294.00
Photograph, Prodigal Son, Sepia, Triptych, Frame, c.1880, 18 x 32 In. 55.00
Photograph, Pulpit Rock, Charles Sawyer, Mat, Frame, c.1905, 16 x 14 In. 187.00
Photograph, Royal Palms, Bermuda, S. Hayward, Frame, c.1920, 13 x 11 In. 39.00
Photograph, Sand & Pebbles, J. Carleton Bicknell, Frame, 1910-20, 21 x 13 In. 55.00
Photograph, Shelburne Birches, Phinney, Signed, Mat, Frame, c.1925, 8 x 6 1/2 In. 66.00
Photograph, Silver Print, 10th Ave. & Santa Fe, Javen Bayer, 17 1/2 x 15 1/2 In. 55.00
Photograph, Silver Print, Harry Houdini, Final Portrait, 1926, 10 x 8 In. 462.00
Photograph, Silver Print, Whale, Platte River, Denver, Javen Bayer, 14 1/2 x 17 In. 11.00

Photograph, Song Of Sea, Fred Thompson, Signed, Mat, Frame, c.1910, 12 x 8 In. 39.00
Photograph, Spring In Meadow, Burrowes, Signed, Mat, Frame, c.1915, 13 x 10 In. 28.00
Photograph, Stonewall Jackson, Salt Print, At Moss Neck, Virginia, 1863, 7 x 5 In. 9200.00
Photograph, Surf At Point Prince, Hand Colored, P. Yates, Frame, c.1925, 10 x 7 1/2 In. 55.00
Photograph, Threshing Scene, Steam Engine, Silver Print, Frame, 9 x 7 In. 59.00
Photograph, To Join Brimming River, C. Sawyer, Frame, 1905-15, 16 x 13 In. 75.00
Photograph, Washing Gold, Vancouver, B.C., Mounted, c.1895, 9 3/4 x 12 In. 430.00
Photograph, Winding Brook, Hand Colored, Gibson, Mat, Frame, c.1915, 7 x 9 In. 17.00
Photograph, Ye Coach Lodge, Hand Colored, Fred Thompson, 1910-20, 7 x 5 In. 176.00
Photograph, York Beach, Maine, Lighthouse, Santilli, Frame, c.1905, 14 x 11 In. 165.00
Photogravure, Chasse Au Renard, Fox Hunt, Le Penne, Frame, c.1879, 36 x 41 In. 275.00
Photogravure, Cheyenne Chief, E.S. Curtis, Mat, Frame, 1927, 29 x 25 In. 978.00
Photogravure, Oasis In Badlands, E.S. Curtis, Mat, Frame, Reprint, 1972, 25 x 30 In. 288.00
Platinum Print, Two Little Crows, No. 996, F.A. Rinehart, c.1898, 7 1/2 x 9 1/2 In. 748.00
Silver Print, Auguste & Louis Lumiere In Laboratory, Card Mount, 7 x 9 In. 235.00
Silver Print, Eskimo Scene, H. Whitney, Mat, Frame, 1909, 13 x 20 In. 1725.00
Silver Print, Harry Houdini, Final Portrait, 1926, 10 x 8 In. 462.00
Silver Print, Lumber Mill, Theodore Fonville Winans, 1940, 11 x 14 In. 1765.00
Silver Print, Oyster, Theodore Fonville Winans, La., c.1939, 14 x 11 In. 2468.00
Silver Print, Swamp Lunch, Theodore Fonville Winans, 1931 .... 2350.00
Slide, Avenger, U.S. Navy, Glass, June 30, 1943, 2 x 2 In. 6.00
Tintype, 2 Union Soldiers, Revolvers, Thermoplastic Case, c.1862, 1/6 Plate 460.00
Tintype, Boy, Union Civil War Uniform, Case, 2 3/4 x 2 1/4 In. 193.00
Tintype, Boy, Union Civil War Uniform, Drum, Sticks, Case, 3 5/8 x 3 1/8 In. 385.00
Tintype, Civil War Cavalryman, Seated, Shell Jacket, Gutta-Percha Case, 4 x 3 In. 115.00
Tintype, Locomotive, Thermoplastic Case, 1860s, 4 x 2 1/2 In. 2415.00
Tintype, Man Playing Violin, 1/6 Plate 160.00
Tintype, Tinted, Young American Soldier, Studio Setting, Oval Mount, Full Plate 499.00
View Finder, Red, Round, Viz Vue, 5 1/2 In. 11.00
Zoetrope, Slotted Red Card Drum, Wood Stem, Oak Base, 11 Strips, 12 In. 323.00
Zograscope, Adjustable Pillar, 4 1/2-In. Lens, Engraved Vue, 9 1/2 x 16 In. 646.00
Zograscope, Mahogany, Brass, Hand Colored Picture, 5 1/2-In. Lens, 18 1/2 In. 764.00

PIANO BABY is a collector's term. About 1880, the well-decorated home had a shawl on the piano. Bisque figures of babies were designed to help hold the shawl in place. They range in size from 6 to 18 inches. Most of the figures were made in Germany. Reproductions are being made. Other piano babies may be listed under manufacturers' names.

Lying On Back, One Foot Up, Hand Touching Foot, Bisque, 7 1/2 x 4 x 3 1/2 In. 250.00
On Stomach, Crawling, Bisque, DEP, 3 1/2 x 6 x 2 1/4 In. 125.00
Reclining, With Rabbit, Unmarked, 9 x 4 1/2 In. 135.00
Twin Girls, Wigs, Rosy Complexion, Blue Eyes, 1 Holding Ball, Victorian, 1900s, 5 x 5 In. 599.00

PICKARD China Company was started in 1898 by Wilder Pickard. Hand-painted designs were used on china purchased from other sources. In the 1930s, the company began to make its own china wares in Chicago, Illinois. The company now makes many types of porcelains, including a successful line of limited edition collector plates.

Bowl, Cherries, Flowers, Gold Exterior & Scrolled Trim, Footed, Maxwell Rean, 9 1/8 In. 945.00
Bowl, Oriental Bird, Parrot, Flowers, Gold Trim & Handles, 6 In. 175.00
Candlestick, Scotch Pattern, 4-Sided, Flared Bottom, Arthur Passoni, 9 x 4 In., Pair 479.00
Charger, Blackberries, Vines, Leaves, Aqua Scrolls, Gold Shaped Rim, Jacob Kiefus, 12 In. 259.00
Coffeepot, Maple Leaves, Green, Red, Tan, Gold Spout & Shaped Handle, 7 3/4 In. 895.00
Creamer, Roses, River Landscape, Heavy Gold Trim, c.1918 .... 90.00
Cup & Saucer, Violets, Gold Trim, Joseph Blaha, Limoges 429.00
Dish, Scallop Shell Shape, Gold Wash, 3 3/4 x 3 1/2 In. 28.00
Pitcher, Cider, Aura Mosaic, Black Ground, Gold Trim, Carl Roessler, 6 x 7 1/2 In. 650.00
Plate, Clover Blossoms, Pink, Green, Gold Scalloped Border, Howard Reury, 8 1/2 In. 149.00
Plate, Floral, Signed, 8 1/4 In. 110.00

Plate, Florida Lagoon, Gold Trim, 6 1/4 In. 195.00
Plate, Hand Painted, Signed, 8 1/2 In. 100.00
Tray, Lake Scene, Italian Garden, Gold Rim & Tab Handles, 8 3/4 In. 285.00
Tray, White, Roses, Rectangular, Pierced Rounded Corners, Eva Maley, 9 3/4 x 7 1/2 In. 295.00
Vase, Gilt, Trailing Vines, 4-Sided, 4 Buttressed Handles, c.1920, 9 3/4 In. 160.00

PICTURE FRAMES are listed in this book in the Furniture category under Frame.

PICTURES, silhouettes, and other small decorative objects framed to hang on the wall are listed here. Sandpaper pictures are black and white charcoal drawings done on a special sanded paper. Some other types of pictures are listed in the Print and Painting categories.

Charcoal & Crayon On Paper, Seated Woman, Fancisco Zuniga, 1974, 22 1/2 x 29 3/4 In. 1770.00
Chromolithograph, Child & Pets, Frame, c.1900, 16 x 20 In. 55.00
Chromolithograph, Smiling Baby, Ida Waugh, c.1900, 9 x 11 In. 5.00
Chromolithograph, Snow Scene, W.H. Chandler, Frame, c.1900, 20 x 16 In. 77.00
Diorama, Carousel, 3 China Figures On Horses, Mirrored Box, 20 x 13 In. 173.00
Drawing, Charcoal, Male Nude In Studio, Frederick Trap Friis, Frame, Late 1800s, 37 x 27 In. 165.00
Engraving, Copper, 4 Equestrian Scenes, Colored, Baron Eisenberg, Frame, 13 x 16 In. 1645.00
Engraving, Declaration Of Independence July 4th 1776, Ormsby, 1800s, 23 1/4 x 32 1/4 In. 1838.00
Engraving, Del Foro Di Nerva, Dei Portici Di Filippo, Luigi Rossini, 18 x 15 In., Pair 1175.00
Engraving, Pharaonic Canopic Jar, Hand Colored, Ivory Mat, Black, Gold Frame, 5 x 4 In. 293.00
Engraving Set, Botanical, Fosseir & Heniquez, Mat, Giltwood Frame, 10 x 7 In., 8 Piece 646.00
Engraving Set, French Costumes, Hand Colored, Frame, Mat, 13 x 9 In., 8 Piece 411.00
Engraving Set, Small Birds, British School, George Edwards, Mat, Frame, 9 3/4 x 8 In. 1645.00
Etching, Abraham Lincoln Statue, Trees, Building, Signed, E.T. Hurley, 12 1/4 x 7 1/4 In. 240.00
Etching, Arch Of Veneventum, Giovanni Battista Piranesi, 18 1/4 x 28 In. 1880.00
Etching, Cincinnati Courthouse, Signed, E.T. Hurley, 11 x 9 In. 300.00
Etching, Garfield Place In Winter, Signed, E.T. Hurley, 12 x 9 In. 360.00
Etching, Mt. Adams Houses, Immaculata Church, Signed, E.T. Hurley, 11 3/4 x 7 1/2 In. 335.00
Etching, Ohio River Scene, Signed, E.T. Hurley, 8 3/4 x 11 3/4 In. 450.00
Etching, Suspension Bridge, Signed, E.T. Hurley, 8 1/2 x 11 3/4 In. 420.00
Etching, Suspension Bridge, Signed, E.T. Hurley, 11 3/4 x 7 3/4 In. 360.00
Etching, Tyler Davidson Fountain, Signed, E.T. Hurley, 12 x 8 In. 300.00
Gouache On Paper, Dawserry Beggar & His Wife, Frame, India, Colonial, 10 x 13 In. 825.00
Graphite & Watercolor On Paper, Standing Nude Model, Chaim Gross, 1937, 18 x 12 In. 1652.00
Hair Wreath, Victorian, Wired Floral Shapes, Walnut Cross Frame, c.1865, 28 x 24 In. 235.00
Hair Wreath, Victorian, Wired Floral Shapes, Walnut Cross Frame, c.1870, 17 x 21 In. 118.00
Ink & Color, On Fabric, Myriad Birds In A River Landscape, 12 x 91 In. 4760.00
Ink & Color, On Fabric, Poet & Attendant, Dong Bangda, Hand Scroll, 12 x 63 In. 1334.00
Ink & Color, On Silk, Mongol Hunting Scene, Frame, Chinese, 1800s, 48 x 22 In. 325.00
Ink On Paper, Chinese Warrior On Horseback, Seifu Tsuda, 15 x 10 3/4 In. 66.00
Ink On Paper, Deity, Japanese School, Early 20th Century, 14 3/4 x 10 3/4 In. 55.00
Memorial, Watercolor, On Ivory, Woman Kneeling, Monument, Locket Frame, 1 3/4 In. 646.00
Memorial, Watercolor, On Paper, Woman Grieving, Monument, c.1815, 12 1/2 x 15 In. 2703.00
Micro Mosaic, Dog, White, Defensive, Round, Grand Tour, Italy, Frame, Late 1800s, 2 3/8 In. 3819.00
Micro Mosaic, Piazza San Pietro, Grand Tour, Italy, Frame, Late 1800s, 2 5/8 x 1 5/8 In. 7638.00
Needlework, Biblical Scene, Jacob Goes To Levin, Poland, c.1935, 32 3/4 x 47 1/4 In. 278.00
Needlework, Chenille, Beadwork, Vase, Flowers, England, Frame, 18 1/4 x 13 3/4 In. 575.00
Needlework, Chenille, Silk, Map, Globe, Americas, Flower Vine, Frame, 17 In. 529.00
Needlework, Deer In Woods, Flame Stitch, Frame, 1800s, 11 x 15 In. 330.00
Needlework, Eagle, Spread Wings, Tree Branch, Flower Border, Frame, 1820, 12 x 14 In. 690.00
Needlework, Embroidered, Flower Vase, Anna R. Conn, Aged 12 Years, c.1835, Frame, 29 x 25 In. 558.00
Needlework, English, Metallic Thread, Red Silk, Birds, Peacock, Roses, 1690, 18 In. 395.00
Needlework, Metallic Thread On Red Silk, Birds, Peacock, Roses, Flowers, 1690, 18 In. 395.00
Needlework, Picture, Chenille On Silk, Elizas Percin Age 8, 1846, 17 x 12 In. 355.00
Needlework, Salon Scene, Hand Painted Accents, Signed, O. Erdmann, Frame, 47 x 58 In. 230.00
Needlework, Show Towel, Linen, Flowers, Birds, Stars, 1830, Cadarina Bechtel, 14 x 48 In. 355.00
Needlework, Silk On Linen, Wrought By Mary Harvey, Verse, Parents, Child, 1800, 11 x 10 In. 800.00
Needlework, Silk, Chenille, Metallic Threads, Ink, Mount Vernon, Early 1800s, 13 x 17 In. 3055.00
Needlework, Silk, Man, Forest, 3 Women, Reverse Painted Glass, Frame, 1800s, 12 x 10 In. 353.00
Needlework, Silk, Memorial, Woman Mourning, Church, Cemetery, 1870s, 17 x 15 In. 2300.00

Picture, Silhouette, Portrait, Anderson Greene Dana, 1791-1861, 4 1/2 x 3 1/2 In.

Picture, Silhouette, Portrait, Hollow Cut, Man, Reverse Painted, Black, 19th Century, 6 1/2 x 5 3/4 In.

Picture, Silhouette, Portrait, Man In Top Hat, 19th Century, 5 1/4 x 4 In.

Needlework, Silk, Watercolor Painted Sky, Coastal Scene, Couple, Dog, Frame, 7 x 9 In. 235.00
Needlework, Silk, Wool, Charles II, Figures, Animals, Birds, Buildings, Frame, 20 x 16 In. 2400.00
Needlework, Wool, British Ship, 3-Masted, Frame, 1835-50, 13 x 17 1/2 In. 805.00
Needlework, Wool, Ship, 3-Masted, British Flag Off Stern, Maple Frame, Late 1800s, 14 x 17 In. .. 705.00
On Ivory, Gentleman, Blue Coat, Purple Guilloche Enamel, Locket, 3 In. 450.00
Optical Engraving, Ansicht Bey Brussel, Hand Colored, 1700s, 12 x 16 In. 235.00
Optical Engraving, La Chancellerie De Grenade, Hand Colored, 1700s, 10 1/2 x 16 In. 235.00
Painted Silk, Man Holding Lobster, Japanese School, 20th Century, 10 1/2 x 9 1/2 In. 11.00
Paper Work, Floral Arrangement, Maple Shadow Box, Myra Bates, 1817, 14 x 12 x 3 In. 243.00
Pastel, Chalk On Sandpaper, Sunnyside, Portrait, Washington Irving, 15 1/4 x 19 In. 295.00
Pastel, Landscape, Lake, Trees, W.H. Chandler, Mat, Frame, c.1900, 10 x 28 In. 110.00
Pastel, Landscape, William H. Chandler, Mat, Frame, c.1900, 28 x 10 In. 88.00
Pastel On Paper, Little Girl In Blue Dress, Seated, Giltwood Frame, c.1840, 26 x 20 In. 5288.00
Pastel On Paper, S.S. United States From Starboard, Paul Maze, Frame, 1952, 16 x 20 In. 4800.00
Pencil, Gouache, June Snow, Yosemite Park, Everett Bryant, Frame, 19 x 29 1/2 In. 4406.00
Sampler, Alphabets, Lettering, Urns Of Flowers, Drucilla Anderson, 1837, 23 x 11 In. 340.00
Sand, Monument Valley, Eugene B. Joe, Frame, 25 x 31 In. 350.00
Scroll, Asian, Silk, 8 Figures In Interior, Rosewood Holders, Signed, 20 x 89 In. 330.00
Scroll, Asian, Silk, Gilded, Women In Courtyard, Rosewood Holders, Signed, 22 x 93 In. 330.00
Scroll, Ink & Colors On Paper, Winter, Ducks, Wang Hsia, Chinese, 1800s, 55 x 22 1/4 In. 2350.00
Scroll, Ink & Colors On Silk, Egrets, Tree, Peony, Rockery, Chinese, 1800s, 56 x 30 In. 825.00
Scroll, Ink & Colors On Silk, Garden, Birds, Chinese, 1800s, 40 1/2 x 15 In. 3525.00
Scroll, Ink & Colors On Silk, Landscape, Boats, Palace, Lake, Chinese, 1800s, 77 x 32 In. 3819.00
Scroll, Ink & Colors On Silk, Spring Cherry Blossoms, Yunen, Japan, c.1910, 43 x 21 In. 590.00
Silhouette, Boy With Book, Louis Henry Maimahon, Birmingham, Frame, 1838, 13 x 10 In. 259.00
Silhouette, Gentleman In Stove Pipe Hat, Cut, Frame, 1800s, 4 x 3 In. 165.00
Silhouette, Gentlemen, Stock Collar, Ink On Paper, Oval Frame, Late 1700s, 5 x 4 In. 323.00
Silhouette, George Wright, Boston Red Stockings, Late 19th Century, 3 7/8 x 2 1/4 In. 137.00
Silhouette, Portrait, Anderson Greene Dana, 1791-1861, 4 1/2 x 3 1/2 In. .... *ILLUS* 115.00
Silhouette, Portrait, Cut, Gentleman, c.1830, 3 1/4 x 2 1/4 In. 350.00
Silhouette, Portrait, Hollow Cut, Girl, Flowers, Eglomise Mat, Gilt Frame, 5 x 5 In. 432.00
Silhouette, Portrait, Hollow Cut, Husband, Wife, Daniel Chase, Sarah Ferrin, 1772-1852, 6 x 5 In. 325.00
Silhouette, Portrait, Hollow Cut, Man, Peale, Embossed Label, 6 3/4 x 5 1/4 In. 144.00
Silhouette, Portrait, Hollow Cut, Man, Pigtail, Peale, Mahogany Veneer Frame, 9 x 8 In. 259.00
Silhouette, Portrait, Hollow Cut, Man, Reverse Painted, Black, 19th Century, 6 1/2 x 5 3/4 In. *ILLUS* 230.00
Silhouette, Portrait, Hollow Cut, Man, Wearing Smoking Cap, Peale's Museum, 6 3/8 In. 200.00
Silhouette, Portrait, Hollow Cut, Young Boy, Gilt Frame, c.1838, 7 x 6 In. 173.00
Silhouette, Portrait, Hollow Cut, Young Woman, Hair Comb, Peale, Frame, 6 1/2 x 5 3/8 In. 115.00
Silhouette, Portrait, Man In Top Hat, 19th Century, 5 1/4 x 4 In. .... *ILLUS* 173.00
Silk, Seasons, Art Nouveau, Allegorical Bust Of Maiden, Wood Frame, 6 x 5 In., 4 Piece 646.00
Spencerian Penmanship, Birds Wreath, Leaves, C.B. Remmington, 1st Prize 18 x 21 In. 104.00
Theorem, Amish Farm Scene, Man, Goose, Dog, Pigs, Velvet, Molded Frame, 17 1/2 x 23 1/2 In. .. 1980.00
Theorem, Bantam Rooster, Yellow Ground, Frame, Bill Rank, 9 3/4 x 7 3/4 In. 413.00

Theorem, Bird, Berry In Beak, Sitting On Flower Stump, Velvet, Frame, D. Ellinger, 7 5/8 x 6 1/4 In. 1705.00
Theorem, Bird, Long Neck, On Flower Branch, Velvet, Block Frame, Bill Rank, 11 1/2 x 9 1/2 In. 413.00
Theorem, Bird, Watercolor, Signed, 1835, 9 x 7 In. 690.00
Theorem, Bouquet Of Flowers & Leaves, Watercolor, Cloth, Giltwood Frame, 9 x 12 In. 115.00
Theorem, Clay Bowl With Fruit, Velvet, Painted Frame, Bill Rank, 18 3/8 x 16 3/8 In. 616.00
Theorem, Compote, Fruit Flowers, Watercolor, On Paper, Giltwood Frame, 6 x 6 1/4 In. 2115.00
Theorem, Flower Vase, Watercolor, Fabric, Giltwood Frame, 21 x 24 1/2 In. 1668.00
Theorem, Flowers, Velvet, Pennsylvania, Early 19th Century, Frame, 13 x 11 In. 2950.00
Theorem, Fruit Basket, 2 Birds With Long Flowing Tails, Velvet, Bill Rank, 13 x 15 In. 330.00
Theorem, Fruit Basket, Melon, Peaches, Pear, Velvet, Frame, Gilt Inner Border, 16 x 19 In. 575.00
Theorem, Fruit Basket, Ribbed Compote, Watercolor, Velvet, Gilt Frame, 8 1/2 x 10 In. 1840.00
Theorem, Fruit Basket, Velvet, Painted Frame, Maine, Calif., Mid 1800s, 14 x 11 In. 6500.00
Theorem, Fruit Basket, Yellow & Brown Bird, Bees, Velvet, Frame, T.J. Graham, 19 3/4 x 24 3/4 In. 1650.00
Theorem, Grape Basket, Bird On Top, Velvet, Frame, D. Ellinger, 1970, 14 x 18 1/2 In. 3410.00
Theorem, Hen On Nest, Eggs Underneath, Velvet, Painted Frame, Bill Rank, 9 3/4 x 11 3/4 In. 303.00
Theorem, Melons, Fruits & Berries, Plinth, Watercolor, Velvet, 19 1/2 x 23 1/2 In. 4113.00
Theorem, Memorial, Watercolor, Stencils, Urn, Willow, Morning Glories, 15 x 13 In. 805.00
Theorem, Oriental Blue & White Porcelain Bowl Of Fruit, Velvet, Gilt Frame, 24 x 28 In. 805.00
Theorem, Pineapple, Velvet, Painted Frame, Bill Rank, 12 5/8 x 14 5/8 In. 224.00
Theorem, Reclining Cat, Oval Blue Rug, Velvet, Painted Frame, Bill Rank, 12 1/2 x 14 1/2 In. 275.00
Theorem, Red Roses, Buds, Green Leaves, White Ground, Red Sponge Frame, 18 x 20 In. 431.00
Theorem, Rooster, On Mound, Tulips, Velvet, Painted Frame, Bill Rank, 17 3/4 x 15 3/4 In. 413.00
Theorem, Roses, Pen & Ink Verse, Stencil, Watercolor, Lucien Courier Nash, N.H., 8 In. 288.00
Theorem, Seashells, On White Velvet, Gilt Frame, 19th Century, 14 1/2 x 20 In. 114.00
Theorem, Small Blossom Bouquet, Watercolor, Velvet, Vermont, 1800s, 7 x 5 In. 235.00
Theorem, Still Life, Basket Of Flowers, Velvet, 1800s, 13 1/2 x 15 1/2 In. 415.00
Theorem, Still Life, Basket, Oil, Stencil, Velvet, c.1820, 21 x 17 1/2 In. 7800.00
Theorem, Still Life, Flower Basket, Watercolor, Mat, Silvered Wood Frame, 11 x 12 In. 1293.00
Theorem, Still Life, Flower Basket, Watercolor, Velvet, Giltwood Frame, 14 x 17 In. 705.00
Theorem, Still Life, Flowers In Urn, Marble Tabletop, Watercolor, Giltwood, 18 x 14 In. 323.00
Theorem, Still Life, Fruit & Flower Basket, Watercolor, Paper, Frame, 10 x 13 1/12 In. 353.00
Theorem, Still Life, Fruit In Basket, Velvet, 1800s, 13 1/2 x 15 In. 550.00
Theorem, Stoneware Jug, Stamped Cowden & Wilcox, Fruit, Frame, Bill Rank, 14 5/8 x 12 5/8 In. . 825.00
Theorem, Strawberry Tree, Small Pot, Velvet, Painted Frame, Bill Rank, 11 1/2 x 9 1/2 In. 220.00
Theorem, Sulky, White Dappled Horse, Rider, Yellow Vest, Frame, Bill Rank, 9 3/4 x 11 3/4 In. 468.00
Tinsel, Fruit In Footed Bowl, Reverse Painted Glass, Multicolored, Foil Back, 11 x 15 In. 411.00
Tinsel, Pink Flower Bouquets, Ribbons, Reverse Painted Glass, Silver Foil, 9 1/2 x 7 1/2 In., Pair .. 288.00
Watercolor, 2 Dogs, Saito Taijin, Japan, Early 1900s, 21 1/2 x 12 In. 118.00
Watercolor, Beach Scene, Sailboat, Hendricks A. Hallett, Frame, 12 x 17 1/2 In. 127.00
Watercolor, Birch Trees & Stream, J.J. Francis, Frame, 8 x 9 3/4 In. 165.00
Watercolor, Brook Trout, W.B. Gillette, Oak Frame, 1800s, 18 x 25 In. 550.00
Watercolor, Cavalier's Quiet Smoke, JZ Aranda, Frame, 1837-1903, 13 1/4 x 9 1/4 In. 1293.00
Watercolor, Chepstow Castle, Wales, Richard Henry Nibbs, 1800s, 25 1/4 x 39 In. 1298.00
Watercolor, Flock Of Sheep, C.E. Cookman, Mat, Gilt Frame, 18 1/4 x 21 In. 230.00
Watercolor, Indian Shooting Arrow From Plateau, C.F. Peters, Frame, 10 3/4 x 13 3/4 In. 374.00
Watercolor, Ink On Paper, Mourning, Calvin & Anna Manning, Frame, c.1840, 8 x 14 In. 508.00
Watercolor, Silk, Memorial, Woman Weeping, Leaning On Urn, Maria Barker, 1819, 22 In. 1150.00
Watercolor, Young Woman, Blue Dress, Pinprick Lace, Frame, 7 x 6 In. 575.00
Watercolor On Ivory, Portrait, Gentleman, In Silvered Pin, 1800s, Miniature 176.00
Watercolor On Ivory, Portrait, Major Stevens, Gilt Locket Frame, Hair, 2 3/8 x 2 In. 5975.00
Watercolor On Ivory, Portrait, Military Officer, Wood Frame, 1 1/2 x 1 1/4 In. 588.00
Watercolor On Paper, 1936 State Fair In Maine, G.A. Hays, Frame, 10 1/4 x 13 1/4 In. 460.00
Watercolor On Paper, Alanson, Michigan, John Keenan, 1975, 11 x 17 1/2 In. 293.00
Watercolor On Paper, Bird Perched, On Branch, Blue Lined Paper, 6 x 4 In. 115.00
Watercolor On Paper, Merritt Road, Ypsilanti, Mich., John Keenan, 1975, 7 x 11 In. 410.00
Watercolor On Paper, Old Red Mill, Signed CHS, Aged 89, Shaker, New Hampshire 405.00
Watercolor On Paper, Still Life, Basket, Fruit, Flowers, Frame, 16 x 20 In. 940.00
Watercolor On Paper, Sunday Morning, Montague Charman, 1900s, 18 1/4 x 22 1/4 In. 263.00
Watercolor On Paper, Woman With Jug By Window, Harry Wooley, 1882, 24 x 18 In. 826.00
Wax, Portrait, Benjamin Franklin, Profile, Fur Hat, Shadow Box Frame, 8 x 7 In. 633.00

PIERCE, see Howard Pierce category.

PIGEON FORGE Pottery was started in Pigeon Forge, Tennessee, in 1946. Red clay found near the pottery was used to make the pieces. Molded or thrown pottery with matte glaze and slip decoration was made. The pottery closed in 2000.

Bowl, Signed, D. Ferguson, 3 1/8 x 7 7/8 In. 35.00
Vase, Signed, Campbell, 3 1/8 In. 9.00

PILKINGTON Tile and Pottery Company was established in 1892 in England. The company made small pottery wares, like buttons and hatpins, but soon started decorating vases purchased from other potteries. By 1903, the company had discovered an opalescent glaze that became popular on the Lancastrian pottery line. The manufacture of pottery ended in 1937. Pilkington's Tiles Ltd. has worked from 1938 to the present.

Vase, Fish, Relief, Frieze, Royal Lancastrian, Richard Joyce, c.1930, 5 In. 207.00
Vase, Red & Yellow Crystalline Glaze, Gourd Shape, 10 1/4 In. 360.00
Vase, Royal Lancastrian Lapis Ware, Bulbous, Feathers, Gladys Rodgers, c.1940, 7 1/2 In. 140.00

PINCUSHION DOLLS are not really dolls and often were not even pincushions. Some collectors use the term *half-doll*. The top half of each doll was made of porcelain. The edge of the half-doll was made with several small holes for thread, and the doll was stitched to a fabric body with a voluminous skirt. The finished figure was used to cover a hot pot of tea, powder box, pincushion, whisk broom, or lamp. They were made in sizes from less than an inch to over 9 inches high. Most date from the early 1900s to the 1950s. Collectors often find just the porcelain doll without the fabric skirt.

Bisque, Shoulder Head, Closed Mouth, Mohair Wig, Victorian Dress, 8 In. 235.00
French Courtesan, 1 Arm Up, Holding Hair, 1 Arm At Waist, Blue Comb, Silk Skirt, 3 1/2 In. 45.00
Nude, Turned Head, Bisque, Painted Eyes, Closed Mouth, Goebel, 6 1/4 In. 235.00
Porcelain, Painted Features, Mohair Wig, Cage Base, Early 1900s, 15 In. 120.00
Swimmer, Nude, Flapper Headdress, Porcelain, Germany, 5 In. 413.00
Woman, Arm Touching Hair, Ruffled Bodice, Hertzwig Germany, 1920s, 3 1/2 In. 42.00
Woman, Bisque, Gown, Low Cut Blouse, Feathered Hat, Fan, Germany, 6 1/2 x 4 1/2 In. 72.00
Woman, Holding Parrot, Waist Up, Bisque, Mohair, Germany, c.1915, 4 1/2 In. 715.00

PINK SLAG pieces are listed in this book in the Slag Glass category.

PIPES have been popular since tobacco was introduced to Europe by Sir Walter Raleigh. Carved wooden, porcelain, ivory, and glass pipes may be listed here.

Black Forest, Carved, Scenic Detail, Silver Mounts, Fitted Case, 19th Century, 19 In. 411.00
Black Forest, Carved, Winged Dragon, Ivory Teeth, Glass Eyes, Silver, c.1900 .... 1410.00
Briar, Scared Black Man Rides Head Of Beast, Bird Claw, 9 1/4 In. 220.00
Burl Wood, Face, Shield, Stars, Stripes, I.O.M., c.1925, 7 1/2 x 3 1/2 In. 92.00
Defiant Black Man, Clay, C. Crop, London, 1870s, 6 1/4 In. 144.00
Iron, Silver, Inlaid, Fish Net, Crescent Moon, Japan, 1800s, 8 In. 518.00
Meerschaum, Angry Man, Beard, Leather & Velvet Case, 1900s, 5 1/2 In. 118.00
Meerschaum, Bearded Turkish Man, Turban, Velvet Lined Case, 6 In. 66.00
Meerschaum, Bearded Warrior, Turkey, Paper, Box, 6 3/4 In. 77.00
Meerschaum, Black Man, Bearded, Amber Stem, Leather Case, Germany, 1890s, 4 1/4 In. 160.00
Meerschaum, Black Man, Germany, 1890s, 5 1/2 In. 213.00
Meerschaum, Devil, Turned Head With Horns, Satin & Velvet Case, Austria, 8 In. 132.00
Meerschaum, High Wheel Bicycle, Uniformed Rider, L. Hartman & E. Wien, Case, 6 1/2 In. 440.00
Meerschaum, Large Head Black Man, 1890s, 5 1/2 In. 190.00
Meerschaum, Uniformed Rider Standing Next To Safety Bicycle, Fitted Case, 4 In. 550.00
Porcelain, 2 Deer In Forest, Hand Painted, Wood, Tassel, 28 In. 121.00
Porcelain, 2 Hunters, Guns, Examining Dead Prey, Hand Painted, Wood, Am Anschufs, 45 In. 55.00
Porcelain, Soldier, Lady Strolling On Path, Signed, Promier Baron Y:13-Anton Gustav, 1893, 22 In. 88.00
Sign, Meerschaum, Briar Pipes, Reverse Silver Leaf, Glue Chip Glass, c.1900, 44 x 14 In. 550.00
PIPE CASE, Kiseruzutsu, Black & Gold Lacquer, Man, Demon, In Clouds, Japan, 1800s 316.00

Kiseruzutsu, Brown Lacquer, Sennin, Riding Carp, Japan, 1800s 978.00
Kiseruzutsu, Carved, Figures, Signed, Yozan, Japan, 1800s 1265.00

PISGAH FOREST pottery was made in North Carolina beginning in 1926. The pottery was started by Walter B. Stephen, who had been making pottery in that location since 1914. The pottery continued in operation after his death in 1961. The most famous kinds of Pisgah Forest ware are the cameo type with designs made of raised glaze and the turquoise crackle glaze wares.

Sugar & Creamer, Glossy, Rose Color, Feldspathic Glaze, 1929-39, 2 In. 66.00
Vase, Blue To Aubergine Glaze, 1950, 5 1/4 x 6 1/2 In. 80.00
Vase, Blue To Aubergine Glaze, Light Crackle Glaze, Mark, 1941, 9 x 5 1/4 In. 288.00
Vase, Bright Blue Crystalline Glaze, Pink Interior, 1938, 4 1/4 x 5 1/2 In. 80.00
Vase, Green, Blue, 3 3/4 In. 25.00
Vase, Oatmeal Glaze, Blue Crystalline Glaze, Cobalt Blue Interior, 1935, 9 3/4 x 7 1/4 In. 920.00
Vase, Turquoise, Crackle Glaze, 5 In. 30.00

PLANTERS PEANUTS memorabilia is collected. Planters Nut and Chocolate Company was started in Wilkes-Barre, Pennsylvania, in 1906. The Mr. Peanut figure was adopted as a trademark in 1916. National advertising for Planters Peanuts started in 1918. The company was acquired by Standard Brands, Inc., in 1961. Standard Brands merged with Nabisco in 1981. Some of the Mr. Peanut jars and other memorabilia have been reproduced and, of course, new items are being made.

Ashtray, Mr. Peanut, Figural, Green Pants, Ceramic, Japan, c.1930, 4 x 3 x 2 1/2 In. 632.00
Bank, Mr. Peanut, Vendor, Yellow, 1/2 Lb. Nuts, Key, Box, 8 x 5 1/4 In. 440.00
Bank, Orange, Plastic, Mr. Peanut Shape, 8 1/2 In. 470.00
Blotter, Gold Standard, Cardboard, 3 3/8 x 6 3/8 In. 210.00
Box, 2-Piece, Chocolate Peanuts, O Boy, 5 Cents, Kid Holding Pack, 7 x 9 In. 1075.00
Box, Cardboard, Candy Bar, Paper Wrapper, 5 1/4 x 10 1/2 x 5 In. 2090.00
Crate, Shipping, Wood, Stencil, Mr. Peanut, Juggling Peanuts, 9 1/4 x 25 1/4 In. 660.00
Display, Cardboard, 24 Bags, 5 Cents, Box, 1930s, 13 x 12 1/2 x 9 In. 6820.00
Display, Jumbo Peanut Block Bars, Good Food, 5 Cents, Tin Lithograph, 12 x 5 x 4 3/8 In. 2530.00
Display, Mr. Peanut Presents Cocktail Peanuts, Cardboard, c.1939, 16 x 15 x 4 In. 1425.00
Display Rack, Peanut Specialties, Z Shape, Tin Lithograph, 4 3/4 x 14 x 7 3/4 In. 1720.00
Jar, Barrel Shape, Original Label, Silver Highlight Paint, 11 1/2 x 8 1/2 In. 525.00
Jar, Cover, 8-Sided, Embossed, 5 Cents, Peanut Finial, c.1936, 13 In. 80.00
Jar, Cover, Mr. Peanut On 3 Sides, Yellow Paint, Pyro, Square, 9 1/2 In. 160.00
Jar, Cover, Salted Peanuts, Football, Peanut Finial, c.1930, 9 In. 250.00
Jar, Cover, Square, Peanut On Each Corner, Peanut Finial, c.1932, 14 In. 160.00
Jar, Mr. Peanut, 8-Sided, Peanut Finial, 13 In. 100.00
Jar Holder, Planters Salted Peanuts, Tin, Die Cut, Jar, Cover, 4 1/2 x 7 1/2 In. 2750.00
Mug, Ceramic, Mr. Peanut In Green Pants, Shell Handle, 1930s, 4 3/4 In. 500.00
Pail, Tin, Yellow Ground, Lithograph, Bail, 1 Lb., 4 x 3 3/4 In. 3960.00
Salt & Pepper, Mr. Peanut, Green Plastic, 3 In. 15.00
Sign, Bag A Day Brings Pep Your Way, Trolley Car Sign, 1920s, 11 x 21 In. 1155.00
Sign, Cocktail Peanuts, 10 Cents, Webster's, Cardboard Lithograph, c.1930, 11 x 21 In. 800.00
Sign, Delicious With Cocktails, Man Holding Tray, Cardboard, Frame, c.1930, 10 x 20 In. 469.00
Sign, Trolley, Good & Big, Cardboard, 16 x 23 7/8 In. 7370.00
Straw, Figural, Mr. Peanut, 1970, 8 In. 13.00
Tin, Planters Salted Peanuts, Mother's Brand, 8 x 6 1/2 In. 9020.00

PLASTIC objects of all types are being collected. Some pieces are listed in other categories; gutta-percha cases are listed in photography, celluloid in its own category.

Bowl, Fruit, Green & White Marble, 5 x 9 x 13 3/4 In. 26.00
Box, Cover, Marbleized Green, Catalin, 6 In. .... *ILLUS* 275.00
Box, Horse Heads, Black Lid, Red Bottom, 3 3/4 x 3 3/4 x 2 In. 68.00
Box, Recipe, Yellow, Hand Painted, Apples, Leaves, Metal Hinges, 1950s, 5 1/4 x 4 x 3 1/2 In. 24.00
Canister Set, Aqua, Cream Knob, Burrough's Mfg. Corp., 1950s, 7-In. Flour, 4 Piece 60.00
Canister Set, Tupperware, Apple Green, 1970s, 4 Piece 25.00

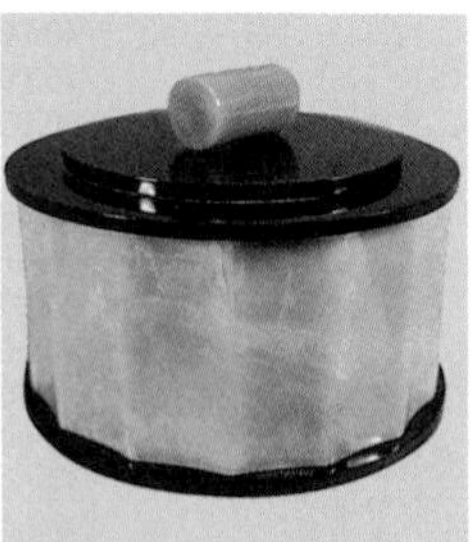
Plastic, Box, Cover, Marbleized Green, Catalin, 6 In.

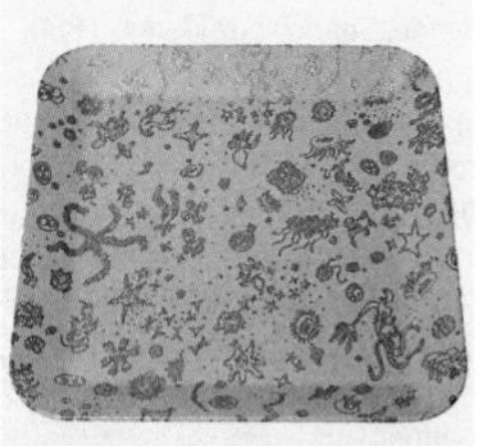
Plastic, Tray, Sea Things, Turquoise, Gold Decoration, Ray Eames, Waverly Products, 20 x 14 In.

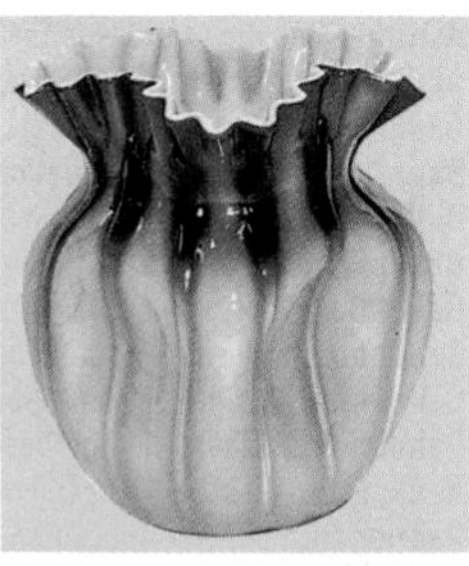
Plated Amberina, Vase, Pinched Sides, Rectangular, 4-Fold Ruffled Rim, 4 In.

Dresser Set, Art Deco, Mirror, Comb, Brush, Box, Lid, Black & Cream, Dupont USA, 1920s 30.00
Facial Massage Kit, Bakelite, 4 Massagers, Instructions, Henry Simons Box 100.00
Ice Bucket, Square, Swivelling Lid, Spherical Compartment, Lucite, 1960s, 6 3/4 In. 566.00
Juice Set, Sunkist Orange Juice, 7 Tumblers, 1970s, 9 3/4-In. Pitcher, 2 3/4-In. Tumbler 28.00
Manicure Set, 10 Tools, Bakelite, Box 353.00
Mixing Bowl, Melmac Spatter Texas Ware, 4 1/2 x 10 In. 35.00
Pitcher, Cover, Pink, White, Speckled, Gray, Vacron Logo, Bopp-Decker Plastics Inc., Mich. 20.00
Platter, Turkey, Thanksgiving, Acorn, Corn & Leaves Border, Red, Brown, Melmac 23.00
Puzzle, Elephant, Multicolor, Gold Colored Keychain, 1950s, 1 x 1 3/4 In. 38.00
Salad Set, Tan & Green, Melamine, Raffiaware, Cover, Server, 4 Piece 30.00
Snack Set, Thermo Temp, Raffiaware, Cups, Trays, 4 Piece 40.00
Thermal Ware Set, Straw-Weave, 4 Glasses, 4 Bowls, 4 Cups, 1950s, 9 1/4-In. Pitcher 65.00
Tray, Babylonia, White, Gray Decoration, Abel Sorenson, Boltabest, 1950s, 10 x 8 In. 300.00
Tray, China Shop, White, Gray, Yellow Decoration, George Nelson, Boltabest, 1950s, 11 x 14 In. ... 390.00
Tray, Sea Things, Turquoise, Gold Decoration, Ray Eames, Waverly Products, 20 x 14 In. .... *ILLUS* 360.00
Tray, White, Gray Stylized Wheels, B. Rudofsky, Boltabest, 1950s, 12 x 16 In. 180.00

PLATED AMBERINA was patented June 15, 1886, by Joseph Locke and made by the New England Glass Company. It is similar in color to amberina, but is characterized by a cream colored or chartreuse lining (never white) and small ridges or ribs on the outside.

Bride's Basket, Inward Crimped Rim, Tufts Silver Plated Holder, 4-Footed, 14 In. 10063.00
Creamer, Applied Amber Handle, 2 1/2 In. 9200.00
Cruet, Bulbous, Tricornered Rim, Applied Amber Handle, Faceted Stopper, 7 In. 6900.00
Pitcher, Bulbous, Tricornered Rim, Applied Amber Handle, 4 1/2 In. 15525.00
Punch Cup, Applied Amber Handle, 2 1/2 In. 2760.00
Punch Cup, Applied Amber Looped Handle, 2 1/2 In. 2588.00
Shaker, Pillar, 4 In. 5175.00
Syrup, Applied Loop Handle, Tufts Silver Plated Caddy, Flip Lid, 6 In. 8625.00
Tumbler, 3 3/4 In. .... 2185.00 to 2415.00
Tumbler, Barrel, 3 3/4 In. 375.00
Vase, Pinched Sides, Rectangular, 4-Fold Ruffled Rim, 4 In. .... *ILLUS* 27600.00
Vase, Pinched Sides, Rectangular, 4-Fold, Ruffled Edge, 4 In. 7475.00
Vase, Trumpet, Ruffled Edge, Tufts Silver Plated Holder, Eagle On Rock, 12 In. 1898.00

POLITICAL memorabilia of all types, from buttons to banners, is collected. Items related to presidential candidates are the most popular, but collectors also search for material related to state and local offices. Memorabilia related to social causes, minor political parties, and protest movements are also included here. Many reproductions have been made. A jugate is a button with photographs of both the presidential and vice presidential candidates. In this list a button is round, usually with a straight pin or metal tab to secure it to a shirt. A pin is brass, often figural, sometimes attached to a ribbon.

Admittance Pass, White House, Franklin D. Roosevelt, Feb. 18, 1933 .... 306.00

Ashtray, Eisenhower, Now Is The Hour, Plastic, 1955, 4 x 4 In. 40.00
Ax, Abraham Lincoln, Rail Splitters Brigade, Shadowbox Frame, 1860, 39 x 16 In. 8725.00
Badge, Emancipation, 1863 .... 3640.00
Bag, Elephant, Republican National Convention, Coke, Plastic, Red, 1960, 12 x 10 In. 25.00
Balloon, Cleveland, Thurman, 1888, 16 x 20 In. 400.00
Ballot Box, Cherry, Brass Handle, 1800s, 9 1/2 In. 25.00
Ballot Box, Pine, Poplar, Dark Stain, Perry County, Ohio, 21 x 26 x 18 In. 85.00
Bandanna, I Like Ike, Rayon Type Material, Elephant Border, 1950s, 28 In. 40.00
Bandanna, McKinley, Hobart, Sound Money, Protection, Frame, 1896, 21 1/2 x 21 1/2 In. 380.00
Bandanna, Win With Ike For President, 27 x 27 In. 86.00
Bank, F.D.R., New Deal, Green Base, Kenton, 5 In. 275.00
Banner, Harrison, Morton, Linen, Multicolored Printing, 1888, 21 x 23 1/2 In. 460.00
Banner, Harrison, Morton, Red, White, Blue, Stars, Frame, 1888, 36 1/4 x 20 1/8 In. 345.00
Banner, Harrison, Reid, Red, White, Blue, Frame, 1892, 31 x 71 In. 355.00
Banner, Progressive Party, Roosevelt, Johnson, 1912, 36 x 60 In. 8720.00
Banner, Vote For Woman Suffrage, Frame, 1916, 19 1/2 x 37 In. 2095.00
Blotter, Eisenhower, Nixon, Lancaster Co., Teen-Age Republican Club, 1952, 3 1/4 x 8 In. 10.00
Booklet, Get The US Out Of Hock, Willkie, Cartoons, Text, 16 Pages 15.00
Booklet, Greatest Show On Earth, Anti-LBJ Cartoons, 7 1/2 x 5 In., 20 Pages 8.00
Booklet, Ike & Nixon, Victory Song, Heavy Stock Paper, Phila., 4 1/2 x 6 In., 4 Pages 11.00
Booklet, Let's Put Robert Kennedy To Work For New York, 11 x 8 1/2 In., 8 Pages 8.00
Booklet, Young Man From Boston, JFK, Pictures, 24 Pages 10.00
Bookmark, Jimmy Carter, Welcome Home, Heavy Stock Paper, Jan. 20, 1981, 8 In. 6.00
Bookmark, LBJ, Welsh, Die Cut Top, Heavy Stock Paper, 8 In. 9.00
Bottle, Bryan, Sewall, In Silver We Trust, Silver Dollar Shape, Amber, 1896, 5 1/8 In. 604.00
Bottle, Embossed Bust Of General MacArthur, Green, 1942, 6 In. 55.00
Bottle Stopper, JFK, Figural, Wood, Painted Cork, 1962, 4 In. 55.00
Bumper Sticker, Sick Of Dick, Vote Democratic, 4 x 7 1/2 In. 5.00
Bust, Stephen A. Douglas, Parian, 8 1/2 In. 1227.00
Bust, Thomas Jefferson, Parian, 11 1/2 In. 427.00
Button, Adam Clayton Powell, Member Powell For Congress Club, Celluloid, 1 In. 182.00
Button, Adlai & Estes, Right Will Prevail, 4-Leaf Clover, 1956, 2 1/4 In. 549.00
Button, Al & Joe, Let's Go, 1928, 1 3/4 In. 2657.00
Button, Al Smith, Derby Hat, Smiling, 1 1/4 In. 855.00
Button, Al Smith, Joe Robinson, Celluloid, Jugate, 1928, 7/8 In. 479.00
Button, Al Smith, Photograph, Black & White, Celluloid, 2 1/8 In. 400.00
Button, Al Smith, President, Enamel, 7/8 In. 36.00
Button, Alfred E. Smith For President, Brown Derby Hat, Photograph, 1928, 1 1/4 In. 879.00
Button, All I Have Left Is A Vote For Willkie, Blue, White, 1 1/4 In. 9.00
Button, All The Way With LBJ, Celluloid, 7/8 In. 11.00
Button, All's Well With Willkie, White Letters, Red & Blue Ground, 7/8 In. 11.00
Button, Another Indian Supports Anderson, President, Red, White, Celluloid, 1 3/4 In. 8.00
Button, Anti-Nixon, Thailand, Celluloid, 1 1/4 In. 10.00
Button, Better Red Than Dead, Red, Black, 1 3/4 In. 15.00
Button, Betty & Gerald Ford, I'm Betting On Betty's Husband, Photo, 1976, 3 In. 365.00
Button, Black Is Beautiful, Panther, Blue Ground, Celluloid, 1 1/4 In. 17.00
Button, Black Panther Party, Black Power, Hand Holding Gun, 1 3/4 In. 27.00
Button, Brotherhood Is Love, Blue, Black & White Handshake, Celluloid, 1972, 2 1/2 In. 10.00
Button, Bryan & His Farm Corn, Oval, William Jennings Bryan, 2 3/8 In. 1587.00
Button, Bryan, 16 To 1 Daisy, Celluloid, Whitehead & Hoag Back Paper, 7/8 In. 65.00
Button, Bryan, Kern, Blue Ground, Celluloid, Jugate Scrolled Frames, 1908, 1 3/4 In. 2905.00
Button, Bryan, Kern, Clean Sweep, Jugate, 1908, 1 1/4 In. 1298.00
Button, Bryan, Kern, Lady Liberty, Jugate, 1908, 1 3/4 In. 3125.00
Button, Bryan, Shaking Hands With Farmer, United We Stand, 1908, 1 3/4 In. 1995.00
Button, Bryan, Stevenson Jugate, NADC, Constitution & Flag, 1900, 1 1/4 In. 50.00
Button, Bryan, Unlimited Silver, High Admiral Cigarettes, Celluloid, 7/8 In. 20.00
Button, Bryan, Whitehead & Hoag Back Paper, Jugate, c.1900, 7/8 In. 86.00
Button, Bull Moose, TR, Teddy Roosevelt, 1912, 7/8 In. 30.00
Button, Bush, Anti Duke, Cartoon, Celluloid, 3 In. 27.00
Button, Bush, Dukakis Is A Greek Tragedy, Celluloid, 2 In. 12.00
Button, Button, Atomic Cloud, 2 1/8 In. 625.00

Button, Carter In '76, 1 3/4 In. 4.00
Button, Carter, Committee Of 51.3% For Jimmy Carter, White, Green, Celluloid, 2 1/2 In. 39.00
Button, Carter, Illinois Federation Of Teachers, Rowlett Coattail, Celluloid, 2 1/2 In. 14.00
Button, Carter, Mondale, 1 1/4 In. 7.00
Button, Carter, Mondale, Universe, Stripes, Phillips Manufacturing, 1976, 4 In. 2289.00
Button, Chelsea Clinton, Vote For My Daddy, Bill Clinton For President, 2 1/4 In. 502.00
Button, Cleaver For President, 1968, 1 1/4 In. 7.00
Button, Clinton, Alexander Country, Clinton, Gore, Oval, Celluloid, 2 1/2 In. 19.00
Button, Clinton, Arkansas Pride, America's Hope, Little Rock, June 23, 1995, 3 1/2 In. 99.00
Button, Clinton, Oregon For Clinton Gore, Celluloid, 1992, 2 In. 32.00
Button, Clinton, Oval Office, Roy Lichtenstein, Celluloid, 2 1/2 In. 204.00
Button, Clinton, Penn State Students Fighting For Our Future, Celluloid, 2 In. 16.00
Button, Clinton, Winning Team, Wisconsin Coattail, Johnson For Congress, Football Shape 25.00
Button, Coolidge, Conn. Club, Cruler, Oval, 7/8 In. 24.00
Button, Coolidge, Dawes, Capitol, Jugate, 1924, 7/8 In. 2986.00
Button, Coolidge, Dawes, Eagle, Lithograph, Jugate, 7/8 In. 322.00
Button, Coolidge, Dawes, Jugate, 1924, 6 In. 12650.00
Button, Cox, Coxsure, Lithograph, J.L. Lynch Co. Reverse, 5/8 In. 34.00
Button, Deadheads For Dukakis, 1988, 2 1/4 In. 305.00
Button, Debs, Seidel, Jugate, 1912, 1 1/4 In. 1020.00
Button, Debs, Stedman, Socialist Party, Red, White, Celluloid, 1920, 7/8 In. 872.00
Button, Dewey & Warren For Prosperity, Jugate, 1948, 6 In. 4478.00
Button, Dewey, Ribbon, Celluloid, 1 1/4 In. 10.00
Button, Dewey, Victory Special, Celluloid, 2 1/2 In. 102.00
Button, Dewey, Warren, Jugate, Celluloid, 3 In. 56.00
Button, Dole, Kansas Cyclone, Celluloid, 3 In. 77.00
Button, Draft Dewey For Governor, Blue, White, 7/8 In. 22.00
Button, Draft Dewey, Bastian Bros., Celluloid, c.1940, 1 In. 20.00
Button, Edith Willkie For First Lady, Photograph, Celluloid, 1940, 1 1/4 In. 40.00
Button, Eisenhower, Nixon, Inauguration Day, 1953, Wyoming, Equality State, Jugate, 3 1/2 In. 750.00
Button, Eisenhower, Nixon, Names On Red Ground, White, Blue, Jugate, 1952, 3 1/2 In. 638.00
Button, Eldridge Cleaver, Black Panthers, Photograph, Celluloid, 1 3/4 In. 14.00
Button, Elephant, Goldwater, Victory, Celluloid, 3 In. 724.00
Button, Enemies Of Special Privilege, 2 1/16 In. 2313.00
Button, Eugene Debs, Ben Hanford, Socialist Candidates, 1904, 1 1/4 In. 747.00
Button, FDR, Brewery Workers Choice, Lucke Badge Co., Celluloid, 1 3/4 In. 842.00
Button, FDR, Celluloid, Phila. Badge Curl, 7/8 In. 96.00
Button, FDR, Democratic Club Of Denver, Photograph, 1 1/4 In. 305.00
Button, FDR, Democratic State Convention, Michigan, Ribbon, Celluloid, c.1936, 1 3/4 In. 894.00
Button, FDR, For Vice President, Celluloid, c.1920, 1 1/4 In. 2540.00
Button, FDR, Happy Birthday, Photograph, Celluloid, 7/8 In. 40.00
Button, FDR, Hello Democrats, Democratic Convention, 1932, 1 3/4 In. 31.00
Button, FDR, Mechanical, Kick Out Depression With A Democratic Vote, c.1932, 2 1/2 In. 109.00
Button, FDR, Okay America, You Bet I'm With You, Celluloid, Ribbon, Pin, c.1933, 2 1/8 In. 460.00
Button, FDR, Re-Elect Roosevelt, 1936, 15/16 In. 660.00
Button, FDR, Sharp Photo, Celluloid, 1 1/4 In. 16.00
Button, FDR, Talking On Phone, 2 1/4 In. 498.00
Button, FDR, Texas For Roosevelt & Truman, Union Label Reverse, 7/8 In. 25.00
Button, FDR, Win What With Willkie, Yellow Ground, Celluloid, 1 1/4 In. 15.00
Button, Ford, Dole, Flasher, 2 1/2 In. 19.00
Button, Ford, Dole, Spirograph, Red, White, Blue, Jugate, 4 In. 94.00
Button, Ford, What America Needs America Had, Celluloid, 1 1/2 In. 10.00
Button, Foster, Ford, Vote Communist, Celluloid, Jugate, 1932, 1 1/4 In. 506.00
Button, Franklin D. Roosevelt For President, Reverse Green Duck, Lithograph, 1 1/4 In. 58.00
Button, Franklin D. Roosevelt, Photograph, Celluloid, 7/8 In. 80.00
Button, Franklin Roosevelt For U.S. Senator, 1914, 7/8 In. 375.00
Button, Franklin Roosevelt, John Nance Gardner, Patriotic Border, Celluloid, Jugate, 1 1/4 In. 1025.00
Button, Furriers For Roosevelt, Photograph, Blue, White, Celluloid, 2 In. 2175.00
Button, Gary Hart, President, We Can't Win 'Em All, 1988, 3 In. 10.00
Button, Gen. Dwight D. Eisenhower, Military Uniform, 1 1/4 In. 9.50
Button, Geraldine Ferraro, America's 1st Woman Vice President, Heart Shape, 1984, 2 3/4 In. 10.00

Button, Glow In Dark, Goldwater, Miller, GOParty, Celluloid, 1964, 1 1/2 In. 125.00
Button, Goldwater In 64, Cold Water In 65, Bread & Water In 66, 3 1/2 In. 10.00
Button, Goldwater, Democrats For Goldwater, Celluloid, 1 1/4 In. 22.00
Button, Goldwater, For Good Roots, Democratic Lyndon Tree, 3 1/2 In. 460.00
Button, Goldwater, For President, Gold Ground, Black Letters, Celluloid, 1 1/2 In. 128.00
Button, Goldwater, Language Key, Portuguese, 1 1/4 In. 40.00
Button, Goldwater, Language Key, Slovak, 1 1/4 In. 14.00
Button, Goldwater, Miller, Stop Socialism, Celluloid, 1 1/2 In. 40.00
Button, Goldwater, Photo, Flasher, Gold Metal Frame, 1 1/4 In. 14.00
Button, Gore, Laborers Take Action, Celluloid, 2000, 2 3/4 In. 13.00
Button, Greeley, Cardboard, 1872, 7/8 In. 550.00
Button, Harding & Kendall Club, Des Moines, Ia., 1 In. 450.00
Button, Harding, Bluetone, Dark Blue Field, Stars, 7/8 In. 610.00
Button, Harding, Coolidge, Jugate, 1920, 7/8 In. 1815.00
Button, Harding, Sepia Fob, c.1920, 1 1/2 In. 305.00
Button, Harrison, Morton, Eagle, Tassel, Mechanical, 1888, 3 1/2 x 2 1/2 In. 419.00
Button, Hoover & Curtis, Elephant, Blue, 7/8 In. 17.00
Button, Hoover, Curtis, Celluloid, Whitehead & Hoag, Back Paper, Jugate, 7/8 In. 205.00
Button, Hoover, Draped Flag, 2 1/4 In. 478.00
Button, Hoover, Full Dinner Pail, Red, White, Blue, Lithograph, 1928, 7/8 In. 666.00
Button, Hoover, Lithograph, 7/8 In. 666.00
Button, Hughes Workers For Law & Liberty, Celluloid, Baltimore Badge, 7/8 In. 26.00
Button, Humphrey, Muskie, 1 1/4 In. 5.00
Button, I Like Ike & Dick, Red, White, Blue, Lithograph, 7/8 In. ....36.00 to 44.00
Button, I Like Ike, Black Ground, Red Letters, Celluloid, 2 1/2 In. 11.00
Button, I'm A Nixon Lodge Volunteer, Celluloid, Oval, 1960, 2 1/8 In. 479.00
Button, I'm An Ike Block Buster, Red, White, 1 1/4 In. 13.00
Button, I'm For Nixon, Celluloid, Picture, 1956, 1 In. 82.00
Button, Ike, Dem-Ike-Crats, Lithograph, 1 1/4 In. 18.00
Button, Ike, Elect A Republican Congress, Lithograph, 1 In. 17.00
Button, Ike, I'm For Keeping Eisenhower, Blue Ground, White Letters, Celluloid, 1956, 3 In. 30.00
Button, Ike, National Citizens For Eisenhower, Outline Of United States, 1 1/2 In. 55.00
Button, James M. Cox, 1 1/4 In. 465.00
Button, James M. Cox, 1920, 7/8 In. 1025.00
Button, JFK, Johnson, Jugate, Vote Democratic, Celluloid, 3 In. 60.00
Button, JFK, Kennedy For President, NG Slater Curl, Celluloid, 1 1/4 In. 14.00
Button, JFK, LBJ, Leadership For The 60s, Jugate, Lithograph, 3 In. 37.00
Button, JFK, LBJ, Stars & Stripes Ground, Flasher, 2 1/2 In. 42.00
Button, JFK, Row All The Way, 1 1/2 In. 801.00
Button, JFK, Royalty, King Olav 5 Norway, 17 Mai, Lenge Leve, Celluloid, 1 1/4 In. 65.00
Button, Joe & I For Willkie, 1940, 1 1/4 In. 460.00
Button, Joe Louis Endorses Willkie, Brown Bomber, Joe & I Want Willkie, 1 1/4 In. 660.00
Button, John F. Kennedy, Youth For Kennedy, Red Writing, 1958, 2 1/4 In. 885.00
Button, John Glenn, Friendship 7, Feb. 20 1962, Celluloid, 1 1/4 In. 170.00
Button, John W. Davis, 2 1/4 In. 11500.00
Button, Johnson, Humprhey, Scientists, Engineers, 1 1/2 In. 7.00
Button, Kennedy & Peace, Photograph, Red, White, Blue, 1968, 7/8 In. 11.00
Button, Kennedy For President In '68, 3 1/2 In. 20.00
Button, Kennedy Is The Remedy, 4 In. 8652.00
Button, Kennedy, Johnson Coattail, New York, Celluloid, 4 In. 40.00
Button, Kennedy, Johnson, Donkey Shape, Tab, 1 In. 25.00
Button, Kennedy, Johnson, Jugate, 2 1/4 In. 54.00
Button, Kennedy, Johnson, Jugate, 4 In. 90.00
Button, Kennedy, Johnson, Red Letters, Celluloid, St. Louis Button Co., Jugate, 7/8 In. 267.00
Button, Kennedy, Vote Democratic, Flasher, 3 In. 39.00
Button, Labor Farm Workers, Grape Boycott, Don't Eat Grapes, Celluloid, 1 1/2 In. 25.00
Button, LaFollette & Wheeler, People's Choice, Celluloid, Jugate, 1924, 1 1/2 In. 1450.00
Button, Landon, Knox, President, Vice President, Jugate, 1936, 7/8 In. 294.00
Button, Landon, Letters In Sunflower, 7/8 In. 11.00
Button, Landon, Sunflower, 1 1/4 In. 12.00
Button, LBJ, Liar, Buffoon, Judas, Gold Color, 1 1/2 In. 66.00

Button, Life Begins In '40, Elephant, Willkie, 7/8 In. 22.00
Button, Long Live The President, GW, Copper, 1789, 1 1/4 In. 4427.00
Button, McCarthy, Blue Ribbon Ground, Photo, 1968, 4 In. 222.00
Button, McCarthy, More Than Ever, 1 1/4 In. 7.00
Button, McGovern, California, Photo, 2 1/2 In. 16.00
Button, McGovern, If I Was 18 I'd Vote For McGovern, Red, Yellow, Celluloid, 1 1/2 In. 17.00
Button, McGovern, Peace Dove, Celluloid, 1972, 1 In. 14.00
Button, McGovern, Peter Max, Celluloid, 1 1/2 In. 377.00
Button, McGovern, Yellow Flower, White Stars, Pink Ground, 1 In. 15.00
Button, McKinley, Back Paper Lists U.S. Presidents, Ohio Badge Co., Celluloid, 2 1/4 In. 121.00
Button, McKinley, Patriotism Prosperity, Draped Flag, Multicolored, 2 1/8 In. 1050.00
Button, McKinley, Portrait, Brass Frame Border, Celluloid, 1 1/4 In. 250.00
Button, McKinley, Roosevelt, Eagle, Rough Rider, Jugate, 1900, 1 3/4 In. 1380.00
Button, McKinley, Roosevelt, Full Dinner Bucket, Jugate, 1900, 1 1/4 In. 3289.00
Button, McKinley, Sepia Cell Image, Carnation At Top, Attached Ribbon, 1 1/4 In. 65.00
Button, McKinley, Sepia Photograph, 1896, 1 1/4 In. 35.00
Button, McKinley, Sound Money, Celluloid, 3/4 In. 15.00
Button, McKinley, Whitehead & Hoag, Back Paper, Patriotic Design, 1 1/4 In. 24.00
Button, Mount Wilson, Above The Clouds, Cartoon Design, Celluloid, 1 1/2 In. 484.00
Button, N.A.A.C.P., White, Brown, Lithograph, 1948, 7/8 In. 56.00
Button, NAACP, Members, Blue Ground, White Letters, Lithograph, 1965, 7/8 In. 22.00
Button, New England Presents Edward M. Kennedy, Vice President, Photograph, 2 In. 80.00
Button, New Yorkers For Ross Perot '92, 1 3/4in. 4.00
Button, Nix On Nixon, Red, White, 1 1/4 In. 5.00
Button, Nixon Bugs Me, 1 1/4 In. 5.00
Button, Nixon, Lodge, Experience Counts, Jugate, Celluloid, 3 In. 11.00
Button, Nixon, Lodge, Stars & Stripes Ground, Flasher, 2 1/2 In. 20.00
Button, Nixon, They Can't Lick Our Dick, 1 3/4 In. 27.00
Button, No Draft Registration, Democratic Convention, Blue, White, 1 3/4 In. 33.00
Button, Of Course It's Romney In '68, 1 1/4 In. 6.00
Button, Oklahoma Territory, Celluloid, 1 1/4 In. 186.00
Button, Palmer, Buckner, Jugate, Gold Democrats, Celluloid, 1 1/2 In. 545.00
Button, Parker, Celluloid, Metal Border, Filled Back, St. Louis, Jugate, 1 1/4 In. 363.00
Button, Parker, Davis, Eagle, Crossed Flags, Sunlight Rays, Celluloid, 1 3/4 In. 799.00
Button, Parker, Davis, Red Border, Flag At Center, Jugate, 1 1/4 In. 487.00
Button, Parker, Davis, Shure Mike, Jugate, 1904, 1 1/4 In. 665.00
Button, Peace, White Dove, Blue Ground, Celluloid, 1 3/4 In. 13.00
Button, Peacemonger, White Letters, Black Ground, 1970s, 1 3/4 In. 25.00
Button, Phooey On Dewey, Celluloid, 1948, 1 1/4 In. 50.00
Button, President Roosevelt Reception, G.G.I.E., 1939, 2 1/4 In. 1000.00
Button, Reagan, Clements, Texas, Celluloid, 1980, 1 3/4 In. 11.00
Button, Reagan, Death Valley Days, Celluloid, 3 In. 21.00
Button, Reagan, The Reagan Bush Bears Bitter Fruit, Celluloid, 1 3/4 In. 30.00
Button, Reagan, Wearing Cowboy Hat, Map Of Minnesota, Blue, White, 1984, 2 1/4 In. 132.00
Button, Reagan, Yuma Area Reagan '84 Teenage Republicans, Celluloid, 1 3/4 In. 30.00
Button, RFK, Kennedy & Peace, Celluloid, 1968, 7/8 In. 22.00
Button, RFK, Not Too Late In '68, White Ground, Blue Letters, Celluloid, 1 1/4 In. 80.00
Button, Ribbon, FDR, Vote Straight Democrat, General Election, Nov. 8, 1938, 3 1/2 In. 175.00
Button, Ribbon, McKinley, Celluloid, 1 3/4 In. 85.00
Button, Ribbon, McKinley, First Voters, 7/8 In. 49.00
Button, Ribbon, Roosevelt, Fairbanks, Lady Liberty, 1904, 2 1/8 x 6 In. 730.00
Button, Ribbon, Roosevelt, We Want FDR, Voting Straight Democratic, 4 In. 164.00
Button, Roosevelt, Eagle Design, J. Florsheim Back Paper, 1 1/4 In. 195.00
Button, Roosevelt, Fairbanks, Baltimore Badge, Celluloid, Jugate, 1904, 1 1/4 In. 187.00
Button, Roosevelt, Fairbanks, Eagle, Ballot Box, Celluloid, Jugate, c.1904, 1 1/4 In. 1738.00
Button, Roosevelt, Fairbanks, Lady Liberty, Jugate, 1 1/4 In. 182.00
Button, Roosevelt, Fairbanks, National Equipment Co., Jugate, c.1904, 7/8 In. 166.00
Button, Roosevelt, Fairbanks, Red, White, Blue, 1 3/4 In. 400.00
Button, Roosevelt, Fairbanks, Sepia, Filled Back, Jugate, 1 1/4 In. 70.00
Button, Roosevelt, Johnson, Progressive, Jugate, 1912, 1 3/4 In. 5420.00
Button, Roosevelt, Labor's Friend, 1 1/4 In. 30.00

Button, Roosevelt, The Winner, Celluloid, c.1912, 2 1/8 In. 738.00
Button, Roosevelt, Theodore, Fairbanks, Flag, Shield, Eagle, Jugate, c.1904, 1 1/4 In. 695.00
Button, Roosevelt, Truman, Tab, 1944, 7/8 In. 25.00
Button, Roosevelt, Wallace, Ear Of Corn, Lithograph, 1940, 7/8 In. 15.00
Button, Roosevelt, Wallace, Lithograph, Geraghty Curl, Jugate, c.1940, 7/8 In. 11.00
Button, Rough Rider, Teddy Roosevelt In Uniform, Celluloid, 2 1/4 In. 1145.00
Button, Save The Constitution, Impeach Nixon, 1 1/2 In. 5.00
Button, Seymour, Ferrotype, 1868, 11/16 In. 742.00
Button, Shield G Man Club, 1 3/4 In. 535.00
Button, Shirley Chisholm, For President, Celluloid, 1972, 1 3/4 In. 19.00
Button, Shirt, Willkie, 1940 .... 245.00
Button, Socialist Party, Debs, Seidel, Jugate, 1912, 1 1/4 In. 1500.00
Button, Solidarnosc, For Reagan, Solidarity, Red, White, 1 3/4 In. 90.00
Button, Stevenson, Labor Supports, Red White Blue, Lithograph, 7/8 In. 15.00
Button, Stevenson, Labor Union, Local 32, I.L.G.W.U., New York, Celluloid, 1 In. 420.00
Button, Stevenson, Precinct Chairman, Stevenson Campaign Committee, Lithograph, 1 1/4 In. 16.00
Button, Stevenson, Sparkman Jugate, Celluloid, 1952, 3 In. 43.00
Button, Taft, Art Nouveau, Jugate, 1 1/4 In. 400.00
Button, Taft, Girl, Blowing Horn, Flag, Art Nouveau, 1908, 1 3/4 In. 2839.00
Button, Taft, Sherman, Celluloid, Jugate, 7/8 In. 19.00
Button, Taft, Sherman, Eagle, Liberty Cap, Celluloid, Jugate, 7/8 In. 900.00
Button, Taft, Sherman, GOP, Elephant Ears, Celluloid, 1908, 1 1/4 In. 6090.00
Button, Taft, Sherman, Stars & Stripes, Jugate, 1908, 1 1/4 In. 460.00
Button, Taft, The Safest, Celluloid, 7/8 In. 17.00
Button, Ted Kennedy For President, Photograph, Red Border, Celluloid, 1968, 7/8 In. 17.00
Button, Teddy Kennedy, Leadership For 80's, Flasher, 1980 .... 17.00
Button, Teddy Roosevelt, Booker T. Washington, Equality, 1904, 1 1/4 In. 4475.00
Button, Teddy Roosevelt, Four Years More, Photograph In Badge, Celluloid, 1 1/4 In. 3090.00
Button, Teddy Roosevelt, Hiram Johnson, Progressives, Jugate, 1912, 1 3/4 In. 11000.00
Button, Teddy Roosevelt, Joseph Weeks Babcock, Coattail, Sepia, Jugate, 1904, 1 1/4 In. 358.00
Button, Teddy Roosevelt, My Hat Is In The Ring, Photograph, Celluloid, 1912, 1 1/4 In. 650.00
Button, Teddy Roosevelt, Our Country's Choice For Another Term, Photograph, 1 1/4 In. 968.00
Button, Teddy Roosevelt, Photograph In Sepia, 1 1/4 In. 50.00
Button, Teddy Roosevelt, Rough Rider, Photograph, Attached Flag Ribbon, 2 1/8 In. 1392.00
Button, Teddy Roosevelt, Shield, Jugate, 1904, 1 1/4 In. 705.00
Button, The Coming Of Carter, Cartoon, Newsweek Cover, Celluloid, 2 1/2 In. 25.00
Button, Together For McGovern, Rainbow, 3 In. 55.00
Button, Truman For Senator, 1940s, 7/8 In. 430.00
Button, Truman, 60 Million People Working, Celluloid, 2 1/4 In. 7315.00
Button, Truman, 60 Million People Working, Why Change, Photograph, Celluloid, 2 In. 7315.00
Button, Truman, Barkley, Jugate, 1948, 7/8 In. 637.00
Button, Truman, Barkley, Lithograph, Bastian Bros. Curl, 7/8 In. 40.00
Button, Truman, Barkley, Red Donkey, 1940s, 1 1/4 In. 575.00
Button, Truman, Jugate, 1 1/4 In. 460.00
Button, V-J Day, Victory Over Japan, World War I, Celluloid, 1 1/4 In. 112.00
Button, Vietnam, Anti War, Patriotic, Honor America, Leave Vietnam, Celluloid, 1 1/4 In. 38.00
Button, Vietnam, Guns For Christ, Celluloid, 1 1/4 In. 22.00
Button, Virginia Loves Grits & Fritz, Red Heart, Green Ground, 1 1/2 In. 10.00
Button, Viva Kennedy, Yellow Ground, Red Sombrero, Lithograph, 1 3/8 In. 27.00
Button, Viva Reagan, Bush, White Letters, Blue Ground, 1 3/4 In. 11.00
Button, Vote Gladly For Adlai, White, Blue, 7/8 In. 13.00
Button, Vote The Kennedy Ticket, Chicago, Red, White, 4 In. 908.00
Button, Vote Truman For President, Easel Back, 1948, 9 In. 1091.00
Button, Vote Truman For President, Photograph, White, Red & Blue Stripes, 3 1/2 In. 1815.00
Button, Votes For Women Suffrage, Purple, Green, Merchants Portrait Co., 1 1/4 In. 799.00
Button, We Need Adlai Badly, Yellow Ground, Celluloid, 4 In. 485.00
Button, We Praise America, Roosevelt Again, Celluloid, 1 3/4 In. 550.00
Button, We Want Mamie, Photograph Of Mamie Eisenhower, 1 1/4 In. 25.00
Button, We Want Willkie, White Ground, Blue Lettering, Red Rim, Celluloid, 1 3/4 In. 10.00
Button, William J. Bryan, For President, Sepia, Photo, 1900, 1 1/2 In. 135.00
Button, William Jennings Bryan, 4 Ears Of Corn, 2 3/8 In. 1587.00

Button, William Jennings Bryan, Corn, Fairview Farm, Oval, 2 3/8 In. 1587.00
Button, Willkie For President, 2 3/4 In. 926.00
Button, Willkie For President, Celluloid, 1 1/4 In. 50.00
Button, Willkie Now Or The Roosevelts Forever, Celluloid, 7/8 In. 30.00
Button, Willkie, Anti Eleanor, Anti New Deal, Outhouse, Lithograph, 1 5/8 In. 40.00
Button, Willkie, Anti Royalty, No Crown For Franklin, Celluloid, 1 1/4 In. 15.00
Button, Willkie, Better Living, 1 1/4 In. 518.00
Button, Willkie, Celluloid, A.G. Trimble Curl, 7/8 In. 26.00
Button, Willkie, Every Buddy For Willkie, In World War I Uniform, Celluloid, 1 In. 158.00
Button, Willkie, For President Will, Attached Metal Key, Celluloid, 7/8 In. 20.00
Button, Willkie, Napoleon Met His Waterloo, Frank You Will Too, Celluloid, 1 1/4 In. 18.00
Button, Willkie, No 3rd Term, The Constitutionists, 1940, 7/8 In. 10.00
Button, Willkie, Perhaps Roosevelt Is All You Deserve, Celluloid, 1 1/4 In. 15.00
Button, Willkie, Red Letters, Gold Ground, 7/8 In. 10.00
Button, Willkie, White Ground, Blue Lettering, Red Rim, Celluloid, 3 In. 14.00
Button, Wilson, Green Edge, Celluloid, 1912, 7/8 In. 45.00
Button, Wilson, Marshall Campaign, Jugate, 1912, 1 3/4 In. 1665.00
Button, Wilson, Marshall, Black, White, Jugate, 1912, 1 3/4 In. 1665.00
Button, Wilson, Marshall, Star, Stripe Panels, Jugate, 1 1/4 In. 830.00
Button, Wilson, Miss Liberty, Jugate, 1 1/4 In. 1265.00
Button, Wilson, Preparedness, Peace, Prosperity, Red, White, Blue, 7/8 In. 20.00
Button, Wilson, Progressive Policies Become Law, Celluloid, 7/8 In. 30.00
Button, Wilson, Scrolled Metal Frame, Wilson Wearing Hat, 1 1/4 In. 80.00
Button, Wilson, Sharp Photo, Celluloid, 1 1/4 In. 40.00
Button, Win With Wilson, Red, White, Blue, Celluloid, 7/8 In. 28.00
Button, Wm. H. Taft For President, Sepia Photograph, 1 1/4 In. 35.00
Button, Wm. J. Bryan, For President, Color Photograph, 1908, 1 1/4 In. 50.00
Button, Woodrow Wilson, Photograph, Stars & Stripes Border, 1 1/4 In. 1425.00
Campaign Print, Currier & Ives, Lincoln, Hamlin, Frame, 1860, 12 x 16 In. 4629.00
Card, Barnes For Supreme Court, Myers For Superior Court, 2 3/4 x 4 In. 9.00
Card, Ben Butler, Riding Presidential Ram, Rides His Own Hobby, 3 x 4 1/2 In. 35.00
Card, Campaign, Hancock, Next President, Diecut, 2 1/2 x 5 3/8 In. 443.00
Card, Eisenhower Volunteers For Northern California, 1952, 2 3/8 x 3 7/8 In. 13.00
Card, Franklin D. Roosevelt Will Speak, Radio Station WMAQ, Tune & Listen 10.00
Card, Garfield, Hancock, Mechanical, 1880 .... 16.00
Card, James Garfield, A&P, Palette Shape, 1880s, 10 1/2 In. 1428.00
Card, Mechanical, Slide Picture, Ike 5.00
Card, Our Favorite Candidate, 4 3/4 x 6 3/4 In. 230.00
Card, Volunteer, Dewey, Warren, October 9, 1948, 2 1/2 x 3 1/2 In. 53.00
Carter, I'm A Bunny For Carter, Pink Ground, Celluloid 18.00
Charm, Cleveland, Thurman Rev, c.1888 .... 135.00
Cigar Band, Teddy Roosevelt, 3 1/2 In. 18.00
Cigar Band, William J. Bryan, Oversized, 5 5/8 In. 32.00
Cigarettes, Bush, 20 In Pack, Unopened, Indents, 1988 .... 27.00
Clicker, Click With Dick, Photograph, White, Blue, 1960, 1 3/4 In. 18.00
Coaster, Goldwater For President, Paper, Round, 1964, 3 1/2 In. 6.00
Cup, Coffee With The Kennedys, Paper, 3 In. 30.00
Cup & Saucer, Roosevelt, Churchill, Champions Of Democracy, Marigold Astoria, Meakin 59.00
Decorated Tumbler, McKinley, Hobart, Etched, 3 3/4 In. 40.00
Decorated Tumbler, The '80 Vote, ABC News, 5 1/2 In. 7.00
Door Hanger, Vote McGovern Democrat, Primary, June 6, 1972, Cardboard 5.00
Drawing, Geo. Washington, On Horseback, Spencerian, Red, Blue Ink, Frame, 21 x 15 In. 978.00
Envelope, Kennedy For Pres., Southern California Headquarters 9.00
Fan, Taft, Cardboard, Red, White, Blue, 6 3/4 In. 27.00
Ferrotype, President Abraham Lincoln, Vice President Andrew Johnson, 15/16 In. 2347.00
Figure, Peaceful Bill & Smiling Jim, Taft & Sherman, Iron, 2-Sided, c.1908, 4 In. 2090.00
Figure Set, Hitler, Mussolini, Tojo, Chalk, Painted, Detailed Facial Expressions, 3 Piece 3950.00
Flag, Garfield & Arthur, 34 Stars, Wool, Hand Sewn, 21 1/2 x 51 In. 2415.00
Flag, M'clellan, Pendleton, Mat, Frame, 1864, 8 1/4 x 13-In. Flag, 13 x 17 In. 12788.00
Flag, McKinley, Hobart, 1896, 19 x 11 In. 5536.00
Flag, Parade, Seymour Blair, Cotton, 36 Stars, Dowel, 12 x 17 1/2 In. 15525.00

Flag, Parade, Wm. J. Bryan, For President, Linen, Wood Dowel, 17 x 13 In. 865.00
Flag, Roosevelt's Rough Riders Reunion, 45 Stars, Frame, 1900, 34 1/2 x 52 1/2 In. 2715.00
Flaglet, Theodore Roosevelt, C.W. Fairbanks, Paper, 1904-12, 2 x 1 1/2 In. 86.00
Flyer, Blot Him Out, Pearl Harbor Day, December 7th, 3 1/2 x 8 1/2 In. 10.00
Flyer, Demos For Willkie National Committee, Uncle Sam, 4 Pages 6.00
Flyer, Indiana Draft Reagan Committee, 8 1/2 x 14, 1968 .... 8.00
Flyer, Kennedy & Labor, RFK, Pictures, 4 Pages 9.00
Flyer, Scranton, Nominee For President, 8 Pages 5.00
Folder, Calvin Coolidge, Sketch Of President, 8 Pages 20.00
Folder, Fugitives From A Brain Gang, 4 Pages, 1940 .... 7.00
Folder, Jesse Jackson For President, 1984, 8 Pages 6.00
Folder, John Glenn For US Senate, 6 Pages 4.00
Folder, Lester Maddox, President Hopeful, 1976, 12 Pages 5.00
Folder, Socialist Hass For President, Blomen For Vice President 20.00
Handkerchief, Hoover, Linen, Embroidered, Republican Elephant, 1928 .... 22.00
Hat, Greeley, Brown, Black, Fabric Band, 1872, 6 x 12 1/2 x 15 In. 6560.00
Hat, Reagan, Bush, Skimmer, 1984, 4 x 12 In. 30.00
Hat Band, Vote Nixon Lodge, Experience Counts, 24 In. 10.00
Helmet, I Like Ike, Plastic, Red, Bobble Head Elephant, 5 In. 55.00
Horn, Lincoln, Hamlin, Metal, Red & White Stripes, Stars, 1860, 13 3/4 In. 2468.00
Ink Blotter, Old Soldiers Never Die, Globe Print Shop Co., 3 1/2 x 6 1/4 In. 12.00
Invitation, President & Mrs. Roosevelt, White House Reception, 1904 .... 40.00
Kerchief, McKinley, Protection To American Industries, Blue Ground, c.1900, 15 x 16 In. 185.00
License Plate Attachment, I Like Ike, Red On White Ground, 1950s, 10 In. 110.00
License Plate Attachment, I Like Ike, Shield Shape, Red, White, Blue, 1950s, 7 In. 49.00
License Plate Attachment, Landon, Glenn, Metal, Geraghty Co., 1936, 11 3/4 In. 354.00
License Plate Attachment, Roosevelt, Aluminum, 10 1/4 In. 215.00
License Plate Attachment, Win With Willkie & McNary, Red, White & Blue, 1940 .... 200.00
License Plate Attachment, Win With Willkie, Metal, 1940, 9 1/2 In. 128.00
Match Safe, Benjamin Harrison, Brass, Hinged Lid, Locking Mechanism 322.00
Matchbook, Goldwater, In 64 .... 13.00
Matchbook, Humphrey, For President 28.00
Medalet, Bryan, Stevenson, Equal Rights, Jugate, 1900, 15/16 In. 72.00
Mirror, I Like Ike, White Ground, Red Strip Top, Blue Strip Bottom, Celluloid, 3 1/2 In. 17.00
Mirror, Wm. H. Taft, For President, Oval, 2 3/4 x 1 3/4 In. 371.00
Mug, Elephant, Nixon, Agnew On Sides, Frankoma Pottery, 1969 .... 22.00
Music Box, Nixon, Dancing, Metal, Windup, 6 In. 161.00
Nodder, Barry M. Goldwater, Campaign Pin, Nemco, Box, 1964, 7 1/2 In. 52.00
Nodder, Dwight Eisenhower, Japan, 6 In. 95.00
Nodder, J.F.K., Football, I Don't Care If You Are Attorney General, Box, Early 1960s, 6 1/2 In. 1206.00
Nodder, John F. Kennedy, Football Players, 1962, 6 In. 1160.00
Nodder, Lyndon B. Johnson, Campaign Pin, Nemco, Box, 1964, 7 1/2 In. 49.00
Oyster Plate, Blue Point, Presidential, Hayes, 1879, 8 5/8 In. 730.00
Pamphlet, LBJ Shaking Hands, I Need William M. Stefanic In Congress, 4 Pages 5.00
Pamphlet, Tom Dewey, Fold-Out, Drake Stadium, 8 Pages 8.00
Paper Doll, Nancy Reagan, Unpunched, 1983 .... 10.00
Parade Torch, Figural, Beaver Hat, Harrison, c.1888, 6 1/2 x 5 3/4 In. 926.00
Pennant, For Our Next President, Hoover, Blue & White, 24 In. 110.00
Pennant, General MacArthur, Yellow & White On Blue Ground, 25 In. 40.00
Pennant, Ike, Nixon, Inaugural, Nixon Pink Hair, Felt, 1957, 3 In. 92.00
Pennant, Suffrage, Votes For Women, Orange & Blue, Felt, Applied White Letters, 1915 .... 1625.00
Pillow, McKinley, Roosevelt, Double Jugate, Square, 1900, 22 In. 1606.00
Pin, Billy Possum, Carrying Golf Club, Symbol For Taft, Metal, Cutout, 3 In. 425.00
Pin, Gold Bug, McKinley, Hobart, Photographs On Wings, Mechanical, 1 5/8 In. 546.00
Pin, Horseshoe, St. John, Prohibition Presidential, Brass, 1884, 1 1/8 In. 430.00
Pin, Ike, Cloth, Sequins, 1956, 1 3/4 In. 33.00
Pin, Ike, Dick, Clutchback, 1 1/4 In. 16.00
Pin, Jack, Shaped Like U.S.A., Enamel, 1 In. 22.00
Pin, JFK, PT Boat Shape, Kennedy 60, 1 1/2 In. 20.00
Pin, McKinley, Hobart, Elephant Shape, Mechanical, Brass, c.1896, 7/8 In. 128.00
Pin, Nixon, Star Shaped, Embroidered Cloth, Dick, 1 1/2 In. 14.00

Pin, Reagan, Sheriff's Badge, Clutchback, 1 1/2 In. 11.00
Pin, Ribbon, Gifford Pinchot, For U.S. Senator, Primary Election, May 18th 1926 .... 165.00
Pin, Rough Rider Hat In The Ring, Metal, Cutout, Red Enameled Ring, 1912, 1 1/4 In. 245.00
Pin, Shoe, Hole In Sole, Adlai Stevenson, Clutchback, 1 In. 16.00
Pin, Taft, Spokane Apple, Sept. 28 1909, Celluloid Novelty Co., Back Paper, 1 1/4 In. 252.00
Pin Dish, Connecticut Citizens For Kennedy, Black, Gold, White, 2 1/2 x 6 In. 35.00
Pipe Bowl, William Howard Taft, 3 In. 80.00
Plate, Abraham Lincoln, Administration, Eagle, Ribbon, Purple Border, Late 1800s, 9 1/2 In. 470.00
Plate, Dessert, Benjamin Harrison, Eagle, Cobalt Blue Rim, Gilt, Limoges, 1892, 7 1/4 In. 920.00
Plate, Dwight D. Eisenhower Center, Past Presidents, Burgundy, Vernon Kilns, 10 1/2 In. 25.00
Plate, Franklin D. Roosevelt, Gold Trim, Blue Border, Imperial China Co., 10 3/4 In. 45.00
Plate, General Jackson, Hero Of New Orleans, Luster Border, 1832, 8 3/4 In. 1015.00
Plate, Grover Cleveland, Ferns, Holly, Ironstone, 8 In. 75.00
Plate, James B. Blaine, Ironstone, Gold Trim, 8 In. 85.00
Plate, Lee & Jackson At Chancellorsville, Last Meeting, May 1, 1863, 1920, 7 In. 50.00
Plate, Presidential, Harrison, 44 Star Border, States Of The Union, Limoges, 9 3/8 In. 549.00
Plate, Soup, Presidential, Lincoln, Haviland Limoges, Purple Border, 1861, 9 3/8 In. 4680.00
Plate, Tom Dewey, N.Y. State Fair, Chamber Of Commerce, Syracuse, 1949, 6 1/4 In. 28.00
Plate, W.H. Harrison, Blue Edge, Center Portrait, Staffordshire, 1840, 10 In. 2415.00
Plate, Winfield S. Hancock, For President, Ironstone, 8 In. 95.00
Postcard, Bryan, Kern, Flag & Shield 32.00
Postcard, Calvin Coolidge For Vice President 75.00
Postcard, Citizens For Goldwater, King County, Charter Member Card, 2 1/2 x 3 1/2 In. 9.00
Postcard, Cracker Jack Bears, No. 7 .... 14.00
Postcard, Cracker Jack Bears, No. 15, Teddy Roosevelt, Treeing Bears, Holding Rifle 18.00
Postcard, FDR Caricature, How My Doin', Inaugural Address Excerpts 25.00
Postcard, FDR, Our Quarterback, In Football Uniform, In Front Of Capitol 14.00
Postcard, Ford, Dole, Steelman, Vote For Texans, 8 1/2 In. 18.00
Postcard, Give Our People Eisenhower, Elephant 9.00
Postcard, Member Of Hoover Committee, Flag, 1932 .... 10.00
Postcard, My Choice Is Wilson For President, Pennant, Portrait 35.00
Postcard, President Taft, At Fort Ticonderoga, July, 1909 .... 18.00
Postcard, President William H. Taft 9.00
Postcard, Teddy Roosevelt, George Washington, Abraham Lincoln, 1909 .... 14.00
Postcard, Teddy Roosevelt, Returns From Africa, Elephant, Wm. H. Taft, c.1910 .... 32.00
Postcard, Truman Holding Chicago Daily Tribune, Black, White, 1992 .... 5.00
Postcard, When President Taft Visited Springfield, Passing Hotel Worthy, 1912 .... 9.00
Poster, All Labor March With Carter, Mondale, Chicago Teachers Union, 8 1/2 x 11 In. 6.00
Poster, Cleveland, Stevenson, Eagle, Flag, Frame, 1892, 19 1/2 x 26 3/4 In. 690.00
Poster, James M. Cox, Frame, 39 x 27 In. 5829.00
Poster, Joe McCarthy, 10 1/2 x 13 In. 92.00
Poster, Landon, Know, Deeds Not Deficits, c.1936, 14 1/2 x 21 1/2 In. 120.00
Poster, McKinley, Hobart, Black, White, 1896, 25 x 29 In. 690.00
Poster, McKinley, Hobart, Republican Nominees, Frame, 1896, 19 1/2 x 25 1/2 In. 711.00
Poster, McKinley, Roosevelt, Prosperity & Patriotism, Frame, 1900, 19 1/2 x 27 1/2 In. 1390.00
Poster, Re-Elect U.S. Senator Kennedy, 1958, 45 x 29 1/2 In. 2178.00
Press Badge, Eisenhower Day, October 1, 1956, Celluloid, Ribbon, 3 In. 89.00
Print, Fremont, N. Currier, Frame, 1856, 12 3/8 x 16 3/8 In. 695.00
Print, Lincoln, Frame, 1860, 12 3/8 x 16 3/8 In. 4628.00
Punchboard, Go To Town With Uncle Sam, WWII, U.S. Defense Bonds, 9 3/4 x 13 In. 230.00
Record, Official Campaign Song For Citizens For Eisenhower, I Go For Ike, Plastic, Red 25.00
Ribbon, Abram Lincoln, Union & Liberty, Paper, 1860, 7 1/2 x 3 1/2 In. 1148.00
Ribbon, Benjamin Harrison, Levi Morton, Paper, 4 1/2 In. 35.00
Ribbon, I Like Ike, White Letters, Blue Ground, 4 1/2 In. 17.00
Ribbon, McKinley, For Governor, Ohio, Pinholes 140.00
Ribbon, McKinley, Women's Club, Ida McKinley Photo, Canton, Oh. c.1896, 9 1/2 In. 218.00
Ribbon, Roosevelt, Johnson, Social & Industrial Justice, Jugate, 1912, 8 1/2 In. 550.00
Ribbon, Taft For President, 1908, 7 In. 120.00
Ruler, Goldwater, A Leader Not A Ruler, List Of Presidents On Back, 1964, 12 In. 19.00
Ruler, Ted Agnew, Fox County Executive, Metal, 12 In. 30.00
Ruler, We Like Ike, Every Inch Of The Way, Ike, Mamie, Cardboard, 6 In. 25.00

Sash, Suffrage, Votes For Women, Early 20th Century, 23 In. 146.00
Scales, Cleveland, Harrison, In American Flags, Ceramic, Wood Lever, 1888, 5 1/4 In. 2039.00
Sheet Music, Don't Let Them Take It Away, Democratic Campaign Song, 1952 .... 22.00
Sheet Music, Eisenhower March, Hike With Ike, Betsy Gay, c.1952 .... 25.00
Sheet Music, Happy Landin' With Landon, c.1936 .... 28.00
Sheet Music, Here's To You, MacArthur, c.1942 .... 25.00
Sheet Music, I Like It, Irving Berlin Music Corp., c.1952 .... 14.00
Sheet Music, Lemke Is The Man, Union Party, c.1936 .... 85.00
Sheet Music, There's FDR In Freedom, c.1942 .... 25.00
Sheet Music, Tie That Binds, Jimmy Is Man For Us, Frame, 1920, 8 1/2 x 5 1/2 In., 4 Pages 805.00
Sheet Music, Wigwam Grand March, Lincoln, Frame, 1860, 13 x 10 In., 3 Pages 2657.00
Snuffbox, Andrew Jackson, 1830s, 3 1/2 In. 3285.00
Snuffbox, Zachary Taylor, Old Rough & Ready, 1840s, 3 1/2 In. 2714.00
Stereo Card, Alaskan Salmon Looks Good To President & Mrs. Harding, Hetiakatin 38.00
Stereo Card, FDR, Behind Desk 35.00
Stereo Card, President McKinley & 8 Chosen Advisors, Underwood & Underwood, c.1902 .... 12.00
Stereo Card, Teddy Roosevelt, At Desk In White House, Sepia 20.00
Stereo Card, Woodrow Wilson & His War Cabinet 15.00
Sticker, Back To Work Quicker With Dewey & Bricker, Shield Shape, 1944, 5 1/4 In. 36.00
Sticker, No Third Term, Red, White, Blue, 5 3/4 In. 31.00
Stickpin, Bryan, 16 To 1 Scales, 7/8 In. 83.00
Stickpin, Bryan, Celluloid, Oval, Fabric Bow, 1 x 2 In. 684.00
Stickpin, Communist, Flag, Karl Marx, Celluloid, 1 3/4 In. 132.00
Stickpin, Flag Shape, Hughes, Fairbanks, 1916, 2 1/2 x 1 1/4 In. 759.00
Stickpin, Hughes, America First, Celluloid, Brass, 1916, 1 x 3/4 x 2 In. 818.00
Stickpin, Karl Marx, Communist, Die Cut, Celluloid Flag, Portrait, c.1933, 1 3/4 In. 132.00
Stickpin, McKinley, Giant Gold Bug 147.00
Stickpin, McKinley, Gold Bug, Heavy Duty Version 284.00
Stickpin, Teddy Bear With Big Stick, Brass, 7/8 In. 245.00
Stickpin, Woodrow Wilson, Gold Metal, Cutout Script, 1912, 2 1/2 In. 69.00
Stocking, Black, Hoover's, Name On Front Of Each, 20 In. 145.00
String Hanger, Labor For McGovern, Paper, 3 3/4 x 8 3/4 In. 7.00
Stud, Bull Moose, Pewter, 1912, 7/8 In. 65.00
Stud, Covered Wagon, Landon, 1 1/4 In. 49.00
Stud, Ike, Enamel, White Letters On Black, 7/8 In. 16.00
Stud, McKinley, Hobart, Jugate, Sepia, Celluloid, c.1896, 7/8 In. 25.00
Stud, McKinley, Jugate, Celluloid, c.1896, 7/8 In. 30.00
Stud, McKinley, Napoleon Hat, c.1896, 7/8 In. 50.00
Stud, McKinley, Pennant, c.1896, 7/8 In. 33.00
Stud, Roosevelt, Bull Moose Founder, c.1912, 7/8 In. 14.00
Stud, Rooster, Cox, Pewter, Embossed, 7/8 In. 16.00
Sugar, W.H. Harrison, Portrait, Log Cabin, Adams Mark, 1840, 4 3/4 x 4 In. 1600.00
Tag, Cardboard, Free Earl Browder, 1941, 4 3/4 In. 613.00
Tankard, George Washington Inaugural, Transfer, 1789, 6 In. 9391.00
Textile, Herbert Hoover, Red, White & Blue Border, Frame, 1928, 20 x 15 In. 42.00
Ticket, Andrew Johnson Impeachment, Unused, 1868, 2 7/8 x 4 3/4 In. 2637.00
Ticket, Democratic Dinner & Rally, Adlai & Estes, November 3, 1956 .... 9.00
Ticket, Democratic National Convention, 11th Session, Press Gallery, Chicago, 1932 .... 20.00
Ticket, Democratic National Convention, Chicago, Stub Attached, 12th Session, 1940 .... 25.00
Ticket, Dewey, Warren Rally, Madison Square Garden, October 30, 1948 .... 24.00
Ticket, FDR Address At Shibe Park, Phila., Oct. 27, 1944 .... 26.00
Ticket, Republican National Convention, 2nd Session, Entertainer, July 14, 1964 .... 7.00
Ticket, Republican National Convention, 4th Session, TV Lounge, Chicago, July 27, 1960 .... 8.00
Tie Clasp, Ike, I Like Ike, Flasher, 1 1/2 In. 11.00
Tin, Tobacco, Garfield, Arthur, Hancock, Mechanical Disk, 1880, 2 1/4 x 3 1/2 In. 1250.00
Tire Cover, Roosevelt & Garner, Return Our Country, Shadowbox Frame, 1932, 35 x 36 In. 4427.00
Toby Mug, F.D. Roosevelt, 2 In. 20.00
Toby Mug, President W.H. Taft, Souvenir Of Washington, Germany, 5 x 4 1/2 In. 235.00
Token, Fremont, Brass, Reverse Eagle, 1856 .... 36.00
Token, Hard Times, Donkey, Tortoise, Anti Jackson, Van Buren 16.00

American postcards from long-gone towns have extra value to collectors. Clean dirty postcards with a piece of white bread. Be sure to cut the crust off first.

Popeye, Toy, Popeye & Olive Oyl, Dancing On Roof, Tin, Windup, Marx, 9 In.

Token, McKinley, Broken Eagle, Mechanical, 1 1/2 In. 44.00
Torch, Harrison Beaver Hat, 1888, 6 1/2 x 5 3/4 In. 926.00
Torch, Lincoln, Eagle, Tin, Brass Plated, 2 Wicks, 1860, 9 x 10 x 3 In. 4427.00
Torch, Lincoln, Wide Awake, 1860, 48 In. 783.00
Tray, Bryan, Stevenson, Lithograph, 1900, 10 In. 1955.00
Tray, Keep Roosevelt In The White House, FDR, 1936, 10 1/2 x 13 1/2 In. 560.00
Tray, McKinley, Roosevelt, Lithograph, 1900, 10 In. 1150.00
Tumbler, Gold, Black Image Of Goldwater, Elephant On Back, Glass, 1964 .... 15.00
Umbrella, McKinley, Roosevelt, Double Jugate, 1900, 33 In. 1685.00
Vase, James Garfield, Pink Luster, 1880, 9 In. 3614.00
Vest, Greeley, Brown, Shadowbox Frame, 1872, 29 1/4 x 19 1/4 In. 3697.00
Vest, I'm A Barry Booster, Cloth, White Ground, Blue Letter, Portrait, 22 In. 54.00
Window Sticker, Stevenson, 7 5/8 In. 7.00
Window Sticker, Willkie, No 3rd Term, 1940, 8 1/2 In. 11.00
Wristwatch, Nixon, Ford, GOP Elephant, Caricature, 1970s 25.00

POMONA glass is a clear glass with a soft amber border decorated with pale blue or rose-colored flowers and leaves. The colors are very, very pale. The background of the glass is covered with a network of fine lines. It was made from 1885 to 1888 by the New England Glass Company. First grind was made from April 1885 to June 1886. It was made by cutting a wax surface on the glass, then dipping it in acid. Second grind was a less expensive method of acid etching that was developed later.

Bowl, Cornflowers, Ruffled Edge, 2nd Grind, 9 In. 290.00
Card Holder, Cornflowers, Shell Shape, Ruffled Edge, 1st Grind, 6 In. 430.00
Cruet, Scalloped Foot, Applied Amber Handle & Stopper, 7 1/2 In. 400.00
Pitcher, Cornflowers, Applied Clear Handle, 1st Grind, 5 1/2 In. 4140.00
Pitcher, Cornflowers, Ruffled Edge, 4-Footed, 1st Grind, 7 1/2 In. 4310.00
Pitcher, Milk, Ball Optic, Amber, Square Rim, 1st Grind, 5 1/2 In. 110.00
Spooner, Cornflowers, Ruffled Edge, 1st Grind, 5 In. 210.00
Sugar & Creamer, Applied Clear Feet, 2nd Grind, 3 1/2 In. & 5 1/2 In. 259.00
Toothpick, Diamond Optic, Cupped Tricornered, 2 In., Pair 375.00
Tray, Rectangular, Ruffled Edge, Flowers, Leaves, 2nd Grind, 12 1/2 x 7 1/2 In. 1265.00
Tumbler, Inverted Thumbprint, Acorn, 1st Grind, c.1885, 3 1/2 In. 35.00
Tumbler, Lemonade, Cornflowers, 1st Grind, 5 3/4 In. 230.00

PONTYPOOL, see Tole category.

POOLE POTTERY was started by Jesse Carter in 1873 in Poole, England. The company specialized in architectural ceramics. In 1908 the company was incorporated as Carter and Company. In 1920 it became Carter & Co. The name Poole Pottery Ltd. was taken in 1963. The company is still in business.

Bowl, Vegetable, Cover, Beige, Brown, 1960s, 5 x 11 In. 180.00

Condiment Set, Tray, Saltshaker, Pepper Pot, Mustard Pot, Beige, Brown, 1960s, 5 x 5 In., 4 Piece 90.00
Creamer, Beige, Brown, 1960s, 4 x 5 In. 34.00
Gravy Boat, Saucer, Beige, Brown, 1960s, 4 x 7 In. 128.00
Plate, Gray, Purple Flowers, Purple Dot Border, 9 In. 20.00
Salt & Pepper, Hand Painted, Aqua, Green, Open Salt, UFW, c.1956, 3 1/2-In. Pepper 25.00
Tea Set, Teapot, Cups, Saucers, Plates, Sugar, Creamer, Cream, Green, Mottled, 1960s, 21 Piece 390.00
Vase, Gazelle, Leaves, Truda Adams, Carter Stabler Adams, Late 1920s, 9 3/4 In. 810.00

POPEYE was introduced to the Thimble Theatre comic strip in 1929. The character became a favorite of readers. In 1932, an animated cartoon featuring Popeye was made by Paramount Studios. The cartoon series continued and became even more popular when it was shown on television starting in the 1950s. The full-length movie with Robin Williams as Popeye was made in 1980. KFS stands for King Features Syndicate, the distributor of the comic strip.

Bank, Daily Quarter, Kalon Mfg., Brooklyn, Box, 5 In. 305.00
Bank, Daily Quarter, Opens At $10.00, Tin Lithograph, 4 1/2 In. 138.00
Bank, Dime Register, Automatic, Locks At First Dime, 1929, 2 1/2 x 2 1/2 In. 125.00
Bank, Mechanical, Tin Lithograph, Metal, Straits, 1935, 3 1/2 x 2 x 1 3/4 In. 1905.00
Bank, Popeye Knockout, Blue, Yellow, Straits Corp. 206.00
Button, Penney's Back To School Days With Popeye, Celluloid, 1 In. 18.00
Button, Popeye Is In The News Bee, Celluloid, Blue, White, 1 In. 38.00
Cap, Sailor, Child's, Fold-Down Earflaps, Chin Strap, Red, White, Blue, 1940s 240.00
Cookie Jar, Printed Scene, 3-Bar Mark Jar, McCoy, 10 3/4 In. 75.00
Costume, Popeye, Hat, Mask, Pipe, Suit, Halco, Box, 1935 70.00
Doll, Plush, Cloth, Stuffed, Felt, 11 In. 168.00
Doll, Wood, Composition, Jointed, KFS, Jaymar, Box, 1935, 8 In. 2066.00
Figure, Popeye, Cloth Body, Molded Rubber Head, Composition Shoes, Corncob Pipe, 17 In. 785.00
Figure, Popeye, Head Goes Up & Down, Celluloid, Japan, c.1935, 5 1/4 In. 448.00
Figure, Popeye, Head Goes Up & Down, Celluloid, Windup, Box, 1929, 8 1/2 In. 595.00 to 950.00
Figure, Popeye, Jointed, Composition, Wood, Ideal, 1935, 14 1/2 In. 550.00
Figure, Popeye, Jointed, Wood, Composition Head, Celluloid Hat Brim, Bag, Chein, 1932, 8 1/2 In. 1120.00
Figure, Popeye, Jointed, Wood, Composition Head, Celluloid Hat Brim, c.1935, 8 In. 392.00
Figure, Popeye, Jointed, Wood, Composition, 14 In. 1792.00
Figure, Popeye, Jointed, Wood, Composition, Rigid Arms, Chein, 1932, 11 In. 450.00
Figure, Popeye, Jointed, Wood, Jeep, Composition Head, Segmented Tail, 1935, 6 In. 1230.00
Figure, Popeye, Jointed, Wood, King Features Syndicate, c.1935, 12 In. 440.00
Figure, Popeye, Motorcycle, Cast Iron, Movable Arms, Hubley, c.1935, 4 3/4 x 4 In. 1008.00
Figure, Popeye, Oilcloth Face, Shoes, Straw Filled, Wire Legs, Wooden Pipe, Japan, c.1935, 10 In. 168.00
Figure, Swee'pea, Sitting, Molded Oilcloth Face, Cloth Body, Clothes, c.1940s, 10 x 8 In. 616.00
Figure, Wimpy, Celluloid, Japan, Box, c.1935, 7 In. 840.00
Game, Bagatelle, Tin, Durable Toy Co., 1935, 14 x 23 In. 195.00
Game, Dexterity, Popeye Juggler, King Features, 1929, 5 In. 94.00
Lamp, Boat, Popeye, Bulb, Aerolux, 1930s, 6 1/2 In. 675.00
Lamp, Electric, Metal, Paper Shade, 9 & 8 In. 225.00
Lunch Box, Metal, No Thermos, 1962 300.00
Pen, Fountain, Popeye & Olive, Green, Lever Fill, 1930s 95.00
Pencil Sharpener, Bakelite, Popeye Holding Pencil Decal, Green, 1929, 1 3/4 In. 85.00
Pencil Sharpener, Tin Lithograph, Tin Tray, Irwin, 1929, 2 3/4 In. 215.00
Printer Set, 8 Popeye Stamps, Thimble Theater Pad, Stampercraft, Box, 1935, 6 3/4 x 9 1/4 In. 95.00
Target, Tin Lithograph, Cardboard Back, Wire Stand, Durable Toy Co., 1935, 14 x 23 In. 2240.00
Toy, Olive Oyl, Ballet Dancer, Spins On Wire, Friction, Linemar, Box, c.1960, 5 1/2 In. 880.00
Toy, Olive Oyl, Pop-Up, Squeaks, Umbrella, Composition, Linemar, 1950s, 7 In. 523.00
Toy, Olive Oyl, Roadster, Tin Lithograph, Friction, Red, Linemar, 1950s, 8 In. 935.00
Toy, Popeye & Baggage, Wheelbarrow, Parrot, Tin, Windup, Marx, Box, 1932, 8 1/4 In. 2240.00
Toy, Popeye & Brutus, Firefighters, Tin, Celluloid, Windup, Marx, Box, c.1935, 10 x 7 In. 1265.00 to 3080.00
Toy, Popeye & Mean Man, Celluloid, Tin, Windup, Linemar, Box, c.1960, 4 In. 2090.00
Toy, Popeye & Olive Oyl, Dancing On Roof, Tin, Windup, Marx, 9 In. *ILLUS* 1008.00
Toy, Popeye & Olive Oyl, Dancing On Roof, Tin Lithograph, Marx, Box, 1936, 10 In. 2800.00
Toy, Popeye & Olive Oyl, Flyers, 2 Airplanes, Tower, Tin, Windup, Marx, 8 x 17 In. 248.00 to 760.00
Toy, Popeye & Olive Oyl, Handcar, Metal, Rubber Figures, Marx, Box, 1935, 6 1/2 In. 840.00

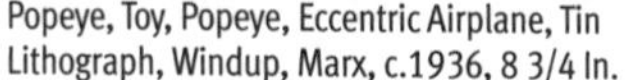
Popeye, Toy, Popeye, Eccentric Airplane, Tin Lithograph, Windup, Marx, c.1936, 8 3/4 In.

Popeye, Toy, Popeye, Parrot On Wheelbarrow, Tin, Celluloid, Windup, Marx, 9 In.

Toy, Popeye & Olive Oyl, Handcar, Stretchy, Pull Toy, Linemar, Box, 1950s, 6 1/2 In. 2200.00
Toy, Popeye & Olive Oyl, Juggling, Tin Lithograph, Linemar, c.1960, 9 In. 1568.00
Toy, Popeye & Wimpy, Walk-A-Way, Plastic, Marx, Box, 1964, 4 1/2 In. ....135.00 to 200.00
Toy, Popeye Aeroplane, Tin Lithograph, No. 47, Marx, Box, c.1935, 8 x 8 1/2 In. ....4400.00 to 4480.00
Toy, Popeye Express, Airplane, Train, Tunnels, Tin Lithograph, Windup, Marx, Box, 9 In. .2036.00 to 2520.00
Toy, Popeye's Big Band, Musical Instruments, Bar Zim, Box, 1933 .... 237.00
Toy, Popeye, Acrobat, Rocking Base, Tin Lithograph, Windup, Linemar, Box, 1950s, 13 In. 5225.00
Toy, Popeye, Bag Puncher, Floor Bag, Chein, 7 1/2 In. 990.00
Toy, Popeye, Bag Puncher, Overhead Bag, Tin, Celluloid, Chein, Box, 1932, 9 x 4 In. .....6050.00 to 6160.00
Toy, Popeye, Barrel Walker, Tin Lithograph, Windup, Chein, 1932, 7 In. ....440.00 to 485.00
Toy, Popeye, Barrel Walker, Tin Lithograph, Windup, Chein, Box, 1932, 7 In. 840.00
Toy, Popeye, Basketball Player, Bounces Ball, Tin, Windup, Linemar, 1950s, 9 In. 1320.00
Toy, Popeye, Boxer, Shadow, Windup, Chein, Box, c.1932, 7 In. 4200.00
Toy, Popeye, Bubble Blowing, Spinach, Pipe, Tin, Battery Operated, Linemar, Box, c.1960, 12 In. .. 1788.00
Toy, Popeye, Champ, Boxing Ring, Celluloid Figures, Windup, Marx, Box, c.1935, 7 In. 3360.00
Toy, Popeye, Dancing On Roof, Tin, Windup, Marx, Repro Box, 1930s, 10 x 4 5/8 x 3 In. 743.00
Toy, Popeye, Dippy Dumper, Tin Lithograph, Celluloid Figure, Windup, Marx, 1940, 9 In. 660.00
Toy, Popeye, Drummer, Tin Lithograph, Chein, 1932, 7 In. ....1760.00 to 2800.00
Toy, Popeye, Eccentric Airplane, Tin Lithograph, Windup, Marx, c.1936, 8 3/4 In. ....*ILLUS* 448.00
Toy, Popeye, Heavy Hitter, Chein, 1932, 11 3/4 In. ....3575.00 to 5880.00
Toy, Popeye, Jack-In-The-Box, Spinach Can, Tin Lithograph, Mattel, Box, 1953, 5 1/2 In. 415.00
Toy, Popeye, Lantern, Tin, Glass, Battery Operated, Linemar, Box, 1950s, 7 1/2 In. ....556.00 to 605.00
Toy, Popeye, Menu Gabutelle, Tin Lithograph, Durable Toys & Novelty, Box, 1935, 21 In. 440.00
Toy, Popeye, Parrot Cages, Carrying, Tin Lithograph, Marx, 1932, 8 1/4 In. ....385.00 to 785.00
Toy, Popeye, Parrot On Wheelbarrow, Tin, Celluloid, Windup, Marx, 9 In. ....*ILLUS* 672.00
Toy, Popeye, Pirate Pistol, Click, Tin Lithograph, Marx, Box, c.1935, 9 In. 935.00
Toy, Popeye, Roadster, Tin Lithograph, Friction, Yellow, Linemar, 1950s, 8 In. 1210.00
Toy, Popeye, Roller Skater, Holding Platter, Tin, Windup, Linemar, 1950s, 6 1/2 In. 496.00
Toy, Popeye, Roller Skater, Holding Platter, Tin, Windup, Linemar, Box, 1950s, 6 1/2 In. 2750.00
Toy, Popeye, Rowboat, Battery Operated, Remote Control, Linemar, Box, c.1960, 10 In. 2200.00
Toy, Popeye, Smoking, On Spinach Can, Tin, Battery, Linemar, Box, 1950s, 9 In. 4950.00
Toy, Popeye, Sparkler, Name On Hat, Tin Lithograph, Chein, c.1935, 6 In. ....195.00 to 224.00
Toy, Popeye, Speedboat, Holding Wheel, Propeller Turns, Windup, Hoge, 1934, 15 In. 3360.00
Toy, Popeye, Spinach Motorcycle, Movable Arms, Cast Iron, Hubley, c.1935, 4 3/4 x 4 In. 560.00
Toy, Popeye, Tumbling, Tin Lithograph, Windup, Linemar, 1950s, 5 In. 525.00
Toy, Popeye, Turnover Tank, Tin Lithograph, Windup, Linemar, 1950s, 4 In. 330.00
Toy, Popeye, Unicyclist, Fat Tire, Tin Lithograph, Windup, Linemar, c.1960, 6 In. 1210.00
Toy, Popeye, Waddler, Name On Hat, Tin Lithograph, Windup, Chein, 6 In. 560.00
Toy, Popeye, Walker, Clenched Fists, Tin Lithograph, Windup, Chein, c.1935, 6 1/4 In. .....149.00 to 385.00
Toy, Popeye, Walker, Red & Blue Outfit, Windup, Celluloid, Irwin, 1930s, 5 1/2 In. 105.00
Toy, Thimble Theatre, Mystery Playhouse, 3 Figures, Harding Products, Box, 1939, 12 In. 5358.00
Toy, Wimpy, Barrel Walker, Tin Lithograph, Windup, Chein, 8 In. 1100.00
Toy, Wimpy, Tricycle, Tin Lithograph, Windup, Linemar, Box, 1950s, 4 In. 1430.00

PORCELAIN factories that are well known are listed in this book under the factory name. This category and the two following list pieces made by the less well-known factories. Porcelain-Contemporary lists pieces made by artists working after 1975. Porcelain-Midcentury includes pieces made from the 1940s to the 1980s.

Apothecary Jar, Hand Painted, Continental, 19th Century, 10 3/4 x 4 1/4 In., Pair 1170.00
Biscuit Barrel, Victorian, Floral Pattern, 19th Century, 5 1/4 x 5 In. 175.00
Bottle, Faceted, Blue Glaze, Squirrel, Grape, Korea, 1800s, 10 1/2 In. 880.00
Bowl, Blue & White Ware, Chinese, c.1900, 2 3/4 In. 120.00
Bowl, Blue & White, Lotus Shape, Peach Lattice Set, Characters, 1700s, 7 1/2 In. 1745.00
Bowl, Blue & White, Shallow, Chinese, 1736-95, 13 1/4 In. 415.00
Bowl, Blue & White, Shallow, Chinese, 1736-95, 17 In. 1770.00
Bowl, Center, Flowers, Footed, C-Scroll Border, Nantgarw, 1820s, 11 1/4 In. 8239.00
Bowl, Center, Maiden, Boy, Fishing Net, Ernst Wahliss, Austria, c.1900, 17 3/4 In. 1225.00
Bowl, Clair-De-Lune, Compressed Globular Shape, 1800s, 7 1/2 In. 708.00
Bowl, Copper Red, Crushed Strawberry Glaze, Chinese, 1875-1908, 7 3/4 In. 826.00
Bowl, Cover, Imari, Birds, Flowers, Finial, Buddha, 12 x 11 In. 880.00
Bowl, Footed, Passion Flower, Handles, Oval, Lobed, Swansea, 1816-26, 13 3/4 In. 9900.00
Bowl, Footed, St. Paul's, Westminster Abbey, Gilt Borders, Oval, Lobed, Swansea, 1816-26, 14 In. 9269.00
Bowl, Glazed Cream, Brown, Maurice Gensoli, 3 1/4 x 9 1/2 In. 1440.00
Bowl, Imperial Yellow Glaze, Opaque Ruby Glaze, Chinese, 6 3/4 x 2 1/2 In., Pair 3658.00
Bowl, Lotus Flower Scrolls, Flaring Rim, Chinese, 1736-95, 5 1/2 In. 1650.00
Bowl, Painted, Waisted Lotus Shape, Painted, Phoenix, Bats, Flowers, Chinese, 7 1/2 In. 270.00
Bowl, Peach Bloom, Steep Sides, Short Foot, Chinese, 1723-35, 6 In. 2125.00
Bowl, Pine, Prunus, Bamboo, Flowers, Comb Foot, Nabeshima Ware, 1800s, 13 1/2 In. 325.00
Bowl, Serpentine, Lotus Shape, Spinach Green, 1900s, 5 In. 135.00
Bowl, Turquoise Ground, Painted, Dancers, Musicians, 1875-1908, 8 In. 440.00
Bowl, Undulating Flared Rim, Harlan House, 1973, 17 1/2 In. 550.00
Bowl, Warriors, Peonies, Blue, White, Chinese, 1662-1722, 9 In. 2596.00
Bowl, Wild Rose, T&V, France, 5 x 9 1/2 In. 189.00
Bowl, Woman Sitting Holding Fan, Bronze Border, Royal Coburg, 10 1/2 In. 800.00
Bowl, Yellow Exterior, Crackle White Interior, Chinese, 1800s, 6 1/4 In. 176.00
Box, Cover, Fukien, Chinese, 1279-1368, 6 In. 415.00
Brush Holder, Landscapes, Waisted, Blue, White, Chinese, 6 1/2 x 7 1/2 In. 1989.00
Brush Washer, Cover, Lotus, Dragon, Blue, White, Chinese, 1662-1722, 4 In. 1060.00
Brush Washer, Peach Bloom, Chinese, 1700s, 4 1/2 In. 415.00
Brushpot, Blue, White, Cylindrical, Figural Landscape, 6 3/4 In. 978.00
Brushpot, Warriors, Famille Verte Colors, Chinese, 1800s, 7 1/2 x 7 1/2 In. 175.00
Bulbpot, Blue & White, Chinese, 19th Century, 2 1/2 x 6 1/4 x 8 3/4 In., Pair 410.00
Bust, Renaissance Nobleman, Feathered Hat, Multicolored, Late 1800s, 26 x 16 In. 880.00
Cachepot, 8-Sided, Carp & Aquatic Plants, Blue, White, c.1885, 8 x 10 In., Pair 470.00
Censer, Animal Shape Feet, Blue Glaze, Upraised Handle, Chinese, 1800s, 6 1/2 In. 440.00
Censer, Blue, White, Calligraphy, Chinese, 1662-1722, 9 In. 945.00
Centerpiece, Putti, Lion's Head Urns, Jardieniers, Multicolored, Flowers, 20 In. 1320.00
Charger, Blue & White, Chinese, 18th Century, 11 In. 530.00
Charger, Blue & White, Chinese, 18th Century, 14 1/4 In. 936.00
Charger, Blue, White, Flower, Scrolling Vine, Japan, 3 x 23 3/4 In. 575.00
Charger, Fitted Case, Chinese, 19th Century, 12 1/2 In. 936.00
Charger, Ming Style, Blue & White, Japanese, 19th Century, 13 1/2 In. 175.00
Charger, Phoenix, Peony Flowers, Japan, 1800s, 17 In. 150.00
Cheese Dish, Landscapes, 6 3/4 In. 115.00
Creamer, Flowers, Leaves, Scrolled Handle, Acanthus Leaf Crest, 5 In. 55.00
Creamer, Scenic, Barnyard Animals, Swans, R.S., 4 In. 70.00
Cup, Stem, Phoenix, Blue & White, Korea, 3 3/4 In. 390.00
Cup & Saucer, Plate, Regimental, 1 Comp Infantry Reg. No. 97, 1907, 9 1/2-In. Plate 420.00
Cup & Saucer, Tea, Blue & White, Chinese, 8 Piece 29.00
Dish, Flowers, 2 Twig Handles, Gilt Borders, Swansea, 1816-26, 12 1/4 In. 9900.00
Dish, Flowers, Castles, Birds, Fruit, Gilt Borders, Square, Nantgarw, c.1818, 9 1/2 In. 8650.00
Dish, Oxblood, Glazed, Shallow Bowl, Ogee Sides, 1736-95, 1800s, 6 In. 1848.00
Dish, Roses, Gilt Highlights, Franz A. Bischoff Painting, 1864-1929, 8 1/2 In. 1170.00

Dish, Seafood, Fired Gold, 3 Shell Patterns, 18 Piece 205.00
Dish, Tiger Lilies, Slip Design, Pink Gray Glaze, Japan, Early 1900s, 7 In. 440.00
Dish, Wine Barrel, Sea Of Wheels, Blue, White, Nabeshima, Japan, 1800s, 6 3/4 In., Pair 805.00
Epergne, Center Tree Trunk, 5 Cups, Painted Flowers, Figures, Gilt Borders, 7 1/2 x 10 In. 430.00
Ewer, Cover, Blanc De Chine, Faceted, Chinese, 17th Century, 6 1/2 In. 1416.00
Ewer, Madame Benzine, Plump Woman, Holding Pitcher, France, c.1900, 11 x 6 In. 1634.00
Figurine, Boy, Kneeling, Dog, Popov, c.1820, 4 In. 3290.00
Figurine, Buddha, Seated, Children, Hand Painted, Signed, Chinese, 12 x 10 In. 40.00
Figurine, Cavalier, Multicolored, Germany, Late 1800s, 22 5/8 x 12 1/4 In. 368.00
Figurine, Cockatoo On Tree, Multicolored Feathers, 13 1/4 In. 235.00
Figurine, Cossack, Popov, Russia, Early 1800, 9 In. 3525.00
Figurine, Dog, Pug, Lying Down, Early 1800s, 2 3/8 In. 1116.00
Figurine, Dog, Pug, Lying Down, On Pillow, Tassels, England, Late 1700s, 3 In. 3055.00
Figurine, Dog, Seated, Chinese, c.1900, 7 x 4 In., Pair 146.00
Figurine, Empress, Scepter, Crown, Yellow, Dragons, Hand Painted, Chinese, 22 In. 1095.00
Figurine, Farmer, Grading Wheat, Biscuit, Popov, Russia, c.1850, 7 1/2 In. 3055.00
Figurine, Flower Girl, Lamb, Sitzendorf, Hand Painted, Germany, 20th Century, 19 In. 440.00
Figurine, Foo Dog, Blanc De Chine, Chinese, 15 In., Pair 530.00
Figurine, Girl, Shawl, Wrap, Lenci, Marked, 11 5/8 In. 805.00
Figurine, Group, Napoleon & Josephine Playing Chess, Multicolored, Germany, 7 1/2 In. 230.00
Figurine, Guanyin, Blanc De Chine, Chinese, 18th Century, 14 In. 1000.00
Figurine, Guanyin, Doucai, Chinese, 1723-35, 18 1/2 In. 2124.00
Figurine, Harvesters, Biscuit, France, 18 1/2 In., Pair 295.00
Figurine, Kuan Ti, Blanc De Chine, Chinese, 19th Century, 8 1/2 In. 560.00
Figurine, Kuan-Yin, Standing On Lotus Bud, Blanc De Chine, Waves, Ming Dynasty, 35 In. 2232.00
Figurine, Lenci, Depicting Madonna Torso, 11 1/2 In. 670.00
Figurine, Man & Woman, Hand Painted, Germany, 10 1/2 x 4 1/2 In. 110.00
Figurine, Napoleon On Rearing Horse, Multicolored, 16 In. 315.00
Figurine, Peasant, Dancing, Biscuit, Popov, Russia, c.1850, 7 1/8 In. 1763.00
Figurine, Peasant, Seated On Bench, Walking Stick, Biscuit, Popov, Russia, c.1845, 5 In. 2703.00
Figurine, Phoenix, Mushrooms, Rockwork, 1800s, 16 x 7 x 5 In., Pair 880.00
Figurine, Quan Yin, Blanc De Chine, Chinese, 1900-10, 22 x 13 1/2 In. 1400.00
Figurine, Rodent, Miklashevskii, Russia, c.1850, 4 In. 1295.00
Figurine, Sancho, Holding Tankard, Bag, c.1860, 6 1/2 In. 4995.00
Figurine, Stallion, Rearing, Kaiser, 13 x 11 In. 410.00
Figurine, Woman, Dancer, Art Deco, Katzhutte, Early 1900s, 10 1/4 In. 145.00
Figurine, Woman, In Dance Pose, Sculpted Hair, Swirling Skirt, Germany, 10 In. 728.00
Figurine, Woman, Kneeling, Arms Outstretched, Rosenthaler, Germany, 6 In. 728.00
Figurine, Woman, Popov, Russia, c.1840, 4 3/4 In. 2940.00
Figurine, Woman, Reclining, Painted Features, Dressel & Kister, Germany, 9 In. 1230.00
Fishbowl, Foo Dogs, Clouds, Grapes, Waves, Chinese, Late 1800s, 11 1/2 x 14 In. 150.00
Foo Dog, Female & Pup, Male & Ball, Plinth Base, Enamel, Chinese, c.1900, 14 In., Pair 470.00
Fruit Basket, La Courtille, Reticulated Paw Footed, Cornflowers, c.1805, 5 x 9 In. 940.00
Ginger Jar, Blue & White, Pheasants On Rockwork, Prunus Ground, Chinese, 13 1/2 In. 295.00
Ginger Jar, Cover, Baluster Shape, Chinese, 17 x 10 In., Pair 410.00
Ginger Jar, Cranes, c.1900, 23 x 15 In. 1287.00
Group, Allegorical Architecture, Frankenthal, c.1775, 5 3/4 In. 3000.00
Group, Galants Couple, Jacob Petit, c.1865, 13 1/2 In. 590.00
Group, Musicians, Stepped Base, Germany, c.1875, 11 In. 1095.00
Hibachi, Cylindrical, Flowering Trees, Stylized Borders, Japan, 12 In. 470.00
Hibachi, Landscape, Flower Border, Ru-Yi Border, Blue, Japan, 16 In. 295.00
Humidor, Geese, Cottage, Boat, Tapestry, Green I&E Wreath Mark, c.1930, 7 3/4 In. 590.00
Humidor, Owl Shape, Glazed Features, Leather Covered, 8 3/4 In. 60.00
Jar, Baluster, Painted, Elephant Head Handles, Birds, Chinese, Early 1900s, 8 1/2 In., Pair 229.00
Jar, Bamboo Shape, Children In Bamboo Grove, Fukagawa, 1868-1912, 6 1/2 In. 1150.00
Jar, Cover, Blue & White, Chinese, 10 In. 266.00
Jar, Cover, Egg Shape, Flower Vases, Blue, White, Chinese, 1662-1722, 7 In. 4130.00
Jar, Cover, Landscape, Prunus Flower Border, Blue, Chinese, 1800s, 17 In., Pair 880.00
Jar, Flowers, Blue & White, Oval, Korea, 3 1/4 x 4 1/4 In. 315.00
Jar, Globular, Leaf Decoration, Blue, White, Korea, Choson Period, 4 In. 825.00
Jar, Phoenix, Garden Design, Blue & White, Meiping Form, Korea, 13 In. 1840.00

Jar, Wood Cover, Carved, Blue & White, Chinese, 19th Century, 8 In., Pair 1416.00
Jardiniere, Egg Shape, Waisted, Gilt Accent, Germany, Late 1800s, 7 1/4 In., Pair 825.00
Jardiniere, Gold, Pink, Blue, Green, Openwork, Ribbed, 46 1/2 In. 865.00
Jardiniere, Oval, Central Band Of Scenes, Cavorting Youths, Handles, 15 In. 325.00
Jardiniere, Peacock, Garden Scene, Chinese, 15 1/2 x 18 In., Pair 350.00
Libation Cup, Blanc De Chine, Chinese, 1750-1800, 4 x 3 1/3 In., Pair 384.00
Mask, Oni Demon, Japan, 19th Century, 6 1/4 x 7 In. 440.00
Medallion, Portrait, Oval, Continental, After Bellini, Painted Doges, 3 x 2 1/2 In., Pair 490.00
Montgolfier Vessel, Blanc De Chine, Hot Air Balloon, Junk, Chinese, 10 3/4 In. 295.00
Mustard Pot, Cover, Flowers, Blue, Gilt, Chinese, 1662-1722, 4 3/4 In. 590.00
Oil Jar, Applied Spout, Chinese, 18th Century, 9 1/2 x 7 1/2 In. 175.00
Pitcher, Cream, Flowers, Leaf, 4-Color, Scrolled Handle, Acanthus Leaf Crest, 5 In. 55.00
Pitcher, Cream, Pink Luster, Mask & Flowers, c.1820, 5 In. 146.00
Pitcher, Grecian Urn, Landscape, Gilt, Enameled, Loop Handle, 1826-32, 9 3/8 In. 4480.00
Pitcher, Hot Milk, White Biscuit, Chinoiserie, Jacob Petit, c.1865, 5 3/4 In. 325.00
Pitcher, Milk, Dressed Frogs, Reading Newspaper, Smoking Pipe, Fishing Pole, 5 1/2 In. 140.00
Pitcher, Milk, Frogs, In Clothing, Reading Newspaper, Fishing Pole, 5 1/2 In. 140.00
Pitcher, Scrolling Gilt, Blue Triangle Mark, Continental, c.1900, 7 In. 100.00
Pitcher, Squat Shape, Raised Overall Scene, Fox Hunt, Lavender Ground, Gilt Rim, 4 In. 58.00
Pitcher, Water, Gilt, Enameled, Landscape, Loop Handle, 1826-32, 9 1/4 In. 8960.00
Plaque, Boys, Eating Fruit, Painted, Oval, Frame, Continental, Late 1800s, 4 3/4 In. 645.00
Plaque, Children Playing Dice, Painted, Oval, Frame, Continental, Late 1800s, 4 3/4 In. 529.00
Plaque, Crowned Christ, Painted, Giltwood Shrine, Oval, Gothic Style Shrine, 37 In. 2115.00
Plaque, Fairy Princess Gliding Over Ocean, Hand Painted, Gilt Frame, Oriental, 17 x 21 In. 145.00
Plaque, Female Portrait, Oval, Gilt Dore Frame, F.Z. Thallmaier, Germany, c.1890, 11 x 8 In. 935.00
Plaque, Fruit, Flowers, Modern Giltwood Frame, England, c.1835, 8 3/4 x 12 In. 8400.00
Plaque, Garland Of Fruit Carried By Putti, Germany, c.1900, 7 x 10 In. 7800.00
Plaque, German Yacht Meteor, Sailboat, Blue, White, Gold Rim, 10 In. 165.00
Plaque, Hand Painted, Young Girl, Hand Painted, 20th Century, 8 x 10 In. 70.00
Plaque, Mary, Girl, Rosa Mystica, Giltwood Frame, France, Late 1800s, 17 x 11 In. 7638.00
Plaque, Penitent Magdalene, Rectangular, Giltwood Frame, Late 1800s, 5 x 7 In. 406.00
Plaque, Portrait, Daphne, Hand Painted, Gilt & Gesso Frame, Fleur-De-Lis 128.00
Plaque, Portrait, Gentleman, In Black Coat, Rectangular, Painted, Frame, 6 x 5 In. 530.00
Plaque, Portrait, Noble Lady, Wooden Frame, Carved Acorn, Leaves, c.1900, 7 In. 825.00
Plaque, Portrait, Transfer, Young Beauties, RPM Germany, Late 1900s, 12 x 14 In., Pair 106.00
Plaque, Putti, Oval, Square Frame, 3 x 2 In., Pair 70.00
Plaque, Queen Louise, Hand Painted, Carved Walnut Frame, c.1900, 4 1/4 In. 206.00
Plaque, Saint, Hand Painted, Florentine Mark, Giltwood Frame, Continental, 7 In. 440.00
Plaque, Scholars In Palace, Molded, Glazed, Frame, Chinese, c.1900, 9 x 5 1/2 In. 765.00
Plaque, Servant Girl, Smiling, Holding Chamberstick, Scrolled Giltwood, 7 x 16 In. 1116.00
Plaque, Sevres Style, 3 Panels, Fan Shaped, Flower Swags, Trophies, 7 x 21 In. 1175.00
Plaque, Vestalin, Woman, Seated, Oil Lamp, Germany, Late 1800s, 7 1/2 x 5 1/2 In. 940.00
Plaque, Vienna, Painted, Court Scene, Suitor Choosing Of 3 Princess' Boxes, 20 In. 3275.00
Plate, Abstract Geometric, Signed, Kasimir Malevich, Russia, 1923, 9 1/2 In. 7080.00
Plate, Armorial, Blue & White, Crichton, Chinese, 18th Century, 9 3/4 In. 1050.00
Plate, Armorial, Clark Of Hereford, Frangas Non Flectes, Flowers, Swansea, 1816-26, 8 1/2 In. 8650.00
Plate, Birds, Butterflies, Insects, Lobed Rim, Nantgarw, c.1822, 8 1/2 In. 5355.00
Plate, Cabinet, Maiden, Grapevines, Art Nouveau, Vienna, 1900s, 9 1/2 In. 1116.00
Plate, Court Scene, Blue, White, Chinese, 1662-1722, 10 1/2 In. 885.00
Plate, Dessert, Ruins, Man, Landscape, Gilt Borders, Swansea, 1815-20, 8 1/4 In. 5150.00
Plate, Dragon, 5-Toe, Chinese, 1800s, 8 1/4 In. 410.00
Plate, Millefleur Design, Gold Ground, Chinese, 1736-95, 13 In. 440.00
Plate, Tobacco Leaf Pattern, Chinese, 18th Century, 9 3/4 In. .....700.00 to 1055.00
Plate, Viennese, Reticulated Edge, Painted Scenic Center, Early 1900s, 9 1/4 In. 175.00
Plate, Woman, Playing Harp, Gilt Border, Cobalt Blue Ground, H. Stadler, Vienna, 1800s, 10 In. 765.00
Plate Set, Bread & Butter, Ambassador, 24 Piece 120.00
Plate Set, Dessert, Reticulated Gilt Rims, Flowers, Austria, 1900s, 5 1/2 In., 6 Piece 59.00
Plate Set, Figural, Painted, Stenciled, 7 1/2 & 9 1/2 & 10 1/2 In., 6 Piece 275.00
Plate Set, Game, Ambassador, 10 1/4 In., 12 Piece 410.00
Plate Set, Scenic, Landscapes, Dessert, Hand Painted, Cobalt Blue Rim, 9 3/8 In., 10 Piece 4115.00
Plate Set, Service, Gold Banded, England, 10 1/2 In., 8 Piece 205.00

Plateau, People Playing Chess, Multicolored, Gilt, Crinoline, Unterweissbach, 17 x 11 In. 205.00
Platter, Blue & White, Chinese, c.1750, 14 In. 500.00
Platter, Blue & White, England, 19th Century, 13 x 17 3/4 In. 120.00
Platter, Strainer, Blue & White, 19th Century, 10 3/8 x 13 1/2 In. 150.00
Pot, Water, Puppy Shape, Blue Decoration, Hirado Ware, Japan, 1800s, 7 In. 1115.00
Punch Bowl, Stand, Grapes, Vines, Leaves, 4 Paw Feet, Acanthus Leaves, 7 x 15 3/4 In. 1955.00
Sauce, Blue & White, Chinese, 4 1/2 x 5 1/4 In., 8 Piece 145.00
Saucer, Blue & White, Chinese, 17th Century, 6 In. 945.00
Screen, 8-Panel, Underglaze, Blue, Multicolored Tiles, Figural, Flowers, Bronze, 24 In. 3220.00
Screen, Table, Relief Flower Vase, Butterfly, Wood Stand, Openwork Leaves, 13 In. 345.00
Tea Set, Figural, Woman, Purple Dress, Red Cape, England, Early 1900s, 8 In., 3 Piece 70.00
Tea Set, Fired Gold, Walbrzych, Poland, 7 x 7 In., 9 Piece 70.00
Tea Set, Royal Chelsea, Golden Rose, England, 19 Piece 175.00
Tea Set, Scrolled Decoration, Translucent Rice Star, 1875-1908, 8 1/2 In. 80.00
Teapot, Cylindrical, Leaf Strap Handle, Strawberry Finial, Chinese, 1700s, 5 In. 410.00
Teapot, Sudlow, Burslem, Gilt Accents, England, 4 In. 120.00
Temple Jar, Cover, Blue & White, Chinese, 23 In. 205.00
Tobacco Canister, Black Boy, Chicken, Basket, Continental, c.1865, 4 1/4 x 5 1/2 In. 880.00
Tray, Bavarian, Water Lilies, Fired Gold Edge, 15 In. 176.00
Tureen, Cover, Stand, 2 Handles, Birds, Branches, Nantgarw, c.1822, 7 1/2 In. 8650.00
Urn, Baluster Shape, Teakwood Stand, Chinese, c.1900, 15 In. 2635.00
Urn, Blue & White, Chinese, 17 x 7 1/2 In., Pair 585.00
Urn, Cover, Naples, c.1880, 16 In. 530.00
Urn, Gilt, Enameled, Flowers, Gold Bands, 2 Handles, 9 3/4 In., Pair 5675.00
Urn, Louis XVI Style, Cobalt Blue, Ormolu Mounted, Putti, Early 1900s, 18 1/2 In. 355.00
Urn, Mantel, Cloisonne Enamel, Paste Mounted, Cover, Gilt Metal Handles, Signed, 12 In. 823.00
Vase, 2 Handles, Painted, Architectural Landscapes, Gilt, Blue Ground, 11 In., Pair 1548.00
Vase, 3 Peacock Head Handles, Blue, Green, Purple Glaze, 16 1/2 In. 489.00
Vase, Baluster, Applied Embossed Dragon, Crackle Glaze, Chinese, 20th Century, 14 In. 82.00
Vase, Baluster, Leaves, Blue, Gilt Accents, Germany, Late 1800s, 10 5/8 In., Pair 588.00
Vase, Baluster, Phoenix, Lotus, Leaves, Wood Cover, Base, Chinese, 1662-1722, 14 1/2 In. 1416.00
Vase, Baluster, Trumpet Mouth, Elephant Head, Ring Handles, Chinese, 11 1/2 In. 760.00
Vase, Blue & White, Chinese, 19th Century, 14 1/2 In. 355.00
Vase, Blue & White, Chinese, Qing Dynasty, 9 In. 295.00
Vase, Blue & White, Dragon, Clouds, Mounted As Lamp, Japan, 28 x 7 3/4 x 37 In. 690.00
Vase, Blue Glaze, Gray, Blue Mouth, Signed, Makuzu Koran, Japan, 4 1/4 In. 410.00
Vase, Bottle, Dragon, Blue, Gilt, Chinese, 1875-1908, 15 1/4 In., Pair 7670.00
Vase, Bulbous, Carp, Blue, White, Chinese, 1662-1722, 15 3/4 In. 1180.00
Vase, Clair-De-Lune, Chinese, Qing Dynasty, 10 In. 325.00
Vase, Clair-De-Lune, Dragon Chasing Pearl, Clouds, Bats, Waves, Chinese, 17 In. 5665.00
Vase, Coalbrookdale, 2 Handles, Urn Shape, Applied Flowers, Leaves, c.1850, 11 1/2 In. 305.00
Vase, Cornucopia, Hand Painted Birds, Roses, Green, France, c.1900, 10 1/2 x 10 In., Pair 2500.00
Vase, Cover, Baluster Shape, Blue & White, Dragons, Flowers, Chinese, 17 1/2 In. 295.00
Vase, Cover, Blue, White, Foo Dog Finial, c.1700, 9 In. 355.00
Vase, Double Gourd Shape, Yellow, Wood Base, c.1850, 7 In. 468.00
Vase, Double Gourd, Elephant Handles, Green Glaze, Iris Flowers, Japan, 15 In. 265.00
Vase, Egg Shape, Apple Green, Chinese, Qing Dynasty, 16 In. 3420.00
Vase, Elephant Handles, Blue, White, Chinese, 8 In. 350.00
Vase, Figures, Tendrils, Blue, Heaped & Piled, Chinese, Early 1900s, 13 1/2 In. 940.00
Vase, Flambe, Foo Dog Heads, Ring Handles, Chinese, 10 1/4 In., Pair 415.00
Vase, Flowers, Pink Ground, Scrolling Leaf Handles, Gilt Edge, 9 1/2 In., Pair 236.00
Vase, Folded Fabric Form, Bronze Waisted Base, Lion Epaulets, Chinese, 7 1/2 In., Pair 1143.00
Vase, Garniture, Neoclassical, White & Gold, Handles, Baluster Shape, Royal Berlin, 12 In. 323.00
Vase, Gourd, Rose Color, Bird, Flowers, 2 Handles, Chinese, 1723-35, 6 In. 530.00
Vase, Green, Crackled, 18th Century, 13 In. 590.00
Vase, Hand Painted, Cupid Plucking Harp Strings, Monogram, Early 1900s, 8 In. 705.00
Vase, Heron, Water Plants, Art Nouveau, Ernest Wahliss, Austria, 1900s, 21 1/2 In. 1880.00
Vase, Mirror Black, Bulbous Body, Elongated Neck, Overgraze Gilt, 18 3/4 In. 600.00
Vase, Monkey In Landscape, Blue Underglaze, Globular, Japan, 20th Century, 10 1/2 x 11 In. 2235.00
Vase, Multicolored Stripes, Oval, Chinese, 18th Century, 9 In. 189.00
Vase, Multicolored, Gilt, Courting Couple, Flower Bouquet, France, c.1850, 21 x 15 In. 705.00

Vase, Multicolored, Gilt, Woman, Putto, 2 Handles, France, c.1850, 20 x 10 3/4 In., Pair 650.00
Vase, Neoclassical, Pyriform, Red Figure Decoration, 2 Handles, Footed, 8 In., Pair 590.00
Vase, Painted, Courting Scene, Baluster Shape, Blue Ground, Handles, 11 In., Pair 940.00
Vase, Persimmon, Blue Leave, Koransha Ware, Japan, 1900s, 11 In. 235.00
Vase, Pomegranate Shape, Lang Yao, Chinese, 1800s, 8 In. 560.00
Vase, Portrait, Iridescent Blue, Medallion, Woman With Flowing Hair, Austria, 7 1/2 In. 115.00
Vase, Red, Globular, Elephant Head Handles, Chinese, 18th Century, 15 In. 1300.00
Vase, Riverscape, Blue, White, Chinese, 1800s, 13 1/2 In. 649.00
Vase, Sang-De-Boeuf, Gourd Shape, Gilt Bronze Base, Lamp Mounted, Chinese, 13 In. 550.00
Vase, Tea Dust, Bottle, Globular, Long Neck, Chinese, 1875-1908, 14 In. 1888.00
Vase, Tea Dust, Broad Shoulder, Meiping, Chinese, 1700s, 9 In. 885.00
Vase, Trefoil Pear Shape, Red Purple Glaze, Kozan Gourd, Japan, Early 1900s, 6 1/2 In. 401.00
Vase, Triple Gourd, Hand Painted, Enamel Dragons, Chinese, 24 x 11 In. 585.00
Vase, Water Pail Shape, Green Glaze, Kozan, Japan, Early 1900s, 9 1/2 In. 499.00
Vase, White Monochrome, Flowering Prunus, Chinese, 17 In. 2360.00
Warming Plate, Coffeepot, Blue & White, Chinese, 18th Century, 9 1/2 In. 295.00
Wine Jar, Cover, Bulbous, Blue & White, Vines, Chinese, Late 1800s, 10 In., Pair 499.00
Wine Pot, Cover, Rope Handle, Flowers, Bird's Head Finial, Red & White, Korea, 4 1/2 In. 978.00
Writing Stand, Dog, Seated, Rochille Base, Jacob Petit, 1800s, 13 x 10 x 9 In. 3510.00

PORCELAIN-CONTEMPORARY lists pieces made by artists working after 1975.

Group, Mother Bird, Babies In Nest, Dahl-Jensen, 1900s, 5 In. 235.00
Platter, China, Pink Border, Aynsley, 11 x 14 In. 53.00

PORCELAIN-MIDCENTURY includes pieces made from the 1940s to about 1980s.

Plaque, Flowers, Hand Painted, Shadow Box, Italy, c.1950, 12 x 14 1/2 In. . . . . 92.00 to 104.00
Teapot, Cat, Dog, c.1950, 8 In., Pair 59.00

POSTCARDS were first legally permitted in Austria on October 1, 1869. The United States passed postal regulations allowing the card in 1872. Most of the picture postcards collected today date after 1910. The amount of postage can help to date a card. The rates are: 1872 (1 cent), 1917 (2 cents), 1919 (1 cent), 1925 (2 cents), 1928 (1 cent), 1952 (2 cents), 1958 (3 cents), 1963 (4 cents), 1968 (5 cents), 1971 (6 cents), 1975 (7 cents), 1976 (9 cents), 1978 (10 cents), March 1981 (12 cents), November 1981 (13 cents), 1985 (14 cents), 1988 (15 cents), 1991 (19 cents), 1995 (20 cents), 2001 (21 cents), 2002 (23 cents), 2006 (24 cents). While most postcards sell for low prices, a small number bring high prices. Some of these are listed here.

Alcazar Hotel, Alligator Border 80.00
Angels, Playing Instruments, Raphael Kirchner 430.00
Bi-Plane Akron Airways, Ken Royce Transportation, Real Photo 184.00
Black Soldier, Machine Gun, Real Photo, Early 1900s 288.00
Bowl, Stuffed Owl, Hand Colored, Billy Owlett, Real Photo 160.00
Butterfly Girl, Samuel L. Schmucker . . . . 345.00 to 546.00
Byrrh, Woman In Black, Javie Gose 115.00
Cats, Fighting, Chimneys, Smoking, Louis Wain 69.00
Clarice, Woman In Cigarette Smoke, Sl.L. Schmucker, Detroit Publishing 80.00
Cypress Point Golf Course, California, 1950s 7.00
Darkey Preacher, 5 1/2 In. 11.00
Elevator Operator, Edward Lund, Real Photo 145.00
European Style Trains, 3 x 5 In. 66.00
Exposition Philatelique, Palais Des Ducs, Dijon, Gerard, France, 1928 . . . . 230.00
Garden Mascot, Cat, Series Oilette, Louis Wain, R. Tuck & Sons 460.00
Glad Thanksgiving Wishes, Indian Woman, Turkey, Pumpkins, Projection, Schmucker 144.00
Glad Thanksgiving Wishes, Woman, Turkeys, Pumpkins, Projection, Schmucker, Winsch 115.00
Good Little Indian, Harrison Fisher, Russia 175.00
Grand Canyon National Park, Shows Guests Arriving, 1912 . . . . 10.00
Greek Girl & Mother, Maurice Manes, Paris, France, 1902 . . . . 200.00
Laughing Waters, Indian Maiden In Pipe Smoke, Detroit Publishing 230.00

Logan Pottery, Logan, Ohio, 1910 Postmark 44.00
Mlle. Gabriel, Living Half Woman, Coney Island, Real Photo 173.00
Moet & Chandon, Woman, Flowers, Alphonse Mucha, Paris 403.00
My Valentine, Think Of Me, Silk Insert, S.L. Schmucker, Winsch 46.00
Old Uncle Joe, Alligator Border 115.00
Railroad, Trains, Color, Black & White, 3 x 5 In. 193.00
Rinehart Cafe Horse Drawn Diner, Real Photo 430.00
Sirene Nude, Real Photo, c.1904 .... 259.00
Society For Benefit Of Austria-Hungary, Alphonse Mucha 518.00
Summer, Woman, Alphonse Mucha 259.00
Thanksgiving Day In South 1912, Schmucker Winsch, John Winson 44.00
Train, Disaster, Boston & Maine Wreck, 6 .... 52.00
Train Engines, B & O, I.C.C.R., Smith & Porter, Northern Pacific, Lackawanna, 11 .... 52.00
Woman, Art Deco, Doudavich 35.00
Zodiac, Woman, Alphonse Mucha 405.00

POSTERS have informed the public about news and entertainment events since ancient times. Nineteenth-century advertising or theatrical posters and twentieth-century movie and war posters are of special interest today. The price is determined by the artist, the condition, and the rarity. Other posters may be listed under Movie, Political, and World War I and II.

American Airlines, Chicago, Pacific Air Lines, Art Deco Style, 1960s, 40 x 30 In. 835.00
Barnum & Bailey Greatest Show On Earth, Acrobats, France, 1900s, 29 1/2 x 37 1/4 In. 675.00
Barnum Museum, Musee Des Barnums De France, Par Le Professeur, Black & White, Paris, 1870s 2415.00
Blue Jeans, You Can't Marry The Gal Cause She's Your Sister, 1900s, 28 x 21 In. 220.00
Carter The Great, Devils, Camel, Sphinx, c.1920, 27 x 41 In. 2637.00
Chicago & North Western Railway, 6 x 14 In. 358.00
Christo Wraps The Museum, Crayon Signature, Frame, 1968, 33 3/4 x 22 3/4 In. 825.00
Clyde Beatty Circus, Lions, Tigers, 1940s, 27 1/2 x 41 In. 920.00
Clyde Beatty-Cole Bros. Circus, World's Greatest Elephant Herd, 29 1/2 x 28 In. 40.00
Clyde Beatty-Cole Brother's Circus, World's Largest, 29 x 28 In. 30.00
Commercial Motor Show, 17th International Motor Transport Exhibit, Frame, 29 x 19 In. 207.00
Concert, Buddy Holly & The Crickets, Liverpool, 1958, 24 x 15 1/2 In. 3615.00
Concert, Woodstock, 3 Days Of Peace & Music, 1969, 36 3/4 x 24 In. 4249.00
Grateful Dead, Riders Of Purple Sage, New Expo Convention Center, 1960s, 29 x 23 In. 390.00
Grateful Dead, Santana, Fillmore West, August 30, September 1, 1968, 21 x 14 In. 569.00
Great Raymond, Noah's Ark, c.1910, 8 Sheet, 88 x 77 In. 10928.00
Hommage A Elsa Schiaparelli, Pavillon Des Arts, Frame, 1984, 65 1/2 x 50 In. 295.00
Houdini, Master Mystifier, Buried Alive, Chromolithograph, Literary Digest, 55 x 78 In. 9200.00
Howling Success The New Baby, Man, Lady, Baby Carriage, c.1900, 28 x 21 In. 208.00
Jamestown Exposition, Bird's-Eye View, Teddy Roosevelt, Frame, 1907, 35 x 22 In. 835.00
Jimi Hendrix Experience, Cobo Arena, Detroit, May 2, 1969, 22 x 14 In. 810.00
Kremotwins, Lithograph, 1940s, 1 Sheet, 37 x 27 In. 230.00
Missouri Pacific Rail, Paper, Lithograph, Frame, 1887, 28 x 9 1/2 In. 935.00
Moby Dick, Gregory Peck, Orson Welles, John Houston, Frame, 20 x 25 In. 259.00
Mon Uncle, P. Etaix, 4-Color, c.1958, 61 x 45 1/4 In. 1200.00
New York, Fly TWA, Neon Theme, 1960s, 40 x 24 1/2 In. 1485.00
Nordini, White Fakir, c.1900, 37 x 27 In. 1761.00
Parker & Watts Circus, Kit Carson, Last Of Famous Scouts, 1930s, 27 x 41 In. 230.00
Ringling Bros. & Barnum & Bailey Circus, Cardboard Lithograph, 37 3/4 x 28 1/4 In. 358.00
Ringling Bros. & Barnum & Bailey Circus, Early 1920s, 19 x 28 In. 1459.00
Ringling Bros. & Barnum & Bailey Circus, Elephant, 1925, 27 1/2 x 47 1/2 In. 690.00
Sells & Gray Circus, Meriden, Columbus Park, July 26, 1973, 28 x 28 In. 40.00
Solanis, Le Magicien Moderne, France, 1945, 37 x 24 1/2 In. 375.00
Union Pacific Railway, Paper, Lithograph, Through Kansas & Nebraska, Frame, 22 x 14 In. 1540.00
United Air Lines, New York, Couple In Horse Drawn Carriage, 1960s, 40 x 25 In. 1330.00
We Can Live Without Another War, Conscientious Objectors, Vietnam Era, 16 1/2 x 22 In. 8.00
Who, Grateful Dead, Fillmore West, 1968, 22 x 28 In. 920.00
Wyoming Bill's Wild West, Almost Endless Procession, Frame, 1913, 24 x 36 In. 2470.00
Yardbirds, Jeff Beck, Carousel Ballroom, Rollarena, Aug. 25 & 26, 1966, 24 x 18 In. 696.00

POTLIDS are just that, lids for pots. Transfer-printed potlids had their heyday from the 1840s to the early 1900s. The English Staffordshire potteries made ceramic containers with decorative lids for bear's grease, shrimp or meat paste, cold cream, and toothpaste. Printed advertising and pictures of historical events, portraits of famous people, or scenic views were designed in black and white or color. Reproductions have been made.

Alas Poor Bruin, Boys Throwing Snow Balls, Man, Bear, Pottery, England, 1845-70, 3 In. 123.00
Burgess's Anchovy Paste, Hythe Road Willesden, London, 1800s, 3 1/4 In. 75.00
Feeding The Chickens, 5 Colors, 1860-80, 4 1/4 In. 275.00

POTTERY and porcelain are different. Pottery is opaque; you can't see through it. Porcelain is translucent. If you hold a porcelain dish in front of a strong light, you will see the light through the dish. Porcelain is colder to the touch. Pottery is softer and easier to break and will stain more easily because it is porous. Porcelain is thinner, lighter, and more durable. Majolica, faience, and stoneware are all pottery. Additional pieces of pottery are listed in this book in the categories Pottery-Art, pottery-Contemporary, Pottery-Midcentury, and under the factory name. For information about pottery makers and marks, see *Kovels' Dictionary of Marks—Pottery & Porcelain: 1650–1850* and *Kovels' New Dictionary of Marks—Pottery & Porcelain: 1850 to the Present.*

Bowl, Center, Abbey Pattern, George Jones & Son, 19th Century, 9 In. 185.00
Bowl, Center, Blanc De Chine, Cherubs, Instruments, Gilt, Moore Bros., c.1890, 17 In. 590.00
Bowl, Low, Marbleized, 5 In. 316.00
Bowl, Marked 408 ABC, American Bowl 'n' Cup, Washington, D.C., 5 1/2 In. 12.00
Bowl, Sevres Style, Painted, Floral Sprays, Sprigs, Booth's, 11 1/2 In. 581.00
Candleholder, Glazed, Crouching Foo Dog, Lotus-Shape Holder, Chinese, 17 x 18 In., Pair 470.00
Charger, Flowers, Band Decoration, Chinese, 13 1/2 In. 235.00
Charger, Woman, Sitting, Sgraffito, Henry Varnum Poor, 1947, 12 3/4 In. 2360.00
Cup, Green Glaze, Mottled Blue & Green Interior, Ozark Pottery, 2 3/4 In. 25.00
Decanter, Figural Bellhop, Holds Whiskey Tumblers, Germany, c.1920, 11 In. .... *ILLUS* 235.00
Dish, Woman, Seated, Cream Glaze, Alexander Archipenko, Arko, 1930s, 6 1/4 In. 265.00
Ewer, Indian Man & Woman, Incised, Signed, Wisecarver, Marked, 10 In. 210.00
Ewer, Indian, Bird On Head, Necklace, Incised, Painted, Signed, Wisecarver, Marked, 10 In. 210.00
Ewer, Phoenix Head, Painted, 3 Colors, Glazed, Chinese, 12 1/2 In. 235.00
Figurine, Chinese Woman, Painted, 3 Colors, Glazed, 12 1/2 In. 235.00
Figurine, Deer, Green, Tan, White, Brown, Incised, Signed, Wisecarver, Marked, 5 1/2 In. 150.00
Figurine, Dog, Mastiff, White Clay, White Glaze, Blue Spots, Crooksville, Ohio, 6 5/8 In. 460.00
Figurine, Dog, Seated, Hand-Tooled Fur, White Clay, Metallic Glaze, Oval Base, 7 3/4 In. 375.00
Figurine, Dog, Spaniel, Seated, White Clay, Blue Running Glaze, Albany Slip, 9 In. 315.00
Figurine, Dog, Spaniel, Seated, Yellow Clay, Shell-Molded Base, 10 1/4 In. 200.00
Figurine, Hand, Fingers Outstretched, Plaster, Paint Remnants, 12 x 28 In. 115.00
Figurine, Horse, Tang Style, Hand Painted, Chinese, 14 x 15 In. 95.00
Figurine, Lion, Lying Down, Glazed, Wood & Caldwell, 1840-60, 3 3/4 x 5 In. 470.00
Figurine, Mud Man, With Token, Glazed, Chinese, 20th Century, 23 In. 70.00
Figurine, Roosters, Hand Decorated, Italy, 17 x 11 In. 175.00
Figurine, Sioux Holy Man, Holding Pipe, Elk Head, Marked, Signed, Wisecarver, 9 1/2 In. 210.00
Incense Burner, Bowl Shape, Pierced Cover, Mandarin Duck Finial, Painted, Kyoto, 10 In. 210.00
Incense Burner, Tri-Glazed, Feet Molded As Lotus Leaves, Mounted As Lamp, 26 In. 1645.00
Incense Stick Holder, Glazed, Chinese, 3 x 3 In. 120.00
Jar, Baluster, Painted, Figural & Floral Reserves, Geometrics, Kyoto, 5 In. 70.00
Jar, Cover, Off-White Ground, Bird & Flower Decoration, Chinese, 13 1/2 In., Pair 235.00
Jug, Grotesque, Edgefield, S.C., 1860s 24725.00
Jug, Shoo Fly, Applied Black Woman, Fly, Semi-Oval, 5 3/4 In. 3520.00
Mug, A Present For Thomas, Child's, 2 1/4 In. 345.00
Mug, Canary Transfer, A Trifle For James, Child's, 2 1/2 In. 460.00
Mug, Cylinder Shape, Ridged Scroll Handle, Yellow, Brown, Green, Wemyss, 5 1/2 In. 2650.00

Pottery, Decanter, Figural Bellhop, Holds Whiskey Tumblers, Germany, c.1920, 11 In.

Pottery, Teapot, Dome Cover, Dolphin Handle, Agateware, c.1750-60, 5 1/2 In.

Mug, Happy The Child Whose Tender Years, Child's, 2 1/4 In. 115.00
Mug, He That Buy The Plough, Transfer Decorated, Child's, 2 1/2 In. 145.00
Mug, Peg In The Ring, Transfer Decorated, Child's, 2 3/4 In. 85.00
Mug, Samuel, Transfer Decorated, Child's, 2 1/2 In. 300.00
Mug, William, Child's, 2 1/2 In. 400.00
Pitcher, Bennington Type, Flint Glazed, Hound Handle, Game Decoration, 8 In. 193.00
Pitcher, Black, Green Panel, Pewter Lid, England, c.1865, 8 In. 115.00
Pitcher, Figural, Punch, Seated, Blue & White Glaze, Hat Lid, 13 In. 170.00
Pitcher, LaBelle, Flow Blue, 1893-1910, Wheeling, 7 x 9 1/2 In. 545.00
Pitcher, Peacock Feather, Green Matte Ground, Tricornered, 1907, 4 1/4 In. 750.00
Pitcher, Pink Tulips, Green Stems & Leaves, Wheeling, c.1900, 7 x 5 1/2 .... 25.00
Plaque, Aesop's Fable, Fox, Stork, Dinner, Circular, Burmantofts, P. Mallet, 1880s, 10 3/4 In. 320.00
Plate, Portrait, Courting Couple, Garden, A.E.G., Wheeling, c.1890, 10 In. 150.00
Plate, Transfer, Present For Going To School, 6 In. 430.00
Platter, Classical Garden Scene, Blue, White, England, 16 In. 115.00
Sugar, Cover, Vining Strawberries, Pink Queen's Roses, Handles, Molded Finial, 5 1/2 In. 145.00
Syrup, Bacchanalian Scenes, Samuel Alcock, c.1850, 7 In. 144.00
Tazza, Tin Glaze, Blue & White Enamel, Cherub Riding Dolphin, Continental, 14 In. 1530.00
Teakettle, Stand, Treacle Glaze, Flowers, Inscription, Measham Bargeware, England, c.1890, 8 In. 355.00
Teapot, Cover, Treacle Glaze, Flower, Fruit, Measham Bargeware, England, c.1891, 13 In. 470.00
Teapot, Cover, Treacle Glaze, Flower, Leaves, Measham Bargeware, England, c.1879, 10 1/2 In. 150.00
Teapot, Cover, Treacle Glaze, Flower, Leaves, Peafowl, Measham Bargeware, c.1890, 14 In. 355.00
Teapot, Cover, Treacle Glaze, Flowers, Inscription, Measham Bargeware, England, c.1894, 15 In. .. 765.00
Teapot, Dome Cover, Dolphin Handle, Agateware, c.1750-60, 5 1/2 In. .... *ILLUS* 10200.00
Teapot, Incised Decoration, Yi-Sing, Chinese, 7 In. 295.00
Urn, Cover, Metallic, Lions, Triangular Base, R.P. Bringhurst, c.1900, 5 1/4 In. 210.00
Urn, Dutch Style, Blue & White, Cover, Chinese, 12 3/4 In., Pair 995.00
Urn, Glazed, 2 Handles, Japan, 8 1/2 x 9 In., Pair 175.00
Vase, Aesthetic Movement, Bottle Shape, Enamel, Faience Mfg., N.Y., Late 1800s, 16 1/2 In. 940.00
Vase, Black, Flowering Prunus, Bamboo, Birds, Mounted As Lamp, Chinese, 31 In., Pair 1870.00
Vase, Blackware, Double Spouted, 13 x 8 1/4 x 7 1/2 In. 750.00
Vase, Buck, Trees, Flattened, Incised, Signed, Wisecarver, Marked, 7 1/4 x 9 In. 150.00
Vase, Daisies, Butterflies, Turquoise Ground, Spherical, John Bennett, c.1878, 8 In. 4995.00
Vase, Earthenware, Enamel, Bird, Flower, Leaves, Cream Ground, Hungary, 1800s, 32 1/4 In. 1765.00
Vase, Egg Shape, Geometric Bands, Birds, Humlebaek, Denmark, 1930s, 14 3/4 In. 265.00
Vase, Explorer, Staff, White Headdress, Feather, Incised, Wisecarver, Marked, 10 1/2 In. 240.00
Vase, Green Glaze, Bulbous, 10 In. 40.00
Vase, Indian Dancing, Antler Headdress, Incised, Signed, Wisecarver, Marked, 9 1/2 In. 210.00
Vase, Owl Sitting On Tree, Painted, Signed, Wisecarver, Marked, 9 1/2 In. 420.00
Vase, Peach Bloom, Lavender Pink, Green, Japan, 20th Century, 11 1/2 In. 150.00
Vase, Ribbed Body, Flared Rim, 3 Openwork Handles, Green & Copper Glaze, 10 In. 495.00
Vase, Stick Neck, Silver Rim, Green Glaze, Chinese, 10 In. 1287.00
Vase, White, 2 Necks, 1 Mouth, Valentine Schlegel, 1954, 16 In. 3120.00
Water Cooler, Dome Cover, Cypress, 8-Sided, Louisiana, 1800s, 22 x 15 In. 1998.00
Whimsy, Woman's Bust, Tan Mottled Alkaline Glaze, c.1900, 3 1/2 In. 22.00
Wine Pot, Fuzan, Figural Reserves, Gold, Blue Ground, Blossoms, Japan, c.1900, 5 1/2 In. 95.00

Pottery-Art, Vase, Brown, Blue, Ivory Crystalline Drip Glaze, Joined Handles, Denbac, 8 1/2 In.

Pottery-Art, Vase, Flattened Lozenge, Opening At Side, Carved Lizard, G. Mettheny, 7 1/2 In.

Pottery-Art, Vase, Naked Woman, Signed, Gres Mougin, Nancy, 18 3/4 In.

POTTERY-ART Art pottery was first made in America in Cincinnati, Ohio, during the 1870s. The pieces were hand thrown and hand decorated. The art pottery tradition continued until the 1930s when studio potters began making the more artistic wares. American, English, and Continental art pottery by less well-known makers is listed here. Most makers listed in *Kovels' American Art Pottery,* such as Arequipa, Ohr, Rookwood, Roseville, and Weller, are listed in their own categories in this book. More recent pottery is listed under the name of the maker or in another pottery category.

Ashtray, Lizard, Figural, Under Blue, Green & Tan Glaze, Signed, Greber, 4 1/2 In. 300.00
Basket, Handle, Marked, C. Greber, 4 1/2 x 4 1/2 In. 165.00
Basket, Hanging, Brown, Green, Black Glazes, Impressed, Avon Faience, 6 1/2 In. 178.00
Ewer, Drip Glaze, Marked, G. Metenier, c.1910-30, 7 3/4 x 4 In. 195.00
Ewer, Le Gaulois, Flowing Glaze, Handle On Top, G. Metenier, 6 x 7 In. 125.00
Jardiniere, Stand, Stylized Trees, Green, Lavender, Green Ground, 1900s, 28 1/2 In. 588.00
Jardiniere, Stylized Trees, Flowers, Incised, Avon Faience, 8 x 13 In. 690.00
Pitcher, Cylindrical, Open Handle, No. 73, Zark, St. Louis, c.1908, 6 3/4 In. 400.00
Urn, Multitoned Brown Crystalline Glaze, Gourd Shape, Curved Handle, Denbac, 9 In. 390.00
Vase, 2 Bacchus Faces, Blue Gray, Moss Green Drip Glaze, Silver Overlay, C. Greber, 6 3/4 In. 265.00
Vase, 2 Lizards, Applied, Sculpted, White Matte Glaze, Gourd Form, 17 In. 900.00
Vase, 3 Indian Heads, Green, Blue Matte, 11 x 4 7/8 In. 230.00
Vase, Arts & Crafts, Tan, Brown, Lavender, Green & Blue Drip Glaze, Handles, Greber, 5 1/2 In. 245.00
Vase, Bamboo Stalks, Blue Heron, Bretby, 11 5/8 In. 145.00
Vase, Black, Blue-Gray Matte, Double Bulbous, France, Maure-Lebret, 1925, 5 3/4 x 3 In. 65.00
Vase, Blue & Tan Crystalline Glaze, Bulbous, 2 Loop Handles, Pierrefonds, 3 In. 60.00
Vase, Blue Matte Glaze, Tan Drip Glaze, Handles, Signed, Maure, France, c.1925, 8 1/2 In. 165.00
Vase, Broad Sculpted Leaves, Blue & Gray Matte Glaze, Bulbous Top, 5 In. 600.00
Vase, Brown Glaze, 5 Openings, 4 Twist Handles, Marked, Avon Faience, 8 3/4 In. 290.00
Vase, Brown Glaze, Bulbous, Rolled Rim, 2 Angular Handles, M. Guillard, Etling, 13 In. 300.00
Vase, Brown Speckled Glaze, White Foot, Short Neck, S. Soudbinine, 1920s, 7 In. 6600.00
Vase, Brown, Blue, Crackled, Glazed, Wide Base, Ernest Chaplet, c.1890, 6 1/2 In. 6000.00
Vase, Brown, Blue, Ivory Crystalline Drip Glaze, Joined Handles, Denbac, 8 1/2 In. .... ***ILLUS*** 420.00
Vase, Brown, White, Ernest Chaplet, c.1900, 7 In. 4800.00
Vase, Copperflake Drip Glaze, Dimpled Body, Double Bulbous, Metenier, 5 1/2 x 4 In. 135.00
Vase, Double Bulbous, 3 Handles, Metenier, France, 7 x 6 In. 250.00
Vase, Flattened Lozenge, Opening At Side, Carved Lizard, G. Mettheny, 7 1/2 In. .... ***ILLUS*** 510.00
Vase, Geometric Hexagonal Pattern, Stoneware, Mougin, 1920s, 10 1/2 In. 189.00
Vase, Glazed, 2 Handles, Stoneware, Henry Van De Velde, Belgium, c.1904, 9 In. 9170.00
Vase, Green, Brown & Blue Crystalline Glaze, Tapered, Indents On Bottom, Denbac, 8 In. 270.00
Vase, Green, Copper Glaze, Ribbed, Flared Rim, Openwork Handles, 10 In. 495.00
Vase, Green, White Crackle Top, Round, Melon Ribs, St. Clement, 4 1/4 In. 390.00
Vase, Heron On Dark Blue Field, France, 8 In. 115.00

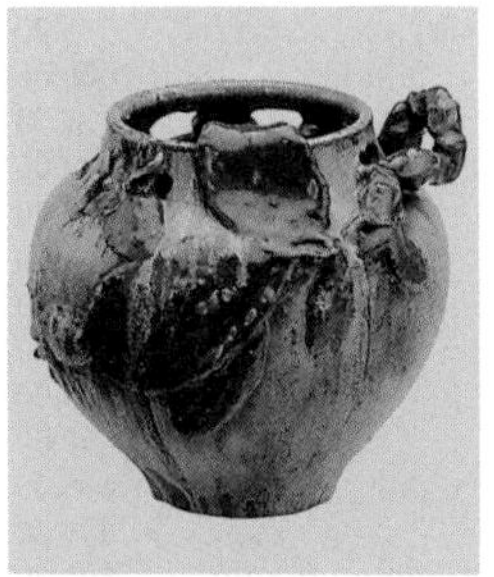
Pottery-Art, Vase, Potbelly, Enameled, Openwork Neck, Figs, Branches, Robalbhen, Apris, 11 3/4 In.

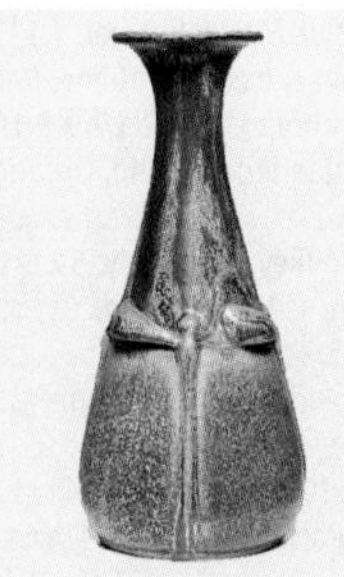
Pottery-Art, Vase, Raised Dragonfly, Blue, Brown, Green, Crystalline Drip Glaze, Denbac, 9 In.

Pottery-Contemporary, Cachepot, Stencilled Scenegio Ponti, Ginori, 1985, 7 1/2 In.

Vase, Mottled Red, Green, Blue, Tan Matte Glaze, Indented Sides, Rolled Rim, Dalpayrat, 12 In. 4200.00
Vase, Multitone Brown Crystalline Glaze, 4 Handles, Denbac, 10 1/2 In. 646.00
Vase, Naked Woman, Signed, Gres Mougin, Nancy, 18 3/4 In. .... *ILLUS* 12960.00
Vase, Potbelly, Enameled, Openwork Neck, Figs, Branches, Robalbhen, Apris, 11 3/4 In. .... *ILLUS* 21600.00
Vase, Raised Dragonfly, Blue, Brown, Green, Crystalline Drip Glaze, Denbac, 9 In. .... *ILLUS* 1560.00
Vase, Ribbed, Green, Tan Glaze, Glatiny, France, Signed, 7 1/2 In. 529.00
Vase, Tapered, White High Glaze, Applied White Decoration, A. Mendini, 12 In. 600.00
Vase, Vertical Geometric Stripes, Blue, Yellow, White, Crackle Glaze, Swollen, Catteau, 10 In. 600.00
Vase, White, Blue & Gray Stripes, Jean Besnard, 17 3/4 In. 6000.00
Vase, Worcester State Hospital, Feathered Brown, Green Glaze, W.J. Walley, 8 x 5 In. 646.00

POTTERY-CONTEMPORARY lists pieces made by artists working after 1975.

Bowl, Verdigris Volcanic Glaze, James Lovera, 3 1/4 x 6 1/4 In. 1060.00
Box, Cover, 2 Girls, Blue, Pink, White, Black, Signed, Pillin, 2 x 8 In. 2990.00
Box, Cover, Woman, Signed, Pillin, 1 3/4 x 4 1/2 In. 1610.00
Cachepot, Stencilled Scenegio Ponti, Ginori, 1985, 7 1/2 In. .... *ILLUS* 480.00
Casserole, Cabbage Shape, Ceramic, Carl Malouf, 1975, 8 1/2 In. 129.00
Charger, Viola Frey, c.1980, 25 1/2 In. 2400.00
Dish, Lid, Mottled Glaze, Ocher, Brown, Stoneware, Arabia, Liisa Hallamaa, 1950s, 6 In. 285.00
Jug, Cylinder, Tapered, Scroll Handle, Stoneware, Arabia, Kyllikki Salmenhaara, 1950s, 12 1/2 In. .. 450.00
Plaque, Branches, Berries, Rectangular, Stoneware, Arabia, Muona, 1950s, 34 1/2 x 9 1/2 In. 565.00
Vase, Ball & Step Form, White Glaze, Matteo Thun, Memphis, 11 In. 450.00
Vase, Brown, Orange, Slender, Tall, Stoneware, Arabia, 1950s, 15 1/4 In. 707.00
Vase, Ceramic, Bennett Bean, c.1975, 14 3/4 In. 3600.00
Vase, Horizontal Black Lines, Mustard Matte Glaze, Stoneware, Peter Voulkos, 4 1/2 In. 823.00
Vase, Mottled, Cylindrical, Tapered, Stoneware, Arabia, Veli Sakari Vapaavuori, c.1960, 10 1/2 In. 285.00
Vase, Mottled, Organic Shape, Slender, Stoneware, Arabia, Toini Muona, 1950s, 16 1/4 In. 1885.00
Vase, Mottled, Square, Tapered, Stoneware, Arabia, Veli Sakari Vapaavuori, c.1960, 16 In. 396.00
Vase, Ocher, Brown, Stoneware, Arabia, Raija Tuumi, 1950s, 9 1/2 In. 320.00
Vase, Ribbed, Cylindrical, Stoneware, Arabia, Francesca Mascitti-Lindh, 1950s, 8 In. 320.00
Vase, White, Brown, Stoneware, Arabia, Raija Tuumi, 1950s, 8 1/2 In. 283.00

POTTERY-MIDCENTURY includes pieces made from the 1940s to about 1975.

Bottle, 2 Handles, Frothy Glaze, Stopper, Gambone, 12 1/4 x 12 In. 5310.00
Bowl, 3-Part, Guido Gambone, Donkey Mark, Italy, 4 x 9 3/4 In. 960.00
Bowl, Blue Matte, Aqua Matte Glaze, Brown High Glaze Interior, 3 1/2 x 6 In. 520.00
Bowl, Blue White Crater Glaze, 1958, 8 x 4 1/2 In. 10800.00
Bowl, Cobalt Blue Glaze, Frosted Blue Ground, Scheier, 3 1/2 x 6 In. 490.00
Bowl, Edwin & Mary Scheier, c.1958, 4 1/4 x 8 1/2 In. 780.00
Bowl, Flared, Mahogany Brown Glaze, Scheier, 3 3/4 x 6 1/2 In. 690.00
Bowl, Green Glaze, Brown Flambe, Scheier, 2 3/4 x 6 1/2 In. 490.00
Bowl, High Walls, Free Flowing Glaze, G. & O. Natzler, c.1958, 3 x 5 1/2 In. 4800.00
Bowl, Volcanic Green & Yellow Glaze, G. & O. Natzler, 1 x 4 5/8 In. 1020.00

Bowl, Woman & Boy, Arms Raised, Incised, Blue Matte, Scheier, 1 1/3 x 7 1/4 In. 575.00
Charger, Geometric, Orange, Green, Manganese, Ivory, Gambone, Italy, 9 In. 2006.00
Charger, Stylized Figures, Yellow, Brown, Gambone, Italy, 2 1/4 x 9 1/4 In. 2125.00
Decanter, Cylindrical, Geometrics, T. & S. Harlander, Brooklin, Ontario, 1950s, 10 1/2 In. 170.00
Dish, Carl Walters, 1928, 11 1/4 In. 1080.00
Figurine, Donkey, Glazed Guido Gambone, Donkey Mark, Italy, 5 x 6 1/2 In. 660.00
Figurine, Panther, Crouching, Red Glaze, France, 1950s, 19 In. 225.00
Jar, Cover, Rose Dodds, c.1958, 14 1/2 In. 600.00
Jug, Cover, Woman, Hat, Flowers, Bjorn Wiinblad, 1963, 10 1/4 In. 575.00
Pitcher, Wash Basin, Blue & White, Italy, 13 1/4 x 13 In. 40.00
Planter, Crimson, David Cressey, Architectural Pottery, No. AP-541, 1955, 10 x 15 In. 195.00
Planter, Green, David Cressey, Architectural Pottery, 1955, 19 3/4 x 16 1/2 In. 330.00
Planter, Organic Designs, Brown, Green & Blue Matte Glaze, Footed, Kahler, 7 x 8 In. 540.00
Vase, 2 Tab Handles, White Glaze, Jean Besnard, 1930s, 5 1/2 In. 6000.00
Vase, Abstract Design, Gray, Brown, Mottled, Stoneware, St. Ives, Bernard Leach, 1950s, 3 1/2 In. 375.00
Vase, Brown Stripes, Brown Leaves, White, Jean Besnard, 1940s, 9 1/2 In. 9600.00
Vase, Caramel Glaze, Closed Mouth, Ribbed Body, Oval, Scheier, 9 x 5 In. 550.00
Vase, Circles, Mottled, Globular, Stoneware, Erica & Kjeld Deichmann, c.1950, 5 In. 396.00
Vase, Feelie, Blue Matte Over Turquoise, Speckle, Cabat, 5 x 4 In. 805.00
Vase, Feelie, Brown Glaze Streaks, Yellow Matte Ground, Cabat, 4 x 2 In. 200.00
Vase, Feelie, Lavender, Violet Matte Glaze, Cabat, 3 1/2 x 1 3/4 In. 175.00
Vase, Feelie, Multicolor Matte Glaze, Cabat, 2 3/4 x 2 1/4 In. 115.00
Vase, Feelie, Silver Gray Streaks, Olive Matte, Cabat, 3 x 2 In. 173.00
Vase, Geometric, Bulbous, Gourd Form, Brown On Brown, Stoneware, Clyde Burt, Signed, 5 3/4 In. 470.00
Vase, Glen Lukens, 3 x 3 1/2 In. 1080.00
Vase, Gold Birds & Flowers, Brown Ground, Bulbous, Flared Rim, Pauline Pottery, 22 In. 2160.00
Vase, Green & Black High Glaze, Incised, Paul Bellardo, 1948, 9 x 3 3/4 In. 316.00
Vase, Lavastone Glaze, Green, G. & O. Natzler, 1957, 6 x 5 1/2 In. 3600.00
Vase, Leaves, Mottled Brown Glaze, Stoneware, T. Kakinuma, c.1957, 13 1/2 In. 377.00
Vase, Mottled Brown & Turquoise, Stoneware, Hilda K. Ross, 1950s, 13 1/4 In. 283.00
Vase, Mottled Glaze, White, Red, Brown, Fantoni, Italy, 1950s, 5 1/4 In. 189.00
Vase, Mottled, Brown, Red, Ocher, Stoneware, Erica & Kjeld Deichmann, 1950s, 7 1/2 In. 1791.00
Vase, Ocher Glaze, Burgundy Glaze Interior, Scheier, 7 x 4 3/4 In. 405.00
Vase, Patchwork Design, Crackled Glaze, Fantoni, Italy, 1950s, 4 3/4 In. 189.00
Vase, Pebble Cream Glaze, Egg Shape, Stoneware, Erica & Kjeld Deichmann, c.1952, 5 1/2 In. 150.00
Vase, Sand Texture, Glazed, Slab Molded, Stoneware, Kanjiro Kawai, c.1960, 9 x 5 In. 11210.00
Vase, Slender, Elongated, Abstract Design, Gambone, Italy, c.1950, 18 3/4 In. 2790.00
Vase, Turquoise, Red, Egg Shape, Stoneware, Erica & Kjeld Deichmann, c.1950, 10 3/4 In. 1885.00
Vase, Turquoise, Red, Mottled, Stoneware, Erica & Kjeld Deichmann, c.1950, 5 In. 189.00

POWDER FLASKS AND POWDER HORNS were made to hold the gunpowder used in antique firearms. The early examples were made of horn or wood; later ones were of copper or brass.

POWDER FLASK, Brass, Birds, Dog, Wreaths, 1800s, 7 In. 116.00
Brass, Copper, Eagle, Arrows, U.S. Military, c.1850, 9 In. 116.00
Brass, Copper, Flowers, Violin Shape, 8 1/2 In. 385.00
Brass, Copper, Shell Design, 8 In. 90.00
Brass, Eagle, U.S. Banner, 9 In. 336.00
Brass, Eagle, U.S. Banner, 10 In. 390.00
Brass, Horses Relief, 8 1/2 In. 170.00
Brass, Hunter, Under Tree, 9 1/2 In. 110.00
Brass, Indian On Horse, Chasing Buffalo, 9 In. 385.00
Brass, Leaves, Vinse, Art Nouveau, J.W. Hawksley, Pre 1900, 8 1/8 x 4 In. 139.00
Brass, Quails, Bag Shape, 6 7/8 In. 90.00
Brass, Shotgun, Butt Shape, Dixon, 8 1/2 In. 165.00
Copper, Brass, Dog, Embossed, 4 Lanyard Rings, Dixon & Sons, 7 5/8 In. 45.00
Copper, Brass, Iron, Rawhide, Dixon, England, 1700s 120.00
Copper, USN Fouled Anchor, Ames, 9 1/2 In. ....770.00 to 798.00
German Silver, Buddha, Brass Chain, Round, 3 1/2 x 2 1/8 In. 90.00
Horn, Coat Of Arms, Woman, Dog, Dteu Etmon Droit, Revolutionary War Era, 5 1/2 In. 460.00
Leather, 2 Curved Horns Shape, German Silver Trim, Persia, 1700s, 10 1/2 x 6 In. 220.00

Leather, Shot Flask, 10 In. 65.00
Metal, Hanging Game Scene, 8 In. 130.00
Metal, Peace, Batty, 8 3/4 In. 358.00
Metal, Peace, Batty, 10 In. 550.00
Metal, Peace, Leather Strap, Ames, 9 1/2 In. 770.00
Metal, Scallops, Flowers, 8 1/2 In. 83.00
Metal, Shell Design, American Flask Co., 5 3/4 In. 132.00
Metal, Sykes Patent, Vine, Leaves, 1800s, 8 1/2 In. 71.00
Silver Hardware, Cylinder, J.W. Hawksley, Sheffield, 4 1/4 x 1 3/8 In. 140.00
Steer Horn, 1/2 Moon Shaped Front, Handmade, 6 1/4 x 3 1/8 In. 61.00
Wood, Banjo Shape, Round Body, Wood Plug, Twisted Cord, 4-In. Neck 220.00
Wood, Leather Cover, Seaman's, Boat, Whale, Cannon, 1700s, 9 3/4 x 6 5/8 In. 289.00
POWDER HORN, Brass Fittings, KLC, 2C, No. 62, Dutch, Late 1700s 88.00
Carved, Brass Tacked, Braided Leather Strap, 9 In. 176.00
Carved, Geometrics, Pinwheel, Turned Tip, 8 1/2 In. 105.00
Eli Howe, Brass Studs, Massachusetts Militia, c.1775, 8 In. 710.00
Engraved, British Coat Of Arms, Royal Artillery, Fort Haldimand, 1779, 13 1/2 In. 1595.00
Engraved, J.H. Tucker Jr., Pine Bluff, Ark., 1899 .... 330.00
Engraved, John Snyder 1691, Designs, 13 In. 8050.00
Engraved, Kimbel Herrick Sequick, Ships, Birds, Trees, Animals, 1830-50, 13 1/2 In. 1980.00
Engraved, Portercal Cove, John Churchill, Peter, Seal Stopper, c.1864, 17 In. 300.00
Engraved, Whaling Motifs, Inscriptions, Flower Urn, Walnut Butt Plug, 18 1/4 In. 705.00
G. & J.W. Hawksley, Remember The Alamo, c.1890, 10 In. 226.00
G. & J.W. Hawksley, Remember The Alamo, Silver Stopper, Charger, c.1865, 10 In. 765.00
Glass, Free Blown, Bird, Initials, Scrolls, Engraved, Curved, Wood Stopper, c.1775, 6 In. 2750.00
Horn, Metal Edge, Eagle, 21 In. 168.00
Isaac Marlow, Civil War Veteran, Caldwell, Ohio, GAR 195.00
Man, Seated, Holding Rifle, Eagle, Snake, Woman, 11 1/2 x 2 1/2 In. 880.00
Map, 2 Rivers, Curved, 1772, 22 In. 1425.00
Map, Hampshire Grants, Thomas Severanse, Sandwich, 1778 .... 578.00
Map, Merimag River, Ft. Weare, Ft. Ticonderoga, Capt. James Osgood, 1777, 16 In. 1128.00
Map, R.D. Brady, Made In Ticonderoga, Jan. 5, 1777, 16 In. 550.00
Navy Gunners Priming, British Flag, Coat Of Arms, England, Early 1800s, 19 In. 1320.00
Scrimshaw, American Eagle Shield, Wood Base, Bone Plug, 1840s, 8 In. 750.00
Scrimshaw, Anchor, Fish, Lady Liberty, 6 In. 690.00
Scrimshaw, Crowned Heart, Man, Woman, Plant, Geese, c.1830, 10 In. 575.00
Scrimshaw, Fish, Duck, Insect, France, 1800s, 18 In. 245.00
Silver Mount, Fort Meigs Map, Eagle, Dan Hanks, September, 1813, 10 In. 1400.00
Tin, Horn, Scenic, Indian Shooting Deer, 12 In. 28.00
Wood, Man Holding Rifle, Dog, Woman Holding Stick, 11 1/2 x 2 1/2 In. 880.00

PRATT ware means two different things. It was an early Staffordshire pottery, cream-colored with colored decorations, made by Felix Pratt during the late eighteenth century. There was also Pratt ware made with transfer designs during the mid-nineteenth century in Fenton, England. Reproductions of the transfer-printed Pratt are being made. More Pratt may be listed in Potlid.

PRATT
FENTON

Figurine, Rooster, Sponge Decorated, Brown, Yellow, Green, 3 1/2 In. 165.00
Figurine, Woman Seated, 10 In. 489.00
Jar, Turkey Dressed As Man, 11 In. 1380.00
Mug, Face, 5 In. .... 195.00 to 330.00
Pitcher, Couple, Children, Dog, Embossed, 4 3/4 In. 165.00
Potlid, Alexandra Palace, Oblong Trefoil, 1800s, 5 3/4 In. 275.00
Potlid, Children Feeding Chickens, Victorian Scene, 5 Colors, 1870, 4 In. 310.00
Potlid, Children Fishing, Round, 1800s, 4 In. 185.00
Potlid, On Guard, Sleeping Night Watchman, Spilled Drink, Jug, Frame, 6 In. 185.00
Snuffbox, Shoe Shape, Screw Lid, Stars, c.1800, 2 x 3 3/4 In. 355.00

PRESSED GLASS was first made in the United States in the 1820s after the invention of glass pressing machines. Hundreds of patterns of pressed glass were made in complete table settings. Although the Boston and Sandwich Works was the most famous of the pressed glass factories, there were about sixteen other factories making pressed glass from 1830 to 1850, and still more from 1850 to 1900, when pressed glass reached its greatest popularity. It is now being widely reproduced. The pattern names used in this listing are based on the information in the book *Pressed Glass in America* by John and Elizabeth Welker. There may be pieces of pressed glass listed in this book in other categories, such as Lamp, Ruby, Sandwich, and Souvenir.

1000-Eye pattern is listed here as Thousand Eye.
Acanthus pattern is listed here as Ribbed Palm.
Acorn, Pitcher, Applied Handle, 7 3/4 x 4 1/8 In. 99.00
Actress, Goblet, 6 1/8 In. 187.00
Admiral Dewey pattern is listed here as Spanish American.
Aquarium, Water Pitcher, U.S. Glass Co., 9 1/4 In. 330.00
Argus, Celery Vase, 6-Sided Knop Stem, 10 3/4 In. 120.00
Argus, Spooner, Pontil, Flint, 4 3/4 x 3 1/2 In. 88.00
Ashburton, Celery Vase, Pleated, Hexagonal Baluster Stem, Flint, 10 x 4 3/4 In. 120.00
Ashburton, Decanter, Bar Lip, Flint, 1/2 Pt., 7 1/4 x 2 1/2 In. 77.00
Ashburton, Eggcup, Fiery Opalescent, 3 1/2 x 2 5/8 In. 745.00
Ashburton, Goblet, Hexagonal Stem, Flint, 6 In. 330.00
Ashburton, Wine, Hexagonal Stem, Flint, 4 1/8 In. 55.00
Baby Face, Spooner, 6 1/2 In. 140.00
Baby Face, Spooner, Frosted Stem, Foot, 6 1/2 In. 110.00
Bakewell Block, Bowl, Amber Stained Blocks, Footed, 3 1/2 x 8 In. 340.00
Balloon & Spearpoint, Compote, Hexagonal Stem, 7 3/4 In. 22.00
Banded Portland, Water Set, Maiden's Blush, Gold Trim, 7 1/2-In. Pitcher, 7 Piece 358.00
Bar & Diamond pattern is listed here as Kokomo.
Barberry, Pitcher, Applied Handle, 9 1/4 x 4 5/8 In. 110.00
Beaded Grape, Sugar, Cover, 8-Sided Bowl, 5 3/4 x 5 In. 154.00
Beaded Thumbprint Block, Spooner, Running Stag, Ruby Stain, 4 1/4 In. . . . . . *ILLUS* 176.00
Beehive, Salt, Scallop & Point Rim, 2 x 2 1/4 In. . . . . . 165.00 to 330.00
Bellflower Double Vine, Decanter, Left & Right Facing Vines, 9 3/4 In. 264.00
Bellflower Double Vine, Decanter, Right Facing Vines, Bar Lip, Flint, Pt., 8 1/2 In. 935.00
Bellflower Double Vine, Pitcher, Left & Right Facing Vines, 9 In. 253.00
Bellflower Double Vine, Pitcher, Left & Right Facing Vines, Flint, 8 1/2 In. 176.00
Bellflower Single Vine, Bowl, Left Facing Vines, Wafer Stem, Footed, Flint, 4 1/2 x 7 3/8 In. . 99.00 to 110.00
Bellflower Single Vine, Champagne, Left Facing Vines, Flint, 5 In. 121.00
Bellflower Single Vine, Goblet, Banded, Flint, 6 1/8 In. . . . . . 22.00 to 33.00
Bellflower Single Vine, Goblet, Looped Vines, Barrel Shape, Flint, 5 1/2 In. 605.00
Bellflower Single Vine, Sauce, Green, Flat Rim, Right Facing Vines, Flint, 4 In. 176.00
Bellflower Single Vine, Spooner, Scallop & Point Rim, Left Facing Vines, Flint, 5 3/4 In. 176.00
Bellflower Single Vine, Tumbler, Coarse Rib, Right Facing Vines, Flint, 3 1/2 x 3 1/8 In. 165.00
Bellflower Single Vine, Tumbler, Whiskey, Left Facing Vines, Flint, 3 x 2 5/8 In. 415.00
Bellflower Single Vine, Wine, Coarse Rib, Straight Sides, Hexagonal Stem, Flint, 4 1/4 In. 385.00
Bellflower Single Vine, Wine, Left Facing Vine, Straight Sides, Flint, 4 In., Pair 120.00
Bellflower Single Vine, Wine, Right Facing Vine, Barrel Shape, Knopped Stem, Flint, 4 In., Pair . . . 120.00
Bird & Strawberry, Spooner, Multicolored Staining, 4 x 3 1/2 In. 145.00
Bird & Tree, Spooner, 5 1/4 x 3 1/2 In. . . . . . *ILLUS* 99.00
Bleeding Heart, Goblet, 6 In. 65.00
Bluebird pattern is listed here as Bird & Strawberry.
Bradford Blackberry, Goblet, Flint, 6 In. 66.00
Bradford Blackberry, Tumbler, Flint, 3 3/4 In. 120.00
Bradford Blackberry, Wine, Flint, 4 In. 110.00
Bradford Grape pattern is listed here as Bradford Blackberry.
Bull's-Eye, Wine, Grooved Knop Stem, Flint, 4 1/2 In. 88.00
Bull's-Eye & Broken Column, Goblet, Short Stem, Flint, 5 1/2 In. 55.00
Bull's-Eye With Diamond Point, Goblet, Flint, 6 3/4 In. . . . . . 145.00 to 165.00
Bullet Emblem, Spooner, 4 In. 88.00
Butterfly Scroll, Salt, Scalloped Rim, Tapered Ends, 1 3/4 x 3 1/4 x 1 3/4 In. 28.00
Cabbage Leaf, Butter, Cover, Frosted, 5 x 6 In. 630.00

Pressed Glass, Beaded Thumbprint Block, Spooner, Running Stag, Ruby Stain, 4 1/4 In.

Pressed Glass, Bird & Tree, Spooner, 5 1/4 x 3 1/2 In.

Cable, Goblet, Flint, 6 1/2 In. .66.00 to 77.00
California pattern is listed here as Beaded Grape.
Candlewick as a pressed glass pattern is properly named *Banded Raindrop*. There is also a pattern called *Candlewick*, which has been made by Imperial Glass Corporation since 1936. It is listed in this book in the Imperial Glass category.
Cane, Pitcher, Blue, 8 1/4 In. ***ILLUS*** 50.00
Carnation, Berry Set, Ruby Stain, Gold Trim, 8 1/2-In. Master, 7 Piece 143.00
Chariot & Horse, Shield, Salt, Scalloped Base, Footed, Band, 1 5/8 x 2 7/8 x 2 1/8 In. 44.00
Classic, Plate, Warrior, 11 1/2 In. 132.00
Coin Spot pattern is listed in this book in its own category.
Colonial Empire, Goblet, Flint, 6 In. 39.00
Colonial With Diamond Point, Goblet, Flint, 6 In. 66.00
Comet, Goblet, Flint, 6 In. 145.00
Comet, Tumbler, Lemonade, Applied Handle, Flint, 3 In. 935.00
Compact pattern is listed here as Snail.
Cord & Drapery, Syrup, Amber, c.1900, 6 3/4 In. 748.00
Cosmos pattern is listed in this book as its own category.
Croesus, Creamer, Emerald Green, Gold Trim, 3 In. ***ILLUS*** 135.00
Croesus, Spooner, Amethyst, Gold Trim, 4 1/4 x 3 1/4 In. ***ILLUS*** 66.00
Cupid & Venus, Berry Set, Footed Master, 9 Piece 66.00
Cupid & Venus, Compote, 12 1/4 In. 77.00
Cupid & Venus, Cruet, Footed, Handle, Checkerboard, Stopper, 8 1/2 In. 176.00
Cupid & Venus, Pitcher, 9 In. 33.00
Cupid & Venus, Pitcher, Milk, 7 5/8 In. 33.00
Curtain, Pitcher, Handle, Footed, 8 3/4 In., Qt. 358.00
Daisy & Button, Celery Dish, Amber, Canoe Shaped, 12 3/4 In. 25.00
Daisy & Button, Pitcher, Amber, 7 3/4 In. 10.00
Daisy & Button, Tray, Water, Amber 95.00
Deer & Oak Tree, Pitcher, 8 3/4 In. 176.00
Delaware, Table Set, Rose Stain, Gold Trim, 4 Piece ***ILLUS*** 242.00
Delaware, Water Set, Rose Stain, Gold Trim, 9 1/4-In. Tankard Pitcher, 4 Piece 143.00
Diamond & Circles, Salt, Swag & Diamond Sides, Oval, 1 1/2 x 3 1/4 In. 33.00
Diamond & Circles, Salt, Swag & Star Burst, 1 1/2 x 3 1/4 x 2 1/4 In. 23.00
Diamond Banding, Salt, Thumbprint Panels, Rectangular, Flared Sides, 3 1/2 x 4 In. 44.00
Diamond In Circle, Salt, Geometric, Footed, 1 5/8 x 3 1/4 x 2 3/8 In. 28.00
Diamond Point, Tumbler, Jelly, Polished Pontil, Flint, 5 3/8 In. 28.00
Diamond Point, Tumbler, Jelly, Polished Pontil, Flint, 6 1/8 In. 39.00
Diamond Star & Scroll, Sauce, Oval, 1830-50, 1 3/4 x 2 1/2 x 3 1/4 In. 154.00
Diamond Thumbprint, Celery Vase, 12-Scallop Rim, Ribbed Stem, Flint, 9 3/4 In. 198.00
Diamond Thumbprint, Champagne, Flint, 5 1/8 In. 770.00
Diamond Thumbprint, Compote, 24-Scallop Rim, Ribbed Stem, Flint, 6 1/4 In. 110.00
Diamond Thumbprint, Compote, 24-Scallop Rim, Ribbed Stem, Flint, 7 In. .88.00 to 132.00
Diamond Thumbprint, Compote, 26-Scallop Rim, Ribbed Stem, Flint, 8 1/4 In. 99.00
Diamond Thumbprint, Goblet, Flint, 6 3/8 In. 880.00
Diamond Thumbprint, Tumbler, Whiskey, Flint, 3 In. 231.00
Diamond Thumbprint, Wine, Flint, 4 3/8 In. 231.00
Diamond With Peg, Sugar & Creamer, Ruby Stain, Engraved 110.00

Pressed Glass, Cane, Pitcher, Blue, 8 1/4 In.

Pressed Glass, Croesus, Creamer, Emerald Green, Gold Trim, 3 In.

Pressed Glass, Croesus, Spooner, Amethyst, Gold Trim, 4 1/4 x 3 1/4 In.

Diamond With Peg, Sugar & Creamer, Ruby Stain, Gold Trim, Engraved 110.00
Dolphin, Spooner, Frosted, 6 1/4 x 3 1/2 In. 121.00
Doric pattern is listed here as Feather.
Double Daisy Chrysanthemum, Pitcher, Applied Handle, 9 3/4 In. 55.00
Double Vine pattern is listed here as Bellflower Double Vine.
Double Wedding Ring pattern is listed here as Wedding Ring.
Dragon, Goblet, 5 5/8 In. 2200.00
Early Moon & Star, Spooner, Plain Rim, Footed, Flint, 5 x 3 1/4 In. 120.00
Early Moon & Star, Tumbler, 14-Point Star Base, Flint, 3 1/2 In. 230.00
Early Thumbprint, Ale, Flint, 6 7/8 In. 240.00
Early Thumbprint, Compote, 32 Scallops, Wafer Stem, Flint, 4 1/2 x 6 In. 176.00
Early Thumbprint, Compote, Double Step Base, 10 3/4 In. 1585.00
Early Thumbprint, Paperweight, Finial Handle, 20-Ray Base, Flint, 3 1/2 In. 358.00
Eight Panel, Tumbler, Cobalt Blue, 1850-70, 3 1/4 In. 176.00
Elongated Honeycomb, Goblet, Flint, 6 3/8 In. 55.00
Esther, Wine, Ruby Stain, 3 3/4 In. 120.00
Excelsior, Eggcup, Double, Flint, 4 1/2 In. 77.00
Excelsior, Tumbler, Flint, 3 3/4 x 3 1/2 In. 99.00
Excelsior, Wine, 4 1/4 x 2 1/2 In. 47.00
Excelsior With Maltese Cross, Goblet, Polished Pontil, Flint, 6 In. 44.00
Fan With Diamond pattern is listed here as Shell.
Feather, Goblet, Amber Stain, 5 3/4 In. 688.00
Fine Cut & Feather pattern is listed here as Feather.
Floral Fence, Plate, Basket Weave Center, Fence Border, 10 In. 22.00
Flying Robin pattern is listed here as Hummingbird.
Fox & Crow, Pitcher, 8 3/4 In. 468.00
Frosted patterns may also be listed under the name of the main pattern.
Frosted Crane pattern is listed here as Frosted Stork.
Frosted Leaf, Goblet, Flint, 5 3/4 In. ..... 77.00 to 88.00
Frosted Stork, Bread Plate, Deer Border, Iowa City, c.1880, 11 1/2 In. 115.00
Frosted Stork, Tray, Water, Oval & Bar Border, 11 x 15 1/2 In. 88.00
Giant Baby Thumbprint, Wine, Flint, 4 In. 28.00
Giant Prism With Thumbprint Band, Ale, Flint, 6 3/4 In. 165.00
Giant Prism With Thumbprint Band, Celery Vase, 18-Scallop Rim, Flint, 9 3/8 In. 110.00
Giant Prism With Thumbprint Band, Champagne, Flint, 5 In. 220.00
Giant Prism With Thumbprint Band, Wine, Flint, 4 In. 209.00
Gibson Girl, Pitcher, 8 3/4 x 5 In. 340.00
Girl With Fan, Goblet, 6 In. 66.00
Gonterman, Spooner, Amber Stained Rim, 6 x 3 In. 358.00
Gothic, Champagne, Plain Foot, Flint, 5 In. 132.00
Gothic, Wine, Plain Foot, Flint, 6 In. 44.00
Grape, see the related pattern Magnet & Grape with Frosted Leaf.
Hairpin, Tumbler, Flip, Amber, 5 1/4 In. 88.00
Hairpin With Thumbprint, Goblet, Flint, 6 In. 66.00

A fresh ink stain on wood can be removed by washing with water and then applying lemon juice.

Pressed Glass, Delaware, Table Set, Rose Stain, Gold Trim, 4 Piece

Hamilton, Tumbler, Lemonade, Applied Handle, Flint, 3 x 2 1/2 In. 165.00
Hand, Cake Stand, 7 1/2 x 9 In. 121.00
Heart With Thumbprint, Goblet, Green, 5 3/4 In. 176.00
Heart With Thumbprint, Syrup, Britannia Lid, 5 1/2 In. 99.00
Heron, Pitcher, 9 x 4 3/8 In. ....253.00 to 275.00
Historical, Mug, Bumper To Flag, Flint, Civil War, 4 x 3 In. 523.00
Historical, Mug, Liberty Bell, Snake Handle, Centennial Exhibit, Gillinder & Sons, 3 5/8 In. 231.00
Historical, Platter, Heroes Of Bunker Hill, Shield Shaped Handles, 9 x 13 In. 323.00
Historical, Platter, Liberty Bell, John Hancock, 100 Years Ago, 9 1/2 x 13 1/4 In. 88.00
Historical, Platter, Teddy Roosevelt, Frosted Profile, Teddy Bear Rim, 7 1/2 x 10 1/2 In. ....143.00 to 176.00
Historical, Tumbler, Campaign, 13-Star Flag, Eagle, 3 1/4 In. 121.00
Historical, Tumbler, Cannon, Flag, Eagle, Flint, Civil War, 4 1/2 In. 385.00
Historical, Tumbler, Cannon, Flag, Eagle, Gold Band, Flint, Civil War, 4 1/2 In. 253.00
Historical, Tumbler, Union Forever, Constitution, Flint, Civil War, 3 1/4 In. ....230.00 to 253.00
Hobnail pattern is in this book as its own category.
Holly, Pitcher, Applied Handle, 8 1/2 x 4 1/4 In. 297.00
Horn Of Plenty, Celery Vase, 12-Scallop Rim, Faceted Knop Stem, Flint, 8 1/2 In. 110.00
Horn Of Plenty, Celery Vase, Footed, Wafer Stem, 8 In. 255.00
Horn Of Plenty, Champagne, Polished Pontil, Flint, 5 1/4 In. 77.00
Horn Of Plenty, Creamer, Applied Handle, 8-Scallop Rim, Footed, 5 1/4 In. 230.00
Horn Of Plenty, Decanter, Bar Lip, Flint, Pt., 8 1/2 x 3 In. 132.00
Horn Of Plenty, Goblet, 5 7/8 In. 44.00
Horn Of Plenty, Goblet, Flint, 6 In. ....39.00 to 66.00
Horn Of Plenty, Pitcher, Applied Handle, 6 7/8 In. 90.00
Horn Of Plenty, Pitcher, Applied Handle, 8-Scallop Rim, 8 1/2 In. 990.00
Horn Of Plenty, Tumbler, Whiskey, Polished Pontil, Flint, 3 x 2 5/8 In. 132.00
Horn Of Plenty, Wine, Polished Pontil, Flint, 4 1/2 In. 88.00
Horse, Cat & Rabbit, Goblet, 3 Panels 978.00
Hummingbird, Pitcher, Milk, 8 In. 154.00
Hunting Dog, Pitcher, 8 3/4 x 4 In. 319.00
Indiana Swirl pattern is listed here as Feather.
Jeweled Moon & Star pattern is listed here as Moon & Star.
Jumbo & Barnum, Spooner, 6 x 3 1/2 In. ....154.00 to 187.00
King's Crown, Pitcher, Ruby Stain, Engraved, 8 In. 88.00
King's Curtain, Goblet, 6 In. 6.00
Kokomo, Wine, Ruby Stain, 3 5/8 In., Pair 88.00
Lacy, Dish, Gothic Arch & Thistle, Oblong, 8-Sided, Midwestern, c.1840, 5 1/4 x 7 In. 44.00
Lacy, Dish, Gothic Arch & Thistle, Oblong, 8-Sided, Midwestern, c.1840, 6 1/2 x 9 In. 120.00
Lacy, Nappy, Cover, Roman Rosette, 1835-50, 3 3/4 x 5 1/2 In. 132.00
Lacy, Nappy, Scrolled Eye, Shell & Circle, Midwestern, 1835-50, 1 1/2 x 9 1/8 In. 468.00
Lacy, Plate, Scroll & Diamond, Yellow Green, Europe, c.1850, 1 x 8 1/8 In. 77.00
Lacy, Plate, Shell & Circle, 12 Bull's-Eye Feet, Midwestern, 1830-40, 1 1/8 x 6 1/8 In. 35.00
Lacy, Tray, Heart & Pinwheel, c.1850, 1 1/8 x 5 3/8 x 8 In. 22.00
Lee, Celery Vase, 8-Scallop Rim, Flint, 9 1/4 x 5 In. 132.00

Pressed Glass, Michigan, Water Set, Maiden's Blush, 7 1/2-In. Pitcher, 8 Piece

Pressed Glass, Saxon, Cake Stand, 7 3/8 x 10 1/4 In.

Pressed Glass, Starred Scroll, Rose Bowl, 5 1/2 In.

Lee, Wine, Polished Pontil, Flint, 4 5/8 In. 39.00
Lily-Of-The-Valley, Wine, 4 In. 143.00
Lincoln Drape, Creamer, Applied Handle, Flint, 6 1/4 x 3 In. 319.00
Lincoln Drape, Goblet, Flint, 6 In. . . . . 88.00 to 110.00
Lion, Bowl, Cover, Oval, Lion Finial, Frosted, 8 x 4 1/2 x 7 3/4 In. 66.00
Lion, Celery Vase, Engraved Leaves, Frosted, 8 3/4 x 4 3/8 In. 55.00
Lion, Compote, Cover, Lion Head Finial, Frosted, 9 1/2 x 6 In. 99.00
Lion, Pickle Jar, Cover, Lion Finial, Frosted, 6 3/4 x 3 1/2 In. 88.00
Lion, Pitcher, Applied Handle, Frosted, 9 x 4 3/4 In. 495.00
Little Samuel, Epergne Base, 8 3/4 x 10 1/2 In. 99.00
Loop, Pitcher, Applied Handle, Flint, 9 3/4 x 5 In. 154.00
Madison, Celery Vase, Hexagonal Bowl, Circular Foot, Flint, 8 3/4 x 4 In. 88.00
Magnet & Grape With American Shield & Frosted Leaf, Goblet, Flint, 6 1/2 In. 209.00
Magnet & Grape With Frosted Leaf, Champagne, Flint, 5 1/8 In. 198.00
Magnet & Grape With Frosted Leaf, Goblet, Flint, 6 1/2 In. . . . . 39.00 to 66.00
Magnet & Grape With Frosted Leaf, Wine, Flint, 4 In. 80.00
Master Argus, Goblet, 6 Panels, Flint, 6 In. 28.00
Michigan, Berry Set, Maiden's Blush, 8 1/2-In. Master, 7 Piece 77.00
Michigan, Lemonade Set, Maiden's Blush, 10 1/4-In. Pitcher, 7 Piece 525.00
Michigan, Pitcher, Maiden's Blush, Gold Trim, 7 1/2 In. 77.00
Michigan, Table Set, Maiden's Blush, Gold Trim, Open Sugar, 4 Piece 209.00
Michigan, Table Set, Maiden's Blush, Gold Trim, Sugar, Cover, 4 Piece 99.00
Michigan, Water Set, Maiden's Blush, 7 1/2-In. Pitcher, 8 Piece . . . . *ILLUS* 286.00
Mirror, Ale, 7 Rows, Plain Stem, Flint, 7 1/2 In. 66.00
Moon & Star, Bowl, Fruit, 7 x 8 In. 59.00
Moon & Stork pattern is listed here as Ostrich Looking At The Moon.
Nail, Goblet, Ruby Stain, 6 3/8 In. 121.00
Nevada, Table Set, Green Stain, Enameled, 4 Piece 635.00
New England Pineapple, Creamer, Applied Handle, Circular Foot, 6 3/4 In. 255.00
Niagara Falls, Tray, Shell Handles, 16 In. 25.00
Nine Flute, Pitcher, Electric Blue, Applied Handle, Toy, 3 x 2 In. 525.00
One-Thousand Eye pattern is listed here as Thousand Eye.
Ostrich Looking At The Moon, Goblet, 5 3/4 In. 154.00
Oval Panels, Goblet, Flint, 6 1/8 In. 77.00
Owl pattern is listed here as Bull's-Eye with Diamond Point.
Owl & Possum, Goblet, 6 In. 145.00
Paneled Grape, Biscuit Jar, Cover, Jenkins 50.00
Paneled Grape, Pitcher, 5 In. 30.00
Paneled Grape, Syrup, 7 In. 95.00
Paneled Wheat, Sugar, Cover, Spoon Slots, 7 3/4 In. 176.00
Peacock Eye Medallion, Salt, Acanthus Leaf Sides, 1835-50, 2 x 2 x 3 1/4 In. 248.00
Petals, Champagne, Flint, 5 1/4 In. 209.00
Pigs In Corn, Goblet, Left Bent Husk, 6 In. 550.00
Pillar, Tumbler, Jelly, Polished Pontil, Flint, 6 In. 50.00

Pressed Glass, Sunk Daisy, Compote, Ruffled Edge, 7 1/2 x 9 1/2 In.

Pressed Glass, Thousand Eye, Mug, Blue

Pressed Glass, Three Face, Compote, Cover, Oval, 12 x 7 1/4 In.

Pinafore pattern is listed here as Actress.
Polar Bear, Goblet, Frosted, Flared Rim, 6 In. 143.00
Polar Bear, Pitcher, Frosted, Applied Handle, 9 1/2 x 5 In. 468.00
Polar Bear, Tray, Water, Frosted Center, 11 x 15 1/2 In. 154.00
Portland With Diamond Point Band pattern is listed here as Banded Portland.
Prism, Salt, Double, Open Loop Handle, Star Bases, c.1885, 3 1/4 x 2 3/8 In. 33.00
Prism & Lobular Loops, Goblet, Flint, 6 1/4 In. 50.00
Prism & Sawtooth, Goblet, Flint, 6 In. 28.00
Punty Quatrefoil & Waffle, Celery Vase, Footed, Flint, 7 3/4 x 5 In. 66.00
Ribbed Clover, Tumbler, Flint, 3 1/2 x 3 In. . . . . 88.00 to 99.00
Ribbed Ivy, Sugar & Creamer, Cover, Applied Handle, 6 1/2 & 8 1/4 In. 253.00
Ribbed Palm, Compote, Open, 26-Scallop Rim, Hexagonal Stem, Flint, 7 3/4 x 8 1/4 In. 275.00
Saxon, Cake Stand, 7 3/8 x 10 1/4 In. . . . . *ILLUS* 43.00
Scarab, Goblet, Rayed Foot, Flint, 6 1/2 In. . . . . 88.00 to 110.00
Scarab, Wine, Rayed Foot, Flint, 4 1/4 In. 143.00
Scroll, Salt, Octagonal, Tapered Sides, Graduated, Tapered Base, 1 1/4 x 3 x 2 1/4 In. 22.00
Scroll & Stag Horn, Salt, Reeded, Tapered Foot, 1 3/4 x 3 x 2 In. 28.00
Scrolling Acanthus Leaf, Salt, 1835-50, 2 1/4 x 3 In. 99.00
Shell, Salt, Silver Platform, France, 1835-50, 2 3/4 x 2 x 3 1/8 In. 66.00
Shell & Hairpin, Salt, 4-Footed, 1830-45, 1 5/8 x 2 x 3 1/8 In. 99.00
Shell & Scrolled Leaf, Salt, Scalloped Rim & Base, 1 1/2 x 3 x 2 1/8 In. 35.00
Shell & Tassel, Plate, Fruit, Shell Feet, 12 1/4 x 12 1/2 In. 308.00
Six Panel Finecut, Compote, Cover, Amber Stain, 12 3/4 In. 209.00
Six Panel Finecut, Tumbler, Cobalt Blue, 3 1/4 x 3 1/4 In. 120.00
Snail, Butter, Ruby Stain, 6 x 7 5/8 In. 198.00
Spanish American, Pitcher, Olympia On Other Side, 9 In. 75.00
Squirrel With Nut, Pitcher, 9 In. 220.00
St. Bernard, Relish, 2 x 5 1/4 x 8 1/8 In. 176.00
Star & Punty pattern is listed here as Moon & Star.
Star & Scroll, Salt, Serrated Edge, Clear, 1 3/4 x 3 1/2 x 2 1/2 In. 28.00
Starred Scroll, Rose Bowl, 5 1/2 In. . . . . *ILLUS* 35.00
Stippled Scroll pattern is listed here as Scroll.
Stork Looking At The Moon pattern is listed here as Ostrich Looking At The Moon.
Strawberry, Pitcher, Applied Handle, 9 1/8 x 4 1/4 In. 176.00
Strawberry Diamond, Salt, Column Corners, Leaf Band, Scalloped Rim, 2 x 3 In. 35.00
Strawberry Diamond, Salt, Leaf Bands, Scalloped Rim, 2 x 3 1/4 x 2 1/4 In. 35.00
Sunk Daisy, Compote, Ruffled Edge, 7 1/2 x 9 1/2 In. . . . . *ILLUS* 25.00
Thousand Eye, Mug, Blue . . . . *ILLUS* 20.00
Three Birds, Pitcher, 9 In. 308.00
Three Face, Cake Stand, 7 x 9 In. 154.00
Three Face, Cake Stand, 8 1/4 x 10 1/2 In. 209.00
Three Face, Champagne, Fern & Berry, Engraving, 5 1/2 x 2 3/4 In. 275.00
Three Face, Champagne, Hollow Stem, 4 x 3 1/2 In. 2530.00
Three Face, Compote, 9 1/2 x 9 1/4 In. 275.00

Pressed Glass, Wildflower, Goblet, Apple Green

Pressed Glass, Wooden Pail, Pitcher, Amber, 8 In.

Three Face, Compote, Cover, Oval, 12 x 7 1/4 In. . . . *ILLUS* 3520.00
Three Face, Compote, Etched Underwater Scene, c.1880, 8 1/2 In. . . . 265.00
Three Face, Compote, Huber Bowl, 8 x 8 1/8 In. . . . 688.00
Three Face, Goblet, 6 1/4 In. . . . 99.00
Three Face, Goblet, Fern Engraving No. 53, 6 3/8 In. . . . 209.00
Three Face, Pitcher, 10 x 4 1/4 In. . . . 358.00
Three Face, Saucer Champagne, 4 5/8 x 3 5/8 In. . . . 303.00
Three Face, Sugar & Creamer, Cover, 9 1/2-In. Sugar . . . 688.00
Three Face, Sugar, Cover . . . 143.00
Three Sisters pattern is listed here as Three Face.
Tree Of Life, Epergne, 6-Petal, Scalloped Rim, 19 x 8 In. . . . 710.00
Tree Of Life, Ice Cream Set, Vaseline, 11 1/2-In. Tray, 13 Piece . . . 286.00
Tree Of Life, Sugar & Creamer, Cover, 7 1/2 & 6 In. . . . 154.00
Tree Of Life With Hand, Compote, Frosted, 9 1/4 x 9 In. . . . 44.00
Tulip & Sawtooth, Decanter, 8 Scallops, Rays, Handle, Stopper, 9 In. . . . 176.00
Tulip & Sawtooth, Goblet, Flint, 6 1/2 In. . . . 66.00 to 99.00
Tulip & Sawtooth, Pitcher, Water, Applied Handle, Circular Foot, 9 In. . . . 715.00
Tulip With Sawtooth, Celery Vase, Scallop & Point Rim, 10 1/2 In. . . . 77.00
Vaulted Smocking, Tumbler, Footed, Apple Green, 8-Scallop Foot, c.1875, 5 In. . . . 99.00
Wading Heron, Pitcher, Water, U.S. Glass Co., 9 1/4 In. . . . 473.00
Waffle & Thumbprint, Celery Vase, Flared Rim, Knop Stem, Flint, 9 1/4 x 4 3/8 In. . . . 132.00
Waffle & Thumbprint, Tumbler, Jelly, Flint, 5 3/8 In. . . . 165.00
Waffle & Thumbprint, Wine, Flint, 4 1/2 In. . . . 50.00
Washington, Goblet, c.1865, 5 1/2 In. . . . 66.00
Wedding Ring, Goblet, Flint, 6 In. . . . 66.00
Westward Ho, Compote, Cover, 9 1/4 In. . . . 468.00
Westward Ho, Spooner, Frosted, Gillinder & Co., 6 1/2 x 3 3/4 In. . . . 99.00
Wildflower, Goblet, Apple Green . . . *ILLUS* 15.00
Windermere's Fan, Spooner, Rosene, 4 1/4 x 2 3/4 In. . . . 39.00
Windflower, Pitcher, Water, Applied Handle, 8 3/4 In. . . . 121.00
Windows Swirled Hobb's No. 326, Spooner, Opalescent, 3 1/2 x 3 In. . . . 50.00
Wooden Pail, Pitcher, Amber, 8 In. . . . *ILLUS* 45.00

PRINT, in this listing, means any of many printed images produced on paper by one of the more common methods, such as lithography. The prints listed here are of interest primarily to the antiques collector, not the fine arts collector. Many of these prints were originally part of books. Other prints will be found in the Advertising, Currier & Ives, Movie, and Poster categories.

Amsden & Cargill, Illinois Schottische, Mat, c.1855, 14 1/4 x 19 1/4 In. . . . 283.00
Antis, Harry E., Bobwhite Quail, Gallery Of N. American Wildlife, Signed, c.1970, 16 x 20 In. . . . 22.00

Audubon bird prints were originally issued as part of books printed from 1826 to 1854. They were issued in two sheet sizes, 26 1/2 inches by 39 1/2 inches and 11 inches by 7 inches. The quadrupeds were issued in 28-by-22-inch prints. Later editions of the Audubon books were done in many sizes, and reprints of the books in the original size were also made. The words *After John James Audubon* appear on all of the prints, including the originals, because the pictures were made as copies of Audubon's original oil paintings. The bird pictures have been so popular they have been copied in myriad sizes by both old and new printing methods. This list includes originals and later copies because Audubon prints of all ages are sold in antiques shops.

J.W.Audubon

Audubon, American Red Pied-Bill Dobchick, Havell, London, Frame, 1835, 25 x 35 In. 1495.00
Audubon, American Sparrow Hawk, 26 x 21 In. 5760.00
Audubon, Black-Billed Cuckoo, R. Havell, 1833, 24 x 35 1/2 In. 8400.00
Audubon, Canvasback Duck, Robert Havell, Frame, 1836, Large Folio, 24 3/4 x 38 In. 1840.00
Audubon, Cedar Bird, R. Havell, 1828, 38 5/8 x 25 3/4 In. 3360.00
Audubon, Columbian Black-Tailed Deer, Males, J.T. Bowen, 1847, 21 1/2 x 27 3/8 In. 3120.00
Audubon, Florida Jay, R. Havell, 1830, 38 5/8 x 25 1/2 In. 12000.00
Audubon, Large-Tailed Skunk, Male, J.T. Bowen, 1846, 27 3/8 x 21 1/8 In. 2880.00
Audubon, Mocking Bird, R. Havell, 1827, 39 1/8 x 26 1/2 In. 26400.00
Audubon, Musk Ox, Males, J.T. Bowen, 1847, 21 1/2 x 27 3/8 In. 2400.00
Audubon, Prong-Horned Antelope, J.T. Bowen, 1846, 21 3/8 x 27 3/16 In. 3360.00
Audubon, Red-Headed Woodpecker, R. Havell, 1827, 39 1/4 x 25 3/4 In. 8400.00
Audubon, Ruffed Grouse, Julius Bien, 1860, 26 5/8 x 38 3/4 In. 3840.00
Audubon, Snowy Heron, Or White Egret, R. Havell, Frame, 1835, 23 x 19 1/4 In. 28800.00
Audubon, Snowy Owl, R. Havell, 1831, 39 1/2 x 26 In. 78000.00
Audubon, Texas Lynx, Female, J.T. Bowen, 1846, 21 1/2 x 27 3/8 In. 2400.00
Audubon, Trumpeter Swan, R. Havell, 1838, 26 x 39 In. 72000.00
Audubon, White-Headed Eagle, R. Havell, 1828, 25 3/8 x 38 3/4 In. 16800.00
Audubon, Winter Hawk, R. Havell, 1829, 26 5/8 x 39 1/2 In. 5760.00
Babcock, Dean, Biloxi Bay, Linocut, On Paper, Signed, 2 3/4 x 4 1/2 In. 28.00
Bisson, Edouard, Love's Capture, Signed, Mat, c.1902, 22 x 32 In. 145.00
Boileau, Philip, Autumn, Mat, New Frame, c.1903, 19 x 15 In. 50.00
Boileau, Philip, Chrysanthemum Girl, Mat, Frame, c.1905, 16 x 12 In. 330.00
Boileau, Philip, Every Breeze Carries A Thought, Mat, Frame, 1905-10, 18 x 14 In. 220.00
Boileau, Philip, Good Little Rogue, Mat, Frame, 1905-10, 18 x 13 In. 44.00
Boileau, Philip, Kimono Girl, New Frame, c.1905, 17 x 13 In. 66.00
Boileau, Philip, My Moonbeam, Mat, Frame, c.1910, 16 x 11 In. 99.00
Boileau, Philip, Summer Girl, New Frame, 1914, 10 x 5 In. 35.00
Christey, Howard Chandler, American Queen, Mat, Frame, c.1912, 20 x 16 In. 39.00
Chromolithograph, Atlantic Salmon, S.A. Kilbourne, Frame, 1878, 21 x 27 In. 220.00
Chromolithograph, Battle Of Chattanooga, Kurz & Allison, Mat, Frame, 1888, 26 x 33 In. 316.00
Chromolithograph, Fish, Schubert, Mat, Frame, Germany, c.1882, 12 x 15 In., 4 Piece 558.00
Chromolithograph, Leaping Brook Trout, S.A. Kilbourne, Frame, 1870s, 14 x 20 In. 330.00
Chromolithograph Set, Canaries & Cage Birds, British School, Cassell, c.1880, 11 x 8 In. 411.00
Crandell, Bradshaw, Accent On Youth, Frame, 1925-35, 11 x 14 In. 27.50
Doench, Eda Soest, Fire-Fly, Signed, c.1919, 18 x 14 In. 198.00
Doench, Eda Soest, Golden Dreams, Mat, c.1925, 19 3/4 x 14 In. 275.00
Doench, Eda Soest, Lucky Dog, Signed, c.1926, 20 x 14 In. 364.00
Doench, Eda Soest, Music Hath Charms, Signed, c.1926, 20 x 14 In. 248.00
Doench, Eda Soest, Special Delivery, Signed, c.1925, 20 x 14 In. 413.00
Eckelberry, Don, Mottled Owl, Frame House Gallery, Signed, c.1972, 18 x 24 In. 16.50
Fox, R. Atkinson, Dawn, Frame, c.1920, 18 x 30 In. 198.00
Fox, R. Atkinson, Enchanted Steps, Signed, 8-Sided Frame, c.1920, 18 x 14 In. 110.00
Fox, R. Atkinson, Garden Of Romance, 8-Sided Frame, 1920-30, 12 x 8 In. 88.00
Fox, R. Atkinson, Glorious Vista, 8-Sided Frame, 1920-30, 14 x 20 In. 154.00
Fox, R. Atkinson, Glorious Vista, Signed, Frame, c.1920, 18 x 30 In. 132.00
Grimball, Meta, Joy Ride, Frame, c.1915, 8 x 10 In. 50.00
Gutmann, Bessie Pease, Awakening, Signed, Frame, c.1918, 14 x 18 In. 28.00
Gutmann, Bessie Pease, Butterfly, Frame, c.1912, 18 x 14 In. .... 88.00 to 110.00
Gutmann, Bessie Pease, Chuckles, Frame, c.1937, 11 x 14 In. .... 77.00 to 220.00
Gutmann, Bessie Pease, Chums, 1918, 18 x 14 In. 198.00
Gutmann, Bessie Pease, First Dancing Lesson, Original Frame, 1923, 19 x 11 In. 523.00
Gutmann, Bessie Pease, Good Morning, 1911, 7 x 5 In. 176.00

Gutmann, Bessie Pease, Hearing 1909, 14 x 11 In. 187.00
Gutmann, Bessie Pease, Hearing, Hand Colored, Signed, Frame, c.1909, 9 x 12 In. 154.00
Gutmann, Bessie Pease, In Disgrace, Frame, c.1935, 20 x 14 In. 121.00
Gutmann, Bessie Pease, Just A Little Bit Independent, 1946, 18 x 14 In. 165.00
Gutmann, Bessie Pease, Lavender & Old Lace, Frame, c.1915, 10 x 12 In. 50.00
Gutmann, Bessie Pease, Little Bit Of Heaven, Frame, 1916, 14 x 18 In. 17.00
Gutmann, Bessie Pease, Little Jack Horner, 1933, 14 x 11 In. 77.00
Gutmann, Bessie Pease, Mighty Like A Rose, Mat, 1915, 14 x 21 In. 38.50
Gutmann, Bessie Pease, On The Up & Up, Frame, 1938, 18 x 14 In. . . . . 77.00 to 165.00
Gutmann, Bessie Pease, Reward, Frame, 1936, 20 x 14 In. 121.00
Gutmann, Bessie Pease, Smile, Smile, Smile, c.1918, 21 x 14 In. 330.00
Gutmann, Bessie Pease, Springtime, 18 x 13 In. 303.00
Gutmann, Bessie Pease, Tasting, Hand Colored, Signed, Frame, c.1909, 12 x 9 In. 132.00
Gutmann, Bessie Pease, To Love & To Cherish, New Frame, 1911, 17 x 13 In. 275.00
H.S. Sadd, T.H. Matteson, Washington Delivering His Inaugural Address, c.1849, 26 x 22 In. 735.00
Harm, Ray, American Eagle, Limited Edition, Signed, c.1970, 30 x 24 In. 77.00
Harm, Ray, Cardinal, Limited Edition, Signed, Frame House Gallery, c.1975, 22 x 26 In. 22.00
Harm, Ray, Meadowlark, Signed, Limited Edition, Frame House Gallery, c.1969, 16 x 20 In. 11.00
Harper, Charles, Red-Bellied Woodpecker, Limited Edition, Signed, Frame, 1970s, 21 x 16 In. 28.00

Icart prints were made by Louis Icart, who worked in Paris from 1907 as an employee of a postcard company. He then started printing magazines and fashion brochures. About 1910 he created a series of etchings of fashionably dressed women and he continued to make similar etchings until he died in 1950. He is well known as a printmaker, painter, and illustrator. Original etchings are much more expensive than the later photographic copies.

Icart, Coup De Vent, Aquatint, Signed, c.1925, 17 3/4 x 21 1/4 In. 1410.00
Icart, La Cachette, Hiding Place, Oval, Frame, 1927, 25 1/2 x 21 In. 969.00
Icart, Look, Aquatint, Signed, 1928, 18 3/8 x 14 In. 1410.00
Icart, Mimi, Frame, 1927, 28 1/2 x 21 3/4 In. 810.00
Icart, Panier De Pommes, Frame, 1924, 17 5/8 x 13 In. 765.00
Icart, Silk Robe, Gold Highlights, Frame, 1920s 145.00
Indiana, Robert, Red Yellow & Orange Love, Lithograph, Signed, 30 x 30 In. 936.00

Jacoulet prints were designed by Paul Jacoulet (1902-1960), a Frenchman who spent most of his life in Japan. He was a master of Japanese woodblock print technique. Subjects included life in Japan, the South Seas, Korea, and China. His prints were sold by subscription and issued in series. Each series had a distinctive seal, such as a sparrow or butterfly. Most Jacoulet prints are approximately 15 x 10 inches.

Jacoulet, 3 Koreans, Trois Coreens, Seoul, Coree, 1935 . . . . 690.00
Jacoulet, After The Banquet, Seoul, Korea, 1951 . . . . 1150.00
Jacoulet, After The Dance, 1940 . . . . 1495.00
Jacoulet, Ancestral Homage, Shinto Priest, 1956 . . . . 1725.00
Jacoulet, Autumn Pilgrimage, 1952 . . . . 604.00
Jacoulet, Awakening, Saipan, Mariana Islands, 1937 . . . . 3105.00
Jacoulet, Basket Weaver, 1948 . . . . 1840.00
Jacoulet, Beauty Of Palao, 1935 . . . . 2400.00
Jacoulet, Beggars' Meal, 1938 . . . . 900.00
Jacoulet, Betel Nut Boy, Yap, 1940 . . . . 2530.00
Jacoulet, Birds Of Paradise, 1937 . . . . 1150.00
Jacoulet, Black Lotus, 1959 . . . . 748.00
Jacoulet, Chinese Mask Seller, 1940 . . . . 805.00
Jacoulet, Daughter Of Chief, 1953 . . . . 2530.00
Jacoulet, Evening Flowers, 1941 . . . . 2300.00
Jacoulet, Geisha, Kiyoka, Tokyo, 1935 . . . . 690.00
Jacoulet, Happy Man, 1955 . . . . 1020.00
Jacoulet, Hokkan-Zan, Seoul, Korea, 1937 . . . . 207.00
Jacoulet, Hunchback, 1952 . . . . 460.00

Jacoulet, In The Private Gardens Of The Palace, Seoul, Korea, 1947 .... 805.00
Jacoulet, Living God, 1952 .... 633.00
Jacoulet, Mandarin With Glasses, 1950 .... 575.00
Jacoulet, Mango Seller, 1939 .... 1150.00
Jacoulet, Miraculous Catch, 1939 .... 575.00
Jacoulet, Mr. Keen & Mr. Lee, 1951 .... 460.00
Jacoulet, New Dress, 1938 .... 1725.00
Jacoulet, North Wind, Korea, 1953 .... 2185.00
Jacoulet, Old South Sea Island Woman, 1942 .... 3738.00
Jacoulet, On Tinian Island, Mariana, 1960 .... 3105.00
Jacoulet, Pearls, Manchuria, 1950 .... 1380.00
Jacoulet, Red Lacquer Mirror, Tokyo, 1938 .... 2990.00
Jacoulet, Salt Merchant, Korea, 1936 .... 920.00
Jacoulet, Sandalwood Smoke, 1948 .... 1150.00
Jacoulet, Scale, 1939 .... 863.00
Jacoulet, Sculptor Of Tokobuei, South Seas, 1954 .... 1265.00
Jacoulet, Shepherds Of High Mountains, 1941 .... 2185.00
Jacoulet, Song Of Waves, 1936 .... 2760.00
Jacoulet, Sunset In Menado, 1938 .... 1035.00
Jacoulet, Tempest Of Heart, 1948 .... 1150.00
Jacoulet, Treasure, 1940 .... 920.00
Jacoulet, Wandering Buddhist Priest, 1948 .... 720.00
Jacoulet, Watermelons, 1939 .... 690.00
Jacoulet, Young Girl Of Polowat, 1948 .... 4313.00

Japanese woodblock prints are listed as follows: Print, Japanese, name of artist, title or description, type, and size. Dealers use the following terms: Tate-e is a vertical composition. Yoko-e is a horizontal composition. The words Aiban (13 by 9 inches), Chuban (10 by 7 1/2 inches), Hosoban (13 by 6 inches), Koban (7 by 4 inches), Nagaban (20 x 9 inches), Oban (15 by 10 inches), Shikishiban (8 x 9 inches), Tanzaku (15 x 5 inches) denote approximate size. Modern versions of some of these prints have been made. Other woodblock prints that are not Japanese are listed under Print, Woodblock.

Japanese, Azechi, Umetaro, Mountain Range, Blue, Gray, Red, Oban, Yoko-e 2530.00
Japanese, Bixler, David, Horse, Landscape, Walnut Frame, 3 3/4 x 3 In. 1430.00
Japanese, Eizan, Kikugawa, 2 Women Standing, c.1850, Oban, Tate-e 189.00
Japanese, Gekko, Ogata, White Rabbit, Seated, Late 19th Century, Aiban 403.00
Japanese, Harunobu, Couple Fleeing Rat-Like Creatures, Mat, Frame, 21 1/4 x 17 1/4 In. 115.00
Japanese, Harunobu, Portraits, Seiro Bijin Awase, Book Pages, 5 1/2 x 8 1/2 In. 325.00
Japanese, Hasui, Kawase, Evening At Tagonoura, Color, 1940, Oban, Tate-e 325.00
Japanese, Hasui, Kawase, Nissaka In Rain, Oban, Yoko-e 403.00
Japanese, Hasui, Kawase, Snow At Mukojima, Oban, Tate-e 920.00
Japanese, Hasui, Kawase, Todoroki Town In Mito, 1946, Oban, Tate-e 633.00
Japanese, Hiroaki, Sailing Ships, Through Pine Tree, c.1935, Chuban 130.00
Japanese, Hiroshige II, Black Ship Off Rocky Coast, Oban, Tate-e 460.00
Japanese, Hiroshige II, Figures On Mountain Path, Oban, Yoko-e 288.00
Japanese, Hiroshige, Ando, Moonlight By River Tama, Mat, Frame, 17 x 21 In. 115.00
Japanese, Hiroshige, Ando, Snow At Shiba Akabane, Frame, 15 x 20 In. 2700.00
Japanese, Hiroshige, Fish Market At Zakoba, c.1835, Oban, Yoko-e 430.00
Japanese, Hiroshige, Kambara, Tokaido Gojusantsugi No Uchi Series, Oban 210.00
Japanese, Hiroshige, Pheasant On Snowy Hillside, c.1845, Aiban 205.00
Japanese, Hiroshige, Rice Market At Dojima, c.1835, Oban, Yoko-e 185.00
Japanese, Hiroshige, Ryogoku In Eastern Capital, Oban, Tate-e 375.00
Japanese, Hiroshige, Sacred Dance At Sumiyoshi Shrine, c.1835, Oban, Yoko-e 144.00
Japanese, Hiroshige, Suijin Grove & Masaki On Sumida River, Frame, 1856 .... 265.00
Japanese, Hiroshige, Travelers Near Inn, Mat, Frame, 17 1/2 x 21 1/4 In. 230.00
Japanese, Inagaki, Tomo, Pumpkins, Orange, Blue, 1955, Oban, Yoko-e 230.00
Japanese, Iwata, Masami, Landscape In Kamakura, 11 x 15 1/2 In. 55.00
Japanese, Kaoru, Kawano, Girl With Flowers In Her Hair, Surimono 132.00
Japanese, Kaoru, Kawano, Sacred Crane, Kakemono 390.00

Japanese, Kasamatsu, Shiro, Carp Swimming Below Cherry Petals, 1956, Oban, Tate-e 1150.00
Japanese, Kasamatsu, Shiro, Harbor, Frame, Oban, Tate-e 290.00
Japanese, Kasamatsu, Shiro, Raccoon In Bamboo Grove, Oban, Tate-e 270.00
Japanese, Kiyokata, Kaburagi, Woman, Measuring Tape, Length Of Cloth, Oban, Yoko-e 120.00
Japanese, Kiyomasu, Man With Fan, Beside 2 Cylindrical Baskets, Early 1700s, Hosoban 460.00
Japanese, Kiyoshi, Kobayakawa, Bijin Applying Make-Up, Frame, Oban, Tate-e 2530.00
Japanese, Kogyo, Fireflies, 1900s, Chuban 400.00
Japanese, Koitsu, Rain At Asakusa Kwannon Temple, Oban, Tate-e 460.00
Japanese, Koitsu, Snow, Farmyard, Sunset, Oban, Tate-e 499.00
Japanese, Koitsu, Tsuchiya, Zozoji Temple In Snow, 1933, Oban, Tate-e 180.00
Japanese, Koitsu, Winter Scene, Water Mill, Mount Fuji, Chuban 150.00
Japanese, Koson, Ohara, 2 White Cranes, c.1910, Hosoban 330.00
Japanese, Koson, Ohara, Egret, Marsh, c.1910, Chuban 220.00
Japanese, Koson, Ohara, Fox, Dancing, Lotus Leaf Hat, c.1910, Hosoban 748.00
Japanese, Koson, Ohara, Mallard Ducks In Marsh, Frame, Hosoban 431.00
Japanese, Kunichika, Courtesans With Attendants, Frame, Triptych 410.00
Japanese, Kunisada II, Samurai & Ladies In Garden, Frame, Diptych 410.00
Japanese, Kunisada II, Scene From A Narrative, Frame, Triptych 206.00
Japanese, Kunisada, Bathers Under Waterfall, Frame, Triptych 375.00
Japanese, Kunisada, Geisha & Komuso, Frame, Oban, Tate-e 270.00
Japanese, Kunisada, Ladies Having Tea In View Of Bay, Frame, Triptych 590.00
Japanese, Kunisada, Sumo Wrestler, Blue Ground, Oban, Tate-e 290.00
Japanese, Kuniyoshi, Battling Figures Beneath Bridge, Oban, Triptych 345.00
Japanese, Kuniyoshi, Woman Mending Fishing Nets, Mount Fuji, Oban, Tate-e 430.00
Japanese, Kuniyoshi, Woman Smoking, Oban, Tata-E 155.00
Japanese, Kuniyoshi, Woman, 2 Children, At Seashore, Wedded Rocks, Frame, Oban, Tate-e 259.00
Japanese, Masanobu, Male & Female Warriors, Early 1700s, Hosoban 2990.00
Japanese, Munakata, Shiko, Seated Female, c.1960, 8 1/4 x 6 In. 2106.00
Japanese, Nakayama, Girl With Sunflower, 1957, Oban, Tate-e 489.00
Japanese, Rikio, Takahashi, Nostalgia Of Kyoto, 24 1/2 x 22 In. 185.00
Japanese, Saito, Kiyoshi, Winter Landscape, Figures, Color, Signed In Pencil, 10 x 15 1/4 In. 556.00
Japanese, Seiko, Blue Bird On Tree Branch, Watching Falling Leaf, Late 19th Century, Aiban 115.00
Japanese, Seitei, Dove On Flowering Tree Branch, Hosoban 288.00
Japanese, Seitei, Watanabe, Mouse Nibbles On Grapes, Early 1900s, Aiban 173.00
Japanese, Shima, Tamami, 4 Horses In Forest, Frame, 1966, Oban, Tate-e 130.00
Japanese, Shoson, Ohara, 2 Flying Herons, 7 x 14 3/4 In. 105.00
Japanese, Sozan, Ito, 3 Swallows On Willow Branch, 1900s, Hosoban 230.00
Japanese, Sozan, Ito, Peacock In Cherry Tree, 1900s, Hosoban 240.00
Japanese, Taisui, Inuzuka, Coleus, Red, Yellow, Gray Ground, 1929, Oban, Tate-e 290.00
Japanese, Taisui, Inuzuka, Dahlias In Ceramic Vase, c.1929, Oban, Yoko-e 330.00
Japanese, Toyoharu, Street, People, Oban, Yoko-e 230.00
Japanese, Toyokuni II, 5 Women, 6 Men, 2 Ferry Boats, River, Frame, Oban Diptych 575.00
Japanese, Toyokuni III, Actor In Role, Frame ....176.00 to 294.00
Japanese, Toyokuni III, Courtesan In Elaborate Kimono, Frame 235.00
Japanese, Toyokuni III, Drummer In Costume, Banners, Mat, Frame, 21 1/4 x 17 1/4 In. 144.00
Japanese, Toyokuni III, Figures In Butterfly Costumes, Frame, Triptych 529.00
Japanese, Toyokuni III, Man, Attendant, Present Gifts To 4 Women, Oban, Triptych 259.00
Japanese, Toyokuni III, Night Scene, Man & Woman, In Rain, Oban, Diptych 230.00
Japanese, Toyokuni III, Woman, Looking In Mirror, Oban, Tate-e 173.00
Japanese, Utamaro, Geisha, Hanamurasaki, Drinking Tea, Oban, Tate-e 1610.00
Japanese, Yoshida, Hiroshi, Parrot In Kurumasaka Zoo, 16 x 10 3/4 In. 429.00
Japanese, Yoshida, Hiroshi, Shalimar Garden, Lahore, Oban, Tate-e 780.00
Japanese, Yoshida, Toshi, Arab In Bagdad, 1954, Oban, Tate-e 240.00
Japanese, Yoshida, Toshi, Benkei, Figures, Beneath Willow Trees, Chuban 184.00
Japanese, Yoshida, Toshi, Seahorses, c.1951, Oban, Tate-e 633.00
Japanese, Yoshitoshi, Jade Rabbit, Monkey & Rabbit, From 100 Aspects Of Moon, Oban, Tate-e 2300.00
Japanese, Yoshitoshi, Kiyomori & 100 Skulls, From 36 Ghosts, Oban, Tate-e 575.00
Japanese, Yoshitoshi, Young Woman Beside Sake Bottle, Oban, Tate-e 150.00
Japanese, Zeshin, Shibata, Crows Flying, Sunset, Hosoban 690.00
Karhu, Clifton, Temple & Rooftops, Oban, Yoko-e 330.00
Keith, Elizabeth, Harbor, Manila, 1924, Oban, Yoko-e 660.00

Keith, Elizabeth, Santa Cruz Church, Manila, Oban, Tate-e, 17 1/4 x 12 1/2 In. 978.00
Keith, Elizabeth, Shigiyama In Hagamoro, Frame, 1936, Oban, Tate-e 690.00
Kellogg, Presidential Series, Madison, Monroe, Adams, Frame, 17 x 13 In. 230.00
Kellogg & Thayer, Promenade, Lithograph, Hand Colored, Frame, c.1850, 10 x 14 In. 44.00
Kittens, Hand Coloring, Molded Wood Frame, Late 19th Century, 10 x 14 In. 355.00
Landacre, Paul, Forest Girl, Frame, 1936, 18 1/2 x 14 1/2 In. 235.00
Lanzedelly, Jupiter & Antelope, Engraved, Hand Colored, Molded Plaster, 26 x 29 In. 110.00
Lithograph, Firefighters, Pulling Wagons, Buchanan & Lyall, Frame, 18 x 23 In. 353.00
Lithograph, Foke-Luste-Hajo, Seminole, J.T. Bowen, Frame, c.1842, 23 x 16 1/2 In. 550.00
Lithograph, Hand Colored, Railroad Line, Horse Drawn Stagecoach, 13 1/2 x 19 1/2 In. 1116.00
Lithograph, Ka-Na-Pi-Ma, Ottawa Chief, Rice & Clark, Frame, c.1842, 23 x 16 1/2 In. 523.00
Lithograph, Monster, Karel Appel, Mat, Frame, 23 1/4 x 18 1/4 In. 259.00
Lithograph, Wa-Kawn, Winnebago Chief, J.T. Bowen, Frame, c.1841, 23 x 16 1/2 In. 550.00
Lithograph, Wakechai, Sukie Chief, Rice & Clark, Frame, c.1842, 23 x 16 1/2 In. 660.00
Max, Peter, Galaxy Lady, Serigraph, Signed, Dated '72, 15 x 17 In. 761.00
Messenger, Ivan, Loaves But No Fishes, San Diego Zoo Bears, Etching, Aquatint, On Paper 55.00

Nutting prints are now popular with collectors. Wallace Nutting is known for his pictures, furniture, and books. Nutting *prints* are actually hand-colored photographs issued from 1900 to 1941. There are over 10,000 different titles. Wallace Nutting furniture is listed in the Furniture category.

Wallace Nutting

Nutting, A Forest Window, Original Frame, 10 x 12 In. 143.00
Nutting, A Hawthorn Bridge, Ireland, Original Frame, 10 x 12 In. 165.00
Nutting, A Lakeside, Belvidere, Italy, Original Frame, 14 x 17 In. 468.00
Nutting, A Porch Tea, Original Frame, 12 x 14 In. 385.00
Nutting, Among The Beeches, Ireland, Original Frame, 20 x 16 In. 110.00
Nutting, An American Garden, Elizabeth Park, Original Frame, 15 x 13 In. 440.00
Nutting, An Amusing Recollection, Original Frame, 13 x 15 In. 198.00
Nutting, An Arbor Arch, Frame, 1930-35, 15 x 19 In. 185.00
Nutting, Ancestral Cradle, Cat, Mat, Frame, 1915-25, 15 x 22 In. 110.00
Nutting, Arlington Hills, Cows, Mat, Frame, 1905-10, 22 x 10 In. 770.00
Nutting, Autumn Grotto, Original Frame, 16 x 20 In. 130.00
Nutting, Autumn Grotto, Signed, Mat, Frame, c.1930, 9 x 11 In. 99.00
Nutting, Bearded Oaks Of Dixie, Original Frame, 14 x 11 In. 250.00
Nutting, Below The Arches, Hand Colored, Signed, Mat, Frame, c.1920, 11 x 14 In. 55.00
Nutting, Berkshire Brook, Signed, Mat, Frame, c.1920, 12 x 16 In. 66.00
Nutting, Bonnie Dale, Signed, Mat, Frame, c.1920, 12 x 10 In. 99.00
Nutting, Brant Daisies, Mat, Frame, 1930-35, 15 x 12 In. 198.00
Nutting, Breakfast Hour, Original Frame, 11 x 17 In. 90.00
Nutting, Brice House, Annapolis, 16 x 13 In. 880.00
Nutting, Bridesmaids' Procession, 12 x 15 In. 165.00
Nutting, Brook & Blossom, Signed, Mat, Frame, c.1920, 17 x 14 In. 99.00
Nutting, Checkered Road, Signed, Mat, Frame, c.1930, 13 x 16 In. 330.00
Nutting, Church By The Stream, Original Frame, 13 x 16 In. 231.00
Nutting, Clouds Over A Mountain Lake, 16 x 20 In. 605.00
Nutting, Cluster Of Zinnias, Mat, Frame, 1930-35, 16 x 13 In. 415.00
Nutting, Cluster Of Zinnias, Original Frame, 16 x 13 In. 605.00
Nutting, Colonial Kitchen, Original Frame, 5 x 7 In. 110.00
Nutting, Come Into The Garden, Original Frame, 11 x 19 In. 187.00
Nutting, Cosmos & Larkspur, Original Frame, 4 x 3 In. 275.00
Nutting, Crossing Of Creek, Signed, Mat, Frame, c.1920, 14 x 16 In. 365.00
Nutting, Decked As A Bride, Signed, Mat, Frame, c.1930, 9 x 11 In. 165.00
Nutting, Dog-On-It, 7 x 11 In. 3630.00
Nutting, Down On The Cape, 8 x 10 In. 145.00
Nutting, Familiar Path, Signed, Mat, Frame, c.1920, 12 x 15 In. 165.00
Nutting, Fleck Of Sunshine, Mat, Frame, 1915-25, 17 x 13 In. 80.00
Nutting, Flowering Time, Signed, Mat, Frame, c.1920, 13 x 16 In. 80.00
Nutting, Franconia Brook, Signed, Mat, Frame, c.1920, 16 x 13 In. 110.00
Nutting, From The Pool's Edge, Original Frame, 13 x 16 In. 550.00
Nutting, Full Summer, Original Frame, 16 x 13 In. 990.00

Nutting, Girl At Vanity, Silhouette, Frame, c.1927, 8 x 7 In. 49.00
Nutting, Girl Plays Piano, Silhouette, 4 x 4 In. 50.00
Nutting, Girl Plays Piano, Silhouette, Frame, c.1927, 7 x 8 In. 39.00
Nutting, Girl Sniffs Flower, Silhouette, Frame, c.1927, 7 x 8 In. 35.00
Nutting, Guardian Mother, Original Frame, 15 x 11 In. 2420.00
Nutting, Half Tide, Cape Cod, Original Frame, 10 x 12 In. 525.00
Nutting, Hawthorne Cottage, Mat, Frame, 1915-25, 14 x 20 In. 55.00
Nutting, Hollyhock Cottage, Original Frame, 14 x 17 In. 110.00
Nutting, Honeymoon Blossoms, Signed, Mat, Frame, c.1920, 11 x 17 In. 77.00
Nutting, Honeymoon Drive, Mat, Frame, c.1915, 11 x 14 In. 55.00
Nutting, In Brave Days Of Old, Frame, 1915-25, 16 x 20 In. 55.00
Nutting, In The Garden Of The Gods, 14 x 17 In. 935.00
Nutting, Inclining Palmettos, Florida, Original Frame, 10 x 16 In. 523.00
Nutting, Italian Cypress Lane, Italy, Original Frame, 12 x 10 In. 248.00
Nutting, Italian Spring, Signed, Mat, Frame, c.1920, 10 x 12 In. 165.00
Nutting, Jersey Blossoms, Signed, Mat, Frame, c.1920, 20 x 16 In. 130.00
Nutting, Joy Path, Mat, Frame, 1930-35, 11 x 9 In. 55.00
Nutting, June Joy, Signed, Mat, Frame, c.1920, 16 x 13 In. 55.00
Nutting, Larkspur, Signed, Mat, Frame, c.1920, 15 x 13 In. 66.00
Nutting, Let's Wade, Cape Cod, Original Frame, 11 x 14 In. 3520.00
Nutting, Listless Day, Holland, Mat, Frame, 1915-25, 11 x 14 In. 88.00
Nutting, Little Washerwomen, Amalfi, Original Frame, 10 x 12 In. 770.00
Nutting, Lough Gill Cottage, Signed, Mat, Frame, c.1920, 10 x 12 In. 132.00 to 165.00
Nutting, Making A Summer Hat, Signed, Mat, Frame, c.1920, 14 x 17 In. 120.00
Nutting, Mary's Little Lamb, Silhouette, Frame, c.1927, 4 x 4 In. 66.00
Nutting, Mary's Well, Nazareth, Palestine, Original Frame, 16 x 10 In. 1045.00
Nutting, Morning Mail, Mat, Frame, 1915-25, 11 x 14 In. 35.00
Nutting, Natural Bridge, 11 x 9 In. 165.00
Nutting, New Hampshire Road, Hand Colored, Signed, Mat, c.1920, 11 x 13 In. 50.00
Nutting, New Hampshire Roadside, Signed, Mat, Frame, c.1905, 11 x 17 In. 90.00
Nutting, Old Drawing Room, Signed, Mat, Frame, c.1920, 10 x 14 In. 55.00
Nutting, On Quinnebaug, Signed, Mat, Frame, c.1920, 13 x 17 In. 66.00
Nutting, On The Heights, Italian Monastery, Original Frame, 17 x 11 In. 385.00
Nutting, Over The Fir Tops, Original Frame, 10 x 12 In. 248.00
Nutting, Pasture Dell, Cows, Original Frame, 13 x 16 In. 825.00
Nutting, Patti's Favorite Walk, England, 14 x 17 In. 275.00
Nutting, Pause At Bridge, Signed, Mat, Frame, c.1930, 16 x 20 In. 532.00
Nutting, Petaled Way, Signed, Mat, Frame, c.1920, 10 x 12 In. 80.00
Nutting, Primrose Cottage, Signed, Mat, Frame, c.1920, 10 x 12 In. 275.00
Nutting, Quilting Party, Original Frame, 13 x 16 In. 99.00
Nutting, Rangeley Landing, Signed, Mat, Frame, c.1930, 8 x 10 In. 145.00
Nutting, Rhododendron Path, Original Frame, 30 x 20 In. 250.00
Nutting, Rhododendron Path, Signed, Mat, Frame, c.1930, 11 x 9 In. 155.00
Nutting, River In Maine, Signed, Mat, Frame, c.1920, 16 x 12 In. 66.00
Nutting, Road To Far Away, Ireland, Original Frame, 12 x 16 In. 300.00
Nutting, Skirting Lake Como, Italy, Original Frame, 14 x 17 In. 880.00
Nutting, Snow At The Bend, 17 x 14 In. 99.00
Nutting, Spring In Dell, Signed, Mat, Frame, c.1920, 16 x 20 In. 90.00
Nutting, St. Mary's In May, Original Frame, 12 x 10 In. 165.00
Nutting, Summer Shore, Signed, Mat, Frame, c.1930, 11 x 9 In. 130.00
Nutting, Swarthmore, Penn., Stream, Trees, 13 x 16 In. 770.00
Nutting, Swimming Pool, Mat, Frame, 1915-25, 13 x 17 In. 66.00
Nutting, Swirling Seas, Original Frame, 20 x 30 In. 110.00
Nutting, Tap At Squire's Door, Mat, Frame, 1905-10, 15 x 12 In. 88.00
Nutting, Time Of Roses, Ireland, Original Frame, 13 x 16 In. 180.00
Nutting, Treasure Bag, Signed, Mat, Frame, c.1920, 13 x 16 In. 45.00
Nutting, Tree At Bridge, Signed, Mat, Frame, c.1920, 13 x 16 In. 220.00
Nutting, Tunnel Of Bloom, Mat, 1915-25, 13 1/2 x 11 In. 35.00
Nutting, Under Ivy Bridge, Signed, Mat, Frame, c.1920, 12 x 14 In. 80.00
Nutting, Under The Mountain, Signed, Mat, Frame, c.1920, 11 x 14 In. 420.00
Nutting, Under The Yosemite, 14 x 9 In. 415.00

Nutting, Vanity & Constancy, Frame, 1930-35, 8 x 10 In. 1045.00
Nutting, Venetian Charm, Signed, Mat, Frame, c.1920, 14 x 11 In. 440.00
Nutting, Warm Spring Day, Frame, 1915-25, 15 x 22 In. 165.00
Nutting, Winter Welcome Home, Original Frame, 16 1/2 x 11 In. 770.00
Nutting, Wrencote, Signed, Mat, Frame, c.1920, 12 x 14 In. 252.00
Orchid, Mat, Frame, Walter Fitch, London, c.1863, Set Of Four, 16 1/2 x 11 1/2 In. 763.00

Parrish prints are wanted by collectors. Maxfield Frederick Parrish was an illustrator who lived from 1870 to 1966. He is best known as a designer of magazine covers, posters, calendars, and advertisements.

Parrish, Air Castles, Frame, c.1904, 14 x 11 In. 154.00
Parrish, Air Castles, Frame, c.1904, 16 x 11 In. 165.00
Parrish, Air Castles, Original Blue & Gold Frame, c.1904, 16 x 12 In. 209.00
Parrish, Canyon, Frame, c.1924, 15 x 12 In. 209.00
Parrish, Cassim, Frame, c.1906, 11 x 9 In. 77.00
Parrish, Circe's Palace, Frame, c.1908, 11 x 9 In. ....110.00 to 121.00
Parrish, Circe's Palace, Mat, Frame, c.1908, 14 x 12 In. 77.00
Parrish, Day Dreaming, Nude Woman, Under Large Tree, Frame, 21 1/2 x 33 1/2 In. 173.00
Parrish, Daybreak, c.1922, 18 x 30 In. 198.00
Parrish, Daybreak, Frame, 21 1/4 x 33 1/4 In. 374.00
Parrish, Daybreak, Frame, c.1923, 10 x 18 In. 143.00
Parrish, Daybreak, Frame, c.1923, 6 x 10 In. 99.00
Parrish, Dinkey Bird, c.1905, 15 x 11 In. 176.00
Parrish, Evening Shadows, Old Birch Tree, Frame, c.1940, 11 x 9 In. 110.00
Parrish, Garden Of Allah, c.1918, 9 x 18 In. 165.00
Parrish, Garden Of Allah, Frame, c.1918, 9 x 18 In. 187.00
Parrish, Golden Hours, Only God Can Make A Tree, c.1938, 8 x 6 In. 66.00
Parrish, Lady Violetta, Frame, c.1925, 12 x 9 In. 88.00
Parrish, Lute Players, Frame, c.1924, 6 x 10 In. 187.00
Parrish, Old King Cole, c.1906, 5 x 19 In. 415.00
Parrish, Primitive Man, c.1921, 9 x 6 1/2 In. 176.00
Parrish, Prince Codadad, Frame, c.1925, 13 x 11 In. 99.00
Parrish, Proserpina & Sea Nymphs, Frame, c.1910, 12 x 9 In. 110.00
Parrish, Romance, c.1925, 11 1/2 x 14 In. 248.00
Parrish, Sunup, Little Brook Farm, Frame, c.1945, 16 x 12 1/2 In. 198.00
Parrish, Twilight Hour, c.1951, 4 x 6 In. 90.00
Parrish, Twilight, Frame, c.1937, 16 x 13 In. 275.00
Parrish, White Birch, Frame, c.1931, 9 x 11 1/2 In. ....33.00 to 66.00
Parrish, Wild Geese, Frame, c.1924, 15 x 12 In. 176.00
Paul Hey, Little Red Riding Hood, Mat, Frame, 20 x 38 In. 28.00
Remington, Pioneers In Canoe, Mat, Frame, c.1908, 10 x 14 In. 80.00
Ritchie, A.H., Lady Washington's Reception, Frame, c.1850, 29 x 42 In. 445.00
Rockland Lake, Cutting Ice, Endicott & Co., Frame, c.1845-49, 12 x 18 In. 300.00
Ruthven, John A., Red Fox, DeSales Limited, Frame, c.1969, 36 x 25 In. 190.00
Ruthven, John A., Roadrunner, Wildlife International, Signed, c.1973, 20 x 25 In. 121.00
Sawyer, Charles, Along The Deerfield River, Mohawk Trail, c.1925, 13 x 16 In. 55.00
Sawyer, Charles, Camden Harbor, Original Frame, 7 x 9 In. 110.00
Sawyer, Charles, Church, Stark Village, N.H., Covered Bridge, c.1930, 8 x 14 In. 715.00
Sawyer, Charles, Majestic Nature, c.1920, 14 x 17 In. 99.00
Sawyer, Charles, Mohawk Trail, c.1935, 6 x 8 In. 130.00
Sawyer, Charles, Surf At Pinnacle Rock, Seascape, c.1925, 6 x 13 In. 66.00
Serigraph, On Paper, Desert In Bloom, Signed, Robert Daughters, 11 1/2 x 14 1/2 In. 290.00
Tadema, Reading From Homer, Mahogany Frame, c.1885, 24 x 45 In. 83.00
Vasarely, Victor, Geometric Abstract, Color, Screen Print, 18 x 18 In. 819.00
William G., Wall, New York From Heights Near Brooklyn, Lithograph, Frame, 20 x 28 In. 2350.00

Woodblock prints that are not in the Japanese tradition are listed here. Most were made in England and the United States during the Arts and Crafts period. Japanese woodblock prints are listed under Print, Japanese.

Woodblock, Baumann, Gustave, Eagle Ceremony At Tesuque Pueblo, 1932, 6 1/2 x 6 1/2 In. 470.00

Purse, Beaded, Floral Garland, Embossed Frame, 10 In.

Purse, Beaded, Floral, Jeweled Metal Frame, 10 In.

Woodblock, Baumann, Gustave, Grandma Battin's Garden, Frame, c.1916, 12 3/8 x 13 1/8 In. 14100.00
Woodblock, Baumann, Gustave, My Garden, Frame, 6 x 7 3/4 In. 8813.00
Woodblock, Baumann, Gustave, Silver Sky, Silver Leaf, On Paper, 12 1/2 x 13 1/2 In. 8800.00
Woodblock, Hiroshige, Chushingura, Act 5, 19th Century, Oban 80.00
Woodblock, Hopkins, Edna Boies, Petunia, Mat, Frame, Chop Mark, 7 x 4 3/4 In. 1880.00
Woodblock, Hyde, Helen, A Rainy Night, Signed, c.1906, 11 1/2 x 5 In. 448.00
Woodblock, Hyde, Helen, Happiness Flower, Signed, 1907, 7 x 2 In. 420.00
Woodblock, Hyde, Helen, In Their Holiday Clothes, Mat, No Frame, Signed, 1914, 13 x 5 In. 300.00
Woodblock, Rice, William, Wave, Rocky California Coast Bay, Mat, Frame, 5 x 7 In. 1998.00
Woodblock, Sandzen, Birger, Pond With Willows, 9 x 11 In. 315.00
Woodcut, Escher, Maurtis, Plane One, Signed, Dated '57, 9 1/4 x 7 In. 1755.00

PURINTON POTTERY COMPANY was incorporated in Wellsville, Ohio, in 1936. The company moved to Shippenville, Pennsylvania, in 1941 and made a variety of hand-painted ceramic wares. By the 1950s Purinton was making dinnerware, souvenirs, cookie jars, and florist wares. The pottery closed in 1959.

Purinton Pottery

Apple, Grease Jar, Cover, 5 1/2 In. 145.00
Apple, Jug, Kent, Pt., 4 1/2 In. 35.00
Apple, Snack Set, Tea & Toast, 8 1/4-In. Plate, 2 Piece 45.00
Bank, Piggy, Hand Painted, Flowers, 2 1/2 x 3 7/8 In. 48.00
Fruit, Cookie Jar, 9 1/4 x 6 In. 100.00
Fruit, Teapot, 4 Cup, 5 In. 55.00
Heather Plaid, Plate, Dinner, 9 3/4 In. 20.00
Heather Plaid, Saucer 5.00
Intaglio, Custard Cup, 4 In. 6.00
Intaglio, Mug, 8 Oz., 4 In. 20.00
Intaglio, Plate, Breakfast, 8 1/2 In. 10.00
Intaglio, Plate, Dinner, 9 3/4 In. 12.00
Intaglio, Plate, Salad, 6 3/4 In. 6.50
Intaglio, Platter, Oval, 12 3/4 In. 25.00
Intaglio, Saucer 4.00
Ivy, Honey Jug, 6 1/4 In. 45.00
Mountain Rose, Teapot, 2 Cup, 4 In. 40.00
Normandy Plaid, Plate, Dinner, 9 3/4 In. 8.00
Normandy Plaid, Salt & Pepper, Jug Shape, Cork Stoppers, 2 1/2 In. 22.00
Shooting Star, Vase, 6 In. 45.00

PURSES have been recognizable since the eighteenth century, when leather and needlework purses were preferred. Beaded purses became popular in the nineteenth century, went out of style, but are again in use. Mesh purses date from the 1880s and are still being made. How to carry a handkerchief and lipstick is a problem today for every woman, including the Queen of England.

Alligator, Bamboo Handle, Leather Interior, Mirror, Gucci, 11 x 8 In. 1530.00
Beaded, 2 Peacocks, Roses, Tassel Fringe, Bakelite Frame, Square Opening, 11 In. 290.00

Purse, Beaded, Seed Bead Strands, Pull String Closure, Victorian

Purse, Fabric, Woman Tending Garden, Applied Plastic Gems, Sequins, 1960s, 12 In.

Beaded, Floral Garland, Embossed Frame, 10 In. .... *ILLUS* 140.00
Beaded, Floral, Jeweled Metal Frame, 10 In. .... *ILLUS* 308.00
Beaded, Floral, Leather Interior, Metal Clasp, Rapps Work Reading, 1837, 9 x 6 In. .... 185.00 to 190.00
Beaded, Sea Fantaseas, Fish, Kathrine Baumann, 7 x 5 In. 999.00
Beaded, Seed Bead Strands, Pull String Closure, Victorian .... *ILLUS* 196.00
Beaded, Sequins, Square, Bulbous, Metal Openwork Trim, Beaded Handle, Tyrolean, 11 x 6 In. 470.00
Caviar Beaded, Sapphire Clasp, Silk Brocade Interior, Mirror, 14K Gold, Gorham, 8 x 9 In. 1410.00
Celluloid, Mauve Silk Back & Sides, Rhinestones, Art Deco, France, 3 x 4 x 2 In. 50.00
Cognac Calfskin, Kelly, Goldtone Hardware, 2 Compartments, Hermes 2940.00
Embroidered, Gold Thread, Tassels, Sage Green Velvet, Scrolls, Flowers, Frame, 16 x 12 In. 690.00
Embroidered, Linen, White, Red Yarn Fringe, Metal Frame, 1832, 10 x 12 In. 630.00
Fabric, Woman Tending Garden, Applied Plastic Gems, Sequins, 1960s, 12 In. .... *ILLUS* 50.00
Folded, Lucky Strike, c.1940, 9 x 13 In. 65.00
Leather, Blue, Goldtone Hardware, Lion's Head, Gucci, 11 1/2 x 5 x 8 1/2 In. 470.00
Leather, Clutch, Blue, Goldtone Metal Hardware, Franzi, 9 1/4 x 1 x 4 3/4 In. 235.00
Leather, Gray, Kelly, Detachable Strap, Silvertone Hardware, Hermes, 11 In. 2235.00
Leather, Shape Of Woman's High Button Shoe, Late 1800s, 6 In. 75.00
Lizard Skin, Box Shape, Taupe, Gilt Brass Handle, Satin Lining, Coin Purse & Mirror, Judith Leiber . 1300.00
Lucite, Bucket Shape, Spun Gold Fiberglass Inclusions, Clear Cut Top & Handle, 11 x 8 In. 105.00
Lucite, Cocoa, Pearlescent Swirl, Iridescent Stone Inclusions, Filigree Trim, 12 x 9 x 5 In. 705.00
Lucite, Coffin Shape, Midnight Blue, Metal Openwork Trim, Handle, Tyrolean, 9 x 8 x 5 In. 176.00
Lucite, Kidney Shape, Black, Clear Cut Geometric Lid, 2 Clear Tube Handles, 9 x 10 In. 146.00
Lucite, Kidney Shape, Gray Marbleized, 2 Tiers, 8 x 7 x 4 In. 350.00
Lucite, Oval, Clear, Chrysanthemum-Cut Sides, Clear Handle, Wilardy, c.1940, 9 x 9 In. 146.00
Lucite, Oval, Clear, Faceted, Rhinestones, Rialto, 8 x 4 x 9 In. 120.00
Lucite, Oval, Midnight Blue, Jewel Inclusions On Lid, c.1950, 9 x 8 x 4 1/2 In. 295.00
Lucite, Spun Gold Fiberglass Marbelized Inclusions, Clear Handle, 12 x 4 x 4 In. 146.00
Lucite, Tortoiseshell, H-Shaped Body, Butterscotch, Round Handle, Wilardy, 11 x 7 x 4 In. 499.00
Lucite, Tube Shape, Black, Rhinestone Trim, Metal Closure, Florida Handbags, 8 x 9 x 3 In. 190.00
Mesh, Art Nouveau, 14K Gold, Sapphire Clasp, Monogram 1755.00
Mesh, Gilt, Flowers, Whiting & Davis, 5 3/4 In. 120.00
Mesh, Multicolored Enamel, Cloisonne Gilt Frame, Signed, Whiting Davis & Co. 355.00
Minaudiere, Foo Dog, Diamante, Cabochon Garnet, Snake Shoulder Chain, Judith Leiber 2820.00
Minaudiere, Rabbit, Gold, Pave Crystal, Arnelian, Snake Shoulder Strap, Judith Leiber 2115.00
Nantucket Basket, Oval, Carved Ivory, Sperm Whale Figure, Swing Handle, 7 x 11 In. 4115.00
Palisades Park, Ford Fairlane, 1956, 13 1/2 x 13 In. 259.00
Petit Point, Unicorn Tapestry, Red Guilloche Enameled Frame, Flowers, Early 1900s 148.00
Seeds, Victorian, Varnished & Strung Apple Seeds, Chain Links, 4 In. 90.00
Silk, Clutch, Gold Thread, Adventurine Quartz, Rock Crystal, Garnet Cabochon, India 106.00
Silk, Rectangular, Abstract Print, Double Rope Chain, Leather Interior, Pucci, 7 In. 470.00
Silk, Silver, Blue, Tourmaline, Emeralds, Amethysts, Topaz, Jacinths, Chain Links, c.1910 .... 940.00
Silver, Gold Coins, Symbols, V.S. Semenov, Russia, c.1910, 4 1/2 x 3 1/4 In. 1000.00
Silver, Gold Mount, Rectangular, Monogram, Art Nouveau, Russia, 1908-17, 5 1/2 In. 440.00

If you hang your quilt like a picture, rotate it once a year and hang it from the opposite end to avoid too much stress on the fabric.

Quezal, Vase, Jack-In-The-Pulpit, Iridescent, Pulled Feathers, Alabaster, 12 3/4 In.

Quezal

QUEZAL glass was made from 1901 to 1924 by Martin Bach, Sr., in Queens, New York. Other glassware by other firms, such as Loetz, Steuben, and Tiffany, resembles this gold-colored iridescent glass. Martin Bach died in 1921. His son-in-law, Conrad Vahlsing, Jr., went to work at the Lustre Art Company about 1920 and his son, Martin Bach, Jr., worked at the Durand Art Glass division of the Vineland Flint Glass Works after 1924.

Bowl, Marigold Iridescent, Oval, 6 1/2 In. 315.00
Candlestick, Blue Iridescent, Baluster Stem, Footed, 7 1/4 In. 290.00
Charger, Gold Iridescent, 10 1/2 In. 690.00
Compote, Shaded Blue, Green Iridescent Rim, Gold Iridescent Foot, 9 1/2 In. 575.00
Lamp, Blue Iridescent, Double Hooked Feather, Gold Tipped, Pinched Waist, 26 In. 2185.00
Perfume Bottle, Iridescent Glass, Ribbed, Original Cap, Melba, 7 1/2 In. 750.00
Sconce, 2 Lily, Green Mottled Highlights, Pulled Feathers, Bronze, 9 In. 1495.00
Shade, Blue Feathers, Gold Border, Ribbed Opal Ground, Gold Iridescent Interior, 6 In. 460.00
Shade, Flower Form, Green & Gold Iridescent, Pulled Feather, c.1902, 7 1/2 In. 190.00
Shade, Flower Form, Iridescent Amber, Green Pulled Feather, 7 1/2 In., Pair 290.00
Shade, Gold Iridescent Wavy Band & Interior, Ivory, Ribbed, Flared, 5 In., 3 Piece 660.00
Shade, Gold Iridescent, White Pulled Feather, Green Tips, c.1910, 4 1/4 In. 323.00
Shade, Green Iridescent Pulled Feather, Ivory Ground, Gold Trim, 6 1/4 In., Pair 335.00
Shade, Platinum Zipper, Green Pulled Feathers, Green Iridescent Ground, Flared, 8 In. 2700.00
Shade, White Ivorine, Wide Ribs, Fluted & Flared Rim, 4 In., Pair 170.00
Vase, Agate, Marbleized Yellow, Green, Red, Blue, Pinched Waist, 5 In. 4600.00
Vase, Blue Iridescent, Baluster, 7 1/2 In., Pair 518.00
Vase, Blue Iridescent, Gold Highlights, Shouldered, 7 In. 575.00
Vase, Bud, Blue Iridescent, Purple Highlights, Ruffled Edge, 11 In. 2300.00
Vase, Flower Form, Alabaster, Green, Gold Waves, Iridescent Gold Interior, Signed, 5 1/2 In. 2875.00
Vase, Flower Form, Green Pulled Feathers, Gold Tips, Scalloped Rim, Opal Ground, 7 1/2 In. 2760.00
Vase, Flower Form, Opal, Green Pulled Feathers, Gold Iridescent Tips, 8 In. 2300.00
Vase, Gold Iridescent Lappets, Green Striated Feathers, Opal Ground, Footed, 4 1/2 In. 4600.00
Vase, Gold Iridescent, Folded Tricornered Rim, Ribbed Body, 1 1/2 In. 259.00
Vase, Gold Iridescent, Optic Ribbed, Tricornered Rim, Signed, 1 3/4 In. 345.00
Vase, Gold Iridescent, Red Highlights, Pinched Waist, 8 In. 173.00
Vase, Green Iridescent Pulled Feathers, Oval, Alabaster, 8 In. 920.00
Vase, Green, White & Gold Iridescent, Pulled Feathers, Signed, c.1905, 6 x 3 1/2 In. 1320.00
Vase, Green, White, Gold, Pulled Feathers, Flared, Ruffled Edge, 8 3/4 In. 3525.00
Vase, Jack-In-The-Pulpit, Gold Iridescent Top, Green Pulled Feathers, 6 5/8 In. x 11 3/4 In. 546.00
Vase, Jack-In-The-Pulpit, Gold Iridescent, 4 1/2 x 6 3/4 In. 980.00
Vase, Jack-In-The-Pulpit, Gold Iridescent, Veining, 13 1/2 In. 7050.00
Vase, Jack-In-The-Pulpit, Iridescent, Pulled Feathers, Alabaster, 12 3/4 In. .... *ILLUS* 8625.00
Vase, Marigold Iridescent, Blue Coil, Signed, 4 3/4 In. 1035.00
Vase, Marigold Iridescent, Shamrock Label, Shouldered, 7 1/2 In. 345.00

Vase, Tangerine Iridescent, Ivory Interior, Baluster, c.1920, 8 In. 388.00

QUILTS have been made since the seventeenth century. Early textiles were very precious and every scrap was saved to be reused. A quilt is a combination of fabrics joined to a filler and a backing by small stitched designs known as quilting. An appliqued quilt has pieces stitched to the top of a large piece of background fabric. A patchwork, or pieced, quilt is made of many small pieces stitched together. Embroidery can be added to either type.

Amish, Alternating Strips, Navy, Tan, Red, Black Border, 69 x 73 In. 230.00
Amish, Diamond In The Square, Center Diamond, Doll's, 15 1/4 x 15 3/4 In. 39.00
Amish, Diamond In The Square, Cotton, Blue, Red, Purple, Stitched Arcs & Stars, 84 x 80 In. 5975.00
Amish, Horizontal Bars, Corner Blocks, Feather Wreath, Lancaster Co., Frame, 39 x 49 In. 770.00
Amish, Pinwheel Blocks, Alternating Blue & Black Square, Ohio, 1910, 65 x 87 In. 865.00
Amish, Red, Black, White, Red Border, Frame, 70 x 85 In. 2300.00
Amish, Squares & Stripes, Blue, Green, Purple, Pink, Cotton, Doll's, 25 x 25 In. 375.00
Amish, Sunshine & Shadow, Multicolored, Rope Stitching, Wool, 80 x 80 In. 7170.00
Amish, Trip Around The World, Brown, Olive, Bronze, Stitched Cables, Stars, Wool, 78 x 76 In. 7768.00
Appliqued, 25 Red, Green Eagles, Yellow Accents, White Ground, Quilted Hearts, 88 x 92 In. 805.00
Appliqued, 36 Orange, Green Pineapples, White Ground, Diamond Quilting, 94 x 102 In. 978.00
Appliqued, 9 Patch, 8-Point Star, Red, Pink, Orange, White Ground, Cotton, 1900s, 84 x 87 In. 235.00
Appliqued, Blue, White Panels, Cherry Tree Branches, Chain Stitched Stems, 76 x 88 In. 345.00
Appliqued, Coxcomb & Tulip, Square, 1850s, 77 In. 1650.00
Appliqued, Cradle, Flowers, Hearts, X's & O's, Printed Fabric, 33 x 35 In. 1000.00
Appliqued, Dresden Plate, Printed Fabric, Wide Border, Floral Back, 38 x 38 In. 580.00
Appliqued, Floral, Red, Blue, Woolwich, Maine, 88 x 90 In. 460.00
Appliqued, Flower Urns, Red, Green, White, Cut Work, Leaves, Flower Quilting, 86 x 86 In. 520.00
Appliqued, Flower, Feather, 90 x 91 In. 430.00
Appliqued, Green, Red, Yellow, Baskets Of Flowers, White Ground, Tulip Border, 82 x 80 In. 375.00
Appliqued, Hawaii, Pink, White, Early 1900s, 75 x 65 In. 546.00
Appliqued, Heart Wreaths, Yellow, Green, Printed Fabric, 80 x 80 In. 245.00
Appliqued, Lily, 34 Blocks, Diagonal, Flowers, Red, Green, Cotton, North Carolina 87 x 86 In. 764.00
Appliqued, Oak Leaf Medallions, Flowers, Cotton, Penn., c.1900, 90 x 90 In. 956.00
Appliqued, Pinwheel, Yellow, White, c.1950, 79 x 81 In. 145.00
Appliqued, Pomegranate, Green Leaves, Scalloped Border, Red, Yellow, Cotton, 76 x 80 In. 460.00
Appliqued, Rose Of Sharon, Medallion, Red, Yellow, Green Calico, 78 x 78 In. 460.00
Appliqued, Tulip & Rose Wreath, Blue, Red, Green, Double Border, 96 x 80 In. 1270.00
Appliqued, Whig Rose, Christmas, c.1890, 79 x 79 In. 875.00
Appliqued, Wreath Of Roses, Quilted Border, 43 1/2 x 44 1/2 In. 1410.00
Appliqued & Embroidered, Birds, Deer, Crosses, Rings, Berry, Leaf Border, Cotton, 74 x 82 In. 2629.00
Crazy, Birds, Fans, Girl, Insects, Silk, Satin, Velvet, April 10, 1883, 66 x 67 In. 630.00
Crazy, Dinosaurs, Schoolhouse, Flowers, F.A.T., 1888, 36 x 47 In. 2420.00
Crazy, Embroidered, 30 Squares, Flowers, State Fair Winner, Vermont, c.1915, 70 x 83 In. 300.00
Crazy, Embroidered, Flowers, Birds, Initials, Silk, Velvet, Black Cotton Back, 64 x 72 In. 290.00
Crazy, First Prize, Louisiana State Fair, 4 Artists, Animals, Fans, 1892 .... 5055.00
Crazy, Friendship, Made In 14 Different States, Dated 1890, 72 x 72 In. 550.00
Patchwork, 9 Patch, Green & Red Stripe Back, Cotton, Penn., c.1900, 80 1/2 x 79 1/2 In. 450.00
Patchwork, 9 Patch, Green, White, 74 x 82 In. 85.00
Patchwork, 9 Patch, Pearl Morgan, Oakville, Indiana, 66 x 78 In. 315.00
Patchwork, 9 Patch, Printed, Cotton, Penn., Early 1900s, 79 1/2 x 82 In. 660.00
Patchwork, 16 Calico Sunbursts, Browns, Red, Blues, Diagonal Stitches, 92 x 90 In. 450.00
Patchwork, Album, Cross, Diamonds & Hex Quilting, Cotton, 76 x 91 In. 290.00
Patchwork, Basket, Red, Yellow, Green, Sawtooth Border, Cotton, 79 x 91 In. 1528.00
Patchwork, Baskets, Green, White, Ludlow Family, Stewartsville, N.J., 76 x 86 In. 195.00
Patchwork, Blue & White, 6-Point Stars, Triangles, 81 x 76 In. 460.00
Patchwork, Broken Star, Blue Ground, Red, Pink, Purple, Yellow, Triple Border, 83 x 82 In. 1270.00
Patchwork, Broken Star, Sawtooth Border, Sunflowers, Cotton, 79 x 81 In. 660.00
Patchwork, Capitol T, Printed Fabrics, Brown Painted Fabric Back, 96 x 98 In. 330.00
Patchwork, Center Block, Crossed Arrows, Lebanon Co., Frame, 34 x 32 1/2 In. 300.00
Patchwork, Charm, 1 Patch, 512 Triangles, Illusion Of Stars, Lancaster, c.1895, 86 x 88 In. 560.00

Patchwork, Compass Star, Indigo Blue, Hearts, Oak Tree Border, 1800s, 73 x 75 In. 770.00
Patchwork, Diamond Design, Multicolored, Red Calico, Brown Plaid Backing, 71 x 72 In. 230.00
Patchwork, Double Irish Chain, Red, Yellow, Green, Cotton, Penn., Early 1900s, 87 x 87 In. 570.00
Patchwork, Double Wedding Ring, Early 20th Century, 56 x 68 In. 176.00
Patchwork, Double Wedding Ring, Leaf Quilting, Cotton, Penn., c.1940, 87 x 92 In. 269.00
Patchwork, Drunkard's Path, 2 Borders, Cotton, 1891, 80 x 82 In. 460.00
Patchwork, Drunkard's Path, Blue & White, 94 x 80 In. 1695.00
Patchwork, Drunkard's Path, Blue Calico, White, Meandering Feather, 75 x 75 In. 460.00
Patchwork, Drunkard's Path, Orange, Red, Sawtooth Border, Cotton, Penn., 75 x 75 In. 3100.00
Patchwork, Duck's Foot, Double Border, Red, Brown Ground, Conn., 1880-1900, 82 x 83 In. 300.00
Patchwork, Flowers, Green, White, Red, Cotton, Early 1900s, 72 x 86 In. 145.00
Patchwork, Geese, Triangles & Blocks, Yellow Lines, Red Blocks, White Floral, 1900, Crib 750.00
Patchwork, Geometric Designs, Red, White, Cotton, c.1900, 56 1/2 x 69 In. 200.00
Patchwork, Handwritten Signatures, 8 Point Stars, Red, Yellow, January 20, 1854, 69 x 83 In. 435.00
Patchwork, Harvest & Star, Red, Green, White, Cotton, Late 1800s, 103 x 101 1/4 In. 390.00
Patchwork, Hexagons, Red Border, Red & Green Stripes, Cotton, Penn., c.1900, 75 x 71 In. 299.00
Patchwork, Irish Chain, Green, Red Calico, White, Black Circles, Flower Stitching, 83 x 84 In. 400.00
Patchwork, Log Cabin, Black & Yellow Diagonal Border, Printed Back, 82 x 80 In. 1160.00
Patchwork, Log Cabin, Courthouse Steps, 6600 Pieces, Calico, c.1850 .... 2200.00
Patchwork, Log Cabin, Pineapple, Double Sawtooth Border, 90 x 91 In. 150.00
Patchwork, Log Cabin, Printed Fabric, Triple Border, Floral Back, 44 1/2 x 42 In. 1040.00
Patchwork, Log Cabin, Printed, Triple Border, Reverse Side Printed On Black, 91 x 74 In. 725.00
Patchwork, Log Cabin, Yellow, Green, Black, Blue, Red, Green Border, Heart, 83 x 83 In. 270.00
Patchwork, Lone Star, Green Ground, Burgundy & Yellow Patches, 88 x 88 In. 215.00
Patchwork, Lone Star, Postage Stamp Ground, Calico, 84 x 84 In. 230.00
Patchwork, Mariner's Compass, Holly Leaf, Red, Green, 79 x 94 In. 825.00
Patchwork, Missouri Puzzle, Cotton, Penn., Early 1900s, 73 x 72 1/2 In. 329.00
Patchwork, Oak Leaf, Blue Chintz Blocks, Printed Fabric, Sawtooth Border, 96 x 96 In. 580.00
Patchwork, Ohio Star, Printed Fabric, Sawtooth Border, 36 x 30 In. 1210.00
Patchwork, Pinwheel, Red, Yellow Calico, Hand Stitched, Penn., 67 1/2 x 67 In. 315.00
Patchwork, Pinwheel, Sawtooth Border, Pink, Yellow, Calico, Cotton, 90 x 90 In. 230.00
Patchwork, Postage Stamp, 6000 Octagonal Pieces, 90 x 93 In. 695.00
Patchwork, Postage Stamp, Printed Fabrics, Red & Yellow Triple Border, 85 x 84 In. 720.00
Patchwork, Prairie Star, Printed Fabric, Wide Border, Printed Back, 88 x 84 In. 345.00
Patchwork, Robbing Peter To Pay Paul, Blue & White, Cotton, 80 x 86 In. 560.00
Patchwork, Rose Of Sharon Wreaths, Red, Green, White, Diamond Stitching, 60 x 89 In. 660.00
Patchwork, Sampler, 5 Rows, Printed Fabric Ground, Flower Blocks, Lancaster Co., 84 x 88 In. 1100.00
Patchwork, Squares Of Triangles, Multicolored, Orange Triangule Border, 88 x 90 In. 1076.00
Patchwork, Star Of Bethlehem, Multicolored, Cotton, Penn., 1900s, 70 x 70 In. 299.00
Patchwork, Star Of Bethlehem, Red, Blue, Green, Orange, Peach, 84 In. 1510.00
Patchwork, Star, Flying Geese, Diamonds, Flowers, Cotton, 68 x 74 In. 259.00
Patchwork, Star, Red Calico, White, c.1900, 37 x 48 In. 85.00
Patchwork, Stripes, Multicolor, Pink Border, Cotton, Penn., 1900s, 76 x 77 In. 359.00
Patchwork, Triangles, Half-Square Printed Fabric, Triple Border, 91 x 80 In. 700.00
Patchwork, Trip Around The World, Cotton, Penn., c.1900, 77 x 75 1/4 In. 269.00
Patchwork, Trip Around The World, Pink Border, Cotton, Penn., 1900s, 76 x 73 In. 478.00
Patchwork, Trip Around The World, Purple, Pumpkin, Maroon, Blue, 1890s, Crib 1455.00
Patchwork, Triple Irish Chain, Red, Green, Yellow, Triple Border, Flower Back, 83 x 82 In. 670.00
Patchwork, Wild Goose Variation, Triangles, Blocks, Yellow Calico, Red, 37 x 37 1/2 In. 750.00
Patchwork, Windmill, Red, Green Calico, 70 x 74 In. 400.00
Patchwork & Appliqued, 56 Squares, Cotton, Chintz, Birds, Animals, Star, 100 x 102 In. 960.00
Patchwork & Appliqued, Birds, Flowers, Yellow Borders, 1800s 798.00
Patchwork & Appliqued, Tulip, 12 Squares, Red, Gold, Green, Red Borders, Cotton, 88 x 68 In. .. 560.00
Patchwork & Embroidered, Birds, Fans, Flowers, Girl, Insects, April 10, 1883, 66 x 67 In. 630.00
Patchwork & Embroidered, Leafy Vine, Flower, Cotton, 1900s, 86 x 90 In. 240.00
Patchwork & Embroidered, Pieced, Sunbonnet, Hand Stitched, Machine Binding, 25 x 34 In. 130.00

QUIMPER pottery has a long history. Tin-glazed, hand-painted pottery has been made in Quimper, France, since the late seventeenth century. The earliest firm, founded in 1685 by Jean Baptiste Bousquet, was known as HB Quimper. Another firm, founded in 1772 by

Francois Eloury, was known as Porquier. The third firm, founded by Guillaume Dumaine in 1778, was known as HR or Henriot Quimper. All three firms made similar pottery decorated with designs of Breton peasants and sea and flower motifs. The Eloury (Porquier) and Dumaine (Henriot) firms merged in 1913. Bousquet (HB) merged with the others in 1968. The group was sold to a United States family in 1984. The American holding company is Quimper Faience Inc., located in Stonington, Connecticut. The French firm has been called Societe Nouvelle des Faienceries de Quimper HB Henriot since March 1984.

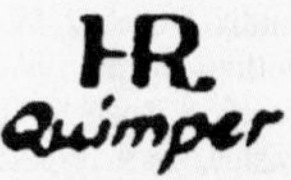

Basket, Blue & White, Delft Style Decoration, Henriot, 9 1/2 x 15 x 7 1/2 In. 1350.00
Charger, Man & Woman, Blue, Yellow & Green Semicircles On Border, c.1875, 12 In. 595.00
Chevrette, Tennis Ball Pattern, Decorative Stripes, Dots, Dashes, Henriot, 9 x 9 In. 495.00
Clock, Woman In Gourse, Carrying Basket Of Eggs, Scrolls, Baroque Shape, 9 1/2 In. 1600.00
Cup & Saucer, Flowers, Blue & Yellow Bands, 4 Sets 350.00
Cup & Saucer, Trefoil Shape, Blue & Green Geometric Pattern, 7-In. Saucer 275.00
Dish, Asparagus, 2 Children Playing With Bird, Shades Of Blue, Porquier Beau, 4 x 13 x 9 In. 3500.00
Dish, Man & Walking Stick, Trees, Oval, Shaped Rim, 11 x 7 In. 195.00
Figurine, Folk Dancers Dancing, 2 Couples, R. Micheau-Vernez, Henriot, 4 1/2 x 7 In. 695.00
Figurine, Man, Carrying Ladder & Broom On Back, Henriot, 4 1/2 In. 225.00
Figurine, Woman, Carrying Basket & Duck-Handled Umbrella, 5 1/2 In. 495.00
Inkstand, Woman Resting, Bread Basket, 2 Pots, Pen Tray, Open Finial, Henriot, 11 x 8 In. 1350.00
Inkwell, Cover, Man Holding Pipe, Tree, 8-Sided, Henriot, 3 x 3 3/4 In. 550.00
Jardiniere, Family Scene, Child Pulling Toy, Flowers, Leafy Scroll Ends, Henriot, 4 x 12 x 6 In. 2500.00
Jardiniere, Man & Woman At Fence, Fleur-De-Lis Shape, Zigzag Bands, Malicorne, 9 x 12 x 6 In. 1900.00
Jardiniere, Woman, Flowers, Coat Of Arms, Scalloped Edge, 4-Footed, Henriot, 6 x 11 x 6 In. 495.00
Pitcher, Horizontal Stripes, Red, Green, Blue, Yellow Ground, Art Deco, Henriot, c.1930, 5 3/4 In. . 225.00
Plate, Man, Woman, Clouds, Birds, Yellow Stripes, Paul Fouillen, Henriot, 7 1/2 In., Pair 595.00
Plate, Old Woman With Walking Stick & Child, Coat Of Arms, Scalloped Rim, Henriot, 10 In. 900.00
Plate, Woman Carrying Milk Jug On Head, Croisille Designs, Henriot, c.1920, 8 In. 295.00
Plate, Yellow Bird, Flowers, Square, Cut Corners, Henriot, 7 1/2 In., Pair 295.00
Platter, Market Scene, Women, Children, Cabbages, Apples, Oval, Shaped Edge, 11 x 17 In. 3900.00
Teapot, Man, Woman, Flower Sprays, Blue Sponge 3-Section Handle, Henriot, 5 1/2 In. 450.00

RADFORD pottery was made by Alfred Radford in Broadway, Virginia, Tiffin and Zanesville, Ohio, and Clarksburg, West Virginia, from 1891 until 1912. Jasperware, Ruko, Thera, Radura, and Velvety Art Ware were made. The jasperware resembles the famous Wedgwood ware of the same name. Another pottery named Radford worked in England and is not included here.

RADURA.

Vase, Brown Flowers, Green Leaves, Dark Green Ground, 22 1/2 In. 600.00

RADIO broadcast receiving sets were first sold in New York City in 1910. They were used to pick up the experimental broadcasts of the day. The first commercial radios were made by Westinghouse Company for listeners of the experimental shows on KDKA Pittsburgh in 1920. Collectors today are interested in all early radios, especially those made of Bakelite plastic or decorated with blue mirrors. Figural advertising radios and transistor radios are also collected.

Advertising, Champion Spark Plug, Transistor, Japan, c.1960, 14 1/2 x 5 In. 100.00
Advertising, Charlie The Tuna, Stand, Box, 1970, 5 In. 68.00
Advertising, Delco Freedom, Battery Shape, Box, Late 1970s ....11.50 to 16.50
Advertising, Dr. Pepper, Cooler Shape, Wood, Electric, 1940s 578.00
Advertising, Gulden's Spicy Brown Mustard, 5 3/8 x 4 1/4 In. 16.50
Advertising, Heinz Ketchup, Bottle Shape, Transistor, AM, Box, 1980s 75.00
Advertising, Little Sprout, AM, Hong Kong, Box, 8 1/4 x 4 3/8 In. 10.50
Advertising, Old Parr Scotch Whiskey, Bottle Shape, 5 1/2 x 2 1/2 In. 42.00
Advertising, Schlitz, Football Shape, Transistor, AM, 1960s, 6 In. 25.00
Advertising, Tide, Tide's In, Dirt's Out, NASCAR, Box, 3 x 4 3/8 In. 24.00

Advertising, Tropicana Pure Premium, Orange Shape, Straw, China, Box, 3 1/2 In. 9.00
Automatic Radio Co., Transistor, Tom Thumb, Red Case, Box, 1955, 6 x 4 In. 136.00
Bendix, Model 526C, Bakelite, Brown, Original Knob, c.1946, 11 x 7 In. 605.00
Bendix, Model 526MC, Green Case, Black Grille, c.1947, 11 In. 550.00
Brother, Aquatron VX-33A, 8 Track Stereo, Head Shape, Portable, 1970s, 12 In. 189.00
Crestline, Model 6T-180, Transistor, Plastic Face, c.1960, 4 1/4 x 2 3/4 In. 122.00
Crosley, Clock, Plastic, Gray, Bronzed Dials, Turners, 1955, 13 In. 310.00
Crown, Model, TR555, Transistor, Plastic, Black & White Grille, Case, c.1960, 4 x 2 1/2 In. 405.00
Fada, Model 115, Bullet, Catalin, Butterscotch, Red, c.1941, 10 1/2 In. 1210.00
Fada, Model 652, Temple, Catalin, Butterscotch Case, Ivory Knobs, c.1946, 11 In. 385.00
Fada, Model 1000, Bullet, Catalin, Maroon, Butterscotch, c.1946, 10 1/2 In. 550.00
Figural, Baseball, Official League Ball, Cushion Cork Center, c.1948 .... 930.00
Gordon Duern & Keith McQuarrie, Electrohome, Circa 711 Bubble Stereo, c.1970, 32 In. 265.00
H. Spencer, Clairtone, Project G Stereo, Rosewood, Globe Speakers, c.1963, 28 x 83 In. 2450.00
Hi-Delity, Model 6T-330, Transistor, Jupiter, Case, Box, 1960, 2 3/8 x 3 5/8 In. 405.00
J. Jensen Bang & Olufsen, Beomaster 3000, Rosewood, Aluminum, 6 Components, c.1970 ..... 615.00
Nordmende, Turnadot, Plastic, 2 Dials, 6 Buttons, AM, FM, 1952, 9 3/4 x 18 1/2 x 11 1/2 In. 355.00
Sony, Model TR-63, Transistor, Yellow, Red Dial, Leather Case, 1957, 4 1/4 x 2 3/4 In. 748.00
Stellar, Model mm-5, Roger Maris, Mickey Mantle, Box, 1962, 7 x 4 5/8 x 4 In. 2900.00
Stewart Warner, Model 63T-36, Marbleized Case, Butterscotch Grill, Knobs, c.1946, 13 In. 525.00
Telefunken, Opus 7 Superheterodyne, Wood Cabinet, Germany, 1950s, Table 390.00
Zenith, Model 705, Tube Operated, Walnut Case, 1933, Table 59.00
Zenith, Royal 800, Transistor, Plastic, Blue, Green, Telescoping Handle, c.1957 .... 230.00
Zephyr, Model ZR620, Transistor, Leather Case, Earphone, Box, 1962, 4 1/4 x 2 1/2 In. 110.00

RAILROAD enthusiasts collect any train memorabilia. Everything is wanted, from oilcans to whole train cars. The Chessie system has a store that sells many reproductions of their old dinnerware and uniforms.

Ashtray, Union Pacific, Utah Parks, Sun Valley, Idaho 18.00
Baggage Cart, Pull, Pine, Omaha 175, c.1898, 72 x 120 In. 3500.00
Bench, Station, Iron, Wood, Plank Seat, Spindle Back, 1800s, 32 x 85 In., Pair 2585.00
Boarding Stool, Venice Simplon Orient-Express, c.1900, 20 x 16 3/4 x 12 1/2 In. 625.00
Button, Baltimore & Ohio, Centenary, Celluloid, 1827-1927, 1 In. 15.00
Key, B & O RR Co. RT 40.00
Key, Brass, N & W, No. 100 .... 30.00
Key, Caboose Door, Brass, B & O 15.00
Key, Switch Lock, Brass, B & O 35.00
Key, Switch Lock, Brass, WMRY 35.00
Lantern, Cast Iron, Porcelain, Glass Globe, 17 In. 250.00
Lantern, Dietz Fitzall, Metal, Green, Label, N.Y. U.S.A., 15 x 8 3/4 In. 80.00
Lantern, Tin, Pierced, Painted, Etched Globe, V.C.C.R., Original Burner, 17 1/2 In. 605.00
Lock, Brass, Heart Shape, CRI & PRR, Hansl Mfg. Co. 75.00
Lock, Brass, P & R, Yale 65.00
Lock, Key, Brass, B & O, Signal Dept., Cumberland Division, Yale & Towne Mfg. Co. 75.00
Lock, Key, Brass, Heart Shape, B & O, Dayton Mfg. Co. 100.00
Lock, Switch, Key, Amtrak 40.00
Lock, Switch, Key, B & O RR, 944 .... 60.00
Lock, Switch, Key, B & O, c.1969 .... 65.00
Lock, Switch, Key, PRR, 1959 .... 60.00
Lock, Switch, WMRY, WMRWY On Key, 1967 .... 70.00
Oil Can, Eagle Soo Line 35.00
Plate, Baltimore & Ohio Railroad, On Incline, Shell Border, Blue, E. Wood & Sons, 9 In. 690.00
Plate, Baltimore & Ohio Railroad, Shell Border, E. Woods & Sons, 10 In. ....750.00 to 1380.00
Poster, Pennsylvania Railroad, Train Schedule, Pittsburgh, 1926, 6 x 18 3/4 In. 20.00
Poster, Pennsylvania Railroad, Train Schedule, Round Trip, Washington, 1926, 5 1/2 x 15 In. 18.00
Poster, See America, Railroads Of U.S., Canada & Mexico, 1939, 37 1/2 x 23 1/4 In. 5358.00
Sign, Eastern Railroad, Portland & Boston, Pullman Cars, Frame, 1872, 24 1/2 x 16 1/2 In. 440.00
Sign, Railroad, Wood, Blue Letters, White Ground, Green Border, 9 1/4 x 54 1/4 In. 55.00
Timetable, Erie Railroad, New York-Buffalo, 6 Panels, Folder, Dec. 6, 1942 .... 12.00
Timetable, N.Y. Central, Mohawk Division, 4 Panels, Folder, Jan. 18, 1938 .... 15.00

RAZORS were used in ancient Egypt and subsequently wherever shaving was in fashion. The metal razor used in America until about 1870 was made in Sheffield, England. After 1870, machine-made hollow-ground razors were made in Germany or America. Plastic or bone handles were popular. The razor was often sold in a set of seven, one for each day of the week. The set was often kept by the barber who shaved the well-to-do man each day in the shop.

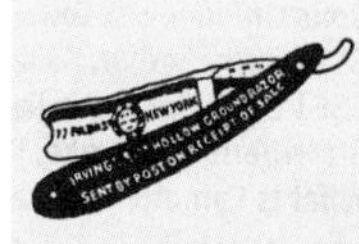

Cattaraugus Cobalt, Straight, Bone Handle, Indian Chief, Box 45.00
Devon Manufacturing, Corn Cobb, Germany 25.00
Display, Gem Double Life Blades, 7 For 50 Cents, Tin, Lithograph, Easel, 24 Holders, 8 x 14 In. . . . 1595.00
Display Board, Marlind Double Edge, Hanging, Die Cut, 20 5 Count Packs, 13 1/2 x 9 In. 150.00
Display Case, Fender's Razor Blades, 6 Columns, Wood, 1950s 70.00
Display Case, Shapleigh Hardware Diamond Edge, 5 Razors, Mahogany, Glass, 14 x 16 In. 396.00
Mirror, Gillette Safety Razor, Round, 2 1/8 In. 30.00
Safety, Clover Leaf, Tin Container, Wedge Blade Type, 2 1/4 x 1 1/2 In. 660.00
Winchester, Straight, No. 8526, Yellow Handle 95.00
Winchester, Straight, No. 8528, Marbled Bakelite Handles, Case 129.00
Winchester, Straight, No. 8531, Bakelite Handles, Leather Case 148.00
Winchester, Straight, No. 8535, Nude Woman, Bakelite Handles, Leatherette Case 253.00

REAMERS, or juice squeezers, have been known since 1767, although most of those collected today date from the twentieth century. Figural reamers are among the most prized.

Cast Aluminum, CK Taiwan, c.1940, 2 1/2 x 8 1/2 In. 28.00
Ceramic, Sailor, 2-Piece, Germany 390.00
Glass, Apple Green, 7 x 8 1/2 In. 32.50
Glass, Crisscross, Green, Hazel Atlas 45.00
Glass, Crisscross, Loop Handle, Hazel Atlas, c.1938 . . . . 26.00
Glass, Draining Holes, Tab Handle, 3 1/4 In. 10.00
Glass, Jadite, 2-Piece, Pitcher Bottom 220.00
Glass, Jadite, McKee, 8 1/2 x 6 1/2 In. 80.00
Glass, Jeannette Glass Co., 3 x 8 In. 10.00
Glass, Jeannette, Pink Jennyware, 3 1/4 x 7 In. 130.00
Glass, Jeannette, Tab Handle, Pink, 7 1/4 In. 36.00
Glass, Ruby Iridescent, 2-Piece, Edna Barnes 48.00
Glass, Sunkist, Embossed, 8 1/2 x 5 3/4 In. 12.50
Glass, Vaseline, 2-Piece, Edna Barnes, 1980s 250.00
Glass, Vertical Ribbing, Ribbed Handle, c.1950, 2 1/4 x 7 3/4 In. 11.50
Glass, Vertical Ribbing, Seed Catcher, 5 In. 11.00
Milk Glass, Sunkist, 1 3/4 x 6 In. 27.50
Milk Glass, Sunkist, Pressed, 8 x 5 3/4 In. 30.00
Plastic, Red, Westland Plastics, Round, 6 In. 7.50
Pottery, Citrus Face, Pink, Napco, Japan, 5 1/4 In. 210.00
Pottery, Clown, Japan, 1940s, 7 3/4 In. 295.00
Pottery, Duck, Japan, 2 1/2 In. 185.00
Pottery, Hall Lettuce, Green Medallion, 3 x 7 In. 490.00
Stoneware, Cobalt Blue Lines, RRP, 4 In. 65.00
Vitrock, 8 3/4 In. 22.00

RECORDS have changed size and shape through the years. The cylinder-shaped phonograph record for use with the early Edison models was made about 1889. Disc records were first made by 1894, the double-sided disc by 1904. High-fidelity records were first issued in 1944, the first vinyl disc in 1946, the first stereo record in 1958. The 78 RPM became the standard in 1926 but was discontinued in 1957. In 1932, the first 33 1/3 RPM was made but was not sold commercially until 1948. In 1949, the 45 RPM was introduced. Compact discs became available in the U.S. in 1982 and many companies began phasing out the production of phonograph records.

10 Li'l Nigger Boys, Marching Nursery Rhyme, Prewar, England, 8 In. 95.00

Del Shannon, Hey Little Girl, Big Top Records, 45 RPM, 1961 . . . . . 35.00
Sons Of Pioneers, Cowboy Classics, Vinyl, Box, 45 RPM, 1948, 3 Records 29.00
SSGT Barry Sadler, Ballad Of Green Berets, RCA Victor, 33 RPM, 1966 . . . . . 12.00
SSGT Barry Sadler, Ballad Of Green Berets, RCA Victor, 45 RPM, 1966 . . . . . 7.00
Strawberry Shortcake, Picture Disc, Cardboard, American Greetings, 45 RPM, 1982 . . . . . 12.00
What Is Communism, Lectures By Dr. Fred C. Schwarz, Case, 33 RPM, c.1966, 4 Records 30.00

RED WING Pottery of Red Wing, Minnesota, was a firm started in 1878. The company first made utilitarian pottery, including stoneware jugs and canning jars. In the 1920s art pottery was made. Many dinner sets and vases were made before the company closed in 1967. Rumrill pottery made by the Red Wing Pottery for George Rumrill is listed in its own category. For more information, see *Kovels' Depression Glass & Dinnerware Price List.*

Advertising, Bean Pot, McCoy & Koll Quality Groceries, Waukesha, Wis. 85.00
Advertising, Beater Jar, McCoy & Koll, Waukesha, Wis. 255.00
Advertising, Beater Jar, Semon's Fair Store Co., Marathon, Wis., Stoneware 225.00
Advertising, Bowl, Stearns & Mc Cormick Bootery, Manchester, Iowa, 7 In. 220.00
Advertising, Bowl, You Have Dollars, Have More Cents, Grondes Store, Wis., 6 In. 155.00
Advertising, Crock, Linden Apiary, Pure Honey, Milwaukee, Wis., 1/2 Gal. 105.00
Advertising, Jug, Beehive, Victoria Sanatorium, Colfax Mineral Springs, 5 Gal. 1350.00
Advertising, Pitcher, Compliments Of August J. Becker, Cherry Band, 1914, Large 775.00
Advertising, Pitcher, Compliments Of Gus Heschke, Oshkosh, Cherry Band 450.00
Advertising, Pitcher, Compliments Of Jacob Pasch, Wis., Cherry Band, 8 1/4 In. 525.00
Advertising, Pitcher, Compliments OK Extract Supply Co., 100% Pure, Cherry Band 400.00
Art Pottery, Bowl, Green Glaze, 3-Footed, Charles Murphy, 3 x 10 1/2 x 5 1/2 In. 10.00
Art Pottery, Bowl, Green, Loop Handle, 5 x 9 1/2 x 6 3/4 In. 25.00
Art Pottery, Candlestick, 2-Light, Magnolia, Eggshell Ivory, Antiqued Brown, 5 1/2 In. 105.00
Art Pottery, Candlestick, Magnolia, Eggshell Ivory, Antiqued Brown, 1 1/2 x 5 x 3 In. 15.00
Art Pottery, Console, Deer Flower Frog, Eggshell Ivory, Antiqued Brown, 10 x 16 In. 75.00
Art Pottery, Ewer, Magnolia, Antiqued Eggshell Ivory, Belle Kogan, 12 1/4 In. 250.00
Art Pottery, Figurine, Parrot, Ivory, 6 In. 59.00
Art Pottery, Jardinere, Cypress Green, Embossed Name, Mid 20th Century, 11 1/2 In. 24.00
Art Pottery, Pitcher, Pink Matte, Scroll Band, Footed, 8 1/4 In. 17.00
Art Pottery, Planter, Reclining Woman With Lyre & Fawn, Yellow, 7 1/2 x 13 In. 45.00
Art Pottery, Planter, Sgraffito, Charles Murphy, 12 x 7 1/2 In. 104.00
Art Pottery, Vase, Cornucopia, Terra-Cotta, 5 x 11 3/4 In. 15.00
Art Pottery, Vase, Ewer, Olive Green, Brown Inside, Handle, Footed, 7 1/4 In. 26.00
Art Pottery, Vase, Fan, Speckled Pink, Gray Inside, Art Deco, 8 In. 12.00
Art Pottery, Vase, Green, Applied Ivy Vine, 9 x 5 1/2 In. 95.00
Art Pottery, Vase, Luster Burgundy & Gray, 9 In. 35.00
Art Pottery, Vase, Magnolia, Eggshell Ivory, Bulbous, Flared Quatrefoil Rim, 6 In. 60.00
Art Pottery, Vase, No. 1230, Magnolia, Boat Shape, Eggshell Ivory, Footed, Belle Kogan 75.00
Art Pottery, Vase, Nokomis Glaze, 8 In. 135.00
Art Pottery, Wall Pocket, Violin, Black Glaze, 13 1/2 x 6 In. 20.00
Ashtray, Fish Shape, No. 1579, 7 In. 35.00
Bob White, Cup & Saucer 20.00
Bob White, Pitcher, Water, 12 In. 28.00
Bob White, Plate, Dinner, 10 3/4 In. 18.00
Bob White, Salt & Pepper 25.00
Capistrano, Bowl, Vegetable, Divided, Cover, Curled Handle, 14 In. 103.00
Capistrano, Plate, Dinner, 10 1/2 In. 20.00
Capistrano, Platter, Irregular Shape, 1953, 15 x 12 In. 36.00
Cattails, Pitcher, Yellow, 8 In. 115.00
Cookie Jar, Baker, Blue 50.00
Cookie Jar, Katrina, Dutch Girl, Blue, 11 In. 80.00
Cookie Jar, King Of Tarts, 9 1/2 In. 650.00
Frontenac, Bowl, Vegetable, Divided, 10 x 8 In. 34.00
Frontenac, Gravy Boat, Attached Underplate 34.00
Frontenac, Platter, Oval, 13 1/4 In. 34.00
Gray Line, Bowl, It Pays To Mix With Barkows Hardware Shoppe, Sponge Band, 6 In. 105.00

Gray Line, Bowl, It Pays To Mix With F. Mands, Phone 100, Sponge Band, 6 In. 125.00
Gray Line, Bowl, It Pays To Mix With T.J. Roberts, Waukesha, Wis., Sponge Band, 6 In. 255.00
Gray Line, Bowl, It Pays To Mix With Wis. Malt Product Co., Sponge Band, 6 In. 105.00
Gray Line, Bowl, It Pays To Trade At HW Berger Co., Random Lake, Sponge Band, 7 In. 160.00
Gray Line, Bowl, Sponge Band, Stoneware, 5 In. 400.00
Gray Line, Bowl, Sponge Band, Stoneware, 8 In. 80.00
Gray Line, Bowl, Sponge Band, Stoneware, 9 In. 115.00
Gray Line, Bowl, Sponge Band, Stoneware, 10 In. 155.00
Gray Line, Casserole, Cover, Sponge Band, Stoneware, Large 80.00
Gray Line, Cookie Jar, Sponge Band 850.00
Gray Line, Mixing Bowl, C.A. Rickeman Co., Helenville, Wis., Sponge Band, 6 In. 175.00
Gray Line, Mixing Bowl, Der Poy Bros., Sheboygan, Wis., Sponge Band, 7 In. 145.00
Gray Line, Mixing Bowl, Marshalls Store, East Troy, Wis., Sponge Band, 6 In. 175.00
Gray Line, Mixing Bowl, McCoy & Koll, Waukesha, Wis., Sponge Band, 6 In. 200.00
Gray Line, Mixing Bowl, R.P. Grabow Co., Knowles, Wis., Sponge Band, 7 In. 155.00
Gray Line, Pitcher, Christmas Greetings, E.W. Guths IGA Store, Sponge Band, Small 450.00
Gray Line, Pitcher, Inter City Fuel Co., 601 N. Fairview NE 1500, Sponge Band, Large 285.00
Greek Key, Bowl, 6 In. 35.00
Greek Key, Bowl, 8 In. 65.00
Gypsy Trail, Salt & Pepper, Yellow, Ball Shape 30.00
Lotus, Cup & Saucer 25.00
Lotus, Dinner Set, Service For 7, 46 Piece 264.00
Lotus, Plate, Dinner, 10 In. 22.00
Lute Song, Platter, Oval, 12 1/2 In. 30.00
Oomph, Bean Pot 75.00
Pink Spice, Cup & Saucer 25.00
Pink Spice, Plate, Dinner, 10 3/4 In. 25.00
Random Harvest, Platter, Oval, 11 In. 30.00
Random Harvest, Sugar & Creamer 26.00
Random Harvest, Tidbit, 2 Tiers, Center Handle, 10 3/4 In. 20.00
Spruce, Cup & Saucer 30.00
Stoneware, Ashtray, Red Wing Club, 1987 .... 85.00
Stoneware, Birch Leaves, Salt Glaze, 6 Gal. 400.00
Stoneware, Bowl, Spongeware, 7 1/2 In. 144.00
Stoneware, Bowl, Spongeware, Blue, Red, 10 In. 115.00
Stoneware, Churn, 4 In. Wing, 5 Gal. 345.00
Stoneware, Churn, Birch Leaf, 2 Gal. 45.00
Stoneware, Churn, Birch Leaf, Ski Oval, 4 Gal. 145.00
Stoneware, Crock, 2 In. Wing & Union Oval, Bail Handle, 5 Gal. 35.00
Stoneware, Crock, 4 In. Wing & Union Oval, 2 Gal. 85.00
Stoneware, Crock, Bail Handle, 8 Gal. 55.00
Stoneware, Crock, Bail Handles, 6 Gal., 15 In. 70.00
Stoneware, Crock, Birch Leaf, 20 Gal. 95.00
Stoneware, Crock, Birch Leaf, Salt Glaze, 5 Gal. 215.00
Stoneware, Crock, Birch Leaf, Ski Oval, 12 Gal. 105.00
Stoneware, Crock, Birch Leaves, Salt Glaze, 5 Gal. 265.00
Stoneware, Crock, Birch Leaves, Salt Glaze, 6 Gal. 315.00
Stoneware, Crock, Butterfly, Salt Glaze, 8 Gal. 2000.00
Stoneware, Crock, Butterfly, Salt Glaze, 12 Gal. 1400.00
Stoneware, Crock, Cover Only, 2 Gal. 50.00
Stoneware, Crock, Elephant Ear & Union Oval, 2 Gal. 50.00
Stoneware, Crock, Elephant Ear & Union Oval, 4 Gal. 35.00
Stoneware, Crock, Large Wing, 10 Gal. 105.00
Stoneware, Crock, Lily, Incised X's, Molded Handle, Salt Glaze, 20 Gal. 1200.00
Stoneware, Crock, Lily, Salt Glaze, 20 Gal. 2900.00
Stoneware, Crock, Single Rib & Target, Salt Glaze, 5 Gal. 315.00
Stoneware, Crock, Union Oval, 5 Gal., 13 In. 40.00
Stoneware, Crock, Union Oval, 10 Gal., 16 In. 17.25
Stoneware, Crock, Union Oval, 20 Gal., 21 In. 69.00
Stoneware, Crock, Union Oval, 30 Gal., 26 In. 201.00
Stoneware, Crock, Union Oval, 40 Gal., 31 In. 345.00

Stoneware, Crock, Willow Farm Products, Fresh Butter, Churned Daily, 3 Lb. 150.00
Stoneware, Jar, Applesauce, 4 In. Wing & Union Oval, 5 Gal. 175.00
Stoneware, Jug, 4 In. Wing & Union Oval, 4 Gal. 65.00
Stoneware, Jug, Beehive, 4 In. Wing & Union Oval, 4 Gal. 500.00
Stoneware, Jug, Beehive, 4 In. Wing & Union Oval, 5 Gal. 300.00
Stoneware, Jug, Beehive, Birch Leaves, 3 Gal. 225.00
Stoneware, Jug, Brown, Red Wing Club, 1978 ..... 775.00
Stoneware, Jug, Brown, Salt Glaze, Dome Top, Gal. 60.00
Stoneware, Jug, Domed Top, 2 Gal. 65.00
Stoneware, Jug, Large Wing, 5 Gal. 35.00
Stoneware, Jug, Red Wing Club, 1981, Mini 225.00
Stoneware, Jug, Spongeware, Gal. 65.00
Stoneware, Jug, Wing, 1/2 Gal. 85.00
Stoneware, Jug, Wing, Gal. 125.00
Stoneware, Mason Canning Jar, Red Wing Club, 1983 ..... 425.00
Stoneware, Mason Fruit Jar, 1/2 Gal. 185.00
Stoneware, Mason Fruit Jar, Qt. 180.00
Stoneware, Measure, Acid Proof, Red Wing Club, 1986 ..... 100.00
Stoneware, Mug, Cherry Band, Red Wing Club, 1982 ..... 395.00
Stoneware, Mug, Malt Syrup 125.00
Stoneware, Pantry Jar, Lid, 5 Lb. 195.00
Stoneware, Pitcher, Cherry Band, Large 100.00
Stoneware, Pitcher, Hamms Bear, Red Wing Club, 2000 ..... 60.00
Stoneware, Plate, Dinner, Red Wing Club, 1988 ..... 55.00
Stoneware, Water Cooler, 2 In. Wing & Union Oval, Bail Handle, 3 Gal. 235.00
Stoneware, Water Cooler, 4 In. Wing, 5 Gal. 325.00
Stoneware, Water Cooler, Birch Leaf, Salt Glaze, Red Wing Club, 1984 ..... 275.00
Stoneware, Water Cooler, Elephant Ear Handle, Red Wing Club, 1985 ..... 325.00
Stoneware, Water Cooler, Lid, 2 Gal. 155.00
Stoneware, Water Cooler, Lid, 4 In. Wing, Bail Handle, 2 Gal. 2900.00
Stoneware, Water Cooler, Lid, 5 Gal. 205.00
Town & Country, Cup & Saucer, Dusk Blue, Eva Zeisel 25.00

REDWARE is a hard, red stoneware that originated in the late 1600s and continues to be made. The term is also used to describe any common clay pottery that is reddish in color.

Bank, Apple, Painted, 2 1/2 x 3 3/4 In. ..... 165.00 to 210.00
Bank, Beehive, Multiglaze, Beaded Band At Neck & Top, 3 1/2 In. 415.00
Bank, Birth, Oval, 3 Birds On Finial, England, c.1888, 10 1/4 In. 605.00
Bank, Birth, Oval, 3 Birds On Finial, Square Base, c.1889, 10 In. 550.00
Bank, Boy's Head, Gold, Black, Signed, Emlek, 3 1/2 In. 155.00
Bank, Boy's Head, Inset Stones For Teeth, Eyes, Lines For Hair, 5 1/4 In. 138.00
Bank, Bulbous, Turkey Finial, 7 1/4 In. 195.00
Bank, Cat, Seated, Punched Eyes, Incised Details, Red, Orange, Black Specks, 5 38 In. 4400.00
Bank, Cradle, African American Baby, Mouth Coin Slot, 19th Century, 6 1/4 In. 4620.00
Bank, Dog, Spaniel, Hand Punched Face Details, c.1760, 6 1/4 In. 1760.00
Bank, Dresser, Cream Glazed Knobs, 19th Century, England, 8 In. 605.00
Bank, Duck, Full-Bodied, Fish In Mouth, Running Brown Glaze, 9 1/2 x 10 In. 405.00
Bank, Hen & Chicks, Olive Glaze, Slots, 5 1/2 In. 165.00
Bank, Hen, Whistle In Tail, Slip Decorated 6056.00
Bank, Incised Flowers, Oval, Button Finial, Yellow, Brown Ground, c.1875, 6 1/2 In. 7700.00
Bank, Log Cabin, Black Glaze, 4 Orange, Woman, Dog Standing, Slot In Top, 1/4 x 5 In. 2200.00
Bank, Log Cabin, Tile Roof, Chimney, Door, Window, Bird On Roof, Coin Slot, 6 1/4 In. 4180.00
Bank, Orange Shape, Dimpled Surface, Painted, 3 1/4 In. 255.00
Bank, Peach, 1800s, 3 x 3 1/4 In. 145.00
Bank, Pear Molded Leaf, Stem, White, 4 1/2 In. 145.00
Bank, Pear, 5 1/2 In. 415.00
Bank, Pig, Salt Glaze, Round Body, Punched Eyes, Incised Snout, England, 4 3/8 In. 220.00
Bank, Santa Claus, Toy Bag, Double Slots, Slip Decorated, Incised, 19th Century 33000.00
Bank, Spaniel Bust, Collar, Chain, Locket, Coin Slot In Head, 3 7/8 In. 95.00
Bank, Stump, Cylindrical, Tree Branch Finial, Incised Bark, Leaves, Applied Knots, 4 3/4 In. 275.00

Bank, Top Hat, Green Glaze, Slot In Top, Earthenware, Incised, c.1905, 4 In. 110.00
Beehive, Multiglaze, Beaded Band, 3 1/2 In. 415.00
Bottle, Brown Glaze, 6 1/2 In. 86.00
Bottle, Glazed, Signed Edwin Rogers Hartford, 15 In., Pair 1035.00
Bowl, Brown Glaze, 2 1/2 In. 60.00
Bowl, Coggled Rim, Tapered Sides, Incised Line, Brown Daubed Glaze, 7 x 3 1/8 In. 405.00
Bowl, Flared Sides, Tooled Band, Brown Daubs, Ocher Ground, 11 x 3 5/8 In. 230.00
Bowl, Manganese Glaze, Footed, c.1840-60, 3 In. 165.00
Bowl, Manganese Splotches, 3 x 6 3/4 In. 80.00
Bowl, Mocha Seaweed, Redware Ground, 1800s 460.00
Bowl, Ovals, Diamonds, Slip Decorated, Glazed, Penn., 1800s, 6 In. 3230.00
Bowl, Slip Decoration, Lead Glaze, Bell Family Attribution, c.1800, 2 5/8 x 8 1/4 In. 1045.00
Bowl, Sugar, Dome Cover, Squat, Splayed Foot, Rope Handles, c.1880, 5 3/4 In. 1760.00
Bust, George Washington, Gilded, Marbleized Socle, Marble Base, 1800s, 15 In. 705.00
Butter Tub, Diamond, Flowers, Coggled Rim, Manganese Glaze, c.1840, 5 1/4 x 10 1/4 In. 880.00
Candleholder, Coggled Rim, Black, Loop Handle, Left Hand, Russell Henry, 1-10-68, 2 In. 165.00
Candleholder, Crimped Rim, Brown Glaze, Ring Handle, Saucer Base, May, 1952, 5 In. 176.00
Candleholder, Ruffled Rim, Barrel, Loop Handle, Brown, R.R. Stahl, May, 1950, 7 In. 415.00
Candleholder, Saucer Base, Ring Handle, Crimped Rim, Brown Glaze, Stahl, 1952, 3 1/2 In. 176.00
Canteen, Round, Tan & Brown Glaze, 7 In. 1150.00
Chamber Pot, New England, 5 1/2 In., Child's 140.00
Charger, Coggled Rim, Slip Decorated, 13 1/2 In. 3100.00
Charger, Coggled Rim, Yellow Slip Line, Comb & Feather Decoration, 11 In. 575.00
Charger, Coggled Rim, Yellow Slip, Berry Sprigs, Polka Dot Bird, 13 3/8 x 2 1/2 In. 865.00
Charger, Peacock, Flower, Slip Decorated, 12 In. 3346.00
Charger, Slip Decorated, Stylized Loops & Flowers, Pennsylvania, 14 In. 4480.00
Charger, Yellow Slip Decoration, Illegible Text, Tankard, 1776, 12 In. 200.00
Compote, Scroddleware, Variegated Red & Yellow Clay, Yellow Glaze, 6 1/2 x 6 In. 230.00
Creamer, Coggled Rim, Manganese Splotches, 8 In. 242.00
Creamer, New Geneva, Flowers, Red, Brown Glaze, 3 1/2 In. 2070.00
Crock, Blue Slip, Lug Handles, Signed, 3 Gal., 13 In. 500.00
Crock, Brown Glaze, 1800s, 9 In. 33.00
Crock, Glazed, Inside, Running Green, Amber Brown, Winchester, Virginia, 7 1/2 In. 690.00
Crock, Storage, Manganese Splotches, 6 1/2 In. 175.00
Cup, Handle, Dark Brown Glaze, 2 1/4 In. 175.00
Cup, Orange Brown Glaze, Footed, 3 x 4 In. 115.00
Cuspidor, Manganese Splotches, Drain Hole, 2 1/2 x 4 1/2 In. 110.00
Dish, Arched Rim Line, 3 Bird-Like Shapes, Glazed, Slip Decorated, 1800s, 13 In. 7770.00
Dish, Coggled Rim, Glazed Slip, Leafy Trailings, 17 x 11 In. 956.00
Dish, Loaf, Slip Decorated, Intersecting Yellow Slip, Glazed Squiggles, 3 x 13 x 15 In. 6465.00
Dish, Maria, Slip Decorated, Round, Coggled Rim, c.1845, 13 1/4 In. 1998.00
Dish, Ruffled Rim, Glazed Slip, White, Brown Bands, Flowers, 7 1/4 In. 2390.00
Dish, Scroll Border, BC Monogram, Impressed Leaves, 1764, 11 In. 2115.00
Doorstop, Dog, Spaniel, Reclining, Rust Glaze, Hand Punched Eyes, 9 1/2 In. 85.00
Figurine, Adam & Eve, Apple Tree, 5 Apples, 1800s, 9 1/2 x 6 In. 4715.00
Figurine, Bird, Manganese, Impressed Eyes, Flared Base, John Maize, 3 1/2 x 3 1/4 In. 2200.00
Figurine, Dog, Spaniel, Seated, Manganese Glaze, Incised Fur, c.1860, 4 1/8 x 3 1/2 In. 2310.00
Figurine, Dog, Spaniel, Seated, With Basket, Incised Fur, 4 1/2 x 4 1/4 In. 3960.00
Figurine, Dog, Whippet, Bennington Glaze, Shenandoah Valley, John Bell, 10 In. 41800.00
Figurine, Ewe & Lamb, Reclining, Shaped Base, 5 x 8 In. 330.00
Figurine, Fox, Brown To Green, 3 1/8 x 4 1/4 In. 1320.00
Figurine, Pig, Ear Of Corn In Mouth, Oval Slab Base, Flower Stamping, 5 1/4 x 3 1/4 In. 8800.00
Figurine, Rocking Horse, Glazed, Hand Molded 5720.00
Figurine, Rooster, Blue Green Glaze, R.R. Stahl, 1948, 4 1/2 In. 265.00
Figurine, Rooster, Blue, Green Glaze, Marked, R.R. Stahl, December 28, 1948, 4 1/2 In. 265.00
Figurine, Salamander, Brown Glaze, Green Splotches, 4 1/2 In. 440.00
Figurine, Sheep, Reclining, Manganese Slip, 4 x 15 1/2 In. 390.00
Flask, Dark Glaze, Flat Sides, Tooled Lip, c.1830-50, 3 In. 300.00
Flowerpot, Applied Loop Hanger, Attached Saucer Base, 5 x 4 3/4 In. 95.00
Flowerpot, Coggled Rim, Attached Undertray, Solomen Bell, 8 In. 1155.00
Flowerpot, Scalloped Midline, Attached Saucer Base, Stahl, 1940, 5 x 6 5/8 In. 297.00

Flowerpot, Scalloped Rim, Brown To Green Glaze, Attached Saucer, Stahl, 4 1/4 x 6 In. 175.00
Flowerpot, Scalloped Rim, Green To Brown Glaze, Attached Saucer, Stahl, 5 x 6 5/8 In. 297.00
Flowerpot, Scalloped Rim, Incised Squiggle Decoration, Attached Saucer, 4 1/4 x 6 In. 175.00
Jar, Apple Butter, Brown Running Glaze At Rim & Shoulder, Oval, 5 3/4 In. 259.00
Jar, Canning, Glazed, Brown Spot At Neck, Incised Lines On Shoulder, 6 x 9 In. 200.00
Jar, Cover, Crackle Finish, Incised Shoulder Line, 8 In. 520.00
Jar, Cover, Cylindrical, Beveled Neck, Green Glaze, Red Speckles, Maine, 8 x 6 1/4 In. 690.00
Jar, Cover, Manganese Glaze, 2 1/4 In. 255.00
Jar, Cover, Orange Glaze, 8 In. 290.00
Jar, Cover, Oval, Tan & Brown Glaze, 10 In. 2875.00
Jar, Cream Slip Flowers, Semi-Oval, Handles, 19th Century, 11 3/8 In. 660.00
Jar, Cream, Multiglaze, Semi-Oval, c.1890, 6 3/8 In. 2640.00
Jar, Flanged Lip, Collar, 8 1/4 In. 550.00
Jar, Footed, Incised Lines, Green, Lead Glaze, 4 3/4 In. 360.00
Jar, Handle, Manganese Slip, Pa., 1800s, 5 In. 305.00
Jar, Incised Decorated, 2 Handles, Baluster Shape, Strap Handles, c.1860, 6 1/8 In. 1880.00
Jar, Lead, Manganese Glaze, Footed, Flaring Collar, Incised Lines, 19th Century, 8 1/4 In. 275.00
Jar, Magnesium Drip, Brown Glaze, Handles, 9 1/4 In. 330.00
Jar, Manganese Glaze, Bulbous, Lip, c.1840-60, 2 In. 155.00
Jar, Manganese Splotches, 6 In. 39.00
Jar, Oval, Pumpkin Glaze, Brown Sponging, Ear Handles, 8 1/2 x 10 In. 690.00
Jar, Oyster, New England, 9 3/4 In. 525.00
Jar, Peach & Brown Glaze, 4 1/4 In. 805.00
Jar, Red Glaze, Brown Decoration, 6 1/2 In. 430.00
Jar, Red Glaze, Brown Spots, 10 In. 230.00
Jar, Ruffled Rim, Applied Double Loop Handles, Yellow Slip, Schoefield, 4 1/4 In. 242.00
Jar, Salve, Manganese Glaze, Flared Lip, Footed, c.1840-60, 2 In. 155.00
Jar, Semi-Oval, Incised Lines, Unglazed, c.1850-80, 8 3/4 In. 165.00
Jar, Storage, Applied Loop Handle, Glazed Interior, 3 3/4 In. 120.00
Jar, Storage, Bulbous, 8 3/4 In. 120.00
Jar, Storage, Bulbous, Manganese Splotches, Incised Lines, 9 In. 525.00
Jar, Storage, Cover, Straight Sides, 7 1/2 In. 250.00
Jar, Storage, Manganese Splotches, Coggled Wheel Incised Lines, 12 1/4 In. 770.00
Jar, Storage, Manganese Splotches, Incised Lines, 6 In. 165.00
Jar, Storage, Manganese Splotches, Incised Lines, Handle, 6 In. 165.00
Jar, Storage, Red & Brown Peppery Glaze, N.Y. State, c.1830, Gal., 8 1/2 In. 145.00
Jar, Storage, Red, Green, Mottled Glaze, 1800s, 10 In. 250.00
Jar, Storage, Ruffled Rim, 3 Applied Loop Handles, Tassel, Schofield, 6 1/4 In. 360.00
Jar, Storage, Splotches, Incised Line, Straight Sides, 5 1/4 In. 198.00
Jug, 3 Tooled Lines On Collar, Pear Shape, 8 1/2 In. 55.00
Jug, Bell Shape, Green Glaze, Orange Spots, 8 1/2 In. 920.00
Jug, Black Glaze, 6 3/4 In. 200.00
Jug, Brown Brush Decoration, Yellow, 8 1/4 In. 805.00
Jug, Brown Glaze, Pear Form, New England, 8 1/2 In. 110.00
Jug, Egg Shape, Handle, 6 1/2 In. 115.00
Jug, Figural, Man Fixing Tie, Billed Cap Is Lid, Running Brown Glaze, 10 3/4 In. 115.00
Jug, Green Alkaline Glaze, L. Johnson, Newstead, N.Y., c.1860, 11 1/2 In. 300.00
Jug, Grotesque, Porcelain Teeth, Applied Ears, Nose, Eyes, Incised Mustache, 6 1/2 In. 358.00
Jug, Harvest, Bulbous, Green, Brown, Yellow Glaze, Nipple, Rosette Terminals, 11 1/4 In. 415.00
Jug, Harvest, Manganese Splotches, Loop Handle, Side Spout, 8 3/4 In. 440.00
Jug, Harvest, Mottled, Bulbous, Flared Base, Green, Brown, Yellow, Loop Handle, 11 In. 415.00
Jug, Incised Rings, Oval, Green Glaze, Orange Spots, Applied Strap Handle, 8 1/4 In. 316.00
Jug, Manganese Accents, c.1830, 10 In. 110.00
Jug, Manganese Glaze, Bulbous, Applied Handle, c.1840, 2 1/2 In. 275.00
Jug, Molded Double Loop Handles, 13 In. 100.00
Jug, Mottled Red, Dark Spots, Running Green Glaze, Applied Strap Handle, 12 3/4 In. 290.00
Jug, New England, Handle, 8 1/2 In. 220.00
Jug, Oblong Shape, Incised Rings, Applied Strap Handles, Orange, Green Glaze, 6 3/4 In. 430.00
Jug, Orange & Brown Spot Decoration, Handle, 8 3/4 In. 748.00
Jug, Orange Spots, Defined Ribs, Oval, Green Glazed, Strap Handle, 9 In. 170.00
Jug, Oval, Brown Manganese Glaze, Applied Ribbed Handle, 6 5/8 In. 230.00

Jug, Oval, Green, Brown Glaze, Orange Brown Halos, Applied Handle, 10 In. 355.00
Jug, Peach Glaze, Brown Specks, 7 In. 85.00
Jug, Red Brown, Thumbprint On Handle, Norcross Attribution, Maine, 6 3/4 In. 1150.00
Jug, Squat, Gray Glaze, 9 In. 175.00
Jug, Storage, Glazed Interior, Applied Loop Handle, 3 3/4 In. 120.00
Jug, Tan Glaze, Brown Spots, 6 1/2 In. 2300.00
Jug, Vinegar, Incised Lines, Oval, Brown Glaze, Applied Reeded Strap Handle, 6 In. 175.00
Jug, Yellow Slip Decoration, Unglazed Lower Half, Handle, 1800s, 10 In. 1210.00
Loaf Pan, Coggled Rim, Yellow 4-Line Wavy Design, Leaf Designs, 15 1/2 In. 978.00
Loaf Pan, Coggled Rim, Yellow Slip Design, 11 x 15 1/4 x 3 1/4 In. 575.00
Loaf Pan, Coggled Rim, Yellow Slip Seaweed, 11 x 15 In. 575.00
Loaf Pan, Coggled Rim, Yellow Slip, Linear Initial G, Conn., 9 3/4 x 15 In. 1265.00
Match Holder, Brown Glaze, 2 1/4 In. 85.00
Match Holder, Interior Brown Glaze, 2 1/2 In. 115.00
Match Holder, Scroddleware, Lyre, Sections, Guitar, Tambourine, 5 1/2 x 6 3/4 In. 120.00
Milk Pan, Red Glaze, 13 In. 115.00
Mug, Manganese Glaze, Incised Lines, Strap Handle, c.1840, 6 1/2 In. 300.00
Mug, Manganese, Applied Handle, c.1840, 2 In. 210.00
Pan, Oval, Orange Glaze, Brown Spots, 13 x 10 1/2 In. 375.00
Pie Plate, 6 Faint Wavy Lines, Yellow Slip, 7 In. 200.00
Pie Plate, Coggled Rim, Yellow Slip Decoration, 4 1/2 In. 490.00
Pie Plate, Coggled Rim, Yellow Slip Decoration, Wavy Lines, 8 In. 430.00
Pie Plate, Coggled Rim, Yellow Slip Design, Wavy Lines, 10 In. 460.00
Pie Plate, Coggled Rim, Yellow Slip, 9 3/4 In. 290.00
Pie Plate, Coggled Rim, Yellow Slip, Ann, 8 In. 980.00
Pie Plate, Coggled Rim, Yellow Slip, Leaves, Wavy Lines, 9 3/4 In. 345.00
Pie Plate, Coggled Rim, Yellow Slip, May, 10 1/4 In. 316.00
Pie Plate, Coggled Rim, Yellow Slip, Wavy Lines, 8 In. 460.00
Pie Plate, Crisscross Yellow Slip Lines, Stamped, 8 1/2 In. 1610.00
Pie Plate, Mustard Glaze, Plymouth, N.H., 10 In. 175.00
Pie Plate, Peacock, Tulip Wreath, Coggled Rim, Mottled Brown Glaze, 8 1/2 In. 748.00
Pitcher, Blue Splotches, New England, c.1850, 5 1/4 In. 660.00
Pitcher, Brown Decoration, Yellow Glaze, Handle, 7 In. 175.00
Pitcher, Bulbous, Mottled Glaze, Flared Base, Stamped, John Bell, 7 3/4 In. 600.00
Pitcher, Cover, Black Speckles, Wavy Line, 8 3/4 x 6 1/2 In. 575.00
Pitcher, Cream Glazed Body, Green & Brown Splotches, Eberly, Shenandoah 4180.00
Pitcher, Egg Shape, Orange Brown, Black Streaks, Applied Handle, 6 1/2 In. 575.00
Pitcher, Manganese Glaze, Bulbous, Pour Spout, Applied Handle, c.1840-60, 2 1/4 In. 230.00
Pitcher, Manganese Glaze, Flared Rim, Applied Handle, 2 1/2 In. 525.00
Pitcher, Manganese Glaze, Pour Spout, Applied Handle, c.1840, 3 In. 465.00
Pitcher, Manganese, Applied Handle, 2 1/4 In. 190.00
Pitcher, Milk, Berry, Squiggle X, Applied Loop Handle, 5 3/4 In. 155.00
Pitcher, Milk, Incised Squiggle Lines, Applied Handle, 6 1/4 In. 176.00
Pitcher, Oval, Applied Corrugated Strap Handle, 1840-60, 5 3/4 In. 330.00
Pitcher, Overglaze, Raised Columns, Panels, Trees, Flowers, Hound Handle, 10 3/4 In. 1210.00
Pitcher, Pig, Pyrographic Facial Features, Leather Clad, 19th Century, 9 3/8 In. 410.00
Pitcher, Raised Anchor, Molded, Lead Glaze, Rising Spout, Thumb Rest, c.1875, 8 1/2 In. 495.00
Pitcher, Ribbed, Strap Handle, M.L. Owens, Seagrove, N.C., 1900s, 9 In. 115.00
Plate, 2 Yellow Squiggle Lines, c.1850, 6 1/4 In. 525.00
Plate, 3 Lines, W. Smith, Womelsdorf, Penn, 7 1/4 In. 715.00
Plate, 6-Line Yellow Slip, c.1850, 6 3/4 In. 275.00
Plate, Coggled Rim, 3 Squiggled Quill Lines, 9 In. 635.00
Plate, Coggled Rim, 3-Band Quill, 10 1/4 In. 660.00
Plate, Coggled Rim, 3-Band Quill, Slip, 12 In. 605.00
Plate, Coggled Rim, Manganese Splotching, 8 In. 110.00
Plate, Coggled Rim, Red Ground, Yellow Wavy Lines, 9 1/2 In. 316.00
Plate, Coggled Rim, Slip Decorated, 3 Squiggled Lines, Quill Lines, 9 In. 635.00
Plate, Coggled Rim, Slip Decorated, 3 Triple Band Quill Decoration, 10 1/4 In. 660.00
Plate, Coggled Rim, Slip Decorated, Center Scroll, 12 1/4 In. 770.00
Plate, Coggled Rim, Yellow Slip Wavy Line, Round, Leaves, Early 1800s, 6 1/4 In. 325.00
Plate, Oval, Lester Breininger, Bicentennial, 15 1/4 x 11 3/8 In. 94.00

Plate, Sheffield Pottery Commemorative, June 17, 1906, 9 3/4 In. 20.00
Plate, Slip Decorated, 3 Squiggled Lines, W. Smith, Womelsdorf, Pa., 7 1/4 In. 715.00
Plate, Slip Decorated, Coggled Rim, Round, James, Early 1800s, 9 1/4 In. 1116.00
Plate, Slip Decorated, Coggled Rim, Squiggle Lines, Round, Anna, Mid 1800s, 10 1/4 In. 1998.00
Plate, Yellow Lines, Penn., c.1800, 11 In. 470.00
Platter, Eternal Vigilance Is Price Of Liberty, Glazed, Slip Decorated, Oval, Penn., 14 In. 900.00
Pot, Brown Glaze, Green Spots, Handle, 6 3/4 In. 290.00
Pot, Stew, Cover, Bulging Neck, Norcross Attribution, Maine, 7 1/2 In. 2358.00
Pot, Stew, Cover, Green, Brown Mottled Glaze, 8 1/4 In. 145.00
Pot, Stew, Green Glaze, Orange Spots, Handle, Cover, 8 1/4 In. 3165.00
Roaster, Cover, Pumpkin Glaze, Cream Band, Interior, Pie Crimped Band, 16 1/2 x 6 In. 85.00
Serving Dish, Coggled Rim, Glazed Slip, 13 1/2 x 8 In. 1075.00
Shaving Mug, Manganese Glaze, 4 5/8 In. 205.00
Stove Feet, Scrolled Form, Resembles Paws, Brown Running Glaze, 3 1/2 In., 4 Piece 145.00
Sugar, Cover, Green Glaze, Incised Lines, I.S. Stahl, November 22, 1940, 5 In. 430.00
Umbrella Stand, Tree Trunk, Sawed Limbs, Twisting Vine, c.1895, 20 3/4 In. 1100.00
Vase, 5 Fingers, Green, Brown Streaks, 7 1/8 In. 990.00
Vase, Eagle, Spread Wings, Shield Breast, Branches, Stars, Jacob Medinger, 11 1/4 In. 1650.00
Vase, Egg Shape, Speckle Green Streaky Glaze, Round Lip, 5 1/2 In. 950.00
Vase, Green & Brown Drip, Mustard Ground, Oval, 4 Twisted Handles, 8 1/8 In. 470.00
Wall Pocket, Applied Flowers, Eberly, Pair 2970.00
Wall Pocket, Coggled Rim, Bird, Blossoms, Leaves, Multiglaze, Splayed Foot, 5 1/2 In. 2970.00
Wall Pocket, Crest, Grape, Leaf, Shaped Rim, 11 In. 80.00
Whimsy, Bird, Brown Slip, 2-Piece Construction, Center Line, 3 1/4 In. 155.00
Whimsy, Fox, Incised Lines, Brown Green Glaze, Rectangular Base, 3 1/8 x 4 1/4 In. 1320.00

REGOUT, see Maastricht category.

RICHARD was the mark used on acid-etched cameo glass vases, bowls, night-lights, and lamps made by the Austrian company Loetz after 1918. The pieces were very similar to the French cameo glasswares made by Daum, Galle, and others.

Vase, Amethyst Flowers, Leaves, Burnt Orange Ground, Bulbous, Flared Rim, 6 In. 805.00
Vase, Brown, Flowers, Leaves, Dragonflies, Orange Ground, Tapered Neck, 4 In. 360.00
Vase, Cobalt Leafy Wisteria, Orange Ground, Cylindrical, Tapered, 15 In. 518.00
Vase, Flowering Vine Design, Cut To Rose Ground, 12 In. 410.00
Vase, Landscape, Lake, Mountain, Sailboats, Purple Over Red, Signed, 6 1/4 In. .... *ILLUS* 330.00
Vase, Leafy Vines, Mauve, Green, Citron, Bulbous, 11 3/4 In. 431.00
Vase, Orange, Stemmed Flowers, Insects, Footed, Early 1900s, 10 In. 440.00
Vase, Sienna, Purple Overlay, Mountain, Castle, Conical, Cushion Foot, c.1900, 12 In. 657.00
Wine, Faceted Clear Stem, Cobalt Blue, Lake, 8 In. 374.00

RIDGWAY pottery has been made in the Staffordshire district in England since 1808 by a series of companies with the name Ridgway. The transfer-design dinner sets are the most widely known product. They are still being made. Other pieces of Ridgway are listed under Flow Blue.

Bowl, Pennsylvania Hospital, Flower Border, c.1820, 9 1/2 In. 4185.00
Creamer, Rutland, Green, 3 1/2 In. 18.00
Cup & Saucer, English Garden, Flowers, Bone China 15.00
Cup & Saucer, Indian Tree, Stoneware, White, Flower Branch Border, 5 5/8-In. Saucer 20.00
Cup & Saucer, Queen Anne 29.00
Cup & Saucer, Royal Vale 16.00
Cup & Saucer, Royal Vale, Pink Flowers, Gold Trim 32.00
Mug, Coaching Days, Black Transfer, 2 Scenes, Catching Mail, Pack Horse, 3 1/2 In. 35.00
Mug, Girl's Face, Silver Luster Handle 69.00
Pin Tray, Windsor, Transfer, Multicolored, 4 3/8 In. 13.00
Plate, Bread & Butter, Espresso Pattern, Ironstone, Brown, Cream Base 5.00
Plate, City Hall, New York, 9 3/4 In. 200.00
Plate, Dinner, Woodland Pattern, Flowers, Castle & Stream, Earthtones 30.00
Plate, Oriental, Arabian Scenes, Blue Transfer, Gold Trim, 5 3/4 In., c.1890 .... 20.00
Platter, Rutland, Flower Bouquet, Green Band, Oval, 12 1/2 x 6 In. 50.00

Sugar, Cover, Aladdin, c.1846, 8 In. 325.00
Tankard, Horse, Bulldog, Earthenware, c.1912, 12 In. 299.00
Teapot, Shakespeare's Country, 6 3/8 x 9 5/8 In. 113.00
Vase, Aesthetic Movement, Cylinder, Transfer, Duck, Flower Stems, c.1900, 8 3/4 In. 118.00

RIFLES that are firearms are not listed in this book. BB guns and air rifles are listed in the Toy category.

RIVIERA dinnerware was made by the Homer Laughlin Co. of Newell, West Virginia, from 1938 to 1950. The pattern was similar in coloring and in mood to Fiesta and Harlequin. The Riviera plates and cup handles were square. For more information, see *Kovels' Depression Glass & Dinnerware Price List.*

Ivory, Butter, 1/2 Lb. 70.00
Ivory, Sauceboat, Fast Stand, 3 x 6 5/8 In. 145.00
Light Green, Plate, Luncheon, 9 In. 14.00
Light Green, Saltshaker 12.00
Mauve, Blue, Tumbler 75.00
Red, Bowl, Vegetable, 8 1/4 In. 30.00
Red, Butter, 1/2 Lb. 125.00
White, Bowl, Dessert, 5 1/4 In. 14.00
Yellow, Creamer 25.00
Yellow, Pitcher, Juice, 5 3/4 In. 195.00
Yellow, Plate, Bread & Butter, 5 In. 10.00
Yellow, Teapot, Cover 185.00

ROCKINGHAM, in the United States, is a pottery with a brown glaze that resembles tortoiseshell. It was made from 1840 to 1900 by many American potteries. Mottled brown Rockingham wares were first made in England at the Rockingham factory. Other types of ceramics were also made by the English firm. Related pieces may be listed in the Bennington category.

Bank, Chest Of Drawers, Early 1900s, 2 3/4 In. 99.00
Bank, Dog, Seated Spaniel, Freestanding Front Leg, 8 1/2 In., Pair 633.00
Bottle, Queen Victoria, Duchess Of Kent, 7 1/2 In. 165.00
Figurine, Dog, Isaac Knowles Attribution, East Liverpool, Ohio, 1856-70, 10 1/2 In. 345.00
Figurine, Dog, Seated, Acanthus Leaves, 12 1/2 In. 345.00
Figurine, Dog, Spaniel, Flint Glazed Enamel, 10 In. 358.00
Figurine, Dog, Spaniel, Seated, Leash, Clay Coleslaw Fur, Rust, 8 1/4 In. 935.00
Figurine, Dog, Spaniel, Seated, Open Front Legs, Curled Tail, Mottled Brown, 10 3/4 In. 385.00
Figurine, Dog, Spaniel, Seated, Scenes Of Dogs, Trees On Base, 12 3/8 In. 1210.00
Figurine, Lion, Lying Down, c.1860, 6 3/4 x 9 In. 300.00
Flask, Book Shape, Glazed, Mid 19th Century, 5 3/4 In. 265.00
Flask, Mermaid, Brown Glaze, c.1860, 8 In. 190.00
Flask, Shoe, Defined Laces, 6 1/4 In. 200.00
Frame, Picture, Glaze, Scalloped Edge, Molded Decoration, Tintype, 12 x 10 1/2 In. 765.00
Group, Deer, Chimney Vase, Rocky Base, Congress Hill Pottery, N.J., 10 In. 4310.00
Inkwell, Court Jester Head, Hat, c.1900, 3 In. 300.00
Jug, Batter, Glazed, Tin Cover, Bail Handle, 10 In. 230.00
Lion, Molded Mane, Standing, Paw On Ball, Grapevine Base, 11 x 10 In. 460.00
Pitcher, Brown Glaze, Yellow Sponging, Relief Hunter, Dogs In Brush, 10 In. 86.00
Pitcher, Flint Glaze, Blue, Acorn, Oak Leaf, Paneled Body, Mid 1800s, 9 In. 460.00
Pitcher, Flint Glaze, Swirl, 9 In. 690.00
Pitcher, Fox Handle, Tan Glaze, Huntsman, Dogs & Horses, 7 In. 115.00
Pitcher, Hound Handle, Brown Glaze, Dogs Hunting Deer, Boar, Scrolls, 7 3/4 In. 259.00
Pitcher, Hound Handle, Embossed Design, Chasing Stag, Scrolling, Glazed, 12 In. 575.00
Pitcher, Hound Handle, Grapevines, Hunt Scene, American Pottery Co., N.J., 10 3/4 In. 460.00
Pitcher, Hound Handle, Grapevines, Hunt Scene, Harker Taylor, 11 In. 1725.00
Pitcher, Hound Handle, Hunt Scenes, East Liverpool, c.1853, 7 1/2 In. 1090.00
Pitcher, Hound Handle, Matte Green Glaze, Grapevines, Dogs Chasing Stag, 10 In. 520.00
Pitcher, Toby, Standing On Grapevines, Taking Snuff, Lid, 9 3/4 In. 85.00
Plate, Dinner, Flowers, Shaped Rim, Shells, Gadroons, 1826-30, 10 In., 12 Piece 1800.00

ROGERS, see John Rogers category.

Richard, Vase, Landscape, Lake, Mountain, Sailboats, Purple Over Red, Signed, 6 1/4 In.

Rookwood, Vase, Black Iris Glaze, Holly Branch, Oval, Sara Sax, c.1906, 6 1/4 x 4 In.

Rookwood, Vase, Scenic Vellum, Hills, Pink Sky, Baluster, Sallie Coyne, c.1916, 11 In.

ROOKWOOD pottery was made in Cincinnati, Ohio, from 1880 to 1960. All of this art pottery is marked, most with the famous flame mark. The R is reversed and placed back to back with the letter P. Flames surround the letters. After 1900, a Roman numeral was added to the mark to indicate the year. The name and some of the molds were purchased in 1984. A few new pieces were made, but these were glazed in colors not used by the original company.

Ashtray, Bird, 1943, 5 x 6 1/2 In. 185.00
Ashtray, Fish, Chinese Turquoise Glaze, 1945, 6 In. 265.00
Ashtray, Rook, Emerald Green Matte Glaze, 1928, 4 x 8 In. 175.00
Bookends, Dutch Boy & Girl, Toohey, 1928, 6 In. 360.00
Bookends, Egyptian Woman, Brown Matte Glaze, McDonald, 1922, 5 1/2 In. 570.00
Bookends, Elephants, Ivory, Trunk Down, William McDonald, 1931, 7 In. .... 415.00 to 460.00
Bookends, Hound Dog, 2-Tone Brown Matte Glaze, Abel, 1927, 5 In. 720.00
Bookends, Hound Dog, Brown Matte Glaze, Abel, 1930, 5 x 6 In. 660.00
Bookends, Hound Dog, Light Blue Matte Glaze, 5 In. 259.00
Bookends, Owl On Closed Book, Green Glaze, 1944, 6 In. 200.00
Bookends, Panther, Ivory High Glaze, McDonald, 1951, 5 1/2 In. 360.00
Bookends, Penguins On Rocks, Shell Base, Dark Brown Matte Glaze, 1934 .... 940.00
Bookends, Rook, Celadon Glaze, McDonald, 1956, 5 In. 420.00
Bookends, Rook, Ivory Matte Glaze, 1939, 5 In. 290.00
Bookends, Rook, Open Book, Plum Matte Glaze, 1926, 6 1/4 x 5 7/8 In. 805.00
Bookends, Schooner Ship, Ivory Matte Glaze, 1936, 5 1/2 In. 230.00
Bowl, Arches, Leaf Spandrels, Compressed, Round, Footed, 1917, 6 1/2 In. 95.00
Bowl, Flowers, Brown & Green Glaze, Virginia Demarest, 1901, 3 1/4 In. 300.00
Bowl, Geometric Border, Mottled, Green, Pink, Round, 1909, 7 In. 95.00
Bowl, Ivory Exterior, Crackled Turquoise Interior, 1919, 6 1/2 In. 170.00
Candlestick, Green Matte Glaze, Anna Valentien, 1902, 4 3/8 In. 7750.00
Candlestick, Pink & Green Matte Glaze, Handles, 1919, 7 In. 420.00
Candlestick, Turquoise Matte Glaze, Embossed Flowers, c.1920, 4 3/4 In., Pair 120.00
Ewer, Butterflies, Gold Neck, Trefoil Spout, Bisque Finish, Mary A. Taylor 750.00
Ewer, Fluted Spout, Serpentine Handle, Standard Glaze, Sallie Toohey, 10 1/2 In. 260.00
Ewer, Leaves, Mahogany, Caramel Ground, Ruffled Mouth, J. Zettel, 1900, 9 x 4 In. 230.00
Figurine, Cat, 1941, 6 3/4 In. 490.00
Fountain, Burgundy Glaze, 15 In. 1265.00
Inkwell, Cover, Blue, 1924, 5 In. 315.00
Jar, Flat Cover, Embossed Flower, Pierced Windows, Rose Matte, 4 x 3 In. 290.00
Jardiniere, Roses, Peach, Mahogany, Crimped Petals, Rolled Edges, 1889, 6 x 8 1/4 In. 635.00
Jug, Black Birds, Branch, Stencil, Silver & Cork Stopper, A. Humphreys, 1882, 5 1/2 In. 500.00
Jug, Stopper, Ear Of Corn, Standard Glaze, 1899, 6 In. 430.00
Jug, Whiskey, Snakes, Grapes, Vine, Silver Overlay, Sterling Stopper, Standard Glaze, 7 1/8 In. 4600.00
Lamp Base, Jewel, Purple Magnolia, Ivory Ground, Brass Fixture, 13 1/2 x 6 1/2 In. 410.00
Mug, Flowers, Mottled Green Glaze, Cylinder, Tapered, 1903, 5 1/2 In. 179.00

Mug, Mottled Green Matte Glaze, 1903, 5 1/2 In. 270.00
Paperweight, Nude Woman, Ivory Matte Glaze, Abel, 1932, 4 In. 185.00
Paperweight, Primate, 1935, 5 3/8 In. 315.00
Paperweight, Rook, Blue Gray, 1930, 4 1/4 x 5 In. 855.00
Paperweight, Rook, Tan Glaze, 1922, 3 x 4 In. 335.00
Paperweight, Squirrel, Mottled Brown, Green Matte Glaze, Toohey, 1928, 4 1/4 In. 900.00
Pencil Holder, Rook, Green Matte Glaze, 1934, 4 3/4 In. 375.00
Pitcher, Bats, Fog, Red Clay Body, Trefoil Mouth, Valentien, 1882, 8 In. 400.00
Pitcher, Blue Matte Glaze, 1933, 5 3/4 In. 180.00
Pitcher, Daisies, Leaves, Yellow, Mahogany Ground, Silver Overlay, 7 x 3 1/2 In. 1840.00
Plaque, Landscape, Birch Trees, Vellum Glaze, Frame, E.T. Hurley, 9 x 5 In. 4780.00
Plaque, Landscape, Trees Along Water, Frame, Carl Schmidt, 1916, 9 1/2 x 7 1/2 In. 8970.00
Plaque, Misty Landscape, Vellum Glaze, Frame, Lorinda Epply, 5 x 9 In. 3585.00
Plaque, Purple Mountains, Pink Sky, Trees, Vellum, Frame, E.T. Hurley, 8 x 10 In. 8813.00
Plaque, River, Large Trees, Water, Vellum Glaze, 1914, 14 x 16 In. 6325.00
Plaque, Snowy Landscape, Vellum, Frame, Elizabeth McDermott, 1918, 5 x 8 In. 5290.00
Plaque, Trees Reflected In Lake, Vellum, Frame, Chas. McLaughlin, 1916, 11 x 9 In. 8815.00
Plaque, Trees, Snow-Capped Mountains, Lake, Frame, Lenore Asbury, 8 1/2 x 4 1/2 In. 6575.00
Plaque, Tropics, Palm Trees, Vellum Glaze, Frame, E.T. Hurley, 1913, 8 x 4 1/4 In. 5875.00
Plaque, Winter Landscape, Frame, Lenore Asbury, 1913, 4 x 8 In. 5089.00
Plaque, Winter Landscape, Vellum Glaze, Frame, Carl Schmidt, 1916, 11 x 9 In. 10000.00
Sconce, Pink, Green Matte Glaze, 1920, 9 In. 590.00
Stein, George Wiedemann Brewing Co., Pewter Lid, 1/2 Liter 215.00
Stein, Harlequin Clown, Glazed, Pewter Lid, Sculpted Hops, McDonald, 1894, 6 In. 3000.00
Tankard, Indian, Brown, Mahogany Ground, Edith Felton, 1900, 7 1/2 x 6 1/2 In. 635.00
Teapot, Orange, Cameo Glaze, 5 5/8 In. 127.00
Tile, 3 White Geese, Verdant Landscape, c.1930, 5 3/4 In. 325.00
Tile, Faience, 3 Carved Seahorses, Circular Center, Oak Frame, 8 In. 3175.00
Tile, Stylized Yellow Rose, Green Leaves, Turquoise Matte Ground, Frame, 4 In. 540.00
Tray, Duck & Crest, Red Matte Glaze, Associated Harvard Clubs, 1929, 3 x 3 1/2 In. 210.00
Tray, Moth, Brown Matte Glaze, 3-Sided, 1929, 6 In. 120.00
Tray, Owl, Wine Madder Glaze, 1951, 4 1/2 x 6 1/2 In. 180.00
Tray, Peacock Feather, Pink & Green Matte Glaze, 1920, 6 1/2 In. 180.00
Tray, Rook, Ivory High Glaze, 1945, 4 1/2 x 8 In. 180.00
Trivet, Basket Of Flowers & Butterflies, Multicolored, Blue Ground, 1926, 6 In. 275.00
Trivet, Basket Of Flowers & Butterflies, Multicolored, Ivory Ground, Frame, 6 In. 305.00
Trivet, Dove, Purple, Pink, Green, Ivory Ground, Frame, 1928, 5 1/2 In. 275.00
Trivet, Potter At Wheel, Green Matte Glaze, 1935, 3 1/2 In. 240.00
Trivet, Woman With Umbrella, Pink, Yellow, Ivory Ground, Frame, 1930, 5 1/2 In. 275.00
Trivet, Yellow Bird On Brown Branches, Ivory Ground, 1929, 6 In. 205.00
Urn, Vellum, Bulbous, Ed Diers, 6 In. 670.00
Vase, Art Deco, Flowers, Vellum, Burgundy, Charles Todd, 1920, 10 x 4 In. 690.00
Vase, Art Deco, Yellow, Embossed, Oval, 1925, 3 3/4 x 4 1/4 In. 175.00
Vase, Arts & Crafts, Turquoise Matte, c.1927, 6 1/4 In. 200.00
Vase, Beaded Border, Mottled Blue Glaze, Egg Shape, Lobed, 1929, 5 In. 179.00
Vase, Berry, Purple Matte Glaze, Cobalt Blue Lined, Sallie Coyne, 1919, 10 x 4 1/2 In. 1610.00
Vase, Bird On Daffodils, Faceted Sides, Shouldered, 1894, 8 In. 575.00
Vase, Black Iris Glaze, Holly Branch, Oval, Sara Sax, c.1906, 6 1/4 x 4 In. .... ***ILLUS*** 4995.00
Vase, Blue Glaze, 1945, 6 1/2 In. 290.00
Vase, Blue, Dandelions, Shouldered, Katherine Elizabeth Ley, c.1945, 6 1/2 In. 645.00
Vase, Bluebells, Squared Shoulder, Mottled Mauve, K. Jones, 1923, 7 1/4 x 3 1/2 In. 920.00
Vase, Branches Of Berries, Leaves, Laura E. Lindeman, c.1899, 5 In. 410.00
Vase, Bud, Mottled, Green, Pink, 1914, 3 1/2 In. 210.00
Vase, Cereus Blooms, Buds, Yellow, Standard Glaze, Albert Valentien, 1894, 13 In. 4845.00
Vase, Cherries, Leaves, Emerald Green, 1920, 5 In. 86.00
Vase, Chrysanthemums, Green, Mahogany Ground, 7 x 4 In. 460.00
Vase, Chrysanthemums, Mahogany Glaze, Harriet Wilcox, 1891, 11 3/4 x 3 1/4 In. 520.00
Vase, Chrysanthemums, Stylized, Yellow Matte, M.H. McDonald, 1933, 7 1/2 x 4 1/2 In. 690.00
Vase, Clover, Iris Glaze, Irene Bishop, 1907, 6 1/2 x 2 1/2 In. 865.00
Vase, Compressed, Greek Key, Mottled, Green, Pink, 1914, 4 In. 300.00
Vase, Crocus, Iris Glaze, Gray, Black Ground, Carl Schmidt, 1908, 9 x 5 In. 978.00

Vase, Daffodils, Vellum, Shouldered, M.H. McDonald, 1919, 6 1/2 x 3 1/2 In. 920.00
Vase, Dragonflies, Burnt Orange, 1926, 6 1/8 In. 345.00
Vase, Egg Shape, Blue Jays, Branches, Flowers, c.1914, 12 1/2 In. 3485.00
Vase, Field Scene, Blue & Green Matte, Ed Diers, 7 In. 3500.00
Vase, Fishermen In Boat, Green Vellum Glaze, Sallie Coyne, 1912, 9 3/8 In. 2530.00
Vase, Flower & Leaf, Yellow Matte Glaze, 1921, 8 3/4 In. 450.00
Vase, Flower Band, Crosshatched Borders, Green Celadon Glaze, 1945, 6 In. 95.00
Vase, Flower, Embossed, Incised Panels, Blue Matte Ground, 1919, 6 1/8 x 3 In. 290.00
Vase, Flowers, Blue & Pink Tinted Glaze, Shouldered, 1920, 10 In. 658.00
Vase, Flowers, Branches, 2 Handles, Howard Altman, 1902, 6 In. 520.00
Vase, Flowers, Brown Branches, Leaves, Mottled Maroon, Blue, 6 x 2 1/4 In. 635.00
Vase, Flowers, Clusters, Maroon, Lined Artwork, Yellow Matte, 8 3/4 x 5 In. 1610.00
Vase, Flowers, Horizontal Ribs, Mottled, 1920, 2 1/4 In. 150.00
Vase, Flowers, Mottled Pink & Blue Ground, Baluster, c.1944, 12 1/2 In. 660.00
Vase, Flowers, Turquoise, Wax Mat, Mottled Cobalt Blue, 1919, 7 1/4 x 5 In. 800.00
Vase, Forget-Me-Nots, Carrie Steinle, 1900, 6 x 4 In. 430.00
Vase, Forget-Me-Nots, Stylized, Elizabeth Barrett, 1923, 6 3/4 x 4 In. 805.00
Vase, Geometric Band, Mottled, Pink, Green, Slender Cylinder, 1909, 5 1/2 In. 170.00
Vase, Geometric Band, Pink, Egg Shape, Shouldered, 1921, 5 1/2 In. 170.00
Vase, Geometric, Green Matte Glaze, Shouldered, William McDonald, 1902, 4 In. 270.00
Vase, Gothic Arches, Pink, Cylindrical, Tapered, 1917, 6 1/4 In. 160.00
Vase, Greek Key, Mottled, Cylindrical, Tapered, 1923, 5 3/4 In. 198.00
Vase, Green, Pink, Egg Shape, Shouldered, 3 Loop Handles, 1934, 5 1/4 In. 265.00
Vase, House, Barn, Vellum Glaze, Logo, Fred Rothenbusch, 1923, 7 7/8 In. 3910.00
Vase, Hydrangea, Bending Down, M.H. McDonald, 1936, 6 1/2 x 5 1/2 In. 865.00
Vase, Iris Bloom, Bud, Vellum Glaze, Carl Schmidt, 1913, 10 1/4 In. 5750.00
Vase, Irises, Textured Glazes, Elizabeth Lincoln, 1920, 22 5/8 In. 9775.00
Vase, Ivy, Mauve Matte, c.1928, 14 In. 560.00
Vase, Jewel Porcelain, Blue Trefoils, Ivory Ground, Jens Jensen, c.1945, 5 3/4 In. 825.00
Vase, Jewel Porcelain, Persian Floral, Arthur Conant, Oval, 1921, 6 1/2 x 3 In. 1528.00
Vase, Leaves & Berries, Flowers, Oval, Sallie Coyne, 1930, 5 3/4 x 5 1/2 In. 1095.00
Vase, Mint Green Matte Glaze, 3 Handles, Marked, 1924, 5 In. 290.00
Vase, Mottled Pink & Green Matte Glaze, Swollen, 1912, 8 In. 330.00
Vase, Peacock Feather, Blue Matte Glaze, Tapered, 1929, 9 In. 540.00
Vase, Peacock Feather, Dark Blue Matte Glaze, Tapered, 1920, 9 1/4 In. 450.00
Vase, Pink Berries, Brown, Blue Ground, Vellum, Egg Shape, Vera Tischler, 7 x 4 In. 705.00
Vase, Pink Matte Glaze, Blue Glaze, Embossed, 1938, 6 1/3 x 3 In. 175.00
Vase, Pink, Yellow Morning Glory, Blue Ground, Vellum, Baluster, 1925, 6 x 4 1/2 In. 1060.00
Vase, Purple, Red Irises, Relief, Yellow Ground, Baluster, Matt Daly, 11 In. 1765.00
Vase, Red, Blue Plums, Mauve Ground, Vellum, Baluster, Rothenbusch, 6 x 3 1/2 In. 940.00
Vase, Sailboats, Water, Gray To Peach Glaze, Oval, 5 3/4 x 3 3/4 In. 2070.00
Vase, Scenic Vellum, Hills, Pink Sky, Baluster, Sallie Coyne, c.1916, 11 In. .... *ILLUS* 1765.00
Vase, Scenic Vellum, Trees In Field, Painted, Ed Diers, c.1922, 5 1/2 x 3 1/4 In. 1175.00
Vase, Swan, Lake, Vellum Glaze, Carl Schmidt, 1904, 6 7/8 In. 8330.00
Vase, Sweet Peas, Vines, Leaves, Baluster, c.1906, 7 1/2 In. 1075.00
Vase, Trees, Lake Shore, Arts & Craft, Vellum Glaze, Kataro Shirayamadani, 1911, 15 In. 8050.00
Vase, Trees, Meadow, Egg Shape, c.1919, 13 In. 3100.00
Vase, Tulip & Flowers, Bending Down, Green Leaves, Delia Workum, 1927, 5 1/4 x 5 In. 920.00
Vase, Tulips, Green Ground, Egg Shape, Shouldered, Sturgis Laurence, 1901, 8 1/4 In. 1885.00
Vase, Tulips, Orange, Elizabeth Lincoln, 1903, 8 1/2 In. 489.00
Vase, Turquoise Matte Glaze, Embossed, c.1925, 9 1/2 In. 380.00
Vase, Turquoise Matte Glaze, Impressed Rooks, 5-Sided, c.1927, 5 In. 325.00
Vase, Water Lily, Blossoms, Iris Glaze, Constance Baker, 1901, 9 x 3 3/4 In. 2415.00
Vase, Wild Roses, Burgundy, Green Branches, Thorns, Leaves, Pronounced Lip, 5 x 7 In. 1035.00
Vase, Woman's Face, Fan, Blue, 1946, 7 1/2 In. 100.00
Vase, Yellow Matte Glaze, 1928, 5 In. 160.00

RORSTRAND was established near Stockholm, Sweden, in 1726. By the nineteenth century they were making English-style earthenware, bone china, porcelain, ironstone china, and majolica. The company is still working. The three crown mark has been used since 1884.

Vase, Egg Shape, Slender, Elongated Neck, Mottled, Carl-Harry Stalhane, Late 1950s, 9 In. 339.00
Vase, Tapered, Brown, Stoneware, Carl-Harry Stalhane, Late 1950s, 16 1/2 In. 710.00
Vase, Vertical Lines, Mottled Turquoise & Red, Stoneware, Gunnar Nylund, 10 3/4 In. 340.00

ROSALINE, see Steuben category.

ROSE CANTON china is similar to Rose Mandarin and Rose Medallion, except no people or birds are pictured in the decoration. It was made in China during the nineteenth and twentieth centuries in greens, pinks, and other colors.

Dish, Shrimp, Celadon Ground, 1800s, 11 In. 147.00
Pitcher, 3 1/4 In. 155.00
Plate Warmer, Late 1800s, 3 x 10 1/4 In. 400.00
Platter, Oval, Late 1800s, 12 1/4 x 9 1/4 In. 300.00
Teapot, Cover, 1800s, 6 1/2 In. 489.00

ROSE MANDARIN china is similar to Rose Canton and Rose Medallion. If the panels in the design picture only people and not birds, it is called Rose Mandarin.

Bowl, Mandarin Figures In Garden, Flower Panels, Wooden Stand, 10 In. 646.00
Bowl, Mandarin Landscape Decoration, Late 18th Century, 10 1/4 In. 1380.00
Bowl, Underplate, Bamboo Sides, Mandarin Scene, Orange Peel, 9 In. & 11 In. 546.00
Box, Cover, Birds, Scenes, Gilt Accents, Orange Peel Glaze, 2 1/2 x 7 1/2 In. 230.00
Bulb Pot, Multicolored Figures, 6 Paneled Sides, 5 Holes, 9 1/4 x 7 1/2 In., Pair 2938.00
Charger, Gold Ring, Alternating Scenes, Birds, Roses, 13 1/2 In. 200.00
Garden Seat, Enamel Decoration, Mandarin Warriors, Flowers, Late 1800s, 18 In. 705.00
Platter, 2 Figures, Landscape, Butterflies, Flowers, Cavetto Border, 11 3/4 x 9 In. 550.00
Platter, Floral Border, Gilt Accents, 12 x 15 In. 1495.00
Punch Bowl, Court Scenes In Reserve, Gilt & Red Glaze, Footed, 5 x 12 In. 2235.00
Punch Bowl, Figural, 20th Century, 17 1/2 In. 1535.00
Punch Bowl, Round Reserve, Courtyard Scene, Landscape, 1800s, 6 x 13 In. 2115.00
Tray, Bronze Stand, 6 3/4 x 12 In. 1610.00
Tray, Figures, Building, Oval, Lobe, c.1825, 8 3/4 x 10 1/4 In. 750.00
Vase, Applied Gilded Salamanders, Ruffled Mouths, 15 In., Pair 1725.00
Vase, Bottle Shape, Figural, Flowers, 19th Century, 17 In. 1535.00
Vase, Courtyard Scenes, Various Images, Gilt Ground, 36 1/2 In. 545.00
Vase, Foo Dogs, Temple, Mandarin Scene, Pheasants & Butterflies, 23 In. 520.00
Vase, Green Fitzhugh, Iron Red, 19th Century, 7 1/4 In. 700.00
Vase, Mythical Creatures On Neck, Mandarin Scenes, Applied Gilt, 42 In. 632.00
Vase, Ruffled Top, Applied Dragon, 14 In., Pair 9775.00
Washbowl, Interior Design, Floral Sprays, 16 1/2 In. 1150.00

ROSE MEDALLION china was made in China during the nineteenth and twentieth centuries. It is a distinctive design with four or more panels of decoration around a central medallion that includes a bird or a peony. The panels show birds and people. The background is a design of tree peonies and leaves. Pieces are colored in greens, pinks, and other colors. It is similar to Rose Canton and Rose Mandarin.

Bowl, 2 Flower & 2 People Reserves, Scalloped Border, c.1840, 9 In. 175.00
Bowl, Butterfly, Bird, Flowers, Scalloped, Pierced, 1800s, 10 In. 413.00
Bowl, Ormolu Mounted, Gilt Bronze Frame & Stand, 8 In. 590.00
Bowl, Ormolu Mounted, Trumpet Stem, Late 1800s, 10 In. 1410.00
Bowl, Scalloped Rim, 19th Century, 2 1/4 x 9 In. 175.00
Box, Cover, 1800s, 3 x 7 x 3 1/2 In. 520.00
Box, Cover, Birds, Flowers, Butterflies, Divided Interior, 2 1/2 x 7 1/2 x 3 1/2 In. 546.00
Candlestick, c.1850, 8 In., Pair 700.00
Candlestick, Figures, Courtyard, Birds, Flowers, Canton, Late 1800s, 8 In., Pair 590.00
Censer, Famille Verte, 8-Sided, Flower Medallion Reserves, Waisted Base, 12 In., Pair 1040.00
Container, Figures, Flowers, Square, c.1840, 5 1/2 x 4 In. 645.00
Dish, Square, c.1840, 9 In. 527.00
Jar, Cover, c.1840, 5 x 5 1/2 In. 410.00
Jardiniere, 1800s, 16 In. 1380.00

Jardiniere, Figures, Court, Flowers, 1800s, 13 x 13 1/2 In. 940.00
Jardiniere, On Stand, c.1850, 9 1/2 x 7 x 9 In. 820.00
Pitcher, Birds, Mountain Village, Molded Leaf Handle End, 6 3/4 In. 290.00
Plate, 1800s, 8 In., 6 Piece 380.00
Plate, Butterflies, Roses, Birds, Flowers 10 1/4 In., 6 Piece 140.00
Plate, Figures, Flowers, 8 In., 8 Piece 470.00
Plate, Serving, Butterflies, Roses, Birds, Fruits, c.1960, 10 3/8 In., 2 Piece 50.00
Plate Warmer, 3 x 10 1/4 In. 400.00
Platter, 19th Century, 17 1/2 In. 590.00
Platter, Bat, Fruit, Butterfly, Flowers, Oval, 1800s, 16 1/2 In. 235.00
Platter, Oval, People, Flowers, Birds, 18 1/4 x 14 3/4 In. 1080.00
Punch Bowl, 13 In. 920.00
Punch Bowl, 1800s, 16 In. 765.00
Punch Bowl, Enameled, 19 Century, 13 1/2 In. 2232.00
Punch Bowl, Flowers, Birds, Figures, 6 1/4 x 14 3/4 In. 1165.00
Punch Bowl, Flowers, Fruits, Butterflies, 1800s, 15 3/4 In. 1175.00
Punch Bowl, Flowers, People, 11 1/2 In. 880.00
Punch Bowl, People, Birds, Flowers, c.1850, 13 1/2 x 5 1/2 In. 1440.00
Sauceboat, On Stand, c.1900, 8 In. 175.00
Serving Dish, Oval Outline Design, Panels Of Figures, 13 In. 610.00
Shrimp Dish, Flowers, People, 1800s, 10 1/2 In. 440.00
Tea Caddy, Figures, Flowers, Square, 3 x 2 1/2 In. 175.00
Tea Set, Teapot, Tea Cups, Saucers, Fitted Wicker Basket, c.1930 .... 200.00
Tea Tray, Quatrefoil Shape, Flowers, Bats, Butterflies, 1800s, 17 3/4 In. 1765.00
Teapot, Cover, 1800s, 2 3/4 In. 290.00
Teapot, Cover, 1800s, 5 3/4 In. 835.00
Teapot, Cover, Bell Shape, 1800s, 4 1/2 In. 520.00
Teapot, Cover, Dome, c.1850, 8 1/4 In. 805.00
Teapot, Strawberry Finial, 6 x 9 In. 750.00
Teapot, Wire Handles, 1800s, 5 In. 125.00
Tureen, Cover, c.1840, 4 x 8 x 9 In. 265.00
Umbrella Stand, Cylindrical, Fluted Sides, Figures, Courtyard, 1800s, 24 1/2 In. 1998.00
Vase, Figures, Courtyard, Flowers, Fruits, Butterflies, Canton, c.1850, 9 3/4 In., Pair 1175.00
Vase, Figures, Courtyard, Flowers, Fruits, Butterflies, Canton, c.1850, 13 In., Pair 3819.00
Vase, Foo Dogs, Fired Gold, 10 x 4 In., Pair 700.00
Vase, Foo Dogs, Scalloped, Flared Lip, Gilt Highlights, 1800s, 24 1/2 In., Pair 3820.00
Washbowl, Multicolored Enamel Decorated, Flower, Figure Panels, c.1870, 16 In. 470.00

ROSE O'NEILL, see Kewpie category.

ROSE TAPESTRY porcelain was made by the Royal Bayreuth factory of Tettau, Germany, during the late nineteenth century. The surface of the porcelain was pressed against a coarse fabric while it was still damp, and the impressions remained on the finished porcelain. It looks and feels like a textured cloth. Very skillful reproductions are being made that even include a variation of the Royal Bayreuth mark, so be careful when buying.

Creamer, Pink, Yellow & White Roses, Blue Mark, 3 1/4 In. 425.00
Dresser Box, Cover, Clam Shape, Roses, Royal Bayreuth Green Mark, c.1919, 5 3/4 In. 475.00
Sugar & Creamer, Small Roses 335.00
Vase, Pink Roses, Blue Mark, 6 In. 350.00

ROSEMEADE Pottery of Wahpeton, North Dakota, worked from 1940 to 1961. The pottery was operated by Laura A. Taylor and her husband, R.I. Hughes. The company was also known as the Wahpeton Pottery Company. Art pottery and commercial wares were made.

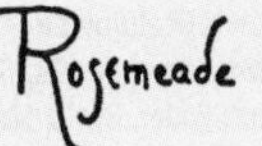

Ashtray, Chicken Dekalb Chix 35.00
Ashtray, Fin & Feather, c.1940s, 7 In. 1880.00
Ashtray, Trout, Green, Figural Trout On Rim, 5 In. 350.00
Candleholder, Square, Brown, Label, 1 5/8 x 3 1/4 x 3 1/4 In., Pair 45.00
Figure, Bird In Tree, Beige, Pink, Green, 6 1/2 In. 125.00
Flower Holder, Bowl, Heron, 8 1/4-In. Bowl, 6 3/4-In. Heron 105.00

Flower Holder, Frog, Blue, 2 3/4 x 3 1/4 In. 40.00
Pitcher, Pink, Citizens State Bank, Big Lake, Minn., 4 In. 40.00
Plaque, Brook Trout, 3 1/2 x 6 In. 205.00
Plaque, Flickertail, 5 1/4 In. 1100.00
Salt & Pepper, Coyote, Howling, 3 1/4 x 2 3/4 In. 275.00
Salt & Pepper, Duck, Black, 2 1/2 In. & 2 1/4 In. 82.00
Salt & Pepper, Flickertail, Tan, 2 1/4 In. 95.00
Salt & Pepper, Mallard Ducks, 2 1/2 In. 75.00
Salt & Pepper, Pheasant, Cork, Label, 3 In. 86.00
Salt & Pepper, Skunk, 3 x 3 3/4 In. 69.00
Spoon Rest, Prickly Pear Cactus, Flower 45.00
Sugar & Creamer, Blue, 2 1/2-In. Sugar, 3 1/4-In. Creamer ....25.00 to 50.00
Tile, Walleyed Pike Les Kouba, Decal, Wooden Frame 75.00
Toothpick, Bowl, Pheasant, Oval, 4 In. 55.00
Wall Pocket, Flower, Blue, Pink Shading, 4 In. 40.00

ROSENTHAL porcelain was made at the factory established in Selb, Bavaria, in 1880. The factory is still making fine-quality tablewares and figurines. A series of Christmas plates was made from 1910. Other limited edition plates have been made since 1971. In 1998 Rosenthal was acquired by the Waterford Wedgwood Group.

Charger, Naked Maiden, Lily Pond, Swans, Pate-Sur-Pate Style, c.1907, 13 1/2 In. 1440.00
Figurine, Ballerina, Green Costume, Aqua Slippers, Signed, 1940s, 9 x 9 1/2 In. 650.00
Figurine, Dog, St. Bernard, Lying Down, Gray, White, F. Diller, 11 3/4 In. 295.00
Figurine, Dog, St. Bernard, Tan, White, F. Diller, 1900s, 11 3/4 In. 355.00
Figurine, Dog, St. Bernard, Tan, White, F. Diller, 1900s, 16 1/4 In. 590.00
Figurine, Spanish Dancer, Deco, 16 1/2 x 9 x 5 In. 2000.00
Figurine, Woman, Blue Draped Skirt, Outstretched Arms, 9 1/2 In. 450.00
Group, Male & Female Lion, M. Herm Fritz, 12 x 19 1/2 In. 1287.00
Plate Set, Ivory, Gold Etched Borders, Early 20th Century, 10 1/2 In., 9 Piece 385.00
Teapot, Cover, Courtship, Pompadour Shape, Ivory, Roses, Gold Trim, 7 1/2 In. 475.00

ROSEVILLE Pottery Company was organized in Roseville, Ohio, in 1890. Another plant was opened in Zanesville, Ohio, in 1898. Many types of pottery were made until 1954. Early wares include Sgraffito, Olympic, and Rozane. Later lines were often made with molded decorations, especially flowers and fruit. Most pieces are marked *Roseville*. Many reproductions made in China have been offered for sale the past few years.

Apple Blossom, Basket, Pink, 2 Handles, 8 3/8 In. 150.00
Apple Blossom, Basket, Pink, 7 1/2 x 12 In. 180.00
Apple Blossom, Jardiniere, Pedestal, Blue, 8 In. 940.00
Apple Blossom, Jardiniere, Pedestal, Blue, 10 In. 645.00
Apple Blossom, Vase, 2 Handles, 10 3/8 In. 150.00
Artcraft, Jardiniere, Pedestal, Mottled Green, Blue Matte, 9 3/4 x 14 In. 2070.00
Aztec, Vase, Blue, Squeezebag, 11 In. 390.00
Baneda, Candlestick, Pink, 5 x 4 In. 400.00
Baneda, Urn, Pink, Cylindrical Neck, Handles, 6 1/2 x 4 In. 440.00
Baneda, Vase, Green, 2 Scrolled Handles At Shoulder, 7 1/2 x 5 3/4 In. .... *ILLUS* 499.00
Baneda, Vase, Green, Flared, Footed, Handles At Bottom, 7 In. 840.00
Baneda, Vase, Green, Shape, 12 In. 1680.00
Baneda, Vase, Orange, Brown, Green Matte, Pumpkin Style, 6 1/4 x 7 In. 690.00
Baneda, Vase, Orange, Brown, Green Matte, Pumpkin Style, 9 1/4 x 5 In. 920.00
Baneda, Vase, Orange, Brown, Green Matte, Pumpkin Style, Handles, 5 1/4 x 4 1/2 In. 460.00
Baneda, Vase, Pink, Bulbous, Stand-Up Rim, Handles, 6 3/4 In. 410.00
Baneda, Vase, Pink, Bulbous, Stand-Up Rim, Handles, 9 In. 940.00
Baneda, Vase, Pink, Footed, Handles, 9 In. 840.00
Bank, Pig, 4 x 5 1/2 In. 260.00
Bittersweet, Jardiniere, Pedestal, Green, Marked, 24 1/2 x 10 In. 660.00
Blackberry, Bowl, Brown, Green Matte, 3 1/4 x 7 1/2 In. 345.00
Blackberry, Bowl, Rectangular, Faceted Sides, Handles, 3 1/2 x 9 3/4 In. 352.00

Roseville, Baneda, Vase, Green, 2 Scrolled Handles At Shoulder, 7 1/2 x 5 3/4 In.

Roseville, Columbine, Vase, Blue Flowers, 10 In.

Blackberry, Candlestick, 5 In., Pair ... 325.00
Blackberry, Vase, Bulbous, Handles, 8 In. ... 315.00 to 570.00
Blackberry, Vase, Handle, 10 1/4 x 7 In. ... 1035.00
Blackberry, Vase, Handle, Black Mark, 5 1/4 In. ... 288.00
Blackberry, Vase, Handles, 6 In. ... 390.00
Blackberry, Vase, Matte, Oval, 6 1/4 x 5 1/2 In. ... 460.00
Blackberry, Vase, Squat, 4 In. ... 259.00
Bushberry, Ewer, Russet, 10 3/8 In. ... 175.00
Bushberry, Jardiniere, Pedestal, Blue, 8 In. ... 1293.00
Bushberry, Pitcher, Ocher Brown Matte Ground, Handle, 10 x 6 In. ... 230.00
Bushberry, Sand Jar, Blue, Footed, Handles, 14 In. ... 880.00
Carnelian I, Vase, Mottled Green & Pink Matte Glaze, Large Shoulder, 13 1/2 In. ... 455.00
Carnelian II, Vase, Foamy Blue & Green, Bulbous, Collared Rim, Handles, 12 In. ... 470.00
Carnelian II, Vase, Green, Purple, Handles, 5 In. ... 90.00
Carnelian II, Vase, Handles, Blue, Green Matte Glaze, 10 1/4 In. ... 518.00
Carnelian II, Vase, Handles, Green Over Rose Glaze, 7 1/8 In. ... 315.00
Carnelian II, Vase, Red Brown, 10 In. ... 310.00
Carnelian II, Wall Pocket, Blue, 8 1/8 In. ... 460.00
Cherry Blossom, Jardiniere, Pedestal, Brown, 11 In. ... 1175.00
Cherry Blossom, Vase, Pink, 4 1/4 x 6 In. ... 345.00
Cherry Blossom, Vase, Pink, Ovoid, Ribbed Bottom, Collared Rim, Handles, 10 1/2 In. ... 825.00
Chloron, Pitcher, Green, 7 1/2 In. ... 440.00
Clemana, Vase, Blue Matte, Globular, 6 1/4 x 7 In. ... 865.00
Clemana, Vase, Brown, Bulbous, Marked, 9 1/2 In. ... 510.00
Columbine, Vase, Blue Flowers, 10 In. ... *ILLUS* 300.00
Cosmos, Jardiniere, Pedestal, Blue, 10 In. ... 1175.00
Dahlrose, Jardiniere, Pedestal, 10 1/2 In. ... 646.00
Dahlrose, Jardiniere, Pedestal, 30 x 14 In. ... 1320.00
Dahlrose, Vase, 8 1/8 In. ... 178.00
Dahlrose, Vase, Bulbous, Paper Label, 10 In. ... 660.00
Dahlrose, Wall Pocket, 10 1/8 In. ... 180.00
Dahlrose, Wall Pocket, Embossed Ivory, Ocher Matte, Handles, 6 3/4 x 8 In. ... 290.00
Dawn, Vase, Green Matte Glaze, Logo, 6 1/4 In. ... 130.00
Dealer's Sign, Scrolled Ivory Letters, Blue Ground, 4 1/2 x 8 In. ... 1765.00
Dealer's Sign, Scrolled Ivory Letters, Pink Ground, 4 1/2 x 8 In. ... 3760.00
Della Robbia, Mug, Dutch Girls, Carved, Multitoned Green Glaze, Signed, 4 In. ... 1135.00
Della Robbia, Teapot, Domestic Scene, Green, Brown Glaze, Wafer Mark, 6 x 7 1/2 In. ... 2030.00
Della Robbia, Teapot, Stylized Flowers, Carved, 2-Tone Green Glaze, Wafer Mark, 7 In. ... 3585.00
Della Robbia, Vase, Incised Rocky Trail Through Forest, Tapered, 10 3/4 In. ... 3525.00
Dogwood II, Jardiniere, Green, Folded-In Rim, 11 In. ... 205.00
Dogwood II, Jardiniere, Pedestal, Green, 28 In. ... 499.00
Donatello, Jardinere, Early 20th Century, 11 1/2 In. ... 120.00
Egypto, Basket, Hanging, Chains ... 140.00
Egypto, Ewer, Green Matte, Mottled, 12 1/2 In. ... 508.00
Egypto, Vase, Aladdin Lamp, Green, Rozane, 4 1/2 In. ... 380.00
Falline, Vase, Blue, Bulbous, Handles, 8 1/4 x 8 1/4 In. ... 2115.00
Falline, Vase, Blue, Bulbous, Ribbed Neck, Scrolled Handles, 7 1/4 In. ... 1175.00

Falline, Vase, Blue, Oval, Stepped Rim, 15 1/2 In. 1880.00
Falline, Vase, Blue, Ribbed Base, Tapered Neck, Handles, 9 1/2 In. 2820.00
Falline, Vase, Blue, Squat, Looped Handles, 6 1/4 x 6 1/2 In. 645.00
Falline, Vase, Blue, Tapered, Handles At Rim, 13 1/2 In. 2938.00
Falline, Vase, Brown, Green, Footed, Handles, 6 In. 330.00
Falline, Vase, Green Matte, Bulbous, Handle, 7 1/2 x 5 1/2 In. 980.00
Ferella, Bowl, Flower Frog, Brown, Flared, 4 1/4 x 10 In. 529.00
Ferella, Planter, Underplate, Red, Pierced, Flared Rim, 5 1/2 x 6 1/2 In. 1060.00
Ferella, Vase, Brown, Spattered, Matte, Chalice Style, 9 1/4 x 4 In. 690.00
Ferella, Vase, Red, Handles, Bulbous, 8 1/4 x 7 In. 1095.00
Ferella, Vase, Red, Maroon Matte, Genie Bottle, 4 1/4 x 6 In. 575.00
Ferella, Vase, Red, Pinched Waist, Handles, 9 1/2 x 6 1/4 In. 1410.00
Florentine, Vase, Brown, c.1924, 8 1/2 In. 80.00
Flower Art, Vase, Green, 15 In. 295.00
Foxglove, Vase, Blue, Handles, 4 1/4 In. 60.00
Foxglove, Vase, Green, Handles, Footed, 15 In. 470.00
Freesia, Basket, Blue, Logo, 8 1/4 In. 150.00
Freesia, Jardiniere Stand, Blue, 17 In. 235.00
Freesia, Jardiniere, Blue, Embossed Logo, 13 In. 265.00
Freesia, Jardiniere, Pedestal, Brown, Marked, 25 x 12 In. 900.00
Freesia, Tea Set, White, Blue Matte, 3 Piece 288.00
Freesia, Vase, Brown, Green, Urn Shape, Handles, Footed, 8 1/4 x 7 In. 120.00
Fuchsia, Pitcher, Brown, Ball Shape, Ice Lip, 8 1/4 In. 176.00
Fuchsia, Vase, Blue, Stretched Handles, 18 In. 765.00
Fuchsia, Vase, Green, 6 3/8 In. 105.00
Fudji, Vase, Art Nouveau, Square, Tapered, Twisted, Squeezebag Poppies, 9 3/4 In. 2115.00
Fudji, Vase, Art Nouveau, Tapered, Slightly Bulbous Neck, 9 In. 2000.00
Fudji, Vase, Pinched Waist, Squeezebag, Stylized Flowers, 10 1/4 In. 2000.00
Fujiyama, Vase, Gourd Shape, Brown Blossoms, Green Leaves, 11 1/2 In. 999.00
Futura, Basket, Hanging, Flared, Leaves, Brown, 8 In. 360.00
Futura, Jardiniere, Brown, Green, Stylized Leaves, Broad Form, Footed, Handles, 7 x 11 In. 270.00
Futura, Vase, Blue, Blue Rays, Rectangular, Flat Sides, 5 In. 175.00
Futura, Vase, Blue, Spherical, Balloon Decorations, Buttressed Base, 8 1/2 In. .... *ILLUS* 1060.00
Futura, Vase, Brown, 4 Bulbs On Footed Base, Flared, 12 In. 780.00
Futura, Vase, Brown, Green, Blue, Footed, 8 1/2 In. 658.00
Futura, Vase, Bud, Tan, 6 In. 250.00
Futura, Vase, Green Blue, Bulbous, Stepped Neck, 12 In. 410.00
Futura, Vase, Green High Glaze, 4-Tiered Neck, Handles, 9 In. 780.00
Futura, Vase, Green, Bulbous, Stepped Neck, 10 In. 840.00
Futura, Vase, Green, Gray, Star Shape, Stepped Foot, 8 In. 590.00
Futura, Vase, Orange Stepped Neck, Green Squat Base, Angular Handles, 7 In. 499.00
Futura, Vase, Pink & Green, Bulbous, Stepped Neck, Paper Label, 8 In. .... 480.00 to 598.00
Futura, Vase, Pink, Green Chevron Design, 4-Sided, Footed, 7 In. 440.00
Futura, Vase, Pink, Purple, Green, Twisted, 8 In. .... 270.00 to 420.00
Futura, Vase, Ribbed, Pink & Green, Footed, 8 In. 360.00
Futura, Vase, Rose Matte, Twisted, 6-Sided, 8 x 4 In. 805.00
Futura, Wall Pocket, Green, Yellow, On Brown, Handles, 8 1/2 In. 420.00
Gardenia, Jardiniere, Pedestal, Gray, 10 In. 590.00
Imperial II, Vase, Blue, Collared Rim, Ivory Stylized Waves, 10 x 5 1/2 In. 1175.00
Imperial II, Vase, Frothy Turquoise, Blue Band & Rim, 7 3/4 x 6 In. 1765.00
Imperial II, Vase, Irregular Incised Bands, Mottled Pink & Blue, 6 x 6 1/2 In. 1410.00
Imperial II, Vase, Mottled Yellow & Lavender, Ribbed, Tapered, 6 1/2 In. 235.00
Imperial II, Vase, Rounded, Rectangles Around Mouth, Yellow Glaze, 5 1/2 In. 865.00
Imperial II, Vase, Sea Form Green, Blue, Barrel Shape, Ribbed Band, 7 1/2 x 6 1/2 In. 750.00
Imperial II, Vase, Turquoise, Yellow Design Around Rim, 7 1/2 In. 600.00
Imperial II, Vase, Yellow Flambe Over Blue, Flared, Ribbed, 9 1/4 x 4 1/2 In. 940.00
Jonquil, Basket, Arched Handle, 6 x 7 3/4 In. 235.00
Jonquil, Candlestick, 4 1/2 In., Pair 355.00
Jonquil, Vase, Brown, Green, Tapered Neck, Flared Rim, Handles, 8 1/4 In. 355.00
Jonquil, Vase, Brown, Ocher Matte, 12 1/4 x 9 1/2 In. 978.00
Jonquil, Vase, Bulbous, Squat, Pinched Rim, 4 1/2 x 6 1/4 In. 265.00

Juvenile, Bowl, Chicks, 4 Chicks, 4 1/4 In. Diam. .... 40.00 to 65.00
Juvenile, Bowl, Chicks, 5 Chicks, 2 3/4 x 6 1/4 In. 105.00
Juvenile, Bowl, Chicks, 5 Chicks, 5 1/2 In. 70.00
Juvenile, Bowl, Duck With Hat, 6 In. .... 20.00 to 45.00
Juvenile, Bowl, Rabbit, 5 1/2 In. 25.00
Juvenile, Bowl, Rabbit, 6 In. .... 12.00 to 40.00
Juvenile, Bowl, Rabbits, 4 1/4 In. 75.00
Juvenile, Chamber Pot, Chicks, No Lid 135.00
Juvenile, Coffee Cup, Skinny Puppy, No. 8 .... 65.00
Juvenile, Creamer, Bear, Ivory, 4 x 4 1/2 In. 430.00
Juvenile, Creamer, Chicks, 3 In. .... 40.00 to 90.00
Juvenile, Creamer, Chicks, 4 In. .... 40.00 to 105.00
Juvenile, Creamer, Chicks, Side Pour, 3 In. 17.00
Juvenile, Creamer, Dog, 3 1/2 In. .... 20.00 to 55.00
Juvenile, Creamer, Duck With Hat, 3 1/2 In. .... 75.00 to 155.00
Juvenile, Creamer, Fat Puppy, 3 1/2 In. 180.00
Juvenile, Creamer, Rabbit, 3 1/2 In. .... 30.00 to 40.00
Juvenile, Creamer, Rabbit, 4 In. 65.00
Juvenile, Creamer, Rabbit, Side Pour, 3 In. 85.00
Juvenile, Creamer, Rabbit, Squat, 2 1/2 In. 120.00
Juvenile, Cup & Saucer, Chicks, 2 x 4 3/4 In. 115.00
Juvenile, Cup & Saucer, Duck With Hat, 2 1/2 x 5 In. 135.00
Juvenile, Cup & Saucer, Duck, With Boots 155.00
Juvenile, Cup & Saucer, Rabbit, 2 1/4 x 5 1/2 In. 150.00
Juvenile, Cup, Chick, Yellow, Handle, 2 1/4 x 4 In. 175.00
Juvenile, Cup, Dog, 2 1/4 In. 100.00
Juvenile, Cup, Rabbit, Ivory, Handle, 3 1/2 x 4 1/4 In. 200.00
Juvenile, Cup, Sunbonnet Girl, 2 1/4 In. 20.00
Juvenile, Dish, Feeding, Chicks, Baby's Plate, 6 1/2 In. .... 65.00 to 135.00
Juvenile, Dish, Feeding, Chicks, Baby's Plate, 7 In. 60.00
Juvenile, Dish, Feeding, Chicks, Baby's Plate, 8 In. 50.00
Juvenile, Dish, Feeding, Chicks, Baby's Plate, Rolled Edge, 7 3/4 In. 40.00
Juvenile, Dish, Feeding, Duck With Hat, Orange Bands, 8 In. .... 130.00 to 170.00
Juvenile, Dish, Feeding, Nursery Rhyme, Baby Bunting, Pigs, Baby's Plate, 8 In. .... 30.00 to 80.00
Juvenile, Dish, Feeding, Nursery Rhyme, Hickory Dickory Dock, Baby's Plate, 7 In. 40.00
Juvenile, Dish, Feeding, Nursery Rhyme, Hickory Dickory Dock, Baby's Plate, 8 In. 75.00
Juvenile, Dish, Feeding, Nursery Rhyme, Higgledy Piggledy, 8 In. 75.00
Juvenile, Dish, Feeding, Nursery Rhyme, Little Bo Peep, Baby's Plate, 8 In. 40.00
Juvenile, Dish, Feeding, Nursery Rhyme, Little Jack Horner, Baby's Plate, 8 In. 65.00
Juvenile, Dish, Feeding, Nursery Rhyme, Old Woman, Baby's Plate, 8 In. .... 55.00 to 110.00
Juvenile, Dish, Feeding, Nursery Rhyme, Tom The Piper's Son, 8 In. 10.00
Juvenile, Dish, Feeding, Nursery Rhyme, Tom The Piper's Son, Baby's Plate, 7 In. 70.00
Juvenile, Dish, Feeding, Rabbit, Turquoise Bands, 8 In. 150.00
Juvenile, Dish, Feeding, Sitting Rabbit, Baby's Plate, 8 In. 70.00
Juvenile, Dish, Feeding, Sunbonnet Girl, 7 In. 55.00
Juvenile, Eggcup, Chicks, 4 In. 60.00
Juvenile, Eggcup, Rabbit, 3 In. 190.00
Juvenile, Mug, Chick, Yellow, Ivory, Handle, 3 1/2 x 4 1/2 In. 145.00
Juvenile, Mug, Chicks, 2 Handles, 3 In. 145.00
Juvenile, Mug, Chicks, 3 In. .... 75.00 to 90.00
Juvenile, Mug, Dog, 2 Handles, 3 In. 110.00
Juvenile, Mug, Duck With Hat, 3 In. .... 40.00 to 90.00
Juvenile, Mug, Rabbit, 3 In. 30.00
Juvenile, Mug, Skinny Puppy, No. 5 .... 85.00
Juvenile, Mug, Sunbonnet Girl, Double Handle, Ivory, 3 x 5 In. 230.00
Juvenile, Plate, Santa Claus, 8 In. 400.00
Juvenile, Potty, Rabbit, 3 1/2 x 7 In. 235.00
Juvenile, Saucer, Chicks, 5 1/2 In. 35.00
Juvenile, Sugar, Cover, Chicks, Art Deco 325.00
Juvenile, Teapot, Cover, Chicks, Art Deco 650.00
Lonhuda, Vase, Pillow, Man Herding Oxen, 4-Footed, Marked, 11 1/2 In. 2990.00

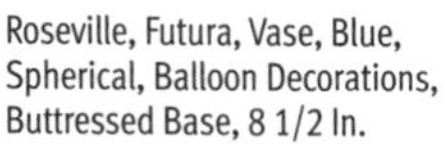

Roseville, Futura, Vase, Blue, Spherical, Balloon Decorations, Buttressed Base, 8 1/2 In.

Roseville, Pine Cone, Pitcher, Blue, Elongated Spout, Branch Handle, 9 In.

Luffa, Jardiniere, Pedestal, Green, 10 In. 825.00
Luffa, Sand Jar, Green, Disc Foot, 14 1/2 In. 470.00
Luffa, Vase, Green, 8 1/2 In. 200.00
Magnolia, Vase, Blue, Red, Handles, 5 x 9 In. 60.00
Magnolia, Vase, Brown, Handles, 12 In. 270.00
Ming Tree, Vase, Turquoise Blue & Brown, c.1947, 8 In. 275.00
Mock Orange, Basket, Orange, Yellow, Marked, 8 1/2 In. 90.00
Moderne, Vase, Turquoise Matte Glaze, Footed, Flared, Handles, Marked, 8 1/2 In. 330.00
Mongol, Vase, Squat, 4 Handles, 6 1/2 In. 890.00
Monticello, Bowl, Brown, Rectangular, Inward-Slanted Sides, Handles, 3 1/2 x 13 In. 265.00
Monticello, Vase, Brown, Bulbous, Squat, Handles, 7 1/2 In. 380.00
Monticello, Vase, Brown, Ovoid, Flared Rim, Handles, 8 1/2 In. 500.00
Monticello, Vase, Green, Looped Handles, 7 In. 360.00
Morning Glory, Bowl, Yellow, Lavender, Squat, 4 x 7 In. 460.00
Morning Glory, Console Set, White, 4 3/4 x 11-In. Bowl, 3 Piece 470.00
Morning Glory, Vase, Bulbous, Green, Tapered Neck, Angular Handles, 10 1/12 In. 1295.00
Morning Glory, Vase, Bulbous, White, Flared Rim, 2 Angular Handles, 6 1/2 x 7 In. 235.00
Morning Glory, Vase, Green, Flared, Buttressed Handles, 14 1/2 x 10 In. 1998.00
Morning Glory, Vase, Lavender, Yellow, Green, Blue, 8 1/2 x 6 3/4 In. 690.00
Morning Glory, Vase, White, Flared, 2 Angular Handles At Foot, 8 In. 265.00
Moss, Bowl, Handle, Ivory To Blue Glaze, 5 3/8 x 7 1/4 In. 145.00
Moss, Jardiniere, Blue, 8 In. 1175.00
Mostique, Vase, Geometric Tulips, Flared, 12 In., Pair 299.00
Mostique, Vase, Geometric Tulips, Flared, 15 1/4 x 8 In., Pair 480.00
Mostique, Vase, Gray, White, Blue, Brown, Aqua, Flared, Handles, 8 In. 150.00
Pauleo, Vase, Red, Wild Roses, Bulbous, 13 In. 600.00
Persian, Jardiniere, Orange Berries, Green Leaves, Inward Folded Rim, 5 x 6 1/2 In. 265.00
Pine Cone, Basket, Blue Matte, Boat Shape, 8 1/4 x 12 In. 518.00
Pine Cone, Basket, Blue, Branch Handle, 9 In. 500.00
Pine Cone, Basket, Brown, Branch Handle, Embossed Cones, Needles, 8 1/2 x 11 In. 520.00
Pine Cone, Basket, Green, 10 In. 259.00
Pine Cone, Bookend Planter, Blue, 5 1/2 In., Pair 1175.00
Pine Cone, Bookend Planter, Brown, 5 1/2 In., Pair 558.00
Pine Cone, Bowl, Blue, Elongated Shape, 14 In. 645.00
Pine Cone, Bowl, Blue, Green, Brown, Handles, 16 1/2 In. 1150.00
Pine Cone, Bowl, Brown, Elongated Shape, 14 In. 410.00
Pine Cone, Candlestick, 3-Light, Blue, 5 1/2 In. 529.00
Pine Cone, Candlestick, Brown Matte, Branch Handle, 4 1/2 x 3 1/2 In., Pair 290.00
Pine Cone, Centerpiece, Brown, Boat Form, 3 1/2 x 15 In. 259.00
Pine Cone, Dish, Double, Green, Center Handle, 13 In. 265.00
Pine Cone, Ewer, Green Matte, Marked, 15 1/2 In. 480.00
Pine Cone, Jardiniere, Blue, Stand-Up Rim, Shaped Handles, 9 In. 380.00
Pine Cone, Jardiniere, Brown, Embossed, Green, Bulbous, 4 1/4 x 6 In. 145.00
Pine Cone, Jardiniere, Brown, Small Twig Handles, 12 1/2 In. 765.00
Pine Cone, Pitcher, Blue, Elongated Spout, Branch Handle, 9 In. .... ***ILLUS*** 880.00
Pine Cone, Tumbler, Green, 5 In., 6 Piece 705.00
Pine Cone, Vase, 3 Buds, Green, 8 3/8 In. 316.00

Pine Cone, Vase, Blue Ground, Handles, 8 1/4 x 7 In. 430.00
Pine Cone, Vase, Blue, Bulbous, Handles, Marked, 11 In. 540.00
Pine Cone, Vase, Blue, Footed, Flared, Handles, Marked, 18 In. 1315.00
Pine Cone, Vase, Blue, Footed, Handles, 10 1/2 In. 600.00
Pine Cone, Vase, Blue, Twig Handles, 14 In. 1058.00
Pine Cone, Vase, Brown High Glaze, Handle, 8 1/4 x 5 1/4 In. 345.00
Pine Cone, Vase, Brown, Flattened, Handles, Marked, 8 1/2 x 9 In. 510.00
Pine Cone, Vase, Brown, Lotus Flower, 3 1/2 x 7 In. 259.00
Pine Cone, Vase, Bud, Brown, Branch Handle, 7 3/4 x 4 In. 230.00
Pine Cone, Vase, Cornucopia, Blue, Footed, Branch Handle, 10 In. 529.00
Pine Cone, Vase, Cornucopia, Blue, Green, 6 1/2 x 8 x 2 3/4 In. 250.00
Pine Cone, Vase, Pillow, Brown, Green, 8 x 9 1/2 In. 460.00
Pine Cone, Wall Pocket, Blue, 4 In. 1645.00
Pine Cone, Wall Pocket, Double Bud, Brown Matte, 4 1/2 x 8 3/4 In. 575.00
Pine Cone, Wall Shelf, Blue, Shape No. 1 .... 500.00
Poppy, Jardiniere, Pedestal, Pink, 8 1/2 In. 825.00
Raymor, Bowl, Ocher Glaze, Pinched Rim, 11 In. 940.00
Rosecraft Panel, Vase, Brown, Art Nouveau Scarf Dancer, Flared Rim, 10 1/2 In. 499.00
Rosecraft Panel, Vase, Fan, Green, Art Nouveau Scarf Dancer, 8 1/2 In. ....590.00 to 765.00
Rosecraft Panel, Vase, Green, Art Nouveau Scarf Dancer, Flared Rim, 10 1/2 In. 590.00
Rozane, Bowl, Yellow, Rose & Green Flowers, Ivory Ground, Handles, c.1917, 9 x 10 In. 90.00
Rozane, Ewer, Yellow, Globular, 6 x 4 1/2 In. 260.00
Rozane, Vase, Brown Glaze, Horse, Signed, Steele, 13 In. 1200.00
Rozane, Vase, Brown, Pansy, 2 Handles, 4 3/4 In. 127.00
Rozane, Vase, Brown, Portrait Of Cavalier, Egg Shape, 17 x 8 1/2 In. 441.00
Rozane, Vase, Poppies, Brown Glaze, Marked, 4 1/4 In. 120.00
Rozane Royal, Vase, Light, White Flowers, Gray To Ivory, Footed, Timberlake, 17 In. 360.00
Russco, Vase, Green & Tan Crystalline Glaze, Footed, 12 1/2 In. 780.00
Silhouette, Vase, Nude Girl, Orange & Brown, Fan Shape, c.1952, 7 In. 385.00
Silhouette, Vase, Nude In White, Flattened, 7 1/2 In. 270.00
Snowberry, Bookends, Coral, 5 In. 325.00
Snowberry, Ewer, Blue Glaze, 15 3/4 In. 315.00
Snowberry, Jardiniere, Pedestal, Pink, 8 In. ....353.00 to 646.00
Sunflower, Bowl, Green Matte, 4 x 7 3/4 In. 690.00
Sunflower, Jardiniere, Green, Brown, Blue, 7 1/2 In. 1135.00
Sunflower, Jardiniere, Yellow, Brown, Green, 7 x 9 In. 660.00
Sunflower, Planter, Spherical, 2 Tiny Handles, 4 1/4 x 5 1/2 In. 380.00
Sunflower, Vase, 2 Long Handles, 5 1/4 x 4 1/2 In. 380.00
Sunflower, Vase, Bulbous, Flat Shoulder, 6 3/4 x 7 In. 705.00
Sunflower, Vase, Multicolored, Handles, 6 1/8 In. 546.00
Sunflower, Vase, Oval, 10 1/4 x 6 In. 2115.00
Sunflower, Vase, Squat, Wide Mouth, 4 1/2 x 7 1/4 In. 705.00
Sunflower, Vase, Textured Green Matte, Semi-Bulbous, 6 1/4 x 5 In. 546.00
Sunflower, Vase, Yellow, Brown, Green, Blue, Handles, 6 In. 570.00
Sunflower, Vase, Yellow, Green Matte, Bulbous, 8 1/2 x 7 In. 2070.00
Sunflower, Window Box, Handles, 3 1/2 x 11 1/2 In. 735.00
Topeo, Vase, Blue Glaze, 7 1/2 In. 200.00
Topeo, Vase, Bulbous, Blue, 9 1/4 In. 441.00
Topeo, Vase, Green & Blue Matte Glaze, Mauve, 15 In. 2030.00
Tourmaline, Candleholder, Blue, 4 5/8 In., Pair 127.00
Tourmaline, Vase, Blue, 8 1/4 In. 185.00
Tourmaline, Vase, Blue, 9 3/8 In. 259.00
Tourmaline, Vase, Blue, Footed, Flared, 8 In. 150.00
Tourmaline, Vase, Blue, Gold Sheeting, 6 1/4 In. 92.00
Tourmaline, Vase, Blue, White Matte Glaze, 5 x 6 1/2 In. 259.00
Tourmaline, Vase, Bulbous, Blue Matte, 7 1/4 x 6 1/2 In. 230.00
Tourmaline, Vase, Pink To Green, Mottled Glaze, 6 In. 80.00
Tuscany, Bowl, Buttressed, Green, Gray Matte, 4 x 6 1/2 In. 90.00
Tuscany, Flower Holder, Pink, 5 1/4 In. 115.00
Tuscany, Wall Pocket, Pink, 7 1/4 In. 290.00
Velmoss, Bowl, Flower Frog, Green Matte Glaze, 8 1/2 In. 120.00

Velmoss, Bowl, Mottled Green, Brown Matte Glaze, Flared, 8 In. 150.00
Velmoss, Jardiniere, Pedestal, Leaves, Brown, Green, 32 1/2 In. 1380.00
Velmoss, Lamp Base, Green, Vertical Leaves, Flared, 12 In. 840.00
Velmoss, Vase, Yellow & Green, Vertical Leaves, Bulbous, 6 In. 540.00
Velmoss, Vase, Yellow Green, Embossed Broad Leaves, Pinched Waist, 12 In. 999.00
Velmoss, Vase, Yellow Green, Embossed Leaves, Flared Rim, 8 In. 590.00
Victorian, Vase, Bulbous, Brown Matte, 4 1/4 x 6 In. 259.00
Victorian, Vase, Gray, Blue, Brown, Footed, Bulbous, 10 In. 720.00
Vista, Basket, 10 1/2 In. 999.00
Vista, Jardiniere, Pedestal, 29 In. 1295.00
Vista, Vase, Green Stems, Blue Ground, 4 Buttresses Around Rim, 17 3/4 In. 705.00
Vista, Vase, Small Angular Handles At Rim, 15 In. 1058.00
Vista, Vase, Stylized Trees, Green & Pink, On Gray Ground, 11 1/2 In. 660.00
Vista, Vase, Stylized Trees, Green & Pink, On Gray Ground, Handles, 10 In. 450.00
Vista, Vase, Trees, Green, Purple Fruit, Swollen Form, 17 In. 1020.00
Vista, Vase, Wide Foot, Flowers, Trees, c.1930, 10 In. 450.00
Vista, Wall Pocket, 9 In. 380.00
Water Lily, Vase, Floor, Brown, Green, Yellow, 14 x 7 1/2 In. 275.00
Water Lily, Vase, Ocher To Brown Matte, Bulbous, Handles, 9 x 7 In. 115.00
Wincraft, Tea Set, Flowers, Tan Glaze, 6 1/2 In., 3 Piece 58.00
Wincraft, Vase, Blue, 10 1/2 x 6 In. 865.00
Wincraft, Vase, Chartreuse, Pinecone, Needles, 6 In. 58.00
Wincraft, Vase, Geranium, Tan Glaze, 10 In. 58.00
Wincraft, Vase, Turquoise Blue, Green Leaves, Shaded To Dark Blue Base, 6 In. 130.00
Windsor, Vase, Green Leaves, Mottled Brown & Red Matte Glaze, Foil Label, 10 In. 890.00
Wisteria, Bowl, Blue, 3 x 8 In. 325.00
Wisteria, Vase, Blue, Globular, Pumpkin Shape, 6 1/4 x 8 In. 865.00
Wisteria, Vase, Blue, Gourd Shape, 6 1/4 In. .... 470.00 to 575.00
Wisteria, Vase, Brown, Angular Handles, 8 1/2 x 8 In. 646.00
Wisteria, Vase, Brown, Blue, Lavender, Green, Flared, Handles At Bottom, 9 In. 1800.00
Wisteria, Vase, Brown, Lavender, Green, Flared, Footed, Lower Handles, Marked, 9 In. 510.00
Zephyr Lily, Ewer, Brown, 10 3/8 In. 127.00
Zephyr Lily, Vase, Handle, Sienna Tan Glaze, 12 1/2 In. 144.00

ROWLAND & MARSELLUS Company is part of a mark that appears on historical Staffordshire dating from the late nineteenth and early twentieth centuries. Rowland & Marsellus is the mark used by an American importing company in New York City. The company worked from 1893 to about 1937. Some of the pieces may have been made by the British Anchor Pottery Co. of Longton, England, for export to a New York firm. Many American views were made. Of special interest to collectors are the plates with rolled edges, usually blue and white.

Cup, Tea, Pink Roses, Blue Floral Garland Rim 9.00
Plate, Dinner, Pink Roses, Blue Floral Garland Rim, 10 In. 18.00
Plate, Elm At Cambridge Mass., A.S. Burbank, Plymouth, Mass., c.1910, 10 In. 65.00
Plate, Federal Hall, Wall St., Where Washington Took Oath Of Office, 9 3/4 In. 95.00
Plate, Souvenir Of Bridgeport Conn., Flow Blue, 10 In. 145.00

ROY ROGERS was born in 1911 in Cincinnati, Ohio. In the 1930s, he made a living as a singer; in 1935, his group started work at a Los Angeles radio station. He appeared in his first movie in 1937. From 1952 to 1957, he made 101 television shows. The other stars in the show were his wife, Dale Evans, his horse, Trigger, and his dog, Bullet. Roy Rogers memorabilia is collected, including items from the Roy Rogers restaurants.

Bank, Boot, Aluminum, American Creative Arts, 6 In. 24.00
Button, Roy Rogers & Trigger, Ribbon, Good Luck Medal, 1950s, 1 3/4 In. 160.00
Button, Roy Rogers, Yellow, White, Black, With Red, White & Blue Ribbon, 1 1/4 In. 53.00
Cap Gun, Bronze Grips & Hammer, RR On Grips, Schmidt, 8 1/2 In. 178.00
Clock, Alarm, Roy Rogers & Trigger, Desert Scene, Ingraham, 1950s, 4 In. 448.00

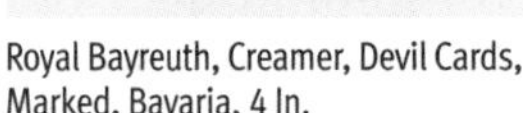
Royal Bayreuth, Creamer, Devil Cards, Marked, Bavaria, 4 In.

Royal Bayreuth, Tea Set, Tomato, 3 Piece

Doll, Pearl Handle Guns, Black Hat, Red Corduroy Pants, Ideal, 1949, 25 In. 185.00
Figurine, Dog, Bullet, Plastic, Hartland, 1950s, 6 1/2 In. 45.00
Gun, BB, Model 1866, No. 9052, Lever Action, Daisy, Sears & Roebuck, 38 1/4 In. 215.00
Gun & Holster Set, Double, Leather, Silver Buckles, Bullets, Schmidt, 10 1/2-In. Guns 565.00
Gun & Holster Set, Nickel, Die Cast, White Grips, 4 Bullets, Kilgore, 8 3/4-In. Gun ....178.00 to 214.00
Holster Outfit, Classy Products, Box, 1940s, 3 1/4 x 12 x 13 In. 750.00
Lunch Box, Dale & Roy, Chow Wagon, Dome Top, Metal, American Thermos Co. 382.00
Lunch Box, Dale & Roy, Double R Bar Ranch, Steel, American Thermos Co., 1955 .... 45.00
Modeling Clay Set, Unopened Clay Packages, Standard Toykraft, Box, 1950s 120.00
Tie Bar, Gold Plated, Roy's Head, Suspended By Chain, Signature On Hat 100.00
Toy, Chuck Wagon & Jeep, Plastic, Fix-It, Ideal, 1950s, 24 In. 358.00
Toy, Nellybelle Jeep & Trailer, Pat Brady, Dog, Ideal Toy Co., 1954, 14 1/2 In. 110.00
Toy, Roy Rogers Fix-It Chuck Wagon & Jeep, Plastic, Ideal, Box 132.00
Wrist Cuffs, Leather, RR Brand In Circle, Chrome Beads, Rivets 85.00

ROYAL BAYREUTH is the name of a factory that was founded in Tettau, Bavaria, in 1794. It has continued to modern times. The marks have changed through the years. A stylized crest, the name *Royal Bayreuth*, and the word *Bavaria* appear in slightly different forms from 1870 to about 1919. Later dishes may include the words *U.S. Zone*, the year of the issue, or the word *Germany* instead of *Bavaria*. Related pieces may be found listed in the Rose Tapestry, Sand Babies, Snow Babies, and Sunbonnet Babies categories.

Basket, White Roses, Cream Ground, Pierced Rim & Handle, 7 3/4 In. 58.00
Bowl, Corinthian Ware, Enameled, Black Transfer, Figures, 1900s, 7 3/4 In. 147.00
Bowl, Embossed Leaf & Flower Mold, 10 1/2 In. 48.00
Bowl, Lobster, Oval, 7 1/2 In. 180.00
Bowl, Pink Roses, Blue, Green, 10 1/2 In. 140.00
Celery Dish, Lobster, 12 In. 125.00
Creamer, Devil Cards, Marked, Bavaria, 4 In. .... *ILLUS* 168.00
Creamer, Fish, c.1910, 4 1/4 In. 80.00
Dinner Service, Off-White Ground, Floral Reserves, Gilt, 84 Piece 820.00
Mustard Jar, Lobster, Open Claw Handled Spoon, Green R B Mark, 4 1/2 In. 250.00
Mustard Jar, Lobster, Spoon 160.00
Pitcher, Dutch Children Waving To Sailboats, 7 3/4 In. 130.00
Pitcher, Lobster, 6 1/2 In. 210.00
Plate Set, Off-White Ground, Gilt Border, Floral Cartouche, 23 Piece 235.00
Sugar & Creamer, Lobster, Cover 200.00
Sugar Cube Tray, Lobster, 5 1/2 In. 90.00
Tea Set, Tomato, 3 Piece .... *ILLUS* 108.00
Vase, Castle & Bathing Women, Brown, Yellow, Orange, 9 1/2 x 26 In. 250.00
Vase, Man Smoking Pipe, Brown, Yellow, Pink, Gold Trim, 9 1/2 x 26 In. 275.00

ROYAL BONN is the nineteenth- and twentieth-century trade name used by Franz Anton Mehlem, who had a pottery in Bonn, Germany, from 1836 to 1931. Porcelain and earthenware were made. The factory was purchased by Villeroy & Boch in 1921 and closed in 1931. Many marks were used, most including the name *Bonn*, the initials *FM*, and a crown.

Clock, Ansonia, K. Montauk, Porcelain, 8-Day, Time & Strike, c.1905, 11 3/4 In. ... 168.00
Clock, Ansonia, La Bretagne, 8-Day, Time & Strike, c.1895, 12 1/2 In. ... 530.00
Clock, Ansonia, La Cerda, 8-Day, Time & Strike, Woman, Holding Mirror, c.1910, 15 In. ... 3250.00
Clock, Ansonia, La Chapelle, 15 In. ... 385.00
Clock, Ansonia, La Lorne, Flowers, 8-Day, Time & Strike, c.1901, 11 1/2 In. ... 616.00
Clock, Ansonia, La Meuse, Dutch Scene, Multicolored, c.1910, 14 1/2 In. ... 1460.00
Clock, Ansonia, La Normandie, Porcelain, 8-Day, Time & Strike, c.1904, 13 1/2 In. ... 300.00 to 880.00
Clock, Ansonia, La Vendee, Shelf, Roses, Green To Aqua, c.1904, 14 1/2 In. ... 1090.00
Clock, Ansonia, La Verdon, 14 In. ... 550.00
Jar, Delft Pattern, Amphora Shape, Scenic Blue & White, 9 1/2 x 7 In. ... 195.00
Urn, Cartouche, Harbor Scene, Scroll Handles, Footed, Blue Underglaze, 29 x 15 In. ... 750.00
Vase, Bulbous Shape, 5 1/2 In. ... 100.00
Vase, Painted Flowers, Curly Leaves, Green, Yellow, Ivory, Bulbous, 7 1/2 In. ... 420.00
Vase, Stylized Flowers, Green, Yellow, Ivory, Handles, Marked, No. 2619, 12 In. ... 510.00

ROYAL COPENHAGEN porcelain and pottery have been made in Denmark since 1775. The Christmas plate series started in 1908. The figurines with pale blue and gray glazes have remained popular in this century and are still being made. Many other old and new style porcelains are made today.

Ashtray, Dragonfly, Spider Web, Oval, Early 1900s, 6 5/8 In. ... 410.00
Ashtray, Lizard, Dragonfly, A. Pedersen, Early 1900s, 5 1/8 In. ... 705.00
Ashtray, Moth, Late 1800s, 5 1/4 In. ... 355.00
Bonbon, Cover, Lizard Finial, 4-Footed, Squat, Circular, Early 1900s, 4 In. ... 1645.00
Bonbon, Monkey On Cover, Early 1900s, 5 In. ... 1295.00
Bonbon, Pigeon On Cover, A. Pedersen, Early 1900s, 10 3/8 In. ... 880.00
Bonbon, Rabbit On Cover, c.1925, 7 1/4 In. ... 440.00
Bowl, Swirls, Mottled Brown Ground, Gerd Bogelund, 1950s, 8 In. ... 265.00
Cachepot, Flora Danica, Flowers, Polychrome, Gilt Edge, 4 3/4 In. ... 878.00
Compote, Flora Danica, Triangular, Serrated Beaded Border, 4 5/8 In. ... 995.00
Creamer, Flora Danica, Cylindrical, Short Spout, Angular Handle, 2 3/4 In. ... 765.00
Cup, Dome Cover, Flora Danica, Flowers, Oval, Crabstock Handle, 3 1/4 In. ... 440.00
Dish, Cover, Flora Danica, Flowers, Oval, Crabstock Handle, 6 1/8 In. ... 1175.00
Figurine, Asian Man Offering Ball To Woman, 9 1/4 In. ... 2235.00
Figurine, Asian Women In Embrace, 9 In. ... 1295.00
Figurine, Bear, Seated, Licking Paw, Stoneware, Knud Kyhn, c.1950, 3 In. ... 189.00
Figurine, Boy With 2 Calves ... 335.00
Figurine, Cat, Crawling, Spots, Liisberg, c.1923, 9 In. ... 940.00
Figurine, Cockerel & Hen, C. Thomsen, c.1980, 9 In. ... 441.00
Figurine, Cow & Calf, K. Kyhn, 1985, 10 1/2 In. ... 382.00
Figurine, Dog, Basset Hound Puppy, Early 1900s, 6 3/4 In. ... 176.00
Figurine, Dog, Bloodhound, Female, c.1941, 9 In. ... 235.00
Figurine, Dog, Bulldog, K. Kyhn, c.1925, 7 3/8 In. ... 880.00
Figurine, Dog, Chewing Bone, C. Thomsen, Early 1900s, 9 In. ... 325.00
Figurine, Dog, Cockerel, C. Thomsen, c.1925, 4 1/8 In. ... 150.00
Figurine, Dog, Collie, Lying Down, c.1970, 11 In. ... 265.00
Figurine, Dog, Dachshund, K. Moller, c.1913, 7 3/4 In. ... 355.00
Figurine, Dog, Danish Bird Dog, J. Grut, c.1930, 10 In. ... 176.00
Figurine, Dog, Great Dane, P. Herold, c.1975, 8 3/4 In. ... 410.00
Figurine, Dog, Poodle, P. Herold, Early 1900s, 9 1/2 In. ... 999.00
Figurine, Elk, c.1970, 9 In. ... 235.00
Figurine, Faun & Owl, 6 1/4 In. ... 130.00
Figurine, Faun & Rabbit, 5 3/4 In. ... 105.00
Figurine, Faun & Snake, 4 1/2 In. ... 90.00

Figurine, Faun Fighting Bear, 6 In. 138.00
Figurine, Faun Playing Pipes, 5 3/4 In. 80.00
Figurine, Faun Riding Goat, 8 In. 207.00
Figurine, Faun Riding Turtle, 3 3/4 In. 104.00
Figurine, Faun Seated On Pedestal, 8 In. 104.00
Figurine, Faun Seated On Pedestal, 18 1/2 In. 115.00
Figurine, Faun With Frog, 4 1/2 In. 104.00
Figurine, Faun With Frog, C. Thomsen, c.1925, 4 1/2 In. 295.00
Figurine, Faun With Rabbit, C. Thomsen, 1953, 8 1/4 In. 206.00
Figurine, Fox On Hollow Mound, E. Nielsen, Early 1900s, 6 In. 765.00
Figurine, Fox, Barking, E. Nielsen, Early 1900s, 10 1/2 In. 295.00
Figurine, Fox, Small Base, C. Thomsen, Early 1900s, 3 3/8 In. 295.00
Figurine, Geese, c.1970, 8 3/4 In., Pair 470.00
Figurine, Girl With Goats . . . . .205.00 to 299.00
Figurine, Goat & Kid, Early 1900s, 7 In. 470.00
Figurine, Gossips, 2 Women, C. Thomsen, c.1960, 11 5/8 In. 294.00
Figurine, Greenland Costumes, Painted, Gilt, C. Martin-Hassen, 13 In., Pair . . . 1935.00
Figurine, Guillemot, Gray, White Belly, Early 1900s, 10 1/2 In. 355.00
Figurine, Guinea Pig, J.A. Heuch, Early 1900s, 3 In. 470.00
Figurine, Jaguar Cub, J. Grut, 8 1/4 In. 355.00
Figurine, Lamb, Seated, K. Kyhn, c.1925, 3 1/4 In. 265.00
Figurine, Leopard, L. Jensen, Early 1900s, 9 1/2 In. 880.00
Figurine, Lioness, L. Jensen, c.1949, 12 In. 235.00
Figurine, Lynx, P. Herold, c.1940, 6 In. 499.00
Figurine, Man Bending To Kiss Nude Woman, Oval Base, 8 1/4 In. 2115.00
Figurine, Marmot, Early 1900s, 7 3/4 In. 825.00
Figurine, Monkey, A. Pederson, c.1930, 5 1/4 In. 265.00
Figurine, Musk Ox, A. Nielsen, Early 1900s, 8 In. 1350.00
Figurine, Orangutans, K. Kyhn, c.1925, 3 1/2 In. 1528.00
Figurine, Owl, Long Eared, c.1970, 13 3/4 In. 558.00
Figurine, Pan On Turtle, C. Thomsen, 1900s, 3 3/4 In. 235.00
Figurine, Pan With Cat, K. Kyhn, Early 1900s, 5 In. 1116.00
Figurine, Pan With Goat, C. Thomsen, c.1935, 5 In. 206.00
Figurine, Pan, Rabbit, C. Thomsen, 1961, 5 In. 176.00
Figurine, Pan, Snake, C. Thomsen, c.1940, 4 1/4 In. 206.00
Figurine, Pan, Wrestling Bear, C. Thomsen, 1965, 6 1/4 In. 295.00
Figurine, Parrot, Blue, White Plinth, Laurel Garland, c.1920, 11 1/2 In. 2115.00
Figurine, Pheasants, A. Nielsen, c.1970, 5 3/4 In. 206.00
Figurine, Pigmy Hippopotamus, c.1930, 14 1/4 In. 1998.00
Figurine, Polar Bear, Roaring, On Haunches, 1900s, 13 In. 235.00
Figurine, Prometheus Kissing Nude Sea Nymph, 1897, 19 In. 999.00
Figurine, Raccoon, W. Timyn, c.1981, 4 1/4 In. 294.00
Figurine, Tiger & Cubs, J. Grut, c.1980, 10 1/8 In. 1763.00
Figurine, Vixen & Cubs, P. Herold, c.1925, 4 1/8 In. 382.00
Figurine, White Mink, Jeanne Grut, c.1980, 7 In. 176.00
Figurine, Woman With Hoe, c.1950, 10 1/2 In. 176.00
Figurine, Woman, Collecting Potatoes, C. Thomsen, c.1975, 10 1/2 In. 295.00
Inkwell, Snake, Frog, Silver Frame, E. Nielsen, Late 1800s, 10 3/4 In. 2350.00
Jar, Cover, Duck Finial, Mottled Brown, Ocher, Knud Khyn, 5 3/4 In. 339.00
Jar, Cover, Flora Danica, Crabstock Handles, 4 1/2 In. 558.00
Plate Set, Dessert, Flora Danica, Flowers, 7 5/8 In., 10 Piece 3175.00
Plate Set, Dinner, Flora Danica, Flowers, 10 In., 10 Piece 4994.00
Plate Set, Side, Flora Danica, Flowers, 5 5/8 In., 10 Piece 2585.00
Sauceboat, Attached Underplate, Flora Danica, Oval, Crabstock Handle, 9 In. . . . 2350.00
Tazza, Flora Danica, Triangular, Rounded Corners, Trumpet Base, 5 In. 940.00
Tureen, Cover, Flora Danica, Egg Shape, Crabstock Handles, Ladle, 11 In. 4995.00
Tureen, Cover, Underplate, Blue, Fluted, 14 In. 1989.00
Vase, Bats, Jenny Meyer, Early 1900s, 21 In. 5875.00
Vase, Bats, Pine Branch, Globular, c.1925, 4 In. 295.00
Vase, Birds, Faces, Square Section, Jorgen Mogensen, 1950s, 9 1/2 In. 285.00
Vase, Bleeding Hearts, Square Bottle Shape, c.1920, 6 1/4 In. 235.00

Vase, Bottle Shape, Green Ground, Silver Mounted, Early 1900s, 9 1/4 In. 470.00
Vase, Butterfly Wings, Early 1900s, 4 In. 880.00
Vase, Chickens, Landscape, c.1925, 13 5/8 In. 646.00
Vase, Crosshatching, Stoneware, Bulbous, Oval, G. Bogelund, c.1950, 6 1/2 In. 320.00
Vase, Daffodils, Square, Footed, Early 1900s, 6 1/2 In. 176.00
Vase, Egg Shape, Shouldered, Ocher Glaze, c.1950, 5 3/4 In. 150.00
Vase, Egrets, Early 1900s, 10 In. 175.00
Vase, Geometrics, Stoneware, Funnel Shape, Gerd Bogelund, c.1950, 4 1/2 In. 265.00
Vase, Iris, Double, c.1937, 12 In. 120.00
Vase, Moths, Pierced Rim, Scalloped Shoulder, Early 1900s, 10 In. 880.00
Vase, Orchid, c.1956, 12 1/4 In. 235.00
Vase, Orchids, 2 Handles, Early 1900s, 13 In. 470.00
Vase, Poppy, Dragonfly, Gray Ground, c.1930, 11 In. 175.00
Vase, Roosters, Stoneware, Oval, Jorgen Mogensen, 1960s, 5 3/4 In. 150.00
Vase, Sheep, Grazing, Landscape, Polychrome, G. Rode, 1933, 22 1/2 In. 1645.00
Vase, Stoneware, Solfatara Glaze, Axel Salto, c.1943, 8 3/8 In. 5400.00
Vase, Water, Farmhouse, Rowboat, K. Sorensen, 1926, 22 3/4 In. 705.00
Vase, White Iris, Blue To White Ground, 17 3/8 In. 1725.00
Vase, Woman's Head, Stoneware, Triangular, Jais Nielsen, 1930s, 2 1/2 In. 66.00

ROYAL COPLEY china was made by the Spaulding China Company of Sebring, Ohio, from 1939 to 1960. The figural planters and the small figurines, especially those with Art Deco designs, are of great collector interest.

Royal
COPLEY

Coaster, Minit-Man Car Wash, Chrome, Pottery, Sticker, 1940s, 4 1/16 In. 27.00
Creamer, Duck, 4 1/2 x 7 In. 40.00
Lamp Base, Begging Spaniel, 9 3/4 In. 35.00
Planter, Brown Bear, Playing Mandolin, Teal Blue Bow, 6 1/2 In. 45.00
Planter, Cocker Spaniel, 8 x 5 In. 90.00
Wall Pocket, Pigtail Girl, 6 3/4 x 4 1/2 In. 28.00

ROYAL CROWN DERBY Company, Ltd., was established in England in 1890. There is a complex family tree that includes the Derby, Crown Derby, and Royal Crown Derby porcelains. The Royal Crown Derby mark includes the name and a crown. The words *Made in England* were used after 1921. The company is now a part of Royal Doulton Tableware Ltd.

Breakfast Set, Imari, 5 3/4-In. Coffeepot, 13 Piece 645.00
Candlesticks, Bone China, Imari, Flower-Form Nozzle, 1900s, 6 In., Pair 440.00
Candlesticks, Imari, Dolphin Head Base, 10 1/2 In., Pair 410.00
Dessert Service, Vine, Plates, Bowls, Teacups, Stands, 36 Piece 265.00
Luncheon Service, Flowers, Porcelain, 47 Piece 380.00
Plate, Town Square, Monuments, People, c.1890, 9 1/2 In. 2530.00
Tureen, Cover, Oval, Undertray, Imari, c.1850, 7 1/2 In. 212.00
Vase, Globular, Scroll Handles, Chinese Lions, Blue Ground, c.1882, 6 3/4 In. 264.00
Vase, Lilies, Leaves, Dragonflies, Bees, Peach, Yellow, Late 1800s, 6 5/8 In. 353.00

ROYAL DOULTON is the name used on Doulton and Company pottery made from 1902 to the present. Doulton and Company of England was founded in 1853. Pieces made before 1902 are listed in this book under Doulton. Royal Doulton collectors search for the out-of-production figurines, character jugs, vases, and series wares. Some vases and animal figurines were made with a special red glaze called flambe. Sung and Chang glazed pieces are rare. The multicolored glaze is very thick and looks as if it were dropped on the clay. Royal Doulton was acquired by the Waterford Wedgwood Group in 2005.

Animal, Dog, Airedale Terrier, HN 1022 .... 260.00
Animal, Dog, Bloodhound, HN 176 .... 650.00
Animal, Golden-Crowned Kinglet, HN 3504, 8 1/4 In. 240.00
Animal, Horse, Pride Of The Shires & Foal, HN 2523, 9 3/4 In. 1210.00
Animal, Tiger Stalking, HN 2646, 5 3/4 x 12 1/2 In. 205.00

Ash Pot, Golfing Scene, 7 1/4 x 8 In. 580.00
Bowl, Flambe Sung, Mottled, Red Ground, 1930s, 6 In. 358.00
Chamber Pot, Scrolling Leaves, 10 1/2 In. 207.00

Royal Doulton character jugs depict the head and shoulders of the subject. They are made in four sizes: large, 5 1/4 to 7 inches; small, 3 1/4 to 4 inches; miniature, 2 1/4 to 2 1/2 inches; and tiny, 1 1/4 inches. Toby jugs portray a seated, full figure.

Character Jug, 'Arriet, D 6236, Small 33.00
Character Jug, Abraham Lincoln, D 6936, 1992, Large 235.00
Character Jug, Athos, D 6452, 1956-91, Small 55.00
Character Jug, Auld Mac, D 5823, 1937-86, Large 95.00
Character Jug, Bacchus, D 6499, 1959-91, Large .... 50.00 to 100.00
Character Jug, Beefeater, D 6206, 1953-87, Large 75.00
Character Jug, Beefeater, D 6233, 1947-53, Small 75.00
Character Jug, Beefeater, D 6251, Miniature .... 44.00 to 55.00
Character Jug, Captain Ahab, D 6500, 1959-84, Large 125.00
Character Jug, Catharine Of Aragon, D 6658, Miniature 125.00
Character Jug, Dick Turpin, D 5485, Large 92.00
Character Jug, Don Quixote, D 6460, 1957-91, Small 90.00
Character Jug, Drake, D 6174, Small 42.00
Character Jug, Fortune Teller, D 6503, 1959-67, Small 335.00
Character Jug, Gaoler, D 6570, Large 69.00
Character Jug, George Washington, D 6669, 1982-94, Large 140.00
Character Jug, Hampshire Cricketer, D 6739, 1985, Small 90.00
Character Jug, Jester, D 5556, 1936-60, Small 95.00
Character Jug, Lobster Man, D 6617, 1968-91, Large 85.00
Character Jug, Merlin, D 6536, 1960-98, Small 110.00
Character Jug, Monty, D 6202, 1946-91, Large 215.00
Character Jug, Neptune, D 6548, 1961-91, Large 110.00
Character Jug, Old Charley, D 5420, 1934-83, Large 100.00
Character Jug, Pied Piper, D 6403, 1954-81, Large 155.00
Character Jug, Poacher, D 6429, 1955-95, Large 110.00
Character Jug, Robinson Crusoe, D 6539, 1960-82, Small 65.00
Character Jug, Sairey Gamp, D 5528, 1935-86, Small 75.00
Character Jug, Smuggler, D 6616, 1966-81, Large 200.00
Character Jug, St. George, D 6618, Large 88.00
Character Jug, Tony Weller, D 5531, Large 35.00
Character Jug, Vicar Of Bray, D 5615, 1936-60, Large 225.00
Character Jug, Viking, D 6502, Small 33.00
Dinner Set, Paneled, Flowers, Blue Ground, Gold Trim, 1900s, 114 Piece 774.00
Dish, Handle, Landscape, 10 1/2 In. 35.00
Figurine, Adrienne, HN 2304, 1964-91 .... 90.00
Figurine, Afternoon Tea, HN 1747, 1935-82 .... 235.00
Figurine, Autumn Breezes, HN 1911, 1939-76 .... 35.00
Figurine, Autumn Breezes, HN 2147, 1955-71 .... 80.00
Figurine, Babette, HN 1423, 1930-38 .... 1210.00
Figurine, Balloon Man, HN 1954, 1940-Present 240.00
Figurine, Belle O' The Ball, HN 1997, 1947-79 .... 240.00
Figurine, Biddy Penny Farthing, HN 1843, 1938-Present 129.00
Figurine, Blithe Morning, HN 2021, 1949-71 .... 69.00
Figurine, Blithe Morning, HN 2065, 1950-73 .... 146.00
Figurine, Bunnykins, Ace, Box, 1986-89, 3 3/4 In. 109.00
Figurine, Bunnykins, Aerobic, Box, 1985-88, 2 3/4 In. 109.00
Figurine, Bunnykins, Australian, Box, 1988, 4 In. 296.00
Figurine, Bunnykins, Daisie Springtime, Box, 1973-83, 3 1/2 In. .... *ILLUS* 150.00
Figurine, Bunnykins, Knockout, Box, 1984-88, 4 In. 118.00
Figurine, Bunnykins, Royal Family, Second Variations, Box, 1990, 5 Piece 2369.00
Figurine, Carpet Seller, HN 1464, 1929-Unknown 235.00
Figurine, Cavalier, HN 2716, 1976-82 .... 129.00 to 145.00
Figurine, Celeste, HN 2237, 1959-71 .... 100.00

The material used to make repairs is warmer to the touch than the porcelain. Feel the surface of a figurine to see if there are unseen repairs.

Royal Doulton, Figurine, Bunnykins, Daisie Springtime, Box, 1973-83, 3 1/2 In.

Figurine, Centurion, HN 2726, 1982-84 . . . . . 105.00
Figurine, Charmain, HN 1948, 1940-73 . . . . . 90.00
Figurine, Darling, HN 1985, 1944-97 . . . . . 35.00
Figurine, Demure, HN 1402, 1930-75 . . . . . 50.00
Figurine, Elegance, HN 2264, 1961-85 . . . . . 115.00
Figurine, Ermine Coat, HN 1981, 1945-67 . . . . . 140.00
Figurine, Fair Lady, HN 2193, 1963-96 . . . . . 69.00
Figurine, Father Christmas, HN, 1992-99 . . . . . 146.00
Figurine, Favourite, HN 2249, 1960-90 . . . . . 115.00
Figurine, Flower Of Scotland, HN 4240, 9 In. 80.00
Figurine, Flower Seller's Children, HN 1342, 1929-93 . . . . . 279.00
Figurine, Gay Morning, HN 2135, 1954-67 . . . . . 129.00
Figurine, Genevieve, HN 1962, 1941-75 . . . . . 115.00 to 160.00
Figurine, Genie, HN 2989, 1983-90 . . . . . 205.00
Figurine, Golliwog, HN 1979, 1945-79 . . . . . 650.00
Figurine, Golliwog, HN 2040, 1949-59 . . . . . 335.00
Figurine, Gossips, HN 2025, 1949-67 . . . . . 222.00 to 335.00
Figurine, Graduate, Male, HN 3017, 1984-92 . . . . . 95.00
Figurine, Granny's Heritage, HN 2031, 1949-69 . . . . . 375.00
Figurine, Herminia, HN 1644, 1934-38 . . . . . 1445.00
Figurine, Jersey Milkmaid, HN 2057, 1950-59 . . . . . 88.00
Figurine, Jester, HN 2016, 1949-97 . . . . . 117.00
Figurine, Lady April, HN 1958, 1940-59 . . . . . 205.00
Figurine, Lily, HN 1798, 1936-71 . . . . . 66.00
Figurine, Lydia, HN 1908, 1939-55 . . . . . 88.00
Figurine, Marguerite, HN 1928, 40-1959 . . . . . 205.00
Figurine, Mask Seller, HN 2103, 1953-95 . . . . . 146.00
Figurine, Maytime, HN 2113, 1953-67 . . . . . 117.00
Figurine, Melanie, HN 2271, 1965-81 . . . . . 65.00
Figurine, Old Balloon Seller, HN 1315, 1929-98 . . . . . 120.00
Figurine, Olivia, HN 1995, 1947-51 . . . . . 355.00
Figurine, Orange Lady, HN 1953, 1940-75 . . . . . 127.00
Figurine, Paisley Shawl, HN 1987, 1946-59 . . . . . 205.00
Figurine, Penelope, HN 1901, 1939-75 . . . . . 175.00 to 240.00
Figurine, Pied Piper, HN 2102, 1953-76 . . . . . 146.00
Figurine, Reflections, HN 1848, 1938-49 . . . . . 466.00
Figurine, Robin Hood, HN 2773, 1985-90 . . . . . 105.00
Figurine, Romeo & Juliet, HN 3113, 1993 . . . . . 838.00
Figurine, Rosemary, HN 2091, 1952-59 . . . . . 290.00
Figurine, Stop Press, HN 2683, 1977-81 . . . . . 129.00
Figurine, Susan, HN 3871, 1997 . . . . . 70.00
Figurine, Sweet & Twenty, HN 1298, 1928-69 . . . . . 205.00
Figurine, Sweet Maid, HN 2092, 1952-55 . . . . . 225.00
Figurine, Thanksgiving, HN 2446, 1972-76 . . . . . 95.00
Figurine, Top O' The Hill, HN 1834, 1937-Present 65.00

Figurine, Top O' The Hill, HN 1849, 1938-75 .... 205.00
Figurine, Town Crier, HN 2119, 1953-76 .... 186.00
Figurine, Winsome, HN 2220, 1960-85 .... 69.00
Jug, Series Ware, Coaching Days, 6 3/4 In. 206.00
Lighter, Toby Jug, Long John Silver, D 6386, 3 1/2 In. 33.00
Loving Cup, Commemorative, 25 Year Reign Of King George, 1953, 10 In. 940.00
Loving Cup, Commemorative, Queen Elizabeth II, 1953, 10 In. 310.00
Pitcher, Series Ware, Early Motoring, Blood Money, 5 In. 520.00
Pitcher, Series Ware, Early Motoring, Deaf, 6 In. 509.00
Planter, Morrisian, Maiden's Playing Instruments, Blue, White, 10 x 12 In. 585.00
Plate, Dinner, Flowers, Cobalt Blue Border, E. Percy, c.1910, 10 1/2 In., 12 Piece 944.00
Plate, Luncheon, Floral Center, Gray Band, 9 1/8 In., 12 Piece 70.00
Plate, Series Ware, Parson, Falconer, Squire, Jester, Mayor, 10 In., 5 Piece 294.00
Toby Jug, Dr. Jekyll & Mr. Hyde, D 7024, Small 70.00
Toby Jug, Falstaff, D 6062, Large 33.00
Toby Jug, Falstaff, D 6385, Small 28.00
Toby Jug, Jester, D 6910, Medium 59.00
Toby Jug, King & Queen Of Diamonds, D 6969, Small 94.00
Toby Jug, Leprechaun, D 6948, Medium 94.00
Toby Jug, Lobster Man, D 6620, Small 28.00
Toby Jug, Merlin, D 6529, Large 33.00
Toby Jug, Old Salt, D 6554, Small 50.00
Toby Jug, Sam Johnson, D 6289, Large 46.00
Toby Jug, Town Crier, D 6920, Medium 70.00
Toby Jug, Walrus & Carpenter, D 6604, Small 44.00
Urn, Emblem, 1937, 10 1/2 In. 345.00
Vase, Chang, Flambe, Crackle, 2 Handles, C.J. Noke, H. Nixon, c.1930, 11 1/2 In. 4713.00
Vase, Flambe, 3 Farmers Harvesting Crop, Daisies, 10 1/2 x 6 In. 259.00
Vase, Flambe, Globular, Compressed, 1920s, 2 3/4 In. 547.00
Vase, Flambe, Sung, Black, Blue & Red Glaze, Bottle Shape, 1930, 8 In. 495.00
Vase, Flambe, Woodcut, Desert Dwellers, Camels, 10 In. 196.00
Vase, Sung, Bird, Egg Shape, Shouldered, Arthur Eaton, 1920s, 4 1/4 In. 1367.00

ROYAL DUX is the more common name for the Duxer Porzellanmanufaktur, which was founded by E. Eichler in Dux, Bohemia, in 1860. By the turn of the century, the firm specialized in porcelain statuary and busts of Art Nouveau–style maidens, large porcelain figures, and ornate vases with three-dimensional figures climbing on the sides. The firm is still in business.

Figurine, Cancan Dancer, Woman, Raised Skirt, Schaff, c.1930, 9 In. 245.00
Figurine, Elephant, Austria, c.1900, 12 x 17 In. 265.00
Figurine, Vide Poche, Maiden, Playing Pipes, Shell, c.1900, 10 1/2 In. 710.00
Group, Clown, 2 Women, c.1930, 18 3/4 In. 710.00
Plaque, Dealer, Gilt Decoration, c.1930, 5 1/2 In. 115.00

ROYAL FLEMISH glass was made during the late 1880s in New Bedford, Massachusetts, by the Mt. Washington Glass Works. It is a colored satin glass decorated with dark colors and raised gold designs. The glass was patented in 1894. It was supposed to resemble stained glass windows.

Biscuit Jar, Flowers, Multicolored, Square, Gold Enameling, Square 5 x 9 1/2 In. 1898.00
Lamp, Kerosene, 8 1/2 In. 550.00
Lamp Base, Garden Of Allah, Desert Scenes, Metal Holder, Collar, 12 In. 1093.00
Pitcher, Blue & Gray Cathedral Window-Style Segments, Mums, 11 In. 6900.00
Tankard, Cathedral Windows, Mums, Leaves, Bulbous, Mt. Washington, 11 1/2 In. 6900.00
Tankard, Medallion, 2 Lions, Scrolls, Crown, Earth Tone Panels, Gold Trim, 12 In. 5250.00
Vase, Circular Suppressed Body, 3 Medallions, Gargoyle, Glowers, 13 In. 3450.00
Vase, Cover, Gold Raised Panels, Amethyst, Red, Brown, Medallions, 10 1/4 In. 4600.00
Vase, Egg Shape, 2 Reed Handles, Gold Medallions, Pansies, Gold Scrolling, 6 In. 2530.00
Vase, Mythological Dragon, Reverse Scrolling Fish, Cranberry Foot, Rim, 13 1/2 In. 9200.00

ROYAL HAEGER, see Haeger category.

ROYAL HICKMAN designed pottery, glass, silver, aluminum, furniture, lamps, and other items. From 1938 to 1944 and again from the 1950s to 1969, he worked for Haeger Potteries. Mr. Hickman operated his own pottery in Tampa, Florida, during the 1940s. He moved to California and worked for Vernon Potteries. The last years of his life he livd in Guadalajara, Mexico, and continued designing for Royal Haeger. Pieces made in his pottery listed here are marked *Royal Hickman* or *Hickman*.

Bookends, Calla Lily, Yellow, Green Leaf, 5 7/8 x 4 3/4 x 4 1/2 In. 65.00
Bowl, Pink, Green & Turquoise Glaze, Raised 6-Petal Flowers, 12 In. 85.00
Compote, Bunches Of Grapes, Mauve Agate, 7 x 15 x 8 In. 38.00
Console, Plum, Mottled Green Accents, Arched Sides, Art Deco, 17 x 7 In. 32.00
Figurine, Horse & Colt, Tan Glaze, Rectangular Tan & Green Base, 9 3/4 x 13 1/2 In. 57.00
Tray, Palm Leaf, Aluminum, 4 Molded Feet, Bruce Fox, 25 x 5 In. 55.00
Vase, Peacock, White Matte Glaze, Gold Tweed Accents, 1949, 16 x 16 In. 21.00
Vase, Pink, Sphere, 3 Applied Plumes, Pink, Blue, Green, 10 1/2 In. 135.00
Vase, Shell, Upturned, Pierced Pedestal Base, Pink, Turquoise Glaze, 10 x 10 3/4 In. 80.00

ROYAL IVY, see Northwood, Royal Ivy

ROYAL RUDOLSTADT, see Rudolstadt category.

ROYAL VIENNA, see Beehive category.

ROYAL WORCESTER is a name used by collectors. Worcester porcelains were made in Worcester, England, from about 1751. The firm went through many different periods and name changes. It became the Worcester Royal Porcelain Company, Ltd., in 1862. Today collectors call the porcelains made after 1862 *Royal Worcester*. In 1976, the firm merged with W. T. Copeland to become Royal Worcester Spode. Some early products of the factory are listed under Worcester.

Bowl, Shell Shape, 9 1/2 In. 100.00
Coffee Set, Coffeepot, Sugar, Creamer, 6 Cups & Saucers, 15 Piece 59.00
Compote, Oval, Scrolled Leaf Handles, Flower, Enamel, Gilt, Early 1900s, 7 5/8 In. 353.00
Condiment Set, Willow, Heart Shape Silver Stand, Dish, Mustard, Shaker 290.00
Cream Jug, Flowers, Gilt, Hand Painted, Late 1800s, 3 In. 69.00
Ewer, Handles, 9 In. 275.00
Ewer, Ivory Ground, Enamel Accented Raised Gold Flowers, 1899, 13 In. 385.00
Figurine, Aberdeen Angus Bull, D. Linder, Oval Fruitwood Base, c.1961, 7 1/2 In. 470.00
Figurine, Belle Masque Ball, 9 In. 176.00
Figurine, Bird, Gray Wagtail On Celandine Mount, Bisque, c.1968, 6 x 7 In. 350.00
Figurine, Boy, With Bundle Of Sticks, 5 In. 179.00
Figurine, Brahman Bull, No. 3821 .... 727.00
Figurine, Chestnut, Collared Longspur, No. 3995 .... 240.00
Figurine, Crabapple & Butterfly, Signed, D. Doughty, 9 1/2 In. 560.00
Figurine, Dairy Shorthorn Bull, No. 3781 .... 708.00
Figurine, Grandmother's Dress, No. 3081 .... 100.00
Figurine, Highland Bull, No. 3999 .... 800.00
Figurine, Jersey Bull, No. 3776B 578.00
Figurine, Parakeet, 6 3/4 In. 129.00
Figurine, Royal Canadian Mounted Policeman, Bisque, 11 1/2 x 9 3/4 In. 644.00
Figurine, Santa Gertrudis Bull, No. 3702 .... 705.00
Goblet, Double Walled, Dots, Blue Honeycomb Body, Pink Ground, 1875, 6 In. 1525.00
Plate, Bread & Butter, Clementine, 6 In. 16.00
Plate, Dessert, Red Starts & Beech, Myrtle Warbler & Cherry, c.1973, 2 Piece 118.00
Plate, Figure, Seated, Wooded Glade, Distant Cliff, Gilt Garland Rim, 9 1/2 In. 968.00
Plate, Gilded, English Landscape, W. Rushton, c.1915, 10 3/4 In., 6 Piece 940.00
Plate, Salad, Dorset, 1967, 8 In. 22.00
Plate Set, Cream Ground, Flowers, 10 1/2 In., 12 Piece 180.00
Platter, Game, Pheasants, Chicks, Blue Transfer Border, c.1894, 17 3/4 In. 765.00
Salt & Pepper, Evesham, 1980, 4 7/8 In. 45.00
Server, Boy, With Boat, 11 In. 505.00
Sugar, Cover, Strawberry Flair, Bee, Butterfly, Rounded, Fluted, c.1974, 4 In. 59.00

Urn, 2 Handles, Fruit & Blossoms, White Ground, F. Parker, c.1906 .... 395.00
Urn, Peach To Yellow, Snake Handles, 1890, 15 x 8 In. 3600.00
Vase, Bamboo, Ivory, Gold & Red, 3 Branch-Form Handles, 1883, 6 3/4 In. 510.00
Vase, Bottle Shape, Parcel Gilt, Flowers, Pierced Handles, c.1889, 12 In. 176.00
Vase, Cover, Globular Shape, Printed, Painted, Flowers, c.1887, 4 1/2 In. 135.00
Vase, Cover, Reticulated, Leaf Panels, Gilt Flowers, Grainger, 1891, 11 In. 4406.00
Vase, Double Wall, Blue Glaze, Honeycomb, 1879, 7 1/8 In., Pair 8815.00
Vase, Double Walled, Gilt Trim, Raised Dots, 1907, 7 In., Pair 2280.00
Vase, Flowers, Hand Painted, Late 1800s, 3 In. 46.00
Vase, Sabrina, Cloudburst, Chicory Blue Glaze, Cobalt Blue Lined, 9 3/4 In. 230.00
Vase, Spill, 1887, 4 3/4 x 3 In. 795.00
Vase, Teardrop Shape, Slender Neck, Gilt Slip, c.1884, 14 1/4 In. 499.00
Wall Sconce, Cornucopia Shape, Acanthus Cresting, Gilt, c.1884, 10 In., Pair 580.00

ROYCROFT products were made by the Roycrofter community of East Aurora, New York, in the late nineteenth and early twentieth centuries. The community was founded by Elbert Hubbard, famous philosopher, writer, and artist. The workshops owned by the community made furniture, metalware, leatherwork, embroidery, and jewelry. A printshop produced many signs, books, and the magazines that promoted the sayings of Elbert Hubbard. Furniture by the Roycroft community is listed in the Furniture category.

Bookends, Copper, Hammered, Embossed Flowers, 4 1/2 x 3 1/4 In. 115.00
Bookends, Copper, Hammered, Molded Edge, Embossed Flowers, 8 1/2 x 5 3/4 In. 200.00
Bookends, Hammered, Tooled Flowers, Mark, 5 1/4 In. 330.00
Candlestick, Copper, Hammered, 4-Sided Stem, Square Top & Base, 8 1/2 In., Pair 1763.00
Candlestick, Copper, Hammered, Twisted Stem, Round Base, Orb & Cross, 13 In., Pair 1880.00
Candlestick, Princess, Copper, Hammered, Twin Stems, Riveted, Square Base, 7 3/4 In., Pair 825.00
Chandelier, Hanging, Copper, Hammered, Cone Shape, 3 Chains, Orb & Cross Mark, 36 In. 8225.00
Lamp, Electric, Hammered Copper, Aurene Glass, Stamped, 15 In. 9600.00
Lamp Shade, Hammered Copper, Clip-On, Helmet Shade, Arts & Crafts, 5 x 6 In. 765.00
Lantern, Green, Purple, Leaded Glass, Hanging Round Cap, Dard Hunter, 16 x 5 In. 10575.00
Tea & Coffee Set, Copper, Hammered, Riveted Brass Band, Orb & Cross Mark, 7 Piece 12925.00
Vase, American Beauty, Copper, Hammered, Flared Rim, Riveted, Orb & Cross Mark, 21 In. 3290.00
Vase, Baluster, Hammered Copper, Flaring Rim, Orb & Cross Mark, 8 1/2 In. 470.00
Vase, Bellflower, Cylindrical, Wavy Rim, Scroll Border, 1920s, 9 1/2 In. 1130.00
Vase, Bud, Holder, Incised Mark, Square Base, 8 1/2 In. 55.00
Vase, Bud, Holder, Incised Mark, Trapezoidal Base, 7 1/2 In. 80.00
Vase, Silvered, Hammered Finish, Early 20th Century, 5 3/4 In. 175.00
Wastepaper Basket, Slatted, Curved Edges, Orb & Cross Mark, 13 x 11 In. 1920.00

ROZANE, see Roseville category.

ROZENBURG worked at The Hague, Holland, from 1890 to 1914. The most important pieces were earthenware made in the early twentieth century with pale-colored Art Nouveau designs.

Cup & Saucer, Orchids, Tulips, Octagonal, 1904, 1910, 5 1/4 In. 780.00
Cup & Saucer, Purple Orchid Spray, Orange Thistle, 1909, 1910, 5 In. 960.00
Ewer, Bird Walking Among Daffodils, Oval, Tapered, Square Base, 1906, 11 In. 4500.00
Jardiniere, Stars, Arches, Leaves, Green Glaze Ground, Bulbous, 1900, 3 1/2 x 8 In. 259.00
Jug, Bird, Long Tail, Spider Chrysanthemum Sprays, Flat Handle, 1900, 7 7/8 In. 3000.00
Jug, Panels, Purple Irises, Leaves, 8 1/2 In. 4800.00
Plaque, Roadway With Workers, Children, Handpainted, Framed, 1890, 15 x 9 In. 880.00
Plate, Flowers, Purple, Magenta, Burgundy, 1910, 5 1/2 In. 935.00
Sugar, Cover, Square, Ocher, Yellow Pansies, 1901, 4 1/4 In. 4800.00
Sugar & Creamer, Cover, Crested Parrot, Scrolling Leaves, Square, 1900, 5 1/8 In. 5400.00
Sugar & Creamer, Cover, Flowers, Leaves, 1906, 4 1/4 In. 4500.00
Tile, 6 To Form Woman Sewing At Window, 1880s, 6 x 6 In. 1410.00
Tile, Landscape, Shepherd Putting His Flock In Shed, 1910, 18 x 11 In. 500.00
Vase, Bird Perched Among Stylized Flowers, Leaves, Square, 2 Handles, 1904, 8 In. 3000.00
Vase, Bird Perched On Branch, Viola Spray, Pansies, 2 Handles, Inverted, 7 In. 6600.00
Vase, Bird Perched On Leafy Stem, Poppy Spray, 1914, 5 3/8 In. 5400.00

Vase, Bird Perched, Wings Spread Among Daisy Stems, 1900, 10 1/2 In. 5400.00
Vase, Bird Under Stylized Vine, Long Tail, 2 Handles, 1903, 8 In. 4800.00
Vase, Butterfly Among Leaves, Baluster, 1913, 4 3/4 In. 1440.00
Vase, Fish, Flared Neck, Angular Handles, Octagonal, Bulbous, 1902, 8 1/2 In. 9000.00
Vase, Flowering Thistle Sprays, Squat, Baluster, 4 1/4 In. 7800.00
Vase, Hawk Perched Below Branches, Curved Handles, 1902, 10 In. 5400.00
Vase, Lilac, Brown Orchid, Baluster, 1903, 5 In. 3000.00
Vase, Nasturtium Sprays, Ocher, Oval, 1904, 6 In. 6000.00
Vase, Orchid, Globular Body, Square Base, 1908, 9 In. 9000.00
Vase, Panels, Purple Irises, Square Neck, 5 3/8 In. 2400.00
Vase, Parrot Perched On Thistle Plant, Flat Handles, 1903, 9 3/4 In. 3900.00
Vase, Peacock, Purple Flowers, Slender Neck, Angular Handles, 1914, 7 1/2 In., Pair 9600.00
Vase, Poppy, Petals, Crimped Edges, Peach Glaze, Cobalt Blue Ground, 3 1/2 x 8 In. 201.00
Vase, Purple Spider Chrysanthemum Sprig, Knopped Neck, Baluster, 1906, 3 3/4 In. 780.00
Vase, Stylized Yellow, Ocher Flower, Square Base, 1901, 7 1/4 In. 7800.00
Vase, Sunflower, Leaves, Handles, Teal Ground, 14 x 13 In. 1725.00
Vase, Tea Service, Pot, Sugar & Creamer, Cover, Yellow Irises, Leaf Sprays, 3 Piece 9600.00
Vase, Tulip, Cascading Arches, Brown, Gourd Shape, 8 1/4 x 7 In. 935.00

RRP or RRP, Roseville, is the mark used by the firm of Robinson-Ransbottom. It is not a mark of the more famous Roseville Pottery. The Ransbottom brothers started a pottery in 1900 in Ironspot, Ohio. In 1920, they merged with the Robinson Clay Product Company of Akron, Ohio, to become Robinson-Ransbottom. The factory is still working.

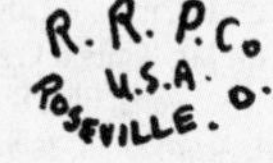

Dog Dish, Cream Glaze, Brown Flecks, Round, Straight-Sided, 2 1/2 x 6 In. 36.00
Jardiniere, Light Green, Blue Green Drip Glaze, Raised Scrolls, 7 x 7 1/4 In. 36.00
Mug, Blue Spongeware, 4 1/4 In. 45.00
Oil Jar, Green Drip Glaze, Urn Shape, Squared Handles, 18 In. 199.00
Planter, Ivory, 2 Blue Stripes, Round, 2 Handles, 3-Footed, 6 1/2 x 8 In. 25.00
Vase, Embossed Flowers, Long Stem & Leaves, Terra-Cotta & Tan Glaze, Flared Rim, Footed, 8 In. .. 49.00

RS GERMANY is part of the wording in marks used by the Tillowitz, Germany, factory of Reinhold Schlegelmilch from 1914 until about 1945. The porcelain was sold decorated and undecorated. The Schlegelmilch families made porcelains marked in many ways. See also ES Germany, RS Poland, RS Prussia, RS Silesia, RS Suhl, and RS Tillowitz.

Basket, Bird & Flowers, Green Mark, 4 1/4 x 5 1/4 In. 125.00
Biscuit Jar, Peach Roses, Green Tones, Handles, 4 3/4 x 8 In. 60.00
Bowl, Cabbage Mold, White Blossoms, White & Green Highlights, 9 1/2 In. 120.00
Candleholder, 4-Sided, Cream, Pink Rose, 10 In., Pair 60.00
Cup, Tea, Peonies, Hand Painted, Gold Trim 25.00
Cup & Saucer, Demitasse, Women Reading Book, Maroon Border 150.00
Cup & Saucer, Different Floral Decoration, 4 Sets 47.00
Flask, Powder, Pink Roses, Light Blue & Cream, 4 3/4 In. 110.00
Hair Receiver & Powder Box, Cotton Plants, 2 1/2 In. 100.00
Jam Jar, Cover, Pink & Yellow Roses, Brown & Yellow, Handles, 5 In. 50.00
Pot, Demitasse, Side Handle, White & Cream, Peach Rose, Satin, 5 1/2 In. 140.00
Relish Tray, Brown, & Yellow, Sheepherder, Cottage, 9 In. 100.00
Syrup, Underplate, Pink & White Roses, Green, Gold Trim 30.00
Toothbrush Holder, White, Pink Roses, Wall Mount, 4 1/2 In. 60.00
Tray, Dresser, Rectangular, Cottage & Flower Field, Signed Hiem, 11 1/2 In. 125.00
Tray, Handles, Heart Shape, Pierced Parrot Handle, Green RSG Mark, 6 3/4 In. 59.00
Vase, Parrot, Figural, Iridescent Purple, Gold Highlights, 7 1/2 In. 90.00
Vase, Yellow, Green, Lady & Peacock, Lady & Doves, 7 1/2 In., Pair 240.00

RS POLAND (German) is a mark used by the Reinhold Schlegelmilch factory at Tillowitz from about 1946 to 1956. After 1956, the factory made porcelain marked PT Poland. This is one of many of the RS marks used. See also ES Germany, RS Germany, RS Prussia, RS Silesia, RS Suhl, and RS Tillowitz.

Biscuit Jar, Cover, Flowers, Red & Green Mark, 7 x 7 In. 325.00

Bowl, Center, Pedestal, Rose Garlands, Gold Beads, Green Ground, 9 x 4 3/8 In. 675.00
Bowl, Footed, Flowers, Hand Painted Highlights, 7 x 3 1/4 In. 350.00
Bowl, Mayonnaise, Footed, Saucer, Hand Painted Hydrangeas, Marked, 8 In. 175.00
Vase, Homecraft, Wreath Mark, 9 1/2 In. 580.00
Vase, Woodland Scene, Chinese Pheasants, 11 In. 1295.00

RS PRUSSIA appears in several marks used on porcelain before 1917. Reinhold Schlegelmilch started his porcelain works in Suhl, Germany, in 1869. See also ES Germany, RS Germany, RS Poland, RS Silesia, RS Suhl, and RS Tillowitz.

Berry Set, Honeycomb Mold, White Luster Finish, Water Lily, Swan, 11 In., 7 Piece 625.00
Berry Set, Icicle Mold, Swans On Lake, 10 3/4 In., 7 Piece 950.00
Berry Set, Medallion Mold, Pink Flowers, Blue Border, Gold Trim, Portraits, 7 Piece 2750.00
Berry Set, Yellow & Blue, Rose & Daisy, 7 Piece 230.00
Biscuit Jar, 2 Handles, Cream & Green, Roses, Gold Stencil Highlights, 5 x 9 In. 175.00
Biscuit Jar, Carnation Mold, Cobalt Blue, 2 Handles, Gold Stencil, 4 1/2 x 9 In. 2100.00
Biscuit Jar, Icicle Mold, 2 Handles, Old Man In The Mountain, Shepherd, 5 x 9 In. 1050.00
Biscuit Jar, Light Green, Handles, 5 x 8 1/2 In. 175.00
Biscuit Jar, Lily, Green, Potocka Portrait, 7 1/2 In. 500.00
Biscuit Jar, Point & Clover Mold, Cream & Green, Glass Bowl, 7 In. 200.00
Biscuit Jar, White & Cream, Wild Flower, Gold Border, 5 x 9 In. 130.00
Bowl, 3 Swans, Blue Birds, Green Wreath Mark, 11 In. 345.00
Bowl, Acorn Mold, Yellow & Green Ground, Pink & Yellow Rose, 10 1/2 In. 230.00
Bowl, Admiral Perry Arctic Expedition, Explorers, Flag, Igloo, 10 In. 7000.00
Bowl, Brown, Castle Scene, 11 3/4 In. 875.00
Bowl, Carnation Mold, Peach & White, Lavender Highlights, Pink Poppy, 10 1/2 In. 170.00
Bowl, Carnation Mold, Pink & Yellow Rose, White, Orange, Green, 8 1/4 In. 70.00
Bowl, Carnation, Cobalt Blue, Gold Highlights, 15 In. 7500.00
Bowl, Cream Ground, Iridescent Tiffany Border, White Poppy, Gold Stencil, 10 3/4 In. 450.00
Bowl, Fruit, Fleur-De-Lis Mold, White, Yellow, Blue, Green, 10 In. 80.00
Bowl, Fruit, White, Cream, Blue, Green, 10 1/2 In. 160.00
Bowl, Green Ground, Winter Season Portrait, White & Blue Trim, 5 1/2 In. 125.00
Bowl, Heart Mold, Pink Roses, Cream & Green, Satin, 10 1/2 In. 160.00
Bowl, Hidden Image, White & Green, Flowers, 10 In. 190.00
Bowl, Iris Mold, Roses, Yellow, Green, Pink, 9 1/4 In. 110.00
Bowl, Iris Mold, White, Gold Highlights, Steeple Mark, 10 1/2 In. 50.00
Bowl, Leaf Mold, White, Tiffany Border, Pink Rose, Gold Highlights, 10 3/4 In. 125.00
Bowl, Leaf Mold, White, Tiffany Finish, Pink & Yellow Rose, Satin, 8 1/2 In. 60.00
Bowl, LeBrun II Portrait, Green Ground, Blue Flowers, Gold Border, 10 1/2 In. 825.00
Bowl, Lily Mold, Green Ground, Recamier Portrait, Bronze Border, 10 1/2 In. 700.00
Bowl, Lily Mold, Green Ground, Recamier Portrait, Iridescent Tiffany Border, 5 3/4 In. 200.00
Bowl, Lily-Of-The-Valley Leaf Mold, White, Green, Tiffany Finish Highlights, 10 1/2 In. 250.00
Bowl, Orange, Yellow, Green Ground, Castle Scene, 10 1/4 In. 225.00
Bowl, Pedestal, Pink Rose, Green, 7 1/2 In. 110.00
Bowl, Pink Poppy, Green Tones, 10 In. 135.00
Bowl, Pink Roses, Blue & Cobalt Blue Domes, Cream Center, 10 1/2 In. 350.00
Bowl, Portrait, Recamier, Green, Brown, Yellow, Maroon Border, Gold Detail, 10 In. 825.00
Bowl, Reticulated, Blue, Yellow, Pink, Maroon, Flowers, 10 1/2 In. 150.00
Bowl, Roses & Daisies, Green & Cream, 10 1/2 In. 100.00
Bowl, Scalloped Mold, Pink Flowers, Green, Green Tones, 10 In. 110.00
Bowl, Schooner, Luster Finish, 10 1/2 In. .... *ILLUS* 225.00
Bowl, Snowball & Rose, Cobalt Blue Domes, Green Trim Highlights, 10 3/4 In. 225.00
Bowl, Snowball & Rose, Cobalt Blue, Green, Gold Trim, Cream Center, 10 1/2 In. 450.00
Bowl, Snowball & Rose, Green Ground, Pink Border, 10 1/2 In. 125.00
Bowl, Square & Jewel, Flowers, Cream, Red Highlights, 11 In. 225.00
Bowl, Steeple Mold, Tiffany Border, Woman & Dog, 10 1/2 In. 775.00
Bowl, Sunflower Mold, White, Green, Tiffany Finish, Pink & Yellow Rose, 9 1/2 In. 150.00
Bowl, Sunflower Mold, White, Tiffany Finish Border, Pink Rose, Satin, 10 3/4 In. 450.00
Bowl, Swag & Tassel, Sheepherder I, 11 In. 450.00
Bowl, Violets, Cream & Green, Footed, 7 In. 60.00
Bowl, White, Green, Brown, Pink Rose, Gold Border, Red Highlights, 9 In. 90.00

RS Prussia, Bowl, Schooner, Luster Finish, 10 1/2 In.

RS Prussia, Plate, Keyhole Charmer, Light Green Ground, Gold Trim, 8 1/2 In.

Bowl, White, Poppies, Tiffany Highlights, Satin, 10 1/2 In. 130.00
Bowl, Yellow, Orange, Lavender, Pink & White Rose, Luster, 10 3/4 In. 130.00
Box, Hidden Image, Heart Shape, Green, Brown Hair, Pink Flowers, 4 1/2 In. 525.00
Bread Tray, Pink & White Roses, Cream Center, Gold Border, 13 In. 130.00
Bread Tray, Plume Mold, Yellow, Lavender, Pink, 16, 13 In. 170.00
Cake Plate, Carnation Mold, Rose, Pink, White, Yellow, Green, 11 In. 140.00
Cake Plate, Fleur-De-Lis Mold, Cobalt Blue, Pink Roses, Cream, Gold Trim, 11 In. 375.00
Cake Plate, Flowers, Handles, Red Mark, c.1900, 11 In. 175.00
Cake Plate, Icicle Mold, 2 Handles, Hanging Basket & Flowers, 11 In. 200.00
Cake Plate, Iris Mold, Autumn Season, Brown Tones, Handles, 10 3/4 In. 1050.00
Cake Plate, Iris Mold, Pink Poppies, Green, Gold Trim, Handles, 11 In. 140.00
Cake Plate, Iris Mold, Tiffany Finish, Pierced Handles, 9 1/2 In. 206.00
Cake Plate, Medallion Mold, 2 Handles, Pink, White Flowers, Portraits, 10 1/2 In. 1400.00
Celery Dish, Floral Mold, Handles, 12 1/2 In. 35.00
Celery Tray, Lily Mold, Cream Center, Pink & Yellow Rose, Tiffany Border, 12 1/2 In. 175.00
Chamberstick, Match Holder, White & Green Luster, Pink Rose, 5 1/2 In. 200.00
Charger, Lily Mold, Green Ground, Potocka Portrait, Bronze Border, 12 In. 350.00
Charger, Orange, Yellow & Green Ground, Cottage Scene, 11 3/4 In. 275.00
Chocolate Pot, 3 Scenes, Swan, Blue Bird, Barnyard, 8 1/2 In. 1300.00
Chocolate Pot, 4 Cups & Saucers, Steeple Mold, Gold Border, Pink Rose, 9 1/2 In. 625.00
Chocolate Pot, Carnation Mold, Cobalt Blue, Gold Stencil, Highlights, 9 1/2 In. 2750.00
Chocolate Pot, Cobalt Blue, Daffodil, Gold Stencil, 9 1/4 In. 500.00
Chocolate Pot, Cobalt, Blue & Yellow Flowers, Gold Trim, Handle & Finial, 12 In. 2300.00
Chocolate Pot, Iris Mold, Pink Poppies, Cream & Green, 9 3/4 In. 150.00
Chocolate Pot Set, Snowbird, 13 Piece 11500.00
Chocolate Set, White Satin, Stylized Swan, Green & Pink, 9 1/2 In., 7 Piece 775.00
Condiment Set, White, Green Highlights, Pink Flower, Mustard, Pepper, Open Salt 400.00
Cup & Saucer, Cobalt Blue, Iris 225.00
Ewer, Green & Yellow, Red Rose, Gold Handle, 7 In. 220.00
Gravy Boat, Underplate, Pink Roses, Cream, Gold Highlights 60.00
Hair Receiver, Cabbage Mold, Tan, Lavender, Green, Rose, Luster Finish, 5 In. 225.00
Hatpin Holder, Spilled Basket Design, Green Ground, 4 1/4 In. 90.00
Humidor, 8-Sided, Pink, Yellow & Green, Glass Bowl, 7 In. 300.00
Match Holder, Pink & Yellow Roses, Pink & White, Wall Mount, 4 1/2 In. 140.00
Mustache Cup, Roses, Blue & White, Beveled Mirror, 3 In. 75.00
Mustard, Brown, White Poppies 95.00
Mustard, Carnation Mold, Pink Poppies, Green Tones 90.00
Mustard, Lily Of The Valley, White & Green 80.00
Mustard, Pink Roses, White, Light Green, Red, Satin 75.00
Pin Tray, Pink Rose, Yellow, Green, Stipple Mold, 5 1/4 In. 120.00
Pin Tray, Roses, Cream, Cobalt Blue Trim, 5 1/2 In. 200.00
Pitcher, Cider, Lily Of The Valley, White, Green Highlights, Satin, 5 1/2 In. 230.00
Pitcher, Lemonade, Carnation Mold, Cobalt Blue, Gold Stencil Highlights, 9 In. 3400.00
Plate, Brown, Swan, 9 In. 200.00
Plate, Cream, Green Ground, Pink & White Rose, Iridescent Tiffany Border, 8 1/2 In. 450.00
Plate, Fruit, Cream, 8 1/2 In. 80.00
Plate, Green, Yellow, Pink, Mill Scene, 8 1/2 In. 120.00

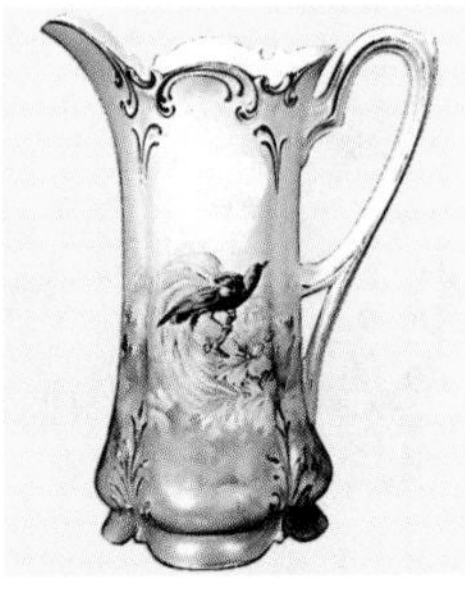

RS Prussia, Tankard, Bird Of Paradise, 2-Tone, Cream Satin Ground, 12 1/2 In.

Rubina, Pitcher, Swirled Panels, Reeded Handle, Overshot, 1870-90, 7 In.

Plate, Keyhole Charmer, Light Green Ground, Gold Trim, 8 1/2 In. .... *ILLUS* 1900.00
Plate, Leaf Mold, Pink Flowers, Green, 10 1/2 In. 110.00
Plate, Lily Mold, LeBrun II Portrait, Green Ground, 8 1/2 In. 250.00
Plate, Lily Mold, Recamier Portrait, Green Ground, 8 1/2 In. 240.00
Plate, Pink & Yellow Roses, White, Lavender, Yellow, 8 1/2 In. 40.00
Plate, Poppies, Tiffany Shading On Yellow, Green Ground, Gold Stencil, 8 3/4 In. 80.00
Plate, Snowball & Rose, Cobalt Blue Dome, 8 1/2 In. 125.00
Plate, Spring Season Scenic, Maroon, Green Border, Gold Greek Key Design, 6 In. 175.00
Plate, Wild Flowers, Cream & Green, White Tapestry, 8 1/2 In. 50.00
Pot, Yellow, Maroon, Blue, Gold Highlights, 7 In. 70.00
Relish Tray, Carnation Mold, White, Peach, Lavender, Pink Rose, 9 1/4 In. 125.00
Relish Tray, Carnation Mold, Yellow & Pink Roses, 9 1/4 In. 70.00
Relish Tray, Fruit, Light Brown, 9 1/2 In. 50.00
Relish Tray, White Poppies, Cream, 9 In. 60.00
Salt & Pepper, Pink Rose, Green 10.00
Serving Dish, White & Green, Flowers 300.00
Shaving Mug, Pink Poppies, Green & Cream 130.00
Shaving Mug, Reflecting Flowers, Yellow, Green 100.00
Sugar & Creamer, Carnation Mold, Green, Peach, White Ground, White Magnolia 110.00
Sugar & Creamer, Fruit, Roses, Green & White 150.00
Sugar & Creamer, Lily Of The Valley, White & Green Highlights 50.00
Sugar & Creamer, Pedestal, Green & White Blossom, Gold Stencil Highlights 175.00
Sugar & Creamer, Pedestal, Orange, Green, Yellow Ground, Castle & Cottage Scene 225.00
Sugar & Creamer, Sunflower Mold, Pink Flowers, Green 75.00
Sugar & Creamer, Sunflower, Light Green 60.00
Syrup, Sunflower Mold, Green, Gold Highlights 70.00
Syrup, Yellow Roses, Pink, Light Yellow 80.00
Tankard, Bird Of Paradise, 2-Tone, Cream Satin Ground, 12 1/2 In. .... *ILLUS* 13000.00
Tankard, Carnation Mold, Pink Poppies, White, Peach, Lavender, Satin, 13 1/2 In. 1000.00
Tankard, Pink & Yellow Roses, White, Peach, Blue, Green, Satin, 10 1/2 In. 240.00
Tankard, Ribbon & Jewel, Snowball & Rose, Green & White, Opal Jewels, 9 1/2 In. 325.00
Tankard, Stipple Flower, c.1900, 13 1/2 In. 290.00
Tankard, Yellow & Green, Pink & White Rose, 11 3/4 In. 1900.00
Tea Set, Carnation Mold, Cobalt Blue, Gold Stencil, 3 Piece 5000.00
Tea Set, White, Cobalt Blue Panels, Cobalt Blue Flowers, Gold Stencil, White, 3 Piece 300.00
Teapot, Demitasse, Pink Poppies, Cream, Blue, Pink, Gold Highlights, 9 In. 195.00
Teapot, Demitasse, Violets, White & Lavender, 9 In. 150.00
Toothpick, Flowers, Green & Yellow, 3 Handles 100.00
Toothpick, Pink Poppies, White, Green, Cream, Handles 125.00
Toothpick, Pink Roses, White, Cream, Green, Footed 50.00
Tray, Bun, Icicle Mold, Flowers, Cream, Cobalt Blue, Gold Border, 12 1/2 x 8 1/2 In. 425.00
Tray, Dresser, Fleur-De-Lis Mold, Green & Lavender, Spring Season Scene, 11 3/4 In. 1250.00
Tray, Swans, Rectangular, Green Wreath Mark, 11 3/4 In. 290.00
Urn, Cover, 2 Handles, Green, Yellow, Lavender, Pink Rose, 9 In. 325.00
Vase, 2 Handles, Green, Yellow, Pink Rose, 9 1/2 In. 250.00
Vase, Jewel Mold, 2 Handles, Green, Mill Scene, 8 1/2 In. 200.00
Vase, Jewel Mold, 2 Handles, Green, Yellow, Pink & White Rose, 10 In. 125.00

Vase, Pedestal, 2 Handles, White, Tiffany Finish, Pink, White Rose, Opal Jewels, 7 3/4 In. 450.00

RS SILESIA appears on porcelain made at the Reinhold Schlegelmilch factory in Tillowitz, Germany, from the 1920s to the 1940s. The Schlegelmilch families made porcelains marked in many ways. See also ES Germany, RS Germany, RS Poland, RS Prussia, RS Suhl, and RS Tillowitz.

Bowl, Footed, Hand Painted, Willow Tree, Medieval Building, 6 1/4 In. 400.00
Charger, Woman, Brown Hair, Signed, Hortense, 11 1/2 In. 275.00
Dinner Set, Art Deco Style, Ohme, Germany, Service For 7, 56 Piece 176.00
Relish, Pink & White Magnolia, Gold Surround Spilling Over Into Dish 85.00
Sugar, Cover, Freesia 45.00
Sugar & Creamer, Cover, 2 1/2 x 4 1/2-In. Creamer, 2 3/4 x 5-In. Sugar 75.00
Tray, Old Ivory, Roses, Elaborate Designs, 4 Marks On The Bottom, 6 1/4 In. 75.00

RS SUHL is a mark used by the Reinhold Schlegelmilch factory in Suhl, Germany, between 1900 and 1917. The Schlegelmilch families made porcelains in many places. See also ES Germany, RS Germany, RS Poland, RS Prussia, RS Silesia, and RS Tillowitz.

Vase, Medallion Scene, Woman Sitting Near Dog, Cream, Maroon Trim, Gold Stencil, 7 In. 130.00
Vase, Melon Eaters Scene, Maroon Ground, Gold Highlights, 9 In. 220.00

RS TILLOWITZ was marked on porcelain by the Reinhold Schlegelmilch factory at Tillowitz from the 1920s to the 1940s. Table services and ornamental pieces were made. See also ES Germany, RS Germany, RS Poland, RS Prussia, RS Silesia, and RS Suhl.

Cake Set, Open Handles, Flowers, Gold Trim, 10 1/4-In. Master Plate, 7 Piece 225.00
Powder Jar, Cover, Melon Eaters, Shadow Flowers, Gold Trim, 4 x 3 In. 350.00
Sugar & Creamer, Cover, Floral, Blue Mark, 3 1/8-In. Creamer, 3 3/4-In. Sugar 80.00

RUBINA is a glassware that shades from red to clear. It was first made by George Duncan and Sons of Pittsburgh, Pennsylvania, about 1885. This coloring was used on many types of glassware. The pressed glass patterns of Royal Ivy and Royal Oak are listed under Northwood.

Pitcher, Swirled Panels, Reeded Handle, Overshot, 1870-90, 7 In. .... *ILLUS* 110.00
Tumbler, Diamond Optic, Victorian, 3 3/4 In. 35.00

RUBINA VERDE is a Victorian glassware that was shaded from red to green. It was first made by Hobbs, Brockunier and Company of Wheeling, West Virginia, about 1890.

Cruet, Polka Dot, Faceted Stopper, 7 In. .... 365.00 to 400.00
Cruet, Polka Dot, Teepee Shape, 7 In. 290.00
Oil Cruet, Polka Dot, Tapered, Vaseline Handle, Faceted Stopper, 8 1/2 In. 460.00
Pitcher, Polka Dot, Applied Reeded Handle, 6 3/4 In. 175.00
Pitcher, Water, Vaseline To Ruby Glass, Coin Spot, Applied Reeded Handle, 6 3/4 In. 173.00

RUBY GLASS is the dark red color of the precious gemstone known as a *ruby*. It was a popular Victorian color that never went completely out of style. The glass was shaped by many different processes to make many different types of ruby glass. There was a revival of interest in the 1940s when modern-shaped ruby table glassware became fashionable. Sometimes the red color is added to clear glass by a process called flashing or staining. Flashed glass is clear glass dipped in a colored glass, then pressed or cut. Stained glass has color painted on a clear glass. Then it is refired so the stain fuses with the glass. Pieces of glass colored in this way are indicated by the word *stained* in the description. Related items may be found in other categories, such as Cranberry Glass, Pressed Glass, and Souvenir.

Berry Set, Flashed, 8 In., 7 Piece 150.00
Bowl, Flashed, 4 1/2 x 8 1/2 In. 70.00
Cordial, Ruby To Clear, Clear Stem & Foot, 3 5/8 In. 33.00

Cruet, Flashed, 5 In. 55.00
Pitcher, Flashed, 8 1/2 In. . . . . 250.00 to 400.00
Pitcher, Milk, Flashed, 8 In. 30.00
Pitcher, Tankard, Flashed, 10 1/4 In. 60.00
Pitcher Set, Water, Flash, 11 Tumblers, 8 1/2 In. 300.00
Sugar & Creamer, Flashed, Individual 50.00
Vase, Optic Ribbed, Applied Glass Swan Handles, c.1950, 6 1/2 In. 118.00

RUDOLSTADT was a faience factory in the Thuringia region of Germany from 1720 to about 1791. In 1854, Ernst Bohne began working in the area. From about 1887 to 1918, the New York and Rudolstadt Pottery made decorated porcelain marked with the RW and crown familiar to collectors. This porcelain was imported by Lewis Straus and Sons of New York, which later became Nathan Straus and Sons. The word *Royal* was included in their import mark. Collectors often call it *Royal Rudolstadt*. Most pieces found today were made in the late nineteenth or early twentieth century. Additional pieces may be listed in the Kewpie category.

Salt Dip Set, Oval, 3 3/4 In., 6 Piece 50.00

RUGS have been used in the American home since the seventeenth century. The oriental rug of that time was often used on a table, not on the floor. Rag rugs, hooked rugs, and braided rugs were made by housewives from scraps of material.

Afghan, Ivory, Red, Blue Design, Rust Ground, 3 Ft. 10 In. x 5 Ft. 5 In. 518.00
Afshar, Blue, Salmon Leaves, Ivory, Dark Brown Border, 4 Ft. 4 In. x 6 Ft. 865.00
Afshar, Boteh Field, Ivory Flowerhead, Blue Ground, c.1925, 5 Ft. 6 In. x 4 Ft. 4 In. 430.00
Afshar, Ivory Stepped Lozenge Medallions, Flowers, Birds, c.1910, 6 Ft. 1 In. x 4 Ft. 2 In. 619.00
Afshar, Multicolored Flowerhead Lattice, Ivory Floral Border, c.1915, 3 Ft. 8 In. x 3 Ft. 105.00
Agra, Green, Ivory, Salmon Medallion, Green Field, c.1940, 12 Ft. 5 In. x 9 Ft. 1429.00
Agra, Stylized Leaves, Burgundy, Beige Ground, 10 x 12 Ft. 1725.00
Art Deco, Geometric, Red, Black, Gold, Taupe, Wool, 14 Ft. 10 In. x 9 Ft. 10 In. 3819.00
Arts & Crafts, Geometric Design, Green Ground, 8 Ft. 3 In. x 10 Ft. 2 In. 460.00
Aubusson, Vase Of Flowers, Beige Field, Pink & Green Border, 6 Ft. 4 In. x 5 Ft. 10 In. 2990.00
Bagface, Baluchi, Northeast Persia, Late 19th Century, 2 Ft. 5 In. x 2 Ft. 2 In. 295.00
Bagface, North West Persia, Trees, Birds, Star Border, c.1920, 1 Ft. 9 In. x 3 Ft. In. 105.00
Bagface, Veramin, North Persia, Early 20th Century, 3 Ft. 2 In. x 1 Ft. 2 In. 646.00
Bahktiari, Blue, Ivory Leaves, Burgundy Border, Ground, 5 Ft. 4 In. x 7 Ft. 11 In. 230.00
Bakhtiari, Teal, Cobalt Blue, Leaves, Border, 9 Ft. 6 In. x 6 Ft. 5 In. 1530.00
Baluchi, Prayer, Northeast, Late 19th Century, 3 Ft. 10 In. x 2 Ft. 5 In. 440.00
Bidjar, Blue Ground, Flower & Leaf, Multiple Borders, 1 Ft. 10 In. x 2 Ft. 8 In. 690.00
Bidjar, Center Medallion, Red Field, Allover Pattern, c.1920, 7 Ft. 7 In. x 11 Ft. 3 In. 7700.00
Bidjar, Central Medallion, Blue Spandrels, Red Ground, 10 Ft. x 14 Ft. 7 In. 6169.00
Bidjar, Red Spandrels, Dark Blue Ground, Borders, 9 Ft. 3 In. x 22 Ft. 4 In. 2645.00
Bokhara, Dark Blue, Brown, Red, 4 Ft. 1 In. x 6 Ft. 7 In. 100.00
Bokhara, Geometric, Red Field, Mat, 3 Ft. 1 In. x 1 Ft. 1 In. 920.00
Bokhara, Ivory, Dark Blue, Burgundy Ground, 2 Ft. 3 In. x 8 Ft. 10 In. 230.00
Bokhara, Persian, Tan Ground, Borders, Mid 1900s, 8 Ft. 4 In. x 10 Ft. 5 In. 440.00
Braided, Mat, Coiled, Sheared, Multicolored, New England, c.1920, 1 Ft. 5 In. Diam. 385.00
Braided, Multicolored, Oval, c.1925, 7 Ft. x 10 Ft. 11 In. 400.00
Braided, Multiple Circle Design, New England, c.1940, 13 Ft. 6 In. x 8 Ft. 4850.00
Braided, Tightly Woven, Earth Tone Colors, Round, New England, c.1900, 4 Ft. 10 In. Diam. 695.00
Caucasian, 3 Star Medallions, Red Ground, Multiple Borders, 7 Ft. x 4 Ft. 1 In. 835.00
Caucasian, Red Field, Geometric, Ivory Border, c.1890, 3 Ft. x 6 Ft. 3 In. 1705.00
Caucasian, Repeating Boteh, Black Field, Blue, Salmon Borders, 3 Ft. 1 In. x 17 Ft. 2 In. 2300.00
Chinese, Art Deco, Center Medallion, Navy Field, Figural Border, Wool, 9 Ft. x 11 Ft. 8 In. 1375.00
Chinese, Art Deco, Flowers, Urns, Red Field, Brown Border, 9 Ft. x 11 Ft. 8 In. 550.00
Chinese, Art Deco, Phoenix Bird, Urn, Tan Ground, Wool, 3 Ft. 2 In. x 4 Ft. 11 In. 110.00
Chinese, Dogwood Blossoms, Medallion, Ivory Field, Blue Border, 5 Ft. 7 In. x 8 Ft. 8 In. 165.00
Chinese, Nichols Style, Phoenix, Black Ground, 12 Ft. 7 In. x 13 Ft. 5 In. 865.00
Drugget, G. Stickley, Geometric, Brown, Oatmeal Field, 110 x 143 In. 940.00

Never treat an old Oriental rug with a stain-resistant product. It will interfere with the natural lanolin in the wool.

Rug, Hooked, Cats, On Branch, Geometrics, Mounted On Frame, Mar. 1934, 40 x 24 In.

Edward Fields, Geometric Pattern, 18 Ft. x 10 Ft. 2000.00
Edward Fields, Swirl Pattern, 6 Ft. x 6 Ft. 8 In. 1180.00
Hamadan, Blue Spandrels, Red Ground, Ivory Border, 4 Ft. 9 In. x 6 Ft. 6 In. 690.00
Hamadan, Geometric Flowers, Blue Ground, Ivory Borders, 7 Ft. 2 In. x 9 Ft. 9 In. 1725.00
Hamadan, Geometric Flowers, Multicolored, Camel Ground & Border, 3 Ft. 7 In. x 13 Ft. 2415.00
Hamadan, Gray, Rust Ground, Camel Border, 3 Ft. 5 In. x 6 Ft. 1 In. 200.00
Hamadan, Multicolored, Brown Ground, 3 Borders, 4 Ft. 2 In. x 6 Ft. 520.00
Hamadan, Persian, Red Field, Medallion, Brown Border, 6 Ft. 8 In. x 4 Ft. 7 In. 118.00
Hamadan, Persian, Salmon Field, Navy Border, 6 Ft. 9 In. x 3 Ft. 1 In. 165.00
Hamadan, Red Field, Floral Arabesques, Pomegranate Border, c.1920, 6 Ft. 9 In. x 3 Ft. 6 In. 460.00
Hamadan, Salmon Field, Blue Medallion, Palmette Border, c.1910, 6 Ft. x 3 Ft. 6 In. 250.00
Hamadan, Sarouk, Salmon Field, 5 Ft. 4 In. x 6 Ft. 3 In. 805.00
Hamadan, Spandrels, Red Ground, Black Border, 3 Ft. 6 In. x 6 Ft. 8 In. 290.00
Heriz, 7 Medallions, Red Ground, Geometric Borders, c.1950, 11 Ft. 1 In. x 2 Ft. 10 In. 518.00
Heriz, Center Medallion, Red Ground, Ivory Corners, 11 Ft. 8 In. x 8 Ft. 2 In. 1495.00
Heriz, Geometric, Red Ground, Multicolored Border, 7 Ft. 4 In. x 8 Ft. 10 In. 470.00
Heriz, Geometric, Red, Blue, Brown, Ivory, Red Ground, 7 Ft. 4 In. x 8 Ft. 10 In. 468.00
Heriz, Geometric, Red, Blue, Green, Ivory, Red Ground, 8 Ft. 9 In. x 12 Ft. 878.00
Heriz, Gorevan Weave, Brick Red Field, Blue, Gold, Green, 8 Ft. 4 In. x 11 Ft. 7 In. 2475.00
Heriz, Ivory Corner, Blue, Pale Olive, 8 Ft. 9 In. x 12 Ft. 1610.00
Heriz, Ivory, Blue Borders, Red Ground, Runner, 1 Ft. 11 In. x 8 Ft. 9 In. 460.00
Heriz, Ivory, Blue Pendant Medallion, Red Field, Blue Palmette Border, 11 Ft. 6 In. x 9 Ft. 1026.00
Heriz, Medallion, Red Ground, Ivory Corners, Decorative Border, 10 Ft. 8 In. x 7 Ft. 9 In. 805.00
Heriz, Northwest Persia, Mid 20th Century, 12 Ft. x 9 Ft. 2 In. 3055.00
Heriz, Persia, Flowers, Medallion, Ivory, Blue, Mustard, Black, 10 x 13 Ft. 1925.00
Heriz, Red & Pink Abrash Ground, Black Border, 8 Ft. 9 In. x 12 Ft. 5 In. 1610.00
Heriz, Red Flower Medallion, Ivory, Cypress Tree, Red Border, 1900s, 6 Ft. 2 In. x 4 Ft. 5 In. 5240.00
Heriz, Rosette Medallion, Red Field, Geometric, Ivory, 7 Ft. 2 In. x 10 Ft. 7 In. 3300.00
Heriz, Serrated Leaves, Red Field, Blue Palmette Border, c.1920, 9 Ft. 9 In. x 7 Ft. 10 In. 2053.00
Hooked, 2 Deer, Multicolored Ground, Mounted, c.1875, 51 x 29 In. 2950.00
Hooked, 2 Reddish Cats In Profile, Maria, Black Border, White Leaf Corners, 30 x 39 In. 290.00
Hooked, 5 Hex Signs, Black Ground, Lancaster County, Pa., 1800s, 27 x 57 In. 495.00
Hooked, Abstract Design, Multicolored, Zigzag Border, Wool, Cotton, 76 1/2 x 45 In. 825.00
Hooked, Bear Cubs, Brown, White Ground, Oval, Border, Frame, 38 x 25 In. 300.00
Hooked, Bird On Branch, E. Ross & Co. Mfr, 22 x 42 In. 450.00
Hooked, Birds, Dog, Chicken, Cat, Fruit, Checkered Pattern, Frame, 31 1/2 x 38 In. 330.00
Hooked, Boston Terrier, Multiple Borders, 31 x 49 In. 489.00
Hooked, Boy With White Goose Being Chased By Large Mother Goose, Tulips, 18 x 36 In. 85.00
Hooked, Brown, St. Bernard Dog, Puppy On Leash, Ears Blowing In Wind, 40 x 40 In. 635.00
Hooked, Candlestick, Candle, Blue Ground, Lobster, Bound Edges, 8 x 38 In. 330.00
Hooked, Cat & Full Moon, N.G.S. Initials, 28 x 28 In. 440.00
Hooked, Cat, Black, Brown Ground, Flower Border, Frame, 27 x 48 In. 550.00
Hooked, Cat, Orange, Black, Perched On Leaf Branch, 39 3/4 x 24 1/2 In. 1485.00
Hooked, Cat, Silhouette, Wearing Bow, Playing Ball, Cardboard Back, 22 x 27 In. 230.00
Hooked, Cats, Black, Brown Ground, Stylized Flower Border, Frame, 27 x 48 In. 550.00
Hooked, Cats, On Branch, Fence, On Frame, Mar., 1934, 24 1/2 x 39 3/4 In. 1485.00
Hooked, Cats, On Branch, Geometrics, Mounted On Frame, Mar. 1934, 40 x 24 In. .... *ILLUS* 1485.00
Hooked, Cattle, Fenced Pasture, Wool, Cotton, 20th Century, 32 x 37 1/2 In. 705.00

Rug, Hooked, Dog, Standing, Red Clovers, Brown Ground, Mounted On Frame, 37 x 18 In.

Rug, Hooked, Penny, Layered Felt Circles, Green Ground, Floral Back, 80 x 40 In.

Hooked, Centennial, American, Center Shield, Arrow, Star Border, Corners, 24 x 36 In. 605.00
Hooked, Center Bouquet, Rose Blossom, Scrolled Leaf Border, Wool, 66 x 43 In. 80.00
Hooked, Chain Link, Green, Tan, Gold Shapes, Band Of Roses, Green, Black, 21 x 32 In. 144.00
Hooked, Cut Pile, Black & White Cat, On Cushion, Board Mounted, 1800s, 24 x 42 In. 1210.00
Hooked, Dazzling Block Pattern, Burgundy, Brown, Blue, Ivory, Black, 35 1/2 x 58 1/2 In. 230.00
Hooked, Diamonds, Red, Green, Tan, Light Blue, Pink, Brown, Borders, Wool, 25 x 48 In. 206.00
Hooked, Dog, Standing, Red Clover Corners, Brown Ground, Frame, 18 x 37 In. 440.00
Hooked, Dog, Standing, Red Clovers, Brown Ground, Mounted On Frame, 37 x 18 In. ...... *ILLUS* 440.00
Hooked, Dog, Yellow, Blue Ground, Border, 24 x 35 In. 28.00
Hooked, Farmhouse, By Stream, Bridge, Olive Green, Black Border, 30 x 51 In. 350.00
Hooked, Flower Center, Ivory Field, Geometric Knot Border, Stretcher, 32 x 54 In. 495.00
Hooked, Flower Medallion, Pink, Green, Yellow, Blue, 15 Blocks, Wool, 31 x 49 In. 235.00
Hooked, Flower Spray, Brown Ground, Frame, 1903, 35 1/2 x 53 In. 198.00
Hooked, Flower Wreath, Braided Edge, Round, 28 In. Diam. 55.00
Hooked, Flowers, Blue Gray Ground, Brown Border, Oval, 35 x 48 In. 110.00
Hooked, Flowers, Brown Ground, Red & Blue Border, Frame, 1903, 35 1/2 x 53 In. 200.00
Hooked, Flowers, Geometric, Alternating Blocks, Wool, Mid 20th Century, 108 x 71 In. 410.00
Hooked, Flowers, Tan Ground, Red Flowers, Black, Tan Borders, 37 x 25 In. 86.00
Hooked, Flowers, Tan, Brown, Oval, c.1950, 112 x 90 In. 330.00
Hooked, Flowers, Vase, Mounted, 1800s, 43 1/2 x 38 1/2 In. 330.00
Hooked, Fluted Urn, Flowers, c.1920, 32 1/2 x 60 1/2 In. 840.00
Hooked, Geometric Designs, 1800s, 44 x 28 In. 690.00
Hooked, Geometric, Multicolored, 8-Point Star, Zigzag Border, Cotton, Frame, 25 x 40 In. 410.00
Hooked, Grenfell Style, Sled, 3 Dogs, Trees, Black Border, 21 1/2 x 27 In. 210.00
Hooked, Grenfell, 3 Puffins, Sand, Rock Covered Round Black Border, 18 x 30 In. 2300.00
Hooked, Grenfell, Dog Sled Team, Figures, 34 x 46 In. 4360.00
Hooked, Grenfell, Labrador, 4 Ducks, Flying, Water, Rosie H., Mat, 53 x 40 In. 2900.00
Hooked, Grenfell, Labrador, Geese, Flying, Nighttime, Evergreens, 26 1/2 x 38 In. 1495.00
Hooked, Hit Or Miss Pattern, Multicolored, Wool, Early 1900s, 45 1/2 x 49 1/2 In. 175.00
Hooked, House, Blue Door, Flower Garden, Trees, 28 1/2 x 41 In. 270.00
Hooked, Lamb, 1930, 24 x 38 In. 395.00
Hooked, Landscape, 1870s, 25 x 35 In. 1250.00
Hooked, Lions, Flowers, Leaves, Brown & Red Striped Border, Wool, Cotton, 32 x 63 In. 4406.00
Hooked, Multicolored Border, New England, 1890, 42 x 26 1/2 In. 2350.00
Hooked, Native American Figures, Forest Setting, Stripe Border, 16 x 68 In. 764.00
Hooked, Noah's Ark, Toy On Wheels, Lamb, Duck, Chick, Elephant, Gray, 25 x 34 In. 250.00
Hooked, Oval Center, Multicolored Flowers, Wool Strips, c.1960, 144 x 108 In. 880.00
Hooked, Penny, Layered Felt Circles, Green Ground, Floral Back, 80 x 40 In. .... *ILLUS* 495.00
Hooked, Quatrefoil Center Medallion, Gray, Green Bands, Orange Flowers, 32 x 62 In. 210.00
Hooked, Red & White House, Trees, Floral Border, Wool, Early 1900s, 32 x 18 In. 118.00
Hooked, Roosters, Blue, Red Combs, Multicolored Tail Feathers, Horse, 31 x 32 In. 2530.00
Hooked, Rose Vine, Barn Swallows, Flowers, 84 x 78 In. 3080.00
Hooked, Roses, Center Leaves, Blue, White Ground, Sawtooth Border, Frame, 45 x 40 1/2 In. 275.00
Hooked, Roses, Leaves, Blue & White Ground, Sawtooth Border, Frame, 45 x 40 1/2 In. 275.00
Hooked, Ruffed Grouse & Chicks, 29 x 42 In. 1150.00
Hooked, Rural Scene, House, Trees, Circular Lane, 26 1/2 x 40 In. 115.00

Hooked, Sailing Vessel, US Shields, Banners, Wool, 1900s, 69 x 56 In. 7200.00
Hooked, Scorpions, 3 Rows, Geometric Border, 32 x 59 In. 415.00
Hooked, Scottie Dog, Multicolored Dog, Gray Ground, c.1930, 22 x 36 In. 220.00
Hooked, Sealife, Lobster, Swordfish, 1940s, 30 1/2 x 43 In. 715.00
Hooked, Ship, The Mayflower, Navy Blue Ground, 1830s, 52 x 30 In. 275.00
Hooked, Squirrels, Oak Tree, Acorns, Owl, Leaf & Acorn Border, 30 x 43 1/2 In. 290.00
Hooked, Stylized Scorpions, Geometric Border, 59 x 32 In. 415.00
Hooked, Tan Field, Bouquet, Meandering Border, c.1930, 30 x 42 In. 165.00
Hooked, Tulips, Hearts, Frame, 1884, 23 x 45 1/4 In. 240.00
Hooked, Waldoboro, Flowers, Oval, Signed, Pearl K. McGowan, 56 1/2 x 33 In. 468.00
Hooked, Waldoboro, Lion Reclining Under Palm Trees, Flower Border, 1940s, 30 x 62 In. 995.00
Hooked, Welcome, Mottled Red, Brown, White Ground, Stripes, 32 x 48 In. 1495.00
Indo Isfahan, Flowers, Blue Double Pendant Medallion, Trellis Field, 7 Ft. 6 In. x 4 Ft. 6 In. 952.00
Indo Isfahan, Red Field, Palmettes, Arabesques, c.1930, 7 Ft. 6 In. x 5 Ft. 3 In. 1810.00
Indo Tabriz, Ivory Ground Floral Field, Guard Borders, c.1930, 13 Ft. 7 In. x 10 Ft. 5 In. 5714.00
Karabagh, Cloud Band Medallions, Red Field, Ivory Crab, c.1915, 10 Ft. 2 In. x 3 Ft. 8 In. 715.00
Karabagh, Cloud Band, Blue Medallions, Salmon Ground, Ivory Border, 4 Ft. 7 In. x 8 Ft. 3680.00
Karabagh, Prayer, Green, Blue Ground, Red Borders, 2 Ft. 11 In. x 5 Ft. 7 In. 1150.00
Karabagh, Striped Ground, Ivory, Red, Blue, Brown, 3 Borders, 4 Ft. x 5 Ft. 5 In. 748.00
Karagashli, Blue Field, Red, Ivory Medallions, Multiple Borders, 5 Ft. 6 In. x 3 Ft. 2 In. 1285.00
Karaja, Northwest Persia, Mid 20th Century, 4 Ft. 8 In. x 3 Ft. 2 In. 590.00
Karaja, Red Ground, Midnight Blue Border, 2 Ft. 1 In. x 9 Ft. 375.00
Kashan, Cobalt Blue, Ivory, Red Central Medallions, Vine Borders, 9 Ft. 5 In. x 13 Ft. 1115.00
Kashan, Flowers Allover, Blue Green Field, Ivory & Pink Border, 8 Ft. 4 In. x 11 Ft. 5 In. 345.00
Kashan, Flowers, Red Ground, Multiple Borders, c.1975, 12 Ft. 6 In. x 9 Ft. 1380.00
Kashan, Ivory Spandrels, Red Ground, Blue Border, 4 Ft. 3 In. x 6 Ft. 6 In. 975.00
Kashan, Red Field, Flower Vines, Multicolored Palmettes, Medallion, 9 Ft. 9 In. x 13 Ft. 2475.00
Kashan, Rust Rosettes, Rust Ground, Borders, 6 Ft. 7 In. x 9 Ft. 9 In. 290.00
Kashan, Stag, Houses, Trees, Mountains, Red Ground & Border, 3 Ft. 8 In. x 5 Ft. 3 In. 1650.00
Kazak, 4 Medallions, Pale Blue Field, 4 Ft. 10 In. x 7 Ft. 4 In. 1610.00
Kazak, Blue, Ivory, Salmon, Gold, Brown, 4 Ft. 1 In. x 7 Ft. 11 In. 345.00
Kazak, Blue, Salmon Central Medallion, Hook Interior Panel, 4 Ft. 8 In. x 6 Ft. 1840.00
Kazak, Caucasus, Blue Field, Octagonal Medallion, Geometric Border, 3 Ft. 4 In. x 5 Ft. 2 In. 440.00
Kazak, Caucasus, Red Field, 3 Diamond Shaped Medallions, Flowers, 6 Ft. 3 In. x 8 Ft. 6 In. 825.00
Kazak, Caucasus, Red Field, 3 Medallions, Flowers, Birds, Runner, 2 Ft. 9 In. x 12 Ft. 3 In. 550.00
Kazak, Cream Center Medallion, 3 Borders, 5 Ft. 1 1/2 In. x 6 Ft. 11 In. 520.00
Kazak, Red & White Medallion, Blue Field, Floral Borders, c.1915, 4 Ft. 5 In. x 2 Ft. 11 In. 135.00
Kazak, Rows Of Botehs, Blue Field, Orange & Red Border, 3 Ft. 8 In. x 11 Ft. 3 In. 1265.00
Kerman, 4 Medallions, Red Ground, Leafy Border, 19 Ft. 2 In. x 13 Ft. 5 In. 9800.00
Kerman, Blue Ground, Red Center Medallion, Red Border, 8 Ft. 8 In. x 10 Ft. 10 In. 649.00
Kerman, Central Medallion, Cream Ground, Flowers, 12 x 22 Ft. 5300.00
Kerman, Central Medallion, Pink Field, Cartouche Border, c.1940, 25 Ft. 4 In. x 12 Ft. 6 In. 950.00
Kerman, Flowers, Burgundy Ground, Ivory Border, 4 Ft. 6 In. x 6 Ft. 10 In. 1150.00
Kerman, Flowers, Pink Ground, Ivory Border, 8 Ft. 11 In. x 11 Ft. 5 In. 3565.00
Kerman, Flowers, Urns, Geometrics, Wide Border, 9 Ft. 4 In. x 11 Ft. 7 In. 1100.00
Kerman, Repeating Flowers, Beige Field, Blue, Salmon Borders, 4 Ft. 6 In. x 6 Ft. 4 In. 1335.00
Khamseh, Abrash, Blue Boteh Field, 3 Floral Borders, 8 Ft. 9 In. x 3 Ft. 6 In. 515.00
Khamseh, Southwest Persia, Early 20th Century, 6 Ft. x 5 Ft. 3 In. 940.00
Kilim, 3 Medallions, Red Ground, Fringe, 1800s, 5 Ft. 7 In. x 9 Ft. 935.00
Kilim, Ivory, Black, Brown, Gold, Salmon, c.1920, 6 x 15 Ft. 1925.00
Kilim, Multiple Diamond Shapes, Hook Edges, Red, Blue, Black, Ivory, 9 Ft. 8 In. x 5 Ft. 430.00
Kilim, Turkey, Orange, Multicolored Stripes, 4 x 4 Ft. 385.00
Kuba, Geometric, Flower Borders, Ivory, Blue Ground, 3 Ft. 2 In. x 5 Ft. 5 In. 403.00
Lavar Kerman, Blue Field, Floral Trellis, Ivory, Tan, Purple, Yellow, c.1900, 7 x 7 Ft. 1619.00
Lavar Kerman, Flowers, Blue, Green, Maroon, Ivory Field, c.1925, 11 Ft. 7 In. x 9 Ft. 2 In. 2670.00
Lavar Kerman, Ivory Field, Flowers, Vining, Flower Border, c.1910, 6 Ft. 8 In. x 4 Ft. 6 In. 1050.00
Lilihan, Medallion, Flowers, Blue Ground, Geometric Flower Borders, 9 Ft. 10 In. x 12 Ft. 440.00
Mahal, 28 Flower Medallions, Red Field, Blue, Ivory, 10 Ft. x 13 Ft. 2 In. 1925.00
Mahal, Abrash Blue Ground, Brick Red Border, 8 Ft. 10 In. x 11 Ft. 9 In. 1208.00
Mahal, Center Medallion, Flowers, Geometrics, 2 Ft. 5 In. x 3 Ft. 10 In. 300.00
Mahal, Flowers, Ivory Field, Green, Red & Orange Border, 8 Ft. 4 In. x 11 Ft. 3 In. 2300.00

Mahal, Red Ground, Ivory & Blue Borders, 9 x 12 Ft. 635.00
Malayer, Blue Herati Field, Salmon Spandrels, Palmettes, c.1920, 6 Ft. 7 In. x 4 Ft. 8 In. 360.00
Malayer, Herati Field, Salmon Palmette Border, Runner, c.1920, 12 Ft. 10 In. x 3 Ft. 7 In. 1050.00
Malayer, Herati, Salmon Field, Ivory Border, c.1920, 6 Ft. x 4 Ft. 9 In. 565.00
Melas, Blue Lattice, Open Red Field, Figural Border, 19th Century, 4 Ft. 3 In. x 2 Ft. 10 In. 1026.00
Meshed, Flowers, Ivory Field, Red Border, 9 Ft. 3 In. x 12 Ft. 3 In. 1925.00
Meshed, Lobed Medallion, Purple Field, Floral Borders, c.1920, 13 Ft. 3 In. x 9 Ft. 5 In. 1230.00
Meshed, Red Medallion, Blue Spandrels, Cream Border, Flowers, 12 Ft. 6 In. x 19 Ft. 2 In. 590.00
Modern, Azeri, Golfers, Golf Course, Figures, Trees, Water & Bridge, 4 Ft. 10 In. x 6 Ft. 11 In. 880.00
Needlepoint Mat, Arts & Crafts, Vine & Buds, Tan Ground, Brown Border, 9 In. Diam. 420.00
Penny, Applied Fabric Circles, Brown, Red Ground, Cotton Backing, 52 x 28 In. 330.00
Penny, Felt, Green Ground, Felt Circles, Flower Print Backing, 40 x 80 In. 495.00
Penny, Trapunto, Daisies, Strawberries, c.1890, 34 1/2 x 54 1/2 In. 795.00
Penny, Wrapped, Tied Yarn, Ribbon, Rags, Hexagonal, Stretcher, 33 1/2 In. Diam. 518.00
Persian, Animals, Birds, Blue Field, Floral Vase Center, Silk, 3 Ft. 4 In. x 4 Ft. 9 In. 880.00
Persian, Farahan, 4 Ft. 4 In. x 6 Ft. 8 In. 3760.00
Persian, Flowers, Geometric, Blue, Black Field, 4 Ft. 2 In. x 6 Ft. 8 In. 1380.00
Persian, Flowers, Spandrels, Red Ground, Violet Border, 4 Ft. 3 In. x 6 Ft. 10 In. 375.00
Persian, Garden, Multicolored Flower Heads, Blue Borders, Silk, 9 Ft. x 5 Ft. 11 In. 2669.00
Persian, Hand Woven, 3 Center Medallions, Geometrics, c.1935, 3 Ft. 6 In. x 5 Ft. 2 In. 605.00
Persian, Lobed Medallions, Ivory, Blue, Red, Blue Field, c.1920, 9 Ft. 11 In. x 6 Ft. 7 In. 950.00
Persian, Oval Central Medallion, Man, Arabic Letters, 2 Ft. 11 In. x 2 Ft. 2 In. 1035.00
Persian, Red, Ivory Geometric, Cobalt Blue Ground, Red, Ivory Border, 4 Ft. 2 In. x 9 Ft. 7 In. 265.00
Persian, Rust Field, Allover Floral, Geometric, Lightning Medallion, 3 Ft. 10 In. x 6 Ft. 9 In. 275.00
Prayer, Kazak, Red Field, Flower Head Lattice, Multiple Borders, c.1915, 5 Ft. 3 In. x 3 Ft. 270.00
Prayer, Red Ground, Lozenge Medallion, Ivory, Red, Borders, c.1910, 5 Ft. 5 In. x 3 Ft. 2 In. 1050.00
Qashqai, Palmette, Lozenge Medallions, Geometric Borders, c.1900, 9 Ft. 2 In. x 5 Ft. 1335.00
Qum, Teal Field Center, Rose Medallion, Border, Silk, 4 Ft. x 2 Ft. 9 In. 220.00
Rag, Check, Orange, Blue, Runner, 11 Ft. 8 In. x 3 Ft. 3 In. 55.00
Rag, Multicolored Stripes, Checks, Runner, 15 Ft. 2 In. x 3 Ft. 6 1/2 In. 33.00
Rag, Plaid, Multicolored, Cotton, Runner, 11 Ft. 7 In. x 3 Ft. 3 In. 165.00
Rya, Abstract Design, Red, Brown, Orange, Danish Design Center, 11 Ft. 5 In. x 7 Ft. 10 In. 265.00
Rya, Danish Modern, Sunburst, Flame Border, Ivory Ground, 9 Ft. x 5 Ft. 9 In. 236.00
Sarouk, Allover Flowers, Blue Field, Floral Borders, Red, Blue, 2 Ft. 1 In. x 4 Ft. 3 In. 205.00
Sarouk, Blue Field, Flower Medallions, Floral Border, 3 Ft. 10 In. x 6 Ft. 10 In. 195.00
Sarouk, Burgundy Ground, Midnight Blue Border, 4 Ft. x 6 Ft. 4 In. 430.00
Sarouk, Camel Spandrels, Abrash Rust Red Ground, Blue Border, 4 Ft. 3 In. x 6 Ft. 6 In. 2875.00
Sarouk, Center Medallion, Flowers, Red, Blue, Ivory, Green, c.1950, 12 Ft. 5 In. x 5 Ft. 2 In. 405.00
Sarouk, Floral, Burgundy Ground, Blue Border, 3 Ft. 4 In. x 4 Ft. 11 In. 690.00
Sarouk, Flowers, Blue, Black Field, Blue, Flower Border, 4 Ft. 4 In. x 6 Ft. 750.00
Sarouk, Flowers, Burgundy Field, 1920s, 4 Ft. 2 In. x 6 Ft. 7 In. 1495.00
Sarouk, Flowers, Red Ground, Multiple Borders, Runner, 6 Ft. 11 In. x 2 Ft. 9 In. 230.00
Sarouk, Flowers, Red, Blue, Green, Ivory, Red Ground, 8 Ft. 10 In. x 11 Ft. 5 In. 585.00
Sarouk, Flowers, Salmon Field, Ivory, Blue, 1920s, 3 Ft. 4 In. x 6 Ft. 7 In. 920.00
Sarouk, Multicolored Floral Lattice, Cartouche Border, c.1940, 21 Ft. 10 In. x 8 Ft. 4 In. 1437.00
Sarouk, Red Field, Blue Floral Border, c.1940, 12 Ft. x 8 Ft. 11 In. 1335.00
Sarouk, Red Ground, Flowers, 8 Ft. 10 In. x 11 Ft. 5 In. 585.00
Sarouk, Red Ground, Flowers, Blue Border, 11 Ft. 9 In. x 16 Ft. 3 In. 4406.00
Sarouk, Repeating Flowers, Salmon Field, Olive, Blue Borders, 8 Ft. 9 In. x 11 Ft. 3 In. 2070.00
Sarouk, Spandrels, Red Ground, Blue Border, 7 Ft. x 9 Ft. 11 In. 1035.00
Serapi, Center Blue Medallion, Red Field, 9 Ft. 3 In. x 1 Ft. 6005.00
Shag, Concepts International, Polo, Circles, Multicolored, Wool, 9 Ft. 11 In. x 6 Ft. 8 In. 1535.00
Shiraz, Animals, Geometrics, Red Ground, Blue Medallion & Spandrels, 5 Ft. x 8 Ft. 6 In. 835.00
Shirvan, Blue Field, Floral Rows, Borders, Ivory Ground, c.1900, 4 Ft. 5 In. x 2 Ft. 10 In. 880.00
Shirvan, Blue Ground, Multicolored Medallions, Ivory Border, 3 x 6 Ft. 290.00
Shirvan, Prayer, Boteh, Blue, Geometric Mirhab, Floral Borders, c.1900, 5 Ft. 5 In. x 2 Ft. 3 In. 860.00
Soumak, Green, Red, Ocher & Gold Ground, 6 Ft. 2 In. x 8 Ft. 7 In. 1295.00
Soumak, Repeating Serrated Diamonds, Ivory, Blue, Salmon Field, 8 Ft. 7 In. x 10 Ft. 2 In. 2185.00
Tabriz, Blue Field, Herati, Palmettes, Guard Borders, c.1920, 7 Ft. 7 In. x 4 Ft. 9 In. 1810.00
Tabriz, Camel Field, Allover Palmettes, Scrolling Leaves, Vines, 9 Ft. 9 In. x 12 Ft. 7 In. 3850.00
Tabriz, Center Medallion, Ivory Field, Flowers, Red, Green, Blue, Tan, 3 Ft. 1 In. x 5 Ft. 550.00

Tabriz, Ivory Spandrels, Red Ground, Blue Border, 6 Ft. 8 In. x 10 Ft. 4 In. 175.00
Tabriz, Ivory, Flowers, Birds Border, Red, Blue, 8 Ft. 5 In. x 11 Ft. 6 In. 750.00
Tabriz, Purple Medallion, Ivory Spandrels, Tree Border, c.1900, 15 Ft. 3 In. x 11 Ft. 5 In. 2050.00
Tekke, Chuval, 3 Rows Of 4 Guls, Rust, Red Field, Tree Borders, c.1900, 3 Ft. 3 In. x 4 Ft. 10 In. 615.00
Tekke, Dark Blue, Orange, Ivory, Burgundy Ground, 3 Ft. 4 In. x 3 Ft. 9 In. 110.00
Tekke Turkoman, Ivory, Rust, Black, Red Ground, 4 Ft. 2 In. x 5 Ft. 1 In. 115.00
Tibetan, Dragons, Yellow, Gold Field, Early 20th Century, 5 Ft. 7 In. x 3 Ft. 1 In. 770.00
Turkish, Central Panel, Repeating Diamonds, Hook Border, 5 Ft. 2 In. x 6 Ft. 9 In. 865.00
Turkish, Prayer, Ivory Field, Columns, Flowers, Silk, c.1900, 5 Ft. 4 In. x 4 Ft. 1 In. 1900.00
William Morris Style, Green, Ocher Vines, Red Ground, Ivory Border, 6 Ft. x 9 Ft. 590.00
William Morris Style, Green, Ocher, Red Vines, Flowers, Ivory Ground, 9 Ft. 2 In. x 12 Ft. 590.00
William Morris Style, Red, Green Vinescroll Pattern, Ivory Ground, 2 Ft. 6 In. x 21 Ft. 9 In. 325.00
William Morris Style, Salmon, Ivory, Ocher, Green Ground, Borders, 10 Ft. 9 In. x 16 Ft. 10 In. 999.00
William Morris Style, Salmon, Ocher, Gray Floral, Ivory & Gray Border, 9 x 12 Ft. 1060.00

RUMRILL Pottery was designed by George Rumrill of Little Rock, Arkansas. From 1933 to 1938, it was produced by the Red Wing Pottery of Red Wing, Minnesota. In 1938, production was transferred to the Shawnee Pottery in Zanesville, Ohio. It was moved again in December of 1938 to Florence Pottery Company in Mt. Gilead, Ohio, where Rumrill ware continued to be manufactured until the pottery burned in 1941. It was then produced by Gouda Ceramic Arts in South Zanesville until early 1943.

Vase, Athenian Nude, Seafoam Green Exterior, White Gloss Interior, 9 1/8 x 6 5/8 In. 695.00
Vase, Fan, Blue, Mottled, 8 x 6 In. 60.00
Vase, Green, Original Sticker Label, 4 1/4 In. 100.00
Vase, Sylvan, Matte, Seafoam Green, Gloss White Interior & Bottom, Red Wing, 1932-37, 8 In. 125.00
Vase, Uranium Glaze, Orange Exterior, White Interior, No. 183, 8 1/4 In. 85.00
Vase, Woman's Head, Blue High Glaze, Art Deco, Marked, 11 In. 510.00

RUSKIN is a British art pottery of the twentieth century. The Ruskin Pottery was started by William Howson Taylor, and his name was used as the mark until about 1899. The factory, at West Smethwick, Birmingham, England, stopped making new pieces in 1933 but continued to glaze and sell the remaining wares until 1935. The art pottery is noted for its exceptional glazes.

Bowl, Lusterware, Mottled Turquoise Glaze, 1921, 5 In., 4 Piece 94.00

RUSSEL WRIGHT designed dinnerwares in modern shapes for many companies. Iroquois China Company, Harker China Company, Steubenville Pottery, and Justin Tharaud and Sons made dishes marked *Russel Wright*. The Steubenville wares, first made in 1938, are the most common today. Wright was a designer of domestic and industrial wares, including furniture, aluminum, radios, interiors, and glassware. Dinnerwares and other pieces by Wright are listed here. For more information, see *Kovels' Depression Glass & Dinnerware Price List*.

Russel Wright MFG. BY STEUBENVILLE

Aluminum, Canape Humidor, 10 1/2 In., Pair 1020.00
Aluminum, Punch Set, Saturn, Wood Knob Handles, 7 Piece 660.00
Aluminum, Sandwich Humidor, Wood Knob Handle, 12 In. 240.00
American Modern, Celery Dish, Granite Gray, 13 In. 35.00
American Modern, Creamer, Coral, 2 3/4 x 7 1/2 In. 15.00
American Modern, Creamer, Granite Gray 8.00
American Modern, Cup & Saucer, Coral, After Dinner 25.00
American Modern, Cup, Tea, Seafoam 17.00
American Modern, Dish, Pickle, Coral, 10 1/2 In. 20.00
American Modern, Gravy Boat, Underplate, Black Chutney 45.00
American Modern, Plate, Dinner, Granite Gray, 10 In. 8.00
American Modern, Platter, Square, Seafoam, 13 1/4 In. 60.00
American Modern, Salt & Pepper, Black Chutney 25.00
American Modern, Salt & Pepper, Cantaloupe, Stoppers 16.00

Pet doors should be less than 6 inches across to keep out small children who might then open a regular door for a burglar.

Russel Wright, Oceana, Bowl, Centerpiece, 1 3/4 x 19 1/2 x 4 1/2 In.

American Modern, Sauceboat, Coral 75.00
American Modern, Soup, Lug, Granite Gray, 9 3/4 In. 16.00
Chrome, Ice Bowl, Chase 85.00
Chrome, Salt & Pepper, Sphere, Chase 30.00
Iroquois Casual, Bowl, Cereal, Ice Blue, 5 In. 12.50
Iroquois Casual, Bowl, Fruit, Sugar White, 5 1/2 In. 10.00
Iroquois Casual, Platter, Oval, Nutmeg Brown, 13 In. 20.00
Iroquois Casual, Salt & Pepper, Stacking, Avocado Yellow 35.00
Iroquois Casual, Skillet, Cover, White, 15 In. 325.00
Iroquois Casual, Soup, Dish, Avocado Yellow, 5 3/8 In. 30.00
Iroquois Casual, Sugar & Creamer, Stacking, Nutmeg Brown 35.00
Lamp, Aluminum, Copper Paint, Chromium-Plated Metal, 1930s, 14 1/2 In. 8400.00
Lamp, Aluminum, Gilt Metal, c.1940s, 64 In., Pair 3600.00
Lamp, Torchere, c.1935, 64 In., Pair 540.00
Lamp, Torchere, Spun Aluminum, Trumpet Shade, Ribbed Shaft, 65 In. 355.00
Oceana, Bowl, Centerpiece, 1 3/4 x 19 1/2 x 4 1/2 In. ..... ***ILLUS*** 4425.00
Oceana, Bowl, Salad, Fluted, Wood, Klise Wood Working Co., 4 x 11 In. 480.00
Oceana, Bowl, Salad, Wave, Wood, Klise Wood Working Co., 4 x 10 x 11 In. 2400.00
Oceana, Relish, 4 Sections, Wood, 2 x 17 1/2 In. 1003.00
Oceana, Relish, Seaweed, Wood, Klise Wood Working Co., 19 x 4 1/2 In. 2400.00
Oceana, Relish, Snail, Wood, Klise Wood Working Co., 10 In. 2700.00
Oceana, Relish, Starfish, Wood, Klise Wood Working Co., 13 1/2 In. ..... 1200.00 to 2280.00
Plastic, Clock, Green & Clear, Chrome Trim, G.E. Telechron, 1950s, 9 In. 125.00
Plastic, Residential, Platter, Turquoise, Melamine, 14 3/4 In. 22.50
Steubenville, Platter, Yellow Green, Square, 13 In. 55.00

SABINO glass was made in the 1920s and 1930s in Paris, France. Founded by Marius-Ernest Sabino (1878–1961), the firm was noted for Art Deco lamps, vases, figurines, and animals in clear, colored, and opalescent glass. Production stopped during World War II but resumed in the 1960s with the manufacture of nude figurines and small opalescent glass animals. The new pieces are a slightly different color and can be recognized.

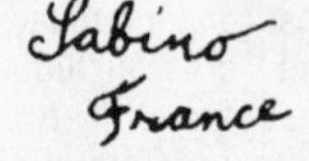

Bottle, Scent, Pomegranate, Opalescent, Signed, 5 1/2 In. 345.00
Bowl, Opalescent, Birds, Berry Branches, Brass Rim, Tab Handles, 3 1/2 x 16 1/2 In. 590.00
Bowl, Opalescent, Flowers, Signed, Vernox Paris, France, 3 x 10 In. 450.00
Figurine, Sea Turtle, Opalescent, Signed In Script, Paris, 2 In. 66.00
Figurine, Turkey, Signed, France, 2 In. 66.00
Plaque, 3 Woman, Classical, Water Fountain, Opalescent, 1920s, 4 3/4 x 12 In. 415.00

SALT AND PEPPER SHAKERS in matched sets were first used in the nineteenth century. Collectors are primarily interested in figural examples made after World War I. *Huggers* are pairs of shakers that appear to embrace each other. Many salt and pepper shakers are listed in other categories and can be located through the index at the back of this book.

Ball Mason Jar, Box, 1988 ..... 10.00

Black Boy On Alligator, Ceramic, 2 1/2 & 4 In. 28.00
Budweiser Beer Bottle, Muth, Buffalo, 4 In. 59.00
Chickens, Nodder 10.00
Fish, Nodder, Tails Up 15.00
Heinz Ketchup, Tray 15.00
Kangaroo & Baby, Nodder, 4 In. 24.00
Mammy & Pappy Yokum, Dogpatch USA, Sadiron Shape, 1958 .... 65.00
Milk Bottle, Warminster Farm Dairies, Hatboro, Pa., Muth, Buffalo, N.Y., 1930s, 3 1/3 In. 55.00
Mother Cow, Calves, Nodder 10.00
Mrs. Gamp & Sam Weller, 1930, 3 In. 14.00
Old Koppitz Beer, Glass, Amber, Metal Tops, Muth, Buffalo, N.Y., 3 1/3 In. 45.00
Olympia Beer, Stein Shape 18.00
Pheasant, Nodder 18.00
Skull, Nodder, 3 1/2 In. 35.00

SALT GLAZE has a grayish white surface with a texture like an orange peel. It is a method of decoration that has been used since the eighteenth century. Salt-glazed pieces are still being made.

Crock, Butter, Cover, S.S. Pierce Co., Boston, Brookline, c.1894, 5 1/2 x 9 1/2 In. 358.00
Match Safe, Blue Base Band, 3 In. 99.00
Pitcher, Cow, Relief, Blue, White, 8 In. 248.00
Pitcher, Gothic Style, Saints, Staffordshire, c.1850, 9 In. 129.00
Pitcher, Grape & Vine, Raised, Gold Decoration, Continental, 6 In. 110.00
Pitcher, Milk, Hound & Hare, Green, 9 In. 205.00
Pitcher, Peacock & Palm Trees, Relief, Blue, White, 8 In. 358.00
Stein, Pewter Lid, Men Drinking, Music Box, 12 In. 330.00

SAMPLERS were made in America from the early 1700s. The best examples were made from 1790 to 1840. Long, narrow samplers are usually older than square ones. Early samplers just had stitching or alphabets. The later examples had numerals, borders, and pictorial decorations. Those with mottoes are mid-Victorian. A revival of interest in the 1930s produced simpler samplers, usually with mottoes.

ABCDE

10 Commandments, Flower Border, Marieanne Lheureux, 1757, Frame, 19 1/2 x 11 1/2 In. 495.00
Adam & Eve, 6 Verse Lines, Embroidered Flowers, Vines, Silk, Linen, 19 1/2 x 14 1/2 In. 920.00
Adam & Eve, Flowers, Ellen Bell 1804, Flying Cherubs, Tree, Snake, Silk On Linen, 19 In. 930.00
Alphabet, Ann Rundle North Salem, 7 1/2 x 4 1/4 In. 805.00
Alphabet, Bible Verse, Berries, Mary Hornblower, 1759, Linen, Silk, Frame, 15 x 11 In. 400.00
Alphabet, Center Poem, Leaves, Flowers, Basket, Sarah Wales, Aged 12, Frame, 20 x 20 In. 495.00
Alphabet, Cross-Stitch, Panels, Flowers, Geometric Half Medallions, Quaker, 12 x 10 1/2 In. 764.00
Alphabet, Double, Numbers, Birds, Flowers, Rabbit, Windmill, Frame, 13 1/4 x 15 1/2 In. 195.00
Alphabet, Eliza Hollister's, Aged 7, Born December 8, 1797, Frame, 11 x 9 In. 275.00
Alphabet, Flower, Star Borders, Off-White Silk Thread, On Linen, Early 1800s, 12 x 10 In. 147.00
Alphabet, Flowerpots, Louis Alexander, January 20, 1833, Frame, 8 3/4 x 8 1/4 In. 220.00
Alphabet, Flowers, Animals, Emma Graybill, 1893, Pa., 25 1/2 x 21 1/2 In. 374.00
Alphabet, Flowers, Elizabeth E. Bomberger, Frame, 1863, 20 1/4 x 17 In. 230.00
Alphabet, House, Trees, Georgina Stubbs, March 10, 1827, Trenton, N.J., 10 x 8 In. 1554.00
Alphabet, Lucinda Spaulding, Age 11, Panels, Tree, Bushes, Baskets, Flowers, 17 1/2 x 12 1/4 In. 1175.00
Alphabet, Mary A. Gilmer, Greensboro, Silk On Silk, c.1842, 18 x 17 In. 1200.00
Alphabet, Numbers, Catherine Cronmillers, Age 18, 1827, Verse, 17 3/4 x 16 1/4 In. 1000.00
Alphabet, Numbers, Marry Ann Jenney, Aged 10 Years, 1826, Frame, 18 x 17 In. 3680.00
Alphabet, Numbers, Rachel Green, 1846, Frame, 7 1/2 x 7 1/2 In. 1250.00
Alphabet, Poem, Catharine Hoff, Mrs. Armstrong's School, Frame, 1813, 13 x 8 1/2 In. 770.00
Alphabet, Potted Flowers, Deer, Peacock, House, Cat, Dog, Frame, 22 1/8 x 19 1/4 In. 489.00
Alphabet, Sally Hemingway, Born 1816, Geometric Flower Border, c.1828, 8 x 17 In. 881.00
Alphabet, Verse, Barbara Ann Donaldson, Octr. The 8, 1811, Berries, Vines, 24 x 21 In. 1438.00
Alphabet, Verse, Birds, Flowers, Lydia Gordon, Massachusetts, c.1797, 23 x 17 In. 8815.00
Alphabet, Verse, Elosia L. Tarvis, 1837, Mahogany Frame, 17 1/4 x 16 1/4 In. 1058.00
Alphabet, Verse, Floral Border, Abigail Stevens, Aged 14, Early 1800s, 19 x 17 In. 920.00
Alphabet, Verse, Flowers, Strawberry Vines, Ruth Cogswell Upham, Age 10, 31 1/2 x 17 3/4 In. .. 1528.00
Alphabet, Verse, Fortitude, Hannah Hall Her Work, 1785, Silk On Linen, 14 x 10 In. 558.00

Alphabet, Verse, Hannah Lee, Age 12 Years, 1793, Linen, 10 1/4 x 9 1/2 In. 1528.00
Alphabet, Verse, Heavenly Love, Mary Burvill, 1800, Silk On Linen, 16 x 20 In. 705.00
Alphabet, Verse, Panels, House, Trees, Vines, Mary Rice, Age 12 Years, 17 1/4 x 18 In. 2000.00
Alphabet, Verse, Panels, Vine, Urns, Harriot Conant, Age 11, 1811, 15 x 21 In. 705.00
Alphabet, Verse, Peacocks, Flowers, Mary Harvey, England, 1800, 11 x 10 In. 800.00
Alphabet, Verse, Sally Mayo, Age 14 Years, Linen Ground, c.1798, Frame, 16 1/4 x 10 1/4 In. 5581.00
Alphabet, Verse, Scenes, Selinda Fales Holden, Aged 10 Years, Frame, 16 1/4 x 16 1/4 In. 3819.00
Alphabet, Verse, Silk On Linen, Mary Noyes Putney, Aged 10 Years, c.1826, 26 x 16 In. 1293.00
Alphabet, Verses, Flowers, Geometric, Abigail Clark Cilley, House, 18 1/2 x 17 1/2 In. 3525.00
Alphabet, Verses, Strawberry Vine, 3 Panels, Sawtooth Border, Nancy Lock, 17 x 17 In. 7638.00
Alphabets, 8-Point Star, Heart, Birds, Cadarina Schmitin, 1798, Frame, 23 1/4 x 23 1/4 In. 288.00
Alphabets, Bible Verses, Strawberries, Mary Hornblower, July 14th, 1759, 15 x 10 In. 750.00
Alphabets, Birds, Baskets, House, Linen, Silk, Polly Semantha Curtis, c.1824, 14 x 14 In. 633.00
Alphabets, Classical Images, Rose Filled Urn, Woman In Robes, c.1810, 18 x 17 1/2 In. 978.00
Alphabets, Crowns, Hearts, Baskets, Birds, Men, Dogs, Pine Tree, 1828, 19 1/2 x 16 In. 863.00
Alphabets, Family Record, Seth Davis, 8 Names, 1828-1836, Silk On Linen, 17 x 21 In. 375.00
Alphabets, Flowers, Hearts Center, Sunburst, Hannah Schell, 1820, 8 x 9 In. 285.00
Alphabets, Grapevine Border, Elizabeth Selby, Aged 16, 1835, Silk, Frame, 20 x 15 In. 1150.00
Alphabets, Numbers, Red, Blue Thread On Linen, Strawberry Border, 1832, 17 x 16 In. 805.00
Alphabets, Numbers, Verse, Flower Border, Huldah N. Potter, 1826, Frame, 18 x 17 1/2 In. 1430.00
Alphabets, Phebe Weeks, 10 Years Old, Phillips Town, 1823, Frame, 11 x 18 In. 660.00
Alphabets, Vining Flowers, ER Bennett March 1845, Blue Tan, Ivory, Frame, 19 x 10 In. 402.00
Basket, House, Birds, Trees, Insects, Wrought By Maria Worts, 1838, 18 x 17 In. 2100.00
Basket Of Fruit, House, Verse, Mary Evans, Born In Ohio 1815, Blue Ground, 16 x 13 In. 510.00
Center Poem, Harriet Pearles, September 18, 1793, Gilt Frame, 15 1/4 x 8 In. 248.00
Flowers, Trees, Birds, Elizabeth Campion, Aged 8 Years, 1832, 19 x 15 1/2 In. 1395.00
Flowers, Vine Border, Demilt Family, 1824, Gilt Frame, 17 3/4 x 14 1/2 In. 440.00
House, People, Animals, Trees, Flowers, M.A. Renouf, Jersey, 1840, Frame, 29 x 30 In. 1380.00
Martha Bowden, Work 1833, Red, Pink, Ivory, Blue, Brown, Silk & Wool On Linen, 12 x 12 In. 1115.00
Memorial, Memory Of Georg E & Grace Hill, Departed 23rd November, 1851, 24 x 27 In. 255.00
Memorial, Monument Surrounded By Weeping Trees, Obediah Fuller, 1834, 20 x 20 In. 575.00
Mourning Verse, Angels, Joanna Francis, Aged 11, 1835, Frame, 17 x 10 In. 1045.00
Pictorial, Elizabeth Morgans, Aged 15 Year, 1868, Wool On Linen, 12 1/2 x 17 In. 441.00
Poem, Eliza Latta Graham, Vine, Flowers, Gilt Frame, 23 x 18 In. 303.00
School Children Fishing, Eleanor Louisa Thompson, 1864, Wool & Linen, 18 x 15 In. 2070.00
Verse, Adam & Eve, Apple Tree, Lions Flanking Crown, 11 3/4 x 11 1/8 In. 375.00
Verse, Emblem Of Industry, Arianna H. Coles, 9th Year Of Her Age, c.1820, 18 x 14 In. 4995.00
Verse, Flower, Birds, Trees Border, Joanna Francis, Aged 11, 1835, 17 x 10 In. 1045.00
Verse, Flowers, Birds, Border, Panel, Anna Bunker Finished This Sampler, 1807, 13 x 12 1/4 In. .. 6900.00
Verse, Flowers, Trees, Dogs, Mary Allagaier, May 3rd, 1810, Frame, 20 x 16 In. 2185.00
Verse, Fruit, Flowers, Animals, Trees, M. Evan's Work, 1840, Frame, 17 1/2 x 21 3/4 In. 575.00
Verse, House, Flowers, Birds, Mary Jackson, In The 8 Year Of Her Age 181-, 18 x 24 In. 1035.00
Verse, House, Trees, Farm Animals, Amelia Franklin's Work, Maine, 1818, 17 x 18 In. 2015.00
Verse, On Youth, Elizabeth Crispe Loose, May 31st, 1836, Ohio, Silk On Linen, 20 x 20 In. 518.00
Verse, Roses, Floral Border, Hannah Elizabeth Condit, c.1834, Aged 12 Y., 16 x 16 In. 575.00
Verse, Ship, Animals, Birds, Butterflies, Susan Musson, Aged 11 Years, 1847, 14 1/4 x 14 1/4 In. 750.00
Verse, Strawberries, Flowers, Fruit, Hannah Lewsey, 1844, Frame, 16 1/2 x 16 1/2 In. 375.00
Verse, Suhelma Brundage Aged 10, Feb 18, 1837, Silk Thread, Frame, 18 x 17 In. 520.00

SAMSON and Company, a French firm specializing in the reproduction of collectible wares of many countries and periods, was founded in Paris in the early nineteenth century. Chelsea, Meissen, Famille Verte, and Chinese Export porcelain are some of the wares that have been reproduced by the company. The firm uses a variety of marks on the reproductions. It is still in operation.

Box, Cover, Armorial Crest, Wood Stands, 8 1/2 x 5 1/2 x 7 1/2 In., Pair 150.00
Figurine, Beggar Child, Eastern Clothes, Imitation Meissen Mark, 4 1/4 In. 400.00
Lamp Base, Urn, Baluster, Lobed, Dome Cover, Flowers, Electrified, c.1900, 14 In., Pair 880.00
Plate, Chinese Armorial, Reticulated, France, c.1880, 9 1/2 In. 200.00
Plate, Flowers In Center, Embossed Border, Hand Painted, Porcelain, Post 1940, 10 In. 19.00
Plate Set, Luncheon, Porcelain, 8 In., 12 Piece 468.00

SANDWICH GLASS is any of the myriad types of glass made by the Boston and Sandwich Glass Works in Sandwich, Massachusetts, between 1825 and 1888. It is often very difficult to be sure whether a piece was really made at the Sandwich factory because so many types were made there and similar pieces were made at other glass factories. Additional pieces may be listed under Pressed Glass and in related categories.

Bowl, Gothic Arch & Tulip, Thistle Base, 1 1/2 x 7 1/2 x 5 1/4 In. 14.00
Bowl, Log Cabin, Ship, Horse, Plow, Scalloped Rim, 6 1/4 In. 55.00
Bowl, Stag Horn, Leaf & Thistle, Cornucopia Bands, Scalloped Rim, 8 In. 25.00
Candlestick, Blown, Clear, Flared, Baluster Stem, Square Base, 9 x 3 In. 105.00
Candlestick, Column, Canary, Stepped Base, 9 1/4 In. 86.00
Candlestick, Hexagonal, Canary, c.1850, 7 1/2 In. 342.00
Candlestick, Hexagonal, Canary, c.1850, 9 In. 468.00
Candlestick, Petal & Loop, Canary, c.1850, 7 In. 99.00
Candlestick, Petal & Loop, Clambroth, c.1850, 7 In., Pair .... 230.00 to 275.00
Candlestick, Petal & Loop, Yellow Green, Clambroth Base, c.1850, 7 In. 1375.00
Cologne, Blue, Opalescent, Corset Waisted, Tooled Lip, c.1860-70, 4 3/4 In. 330.00
Cologne, Cranberry Cut To Clear, Cane, Stopper, 7 1/2 In. 450.00
Cologne, Heart, Cobalt Blue, Flat Top Pressed Stopper, 6 3/4 In. .... *ILLUS* 3850.00
Cologne, Panels, Cobalt Blue Cut To Clear, Bulbous Base, Stopper, 5 1/2 In. 358.00
Cologne, Ribbed, Cobalt Blue, Tam-O'-Shanter, Stopper, 6 1/2 In. 275.00
Compote, Fruit Basket, Princess Feather, Canary, 1835-60, 6 x 11 In. 33460.00
Compote, Loop Leaf, Open, 6-Sided Knop Stem, c.1850, 7 1/2 In. 154.00
Compote, Morning Glory, Plain Rim, 9-Sided Stem, 7 3/4 x 9 In. 176.00
Creamer, Arched Panels, Scalloped Rim, Applied Handle, 3 1/4 x 4 1/2 In. 61.00
Creamer, Heart & Scale, Molded Handle, Circular Foot, 1835-50, 4 1/2 x 3 In. 80.00
Curtain Tieback, Fiery Opalescent, 3 1/4 In., Pair 45.00
Decanter, Diamond Diaper, 3 Rigaree Rings, Blown Ribbed Ball Stopper, 9 In. 125.00
Decanter, Diamond Diaper, Ribbed Base, 3-Piece Mold, Blown Diamond Stopper, Pt., 8 1/4 In. 99.00
Decanter, Sandwich Star, Bar Lip, c.1865, 10 3/4 In. 66.00
Finger Bowl, Cut, Ruby Beaded Rim, 5 1/4 In., Pair 55.00
Finger Bowl, White Cut To Ruby, 2 3/4 x 4 1/2 In. 77.00
Furniture Knob, Lacy, Crosshatch Pointed Ovals & Stars, Opaque Blue, 1829-40, 3 1/4 In. 470.00
Goblet, Colonial, Fiery Opalescent, Hexagonal Stem, 1850-70, 6 x 3 1/4 In. 3300.00
Goblet, Lattice & Ovals, Flat Diamond & Panel, Applied Handle, Flint, 6 1/4 In. 2860.00
Hat, Sunburst & Diamonds, 3-Piece Mold, Rayed Base, 1825-40, 2 1/4 x 2 In. 80.00
Ink Bottle, Red & White Stripes, Swirled To Left, Ground Mouth, Hinged Pewter Lid, Pontil, 2 3/4 In. 1980.00
Jar, Grease, Black Amethyst, Pressed Body, 1840-50, 4 In. 465.00
Jar, Pomade, Bear, Clambroth, Embossed, F. B. Strouse, N.Y., 1840-1850, 4 3/4 In. .... 825.00 to 1760.00
Lamp, Kerosene, Banquet, Quatrefoil Font, Blue Cut To Clear, 1860-75, 20 3/4 In. 9900.00
Lamp, Kerosene, Banquet, Quatrefoil Font, Teal Green Cut To Clear, 1860-75, 20 1/4 In. 6050.00
Lamp, Kerosene, Dillaway Patent Font, Wavy Shoulder, Handle, 1871-87, 3 1/8 x 3 3/8 In. 120.00
Lamp, Kerosene, Eaton, Onion Font, Heliotrope, Ribs, 1865-80, 12 In. .... *ILLUS* 5060.00
Lamp, Kerosene, Moorish Window Font, White Cut To Ruby, Marble Base, 1860-75, 9 3/4 In. 385.00
Lamp, Kerosene, Punty & Oval Font, Cobalt Blue Cut To White Cut To Clear, 1860-75, 12 In. 1155.00
Lamp, Kerosene, Quatrefoil Font, Cobalt Blue Cut To Clear, Brass, Oregon Shade, 1860-80, 14 In. 3410.00
Lamp, Kerosene, Quatrefoil Font, White Cut To Green, Gold, Baroque Base, 1865-75, 12 In. 1870.00
Lamp, Kerosene, Ruby, Overshot Font, Brass Collar, 1870-87, 8 1/2 In. 2200.00
Lamp, Kerosene, Swirled Latticinio Font, Cobalt Blue & White Stripes, 1870-87, 10 In. 3410.00
Lamp, Oil, Amethyst, Oval Panels, Metal Burner, Finger, c.1850, 3 1/2 In. 460.00
Lamp, Oil, Clear, Double Pewter Burner, 6 1/2 In. 220.00
Lamp, Oil, Clear, Hearts, 6-Sided Base, 8 1/4 In. 55.00
Lamp, Oil, Fluted & Diamond Pattern, Clear, 9 In., Pair 165.00
Lamp, Oil, Star Pattern, 10 In. 77.00
Lamp, Oil, White Swirl, Brass Connector, Milk Glass Base, 10 In. 495.00
Lamp, Oil, White Swirled, Brass Connector, Marble Base, 9 In. 469.00
Lamp, Whale Oil, Blown Font, Clear, Globular, 12 Broad Flutes, 1827-35, 4 1/4 In. 715.00
Lamp, Whale Oil, Blown Font, Clear, Stepped Square Base, Pewter Collar, c.1835, 12 In. 330.00

Sandwich Glass, Cologne, Heart, Cobalt Blue, Flat Top Pressed Stopper, 6 3/4 In.

Sandwich Glass, Lamp, Kerosene, Eaton, Onion Font, Heliotrope, Ribs, 1865-80, 12 In.

Sandwich Glass, Pitcher, Comet, Cut Thumbprints & Honeycomb, c.1865, 10 In.

Lamp, Whale Oil, Cable Font, 6-Sided Base, 2-Tube Burner, 1845-65, 7 3/4 x 3 1/2 In. 198.00
Lamp, Whale Oil, Cable With Ring Font, Brass Collar, Handle, 1850-70, 2 3/4 x 2 1/8 In. 286.00
Lamp, Whale Oil, Cable With Ring Font, Clearh, Handle, 2-Tube Burner, 4 1/2 In. 578.00
Lamp, Whale Oil, Circle & Ellipse Font, Canary, Pewter Collar, 1840-60, 10 1/4 In. 1045.00
Lamp, Whale Oil, Clear, Bulbous, Blown Baluster, Ringed, 10 3/4 In. 358.00
Lamp, Whale Oil, Cut Font, Clear, Applied Wafers, Blown Baluster Stem, Burner, 13 In. 4950.00
Lamp, Whale Oil, Giant Sawtooth Font, Clear, 10 3/4 In., Pair 345.00
Lamp, Whale Oil, Harp Lyre Font, Clear, 2-Tube Burner, Brass Collar, 5 x 4 In. .... 305.00 to 385.00
Lamp, Whale Oil, Horn Of Plenty Font, Comet, Clear, 10 1/4 In. 195.00
Lamp, Whale Oil, Punty & Star Font, Clear, 6-Sided Base, Brass, Handle, 9 1/2 In. .... 88.00 to 120.00
Lamp Shade, Cut Frosted & Bright, Grapes, 7 1/4 In., Pair 440.00
Mug, Daisy, Flared Rim, Scrolled Handle, Octagonal Base, 3 1/4 x 4 1/2 In. 22.00
Mustard, Cover, Underplate, Peacock Eye, Spoon Slot, 1830-45, 2 1/2 In. 275.00
Nappy, Diamonds, Ribbed, Flared & Folded Rim, Diamond Ray Base, 1825-40, 1 1/4 x 5 In. 66.00
Nappy, Shield & Acanthus Leaf, Scalloped Rim, 1830-45, 1 7/8 x 9 1/2 In. 66.00
Nappy, Tulip & Acanthus Leaf, 1830-45, 2 x 9 1/2 In. 110.00
Newel Post, Punty, Red Cut To White Cut To Clear, Brass Fitting, 6 1/2 In. 440.00
Pitcher, Comet, Cut Thumbprints & Honeycomb, c.1865, 10 In. .... *ILLUS* 3740.00
Pitcher, Milk, Diamond Thumbprint, Bulbous, 8 3/4 In. 2530.00
Pitcher, Milk, Mercury Glass, Clear Handle, 6 In. 173.00
Pitcher, Overshot, Blue, Amber Rigaree & Reeded Handle, Flared Foot, 10 In. 290.00
Pitcher, Ribbed Palm, Applied Handle, 9 In. 192.00
Plate, Eye & Scale, Canary, Rayed Base, 1830-45, 3/4 x 4 1/2 In. 176.00
Plate, Quatrefoil & Feather, Scalloped Rim, Stippled Center, 1830-45, 1 x 9 3/4 In. 130.00
Salt, Basket Of Flowers, Peacock Green, Groove & Diamond Base, 3 In. .... *ILLUS* 8800.00
Salt, Beaded Scroll & Basket Of Flowers, Opalescent, Beaded Circle Base, 2 x 3 1/4 In. 198.00
Salt, Boat, Rope & Strawberry-Diamond Bands, Plain Base, 1 3/4 x 4 In. 155.00
Salt, Crown, Crescent Edge, Diamond Fan Base, 4 Scroll Feet, 2 1/8 x 3 1/8 In. 66.00
Salt, Eagle & Shield, Eagle Corners, 12-Petal Base, 4-Footed, 2 1/8 x 3 1/4 In. .... 155.00 to 176.00
Salt, Eagle & Shield, Eagle Corners, 12-Ray Base, 4-Footed, 2 1/8 x 3 1/4 In. 155.00
Salt, Eagle & Shield, Eagle Corners, 12-Ray Base, Fiery Opalescent, 4-Footed, 2 1/8 x 3 1/4 In. 825.00
Salt, Eagle & Stippled Shield, Eagle Corners, 12-Ray Base, 4-Footed, 2 1/8 x 3 1/4 In. 605.00
Salt, Oval, Cornucopia & Diamond Scroll, Serrated Scalloped Rim, 1835-50, 2 3/8 x 3 3/8 In. 45.00
Salt, Peacock Eye, Oval, Roped Eyes, Rayed Base, 1 3/8 x 3 x 3 3/4 In. 230.00
Salt, Strawberry Diamond, 6-Point Stars, Cobalt Blue, Scallop & Point Rim, 2 x 3 In. 385.00
Smoke Bell, Blown, Engraved Punty & Star, Frosted, Ruffled Cobalt Rim, 1860-87, 9 1/2 In. 358.00
Smoke Bell, Blown, Fiery Opalescent, Ruffled Ruby Rim, 1860-87, 8 1/4 In. 255.00
Smoke Bell, Blown, Opal, Painted Flowers, Pink, Metal Cap, 1865-87, 3 1/4 In. 198.00
Smoke Bell, Blown, Opal, Painted Marsh Grass, Salmon Bands, 1865-87, 3 x 3 1/4 In. 198.00
Smoke Bell, Blown, Opal, Ruffled Cobalt Rim, Clear Glass Ring, 1860-87, 7 1/2 In. .... 55.00 to 66.00
Smoke Bell, Blown, Opal, Ruffled Ruby Rim, Metal Cap, 1865-87, 3 1/2 In. 99.00
Spoon Holder, Hexagonal, Pale Blue, Toy, 1850-70, 1 3/4 x 1 1/4 In. 120.00
Spooner, Cut Frosted & Bright, Beaded Ruby Band, Parker & Casper Stand, c.1880, 3 In. 230.00
Sugar, Cover, Cornucopia, Scallop & Star Medallion, Flared Base, 6 1/2 x 5 1/2 In. 55.00

Sandwich Glass, Salt, Basket Of Flowers, Peacock Green, Groove & Diamond Base, 3 In.

Sandwich Glass, Vase, Elongated Loop, Bisecting Lines, Red, White Streaks, 6-Sided, 6 7/8 In.

Sandwich Glass, Vase, Sawtooth, Clambroth, Jade Green, Folded Scalloped Rim, 9 In.

Sugar, Cover, Cornucopia, Star Medallion, Flared Base, 6 1/2 x 5 1/2 In. 55.00
Sugar, Cover, Gothic Arch, Canary, Octagonal Foot, 1840-50, 5 1/2 x 4 5/8 In. 605.00
Sugar Shaker, Ruby Stain, 10 Panels, Tapered, Threaded & Ground Mouth, Brass Lid, 5 1/2 In. 247.00
Toy, Flat Iron, 1 3/8 In. 318.00
Toy, Flat Iron, Amethyst, 1800s, 1 3/8 In. 460.00
Tray, Butterfly & Pinwheel, 1835-50, 4 3/8 x 6 7/8 In. 66.00
Tumbler, 9 Panels, Pontil, Toy, 1845-70, 1 3/4 x 1 5/8 In. 22.00
Tumbler, Panel & Bull's-Eye, Cobalt Blue, Hexagonal, 3 1/2 In. 35.00
Vase, 4 Printie Block, 8-Scallop Rim, 6-Sided Stem, Flint, 9 3/4 In. 99.00
Vase, Cobalt Blue & White Cut To Clear, Gold Enameled, 5 3/4 In. 165.00
Vase, Elongated Loop, Bisecting Lines, Red, White Streaks, 6-Sided, 6 7/8 In. .... ***ILLUS*** 7700.00
Vase, Hyacinth, Blue Green, 8 1/8 In. 112.00
Vase, Icicle, Cylindrical, Prussian Blue, Enameled Grass, Rigaree Rim, 7 1/2 In. 405.00
Vase, Overshot Wheel, Icicle, Prussian Blue, Enameled Grass, Rigaree Rim, 7 1/2 In. 405.00
Vase, Sawtooth, Clambroth, Jade Green, Folded Scalloped Rim, 9 In. .... ***ILLUS*** 990.00
Vase, Trumpet, Cobalt Blue, 4 Printie Block, Ruffled Edge, Hexagonal Foot, 11 3/4 In. 1840.00
Vase, Trumpet, Tappan, Deep Teal Blue, Disc Foot, 10 1/4 In. 336.00
Vase, Tulip, Violet Blue, White Striations, Octagonal Base, 1845-65, 10 1/4 x 5 5/8 In. 22000.00
Vase, White Cut To Green, Gold Enameled, Flared, 16 1/4 In. 495.00
Wine, Gold Rim, Canary, 4 1/2 In. 55.00

SARREGUEMINES is the name of a French town that is used as part of a china mark. Utzschneider and Company, a porcelain factory, made ceramics in Sarreguemines, Lorraine, France, from about 1775. Transfer-printed wares and majolica were made in the nineteenth century. The nineteenth-century pieces, most often found today, usually have colorful transfer-printed decorations showing peasants in local costumes.

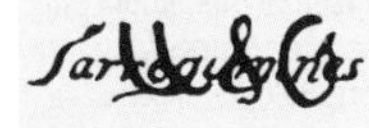

Holder, Placecard, Shell & Coral, Majolica, 2 1/4 In. 196.00
Stein, Birds, Transfer, 1/4 Liter, 5 1/2 In. 218.00
Stein, Man Feeding Baby At Table, No. 2889, Stoneware, Pewter Lid, 1/2 Liter 845.00
Urn, Cover, Majolica, Bronze, France, c.1850, 17 x 10 In. 3745.00
Vase, Dolphin & Shell, No. 948, 15 In. 504.00

SASCHA BRASTOFF made decorative accessories, ceramics, enamels on copper, and plastics of his own design. He headed a factory, Sascha Brastoff of California, Inc., in West Los Angeles, from 1953 until about 1973. He died in 1993. Pieces signed with the signature *Sascha Brastoff* were his work and are the most expensive. Other pieces marked *Sascha B.* or with a stamped mark were made by others in his company. Pieces made by Matt Adams after he left the factory are listed here with his name.

Vase, Pottery, Glazed, Gilt, Marked, 1950s, 19 1/4 In. 60.00

SATIN GLASS is a late-nineteenth-century art glass. It has a dull finish that is caused by hydrofluoric acid vapor treatment. Satin glass was made in many colors and sometimes has applied decorations. Satin glass is also listed by factory name, such as Webb, or in the Mother-of-Pearl category in this book.

Bowl, 6 Curved Petals, Pale Green, 3 1/4 x 6 In. 69.00
Compote, Green, Tiara, 16 x 5 1/2 x 4 1/2 In. 40.00
Dresser Jar, Art Deco, Green, Footed, Durmay, c.1930, 6 x 4 1/2 In. 235.00
Lamp, Fairy, Pink To White, White Lining, Matte Finish, 4 In., Pair 290.00
Rose Bowl, Yellow, White, 4 In. 45.00
Shade, Beaded Fringe, Art Nouveau, Mother-Of-Pearl, 4 x 5 1/2 In. 85.00
Vase, Lavender, 4 5/8 In. 4.00
Vase, Pink & White Swirl, Ruffled Edge, 10 In. 345.00
Vase, Seahorse Handles, 7 1/4 x 5 In. 36.00

SATSUMA is a Japanese pottery with a distinctive creamy beige crackled glaze. Most of the pieces were decorated with blue, red, green, orange, or gold. Almost all Satsuma found today was made after 1860, especially during the Meiji Period, 1868–1912. During World War I, Americans could not buy undecorated European porcelains. Women who liked to make hand painted porcelains at home began to decorate plain Satsuma. These pieces are known today as *American Satsuma.*

Bowl, Flowers, 8 In. 118.00
Bowl, Gilt Highlights, c.1900, 11 In. 94.00
Bowl, Landscape, Dragons, Crane, Octopus, Crab, Turtle, Ivory, 7 x 14 In. 185.00
Bowl, Lohan, Buddhist Saints, Karako, Small Boy, Crane, c.1860, 5 1/2 In. 375.00
Bowl, Women, Landscape, Lavender Wisteria, Vines, Ryokuzan, 5 In. 4315.00
Censer, 100 Wise Men, Double Gourd Shape, Foo Dog Finial, 1800s, 5 1/2 In. 325.00
Censer, Battle Scenes, Armor Box, Helmet On Top, 1800s, 7 In. 2350.00
Censer, Silver Cover, Chrysanthemum, Ruyi Feet, Japan, 19th Century, 4 1/2 In. 1410.00
Censer, Silver Flowers, Warriors, Poets, Blue Ground, Kinkozan, c.1900, 4 1/4 In. 1880.00
Censer, Women, Village, Ducks, Diamond, Indented, Kinkozan, 1800s, 6 x 8 In. 3819.00
Charger, Samurai, Early 1900s, 15 In. 265.00
Chawan, Tea Bowl, Peony Shape, Dragon, Raised Foot, 4 3/4 In. 780.00
Cup & Saucer, Woman, Children, Tozan, Early 1900s 59.00
Cup & Saucer Set, Demitasse, Earthenware, 23 Piece 176.00
Dish, Oval, Lute Player, Noblemen, In Boat, Dragon Border, 24 1/2 In. 720.00
Figurine, Woman, On Platform, Playing Koto, Early 1900s, 6 1/4 In. 240.00
Incense Box, Room Interior, Early 1900s, 3 1/4 In. 176.00
Incense Burner, Square, Chrysanthemum, Waterfall, Pierced Dome Cover, Kozan, 5 In. 805.00
Jar, Baluster, Koshuzan, Painted, Rakan, Carved, Dragon, Japan, 1800s, 7 In. 105.00
Jar, Cover, Exotic Bird, Flower, Leaf Ground, Early 1900s, 8 1/2 In. 405.00
Plate, 100 Wise Men, Dragon, 1800s, 9 1/2 In. 646.00
Plate, Flower-Form Cartouche, Blue & Gold Ground, Kinkozan, 6 In. 720.00
Tea Caddy, Buddhist Wise Men In Gilt Costumes, Dragon, Star-Filled Sky, 7 x 5 1/2 In. 390.00
Tea Caddy, Cover, 4 x 3 In. 700.00
Tokuri, Sake Bottle, Double Gourd Shape, Dragon & Cloud, Ceramic Stopper, Kinkozan, 13 In. 230.00
Tureen, Enamel Parrots & Chrysanthemums, Oval, Urn Foot, Domed Cover, 12 In. 705.00
Urn, Cover, Gilt, Multicolored, Baluster, Buddha, 8 Immortals, Kyoto, c.1900, 17 x 13 In. 470.00
Urn, Red Ground, Gold Decoration, Double Handle, 21 x 12 In. 235.00
Vase, 8-Sided, Lohan, Buddhist Saints, Black Mark Signature, 6 In. 290.00
Vase, Baluster, Animal Head Handles, c.1900, 9 1/2 x 5 1/2 In., Pair 1410.00
Vase, Bamboo, Cylindrical, Bulging Base, 3-Footed, 4 1/4 x 3 3/4 In. 86.00
Vase, Birds, Peonies, Bulbous, Tubular Neck, Multicolor Enamels, Gilding, 12 In. 323.00
Vase, Bucket Shape, Women, Children, 7 1/4 In. 2470.00
Vase, Buddhist Saints, Brocade Panels, Lobated Form, 6 In. 1293.00
Vase, Buddhist Saints, Signed, Gyokusen, c.1900, 6 In. 590.00
Vase, Buddhist Saints, Square, Flaring Mouth & Neck, Late 1800s, 8 In., Pair 470.00
Vase, Courtiers, Birds, Flowers, Fans, Egg Shape, Tall Neck, Japan, Late 1800s, 30 1/2 In. 411.00

Vase, Cover, Flowers, Oval, 18 In., Pair 717.00
Vase, Cylinder, Butterfly Dancers, Late 19th Century, 9 1/2 In. 633.00
Vase, Cylindrical, 3-Footed, Dragon, 7 Sages, Wood Stand, Late 1800s, 3 3/4 In. 440.00
Vase, Dragon, Flowers, Double Gourd Shape, Relief, 8 In., Pair 353.00
Vase, Fans, Flowers, Lamp Mount, Early 1900s, 16 In. 176.00
Vase, Festival, Millefleur, Broad Borders, Early 1900s, 6 1/4 In. 294.00
Vase, Figures, Inverted Pear Shape, Brocade Ground, Late 1800s, 7 In. 230.00
Vase, Figures, Slender Neck, Late 19th Century, 4 1/2 In., Pair 325.00
Vase, Immortals, Dragon, Baluster Form, 12 In. 956.00
Vase, Lake Biwa, Brocade Shoulder, Kinkozan, 9 3/4 In. 2760.00
Vase, Lake Biwa, Flowers, Geometrics, Silver Cover, Yabu Meizan, 8 1/2 In. 16100.00
Vase, Landscape, Figures, Bird, Flower, Rectangular, Late 1800s, 9 1/2 In. 430.00
Vase, Landscape, Mallet Shape, Red Mark, Early 1900s, 3 3/4 In., Pair 150.00
Vase, Lohan, Buddhist Saints, Inverted Pear Shape, c.1870, 5 3/4 In. 345.00
Vase, Moriage, Cinnabar Lacquer, 19th Century, 16 In. 120.00
Vase, Moriage, Trumpet Mouth, Leaf Handles, Early 1900s, 18 In. 235.00
Vase, People, Birds, Flowers, Globular, Trumpet Mouth, c.1900, 5 In. 176.00
Vase, Processional Scene, Slender, Shoulder, Kinkozan, 5 In. 1380.00
Vase, Scholars, Flowers, Hexagonal, Early 1900s, 15 3/4 In. 120.00

SATURDAY EVENING GIRLS, see Paul Revere Pottery category.

SCALES have been made to weigh everything from babies to gold. Collectors search for all types. Most popular are small gold dust scales and special grocery scales.

Advertising, Wrigley's Pressed Tin, Brass, 9 1/2 In. 275.00
Advertising, Wrigley's Spearmint Pepsin Gum, Brass, Dial & Pan, Painted, 9 1/2 x 7 In. 715.00
Balance, Analytical Beam, Becker & Sons, Brass, Mahogany Case, 23 In. 176.00
Balance, Analytical Beam, Seederer Kohlbusch, Brass, Mahogany Case, 15 1/2 In. 90.00
Balance, Analytical, Christian Becker, Chain-O-Matic, Spatulas, Weights 470.00
Balance, Beam, Brass, Steel Arm, Hoop Stirrups, 27 In. 120.00
Balance, Beam, Fairbanks, No. 8, Burgundy Paint, Decals, Pinstripes, 6 x 13 In. 145.00
Balance, Coin, W & T Avery, Brass, Steel Beam, 10 Weights, Oak Case, 7 1/2 In. 145.00
Balance, Day & Milt Ward, Brass, Wood, England, 14 x 15 x 7 In. 99.00
Balance, E.H. Sargent & Co., Chicago, c.1900 .... 245.00
Balance, Henry Troemner, Phila., Marble Top, Wood Base, 17 Weights, c.1890, 7 x 16 In. 310.00
Balance, Howe Mfg. Co., Iron, Brass, Oak, c.1880, 29 x 28 In. 1400.00
Balance, R & J Templeton, Ltd., Brass, Cast Iron, Scotland, 32 1/4 x 23 In. 425.00
Balance, Torsion, Henry Troemner, Oak Case, Early 1900s 350.00
Balance, Trade, Nickel-Plated Iron, Brass, Marble Base, Weigh Pan, 9 1/2 In. 895.00
Balance, Traveling, Pharmacist, Walnut Case, 9 x 4 In. 360.00
Balance, Wet Averty Ltd. Portsmouth, Class C To Weigh 28 Lb., Copper Pans, Chains 115.00
Candy, Cast Iron, Nickel Over Brass Weighing Scoop, 11 x 12 x 4 In. 635.00
Candy, Howe, Maroon, Gold Details, Weighs Up To 2 Lbs., 17 In. 440.00
Candy, Toledo, Scoop Pan, Gold Paint, 3 Lb., 20 x 20 In. 110.00
Candy, Wrigley's Spearmint Pepsin Gum, Brass Dial & Pan, 4 Lb., 9 1/2 In. 495.00
G. Harding & Sons, Ltd., England, Brass Pan, Scoop, Cast Metal, 10 In. 59.00
Gold, Miner's Improved, California, Weights, Case, c.1850, 3 1/4 x 5 3/4 x 1 1/4 In. 590.00
Gold, Wells Fargo & Co., W.F. & Co., Assayer Office No. 1147, Box 77.00
Meat, Toledo, Porcelain, Nickel, 30 1/2 In. 6.00
Pharmacy, Henry Troemner, Wood, Marble, Pewter Pans, c.1850, 7 x 19 x 9 In. 176.00
Postal, Brass, Oak, England, c.1900, 3 x 7 In. 99.00
Postal, Foyer Manufacturing Co., Cast Iron, Brass Arm, Sliding Poise, 5 1/2 In. 95.00
Scientific, W.M. Ainsworth & Sons, Metal, Brass, Case, Early 1900s, 19 x 20 x 10 In. 176.00
Scientific Material Co., Nickel Plated Pans, Cherry Case, 2 Weight Sets, 13 In. 175.00
Scientific Materials Co., Nickel Plated Pans, Marble Platform, Cherrywood Case, 13 In. 170.00
Steelyard, For Furs & Commodities, 19 1/2 In. 11.00
Weighing, Coin-Operated, 1 Cent, Mahogany, Porcelain, Upright, Columbia, 70 In. 550.00
Weighing, Coin-Operated, Fortune, 1 Cent, Sidewalk, Watling 110.00
Weighing, Coin-Operated, Horoscope Astrology, C.R. Kirk & Co., 1930s, 62 x 21 x 28 In. 225.00
Weighing, Coin-Operated, Metal, White Porcelain Base, Mirrors, Columbia 475.00
Weighing, Peerless, Aristocrat, Porcelain, Blue, Lollipop, Sidewalk, 1 Cent, c.1918 .... 840.00

Weight Set, Arthur H. Thomas, Germany, Bronze, Fitted Wood Box, 17 Piece 175.00

SCHAFER & VATER, makers of small ceramic items, are best known for their amusing figurals. The factory was located in Volkstedt-Rudolstadt, Germany, from 1890 to 1962. Some pieces are marked with the crown and R mark, but many are unmarked.

Ashtray, Skinny Woman, Sitting In Chair, Legs Crossed, Match Holder On Side, 4 In. 225.00
Creamer, Cow's Head, Blue Glaze, 3 1/4 In. 295.00
Figurine, Bathing Beauty, Wearing Beaded Chemise, Black Stockings, 3 1/4 In. 131.00
Hair Receiver, Green Jasperware, 2 Lavender Cameos, Wreaths, Oval, 4 1/2 x 3 In. 140.00
Hair Receiver, Green Jasperware, Classical Figures, Garlands, Rectangular, 4 1/2 x 3 In. 125.00
Hair Receiver, Pink Jasperware, Embossed Woman's Head, Faux Jewels, 4 x 3 In. 250.00
Match Holder, Nodder, Monkey Holding Apple, Eve, 4 1/4 In. 175.00
Pitcher, Figural, Peasant Holding Water Jar, Basket On Back, 5 1/2 In. 195.00
Pitcher, Mr. Bear, Wearing Green Bathrobe, Fur Muff, 5 In. 295.00
Pitcher, Trunk Shape, Green Branches, Dove, Snow-Like Glaze, 3 1/4 In. 95.00
Toothpick, Monk, Brown Robes, Painted, 5 1/4 In. 180.00
Vase, Blue Jasperware, Classical Couple Walking, Urn Shape, Buttressed Handles, 8 In. 75.00

SCHNEIDER Glassworks was founded in 1917 at Epinay-sur-Seine, France, by Charles and Ernest Schneider. Art glass was made between 1917 and 1930. The company still produces clear crystal glass. See also Le Verre Français.

Bowl, Blue, Mottled, Metal Holder, 3 Ball Feet, Leaves, Shallow, 6 1/2 In. 175.00
Bowl, Red, Yellow, Mottled, Leaf Shape, Wrought Iron Holder, 5 In. 230.00
Ewer, Orange, Mottled Raspberry, Applied Shaped Purple Handle, Pinched Neck, 7 In. 750.00
Jardiniere, 8-Sided, Blown Into Iron, Mottled, c.1900, 6 3/4 x 13 1/2 In. 660.00
Vase, Amethyst & Yellow Leaves, Frosted Mottled Ground, Footed, Cameo, 5 1/2 In. 1560.00
Vase, Mottled Orange, Maroon, Yellow, Amethyst Handles, Squat, France, 6 1/2 In. 1150.00
Vase, Shouldered, Red, Yellow, Blue, Mottled, 12 In. 805.00
Vase, Stylized Berries, Red Overlay, Cushion Foot, Charder, c.1920, 16 In. 1673.00

SCIENTIFIC INSTRUMENTS of all kinds are included in this category. Other categories such as Barometer, Binoculars, Dental, Nautical, Medical, and Thermometer may also price scientific apparatus.

Aneroid Altimeter, Th. Usteri-Reinacher, No. 1576, Brass Casing, 1 3/4 In. 410.00
Chrondrometer, Dring & Fage, Brass Arm, Sliding Poise, 5 1/2 In. 206.00
Chrondrometer, Dring & Fage, Grain Measure, London, Case, 5 1/2 In. 206.00
Circumferentor, J. Hale, Brass, Ebonized Case, 1886 Patent, 14 In. 765.00
Compass, Eames, Improved Patent, 1835 Patent, 11 3/4 x 7 1/2 In. 1175.00
Compass, Hutton's Pelorus, Kelvin & James White, Mahogany Case, 11 In. 176.00
Compass, Surveyor's, Benjamin Pike & Sons, Lacquered Brass, 16 In. 1175.00
Compass, Surveyor's, Benjamin Platt, Conn., c.1800, 14 3/4 In. 6465.00
Compass, Surveyor's, E. Draper, Brass, 4-In. Dial, 11 In. 705.00
Compass, Surveyor's, Edmund Blunt, Oak Staff, Early 1800s, 15 In. 3410.00
Compass, Surveyor's, George Adams, London, Mahogany, 14 1/2 In. 1115.00
Compass, Surveyor's, J. Hanks, Brass, 5 3/4-In. Dial, 15 In. 2235.00
Compass, Surveyor's, J. Hanks, Brass, Silver Dial, Socket Mount, 15 In. 2235.00
Compass, Surveyor's, T. Kendally, Brass, Tripod, Mahogany Case, 12 In. 1880.00
Compass, Table, Brass Dial, Steel Needle, Pierced N, 6 In. 470.00
Compass & Sundial, Fruitwood Case, France, 2 In. 118.00
Compass Sundial, Butterfield, Paris, 8-Sided, Silver Plated, Brass Box, 3 In. 999.00
Cyclo-Stormograph, Tycos, T. Tweedale Whipp, Print Out Sheet, 14 1/2 In. 260.00
Drafting Instruments, P. Hill, Edinburgh, Fishskin Covered Etui, 7 In. 206.00
Drawing Set, Canivet A La Sphere A Paris, France, Brass, Pine Case, 12 In. 150.00
Edison Electric Pen, Iron Frame, Steel Shaft, 4 x 5 1/2 In. 8225.00
Electric Current Meter, W. & L.E. Gurley, No. 1524, Nickel Plated, Wood, 15 In. 129.00
Electric Motor, Perret's Patent, Elektron Mfg., c.1890, 21 x 14 In. 3525.00
Equinoctial Ring Dial, C. Metz Fecit, Brass Loop, 3 1/4 In. 1998.00
Equinoctial Ring Dial, George Adams, London, Brass Ring, 4 In. 4585.00
Field Glass, Hensoldt, Wetzlar, Prism, Monocular 955.00
Fowler's, Scale Calculator, Paper Scale, Nickel Plated Case 176.00

G. Caradi, Integraph Machine, 2 Scale Indices, Walnut Case, 17 In. 1295.00
Galvanometer, Silver Dial, Steel Needle, Mahogany Hoop, 15 In. 176.00
Galvanometer, Steel Needle, Mahogany Hoop, 4 1/2-In. Dial, 15 In. 176.00
Gyroscope, Brass, 3 1/2-In. Flywheel, Mahogany Base 1528.00
Gyroscope, C. Becker, London, Brass, Mahogany Case, 9 1/2 In. 646.00
Hydrometer, Dring & Fage, Sikes 88.00
Integraph Machine, G. Caradi, Zurich, Walnut Case, 17 In. 1295.00
Magnifying Glass, Silver Mounted, Pistol Grip Handle, London, 1888, 9 In. 265.00
Microscope, Bate, London, Compendium, Solar, Brass, Case, 15 1/2 In. 3819.00
Microscope, Bausch & Lomb, Lacquered Brass, Gutta-Percha Stage, 14 In. 705.00
Microscope, Bausch & Lomb, Nickel Plated, Brass Stage, Case, 12 In. 380.00
Microscope, Compound, Nachet Et Fils, Lacquered Brass, 9 In. 385.00
Microscope, Dissecting, Pocket, Brass Pillar, Stage, Walnut Case, 3 1/2 In. 380.00
Microscope, Duboscq, Paris, Projecting, Tripod Base, Walnut Case, 18 In. 2115.00
Microscope, Ellis Pattern, Lacquered Brass, Case, 4 1/4 In. 705.00
Microscope, Gould Type, Lacquered Brass, Mahogany Case, 7 x 3 3/4 In. 470.00
Microscope, Henry Crouch, Binocular, Student's, Accessories, Case, 14 1/2 In. 880.00
Microscope, J. Swift, Compound, Brass, Mahogany Case, 13 1/2 In. 235.00
Microscope, Leitz, Wetzlar, No. 305801, Polarizing, Case, c.1930, 13 3/4 In. 485.00
Microscope, Leitz, Wetzlar, No. 370020, Bright Field, Accessories, Box, 1946 .... 308.00
Microscope, Martin Pattern, Drum, Brass, Rosewood Case, 10 In. 470.00
Microscope, Newton & Co., London, Compound, Mahogany Case, 14 In. 880.00
Microscope, Nuremberg Culpeper Type, 1800s, 13 In. 1410.00
Microscope, W & S Jones, London, Solar, Brass, Mahogany Case, c.1800, 11 1/2 In. 1880.00
Microscope, Witzlar E. Keitz, Mahogany, Brass, Monocular, c.1890, 5 x 12 1/2 In. 140.00
Microscope, Zeiss, No. 17345, 2 Objectives, Brass, Lacquered, Case 264.00
Octant, Radius, Spencer, Browning & Rust, Bone Scale, 13 In. 705.00
Octant, Vernier, Ebony, 16 In. Radius, Brass Index Arm, Brass Feet 206.00
Pantograph, Dollond, Brass, Engraved, Bone, Leather, Mahogany Case 295.00
Planetarium, Brass, Double Geared Mechanism, 8 Arms, Ebonized Column, 15 1/2 In. 1765.00
Quadrant, Surveyor's, Colonial, Walnut, Pewter Scale, 8 1/2 In. 590.00
Quadrant, Surveyor's, John Kennard, Oak Case, Early 1800s, 9 In. 2585.00
Quadrant, T.R. Hoyt, Oak, 1876, 14 In. 940.00
Semi Circumferentor, Brass, Compass, Engraved, Mahogany, 7 1/2 In. 355.00
Slide Rule, Calculating, Fuller's, Stanley, Mahogany Case, London, 17 In. 380.00
Slide Rule, Fuller's, 2 Cylinders, Tables Of Power & Roots, Stanley, 17 In. 380.00
Slide Rule, Thacher's, Mahogany Case, Calculating, Cylindrical, 7 1/2 x 24 In. 765.00
Surveyor's Level, Troughton & Simms, Brass, Case, 14-In. Telescope, 8 In. 176.00
Sykes Hydrometer, W.R. Loftus, Weights, Thermometer, Box, 2 x 8 x 4 In. 480.00
Sympiesometer, Tarelle, No. 2228, Rotating Scale, Thermometer, 23 In. 2115.00
Teaching Model, Marine Leech, L.&R. Blashka, Blown Glass, 1800s, 5 x 3/4 In. 1150.00
Telegraph, Brass, Twin 10-In. Illuminated Dials, 2 Levers, Brass Pillar, 44 In. 1410.00
Telegraph, Durkee Marine, Lenox, Brass, Reverse Painted Glass, 1900s, 45 In. 805.00
Telegraph Key, Menominee, Steel Lever, Ebonite Knob, Mahogany Base, 7 In. 71.00
Telegraph Key, Mesco, 5 Ohm, Steel Lever, Ebonite Knob, 7 In. 59.00
Telegraph Key & Sounder, Menominee, Steel Lever, Mahogany, 7 In. 71.00
Telegraph Key & Sounder, Mesco, 5 Ohm, Steel Lever, Wood, 7 In. 59.00
Telescope, 2 Draw, Dolland, Refracting, Mahogany, London, 14 In. 325.00
Telescope, 2 Draw, Yeates & Son, Brass, Stand, Dublin, 15 x 38 1/4 In. 575.00
Telescope, 3 Draw, Brass, Tripod Base, 26 In. 750.00
Telescope, 3 Draw, Dolland, Day Or Night, 10 In. Mahogany Tube, Shade, Eyepiece 295.00
Telescope, 3 Draw, Mahogany Tube, Pasteboard Case, Pocket, 1 x 4 In. 148.00
Telescope, 3 Draw, Plossl, Brass, Wood, Vienna, c.1830, 8 1/4-In. Closed 440.00
Telescope, 3 Draw, Steinheil, Brass, Wood, Munich, c.1850, 31 In. 380.00
Telescope, 3 Draw, Ultzschneider, Benedictbeuren, Brass, Pre 1816, 32 In. 380.00
Telescope, 4 Draw, Brass, Leather Cover, Sliding Shade, Carrying Case, 9 3/4 x 1 3/4 In. 248.00
Telescope, 7 Draw, Dixey, Shagreen Covered Tube, Pocket, 1 1/8 x 4 In. 590.00
Telescope, Alvan Clark & Sons, Astronomical Refracting, 1871, 63 In. 5290.00
Telescope, Brass, Hand Held, 19th Century, 30 x 3 In. 295.00
Telescope, Observatory, 2-In. Refraction, Lacquered Brass, 18 1/2-In. Tube 2235.00
Telescope, Questar, Catadioptric, Apochromatic, Zoom Eyepieces, Case 920.00

Telescope, Single Draw, 2-In. Refraction, 18-In. Mahogany Tube 470.00
Telescope, Single Draw, Engraved, 33-In. Mahogany Tube, Dust Slide 825.00
Telescope, Single Draw, Refracting, Reverse Taper, England, Late 1700s, 47 In. 1295.00
Telescope, W & D Mogey, Astronomical, Refracting, Lacquered Brass, 62 In. 2350.00
Tellurium, Jan Felkl, Globe, Iron Base, Czechoslovakia, 15 1/2 x 2 1/2 In. 2940.00
Theodolite, Caleb Leach, Mahogany Case, 1792, 6 In. 2468.00
Theodolite, Dearborne, Brass, Pocket, 8 In. 1175.00
Theodolite, Edmund Draper, 13-In. Telescope, Lacquered Brass, 9 1/2 In. 2350.00
Theodolite, J.T. Hobby, Lacquered Brass, Mahogany Case, N.Y., 12 In. 825.00
Theodolite, Wm. J. Young & Co., No. 4124, Brass, Mahogany Case, 12 In. 705.00
Theodolite, Young & Sons, No. 7409, Brass, Mahogany Case, 13 In. 646.00
Thermograph, Short & Mason, Walnut Case, England, 14 1/2 In. 1058.00
Transit, Heller & Brightly, Auxiliary Telescopic Solar, 1871 .... 1750.00
Transit, Surveyor's, Troughton & Simms, London, Brass, Case, 1800s, 19 In. 345.00
Universal Science Lantern, Newtonian, No. 518, Mahogany, Newton & Co., 14 1/2 In. 3818.00
Waywiser, James Beers, Spoked Wheel, 21-In. Diameter, 1875, 64 In. 3290.00
Wye Level, Sawyer & Hobby, 17-In. Telescope, Brass, 9 In. 205.00
Wye Level, W. & L.E. Gurley, Troy N.Y., Brass, Mahogany Case, 18 In. 355.00

SCRIMSHAW is bone or ivory or whale's teeth carved by sailors and others for entertainment during the sailing-ship days. Some scrimshaw was carved as early as 1800. There are modern scrimshanders making pieces today on bone, ivory, or plastic. Other pieces may be found in the Ivory and Nautical categories.

Board, Cribbage, Geometrics, Fish, 6 In. 263.00
Ditty Box, Baleen, Oval, American Ships, Buildings, 19th Century, 7 1/2 x 5 1/2 In. 316.00
Letter Opener, Walrus Tusk, Whale Fishing, Outward Bound, Home, 14 In. 489.00
Powder Horn, Sailing Ship, Flowers, John Barns, 1804, 12 1/2 In. 247.00
Sperm Whale's Tooth, Tropical Seascape, Palm Trees, Sandy Shore, Flag, Boats, 6 In. 1150.00
Tusk, Ancestor Figure, Geometric Bands, Central Kneeling Figure, Africa, 20 In. 250.00
Tusk, Carved, Apple Merchant, 10 Monkeys, Inset Hardstone Chopmark, 1900s, 12 1/4 In. 999.00
Tusk, Daughter Of Sea King, Dragons, Japan, 1800s, 8 1/2 In. 4406.00
Tusk, Dragon, Sunken Relief, Wood Stand, Kogyoku, Japan, Early 1900s, 23 In. 3000.00
Tusk, Elephant Train, Crocodile Head, India, 23 In. 350.00
Tusk, Elephant, 22 In. 525.00
Tusk, Incised Oriental Court Scenes, Square Base, 43 1/2 x 12 In., Pair 294.00
Tusk, Letter Opener, Elephant Finial, India, 22 1/8 In. 265.00
Whale's Jaw, Ship, Woman, Waves, 2-Sided, 1800s, 19 In. 4474.00
Whale's Tooth, Eagle, Inlaid Eyes, Japan, 1800s, 5 1/2 In. 1880.00
Whale's Tooth, Engraved, 3-Masted Ship, Early 1800s, 7 3/4 In. 4994.00
Whale's Tooth, Engraved, Boston View, Waterfront, Signed D. Waring, 6 1/2 In. 575.00
Whale's Tooth, Engraved, Male Portrait, Fashionable Amuse't, Dapper Peer, 6 1/2 In. 4994.00
Whale's Tooth, Man In Long Coat, Standing By Chair, 19th Century, 4 1/2 In. 374.00
Whale's Tooth, Victorian Woman, War Heroes, Joseph Warren, Ellsworth, 3 1/2 x 2 In. 1955.00

SEG, see Paul Revere Pottery category.

SEVRES porcelain has been made in Sevres, France, since 1769. Many copies of the famous ware have been made. The name originally referred to the works of the Royal Porcelain factory. The name now includes any of the wares made in the town of Sevres, France. The entwined lines with a center letter used as the mark is one of the most forged marks in antiques. Be very careful to identify Sevres by quality, not just by mark.

Bottle, Cover, Pate-Sur-Pate Medallion, Taxile Doat, 1903, 13 3/4 In. .... *ILLUS* 54720.00
Bust, Dante With Headdress, 12 In. 2468.00
Bust, Louis XVI, Marie-Antoinette, Biscuit Porcelain, 1861, 12 1/2 In., Pair 880.00
Bust, Parian, Young Woman, Stepped Square Base, Agathon Leonard, c.1903, 18 1/2 In. 1355.00
Candelabrum, 5-Light, Ormolu, Urn Shaped Standards, 1800s, 26 x 8 In., Pair 2585.00
Candelabrum, 5-Light, Spiraled Urn, Cobalt & White, Gilt Leaves, Stepped Base, 18 In., Pair 2415.00
Casket, Cover, Lovers Under Tree, Heart Shape, Gilt Brass, Painted, c.1900, 9 1/2 In. 680.00
Clock, Bronze Mounted, 1800s, 13 x 7 In. 410.00

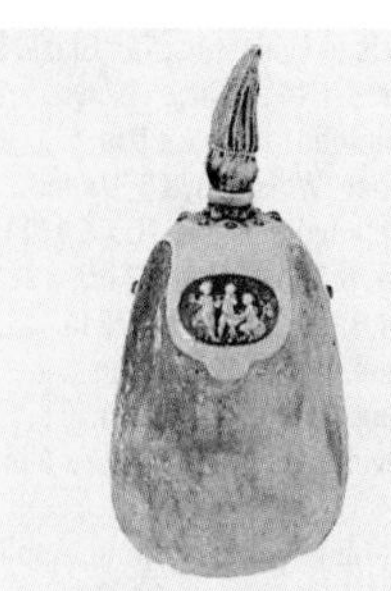

Sevres, Bottle, Cover, Pate-Sur-Pate Medallion, Taxile Doat, 1903, 13 3/4 In.

Sewing, Tape Measure, Billiken, Metal, Windup, Full Tape

Compote, Petit Fours, 9 In. 35.00
Cup & Saucer, Leticia Bonaparte, Gilt Bonaparte Bees, Green Ground, 2 Piece 470.00
Cup & Saucer, Portrait, Napoleon, Gilt Border Against Blue Ground, 1800s, 3 1/2 In. 440.00
Dish, Enameled, Putti In Various Pursuits, Burnished Gilt, Blue Surround, 1800s, 12 In., Pair 510.00
Dresser Box, Courting Couple, Squat, Cobalt, Gold Floral Band, 1875, 5 3/4 In. 590.00
Ewer, Pedestal, 12 In., Pair 350.00
Figurine, Woman, Nude, Holding Flowers, Antoine Orlandini, 23 1/2 In. 1980.00
Jardiniere, Egg Shape, Flowers, Wreaths, Musical Instruments, Birds, 1844, 12 3/4 In. 2470.00
Lamp, Porcelain, Chromed Steel, c.1930, 12 x 12 1/2 In. 2620.00
Plate, Courting Scene, Louis XVI, 19th Century, 9 In., Pair 90.00
Plate, Louis Philippe Service, Pink Border, Flowers, c.1845, 7 In. 146.00
Plate, Madame Elisabeth, Cherubs, 9 1/2 In, Pair 470.00
Plate, Man & Woman, Wooded Landscape, Gilt, Metal Mounts, Signed, Geo. Rochette, 11 3/8 In. 585.00
Plate, Paneled Center, Lavender Garlands, Reticulated Border, 9 1/2 In., Pair 300.00
Plate, Topographical, Landscape, Nice & Perigueux, c.1864, 9 1/2 In., Pair 3000.00
Plate Set, Portrait, 19th Century, 9 3/4 In., 4 Piece 700.00
Plate Set, Putto, Crowned Monogram, Gilt Leaf Scrolls, 10 1/2 In., 12 Piece 825.00
Tazza, Courting Couple, Flowers, Gilt Metal Mount, Painted, Central Panel, Tilt, 12 In. 615.00
Tea Bowl & Saucer, Green Ground, Birds, Gilt Details, c.1765, Pair 8650.00
Tea Service, Flowers, Putti, Gold Family Crest, 9 Piece 660.00
Tureen, Cover, Underplate, Floral Reserves, Blue Celeste Ground, Gilt Trim, 16 x 23 In. 1880.00
Tureen, Cover, Underplate, Flowers, White Bands, Blue Ground, Leaf Handles & Finial, 16 In. 1530.00
Urn, Boy & Girl Fishing, Hand Painted, Bronze, Square Base, 1800s, 16 1/2 x 4 In. 275.00
Urn, Continuous Relief Figures, Cobalt Blue & Multicolored, Footed, 22 x 13 In. 1410.00
Urn, Cover, Napoleonic, Green, Gold Enamel Crest, Serpent Handles, 14 In. 1100.00
Urn, Cover, Romantic Scene Of Couple, Hand Painted, 19th Century, 11 1/2 In. 190.00
Urn, Landscape, Potpourri, Ormolu Mounted, Tapered Egg Shape, Late 1800s, 17 In. 380.00
Urn, Purple, 3-Footed, Triangular Base, 1800s, 4 1/4 x 4 In., Pair 295.00
Urn, Rams Head, Pair 240.00
Vase, Blue, Gold Stylized Birds & Insects, Shouldered, 24 In. 120.00
Vase, Bottle, Matte, Stoneware, Green, White, Pate-Sur-Pate, Taxile Doat, 1901, 13 1/4 In. 4500.00
Vase, Brown, Oval, Footed, Green Mark, 1887, 7 1/4 In., Pair 750.00
Vase, Flowers, Landscape, 12 1/2 In., Pair 390.00
Vase, Lid, Porcelain, Bronze Mounted, Painted Scene, Loop Handles, 19th Century, 16 In. 2635.00
Vase, Snake & Lizards, Green, Bulbous, Metal Foot, Rim, 5 In. 1060.00

SEWER TILE figures were made by workers at the sewer tile and pipe factories in the Ohio area during the late nineteenth and early twentieth centuries. Figurines, small vases, and cemetery vases were favored. Often the finished vase was a piece of the original pipe with added decorations and markings. All types of sewer tile work are now considered folk art by collectors.

Bank, Rabbit, Crouched, 6 1/4 x 10 1/2 In. 115.00
Doorstop, Lion, Reclining, Rectangular Base, 19th Century, 10 In. 30.00
Face, Hand Molded, Protruding Eyes, Dark Glaze, 5 In. 115.00
Figure, Dog, Seated, Fur Detail, Ohio, 5 In. 489.00
Figure, Dog, Spaniel, Incised Fur, Punched Eyes, Nostrils, Collar, Locket, 19th Century, 10 In. 550.00

Figure, Dog, Spaniel, Seated, Wide Eyes, Incised Eyelashes, Tan Glaze, 9 1/4 In. 1150.00
Figure, Frog, Smiling, Hand Tooled, 4 1/2 x 6 3/4 In., Pair 430.00
Figure, Lion, Reclining, Fluted Base, Hand Molded, 10 1/2 x 5 In. 345.00
Figure, Lion, Reclining, Hand Incised Eye, Nose, Whiskers, 15 3/4 In. 300.00
Figure, Lion, Reclining, Handed Molded, Rectangular Base, 10 x 6 1/2 In. 316.00
Figure, Lion, Reclining, Scalloped Edge Base, 5 1/2 x 9 x 4 1/2 In. 115.00
Figure, Lion, Reclining, Smiling, Rectangular Base, 9 5/8 x 6 1/2 In. 518.00
Figure, Pig, Free Standing, Muscular Physique, 14 x 7 1/2 In. 805.00
Figure, Squirrel, Bushy Tail, Tooled Fur, Eating Walnut, 11 1/2 In. 115.00
Jar, Cover, Hand Tooled Bark, Applied Grapevines, Handles, 6 1/2 x 5 In. 230.00
Match Holder, Tree Stump Shape, c.1909, 4 1/4 In. 145.00
Pitcher, Hand Tooled, Bark, Branch Stumps, Minerva Head Spout, Applied Design, 7 In. 145.00
Vase, Flared Pinched Rim, Folky Flowers, Red, Green Paint, 6 1/2 In., Pair 145.00

SEWING equipment of all types is collected, from sewing birds that held the cloth to tape measures, needle books, and old wooden spools. Sewing machines are included here. Needlework pictures are listed in the Picture category.

Basket, 2 Handles, 2 Colors, Porcupine Decoration, 10 x 11 In. 50.00
Basket, Splint, Ash, Oval, Carved Bentwood Handles, Multicolored Bands, 6 x 16 x 11 3/4 In. 300.00
Bird, Pincushion Top, Red Velvet, Iron Bird Shaped Clamp, Heart Shaped Screw, 6 x 4 In. 330.00
Bottle, Pfaff Sew Machine Oil, Spanish, Italian & Dutch Label, Germany, c.1862, 4 1/2 In. 15.00
Bottle, Singer Manufg. Co., Sewing Machine Oil, Sun Purple, Pre 1906, 5 In. 32.00
Bottle, Singer Oil, Dome, Pointed Spout, 3 x 2 In. 25.00
Box, Abalone Shell Inlay, Center Medallion, Chamfered Lid, Butterfly, 8 x 13 1/2 x 8 In. 308.00
Box, Black Lacquer, Chinoiserie, Fitter Tray, Gilt Paw Feet, George III, 5 x 11 In. 265.00
Box, Chest Of Drawers Shape, Hearts, Flowers, Stars, Nancy Hanks Owner, 1800s, 16 x 9 In. 825.00
Box, Lift Lid, Hear Handle, Sponge Decorated, c.1825, 9 x 10 1/4 x 10 In. 7700.00
Box, Mixed Woods, Painted, Birds, Drawer, Pa., 11 3/4 x 6 x 5 1/2 In. 495.00
Box, Papier-Mache, Mother-Of-Pearl Inlay, Flowers, Village, England, 1800s, 12 In. 590.00
Box, Pincushion Lid, Flowers, Geometrics, Wallpaper, Oval, 5 3/4 x 9 1/4 x 6 In. 198.00
Box, Prison Art, Fannie, Abalone Shell Inlay, Butterfly, Chamfered Lid, 8 x 13 1/2 In. 308.00
Box, Rosewood, Stepped Lid, Divided Interior, Gilt Bronze Handles, 5 x 18 x 13 In. 410.00
Box, Spool Holder, Book Shape Base, Sliding Drawer, Hearts, Birds, 1800s, 12 In. 5143.00
Box, Straw, Canterbury Shaker, Original Cardboard Box 635.00
Box, Wallpaper Covered, Flowers, Geometric, Pincushion On Lid, Oval, 5 3/4 x 9 1/4 x 6 In. 198.00
Box, Wood, Paper Lined, Gymnast Painted Inside, Lift-Out Tray, Handle, 6 x 11 x 8 In. 358.00
Box, Wood, Raised Paneled Lid, Lift-Out Tray, Flowers, Shield, Pin Stripes, 6 x 11 x 7 In. 1045.00
Cabinet, Spool, see Advertising category under Cabinet, Spool.
Case, Cloth, Folding, Black, Flowers, Thimble & Needle Holders, 3 x 2 In. 80.00
Darner, Hardwood, Turned, Club Shape, Flared End, Incised Banding, 7 1/2 x 1 1/2 In. 6.00
Darner, Turned, Club Form, Flared End, Incised Banding, 7 1/2 x 1 1/2 In. 6.00
Darning Egg, Glass, Blown, Pale Green, Open Pontil, c.1825, 3 1/4 x 2 1/2 In. 110.00
Distaff, Pine, Multicolored, Carved, Painted, Russia, 1800s, 41 In. 518.00
Dressmaker's Dummy, Vinyl, Canvas, British Royal Crest, James Hogan, 1900s, 64 In. 708.00
Kit, Leather, Brass Thimble, Needle Case, Scissors, 3 1/2 x 1 1/2 In., 2 Piece 105.00
Knitting Ball, Sterling Silver Handle, c.1870, 5 1/2 In. 35.00
Machine, Chain Stitch, Hand, Serpentine Arm, Gilt Transfers, Clamp, 8 In. 1116.00
Machine, Chain Stitch, Serpentine Arm, Stitch Plate, Wheel, 8 In. 1116.00
Machine, Franklin, Treadle, Oak Case, c.1920, 30 x 20 In. 80.00
Machine, Singer, Featherlite, Leather Case, Simanco U.S.A. 45713, No. AG881346 .... 350.00
Machine, Singer, Stand, Stool, Flip Top, Art Deco, 31 In. 299.00
Mannequin, Wooden Stand, Singer Sewing Machine Co., 52 3/4 In. 25.00
Necessaire, Music, Box, Empire, Mahogany, Bordier Movement, Piano Shape, 12 In. 1645.00
Needle Book, Happy Home, 21 Needles & Threader, c.1950, 5 x 3 1/2 In. 15.00
Needle Case, Bamboo, Ivory Caps, Procession Of Nobles, Chinese, Late 1800s, 4 1/2 x 3/4 In. 400.00
Needle Case, Wood, 2 Needles, Cylindrical, Late 1790s 195.00
Needle Case, Wood, Boye, 2 1/2 x 5/8 In. 8.00
Niddy Noddy, Glass, Carved Wood Cap, Silk Thread, 6 3/8 To 8 In., 4 Piece 588.00
Pin Holder, Lion, Globe, Round, Kemp & Burpee, Pin Your Faith To Success Spreaders 37.00
Pin Holder, Round, 2-Sided, Success Spreader, Fertilizes The Earth, Kemp, Burpee 31.00

Sewing, Tape Measure, Dog With Hat, Porcelain, Full Tape

Sewing, Tape Measure, Rabbit, Metal, Celluloid Body, Windup, Short Tape

Pin Holder, Tin, Round, Pioneer Spices, J.A. Folger & Co., San Francisco, 1 1/2 In. 209.00
Pincushion, Apple, Velvet, 3 1/2 In. 209.00
Pincushion, Ball, Needlework, Flower, I.M., 1807, 2 1/2 In. 385.00
Pincushion, Carrot, Leaf Top, Velvet, 10 In. 88.00
Pincushion, Carrot, Velvet, 7 In., 2 Piece 330.00
Pincushion, Clamp, Crazy Quilt Top, Blue Skirt, Brass Screw, Wood Base, 5 1/2 x 4 In. 195.00
Pincushion, Clamp, Felt Top, Green Sawtooth Banding, Turned Wood Base, 6 x 4 In. 385.00
Pincushion, Clamp, Felt Top, Turned Wood Base, Screw, 6 x 4 x 2 In. 385.00
Pincushion, Clamp, Iron Bird, Red Velvet Top, Heart Shape Screw, 6 x 4 x 1 In. 330.00
Pincushion, Clamp, Table Top, Turned Burl Base, Screw, 7 x 2 In. 154.00
Pincushion, Clamp, Turned Burl Base, Screw, 4 1/4 x 2 1/2 In. 154.00
Pincushion, Clamp, Wallpaper Box, Barrel Shape, Diamond Fabric, Hinged Lid, 8 In. 440.00
Pincushion, Clamp, Wallpaper Box, Hinged Lid, Barrel Form, Teardrop Screw, 8 In. 440.00
Pincushion, Pillow, Silk Embroidered, Metallic Thread, Portrait Panels, c.1640, 12 x 8 In. 1200.00
Pincushion, Quilt Top, Blue Skirt, Wood Base, Brass Screw, 5 1/2 x 4 x 2 In. 195.00
Pincushion, Red Velvet, Sterling Silver Openwork Holder, Round, 3 1/2 In. 70.00
Pincushion, Silver, Shoe Form, Bow, Burgundy Velvet Interior, 3 In. 29.00
Pincushion, Velvet, Frog Shape, Green, Glass Eyes, Early 19th Century, 3 In. 700.00
Pincushion, Velvet, Gold Thread, Tassels, 1880, 5 In. 146.00
Pincushion Dolls are listed in their own category.
Pocket, Cloth, Deer, Hearts, Dog, 1852, 10 x 6 3/4 In. 415.00
Shears, Tailor, Brass, SI22, Beryl Co., 14 1/2 In. 45.00
Sign, Singer Sewing Machines, Large Red S, Green Ground, Porcelain, 24 x 16 In. 770.00
Spool Cabinets are listed here or in the Advertising category under Cabinet, Spool.
Tape Loom, Pine, Dovetailed Base, Shuttle, 14 x 19 x 10 In. 230.00
Tape Loom, Pine, Walnut Teeth, Red Wash, Heart Cutout, Wood Gears, 24 x 15 In. 489.00
Tape Loom, Wood, 1800s, 19 x 18 1/2 x 7 1/2 In. 470.00
Tape Loom, Wood, 19 1/2 x 4 3/4 In. 805.00
Tape Measure, Alligator, Celluloid, Yellow Cloth Tape, 7 1/2 In. 185.00
Tape Measure, Baseball Player, Boy, Holding Bat, Celluloid, Cloth Tape, 2 1/2 In. 250.00
Tape Measure, Bear, Holding Stick, Bronze, Glass Eyes, England, 2 1/2 In. 495.00
Tape Measure, Billiken, Metal, Windup, Full Tape .... *ILLUS* 196.00
Tape Measure, Bowl Of Fruit, Pedestal Base, Celluloid, 1 1/2 x 1 3/4 In. 160.00
Tape Measure, Chick, Yellow, Celluloid, 2 1/2 In. 59.00
Tape Measure, Clermont Shirts & Pajamas, Celluloid, Round, 1 1/2 In. 78.00
Tape Measure, Dog With Hat, Porcelain, Full Tape .... *ILLUS* 140.00
Tape Measure, Ivory, Spindle Shape, Turned & Pierced, 2 1/2 In. 69.00
Tape Measure, Parrot's Head, Painted, Celluloid, 1 1/2 In. 320.00
Tape Measure, Petit Point On Silk, Purple Flowers, Blue Ground, Round, Germany, 2 In. 46.00
Tape Measure, Pig, Buffalo Ranch, Oklahoma, Celluloid, 3 1/2 In. 45.00
Tape Measure, Pig, Pink, Celluloid, 2 1/2 x 1 1/4 In. 58.00
Tape Measure, Rabbit, Metal, Celluloid Body, Windup, Short Tape .... *ILLUS* 168.00
Tape Measure, Vacuum Cleaner, Hoover, Cannister Sytle, Plastic, 2 In. 45.00
Tape Measure, Zeppelin Shape, Crank Handle, Aluminum, Metal Tailplanes, Germany 870.00
Tip Tray, Round, Home Sewing Machine, Grandma Sewing Pants, Boy Still In Them 150.00
Yarn Winder, 4-Arm, Blue Paint, Splayed, Chamfered Legs, 39 In. 145.00
Yarn Winder, Wood, Octagonal Shaft, Blue Paint, 1800s, 46 x 27 In. 295.00

SHAKER items are characterized by simplicity, functionalism, and orderliness. There were many Shaker communities in America from the eighteenth century to the present day. The religious order made furniture, small wooden pieces, and packaged medicines, herbs, and jellies to sell to *outsiders*. Other useful objects were made for use by members of the community. Shaker furniture is listed in this book in the Furniture category.

Apothecary Jar Set, Hand Blown, Tin Lid, Open Pontil, c.1860, 7 To 10 In., 4 Piece 1055.00
Basket, Berry, Round, Cut Side Staves, Pine Base, Tin Banded, Nails, 4 x 4 3/8 In. 130.00
Basket, Berry, Splint, Round, Cut Side Staves, Pine Base, Tin Bands, 4 x 4 3/8 In. 130.00
Basket, Berry, Splint, Round, Stave Sides, Wood Base, 2 3/4 x 4 7/8 In. 145.00
Basket, Berry, Splint, Splint Stave Sides, Nail Construction, Wood Base, 2 3/4 x 4 7/8 In. 145.00
Basket, Black Ash, Double Wrapped Rim, Carved Inset Handles, c.1850, 16 1/2 x 24 In. 205.00
Basket, Gathering, Splint, Black Ash, Double Wrapped Rim, Hoop Handle, 14 x 12 In. 760.00
Basket, Oval, Black Ash, Single Wrapped Rim, Carved Outset Handles, 11 x 30 x 24 In. 410.00
Basket, Rattan, Woven, Round, Nailed Rim, Stenciled Letters, Carved Double Handle, 21 In. 468.00
Basket, Rectangle, Black Ash, Wrapped Rim, Carved Handles, c.1850, 10 x 19 In. 235.00
Basket, Rectangle, Black Ash, Wrapped Rim, Carved Handles, Openwork, 9 x 16 In. 410.00
Basket, Sewing, Splint, Black Ash, 8 Interior Baskets, Carved Handles, 6 x 14 In. 3276.00
Basket, Splint, Woven, 2 Bentwood Rim Handles, 5 1/4 x 3 1/4 In. 200.00
Basket, Splint, Woven, Kentucky, c.1840, 11 x 15 x 9 In. 850.00
Bedpan, Shaped Tin, Short Turned Handle, Canterbury, N.H., c.1850, 24 In. 470.00
Bell, School, Long Walnut Handle, Turned, Flared Brass, Iron Clapper, c.1850, 28 In. 2457.00
Bench, Pine, Blue Paint, Single Board Top, Bootjack Arched Flat Legs, 8 1/2 x 18 1/2 In. 1870.00
Bench, Woodworker's, Hardwood, Pine, 5 Drawers, 2 Vises, c.1860, 32 x 138 In. 8485.00
Bonnet, Black Fabric, Ribbon Tie, Wooden Head Form 145.00
Box, 2-Finger, Oval, 1 1/2 x 4 x 2 1/2 In. 460.00
Box, 2-Finger, Oval, Maple, Pine, Stained Finish, Copper Nails, c.1840, 1 1/2 x 5 3/4 In. 760.00
Box, 2-Finger, Oval, Pine Bottom, Red Paint, 2 x 6 1/4 x 4 In. 2645.00
Box, 2-Finger, Oval, Swallowtail Fingers, Red Paint, 6 x 2 In. 605.00
Box, 3-Finger, Bentwood, Oval, Copper Tacks, 4 3/4 x 8 1/2 x 12 In. 630.00
Box, 5-Finger, Oval, Maple, Pine, Copper Tacks, 5 x 13 1/2 In. 1315.00
Box, Band, Finger Joints, Copper Nail Fasteners, Oval, 2 1/4 x 4 1/4 In. 105.00
Box, Band, Finger Joints, Copper Tack Fasteners, 1 5/8 x 5 1/4 In. 120.00
Box, Band, Finger Joints, Copper Tack Fasteners, 1857, 1 5/8 x 4 In. 45.00
Box, Band, Finger Joints, Copper Tack Fasteners, Cloth Strainer, 1 1/2 In. 85.00
Box, Band, Finger Joints, Copper Tacks, Stenciled, 2 1/8 x 7 1/4 In. 154.00
Box, Band, Finger Joints, Nail Fasteners, 2 3/4 x 6 1/4 In. 297.00
Box, Band, Finger Joints, Nail Fasteners, Clothespins, Oval, 1 1/2 x 4 In. 143.00
Box, Band, Finger Joints, Nail Fasteners, Oval, 2 x 6 In. 88.00
Box, Band, Wood, Oval, Finger Joints, Copper Nail Fasteners, 2 x 4 3/4 In. 660.00
Box, Cutlery, Birch, Pine, Oak Handle, Brass Hinged Lids, Applied Lip Closing, 5 x 12 In. 700.00
Box, Kindling, Pine, Chestnut Brown Paint, Hoop Handle, Inset Screws, 14 x 20 x 12 In. 7605.00
Box, Map, Poplar, Meeting House Blue Paint, 1 Board Top, Molded Edge, 9 x 49 x 11 In. 3745.00
Box, Nesting, Oval, Finger Jointed, Beechwood, Pine, 2 3/4 x 6 x 4 1/2 In., 3 Piece 690.00
Box, Oval, Green Paint, Pine Top, Bottom, Maple Sides, Lapped Fingers, 2 x 5 In. 825.00
Box, Oval, Wood Pegged Construction, c.1867, 6 In. 90.00
Box, Pantry, 1-Finger, Iron Tacks, Tan Paint, 3 1/4 x 1 3/4 In. 1265.00
Box, Pantry, 3-Finger, Oval, 10 1/2 In. 350.00
Box, Pantry, 4-Finger, Oval, Maple, Pine, Square Nails, 6 1/2 x 4 1/4 x 2 1/2 In. 650.00
Box, Pantry, Oval, Fingered, Green Paint, Branded, 7 1/2 x 10 1/2 x 4 In. 748.00
Box, Pantry, Oval, White Paint, 6 x 9 1/2 x 3 1/2 In. 520.00
Box, Storage, 4 Compartments, New Lebanon, N.Y., c.1840, 3 In. 2100.00
Box, Storage, Pine, Light Ocher Stain, Hinged Lift Lid, Side Handles, 19 x 36 x 16 In. 645.00
Box Stack, Oval, Maple, Pine, Oak, 3- & 4-Finger Graduated Sizes, 4 3/4 To 10 In., 6 Piece 2100.00
Broom, Flat, Pine Handle, Nailed Tin Plate Secures Corn, 53 In. 145.00
Broom, Oak Handle, Corn Flat, Wire Top, Tole Dustpan, Long Poplar Handle 410.00
Bucket, Berry, Pine, Green Paint, 2 Blue Hoops, Wire Swing Handle, Wood Grip, 6 x 5 In. 220.00
Bucket, Cover, Yellow, Brown, Wire Handle, 2 Iron Straps, Enfield, N.H., 9 1/2 x 12 In. 720.00
Bucket, Mustard Paint, No. 4, Kitchen On Bottom, Bail Handle, Canterbury, N.H. 2590.00

Bucket, Pine Staves, Yellow, Bottom, Iron Hoops, Bail Plates, Diamond Shape, 6 1/4 x 8 1/8 In. . . . 1880.00
Bucket, Pine, Black Ash Swing Handle, Other Oak Swing Handle, Fingered Lid, 13 x 10 In. 645.00
Butter Churn, Mechanical, Signed D.P., N.H., 37 In. 805.00
Candlestand, Maple, Birch, Brown Stain, 2 Candle Bar, Lipped Tray, c.1810, 34 x 12 In. 5850.00
Carrier, 4-Finger, Maple, Pine, Varnish Finish, Swing Handles, 7 1/2 x 10 3/4 In., Pair 820.00
Carrier, Cherry, Pine, Natural Varnish, Canted, Hoop Handle, Iron Clasp, 7 x 12 1/2 In. 645.00
Carrier, Sewing, 4-Finger, Oval, Maple, Swing Handle, Pine Base, Satin Ribbons, 8 x 9 In. 470.00
Cloak, Sister's, Blue Wool, Collar Liner, Blue Check Gingham, Hooded, c.1890, 52 In. 585.00
Coffeepot Set, Tin, Side Handle, Spout, Hinged Lid, Graduated Sizes, 6 To 18 In., 10 Piece 375.00
Darner, Maple, Round, Moving Center Ball, Mt. Wachusett, 2 1/2 x 2 1/2 In. 35.00
Darner, Turned Wood, Needle Holder, Needle Case, 6 1/2 x 2 1/8 In. 19.00
Darner & Needle Holder, Turned Wood, Egg Shape Top, Removable Handle, 6 1/2 x 2 In. 19.00
Doorstop, Maple, Pine, Wedge Shape Box, Scene, Oil Paint, Sand Filled, 5 x 7 x 5 In. 760.00
Dress, Bertha, Purple Wool, Gold Buttons, Collar, Blue Silk, Inside Trim, Maple Hanger 350.00
Dry Measure, Maple, Pine, Red Paint, Nailed Lap Closure, c.1840, 3 x 4 1/2 In. 1170.00
Dry Measure, Maple, Pine, Yellow Painted Finish, Nailed Lap Closure, c.1840, 3 1/2 x 6 In. 3218.00
Duster, Maple, Turquoise, Pink, Orange Wool, Black Handle, Wire Hanger, 24 In. 819.00
Hanger Set, Garment, Maple, String For Hanging On Pegs, 16 In., 24 Piece 380.00
Hay Fork, Black Ash, 3 Shaped Tines, 3 Tine Spreaders, Turned, Graduated, 5 In. 176.00
Kerchief, Linen, Woven, White, Blue Line Edge, Initials J.E., Caroline, Frame, 20 x 23 In. 470.00
Kerchief, Sister's, Rose Pink Silk, Striped Borders, Black, Magenta, Frame, 36 x 36 In. 1990.00
Lamp, Hanging, Holder, Ventilation Funnel, South Union, Ky., c.1870, 24 x 10 In. 4390.00
Lamp Filler, Tin, Cone Shape, Applied Strap Handle, 19th Century, 6 1/2 In. 120.00
Lumber Measure, Cherry, Patina, Calibrated Board, Adjustable Lower Arm, 41 In. 295.00
Paint Can, Tin, Maple Handle Brush, Horsehair Bristles 440.00
Print, Shakers At Meeting House Dance, Birch Frame, Red Paint, 9 1/2 x 13 1/2 In. 644.00
Rake, Black Ash, Yellow Painted Finish, Shaped Tines, Bentwood Brace, c.1850, 59 In. 410.00
Rug, Braided, 3 Circles, Wool, Radiating Ovals, Alternating Colors, 151 x 110 In. 2225.00
Rug, Braided, 7 Circles, Scalloped Edges, 57 1/2 In. 700.00
Rug, Braided, 9 Circles, Diamond Shape, 98 x 64 In. 1346.00
Rug, Braided, 11 Joined Circles, Brown Shades, Wool, Runner, 30 x 202 In. 1210.00
Rug, Braided, Octagonal, Coiled Gray Center, Alternating Light & Dark, 36 In. 2106.00
Rug, Braided, Oval, Wool, Mustard, Olive, Tongue Border, 55 x 44 In. 350.00
Rug, Braided, Wool, Cotton, Multiple Circles, c.1930, 54 x 34 In. 820.00
Rug, Confetti, Alternating Ivory Rows, Multicolored Concentric Squares, 52 x 50 In. 295.00
Rug, Confetti, Multicolored Interior, Concentric Red Border, 48 x 24 In. 2925.00
Rug, Confetti, Multicolored Squares, 8 Braided Rows, Mounted, c.1900, 26 x 46 In. 1815.00
Rug, Geometric, Punched Wool, Tongue Shaped Border, Burlap Backing, 39 x 24 In. 350.00
Rug, Penny, Hexagonal, Radiating Star, Wool Back, 14 x 15 1/2 In. 585.00
Rug, Rag, Confetti, Wool, Knitted Cotton String, Red, Green Borders, c.1920, 41 x 26 In. 470.00
Rug, Rag, Loom Woven, Wool, Cotton, Olive Green, Hand Dyed, 24 Ft. 7 In. x 2 Ft. 10 In. 2460.00
Rug, Spiral Shape, Knitted Cotton String, Red Center, Black, Turquoise, Burgundy, 32 In. 819.00
Rug, Starburst, Cotton, Wool, Knitted, 6 In. Striped Border, c.1900, 44 In. 1346.00
Rug, Striped, Wool, Cotton Back, 43 x 30 In. 235.00
Rug, Table, Woven, Bars, 45 x 26 In. 410.00
Runner, Braided, 6 Circles, Colorful Interior, Black Border, 2 Ft. 6 1/2 In. x 9 Ft. 5 In. 1465.00
Scoop Set, Maple, Carved, Shaped Handles, Graduated Sizes From 7 To 15 In., 4 Piece 585.00
Seed Box, Pine, Red Paint, Original Labels, Mt. Lebanon, 3 1/2 x 24 In. 5850.00
Seed Spreader, Tin, Red Paint, Iron, Crank, Wood Handle, Strap, c.1870, 4 x 120 In. 819.00
Spinning Wheel, Oak, Maple, Pine, Original Finish, Canterbury, N.H., 1830, 33 In. 750.00
Theorems, Stenciled, Hand Worked, Watercolor, Floral, 3 x 3 1/4 In., 40 Piece 5465.00
Tub, Lid, Pine, Oak Interwoven Wraps, Copper Tack Closures, 12 1/2 & 14 In., Pair 1055.00
Tub, Pine Bottom, Staves, Hickory Wraps, Round, Carved Handles, 8 1/2 x 11 3/4 In. 320.00
Work Frock, Hanger, Cotton, Neck & Wrist Gathers, Glass Buttons, Initials, c.1890, 42 In. 530.00
Yarn Winder, Pine, Maple, Red Paint, Hexagonal Spoke Wheel, 39 1/2 x 24 In. 500.00

SHAVING MUGS were popular from 1860 to 1900. Many types were made, including occupational mugs featuring pictures of men's jobs. There were scuttle mugs, silver-plated mugs, glass-lined mugs, and others.

2 Horses, Signed Limoges France, c.1914, 4 In. 280.00

4 Frogs Riding High Wheel Bicycles, Channing, T & V, France, 3 5/8 In. 270.00
Black Men, Close Shave, c.1880, KPM 550.00
Eagle & Shield, J.H. Reock, 3 3/8 In. 288.00
Fraternal, Ancient Order Of United Workman Emblem, C. Buttman, 3 3/4 In. 90.00
Fraternal, Black Cat In Oval, Hoo-Hoo, No. 93, 1889-1925, 3 1/2 In. 950.00
Fraternal, Brotherhood Of Railroad Trainmen, K. Carven, W.G. & Co. Limoges, France, 3 5/8 In. 155.00
Fraternal, Machine Tools, I.M. Of A., J. McClennan, Limoges, France, 3 5/8 In. 476.00
Fraternal, Mason, Signed CFM, France, 3 3/4 In. 110.00
Fraternal, Masons Emblem, F. Bonda, 3 5/8 In. 55.00
Fraternal, Medal, Elk's Head, P.C.R., A.O.F., U.B.C., K. Wettufer, 3 5/8 In. 134.00
Fraternal, Medal, Sons Of Veterans, H.E.L Jeffers, 1885-1925, 3 1/2 In. 180.00
Frog Fishing, John A. Fulmey, 3 1/4 In. 255.00
Horse & Buggy, 3 3/4 In. 56.00
Horse & Rider, Signed, A. Kern, 4 In. 56.00
Horseshoe, Signed E.J. Mooney, 3 1/2 In. 28.00
Hunting Scene, Signed, Koken, 3 1/2 In. 85.00
Hunting Scene, Signed, T & V Limoges, France, 3 1/2 In. 196.00
Irish Immigrant Being Welcomed By Uncle Sam, Nancey Rile, 3 7/8 In. 545.00
Occupational, 2 Men, Hanging Wallpaper, H.A. Long, 3 7/8 In. 950.00
Occupational, 2 Men, In Lumberyard, Loading Horse Drawn Wagon, J.F. Bernardin, 3 3/4 In. 660.00
Occupational, 2 Men, Printing Press, Green Wrap, Ott Bros., 3 5/8 In. 336.00
Occupational, 2 Men, Sailing Schooner, Michael Hayes, 3 7/8 In. 1232.00
Occupational, 2 Men, Singing Duet, Robert Quhl, 3 1/4 In. 138.00
Occupational, 5 Brick Masons Working, A. Strempel, 3 1/2 In. 440.00
Occupational, Accountant's Office, Wm. Bert, Aug. Kern Barber Supplies, 3 7/8 In. 403.00
Occupational, Accountant, Writing In Ledger, Austin D. Shaffer, 3 5/8 In. 575.00
Occupational, Artist Pallet, K. Harvey, 3 5/8 In. 175.00
Occupational, Automobile, Driver, John F. Murray, Blue, Red, Green, 3 5/8 In. 805.00
Occupational, Automobile, Ray T. Burson, Germany, 3 3/4 In. 470.00
Occupational, Baker's Shop, Flower Border, G. Sturm, 3 5/8 In. 460.00
Occupational, Baker, By Oven, F. Cook, 3 5/8 In. 715.00
Occupational, Baker, Putting Bread In Oven, Friedrich Finkbeiner, T & V Limoges, France, 3 5/8 In. 275.00
Occupational, Bar Scene, Bartender, 3 Men, W.W. Brabon, P. Germany, 3 3/4 In. 300.00
Occupational, Bar Scene, Michael Crossin, T & V, France, 3 5/8 In. 145.00
Occupational, Bar Scene, S.M. Mohler, Marked, CFH GDM, 3 1/2 In. 336.00
Occupational, Barber, Shaving Man, C.S. Bickock, 1885-1925, 3 1/4 In. 728.00
Occupational, Barrel Wagon, Horses, Driver, Jos F. May, D&Co, 3 1/2 In. 518.00
Occupational, Baseball Players, 3 Links Of Odd Fellows, Inscribed, H.J. Heisey 3450.00
Occupational, Baseball, 12 Players, Grandstand, R.R. Tinney 7475.00
Occupational, Baseball, Wood Bat, Ball, Hand Painted, 4 x 3 3/4 In. 1265.00
Occupational, Bicycle, Cattails, J.M. Roger, 3 1/2 In. 518.00
Occupational, Black Boot, S. Morse, 3 7/8 In. 258.00
Occupational, Black Man, Banjo, Sitting In Crescent Moon, T.P. Crogan, 3 7/8 In. 375.00
Occupational, Blacksmith, Anvil, Joe Tolley, O.&E.G. Royal Austria, 3 7/8 In. 259.00
Occupational, Blacksmith, Horse Looking At Man, D.G. Mabery, 3 5/8 In. 880.00
Occupational, Blacksmith, Shoeing Horse, E. Esselborn, 3 7/8 In. 375.00
Occupational, Blacksmith, Shoeing Horse, P.M. Brooks, GDA France, 3 5/8 In. 230.00
Occupational, Brick Mason, Building Wall Of House, Cornelius Kievit, V&D Austria, 3 1/2 In. 660.00
Occupational, Brick Mason, Building Wall, 3 1/2 In. 345.00
Occupational, Bricklayer, Working On A Building Corner, N. Matthews, 3 5/8 In. 504.00
Occupational, Butcher, Cutting Meat, Royal Austria, St. Louis, 3 7/8 In. 374.00
Occupational, Butcher, M.A. Mather, Maroon Wrap, 3 7/8 In. 375.00
Occupational, Butcher, Steer's Head, Tools, John A. Fischer, T & V Limoges, France, 3 5/8 In. 207.00
Occupational, Cabinetmaker, Planing Board At Bench, Hermann Seeck, T & V, 3 5/8 In. 220.00
Occupational, Cabinetmaker, Planing Board At Bench, W. Watson McLain, JHK, 3 3/4 In. 220.00
Occupational, Caboose C. & R.R.R. 643, Gilt Scrolls, J.W. Francis, 3 5/8 In. 345.00
Occupational, Caboose, Boxcar, A.W. Rickey, B. Of R.R.C., 3 1/2 In. 430.00
Occupational, Carpenter's Tools, F.M. Reeves, 4 In. 100.00
Occupational, Carriage, Horse Drawn, Passengers, C.M. Ford, 3 3/4 In. 405.00
Occupational, Cigar Box, Gattschalk Pinks, G.W. Bastian, 3 7/8 In. 469.00
Occupational, Cobbler, Working On Shoe, Morris Friedman, 3 3/4 In. 230.00

Occupational, Coffin, Black, Open Lid, D.C. Morton, 1885-1925, 3 1/2 In. 1430.00
Occupational, Cowboy, On Horse, Hand Painted, Germany, 4 x 3 3/4 In. 275.00
Occupational, Delivery Wagon, Fred Rappold, Germany, 1885-1925, 3 5/8 In. 660.00
Occupational, Delivery Wagon, Horse Drawn, Bakery, C. Cavallaro, 3 3/4 In. 120.00
Occupational, Delivery Wagon, Horse Drawn, Pure Milk, H. Danehower, 3 7/8 In. 440.00
Occupational, Dry Cleaner, Ironing Trousers, Max Jacobowik, 3 5/8 In. 1345.00
Occupational, Engine, S. Aguila, 3 5/8 In. 110.00
Occupational, Factory, Water, Railroad Cars, K.M. Keggen, 1885-1925, 4 In. 1345.00
Occupational, Farmer, Plowing Field, 2-Horse Team, H. Brosman, T & V, France, 4 1/8 In. 358.00
Occupational, Farrier, Shoeing Horse, Harry T. Griffith, Stamped, T & V Limoges, France, 3 5/8 In. . . 319.00
Occupational, Fire Engine, Steam, F. Horn, Rescue S.F.E.H.C. No. 4, 3 3/4 In. 1045.00
Occupational, Fire Engine, Steam, Pulled By 2 Horses, Wick C. Osborn, 3 3/4 In. 1210.00
Occupational, Fire Hose Reel Wagon, J.R. Menapace, T & V Limoges, France, 3 5/8 In. 770.00
Occupational, Fireman, 4 In. 56.00
Occupational, Fireman, Holding Hose, Pointing At Fire, D. Green, 4 In. 550.00
Occupational, Fireman, On Horse Drawn Steam Pumper, C.D. Dorgan, 3 1/4 In. 1150.00
Occupational, Football, 2 Players In Tackle, Chas. A. Donachy, B.H.S. '04 .... 5290.00
Occupational, Foundry Worker, Working With Floor Mold, G.W. Thompson, 3 5/8 In. 1100.00
Occupational, Fraternal, Railroad Box Car, 1885-1925, 3 5/8 In. 125.00
Occupational, Freight Wagon, Horse Drawn, C.K. Becker, 1885-1925, 3 5/8 In. 560.00
Occupational, Frothy Beer Mug, Kessler, 3 3/8 In. 258.00
Occupational, Grocery Store Scene, John Miller, Cleveland, Ohio, 3 3/4 In. 728.00
Occupational, Grocery Store, Front Door, W.R Shags, 1885-1925, 3 1/2 In. 336.00
Occupational, Hardware Store, 4 x 3 3/4 In. 495.00
Occupational, Harness Maker, At His Bench, W.F. Rhoades, 3 3/4 In. 420.00
Occupational, Hay Wagon, E.R. Abeling, 3 1/4 In. 715.00
Occupational, Hearse, 2-Horse Team, G. Baker, 3 7/8 In. 605.00
Occupational, Horse Drawn Steam Fire Engine, Jno. K. Culp, 4 In. 896.00
Occupational, Horse In Pasture, L.C. Hill, 3 5/8 In. 290.00
Occupational, House Painter, On Lift, Between 2 Windows, J.H. Morgan, 4 In. 728.00
Occupational, House, Purple Wrap, N. Robillard, 3 5/8 In. 670.00
Occupational, Hunter & Bird Dog, In Skiff, Wm. Grossmann, 3 5/8 In. 230.00
Occupational, Ice Wagon, Horse Drawn, Union Ice Co., Thos. Kulpin, 3 7/8 In. 448.00
Occupational, Jockey, Riding Horse, Flowers, D. Slidgell, 3 7/8 In. 530.00
Occupational, Leather Worker, J.W. Fry, Leonard Vienna, Austria, 3 5/8 In. 460.00
Occupational, Livery Stable Scene, G.W. Liten Jr., 3 7/8 In. 360.00
Occupational, Locomotive & Tender, Jacob Kalb, Royal China International, 3 5/8 In. 135.00
Occupational, Locomotive & Tender, Wm. Adolph, N.Y.C. & H.R.R.R., 3 5/8 In. 476.00
Occupational, Locomotive, Tender, 2 Passenger Cars, Frank Colvin, 3 5/8 In. 520.00
Occupational, Locomotive, Tender, Country Track, P.H. Foltz, 3 3/4 In. 490.00
Occupational, Locomotive, Tender, Wm. Mitchell, 3 3/4 In. 320.00
Occupational, Lumber Dealer, Limoges, 3 1/2 x 3 1/2 In. 690.00
Occupational, Luxury Touring Car, J.W. Skene, 1885-1925, 3 5/8 In. 1120.00
Occupational, Machinist, Drill Press, Ed Herkman Jr., 3 3/8 In. 635.00
Occupational, Machinist, Lathe, Andy Hjerpe, 3 1/2 In. 375.00
Occupational, Machinist, Stationary Engine, LeRoy H. Smeltzer, 3 1/2 In. 400.00
Occupational, Mailman, Horse Drawn Mail Wagon, J.R. Porter, 4 In. 896.00
Occupational, Man, Boxing Cigars, C.D. Starr, 1885-1925, 3 7/8 In. 670.00
Occupational, Man, Cutting Cloth, E. Gronotte, 3 1/2 In. 715.00
Occupational, Man, Driving Funeral Hearse, Horse Drawn, A.W. Green, 3 5/8 In. 1345.00
Occupational, Man, Driving Horse Drawn Buggy, A.F. Jenkins, O. & E.Q. Royal Austria, 3 7/8 In. ... 100.00
Occupational, Man, Driving Horse Drawn Delivery Cart, John McGarth, 4 In. 410.00
Occupational, Man, Driving Horse Drawn Delivery Wagon, National Express, Name, 3 7/8 In. 715.00
Occupational, Man, Driving Horse Drawn Delivery Wagon, P.H. Hussey, T & V, France, 3 5/8 In. 330.00
Occupational, Man, Driving Horse Drawn Omnibus, Fred A. Phelps, 3 3/8 In. 1340.00
Occupational, Man, Driving Phaeton, Country Road, 2 Horses, D.A. Davis, 3 1/2 In. 345.00
Occupational, Man, Driving Red Wagon, 2 Horses, Jos. D. Minier, 3 5/8 In. 316.00
Occupational, Man, Driving Touring Car, Robert Dickemann, Footed, 1919, 4 In. 896.00
Occupational, Man, Rolling Cigars At Table, S. Burger, 3 3/4 In. 715.00
Occupational, Man, Sitting In Milk Wagon, Ladling Milk Into Pitcher, F.W. Stratton, 3 1/2 In. 330.00
Occupational, Man, Telegraph Operator, V.G. Durant, Kern B.S. Co., St. Louis, 4 In. 840.00

Occupational, Man, Working At Lathe, J.G. Polk, Felda China Germany, 3 5/8 In. 495.00
Occupational, Man, Working At Sewing Machine, M. Jeanson, V&D Austria, 3 1/2 In. 725.00
Occupational, Men, Bowling Alley, Joe Hill, 1885-1925, 3 3/4 In. 2130.00
Occupational, Men, Working On Boiler, M.J. Caverty, 1885-1925, 3 1/2 In. 670.00
Occupational, Mortar & Pestle, Skull & Crossed Bones, T.C. Schmaler, T & V, France, 3 5/8 In. 297.00
Occupational, Motorcar, Flowers, D.A. Matheson, T & V, Limoges, France 2350.00
Occupational, Oil Derrick, Olie. Oleson, 3 1/2 In. 728.00
Occupational, Painter, 3 1/2 In. 56.00
Occupational, Pharmacy, J.R. Sturgis, 3 7/8 In. 1438.00
Occupational, Plumber, Working On Boiler, Sam Anadio, Germany, 3 3/4 In. 530.00
Occupational, Policeman, Chasing Pig, K. Shierloh, 1885-1925, 3 1/2 In. 730.00
Occupational, Printing Press, W.J. Martin, Deckleman Bros. Barber Supplies, 4 In. 508.00
Occupational, Produce Dealer, Hand Painted, 4 x 4 In. 440.00
Occupational, Railroad Brakeman, John Behrandt, C.A. Smith Barber Supplies, 3 3/4 In. 1100.00
Occupational, Railroad Car, C.E. Pender, 3 1/2 In. 330.00
Occupational, Rowboat, Lake, F.J. Baker, Germany, 3 5/8 In. 80.00
Occupational, Skeleton, M.F. Carnes, 3 1/2 In. 110.00
Occupational, Soda Fountain, Clerk, Holding Up Glass, Fred. Stern, 3 3/8 In. 2750.00
Occupational, Stone Cutter, F.D. Kering, O & AG, Austria, 3 1/2 In. 225.00
Occupational, Stonecutter's Shop, H.O. Reeder, Herold Bros., 3 1/2 In. 978.00
Occupational, Surveyor's Scope, Civil Engineer City Surveyor, T & V Limoges, 3 5/8 In. 2970.00
Occupational, Tailor, Measuring Man For Suit, J. Kilchenstein, D & Co., 3 1/2 In. 660.00
Occupational, Telegraph Key, V. A. Rowley, 3 1/2 In. 495.00
Occupational, Telephone Lineman, Climbing Pole, G.W. Frost, 1885-1925, 3 1/2 In. 2016.00
Occupational, Tinsmith, Hand Painted, Limoges, 4 x 3 3/4 In. 187.00
Occupational, Tinsmith, Making Piping, W.F. Bishop, 1885-1925, 3 5/8 In. 730.00
Occupational, Tinsmith, Working At Bench, Making Pan, B.F. Clemett, 4 In. 660.00
Occupational, Train Car, P.J. Kelley, T & V, France, 3 5/8 In. 469.00
Occupational, Trolley, Open Sides, Electric, On Tracks, George Carson, 3 7/8 In. 476.00
Occupational, Trotter & Sulky On Dirt Road, John Beck, D&Co., France, 3 1/2 In. 60.00
Occupational, Trout Fisherman, Gilt Scrolls, Clint. Dye, V&D Austria, 3 7/8 In. 1785.00
Occupational, Upholsterer, Working On Parlor Chair, Wm. Claus, 3 1/2 In. 2200.00
Occupational, Vintner, Casks, Chas. B. Keller, 3 1/2 In. 1150.00
Occupational, Wagon, Water Sprinkler, Horse Drawn, Geo. B. Marshall, 3 5/8 In. 1870.00
Occupational, Wall Telephone, John Brown, 1885-1925, 3 5/8 In. 990.00
Patriotic, Eagle, Shield, Crossed Flags, T & V Limoges, France, 3 1/2 In. 165.00
Shield & Crossed Flags, Italian & American, Ignazio Spicuzzo, 3 7/8 In. 365.00
Train, Marked T & V, 3 1/2 In. 225.00
Western Campfire Scene, 4 In. 56.00

SHAWNEE POTTERY was started in Zanesville, Ohio, in 1937. The company made vases, novelty ware, flowerpots, planters, lamps, and cookie jars. Three dinnerware lines were made: Corn, Lobster Ware, and Valencia (a solid color line). White Corn pattern utility pieces were made in 1945. Corn King was made from 1946 to 1954; Corn Queen, with darker green leaves and lighter colored corn, from 1954 to 1961. Shawnee produced pottery for George Rumrill during the late 1930s. The company closed in 1961.

Bank, Smiley Pig, 10 1/4 In. 475.00
Bowl, Corn King, 6 1/2 In. 60.00
Bowl, Corn King, 8 In. 55.00
Butter, Cover, Corn King 135.00
Casserole, Corn King, 11 x 5 1/4 In. ....75.00 to 125.00
Cookie Jar, Drum Major, 1940s, 10 In. 300.00
Cookie Jar, Dutch Girl, Blue, White, Brown Hair & Eyes, 10 1/4 x 7 1/2 In. 290.00
Cookie Jar, Lucky Elephant, 12 In. 26.00
Cookie Jar, Muggsy, Blue Scarf, 11 3/4 In. 645.00
Cookie Jar, Puss 'n Boots, Red Bow, Yellow Bird On Hat, 10 1/4 In. 295.00
Cookie Jar, Smiley Pig, Chrysanthemums, 11 1/2 In. 350.00
Cookie Jar, Smiley Pig, Shamrocks, Green Scarf, 11 1/4 In. 295.00
Cookie Jar, Smiley Pig, Tulips, 11 1/4 In. 40.00

Creamer, Elephant, 5 In. 75.00
Creamer, Puss 'n Boots, 4 3/4 In. 175.00
Creamer, Puss 'n Boots, Gold Trim, 4 3/4 In. 285.00
Creamer, Smiley Pig, Embossed, 4 1/2 In. 300.00
Figurine, Tumbling Bear, c.1950, 3 In. 59.00
Lamp, Stagecoach, Original Shade, 9 x 7 In. 250.00
Pie Bird, Blue, 5 In. 87.00
Pitcher, Bo Peep, 1940s, 8 In. ....125.00 to 175.00
Pitcher, Chanticleer, Red, Green & Brown Trim, 1940s, 7 1/2 In. ....150.00 to 185.00
Pitcher, Corn King No. 70 .... 75.00
Pitcher, White Corn, 8 In. 125.00
Salt & Pepper, Charlicleer, 1940s, 5 In. 58.00
Salt & Pepper, Corn King, 5 In. 55.00
Salt & Pepper, Dutch Boy & Dutch Girl, 5 In. ....70.00 to 95.00
Salt & Pepper, Muggsy, 3 1/4 In. 125.00
Salt & Pepper, Muggsy, 5 In. ....245.00 to 350.00
Salt & Pepper, Winking Owl, Paper Label, Souvenir Of Leavenworth, Kans., Corks, c.1950, 3 In. .. 36.00
Salt & Pepper, Winnie Pig, 3 In. 74.00
Sugar, Cover, Corn King, No. 78, 5 1/2 In. 50.00
Teapot, Burgundy Flowers, Gold Trim, 6 1/2 x 9 1/2 In. 90.00
Teapot, Cover, Corn King, 10 Oz. 395.00
Teapot, Granny Ann, 1940s, 8 1/2 In. ....139.00 to 165.00
Teapot, Tom Tom The Piper's Son 110.00
Vase, Fluted, 2 Birds Embossed On Sides, 9 In. 95.00

SHEARWATER pottery is a family business started by Mr. and Mrs. G. W. Anderson, Sr., and their three sons. The local Ocean Springs, Mississippi, clays were used to make the wares in the 1930s. The company is still in business.

Bowl, Figures, Running, 1981, 4 1/4 x 7 1/4 In. 3760.00
Bowl, Flambe Glaze, c.1930, 3 1/4 x 5 3/4 In. 410.00
Creamer, Purple, Rutile Glaze, No. 10, c.1940, 5 1/4 x 5 3/4 In. 206.00
Cup, Woodpecker, Bronze Glaze, Handle, 3 3/4 x 5 1/8 In. 176.00
Figurine, Black Man, Playing Accordion, Seated, 3 1/2 In. 40.00
Figurine, Goose, Head Down, c.1940, 4 5/8 x 9 1/4 x 5 1/8 In. 825.00
Figurine, Mammy, Cradling Infant, c.1950, 6 1/2 x 6 x 5 3/4 In. 499.00
Figurine, Stevedore, Woman Carrying Bundle, Man, Bale On Shoulder, 6 1/2 & 4 1/2 In., Pr. 125.00
Goblet, Brown, Purple, Rutile Glaze, 4 5/8 x 3 1/8 In. 265.00
Goblet, Purple Rutile Glaze, c.1935, 4 1/4 x 3 3/4 In., Pair 235.00
Pitcher, Alkaline Blue, c.1928, 6 x 6 1/4 In. 90.00
Plate, Chicken, c.1940, 10 1/4 In. 3820.00
Plate, Deer, c.1940, 6 In. 1880.00
Plate, Fish, c.1940, 10 In. 5200.00
Porringer, Brown, Purple, Rutile Glaze, c.1970, 1 3/8 x 5 1/2 x 4 In., Pair 147.00
Vase, Baluster, 1930s, 7 x 3 3/4 In. 150.00
Vase, Green, Gunmetal Gray, Metallic Glaze, 5 3/8 In. 120.00
Vase, Mottled, Turquoise, Over Tan, 2 Handles, 2 3/4 x 4 3/4 In. 310.00
Vase, Rings, Dripped Glaze, Gray, Blue, Rainbow Shaped Stamp, 10 1/2 x 4 In. 170.00
Vase, Turquoise Glaze, c.1928, 6 x 6 1/4 In. 235.00

SHEET MUSIC from the past centuries is now collected. The favorites are examples with covers featuring artistic or historic pictures. Early sheet music covers were lithographed, but by the 1900s photographic reproductions were used. The early music was larger than more recent sheets, and you must watch out for examples that were trimmed to fit in a twentieth-century piano bench.

Ac-Cent-Tchu-Ate The Positive, J. Mercer & H. Arlen, E.H. Morris & Co., 1944, 4 Pages 7.00
Anchors Aweigh, C.A. Zimmermann, 1942, 2 Pages 7.00
Don't Fence Me In, C. Porter, Harms, N.Y., 1944, 2 Pages 6.00
Everyone's Gone To The Moon, Astronauts, JFK, c.1965 .... 14.00
Father Of The Land We Love, George M. Cohan, 1931 .... 55.00

Greenbacks, Dan. D. Emmett, c.1868, 13 x 10 1/2 In., 4 Pages 420.00
Hair, Natoma Productions, Psychedelic Cover, Copyright 1968 ..... 15.00
High School Cadets March, J.P. Sousa, Calumet Music Co., 1947, 3 Pages 6.00
Is You Is Or Is You Ain't My Baby, Billy Austin, L. Jordan, Leeds Music, 1944 ..... 7.00
My One & Only Highland Fling, Ira Gershwin, Harry Warren, 1949 ..... 15.00
Plantation Melodies, 6 Songs, Geo. P. Reed, Boston, Mass, 1847, 14 x 11 In. 748.00
Three Little Words, Check & Double Check, Amos 'n' Andy, 1930 ..... 28.00
Tie A Yellow Ribbon Round The Ole Oak Tree, I. Levine & R. Brown, 1972 ..... 7.00 to 11.00
Yellow Kid On Parade, C.E. Vandersloot, Frame, 13 1/2 x 10 3/8 In. 974.00
Yellow Kid On Parade, Singing, Dancing, 21 x 16 In. 1075.00
You'll Be There To Meet Them When The Boys Come Home, Uncle Sam, 1915 ..... 20.00
You're A Grand Old Flag, G.M. Cohan, Vogel Music Co., 1933, 3 Pages 10.00

SHEFFIELD items are listed in the Silver Plate and Silver-English categories.

SHIRLEY TEMPLE, the famous movie star, was born in 1928. She made her first movie in 1932. Thousands of items picturing Shirley have been and still are being made. Shirley Temple dolls were first made in 1934 by Ideal Toy Company. Millions of Shirley Temple cobalt blue glass dishes were made by Hazel Atlas Glass Company and U.S. Glass Company from 1934 to 1942. They were given away as premiums for Wheaties and Bisquick. A bowl, mug, and pitcher were made as a breakfast set. Some pieces were decorated with the picture of a very young Shirley, others used a picture of Shirley in her 1936 *Captain January* costume. Although collectors refer to a cobalt creamer, it is actually the 4 1/2-inch-high milk pitcher from the breakfast set. Many of these items are being reproduced today.

Carriage, Wood, Leatherette Sunshade, Metal Grip, Wire Wheels, F.A. Whitney, 26 x 12 In. 3960.00
Display, Box, Pitcher, Wheaties, Diecut, 1930s, 3 1/4 x 17 x 17 In., 12 Piece 1495.00
Doll, Composition, Sleep Eyes, 5-Piece Body, Dress Tag, Ideal, 22 In. 770.00
Fan, R.C. Cola, 1944 ..... 35.00
Pastime Box, Set No. 1732, 4 Books, Saalfied Co., 1937 ..... 175.00
Soap Set, Soapy Theater, Blue & Red Ribbon, Box, Kerk Guild Bath Prod., 6 x 9 In. 170.00

SHRINER, see Fraternal category.

SILVER DEPOSIT glass was first made during the late nineteenth century. Solid sterling silver is applied to the glass by a chemical method so that a cutout design of silver metal appears against a clear or colored glass. It is sometimes called silver overlay.

Decanter, Clear Glass, Flowers & Leaves, Overlay, Faceted Stopper, Tuthill, 13 1/2 In. 604.00
Decanter, Glass, Scrolling Vine Overlay, Egg Shape, Alvin, c.1900, 9 In. 470.00
Vase, Bud, Cranberry Glass, Flowers & Bows Overlay, Art Nouveau Style, Alvin, 8 In. 865.00
Vase, Emerald Glass, Hemming, Montreal, c.1900, 5 In. 234.00
Vase, Glass, Flowers, Leaves, Silver Leaf & Flower Overlay, Alvin, R.I., c.1900 ..... 660.00
Vase, Serpentine Shape, Flower Vines, Art Nouveau, Alvin, Early 1900s, 8 In. 410.00

SILVER FLATWARE includes many of the current and out-of-production silver and silver-plated flatware patterns made in the past eighty years. Other silver is listed under Silver-American, Silver-English, etc. Most silver flatware sets that are missing a few pieces can be completed through the help of one of the many silver matching services that advertise in many of the national publications.

SILVER FLATWARE PLATED, Adoration, Tomato Server, 1847 Rogers Bros., 7 In. 45.00
Alhambra, Serving Fork, International, Anchor Rogers Backstamp, 8 1/2 In. 39.00
Alton, Cold Meat Fork, International W. F. Rogers, c.1901, 7 1/2 In. 29.00
Always, Tablespoon, Oneida, 1958 ..... 9.00
Anniversary Rose, Serving Fork, International Silver, 8 15/16 In. 29.00
Chester, Fork, Monogram H, Towle, 6 Piece 65.00
Elberon, Punch Ladle, Monogram, Wm. A. Rogers, c.1897 ..... 100.00
Eternally Yours, Carving Fork, 1847 Rogers 59.00
Fiddle, Butter Knife, Twist Handle, 1847 Rogers, 1850s 35.00
First Colony, Cake Server, Pierced Handle, Oneida, 1975 ..... 13.00

Floral, Cold Meat Fork, Wallace, 8 In. 35.00
Her Majesty, Dinner Knife, International, 1847 Rogers Bros., c.1931, 5 Piece 70.00
Holly, Gravy Ladle, Patent Dated 1904 .... 110.00
La Vigne, Sugar Spoon, 1881 Rogers A1, c.1908, 6 x 1 1/2 In. 35.00
Lancaster, Serving Fork, Alvin, c.1923, 8 1/2 In. 32.00
Le Louvre, Dinner Fork, Scrolls, Leaves, Shell, Reed & Barton, c.1888, 6 Piece 100.00
Lorne, Ice Tongs, Rogers, 8 In. 125.00
Louis XVI, Strawberry Fork, Community Plate, M Monogram, 5 In. 30.00
Magnolia, Sugar Shell, Wm. Rogers, 6 In. 32.00
New Century, Serving Fork, Gold Wash, International, 1898 Patent, 8 3/8 In. 32.00
Orange Blossom, Dinner Fork, International, Rogers & Bro., c.1910, 6 Piece 120.00
Orange Blossom, Meat Fork, International, Rogers & Bro., c.1910 .... 45.00
Orange Blossom, Tomato Server, International, Rogers & Bro., c.1910 .... 38.00
Oxford, Serving Spoon, Wm. Rogers & Son, Patented 1901, 8 1/2 In. 49.00
Princess, Butter Knife, Twist Handle, 1847 Rogers Bros., c.1879, 7 3/8 In. 28.00
Queen Bess, Pie Server, Oneida, c.1946, 9 1/2 In. 30.00
Queen Bess, Salad Fork, Community Plate, Pierced Tine, 6 1/2 In., 6 Piece 49.00
Royal Victorian, Soup Ladle, Wm. Rogers, c.1919, 6 1/4 In. 30.00
Seville, Butter Knife, Twist Handle, International, c.1898, 7 In. 29.00
Shelton, Fork Set, Wm. A. Rogers A1X, c.1935, 4 Piece 45.00
Sweet Briar, Cocktail Fork, Oneida, c.1948, 8 Piece 48.00
Troy, Butter Knife, Twist Handle, R. Wallace, c.1902, 7 1/2 In. 36.00
Vintage, Berry Spoon, 1847 Rogers Bros., c.1904, 9 In. 52.00
Vintage, Soup Ladle, International, 1847 Rogers Bros., c.1904, 11 In. 95.00
Woodsong, Salad Servers, Holmes & Edwards, c.1958 .... 30.00
SILVER FLATWARE STERLING, Acorn, Salad Set, Georg Jensen, 2 Piece 497.00
Acorn, Serving Set, Fork, Tongs, Georg Jensen, Case 265.00
Alhambra, Soup Ladle, Gold-Washed Bowl, Whiting, 12 5/8 In. 600.00
Angelo, Soup Ladle, Wood & Hughes 650.00
Arabesque, Cream Ladle, Gilt Bowl, Monogram, 5 3/8 In. 300.00
Athenian, Toast Fork, Whiting 375.00
Bridal Rose, Butter Pick, Monogram, Alvin, 6 1/2 In. 125.00
Bridal Rose, Fish Set, Roses, Leaves, Monogram, Alvin Co., c.1903, 9 3/4 In. 956.00
Bridal Rose, Ice Cream Fork, Alvin 140.00
Bridal Rose, Sugar Shell, Alvin, 6 1/4 In. 145.00
Buckingham, Salad Fork, Pierced Bar, Gorham, 6 1/4 In. 75.00
Buckingham, Soup Spoon, Oval, Gorham, 7 In. 50.00
Buttercup, Punch Ladle, 13 5/8 In. 1300.00
Buttercup, Sardine Tongs, 4 In. 295.00
Cashmere, Punch Ladle, Wood & Hughes, Late 19th Century, 12 3/4 In. 206.00
Celestial, Serving Spoon, Wood & Hughes, c.1870, 8 1/4 In. 265.00
Chrysanthemum, Butter Spreader Set, Flat, W.B. Durgin, 6 Piece 630.00
Chrysanthemum, Jelly Server, Gold Washed Bowl, W.B. Durgin, 7 1/2 In. 450.00
Chrysanthemum, Salt Spoon, Master, Monogram, W.B. Durgin, 3 3/4 In. 100.00
Chrysanthemum, Waffle Server, Scalloped, Pierced, W.B. Durgin, 9 1/4 In. 1015.00
Cloeta, Asparagus Server, Pierced, International, c.1904, 4 1/2 In. 215.00
Cordova, Lettuce Fork & Spoon Set, Towle 275.00
Corinthian, Gravy Ladle, Shiebler 265.00
Corinthian, Ice Cream Serving Spoon, Gold Wash, Monogram, 10 1/4 In. 399.00
Courtship, International, Service For 12, 78 Piece 527.00
Cupid, Serving Spoon & Fork, Long Handle, Dominick & Haff, 11 1/2 In. 410.00
Dresden, Salad Set, Gilt End, Repousse, Whiting, c.1896, 11 3/4 In. 508.00
Du Barry, Cheese Scoop, Leaves, Monogram, Durgin, c.1901, 7 1/4 In. 299.00
Eva, Pickle Fork & Knife, Gorham 265.00
Fiddleback, Jelly Server, Old Newbury Crafters, Early 1900s, 7 1/4 In. 60.00
Fleury, Ladle, Gilt Interior, Arched Handle, Flowers, Gorham, c.1909, 10 1/2 In. 149.00
Florence Nightingale, Soup Ladle, Alvin, c.1919, 12 In. 625.00
Francis I, Gravy Ladle, Reed & Barton, 6 1/2 In. 70.00
Francis I, Serving Set, Reed & Barton, 10 Piece 527.00
Francis I, Stuffing Spoon, Reed & Barton, 13 1/2 In. 295.00
Golden Scroll, Silver & Gold Plate, Gorham, c.1977, 90 Piece 1400.00

Hizen, Ice Cream Slice, Fish, Crane, Bamboo, Gorham, c.1880, 12 In. 2150.00
Hyperion, Fish Serving Set, Knife, Fork, Monogram, Whiting 1495.00
Hyperion, Macaroni Server, Whiting, 9 3/4 In. 685.00
Imperial Chrysanthemum, Pie Server, Gorham, 9 In. 325.00
Imperial Queen, Punch Ladle, Whiting, c.1900, 12 In. 205.00
Iris, Gravy Ladle, Monogram, W.B. Durgin, c.1900, 7 In. 390.00
Kings III, Sauce Ladle, D Monogram, Gorham, 7 In. 175.00
Lily, Berry Spoon, Gilt Washed Interior, Scalloped Rim, Whiting, c.1902, 9 In. 388.00
Lily, Iced Tea Spoon Set, Whiting, 8 Piece 650.00
Lily Of The Valley, Sugar Shell, Whiting, 6 3/4 In. 200.00
Love Disarmed, Salad Set, Spoon & Fork, Reed & Barton, 10 In. 375.00
Love Disarmed, Serving Spoon & Fork, Reed & Barton, 10 1/2 In. 558.00
Marguerite, Oyster Server, Scalloped, Wood & Hughes, c.1880, 10 1/4 In. 310.00
Medallion, Berry Server, Gilt, Scallop Bowl, Gorham, c.1864, 9 In. 450.00
Medallion, Cream Soup Spoon Set, Shiebler, c.1880, 12 Piece 1200.00
Medallion, Fried Oyster Server, Gorham, c.1864, 9 1/2 In. 420.00
Medallion, Macaroni Server, Pierced, Monogram, Gorham, c.1864, 10 In. 960.00
Medallion, Serving Spoon, Roman Warrior, Gorham, Box, c.1865, 9 1/2 In. 499.00
Medici, Soup Ladle, Scalloped, Scrolls, Flowers, Dog, Gorham, c.1880, 13 In. 450.00
Mythologique, Knife, Blunt Hollow Handle, Gorham, 8 1/2 In. 100.00
Napoleon, Berry Spoon, Parcel Gilt, Wreath, Scalloped Bowl, Late 1800s, 9 1/2 In. 108.00
New King, Demitasse Spoon Set, Dominick & Haff, 8 Piece 240.00
New King, Punch Ladle, Oval Bowl, Dominick & Haff, 13 In. 265.00
New King, Vegetable Fork, Dominick & Haff, 8 7/8 In. 265.00
No. 10, Fork Set, Dominick & Haff, c.1900, 6 In., 12 Piece 265.00
Old English, Macaroni Server, Goldwashed Tines, Towle, 9 7/8 In. 575.00
Old King, Asparagus Server, Whiting, 9 3/4 In. 450.00
Orange Blossom, Punch Ladle, Alvin, 20th Century, 18 In. 265.00
Oval Twist, Jelly Knife, Whiting, 8 1/4 In. 159.00
Oval Twist, Mustard Ladle, Gold Washed Bowl, Whiting, 4 5/8 In. 135.00
Oval Twist, Soup Ladle, Whiting, 10 1/4 In. 390.00
Phoebe, Almond Spoon, Pierced, Watson, 6 In. 400.00
Poppy, Ladle, Flared Rim, Gilt Wash Interior, Gorham, c.1902, 10 3/4 In. 275.00
Raphael, Cucumber Server, Flowers, Woman, Alvin Corp., c.1902, 6 1/4 In. 780.00
Regent, Salad Servers, W.B. Durgin, 1900s, 9 3/4-In. Fork, 9 5/8-In. Spoon 765.00
Repousse, Berry Spoon, S. Kirk & Son, c.1950, 9 1/4 In. 235.00
Rococo, Cold Meat Fork, Dominick & Haff 138.00
Rococo, Demitasse Spoon Set, Dominick & Haff, 5 Piece 150.00
St. Cloud, Fish Slice, Gorham, c.1885, 11 3/4 In. 800.00
St. Cloud, Serving Spoon & Fork, Gorham, c.1885, 11 1/4 In., 2 Piece 1015.00
Stieff Rose, Salad Servers, Kirk Stieff, 9 1/8-In. Fork, 9-In. Spoon 355.00
Trajan, Lettuce Fork, 3 Tines, Reed & Barton, c.1892, 9 1/2 In. 84.00
Versailles, Berry Spoon, Gorham 110.00
Versailles, Coffee Spoon, Gorham, 5 1/8 In. 25.00
Versailles, Teaspoon, Gorham, 5 7/8 In. ....40.00 to 45.00
York, Ice Cream Knife, Scimitar Blade, Engraved, Old Newbury Crafters, 9 1/2 In. 379.00

SILVER PLATE is not solid silver. It is a ware made of a metal, such as nickel or copper, that is covered with a thin coating of silver. The letters *EPNS* are often found on American and English silver-plated wares. Sheffield is a term with two meanings. Sometimes it refers to sterling silver made in the town of Sheffield, England. In this section, Sheffield refers to a type of silver plate, usually English.

E P N S

Basket, Handle, Rounded Rectangular, Old Sheffield, 7 3/4 x 10 x 7 3/4 In. 81.00
Basket, Oval, Reticulated, Reeded Rim, Swing Handle, Footed, Sheffield, 12 x 14 In. 590.00
Basket, Vase Shape, Fluted & Reticulated Sides, Footed, c.1920, 18 1/2 In. 440.00
Basket, Vase Shape, Reticulated Sides & Foot, No. 6650, Reed & Barton, c.1920, 21 In. 270.00
Biscuit Box, Military Drum Form, Crossed Drumsticks, Edwardian, 5 1/2 x 5 1/2 In. 350.00
Biscuit Box, Shell Shape, Chased Leaf Scrolls, On Shells, England, 10 1/2 In. 490.00
Bowl, Center, 3 Classical Figures Holding Basket, 3-Scroll Pedestal Base, 24 In. 5580.00
Bowl, Center, Flower Basket, Glass Bowl, Meriden, c.1880, 10 1/2 x 9 1/4 In. 110.00

Bowl, Center, Victorian, Etched, Frosted Bowl, Pierced Basket, Late 1800s, 10 In. 195.00
Bowl, Vegetable, Domed Ribbed Cover, 8 1/2 In. 265.00
Bread Tray, Pine Cone Design, Christofle, 14 In. 120.00
Cake Basket, Chased Scrolls, Fluted Swirls, Lobed, Spread Foot, Ellis-Barker, 8 1/2 In. 240.00
Cake Basket, Glass, Ivory Enamel, Middletown Plate Co., Conn., c.1870, 10 3/4 In. 120.00
Cake Basket, Lobed, Chased, Leafy Edge, Swing Handle, Ellis-Barker, 8 x 10 In. 50.00
Cake Plate, Gadroon Border, 4 Scroll Supports, 4 1/2 x 19 In. 410.00
Candelabrum is listed in its own category.
Candlesticks are listed in their own category.
Candy Dish, Worthington, Glass, Victorian, c.1900, 4 x 6 In. 350.00
Chafing Dish, 3 Removable Dividers, Rectangular, 8 x 20 x 14 In. 105.00
Chafing Dish, Dome Lid, Tiered, Gadroon Handle, Oblong, Late 1800s, 13 1/2 In. 176.00
Champagne Cooler, Neptune's Head, Seashells, Signed, Figura Piero, 18 3/4 x 12 In. 5465.00
Cigar Box, Man, Steering Wheel, Goddess Of Speed, 1915-20, 2 1/2 x 9 x 5 1/2 In. 390.00
Cigar Holder, Automobile, Match Holder, Electroplate, England, c.1900, 5 x 9 x 4 In. 1799.00
Cigarette Box, Enamel, Figural Decoration, Early 1900s, 8 1/4 x 5 x 2 3/4 In. 205.00
Claret Jug, Bulbous, Slender Neck, Grapevines, Leaves, F. Hess, 1800s, 13 1/2 In. 780.00
Claret Jug, Cut Glass, Pear Shape Body, Fish Scale Neck, 9 In. 90.00
Cocktail Shaker, Gold Design, Relief, Apollo, 12 1/2 In. 345.00
Cocktail Shaker, Lighthouse Shape, 18 x 6 In. 3120.00
Coffee Set, George III Style, Baluster, Ellis-Barker, 12 In., 3 Piece 118.00
Coffeepot, Dome Lid, Swirl Lobed Lower, C-Scroll Handle, 6 x 9 1/2 x 5 In. 155.00
Compote, Crystal Bowl, 3-Footed, Sheffield, Henry Wilkinson & Co., c.1880, 13 In. 439.00
Cover, Meat, Acanthus Scroll, Fruit Handle, Lobed Oval Body, Sheffield, c.1825, 14 In. 629.00
Cover, Meat, Motto, Winged Spurs Crest, Cast Handle, England, 20 1/2 In. 405.00
Cover, Meat, Victorian, Old Sheffield, Oval, Chased Acanthus, c.1840, 7 x 19 In. 645.00
Crumber, Louis XVI Style, France, c.1885, 9 1/2 x 10 In., 2 Piece 205.00
Decanter Stand, Victorian, 3 Cut Glass Bottles, Fenton Brothers, c.1880, 14 x 9 1/2 In. 1000.00
Desk Ornament, Car, Woman Driver, Over Brass, c.1902, 4 3/4 x 2 1/2 In. 259.00
Dessert Spoon, Down-Curved Fiddle Handle, Louis Boudo, Charleston, c.1825, 8 1/2 In. 470.00
Dish, Art Nouveau Flowers In Relief, Openwork Sides, Meriden, 18 x 8 In. 230.00
Dish, Entree, Cover, Copper, Early 20th Century, 14 1/4 In., Pair 145.00
Dish, Entree, Cover, Oval, Strapwork, Reeded Rims, Late 1800s, 12 In. 105.00
Dish, Entree, Handle, Cover, Sheffield, 6 x 8 1/2 In., Pair 235.00
Dish, Entree, Sheffield, c.1920, 5 x 10 In., Pair 175.00
Drink Dispenser, Rocket Ship Shape, Glass Liner, Rogers & Co., c.1930, 14 1/4 In. 1980.00
Egg Nipper, Chicken Shape, E.D. Wusthof, Soligen, Germany, 5 In. 85.00
Epergne, 3-Footed, Putti, Hamilton & Laidlaw, Scotland, c.1863, 11 In., Pair 715.00
Epergne, Openwork, Hanging Baskets, Robert Scott, Glasgow, Scotland, 19 In. 460.00
Epergne, Reed & Barton, 14 x 17 In. 1404.00
Fish Platter, Jugenstil, Oval, Shaped Rim, Cast, Band Of Fish, Early 1900s, 20 In. 588.00
Fish Server, Scimitar Blade, Pierced, Engraved Fish, Bone Handle, 13 In., Pair 88.00
Fish Servers, Case, Fisherman, Rod, In Stream, 12 1/2 & 9 3/4 In. 215.00
Fish Set, Mother Of Pearl, Sheffield, 12 Knives, 12 Forks, Case, c.1870 .... 468.00
Fish Set, Pearce & Sons, Fan Border, Oak Case, Victorian, 26 Piece 355.00
Fish Set, Prince's Plate, Mappin & Webb, Fitted Oak Case, 24 Piece 205.00
Frame, Flowers, Birds, Matte Ground, Rectangular, 9 1/2 x 7 In. 325.00
Frame, Serpentine Sides, Chrysanthemums, Rectangular, 12 1/2 x 10 In. 295.00
Hot Water Urn, Dome Top, Lion Mask, Ring Handles, Ball Feet, Sheffield, 21 x 11 In. 330.00
Hot Water Urn, Egg Shape, Scalloped, Gadroon Rim, Dome Top, Sheffield, 1800s, 17 In. 529.00
Hot Water Urn, George III, Sheffield 413.00
Hot Water Urn, Melon Lobed, Acanthus Scrolls, Spigot, Melon Finial, Footed, Handles, 16 In. 998.00
Ice Bucket, Wilcox International, c.1960, 15 In., Pair 410.00
Kettle, Stand, Goblet, Quadruple Plated, Reed & Barton, 19 1/2 In. 288.00
Kettle, Stand, Pyriform, Elkington Mason & Co., Birmingham, c.1854, 17 In. 410.00
Kettle, Stand, Whiplash Handle, Scrolled Stretchers, Art Nouveau, c.1900, 10 3/4 In. 1037.00
Kettle, Warming Base, Sheffield, c.1820, 14 1/2 x 10 In. 700.00
Mirror, Dressing, Art Nouveau, Columns, Flowers, Maidens, c.1900, 20 1/4 In. 700.00
Mirror, Dressing, Cherubs, Ribbons, Rouge Marble Plinth, Oval, 16 1/2 In. 700.00
Mirror, Vanity, Swivel Stand, Sheffield, c.1900, 20 x 15 In. 585.00
Napkin Rings are listed in their own category.

Pitcher, Angular & Ball Handle, King's College, Elkington & Co., England, 6 5/8 In. 115.00
Pitcher, Water, Aesthetic Style, Cylindrical, Tapered, Reed & Barton, 1886, 13 1/2 In. 325.00
Platter, Dome Lid, Venison, Well & Tree, Leaf Scroll Feet, 14 x 26 In. 1998.00
Punch Ladle, H&S, Sheffield, England, c.1930, 13 In. 59.00
Punch Set, Grapevine Rims, Footed, Sheridan Silversmiths, Taunton, 15 Piece 355.00
Server, Bacon, Cover, Hinged Dome, Acanthus Handle, Old Sheffield, 5 x 12 x 7 3/4 In. 201.00
Server, Bowl, Tray Inserts, Acanthus, Fruit, Old Sheffield, 7 x 15 3/4 x 10 In., Pair 1380.00
Server, Cover, Oval, Reed, Flowers, Bands, Bowl, Tray Insert, Old Sheffield, 8 x 14 In. 1495.00
Server, Cover, Scroll, Flower Handle, Bowl, Tray, Old Sheffield, 7 x 13 1/2 x 9 1/2 In. 635.00
Serving Spoon, Continental, Victorian, 14 & 15 In., Pair 80.00
Serving Spoon, Shell Shape Bowl, Flowers, James Dixon & Sons, c.1870, 10 1/4 In., Pair 155.00
Spoon, Souvenir, see Souvenir category.
Stand, Japonesque, Fans, Simpson, Hall, Miller & Co., Late 1800s, 7 x 9 1/2 In. 25.00
Sweetmeat Basket, Ladle, c.1910, 6 1/2 x 7 In., Pair 644.00
Tea & Coffee Set, Neoclassical, Oval, William Adams, England, 1900s, 8 1/4 In., 5 Piece 110.00
Tea & Coffee Set, Repousse, Chinoiserie Landscape, John Chandler Moore, N.Y., 4 Piece 6760.00
Tea & Coffee Set, Skyscraper, Stepped Squared Covers, Black Handles, 3 Piece 3360.00
Tea Set, Aesthetic Movement Style, Wrapped Bamboo Handles, Christofle, 7 Piece 1840.00
Tea Set, Chased, Hound Finials, Stag Feet, Meriden, 1880-1910, 4 Piece 320.00
Tea Set, Christopher Wren Pattern, Wallace, 5 Piece 235.00
Tea Set, Sphinx Finials, Hoof Feet, Elk Heads, Middleton Plate Co., Victorian, 7 Piece 110.00
Tea Set, Victorian, Engraved, Lion Head, Reed & Barton, 7 Piece 220.00
Teapot, Bright Cut Decoration, Ribbed, Pearwood Handle, Sheffield, 1780-1800, 6 In. 330.00
Teapot, Ribbed, Wood Handle, Ilonka Karasz, Paye & Baker, 1928, 5 x 6 x 4 In. 3300.00
Toiletry Kit, Traveling, Gentleman's, Cartier, Early 20th Century 236.00
Tongs, Kings Plate Pattern, Initial H, William Hutton & Sons, Late 19th Century 50.00
Tray, Angler's Club Of New York, Etched, International Silver Co., c.1950, 12 x 9 In. 550.00
Tray, Footed, Vintage Border, c.1940, 17 In. 35.00
Tray, Navette Shape, Gadroon, Acanthus, Shell, Webster & Son, 16 x 8 1/2 In. 120.00
Tray, Octagonal, Early 20th Century, 14 In., Pair 100.00
Tray, Scalloped Sides, Round, Ilonka Karasz, Paye & Baker, 1928, 1 x 12 In. 4500.00
Tray, Serving, Cheltenham & Co., Hand Chased, 15 1/2 x 26 In. 410.00
Tray, Victorian, Rococo Style, Circular, Footed, Scottish Crest, Motto, 2 x 20 In. 120.00
Tureen, Dome Lid, Bombe Shape, Shaped Rim, Cartouches, Footed, Pear Finial, 10 x 8 In. 1060.00
Tureen, Dome Lid, Oval, Scroll Handles, Martin Hall, Sheffield, Late 1800s, 10 1/4 x 14 In. 240.00
Tureen, Old Sheffield, Acanthus Scroll, William IV, c.1835, 10 x 10 x 16 In. 2820.00
Vase, Poppies, Molded, Raised, Circular Foot, Art Nouveau, 10 1/2 In. 127.00
Vase, Victorian, Faux Bamboo Legs, Cherry Stems, Blown Glass Trumpet Vase, 18 In. 265.00
Waiter, 2 Handles, George IV Style, Armorial, Motto, c.1935, 4 x 28 x 17 In. 1645.00
Warming Dish, Cover, Sheffield Plate, 2 Handles, Oval, c.1810, 18 In. 666.00
Wine Coaster, Pierced, Scrolls, Swags, Flared Rim, Scroll & Floral Border, 5 x 8 In. 978.00
Wine Cooler, Greek Key Bands, Stag's Head Handles, England, 11 In., Pair . . . . .2115.00 to 2645.00
Wine Cooler, Melon Lobed, Flared Collar & Rim, Scalloped Foot, 9 x 9 3/4 In., Pair 3525.00
Wine Cooler, Sheffield, Oval, Vertical Reeding, Trumpet Foot, c.1800, 9 1/2 In., Pair 2585.00
Wine Trolley, Cannon Shape, Scrolled & Leaf-Carved Carriage & Wheels, Pair 1440.00

SILVER, SHEFFIELD, see Silver Plate; Silver-English categories.

SILVER-AMERICAN. American silver is listed here. Coin and sterling silver are included. Most of the sterling silver listed in this book is subdivided by country. There are also other pieces of silver and silver plate listed under special categories, such as Candelabrum, Napkin Ring, Silver Flatware, Silver Plate, Silver-Sterling, and Tiffany Silver. For information about makers and marks, see *Kovels' American Silver Marks: 1650 to the Present.*

SILVER-AMERICAN, Almond Dish, Narragansett, Oyster Shell Shape, Gorham, c.1888, 4 3/4 In. . 1076.00
Basket, Egyptian Pattern, Handle, Oval, Ford & Tupper, c.1870, 7 3/4 x 6 3/4 In. 895.00
Basket, Reticulated, Boat Shape, C-Scroll Cartouche, Gorham, 9 In., Pair 499.00
Basket, Shell Shape, 3 Dolphin Feet, Pierced, Handle, c.1910, 10 1/2 In., Pair 5400.00
Basket, Swing Handle, Repousse Grape & Leaf, Cupids, Ball Feet, Theodore Starr, 7 x 10 In. 345.00
Beaker, Cylindrical, Flared Sides, Rim, Monogram, Kalo, 4 x 3 1/8 In. 475.00
Berry Bowl, Fruit Pattern, Monogram, Gorham, c.1868, 10 In. 405.00

Berry Spoon, Gilt Wash Bowl, Birds, Spread Feathers, Whiting, c.1866, 10 In. 1315.00
Bonbon, Openwork, Scroll Edge, Oval, Shell Ends, Gorham, 1953, 8 3/4 x 5 In. 35.00
Bonbon Spoon, Gold Washed Bowl, Leaves, Gorham, Late 1800s, 5 In. 106.00
Bowl, 4 Scroll Legs, Repousse Shells, Seaweed, Partial Gilt, Whiting, 7 x 12 In. 5558.00
Bowl, Art Nouveau Leaves, Flowers, Footed, Monogram, International, c.1920, 6 x 10 In. 335.00
Bowl, Arts & Crafts, Hammered, Egg Shape, F. Novick, 10 In. 1116.00
Bowl, Boat Shape, Angular Handles, Trumpet Foot, Durgin, 1900s, 8 3/8 x 17 In. 825.00
Bowl, Center, Martele, Round, Wavy Border, Gorham, c.1912, 15 1/2 In. 10800.00
Bowl, Center, Salem Pattern, Reed & Barton, 1952, 3 x 12 x 8 In. 645.00
Bowl, Center, Virginia Pattern, Dominick & Haff, 14 1/4 In. 275.00
Bowl, Child's, Ruffled Rim, Flowers, Inscription, c.1897, 2 1/2 x 5 In. 4480.00
Bowl, Classical Style, Oval, Open Loop Handles, Trumpet Foot, Gorham, 14 In. 470.00
Bowl, Cut Glass, Hemispherical, Gadroons, Flutes, Gorham, c.1898, 4 x 9 In. 820.00
Bowl, Egg Shape, Flowers, Acanthus Feet, Gorham, c.1904, 16 1/2 In. 3525.00
Bowl, Egg Shape, Low Foot, Flared Rolled Rim, Arthur J. Stone, 1908-37, 8 1/4 In. 470.00
Bowl, Egg Shape, Trumpet Foot, Greek Key Rim, Gorham, c.1875, 8 1/4 In. 999.00
Bowl, Flat Bottom, Flared Side, Turned In Rim, K. F. Leinonen, 2 x 4 In. 325.00
Bowl, Flat Bottom, Flared Side, Turned In Rim, K. F. Leinonen, 2 1/2 x 7 1/2 In. 695.00
Bowl, Flat Bottom, Fluted, Applied Wire To Rim, Rounded Sides, Kalo, 2 1/2 x 8 In. 1050.00
Bowl, Flat Bottom, Fluted, Flared Side, Flower Blossom, K. F. Leinonen, 2 x 5 In. 395.00
Bowl, Flat Bottom, Fluted, Turned In Rim, Applied Wire, Kalo, 2 3/4 x 9 In. 875.00
Bowl, Flowers, Repousse, S. Kirk & Son Co., 4 1/2 x 10 1/2 In. 1285.00
Bowl, Fruit, Reticulated, Boat Shape, C-Scrolls, Gorham, 1894, 12 1/2 In. 645.00
Bowl, Fruit, Reticulated, Stamped, C-Scrolls, Pierced, Monogram, c.1894, 12 1/2 In. 470.00
Bowl, Fruit, Scalloped, Egg Shape, 3 Scroll Feet, Tuttle, 1900s, 8 1/2 x 5 In. 295.00
Bowl, Georgian, Egg Shape, Leaves, Rocaille, Reed & Barton, 1937, 11 In. 1116.00
Bowl, Hammered, Flared Rim, Rose Vine, Graff Washbourne & Dunn, 8 5/8 In. 470.00
Bowl, Hammered, Monogram, GW, Scalloped Rim, Copper Foot, G.C. Gebelein, Boston, 9 In. 765.00
Bowl, Hand Hammered, DeMatteo, 1923-88, 4 1/2 In. 405.00
Bowl, Oval, Floral Repousse Design, Gorham, 1899, 10 In. 405.00
Bowl, Pedestal, Chased, Flared Sides, Applied Wire Rim, F. Novick, 4 1/2 x 10 In. 2900.00
Bowl, Pierced Flower Border, Relief Flowers, J.E. Caldwell & Co., 2 1/2 x 12 In. 520.00
Bowl, Poppies On Rim, Monogram, Round, Unger Bros., No. 0848, 3 x 10 In. 345.00
Bowl, Repousse Flower, Oval, Gorham, 1899, 1 3/4 x 10 1/4 x 7 3/4 In. 400.00
Bowl, Repousse Flowers, Dragonfly, Mauser, c.1900, 5 1/2 In. 170.00
Bowl, Repousse, Village, Flowers, Sawtooth Rim, S. Kirk & Son, 5 1/2 x 6 In. 556.00
Bowl, Ring Foot, Applied Wire Rim, Chased, Arthur J. Stone, 2 x 6 In. 1700.00
Bowl, Royal Danish, Pierced Leaf Corners, International Silver Co., 9 1/4 x 12 1/2 In. 58.00
Bowl, Salem Pattern, Round, Lobed Rim, Footed, Reed & Barton, 1941, 11 3/4 In. 295.00
Bowl, Scalloped Shape, Kalo, 6 1/2 In. 420.00
Bowl, Shallow, Egg Shape, Tiered Foot, Watson, 1900s, 9 5/8 In. 176.00
Bowl, Spoon, Japanese Style, Copper, Hammered, 3-Footed, Gorham, 1883, 8 1/2 In. 7800.00
Bowl, Undertray, Fluted, Monogram, Randahl, 3 & 9 In. 2300.00
Bowl, Vegetable, Gadroon Edge, Jacobi & Jenkins, 11 1/2 In., Pair 635.00
Bowl, Vegetable, Gorham, 10 1/2 In., Pair 175.00
Bowl, Windsor Pattern, Oval, Lobed, Reed & Barton, 15 x 10 1/2 In. 765.00
Bowl & Plate, Squat, Egg Shape, Alphabet, Gorham, c.1905, Child's, 8 1/8-In. Plate 880.00
Bread Plate, Francis I, Reed & Barton, 7 In. 295.00
Bread Tray, 2 Handles, Gorham, 13 1/2 In. 219.00
Bread Tray, Francis I, Oval, Reed & Barton, 12 x 7 1/2 In. .... 440.00 to 646.00
Bread Tray, Hammered, Chased, Oval, Fruit, Vine Handles, Watson, Mass., 11 1/4 In. 58.00
Bread Tray, Oblong, Repousse, Water Lilies, Art Nouveau, Mauser, 12 1/2 In. 265.00
Bread Tray, Reticulated, Pierced, Guilloche, Flowers, Whiting, c.1900, 12 1/4 In. 175.00
Cake Basket, Oval, Reticulated Rim, Swags, Redlich & Co., Early 1900s, 10 5/8 In. 206.00
Cake Knife, Geometric Pattern, Flowers, Shultz & Fischer, Case, c.1875, 11 1/4 In. 600.00
Cake Plate, Dolores, Footed, Hammered Rim, Shreve, 12 In. 105.00
Cake Plate, Flower Sprays, Low Foot, Concord Silversmiths, c.1935, 10 1/2 In. 150.00
Cake Plate, Flower Vines, Trumpet Foot, Meriden Britannia, Early 1900s, 12 In. 440.00
Cake Plate, S. Kirk & Son, 10 In. 295.00
Cake Stand, Dominick & Haff, c.1920, 2 1/2 x 10 In. 176.00
Cake Stand, Raised Foot, Wire Rim, 4 Flutes, Lebolt & Co., 1 x 10 1/2 In. 875.00

Candelabrum is listed in its own category.
Candle Snuffer, Francis I, Vermeil, Reed & Barton, 8 1/2 In. 235.00
Candlesticks are listed in their own category.
Cann, Cup, Baluster, Double Scroll Handle, Leaf Terminal, Crest, c.1775, 5 In. 3068.00
Cann, Cup, C-Scroll Handle, William Hackle, Baltimore, Coin, c.1770, 5 x 5 1/2 In. 6580.00
Card Tray, Repousse Flower Border, Kirk, 6 In. 316.00
Castor, Aesthetic Movement, Baluster, Copper Man, Pipe, Butterfly, Gorham, 4 In. 705.00
Celery Vase, Cylindrical, Butterflies, Bamboo, Gorham, c.1876, 8 1/2 In. 1135.00
Chalice, Bucket Shape Bowl, Grapevine, Trumpet Foot, Coin, c.1850, 6 1/4 In. 295.00
Charger, Openwork Border, Flowers, Leaves, Theodore B. Starr, c.1910, 9 3/4 In. 625.00
Cheese Knife, Curved Blade, Family Crest, Leaves, Flowers, Gorham, 1800s, 8 1/2 In. 210.00
Cheese Scoop, Beading, Face, Wood & Hughes, Coin, c.1880, 9 1/4 In. 780.00
Cheese Scoop, Curving, Roses, Scrolls, Monogram, Whiting, c.1890, 8 In. 287.00
Chocolate Set, Japonisme, Organic Shape Tray, Gorham, c.1887, 3 Piece 2468.00
Cigar & Cigarette Box, Hinged Cover, Coat Of Arms, Leaf Pierced, 3 x 18 x 10 In. 7800.00
Cigar Box, Rectangular, Wood Lining, John Chattellier, c.1935, 9 1/2 In. 440.00
Cigarette Box, Dome Lid, Clemens Friedell, 3 x 10 1/2 x 3 1/2 In. 1350.00
Cigarette Case, Enamel, NYNH & H Steam Engine, c.1906, 4 x 3 In. 1265.00
Cigarette Cutter, Bacchus, Grapes, Art Nouveau, William Kerr, Baltimore, 2 In. 175.00
Cigarette Urn, Francis I, Reed & Barton, 2 1/4 In., Pair 235.00
Claret Ladle, Wavy Rim, Gilt Wash Bowl, Twisted Stem, Gorham, c.1900, 14 1/4 In. 896.00
Cocktail Set, Shaker, Strap Handle, Goblets, Lebolt, 8 1/2 & 4 1/2 In., 13 Piece 3400.00
Cocktail Shaker, Crest, Boar, Motto, Shreve, Crump & Low, 1920s, 9 1/4 In. 650.00
Cocktail Shaker, Presentation, Egg Shape, Taper, Manchester, c.1941, 11 In. 235.00
Coffee Set, Baluster Shape, Engraved Initial, Dome Lid, Watson Co., 3 Piece 690.00
Coffee Set, Baluster Shape, Open Sugar, Ivory Handle, Gorham, c.1906, 4 Piece 11165.00
Coffee Set, Hepplewhite Pattern, Reed & Barton, c.1930, 10 In., 3 Piece 945.00
Coffee Set, Landscapes, Spiral Finials, Scroll Supports, Coin, 4 Piece 6756.00
Coffee Set, Pear Shape, Scroll Rim, Graff, Washbourne & Dunn, 3 Piece 558.00
Coffee Set, Pot, Sugar, Creamer, Ivory Insulators, 3 Piece, 10 & 4 & 4 In. 3400.00
Coffee Set, Queen Anne, Richard Dimes Co., 1900s, 9 1/4-In. Pot, 3 Piece 295.00
Coffeepot, Double Dome Lid, Baluster, Scroll Spout, Wood Handle, 11 In. 11400.00
Coffeepot, ES Monogram, Wood Handle, Gorham, 1 1/2 Pt., 7 1/2 In. 148.00
Coffeepot, Fairfax, Paneled, Vasiform, Gorham, 1900s, 7 1/4 In. 705.00
Coffeepot, Hinged Cover, Cone, Ivory Insulators, Shiebler, 12 In. 1300.00
Coffeepot, Lighthouse, William Calder, 11 In. 405.00
Coffeepot, Louis XIV Pattern, Towle, c.1930, 10 1/2 In. 350.00
Coffeepot, Oval Wreaths, Urn Shape, Acorn Finial, Dominick & Haff, 12 In. 450.00
Coffeepot, Persian Style, Pear Shape, Reed & Barton, Early 1900s, 14 In. 880.00
Compote, 3 Sphinx, Gilt Lined Bowl, Gorham, c.1904, 14 3/4 x 12 In. 5079.00
Compote, Berry & Vine Rim, Monogram, T.B. Starr, c.1900, 2 3/4 x 7 1/2 In., Pair 810.00
Compote, Cupid, Lion, Ball, Black & Co., N.Y., 4 1/4 x 9 In. 635.00
Compote, Dolphin, Stemmed, Shreve, Crump & Low, Mid 1900s, 4 5/8 In. 470.00
Compote, Flowers, Pear Shape Stem, Gorham, c.1904, 4 3/4 x 10 In., Pair 1880.00
Compote, Octagonal, Panels, Hammered, Lebolt & Co., 6 In. 995.00
Condiment Server, Arts & Crafts, Hammered, 3 Dishes, Robert Sturm, c.1915, 5 In. 835.00
Cream Jug, Vase Shape, Stepped Round Foot, Beaded Borders, c.1800, 6 In. 480.00
Cream Ladle, Gilt Wash, Twig Handle, Bird, Nest, Engraved Name, c.1865, 6 1/2 In. 1315.00
Creamer, Oval Foot, Lobed Body, Monogram, G. Lenhart, c.1845, 6 1/2 In. 1016.00
Creamer, Pear Shape, Repousse, Coin, Samuel Wilmot, Ga., c.1845, 4 1/4 x 3 1/3 In. 940.00
Cruet Tray, Oval, 4 Scrolled Feet, Garlands, Coin, c.1900, 3 1/4 x 10 In. 239.00
Crumber, Flat Blade, Curved Back, Kings Pattern, Shells, Scrolls, c.1910, 12 In. 120.00
Cup, 8-Sided, Acanthus Leaves, Coin, Tifft & Whiting, c.1854, 3 1/2 In. 470.00
Cup, 8-Sided, Repousse, Monogram, Alexander McGrew, 1800s, 3 1/2 In. 508.00
Cup, Flared Rim, Sea Shells, Engraved Grapevines, Coin, c.1832, 3 1/8 In., Child's 259.00
Cup, Handle, Leaf, Scroll, Presentation, Bailey, Banks & Biddle, 1800s, 3 1/8 In. 295.00
Cup, Loop Handle, Molded & Beaded Lip, Coin, Wood & Hughes, c.1850, 3 x 4 In. 295.00
Cup, Presentation, Etched, Oak Branches, Acorns, Wm. B. Kerr & Co., c.1918, 7 In. 235.00
Cup, Seamed Sides, Beaded Bands, Coin, Mead & Co., c.1850, 3 3/8 x 2 3/4 In. 735.00
Cup, Tapered, Seamed Sides, Beaded Lip, Coin, E. Jaccard, 3 3/8 x 2 3/4 In. 490.00
Demitasse Pot, Pear Shape, Gadroon, Wood Handle, Currier & Roby, 1900s, 8 3/8 In. 118.00

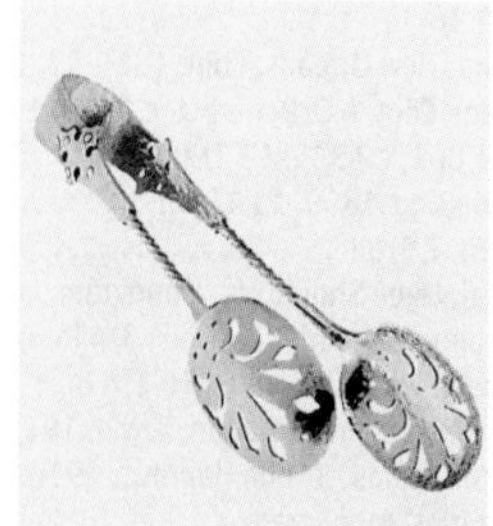
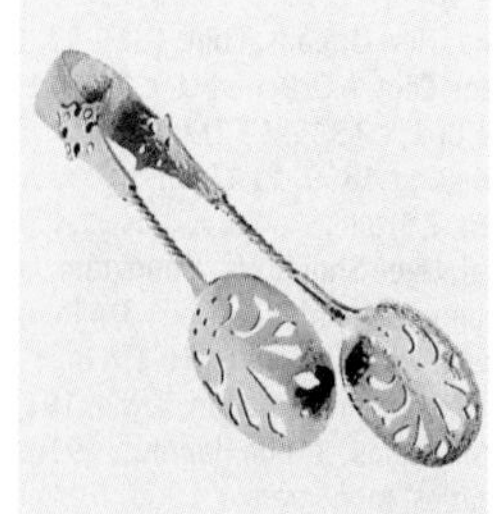

Silver-American, Ice Tongs, Fourteenth Century Pattern, Shreve & Co., c.1914, 6 1/2 In.

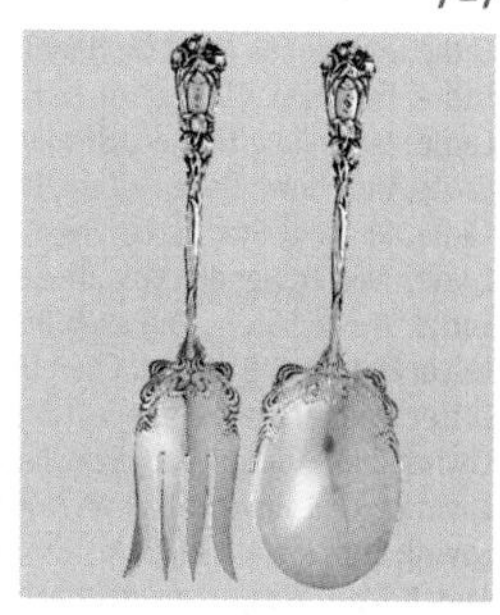

Silver-American, Salad Servers, Iris Pattern, Gilt Bowl, Tines, Durgin, c.1900, 9 In., 2 Piece

Demitasse Set, Pot, Sugar & Creamer, 4 Shell Shape Dishes, Whiting, c.1910 .... 265.00
Dinner Service, Hammered, Squared Ends, Allan Adler, For 12, 81 Piece 9400.00
Dish, Entree, Dome Lid, Hammered Edge, Claw Feet, Ivory Finial, Shreve, 11 x 8 In. 2629.00
Dish, Francis I, Oval, Reed & Barton, 11 3/4 In. 546.00
Dish, Francis I, Reed & Barton, 7 In., Pair 645.00
Dish, Indian Chief, Feathers, Unger Bros., c.1900, 4 1/4 In. 1790.00
Dish, Repousse Rose Border, S. Kirk & Sons, 7 x 5 1/4 In., Pair 345.00
Dish, Reticulated, Gorham, c.1895, 3 1/2 x 6 1/4 In. 320.00
Dish, Ring Foot, Hammered, Applied Rim, Frans Gyllenberg, 1 3/4 x 10 1/4 In. 550.00
Ewer, Ball, Black & Company, New York, c.1880, 12 1/2 In. 679.00
Ewer, Hammered, Ivory Handle, Cartier, Art Deco, c.1940, 14 3/4 x 6 1/8 In. 3950.00
Ewer, Pear Shape, Short Spout, Flowers, Coin, Cann & Dunn, N.Y., c.1860, 12 1/4 In. 1116.00
Ewer, Repousse, Beaded Waist, Acanthus Loop Handle, George Sharp, 15 In. 4110.00
Ewer, Slender, Curved Handle, Step Foot, Reed & Barton, c.1890, 15 1/2 In. 436.00
Fish Serving Fork, Pierced, Bright Cut, Twisted Handle, Monogram, Coin, 10 1/4 In. 1000.00
Fish Slice, Parcel Gilt, Ivory Handle, Ajoure, Whiting, c.1900, 14 1/4 In. 956.00
Fish Slice, Scimitar Shape, Flowers, Shells, N.G. Wood & Sons, Boston, c.1870, 11 In. 264.00
Flask, Etched, Enameled Scene, German Shepherds, Towle-Blackington, Pt., 7 1/2 In. 95.00
Flask, Rectangular, Canted Corners, Engraved Flowers, Early 1800s, 7 3/4 In. 360.00
Flask, Shaped Body, Enameled, Classical Maiden, Landscape, c.1905, 4 In. 666.00
Flower Arranger, Cover, Wedgwood Pattern, International, 5 1/2 x 13 In. 556.00
Frame, Fourteenth Century Pattern, Shreve, c.1914, 7 x 9 1/2 In. 690.00
Fruit Bowl, Wide Flared Rim, Flowerhead Edge, Trumpet Foot, International, 11 In. 118.00
Goblet, Grapevine Rim, William Webber, c.1800, 4 1/2 In. 207.00
Gravy Boat, Undertray, Repousse Pattern, S. Kirk & Son, No. 50 R 385.00
Ice Bucket, Arts & Crafts, Tapered, Egg Shape, Shreve & Co., c.1915, 6 1/8 In. 1528.00
Ice Cream Slice, Flowers, Medallion, Coin, Shulz & Fisher, c.1870, 9 3/4 In. 896.00
Ice Cream Slice, Parcel Rose Gilt, Leaves, Flowers, Gorham, c.1865, 10 3/4 In. 1016.00
Ice Tongs, Fourteenth Century Pattern, Shreve & Co., c.1914, 6 1/2 In. .... *ILLUS* 1315.00
Ideal Olive, Gilt Wash, Leaf Shape Spoon, Twig Handle, Gorham, c.1880, 11 3/4 In. ......840.00 to 896.00
Ideal Olive, Parcel Gilt, Leaf Shape Spoon, Spiral Handle, Gorham, c.1890, 9 3/4 In. 896.00
Ideal Olive, Scalloped Spoon, Gilt Wash, 2 Tine Fork, Coin, c.1870, 12 1/2 In. 418.00
Ink Blotter, 8-Point Star, Fleur-De-Lis Corners, Scrolls, Button Handle, Shiebler, 5 In. 940.00
Jug, Acid Etched, Military Carriage, Horse, Scalloped Rim, Whiting, Late 1800s, 8 In. 825.00
Jug, Hot Water, Hinged Cover, Spiral Flame Finial, Handle, K. F. Leinonen, 9 3/4 In. 1000.00
Jug, Milk, Coin, H. Salisbury & Co., N.Y., c.1830, 6 1/2 x 5 1/4 In. 350.00
Jug, Thermos, Handle, Stopper, Mercury Glass Bottle, Lebolt & Co., 7 x 5 In. 2100.00
Julep Cup, Coin, A.C. Hallack, Paris, Kentucky, c.1853, 3 1/2 In. 1670.00
Julep Cup, Coin, E. & D. Kinsey, c.1850, 3 5/8 In. 575.00
Julep Cup, Coin, Henderson Union & Hopkins, c.1880, 3 5/8 In. 1150.00
Julep Cup, Coin, John B. Akin, Danville, Ky, 3 5/8 In. ....345.00 to 978.00
Julep Cup, Coin, Poindexter, Lexington, Kentucky, 3 1/2 In. 1150.00
Julep Cup, Engraved C. Fowler, Willey & Blakesley, 3 1/2 In. 575.00
Julep Cup, Engraved Name, Coin, A.R. Sale, Williams, 3 1/2 In., Pair 635.00
Julep Cup, Molded Rim, Samuel Kirk & Son, c.1925, 6 Piece 2115.00
Kettle, Hot Water, Stand, Fluted Melon Shape, Ivory Insulators, A.J. Stone, 13 In. 2700.00
Kettle, Stand, Bullet Shape, Swing Handle, Monogram, Gorham, 1894, 10 1/2 In. 880.00

Ladle, Anthemion Motif On Handle, 12 3/4 In. 266.00
Ladle, Fiddle, CB Monogram, H. Harland, New Orleans, Coin, 1815-32, 14 1/8 In. 2115.00
Ladle, Medallion, Twisted, Beaded Stem, Coin, A.C. Benedict, c.1840, 11 In. 325.00
Ladle, Oval Bowl, Bead Pattern, Platt & Bro., c.1825, 13 1/2 In. 485.00
Ladle, Shallow, Grapes, Leaves, A. Hews Jr., c.1850, 11 1/4 In. 175.00
Ladle, Twisted Handle, Coin, H. Semken, 7 5/8 In. 850.00
Ladle, Twisted Stem, Engraved Terminal, Ogee Shoulders, Monogram, Coin, 10 In. 150.00
Letter Holder, 4 Ball Feet, Cherubs, Monogram, Shiebler, 3 x 4 3/4 In. 450.00
Letter Opener, Sword Shape, Gold Queen Victoria Handle, 10 1/4 In. 206.00
Loving Cup, Art Nouveau, Egg Shape, Flowers, Presentation, Towle, 1911, 13 In. 2115.00
Loving Cup, Cylindrical, Chrysanthemum Stems, 3 Loop Handles, 1910, 10 3/8 In. 1410.00
Loving Cup, Repousse, Baluster, 3 Handles, Monogram, c.1900, 6 1/4 In. 390.00
Match Safe, Wall, Triangular Backplate, Flowers, 2 Hooks, Shiebler, c.1900, 4 In. 295.00
Meat Fork, Art Nouveau Style, 4 Tines, Poppy, Woman, Alvin, c.1902, 7 3/4 In. 895.00
Medal, Peace, Andrew Jackson, c.1830, 3 In. 19500.00
Mirror, Hand, Flowers, Monogram, Whiting, c.1880, 11 In. 508.00
Mug, Bulbous, Scrolled Handle, Coin, 5 1/4 In. 2760.00
Mug, Cylindrical, Reed Borders, Strap Handle, Nathaniel Vernon, c.1810, 3 In. 960.00
Mug, Flared Rim, Incised Line, Coin, Stephen Emery, 5 1/2 x 6 x 4 1/4 In. 2415.00
Napkin Rings are listed in their own category.
Nappy, Art Nouveau Style, Flowers, Square, Simpson, Hall, Miller, c.1895, 5 1/2 In. 240.00
Nut Dish, 4 Ball Feet, Shell & Scroll Rim, Gorham, 1900s, 4 1/2 In., Pair 125.00
Nut Dish, Francis I, Reed & Barton, 1955, 3 1/4 In. 94.00
Nut Dish, Lobed, Oval, Embossed Poppies, 3 1/2 x 4 1/4 In., Pair 146.00
Nut Dish Set, Francis I, W Monogram, Reed & Barton, 12 Piece 750.00
Nut Server, Parcel Gilt, Pierced Bowl, Squirrel Terminal, Late 1800s, 9 3/4 In. 1554.00
Paper Knife, Oblong Blade, Fox Head, S. Kirk & Son, 1932-61, 12 In. 529.00
Pastry Server, Samuel Kirk & Son, 9 1/4 In. 176.00
Pickle Fork, Estruscan Handle, 3 Tines, Shiebler, N.Y., c.1880, 7 3/4 In. 508.00
Pie Server, Japanese Style, Bird, Butterfly, Monogram, Wood & Hughes, c.1870, 9 In. 560.00
Pill Box, Dome Lid, Wire, Monogram, Arthur J. Stone, 1 x 2 1/2 In. 595.00
Pitcher, Bulbous, Squat, Flared Spout, Looping Handle, Randahl, 7 In. 2500.00
Pitcher, Cover, Repousse Birds & Flowers, Ivory Accents, Coin, Samuel Kirk, 6 In. 805.00
Pitcher, Egg Shape, Raised Leaves, Randahl, 10 In. 633.00
Pitcher, Helmet Shape, Gadroon Border, C-Shaped Handle, Coin, F. Woods, 6 In. 2300.00
Pitcher, Looping Handle, Spout, Squat, Monogram, Lebolt & Co., 7 x 8 1/4 In. 2200.00
Pitcher, Presentation, Squat, Egg Shape, Scroll Handle, Howard & Co., 1889, 6 1/2 In. 499.00
Pitcher, Repousse Rose, Scrolls, Footed, S. Kirk & Son, c.1868, 10 1/4 In. 1795.00
Pitcher, Water, Applied Scroll Handle, Flared Spout, Monogram, Wallace, 8 3/4 In. 165.00
Pitcher, Water, Baluster, Double Scroll Handle, c.1940, 9 1/2 In. 354.00
Pitcher, Water, Baluster, Scrolled Handle, Leaf, International, c.1950, 9 In. 325.00
Pitcher, Water, Baluster, Short Spout, Scrolled Handle, Leaf, International, c.1950, 9 In. 323.00
Pitcher, Water, Botticelli Pattern, Frank Whiting Co., 1939, 7 5/8 In. 529.00
Pitcher, Water, Bulbous, Hand Hammered, Branch Handle, Gorham, c.1912, 9 In. 1016.00
Pitcher, Water, Flowers, Scrolls, Bulbous, Redlich, c.1900, 10 1/2 In. 2270.00
Pitcher, Water, Helmet Shape, Angular Handle, W.B. Durgin, Early 1900s, 2 1/2 In. 205.00
Pitcher, Water, Paneled Pear Shape, Short Spout, F.M. Whiting, Early 1900s, 8 5/8 In. 355.00
Pitcher, Water, Paneled Vase Shape, Short Spout, Reed & Barton, 1900s, 10 5/8 In. 470.00
Pitcher, Water, Rococo, Scroll Handle, Repousse, Coin, Cann & Dunn, N.Y., c.1850, 13 In. 1880.00
Pitcher, Water, Seville Pattern, Towle, c.1920, 10 1/2 In. 440.00
Pitcher, Water, Urn Shape, Short Spout, Dome Foot, Meriden Britannia, 1900s, 10 In. 235.00
Pitcher, Water, Vase Shape, Flared Spout, Lebolt & Co., 9 x 8 1/2 In. 2800.00
Pitcher, Water, Vase Shape, Laurel Band, Trumpet Foot, W.B. Durgin, 9 1/2 In. 350.00
Plate, Crystal Center, Francis I Silver Rims, Reed & Barton, 7 In., Pair 290.00
Plate, Francis I Pattern, Reed & Barton, Mass., 11 In. .... 1057.00 to 1175.00
Plate, Francis I Pattern, Reed & Barton, Taunton, Mass., c.1907, 11 1/2 In., Pair 2230.00
Plate Set, Marcus & Co., Ogee Shape, Reeded Rim, Band, 6 3/8 In., 10 Piece 410.00
Plateau, 3 Segments, Pierced Scrolled Rim, Eli's Studio, 17 x 50 In. 6168.00
Platter, Oblong, Ogee Rim, Frank W. Smith, 1900s, 19 3/4 In. 499.00
Platter, Oval, Gorham, c.1915, 16 In. .... 530.00 to 645.00
Platter, Oval, Tuttle, c.1950, 18 1/4 In. 499.00

Porringer, Keyhole Pierced Handle, Wire Rim, Engraved, J.T. Woolley, 2 x 7 In. 395.00
Porringer, Pierced Handle, Gebelein Silversmiths, c.1935, 7 1/4 In. 150.00
Porringer, Pierced Handle, Monogram, Inscription, Arthur J. Stone, c.1919, 7 1/8 In. 558.00
Porringer, Raised Flowers, J.E. Caldwell, 9 In. 518.00
Porringer, Repousse Pattern, S. Kirk & Sons, No. 27, 7 In. 410.00
Porringer, Round, Keyhole Handle, Engraved, Jonathan Clarke, 1700s, 7 In. 2400.00
Postal Scales, Molded, Leaves, Ivorine Panels For Rates, Gorham, 3 1/4 In., Pair 295.00
Punch Bowl, Flaring, Inscription, Holland Furnace Co., Wallace, c.1959, 6 5/8 x 13 In. 460.00
Punch Bowl, Neoclassical, Pedestal Foot, 2 Handles, J.E. Caldwell, c.1906, 21 In. 9600.00
Punch Bowl, S. Kirk & Son, Baltimore, c.1900, 10 x 9 In. 2478.00
Punch Bowl, Swirls, Waisted Foot, Black, Starr & Frost, Late 1800s, 8 x 14 In. 3290.00
Punch Ladle, Double Pouring Lip, Gilt Wash Bowl, Satyr, Gorham, c.1860, 12 In. 1015.00
Punch Ladle, Parcel Gilt, Monogram, Gorham, c.1880, 15 In. 720.00
Punch Ladle, Stieff, Baltimore, c.1910, 14 In. 470.00
Ramekin Set, Porcelain, Watson, 12 Piece 770.00
Relish, Cover, Canister, Pierced Sides, Glass Liner, Arthur J. Stone, 4 x 4 1/4 In. 2700.00
Salad Servers, Fourteenth Century Pattern, Hammered, Shreve & Co., Ca., c.1909, 16 1/2 In. 1910.00
Salad Servers, Fourteenth Century Pattern, Shreve & Co., Ca., c.1914, 10 In., 2 Piece 1555.00
Salad Servers, Iris Pattern, Gilt Bowl, Tines, Durgin, c.1900, 9 In., 2 Piece .... *ILLUS* 1016.00
Salad Servers, Scalloped, Shells, Flowers, c.1890, 10 In. 190.00
Salad Tongs, Louis XIV, John Polhemus, Coin 995.00
Salt, 1/2 Barrel, 2 Putti, Gilt Wash Interior, 2 x 3 1/2 In., Pair 598.00
Salt, Aesthetic Movement, Cupped Leaf Shape, Shiebler, Late 1800s, 2 1/8 In., Pair 235.00
Salt, Bird & Twig Handles, Oval, Pedestal, Gorham, c.1865, 2 1/4 x 4 3/4 In., Pair 780.00
Salt, Gilt Interior, Lion, Crown Family Crest, 3 1/4 x 5 1/2 x 2 1/4 In., Pair 2070.00
Salt, Japanese Pattern, Birds, Bamboo, Flowers, Late 1800s, 2 x 2 1/4 In., Pair 480.00
Salt, Master, Renaissance, Dominick & Haff, 3 1/4 In. 75.00
Salt & Pepper, Flowers, Colored Enamel, Old Newbury Crafters, 2 1/2 x 2 3/4 In. 450.00
Salt & Pepper, Francis I Pattern, Reed & Barton, 1954, 4 1/2 In. 499.00
Salt & Pepper Sets, Dunkirk, Boxed, Mid 20th Century, 2 1/4 In., Set Of 12 .... 95.00
Salt Cellar, Renaissance Revival, Glass Lining, Gorham, c.1891, 3 1/8 In., 4 Piece 558.00
Salver, Chippendale, Oval, Ogee Rim, Monogram, Black, Starr & Gorham, 12 In. 176.00
Salver, Gadroon Border, Engraved, Footed, F. Marquand, N.Y., 18 In. 1785.00
Salver, Lobed Border, Hammered Surface, c.1930, 9 3/4 In. 385.00
Salver, Square, Round Corners, Reeded Edge, Monogram, Dominick & Haff, 1883, 10 In. 325.00
Sandwich Server, Ring Foot, Applied Rim, Pierced Handles, 1 1/2 x 12 3/4 In. 650.00
Sauce Ladle, Bright Cut, Armorial Crest, Richard Humphreys, 1749-1832, 7 1/2 In. 635.00
Sauceboat, Flat Bottom, Flared Rim, Wood Handle, Porter Blanchard, 2 x 5 3/4 In. 375.00
Sauceboat, Husk Roundels, Bailey, Banks & Biddle, 9 1/2 In., Pair 355.00
Sauceboat, Ladle, Oval, Pedestal, Flared Rim, Monogram, Lebolt & Co., 3 & 7 1/2 In. 1100.00
Sauceboat, Scalloped Rim, Scroll Handle, Scroll & Shell Feet, Low, Ball & Co., 7 In. 748.00
Sauceboat, Scrolled Handle, Gadroon & Leaf Edge, Howard & Co., 1900s, 8 3/4 In. 295.00
Server, Hammered, Applied Pattern, Typt Handle, Leaves, Berries, Gorham, 11 In. 980.00
Server Set, Dessert, Chased Leaves, Underplates, Holders, Reed & Barton, 12 Piece 380.00
Serving Dish, Stradivari, Wallace, 10 In. 145.00
Serving Spoon, Cattail, Parcel Gilt Bowl, Shell Shape, Ivy Leaves, Late 1800, 8 In. 657.00
Serving Spoon, Monogram, Arthur J. Stone, 12 In. 138.00
Serving Spoon & Fork, Scallop Rim, Raspberries, Vines, Whiting, c.1880, 9 1/2 In. 538.00
Shoe Buckles, Oval, Iron Hasps, William Roe, Kingston, N.Y., c.1795, 2 3/8 In. 120.00
Shrimp Pick Set, Fourteenth Century Pattern, Shreve & Co., Ca., 1 3/4 In., 6 Piece 956.00
Soup Ladle, Coin, G.K. Lentz 290.00
Soup Ladle, Egyptian Revival, Gilt Interior, Wm. Gale Jr., c.1866, 14 3/4 In. 3885.00
Soup Ladle, Greenawalt & Cover, c.1840, 14 In. 290.00
Spoon, Colonial, Rattail, Oval Bowl, Monogram, Jacob Hurd, Boston, c.1750, 7 1/4 In. 598.00
Sugar, Cover, Bulbous, Double Handles, Footed, Rosette Band, c.1820, 8 In. 470.00
Sugar, Dome Lid, Flattened, Spherical, Goodnow, c.1900, 3 x 6 1/2 In. 265.00
Sugar, Rocaille Cartouches, Monogram, Black, Starr & Frost, Late 1800s, 4 3/8 In. 206.00
Sugar & Creamer, Aesthetic, Hammered, Wood & Hughes, 4 In. 355.00
Sugar & Creamer, Baltimore Federal, Reeded Handles, Early 1800s, 9 1/2-In. Sugar 5288.00
Sugar & Creamer, Flat Topped Ear Handles, Scrolls, Gorham, c.1942, 3 Piece 118.00
Sugar & Creamer, Geometric Cutouts, Strap Handle, Randahl, 2 3/4 In. 600.00

Sugar & Creamer, Monogram, Gorham, c.1910 .... 205.00
Sugar & Creamer, Repousse Flowers, Coin, Gorham & Thurber, 8 1/4 In. 748.00
Sugar & Creamer, Repousse, Chased Leaves, Beaded Trim, Monogram, Coin, 7 In. 405.00
Sugar & Creamer, Squat, Inverted Pear Shape, Leaves, S. Kirk & Son, c.1910, 2 1/2 In. 470.00
Sugar Sifter, Fiddle & Thread, Pierced Fluted Bowl, Coin, 1850, 7 7/8 In. 275.00
Sugar Sifter, Pierced, Gilt Bowl, Bird, Nest, Gorham, c.1865, 6 1/2 In. 1795.00
Sugar Spoon, Gilt Wash Bowl, Twig Handle, Bird, Nest, Gorham, c.1865, 5 3/4 In. 1135.00
Sugar Urn, Cover, Beaded Square Foot, Border, Engraved Shield, c.1790, 11 In. 2400.00
Syrup, Hinged Lid, Undertray, Vase Form, Hammered, Lebolt & Co., 4 3/4 & 5 1/8 In. 1000.00
Table Set, Bowl, Candlesticks, Vases, La Paglia, International, 5 Piece 2300.00
Tablespoon, Downcurved Fiddle Handle, Coin, Louis Muth, New Orleans, 8 3/4 In. 70.00
Tankard, Flared, Molded Foot, Scroll Handle, Dome Lid, Jacob Hurd, Boston, 8 In. 19720.00
Tankard, Tapering Cylindrical, Scroll Handle, John Edwards, c.1730, 8 In. 8400.00
Tazza, 3 Grotesque Supports, Round Stepped Base, Gorham, 1910, 6 x 10 In. 2325.00
Tazza, Openwork Scrolled Leaf, Monogram, Howard & Co., 5 1/4 x 14 In. 1725.00
Tazza, Reticulated, Applied Openwork Rim, Howard & Co., Early 1900s, 8 3/4 In. 325.00
Tazza, Shallow, Knopped Stem, Square Supports, Wallace, Conn., 4 1/2 In., Pair 86.00
Tea & Coffee Set, Cylindrical, Plated Tray, Tuttle, 1900s, 27-In. Tray, 4 Piece 765.00
Tea & Coffee Set, Egg Shape, Paneled, Angular Handle, Gorham, c.1920, 6 Piece 2115.00
Tea & Coffee Set, Engraved, Laurel Wreath, Angular Handles, W.B. Durgin, 6 Piece 940.00
Tea & Coffee Set, Flowerhead Pendants, Urn Finials, International, 7 Piece 3819.00
Tea & Coffee Set, Lord Robert, International Silver Co., 1900s, 9 1/4-In. Pot, 4 Piece 1058.00
Tea & Coffee Set, Medallion, Classical Profile, Engraved, 11 3/4 In., 5 Piece 9400.00
Tea & Coffee Set, Medallion, Pear Shape, c.1865, 10 5/8-In. Coffeepot 4995.00
Tea & Coffee Set, Pear Shape, Mulford & Wendell, Albany, c.1840, 13 1/4 In., 5 Piece 3525.00
Tea & Coffee Set, Plymouth Pattern, Monogram, Theodore Starr, Gorham, 6 Piece 1495.00
Tea & Coffee Set, Queen Anne, Sugar, Creamer, Waste Bowl, 6 Piece, 11 In. 1060.00
Tea & Coffee Set, Queen Charlotte Pattern, Gorham, 1927, 5 Piece 1140.00
Tea & Coffee Set, Repousse, Engraved, Flutes, Providence, R.I., c.1902 .... 2516.00
Tea & Coffee Set, Simons, Bro. & Co., Early 1900s, 9 1/2-In. Coffeepot, 6 Piece 880.00
Tea & Coffee Set, Squat, Pear Shape Pots, Dominick & Haff, c.1910, 7 Piece 12925.00
Tea & Coffee Set, Sugar Tongs, Hampton Court, Reed & Barton, 6 Piece 878.00
Tea Caddy, Hinged Lid, Oval Canister, Spiral Finial, DeMatteo, 4 3/4 x 3 3/4 In. 385.00
Tea Set, Art Nouveau, Black, Starr & Frost, c.1905, 9 1/2-In. Teapot 1320.00
Tea Set, Egg Shape, Pedestal Base, Gadroon Border, Coin, Caleb Warner, 8-In. Pot 1840.00
Tea Set, Embossed, Chased, Buildings, Bud Finials, S. Kirk & Son, c.1860, 4 Piece 4800.00
Tea Set, Federal, Squat, Egg Shape, Coin, c.1812, 7 1/2-In. Teapot, 3 Piece 1410.00
Tea Set, Federal, Squat, Egg Shape, Coin, Lewis & Smith, c.1805, 8 1/2 In., 5 Piece 2468.00
Tea Set, Flower Finials, Marquand & Brother, c.1832, 9-In. Teapot, 3 Piece 935.00
Tea Set, Grapevine Chased Band, Melon Shape, Footed, S. Williamson, 4 Piece 2868.00
Tea Set, Inverted Pear Shaped Pot, Concord Silversmiths, c.1935, 8 1/4-In. Pot, 5 Piece 1765.00
Tea Set, Lotus, Monogram, Whiting, 4 Piece 936.00
Tea Set, Medallion Pattern, Classical Bust, Greek Key, Wood & Hughes, 5 Piece 7050.00
Tea Set, Melon Shape Teapot, Scroll Feet, Shreve, Crump & Low, 1900s, 12 In. 1295.00
Tea Set, Peaked Lids, Reeded Handles, Gorham, c.1916, 8 1/4-In. Pot, 4 Piece 1175.00
Tea Set, Pear Shape Pot, Sugar & Creamer, La Paglia, International, c.1950, 4 Piece 3290.00
Tea Set, Repousse, Flowers, c.1900, 9 1/4-In. Water Pot, 5 Piece 4780.00
Tea Set, Rococo, Grapes, Leaves, Coin, Clark & Co., 9-In. Teapot, 4 Piece 2585.00
Tea Set, Scroll, Flowers, Gold Wash Interior, Monogram, Gorham, 3 Piece 450.00
Tea Set, Shaped Oval, Facet, Beaded Borders, Engraved, c.1810, 4 Piece 2280.00
Tea Set, Squat, Beaded Rims, Angular Handles, Gorham, 1903, 7-In. Pot, 4 Piece 765.00
Tea Set, Sterling, Hammered, Dome Lid, Tassel Finials, Gorham, 3 Piece 1060.00
Tea Set, Sugar Tongs, Dinner Bell, Repousse, S. Kirk & Son Co., 5 Piece 1400.00
Tea Set, Urn Shape, Squared C-Shaped Handle, Reed & Barton, 9 1/2-In. Pot, 5 Piece 690.00
Tea Urn, Pear Shape, Beaded Rim, Leaves, Loop Handles, Gorham, c.1866, 17 3/4 In. 2820.00
Teapot, Chased Decoration, Towle, 10 In. 175.00
Teapot, Lighthouse, William Calder, 7 1/2 In. 290.00
Teapot, Pear Shape, J. Danforth, 8 In. 1380.00
Teapot, Urn Shape, Footed, Monogram, Bone Handle, Frank W. Smith, 9 In. 165.00
Teapot & Sugar, Lobed, Scrolled Handle, W. Gale & Sons, 1853, 8 1/2 In., 2 Piece 590.00
Tray, 4 Shell Feet, Flared Rim, Scroll & Shell Handles, Coin, c.1850, 31 In. 3585.00

Tray, Chippendale Pattern, Monogram, International, 14 In. 230.00
Tray, Chippendale Pattern, Piecrust Rim, Monogram, Coin, Frank W Smith, 1 x 14 In. 358.00
Tray, Footed, Leaf Shape, Applied Branches, Wood & Hughes, c.1880, 6 3/4 In. 598.00
Tray, Footed, Oval, Beaded, Monogram, Geometrics, 4 Fluted Legs, S. Kirk & Son, 7 In. 305.00
Tray, Fourteenth Century Pattern, 8-Sided, Hammered, Monogram, Shreve, c.1900, 14 1/2 In. 1912.00
Tray, Fourteenth Century Pattern, Strapped, Hammered, Shreve, c.1900, 16 1/2 x 12 1/4 In. 2270.00
Tray, Louis Nouveau Pattern, Barbour, International, c.1910, 31 x 22 In. 1295.00
Tray, Monogram, Shaped Edge, Reed & Barton, 12 In. 295.00
Tray, Oval, 4-Footed, Acanthus Leaves, Inscription, Gadroon Edge, Gorham, c.1860, 6 In. 1076.00
Tray, Oval, Chased, Raised Border, Monogram, J.E. Caldwell, 16 3/4 x 9 1/4 In. 690.00
Tray, Oval, Flower, Leaves, Tendrils, Raised Border, Elverhoj Craft, 11 1/2 x 8 1/2 In. 1250.00
Tray, Round, Applied Hammered Rim, Faux Rivets, Heinrich Eicher, 14 In. 1400.00
Tray, Round, No. 2212, G Monogram, Spaulding & Co., 1 x 12 In. 530.00
Tray, Serving, Figures, Flowers, Reticulated, Footed, Monogram, 1 1/4 x 11 1/2 In. 220.00
Trivet, Glass, Round, Pierced, Flower Scrolls, 3-Footed, c.1900, 12 In. 765.00
Trivet, Pine Cone, Pierced, Chased, Round, Hammered, Ball Feet, Emily A. Day, 5 In. 395.00
Trophy Bowl, Rococo Revival, Oblong, Chased, Howard & Co., Late 1800s, 4 In. 150.00
Trophy Cup, Handles, Step Foot, Hammered, Gorham, c.1926, 12 In. 780.00
Tureen, Gadroon, Shell Borders, Paw Feet, Winged Terminals, 5 x 9 1/4 x 5 1/4 In. 690.00
Urn, Cover, Scallop Rim, Acanthus Bands, Scroll Handles, Coin, c.1850, 9 1/2 In. 375.00
Urn, Trophy, Kentucky State Fair Roadster Championship, 1938, 16 In. 4320.00
Vase, Aesthetic Movement, Engraved, Baluster Shape, Gorham, c.1880, 7 In. 1528.00
Vase, Bud, Trumpet, Ruffled Rim, Hammered, Round Base, Clemens Friedell, 7 In. 535.00
Vase, Chased, Engraved, Roger Williams Silver Co., Providence, c.1900, 18 In. 5400.00
Vase, Cone Shape, Reticulated Vine, FML Monogram, Reed & Barton, 14 3/4 In. 400.00
Vase, Crystal Flower-Form Liner, Daffodils, Gorham, 10 In. 195.00
Vase, Flower-Form, Roses, Repousse, Black, Starr & Frost, c.1876, 22 3/4 In. 9560.00
Vase, Flowers, 8-Sided, Flared, Gorham, Early 1900s, 20 In. 1495.00
Vase, Squared Baluster, Applied Copper Designs, Flared Rim, Gorham, 4 x 3 In. 275.00
Vegetable Fork, Quatrefoil, 5 Tines, Egyptian Pharoah, Coin, c.1870, 9 1/2 In. 1315.00
Waffle Server, Gilt Wash, Scalloped Tip, Iris Handle, W.B. Durgin, c.1900, 8 1/2 In. 995.00
Wine, Melon Shape, Fluted, Flower Heads, Acanthus Leaves, Handles, Pair 3525.00
SILVER-AUSTRIAN, Box, Rococo, 1800s, 2 1/2 x 3 1/2 In. 205.00
Box, Sweetmeats, Oblong, Inscription, Gilded Inside, c.1825, 3/4 x 3 3/4 x 2 1/2 In. 558.00
Chocolate Set, Ribbed, Rozet & Fischmeister, c.1900, 24 Piece 2030.00
Cigarette Case, Enamel, 3 Graces, Sepia, Blue Border, c.1900, 3 1/2 In. 1355.00
Tea & Coffee Set, Art Deco, Melon Shape Teapot, Lobed, 1920s, 5 Piece 2470.00
SILVER-CANADIAN, Bowl, Footed, Berries, Leaves, Poul Petersen, Montreal, 1935-53, 1 3/4 In. . . 189.00
Cigarette Box, Leaf Borders, Poul Petersen, Montreal, 1935-53, 4 3/4 In. 339.00
Compote, Hammered, Berry & Leaf Stem, Poul Petersen, Montreal, 1935-53, 5 In. 339.00
Dresser Set, Edwardian Style, Monogram, Roden Bros., Toronto, 3 Piece 235.00
Goblet, U-Shape, Repousse, Engraved, Flowering Leaves, c.1860, 6 In. 3070.00
Plate, Molded Rim, Douglas Boyd, Toronto, 1942, 10 1/4 In. 330.00
Ragout Spoon, Douglas Boyd, Richmond Hill, 1969, 15 In. 245.00
Salt Cellar, Shell, Circular Base, Poul Petersen, Montreal, 1935-53, 4 In., Pair 226.00
Tea & Coffee Set, Ebony Handles, Poul Petersen, Montreal, 1935-53, 6 Piece 3395.00
Tea & Coffee Set, Engraved, Scrolling Leaf Band, Montreal, c.1929, 6 Piece 2516.00
Trowel, Presentation, Wooden Handle, Engraved Inscription, c.1859, 13 In. 2516.00
SILVER-CHINESE, Bonbon Basket, Wire, Grapevine Handle, Wing On Co., Early 1900s, 5 In., Pair . 705.00
Bowl, Vegetable, Cover, Loop Handles, Garlands, Oval, Wang Hing, Late 1800s, 14 In. 450.00
Cigarette Box, Dragon, Wood Lining, Wang Hing & Co., Early 1900s, 6 3/8 In. 705.00
Cigarette Case, 2 Dragons, Raised Pearl, 4 In. 190.00
Frame, Cherry Blossoms, Round, Early 1900s, 7 1/4 In. 390.00
Serving Spoon, Dragon Handle, Bone Scoop, c.1890, 12 3/4 In. 390.00
Tea Set, Egg Shape, Acanthus Leaves, Khecheong, Canton, c.1850, 3 Piece 3995.00
Tea Set, Tree Trunk Bodies, Prunus, Twig Handles, Finials, Early 1900s, 3 Piece 670.00
SILVER-CONTINENTAL, Basket, Classical, Reticulated, Egg Shape, Husk Swag, c.1900, 11 3/8 In. . 825.00
Bowl, Rococo Revival, Reticulated, Early 1900s, 10 5/8 In. 499.00
Box, Cello Shape, Repousse, Pastoral Scene, 1800s, 5 In. 200.00
Box, Enamel, Painted, Pastoral Scene, c.1900, 2 1/2 In. 265.00
Charger, Raised Lobes, Strapwork, Scrolls, Round, c.1900, 18 1/2 In. 770.00

Silver-Danish, Candelabrum, 5-Light, Grape Pattern, Marked, 1945-77, 10 1/2 In., Pair

Silver-Danish, Candlestick, Grape Pattern, 1945-77, Georg Jensen, 11 1/2 In., Pair

Cigarette Case, Enamel, Seminude Woman, c.1930, 3 1/4 In. 945.00
Cigarette Case, Gilt, Fan, Paste Cabochon, 1940s, 3 1/4 In. 130.00
Compote, Cover, Horse Finial, c.1880, 6 1/2 x 5 1/2 x 7 In. 322.00
Compote, Repousse Flowers, 4 x 8 In. 220.00
Cork, 19th Century, 4 1/4 In. 50.00
Dresser Box, Floral Swags, Navette Ground, Hinged Lid, Late 1800s, 9 In. 1116.00
Figurine, Owl, Detachable Head, Feathers, Glass Eyes, On Stump, 10 x 3 3/4 In. 2760.00
Goblet, Gilded, Mixed Metal, Neillo, Hallmark, 7 1/2 x 2 1/2 In. 330.00
Ladle, Stamped 90, 13 1/2 In. 40.00
Salt, Open, Shell Shape, 3 Dolphin Feet, 2 1/2 x 2 1/4 x 1 1/2 In., 6 Piece 495.00
Salt, Renaissance Revival Style, Triangular, Cherubs, Flowers, Late 1800s, 4 In. 470.00
Spoon, Apostle Style, Crucifix Topped, Oval Bowl, Cherub Shoulders, 8 In. 880.00
Sugar Box, Dome Lid, Egg Shape, Rope Twist Legs, J. Nowotny, c.1865, 5 1/4 In. 410.00
Sugar Tongs, Wire Work, Scroll Designs, 5 1/2 In. 47.00
Taperstick, Neoclassical Style, Bell Shape Sconce, Ionic Capital, 7 In., Pair 206.00
Tea & Coffee Set, Pear Shape, 1900s, 11 3/4-In. Coffeepot, 5 Piece 2700.00
Tea Caddy, Tiered Lid, Acorn Finial, Engraved Ground, Late 1800s, 6 In. 940.00
Tray, Rectangular, Reticulated Guilloche, Patera Gallery, Handles, 22 In. 4115.00
Vase, Repousse, Egg Shape, Flowers, Stippled Ground, 11 3/4 In., Pair 825.00
Wedding Cup, Gilt, Woman Holding Pivoted Bowl Over Head, 1800s, 8 1/2 In. 485.00
SILVER-DANISH, Bowl, Footed, Bud & Scrolling Leaf, Johan Rohde, Georg Jensen, Post 1945, 5 1/4 In. 1884.00
Bowl, Hammered Bowl, Leaves, Buds, Spreading Foot, 1933-44, 4 1/8 In. 705.00
Bowl, No. 461A, Egg Shape, Hammered, Georg Jensen, Post 1945, 7 1/2 In. 940.00
Bowl, No. 461B, Egg Shape, Hammered, Georg Jensen, Post 1945, 9 1/2 In. 1765.00
Burner, Openwork, Beaded Border, Pear Shape, Georg Jensen, 3 3/4 x 5 1/4 In. 1150.00
Cake Knife, Acorn Pattern, Stainless Steel Blade, Georg Jensen, c.1945, 11 In. 206.00
Candelabrum, 5-Light, Grape Pattern, Marked, 1945-77, 10 1/2 In., Pair .... *ILLUS* 72000.00
Candlestick, Grape Pattern, 1945-77, Georg Jensen, 11 1/2 In., Pair .... *ILLUS* 22800.00
Cigar Lamp, Georg Jensen, 1915-30, 5 1/4 In. 1600.00
Cigar Lamp, Roman Oil Lamp Shape, 10-Sided Base, Georg Jensen, 1915, 5 In. 1900.00
Coffee Set, Egg Shape, Hammered, Bead Borders, Georg Jensen, Post 1945, 3 Piece 3016.00
Coffee Set, Solitaire, Squat Baluster Shape, Ivory Handles, Georg Jensen, 3 Piece 1470.00
Compote, Hammered Finish, Fruit, Vines, Georg Jensen, Post 1915, 10 1/2 In. 8484.00
Creamer, Ebony Handle, Tapio Wirkkala, c.1955, 3 1/2 x 3 1/2 x 2 1/2 In. 600.00
Demitasse Set, Blossom, Georg Jensen, 1933-44, 6 1/4 In., 3 Piece 4700.00
Demitasse Set, Egg Shape, Tapered, Wood Handles, 1900s, 6 In., 3 Piece 529.00
Dresser Set, Dolphins, Harald Nielsen, Georg Jensen, Post 1945, 9 In., 3 Piece 424.00
Dresser Set, Inscription, Georg Jensen, c.1963, 6 Piece 4255.00
Fruit Bowl, Leaves, Berries, Openwork, Flared, Post 1945, 8 x 9 1/2 In. 7605.00
Gravy Ladle, Leaf & Berry, Georg Jensen, c.1930, 8 In. 655.00
Hand Mirror, Flower Filigree Cartouche, Georg Jensen, 10 1/4 In. 430.00
Jelly Spoon, Coral Set, Hammered Oval Bowl, Georg Jensen, c.1930, 7 In. 440.00
Pepperette, Spherical, Harald Nielsen, Georg Jensen, Post 1945, 1 3/4 In., Pair 380.00
Pitcher, Angled Spout, Ebony Handle, Johan Rohde, Georg Jensen, Post 1945, 8 3/4 In. 4148.00
Pitcher, Cosmos Pattern, Wood Handle, Georg Jensen, Post 1945, 9 1/2 In. 4600.00
Pitcher, Modernist, Slender, Short Spout, A. Michelsen, c.1950, 9 5/8 In. 2350.00
Salad Servers, No. 83, Flower Tip, Georg Jensen, c.1914, 7 1/2 In. 1555.00

Salt Cellar, Bud & Leaf Base, Georg Jensen, Post 1945, 1 1/2 In. 320.00
Sauce Ladle, Cactus, Egg Shape, 2 Spouts, Georg Jensen, 1900s, 6 In. 235.00
Spoon, Cocktail, Blossom, Hammered, Georg Jensen, 8 1/2 In. 460.00
Spoon, Cocktail, Blossom, Marked, Georg Jensen, 1944, 8 1/2 In. 460.00
Sugar & Creamer, Squat, Turned Handle, Circular Foot, Lettner, c.1950, 8 In. 380.00
Tea & Coffee Set, Cosmos Pattern, Georg Jensen, Post 1945, 9 1/2-In. Pot, 4 Piece 5750.00
Tea & Coffee Set, Ebonized Wood, Hans Bunde, c.1955, 6 Piece 2160.00
Tea Set, Onion Shape, Sugar, Creamer, Wood Finial, Georg Jensen, 3 Piece 6900.00
Tea Strainer, Carved Ivory Handle, Georg Jensen, c.1944, 5 1/4 x 1 1/2 In. 760.00
Tray, Blossom Pattern, 2 Handles, Oval, Georg Jensen, Post 1945, 22 In. 8955.00
Tray, Blossoms, Pod Handles, Hammered, Georg Jensen, Denmark, 13 3/4 x 11 In. 6325.00
Tray, Handles, Poul Petersen, c.1920, 17 x 28 1/2 In. 4388.00
Tray, Silver Blossom, Georg Jensen, 1900s, 13 1/4 In. 7768.00
SILVER-DUTCH, Bowl, Brandy, Oval, Openwork Handles, Pedestal, Repousse, Late 1800s, 9 In. 348.00
Box, Hinged, Cedar Bottom, 1 1/2 x 4 x 5 In. 176.00
Censer, Pheasant, Glass Eyes, Removable Head, c.1919, 9 x 24 1/4 In. 775.00
Demitasse Pot, Baluster Shape, Domed Lid, Serpentine Spout, Handle, 7 In. 176.00
Gravy, Repousse Flower, Swag, Ribbon, Family Crest, 1893, 5 x 8 x 3 1/2 In. 290.00
Jug, Hot Water, Oval, Short Spout, Flat Lid, Angular Wood Handle, 1800s, 5 1/2 In. 1058.00
Teapot, Oval, D.L.D. Van Reutelen, Amsterdam, 1802 . . . . . . 1170.00
Tongs, Scalloped Handles, Leaf Scrolls, Knop Finial, c.1900, 11 3/4 In. 205.00
Tray, Oval, Pierced Gallery, Beaded Border, Oval, VS, H, 14 3/8 In. 700.00

SILVER-ENGLISH. English sterling silver is marked with a series of four or five small hallmarks. The standing lion mark is the most commonly seen sterling quality mark. The other marks indicate the city of origin, the maker, and the year of manufacture. These dates can be verified in many good books on silver.

SILVER-ENGLISH, Asparagus Tongs, Arthur's Club, W. Eley & W. Fearn, George III, 1779, 9 3/4 In. 590.00
Basket, Bateman, London, George IV, c.1829, 4 3/4 x 10 3/4 x 16 In. 5850.00
Basket, Oval, Pierced, Repousse, Engraved, Scrollwork, Edwardian, c.1910, 16 In. 1160.00
Basket, Reticulated, Quatrefoil Bowl, WS Maker, Sheffield, 1913, 12 3/8 In. 590.00
Basket, Rococo Revival, Chinoiserie, Egg Shape, Crichton Bros., 1917, 15 In. 3290.00
Basting Spoon, Hanoverian, London, George II, c.1732 . . . . . . 445.00
Beaker, Flared Rim, Vermeil Interior, Engraved Motto, Robertson, c.1764, 3 In. 635.00
Beaker, Flared Rim, Vermeil Interior, Monogram Shield, Ribbon, 3 3/4 In. 1955.00
Beaker, London Hallmarks, William Caldecott, Vermeil Interior, c.1763, 3 In. 920.00
Beaker, London Hallmarks, William Sheen, Engraved Armorial Crest, c.1766, 4 In. 920.00
Beer Jug, Pear Shape, Scroll Handle, Thomas Whipham, George II, 1756, 6 In. 2160.00
Bottle Coasters, Bellied Circular Shape, Molded Rims, c.1984, 5 In., Pair 245.00
Bowl, Center, Pierced, Flowers, Scrolls, Repousse, E & Co., c.1904, 5 1/2 x 15 1/2 In. 529.00
Bowl, Center, Vermeil, c.1900, 9 In. 265.00
Bowl, Egg Shape, Pierced Sides, Engraved, C.S. Harris, Edward VII, 1903, 11 In., Pair 765.00
Bowl, Footed, Shell & Cherub Rim, Drapery, Lion Handles, c.1897, 7 1/2 x 10 1/4 In. 1495.00
Bowl, Pedestal Foot, Adie Bros. Ltd., c.1961, 9 1/4 In. 580.00
Bowl, Round, Foot, Raised Gadrooning, Hallmarks, c.1827, 10 3/4 x 6 1/2 In. 1035.00
Box, Birmingham, George III, c.1815, 1 x 1 7/8 In. 410.00
Box, Birmingham, Victorian, c.1900, 1 x 1 1/2 x 5 In. 145.00
Box, Cover, Oval, Geometrics, Flowers, Leaves, London, 1800s, 1 1/8 x 2 5/8 In. 145.00
Box, Monogram, Birmingham, Early 1800s, 3/4 x 2 x 3 1/2 In. 145.00
Brandy Warmer, Bulbous, Single Lip, Domed Bottom, Wood Handle, George III, 2 x 3 In. 1060.00
Butter Shell, George III Style, Reeded Borders, Shell Feet, 1921, 5 In., Pair 266.00
Caddy Spoon, William IV, John Henry & Charles Lias, London, c.1831, 3 3/4 In. 35.00
Calling Card Case, Cathedral, Hilliard & Thomason, c.1851, 2 1/2 x 3 1/2 In. 996.00
Candelabrum is listed in its own category.
Candle Extinguisher, Scissors, Shell Stems, George III, c.1815, 7 In. 325.00
Candlesticks are listed in their own category.
Candy Dish, Shell Shape, CB&S, 1913-14, 5 1/4 x 6 In., Pair 146.00
Card Case, Enamel, Peacock, Flowering Branch, 3 x 2 3/4 In. 1058.00
Card Tray, Footed, Crichton Bros., London, c.1930, 7 3/4 In. 145.00
Chalice, Archibald Knox, 1900, 7 1/2 In. 7645.00

Chalice, Archibald Knox, 1905, 8 1/4 In. 8299.00
Chalice, Engraved Animals, Vermeil Interior, 1766, 6 In. 1850.00
Chalice, Victorian, Tapering Bowl, Knopped Stem, Lobed Base, c.1893, 6 In. 1536.00
Chamberstick, Removable Nozzle, Loop Handle, George III, c.1802, 6 3/8 In. 705.00
Cheese Scoop, Crested, Initialed, George III, c.1812 .... 230.00
Chocolate Pot, Bulbous, Crest, Cylindrical Neck, E. Feline, London, c.1739, 8 In. 5079.00
Cigarette Box, Rectangular, Mahogany-Lined Interior, London, 1924, 9 In. 380.00
Cigarette Box, Shagreen, Cedar Lining, Archibald Knox, 1901, 9 In. 13105.00
Cigarette Case, Embossed Waves, Rectangular, Birmingham, 1903, 3 x 3 1/2 In. 176.00
Cigarette Case, Enamel, Blue Engine Turned Decoration, 1927, 3 1/2 In. 135.00
Claret Jug, Edwardian, Pierced Thumb Piece, Diamond & Star Band, c.1904, 10 In. 1160.00
Claret Jug, Victorian, Shouldered, Repousse, Engraved, Scrolling, c.1886, 11 In. 2129.00
Coffee Tray, 2 Handles, Reeded Border, Oval, Elizabeth Jones, George III, 1792, 18 In. 4800.00
Coffeepot, 8-Sided, Queen Anne Style, Chester, 1930, 7 1/2 In. 295.00
Coffeepot, Baluster Body, Repousse, Engraved, George III, c.1773, 11 In. 968.00
Coffeepot, Baluster, Engraved Arms, Francis Page, George II, 1742, 8 5/8 In. 2700.00
Coffeepot, Barnard, London, Victorian, 1895-96, 9 1/2 In. 410.00
Coffeepot, Bulbous, Flowers, Shell, Leaf, Repousse, George III, 1781, 9 1/2 In. 915.00
Coffeepot, Dome Lid, Cylindrical, Tapered, Thomas Whipham, George II, 1739, 9 In. 2160.00
Coffeepot, Flower & Scroll Repousse, William Grundy, George II, 1757, 8 3/4 In. 1037.00
Coffeepot, Flower Repousse, London, George III, 1763, 11 1/2 In. 1159.00
Coffeepot, Flowers, Bulbous, Ribbed, Wood Handle, John Robertson, c.1800, 11 3/4 In. 1315.00
Coffeepot, Lid, Hinge, Acorn Finial, Treen Handle, George III, 1800, 12 In. 2240.00
Coffeepot, Lighthouse Shape, 8-Sided Spout, Benjamin Pyne, George I, 1719, 9 In. 7200.00
Coffeepot, Monogram, George IV, 1827, 9 1/2 In. 978.00
Coffeepot, Oval, Tiered Lid, Oval Finial, Serpentine Handle, George II, c.1747, 9 In. 1410.00
Coffeepot, Pear Shape, Dome Lid, Bud Finial, Wood Handle, George III, 10 1/2 In. 690.00
Coffeepot, Pear Shape, Dome Lid, Serpentine Wood Handle, George III, 1775, 11 3/4 In. 2115.00
Coffeepot, Tapered Egg Shape, John Wirgman, George II, 1753, 9 3/8 In. 1528.00
Coffeepot, Thomas Morse, London, George III, 1803, 8 1/2 In. 1287.00
Coffeepot, Urn Shape, Reeded Borders, Acorn Finial, John Emes, George III, 1799, 13 In. 1320.00
Compote, Double Walled, Reeded, Lion Head Handles, Vine Rim, c.1804, 4 1/4 In. 545.00
Cream Jug, Marks, George I, c.1726, 4 3/4 In. 295.00
Cream Jug, Pedestal, S-Scroll Handle, Round Foot, George III, c.1777, 5 1/4 In. 195.00
Creamer, Helmet Shape, Flared Spout, Reeded Loop Handle, 6 1/2 x 4 3/4 x 2 In. 1725.00
Creamer, Helmet Shape, John Moore, London, 1793 .... 320.00
Creamer, Pear Shape, Short Spout, Serpentine Handle, George I, 1727, 3 In. 1410.00
Cup, Caudle, Presentation, Victorian, Edward VII, Pear Shape Body, c.1900, 4 In. 235.00
Cup, Caudle, Reeded Ear Handles, Beaded Girdle, George II, c.1759, 5 In. 470.00
Cup, Cover, Queen Anne Style, Strapwork, 2 Handles, Crichton, 1929, 11 3/4 In. 3900.00
Cup, Presentation, Cover, Mark, Girdled Urn Body, Scrolled Handles, 12 In. 940.00
Desk Tray, Enamel, Turquoise Cabochon, Archibald Knox, 1906, 7 3/4 In. 10485.00
Dish, Circular, 3-Part, Sheffield, Matthew Boulton, Georgian, c.1810, 6 1/2 x 10 1/2 In. 295.00
Dish, Entree, Cover, Gadroon Border, Robert Garrard I, Regency, 12 In., Pair 8400.00
Dish, Entree, Cover, Octagonal, Reeded Borders, Crested, George III, c.1798, 12 In. 350.00
Dish, Entree, Cover, William Bennett, George III, 1804, 11 1/4 In., Pair 6600.00
Dish, Shell Shape, Snail Supports, Edward Aldridge, c.1771, 5 1/4 x 4 5/8 In., Pair 1300.00
Dresser Box, Scrolls, WN Monogram, W. Comyn & Sons, London, 1882, 2 3/4 x 3 1/2 In. 118.00
Ewer, Footed, Paisley, Garlands, Flowers, Gilt Wash, Frederick Elkington, c.1874, 13 1/2 In. 956.00
Ewer, Sterling, Round, Bulbous, Scroll Handles, Flowers, Repousse, 1880, 12 In. 645.00
Fish Knives & Forks, Victorian, Engraved, Fish, Ivory Handles, c.1865, 6 Piece 270.00
Fish Slice, 3 Fish, Garlands, Deer, Thistle, George Ferris, c.1817, 10 3/4 In. 310.00
Fish Slice, Fiddle & Shell, Pierced, Engraved, George III, c.1817 .... 270.00
Fish Slice, Fiddle, Pierced, Scimitar Shape, Crest, George IV, 1825, 11 5/8 In. 475.00
Fish Slice, Openwork Blade, Scrolls, Arabesques, Shell Terminal, George II 2478.00
Fish Slice, Pierced, Engraved Shaped Blade, Ivory Handle, George III, 1801 .... 225.00
Fruit Set, Mother-Of-Pearl, 20th Century, 12 Piece 295.00
Fruit Set, Victorian, Fruiting Vine Handles, Red Leather Case, 1856, 3 Piece 666.00
Goblet, Family Armorial, Motto, Burwash & Sibley, George III, c.1807, 6 In. 2000.00
Goblet, Grapes, Leaves, Robert Hennell, London, George IV, 1826-27, 8 In. 1287.00
Goblet, London, George III, c.1815, 6 3/4 In. 470.00

Hot Water Urn, Vase Shape, Pedestal, Beaded Border, Loop Handles, George III, 15 1/2 In. 1121.00
Hot Water Urn, Vase Shape, Ram Heads, John Robins, George III, 1791, 17 1/2 In. 2700.00
Inkstand, Inscription, 2 Crystal Inkwells, H.W. & Co., c.1842, 5 1/2 x 10 1/2 In. 1560.00
Inkstand, Oval, 4 Supports, Ring Handle, Candlestick, Snuffer, George III, 5 1/2 In. 920.00
Inkwell, Figural, Donkey, Carrying Double Baskets, Hinged Reservoirs, 1800s 865.00
Jug, Hot Water, Cymric, Ivory Handle, Archibald Knox, 1904, 7 In. 4370.00
Jug, Hot Water, Fluted, Oval, Baluster, Charles Kandler, George II, 1727, 8 1/4 In. 7200.00
Jug, Hot Water, Tudric, Basket Handle, Archibald Knox, 1902-05, 12 In. 2075.00
Jug, Lid, Hinges, Vasiform, Waisted Body, Cane Covered Handle, George III, 12 In. 1890.00
Jug, Milk, John Robins, London, George III, c.1803, 9 In. 500.00
Kettle, Stand, Egg Shape, Chased, Embossed, Dome Lid, C.S. Harris, 1899, 11 3/8 In. 380.00
Kettle, Stand, Inverted Pear, George II, Peze Pilleau, 1754, 15 1/4 In. 4800.00
Ladle, Cherub Stem, Cast, Engraved, Husk, Stippled Ground, c.1769, 13 In. 590.00
Ladle, Fiddle Handle, Rampant Lion, William Chawner, 1826, George IV, 13 In. 175.00
Ladle, Fiddle Handle, Wolf Armorial, Randall Challerton, London, 1827, 13 1/4 In. 175.00
Ladle, Onslow Handle, Shell Shape Bowl, Inscribed, George III, 13 1/4 In. 690.00
Ladle, Oval Handle, Bowl, Downturned Tipt Back, Family Crest, George III, 1792, 13 In. 315.00
Mug, Bombe, S-Scroll Handle, John Langland I, Newcastle, George II, 1757, 5 3/8 In. 660.00
Mug, Cylinder Shape, Angled Scroll Handle, Reeded Bands, George IV, c.1822, 3 In. 155.00
Mug, Cylindrical, Scroll Handle, Hoops, Alice Sheen, Queen Anne, 1702, 3 3/4 In. 5100.00
Mug, Cylindrical, Tapered, S-Scroll Handle, Isaac Dighton, William III, 1700, 3 1/4 In. 2700.00
Mug, Pear Shape, Paul De Lamerie, London, George II, 1749, 4 1/2 In. 8625.00
Mug, Provincial, Tapered, S-Scroll Handle, George II, c.1759, 6 In. 820.00
Mustard Pot, Cylindrical, Beaded Rims, Ear Handle, Thomas Daniel, George III, 1785, 3 In. 940.00
Mustard Pot, Hexagonal, Handles, Pierced Panel, George III, 1786, 4 5/8 In. 1755.00
Napkin Rings are listed in their own category.
Open Salt Set, 3-Footed, Georgian, 18th Century, 1 1/2 x 2 3/4 In., 4 Piece 350.00
Pap Boat, Oval, London, George III, c.1769, 4 1/4 In. 230.00
Pastry Server, Mother-Of-Pearl, George Smith, George III, c.1797, 9 7/8 In. 115.00
Patch Box, Thomas Nickolson, Birmingham, 1820, 1 1/2 x 2 3/4 In. 350.00
Pill Box, Joseph Willmore, Birmingham, George III, c.1810, 1 1/8 In. 115.00
Pitcher, Bulbous, Slender Neck, Flowers, Angels, Shells, Martin Hall & Co., c.1862, 14 In. 2270.00
Plate, Cast Gadroon Rims, John Wakelin & William Taylor, c.1777, 10 In., Pair 1955.00
Plate, Grape & Leaf Border, Reticulated, Footed, CB & S Co., 1 1/2 x 10 In. 360.00
Plate, Second Course, William Elliott, George IV, 1823, 12 In., Pair 3000.00
Plate Set, Grape, Vine Reeded Borders, Crest, George III, 1817, 9 1/2 In., 11 Piece 6440.00
Plate Warmer, Revolving, Sheffield, 9 x 12 In. 176.00
Platter, Armorial, Elkington & Co., Fluted Inner Rim, Stippled Ground, c.1867 .... 5875.00
Platter, Meat, Oval, Molded Rim, Frederick Kandler, George II, 1744, 15 1/2 In. 2400.00
Platter, Meat, Oval, Molded Rim, Frederick Kandler, George II, 1744, 20 1/2 In. 4200.00
Punch Bowl, Embossed Flowers, Swags, Sheffield, Hallmark, c.1900, 9 x 6 In. 430.00
Punch Bowl, Monteith Style, S-Scroll, Shell Rim, BB Maker, Edward VII, 1903, 8 x 10 In. 1880.00
Punch Bowl, Repousse Flowers, J.B. Chatterley, Carrington & Co., 1891, 11 In. 920.00
Rattle, Coral, Baluster Shape, Embossed Flowers, Leaves, c.1900, 5 1/4 In. 323.00
Rattle, Repousse Flowers, Whistle, Bells, 1862, 6 In. 490.00
Rattle, Repousse Flowers, Whistle, Bells, Coral, c.1862, 6 1/4 In. 200.00
Rose Bowl, Chased, Embossed, Scrollwork, Leaves, c.1932, 10 In. 720.00
Rose Bowl, Fire Opals, Bernard Cuzner, 1901, 3 1/2 In. 2620.00
Rose Bowl, Opals, Bernard Cuzner, 1904, 7 1/4 In. 6115.00
Salt, Open, Oval, Fluted, Gadroon Border, Paul Storr, George III, 1811, 5 In. 910.00
Salt, Pedestal, Circular, Flowers, Anne Tanqueray, George II, 3 1/2 In., Pair 4800.00
Salt Set, Peacock, Silver, Cast, Engraved, Spread Tails Shape Bowl, 6 In., 4 Piece 1065.00
Salver, Circular, Gadroon & Shell Rim, 3-Footed, Richard Rugg, George III, 1763, 13 In. 5100.00
Salver, Circular, Gadroon Border, 3 Hoof Feet, R. Peaston, George III, 1774, 6 1/8 In. 460.00
Salver, John Carter II, London, George II, c.1770, 9 1/2 In. 1290.00
Salver, Molded Ogee Edge, S-Scroll & Shell Rim, R. Rugg, George III, 1763, 15 1/2 In. 3819.00
Salver, Molded Rim, 4-Footed, Oval, T. Hannam, J. Crouch II, George III, 1805, 22 In. 3000.00
Salver, Ogee Molded Rim, Monogram, Crichton Bros., George V, 1916, 10 1/8 In. 175.00
Salver, Reeded, Beaded, 4 Shell Feet, Oval, John Scofield, George III, 1788, 18 3/8 In. 3000.00
Salver, Round, Molded Bead Rim, 3 Panel Feet, George III, 1871, 11 In. 1160.00
Salver, Shell & Scroll Border, Armorials, 3 Scroll Legs, R. Rugg, George III, 1762, 12 In. 1170.00

Sauce Ladle, Backtipt Handle, Crest, Hester Bateman, George III, 1786, 7 1/8 In. 380.00
Sauceboat, Egg Shape, Wide Spout, Ogee Rim, R. Cox, George II, 1753, 8 3/8 In. 705.00
Sauceboat, Fras. Crump, London, George III, 1770-71, 4 1/2 x 6 3/4 In. 527.00
Saucepan, Baluster, Turned Wood Handle, Thomas Folkingham, George I, 1716, 8 3/4 In. 3300.00
Saucepan, Brandy, Paul Hanet, London, George I, 1722, 5 1/2 x 3 x 7 1/4 In. 290.00
Saucepan, Bulbous, Side Wood Handle, Ed Malluson, George II, 1744 .... 439.00
Server, Round, Threaded Handle, Bird, Olive Branch, George W. Adams, c.1845, 10 In. 78.00
Serving Spoon, Fiddle & Thread, William IV, c.1833, 11 1/4 In. 206.00
Serving Spoon, Fiddle Pattern, Crested, Thomas Barker, George III, c.1815, Pair 230.00
Skewer, Poultry, Lion Crests, George III, c.1780, 5 Piece 177.00
Snuffers Stand, Hourglass Shape, Scroll Handle, Paul Crespin, George II, 1740, 7 In. 3900.00
Soup Ladle, Fiddle, Double Lipped Bowl, England, George IV, c.1829 .... 184.00
Soup Ladle, Rampant Lion, Cross, Monogram, Charles Eley, c.1825, 12 1/2 In. 285.00
Spoon, Rounded Handle, Downturned Tipt, Oval Bowl, George III, 1773, 8 1/2 In., Pair 520.00
Spoon, Seal Top, Teardrop Bowl, Richard Osborne, Elizabeth I, 6 1/4 In. 2700.00
Stuffing Spoon, Backtipt, Crest, Hester Bateman, George III, 1787, 11 1/2 In. 38.00
Stuffing Spoon, Onslow, Scroll Terminal, Family Crest, George II, 1752, 11 1/8 In. 750.00
Sugar & Creamer, Bulbous, Fluted, William Elliott, George IV, 1822 .... 410.00
Sugar Basket, Boat Shaped, Bail Handle, Pedestal Foot, George III, 5 1/2 In. 649.00
Sugar Castor, BD Mark, Birmingham, Edward VII, 1904, 8 In. 295.00
Sugar Castor, Elkington & Co., Birmingham, 1935-36, 7 In. 295.00
Sugar Castor, Footed, Bulbous, Collared Neck, Thomas Bamford, c.1720, 7 1/4 In. 840.00
Sugar Castor, London, George IV, c.1826, 4 In. 468.00
Sugar Castor, Sam Wood, London, George II, 1755 .... 936.00
Sugar Castor, Victorian, Baluster Shape, Repousse, Engraved, Leaf Scroll, 1886, 9 In. 266.00
Syrup, Cover, C-Scrolls, Flowers, Leaves, Scroll Handle, London, 1855, 8 1/4 In. 920.00
Tablespoon, Chasing, Embossing, Hester Bateman, c.1780, 8 In., Pair 175.00
Tablespoon, JMA Monogram, Hester Bateman, 1780, 8 1/8 In. 275.00
Tankard, C-Scroll Handle, Tapered, Banded, Edwardian, c.1908, 4 1/4 x 5 1/4 In. 205.00
Tankard, Cymric, Enamel, Archibald Knox, 1903, 5 3/8 In. 5678.00
Tea & Coffee Set, Shell Decoration, Ribbed, Carrington & Co., London, c.1919, 6 Piece 5175.00
Tea & Coffee Set, Victorian, Adam Style, Tapered Oval, Swags, c.1873 .... 3485.00
Tea Caddy, Sheffield, Arkins Brothers Hallmark, 3 3/4 In. 140.00
Tea Set, Edward VII, Rococo Revival, Chased, Embossed, c.1904, 3 Piece 705.00
Tea Set, Egg Shape, Flowers, R. & D. Hennell, George III, 1800, 10-In. Pot, 3 Piece 1175.00
Tea Set, Hepplewhite Style, London, Victorian, 1870-71, 3 Piece 530.00
Tea Set, Queen Anne Style, Melon Shape, Teapot, Surgar, Creamer, 6 In., 3 Piece 635.00
Tea Set, Squat, Melon Shape, Gold Wash Interior, E. Farrell, George IV, 1828, 6 In., 3 Piece 588.00
Tea Set, Wood Handle, 8-Sided Body, E & Co., c.1935-37, 3 Piece 518.00
Tea Urn, Dome & Finial Top, Burner, Henry Greenway, London, 1796, 19 In. 6038.00
Teapot, Apple Shape, Engraved Arms, Nathaniel Gulliver, George I, 1722, 4 1/2 In. 3600.00
Teapot, Bulbous, Fluted, Squat, John Angell, George IV, 1825, 5 1/4 In. 936.00
Teapot, Chased Flowers, Lobed, Dome Lid, Flower Finial, D. Hennell, 7 In. 130.00
Teapot, Egg Shape, Straight Spout, Wood Handle, A. Fogelberg, George III, 1796, 6 In. 410.00
Teapot, Ivory Handle, Cymric, Archibald Knox, 1904, 5 3/4 In. 1747.00
Teapot, Ivory, Glass Cabochon, Archibald Knox, 1902, 6 1/8 In. 8736.00
Teapot, Lobed Compressed Round Shape, Squash Finial, George IV, c.1834, 6 In. 580.00
Teapot, Oval Shape, Scroll Handle, Spout, Engraved, Leaves, George III, 1799, 7 In. 666.00
Teapot, Pear Shape, Dome Lid, Gold & Silversmiths Co., George V, 1934, 7 3/4 In. 325.00
Teapot, Queen Anne Style, Pear Shape, Footed, Birmingham, 1928, 4 In. 145.00
Teapot, Queen Anne, Pear Shape, Swan-Neck Spout, Edward Pearce, 1712, 5 1/2 In. 300.00
Teapot, Spherical, Molded Foot, Alexander Johnston, George III, 1760, 7 In. 1680.00
Toasted Cheese Dish, Gadroon Rim, William Stroud, George III, 1805, 9 3/8 In. 1080.00
Toasting Fork, 3 Tines, Open Scrollwork Handle, George III, c.1770 .... 708.00
Tobacco Box, William Parker, Serpentine Handle, George III, c.1807, 6 1/2 In. 1528.00
Tongs, Kings Pattern, 6 In. 80.00
Tray, 2 Loop Handles, Molded Rim, Crichton, 1929, 27 In. 3600.00
Tray, Edwardian, Cartouche Shape, Repousse, Costumed Figures, Putti, 1903, 12 In. 287.00
Tray, Flowers, W. Comyns & Sons, London, 1889-90, 4 3/4 x 13 In. 295.00
Tray, Footed, Scalloped Edge, Mappin & Webb, Sheffield, c.1917, 10 In. 470.00
Tray, Liquor, Wolf's Head, Animo Non Astutia, Sheffield, 1800-30, 2 1/4 x 21 3/4 In. 690.00

Tray, Ogee Molded Rim, Oblong, C.S. Harris, Edward VII, 1903, 27 3/4 In. 3175.00
Tray, Presentation Inscription, 3-Footed, Scalloped Rim, c.1836, 6 1/4 In. 478.00
Tray, Round, Atkin Brothers, Sheffield, 1911-12, 15 1/2 In. 585.00
Tray, Shell & Scroll Border, George III, 1802, 17 1/2 In. 2760.00
Tureen, Oval, Reeded Oval, Acanthus, Paw Feet, Victorian, c.1847, 18 x 13 In. 16450.00
Urn, 2 Open Handles, Armorial Decoration, William Abdy, George III, 16 In. 1870.00
Vase, Cymric, Enamel, Archibald Knox, 1902, 6 3/8 In. 8299.00
Vinaigrette, Agate, Joseph Taylor, Birmingham, George III, c.1799, 1 1/4 In. 235.00
Vinaigrette, Edward Smith, Birmingham, George III, c.1827, 1 1/4 In. 265.00
Vinaigrette, John Bettridge, Birmingham, George III, c.1820, 1 1/8 In. 205.00
Vinaigrette, Perfume, Victorian, Hunting Horn Shape, c.1870, 4 In. 470.00
Vinaigrette, Samuel Pemberton, Birmingham, George III, c.1812, 1 1/2 In. 175.00
Vinaigrette, William IV, Francis Clark, Birmingham, c.1833, 1 3/8 In. 205.00
Waiter, Round, Molded Leaf & Shell Border, 3 Panel Feet, 1851, 7 In. 510.00
Waiter, Shell & Scroll Rim, 3-Footed, William Peaston, George II, 1747, 7 In., Pair 4200.00
Warming Dish, 2 Handles, Dome Lid, Crest, Cast Iron Handle, 15 x 23 In. 4110.00
Wine Coaster, Gothic Revival, Leaftip Borders, William IV, c.1838, 6 In., Pair 3525.00
Wine Coaster, Urns, Pierced, Scroll Border, Wood Base, 1780, 4 3/4 In., Pair 6000.00
Wine Cooler, Lion Mask, Loose Ring Handles, Collars, Liners, 8 In., Pair 1035.00
Wine Cooler, Oval Body, Chased, Embossed, Leaves, Beading, Victorian, 7 In. 765.00
Wine Cooler, W. Fountain, Urn Shape, Reeded Handles, George III, c.1804, 9 In. 7638.00
Wine Funnel, 4 Applied Ribs, Strainer Base, Monogram, George III, 1802, 6 7/8 In. 999.00
Wine Funnel, Reeded Details, Alexander Hewat, c.1830, 4 3/4 x 3 1/4 In. 538.00
Wine Funnel, Stand, Thumbpiece, George III, c.1800 .... 826.00
SILVER-FRENCH, Basket, Rococo, Reticulated, Boat Shape, Cherubs, Flowers, Late 1800s, 16 In. . 940.00
Cake Stand, Wild Roses, Scroll, 1800s, 8 1/2 In. 265.00
Coffeepot, Oval, Leaf & Dart Borders, Bud Finial, Horse Head Spout, c.1838, 10 In. 1435.00
Compote, Crystal Dish, Christofle, c.1880, 7 3/4 x 6 1/2 In. 878.00
Cream Jug, Oval, High Handle, c.1810, 5 In. 385.00
Cruet, Stand, Female Figural, Classical Empire Style, Basket Handle 1100.00
Cup & Saucer, Renaissance Revival, Winged Herm Handle, c.1875, 4 In. 999.00
Decanter, Cut, Etched Glass, Stoppers, Repousse, Engraved, Late 1800s, 10 In., Pair 580.00
Jug, Hot Water, Bulbous, 1800s, 7 1/2 In. 235.00
Ladle, Fiddle, France, c.1849, 14 In. 184.00
Salt, Open, Navette Shape Base, Gadroon Rim, Glass Well, Late 1800s, 4 1/8 In., Pair 176.00
Salt Cellar, Double, Louis Philippe, Embossed Acanthus Scrolls, 5 x 5 x 3 In. 528.00
Tazza, Hammered, Jean Despres, 1900s, 1 3/8 x 7 7/8 In. 8540.00
Tazza, Poppies, Puiforcat, 2 x 9 1/2 In., Pair 4036.00
Tea & Coffee Set, Fruit Finial, DR Paris Sterling, 10-In. Coffeepot, 5 Piece 2760.00
Tea Set, Enamel, Towle, c.1900, 5 Piece 24570.00
Teapot, Exotic Wood, c.1930, Art Deco Style, Squat, Black Handle, Tirbour, 4 In. 2640.00
Tray, Round, Scalloped Edge, Crest, Aix-En-Provence, c.1756, 12 In. 1195.00
SILVER-GERMAN, Basket, Garlands, Flared, Swing Handle, Pierced, Repousse, c.1900, 16 In. ... 870.00
Basket, Neoclassical Style, Reticulated, Oblong, Early 1900s, 8 3/8 In. 265.00
Bowl, Oval, Reticulated Sides, Gadroon Edges, Footed, Glass Liner, 6 1/4 x 15 1/2 In. 556.00
Box, Victorian, Ribbed, Footed, Flower Finial, Lock, 5 x 6 In. 385.00
Compote, Art Nouveau, Figural, Marked Friedlander, c.1900, 18 x 14 In., Pair 10030.00
Ewer, Egg Shape, Slender Neck, Short Spout, Loop Handle, Early 1900s, 8 3/4 In. 355.00
Figure, Knight, Chased, Ivory Face, Glass Cabochons, Oval Base, Gadroon, 16 In. 2820.00
Punch Ladle, WMF, Art Deco, Oval Handle, Gilt Interior, Flattened Round Bowl, 12 In. 80.00
Salt & Pepper, Cupid Finial, c.1900, 4 7/8 In. 295.00
Serving Dish, Rococo Revival, Navette Shape, Eugen Marcus, 13 1/8 In., Pair 940.00
Sugar Castor, Embossed Neoclassical Designs, 8-Sided, Tapered, 8 In., Pair 350.00
SILVER-INDIAN, Cup, Pedestal, Reeded Handle, Grapes, Flowers, Acorns, Leaves, c.1810, 5 In. ... 538.00
Incense Burner, Chased, Repousse Flowers, 8 In. 266.00
Vase, 4 Oval Reserves, Flowers, Bird, 7 1/2 In. 266.00
Vase, Repousse Cartouches, Flowering Branch, 6 1/2 In., Pair 266.00
Vase, Repousse, Oval Reserves, Flowers, 6 In. 385.00
SILVER-IRISH, Basket, Stepped Navette Shape, Reeded Swing Handle, George III, c.1790, 6 In. .. 1025.00
Bonbon, Circular, Footed, Dublin, George III, 1811, 3 3/8 In. 185.00
Coffeepot, Baluster, Twist Turned Finial, Gadroon Lip, Wood Loop Handle, 1774, 11 In. 880.00

Creamer, Helmet Shape, Molded Girdle, Waved Rim, Dublin, c.1750, 5 In. 1440.00
Fish Slice, Flat Chased, Pierced Blade, Feathered Edge, Stag Crest, George III 2478.00
Salt, Gilt Interior, 3-Footed, 3 Engraved Crests, Michael Walsh, c.1750, 3 In., 4 Piece 2280.00
Sauceboat, Oval, Waved Rim, 3 Scroll Feet, Thomas Walker, c.1755, 9 In. 3000.00
Sauceboat, Waved Rim, 3 Scroll Feet, George Hodder, c.1760, 9 In., Pair 7800.00
Serving Spoon, James Scott, George III, 1819, 9 In., Pair 205.00
Spoon Tray, Oval, Scalloped Sides, Engraved Crest, John Williamson, c.1740, 6 1/2 In. 3900.00
Sugar, Flaring, Molded Rim, Base Band, Jane Daniell, Dublin, c.1740, 4 1/4 In. 3600.00
Sugar Castor, Baluster, Double Girdle, Pierced Ribbed Cover, Dublin, 1714, 6 1/2 In. 3600.00
SILVER-ITALIAN, Bowl, Center, Repousse, Engraved, Scrolls, Shells, Leaves, 1900s, 19 In. 4505.00
Bowl, Flared, Beaded Oval Medallions & Bands, 3 Ball Feet, Draraffman, 9 3/8 In. 540.00
Dish, Egg Shape, Ribbon Wrapped Reeded Rim, M. Buccellati, 1900s, 15 In. 1528.00
Dish, Shell Shape, Inner Scrolled Handles, 4 Conch Feet, Buccellati, 2 x 9 x 7 In. 960.00
Ewer, Neoclassical, Paneled Helmet Shape, Engraved, C-Scroll Handle, 8 In. 2585.00
Tray, Serving, Oval, Molded Leaf & Dart Rim, 2 Beaded Leaf Handles, 1900s, 22 In. 580.00
SILVER-JAPANESE, Box, Wheeled Cart Shape, Ho Bird Engraving, Late 19th Century, 8 In. 390.00
Censer, Phoenixes, Japan, 19th Century, 5 1/4 In. 4994.00
Cigarette Box, Bamboo, Stippled Ground, Wood Lining, Early 1900s, 6 1/2 x 3 3/4 In. 705.00
Cosmetic Box, Bat, Seal, Calligraphy, 1900s, 2 1/4 In. 259.00
Cup, Cylindrical, Battle Scene, Gilt Wash Interior, c.1868, 3 1/2 In. 660.00
Decanter, Triform Vessel, Dimpled, Stylized Flowering Leaves, c.1920, 9 In. 390.00
Dish, Reeded Handle, Shallow, Circular, Bamboo Leaf Designs, 4 3/4 x 8 1/8 In. 330.00
Salt & Pepper, Flower Cart, Movable Wheels, 1900s, 2 3/4 In. 185.00
Salt & Pepper, Hair Comb Shape, Bamboo, Prunus, Kozan, 1900s, 2 In. 160.00
Salt & Pepper, Hanging Lanterns, 1900s, 3 3/4 In. 196.00
Salt & Pepper, Mount Fuji, Temple, Flower, 1900s, 3 1/4 In. 160.00
Salt & Pepper, Pagoda Shape, 1900s, 3 3/4 In. 127.00
Salt & Pepper, Palanquin Shape, 1900s, 3 3/4 In. 175.00
Salt & Pepper, Temple Gates, 1900s, 2 3/4 In. 127.00
Salt & Pepper, Umbrella On Geta, 1900s, 3 1/2 In. 219.00
Tea & Coffee Set, Arthur & Bond, Yokohama, Early 20th Century, 7 Piece 9000.00
SILVER-LATVIAN, Cigarette Case, Eagle, Repousse, Gem Thumb Press, Gilt Wash, 3 1/4 x 4 In. ... 239.00
SILVER-MEXICAN, Bowl, Chased Stylized Flowers, Lobes, 3 Ball Feet, Sanborns, 4 3/8 x 6 1/2 In. . 765.00
Bowl, Oval, Ribbed, Gadroon Sides, Dome Lid, Twisted Ring Handle, Tane, 6 In. 410.00
Bowl, Round, Fluted, 3 Ball Feet, 10 3/4 x 4 1/2 In. 176.00
Bowl, Round, Shaped, Mexican Medallion, 18 3/4 x 3 In. 527.00
Box, Cover, Circular, Rope Twist Border, 3 1/4 In. 58.00
Coffeepot, Drapery Pattern, Wood Finial, Spratling, Taxco, c.1967, 8 3/4 In. 1680.00
Dish, Underplate, Hand Wrought, 20th Century, 5 1/2 x 7 In. 120.00
Fish Serving Set, Owl, Engraved, Sanborns, 9 1/2 & 12 1/2 In., 2 Piece 80.00
Fruit Bowl, Circular, Lobed Sides, Chased Roses, Ortega, 1900s, 12 In. 560.00
Goblet, Dome Foot, Knobbed Stem, Flowers, Sanborns, Early 1900s, 5 1/2 In., 12 Piece 598.00
Judaic Bible Cover, 5 3/8 x 3 3/4 In. 235.00
Pitcher, Sangria, Hammered, Built-In Strainer, Strap Handle, Spratling, 7 1/2 In. 4360.00
Server Group, Wood, William Spratling, Taxco, c.1967, 10 Piece 6600.00
Serving Dish, Sloping Sides, Scalloped Rim, 1800s, 11 1/2 In. 598.00
Tea & Coffee Set, Chased, Embossed, Rosehead Band, 8 1/2 In., 4 Piece 558.00
Tea & Coffee Set, Stylized Flowers, Urn Shape, Lobed, Acorn Finial, Sanborns, 6 Piece 1528.00
Tea & Coffee Set, Tray, Jaguar Finials, Scroll, Ball Handle, Spratling, c.1967, 5 Piece 24000.00
Tea & Coffee Set, Urn Shape, Ortega, 1900s, 10 3/4-In. Coffeepot, 5 Piece 2820.00
Tea Set, Ribbed, Myers, 1900s, 26 1/4 In., 5 Piece 1135.00
Teapot, Stand, Burner, Melon Shape, Flower Finial, Early 1900s, 13 1/4 In. 840.00
Tequila Server, Sombrero Shape, Flower Shapes, Shot Glasses, Bottle Holder, 17 In. 1180.00
SILVER-NORWEGIAN, Bowl, Guilloche Enamel, Atom Center, Black, 1950s, 6 3/4 In. 358.00
Dish, Turquoise Guilloche Enamel, 1950s, 6 1/4 In. 265.00
Fish Server, Reticulated Handle, Fish, Rosette, 2 Tines, David Anderson, 9 1/2 In., Pair 120.00
Salad Servers, Birds & Leaves, David Andersen, 2 Piece 120.00
SILVER-PERSIAN, Tankard, Repousse, Animal Head Handle, Flowers, Scrolls, 4 1/2 x 4 In. 385.00
SILVER-PERUVIAN, Bowl, Hand Hammered, Round, 2 Swing Handles, Welsch, 3 x 10 In. 420.00
Skewer, Sword Shape, Camusso, 1900s, 10 3/4 In., 6 Piece 140.00
Tea Set, Ribbed, Scroll Handles, 4 Ribbed Feet, Gilt Wash, Camusso, 13 1/2 In., 6 Piece 1058.00

Tray, Classical Revival, Egg Shape, Reeded Handles, 1900s, 25 In. 645.00
SILVER-PORTUGUESE, Toothpick Holder, Figural, Man, With Staff, Bag, 19th Century, 6 In. 940.00
Tray, Serving, 2 Handles, Rectangular, Molded, Repousse Scroll Rim, 31 In. 2615.00

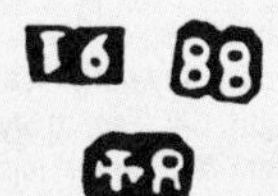

SILVER-RUSSIAN. Russian silver is marked with the Cyrillic, or Russian, alphabet. The numbers 84, 88, or 91 indicate the silver content. Russian silver may be higher or lower than sterling standard. Other marks indicate maker, assayer, or city of manufacture. Many pieces of silver made in Russia are decorated with enamel. Faberge pieces are listed in their own category.

SILVER-RUSSIAN, Bowl, Enamel, Bear Head Handles, Scrolling Leaves, F. Ruckert, 1908-17, 5 3/4 In. 11750.00
Case, Cheroot, Niello, Oblong, Decorated, St. Basil's Basilica, 3 x 3 1/2 In. 389.00
Cigar Case, Applied BJ Monogram, Gilt Lined, Inscription, c.1882, 3 1/2 x 5 3/4 In. 538.00
Cigarette Case, Diamond Pattern, Niello, Monogram, 2 3/4 x 4 3/4 In. 160.00
Cigarette Case, Gold Mount, Rectangular, Flowers, Presentation, c.1900, 4 3/4 In. 499.00
Cigarette Case, Miniature On Ivory, Nude Woman, c.1917, 3/4 x 4 1/2 x 3 1/2 In. 2860.00
Cigarette Case, Rectangular, Rounded Corners, Warrior, Horse, 1908-17, 4 5/8 In. 380.00
Cigarette Case, St. Petersburg, Late 19th Century, 1 5/8 x 2 3/8 In. 320.00
Desk Set, Real Horse's Hoof, Cut Glass Ink Bottles, Monogram, MTC, 5 3/4 In. 558.00
Egg, Raised Flowers, Leaves, Gold Washed Bees, Amethysts, Bird Feet, 3 1/4 In. 556.00
Kovsh, Enameled, 1880-84, 2 x 6 x 3 In. 2185.00
Kovsh, Gold Washed, Enamel, Overall Multicolor Flowers, c.1917, 7 In. 3408.00
Ladle, Gold Washed Bowl, 14 In. 385.00
Spoon, Enamel, 11th Artel, H.F.H. Inscription, 5 1/2 In. 410.00
Table Ornament, Filigree, Baby Carriage Shape, Open Wirework, 4 1/4 In. 470.00
Tray, Neoclassical, Swan Corners, 2 Handles, P.F. Sazikov, 1833, 26 1/4 In. 2938.00
SILVER-SCOTTISH, Box, Early Victorian, J. Nasmyth & Co., Edinburgh, 1 3/8 x 3 3/4 In. 645.00
Cann, Cup, Monogram T, Decorated Border, Lothian & Robertson, c.1764, 3 In., Pair 1990.00
Coffeepot, Stand, Squat, Egg Shape, Dome Lid, Frs. Howden, George III, 1810, 12 In. 940.00
Jug, Hot Water, Oval Body, Bud Finial, Scroll Handle, George III, c.1807, 12 In. 1935.00
Jug, Water, Victorian, Chased, Engraved, Scrolling, Leaves, c.1842, 12 In. 1160.00
Tea & Coffee Set, Faceted Oval Shape, Scroll Rims, Edwardian, c.1910 .... 968.00
Toddy Ladle, Fiddle Back, Armorial, William Jamieson, Aberdeen, 6 In., 6 Piece 646.00
Toddy Ladle, Plain Oval Bowl, Volute Whalebone Handle, George III, 13 1/2 In. 185.00
SILVER-SOUTH AMERICAN, Asparagus Server, Cartouche, Plata Imperio, c.1920, 5 In., 8 Piece .. 205.00

SILVER-STERLING. Sterling silver is made with 925 parts silver out of 1,000 parts of metal. The word *sterling* is a quality guarantee used in the United States after about 1860. The word was used much earlier in England and Ireland. Pieces listed here are not identified by country. Other pieces of sterling quality silver are listed under Silver-American, Silver-English, etc.

SILVER-STERLING, Bonbon Set, Reticulated, Heart Shape, Ball Feet, 8 Piece 558.00
Bottle, Perfume, Scrolling Iris Flowers On Green Glass, 1920, 4 In. 400.00
Bowl, Center, Applied Grapevine & Rim, Footed, Arts & Crafts, 5 x 8 In. 1348.00
Bowl, Center, Flaring, Fluted Sides, Wire Work Flower Frog, c.1950, 12 1/2 In. 265.00
Bowl, Center, Glass Bowl, Sheffield, c.1830, 21 3/4 In. 439.00
Bowl, Floral Decoration, Boat Shape, Flower Heads, Monogram, Late 1800s, 10 In. 120.00
Bowl, Vegetable, Squat, Oval, Flowers, Scroll Rim, Embossed, 11 1/2 In. 1175.00
Bread Tray, Hand Wrought, 12 1/4 In. 265.00
Candelabrum is listed in its own category.
Candlesticks are listed in their own category.
Crosier, Bishop's, Cased, Acanthus Leaves, Gilded Silver Figure, Silk Lined Case, 71 In. 1060.00
Dish, Danish Modern, Leaf Shaped, Acanthus Handle, c.1940, 1 3/4 x 10 1/2 In. 765.00
Figure, Swan, 14 x 6 x 15 In. 2925.00
Frame, Photograph, Asian Style, Serpentine, Embossed Dragons, 13 x 10 In. 380.00
Inkstand, Rococo Revival, Diapered Cartouche, Cut Glass Inkwells, 8 In. 999.00
Ladle, Shell Shape Bowl, Leaf Scrolled Handle, 12 In. 266.00
Napkin Rings are listed in their own category.
Pitcher, Water, Baluster, Double Scroll Handle, c.1950, 9 1/2 In. 385.00
Plate Set, Stamped Rim, Ovolo Band, 20th Century, 6 1/4 In., 12 Piece 355.00

Punch Bowl, Relief Stag's Head Cartouche, Repousse Flowers, Swags, Footed, 9 x 11 In. 3450.00
Rattle, Baseball, Bat, 1890s 1045.00
Rattle, Mother Of Pearl, Victorian, Late 19th Century, 2 1/4 x 4 1/4 In. 527.00
Ruler, Early 20th Century, 4 1/2 In. 59.00
Salt & Pepper, Repousse Flowers, 3-Footed, 5 In. 180.00
Spoon, Souvenir, see Souvenir category.
Sugar, Gilt, Empire Style, Palmette Banding, Handles, Mid 1900s, 10 x 5 1/2 In. 145.00
Sugar & Creamer, Japonisme, Hammered, Crabstock Handle, 3 3/4 In. 558.00
Syrup, No. 500, Monogram PLM, Angular Handle, 4 1/2 In. 146.00
Tea & Coffee Set, 11-In. Coffeepot, 5 Piece 750.00
Tea & Coffee Set, Classical Revival, Roger Williams, Mid 1900s, 5 Piece 705.00
Tea & Coffee Set, Georgian Style, Ear Handles, 1900s, 8 1/2 In., 4 Piece 410.00
Trophy Bowl, Rococo Revival, Embossed, Howard & Co., Late 19th Century, 4 In. 147.00
Tureen, Soup, Dome Lid, Acanthus Handles, Engraved, 16 x 9 1/2 x 10 In. 13200.00
Vase, Trumpet, Crystal, No. 4297, 10 1/2 x 6 In. 88.00
Wedding Beaker, Woman, Cup On Head, Repousse, Gold Wash Interior, c.1850, 12 In. 1690.00
SILVER-SWEDISH, Vase, Trumpet, Hammered Surface, Vines, Rocaille, c.1931, 10 1/8 In. 325.00
SILVER-SWISS, Cigarette Case, Striped, Hinged, Clock, Gilt Wash, Monogram, 3 1/2 x 2 1/4 In. .. 137.00
SILVER-TIBETAN, Ewer, Cover, Dragon Handle, Spout, Repousse Buddhist Symbols, 7 In. 236.00
Vase, Covers, Repousse, Petal Shape Reserves, Buddhist Symbols, 10 In., Pair 325.00
Vase, Repousse Reserves, Animal, Scrolling Leaf Ground, 9 1/2 In. 177.00
Vase, Repousse, Buddhist Symbols, Foo Dog, Ring Handles, 8 In. 189.00

SINCLAIRE cut glass was made by H.P. Sinclaire and Company of Corning, New York, between 1905 and 1929. He cut glass made at other factories until 1920. Pieces were made of crystal as well as amber, blue, green, or ruby glass. Only a small percentage of Sinclaire glass is marked with the S in a wreath.

Basket, Hobstar & Honeycomb, Triple Notched Handle, Signed, 8 x 6 In. 1100.00
Bowl, Engraved Fish In Water, Signed, 9 1/2 In. 715.00
Dish, Brussels Pattern, Oval, 7 3/4 In. 413.00
Punch Set, Hobstar Chain With Cane, Strawberry Diamond, Punty & Fan, 6 Piece 495.00
Teapot, Flower Petals With Silver Thread & Hobstar, 6 x 9 1/2 In. 1375.00
Tray, Hobstar & Intaglio Thistle, Signed, 9 3/4 x 12 1/2 In. 2420.00

SKIING, see Sports category.

SLAG GLASS resembles a marble cake. It can be streaked with different colors. There were many types made from about 1880. Caramel slag is the incorrect name for Chocolate glass. Pink slag was an American Victorian product made by Harry Barstow and Thomas E.A. Dugan at Indiana, Pennsylvania. Purple and blue slag were made in American and English factories. Red slag is a very late Victorian and twentieth-century glass. Other colors are known but are of less importance to the collector. New versions of chocolate glass and colored slag glass are being made.

Purple, Bowl, Hobnail, 3 x 7 1/2 In. 47.00
Purple, Butter, Cover, Figural, Rabbit, Bird, Chicken, 5 In., 3 Piece 59.00
Purple, Cruet Set, Vinegar, Oil, 6 1/2 In., 4 Piece 59.00

SLEEPY EYE collectors look for anything bearing the image of the nineteenth-century Indian chief with the drooping eyelid. The Sleepy Eye Milling Co., Sleepy Eye, Minnesota, used his portrait in advertising from 1883 to 1921. It offered many premiums, including stoneware and pottery steins, crocks, bowls, mugs, and pitchers, all decorated with the famous profile of the Indian. The popular pottery was made by Western Stoneware, Weir Pottery Company, and other companies long after the flour mill went out of business in 1921. Reproductions of the pitchers are being made today. The original pitchers came in only five sizes: 4 inches, 5 1/4 inches, 6 1/2 inches, 8 inches, and 9 inches. The Sleepy Eye image was also used by companies unrelated to the flour mill.

Bowl, Salt, Stoneware 265.00
Cigar Box 500.00
Crock, Butter, Blue & Gray, Old Sleepy Eye, Village Scene 360.00
Crock, Butter, Stoneware, 5 In. 205.00
Fan 450.00
Mug, Old Sleepy Eye, Blue & White, 4 1/4 In. 260.00
Paperweight, Bust Of Indian, Bronze .... 400.00 to 500.00
Pitcher, Blue & Gray, No. 1, 4 In. 350.00
Pitcher, Blue & White, No. 1, 4 In. 150.00
Pitcher, Blue & White, No. 3, 6 1/2 In. 550.00
Pitcher, Blue & Yellow, No. 2, 6 In. .... 150.00 to 213.00
Pitcher, Blue & Yellow, No. 3, 6 1/2 In. 640.00
Pitcher, Blue Rim, No. 2 .... 1500.00
Pitcher, Blue Rim, No. 5, 9 In. .... 450.00 to 770.00
Pitcher, Brown & White, No. 4, 8 In. 4000.00
Pitcher & Mug Set, Green, Brown, Tan, Trees, Teepees, 8 1/2-In. Pitcher, 7 Piece 564.00
Postcard, 5 Piece 200.00
Salt Bowl, Blue & Gray, Stoneware, 4 In. 355.00
Stein, Blue & Gray, 7 1/2 In. .... 500.00 to 600.00
Stein, Blue & Gray, Flemish, Western Stoneware, Monmouth, Ill., 7 1/2 In. .... 154.00 to 350.00
Stein, Western Stoneware, 1979 .... 355.00
Sugar & Creamer, Blue & White 406.00
Vase, Cattails, Indian, Stoneware, 8 1/2 In. .... 245.00 to 310.00
Vase, Old Sleepy Eye, Cattails, Dragonfly, Blue & White, Cylindrical, 8 1/2 In. .... 179.00 to 238.00
Vase, Pillow Case 550.00

SLOT MACHINES are included in the Coin-Operated Machine category.

SMITH BROTHERS glass was made after 1878. Alfred and Harry Smith had worked for the Mt. Washington Glass Company in New Bedford, Massachusetts, for seven years before going into their own shop. They made many pieces with enamel decoration.

Smith Bros. Co.

Biscuit Jar, Pink Flowers, Green Stems, Blue & Cream Ground, Melon Ribbed, 8 In. 375.00
Biscuit Jar, Pink Roses, Green Leafy Stems, Melon Ribbed, Red Lion Mark, 8 In. 430.00
Biscuit Jar, Water Lilies, Leaves, Melon Ribbed, Silver Plated Collar, Handle, 9 In. 430.00
Dish, Sweetmeat, Water Lily, Leaves, Melon Ribbed, Metal Top, 5 1/2 In. 200.00
Jar, Cover, Blue, Red Flowers, Leafy Stems, Melon Ribbed, Signed, 3 1/2 In. 145.00
Sugar & Creamer, Yellow Daisies, Leafy Stems, Melon Ribbed, Signed, 3 In. 145.00
Syrup, Enameled, Violets, Satin Ground, 5 In. 259.00
Syrup, Gold Prunus Flower, Opaque, Melon Ribbed, 6 In. 290.00
Vase, Roses, Blue Ribbon, Leaves, Melon Ribbed, Bulbous Neck, 9 In. 430.00
Vase, Wisteria, Green & Gold Vines, Gold Dotted Rim, Melon Ribbed, 9 In. 460.00

SNOW BABIES, made from bisque and spattered with glitter sand, were first manufactured in 1864 by Hertwig and Company of Thuringia. Other German and Japanese companies copied the Hertwig designs. Originally, Snow Babies were made of candy and used as Christmas decorations. There are also Snow Babies tablewares made by Royal Bayreuth. Copies of the small Snow Babies figurines are being made today and can easily confuse the collector.

Candleholder, Shieldback, Royal Bayreuth, 4 3/4 In. 150.00
Figurine, 2 Babies On Snowy Ledge, Germany, 2 1/2 In. 300.00
Figurine, 2 Babies On Toboggan, Germany 195.00
Figurine, Girl, On Sled, Pink Skirt, Black Shoes, White Coat & Hat, Germany, Early 1900s 107.00
Figurine, Peary & Cooke, North Pole Dispute, Globe, Germany, 5 1/8 In. 2475.00
Figurine, Snow Baby, 2 Huskies Pulling Baby, Germany, 2 3/4 In. 165.00
Figurine, Snow Baby, Feeding Baby Seal, Germany, 2 In. 195.00
Figurine, Snow Baby, Hiding From Polar Bear, Germany, 2 In. 330.00
Figurine, Snow Baby, Mother Pushing Twins, Germany, 2 1/2 In. 358.00
Figurine, Snow Baby, Seal, Ball, Bisque, Germany, 2 In. 195.00
Figurine, Standing, Arms Outstretched, c.1920, 1 1/2 In. 45.00
Figurine Set, Band, Saxophone, Drum, Trumpet, U.S. Zone, Germany, 2 In., 3 Piece 65.00

SNUFF BOTTLES are listed in the Bottle category.

SNUFFBOXES held snuff. Taking snuff was popular long before cigarettes became available. The gentleman or lady would take a small pinch of the ground tobacco or snuff in the fingers, then sniff it and sneeze. Snuffboxes were made of many materials, including gold, silver, enameled metal, and wood. Most snuffboxes date from the late eighteenth or early nineteenth centuries.

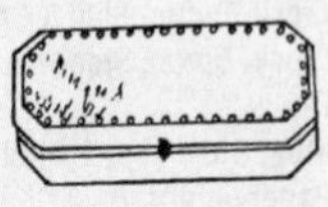

Agate, Victorian, 19th Century, 5/8 x 1 1/2 x 2 In. 146.00
Enamel, Farmers, Butterflies, Leaves, Double, Hinged Cover, France, 1800s, 3 1/4 In. 295.00
George III Bust, Tortoiseshell, c.1800, 2 1/4 In. 825.00
Gilt Copper, Tortoiseshell, Round, Hinged, Inlaid Flowers, Continental, 2 In. 135.00
Horn, Cornucopia Shape, Sterling Silver Mount, Thistles, Scotland, 4 In. 558.00
Horn, Ivory Inlay, Curved Shape, Hinged Lid, Scotland, 1 1/2 x 4 1/2 In. 345.00
Papier-Mache, Border, Lid Medallion, 19th Century, 3/4 x 2 1/2 x 1 1/4 In. 95.00
Porcelain, Scrolled, Gilded Leaves, Enamel, Seaside Landscape, 1800s, 3 1/4 In. 940.00
Silver, Agate, Armorial Crest, Inscription, Norway, Late 1700s, 2 1/4 x 1 x 2 In. 710.00
Silver, Agate, Cartouche Shape, Leaves, Continental, c.1740, 3 In. 1000.00
Silver, Agate, Motto, Let The Deed Shaw, Scotland, George II, c.1760, 2 1/2 In. 580.00
Silver, Gold Plated Edges, Continental, 3/4 x 1 1/2 x 3 In. 235.00
Silver, Oblong, Cast Cover Horse Racing Scene, England, George IV, c.1828, 3 1/2 In. 666.00
Silver, Oblong, Hinged Cover, Cartouche, Decoration, France, Early 1800s, 3 1/4 In. 155.00
Steel, Presentation, Inscription, John Brockford, Lighterman, Surry, 1735, 3 1/4 x 1 1/4 In. 470.00
Tortoiseshell, Burl Walnut, Landscape Print Under Glass, 3 1/4 In. 236.00
Tortoiseshell, Round, Portrait, Washington In Military Uniform, 2 3/4 In. 2415.00
Tortoiseshell, Silver, Mother-Of-Pearl, Scottish Dancing Scene, Oval, Early 1700s, 3 1/4 In. 530.00
Wood, Black Lacquer, Baseball Batter, 1800s, 2 1/2 x 1 1/2 In. 1740.00
Wood, Shoe Shape, Carved, Signed, R, 1 3/4 x 4 1/2 In. 265.00

SOAPSTONE is a mineral that was used for foot warmers or griddles because of its heat-retaining properties. Soapstone was carved into figurines and bowls in many countries in the nineteenth and twentieth centuries. Most of the soapstone seen today is from China or Japan. It is still being carved in the old styles.

Brush Washer, Lotus Leaf & Flower, Yellow, Chinese, 1800s, 2 1/2 In. 380.00
Figurine, Girl Feeding Goose, Chinese, 20th Century, 2 In. 205.00
Figurine, Manjushii On Lion, Chinese, 1800s, 9 In. 1116.00
Figurine, Musicians Playing Instruments, 5 1/2 x 3 1/4 In. 180.00
Figurine, Quan Yin, Chinese, 11 In. 90.00
Group, Quan Yin Riding Horse, Chinese, 12 In. 980.00
Group, Water Buffalo, Chinese, 8 In. 290.00
Incense Burner, Hand Carved, Green, Cover, Chinese, 18 x 20 In. 410.00
Seal, Scholars, Mountain, T'ien Huang Stone, Chinese, Early 1900s, 2 1/4 In. 880.00

SOFT PASTE is a name for a type of pottery. Although it looks very much like porcelain, it is a chemically different material. Most of the soft-paste wares were made in the early nineteenth century. Other pieces may be listed under Gaudy Dutch or Leeds.

Bowl, Blue & White, Oriental Design, Bridge, Leaves, 8 1/2 x 3 3/4 In. 200.00
Cup & Saucer, King's Rose, Queen's Rose & Vine Border, Handleless 165.00
Figurine, Girl, On Pillar, Industry, Idleness, France, c.1900, 10 1/4 In., Pair 700.00
Mug, Child's, Child On Dog, Mother, Transfer, Victorian, Child's 185.00
Plate, King's Rose, Scalloped Rim, 9 1/4 In. 193.00
Plate, Scalloped Rim, King's Rose, 9 1/4 In. 145.00
Soup, Dish, Flowers, Stencil, 9 In. 50.00
Sugar, Cover, Blue Swag & Flowers, 4-Sided 80.00
Sugar, Cover, Flower & Trailing Vine, Ribbed, Scalloped, 1700s, 6 In. 300.00

SOUVENIRS of a trip—what could be more fun? Our ancestors enjoyed the same thing and souvenirs were made for almost every location. Most of the souvenir pottery and porcelain pieces of the nineteenth century were made in England or Germany, even if the picture showed a North American scene. In the twentieth century, the souvenir china business seems to have gone to the manufacturers in Japan, Taiwan, Hong Kong, England, and America. Another popular souvenir item is the souvenir spoon, made of sterling or silver plate. These are usually made in the country pictured on the spoon. Related pieces may be found in the Coronation and World's Fair categories.

Accordion Folder, Bear Mountain Duson River Bridge, East Approach, 1920s 15.00
Accordion Folder, Fort Ticonderoga, N.Y., 1947 .... 15.00
Accordion Folder, Scenic Folder Of Ausable Chasm, N.Y., Curt Teich & Co., Chicago 12.00
Bank, Ceramic, Chicago World's Fair, Round, 5 1/2 x 5 1/2 In. 1020.00
Button, Buffalo Bill, Pawnee Bill, Wild West Shows, Celluloid, 1913, 7/8 In. 920.00
Creamer, Sandstone, Minnesota, Carnival Glass, Near Cut, Marigold 75.00
Fan, Robert Houdini, Boulevart Des Italiens, Black & White, Wood, c.1860 .... 5606.00
Jug, Stoneware, Souvenir Seattle Washington, Wood & Wore Bail Handle, 4 In. 135.00
Mirror, Olympics, 1980, Lake Placid, Winter Games, 3 In. ....7.00 to 9.00
Paperweight, Charleston & West Indian Expo, Negro Building, Glass, 1901-02, 4 x 2 1/2 In. 41.00
Pin, Olympic, 1956, Melbourne, Kenya Team, Multicolored 300.00
Skillet, Smith's Opening 1900, 3 5/8 x 2 5/8 In. 145.00
Spoon, Alaska, Woodsman, Ram, Moose, Prospector, Huskie, Sterling Silver, 4 In. 45.00
Spoon, Angels, California, Mining Theme, Shovel Shape, Gold Pan, c.1930, 3 1/2 In. 345.00
Spoon, Charleston & West Indian Expo, Sterling Silver, Palm Tree, 1901-02, 5 1/2 In. 35.00
Spoon, Grant's Tomb, Inscription, Dedicated April 27, 1897 .... 36.00
Spoon, Pomona, California, Sterling Silver 40.00
Tape Measure, Goose, Niagara Falls, Celluloid, Made In Germany, 1930s, 1 1/2 In. 106.00
Tumbler, Charleston & West Indian Expo, Woman, Seated Robed, 1901-02, 3 1/2 In. 33.00
Tumbler, Spirit Of St. Louis, Pictures Of Statue Of Liberty, Eiffel Tower, Milk Glass, 4 In. 150.00

SPANGLE GLASS is multicolored glass made from odds and ends of colored glass rods. It includes metallic flakes of mica covered with gold, silver, nickel, or copper. Spangle glass is usually cased with a thin layer of clear glass over the multicolored layer. Similar glass is listed in the Vasa Murrhina category.

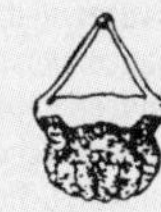

Basket, Cased Yellow, Butterscotch & Silver Mica, Clear Reeded Handle, 6 x 4 1/2 In. 55.00
Basket, Opal, Cranberry, Silver Mica, Crystal Rigaree Rim, Thorn Handle, 8 x 11 In. 375.00
Bottle, Dresser, Blue, Bird, Grass, Enamel, Faceted Stopper, 8 1/2 In. 173.00
Cruet, Cranberry Spatter, Gold Mica, Applied Handle, Faceted Stopper, 5 3/4 In. 175.00
Pitcher, Pink & Green Spatter, Silver Mica, Clear Reeded Handle, 8 3/4 In. 200.00
Pitcher, White, Apricot Spatter, Silver Mica Highlights, Star Crimped Rim, 8 1/2 In. 130.00
Rose Bowl, Cranberry Shaded To White, Silver Mica, Folded Rim, Hobbs Brockunier, 4 In. 110.00
Rose Bowl, End Of Day, Brown, Green, Ruffled Rim, 4 Clear Feet, 4 x 5 In. 325.00
Rose Bowl, Pink Over White, Case, Silver Mica Flakes, Victorian, 4 3/4 In. 58.00
Vase, Brown Cased, Multicolored Spatter, Mica Flecks, 9 1/2 In. 58.00
Vase, Pink Cased, Pink Mica, Twisted Crystal Rigaree, Flared Ruffled Rim, 9 1/2 In. 365.00

SPATTER GLASS is a multicolored glass made from many small pieces of different colored glass. It is sometimes called *End-of-Day* glass. It is still being made.

Cruet, Blue, 6 In. 75.00
Pitcher, Blue & White, Ribbed, 8 1/4 In. 175.00
Sugar Shaker, Cranberry, Opal, Late 1800s, 4 1/2 In. 173.00

SPATTERWARE is the creamware or soft paste dinnerware decorated with colored spatter designs. The earliest pieces were made in the late eighteenth century, but most of the spatterware found today was made from about 1800 to 1850, or it is a form of kitchen crockery with added spatter designs, made in the late nineteenth and twentieth centuries. The early spatterware was made in the Staffordshire district of England for sale in America. The later kitchen type is an American product.

Basket, Cased, Applied Clear Thorn Handle, 1900s, 6 1/2 In. 115.00

Bowl, Crescent Moon, Blue, Brown Flowers, 4 In. 35.00
Bowl, Holly Berry, Purple, Paneled, 4 In. 176.00
Bowl, Peafowl, 10 1/2 In. 910.00
Bowl, Sauce, Peafowl, Red, Purple, 5 In. 300.00
Bowl, Umbrella, Blue Paneled Border, 10 1/4 In. 3190.00
Creamer, Acorn, Red, Square Handles, Elongated Spout, 5 In. 470.00
Creamer, Fort, Green Flowers, Blue Ground, Paneled, 5 In. 330.00
Creamer, Peafowl, Blue, Paneled Baluster, Staffordshire, c.1840, 6 In. 390.00
Creamer, Rainbow, Red, Blue, Green, Bulbous, Loop Handle, 3 3/4 In. 110.00
Creamer, Rainbow, Red, Blue, Green, Scrolled Handle, Elongated Spout, 4 3/4 In. 330.00
Creamer, Tulip, Blue, Scrolled Handle, Elongated Spout, 1934, 5 3/4 In. 415.00
Creamer, Tulip, Purple, Red, Blue Tips, 5 3/4 In. 440.00
Cup, Crisscross, Strawberry, Blue Spatter, Applied Loop Handle, Child's, 2 3/4 In. 770.00
Cup, Mush, Peafowl, Green Splotches, 2 3/4 In. 155.00
Cup & Saucer, 4-Petal Flower, Blue, Red Border, Handleless 495.00
Cup & Saucer, 6-Point Star, Blue, Handleless 145.00
Cup & Saucer, Acorn, Blue Border, Handleless 2750.00
Cup & Saucer, Acorn, Red Border, Handleless 1375.00
Cup & Saucer, Bull's-Eye, Rainbow, Christmas Colors 405.00
Cup & Saucer, Christmas Ball, Red, Green, Handleless 3300.00
Cup & Saucer, Cluster Of Buds, Blue Flower Panels, Impressed Harvey 110.00
Cup & Saucer, Dot, Purple & Red Spatter, Handleless 415.00
Cup & Saucer, Peafowl, 4-Color, Green Surround, Brown Spatter, Handleless 635.00
Cup & Saucer, Peafowl, Blue, Green & Red, Handleless, Demitasse 310.00
Cup & Saucer, Peafowl, Red 165.00
Cup & Saucer, Peafowl, Teal, Handleless 195.00
Cup & Saucer, Rainbow, Red, Yellow, Handleless, Child's 935.00
Cup & Saucer, Red, Applied Loop Handle, Child's 55.00
Cup & Saucer, Red, Parrot, 3 Colors, Handleless 550.00
Cup & Saucer, Rose, Black, Brown, Handleless ....195.00 to 300.00
Cup & Saucer, Rose, Red, Black & Brown Border, Handleless 300.00
Cup & Saucer, School House, Blue, Paneled, Handleless 495.00
Cup & Saucer, School House, Red, Handleless 1045.00
Cup & Saucer, Thistle, Rainbow, Red, Yellow, Handleless 2090.00
Cup & Saucer, Tulip Variant, Purple, Green, Handleless 5775.00
Cup & Saucer, Tulip, Red, Blue Spatter, Impressed Anchor, Handleless 415.00
Cup & Saucer, Tulip, Red, Yellow Border, Handleless 990.00
Cup & Saucer, Tulip, Yellow, Handleless 990.00
Cup Plate, 4-Petal Flower, Brown, Staffordshire, c.1840, 4 In., Pair 1076.00
Cup Plate, Bull's-Eye, Rainbow, Pink, Green, Staffordshire, c.1840, 4 In., Pair 191.00
Cup Plate, School House, Red, Blue, Green, 4 3/4 In. 110.00
Cup Plate, Tulip, Blue Spatter, 4 1/8 In. 121.00
Mug, Rainbow, Brown & Blue, Straight Sides, Loop Handle, 5 In. 1045.00
Mug, Strawberry, Crisscross, Blue, Loop Handle, Child's, 2 1/4 In. 880.00
Pepper Pot, Blue, Bulbous, Footed Base, 3 3/4 In. 94.00
Pepper Pot, Dome Cover, Rainbow, Red, Blue, Button Finial, 5 In. 1980.00
Pitcher, Acorn, Purple Spatter, Paneled, Squared Handle, Elongated Spout, 7 1/2 In. 4400.00
Pitcher, Building, Trees, Grass, Blue, Staffordshire, c.1840, 7 1/2 In. 295.00
Pitcher, Cream, Tulip, Blue Spatter, Paneled, Scrolled Handle, 1934, 5 3/4 In. 413.00
Pitcher, Cream, Tulip, Blue, Paneled, Square Handle, 5 1/4 In. 415.00
Pitcher, Flower Buds Cluster, Blue, Red, Green, 8 5/8 In. 633.00
Pitcher, Fort, Blue, Molded Spout, Handle, Fortress Design, 7 1/4 In. 115.00
Pitcher, Peafowl, Blue, Staffordshire, c.1840, 6 In. 657.00
Pitcher, Rainbow, 5-Color, Bulbous, Embossed Swag, Scroll Handle, 8 3/4 In. 4675.00
Pitcher, Rose, Blue, Paneled, Loop Handle, 9 3/4 In. 605.00
Pitcher, School House, Blue, Baluster, Flaring Spout & Foot, c.1835, 10 1/4 In. 5378.00
Pitcher, Water, Peafowl, Blue, Loop Handle, 10 1/4 In. 330.00
Pitcher & Bowl, Fort, Blue, Square Handle, Elongated Spout, 12 & 13 1/2 In. 715.00
Plate, Acorn, Purple Paneled Border, 8 1/4 In. 2200.00
Plate, Acorn, Purple, Paneled, 9 1/4 In. 935.00
Plate, Bull's-Eye, Rainbow, Red, Green, 9 1/2 In. 176.00

Plate, Cockscomb, Yellow Paneled Border, 9 3/4 In. 2750.00
Plate, Cup, Tulip, Blue, 4 1/8 In. 121.00
Plate, Dahlia, 2-Color Flower, Purple Paneled Border, 8 1/4 In. 495.00
Plate, Dahlia, Rainbow, Blue, Green, Paneled, 8 1/4 In. 1540.00
Plate, Dahlia, Red, 8 In. 660.00
Plate, Fort, Blue Paneled Border, 8 In. 715.00
Plate, Hex Sign, Red Border, 9 In. 165.00
Plate, Peafowl, 4 Colors, Blue Paneled Border, 7 1/2 In. 495.00
Plate, Peafowl, 4 Colors, Red Paneled Border, 8 1/2 In. 880.00
Plate, Peafowl, Blue, 9 1/2 In. 248.00
Plate, Peafowl, Blue, Paneled, 9 1/2 In. 413.00
Plate, Peafowl, Blue, Paneled, 10 7/8 In. 115.00
Plate, Peafowl, Folky, 4 Colors, Blue Border, 8 3/4 In. 770.00
Plate, Peafowl, Green Tree, Impressed Heart, England, 9 5/8 In. 978.00
Plate, Peafowl, Green, 4 Colors, 9 1/8 In. 550.00
Plate, Peafowl, Green, Spray, 8 1/2 In. 880.00
Plate, Peafowl, On Branch, Red, Yellow, Blue, 8 1/2 In. 465.00
Plate, Peafowl, Red, 4 Colors, 8 1/2 In. 330.00
Plate, Peafowl, Red, Paneled, 7 1/2 In. 193.00
Plate, Rainbow, Concentric Circles, Red, Blue, Green, Scalloped Edge, 9 1/2 In. 575.00
Plate, Rainbow, Mulberry, Green, Yellow, Black, 8 1/4 In. 4600.00
Plate, Rainbow, Red, Blue, Green, Scalloped Edge, Impressed Adam, 7 1/4 In. 264.00
Plate, Rainbow, Scalloped Rim, Red, Blue, Green, 7 1/4 In. 264.00
Plate, Rose, Red, Green Leaves, Blue Paneled Border, 9 5/8 In. 413.00
Plate, Rosebud, Blue Border, Paneled, 9 1/2 In. 360.00
Plate, School House, Blue Building, Red Over Brown, Green Flowers, 8 In. 3300.00
Plate, School House, Green, Staffordshire, c.1840, 8 1/4 In., Pair 10755.00
Plate, School House, Red Building, Green Border, 7 5/8 In. 3190.00
Plate, School House, Red, Yellow Roof, Blue Paneled Border, 8 1/4 In. 3960.00
Plate, Thistle, Rainbow, Paneled, Red & Green Vertical Bands, 7 1/8 In. 605.00
Plate, Thistle, Red, Black, Staffordshire, c.1840, 8 1/4 In. 9560.00
Plate, Toddy, Swag, Rainbow, Yellow, Red, Green, Staffordshire, c.1840, 5 In. 7170.00
Plate, Toddy, Thistle, Alternating Red & Blue Border, 6 1/4 In. 1375.00
Plate, Tulip, Blue & Green Rainbow, Staffordshire, c.1840, 7 In. 7170.00
Plate, Tulip, Blue, Red, Purple & Black Rainbow Paneled Border, 9 1/4 In. 550.00
Plate, Tulip, Red, Blue Tips, Red Paneled Border, 7 1/4 In. 248.00
Plate, Tulip, Red, Purple Paneled Border, 8 1/4 In. ....1320.00 to 1595.00
Plate, Tulip, Yellow, Red, Green, Paneled, 8 5/8 In. 5225.00
Plate Set, Acorn, Purple, Staffordshire, c.1840, 8 In., 8 Piece 6573.00
Plate Set, Dinner, Peafowl, Blue, Paneled, Staffordshire, 9 1/4 In., 4 Piece 1315.00
Platter, Bull's-Eye, Rainbow, Purple, Black, Bands, 13 3/8 In. 7150.00
Platter, Horses, Blue, Red Transfer Scene, 16 In. 440.00
Platter, Peafowl, Brown & Yellow, Green Tree, 15 x 11 In. 1610.00
Platter, Peafowl, Green Tree, Brown, Yellow, 1 3/8 x 15 x 11 1/4 In. 1610.00
Platter, Peafowl, Red, Adams, Staffordshire, c.1840, 15 In. 1793.00
Platter, Peafowl, Red, Staffordshire, c.1840, 13 1/2 In. ....1434.00 to 2629.00
Platter, Thistle, Blue, 8-Sided, Staffordshire, c.1840, 14 1/2 In. 5378.00
Sauce, Peafowl, 4 Colors, Red, 5 In. 303.00
Saucer, Cluster Of Buds, Red Border, Impressed Harvey 121.00
Saucer, Peafowl, Green, 4 Colors 61.00
Saucer, Tulip, Blue Border 94.00
Spoon Rest, Tulip, Blue, Elongated Shell Shape, 8 3/4 In. 3190.00
Sugar, Brown, Rose, 6 In. 330.00
Sugar, Cover, Blue, Shed, Rosette Finial, 9 1/2 In. 990.00
Sugar, Cover, Dahlia, Blue 55.00
Sugar, Cover, Fort, Blue, Bulbous, 4 1/2 In. 303.00
Sugar, Cover, Holly Berry, Bulbous, Purple, 5 3/4 In. 165.00
Sugar, Cover, Rainbow, Red & Green, 4 1/4 In. 205.00
Sugar, Cover, Rose, Blue, 4 In. 110.00
Sugar, Cover, Vertical Bands, Red, Green, 4 1/8 x 4 1/2 x 4 1/2 In. 460.00
Sugar, Rooster, Red, 4 Colors, Embossed Floral Finial On Lid, 4 1/2 In. 550.00

Sugar, Thistle, Yellow Spatter, Paneled, Shell Shape Handles, 7 3/4 In. 2640.00
Tea Bowl & Saucer, Peafowl, Blue, Staffordshire, c.1840, 2 Each ....418.00 to 657.00
Tea Bowl & Saucer, Peafowl, Pink & Blue Rainbow, Staffordshire, c.1840 .... 2271.00
Teapot, 4-Petal Flower, Red, 6 1/2 In. 413.00
Teapot, Peafowl, Blue, Staffordshire, c.1840 .... 568.00
Teapot, Peafowl, Red, c.1840, 6 1/4 In. 717.00
Teapot, Peafowl, Red, Staffordshire, c.1840, 7 In. ....896.00 to 2390.00
Teapot, Peafowl, Scrolled Handle, Gooseneck Spout, 7 3/4 In. 578.00
Teapot, Rainbow, Paneled Shape, Black, Purple 10 1/2 In. 345.00
Teapot, Thistle, Red, Staffordshire, c.1840, 7 In. 2868.00
Teapot, Tree, Red, c.1850, 6 1/2 In. 3466.00
Teapot, Tulip, Blue Border, Gooseneck Spout, Scroll Handle, 5 3/4 In. 330.00
Teapot, Tulip, Blue, Paneled, Square Handle, Gooseneck Spout, 7 3/4 In. 660.00
Toddy Plate, Castle, Blue, c.1840, 5 In., Pair 508.00
Vase, Egg Shape, Blue & Green Leaves, 1800s, 9 1/2 In. 115.00
Washbowl, Pitcher, Rainbow, Green, Red, Bulbous Pitcher, 11 3/4 & 13 1/2 In. 3450.00
Waste Bowl, Peafowl, Red, Staffordshire, c.1840, 6 1/2 In. 448.00
Waste Bowl, Red, Primrose Pattern, Yellow Center, Purple Flower, 3 x 5 In. 1210.00

SPELTER is a synonym for a zinc alloy. Figurines, candlesticks, and other pieces were made of spelter and given a bronze or painted finish. The metal has been used since about the 1860s to make statues, tablewares, and lamps that resemble bronze. Spelter is soft and breaks easily. To test for spelter, scratch the base of the piece. Bronze is solid; spelter will show a silvery scratch.

Figure, Bird Dog, Cast, 7 x 17 In. 100.00
Figure, Dancer, Headdress, Patinated, Painted, Marble Base, Continental, 1920s, 14 1/2 In. 755.00
Figure, Lady, Holding Orb Clock, Hollow Cast, Bronze Patina, 39 In. 1323.00
Figure, Stag, Cast, 8 In. 70.00
Figure, Toad, Green Surface, 2 1/2 In. 115.00
Figure, Woman, Seated, Classical Style, 10 1/2 x 10 In. 88.00
Statue, Boy In Robe, 25 In. 295.00

SPINNING WHEELS in the corner have been symbols of earlier times for the past 100 years. Although spinning wheels date back to medieval days, the ones found today are rarely more than 200 years old. Because the style of the spinning wheel changed very little, it is often impossible to place an exact date on a wheel.

Canted Legs, Tulip Feet, Multicolored, 47 1/2 x 31 In. 495.00
Carved, Turned, 19th Century, 59 1/2 In. 115.00
Mixed Woods, Turned Spindles, Phila., 19th Century, 39 In. 265.00

SPODE pottery, porcelain, and bone china were made by the Stoke-on-Trent factory of England founded by Josiah Spode about 1770. The firm became Copeland and Garrett from 1833 to 1847, then W.T. Copeland or W.T. Copeland and Sons until 1976. It then became Royal Worcester Spode Ltd. The word *Spode* appears on many pieces made by the factories. Most collectors include all the wares under the more familiar name of Spode. Porcelains may be listed in this book by the name that appears on the piece. Related pieces may be listed under Copeland, Copeland Spode, and Royal Worcester.

Bowl, Fairyland Luster, Raspberry Ground, Gilt Chinoiserie Decoration, 5 x 10 In. 936.00
Dinner Service, Kensington, 154 Piece 1638.00
Fruit Cooler, Cover, Liner, Flowers, Footed, c.1815, 12 In., Pair 5100.00
Mug, Imari Style Decoration, 2 1/2 In. 90.00
Plate, Apple Green Ground, Flowers, c.1810, 8 1/2 In., 14 Piece 5700.00
Plate, Molded Edge, Painted, Green, Gilt, Flower Sprays, c.1820, 12 Piece 195.00
Plate, Salad, Camilla, Blue, 6 1/2 In. 14.00
Platter, Blue Transfer, Castle, Cows, Bridges, Trees, Birds, 19 In. 330.00
Platter, Imari, 19th Century, 14 5/8 x 10 7/8 In. 460.00
Tea Set, Japan Pattern, Geometrics, Leaves, England, c.1815, 22 Piece 646.00

Tureen, Cover, Underplate, Green, c.1840, 6 1/2 x 7 1/2 In. 205.00

SPONGEWARE is very similar to spatterware in appearance. The designs were applied to the ceramics by daubing the color on with a sponge or cloth. Many collectors do not differentiate between spongeware and spatterware and use the names interchangeably. Modern pottery is being made to resemble the old spongeware, but careful examination will show it is new.

Bowl, Green, White, 2 Blue Bands, 12 1/2 In. 35.00
Bowl, Vegetable, Blue, White, 9 3/4 In. 121.00
Bowl Set, Maple Leaf, Multicolored, Portneuf, 8 1/2 In., 6 Piece 362.00
Charger, Rabbit & Frog Border, Vines, Stick Spatter Flowers, Red, Green, Blue, 13 In. 575.00
Creamer, Blue, Tulip, Square Handle, Elongated Spout, 5 1/4 In. 413.00
Creamer, Cow, 4 Colors, Oval Base, Blue Sponge, Yellow Ground, 4 1/4 x 6 1/2 In. 440.00
Creamer, Cow, Blue, Yellow Ground, 4 1/4 x 6 1/2 In. 440.00
Crock, Butter, Wood Cover, Blue, White, Bail Handle, 6 1/4 In. 70.00
Cup & Saucer, Center Black Stag, Handleless 1100.00
Cup & Saucer, Cluster Of Buds, Green, Handleless 95.00
Cup & Saucer, Rainbow, Blue, Red, Green, Concentric Circles, Ear Handle 85.00
Cup & Saucer Set, Rosette, Red, Green, Portneuf, 3 In., 6 Piece 152.00
Figurine, Dog, Boxer, Molded, Blue, Dotted Eyes, Hollow, 6 1/2 In. 1265.00
Mixing Bowl, Blue, White, Blue Bands, 11 In. 137.00
Mug, Bull's-Eye, Brown, Yellow Dot Corners, Band, 4 1/2 In. 275.00
Pitcher, 3 Bands, Gunmetal Brown, Green, Amber Ground, 8 3/4 x 5 In. 6465.00
Pitcher, Blue, White, 8 1/4 In. 360.00
Plate, Rabbit & Frog Border, Red & Blue Blooms, Red Vines, Green Leaves, 9 1/4 In. 200.00
Plate Set, Rosette Pattern, Red, Green, Portneuf, 8 1/2 In., 8 Piece 305.00
Soup, Dish, Underplate, Blue, White, 8 1/4 In. 33.00
Tankard, 19th Century, 9 In. 250.00

SPORTS equipment, sporting goods, brochures, and related items are listed here. Items are listed by sport. Other categories of interest are Advertising, Bicycle, Card, Fishing, Sword, Toy, and Trap. Kentucky Derby glasses are listed in the Decorated Tumblers category.

Auto Racing, Pennant, Indianapolis 500, Green With Red Border, Car & Driver 300.00
Auto Racing, Program, National Championship Classic, L.A., Thanksgiving Day, 1923 .... 40.00
Auto Racing, Race Suit, Mario Andretti, Grand-Prix Used, 1993 .... 1624.00
Auto Racing, Tire, Autographed, Davey Allison, Daytona 500 Used, 1992 .... 1044.00
Baseball, Ball, Autographed, Atlanta Braves, N.L. Champions, 1991 .... 340.00
Baseball, Ball, Autographed, Billy Martin 410.00
Baseball, Ball, Autographed, Casey Stengel 2039.00
Baseball, Ball, Autographed, Cincinnati Reds, 1940 .... 1540.00
Baseball, Ball, Autographed, Connie Mack 2826.00
Baseball, Ball, Autographed, Detroit Tigers, Owned By Clubhouse Mgr., 1955 .... 175.00
Baseball, Ball, Autographed, Early Wynn 175.00
Baseball, Ball, Autographed, Hank Greenberg 1086.00
Baseball, Ball, Autographed, Honus Wagner, 1944 .... 4815.00
Baseball, Ball, Autographed, Lefty Gomez 500.00
Baseball, Ball, Autographed, Lefty Grove 3300.00
Baseball, Ball, Autographed, Memphis Red Sox, Negro League, 1955 .... 300.00
Baseball, Ball, Autographed, New York Giants, 1954 .... 750.00
Baseball, Ball, Autographed, New York Yankees, 26 Signatures, 1948 .... 2088.00
Baseball, Ball, Autographed, Oakland Athletics, A.L. Champions, 1990 .... 212.00
Baseball, Ball, Autographed, Reggie Jackson 493.00
Baseball, Ball, Autographed, Sandy Koufax 449.00
Baseball, Ball, Autographed, Satchel Paige .... 1160.00 to 3511.00
Baseball, Ball, Autographed, St. Louis Cardinals, 34 Signatures, 1949 .... 812.00
Baseball, Ball, Autographed, Ty Cobb, 4/24/59 .... 3190.00
Baseball, Ball, Figure Eight Style, c.1870 .... 555.00
Baseball, Ball, Goose Tatum Home Run, 1946-47 .... 1210.00
Baseball, Ball, Lemon Peel, c.1840 .... 1086.00

Baseball, Bandanna, Boston Braves, Mat, Frame, 1914, 23 x 23 1/2 In. 1508.00
Baseball, Banner, Louisville Slugger, c.1940, 36 x 56 In. 523.00
Baseball, Bat Rack, Hillerich & Bradsby, Metal, 12 Holders, 1940s, 47 x 18 x 23 In. 1853.00
Baseball, Bat Rack, Spalding, Wood, c.1910-15, 72 In. 3850.00
Baseball, Bat Rack, Worth, World's Largest Manufacturer, 48 Holders, 1960s, 54 In. 690.00
Baseball, Bat, Autographed, Cal Ripken Jr., Louisville Slugger, 1985 .... 543.00
Baseball, Bat, Autographed, Hank Aaron, Hillerich & Bradsby, Model A99, 1965-68, 35 In. 3190.00
Baseball, Bat, Autographed, Joe DiMaggio, Louisville Slugger 740.00
Baseball, Bat, Autographed, Lou Brock, Louisville Slugger, 1977-79, 34 1/2 In. 1485.00
Baseball, Bat, Autographed, Pee Wee Reese, Hillerich & Bradsby, Model S100, 1954, 33 In. 1508.00
Baseball, Bat, Autographed, Rickey Henderson, Louisville Slugger, 1984 .... 449.00
Baseball, Bat, Autographed, Stan Musial, Adirondack, Model 57B, 1958-60, 34 1/4 In. 3480.00
Baseball, Bat, Autographed, Ted Williams, Louisville Slugger 505.00
Baseball, Bat, Brooks Robinson, Adirondack, Game Used, 1971-79 .... 985.00
Baseball, Bat, Eddie Collins Decal, c.1910-15, 18 In. 575.00
Baseball, Bat, Eddie Murray, Cooper, Pro 100, Game Used, 1969-70 .... 458.00
Baseball, Bat, Harry Gowdy Decal, c.1910-15, 35 1/2 In. 990.00
Baseball, Bat, Honus Wagner Decal, c.1910-15, 12 In. 2090.00
Baseball, Bat, Jim Delahanty Decal, 1910, 34 1/2 In. 1925.00
Baseball, Bat, Joe Jackson Decal, c.1910-15, 33 In. 2860.00
Baseball, Bat, Oakland, World Series Champions, Louisville Slugger, 1989 .... 35.00
Baseball, Bat, Pete Rose, Hillerich & Bradsby, Game Used, 1969-70 .... 2120.00
Baseball, Bat, Reggie Jackson, Adirondack, Model 288RJ, Game Used, 1980-82, 34 1/2 In. 930.00
Baseball, Bat, Ty Cobb Decal, c.1910, 34 1/2 In. 5500.00
Baseball, Bat, Ty Cobb Decal, c.1910-15, 14 In. 1760.00
Baseball, Bat, Victor, No. 94, Model 2, 1910s, 31 1/2 In. 1606.00
Baseball, Bat, Winchester, No. 2400, 33 3/4 In. 150.00
Baseball, Booklet, Science Of Batting, Ty Cobb On Cover 1650.00
Baseball, Button, 1927 Yankees, Murderers Row, Celluloid, 1929, 1 1/8 In. 2900.00
Baseball, Button, Detroit Tigers, Champions, 4 Players, Orange Ground, 1934, 1 3/4 In. 1045.00
Baseball, Button, Lou Gehrig, Never Forgotten, Ball, Bat, Plastic, 1940s, 1 5/8 In. 1765.00
Baseball, Button, Mantle, Ruth, Maris, Greatest Home Run Hitters, 1961, 6 In. 1275.00
Baseball, Button, Mickey Mantle Fan Club, Celluloid, 1952, 1 1/4 In. 5800.00
Baseball, Button, Miller Huggins, Diamond Gum, 1900, 7/8 In. 418.00
Baseball, Button, Philadelphia Athletics, Celluloid, 7/8 In. 65.00
Baseball, Button, Philadelphia Athletics, World Champions, U.S. Flag Ribbon, 1913, 2 3/4 In. 1275.00
Baseball, Cap, Autographed, Cal Ripken Jr., Baltimore Orioles, Game Used 2120.00
Baseball, Cap, New York Yankees, 1932 .... 1900.00
Baseball, Cap, Philadelphia A's, Royal Blue, Spalding, Mitchel & Ness Tag, c.1949 .... 360.00
Baseball, Catcher's Chest Protector, Canvas, Shoulder Straps, Leather Neck Pad, c.1900 .... 1100.00
Baseball, Catcher's Mask, Birdcage, 1890s, 11 x 6 In. 679.00
Baseball, Catcher's Mask, Leather Chin, Forehead Padding, c.1890-1910 .... 385.00
Baseball, Catcher's Mask, Steel Wire, Leather Padding, c.1900 .... 315.00
Baseball, Display, Homerun Derby, Mantle & Maris Race, Card Stock, 12 x 52, c.1961 .... 1650.00
Baseball, Fan, Christy Mathewson, A Fan For A Fan, c.1910 .... 1928.00
Baseball, Fan, Scorecard, Major League Managers, Cardboard, c.1910, 14 In. 550.00
Baseball, Figure, Ernie Banks, Hartland, Box, Tag 610.00
Baseball, Figure, Harmon Killebrew, Box 740.00
Baseball, Glove, Autographed, Tom Seaver, Rawlings, Wingtip, 1979-84 .... 3615.00
Baseball, Glove, Babe Ruth Home Run Special, A.J. Reach, Box, 8 1/2 x 9 1/2 In. 3614.00
Baseball, Glove, Don Drysdale Model, Spalding, Box, 1960s 815.00
Baseball, Glove, Fielder's, Dizzy Dean Model, A.J. Reach, Box, 9 1/4 x 8 1/4 In. 1045.00
Baseball, Glove, Winchester, Youth, No. 2144, Left Hand Model 615.00
Baseball, Helmet, Autographed, Mickey Mantle 670.00
Baseball, Helmet, Chicago Cubs, Game Used, 1970s 725.00
Baseball, Home Plate, Autographed, Mickey Mantle 610.00
Baseball, Jersey, Andre Dawson, Chicago Cubs, Home, Game Used, 1988 .... 1485.00
Baseball, Jersey, Autographed, Joe DiMaggio 2530.00
Baseball, Jersey, Bob Gibson, St. Louis Cardinals, Home, Game Used, 1971 .... 5538.00
Baseball, Jersey, Ryne Sandberg, Chicago Cubs, Home, Game Used, 1983 .... 5656.00
Baseball, Leather, Frank Baker, 1911, 11 3/4 x 9 3/4 In. 5824.00

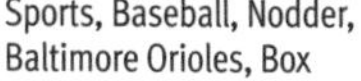
Sports, Baseball, Nodder, Baltimore Orioles, Box

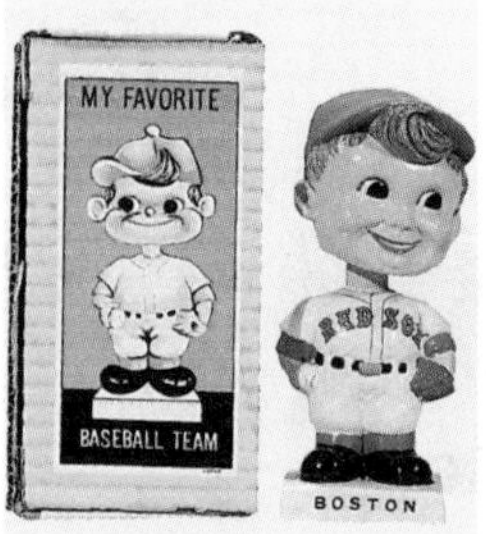

Sports, Baseball, Nodder, Boston Red Sox, Box

Sports, Baseball, Nodder, Cleveland Indians, Box

Baseball, Leather, Walter Johnson, 1912 .... 22040.00
Baseball, Letter, Autographed, Ty Cobb, Personal Stationery, Dated April 26, 1937 .... 3800.00
Baseball, Letter, Connie Mack, Regarding Joe Cronin, Handwritten, Signed, April, 1944 .... 415.00
Baseball, Letter, Connie Mack, To Jimmie Dykes, Typewritten, 1922 .... 140.00
Baseball, Mask, Babe Ruth, Feen-A-Mint, 1933, 6 1/2 x 9 1/2 In. 1160.00
Baseball, Nodder, Baltimore Orioles, Box .... *ILLUS* 140.00
Baseball, Nodder, Boston Red Sox, Box .... *ILLUS* 224.00
Baseball, Nodder, Chicago Cubs, Black Player, 1962-66 .... 1160.00
Baseball, Nodder, Cleveland Indians, Box .... *ILLUS* 196.00
Baseball, Nodder, Roberto Clemente, 1961-63 .... 2090.00
Baseball, Nodder, Roger Maris, N.Y. Decal, Mr. Home Run, Box, 1961-63 .... 1855.00
Baseball, Nodder, Washington Senators, Black Player, 1962-66 .... 696.00
Baseball, Pants, Autographed, Willie Mays, San Francisco Giants, 1969 .... 2285.00
Baseball, Pennant, Baltimore Orioles, Orange & Black, Full Size, 1971 .... 135.00
Baseball, Pennant, Brooklyn Dodgers, Da Bums, Felt, Green Ground, 1956, 28 1/2 In. 695.00
Baseball, Pennant, Chicago White Sox, c.1910, 33 In. 2985.00
Baseball, Pennant, Connie Mack, Philadelphia Athletics, World's Series, c.1929 .... 3410.00
Baseball, Pennant, Joe Tinker, ChiFeds, Felt, 1914-15, 36 In. 3658.00
Baseball, Pennant, New York Giants, Polo Grounds, Felt, Black, Orange, 1950s, 30 1/2 In. 95.00
Baseball, Pennant, New York Yankees, Stadium, Blue, White, Felt, 1950s, 34 In. 55.00
Baseball, Photograph, Autographed, Roger Maris, Black & White, 10 x 8 In. 1170.00
Baseball, Photograph, Autographed, Roger Maris, Color, Frame, 16 x 14 In. 1606.00
Baseball, Photograph, Autographed, Satchel Paige, Black & White, 8 x 10 In. 605.00
Baseball, Photograph, Effa Manley, Matte Finish, 10 x 13 In. 110.00
Baseball, Photograph, International League Champions, Utica, 1886, 16 x 20 In. 1320.00
Baseball, Photograph, Louisville Colonels, 1938, 11 x 18 In. 495.00
Baseball, Photograph, Philadelphia Athletics, Shibe Park, Black & White, 1931 .... 275.00
Baseball, Photograph, Satchel Paige, Goose Tatum, Black & White, c.1940, 11 x 12 In. 250.00
Baseball, Photograph, Ted Williams & Babe Ruth Shaking Hands, Signed J. Dempsey 375.00
Baseball, Pitcher's Mound Tamper, Wooden Plinth, Cast Iron Bracket, 32 In. 2530.00
Baseball, Plate, Philadelphia Athletics, World's Champions, Florence Cook, 1911, 10 In. 810.00
Baseball, Pocket Mirror, Pittsburg Pirates, NL Champions, Celluloid, 1909, 2 1/4 In. 1160.00
Baseball, Poster, Louisville Slugger, Famous Sluggers Of 1930, 24 x 18 In. 1980.00
Baseball, Poster, N.Y. Black Yankees vs. Indianapolis Clowns, c.1956, 22 1/4 x 14 In. 2015.00
Baseball, Program, 1911 World Championship Series, Giants vs. Athletics 1625.00
Baseball, Program, 1915 World Series, Red Sox vs. Philadelphia 2320.00
Baseball, Program, 1919 World Series, Golden Jubilee, Cincinnati Reds, 1869-1919, 50 Pages 510.00
Baseball, Program, 1928 World Series, Yankees vs. Cardinals 2610.00
Baseball, Scoreboard, Wood, National, American Leagues, c.1900-20, 22 x 64 In., 2 Piece 2310.00
Baseball, Scorecard, Brooklyn Federal League, 1915, 9 x 6 In., 12 Pages 1327.00
Baseball, Season Pass, 1925, National League Golden Jubilee, Original Leather Case 1650.00
Baseball, Season Pass, 1925, Sterling Silver, Marked Lambert Bros., N.Y. 770.00
Baseball, Seat, Ebbets Field, Cast Iron Frame, Wood, Dodger Blue, Double 4024.00
Baseball, Sheet Music, Base Ball Gallop, Lyon & Healy Base Ball Club, c.1870 .... 1510.00
Baseball, Sheet Music, Base Ball Quadrille, Henry Von Gudera, 1867 .... 9280.00

Game-worn All-Star uniforms and shoes are the best things to collect from an All-Star Game. Other collectibles are mass-produced and widely available.

Sports, Baseball, Ticket Stub, 1923 World Series, Giants At Yankees, Game 5

Baseball, Silk, 1911 New York Giants, Tobacco Premium, Beige, 30 In. 1100.00
Baseball, Silk, 1911 Philadelphia Athletics, Tobacco Premium, Purple, 30 In. 495.00
Baseball, Silk, 1912 Boston Red Sox, Tobacco Premium, Red, 30 In. 2420.00
Baseball, Sled, Mike King Kelley, Wood, Cast Iron Runners, c.1888 . . . . 4950.00
Baseball, Spikes, Ryne Sandberg, Game Used, 1984 . . . . 410.00
Baseball, Spikes, Willie Mays, Autographed, Game Used, 1971 . . . . 5140.00
Baseball, Ticket Stub, 1923 World Series, Giants At Yankees, Game 5 . . . . *ILLUS* 400.00
Baseball, Ticket Stub, Pittsburgh Pirates vs. New York Giants, Sept. 29, 1957, 3 Piece 825.00
Baseball, Turnstile, Cincinnati Crosley Field, Iron, Brass Cap, 41 x 42 In. 4510.00
Baseball, Umpire Mask, 1930s 305.00
Baseball, Uniform, Andre Dawson, Chicago Cubs, Road, 1991 . . . . 2320.00
Baseball, Uniform, Kansas City Monarchs, Negro League, 1924 . . . . 248.00
Baseball, Uniform, New York Cubans, Negro League 550.00
Baseball, Wheaties Box, Joe DiMaggio, 1930s 580.00
Baseball, Wristwatch, Babe Ruth, Ball-Shape Container, Exact Time Corp., Box, 1949 . . . . 2140.00
Baseball, Wristwatch, Babe Ruth, Sultan Of Swat, Book, c.1948 . . . . 500.00
Baseball, Yearbook, Cincinnati Reds, Pat Moran, 1919, 46 Pages 1044.00
Basketball, Ball, Autographed, Bill Russell, Spalding 342.00
Basketball, Ball, Autographed, Michael Jordan, Chicago Bulls, Spalding, Black, Red 610.00
Basketball, Ball, Winchester, Official Playground, No. 3756, Cowhide, 9 In. 7245.00
Basketball, Jersey, Clem Haskins, Chicago Bulls, Home, Game Used, 1967-68 . . . . 1045.00
Basketball, Jersey, Darryl Dawkins, 76ers, Home, Game Used, 1976-77 . . . . 1230.00
Basketball, Jersey, Jerry Sloan, Chicago Bulls, Home, Game Used, 1970, Size 42 . . . . 1530.00
Basketball, Jersey, Kareem Abdul Jabbar, Lakers, Game Used, Early 1980s 8110.00
Basketball, Jersey, Michael Jordan, Bulls, Road, Red, 1992-93, Size 46 . . . . 4060.00
Basketball, Photograph, Autographed, Pistol Pete Maravich, Matte, Frame, 10 x 8 In. 1330.00
Basketball, Photograph, Autographed, Pistol Pete Maravich, Oversize 658.00
Basketball, Shoes, Autographed, Charles Barkley, Philadelphia 76ers, Game Used, Nike 235.00
Basketball, Shoes, Autographed, Robert Parrish, Boston Celtics, Game Used, Avia 190.00
Boxing, Ashtray, Joe Louis, Figural, Brown Bomber, Chalkware, Ashtray By Foot, 1940s 610.00
Boxing, Button, Jack Johnson, James Jeffries, U.S. Button & Novelty, c.1910, 1 1/2 In., Pair 2465.00
Boxing, Button, Joe Louis, World's Heavyweight Champion, Celluloid, 1 1/4 In. 45.00
Boxing, Cabinet Card, Black Boxer, Late 1800s, 6 1/2 x 4 1/2 In. 405.00
Boxing, Cabinet Card, John L. Sullivan, 1880s, 6 1/2 x 4 1/4 In. 1350.00
Boxing, Figurine, Joe Louis, Brown Bomber, 3 1/2 x 4 x 12 In. 608.00
Boxing, Photograph, Autographed, Abe Attell, Inscription, 10 x 8 In. 310.00 to 580.00
Boxing, Photograph, Autographed, Joe Louis, Black & White, 1940s, 9 1/2 x 7 1/2 In. 465.00
Boxing, Photograph, Autographed, Joe Louis, Inscription, Frame, 1930s, 17 1/2 x 15 In. 1013.00
Boxing, Photograph, Autographed, Muhammad Ali, Inscription, 1984, 10 x 8 In. 645.00
Boxing, Photograph, Autographed, Muhammed Ali, Black & White, Inscription, 10 x 8 In. 1508.00
Boxing, Postcard, Jim Jeffries Waiting For Gong, Photograph 175.00
Boxing, Poster, Cassius Clay vs. George Logan, April 23, 1962 . . . . 10749.00
Boxing, Program, Cassius Clay, Sonny Liston, 1964 . . . . 1065.00
Boxing, Program, Max Schmeling vs. Joe Louis, Yankee Stadium, June 18, 1936 . . . . 670.00
Boxing, Ring Bell, Autographed, Muhammad Ali, On Board, 14 1/2 In. 825.00
Boxing, Trunks, Autographed, Muhammed Ali, White, Black Trim 369.00

Football, Ball, A.J. Reach Co., Official, Box, c.1930 .... 610.00
Football, Ball, Autographed, Chicago Bears, World Champions, 1946 .... 815.00
Football, Ball, Autographed, Cleveland Browns, 1953 .... 416.00
Football, Ball, Autographed, Detroit Lions, World Champions, 1957 .... 416.00
Football, Ball, Autographed, Green Bay Packers, World Champions, 1961, 35 Signatures 2245.00
Football, Ball, Bill Wade Model, Spalding, Box, 1960s 140.00
Football, Ball, Melon Style, c.1900 .... 256.00
Football, Button, Red Grange Homecoming, U. Of Illinois, Celluloid, 2 Ribbons, c.1934, 7 In. 450.00
Football, Cleats, 1926 .... 310.00
Football, Helmet, Alan Page, Minnesota Vikings, Game Used, 1975, Size 7 1/2 .... 1045.00
Football, Helmet, Charlie Trippi, Chicago Cardinals, Game Used, 1940s 1265.00
Football, Helmet, Chicago Bears, Wilson, Game Used, 1960s 690.00
Football, Helmet, Chicago Bears, Wilson, Game Used, 1980s 315.00
Football, Helmet, Green Bay Packers, Game Used, 1960s 880.00
Football, Helmet, Jerry Sisemore, Philadelphia Eagles, Game Used, 1980s 458.00
Football, Helmet, Leather, Goldsmith, 1940s 369.00
Football, Helmet, Leather, Lucite Face Mask, 1930s, Size 6 3/4 .... 345.00
Football, Helmet, Louis Wright, Denver Broncos, Game Used, 1980s 235.00
Football, Helmet, Red Grange Model, Wilson, Dog Ears, 1926 .... 626.00
Football, Jersey, Dan Marino, Game Used, 1990 .... 3285.00
Football, Jersey, Dick Butkus, Chicago Bears, Home, Game Used, 1960s 17986.00
Football, Jersey, Joe Namath, New York Jets, Road, Game Used, 1971-73, Size 52 .... 9860.00
Football, Nodder, Dallas Cowboys, Black Player, Toes Up, 1962-64 .... 1625.00
Football, Nodder, LSU College Mascot, Tiger, 1962 .... 2900.00
Football, Pennant, Green Bay Packers, Brown Ground, 1960s 160.00
Football, Pennant, University Of Illinois, Red Grange, Fighting Illini, 1920s, 29 1/4 In. 750.00
Football, Poster, Kansas City Chiefs, Silver Anniversary, 1960-1984, Frame, 16 x 20 In. 50.00
Football, Program, AFL-NFL Champ., Super Bowl I, Green Bay vs. Kansas City, L.A., 1967 .... 545.00
Football, Program, Chicago Bears vs. Hammond Pros, 1923, 10 x 7 In., 16 Pages 2355.00
Football, Program, Chicago Bears vs. Washington Redskins, Championship, 1940 .... 2285.00
Football, Program, Chicago Bears, vs. Chicago Cardinals, Oct., 1926, 11 x 7 In., 20 Pages 1330.00
Football, Program, Dallas Texans vs. Oakland Raiders, 1960, 10 1/2 x 7 3/4 In., 44 Pages 345.00
Football, Program, Minneapolis Red Jackets vs. Green Bay Packers, 10 Cents, Oct. 20, 1929 .... 815.00
Football, Program, Princeton vs. Yale, 50 Cents, Football Shape, Nov. 15, 1919 .... 210.00
Football, Shoes, Autographed, Eric Dickerson, Game Used, Nike 340.00
Football, Shoes, Autographed, Reggie White, Game Used, Nike 555.00
Football, Stereoview Card, Princeton, 1893 .... 140.00
Golf, Ball, Leather Cover, Hemp Core, c.1680 .... 650.00
Golf, Club, Mashie Nibic, Winchester Braeburn, No. 6699, Oak Shaft, Leather Grip 90.00
Golf, Club, Putter, Babe Didrikson Zaharias, Tournament Used, 1940s, 36 In. 950.00
Golf, Club, Putter, Jack Hutchinson, Winchester, No. 9, Oak Shaft, Leather Wrap Grip 175.00
Golf, Club, Sand Wedge, Steve Ballesteros, Tournament Used, Wilson, 1981, 56 In. 470.00
Golf, Shoes, Autographed, Michelle Wie 380.00
Hockey, Helmet, Autographed, Pittsburgh Penguins, World Champions, CCM, 1990s 380.00
Hockey, Jersey, Bobby Orr, Boston Bruins, Road, Game Used, 1969-71 .... 19785.00
Hockey, Stick, Autographed, Bobby Hull, Chicago Blackhawks, Game Used, Northland, 1960s 1635.00
Hockey, Stick, Autographed, Bobby Orr, Boston Bruins, Game Used, Victoriaville Pro, 1970s 1980.00
Hockey, Stick, Autographed, Gretzky, L.A. Kings, Aluminum Handle, Used, Easton, c.1990 .... 1392.00
Hockey, Stick, Autographed, Stan Mikita, Chicago Blackhawks, Game Issued, CCM, Late 1960s 175.00
Hockey, Stick, Bobby Orr, Boston Bruins, Game Issued, Northland, c.1968 .... 406.00
Horse Racing, Tumbler, Kentucky Derby, 1952 .... 155.00
Hunting, Cartridge Box Insert, UMC, 22 Caliber, Big Horn Sheep, Target, 2-Sided, 3 1/2 In. 985.00
Hunting, Cartridge Box Insert, UMC, 22 Caliber, Game Birds, Target, 2-Sided, 3 1/2 In. 930.00
Hunting, Cartridge Box, Browning 35 Power Shotgun Shells, 410 Gauge, Contents 144.00
Hunting, Cartridge Box, Dominion Cartridge Co., Falcon, 12 Gauge, Montreal, Canada 185.00
Hunting, Cartridge Box, Peters Rustles High Velocity Shotgun Shells, 20 Gauge, Contents 780.00
Hunting, Cartridge Box, Peters Victor Shotgun Shells, 20 Gauge, Contents 26.00
Hunting, Cartridge Box, Remington, Dupont, Rim Fire Magnum, Contents 55.00
Hunting, Cartridge Box, Robin Hood Ammunition Co., Game Getter, Round Ball, Contents 945.00
Hunting, Cartridge Box, Sears Roebuck & Co., Pro-Tex-Bor, Contents 100.00
Hunting, Cartridge Box, U.S. Cartridge Co. Defiance Shotgun Shells, 12 Gauge, Contents 50.00

Hunting, Cartridge Box, Winchester Repeater Loaded Shotgun Shells, 20 Gauge, Contents 1469.00
Hunting, Cartridge Box, Winchester, 32 Smith & Wesson, Partial Contents 23.00
Hunting, Deer Call, Herter's, Master, No. 903, Box 19.00
Hunting, Duck Call, Faulk's, Model SC-77, Supreme, Box, 5 1/8 In. 25.00
Hunting, Game Call, Herter's, Call Of The Wild, 2 Records, Wightman Electronics, Box, c.1945 .... 148.00
Hunting, Game Call, Marble's Arms Corp., 2 Records, 7 3/4 x 7 3/8 In. 30.00
Hunting, Gun Rack, Antler, Oak Medallion Back, Wood Deer Head, Glass Eyes, 40 x 28 In......... 805.00
Hunting, Horn, Carved, Fox Hunting Scene, c.1870, 24 In. 1150.00
Hunting, Target, Cast Iron, Rimfire Rifles & Pistols, 9 1/4 In.................................. 198.00
Hunting, Target, Ram Shape, Iron Plate, 27 x 32 In., Pair 880.00
Hunting, Targets, Clay, Western White Flyer, 1940s, Full Case 42.00
Hunting, Tin, Fairlawn Gunpowder, Multicolored Label, DuPont, 1/2 Lb. 1100.00
Hunting, Tin, Mathewson's Gun Powder, Screw Lead Cap, 6 3/4 x 3 3/4 In. 80.00
Hunting, Tin, Outers Gun Oil, Ducks, Plastic Spout, No. 445A 40.00
Hunting, Tin, Remington Oil, Stencil Printed, Lead Spout, Cap, 3 Oz. 60.00
Hunting, Tin, Remington Powder Solvent, 3 Oz. 270.00
Hunting, Tin, Winchester New Gun Oil, Lead Spout, Cap 40.00
Hunting, Tin, Winchester No. 9115, Split Buck, Celluloid 250.00
Rodeo, Bull Rider's Groin Protector, Leather, Early 1900s, 33 x 21 In. 120.00
Roller Polo, Postcard, Schenectady, Champions, 1913-14 .... 175.00
Snowshoes, Yukon Style, Leather Bindings, C.A. Lund Co., Minn., Size 10 x 54 .... 105.00
Soccer, Jersey, Autographed, Pele, New York Cosmos 380.00
Soccer, Jersey, Autographed, Pele, No. 10, Yellow, Green Letters & Numbers 545.00

STAFFORDSHIRE, England, has been a district making pottery and porcelain since the 1700s. Hundreds of kilns are still working in the area. Thousands of types of pottery and porcelain have been made in the many factories that worked and still work in the area. Some of the most famous factories have been listed separately, such as Adams, Davenport, Ridgway, Rowland & Marsellus, Royal Doulton, Royal Worcester, Spode, Wedgwood, and others. Some Staffordshire pieces are listed under categories like Fairing, Flow Blue, Mulberry, Shaving Mug, etc.

Bowl, Fair Mount Near Philadelphia, Joseph Stubbs, c.1820, 12 In. 1554.00
Bowl, Fruit, Stand, Landing Of General Lafayette, E. Wood & Sons, c.1825, 6 x 11 In............ 4780.00
Bowl, Landing Of General Lafayette, Blue, Flower Border, 8 3/4 In. 575.00
Bowl, Manchu, Enameled Decoration, Keeling & Co., c.1920, 9 1/2 In. 35.00
Bowl, Scenic, Byran Gallery, 6 1/4 x 8 In. 175.00
Bowl, Scenic, Select Views, Boughton House Northhamptonshire, R. Halls, 11 In. 345.00
Bowl, Vegetable, Arms Of Georgia, Blue Transfer, c.1829, 11 3/4 x 9 1/4 In. 10158.00
Bowl, Vegetable, Cover, Highbury College, London, Blue Transfer, 12 1/8 x 6 In. 115.00
Bowl, Vegetable, Cover, Landing Of General Lafayette, E. Wood & Sons, c.1825, 9 3/4 In. 1910.00
Bread & Butter, Green Transfer, Red Border, 5 3/4 In. 75.00
Bust, Alexander I, Wood & Caldwell, Burslem, 19th Century, 12 In. 2480.00
Bust, George Washington, Sponge Blue Coat, Marbleized Base, 8 In. ....230.00 to 375.00
Bust, Lord Byron, Parian, Waisted Round Socle, 19th Century, 13 In. 265.00
Bust, Man, Marble Plinth, 12 1/2 In. 460.00
Bust, Neptune, 14 3/4 In. 1035.00
Coffeepot, Blue & White, Transfer Decorated, Baluster Shape, c.1820, 11 1/4 In. 235.00
Coffeepot, Lafayette At Franklin's Tomb, c.1825, 11 1/2 In. ....956.00 to 1910.00
Cottage, Pink, Green, Gilt, 1800s, 8 1/4 In. 140.00
Creamer, Cover, Cow, 1800s, 7 In. 330.00
Creamer, Cow, c.1840, 4 3/4 x 6 3/4 In. 295.00
Creamer, House, Bridge, Country, Blue, c.1840, 9 In. 175.00
Creamer, Lafayette At Franklin's Tomb, Flower Border, c.1825, 5 In. 359.00
Cup, Pug Head, Lead Glaze, Pearlware, Late 1700s, 3 1/4 In. 2585.00
Cup & Saucer, Crown, Demitasse, 24 Piece 50.00
Figurine, 2 Dogs, Stag, 7 In. 345.00
Figurine, Benjamin Franklin, Mid 19th Century, 15 In. 1495.00
Figurine, Cat, Luster, White, Red & Black Detail, c.1940, 8 x 6 In., Pair 205.00
Figurine, Cat, Seated On Cushion, Green Spots, Pink Luster Ribbon, 7 1/4 In., Pair 630.00

Figurine, Cat, Seated, c.1850, 7 In. 295.00
Figurine, Cats, Green, Rust Pillow, 7 In. 325.00
Figurine, Couple, With Dogs, 6 1/2 In. 230.00
Figurine, Cow & Calf, 1800s, Oversize, Pair 805.00
Figurine, Dog, Green, White, 9 1/2 In., Pair 630.00
Figurine, Dog, Pillow Base, Lead Glaze, Pearlware, c.1800, 3 3/8 In., Pair 2350.00
Figurine, Dog, Poodle, 19th Century, 6 1/4 x 11 3/4 In., Pair 500.00
Figurine, Dog, Poodle, 2 Pups, Coleslaw, Oval Cobalt Blue Base, 8 In. 250.00
Figurine, Dog, Spaniel, 2 3/4 In. 90.00
Figurine, Dog, Spaniel, Black Glaze, Gold, Mounted As Lamp Base, Pair, 12 1/2 In. 300.00
Figurine, Dog, Spaniel, Black Spots, Yellow Eyes, Red Collar, 11 3/4 In., Pair 170.00
Figurine, Dog, Spaniel, Black, Red, Gold, c.1850, 13 1/2 In., Pair 390.00
Figurine, Dog, Spaniel, Comforter, Gilt Decoration, c.1850, 10 1/2 In., Pair 355.00
Figurine, Dog, Spaniel, Pink & Copper Luster, 1800s, 13 1/2 In. 175.00
Figurine, Dog, Spaniel, Seated, Copper Luster Accents, Black Muzzles, 8 1/8 In., Pair 489.00
Figurine, Dog, Spaniel, Seated, Luster, Painted, 1800s, 4 5/8 In., Pair 170.00
Figurine, Dog, Spaniel, Seated, Orange, Black, Gold, Lustre, c.1850, 12 1/4 In., Pair 750.00
Figurine, Dog, Spaniel, Seated, Yellow Eyes, Gilt Chains, 14 5/8 In., Pair 430.00
Figurine, Dog, Spaniel, White, Black & Gold Highlights, 1800s, 14 1/2 In., Pair 230.00
Figurine, Dog, Spaniel, White, Glass Eyes, c.1890, 13 1/2 In., Pair 259.00
Figurine, Dog, Whippet, 8 3/4 3 x 10 In., Pair 210.00
Figurine, Dog, Whippet, 9 1/2 x 3 1/2 x 11 In. 118.00
Figurine, Dog, Whippet, Dead Rabbit, Scrolled Base, Multicolored Enamel, 10 3/4 In. 345.00
Figurine, Dog, Whippet, With Rabbit In Mouth, Multicolored Enamel, 6 x 6 In., Pair 345.00
Figurine, Dogs, Pekinese, Hand Painted, 19th Century, 9 1/2 In., Pair 175.00
Figurine, Dogs, Reclining, Late 19th Century, 3 1/2 x 4 3/4 In., Pair 468.00
Figurine, Elijah & Raven, 9 1/2 In. 175.00
Figurine, Fishmonger, Man, Woman, Enamel, 1800s, 13 & 13 1/2 In., Pair 264.00
Figurine, Gin & Water, Temperance, 2-Sided, 8 3/8 In. 259.00
Figurine, Girl & Sheep, 1800s, 9 In. 415.00
Figurine, Hen On Nest, Matte Finish, 6 1/4 x 7 1/4 In. 275.00
Figurine, Highland Jessie, Woman, Soldier, Victorian, 9 In. 195.00
Figurine, Highland Soldier, Holding Flag, Polychrome, 1800s, 16 In. 325.00
Figurine, Huntsman, On Horse, Dead Stag, 1800s, 14 1/2 In., Pair 175.00
Figurine, Lamb, Lying Down, Long Tail, Flowering Shrub, 2 3/4 In., Pair 430.00
Figurine, Lion Slayer, 15 1/2 In. 165.00
Figurine, Lion Slayer, Scotsman, 16 1/8 In. 405.00
Figurine, Lion, Yellow, Brown Mane, 3 In. ....110.00 to 130.00
Figurine, Man & Woman Riding Goats, c.1900, 7 1/4 In., Pair 175.00
Figurine, Man & Woman, Seated, With Sheaves Of Wheat, 14 1/2 In. 175.00
Figurine, Man, Striped Knickers, Holding Calico Cat, 7 3/4 In. 230.00
Figurine, Milkmaid With Cow, 6 In., Pair 180.00
Figurine, Naughty Barmaid, Bottle Of Wine, 8 1/8 In. 345.00
Figurine, Obediah Sharette, Woman, Child Seated, 11 3/8 In. 1020.00
Figurine, Sheep, Flowers, Leaves, Marked Salt, 6 1/4 In. 275.00
Figurine, Sheep, Flowers, Leaves, Marked Walton, 6 1/2 In. 220.00
Figurine, Uncle Tom & Eva, 1800s, 8 1/2 In. 330.00
Figurine, Woman Carrying Sickle & Wheat, Autumn, c.1800-10, 7 In. 395.00
Figurine, Zebra, With Reins, Prancing, 8 1/2 In., Pair 1265.00
Group, Boy & Girl, At Well, 1800s, 10 In. 80.00
Group, Boy & Girl, Clock, 1800s, 8 In. 69.00
Group, Courtship Couple, 9 3/4 In. 115.00
Group, Joan & Darby, Having Drink, 5 5/8 In. 85.00
Group, Prince & Princess, Pony Cart, Gilt Accents, 7 1/4 In. 200.00
Group, Red Riding Hood, Wolf, 1800s, 10 In. 130.00
Group, Sailor, Woman, Dog, Late 1800s, 10 In. 150.00
Group, Uncle Tom & Little Eva, c.1850, 7 1/2 In. 470.00
Jug, Scandaga & Hudson Rivers, Black Transfer, c.1825, 6 In. 585.00
Meat Drainer, English Castle Rural Scene, Blue & White, 13 In. 220.00
Mug, Boy, Drum, Polychrome, 3 In., Child's 140.00
Mug, E & F, Man, Lion, Multicolored, Child's, 2 1/2 In. 140.00

Mug, Hop Gatherer, Multicolored, 2 1/2 In., Child's 65.00
Mug, I & J, Cobbler, Multicolored, 2 3/4 In., Child's 275.00
Mug, Landing Of General Lafayette, Castle Garden, E. Wood & Sons, c.1825, 4 3/4 In. 6575.00
Penholder, Dog, Whippet, Lying Down, 6 1/2 x 2 3/4 x 5 In., Pair 325.00
Pepper Pot, Landing Of General Lafayette, Castle Garden, J.&R. Clews, c.1825, 4 In. ....1435.00 to 1795.00
Pitcher, Admiral Nelson, 1800s, 11 1/4 In. 196.00
Pitcher, Animals, Pink Luster, Underglaze Decorations, Pearlware, c.1800, 8 In. 1170.00
Pitcher, Boston State House, Blue & White, 9 1/4 In. 440.00
Pitcher, Dog, Spaniel, Sitting Up, Tricornered Hat, 1900s, 10 In. 105.00
Pitcher, Egg Shape, Eagle, E Pluribus Unum, William Adams, c.1825, 6 1/2 In. 3110.00
Pitcher, Fruit, Bird Decoration, Dark Blue, 5 1/2 In. 345.00
Pitcher, Game Bird Decoration, 8 1/2 In., Pair 405.00
Pitcher, Geneva Pattern, Blue, White, Davenport, 9 In. 330.00
Pitcher, Lafayette & Washington, c.1825, 5 1/2 In. 1075.00
Pitcher, Lafayette At Franklin's Tomb, Blue, Bulbous, 6 In. 520.00
Pitcher, Lafayette At Franklin's Tomb, Egg Shape, E. Wood & Son, c.1825, 6 1/4 In. 956.00
Pitcher, Lafayette At Franklin's Tomb, Enoch Wood & Sons, c.1825, 6 3/4 In. 1795.00
Pitcher, Landing Of General Lafayette, Castle Garden, E. Wood & Sons, c.1825, 7 In. 1675.00
Pitcher, Shepherd Scene, E&G Philips, Longport, Dark Blue, 6 3/4 In. 1035.00
Pitcher, Views Of The Erie Canal, Dark Blue, Flowers, 9 In. 2875.00
Pitcher, Welcome Lafayette, Egg Shape, Scalloped Edge, J.&R. Clews, c.1825, 7 In. .....2030.00 to 2390.00
Pitcher & Washbowl, Upper Ferry Bridge, Joseph Stubbs, c.1815, 8 3/4 x 11 1/2 In. 2510.00
Plate, America & Independence, States Border, Clews, 9 In. ....288.00 to 345.00
Plate, Antislavery, Blue Transfer, Constitution Quotes, Medallions, 9 1/2 In. 705.00
Plate, Arms Of Rhode Island, Blue Transfer, Compass Star Border, c.1829, 8 5/8 In. 590.00
Plate, Arms Of South Carolina, Blue Transfer, c.1829, 7 3/8 In. 558.00
Plate, Bank Of United States, Philadelphia, Blue Transfer, Eagle Border, 10 1/8 In. 430.00
Plate, Boston State House, 10 In. 173.00
Plate, Boston State House, Reticulated Edge, John Rogers & Son, c.1820, 18 In. 660.00
Plate, Capital At Washington, Blue Transfer, 10 In. 315.00
Plate, Chapelle De Guillaume Tell, Blue, 6 1/2 In. 86.00
Plate, Chief Justice Marshall Troy, Dark Blue, Woods, 8 1/4 In. 468.00
Plate, City Hotel, New York, Oak Leaf Border, 8 3/4 In. 460.00
Plate, City Of Albany, State Of New York, Shell Border, Blue, E. Wood & Sons, 10 In. 460.00
Plate, City Of Albany, State Of New York, Shell Border, E. Woods & Sons, 10 In. 288.00
Plate, Cowes Harbor, Blue, Shell Rim Decoration, Scalloped Rim, 6 1/2 In. 330.00
Plate, Dinner, Armorial, Duke & Duchess Of Marlborough, 10 1/2 In. 176.00
Plate, Dr. Syntax Taking Possession Of His Living, Blue Transfer, 10 1/2 In. 220.00
Plate, Fairmount Near Philadelphia, Eagle Border, 10 1/4 In. ....173.00 to 316.00
Plate, Fall Of Montmoranci, E. Pluribus Unum Eagle & Shell Border, Dark Blue, 9 In. 275.00
Plate, Fishermen By Creek, Castle, Blue Transfer, Clews Warranted, 9 In. 248.00
Plate, Flowers, Multicolored, Scalloped Rim, 10 In., Pair 127.00
Plate, Fruit Center, Flower Border, 10 In. 275.00
Plate, Hollywell Cottage, Cavan-Kely, 10 In. 85.00
Plate, Hospital Boston, Blue Transfer, Leaf Border, 9 In. 430.00
Plate, Hospital, Boston, Jefferson, Lafayette, R. Stevenson & Williams, c.1820, 8 1/2 In. 9560.00
Plate, Landing Of General Lafayette, Blue, Floral Border, 8 7/8 In. 375.00
Plate, Landing Of General Lafayette, Dark Blue, Clews, 6 3/4 In. 385.00
Plate, Landing Of General Lafayette, Dark Blue, Clews, 8 3/4 In. ....200.00 to 345.00
Plate, Landing Of General Lafayette, Dark Blue, Clews, 10 In. ....330.00 to 400.00
Plate, Landing Of General Lafayette, Flower Border, Blue, 7 3/4 In. 173.00
Plate, Marine Hospital, Louisville, Kentucky, Shell Border, E. Wood & Sons, 9 In. ....430.00 to 546.00
Plate, Marine Hospital, Louisville, Kentucky, Shell Border, Marked, 8 In. 690.00
Plate, Mount Vernon, Black Transfer, 7 In. 55.00
Plate, Napoleon Bonaparte, Half Body Image, Name In Banner, Black Transfer, 10 In. 138.00
Plate, New York From Brooklyn Heights, Andrew Stevenson, c.1820, 10 In. 239.00
Plate, Oriental Scenes, Rider On Zebra, Flower Borders, 9 1/2 In., Pair 747.00
Plate, Pastoral Pattern, Dark Blue, Marked, E. & G. Phillips, Longport, 7 1/2 In. 55.00
Plate, Pomegranate, Scalloped Rim, Multicolored, 10 1/2 In. 105.00
Plate, President's House, Washington, Blue Transfer, 10 3/8 In. 235.00
Plate, Soup, Harvard College, Dark Blue, Oak Leaf & Acorn Border, Marked, 10 In. 345.00

Plate, Soup, Table Rock, Niagara, Shell Border, Dark Blue, Marked, 10 In. 460.00
Plate, Tae Mouth Castle, Perthshireby Riley, 10 In. 86.00
Plate, Toddy, Scenic, R Halls Dreghorn House Scotland 60.00
Plate, Toddy, Winter View Of Pittsfield Mass., Blue, 6 3/4 In. 546.00
Plate, Trenton Falls, Seashell Border, 7 1/2 In. 315.00
Plate, Union Line, Steamship, Shell Border, Blue, Wood & Sons, 9 1/8 In. 546.00
Plate, Upper Ferry Bridge Over River Schuykill, 8 3/4 In. 220.00
Plate, Valentine, Dark Blue, 8 3/4 In. 192.00
Plate, View Near Conway, New Hampshire, Red Transfer, 9 1/4 In. 155.00
Plate, Washington, Lafayette, Canal, R. Stevenson & Williams, c.1825, 8 1/2 In. 9560.00
Plate, Washington, Lafayette, Hotel, R. Stevenson & Williams, c.1825, 8 1/2 In. 5676.00
Platter, Bay Of New York From Staten Island, Enoch Wood & Sons, 18 1/2 x 15 1/2 In. 1495.00
Platter, Blantyre Pattern, Castle, People, Blue Transfer, 16 x 12 1/2 In. 105.00
Platter, Chesapeake & Shannon, Naval Battle, John Rogers & Son, c.1815, 19 In. 3585.00
Platter, Dr. Syntax, Advertisement For A Wife, Clews, Early 1800s 880.00
Platter, Fairy Villa, Ironstone, Blue Transfer, Printed, 1 3/4 x 19 1/2 In. 350.00
Platter, Flowers, Multicolored, Impressed Eagle, 15 x 11 5/8 In. 250.00
Platter, Halls Quadruped, Dark Blue, 15 x 12 In. 1440.00
Platter, Landing Of General Lafayette, Castle Garden, J.&R. Clews, c.1825, 15 1/4 In. ....960.00 to 1675.00
Platter, Landing Of General Lafayette, Castle Garden, J.&R. Clews, c.1825, 17 1/4 In. ...1795.00 to 2030.00
Platter, Landing Of General Lafayette, Castle Garden, J.&R. Clews, c.1825, 19 In. 2270.00
Platter, Medina Pattern, Blue, White, 1800s, 15 In. 58.00
Platter, Mediterranean Scene, Blue, White, Riley, 18 1/2 In. 200.00
Platter, North Carolina State Arms, Flower Border, 14 In. 1955.00
Platter, People, Lake, Castles, Blue, White, 15 1/4 x 12 In. 375.00
Platter, Plate, Almshouse, Boston, Sancho Panza, 11 x 14 & 10 In. 590.00
Platter, Port Scene, Sailing Ship, Shell & Flower Border, Blue, 15 x 11 3/4 In. 1045.00
Platter, Rural Scene, Castle Bridge, Moat, 3 Figures, Cattle, Flower Border, 16 3/4 x 21 In. 630.00
Platter, Sancho Panza & The Duchess, Floral Border, 15 x 18 1/2 In. 375.00
Platter, Sandusky Ohio, c.1840, 16 1/2 In. 5079.00
Platter, Sheltered Peasants, Dark Blue Transfer, c.1835, 17 In. 1095.00
Platter, Tempest, Act 1, Scene 2, Blue, 15 In. 220.00
Platter, Upper Ferry Bridge Over River Schuylkill, Joseph Stubbs, c.1815, 18 3/4 In. 2270.00
Platter, Vue Du Chateau Ermenonville, Flowers, Grapevine Border, Wood, 12 In. 460.00
Platter, Well & Tree, Upper Ferry Bridge, Joseph Stubbs, c.1815, 18 3/4 In. 2870.00
Platter, Wild Rose Roma, Blue, White, 12 1/2 x 15 7/8 In. 230.00
Platter, Wild Rose, Men In Boats, House, Blue Transfer, 15 1/2 x 12 1/4 In. 200.00
Platter, Winter View Of Pittsfield, Mass., J.&R. Clews, 14 1/2 In. 2390.00
Pot, Chameleon Ware, Mae West, Clews, c.1930, 2 5/8 x 4 1/4 In. 120.00
Sauceboat, St. Patrick's Cathedral, Mott Street, Ralph Stevenson, c.1820, 8 In. 2870.00
Serving Dish, Cover, Seashell Pattern, Blue Transferware, c.1825, 9 x 9 In. 1528.00
Soup, Cream, Man Fishing, Seated Ladies, Buildings, Blue, Impressed, 9 3/4 In. 138.00
Stirrup Cup, Fox Head, Grapevines, 4 3/4 In. 230.00
Sugar, Cover, Lafayette At Franklin's Tomb, Flower Border, c.1825, 7 In., Pair 540.00
Sugar & Creamer, Washington At Tomb, E. Wood & Sons, c.1825, 6 1/4-In. Creamer 1135.00
Tea Bowl, Saucer, Neptune, Transfer, Decorated, Seashell Borders, c.1834, 2 3/8 In. 235.00
Tea Set, Girl With Goat, Black, White Transfer, Child's, 14 Piece 995.00
Tea Urn, Cover, Stoneware, Buff Color, White Leaves, Royal Crest, Late 1800s, 23 In. 295.00
Teapot, Cover, Sailing Boat On Lake, Shell Border, Dark Blue Transfer, 6 In. 345.00
Teapot, Flowers, Blue, 12 In. 330.00
Teapot, Globular, Crabstock Handle, Spout, Bird, Flowers, Salt Glaze, c.1760, 4 In. 590.00
Teapot, Globular, Crabstock Handle, Spout, Bird, Flowers, Salt Glaze, c.1760, 6 In. 355.00
Teapot, Lafayette At Franklin's Tomb, Flower Border, c.1825, 8 In. 538.00
Toby Jugs are listed in their own category.
Tray, Scenic, Oxburgh Hall Norfolk, Dark Blue, 10 x 8 In. 290.00
Tureen, Cover, Blue, Man & Woman, Donkey, Church, Floral Border, 7 x 10 In. 165.00
Tureen, Sauce, Cover, Landing Of General Lafayette, J.&R. Clews, c.1825, 8 1/2 In. 956.00
Tureen, Soup, Ladle, Landing Of General Lafayette, J.&R. Clews, c.1825, 10 x 17 In. 19120.00
Tureen, Soup, Tray, Fairmount Near Philadelphia, Joseph Stubbs, c.1815 .... 8965.00
Vase, Brown, Classical Transfer, Orange Red Ground, 1800s, 10 3/4 In. 355.00
Vase, Chameleon Ware, African Shield, Beige Ground, Clews, 6 x 4 1/2 In. 245.00

Vase, Chameleon Ware, Blue Flame, Blue Ground, Clews, 6 3/4 x 3 1/2 In. 195.00
Vase, Chameleon Ware, Blue Flame, Squat, Pinched Neck, Clews, c.1930, 2 3/4 In. 115.00
Vase, Chameleon Ware, Green Flame, Clews, c.1930, 4 x 3 1/2 In. 155.00
Vase, Chameleon Ware, Holly Leaf, Clews, c.1940, 6 1/2 x 3 In. 190.00
Vase, Chameleon Ware, Leaves, Geometric Band, Sponged Ground, Clews, c.1935, 14 1/4 In. 452.00
Vase, Enamel, Classical Subjects, Black Ground, 1800s, 19 In. 235.00
Vase, Man, Woman, Basket, Grapes, 1800s, 11 In. 80.00
Vase, Spill, Figural, Robin Hood & Little John, Spaniel, 12 In. 896.00
Warming Dish, Flower Basket, Blue, 9 3/4 In. 55.00
Washbasin, Ironstone, Brown Transfer, Urn, Classical Revival, 1800s, 15 1/4 In. 235.00
Waste Bowl, Bird Pattern, Dark Blue, Marked Stone China, 3 1/2 In. 345.00
Waste Bowl, Lafayette At Franklin's Tomb, E. Wood & Son, c.1825, 3 x 6 In. 448.00
Watch Hutch, Shed With Cats, Birds, 8 1/4 In. 575.00

STANGL Pottery traces its history back to the Fulper Pottery of New Jersey. In 1910, Johann Martin Stangl started working at Fulper. He left to work at Haeger Pottery from 1915 to 1920. Stangl returned to Fulper Pottery in 1920, became president in 1926, and changed the company name to Stangl Pottery in 1929. Stangl acquired the firm in 1930. The pottery is known for dinnerware and a line of bird figurines. Martin Stangl died in 1972, and the pottery was sold to Frank Wheaton, Jr., of Wheaton Industries. Production continued until 1978, when Pfaltzgraff Pottery purchased the right to the Stangl trademark, and the remaining inventory was liquidated. A single bird figurine is identified by a number. Figurines made up of two birds are identified by a number followed by the letter "D" indicating "Double."

Apple Delight, Bowl, Vegetable, Divided, Oval, 10 1/2 In. 20.00
Bird, Bird Of Paradise, No. 362S, 13 1/2 In. 1293.00
Bird, Blue Jay With Peanut, No. 3715, 10 1/4 In. 380.00
Bird, Blue Jay, Double, No. 3717D, 12 1/2 In. 1293.00
Bird, Crossbill, Double, No. 3727D, 7 1/2 In. 2115.00
Bird, Crossbill, No. 3726, 5 1/2 In. 3760.00
Bird, European Finch, No. 3922, 5 1/2 In. 1116.00
Bird, Fish Hawk, No. 3459, 9 1/2 In. 5290.00
Bird, Flying Blue Jay With Leaf, No. 3716, 10 1/4 In. 380.00
Bird, Golden-Crowned Kinglet, Double, No. 3853D, 5 1/2 In. 440.00
Bird, Magnolia Warbler, No. 3925, 5 1/2 In. 2235.00
Bird, Magpie-Jay, No. 3758, 10 3/4 In. 940.00
Bird, Mountain Bluebird, No. 3453, 6 In. 646.00
Bird, Passenger Pigeon, No. 3450, 9 x 18 In. 1645.00
Bird, Penguin, No. 3274, 6 In. 470.00
Bird, Pheasant, No. 3457, 7 1/4 x 15 In. 2468.00
Bird, Pheasant, No. 3586, 9 x 15 1/2 In. ....646.00 to 1410.00
Bird, Quail, No. 3458, 7 1/2 In. 1295.00
Bird, Red-Headed Woodpecker, Double, No. 3729D, 7 3/4 In. 2938.00
Bird, Red-Headed Woodpecker, No. 3725, 7 In. 2115.00
Bird, Robin, No. 3741, 9 1/2 In. 3760.00
Bird, Rooster, No. 3273, 5 3/4 In. 440.00
Bird, Rooster, No. 3435, 16 1/2 In. 8225.00
Bird, Scarlet Tanagers, Double, No. 3724D, 7 1/2 In. 2115.00
Bird, Scissor-Tailed Flycatcher, No. 3757, 11 In. 646.00
Bird, Shoveler, No. 3455, 12 1/4 x 14 In. 999.00
Bird, Summer Tanager, No. 3868, 4 In. 529.00
Bird, Vermillion Flycatcher, No. 3923, 5 3/4 In. 2705.00
Bird, Western Tanager, No. 3749, 4 3/4 In. 325.00
Bird, White Wing Crossbill, Double, No. 3754D, 8 3/4 In. 646.00
Bird, White Wing Crossbill, No. 3754, 3 1/2 In. 3525.00
Bird, Willow Ptarmigan, No. 3451, 11 In. 3760.00
Bird, Yellow-Headed Verdin, No. 3921, 5 In. 1410.00
Bird, Yellow-Throated Warbler, No. 3924, 5 1/2 In. 440.00
Blueberry, Cup & Saucer 14.00

Blueberry, Plate, Dinner, 10 In. 9.00
Blueberry, Sugar, Cover 20.00
Country Garden, Bowl, Vegetable, Divided, Oval, 10 1/2 In. 29.00
Country Garden, Cup & Saucer 24.00
Country Garden, Plate, Dinner, 10 In. 36.00
Country Garden, Tidbit, Center Handle, 10 In. 30.00
Dogwood, Plate, Bread & Butter, 6 In. 3.00
Festive Fruit, Sugar & Creamer 14.00
Fruit, Tidbit, Center Handle, 10 In. 15.00
Garden Flower, Eggcup 20.00
Garland, Sugar, Cover 19.00
Golden Blossom, Plate, Salad, 8 In. 7.00
Golden Harvest, Bowl, Salad, 12 In. 40.00
Golden Harvest, Chop Plate, 14 1/2 In. 34.00
Golden Harvest, Creamer 35.00
Golden Harvest, Platter, Oval, 14 3/4 In. 35.00
Magnolia, Chop Plate, 12 1/2 In. 18.00
Orchard Song, Plate, Dinner, 10 In. 18.00
Orchard Song, Plate, Salad, 8 In. 8.00
Orchard Song, Platter, Oval, 14 3/4 In. 45.00
Orchard Song, Tidbit, Center Handle, 10 In. 36.00
Pitcher, Franklin D. Roosevelt, Happy Days Are Here Again, 7 1/2 x 10 1/2 In. 345.00
Ranger, Plate, Cowboy, Cactus, 10 In. 540.00
Sculptured Fruit, Bowl, Fruit, 5 1/2 In. 9.00
Sculptured Fruit, Mug, 4 In. 25.00
Sculptured Fruit, Plate, Dinner, 10 In. 18.00
Sculptured Fruit, Plate, Salad, 8 In. 14.00
Sculptured Fruit, Saucer 5.00
Sculptured Fruit, Soup, Dish, 7 3/4 In. 16.00
Thistle, Pitcher, 5 3/8 In. 33.00
Thistle, Plate, Dinner, 10 In. 22.00
Thistle, Plate, Luncheon, 9 1/2 In. .... 18.00 to 22.00
Thistle, Plate, Salad, 8 In. 18.00
Town & Country, Bowl, Cereal, Blue 27.00
Town & Country, Gravy Boat, Underplate, Blue, 8 1/2 In. 12.00
Trinidad, Tidbit, Center Handle, 10 In. 15.00
Wild Clover, Plate, Bread & Butter, 6 In. 18.00
Wild Rose, Bowl, Vegetable, Oval, Divided, 10 1/2 In. 35.00

STAR TREK AND STAR WARS collectibles are included here. The original television series *Star Trek* ran from 1966 through 1969. The series spawned an animated series, three sequels, and a prequel, which is still in production. The first Star Trek movie was released in 1979 and eight others followed, the most recent in 2002. The movie *Star Wars* opened in 1977. Sequels were released in 1980 and 1983, and prequels in 1999, 2002, and 2005. Other science fiction and fantasy collectibles can be found under Batman, Buck Rogers, Captain Marvel, Flash Gordon, Superman, Movie, and Toy.

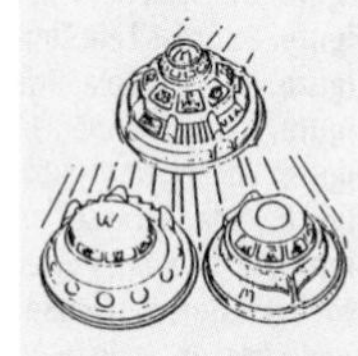

STAR TREK, Calendar, Next Generation, Pocket Books, 1993 .... 15.00
Calendar, Star Trek Celebration, Pocket Books, Unopened, 1988 .... 13.00
Comic Book, Enterprise Logs, Vol. 2, 1976, Golden Press, 1976, 224 Pages 34.00
Comic Book, Issue No. 31, Gold Key, July, 1975 .... 20.00
Dolls, Barbie & Ken, Star Trek Outfits, Mattel, Box, 1996, 12 In., Pair 85.00
Figure, Borg, No. 6010, Stock No. 6055, On Card, Playmates, 1992, 4 1/2 In. 8.00
Figure, Captain Kirk, Posable, Soft, Knickerbocker, Box, c.1979, 12 In. 82.00
Figure, Captain Picard, Romulan Costume, No. 6070, No. 6032, On Card, Playmates, 1994, 4 In. 8.00
Figure, Dr. Beverly Crusher, No. 6950, Stock No. 6961, On Card, Playmates, 1994-95, 4 1/2 In. 8.00
Figure, Q, Talking, 3 Phrases, Accessories, Playmate, Box, Unopened, 1995, 7 In. 19.00
Figure, Quark, Deep Space 9, No. 6200, Stock No. 6203, On Card, Playmates, 1993, 4 1/2 In. 8.00
Jigsaw Puzzle, Journey To Undiscovered Country, R. Peak, Springbok, Box, 1993, 24 x 30 In. 30.00
Lunch Box, Dome Top, Metal, Aladdin, 1968, 9 In. 840.00

Lunch Box, Dome Top, Metal, No Thermos, Aladdin, 1968, 9 In. ....280.00 to 575.00
Lunch Box, Motion Picture, Metal, Plastic Bottle, King Seeley Thermos Co., 1979 .... 48.00
Magazine Advertisement, Star Trek Movie, Full Page, Color, 1979 .... 12.00
Mug, Captain Kirk, Box, c.1980 .... 50.00
Mug, Lt. Cmdr. Geordi La Forge, Applause, Box, 1994 .... 15.00
Mug, Star Trek Logo, Pfaltzgraff, 1994, 3 3/4 In. 16.00
Ornament, Captain James Tiberius Kirk, Hallmark, Box, 1995 .... 15.00
Ornament, Enterprise, 25th Anniversary, Blinking Lights, Hallmark, Box, 1991 .... 97.00
Ornament, Romulan Warbird, Hallmark, Box, 1995 .... 23.00
Pin, 25 Year Anniversary, 1 x 5/8 In. 35.00
Poster, Generations, Voyage Continues, Signed, Sonia Hillios, c.1994, 22 x 34 In. 28.00
Record, Touch Of Leonard Nimoy, 11 Songs, DOT Records, 33 RPM, 1969 .... 40.00
Toy, USS Enterprise, Die Cast Metal, No. 358, Dinky, Box, 1979, 7 3/4 x 10 In. 124.00
Toy, USS Enterprise, Light-Up, Captain Picard's Voice, Playmates, 1994, 15 In. 80.00
Tumbler, Captain Kirk, Shooting Ray Gun, Dr Pepper, 1978, 6 1/4 In. 26.00
Tumbler, Dr. Leonard McCoy, Dr Pepper, 1976, 6 1/4 In. 11.50
Tumbler, Fal-Tor-Pan, Search For Spock, Taco Bell, 1984, 5 1/2 In. 8.00
Tumbler, Lord Kruge, Search For Spock, Taco Bell, 1984, 5 1/2 In. 8.00
STAR WARS, Bottle, Galactic Shampoo, C-3PO, Unopened, Minnetonka Brands, 1999, 8 1/4 In. ... 15.00
Comic Art, Star Wars, No. 76, Page 2, Ron Frenz, Tom Palmer, 1983, 15 x 10 In. 165.00
Comic Art, Star Wars, No. 102, Page 9, Sal Buscema, Pat Boyette, 1985, 15 x 10 In. 110.00
Figure, A-Wing Pilot, Coin, Power Of The Force, On Card, 1985, 3 3/4 In. 125.00
Figure, Ben Obi-Wan Kenobi, Green No. 1, On Card, Kenner, 1998, 3 3/4 In. 10.00
Figure, C-3PO, Kenner, 1978-79, 3 3/4 In. ....8.00 to 15.00
Figure, C-3PO, On Card, Kenner, 1978-79, 3 3/4 In. 200.00
Figure, C-3PO, Plastic, Jointed, 1979-80, 12 In. 115.00
Figure, Chewbacca, Coin, Power Of The Force, On Card, Kenner, 1985, 4 1/4 In. 85.00
Figure, Darth Vader, 1978-79, 3 3/4 In. ....10.00 to 14.00
Figure, Darth Vader, Kenner, Box, 1977, 15 In. 216.00
Figure, Darth Vader, On Card, Kenner, 1978-79, 3 3/4 In. 410.00
Figure, Han Solo, Small Head, On Card, Kenner, 1978-79, 3 3/4 In. 500.00
Figure, Lando Calrissian, Skiff Guard, On Card, Kenner, 1983 .... 47.00
Figure, Luke Skywalker, Box, Kenner, 1979-80, 12 In. 220.00
Figure, Luke Skywalker, Hoth Gear, On Card, Kenner, 1982, 3 3/4 In. 115.00
Figure, Luke Skywalker, Jedi Knight, Blue Lightsaber, On Card, Kenner, 1983, 3 3/4 In. 110.00
Figure, Luke Skywalker, Kenner, 1978-79, 3 3/4 In. ....24.00 to 30.00
Figure, Luke Skywalker, On Card, Kenner, 1978-79, 3 3/4 In. 480.00
Figure, Luke Skywalker, Stormtrooper Disguise, Green No. 2, On Card, Kenner, 1997 .... 10.00
Figure, Obi-Wan Kenobi, Kenner, Box, 1979-80, 12 In. 270.00
Figure, Princess Leia Organa, Kenner, Box, 1979-80, 12 In. 220.00
Figure, Princess Leia, Prisoner, Green No. 1, On Card, Kenner, 1998, 3 3/4 In. 10.00
Figure, R2-D2, Kenner, 12-Back Card, 1977, 2 1/4 In. 308.00
Figure, Wicket, Return Of The Jedi, Kenner, 1984 .... 25.00
Figure, Yoda, Accessories, On Card, Kenner, c.1981 .... 170.00
Figure, Yoda, Coin, Power Of The Force, On Card, Kenner, 1985 .... 350.00
Movie Poster, Anniversary, Re-release, 20th Century Fox, 1978, 41 x 27 In. 1298.00
Movie Poster, Style D, 20th Century Fox, 1977, 41 x 27 In. 180.00
Playset, Death Star Space Station, Star Wars Movie, Box, 1979, 23 In. 160.00
Toy, Darth Vader's Star Destroyer, Kenner, Box, 1980, 13 x 21 x 7 In. 246.00
Toy, Imperial TIE Fighter, Kenner, Box, 1978, 11 x 12 1/2 x 4 1/4 In. 340.00
Toy, Jawa Sandcrawler, Radio Controlled, Kenner, Box, 1979, 9 x 17 x 7 In. 420.00

STEINS have been used by beer and ale drinkers for over 500 years. They have been made of ivory, porcelain, stoneware, faience, silver, pewter, wood, or glass in sizes up to nine gallons. Although some were made by Mettlach, Meissen, Capo-di-Monte, and other famous factories, most were made by less important German potteries. The words *Geschutz* or *Musterschutz* on a stein are the German words for *patented* or *registered design*, not company names. Steins are still being made in the old styles. Lithophane steins may be found in the Lithophane category.

Brewery, Brauerei Zum Munchener Kindl, Stoneware, Pewter Lid, 2/5 Liter 360.00
Brewery, Independent Brewery Association Prima, Glass, Pressed, Inlaid Lid, 1/2 Liter 135.00
Brewery, Kochelbrau, Ernst Erich, Munchen, Enamel, Stoneware, Pewter Lid, 1/2 Liter 330.00
Brewery, Kulmacher Export Bierbrauerie Vorm, Carl Petz, Pottery, Relief Pewter Lid, 1/2 Liter 485.00
Brewery, Mannheimer Actien-Brauerei, Enamel, Pottery, Relief Pewter Lid, 1/3 Liter 485.00
Brewery, Otto Huber Brewery, New York, Enamel, Stoneware, Relief Pewter Lid, 1/2 Liter 220.00
Brewery, Russian Bavaria Beer, St. Petersburg, Etched, Stoneware, Pewter Lid, 1/2 Liter 600.00
Brewery, Sorietats Brauerei Gorkau, Glass, Pressed, Pewter Lid, No. 971, 1/3 Liter 120.00
Brewery, St. Georgenbrau Buttenheim, Stoneware, Transfer, Enameled, Pewter Lid, 1 Liter 127.00
Brewery, Ulmer Brauerei-Gesellschaft, Pottery, Transfer, Enamel, Pewter Lid, 3 Liter 845.00
Brewery, Wurzburger Hofbrau, Transfer, Engraved Pewter Lid, 1/2 Liter 128.00
Character, Artillery Shell, German Soldiers, Pewter, Eagle Thumblift, 1/2 Liter 250.00
Character, Artillery Shell, Iron Cross & Flowers, Screw-Off Lid, Stoneware, Signed, TOH, 1/2 Liter .. 385.00
Character, Artillery Shell, Iron Cross, Dir Sorgen, Aus Diesem, Stoneware, 1/2 Liter 230.00
Character, Artillery Shell, Lion & Shield, Pewter, Iron Cross Thumblift, 1/2 Liter 200.00
Character, Artillery Shell, Porcelain, Bisque Painted Finish, Inlaid Lid, 1/2 Liter 375.00
Character, Artillery Shell, Prussian Eagle & Flags, Stoneware, 1 Liter 240.00
Character, Artillery Shell, Prussian Eagle, Iron Cross Thumblift, Stoneware, 1/2 Liter 220.00
Character, Artillery Shell, Red, White, Gold, Lithograph, Porcelain, 1/2 Liter 305.00
Character, Artillery Shell, Silver Plate, 1/2 Liter 835.00
Character, Artillery Shell, Tan, Yellow, Gray, Gold, Lithograph, Porcelain, 1/2 Liter 275.00
Character, Artillery Shell, Wilhelm I & II, Pewter, Eagle Thumblift, 1/2 Liter 175.00
Character, Beehive, No. 1384, Pottery, Inlaid Lid, 1/2 Liter 315.00
Character, Berlin Bear, Inscribed Shield, Porcelain, Inlaid Lid, Schierholz, 1896, 1/2 Liter 1690.00
Character, Bismarck Radish, Porcelain, Schierholz, 1/2 Liter 440.00
Character, Bismarck, Porcelain, Lid, Schierholz, 1/2 Liter 374.00
Character, Bismarck, Porcelain, Porcelain Lid, Schierholz, 1/2 Liter 184.00
Character, Bowling Ball, Relief Bowling Pins Around Body, Porcelain, Inlaid Lid, 1/2 Liter 468.00
Character, Bowling Pin, Porcelain, Inlaid Lid, 1/2 Liter 845.00
Character, Bowling Pin, Pottery, Inlaid Lid, 1/2 Liter ....95.00 to 200.00
Character, Bowling Pin, Pottery, Inlaid Lid, 2 Liter 450.00
Character, Bowling Pin, Pottery, Lid, No. 1139, 1/2 Liter 195.00
Character, Bustle Lady, Flower Panels, Threaded Relief, Woman & Umbrella Thumblift, 1/2 Liter .. 525.00
Character, Bustle Lady, Stoneware, Pewter Lid, HR Mark, 1/2 Liter 620.00
Character, Cat, Music Box Base, Pottery, Inlaid Lid, No. 632, 1/2 Liter 669.00
Character, Clown, Pottery, Inlaid Lid, Diesinger, No. 795, 1/2 Liter 140.00
Character, Dwarf, Inlaid Lid, Diesinger, No. 694, Pottery, 1/2 Liter 545.00
Character, Fox, Stoneware, Inlaid Lid, 1/2 Liter 390.00
Character, Girl, Holding Baby Rattle, Stoneware, Pewter Lid, 5 In. 360.00
Character, Guitar Player, Outdoor Table Scene, Inlaid Lid, JW Remy, No. 962, 2 1/2 Liter 265.00
Character, Happy Radish, Porcelain Inlaid Lid, Porcelain, Schierholz, 1/2 Liter 380.00
Character, Hops Lady, Porcelain, Lid, Schierholz, 1/2 Liter 725.00
Character, Judge, Porcelain, Inlaid Lid Of Funnel, Schierholz, 1/2 Liter 966.00
Character, Knight, Pottery, Majolica Glaze, Pewter Base Ring & Lid, 1/2 Liter 518.00
Character, Knight, Pottery, White, Blue, Black, 3 1/4 In. 145.00
Character, Man, Riding High Wheel Bicycle, Cast Pewter Lid, Stoneware, 1/2 Liter 3188.00
Character, Man, Wearing Military Hat, Stoneware, Inlaid Lid, 1/2 Liter 559.00
Character, Monk Looking At Wine Glass, Eating, Monk Reading, Porcelain, Inlaid Lid, 1 Liter 2325.00
Character, Monk, Stoneware, Inlaid Lid, Merkelbach & Wicke, 1 Liter 175.00
Character, Monkey, Sitting On Barrel, Porcelain, Inlaid Lid, Schierholz, 1/2 Liter 362.00
Character, Munchen, Munich Child, Pottery, Inlaid Lid, J. Reinemann, 1/2 Liter 725.00
Character, Munchen, Porcelain, Porcelain Inlaid Lid, J. Reinemann, 1/3 Liter 159.00
Character, Munich Child, Barrel, Bock, Porcelain, 4 1/2 In. 345.00
Character, Munich Child, Black Robe, Porcelain, Inlaid Lid, 1/2 Liter 339.00
Character, Munich Child, Brown Robe, Pointed Hood, Porcelain, Inlaid Lid, 1/2 Liter 301.00
Character, Munich Child, City Scene Of Munchen, Pewter Lid, Hauber & Reuther, 1/2 Liter 376.00
Character, Munich Child, Hofbrauhaus & Bavaria, Relief, Pottery, Pewter Lid, 1 Liter 130.00
Character, Munich Child, On Barrel, Porcelain, Inlaid Lid, Schierholz, 1/2 Liter 1277.00
Character, Munich Child, Porcelain, Inlaid Lid, 1/4 Liter 156.00
Character, Munich Child, Pottery, Inlaid Lid, No. 554, 1/3 Liter 517.00
Character, Munich Child, Relief, Pewter Lid, Martin Pauson Workshop, Pottery, 1/8 Liter, 4 1/4 In. 139.00

Character, Munich Child, Stoneware, Pottery Inlaid Lid, No. 1585, 1/2 Liter 485.00
Character, Munich Child, Transfer, Enamel, Lithophane, Pewter Lid, Martin Pauson, 5 1/2 In. 165.00
Character, Nurnberg Tower, Pewter, Pewter Lid, 1/4 Liter, 6 In. 173.00
Character, Nurnberg Tower, Stoneware, Pewter Lid, Marked, HR, 5 In., 1/8 Liter 210.00
Character, Nurnberger Trichter, Jester Handle, Porcelain, Inlaid Lid, Schierholz, 1/2 Liter 1065.00
Character, Owl, Inlaid Lid, Pottery, 1/2 Liter 300.00
Character, Owl, Pottery, Music Box, Inlaid Lid, 1/2 Liter 966.00
Character, Owl, Stoneware, Inlaid Lid, 1/2 Liter 195.00
Character, Rich Man, Pottery, Inlaid Lid, No. 8669, 1/2 Liter 563.00
Character, Sad Radish, Porcelain, Inlaid Lid, Schierholz, 1/2 Liter 185.00
Character, Sad Radish, Porcelain, Inlaid Lid, Schierholz, 1/3 Liter 240.00
Character, Sad Radish, Porcelain, Schierholz, 1/2 Liter 176.00
Character, Schutzenliesl Inside Barrel, Porcelain, Lid, Clown With Target, Schierholz, 1/2 Liter 3230.00
Character, Skull, Porcelain, Inlaid Lid, E. Bohne & Sohne, 1/2 Liter ....189.00 to 405.00
Character, Sleeping Hunter, Porcelain Lid, Bauer, 1/2 Liter 725.00
Character, Student, Porcelain, Inlaid Lid, 1/2 Liter 1810.00
Character, Tower, Postwar, Rastal, Stoneware, 1 Liter 90.00
Character, Von Moltke, Porcelain, Lid, Schierholz, 1/2 Liter 1208.00
Character, Wilhelm, Stoneware, Inlaid Lid, No. 934, 1/2 Liter 278.00
Character, Woman, Pottery, Inlaid Lid, No. 724, 1/2 Liter 290.00
Character, Woman, Smiling, Porcelain, Pewter Lid, Schierholz, 1/2 Liter 440.00
Delft, Dutch Windmill & Sailboat, Hand Painted, Inlaid Lid, 1/2 Liter 145.00
Faience, Fish, Hannau Style, Pewter Base Ring & Lid, c.1900, 1/2 Liter, 7 3/4 In. 175.00
Faience, Pewter Lid, Potsdam Factory, Floral & Sponge Manganese, 1/2 Liter 525.00
Glass, Blown, Amber, Applied Blue Glass Prunts, Pewter Lid, 1/2 Liter 138.00
Glass, Blown, Amber, Birds, Enameled, Pewter Lid, 1 1/2 Liter 120.00
Glass, Blown, Amber, Coin Spot, Pewter Base & Relief Lid, Inscribed, Andreas Huber, 1/2 Liter 220.00
Glass, Blown, Amber, Coin Spot, Pewter Relief Overlay & Lid, 1/2 Liter 395.00
Glass, Blown, Amber, Enameled Crest, Sachsen, Pewter Lid, 1/2 Liter 230.00
Glass, Blown, Amber, Green Prunts, Faceted Body, Pewter Base & Filigree Lid, 1/2 Liter 176.00
Glass, Blown, Amber, Pewter Relief Overlay & Lid, 1/2 Liter 330.00
Glass, Blown, Amber, Pewter Relief Overlay & Lid, 3/10 Liter 160.00
Glass, Blown, Applied Pink Glass Prunts, Pewter Lid, Dwarf Thumblift, 3 Liter 345.00
Glass, Blown, Barrel Shape, Cobalt Blue, Pewter Lid, c.1820, 5 In. 290.00
Glass, Blown, Blue Glass Layer, Fluted, Flowers, Gold, Silver Mounts, Inlaid Lid, 1/2 Liter 375.00
Glass, Blown, Cut & Polished, Pewter Lid, 1/2 Liter 110.00
Glass, Blown, Cut Design, Woman, Transfer, Silver Plated Lid, 1/2 Liter 325.00
Glass, Blown, Dog, Running, Forest, Engraved, Yellow Stain, Glass Inlaid Lid, c.1850, 2 3/4 In. ... 340.00
Glass, Blown, Dwarf Playing Bass Finial, Playing Fiddle Thumblift, Pewter Lid, 1/2 Liter 120.00
Glass, Blown, Enameled Castle, Pink, White Glass Overlay, Inlaid Lid, c.1850, 1/2 Liter 750.00
Glass, Blown, Enameled Flowers, Wedding Design, Pewter Lid, c.1850, 3/4 Liter 485.00
Glass, Blown, Enameled, Cherub In Flower, Pewter Lid, Closed Hinge, 1/2 Liter 350.00
Glass, Blown, Facet Cut, Brass Helmet Finial Lid, Eagle Thumblift, Engraved, 1909, 1/2 Liter 250.00
Glass, Blown, Facet Cut, Brass Lid, Helmet Finial, Cannon Thumblift, 1/2 Liter 220.00
Glass, Blown, Facet Cut, Carved Horn Lid & Thumblift, Pewter Lid, 1/2 Liter 358.00
Glass, Blown, Green, Enameled Flower, Pewter Lid, 1/2 Liter 180.00
Glass, Blown, Green, Ribs, Gold Paint, Pewter Lid, 1 1/2 Liter, 16 1/2 In. 60.00
Glass, Blown, Green, Thumbprint, White Enameled Woman, Glass Inlaid Lid, 5 1/2 In. 145.00
Glass, Blown, Man & Woman, Enamel, Fritz Heckert, 1/2 Liter, 4 x 4 1/2 In. 230.00
Glass, Blown, Marktbrun Spa Building, Facet Cut, Hourglass, Pedestal Base, Engraved, SW, 1/2 Liter 176.00
Glass, Blown, Musical Instruments, Verse, Transfer, Enameled, Pewter Lid, 1 Liter 230.00
Glass, Blown, Prosit Papa., Cut Design, Glass Inlaid Lid, c.1850, 1/2 Liter 75.00
Glass, Blown, Red, Deer In Forest, Engraved, Inlaid Lid, c.1850, 3/4 Liter, 7 In. 660.00
Glass, Blown, Sprudel I. Karlsbad, Fluted, Glass Inlaid Lid, c.1850, 3 1/4 Liter 265.00
Glass, Blown, Stags In Forest, Enamel, Facet Cut, Pedestal Base, Pewter Lid, 1/2 Liter 248.00
Glass, Blown, Threading, Pewter Lid, 16 In., 1 1/2 Liter 80.00
Glass, Blown, Uranium, Yellow, Interior Fluted Body, Relief Pewter Base & Lid, 1/2 Liter 250.00
Glass, Blown, Wilhelm I, Transparent Enamel, Facet Cut, Prism Lid, 1/2 Liter 265.00
Ivory, Battle Scene, Hand Carved, Brass Base Top Rim, Handle, Lid, Soldier Finial, 1900, 8 In. 875.00
Majolica, Blue Glaze, Relief, Austria, 1/4 Liter 90.00
Majolica, Olive Green Glaze, Relief, Austria, 1/4 Liter 90.00

Mettlach steins are listed in the Mettlach category.
Military, 3 Panels Of Soldiers, Pottery, Pewter Lid, 1/2 Liter . . . 90.00
Military, 3rd BN. 16th Arty. Baumholder, Porcelain, Pewter Lid, 1/2 Liter . . . 95.00
Military, 15th Army Postal Unit Zweibrucken, Transfer, Enamel, Pottery, Pewter Lid, 1 Liter . . . 145.00
Military, 83rd Eng. BN. H/S Co. Bussac-France, 1955-57, Porcelain, Pewter Lid, 1/2 Liter . . . 145.00
Military, 7425th. Support Group Hahn Airbase, 1953-55, Porcelain, 1/2 Liter . . . 115.00
Military, Cannoniers, Franco-Prussian Helmet Finial, Merkelbach & Wick, POG, 1897, 1 Liter . . . 468.00
Military, Fat Soldier, Stoneware, Pewter Lid, Signed, Franz Ringer, 1/2 Liter . . . 385.00
Military, Glass, Blown, Silver Plated Lid, Helmet Finial, Wurttemberg Crest, c.1914, 1/2 Liter . . . 720.00
Military, Reservilt Krieger, Lithophane, Germany, Early 1900s, 7 In. . . . 175.00
Military, S.M.S. Kaiser Barbarossa, Pottery, 1/2 Liter . . . 220.00
Military, Soldier & Shields, Franco-Prussian Helmet Lid, Porcelain, Lithograph, 1/2 Liter . . . 495.00
Military, Soldiers, Konigl, Bayer, Infanterie Leib-Regiment, 1814-1914, Relief Pewter Lid, 1/2 Liter 165.00
Military, Vietnam Jun 64-Nov. 65 Magnus Amator Mulierum, Glass, 1/4 Liter . . . 120.00
Military, Wilhelm I & II, Iron Cross Relief Pewter Lid, Kaisers On Thumblift, Porcelain, 1/2 Liter . . . 100.00
Military, Wilhelm I & II, Porcelain, Lithograph, Pewter Lid, 1/2 Liter . . . 149.00
Occupational, Baker, Rampant Lions, Bakers Shield, Porcelain, Lithograph, Pewter Lid, 1/2 Liter . 300.00
Occupational, Beer Brewer, Porcelain, Pewter Lid, 1929, 1/2 Liter . . . 360.00
Occupational, Belgium Rabbits, Transfer, Enamel, Lithophane, Pewter Lid, 1/2 Liter . . . 390.00
Occupational, Builder, Men Building House, Pottery, Lithograph, Pewter Lid, 1/2 Liter . . . 230.00
Occupational, Butcher, Engraved, Pewter, 3 Ball Feet, 13 In. . . . 385.00
Occupational, Butcher, Porcelain, Transfer, Enamel, Pewter Lid, 1/2 Liter . . . 242.00
Occupational, Carpenter, Karl Metzger, Porcelain, Transfer, Enamel, Lion Thumblift, 1/2 Liter . . . 370.00
Occupational, Farmer Plowing In Hot Sun, Porcelain, Lithograph, Pewter Lid, 1/2 Liter . . . 220.00
Occupational, Firefighting Scenes, Stoneware, Relief Pewter Lid, POG, 1/2 Liter . . . 176.00
Occupational, Master Plasterer, Jakob Knoch, Porcelain, Lithophane, Pewter Lid, 1/2 Liter . . . 450.00
Occupational, Printer, Saxa Loquunture, Lithographer, Porcelain, Pewter Lid, 1/2 Liter . . . 276.00
Occupational, Socialist Traveling Mason, Porcelain, Transfer, Enamel, Pewter Lid, 1/2 Liter . . . 604.00
Pewter, 4F Shield, Fireman Helmet Finial & Thumblift, 1/2 Liter . . . 140.00
Pewter, Eagle, Relief, Pewter Lid, 2 1/2 Liter . . . 240.00
Pewter, Flower Wreath, Engraved, Smooth Finish, Lid, c.1820, 1/2 Liter . . . 145.00
Pewter, Lion Masks, Barrel Shape Thumblift, Josf Msel, Germany, c.1690, 9 1/2 In. . . . 210.00
Pewter, Pillow Fight Of French & Germans, Relief, 1/2 Liter . . . 525.00
Pewter, Raised Faces, Pineapple Finial, Face Thumblift, Christmas, 1896, 1/2 Liter . . . 120.00
Porcelain, Animals, Inlaid Lid Of Hunter, 1/2 Liter . . . 180.00
Porcelain, Gruss Aus Rothenberg, Transfer, Enamel, Pewter Lid, 1/4 Liter . . . 95.00
Porcelain, King Ludwig, Pewter Lid, Strap, 1/2 Liter . . . 86.00
Porcelain, Ludwigsburg., Chinoiseries, Porcelain Inlaid Lid, 1/2 Liter, 5 1/2 In. . . . 1610.00
Porcelain, Man & Woman, Verse, Lithophane, 1/2 Liter . . . 110.00
Porcelain, Man Drinking, Pewter Lid, Etched, Tapestry, Hauber & Reuther, 1/2 Liter . . . 145.00
Porcelain, Reichenhall, Transfer, Enameled, Pewter Lid, 1/4 Liter, 5 1/2 In. . . . 80.00
Porcelain, Tapestry, Man Drinking, No. 157, Pewter Lid, Hauber & Reuther, 1/2 Liter . . . 210.00
Porcelain, Tapestry, Man Feeding Fish To Cat, No. 178, Pewter Lid, Hauber & Reuther, 1/2 Liter . . . 169.00
Porcelain, Trees, Birds, Hand Painted, Gold, Lithophane, Pewter Lid, 1/3 Liter . . . 138.00
Pottery, 4F Shield, Turner, Skyline Of Munchen, Transfer, Enamel, Pewter Lid, 1/8 Liter . . . 105.00
Pottery, Alt Heidelberg Du Feine, Transfer, Enamel, Pewter Lid, Perkeo, 2 1/2 In. . . . 70.00
Pottery, Bayreuth, City Scenes, Pewter Lid, No. 414, Thewalt, 1/2 Liter . . . 130.00
Pottery, Bird, Brown W, George Wiedemann Brewing Co., Relief, Pewter Lid, Rookwood, 1/2 Liter . . 220.00
Pottery, Card Playing Scene, Relief, No. 1403, Pewter Lid, 1/2 Liter . . . 270.00
Pottery, Cards, Etched, No. 1255A, Pewter Lid, 1/2 Liter . . . 138.00
Pottery, Cherubs & People, Relief, Pewter Lid, No. 353, 2 1/2 Liter . . . 135.00
Pottery, Child With Snail, Birdhouse, 2 Birds, Transfer, Pewter Lid, 4 1/2 In. . . . 240.00
Pottery, Couple At Table, Threading, Pewter Lid, Diesinger, 1/2 Liter . . . 145.00
Pottery, Drinking Scene Around Body, Relief, Pewter Lid, 2 1/2 Liter . . . 120.00
Pottery, Dwarf Adjusting Clock, Pewter Lid, Diesinger, 1/2 Liter . . . 158.00
Pottery, Dwarfs Playing Dice On Toadstools, Multicolored, Relief, 1/2 Liter . . . 120.00
Pottery, Falstaff & Bardolph, Etched, Pewter Lid, Birmscheid, 1/2 Liter . . . 115.00
Pottery, Falstaff, Relief, Pewter Lid, No. 571, 1 Liter . . . 240.00
Pottery, Fish, Etched, Pewter Lid, Merkelbach & Wick, 1/2 Liter . . . 295.00
Pottery, Flowers, Relief, Pewter Lid, No. 572, Gerz, 21 In. . . . 290.00
Pottery, Gasthaus Scene, Etched, Inlaid Lid, No. 717, JWR, 1 Liter . . . 220.00

Pottery, Gasthaus Scene, Etched, Pewter, 2 Liter 230.00
Pottery, Germans Meeting Romans, Pewter Lid, 1/2 Liter 90.00
Pottery, Goose Man Fountain, Gruss Aus Nurnberg, Transfer, Pewter Lid, 1/8 Liter, 3 1/2 In. 94.00
Pottery, Greek Scene, Relief, No. 1272, Pewter Lid, Steinzeugwerke, 1/2 Liter 220.00
Pottery, Gruss Aus Frankfurt A.M., Transfer, Enamel, Pewter Lid, 1/8 Liter 58.00
Pottery, Hunter & Maiden, Relief, 3-D Figural Dwarfs On Barrel Lid, Signed, KB, 1/2 Liter 120.00
Pottery, Hunter, Relief, Pewter Lid, No. 6, 1 1/2 Liter 121.00
Pottery, Hunting Scene, Fox Handle, Pewter Lid, 2 Liter 85.00
Pottery, Innkeeper At Barrel, Relief, Pewter Lid, 1/2 Liter 90.00
Pottery, Man & Woman, Relief, Pewter Lid, Diesinger, 1/2 Liter 145.00
Pottery, Man Lifting Dumbbells, 100 Lb. Weight Thumblift, Relief Pewter Lid, POG, 2/5 Liter 132.00
Pottery, Man Riding Standard Bicycle, Relief, Pewter Lid, 1/2 Liter 200.00
Pottery, Man, 2 Women, Dog, Etched, Pewter Lid, 1/2 Liter 110.00
Pottery, Men & Boy, Pewter Lid, JWR, 1/2 Liter 158.00
Pottery, Men At Table Gambling, Etched, No. 527, HR, 1/2 Liter 275.00
Pottery, Men On Horseback, Etched, No. 1621, Pewter Lid, Marzi & Remy, 1/2 Liter 230.00
Pottery, Monk & Stein, POG, Manning Bowman, 1/2 Liter 85.00
Pottery, Monkey & Shield, Cream, Red, Brown, 1/2 Liter 80.00
Pottery, Monkeys, Pewter Lid, Dumler & Breiden, 1/2 Liter 120.00
Pottery, Monks, Soldiers, Falstaff, Relief, Pewter Lid, No. 103, 4 Liter 259.00
Pottery, Munchen City Scene, Relief, Glazed Finish, Pewter Lid, 1/2 Liter 165.00
Pottery, Musical Harp & Cupid, Harp Pewter Relief Lid & Thumblift, POG, 1/2 Liter 110.00
Pottery, Night Watchman Chasing Fraternal Students Home, 1/2 Liter 314.00
Pottery, Nurnberg, City Scenes, Relief, Pewter Lid, 1/2 Liter 159.00
Pottery, Outdoor Scene, Etched, Hanke, 1/2 Liter 110.00
Pottery, People Around Water Pump, Relief, Pewter Lid, No. 456, Hauber & Reuther, 1/2 Liter 240.00
Pottery, Schutzenliesl, Relief, Pewter Lid, 1914, 2 1/2 Liter, 15 1/4 In. 236.00
Pottery, Socialist, Dumler & Breiden, Marx, Lassalle, Bebel & Liebknecht, 1/2 Liter 690.00
Pottery, Souvenir Scenes Of Boston, POG, Pewter Lid, 1/4 Liter 85.00
Pottery, St. Nickolas Society Meeting, December 5, 1900, Blue Underglaze, Holland, 1/2 Liter 130.00
Pottery, Stoneware, Card Game In Gasthaus & Priest, Pewter Lid, Hauber & Reuther, 1/2 Liter 220.00
Pottery, Tavern Scene, 3 People Sitting At Table, Multicolored, Relief, Pewter Lid, 1 Liter 110.00
Pottery, Tavern Scene, Woman Figural Handle, Pewter Lid, 1/2 Liter 110.00
Pottery, Trumpeter Of Sackingen, Inlaid Lid, Etched, Relief, 1/2 Liter 195.00
Pottery, Trumpeter Of Sackingen, Relief, Pewter Lid, Diesinger, 1/2 Liter 195.00
Pottery, Von Hindenburg In Wreath, Soldiers, Pewter Lid, Iron Cross Thumblift, 1/2 Liter 150.00
Pottery, Warriors Drinking, Pewter Lid, Thick Relief, 1 Liter 305.00
Regimental, 1. Kgl. Sachs. Lieb-Gren, Rgt. Nr. 100. 4. Comp. Dresden 1910-12, 1/2 Liter 330.00
Regimental, 3 Comp Infantry, 7 Wurttb., No 125 Stuttgart 1895-97, 1/2 Liter, 9 In. 316.00
Regimental, 4 Co. Kgl. Bayr. 4 Infantry Rgt. Metz 1896-98, 1/2 Liter, 10 1/2 In. 280.00
Regimental, Campfire & Native Scenes, Pewter, 5 1/4 In. 265.00
Regimental, Eagle Thumblift, Porcelain, 1/2 Liter, 8 1/2 In. 270.00
Regimental, Medical Scenes, Roster, Lion Thumblift, Porcelain, 1/2 Liter, 11 3/4 In. 1058.00
Regimental, Roster, 1 Esc. 1. Garde Ulanen Regt. Potsdam 1901-04, 1/2 Liter, 11 In. 828.00
Regimental, Roster, 1 Gr. Hess. Infantry Reg. No 115, 2 Comp Darmstadt 1898-1900, 1/2 Liter 478.00
Regimental, Roster, 2 Battr. Field Artillerie Nr 39 Perleberg 1908-10, 1/2 Liter, 12 In. 410.00
Regimental, Roster, 16 Infantry 4 Comp. Landshut 1908-10, Stoneware, 1/2 Liter, 12 In. 470.00
Regimental, Roster, Eagle Thumblift, 1/2 Liter, 11 1/4 In. 605.00
Regimental, Roster, Eagle Thumblift, 1/2 Liter, 12 In. 1093.00
Regimental, Roster, Eagle Thumblift, Porcelain, 1/2 Liter, 11 In. 485.00
Regimental, Roster, Griffin Thumblift, Horse, Rider Finial, Porcelain, 1/2 Liter, 13 1/4 In. 605.00
Regimental, Roster, Griffin Thumblift, Porcelain, 1/2 Liter, 10 3/4 In. 665.00
Regimental, Roster, Kgl. Bayr. 5 Infantry 7 Comp Bamberg 1909-11, 1/2 Liter, 12 1/4 In. 2415.00
Regimental, Roster, Lion Thumblift, Glass Prism Inlaid Lid, 1/2 Liter, 9 1/2 In. 348.00
Regimental, Roster, Porcelain, Pewter Lid, 1/2 Liter, 9 1/2 In. 255.00
Regimental, Roster, Winged Wheel Thumblift, Stoneware, 1/2 Liter 7005.00
Salt Glaze, Springer Spaniel, Standing Nude, Sunset Beach, White's, Utica, 6 3/4 In. 580.00
Stoneware, 12 Apostles, Fired Multicolored Enamel, Pewter Lid, Creussen, c.1900, 1/2 Liter 356.00
Stoneware, Art Nouveau, Pewter Lid, Jacob Julius Scharvogel, 1/2 Liter 315.00
Stoneware, Barmaid Carrying Many Steins, Speckled Brown Body, POG, 1 Liter 138.00
Stoneware, Blue Flowers, Oberstdorf, Enamel, Relief Pewter Lid With Edelweiss, 1/8 Liter 98.00

Stoneware, Character, Monk, Merkelbach & Wick, 1/2 Liter 248.00
Stoneware, Defregger Gasthaus Scene, Transfer, Pewter Lid, Martin Pauson Shop, 1 Liter 330.00
Stoneware, Defregger Pipe Scene, Men In Kitchen With Women, Pewter Lid, 3 Liter 575.00
Stoneware, Deutsches Bundesschiessen 1927, Officieller Festkrug, POG, 1/2 Liter, 18 In. 198.00
Stoneware, Edm. V. Konig Heidelberg, No. 5173, Alt Heidelberg Due Feine, 1/2 Liter 300.00
Stoneware, Flowers & Verse, Porcelain Inlaid Student Shield, Relief, 1/2 Liter 110.00
Stoneware, Flowers, Block, Hand Engraved, Pewter Lid, Westerwald, 1700s, 1/2 Liter, 8 1/4 In. .. 605.00
Stoneware, Funnel, Verse, Gruss Aus Nurnberg, Pewter Lid, F. Ringer, 1/8 Liter 290.00
Stoneware, Germania, Bavaria & Munich Child, Cupid Pewter Relief Lid, 1 Liter 130.00
Stoneware, Hand Engraved Pattern, Pewter Lid, Westerwald, 1 Liter, 8 In. 320.00
Stoneware, Hanswurst., Inlaid Lid, F. Ringer, 6 In. 578.00
Stoneware, Heads & Prosit, Blue & White, Relief, Pewter Lid, 1/4 Liter 35.00
Stoneware, Hunter & Barmaid, Etched, Stoneware Lid, Girmscheid, 1 Liter 140.00
Stoneware, Hunter & Song Notes, Etched, Inlaid Lid, Marzy & Remy, No. 1614, 1/2 Liter 300.00
Stoneware, Koln Cathedral, Relief, Pewter Lid, 1/2 Liter 130.00
Stoneware, Koln Cathedral, Relief, Pewter Lid, Monk Finial, 1/2 Liter 195.00
Stoneware, Man Playing Lyre, Transfer, Enamel, Pewter Lid, 1/2 Liter 85.00
Stoneware, Men Drinking, Pewter Lid, No. 35, White's, N.Y., 1/3 Liter 120.00
Stoneware, Men Riding High Wheel Bicycles, Relief, Pewter Lid, 1/2 Liter 195.00
Stoneware, Musicians, Relief, Blue & White, Frog On Bottom, 1/2 Liter 90.00
Stoneware, Night Watchman & Innkeeper, Pewter Lid, Girmscheid, 1 1/2 Liter 155.00
Stoneware, Night Watchman, Transfer, Enameled, Pewter Lid, 1 Liter 206.00
Stoneware, Noah & Ark, King David Playing Harp, Relief, Inlaid Lid, Gerz, 1/2 Liter 70.00
Stoneware, People, Pressed, Relief, Cream, Porcelain Inlaid Lid, Pewter, 1/2 Liter 90.00
Stoneware, Prince Of Pilsen, Silver Plated Lid, White's, Utica, N.Y., 1/2 Liter 180.00
Stoneware, Saul Holofernes, Sanherib, Relief, Blue Salt Glaze, 2 Liter 38.00
Stoneware, Scene Commemorating 10 Years Of Song Club, 1924-34, POG, Woman, 1/2 Liter 88.00
Stoneware, Shooting Festival, 18 Deutsches Bundesschiessen Munchen, 1927, 1 Liter 435.00
Stoneware, Shooting Festival, Man Shooting Rifle, Germania, Transfer, Pewter Lid, 1/2 Liter 250.00
Stoneware, Trumpeter Of Sackingen, Pewter Lid, Relief, 4 1/4 In. 79.00
Stoneware, Union Station St. Louis, Mo., Pewter Lid, White's, New York, 1/3 Liter 966.00
Stoneware, Verse, Hand Painted, Pewter Lid, Saltzer, c.1893, 1 Liter 300.00
Stoneware, Warriors & Knights At War, Relief, 2 Liter 165.00
Stoneware, Woman, Pewter Lid, White's, N.Y., 3/4 Liter 220.00
Wood, Wheat, Hops, Oak Leaves, Hand Carved, Handle, Lid, Worm Holes, 1 Liter, 11 In. 970.00

STEREO CARDS that were made for stereoscope viewers became popular after 1840. Two almost identical pictures were mounted on a stiff cardboard backing so that, when viewed through a stereoscope, a three-dimensional picture could be seen. Value is determined by maker and by subject. These cards were made in quantity through the 1930s.

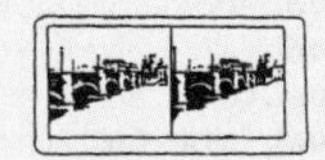

Admiral Sampson's Fleet At Blockade, Havana, James M. Davis, c.1898 .... 12.00
Basillo Street, Poor Quarter, Santiago, Cuba, Underwood & Underwood, c.1899 .... 9.00
Curley, Sole Survivor Of Custer Massacre, F.A. Rinehart, 1900 .... 380.00
Fishermen Of Siasconset, Nantucket, No. 1232, Kilburn 80.00
French Colonial Cavalry In Paris, Keystone View Co. 8.00
Going Up Yukon River By Moonlight To Dawson City, Alaska, 1898, 3 1/2 x 7 In. 108.00
Libby Prison, Richmond, Virginia 175.00
London Bridge, London, England, Underwood & Underwood, c.1901 .... 12.00
Music Day In The Park, Central Park, No. 7245, Anthony 127.00
Onward & Upward Over Chilcoot Pass, James M. Davis, Kilburn, 1898, 3 1/2 x 7 In. 145.00
Our Grand Battleship Oregon, Underwood & Underwood, c.1898 .... 15.00
Plunder Captured From The Russians, T.W. Ingersoll, c.1905 .... 8.00
Railroad Trestle Works, Nevada County, Cal., No. 201, J.J. Reilly 288.00
Recreation In A Japanese Army Camp, T.W. Ingersoll, c.1905 .... 7.00
Royal Guard On Duty, Windsor Palace, Windsor, England, Stereo-Travel Co., c.1908 .... 12.00
Scene Of Late Fire, H.A. Kimball, Concord, N.H., c.1869 .... 52.00
Ste. Marie Shiop Canal, In Locke, No. 494, C.B. Brubaker, Marquette, Mich. 196.00
Steamer Darlington At Enterprise, No. 86, Wood & Bickle, Jacksonville, Florida 86.00
Studio, Tilden Ladies Seminary, W. Lebanon, N.H., W.W. Culver 86.00

U.S. Troops Leaving San Francisco For Manila, Griffith & Griffith, c.1898 .... 14.00
Uncle Sam Remembers Dewey Day, Griffith & Griffith, c.1898 .... 14.00
War Chief Of Zuni Indians, Wheeler Expedition, T.H. O'Sullivan, 1873 .... 288.00
Winter View From My Window, Carl Meinerth, Newburyport, Mass. 449.00
Wrecked Building In Amiens, France, Keystone View Co. 8.00
Zuni Indian Girl With Water Olla, No. 17, Wheeler Expedition, T.H. O'Sullivan, 1873 .... 196.00

STEREOSCOPES were used for viewing stereo cards. The hand viewer was invented by Oliver Wendell Holmes, although more complicated table models were used before his was produced in 1859. Do not confuse the stereoscope with the stereopticon, a magic lantern that used glass slides.

Becker, Stereo Double Viewer, Walnut, 2 Lens Sets, 1857 Patent, 15 In. 880.00
Brewster Form, Biedermeier Style, Fruitwood, Table Top, Late 1800s, 9 3/4 In. 429.00
Brewster Pattern, Mahogany Body, Glass Screen, Brass, 14 1/2 In. 529.00
H.C. White, Perfecscope, 22 Cards, Case, 14 In. 295.00
Keystone, Tour Of The World, 7 Slip Cases, 1600 Views 863.00
P. Spruit, Focusable Eyepieces, Wood, For 9 x 18 cm, Helder 411.00
Schneck Pattern, Reversible, Nickel Plated, Baluster Stand, No Lens, 13 In. 295.00
Stereo-Graphoscope, Walnut, Folding Stereo Lenses, France, 4 1/2-In. Lens, 16 In. 295.00
Stereopticon, 50 Photo Cards, Celluloid Card Holder 173.00
Stereoscope, Ernemann, Wood Case, 1913, 15 1/3 In., 5 Magazines 1175.00
Verascope, Folding, Hand-Held, For 45 x 107, Leather Case, c.1909, 16 Slides 617.00
Verascope, Wood, Paternoster Mechanism, 20 Boxes Of Slides, c.1900, 15 1/2 In. 1762.00

STERLING SILVER, see Silver-Sterling category.

STEUBEN glass was made at the Steuben Glass Works of Corning, New York. The factory, founded by Frederick Carder and T.G. Hawkes, Sr., was purchased by the Corning Glass Company. They continued to make glass called *Steuben*. Many types of art glass were made at Steuben. The firm is still making exceptional quality glass but it is clear, modern-style glass. Additional pieces may be found in the Aurene, Cluthra, and perfume bottle categories.

Basket, Green Jade, Alabaster Handle, 8 In. 805.00
Bowl, Acid Cut, Green Jade Over Alabaster, 2 3/4 x 10 In. 635.00
Bowl, Acid Cut, Nedra, Rosaline Over Alabaster, 6 1/2 x 8 In. 1150.00
Bowl, Acid Cut, Sea Holly, Mirror Black Over Alabaster, 10 In. 4370.00
Bowl, Calcite, Blue Aurene Interior, 2 3/4 x 8 In. 430.00
Bowl, Calcite, Blue Aurene Interior, Flaring Rim, 9 In. 920.00
Bowl, Calcite, Gold Aurene Interior, Footed, 10 In. 375.00
Bowl, Calcite, Gold Aurene Interior, Stepped, Rolled Curved Rim, c.1900, 12 In. 418.00
Bowl, Crystal, Calyx, No. 8115, Donald Pollard, Signed, 9 1/2 In. 230.00
Bowl, Crystal, Leafy Base, James McNaughton, c.1937, 6 3/4 x 8 1/4 In. 235.00
Bowl, Crystal, Triple Loop Base, Footed, 3 1/4 x 7 3/4 In. 120.00
Bowl, Millefiori, Flowers, Vines, Leaves, Scalloped Rim, 2 1/16 x 3 7/8 In. 1725.00
Bowl, Openwork Cover, Topaz, Celeste Blue Foot, Folded Leaf Finial, 10 In. 1095.00
Candleholder, Celeste Blue Loop Handle, Green Disc Foot, No. 5146, Label, 4 1/2 In. 489.00
Candlestick, 2-Light, Ivrene, Flower Shape Cups, Round Foot, c.1920, 10 1/2 In. 720.00
Candlestick, Amethyst Cut To Crystal, Swirled Body, 8 In., Pair 1150.00
Candlestick, Amethyst, Optic Ribbed, c.1924, 7 15/16 In. .... *ILLUS* 478.00
Candlestick, Celeste Blue Top & Fluted Foot, Clear Rope Twist Stem, c.1920, 9 3/4 In. 508.00
Candlestick, Celeste Blue, Amethyst Cup, Applied Prunts, Teardrop Stem, 12 In., Pair 2875.00
Candlestick, Pomona Green, Amber Foot, Cup, Fluted, c.1920, 12 In., Pair .... *ILLUS* 717.00
Candlestick, Pomona Green, Ribbed, Double Ball Knop, 10 In., Pair 575.00
Candy Dish, Cover, Crystal, Ram's Head Finial, Signed, No. 7936, 1949, 6 In. 489.00
Champagne, Clear Bowl, Rose Stem, Etched, 6 1/2 In., 6 Piece 1112.00
Cigarette Holder, Crystal, 5 In. 80.00
Cocktail, Amber, Ribbed, Celeste Blue Twist Stem, 5 1/2 In. 290.00
Compote, Amber Oval Bowl, Optic Ribbed, Pomona Green Swirled Foot, 7 x 9 In. 518.00
Compote, Amethyst, Footed, 5 1/4 x 12 In. 375.00
Compote, Cover, Jade Yellow, Pear Finial, Knopped Stem, Flared Rim, c.1920, 7 1/4 In. 657.00

Steuben, Candlestick, Amethyst, Optic Ribbed, c.1924, 7 15/16 In.

Steuben, Candlestick, Pomona Green, Amber Foot, Cup, Fluted, c.1920, 12 In., Pair

Steuben, Perfume Bottle, Blue, Teardrop Body, Footed, Green Apple Stopper, 10 1/2 In.

Compote, Cover, Rosaline, Alabaster Finial, Stem, 7 1/2 In. 635.00
Compote, Gold Aurene, Calcite, Intaglio Band Of Flowers On Inside, 8 In. 920.00
Compote, Gold Aurene, Calcite, Trumpet Bowl, Flared Rim, 6 In. 345.00
Compote, Pomona Green, Deep Bowl, c.1925, 7 1/4 x 9 1/4 In. 179.00
Compote, Ruby Selenium, Disc Foot, Signed, 5 1/4 In. 690.00
Console, Celeste Blue, Ribbed, Amethyst Base, 6 x 12 In. 575.00
Console Set, Amethyst, Clear Wafer In Candlestick, 7 3/4-In. Candlestick, 3 Piece 865.00
Creamer, Crystal, No. 7778, Ball Knop, Shaped Rim & Handle, 6 1/2 In. 201.00
Creamer, Rosaline, Applied Alabaster Handle, 1 3/4 In. 259.00
Cup & Saucer, Rosaline, Applied Alabaster Handle, c.1910, 4 1/2 In. 345.00
Decanter, Crystal, 3-Ring Neck, Flattened Oval Stopper, Signed, 10 3/4 In. 350.00
Decanter, Crystal, Air Twist Stopper, 9 1/4 In. 69.00
Figurine, Apple, 4 1/2 In. 205.00
Figurine, Chick, 3 1/4 x 5 In. 235.00
Figurine, Grape Bunch, 7 In. 527.00
Figurine, Mirror Black, c.1928, 5 3/4 In. 1495.00
Figurine, Owl, Donald Pollard, 1955, 5 In. 439.00
Figurine, Penguin, 3 3/4 x 2 3/4 In. 265.00
Figurine, Pigeon, No. 6824, Signed, 6 1/2 In. 1380.00
Figurine, Whale, 2 3/4 x 4 3/4 In. 234.00
Goblet, Amethyst Cintra Lip Wrap On Foot & Rim, 6 1/2 In. 290.00
Goblet, Clear Bowl, Rose Stem, Etched, 8 In., 6 Piece 1404.00
Goblet, French Blue, Translucent Stem, Threading, 9 In., 4 Piece 316.00
Goblet, Green Jade, Knopped Stem, c.1920, 5 1/4 In. 120.00
Goblet, Internal Twisted Stems, 18 In., Pair 690.00
Jar, Cover, Flemish Blue, Pear & Leaf, Finial, 5 3/4 In. 2070.00
Lamp, Acid Cut, Black Amethyst, Ribbed, Gilt Foot, Chinese-Style, Brass Cap, 2 Sockets, 24 1/2 In. 1150.00
Lamp, Acid Cut, Flowers, Blue Aurene, Cast Swans Base, Silk Shade, 24 In. 2300.00
Lamp, Acid Cut, Green Jade, Silver Base & Fittings, c.1920, 27 In. 956.00
Lamp, Acid Cut, Yellow Jade, Chrysanthemum, Rectangular, Greek Key Base, 5 3/4 x 4 In. 2070.00
Lamp, Baluster Shade, Onion Skin Pattern, Metal Base, c.1900, 14 1/4 In. 1195.00
Lamp, Ceiling, Bell Shape, Gold Aurene Shade, Single Drop Chain, Signed, 8 In. 1200.00
Lamp Base, Acid Cut, Green Jade, Gold Aurene, Lava Drip, Flask Shape, 10 In. 1150.00
Lamp Base, Yellow Jade, Applied Blue Aurene Branch, Double Gourd, 11 In. 1265.00
Liqueur Set, Teardrop, Samuel Ayres, c.1937, 2 3/4 In., 12 Piece 500.00
Parfait, French Blue, Translucent Stem, Threading, 5 1/2 In. 316.00
Perfume Bottle, Blue, Teardrop Body, Footed, Green Apple Stopper, 10 1/2 In. .... *ILLUS* 478.00
Pitcher, Venetian, Clear, Pink Threads, No Stopper, 8 1/2 In. 185.00
Plate, Blue Cut To Clear, Poussin Pattern, Signed, 10 1/2 In. 805.00
Plate, Crystal Scroll, No. 8025, Signed, 8 5/8 In. 230.00
Plate, Rouge Flambe, Swirling Ribs, 8 1/2 In. 748.00
Salt, Calcite, Gold, Aurene Interior, Flared Rim, 1 1/2 In. 230.00
Salt, Green Jade, Alabaster, Footed, Flared Rim, 1 1/2 In. 345.00
Sculpture, Crystal, 2 Silver Gulls On Rock, Leather Box, 8 1/2 In. 2280.00

Sculpture, Crystal, 4 Seasons Panels, Wood Frame, Lucite Base, 11 1/4 In. 6900.00
Sculpture, Crystal, Egg Sliced Open, Gold Lilies, Translucent White Enamel, 5 In. 2300.00
Sculpture, Crystal, Guardian Angel, Outstretched Wings, Metal Halo, Leather Case, 6 In. 1265.00
Sculpture, Crystal, Luminor, Nude Woman, Black Glass Base, 12 1/2 In. 1380.00
Sculpture, Crystal, Narcissus Reclining At Pool, Touching Water, Leather Case, 11 In. 2875.00
Shade, Calcite, Green Pulled Feathers, Gold Aurene Tips, F. Carder, 7 In. 288.00
Shade, Gold Aurene, Green Drape, Stretched, Ruffled Edge, 6 In. 805.00
Shade, Gold Aurene, Pink, Blue Highlights, Green Pulled Feathers, 5 1/4 In. 290.00
Shade, Iridescent Ivory, Gold Aurene Hearts, Raised Vines, Bulbous, 4 3/4 In. 287.00
Shade, Lily Shape, Calcite, 5 In., Pair 325.00
Sherbet, Calcite, Gold Aurene Interior, Signed, 4 In. 230.00
Tumble-Up, Amber, Celeste Blue Handle, Lip Wrap, Tumbler, 5 1/4 & 3 1/2 In. 345.00
Tumbler, Highball, Crystal, No. 7940, Signed, George Thompson, 1947, 5 1/2 In., 16 Piece 705.00
Tumbler, Iced Tea, Crystal, Cylindrical, Flared Rim, Signed, 5 3/4 In., Pair 546.00
Urn, Aquamarine, 8 5/8 In. 290.00
Urn, Iridescent Gold, 2 1/2 In. 575.00
Vase, 2 Handles, Green Jade, c.1900, 10 x 8 In. 2106.00
Vase, 3 Bulbous Prongs, Ivory, Bulbous Knop, Disc Foot, No. 7321, 7 1/2 In. 1610.00
Vase, Acid Cut, Geisha, Birds, Mountains, Black, Blue, Aurene, Mary Alice Hawke, 10 1/4 In. 1380.00
Vase, Acid Cut, Green Jade Over Alabaster, Birds, c.1924, 9 In. 1150.00
Vase, Acid Cut, Green Jade Over Alabaster, Chinese Pattern, Carder, c.1915, 10 In. 765.00
Vase, Acid Cut, Ivory, Gazelles, Bulbous, Flared Rim, 10 1/2 In. 2530.00
Vase, Acid Cut, Rosaline Over Alabaster, Chinese Style, Egg Shape, 10 In. 3884.00
Vase, Acid Cut, Rosaline Over Alabaster, Peony, 6 3/8 In. 528.00
Vase, Acid Cut, Vines, Grape Pods, Cobalt Blue, Gold Aurene, White Ground, 11 1/4 In. 489.00
Vase, Alabaster, Gold Aurene Hearts, Vines, Inverted Baluster, 6 1/2 In. 230.00
Vase, Amethyst, Ribbed, Faint Diagonal Swirl, Bowl Shape, Flared Rim, 4 x 7 1/2 In. 489.00
Vase, Amethyst, Silverina, Tapered Cylinder, Flared Rim, Applied Webbing, 7 In. 865.00
Vase, Bud, 3-Sided, Dark Amethyst, Disc Foot, Art Deco, No. 6873, 10 1/2 In., 3 Piece 1725.00
Vase, Bud, Crystal, Applied Teardrops On Base, Signed, 8 1/2 In., Pair 316.00
Vase, Bud, Rosaline, Alabaster Foot, 8 1/4 In., Pair 635.00
Vase, Bud, Triangular, Green Jade, Single Stem, Alabaster Foot, 8 In. 290.00
Vase, Calcite, Egg Shape, Shouldered, 8 In. 265.00
Vase, Canary Yellow, Diagonal Swirl, 6 In. 145.00
Vase, Celeste Blue, Flared Rim, Footed, 11 In. 518.00
Vase, Cintra, Pink, Bulbous, 6 3/4 In. 605.00
Vase, Cintra, Pink, Frosted, Mottled, Shouldered, 13 1/2 In. 978.00
Vase, Cluthra, Shouldered, Rose Color, 8 1/4 In. 1495.00
Vase, Cornucopia, Ivory, Flared Rim, Black Amethyst Foot, 8 In. 460.00
Vase, Cornucopia, Optic Ribbed, Green, Amber Foot, 8 1/4 In. 316.00
Vase, Crystal, Rounded Cone, Scrolled Feet At Sides, 6 x 4 In. 115.00
Vase, Crystal, Spiral Stem, No. 8058, Signed, 6 1/2 In. 175.00
Vase, Fan, Amber, Optic Ribbed, Pomona Green Disc Foot, 8 3/4 In. 345.00
Vase, Fan, Green Jade, Alabaster Foot, 8 In. 460.00
Vase, Fan, Yellow, Flowers, 2-Knop Stem, Pomona Green Disc Foot, c.1928, 10 3/4 In. 450.00
Vase, Green Jade, Alabaster, Pulled Swirl, 9 1/2 In. 120.00
Vase, Green Jade, Urn Shape, Applied Alabaster Handles, 10 In. 1725.00
Vase, Grotesque, Ivory, 6 1/2 x 12 In. 345.00
Vase, Grotesque, Wisteria, Footed, 9 1/2 In. 1495.00
Vase, Heritage, Engraved Gazelle, 7 1/2 In. 1320.00
Vase, Ivorene, Ribbed, Flared Rim, 5 In. 175.00
Vase, Ivory, Egg Shape, Shouldered, 10 1/2 In. ....450.00 to 635.00
Vase, Ivrene, Bulbous, 8 In. 316.00
Vase, Ivrene, Shouldered, 6 In. 230.00
Vase, Jack-In-The-Pulpit, 3-Prong, Ivrene, 12 In. 2185.00
Vase, Moss Agate, Raspberry, Gray, Blue, Yellow, Cobalt Blue, 8 3/4 In. 4600.00
Vase, Silverina, Mica Flecks, Lattice Pattern, Shouldered, Flared Rim, 6 1/2 In. 865.00
Vase, Silverina, Slight Flaring, 7 In. 518.00
Vase, Tree Trunk, 3 Prong, Amber, 6 1/4 In. 345.00
Vase, Tree Trunk, 3 Prong, Amber, Pomona Green Base, 6 In. 978.00
Vase, Tree Trunk, 3 Prong, Amethyst, 6 1/4 In. 460.00

Vase, Tree Trunk, 3 Prong, Aquamarine, 6 1/4 In. 460.00
Vase, Tree Trunk, 3 Prong, Celeste Blue, 6 1/4 In. 635.00
Vase, Tree Trunk, 3 Prong, Green Jade, 5 3/4 In. 115.00
Vase, Tree Trunk, 3 Prong, Pomona Green, 6 1/4 In. 518.00
Vase, Tree Trunk, 3 Prong, Rosaline, Alabaster Disc Foot, 6 1/2 In. 1035.00
Vase, Tree Trunk, 3 Prong, Wisteria, Disc Foot, Signed, 6 1/2 In. 2185.00
Vase, Triangular, Black, Single Stem, Oval Foot, 8 1/2 In. 748.00
Water Set, Green Jade, Swirls, Applied Alabaster Handle, Mugs, 9 1/2 In., 7 Piece 865.00
Wine, Clear, Rose Colored Stem, Etched, 5 3/4 In., 6 Piece 1112.00
Wine, French Blue, Translucent Stem, Threading, 6 1/2 In. 290.00
Wine, Poppy, Pink, Clear Stem, Opalescent Rim, 6 In. 390.00

STEVENGRAPHS are woven pictures made like fancy ribbons. They were manufactured by Thomas Stevens of Coventry, England, and became popular in 1862. Most are marked *Woven in silk by Thomas Stevens* or were mounted on a cardboard that tells the story of the Stevengraph. Other similar ribbon pictures have been made in England and Germany.

Bookmark, A Birthday Gift, Silk, Multicolored, 6 In. 30.00
Bookmark, A Birthday Wish, Silk, Multicolored, Tassel, No. 301, 12 In. 25.00
Bookmark, A Dear Friend's Wish, Silk, Multicolored, No. 321, 9 In. 14.00
Bookmark, A Merry Christmas To You, Silk, Multicolored, No. 398, 9 In. 40.00
Bookmark, Busy Bee, Silk, Multicolored, No. 675 .... 52.00
Bookmark, Coventry & Midland Mfg. & Art Industrial, June, 1867, 13 x 2 In. 35.00
Bookmark, G. Washington, July 4, Silk, Pan American Exposition, Buffalo, 1901, 10 x 2 In. 85.00
Bookmark, George Washington, Centennial, 1876, 8 1/2 x 2 1/8 In. 88.00
Bookmark, Little Bo-Peep, Silk, Multicolored, No. 530 .... 69.00
Bookmark, Little Red Riding Hood, Silk, Multicolored, 1872, 6 x 1 3/4 In. 58.00
Bookmark, May Happiness Be Ever Thine, Tassel, 5 1/2 x 1 1/4 In. 58.00
Bookmark, Mizpah, Verse, Silk, Multicolored, 6 In. 27.00
Bookmark, Royal Wedding, Albert & Alexandra, 1863, Silk, Multicolored, 8 In. 62.00
Bookmark, Shakespeare, Tercentenary, April 23, 1864, Silk, Tassel 50.00
Bookmark, Signing Of The Declaration Of Independence, July 4th, 1776, 2 x 7 In. 125.00
Picture, Betsy Ross Making Flag, Silk, Anderson Bros., Patterson, N.J., Frame, 7 5/8 x 4 1/2 In. 54.00
Picture, Crystal Palace, Frame, 1880s, 2 1/2 x 5 1/4 In. 300.00
Portrait, J. M. Jacquard, Silk, Signed, Didier Petit, 10 1/2 x 8 1/2 In. 230.00
Portrait, Late Earl Of Beaconsfield, Silk, Frame, 8 1/2 x 6 1/2 In. 35.00
Postcard, S.S. Arabic, Silk 60.00
Ribbon, Centennial, Geo. Washington, Thomas Stearns, Frame, England, 1876, 12 x 4 In. 275.00
Ribbon, Lady Godiva Procession, Silk, Frame, 2 x 6 In. 110.00

STEVENS & WILLIAMS of Stourbridge, England, made many types of glass, including layered, etched, cameo, and art glass, between the 1830s and 1930s. Some pieces are signed *S & W.* Many pieces are decorated with flowers, leaves, and other designs based on nature.

Bowl, Lily, Cranberry, Green Petal Foot, Twisted Leaves, Bulbous, 12 In. 660.00
Bowl, Pompeiian Swirl, Caramel Exterior, Blue Interior, 7 In. 290.00
Decanter, Green Cut To Clear, Flowers, Swirling Leaves, Clear Handle, 10 In. 2875.00
Finger Bowl, Underplate, Pompeiian Swirl, Red Shaded To Amber, Blue Inside, 4 1/2 In. 1495.00
Rose Bowl, Applied Pink, White Flowers, Amber Stems, Leaves, Cream Ground, 6 In. 180.00
Rose Bowl, Green, Pink Diagonal Bands, Frosted Ground, Leaves, Buds, Flowers, 5 1/2 In. 575.00
Vase, Double Gourd, 3 Looping Rigaree Feet, Pulled Wave, John Northwood, 8 In. 775.00
Vase, Flower Shape, White, Amber Stem, Leaves, Peachblow, Ruffled Rim, 3 1/2 x 5 In. 72.00
Vase, Funeral, Crimped Rim, Crimson & Orange Bands, Peach Ground, John Northwood, 7 In. 690.00
Vase, Mother-Of-Pearl, 4-Footed, Brown Pulled Zipper, Pink, John Northwood, 10 1/2 In. 2300.00
Vase, Osiris, Rose Amber, Tapering Oval, 5 1/2 In. 690.00
Vase, Peachblow, Applied Cherries, Leaves, Amber Base, 8 1/4 In. 520.00
Vase, Peachblow, Applied Oak Leaves, Acorns, Ruffled Edge, Amber Foot, 10 1/4 In., Pair 145.00
Vase, Pompeiian Swirl, Amber To Pink, Blue Interior, Ruffled Edge, 5 In. 845.00
Vase, Pompeiian Swirl, Pink Satin, Oval, Acid Stamp, 4 In. 345.00
Vase, Pompeiian Swirl, Rose Shaded To Green, Shouldered, Flared Rim, 14 In. 3795.00

Vase, White, Pink Interior, Applied Leaves, Amber Foot, 6 1/2 In., Pair 250.00
Vase, Wine Red, Flower Cuttings, Egg Shape, Rolled Rim, 4 1/4 In. 805.00
Vase, Yellow, Applied Glass Cherries & Leaves, Ruffled Edge, 10 1/2 In. 150.00

STIEGEL TYPE glass is listed here. It is almost impossible to be sure a piece was actually made by Stiegel, so the knowing collector refers to this glass as *Stiegel type.* Henry William Stiegel, a colorful immigrant to the colonies, started his first factory in Pennsylvania in 1763. He remained in business until 1774. Glassware was made in a style popular in Europe at that time and was similar to the glass of many other makers. It was made of clear or colored glass and was decorated with enamel colors, mold blown designs, or etching.

Bottle, Enameled Daisy, Pewter Screw Top, 7 1/4 x 3 1/8 x 2 1/2 In. 55.00
Bottle, Enameled Rabbit & Dog, Flower Panels, Screw Top, Clear, 6 x 3 1/4 x 2 1/4 In. 55.00
Bottle, Engraved Devils Dancing Around Fire, Stopper, Pontil, 8 1/2 In. 165.00
Bowl, Cobalt Blue, Tapered, Mold Blown, Ribbed, 3 3/8 x 3 1/2 In. 165.00
Creamer, Blue, Diamond Optic, Applied Foot, C-Shaped Handle, 3 3/4 x 2 3/4 x 2 In. 275.00
Salt, Diamond Optic, Scalloped Base 143.00
Salt, Diamond Optic, Scalloped Base, Master 143.00
Tumbler, Engraved Flowers, Cut Flutes At Base, Tapered, c.1800, 4 1/4 x 3 5/8 In. 440.00
Tumbler, Engraved, Ovals, Stars, Cut Flutes At Base, c.1800, 3 5/8 In. 99.00
Tumbler, Engraved, Sprig & Oval Band At Rim, Flowers, Stars, Tapered, c.1800, 3 1/2 In. 110.00
Tumbler, Engraved, Sprigs, Ovals, Stars, Tassels, Cut Basal Flutes, c.1800, 3 1/2 In. 198.00
Tumbler, Engraved, Swags, Tassels, Flared Rim, c.1800, 3 1/4 x 2 3/4 In. 66.00
Tumbler, Flip, Blown, 10 Cut Panels Around Base, c.1800, 4 x 3 1/4 In. 77.00
Tumbler, Flip, Engraved, Basket, Leaves, Flowers, Tapered, c.1800, 6 1/4 x 4 5/8 In. 175.00
Tumbler, Flip, Glass, Blown, 12 Vertical Lower Panels, c.1800, 4 3/8 x 3 1/2 In. 90.00
Tumbler, Flip, Glass, Blown, 12 Vertical Lower Panels, c.1800, 6 x 4 3/8 In. 110.00
Tumbler, Flip, Tapered, c.1800, 5 1/4 x 4 1/8 In. 110.00
Tumbler, Green, Engraved, Wavy Line, Diamond, Flared, Monogram, c.1800, 3 3/4 In. 330.00
Tumbler, Tapered, 26 Lower Vertical Panels, c.1800, 3 3/4x 3 In. 120.00
Tumbler, Tapering, 12 Lower Vertical Panels, c.1800, 2 3/4 x 2 3/8 In. 90.00
Wine, Conical Bowl, Engraved, Crosshatch, Flowers, Bird, Footed, Folded Rim, c.1800, 4 In. 264.00
Wine, Conical Bowl, Engraved, Garland, Ovals, Stars, c.1800, 5 In. 240.00
Wine, Conical Bowl, Engraved, Lily-Of-The-Valley, c.1800, 4 3/4 In. 90.00
Wine, Conical Bowl, Engraved, Ovals, Leaves, Stars, c.1800, 5 1/4 In. 120.00
Wine, Conical Bowl, Engraved, Stars, Facet Cut Stem, c.1800, 4 3/4 In. 120.00

STONE includes those articles made of stones, coral, shells, and some other natural materials not listed elsewhere in this book. Micro mosaics (small decorative design, made by setting pieces of stone into a pattern), urns, vases, and other pieces made of natural stones are listed here. Alabaster, Jade, Malachite, Marble, and Soapstone are in their own categories. Stoneware is pottery and is listed in the Stoneware category.

Bowl, Rose Quartz, 5 x 9 In. 998.00
Cross, Micro Mosaic, Bronze, Silver Portrait, Pope Pius X, Grand Tour, 6 x 4 In. 560.00
Cross, Micro Mosaic, Polished Nickel, Cartouche Terminals, Church Landmarks, 8 1/4 In. 558.00
Crucifix, Micro Mosaic, Tour, Nickel, Silvered Corpus, Churches, Italy, c.1915, 5 1/2 In. 323.00
Eagle, On Rocky Outcrop, Cast, Gray, 8-Sided Plinth, 33 x 9 In., Pair 411.00
Figure, Buddha, Standing, Chinese, Early 1900s, 22 In. 176.00
Figure, Elephant, African, Upturned Trunk, Rock Crystal, Wood Base, Chinese, 6 In. 235.00
Figure, Female Immortal, Holding Flower Bowl, Branches, Birds, Amethyst, Chinese, 8 In. 763.00
Figure, Female Immortal, Robe, Holding Vase, Branches, Bird, Agate, Chinese, 7 1/2 In. 499.00
Figure, Foo Dog, Rectangular Plinth Base, Chinese, 20 In., Pair 1298.00
Figure, Foo Dog, Rolling Balls In Mouth, 19 1/2 x 18 1/2 In., Pair 978.00
Figure, Pear, Painted Fly Speck, Early 1900s, 6 x 4 In. 850.00
Figure, Putto, Holding Shell, Square Base, Italy, 1800s, 43 x 16 In. 2820.00
Figure, Stag, Lying Down, Terra-Cotta Tint, 29 x 33 In. 940.00
Figure, Woman, Standing, Turquoise, Carved, Wooden Stand, Chinese, 5 x 3 In. 146.00
Fruit, Cantaloupe, Wooden Stem, 4 1/2 In. 431.00

Fruit, Fig Half, Carved, Painted, 19th Century, 6 1/4 In. 1645.00
Fruit, Tomato, Yellow Pepper, Wooden Stems, 3 1/2 In. 230.00
Group, Woman, Robed, Fan, Leaves, Flowers, Bird, Coral, Wooden Stand, Chinese, 7 In. 940.00
Group, Woman, Standing, Flowing Robes, Flower Basket, Dove, Children, Carved, Stand, 10 In. 2585.00
Madonna, Micro Mosaic, Mounted, Gilded Frame, Italy, 19th Century, 3 x 2 1/4 In. 325.00
Plaque, Architectural Street Scene, Pietra Dura, Frame, R. Casini, Italy, c.1900, 11 x 8 3/4 In. 2938.00
Plaque, Depicting The Crucifixion, Mosaic, Pietra Dura, Italy, 1800s, 18 x 11 In. 3055.00
Plaque, Flowers, Black Ground, Hinged Cover, Oval, Pietra Dura, Wire Easel, 3 1/2 x 2 1/4 In. 173.00
Plaque, Maiden Carrying Basket Of Eggs & Chicken, Pietra Dura, Frame, 9 x 5 In. 780.00
Plaque, St. Peter's Square, Micro Mosaic, Frame, Italy, c.1875, 5 1/4 x 7 In. 4800.00
Scroll Press, Foo Dogs, Birds, Flowers, Black, 5 1/8 x 8 3/4 In. 403.00
Urn, Classical Shape, Basalt, Applied Handles, Gargoyle Mounts, Victorian, 9 3/4 x 4 In. 385.00
Urn, Patinated Bronze, Maidens, c.1865, 15 x 7 x 6 1/4 In., Pair 588.00

STONEWARE is a coarse, glazed, and fired potter's ceramic that is used to make crocks, jugs, bowls, etc. It is often decorated with cobalt blue decorations. In the nineteenth and early twentieth centuries, potters often decorated crocks with blue numbers indicating the size of the container. A "2" meant 2 gallons. Stoneware is still being made. American stoneware is listed here.

Batter Jug, Flower, Cobalt Blue, Bail Handle, Gal. 195.00
Batter Jug, Impressed No. 4, Ottman Bros. & Co., Ft. Edward, N.Y., 1872-92, 9 1/4 In. 110.00
Batter Jug, Tulip, Leaf Design, Cobalt Blue, Tin Lid, Bail Handle, Cowden & Wilcox, 8 1/4 In. 3120.00
Batter Pail, Blue Accents, Bail Handle, c.1865, Gal., 8 In. 165.00
Batter Pail, Blue Accents, Lug Handle, Roberts, Binghamton, c.1860, Gal., 8 1/2 In. 165.00
Batter Pail, Brushed Plume, Lug Handle, Harrisburg, c.1870, 1 1/2 Gal., 9 1/2 In. 965.00
Batter Pail, Flower, Blue, Bail Handle, Tin Spout Lid, c.1860, 9 In. 745.00
Batter Pail, Flowers, Stem, Cobalt Blue, Oval, Wire, Wood Handle, c.1870, 9 In. 385.00
Batter Pail, Tin Lid, Tulips, Leaves, Cobalt Blue, Bail Handle, c.1880, 8 1/4 In. 1870.00
Bean Pot, Brown, Cream, No. 2, E. Swasey & Co., Portland, Maine 48.00
Bean Pot, Enoch Plann, General Merchandise & Fresh Meats, I.G.A., Wis., 1/2 Gal. 129.00
Birdhouse, Unglazed, Squiggly Lines, Wire Hanger, B.B. Craig, 7 3/4 x 7 1/2 In. 230.00
Bottle, BF & CC Haley, California Pop Beer, Blue Spout, 1895, 9 In. 300.00
Bottle, C. Shaw Impressed On Shoulder, 3 1/2 In. 330.00
Bottle, Cobalt Blue Accents, Hand Formed, 6 1/2 In. 630.00
Bottle, Cobalt Blue Decorated Shoulder, Paterson, N.J., c.1870, 10 In. 120.00
Bottle, Cobalt Blue Wash At Neck, P. Pfannebecker, 9 1/2 In. 110.00
Bottle, Crushed-Glass Glaze, Cobalt Blue Neck, Pinch, E.A. Hilton Shop, c.1930, 10 In. 220.00
Bottle, Impressed Shoulder, Moses Fairbanks & Co., c.1872, 9 In. 80.00
Bottle, Impressed, D.W. DeFreest, Troy, N.Y., c.1874, 10 In. 90.00
Bottle, Impressed, G.N. Cox, Mottled, 9 In. 70.00
Bottle, Initials, Blue Script, Tan Alkaline Glaze, 10 In. 175.00
Bottle, Pig, Albany Slip Glaze, Brown, Hole In Tail, 7 1/4 In. 3740.00
Bottle, Poland Springs, Me., Souvenir, Gold Decoration, 1880-1900, 5 1/4 In. 59.00
Bottle, Smith Whiteroot, Pat July 17, 66, ITD & Co., 1876, 9 1/2 In. 130.00
Bottle, Whiskey, Iron Cross, Impressed, Salt Glaze 69.00
Bottle, Whiskey, J.C. Schnell's Sour Mash Kiln Dried Grain, Incised, 8 1/2 In. 69.00
Bowl, Brushed Leaves, Cobalt Blue, Slanted Sides, 2 Handles, Spout, 9 1/2 x 5 1/2 In. 200.00
Bowl, Ivory, Brown, Raija Tuumi, 1950s, 11 1/2 In. 615.00
Bowl, Lid, Stylized Designs, Brown, Gray Ground, Clyde Burt, 7 1/2 x 4 1/2 In. 441.00
Bowl, Triangles, Stylized Flowers, Blue, Yellow, Morocco, 2 3/4 x 11 5/8 In. 400.00
Chicken Waterer, Blue Accents, c.1860, 1/2 Gal., 7 1/2 In. 800.00
Churn, Albany Slip Glaze, Incised No. 6, 2 Handles, J.P. Reid, Early 1900s, 18 In. 770.00
Churn, Bird On Branch, Fantail, Cobalt Blue, Impressed White's, Utica, 9 In. 460.00
Churn, Bird On Plume, Blue, Dotted, N.Y. Stoneware Co., Fort Edward, N.Y., c.1870, 5 Gal., 18 In. .. 1020.00
Churn, Bird, Blue, Haxtun & Co., Fort Edward, N.Y., 5 Gal. 1210.00
Churn, Bird, Long Tail, Flowering Tree, White's, Utica, c.1865, 5 Gal., 18 In. 4070.00
Churn, Cabbage Flower, Dasher Guide, J. Burger Jr., Rochester, c.1885, 4 Gal., 16 In. 1020.00
Churn, Clover Plant, Cobalt Blue, Wooden Dasher, Guide, c.1875, 12 5/8 In. 1430.00
Churn, Cobalt Blue Strokes, Yellow, Egg Shape, Wood Dasher, Stanly & Beman, 1837, 9 1/2 In. 175.00
Churn, Flower, Blue, Applied Handles, Flared Rim, 14 3/4 In. 470.00

Churn, Flower, Cobalt Blue, Salt Glaze, 3 Gal., 13 In. 375.00
Churn, Flower, Leaves, Blue, 4 Gal. 165.00
Churn, Glossy, Albany Slip, Incised No. 5, 2 Handles, M. Hewell, Gillsville, Ga., 18 1/2 In. 440.00
Churn, Green Glaze, Oval, Thin Handle, Large Ear, Wooden Dasher, 17 In. 175.00
Churn, Line, Stencil Mark, Cobalt Blue, Augustus Hille General Mds'e, Ohio, 15 In. 1150.00
Churn, Lion, Spotted Body, Speckled Ground, Tree, J. Burger, Rochester, N.Y., 8 Gal. 31900.00
Churn, Lion, Tree, Curving Trunk, Shrubbery, Cobalt Blue, 8 Gal., 22 1/2 In. 220.00
Churn, Medium Olive Alkaline Glaze, Double Stamped, 18 x 10 3/4 In. 230.00
Churn, Morning Glory Vine, Slip Trailed Lines, Guide, Wooden Dasher, 1878, 4 Gal., 16 1/4 In. 2090.00
Churn, Partridge Under Tree, J. Burger, Rochester, N.Y. 26400.00
Churn, Ribbed Stylized Leaf, Haxstun Ottman & Co., c.1870, 4 Gal., 16 In. 220.00
Churn, Salt Glaze, Tooled Collar, Drain Hole, Wooden Dasher, Guide, 6 Gal., 21 In. 300.00
Churn, Speckled Brown Glaze, Applied Strap, Lug Handles, 1880s, 15 1/2 In. 120.00
Churn, Stylized Flowers, W. Roberts, Binghamton, N.Y., c.1860, 6 Gal., 19 In. 550.00
Churn, Tree, Blue Slip, C.W. Braun, Buffalo, N.Y., c.1870, 4 Gal., 16 In. 4510.00
Churn, Vines, Blue Slip, L. & B.G. Chace, Somerset, c.1856, 2 Gal., 13 In. 250.00
Cooler, Sheaf Of Wheat, Double Pulled Handles, Ohio, 1930s, 15 In. 1150.00
Cream Pot, Bird, Tree Stump, O.L. & A.K. Ballard, Burlington, c.1870, 5 Gal., 13 1/2 In. 1760.00
Cream Pot, Birds, Jack & Jill, Blue, Clark & Fox, Athens, N.Y., c.1830, 3 Gal., 13 In. 5500.00
Cream Pot, Bowtie, Blue, Applied Handles, New York, c.1840, 3 Gal., 12 In. 250.00
Cream Pot, Brushed Flower, Jones Factory, Pa., c.1870, Gal., 7 1/2 In. 70.00
Cream Pot, F.H. Cowden, Harrisburg, Pa., c.1890, 1/2 Gal., 6 1/2 In. 45.00
Cream Pot, Flower & Leaf, Blue, D. Roberts & Co., Utica, c.1828, Gal., 6 1/2 In. 300.00
Cream Pot, Flower, Blue, Whittemore, Havana, N.Y., c.1870, Gal., 7 1/2 In. 360.00
Cream Pot, Flower, Brushed, H. & G. Nash, Utica, c.1832, 2 Gal., 9 In. 145.00
Cream Pot, Man In Moon, Cowden & Wilcox, Harrisburg, Pa., c.1870, 1 1/2 Gal., 8 1/2 In. 7150.00
Cream Pot, Parrot On Plume, Blue, F.B. Norton & Co., Mass., c.1886, 2 Gal, 10 1/2 In. 2200.00
Cream Pot, Robin, Blue, c.1850, 2 Gal., 10 In. 470.00
Cream Pot, Squat, Ear Handles, S.S. Perry, Troy, c.1830, Gal., 5 1/4 In. 250.00
Cream Pot, Star, Blue, New York, c.1850, Gal., 8 1/2 In. 165.00
Cream Pot, Stenciled Snowflake, Blue Accent, F.H. Cowden, c.1870, 4 Gal., 13 1/2 In. 165.00
Cream Pot, Sunflower, Blue, N. Clark & Co., Rochester, N.Y., c.1850, 2 Gal., 11 1/2 In. 1595.00
Creamer, Blue Incising, Salt Glaze, Applied Handle, E.M. Frasier, c.1880, 4 In. 550.00
Creamer, Blue Splotches, Applied Handle, c.1840-1860, 4 In. 1045.00
Creamer, Vines, Dashes, Lines, Albany Glaze, Tan, c.1870, Qt., 8 In. 690.00
Crock, 4 Tulips & Leaves, Cobalt Blue, Tooled Band, Applied Handles, 10 x 9 In. 259.00
Crock, Alkaline Glaze, Impressed No. 1 & 2, Signed D.H., c.1850, 9 1/4 In. 770.00
Crock, American Eagle, Salt Glaze, Closed Handles, Gardner, Mass., 4 Gal., 11 1/2 In. 110.00
Crock, Bird On Branch, Blue, 2 Gal., 9 1/4 In. 190.00
Crock, Bird On Branch, Blue, Handles, 2 Gal. 250.00
Crock, Bird On Branch, Blue, Handles, New York Stoneware Co., Ft. Edward, N.Y., Gal. 385.00
Crock, Bird On Branch, Blue, Satterlee & Mory, Fort Edward, N.Y., 4 Gal. 300.00
Crock, Bird On Branch, Body Dot, Extended Tail, 6 Gal., 14 In. 880.00
Crock, Bird On Branch, Cobalt Blue, c.1870, 5 Gal., 11 7/8 In. 1100.00
Crock, Bird On Branch, Dog's Head, Cobalt Blue, Handles, 3 Gal., 10 1/2 In. 440.00
Crock, Bird On Branch, Mushroom Finial, Handles, Wilcox & Cowden, 12 In. 7920.00
Crock, Bird On Fence, Blue, N. Clark Jr., Athens, N.Y., 4 Gal. 1210.00
Crock, Bird On Fern Branch, Blue, 4 Gal., 11 1/2 In. 525.00
Crock, Bird On Fern Branch, Cobalt Blue, F.B. Norton Sons, Worcester, Mass., 12 1/4 In. 630.00
Crock, Bird On Stump, Blue, F.T. Wright & Son, Taunton, Mass., 4 Gal. 1320.00
Crock, Bird, 2 Gal., 7 x 7 1/2 In. 1250.00
Crock, Bird, Cherry Branch, Freehand Blue Slip, Ear Handles, 4 Gal., 12 x 11 In. 175.00
Crock, Bird, Cobalt Blue, 1800s, 1 1/2 Gal. 105.00
Crock, Bird, Cobalt Blue, West Troy Pottery, N.Y., 1800s, 2 Gal. 175.00
Crock, Bird, Harmon & Dearden, Springfield, Mass., c.1870, 10 1/2 In. 385.00
Crock, Black Stencil, Richmond Portable Battery Fan, c.1910, 6 1/2 In. 35.00
Crock, Blue Accents, Egg Shape, Chollar & Darby, Cortland, c.1840, 5 Gal., 15 In. 630.00
Crock, Blue Decoration, Accent At Handle, Oval, 13 1/4 In. 308.00
Crock, Blue Highlights, Egg Shape, Double Handles, S. Purdy, Portage Co., Ohio, 16 In. 750.00
Crock, Blue Stencil, Hamilton & Jones, Greensboro, Pa., c.1870, 10 Gal., 21 In. 468.00
Crock, Blue Stenciled Designs, A.P. Donaghho, Parkersburg, c.1800, 5 Gal., 13 In. 550.00

Crock, Brushed Cobalt Blue Accents, No. 4, Oval, 2 Handles, Bennage 1837, 13 x 15 In. 400.00
Crock, Brushed Flower, Blue, Taunton, Mass., c.1840, Pt., 5 In. 1595.00
Crock, Butter, Cover, Ev-Re-Day Oleomargarine, Milwaukee, Wis. 125.00
Crock, Butter, Cover, Leaves, Brushwork, Cobalt Blue, Handles, 1865, 9 3/4 In. 385.00
Crock, Butter, Cover, Tulips, Horizontal Stems, Leaves, Cobalt Blue, Handles, 8 3/4 In. 520.00
Crock, Butter, Lid, Bail Handle, Marvel, Reed & Tyerman Co., Chicago, Ill. 85.00
Crock, Butter, Swags, Cobalt Blue, Handles, c.1875, Gal., 10 1/2 In. 330.00
Crock, Butter, Swags, Flower, Incised Shoulder, Ribbed Handles, c.1865, 8 1/4 In. 358.00
Crock, Butterine, From Your Old Friend, C.W. Townson, 1/2 Gal., 6 1/2 In. 269.00
Crock, Cake, Bird, A.O. Whittemore, Havana, N.Y., c.1870, 4 Gal., 8 1/2 x 14 In. 2750.00
Crock, Cake, Clover Plant, Cobalt Blue, Handles, c.1860, 2 Gal., 5 7/8 x 12 1/4 In. 495.00
Crock, Cake, Flower, Incised Lines, Cobalt Blue, Applied Handles, 10 3/4 x 7 In. 690.00
Crock, Cake, Lid, 3, Hand-Brushed, Cobalt Blue, Tulips, 6 3/4 x 5 In. 635.00
Crock, Cake, Lid, Flowers, Blue, Salt Glaze, c.1850, 6 x 10 In. 880.00
Crock, Cake, Lid, Swag, Flower, Cobalt Blue, Handles, c.1870, 1 1/2 x 11 1/4 In. 385.00
Crock, Canning, Feather, Cobalt Blue, Gray Ground, Wax Seal Rim, 2 Gal., 11 x 7 1/2 In. 235.00
Crock, Chicken Pecking Corn, N.Y. Stoneware Co., Fort Edward, N.Y., c.1870, 4 Gal., 11 1/2 In. 1155.00
Crock, Cobalt Blue Brushed Accent, Double Ribbed Handles, Oval, 15 In. 805.00
Crock, Cobalt Blue Spirals, No. 6, Applied Handles, Incised Bands, 6 Gal., 16 In. 230.00
Crock, Cobalt Blue Stencil, Band, A. Conrad, New Geneva, 10 In. 405.00
Crock, Cobalt Blue Stencil, Buckeye Pottery Co., Macomb, c.1880, 6 Gal., 14 In. 145.00
Crock, Cobalt Blue Stencil, Gray, John W. Carder & Son, Old Town, Md., 10 In. 728.00
Crock, Cobalt Blue Stencil, Hamilton & Jones, Greensboro, Penn., 2, 9 x 10 In. 230.00
Crock, Cobalt Blue Stencil, Williams & Reppert, Greensboro, Pa., 2 Gal., 11 3/4 In. 345.00
Crock, Cobalt Blue, Egg Shape, C. Crolius, N.Y., c.1800, 2 Gal., 12 1/2 In. 1540.00
Crock, Cobalt Blue, Flowers, Handles, 4 Gal., 10 1/2 In. 330.00
Crock, Cobalt Blue, Gray, Thompson Williams Co., Morgantown, Ear Handles, 16 Gal. 2240.00
Crock, Cobalt Blue, Salt Glaze, Applied Lug Handles, 3 Gal., 10 3/4 In. 676.00
Crock, Cobalt Blue, Script No. 4, Oval, Handles, Porter, 4 Gal. 400.00
Crock, Compliments Of D.S. Corsaw, Moxley's Daisy Oleomargarine, Pa., 7 1/2 In. 150.00
Crock, Compliments Of E.A. Volkwein, Allegheny Ave., Oakmont, Pa., 1/2 Gal. 169.00
Crock, Crown, Dotted, Blue Slip, Tyler & Co., Troy, N.Y., c.1860, 3 Gal., 15 1/2 In. 550.00
Crock, Deer, Reclining, Blue, Edmands & Co., c.1870, 3 Gal., 10 In. 5500.00
Crock, Double Tulips, Striped Leaves, Blue, Impressed No. 3, Applied Handles, 13 In. 775.00
Crock, Drop 8, Cobalt Blue, Salt Glaze, 5 Gal., 13 In. 219.00
Crock, Dry River Pottery, John Heatwole, Rockingham County, Va., 1876, 3 Gal. 13750.00
Crock, Eagle, Flower, Blue, Stencil, T.F. Reppert, Greensboro, c.1880, Gal., 8 1/2 In. 220.00
Crock, Fern, Flowers, Flower Swags, Applied Handles, 6 In. 330.00
Crock, Fish Around Rim, Incised, Salt Glaze, Ear Handles, c.1780, 10 1/2 In. 165.00
Crock, Flower & Script, Cobalt Blue, H. & G. Nash, Utica, 2 Gal. 165.00
Crock, Flower & Vine, Blue, Gray Salt Glaze, Handles, 14 1/2 In. 330.00
Crock, Flower Basket, Blue, White's, Utica, c.1865, 4 Gal., 11 In. 935.00
Crock, Flower Spray, Ballard, Burlington, Vt., Civil War Era, 5 Gal. 365.00
Crock, Flower Swags, Blue, Impressed No. 2, Applied Handle, 11 3/4 In. 360.00
Crock, Flower, Blue, Bristol Glaze, Albany Slip Interior, 1885-1900, 10 1/4 In. 130.00
Crock, Flower, Blue, J. Burger Jr., Rochester, N.Y., c.1885, 2 Gal., 9 1/2 In. 635.00
Crock, Flower, Blue, Light Blue Wash, J. Burger Jr., Rochester, c.1880, 4 Gal., 11 In. ....165.00 to 385.00
Crock, Flower, Blue, Sideways, Ottman Bros. & Co., 4 Gal. 250.00
Crock, Flower, Cobalt Blue, F.A. Plaisted & Co., Gardiner, Me., 4 Gal., 12 x 12 In. 345.00
Crock, Flower, Cobalt Blue, No. 5, Applied Handles, Cedar Falls, 1800s, 5 Gal., 13 In. 765.00
Crock, Flower, Cobalt Blue, Slip Trailed, 6 Flourishes, Handles, 6 Gal., 13 1/2 In. 220.00
Crock, Flower, Double, Blue, c.1870, 3 Gal., 9 In. 110.00
Crock, Flower, Freehand Blue Slip, 4, Ear Handles, 4 Gal., 11 x 11 1/2 In. 290.00
Crock, Flower, Leafy Stem, Large Leaf, Cobalt Blue, Handles, 5 Gal., 12 5/8 In. 385.00
Crock, Flower, Slip Trailed, Script, c.1880, 2 Gal., 9 3/8 In. 198.00
Crock, Flowering Tree Branch, Cobalt Blue, F.B. Norton & Co., Worcester, Mass., 2 Gal. 265.00
Crock, Flowers, 2 Stems, Impressed, Blue, 1 1/2 In. 275.00
Crock, Flowers, Blue, Lyons, Gal. 190.00
Crock, Flowers, Blue, Salt Glaze, Applied Ear Handles, c.1850, 10 In. 440.00
Crock, Flowers, Cobalt Blue, Cream, J.M. Pruden, Eliz-Town, N.J., Gal. 330.00
Crock, Flowers, Cobalt Blue, F.T. Wright & Son, Taunton, Mass., 1800s, 3 Gal. 430.00

Crock, Flowers, Cobalt Blue, Gray, Salt Glaze, Double Handles, 4 Gal., 13 In. 280.00
Crock, Flowers, Cobalt Blue, N.Y. Stoneware Co., Gal. 325.00
Crock, Flowers, Cobalt Blue, Slip Trailed, c.1885, 3 Gal., 10 In. 330.00
Crock, Flowers, Cobalt Blue, Slip Trailed, Handles, c.1885, Gal., 6 7/8 In. 165.00
Crock, Flowers, Cobalt Blue, West Troy Pottery, N.Y., 1800s, 2 Gal. 220.00
Crock, Flowers, Swags, Blue, 13 In. 220.00
Crock, Freehand Blue Slip Lines, Ear Handles, No. 6, Hamilton & Jones, Pa., 11 x 17 In. 430.00
Crock, Hand-Brushed Cobalt Blue, No. 3, Harmell & Smyth, Ohio, 12 1/2 In. 345.00
Crock, House, Flag, Whittemore, Havana, N.Y., 4 Gal. 10450.00
Crock, Leaf & Flower, Cobalt Blue, 1800s, 4 Gal. 200.00
Crock, Leaf, Blue, Salt Glaze, Ear Handles, c.1850, 10 In. 300.00
Crock, Leaf, Cobalt Blue, J.B.C.A. RE & Co., Poughkeepsie, New York, 1800s, 2 Gal. 145.00
Crock, Leaves, Flowers, Swags, Cobalt Blue, Hand Brushed, Applied Handles, 9 1/8 In. 430.00
Crock, Lid, Antlers, Blue, Egg Shape, c.1841, 2 Gal., 11 In. 580.00
Crock, Lid, Brown, N. & A. Seymour, Rome, 2 Closed Handles, 1880-95, 6 5/8 In. 160.00
Crock, Lid, Spray Of Flowers, Center Lift Handle, 5 1/4 x 7 3/4 In. 95.00
Crock, Man With Cane & Top Hat, Cobalt Blue, Handles, 2 Gal., 9 7/8 In. 2970.00
Crock, Oak Leaf, Blue, White's, Utica, c.1865, Gal., 7 1/2 In. 300.00
Crock, Parrot On Branch, Cobalt Blue, Handles, 5 Gal., 12 1/2 In. 1210.00
Crock, Parrot, Double Plume, F.B. Norton & Co., Mass., c.1886, 6 Gal., 13 1/2 In. 660.00
Crock, Parrot, Flower, Cobalt Blue, Stenciled, Ribbed Handles, 17 1/4 In. 1375.00
Crock, Peacock, Fancy Tail Feathers, T. Harrington, Lyons, c.1850, 3 Gal., 10 In. 10750.00
Crock, Plume, Cobalt Blue, Adam Caire, Po'keepsie, N.Y., 3 Gal. 138.00
Crock, Plume, D. Weston, Ellenville, N.Y., c.1860, 1 1/2 Gal., 8 In. 330.00
Crock, Prancing Zebra, W.A. Macquoid & Co. Pottery Works, N.Y., c.1870, 9 1/2 In. 8250.00
Crock, Quail & Plume, Blue, J. Burger Jr., Rochester, N.Y., c.1885, 4 Gal., 11 1/2 In. 1595.00
Crock, Ribbed Flower, Blue, No. 2, Harrington & Burger, c.1853, 2 Gal., 9 In. 745.00
Crock, Robin On Twig, Blue, Hudson, N.Y., c.1868, 4 Gal., 11 In. 468.00
Crock, Rooster, Flowering Plant, Wreath, Stencil, Handles, 6 Gal., 13 5/8 In. 120.00
Crock, Rose, Cobalt Blue, Gray, Tan, Salt Glaze, Double Handles, 3 Gal., 10 1/4 In. 168.00
Crock, Sideways Tulip, M. Tyler, Albany, 3 Gal. 165.00
Crock, Singing Bird, No. 2, S. Hart Fulton, c.1875, 2 Gal., 9 In. 468.00
Crock, Singing Bird, Song Notes, New York State, c.1870, 2 Gal., 11 1/2 In. 360.00
Crock, Spray Of Flowers, Blue Stencil, Applied Handles, Jas. Hamilton & Co., 13 In. 300.00
Crock, Spray Of Flowers, Blue, 3 Gal., 11 1/4 In. 415.00
Crock, Stenciled Cobalt Blue Label, Wavy Lines, Applied Handles, 11 1/2 x 14 In. 805.00
Crock, Stenciled, C.L. Williams & Co., Lug Handles, 8 Gal., 20 1/4 In. 1430.00
Crock, Tulip, Double, Ocher, Elmira, N.Y., c.1870, 1 1/2 Gal., 8 In. 1018.00
Crock, Tulips, Cobalt Blue, Straight Sides, c.1865, Gal., 10 1/2 In. 275.00
Crock, Tulips, Swags, Cobalt Blue, 2 Ear Handles, R.C.R., Philadelphia, 1859, 16 In. 1355.00
Crock, V-Shape Wreath, Mottled Clay Color, Pail Shape, c.1850, Gal., 7 1/4 In. 300.00
Crock, Wreath, Blue, Burger & Co., Rochester, N.Y., c.1877, 3 Gal., 10 In. 415.00
Cuspidor, Flower, Stem, Cobalt Blue, Carved Hole, Cylindrical, c.1815, 3 1/4 x 7 1/4 In. 440.00
Cuspidor, Flower, Stem, Cobalt Blue, Carved Hole, Cylindrical, c.1850, 3 3/8 x 7 3/8 In. 1045.00
Cuspidor, Flowers, Cobalt Blue, Ribbed Foot, Lug Handles, c.1880, 11 3/8 x 6 3/8 In. 275.00
Cuspidor, Leaves, Blue, Mottled, c.1840, 3 1/4 x 7 1/2 In. 198.00
Cuspidor, Ohio, c.1850, 4 1/2 x 9 1/2 In. 55.00
Cuspidor, Shield, Vines, Bristol Glaze, Relief, Blue Accents, 4 1/4 x 8 1/2 In. 145.00
Cuspidor, Tulips, Leaves, Brown Freehand Slip, Red Clay, Gray Brown Glaze, 9 x 4 In. 1302.00
Decanter, Eagle, Removable Head, M & W, GR, c.1876, 10 1/2 In. 2200.00
Dish, Flower, Swirling Border, Circles, Curves, Morocco, 3 x 13 1/2 In. 635.00
Figurine, Buddha, Seated On Lotus Throne, Gold, Green, 14 1/2 In. 1100.00
Figurine, Dog, Poodle, Seated, Green, Brown Alkaline Glaze, Coleslaw Fur, c.1850, 7 In. 2090.00
Figurine, Dog, Spaniel, Brown Glaze, Incised Facial Detail, 6 1/8 In. 660.00
Figurine, Dog, Spaniel, Molded, Vent Hold, Albany Slip, 19th Century, 4 1/4 In. 95.00
Figurine, Joi Tei & Bag Of Wealth, Ash Glaze, Bizen Ware, Japan, 9 1/2 In. 120.00
Figurine, Rooster, Runny, Olive Alkaline Glaze, Edwin Meaders, 15 x 7 1/2 x 5 In. 575.00
Figurine, Sphinx, Reclining, Cast, Black, Late 1800s, 5 1/2 In., Pair 825.00
Flask, Birds & Flowers, Blue Highlights, Embossed, 3 1/4 In. 55.00
Flask, Flower Head, Cobalt Blue, Rounded Spout, Footed Base, 18th Century, 6 3/4 In. 2970.00
Flask, Flowers, Brushed Cobalt Blue, 6 3/4 In. 2970.00

Flask, Tree & Leaf, Cobalt Blue, Reeded Neck, c.1800, 8 In. 1650.00
Flowerpot, Applied Drain Dish, Ocher, Fort Edward Factory, c.1870, 2 Gal., 9 1/2 In. 275.00
Flowerpot, Flowers, Blue, Underplate, c.1890, 7 1/2 In. 175.00
Flowerpot, Tulip, Brown Slip, Grayware, Geneva, 5 1/4 x 5 1/2 In. 290.00
Grave Marker, Repeated Asterisks, Salesman Sample, c.1860, 12 In. 8800.00
Humidor, Hunting Dog, Relief, Blue Accented, Salt Glaze, 7 In. 190.00
Jar, 2 Incised Shoulder Lines, Impressed No. 2, 2 Lug Handles, c.1785, 13 3/4 In. 715.00
Jar, 3 Applied Shoulder Ornaments, Swirl, Brown, Yellow, 14 1/2 x 8 3/4 In. 430.00
Jar, 3 Incised Lines, Cobalt Blue, Clark & Fox, Athens, N.Y., c.1838, 3 Gal., 15 In. 470.00
Jar, Accent Lines, Blue, Cylinder, Pottery IXL Havens, c.1870, 3 Gal., 13 1/2 In. 220.00
Jar, Alkaline Glaze, Bulbous, D. Hartzog Attribution, c.1850, 14 1/2 In. 605.00
Jar, Alkaline Glaze, Glossy, 2 Handles, Stone-Penland Shop, c.1875, 8 In. 80.00
Jar, Alkaline, Streaked Glaze, Oval, Tab Handles, 15 In. 440.00
Jar, Bird On Stump, Blue, 2 Gal. 275.00
Jar, Blue Slip Bands, Stencil, Jas. Hamilton & Co., Greensboro, Pa., 7 1/2 x 8 In. 200.00
Jar, Blue Slip Shoulder Band, Stencil, Jas. Hamilton & Co., Greensboro, Pa., 10 In. 259.00
Jar, Brown Alkaline Glaze, J. Heiser, Buffalo, N.Y., c.1852, Gal., 9 In. 35.00
Jar, Brown Bands, Loop Handles, Edmands & Burroughs, Charlestown, Mass., c.1850, 14 In. 1175.00
Jar, Brown Glaze, Manganese Drips, Splashes, Shaped Foot Ring, 10 x 8 1/2 In. 180.00
Jar, Brown, Running Black Glaze, Applied Handles, 10 1/2 In. 200.00
Jar, Canning, Alkaline Glaze, Impressed No. 1, Signed S.L.H., c.1885, 8 3/4 In. 605.00
Jar, Canning, Alkaline Glaze, Slave Made, B.F. Landrum Shops, Signed, c.1820, 7 3/4 In. 5500.00
Jar, Canning, Asterisk, Salt Glaze, J.D. Craven, c.1875, 8 In. 415.00
Jar, Canning, Bird, Running, White's, Utica, c.1865, 3 Gal., 12 1/2 In. 300.00
Jar, Canning, Bull's-Eye, Stylized, Blue, West Troy, c.1880, 3 Gal., 13 In. 220.00
Jar, Canning, Cabbage Flower, John Burger, Rochester, c.1855, 2 Gal., 11 1/2 In. 580.00
Jar, Canning, Currant Jelly, Blue, RMC, c.1850, Qt., 8 In. 3410.00
Jar, Canning, D & D, The Best, Bulbous, N.C., Late 1890s, 10 1/2 In. 1760.00
Jar, Canning, Elephant Ear, Blue, Stylized, c.1860, 1/2 Gal., 7 1/4 In. 248.00
Jar, Canning, Flower & Leaf, Blue, Dotted, J. Heiser, Buffalo, N.Y., c.1852, 3 Gal., 11 In. 330.00
Jar, Canning, Flower, 4 Buds, Blue, Pottery Works, N.Y., c.1870, 4 Gal., 15 1/2 In. 358.00
Jar, Canning, Flower, Blue, Double, J. McBurney, Jordan, c.1855, 3 Gal., 13 In. 495.00
Jar, Canning, Flower, Blue, G. Hart, Fulton, c.1875, 2 Gal., 10 In. 99.00
Jar, Canning, Flower, Burger Bro's & Co., Rochester, N.Y., c.1869, 2 Gal., 12 In. 300.00
Jar, Canning, Flower, Double, Brushed, Homes & Purdy, Dundee, 1850, 2 Gal., 10 1/2 In. 385.00
Jar, Canning, Flower, Double, F. Stetzenmeyer, Rochester, c.1855, 3 Gal., 13 1/2 In. 4180.00
Jar, Canning, Flower, Ribbed, F. Stetzenmeyer & Co., Rochester, c.1855, 2 Gal., 12 In. 2145.00
Jar, Canning, Flowers, Blue, Hamilton & Jones, Greensboro, Pa., c.1870, Gal., 10 In. 120.00
Jar, Canning, Hunting Dog, Cowden & Wilcox, Harrisburg, c.1870, 4 Gal., 13 In. 9625.00
Jar, Canning, Leaf, Blue, A.B. Wheeler & Co., Boston, c.1880, 2 Gal., 11 1/2 In. 175.00
Jar, Canning, Leaf, Cobalt Blue, Gal. 80.00
Jar, Canning, Leaf, Triple, Blue, Pliny Thayer, Lansinburgh, c.1850, 2 Gal., 11 In. 385.00
Jar, Canning, Lid, Flowerpot, Dotted Leaves, Blue Accents, c.1860, 2 Gal., 11 In. 468.00
Jar, Canning, Lid, Flowers, Blue, c.1850, Gal., 8 1/2 In. 495.00
Jar, Canning, Lid, Walk Of The Cock, Blue, W.A. MacQuoid, N.Y., c.1870, 2 Gal., 12 In. 11550.00
Jar, Canning, Pear, Cobalt Blue Stencil, Palatine Pottery Co., 8 1/2 In. 375.00
Jar, Canning, Pear, Cobalt Blue Stenciled Label, 8 1/8 In. 230.00
Jar, Canning, Plume, Brushed, Reddish Clay, c.1850, 1/2 Gal., 8 1/2 In. 275.00
Jar, Canning, Stencil, Top Hat Shape, A.P. Donaghho, Parkersburg, Va., c.1860, 5 1/2 In. 578.00
Jar, Canning, Stenciled Mark, Shield, T.F. Reppert, Greensboro, c.1880, Gal., 10 In. 110.00
Jar, Canning, Strawberry & Apple, Paper Label, Logan Johnson & Co. 22.00
Jar, Canning, Swags, Blue, Cylindrical, c.1850, Gal., 10 In. 300.00
Jar, Canning, Tulip, Blue Dots, Tin Lid, Cortland, c.1860, Gal., 9 In. 440.00
Jar, Cobalt Blue, Salt Glazed, Oval, Applied Lug Handles, Incised 1840, 15 1/4 In. 999.00
Jar, Cobalt Blue, Tall Collar, Handles, Oval, 1830, 12 3/4 In. 715.00
Jar, Cobalt Blue, Wide Mouth, Nathan Clark Jr., c.1829, 3 Gal., 10 1/8 In. 765.00
Jar, Coggle Bird, Leaf, Oval, Impressed, Stamped, 1820, 14 1/2 In. 880.00
Jar, Coggle No. 2, Salt Glaze, 2 Handles, A.L. Moody, c.1900, 14 In. 1045.00
Jar, Coggle No. 5, Salt Glaze, 2 Handles, W.H. Hancock, c.1875, 17 1/2 In. 385.00
Jar, Crushed-Glass Glaze, 2 Handles, Hilton Pottery Co. Attribution, c.1925, 12 1/2 In. 165.00
Jar, Double Slip Loops, Celadon Highlights, Olive Alkaline Glaze, Edgefield, 16 1/2 x 13 1/4 In. 2530.00

Jar, Fitted Wooden Lid, Blue Plume, No. 2, Oval, N. Clark & Co, Rochester, c.1850, 11 In. 275.00
Jar, Flower Band, 10 3/4 In. 195.00
Jar, Flower, Blue, Egg Shape, Chollar Darby & Co., Homer, N.Y., c.1840, 4 Gal., 12 1/2 In. 385.00
Jar, Flower, Cobalt Blue, Hasting & Belding, Ashfield, Mass., 2 Gal. 440.00
Jar, Flower, Cobalt Blue, Oval, Collar, Foot, Handles, 1 1/2 Gal., c.1865, 10 3/8 In. 190.00
Jar, Flower, Cobalt Blue, Oval, Open Loop Handles, 1824, 1/2 Gal., 8 3/8 In. 1650.00
Jar, Flower, Cobalt Blue, Slip Trailed, Brushed, Tall Collar, Handles, c.1855, 3 Gal., 12 In. 330.00
Jar, Flower, Leaves, Cobalt Blue, Gal. 110.00
Jar, Flowers, Cobalt Blue, Manganese, Oval, Open Handles, 14 In. 4840.00
Jar, Flowers, Handles, O.L. & A.K. Ballard, Burlington, Vt., 2 Gal. 250.00
Jar, Flowers, Swags, Cobalt Blue, Oval, Tab Handles, c.1845, 1/2 Gal., 8 1/8 In. 358.00
Jar, Fruit, Hamilton & Jones, Greensboro, Pa., Gal. 275.00
Jar, Grape Cluster, Blue, T. Harrington, 2 Gal. 935.00
Jar, Grapes, Branch, Cobalt Blue, c.1870, 1/2 Gal., 8 7/8 In. 605.00
Jar, Green Glaze, Blue Flowers, Oribe Style, Baluster, Japan, 19th Century, 9 3/4 In. 265.00
Jar, Green, Alkaline Glaze, Flared Lip, 1865-1900, 9 3/4 In. 300.00
Jar, Greyhound, Slip Trailed, Cobalt Blue Dots, Handles, c.1870, 3 Gal., 12 1/4 In. 4950.00
Jar, Home Made Preserves, Bail Handle, H.A. Johnson & Co., Boston 22.00
Jar, Impressed Bird, Oval, Handles, Collar Ribbing, Footed Base, c.1820, 9 In. 1650.00
Jar, Impressed No. 2, Downward Rolled Rim, 2 Handles, Signed JAC, 1840-60, 11 3/4 In. 3080.00
Jar, Impressed No. 2, Streaked Alkaline Glaze, 2 Handles, J.F. Seagle, 1850-80s, 12 3/4 In. 2420.00
Jar, Incised Flower, Cobalt Blue, Applied Loop Handles, Jonathan Fenton, 14 1/2 In. 1410.00
Jar, Incised Flowers, Cobalt Blue, Tall Collar, Footed Base, Loop Handles, 1830, 12 In. 140.00
Jar, Incised Flowers, Mottled Brown Glaze, Round, Tapered, Lanier Meaders, 14 1/2 x 6 1/2 In. 1495.00
Jar, Incised Lines, Mottled, Medium Olive Alkaline Glaze, Lanier Meaders, 13 1/2 x 8 3/4 In. 230.00
Jar, Incised Lines, Salt Glaze, 2 Flat Lug Handles, J.M. Hays, c.1875, 14 1/4 In. 1485.00
Jar, Incised Shoulders, Straight Sides, Square Rim, Warne & Letts, 1906, 9 In. 4400.00
Jar, Incised Wavy Line, Mottled Dark Brown Glaze, Cylindrical, 19th Century, 9 7/8 In. 275.00
Jar, Incised, Brushed Dashes, Cobalt Blue, c.1850, 12 3/8 In. 275.00
Jar, Leaf Sprays, Blue, 8 3/4 In. 165.00
Jar, Lid, Blue, Tencil, Mushroom Finial, Cowden, Harrisburg, 9 1/2 In. 880.00
Jar, Lid, Brown Sponge Decoration, 8 1/2 In. 259.00
Jar, Lid, DeMuth's Snuff, Blue Stencil, Lancasater, Pa., Cowden, 9 1/2 In. 880.00
Jar, Oak Leaf, Blue Accents, Relief, Bristol Glaze, Qt., 4 3/4 In. 385.00
Jar, Olive, Incised No. 3, Rounded Handle, Alabama, c.1900, 15 1/2 In. 165.00
Jar, Olive, Incised No. 4, 2 Handles, Alabama, c.1900, 15 In. 330.00
Jar, Oyster, Brown, White, Glaze, Stencil, Swasey & Co., Portland, Me., c.1900, 6 1/2 In. 65.00
Jar, Parrot On Branch, Cobalt Blue, 2 Gal., 11 1/2 In. 2090.00
Jar, Pie-Crimped Half-Circles, Cobalt Blue, Applied Handle, Oval, 11 1/2 In. 690.00
Jar, Plume, Double, Cobalt Blue, J. McBurney, Jordan, c.1855, 2 Gal., 10 1/2 In. 415.00
Jar, Poppy, Center Bud, Slip Trailed, Stem, c.1866, 3 Gal., 16 In. 330.00
Jar, Runny Alkaline Glaze, Marked, 12 1/4 x 6 3/4 In. 200.00
Jar, Salt Glaze, Bulbous, Impressed No. 5, 2 Handles, J.D. Craven, 17 1/2 In. 1045.00
Jar, Salt Glaze, Impressed No. 5, 2 Handles, J.T. Boggs, 1820-80, 14 3/4 In. 5060.00
Jar, Snowflake, Face, Harrington, Lyons, N.Y., 2 Gal. 11550.00
Jar, Snuff, Figural, Old Woman Snorting Snuff, Vine Borders, Tin Cover, 10 In. 190.00
Jar, Speckled Brown, Blue Alkaline Glaze, J.H. Stone, 5 Gal., 20 1/4 In. 805.00
Jar, Spray Of Flowers, Blue, 8 3/4 In. 165.00
Jar, Streaked Alkaline Glaze, Egg Shape, Lug Handles, Seagle Attribution, c.1850, 14 In. 1375.00
Jar, Stylized Leaves, Incised Triangle, Cobalt Blue, Oval, c.1830, 2 Gal., 11 1/2 In. 165.00
Jar, Swirl, Gray, Cream, B.B. Craig, 16 3/4 x 11 1/4 In. 489.00
Jardiniere, Dots & Lines, Blue, J. Weaver, c.1850, 3 Gal., 12 1/2 In. 660.00
Jardiniere, Vine & Flower, Kiln Burns, c.1830, Gal., 8 1/2 In. 305.00
Jug, 2 Incised Bands, Brown Glaze, Applied Handle, Oval, Culpeper, Virginia, 14 In. 115.00
Jug, 2-Stem Flowers, Blue, F.H. Cowden, Harrisburg, Penn., 10 3/4 In. 330.00
Jug, 3-Petal Flower, Leafy Stem, Cobalt Blue, Handles, c.1870, 3 Gal., 14 1/2 In. 1155.00
Jug, Albany Slip Glaze, R.H. Parker, 19th Century, 3 In. 70.00
Jug, Alkaline Glaze, 2 Handles, Propst Shop Attribution, Early 1900s, 17 In. 550.00
Jug, Alkaline Glaze, Beehive Shape, Handle, Washington Becham, Ga., c.1865, 8 1/4 In. 3300.00
Jug, Alkaline Glaze, Handle, Signed NB, c.1865, 15 1/2 In. 2200.00
Jug, Alkaline Glaze, Kaolin Slip, Handle, T. Chandler, 2 Gal., 14 1/2 In. 7150.00

Jug, Armorial Medallions, Pewter Mount, Oval, Strap Handle, c.1594, 14 In. 3568.00
Jug, Basket Of Flowers, Nichols & Boynton, Burlington, Vt., 1 1/2 Gal. 1320.00
Jug, Beck Pottery Parish, Iowa, No. 3, Brown, 19th Century, 3 Gal., 15 In. 175.00
Jug, Bidwell & Co., Woodbridge, Blue Slip, Salt Glaze, Egg Shape, c.1810, 12 3/4 In. 550.00
Jug, Bird In Hand, Cobalt Blue, Applied Strap Handle, 11 1/4 In. 575.00
Jug, Bird On Branch, Applied Handle, 2 Gal., 14 x 9 In. 1210.00
Jug, Bird On Branch, Cobalt Blue, Strap Handle, West Troy Pottery, 12 In. 520.00
Jug, Bird On Branch, Paddle Tail, Blue, N.A. White & Son, Utica, N.Y., 5 Gal., 12 In. 495.00
Jug, Bird On Branch, Paddle Tail, Wreath, Cobalt Blue, N.A. White & Son, Utica, N.Y., 16 1/2 In. 1058.00
Jug, Bird On Plume, J.A. & C.W. Underwood, Fort Edward, N.Y., c.1865, 2 Gal., 13 1/2 In. 880.00
Jug, Bird On Twig, Blue, N.Y. Stoneware Co., Fort Edward, N.Y., c.1880, 2 Gal., 14 In. 635.00
Jug, Bird, Blue, Script No. 3, c.1870, 3 Gal., 15 In. 605.00
Jug, Bird, Blue, West Troy, N.Y., c.1880, Gal., 11 1/2 In. 1540.00
Jug, Bird, Blue, White's, Utica, c.1865, Gal., 11 In. 300.00
Jug, Bird, Cobalt Blue, Rogers & Co., Boston, 1 1/2 Gal. 115.00
Jug, Bird, Cobalt Blue, Straight Sides, Slope Shoulders, c.1905, 5 Gal., 19 In. 705.00
Jug, Bird, Incised, Daniel Goodale Jr., Benton & Stewart Pottery, c.1822, 12 In. 2115.00
Jug, Birds, Blue, Dotted, Hubbell & Chesebro, Geddes, N.Y., c.1870, 5 Gal., 17 In. 5500.00
Jug, Blue 3-Bud Flower, Oval, Thompson & Co., Gardiner, c.1840, Gal., 11 1/2 In. 410.00
Jug, Blue Accents, Oval, D. Goodale, Hartford, c.1826, 2 Gal., 15 1/2 In. 300.00
Jug, Blue Date, Dots, Egg Shape, E.S. Fox, Athens, 1838, c.1838, 12 1/2 In. 908.00
Jug, Blue Decoration, Gray, Egg Shape, Handle, 1830, 8 In. 550.00
Jug, Blue Incised Line, Egg Shape, J. Remmey, Manhattan, c.1790, 3 Gal., 15 1/2 In. 2420.00
Jug, Blue No. 2, Egg Shape, S. Addington, Utica, c.1830, 2 Gal., 13 In. 300.00
Jug, Blue Script, J.J. O'Connor, E.W. Farrington, Elmira, N.Y., c.1890, Gal., 11 1/2 In. 99.00
Jug, Blue Script, M.J. Skelly, E.W. Farrington, Elmira, N.Y., c.1890, Gal., 10 In. 248.00
Jug, Blue Underlined No. 2, Oval, Nathan Clark, Mount Morris, c.1835, 12 1/2 In. 248.00
Jug, Blue Wash, Clark & Co., Lyons, N.Y., c.1830, 2 Gal., 13 1/2 In. 305.00
Jug, Blue, M. Schwartzkopf, Scranton, Pa., 18 1/2 In. 440.00
Jug, Brown Glaze, Egg Shape, c.1850, 16 1/2 x 9 In. 150.00
Jug, Brown Salt Glaze, Hand-Brushed Cobalt Blue, No. 4, Applied Handles, 14 1/4 In. 115.00
Jug, Brown, Cream Glaze, Black Stencil, When I Am Empty, Fill Me Up, Qt. 89.00
Jug, Brown, Cream Glaze, Cobalt Blue Stencil, 6-Pointed Star, E. Block & Co., Qt. 79.00
Jug, Brushed Blue Flower, Sipe & Sons, c.1870, Gal., 11 In. 165.00
Jug, Brushed Flower, Cylinder, J.B. Magee, Ithaca, c.1853, Gal., 11 In. 165.00
Jug, Bull's-Eye Leaf, Blue, F.B. Norton & Co., Worcester, Mass., c.1870, Gal., 10 1/2 In. 154.00
Jug, C.D. Coons, Nunda, N.Y., Blue Script, E.W. Farrington, Elmira, c.1890, Gal., 10 1/2 In. 520.00
Jug, Casey Whiskey, Man Turning Crank, Cobalt Blue, Twig Handle, 7 7/8 In. 330.00
Jug, Charlestown, Impressed, Oval, 2 Gal. 190.00
Jug, City Wine Store, Brown, Cream Glaze, Stencil, Montpelier, Qt. 90.00
Jug, Cobalt Blue Decoration, Salt Glaze, H.R. Pfaltzgraff, 11 In. 290.00
Jug, Cobalt Blue Decoration, Salt Glaze, Lowden & Wilcox, 11 In. 259.00
Jug, Cobalt Blue Stencil, Tooled Spouts, Rainbow Handle, Domed, c.1875, 15 3/8 In. 2640.00
Jug, Cobalt Blue, Oval, Applied Strap Handle, 1830, Gal., 11 3/8 In. 140.00
Jug, Cobalt Blue, Slope Shoulders, Straight Sides, Applied Strap Handle, c.1865, 11 In. 380.00
Jug, Compliments Of John J. Stump & Co., Cumberland, Md., 5 1/4 In. 89.00
Jug, Compliments Of The O.L. Gregory Vinegar Co., St. Louis, Mo., Mini 50.00
Jug, Cornucopia Of Flowers, Fort Edward, N.Y., 2 Gal., 14 1/2 In. 220.00
Jug, Crossed Birds, Cobalt Blue Wings, Dots, c.1860, 3 Gal., 14 1/8 In. 5500.00
Jug, Daisy, Leaf Wreath, Cobalt Blue, Semi-Oval, c.1870, 3 Gal., 16 1/4 In. 1320.00
Jug, Daisy, Light Blue Wash, Burger & Lang, Rochester, N.Y., c.1870, 2 Gal., 14 1/2 In. 220.00
Jug, Detrick Distilling Co., I Am Always Welcome Wherever I Go, Dayton, O., 4 1/2 In. 25.00
Jug, Doran., 92 West Main St., Rochester, Wood Stopper, c.1880, 11 In. 175.00
Jug, Drape, Blue, Mottled Glaze, Crolius, New York, c.1830, 2 Gal., 12 1/2 In. 880.00
Jug, Egg Shape, T. Crafts, Nashua, Gal. 220.00
Jug, Face, 3 Openings, 7 Teeth, Drizzling Bottle-Green Glaze, A.G. Meaders, 11 3/4 In. 560.00
Jug, Face, Bearded Devil, Shard Teeth, 2 Handles, Oval, Hussey, 23 1/2 In. 575.00
Jug, Face, Broken China Teeth, Runny Medium Olive Alkaline Glaze, 8 x 6 In. 375.00
Jug, Face, Broken China Teeth, Swirl, B.B. Craig, 6 1/2 x 5 In. 430.00
Jug, Face, Bulging Eyes, Ceramic Teeth, Runny Olive Alkaline Glaze, 8 1/2 x 7 In. 920.00
Jug, Face, Cobalt Blue Highlights, 1900s, 8 1/2 In. 220.00

Jug, Face, Devil's Head, Brown Glaze, Snakes, Albert Hodge, N.C., 13 In. 115.00
Jug, Face, Grotesque, Meaders Potter, 7 1/4 In. 90.00
Jug, Face, Grotesque, Molded Features, White Shard Teeth, Albany Slip Glaze, 7 1/2 In. 805.00
Jug, Face, Medium Brown Glaze, Flossie Meaders, 9 1/2 x 9 3/4 In. 400.00
Jug, Face, White Teeth, Eyes, Green Ash Glaze, Lanier Meaders, 10 In. 1265.00
Jug, Fault & Sass Pure Wines, Brown Glaze, Incised Label, 16 1/2 In. 200.00
Jug, Fish, Cherries, Blue, Egg Shape, Old Bridge Pottery, N.J., c.1810, 7 1/2 In. 1265.00
Jug, Flamingo, Blue, White's, Utica, 2 Gal. 275.00
Jug, Flower & Leaf, Ribbed, Mantell & Thomas, Penn Yan, N.Y., c.1853, 2 Gal., 14 1/2 In. 495.00
Jug, Flower Slip, Applied Handle, 2 Gal., 13 1/2 In. 605.00
Jug, Flower Spray, Haxstun & Co., Fort Edwards, N.Y., 2 Gal. 190.00
Jug, Flower Vine, Blue, Dark Tan Clay, E.H. Farrar, North Bay, c.1851, Gal., 12 In. 275.00
Jug, Flower, Blue, Ball Shape, Clark & Fox, Athens, N.Y., c.1830, 12 1/2 In. 855.00
Jug, Flower, Blue, Ball Shape, S. Fox, Athens, N.Y., c.1840, 2 Gal., 12 1/2 In. 468.00
Jug, Flower, Blue, Egg Shape, P. Mugler & Co., Buffalo, N.Y., c.1850, 3 Gal., 16 In. 440.00
Jug, Flower, Blue, Gray, Applied Ear Handles, Interior Glaze, Debossed, c.1850, 9 1/4 In. 1430.00
Jug, Flower, Blue, J.B. Magee, Ithaca, c.1853, 2 Gal., 12 1/2 In. 165.00
Jug, Flower, Blue, New York Stoneware Co., Fort Edward, c.1880, 2 Gal., 13 1/2 In. 248.00
Jug, Flower, Blue, Ribbed, John Burger, c.1865, 2 Gal., 14 In. 1075.00
Jug, Flower, Blue, S. Hart, Fulton, c.1875, 2 Gal., 12 1/2 In. 248.00
Jug, Flower, Cobalt Blue, High Shoulder, Narrow Neck, Applied Handle, c.1850, 15 x 19 In. 355.00
Jug, Flower, Cobalt Blue, White's, Utica, Gal. 65.00
Jug, Flower, F. Stetzenmeyer & Co., Rochester, c.1855, 2 Gal., 14 In. 1650.00
Jug, Flower, Leaves, Incised, Blue Decoration, Salt Glaze, Oval, Handle, c.1843, 11 In. 2750.00
Jug, Flower, Ribbed, F. Stetzenmeyer, Rochester, c.1855, 3 Gal., 16 1/2 In. 2860.00
Jug, Flower, Triple, Blue, Beehive Shape, W. Hart, Ogdensburgh, c.1860, 3 Gal., 13 1/2 In. 165.00
Jug, Flowering Plume, Blue, A. & B.G. Chace, Somerset, c.1860, 3 Gal., 16 In. 385.00
Jug, Flowers, Blue Slip, Applied Handle, D.P. Shenfelder, Reading, Pa., 2 Gal., 13 1/2 In. 605.00
Jug, Flowers, Blue, D.W. Graves, Westmoreland, 3 Gal., 15 1/2 In. 275.00
Jug, Flowers, Cobalt Blue, J.S. Taft & Co., Keene, N.H., Gal. 550.00
Jug, Flowers, Cobalt Blue, Oval, Stamped, E.S. Fox, Athens, c.1835, 10 1/2 In. 195.00
Jug, Flowers, D.W. Westmoreland, 3 Gal., 15 1/2 In. 275.00
Jug, Flowers, Incised Shoulders, Oval, Ribbed Handle, 2 Gal., 13 5/8 In. 220.00
Jug, Flowers, Riedinger & Caire, Po'keepsie, N.Y., 13 1/2 In. 250.00
Jug, Flowers, Stylized, E. E. Hall & Co., Gal., 11 1/4 In. 176.00
Jug, Freehand Design, Hamilton & Jones, Greensboro, Pa., c.1870, 3 Gal., 16 In. 578.00
Jug, Freehand Feather Design, Cobalt Blue, Impressed No. 2, Strap Handle, 13 In. 145.00
Jug, French Wine House, Brooklyn, N.Y., Blue Stencil, 5 Gal., 18 In. 70.00
Jug, Fuchsia Vine, Cobalt Blue, Oval, Stenciled Foell & Alt, c.1860, 2 Gal., 13 3/4 In. 825.00
Jug, Gemel, Albany Slip Glaze, Black, Center Handle, c.1880, 10 In. 195.00
Jug, Gillett Snow & Thayer, Dealers In Dry Goods, Bird, Blue, Mass., c.1870, 2 Gal., 11 1/2 In. 220.00
Jug, Good Old O.C.B. Whiskey, Winchell & Davis Imp., Albany, N.Y., 4 1/4 In. 89.00
Jug, H. Armour, Paterson, Union Pottery, Newark, N.J., 2 Gal. 220.00
Jug, Harvest, Script, Blue, Cinnamon Clay, c.1850, 1 1/2 Gal., 11 1/2 In. 358.00
Jug, Hayes & Co. Liquor Dealers, Manchester, N.H., Cobalt Blue Decoration, Gal. 99.00
Jug, Horkhelmer Bro's., Wine, Brandies, Whiskies, Stencil, Wheeling, W.Va., 11 1/2 In. 290.00
Jug, Impressed Flower Blossoms, Cobalt Blue, Applied Reeded Handle, 8 In. 470.00
Jug, Incised Lines, Applied Strap Handle, Oval, Maker's Mark, Charlestown, 12 In. 470.00
Jug, Incised Shoulder Line, Salt Glaze, Handle, B.C. Milburn, Early 1840s, 9 In. 250.00
Jug, Insect, Wings, Dotted, W. Roberts, Binghamton, c.1860, Gal., 11 In. 145.00
Jug, J Potts & Son Grocers, Alkaline Glaze, Handle, 1890-1910, 7 7/8 In. 150.00
Jug, J.B. Doherty & Co., Dudley & Adam Sts., Roxbury, Mass., 1/2 Gal. 80.00
Jug, J.J. Donnelly, Paterson, N.J., 2 Gal., 13 1/2 In. 248.00
Jug, J.R. Watkins Med. Co., Winona, Minn., U.S.A., Established 1868, Gal. 195.00
Jug, James Slevin, Greenwich St., New York, Impressed, c.1890, 5 Gal., 17 1/2 In. 90.00
Jug, John Driscoll, Bridgeport, Conn., Blue Script, 11 In. 300.00
Jug, John H. Walsh & Co., Haymarket Sq., Boston, Mass., Gal., 11 In. 52.00
Jug, Jorum Roderick Old Highland Whisky, Wright & Greig Ltd., Glasgow, 4 In. 45.00
Jug, Leaf, Cobalt Blue, Estabrook & Robinson, Boston, 1800s, Gal. 130.00
Jug, Leaping Rabbit, Cobalt Blue, Ribbed Handle, c.1840, 13 5/8 In. 3740.00
Jug, Leaves, Stylized Tree, Blue, Edmands & Co., c.1870, 2 Gal., 14 In. 578.00

Jug, Lewis Fischer & Bro., Early 1900s, 3 Gal. 250.00
Jug, Marshall Pottery Products, Contain Nothing Harmful, Glazed, c.1910, Gal., 11 In. 248.00
Jug, Masonic Emblem, Salt Glaze, Handle, J.F. Brower, 2 Pt., 9 In. 605.00
Jug, Matewan's Old Time Maple Syrup, Fresh From The Still, 1/2 Pt., 6 1/4 In. 59.00
Jug, May's, Pittsburgh, Pa., Brown, Cream, Blue Letters, Pt. 50.00
Jug, Monkey, Alkaline Glaze, 2 Chambers, Propst Shop Attribution, Early 1900s, 9 1/4 In. 415.00
Jug, Moore & Hubbard, Syracuse, N.Y., 2 Gal. 450.00
Jug, Morning Dove On Branch, Cobalt Blue, 2 Gal., 13 3/4 In. 2310.00
Jug, Mottled Black, Brown Glaze, Edward Leslie Stork, 15 1/4 x 9 3/4 In. 635.00
Jug, Mottled Green & Brown, Gourd Shape, Louis Lourioux, 1930s, 7 1/4 In. 285.00
Jug, Mottled, Runny Olive Alkaline Glaze, Timmerman, 9 1/2 In. 290.00
Jug, Ocher Accents, Applied Loop Handles, Charlestown, c.1850, Gal., 10 In. 605.00
Jug, Old Continental Whiskey, Acorn, Blue Stencil, Brown, Tan, 3 1/2 In. 39.00
Jug, Olive Alkaline Glaze, Applied Handles, 16 3/4 x 12 In. 375.00
Jug, Olive Alkaline Glaze, Speckled, Edgefield, 16 1/2 x 12 In. 489.00
Jug, Olive Green, Mottled Gray, No. 1, Handle, Daniel Anderson, Ill., 1900s, 8 1/2 In. 265.00
Jug, Olive, Alkaline Glaze, 2 Handles, H. Craven Attribution, c.1875, 17 1/4 In. 935.00
Jug, Parrot, Plume, F.B. Norton & Co., Worcester, Mass., c.1870, 3 Gal., 14 1/2 In. 745.00
Jug, Patriotic Shield, Flags, Blue Plume, Cowden & Wilcox, c.1870, 4 Gal., 18 In. 8800.00
Jug, Peabody Club Whiskey RM Redfearn, Bolivar, Tenn., Mini 105.00
Jug, Peacock, Long Neck, On Stump, c.1865, 3 Gal., 15 In. 635.00
Jug, Pine Tree, N.A. White & Son, Utica, c.1870, Gal., 11 In. 175.00
Jug, Pinwheel Flower, Blue, N. Clark, Rochester, N.Y., c.1850, 2 Gal., 14 1/2 In. 3520.00
Jug, Plume, Blue, J. Fisher, Lyons, N.Y., c.1880, 2 Gal., 13 1/2 In. 165.00
Jug, Rabbit, Running, Blue, c.1870, 2 Gal., 14 In. 1760.00
Jug, Raised Rings, Brown Glaze, Applied Strap Handle, Stamped, 12 1/2 In. 400.00
Jug, Rings, Salt Glaze, Impressed No. 2, Masonic Emblem, Handle, H. Fox, c.1875, 14 1/4 In. 3740.00
Jug, Rose, Stencil, Freehand Lines, Rager Lloyd & Co., c.1875, 4 Gal., 18 In. 330.00
Jug, Roses, Stencil, Jas. Hamilton & Co., Greensboro, Pa., c.1870, 16 In. 275.00
Jug, Rosette, Horizontal Lines, Alkaline Glaze, Kaolin Slip, Handle, c.1854, 14 1/4 In. 5500.00
Jug, Runny Olive Alkaline Glaze, Handles, Henry Long, 18 1/2 x 12 1/2 In. 460.00
Jug, Runny Olive Glaze, Applied Strap Handles, Jack N. Merrett, 15 1/2 x 10 In. 635.00
Jug, S. Reals, Lyons, N.Y., Blue Script, c.1880, Gal., 11 In. 130.00
Jug, Salt Glaze, Egg Shape, Handle, J.M. Yow, Erect, N.C., Late 1800s, 9 1/2 In. 2860.00
Jug, Salt Glaze, Groove Top Handle, E.S. Craven, c.1875, 8 3/4 In. 1430.00
Jug, Salt Glaze, Handle, M.W. Owens, 9 3/4 In. 550.00
Jug, Salt Glaze, Handle, T. Gay, c.1875, 12 In. 1540.00
Jug, Salt Glaze, Incised No. 2, Flat Handle, W.F. Outen Attribution, c.1900, 15 1/2 In. 65.00
Jug, Scranton Wine & Liquor Co., Brown Slip Glaze, 11 1/2 In. 248.00
Jug, Scranton Wine & Liquor Co., Brown Slip, James Ryan, Pittston, Pa., 11 1/2 In. 250.00
Jug, Script, Blue, Calvin Higgins, Made July 25, 1882, 1/2 Gal., 7 1/2 In. 745.00
Jug, Senesac Bros., Dealers In Dry Goods, Readimade Clothing, Quebec, 2 Gal. 650.00
Jug, Shenfelder, Reading, Oval, Gal. 730.00
Jug, Shoofly, Applied Stylized Black Woman, Erotic Decoration, 5 7/8 In. 3525.00
Jug, Songbird Perched On Branch, Cobalt Blue, Stamped, W. Roberts, 11 1/8 In. 550.00
Jug, Sunflower, Blue, John Burger, Rochester, N.Y., c.1865, 2 Gal., 13 1/2 In. 385.00
Jug, Syrup, Blue Letters, M.H. Brown, Brookfield, N.Y., c.1880, 1/2 Gal., 7 1/2 In. 600.00
Jug, Syrup, C.E. Orr, 45 Cts., Camden, N.Y., Bristol Glaze, c.1880, Gal., 9 1/2 In. 250.00
Jug, Teardrops & Diamonds, Blue, White, Pewter Lid, No. 1769, R. Merkelbach, 9 1/2 In., 3 Liter .. 770.00
Jug, Tornado, Blue, D.W. Graves, Westmoreland, c.1860, 2 Gal., 13 In. 130.00
Jug, Tree Of Life, Blue, Cylindrical, Cream Glaze, c.1880, 1/2 Gal., 7 1/2 In. 198.00
Jug, Tree, Stylized, Oval, Ribbed Handle, 3 Gal., 14 3/4 In. 165.00
Jug, Trophy, Crossed Arrows, Blue, Webster & Bergen, North Bay, c.1851, 2 Gal., 14 In. 550.00
Jug, Tulip, Blue, J. Fisher, Lyons, N.Y., c.1880, 3 Gal., 14 1/2 In. 130.00
Jug, Tulip, Cobalt Blue, Egg Shape, Strap Handle, 2 Gal., 13 1/2 In. 316.00
Jug, Tulip, Triple, Cortland, c.1860, 2 Gal., 13 In. 525.00
Jug, Wetts Bros., Akron, O., Dark Brown Glaze, Handle, 1890-1910, 8 In. 45.00
Jug, Whiskey, Brown Albany Slip Glaze, 9 3/4 x 7 1/2 x 7 In. 430.00
Jug, Whittmore, Havana, N.Y., c.1850, 2 Gal. 120.00
Jug, Wreath, Blue, Tan Clay, Burger & Co., Rochester, N.Y., c.1877, 2 Gal., 13 1/2 In. 275.00
Jug, Wreath, Cobalt Blue, 1850, 12 1/2 In. 495.00

Milk Pan, Leaves, Cobalt Blue, Handles, Spout, c.1865, 12 3/4 In. 490.00
Mug, Blue Accents, Impressed, Salt Glaze, 25 Bezirks Turnfest, N.Y., c.1894, 5 In. 90.00
Mug, Blue Bands, Tooled, Cobalt Blue Flowers On Handle, Impressed, John Wiggand, 6 1/4 In. ... 65.00
Mug, Grapes, Band, Blue, Embossed, 4 3/4 In. 65.00
Mug, Tree Bark Design, Applied Clay Branches, Alkaline Glaze, c.1860, 3 1/2 In. 55.00
Mug, Wide Blue Bands, Barrel Form, 4 1/2 In. 80.00
Pitcher, 3 Accent Rings, Blue Accents At Handle, Stamped, 1 1/2 Gal., 12 1/2 In. 1000.00
Pitcher, 4 Flowers, Sprays, Blue, Bulbous, 10 1/2 In. 798.00
Pitcher, 5 Accent Rings, Blue Accents At Handle, Gal., 11 1/4 In. 450.00
Pitcher, 6 Flowers, 5 Accent Rings, Blue Accents At Handle, Remmey, Gal., 11 In. 3360.00
Pitcher, Accent Neck Ring, Blue Accents At Handle, 1/2 Gal., 9 In. 450.00
Pitcher, Albany Slip Glaze, Gordy Shop Attribution, Early 1900s, 7 3/4 In. 65.00
Pitcher, Alkaline Glaze, Cheever Meaders Attribution, c.1950, 6 In. 195.00
Pitcher, Dogwood Blossom, Crushed-Glass Glaze, Hilton, Late 1930s, 6 1/4 In. 550.00
Pitcher, Face, Runny Brown Glaze, 7 3/4 x 7 1/2 In. 430.00
Pitcher, Flatiron Building, Lady, Blue & White Stripes, Robinson Pottery, Akron, Ohio, 8 1/2 In. ... 250.00
Pitcher, Flower Spray, Blue, Bulbous, Applied Handle, 10 1/2 In. 745.00
Pitcher, Flower Sprig, Cobalt Blue, Incised, Inscription, c.1835, 8 1/4 In. 12925.00
Pitcher, Flower, Blue, Applied Handle, Wingender, Haddonfield, N.J., 7 1/4 In. 300.00
Pitcher, Flower, Cobalt Blue, Impressed No. 3, Ring Near Top, Strap Handle, 14 1/2 In. 690.00
Pitcher, Flower, Double, 3 Accent Rings, Blue Accents At Handle, Remmey, 10 1/2 In. 2240.00
Pitcher, Flower, Drop Swag, Blue Decoration, 11 In. 415.00
Pitcher, Flower, Leaves, Swag Around Rim, Cobalt Blue, 9 In. 1290.00
Pitcher, Flower, Ribbed & Brushed, J. Mantell, Penn Yan, N.Y., c.1860, Gal., 9 1/2 In. 990.00
Pitcher, Flower, Stylized, Blue Decoration, White's, Binghamton, 10 In. 825.00
Pitcher, Flowers, Cobalt Blue, Embossed, White's, Utica, 6 1/2 In. 55.00
Pitcher, Flowers, Cobalt Blue, Flared Collar, Ribbed Handle, Oval, c.1865, 3 3/8 In. 1980.00
Pitcher, Flowers, Cobalt Blue, Tall Collar, 1870, Gal., 10 5/8 In. 880.00
Pitcher, Flowers, Salt Glaze, Tooled Neck, Applied Handle, Thumb Rest, c.1850, 8 3/4 In. 1320.00
Pitcher, Flowers, Vine, Swag & Dot, Brown Brushstrokes, 7 In. 1210.00
Pitcher, Flying Dove, Incised, Ohio, c.1830, 2 Gal., 12 1/2 In. 1018.00
Pitcher, Fuchsia Vine, Dashes, Swags, Tan, Tall Collar, c.1880, 8 1/2 In. 605.00
Pitcher, Fuchsia Vine, Incised, Tan, Striped Handle, Semi-Oval, c.1880, 5 3/4 In. 605.00
Pitcher, Fuchsia Vine, Swags, Tan, 8 1/2 In. 605.00
Pitcher, Lid, Salt Glaze, Finger-Groove Handle, c.1885, 8 3/4 In. 250.00
Pitcher, Olive, Alkaline Glaze, Cheever Meaders Attribution, c.1960, 8 1/2 In. 120.00
Pitcher, Relief Shield, Blue & White Salt Glaze, 8 In. 165.00
Pitcher, Roses, Applied, Branch, Leaves, Molded Rim, Shoulder, Tankard Form, 8 3/4 In. 1540.00
Pitcher, Salt Glaze, Squat Belly, 19th Century, 8 5/8 In. 165.00
Pitcher, Squiggle Lines, Blue, Gray Salt Glaze, Applied Handle, c.1850, 7 1/2 In. 300.00
Pitcher, Stylized Plant, Flowerhead, Cobalt Blue, Oval, Flared Collar, c.1860, 10 In. 385.00
Pitcher, Swirlware, Crushed Glass Glaze, Propst, North Carolina, c.1925, 7 In. 990.00
Pitcher, Tulip, Double, Cobalt Blue, Gal., 11 In. 578.00
Pitcher, Tulips, Vines, Brown Matte Glaze, Albany Slip, 7 In. 290.00
Pitcher, Watch Spring, Blue, Speckled Clay, c.1860, Qt., 7 In. 715.00
Pitcher Set, Graduated, England, c.1870, 6 1/4 x 8 1/2 In., 3 Piece .... 150.00 to 189.00
Punch Bowl, Bardwell's Root Beer, Blue Accents, Salt Glaze, White's, Utica, 10 x 20 In. 3080.00
Shaving Mug, Brown Glaze, 4 3/4 In. 230.00
Strainer, Brown Alkaline Glaze, Handle, New York State, c.1880, 11 In. 70.00
Strainer, Pierced Holes, Handles, 20th Century, 6 Qt., 15 In. 59.00
Sugar & Creamer, Dogwood Blossom, Crushed-Glass Glaze, Hilton, Late 1930s, 3 3/8 In. 358.00
Tankard, Blue Brushed Bands, 7 In. 70.00
Teapot, Cover, 6-Sided, Red, Molded Panels, Chinoiserie, c.1760-65, 3 7/8 In. .... ***ILLUS*** 5400.00
Teapot, Cover, Glazed, Bamboo Handle, 7 In. 350.00
Vase, Albany Slip Glaze, Glossy, Trophy Style, Brown Shop Attribution, Ga., 1920s, 15 In. 66.00
Vase, Art Nouveau, Vines, Fruit, Baluster, c.1900, 5 1/2 In. 339.00
Vase, Olive Green, Dragon Handles, Jump Rings, Chinese, 5 1/4 In. 1175.00
Vase, Swimming Fish, Sea Plants, Unglazed Outline, Tapered, 14 3/4 x 8 In. 1175.00
Water Cooler, Blue Band, Crown No. 6, 6 Gal., 21 In. 147.00
Water Cooler, Cobalt Blue, Lug Handles, Spout, 1835, 3 Gal., 15 1/2 In. 1100.00
Water Cooler, Cover, Blue Decoration, Spout, Early 1900s, 4 Gal. 295.00

Stoneware, Teapot, Cover, 6-Sided, Red, Molded Panels, Chinoiserie, c.1760-65, 3 7/8 In.

Superman, Lunch Box, Robot, Action Pictures, Metal, Universal Industries, 1954

Water Cooler, Flower, Cobalt Blue, Semi-Oval, Hole, Metal Spigot, 1886, 14 1/8 In. 220.00
Water Cooler, Flower, Hash Marks, Cobalt Blue, Spigot, 3 Gal., 15 3/4 In. 1980.00
Water Cooler, Flowers & Fruit, Blue, Egg Shape, c.1800, 1 1/2 Gal., 12 1/2 In. 688.00
Water Cooler, Flowers, Blue, Applied Handles, 2 Gal., 12 3/4 In. 550.00
Water Cooler, Leaves & Pineapple, Blue, Goodwin & Webster, Hartford, c.1810, 19 In. 5500.00
Water Cooler, Relief Flowers & Bouquet, Ice Water, 15 In. 231.00
Water Cooler, Tulips, Cobalt Blue, Ribbed Handles, Bung Hole, 1865, 2 Gal., 13 In. 550.00

STORE fixtures, cases, cutters, and other items that have no advertising as part of the decoration are listed here. Most items found in an old store are listed in the Advertising category in this book.

Bin, Stenciled Fresh Roasted Coffee, Tin, Painted, Slanted Lid, Glass Front, 17 x 18 In. 248.00
Cabinet, Hardware, 2 Recessed Panel Doors, 20 Drawers, 1800s, 51 1/2 x 49 In. 2750.00
Cabinet, Jeweler's, Softwood, Grain Painted, Slanted Top, 6 Drawers, Door, 38 x 40 In. 990.00
Cabinet, Pharmacy, Oak, Sliding Glass Doors, 2 Parts, Brass Plaque, 96 x 22 x 91 In. 2300.00
Case, Mahogany, Glass, Twin Tower, Show Case Works, Mo., Early 1900s, 38 x 96 In. 1696.00
Case, Oak Top, 4 Sliding Mirrored Doors, 1890-1900, 15 x 69 x 28 In. 220.00
Case, Oak, Glass, Excelsior Show Case Co., Quincy, Ill., Early 1900s, 38 x 37 In. 3029.00
Case, Oak, Glass, Show Case Works, Quincy, Ill., Early 1900s, 20 x 92 x 29 In. 452.00
Cigar Lighter, Country Store, Counter 130.00
Cigarette Dispenser, Flapper Girl Head, Feathers, Jewels, 7 In. 360.00
Coffee Grinders are listed in their own category.
Cork Press, Alligator, Cast Iron, Holes In Feet, 11 1/2 In. 330.00
Counter, Basswood, Poplar, Yellow Paint, 6 Drawers, Paneled Door, 83 x 31 In. 2415.00
Counter Window, U.S. Postal Sub Station, Maple, Barred Window, c.1900, 42 x 40 In. 1057.00
Cupboard, Hardware, 8 Chamfered Face Drawers, Blue Paint, 38 x 26 x 21 In. 1980.00
Dispenser, Sugar, Purple Glass, Metal Lid, Pat. Nov. 10, 1914, Bracket & Holder, 10 1/2 In. 190.00
Display, Toothbrush, 1930s, Tabletop 325.00
Mannequin, Head, Torso, Wood, Polychrome, Glass Eyes, Blond, 1700s, 12 x 8 x 8 In. 3173.00
Meat Slicer, No. 7317, Winchester, 17 1/2 In. 115.00
Sign, Bullet, Carved, Gold End, 14 1/2 x 5 In. 115.00
Sign, Cigars & Tobacco, Pipes, Pipe Repairing, Painted Glass, Gold Letters 110.00
Sign, Clothespin Shape, Oak, Carved, Early 20th Century, 24 In. 590.00
Sign, Directory, 2nd Floor, Reverse Painted Glass, Black Ground, Gilt Lettering, 27 x 72 In. 8813.00
Sign, F.L. Thorndike, Hatmaker, Wood, Gold Letters, Sand Paint, 10 x 69 In. 360.00
Sign, Fish Shape, Wood, Painted, 35 1/4 In. 470.00
Sign, Fish, Tin, Hollow Body, Painted, 36 1/2 In. 275.00
Sign, Horseshoe, Carved, Wood, Forged Iron, O.R. Forsythe, 46 x 40 In. 3738.00
Sign, Hotel Entrance, Forest Green, Gilded Relief Carved Lettering, Wood, 10 x 98 In. 880.00
Sign, Ice Cream Cone, Brown, Pink, Tan, Papier-Mache, Wood Base, c.1930, 72 In. 275.00
Sign, Keys & Locksmithing, Sharpening & Grinding, Key Shape, Painted, 61 In. 605.00
Sign, Meals & Lodging, Jitney Service, 2-Sided, Multicolored, 12 3/4 x 48 In. 1320.00
Sign, Pocket Watch, Zinc, Painted, 11 In. 715.00
Sign, Rooms For Tourists, Silver Block Letter, Green Ground, 13 3/4 x 73 1/2 In. 748.00
Sign, Shoe Repairing, Shoe Shape, Tin, Early 1900s, 44 In. 165.00
Sign, Shoe, Repair, Shine, Tin, 2-Sided, 1880-1910, 54 x 28 In. 3200.00
Sign, Shop, Oval, Profile Of 18th Century Gentleman, Multicolored, 16 x 12 1/2 In. 968.00

Sign, Signs, Reverse On Glass, Painted, 43 In. 660.00
Sign, Soda Fountain Luncheonette, Sheet Metal, Wood, Gilt Lettering, 22 x 72 In. 1880.00
Sign, Watch, Cast Iron, Painted, 2 Father Time Winged Figures, With Scythes, 30 In. 355.00
Spool Cabinet, 6-Cord, Soft Finish Spool Cotton, Oak, Glass, Cylinder, Victorian 360.00
Stand, Bank, Brass, Glass, Pen Stands, Perpetual Calendar, c.1920, 11 x 36 x 11 In. 645.00
Stand, Slot Machine, Oak, Cast Iron, Caille, 32 In. 3850.00
Strawholder, Amber Glass, Metal Lid & Insert, 10 1/2 In. 360.00
Strawholder, Blue Glass, Metal Lid & Insert, 10 1/2 In. 360.00
Strawholder, Glass, Metal Lid & Insert, Late 19th Century, 12 In. 330.00
Strawholder, Green Glass, Metal Lid & Insert, 10 1/2 In. 330.00
Strawholder, Green Pressed Glass, Domed Metal Lid & Insert, 12 In. 440.00 to 550.00
Strawholder, Green Pressed Glass, Metal Lid & Insert, 11 In. 358.00
Strawholder, Heavy Pressed Glass, Block Pattern, Sawtooth Lip, Dome Lid, 13 In. 358.00
Strawholder, Heavy Pressed Glass, Linked Chain Design, Metal Lid & Base, 11 1/2 In. 255.00
Strawholder, Heavy Pressed Glass, Purple Tint, Block Pattern, Sawtooth Lip, Dome Lid, 13 In. 470.00
Strawholder, Heavy Pressed Glass, Quilted Star Pattern, Flared Bottom, Domed Lid, 13 In. 410.00
Strawholder, Heavy Pressed Glass, Zigzag Pattern, Metal Lid, Square Base, Angled Corners, 11 In. 715.00
Strawholder, Pressed Glass, Linked Chain, Chrome Base, Lid, Swivel Insert, 11 In. 660.00
Strawholder, Pressed Glass, Metal Dome Lid & Base, 1918, 12 In. 165.00
Strawholder, Pressed Glass, Silver Plated Lid, Utilities Specialties, Jersey City, N.J., 11 x 6 In. 550.00
Stringholder, Beehive, Hubley, 1900s 475.00
Tally Board, Shopkeeper's, Walnut, 18th Century 195.00
Tobacco Cutter, Horse Shape, Wood Tail Handle, Wood Base, Late 1800s 325.00
Tobacco Cutter, Iron Blade, Walnut Board, Tombstone Shape, E.H.D., 1861, 16 1/2 In. 345.00

STOVES have been used in America for heating since the eighteenth century and for cooking since the nineteenth century. Most types of wood, coal, gas, kerosene, and even some electric stoves are collected.

Art Andes No. 4, Base Burner, Cast Iron 1000.00
Base Burner, Sterling, Cast Iron 1600.00
Box, Cherubs, Cast Iron 700.00
Bridge Beach & Co., Iron Mountain, Step Back, Cast Iron, 1858, 53 x 46 x 38 In. 230.00
Buck Water Stove Co., Ring Old No. 9, Nickel, 6 Tiles, 46 In. 1700.00
Castle, G.W. Eddy Troy, Pat. 1853 1400.00
E.M. Pratt, 2 Columns, 1840 1000.00
Favorite Stove & Range Co., Cast Iron, Scrolled, Embossed, 25 x 19 1/2 In. 1760.00
Fuller & Warran Co., Globe, Sail Ships, Birds 3900.00
Gothic Pattern, No. 5, Cast Iron, 32 x 29 x 23 In. 138.00
Jewel Range, Detroit Stove Works, 6 Burners, 2 Piece Reservoir, Cast Iron, 16 x 18 In. 1760.00
Karr Qualified Range, Porcelain, Blue Speckled, Nickel Plate, Rolled Lid, Belleville, Il., 21 x 13 In. 4290.00
Laboratory, Jiffy, Enamel On Steel, Serelco, 1925, 21 x 10 x 14 3/4 In. 235.00
Laundry, Great Western Stove Company, Cast Iron, Early 1900s, 27 x 31 x 19 In. 81.00
Parlor, Atlantic, Cast Iron 675.00
Parlor, Bent. Griffith & Co., No. 3 Portable Grate, Cast Iron, Mass., 1862, 31 x 24 In. 230.00
Parlor, Cast Iron, Chrome, Mica Panels, Bangor, Me., 1893, 26 x 26 In. 413.00
Parlor, Morrison & Willard, Andirons, Basket, Screen 2900.00
Parlor, Venetian Franklin Vose Co., No. 4 2500.00
Pratt Weeks & Co., Model No. 2, Cast Iron, Embossed, Boston, c.1857, 36 x 27 In. 165.00
Railroad, Cast Iron, Acorns 750.00
Range, Eagle, Cast Iron, Utensils, 4 x 7 1/2 x 4 In. 25.00
Range, Gas, Porcelain, c.1920, 51 x 40 x 24 In. 69.00
Zoar, Cast Iron, Raised Leaf Panel, Cabriole Feet, Tin Ash Hopper, 44 In. 230.00

SULPHIDES are cameos of unglazed white porcelain encased in transparent glass. The technique was patented in 1819 in France and has been used ever since for paperweights, decanters, tumblers, marbles, and other type of glassware. Paperweights and Marbles are listed in their own categories.

Bowl, Horse-Drawn Wagon, Green, Applied Ruffled Crystal Trim, 1950s, 9 1/2 In. 145.00
Carafe, Bust, Gentleman, White, Clear Glass, Flattened Lip, Footed, 5 In. 13.00

SUMIDA is a Japanese pottery that was made from about 1870 to 1941. Pieces are usually everyday objects—vases, jardinieres, bowls, teapots, and decorative tiles. Most pieces have a very heavy orange-red, blue, brown, black, green, purple, or off-white glaze, with raised three-dimensional figures as decorations. The unglazed part is painted red, green, black, or orange. Sumida was sometimes mistakenly called *Korean Pottery* or *Poo Ware* in the past.

Bowl, 3-Sided, Boy Leaning Over Edge, c.1900, 6 1/4 x 4 1/4 In. 295.00
Bowl, Round, 2 Children Looking Over Rim, Seated Buddha, Signed, Ryosai, c.1890, 6 1/2 In. 895.00
Bowl, Round, Irregular Folds, Woman Looking Over Edge, c.1900, 3 1/2 x 5 1/4 In. 495.00
Brush Washer, Monkey Gazing Into Lotus Pool, Irregular Shape, 2 1/2 x 4 1/2 In. 225.00
Flower Dish, Figures, Looking Into Bowl, 1800s, 2 x 5 x 7 In. 760.00
Mug, Devil, Child, Red Ground, Multicolored Drip Glaze, 4 3/4 x 3 1/4 In. 350.00
Tobacco Jar, Figural, Okame, Patron Goddess Of Theater, c.1910, 6 1/2 x 4 In. 1295.00
Vase, Baluster, Boys Playing, Red Ground, Green Drip Glaze, Signed, 9 In. 500.00
Vase, Moon Shape, Boys Playing, Inset House, Ryosai Mark, c.1915, 11 1/2 x 10 In. 2150.00
Vase, Shouldered, Mother & 2 Children Playing, Koko Gourd Mark, c.1910, 11 In. 2850.00
Vase, Tapered, Pinched Neck, Woman Cooking, Signed, Koko, 7 In. 550.00

SUNBONNET BABIES were first introduced in 1900 in the book *The Sunbonnet Babies*. The stories were by Eulalie Osgood Grover, illustrated by Bertha Corbett. The children's faces were completely hidden by the sunbonnets. The children had been pictured in black and white before this time, but the color pictures in the book were immediately successful. The Royal Bayreuth China Company made a full line of children's dishes decorated with the Sunbonnet Babies. Some Sunbonnet Babies plates have been reproduced, but are clearly marked.

Bell, Ironing, Gold Trim, Wood Clapper, 3 x 3 In. 195.00
Card, Bergman, c.1916 .... 10.00
Card, Tuesday, Ironing, Ullman, c.1905 .... 15.00
Creamer, Mopping, Cleaning Windows, 3 1/2 x 3 1/2 In. 225.00
Pitcher, Friday, Sweeping, 1974, 4 1/2 In. 400.00
Pitcher, Sunday, Fishing, 5 1/4 In. 375.00
Plate, Monday, Washing, 1974, 6 In. 325.00
Postcard, Friday, Sweeping, No. 1492, Ullman Mfg. Co., N.Y., 1906 .... 8.00
Postcard, See Saw Margery Daw, 1906 .... 10.00

SUNDERLAND luster is a name given to a special type of pink luster made by Leeds, Newcastle, and other English firms during the nineteenth century. The luster glaze is metallic and glossy and appears to have bubbles in it. Other pieces of luster are listed in the Luster category.

Cup, 2 Handles, Hand Painted, Nautical Design, 3 1/2 x 5 1/2 In. 715.00
Mug, Scuttle, Black Transfer, Ship, Sailor's Poem, 4 In. 60.00
Pitcher, 3 Black Transfers, West View Of The Iron Bridge At Sunderland, 8 3/8 In. 860.00
Pitcher, Garden Arms, Verse, Loop Handle, 5 3/4 In. 300.00
Plaque, 3-Mast Ship, May Peace & Plenty, England, 8 1/2 x 9 1/2 In. 315.00
Plaque, Peace & Plenty Verse, Transfer, Enameled Corners, 8 x 9 In. 175.00

SUPERMAN was created by two seventeen-year-olds in 1938. The first issue of *Action* comics had the strip. Superman remains popular and became the hero of a radio show in 1940, cartoons in the 1940s, a television series, and several major movies.

Badge, Superman Junior Defense League, Brass, Enamel, c.1941, 1 1/4 In. 105.00
Bank, Dime Register, Tin Lithograph, Square, c.1940, 2 1/2 In. 110.00
Bottle Cap, 7Up, Superman Sweepstakes, Crown, Canada, 1978 .... 10.00
Costume, Official, Ben Cooper, Box, Early 1950s, 10 x 12 In. 165.00
Doll, Superman, Composition, Wood, Jointed, Ideal, Box, 1940, 13 In. 1760.00
Doll, Superman, Composition, Wood, Jointed, Painted, Ideal, 1940, 13 In. 280.00
Figure, Superman, Die Cast Metal, On Card, Mego, 1979, 5 1/2 In. 55.00

Game, Calling Superman, Transogram, 1954 .... 139.00
Kryptonite Rock, Glows In Dark, Pro Arts, Box, 1977, 3 x 3 In. 100.00
Lunch Box, Metal, Bottle, Universal Industries, 1954 .... 4649.00
Lunch Box, Robot, Action Pictures, Metal, Universal Industries, 1954 .... *ILLUS* 879.00
Milk Bottle, Warner Bros., Only 8016 Made, Multicolor ACL, Square, Qt. 35.00
Poster, Movie Serial, Linen, Kirk Alyn, Columbia, 1948, 27 x 41 In. 1800.00
Ring, F87 Jet Plane, Brass, Metal Plane, c.1948 .... 80.00
Toy, Krypto Raygun, Steel, 7 Filmstrips, Battery Operated, Daisy, Box, 1940 .... 1265.00
Toy, Superman & Airplane, Rollover, Tin, Windup, Marx, 1940, 6 In. 1100.00
Toy, Tank, Tin, Battery Operated, Linemar, Box, c.1960, 11 In. 4510.00
Trading Card Set, Topps, 1966, 66 Cards 2590.00
Wallet, Yellow, Vinyl, Standard Plastics, 1966 .... 95.00

SUSIE COOPER began as a designer in 1925 working for the English firm A.E. Gray & Company. In 1932 she formed Susie Cooper Pottery, Ltd. In 1950 it became Susie Cooper China, Ltd., and the company made china and earthenware. In 1966 it was acquired by Josiah Wedgwood & Sons, Ltd. The name Susie Cooper appears with the company names on many pieces of ceramics.

Bowl, Vegetable, Dresden Spray, Oval, 1930s, 7 x 10 In. 56.00
Breakfast Service, Honeymoon, Concentric Circles, 10 Piece 500.00
Casserole, Cover, Handles, Label, Burslem, England, British Patent, 10 1/2 In. 95.00
Coffee Cann, Saucer, Printemps, Blue 85.00
Gravy Boat, Brown Rose, Pink Beige, White, Gold Trim 160.00
Muffin Dish, Cover, Flowers 145.00
Plate, Abstract Design, Earthenware, Gray's Pottery, c.1929, 9 In. 375.00
Plate, Dinner, Panel Spray, 10 In. 195.00
Platter, Dresden, Pink, 18 1/2 x 14 1/2 In. 70.00
Tea Set, Art Deco, Crown Works, Burslem, England, c.1940, 3 Piece 320.00
Teapot, Spiral, Endon 95.00
Tureen, Vegetable, Cover, Clematis, Art Deco, 1930s, 5 1/2 x 10 1/2 In. 90.00

SWANKYSWIGS are small drinking glasses. In 1933, the Kraft Food Company began to market cheese spreads in these decorated, reusable glass tumblers. They were discontinued from 1941 to 1946, then made again from 1947 to 1958. Then plain glasses were used for most of the cheese, although a few special decorated Swankyswigs have been made since that time. A complete list of prices can be found in *Kovels' Depression Glass & Dinnerware Price List.*

Antique No. 1, Black, 1954, 3 1/4 In. 7.00
Antique No. 1, Green, 1954, 3 3/4 In. 5.00
Antique No. 1, Orange, 1954, 3 3/4 In. 10.00
Antique No. 1, Red, 1954, 3 1/4 In. 7.00
Bustlin' Betsy, Green, 1953, 3 1/4 In. 7.00
Bustlin' Betsy, Orange, 1953, 3 3/4 In. 5.00
Bustlin' Betsy, Red, 1953, 3 3/4 In. .... 5.00 to 10.00
Bustlin' Betsy, Yellow, 1953, 3 3/4 In. 12.00
Forget-Me-Not, Red, 1948, 3 1/4 In. 7.00
Kiddie Kup, Bear & Pig, c.1956, 3 3/4 In. .... 7.00 to 8.00
Kiddie Kup, Elephant & Bird, Red, c.1956 .... 7.00
Posy Cornflower No. 1, 1941, 3 1/4 In. 8.00
Posy Violet, Blue, 1941, 3 1/2 In. 8.00

SWORDS of all types that are of interest to collectors are listed here. The military dress sword with elaborate handle is probably the most wanted. A *tsuba* is a hand guard fitted to a Japanese sword between the handle and the blade. Be sure to display swords in a safe way, out of reach of children.

Cavalry, Officer's, U.S., Sharkskin Grips, Engraved, Gaylord Mfg., Chicopee, Mass., c.1860 .... 560.00
Cavalry Officer's, Bavaria, M.1826, Etched, Leather Grip, c.1835, 36-In. Curved Blade 545.00
Centurion Handle, Chicago, Sheath, Wabhams & Roundy, 30-In. Blade 315.00

Dress, U.S. Army, Model 1910, Etched Blade, Eagle, Liberty Shield, Scabbard, 32-In. Blade 145.00
Executioner's, Indo-Persian, Curved Blade, Iron Hilt, Disk Pommel, c.1725, 27 1/4-In. Blade 775.00
Foot Officer's, Germany, Iron Knuckle Guard, Wood Grip, Scabbard, 1870s, 35 1/2-In. Blade 130.00
Foot Officer's, U.S. Model 1851, Scabbard, 27-In. Blade 240.00
Horseman's, Indo-Persian, Curved Blade, Iron Hilt, Scabbard, c.1700, 32-In. Blade 545.00
Imperial Russia, Engraved Spine, c.1837, 41 1/4 In. 2820.00
Indonesia, Carved Hilt, Wood Scabbard, Brass Mounts, 1800s, 28 1/2 In. 646.00
Infantry, Savoyard Soldier, Brass Hilt, Crested Pommel, Ribbed Grip, 23 3/4 In. 650.00
Infantry, Savoyard Soldier, Brass Hilt, Leather Scabbard, Brass Mounts, 24 1/2 In. 650.00
Infantry Officer's, Cavalry, Saber, Brass Hilt, Back Strap, Curved Blade, 30 In. 485.00
Infantry Officer's, England, M.1796, Wire Grip, Straight Blade, 31 1/2-In. Blade 850.00
Japan, Brass Hand Guard, Handle, Nickel Plated Scabbard, 36 In. 110.00
Japan, Crayfish Shaped Copper Mountings, Rosewood Hilt & Scabbard, 1800s, 22 In. 2115.00
Kaskara, Sudan, Double Edged Blade, Cruciform Hilt, Leather Scabbard, 1800s, 40 In. 205.00
Katana, Japan, Ho Bird Mount, Gold Lacquer Saya, 1800s, 26 1/2 In. 3105.00
Katana, Japan, Lacquered Wood Saya, Iron Tsuba, 1614-1868, 29 1/2-In. Blade 2715.00
Military Officer's, Germany, Bronze Hilt, Diamond Section Blade, c.1760, 31 1/2-In. Blade 1125.00
Model 1852, U.S., Etched, Eagle, Liberty Shield, Tiffany, N.Y., 32-In. Blade 980.00
Musician's, U.S., Etched Blade, Liberty Eagle, Scabbard, 30-In. Blade 290.00
Naval Officer's, Model 1852, Schuler Hartley & Graham, 30 1/2-In. Blade ....220.00 to 785.00
Naval Officer's, U.S. Model 1852, Etched, Scabbard, 1900-20, 27 3/4-In. Blade 330.00
Naval Officer's, U.S. Model 1852, Etched, Scabbard, 1900-20, 30-In. Blade 249.00
Officer's, American Eagle Head, Curved Blade, Iron Guard, Bone Grip, c.1812, 28-In. Blade 1150.00
Officer's, British Royal Navy, Model 1822, Pipeback, Double Edge, Hatchet Point, 29-In. Blade ... 415.00
Officer's, Model 1902, Etched, Scabbard, 29 1/2-In. Blade 345.00
Officer's, RAF, George V Cipher, Wilkinson & Co., Engraved, 32 In.-Blade, 38 1/2 In. 666.00
Officer's, Staff & Field, Shark Skin Handle, Lieut. Col. Rader, Scabbard, c.1850, 32-In. Blade 1495.00
Officer's, U.S., Blued, Gold Oak Leaf, Eagle Handle, Scabbard, c.1820, 30 1/2-In. Blade 520.00
Presentation, U.S. Model 1852, B.M. Flint, 6th Reg. Maine, Scabbard, Ames, 30 1/2-In. Blade ... 2645.00
Quill Back Blade, Iron Guard, Sharkskin Grip, c.1842, 32 1/2-In. Blade 445.00
Rapier, Germany, Slightly Concave Surfaces, c.1670, 32 1/4-In. Blade 3100.00
Rapier, Spain, Slender Blade, Etched, Motto, Leaves, c.1660, 35-In. Blade 3400.00
Saber, American Eagle Head Hilt, Brass Hilt, Bone Grip, Early 1800s, 29-In. Blade 510.00
Saber, Cavalry, British Army, India Issue, Iron Hilt, Leather Grip, 32-In. Curved Blade 325.00
Saber, U.S. Cavalry Officer's, Model 1872, Scabbard, Curved, H.V. Ailifn & Co., France, 40 In. 826.00
Scottish Regimental Broadsword, Germany, 1800-20, 31 1/2-In. Blade 2600.00
Shamshir, Indo-Persia, Bronze Hilt, Curved Blade, 1750-1800, 30-In. Blade 525.00
Short, Ivory Handle, Ivory Sheath, Men, Warriors, Oriental, 10 1/4-In. Blade, 17 In. 115.00
Short, Persia, Curved Blade, Silver Mounted, Scabbard, c.1850, 23-In. Blade 640.00
Single-Edged Blade, Flared Point, Horn Hilt, Sumatra, 1800s, 24 In. 530.00
Single-Edged Curved Blade, Fluted Ivory Hilt, Indonesia, 1800s, 25 3/4 In. 765.00
Small, Double Edge, Iron Facet Cut Grip, Europe, 1700s, 30-In. Blade 355.00
Small, Iron, Diamond Shaped Blade, Brass Hilt, Dutch, c.1750, 31 1/2 In. 600.00
Small, Military, France, Scrolls, Leaves, Wire Wrapped Grip, c.1780, 31 1/4-In. Blade 1325.00
Staff Officer's, U.S., Sharkskin Grips, Japanned Scabbard, Brass Mounts, c.1860 .... 730.00
Tsuba, Japan, Copper, Naga-Maru-Gata, Sage, 2 Children, Bamboo, Somin, c.1800, 2 3/4 In. 600.00
Tsuba, Japan, Copper, Shin No Maru-Gata, Geese, Shakudo, Tree, 1800s, 3 1/4 In. 690.00
Tsuba, Japan, Gilt Inlay, Lacquered Saya, Early 20th Century, 38 In. 380.00
Tsuba, Japan, Iron, Applied Dragon Head, 2 3/4 x 2 1/2 In. 130.00
Tsuba, Japan, Iron, Mokko Form, Geese, Flying, Marsh, Mount Fuji, Masatsugu, c.1800, 3 In. 550.00
Tsuba, Japan, Iron, Mokko Form, Sukashi Bamboo, Gilt Highlights, 1700s, 3 1/4 In. 460.00
Tsuba, Japan, Iron, Nade Goku Hokei, Silver & Gold Plum Tree, c.1800, 2 1/2 In. 690.00
Wakizashi, Japan, Lacquered Wood Saya, Iron Tsuba, c.1860, 17 1/2-In. Blade 1535.00
Warrior's, Japan, Mounting, Bone, Carved, 1868-1911, 24 In. 645.00
Yataghan, Ottoman, Gold Inlaid Blade, Repousse Silver Scabbard, Niello Hilt, 1800s, 25 In. 1175.00

SYRACUSE is a trademark used by the Onondaga Pottery of Syracuse, New York. The company was established in 1871. It is still working. The name became the Syracuse China Company in 1966. It is known for fine dinnerware and restaurant china.

Avalon, Creamer, Virginia Shape, White Rose, Green Leaves, Gold Trim, 3 1/8 x 5 1/2 In. 26.00

Avalon, Serving Bowl, Virginia Shape, White Rose, Green Leaves, Gold Trim, 9 In. 50.00
Briarcliff, Bowl, Vegetable, Federal Shape, Oval, Gold Trim, 3 x 10 3/4 In. 38.00
Charm, Plate, Bread & Butter, Berkeley Style, Platinum Trim, 6 3/8 In. 12.00
Concord Rose, Bowl, Vegetable, Divided, Carefree Shape, Oval, 2 1/8 x 8 1/4 x 10 In. 30.00
Concord Rose, Cup & Saucer, Carefree Shape, Coupe 7.00
Coralbel, Gravy Boat, Attached Underplate, Winchester Shape, Green & Silver Trim, 3 x 9 In. 45.00
Countess, Sugar, Cover, Carolina Shape, Silver Trim, 3 1/2 In. 35.00
Coventry, Bowl, Vegetable, Virginia Shape, Flowers, Gold Trim, Oval, 2 1/4 x 10 1/2 In. 17.50
Debonair, Bowl, Vegetable, Silhouette Shape, Oval, Gold Trim, 2 1/4 x 10 In. 45.00
Dorian, Cup & Saucer, California Shape, Gray Cup, White Saucer, Gold Trim 15.00
Finesse, Bowl, Vegetable, Divided, Carefree Shape, Rust & Blue Flowers 18.00
Flame Lily, Coffeepot, Carefree Shape, Copper Top, China Knob, 9 1/2 In. 38.00
Flame Lily, Serving Bowl, Carefree Shape, White, Pink Lilies, Gray Stems, 8 In. 50.00
Graymont, Sugar, Cover, Paul Revere Shape, 3 1/2 x 6 1/4 In. 30.00
Harvest Gold, Platter, Oval, Carefree Shape, 10 x 11 1/2 In. 24.00
Jefferson, Gravy Boat, Underplate, 3 1/4 x 7 5/8 In. 38.00
Lilac Rose, Bowl, Fruit, Berkeley Shape, Flowers, Gold Trim, 1 3/8 x 4 5/8 In. 16.00
Lilac Rose, Soup, Cream, Berkeley Shape, Flowers, Gold Trim 35.00
Madame Butterfly, No. 12, Platter, Virginia Shape, Oval, Ivory, 1952, 14 1/8 In. 65.00
Madame Butterfly, Sugar, Cover, Virginia Shape, Gold Trim, c.1950, 3 1/8 In. 15.00
Nimbus Platinum, Serving Bowl, Virginia Shape, 3 Platinum Bands, Round 48.00
Seville, Cup & Saucer, Carefree XL Shape, Yellow, Orange & Green Border 8.50
Seville, Platter, Round, Carefree XL Shape, Festive Yellow, Orange & Green Border 24.00
Shelledge, Plate, Bread & Butter, Flower, 6 1/4 In. 9.00
Sherwood, Gravy Boat, Attached Underplate, Virginia Shape 35.00
Somerset, Plate, Salad, Mayflower Shape, Flowers, Gray & White Border, Bird, Gold Trim. 12.50
Victoria, Bowl, Vegetable, Federal Shape, Rosebuds, Ivory Ground, Gold Trim, Oval, 10 3/4 In. 35.00
Victoria, Gravy Boat, Attached Underplate, Federal Shape, Rosebuds, Ivory Ground, 9 In. 63.00
Windswept, Cup, Carefree Shape, Pink & Brown Flowers 5.00
Windswept, Plate, Dinner, Carefree Shape, 10 In. 12.00
Woodbine, Bowl, Vegetable, Carefree Shape, Leaves, Vines, Flowers, Round, 9 1/2 In. 20.00
Woodbine, Plate, Dinner, Carefree Shape, Leaves On Vine, Flowers, 10 1/4 In. ....7.00 to 10.00

TAPESTRY, PORCELAIN, see Rose Tapestry category.

TEA CADDY is the name for a small box made to hold tea leaves. In the eighteenth century, tea was very expensive and it was stored under lock and key. The first tea caddies were made with locks. By the nineteenth century, tea was more plentiful and the tea caddy was larger. Often there were two sections, one for green tea, one for black tea.

Apple Wood, Apple Shape, English, Early 19th Century, 4 1/2 In. 3875.00
Black Lacquer, Chinoiserie, Carved Gilt Paw Feet, George III, 5 x 7 1/2 In. 295.00
Black Lacquer, Gilt Court Scenes, Dragons, 8-Sided, Gilt Paw Feet, 5 1/4 x 9 1/4 In. 1116.00
Black Lacquer, Gilt, 2 Tea Canisters, Giltwood Feet, Chinese, c.1835, 6 x 9 x 6 In. 3525.00
Black Lacquer, Gilt, 2 Tea Canisters, Giltwood Feet, Chinese, c.1835, 7 x 12 x 9 In. 2820.00
Burled Walnut, 6 Glass Jars, George III, Early 19th Century, 8 In. 410.00
Burlwood, Dome Lid, Brass Mounted, Bagshaw & Sons, Liverpool, 6 x 9 x 5 In. 765.00
Coffer Shape, Red Paint, Stencil, Cast Feet, 1800s, 4 1/2 x 5 1/4 In. 956.00
Cover, Blue & White, Flowering Tree, Riverscape, Rouleau Form, Chinese Export, Pair 590.00
Cover, Grisaille Floral Pattern, Chinese Export, Early 19th Century, 6 In. 315.00
Cube Parquetry, Brass Mounted, Lead Lining, 1800s, 4 1/4 x 7 1/4 x 5 In. 529.00
Ebony, Coromandel Veneer, Brass Inlaid, Monogram, Hinged, Regency, 10 x 5 In. 235.00
Light Wood, Dark Wood Edge, Coffin Shape, 2 Compartments, Inlaid, Key, 4 1/2 x 7 In. 345.00
Mahogany, Dome Lid, Inlaid, Leaves, Flowers, 2 Compartments, Early 1800s, 6 x 7 In. 2629.00
Mahogany, George III, c.1800, 12 x 6 x 6 In. 445.00
Mahogany, Hinged Lid, Inlaid Conch Shell, 2 Compartments, 6 x 12 x 6 In. 1035.00
Mahogany, Whalebone Inlay, Bun Feet, 5 1/2 x 10 x 5 1/2 In. 316.00
Papier-Mache, Mother-Of-Pearl, Hinged Lid, Victorian, c.1865, 5 x 7 1/2 x 4 1/2 In. 660.00
Porcelain, Flowers, Silver Lid, Chinese Export, 6 x 3 1/4 In. 290.00
Rosewood, Arched Lid, Brass Medallions & Escutcheon, 7 x 9 x 5 In. 380.00

Rosewood, Beaded, 2 Box Interior, Coffin Shape, Regency, c.1815, 7 x 12 In. 518.00
Rosewood, Brass Inlaid Scrolls, Coffin Shape, Lead Lined, William IV, 9 x 14 In. 705.00
Rosewood, Brass Stringing, Ring Handles, Coffin Shape, 3 Compartments, 9 x 13 In. 1125.00
Rosewood, Brass, Cut Glass Bowl, 2 Hinged Lid Boxes, England, 9 x 13 x 6 1/4 In. 1035.00
Rosewood, Diamond Shape, Mother-Of-Pearl Inlay, Reeded Bands, 9 x 5 In. 315.00
Rosewood, Parquetry, Diamonds, Coffin Shape, Fitted Interior, 8 x 12 3/4 In. 675.00
Rosewood, Tea Bowl, 2 Compartments, England, 8 1/2 x 13 1/2 x 7 In. 518.00
Rosewood Veneer, Canted Sides, Mother Of Pearl Keyhole Escutcheon, 8 x 5 x 5 In. 175.00
Shell, Bone Feet, Bombe, 2 Compartments, England, c.1800s, 6 x 7 1/2 x 4 1/2 In. 1610.00
Silver, 8-Sided, Sliding Lid, Engraved Arms, FA Mark, London, 1714, 5 In. 3900.00
Silver, Classical Scene, Centaur, Birmingham, Victorian, c.1900, 4 1/4 x 5 In. 468.00
Silver, Cut Corners, Engraved Arms, Thomas Ash, London, 1710, 4 1/2 In. 3000.00
Silver, Cylindrical, J.H., London, Victorian, c.1900, 3 3/4 In. 410.00
Silver, Dome Lid, Bright Cut, Hester Bateman, George III, c.1786, 4 3/4 x 5 x 3 5/8 In. 5288.00
Silver, Oval, Gadroon Border, Engraved Arms, Michael Plummer, London, 1794, 6 In. 3900.00
Silver, Oval, Slip On Cap, Rocailles, Samuel Taylor, London, 1751, 5 1/4 In. 3900.00
Specimen Wood, Marquetry Inlaid, Coffin Shape, Handles, Regency, 8 x 12 In. 999.00
Tortoiseshell, Blond, 3 Compartments, Regency, England, c.1835, 5 1/4 x 11 In. 2350.00
Tortoiseshell, Blond, Nickel, Silver, 2 Compartments, Regency, England, c.1835, 6 x 7 In. 2000.00
Tortoiseshell, Chocolate, Mother-Of-Pearl Canted Corners, 8-Sided, Bun Feet, 6 x 8 In. 3760.00
Tortoiseshell, Dome Lid, 2 Compartments, Monogram Plate, England, c.1835, 5 x 6 In. 2000.00
Tortoiseshell, Lid, Brass Label, Mother-Of-Pearl Flower Finials, 2 Sections, 5 x 8 x 4 In. 1725.00
Tortoiseshell, Russet, Nickel, Silver, Mother Of Pearl, 2 Compartments, c.1835, 5 x 8 In. 3525.00
Tortoiseshell, Silver & Silver Plate Mounted, 2 Compartments, c.1815, 5 3/8 x 7 In. 3525.00
Turned Wood, Barrel Shape, 5 1/4 x 3 1/2 In. 146.00
Walnut, Brass Bound, Rectangular Shape, Strapwork, Zinc Lined, Victorian, 10 x 10 In. 510.00
Yew, Brass Mounted, Coffin Shape, 3 Compartments, England, c.1835, 7 1/2 x 12 In. 1530.00

TEA LEAF IRONSTONE dishes are named for their decorations. There was a superstition that it was lucky if a whole tea leaf unfolded at the bottom of your cup. This idea was translated into the pattern of dishes known as *tea leaf*. By 1850, at least twelve English factories were making this pattern, and by the 1870s, it was a popular pattern in many countries. The tea leaf was always a luster glaze on early wares, although now some pieces are made with a brown tea leaf. There are many variations of tea leaf designs, such as Teaberry, Pepper Leaf, and Gold Leaf. The designs were used on many different white ironstone shapes, such as Bamboo, Lily of the Valley, Empress, and Cumbow.

Bowl, Vegetable, Cover, Cable, Shaw .... 150.00 to 175.00
Bowl, Vegetable, Cover, East End 55.00
Bowl, Vegetable, Cover, Fishhook, Meakin 15.00
Bowl, Vegetable, Cover, Gothic Thistle 150.00
Brush Vase, Mayer 110.00
Brush Vase, Moss Rose, Meakin 130.00
Brush Vase, Scalloped, Meakin 95.00
Brush Vase, Wedgwood .... 150.00 to 175.00
Butter, Basketweave, Shaw 425.00
Butter, Cable, Shaw 195.00
Butter, Grindley Favorite 100.00
Cake Plate, Brocade, Meakin 110.00
Cake Plate, Prairie Flowers, Powell & Bishop 130.00
Cake Plate, Washington, Powell & Bishop 325.00
Chamber Pot, Grape Octagon, Walley 130.00
Child's Set, Moss Rose, G. Scott 575.00
Coffeepot, Hearts, Mellor Taylor 100.00
Coffeepot, Lily Of The Valley, Shaw 275.00
Compote, Luster Band, Livesley & Powell & Co., 9 In. 575.00
Creamer, Brocade, Meakin 130.00
Creamer, Chelsea, Johnson Bros. 90.00

Creamer, Cockscomb, J. Furnival 150.00
Creamer, Gothic, Livesley & Powell 115.00
Creamer, Grand Loop, J. Furnival 375.00
Creamer, Grindley Favorite 90.00
Cuspidor, Tobacco Leaf, Elsmore & Forster 400.00
Ewer, Cable, T. Furnival 105.00
Ewer, Chelsea, Meakin 160.00
Gravy Boat, Cable, Shaw 35.00
Gravy Boat, Chelsea, Meakin 160.00
Ladle, Sauce, Cable, Shaw 255.00
Ladle, Sauce, Meakin 250.00
Milk Jug, Daisy, Shaw 150.00
Mug, Maiden Hair Fern, Wilkinson 400.00
Pitcher, Daisy 'n Chain, Wilkinson 125.00
Pitcher, Hawthorn, Wilkinson 95.00
Pitcher, Hot Water, Mayer 200.00
Pitcher, Milk, Fishhook, Meakin 150.00
Posset Cup, Lily Of The Valley, Shaw ....275.00 to 300.00
Powder Dish, Cover, Johnson Bros. 210.00
Punch Bowl, Primrose Scroll, Livesley, Powell & Co. 600.00
Punch Bowl, Reeded, Round, Burgess 1100.00
Relish, Elegance, Teaberry, Clementson Bros. 500.00
Soap Dish, Chinese, Shaw 250.00
Sugar, Arched Forget-Me-Not, Elsmore & Forster 80.00
Sugar, Ceres, Elsmore & Forster 250.00
Sugar, Lily Of The Valley, Shaw 275.00
Sugar, Pagoda, Burgess 110.00
Sugar, Panelled Grape, Clementson 200.00
Teapot, Fig Cousin, Davenport 300.00
Teapot, Gothic Panel, Shaw 175.00
Teapot, Pagoda, Burgess 275.00
Teapot, Rondeau, Davenport 110.00
Teapot, Scroll, Meakin 140.00
Teapot, Square Ridged, Burgess 80.00
Tureen, Soup, Bamboo, Meakin 110.00
Tureen, Soup, Cable, Shaw ....100.00 to 150.00

TECO is the mark used on the art pottery line made by the American Terra Cotta and Ceramic Company of Terra Cotta and Chicago, Illinois. The company was an offshoot of the firm founded by William D. Gates in 1881. The Teco line was first made in 1885 but was not sold commercially until 1902. It continued in production until 1922. Over 500 designs were made in a variety of colors, shapes, and glazes. The company closed in 1930.

TECO

Bookends, Gnomes, Green, Brown Matte Glaze, 9 In. 823.00
Chamberstick, Angular Handle, Green Matte Glaze, Gray Highlights, 2 1/4 x 5 In., Pair 570.00
Pitcher, Green Matte Glaze, 8 7/8 In. 403.00
Vase, 2 Handles, Green Matte Glaze, 9 3/8 In. 1150.00
Vase, 2 Looped Handles, Semi-Bulbous, Matte Green Glaze, 9 1/4 x 5 1/2 In. 2185.00
Vase, 3 Handles, Ribbed Shape, Green Matte Glaze, Charcoal Highlights, 6 1/2 In. 1765.00
Vase, 4 Lobes, Green, 15 3/4 In. 2645.00
Vase, Angular Buttressed Handles, Green Matte Glaze, Charcoaled Edges, 11 x 5 In. 1645.00
Vase, Bulbous, Multitone Green Matte Glaze, W.D. Gates, 4 3/4 In. 660.00
Vase, Green Matte Glaze, Charcoal Highlights, 3 1/4 In. 1080.00
Vase, No. 172, Tapered, 4 Curved Handles, Green Matte Glaze, Charcoal Highlights, 14 1/2 In. ... 8970.00
Vase, No. 233, Rolling Top Rim, Matte Green Glaze, Factory Mark, 5 x 4 1/2 In. 600.00
Vase, Ribbed, Paneled, Green Matte Glaze, Hugh Garden, 12 In. 7770.00
Vase, Tapered, 4-Sided, 4 Open Handles On Top, Green Matte Glaze, Fritz Albert, 14 In. 16750.00
Vase, Tulips, Overlapping Leaves, Green Matte Glaze, William Dodd, 11 In. 4190.00

TEDDY BEARS were named for a president of the United States. The first teddy bear was a cuddly toy said to be inspired by a hunting trip made by Teddy Roosevelt in 1902. Morris and Rose Michtom started selling their stuffed bears as *teddy bears* and the name stayed. The Michtoms founded the Ideal Novelty and Toy Company. The German version of the teddy bear was made about the same time by the Steiff Company. There are many types of teddy bears and all are collected. The old ones are being reproduced. Other bears are listed in the Toy section.

Baby, Mohair, Jointed, Velvet Lined Open Mouth, Felt Teeth, 1929 Replica, 1995, 14 In. 115.00
Black Lacy Outfit, Hat, Umbrella, Jointed, Glass Eyes, c.1920, 24 In. 350.00
Chiltern, Plush, Sandy Brown, Fully Jointed, 12 In. 69.00
Growler, Mohair, Blond, Shoebutton Eyes, Stitched Nose, 1910, 16 In. 4030.00
Hairless, Fully Jointed, c.1920, 14 In. 35.00
Hairless, Fully Jointed, Glass Eyes, Early 1900s, 8 1/2 In. ....195.00 to 196.00
Mohair, Brown Trousers, Early 1900s, 16 In. 69.00
Mohair, Brown, 4 Wheels, Germany, 1920s, 8 x 11 1/2 In. 220.00
Mohair, Felt Feet, Large Hump, Fully Jointed, Glass Eyes, 16 In. 1320.00
Mohair, Fully Jointed, Early 1900s, 12 In. 130.00
Mohair, Fully Jointed, Early 1900s, 18 In. 69.00
Mohair, Fully Jointed, Glass Eyes, Early 1900s, 16 In. 69.00
Mohair, Fully Jointed, Glass Eyes, Germany, Early 1900s, 14 In. 127.00
Mohair, Glass Eyes, Early 1900s, 12 In. 127.00
Mohair, Gold, Long Arms, Hump, Nose, Velvet Pads, Plastic Eyes, 17 In. 90.00
Mohair, Golden, Fully Jointed, Glass Eyes, 12 In. 69.00
Mohair, Jointed, Hump, Restitched Nose, Glass Eyes, 16 In. 345.00
Mohair, Straw Filled, 20 In. 110.00
Mohair, Straw Stuffed, Longer Limbs, Felt Pads, Jointed, Shoebutton Eyes, 17 1/2 In. 495.00
Mohair, Tipped Mohair, Open Mouth, Fully Jointed, Velvet Mouth, Jointed, 19 In. 115.00
Mohair, White, Brown Stitched Nose, Shoebutton Eyes, Germany, Early 1900s, 13 In. 1210.00
Mohair, White, Fully Jointed, Glass Eyes, Germany, 1920s, 11 In. 550.00
Plush, Cinnamon Cotton, Restitched Nose, Glass Eyes, Jointed, 20 & 22 In., Pair 145.00
Plush, Cotton, White, Fully Jointed, Googly Eyes, Late 1930s, 14 In. 305.00
Plush, Honey Brown, Jointed, Shoebutton Eyes, Music Box, Germany, c.1930 .... 105.00
Schuco, Janus, Mohair, 2 Faces, 1950s, 4 In. 410.00
Schuco, Yes, No, Mohair, Embroidered Nose, Mouth, Claws, Glass Eyes, 1920s, 13 In. 235.00
Steiff, Cinnamon, Jointed Shoulder & Hips, Black Shoebutton Eyes, 10 In. 1430.00
Steiff, Collector's Edition, 1978, 14 In. 69.00
Steiff, Felt Pad Feet, Hump Back, Early 1900s, 12 In. 375.00
Steiff, Fully Jointed, Shoebutton Eyes, Button In Ear, c.1920, 9 In. 489.00
Steiff, Gift Set, Nimrod, Mohair, White, Caramel, Brown, Limited Edition, c.1983, 8 In. 175.00
Steiff, Growler, Mohair, Beige, Curly, Embroidered Nose, Mouth, Claws, Jointed, 20 In. 570.00
Steiff, Growler, Mohair, Blond, Curly, Embroidered Nose, Mouth, Claws, Jointed, 26 In. 590.00
Steiff, Hello-Goodbye, Mohair, Pink, Blue, Jointed, Glass Eyes, Box, 8 In., Pair 105.00
Steiff, Mohair, Beige, Embroidered Nose, Claws, Jointed, Glass Eyes, Felt Pads, 16 In. 120.00
Steiff, Mohair, Beige, Embroidered Nose, Stuffed, Jointed, Steel Eyes, 3 1/2 In. 70.00
Steiff, Mohair, Blond, Cotton Floss Nose, Shoebutton Eyes, 16 In. 3430.00
Steiff, Mohair, Blond, Embroidered Mouth, Nose, Claws, Felt Pads, Glass Eyes, 20 In. 1885.00
Steiff, Mohair, Blond, Embroidered Nose, Claws, Felt Pads, Jointed, Glass Eyes, 14 In. 264.00
Steiff, Mohair, Blond, Embroidered Nose, Claws, Felt Pads, Jointed, Steel Eyes, 12 In. 590.00
Steiff, Mohair, Blond, Embroidered Nose, Claws, Jointed, Glass Eyes, 1930s, 13 1/2 In. 176.00
Steiff, Mohair, Brown, Leather Collar, Glass Eyes, Teddy Baby Tag, 10 In. 1375.00
Steiff, Mohair, Brown, Pointed, Embroidered Nose, Jointed, Glass Eyes, c.1950, 30 In. 1904.00
Steiff, Mohair, Brown, Shoebutton Eyes, Button In Ear, Germany, 16 In. 4950.00
Steiff, Mohair, Golden Blond, Embroidered Nose, Glass Eyes, c.1950, 20 In. 1880.00
Steiff, Mohair, Golden, Embroidered Nose, Hip Jointed, Shoebutton Eyes, 16 In. 2128.00
Steiff, Mohair, Jointed At Neck, Shoulders, Curved Legs, Button, Ear Tag, 17 In. 69.00
Steiff, Mohair, Silver, Felt Paw Pads, Shoe Button Eyes, Germany, Early 1900s, 10 In. 770.00
Steiff, Mohair, White, Embroidered Nose, Claws, Felt Pads, Shoebutton Eyes, 10 In. 325.00
Steiff, On Wheels, Glass Eyes, Straw Stuffed, Early 1900s 950.00
Steiff, Sandy Brown, Fully Jointed, Glass Eyes, Post 1945, 8 In. 35.00
Steiff, Teddy Baby, Mohair, Swivel Neck, Jointed, Glass Eyes, c.1950, 3 3/4 In. 468.00

Tea Cozy, Mohair, White, Felt Collar, Shoebutton Eyes, 11 x 12 In. 3850.00

TELEPHONES are wanted by collectors if the phones are old enough or unusual enough. The first telephone may have been made in Havana, Cuba, in 1849, but it was not patented. The first publicly demonstrated phone was used in Frankfurt, Germany, in 1860. The phone made by Alexander Graham Bell was shown at the Centennial Exhibition in Philadelphia in 1876, but it was not until 1877 that the first private phones were installed. Collectors today want all types of old phones, phone parts, and advertising. Even recent figural phones are popular.

Booth, Oak, Lights, Telephone, 1930s, 83 In. 728.00
Busch Beer, Can Shape, 1983, 6 1/2 x 2 1/2 In. 25.00
Candlestick, Black, Nickel, Pressed Steel, 13 In. 66.00
Ericsson, Ericofon, Cobra, ABS Plastic, Pink, Gosta Thames, c.1950, 8 1/4 In. 60.00
Henry Dreyfuss, Model No. 302, Metal, Bakelite, c.1937, 5 1/2 x 9 x 7 1/2 In. 2700.00
Kellogg, Candlestick, Oak Ringer Box, Early 1900s, 12 In. 115.00
Kellogg, Wall, Oak, c.1901, 32 In. ....260.00 to 450.00
Northern Electric Company, Wall, Oak, Early 1900s, 21 In. 176.00
Paperweight, Bell System, New York Telephone Co., Glass, Cobalt Blue, 3 In. 35.00
Pay, 1950s, 34 In. 225.00
Pay, Black, Wall Mounted, 5, 10, 15 Cents 70.00
Sign, American Telephone & Telegraph Co., NY Bell System, Porcelain, Round, 8 In. 358.00
Sign, Bell Systems Public Telephone, Metal, 1930s 225.00
Sign, Independent Telephone, Local & Long Distance, 2-Sided, Porcelain, Flange, 18 x 17 In. 255.00
Sign, New England Tel. & Tel. Co., Phone Booth, Please Do Not Smoke, 3 x 6 1/2 In. 525.00
Sign, New England Tel. & Tel. Co., Public Telephone Station, Porcelain, 10 x 18 In. 468.00
Sign, Public Telephone, Pacific Telephone & Telegraph, 5 1/2 x 19 In. 605.00
Stromberg-Carlson, Wall, Oak, c.1894, 19 In. ....250.00 to 450.00
Wall, Chicago Telephone Supply Co., Bells, Patina, Metal Plate, 27 In. 375.00
Wall, Crank, Oak, Adjustable Mouthpiece, 1930s, 36 In. 448.00
Western Electric, Bell System, Pay, 5, 10 & 25 Cents, Cast Iron Bracket, Porcelain 260.00

TELEVISION sets are twentieth-century collectibles. Although the first television transmission took place in England in 1925, collectors find few sets that pre-date 1946. The first sets had only five channels, but by 1949 the additional UHF channels were included. The first color television set became available in 1951.

Motorola, Bakelite, On Stand, c.1945, 20 x 22 x 19 In. 66.00
Philco, Predicta, On Stand, Canada, c.1948, 41 x 11 x 26 In. 707.00
Pilot Radio Corp., Model TV37, Receiver, Portable, c.1940, 9 1/2 x 14 x 14 1/2 In. 245.00

TEPLITZ refers to art pottery manufactured by a number of companies in the Teplitz-Turn area of Bohemia during the late nineteenth and early twentieth centuries. Two of these companies were the Alexandra Works and The Amphora Porcelain Works, run by Reissner, Stellmacher, and Kessel. Ernst Wahliss, connected with the RS & K wares, started his own factory after 1900.

Biscuit Barrel, Fox & Hen House, Globular, Bird Medallions, Amphora, c.1920, 9 In. 195.00
Bust, Woman, Roses In Hair & On Bust, Amphora, 16 In. 1440.00
Centerpiece, Green Man, Stylized Tree Trunk, Vines, Painted, Amphora, c.1900, 13 1/2 In. 310.00
Ewer, Birds, Landscape, Dragon Handles, Gilt Decorated, Enamels, Amphora, 9 In., Pair 629.00
Figurine, 2 Owls, Perched On Branch, Simulated Wood, Amphora, c.1900, 12 In. 680.00
Figurine, Dancing Maiden, Yellow Gown, 16 1/2 In., Pair 1800.00
Figurine, Man Holding Pitcher, Blue Printed, 11 1/2 x 4 x 4 3/4 In. 5320.00
Figurine, Peasant Woman, Hunched, Baskets, Amphora, c.1900, 16 In. 700.00
Humidor, Teepee, Indian Peeking Out, Painted, Amphora, c.1900, 10 1/2 In. 1355.00
Jardiniere, Gothic, Square, Low Relief, Figures, Spiral Columns, Amphora, c.1900, 16 In. 250.00
Jardiniere, Spiraling, 3 Leaf Handles, 6 1/2 x 11 In. 105.00
Lamp, Esmarelda, Bust, Woman, Art Nouveau Style, Paints, Gilt, Amphora, c.1900, 24 In. 4355.00

Lamp, Hydrangea, Jeweled Handles, High Relief, Painted, Gilt, Amphora, c.1900, 28 In. 290.00
Pitcher, Dandelion, Painted, Gilt, 3 Jeweled Handles, Amphora, c.1900, 7 3/4 In. 385.00
Planter, Carved Designs, Multitone Green Glaze, Orange, Footed, Amphora, 12 x 4 1/2 In. 765.00
Plaque, Putto, Riding Sea Monster, Painted, Gilt, Amphora, c.1890, 12 In. 680.00
Vase, Apple & Leaf, Painted, Crackled, Twisted Oval Shape, Amphora, c.1900, 8 1/2 In. 250.00
Vase, Art Nouveau Style, Stylized Flowers, Gilt, 2 Handles, Amphora, c.1900, 12 1/2 In. 1740.00
Vase, Art Nouveau Women, Flowing Hair, Flowers, Green & Rose Ground, 7 In., Pair 1035.00
Vase, Bunnies, Seated, Leaves, Mottled Green Glaze, Amphora, c.1900, 6 1/2 In. 348.00
Vase, Cat, Jeweled, Painted, Gilt, 4 Handles, Amphora, c.1900, 17 1/2 In. 2905.00
Vase, Confetti, Low Relief, Painted, Gilt, Mottled Panels, Amphora, c.1900, 8 In. 970.00
Vase, Cover, Floral Garlands, Low Relief, Urn Shape, Ivory Ground, Amphora, c.1900, 11 In. 194.00
Vase, Dandelion, Scrolling Tendrils, Relief, Leaves, Painted, Amphora, c.1900, 15 In. 240.00
Vase, Dandelions, Jeweled Flowers, Leaves Band, Painted, Gilt, Amphora, c.1900, 5 1/2 In. 919.00
Vase, Dragon, Winged, Around Rim, Painted, Green, Blue, Amphora, c.1900, 14 1/2 In. 10160.00
Vase, Earthenware, 2 Handles, Amphora Shape, Amphora, c.1900, 13 3/4 In. 360.00
Vase, Enamel Decorated, 3 Birds, Branch, Mottled Ground, 2 Handles, 20 1/2 x 7 1/2 In. 558.00
Vase, Enameled Jewel, Spider Web, Butterfly, Fly, 7 In. 1670.00
Vase, Espaniola, Goblet Shape, Loop Handles, Enamel, Amphora, c.1900, 7 In. 265.00
Vase, Fish, Swimming, In Seaweed, Green, Blue Glaze, Mark, Amphora, c.1900, 11 1/4 In. 485.00
Vase, Gilt Highlights, Cobalt Blue Neck, Hand Painted Flowers, 2 Handles, 7 1/2 In. 115.00
Vase, Girl & Goats, Dutch Costume, Painted, Gilt, Amphora, c.1900, 16 In. 445.00
Vase, Grape Cluster, Leaves, Amphora, 14 7/8 In. 288.00
Vase, Grapes & Leaves, 4 Angular Handles, Painted Ivory, Gilt, Amphora, c.1900, 8 In. 195.00
Vase, Jeweled, 4 Handles, Painted, Gilt, Flower, Leaves, Amphora, c.1900, 13 1/2 In. 485.00
Vase, Jeweled, Tapering Cylinder, Leaf & Grape Band, Amphora, c.1900, 9 1/2 In. 677.00
Vase, Mermaid, Holding Net, Ribbed Ground, Painted, Gilt, Amphora, c.1900, 18 1/2 In. 775.00
Vase, Mini Monster, Dimpled, Oval Body, High Relief, Painted, Amphora, c.1900, 7 In. 775.00
Vase, Moonlit Landscape, Trees, Enameled Flowers, Blue Ground, 8 1/8 x 4 3/4 In. 405.00
Vase, Mucha Lady, Profile, Wooded Landscape, Painted, Gilt, Amphora, c.1900, 5 1/2 In. 1450.00
Vase, Mushrooms, Painted, Raised, Gourd Form, Signed, Paul Daschel, 7 In. 1765.00
Vase, Organic Shape, 4 Handles, Drip Glaze, Crown, Swastika Mark, Amphora, 17 1/2 In. 6000.00
Vase, Organic Shape, Green, Pink, Brown, Ivory Glaze, Amphora, c.1900, 11 In. 405.00
Vase, Peasant Boy, Girl, Tree Trunk, Amphora, c.1900, 16 In., Pair 755.00
Vase, Pedestal, Red Cherries, Golden Leaves, Branch Like Handles, Amphora, 13 5/8 In. 375.00
Vase, Pheasant, Branches, Green, Blue Glaze, Gilt, Amphora, c.1900, 16 1/2 In., Pair 3290.00
Vase, Pheasant, Branches, Mottled Brown, Green, Blue Glaze, Gilt, Amphora, c.1900, 17 In. 629.00
Vase, Pierced Spiral Handles, Painted, Gilt, Flowers, Amphora, c.1900, 10 In. 250.00
Vase, Ram's Heads, Floral Garlands, Wooded Landscape, Low Relief, Amphora, c.1900, 9 In. 1258.00
Vase, Red Printed, Amphora, 8 x 4 1/2 In. 2070.00
Vase, Vine, Leaves, Geometric Bottom, Amphora, 11 1/2 In. 180.00
Vase, Vines, Fruit, 2 Handles, Amphora Shape, Amphora, c.1900, 13 1/2 In. 435.00
Vase, Water Lily, Flower Tendrils, Painted, Urn Shape, Amphora, c.1900, 14 3/4 In. 290.00

TERRA-COTTA is a special type of pottery. It ranges from pale orange to dark reddish-brown in color. The color comes from the clay, which is fired but not always glazed in the finished piece.

Bust, Classical Style, Gilt Metal Laurel Wreath, 20th Century, 31 1/2 In. 410.00
Bust, Julius Caesar, Raised Relief, Continental, 23 x 15 x 9 In. 645.00
Bust, Woman, Holly In Hair, Caesar Ceribelli, Late 1800s 765.00
Capital, George Grant Elmslie, c.1936, 22 3/4 x 15 3/4 x 8 In., Pair 600.00
Cornice Panel, George Grant Elmslie, c.1936, 13 1/2 x 27 1/4 x 5 5/8 In. 600.00
Group, Equestrian, Mounted Arab Hunter, Wood Finished, Late 1800s, 25 x 17 In. 590.00
Group, Nymph & Satyr, A. Carrier-Belleuse, Mid 1800s, 21 In. 7800.00
Jar, Olive, Egg Shape, Flared Lip, Yellow Interior, St. Remy, 1800s, 28 x 15 In. 1530.00
Jar, Water, Hand Coiled, Geometric, Black, Orange, White Ground, c.1900, 10 1/2 x 8 In. 3195.00
Ornament, Scrolling Leaves, Mask Of Mercury, c.1900, 12 1/4 x 40 1/4 In. 826.00
Planter, Bacchic Friezes, Putto, Dolphin Borders, Louis XVI Style, 27 x 32 In., Pair 3290.00
Plaque, Crowned Virgin Mary, Christ Child, Della Robbia Style, Cantagalli, 36 In. 580.00
Plaque, Frolicking Putti, On Dolphins, Gadroon Border, Neoclassical Style, 21 3/4 In. 235.00
Urn, Replica Of Greek Blackware, Figural Vase, 10 1/2 x 6 In., Pair 99.00
Vase, Archaic Greek, Black Decoration, 5 1/4 In. 205.00

TEXTILES listed here include many types of printed fabrics and table and household linens. Some other textiles will be found under Clothing, Coverlet, Quilt, Rug, etc.

Banner, Great Seal Of The Commonwealth Of Mass., Silk, 1800s, 45 1/2 x 41 1/2 In. 825.00
Bed Cover, Cotton, Blue, White Plaid, 74 x 55 In. 138.00
Bed Cover, Homespun, Cotton, Blue, White Plaid, 132 x 56 In. 140.00
Bed Cover, Homespun, Cotton, Blue, White Plaid, 68 x 57 In., 2 Piece 165.00
Bed Cover, Homespun, Cotton, White, Blue Checked, 78 x 78 In. 45.00
Bed Cover, Homespun, Linen, Checked, Blue, White, Tape Loom Ties, 64 x 54 In. 165.00
Bed Cover, Silk, Yellow, Stripes, Embroidered Flowers, France, Late 1800s, 80 x 64 In. 1765.00
Bed Cover, Woven, Medallions, Rose Vine Border, Green, Blue, Red, Wool, 1845, 76 x 76 In. 510.00
Bed Sheet, Homespun, Cotton, Warp & Weft Threads, Arcadian, c.1890, 86 x 72 In. 470.00
Bed Sheet, Homespun, Natural Cotton Warp & Weft, Arcadian, c.1890, 90 x 68 In. 765.00
Bed Sheet, Linen, Homespun, Cotton, Blue, White Plaid, 2 Piece, Sewn, 102 x 59 In. 28.00
Bedspread, Chintz, Multicolored Floral Print, Brown Ground, 2-Sided, 84 x 82 In. 195.00
Bell Pull, Needlepoint, Charles X Style, Dolphins, Brass Mounts, Silk Damask, 72 x 3 In. 355.00
Bell Pull, Silk Ribbon, Ormolu, Flowers, Leaves, Gilt Hardware, France, c.1830, 61 x 3 3/4 In. 295.00
Blanket, Homespun, Cotton, Indigo, Mulberry, Natural, Stripes, Arcadian, c.1900, 86 x 74 In. 1410.00
Blanket, Hudson Bay, 4-Point, Red, Black Stripe, Tag, England, c.1925, 84 x 68 In. 175.00
Blanket, Hudson Bay, 4-Point, White, 4 Stripes, Tag, England, c.1925, 89 x 71 In. 345.00
Blanket, Irony, Brown, Red, 2 Diamond Center, Gray Field, c.1920, 92 x 55 In. 660.00
Blanket, Patchwork, Appliqued, Memory, Denim Squares, Frame, c.1970, 66 x 44 In. 165.00
Blanket, Pendleton, Royal Blue, Beaver State, Chevron, Indian Motif, 64 x 80 In. 140.00
Blanket, Wool, White, Blue Plaid, 74 x 68 In. 165.00
Blanket, Wool, Woven, Blue & Tan, 72 x 72 In. 290.00
Bread Sack, Cotton, Knitted, Slave Made, Confederate, Civil War, 8 x 8 In. 336.00
Curtain, Overdoor, Silk, Cotton, Mauve, Green Floral Tile Design, Celadon Center, 90 x 44 In. 1410.00
Dish Cloth, Roosters, Trees Of Life, Cross-Stitch, B.S., Amish, 1871, 10 x 9 In. 175.00
Doll Pattern, Art Fabric Mills, Cloth Printed, Patented Feb.13, 1900, 22 In. 56.00
Embroidery, Silk, Eagle, On Pine Limb, Carved Teakwood Frame, 52 x 27 In., Pair 230.00
Fabric, Manhattan No. 490, A. Girard, Herman Miller, c.1958, 20 Yards 3360.00
Fabric Panel, Love, Alexander Girard, Herman Miller, Frame, c.1960, 14 1/2 x 14 1/2 In. 420.00
Flag, American, 13 Stars, Wool Bunting, Machine Sewn, c.1876, 44 x 28 In. 1770.00
Flag, American, 33 Stars, Cotton, 1859, 14 x 9 In. 2185.00
Flag, American, 37 Stars, Hung In Independence Hall In The Late 1860s, Cloth, 12 x 7 In. 785.00
Flag, American, 38 Stars, Linen, Cotton, Appliqued Stars, Home Made, c.1876, 73 x 46 In. 690.00
Flag, American, 38 Stars, Wool, 8-8-6-8-8 Star Pattern, 1876, 80 x 50 In. 1415.00
Flag, American, 42 Stars, Cotton, c.1890, 24 x 18 1/4 In. 518.00
Flag, American, 42 Stars, Cotton, Cut From Bolt Of Flags, 1889, 23 3/4 x 18 1/2 In. 355.00
Flag, American, 44 Stars, Linen, Home Made, 1890, 80 x 43 In. 552.00
Flag, American, 44 Stars, Wool Bunting, 1890, 168 x 84 In. 470.00
Flag, American, 45 Stars, Wool Bunting, Machine Sewn, 1896, 60 x 36 In. 776.00
Flag, Civil War Battle, Confederate, White Cross, Blue Ground, Attached Letter, 52 x 41 In. 1845.00
Flag, Naval, 24 Stars, State Of Missouri, 1822, 108 x 204 In. 7350.00
Gujarat Cloth, Beaded, Krishna, Cattle, India, Frame, 1800s, 24 x 22 In. 295.00
Hand Towel, 4 Panels, Birds, Flowers, Fringe, Maria Landis, 1836, 68 x 17 1/2 In. 798.00
Hand Towel, Birds, Initials IHND, 1844, 54 x 13 1/2 In. 358.00
Hand Towel, Catrine Gass, 1836, 33 x 14 3/4 In. 240.00
Hand Towel, Flowers, Hanna Kaufman, 1842, 54 x 16 In. 935.00
Handkerchief, Birds, 9 Vignettes, 4 Sections, 33 x 30 In. 105.00
Handkerchief, Birds, Eagle Center, Red, White, 12 x 12 In. 90.00
Handkerchief, Cotton, Flowers, Blue, Red, White Ground, Sears Roebuck, 1960s, Box, 4 Piece 15.00
Handkerchief, Grenadier Guards, First Regiment Of Life Guards, Horse Artillery, 11 x 8 In. 90.00
Handkerchief, Kids Playing Cricket, S.H. Greene & Sons, Washington, 12 1/2 x 12 1/2 In. 90.00
Handkerchief, Kids Playing Hopscotch, S.H. Greene & Sons, Washington, 13 1/2 x 12 In. 105.00
Hat, Woman's, Floppy, Black Velvet, 3-Inch Brim, Red Satin Bow, Lined, 1940s 55.00
Homespun, Cotton, Blue, White Plaid, 160 x 25 1/2 In. 66.00
Linen, Homespun, Blue & White Checked, 33 x 20 1/2 In. 120.00
Linen, Homespun, Blue & White Checked, 82 x 72 In. 55.00
Linen, Homespun, Bolster Case, Blue & White Checked, 61 x 19 In., Pair 575.00

Linen, Homespun, Brown & White Plaid, 128 x 37 In. 1330.00
Linen, Homespun, Brown, White, 27 x 23 1/2 In. 165.00
Map, Embroidered, Europe, Oval Medallion, Silk, Linen, 1801, 27 1/2 x 24 In. 805.00
Mask, Elephant, 2 Long Flaps, Ovoid Ears, Geometric Beads, Grasslands, 47 In. 267.00
Mattress Cover, Blue & White Checked, Cloth Ties, 70 x 58 In. 160.00
Mattress Cover, Red, White, Blue Plaid, Cotton, Cloth Covered Metal Buttons, 70 x 45 In. 115.00
Needlepoint, Church, Weeping Willows, Verse, Scrolled Flowers, 1832, 16 1/2 x 16 1/2 In. 7375.00
Needlepoint, Uncle Tom & Little Eva, Giltwood Frame, c.1850, 32 x 25 In. 1595.00
Needlework, 4 Figures In Pavilion, Flower Border, Gold, Chinese, 29 x 22 In. 375.00
Needlework, American Eagle Shield, Flags, Silk, Frame, 19 1/2 x 19 1/2 In. 575.00
Needlework, Embroidered, Pictorial Panels, Homespun, Wool Thread, 1840s, 25 x 18 In. 4945.00
Needlework, Horn Of Plenty, Silk, Frame, 17 1/2 x 15 In. 127.00
Panel, Cotton, 3 Flower Roundels, India, 19th Century, 115 x 35 1/2 In. 825.00
Panel, Embroidered Scene, Castle Town, Boats, Gold Thread, Japan, c.1800, 33 x 27 In. 4406.00
Panel, Embroidered, Birds, Flowers, Japan, 19th Century, 54 x 34 In. 235.00
Panel, Embroidered, Flowers, Metal Threads, Lace, Multicolored, Turkey, 1800s, 70 x 50 In. 1058.00
Panel, Embroidered, Stylized Lotus Flowers, Yellow Ground, Chinese, 1700s, 62 x 45 In. 1880.00
Panel, Silk, Embroidered, Dragons, c.1800, 65 x 65 In. 3540.00
Panel, Silk, Embroidered, Green, Gold Thread, Dragons, 19th Century, 65 x 46 In. 649.00
Panel, Silk, Embroidered, Peonies, Pheasants, Pastels, Black Ground, 68 x 46 In. 509.00
Panel, Silk, Hand Woven, Stitched, Blue, Red, Green, Brown, Linen Field, 56 x 54 In. 259.00
Pillow, Cover, Geometric, Hand Sewn, 18 x 17 In. 55.00
Pillow, Needlepoint, Petit & Gros Point, Vase Of Flowers, Tassels, 1800s, 26 x 22 In. 940.00
Pillow, Needlepoint, Petit Point Cover, Flower Basket, Leaves, Tassel, 28 x 20 In. 195.00
Pillow, Silk, Brown, Flowers, Embroidered, Brocade, China, 18th Century, 10 x 8 In. 825.00
Place Mat, Homespun, Linen, Brown, White, Checked, Fringed Edges, 16 x 13 In., 7 Piece 358.00
Pot Holder, Chicken, 6 1/2 x 6 In. 6.00
Pouch, Leather, Silk Needlework, Dragon, Mount Fuji, Japan, 1800s, 5 1/2 In. 115.00
Saddlecloth, Goatskin, General Officer Of Hussars, Red, England, 1810-20, 83 x 63 In. 7986.00
Table Rug, Appliqued, Embroidered, Animals, Insects, Triangles Border, 49 x 34 In. 9775.00
Table Rug, Penny, Scalloped Skirt, Applied Felt, Fabric Circles, Needlework, 53 x 20 In. 50.00
Table Runner, Embroidered Poppy, Daisy, Wheat, Gold Card, Arts & Crafts, 26 x 54 In. 59.00
Table Runner, Woven, Cotton, Blue, Black, Green, Orange, White Plaid, 11 Ft. x 5 1/2 In. 329.00
Table Runner, Woven, Cotton, Blue, Black, Yellow, Green Plaid, 15 Ft. x 3 Ft. 4 In. 269.00
Table Scarf, Gustav Stickley, Zinnia, c.1910, 69 x 19 In. 6600.00
Tablecloth, Arts & Crafts, Jacquard Weave, Flowers, Hearts, 1910, 116 x 62 In. 510.00
Tablecloth, Hand Stitched, Paisley Border, Fringe Edge, 1900-10, 72 x 72 In. 140.00
Tablecloth, Homespun, Linen, Blue, White Plaid, 72 x 67 In. 50.00
Tablecloth, Lace, Off-White, Flowers, Fruit, Thanksgiving Scene, Quaker, 108 x 70 In. 130.00
Tablecloth, Linen, Homespun, Cotton, Blue, White, Metal Snaps, 62 x 37 In. 130.00
Tablecloth, Linen, Homespun, White, 44 x 44 In. 37.00
Tablecloth, Velvet, Embroidered, Flowers, Leaves, 93 x 54 1/2 In. 175.00
Tapestry, 4 Stages Of Romance, Petit Point, France, Frame, 1800s, 41 x 10 1/2 In. 410.00
Tapestry, After Guido Reni's Aurora, 10 Figures, 3 Horses, 116 x 72 In. 605.00
Tapestry, Aubusson, Forest, 1600s, 74 3/4 x 63 In. 4425.00
Tapestry, Aubusson, Musical Theme, Flowers, Cream Ground, Gold Border, 100 x 48 In. 2350.00
Tapestry, Aubusson, Soldiers, Temple Of Venus, Garland Border, 111 x 70 In. 5875.00
Tapestry, Aubusson, Woman On Swing, Floral Garlands, Drapery, 87 x 70 In. 3819.00
Tapestry, Court Scene, Woven, France, Early 1900s, 39 x 38 In. 58.00
Tapestry, Men & Women At River, Fishing, Leaf Border, Belgium, 1800s, 61 x 44 In. 110.00
Tapestry, Monkeys In Trees, Wool, Hooked, Tab Top, Evelyn Ackerman, 49 x 19 In. 540.00
Tapestry, Shepherd, By Tree, Blue, Tan, Brown, Belgium, 1700s, 65 x 27 In. 550.00
Tapestry, Sirens, Woven, Jean Van Vlasselaer, Royale G. Dewit, c.1969, 80 x 45 In. 3422.00
Tapestry, Woven, Paris Street Scene, c.1900, Belgium, 33 x 25 In. 24.00
Towel, Show, Crowns, Flowers, Women, Heart, Star, Fringe, Linen Loops, 38 x 17 In. 110.00
Towel, Show, Embroidered, Leaping Stags, Tulip In Urn, Elizabeth Bransteterin, 1809 .... 210.00
Towel, Show, Homespun, Linen, Alphabet, Potted Flowers, Birds, 1840, 68 x 19 1/2 In. 415.00
Towel, Show, Homespun, Linen, Flowers, Birds, Stars, Cadarina Bechtel, 1830, 48 x 15 In. 358.00
Towel, Show, Homespun, Linen, Stylized Flowers, Stars, Fringe, 56 x 12 In. 120.00
Towel, Show, Homespun, Linen, Tatting, Knotted Fringe, 43 x 16 In. 90.00
Towel, Show, Linen, Homespun, Alphabet, Flowers, Birds, Sarah Ann Kline, c.1842, 68 x 20 In. 413.00

Towel, Show, Needlework, Birds, Flowers, Stars, Hearts, Red, Blue, Yellow, 62 x 17 1/2 In. 95.00
Towel, Show, Needlework, Crowns, Flowers, Women, Maria Bambergerin, 38 x 17 In. 110.00
Towel, Show, Needlework, Drawn, Fringe, 38 x 14 In. 66.00
Towel, Show, Needlework, Flowers, Birds, Stars, Cadarina Bechtel, 1830, 48 x 14 1/2 In. 358.00
Towel, Show, Needlework, Yellow, 17 1/2 x 38 In. 90.00
Valance, Toile, Purple, Scenic, King & Queen, Peasants, Castle, 58 x 20 1/2 In. 175.00

THERMOMETER is a name that comes from the Greek word for heat. The thermometer was invented in 1731 to measure the temperature of either water or air. All kinds of thermometers are collected, but those with advertising messages are the most popular.

7Up, Oval, Metal, Fresh Up, Ca Ravigote, 15 In. 30.00
Abbotts Bitters, Rapkey & Co. Ltd., Tin, Brass, Glass, 9 In. Diam. 222.00
Beattie's Eye Service, Optometrists, Eye, White, Blue, Wood, 21 x 5 In. 220.00
Borden's Ice Cream, Very Big On Flavor, Elsie, Blue, Yellow, Red, Metal, 26 x 10 In. 605.00
Calumet Baking Powder, Wood, 6 x 10 1/4 In. 170.00
Carter Inx, Porcelain, 34 In. 224.00
Clark Bar, Clark Bar O'Clock, 4 P.M., Wood, 5 1/2 x 19 In. ....310.00 to 500.00
Cutlery By Remington, DuPont, Razor Sharp, Porcelain, 39 x 8 In. 498.00
Dad's Root Beer, Just Right For Dads, Tastes Like Root Beer Should, Tin Litho, 27 x 7 In. 265.00
Daily News, Chicago, Porcelain, Tin, 1910s, 38 1/2 x 8 1/4 In. 450.00
Dr Pepper, When Hungry, Thirsty Or Tired, Tin, 9 1/2 x 25 1/2 In. 280.00
Dr. A.C. Daniels, Famous Veterinary Medicines, Wood, White Paint, 21 In. 290.00
Drink Barq's, 9 3/4 x 25 1/2 In. 196.00
Dunham's Shredded Coconut, Country Store Dial, 11 3/4 x 1 1/8 In. 440.00
Ex-Lax, The Chocolate Laxative, Porcelain, Enamel, 1 1/4 x 8 x 36 In. 252.00
Fatima Cigarette, 20 For 15 Cents, Yellow, White, Red, Porcelain, 27 x 7 1/2 In. 470.00
Frostie Root Beer, Tin, 8 3/4 x 36 In. 196.00
Hills Bros. Coffee, Coffee Drinker, Red, Yellow, Porcelain, Lithograph, 21 x 9 In. 300.00
J. McAllister & Co., Philadelphia, Mahogany, Bowed Glass, 15 3/4 In. 1675.00
Keen Kutter, Simmons Hardware, Walnut Base, 7 1/4 x 1 1/2 In. 115.00
Koch Bros. Clothiers, Man & Boy, Allentown, Pa., 21 x 5 1/4 In. 385.00
Mail Pouch Tobacco, Porcelain, 8 1/4 x 39 In. 168.00
Mail Pouch Tobacco, Treat Yourself To The Best, Blue, Yellow, Porcelain, 38 1/2 In. 275.00
Morton's Salt, Umbrella Girl, When It Rains It Pours, 1950s, 16 x 6 In. ....85.00 to 95.00
Nature's Remedy, Tablets, Feel Like A Million, Blue, White, Red, Tin, Glass, 9 In. Diam. 70.00
Nature's Remedy, To-Night, Come In, Blue, White, Red, Porcelain, 27 x 7 In. ....220.00 to 495.00
Nesbitt's, Tin Lithograph, 7 3/4 x 17 1/2 In. 196.00
Oasis Cigarette, Refreshes You More, Embossed, Pressed Tin, 13 In. 44.00
Pabst Blue Ribbon, J.A. Conkling, Yankton, S.D., 1959, 12 x 5 1/2 In. 140.00
Park & Pollard Co., Lay Or Bust Feeds, Chickens, Porcelain, 27 1/4 x 7 In. 910.00
Peter's Shoes, Diamond Brand, Porcelain, 27 1/4 In. 660.00
Pewter Baseball Player, Pairpoint, Bakelite Mount, Late 1800s, 7 x 4 1/2 In. 930.00
Polarine, Red Crown Gasoline, For Power Mileage, Porcelain, 73 1/4 x 19 In. 2750.00
Pollack Wheeling Stogies, Crowns, Melo-Crown Experts, Blue, Porcelain, 39 In. 440.00
Ramon's Brownie Pills, Pink Pills, Little Doctor, Yellow, Tin Lithograph, 21 In. 440.00
Ramon's Brownie Pills & Pink Pills, Little Doctor, Enamel On Metal, 21 x 9 In. 1045.00
Ramon's Pills, Brownie For Kidneys, Pink For Liver, Wood, White, Red, Green, 21 In. 520.00
Remember To Buy Grapette, Thirsty Or Not, 1950s, 14 x 6 In. 50.00
Royal Baking Powder, Porcelain, 27 1/8 x 7 In. 4290.00
Royal Chinook Shoes, Goodman Bros., Fish Shape, Wood, 15 3/4 x 5 In. 468.00
Sanilac Cattle Spray, Socony Vacuum Oil Co., Cows, Landscape, Wood, 19 In. 660.00
Sauer's Flavoring Extracts, Wood, 24 x 7 In. 1155.00
Sprague Funeral Home, Pressed Tin, Governor, New York, 16 In. 55.00
Stephen's Inks, Porcelain, 61 x 12 In. 800.00
Vodka, Wolfschmidt, Pressed Tin, Glass, 12 1/2 In. 28.00
Ward's Vitovim Bread, Porcelain, Child Eating Bread, 20 3/4 x 8 3/4 In. 2200.00

TIFFANY is a name that appears on items made by Louis Comfort Tiffany, the American glass designer who worked from about 1879 to 1933. His work included iridescent glass, Art Nouveau styles of design, and original contemporary styles. He was also noted for stained glass windows, unusual lamps, bronze work, pottery, and silver. Other types of Tiffany are listed under Tiffany Glass, Tiffany Gold, Tiffany Pottery, or Tiffany Silver. The famous Tiffany lamps are listed in this section. Tiffany jewelry is listed in the jewelry and wristwatch categories. Some Tiffany Studio desk sets have matching clocks. They are listed here. Clocks made by Tiffany & Co. are listed in the Clock category. Reproductions of some types of Tiffany are being made.

Louis C. Tiffany

Ash Stand, Etched, Bronze, 29 x 9 In. 1058.00
Ashtray, Bronze, Gold Dore, Nesting, Ribbed, Oval, Signed, 4 Piece 350.00
Ashtray, Bronze, Gold Dore, Ribbed Handles, 1 x 4 In. 150.00
Ashtray, Match Holder, Pine Needle, Green Slag Glass, Bronze, Signed, 4 1/2 x 5 1/4 In. 650.00
Blotter, Abalone, Bronze, Gold Dore, 5 3/4 x 3 In. 450.00
Blotter, American Indian, Bronze, 5 1/2 x 3 In. 650.00
Blotter, Graduate, Bronze, Gold Dore, 5 1/2 x 2 3/4 In. 350.00
Blotter, Grapevine, Amber Slag Glass, Bronze, 5 7/8 x 3 In. 144.00
Blotter, Grapevine, Green Slag Glass, Bronze, Dark Patina, Signed, 6 x 3 In. 650.00
Blotter, Pine Needle, Amber Slag Glass, Bronze, Gold Dore, 1 1/2 x 6 x 3 In. 550.00
Blotter, Zodiac, Bronze, Gold Dore, 2 x 2 3/4 x 5 1/2 In. 400.00
Blotter Ends, Abalone, Bronze, Gold Dore, 12 x 2 1/2 In., Pair 550.00
Blotter Ends, Adam, Bronze, Gold Dore, 19 x 2 In., Pair 350.00
Blotter Ends, Grapevine, Bronze, 19 x 2 In., Pair 90.00
Blotter Ends, Pine Needle, Bronze, 12 x 2 In., Pair 350.00
Blotter Ends, Zodiac, Bronze, 3 1/2 x 4 In., 4 Piece 400.00
Blotter Ends, Zodiac, Bronze, Gold Dore, Signed, 19 x 2 In., Pair 250.00
Bookends, Abalone, Bronze, Gold Dore, Iridescent, Leaf & Line, 5 1/2 x 5 1/2 In. 3000.00
Bookends, Bookmark, Gold Dore, 14K Gold Plate, Trees, Branches, Scrolls, 6 x 5 In., Pair 2500.00
Bookends, Peacock Portal, Bronze, Gold Dore, 6 x 4 1/2 In. 1800.00
Bookends, Venetian, Multicolored Enameled, Bronze, Gold Dore, Signed, 6 x 5 In. 2500.00
Bookends, Zodiac, Bronze, Gold Dore, Signed, 6 In. .... 471.00 to 837.00
Bookrack, Grapevine, Bronze, Gold Dore, Amber Slag Glass, 6 x 5 3/4 x 14 To 23 In. 3000.00
Bowl, Blue Iridescent, Wavy Rim, Favrile, 1900-19, 3 1/4 x 8 1/2 In. 1495.00
Bowl, Bronze, Gold Dore, Embossed Rim, Shallow, 1920s, 9 In. 285.00
Bowl, Bronze, Rolled Edge, Signed, 1 3/4 x 5 1/2 In. 350.00
Bowl, Centerpiece, Bronze, Gold Dore, Enameled, Favrile Glass Inset, Footed, 4 1/2 x 8 In. 2500.00
Box, Bronze, Grapevine, Green Slag Glass, Bronze, Brown Patina, 8 x 8 x 2 1/2 In. 1725.00
Box, Card, Grapevine, Green Slag Glass, Bronze, 4 1/2 x 3 x 2 In. 2500.00
Box, Chinese, Bronze, Gold Dore, Cedar Lined, 5 1/4 x 8 In. 1800.00
Box, Grapevine, Green Slag Glass, Bronze, Beaded Edge, 4 Ball Feet, 1 3/4 x 4 1/2 x 3 In. 850.00
Box, Handkerchief, Grapevine, Green Slag Glass, Bronze, 2 1/2 x 8 In. 3000.00
Box, Hinged Cover, Abalone, Bronze, Gold Dore, Leaf & Flower, 5 1/4 x 3 1/2 In. 950.00
Box, Hinged Cover, American Indian, Bronze, Raised Mask, Signed, 2 x 5 1/2 x 3 In. 650.00
Box, Hinged Cover, Bookmark, Bronze, Gold Dore, Trees, Scroll, 1 x 5 x 3 In. 950.00
Box, Hinged Cover, Bronze, Geometric Red & Black Enamel, Art Deco, 1 3/4 x 6 1/4 In. 950.00
Box, Hinged Cover, Enameled Bronze, Beaded Edge, 2 x 6 1/4 x 4 In. 1500.00
Box, Hinged Cover, Enameled Bronze, Gold Dore, 2 3/4 x 6 x 5 In. 1500.00
Box, Hinged Cover, Glass, Bronze, Half Moons, Ribs, 6-Sided, Favrile, 2 In. 4500.00
Box, Hinged Cover, Grapevine, Green Slag Glass, Bronze, Beaded Edge, Ball Feet, 1 x 3 In. 850.00
Box, Hinged Cover, Pine Needle, Amber Slag Glass, Bronze, Dore, Ball Feet, 4 x 6 1/2 In. 2500.00
Box, Pine Needle, Green Slag Glass, Bronze, Beaded Edge, Ball Feet, 2 x 5 1/2 x 3 In. 900.00
Box, Stamp, Hinged Cover, Grapevine, Amber Slag Glass, Bronze, 3 1/4 x 4 1/2 In. 288.00
Box, Stamp, Hinged Cover, Pine Needle, Green Slag Glass, Bronze, 3 Sections, 2 1/4 x 4 In. 800.00
Box, Stamp, Hinged Cover, Zodiac, Bronze, Gold Dore, 3 Sections, Signed, 3 3/4 x 2 1/4 In. 600.00
Box, Zodiac, Entwined Line, Hinged Cover, 1 x 5 1/4 x 3 1/2 In. 650.00
Calendar, Adam, Gold Dore, Seal, 6 x 6 1/2 In. 1200.00
Calendar, Graduate, Bronze, Gold Dore, Easel Back, 6 1/4 x 5 1/2 In. 750.00
Calendar, Grapevine, Carmel Slag Glass, Curved Panels, 4 1/2 x 3 1/2 In. 115.00
Calendar, Pine Needle, Slag Glass, Bronze, Easel Back, 4 1/2 x 6 In. 750.00
Calendar, Venetian, Bronze, Gold Dore, Line & Scrolls, Raised Minks, Perpetual, Signed 1500.00
Candelabrum, 3-Light, Bronze, c.1910, 14 1/4 In. 4800.00
Candelabrum, 6-Light, Bronze, c.1910, 15 x 22 1/4 In. 9000.00

Candle Lamp, Bronze, Jeweled, Gold Iridescent, Candle Cup, 3 Ball Feet, 14 1/2 In. 2875.00
Candle Lamp, Bronze, Pulled Feather Glass, 3 Lily Pad Feet, Snuffer, 16 In. 7475.00
Candleholder, Bronze, Gold Dore, Handle, Signed, 5 1/4 Diam. 550.00
Candleholder, Bronze, Urn Candle Cup, Quatrefoil Base, Thumb Rest, c.1920, 7 1/4 In. 1076.00
Candlestick, 2-Light, Bronze, Gold Dore, Stylized Flower, Stem, Bud, 9 1/4 In. 1150.00
Candlestick, Bronze, Glass Insert, c.1910, 15 In. 1680.00
Candlestick, Bronze, Green Glass Jewels, Removable Bobeche, Footed, 12 1/2 In., Pair 3055.00
Candlestick, Bronze, Iridescent Lily Glass Shade, Pulled Feathers, 5 x 21 In. 1380.00
Candlestick, Bronze, Urn Candle Cup, 4 Legs, Quatrefoil Base, c.1900, 11 In., Pair 2151.00
Canister, Cover, Bronze, Gold Dore, Embossed Sailboat, 3 1/2 x 3 In. 450.00
Clip, Zodiac, Bronze, Gold Dore, Signed, 3 3/4 x 2 3/4 In. 360.00
Clock, American Indian, Bronze, Patina, c.1910, 5 3/8 x 4 1/4 x 2 1/8 In. 5280.00
Clock, Heraldic, Enameled, Bronze, Gold Dore, c.1910, 7 7/8 x 6 x 3 In. 6000.00
Clock, Louis XVI, Enameled, Bronze, Gold Dore, c.1910, 6 7/8 x 4 3/8 x 2 7/8 In. 4200.00
Clock, Pine Needle, Green Slag Glass, Bronze, 4 1/2 x 3 1/2 In. 3000.00
Clock, Venetian, Bronze, Gold Dore, 1 3/4 x 4 1/4 In. 3000.00
Compote, Bronze, Abalone, Silver Finish, Curved Leaf Pattern, Signed, 3 1/4 In. Diam. 650.00
Compote, Bronze, Gold Dore, 3 1/2 x 6 In. 550.00
Compote, Bronze, Gold Dore, Enameled Flowers, Vines, Footed, Handles, 13 1/2 In. 478.00
Compote, Bronze, Gold Dore, Enameled, Footed, Flower Border, 3 x 10 In. 1500.00
Compote, Bronze, Gold Dore, Sunburst Lines, Footed, Signed, 3 1/2 x 6 In. 450.00
Desk Set, Grapevine Pattern, Slag Glass, Bronze, c.1906, 6 Piece 2032.00
Desk Set, Venetian, Bronze, 8 Piece 5875.00
Dish, Bronze, Gold Dore, Enameled, Red, Blue, Green, Signed, 1 x 8 In. 1500.00
Flower Holder, Bronze, Gold Dore, 5 Glass Tube Holders, 4 x 4 In. 2500.00
Frame, Abalone, Bronze, Gold Dore, Leaves & Flowers, Signed, 10 1/4 x 7 1/4 In. 4000.00
Frame, Adam, Bronze, Gold Dore, Dark Patina, Ovals, Folds, Lines, Swags, 12 x 9 In. 2500.00
Frame, Bronze, Gold Dore, Blue Enamel, 7 1/2 x 6 1/4 In. 1500.00
Frame, Bronze, Patina, Monogram, Favrile, 9 1/2 x 15 5/8 In. 7200.00
Frame, Chinese, Bronze, Easel Back, 7 1/4 x 8 3/4 In. 950.00
Frame, Grapevine, Green Slag Glass, Bronze, Easel Back, Signed, 7 x 6 1/2 In. ....2100.00 to 3000.00
Frame, Pine Needle, Green Slag Glass, Bronze, Brown Patina, Signed, 7 1/2 x 9 1/4 In. 2875.00
Frame, Pine Needle, Green Slag Glass, Bronze, Easel Back, 8 1/2 x 7 In. 3000.00
Frame, Pine Needle, Oval Opening, Amber Slag Glass, Bronze, 9 1/2 x 11 1/2 In. 1725.00
Frame, Venetian, Geometric, Curved Lines, Bronze, Gold Dore, 12 x 9 In. 3000.00
Frame, Zodiac, Bronze, Gold Dore, 11 x 9 In. 2000.00
Frame, Zodiac, Bronze, Gold Dore, Signed, 7 x 8 In. ....1000.00 to 1200.00
Glass, Compote, Blue Iridescent, Stretch Rim, Blue To Purple Base, Signed, 4 1/2 x 8 In. 3000.00
Hatpin Holder, Bronze, Twisted, 3 1/2 In. 403.00
Humidor, Hinged Cover, American Indian, Bronze, Dark Patina, Cedar Lining, 8 x 2 3/4 In. 2500.00
Inkstand, 3 Men & Chest, Bronze, Patina, Favrile Glass Cabochons, c.1910, 3 x 10 In. 7200.00
Inkwell, Abalone, Bronze, Gold Dore, 8-Sided, 3 1/2 In. 750.00
Inkwell, American Indian, Geometric Lines, Bronze, Glass Insert, 5 1/2 In. 950.00
Inkwell, Beehive Shape, Bronze, Glass Inset, 7 1/2 In. 7670.00
Inkwell, Bookmark, Bronze, Gold Dore, 8-Sided, 2 1/2 x 4 1/2 In. 1200.00
Inkwell, Bookmark, Bronze, Gold Dore, Square, Canted Corners, 2 1/2 x 3 In. 750.00
Inkwell, Cover, Modelled, Bronze, Gold Dore, 2 1/2 x 3 1/2 In. 550.00
Inkwell, Dome Cover, Dore Bronze, Textured, Favrile Insert, 4 1/2 In. 3508.00
Inkwell, Graduate, Gold Dore, Glass Insert, Square, 2 x 4 In. 550.00
Inkwell, Grapevine, Green Slag Glass, Bronze, Patina, Glass Insert, Ball Feet, 3 1/2 x 4 In. 950.00
Inkwell, Grapevine, Green Slag Glass, Bronze, Patina, Glass Insert, Signed, 2 1/2 x 3 3/4 In. 650.00
Inkwell, Hinged Cover, Adam, Bronze, Gold Dore, 2 1/2 x 4 x 3 In. 750.00
Inkwell, Hinged Cover, American Indian, Bronze, Glass Insert, 5 1/2 x 3 1/2 In. ....950.00 to 1100.00
Inkwell, Hinged Cover, Bookmark, Bronze, Gold Dore, 8-Sided, Glass Insert, 4 1/2 In. 1200.00
Inkwell, Hinged Cover, Bookmark, Bronze, Gold Dore, Glass Insert, Signed, 2 1/2 x 3 In. 750.00
Inkwell, Hinged Cover, Pine Needle, Bronze, Glass Inset, 7 In. 2000.00
Inkwell, Hinged Cover, Zodiac, Bronze, Glass Insert, 6 1/4 In. 1800.00
Inkwell, Hinged Cover, Zodiac, Bronze, Gold Dore, 6-Sided, Glass Insert, Signed, 4 In. 750.00
Inkwell, Hinged Cover, Zodiac, Bronze, Gold Dore, 8-Sided, Glass Insert, Signed, 2 In. 550.00
Inkwell, Oak Leaf, Green Slag Glass, Beaded Edge, Bronze, Dark Patina, 6-Sided, 3 x 6 In. 2500.00
Inkwell, Pine Needle, Bronze, Gold Dore, 3 1/2 x 4 In. 950.00

Tiffany, Lamp, Geometric Shade, Dichroic, Green, Yellow, Bronze, 24 x 18 In.

Tiffany, Lamp, Geometric Shade, Green, Mottled, Raised Dots, Favrile, 22 x 16 In.

Tiffany, Lamp, Poinsettia Shade, Dichroic, Leaded Glass, Bronze Base, 26 1/2 x 18 In.

Inkwell, Pine Needle, Bronze, Gold Dore, 3 x 3 1/2 In. .450.00 to 650.00
Inkwell, Tray, Zodiac, Bronze, 10 3/4-In. Tray 2500.00
Jewelry Box, Bronze, Chinese, Gold Dore Finish 2500.00
Jewelry Box, Grapevine, Green Slag Glass, Bronze, Trays, 6 x 9 x 3 In. 3105.00
Jewelry Box, Hinged Cover, Bronze, Antique Gold, Pale Green Enamel, 3 x 8 x 3 3/4 In. 3900.00
Jewelry Box, Hinged Cover, Byantine, Bronze, Gold Dore, Casket, Signed, 3 x 5 1/2 In. 2200.00
Jewelry Box, Pine Needle, Bronze, Gold Dore, 3 x 6 1/2 x 4 In. 2500.00
Lamp, 10-Sided, Mesh Shade, Bronze, 23 x 16 In. 3024.00
Lamp, Acorn Shade, Green Slag Glass, Bronze, Gold Dore, Double Harp, Lily Pad Feet, 58 In. 9775.00
Lamp, Acorn Shade, Green Slag Glass, Yellow, Cream Ground Panels, Bronze Base, 17 In. 9775.00
Lamp, Blue, Green Iridescent Shade, Queen Anne's Lace Base, Bronze, Gold Dore, 16 In. 1955.00
Lamp, Bronze, Amber Glass Shade, 3 Ovals, Urn Base, Ribbed Feet, 16 1/2 In. 3500.00
Lamp, Clematis Shade, Bronze Base, c.1920, 22 1/2 In. 8963.00
Lamp, Daffodil Shade, Bronze Base, 24 1/2 x 20 In. 34500.00
Lamp, Desk, Damascene Shade, Bronze, Ribbed Base, 2 Curved Arms, c.1900, 13 In. 5079.00
Lamp, Desk, Damascene Shade, Ribbed, Gold Iridescent Waves, Bronze Harp Base, 13 In. 1725.00
Lamp, Desk, Damascene, Blue, Purple, Gold Iridescent, Bronze, 3 Sockets, Favrile, 16 In. 6038.00
Lamp, Desk, Green Pulled Feather Shade, Blue Iridescent, Bronze Harp Base, 17 1/2 In. 6038.00
Lamp, Desk, Iridescent Jewels, Bronze Base, 3 Ball Feet, Curved Legs, 14 1/2 In. 2875.00
Lamp, Desk, Nautilus Shell, Leaded Glass, Bronze, Patina, c.1915, 13 3/8 In. 2350.00
Lamp, Desk, Pine Needle, Bronze, Gold Dore, 19 In. 2760.00
Lamp, Desk, Zodiac, Gold Pulled Feather Shade, Ivory, Bronze, Signed, 18 In. 4500.00
Lamp, Geometric Shade, Bronze Base, 3 Sockets, 4-Footed, c.1890, 21 1/2 In. 10158.00
Lamp, Geometric Shade, Dichroic, Green, Yellow, Bronze, 24 x 18 In. ***ILLUS*** 34500.00
Lamp, Geometric Shade, Green, Mottled, Raised Dots, Favrile, 22 x 16 In. ***ILLUS*** 89125.00
Lamp, Greek Key, Leaded Glass, Conical, Bronze Base, 1916, 26 x 20 1/2 In. 39100.00
Lamp, Hanging, Butterfly, Leaded Glass, c.1910, 7 x 10 In. 7200.00
Lamp, Hanging, Moorish, 12 Green Slag Glass Tiles, 12 3/4 In. 5900.00
Lamp, Hanging, Opalescent, Pulled Iridescent Over Blue, Bronze Frame, Signed, 18 In. 8225.00
Lamp, Harp, Gold Iridescent Shade, Bronze Base, Brown Patina, 13 In. 1323.00
Lamp, Kerosene, Damascene Shade, Urn Base, 4 Legs, Paw Feet, Bronze Saucer, 7 1/4 In. 9220.00
Lamp, King Tut Shade, Tulip, Blue Iridescent, Bronze, Gold Dore, Pillar Base, 14 3/4 In. 3163.00
Lamp, Lily, 3-Light, Twisting Stems, Scrolled Finial, Favrile, 16 In. 7475.00
Lamp, Lily, 3-Light, Zephyr Shades, Bronze, 12 3/4 In. 1840.00
Lamp, Lily, 5-Light, Iridescent, Blue Highlights, 16 In. 1150.00
Lamp, Lily, 12-Light, Bronze, Gold Dore, c.1910, 21 1/4 In. 26400.00
Lamp, Linenfold Shade, 10 Panels, Green, Bronze Base, 1938, 19 x 8 In. 11210.00
Lamp, Mosque, Opalescent, Green Pulled Feather, Gold Iridescent, Bronze Base, 8 1/2 In. 5500.00
Lamp, Mosque, Yellow Shade, Gold Iridescent Pulled Feathers, Wooden Base, 8 1/4 In. 4600.00
Lamp, Mushroom Shade, Green Leaded Glass, Bronze Base, 6 x 14 In. 8050.00
Lamp, Poinsettia Shade, Dichroic, Leaded Glass, Bronze Base, 26 1/2 x 18 In. ***ILLUS*** 46000.00
Lamp, Spider & Web Shade, Bronze Mushroom Base, c.1910, 17 5/8 In. 60000.00
Lamp, Student, Damascene Shade, Bronze Base, Patina, Adjustable, Signed, 10 x 24 In. 8400.00
Lamp, Student, Hooked Feather Shade, Orange To Cream, Bronze Base, 24 1/2 In. 4313.00

Lamp Base, 3 Lily Pad Feet, Bronze, Brown Patina, Green Highlights, Harp, 55 In. 1955.00
Letter Holder, Abalone, Bronze, Gold Dore, 2 Sections 1500.00
Letter Holder, Adam, Bronze, Gold Dore, 2 Sections, 6 x 9 1/4 x 2 1/4 In. 900.00
Letter Holder, Bookmark, Bronze, Gold Dore, 6 x 9 In. 1500.00
Letter Holder, Chinese, Bronze, 3 Sections, 8 x 12 x 3 1/2 In. .... 700.00 to 1500.00
Letter Holder, Etched Metal, Amber Slag Glass, Bronze, Dore, 3 Sections, c.1910, 6 x 10 In. 999.00
Letter Holder, Graduate, Bronze, Gold Dore, 2 Sections, 5 1/4 x 9 1/2 x 2 3/4 In. 850.00
Letter Holder, Grapevine, Carmel Slag Ground, Bronze, Signed, 10 x 6 1/4 In. 575.00
Letter Holder, Grapevine, Green Slag Glass, Bronze, 10 x 6 1/4 In. 1268.00
Letter Holder, Grapevine, Green Slag Glass, Bronze, 2 Sections, 6 1/2 x 10 x 2 1/2 In. 1500.00
Letter Holder, Pine Cone, Bronze, 4 1/2 x 6 1/4 In. 1287.00
Letter Holder, Pine Needle, Green Slag Glass, Bronze, 3 Sections, c.1920, 6 1/4 x 10 In. 848.00
Letter Holder, Pine Needle, Green Slag Glass, Bronze, 5 1/2 x 6 1/4 In. 1500.00
Letter Holder, Venetian, Bronze, Gold Dore, 2 Sections, Signed, 4 1/2 x 6 1/4 In. 1500.00
Letter Holder, Zodiac, Bronze, 9 1/2 x 6 1/4 In. 230.00
Letter Opener, Abalone, Bronze, Gold Dore, 10 In. 650.00
Letter Opener, Adam, Bronze, Gold Dore, Curved Handle, 9 In. 500.00
Letter Opener, Chinese, Bronze, Gold Dore, 11 In. 500.00
Letter Opener, Grapevine, Amber Slag Glass, Bronze, Gold Dore, 9 1/4 In. 650.00
Letter Opener, Grapevine, Green Slag Glass, Bronze, Dark Patina, 9 1/4 In. 650.00
Letter Opener, Grapevine, Slag Glass, Bronze, Signed, 9 1/2 In. 173.00
Letter Opener, Pine Needle, Amber Slag Glass, Bronze, Gold Dore, 9 1/4 In. 650.00
Letter Opener, Pine Needle, Green Slag Glass, Bronze, Dark Patina, 9 1/4 In. 650.00
Letter Opener, Spanish, Bronze, Gold Dore, 8 3/4 In. 850.00
Magnifying Glass, Abalone, Bronze, Gold Dore, 9 x 4 In. .... 1800.00 to 2000.00
Magnifying Glass, Adam, Bronze, Dark Patina, Beaded Edge, Signed, 4 x 8 1/4 In. 1500.00
Magnifying Glass, American Indian, Bronze, Gold Dore, 8 1/2 x 4 In. 1500.00
Magnifying Glass, Bookmark, Bronze, Gold Dore, 8 3/4 x 4 In. 1500.00
Magnifying Glass, Grapevine, Amber Slag Glass, Bronze, Gold Dore, Signed, 8 In. .... 1800.00 to 2000.00
Magnifying Glass, Pine Needle, Green Slag Glass, Bronze, Beaded Edge, Signed, 8 In. 2000.00
Magnifying Glass, Venetian, Bronze, Dark Patina, 8 3/4 x 4 In. 1500.00
Magnifying Glass, Venetian, Bronze, Gold Dore, 8 3/4 x 4 In. 1500.00
Magnifying Glass, Zodiac, Bronze, Dark Patina, Signed, 4 x 8 3/4 In. 1500.00
Magnifying Glass, Zodiac, Bronze, Gold Dore, Signed, 4 x 8 3/4 In. 1500.00
Match Safe, Bronze, Gold Dore, Rectangular, 4 1/2 x 3 3/8 x 3 1/2 In. 345.00
Match Safe, Zodiac, Bronze, Gold Dore, 3/4 x 2 1/2 x 1 3/4 In. .... 390.00 to 450.00
Notepad Holder, Bookmark, Bronze, Gold Dore, 4 1/2 x 7 1/2 In. 950.00
Notepad Holder, Venetian, Bronze, Gold Dore, Signed, 7 1/2 x 4 1/2 In. 750.00
Paper Clip, Abalone, Bronze, Gold Dore, 2 x 2 1/4 In. 650.00
Paper Clip, American Indian, Bronze, 2 1/2 x 4 In. 600.00
Paper Clip, Bookmark, Bronze, Gold Dore, 3 1/4 x 2 1/4 In. 650.00
Paper Clip, Chinese, Bronze, 2 3/4 x 4 In. 600.00
Paper Clip, Grapevine, Amber Slag Glass, Bronze, 2 3/4 x 3 3/4 In. 316.00
Paper Clip, Grapevine, Bronze, Gold Dore, 2 1/2 x 3 3/4 In. 650.00
Paper Clip, Grapevine, Green Glass Slag, Beaded Edge, Bronze, Dark Patina, 3 3/4 In. 650.00
Paper Clip, Pine Needle, Amber Glass, Bronze, Gold Dore, 2 1/2 x 3 3/4 In. 650.00
Paper Clip, Zodiac, Bronze, Gold Dore, 2 1/2 x 4 In. .... 550.00 to 650.00
Paperweight, Grapevine, Green Slag Glass, Bronze, Dark Patina, Signed, 3 3/4 In. 650.00
Paperweight, Zodiac, Bronze, 3 1/2 x 2 In. 550.00
Pen Brush, Abalone, Bronze, Gold Dore, 2 x 2 1/4 In. 650.00
Pen Brush, American Indian, Bronze, Dark Patina, Signed, 1 3/4 In. 650.00
Pen Brush, Bookmark, Bronze, Gold Dore, 2 1/2 x 3 In. 750.00
Pen Brush, Grapevine, Green Glass, Bronze, Dark Patina, Signed, 1 1/2 x 2 1/4 In. 650.00
Pen Brush, Pine Needle, Bronze, Gold Dore, 2 1/2 x 2 1/2 In. .... 500.00 to 650.00
Pen Brush, Venetian, Bronze, Gold Dore, 8-Sided, Signed, 2 1/4 x 3 In. 650.00
Pen Holder, Bronze, Gold Dore, Geometric Red & Black Enamel, Art Deco, 3 3/4 x 3 1/4 In. 650.00
Pen Holder, Grapevine, Carmel Slag Glass, Bronze, 5 1/4 x 4 In. 575.00
Pen Holder, Modelled, Bronze, Gold Dore, 2 Holes, 8 x 4 In. 1500.00
Pen Tray, Chinese, Bronze, 9 1/2 x 3 In. 350.00
Pen Tray, Zodiac, Bronze, Gold Dore, Signed, 3 x 9 3/4 In. 250.00
Platter, Bronze, Gold Dore, Cupped Up Edge, Round, 8 In. 195.00

Platter, Bronze, Gold Dore, Geometric & Curved Border, 1 1/4 x 9 In. ....350.00 to 400.00
Postage Scale, Grapevine Pattern, Bronze, Green Slag Glass, 3 x 1 1/2 x 3 In. 1500.00
Postage Scale, Pine Needle, Bronze, Green Slag Glass, 3 x 2 x 3 In. 1500.00
Postage Scale, Zodiac, Bronze, 3 1/4 x 3 x 1 1/2 In. 1500.00
Sconce, 6 Lily Shades, Gold Iridescent, Vertical Ribs, Bronze, Curved Arms, Patina, 19 In. 7475.00
Sconce, Artichoke, Tulip Shades, Gold Iridescent, 2 Arms, Bulbous Center, Favrile, 18 In. 4025.00
Smoking Set, Enameled, Geometric, Bronze, Gold Dore, 12-In. Tray, 4 Piece 3500.00
Smoking Stand, Enameled, Bronze, Gold Dore, Match Safe, Scrolled Edge, 25 x 10 In. 1800.00
Tazza, Bronze, Gold Dore, Enamel, 3 x 10 In. 323.00
Tazza, Bronze, Gold Dore, Enameled, Favrile Glass Insert, Gold Dore, 6 1/4 x 7 In. 3500.00
Tea Screen, Bronze, Green Slag Glass, 3 Section, 7 x 12 In. 4500.00
Thermometer, Zodiac, Bronze, Easel Back, Signed, 8 x 4 In. 2000.00
Tray, Bronze, Enameled, Peacock Feather Border, Round, 6 1/2 In. 550.00
Tray, Bronze, Gold Dore, Entwined Line Border, 12 x 15 In. 1500.00
Tray, Zodiac, Bronze, Gold Dore, Signed, 10 In. 270.00
Vase, Bronze, Dark Patina, Curved Wreath, Raised Berries, Fluted Edge, 3 1/2 x 4 1/2 In. 1500.00
Vase, Bud, Bronze, Gold Dore, Green & Yellow Enameled Base, Favrile, 13 In. 920.00
Vase, Reverse Trumpet, Blue Iridescent, Favrile, 10 In. 1380.00
Vase, Trumpet, Blue Iridescent, 6-Sided, Knopped Stem, Footed, 8 In. 2185.00
Window, Leaded Glass, Demilune, Peacock, Cornucopia, Use As Light Fixture, 23 x 44 In. 17625.00
TIFFANY GLASS, Bonbon, Gold Iridescent, Ribbed, Flared Rim, Stretched, Signed, 2 1/2 x 6 In. 650.00
Bonbon, Gold Iridescent, Ruffled, 8-Pointed Edge, Favrile, 2 x 5 1/2 In. 400.00
Bowl, Blue Iridescent, Blue Center, Ruffled Edge, Ribbed, Cupped Rim, 2 x 9 1/2 In. 1500.00
Bowl, Blue Iridescent, Favrile, c.1919, 8 1/2 In. 1040.00
Bowl, Centerpiece, Attached Flower Frog, Blue Iridescent, Gold, Favrile, 13 In. 5750.00
Bowl, Centerpiece, Attached Flower Frog, Gold Iridescent, Green Vine, Favrile, 12 In. 1840.00
Bowl, Centerpiece, Attached Flower Frog, Gold Iridescent, Hearts & Vines, 11 In. 2013.00
Bowl, Centerpiece, Blue Iridescent, Green Lily Pads, Leaves, Rolled Edge, 12 In. 4000.00
Bowl, Centerpiece, Blue Iridescent, Lily Pads, Leaves, Favrile, 1 1/2 x 11 1/2 In. 4000.00
Bowl, Centerpiece, Gold Iridescent, Optic Ribbed, Scalloped Rim, Favrile, 9 x 2 1/2 In. 920.00
Bowl, Centerpiece, Peacock Blue, Footed, Favrile, 3 x 11 1/4 In. 3000.00
Bowl, Gold Iridescent, Brown Pulled Feather, Tricornered, Favrile, 2 1/4 In. 450.00
Bowl, Gold Iridescent, Crackled, Favrile, 10 1/2 In. 719.00
Bowl, Gold Iridescent, Intaglio Cut, Leaf & Vine, Ruffled Edge, Favrile, 2 1/2 x 7 In. 1500.00
Bowl, Gold Iridescent, Optic Ribbed, Flared, Scalloped Rim, Favrile, 6 1/2 In. ....460.00 to 1035.00
Bowl, Gold Iridescent, Pink, Purple Highlights, Swirled Ribs, Fluted Rim, 7 3/4 In. 920.00
Bowl, Gold Iridescent, Ruffled Edge, Favrile, 4 1/4 In. 354.00
Bowl, Gold Iridescent, Swirled, Favrile, 1892-1928, 3 x 7 In. 1495.00
Bowl, Morning Glory, Favrile, c.1915, 4 3/4 x 9 5/8 In. 1410.00
Bowl, Peacock Blue Iridescent, Gold, Green Highlights, 4 1/2 In. 633.00
Bowl, Peacock Blue Iridescent, Green, Purple, Gold, Ribbed, Ruffled Edge, 6 1/4 In. 920.00
Bowl, Pink Pastel, Rolled Scalloped Rim, Favrile, 9 In. 460.00
Bowl, Pulled Feather, Iridescent, Opalescent, Flared Rim, 3 1/2 x 7 3/4 In. 1265.00
Bowl, Transparent Green, Red Pulled Feather, Favrile, 9 1/4 In. 316.00
Bowl, Underplate, Gold Iridescent, 8-Point, Ruffled Edge, Stretched, 2 1/2 x 6 In. 750.00
Candle Lamp, Gold Iridescent, Twisted Stem, Ruffled Shade, Favrile, Electrified, 11 In. 1668.00
Candle Lamp, Ivory, Twisted Stem, Ivory, Gold Ruffled & Stretched Shade, 13 1/2 In. 863.00
Candle Lamp, Peacock Blue Iridescent, Favrile, 14 In. 6000.00
Candle Lamp, Twisted Rib, Platinum, Blue Iridescent, Ruffled Shade, Electrified, 12 In. 1380.00
Candlestick, Flower Shape, Amethyst, Quatrefoil Cup, Clear Foot, 3 1/2 In., Pair 1315.00
Candlestick, Gold Iridescent, Twisted Stem, Flanged Cup, Favrile, 5 1/4 In., Pair 1200.00
Candlestick, Gold Iridescent, Twisted Stem, Lobed Base, Favrile, 6 x 4 In. 499.00
Candlestick, Green Cup, Stretched Rim, Ribbed, Opalescent, Footed, 11 1/2 In. 690.00
Compote, Amber Iridescent, Fruit Vines, Favrile, c.1900, 3 1/4 In. 320.00
Compote, Blue Iridescent, Diamond Optic, Ribbed Foot, Purple, Favrile, 5 3/4 In. 920.00
Compote, Blue Iridescent, Pedestal Base, 4 1/2 x 8 In. 3000.00
Compote, Chinese Gold, Ruffled & Cupped Bowl, Pedestal Base, 5 3/4 x 4 In. 800.00
Compote, Flower Shape, Gold Iridescent, Footed, Favrile, c.1908, 5 In. 1725.00
Compote, Gold Iridescent, Amethyst Highlights, Onion Skin Rim, Favrile, 6 In. 1610.00
Compote, Gold Iridescent, Flared Rim, Stretched, Favrile, 5 x 11 3/4 In. 1668.00
Compote, Gold Iridescent, Gold Foot, Blue Highlights, 8 1/4 x 4 In. 431.00

Compote, Gold Iridescent, Red, Green Highlights, 8 1/4 x 4 1/2 In. 633.00
Compote, Gold Iridescent, Ribbed Foot, Platinum, Pink, Blue, Favrile, 8 In. 546.00
Compote, Gold Iridescent, Scalloped Rim, Ribbed, 6 In. 805.00
Compote, Violet Stretched Rim, Opalescent Edge, Signed, 2 x 5 1/4 In. 850.00
Compote, Yellow Pastel Iridescent, Favrile, 2 x 2 1/2 In. 850.00
Cordial, Gold Iridescent, Pinched, Signed, 1 3/4 In., Pair 345.00
Creamer, Blue Iridescent, Platinum, Gold Highlights, Handle, Favrile, 6 1/2 In. 920.00
Decanter, Gold Iridescent, Pear Shape, Circular Neck, Chain, Stopper, Favrile, 11 In. 2128.00
Decanter, Gold Iridescent, Pinched, Footed, Stopper, Favrile, 10 In. 633.00
Dish, Sweetmeat, Gold Iridescent, Pulled Blue Feathers, Ruffled Edge, 3 1/4 In. 1131.00
Dish, Sweetmeat, Gold Iridescent, Ribbed, Favrile, c.1915, 2 x 6 5/8 In. 1175.00
Finger Bowl, Underplate, Blue Iridescent, Purple, Gold Highlights, Signed, 4 1/4 In. 863.00
Finger Bowl, Underplate, Gold Iridescent, Blue, Purple, Ruffled Edge, 6 1/4 In. 1205.00
Finger Bowl, Underplate, Gold Iridescent, Leaf, Vine, Millefiori Flowers, Signed, 5 In. 1150.00
Finger Bowl, Underplate, Gold Iridescent, Ruffled Edge, Favrile, Signed, 4 1/2 In. 460.00
Finger Bowl, Underplate, Green, Ribbed, Scalloped Rim, Favrile, 6 1/2 In. 1035.00
Flower Frog, Gold Iridescent, Mushroom Shape, Scalloped Foot, Favrile, 5 In. 403.00
Goblet, Gold, Iridescent, Rainbow Highlights, 3 1/2 In., 6 Piece 1725.00
Goblet, Pastel, Lavender Stripe Stem, Opalescent Foot, Favrile, 6 1/2 In. 1035.00
Jar, Cover, Gold Iridescent, Sunburst, Rounded, Favrile, 7 1/2 x 4 In. 1800.00
Jar, Cover, Gold Iridescent, Waves, Enameled, Favrile, 3 1/2 x 5 In. 1200.00
Lamp, Damascene, Evergreen Shape, Pulled Zigzag, Cut Insects, Favrile, 20 x 10 In. 3173.00
Lamp, Gold & Blue Iridescent Twisted Base, Green Leaves, Ruffled Shade, 12 In. 2350.00
Lamp, Gold Iridescent, King Tut Shade, Cushion Foot, c.1900, 13 In., Pair 4183.00
Loving Cup, Gold Iridescent, Green Leaf, Vine, 3 Handles, Favrile, 5 In. ....1440.00 to 2200.00
Mint Dish, Ivory Iridescent, Peacock Blue Border, Favrile, 7 In. 550.00
Mug, Gold Iridescent, Green Zigzag Bands, Reeded Handle, Favrile, 2 1/2 In. 335.00
Nut Dish, Gold Iridescent, Scalloped Rim, Favrile, 5 In. 575.00
Ornament, Jewel, Blue Iridescent, Favrile, 2 In. 350.00
Ornament, Jewel, Gold Iridescent, Favrile, 2 In. 325.00
Ornament, Rondel, Blue Iridescent, Shading To Purple Iridescent Center, 16 1/2 In. 4600.00
Ornament, Scarab, Red Iridescent, Favrile, 3/4 In. 150.00
Paperweight, Green Spots, Amber Ground, 2 1/2 x 2 3/4 In. 489.00
Paperweight, Turtleback, Iridescent, 5 3/4 x 4 1/2 In. 2500.00
Parfait, Moonlight, Opalescent White, Favrile, c.1915, 6 1/2 In. 499.00
Plate, Alabaster, Gold Iridescent, Favrile, 9 1/2 In. 3738.00
Plate, Coupe, Ceruean Blue, Iridescent, Pulled Feather, Favrile, c.1900, 7 3/4 In. 374.00
Plate, Green Pastel, Optic Ribbed, Stretched Rim, Favrile, 8 In. 460.00
Salt, Blue Iridescent, Ruffled Edge, Favrile, 3 In. ....150.00 to 430.00
Salt, Gold Iridescent, Favrile, c.1900, 2 3/4 In. 201.00
Salt, Gold Iridescent, Flared Rim, 4-Footed, Favrile, 1 1/4 x 2 1/4 In. 300.00
Salt, Gold Iridescent, Ruffled Edge, Favrile, 2 3/4 In. ....200.00 to 259.00
Shade, Ascot, Gold Iridescent, Pink, Blue, Ribbed, Red Ruffled Edge, Favrile, 5 1/4 In. 1150.00
Shade, Gold Iridescent, Ribbed, Ruffled Edge, Favrile, 5 1/8 x 2 1/4 In. 604.00
Shade, Lily, Amber Iridescent, Ribbed, White Opalescent, Ruffled Edge, 4 1/2 In. 2013.00
Shade, Lily, Gold Iridescent, Purple, Pink, Blue, Ribbed, Ruffled Edge, 4 1/4 In. 2128.00
Shade, Lily, Red, Ribbed, 4 1/4 In. 1955.00
Shade, Lily, Yellow, Green Pulled Design, 4 1/2 In. 1495.00
Shade, Lily, Yellow, Orange & Yellow Pulled Design, Bulbous, 4 1/4 In. 1783.00
Shade, Tulip, Gold Iridescent, Favrile, 5 1/4 x 2 1/4 In. 863.00
Tile, Turtleback, Amethyst Iridescent, Bronze Mount, Favrile, 6 x 5 In. 1150.00
Tumbler, Gold Iridescent, Corset Shape, Favrile, 4 In. 403.00
Tumbler, Gold Iridescent, Pigtail Prunts, Favrile, 3 In. 403.00
Tumbler, Whiskey, Gold Iridescent, Violet Highlights, Twisted Prunts, 1 3/4 In. 300.00
Vase, Agate, Brown Ground, Gold, Veining, Favrile, 6 3/4 In. 9200.00
Vase, Black, Pulled Blue Design, Favrile, Signed, 14 In. 3450.00
Vase, Blue Iridescent, Bronze Base, Favrile, Signed, 14 1/2 In. 1998.00
Vase, Blue Iridescent, Bronze, Platinum Pulled Swirl, Signed, 5 1/4 x 4 1/2 In. 5175.00
Vase, Blue Iridescent, Egg Shape, Handles, 3 In. 633.00
Vase, Blue Iridescent, Gold Highlights, Gourd Shape, Ribbed, Favrile, 3 In. 805.00
Vase, Blue Iridescent, Green Highlights, Bulbous, Ribbed, Favrile, c.1900, 2 3/4 In. 1016.00

Vase, Blue Iridescent, Green Pulled Heart, Vine, Favrile, Signed, 5 3/4 In. 2300.00
Vase, Blue Iridescent, Knopped Stem, Flared Rim, Favrile, c.1916, 10 In. 1150.00
Vase, Blue Iridescent, Optic Ribbed, Favrile, Signed, 3 In. 518.00
Vase, Blue Iridescent, Ribbed, Waisted Collar, Purple & Green, Flared Rim, 7 In. 633.00
Vase, Blue Iridescent, Silver, Green, Gold Chain, Favrile, 8 3/4 In. 633.00
Vase, Blue Shaded To Gold Iridescent, Elongated Neck, Favrile, Marked, 8 In. 1116.00
Vase, Blue, Black, Gold Iridescent, Squat, Urn Shape, Favrile, Signed, 4 1/4 In. 4888.00
Vase, Blue, Green, Egg Shape, Footed, c.1900, 5 1/2 In. 837.00
Vase, Blue, Purple Iridescent, Ribbed, Cupped Rim, Favrile, 5 1/2 In. 1800.00
Vase, Brown, White, Gold Iridescent Pulled Feathers, Favrile, 8 3/4 In. 3163.00
Vase, Bud, Gold Iridescent, Blue Highlights, Ribbed, 8 1/2 In. 776.00
Vase, Bud, Gold Iridescent, Green Pulled Leaf, Favrile, 10 1/2 In. 2000.00
Vase, Bud, Gold Iridescent, Pairpoint Silver Plated Stand, Favrile, 11 1/2 In. 622.00
Vase, Bud, Gold Iridescent, Ribbed, Flared Rim, Favrile, 10 x 3 1/2 In. 1410.00
Vase, Bud, Opal, Gold Iridescent Feathers, Favrile, 6 1/4 In. 575.00
Vase, Bud, Purple & Gold Iridescent, 8-Sided, Tapered, Flared Base, 7 x 2 In. 764.00
Vase, Cypriote, Black Iridescent, Silver, Favrile, 5 1/2 In. 6043.00
Vase, Cypriote, Gold Iridescent, Purple, Green Flashes, Signed, 7 1/2 x 8 In. 5175.00
Vase, Cypriote, Seafoam, Swirls, 3-Sided, Cushion Foot, c.1900, 7 1/2 In. 2868.00
Vase, Egyptian Chain, Green, Gold Iridescent Collar, Favrile, 9 1/2 In. 5463.00
Vase, Egyptian Shape, Gold Iridescent, Shouldered, Scrolled Handles, Favrile, 6 In. 1725.00
Vase, Flower Shape, Baluster, Striated Feathers, Ruffled Edge, Ribbed Base, 13 1/2 In. 9775.00
Vase, Flower Shape, Blue Iridescent, Favrile, 5 3/8 In. 2588.00
Vase, Flower Shape, Blue Iridescent, Favrile, c.1916, 4 3/4 In. 1668.00
Vase, Flower Shape, Blue Iridescent, Knopped Optic Ribbed Stem, Favrile, 11 1/2 In. 2530.00
Vase, Flower Shape, Gold Iridescent, Favrile, 1905, 9 7/8 In. 1350.00
Vase, Flower Shape, Gold Iridescent, Fuchsia, Green Highlights, Ribbed, 9 In. 1380.00
Vase, Flower Shape, Gold Iridescent, Optic Ribbed Body, Scalloped Rim, Favrile, 10 In. 863.00
Vase, Flower Shape, Gold Iridescent, Ruffled Edge, Favrile, c.1905, 11 1/2 In. 6613.00
Vase, Flower Shape, Green Pulled Feathers, Knopped Stem, Opalescent Foot, 12 In. 6900.00
Vase, Flower Shape, Green, Purple, Gold Iridescent, Ribbed, Ruffled Edge, 10 3/4 In. 2300.00
Vase, Flower Shape, Iridescent, 2 Rows Applied Lily Pads, Applied Foot, 12 1/4 In. 5463.00
Vase, Flower Shape, Opal, Gold Iridescent Foot, Pulled Feathers, Favrile, 4 1/4 In. 1495.00
Vase, Flower Shape, Opal, Green Iridescent Feathers, Amber Foot, Ruffled Edge, 5 In. 2588.00
Vase, Flower Shape, Opalescent, Pulled Chartreuse Leaves, Ruffed Edge, 4 7/8 In. 1955.00
Vase, Flower Shape, Pearly Opalescent, Striated Feathers, Ruffled Edge, 10 1/2 In. 3162.00
Vase, Flower Shape, Yellow, White, Opalescent, Clear Stem, Foot, Favrile, 1910, 9 In. 1115.00
Vase, Gold Iridescent & Alabaster, Green Pulled Design, Ribbed, Bulbous, 6 1/2 In. 4313.00
Vase, Gold Iridescent Pulled Zipper Pattern, Favrile, c.1927, 5 3/4 In. 2243.00
Vase, Gold Iridescent, Applied Green Leaves, Flared Rim, Favrile, 10 1/2 In. 2000.00
Vase, Gold Iridescent, Applied Raised Zipper, Bulbous, Favrile, 4 x 6 In. 1800.00
Vase, Gold Iridescent, Baluster Shape, Scalloped Rim, c.1900, 9 In. 1370.00
Vase, Gold Iridescent, Blue, Magenta, Dimpled Sides, c.1900, 2 3/4 In. 335.00
Vase, Gold Iridescent, Blue, Pink Highlights, Ribbed, Signed, 2 3/4 In. 546.00
Vase, Gold Iridescent, Blue, Red Highlights, Flared Foot, Rim, 4 3/4 In. 690.00
Vase, Gold Iridescent, Brown, Favrile, Signed, 4 1/4 In. 2588.00
Vase, Gold Iridescent, Bulbous Top, Pedestal Base, Favrile, 3 3/4 In. 950.00
Vase, Gold Iridescent, Dimpled Shoulder, Shaped Rim, Favrile, Signed, 3 1/2 In. 978.00
Vase, Gold Iridescent, Egg Shape, Pulled Handles, Footed, Favrile, c.1900, 3 3/4 In. 498.00
Vase, Gold Iridescent, Gold Heart, Favrile, Signed, 4 In. 4888.00
Vase, Gold Iridescent, Green & Gold Waves, Favrile, 5 3/8 In. 2875.00
Vase, Gold Iridescent, Green & Silver Pulled Feather, Bulbous, c.1929, 1 3/4 In. 809.00
Vase, Gold Iridescent, Green Ground, Pulled Feathers, Ribbed Bottle Shape, 8 In. 690.00
Vase, Gold Iridescent, Green Hearts, Vines, Signed, 2 1/2 x 3 1/2 In. 2013.00
Vase, Gold Iridescent, Green Trailings, Millefiori Flower, Favrile, 5 1/2 In. 4313.00
Vase, Gold Iridescent, Green, Blue Iridescent, Wavy Ribbon, 8 In. 4025.00
Vase, Gold Iridescent, Hooked Feathers, Baluster, Ruffled Edge, Favrile, 3 1/4 In. 978.00
Vase, Gold Iridescent, Hooked Feathers, Green Tips, Favrile, 1 1/2 In. 1093.00
Vase, Gold Iridescent, Intaglio Cut, Flower Swags, Coil Handles, Favrile, 6 1/4 In. 2300.00
Vase, Gold Iridescent, Magenta Highlights, Flanged Rim, Ribbed, 5 1/2 In. 1035.00
Vase, Gold Iridescent, Optic Ribbed, Bulbous, Footed, Favrile, 8 1/4 In. 805.00

Vase, Gold Iridescent, Optic Ribbed, Bulbous, Iridescent, Favrile, 8 1/4 In. 748.00
Vase, Gold Iridescent, Pulled Hearts & Vines, Round, Favrile, 2 1/2 In. 2200.00
Vase, Gold Iridescent, Red, Pink, Blue Highlights, Bulbous, 3 1/2 In. 748.00
Vase, Gold Iridescent, Ribbed, Red & Blue Highlights, Ruffled Edge, Favrile, 18 In. 2500.00
Vase, Gold Iridescent, Ribbed, Waisted, Green, Blue Flashes, Favrile, 8 In. 1121.00
Vase, Gold Iridescent, Ribs, Dimples, Rose & Blue Interior, Scalloped Rim, 4 1/2 In. 950.00
Vase, Gold Iridescent, Small Bottom, Bulbous, Rolled Rim, Pedestal Base, Favrile 950.00
Vase, Gold Iridescent, Translucent, Olive Green, Vertical Zipper, 8 In. 1294.00
Vase, Gold Top, Green Leaf Base, Favrile, c.1915, 11 3/4 In. 2350.00
Vase, Gold, Melon, Ribbed, Favrile, Signed, 2 3/4 In. 403.00
Vase, Green Hooked Feathers, Gold Iridescent, Urn Shape, Footed, Favrile, 4 In. 863.00
Vase, Green Iridescent, Pulled Zigzag, Baluster, c.1900, 7 1/2 In. 2739.00
Vase, Green, Blue Wave, Label, Favrile, 10 In. 316.00
Vase, Green, Bottle Shape, Favrile, c.1900, 10 In. 1315.00
Vase, Green, Gold Iridescent, Pulled Feathers, 2 1/4 In. 2875.00
Vase, Jack-In-The-Pulpit, Blue Iridescent, Ribbed, Footed, Favrile, c.1910, 13 1/4 In. 10925.00
Vase, Jack-In-The-Pulpit, Gold Iridescent, Pink Highlights, Signed, 9 In. 3738.00
Vase, Jack-In-The-Pulpit, Gold Iridescent, Raspberry Iridescent Center, 10 1/4 In. 5750.00
Vase, Jack-In-The-Pulpit, Gold, Iridescent Rainbow Highlights, Favrile, 13 1/2 In. 7475.00
Vase, Morning Glory, Yellow, Opal Veins, Ribbed, Flared Rim, 6 7/8 In. 690.00
Vase, Opal, Brown & Gold Pulled Feathers, c.1905, 2 1/2 In. 1035.00
Vase, Opalescent, Gold Iridescent Pulled Feather, Favrile, 1905, 10 In. 1227.00
Vase, Orange, Pulled Feathers, Double Gourd Shape, Pedestal Base, Favrile 3450.00
Vase, Paperweight, Flowers, Leaves, Gourd Shape, c.1900, 6 1/2 In. 5975.00
Vase, Peacock Blue, Ribbed, Pinched Rim, Favrile, 5 In. 1800.00
Vase, Platinum Iridescent, Blue, Purple, Green, Ribbed, Silver Neck, Rim, 4 1/2 In. 1035.00
Vase, Platinum, Gold Iridescent, Blue Highlights, Favrile, 8 In. 575.00
Vase, Purple Iridescent, Ruffled Edge, Favrile, 14 1/4 In. 805.00
Vase, Red Luster, Bulbous Midsection, Favrile, c.1906, 11 In. 6613.00
Vase, Red, Orange, Button Pontil, Favrile, 11 1/4 In. 5175.00
Vase, Stick Wisteria, White Opalescent, Favrile, 9 1/8 In. 2185.00
Vase, Tel El Amarna, Egyptian Chain, Blue Midsection, Black Neck, Favrile, 8 3/4 In. 8050.00
Vase, Transparent Green, Red & Gold Pulled Feathers, Signed, 5 7/8 In. 863.00
Vase, Trumpet, Blue Iridescent, Pulled Feather, Bronze Base, c.1915, 17 In. 1175.00
Vase, Trumpet, Gold Iridescent, 6-Sided, Favrile, c.1915, 7 5/8 In. 1057.00
Vase, Trumpet, Gold Iridescent, Favrile, 1910, 12 1/4 In. 2243.00
Vase, Trumpet, Gold Iridescent, Footed, Flaring Rim, Knopped Stem, Favrile, 8 In. 575.00
Vase, Trumpet, Gold Iridescent, Pink, Green, Blue Highlights, Flared Foot, 8 In. 460.00
Vase, Trumpet, Gold Iridescent, Ribbed, Favrile, c.1915, 10 5/8 In. 1175.00
Vase, Trumpet, Green, Leaf, Vine, Ribbed Applied Foot, Signed, 16 In. 3335.00
Vase, Yellow Over White, Egg Shape, Stand, Favrile, 6 In. 575.00
Wine, Gold Iridescent, Optic Ribbed Foot, Twisted Stem, Favrile, 7 In., Pair 1725.00
Wine, Green, Opalescent Foot, Ribbed Stem, Favrile, 7 1/4 In. 1093.00
TIFFANY GOLD, Frame, 14K Gold, BPA Monogram, Easel Back, 3 x 3 1/2 In. 633.00
TIFFANY POTTERY, Vase, Embossed Leaves & Vines, Unglazed, Bisque, 10 x 6 1/2 In. 4000.00
Vase, Embossed Leaves, Unglazed, Bisque, Bulbous, 4 1/2 x 3 In. 1500.00
Vase, Organic Design, Mustard Exterior, Mottling, 3 x 3 1/4 In. 3500.00
TIFFANY SILVER, Basket, Swing Handle, Acid Etched, Rose, Flowers, 1907-38, 8 1/4 In. 558.00
Berry Spoon, Flemish Pattern 175.00
Berry Spoon, Openwork, Strawberry Handle, Kidney Shape Bowl, 1900s, 9 1/2 In. 588.00
Bonbon, Openwork, Parcel Gilt Bowl, Prince Of Wales Feathers, c.1870, 12 In. 1195.00
Bonbon, Shallow Bowl, Scalloped Rim, Monogram, Woman Handle, c.1900, 5 1/4 In. 777.00
Bowl, Caviar, Sturgeon, Waves, Seagulls, Aesthetic Movement, c.1910, 8 In. 3346.00
Bowl, Centerpiece, Gold Wash Interior, Classical Woman, Cornucopia, 17 1/2 In. 9400.00
Bowl, Egg Shape, Rolled Rim, 4 Diapered Cartouches, 1902-07, 15 In. 1998.00
Bowl, Flared, Notched Rim, Art Deco, c.1930, 4 1/2 x 9 3/8 In. 960.00
Bowl, Fluted, HEW Monogram, 2 x 9 3/4 In. 748.00
Bowl, Fruit, Clover, Flowers, c.1850, 9 In. 837.00
Bowl, Fruit, Egg Shape, Acanthus Scrolls, Flower Urns, Dogs, Footed, 6 x 9 In. 1763.00
Bowl, Fruit, Egg Shape, Scalloped Edge, Acanthus Cartouches, 1907-38, 11 3/8 In. 470.00
Bowl, Gilt, Hammered, Stepped & Domed Foot, Engraved, c.1877, 7 1/2 In. 4800.00

Bowl, Lobed, Scalloped Edge, 2 1/4 x 5 3/4 In. 81.00
Bowl, Lotus Leaf Design, Art Deco, Tapering Sides, 1907-38, 6 In. 529.00
Bowl, Paneled, c.1940, 3 1/2 x 9 1/4 In. 1560.00
Bowl, Revere, Footed, 3 3/4 x 7 3/4 In. 240.00
Bowl, Revere, Footed, 5 x 10 In. 510.00
Bowl, Revere, Low Foot, Everted Rim, Horizontal Band, 1907-38, 5 5/8 In. 235.00
Bowl, Ring Foot, Fluted, Applied Wire Rim, Hammered, 2 1/2 x 9 1/2 In. 1000.00
Bowl, Scalloped Border, 7/8 x 5 1/4 In. 115.00
Bread Basket, Angular Handles, Engraved Rim, Low Foot, 1850s, 12 In. 382.00
Cake Plate, Ring Foot, 12 Flutes, Monogram, 1 x 10 1/4 In. 1400.00
Cake Plate, Sterling, c.1956, 10 3/4 In. 819.00
Candlestick, Chrysanthemum, 4 1/2 In., Pair 1035.00
Candlestick, Chrysanthemum, 9 1/2 In., Pair 4600.00
Candlestick, Leaves, Monogram, c.1902, 10 1/4 In., Pair 4358.00
Candlestick, Sunflowers, 9 1/4 In., Pair 4346.00
Chalice, Flower & Leaves, Gorsjen & Woodward, c.1853, 6 1/2 In., Pair 1380.00
Cheese Scoop, Stilton, Olympian, 7 1/2 In. 650.00
Chip Server, Saratoga Pattern, Ailanthus, Pierced Bowl, Clover, Monogram, c.1899, 8 3/4 In. 1912.00
Coffeepot, Repousse, Presentation, Tapered, c.1890, 8 3/4 In. 1528.00
Cup, Leather Case, 4 1/4 In. 176.00
Demitasse Set, Baluster, Berries, Round Salver, c.1950, 9 3/8-In. Pot, 4 Piece 1116.00
Dresser Set, Berry, Leaves, Acid Etched, Monogram, 1907-38, 11-In. Mirror, 9 Piece 764.00
Entree Server, Cover, Chrysanthemum, Oval, c.1907, 5 x 10 3/4 In., Pair 6573.00
Ewer, Baluster, Claw Feet, Flowers, Scroll, c.1892, 22 1/4 In. 4481.00
Fish Platter, Urn Decorated Ends, EF Monogram, Oval, 26 3/4 x 11 1/4 In. 2530.00
Flatware Set, Colonial Pattern, Early 20th Century, 127 Piece 4096.00
Flatware Set, English King Pattern, 81 Piece 6300.00
Flatware Set, Nursery Rhyme, Child's, 7 1/2 In., 3 Piece 230.00
Flatware Set, Olympian Pattern, Gilt, Late 20th Century, 25 Piece 1800.00
Flatware Set, San Lorenzo Pattern, Box, Mid 1900s, 112 Piece 9000.00
Flatware Set, Shell & Thread, 127 Piece 5265.00
Fork, Cold Meat, Grapevine, 9 In. 495.00
Goblet, Bell Shape Bowl, Slender Stem, 1907-38, 5 In. . . . . .176.00 to 206.00
Goblet, Bulbous, Flower, Leaf, Bowknot, Gilt Interior, 1870-75, 7 1/2 In., Pair 1287.00
Grooming Set, CCH Initials, 10 Piece 322.00
Ice Cream Server, Grapevine, Monogram, Gold Wash, c.1880, 10 3/4 In. . . . . .591.00 to 777.00
Ice Cream Slice, Persian, Scalloped Back, Monogram, c.1872, 12 1/4 In. 568.00
Jewelry Box, Racing Boat, c.1935, 7 5/8 x 3 3/8 x 2 1/8 In. 1945.00
Jug, Helmet Shape, Pedestal, Strap Handle, Monogram, 5 x 3 1/2 In. 975.00
Jug, Presentation, Baluster, Rope Band, Handle, Leaves, Poseidon Mask, 11 In. 9000.00
Julep Cup, Tapering, Waisted, Cylindrical, Footed, 1912, 12 Piece 5060.00
Loving Cup, Embossed Nude Woman, Sea Creature, Wreath, Scroll Handles, 8 1/2 In. 7480.00
Loving Cup, Presentation, Acid Etched Figure, 3 Handles, 1891-1902, 8 5/8 In. 2233.00
Loving Cup, Vase Shape, Everted Rim, Loop Handles, Trumpet Foot, Monogram, 9 In. 823.00
Mug, Chrysanthemum, Acid Etched, Cylindrical, 1875-91, 3 3/8 In. 588.00
Mug, Egg Shape, Ear Handle, Acanthus Leaf, Trumpet Foot, Moore, 4 3/8 In. 411.00
Mug, Japonisme Style, Geometric, Monogram, Gold Wash, c.1880, 3 3/4 In. 1293.00
Mug, Repousse Handle, Coin, 3 3/4 In. 220.00
Mustard Pot, Flat Lid, Repousse, Teardrop Thumbpiece, c.1891, 3 3/8 In. 294.00
Pastry Server, Grapevine, Triangular Blade, c.1872, 11 1/4 In. 809.00
Pick Set, Butter Or Seafood, Monogram, c.1861, 5 In., 11 Piece 205.00
Pitcher, Egg Shape, Short Spout, Flowers, Moorish Style Foliate, Ear Handle 3820.00
Pitcher, Frank Lloyd Wright, 1918 Design, Hexagonal Body, c.1985, 10 In. 4500.00
Pitcher, Hammered, Applied Copper Fish, 9 x 5 1/4 In. 62093.00
Pitcher, Presentation, Helmet Shape, Matte, Acanthus, 1871 Pigeon Club, 13 3/4 In. 1380.00
Pitcher, Repousse, Flowers, Egg Shape, Cylindrical Neck, Short Spout, 1875-91, 7 In. 3819.00
Pitcher, Water, Pinched Rim, C-Shaped Handle, Spreading Base, 1907-47, 7 1/2 In. 1058.00
Plate, Sports, Round, 9 3/4 In. 3335.00
Platter, Meat, Urn Decorated Ends, EF Monogram, Oval, 22 1/2 x 14 1/4 In. 2300.00
Preserve Spoon, English King, c.1890, 7 1/2 In. 191.00
Preserve Spoon, Grapevine, 8 7/8 In. 495.00

Never store silver in plastic wrap or newspapers or with rubber bands. They will all cause discoloration.

Tiffany Silver, Sardine Fork, Wave Edge, Parcel Gilt Tines, c.1884, 5 1/2 In.

Salad Set, Tomato, Leaves, Monogram, Gilt Bowls, c.1910, 9 3/4 In., 2 Piece 568.00
Salt, Georgian Style, Oblong, Gadroon, Acanthus, Flowers, 1875-91, 3 5/8 In., Pair 470.00
Salt, Persian Band, Flower Style Rim, Conical Foot, c.1875, 1 1/2 x 2 3/4 In. 717.00
Salver, Armorial & Flower Border, Husk Molded Edge, 3 Beaded Feet, 10 In. 441.00
Salver, Pierced Gallery, Square, Concave Corners, 1891-1902, 12 1/4 In. 1998.00
Salver, Rocaille Scrolls Rim, Square, Canted Corners, Monogram, 1875-91, 11 In. 1293.00
Sardine Fork, Wave Edge, Parcel Gilt Tines, c.1884, 5 1/2 In. .... *ILLUS* 359.00
Sauce Ladle, Japanese Pattern, Scalloped Rim, Monogram, c.1871, 8 1/2 In. 1135.00
Sauce Ladle, Vine, Grapevine, Monogram, 1872-91, 7 1/2 In. 411.00
Serving Fork, 4 Tines, Scalloped Edge, Peapod Pattern, c.1872, 8 3/4 In. 1121.00
Serving Spoon, Gold Washed Bowl, Apple Stem, Art Deco, c.1925, 9 1/2 In. 470.00
Stuffing Spoon, Saratoga Pattern 950.00
Sugar & Creamer, Oval, Short Spout, Swing Handle, c.1938, 3 3/4 In. 235.00
Sugar Sifter, Broom Corn, Openwork Bowl, c.1890, 7 In. 388.00
Tazza, Downswept Rim, Scrolls, Bellflowers, Acanthus, Ferns, Spreading Foot, 9 In. 705.00
Tea & Coffee Set, Edward C. Moore, c.1865, 9 1/2 x 30 In. 6000.00
Tea & Coffee Set, Flowers, Scrolls, Claw Feet, Monogram, c.1892, 6 Piece 3884.00
Tea Caddy, Rosettes, Asian Swags, Enameled, c.1891, 4 1/4 In. 19200.00
Tea Set, Repousse, Flower & Leaf, 5 1/2-In. Teapot, 4 Piece 2070.00
Tea Set, Squat, Egg Shape, Peaked Lids, 1902-07, 12 3/4-In. Teapot, 4 Piece 2350.00
Tea Set, Tete-A-Tete, Squat, Vase Shaped, Helmet Creamer, 1907-38, 6-In. Pot, 3 Piece 646.00
Tea Strainer, Bead & Scroll Design Rim, Ivory Handle, 1880, 6 1/2 In. 415.00
Tongs, Asparagus, Wave Edge, Gilt Blades, Pierced, c.1884, 7 1/2 In. 1554.00
Tongs, Sugar, Japanese Pattern, Bird, Reeds, Flowers, c.1910, 4 1/4 In. 436.00
Tray, 6-Sided, Hand Hammered, B Monogram, 16 1/2 In. 2875.00
Tray, Gadroon Rim, Oval, 1921-47, 22 x 16 In. 2400.00
Tray, Ribbed Edge, Round, EF Monogram, 13 In. 920.00
Tray, Triangular Petal Shape, Rolled Edge, 3 Ball Feet, 1 1/2 x 7 In. 288.00
Trophy, Yachting, Chased, Leaves, Tridents, Classical Scenes, c.1892, 16 In. 36000.00
Tureen, Dome Cover, Egg Shape, Chased, Embossed, Acanthus, 1875-91, 10 1/2 In. 1880.00
Tureen, Oblong, Acanthus, Oblong, Monogram, 1875-91, 4 1/2 x 8 x 7 3/4 In. 1410.00
Vase, Figures, Flowers, Footed, Handles, 17 1/2 In. 4388.00
Vase, Raised Palmette Band, Round Stepped Foot, Monogram, 12 In. 1762.00
Vase, Trumpet, Horizontal Band, Anthemion Lappets, 1907-38, 12 In. 1175.00

TIFFIN Glass Company of Tiffin, Ohio, was a subsidiary of the United States Glass Co. of Pittsburgh, Pennsylvania, in 1892. The U.S. Glass Co. went bankrupt in 1963, and the Tiffin plant employees purchased the building and the inventory. They continued running it from 1963 to 1966, when it was sold to Continental Can Company. In 1969, it was sold to Interpace, and in 1980, it was closed. The black satin glass, made from 1923 to 1926, and the stemware of the last twenty years are the best-known products.

Arcadian, Plate, Bread & Butter, Pink, 6 In. 7.00
Arcadian, Plate, Salad, Pink, 8 In. 12.00
Byzantine, Cocktail, 3 Oz. 29.00
Cerise, Ashtray, 8-Sided, Handles, 3 3/4 In. 40.00
Cherokee Rose, Champagne, 6 Oz. 17.00

Cherokee Rose, Cocktail, 3 Oz., 5 1/4 In. 60.00
Chipperfield, Dresser Set, Green, 3 Piece 135.00
Empress Modern, Bowl, Blue, Pulled Wings, 7 3/4 x 13 In. 135.00
Flanders, Plate, Pink, 8 In. .... 32.00 to 35.00
Flanders, Tumbler, Iced Tea, Footed, 5 3/4 In. 100.00
Flanders, Tumbler, Pink, Footed, 10 Oz., 4 3/4 In. 65.00
Flanders, Tumbler, Soda, Pink, Footed, 5 Oz., 3 7/8 In. 70.00
Flanders, Vase, Pink, Flared Rim, Footed, 8 In. 675.00
Flower Garden, Candlestick, Black, 6 1/2 In. 238.00
Fontaine, Console, Rose Pink, Etched Birds & Birdcages, Rolled Rim, 13 In. 80.00
Franciscan Ondine, Goblet, Water, 10 Oz. 100.00
Fucshia, Candlestick, 2-Light, Pair 125.00
Fucshia, Console, Footed, 12 In. 57.00
Fucshia, Vase, Bud, 10 1/12 In. 38.00
June Night, Bowl, 11 In. 68.00
June Night, Tumbler, Iced Tea, Footed, 10 1/2 Oz., 6 3/4 In. 23.00
King's Crown, Bowl, Wide Flat Rim, 12 In. 85.00
King's Crown, Goblet, Amethyst, 4 3/8 In. 10.00
King's Crown, Wedding Bowl, Cover, Ruby Stain, Pedestal Base 175.00
Laurel, Goblet, Wine, Gold Encrusted, 6 1/4 In. 40.00
Liege, Goblet, Wine, 3 7/8 In. 18.00
Majesty, Champagne, 6 Oz. 10.00
Milady, Dresser Set, Pink Satin, 5 Piece 350.00
Mirage, Goblet, 10 Oz., 6 3/4 In. 25.00
Modern, Vase, Copen Blue, Cylindrical, 12 x 4 In. 140.00
Modern, Vase, Flip, Blue, 8 In. 85.00
Mystic, Goblet, 9 Oz., 5 3/4 In. 45.00
Oak Lawn, Goblet, 10 Oz., 6 3/4 In. 25.00
Paula, Goblet, 10 Oz., 7 3/4 In. 29.00
Persian Pheasant, Champagne, 6 Oz. 29.00
Persian Pheasant, Cocktail, 3 Oz. 34.00
Poppy, Vase, Black, Satin, 5 1/2 x 4 In. 35.00
Princess, Pitcher, 8 1/2 In. 175.00
Princess, Sherbet, 6 Oz. 13.00
Princess, Tumbler, Whiskey, 2 Oz. 18.00
Princess, Wine, 3 1/2 Oz., 4 1/2 In. 25.00
Queen Astrid, Dish, Mayonnaise, Underplate 40.00
Rambler Rose, Dish, Mayonnaise, Pink, Gold Encrusted 40.00
Rambler Rose, Tumbler, Pink, Gold Encrusted, 3 7/8 In. 23.00
Shooting Star, Champagne, 6 Oz., 4 1/2 In. 20.00
Spiral Optic, Plate, Salad, Green, 7 1/2 In. 8.00
Swedish Optic, Pitcher, Footed, No. 5935 .... 71.00
Swedish Optic, Rose Bowl, 4-Footed .... 71.00 to 100.00
Twilight, Bowl, 4 Scroll Feet, 4 x 10 x 6 1/4 In. 290.00
Twilight, Bowl, Flared, Wide Ruffled Edge, 4 x 12 In. 140.00
Twilight, Rose Bowl, Scalloped Rim, 3 1/2 x 5 1/2 In. 65.00
Twilight, Vase, Cornucopia, 2-Footed 195.00
Twilight, Vase, Flared Ruffled Edge, 4 3/4 x 5 3/4 In. 68.00
Twilight, Vase, Folded Sides, Rounded Square Rim, 7 x 5 1/2 In. 240.00
Valencia, Wine, Rose, Gold Encrusted, 6 3/4 In. 30.00
Wisteria, Vase, 4 Scroll Feet, 7 5/8 x 4 1/4 In. 145.00

TILES have been used in most countries of the world as a sturdy building material for floors, roofs, fireplace surrounds, and surface toppings. The cuerda seca (dry cord) technique of decoration uses a greasy pigment to separate different glaze colors during firing. In cuenca (raised line) decorated tiles, the design is impressed, leaving ridges that separate the glaze colors. Many American tiles are listed in this book under the factory name. Many of the American tiles are listed in this book under the factory name.

3 Men, Wearing Sombreros, Cock Fight, Multicolored Glaze, Cuerda Seca, Rustic Frame, 6 In. 470.00

Birds, Cobalt Blue Scrolls, Pottery, Multicolored, Qajar, Persia, c.1785, 6 x 7 In., Pair 295.00
Calla Lilies, White, Stylized, Blue Heart, Green Ground, Boizenburg, Cuenca, 6 In., 4 Piece 235.00
Embossed Putti, Goat, Emerald Green Glaze, Art Pottery, 1900s, 11 1/2 x 6 In. 80.00
Eucalyptus Tree, Windmill, Mountain Landscape, Claycraft, Arts & Crafts Frame, 16 x 4 In. 1295.00
Figures, Kneeling, Praying, Incised, Outlined, Stylized Sun, Harding, Black, c.1945, 5 1/2 In. 705.00
Flower, Stylized, Red, Gold, Geometric Indigo, Blue, Cuenca, Rohn, 6 In., 6 Piece 645.00
Forest Landscape, Deer, W. Georges, Frame, c.1900, 23 1/2 x 13 3/4 In. 527.00
Frieze, Hilly Landscape, Stylized, Herman Mueller, Arts & Crafts Frame, 6 x 24 In., 4 Piece 3525.00
Frieze, Leaves, Barries, Celadon, Amber, Green, Blue & Amber Border, 6 In., 6 Piece 235.00
Frieze, Majolica, Swans, Water Lilies, Cattails, Dragonflies, Multicolored, 5 3/4 In., 8 Piece 410.00
Frieze, New York City Panorama, Harris Strong, Frame, 9 1/2 x 40 In., 6 Piece 325.00
George Washington Bookplate, Crest, Result Justifies The Deed, Square, Wheeling, 6 In. 95.00
Leaves, Berries, Green, Encaustic Tile Co., Square, 6 In. 120.00
Man, Woman, Child, Kneeling, Flowers, Pottery, Blue Ground, Persia, 8 1/2 x 8 1/2 In. 585.00
Mission, Incised, Outlined, Multicolored Matte Glazes, Harding, Black, c.1945, 5 1/2 In. 880.00
Parrot, Green, Pink & Blue Ground, Cuenca, Slon & Schlemme, Arts & Crafts Frame, 5 In. 235.00
Persian Antelope, Old Ivory, Green Glaze, Moravian, 7 x 6 In., Pair 529.00
Viking Ship, Molded, Franklin, Matte, Glossy, Multicolored, 8 In. 235.00
Windmill Landscape, Farm Cottage, Molded, Rustic Period Frame, 6 In., Pair 529.00

TINWARE containers for household use have been made in America since the seventeenth century. The first tin utensils were brought from Europe, but by 1798, tin plate was imported and local tinsmiths made the wares. Painted tin is called *tole* and is listed separately. Some tin kitchen items may be found listed under Kitchen. The lithographed tin containers used to hold food and tobacco are listed in the Advertising category under Tin.

Basket, Woven, Intertwining Banding, Applied Ring Corners, Handle, 5 3/4 x 4 x 3 1/2 In. 440.00
Cheese Strainer, Heart Shape, Punched, 1 5/8 x 4 x 3 3/4 In. 110.00
Cheese Strainer, Heart Shape, Punched, Holes, Slots, Scroll Feet, Handle, 3 3/4 x 7 1/4 In. 220.00
Cheese Strainer, Heart Shape, Straight Feet, 3 3/4 x 4 1/2 x 4 1/2 In. 120.00
Coffeepot, Cone Shape, Scroll Work, C-Shaped Handle, Straight Spout, 10 1/2 x 6 In. 165.00
Coffeepot, Punched, Tulips, Chain Banding, Hinged Lid, Gooseneck Spout, 11 x 7 In. 1210.00
Coffeepot, Punched, Tulips, Intertwined Lines, Brass Finial, 11 In. 230.00
Infant Feeder, Loop Handle, 4 In. 210.00
Mold, Candle, 36 Tube, Gray Paint, 11 x 8 In. 175.00
Pattern, Weather Vane, Prancing Horse, Pierced Eye, 17 1/2 x 22 In. 165.00
Roaster Oven, Wrought Iron Spit, Side Drip Spout, 18 1/4 x 9 1/2 In. 86.00
Sconce, 3-Light, Arched Shape, Crimped Crest, Punched Hanging Hole, 13 In. 390.00
Sconce, Candle, Mirrored, Oval Reflector, Crimped Rim, 11 In., Pair 2468.00
Sconce, Candle, Punched, Crimped Reflectors, Painted, Early 1900s, 10 To 13 In., 7 Piece 880.00
Tea Caddy, Cover, Painted, Red, Yellow Orange, Green Flowers, Early 1800s, 5 In. 235.00

TOBACCO CUTTERS may be listed in either the Advertising or Store categories.

TOBACCO JAR collectors search for those made in odd shapes and colors. Because tobacco needs special conditions of humidity and air, it has been stored in special containers since the eighteenth century.

Baseball Team, Georgetown University Crest, Ceramic, c.1890, 5 1/2 x 4 3/4 In. 1160.00
Black Man, Top Hat Cover, Ceramic, 7 1/2 In. 69.00
Glass, Amber, Wm. S. Kimball & Co., Rochester, N.Y., 6 In. 20.00
Humidor, Black Girl, Scarf, White, Pink & Green Stripes, Hand Painted, Porcelain, 5 In. 232.00
Humidor, Chinese Man, Hand Painted, Porcelain, 4 1/2 In. 110.00
Humidor, Cover, 1700's Fishing Scene, Adnian Reg., England, 5 x 5 In. 110.00
Humidor, English Spaniel, 2-Sided, Hand Painted, Porcelain, 6 In. 75.00
Man's Head, Black Hat, Ceramic, 7 1/2 In. 60.00
Woman's Head, Art Nouveau, Pottery, Czechoslovakia, 9 In. 106.00

TOBY JUG is the name of a very special form of pitcher. It is shaped like the full figure of a man or woman. A pitcher that shows just the top half of a person is not correctly called a toby. More examples of toby jugs can be found under Royal Doulton and other factory names.

Tole, Box, Document, Dome Top, Red Fruit, Leaves, Tin Hasp, 2 7/8 x 4 x 2 3/4 In.

Tole, Box, Document, Painted Fruit, Black Ground, Tin Hasp, 5 5/8 x 9 x 4 1/2 In.

Andrew Harding, 1940s, Miniature, 2 In. 20.00
Duke Of Wellington, Brown Flint Glaze, England, 8 In. 90.00
English Man, Beer Stein, Cigar, Green Coat, Yellow Vest, Black Hat, Miniature 60.00
Gentleman, With Claret Glass, Jug, Allertons, 4 1/2 x 4 1/4 x 3 3/4 In. 225.00
Long John Silver, Parrot On Shoulder, Shorter & Son Ltd., England, 1940s, 9 3/4 In. 385.00
Man, Blue Sponging Over White, Initialed AG, 5 1/4 In. 230.00
Man, Tricorner Hat, Pint Of Ale & Cigar, Devonmoir, 7 x 4 1/4 x 6 1/4 In. 175.00
Mr. Pickwick, Standing, W. Kent Potteries, Staffordshire, England, 1890s, 7 1/2 In. 180.00
Napoleon, Alfred Evans, Late 1800s, 8 1/2 In. 60.00
Old Lady, Burlington Ware, J. Shaw Potteries, Staffordshire, England, 6 In. 56.00
Pink Luster Trim, Allertons, England, 1800s, 5 1/4 In. 127.00

TOLE is painted tin. It is sometimes called *japanned ware, pontypool*, or *toleware*. Most nineteenth-century tole is painted with an orange-red or black background and multicolored decorations. Many recent versions of toleware are made and sold. Related items may be listed in the Tinware category.

Basket, Woven, Intertwining Bands, Applied Ring Corners, Handle, 5 3/4 x 4 x 3 1/2 In. 440.00
Box, Document, Dome Lid, Drapery, Flowers, Leaves, Wire Ring, Tin Hasp, 5 x 9 x 4 3/4 In. 115.00
Box, Document, Dome Lid, Multicolored Flowers, Stenciled, Brass Bail Handle, 1800s, 9 1/2 In. .. 55.00
Box, Document, Dome Lid, Wire Pull, Japanned, Flowers, Pin Stripes, 5 1/2 x 9 x 4 1/2 In. 440.00
Box, Document, Dome Lid, Wire Ring, Black Ground, Red Fruit, Yellow, Green, 4 x 3 In. 115.00
Box, Document, Dome Lid, Yellow Swags, White Band, Red Roses, Tin Hasp, 9 x 4 1/4 In. 635.00
Box, Document, Dome Top, Red Fruit, Leaves, Tin Hasp, 2 7/8 x 4 x 2 3/4 In. .... ***ILLUS*** 115.00
Box, Document, Japanned, Yellow, Red Swags, Pomegranate, Wire Ring Handle, 8 x 4 In. 430.00
Box, Document, Painted Fruit, Black Ground, Tin Hasp, 5 5/8 x 9 x 4 1/2 In. .... ***ILLUS*** 431.00
Box, Document, Peaked Lid, Flower, Decal, Woman, Wire Handle, Red, Oval, 7 3/4 x 10 In. 415.00
Box, Document, Red & Green Flowers, Leaves, Black, Japanned, Tin Hasp, 5 1/2 x 8 3/4 x 5 In. 173.00
Box, Document, Red, Blue & Yellow Flowers, White Band, Japanned, Bail Handle, 5 x 8 1/2 In. 630.00
Box, Document, Stylized Flower, Japanned Black, Multicolored, Wire Pull, 5 1/2 x 9 In. 275.00
Box, Flowers, Oval, Wire Pull, Japanned Black, White Band, Multicolored, 6 1/4 x 9 x 6 1/2 In. 440.00
Box, Oval, Red & Yellow Flowers, Green Leaves, Yellow Ground, 4 7/8 x 7 x 5 In. .... ***ILLUS*** 201.00
Box, Oval, Yellow Ground, Red & Yellow Flowers, Buckley Maine, 7 x 5 1/4 x 5 In. 3165.00
Box, Red Ground, Black, Red, Yellow Flowers, Curlicues, Tin Hasp, Handle, Oval, 4 x 6 x 4 In. 430.00
Box, Seminude Woman, Oval, 18th Century, 7/8 x 3 1/2 x 5 1/2 In. 820.00
Box, Shoeshine, Polychrome, Cast Iron Shoe Rest, 1800s, 9 x 10 In. 2585.00
Bread Tray, Fruit, Flowers, Late 1800s, 13 1/2 In. 259.00
Bread Tray, Fruit, Wreath, Flared Ends, Tapered Sides, 3 3/4 x 13 1/2 x 8 1/2 In. 95.00
Bread Tray, Japanned Black, Flowers, S Banding, Flared Ends, 2 1/4 x 13 1/4 x 7 1/4 In. 110.00
Bread Tray, Multicolored Flowers, Flared Ends, Japanned, 2 1/4 x 13 1/4 x 7 1/4 In. 110.00
Candlestick, Yellow, Flared Rim, Loop Carry Handle, Saucer Base, 1 1/2 In. 138.00
Canister, Dome Lid, Japanned Black, Green, Yellow, Red Flowers, 3 x 2 7/8 In., Pair 20.00
Canister, Flowers, Leaves, Yellow Highlights, 19th Century, 7 1/4 In. 200.00

Tole, Box, Oval, Red & Yellow Flowers, Green Leaves, Yellow Ground, 4 7/8 x 7 x 5 In.

Tole, Tray, Red, Yellow, Green Flowers, Yellow Swags, Black Ground, 7 3/4 x 13 1/2 In.

Canister, Spice, Dome Lid, Japanned, 3 x 2 7/8 In., Pair 20.00
Canister, Tea, Black Ground, Gilt Stencils, Merchant Scenes, Round Lid, 21 x 12 In., Pair 4115.00
Canister, Tea, Peach, Black Ground, Green Leaves, Yellow Pinstripe, Cylindrical, 6 3/4 In. 178.00
Clock, Bronze Rim, France, 19th Century, 14 In. 468.00
Coal Hod, Black, Flowers, Cast Iron Feet, Removable Inner Bucket, 24 x 15 x 10 In. 290.00
Coffeepot, Cone Shape, Leaf Swags, Berries, Leaves, Pa., 1800s, 9 In. 3885.00
Coffeepot, Cone Shape, Red, Flowers, Swags, Band Border, Pa., 1800s, 11 In. 3000.00
Coffeepot, Cone Shape, Straight Spout, Flowers, Pa., 1800s, 8 3/4 In. 1435.00
Coffeepot, Dome Lid, Red, Yellow, Crosshatched Flowers, Fruit, Black Ground, 10 1/2 In. 805.00
Coffeepot, Dome Top, Cone Shape, Fruit, Striped Band, Penn., 1800s, 11 In. 1675.00
Coffeepot, Flowers, Black, Red, Yellow, Green, 19th Century, 8 1/2 In. 3450.00
Coffeepot, Fruit, Black, Red, Yellow, 19th Century 6325.00
Coffeepot, Lighthouse Shape, Hinged Dome Lid, Strap Handle, Fruit, Leaves, 11 1/4 In. 2350.00
Coffeepot, Red, Flowers, Fruit, Swag Design Rim, Straight Spout, Loop Lift, 9 In. 910.00
Coffeepot, Strap Handle, Gooseneck Spout, Green, Yellow Flowers, 10 1/2 In. 3680.00
Coffeepot, Yellow Fruit, Leaves, Red, Spout, 10 3/4 x 9 x 6 1/2 In. 345.00
Creamer, Red, Green, Yellow Flowers, Japanned Ground, Loop Handle, Scrolled Finial, 4 In. 485.00
Cup, Pomegranate, C-Shaped Handle, Yellow Ground, Child's, 2 7/8 x 2 1/4 In. 330.00
Cup, Pomegranate, Yellow Ground, Red, White, Green, C-Shaped Handle, Child's, 3 x 2 1/4 In. 330.00
Fish Horn, Red, Green & Yellow Swag, 19 3/4 In. 336.00
Kindling Bin, Tin, Painted, 19th Century, 19 x 19 x 13 1/2 In. 205.00
Lantern, Conical Lid, Looped Handle, Hinged Door & Clasp, Punched, Gold, 8 1/2 x 3 3/4 In. 193.00
Match Safe, John J. Perley, Jr., Nov.18, 1859 .... 85.00
Mug, Pomegranate, Black Ground, Red Yellow Leaves, C-Shaped Handle, 4 1/2 x 3 1/4 In. 110.00
Pail, Flowers, Embossed Band, Pressed, Tapered Sides, Wire Bail Handle, 3 x 2 1/2 In. 95.00
Pail, Flowers, Pressed Tin, Wire Bail Handle, Embossed Bands, Red Ground, 3 x 2 1/2 In. 95.00
Pail, Pomegranate, Tapered Sides, Wire Bail Handle, Footed Base, Green Ground, 2 5/8 In. 605.00
Pail, Stylized Yellow Pomegranate, Wire Bail Handle, Footed Base, Green, 2 5/8 x 2 1/2 In. 605.00
Pin & Ink Sander, Black, Leaf Band, Yellow, Green, Red, Cylindrical, 2 1/2 x 2 3/4 In. 10.00
Plate Warmer, Domed Lid, Hinged Door, Floral Ground, Paw Feet, 1900, 30 x 18 In. 510.00
Pot, Gooseneck Spout, Yellow Birds, Pennsylvania, 1800s, 10 1/2 In. 825.00
Sconce, Candle, Miniature, 5 In. 1840.00
Spice Box, Cloves, Slant Lid, 10 x 6 3/4 In. 200.00
Spice Chest, 8 Drawers, Molded Top, Flowers, Fruit, Pinstripe, 13 1/4 x 9 x 3 1/2 In. 220.00
Stand, 2 Tiers, Removable Trays, Yellow Ground, Black Transfer, 23 1/4 x 19 x 14 In. 546.00
Sugar, Cover, Black, Red Flower, Double Scroll Lift, 3 1/2 In. 195.00
Sugar, Cover, Fruit & Tulips, White Band, Japanned Ground, 4 x 3 3/4 In. 575.00
Syrup, Strap Handle, Stylized Flowers, Blossom, Brushstrokes, 4 In. 646.00
Tea Caddy, Black, Stenciled, Hand Painted Birds, Flowers, Fruit, Acorn Finial, 7 x 4 1/2 In. 80.00
Tea Caddy, Flowers, Yellow Leaf Sprays, 5 x 3 1/2 In. 525.00
Tea Caddy, Flowers, Yellow Leaves, 5 x 3 1/2 In. 525.00
Tea Caddy, Fruit, Yellow, Red, Green, 6 3/4 In. 5290.00
Tea Caddy, Red & Green Flowers, Yellow Swags, White Band, Black Ground, 5 3/4 In. 172.00

Teapot, Red & Yellow Design, Black Ground, Hinged Lid, Straight Spout, 5 1/2 In. 259.00
Tray, Apple, Crystallized Center, Red & Green Flowers & Berries, Flared Ends, 2 1/2 x 13 1/4 x 8 In. 390.00
Tray, Birds, Rocaille, Gilt Stencil, Black Ground, Trestle Stand, 1800s, 20 x 28 x 22 In. 470.00
Tray, Black, Fruit & Flowers, Crystallized Center, Octagonal, 12 1/4 x 8 3/4 In. 385.00
Tray, Flowers, Birds, Scalloped Rim, 25 x 19 In. 450.00
Tray, Flowers, Fruit, Loops, Flared Sides, Octagonal, 12 1/4 x 8 3/4 In. 660.00
Tray, Flowers, Leaves, Black Ground, Red Striped Borders, Rectangular, 20 1/4 x 28 In. 230.00
Tray, Flowers, Yellow, Green, Black Ground, Octagonal, 18 x 11 3/4 In. 50.00
Tray, Hilly Landscape, Buildings, Gold Color Border, Victorian, 18 1/4 x 24 1/2 In. 4200.00
Tray, Japanned, Red Tulips, Blue Flowers, Zachariah Stevens, Maine, 7 1/2 x 13 In. 374.00
Tray, Man, Smoking Pipe, Flowers, Vine Border, Victorian, Late 1800s, 28 In. 176.00
Tray, Oval, Reticulated Rim, Punched Handholds, Flower Spray, Black Ground, 29 3/4 In. 355.00
Tray, Peaches, Leaves, Cut Corner, c.1825, 17 1/4 x 11 3/4 In. 210.00
Tray, Peacock, Flowers, Black Ground, Round Corners, Cutout Handles, 18 x 24 1/4 In. 190.00
Tray, People, Livestock, Water, House, Statue, Oval, 19 1/2 x 25 1/4 In. 550.00
Tray, Pontypool, Parrot & Leaves, Multicolored, Parcel Gilt, Late 1800s, 25 x 19 In. 325.00
Tray, Pressed Tin, Yellow Ground, Green, White, Red, Metallic Flowers, 6 x 5 5/8 In. 825.00
Tray, Red Bird, Leaves, 1800s, 12 1/2 x 8 1/2 In. 525.00
Tray, Red, Yellow, Green Flowers, Yellow Swags, Black Ground, 7 3/4 x 13 1/2 In. .... *ILLUS* 230.00
Tray, Reticulated Gallery Rim, Neoclassical, En Grisaille, Fortune Reserve, 26 x 18 In. 765.00
Tray, Roses, Leaves, Black Ground, Gold Feather Edge, 12 In. 450.00
Tray, Scalloped Edge, Flowers, Mother-Of-Pearl, On Stand, Regency Style Stretcher, 19 x 32 In. ... 490.00
Tray, Steam Engine, Tender, Box Cars, Flowers, Stamped Cross, Shaped Rim, 12 x 8 3/4 In. 60.00
Tray, Yellow & Red Swags, White & Red Flowers, Black, Japanned, 7 3/4 x 14 1/4 In. 345.00
Urn, Chestnut, Black, Gilt Chinoiserie, Spire Lid, Lion Mask Handles, 11 3/4 In., Pair 2585.00
Vase, Garniture, Baluster, Goat Masque, Grisaille, Brass Mount, Restauration, 8 3/4 In., Pair 822.00
Vase, Urns, Goddesses, Flared Rim, Paw Feet, Square Base, France, 13 x 7 3/8 In. 120.00
Waiter, Bird, Flowers, Scroll Border, 1800s, 27 3/4 x 20 3/4 In. 145.00
Wall Box, Blue Paint, 9 In. 518.00
Wall Sconce, Candleholder, Drip Pan, Punch Reflector, 8 x 8 x 4 1/2 In. 28.00
Wall Sconce, Circular Crest, Crimped Rim, Half Moon Base, Electrified, 13 3/4 x 5 In., Pair 138.00
Wall Sconce, Crimped Circle Crest, Half Moon Base, Electrified, 13 3/4 x 5 1/4 In. 55.00
Wall Sconce, Fan Crest, Punched, Reeded, Half Moon Base, Painted, Electrified, 13 3/4 x 5 In. ... 110.00
Washbasin, Faucet Front, Flowers, Mustard Ground, France, c.1890, 30 x 14 In. 295.00
Watering Can, Gooseneck Spout, Footed, Swivel Bail Handle, 3 x 2 5/8 In. 83.00
Watering Can, Gooseneck Spout, Tapered Sides, Footed, Red, 3 1/4 x 2 5/8 In. 83.00

TOM MIX was born in 1880 and died in 1940. He was the hero of over 100 silent movies from 1910 to 1929, and 25 sound films from 1929 to 1935. There was a Ralston Tom Mix radio show from 1933 to 1950, but the original Tom Mix was not in the show. Tom Mix comics were published from 1942 to 1953.

Badge, Ranch Boss, Brass, 1938, 1 7/8 In. 315.00
Booklet Set, Tom Mix Adventure Stories, National Chicle, Wrapper, 1934, 48 Cards 4930.00
Button, Miracle Rider, 1935, 1 1/4 In. 480.00
Button, Tom Mix Circus, Color, 1936-37, 1 3/4 In. 85.00
Decoder, Secret Code, Cardboard, Center Rivet, From Secret Ink Writing Kit, 1938, 3/4 In. 56.00
Gum Wrapper, Tom Mix Adventure Stories, Deputy Ring Offer, c.1935, 5 x 5 3/4 In. 100.00
Gun, Wood, Logo & Name On Grips, 1930s, 8 In. 100.00
Lariat, Humming, On Cardboard, 1935, 2 1/2 x 4 In. 85.00
Spurs, Cowboy, Glow In Dark, Aluminum, Plastic Rowels, Box, c.1949, 1 1/4 x 3 x 5 In. 154.00
Television, Film Viewer, 5 Films, R.C.A. Victor, Mailer, 1949-50 .... 165.00
Wristwatch, Metal Link Band, Ingersoll, 1935, 1 1/4-In. Dial, 5 1/2-In. Band 3390.00

TOOLS of all sorts are listed here, but most are related to industry. Other tools may be found listed under Iron, Kitchen, Tinware, and Wooden.

Bench, Cabinetmaker's, 3 Drawers, Wooden Screw Vise, Square Holes, 108 In. 1695.00
Book Press, Iron, Painted, Maroon, Black Japanned Finish, Gilt Transfers, c.1890, 25 In. 295.00
Bootjack, Cod Shape, Wood, 1800s, 19 In. 55.00
Brace, Jennings & Co., Rosewood Head & Handle, Sweep Patented, 1892, 13 1/2 In. 65.00
Branding Iron, Flared Shaft, Letters MD, 16 1/2 In. 72.00

Branding Iron, S7 Logo, Hand Forged, c.1900, 21 In. 23.00
Caliper, Stevens & Co., Threaded, Spring Joint, 4 1/2 In. 45.00
Caliper Rule, Lufkin, No. 455 EM, Pocket Slide, Box, 5 In. 75.00
Carrier, Cobbler's, Wood, Dovetailed, Chamfered Edges, New England, c.1925, 20 x 16 In. 1450.00
Chest, Tool-Maker's, George III, Pine, Iron Bound, Fitted Interior, 27 x 37 x 20 In. 2115.00
Chisel, Buck Bros., 1/2-In. Crank Neck, Fruitwood Handle, 12 1/2 In. 75.00
Chisel, Buck Bros., Millbury, Mass., Crank Neck, 1 1/4 x 14 In. 75.00
Chisel, Socket, Stanley, No. 750, 1/2-In. Bevel Edge, 9 In. 45.00
Chisel, Woon Edge Co., Woonsocket, R.I., Patented January, 1888, 12 1/2 In. 115.00
Countersink, Wells Bros. & Co., No. 3, Machinist's, 6 In. 35.00
Cutter, Chicago Automatic Machine Co., Star, Black, Patented, c.1907, 8 1/2 x 14 In. 45.00
Drill, Breast, Ayer's Patent, Speed, Forged Square Chuck, June 1868 .... 160.00
Drill, Radio, Millers Falls Co., No. 86, Box, 12 1/2 In. 145.00
Engraving, Chas. T. Mantz, Numbered 1-24, Mahogany Box, Nanuet, N.Y., 6 x 6 x 3 In. 310.00
Engraving Machine, Wight's Patent, Iron, Transfer Decoration, No. 465, Mahogany, 21 In. 705.00
Flashlight, Franco, Miner's, 2 Cell Globe Lens, Nickel Plated, 1915 .... 24.00
Flashlight, Winchester, 6 D Cell Batteries, 8-Sided Bezel, Ribbed Body, 3-In. Lens, 15 In. 52.00
Flashlight, Winchester, Bull's Eye Lens, Red Paint, 2 D Batteries, 7 In. 35.00
Flashlight, Winchester, Chrome Plated, 3 D Batteries, 1 3/4-In. Lens 27.00
Flashlight, Winchester, No. 2745P, Safety, 2 D Batteries 89.00
Flashlight, Winchester, No. 6411, Standard Junior, Nickel, Brass, Bull's-Eye Lens, 5 1/2 In. 23.00
Flashlight, Winchester, No. 7021, 2 Cell, Vest Pocket 148.00
Flashlight, Winchester, No. 7031, 2 Cell, Mazda Bulb, Vest Pocket 149.00
Flashlight, Winchester, Torpedo Style, 7 1/4 In. 25.00
Flax Hackle, David Rode, H.B., Punched Tulip Decoration, Pa., 1833, 3 5/8 x 12 x 3 In. 149.00
Fruit Press, Oak, Pegged Tenons, c.1900, 41 x 27 x 14 In. 430.00
Garden Tiller, Oak Handle, Iron Tines, Blacksmith Made, 1700s 395.00
Gauge, Brown & Sharpe, No. 694, Original Sleeve, 3 1/2 In. 25.00
Gauge, Butt, Winchester, No. 9778 .... 35.00
Gauge, Marking, Stanley, No. 64 1/4, Beechwood, c.1915, 8 In. 575.00
Gauge, Marking, Stanley, No. 72, Beechwood, Double Scribe, 8 In. 45.00
Grinding Machine, Mamod, Pressed Steel, Box, 4 In. 39.00
Hacksaw, Millers Falls Co., Jeweler's, Tropical Wood Handle, c.1887, 12 In. 95.00
Hacksaw, Winchester, No. 8020 .... 55.00
Hammer, Cobbler's, Long Wings, c.1760 .... 185.00
Hammer, Osborne & Co., No. 5, Leatherworking, Rosewood Handle, 11 In. 135.00
Hoe, Iron, Heart Shape Head, Penn., 1790-1830 .... 395.00
Ladder, Fruit Picker's, Split Rail, 197 In. 55.00
Lampfiller, Nickel Plated, Long Spout, Pump, Scroll Handle, c.1875, 5 1/4 x 2 3/4 In. 286.00
Lathe, Watchmaker's, American Watch Tool Company, c.1900, 4 x 11 x 14 In. 748.00
Level, Bubble, Stanley Rule & Level Co., Wood & Brass, 1820 Patent, 24 In. 440.00
Level, Carpenter's, Keen Kutter, Model KK30, Wood, Brass, 30 In. 20.00
Level, Disston & Sons, No. 70, Brass Bound, Pat. Oct. 29, 1912, 12 In. 265.00
Level, Disston & Sons, No. KK 104, Keen Kutter, Cherry Wood, Simmons Hardware Co., 12 In. 75.00
Level, L.S. Starrett Co., Double Plumb, Cast Iron, 6 In. 75.00
Level, Rule, Square, L.L. Davis, No. 37 1/2 .... 75.00
Level Indicator, Warren Knight, Precision, Carrying Case, Philadelphia, 12 x 8 In. 66.00
Light Bulb, Mazda B, General Electric, 1915-19, 5 1/4 In. 23.00
Mold, Spoon, 2 Sections, 9 In. 290.00
Monkey Wrench, Peck, Stow & Wilcox, Solid Bar, 6 In. 65.00
Monkey Wrench, Whitman & Barnes, Twist Handle, Pat. Feb. 27, 1883, 4 3/4 In. 95.00
Motor, Electric, Electro-Dynamic Co., Philadelphia, Box, 1880 Patent 1998.00
Noisemaker, Wood, Hand Crank, Nail & Screw, 11 x 22 x 10 In. 72.00
Nut Wrench, Gordon Automatic, Schultz, No. 493, Spring Loaded, 7 1/4 In. 125.00
Pantograph, Schmalcalder, Brass, Bone Wheels, Mahogany Case, London, 27 In. 295.00
Pipe Wrench, Peck, Stow & Wilcox, Walworth Mechanism, Blue Handle, 10 In. 65.00
Plane, Block, Millers Falls Co., No.75, Box, 7 In. 125.00
Plane, Block, Stanley, No. 65, Low Angle, Knuckle Joint Cap, 7 1/4 In. 175.00
Plane, Circular, Stanley, No. 113, 1877-1942, 10 In. 85.00
Plane, Compass, C.F. Moll, Charff F.N., Punchwork, Scrolling Handle, 1834, 6 In. 120.00
Plane, Cove Molding, A. Fish, Lowell, Mass., 9 1/2 In. 75.00

Plane, Dado, Winchester, No. 3062 .... 175.00
Plane, Jack, Bed Rock, Stanley, No. 605, 14 In. 295.00
Plane, Jack, Stanley, No. 5, Rosewood Handle, 1930s, 14 In. 115.00
Plane, Jointer, Stanley, No. 608C, c.1910, 24 In. 425.00
Plane, Molding, Carved Finger Grips, Heart, Chamfered Heel, 1673, 9 1/2 In. 235.00
Plane, Molding, Ovolo & Astragal, S. Rowell, c.1830, 9 1/2 In. 325.00
Plane, Nosing, Auburn Tool Co., No. 189, Double Iron, 9 1/2 In. 75.00
Plane, Ogee, Mockridge & Francis, Newark, N.J., 1835-69, 6 x 16 In. 225.00
Plane, Rabbet & Dado, Stanley, No. 45, Sweetheart Logo, Fitted Box, 9 In. 285.00
Plane, Rabbet, Stanley, No. 289, Skew-Blade, 8 1/2 In. 395.00
Plane, Scraper, Stanley, No. 12 1/2, Adjustable, Rosewood Bottom, 6 In. 245.00
Plane, Smoothing, Stanley, No. 4, Rosewood Handle, Box, 9 In. 135.00
Plane, Toothing, Hegny & Hollerman, New York, 6 1/2 In. 225.00
Pliers, Crimping, Sargeant & Co., Bernard's Patent, 7 In. 65.00
Pliers, Cruso, Combination, Screwdriver, Nail Puller, 6 In. 15.00
Pliers, Fencing, M. & M., Pat. May 22, 1900, 10 In. 105.00
Plumb Bob, Brown & Sharpe, No. 790, Mercury Filled, Wood Box, 5 1/2 In. 95.00
Rake, Clam, Cast Iron, Curved Tines, Long Wooden Shaft Handle, Early 1800s, 51 x 11 In. 295.00
Rake, Cranberry, Wood, 20 x 21 x 6 In. 518.00
Ripsaw, Richardson Saw Co., Newark, N.J. 25.00
Router, Door Trim, Stanley, No. 171, 3 Cutters, 11 1/2 In. 585.00
Router, Mockridge & Francis, Double, Newark, N.J. 150.00
Rule, Folding, Evans Rule Co., Gold Tip, No. X40, Holster, Belt Clip, Box 55.00
Rule, Folding, Stanley, No. 506, Zigzag, Pat. May 14, 1912, 72 In. 115.00
Rule, L.C. Stephens, No. 036, Inclinometer, Folding, 1858 Patent, 12 In. 2750.00
Rule, Parallel, Keuffel & Esser, New York, No. 1797, Ebony, Leather Case, 18 In. 315.00
Rule, Trammel Points, Combination, E.S. Smith & Co., 24 In. 675.00
Safe, Black, Stencil, Pinstripe, Dr. Clarence A. Race, Morris Ireland, Boston, 32 x 21 In. 165.00
Safe, Green, Central Combination Dial, Wheels, E. W. Coffin, Worcester, Early 1900s 250.00
Safe, Wood, Black Paint, Recessed Paneled Top, Sides, Hinged Door, 15 x 14 In. 175.00
Saw, Dovetail, Buck & Ryan, London, Octagonal Boxwood Handle, 13 In. 115.00
Saw, Fret, Millers Falls Co., No. 2, Deep Throat, Nickel Plated, 12 In. 85.00
Saw, Miter Box, Shapleigh Hardware, Diamond Edge, Wood Handle, Iron Blade, 20 In. 14.00
Saw, Panel, Keystone, Disston & Sons, No. 150, Orange & Black Handle, 1920s, 19 1/2 In. 35.00
Saw, Plumber's Friend, Brass Fixing Screw, Pivot Handle, Patented Dec. 31, 1895, 11 1/2 In. 115.00
Saw, Turning, Richardson Bros., Newark, N.J. 45.00
Saw, Turning, W. Johnson, Newark, N.J. 15.00
Screwdriver, Archimedian Push, A.H. Reid, Philadelphia, Pat. Dec. 12, 1882, 16 1/2 In. 75.00
Screwdriver, H.D. Smith Co., Perfect Handle, Triple Lever, 9 In. 135.00
Screwdriver, Millers Falls Co., No. 850, Phillips Head No. 4, Permaloid Plastic Handle, 1930s 10.00
Screwdriver, S.F. Bowser & Co., Spiral Ratchet, 13 1/2 In. 145.00
Screwdriver, Stanley, No. 2703, Phillips Head, No. 3 .... 15.00
Screwdriver, Young Mfg. Co., Hartford, 4 Retractable Blades, 7 1/2 In. 85.00
Shoehorn, Rattail Handle, Whitesmithed, 1800s, 9 1/2 In. 99.00
Shovel, Grain, Maple, 1800s, 34 1/2 In. 165.00
Shovel, Grain, Pine, Hand Carved, Wide Blade, Short Handle, Stained, 34 1/2 x 10 In. 250.00
Shovel, Maple, 19th Century, 36 In. 65.00
Slide Rule, Novotni Slide Rule Co., Weight, For Blacksmiths, 13 1/2 In. 345.00
Slide Rule, Slide Rule & Scale Engineering Co., No. 796, Original Case, 8 In. 15.00
Spokeshave, Stanley, Razor Edge, No. 72, 11 In. 325.00
Square, Bruin & Co., Folding, Boxwood, 18 In. 135.00
Square, Level, Combination, Stanley, No. 122, Defiance, 12 In. 65.00
Square, Machinist's, Combination, L.S. Starrett Co., Center Head, 6 In. 65.00
Square, Protractor Head, Machinist's, Combination, Lufkin Rule Co., 12 In. 165.00
Square, Try, Millers Falls Co., Locking Screw, Original Scribe, 6 In. 45.00
Square, Try, Winchester, No. 9706, Walnut Grip, Brass Hardware, 6 In. 35.00
Straightedge, Walnut, Cut Out Hearts, c.1800s, 18 7/8 x 2 1/8 In. 154.00
Stretcher For Barbed Wire Fencing, c.1900, Handle 3 In. 50.00
Tape Measure, Stanley, No. 556, Pull-Push, Art Deco Script, Box, 72 In. 95.00
Tobacco Slicer, Iron, John Blaul, Burlington, Iowa, c.1900, 16 In. 115.00
Trammel, Sawtooth, Ratchet Mechanisms, Slipper Shaped Catch, 33 x 7 x 2 In. 260.00

Trammel, Wrought Iron, Ratchet Mechanism, Scrolled Top, Adjusting Device, 39 1/2 In. 104.00
Vise, Bench, Vindex, Cast Iron, Painted, Green, Working Model, Lever, 5 3/4 In. 138.00
Vise, North Bros., No. 991, Yankee, Machinist's, Jaw Insert, Box, 5 In. 225.00
Wedge, Nickel Plated, Key Wind, Scroll Work Sides, Patent July 27 1875, 5 x 4 3/4 In. 138.00
Wheelbarrow, Wood, Red Paint, Spoked Wheel, Iron Band, Steel, 1800s, 24 x 69 In. 182.00
Wood Scribe, Winchester, No. W26, Green & Red Label 85.00
Wrench, Acme, Pat. Feb. 27, 1882, Twist Handle, 21 In. 425.00
Wrench, Alligator, Climax No. 2, Double Jaw, 10 In. 145.00
Wrench, Combination, Pipe, Nut, Erie Tool Works, 11 In. 145.00
Wrench, Elgin, Schultz, No. 35B, Pat. June 8, 1897, 7 In. 95.00
Wrench, Winchester, No. 1514, S Shape, 1/2 x 5/8 In. 34.00
Wrench, Winchester, No. W 23, Box End, 1/4 & 3/16 In. 90.00

TOOTHBRUSH HOLDERS were part of every bowl and pitcher set in the late nineteenth century. Most were oblong covered dishes. About 1920, manufacturers started to make children's toothbrush holders shaped like animals or cartoon characters. A few modern toothbrush holders are still being made.

3 Little Pigs, Bisque 85.00
Bonzo, Lustreware, Blue, Japan, Prewar, 5 1/2 In. 248.00
Kayo, Wall Hanger, F.A.S., Japan, 1930s, 5 In. 245.00
Skippy, Movable Arm, 1930s, 5 1/2 In. 165.00
Smitty, Tin, Prophylactic, Listerine, King On Foot, 6 In. 120.00
Uncle Willie & Emmy, Bisque, Japan, 3 7/8 In. 95.00

TOOTHPICK HOLDERS are sometimes called *toothpicks* by collectors. The variously shaped containers used to hold small wooden toothpicks are made of glass, china, or metal. Most of the toothpick holders are Victorian. Additional items may be found in other categories, such as Bisque, Silver Plate, Slag Glass, etc.

Acorn, Rose Blush 80.00
Amberina, Silver Plated Holder 500.00
Beaded & Scroll 30.00
Beveled Star, Green 50.00
Big Wheel 60.00
Blue Cut To White Cut To Clear, 2 3/4 In. 90.00
Boy With Pack, Amber 60.00
Brazilian 25.00
Buckingham 25.00
Chrysanthemum Leaf 100.00
Chrysanthemum Leaf, Gold Trim 105.00
Chrysanthemum Sprig, Custard Glass 75.00
Church Windows, Maiden's Blush 50.00
Collector's Society, 1977, Ruby Stain 45.00
Croesus, Amethyst, Gold Trim 90.00
Croesus, Green, Gold Trim 80.00
Diamond Peg, Custard Glass 50.00
Diamond Spearhead, Canary Opalescent 70.00
Diamond Spearhead, Dark Blue Opalescent 130.00
Doric 90.00
Edgewood 45.00
Empress, Green, Gold Trim 140.00
Figural, Book ....85.00 to 95.00
Figural, Frog On Lily Pad 70.00
Figural, Indian, Stag Horn, Ormolu Mounted, c.1900, 4 In. 59.00
Figural, Rooster & Barrel, Silver Plate 80.00
Flora, Blue Opalescent 400.00
Florene, Gold Trim 40.00
Frazier, Gold Trim 40.00
Geneva, Custard, Green & Gold 220.00
Georgia Gem, Green, Gold Trim 90.00

Hat, Cobalt Blue, Blown Glass 25.00
Holly Amber 300.00
Homestead 45.00
Intaglio Sunflower 25.00
Iris With Meander, Turquoise Blue 55.00
Jefferson 150.00
Jefferson Optic, Amethyst 60.00
Jefferson Optic, Enamel 10.00
Juno 30.00
Kewpie 35.00
Kittens, Marigold Carnival 165.00
Klondike 115.00
Klondike, Frosted, Amber Stain 375.00
Ladders With Diamonds, Ruby Stain, Gold Trim 50.00
Leaf Mold, Yellow, Pink & White Spatter 130.00
Louis XV, Custard Glass, Blue 50.00
Majestic, Ruby Stain 130.00
Manhattan 30.00
Maryland 200.00
Medallion Sprig, Green Trim 350.00
Michigan, Ruby Stain 80.00
Nevada 45.00
Nevada, Flower 85.00
New Hampshire 25.00
Oregon 65.00
Orinda 35.00
Pennsylvania 25.00
Pleating, Ruby Stain 75.00
Prince Of Wales Plumes, Gold Trim 95.00
Punty & Diamond Point 230.00
Punty Band, Custard Glass 25.00
Reverse Swirl, Vaseline, Opalescent 85.00
Ribbed Spiral 60.00
Ribbed Spiral, Canary Opalescent 80.00
Ring & Beads, Custard Glass 45.00
Royal Bayreuth, Rose Tapestry, Porcelain 395.00
Royal Bayreuth, Sunbonnet Babies Sweeping, Porcelain 385.00
Royal Doulton, Welsh Ladies, Porcelain 130.00
RS Prussia, Roses, Gold Trim, 2 Handles 85.00
S Repeat, Apple Green, Gold Trim 75.00
Scalloped Panel, Green 25.00
Scroll With Cane Band, Amber Stain .... 60.00 to 80.00
Scroll With Cane Band, Ruby Stain 80.00
Shamrock, Ruby Stain .... 50.00 to 60.00
Star & Feather 60.00
Stippled Fans 25.00
Sunflower Patch, Gold Trim 200.00
Swan, Milk Glass 8.00
Swirl 30.00
Truncated Cube, Ruby Stain .... 35.00 to 60.00
Umbrella, Multicolor, Green Rim, Paperweight Base, Millville, 5 1/2 x 3 In. .... 1183.00 to 1320.00
Virgo, Etched 50.00
Wedding Bells 35.00
Wild Bouquet, Opalescent 145.00
Wreath & Shell, Blue Opalescent 200.00

TORQUAY is the name given to ceramics by several potteries working near Torquay, England, from 1870 until 1962. Until about 1900, the potteries used local red clay to make classical-style art pottery vases and figurines. Then they turned to making souvenir wares. Items were dipped in colored slip and decorated with painted slip and sgraffito designs. They often had mottoes or proverbs, and scenes of cottages, ships, birds, or flowers. The *Scandy* design was a symmetrical arrangement of brushstrokes and spots done in colored slips. Potteries included Watcombe Pottery (1870–1962); Torquay Terra-Cotta Company (1875–1905); Aller Vale (1881–1924); Torquay Pottery (1908–1940); and Longpark (1883–1957).

TORQUAY

Dish, Cover, Lands End 13.00
Dish, Handles, Actions Speak Louder Than Words 3.00
Eggcup, Laid Today 22.00
Eggcup, New Laid 22.00
Milk Pan, Fresh From The Dairy, 4 In. 15.00
Mug, Boscastle, 4 In. 15.00
Pitcher, Rooster, 4 1/2 In. 25.00
Plate, First Deserve, 5 1/4 In. 15.00
Sugar & Creamer, 2 1/2 In. 32.00

TORTOISESHELL is the shell of the tortoise. It has been used as inlay and to make small decorative objects since the seventeenth century. Some species of tortoise are now on the endangered species list, and old and new objects made from these shells cannot be sold legally.

Box, Geometric Paneled Lid, Hinged, Early 19th Century, 1 1/4 x 2 3/8 x 1 1/4 In. 380.00
Box, Gold, Silver Inlaid, Victorian, 19th Century, 1 1/4 x 2 7/8 x 3 1/2 In. 205.00
Box, Hinged, Oval, England, 19th Century, 1 1/4 x 2 1/4 x 4 1/2 In. 234.00
Calling Card Case, Silver, Gold, Victorian, 19th Century, England, 2 x 3 In. 325.00
Cigarette Box, Round, Reeded Edge, Central Patera, Brass Frame, France, 1 1/2 x 4 In. 205.00
Comb, Double Sided, Carved, Hollow Center, Secret Opening, 17th Century 650.00
Memoire, Aide, Rectangular, Initialed Silver Clasp, Ivory Pages, Pencil, 4 In. 80.00
Page Cutter, Repousse Silver Handle, Colonial Couple, Green Man, 17 7/8 In. 575.00
Spoon, Mid 19th Century, 10 1/2 In. 140.00
Vase, Squirrels, Grapevines, Reticulated, Flattened Double Gourd, Chinese, 7 In. 998.00

TOY collectors have special clubs, magazines, and shows. Toys are designed to entice children, and today they have attracted new interest among adults who are still children at heart. All types of toys are collected. Tin toys, iron toys, battery operated toys, and many others are collected by specialists. Dolls, Games, Teddy Bears, and Bicycles are listed in their own categories. Other toys may be found under company or celebrity names.

Acrobat, Celluloid, Somersaults, Articulated Arms, Steel Trapeze, Clockwork, 7 1/2 In. 82.00
Acrobat, Gray Outfits, Red Details, Tumbling Action, Crank Handle, Lithograph, Meier, Pair 1604.00
Acrobatic Monkeys, Clown, On Motorcycle, Windup, Wyandotte 475.00
Acrobatic Monkeys, Clown, On Motorcycle, Windup, Wyandotte, Box 675.00
Airplane, 2 Airplanes On Stand, Flag On Top, Brown Ribbed Base, Tin, Germany 411.00
Airplane, 2 Propellers, Windup, Friction, Silver, Black, Huki, c.1948 . . . . . 100.00
Airplane, 3 Airplanes Whirling, Tin, Red, Blue, Stamped, DRGM, Germany 411.00
Airplane, 4 Engine, Tin, Windup, U.S. Zone Germany, 1940s, 10 1/4-In. Wingspan 220.00
Airplane, 4 Propellers, Tin, Battery Operated, Stop & Go, Wing Lights, Japan, 1950s, 16 1/2 In. . . 245.00
Airplane, Aero No. 546, Tin, Windup, U.S. Zone Germany, 5 1/4 In. 55.00
Airplane, Aero-Dawn, Mono, Red, Tootsietoy, 1928, 4 In. 125.00
Airplane, Air Service, Pressed Steel, Green Wings, Red Disc Wheels, American Flyer, 24 In. 1540.00
Airplane, America, Cast Iron, 17-In. Wingspan 2016.00
Airplane, Army Bomber, Mechanical Propellers, 1930-40, 24 In. 550.00
Airplane, Autogiro, Green, Yellow, Tootsietoy, 4 1/2-In. Wingspan 225.00
Airplane, Big Bang, Cast Iron, Guarantee, Box, 13 In. 560.00
Airplane, Biplane, German Fighter, Tipp & Co., 11 In. 1995.00
Airplane, Bremen Junkers, Cast Rib Design, Embossed Wings, Cast Iron, Green, Hubley, 10 In. 2475.00
Airplane, Cast Iron, Hubley, 6 In. 225.00
Airplane, Cast Iron, Nickel Plated Wheels, Propeller, Figures, Hubley, 7 In. 1064.00
Airplane, China Clipper, Tin, Wyandotte, Box, 13-In. Wingspan 358.00
Airplane, Circles Hangar, Tin Lithograph, Clockwork, Germany, c.1920, 6 x 5 1/2 In. 294.00

Airplane, Convair, Die Cast, Silver Color, Blue Propellers, Tootsietoy 75.00
Airplane, Dagwood As Pilot, Tin Lithograph, Louis Marx, c.1935, 9 In. 715.00
Airplane, Fighter, Heinkel, Nazi, Lehmann, Germany, 1930s 450.00
Airplane, Fighter, Jet, Tin, Battery Operated, USAF FW 996, TN, Box, 1950s 110.00
Airplane, Fighter, Tin, Battery Operated, KO, Box, 10 1/2 In. 175.00
Airplane, Flyin' Fool, Metal, Enmert-Hammes Inc., 1940s, 16-In. Wingspan 88.00
Airplane, Flying Tiger, Tin, Friction, Tan, Orange, Marx, 6 In., 7-In. Wingspan 125.00
Airplane, Giroplane, Green, Hubley, 4 1/2 In. 325.00
Airplane, Honeymoon Express, Circling, Tin Lithograph, Clockwork, Marx, Original Box 275.00
Airplane, Jet, Navy, Douglas Sky Rocket, Silver & Red, Bandai, 10-In. Wingspan 165.00
Airplane, Jetstar, Lockheed, Tin, Friction, Japan, Box, 12-In. Wingspan 77.00
Airplane, Lindy, Aluminum, Hubley, 5 In. 275.00
Airplane, Lindy, Cast Iron, Hubley, 9 1/2 In. 168.00
Airplane, Lockheed Sirius Monoplane, Orange, Black, Tootsietoy, 3 1/2-In. Wingspan 125.00
Airplane, Lockheed Sirius, Pressed Steel, Painted Black, Orange Wing, Tail, Steelcraft, 21 In. 1045.00
Airplane, Lockheed Sirius, Pressed Steel, Painted White, Red Wings, Steelcraft, 21 In. 990.00
Airplane, Lockheed Vega, Black, Orange, Wyandotte, 12 In., 18-In. Wingspan 135.00
Airplane, Monoplane, Windup, Paya, 1920s, 15 In. 425.00
Airplane, Mystery, Cast Iron, Painted, Blue, Embossed Wings, White Lettering, 6 In. 525.00
Airplane, Paper, Tin, Henley, Box, 1919, 7-In. Wingspan 250.00
Airplane, Patrol Plane, Tin, Friction, Momoya, Japan, Box, 14 In. 195.00
Airplane, Pilot, Tin, U.S. Zone 47.00
Airplane, Right Plane, Blue, White, Trade Mark Applied For, No. 20, 1920s, 30 x 27 In. 370.00
Airplane, Rookie Pilot, Tin, Windup, Marx, 8 In. 550.00
Airplane, Scout, Pressed Steel, Steelcraft, 23 In. 550.00
Airplane, Sea Gull, Cast Iron, Wing Mounted Nickel Motor, Propeller, Kilgore, 8 In. 468.00
Airplane, Seaplane, Friendship, Cast Iron, Yellow Paint, Blue Letters, Hubley, 13 In. 2750.00
Airplane, Strato Jet, Tin, Battery Operated, TN, Box, 14-In. Wingspan 83.00
Airplane, Stratocruiser, Die Cast, Silver Color, Blue Propellers, Tootsietoy 125.00
Airplane, Super Constellation, Tin Friction, Joustra, France, Box, 1950s, 19-In. Wingspan 330.00
Airplane, Swissair, Jet, Tin, Cable Driven, Arnold, Box, 1960s, 14 1/2-In. Wingspan 165.00
Airplane, Tri-Motor, Pressed Steel, Propellers, Rubber Tires, Kingsbury, 15 In. 385.00
Airplane, Tri-Motor, Pressed Steel, Rubber Tires, Keystone, 23-In. Wingspan 523.00
Airplane, Tri-Motor, Tin, Pressed Steel, American Flyer, 23-In. Wingspan 448.00
Airplane, Twin Engine, Twin Tail, Wyandotte, 6 1/4 In. 66.00
Airplane, U.S. Army, Wood Hubs, Folding Wheels, Blue, Silver, Hubley, 1939, 8-In. Wingspan 175.00
Airplane, United Airlines, Tin, Friction, Japan, Box, 11-In. Wingspan 165.00
Airplane, United Boeing, Green, Nickel Plate, Arcade, 5-In. Wingspan 275.00
Airplane-Go-Round, 2 Airplanes, Tin, U.S. Zone, Box 235.00
Airplane-Go-Round, 3 Airplanes, Tin & Celluloid, U.S. Zone 94.00
Airport Service Set, Jeep, Ser-Vi-Car, Tractor, Baggage Wagons, Tonka 303.00
Airship, Silver, Kenton, 6 In. 350.00
Alabama Coon Jigger, Tin, Windup, Lehmann, Box, 1912, 10 In. ....880.00 to 1650.00
Alligator With Baby On Back, Green, Beige, Tin, Occupied Japan 30.00
Ambulance, Chevrolet SW, Cream, Japan, 1958, 8 In. 145.00
Ambulance, Driver, Passenger, Person On Stretcher, Tonka, 19 In. 75.00
Ambulance, Metal, Lupor, Box, 1950s, 7 In. 145.00
Ambulance, Police, City Of London, Driver, Crew, Blue Uniforms, Lithographed, Georg Fischer 1835.00
Ambulance, Pressed Steel, Closed Van Body, White, Red Cross Emblem, Sturditoy, 26 1/2 In. 10450.00
Ambulance, Pressed Steel, Keystone, 1930s, 27 In. 2420.00
Ambulance, White, Red, Blue, Red Cross, Tin, Stamped, 343, Germany 80.00
Animal Set, Zebra, Lion, Horse, Giraffe, Carved, Painted, Articulated Limbs, Schoenhut, 11 In. 2400.00
Apollo 11 Eagle Lunar Module, Battery Operated, DSK, Japan, Box, c.1970, 10 In. 105.00
Apollo Explorer, Flying Spaceman, Remco, Box, c.1969, 8 In. 99.00
Astronaut, Super, Battery Operated, S.H., Japan, Box, c.1950, 12 In. 145.00
Baby, Crawling, Wheels In Knees, Articulated Arms Simulate Crawling, Cast Iron, Ives, 5 In. 413.00
Baby Bertha, Tin, Vinyl, Battery Operated, Mego, Box, 12 1/2 In. 425.00
Badge, Sgt. Preston Mountie, Brass, Embossed, 2 1/8 In. 400.00
Balky Mule, Tin Lithograph, Windup, Lehmann, Box, c.1900, 7 1/2 In. ....460.00 to 585.00
Balloon Vendor, Tin, Windup, Distler, 6 1/2 In. 750.00
Banjo Player, Celluloid, Cloth Fabric, Box, Occupied Japan 47.00

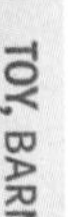

Toy, Barney Google, Riding Sparkplug, Windup, Tin, Nifty Co., Germany, 8 In.

Toy, Bell Ringer, Clown Riding Tree Branch, Watrous Mfg. Co., 7 In.

Barn, Pine, Wallpaper, Painted, Germany, c.1900, 28 x 32 In. 230.00
Barney Google, Riding Sparkplug, Windup, Tin, Nifty Co., Germany, 8 In. .... *ILLUS* 728.00
Barnyard Set, Ohio Art, Box 55.00
Baseball Catcher, Looking Up, Celluloid, Occupied Japan 41.00
Bears are also listed in the Teddy Bears category.
Bear, Barney, Drummer Boy, Battery Operated, Remote Control, Alps, Box, 11 In. 295.00
Bear, Blacksmith, Tin, Fabric, Plush, Battery Operated, A-1, Box, 9 1/2 In. 330.00
Bear, Busy Housekeeper, Battery Operated, Alps, Box, 9 In. 90.00
Bear, Busy Housekeeper, Tin, Fabric, Plush, Battery Operated, Alps, Box, 9 1/2 In. 214.00
Bear, Busy Housekeeper, Vacuum Cleaner, Battery Operated, Alps, Box, 9 1/2 In. 395.00
Bear, Cutie Cook, Tin, Vinyl, Cloth, Battery Operated, Y Co., Box, 10 In. 434.00
Bear, Fishing, Light-Up Eyes, Tin, Battery Operated, White, Brown 275.00
Bear, Grandpa Bear, Mixed Material, Battery Operated, Alps, Box, 9 In. 425.00
Bear, Jolly, Peanut Vendor, Tin, Fabric, Plush, Battery Operated, TN, Box, 8 In. 240.00
Bear, On Wheels, Plush, Straw Stuffed, Early 1900s, 11 In. 425.00
Bear, Picnic, Drinks Cola, Battery Operated, Alps 145.00
Bear, Picnic, Tin, Plush, Battery Operated, Alps, Box, 9 1/2 In. 225.00
Bear, Shoemaker, Tin, Fabric, Plush, Battery Operated, TN, Box, 8 1/2 In. 165.00
Bear, Skier, Cloth Suit, Legs Move Back & Forth, Windup, 7 In. 225.00
Bear, Sneezing, Tin, Plush, Battery Operated, Linemar, Box, 9 In. 275.00
Bear & Rowboat, Tin, Windup, Japan, Box, 1950s, 10 In. 395.00
Bears, Papa, Mama, Baby, Bisque, Japan, Box, 5 In., 4 In., 3 In., Set 448.00
Bed, Doll's, Blue, Gray, 8 Slats, Ticking Mattress, Late 1800s, 14 x 19 1/2 x 17 In. 59.00
Bed, Doll's, Cannonball, Rope, Cherry, Four-Poster, Shaped Headboard, 29 x 17 1/2 In. 175.00
Bed, Doll's, Mission Style, Mixed Hardwoods, Red Mahogany Stain, Castors, 24 In. 58.00
Beetle, Crawling, Lehmann, Box, c.1900 .... 275.00
Beetle Set, Lithograph, 4-Legged, 4-Wheel Trolley Bases, Disc Wheels, Kellermann, 3 Piece 459.00
Bell, Monkey, Cast Iron, J & E Stevens 280.00
Bell, Rocking, Eagle, Cast Iron, Brass Bell, 1890s, 4 3/4 x 3 1/2 In. 220.00
Bell, Rocking, Prancing Horse, Red White & Blue Shield, 1890s, 4 1/2 In. 300.00
Bell Pull, Elephant, Iron, East Hampton, Conn., Late 1800s, 6 1/2 In. 715.00
Bell Ringer, Acrobats, Gong Bell Mfg., c.1890, 6 In. 1840.00
Bell Ringer, Alligator, c.1880, 8 In. 1500.00
Bell Ringer, Black Heads Ring Bells, Iron, Heart Wheels, Nickel Plated 465.00
Bell Ringer, Boy Fishing, Red Spoke Wheels, N.N. Hill Brass Co., 8 In. 3300.00
Bell Ringer, Clown Riding Tree Branch, Watrous Mfg. Co., 7 In. .... *ILLUS* 1035.00
Bell Ringer, Columbia, Patriotic Figure, Shell Cart, Gong Bell, Cast Iron, c.1880, 7 1/2 In. 1650.00
Bell Ringer, Ding Dong, 2 Nursery Rhyme Figures, Pussy's Not In Well, c.1903, 9 In. 770.00
Bell Ringer, Ding Dong, Pussy's Not In Well, Gong Bell Mfg, c.1890 .... 4370.00
Bell Ringer, Harold Lloyd, Squeeze, Germany, 1930s 375.00
Bell Ringer, Harold Lloyd, Tin Plated Face, Lithograph, Articulated, Germany, 12 In. 646.00
Bell Ringer, Landing Of Columbus, 1893, 7 1/4 In. 679.00
Bell Ringer, Man & Raccoon, Figure Crawling In Log, Gong Bell, Cast Iron, c.1900, 8 1/2 In. 3025.00
Bell Ringer, Miss Liberty, Raises Flag, Cast Iron, Kyser & Rex, 8 In. .... *ILLUS* 14950.00
Bell Ringer, Monkey & Coconut, Wheeled Log, N.N. Hill, c.1905, 6 In. 330.00
Bell Ringer, Monkey, Articulated, Open Cart, Red Spokes, Cast Iron, Kyser & Rex, c.1890 .... 715.00
Bell Ringer, Monkey, Jim-Along-Jose, Open Carriage, Cast Iron, Kyser & Rex, c.1881, 7 In. 468.00

Toy, Bell Ringer, Miss Liberty, Raises Flag, Cast Iron, Kyser & Rex, 8 In.

Toy, Bell Ringer, Uncle Sam & The Don, Exchange Hits, Cast Iron, Gong Bell Co., 7 In.

Bell Ringer, Pony & Carriage, Green, Boy In Red Coat, Cast Iron Cart, Gong Bell, c.1905, 6 In. 220.00
Bell Ringer, Poodle Dog, Clown Figure, Leash Spins Dog, Cast Iron, 8 In. 715.00
Bell Ringer, Running Monkey, No. 49 Monkey, Gong Bell, Oval Base, c.1905, 6 In. 880.00
Bell Ringer, Teddy Bear, Cast Iron, Red Coat, 6 1/2 In. 605.00
Bell Ringer, Turtle, Frog On Back, 1880s 1800.00
Bell Ringer, Uncle Sam & The Don, Exchange Hits, Cast Iron, Gong Bell Co., 7 In. ..... ***ILLUS*** 4312.00
Bicycles that are large enough to ride are listed in their own category.
Billy Goat, Hide Covered, Wood Pull Frame, Head Moves, Voice Box, Glass Eyes, 16 x 6 In. 920.00
Bimbo Orchestra, Violin, Accordion, Tuba, Bisque, Fleischer Studios, Borgfeld, Box, 3 Piece 560.00
Bimbo The Drumming Clown, Battery Operated, Tin, Plastic, Cragstan, Box, 9 1/2 In. 55.00
Bird On Roof, Wire Legs, Applied Felt Wings, Feather Tail, Squeak, 5 1/2 In. 155.00
Birds, Kissing, Tin Lithograph, Animated, Wood Base, Bellows, Germany, 3 1/4 x 4 3/4 In. 95.00
Black Dancer By Street Sign, Celluloid, Windup, Japan 275.00
Black Mailman, Pulled By Ostrich, Lead Fly-Wheel Mechanism, Lehmann, 1889-1916 ..... 650.00
Black Man, Cast Iron, Wood Rollers, Extra Clothes, Ives Secor, 9 1/2 In. 2310.00
Black Man Playing Banjo, Tapping Foot, Wood, Metal Crank, W.J. Wallace, 1978, 16 In. 345.00
Black Oscar, Porter Peddles 3-Wheel Baggage Cart, Friction, Head Moves, France 485.00
Black Porter, Tin, Windup, Marx, 9 In. 336.00
Blacksmith, Tin, Windup, Showa, Box, 5 1/2 In. 402.00
Block Village, Wood, Cardboard Lithograph, Buildings, Cars, Keystone, Box, 15 x 22 In. 110.00
Blocks, ABC, Nesting, Paper Lithograph On Wood, c.1900, 19 1/4 In. 150.00
Blocks, Building, Arquitectura Moderna, Early 1900s 125.00
Blocks, Picture, 30 Blocks, Paper Lithograph, Wood, Germany, 9 1/2 x 11 1/2 In. 65.00
Blocks, Picture, Scenes, Numbers, Letters, Paper Lithograph, Wood, Box 65.00
Boat, Aircraft Carrier, Wood, Battery Operated, Tsukuda, Occupied Japan, Box, 23 1/2 In. 440.00
Boat, Battery Operated, Straco, Cardboard Store Pack, 9 In. 45.00
Boat, Battleship, Dreadnought, 3-Funnel, Lithograph, Gray, White Deck Pennants, Meier 920.00
Boat, Battleship, Hillclimber, Painted Tin, Wood Components, Cast Iron Wheels, 18 In. 330.00
Boat, Battleship, New York, White, Orange Deck, 3 Black Stars, Embossed, Dent, c.1905, 20 In. 1430.00
Boat, Battleship, Pressed Steel, Green & White Hull, Orange Guns, Friction, Dayton, 15 In. 165.00
Boat, Battleship, Sailor, Rigging, Smoke Stacks, Wood, Paper Lithograph, 20 In. 880.00
Boat, Battleship, Thunderer, 3-Funnel, Flywheel, Lithograph, Black Disc Wheels, Georg Fischer 344.00
Boat, Battleship, USS Washington, Tin, Windup, 15 In. 325.00
Boat, Battleship, Valiant, Tin, Windup, Sutcliffe, Box, 12 In. 190.00
Boat, Cabin Cruiser, Chris Craft, Cast Iron, Yellow, Green, Kilgore, 11 In. 4400.00
Boat, Cabin Cruiser, Outboard Motor, Linemar, Box, 12 1/2 In. 305.00
Boat, Carrier, Battery Operated, Marx, Japan, 1950, 21 In. 295.00
Boat, Commander, B-510, Japan, 1950s, 8 1/2 In. 120.00
Boat, Commodore Cruiser, Tin, Windup, Sutcliffe, Box, 12 In. 45.00
Boat, Cruiser, 2 Stacks, Rigging, Gun Mounts, U.S. Flag, Wood, Paper Lithograph, 31 1/2 In. 1540.00
Boat, Flywheel Drive, Germany, c.1915, 7 In. 195.00
Boat, Hawk, Tin, Clockwork, Sutcliffe, Box, 13 In. 130.00
Boat, Jet Patrol, Tin Lithograph, Japan, 1950s, 11 In. 110.00
Boat, Jupiter, Ocean Pilot, Tin, Windup, Sutcliffe, Box, 9 In. 85.00
Boat, Metal, Windup, Arnold, Germany, US Zone, 1948, 8 In. 275.00
Boat, Miami Sea Sled, Big Boat Tows Little Boat, Pressed Tin, Wheels, Strauss, 15 In. 176.00
Boat, Motor, Chester A. Pimmer, 7 In. 176.00

Boat, Motor, Evinrude, Box, 6 In. 305.00
Boat, Motor, Gas, Allyn Seafury, Los Angeles, 5 1/2 In. 99.00
Boat, Motor, N.B.K., Box, 4 In. 88.00
Boat, Motor, Plastic, Electric, Schilling, Box, 14 In. 90.00
Boat, Motor, Sea Horse, Johnson's, Box, 5 In. 305.00
Boat, Ocean Liner, 2 Funnels, Lithograph, Cream, Green Hull, Yellow Deck, Disc Wheels, Distler 575.00
Boat, Outboard Motor, Johnson Sea Horse, 30 HP, Brown, White, Paperwork, Box 358.00
Boat, Outboard Motor, Mercury Mark 55, Thunderbolt, Green, Silver, Box 358.00
Boat, Outboard Motor, Wizard, Box, 9 In. 80.00
Boat, Paddle, New York, Cast Iron, Painted, Wilkins, 15 In. 1330.00
Boat, Phillips 66, Plastic, Box, 15 In. 110.00
Boat, Pilot, Chesapeake Bay, Hinged Windows, Removable Roof, Steering Wheel, 1920, 66 In. 649.00
Boat, Pinnace, Lithograph, Yellow, Red Edging, Eagle Bowsprit, Pennants, Standing Sailor 1375.00
Boat, Pressed Steel, Windup, Stand, Lionel, 18 In. 880.00
Boat, PT, Tank, Cargo Holder, Soldiers, Pressed Steel, Buddy L, 14 In. 248.00
Boat, Racer 1, Tin, Sutcliffe, Box, 10 In. 99.00
Boat, Racing Sailboat, Wood, Keystone, Box, 17 In. 120.00
Boat, Racing, Plastic, Battery Operated, Ideal, Box, 13 In. 110.00
Boat, Riverboat, Side-Wheel, Cast Iron, Nickel Plated, Floor Toy, 7 1/2 In. 165.00
Boat, Riverboat, Side-Wheel, Cast Iron, Walking Beams, 15 In. 300.00
Boat, Rowboat, Indian, Celluloid, 6 In. 95.00
Boat, Safety, Tin, Friction, Haji, Japan, 1950s, 6 1/2 In. 95.00
Boat, Sail, Peggy Ann, Tin, Cloth, Celluloid, Windup, Green, Red, Yellow, Chein 40.00
Boat, Sail, Wood, Paper Lithograph, 17 In. 1540.00
Boat, Scull, 4 Rowers, Wood, Hustler, 14 In. 55.00
Boat, Side-Wheeler, Puritan, Cast Iron, White, Black Stack, Wheels, Stencil, Wilkens, 11 In. 468.00
Boat, Speedboat, Cast Iron, Hubley, 4 In. 99.00
Boat, Speedboat, Lady Driver, No. 4, Lithograph, Cream, Red, Blue, White Stern Flag, Meier 1605.00
Boat, Speedboat, Lionel, Box, 16 1/2 In. 978.00
Boat, Thunderbolt, Fleet Line, Box, 12 1/2 In. 99.00
Boat, Tin, Windup, Arnold, West Germany, 5 In. 78.00
Boat, Torpedo, Motor, Victor, Tin, Windup, Sutcliffe, Box, 9 In. 88.00
Boat, Trailer, Meteor, Plastic, Metal, No. 48, White, Red, Matchbox, Box, 2 3/4 In. 105.00
Boat, Tugboat, Railed Cabin, Decal On Funnel, Searchlight, Pressed Steel, Red, Buddy L, 27 In. 30800.00
Boat, Viking, Plastic, Johnson Motor, Fleetline, Box, 10 In. 110.00
Boat, Water Skiing, Skier, Pressed Tin, Plastic, Haji, Box, 14 In. 248.00
Boat, Wheel, Pioneer, Paper Lithograph On Wood, Late 1800s, 10 1/2 x 24 1/4 In. 1295.00
Boat, Wood, Battery Operated, Linemar, Box, 11 In. 110.00
Boat, Wood, Electric, Rico, Box, 10 In. 99.00
Boat, Wood, Keystone, 10 In. 99.00
Boat, Wood, Union, Box, 13 1/2 In. ....66.00 to 110.00
Boat, Yacht, Plastic, Ideal, 15 In. 45.00
Boat, Yacht, Power, Marina, Phillips 66, Box, 1965 .... 120.00
Boat, Zephyr, Plastic, Battery Operated, Fleetline, Box, 10 In. 120.00
Boat House, Sailboat, Speedboat, Ocean Wave Display Canal, Keystone, 9 x 13 In. 190.00
Boat Ride, Pressed Tin, Windup, Unique Art, 9 In. 190.00
Bobsled, Wood Slat, Steering Wheel, Hand Brake, Running Boards, 48 1/2 In. 165.00
Bomber Pilot, Tin, Battery Operated, KO, Japan, Box, 10 1/2 In. 110.00
Boob McNutt, Waddles, Windup, Strauss, Co., 1925 .... 650.00
Box, For Dapper Dan, Carter's Coon Jigger, Marx, 1910, 7 In. 275.00
Box, Treasure Chest, Hubley, 1930s, 11 1/2 x 16 In. 110.00
Boxers, Articulated Arms, Tin Platforms, Disc Wheels, Spring Connection, 6 In. 50.00
Boxers, Cloth Dressed, Clockwork, Wood Base, Hides Mechanism, Ives, 1876, 8 1/4 In. 4950.00
Boxers, Knock-Out, Champion Prize Fighters, Tin, Windup, Strauss, Box, 5 1/2 In. 330.00
Boy, Butterfly Net, White Striped Sailor Suit, Spring Action, Lithograph, Blue, Georg Fischer 229.00
Boy & Dog, Boy Eating Watermelon, Dog Bites Him, Celluloid, Clockwork, 5 7/8 In. 220.00
Boy On Sled, Lithograph, Gray Jacket, Stockings, Brown Britches, Black Wheels, Distler 345.00
Boy On Sled, Lying Down, White Jacket, Black Boots, Tin, Ges Gesch, Meier Trademark, Germany .. 620.00
Boy On Sled, Lying Down, White Jacket, Red Pants, Carved Rungs, Tin, Germany 410.00
Boy On Sled, Sitting, White Jacket & Pants, Tin, Meier Trademark 499.00
Boy On Trapeze, J. Barton & Smith Co., Philadelphia, Pa., 1891 .... 4800.00

Boy On Tricycle, Bisque Head, Painted Features, Metal Tricycle, Vichy, France, c.1860, 8 In. 2910.00
Boy With Newspaper, Rings Bell, Red Hat, Stars & Stripes Outfit, Tin, Occupied Japan 47.00
Bringing Up Father Set, Accessories, Schoenhut, Box, c.1924 .... 3080.00
Bubble Bear, Tin, Battery Operated, Modern Toys, Box, 9 1/2 In. 350.00
Bubbler Set, Midget, Happy Hours With Bubbles, 3 Wind Pipes, Box, 6 In. 11.00
Bucking Bronco, Rider, Brown Horse, Black Mane, Tail, Lehmann, c.1906 .... 1350.00
Buffalo, Wood, Jointed, Carved Beard, Mane, Leather Horns, Schoenhut, 7 1/2 In. 165.00
Bulldozer, Caterpillar, Pressed Tin, Marx, 11 In. 90.00
Bulldozer, Metal, Japan, 1950s, 8 In. 55.00
Bulldozer, Metal, Plastic, Japan, 1960s, 10 In. 75.00
Bulldozer, Mighty, No. 3907, Tonka, Box, 10 In. 121.00
Bulldozer, Stop & Go, Japan, 1960s, 9 In. 95.00
Bulldozer, Tiger Tractor, Tin, Windup, Friction, Japan, Box, 6 1/4 In. 90.00
Bulldozer, Tru-Matic, Sit 'n' Ride, Working Blade, Red Body, 1940s, 23 In. 150.00
Bunny Rabbit Express, Pressed Tin, Chein, 11 1/2 In. 120.00
Bus, Arcade, 1930s, 8 In. 495.00
Bus, Double-Decker, 2 People, Cast Iron, Arcade, 8 In. 485.00
Bus, Double-Decker, City, Green, Gold Trim, Arcade, 14 In. 3500.00
Bus, Double-Decker, City, Red, Green Trim, Kenton, 10 In. ....1000.00 to 1350.00
Bus, Double-Decker, Green, Arcade, 1939, 8 In. 595.00
Bus, Double-Decker, Inter-State, Green, Strauss, c.1930, 10 1/2 In. 1250.00
Bus, Double-Decker, Lithograph, Red, Gold, Black, Embossed Passengers, Georg Fischer 2292.00
Bus, Double-Decker, Open Cab, Driver, Lithograph, Yellow, Brown, Blue Wheels, Dico 690.00
Bus, Double-Decker, Open Cab, Driver, Yellow, Red, Lithograph, Distler 1375.00
Bus, Express, Tin, Push Down, Wolverine, Box, 1950s, 14 In. 345.00
Bus, Fageol, Cast Iron, Painted, Green, Gold Stripe, Nickel Disc Wheels, Arcade, 8 In. 165.00
Bus, Flivver, Pressed Steel, Green, Decal Striping, Spoke Wheels, Cowdery Toy Works, 16 1/2 In. .. 1320.00
Bus, GMC, Coast To Coast, Cast Iron, Blue & White, Rubber Tires, Arcade, 8 3/4 In. 330.00
Bus, Greyhound, Cast Aluminum, No. 101, Realistic Toys, 1947, 8 3/4 In. 210.00
Bus, Greyhound, Coast-To-Coast, Platform, Tin, Chein, 1920s, 9 In. 225.00
Bus, Greyhound, Door Opens, Bell Rings, Steel, Windup, Blue, White, Buddy L, 1930s, 16 In. 415.00
Bus, Greyhound, Ertl Co. Inc., Signed, Box, 1950s 425.00
Bus, Greyhound, GMC Scenicruiser, Blue, White, Die Cast, Tootsietoy, 1955, 7 In. 45.00
Bus, Greyhound, Great Lakes Expo, Tandem, Cast Iron, Blue, White, Stenciled, Arcade, 6 3/4 In. .. 385.00
Bus, Greyhound, Motor Driven, Pressed Steel, 2-Tone, Beige, White, Kingsbury, 1930s, 18 In. 630.00
Bus, Greyhound, Moving Passengers, Tin, Friction, Blue, White, Cragston, Box, 1950s, 11 3/4 In. . 448.00
Bus, Greyhound, Passengers In Windows, Tin, Friction, Multicolored, Marusan, Box, 1950s 140.00
Bus, Greyhound, Pressed Steel, Battery Operated, Push-Down, Buddy L, 16 In. 358.00
Bus, Greyhound, Scenicruiser, Tin, Battery Operated, KKK, Japan, Box, 1950s, 7 1/4 In. 149.00
Bus, Greyhound, Scenicruiser, Tin, Japan, 1950s, 7 1/2 In. 75.00
Bus, Greyhound, Scenicruiser, Tootsietoy, 7 In. 250.00
Bus, Greyhound, Tin, Battery Operated, Japan, Box, 1950s, 8 In. 75.00
Bus, Greyhound, Tootsietoy 35.00
Bus, Greyhound, Tootsietoy, On Card, 6 In. 135.00
Bus, Greyhound, White Passengers, Black In Rear, Tin, Friction, Marusan, Japan, 1930s, 12 In. ... 950.00
Bus, Intercity, Pressed Steel, 23 In. 468.00
Bus, Intercity, Pressed Steel, Boycroft, 24 In. 550.00
Bus, Interstate, Driver, Windup, 1920, 10 In. 575.00
Bus, Long Distance, Royal Tiger Coach, No. 40, Silver, Plastic Tires, Matchbox, Lesney, Box, 1961 .. 30.00
Bus, Modern, Cast Iron, Painted, Red, Silver Highlights, Tin Base, Rubber Tires, Hubley, 7 1/2 In. .. 248.00
Bus, National Park, Tin, Friction, Daiya, Japan, 1950s, 14 In. 145.00
Bus, New York World's Fair, Cast Iron, Arcade, 6 1/2 In. 325.00
Bus, Omnibus, Double-Decker, Electric, Lithograph, Embossed Figures, Meier 1834.00
Bus, Omnibus, Grand Hotel, Horse Drawn, Lithograph, Dapple Gray, Meier 575.00
Bus, Omnibus, Hotel, Bright Blue, Red, Gold Wheels, Spirit Painted, Meier 575.00
Bus, Overland Stage Lines, Pressed Steel, Box, 32 In. 1540.00
Bus, Packard Decal, Pressed Steel, Blue, Cream Roof, Hinged, Keystone, 31 In. 3850.00
Bus, Pickwick Nite Coach, Cast Iron, Painted, Red, Green Stripe, Disc Wheels, Kenton, 11 In. 1980.00
Bus, Pickwick Stages System, Pressed Steel, Box 660.00
Bus, Pressed Steel, Blue, Orange Stripe, Clockwork, Rubber Tires, Kingsbury, 16 In. 825.00
Bus, Pressed Steel, Cor-Cor, 24 In. 440.00

Bus, School, Die Cast, Decal Sheet, Hubley, Box, 1961, 4 1/2 In. 145.00
Bus, School, Holgate, 10 In. 75.00
Bus, Trolley, Tin, Friction, Japan, 1950, 12 1/2 In. 295.00
Bus Terminal, Wood, 2 Buses, Arcade, Box, 1943, 30 In. 5720.00
Busy Delivery, Black Figure, Pushing Cart, Tin, Windup, Marx, 1939, 9 In. 505.00
Busy Lizzie, Sweeps Floor, Windup, Germany, 1920s 550.00
Butcher Shop, Papier-Mache Meat, Metal Butcher, Paper Lithograph On Wood, 8 In. 355.00
Buttercup & Spareribs, Tin, Pull, Nifty Co., 1920s, 7 1/2 In. ....850.00 to 975.00
Butterfly, Apollo, Lithograph, Naturalistic Colors, Moving Wings, Gold Wheels, Georg Fischer 640.00
Calculator, Multiplication, Child's, Tin, Cylindrical, 1898, 9 In. 95.00
Calypso Joe, Drummer, Tin, Windup, Linemar, 1950s 485.00
Camel, Double Hump, Swivel Neck, Glass Eyes, Wood, Leather Ears, Rope Tail, Schoenhut, 8 In. 1650.00
Camel, Man On Back, Tin, U.S. Zone, Box 265.00
Cannon, Tin, Blue & White, Chein 35.00
Cap Gun, 2 Monkeys, Bang Into Each Other, Cast Iron, 3 5/8 x 4 1/4 In. 495.00
Cap Gun, Automatic, Cast Iron, National, 1920, 3 5/8 In. 170.00
Cap Gun, Buccaneer Flintlock, Cast Metal, Plastic Grips, Nichols, 3 1/2 In. 18.00
Cap Gun, Buck, Cast Iron, Single Shot, Single Action, Revolver Style, Hubley, 3 1/4 In. 100.00
Cap Gun, Buckaroo, Single Shot, Chess Piece Grips, Nickel, Actoy, 7 1/2 In. 55.00
Cap Gun, Buffalo Bill, Long Barrel, Kenton, 1923, 11 3/8 In. 130.00
Cap Gun, C-Boy, Cast Iron, Faux Pearl Grips, Kenton, 6 In. 46.00
Cap Gun, Chief, Silver, Hubley, 7 1/2 In. ....12.00 to 47.00
Cap Gun, Die Cast, Nickel Plated, Paladin Leslie Henry, 9 3/4 In. 358.00
Cap Gun, Fanner 50, Mattel, Box 130.00
Cap Gun, Frontier Smoker, PE Co., Box, 9 In. 169.00
Cap Gun, Hero, Cast Iron, Nickel Plated, Stevens 50.00
Cap Gun, Monkey & Coconut, Figural, Cast Iron, 4 x 4 1/8 x 3/4 In. 495.00
Cap Gun, Mountie, Silver Color, Hubley, 8 In. 12.00
Cap Gun, Pirate, Double Shot, Hubley, Box, 9 1/2 In. 99.00
Cap Gun, Punch & Judy, Ives 3565.00
Cap Gun, Repeating Pistol, Dick, Hubley, Box 35.00
Cap Gun, Ric-O-Shay Jr., Nickel, Horse Head Grips, Hubley, 9 1/2 In. 124.00
Cap Gun, Rodeo, Silver, White Plastic Grips, Hubley, 9 In. 40.00
Cap Gun, Single Shot, Single Action, Derringer, Cast Iron, Stevens, 1882, 3 1/4 In. 120.00
Cap Gun, Super Cowboy, Die Cast, Revolving Cylinder, Wood Grips, Crescent Toys, 9 1/4 In. 28.00
Cap Gun, Super Nu-Matic, 2 Boxes Of Cap Rolls, Louis Marx, 6 1/4 In. 40.00
Cap Gun, Sure Shot, Hubley, Box, 7 In. 159.00
Captain Hook, Tin, Fabric, Battery Operated, Marusan, 10 1/2 In. 1429.00
Captain Video Spaceship Set, Lido, Box, 1950s 797.00
Car, Airflow, Coupe, Cast Iron, Nickel Bumpers, Rubber Tires, Hubley, 7 1/4 In. 728.00
Car, Airflow, Coupe, Yellow, Wyandotte, 1930s, 6 In. 285.00
Car, Airflow, Pressed Steel, Electric Lights, Windup, Kingsbury, 1930s, 14 In. 415.00
Car, Airflow, Pressed Steel, Windup, Kingsbury, 12 In. 770.00
Car, Airflow, Sedan, 1934 Decal On Roof, Cast Iron, Gray, Nickel Plated Grille, Arcade, 4 In. 330.00
Car, Airflow, Sedan, Electric Light, Cast Iron, Hubley, 7 1/4 In. 670.00
Car, Andy Gump, Cast Iron, Arcade, 1923, 8 In. 450.00
Car, Andy Gump, Cast Iron, Painted Figure, Arcade, 1924 .... 1400.00
Car, Armored, Gray, Tootsietoy, 1938, 4 In. 225.00
Car, Armored, Silver, Tootsietoy, 1938, 4 In. 175.00
Car, Aston Martin, James Bond, Tin, Battery Operated, Gilbert, Box, 11 In. 745.00
Car, Austin Healy, Sedan, Windshield, Driver, Yellow, Dinky Toys, 1957, 3 1/2 In. 75.00
Car, Austin, Hot Rod Roadster, Blue, Arcade, 3 3/4 In. 250.00
Car, Austin, Nickel Wheels, Arcade, 3 3/4 In. 275.00
Car, Benz, Mystery Action, Tin, Battery Operated, TN, Japan, 10 1/2 In. 220.00
Car, Blue, White Lining, Driver, Blue Uniform, Driver Cog On Rear Axle, Germany 206.00
Car, Boat, Trailer, Convertible, Pressed Tin, Haji, 16 In., 3 Piece 176.00
Car, Brevete, No. 2002, 2 Door, Windup, France, 5 1/2 In. 55.00
Car, Buick, 2-Tone, Brown, Beige, Tin, Friction, Japan, 8 In. 175.00
Car, Buick, Black, ATC, 1958, 14 In. 2300.00
Car, Buick, Century Wagon, Remote Control, Battery Operated, Tin, IRCO, Japan, 8 1/2 In. 130.00
Car, Buick, Fire Chief, Metal, Ichiko, 1959, Japan, Box, 11 1/2 In. 295.00

Car, Buick, Riviera, Door-Matic, Japan, 1962, 11 In. 395.00
Car, Bumper, Tin Lithograph, Windup, Jiggs Midway, Germany, c.1925, 5 1/4 In. 8960.00
Car, Cadillac, 1941 Model, Toytown Estate Wagon, Wyandotte, 21 In. 195.00
Car, Cadillac, 1950s Model, Plastic, Green, Kahn, 9 1/4 In. 50.00
Car, Cadillac, 1957 Model, 4 Doors, Hardtop, Friction, Marusan, Japan, Box, 15 In. 280.00
Car, Cadillac, Metal, Battery Operated, Korea, Box, 1960s, 13 In. 175.00
Car, Cadillac, Red, Japan, 1965, 25 In. 475.00
Car, Cadillac, Sedan, Silver Grille, Cream, Plastic Wheels, No. 27, Matchbox, Box, 1960, 2 3/4 In. .. 105.00
Car, Cadillac, Tin, Friction, Red, Japan, 1960s, 8 In. 120.00
Car, Camaro, Tin, Friction, Japan, Box, 1967, 13 In. 395.00
Car, Campus Express, Tin, Friction, Linemar, Japan, 9 In. 195.00
Car, Cast Iron, Painted Black, Cast Headlamps, Silver Trim, Cast Driver, Hubley, 7 In. 525.00
Car, Celica, Tin, Friction, Ichiko, Japan, Box, 14 In. 195.00
Car, Chevrolet Impala, 007 Secret Agent, Joy Toy Co., Japan, Box, 1963, 15 In. 625.00
Car, Chevrolet, Corvair, Hub Caps, Metal Friction, Japan, Box, 9 In. 175.00
Car, Chevrolet, Coupe, 1928 Model, Cast Iron, Arcade, 8 In. 1250.00
Car, Chevrolet, Coupe, Arcade, c.1935, 8 In. 1725.00
Car, Chevrolet, Coupe, Cast Iron, Gray, Black, Nickel Disc Wheels, Spare On Trunk, Arcade, 8 In. ... 715.00
Car, Chevrolet, Coupe, Tootsietoy, 3 In. 30.00
Car, Chevrolet, Highway Patrol, Convertible, Daiya, Japan, 14 In. 250.00
Car, Chevrolet, Ichiko, Japan, Box, 1963, 8 1/2 In. 175.00
Car, Chevrolet, Impala, Blue, Tinted Windows, No. 57, Matchbox, 1961, 2 3/4 In. 85.00
Car, Chevrolet, Sedan, Cast Iron, Arcade, 1925, 7 In. 168.00
Car, Chevrolet, Sedan, Cast Iron, Arcade, 1928, 9 In. 2800.00
Car, Chrysler, Airflow, Pink, Nickel Grill, Chassis, Rubber Spare On Trunk, Hubley, 4 1/2 In. 195.00
Car, Chrysler, Airflow, Sedan, Pressed Steel, Painted, Red, Nickel Grill, Bumpers, Cor-Cor, 16 In. ... 1650.00
Car, Circus Clown, Tin, Windup, Japan, Box, 1950, 6 In. 345.00
Car, Convertible, Tin, Wood Wheels, Marx, 6 1/2 In. 120.00
Car, Corvette, Fire Chief, Battery Operated, Tin, Taiyo, Japan, 1971, 10 In. 80.00
Car, Coupe, Cast Iron, Blue, Nickel Plated Grill, Kilgore, 3 3/4 In. 110.00
Car, Coupe, Cast Iron, Detachable Body, Orange & Green, Hubley, 5 In. 330.00
Car, Coupe, Cast Iron, Detachable Body, Yellow & Black, White Roof, Hubley, 5 In. 165.00
Car, Coupe, Cast Iron, Orange, Metal Wheels, Kilgore, 3 1/4 In. 65.00
Car, Coupe, Cast Iron, Yellow, Black, Nickel Plated Grille, Hubley, 3 3/4 In. 110.00
Car, Coupe, Convertible, Pressed Steel, Windup, Kingsbury, 12 1/2 In. 880.00
Car, Coupe, Pressed Steel, Green Body, Tan Roof, Running Boards, Marklin, 14 3/4 In. 715.00
Car, Dan, Dipsy, Tin, Windup, Marx, Box, 5 1/2 In. 165.00
Car, DeSoto, Airflow, Green, Hubley, 4 1/2 In. 425.00
Car, DeSoto, Airflow, Rose, Hubley, 6 1/4 In. 750.00
Car, DeSoto, Airflow, Windup, Cor-Cor, 17 In. 660.00
Car, Driver, Blue Uniform, Flywheel, Lithograph, Red, Black Details, Germany 230.00
Car, Driver, Flywheel Drive, Lithograph, Red, Yellow, White Lining, Georg Fischer 573.00
Car, Driver, Passenger, Lithograph, Red, Gold, Black, Red, No. 45, Georg Fischer 1605.00
Car, Driver, Tin, Metal, Windup, Gunthermann, Germany, 14 In. 560.00
Car, Ferrari, Berlinetta, Light Green, No. 75, Matchbox, Lesney, Box, 1965 .... 38.00
Car, Ferrari, Racing, 365GT BB, Bump & Go, Tin, Battery Operated, Japan, Box, 1960s, 9 In. 75.00
Car, Fiat 1500, Pea Green, Brown Luggage On Roof, No. 56, Matchbox, Lesney, Box, 1965 .... 20.00
Car, Fire Chief, Pressed Steel, Battery Operated, Windup, Hoge, 14 In. 495.00
Car, Fire Chief, Pressed Tin, Siren, Marx, 15 In. 440.00
Car, Fire Chief, Pull, c.1940, 8 In. 195.00
Car, Fire Chief, Tin, Windup, Courtland, U.S.A., 1950, 7 1/2 In. 95.00
Car, Flivver, Pressed Steel, Black, Flat Hardtop, Spoke Wheels, Buddy L, 11 In. 660.00
Car, Flivver, Sedan, Center Door, Pressed Steel, Black, Red, Cowdery Toy Works, Box, 11 In. 935.00
Car, Flywheel, Driver, Blue Uniform, Red, Lithograph, Meier 459.00
Car, Ford, 1958 Model, Skyliner, Open & Close Top, Tin, Friction, TN, Japan, Box, 8 In. 120.00
Car, Ford, Convertible, Tin, Friction, Red, 1957, 7 1/2 In. 120.00
Car, Ford, Convertible, Top Goes Up & Down, Tin, Friction, Japan, 1958, 8 In. 120.00
Car, Ford, Country Sedan, Promo, Plastic, Green, Hubley, Box 120.00
Car, Ford, Country Squire, Station Wagon, Tin, Friction, Japan, Box, 1963, 10 In. 195.00
Car, Ford, Coupe, Cast Iron, Arcade, 1925, 7 In. 392.00
Car, Ford, Coupe, Gray, Iron, c.1924, 8 1/2 In. 206.00

Car, Ford, Custom 300, Micro Racer, Tin, Windup, No. 1045, Schuco, Box, 4 3/4 In. 110.00
Car, Ford, Fairlane, 2 Door, Tin, Friction, Blue & White, Steerable Front Wheels, Marusan, 13 In. 255.00
Car, Ford, Fairlane, Fire Chief, Ivory Interior, Plastic Tires, No. 59, Matchbox, 2 1/2 In. 80.00
Car, Ford, GT Racer, White, Yellow Hubcaps, No. 41, Matchbox, Lesney, Box, 1966 .... 36.00
Car, Ford, Model A, Coupe, A.C. Williams, 3 3/4 In. 250.00
Car, Ford, Model T, Coupe, Black, Hubley, 4 In. 250.00
Car, Ford, Model T, Coupe, Gray, Nickel Wheels, Kilgore, 6 1/2 In. 500.00
Car, Ford, Model T, Hot Rod, Yellow, Battery Operated, Alps, Box, 1950s, 11 1/2 In. 350.00
Car, Ford, Model T, Orange, Tootsietoy 55.00
Car, Ford, Model T, Sedan, Cast Iron, Black, Gold Side Stripe, Nickel Driver, Arcade, 1926, 6 In. 880.00
Car, Ford, Model T, Sedan, Cast Iron, Black, Spoke Wheels, Cast Driver, Dent, 6 3/8 In. 165.00
Car, Ford, Model T, Sedan, Center Door, Black, Hubley, 6 1/2 In. 650.00
Car, Ford, Mustang, Mach I, Battery Operated, 1960s, 10 1/2 In. 80.00
Car, Ford, Prefect, Metal Wheels, Silver Grille, Tow Hook, No. 30, Matchbox, Box, 2 1/4 In. 99.00
Car, Ford, Sedan, Tootsietoy, 1935, 3 In. 65.00
Car, Ford, Skyliner, Battery Top Open, Japan, Box, 1958, 9 1/4 In. 225.00
Car, Ford, Thunderbird, 1955, 11 In. 595.00
Car, Ford, Zodiac Mk IV, Metallic Blue, Hood Opens, Spare, No. 53, Matchbox, Lesney, Box, 1968 .. 30.00
Car, Franklin, Cream, Japan, 1931, 8 In. 85.00
Car, G-Man Pursuit, Pressed Tin, Marx, 14 1/2 In. 525.00
Car, G-Man Pursuit, Red, Blue, Windup, Marx, 14 In. 385.00
Car, Graham, Pressed Steel, Cor-Cor, 20 In. 660.00
Car, Graham, Sedan, Pressed Steel, Blue, Electric Lights, Spare On Trunk, Cor-Cor, 1933, 19 In. 1760.00
Car, Headquarters Staff, Pressed Tin, Marx, 14 1/2 In. 2310.00
Car, Hi-Way Henry, Tin Lithograph, Doghouse Hood, Clockwork, Fischer, Germany, 8 In. 880.00
Car, Highway Patrol, Arm Goes Up & Down, Tin, Battery Operated, Daiya, Japan, Box, 1950s, 10 In. 275.00
Car, Hill Climber Roadster, Flywheel Drive, Schiebel, 1920s, 20 In. 475.00
Car, Hot Dog Rod, Friction, Masuya, Japan, 9 In. 185.00
Car, Hot Rod, Friction, Japan, Box, 1950s, 7 1/2 In. 175.00
Car, Hot Rod, Lightening, Driver, Battery Operated, Japan, Box, 1950s, 10 1/2 In. 295.00
Car, Indian, Crash Car, Motorcycle Front, Accessories, Hubley, 11 1/2 In. 3300.00
Car, Jaguar, Mark 10, Metallic Beige, Hood Opens, No. 28, Matchbox, Lesney, Box, 1964 .... 35.00
Car, Jaguar, Pressed Steel, Doepke, 18 In. 415.00
Car, Jaguar, Silver, Red, Tin Lithograph, Battery Operated, 1950s, 7 In. 150.00
Car, Jaguar, Stunt, TM, Japan, 9 1/2 In. 195.00
Car, Jalopy, Comic, Tin, Linemar, 1950s, 5 In. 125.00
Car, Jalopy, Tin, Friction, Linemar, Box, 1950s 150.00
Car, Jalopy, Tin, Windup, Marx, Box, c.1935, 7 In. 250.00
Car, Jupiter Space, Tin, Red, Yellow, Turquoise, Friction, TN, 5 In. 1176.00
Car, Komikal Kop, Marx, 1930s 650.00
Car, Krazy Kar, Unique Art, c.1921, 7 1/2 In. 450.00
Car, Leaping Lena, Tin, Windup, Strauss, 8 1/2 In. 248.00
Car, Limousine, Cast Iron, Painted, Black, Red Spoke Wheels, Hubley, 6 3/4 In. 195.00
Car, Limousine, Chauffeur, Family, Lithograph, Red, Yellow, 6-Light, Georg Fischer 800.00
Car, Limousine, Driver, Tin Lithograph, Clockwork, England, 1920s, 8 5/8 In. 235.00
Car, Limousine, Tin, Painted, Carette, 20th Century, 15 In. 3680.00
Car, Limousine, Tin, Painted, Carl Bubb, 11 In. 690.00
Car, Limping Lizzie, Driver, Windup, Marx, Box, 1930s 495.00
Car, Lincoln, Cosmopolitan, Red, Black, Japan, 1953, 11 1/2 In. 2200.00
Car, Lincoln, Coupe, Japan, 1956, 9 1/2 In. 195.00
Car, Lincoln, Ed, Black, Yonezawa, 1955, 13 In. 3200.00
Car, Lincoln, Orange, White, Ichiko, 1957, 12 1/2 In. 2300.00
Car, Lincoln, Zephyr, Cast Iron, Nickel Grille, Bumpers, Painted Blue, Hubley, 7 In. 825.00
Car, Lo-Lo, Tin, Windup, Lehmann, 4 In. .... *ILLUS* 336.00
Car, Luggage Rack & Chauffeur, Windup, Orange & Black, G & K, Germany 550.00
Car, Magic, Tin, Friction, T.M. Co., Japan, 1950s, 5 1/2 In. 95.00
Car, Magnette, Tin, Friction, Japan, 8 1/2 In. 295.00
Car, Mazda, Cosmo, Sedan, Tin, Friction, TN, Japan, Box, 14 1/2 In. 195.00
Car, Mechanical, Animal, Driver, Painted, Pressed Steel, Dayton, 14 1/2 In. 175.00
Car, Mercedes-Benz, 2/9, Tin, Friction, Green, Japan, 1950s, 8 In. 95.00
Car, Mercedes-Benz, 250SE, Tin Friction, Japan, Box, 7 In. 55.00

Toy, Car, Lo-Lo, Tin, Windup, Lehmann, 4 In.

Toy, Cat, Happy Tabby, Paper Lithograph On Wood, All Fair, No. 283, Box, 10 In.

Car, Mercedes-Benz, 300, Die Cast, Windup, Germany, 5 1/2 In. 154.00
Car, Mercedes-Benz, 300SL, Marklin, Germany, Box, 13 In. 220.00
Car, Mercedes-Benz, 300SS, Tin, Friction, Box, 24 In. 55.00
Car, Mercedes-Benz, Bump & Go, Battery Operated, Tin, Taiyo, Japan, 10 1/2 In. 20.00
Car, Mercedes-Benz, Bump & Go, Battery Operated, Tin, Taiyo, Japan, Box, 10 1/2 In. 80.00
Car, Mercedes-Benz, Coach, White, Plastic Wheels, No. 68, Matchbox, Box, 1970, 2 3/4 In. 94.00
Car, Mercedes-Benz, Model Kit, Schuco Studio, Box, 1930s 460.00
Car, Mercedes-Benz, Pressed Tin, Chiko, Box, 24 In. 248.00
Car, Mercedes-Benz, SS, Sedan, Head Lights, Tin, Battery Operated, Japan, Box 33.00
Car, Mercury, Sedan, 1949 Model, Blue, Red Seats, Teckno, 4 1/2 In. 185.00
Car, Mercury, Station Wagon, Metallic Lime Green, Dogs, No. 73, Matchbox, Lesney, Box, 1968 .... 45.00
Car, Metal, Windup, Marx, Box, 1950s, 11 In. 195.00
Car, Metal, Windup, Red, Germany, 1950s, 10 In. 145.00
Car, MGA, Sports Roadster, Tin, Remote Control, Battery Operated, Japan, 7 In. 145.00
Car, Milton Berle, Caricature, Tin Lithograph, Windup, Marx, 1950s, 6 In. 550.00
Car, Milton Berle, Tin, Windup, Marx, Box, 6 1/2 In. 440.00
Car, Monkee-Mobile, Plays Tunes, Tin, Battery Operated, Friction, ASC, Box, 12 In. 150.00
Car, Motor Kutsche, Lehmann, Box, c.1914 .... 2275.00
Car, Nash, Tin, Friction, Japan, 1950s, 8 In. 120.00
Car, Nazi Command, 9 Soldiers, Windup, Tipp Co., 1930 .... 950.00
Car, New Drive, Tin Lithograph Bottom, Japan, Original Box, c.1955 .... 59.00
Car, Oldsmobile, Curved Dash, Steel, Black, Crank Wind, Hafner, Early 1900s, 10 1/2 In. 355.00
Car, Oldsmobile, Gray Blue, Orange Roof, 1958, 12 In. 425.00
Car, Oldsmobile, Tin, Friction, Driver, Japan, 14 In. 500.00
Car, Oldsmobile, Tin, Remote Control, Red, Cream, Green, Japan, 8 1/2 In. 135.00
Car, Open, Driver, Tin Plated, Windup, Fischer, c.1910-20, 5 3/4 In. 425.00
Car, Packard, Phaeton, Steel Plate, Friction, Red, Green, Disc Wheels, Schieble, 1920, 12 1/2 In. 395.00
Car, Packard, Red, 1930s, 13 In. 85.00
Car, Packard, Sedan, Straight 8, Iron, Green Body, Black Roof, Running Boards, Hubley, 11 In. 24200.00
Car, Pierce Arrow, Sedan, Cast Iron, Arcade, 1935, 7 In. ....1100.00 to 1250.00
Car, Plymouth, Convertible, Tin, Friction, Bandai, Japan, Box, 8 1/4 In. 415.00
Car, Plymouth, Valiant, Tin, Friction, SAN, Japan, Box, 9 1/2 In. 80.00
Car, Police, Buick, Tin, Friction, Japan, 14 1/2 In. 145.00
Car, Police, Buick, Tin, Friction, Japan, 1959, 11 1/2 In. 195.00
Car, Police, Chevrolet, Battery Operated, Cap Firing, Cragstan, 12 In. 425.00
Car, Police, Convertible, 2 Policemen, Battery Operated, Daiya, Box, 1963, 14 In. 325.00
Car, Police, Ford, Yonezawa, Japan, 1957, 16 In. 350.00
Car, Police, Mercury, Tin, Friction, Japan, 1958, 11 1/2 In. 275.00
Car, Police, New Siren, VW, Tin, Taiyo, Japan, 1970s, 9 3/4 In. 100.00
Car, Police, Tin, Friction, Green, Marx, U.S.A., 1930s, 8 In. 245.00
Car, Pontiac, Convertible, Yellow, Silver Grille, White Interior, No. 39, Matchbox, 2 3/4 In. 110.00
Car, Pontiac, Metal, Japan, 1962, 8 1/2 In. 175.00
Car, Pontiac, Safari, Station Wagon, Blue, White, Tootsietoy, c.1955, 7 In. 290.00
Car, Pontiac, Tin, Friction, Japan, 1962, 8 1/2 In. 225.00
Car, Prop-Rod, Thimble-Drome, Box, 1960s, 12 1/2 In. 220.00
Car, Racing, 2 Cars, Red, Blue, Round Track, Tin, U.S. Zone, Box 176.00
Car, Racing, 2-In-1, Turnover, Metal, Friction, TM, Japan, Box, 1950s, 8 1/2 In. 245.00

Car, Racing, Articulated Exhaust Flames, Cast Iron, Cast Driver, Yellow, Red, Hubley, 8 1/2 In. 1760.00
Car, Racing, Blue Bird, Tin, Friction, SAN, Japan, 1950s, 12 In. 295.00
Car, Racing, Boat Tail, Metal, Windup, England, 1930s, 12 In. 475.00
Car, Racing, Boat Tail, Penny, Tin, Germany, 4 1/2 In. 220.00
Car, Racing, Champion Road Racer Of 1927, Tin Lithograph, Friction, Box, 1960s, 3 x 8 In. 620.00
Car, Racing, Crouching Driver, Flywheel Drive, Lithograph, Cream, Black, Red Details, Distler 3095.00
Car, Racing, Driver, Cast Iron, 12 Moving Cylinders, c.1930s, 10 3/4 In. 1568.00
Car, Racing, Electric Headlight, Iron, Painted, Blue, Cast Driver, Rubber Tires, Hubley, 6 1/2 In. 2200.00
Car, Racing, Gordon Bennet, Flywheel Drive, Single Seat, Lithograph, Cream, No. 948 ..... 1835.00
Car, Racing, Haul-A-Car, No. 7, Wyandotte 110.00
Car, Racing, Hot Rod, Honey Chile, No. 5, Lupor, Box, 7 In. 165.00
Car, Racing, Hubley, 1930s 250.00
Car, Racing, Indy Car, Gas Powered, Testors, Plastic, Original Box, 12 In. 84.00
Car, Racing, Loop The Loop, Tin, U.S. Zone 82.00
Car, Racing, Mercedes, Tin, Friction, Cragstan, Japan, 1950, 8 1/2 In. 125.00
Car, Racing, Metal, Windup, Canada, 1930s, 22 In. 295.00
Car, Racing, Metal, Windup, U.S.A., 1950s, 16 In. 175.00
Car, Racing, Mobilgas, Pegasus, No. 65, 12 In. 66.00
Car, Racing, Pressed Steel, Mark, 1930s, 13 In. 275.00
Car, Racing, Race Master, Tin, Windup, Lupor, Box, 11 1/2 In. 138.00
Car, Racing, Rocket, Pressed Tin, Friction, Bandai, 7 In. 77.00
Car, Racing, Silver Bullet, Tin, Windup, Wood Wheels, Buffalo, 12 1/2 In. 193.00
Car, Racing, Tin, France, 1930, 10 In. 195.00
Car, Racing, Tin, Friction, Japan, 1950s, 11 In. 145.00
Car, Racing, Tin, Friction, No. 18, Linemar, Japan, 1950, 11 In. 295.00
Car, Racing, Tin, Windup, 1930, 6 1/2 In. 175.00
Car, Racing, Tin, Windup, Ingap, Italy, c.1950, 5 1/2 x 9 In. 3136.00
Car, Roadster, Art Deco, Marx, 6 In. 150.00
Car, Roadster, Battery Operated, Daiya, Japan, 1950s, 12 In. 375.00
Car, Roadster, Cast Aluminum, Faith Mfg. Co., 1930s, 11 In. 475.00
Car, Roadster, Cast Iron, Gray, Black, Nickel Plated Grille, Hubley, 3 3/4 In. 110.00
Car, Roadster, Cast Iron, Red, Open Rumble Seat, Rear Spare, Driver, Kilgore, c.1928, 8 In. 495.00
Car, Roadster, Dayton, Driver, Tin, 7 In. 303.00
Car, Roadster, Driver, Tin, Painted, Carette, 10 1/2 In. 1955.00
Car, Roadster, Driver, Yellow, Black, Cast Iron, Nickel Plated Grille, Detachable Body, Hubley, 6 In. . 550.00
Car, Roadster, Graham, Red, Black, Tootsietoy, 4 In. 175.00
Car, Roadster, Mechanical, Metal, Windup, Marx, Box, 1940s, 11 In. 195.00
Car, Roadster, Open, Terraplane, Cast Iron, Painted Red, Black Chassis, Nickel Grille, c.1934, 6 In. . 415.00
Car, Roadster, Orange, Black, A.C. Williams, 4 1/2 In. 250.00
Car, Roadster, Packard, Pressed Steel, Hood, Radiator Vents, Windshield Visor, Tan Top, 26 In. 770.00
Car, Roadster, Pressed Steel, Structo, 1930, 16 In. 270.00
Car, Roadster, Red, Schieble, 1920s, 18 In. 425.00
Car, Roadster, Running Boards, Cast Iron, Red, Nickel Plated Grille, Kilgore, 4 In. 99.00
Car, Roadster, Running Boards, Electric Headlights, Steel, Yellow, Brown, Clockwork, 15 In. 990.00
Car, Roadster, Steel, Windshield Side Flaps, Tonneau Cover, Dayton, 13 In. 550.00
Car, Roadster, Stutz Model, Open, Cast Iron, Painted, Lavender, Red, Kilgore, 10 1/2 In. 1650.00
Car, Roadster, Tin, Painted, Bing, 11 In. 2300.00
Car, Roadster, Tin, Painted, Converse, 15 In. 2990.00
Car, Roadster, Tin, Painted, Germany, 9 In. 1265.00
Car, Roadster, Wood, Painted, 38 In. 1150.00
Car, Rocket Racer, Red, Green, Black, White Rubber Tires, Wyandotte, 1935, 6 In. 95.00
Car, Rocket Ranger, Tin, Friction, Crank, Marusan, Box, Early 1950s, 6 In. 830.00
Car, Roll Car, Speed King, Tin, Windup, Marx, 1930s, 16 In. 295.00
Car, Rolls-Royce, Silver Cloud Convertible, Tin, Friction, Bandai, 12 In. 250.00
Car, Rolls-Royce, Silver Cloud Sedan, Tin, Friction, Bandai, 12 In. 240.00
Car, Rolls-Royce, Silver Cloud, Metal Wheels, No. 44, Matchbox, Moko Lesney, Box, 1958 ..... 145.00
Car, Rolls-Royce, Silver Shadow, Metallic Red, No. 24, Matchbox, Lesney, Box, 1967 ..... 30.00
Car, Rolls-Royce, Tin, Friction, Black, Japan, 1950s, 8 1/2 In. 145.00
Car, Saloon, Blue Fenders, Roof, Lithograph, England, 1920s, 9 In. 295.00
Car, Saloon, Tin Lithograph, Clockwork, Bub, c.1912, 9 3/8 In. 645.00
Car, Scarab, Pressed Steel, Ny-Lint, 14 In. 132.00

Car, Scarab, Pressed Steel, Windup, Paperwork, Buddy L, 10 In. 440.00
Car, Seated Figures, 2 Seat, Open, Cast Iron, Red, Clockwork, Kenton, 7 In. 440.00
Car, Sedan, 4 Door, Cast Iron, Painted, Green, Black Disc Wheels, Skoglund & Olsen, 7 1/2 In. 825.00
Car, Sedan, 4 Door, Painted Red, Black Roof, Silver Trim, Nickel Disc Wheels, Dent, 7 1/2 In. 660.00
Car, Sedan, Blue, Schieble, 1920s, 18 In. 495.00
Car, Sedan, Blue, Wyandotte, 1930s, 6 In. .... 175.00 to 250.00
Car, Sedan, Cast Iron, Green, Nickel Plated Grille, Champion, 4 In. 192.00
Car, Sedan, Driver, Windup, Gunthermann, 1930s, 9 1/2 In. 475.00
Car, Sedan, Light Bulbs, Green, Wyandotte, 1930s, 9 In. 375.00
Car, Sedan, Pressed Steel, Turner, 29 In. 1980.00
Car, Sedan, Red, Black, A.C. Williams, 4 1/2 In. 250.00
Car, Sedan, Windup, C. Rossignol, France, 8 In. 450.00
Car, Sedan, Yellow, Wyandotte, 1930s, 6 In. 250.00
Car, Space Patrol, 1950s Model, Tin, Friction, Blue, Japan, 5 1/2 In. 1120.00
Car, Space Patrol, Tin, Friction, Ichiko, Box, 8 In. 5800.00
Car, Sport Roadster, Driver, Rumble Seat, Red, Kilgore, 8 In. 750.00
Car, Sports, 2-Seater, Driver In Tan Overcoat, Lithograph, Brown, Red, Yellow, Georg Fischer 1260.00
Car, Steer-O-Car, Plastic, Original Box, 12 In. 110.00
Car, Stock Car, Pressed Steel, Red, Slat Side, Buddy L, 20 In. 715.00
Car, Stutz, Cast Iron, Kilgore, 10 1/4 In. 1450.00
Car, Stutz, Pressed Steel, Transmission, Steering, Structo, 16 In. 990.00
Car, Take Apart, Cast Iron, Hubley, 6 1/8 In. 110.00
Car, Tin, Push Down On Back, Friction, Daiya, Japan, 8 1/4 In. 275.00
Car, Tin, Windup, Gama Patent, Schuco, U.S. Zone Germany, 6 1/2 In. 220.00
Car, Touring, Cast Iron, Kenton, 9 1/2 In. 550.00
Car, Touring, Cast Iron, Kenton, 12 In. 775.00
Car, Touring, Cast Iron, Removable Pressed Steel Canopy, Blue, Gold, Hubley, c.1911, 10 In. 1210.00
Car, Touring, Chauffeur, Windup, Lehmann, 1924, 10 In. 1750.00
Car, Touring, Open, Cast Iron, Blue, Silver, Yellow Spoke Wheels, Jones & Bixler, 8 3/4 In. 360.00
Car, Touring, Passengers, Cast Iron, Dent, 9 1/2 In. 660.00
Car, Vauxhall, Sedan, Red, Cream, Tow Hook, No. 22, Matchbox, Box, 1957, 2 1/2 In. 72.00
Car, Vauxhall, Victor, Yellow, No. 45, Matchbox, Lesney, Box, 1958 .... 80.00
Car, Volkswagen, 1500 Saloon, White, No. 15, Matchbox, Lesney, Box, 1968 .... 35.00
Car, Volkswagen, 1500, Tin, Friction, Maroon, Japan, 8 In. 225.00
Car, Volkswagen, 1600 TL, Red, No. 67, Matchbox, Lesney, Box, 1967 .... 35.00
Car, Volkswagen, Beetle, Turquoise, No. 154, Tonka, Box, 8 1/2 In. 66.00
Car, Volkswagen, Tin, Friction, KO, Japan, Box, 1960s, 9 1/2 In. 95.00
Car, Volvo, The Saint, P-1800, White, Corgi, 3 3/4 In. 65.00
Car, Woody, Tin, Windup, Marx, 1950s, 7 1/2 In. 110.00
Car, X-Car, Woman Driver, Windup, Japan, 1940s, 5 In. 95.00
Car & House Trailer, Green, Tootsietoy, 1935 .... 175.00
Car & Trailer, Lincoln Zephyr, Kingsbury, 1930s, 23 In. 1540.00
Carousel, Aerial Gnomes, 3 Trapezes, String Pull, Lithograph, Blue Circular Tilt, Distler 1375.00
Carousel, Airplanes, Ducks, Tin, Crank, Wyandotte, U.S.A. 245.00
Carousel, Swans, Airplanes, Windup, Wyandotte, 1930s, 6 In. 350.00
Carousel, Tin Lithograph, Zeppelins, Planes, Hot Air Balloons, Clockwork, Germany, 11 1/2 In. 5500.00
Carousel, Tin, Boys Riding Boats, Painted, Clockwork, Muller & Kadeder, Germany 1760.00
Carriage, 3 Wheel, Painted Wood Seat, Metal Frame, Tufted Upholstery, Bonnet, 23 In. 115.00
Carriage, Doll's, Lithograph, Cream, Scenes, Boys & Girls, Folded Hood, Quilt, Baby, Distler 415.00
Carriage, Doll's, Painted, Cream, Pink Fabric Lining, Lace, Bisque Baby, Germany 185.00
Carriage, Doll's, Wood, Metal Frame, Oil Cloth Hood, Rubber Rim Wheels, 17 In. 58.00
Carriage, Doll's, Wood, Painted, 3 Wheels, 1800s 300.00
Carriage, Doll's, Wood, Rubber Tires, Spoke Wheels, Folding Top, F.W. Whitney, 33 In. 66.00
Carriage, Doll's, Wood, Spoke Wheels, Cast Iron Top, 31 In. 248.00
Carriage, Horse Drawn, Brake, 3 Seat, Driver, 5 Passengers, Hubley, c.1900, 18 In. 7150.00
Carriage, Lady Driver, Cast Iron, Open Cart, Spoke Wheels, Japanned Horse, 9 1/2 In. 165.00
Carriage, Landau, 2 Passenger, Black, 2 Prancing Horses, Wilkens, c.1895, 15 In. 385.00
Carriage, Oxford Trap, Back-To-Back Seats, Graphics, Black, Silver Horses, Kenton, c.1911, 15 In. 2200.00
Carriage, Phaeton, Open, Black, Tufted Seat, Mat, Horse, Pratt & Letchworth, c.1883, 17 In. 935.00
Carriage, Phaeton, Seated Driver, Cast Iron, Pressed Steel, Open, Clockwork, Wilkens, 10 In. 550.00
Carriage, Phaeton, Spider, Driver, Cast Iron, Blue Open Top, Embossed Seats, Hubley, 13 1/2 In. 2475.00

Carriage, Quilt, Wood, Metal Hinges, Painted, Stenciled, Fringe, 27 In. & 27 x 28 In. 115.00
Carriage, Trap, Horse Drawn, Lithograph, Black & White Dappled Horse, Dos-A-Dos, Driver, Meier . 413.00
Cart, 2 Oxen, Softwood, Painted, Wood Wheels, 5 3/4 x 18 x 5 1/2 In. 330.00
Cart, Barrel, Horse Drawn, Wood, Pull Toy, 29 In. 510.00
Cart, Donkey Drawn, Cast Iron, Black, Red Highlights, Welker & Crosby, c.1883, 11 x 5 1/2 x 4 In. . . 360.00
Cart, Gloomy Gus, Blue Tin, Cast Iron, Black Donkey, Red Spoke Wheels, 7 1/4 In. 220.00
Cart, Gloomy Gus, Driver, Donkey, Cast Iron, Open Stake Side Body, Harris, 13 In. 415.00
Cart, Horse Drawn, Black Driver, Cast Iron, Kenton, 15 In. 560.00
Cart, Horse Drawn, Buckboard, Tin, Geo. Brown Co., 6 In. 220.00
Cart, Horse Drawn, Chester Gump, Arcade, 7 In. 395.00
Cart, Horse Drawn, Coal, Figure, Dent, 13 1/2 In. 850.00
Cart, Horse Drawn, Walking, Articulated Legs, Open Cart, Spoke Wheels, Cast Iron, Ives, 9 1/2 In. . . 825.00
Cart, Hose Reel, Open Bench Seat, Driver, Spoke Wheels, Nickeled Cast Iron, Shimer, 10 In. 495.00
Cart, Ice Cream, Plastic, Wyandotte, 1950, 4 1/2 In. 120.00
Cart, Mule Drawn, c.1900 .... 350.00
Cart, Mule, Articulated, Open Bed, Cast Iron, Red, Black Spoke Wheels, Ives, 14 In. 990.00
Cart, Ox Drawn, Black Driver, Pull Toy, Cast Iron, 12 In. 550.00
Cart, Ox Drawn, Driver, c.1900 .... 1250.00
Cart, Ox Drawn, Silver Ox, Cast Iron, Blue Open Bed Cart, Red Spoke Wheels, Harris 90.00
Cart, Pig Pulling Clown, Bell Toy, Cast Iron, Painted 485.00
Cart, Pony, Driver Whipping Horse, Articulated Action, Cast Iron, Wilkens, 7 1/2 In. 66.00
Cart, Produce, Man, Sheep, Circular Pad, Rotates, Side Crank, 3 x 4 1/4 In. 110.00
Cart, Rabbit Pulling, Tin, Chein, 7 3/4 x 11 In. 135.00
Cart, Rabbit, Open Bench, Spoke Wheels, Cast Iron, Painted, Kenton, 5 1/4 In. 275.00
Cart, Wood, Metal Wheels, 30 x 11 In. 30.00
Cart, Woven Wicker, Upholstered, Double Seated, Mechanical, Papier-Mache Goats, 26 In. 7700.00
Cart & Driver, Scalloped, Red, 2 Black Galloping Horses, Patent Dates, Carpenter, c.1885 .... 550.00
Castle & Swans, Steam Accessory Toy, Fleischmann, Germany, 6 1/4 In. 440.00
Cat, Felix, Chasing Mice, Tin Lithograph, Wheeled Platform, Pull Toy, 7 1/4 In. 1430.00
Cat, Felix, Riding Scooter, Tin, Chein 260.00
Cat, Felix, Squeeze Toy, Germany, 1920s 385.00
Cat, Felix, Wood Jointed, Leather Ears, Schoenhut, 1924, 8 In. 115.00
Cat, Felix, Wood, Jointed, Schoenhut, 8 In. ....475.00 to 550.00
Cat, Felix, Wood, Mechanical, Push Toy, Schoenhut, 12 x 18 In. 560.00
Cat, Felix, Wood, Pat Sullivan, 8 In. 248.00
Cat, Felix, Wood, Rubber, Jointed, King Features, 9 1/2 In. 504.00
Cat, Happy Tabby, Paper Lithograph On Wood, All Fair, No. 283, Box, 10 In. .... *ILLUS* 448.00
Cat, Pouncing, Lithograph, Gray, Black, Red Collar, Green Base, Red Disc Wheels, Meier, c.1910 . . 321.00
Cat, Tabby, Crouching, Lithograph, Brown, Cream, Moving Spring Tail, Georg Fischer 688.00
Cat, Tin Lithograph, Leatherette Ears, Wood Ball, Clockwork, Germany, 1930s, 8 3/8 In. 118.00
Cat & Dog, Fighting, Lithograph, Cream, Gray, Red Base, Gold Wheels, Meier 415.00
Chair, Doll's, Balloon Back, Scalloped Crest, Cane Seat, Painted, 6 x 13 1/2 In. 145.00
Chair, Doll's, Carved Wood, Spindles, Legs, Cushions, 11 In. 935.00
Chair, Doll's, Painted, Wood, Spindles, Upholstered, c.1885, 15 In. 605.00
Chairboat, 2 Children, Tin Lithograph, Wood Base, Pickwick Toys, 5 1/2 In. 206.00
Chariot, 3 Horses, Hubley, 10 In. 633.00
Charleston Trio, Tin, Windup, Marx, Box, 9 1/2 In. 1980.00
Charley Weaver Bartender, Battery Operated, Box, c.1950, 12 In. ....55.00 to 69.00
Charlie The Drumming Clown, Battery Operated, Tin, Cragstan, Japan, 9 In. 55.00
Cheery Cook, Windup, Celluloid, Box, Occupied Japan 106.00
Chemical Set, Chemcraft, Gilbert, Box, 1917 .... 50.00
Chest, Mahogany, Satinwood Veneer, Bracket Feet, Brass Knobs, 7 Drawers, England, 22 In. 2530.00
Chester Gump, In Cart, Horse Drawn, Cast Iron, 1900 .... 385.00
Chicken & Chicks, Lithograph, Brown, Black, Yellow, Green Base, Red Wheels, Meier 690.00
Chicken Snatcher, Figure Holding Chicken, Dog Bites Him, Tin Lithograph, c.1927, 8 1/2 In. 1100.00
Chickens, Rotate As They Touch Wheels, Wood, 9 x 13 x 11 In. 115.00
Chinese Man, On Buckboard, With Parasol, Lithograph, Blue, Red, Yellow Tunic, Disc Driven 575.00
Circus, Humpty Dumpty, Big Top, Trapeze, Clowns, Ring Master, Animals, Acrobats, 36 x 24 In. ... 4995.00
Circus, Humpty Dumpty, Wood, Schoenhut, Box, 1930s 300.00
Circus, Lady Rider, Painted Head, Carved Hair, Schoenhut, 8 In. 165.00
Circus, Overland, Bear, Kenton, 1930s 950.00

Circus Boy Hawker, Japan, 1950s, 6 In. 185.00
Circus Car & Trailer, Pressed Tin, Wyandotte, 20 In. 825.00
Circus Clown, Tin, Celluloid, Cloth, Windup, Cragston, 9 In. 395.00
Circus Set, Bimbo Barany, Wood, Tractor, Music Wagon, Semi Truck, Animals, Tent, 40 In. 56.00
Circus Train Set, Elephant, Calliope, Lion, Giraffe, Bengal Tiger, Dickie Bears, Steiff 748.00
Clicker, Mammy Scrubs Baby, Embossed, Tin, Germany, 3 1/2 x 2 1/4 In. 145.00
Climbing Linesman, Battery Operated, T.P.S., c.1957, 24 In. 425.00
Climbing Tractor, Driver, Tin, Windup, Marx, 10 In. 80.00
Clown, Artist, At Easel, Sketches Picture, Mechanical, Vielmetter, Germany, c.1885 .... 3025.00
Clown, Balanced Teeter-Totter, Plink Plunk Music, Clockwork, c.1915, 8 x 8 In. 1650.00
Clown, Bozo, Steaming, Sweeps, Tin, Vinyl, Fabric, Battery Operated, TN, Box, 14 In. 165.00
Clown, Charlie, Tin, Vinyl, Fabric, Battery Operated, Alps, Box, 9 In. 220.00
Clown, Flip Action, 2 Figures, Lithograph, Spring Sticks, Sitting On Sliding Beams, Germany 920.00
Clown, Good Time Charlie, Mixed Material, Windup, Alps, Box, 12 1/2 In. 275.00
Clown, Holding Umbrella, Penny, Tin Lithograph, Bing, 12 In. 50.00
Clown, In Cart, Mule, Windup, Lehmann, Box, 1897-1938 .... 650.00
Clown, Inside Barrel, Tin, DRGM, Germany 590.00
Clown, Juggles 4 Balls, Windup, Schuco, Germany 250.00
Clown, Jumping, Windup, Minkuni, Box, 1950s, 6 1/2 In. 165.00
Clown, Ko-Ko, Max Fleischer, Schoenhut, 1920, 10 In. 3920.00
Clown, Moves On Donkey, Windup, Gama, Germany, 1920s 395.00
Clown, Musician Trio, Felt Costumes, Drum, Symbols, Violin, 4 In. 410.00
Clown, On Cantering Pig, Rocking Action, Lithograph, Pink Pig, Green Base, Georg Fischer 3440.00
Clown, On Platform, Strums Guitar, Head Bobs, Windup, Distler, Germany, 8 1/2 In. 475.00
Clown, On Tightrope, Tin, Painted, Clockwork, Stencil D.R.G.M., Germany, 16 x 8 In. 1650.00
Clown, Pig Cart, Lithograph, Polka Dot Outfit, Red Card, Meier 920.00
Clown, Riding Backwards On Pig, Red & White Polka Dot Outfit, Lithograph 11460.00
Clown, Roller Skating, Tin, Windup, T.P.S., 6 In. 220.00
Clown, Roly Poly, Double Fronted, Yellow, Turquoise, Hemisphere Base, Lithograph, Germany 415.00
Clown, Spins, Papier-Mache, Long Nose, Painted, Clown Makeup, Germany, 1910, 9 In. 120.00
Clown, Standing With Umbrella, Looking Up, Tin, Celluloid, Chein 235.00
Clown, Tambourine, Windup, NGT, Box, 1950s, 7 1/4 In. 235.00
Clown, Tumbling, Lithograph, Red, Yellow Harlequin Clown, Pull Toy, Distler 229.00
Clown, Walking Behind Donkey, Tin, Ges Gesch, Meier Trademark, Germany 500.00
Clown, Weight Lifter, Bends Down, Lifts Weights With Teeth, Windup, 1920s 950.00
Clown, With Banjo, Tin, Round Base, Clockwork, Gunthermann, Germany, 6 1/2 In. 385.00
Clown Dancers, Wood Jointed Figures, Wood Base, Clockwork, 10 In. 1430.00
Clown Trio, Felt Costumes, Drums, Cymbals, Violin, Schuco, 4 In. 410.00
Clowns, Performing, Twirling Barrel, Plays Banjo, Tin, Painted, 8 3/4 x 7 1/4 In. 2200.00
Coach, Coronation, Die Cast, Lesney, England, Box, 15 1/2 In. 220.00
Coach, Driver, Windup, Lehmann 450.00
Coach, Fageol Safety, Cast Iron, Arcade, 12 In. 336.00
Coach, Fageol Safety, Cast Iron, Blue, Gold Strip, Nickel Driver, Rubber Tires, Arcade, 12 In. 248.00
Coach, Fageol Safety, Cast Iron, Orange, Black Roof, Embossed Public Service, Dent, 13 In. 6050.00
Coach, Horse Drawn, Open, Landau, Tin, Painted, Bench Seat, 14 1/2 In. 1760.00
Coach, Horse Drawn, Post, Lithograph, Spirit Painted, Dapple Gray, Driver, 1890s 1146.00
Coal Elevator, Buddy L, 38 1/4 In. 430.00
Cockerel, Lithograph, Cream, Brown, Red, Turquoise, Green Base, Red Disc Wheels, Meier 275.00
Coco, Native Climbs Palm Tree, Lehmann, 1889-1935 .... 2500.00
Combine, Case, Cast Iron, Silver, Red, Revolving Cutter Reel, Spoke Wheels, Vindex 3850.00
Construction Set, DUX Metal Aeroplane, Germany, Box 165.00
Cop, Pressed Tin, Windup, TN, Japan, 6 1/2 In. 99.00
Cow, Elsie, Wood, Pop-Up, Green Base, 6 In. 165.00
Cow, Josie, Walking, Tin, Vinyl, Plush, Battery Operated, Rosko, Box, 14 In. 138.00
Cow, Papier-Mache, Bellows In Head, Pull Toy, Late 1800s .... 550.00 to 825.00
Cradle, Doll's, Carved Edges, Rockers, Peaked Hood, Acorn Finial, Side Panels, 10 x 13 x 8 In. 220.00
Cradle, Doll's, Hooded, Pine, Painted, House, Barn, Pillsbury, Ohio, 1864, 22 x 10 In. 920.00
Cradle, Jenny Lind, Hardwood, Turned Spindle Side Rails, Legs, Rockers, 37 x 20 In. 29.00
Crane, Pressed Steel, Doepke, 28 In. 300.00
Crane, Wrecking, Locomotive, Boom, Shovel Bucket, Pressed Steel, 18 In. 2475.00
Crane, Wrecking, Locomotive, Hook, Pressed Steel, Buddy L, 18 In. 4070.00

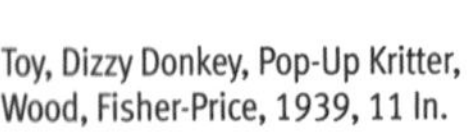

Toy, Dizzy Donkey, Pop-Up Kritter, Wood, Fisher-Price, 1939, 11 In.

Toy, Dog, Hoppel-Dackel, Wheeled Cart, Steiff, Button, Tag, 1950s, 7 x 10 In.

Crocodile, Windup, Legs Move, Mouth Opens, Lehmann, Germany, 1898-1945 .... 550.00
Cupboard, Doll's, Stepback, Panels, Drawers, Wood Knobs, 3 Shelves, 22 In. 1650.00
Cycling Daddy, Tin, Plastic, Fabric, Battery Operated, Bandai, Box, 10 In. 165.00
Cyclist, Kiddy, Tin, Windup, Unique Art, Box, 8 1/2 In. 385.00
Cyclist, Tin Lithograph, Windup, Unique Art, 8 1/2 In. 118.00
Dagwood The Driver, Tin, Marx, Box, 1935, 8 In. 2200.00
Dancer, Hanging, Jointed Wood Figure, Stage, Curtain Hides Clockwork, c.1885, 8 3/4 In. 605.00
Dancing Black Boy, Jointed, Tin, Painted, French Cut, 19th Century, 17 1/2 In. 220.00
Dancing Black Man, Wood, Carved, Jointed Limbs, Painted Black, Mounted On Stand, 14 In. 956.00
Dancing Sam, Tin, Windup, Japan, Original Box, 9 In. 225.00
Dapper Dan, Tin, Windup, Marx, Box, c.1910, 10 In. 1650.00
Dirigible, Silver, Kenton, 6 In. 350.00
Dirigible, String Operated, Lithograph, Yellow Fuselage, Blue Banding, Red Gondola, Distler 1835.00
Dizzy Donkey, Pop-Up Kritter, Wood, Fisher-Price, 1939, 11 In. .... ***ILLUS*** 55.00
Dog, Astro, Tin, Plastic, Plush, Battery Operated, Remote Control, Y Co., Box, 11 In. 195.00
Dog, Boxer, Tin, U.S. Zone 590.00
Dog, Bubbling Pup, Tin, Plush, Battery Operated, Linemar, Box, 7 1/2 In. 220.00
Dog, Buttons, Puppy With A Brain, Battery Operated, 12 In. 80.00
Dog, Buttons, Puppy With A Brain, Tin, Plush, Battery Operated, Marx, Box, 12 In. 330.00
Dog, Chases Cat Around Dog House, Kennel Frolics, Celluloid, Tin, Windup, Japan 225.00
Dog, Dachshund, Long Haired, Green Collar, Waldie Name Tag, Button In Ear, Steiff, 14 1/2 In. 35.00
Dog, Dachshund, Short Haired, Red Collar, Tag, Button In Ear, Steiff, 14 In. 35.00
Dog, Dachshund, Standing, Lithograph, Gray, Black, Tan, Spring Tail, Gray Wheels, Distler 459.00
Dog, Fido, Xylophone Player, Tin, Plush, Battery Operated, Alps, Box, 9 In. 165.00
Dog, Hoppel-Dackel, Wheeled Cart, Steiff, Button, Tag, 1950s, 7 x 10 In. .... ***ILLUS*** 504.00
Dog, Hot Dog, 3 Sections, Tin, Windup, SAE, Japan, 11 In. 65.00
Dog, Irish Setter, Golden Mohair, Painted Features, Swivel Head, Steiff, 1920, 11 In. 615.00
Dog, Mr. Strongpup, Mighty Weightlifter, Tin, Fabric, Plush, Battery Operated, Alps, Box, 9 In. 220.00
Dog, Party Guest, Monkey Attendant, Push Along, Lithograph, Dog In Long Blue Dress, Meier 4585.00
Dog, Police, Celluloid, Articulated Head, France, c.1920, 4 3/4 In. 235.00
Dog, Police, Gendarme, Articulated Head, Molded Arms, France, c.1920, 5 In. 235.00
Dog, Pop-Up, Red Base, Wakouwa, 6 In. 20.00
Dog, Scotty, Tin, Windup, Marx, 1930s 145.00
Dog, Sitting, Mohair, Excelsior Stuffed, Glass Eyes, Cotton Floss Nose, Steiff, 8 In. 550.00
Dog, Space, Tin, Windup, KO, Box, 7 1/2 In. 550.00
Dolls are listed in their own category.
Dollhouse, 1 Room, Wood, Painted, Gable, Glass Windows, Mesh Grates, 22 x 9 1/2 x 18 In. 200.00
Dollhouse, 2 Rooms, Glass Windows, Lace Curtains, Lithograph On Wood, 24 x 18 x 11 In. 8250.00
Dollhouse, 2 Story, 3 Rooms, Wood, Glass Windows, 18 x 12 1/2 In. 259.00
Dollhouse, 2 Story, Wood, Tin, Painted, Brick, Mansard Roof, 19th Century, 33 x 19 1/2 In. 1910.00
Dollhouse, 3 Story, Painted, Sand, Wood, Lace, Grass, Cut Colored Paper, 21 7/8 x 20 In. 460.00
Dollhouse, Colonnade Portico, Lithograph On Wood, Glassine Windows, Reed, 13 In. 1650.00
Dollhouse, Lithograph On Wood, Glassine Windows, Lace Curtains, Dormer, Bliss, 14 1/2 In. 495.00
Dollhouse, Newlyweds Bathroom, Tub, Toilet, Sink, Stool, Tin, Marx, Box, c.1930, 5 In. 165.00
Dollhouse, Pine, 2 Removable Panels, Wallpaper, Painted, 19th Century, 32 x 43 x 19 In. 1725.00
Dollhouse Furniture, Bedroom Set, Bed, Dresser, 2 Chairs, Night Stand 695.00
Dollhouse Furniture, Bedroom, Victorian, Yellow Cherry, Schneegas, 1880s, 6 Piece 295.00

Dollhouse Furniture, Canopy Bed, Side Table, Piano, Settee, Chairs, Gottschalk, c.1885 .... 575.00
Dollhouse Furniture, Living Room, Sofa, Chairs, Table, Tynie Toy, 1940s, 1-In. Scale, 7 Piece 590.00
Donkey, Lithograph, Gray, Green Base, Red Wheels, Meier, c.1920 .... 275.00
Donkey, Standing, Lithograph, Gray, Collar, Harness, Tack, Articulated Head, Georg Fischer 250.00
Dr. Richter Architectural Building Bricks, Oak Box, N.Y., c.1897, 17 In. 590.00
Dragon, Snappy, Tin, Plastic, Plush, Battery Operated, TN, Box, 30 In. 3520.00
Dresser, Doll's, Mirror, 6 Drawers, Cheval Mirror, Mixed Wood, 16 In. 115.00
Drum, 5 War Scenes, Tin, World War II Era, 7 1/2 In. 125.00
Drum, Child's, 2-Sided Eagle, Embossed, American Flag, Red Ground, 7 x 8 In. 695.00
Drum, Snare, Parade, 1880, 12 1/2 x 16 In. 1200.00
Drum, Tom-Tom, 7 Dancing Black Children Circle Drum, 1930s, 7 In. 110.00
Drum Major, No. 27, Tin, Windup, Wolverine, 1930s, 14 In. 138.00
Drum Major, Tin, Windup, Wolverine, Box, 14 In. 440.00
Drum Set, Complete Trap Set, Rainbow Band, No. 3000, Chein, Box 50.00
Drummer, Pressed Tin, Marx, 9 In. 105.00
Drummer Boy, Red Jacket, Blue Pants, Tin, Chein 295.00
Drummer Boy, Windup, Handle, Japan, Box, 1930s, 11 3/4 In. 225.00
Dry Sink, Doll's, Country, Red Paint, Late 1800s, 12 x 22 x 11 In. 880.00
Duck Decoy, Wood, Red Paint, Glass Eyes, Steering Handle, 4 Rubber Tires, Pull Toy, 15 x 16 In. ... 575.00
Dump 'n Dozer, No. 1516, Hubley, Box, 13 In. 35.00
Dump Rake, Horse Drawn, Cast Iron, Red, Yellow, Green Seat, Spoke Wheels, Arcade 495.00
Dynarama, Monster Scene, Metal, Plastic Figures, Wood Base, Lights Up, 16 x 20 In. 390.00
Dynarama, Munsters, Coach, Dragster, Figures, Wood, Plastic, Rubber, 16 x 20 In. 165.00
Earth Hauler, Allis Chalmers, Cast Iron, Orange, Cast Driver, Side Lever, Arcade, 12 1/2 In. 165.00
Earth Hauler, Euclid, Pressed Steel, Doepke, 27 In. 275.00
Earth Hauler, Wooldridge, Pressed Steel, Doepke, 27 In. 330.00
Elephant, Cast Iron, 3 Bells, Pull Toy, Early 1900s, 11 In. 90.00
Elephant, Japan, 1950s 35.00
Elephant, Jointed Wood Body, Glass Eyes, Leather Ears, Trunk, Rope Tail, Schoenhut, 9 In. 110.00
Elephant, Mambo Jolly Drumming, Tin, Plush, Battery Operated, Alps, Box, 9 In. 325.00
Elephant, Trumpeting, Lithograph, Gray, Spring Trunk, Green Base, Red Wheels, Distler 345.00
Elsie, Cow Jumped Over Moon, Wood, Pull Toy, Wood Commodities Corp., 10 x 7 In. 320.00
Erector Set, No. 2, Meccano, Box 99.00
Erector Set, No. 4, Electric Motor, Wheels, Booklet, A.C. Gilbert, Wood Box 165.00
Erector Set, No. 7 1/2, White Truck Set, Gilbert Toys, Wood Box, 1926 .... 275.00
Erector Set, No. 8 1/2, Pressed Steel, Ferris Wheel, Circus, Instructions, Box 75.00
Erector Set, No. 10051, Pressed Steel, Gilbert, Box 65.00
Etch A Sketch, Ohio Art, Box, 1960 .... 170.00
Evel Knievel, Escape From Skull Canyon, Ideal, Box, 1975, 17 x 13 In. 16.00
Felix, Whirligig, El Gato, Tin Lithograph, Clockwork, La Isla, Spain, 7 3/4 In. 1540.00
Ferdinand The Bull, Bull Fighter Opposing The Bull, Windup, Marx, 1935, 8 1/2 In. 315.00
Ferdinand The Bull, Tin, Windup, Marx, Box, 1938, 6 1/2 In. .... 440.00 to 550.00
Ferris Wheel, 12 Cars, Ticket Stand, Mechanical, Carved, Painted, c.1940, 36 1/2 x 30 In. 316.00
Ferris Wheel, Metal, Chein, Box, 1950s, 18 In. 375.00
Ferris Wheel, Steam Accessory Toy, Open Frame, Railed Seats, Riders, Germany, 29 In. 9350.00
Ferris Wheel, Tin, Mechanical, Windup, Chein, Box, 1930s, 17 In. 550.00
Ferris Wheel, Tin, Painted, c.1920, 35 In. 180.00
Figure, Movie, Quo Vadis, John Hill Co., England, Box, 9 x 11 In., 10 Piece 1127.00
Finch, Bobbing, Lithograph, Naturalistic Colors, Action Driven, Yellow Base, Georg Fischer 459.00
Finnegan The Porter, Drives Baggage Card, Windup, Unique Art, 13 1/2 In. 225.00
Fire Brigade Set, Spirit Painted, Horse Drawn Vehicles, Tender, Ladder Wagon, Pump, Meier 4585.00
Fire Crew Tender, No. 58, Flywheel Drive Motor, Open Cab, Lithograph, Georg Fischer 1375.00
Fire Hydrant, Cast Iron, 2 1/2 In. 90.00
Fire Patrol, 2 Horses, 4 Firemen, Gong Bell, Hubley, 1915, 19 In. 1595.00
Fire Patrol, Horse Drawn Wagon, Dent, 1910 .... 3200.00
Fire Patrol, Horse Drawn, Cast Iron, Painted, Red, Spoke Wheels, Bench Seat, 12 1/2 In. 275.00
Fire Patrol, Phoenix, Black Running Horse, 8 Figures, Ives, c.1895, 18 In. 1430.00
Fire Pumper, 2 Horses, 2 Firemen, Gong Bell, Pratt & Letchworth, 1883, 17 In. 3295.00
Fire Pumper, 2 Horses, Gong Bell, Dent, 1905, 19 1/4 In. 1095.00
Fire Pumper, 2 Horses, Painted, Red, Black, Driver, Cast Iron, Welker & Crosby, c.1883, 17 1/2 In. 1650.00
Fire Pumper, 3 Horses, Cast Iron, Driver, Wilkins, 12 1/2 In. 325.00

Fire Pumper, 3 Horses, Cast Iron, Ideal, 22 In. . . . 1955.00
Fire Pumper, 3 Horses, Driver, Harris, 1903, 15 In. . . . 750.00
Fire Pumper, Aerial Ladder, Keystone . . . 5400.00
Fire Pumper, Cast Iron, Driver, Kenton, 10 In. . . . 250.00
Fire Pumper, Cast Iron, Electric Light, Hubley, 9 3/4 In. . . . 250.00
Fire Pumper, Cast Iron, Nickel Plated Bumper, Accessories, Tires, Hubley, 8 3/8 In. . . . 225.00
Fire Pumper, Cast Iron, Nickel Plated Bumper, Hubley, 11 1/2 In. . . . 168.00
Fire Pumper, Cast Iron, Open Frame, Vertical Boiler, Spoke Wheels, Carpenter, 17 1/2 In. . . . 880.00
Fire Pumper, Double Team, Cast Iron, Nickel, Kenton, Early 1900s, 20 1/4 In. . . . 355.00
Fire Pumper, Double Team, Cast Iron, Steel, Wilkins, c.1900, 16 3/4 In. . . . 470.00
Fire Pumper, Driver, Fireman, Cast Iron, Phoenix, Ives, 18 In. . . . 748.00
Fire Pumper, Horse, Driver, Cast Iron, Painted, c.1880s . . . 2400.00
Fire Pumper, Ives, 1880s . . . 2400.00
Fire Pumper, Phoenix Pumper, 2 Horses, 2 Firemen, Ives, 1890s, 19 In. . . . 2195.00
Fire Pumper, Threaded Hose, Original Wax Paper, Hydrant, No. 5, Tonka, 1956 . . . 440.00
Fire Set, Tin, Windup, Japan, 1950s . . . 65.00
Fire Truck, 4 Firemen, Tin, Windup, Mettoy, England, Box, 1930s, 13 In. . . . 575.00
Fire Truck, Aerial Ladder, Doepke, Box, 34 In. . . . 605.00
Fire Truck, Aerial Ladder, Packard, Keystone, 1924, 31 In. . . . 850.00
Fire Truck, Aerial Ladder, Pressed Steel, Buddy L, 39 In. . . . 1045.00
Fire Truck, Aerial Ladder, Pressed Steel, Doepke, 32 In. . . . 248.00
Fire Truck, Aerial Ladder, Red, Tonka, 1956, 32 In. . . . 325.00
Fire Truck, Aerial Ladder, Wood, Brio, Ladder Extends To 6 Ft. . . . 330.00
Fire Truck, Buddy L, U.S.A., 1930s, 12 In. . . . 65.00
Fire Truck, Cast Iron, Hubley, 6 1/4 In. . . . 90.00
Fire Truck, Circus, Clown Fireman Driver, Tin, Plastic, Battery Operated, MT Mark, Box, 11 In. . . . 165.00
Fire Truck, Diamond T, Red, Nickel Grille, Hubley, 6 1/2 In. . . . 300.00
Fire Truck, Fire Hose, Center Hose Stand, Red, No. 38, Buddy L, 21 3/4 In. . . . 115.00
Fire Truck, Fire Station, Fire Pumper, Pressed Steel, 19 1/2 In. . . . 1045.00
Fire Truck, Hook & Ladder, 2 Horses, 2 Firemen, 2 Ladders, Gong Bell, Hubley, 1910, 24 In. . . . 1295.00
Fire Truck, Hook & Ladder, 2 Horses, 2 Firemen, 3 Ladders, Bell, Jones & Bixler, 1908, 31 In. . . . 3100.00
Fire Truck, Hook & Ladder, 2 Horses, 2 Firemen, 4 Ladders, Iron Bucket, Carpenter, 1880s, 25 In. . . 2195.00
Fire Truck, Hook & Ladder, 3 Horses, Cast Iron, Steel Frame, Hubley, 20 1/2 In. . . . 380.00
Fire Truck, Hook & Ladder, 3 Horses, Cast Iron, Steel Ladders, Williams, Early 1900s, 16 3/4 In. . . 235.00
Fire Truck, Hook & Ladder, Aerial, No. 880, Ny-Lint, Box . . . 165.00
Fire Truck, Hook & Ladder, Gong Bell, 3 Articulated Horses, Dent, 1905, 26 In. . . . 1395.00
Fire Truck, Hook & Ladder, No. 10, Pressed Steel, Wyandotte, 25 In. . . . 110.00
Fire Truck, Ladder, Carpenter Fire Department, 1883 . . . 2800.00
Fire Truck, Ladder, Doepke, 1853-56, 33 1/2 In. . . . 375.00
Fire Truck, Ladder, Lithograph, Red, Black Edge Gold Lining, Ladder, Driver, Georg Fischer . . . 575.00
Fire Truck, Ladder, Metal, Windup, Mettoy, England, Box, 1930s, 15 In. . . . 475.00
Fire Truck, Ladder, Open Cab, Vertical Boiler, Lithograph, Georg Fischer . . . 688.00
Fire Truck, Ladder, Pressed Steel, Buddy L, Box, 1930s, 22 In. . . . 495.00
Fire Truck, Ladder, Silver, Red, Hubley, 5 In. . . . 200.00
Fire Truck, Pressed Steel, Doepke, 19 In. . . . 360.00
Fire Truck, Pressed Steel, Ladders, Gerard, U.S.A., 1920s, 12 In. . . . 175.00
Fire Truck, Pressed Steel, Metal Ladder, Canadian Lincoln, 1940s, 16 In. . . . 245.00
Fire Truck, Texaco, Fire Chief, Pressed Steel, Buddy L, 26 In. . . . 120.00
Fire Truck, Texaco, Tin Body, Plastic Wheels, Buddy L, Box, 25 1/2 In. . . . 66.00
Fire Truck, Water Tower, Pressed Steel, Keystone, 32 In. . . . 1760.00
Fire Truck, Water Tower, Pressed Steel, Sturditoy, 34 In. . . . 2530.00
Fire Wagon, Hook & Ladder, 2 Horses, 2 Firemen, Phoenix, Ives, 26 In. . . . 1595.00
Fire Wagon, Hook & Ladder, 2 Horses, Driver, Steerer, Painted, Cast Iron, Dent . . . 3910.00
Fire Wagon, Hook & Ladder, 3 Horses, Driver, Fireman, 3 Ladders, Painted, Kenton . . . 575.00
Fire Wagon, Hook & Ladder, 3 Horses, Firefighters, Gallops, Pressed Steel, Hubley, 20 1/2 In. . . . 380.00
Fire Wagon, Hook & Ladder, 3 Horses, Spoke Wheels, Ladder Brackets, Cast Iron, 18 In. . . . 235.00
Fire Wagon, Hook & Ladder, 3 Horses, Spoke Wheels, Silver Tires, Cast Iron, Williams, 16 3/4 In. . 235.00
Fire Wagon, Hook & Ladder, Driver, Pressed Steel, Buddy L, 25 In. . . . 546.00
Fire Wagon, Hook & Ladder, Horses, 2 Firemen, Kenton, 1910, 16 3/4 In. . . . 750.00
Fire Wagon, Hook & Ladder, Horses, Cast Iron, Dent, 28 In. . . . 460.00
Fire Wagon, Hook & Ladder, Horses, Firemen, 3 Wood Ladders, Gong Bell, 1911, 28 In. . . . 1995.00

Fire Wagon, Horse, Driver, Hose Reel, Hubley, 1915, 12 1/4 In. 725.00
Fire Wagon, Hose Reel, 2 Horses, Gong Bell, Brass Hose Nozzle, Hubley, 1910, 19 1/2 In. 1750.00
Fire Wagon, Hose Reel, 2 Horses, Gong, Driver, 19 1/2 In. 635.00
Fire Wagon, Hose Reel, Fire Department, Carpenter, 1883 .... 2800.00
Fire Wagon, Hose Reel, Green, Woven Cotton Hose, Bell, Horse, Pratt & Letchworth, c.1890 ...... 1430.00
Fire Wagon, Hose Reel, Horse, Driver, Cast Iron, Painted, Carpenter, c.1883 .... 2800.00
Fire Wagon, Hose Reel, Painted Nickel, Cast Iron, Seated Driver, Red Spoke Wheels, Shimer, 14 In. 1320.00
Fire Wagon, Hose Reel, Standing Fireman, Seated Driver, Open Frame, Platform 4600.00
Fire Wagon, Hose, 2 Horses, Driver, Wilkins, 14 In. 1265.00
Fire Wagon, Ladder, 3 Horses, Driver, Dent 3162.00
Fire Wagon, Patrol, 2 Horses, Driver, 4 Firemen, Spoke Wheels, Cast Iron, Hubley 1265.00
Fire Wagon, Patrol, 6 Firemen, 2 Hanging On Platform, Phoenix, Ives 1840.00
Fire Wagon, Patrol, Horse Drawn, Dent, c.1910, 19 In. 3200.00
Fire Wagon, Pumper, Double Team, Nickel, Cast Iron, 22 In. 235.00
Fire Wagon, Pumper, Double Team, Nickel, Wheels, Firemen, Hose, Cast Iron, Kenton, 20 3/8 In. .. 355.00
Fire Wagon, Pumper, Double Team, Painted, Cast Iron, Wood Air Chambers, Cylinders, 16 3/4 In. . 470.00
Fire Wagon, Pumper, Painted Steel, Wood Air Chambers, Cylinders, Rubber Tires, 9 3/4 In. 440.00
Fireman, Metal, Plastic, Marx, 1950s 145.00
Fireman, Walking, Climbing, Tin, Battery Operated, Sonsco, Box, 24 In. 745.00
Fishing Boy, Battery Operated, Plastic, Japan, Box, 1960s, 9 In. 20.00
Fix-It Car Of Tomorrow, XP-600, Plastic, Ideal, Original Box, 16 In. 140.00
Flintstones, Dino On Tricycle, Tin, Celluloid, Marx, Box, 4 1/2 In. 750.00
Flintstones, Dino The Dinosaur, Mechanical, Louis Marx, Box, 1961, 5 5/8 x 7 1/2 In. 569.00
Flintstones, Dino, Walks, Opens Mouth, Tin, Windup, Linemar, Box, 1961, 6 In. 440.00
Flintstones, Flivver, Fred Drives, Vinyl Head, Tin, Friction, Marx, 1963, 6 3/4 In. 195.00
Flintstones, Flivver, Tin, Battery Operated, Remote Control, Marx, Box, 7 In. 468.00
Flintstones, Fred Flintstone's Bedrock Band, Battery Operated, Alps, Box, 1962, 9 In. 435.00
Flintstones, Fred On Dino, Dino Walks, Tin, Vinyl, Windup, Marx, 1962, 8 In. 166.00
Flintstones, Fred On Dino, Tin, Vinyl, Plush, Battery Operated, Marx, Box, 21 In. 715.00
Flintstones, Fred On Dino, Walks, Whistles, Battery Operated, Marx, Box, 1961 .... 625.00
Flintstones, Fred, Xylophone, Fisher-Price, 1962, 8 In. .... *ILLUS* 448.00
Flintstones, Rubble's Wreck, Barney Drives, Vinyl Head, Tin, Friction, Marx, 1962, 7 In. 220.00
Flintstones, Tank, Turnover, Linemar, 1950s, 4 In. 325.00
Flintstones, Tank, Turnover, Rolls, Stops, Lifts, Tin, Windup, Linemar, 4 In. 680.00
Flintstones, Tricycle, Fred Drives, Bell Rings, Tin, Celluloid, Windup, Marx, 4 In. 165.00
Flintstones, Tricycle, Wilma, Bell Rings, Tin, Celluloid, Windup, Marx, Box, 1962, 4 In. ....115.00 to 330.00
Flip The Frog, Green, Tan, Brown Shoes, Stuffed, Tag, Chiltern Toys, England, 1930s, 6 1/4 In. 455.00
Flying Saucer, Space Pilot, Tin, Battery Operated, K-O, Japan, 7 1/2 In. 195.00
Flying Saucer, Tin, Battery Operated, KO, Japan, Box, 1950s 295.00
Flying Saucer, Z-101, Tin, Friction, Masudaya, Box, 6 1/2 In. 405.00
Football Player, Balances Ball On Head, Sways To Side, Papier-Mache, Germany, 1920, 11 In. 176.00
Football Player, Kicking Ball, Cast Iron, Red, Yellow, Green Base, Lever Kicks Ball, 8 In. 660.00
Football Player, Sandy Andy Fullback, Tin, Celluloid Ball, Wolverine, Box, c.1919, 8 In. 2860.00
Footstool, Frog, Stuffed, Steiff, 11 1/4 x 22 x 15 In. 410.00
Fort Set, U.S. Coast Defense, Ship, Plane, Soldiers, Layout Board, Box, 11 1/2 x 23 In. 195.00
Fox, Magician, Mixed Material, Windup, Nomura, Box, 7 In. 165.00
Foxy Grandpa, Composition, Clothes, Lead Feet, Windup, Germany, c.1915, 6 In. 616.00
Foxy Grandpa, Composition, Squeeze, Cardboard Hat, Wood Hands, Feet, Germany, 10 1/2 In. ... 390.00
Foxy Grandpa, Roly Poly, Movable Head, Schoenhut, c.1915, 11 In. 670.00
Foxy Grandpa, Roly Poly, Papier-Mache, 1900s, 9 1/2 In. 650.00
Foxy Grandpa, Tin, Windup, Painted, Germany, c.1910-15, 8 1/2 In. 616.00
Frankenstein, Ball Toss, 3 Styrofoam Balls, Cardboard, 20 x 20 In. 196.00
Frankenstein, Battery Operated, Nippon/Morimura, Japan, 1960s, 13 1/2 In. 350.00
Frankenstein, Bust, 21 In. 225.00
Frankenstein, Robot, Tin, Vinyl, Battery Operated, Remote Control, Marx, Box, 12 1/2 In. 3080.00
Frankenstein, Rubber, Alton, 18 In. 336.00
Frankenstein, Tin, Vinyl Head, Cardboard Inserts, Battery Operated, Marx, Box, 13 In. 1120.00
Frankenstein, Tin, Vinyl, Cloth, Battery Operated, TN, Box, 13 In. 305.00
Frankenstein, Walks, Bends Over, Raises, Lowers Arms, Tin, Vinyl, Battery, Marx, 12 In. 2115.00
Furniture, Newlyweds Library, Bookcase, Sofa, Table, Chairs, Radio, Tin, Marx, Box, c.1930, 5 In. . 165.00
Furniture, Settee, Shaped Crest, Red-Brown Paint, Flowers, Yellow Highlights, 19th Century, 24 In. 1375.00

G.I. Joe, Blond Hair & Beard, Orange Jumpsuit, Sun In Shoulder Rig, 1970s 140.00
G.I. Joe, Bouncing Jeep, Tin Lithograph, Clockwork, Unique Art, Patent Apr. 11, 1944, 8 In. 118.00
G.I. Joe, Hat, Boots, Dog Tags, Decals, Hasbro, Box, 12 In. 390.00
G.I. Joe, K-9 Pups, Tin, Windup, Unique Art, Box, 9 In. 275.00
G.I. Joe, Scarface, Marine Manual, Shoes, Belt, Blond Hair, Pat. Pending 195.00
Games are listed in their own category.
Gamecock, Squeak, Standing Figure, Papier-Mache, Wirework Legs, Bellows, Painted, 9 x 8 In. 705.00
Garage, 2 Car, Keystone, Box, 8 x 24 x 11 In. 110.00
Garage, 2 Car, Penny, 2 1/2 In. 220.00
Garage, 2 Car, Pressed Tin, Battery Operated, Windup, TCO, Germany 2970.00
Garage, 2 Car, Tin Lithograph, Wyandotte 190.00
Garage, 2 Levels, Elevator, Wood, Paper Lithograph, Masonite Base, Keystone, 8 x 22 x 16 In. 66.00
Gas Pump, Pressed Steel, Black, Red, Electric Light In Globe, Celluloid, Bell Ringer, 13 In. 358.00
Gas Station, 1 Bay, 2 Levels, Wood, Paper Lithograph, Keystone, 8 x 21 x 12 In. 35.00
Gas Station, 2 Bays, Plasticville, 5 1/2 x 12 x 6 In. 22.00
Gas Station, Complete Car Service, Firestone, Roof Parking, Elevator, Tin Lithograph, 11 x 23 In. .. 140.00
Gas Station, Esso, Playmobile, Plastic, 2 Gas Pump Islands, Sign Island, 2 Cars 22.00
Gas Station, Gulf Oil, Tin Lithograph, Marx, 3 1/2 x 17 x 11 In. 155.00
Gas Station, Midtown Service, 24 Hours, Tin Lithograph, Marx, 15 x 27 x 15 In. 90.00
Gas Station, Sears Service Center, Car, Gas Pumps, Oil Can Rack, Tin Lithograph, 8 x 27 x 16 In. .. 55.00
Gas Station, Shell, 5 Cars, 2 Gas Islands, Pole, Plasticville, 2 x 6 x 3 1/2 In. 33.00
Gasoline Truck, Richfield, Pressed Steel, Mack Cab, Decals, American National, 28 In. 4125.00
Gasoline Truck, Texaco, Cast Iron, Painted, Red, Semitrailer, Embossed, Kenton, 1933, 9 In. 440.00
Geese, Pecking, Crank Handle, Lithograph, 2 White Heads, Wood Simulated Hutch 229.00
General Grocery, Shelves, Swing Open Doors, Counter, Scale, Wolverine, 1940s 600.00
Gig, Cast Iron, Painted, White, Red Spoke Wheels, Black Horse, Wilkens, c.1911, 11 1/2 In. 550.00
Gig, Horse Drawn, Cast Iron, Kenton, Late 1800s, 9 In. 150.00
Gig, Open, Gentlemen's, Nickel Plate Gig, Prancing Horse, Shimer, c.1890, 10 In. 220.00
Gino, Balloon Blower, Man With Tank Blows Up Balloons, Rasho, Japan, Box, 1950s, 10 In. 145.00
Giraffe, Painted, Wood, Rope Tail, Leather Ears, Jointed Neck, Limbs, Schoenhut, 11 1/4 In. 275.00
Giraffe, Wood, Pop-Up, Red Base, Wakouwa, 6 In. 28.00
Glide-A-Ride, Greyhound, Friction, Tin, Japan, 9 In. 120.00
Go Round, Zeppelins, Airplanes, Tin, Painted, Germany, c.1900, 11 In. 1840.00
Go Round, Zeppelins, Airplanes, Tin, Painted, Muhler & Kadater, 22 In. 5290.00
Goat, Articulated Legs, Cast Iron, Japanned Finish, Ives, 6 3/4 In. 825.00
Goat, Standing, Gray, Cream, Red Collar, Bell, Green Base, Red Disc Wheels, Meier 275.00
Godzilla, Tin, Windup, Billiken, Japan, Box, 7 1/2 In. 176.00
Gondola, Tin, Windup, Alps, Japan, 1950s 245.00
Gorilla, Tin, Plush, Brown, Battery Operated, Remote Control, TN, Box, 9 In. 305.00
Gorilla, Tin, Plush, White, Battery Operated, Remote Control, TN, Box, 9 In. 330.00
Grader, Adams Motor, Pressed Steel, Doepke, Box, 26 In. 330.00
Grader, Mighty, No. 3945, Tonka, Box, 24 In. 145.00
Grader, Pressed Steel, Doepke Adams, 26 In. 209.00
Gun, 105mm Howitzer, Tin, Elastolin Hausser, Germany, 13 In. 295.00
Gun, Atomic Disintegrator, Red Grips, Hubley, 8 1/2 In. 170.00
Gun, Badge, Deputy, No. 254, Hubley, Box 110.00
Gun, Billy The Kid, Repeating, Black Grips, Stevens, Box, 8 In. 156.00
Gun, Buckle, Derringer, Gun In Belt Buckle, Mattel, Box, 3 In. 119.00
Gun, Cast Iron, Kilgore, 1912, 5 In. 198.00
Gun, Derringer, Die Cast, White Grips, Halco, 3 1/2 In. 13.00
Gun, Derringer, Dyna-Mite, Cast Metal, White Grips, Nichols, 3 1/2 In. 8.00
Gun, Derringer, Silva-Mite, Nickel Finish, Blue Grips, Die Cast, Crescent, England, 3 1/2 In. 14.00
Gun, Luger, Desert Patrol, Plastic, Bullets, Marx, 10 1/2 In. 119.00
Gun, Machine, Ronson, 23 In. 121.00
Gun, Machine, Soldier, Tin, Crank, Prewar China, 5 1/2 In. 95.00
Gun, Machine, Tin, Windup, Marx, Box, 5 In. 248.00
Gun, Mobile, Military, Driver, 2 Gunners, Gray Uniform, Red Wheels, Lithograph, Meier 370.00
Gun, Mobile, No. 38, Lithograph, Gray, Red, Modeled As Gunboat, Germany 185.00
Gun, Police Chief, Nickel Finish, Kenton, 1938, 4 5/8 In. 67.00
Gun, Red Ryder, 1000 Shot Carbine, Iron Lever, Daisy, Box, 1940, 35 In. 129.00
Gun, Rifle, M-16, Plastic, Mattel, 31 1/4 In. 14.00

Toy, Flintstones, Fred, Xylophone, Fisher-Price, 1962, 8 In.

Toy, Hangover Pete, Push-Up, Wood, Kohner Bros., 6 In.

Toy, Jeep, Jumpin', Tin Lithograph, Windup, Marx, Box, 6 In.

Gun, Rifle, Rolling Block, Plastic, Die Cast, Mattel, 29 1/2 In. 30.00
Gun, Space, Pop, Red, Black, Pressed Steel, All Metal Products, 1930s, 7 In. 128.00
Gun, Space, Super Jet, Sparks, Tin, Plastic, KO, Japan, 1950s, 9 In. 100.00
Gun, Space, Turquoise, Red, Tin, Friction, TN, Box, 4 In. 1792.00
Gun, Sparkler, Ringling Bros. & Barnum & Bailey, Red, Clear Windows 17.00
Gun, Target, Spring Action Peashooter, Altazimuth Mount, Lithograph, HMN 185.00
Gun, Tom Corbett Space Cadet, Sparking, Plastic, Box, 22 1/2 In. 468.00
Gun & Holster, Buffalo Bill, Double, 6 Red Bullets, Leather Belt, Fringe, 7 1/2-In. Guns 300.00
Gun & Holster, Buffalo Bill, Double, Keystone, Box, 1940s 825.00
Gun & Holster, Buffalo Bill, Leslie Henry, Halco, Unopened Package, 8-In. Gun 50.00
Gun & Holster, Double, Cast Iron, Beasley Steer Head Grips, Tex Hurley, 8-In. Guns 190.00
Gun & Holster, Kit Carson, Nickel Plated, Die Cast, Black Grips, Leather, Kilgore, 10-In. Gun 85.00
Gun & Holster, L'il Smoky, Tiny Tot, Halco 39.00
Gun & Holster, Pony Boy, Hand Cuffs, Esquire Novelty, Unused, Box, 1944 . . . . . . 450.00
Gun & Holster, Wyatt Earp, Double, Buntline Special, Stag Handles, Plastic Bullets, 10-In. Guns . . 200.00
Gun & Holster, Wyatt Earp, White Plastic Grips, Leather, Actoy 115.00
Gun & Target Set, Air Blaster, Wham-O, Box, 1963, 12 x 14 In. 180.00
Gun Set, Sixfinger, Spy Gun, 6 Projectiles, Card, Topper, 1965, 7 3/4 x 11 In. 240.00
Gyro-Cycle, Rider, Metal, Celluloid, Pull Toy, Tri-Ang Co., London, Box, 1939 . . . . . . 350.00
Ham & Sam, Minstrel Team, 2 Black Figures, Piano, Tin Lithograph, Clockwork, Strauss, 7 In. 646.00
Ham & Sam, Plays Piano, Dances, Tin, Windup, Linemar, Box, 5 1/2 In. 1176.00
Hammer, Bear & Black Man, Double Hammer, Cast Iron, Painted 525.00
Hand Truck, Arcade, 5 In. 85.00
Handcar, Metal, Windup, Girard, 1930s, 6 In. 145.00
Handcar, Moon Mullins & Kayo, Tin Lithograph, Windup, Louis Marx, 1930s 1250.00
Hangover Pete, Push-Up, Wood, Kohner Bros., 6 In. . . . . . *ILLUS* 44.00
Hansom Cab, Articulated Horse, Painted, Tin Carriage, Silk Interior, c.1890, 17 In. 1650.00
Hansom Cab, Black, Coachman's High Seat, Cast Iron, Painted, Pratt & Letchworth, 11 In. 495.00
Hansom Cab, High Coachman's Seat, Cast Iron, Clockwork, Painted, Black, Ives, 11 1/4 In. 2750.00
Hansom Cab, Horse Drawn, Dapple Gray Trotting Horse, Green Cab, Driver, Lithograph, Meier 415.00
Hansom Cab, Horse, Coachman, Cast Iron, Pratt & Letchworth, 19th Century, 12 In. 295.00
Hansom Cab, Tin, Red, Black, Converse, c.1895 . . . . . . 1750.00
Hansom Cab, Tin, Spoke Wheels, Rubber Tires, Cast-Iron Horse, 14 In. 120.00
Happy Hooligan, Goat Cart, Nickeled Cast Iron, Pressed Steel, Spoke Wheels, Kenton, 7 1/2 In. . . 110.00
Happy Hooligan, Nodder, Yellow Carriage, Red Wheels, Kenton, 10 x 8 1/2 In. 415.00
Happy Hooligan, Racer, Comical, Cast Iron, Spoke Wheels, N. N. Hill Brass & Watrous Mfg. 470.00
Happy Hooligan, Roly Poly, Schoenhut, c.1910 . . . . . . 210.00
Happy Hooligan, Schoenhut, Box, 1924, 8 1/2 In. 2800.00
Happy Hooligan, Tin, Windup, Chein, 1930s 750.00
Happy Hooligan, Walker, Tin Lithograph, Clockwork, Chein, 6 1/2 In. 360.00
Happy Hooligan, Walker, Windup, Chein, 1930s 475.00
Hay Loader, John Deere, Cast Iron, Red, Green, Yellow Spoke, Decal, Vindex, 9 In. 2750.00
Hay Wagon, Cast Iron, Painted, Green, Foldable Stake Side Ends, Low Rails, Vindex, 8 In. 990.00
Hee-Haw The Balky Mule, Windup, Marx 120.00
Helicopter, Auto Gyro, Blue, Sheet Steel, Occupied Japan 188.00

Helicopter, Police, Tin, Windup, Korea, Box, 8 In. 45.00
Helicopter, Vertical Liner, Tin, Battery Operated, Go & Stop, Sears, Japan, Box, 19 In. 395.00
Hen, Pecking, Spring Action, Lithograph, Yellow, Red, Blue Hen, Candy Container Box, Fischer 275.00
Hen & Egg, Spring Action, Lithograph, Yellow, Red, Black, Pecking Action, Georg Fischer 459.00
Hen & Rooster, In Cage, Pip-Squeak, Paper Lithograph Roof, Painted Papier-Mache, 8 x 7 x 5 In. 80.00
Henry, Celluloid, Windup, Tin Lithograph Suitcase, Japan, c.1935, 4 1/2 In. 1345.00
Henry & Henrietta, Running Away, Celluloid, Tin Lithograph Suitcase, Windup, 7 1/2 In. 2128.00
Henry & Mahout, Ride Elephant, Celluloid, Windup, 1930s 950.00
Henry & Porter, Celluloid, Tin Platform, Clockwork, Geo. Borgfeldt, Box, 6 1/2 In. 1430.00
Henry On Elephant, Celluloid, Box, 8 In. 1320.00
Hi-Jinks, Clown, Monkey, Cymbals, Cragstan, Box 176.00
Hillclimber, Cast Iron, Painted, Orange, Nickel Spoke Wheels, Rubber Tires, Hubley, 5 1/2 In. 495.00
Hillclimber, Electric Friction Runabout, Cast Iron, Sheet Metal, c.1902, 6 In. 248.00
Hippo, Painted Eyes, Wood Jointed Body, Leather Tusks, Open Mouth, Schoenhut, 9 1/2 In. 415.00
Hit & Miss, Wood, Push-Up, Round Base, Box, 6 In. 35.00
Hobbyhorse, Birch, Curved, Red Ball Head, Creative Playthings, 1960s, 19 x 25 In. 330.00
Hobbyhorse, Prancing, Wood Frame, Brown, Horsehair Mane & Tail, 1900, 44 In. 570.00
Hobbyhorse, Wood, Multicolored, Articulated, Folk Art, 16 x 25 In. 80.00
Hobo, Squeeze, Rempel, 6 In. 39.00
Hobo, Wood, Jointed, Brown Felt Coat, Hat, Leather Ears, Schoenhut, 8 In. 195.00
Honeymoon Express, Tin, Windup, Marx, Original Box 110.00
Hootin Hollow Haunted House, Tin, Battery Operated, Marx, Box, 11 In. 1456.00 to 1595.00
Horse, Armored, Noble Knight Series, Marx, Box, 13 1/2 In. 35.00
Horse, Felt, Leather Harness, Wood Platform, Pull Toy, 14 1/2 x 15 In. 660.00
Horse, Felt, Wood Platform, Iron Wheels, Pull Toy, 18 1/2 x 19 In. 575.00
Horse, Gliding, Wood, Painted, Leather Saddle, Brass Tacks, Metal Eyes, Flax Mane, Tail, 40 In. 235.00
Horse, On Platform, Papier-Mache, Mohair Fabric, Horsehair Tail, Metal Wheels, 14 In. 169.00
Horse, On Platform, Wheels, Germany, c.1900, 13 In. 385.00
Horse, Papier-Mache, Germany, 4 1/2 In. 65.00
Horse, Plush, Wood Base, Tin Wheels, Pull Toy, 1800s, 8 1/2 In. 220.00
Horse, Prancing, Iron, Pierced Eyes, Applied Ears, Bolted Legs, 27 x 38 In. 660.00
Horse, Push & Pull, Prancing, Wood Platform Base, 12 x 12 In. 165.00
Horse, Push & Pull, Tin, Stamped, Painted, Spoke Wheels, c.1875, 6 1/2 In. 448.00
Horse, Racing, Arabian, Cart, Driver, Windup, Germany, 1950, 7 In. 195.00
Horse, Riding, Wood, Carved, Painted, Dapple Gray, Spoke Wheels, Saddle, 26 x 19 In. 353.00
Horse, Rocking, Carved, Painted, 28 x 22 In. 546.00
Horse, Rocking, Carved, Painted, Horsehair Tail, Mane, 19th Century 1265.00
Horse, Rocking, Converts To Roller, Red Paint, Early 1900s, 27 x 20 x 14 In. 1250.00
Horse, Rocking, Dapple Gray, Painted Glider Frame, Leather Saddle, 25 x 31 In. 575.00
Horse, Rocking, Dapple Paint, Bridle, Saddle, 1800s 550.00
Horse, Rocking, Dapple, Green Rocker Base, No Tail, Victorian, 33 x 62 x 14 In. 978.00
Horse, Rocking, Pine Planks, Silhouetted Head, Multicolored Paint, 23 x 49 In. 323.00
Horse, Rocking, Platform, Wood, Painted, Stenciled, Cloth Covered, Glass Eyes, 35 In. 660.00
Horse, Rocking, Smoke, White Ground, Leather, Wood Saddle, 38 x 44 1/4 x 16 1/2 In. 660.00
Horse, Rocking, Wood, Smoke Decorated, Whitney Reed Chair Co., Mass., 38 x 44 In. 660.00
Horse, Sparkplug, Walker, Blanket, Wood, King Features, 10 1/2 In. 248.00
Horse, Spring, Rearing Position, Scrolled Spring, Shaped Base, Later Paint, 44 x 57 In. 935.00
Horse, Tin, Stamped, Painted, Platform Base, 4 Wheels, G. Brown, Connecticut, c.1875, 9 In. 657.00
Horse, Walking, Saddle, Red Wool Blanket, Articulated, Ives, c.1890, 10 In. 7700.00
Horse & Cart, Cowboy, Celluloid, Box, Occupied Japan 141.00
Horse & Wagon, 2 Horses, Best Family Flour, Iron Wheels, Pull Toy, 10 1/2 x 29 x 8 In. 550.00
Horse & Wagon, 2 Horses, Boy & Company, Tin Lithograph, Converse, 22 In. 825.00
Horse & Wagon, 2 Horses, City Delivery, Green, Gold, Red, Yellow Wheels, Harris, c.1895, 16 In. 2475.00
Horse & Wagon, 2 Horses, Log, Driver, Cast Iron, Kenton 850.00
Horse & Wagon, 2 Horses, Supply, III Armee Korps, Driver, Lithograph, Georg Fischer 415.00
Horse & Wagon, Articulated, Red Wagon, Cast Iron, Tin, Wood, Spoke Wheels, Ives, 13 In. 1760.00
Horse & Wagon, Borden's Milk, Wood, 13 1/2 x 28 1/2 In. 250.00
Horse & Wagon, Dairy, Toylands, Tin Lithograph, Marx, Early 1900s, 11 In. 88.00
Horse & Wagon, Dapple Gray Horse, Collar Harness, Yellow Wagon, Lithograph, Meier 735.00
Horse & Wagon, Driver, Barrels, Dent, 1905, 12 In. 375.00
Horse & Wagon, Hay, Cast Iron, Stake Racks, Red, Spoke Wheels, Vindex, 14 1/2 In. 1210.00

Toy, Kangaroo, Steiff, Button In Ear, 20 In.

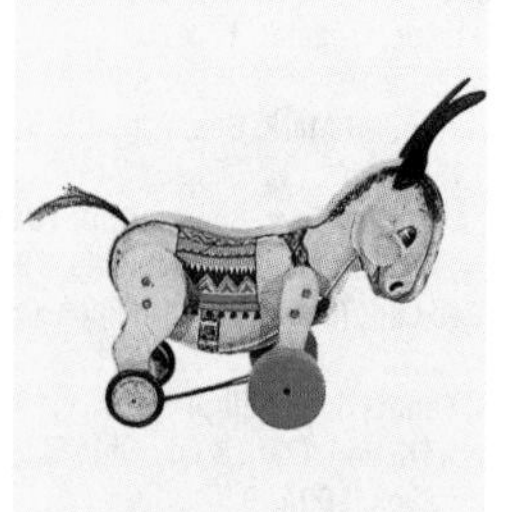
Toy, Kicking Donkey, Fisher-Price, 1937, 10 In.

Toy, Moose, Steiff, Button In Ear, Tag, 9 In.

Horse & Wagon, Ladder, Black Open Frame, Spoke Wheels, Cast Iron, Carpenter, 24 In. 525.00
Horse & Wagon, Military Pontoon, Black & White Horses, Driver, Lithograph, Meier 415.00
Horse & Wagon, Milk, Covered, Elmside Farms, Cast Iron, Painted, White, 13 In. 230.00
Horse & Wagon, Milk, Driver, Cast Iron Tires, Moving Wheels, Kenton, 13 1/2 In. 120.00
Horse & Wagon, Pull, Cloth, Leather Straps, Wooden Base, Iron Wheels, 10 1/2 x 29 x 8 In. 550.00
Horse & Wagon, Sheffield Farms Co., c.1920, 21 In. 305.00
Horse & Wagon, Spirited Hide Covered, Mane & Horsehair Tail, Wood Pull Base, 26 In. 635.00
Horse & Wagon, U.S. Express, Tin Lithograph, 15 1/8 In. 82.00
Hose Carriage, Cast Iron, Ives, c.1900, 15 1/2 In. 470.00
Hott & Tott, Tin, Windup, Unique Art, 8 In. 770.00
Humphrey Mobile, Tin, Windup, Wyandotte, 8 1/2 In. 365.00
Humphrey Mobile, Tin, Windup, Wyandotte, Box, 8 1/2 In. 550.00
Ice Cream Cart, Man Pushing, Tin, Windup, Courtland, 1948 . . . . 475.00
Ice Cream Vendor, Windup, Sheet Steel, Box, Occupied Japan 83.00
Indian, Crawling, Tin, Windup, Ohio Art, 1950s, 8 In. 95.00
Indian Joe, War Drum, Tin, Plastic, Battery Operated, Alps, Japan, Box, 10 1/2 In. 45.00
Ironing Board, Iron, Little Bo-Peep, Wolverine, 1950s, 20 In. 50.00
J.F.K. & Rocking Chair, Kamar, Japan, Box, 1963, 11 In. 325.00
Jazzbo Jim, Dancing On Roof, Black Banjo Player, Tin Lithograph, 10 x 5 In. 382.00
Jazzbo Jim, Marx, 9 1/2 In. 330.00
Jazzbo Jim, Song & Dance Man, White Men, Tin, Windup, Linemar, 6 1/2 In. 1020.00
Jeep, Convertible, Tin Friction, GW, Japan, Box, 7 1/2 In. 66.00
Jeep, Flying, U.S. Army, Tin, Friction, Wheels Spin, Daiya, Box, 8 1/2 In. 1176.00
Jeep, Jolly Joe, Tin, Windup, Marx, 5 1/2 In. 305.00
Jeep, Jumpin', Tin Lithograph, Windup, Marx, Box, 6 In. . . . . ***ILLUS*** 224.00
Jeep, Trailer, Willys, Pressed Steel, Marx, Box, 23 In. 330.00
Jeep, U.S. Armed Forces, Radio Jeep, No. 877, Marx, Box, 1950s 425.00
Jeep, U.S. Army, Tin, Friction, Converts To Gunship, Box, 7 1/2 In. 200.00
Jeep, Yellow, Red Nose, Bow, Composition, Jointed, KFS, 1935, 13 In. 1067.00
Jenny The Balking Mule, Tin, Windup, Strauss, Box 575.00
Jiggs, Driving Jazz Car, Tin Lithograph, Germany, 1932, 6 x 6 In. 2128.00
Jiggs, Riding Bumper Car, Tin Lithograph, Germany, c.1925, 5 1/4 x 3 1/2 In. 8960.00
Jocko The Climbing Monkey, Tin, Linemar 15.00
Joe Lewis & M. Schmelling, Move Back & Forth, Arms Swing, Germany, 1930s, 6 In. 270.00
Jonah & The Whale, Boat & Figures, Shepard Hardware Co. 785.00
Juggler, Black Man, Paper On Wood, Toys Incorporated, Md., 11 3/4 In. 95.00
Kangaroo, Steiff, Button In Ear, 20 In. . . . . ***ILLUS*** 252.00
Kicking Donkey, Fisher-Price, 1937, 10 In. . . . . ***ILLUS*** 224.00
Kiddy Cyclist, Boy On Tricycle, Tin Lithograph, Windup, Unique Art, 8 1/2 In. 118.00
Kodatoy, 16mm Projector, Hand Crank, 2 Rolls Of 16mm Film, Eastman Kodak Co., 1931 . . . . 125.00
Krazy Kat, On Scooter, Tin, Windup, Nifty, Germany, 1920s, 7 1/2 In. . . . . .650.00 to 685.00
Lamb, Baby, Steiff, c.1920, 8 In. 375.00
Lamb, Pee Wee The Astrakhan, Black, Rubber Form Stuffed, Vogue, 1950s, 9 In. 155.00
Lamb, Wool & Muslin, Wood Wheels, Pull Toy, c.1875, 13 x 10 In. 3350.00
Laurel & Hardy, Plunger Toy, Picnic Basket, Tin Lithograph, La Isla, Spain, 1930s, 19 In. 935.00

Li'l Abner Dogpatch Band, 4 Musicians, Piano, Tin Lithograph, Windup, Unique Art, 1945 382.00 to 550.00
Lido Steam Shovel, Construction Kit, Plastic, Original, 12 x 18 In. 56.00
Lincoln Logs & Bricks, J.L. Wright, Box, Early 1920s 250.00
Lion, Bubble Blowing, Tin, Battery Operated, MT Mark, Box, 7 In. 138.00
Lion, Bubble, Masudaya, Japan, Box, 1959, 8 In. 225.00
Little Logging Set, Tractor, Log Trailer, Animated Toys, Box, c.1930, 10 In. 185.00
Locomotive, Hillclimber, Flywheel Drive, Red, Green, Gold, Schieble, 1909, 10 In. 295.00
Locomotive, Ride 'Em, Pressed Steel, Red Cab, Tender, Seat On Roof, Keystone, c.1928, 27 In. 248.00
Locomotive, Wood, Friction, Dayton Toy Co. 330.00
Locomotive, Wood, Red, Green, Yellow, Connecting Chain, Folk Art, c.1900, 19 x 27 x 12 In. 440.00
Locomotive & Tender, Iron, Tin, Painted, Friction, Clark & Co., Ohio 275.00
Maggie & Jiggs, Accessories, Schoenhut, Box, 1924, 9 In. 3080.00
Maggie & Jiggs, Fighting, Tin Lithograph, Squeeze, Germany, 5 1/2 x 8 In. 1008.00
Maggie & Jiggs, Tin Lithograph, Strip Spring Makes Figures Jump, Germany, 1920s, 6 3/4 In. 940.00
Maggie & Jiggs, Wood, Jointed, Painted Faces, Schoenhut, 7 & 9 In. 358.00
Magic Set, Adams Rare Triple-Decker, Germany, 1920s 1975.00
Magic Set, Box, France, 1870s, 7 x 10 x 2 In. 1940.00
Magic Set, Der Zauberer, Germany, Red Box, c.1890 .... 285.00
Magic Set, Gilberto Mysto Magic, No. 2001, 1916 .... 230.00
Magic Set, James Bond, 007 Spy Tricks, Gildrose Productions Ltd., c.1965, 14 x 20 x 2 In. 1495.00
Magic Set, Martian Magic Tricks, Gilbert, 1964 .... 259.00
Magic Set, Neuer Taschlerspieler Apparaf, Box, Germany, 1870s 1940.00
Magic Set, Spears Box Of Card Tricks, Germany, 1930 .... 346.00
Magic Set, Spears Conjuring Tricks, Red Box, c.1935 .... 170.00
Mama Katzenjammer, Spanking Toy, Kenton, 1905 .... 6500.00
Mammy, Windup, Lindstrom, Tin, 8 In. 225.00
Man Playing Xylophone, Windup, Celluloid, Occupied Japan 41.00
Man Standing At Hollywood & Vine, Celluloid, Occupied Japan 130.00
Manure Spreader, Case, Cast Iron, Painted, Red, Yellow, Spoke Wheels, Vindex, 11 1/2 In. 1870.00
Marionette Theater, Celluloid Figures, Articulated Legs, Stage, Canopy, Karamochi, 9 3/4 In. 235.00
Marionette Theater, Tin, Celluloid, Windup, Prewar Japan, Box, 1930s, 11 In. 895.00
Mary & Lamb, Celluloid, Windup, Articulated Arm With Leash, Nodding Head, Japan, 9 In. 206.00
Mary & Lamb, Wheeled Platforms, Celluloid, Windup, Box 375.00
Mary & Lamb, Windup, Celluloid, Occupied Japan 676.00
Mechanical, Zeppelins, Airplanes, Tin, Painted, Muhler & Kadater, 22 In. 5290.00
Merry-Go-Round, Canopy Top Carnival Ride, Children On Horses, Tin, Painted, 11 In. 550.00
Merry-Go-Round, Horses, Airplanes, Tin, Lever Action, Wolverine, 1930s 395.00
Merry-Go-Round, Nickeled Cast Iron, Revolves On Base, Gray Iron Casting Co., 4 5/8 In. 523.00
Merry-Go-Round, Playland, Tin, Windup, Chein, 1930s, 10 In. 415.00
Merry-Go-Round, Tin, Windup, Wolverine, 1930s, 11 In. 255.00
Mexicali Pete, Drum Player, Tin, Vinyl, Fabric, Battery Operated, Alps, Box, 11 In. 105.00
Mice, Playing, 2 Mice Race Down Spiral Rod, Iron, Lehmann, 1898-1926, 14 In. 125.00
Mighty Kong, Tin, Fur, Battery Operated, Marx, 11 In. 560.00
Milk Carrier, Sealtest, 8 Wood Bottles 50.00
Minstrel Duo Musicians, Tin, Painted, Clarinet, Accordion, Gunthermann, Germany, 8 x 9 In. 2475.00
Mobile, Peter Rabbit, Chick, Windup, Key, Bell Rings, Lionel, c.1930s 685.00
Model Kit, Tom Corbett Space Cadet, Model Craft, Box, 1950s, 11 x 16 In. 105.00
Model Kit, Visible Man, Unused, Renwal, Box, 1959 .... 85.00
Model Kit, Visible Woman, Miracle Of Creation, Renwal, Box, 1960 .... 170.00
Model Kit, Wells Fargo Overland Stagecoach, Lindberg Toys, Box, 1979 .... 275.00
Monkey, Baseball Batter, Tin, Plastic, Windup, Yoneya, 7 In. 165.00
Monkey, Climbing, Pressed Tin, Lehmann, Box, 8 In. 220.00
Monkey, Standing On All Fours, Lithograph, Gray, Brown, Spring Tail, Green Base, Distler 320.00
Monkey, Traveling, Felt Clothing, Tin Lithograph Suitcase, Windup, Schuco, 4 1/2 In. 145.00
Monoplane, Gliding, 4 Side Facing Propellers, Lithograph, Yellow Wings, Gold Green, Meier 1948.00
Monorail, Tin, U.S. Zone, Box 235.00
Monster, Great Son Of Garloo, Tin, Plastic, Windup, Marx, Box, 6 In. 330.00
Moon Explorer, Tin Lithograph, Windup, Friction Motor, Japan, Box, 3 x 3 1/2 x 7 1/4 In. 665.00
Moon Explorer, Windup, Crank Type Friction Motor, Yoshiya, Box, 1960s, 3 x 3 1/2 x 7 In. 665.00
Moon Mullins, Kayo Track Toy, c.1930, 6 1/2 In. 675.00

Toy, Motorcycle, Driver, Tin Lithograph, Head Light, Germany, 4 In.

Toy, Mule On Platform, Tin Lithograph, Gold Wash Wheels, Germany, 3 In.

Moon Mullins Set, Kayo, Uncle Willy, Emmy, Bisque, Japan, Box, 3 In. & 2 In. 224.00
Moose, Steiff, Button In Ear, Tag, 9 In. . . . . . *ILLUS* 196.00
Motor Home, Winnebago, Tin, Plastic, Mighty Tonka, 22 1/2 In. 80.00
Motorcycle, Cast Iron, Rubber Tires, A.C. Williams, 7 In. 450.00
Motorcycle, Cop, Cast Iron, Champion, 5 In. 175.00
Motorcycle, Cop, Cast Iron, Champion, 7 In. 285.00
Motorcycle, Cop, Cast Iron, Hubley, 4 1/4 In. 160.00
Motorcycle, Cop, Cast Iron, Hubley, 6 1/2 In. 285.00
Motorcycle, Cop, Sidecar, Nickel Wheels, Hubley 275.00
Motorcycle, Driver, Tin Lithograph, Head Light, Germany, 4 In. . . . . . *ILLUS* 1456.00
Motorcycle, Harley-Davidson, Cast Iron, Hubley, 5 1/2 In. 196.00
Motorcycle, Harley-Davidson, Driver, Cast Iron, Hubley, 6 In. 505.00
Motorcycle, Harley-Davidson, Parcel Post, Driver, Cast Iron, Hinge Door, 9 1/4 In. 840.00
Motorcycle, Mac 700, Tin, Windup, Arnold, 8 In. 369.00
Motorcycle, Motodrill 1006, Tin, Windup, Schuco, U.S. Zone Germany, Box, 5 In. 275.00
Motorcycle, Patrol, Cast Iron, Orange, 6 1/2 In. 280.00
Motorcycle, Patrol, Cast Iron, Red, 6 1/2 In. 170.00
Motorcycle, Police Siren Squad, Tin, Windup, Marx, 8 1/2 In. 165.00
Motorcycle, Police, Sidecar, Tin, Windup, Marx, 8 1/2 In. 360.00
Motorcycle, Sidecar, Battery Operated, Sunbeam, SAN, Japan, Box, 10 1/2 In. 1045.00
Motorcycle, Sidecar, Harley-Davidson, Spoke Wheels, No. 66, Matchbox, Lesney, Box, 1962 . . . . . 149.00
Motorcycle, Sidecar, Police Driver, Rider, Electric Light, Cast Iron, Red, Rubber Tires, Hubley, 9 In. . . 1320.00
Motorcycle, Sidecar, Police Riders, Cast Iron, Painted, Red, Rubber Tires, Decal, Hubley, 9 In. 715.00
Motorcycle, Tin, Windup, Technofix, 7 1/2 In. 138.00
Motorcycle, Triumph, 1-Cylinder, Lithograph, Blue, Black Details, Rider, Passenger, Meier 2520.00
Motorcycle, Triumph, Driver, 1-Cylinder, Lithograph, Blue, Black Details, Meier 1100.00
Mouse, Ignatz, Wood, 5 1/2 In. 248.00
Mule On Platform, Tin Lithograph, Gold Wash Wheels, Germany, 3 In. . . . . . *ILLUS* 616.00
Mysto Magic Exhibition Set, Gilbert, Box, 1909 . . . . . . 332.00
Noah's Ark, 9 Animals, Alphabet Blocks, Paper Lithograph, 1800s, 12 In. 275.00
Noah's Ark, 16 Animals, Pine, Stenciled, Wood Wheels, Cass, 1920s, 6 3/4 x 4 x 14 In. 150.00
Nodder, Foxy Grandpa, Composition, Papier-Mache, c.1920, 8 1/2 In. 165.00
Nodder, Foxy Grandpa, Composition, Wood Base, Fur Hair Tufts, Germany, c.1915, 8 1/2 In. 56.00
Nodder, Harold Lloyd, Composition, Germany, Box, 1930s, 8 In. 470.00
Noise Maker, 4 Frogs, Tin, Windup, Chein, 3 In. 50.00
Nucar Transport, 2 Sections, Cast Iron, Painted, Red, Auto Ramp, Hubley, 16 In. 605.00
Nutty Mad Tricycle, Pedals Bike, Bell Rings, Tin, Celluloid, Windup, Marx, Box, 4 1/4 In. 280.00
Oliver Plow, Cast Iron, Painted, Red, Silver Blades, Stenciled, Arcade, 6 1/2 In. 415.00
Organ, Crank, Tin Lithograph, Germany, c.1910, 7 1/4 x 3/4 x 5 In. 135.00
Paddy & Pig, Tin, Windup, Lehmann, 6 In. 715.00
Pail, Children, Beach Scene, T. Bros., c.1910, 4 1/4 In. 225.00
Pail, Embossed, Original Handle, Early 1900s, 4 1/4 In. 195.00
Pail, Seaside, c.1900, 3 1/4 In. 275.00

Paint Set, Big Show Circus, Box, c.1940, 18 x 21 In. 130.00
Paint Set, Green Hornet, Oil, Green Plastic Frame, Hasbro, Greenway Productions, 1966 .... 610.00
Panorama, Monarch, Boer Prisoners, Wounded, Gold Lacquer, Theatre Proscenium, Walker 415.00
Parrot, Pretty Peggy, Tin, Plush, Battery Operated, TN, Box, 11 In. 190.00
Parrot & Gnome, Gnome Offering Bowl To Parro, Lithographt, Meier 1375.00
Parrots, Pecking, Lithograph, Lever Action, Candy Container Box, Georg Fischer 229.00
Peacock, Rocking, Wood, Painted, Child's, 24 x 36 In. 168.00
Peacock, Tin, Windup, Eberle, Germany, 9 1/2 In. 1050.00
Pedal Car, Airplane, Air Mail, Pressed Steel, Steelcraft, 46 In. 1980.00
Pedal Car, Airplane, Pursuit, Gray, Blue, Yellow, 3 Wheels, Steel, Steelcraft, c.1946, 48 In. 259.00
Pedal Car, Airplane, Supersonic Jet, Pressed Steel, Murray, 48 In. 430.00
Pedal Car, Airplane, U.S. Airpatrol, Pressed Steel, 48 In. 1540.00
Pedal Car, American National Packard, Early 1920s 14210.00
Pedal Car, Austin Healey, Dummy Spark Plugs, 60 In. 2800.00
Pedal Car, Boat, Outboard Motor Speed, Pressed Steel, c.1950, 46 In. 1095.00
Pedal Car, Car, Buick Torpedo, Black, Chrome, Pressed Steel, Murray, 1953, 39 In. 374.00
Pedal Car, Casey Jones, Cannonball Express, Pressed Steel, 40 In. 935.00
Pedal Car, Chrysler, Steelcraft, 1941, 37 In. 4125.00
Pedal Car, Dump Truck, Pressed Steel, American National Co., Early 1900s, 56 In. .... *ILLUS* 1840.00
Pedal Car, Fire Chief's, Pressed Steel, Red, White, Bell, Rubber Tires, American National, 44 In. 3575.00
Pedal Car, Ford, Pressed Steel, Maroon, Upholstered Seat, Nickel Trim, Steelcraft, 1936, 37 In. 825.00
Pedal Car, Kidillac, Pressed Steel, Garton Toy Co., 48 In. 375.00
Pedal Car, Moonlight Woodies, No. 6, Maroon, Leather Top, George Benson 880.00
Pedal Car, Oldsmobile, Steel, Wood, Leather, Gendron, Early 1920s, 33 In. 470.00
Pedal Car, Ranch Wagon, Pressed Steel, Chain Drive, Electric Lights, Garton, 1950s, 45 In. 165.00
Pedal Car, Ranch Wagon, Pressed Steel, Murray, 1940s, 48 In. 210.00
Pedal Car, Speedboat, Red, 3 Wheels, Pressed Steel, Mid 20th Century, 46 In. 1092.00
Pedal Car, Sulky, Pony, Pressed Steel, Wood Slats, England, 1940s, 39 In. 150.00
Pedal Car, Tractor, Allis Chalmers, Model C, Type 1, Cast Aluminum, Eska, c.1950, 35 In. 489.00
Pedal Car, Tractor, Allis Chalmers, Model XT-190, Cast Aluminum, Ertl, c.1966, 37 In. 105.00
Pedal Car, Tractor, Case, Model 30, Pleasure King, Cast Aluminum, Ertl, c.1965, 39 In. 259.00
Pedal Car, Tractor, Ford, Model 8000, Cast Aluminum, Ertl, c.1968, 36 In. 105.00
Pedal Car, Tractor, IH Farmall, Model 806, Cast Aluminum, Ertl, c.1964, 36 In. 150.00
Pedal Car, Tractor, IH Farmall, Model H, Type 2, Cast Aluminum, Eska, c.1949, 34 In. 345.00
Pedal Car, Tractor, IH Farmall, Model M, Cast Aluminum, Eska, c.1953, 39 In. 345.00
Pedal Car, Tractor, John Deere, Model 3010, 3-Hole, Cast Aluminum, Ertl, c.1962, 37 In. ....210.00 to 259.00
Pedal Car, Tractor, John Deere, Model 40, Cast Aluminum, Ertl, c.1978, 37 In. 90.00
Pedal Car, Tractor, John Deere, Model 60, Cast Aluminum, Eska, c.1952, 35 In. 375.00
Pedal Car, Tractor, John Deere, Model 620, Cast Aluminum, Eska, c.1956, 38 In. 489.00
Pedal Car, Tractor, Massey Harris, Model 44, Type I, Cast Aluminum, Eska, c.1954, 37 In. 920.00
Pedal Car, Tractor, Oliver Model 1855, White, Cast Aluminum, Ertl, c.1972, 38 In. 375.00
Pedal Car, Tractor, Oliver Model 88, Open Grill, Cast Aluminum, Eska, c.1949, 32 In. 1265.00
Pedal Car, Tractor, Oliver Model 880, Cast Aluminum, Eska, c.1958, 39 In. 460.00
Pedal Truck, Hook & Ladder, Pressed Steel, Red, Low Cab, Open Bed, Hose Reel, c.1926, 25 In. 1430.00
Pedal Truck, Insurance Patrol, Pressed Steel, Open Seat, Railed Body, Buddy L, 27 In. 7700.00
Pedal Truck, Ladder, Pressed Steel, Red, Full Running Boards, Kingsbury, c.1926, 26 In. 1980.00
Pedal Truck, Ladder, Pressed Steel, Red, Side Ladder, Open Bed, Buddy L, 25 1/2 In. 715.00
Pedal Truck, Pumper Engine, Pressed Steel, Open Seat, Boiler Flywheels, Buddy L, 23 In. 1540.00
Pelican, Strolling, Tin, Celluloid, Windup, Nomura, Occupied Japan, Box, 5 1/4 In. 745.00
Penguin, Cyclist, Tin, Fabric, Battery Operated, Remote Control, K, Box, 6 1/2 In. 435.00
Penguin, Ramp Walker, Wood, 4 In. 11.00
Perambulator, Horse Drawn, Glass Eyes, Flax Mane, Leather Tack, Early 1900s, 55 In. 2585.00
Piano, Baby, Open Bottom, Girl In Green Hat, Feeding Dog, Germany, 7 In. 69.00
Piano, Grand, 22 Keys, Schoenhut, c.1900, 18 x 24 x 21 1/4 In. 425.00
Piano, Music Box, 2 Tunes, Schoenhut, Early 1900s 375.00
Piano, Upright, Harp & Angels Decoration, Hinged Lid, Schoenhut, 22 In. 90.00
Pig, Cutie Cook, Tin, Vinyl, Cloth, Battery Operated, Y Co., Box, 10 In. 495.00
Pink Panther, 1 Man Band, Plastic, Tin, Plush, Battery Operated, Illco, Box, 10 In. 120.00
Playing Dog, Dog With Shoe, Tin, Celluloid, Box, Occupied Japan 130.00
Playland Octopus, Amusement Ride, Tin, Battery Operated, Remote Control, Alps, 20 In. 770.00
Playland Whip, Tin, Windup, Chein, Box, 20 In. 1210.00

Toy, Pedal Car, Dump Truck, Pressed Steel, American National Co., Early 1900s, 56 In.

Toy, Space Ride, Tin Lithograph, Chein, Box, 10 In.

Playset, Cape Canaveral, Box, Marx, Box, 14 x 24 In. 170.00
Playset, Super Circus, Tin, Plastic Box, Marx, Box, 12 x 28 In. 195.00
Pond Boat, Wooden, Blue Paint, 30 1/2 In. 145.00
Pond Boat, Wooden, Green Paint, 36 In. 145.00
Pool Player, Player In Tailcoat, Wood Table, Lithograph, Painted, Spain 265.00
Pool Player, Tin Lithograph, Clockwork Motor, Articulated Arm, Kico, c.1910, 6 1/2 In. 355.00
Pool Player, Tin, Windup, Germany, 6 In. 250.00
Poor Pete, Black Man, With Dog, Windup, Celluloid, 6 In. 336.00
Pop-Up Critter, Cat, Black, Yellow Face, Red Base, 11 In. 39.00
Pop-Up Critter, Dizzy Donkey, Wood, 11 In. ....45.00 to 55.00
Pop-Up Critter, Elephant, Wood, Red, Blue Base, 10 In. 248.00
Pop-Up Critter, Lucky Louis, Wood, 11 In. 176.00
Pop-Up Critter, Ostrich, Wood, 11 In. 275.00
Porky Pig, Cowpunch, Lasso Spins, Tin, Windup, Marx, 1949, 8 1/2 In. 470.00
Porky Pig, Holding Umbrella, Tin Lithograph, Windup, Leon Schlesinger, c.1939, 8 1/2 In. 165.00
Porky Pig, Twirls Umbrella, Windup, Marx, 1939 .... 375.00
Pram, Victorian, Painted, Blue, 19th Century 575.00
Praxinoscope, Kinetoscope, Tin, 8 Piece Mirror, Iron Base, Germany, c.1900, 5 3/4 In. 1765.00
Praxinoscope, Wood Box, 8 Picture Strips, Ernst Plank, Germany, c.1903, 8 x 8 1/2 In. 4110.00
Preacher At The Pulpit, Full Robe, Wood Podium & Base, Clockwork, Ives, 10 1/2 In. 2750.00
Printing Set, Favorite Funnies, No. 4085, Complete, Stamperkraft, Box, c.1935 .... 110.00
Puffy Morris, Tin, Vinyl, Fabric, Battery Operated, Y Co., Box, 10 In. 138.00
Pump, Gas, Cast Iron, Arcade, 7 In. 616.00
Puppet Theater, Folding, le Blot Til Lyst, Paper, Wood, 1800s, 33 x 25 1/2 In. 69.00
Putty, Green Hornet Print Putty, Bounces, Stretches, Card, Colorforms, 1966, 6 1/4 x 8 In. 84.00
Rabbit, Easter, Astride Egg, Lithograph, White Rabbit, Red Tailcoat, Yellow & Blue Egg, Meier 2750.00
Rabbit, Easter, Delivery Cycle, Push Toy, Wyandotte, 1930, 5 In. 240.00
Rabbit, Playing Guitar, Sitting On Stump, Celluloid, Occupied Japan 83.00
Rabbit, Telephone, Plush, Tin, Battery Operated, Modern Toy, Box, 10 In. 350.00
Raceway, Green & White, 2 Red Cars, Tin, U.S. Zone, Box 55.00
Railway Porter, Lithograph, Blue Jacket, Gold Trousers, Red Cap, Candy Container Trunk, Meier 920.00
Range Rider, Tin, Windup, Marx, 9 1/2 In. 225.00
Rickshaw, Plastic, Battery Operated, Hong Kong, 1960s, 9 In. 150.00
Ring, Flicker, Fantastic Four, Multicolored, Silver, 1966 .... 69.00
Ring, Flicker, Iron Man, Multicolored, Silver, 1966 .... 40.00
Ring, Green Hornet, Secret Compartment, Flyer, Mailer, 1947 .... 690.00
Road Roller, Robby, Tin, Battery Operated, Daiya, 9 In. 2200.00
Road Roller, Standing Figure, Cast Iron, Painted, Green, Red Spoke Wheels, Hubley, 14 In. 1760.00
Road Runner, No. 2110, Ny-Lint, Box, 1960s, 9 In. 66.00
Road Scraper, Cast Iron, Kenton, Box, 7 1/2 In. 2128.00
Roadside Rest Service Station, Motor Oil Lubster, Water Can, Tin, Pump, Marx 195.00
Robot, Change Man, Head Splits, Walks, Tin, Plastic, Battery, Remote, Horikawa, 13 1/2 In. 12320.00
Robot, Earth Man, Walks, Fires Gun, Lights Flash, Tin, Battery, Remote, Nomura, Box, 9 In. 1680.00

Robot, Fighting Spaceman, Tin, Plastic, Battery Operated, Horikawa, Japan, Box 225.00
Robot, Hopping Rosey, Walks, Hops, Tin, Windup, Marx, Japan, Box, 5 In. 815.00
Robot, Lost In Space, 1 Chrome Hand, 1 Clear Hand, Battery Operated, Remco, Box, 12 In. 725.00
Robot, Lost In Space, Battery Operated, Remco, Box, 12 In. 728.00
Robot, Mechanical Walking, Sparking, Tin, Plastic, Windup, Linemar, Box, 5 3/4 In. 645.00
Robot, Mego-Man, Walks, Opens Mouth, Bell Rings, Gears, Tin, Windup, Yoneya, Box, 6 1/2 In. 1176.00
Robot, Mighty Atom, Tin, Battery Operated, Japan, Box, 12 In. 385.00
Robot, Mighty Atom, Tin, Windup, Billiken, Japan, Box, 9 In. 110.00
Robot, Minirobo, Moves, Fires Gun, Tin, Plastic, Battery Operated, TN, Box, 4 1/2 In. 1090.00
Robot, Moon Explorer, Windup, Crank Type Friction, Red Body, Yoshiya, Box, 1950s, 3 In. 665.00
Robot, Moves, Hits Changes Direction, Lights, Tin, Battery Operated, Yonezawa, Box, 11 In. 1400.00
Robot, Mr. Mercury, Tin, Battery Operated, Remote Control, Linemar, Box, 13 In. 525.00
Robot, Mr. Robot, Bump & Go, Lights, Antenna Spins, Tin, Battery Operated, Yonezawa, Box, 11 In. 70.00
Robot, Mr. Robot, Tin, Plastic, Battery Operated, Cragstan, 11 In. 525.00
Robot, Planet Action, Tin, Windup, Box, 1958 .... 375.00
Robot, Radicon, Lights Blink, Antennas Turn, Tin, Battery, Remote, Masudaya, Box, 20 In. 11200.00
Robot, Ranger, Walks, Visible Inner Workings, Tin, Plastic, Battery, Daiya, Box, 10 1/2 In. 1770.00
Robot, Ratchet, Walks, Tin, Windup, Nomura, Box, 8 In. 1090.00
Robot, Robby, Mechanized, Walks, Head Lights, Tin, Battery Operated, Nomura, Box, 13 In. 925.00
Robot, Robert The Robot, Tin Lithograph, Japan, 1950s, 5 In. 55.00
Robot, Rocket Man, Antenna, 2 Missiles, Remote Control, Rosko, Box, 14 In. 1456.00
Robot, Roto, Battery Operated, S.H., Japan, Box, c.1950, 8 1/2 In. 175.00
Robot, See-Thru, Plastic, Battery Operated, HK, Box, 12 1/2 In. 965.00
Robot, Smoking, Tin, Battery Operated, Green, Y Co., 12 In. 2695.00
Robot, Space Conqueror, Tin, Battery Operated, Daiya, 12 In. 815.00
Robot, Spaceman, Antenna Spins, Walks, Arms Up & Down, Tin, Windup, Yoneya, Box, 8 1/2 In. .. 560.00
Robot, Sparking, Tin, Windup, Box, 6 1/2 In. 350.00
Rock Crusher, Pitmaster, Portable Crushing Plant, Cedar Rapids, Iowa Mfg. Co., 1/24 In. Scale 990.00
Rocket, Art Deco, Wheels, Tin, Wyandotte, 6 1/2 In. 90.00
Rocket Ride, Chein, 1950s, 18 In. 295.00
Rocket Ride, Mechanical, Tin, Windup, Chein, Box, 18 In. 780.00
Rocket Ship, Astro Mobil, Driver, Tin, Vinyl, Friction, Marubishi, 8 1/4 In. 1120.00
Rocky, Ax, Battery Operated, Box, 1960s 225.00
Roller Coaster, Tin, Windup, Chein, 1938, 19 In. 175.00
Roller Coaster, Tin, Windup, Chein, 1950s, 19 In. 175.00
Rolling Pin, Palmer Cox, 1890s, 8 In. 350.00
Roly Poly, British Man, Tin, Mayo, 7 In. 185.00
Roly Poly, Chinese Boy, Papier-Mache, 4 In. 125.00
Roly Poly, Clown, Papier-Mache, 5 1/2 In. 125.00
Roly Poly, Clown, Schoenhut, 1920s, 5 1/2 In. 175.00
Roly Poly, Elephant, c.1920s, 7 In. 275.00
Roly Poly, Indian Baby, Papier-Mache, 4 In. 125.00
Roly Poly, Keystone Kop, Papier-Mache, 4 In. 125.00
Rooster, Push Toy, Steel Wings, Wood Body, Iron Wheels, c.1890 .... 365.00
Roundabout, 4 Sleds, Tin Figures, Open Sleds, Pedestal Base, V & R, Germany, 12 3/4 In. 825.00
Roundabout, Double Seat, 6 Seat, Tin, Clockwork, Germany, 11 1/4 In. 1045.00
Rudolph The Red Nosed Reindeer, Yellow, Brown, Red Bowtie, Occupied Japan 24.00
Runabout, Painted, Red, Wood, Pressed Steel, Spoke Wheels, Arcade, c.1908, 9 In. 470.00
Safari Hunt, Ford Bronco, Trailer, No. 8800, Ny-Lint, Box, 25 In. 190.00
Sam, City Gardner, Pushes Cart, Tools, Windup, Marx, Box 295.00
Sambo, Monkey, Playing Ukulele, Tin, Composition, Fabric, Windup, Alps, 9 1/2 In. 360.00
Sand Loader, Barber Greene, Pressed Steel, 18 In. 210.00
Sand Loader, Barber Greene, Pressed Steel, Doepke, 18 In. 165.00
Sand Loader, Barber Greene, Pressed Steel, Doepke, Box, 18 In. 470.00
Sand Loader, Cast Iron, Red, Yellow, Cast Figure, Spoke Wheels, Arcade, c.1928, 8 3/4 In. 1980.00
Sand Loader, Pressed Steel, Buddy L, 18 In. 300.00
Sand Sifter, Tin Lithograph, E.E. Hileman Scenes, Ohio Art, 1930s, 8 In. 59.00
Sandwich Man, Eat At Joe's, Mixed Material, Windup, KO, Box, 8 In. 175.00
Sandy Andy, Tin, Windup, Wolverine, Box, 14 In. 120.00
Satellite Launcher, 4 Launching Discs, Plastic, Original Box, 17 In. 308.00
Scooter, 2 Wheels, Red, 32 x 36 1/2 In. 140.00

Scooter, Kid Flyer, Tin Lithograph, Crate Front, Clockwork, Behrend & Rothschild, 6 1/2 In. 770.00
Scooter, Pressed Steel, Wood Seat, American National Co., Early 1900s, 32 In. 184.00
Scottish Dancers, Wood Jointed Figures, Wood Stage Base, Clockwork, Ives, c.1885, 10 In. 990.00
Scraper, Mini-Tonka, No. 1091, Box, 13 1/2 In. 65.00
Secretary, Slant Front, Paneled Cupboard, Leather Writing Surface, Pigeon Holes, 21 In. 1540.00
Service Center, Sears, Tin Lithograph, Plastic Cars, Marx, Box, 15 x 23 In. 55.00
Service Center, Sky-View, Tin Lithograph, Marx, 11 x 25 x 15 In. 130.00
Service Station, 1 Bay, Tin Lithograph, 5 1/2 x 12 x 8 In. 35.00
Service Station, Car, Lift Jack, Gas Pumps, Die Cast, Tootsietoy 130.00
Service Station, Day & Night, 2 Bay, Roof Parking, Tin Lithograph, Plastic, Marx, 11 x 26 x 14 In. . . 99.00
Service Station, Parking Garage, 3 Levels, Gas Pumps, Vehicles, Tin Lithograph, 16 x 26 x 15 In. . . 75.00
Service Station, Texaco, Accessories, 24 In. 415.00
Service Station, Wood, Arcade, 12 1/2 In. 1100.00
Service Station, Wood, Paper Lithograph, 2 Levels, 2 Bays, Elevator, Keystone, 8 x 22 x 12 In. 66.00
Sewing Box, Contents, Celluloid 150.00
Sewing Machine, Crank, Muller Toy, c.1910 . . . . 275.00
Sewing Machine, Hand Crank, Cast Iron, Midget, Early 1900s 425.00
Sewing Machine, Hand Crank, Model 20, Singer, Box, c.1915 . . . . 95.00
Sewing Machine, Instructions, Trade Cards, 3 Dollars Original Price, Singer, Box 209.00
Sewing Machine, Little Comfort, Improved Toy, Box, 6 3/4 In. 206.00
Sewing Machine, Little Seamstress, Casige, W. Germany, Box, 8 x 8 1/2 In. 250.00
Sewing Machine, Metal Lithograph, Gold Highlights, Germany, Early 1900s, Miniature 195.00
Sewing Machine, Pansy, Cast Iron, Gold Painted Open Work, C.J. Bailey, 8 3/4 In. 1880.00
Sewing Machine, Singer, Lockstitch Action, Japanned Finish, 6 1/2 In. 50.00
Sewing Machine, Singer, Sew Handy, No. 20, Girl Holding Machine On Box, 6 x 7 In. . . . . .165.00 to 308.00
Sewing Machine, Singer, Wood Handle, Marked, Singer Mfg., c.1920, 6 1/2 x 7 1/8 In. 175.00
Sewing Room, Shaker Style Furniture, Pine, Seamstress, Box, c.1950, 10 x 15 1/2 x 12 1/2 In. . . . 353.00
Sheep, Wooly, Papier-Mache, Painted, Germany, Late 1800s, 3 1/2 x 3 In., 13 Piece 380.00
Sheep & Lamb, Wood & Composition, Cotton, Pink Ribbon, Pull Toy, Stamped Germany, 5 In. 375.00
Sheep & Rabbit, In Pen, White Sheep, Lying Rabbit, Fencing, Lithograph, Kellermann 575.00
Shepherd Set, Blue Jacket, Red & Yellow Spotted Trousers, Terrier, 3 Sheep, Lithograph, Meier . . . 920.00
Sheriff, 2 Guns, Tin, Vinyl, Fabric, Battery Operated, Remote Control, Y Co., Box, 10 In. 165.00
Shoe, Horse Drawn, Cupid, Cast Iron, Painted, Kenton, 8 1/2 In. 305.00
Shoe Shine Joe, Battery Operated, Japan, Box, 1950s, 9 1/2 In. 120.00
Shooting Range, Outer Space, Targets, Pellets, Tin Lithograph, Plastic, Windup, Marx, Box, 19 In. 2300.00
Sign, Don't Park Here, Cast Iron, Tropical Paint & Oil Co., 4 3/4 In. 220.00
Sign, Don't Park Here, Police Department, Cast Iron, 4 3/4 In. 250.00
Sign, No Parking, Not Even Buicks, 4 1/4 In. 220.00
Silversmith Shop, Hinges, Front, Glass Windows, Shelves, Table, Chair, Silverware, 17 In. 5775.00
Sink, Functioning Faucets, Drain Pan, No. 22, Renwal 60.00
Ski Boy, Tin, Windup, Chein, Box, 1940s, 7 1/2 In. 195.00
Skier, Cross-Country, White & Gray Jersey, Cap, Gloves, Red Britches, Lithograph, Meier 1100.00
Sky Rail Set, Inserts, Kenner, Box, 1961 . . . . 110.00
Sled, 1 Board Seat, Metal Runners, Child's, 31 In. 80.00
Sled, Horse, Wood, Painted, Late 19th Century, 32 In. 190.00
Sled, Push, Red & Blue, Yellow Stenciling, Late 19th Century, 36 1/2 In. 209.00
Sled, Reindeer, Cast Iron, Painted, 19th Century, 55 In. 1495.00
Sled, Trail, Wood, Metal Runners, Red & Blue Paint, New England, 31 x 14 In. 316.00
Sled, Volunteer, Painted, Polychrome, Wood, Iron, Iron Strap Runners, c.1880, 6 1/2 x 12 In. 1998.00
Sled, Wood, Carved, Painted, Woman Standing, Cat, Iron Rails, 16 x 9 x 22 In. 230.00
Sled, Wood, Good Luck, Horse Shoe, Iron Capped Runners, No. 54, Paris Mfg., Me., 12 x 34 In. . . . 330.00
Sled, Wood, Green Paint, Iron Capped Runners, Fireman, Father, 1882, 6 x 34 x 13 In. 635.00
Sled, Wood, Iron, Painted Seat, 1800s, 36 In. 259.00
Sled, Wood, Metal Runners, Stenciled Scene Of Lake & Trees, 1910, 40 In. 675.00
Sled, Wood, Painted, Double Runner, No. 20, Sheffield Mfg., Burr Oak, Mich., c.1900, 40 In. 220.00
Sled, Wood, Painted, Fireman Holding Speaking Trumpet, Iron Capped Runners, 6 x 34 x 13 In. . . . 635.00
Sled, Wood, Painted, Green, Stenciled, Capped Runners, Mortised, 6 x 26 x 12 In. 660.00
Sled, Wood, Painted, Horseshoe, Clover, Good Luck, Rosettes, 11 1/2 x 33 1/2 x 11 1/4 In. 330.00
Sled, Wood, Painted, Sailboats, Late 1800s, Child's 550.00
Sled, Wood, Painted, Swan Head, Flower, Pin Stripes, Iron Capped Runners, 14 x 36 x 15 1/2 In. . . 305.00
Sled, Wood, Red Flowers, Metal Runners, Patina, New England, c.1880, 27 x 12 In. 4850.00

Sled, Wood, Swan Head Terminals, Flowers, Pin Stripe, Iron Capped Runners, 14 x 36 x 16 In. 303.00
Sled, Wood, V-Shape, Dragon Head Terminals, Metal Runners, Panel Seat, 12 x 30 x 13 In. 165.00
Sled Truck, U.S. Mail, Flivver, Pressed Steel, Painted Green, Cowdery Toy Works, 11 1/2 In. 1980.00
Sleigh, 2 Seats, Hobbyhorses, Carved, Painted 545.00
Sleigh, Horse Drawn, Hubley, c.1906 .... 2800.00
Sleigh, Horse, Flowers, Carved, Painted, Red Runners 1610.00
Sleigh, Open, 1 Horse, Woman Driver, Green, Gold, White Horse, Embossed Seat, Hubley, 15 In. .. 275.00
Sleigh, Push, Boat Shape, Painted, Plank Seat, Dutch, 1723, 38 x 46 x 20 In. 3740.00
Smitty, Riding Scooter, Removable, Tin Lithograph, Windup, Marx, 6 & 5 x 4 1/2 In. 1680.00
Snowflake & Buttercup, Wheeled Platform, Tin Lithograph, Blue Disc Wheels, 7 1/2 In. 440.00
Snowmobile, Metal, Battery Operated, TN, Japan, Box, 1950s, 8 In. 375.00
Soccer Player, Ball On Head, Papier-Mache, Clockwork, Germany, c.1920, 11 In. 176.00
Soldier, Gun, Reclining, Green Uniform, Celluloid, Occupied Japan 41.00
Soldier, Ramp Walker, Wood, 4 In. 28.00
Soldier Set, Artillerie, Lead, Heyde, Box, 1900-20, 2-In. Figures, 10 3/4 x 5 1/2 In. 235.00
Soldier Set, Bulgarian Infantry, No. 172, Britains, 8 Piece 560.00
Soldier Set, Butterscotch Uniforms, Machine Gunners, No. 194, Britains, c.1920, 6 Piece 112.00
Soldier Set, Cavalry & Infantry, Lead, Heyde, 1900-20, 2-In. Figures, 13 x 10 In. 588.00
Soldier Set, City Imperial Volunteers, No. 104, Britains, c.1900, 10 Piece 672.00
Soldier Set, Crescent Knights, In Armor, Postwar, 8 Piece 335.00
Soldier Set, Dublin Fusiliers, Olive Drab Uniforms, No. 109, Britains, c.1930s, 8 Piece 390.00
Soldier Set, First Madras Native Infantry, No. 67, Britains, Round Base, c.1900, 8 Piece 560.00
Soldier Set, Grenadier Guards, No. 312, Britains, c.1920, 8 Piece 110.00
Soldier Set, Musik Band, Lead, Heyde, Box, 1900-20, 2 1/4-In Figures, 10 Piece 235.00
Soldier Set, Russian Infantry, No. 133, Britains, c.1920, 8 Piece 500.00
Soldier Set, Turcos, Baby Blue Uniforms, No. 191, Britains, Early 1910s, 8 Piece 450.00
Soldier Set, U.S. White Jackets, No. 1253, Britains, c.1920, 8 Piece 280.00
Soldiers, Infantrymen, Zouave, French, Italian, Austro-Hungarian Officer, Mounted, Meier 345.00
Soldiers Of Fortune, Marx, Box, 1940s 195.00
Somstepa Coon Jigger, Tin, Windup, Marx, 1926, 7 3/4 In. 468.00
Space Capsule, Astronaut On Space Walk, Tin, Plastic, Battery Operated, Horikowa, Box, 6 In. 3640.00
Space Capsule, Carrousel, Glenn, Schirra, Shepard, Tin, Celluloid, ATC, Box, 6 1/2 In. 4950.00
Space Capsule, Floating Astronaut, Tin, Friction, Kanto, Box, 6 In. 330.00
Space Capsule, Friendship 7, Astronaut, Tin Lithograph, Friction, Horikowa, Box, 6 1/2 In. 3584.00
Space Capsule, Friendship 7, Tin, Friction, SH, Box, 7 In. 330.00
Space Capsule, Gemini, 2 Astronauts, Tin Lithograph, Friction, Horikowa, Box, 6 In. 1680.00
Space Capsule, Mercury, Friendship 7, Tin Lithograph, Friction, Horikowa, Box, 9 In. 1736.00
Space Helmet, Space Patrol, Adult Size, Box, 12 In. 308.00
Space Patrol, Holster, Dart Gun, Raised Grip Design, U.S. Plastic Co., Box, 1950s, 7 x 12 In. 2200.00
Space Patrol, NASA, Tin, Friction, MT Mart, Box, 7 In. 308.00
Space Pistol, Tom Corbett, Tin Lithograph, Marx Toys, Box, 10 In. 935.00
Space Ride, 4 Rockets, Tin, Windup, Chein 295.00
Space Ride, Tin Lithograph, Chein, Box, 10 In. .... *ILLUS* 672.00
Space Ride, Tin, Battery Operated, Alps, Japan, 4 In. 615.00
Space Tank, Mars, Graphics, Clockwork, Marx Toys, Box, 12 In. 1045.00
Space Tank, Robby, Tin, Battery Operated, Yoshiya, Box, 6 In. 1155.00
Space Trip, Tin Lithograph, Battery Operated, Modern Toy, Box, 1950s, 7 3/4 x 19 In. 835.00
Spaceship, Mercury Explorer, Tin, Plastic, Battery Operated, T.P.S., Box, 8 In. 195.00
Spaceship, Sparking, Tom Corbett, Tin Lithograph, Graphics, Clockwork, Box, 12 In. 1210.00
Spaceship, X-7, Tin, Battery Operated, Japan, 1950s, 8 In. 95.00
Sparkler, Andy, Taxi Hat, Eyes Light Up, Embossed, Tin Lithograph, Germany, 6 1/2 x 3 In. 412.00
Sparklers, Amos 'n' Andy, Tin Lithograph, Germany, 6 1/2 In. 1760.00
Spic & Span, Tin, Windup, Marx, Box, 10 In. 4125.00
Spirograph, Kenner, Factory Sealed, Box, 1967, 10 x 13 In. 110.00
Spreader, Oliver Superior, Cast Iron, Painted, Yellow, Black Trim, 3 Rotating Shafts, Arcade 250.00
Squirrel, Red, Seated, Lithograph, Green Base, Gold Wheels, Meier, c.1910 .... 459.00
Stagecoach, Overland, Tin, Battery Operated, Ichita Co., Japan, 18 In. 165.00
Stagecoach, Overland, Tin, Plastic, Battery Operated, MT Mark, Box, 18 In. 190.00
Stagecoach, Winner Of West, Wells Fargo, Tin, Battery Operated, Alps, Box, 18 In. 825.00
Steam Engine, Cast Iron, Pressed Steel, Stuart, 8 1/2 In. 187.00
Steam Engine, Working Model, Corliss, 26 In. 2090.00

Steam Engine, Working Model, Cretor's & Co., May 1906 Patent, 20 In. 2310.00
Steam Excavator, Open Cab, Black, Movable Boom, Clamshell Bucket, Kelmet, 25 x 15 In. 3575.00
Steam Shovel, Buddy L, Piston Version, Pressed Steel, Black, Red Roof, Boom, 27 1/2 x 15 In. 1320.00
Steam Shovel, Pressed Steel, $2.98 Price Tag, Turner, 20 In. 385.00
Steam Shovel, Pressed Steel, Keystone, 26 In. .... 120.00 to 187.00
Steam Shovel, Pressed Steel, Structo, 21 In. 99.00
Steamroller, Pressed Steel, Keystone, 20 In. 275.00
Steamroller, Pressed Steel, Steelcraft, 17 In. 275.00
Steamroller, Pressed Steel, Steelcraft, 1920s, 11 In. 795.00
Stinkey The Skunk, Windup, Japan, Box, 1950s, 6 1/2 In. 35.00
Stove, 4 Burners, Lids, Water Reservoir, Coal Scuttle, Lifter, Cabriole Legs, Cast Iron, Kenton, 9 In. 235.00
Stove, Accessories, Tin, Embossed, Schlesinger, c.1900, 8 3/4 x 7 3/8 x 5 In. 264.00
Stove, Bucks Stoves & Ranges, Nickel, 23 In. 3080.00
Stove, Bucks Stoves & Ranges, Wood Burning, 23 In. 3025.00
Stove, Burners, 2 Ovens, Coal Door, Chimney, Knobs, Cookware, Cast Iron, France, 14 In. 1540.00
Stove, Burners, Chimney, Oven Doors, Dishes, Cups, Lids, Embossed Tin, Schlesinger, 9 x 7 x 5 In. 265.00
Stove, Cast Iron, Arcade, 6 In. 325.00
Stove, Cast Iron, Baby, 6 Burners, Range, Reservoir, 15 x 18 In. 550.00
Stove, Cast Iron, Dictator, 4 Burners, Detroit Stove Works, c.1870, 9 x 10 x 11 In. 385.00
Stove, Cast Iron, Grey Iron Casting Co., Box 950.00
Stove, Crescent, Cast Iron, c.1900s 495.00
Stove, Crescent, Nickel Plated Cast Iron, Port & Coal Scuttle, 12 In. 280.00
Stove, Eagle, 4 Burners, Chimney Cover, Cast Iron, Lancaster, Pa., Hubley, 13 x 14 In. 130.00
Stove, Enameled Front, Brass Legs, Trim, Doors, 4 Copper Clad Accessories, 14 x 9 In. 115.00
Stove, Great Majestic Jr., 16 x 27 In. 3200.00
Stove, Ideal No. 6 .... 610.00
Stove, Image Of Seated Children On Back Plate, Tin, 8 1/2 In. 17.00
Stove, Isabella Furnace, 20 x 24 In. 345.00
Stove, Majestic Junior, Great Majestic, St. Louis, 2 Doors, Cast Iron, c.1900, 31 x 18 1/2 In. 8020.00
Stove, Perfection Toy, 7 x 8 1/8 In. 150.00
Stove, Pots, Pans, Accessories, Cast Iron 375.00
Stove, Pressed Steel Body, Painted, Black, Nickel Finish Top, Teapot, Child's, 9 x 12 1/2 In. 220.00
Stove, Queen Toy Stove, Cast Iron, 11 In. 90.00
Stove, Range, Cast Iron, Karr Co. 1450.00
Stove, Range, Cast Iron, MAF, Engman Matthews 4100.00
Stove, Royal Toy, 2 Skillets, Cast Iron, Kenton, 15 In. 1320.00
Stove, Royal, 6 Burners, Reservoir, Ornate Chimney Cover, 2 Doors, Nickel Plated, Iron, 11 x 12 In. 935.00
Stove, Royal, Accessories, Cast Iron, Kenton, 9 In. 235.00
Stove, Tin, Cast Iron, 7 x 9 x 6 1/2 In. 110.00
Stove, Water Pump, Pots, Pans, Tin, Painted, 1800s, 7 x 13 x 5 1/2 In. 176.00
Stove, With Chimney, Shelves, Food Chopper, Dish, Mug, Tin, Painted, 6 1/2 x 5 5/8 In. 120.00
Stove, Yale Brand Air Tight, Metal, Cast Iron, 6 1/2 x 4 1/2 In. 1485.00
Street Corner Dancer, Lenox & 125th St., Tin, Celluloid, Occupied Japan 323.00
Street Roller, Jumbo, No. 2050, Ny-Lint, Box, 16 In. 110.00
Street Sweeper, Elgin, Painted, Gray, Seated Driver, Hubley, c.1930, 8 1/2 In. 3025.00
Stroller, Doll's, Painted, Surrey Top, Fringe, Victorian 525.00
Submarine, Pressed Steel, Windup, Wolverine, 1930, 13 In. 110.00
Submarine, Sea Wolf Atomic, Pressed Tin, Key, Sutcliffe, Box, 10 In. 190.00
Submarine, Sea Wolf, Atomic, Sutcliffe, Box, 9 In. 35.00
Sulky, Black Horse, Cast Iron, Kenton, 7 1/2 In. 150.00
Sulky, Buffalo Brand, Black, Orange Wheels, Pull Toy, Welker & Crosby, c.1883, 8 1/4 In. 415.00
Sulky, Pacing Horse, Jockey, Silver Mane, Cast Iron, Kenton, 7 1/2 In. 150.00
Superjet Mouse, Cape, Walks, Tin, Vinyl, Japan, Box, 9 In. 1400.00
Surrey, Cast Iron, 2 Seat, Open Wagon, Spoke Wheels, Pratt & Letchworth, c.1900, 14 In. 935.00
Surrey, Cast Iron, Open Slat Floor Bed, 1 Horse, Driver, Passenger, Shimer, 12 In. 195.00
Surrey, Cast Iron, Steel, Open Wagon, Red Spoke Wheels, White Horse, Pratt & Letchworth 330.00
Surrey, Horse Drawn, Fringed, Driver, Passenger, Spoke Wheels, 12 In. 1756.00
Surrey, Horse Drawn, Fringed, Driver, Woman, Kenton, 13 In. 475.00
Surrey, Single Seat, Pressed Steel Cart, Spoke Wheels, Cast Iron, Pratt & Letchworth, 15 In. 605.00
Surrey, Wood, Iron, Victorian, Plaid, Black Carriage, Red Frame, 41 x 45 In. 2185.00
Suzy Bouncing Ball, Tin, Windup, T.P.S., Japan, Box, 1950s 95.00

Sweeper, Little Handi-Aid, Norstar 25.00
Sweeping Betty, Tin, Windup, Lindstrom, 1930s, 8 In. 275.00
Sweeping Mammy, Tin, Windup, Lindstrom, Box, 1930s, 8 In. .... 385.00 to 523.00
Swim Queen, Celluloid, Box, Occupied Japan 265.00
Tailspin Tabby, Pop-Up Kritter, Wood, Fisher-Price, 1931, 11 In. .... *ILLUS* 39.00
Tailspin Tabby, Pop-Up, Wood, Red Base, Fisher-Price 165.00
Talking Machine, Scottish Dancer, 8 In. 55.00
Talking Machine, Uncle Rastus, Box, 8 In. 187.00
Talking Teeth, Windup, Box 11.00
Tango Two, Man & Woman, Dancing, Pressed Tin, Cardboard, Box, 5 In. 176.00
Tank, Camouflage, Animated, Box, 1918, 2 1/2 x 1 1/4 In. 140.00
Tank, Cap Firing, Tin, Friction, Box, 9 In. 200.00
Tank, Casper Ghost, Turns Over, Tin, Windup, Linemar, Box, 3 3/4 In. 395.00
Tank, Mighty Explorer, Mystery Action, Pistons, Light, Tin, Battery Operated, Yonezawa, Box, 6 In. .. 1120.00
Tank, Pop Out Soldier, Tin, Windup, Germany, 1920s, 6 In. 145.00
Tank, Saladin Armored Car, Green, Plastic Wheels, No. 67, Matchbox, Lesney, Box, 1959 .... 58.00
Tank, Space Explorer, Astronaut, Bump & Go, Tin, Crank, Yoshiya, Box, 6 In. 185.00
Tank, Space, Rex Mars Planet Patrol, Tin, Windup, Marx, Box, 10 In. 450.00
Tank, WWI, German Decals, Camouflage, Clockwork Motor, 14 1/2 In. 225.00
Tank, X-7 Space Tank, Bump & Go, Tin, Plastic, Friction, Crank, Yoshiya, 5 3/4 In. 1230.00
Taxi, Amos 'n' Andy, Fresh Air, Windup, Marx, 8 In. .... 440.00 to 1075.00
Taxi, Cast Iron, Orange, Black, Hubley, 8 In. 775.00
Taxi, Flat Top, Cast Iron, Orange, Black, Nickel Lights, Disc Wheels, Arcade, 8 In. 5225.00
Taxi, For Hire, Lithograph, Red, Yellow, Gold Wheels, Georg Fischer 690.00
Taxi, Old Timer, Battery Operated, Japan, Box 135.00
Taxi, Yellow Cab, Black, Tin, Windup, Chein 155.00
Taxi, Yellow Cab, Cast Iron, Arcade, Early 20th Century, 9 In. 410.00
Taxi, Yellow Cab, Cast Iron, Orange, Black Roof, White Disc Wheels, Kenton, 6 1/2 In. 880.00
Taxi, Yellow Cab, Cast Iron, Painted Orange, Black Roof, Hood, Running Boards, Arcade, 8 In. 385.00
Taxi, Yellow Cab, Cast Iron, Painted Orange, Black Trim, Spare Tire, Hubley, 8 In. 825.00
Tea Set, China, Teddy Bear, Germany, c.1910, 10 Piece 225.00
Tea Set, Play Time, Tin Lithograph, J. Chein, Box, 1950s 125.00
Teddy Bears are also listed in the Teddy Bear category.
Telegraph Set, Tri-Signal, Pressed Tin, Box 35.00
Thresher, McCormick Deering 10-20, Orange, Blue Wheels, Nickel Driver, Kilgore, 5 3/4 In. 440.00
Thresher, McCormick Deering, Cast Iron, Arcade 720.00
Thresher, McCormick Deering, Cast Iron, Gray, Silver, Yellow Spoke Wheels, Arcade, 12 In. 250.00
Tiger, Bengal, Tin, Vinyl, Plush, Battery Operated, Remote Control, Marx, Box, 17 In. 149.00
Tiger, Glass Eyes, Hide Covered, Attached Ears, Painted Nose, Mouth, Windup, 15 In. 345.00
Tiger, Walker, Bouquet, Windup, Marx, Box, 8 In. 235.00
Tiger Cage, Royal Circus, Hubley, 1910 .... 2900.00
Tiller Car, Open, Cast Iron, Painted Black, Red Embossed Panels, Driver, Hubley, 3 7/8 In. 360.00
Toddling Babe, Windup, Celluloid, Box, Occupied Japan 41.00
Toilet, World's Smallest Receiver, H. Fishelov Co., Tootsietoy, Box, c.1925 .... 75.00
Tom Tom Canoe, 2 Men, Wearing Indian Headdress, Tin, Friction, Japan, Box, 1950s, 9 1/2 In. ... 295.00
Tombo, Alabama Coon Jigger, Tin Lithograph, Clockwork, Strauss, 1910, 10 In. .... 880.00 to 1100.00
Tool Chest, Tools, Wood Box, Mason & Parker, 1920s 36.00
Tool Chest, Wood, Carrying Stray, Buddy L, 23 In. 45.00
Tool Chest, Wood, Instructions, Saw, Carrying Tray, Buddy L, 23 In. 660.00
Toonerville Trolley, Tin, Marked Fountain Fox, Germany, Cracker Jack, c.1922, 1 7/8 In. 725.00
Toonerville Trolley, Tin, Windup, Dent, Box, 7 In. .... 750.00 to 1430.00
Toonerville Trolley, Windup, Nifty Co., Germany, 1922 .... 495.00
Top, Pirates, Tin, Ohio Art, 5 In. 90.00
Top, Spinner, Lion Chases 5 Exaggerated Blacks On Assorted Animals, 1920s, 7 1/2 In. 360.00
Top, Tulip, Fascinating Action, Tin, Chein, Box 40.00
Topo Gigio, Playing Xylophone, Tin, Vinyl, Plush, Battery Operated, TN, Box, 10 1/2 In. 1789.00
Topo Gigio, Walker, Swings Arms, Tin, Vinyl, Fabric, Squeaks, Japan, 11 In. 550.00
Tracks, Pressed Steel, Black, Decals, Buddy L, Box, 48 In., 12 Piece 440.00
Tractor, Accessories, True Scale, Cast Metal 110.00
Tractor, Blue, Red, Gescha, Germany, 1950s, 6 In. 245.00
Tractor, Caterpillar, Ten, Cast Iron, Painted, Green, Chain Tracks, Arcade, c.1929, 5 1/2 In. 770.00

Toy, Tailspin Tabby, Pop-Up Kritter, Wood, Fisher-Price, 1931, 11 In.

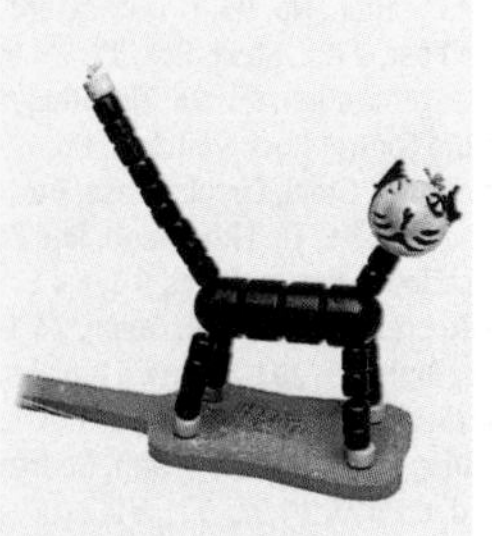

Toy, Train, Engine, Tin Lithograph, Germany, 4 In.

Tractor, Climbing, Highboy, Driver, Marx, Box 295.00
Tractor, Climbing, Highboy, Tin, Windup, Marx, Box, 10 1/2 In. 195.00
Tractor, Climbing, Metal, Windup, Marx, Japan, 8 In. 65.00
Tractor, Climbing, Midget, Tin Lithograph, Windup, Marx, 1930s, 5 In. 140.00
Tractor, Crop, Oliver 70 Row, Cast Iron, Green, Decals, Nickel Driver, Arcade, 7 1/4 In. 470.00
Tractor, Farmall, Regular, Cast Iron, Painted, Red, Gold Trim, Painted Driver, Arcade, 6 In. 415.00
Tractor, Fordson, Cast Iron, Painted, Gray, Nickel Driver, Red Spoke Traction Wheels, 1930s, 6 In. .. 110.00
Tractor, Giant Reversing, Tin, Windup, Marx, Box, 14 In. 300.00
Tractor, International Farmall, Model M, Cast Iron, Red, Decals, Nickel Driver, Arcade, c.1940 .... 305.00
Tractor, John Deere, Cast Iron, Painted, Green, Spoke Wheels, Vindex, c.1988, 6 1/2 In. 605.00
Tractor, John Deere, Model A, Cast Aluminum, c.1950, 7 1/2 In. 90.00
Tractor, Marvelous Mike, Tin, Battery Operated, Saunders, Box, 13 In. 240.00
Tractor, McCormack Deering, Driver, Cast Iron, Arcade, 7 1/4 In. 196.00
Tractor, Motor Express, Red, Silver, Hubley, 7 1/2 In., 2 Piece 500.00
Tractor, Mystery, Light, Japan, 1950s, 11 In. 120.00
Tractor, Road Roller, Tin, Windup, Marx, 12 In. 145.00
Tractor, Wagon, Cast Iron, Painted, Red, Cast Driver, Nickel Spoke Wheels, Arcade 220.00
Tractor, Wagon, Fordson, Cast Iron, Blue, Red Wheels, Driver, Skoglund & Olson, 14 1/2 In. 1540.00
Traffic Light, Marx, Box, 8 In. 55.00
Trailer, Pony, Yellow, Green Base, Plastic Wheels, 2 Horses, No. 43, Matchbox, Lesney, Box, 1968 . 25.00
Trailer, Travel, Silver, Tootsietoy, 1935, 3 In. 175.00
Train, Althof Bergmann, Locomotive & Tender, Tin, Cast Iron Wheels, Clockwork, 16 In. 2200.00
Train, Althof Bergmann, Locomotive, Painted, Stenciled, Cast Iron Wheels, 17 In. 770.00
Train, America, Locomotive, Painted, Stenciled, Tin, Cast Iron Wheels, Clockwork, 11 In. 770.00
Train, American Profile, Locomotive, Tender, Electrified, 48 x 9 1/2 In. 8800.00
Train, Aster, Steam Locomotive, Tender, Display Block, Instructions, Box, c.1977, 24 In. 3025.00
Train, Buddy L, Engine, Tender, Pressed Steel, 42 In. 1320.00
Train, Buddy L, Engine, Tender, Pressed Steel, Push Toy, 42 In. 2475.00
Train, Buddy L, Locomotive, Tender, Pressed Steel, Black Paint, Brass Rail Boiler, 42 1/2 In. 2200.00
Train, Buddy L, Locomotive, Wrecking Crane, Pressed Steel, Black Red Roof, 27 x 20 In. 3025.00
Train, Carette, No. 2350, Steam Locomotive, Tender, Enameled, 24 In. 1430.00
Train, Dewey, Locomotive, Coal Car, Flat Car, Early 20th Century, 8, 5, 3 5/8 In. 120.00
Train, Engine, Tin Lithograph, Germany, 4 In. .... *ILLUS* 224.00
Train, George Brown, Locomotive, Painted, Stenciled, Tin, Clockwork, 14 In. 3850.00
Train, Hartland, Locomotive, Tender, Metal, Plastic, Box, 22 In. 330.00
Train, Ives, Locomotive, Painted, Cast Iron Wheels, Japanned, Clockwork, 12 In. 2200.00
Train, Ives, No. 3251, No. 60, No. 61, No. 67, O Gauge, 1920s, 7-In. Engine, 4 Piece 355.00
Train, LGB Denver, Rio Grande, Coaches, Box, 17 1/2 In., 6 Piece 385.00
Train, Locomotive, Tender, Cast Iron, Painted, No. 178, 7 1/2 In. 120.00
Train, Meier, Locomotive, Integral Tender, Lithograph, Red Livery, No. 950, JPM On Tender 459.00
Train, Meier, Locomotive, Tender, Lithograph, Green, Red Livery, No. 960, British Market 1146.00
Train, Ohio Art, Tin Lithograph, c.1920s, 3 Piece 75.00
Train, Whistle Train, Monkey Driver, Smoking Action, Battery Operated, Box, 9 In. 6.00
Train Accessory, American Flyer, Block Signal, No. 2218, Steel, Box 65.00
Train Accessory, American Flyer, Danger Signal, Ringing, Box, 11 1/2 In. 440.00
Train Accessory, American Flyer, Danger Signal, Steel, Box, 10 3/4 In. 165.00
Train Accessory, American Flyer, Flag Pole, Old Glory, Silk Flag, 22 1/2 In. 1045.00

Train Accessory, American Flyer, Freight Station, No. 95, Tin Lithograph, 12 In. 195.00
Train Accessory, American Flyer, Lamp Post, 2 Arc, Steel, Box, 11 3/4 In. 140.00
Train Accessory, American Flyer, Passenger Station, No. 96, Tin Lithograph, Green Roof, Box 385.00
Train Accessory, American Flyer, Remote Control Track Switches, No. 720, Box 40.00
Train Accessory, American Flyer, Semaphore, Steel, Circular Base, Box, 9 3/4 In. 220.00
Train Accessory, American Flyer, Station, No. 96, Tin Lithograph, Red Roof, 10 In. 45.00
Train Accessory, American Flyer, Switch Tower House, Steel, 9 1/4 x 12 In. 770.00
Train Accessory, American Flyer, Trestle Bridge, Steel, Red, Green, 24 1/2 In. 88.00
Train Accessory, American Flyer, Water Tank, No. 2020, Mack's Junction, Tin, Box, 9 1/4 In. 1320.00
Train Accessory, American Flyer, Whistling Billboard, Ringling Bros. Circus, Light-Up, 7 1/4 In. . . . 35.00
Train Accessory, Bing, Railway Ticket Dispenser, Tin Lithograph, Germany, 6 5/8 In. 140.00
Train Accessory, Bing, Station, Painted, c.1910, 13 In. 1250.00
Train Accessory, Carette, Station, 2 Buildings, Tin Roof, Platform, Tower, 10 x 12 x 11 In. 3850.00
Train Accessory, Carette, Station, Canopies, Red Roof, Platforms, Embossed Tin, 19 x 12 In. 880.00
Train Accessory, Ives, Electrical Block Signal, Box, 13 In. 140.00
Train Accessory, Ives, Grand Central Station, Tin Lithograph, 22 In. 2475.00
Train Accessory, Ives, Semaphore, Platform, 2 Arms, 13 In. 165.00
Train Accessory, Ives, Semaphore, Single Arm, Box, 11 In. 220.00
Train Accessory, Ives, Ticket Office, No. 114, Box, 11 1/2 In. 1430.00
Train Accessory, Ives, Ticket Office, Tin Lithograph, 11 1/2 In. 55.00
Train Accessory, Ives, Water Tank, Pressed Steel, Orange, 9 1/4 In. 140.00
Train Accessory, Lionel, Beacon, Rotates, No. 494, Box 50.00
Train Accessory, Lionel, City Station, Red Window Frames, Lamps, Doors, Skylights, 9 x 19 1/2 In. 850.00
Train Accessory, Lionel, Figure Set, No. 550, Box, 13 In., 6 Figures 385.00
Train Accessory, Lionel, Freight Station, No. 155, Box, 11 x 18 In. 468.00
Train Accessory, Lionel, Lamp Post, No. 71, Box 6.00
Train Accessory, Lionel, Panel Board, No. 439, Steel, Red, Black, 8 1/4 In. 110.00
Train Accessory, Lionel, Power Station, No 436, Steel, Box, 9 1/8 x 7 In. 440.00
Train Accessory, Lionel, Signal Bridge, No. 440, Box, 14 x 20 1/2 In. 220.00
Train Accessory, Lionel, Station, No. 113, Steel, Terra-Cotta Base, 8 1/2 x 13 3/4 In. 193.00
Train Accessory, Lionel, Station, No. 121, Pressed Steel, 10 1/2 x 13 1/2 In. 110.00
Train Accessory, Lionel, Station, No. 126, Lionelville, Steel, 7 1/2 x 10 In. 110.00
Train Accessory, Lionel, Stockyard Train Station, No. 3656, 18-In. Track, 10 x 5-In. Station 23.00
Train Accessory, Lionel, Trainmaster Transformer, Type ZW, 275 Watts, 115 Volts, Box 140.00
Train Accessory, Marklin, Double Station, Canopy, Removable Roof, 10 1/2 x 8 x 15 In. 5500.00
Train Accessory, Marklin, Station, Enameled Tin, Stained Glass, Doors, 10 1/2 x 9 x 5 1/2 In. . . . 4400.00
Train Accessory, Platform, Covered, Marklin O, 22 x 16 In. 1380.00
Train Accessory, Schuco, Bridges, Tin 70.00
Train Car, American Flyer, Caboose, No. 3017, Box 77.00
Train Car, American, Locomotive, Painted, Stenciled, Tin, Cast Iron Wheels, Clockwork, 8 3/4 In. . . 4400.00
Train Car, Bassette-Lowke, Baggage Car, Track 1260.00
Train Car, Bing, Reefer, Pabst Blue Ribbon, O Gauge 1925.00
Train Car, Bing, Tank Locomotive, Gauge 10-6-2 . . . . . 4410.00
Train Car, Buddy L, Box Car, Pressed Steel, Painted, Red, Sliding Side Door, 20 1/2 In. 1210.00
Train Car, Buddy L, Flat Car, Pressed Steel, Decals, 20 In. 440.00
Train Car, Buddy L, Hopper, Pressed Steel, 2 Dump Ports, 20 In. 825.00
Train Car, Buddy L, Outdoor Caboose, Pressed Steel, Decals, 19 In. 825.00
Train Car, Buddy L, Outdoor Tank Car, Yellow, Pressed Steel, Back Frame Straps, 17 1/2 In. 1540.00
Train Car, Ives, Caboose, No. 67, Tin Lithograph, Red, Gray Roof, Box, 6 1/2 In. 66.00
Train Car, Ives, Locomotive, Bicycle Wheel 1100, Steam, O Gauge 2000.00
Train Car, Ives, Union Line Merchandise Car, No. 64, Tin Lithograph, Box, 6 1/2 In. 275.00
Train Car, Ives, Wannamaker Locomotive, No. 3243 . . . . . 7810.00
Train Car, Lionel, No. 400E, Locomotive & Tender, Red Stripe, Box, 2 Piece 17600.00
Train Car, Lionel, No. 675, Locomotive, Smoke Chamber, Box 145.00
Train Car, Lionel, No. 2046w, Tender, Whistle, Box 110.00
Train Car, Lionel, No. 2955, Tank, Shell, Zinc Die Cast, O Gauge, c.1940, 9 In. 220.00
Train Car, Lionel, No. 2956, Hopper, B&O, Zinc Alloy, c.1940, O Gauge, 10 1/2 In. 220.00
Train Car, Lionel, No. 2967, Caboose, Magnesium Alloy Die Cast, c.1940, 8 3/4 In. 195.00
Train Car, Lionel, No. 6457, Caboose, Box 85.00
Train Car, Lionel, No. 6462, Gondola Car, Box 25.00
Train Car, Lionel, No. 6465, Tank Car, Box 25.00

Train Car, Lionel, No. 6472, Refrigerator Car, Box 50.00
Train Car, Lionel, No. 6520, Electric, Searchlight, Cast Iron, Box 40.00
Train Car, Lionel, No. 6656, Stock Car, Box 40.00
Train Car, Lionel, No. X2954, Boxcar, Tuscan, Plastic, O Gauge, c.1940, 10 3/4 In. 165.00
Train Car, Locomotive, Painted, Tin, Hull & Stafford, 1870s, 11 In. 705.00
Train Car, Passenger, Railway Express Line City Of New Bedford, Late 1800s, 9 3/4 In. 155.00
Train Car, Steam Engine, Tin, Pulley Operated, Germany, 6 1/2 In. 106.00
Train Car, Tick-Tack-Express, Tin, U.S. Zone, Box 35.00
Train Set, Alpine Express, Tin, Technofix, Box, 20 In. 88.00
Train Set, American Flyer, Blue Bird Passenger, O Gauge, 4 Cars, Box, 6 1/2 In. 935.00
Train Set, American Flyer, Clockwork, Original Box, c.1923 .... 525.00
Train Set, American Flyer, Hiawatha Passenger, Sheet Metal, 5 Cars, O Gauge, Box, c.1936 .... 1540.00
Train Set, American Flyer, Hiawatha Passenger, Sheet Metal, 6 Cars, O Gauge, Box, c.1936 .... 2090.00
Train Set, American Flyer, Jeffersonian Passenger, 4 Cars, Box, 9 1/2 In. 1980.00
Train Set, American Flyer, Major Leaguer Freight, Tin Lithograph, Box, c.1930, 7 Piece 770.00
Train Set, American Flyer, Montgomery Ward Passenger, 4 Cars, O Gauge, Box 3300.00
Train Set, American Flyer, New Potomac Passenger, O Gauge, Box, c.1931, 8 1/4 In. 605.00
Train Set, American Flyer, No. 505WT, 1950-60 .... 878.00
Train Set, American Flyer, Oriental Passenger, 4 Cars, O Gauge, Box, 6 1/2 In. 195.00
Train Set, American Flyer, Passenger, 3 Cars, O Gauge, Box, c.1922, 5 1/2 In. 220.00
Train Set, American Flyer, Passenger, Tin Lithograph, Green, 4 Cars, O Gauge, Box 880.00
Train Set, Crescent Woodbine & Belmont, Engine, Cast Iron, 3 Cars, 10 In., 5 Piece 170.00
Train Set, Grey Iron, Nickel, Copper Plate, Locomotive, Tender, Coaches, 1920s, 4 Piece 300.00
Train Set, Ives, Black Diamond Passenger, 5 Cars, Box, 10 In. 4125.00
Train Set, Ives, Limited Vestibule Express Passenger, 5 Cars, O Gauge, Box, 8 3/4 In. 1210.00
Train Set, Ives, Patriot Passenger, 4 Cars, O Gauge, Box 935.00
Train Set, Ives, Red Hawk Special Passenger, Electric, 4 Cars, O Gauge, Box, 8 In. 660.00
Train Set, Ives, Sunbeam Limited Passenger, 5 Cars, O Gauge, 7 3/4 In. 605.00
Train Set, Ives, Universal Fast Freight, 5 Cars, O Gauge, Box, 9 In. 440.00
Train Set, Lehmann, LGB Passenger Coach, Electric Engine, Tender, Box 495.00
Train Set, Lehmann, LGB, Freight, Electric Engine, Box Car, Gondola 415.00
Train Set, Lionel, Commodore Vanderbilt, O Gauge, Box, 1930s, 5 Piece 560.00
Train Set, Lionel, Engine, No. 347, Observation Car, Pullman Car, Standard Gauge, Box, 1920s 420.00
Train Set, Lionel, Locomotive, Tender With Whistle, Pullmans, Observation, Box, 1930s 560.00
Train Set, Lionel, Locomotive, Tender, Gondola, Tanker, Caboose, Gate, Signal Switch, 1930s 410.00
Train Set, Lionel, No. 2511W, No. 3252 EP-5 Locomotive, 5 Freight Cars, Boxes, 1958 .... 7810.00
Train Set, Lionel, Pink Engine & Tender, Pink Gondola, Lilac Hopper, Blue Caboose, Girl's 2070.00
Train Set, Marx, Engine, 2 Cars, Caboose, Track, Platform, Tin, Windup, 13 x 23 In. 140.00
Train Set, Santa Fe & Erie, Granague Coaches, Cast Iron, Nickel Finish, Kenton, 28 In. 138.00
Train Set, Sears, Halloween, Orange & Black Locomotive, Box, Early 1960s 7150.00
Train Set, SMJ, Steam, Spirit Painted, Gold, Red, Blue, Green Coaches, Original Box 460.00
Train Set, Virginian Rectifier, No. 2513W, No. 6556 Katy Stock Car, No. 6427 Caboose, 1957 .... 6480.00
Train Set, Wekler & Crosby, Floor, Locomotive, Tender, Cast Iron, Wood, Coaches, 28 In. 880.00
Train Set, Wilkens, Engine, Tender, 3 Cars, Cast Iron, 7 In., 5 Piece 140.00
Train Station, Ives, Grand Central, Lithograph, 22 x 10 In. 980.00
Train Station, Lionel, No. 116, City, Tin, O Gauge, 9 x 19 1/2 In. 850.00
Train Station, Marklin O, 1930-40, 22 x 16 In. 345.00
Train Station, Toy Town, Ticket Office, Red, Yellow, Green, Blue, Tin, Chein 35.00
Treasure Chest, Tin Lithograph, Wolverine, 25 In. 90.00
Trencher, No. 1089, Tonka, Box, 17 In. 45.00
Tricycle, Cast Iron, Steel, Rubber Tired, Spoke Wheels, Leather Seat, Wood Grips, 31 In. 1760.00
Tricycle, Horse Form, Carved, Painted, 19th Century, 32 x 35 In. 1840.00
Tricycle, Horsehead Finial, Carved, Painted, 19th Century, 32 x 35 In. 3680.00
Tricycle, Ice Cream, Stop Me & Buy One, Lithograph, Blue, Uniformed Vendor, Kellermann 2290.00
Tricycle, Motor, Vee-Twin, Lithograph, Red, Yellow, Tiller Steering, Driver, Passenger, Kellermann 1145.00
Tricycle, Patrol Auto, Tin, Battery Operated, Travels In Figure 8, TN, Box, 10 In. 315.00
Tricycle, Pluto, Tin, Celluloid, Windup, Linemar 650.00
Tricycle, Tiller, Metal, Cast Iron, Upholstered Seat, Victorian, 45 In. 275.00
Trolley, 270 Broadway, Tin, Green, Blue, Yellow, Red, Chein 130.00
Trolley, Cast Iron, Blue, Red Panels, Embossed, Harris, c.1900, 7 1/2 In. 360.00
Trolley, Hillclimber, Yellow, Red, Fly Wheel Drive, Dayton, 1912, 16 In. 275.00

Trolley, Horse Drawn, Cast Iron, Red, Yellow Clerestory, Cupola Roof, Wilkins, c.1895, 18 In. 385.00
Trolley, Ives, No. 809, Electric, Tin Lithograph, Painted Roof, 8 In. 990.00
Trolley, Opening, Closing Door, Conductor, Tin, Windup, Nifty, 1925, 9 In. 525.00
Trotter, Driver, Whips Horse, Red Carriage, Ives, Cuzner, c.1890, 11 In. 3300.00
Truck, American Oil, Mack, Cast Iron, Red, Black, Blue, Embossed, Spoke Wheels, Dent, 15 In. ... 7150.00
Truck, Army National, L. Mack, Die Cast Cab, Open Bed Body, Army Drab, Tarp, Smith-Miller 600.00
Truck, Army Transport, Pressed Steel, Buddy L, 1940s, 21 In. 175.00
Truck, Army, Electronic Cannon, Rockets, Ny-Lint, 22 In. 110.00
Truck, Army, Pressed Steel, Canvas, Steelcraft, Box, 1930s, 23 In. 1980.00
Truck, Army, Pressed Steel, Structo, 13 In. 50.00
Truck, Army, Search Light, Soldiers, Windup, Wells Of London, Box, 1940s 450.00
Truck, Army, Tin, Windup, U.S.A., 1930, 10 1/2 In. 375.00
Truck, Auto Express, Cast Iron, Pressed Steel Canopy Roof, Spoke Wheels, 9 1/2 In. 770.00
Truck, Baggage Ride 'Em, Pressed Steel, Electric, Green, Rubber Tires, Buddy L, 26 1/2 In. 1760.00
Truck, Banner Toy, 12 1/2 In. 295.00
Truck, Barrel, Lithograph, Open Frame Back Body, Barrel Load, Driver, Motor, Georg Fischer 690.00
Truck, Bedford Evening News, Yellow, Silver Grille, No. 42, Matchbox, Box, 1957, 2 1/4 In. 95.00
Truck, Bell Telephone, Accessories, Cast Iron, Hubley, 9 In. 650.00
Truck, Bell Telephone, Boom, Auger, Log Carrier, Log, Ladders, Tools, Tires, Cast Iron, Hubley, 9 In. 670.00
Truck, Bell Telephone, Cast Iron, Red, Accessories, Log Carrier 390.00
Truck, Bell Telephone, Nickel Wheels, Ladders, Tools, Cast Iron, Hubley, 7 In. 950.00
Truck, Bell Telephone, Pole Wagon, Tools, Cast Iron, Hubley, 9 In. 575.00
Truck, Boat, Buddy L, 1959 .... 425.00
Truck, Breyers Ice Cream, Cast Iron, Painted, Orange, Black Roof, Blue Striping, Dent, 8 1/2 In. ... 880.00
Truck, Bucket Loader, Barber Greene, Pressed Steel, 24 In. 305.00
Truck, Bulldog Shape, Tin, Friction, Hishimo, 8 In. 275.00
Truck, Cadillac, Delivery, Tootsietoy, 3 1/4 In. 65.00
Truck, Camper, Ford Pickup, AM Radio, Ny-Lint, 16 In. 300.00
Truck, Canopy, Cast Tin, Red, Yellow, Green, A.R., France, 1930s 135.00
Truck, Car Carrier, Pullmore, Die Cast, Dinky Toys, Box, 10 In. 145.00
Truck, Cargo King, Red, Silver, Tonka, 1956, 24 In. 225.00
Truck, Caterpillar, DW-20, No. 1, Matchbox, Box, 4 3/4 In. 105.00
Truck, Cattle Trailer, Plastic, Hubley, 12 1/2 In. 65.00
Truck, Cement Mixer, Cast Iron, Painted, Orange, Red, Green, Aluminum Trim, Kenton, 9 1/2 In. ... 275.00
Truck, Cement Mixer, No. 77, Tonka, Box, 1960s, 9 In. 65.00
Truck, Cement Mixer, Pressed Steel, Green Frame, Base, Hopper, Mixing Drum, Buddy L, 11 In. ... 138.00
Truck, Cement Mixer, Pressed Steel, Structo, 20 In. 155.00
Truck, Cement Mixer, Turbine, Yellow, Tonka, 1970, 14 In. 110.00
Truck, Cement, Pressed Steel, Canadian Lincoln, 1950, 14 In. 245.00
Truck, Chevrolet, Heinz 57, Yellow Cab, Wood Stake Sides, Flooring, Decals, Smith-Miller 330.00
Truck, Circus Cage, Overland, White, Disc Wheels, Driver, Lion, Kenton, 9 In. 880.00
Truck, Circus, Buddy L, 1960s 425.00
Truck, Circus, Overland, Driver, Lion, Cast Iron, Kenton, 9 In. 1075.00
Truck, Circus, Pressed Steel, Blue Cages, Electric Lights, Lithograph, Keystone, 26 In. 6600.00
Truck, Circus, Wyandotte, 1930s 750.00
Truck, City, Red Stake Wagon, Silver Insert, Yellow Spoke Wheels, c.1903, 15 In. 440.00
Truck, Civilian Defense, Gun, Plastic, Tin, Friction, Marx, 12 In. 130.00
Truck, Coal, Packard, Pressed Steel, Front Crank, Decals, Rubber Tires, Keystone, 27 In. 825.00
Truck, Coal, Pressed Steel, Black Cab, Orange Coal Bed, Side Chute, Sturditoy, 26 In. 1540.00
Truck, Coal, Pressed Steel, Doorless Cab, Chute Slide Interior Bed, American National, 25 In. 3850.00
Truck, Coal, Red, Green, Marx, 6 1/4 In. 250.00
Truck, Commer, 30 CWT, Maroon, Nestle's Decal, No. 69, Matchbox, Box, 1959, 2 1/4 In. 99.00
Truck, Construction, Orange, Ny-Lint Pettibone, 19 In. 175.00
Truck, Crane, Pressed Steel, Smith-Miller 715.00
Truck, Crane, Red, Blue, Yellow, Bucket, Turner, 19 In. 425.00
Truck, Decker's Iowana, Pressed Steel, White, Embossed Roof Vent, Metalcraft, 13 In. 1430.00
Truck, Delivery, Cottonwood Acres, Hap's Oil Company, Standard Oil, R-190, 17 In. 250.00
Truck, Delivery, Deluxe Rider, Ride On, Pull Bar, Pressed Steel, Buddy L, 23 In. 605.00
Truck, Delivery, Kaufmann & Baer, Tin Lithograph, Friction, Turner Toys, 13 In. 1045.00
Truck, Delivery, Motor, Driver, GF 91, Lithograph, Yellow Over Red, Georg Fischer 345.00
Truck, Delivery, New York Truck Co., Green, Red Rims, Electric Headlights, Steelcraft, 1930s 355.00

Truck, Delivery, Panel, Pressed Steel, Yellow, Marx, 5 1/2 In. 120.00
Truck, Delivery, Penny, Tin, Germany, 3 3/4 In. 220.00
Truck, Delivery, Pressed Steel, Aluminum Spoke Wheels, Buddy L, 24 In. 660.00
Truck, Delivery, Sack & Box Load, Flywheel Drive, Motor Cart, Lithograph, Georg Fischer 1145.00
Truck, Delivery, Stake, Blue, Red, Cast Iron, Nickel Plated Grille, Arcade, 4 1/2 In. 165.00
Truck, Delivery, Stake, Red, Green, Cast Iron, Nickel Plated Grille, Kenton, 7 In. 220.00
Truck, Dugan's Bakers, Tin, Friction, HTC, 7 1/4 In. 390.00
Truck, Dump, Black, Open Bed, Open Cab, Rubber Wheels, Kelmet, 25 In. 605.00
Truck, Dump, Blue, Red, Nickel Wheels, Kilgore, 6 In. 325.00
Truck, Dump, Buddy L, 23 In. 240.00
Truck, Dump, Cast Iron, Arcade, 7 1/4 In. 450.00
Truck, Dump, Cast Iron, Hubley, 7 1/2 In. ....85.00 to 112.00
Truck, Dump, Cement Mixer, Dodge, Yellow, Tonka, 1970, 19 In. 75.00
Truck, Dump, Chain Drive, Pressed Steel, Open Cab, Tilt Body, Buddy L, 25 In. 770.00
Truck, Dump, Dodge, 1959 Model, Hydraulic, Red, Blue, Tin, Japan, 24 In. 125.00
Truck, Dump, Dodge, Pressed Steel, Turner, 28 In. 495.00
Truck, Dump, Enclosed IG Cab, Nickel Driver, Cast Iron, Painted, Green, Arcade, 10 In. 715.00
Truck, Dump, Gondola, Pressed Steel, Doorless Cab, Black, Swing Body, Sturditoy, 24 In. 3300.00
Truck, Dump, Grit Spreader, Red, Yellow, Gray Pull, No. 70, Matchbox, Lesney, Box, 1966 .... 26.00
Truck, Dump, Heavy Duty, No. 2083, Marx, 1958, 20 In. 385.00
Truck, Dump, High Lift, Structo, 1951, 12 1/2 In. 95.00
Truck, Dump, Hoveringham Tipper, 8 Wheels, No. 17, Matchbox, Lesney, Box, 1963 .... 45.00
Truck, Dump, Hydraulic Dumper, Pressed Steel, Buddy L, 1940s, 21 In. 145.00
Truck, Dump, Hydraulic, Pressed Steel, Ride On, Handle, Buddy L, Box, 27 In. 2860.00
Truck, Dump, Hydraulic, Shovel, Buddy L, Box, 11 1/2 In. 175.00
Truck, Dump, Hydraulic, Tonka, 1963, 13 In. 99.00
Truck, Dump, International, Cast Iron, Red, Silver, Arcade, 11 In. 365.00
Truck, Dump, International, Green, Red, Arcade, 10 3/4 In. ....2000.00 to 2250.00
Truck, Dump, International, Red, Yellow, Buddy L, 1948, 21 In. 325.00
Truck, Dump, Junior, Pressed Steel Cab, Black, Running Boards, Red Body, Buddy L, 20 1/2 In. 2475.00
Truck, Dump, Lumar Construction, Lithograph, Red, Yellow, Marx, 1950s, 12 In. 85.00
Truck, Dump, Mack, C Cab, Cast Iron, Gray, Nickel Load Bar, Disc Wheels, Kenton, 11 In. 990.00
Truck, Dump, Mack, Green, Arcade, 8 1/2 In. 1250.00
Truck, Dump, Mack, Hydraulic Pump, Driver, Cast Iron, Arcade, 12 In. 750.00
Truck, Dump, Mack, Iron Wheels, Green, Arcade, 8 1/2 In. 1350.00
Truck, Dump, Mack, Model B-61, First Gear, C.P. Ward Inc., Box, 1960 .... 65.00
Truck, Dump, Mack, Pressed Steel, Red, C Cab Design, Open Bed Body Tilts, Steelcraft, 26 1/2 In. 990.00
Truck, Dump, MIC, Pressed Steel, Smith-Miller, 17 In. 770.00
Truck, Dump, Model T, Pressed Steel, Buddy L, 12 In. ....805.00 to 1265.00
Truck, Dump, Nickel Grille, Cast Iron, Painted, Green, Red, Rubber Tires, Arcade, 10 In. 880.00
Truck, Dump, Nickel Wheels, Blue, Red, Kilgore, 6 In. 325.00
Truck, Dump, Oh Boy, Pressed Tin, 19 In. 175.00
Truck, Dump, Open Bed, Black, Anthony Dump Body, Tailgate, Nickel Driver, Arcade, 8 1/2 In. 935.00
Truck, Dump, Pointer, No. 51, Matchbox, Lesney, Box, 1969 .... 29.00
Truck, Dump, Pressed Steel, Buddy L, c.1925, 24 In. 660.00
Truck, Dump, Pressed Steel, Burdett-Murray White, 25 In. 935.00
Truck, Dump, Pressed Steel, Green, Black Running Boards, Open Bed, Rubber Tires, 27 1/2 In. 1430.00
Truck, Dump, Pressed Steel, Painted, Red, Black, Open Body, Clockwork, Structo, 18 In. 1430.00
Truck, Dump, Pressed Steel, Steelcraft, 27 In. 550.00
Truck, Dump, Pressed Steel, Tonka, 1955, 13 In. 110.00
Truck, Dump, Red Baby, Cast Iron, Arcade, 10 1/2 In. 475.00
Truck, Dump, Red Baby, Iron Wheels, Arcade, 10 3/4 In. 650.00
Truck, Dump, Red, Green, Tonka, 1955, 13 In. 195.00
Truck, Dump, Red, Wyandotte, 1930s, 6 In. 195.00
Truck, Dump, Ride-Er-Dumper, Copper, White, Structo, 1960s, 20 In. 80.00
Truck, Dump, Sand, Marx, 10 1/2 In. 225.00
Truck, Dump, Spring, Cast Iron, Arcade, 8 1/4 In. 140.00
Truck, Dump, Steel, Red, Blue, Yellow Gate, Marx, Early 1950s, 21 In. 235.00
Truck, Dump, Tin, Friction, Japan, 1950s, 9 In. 45.00
Truck, Dump, Yellow, Wooldridge, Doepke, 1946, 25 In. 295.00
Truck, Emergency Searchlight Unit, Pressed Steel, Rossmoyne, 19 In. 2970.00

Truck, Emergency Spotlight, Pressed Tin, Marx, 19 In. 154.00
Truck, Enclosed Cab, Blue, Orange Stake Side, Motor Driven, Kingsbury, 1926, 23 1/2 In. 4675.00
Truck, Express Freight, Metal, Friction, 1950s, Japan, Box, 9 1/2 In. 95.00
Truck, Express Line, Pull Cord, Buddy L, 25 In. 1760.00
Truck, Express, 1 Ton, Pressed Steel, Black, Enclosed Cab, Open Body, Buddy L, 14 In. 3025.00
Truck, Express, Doors, Pressed Steel, Open Bed Body, Rear Gate, Rubber Tires, Buddy L, 25 In. 6050.00
Truck, Express, Pressed Steel, Rear Doors, Gate, Aluminum Disc Wheels, Buddy L, 24 In. 825.00
Truck, Express, Red, Dent, 5 In. 450.00
Truck, Express, Toledo Bulldog Mack, Open Cab, Black, 3 Panel Screen, c.1926, 26 In. 2090.00
Truck, Fixed Bed, Red, Cast Iron, Red & White Disc Wheels, Nickel Driver, Arcade, 10 In. 660.00
Truck, Fleet Set, Tin, Windup, Ranger, Box 425.00
Truck, Flywheel Drive, Lithograph, Red, Yellow Panels, Gray Cab, Driver, Georg Fischer 459.00
Truck, Ford, 3 Seat, Tin, Friction, 19 In. 375.00
Truck, Ford, Pickup, 1956 Model, Blue, Tin, Friction, Japan, 12 In. 295.00
Truck, Fork-Lift, Red, Silver, Windup, Ny-Lint, 1947, 11 In. 125.00
Truck, Frosty Bar, Friction, White, Orange Trim, Japan, 7 In. 165.00
Truck, Fuel, Aviation, Cast Iron, Red, Yellow Chassis, Nickel Spoke Wheels, Kilgore, 12 In. 5225.00
Truck, Fuel, International, Tin, Friction, San Japan, 1950, 9 1/2 In. 95.00
Truck, Future, Tin, Friction, Linemar, Japan, 1950s, 8 1/2 In. 275.00
Truck, Garbage, Dept. Of Street Cleaning, Wood Wheels, Wyandotte, 1930s, 11 In. 400.00
Truck, Goodrich Silver Town Tires, Pressed Steel, Metalcraft, 1930s, 12 In. 248.00
Truck, Green Giant, White, Tonka, 1955, 24 In. 395.00
Truck, Grocery, Tin Plated, Windup, Chein, 5 3/4 In. 275.00
Truck, Hap's Oil Company, Standard, Pressed Steel, 17 In. 413.00
Truck, Hauler, Livestock Trailer, Marcrest Farms, Tin, Plastic, Animals, Marx, Box, 16 1/2 In. 138.00
Truck, Heinz 57, Delivery, Electric Headlights, Painted, White, Pressed Steel, Metalcraft, 12 In. 275.00
Truck, Heinz 57, For Pickles It's Heinz, White, Metal, Rubber Tires, Box, 10 x 29 In. 585.00
Truck, Horse Van, No. 6300, Ny-Lint, Box 385.00
Truck, Hose, Cast Iron, Painted, Yellow, Nickel Bumper, Disc Wheels, Kenton, 9 In. 660.00
Truck, Ice Cream, Chevrolet, Bell, Nomura, Japan, 8 In. 275.00
Truck, Ice Cream, Chevrolet, Japan, 1959, 8 In. 175.00
Truck, Ice Cream, Delicious Ice Cream, Driver, Bell Rings, Tin, Friction, Nomura, 9 3/4 In. 125.00
Truck, Ice Cream, Driver, Tin, Friction, Japan, 1950s, 7 1/2 In. 175.00
Truck, Ice, Cast Iron, Nickel Grille, Accessories, Tongs, Arcade, 6 3/4 In. 224.00
Truck, Ice, Doors, Pressed Steel, Rubber Tires, Black Cab, Yellow Body, Tarp, Buddy L, 26 1/2 In. 8250.00
Truck, Indian Head Express, Box, Linemar, Japan, 1960s, 11 1/2 In. 120.00
Truck, Kraft Cheese, GMC, Pressed Steel, Smith-Miller, 1950s, 14 In. 230.00
Truck, Ladder, Aerial, No. 2960, Tonka, Box, 1970s 55.00
Truck, Ladder, Aerial, Pressed Steel, Aluminum Disc Wheels, Buddy L, 40 In. 660.00
Truck, Ladder, Cast Iron, Open Truck, Cast Driver, Nickel Ladder Supports, Kenton, 8 3/4 In. 330.00
Truck, Ladder, Cast Iron, Painted, Red, Silver Chassis, Nickel Grille, Cast Lights, Hubley, 8 In. 220.00
Truck, Ladder, Hill Climber, Steel, Flywheel Friction, Driver, 12 In. 360.00
Truck, Ladder, Tandem, Cast Iron, Open Truck, Cast Figures, Nickel Hose Reel, Arcade, 18 1/2 In. 385.00
Truck, Loader, Wheel, Ripper, Caterpillar 950, Gescha, Box 165.00
Truck, Loader, Woodrige, Pressed Steel, Doepke, 24 In. 155.00
Truck, Log Hauler, Tonka, 1954, 23 In. 250.00
Truck, Log, Mack, Red Tractor, Black Fenders, Open Frame Body, Log Load, Smith-Miller 415.00
Truck, Log, Trailer, Metal, Wood Load, Metal Chains, Smith-Miller, 35 In. 336.00
Truck, Long Distance Moving, Wood, Buddy L, 27 In. 248.00
Truck, Lumber, Miniature, Operation, Cari-Car, Swan Hill, Box, 7 1/2 In. 165.00
Truck, Lumber, Pressed Steel, Buddy L, 25 In. 4950.00
Truck, Lumber, Pressed Steel, Doorless Cab, Black, Red Cargo Bed, Buddy L, c.1925, 24 In. 2090.00
Truck, Mack, A & P, Semi, Red, Tootsietoy 250.00
Truck, Mack, Army, Tan, Red, Steel, Canvas, Steelcraft, 1927, 22 In. 340.00
Truck, Mack, Cast Iron, Stenciled, A. Rigel & Sons Inc., White, Red Chassis, Arcade, 12 In. 4400.00
Truck, Mack, Dump Bed, Tootsietoy, 3 1/4 In. 35.00
Truck, Mack, Lubrite Gasoline, Driver, Cast Iron, Arcade, 13 In. 1250.00
Truck, Mack, Railway Express Semi, Orange, Green, Tootsietoy 250.00
Truck, Mack, Transport, Carrying 4 1928-Model Buicks, Tootsietoy, 10 3/4 In. 275.00
Truck, Mack, US Airmail, Red, Olive, Tootsietoy, 3 In. 175.00
Truck, Mail, Olive Green, Yellow Top, Buddy L, 1941 .... 395.00

Truck, Mail, Pressed Steel, Keystone, 1930s, 27 In. 1650.00
Truck, Military, 10 Soldiers, Tin, Windup, England, Wells, 1940s, 12 1/2 In. 295.00
Truck, Milk Delivery, Junior, Black, Green Tank, Red Chassis, Buddy L, c.1932, 24 In. 1760.00
Truck, Milk, Borden's, Cast Iron, White, Embossed, Red, White Rubber Tires, Hubley, 6 In. 990.00
Truck, Milk, Driver, Tin, Friction, Japan, 1950, 7 In. 95.00
Truck, Milk, Federal, White, Tootsietoy, 3 In. 225.00
Truck, Mobile Repair It, Pressed Steel, Tool Box, Buddy L, 1950s, 27 In. 303.00
Truck, Model A, Side Dump Trailer, Painted, Green, Red Frame, Cast Iron, Arcade, 13 In. 770.00
Truck, Moving Van, U-Haul, Maxi-Mover, Ny-Lint, Box, 19 In. 143.00
Truck, Moving Van, United Van Lines Inc., Tin, Friction, Cragstan, Japan, Box, 9 1/2 In. 121.00
Truck, Moving Van, White, Cast Iron, Embossed, Tan, Red Hood, Rubber Tires, Arcade, 13 In. 8350.00
Truck, Moving, Allied Van Lines, Buddy L, 1940s 4865.00
Truck, Moving, North American Van Lines, Friction, Japan, 13 In. 225.00
Truck, Packing, First Prize Ham, Electric Headlights, Pressed Steel, Metalcraft, 13 In. 1540.00
Truck, Panel, White, Cast Iron, Blue, Cast Headlights, Nickel Disc Wheels, Arcade, 8 In. 2750.00
Truck, Parcel Post, Pressed Steel, Sonny, 1930s, 26 In. 1210.00
Truck, Payless Drug Stores, Private Label, White, Blue, Structo, 1963, 12 In. 165.00
Truck, Pickup, Commer, Silver Grille, No. 50, Matchbox, Box, 2 1/2 In. 88.00
Truck, Pickup, Corvair, Tin, Friction, KTS, Box, 8 In. 304.00
Truck, Pickup, Pressed Steel, Tonka, 1956, 12 1/2 In. 198.00
Truck, Pickup, Tonka, Box, 1961, 13 In. 248.00
Truck, Plee-Zing Quality Products, Metalcraft, 11 In. 275.00
Truck, Polish Your Car With Rain Proof Finish, Pressed Steel, Metalcraft, 12 1/2 In. 825.00
Truck, Pure Ice, Pressed Steel, American National, 29 In. 770.00
Truck, Pure Oil Co., Pressed Steel, Electric Light, Metalcraft, 15 In. 1430.00
Truck, Quarry, Euclid, 10 Wheel, Yellow, No. 6, Matchbox, Lesney, Box, 1964 .... 34.00
Truck, Radio Rentals, White, Yellow, No. 62, Matchbox, Lesney, Box, 1963 .... 98.00
Truck, Railroad Transfer, Stake Body, 20 Tone, Red & Yellow, Buddy L, 1940s, 23 In. 415.00
Truck, Railway Express, Green, Hubley, 6 1/2 In. 500.00
Truck, Railway Express, Ice Cream, Pressed Steel, Buddy L, 1950s, 22 In. 468.00
Truck, Railway Express, Pressed Steel, Open Cab, Van Body, Buddy L, 25 In. 2750.00
Truck, Railway Express, Pressed Steel, Sturditoy, 26 1/2 In. 1760.00
Truck, Railway Express, Wrigley's Gum Ad, Pressed Steel, Green, Yellow, Buddy L, 26 In. 2475.00
Truck, Ranch, Ford, No. 4500, Ny-Lint, 1950s, 14 In. 88.00
Truck, RCA NBC Television, Tin, Battery Operated, Linemar, Box, 9 In. 1210.00
Truck, REA Express, Delivery Step, Green, Spring Suspension, Buddy L, 1964, 11 1/2 In. 121.00
Truck, Semi-Trailer, Grain, Ralston, Box, 8 In. 193.00
Truck, Semi-Trailer, Green Giant, Tonka, 1955, 24 In. 395.00
Truck, Semi-Trailer, Long Hauler, Tonka, 1956, 23 1/2 In. 193.00
Truck, Semi-Trailer, Sparkling, Marbrook Farms, Tin, Windup, Marx, Box, 21 In. 248.00
Truck, Shell Chemicals Limited, Die Cast, Dinky Toys, Box, 6 In. 130.00
Truck, Shell Oil, Pressed Steel, Orange, Red, Duo Tone, Side Rails, Buddy L, 29 In. 6600.00
Truck, Shovel Loader, Flatbed, Structo, Box, 8 1/2 & 9 1/4 In. 195.00
Truck, Smile, Pressed Steel, Electric Headlights, Stake Body, Metalcraft, 12 In. 440.00
Truck, Soda, Crown, Tin, Friction, TK, Japan, Box, 1950s, 7 1/2 In. 175.00
Truck, Speed, Pressed Steel, Enclosed Cab, Painted, Cream, Green, Keystone, c.1938, 23 1/2 In. 440.00
Truck, Stake, 5 Ton, Cast Iron, Painted, Green, Seated Driver, Embossed Panels, Hubley, 17 In. 990.00
Truck, Stake, Cast Iron, Freidag, 7 3/4 In. 1456.00
Truck, Stake, Diamond T, Cast Iron, Painted, Green, Nickel Bumper, Rubber Tires, Hubley, 7 In. 195.00
Truck, Stake, Dough Boy Feeds, Tonka, 1959, 15 In. 99.00
Truck, Stake, Ford Model T, Red, Arcade, 6 3/4 In. 325.00
Truck, Stake, Ford, Chase & Sandborn Coffee, Ny-Lint, 14 1/2 In. 130.00
Truck, Stake, International, Pressed Steel, Buddy L, Box, 25 In. 2200.00
Truck, Stake, Mack Express, Green, Tootsietoy, 5 1/2 In. 275.00
Truck, Stake, Take Apart, Cast Iron, Yellow Body, Black Chassis, A.C. Williams, 7 1/4 In. 330.00
Truck, Stake, Tinted Windows, No. 4, Matchbox, 1967, Box, 2 3/4 In. 143.00
Truck, Stake, Tinted Windows, No. 4, Matchbox, 1968, Box, 2 3/4 In. 130.00
Truck, Steam Pumper, Diamond T, Red, Nickel Grille, Boiler, Hubley, 6 1/2 In. 400.00
Truck, Sunshine Biscuit, Pressed Steel, Painted, Yellow, Decals, Metalcraft, 12 1/2 In. 385.00
Truck, Tanker, Dan Dugan, 18-Wheel, Die Cast, Ralstoy, Box, c.1958, 9 In. 175.00
Truck, Tanker, Domaco Gasoline & Oils, Orange, Green, Tootsietoy, 5 1/2 In. 350.00

Truck, Tanker, Ford, SuCrest, Die Cast, Ralstoy, Box, c.1958, 8 In. 175.00
Truck, Tanker, Gas & Oil, Mack, Green, Red, Tootsietoy 250.00
Truck, Tanker, Gas, Pressed Steel, Sinclair, 17 In. 495.00
Truck, Tanker, Gas, Shell BP, Pressed Steel, Tri-Ang, 24 In. 186.00
Truck, Tanker, Gas, Texaco, Pressed Steel, Buddy L, 24 In. 65.00
Truck, Tanker, Gasoline, Mack, Cast Iron, Light Blue, Fuel Tank, Seated Driver, Arcade, 13 In. 1320.00
Truck, Tanker, Gasoline, Mack, Domaco Gas & Oil, Orange, Red, Tootsietoy, 5 1/2 In. 200.00
Truck, Tanker, Gasoline, Mack, Hose, Driver, Cast Iron, Arcade, 1929, 12 1/2 In. 1550.00
Truck, Tanker, Jet Fuel, Texaco, AMF, Box, 23 1/2 In. 130.00
Truck, Tanker, Little Audrey, Die Cast, Ralstoy, Box, c.1958, 9 In. 175.00
Truck, Tanker, Mobilgas, Red, Heavy Duty Carrier, Tin, Friction, Hayashi, Box, 1960s, 8 In. 400.00
Truck, Tanker, Oil, Pressed Steel, Tandem, Red, Doorless Cab, Decals, Spigot, Sturditoy, 34 In. 2750.00
Truck, Tanker, Red Lion, Pressed Steel, Gilmore, 27 In. 2090.00
Truck, Tanker, Shell Motor, Pressed Steel, 8 Oil Cans, Metalcraft, 1930s, 12 In. ....176.00 to 385.00
Truck, Tanker, Shell, Tootsietoy 65.00
Truck, Tanker, Sinclair, Tootsietoy 55.00
Truck, Tanker, Tanker & Pup, Terrible Herbst Oil Co., Pressed Steel, Smith-Miller, 36 In. 935.00
Truck, Tanker, Texaco, Tootsietoy 66.00
Truck, Tanker, Toledo Bull Dog, Pressed Steel, Embossed Doorless Cab, Black, Red, 26 1/4 In. 3850.00
Truck, Tanker, Tydol, Red, Friction, Londontoy, 1948, 6 In. 50.00
Truck, Telephone, Unassembled, Structo, Box, 1950s, 12 In. 220.00
Truck, Tow, AAA, Tonka, 1956 .... 275.00
Truck, Tow, Auto Wrecking, Pressed Steel, Black Open Seat Cab, Red, Buddy L, 26 1/2 In. 4125.00
Truck, Tow, Blue, Red Boom, Wyandotte, 21 In. 245.00
Truck, Tow, Cast Iron, Painted, White, Red Boom, Disc Wheels, Sloglund & Olsen, 10 In. 935.00
Truck, Tow, Diamond T, Nickel Grille, Red, Hubley, 9 In. 750.00
Truck, Tow, Dodge, BP, Yellow Cab, Green Body, No. 13, Matchbox, Lesney, Box, 1965 .... 112.00
Truck, Tow, Dodge, BP, Yellow Cab, Green Body, Red Hook, No. 13, Matchbox, Lesney, Box, 1965 .. 63.00
Truck, Tow, Fix-All, Plastic, Marx, Box, 9 1/2 In. 72.00
Truck, Tow, Ford, Red, Tootsietoy, 1935, 3 In. 125.00
Truck, Tow, Goodrich Silver Town, Electric Lights, Metalcraft, 1930s, 13 In. 495.00
Truck, Tow, Graham, Yellow, Black, Tootsietoy, 4 In. 150.00
Truck, Tow, JMB, Tin, Motor, Hoist, France, 1940-50s, 14 In. 595.00
Truck, Tow, Lil Beaver, Pressed Steel, Canada, 13 1/2 In. 175.00
Truck, Tow, Nickel Grille, Red, Black, Hubley, 4 1/2 In. 375.00
Truck, Tow, Pressed Steel, Keystone Packard, 26 In. 1760.00
Truck, Tow, Pressed Steel, Keystone Packard, 27 In. 1650.00
Truck, Tow, Pressed Steel, Open Cab, Red, Hand Cranking Crane, Keystone, 28 In. 1650.00
Truck, Tow, Pressed Steel, Sturditoy, 31 In. 1650.00
Truck, Tow, Red, Black, Nickel Grille, Hubley, 4 1/2 In. 375.00
Truck, Tow, Red, Cast Boom, Service Bed, Nickel Spoke Wheels, Arcade, 8 1/2 In. 165.00
Truck, Tow, Red, Green, Marx, 12 In. 275.00
Truck, Tow, Repair-It Unit, Red, White, Buddy L, 1950, 22 1/2 In. 410.00
Truck, Tow, Tin, Wyandotte, 14 In. 145.00
Truck, Tow, Weaver Boom, Cast Iron, Arcade, 11 In. 660.00
Truck, Toytown Ice, Green, White, Wyandotte, 11 1/4 In. 130.00
Truck, Tractor Shovel, Hatra, Orange, Movable, Plastic Tires, No. 69, Matchbox, Box, 1965, 3 In. .. 45.00
Truck, Trailer, Double Van, PIE, Tin, Friction, Japan, Box, 24 In. 140.00
Truck, Trailer, Motor Express, Red, Silver, Green, Hubley, 7 1/2 In., 2 Piece 500.00
Truck, Trailer, Safeway Food Store, Tin, Friction, Box, 15 In. 85.00
Truck, Transport, Mack, 3 Buicks, 1928 Models, Tootsietoy 350.00
Truck, Transport, Marx, Box, 23 1/2 In. 475.00
Truck, Traveling Store, Sturditoy, Pressed Steel, Open Cab, Orange, Box, 26 In. 4620.00
Truck, U.S. Army, Brown, White Rubber Tires, Barclay, 1929, 2 1/2 In. 35.00
Truck, U.S. Army, Pressed Steel, Canvas, Keystone, 1930s, 27 In. 990.00
Truck, U.S. Army, Pressed Steel, Sonny, 26 In. 660.00
Truck, U.S. Mail, Black, Doorless Cab, Red Chassis, Disc Wheels, Keystone, Box, 26 In. 4950.00
Truck, U.S. Mail, Pressed Steel, Buddy L, 1940s, 25 In. 330.00
Truck, Utility, City Of Toyland, No. 7, Pressed Steel, Structo, 18 1/4 In. 105.00
Truck, Utility, Pressed Steel, Accessories, Lumar, 20 In. 305.00
Truck, VW, Ice Cream, Metal, Friction, Japan, Box, 1950s, 8 1/2 In. 475.00

Truck, Werk's Tag Soap, Pressed Steel, Metalcraft, 1930s, 11 In. 305.00
Truck, West Coast, Mack, Red Cab, Black Fenders, Gray Van, Decals, Smith-Miller 550.00
Truck, Wild Animal Circus, Pressed Steel, Buddy L, Box, 26 In. 605.00
Truck, World Circus, Friction, Peek-A-Boo Animals, 1950s, 10 In. 225.00
Truck, Wrigley Gum, Buddy L, Advertising On Sides, 7 1/4 x 14 1/2 x 6 In. 468.00
Truck, Wyandotte, 1930s, 6 In. 195.00
Truck & Car Set, Stake, Dump & Wrecker Trucks, Sedan, Arcade, Cast Iron, Box, 12 In. 4400.00
Truck Set, Air Defense, Pressed Steel, Electronic Speaker, Buddy L, Box, 15 x 25 In. 715.00
Truck Set, Army Combination, Field Hospital, Pressed Steel, Buddy L, Box, 10 x 20 In. 825.00
Trunk, Doll's, Dome Top, Paper Litho Over Wood, Tray, Paper Lining, 14 x 8 1/2 x 6 In. 155.00
Trunk, Doll's, Dome Top, Paper Litho, Wood, Leather Straps, Tray, Clothing, Dolls, 18 x 10 In. 259.00
Trunk, Doll's, Pine, Metal Banded, Tray, Calico Cloth Lining, 12 x 7 x 7 In. 201.00
Turkey, Lucky, Stuffed Mohair, Steiff, Tag, 1950, 4 In. 85.00
Typewriter, Blue, Buddy L, 1976 .... 45.00
Typist Miss Friday, Tin, Battery Operated, 7 1/2 In. 220.00
U-Haul Set, Multi-Mover, No. 4310, Ny-Lint, Box 110.00
U-Haul Set, Truck, 2 Trailers, Orange, White, Ny-Lint, 1960, 32 In. 165.00
Uncle Wiggily Crazy Car, Tin Lithograph, Open, Cane, Briefcase, Clockwork, 1920s, 9 1/2 In. 3300.00
Uniform Set, Army, Peaked Cap, Holsters, Belt, Puttees, Gun, Boys-D-Lite, c.1940 .... 125.00
Velocipede, Zigzag Motion, Composition Doll Head, Stevens & Brown, c.1870, 10 x 9 In. 1760.00
View Finder, International Exposition, San Francisco, Cinevue, Box, c.1939 .... 55.00
Village, Wood Black, Set No. 718, Keystone, Box, 1930s, 23 x 15 In. 375.00
Wagon, Artillery, Horse Drawn, Yellow, Driver, Pulls Cannon, Iron, Wilkens, 18 1/2 In. 770.00
Wagon, Barrel, 2 Horses, Galloping Motion, Red, Black Wagon, Carpenter, c.1883, 16 1/2 In. 220.00
Wagon, Brewery, Open Bed, Driver, Cast Iron, Flared Sides, Embossed, Ives, 18 In. 1760.00
Wagon, Cannon Ball Jr., Orange & Green Paint, Wood, Metal, 12 x 33 In. 77.00
Wagon, Circus, Bear Cage, Overland, Cast Iron, Red, Roof Seat, Spoke Wheels, Kenton, 14 In. 165.00
Wagon, Circus, Cage, Cast Iron, Marquee Sides, Royal Circus, Spoke Wheels, Hubley, 15 1/2 In. 1540.00
Wagon, Circus, Cast Iron, Kenton, 14 1/2 In. 220.00
Wagon, Circus, Overland, Bear, Cast Iron, Kenton, 14 In. 250.00
Wagon, Circus, Overland, Cast Iron, Kenton, 15 In. 275.00
Wagon, Circus, Overland, Driver, Horses, Lion, Red, Yellow Cage, Hitch, Cast Iron, Kenton, 14 In. 748.00
Wagon, Circus, Overland, Driver, Tailgate, Spoke Wheels, Kenton, c.1952, 7 1/2 In. 235.00
Wagon, Circus, Overland, Kenton Hardware, Red, Polar Bear, 2 White Horses, Driver, 14 In. 375.00
Wagon, Circus, Tin, Wyandotte, Clown, 3 Animals, 18 In. 168.00
Wagon, Coal & Wood, Cast Iron, Green, Stenciled, Spoke Wheels, Seated Driver, Harris, 12 In. 770.00
Wagon, Coal, 2 Horses, Cast Iron, Open Bed, Black, Gold Trim, Bench Seat, Hubley, 18 In. 715.00
Wagon, Coal, Donkey Drawn, Lithographed Paper-On-Wood, Tin Spoke Wheels, 14 In. 147.00
Wagon, Coal, Open Bed, Standing Driver, Yellow Spoke Wheels, Mule, Cast Iron, Ives, 17 In. 635.00
Wagon, Dairy, Horse Drawn, Marx, Tin Lithograph, 10 7/8 In. 90.00
Wagon, Detroit Free Press, Wood, Stenciled, Metal Pull Handle, Rubber Tires, 35 1/2 In. 65.00
Wagon, Dray, 2 Black Horses, Cast Iron, Posts, Red, Yellow Spoke Wheels, Wilkens, 20 1/2 In. 550.00
Wagon, Dray, Horse Drawn, Cast Iron, 2 Wood Barrels, Kenton, 15 In. 145.00
Wagon, Dray, Horse Drawn, Open Wagon, Stenciled Express, Cast Iron, Tin, Wood, Ives, 17 In. 415.00
Wagon, Dray, Horse Drawn, Stakes, c.1883, 15 In. 770.00
Wagon, Dump, Contractors, Open Bed, Embossed Sides, Spoke Wheels, Kenton, 15 In. 220.00
Wagon, Express, Open Bed, Rail Sides, Cast Iron, Nickel Galloping Horse, Jones & Bixler, 16 In. 275.00
Wagon, Farm, Carved, Painted, c.1900, 20 1/2 x 44 1/2 In. 450.00
Wagon, Farm, Cast Iron, Open Bed Box, Red, Spoke Wheels, Seated Driver, Kenton, 14 In. 275.00
Wagon, Ice, Cast Iron, Red, Embossed ICE, Black Spoke Wheels, Black Horse, Ives, 11 In. 360.00
Wagon, Log, Cast Iron, Seated Plantation Figure, Yellow Hitch Frame, Hubley, 15 In. 935.00
Wagon, Log, Flat Bed, Pressed Steel, Painted Green, Yellow Spoke Wheels, Arcade, 12 1/2 In. 275.00
Wagon, Milk, Eagle, Cast Iron, White Van Body, Red Spoke Wheels, Black Horse, Hubley, 13 In. 770.00
Wagon, Milk, Horse Drawn, Cast Iron, Kenton, 13 1/2 In. 120.00
Wagon, Milk, Horse, Tin, Windup, Marx, 1930s, 9 1/2 In. 275.00
Wagon, Motor, Lithograph, Driver, Gray, Red Details, Gold Coal Scuttle Bonnet, Meier 550.00
Wagon, Open Bed, Adams Express, Cast Iron, Green, Bench Seat, Driver, Ives, 18 1/2 In. 770.00
Wagon, Patrol, 3 Horses, Driver, 4 Cops, Cast Iron, Red, White, Blue, 21 1/4 In. 605.00
Wagon, Patrol, Black, Open Wagon, Bench Seating, Spoke Wheels, Cast Iron, Shimer, 21 In. 1760.00
Wagon, Patrol, Open Bed, Bench Seat, Rail Sides, Cast Lanterns, Cast Iron, Ideal, 20 In. 605.00
Wagon, Pedal, Pioneer Flyer, Wood, Green, Red, Handle Bars, Spoke Wheels, 28 x 23 1/2 In. 470.00

Wagon, Pickfords, Removals & Warehousing, Domed, 15 1/2 x 26 In. 980.00
Wagon, Police Patrol, 2 Horses, 3 Policemen, Driver, Hubley, 1910, 19 In. 975.00
Wagon, Police Patrol, 2 Horses, 6 Policemen, Driver, Cast Iron, Hubley, 28 In. 920.00
Wagon, Police Patrol, Pressed Steel, Sonny, 28 In. 978.00
Wagon, Royal Circus, Horses, Rhinoceros, Bear, Driver, Hubley, Cast Iron, 1920, 16 In. 805.00
Wagon, Sand & Gravel, 2 Horses, Cast Iron, White, Black, Green & Red Wagon, 15 1/2 In. 173.00
Wagon, Stake, Cast Iron, Pressed Steel, Seated Driver, Yellow, Red, Wilkens, 15 In. 385.00
Wagon, U.S. Mail, Black Horse, Silver, Red Spoke Wheels, 6 1/4 In. 110.00
Wagon, U.S. Mail, Tin, Labels, Metal Spoke Wheels, Lithographed Paper-On-Wood, 12 1/2 In. 118.00
Wagon, Wood, Pull Toy, Fold-Up Handle, 1800s, 26 x 13 In. 230.00
Wagoneer, Trailer, No. 1080, Tonka, Box, 17 In. 110.00
Walker, Amos 'n' Andy, Windup, Marx 875.00
Walker, Barnacle Bill, Tin, Windup, Chein, 6 1/2 In. .... 303.00 to 425.00
Walker, Happy Hooligan, Windup, Chein, 1930s 475.00
Walking Little Lady, Japan, Box, 9 1/2 In. 20.00
Waltzing Couple, Automation, Man In Tails, Lady In Gown, Gunthermann, 8 In. 1150.00
Wandering Chimpanzee, Tin, Cloth, Box, Occupied Japan 30.00
Warehouse, Wood, Keystone, 15 x 14 In. 168.00
Washing Machine, Cast Iron, Thor, Arcade, 6 In. 145.00
Washing Machine, Dolly's Washer, Pressed Tin, 9 In. 120.00
Washing Machine, Queen, Wood, J.H. Knoll, 9 1/2 x 9 In. 4620.00
Washing Machine, Wringer, Gold & Cream, Sunny Suzy, 10 1/2 x 10 In. 200.00
Water Tower, Hose, Bracket, 3 Horses, Gallops, Rider, Bell, Cast Iron, 26 In. 499.00
Water Tower, Pressed Steel, Red, Pump, Open Frame, Horn, Keystone, Box, 30 In. 1430.00
Water Tower Wagon, Cast Iron, Ratchet Action Tower, 3 Horses, 26 In. 499.00
Water Tower Wagon, White Extension Water Tower, Nozzle, Driver, Cast Iron, Kenton, 20 In. 660.00
Watering Can, Embossed, Boy Holding Sailing Ship, c.1900, 5 1/2 In. 325.00
Watering Can, Little Girl, Flowers, Picket Fence, Birdhouse, Chein, 1950s, 9 3/4 In. 135.00
Weber Wagon, Cast Iron, McCormick Deering, Open, Removable Seat, Spoke Wheels, 12 In. 330.00
Wheelbarrow, Painted, c.1890, 33 In. 550.00
Wheelbarrow, Pressed Steel, Blue, Yellow Wheel, Marx, 9 In. 45.00
Whistle, Black Girl, Terra-Cotta, Painted, Holds Flower, Basket, Germany, 1900, 2 In. 75.00
Wolfman Monster, Ceramic, Tuscany Studios, 1973, 19 In. 560.00
World Flyers, Tin, Windup, Bavaria, Bing, Box, 8-In. Wingspan 165.00
Xylophone, Clown, Tin, Windup, Wolverine, 8 In. 385.00
Yeti, Battery Operated, Marx, 11 In. 1345.00
Zeppelin, Graf, Aluminum, Windup, c.1940, 9 In. 45.00
Zillograph, Funny Shadow Theatre, 8 Figures, Germany, Box, c.1890, 12 1/4 In. 875.00
Zilotone, Clown Plays Xylophone, Pressed Steel, Tin, Windup, Wolverine, 8 In. 460.00

TRAMP ART is a form of folk art made since the Civil War. It is usually made from chip-carved cigar boxes. Examples range from small boxes and picture frames to full-sized pieces of furniture.

Birdcage, Carved Wood, Crown-Of-Thorns Pattern, Hinged Door, 1885, 13 In. 200.00
Box, Wood, Chip Carved, Stepped Pyramid Design, 6 x 10 1/2 x 7 1/2 In. 69.00
Chair, Doll's, Upholstered, Button Cushion, 15 x 9 1/2 x 9 In. 325.00
Cupboard, Hanging, Carved Tiers, Black Paint, Door, Arched Panel, Flared Base, 24 In. 2640.00
Doll Cradle, Chip Carved Edges, Peaked Hood, Acorn Finals, 10 x 13 x 8 In. 220.00
Dresser Box, Notched Tier, Mirrored Lid, Velvet, 6 1/4 x 10 3/4 x 7 1/4 In. 120.00
Dresser Box, Notched Tiers, Star, Brass Handles, Zum Andenken, 1913, 5 x 8 1/4 In. 130.00
Dresser Box, Shelves, Triangular Mirrored Crest, 4 Drawers, Brass Pulls, 13 x 21 In. 400.00
Frame, Carved Tiers, Gold Painted Accents, 22 1/2 x 13 1/4 In. 80.00
Frame, Carved Tiers, Pyramid Corners, 9 1/2 x 10 In. 105.00
House, Wood, Carved, 4 Gables, Stepped Chip Carved Windows, 23 x 17 x 15 In. 588.00
Jewelry Box, Lift Lid, Pedestal Base, 5 x 7 1/2 In. 115.00
Letterbox, Chip Carved, Painted Decoration, Hanging, Early 20th Century, 15 In. 240.00
Mirror, Chip Carved, Stepped Diamonds & Hearts, Painted Red, White, Blue, 12 x 10 In. 1195.00
Mirror, Chip Carved, Stepped Geometric Frame, Brown, Orange Border, 40 x 35 1/2 In. 530.00
Table, Painted, Rustic Hickory, Twigs, Medial Shelf, 20th Century, 42 x 21 x 14 In. 235.00
Wall Box, 3 Pockets, Heart Shape, Geometric Patterns, Chip Carved, 13 1/2 x 7 3/4 In. 130.00
Wall Pocket, Wood, Carved, Painted, Shaped Backboard, Kissing Birds, 18 x 13 In. 880.00

TRAPS for animals may be handmade. One of the most unusual is the mousetrap made so that when the mouse entered the trap, it was hit on the head with a mallet. Other traps were commercially manufactured and often are marked with the name of the manufacturer. Many traps were designed to be as humane as possible, and they would trap the live animal so it could be released in the woods.

Animal, Charles Birdell Escape Proof, No. 1, Crisfeild, Md., Animal Trap Co. 45.00
Animal, Cortland Trap Co., No. 1, 12 Teeth, Cut Away Base, Cast Pan, Link Chain, Cortland, N.Y. 170.00
Animal, Diamond No. 21, Long Spring, 8 x 3 x 2 3/8 In. 12.00
Animal, Hand Forged, Oval Base, Mascal Type Spring, 6 Teeth, I.H. Schilckei, 9 1/2 In. 83.00
Animal, No. 0, S. Newhouse, Flat Link Chain, Ring, Wedge, L.S. Oneida, c.1902 .... 105.00
Animal, Pratt, No. 2, Double L.S., Circular Base, Hay Manufacturing Co., Racine, Wisc. 225.00
Bear, No. 5, Teeth, Long Chain, Oneida Community 825.00
Bear, Wrought Iron, Rope Ring, c.1800, 40 x 14 In. 765.00
Fly, Mold Blown, Pale Green, 3 Applied Feet, Stopper, 9 x 6 1/2 In. 295.00
Fly, Tin, Wire Screen, Tin Lid, Ring Pull, Tapered Sides, 3 Iron Legs, 19 x 10 In. 175.00
Fox, No. 21, Blake & Lamb, Hawkings, South Britain, Conn., 2-In. Pan 27.00
Herters, No. 121, Steel, Double Jaws, Hudson Bay 165.00
Mole, Spear Type, Reddick, Niles, Mich., 17 In. 17.00
Mole, Victor, Animal Trap Co. 14.00
Mouse, Wood, Metal, Catchemalive, Animal Trap Co., Pa., c.1920, 2 1/2 x 6 x 5 1/4 In. 123.00

TREEN, see Wooden category.

TRENCH ART is a form of folk art made by soldiers. Metal casings from bullets and mortar shells were cut and decorated to form useful objects, such as vases.

Ashtray, Bullets, World War II, 1942 .... 50.00 to 75.00
Bottle Opener, Machine Gun Round, 50 Caliber, World War II, 5 1/2 In. 42.00
Lamp, Military Shell, Made On Ship Kentucky, 8 In. 24.00
Letter Opener, Bullet Handle, Sword Shape, Military Button, Brass, LENS, 7 In. 24.00
Lighter, Table, Royal Montreal Regiment Badge, 50 Cal. Shell, Canada, 1945, 7 1/2 In. 63.00
Match Holder, Shell Case, Insignia, Mahogany Base, World War I, 2 3/4 In. 11.00
Pencil Holder, World War I, 4 3/8 x 3 1/2 In. 95.00
Vase, Shell, Brass Casing, M 105 mm M14, World War II, 12 x 7 In. 225.00
Vase, Shell, Brass, Maple Leaf, Beaver, Arras & Amiens, Canada, c.1917, 9 x 3 1/2 In. 165.00
Vase, Shell, Shield, St. Mihiel, AEF, 1918, 13 1/2 x 4 In. 57.00

TRIVETS are now used to hold hot dishes. Most trivets of the late nineteenth and early twentieth centuries were made to hold hot irons. Iron or brass reproductions are being made of many of the old styles.

Brass, Colonial Revival, George Washington, Bust, 2 x 9 1/2 In. 48.00
Brass, Georgian Style, 15 x 17 In. 480.00
Brass, Iron, D-Shape, 3 Legs, Turned Wood Handle, 10 1/2 In. 143.00
Brass, Iron, Engraved Skirt, 2-Headed Eagle, Cabriole Legs, Penny Feet, 9 x 9 In. 350.00
Iron, Borough Hall Unicast Outlet Store, Boyerstown, Pa., June 15, 1975, 4 3/16 In. 48.00
Iron, Cathedral, 3 1/16 In. 18.00
Iron, Griswold, Cathedral, 5 1/2 In. 12.00
Iron, Griswold, Cathedral, 8 13/16 In. 12.00
Iron, Griswold, Circles In Star, 9 1/4 In. 18.00
Iron, Griswold, Classic 60.00
Iron, Griswold, Double Broom, 8 1/8 In. 12.00
Iron, Griswold, Eagle In Wreath, 8 5/8 In. 24.00
Iron, Griswold, Floral Scroll, 7 1/2 In. 12.00
Iron, Griswold, Lacy Round, 4 3/4 In. 165.00
Iron, Griswold, Small Eagle In Wreath, 5 3/16 In. 24.00
Iron, Griswold, Star In Circle, 7 1/8 In. 12.00
Iron, Griswold, Tree, 8 5/8 In. 18.00
Iron, Running Wheel, Hex Designs, Crosshatched Handle, Pa., 1800s, 10 1/4 In. 27.50
Iron, Sand Cast, Heart Center, Heart Handle, 1800s, 11 In. 61.00

Iron, Tree Of Life, 1800s, 9 In. 50.00
Iron, Tulip Tree, Sand Mold Made, c.1850, 7 1/2 In. 72.00
Iron, Wilton, Hearts, Hex, Running Wheel, 12 1/2 In. 61.00
Iron, Wrought, Heart Shape, 3 Legs, c.1800, 2 x 6 3/4 x 4 1/2 In. 253.00

TRUNKS of many types were made. The nineteenth-century sea chest was often handmade of unpainted wood. Brass-fitted camphorwood chests were brought back from the Orient. Leather-covered trunks were popular from the late eighteenth to mid-nineteenth centuries. By 1895, trunks were covered with canvas or decorated sheet metal. Embossed metal coverings were used from 1870 to 1910. By 1925, trunks were covered with vulcanized fiber or undecorated metal. Suitcases are listed here.

Camphorwood, Brass Strapped Corners, Side Bail Handles, 19 1/2 x 37 x 21 In. 345.00
Camphorwood, Brass Strapped Edges, Ring Pull Handle, Oriental, 12 x 30 In. 175.00
Camphorwood, Brassbound, Brass Bail Handles, Late 1800s, 13 x 37 x 20 In. 345.00
Camphorwood, Brassbound, Green Leather, 1800s, 18 x 39 x 20 In. 600.00
Dome Top, Pine, Dovetailed, Blue Paint, 19th Century, 30 In. 165.00
Dome Top, Pine, Painted Flowers, 12 x 13 1/4 x 18 1/2 In. 605.00
Dome Top, Pine, Painted, 1800s, 10 1/2 x 24 x 11 1/2 In. 300.00
Dome Top, Pine, Repousse Metal Straps, Putti, Nymph, Continental, c.1700, 24 x 50 1/4 In. 560.00
Dome Top, Rosewood, Grain Painted, Maine, 11 x 24 3/4 x 12 1/2 In. 115.00
Dome Top, Strap Hinges, Charcoal Black Paint Over Blue, 18th Century, 15 In. 310.00
Dome Top, Wooden Slat, Metal Mounts, Early 20th Century, 32 x 21 x 26 In. 90.00
Elm, Multicolored, Flowers, 13 1/2 x 30 x 17 In. 230.00
Elm, Multicolored, Scholar's Objects, Chinese, 1600s, 28 x 39 x 25 In. 1062.00
Hinged Top, Multicolored, Panel, Flower, Vase, Mongolia, 14 x 32 x 18 In., Pair 415.00
Immigrant's, Pine, Red, Dome Top, Canted Sides, Brass Straps, Bail Handles, 22 x 38 In. 230.00
Louis Vuitton, Canvas Cover, Leather Straps, 15 x 24 x 15 In. 1960.00
Louis Vuitton, Canvas, Brown, Leather Trim, Wood Bands, Early 1900s, 15 1/2 x 41 x 24 In. 1415.00
Louis Vuitton, Canvas, Tan, Leather Trim, Wood Bands, 1900s, 22 1/2 x 43 1/2 x 22 In. 2240.00
Louis Vuitton, Steamer, Calfskin, Orange & Brown, Impressed Gold Initials, 1940s 6000.00
Louis Vuitton, Steamer, Wood Straps, Leather, Early 1900s, 23 x 36 x 21 In. 2700.00
Louis Vuitton, Suitcase, Brassbound, Leather Trim, Interior Tray, 24 x 15 x 8 In. 765.00
Louis Vuitton, Wood Straps, Leather Cover, Early 1900s, 22 x 31 x 20 In. 3175.00
Louis Vuitton, Wood Straps, Metal Mounted, 2 Side Handles, Label, 21 x 23 x 18 In. 1290.00
Military, Wood, Graphic Decoration, Corp. Mark O. Hemphill, 32 x 16 In. 290.00
Necessaire De Voyage, Victorian, Rosewood, Brass Bound, 11 3/4 x 6 3/4 In. 413.00
Pigskin, Lacquer, Brass Mouth, Inscribed, Chinese, 10 x 26 x 16 1/2 In. 180.00
Pigskin, Red Lacquer, Chinese, 10 1/2 x 28 x 17 3/4 In. 210.00
Pine, Comb Painted, Multicolored, Chevrons, Bands, Leaves, 1900s, 15 x 26 In. 295.00
Pine, Hide Covered, Brass Tacks, Leather Trim, Wallpaper Lining, 7 x 20 x 9 1/2 In. 92.00
Pine, Vinegar Decoration, Brown Fans, Circles, Yellow Ground, 28 x 14 x 10 In. 375.00
Storage, Walnut, Moore 14 Mile Island Lake George Via Caldwell, 1800s, 18 x 36 In. 58.00
Walnut, Multicolored, 2 Reserves, Flower, Vases, Mongolia, 15 x 35 x 31 In. 200.00

TYPEWRITER collectors divide typewriters into two main classifications: the index machine, which has a pointer and a dial for letter selection, and the keyboard machine, most commonly seen today. The first successful typewriter was made by Sholes and Glidden in 1874.

Franklin, No. 7, Curved Keyboard, 3 Rows, Gilt Transfers, 1891 Patent 645.00
Hall, No. 5767, Mahogany Case, 1881 Patent, 15 In. 355.00
Hammond, Model 1, Curved Keyboard, Piano Keys, Bentwood Case, 1883, 13 In. 1295.00
Hammond, Multiplex, Model 26, 3 Row Keyboard, Oak Bentwood Case, 14 In. 118.00
Odell's, Circular Nickel Plated, Sliding Type Selector, 1890, 10 In. 325.00

TYPEWRITER RIBBON TINS are now being collected. The lithographed tin containers have been used since the 1870s. Most popular with collectors are tins with pictorial graphics.

Allied, Bird Flying Over Water, Allied Cabon & Ribbon Mfg., N.Y. 34.00
American Brand, Cobalt Blue, Silver, 4-Sided, 2 1/2 In. 10.00
Amneco, Blue, White, 4-Sided 18.00

Burroughs, White, Orange, Brown 9.00

Carnation, Red, White, Blue, 2 5/8 In. 6.00

Carter's Midnight, Stars, Saturn, Blue, White 12.00

Codo, Super Fiber, Silhouette Of Lady Typing, 2 5/8 In. 6.00

Columbia Silk Gauze, Blue, White, 4-Sided, 2 1/2 In. 10.00

Court House Ribbon, Lithograph, Stationers Inc., 2 1/8 In. 550.00

Ditto, Art Deco, Black, Silver, 4-Sided 10.00

Duro-Flex, Red, Blue, White, 2 1/2 In. 13.00

Gibraltar, Rock, Sun, 2 1/2 In. 60.00

Great Lakes, Lakes, Red, Black, Blue, Cleveland, Ohio, 2 1/2 In. 10.00

Hallmark, White, Blue, Cameron Mafg., Dallas, Texas, 2 1/2 In. 20.00

KeeLox, Burroughs Typewriter, Black, Red, 2 x 1 1/4 In. 12.00

KeeLox, Red, 2 1/2 In. 13.00

KeeLox, Red, White 18.00

KeeLox, Underwood, Red, 4-Sided, 2 1/4 x 2 1/4 In. 10.00

KeeLox Mfg. Co., Geisha Girl, Golden Skin, 2 1/2 In. 15.00

M & M, Mittag & Volger Inc., Green, 2 1/2 In. 8.00

Miller Line, Green, Cream, c.1960 .... 5.00

Old Town, Blue, Red, White, 2 5/8 In. 6.00

Park Avenue, Dark Blue, 2 1/2 In. 12.00

Plenty Copy, Yellow 10.00

Remtico Paragon, Remington Typewriter, 4-Sided, 1 3/4 x 2 x 1 5/8 In. 6.00

Royal Typewriter Co., Vogue, Green, Blue, Red & Yellow Flowers, 2 1/2 In. 13.00

Type Bar, Smith-Corona Co., Red, Black, White, Art Deco 12.00

Type Bar Brand, LC Smith Corona Typewriters Inc., 4-Sided 14.00

Vertex Roytype, 2 1/2 In. 12.00

Webster Star, Star, 4-Sided, 2 1/4 x 2 1/4 In. 20.00

Western Union, 4-Sided, Eaton Carbon & Ribbon Corp., Box 12.00

UHL pottery was made in Evansville, Indiana, in 1854. The pottery moved to Huntingburg, Indiana, in 1908. Stoneware and glazed pottery were made until the mid-1940s.

Casserole, Cover, Brown, Round, 3 1/2 x 8 In. 29.00

Crock, Huntingsburg Indiana Acorn Wares, c.1908-44, 7 3/4 x 7 1/2 In. 145.00

Figurine, Dog, Cocker Spaniel, Miniature, 1 5/8 In. 99.00

Pitcher, Grape Pattern, Brown, Cream Interior, 8 1/4 In. 89.00

UMBRELLA collectors like rain or shine. The first known umbrella was owned by King Louis XIII of France in 1637. The earliest umbrellas were sunshades, not designed to be used in the rain. The umbrella was embellished and redesigned many times. In 1852, the fluted steel rib style was developed, and it has remained the most useful style.

Bakelite Handle, Tips, Cloth Wrist Handle, Black Ground, Blue & Red Designs, 24 In. 60.00

Bamboo, Folding, Purple Fabric, Flowers, Pink Threads, Oriental 30.00

Black Nylon, Carved Lucite Handle, Crosshatched Tip, Japan, 31 1/2 x 35 In. 29.00

Ivory & Gilt Metal Handle, Wood Shaft, Black, S Fox & Co., England, 35 In. 180.00

Parasol, Black Silk, Ruffled, Wood, Black Lacquered Handle, Silk Flower, 35 3/4 In. 195.00

Parasol, Carved Red Bakelite Handle, Circles, Art Deco Design 110.00

Parasol, Linen, Lace Insert, Knotty Wood Handle, Tassel, Wood Bead, Victorian, 36 1/2 In. 395.00

Parasol, Painted, Birds, Roses, 23 x 35 In. 72.00

Parasol, Silk, Black, Victorian, 29 x 29 In. 100.00

Parasol, Tambour Lace, Cotton, Wood Handle, 1870s, 26 1/2 x 19 In. 195.00

Plastic, Leafy Handle, 2-Tone Rose, Wrist Chain, Red Fabric 35.00

Silk, Pink Flowers, White Pearlized Bakelite Handle 6.95

UNION PORCELAIN WORKS was established at Greenpoint, New York, in 1848 by Charles Cartlidge. The company went through a series of ownership changes and finally closed in the early 1900s. The company made a fine quality white porcelain that was often decorated in clear, bright colors.

Creamer, Eagle, Holding Serpent In Beak, White 100.00

Match Holder, Striker, Plant System Railroad 375.00

UNIVERSITY CITY POTTERY, of University, Missouri, worked from 1909 to 1915. Well-known artists, including Taxile Doat, Adelaide Alsop Robineau, and Frederick Hurten Rhead, worked there.

Vase, Cylindrical, Ivory, Yellow, Green Crystalline Glaze, 1913, 3 1/2 In. 1530.00

UNIVERSITY OF NORTH DAKOTA, see North Dakota School of Mines category.

VAL ST. LAMBERT Cristalleries of Belgium was founded by Messieurs Kemlin and Lelievre in 1825. The company is still in operation. All types of table glassware and decorative glassware have been made. Pieces are often decorated with cut designs.

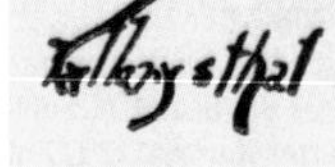

Bowl, Triangular, Radiating Lines, Red, Clear, 1960s, 8 1/2 In. 75.00
Vase, 4 Embossed Soccer Players, Art Deco, 8 3/4 In. 175.00
Vase, Allover Diamond Cut, 9 In. 70.00
Vase, Blue Flowers & Leaves, Cameo, Frosted, Flattened Bottle Shape, 6 In. 345.00
Vase, Blue Iridescent, Abstract, 6 1/2 In. 1058.00
Vase, Bottle Shape, Tapered Neck, Cranberry Cut To Clear, Marked, 6 1/2 In. 145.00
Vase, Cranberry Cut To Clear, 16 In. 575.00
Vase, Green To Amber, Horizontal Band, Grapes, Leaves, Cameo, 14 In. 2645.00
Vase, Orchids, Cranberry To Vaseline, Cameo, 9 In. 575.00
Vase, Oval, Etched Mythological Horse, Star, 5 In. 225.00

VALLERYSTHAL Glassworks was founded in 1836 in Lorraine, France. In 1854, the firm became Klenglin et Cie. It made table and decorative glass, opaline, cameo, and art glass. A line of covered, pressed glass animal dishes was made in the nineteenth century. The firm is still working.

Vase, Pink & Amber Opalescent, Mythological Scene, Oval, Cameo, Signed, 8 In. 2590.00

VAN BRIGGLE pottery was started by Artus Van Briggle in Colorado Springs, Colorado, after 1901. Van Briggle had been a decorator at Rookwood Pottery of Cincinnati, Ohio. He died in 1904 and his wife took over managing the pottery. His wares usually had modeled relief decorations and a soft, dull glaze. The pottery is still working and still making some of the original designs.

Bowl, Acorns, Oak Leaves, Squat, Circular, 1920s, 6 1/4 In. 141.00
Bowl, Leaves, Double, Aqua Blue Matte Glaze, Globular, Incised, 2 1/4 x 3 1/4 In. 175.00
Bowl, Leaves, Globular, Aqua Matte Glaze, 4 1/2 x 7 In. 315.00
Candlestick, Mulberry, Maroon & Blue Matte Glaze, Marked, 10 In. 80.00
Figurine, Donkey, Black Glaze, Anna Van Briggle, 4 In. 30.00
Lamp, Butterfly, Blue, 7 x 4 In. 225.00
Plate, Mermaid, Turquoise Matte Glaze, Signed, 9 x 10 1/2 In. 90.00
Tile, Architectural, Relief Design, Stylized Blossoms, Gray, Celadon, Frame, 6 In. 705.00
Vase, 3 Graces, Turquoise Matte Glaze, Signed, TE, 16 In. 275.00
Vase, 3-Headed Indian, Purple Matte Glaze, Signed, 12 In. 265.00
Vase, 3-Headed Indian, Teal Blue Matte Glaze, Signed, 12 In. 310.00
Vase, 3-Headed Indian, Turquoise Matte Glaze, Signed, MP, 12 In. 275.00
Vase, Blue Matte Glaze, Incised Logo, 4 1/2 x 3 3/4 In. 1380.00
Vase, Dragonfly, Aqua Blue Matte Glaze, 1915-20, 6 3/4 x 3 In. 460.00
Vase, Flower, Long Stem, Petals Around Mouth, Blue Glaze, 7 1/2 x 3 1/2 In. 259.00
Vase, Flowers Under Green Matte Glaze, Gourd, Incised Mark, 1907-12, 3 1/2 In. 660.00
Vase, Flowers, Mulberry Glaze, Incised, 4 3/4 In. 115.00
Vase, Flowers, Textured & Multitoned Brown Matte Glaze, 1907-12, 9 1/4 In. 1075.00
Vase, Flowers, Textured Green Matte Glaze, Bulbous, Marked, 1903-12, 3 In. 1795.00
Vase, Green Textured Glaze, Flecks, Bulbous, Signed, 1907, 5 x 6 In. 920.00
Vase, Lady Of The Lily, Persian Rose Glaze, 1930s, 11 In. 1528.00
Vase, Lady Of The Lily, Turquoise Matte Glaze, Signed, LS, 15 In. 265.00
Vase, Leaf & Bud, Shouldered, Carved, Green Matte Glaze, 1907-12, 5 1/2 In. 1555.00
Vase, Leaf, Mulberry Glaze, 5 1/2 In. 98.00
Vase, Leaves, Swirled, Gourd, Turquoise & Purple Matte Glaze, Incised Mark, 1903, 6 In. 2750.00
Vase, Leaves, Turquoise Matte Glaze, Bulbous, Signed, HVM, 9 In. 145.00
Vase, Lorelei, Turquoise Matte Glaze, Signed, 11 In. ....165.00 to 330.00

Vase, Organic, Swollen, Mottled Gunmetal To Green Matte Glaze, Marked, c.1910, 4 1/2 In. 900.00
Vase, Poppies, Blue Matte Glaze, Marked, 3 3/4 In. 58.00
Vase, Poppies, Shouldered, Charcoal Matte Glaze, Marked, c.1902, 4 In. 2510.00
Vase, Shouldered, Blue Matte Glaze, Incised Mark, 1905, 7 In. 1017.00
Vase, Shouldered, White To Gray Matte, c.1906, 6 1/2 In. 940.00
Vase, Spider, Bulbous, Charcoal Matte Glaze, Incised Mark, 1902, 4 3/4 In. 2510.00
Vase, Stylized Flowers, Maroon Matte Glaze, Marked, 10 In. 633.00
Vase, Stylized Leaves, Blue Matte Glaze, Marked, 4 3/8 In. 69.00
Vase, Swan, Turquoise Matt Glaze, Signed, VR, 8 1/2 In. 60.00

VASA MURRHINA is the name of a glassware made by the Vasa Murrhina Art Glass Company of Sandwich, Massachusetts, about 1884. The glassware was transparent and was embedded with small pieces of colored glass and metallic flakes. The mica flakes were coated with silver, gold, copper, or nickel. Some of the pieces were cased. The same type of glass was made in England. Collectors often confuse Vasa Murrhina glass with aventurine, spatter, or spangle glass. There is uncertainty about what actually was made by the Vasa Murrhina factory. Related pieces may be listed under Spangle Glass.

Basket, Crimped Top, Triple Cased, Applied Pastel Handle, Pontil, England, 8 x 5 In. 325.00
Basket, Teal Blue, Ruffled Edge, Reeded Handle, Victorian, 8 x 6 In. 265.00
Cruet, Rose & Yellow Spatter, Gold Spangle, Clear Handle, Faceted Stopper, 7 In. 175.00

VASELINE GLASS is a greenish-yellow glassware resembling petroleum jelly. Some vaseline glass is still being made in old and new styles. Pressed glass of the 1870s was often made of vaseline-colored glass. Additional pieces of vaseline glass may also be listed under Pressed Glass in this book.

Bowl, Pedestal, 9 1/2 In. 89.00
Candlestick, Petal Shape Cup, Hexagonal Stem, Flared Base, 7 1/4 x 4 1/4 In. 165.00
Candlestick, Thumbprint, Petal Top, Flared Base, 7 x 4 3/8 In., Pair 200.00
Oil Lamp, Match Holder & Striker Base, 8 In. 440.00
Sugar, Cover, Gothic Arch Panels, Octagonal, Round Base, 5 1/4 x 4 3/4 In. 468.00
Syrup, Hobnail, Pewter Top, Hobbs, c.1883, 7 In. 290.00
Table Set, Gold Enameled, Butter, Cover, Creamer, Sugar, Waste, c.1900, 5 In. 205.00
Tumbler, Mold Blown, Thumbprint Facet Sides, Flared Foot, 7 1/2 In., 8 Piece 660.00
Vase, Circle & Oval Paneled Sides, Scalloped, Flared Rim, Hexagonal Base, 7 1/2 In. 149.00
Vase, Scalloped Rim, Thumbprint, Panels, Flared Base, 9 1/2 x 4 1/3 In. 265.00
Vase, Scalloped, Flared Rim, Circle, Oval Panels, Hexagonal Base, 7 1/2 x 3 1/4 In. 149.00
Vase, Three Printie Block, New England, 9 7/8 In. 360.00
Vase, Thumbprint Paneled Sides, Scalloped Rim, Flared Base, 9 1/2 x 4 1/2 In. 265.00
Wig Stand, Blown, 4 1/2 In. 165.00

VENETIAN GLASS, see Glass-Venetian category.

VERLYS glass was made in Rouen, France, by the Societe Holophane Francais, a company that started in 1920. It was made in Newark, Ohio, from 1935 to 1951. The glass is either blown or molded. The American glass is signed with a diamond-point-scratched name, but the French pieces are marked with a molded signature. The designs resemble those used by Lalique.

Bowl, Centerpiece, Fantail Goldfish, Opalescent, Handles, Signed, 5 x 19 x 7 In. 1175.00
Vase, Wildflowers, White Opalescent, Signed, 7 1/2 In. 125.00

VERNON KILNS was the name used by Vernon Potteries, Ltd. The company, which started in 1931 in Vernon, California, made dinnerware and figurines until it went out of business in 1958. The molds were bought by Metlox, which continued to make some patterns. Collectors search for the brightly colored dinnerware and the pieces designed by Rockwell Kent, Walt Disney, and Don Blanding. For more information, see *Kovels' Depression Glass & Dinnerware Price List*.

Arcadia, Plate, Dinner, 10 1/2 In. 24.00

Beverly, Teapot, Melinda Shape 125.00
Brown Eyed Susan, Chop Plate, 12 1/4 In. 25.00
Brown Eyed Susan, Gravy Boat, White, 7 x 4 In. 25.00
Brown Eyed Susan, Salt & Pepper, 3 x 2 1/2 In. 19.00
Brown Eyed Susan, Soup, Dish, Rim, 8 1/8 In. 14.00
Brown Eyed Susan, Teapot 95.00
Casual California, Creamer 15.00
Casual California, Sugar, Cover 18.00
Coronado, Coffee Server, Turquoise Blue 39.00
Dolores, Plate, Dinner, 10 1/2 In. 18.00
Gingham, Plate, Bread & Butter, 6 1/2 In. 5.00
Gingham, Plate, Dinner, 10 1/2 In. 15.00
Gingham, Plate, Luncheon, 9 1/2 In. 12.00
Hawaiian Coral, Pitcher, Water, 12 In. 60.00
Hawaiian Coral, Sauceboat 20.00
Hawaiian Coral, Sugar & Creamer 25.00
Homespun, Bowl, Vegetable, 9 In. 20.00
Homespun, Casserole, Cover, Handles, 8 In. 45.00
Homespun, Cup & Saucer 15.00
Homespun, Platter, 10 1/2 In. 23.00
Homespun, Sauceboat, 8 In. 20.00
Linda, Bowl, Fruit, 5 1/2 In. 10.00
Linda, Chop Plate, 12 In. 31.00
Linda, Plate, Bread & Butter, 6 1/2 In. 10.00
May Flower, Cup & Saucer .... 15.00 to 28.00
May Flower, Plate, Bread & Butter, 6 1/2 In. 15.00
May Flower, Plate, Luncheon, 9 1/2 In. 8.50
May Flower, Salt & Pepper 20.00
May Flower, Saucer 8.00
Modern California, Chop Plate, 14 In. 49.00
Modern California, Plate, Luncheon, Pistachio, 8 1/2 In. 15.00
Monterey, Sauceboat 25.00
Monterey, Saucer 4.00
Monterey, Teapot, 6 Cup 90.00
Organdie, Butter 35.00
Organdie, Chop Plate, 12 In. 25.00
Organdie, Chop Plate, Poppytrail, 12 In. 15.00
Organdie, Coffeepot, 10 Cup 65.00
Organdie, Creamer 7.00
Organdie, Cup & Saucer 12.00
Organdie, Mixing Bowl, 9 In. 45.00
Organdie, Plate, Dinner, 10 1/2 In. 7.00
Organdie, Plate, Luncheon, 9 1/2 In. 9.00
Organdie, Platter, 14 x 10 In. 18.00
Organdie, Salt & Pepper 18.00
Organdie, Sauceboat 35.00
Organdie, Saucer 2.00
Raffia, Butter 35.00
Raffia, Creamer 12.00
Raffia, Cup & Saucer 8.00
Raffia, Sauceboat 17.00
Sherwood, Pitcher, 2 Qt., 10 In. 38.00
Sierra Madre, Chop Plate, 12 In. 12.00
Souvenir, Cup & Saucer, Statue Of Liberty, Melinda Shape 35.00
Souvenir, Plate, 48th National Convention Of Postmasters, 1952 .... 25.00
Souvenir, Plate, Arkansaw Traveler, 10 In. 76.00
Souvenir, Plate, Carslbad Caverns, 10 1/2 In. 30.00
Souvenir, Plate, Durango, Colorado, San Juan Train, 10 1/2 In. 65.00
Souvenir, Plate, Endless Caverns, Virginia, 10 1/2 In. 18.00
Souvenir, Plate, Grand Canyon National Park, 10 1/2 In. 42.00
Souvenir, Plate, My Maryland, Landmarks, 10 1/2 In. 24.00

Souvenir, Plate, Nevada, Landmarks, 10 1/2 In. 20.00
Souvenir, Plate, New Orleans, 10 1/2 In. 28.00
Souvenir, Plate, Pennsylvania Turnpike, Howard Johnson's, 10 1/2 In. 35.00
Souvenir, Plate, St Louis, Missouri, Map, 1948, 10 1/2 In. 25.00
Souvenir, Plate, Washington, D.C., 10 1/2 In. 28.00
Tweed, Casserole, Cover, Handles, 5 1/4 x 11 In. 65.00
Tweed, Creamer 15.00
Tweed, Cup & Saucer 13.00
Tweed, Plate, Bread & Butter, 6 1/2 In. 4.00
Tweed, Plate, Dinner, 10 1/2 In. 10.00
Tweed, Platter, 14 In. 42.00

VERRE DE SOIE glass was first made by Frederick Carder at the Steuben Glass Works from about 1905 to 1930. It is an iridescent glass of soft white or very, very pale green. The name means *glass of silk*, and it does resemble silk. Other factories have made verre de soie, and some of the English examples were made of different colors. Verre de soie is an art glass and is not related to the iridescent, pressed, white carnival glass mistakenly called by its name. Related pieces may be found in the Steuben category.

Vase, Baluster, 2 Applied Handles, Opalescent Finish, Early 1900s, 10 x 7 In. 823.00
Vase, Bulbous, Tall Ribbed Neck, Flared Rim, 14 In. 405.00
Vase, Diamond Quilted, Pink Rim Threading, 6 In. 145.00
Vase, Diamond Quilted, Ruffled Rim, 8 In. 230.00
Vase, Nude Youths Kneeling, Amethyst Vines, Pods, Bronze Base, 5 x 9 x 6 1/2 In. 207.00

VIENNA, see Beehive category.

VILLEROY & BOCH Pottery of Mettlach was founded in 1836. The firm made many types of wares, including the famous Mettlach steins. Collectors can be confused because although Villeroy & Boch made most of its pieces in the city of Mettlach, Germany, they also had factories in other locations. The dating code impressed on the bottom of most pieces makes it possible to determine the age of the piece. Additional items, including steins and earthenware pieces marked with the famous castle mark or the word *Mettlach,* may be found in the Mettlach category.

Bowl & Pitcher, Gold Banded Rim, No. 9046, c.1900, 11 1/2 In. 81.00
Charger, Baseball, Batter, Catcher, 1880s, 12 1/2 In. 1392.00
Ewer, White Roses, Putti, Silver Highlights, c.1890, 13 In. 324.00
Pitcher, Arts & Crafts Design, 8 3/4 In. 40.00
Tile, Woman In Flowers, Dresden, 12 1/2 x 19 1/2 In. 290.00
Vase, Bulbous, Lions, Geometric, 10 x 9 1/2 In. 354.00
Vase, Cobalt Drip Glaze, Protruding Neck, Green Ground, Oval, 10 1/2 x 8 In. 633.00
Vase, Satyrs Playing Flutes, Green, Brown, Blue, 10 3/4 x 3 3/4 In. 413.00

VOLKMAR pottery was made by Charles Volkmar of New York from 1879 to about 1911. He was associated with several firms, including the Volkmar Ceramic Company, Volkmar and Cory, and Charles Volkmar and Son. Volkmar had been a painter, and his designs often look like oil paintings drawn on pottery.

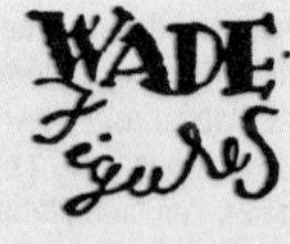

Bowl, Flaring, Modeled Flowers, Blue Crackled Persian Glaze, Durant Kilns, 3 x 9 In. 441.00
Vase, Baluster, Barbotine, Cows In Landscape, 14 1/2 x 7 1/2 In. 2000.00

WADE pottery is made by the Wade Group of Potteries started in 1810 near Burslem, England. Several potteries merged to become George Wade & Son, Ltd. early in the twentieth century, and other potteries have been added through the years. The best-known Wade pieces are the small figurines given away with Red Rose Tea and other promotional items. The Disney figures are listed in this book in the Disneyana category.

WADE
Figures
c. 1936+

Bank, Pig, Lady Hillary, Rubber Stopper, National Westminster Bank, 7 In. 75.00

Figurine, Bear, Grizzly, North American Animals Series ... 75.00
Figurine, Policeman, 1993, 3 3/4 In. ... 68.00
Figurine, Rabbit, 1930s, 2 3/4 In. ... 65.00
Tray, Kidney Shape, Black, Gray Squirrel, Squirrel Whimsie-Land Tray, c.1987, 4 1/2 x 3 5/8 In. ... 50.00
Trinket Box, Treasure Chest, Removable Top, Miniature ... 65.00

WAHPETON POTTERY, see Rosemeade category.

WALL POCKETS were popular in the 1930s. They were made by many American and European factories. Glass, pottery, porcelain, majolica, chalkware, and metal wall pockets can be found in many fanciful shops.

Black Lacquer, Green Paint, Rounded Back, Scalloped Edge, 3 x 5 3/4 x 2 3/4 In. ... 12.00
Copper, Hand Chased, Silvered, Brass Base, Flared Top, Rolled Rim, 9 x 7 In., Pair ... 220.00
Cowboy Boot, 7 In. ... 12.50
Duck, Flying, Red, Green Cattails, Ohio Porcelain Company, 1940-56, 6 x 5 1/2 In. ... 16.00
Flowering Tree, Magenta, Green, Yellow, Brown, 5 1/4 x 5 In. ... 30.00
Frog, Playing Accordion, High Glaze, Japan, Pre-1940, 5 x 3 3/4 x 2 1/2 In. ... 55.00
Orange Shape, Chalkware, 7 1/2 x 6 In. ... 28.00
Parrot, Blue Head, 7 In. ... 100.00
Star, Half-Moon Cutouts, Pine, Old Red Brown Paint, Late 1800s, 22 In. ... 55.00
Teapot Shape, Maurice Of California, Marked, 7 x 9 In. ... 13.00

WALLACE NUTTING photographs are listed under Print, Nutting. His reproduction furniture is listed under Furniture.

WALRATH was a potter who worked in New York City; Rochester, New York; and at the Newcomb Pottery in New Orleans, Louisiana. Frederick Walrath died in 1920. Pieces listed here are from his Rochester period.

Scarab, Gray Green Matte Glaze, 3 3/4 In. ... 360.00
Vase, Blue Matte Glaze, Black Speckling, 4 x 3 1/4 In. ... 978.00

WALT DISNEY, see Disneyana category.

WALTER, see A. Walter category.

WARWICK china was made in Wheeling, West Virginia, in a pottery working from 1887 to 1951. Many pieces were made with hand painted or decal decorations. The most familiar Warwick has a shaded brown background. The name *Warwick* is part of the mark and sometimes the mysterious word *IOGA* is also included.

Compote, Acorns, Pinecones, Brown Ground, 1887, 4 3/4 x 7 1/4 In. ... 30.00
Gravy Boat, Attached Undertray, Flowers, Lobed Rim, White Ground ... 16.00
Mug, Indian, Osiris Temple A.O.N.M.S., Wheeling, W.Va., Atlantic City, 1904, 5 In. ... 145.00
Vase, Pine Cone, 2 Handles, IOGA USA, 8 In. ... 150.00
Vase, Portrait, Woman, 2 Twisted Handles, 10 1/2 In. ... 200.00
Vase, Red Poinsettias, Ruffled Top, 11 1/2 x 5 1/4 In. ... 100.00
Vase, Urn, Portrait, Woman, Bust, 10 1/4 x 5 In. ... 275.00

WATCH pockets held the pocket watch that was important in Victorian times because it was not until World War I that the wristwatch was used. All types of watches are collected: silver, gold, or plated. Watches are arranged by company name or by style. Wristwatches are a separate category.

Abercrombie & Fitch, Stop, N.Y., Box, c.1930, 2 1/2 In. ... 509.00
Arnex, Hebdomas, Hunting Case, 8-Day, Girl, Dove, Fawn Doe, c.1950, Size 13, Pocket ... 173.00
Ball Watch Co., 21 Jewel, Railroad Standard, Gold Case, No. 16 Size, Pocket ... 475.00
Ball Watch Co., 23 Jewel, Railroad, Open Face, Gold Filled Case, Size 16, Pocket ... 872.00
Bulova, Open Face, 21 Jewel, 14K Gold Case, Size 10, Pocket ... 80.00
Cartier, Pendant, Platinum, Diamond, 18 Jewel, On Black Cord, Art Deco, 26 In. ... 6465.00
Columbus, Railway King, 21 Jewel, Silveroid, Double Sunk Dial, Size 15, Pocket ... 259.00
Crawford, 14K Yellow Gold, 17 Jewel, Swiss ... 100.00
E. Howard, Open Face, 23 Jewel, 14K Gold Filled Case, c.1912, Size 13, Pocket ... 218.00

Elgin, B.W. Raymond, Railroad, Open Face, 21 Jewel, Size 16, Pocket 260.00
Elgin, Hunting Case, Father Time, 21 Jewel, 14K Gold, Porcelain Dial, Size16 .... 400.00
Elgin, Open Face, 17 Jewel, 673 Movement, 10K Gold Case, Size 13, Pocket 99.00
Elgin, Open Face, 17 Jewel, Yellow Gold, Porcelain Face, Size 13, Pocket 110.00
Elgin, Open Face, Nickel Case, Elk, Standing, Sunk Dial, 17 Jewel, c.1905, Size 16, Pocket 173.00
Elgin, Railroad, Double Back, Veritas Wind Indicator, 21 Jewel, Size16 .... 1440.00
Golay Fils Et Stahl, Pendant, Enamel, Diamond, Silvertone Dial, Enamel Case, Edwardian 2115.00
Golay Leresche, Hunting Case, Scenes, Key Wind, 18K, Swiss, c.1850, Size 13, Pocket 374.00
Haas Neveux & Cie, Pendant, Enamel, Diamond, Carved Gold Water Lily 12500.00
Hamilton, Gold Filled Case, Porcelain Double Sunk Dial, Grade 950B, 23 Jewel, Size 16 .... 835.00
Hamilton, Open Face, Yellow Gold, 17 Jewel, Porcelain Dial, Size 13, Pocket 66.00
Hamilton, Railroad, 992, Railway Special, Open Face, 21 Jewel, c.1911, Size 13 .... 403.00
Hamilton, Railroad, Gold Filled Case, Porcelain, Double Sunk Dial, 21 Jewel, 950B, Size 16 ...... 300.00
Hamilton, Railroad, Open Face, 21 Jewel, Porcelain Face, Size 16, Pocket 359.00
Hampden, Hunting Case, Molly Stark, Woman's, 7 Jewel, Yellow Gold Case, Size 4/0 .... 45.00
Howard, 23 Jewel, 14K Gold, Polished Case, Double Sunk Dial, Size16 .... 1035.00
Hunting Case, Chain, Fob, Gold, 14K Yellow, Curb Link, 1895 & 1896 Awards, c.1900 .... 4465.00
Illinois, 7 Jewel, Key Wind, Dubber Silverine Case, Size 18, Pocket 155.00
Illinois, Railroad, Bunn Special, 21 Jewel, 60 Hour, Model 161A, Porcelain Dial, Size 16 .... 635.00
Illinois, Sangamo Special, 23 Jewel, Checkerboard, Damascene, Gold Filled Case, Size 16 .... 748.00
Illinois Watch Co., Open Face, 21 Jewel, 14K White Gold, 8-Sided Case, Size 7 .... 80.00
Jaeger LeCoultre, Open Face, 15 Jewel, 18K White Gold, Box, Pocket 754.00
John Forrest Hopper, Key Wind, 18K Gold, Late 1800s, Pocket, 2 In. 527.00
L. Audemars, Open Face, Repeating, Enamel Dial, Nickel Movement, Pocket, 2 In. 4115.00
Lapel, 14K Gold, Rose Tone Metal Dial, Arabic Numbers, C-Scrolls, Scrolling Tendrils, 2 In. 2470.00
Liptrot, Silver, Fusee, Double Case, Key Wind, Roman Numerals, London, c.1700, Pocket 1553.00
Longines, Chronometer, Rally, Stainless Steel, 21 Jewel, Leather Case, 1950s 2635.00
Longines, Woman's, 18K Gold, Inset Minute Dial, Art Nouveau Style, 1 1/4 In. 380.00
M.J. Tobias & Co., Pair Case, Fusee, Flowers, 18K Gold, Liverpool, c.1815 .... 1175.00
Movado, Woman's, Diamond, 14K White Gold, 17 Jewel, No. 4561 .... 450.00
New England Watch Co., Baseball, Silver Case, Pocket, 2 5/8 x 2 In. 3300.00
Patek Philippe, American Watch & Clock, Open Face, 18K Gold, Art Deco, 1891, Pocket, 1 3/4 In. . 765.00
Patek Philippe, Engraved Case, 18K Gold, 1891, Pocket, 2 3/4 In. 2233.00
Pendant, Silver, Black, Pink Enamel, Art Deco, 18 In. 29.00
R. Roskell, Open Face, Enamel Dial, Fusee, 18K Gold, Liverpool, c.1818, 2 In. 881.00
R.H. Taylor, Open Face, 13 Jewel, 18K Gold, Engraved Flowers, Monogram, Pocket, 2 1/8 In. 823.00
Rock Island, 21 Jewel, Security Regulation, Hinged Back, c.1900, Size 17, Pocket 115.00
Rockford, Hunting Case, Enameled Dial, 15 Jewel, 14K Gold, c.1912, Size 0, Pocket 201.00
Samuel Hammond, Open Face, 15 Jewel, Separate Second & Hour Face, Pocket 59.00
South Bend, Railroad, 17 Jewel, Scepter Case, Star Case Co., Size 16, Pocket 89.00
South Bend, Railroad, 21 Jewel, Open Face, 21 Jewel, 10K Gold Case, Pocket 120.00
Stephen Houghton, Chester, Hunting Case, Side Winder, England, Pocket, c.1872, 2 In. 110.00
T.B. & Co., Open Face, Goldtone Dial, River, Fusee, Engine Turned Case, 18K Gold, 2 In. 235.00
Thos. Moss, Pair Case, Enamel Dial, Fusee Movement, 18K Gold, London, c.1830, Pocket, 2 In. 823.00
Tiffany & Co., Open Face, 18K Gold, Nickel Movement, Pocket, 1 3/4 In. 823.00
W.J. Cartier, Open Face, Sterling Silver, 17 Jewel, Nickel Lever, Arctic, R.I., 2 In. 705.00
Waltham, Canadian Railway Times Service, 17 Jewel, Glass Back Display, Size 16 .... 480.00
Waltham, Chronometro Victoria, 18 Jewel, Silverplated Case, Size 16 .... 129.00
Waltham, Hunting Case, 14K Gold, AK Monogram, White Dial, c.1881 .... 660.00
Waltham, Hunting Case, 14K Gold, Engraved Intertwined B's, 2 Gilt Fobs, 2 In. 499.00
Waltham, Hunting Case, 17 Jewel, 14K Gold Case, Size 19, Pocket 745.00
Waltham, Hunting Case, Buck, Flowers, 14K Gold Chain, Pocket 764.00
Waltham, Hunting Case, Crescent St. Movement, 14K Gold, Size 18, Pocket 660.00
Waltham, Open Face, 17 Jewel, Nickel Movement, 14K Gold, 1 3/4 In. 380.00
Waltham, P.S. Bartlett, Hunting Case, Multicolored 14K Gold, Stag, 17 Jewel, Size18 .... 1380.00
Waltham, Premier 16S, 21 Jewel, RR, 10 K Rolled Gold Case, Size 13, Pocket 214.00
Waltham, Railroad, Case, Vanguard, 23 Jewel, Up/Down Indicator, Lossier Spring, Size16 .... 863.00
Waltham, Silver Hunting Case, Key Wind, c.1879, Size 16, Pocket 173.00
Waltham, Silverine Case, 7 Jewel, White Porcelain Dial, Size 19, Pocket 66.00
Waltham Vanguard, Railroad, 23 Jewel, Illinois Watch Gold Case, Size 16, Pocket 482.00
William Renwick, Open Face, 14K Gold, Pocket, 1 7/8 In. 234.00

WATCH FOBS were worn on watch chains. They were popular during Victorian times and after. Many styles, especially advertising designs, are still made today.

Bulldog, Cigar Clipper, John Merriam's Real Habana Cigars, 1 3/4 x 1 1/2 In. 330.00
Dead Shot Powder, Celluloid Center, Falling Duck, Embossed Hunting Scene 459.00
Dead Shot Powder, Celluloid Center, Falling Duck, Strap, Round .... 120.00 to 128.00
E.C. Simmons Keen Kutter, Celluloid, Leather Band, 1 3/4 In. 154.00
Etruscan Revival, 22K Gold, Double Trace Link Chain, Fox Tail Fringe, Ewer, 10 1/2 In. 700.00
Old Crane Whiskey, Bachrach & Co., San Francisco, California, 1 1/2 x 1 3/4 In. 139.00
Savage Arms Co., Sterling Silver, Leather Strap, Indian, Headdress, 1 3/8 In. 285.00
Savage Rifles, Copper, Strap, Indian, Headdress, Open Mouth, 1 1/2 In. 285.00
Shoot Western Ammunition, Metal, Enamel, Hunter, Dog, Oval, No Strap 360.00

WATERFORD type glass resembles the famous glass made from 1783 to 1851 in the Waterford Glass Works in Ireland. It is a clear glass that was often decorated by cutting. Modern glass is being made again in Waterford, Ireland, and is marketed under the name *Waterford*. Waterford merged with Wedgwood in 1986 to form the Waterford Wedgwood Group.

Biscuit Jar, Cover, 6 x 5 In. 70.00
Biscuit Jar, Cover, Glandore, 6 In. 175.00
Bud Vase, Lismore, Flashed Fans At Top, 16-Point Star Base, 7 In. 198.00
Candleholder, Marquis, 2 1/2 x 4 In., Pair 150.00
Candlestick, Marquis, 6-Sided Stems, 6-Panel Base, 10 In., Pair 100.00
Champagne, Curraghmore, 5 1/2 In. 74.00
Creamer, Lismore, Footed, 4 1/4 In. 95.00
Decanter, Diamond Cross, Prism Stopper, 11 In. 325.00
Decanter, Stopper, Kilmore, 13 In. 88.00
Decanter, Stopper, Ship's, 10 In. 235.00
Goblet, Alena, 7 3/4 In., 10 Piece 350.00
Knife Rest, Marked, 2 1/2 x 3 1/4 In. 145.00
Liquor Set, Lismore, 3 1/2 In., 10 Piece 150.00
Music Box, Songs Of Christmas, Jingle Bells, 1997 .... 100.00
Plate, 12 Days Of Christmas, 3 Three French Hens, Box, 1986 .... 199.00
Rose Bowl, Glandore, 6 In. 90.00
Sugar & Creamer, Lismore Pattern 129.00
Vase, Thistle Shape, Hobnail Panels, Engraved, King David With Harp, 11 In. 204.00
Water Set, Pitcher, Goblets, Sheila, 14 Piece 468.00
Wine, Glenmore, 5 1/2 In., 8 Piece 176.00

WATT family members bought the Globe pottery of Crooksville, Ohio, in 1922. They made pottery mixing bowls and tableware of the type made by Globe. In 1935 they changed the production and made the pieces with the freehand decorations that are popular with collectors today. Apple, Starflower, Rooster, Tulip, and Autumn Foliage are the best-known patterns. Pansy, also called Rio Rose, was the earliest pattern. Apple, the most popular pattern, can be dated from the leaves. Originally, the apples had three leaves; after 1958 two leaves were used. The plant closed in 1965. For more information, see *Kovels' Depression Glass & Dinnerware Price List*.

Animal Dish, Green, Raised Letters DOG, 2 Dogs, No. 7, 3 x 7 In. 40.00
Animal Dish, Mink Chow, Green, 9 In. 10.00
Animal Dish, Spaniel, Yellow, No. 504 .... 35.00
Apple, Baker, Cover, 2-Leaf, No. 67, 6 1/2 x 8 1/2 In. 20.00
Apple, Baker, Cover, No. 110, 6 3/4 x 8 1/2 In. 165.00
Apple, Baker, Cover, State Bank Of Wabeno, Wabeno, Wis., No. 601, 6 1/2 x 8 3/4 In. 30.00
Apple, Baker, Farmers Co-Op Creamery, Albert City, Iowa, No. 66 .... 35.00
Apple, Baker, No. 94, 1 3/4 x 6 In. 25.00
Apple, Baker, Open, Farmers State Bank Minnewaukan, North Dakota, No. 96, 8 1/2 In. 30.00
Apple, Baker, Ribbed, Allison, Iowa, No. 604, 2 1/2 x 6 3/4 In. 50.00

Apple, Baker, Ribbed, No. 602, 1 3/4 x 4 3/4 In. 30.00
Apple, Baker, Ribbed, No. 603, 2 x 5 3/4 In. 45.00
Apple, Baker, Ribbed, Overland Hatchery, Postville, Iowa, No. 604, 2 1/2 x 6 3/4 In. 40.00
Apple, Bean Cup, No. 75, 2 1/4 x 3 1/2 In. 155.00
Apple, Bowl, 2-Leaf, No. 55, 4 x 11 3/4 In. 150.00
Apple, Bowl, Brilion, Wis., No. 53, 3 x 7 1/2 In. 15.00
Apple, Bowl, Cereal, No. 23, 5 3/4 In. 18.00
Apple, Bowl, Cereal, No. 68, 5 In. 40.00
Apple, Bowl, Cereal, No. 74, 5 1/4 In. 35.00
Apple, Bowl, Cereal, Rock Rapids, No. 74, 5 1/2 In. 35.00
Apple, Bowl, Cover, Readlyn, Ia., No. 66, 5 1/2 x 7 1/2 In. 60.00
Apple, Bowl, Montello, Wis., No. 60, 2 3/8 x 6 1/4 In. 50.00
Apple, Bowl, Nappy, No. 04, 2 x 4 1/4 In. .... 20.00 to 70.00
Apple, Bowl, No. 1, 2 1/4 x 5 3/4 In. 65.00
Apple, Bowl, Salad, 2-Leaf, No. 73, 9 1/2 In. 13.00
Apple, Bowl, Salad, Cover, Algoma Feed Store, No. 73, 9 1/2 In. 50.00
Apple, Bowl, Salad, Footed, No. 106, 3 1/2 x 10 3/4 In. 125.00
Apple, Bowl, Salad, No. 73, 9 1/2 In. .... 20.00 to 35.00
Apple, Bowl, Spaghetti, 2-Leaf, No. 39, 3 x 13 In. 60.00
Apple, Bowl, Spaghetti, Individual, No. 44, 8 In. 40.00
Apple, Casserole, 8 1/2 In. 75.00
Apple, Casserole, Cover, 2-Leaf, Stick Handle, No. 18, 3 3/4 x 5 In. 45.00
Apple, Casserole, Cover, Large Knob, No. 96, 2 3/4 x 8 1/2 In. 55.00
Apple, Casserole, Cover, Tab Handles, No. 18, 4 x 5 In. 125.00
Apple, Chop Plate, No. 31, 15 In. 35.00
Apple, Cookie Jar, No. 503, 8 x 6 1/2 In. 185.00
Apple, Creamer, 2-Leaf, No. 62, 4 1/4 In. 55.00
Apple, Creamer, Dale Neucomer Auto, Buick, Wessington Springs, No. 62, 4 1/4 In. 125.00
Apple, Creamer, Pecks Corners Food & Liquors, Lester & Shirley Huber, No. 62, 4 1/4 In. 55.00
Apple, Creamer, Wessington Springs, S.D., No. 62, 4 1/4 In. 95.00
Apple, Dutch Oven, Cover, No. 73, 6 x 9 1/2 In. 115.00
Apple, Grease Jar, Cover, No. 01, 3 1/2 x 5 In. 500.00
Apple, Grease Jar, Menno, S.D., No. 01, 5 In. 200.00
Apple, Ice Bucket, Cover, No. 59, 7 x 7 1/2 In. 50.00
Apple, Ice Bucket, Tripp, S.D., No. 59, 7 x 7 1/2 In. 35.00
Apple, Mixing Bowl, 2-Leaf, No. 63, 4 1/4 x 6 1/2 In. 30.00
Apple, Mixing Bowl, Bancroft, Iowa, Wide Lip, No. 7, 4 x 7 In. 30.00
Apple, Mixing Bowl, Ribbed, First State Bank, Thornton, Meservey, Swaledale, No. 06 .... 40.00
Apple, Mixing Bowl, Wide Lip, Canby Dairy, Canby, Minn., No. 6, 3 1/2 x 6 In. 35.00
Apple, Mixing Bowl, Wide Lip, No. 6, 3 1/2 x 6 In. 30.00
Apple, Mixing Bowl, Wide Lip, No. 8, 4 1/2 x 8 In. 200.00
Apple, Mug, Beer, No. 501, 4 1/2 In. 180.00
Apple, Mug, No. 121, 3 1/4 In. 105.00
Apple, Mug, No. 701, 3 3/4 In. 300.00
Apple, Nappy, Cover, Ribbed, No. 05, 2 1/2 x 3 1/2 In. 35.00
Apple, Nappy, Cover, Ribbed, Thornton Hatchery & Produce, No. 05, 2 1/2 x 5 In. 40.00
Apple, Pie Plate, Becker Lumber Co., No. 33, 9 1/4 In. 105.00
Apple, Pie Plate, First State Bank, Thornton, Iowa, No. 33, 9 1/4 In. 75.00
Apple, Pie Plate, Frudden Lumber Co., Ft. Atkinson, Iowa, No. 33, 9 1/4 In. 65.00
Apple, Pie Plate, No. 33, 9 1/4 In. .... 45.00 to 50.00
Apple, Pie Plate, Trimont, Minn., No. 33, 9 1/4 In. 90.00
Apple, Pitcher, 2-Leaf, No. 16, 6 1/2 In. 95.00
Apple, Pitcher, Anderson Elevator, Rossie, Iowa, No. 16, 6 1/2 In. 60.00
Apple, Pitcher, Compliments Of Your Skelly Tank Man, R.C. Baber, No. 15, 5 1/4 In. 65.00
Apple, Pitcher, Cowan's, No. 16, 6 1/2 In. 50.00
Apple, Pitcher, Dane Cty. Farmco Service Co-Op, Vern Johnson, Your Oil Man, No. 15, 5 1/4 In. 60.00
Apple, Pitcher, Fairfax Co-Op Creamery Co., Use More Butter, Fairfax, Minn., No. 15, 5 1/4 In. 95.00
Apple, Pitcher, Farmers Co-Op Elevator, Panora, IA, No. 15, 5 1/4 In. 55.00
Apple, Pitcher, Ice Lip, No. 17, 8 In. .... 85.00 to 165.00
Apple, Pitcher, Kewaunee Co-Op Store, No. 15, 5 1/4 In. 65.00
Apple, Pitcher, Liquidgas, Windom-Jackson, No. 15, 5 1/4 In. 70.00

Apple, Pitcher, Orange City, Iowa, No. 16, 6 1/2 In. 105.00
Apple, Pitcher, Refrigerator, Square, 2-Leaf, No. 69, 8 In. 300.00
Apple, Pitcher, Rock Rapids, No. 15, 5 1/4 In. 85.00
Apple, Pitcher, Swansons Bros., Hawarden, Iowa, No. 15, 5 1/4 In. 20.00
Apple, Plate, Dinner, Lewisville, Minn., No. 29, 9 1/2 In. 40.00
Apple, Salt & Pepper, Hourglass, No. 117 & 118, 4 3/4 In. 215.00
Apple, Salt & Pepper, Hourglass, Rock Rapids, IA., No. 117 & 118, 4 3/4 In. 145.00
Apple, Salt & Pepper, Hourglass, Tyler Feed Store, Suymon, Okla., No. 117 & 118, 4 3/4 In. 165.00
Apple, Sugar, Ackley, Iowa, No. 98, 4 1/4 In. 135.00
Apple, Teapot, No. 112, 6 Cup, 6 In. 1400.00
Autumn Foliage, Baker, No. 94, 1 3/4 x 6 In. 10.00
Autumn Foliage, Bean Pot, Peshtigo Feed Mill, No. 76, 6 1/2 x 5 1/2 In. 20.00
Autumn Foliage, Bowl, Clarksville, Iowa, 1961, No. 7, 2 3/4 x 7 In. 50.00
Autumn Foliage, Bowl, Dip, No. 120, 2 x 5 In. 20.00
Autumn Foliage, Bowl, No. 7, 2 3/4 x 7 In. 20.00
Autumn Foliage, Bowl, Salad, No. 106, 3 3/4 x 10 3/4 In. 65.00
Autumn Foliage, Casserole, Cover, Metal Stand, No. 110, 8 1/2 In. 10.00
Autumn Foliage, Casserole, Cover, Tab Handles, No. 18, 3 3/4 x 5 In. 105.00
Autumn Foliage, Creamer, No. 62, 4 1/4 In. 15.00
Autumn Foliage, Dip Bowl, No. 120, 2 x 5 In. 10.00
Autumn Foliage, Mixing Bowl, Cold Spring Cheese Factory, 1960, No. 9, 9 In. 40.00
Autumn Foliage, Mug, Hourglass, No. 121, 3 3/4 In. 75.00
Autumn Foliage, Nappy, Ribbed, Unkrich Swifts Feed, No. 600, 3 x 7 3/4 In. 55.00
Autumn Foliage, Pitcher, No. 15, 5 1/4 In. .... 30.00 to 50.00
Autumn Foliage, Pitcher, No. 16, 6 1/2 In. 30.00
Autumn Foliage, Salt & Pepper, Hourglass, No. 117 & 118, 4 3/4 In. 75.00
Autumn Foliage, Sugar, No. 98, 4 1/4 In. 45.00
Cherry, Baker, No. 54, 3 1/4 x 8 1/4 In. 60.00
Cherry, Bowl, Ely, Solon, Rowley, Walker, No. 8, 8 In. 50.00
Cherry, Bowl, Salad, No. 52, 2 1/4 x 6 1/4 In. .... 15.00 to 45.00
Cherry, Bowl, Spaghetti, No. 25, 3 1/2 x 15 In. 85.00
Cherry, Bowl, Spaghetti, No. 39, 3 1/4 x 13 In. 20.00
Cherry, Chop Plate, No. 31, 15 In. 65.00
Cherry, Chop Plate, No. 49, 12 In. 95.00
Cherry, Cookie Jar, No Cover, No. 21, 6 x 7 In. 25.00
Cherry, Mixing Bowl, Rim, No. 6, 6 In. 30.00
Cherry, Mixing Bowl, Rim, No. 7, 7 In. 30.00
Cherry, Pitcher, No. 16, 6 1/2 In. 65.00
Cherry, Saltshaker, No. 45, 4 In. 45.00
Corn Row, Pitcher, Pink, No. 15, 5 1/4 In. 10.00
Daisy, Baker, 7 In. 25.00
Daisy, Casserole, No Cover, No. 8, 8 3/4 In. 10.00
Daisy, Mixing Bowl, Wide Lip, No. 6, 6 In. 75.00
Daisy, Mixing Bowl, Wide Lip, No. 9, 9 In. 75.00
Daisy, Plate, Luncheon, 8 1/2 In. 30.00
Double Apple, Baker, Cover, Large Knob, No. 96, 2 3/4 x 8 1/2 In. 95.00
Double Apple, Bowl, Salad, No. 73, 4 x 9 In. 5.00
Double Apple, Creamer, No. 62, 4 1/4 In. 195.00
Double Apple, Mixing Bowl, Deep, No. 63, 4 1/4 x 6 1/2 In. .... 50.00 to 55.00
Double Apple, Nappy, Ribbed, No. 05, 2 1/2 x 5 In. 100.00
Double Apple, Pitcher, No. 15, Pt., 5 1/4 In. 65.00
Dutch Apple, Bean Pot, No. 76, 6 1/2 x 5 1/2 In. 60.00
Dutch Apple, Canister, Large, No. 72, 9 x 7 1/4 In. 195.00
Dutch Apple, Casserole, Cover, French Handles, No. 18, 4 x 5 In. 95.00
Dutch Apple, Cheese Crock, No Cover, No. 80, 8 1/2 In. 55.00
Dutch Apple, Plate, Dinner, Divided, 3 Sections, Experimental, 10 1/2 In. 700.00
Dutch Tulip, Baker, Cover, No. 66, 3 1/2 x 7 1/4 In. 55.00
Dutch Tulip, Creamer, No. 62, 4 1/4 In. 115.00
Dutch Tulip, Nappy, Cover, Round Knob, No. 05, 2 1/2 x 5 1/4 In. 30.00
Dutch Tulip, Pitcher, Adel, Iowa, No. 15, Pt., 5 1/4 In. 245.00

Dutch Tulip, Pitcher, Ice Lip, Square, No. 69, 8 In. 130.00
Dutch Tulip, Pitcher, No. 15, Pt., 5 1/4 In. 100.00
Dutch Tulip, Pitcher, No. 16, 2 Pt., 6 1/2 In. ....45.00 to 50.00
Eagle, Mixing Bowl, No. 12, 12 In. 55.00
Eagle, Mixing Bowl, Ribbed, No. 5, 5 In. 75.00
Eagle, Mixing Bowl, Ribbed, No. 6, 6 In. 65.00
Esmond, Canister Set, 4 Sections, Wood Lazy Susan Base, Covers, No. 32, 10 1/2 x 10 1/4 In. 25.00
Eve-N-Bake, Casserole, Brown Spray Bands, 8 In. 10.00
Eve-N-Bake, Pitcher, Brown Spray Bands, 7 In. 45.00
Kitch-N-Queen, Mixing Bowl, Ribbed, Bristow Grocery & Locker, No. 7, 2 3/4 x 7 In. 35.00
Kitch-N-Queen, Mixing Bowl, Ribbed, Dumont, No. 6, 6 In. 35.00
Kitch-N-Queen, Mixing Bowl, Wide Lip, No. 10, 10 In. 75.00
Kitch-N-Queen, Mixing Bowl, Wide Lip, No. 12, 12 In. 75.00
Kitch-N-Queen, Pitcher, Ice Lip, No. 17, 5 Pt., 8 In. 65.00
Kolor Kraft, Mixing Bowl, Wide Lip, Aqua, No. 7, 7 In. 12.50
Moonflower, Berry Bowl, Black, No. 22, 2 x 5 1/2 In. 30.00
Moonflower, Bowl, Green, No. 4, 1 3/4 x 5 In. 20.00
Moonflower, Casserole, Cover, Green, 8 In. 25.00
Moonflower, Casserole, Cover, Stick Handle, Black, No. 18, 4 x 5 In. 20.00
Moonflower, Cookie Jar, Black, No. 21, 7 1/2 x 7 In. 10.00
Moonflower, Plate, Dinner, Black, No. 101, 10 In. 65.00
Morning Glory, Baker, No. 94, 1 3/4 x 6 In. 95.00
Morning Glory, Cookie Jar, No Cover, No. 95, 7 1/2 In. 50.00
Morning Glory, Creamer, No. 97, 4 1/4 In. 425.00
Morning Glory, Mixing Bowl, No. 7, 7 In. 80.00
Morning Glory, Pitcher, Ice Lip, No. 96, 8 x 8 1/2 In. 65.00
Morning Glory, Sugar & Creamer, No. 98, 4 1/2 In. 345.00
Oven Ware, Pie Plate, Yellow, Arcs, 9 1/4 In. 9.00
Pansy, Baker, Open, Crosshatch, 8 3/4 In. 13.00
Pansy, Baker, Open, Raised, 8 In. 8.00
Pansy, Berry Bowl, Bullseye, No. 22, 5 1/2 In. 20.00
Pansy, Berry Bowl, No. 22, 2 x 5 1/2 In. 10.00
Pansy, Bowl, No. 1, 2 1/4 x 5 3/4 In. 25.00
Pansy, Bowl, No. 4, 1 3/4 x 5 In. 45.00
Pansy, Bowl, Rio Rose, No. 4, 1 3/4 x 5 In. 5.00
Pansy, Bowl, Rio Rose, No. 23, 1 1/2 x 5 5/8 In. 15.00
Pansy, Bowl, Spaghetti, Bullseye, No. 25, 3 1/2 x 15 In. 10.00
Pansy, Bowl, Spaghetti, Crosshatch, No. 24, 2 1/2 x 11 In. 165.00
Pansy, Bowl, Spaghetti, Crosshatch, No. 39, 3 1/4 x 13 In. 20.00
Pansy, Casserole, Cover, Lug Handle, Raised, No. 18, 4 x 5 In. 15.00
Pansy, Casserole, Cover, Rio Rose, No. 18, 4 x 5 In. 13.00
Pansy, Chop Plate, Bullseye, Cut-Leaf, No. 31, 15 In. 60.00
Pansy, Chop Plate, Crosshatch, No. 31, 15 In. 105.00
Pansy, Chop Plate, Cut-Leaf, No. 31, 15 In. ....30.00 to 45.00
Pansy, Chop Plate, No. 31, 15 In. 10.00
Pansy, Cookie Jar, Crosshatch, No. 21, 7 1/2 x 7 In. 200.00
Pansy, Cookie Jar, No Cover, Raised, No. 21, 6 x 7 In. 15.00
Pansy, Cookie Jar, Rio Rose, No. 21, 7 1/2 x 7 In. 105.00
Pansy, Cup & Saucer, Bullseye, Large 20.00
Pansy, Cup & Saucer, Crosshatch, No. 40 .... 135.00
Pansy, Cup & Saucer, Rio Rose, No. 27 .... 10.00
Pansy, Mixing Bowl, Cut-Leaf, No. 5, 5 In. 17.00
Pansy, Pie Plate, Crosshatch, No. 33, 9 1/4 In. 175.00
Pansy, Pitcher, Cover, Raised, 5 1/4 In. 90.00
Pansy, Pitcher, Cover, Raised, 6 1/2 In. 45.00
Pansy, Pitcher, Cover, Raised, 8 In. 10.00
Pansy, Pitcher, Crosshatch, No. 16, 6 1/2 In. 315.00
Pansy, Pitcher, Ice Lip, Square, Cover, Raised, No. 69, 8 In. 110.00
Pansy, Pitcher, No. 15, 5 1/4 In. 40.00
Pansy, Pitcher, No. 17, 8 In. 105.00

Pansy, Pitcher, Old Style, Crosshatch, 4 Pt., 7 In. 175.00
Pansy, Pitcher, Old Style, Raised, 4 Pt., 7 In. 45.00
Pansy, Plate, Dinner, No. 101, 10 In. 40.00
Pansy, Plate, Luncheon, Crosshatch, No. 43, 8 3/4 In. 175.00
Pansy, Plate, Salad, Bullseye, No. 28, 7 1/2 In. 20.00
Pansy, Plate, Snack, Bullseye, No. 30, 11 1/2 In. 30.00
Pansy, Sandwich Plate, No. 49, 12 In. 30.00
Pansy, Saucer, Crosshatch 40.00
Pansy, Snack Plate, Cup, Bullseye, 11 1/2 In. 25.00
Pansy, Soup, Dish, No. 44, 8 In. 15.00
Pansy, Sugar & Creamer, Bullseye 35.00
Peedeeco, Bean Pot Set, 3 Bean Cups, 6 3/4-In. Pot 5.00
Rio Rose, see Pansy
Rooster, Baker, Rectangular, Tab Handles, No. 85, 5 1/2 x 9 In. 375.00
Rooster, Casserole, Cover, French Handle, No. 18, 4 x 5 In. 50.00
Rooster, Creamer, No. 62, 4 1/4 In. .... 125.00 to 195.00
Rooster, Mixing Bowl, Wide Lip, Dekolb Dolton, S.D., No. 8, 8 In. 65.00
Rooster, Pitcher, No. 15, Pt., 5 1/4 In. .... 65.00 to 115.00
Rooster, Pitcher, No. 16, 2 Pt., 6 1/2 In. .... 95.00 to 135.00
Rooster, Pitcher, Refrigerator, No. 69, 8 In. 300.00
Rooster, Salt & Pepper, Hourglass, Clarinda, No. 117 & 118 .... 125.00
Silhouette, Casserole, Cover, No. 18, 5 In. 7.50
Silhouette, Casserole, Cover, Tab Handles, No. 18, 3 3/4 x 5 In. 45.00
Silhouette, Cookie Jar, No. 21, 7 1/2 x 7 In. 165.00
Silhouette, Pitcher, No. 16, 2 Pt., 6 1/2 In. 195.00
Starflower, Baker, Cover, No. 96, 8 1/2 In. 23.00
Starflower, Baker, No. 60, 2 3/8 x 6 1/4 In. 20.00
Starflower, Baker, No. 68, 4 x 5 1/4 In. 5.00
Starflower, Bean Cup, No. 75, 2 1/4 x 3 1/2 In. 40.00
Starflower, Bean Pot, No. 76, 6 1/2 x 5 1/2 In. 85.00
Starflower, Bowl, No. 4, 1 3/4 x 5 In. 10.00
Starflower, Bowl, Salad, No. 52, 2 1/4 x 6 1/4 In. 15.00
Starflower, Bowl, Spaghetti, No. 39, 3 1/4 x 13 In. .... 25.00 to 50.00
Starflower, Canister, No Cover, No. 82, 5 In. 65.00
Starflower, Casserole, Cover Only, No. 18 .... 13.00
Starflower, Casserole, Cover Only, No. 53 .... 18.00
Starflower, Casserole, Individual, Cover, No. 18, 5 In. .... 10.00 to 25.00
Starflower, Creamer, No. 62 .... 85.00 to 200.00
Starflower, Mixing Bowl, Lipped, Renville, Minn., No. 7, 7 In. 75.00
Starflower, Mug, Beer, 4-Petal, No. 501, 4 1/2 In. .... 30.00 to 60.00
Starflower, Nappy, Ribbed, No. 04, 2 x 4 1/4 In. 30.00
Starflower, Pie Plate, 4-Petal, Renville, Minn., No. 33, 9 1/4 In. 325.00
Starflower, Pitcher, 4-Petal, No. 16, 2 Pt., 6 1/2 In. 100.00
Starflower, Pitcher, No. 15, 5 1/4 In. .... 23.00 to 105.00
Starflower, Pitcher, No. 16, 2 Pt., 6 1/2 In. .... 25.00 to 35.00
Starflower, Pitcher, No. 17, 5 Pt., 8 In. 20.00
Starflower, Salt & Pepper, Barrel, No. 45 & 46 .... 105.00
Tear Drop, Baker, Cover, No. 66, 5 1/2 x 7 1/4 In. 20.00
Tear Drop, Baker, Cover, Oval, No. 86, 10 In. 195.00
Tear Drop, Baker, Rectangular, No. 85, 5 1/2 x 9 In. 210.00
Tear Drop, Bean Cup Set, No. 75, 8 Oz., 4 Piece 22.50
Tear Drop, Bean Cup, No. 75, 8 Oz. 10.00
Tear Drop, Bowl, No. 68, 4 x 5 1/4 In. 30.00
Tear Drop, Canister, Cover, No. 72, 9 x 7 1/4 In. 200.00
Tear Drop, Casserole, Cover, French Handles, No. 18, 4 x 5 In. 65.00
Tear Drop, Crock, Cheese, Cover, No. 80, 8 x 8 1/2 In. 135.00
Tear Drop, Mixing Bowl, Deep, Tracy, Minn., No. 64, 4 3/4 x 7 1/2 In. .... 40.00 to 45.00
Tear Drop, Nappy, Ribbed, No. 05, 2 1/2 x 5 1/4 In. 20.00
Tear Drop, Nappy, Ribbed, No. 06, 3 x 6 1/4 In. 35.00
Tear Drop, Nappy, Ribbed, No. 07, 3 3/4 x 7 1/4 In. 38.00

Tear Drop, Pitcher, No. 15, 5 1/4 In. .... 13.00 to 70.00
Tear Drop, Pitcher, No. 16, 2 Pt., 6 1/2 In. 35.00
Tear Drop, Salt & Pepper, Barrel, No. 45 & 46 .... 265.00
Tear Drop, Salt & Pepper, Hourglass, No. 117 & 118 .... 135.00
Tulip, Casserole, Cover, Ribbed, No. 600, 3 x 7 3/4 In. 85.00
Tulip, Creamer, No. 62, 4 1/4 In. 105.00
Tulip, Mixing Bowl, Deep, No. 63, 4 1/4 x 6 1/2 In. 35.00

WAVE CREST glass is an opaque white glassware manufactured by the Pairpoint Manufacturing Company of New Bedford, Massachusetts, and some French factories. It was decorated by the C.F. Monroe Company of Meriden, Connecticut. The glass was painted in pastel colors and decorated with flowers. The name *Wave Crest* was used after 1898.

WAVE CREST WARE

Biscuit Jar, 2 Handles, 8 In. 325.00
Biscuit Jar, Rococo Mold, Flowers, C.F.M. Co. Cover, 8 1/4 In. 290.00
Bowl, Zinnia, Cream Ground, Brass Foot & Rim, 8 1/4 x 6 In. 405.00
Box, Baroque Shell Mold, Pink & White Flowers, Round, 7 In. 345.00
Box, Egg Crate Mold, Flowers, Orange Ground, Metal Base, Lion Head Feet, 7 x 3 3/4 x 5 In. 630.00
Creamer, Flowers, Leaves, Cream Ground, 3 x 5 In. 175.00
Dresser Box, Baroque Shell Mold, Enameled Blossoms, 7 1/4 In. 430.00
Dresser Box, Flowers, Painted, 7 In. 410.00
Dresser Box, Helmschmied Swirl, Blue & Pink Flowers, Leaves, 7 In. 345.00
Dresser Box, Round, Hinged, 7 In. 375.00
Dresser Box, Swirl Mold, Enameled Flowers, 4 1/2 In. 70.00
Pomade Jar, Cover, Flowers, Red Banner Mark, 2 x 2 In. 245.00
Salt & Pepper, Opera Glass Frame, Flowers 460.00
Vase, Flower Reserve, Gold Enameled Satin Ground, Ormolu Mounts, 6 1/2 In. 200.00

WEAPONS listed here include instruments of combat other than guns, knives, rifles, or swords. Firearms are not listed in this book. Knives and Swords are listed in their own categories.

Battle Ax, Iron Head, Hammer Back, Leaf Panels, Lacquered Shaft, 1700s, 39 1/2 In. 475.00
Bludgeon, Officer's, Continental, Cylindrical, Cruciform Blade, Leather, c.1890, 25 1/2 In. 245.00
Cannon, Cast Iron, Wooden Carriage, Black, White, 24 1/2 x 45 In. 805.00
Jambiya, Crested Pommel, Silver-Faced Scabbard, Morocco, c.1850, 9 1/4-In. Blade 550.00
Kris, Wavy Damascus Blade, Coral Handle, Wood Sheath, Philippines, 1800s, 19 In. 144.00
Shield, Metal, Hammered, Leather Appearance, Brass Mounts, Ethiopia, 20 In. 355.00

WEATHER VANES were used in seventeenth-century Boston. The direction of the wind was an indication of coming weather, important to the seafaring and farming communities. By the mid-nineteenth century, commercial weather vanes were made of metal. Today's collectors often consider weather vanes to be examples of folk art, even though they may not have been handmade.

Angel, Blowing Horn, Orange, Yellow, Carved Wood, 1930s, 22 x 70 In. 2415.00
Angel, Blowing Trumpet, Sheet Iron, Painted, Weathered, 23 1/2 In. 1435.00
Arrow, Pine, Wrought Iron, Heart Shape Tail, Late 1800s, 42 In. 4800.00
Automobile, Zinc, Cast Iron Directional, c.1900, 10-In. Car, 22 1/2 In. 440.00
Banner, Arrow, Ball & Spike Finial, Verdigris Patina, Custom Stand, 41 x 23 In. 1210.00
Banner, Arrow, Fleur-De-Lis, Gilt Surface, 19 x 48 In. 1540.00
Banner, Arrow, Red Paint, Gilt, Custom Stand, 101 x 70 In. 4730.00
Banner, Circular Cutouts, Verdigris Patina, Custom Stand, 77 x 58 In. 1320.00
Banner, Smith Cutout, Copper, On Base, 26 x 37 In. 690.00
Banner, Wrought Iron, Pierced Compass Star, Lead Counterweight, 22 In. 1725.00
Banner & Hand, Gilt Patina, 29 x 36 In. 3960.00
Bicycle, High Wheel, Copper, Brass Directionals, Arrow, 33 x 19 In. 66.00
Bull, Copper, Hollow Body, Applied Ears & Horns, Iron Base, 25 x 13 In. 8912.00
Cow, Copper, Full-Bodied, Cast Zinc Horns, Waltham, Mass., c.1880, 28 x 16 1/2 In. 16500.00
Cow, Copper, Gilding Trace, Patina, Verdigris, Iron Face, 26 1/2 x 16 In. 6325.00
Cow, Copper, Hollow, Early 1900s, 28 In. 605.00
Cow, Hollow, Cast Iron Arrow, Tin, Early 20th Century, 28 In. 145.00

Eagle, Grasping Serpent, Copper, Finders, 38 In. 4255.00
Eagle, Spread Wings, Copper, 24 In. 980.00
Fireman, Sheet Iron, Silhouette, New England, Early 1800s, 20 1/2 x 11 In. 2645.00
Fish, Metal, Directionals, Weirs Beach, 18 In. 750.00
Fish, Sheet Iron, Weathered, 10 x 21 3/4 In. 1435.00
Flag, Copper, Painted, Cutout Stars, c.1950, 23 1/2 x 34 1/2 In. 780.00
Halley's Comet, Blue Glass Panel, Iron Directional, Late 1800s, 22 1/2 In. 525.00
Hamburg Rooster, Gilded Copper, Late 1800s, 29 x 27 In. 20500.00
Horse, 3-Dimensional, Directional Markers, Copper, 13 x 24 In. 605.00
Horse, Ethan Allen, Copper, Zinc Head, Red Paint, 29 3/4 x 17 In. 3738.00
Horse, Running, Copper, Cast Zinc Ears, Black Hawk, J.W. Fiske, 27 x 20 In. 6900.00
Horse, Running, Copper, Full-Bodied, Gilt, J. Harris & Son, Boston, 15 x 32 In. 770.00
Horse, Running, Copper, Gilt, 17 x 62 In. 748.00
Horse, Running, Copper, Green Patina, Cushing & White, 43 In. 14950.00
Horse, Running, Copper, Patina, Hollow, Iron Mounting Rod, 17 x 30 In., 2 Piece 1840.00
Horse, Running, Dexter & Jockey, J.W. Fiske, Copper, Zinc Horse Head, 32 x 18 In. 7765.00
Horse, Running, Flying Tail, New Rod, Copper, Wood Base, 51 x 31 In. 200.00
Horse, Running, Molded Copper, Cast Zinc, Full-Bodied, Verdigris, 13 x 29 In. 11750.00
Horse, Running, Molded Sheet Copper, Verdigris, 19th Century, 20 1/2 x 31 In. 5875.00
Horse, Running, Smuggler, Molded Copper, Stand 3345.00
Horse, Running, Verdigris, Smuggler, c.1890, 32 In. 7600.00
Horse, Running, Wood, Painted, Carved, Mid 1800s, 27 x 15 In. 9800.00
Horse, Standing, Cast Iron Head, Molded Vane, Flat Tail, 26 x 33 In. 28750.00
Horse, Standing, Wood, Painted White, Black Mane, Tail, 25 in. 290.00
Horse, Trotting, Dan Patch, Wrought Iron Indicators, Violet Glass Ball, Wood Base, 75 In. 2585.00
Horse, Trotting, Sheet Iron, Forged Rivets, Black Paint, c.1860, 19 1/2 x 26 1/2 In. 4500.00
Horse, Wood, Painted, 15 x 22 In. 633.00
Horse & Sulky, Copper, 31 In. 46.00
Horse & Sulky, Copper, Applied Green Patina, 18 x 32 In. 288.00
Horse & Sulky, Driver, Wood, Steel, Wire, Mounted Flywheel & Pulley, 66 x 38 In. 1150.00
Horse & Sulky, Verdigris Patina, Harris & Co. Attribution, 18 x 28 In. 11500.00
Indian, Kneeling, Drawing Bow & Arrow, Pine, Tin, Carved, 2-Sided, 52 x 50 In. 18800.00
Indian, Standing, Wearing Headdress, Iron, Pine, 67 x 52 x 62 1/2 In. 6463.00
Lovebird, On Arrow, 2 Copper Sheets, Riveted, Folded Edges, Bullet Holes, 36 In. 935.00
Man, Playing Trumpet, Painted, Wood, Iron Directionals, 1900s, 59 x 42 1/2 In. 235.00
Man, With Bow & Arrow, Sheet Metal, Old Paint, 19th Century, 22 1/2 x 23 In. 1045.00
Pig, Copper, Cast Iron Directional, 9-In. Pig, 21 In. 550.00
Pigeon, On Ball, On Arrow, Copper, Verdigris Patina, J.W. Fiske, 16 1/2 x 24 1/2 In. 8625.00
Quill, Directionals, Presque Isle Maine, 36 In. 1955.00
Rooster, Banner, Custom Stand, 76 x 77 In. 1155.00
Rooster, Cast Zinc, Copper Legs & Tail, Folk Art, 12 3/4 x 14 1/2 x 3 In. 9775.00
Rooster, Copper Body, Zinc Legs, Black Wooden Base, 40 In. 1904.00
Rooster, Copper, Maine, 18 In. 3165.00
Rooster, Copper, Molded Sheet, Flattened Full-Bodied, Copper Arrow, 22 x 23 In. 1645.00
Rooster, Gilt Cast Iron, Sheet Iron, Rochester Iron Works, N.H., 32 1/2 x 35 1/2 In. 8225.00
Rooster, Molded Sheet Copper, Riveted, Verdigris, Mustard Paint, 21 x 20 In. 764.00
Rooster, Sheet Copper, Full-Bodied, Cast Zinc Feet, Verdigris, Early 1900s, 23 In. 2350.00
Rooster, Sheet Iron, Black Paint, Stylized, High Comb, Directionals, 30 In. 290.00
Rooster, Sheet Iron, Bullet Hole Eye, Directional Arrow, 27 1/2 In. 288.00
Rooster, Stamped Metal, Late 1800s, 24 x 24 In. 10530.00
Rooster, Wood, Full-Bodied, Carved Tail, Wings, Painted, 1800s, 19 x 14 1/2 In. 1116.00
Rooster, Zinc, Iron, James Directional, Early 1900s, 14-In. Rooster, 32 In. 495.00
Schooner, 2-Masted, Gilt Decorated, 59 x 64 In. 2015.00
Ship, 3-Masted, Copper, 19 Sails, 1950s, 70 x 67 In. 1495.00
Ship, 3-Masted, Copper, Signed Felix, 1950s, 72 In. 1495.00
Ship, 3-Masted, Molded Sheet Copper, Copper Wire Rigging, 39 x 36 In. 5875.00
Ship, Wood, Copper Rigging, Sails, c.1900, 39 In. 145.00
Spire, Ball, Atop Quill, Gilded Molded Sheet Copper, 23 1/2 x 35 1/4 In. 3290.00
Swordfish, Wood, Painted, Early 1900s, 26 1/2 In. 175.00

WEBB glass was made by Thomas Webb & Sons of Ambelcot, England. Many types of art and cameo glass were made by them during the Victorian era. Production ceased by 1991, and the factory was demolished in 1995. Webb Burmese and Webb Peachblow are special colored glasswares of the Victorian era. They are listed at the end of this section. Glassware that is not Burmese or Peachblow is included here.

Webb

Bowl, Optic Ribbed, Ruffled Rim, Alexandrite, 2 In. 980.00
Bowl, Satin, Prunus Blossoms, Ribbon Pattern, Tricornered Rim, Footed, 3 In. 315.00
Bowl, White Over Ruby, Flowers, Butterfly, 5 1/8 In. 705.00
Finger Bowl, Underplate, Alexandrite, Ruffled Edge, 6 In. ....1955.00 to 2530.00
Finger Bowl, Underplate, White Flowers, Yellow Ground, Butterfly, Cameo, 4 1/2 In. 1800.00
Plaque, Cherries, Leaves, Pie Crust Edge, Leather Case, c.1900, 4 x 4 1/2 In. 5079.00
Plate, Flowers, White, Powder Blue Translucent Ground, Acid Etched, Cameo, 7 1/2 In. 7190.00
Scent Bottle, Blue, White Flower Overlay, Gilt Silver Collar & Lid, c.1884, 3 3/4 In. 1135.00
Scent Bottle, Ivy Leaves, Blue Ground, Ivory Overlay, Silver Top, Tapered, c.1900, 5 In. 1315.00
Scent Bottle, Mother-Of-Pearl Satin, Peacock Eye, Globe Shape, Silver Mounted, c.1902, 4 x 3 In. . . 805.00
Urn, Ivory, Geometric & Flowers, Cameo, 4 In. 1725.00
Vase, Alexandrite, Honeycomb, Oval, 6-Sided Rim, 2 3/4 In. 1095.00
Vase, Amber, Stems, Flower, Fuchsias, Reverse Morning Glory, Oval, Cameo, 7 In. 1035.00
Vase, Bellflowers, Leaves, Citrine Ground, Butterfly, Cameo, 11 In. 2300.00
Vase, Blue, Flowers, Butterfly, Cameo, Bulbous, Flared Rim, 4 1/2 In. 865.00
Vase, Cameo, Ivory, Oval, 6-Sided Rim, Birds, Insects, Flowers, Leaves, 4 1/4 In. 635.00
Vase, Cameo, Prussian Blue, Oval, Rolled Rim, Flowers, 8 In. 2990.00
Vase, Cameo, Red, Opaque Overlay, Cased In Clear, Raspberry Design, 10 3/4 In. 2300.00
Vase, Cranberry To Peach, Ivory Overlay, Oval, Flared Rim, c.1890, 4 1/4 In. 1554.00
Vase, Dragon Blood Cased, Gold & Silver Scrolls, Bulbous, 10 3/4 In. 290.00
Vase, Flowers, Dragonfly, Cranberry Ground, Ivory Overlay, Globular, Cameo, c.1900, 1 In. 478.00
Vase, Flowers, Leaves, Butterfly, Amber Ground, Squat, Cameo, 3 1/4 In. 630.00
Vase, Flowers, Leaves, Stems, Butterfly, Citrine Ground, Flared Neck, Cameo, 9 In. 690.00
Vase, Honeysuckle, Yellow Ground, Cranberry & Ivory Overlay, Oval, c.1890, 6 1/2 In. 2868.00
Vase, Irises, Duck, Chipped Ice Ground, Oval, Rolled Rim, Cameo, Corbett, 12 In. 1610.00
Vase, Lilac, Scalloped Rim, Blue To Pink, Flowers, Leaves, Oval, 2 1/2 In. 1438.00
Vase, Nasturtiums, Lemon Yellow Ground, Ivory Overlay, Bulbous, c.1890, 5 In. 1315.00
Vase, Opal, Flowers, Leafy Stems, Green Ground, 18 In. 260.00
Vase, Ovals, Diamonds, Triangles, Birds, Ivory, Gourd Shape, Cameo, 6 3/4 In. 1035.00
Vase, Poppy, Leaves, Buds, Butterfly, Citrine Ground, Cameo, 5 1/4 In. 1380.00
Vase, Silveria, Stringing, Multicolored, c.1900, 13 1/2 In. 5080.00
Vase, Stick, Citron, Shells, Leaves, Seaweed, Stalactite Border, Bulbous Base, Cameo, 8 1/2 In. . . . 2300.00
Vase, Trumpet, Cranberry, Flowers, Leaves, Ivory Overlay, Flared Base, Cameo, c.1890, 14 3/4 In. . 1135.00
Vase, White To Red Flowers, Leaves, Vines, Yellow Ground, Butterfly, Cameo, 5 In. 1610.00
Vase, Wild Rose, Yellow Ground, Cranberry Overlay, Cameo, Bulbous, Cameo, c.1890, 3 3/4 In. . . . 1910.00

WEBB BURMESE is a colored Victorian glass made by Thomas Webb & Sons of Stourbridge, England, from 1886.

Condiment Set, Flowers, Butterflies, Spoons, 5 3/4 In., 3 Piece 6440.00
Fairy Lamp, 3 3/4 In. 230.00
Fairy Lamp, 4-Fold Base, Clarke Burner, 5 In. 575.00
Fairy Lamp, Clear Insert, Ruffled Base, 5 In. 460.00
Pitcher, Oval, Applied Handle, 3-Footed, 5 1/2 In. 635.00
Rose Bowl, Enameled Berry & Leaf, Glossy, Folded & Ruffled Edge, 2 3/4 x 2 In. 290.00
Rose Bowl, Enameled Flowers, Fluted Rim, 2 3/4 In. 259.00
Rose Bowl, Oval, Rolled Ruffled Rim, Glossy, 3 In. 290.00
Salt, Glossy, Silver Plated Frame 460.00
Salt, Open, Silver Plate Holder, Ribbed, 1 1/4 x 2 1/2 In. 520.00
Vase, Hawthorn, Stick, Bulbous Base, Ruffled Edge, 3 1/4 In. 175.00

WEBB PEACHBLOW is a colored Victorian glass made by Thomas Webb & Sons of Stourbridge, England, from 1885.

Biscuit Jar, Cover, Gold Peacock On Branch, 7 In. 345.00
Bowl, Coralene, Yellow Seaweed, Notched Rim, Crimson Interior, 7 In. 400.00
Celery Vase, Gold Trim, Stemmed Flowers, 4-Fold Ruffled Edge, 5 3/4 In. 175.00
Lamp, Oil, Satin, 13 In. 1000.00

Pitcher, Branch & Blossom, Gold Enameled, Tricornered Lip, Satin Handle, 9 1/2 In. 325.00
Pitcher, Coralene Design, 7 1/4 In. 600.00
Vase, Butterfly, Flowers, Amber Handles, Flat Sides, Ruffled Edge, 4 In. 200.00
Vase, Cased, 4 3/4 In. 200.00
Vase, Gold & Silver Gingko Branches, Gold Trim, Shouldered, 6 In., Pair 460.00

WEDGWOOD, one of the world's most successful potteries, was founded by Josiah Wedgwood, who was considered a cripple by his brother and was forbidden to work at the family business. The pottery was established in England in 1759. A large variety of wares has been made, including the well-known jasperware, basalt, creamware, and even a limited amount of porcelain. There are two kinds of jasperware. One is made from two colors of clay, the other is made from one color of clay with a color dip to create the contrast in design. The firm is still in business. Other Wedgwood pieces may be listed under Flow Blue, Majolica, Tea Leaf Ironstone or in other porcelain categories. In 1986 Wedgwood and Waterford Crystal merged to form the Waterford Wedgwood Group.

WEDGWOOD

Bidet, Queen's Ware, In Maple Stand, Early1800s, 13 5/8 x 21 3/4 x 15 1/4 In. 470.00
Biscuit Jar, Blue & White, Silver Plated Lid, Bail, Signed, 6 1/2 In. 240.00
Biscuit Jar, Blue, Classical Scenes, Sheffield Mounts, Early 1900s, 7 1/2 In. 106.00
Biscuit Jar, Cover, Jasper Dip, Black, Egyptian Motif, 6 1/4 In. 705.00
Biscuit Jar, Cover, Jasper Dip, Black, Grapevine Festoons, Lion Masks, Rings, 5 7/8 In. 529.00
Biscuit Jar, Jasperware, Blue, Early 1900s, 5 1/4 In. 200.00
Bowl, Butterfly Luster, Flying Crane, Waso-Byo-Ye, Octagonal, Cream, Blue Border, 9 In. 920.00
Bowl, Dragon Luster, Octagonal, Cobalt Blue, Flying Crane, Waso-Byo-Ye, Temple, 8 In. 805.00
Bowl, Fairyland Luster, Bronze, Coral, Willow Pattern, Octagonal, 8 In. 3450.00
Bowl, Fairyland Luster, Butterflies, Octagonal, Daisy Makeig-Jones, 1920s, 7 In. 358.00
Bowl, Fairyland Luster, Dana, Panels, Village Scene, Water, Mountains, Elves, 3 1/2 In. 4888.00
Bowl, Fairyland Luster, Garden Of Paradise, D. Makeig-Jones, 1920s, 5 3/4 In. 4150.00
Bowl, Fairyland Luster, Geisha, Black Ground, Octagonal, c.1920, 6 1/4 In. 8225.00
Bowl, Fairyland Luster, Imperial, Poplar Tree, Interior Woodland Bridge, 10 1/2 In. 6325.00
Bowl, Fairyland Luster, Landscape, 8 Panels, 4 1/2 x 9 3/8 In. 3450.00
Bowl, Fairyland Luster, Panels, Gold Cranes, Hummingbird, Birds, 4 x 2 1/2 In. 345.00
Bowl, Fairyland Luster, Poplar Tree, Blue Ground, Elves, Bridge, 10 3/4 In. 5175.00
Bowl, Fairyland Luster, Poplar Trees, Woodland Bridge, 1920s, 11 In. 5100.00
Bowl, Fairyland Luster, Queen In Woods, Wilton Ware, England, 9 1/2 In. 978.00
Bowl, Fairyland Luster, Woodland Bridge, Picnic By River, 1920s, 8 1/4 In. 5700.00
Bowl, Grape & Wicker, Twig Handle, Cobalt Blue Center, 11 3/4 In. 950.00
Bowl, Jasper Dip, Crimson, Classical Figures, c.1920, 4 1/4 In. 940.00
Bowl, Luster, Mythological Figures, Stylized Spider In Bottom, 2 1/4 In. 259.00
Bowl, Vegetable, Majolica, Footed, Cobalt Blue Lobster, 10 3/4 x 5 1/4 In. 1095.00
Bowl, Yellow Luster, Pheasants In Flight, Resting, Octagonal, 8 In. 1785.00
Bowl & Pitcher, Willow, Blue Transfer, Etruria England, c.1900, 11 1/4 x 16 In. 259.00
Bust, Wesley, Black, Basalt, c.1850, 8 1/8 In. 646.00
Butter Pat, Majolica, Argenta Chrysanthemum 230.00
Butter Pat, Majolica, Ocean 207.00
Button, People, Dog, Under Tree, White On Blue Ground, 1700s, Large 410.00
Candlestick, Classical Figures, Medium Blue Ground, 9 3/4 x 5 1/2 In., Pair 259.00
Candlestick, Jasper Dip, Tricolor, Lilac Classical Figures, Green Leaves, Border, 5 In., Pair 1410.00
Candlestick, Jasperware, Blue, Classical Scenes, c.1900, 6 In., Pair 145.00
Candlestick, Moonlight Luster, Cylindrical, Flared Foot, Gilt Trim, c.1810, 8 In., Pair 1410.00
Candlestick, Putti Cattail, 10 In. 560.00
Charger, Mared Pattern, Reticulated Insert, Blue Feather Edges, 11 1/4 In. 460.00
Cheese Bell, Jasperware, Blue, Relief Classical Figures, Oak Leaf & Acorn Borders, 9 1/2 In. 489.00
Cheese Dish, Blue & White, Black Handle, 6 x 9 In. 120.00
Cheese Dish, Green, Jasper Dip, Cover, Round, White Relief Classical Figures, 11 In. 270.00
Cheese Dish, Jasperware, Blue, White Ferns, Pine Branches, 11 x 12 1/2 In., Pair 1410.00
Coffee Cann & Saucer, Jasperware, Tricolor, Leaves, Flower Garland, c.1850, 4 3/4 In. 1293.00
Coffee Set, Jasper Dip, Blue, Creamer, Sugar, Cover, 3 Piece 999.00

Cologne Bottle, Jasperware, Black, Cover, Late 19th Century, 8 In., Pair 380.00
Compote, Fairyland Luster, Elves, Mushrooms, Brown Fairies, 4 3/4 x 3 1/4 In. 4600.00
Compote, Moonlight Luster, Nautilus Shell, Stand, c.1820, 7 1/2 In. 2468.00
Compote, Moonlight Luster, Oval, Loop Handles, Raised Base, c.1820, 5 1/2 In. 999.00
Cruet, Majolica, Mottled, Pewter Top, 6 1/2 In. 168.00
Cup, Cover, Jasper Dip, Green, Cylindrical Shape, Rope Twist Handle, Lattice, 2 1/2 In. 2700.00
Cup, Pierced Cover, Jasper Dip, White, Rope Twist Handle, Lattice, 18th Century, 2 1/2 In. 2585.00
Cup & Saucer, Mustache, Majolica, Argenta Ocean 196.00
Dish, Man, Woman, Child, Polychrome, Scalloped Rim, E. Lessore, 7 3/8 x 9 1/4 In. 940.00
Dish, Queen's Ware, Puce, Leaf Border, Flower, Octagonal Shape, c.1800, 9 3/4 In., Pair 1528.00
Dish, Shell, Woman Reading To Children, Landscape, E. Lessore, c.1861, 8 5/8 In. 999.00
Ewer, Wine, Rosso Antico, Leaf Spout, Loop Handle, Early 1800s, 17 1/2 In. 3525.00
Figurine, Bear, Black, Basalt, c.1913, 4 3/4 In. 705.00
Figurine, Kangaroo, Celadon, Green Glaze, c.1927, 8 1/4 In. 940.00
Figurine, Polar Bear, Skeaping, Cream, Wood Base, c.1927, 7 In. 235.00
Figurine, Pug Dog Head, Smoking Pipe, Pink Collar, 1880, 3 1/2 In. 9400.00
Figurine, Taurus The Bull, Arnold Machin Model, Basalt, c.1966, 14 1/2 In. 264.00
Figurine, Tiger & Buck, Moonstone Glaze, c.1927, 8 In. 295.00
Figurine, Venus, Black Basalt, 19th Century, 20 3/4 In. 1645.00
Fruit Basket, Underplate, Oval, Pierced Border, c.1850, 9 In., Pair 529.00
Garden Pot, Majolica, Cobalt Blue, Blackberry, c.1868, 10 1/2 In. 805.00
Garden Seat, Majolica, Bird, Fan, Blue, Green Ground, Fans, Birds On Branches, 17 In. 2300.00
Garden Seat, Muses, Earthenware, Majolica Glazes, Hexagonal, 17 1/2 In. 2235.00
Jam Jar, Glazed Pottery, Brass, 19th Century, 2 x 4 1/2 In. 40.00
Jardiniere, Jasper Dip, Black, Applied White Classical Relief, 19th Century, 10 1/4 In. 410.00
Jug, Caneware, Molded Collar, Handle, Boys, Feathered Crown, Enamel Trim, 7 3/4 In. 2468.00
Jug, Caterer, Majolica, Frederick Bret Russel, c.1867, 11 In. 690.00
Jug, Caterer, Majolica, Multicolored, Jeweled Medallions, c.1890, 7 3/8 In. 325.00
Jug, Jasper Dip, Crimson, White Relief Florets, Pewter Rim, Hinged Cover, c.1920, 9 In. 2940.00
Jug, Jasper Dip, Yellow, Rope Twist Handle, Classical Figures, Grapevine Border, 6 1/2 In. 382.00
Jug, Jasper Dip, Yellow, Tapered, Black Classical Figures, Grapevine Border, 7 1/2 In. 588.00
Jug, Syrup, Jasperware, Tricolor, Rope Twist Handles, Green Ground, 7 3/4 In. 645.00
Lantern, Jasper Dip, Blue, Brass Mounted, Oval Medallions, Cylindrical, 11 In. 646.00
Medallion, Jasper Dip, Blue, Oval, White Relief Muse, Bentley, c.1775, 3 x 4 In. 1410.00
Medallion, Jasper Dip, Blue, Portrait, Shakespeare, Bentley, 2 3/4 x 3 3/4 In. 1410.00
Medallion, Jasper Dip, Blue, White Portrait, Sobieski, Oval, 2 3/4 x 3 3/4 In. 529.00
Medallion, Jasperware, Classical Figure, Blue, White, Frame, 2 3/4 x 1 1/4 In. 380.00
Mug, Investiture, Welsh Dragon, Prince Of Wales Feathers, Richard Guyatt, c.1969, 4 In. 95.00
Oyster Plate, Green, Pink, 9 x 7 1/2 In. 345.00
Oyster Plate, Majolica, St. Louis Pattern, Oriental Floral Motif, 9 In. 245.00
Pin, Fairyland Luster, Gilt Coil, Oriental Dragon, Round, 1920s, 2 In. 460.00
Pin, Jasper Dip, Blue, Medallion, Applied Flower, Clock Dial, 14K Gold, 1 1/4 In. 355.00
Pitcher, Jasperware, Classical Figural, White, Mauve Borders On Green, 8 In. 127.00
Pitcher, Table, Jasperware, Blue, Classical Scenes, Silvered Lid, c.1890, 6 1/4 In. 435.00
Plant Stand, Flow Blue, 20th Century, 20 x 9 3/4 In. 475.00
Planter, Cameo Figures, Classical, Swags, Basalt, 7 x 8 In. 410.00
Planter, Jasper Dip, Blue, White Relief Classical Figures, Arts, Lion's Masks, 5 1/2 In. 215.00
Plaque, Black, Dancing Hours, Basalt, Frame, 1800s, 5 x 15 In. 468.00
Plaque, Earthenware, Romeo, Raised Gilt Ground, Round, Thomas Allen, c.1881, 15 In. 1295.00
Plaque, Fairyland Luster, Fairies, Bat, Multicolored, 10 1/2 x 11 3/4 In. 8625.00
Plaque, Jasper Dip, Blue, White Relief, Round, c.1880, 5 In. 2350.00
Plaque, Jasper Dip, Green, Offering To Peace, c.1850, 6 x 12 In. 765.00
Plaque, Jasper Dip, Green, White Relief Children, Rectangular, 5 1/2 x 11 1/4 In. 1410.00
Plaque, Jasper Dip, Lilac, Applied Relief, Women With Tambourines, Oval, 5 1/2 x 7 3/4 In. 440.00
Plaque, Jasper Dip, Lilac, Applied White Relief Venus, Frame, Oval, 6 3/4 x 9 1/4 In. 4406.00
Plaque, Jasper Dip, Lilac, Winged Angel Holding Garland, Urn Of Fire, Oval, 4 1/2 x 6 In. 1060.00
Plate, Botanical, Reticulated Rim, 8 1/2 In. 170.00
Plate, Cauliflower, 8 1/4 In. 225.00
Plate, Dessert, Florentine, Polychrome Flower Spray, Blue Border, 8 3/4 In. 180.00
Plate, Fish, Majolica, Turquoise, Triple, 9 In. 690.00

Plate, Formosa, Signed, 9 1/4 In. 80.00
Plate, Fort Ticonderoga Bicentennial, 1755-1955, Rose Tones 50.00
Plate, Grape & Strawberry, Turquoise Ground, 9 In. 252.00
Plate, Grape Leaf, Strawberry, Yellow Ground, 9 In. 250.00
Plate, Majolica, Cobalt Blue, Botanical, Reticulated Rim, 8 3/4 In. 345.00
Plate, Majolica, Cobalt Blue, Lobster, Vegetable Border, 8 1/2 In. .... 750.00 to 1840.00
Plate, Majolica, Ocean, Center Shell & Seaweed Sprig, Waves Border, 9 In., 8 Piece 805.00
Plate, Majolica, Stork, In Marsh, Reticulated Rim, 9 In. 1006.00
Plate, Majolica, Water Lily, Dragonfly, 8 3/4 In. 196.00
Plate, Scalloped, Pink Luster Star Design, Fruit Basket, 9 1/8 In., 12 Piece 230.00
Plate, Schooner & Rope Knot Design, 7 In. 25.00
Plate, Shells, Sea Life, Pearlware, Feather Edges, Green Ribbon Borders, 7 3/4 In., 4 Piece 345.00
Plate, Trophy, Jasper Dip, Black, Flower Border, Classical Figures, Late 1800s, 8 3/4 In. 1175.00
Plate, Williamsburg, Capitol Scene, Governor's Palace, Raleigh Tavern, 12 Piece 130.00
Platter, Blue & White, Yale College & State House, 16 In. 205.00
Platter, Majolica, Argenta, Strawberry, Ribbon, Bow, 16 1/2 In. 219.00
Potpourri, White Smear Glaze, Squat, Upturned Loop Handles, Early 1800s, 4 In. 380.00
Punch Bowl, Lahore Design, Swags, Hanging Lanterns, Yellow Ground, Footed, 11 In. 8625.00
Sardine Box Base, Argenta, Majolica, Basketweave & Fruit 11.00
Slave Medallion, Jasperware, Man, Kneeling, Am I Not A Man & Brother?, c.1787 .... 2056.00
Sugar Shaker, Jasperware, Blue, Classical Figures, Dome Top, c.1900, 6 1/2 In. 290.00
Sweetmeat Set, Blue & White, Silver Plate Frame, 4 x 6 In. 130.00
Tazza, Majolica, Louis XV, Deer, Pierced Border, 3 Paw Feet, c.1878, 9 In. 355.00
Teapot, Cover, Jasperware, Tricolor, Diceware, Drum Shape, c.1850, 4 1/4 In. 3175.00
Teapot, Jasperware, Lavender, 3 3/4 x 4 1/2 In. 610.00
Tobacco Jar, Dome Cover, Jasper Dip, Black, Cylindrical, Lion Mask, Ring Handles, 6 1/4 In. 470.00
Tray, Argenta, Pastel, Wicker, Reticulated Rim, 10 In. 645.00
Tray, Majolica, Swimming Seal, Seal Handles, 17 In. 316.00
Umbrella Stand, Majolica, Cobalt Blue, Peacock Feather, Yellow Ribbon, 21 3/4 In. 6325.00
Urn, 2 Covers, Pearlware, Handle, Bulbous, Allegorical Decoration, 9 3/4 x 7 1/2 In. 235.00
Urn, Cover, Cameo, Basalt, 1800s, 9 In. 468.00
Urn, Creamware, Chestnut, 2 Part, Applied Handles, Ribbed, Beaded, 9 x 4 1/2 In. 550.00
Urn, Jasperware, Blue, Applied Women Carrying Fruit, Garlands, Wreaths, 10 3/4 In., Pair 1150.00
Vase, Black Basalt, Lion & Mask Handle, Bottle Shape, Marked, 1868, 14 In. 1295.00
Vase, Black Basalt, Raised Goat Mask Handles, 20th Century, 7 1/2 In., Pair 881.00
Vase, Black, White, Basalt, Portland, 9 1/2 x 7 In. 556.00
Vase, Butterfly Luster, Mottled Blue, Double Bulbous, 6 1/2 In. 460.00
Vase, Cover, Jasper Dip, Black, Classical Figures, Medallions, Zodiac, Leaf Borders, 12 1/2 In. 2233.00
Vase, Cover, Jasper, Light Blue, 3 Persians, Medallion, Garlands, Zodiac, 16 In. 7050.00
Vase, Dragon Luster, Dragon, Green Mottled Ground, 11 1/4 In. 3680.00
Vase, Dragon, Gilt, Magenta Ground, Luster, 9 In. 450.00
Vase, Fairyland Luster, Argus, Pheasant, Birds, Flowers, Tapered, Footed, 12 In. 6325.00
Vase, Fairyland Luster, Brown Goblins, Butterflies, Fairies, 8 1/2 In. 7475.00
Vase, Fairyland Luster, Butterfly Woman Seated In Tree, Gold Accents, 8 In. 2185.00
Vase, Fairyland Luster, Fairies Under Bridge, Seated On Cliff, Spider, Web, 8 In. 345.00
Vase, Fairyland Luster, Imps On Bridge, Boy With Wings, Bird, 10 1/2 In. 7475.00
Vase, Fairyland Luster, Sky, c.1920, 13 3/4 In. 7638.00
Vase, Fairyland Luster, Tree Serpent, Flame Luster Sky, Flared Base & Rim, 11 In. 7475.00
Vase, Gilded Foo Dog Mask, Ring Handles, Courtesans, Japonesque, 6 1/4 In., Pair 1765.00
Vase, Jasper Dip, Black, Bottle Shape, Infant Academy, Early 1800s, 7 1/2 In. 1528.00
Vase, Jasper Dip, Black, Man Wearing Phrygian Cap, 10 1/4 In. 2585.00
Vase, Jasperware, Tricolor, Applied Leaves, Garlands, Early 1800s, 5 1/8 In., Pair 2705.00
Vase, Jasperware, Tricolor, Lilacs, Leafy Vines, Garland, Lion Masks, Late 1800s, 5 In. 590.00
Vase, Leaves, Fruits, Gilded, Auro, Black, Basalt, c.1885, 9 In. 1998.00
Vase, Pot, Cover, Willow, Flame Luster Ground, 8 1/2 In. 3738.00
Vase, Queen's Ware, Dragon, Polychrome Enamel, 1872, 9 In., Pair 1116.00
Vase, Sleeping Sea Lion, Green Glaze, Marked, 1927, 7 3/4 In. 530.00
Vase, Trumpet, Fairyland Luster, Black, Butterfly Women, c.1920, 8 In. 2705.00
Veilleuse, Queen's Ware, Cylindrical, Pierced, Covered Teapot, c.1790, 10 3/4 In. 259.00

WELLER pottery was first made in 1872 in Fultonham, Ohio. The firm moved to Zanesville, Ohio, in 1882. Artwares were introduced in 1893. Hundreds of lines of pottery were produced, including Louwelsa, Eocean, Dickens Ware, and Sicardo, before the pottery closed in 1948.

LOUWELSA
WELLER

Ansonia, Vase, 11 In. 65.00
Ardsley, Bowl, Flower Frog, Twisted Rim, 14 1/2-In. Bowl 441.00
Ardsley, Vase, Double, Cattails, Water Lilies, 10 In. 115.00
Ardsley, Vase, White Flowers, Cattails, Flared, 12 In. 185.00
Art Nouveau, Vase, Sculpted Iris, Orange, Green, Brown, 9 In. 960.00
Assyrian, Vase, Egyptian Design, Cylindrical, 9 1/2 In. 360.00
Aurelian, Mug, Mountain Ash Seed Pods, 6 1/4 In. 184.00
Aurelian, Vase, Dandelions, Brown Glaze, Twisted Form, Marked, Signed, 12 In. 300.00
Aurelian, Vase, Irises, Yellow, Red, 14 3/8 In. 1150.00
Aurelian, Vase, Purple, Golden Grapes, Incised, 20 In. 920.00
Aurelian, Vase, Roses, Signed, H. Haubrick, 17 In. 1015.00
Baldin, Jardiniere, Pedestal, Marked, 35 x 15 In. 1017.00
Baldin, Vase, Apples, Embossed, Blue Matte Ground, 9 3/4 x 5 1/2 In. 489.00
Barcelona, Console Set, Handled Bowl, Candle Stands, Early 1900s, 8 In., 3 Piece 175.00
Barcelona, Ewer, Hand Thrown, Marked, 9 In. 120.00
Barcelona, Vase, Hand Thrown, Handles, Marked, 8 In. 150.00
Barcelona, Vase, Hand Thrown, Handles, Marked, 18 In. 960.00
Bedford, Vase, Molded Flowers, Glossy, 8 1/4 In. 104.00
Blue Drapery, Wall Pocket, 9 x 5 1/2 In. 206.00
Camelot, Compote, Yellow, Greek Key Design, 4 1/2 x 8 In. 645.00
Chase, Vase, Tan Matte Glaze, White Design, Bulbous, Marked, 5 1/2 In. 300.00
Claywood, Bowl, Running Mice, Incised, Brown Ground, 2 x 3 1/4 In. 105.00
Coppertone, Bowl, Flower Frog, Frog, Lily Pads, Stamped, 16 In. 600.00
Coppertone, Bowl, Frog, Lotus Blossom, Pads, Marked, 15 1/2 x 10 1/4 In. 460.00
Coppertone, Bowl, Lily Pad, Rock Shaped Flower Frog, 12 1/2 In. 345.00
Coppertone, Figurine, 2 Dancing Frogs, On Lily Pad, Marked, 16 1/2 x 11 1/2 In. 8225.00
Coppertone, Figurine, 2 Frogs Embracing, Signed, 16 1/2 x 12 In. .... *ILLUS* 7780.00
Coppertone, Figurine, Frog, Cement Filled, 6 In. 480.00
Coppertone, Figurine, Turtle, Brown, Green Splotches, 6 1/4 In. 510.00
Coppertone, Vase, 2 Frogs Perched On Sides, Marked, Paper Label, 7 1/2 In. 1560.00
Coppertone, Vase, Flared Mouth, Square Base, 6 3/4 In. 115.00
Coppertone, Vase, Frog Holding Lotus Flower, 4 1/4 x 4 1/2 In. 230.00
Coppertone, Vase, Pedestal, Green Matte Ground, Bronzed, 8 1/2 x 5 3/4 In. 230.00
Cornish, Vase, Blue Glaze, 10 3/8 In. 316.00
Cottonwood, Urn, c.1920, 14 x 9 In. 1989.00
Crab, Flower Frog, 2 x 6 In., Pair 118.00
Creamware, Candlestick 95.00
Dickens Ware, Ewer, 2 People At Water Pump, Marked, No. 580, 11 1/2 In. 956.00
Dickens Ware, Vase, Chief Hollow Horn Bear, Edwin Pickens, 10 1/4 In. 1528.00
Dickens Ware, Vase, David Copperfield, Street Scene, Quote, 17 In. 820.00
Dickens Ware, Vase, Pillow, 2 Men Playing Checkers, John Herold, 8 7/8 In. 630.00
Dickens Ware, Vase, Pillow, 4 Kittens, Painted, Carved, 4-Footed, Marked, 9 1/2 x 10 In. 2990.00
Dickens Ware, Vase, Satan Cast From Heaven, Archangel Michael, 16 1/4 In. 3785.00
Dickens Ware, Vase, Shouldered, 4-Fold Rim, Ghost Bull, 8 1/2 In. 748.00
Dickens Ware, Vase, Woman Golfer, 2 Round Handles Blend Into Rim, 10 1/4 In. .... *ILLUS* 1528.00
Eocean, Vase, Bud, Flowers, 5 1/4 In. 127.00
Eocean, Vase, Iris, Magenta, Lavender, Black To Gray Ground, Signed, 9 1/4 x 4 1/2 In. 2070.00
Eocean, Vase, Ruby Nasturtium, 5 1/4 In. 210.00
Eocean Rose, Vase, 5 Flowers Around Shoulder, Short Neck, c.1900, 6 In. 215.00
Etched Matte, Vase, Flowers, Outlined, Tan Matte Ground, 12 1/4 In. 1380.00
Etna, Vase, Blue Pansy, Yellow Stamen, Gray Ground, Impressed, 5 1/4 x 5 1/2 In. 200.00
Etna, Vase, Embossed Red Roses, Marked, 10 In. 185.00
Etna, Vase, Flower, 6 In. 85.00
Flemish, Vase, Plums, 12 In. 280.00
Florenzo, Vase, 6 1/2 In. 80.00

Weller, Coppertone, Figurine, 2 Frogs Embracing, Signed, 16 1/2 x 12 In.

Weller, Dickens Ware, Vase, Woman Golfer, 2 Round Handles Blend Into Rim, 10 1/4 In.

Weller, Hudson, Vase, Pink & Yellow Flowers, Blue Shaded To Green Ground, Flared Rim, 8 In.

Floretta, Vase, Poppies, Red, Green, Gray Shaded To White, Bulbous, 12 1/4 In. 390.00
Forest, Jardiniere, Pedestal, Landscape, 27 x 11 In. 960.00
Forest, Planter, 6 1/2 x 17 In. 1020.00
Forest, Umbrella Stand, 22 In. 588.00
Forest, Vase, Cylindrical, Marked, 19 In. 840.00
Frosted Matte, Vase, Curdled Yellow Green, Brown Ground, Flared Rim, 13 x 6 In. 2115.00
Gardenware, Duck, Figurine, Hollow, Glazed Exterior, Painted Bill, Feet, Eyes, 9 1/2 x 5 In. 110.00
Gardenware, Figurine, Girl Holding Duck, Bisque, 14 In. 269.00
Glendale, Vase, Bird Near Nest, Speckled Eggs, 6 3/8 In. 374.00
Glendale, Vase, Embossed Flowers, Birds, Butterflies, 12 In. 705.00
Golden Glow, Vase, Yellow, Brown, Handles, Footed, c.1920, 8 1/2 In. 80.00
Greenbrier, Ewer, 12 In. 35.00
Greora, Pot, Strawberry, 8 1/4 In. 259.00
Greora, Vase, Flared, Green Design, Rust Shaded To Blue Ground, Footed, 9 In. 410.00
Hobart, Flower Frog, 2 Ducks, Ivory Matte Glaze, Marked, 6 1/2 x 9 In. 185.00
Hobart, Vase, Woman, Holding Her Dress, Lilac Faded To Green, Stamped, 11 In. 155.00
Hudson, Jug, Ear Of Corn, Blue Ground, Signed, Leffler, 9 In. 1915.00
Hudson, Lamp Base, Roses, Blue Ground, 22 1/2 In. 330.00
Hudson, Vase, Berries, Leaves, Blue Ground, 10 In. 230.00
Hudson, Vase, Blue, White Wild Roses, Gray To Blue Matte Ground, Signed, 8 x 4 In. 489.00
Hudson, Vase, Bud, Blooming Blackberry Plant, Blue Ground, 10 In. 185.00
Hudson, Vase, Cherry Blossom, Pink To Green Ground, Signed, M. Laughlin, 13 x 4 1/2 In. 748.00
Hudson, Vase, Daisy, Gray To Ivory Matte Ground, 9 3/4 x 5 In. 430.00
Hudson, Vase, Dogwood Flowers, 2-Tone Red Matte Glaze, Marked, 9 1/2 In. 1915.00
Hudson, Vase, Dogwood Flowers, Green Leaves, Morris, 7 1/4 In. 575.00
Hudson, Vase, Iris, Shouldered, Signed, Marked, 15 In. 1435.00
Hudson, Vase, Lilac, Blue To Tan Matte Ground, 12 x 4 1/2 In. 2875.00
Hudson, Vase, Lily Of The Valley, Blue Ground, Oval, Sarah Timberlake, 9 x 4 In. 558.00
Hudson, Vase, Lily Of The Valley, Pillsbury, 9 In. 805.00
Hudson, Vase, Peonies, Pink, White, Gold, Marked, 23 1/8 In. 4830.00
Hudson, Vase, Pink & Yellow Flowers, Blue Shaded To Green Ground, Flared Rim, 8 In. ..... *ILLUS* 440.00
Hudson, Vase, Tapering, High Shoulder, Pink Tulips, Green Leaves, Matte Glaze, 10 1/4 In. 316.00
Hudson, Vase, White, Red, Blue Flowers, Leaves, Gray To Pink Matte Glaze, Walch, 10 3/4 In. 600.00
Jap Birdimal, Hair Receiver, Viking Ships, Blue Ground, 2 x 4 In. 646.00
Jap Birdimal, Jardiniere, Moonlit Scene, Trees, Impressed, 7 3/8 x 9 In. 58.00
Jardiniere, Bulbous, Fruit, Leaves, Pedestal, Ivory Ground, Brown Wash, 39 In., Pair 2300.00
Jewel, Umbrella Stand, White Shaded To Green Shaded To Blue, 22 1/2 In. 705.00
Jewell, Vase, Woman Picking Apples, Incised, Marked, 12 3/4 In. 1015.00
Kenova, Vase, Applied Turtle, Multitoned Green Matte Glaze, Marked, 5 In. 1320.00
Kenova, Vase, Organic Design, Green & Brown Matte Glaze, Cylindrical, Marked, 9 In. 206.00
Klyro, Wall Pocket, Roses, Grapes, 7 1/2 In. 115.00
Knifewood, Vase, Daisies & Butterflies, Black Ground, 4 1/4 x 4 1/4 In. 353.00
L'Art Nouveau, Umbrella Stand, Marked, 24 In. 1020.00
L'Art Nouveau, Vase, Orange Flowers, Flowing Leaves, 8 3/4 In. 206.00

LaSa, Vase, Landscape, Pine Trees, Lake, Mountains, Iridescent, 8 1/2 In. 489.00
LaSa, Vase, Landscape, Red, Gold, Signed, 8 5/8 In. 549.00
LaSa, Vase, Rounded, Palm Trees, Mountains, Water, 3 1/2 In. 115.00
LaSa, Vase, Tropical Landscape, Iridescent Glaze, Shouldered, 10 In. 420.00
LaSa, Vase, Tropical Scene, 9 1/4 In. 980.00
Lonhuda, Ewer, Ed Abel, c.1895, 8 7/8 In. 805.00
Lonhuda, Powder Box, 2 1/2 In. 489.00
Lorber, Vase, Woman Picking Apples, 11 1/2 In. 1700.00
Loru, Vase, Flower Form, Slender, Red To Purple, 10 In. 69.00
Louwelsa, Ewer, Geraniums, Brown Glaze, Marked, Signed, M. Mitchell, 22 In. 540.00
Louwelsa, Ewer, Indian Portrait, Feather In Hair, Signed, 12 1/2 In. 2400.00
Louwelsa, Ewer, Indian Portrait, Headdress, Turquoise Necklace, Brown Glaze, 12 1/2 In. 1795.00
Louwelsa, Jug, Mouse On Corncob, Brown Glaze, Signed, Abel, Marked, 8 In. 1795.00
Louwelsa, Lamp, Kerosene, Flowers, Round, Red Glass Shade, Signed, Marked, 25 In. 300.00
Louwelsa, Rembrandt Portrait, Brown Glaze, Gallant Cavalier, Early 1900s, 14 In. 825.00
Louwelsa, Tankard, Monk, Brown Glaze, Signed, L. J. Burgess, 11 In. 1912.00
Louwelsa, Vase, Berries, Handles, Brown Glaze, Marked, 4 1/2 In. 90.00
Louwelsa, Vase, Berries, Leaves, Brown Glaze, Bulbous, Slender Neck, No. 109, 4 In. 150.00
Louwelsa, Vase, Buttercups, Brown Glaze, Marked, 3 3/4 In. 90.00
Louwelsa, Vase, Cavalier Man, 14 1/4 In. 489.00
Louwelsa, Vase, Clovers, Brown Glaze, Gourd, Marked, No. 468, 5 1/4 In. 120.00
Louwelsa, Vase, Dog, 12 1/4 In. 1150.00
Louwelsa, Vase, Nasturtium, Cobalt Blue Ground, 8 1/2 x 3 3/4 In. 1150.00
Louwelsa, Vase, Native American, 1901, 13 5/8 In. 2185.00
Louwelsa, Vase, Owl To Pounce On Mice, 15 1/8 In. 2990.00
Louwelsa, Vase, Pansy, Brown Glaze, Squat, 2 3/4 In. 90.00
Louwelsa, Vase, Wheat, Handles, Brown Glaze, Marked, 4 1/2 In. 120.00
Louwelsa, Vase, White Violets, Brown Glaze, Ruffled Rim, Marked, 3 1/2 In. 150.00
Louwelsa, Vase, Yellow Daffodils, H.M., 11 In. 660.00
Louwelsa, Vase, Yellow Flowers, Ruffled Rim, Brown Glaze, 3 1/2 In. 120.00
Marengo, Vase, Palm Trees, Orange Ground, 6-Sided, 11 1/2 In. 294.00
Marvo, Pitcher, Brown Glaze, 8 In. 115.00
Muskota, Flower Frog, Nude & Swan, 7 1/2 x 7 1/2 In. 275.00
Orris, Wall Pocket, Embossed Flowers & Columns, Brown & Green Glaze, 8 x 4 1/2 In. 120.00
Roma, Vase, Ivory, Bottle Shape, Squat Base, Elongated Neck, 13 1/2 In. 176.00
Roma, Vase, Stylized Dogwood, Marked, 10 In. 185.00
Roma, Wall Pocket, Dupont Design, 10 1/4 x 5 In. 206.00
Sabrinian, Vase, Lavender Glaze, Seahorse Handles, 10 1/4 x 5 In. 315.00
Sicardo, Bowl, Swirling Flowers, Art Nouveau, 4 x 8 In. 460.00
Sicardo, Bowl, Swirling Flowers, Footed, Art Nouveau, 4 x 8 In. 315.00
Sicardo, Plaque, Spider In Web, Berry Vine, Leaves, 15 1/4 In. 7475.00
Sicardo, Vase, Clovers, Green, Blue, Pink, Yellow Iridescent, Double Gourd, Signed, 7 1/4 In. 1320.00
Sicardo, Vase, Flowers, Purple Metallic Glaze, Iridescent, Pillow Form, Footed, Signed, 7 1/2 x 8 In. 1920.00
Sicardo, Vase, Flowers, Purple, Green, Blue Iridescent, Double Gourd, Signed, 10 In. 1680.00
Sicardo, Vase, Leaves, Blue, Brown, Red, Purple Iridescent, Twisting Form, Signed, 8 In. 389.00
Sicardo, Vase, Luster, Leaves, Fruit, Iridescent Gold, Jacques Sicard, 1902-07, 5 In. 490.00
Sicardo, Vase, Purple, Red, Gold, Green, Gold Clover, Bulbous, Twisted, Signed, 5 1/4 In. 940.00
Sicardo, Vase, Stylized Flowers, Double Gourd, Ruffled Rim, Signed, Marked, 7 In. 1680.00
Sicardo, Vase, Stylized Flowers, Gourd, Signed, 5 1/4 In. 600.00
Silvertone, Vase, Basket, Ruffled Rim, Embossed, Silver Over Green Matte, 9 x 8 1/2 In. 175.00
Silvertone, Vase, Embossed Iris, Bulbous, Flared Rim, 5 1/2 In. 380.00
Silvertone, Vase, Embossed Yellow Flowers, Bulbous, Twisted Handles, 7 x 6 1/2 In. 294.00
Silvertone, Vase, White Flowers, Green, Purple, Flared Neck, Marked, 11 1/2 In. 390.00
Sydonia, Vase, Green, Molded Marsh Plants, 9 In. 46.00
Warwick, Candleholder, Paper Label, 2 1/4 x 5 1/8 In., Pair 198.00
Warwick, Planter, Berry Branch, Leaves, Ink Stamp, 5 7/8 x 6 5/8 In. 220.00
Warwick, Planter, Double, Center Handle, Ink Stamp, 4 3/4 x 5 3/4 In. 185.00
Warwick, Potpourri Jar, Cover, 5 x 6 1/2 In. 147.00
Warwick, Sugar, Cover, 5 In. 69.00
Warwick, Vase, Round Handle, Ink Stamp, 6 3/4 x 7 In. 188.00
Water Lily, Umbrella Stand, Cylindrical, Brown Glaze, 21 1/2 In. 390.00

Water Lily, Umbrella Stand, Molded, Multicolored Drip Glaze, 18 In. 210.00
Woodcraft, Basket, Hanging, Owls In Apple Tree, 5 x 9 3/4 In. 294.00
Woodcraft, Bowl, Oak Leaf, Squirrel, J. Butterworth, 4 3/4 x 7 In. 115.00
Woodcraft, Jardiniere, Cats, Birds, Flowers, 8 1/2 x 10 In. 660.00
Woodcraft, Planter, Brown, Green, Footed, 5 x 11 In. 210.00
Woodcraft, Planter, Cows, Landscape, Impressed Mark, 6 1/2 x 11 1/2 In. 920.00
Woodcraft, Vase, 3 Foxes, Cylindrical, Impressed Mark, 4 1/2 x 7 1/2 In. 269.00
Woodcraft, Vase, Bud, Yellow, Green, Brown, 10 1/2 In. 88.00
Woodcraft, Vase, Tree Trunk Foot, 9 3/8 In. 201.00
Woodcraft, Wall Pocket, Birds & Flowers, 15 x 11 1/2 In. 1320.00
Woodrose, Bowl, 7 In. 46.00
Woodrose, Pottery Group, 3-Handled Jardineres, Mid 20th Century, 3 1/2 To 6 In. 106.00
Zona, Dish, Baby, Bird, Bunny 40.00
Zona, Dish, Baby, Ducks 40.00
Zona, Pitcher, Paneled, Kingfisher, Landscape, Leaf Spout, Branch Handle, 8 1/4 In. 264.00

WEMYSS ware was made by Robert Heron in Kirkaldy, Scotland, from 1850 to 1929. It is a colorful peasant-type pottery that is occasionally found in the United States.

Figure, Pig, Seated On Haunches, Pink, Green Berries, Leaves, Bovey Tracey, Plichta, 17 In. 2129.00

WESTMORELAND GLASS was made by the Westmoreland Glass Company of Grapeville, Pennsylvania, from 1890 to 1984. They made clear and colored glass of many varieties, such as milk glass, pressed glass, and slag glass.

3 Bears, Plate, Milk Glass, 7 1/2 In. 12.00
3 Kittens, Plate, Milk Glass, 7 1/2 In. 14.00
3 Owls, Plate, Milk Glass, 7 1/2 In. 8.00
Animal Dish, Cat Cover, On Lacy Base, Milk Glass 150.00
Animal Dish, Hen Cover, On Basket Weave Base, Almond, 8 In. 145.00
Animal Dish, Lion Cover, Blue Milk Glass, 6 x 7 1/2 In. 250.00
Balking Mule, Plate, Milk Glass, 7 1/2 In. 14.00
Cherry & Cable, Cookie Jar, Cover, Milk Glass, Footed, 11 3/4 In. 225.00
Della Robbia, Candy Dish, Cover, 4 5/8 x 6 3/8 In. 130.00
English Hobnail, Basket, Milk Glass, 9 x 5 1/4 In. 58.00
English Hobnail, Bowl, Fruit, Green, Flared Rim, 2 3/4 x 9 3/4 In. 65.00
English Hobnail, Compote, Green, Flared Rim, 8-Sided Base, c.1930, 5 x 8 1/4 In. 138.00
English Hobnail, Pitcher, Milk, c.1930, 5 1/4 x 4 3/4 In. 125.00
English Hobnail, Punch Set, 14-In. Bowl, 20 1/2-In. Underplate, 14 Piece 445.00
English Hobnail, Vase, Pinched Neck, Green, 7 1/4 In. 135.00
Old Quilt, Bowl, Footed, Crimped Rim, 2 x 12 In. 165.00
Paneled Grape, Basket, Crimped Rim, 6 x 7 5/8 In. 100.00
Paneled Grape, Basket, Laurel Green, 11 x 7 1/4 In. 175.00
Paneled Grape, Compote, Ruby Stain, Ruffled Edge, 6 3/8 In. 110.00
Paneled Grape, Egg Set, Deviled Egg Plate, Condiment Dish, 13-In. Tray, 2 Piece 275.00
Paneled Grape, Epergne, 1-Lily, Milk Glass .... 275.00 to 345.00
Paneled Grape, Soap Dish, 6 3/4 x 5 3/16 In. 145.00
Paneled Grape, Torte Plate, Milk Glass, Scalloped Rim, 14 1/2 In. 128.00
Plate, Cupid & Psyche, Milk Glass, 7 1/2 In. 10.00
Plate, Easter Chicks, Milk Glass, 7 1/2 In. 11.00
Thousand Eye, Basket, Oval, Ruby Stain, 8 3/4 x 12 In. 295.00
Waterford, Urn, Cover, Ruby Stain, 15 In. 135.00

WHEATLEY Pottery was established in 1880. Thomas J. Wheatley had worked in Cincinnati, Ohio, with the founders of the art pottery movement, including M. Louise McLaughlin of the Rookwood Pottery. Wheatley Pottery was purchased by the Cambridge Tile Manufacturing Company in 1927.

Tile, Carved, Gray Ground, Square, c.1915, 6 In. 450.00
Tile, Knight On Horse, Tan, Blue Shield, Square, Arts & Crafts Oak Frame, 3 In. 420.00
Tile, Large Raised Leaf, Green Matte Glaze, Arts & Crafts Oak Frame, 6 In. 510.00

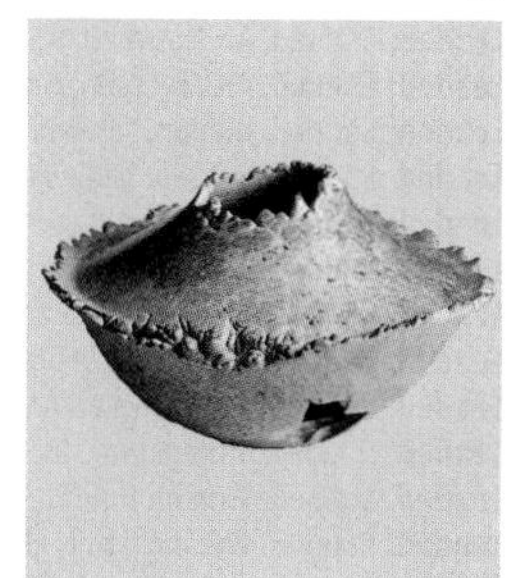

Willow, Pitcher, Bulbous, Wide Spout, Doulton Burslem, 11 In.

Wood Carving, Vessel, Maple Burl, Broad Leaf, Torn Rim, Center, Elliott, 1989, 11 1/2 x 17 In.

Tile, No. 1104, Ribbon, Gunmetal Black, Multicolored Glaze, c.1925, 4 1/4 In. 230.00
Tile, Stylized Grapes & Leaves, Matte Glaze, Cream, Green, Dark Blue, Square, c.1920, 4 In. 325.00
Tile Set, Raised Outline, Flowers, Geometric, Multicolored Matte, 4 In., 8 Piece 353.00
Vase, Barbotine Painting, Applied Leaves, Flowers, 1880s, 7 x 7 1/2 x 3 1/2 In. 1100.00
Vase, Bulbous, Footed, Frothy Green Matte Glaze, Stamped WP, 8 1/2 x 6 1/2 In. 588.00
Vase, Green Matte, Organic Design, 4 Handles, 14 In. 2400.00

WILLETS Manufacturing Company of Trenton, New Jersey, began work in 1879. The company made Belleek in the late 1880s and 1890s in shapes similar to those used by the Irish Belleek factory. They stopped working about 1912. A variety of marks were used, all including the name Willets.

Biscuit Jar, Roses, Forget-Me-Nots, Red, Pink, Signed, MB Mchand, 1909, 5 x 9 3/4 In. 395.00
Bowl, Roses, Mrs J Brucken, 1885-1909, 5 x 13 1/2 In. 1895.00
Mug, Flowers & Leaves, Dragon Handle, Signed, E. Meier, c.1905 .... 250.00
Mug, Portrait, Hinz Ceramic Photo Co., Detroit, Mich., c.1900, 5 1/2 In. 115.00
Pitcher, Milk, Grapes, Hand Painted, 7 In. 295.00
Pitcher, Tankard Style, Dragon Handle, Face Spout, 9 1/4 In. 425.00
Plate, Lily Pattern, Pink, Yellow, Scalloped Edge, Gold Splatter, 10 In. 50.00
Salt Cellar, Coiled Snake, Green Exterior, White Interior, 1 3/8 x 1 3/4 In. 55.00
Vase, Cylindrical, Green, 2 Cranes, 15 1/4 In. 635.00
Vase, Cylindrical, Herons, Woods, Hand Painted, 16 x 5 1/4 In. 1595.00
Vase, Daisies, Hand Painted, Belleek, 12 x 4 In. 265.00
Vase, Lilacs, Hand Painted, Ruffled, Gilded Top, c.1900, 11 In. 665.00
Vase, Pink Roses, High Gloss, 15 3/4 In. 1895.00
Vase, Rose Pattern, Hand Painted, Fire Gold Rim, Belleek, 18 1/2 x 8 In. 527.00
Vase, Roses, Hand Painted, Gilded Top Lip, 14 1/2 In. 1100.00
Vase, Storks On Branch, Hand Painted, Belleek, 12 1/4 In. 468.00

WILLOW pattern has been made in England since 1780. The pattern has been copied by factories in many countries, including Germany, Japan, and the United States. It is still being made. Willow was named for a pattern that pictures a bridge, birds, willow trees, and a Chinese landscape. Most pieces are blue and white.

Pitcher, Bulbous, Wide Spout, Doulton Burslem, 11 In. .... *ILLUS* 690.00
Platter, Well & Tree, Gold Highlighted Rim, Footed, Flow Blue, Crown Mark, 22 x 18 In. 805.00
Tea Set, Child's, 15 Piece 55.00

WINDOW glass that was stained and beveled was popular for houses during the late nineteenth and early twentieth centuries. The old windows became popular with collectors in the 1970s; today, old and new examples are seen.

Leaded, Bonded, 2 Rows Of Bull's-Eyes, Clear, Pine Frame, 60 x 9 In., 4 Piece 605.00
Leaded, Frank Lloyd Wright, Opalescent, Gilded, Zinc Cames, c.1909, 32 x 16 In. 6000.00
Leaded, Maiden, Long Hair, Swinging, Crescent Moon, Amber, Blue Green, 32 x 25 In. 4994.00
Leaded, Slag, Violet, Lime, Fleur-De-Lis Corners, Wood Frame, c.1900, 17 x 32 In. 275.00
Leaded, Stained, 3 Figures, 1 Figure Kneeling With Water Urn, Frame, 100 x 45 In. 2070.00

Leaded, Stained, Art Nouveau, Apothecary, Mortar & Pestle, Ivy, Frame, 24 x 36 1/2 In. 978.00
Leaded, Stained, Arts & Crafts, Glasgow Roses, Swag, Medallion, Jewel Tones, Frame, 28 x 43 In. . 352.00
Leaded, Stained, Bishop, Flowers, Geometric Borders, Steel Frame, 100 x 45 In. 2070.00
Leaded, Stained, Cafe For Ladies & Gents, 93 x 43 1/2 In. 719.00
Leaded, Stained, Christ Holding Bible, Behold, Stand At The Door & Knock, 50 x 11 In. 717.00
Leaded, Stained, Geometric, Poppies, Frame, 39 x 27 In. 527.00
Leaded, Stained, Scrolled Decoration, c.1900, 44 x 20 In. 294.00
Leaded, Stained, St. Francis, 3 Sections, c.1880, 39 x 38 & 40 x 35 & 40 x 35 In. 527.00
Leaded, Stained, Tree, Jeweled Amber, Geometrics, Flower Borders, 89 x 44 In. 1840.00
Leaded, Stained, Variegated Opalescent, Scrolled Designs, c.1900, 80 x 50 In. 588.00
Leaded, Stained, Woman Holding Cross, Flowers, Geometric Borders, Arched, 100 x 45 In. 2070.00
Leaded, Stained, Woman Saint, Flowers, Geometric Borders, Steel Frame, 100 x 45 In. 2070.00
Stained Glass, Wreath, Ribbons, Jewels, 1900s, 20 x 68 1/2 In. 413.00

WOOD CARVINGS and wooden pieces are listed separately in this book. Many of the wood carvings are figurines or statues. There are also wooden pieces found in other categories, such as Kitchen.

2 Deer, Glass Eyes, Germany, c.1940, 18 1/2 x 16 In. 1208.00
Acolyte, Shoulder Scarf, Necklace, Lacquered, Multicolored, 20 1/2 In. 328.00
Angel, Holding Papal Tiara, Multicolored, Gilded, 20th Century, 21 In. 529.00
Angel, Musical, Giltwood, Multicolored, 20th Century, 17 In. 295.00
Angel, Pine, Pleated Skirts, Winged Man, Platform Base, 13 x 8 In., Pair 1438.00
Angel, Playing Violin, Germany, 10 In. 150.00
Angel, Robe, Glass Eyes, Multicolored, Continental, 21 x 11 1/2 In., Pair 880.00
Antelope Head, Painted, Oval Plaque, 38 x 21 In. 1150.00
Bald Eagle, Stylized, Glass Eyes, Painted, Stippled, Pine Base, Ohio, 26 3/8 In. 4115.00
Bird, Baltimore Oriole, Early 1900s, 7 1/2 In. 77.00
Bird, Painted, Square Base, 2 3/4 In. 896.00
Blackamoor, Painted, Gilt, Italy, c.1900, 30 In. 1535.00
Boar Head, Germany, c.1920, 19 x 16 1/2 In. 460.00
Bowl, Oblong, Flared, Rosewood, Marked, Aubock, 2 1/4 x 9 1/4 x 3 In. 360.00
Boy's Head, Stand, Italy, 7 In. 384.00
Buddha, Gilt, Red Lacquered Plinth Stand, 21 x 9 In. 350.00
Buddha, Giltwood, Burma, 19th Century, 13 In. 165.00
Buddha, Robes, Lotus Base, Paint, Gilt, Oriental, 37 1/4 In. 978.00
Bust, Child, Signed, Gennarelli, 17 In. 390.00
Bust, Lady Liberty, Flowing Hair, Flower Wreath, 11 x 8 1/2 In. 720.00
Bust, Mephistopheles, Oak, Pierced, Scrolled Leafy Crest, 35 x 13 In. 441.00
Bust, Saint, Male, Head Tilted Back, Eyes Shut, Beard, Spain, 1800s, 11 1/2 In. 560.00
Candleholder, Samurai Figures, Inlaid Eyes, Japan, 18th Century, 19 In., Pair 235.00
Card Case, Merchants Card, Chinese, 4 1/2 x 3 In. 127.00
Cat, Seated, Tail Curved To Front, Painted, Pa., 14 1/2 x 11 In. 575.00
Centaur, Fighting, 8 1/4 x 8 1/4 In. 805.00
Cherub, Incised Wing, Hair, Glass Eyes, Painted, 7 x 4 1/4 x 22 In. 220.00
Cup, Hardwood, Open Blossom, Flowering Branches, Chinese, c.1800, 4 1/4 In. 325.00
Davy Crocket, Redwood, Bill Baker, California, Early 1900s, 77 In. 660.00
Deer, Standing, Softwood, Oversized Ears, Tack Eyes, Applied Tail, 6 3/4 x 9 In. 495.00
Deer, Standing, Softwood, Painted, Tack Eyes, 6 3/4 x 9 In. 495.00
Dog, Standing, Natural, Hatch Carved, 4 1/4 x 5 1/2 In. 195.00
Dragon, Ma Lung, Glass Eyes, Lacquered Surface, Chinese, 1800s, 19 In. 1880.00
Drummer, English Military Uniform, c.1925, 37 x 24 In. 690.00
Duck, Painted, Driftwood Base, 2 x 6 x 2 In. 413.00
Eagle, Banner, Independence, Now & Forever, Lucien Green, Me., 7 1/2 x 49 In. 4025.00
Eagle, Painted, Glass Bead Eyes, Square Base, Signed, G.M.H. 1916, 3 3/8 In. 588.00
Eagle, Pine, Spread Wings, Painted, Aaron Mountz, Penn., 8 x 12 In. 4200.00
Eagle, Pine, Spread Wings, Shield, Arrows, Boston, 43 In. 6500.00
Eagle, Spread Wings, Gilt, 1800s, 16 x 36 In. 1265.00
Eagle, Spread Wings, Holding Banner, Flag, Blue, Red, Gold, 21 x 82 In. 2760.00
Eagle, Spread Wings, Ribbon Banner, Wreath, Berry, 20 x 32 1/2 In. 440.00
Eagle, Spreadwings, Feather Details, Gilt, 29 x 34 In. 1410.00
Emperor Penguin, Standing, Iron Tack Eyes, Applied Flippers, c.1931, 9 In. 5581.00

Gnome, Parrot On Arm, Painted, 1910-20, 17 x 11 x 6 In. 235.00
Group, 11 Birds, Driftwood Base, Painted, Stick Pin Bases, 15 1/2 In. 230.00
Gun Boat, Men Wearing Clogs, In Rowboat, Painted, Found Items, 1884, 16 In. 978.00
Head, Burl, Natural Surface, Nova Scotia, 11 x 15 In. 1783.00
Horse, Brown, Black Sponging, Red Blanket, Hair Mane, 13 x 10 In., Pair 805.00
Horse Head, Glass Eyes, Leather Ears, Horse Hair Mane, 10 x 16 x 3 In. 83.00
Humpback Whale, Silhouette, Clark Vorrheees, 37 In. 1300.00
Infant Christ, Robe, Parcel Gilt, Polychrome, Spanish Colonial, c.1815, 35 1/4 In. 3995.00
Kui Xing, Striding On Dragon, Coiled, 19th Century, Chinese, 27 1/2 In. 2286.00
Lion, Painted, Gilt, Ebonized Wood Base, Southeast Asia, 25 In. 763.00
Lion, Painted, Open Mouth, Wood Platform Mount, 1800s, 8 x 6 x 13 In. 940.00
Lion, Reclining, Front Legs Extended, Ebonized Base, 44 x 12 In., Pair 1880.00
Lion, Walnut, Glass Eyes, Folk Art, c.1900, 10 In. 35.00
Lobi, Kneeling Ancestor Figure, Mother & Child, Upper Volta, 23 1/2 In. 493.00
Mackerel, Painted, Hanging Chains, John Caldwell, 68 x 24 In. 2070.00
Madonna, Painted, Blue Shawl, Square Pedestal Base, 23 In. 3173.00
Madonna & Child, Ivory Face, Hands & Child, Heuvelmans, 12 3/4 In. 978.00
Man, Limbs Akimbo, Root, Nailhead Eyes, Southern U.S., 26 x 25 x 5 In. 4465.00
Man, Praying, Standing On Cloud, Angels, Cherubs, 19 1/2 x 7 1/2 In. 1093.00
Man, With Pipe, Wearing Hat, Pennsylvania, c.1925, 20 x 10 In. 1500.00
Man's Head, Joined Segments, Black Painted Stand, Folk Art, 14 1/2 In. 705.00
Mary Magdalene, Multicolored, Gilding, Continental, 32 3/4 In. 1150.00
Mask, Guro, Curved Horns, Ivory Coast, c.1900, 19 x 13 x 9 1/4 In. 410.00
Mask, Horns, Triangles, Guro, Ivory Coast, c.1950, 12 x 6 1/4 x 5 1/2 In. 410.00
Mask, Mende, Carved Hair, Finial, Sierra Leone, c.1950, 16 x 9 x 10 In. 4230.00
Mother & Child, Kneeling, Newborn Held To The Hip, Ivory Coast, 14 In. 165.00
Neck Rest, Africa, c.1950, 7 x 9 3/8 In. 176.00
Noisemaker, Turk's Head On Handle, Clacker, Oak, Walnut, Macrame, 8 x 6 In. 220.00
Osprey, Spread Wings, Clutching Fish, Painted, 17 x 9 In. 2015.00
Oxen, In Yoke, Stick Legs, Painted, 4 3/4 x 8 1/2 In., Pair 275.00
Oxen & Cart, Painted, Yoke, Wooden Wheels, 5 3/4 x 18 In. 330.00
Pagoda, Chinese, 3 Tier Temple, Tiled Roof, Carved Balustrade, 1800s, 24 1/2 In. 590.00
Panel, Landscape, Birds, Animals, Woman, Bagpipe Player, Chestnut, 46 x 31 In. 2480.00
Parrot, On Perch, Black Paint, Gilt, Square Base, Continental, 34 x 12 x 13 In. 635.00
Plaque, Classical, Demilune, Gilt, Urn, Putti, Griffins, 25 x 48 x 1 1/2 In. 330.00
Plaque, Cow, Relief, Black, White, A. Coursol, 1900s, 12 3/4 x 17 In. 230.00
Plaque, Eagle, Arrow, American Flag, Shield, Painted, c.1900 .... 22425.00
Plaque, Freedom Of America, Liberty, Flag, Griffins, Putto, 38 x 61 1/2 In. 3055.00
Plaque, George & Martha Washington Bust, Relief, Oval, 25 1/2 x 18 1/2 In., Pair 705.00
Plaque, Lion Head, Carnival, Deep Relief, Early 20th Century, 12 x 8 1/2 In. 470.00
Plaque, Lion Of Lucerne, Oak, After Bertel Thorvaldsen, Inscribed, 10 1/2 x 14 In. 230.00
Portrait, President McKinley, Poplar Board, 27 x 20 In. 1380.00
Putti, Holding Brush, Palette, Europe, 19th Century, 23 In. 400.00
Putto Head, Baroque, Lindenwood, Gesso, Austro-Germany, 1700s, 10 In. 205.00
Shield, Patriotic, Pine, Red Stripes, 13 Stars, Original Battens, c.1875, 32 1/2 In. 3450.00
Shield, Stars, Stripes, Red, White, Blue, Henry Cole, 1800s, 8 3/4 x 6 1/2 In. 1150.00
Ship, 8 Immortals, Chinese, 20th Century, 10 x 6 In. 120.00
Shorebird, Painted, Iron Stand, Marked, B, 8 1/2 In. 55.00
Sign, Lion Patrol, Rustic, Rough Cut, Mid 1900s, 8 1/2 x 25 In. 76.00
Sign, Rooster, Painted, 2-Sided, Panels, Sheet Metal Borders, 33 x 31 In. 410.00
Snail, On Bent Piece Of Grass, Japan, Early 1900s 69.00
Soldier, Blue & Red Coat, Tricornered Hat, Hands Crossed, c.1925, 68 1/2 In. 4800.00
St. John, Evangelist, Eagle At Feet, Multicolored, Continental, 24 x 12 x 10 In. 865.00
Stagecoach, Red & Yellow Paint, Varnished Horses, Wood Base, 18 In. 115.00
Trout Diorama, Painted Background, Frame, 28 1/2 x 23 In. 978.00
Vessel, Maple Burl, Broad Leaf, Torn Rim, Center, Elliott, 1989, 11 1/2 x 17 In. .... *ILLUS* 1298.00
Virgin Mary, Flower Basket, Fruitwood, Enamel, 8 In. 1293.00
Warrior, On Horse, Multicolored, Chinese, 28 x 34 In. 265.00
William Tell & Son, Carrying Cross Bow, Switzerland, c.1920, 17 In. 965.00
Woman, Mossi, Standing, Hands Held At Waist, Conical Breasts, 10 In. 205.00
Woman, Peasant, Walking Against Wind, Holding Bundle, 40 In. 236.00

WOODEN wares were used in all parts of the home. Wood was used for many containers and tools. Small wooden pieces are called *treenware* in England, but the term woodenware is more common in the United States. Additional pieces may be found in the Advertising, Kitchen, and Tool categories.

Airplane Propeller, Mahogany, Laminated, Copper Edge Tips, Gardner, 1900, 96 In. 940.00
Barrel, Lid, Stave Construction, Oak, Hickory, Gray Paint, New England, 18 1/2 x 29 In. 345.00
Bell, Liberty, Turned, Old Bronze Paint, Late 19th Century, 32 x 33 In. 705.00
Birdhouse, Joseph Lehn, Lancaster County, c.1875, 22 x 23 x 16 In. 965.00
Biscuit Jar, Oak, England, 6 1/4 x 5 1/2 In. 117.00
Bowl, Burl, Carved, Tapered Sides, 6 1/2 x 5 3/4 In. 358.00
Bowl, Feathers, Red Ground, Treen, 1800s, 5 x 17 1/2 In. 556.00
Bowl, Turned, James Prestini, c.1948, 2 1/2 x 7 In. 840.00
Bowl, Walnut, Plywood, Bent, James Prestini, c.1954, 6 x 15 3/4 In. 6600.00
Bowl Set, Salad, Teak, Finn Juhl, 1950s, 14 x 15-In. Serving Bowl, 13 Piece 9000.00
Brush Pot, Rosewood, Hardstone Decoration, Bird, Flowering Plum Tree, Chinese, 7 In. 3055.00
Bucket, Cover, 13 x 8 1/2 In. 520.00
Bucket, Cover, Red Paint, Multicolored Bands, Lancaster County, 10 x 11 1/2 In. 3300.00
Bucket, Cover, Stave Construction, Bentwood Laced Bands, Stencil Label, 16 In. 92.00
Bucket, Grain Painted, Wire Band, Bail Handle, 12 In. 55.00
Bucket, Kerosene, Stave Construction, Spigot, 4 Gal., 13 In. 395.00
Bucket, Old Yellow Paint Over Salmon, Stave Construction, Wire Bail Handle, 4 1/2 In. 259.00
Bucket, Peat, George III Style, Mahogany, Inlaid, Flared Slats, Tripod Base, 18 In. 265.00
Bucket, Peat, Mahogany, 3 Brass Bands, 2 Openwork Handles, Georgian, 10 x 25 1/2 In. 1528.00
Bucket, Peat, Mahogany, Brass Bands, George III, Late 1700s, 12 1/2 x 13 In. 2160.00
Bucket, Peat, Neoclassical, Mahogany, Brass, Waisted, Dutch, Early 1800s, 17 In. 529.00
Bucket, Peat, Oak, Brass Bands, Oval, Swing Handle, England, 11 1/2 x 15 In. 646.00
Bucket, Pine, Old Blue Paint, Bentwood Swing Handle, 3 Wood Bands, 14 In. 230.00
Bucket, Red Paint, Stamped Circles, 22 Staves, Wire Bail Handle, Penn., 7 3/4 In. 5175.00
Bucket, Stave Construction, Tapered, Wire Bail, Wood Handle, 12 1/2 x 10 1/4 In. 230.00
Bucket, Sugar, Cover, Blue Paint, Stave Construction, Bentwood Bands, Handle, 12 In. 400.00
Bucket, Sugar, Gray Paint, Stave Construction, Steel Tacks, Bentwood Handle, 13 In. 375.00
Bucket, Sugar, Old Green Paint, 8 1/2 In. 247.00
Bucket, Yellow Ground, Stave Construction, Wood Grain Stencil, Bail Handle, 12 x 9 In. 460.00
Bucket, Yellow Paint, 8 x 6 In. 1093.00
Bust, Man's Head, Beard, Mustache, Classical Style, Round Base, 1908, 8 In. 805.00
Canon, Parade, Black Paint, Olive Green, Red Stripes, Iron Strap Wheels, 20 x 20 In. 881.00
Canteen, Painted, 2 Iron Bands, Wood Plug, Impressed, N. Young, 19th Century, 9 1/2 In. 192.00
Carnival Gaming Pin, Painted Face, 15 x 3 1/4 In. 248.00
Carrier, Bentwood, Cover, Lapped Seams, Iron Tacks, Wire Bale Handle, 11 x 6 In. 460.00
Cheese Coaster, Mahogany, Boat Shape, Divider, Castors, Late 1700s, 17 1/4 In. 794.00
Cheese Tray, Mahogany, Crescent Bowl, Scrolled Ends, Georgian, England, 1800s, 17 In. 499.00
Cup, Turned, Painted, Treen, Joseph Long Lehn, Lancaster County, Penn., 1889, 3 1/4 In. 1315.00
Dish, Cherry Wood, 18th Century, 12 In. 395.00
Dish, Laminated Birch, Leaf, Tapio Wirkkala, Finland, c.1954, 11 1/2 In. 3276.00
Figurine, Geisha, Double Gourd Wine Flask, Japan, c.1900, 15 1/2 In. 1140.00
Firkin, Black Paint, 6 1/2 In. 290.00
Firkin, Blue Paint, Stave & Lapped Hoop Construction, Carved Wing Handle, 14 1/2 In. 705.00
Firkin, Blue Paint, Swing Handle, 14 In. 385.00
Firkin, Cover, Brown, 1800s, 12 x 11 In. 115.00
Firkin, Cover, Green Paint, Rosehead Nails, S. Weymouth, Mass., c.1800, 10 1/2 x 11 In. 1430.00
Firkin, Red Paint, Bail Handle, Marked, Geo. P. Lane & Son, Marlboro Depot, N.H., 9 3/4 In. 297.00
Firkin, Red Paint, Wood Bands, Swing Handle, 14 In. 330.00
Foot Warmer, Maple, Diamond & Circle Piercing, Painted, Wire Swing Handle, 6 x 10 In. 382.00
Game Rack, Pine, Gray Green Paint, Scalloped Crest, Iron Hooks, 14 x 25 In. 115.00
Gazebo, Gray Paint, Red Trim, Octagonal, 2 Benches, Miniature, 12 3/4 x 12 In. 1410.00
Hibachi, Keyaki Wood, 3 Drawers, Copper-Lined Burner, Japan, c.1900, 11 1/2 x 25 In. 115.00
Hibachi, Kiriwood, 2 Drawers, Copper Liner, Japan, Early 1900s, 12 x 26 In. 230.00
Humidor, Bear, Walking Stick, Brass Pan, Glass Eyes, Hinged Neck, Swiss, c.1900, 15 x 7 1/2 In. . . 2656.00

Jar, Cover, Camphorwood, Incised Rings, Raised Rings On Lid, 6 x 10 In. 518.00
Jar, Cover, Sponge Decoration, Red Over Yellow, Treen, 3 5/8 x 3 3/4 In. 865.00
Jardiniere, Regency Style, Mahogany, Slatted, Brass Handle, 3 Legs, 47 x 14 In., Pair 1000.00
Jardiniere, Regency Style, Mahogany, Slatted, Brass Handle, Liner, 21 x 14 In., Pair 880.00
Letter Holder, Victorian, Mahogany, 2 Shelves, c.1880, 15 x 8 x 9 In. 115.00
Mannequin, Artist's, Pine, Carved, Articulated Limbs, Stamped, RMS, 12 1/2 In. 518.00
Mirror, Maple, Molded, Round, Turned Handle, 19th Century, 14 x 8 In. 120.00
Mirror, Traveling, Hepplewhite, Mahogany Veneer, String Inlay, 9 5/8 x 6 1/2 In. 115.00
Piggin, Painted, 6 In. 259.00
Piggin, Painted, 7 In. 200.00
Platter, Turned, Black Walnut, Bob Stocksdale, Ca., 11 In. 840.00
Platter, Turned, James Prestini, c.1948, 16 1/2 In. 3600.00
Salt, Lehnware, Pink Paint, Strawberries, Treen, 2 In. 1725.00
Sugar, Cover, Green Paint, Early 19th Century, 6 x 9 In. 410.00
Tankard, Hinged Cover, Tapered, Burl, Footed, 3 Bun Feet, Continental, 7 x 7 In. 1725.00
Tray, Apple, Pine, Blue Paint, Cutout Handles, Pa., 1800s, 20 x 14 In. 715.00
Tray, George III, Mahogany, Oval, Late 1700s, 31 1/4 x 20 1/4 In. 2700.00
Tray, Inlaid Satinwood Butterfly, Sterling Silver Handles, Gallery, Oval, 2 1/2 x 18 1/2 In. 440.00
Tray, Marquetry, Stemmed Dogwood Buds, Flowers, Signed, Galle, 20th Century, 17 In. 149.00
Tray, Pine, Cutout Handholds, Dovetailed, Rose Head Nails, 44 x 18 In. 405.00
Tray, Serving, Federal, Mahogany, Figured, Oval, c.1800, 2 3/4 x 28 1/2 In. 3300.00
Tray, Sheraton, Mahogany, Shell Design, England, c.1900, 15 x 24 In. 235.00
Tray, Triangular, Morning Glories, Yellow Ground, Blue & Purple Overlay, Galle, c.1900, 5 In. 510.00
Trencher, Blue Paint, 1800s, 3 3/4 x 19 1/2 In. 468.00
Trencher, Hand Hewn, Aqua Green Paint, Scrubbed Interior, Maryland, 12 x 21 In. 430.00
Trencher, Hand Hewn, Green Paint, Scrubbed Interior, 11 x 19 1/2 In. 175.00
Wagon Wheel, Bittersweet Orange Paint, 48 In., Pair 385.00

WORCESTER porcelains were made in Worcester, England, from 1751. The firm went through many name changes and eventually, in 1862, became The Royal Worcester Porcelain Company Ltd. Collectors often refer to *Dr. Wall*, *Barr*, *Flight*, and other names that indicate time periods or artists at the factory. It became part of Royal Worcester Spode Ltd. in 1976. Related pieces may be found in the Royal Worcester category.

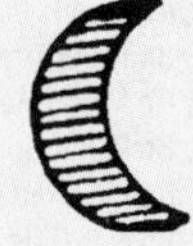

Basket, Round, Pierced Arched Sides, Center Crest, Handles, Early 1800s, 11 1/4 In. 2129.00
Beaker, Fruit, Gilt Edged Panel, Pink Ground, Flight & Barr, c.1800, 4 In. 3900.00
Biscuit Jar, Cover, Notched Underplate, Melon Shape, 5 1/4 x 6 1/4-In. Jar, 7 1/2-In. Plate 495.00
Bowl, Vegetable, Cover, Verona, Gold Trim, 2 7/8 x 8 In. 65.00
Bowl, Vegetable, Evesham, Oval, 2 1/8 x 9 5/8 x 6 3/4 In. 40.00
Butter, Cover, Flowers, Blue Transfer, c.1890 .... 95.00
Cake Plate, Flowers, White Ground, 11 In. 20.00
Cup & Saucer, Clementine 25.00
Cup & Saucer, Demitasse, Art Nouveau, Jeweled, Black Ground, Trees, Fruit, c.1915 .... 450.00
Cup & Saucer, Demitasse, Flowers, Pink Transfer, Gilt Edge, c.1889 .... 75.00
Cup & Saucer, Evesham 20.00
Egg Coddler, Flowers, 5 x 3 1/2 In. 60.00
Figurine, Giraffe, Lying Down, Manganese Spots, Grainger Lee & Co., 1820-37, 4 1/2 In. 3600.00
Figurine, Pied Woodpeckers, No. 3363, 4 In., Pair 150.00
Gravy Boat, Flowers, 4 x 7 3/4 In. 500.00
Jam Pot, Evesham, Apples, Berries, Cherries, 4 In. 45.00
Pie Server, Country Kitchen, Herbs & Spices, 10 3/8 In. 24.00
Pin Dish, Shell Shape, Applied Flowers, 1955 .... 58.00
Pitcher, Cream, Dr. Wall, Blue, White, 1700s, 3 1/2 In. 99.00
Pitcher, Dr. Wall, Blue, White, 1700s, 9 1/2 In. 468.00
Pitcher, Lemonade, Flower, Gilt Edge, c.1890, 7 1/4 In. 110.00
Plate, Dessert, Dr. Wall, Flowers, c.1790, 10 In. 950.00
Plate, Dinner, Woburn, Plumes & Flowers, Rope Edge, 10 1/2 In. 140.00
Plate, Hay Church, Wales, Signed, George Johnston, 1900, 8 1/2 In. 395.00
Plate Set, Dinner, Chamberlain & Co., Blue Border, Gilt Edge, 10 1/4 In., 9 Piece 560.00

World War I, Poster, Our Boys Need Sox, Knit Your Bit, American Red Cross, 30 x 20 In.

World War I, Poster, Treat 'Em Rough, Join The Tanks, U.S. Tank Corp., 19 1/4 x 14 In.

Sugar, Flowers, Gold Trim, 3 3/4 x 4 1/2 In. 300.00
Teapot, Flowers, 5 1/4 x 7 1/4 In. 500.00
Tureen, Underplate, Dr. Wall, 10 1/2 x 13 1/4 In. 80.00

WORLD WAR I and World War II souvenirs are collected today. Be careful not to store anything that includes live ammunition. Your local police will tell you how to dispose of the explosives. See also Sword and Trench Art.

WORLD WAR I, Beat Back The Hun With Liberty Bonds, Frame, 1918, 30 1/4 x 20 In. 86.00
Boots, U.S. Cavalry, Leather, Brown, 16 In. 77.00
Grenade Apron, Khaki, U.S. Army 22.00
Leggings, U.S. Army, Canvas, 6 Hooks, Size 3, Pair 18.00
Postcard, Camp Lee, Va., Bayonet Combat, Thompson Illustragraph, c.1918 .... 3.00
Postcard, Camp Lee, Va., Mess Time, Thompson Illustragraph, c.1918 .... 3.00
Poster, Americans All!, Victory Liberty Loan, H.C. Christy, 1919, 40 x 26 In. 462.00
Poster, Avez Vous Place Dans Votre Coeur Pour Nous?, DeMaris, France, 30 x 20 In. 358.00
Poster, Bank Fur Tirol Und Vorarlberg, W. Kuhn, Germany, 1918, 41 1/2 x 27 In. 165.00
Poster, Be A U.S. Marine, Man, American Flag Ground, J.M. Flagg, c.1918, 41 x 28 In. 1115.00
Poster, Be Ready, Join Now, England, 39 1/4 x 24 3/4 In. 99.00
Poster, Belgian Red Cross Donations May Be Sent, C. Buchel, England, 30 x 20 In. 220.00
Poster, Boys & Girls, You Can Help Uncle Sam, J.M. Flagg, 1918 .... 905.00
Poster, Come On!, Let's Finish The Job, Buy Victory Bonds, Canada, 36 x 24 In. 110.00
Poster, Halt!, Who Goes There?, Join British Ranks, London, 39 1/2 x 23 3/4 In. 110.00
Poster, Help Them, Keep Your War Savings Pledge, Casper Emerson Jr., 30 x 20 In. 145.00
Poster, Hygiene De Guerre, V. Prouve, France, 1918, 25 1/2 x 19 1/2 In. 110.00
Poster, Industrial Expansion, Buy Victory Bonds, Arthur Keelor, Canada, 36 x 24 In. 360.00
Poster, Jobs For Fighters, Soldier At Door, U.S. Employment Service, 25 x 15 In. 115.00
Poster, Keep Him Free, Buy War Savings Stamps, C.L. Bull, 1918, 30 x 20 In. 995.00
Poster, Our Boys Need Sox, Knit Your Bit, American Red Cross, 30 x 20 In. .... *ILLUS* 108.00
Poster, Rivets Are Bayonets, Drive Them Home!, J.E. Sheridan, 39 x 25 In. 138.00
Poster, See Him Through, Help Us To Help The Boys, Nov. 1918, 30 x 20 In. 66.00
Poster, Teamwork Builds Ships, U.S. Shipping Board, W.B. Stevens, 36 x 50 In. 2530.00
Poster, Together We Win, J.M. Flagg, 1917, 38 1/2 x 28 1/2 In. 690.00
Poster, Treat 'Em Rough, Join The Tanks, U.S. Tank Corp., 19 1/4 x 14 In. .... *ILLUS* 3884.00
Poster, Uncle Sam, I Want You For U.S. Army, James Flagg, February, 1917, 40 x 30 In. .... *ILLUS* 3107.00
Poster, Victory Liberty Loan, Lady Liberty With Flag, 1919, 38 x 26 In. 205.00
Saddle, Cavalry, McClellan, U.S., 1918 .... 259.00
Sheet Music, After The War Is Over, N. Andrieu, Pourmon, Woodruff, 1918, 2 Pages 8.00
Sheet Music, Good Bye Broadway, Hello France, 1917 .... 15.00
Sheet Music, We're Bound To Win With Boys Like You, c.1918 .... 25.00
Stereo Card, Victory Day Celebration, Arch Of Triumph, Keystone View Co., c.1919 .... 8.00
WORLD WAR II, Belt, Web, Khaki, Officer's Buckle, Brass, 1943, Size 36, 1 1/4 In. 16.00
Breeches, U.S. Army, Enlisted Man, Khaki, Twill, Plastic Buttons, Size 29W x 24L 22.00
Bucket, Canvas, Olive Drab, U.S. Army, 8-In. Diam. 15.00
Button, Buy War Bonds, Kilroy Was Here, 1 1/4 In. 25.00
Button, Churchill, Roosevelt, Victory Celebrations, 1 1/4 In. 400.00
Button, Let's Clean Out The Rats, 1 1/2 In. 7.00

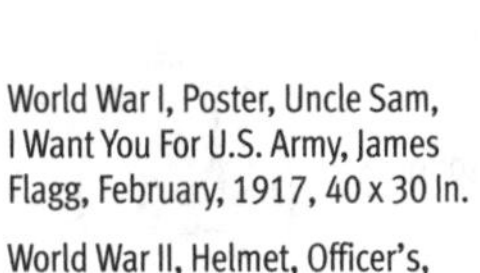

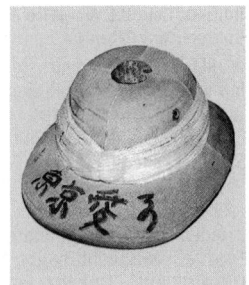

World War I, Poster, Uncle Sam, I Want You For U.S. Army, James Flagg, February, 1917, 40 x 30 In.

World War II, Helmet, Officer's, Cloth, Japan

Button, Pack Up Japan The Yanks Are Coming, 1 1/4 In. 20.00
Button, Remember Pearl Harbor, Uncle Sam, 1 1/4 In. 38.00
Button, To Hell With Hitler, Black, White, 1 1/4 In. 50.00
Card, Togo, Careless Matches Aid The Axis, Prevent Forest Fires, 5 x 3 In. 8.00
Certificate, Japanese Hunting License, Japanese Soldier As Skunk, 6 x 9 In. 30.00
Coat, Service Dress, Navy Wool, Lieutenant Sleeve Stripes, U.S. Navy, Size 38 55.00
Coat, U.S. Army Officer, Wool, Olive Drab, Belt, 1942, Size 34R 47.00
Flag, Japanese, Frame, 12 x 17 1/2 In. 44.00
Garrison Cap, Khaki, Artillery, Size 7 7.00
Handkerchief, U.S. Army Air Forces, Winged Prop, Stain, Purple, Embroidered, 9 x 9 In. 10.00
Helmet, Luftwaffe, M40, 2 Decals, Aluminum Liner Band, M31 Liner, Neck Guard 748.00
Helmet, Officer's, Cloth, Japan *ILLUS* 322.00
Life Vest, Aviator's, CO2 Inflatable, Blue, U.S. Navy 60.00
Medal Set, Combat, U.S. Military, Frame, Under Glass, c.1944, 15 x 9 In., 17 In. 205.00
Mittens, U.S. Army, Cotton, Wool Lining, Olive Drab 14.00
Overcoat, Enlisted Man's, U.S. Marine Corps, 1942, Size 3L 55.00
Pennant, U.S. Coast Guard, Insignia, Felt, Red, Screened, 9 x 26 In. 15.00
Pin, Exterminate These 3 Rats, Celluloid, Round, 1 1/2 In. 24.00
Pin, Let's Go, U.S.A., Keep 'Em Flying, 3 Bombers, Celluloid, Round, 1 1/2 In. 15.00
Pin, Let's Pull Together, Uncle Sam, Hanging Hitler, Mechanical, 1 1/2 In. 99.00
Pin, No Jim Crow In The Armed Forces, Ribbon, 1940, 2 3/4 x 7/8 In. 2556.00
Pin, V For Victory, Red, White, Blue, Celluloid, Round, 1 1/2 In. 11.00
Pin Dish, Milk Glass, Keep Em Flying, Buy Another Savings Bond Today, 3 1/2 In. 35.00
Poster, A Careless Word, A Needless Sinking, Anton Otto Fischer, 37 x 28 In. 69.00 to 81.00
Poster, A Careless Word, Another Cross, Memorial, John Atherton, 38 x 28 In. 69.00
Poster, Americans Fight For Liberty, 1778 & 1943 Army Graphic, 40 x 28 1/4 In. 64.00
Poster, Attack, Attack, Attack, Buy War Bonds, Soldiers, Planes, 38 x 28 In. 92.00 to 161.00
Poster, Avenge, December 7, Sailor, Sinking Ship, Bernard Perlin, 40 x 28 In. 219.00
Poster, Buy War Bonds, Don't Let That Shadow Touch Them, 40 x 28 In. 148.00
Poster, Can I Tell 'Em You're Still With Us, Next Stop Tokyo, Navy, J. Falter, 40 x 29 In. 58.00
Poster, Careless Talk Got There First, Henry Moore, 38 x 28 In. 230.00
Poster, Careless Talk Got There First, Ray Prahaska, 38 x 28 In. 105.00
Poster, Doing All You Can, Brother, Buy War Bonds, Robert Sloan, 38 x 28 In. 105.00
Poster, Get The Jap & Get It Over, Allen Saalburg, 1945, 29 x 21 In. 550.00
Poster, Remember Dec. 7th, Tattered Flag, Smoke, Flames, A. Saulburg, 40 x 28 1/2 In. 80.00
Poster, Someone Talked, Drowning Sailor, Siebel, 38 x 28 In. 104.00
Poster, That's The One To Hit, Admiral Chester Nimitz, J. Falter, 39 x 28 In. 69.00
Poster, Together We Win, Get Behind Labor Management Committee, 40 x 28 In. 45.00
Poster, Uncle Sam, Liberty Loan, Linen Backed, Dan Sayre Grosebeck, 29 x 20 In. 206.00
Punchboard, Go To Town With Uncle Sam, 13 1/4 x 9 3/4 In. 230.00
Sheet Music, Any Bonds Today?, I. Berlin, 1941, 11 x 8 1/2 In., 4 Pages 9.00
Sheet Music, Fellow On Furlough, B Worth, Martin Block Pub., 1943, 2 Pages 6.00
Sheet Music, Hot Time In Town Of Berlin, Sinatra, Bushkin & De Vries, 1943, 2 Pages 8.00
Sheet Music, Praise The Lord & Pass The Ammunition, F. Loesser, 1942, 3 Pages 7.00
Sleeping Bag, Wool, Olive Drab, Case, U.S. Army 45.00
Surgeon's Kit, Wood Case, Medical Instruments, Japan, 3 1/2 x 13 1/2 x 10 In. 267.00
Telephone, Military Defense Plant, Fairchild Republic 950.00

Trousers, Field, U.S. Army, Wool Serge, Olive Drab, Size 30 x 31 In. 30.00
Trousers, Navy Gabardine, Zipper Fly, Officer, U.S. Navy, 29 x 33 In. 28.00

WORLD'S FAIR souvenirs from all of the fairs are collected. The first fair was the Great Exhibition of 1851 in London. Some other important exhibitions and fairs include Philadelphia, 1876 (Centennial); Chicago, 1893 (World's Columbian); Buffalo, 1901 (Pan-American); St. Louis, 1904 (Louisiana Purchase); San Francisco, 1915 (Panama-Pacific); Philadelphia, 1926 (Sesquicentennial); Chicago, 1933 (Century of Progress); Cleveland, 1936 (Great Lakes); San Francisco, 1939 (Golden Gate International); New York, 1939 (World of Tomorrow); Seattle, 1962 (Century 21); New York, 1964; Montreal, 1967; New Orleans, 1984; Tsukuba, Japan, 1985; Vancouver, B.C., 1986; Brisbane, Australia, 1988; Seville, Spain, 1992; and Genoa, Italy, 1992; Seoul, Korea, 1993; and Lisbon, Portugal, 1998. Memorabilia of fairs include directories, pictures, fabrics, ceramics, etc. Memorabilia from other similar celebrations may be listed in the Souvenir category.

Bank, 1893, Chicago, Columbia Magic, Building, Nickel Plated, 5 1/4 In. 385.00
Bank, 1893, Chicago, Locomotive, Ceramic, My Expenses Too, 5 1/2 x 5 1/2 In. 1020.00
Bank, 1926, Philadelphia, Liberty Bell, 7 1/4 x 3 1/2 x 4 3/4 In. 72.00
Bank, 1939, New York, Libby's Treasure Ship, Tin Can, 3 1/2 In. 55.00
Banner, 1926, Philadelphia, Welcome To Philadelphia, 12 x 8 1/2 In. 29.00
Booklet, 1898, Trans-Mississippi Exposition, Buildings Photos, 58 Pages 40.00
Booklet, 1898, Trans-Mississippi Exposition, Grounds, Buildings, Photographs, 32 Pages 66.00
Booklet, 1898, Trans-Mississippi Exposition, Pictures, Administration Arch, 32 Pages 72.00
Booklet, 1926, Philadelphia, Pennsylvania Railroad, 46 Pages 18.00
Booklet, 1926, Philadelphia, Pictorial Record, 64 Pages 26.00
Bottle, 1939, New York, Milk Glass, Globe Shape, Lid, 9 1/4 In. 55.00
Bus, 1933, Chicago, Century Of Progress, GMC, Greyhound Lines, 12 In. 305.00
Coffee Set, Sugar & Creamer, 1939, New York 440.00
Coin, 1901, Buffalo, Aluminum, Woman Shaking Hands 15.00
Coin, 1901, Buffalo, Center Hole, Horseshoes, 1 1/2 In. 18.00
Cup & Saucer, 1893, Chicago, Satsuma, Fisheries, Demitasse, 4 1/4 In. 368.00
Decanter, 1939, New York, Globe Shaped Base, Banner, White, 9 In. 45.00
Display, 1939, New York, Longines Wittnauer Time & Space Building, Plaster, 9 x 12 In. 2140.00
Figurine, 1901, Buffalo, Embossed Buffalo, 2 x 2 1/2 In. 72.00
Ink, 1939, New York, Administration Building, Paneled Glass, 1 1/2 In. 99.00
Inkwell, 1915, San Francisco, Panama Pacific, Baseball, Gold Color, 4 1/4 In. 465.00
Jewel Box, 1876, Philadelphia, Oval, Beveled, Scenes, 3 1/4 x 2 1/4 x 1 1/4 In. 341.00
Lamp, 1939, New York, Trylon & Perisphere, Glass, Chrome, 5 1/2 In. .... *ILLUS* 266.00
Matchbook, 1939, New York, Schlitz, Milwaukee, Wisc. 2.00
Mug, 1901, Buffalo, Green Glass, 2 3/4 x 3 1/2 In. 39.00
Pamphlet, 1893, Chicago, California Fig Syrup Co. 15.00
Paper Clip, Bookmark, 1926, Philadelphia, Metal, Box 26.00
Paperweight, 1901, Buffalo, Electric Tower, Faux Leather, 4 x 2 1/2 In. 28.00
Pillow Cover, 1904, St. Louis, Festival Hall, Blue, 21 1/2 x 18 In. 42.00
Pin, 1901, Buffalo, 2 Women, North, South America, 1 1/4 In. 13.00
Pin, 1901, Buffalo, Celluloid, Ceresota Flour, 2 In. 30.00
Pin, 1901, Buffalo, Celluloid, Liberty, Peace, 1 1/4 In. 24.00
Pin, 1901, Buffalo, Celluloid, New York State Grange Day, 1 1/4 In. 26.00
Pin, 1904, St. Louis, Celluloid, Liberty Bell, White, Blue, Sepia 11.00
Plate, 1904, St. Louis, Multicolored, Washington, Jefferson, Lafayette, Napoleon, 10 3/8 In. 28.00
Pocket Knife, 1904, St. Louis, Louisiana Purchase, 2 Blades, Medallion, 2 3/4 In. 50.00
Poster, 1901, Buffalo, Maid Of Mist, Frame, 51 x 27 In. 3615.00
Poster, 1904, St. Louis, Alphonse Mucha, 40 x 29 In. 3910.00
Poster, 1933, Chicago, Weimer Pursell, 40 3/4 x 27 In. 1115.00
Poster, 1936, San Francisco, Golden Gate, 34 x 27 In. 825.00
Poster, 1937, Paris, Ates Et Techniques, Leonetto Cappiello, Frame, 66 x 49 In. 1684.00
Poster, 1939, New York, Nembhard Culin, Frame, 39 x 28 In. 9380.00
Purse, 1893, Chicago, Mother-Of-Pearl, Agriculture Building, 3 In. 115.00
Radio, 1939, New York, RCA, Trylon-Perisphere, 5 Tubes, 7 x 9 x 6 In. 1855.00

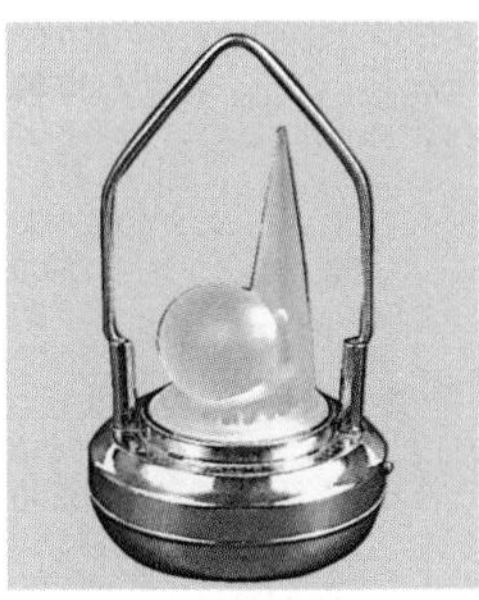
World's Fair, Lamp, 1939, New York, Trylon & Perisphere, Glass, Chrome, 5 1/2 In.

World's Fair, Ribbon, 1893, Chicago, Administration Building, Star Spangled Banner, 8 1/2 In.

World's Fair, Thermometer, 1933, Chicago, Havoline Tower, Gold Plastic, 4 1/2 In.

Ribbon, 1893, Chicago, Administration Building, Star Spangled Banner, 8 1/2 In. .... *ILLUS* 287.00
Safe, 1901, Buffalo, Woman, Spirit Of Niagara, 3 3/4 In. 44.00
Smoking Stand, 1933, Chicago, Art Deco, Glass, Aluminum, Illuminated, 31 In. 2851.00
Spoon, 1893, Chicago, Demitasse, Columbus, 4 1/4 In. 39.00
Spoon, 1893, Chicago, Sterling Silver, Ship, Stars, Stripes, Eagle, 5 3/4 In. 99.00
Spoon, 1904, St. Louis, Sterling Silver, Train, Covered Wagon, Buffaloes, Riders, 5 7/8 In. 33.00
Spoon, 1933, Chicago, Fort Dearborn, Silver Plate 32.00
Thermometer, 1933, Chicago, Havoline Tower, Gold Plastic, 4 1/2 In. .... *ILLUS* 35.00
Tip Tray, 1901, Buffalo, Brass, 5 1/2 x 3 1/4 In. 28.88
Toy, 1933, Chicago, Bus, Century Of Progress, Arcade, 10 1/4 In. 330.00
Toy, 1958, Brussels, Helicopter, Flies Around Satellite, Metal, Plastic, Windup, Box 125.00
Tumbler, 1904, St. Louis, Milk Glass, Pictures, 5 In. 18.00
Tureen, Cover, 1851, London, Pictures Inside, Outside, Staffordshire, 11 3/4 x 7 In. 275.00
Vase, 1904, St. Louis, Flow Blue, Palace Of Machinery, 9 x 5 1/2 x 4 In. 165.00

WPA is the abbreviation for Works Progress Administration, a program created by executive order in 1935 to provide jobs for millions of unemployed Americans. Artists were hired to create murals, paintings, drawings, and sculptures for public buildings. Pieces are marked WPA and may have the artist's name on them.

Book, Maryland, American Guide Series, 1946 .... 12.00
Book, San Antonio, Authoritative Guide, Writer's Project, First Edition, 1938, 106 Pages 60.00
Doll, Dutch Boy & Girl, Cloth, Handicraft Project No. 7040, Milwaukee, Wisc., 19 In., Pair 510.00
Folk Tunes, Square & Round Dances, Writer's Project, Ill., First Edition, 1942, 114 Pages 79.00
Lithograph, Catholic Church At Waterville, Adolph Dehn, 1932, 16 x 11 1/2 In. 178.00
Lithograph, Harbor Dock Wharf Fishing Scene, Malvin Marr Albright, Frame, 21 x 17 In. 55.00
Painting, Oil On Board, Winter Farm Scene, Edward Carlson, Frame, c.1940, 21 1/2 x 26 In. 295.00
Painting, Watercolor On Paper, Construction Workers, Irving G. Lehman, Frame, 1930s, 20 x 17 In. 250.00
Playing Cards, Super Materiam Ignis Triumphans, 1 Used, 1 Unopened, Box, 1945, 2 Decks 30.00
Poster, Use The Flushing Bar, Protect Game, Penn. Game Commission, 20 x 14 In. 205.00
Print, Woodblock, Flood, William Jacobs, Chicago, 1938, 9 3/4 x 7 1/2 In. 115.00
Print, Woodblock, Undeclared War, William Jacobs, Chicago, 1938, 9 3/4 x 7 1/2 In. 68.00
Stunt Songs, Writer's Project, Pictorial Wrappers, Illinois, First Edition, 1940, 55 Pages 1525.00
Watercolor, Grain Silos, Farmland, Helen Lane, Frame, 1940s, 23 x 19 In. 66.00
Watercolor, Tenement, Family, On Heavy Paper, David Phillip Levine, 14 x 20 3/4 In. 675.00

WRISTWATCHES came into use during World War I. Wristwatches are listed here by manufacturer or as advertising or character watches. Wristwatches may also be listed in other categories. Pocket watches are listed in the Watch category.

Abercrombie & Fitch, Woman's, Reverse Crystal, Horse, 15 Jewel, 14K Gold, 7 3/4 In. 1765.00
Baume & Mercier, Woman's, Black Face, 18K Gold, 7 In. 1840.00
Boucheron, Woman's, Leather Band, Quartz, Diamond, 18K Gold, Fitted Case 7285.00
Bulova, 21 Jewel, 10K Gold Filled Case, 1930s 90.00

Bulova, Woman's, Synthetic Blue Sapphire Melees, White Gold Plated Band, 6 In. 200.00
Cartier, Woman's, Classic Tank, 18K Gold, Quartz Movement, Leather Band, Box 2350.00
Cartier, Woman's, Santos, Ivorytone Dial, Stainless Steel, 18K Gold, Brickwork Links, Box 1998.00
Cartier, Woman's, Tank Francaise, Stainless Steel, Quartz Movement, Box 1998.00
Cartier, Woman's, Tank, Roman Numerals, Diamond, 18K Gold, Brickwork Links 10575.00
Character, Hawaiian Punch, Punchy, White Face, Red Band, 1971 . . . . . . 25.00
Concord Woman's, Lapis Face, Calf Skin Band, 18K Gold, Swiss, 8 In. 660.00
Corum, Admiral's Cup, Ivorytone Dial, Stainless Steel, Quartz, 18K Gold 823.00
Corum, Woman's, 18K Gold, 17 Jewel, Manual Wind, Braided Band, 7 In. 705.00
Gerard Perregaux, Woman's, Diamonds, Woven Gold Band, 14K Gold, 6 1/2 In. 646.00
Gisiger Greder Son, 17 Jewel, Single Disc Display, Stainless Steel Case 130.00
Gruen, Woman's, Diamonds, Platinum, Art Deco, 17 Jewel, Swiss 2130.00
Gubelin, Woman's, Ivorytone Dial, 17 Jewel, Ribbed Bezel, Woven Band, c.1960 . . . . . . 265.00
Gubelin, Woman's, Platinum, Diamond, Arabic Numerals, 18 Jewel, Art Deco 1880.00
Hamilton, Woman's, Platinum, Diamond, Ivorytone Dial, 17 Jewel, 6 1/2 In. 940.00
Hamilton, Woman's, Platinum, Diamond, Ivorytone Dial, 5 3/8 In. 1528.00
Hermes, Woman's, Rallye, Stainless Steel, Quartz Movement, Leather Band, Box 765.00
Hublot, Chronograph Superb, Stainless Steel, Automatic Movement, Rubber Band 2350.00
Hublot, Woman's, Mother-Of-Pearl Dial, Diamonds, 18K Gold, Rubber Band, Box 2115.00
Jaeger LeCoultre, Woman's, 17 Jewel, 18K Gold Case 285.00
Juvenia, 17 Jewel, Automatic Wind, Gold Hands, 18K Gold Case 1015.00
Kelbert, Inscription, Mesh Band, Square Face, 14K Gold, 7 1/2 In. 480.00
LeCoutre, Woman's, Mystery, 17 Jewel, Diamond Numerals, 1950s 525.00
Longines, Sterling Silver, Leather Band, Serge Manzon, c.1972, 1 1/2 x 8 1/2 In. 765.00
Longines, Woman's, 14K White Gold, Diamond, 17 Jewel, Manual Wind, 6 1/4 In. 440.00
Longines, Woman's, Art Deco, Platinum, Diamond, 18 Jewel, 6 3/8 In. 880.00
Milus, Woman's, 2 O'Clock II, Quartz, Stainless Steel Case, Mesh Band, Paul Junod 150.00
Montblanc, Quartz Movement, Steel Hands, Black Dial, Date Aperture 510.00
Movado, Woman's, 17 Jewel, White Gold Hands, Platinum Case, Diamonds 870.00
Movado, Woman's, Ivorytone Dial, Platinum, Diamond, 17 Jewel 3175.00
Patek Philippe, 18 Jewel, Gold Hands, Brushed Gold Dial, 1970s 2765.00
Patek Philippe, Calatrava, 18K Gold, Manual Wind, Leather Band, 1950s 4115.00
Patek Philippe, Manual Wind, Leather Band, 18K Rose Gold, 1940s 7050.00
Patek Philippe, Woman's, 18K Gold, Round Head, Gold Snake Band 1320.00
Patek Philippe, Woman's, Nickel Movement, Flexible Band, 18K Gold, 6 3/4 In. 1998.00
Piaget, Woman's, Jade, Diamond, Emerald, 18K Gold, Manual Wind, Mesh Band, 6 3/4 In. 3645.00
Piaget, Woman's, Quartz Movement, Mesh Band, Blue Metal Dial, Roman Numerals, 18K Gold . . . 1295.00
Raymond Yard, Woman's, Aquamarine, Diamond, Silvertone Dial, c.1940, 7 3/8 In. 2938.00
Renaud, Woman's, Diamond, 18K White Gold, Brickwork Links, 6 In. 880.00
Rolex, Oyster Perpetual Chronometer, Ivorytone Dial, 14K Rose Gold, 1940s 3525.00
Rolex, Oyster Perpetual Date Superlative Chronometer, 18K Gold 5465.00
Rolex, Oyster Perpetual Date, Stainless Steel, Blue Metal Dial, 14K Gold 2115.00
Rolex, Oyster Perpetual, Datejust, 14 & 18K Gold, Silvertone Dial, Stainless Steel, Box 1295.00
Rolex, Oyster Precision, Stainless Steel, Black Dial, Manual Wind, c.1960 . . . . . . 825.00
Rolex, Tudor Prince, Oysterdate, Box 316.00
Rolex, Tudor Prince, Oysterdate, Self-Winding, Stainless Steel Case 345.00
Rolex, Tudor Prince, Oysterdate, Stainless Steel Case, Band, Box 290.00
Rolex Cellini, 19 Jewel, 18K Gold Case, c.1969 . . . . . . 920.00
Universal Geneve, Compax, Black Metal Dial, Leather Band, Box 940.00
Vacheron & Constantine, Silver Dial, 17 Jewel, Model 6355, 18K 1840.00
Vacheron & Constantine, Woman's, 18K Yellow Gold Case, Mesh Band, 1975 . . . . . . 580.00

YELLOWWARE is a heavy earthenware made of a yellowish clay. It varies in color from light yellow to orange-yellow. Many nineteenth- and twentieth-century kitchen bowls and jugs were made of yellowware. It was made in England and in the United States. Another form of pottery that is sometimes classed as yellowware is listed in this book in the Mocha category.

Bank, Bulbous, Elongated Spear Finial, Mottled Glaze, 5 In. 440.00
Bank, Cat Head, Yellow, Brown, c.1870, 3 1/4 In. 468.00
Bank, Cat Head, Yellow, c.1870, 3 1/4 In. 413.00

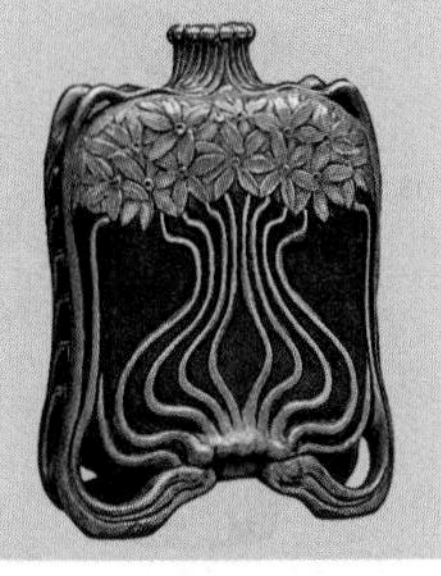

Zsolnay, Cachepot, Red Flowers, Blue Iridescent Panels, Marked, 7 3/4 x 7 In.

Zsolnay, Flask, Art Nouveau, Red, Green, Blue, Eosin Glaze, Marked, 9 3/4 x 7 In.

Bank, Hen On Nest, Mottled Yellow, Brown, c.1860, 3 1/2 In. 550.00
Bowl, Bands, 4 In. 75.00
Bowl, Seaweed, Blue, On Cream Band, Brown Bands, Footed, 2 3/4 x 5 1/4 In. 259.00
Bowl, Seaweed, Blue, On White Band, Blue Band, Footed, 6 x 12 1/4 In. 403.00
Bowl, Vegetable, Oval, 11 x 8 In. 50.00
Butter, Cover, White Bands 130.00
Chamber Pot, 2 White Slip Bands, Brown Slip Bands, Loop Handle, 1 1/2 In. 94.00
Chamber Pot, Lid, Blue Sponge 30.00
Chamber Pot, Seaweed, 1800s, 5 x 8 In. 230.00
Chamber Pot, White, Brown Slip Bands, Loop Handle, 1 1/2 In. 95.00
Dish, Rabbit, Molded Garland Base, Rabbit With Petal Handle, 12 x 5 1/2 In. 315.00
Jug, Amber Brown Glaze, Molded Grapes, Roses, Masks, Woman Playing Lyre, 8 1/4 In. 575.00
Mixing Bowl, Reinforced Rim, 7 x 15 1/2 In. 220.00
Mixing Bowl Set, Pink & Blue Bands, c.1900, 8 To 9 1/2 In. 94.00
Mold, Lamb, 2 Sections, Handles, Yellow Glaze, Green, 13 1/2 x 7 In. 200.00
Mug, Salt Glaze Finish, Blue Bands, Ribbed Handle, 1800s, 2 3/4 In. 115.00
Mug, Seaweed, 4 In. ....385.00 to 660.00
Mug, Seaweed, Blue, 3 1/2 In. 305.00
Pail, Clam, Black Slip Bands, Center Finger Hold, Barrel, 5 1/2 In. 28.00
Pitcher, Bands, 7 In. 330.00
Pitcher, Brown Sponge, 17 In. 45.00
Pitcher, Peacock, Brown Drip, Stoneware 65.00
Pitcher, Seaweed, Blue, Green, Brown, On Ivory Shoulder Band, Brown Rings, 6 In. 345.00
Pitcher, Seaweed, Green & Brown Design, Brown Rings, 6 In. 435.00
Rolling Pin, Wood Handles, 15 In. 550.00
Salt, Blue Bands, Footed, c.1865, 2 x 3 In. 198.00
Syrup, c.1850, 7 In. 175.00

ZANESVILLE Art Pottery was founded in 1900 by David Schmidt in Zanesville, Ohio. The firm made faience umbrella stands, jardinieres, and pedestals. The company closed in 1962. Many pieces are marked with just the words *La Moro.*

LA MORO

Jardiniere, Green, Brown Glaze, Red Flowers, Tulips, c.1900, 17 In. 353.00
Vase, Baluster Shape, Green Matte Glaze, No. 37, 12 In. 60.00
Vase, Baluster Shape, Thick Neck, Blue Glossy Glaze, 10 3/4 In. 35.00
Vase, Embossed Daffodils, Green Matte Glaze, 8 3/4 In. 60.00

ZSOLNAY pottery was made in Hungary after 1862 and was characterized by Persian, Art Nouveau, or Hungarian motifs. A series of new Zsolnay figurines with green-gold luster finish is available in many shops today. Early Zsolnay was not marked, but by 1878 the tower trademark was used.

Bowl, Seminude Woman, Seated On Edge, Raised Water Drops, 4 1/2 x 4 1/2 In. 1560.00
Bowl, Sunburst Ground, Iridescent Glaze, Stylized Clouds, 7 In. 9200.00
Cachepot, Red Flowers, Blue Iridescent Panels, Marked, 7 3/4 x 7 In. .... *ILLUS* 460.00
Cigarette Box, Woman Smoking, Smoke Swirls, Peacock Eosin Glaze, 3 x 2 x 1 1/4 In. 660.00
Cruet, Mottled Metallic Glaze, Logo, 4 1/4 In. 403.00
Figurine, Bust, Woman With Flowing Scarf, Hand To Breast, Blue Eosin, 5 In. 805.00

Zsolnay, Pitcher, Double Walled, Cutout Outer Layer, Twisted Rope Handle, Marked, 1886, 8 In.

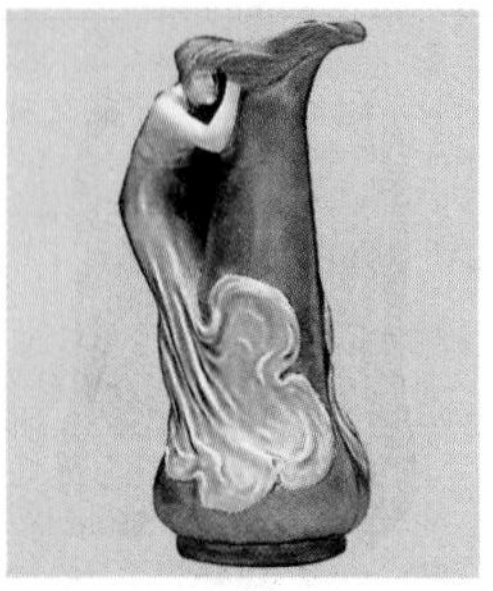

Zsolnay, Pitcher, Lady Forms Handle, Eosin Glaze, Art Nouveau, Marked, 8 1/2 In.

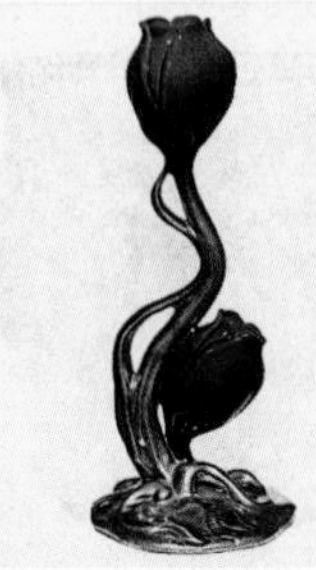

Zsolnay, Vase, Tulip Shape, Iridescent Green Leaves, Goldstems, Marked, 10 In.

Figurine, Cello Player, Red Tuxedo, Yellow Cummerbund, Art Deco, 8 In. 345.00
Figurine, Fox, Blue Green Glaze, Logo, 4 In. 81.00
Figurine, Fox, Stylized, Green Eosin Glaze, 5 1/2 x 4 1/2 In. 115.00
Figurine, Nude Woman, Kneeling, Hands Behind Head, Iridescent Green Glaze, 9 In. 330.00
Figurine, Scribe, Hood, Seated, Book, Pen, Iridescent, Luster Glaze, 1930s, 8 1/4 In. 471.00
Figurine, Seminude Woman, Draped Skirt, Eosin Glaze, 14 In. 1438.00
Figurine, Woman, Draped Cloth, Green Iridescent Glaze, Signed, A. Jehring, Marked, 14 In. 1140.00
Flask, Art Nouveau, Red, Green, Blue, Eosin Glaze, Marked, 9 3/4 x 7 In. .... *ILLUS* 9200.00
Jardiniere, Luster, Spiral Lobes, Roses, Reticulated Rim, c.1890, 15 In. 9600.00
Jug, Sun Setting Behind Ocean, Red Ground, Iridescent Blue, Handle, 10 1/2 In. 7190.00
Pitcher, Double Walled, Cutout Outer Layer, Twisted Rope Handle, Marked, 1886, 8 In. .... *ILLUS* 575.00
Pitcher, Lady Forms Handle, Eosin Glaze, Art Nouveau, Marked, 8 1/2 In. .... *ILLUS* 3720.00
Plate, Trees Against Red Water & Sky Ground, 9 In. 660.00
Vase, Baluster, Woman Seated On Shoulder, Flowers, Clouds, Luster, c.1905, 9 In. 8400.00
Vase, Cobalt Blue Ground, Stylized Flowers, Leaves, Green, Yellow, 5 1/4 In. 510.00
Vase, Doe Peeking Out, Reticulated Trees, Purple, Gold, Green Glaze, 18 x 7 In. 15275.00
Vase, Egg Shape, Bulbous Neck, Mottled, Luster Glaze, 1930s, 15 1/4 In. 340.00
Vase, Eosin Labrador Glaze, Purple, Silver, Gold, 4 In. 270.00
Vase, Fern Leaf, Red Flowers, Mottled Green Ground, 5 In. 1093.00
Vase, Green Iridescent, Melon Ribs, 6 In. 225.00
Vase, Hammered Texture, 4 Handles, Gold, Green Eosin Glaze, 8 3/4 In. 3120.00
Vase, Iridescent Blue Glaze, Green, Purple, Wide Mouth, Tapered, 9 In. 1208.00
Vase, Iridescent Gold, Nautical Scene, Maroon Ground Glaze, 5 1/4 In. 978.00
Vase, Iridescent Millefiori, Handles, Heart Shape Leaf, Multicolored Iridescent Glaze, 9 1/2 In. 8280.00
Vase, Ivory, Pink, Gray & Black Organic Designs, 13 In. 210.00
Vase, Metallic Flowers, Ribs, Pierced Handles, Foot, 11 3/4 In. 476.00
Vase, Metallic Glaze, Iridescent, Wafer Mark, 4 Handles, 14 1/4 In. 4700.00
Vase, Monumental, Swirling Silver, Blue, Eosin Labrador Glaze, Gold Interior, 19 In. 1725.00
Vase, Secessionist, Silver, Blue, Copper Eosin Ground, 11 1/2 In. 5175.00
Vase, Shell Form, Flowers, Pierced, Painted, Footed, Numbered, 13 In. 180.00
Vase, Stylized Flowers, Gold Swirls Ground, 7 3/4 In. 630.00
Vase, Stylized Flowers, Vines, Iridescent Gold To Blue Ground, 10 1/4 In. 4428.00
Vase, Stylized Landscape, Crescent Moon, Iridescent, 9 1/4 In. 4600.00
Vase, Stylized Leaves, Vines, Green Ground, 11 3/4 In. 870.00
Vase, Tulip Shape, Iridescent Green Leaves, Goldstems, Marked, 10 In. .... *ILLUS* 1800.00

INDEX

This index is computer-generated, making it as complete as possible. References in uppercase type are category listings. Those in lowercase letters refer to additional pages where pieces can be found. There is also an internal cross-referencing system used in the main part of the book, so if you look for a Kewpie doll in the Doll category, you will be told it is in its own category. There is additional information at the end of many paragraphs about where to find prices of pieces similar to yours.

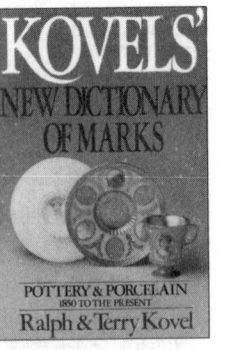

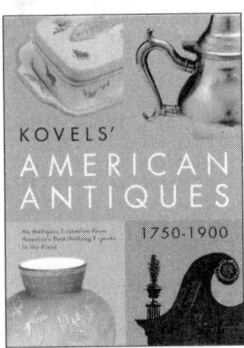

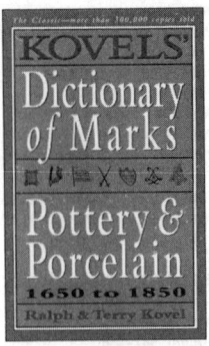

BUSINESS REPLY MAIL

FIRST CLASS PERMIT NO. 191 FLAGLER BEACH, FL

POSTAGE WILL BE PAID BY ADDRESSEE

KOVELS ON ANTIQUES AND COLLECTIBLES

P.O. BOX 420349

PALM COAST, FL 32142-9655